Wine^{Pro} Italy app B2B for the Italian wine market

P9-CLU-472

New business opportunities, time reduction between supply and demand, great temporary offers and requests for specific products.
All of this is summarized in **Wine^{Pro} Italy**.

Wine^{Pro} Italy

FREE download!

www.wineproitaly.com

Umani Ronchi winemakers
in Marche and Abruzzo.

Castelli di Jesi

Conero

Abruzzo

Verdicchio, Montepulciano and other typical grapes of the Adriatic coast.

UMANI RONCHI

Italian Wines

2016

VINI D'ITALIA 2016
GAMBERO ROSSO®

Gambero Rosso S.p.A.
via Ottavio Gasparri, 13/17 - 00152 Roma
tel. 06/551121 - fax 06/55112260
www.gamberorosso.it
email: gambero@gamberorosso.it

Senior Editors
Gianni Fabrizio
Eleonora Guerini
Marco Sabellico

Co-editor
Giuseppe Carrus

Special Contributors
Antonio Boco
Paolo De Cristofaro
Lorenzo Ruggeri
Paolo Zaccaria

Regionali Coordinators
Nino Aiello
Alessandro Bocchetti
Nicola Frasson
Massimo Lanza
Giorgio Melandri
Gianni Ottogalli
Nereo Pederzolli
Pierpaolo Rastelli

Contributors
Giovanni Angelucci
Stefania Annese
Francesco Beghi
Sergio Bonanno
Michele Bressan
Pasquale Buffa
Dionisio Castello
Giacomo Mojoli
Franco Pallini
Alessio Pietrobattista
William Pregentelli
Leonardo Romanelli
Maurizio Rossi
Giulia Sampognaro
Herbert Taschler
Cinzia Tosetti

Other Contributors
Filippo Apollinari
Elena Bardelli
Enrico Battistella
Alexandre Bronzatto
Camilla Bianchin
Sergio Ceccarelli
Lucio Chiesa
Francesca Ciancio
Mario Demattè
Valentina Faccia
Pierluigi Fais
Maurizio Fava
Pierluigi Giuliani
Leonardo Marco
Nicola Massa
Enrico Melis
Michele Muraro
Nicola Piccinini
Massimo Ponzanelli
Walter Pugliese
Carlo Ravanello
Lorenzo Rondinelli
Riccardo Rossetti
Simona Silvestri

Andrea Sponsilli
Paolo Trimani
Vincenzo Verrastro
Stefano Zaghini
Liliana Zanellato

Editorial Secretary
Giulia Sciortino

Coordination and Layout
Marina Proietti

Managing Editor Books
Laura Mantovano

Graphics
Chiara Buosi

Commercial Director
Francesco Dammicco

Editorial Product Sales Manager
Gianpiero Ciorra

Production
Angelica Sorbara

Distribution
Eugenia Durando

Translation Coordinator
Angela Arnone

Translators and Revisors
Angela Arnone
Anthony Green
Sarah Ponting
Simon Tanner
Ailsa Wood

Publisher
Gr Usa Corp c/o Csc Services of Nevada Inc
2215-B RENAISSANCE DR
Las Vegas , NV 89119
email: gamberousa@aol.com

Distribution
USA and Canada
by Antique Collector's Club, Eastworks, 116
Pleasant St #18, Easthampton, MA 010207, USA;
UK and Australia by Antique Collector's Club Ltd
Sandy Lane, Old Martlesham, Woodbridge,
Suffolk IP12 4SD - United Kingdom

The final edit of Italian Wines was completed on
5 September 2015

ISBN 9781890142179

Printed in Italy for Gambero Rosso S.p.A.
in November 2015 by
REVELOX - soluzioni tipografiche
V.le Charles Lenormant 112 - 00119 (RM)
www.revelox.it

SUMMARY

REGIONS

INDEXES

THE GUIDE

Welcome to the 29th edition of this Guide. With the world changing ever faster, even within the close confines of our little oenological universe, 29 might seem an eternity, to be measured more in terms of geological ages than in years. While everything around us has changed out of all recognition, we have tried to abide by our principles, our inspiration, and our working methods, simply fine-tuning them over the years. Italian Wines has remained true to its mission of sharing with the most judicious and passionate wine buffs all the complexity and charm of the Italian wine scene, probably the most intricate and intriguing anywhere in the world. Nowhere else is there such a variety of terroirs, winemaking techniques both modern and traditional, and a native grape heritage of such excellence, all of which are key factors in making our oenological scenario such an incredibly multicoloured and variegated mosaic. As the crow flies, Passito di Pantelleria and Passito di Chambave may be vinified over 1,000 kilometres from each other, using very different techniques and varietals, from two terroirs – Mediterranean and Alpine, respectively – that could scarcely be further apart. That said, if we read them as we should (or should we say breath in deeply from the glass) and recap their histories, we come to realize that they are products of a single civilization, of the same culture, of which we are the heirs and guardians. Despite some obvious differences, their DNAs, if you like, largely overlap. And though they have different accents, they still speak the same language. So this is our mission, to tell the stories of Italian wines and winegrowers large and small in a simple and easy-to-understand style, as they are one of the driving forces of our economy, working with passion to preserve all that is best about our countryside. They are its true custodians, and we are proud and pleased to bring the fruits of their toils to the attention of the rest of the world. And we do all this without any sectarian bias, with great open-mindedness, with no ideological barriers or obstacles: here there are both large-scale and boutique producers, industrial concerns churning out millions of bottles and small-scale winemakers, international brands but also biodynamic wines, orange wines created by macerating skins, others aged in small wood, or else in amphorae as our forefathers did some 2,000 years ago. Here in these pages there is some of the best of everything, carefully selected with intellectual honesty and secular spirit. Among the changes introduced in this edition, as well as an indication of the type of production (conventional, organic or biodynamic), there is also an indication of which wineries follow strict sustainability criteria. This is an area to which we are particularly committed and our faith in sustainability shines through, as can be seen in our role in the new Forum per la Sostenibilità Ambientale del Vino (www.vinosostenibile. org), which has published an online report referred to the sustainability of Italian wine. Now, after interviewing over 1,000 wineries, it is about to publish a second and to do this, we brought together a team of outstanding experts, 60 people united by their skill and passion who, in the space of just a few months, have travelled the length and breadth of Italy, tasting all of the wines reaching the market, no less than 45,000 labels, drafting tasting notes and scores. As happens every year, the best wines selected during the regional selections all headed off to Rome's Città del Gusto for the final tastings, where almost 1,500 samples were examined by a panel of three curators, plus the delegates from each area, to assign the Tre Bicchieri awards. Of course one of the reasons for the success of the Guide lies in the simplicity of the points system: good wines which we recommend are given Un Bicchiere, whereas Due Bicchieri are for the best expressions of the territory, and a Tre Bicchieri, which has now become an international trademark, goes to great wines and is now universally recognized as a symbol of Italian winemaking excellence. Wines can also be given two red glasses, where they went forward for the final tastings. Both for local panels and during finals, all tastings are rigorously blind. This year, at the end of our work we had awarded prizes to 421 wines, more or less the same number as last time round, though the number of wines we tasted and reviewed was a lot higher this year. We have reached the figure of over 22,000 wines from 2,400 winemakers, a gargantuan task, creating an extremely useful tool both for wine lovers and for wine professionals all over the world. As well as assessing all the wines we reviewed (together with their price range), this Guide also provides in-depth profiles of the winery and its winemaking philosophy, giving the reader a wide variety of useful information, from style notes for the wines to the number of hectares under vine, to the production figures, to information on the type of winegrowing, whether traditional, organic or biodynamic. Each profile is completely rewritten every year, rather than just updated. This explains its huge success on an international scale because as well as the Italian version, for years now been we have publishing translations into English, German, Chinese and Japanese, making this the world's most popular publication on Italian wines. The reputation grown by Gambero Rosso with years of work also enables us to stage 30 different international events every year, starring the best wines of Italy. These events continue to be a huge boost for our wine exports, and a firm date on the calendars of wine lovers the world over, who throng events and make them a runaway success. At the end of another year of tastings, it is time to draw a few conclusions. In this edition we have seen a few classic terroirs come to the fore, such as Montalcino, with great 2010 vintages, or Chianti Classico with its excellent Gran Selezione wines and much more. King of the Langhe remains the Barolo with over 30 wines earning a prize, the north-east submitted some fine 2014 whites, Veneto reds are on great form, while the general improvement among southern wines and the ever-more dynamic Lambrusco mean there is always plenty to write about, from both large- and small-scale designations. Just like every year, our special prizes say it all. Red of the Year is an outstanding Etna Rosso Vigna Barbagalli 2012 from Pietradolce. Alongside is a "venerable" white now once again bathing in glory: the Collio Friulano 2014 from Schiopetto. Sparkler of the Year and the 40th Tre Bicchieri of all time are just reward for decades of effort from Ca' del Bosco and Maurizio Zanella, who have come up with a very elegant, complex Franciacorta Vintage Collection Dosage Zéro Noir Riserva 2006. The quartet is brought to a close by a sweet mountain wine of refined elegance and great intensity, Valle d'Aosta's Chambave Moscato Passito Prieuré 2013, from La Crotta di Vegneron. Winery of the Year is Allegrini from Fumane, whose alluring Amarones reach all four corners of the globe. Grower of the Year is Giulio Grasso, head of Ca' del Baio, the creator of great Barbarescos. Up-and-Coming Winery is a vibrant Bolgheri cellar, the Scienza family's Guado al Melo. Best Value For Money goes to a Campanian wine, the persuasive Falanghina del Sannio Svelato 2014, from the comparatively new Terre Stregate winery. Last but not least, Sustainable Viticulture Award was deservedly won by the Manincor winery from Alto Adige, which has long made the environment a priority. There are also no less than 80 Tre Bicchieri Verdi awards, for certified organic and biodynamic wineries. And lastly there are 111 award-winning wines available at your local stores for under 15 euros a bottle.

We would like to thank Bolzano EOS, Cagliari and Perugia chambers of commerce, the Oltrepò Pavese Quality Wine District association, the coordinators of Umbria's wine and oil trails, the Strada dei Vini di Arezzo wine trail, the Istituto Marchigiano di Tutela Vini di Jesi (IMT), and VINEA of Offida, Picenos – Consorzio Vini Piceni, ERSA Friuli Venezia Giulia, the Istituto Agronomico Mediterraneo of Valenzano, the Ente Vini Bresciani, the Municipality of Cairo Montenotte (Savona), Comitato Grandi Cru della Costa Toscana, Assovini Sicilia, Pro.vi.di. – association of Sicilian Wine- and Spirit-makers, the E. del Giudice Centro per l'Innovazione della Filiera Vitivinicola in Marsala. Also, the protection consortiums of Gavi, Barolo, Barbaresco, Alba, Langhe and Roero, Vini Colli Tortonesi, Nebbiolo dell'Alto Piemonte, Caluso, Carema and Canavese, Oltrepò Pavese, Vini di Valtellina, Franciacorta, Valcalepio and Vini Mantovani, Lugana, Conegliano Valdobbiadene, Soave, Consorzio Vini Trentini, Bolgheri, Brunello di Montalcino, San Gimignano, Montepulciano, Colli Fiorentini, Chianti Rufina, Morellino di Scansano, Montecucco, Carmignano, Chianti Classico, Orvieto, Montefalco, and finally the Consorzio di Tutela Vini DOC Sicilia. We also thank the regional wine cellars of Ovada, Monferrato and Roero; provincial wine cellars of Turin, Nizza Monferrato, Canelli and Astesana; Cantina Comunale I Söri in Diano d'Alba, Bottega del Vino in Dogliani, the Millésimes wine merchants in Collegno, University of Bologna – Degree Course in Viticulture and Oenology, Terre Naldi in Tebano, the Carpe Diem restaurant in Montaione, the Calidarium in Venturina, the Città del Gusto of Rome and Naples, the regional wine cellar of Basilicata in Venosa, La Réserve in Caramanico, Caneva in Mogliano Veneto, the Bouchon restaurant in Messina, and Acqua San Martino of Codrongianos.

And last but not least, we would like to thank each and every one of our great team, whose passion in creating this Guide, from the local tastings to writing the profiles and putting together the entire volume has won through, with special thanks to Giuseppe Carrus, our truly irreplaceable co-editor.

Gianni Fabrizio, Eleonora Guerini, Marco Sabellico

TRE BICCHIERI 2016

VALLE D'AOSTA

Valle d'Aosta Chambave Moscato Passito Prieuré '13	La Crotta di Vegneron	27
Valle d'Aosta Chardonnay Cuvée Bois '13	Les Crêtes	27
Valle d'Aosta Petite Arvine '14	Elio Ottin	30
Valle d'Aosta Pinot Gris '14	Lo Triolet	29
Valle d'Aosta Pinot Noir Semel Pater '13	Maison Anselmet	26
Valle d'Aosta Syrah '13	Rosset Terroir	31

PIEDMONT

Alta Langa Brut Zero Cantina Maestra '09	Enrico Serafino	163
Barbaresco Albesani S. Stefano '12	Castello di Neive	79
Barbaresco Asili '12	Ca' del Baio	63
Barbaresco Asili '12	Bruno Giacosa	106
Barbaresco Boito Ris. '10	Rizzi	150
Barbaresco Crichët Pajé '06	I Paglieri - Roagna	135
Barbaresco Gallina '11	Piero Busso	62
Barbaresco Marcorino '12	Cantina del Glicine	66
Barbaresco Ris. '10	Sottimano	165
Barbaresco Serraboella '11	F.lli Cigliuti	85
Barbera d'Asti Pomorosso '12	Coppo	91
Barbera d'Asti Sup. Genio '12	Gianni Doglia	96
Barbera d'Asti Sup. La Mandorla '13	Luigi Spertino	166
Barbera d'Asti Sup. Nizza '12	Tenuta Olim Bauda	134
Barbera d'Asti Sup. Nizza A Luigi Veronelli '12	Brema	57
Barbera d'Asti Sup. Nizza La Court '12	Michele Chiarlo	83
Barbera del M.to Sup. Bricco Battista '12	Giulio Accornero e Figli	36
Barbera del M.to Sup. Le Cave '13	Castello di Uviglie	81
Barolo '11	Bartolo Mascarello	122
Barolo Acclivi '11	G. B. Burlotto	61
Barolo Bric dël Fiasc '11	Paolo Scavino	160
Barolo Bricco Rocche '11	Ceretto	83
Barolo Broglio '11	Schiavenza	161
Barolo Brunate '11	Mario Marengo	120
Barolo Brunate '11	Giuseppe Rinaldi	149
Barolo Bussia '11	Giacomo Fenocchio	98
Barolo Cannubi '11	Poderi Luigi Einaudi	97
Barolo Cannubi '11	Marchesi di Barolo	119
Barolo Cannubi '11	E. Pira & Figli - Chiara Boschis	142
Barolo Cannubi Boschis '11	Luciano Sandrone	157
Barolo Cerviano '10	Abbona	34
Barolo Gallinotto '11	Mauro Molino	125
Barolo Gattera '11	Gianfranco Bovio	55
Barolo Giachini '11	Giovanni Corino	91
Barolo Gramolere '11	F.lli Alessandria	37
Barolo Liste '10	Giacomo Borgogno & Figli	53
Barolo Marenca '11	Luigi Pira	141
Barolo Monfortino Ris. '08	Giacomo Conterno	89
Barolo Monprivato '10	Giuseppe Mascarello e Figlio	123
Barolo Ornato '11	Pio Cesare	141
Barolo Parafada '11	Massolino	123

Franciacorta Dosage Zéro Noir		
Vintage Collection Ris. '06	Ca' del Bosco	225
Franciacorta Dosage Zero Secolo Novo Ris. '08	Le Marchesine	241
Franciacorta Dosaggio Zero Ris. '08	Lo Sparviere	251
Franciacorta Extra Brut '09	Ferghettina	235
Franciacorta Extra Brut Extrême Palazzo Lana Ris. '07	Guido Berlucchi & C.	219
Franciacorta Extra Brut Vittorio Moretti Ris. '08	Bellavista	218
Franciacorta Nature	Enrico Gatti	237
Lugana Molin '14	Cà Maiol	224
OP Pinot Nero Brut 1870 '11	F.lli Giorgi	238
OP Pinot Nero Giorgio Odero '12	Frecciarossa	237
OP Pinot Nero Noir '12	Tenuta Mazzolino	241
Pinot Nero Brut 64 '11	Calatroni	227
Valtellina Sfursat 5 Stelle '11	Nino Negri	245
Valtellina Sfursat Fruttaio Ca' Rizzieri '11	Aldo Rainoldi	248
Valtellina Sup. Dirupi Ris. '12	Dirupi	234
Valtellina Sup. Sassella Rocce Rosse Ris. '05	Ar.Pe.Pe.	217
Valtellina Sup. Sassella Sommarovina '13	Mamete Prevostini	240

TRENTINO

San Leonardo '10	Tenuta San Leonardo	285
Trentino Müller Thurgau V. delle Forche '14	La Vis/Valle di Cembra	280
Trento Brut Altemasi Graal Ris. '08	Cavit	275
Trento Brut Domini Nero '10	Abate Nero	272
Trento Brut Dosaggio Zero Opera Ris. '08	Opera Vitivinicola in Valdicembra	282
Trento Brut Methius Ris. '09	F.lli Dorigati	277
Trento Dosaggio Zero Ris. '10	Nicola Balter	273
Trento Extra Brut Lunelli Ris. '07	Ferrari	278
Trento Riserva del Fondatore 976 '05	Letrari	280
Vino Santo Arèle '06	Pravis	284

ALTO ADIGE

A. A. Cabernet Sauvignon Cor Römigberg '11	Alois Tenutae Lageder	317
A. A. Cabernet Sauvignon Lafòa '12	Cantina Produttori Colterenzio	296
A. A. Gewürztraminer Auratus Crescendo '14	Tenuta Ritterhof	312
A. A. Gewürztraminer Brenntal Ris. '12	Cantina Produttori Cortaccia	297
A. A. Lago di Caldaro Cl. Sup. Leuchtenburg '14	Erste+Neue	299
A. A. Lagrein Abtei Muri Ris. '12	Cantina Convento Muri-Gries	309
A. A. Lagrein Castel Ringberg Ris. '11	Elena Walch	321
A. A. Lagrein Staves Ris. '12	Tenuta Kornell	305
A. A. Lagrein Taber Ris. '13	Cantina Bolzano	293
A. A. Moscato Giallo Passito Serenade '12	Cantina di Caldaro	295
A. A. Müller Thurgau Feldmarschall von Fenner zu Fennberg '13	Tiefenbrunner	318
A. A. Pinot Bianco Praesulis '14	Gumphof - Markus Prackwieser	302
A. A. Pinot Bianco Sirmian '14	Cantina Nals Margreid	310
A. A. Pinot Bianco St. Valentin '13	Cantina Produttori San Michele Appiano	314
A. A. Pinot Bianco Tyrol '13	Cantina Meran Burggräfler	309
A. A. Pinot Nero Trattmann Mazon Ris. '12	Cantina Girlan	300

Verdicchio dei Castelli di Jesi Cl. Sup. Il Priore '13	Sparapani - Frati Bianchi	721
Verdicchio dei Castelli di Jesi Cl. Sup. Misco '14	Tenuta di Tavignano	723
Verdicchio dei Castelli di Jesi Cl. Sup. Podium '13	Gioacchino Garofoli	710
Verdicchio dei Castelli di Jesi Cl. Sup. Qudì '13	Roberto Venturi	726
Verdicchio dei Castelli di Jesi Cl. Sup. Vecchie Vigne '13	Umani Ronchi	724
Verdicchio di Matelica Cambrugiano Ris. '12	Belisario	696
Verdicchio di Matelica Collestefano '14	Collestefano	704

UMBRIA

Cervaro della Sala '13	Castello della Sala	741
Montefalco Sagrantino '12	Fattoria Colleallodole	743
Montefalco Sagrantino '11	Perticaia	750
Montefalco Sagrantino '11	Romanelli	752
Montefalco Sagrantino '10	Scacciadiavoli	753
Montefalco Sagrantino Campo alla Cerqua '11	Giampaolo Tabarrini	754
Montefalco Sagrantino Collenottolo '11	Tenuta Bellafonte	737
Montefalco Sagrantino Collepiano '11	Arnaldo Caprai	739
Spoleto Trebbiano Spoletino Trebium '14	Antonelli - San Marco	736
Torgiano Rosso V. Monticchio Ris. '10	Lungarotti	747

LAZIO

Antium Bellone '14	Casale del Giglio	763
Baccarossa '13	Poggio Le Volpi	770
Fiorano Bianco '13	Tenuta di Fiorano	771
Frascati Sup. Eremo Tuscolano '13	Valle Vermiglia	772
Grechetto '14	Trappolini	772
Grechetto Poggio della Costa '14	Sergio Mottura	767
Montiano '13	Falesco	766

ABRUZZO

Abruzzo Pecorino '14	Tenuta I Fauri	786
Montepulciano d'Abruzzo '13	Tiberio	791
Montepulciano d'Abruzzo Cerasuolo Le Cince '14	Nicoletta De Fermo	784
Montepulciano d'Abruzzo Colline Teramane Adrano '12	Villa Medoro	795
Montepulciano d'Abruzzo Colline Teramane Pieluni Ris. '10	Dino Illuminati	787
Montepulciano d'Abruzzo Mo Ris. '11	Cantina Tollo	792
Montepulciano d'Abruzzo Malandrino '13	Luigi Cataldi Madonna	781
Montepulciano d'Abruzzo Marina Cvetic '13	Masciarelli	787
Montepulciano d'Abruzzo Nativae '14	Tenuta Ulisse	793
Montepulciano d'Abruzzo Podere Castorani Ris. '10	Castorani	780
Montepulciano d'Abruzzo S. Clemente Ris. '12	Ciccio Zaccagnini	795
Montepulciano d'Abruzzo Spelt Ris. '11	La Valentina	793
Trebbiano d'Abruzzo '12	Valentini	794
Trebbiano d'Abruzzo V. di Capestrano '13	Valle Reale	794

MOLISE

Molise Rosso Don Luigi Ris. '12	Di Majo Norante	801

CAMPANIA

Costa d'Amalfi Bianco Per Eva '13	Tenuta San Francesco	824
Costa d'Amalfi Bianco Puntacroce '14	Raffaele Palma	820
Costa d'Amalfi Furore Bianco Fiorduva '14	Marisa Cuomo	809
Falanghina del Sannio Biancuzita '12	Torre a Oriente	829
Falanghina del Sannio Janare '14	La Guardiense	815
Falanghina del Sannio Svelato '14	Terre Stregate	828
Falanghina del Sannio Taburno '14	Fontanavecchia	813
Fiano di Avellino '14	Colli di Lapio	807
Fiano di Avellino '13	Rocca del Principe	824
Fiano di Avellino 22 '13	Villa Raiano	831
Fiano di Avellino Clos d'Haut '13	Villa Diamante	830
Greco di Tufo '13	Fonzone	814
Greco di Tufo '14	Pietracupa	822
Greco di Tufo Claudio Quarta '13	Sanpaolo	
	Magistravini di Claudio Quarta	825
Greco di Tufo V. Cicogna '14	Benito Ferrara	812
Le Sèrole Pallagrello Bianco '13	Terre del Principe	827
Pallagrello Bianco Caiatì Morrone '13	Alois	804
Pian di Stio '14	San Salvatore	825
Taurasi '10	Contrade di Taurasi	808
Taurasi '07	Perillo	821
Terra di Lavoro '13	Galardi	815

BASILICATA

Aglianico del Vulture Il Repertorio '13	Cantine del Notaio	842
Aglianico del Vulture Serpara '10+	Re Manfredi - Terre degli Svevi	846
Aglianico del Vulture Titolo '13	Elena Fucci	844

PUGLIA

Castel del Monte Rosso V. Pedale Ris. '12	Torrevento	865
Gioia del Colle Primitivo 17 Vign. Montevella '12	Polvanera	861
Gioia del Colle Primitivo Et. Nera Contrada San Pietro '13	Plantamura	861
Gioia del Colle Primitivo Marpione Ris. '11	Tenuta Viglione	867
Gioia del Colle Primitivo Muro Sant'Angelo Contrada Barbatto '12	Chiaromonte	854
Masseria Maime '12	Tormaresca	864
Negroamaro '13	Carvinea	853
Primitivo di Manduria Raccontami '13	Futura 14	856
Primitivo di Manduria Talò '13	Cantine San Marzano	853
Primitivo di Manduria Zinfandel Sinfarosa '13	Racemi	862
Salice Salentino Rosso Per Lui Ris. '13	Leone de Castris	858
Salice Salentino Rosso Selvarossa Ris. '12	Cantine Due Palme	855
Torre Testa '13	Tenute Rubino	863

CALABRIA

Grisara '14	Roberto Ceraudo	876
Magno Megonio '13	Librandi	878
Moscato Passito '14	Luigi Viola	881

SICILY

Cerasuolo di Vittoria Cl. Dorilli '13	Planeta	902
Cerasuolo di Vittoria Giambattista Valli Paris '11	Feudi del Pisciotto	893
Contea di Sclafani Riserva del Conte '10	Tasca d'Almerita	906
Etna Bianco A' Puddara '13	Tenuta di Fessina	893
Etna Rosso Arcurìa '13	Graci	897
Etna Rosso Calderara Sottana '13	Tenuta delle Terre Nere	907
Etna Rosso San Lorenzo '13	Girolamo Russo	904
Etna Rosso V. Barbagalli '12	Pietradolce	901
Etna Rosso Zottorinoto Ris. '11	Cottanera	890
Faro '13	Le Casematte	889
Harmonium '13	Firriato	895
Lorlando '14	Alliata	887
Marsala Sup. Semisecco Targa 1840 Ris. '04	Cantine Florio	896
Saia '13	Feudo Maccari	894
Sicilia Bianco Maggiore '14	Rallo	903
Sicilia Deliella '13	Feudo Principi di Butera	895
Sicilia Noà '13	Cusumano	891
Sicilia Rosso Ramione '13	Baglio di Pianetto	888
Tancredi '11	Donnafugata	891
Timperosse Mandrarossa '14	Settesoli	905

SARDINIA

Barrua '12	Agricola Punica	930
Cannonau di Sardegna Cl. D53 '12	Cantina Dorgali	923
Cannonau di Sardegna Cl. Dule '12	Giuseppe Gabbas	924
Cannonau di Sardegna Mamuthone '12	Giuseppe Sedilesu	932
Capichera '13	Capichera	920
Carignano del Sulcis Buio Buio Ris. '12	Mesa	927
Carignano del Sulcis Sup. Terre Brune '11	Cantina di Santadi	931
Turriga '11	Argiolas	920
Vermentino di Gallura Canayli V. T. '14	Cantina Gallura	924
Vermentino di Gallura Sup. Maìa '14	Siddùra	933
Vermentino di Gallura Sup. Monteoro '14	Tenute Sella & Mosca	933
Vermentino di Gallura Sup. Sciala '14	Vigne Surrau	935
Vermentino di Sardegna Stellato '14	Pala	929

THE BEST

RED OF THE YEAR
ETNA ROSSO V. BARBAGALLI '12 – PIETRADOLCE

WHITE OF THE YEAR
COLLIO FRIULANO '14 - SCHIOPETTO

SPARKLER OF THE YEAR
FRANCIACORTA DOSAGE ZÉRO NOIR VINTAGE COLLECTION RIS. '06 – CA' DEL BOSCO

SWEET OF THE YEAR
VALLE D'AOSTA CHAMBAVE MOSCATO PASSITO PRIEURÉ '13 – LA CROTTA DI VEGNERON

WINERY OF THE YEAR

ALLEGRINI

BEST VALUE FOR MONEY

FALANGHINA DEL SANNIO SVELATO '14 - TERRE STREGATE

GROWER OF THE YEAR

GIULIO GRASSO

UP-AND-COMING WINERY

GUADO AL MELO

AWARD FOR SUSTAINABLE VITICULTURE

MANINCOR

TRE BICCHIERI VERDI

The Tre Bicchieri Verdi award is applicable to wines produced with grapes from official organic and biodynamic certified plots. This year we have 80 such wines, accounting for just under 20% of our total listings. An important datum testifying how Italy's top wineries are now fully committed to the environmental process. There are more complex aspects, however, given that many wineries apply similar criteria but do not request certification, and that sustainability protocols are increasingly common among growers. From this year, we will be indicating those wineries by including the wording "Sustainable Winery" in their profiles.

A. A. Cabernet Sauvignon Cor Römigberg '11	Alois Tenutae Lageder	**Alto Adige**
A. A. Terlano Sauvignon Tannenberg '13	Manincor	**Alto Adige**
A. A. Valle Isarco Sylvaner '13	Garlider - Christian Kerschbaumer	**Alto Adige**
Aglianico del Vulture Il Repertorio '13	Cantine del Notaio	**Basilicata**
Amarone della Valpolicella Cl. Vign. di Ravazzol '11	Ca' La Bionda	**Veneto**
Amarone della Valpolicella Cl. Vign. Sant'Urbano '11	Viticoltori Speri	**Veneto**
Barolo Bricco Rocche '11	Ceretto	**Piedmont**
Barolo Cannubi '11	E. Pira & Figli - Chiara Boschis	**Piedmont**
Barolo Ravera '11	Elvio Cogno	**Piedmont**
Barolo Resa 56 '11	Brandini	**Piedmont**
Barolo Sarmassa '11	Giacomo Brezza & Figli	**Piedmont**
Barolo Villero '11	Brovia	**Piedmont**
Bolgheri Rosso Sup. Grattamacco '12	Podere Grattamacco	**Tuscany**
Bolgheri Rosso Sup. Atis '12	Guado al Melo	**Tuscany**
Brunello di Montalcino '10	Le Chiuse	**Tuscany**
Brunello di Montalcino '10	Poggio di Sotto	**Tuscany**
Brunello di Montalcino V. V. '10	Le Ragnaie	**Tuscany**
Castel del Monte Rosso V. Pedale Ris. '12	Torrevento	**Puglia**
Castelli di Jesi Verdicchio Cl.		
Il Cantico della Figura Ris. '12	Andrea Felici	**Marche**
Castelli di Jesi Verdicchio Cl. Villa Bucci Ris. '13	Bucci	**Marche**
Chianti Cl. '13	Badia a Coltibuono	**Tuscany**
Chianti Cl. '13	Bandini - Villa Pomona	**Tuscany**
Chianti Cl. '13	Castello di Volpaia	**Tuscany**
Chianti Cl. '12	Le Cinciole	**Tuscany**
Chianti Cl. '12	Villa Le Corti	**Tuscany**
Chianti Cl. '12	Podere Val delle Corti	**Tuscany**
Chianti Cl. Bugialla Ris. '12	Fattoria Poggerino	**Tuscany**
Colline Lucchesi Tenuta di Valgiano '12	Tenuta di Valgiano	**Tuscany**
Costa d'Amalfi Bianco Puntacroce '14	Raffaele Palma	**Campania**
Do ut des '12	Fattoria Carpineta Fontalpino	**Tuscany**
Duemani '12	Duemani	**Tuscany**
Etna Rosso Arcuria '13	Graci	**Sicily**
Etna Rosso Calderara Sottana '13	Tenuta delle Terre Nere	**Sicily**
Etna Rosso San Lorenzo '13	Girolamo Russo	**Sicily**
Faro '13	Le Casematte	**Sicily**
Fiano di Avellino '14	Colli di Lapio	**Campania**
Fiano di Avellino 22 '13	Villa Raiano	**Campania**
Fiano di Avellino Clos d'Haut '13	Villa Diamante	**Campania**
Flaccianello della Pieve '12	Fontodi	**Tuscany**
Franciacorta Brut Extreme Palazzo Lana Ris. '07	Guido Berlucchi & C.	**Lombardy**
Franciacorta Brut Naturae '11	Barone Pizzini	**Lombardy**
Gioia del Colle Primitivo 17 Vign. Montevella '12	Polvanera	**Puglia**
Gioia del Colle Primitivo Et. Nera		
Contrada San Pietro '13	Plantamura	**Puglia**
Gioia del Colle Primitivo Marpione Ris. '11	Tenuta Viglione	**Puglia**
Gioia del Colle Primitivo Muro Sant'Angelo		
Contrada Barbatto '12	Chiaromonte	**Puglia**

Grechetto Poggio della Costa '14	Sergio Mottura	Lazio
Grisara '14	Roberto Ceraudo	Calabria
Harmonium '13	Firriato	Sicily
Maremma Toscana Sangiovese		
Podere San Cristoforo '13	Podere San Cristoforo	Tuscany
Masseria Maime '12	Tormaresca	Puglia
Molise Rosso Don Luigi Ris. '12	Di Majo Norante	Molise
Montecucco Sangiovese Lombrone Ris. '11	Colle Massari	Tuscany
Montepulciano d'Abruzzo Cerasuolo Le Cince '14	Nicoletta De Fermo	Abruzzo
Montepulciano d'Abruzzo Spelt Ris. '11	La Valentina	Abruzzo
Moscato Passito '14	Luigi Viola	Calabria
Negroamaro '13	Carvinea	Puglia
Nobile di Montepulciano Salco '11	Salcheto	Tuscany
Offida Pecorino Donna Orgilla '14	Fiorano	Marche
Pian di Stio '14	San Salvatore	Campania
Piceno Morellone '10	Le Caniette	Marche
Roero Mompissano Ris. '12	Cascina Ca' Rossa	Piedmont
Romagna Sangiovese Sup. Avi Ris. '11	San Patrignano	Emilia Romagna
Salice Salentino Rosso Selvarossa Ris. '12	Cantine Due Palme	Puglia
Sicilia Bianco Maggiore '14	Rallo	Sicily
Soave Cl. Ca' Visco '14	Coffele	Veneto
Soave Cl. Calvarino '13	Leonildo Pieropan	Veneto
Soave Cl. Staforte '13	Graziano Prà	Veneto
Spoleto Trebbiano Spoletino Trebium '14	Antonelli - San Marco	Umbria
Taurasi '10	Contrade di Taurasi	Campania
Terra di Lavoro '13	Galardi	Campania
Terre di Pisa Nambrot '12	Tenuta di Ghizzano	Tuscany
Torgiano Rosso V. Monticchio Ris. '10	Lungarotti	Umbria
Trebbiano d'Abruzzo V. di Capestrano '13	Valle Reale	Abruzzo
Trentino Müller Thurgau V. delle Forche '14	La Vis/Valle di Cembra	Trentino
Valdobbiadene Brut Prior '14	Bortolomiol	Veneto
Valpolicella Sup. '13	Musella	Veneto
Verdicchio dei Castelli di Jesi Cl. Sup.		
Vecchie Vigne '13	Umani Ronchi	Marche
Verdicchio di Matelica Collestefano '14	Collestefano	Marche
Vernaccia di S. Gimignano Carato '11	Montenidoli	Tuscany
Vernaccia di S. Gimignano l'Albereta Ris. '12	Il Colombaio di Santa Chiara	Tuscany

TABLE OF VINTAGES
FROM 1990 TO 2014

	BARBARESCO BAROLO	AMARONE	CHIANTI CLASSICO	BRUNELLO DI MONTALCINO	BOLGHERI	TAURASI	MONTEPULCIANO D'ABRUZZO
1990	5	4	4	5	5	5	4
1995	2	5	4	4	4	4	5
1996	5	3	3	2	3	5	5
1997	3	4	4	5	4	4	5
1999	4	3	5	5	5	5	2
2000	4	4	4	3	3	2	4
2001	5	4	4	5	5	4	4
2003	2	2	2	2	1	3	3
2004	5	4	4	4	4	4	4
2005	3	4	3	3	4	3	4
2006	5	4	4	5	5	3	3
2007	4	5	4	4	5	4	4
2008	4	4	4	4	5	4	4
2009	4	4	4	3	5	4	2
2010	5	5	5	5	4	2	2
2011	4	3	3		4		4
2012	3		3		4		3
2013			4				

	ALTO ADIGE BIANCO	LUGANA SOAVE	FRIULI BIANCO	VERDICCHIO DEI CASTELLI DI JESI	FIANO DI AVELLINO	GRECO DI TUFO
2004	4	4	4	5	4	4
2005	4	3		4	3	1
2006	3	3	5	5	4	4
2007	3		4	4	3	
2008	3	3		4	4	4
2009	4	4	4	4	4	4
2010	5	3	3		4	4
2011	3	3	3	1	3	3
2012	3	3	3	4	4	4
2013	4	3	4	4	4	4
2014	3		3	3	4	3

STARS

Stars are awarded to wineries that have won a Tre Bicchieri at least ten times. There are currently 209 "stellar cellars" across the Guide's 29 editions. These are the elite of Italian oenology, a ranking led for years by Angelo Gaja, who now has 53 awards under his belt. He is followed by Ca' del Bosco, scoring its fourth star along with the Sparkler of the Years prize. Behind them we find La Spinetta (38), Elio Altare (34). Still at three stars, Allegrini, Castello di Fonterutoli and Valentini. We welcome new entries to the club of stars: Abate Nero, Giulio Accornero e Figli, Ca' del Baio, Cavalchina, F.lli Cigliuti, Eugenio Collavini, Cantina Produttori di Cortaccia, Elena Fucci, Ettore Germano, Franz Haas e Köfererhof – Günther Kerschbaumer, Mamete Prevostini, Monchiero Carbone, Cantina Nals Margreid.

★★★★★
53
Gaja (Piedmont)

★★★★
40
Ca' del Bosco (Lombardy)

★★★
38
La Spinetta (Piedmont)
34
Elio Altare (Piedmont)
31
Allegrini (Veneto)
Castello di Fonterutoli (Tuscany)
Valentini (Abruzzo)

★★
28
Fattoria di Felsina (Tuscany)
27
Giacomo Conterno (Piedmont)
Jermann (Friuli Venezia Giulia)
Masciarelli (Abruzzo)
Tenuta San Guido (Tuscany)
Cantina Produttori San Michele Appiano
(Alto Adige)
26
Bellavista (Lombardy)
Castello della Sala (Umbria)
Ferrari (Alto Adige)
Planeta (Sicily)
25
Poliziano (Tuscany)
Tasca d'Almerita (Sicily)
Vie di Romans (Friuli Venezia Giulia)
24
Marchesi Antinori (Tuscany)
Castello di Ama (Tuscany)
Feudi di San Gregorio (Campania)
Cantina Tramin (Alto Adige)
23
Livio Felluga (Friuli Venezia Giulia)
Bruno Giacosa (Piedmont)
Gravner (Friuli Venezia Giulia)
Ornellaia (Tuscany)
Leonildo Pieropan (Veneto)
22
Argiolas (Sardinia)
Domenico Clerico (Piedmont)

Fontodi (Tuscany)
Paolo Scavino (Piedmont)
Villa Russiz (Friuli Venezia Giulia)
21
Cantina Bolzano (Alto Adige)
Arnaldo Caprai (Umbria)
Nino Negri (Lombardy)
Schiopetto (Friuli Venezia Giulia)
20
Barone Ricasoli (Tuscany)
Cascina La Barbatella (Piedmont)
Michele Chiarlo (Piedmont)
Dorigo (Friuli Venezia Giulia)
Falesco (Umbria)
Isole e Olena (Tuscany)
Tenute Sella & Mosca (Sardinia)
Cantina Terlano (Alto Adige)
Elena Walch (Alto Adige)

★
19
Ca' Viola (Piedmont)
Cantina di Caldaro (Alto Adige)
Castello del Terriccio (Tuscany)
Cantina Produttori Colterenzio (Alto Adige)
Montevetrano (Campania)
Tenuta San Leonardo (Alto Adige)
Venica & Venica (Friuli Venezia Giulia)
Vietti (Piedmont)
18
Castello Banfi (Tuscany)
Matteo Correggia (Piedmont)
Les Crêtes (Valle d'Aosta)
Cusumano (Sicily)
Gioacchino Garofoli (Marche)
Elio Grasso (Piedmont)
Mastroberardino (Campania)
Ruffino (Tuscany)
Luciano Sandrone (Piedmont)
Serafini & Vidotto (Veneto)
Franco Toros (Friuli Venezia Giulia)
Volpe Pasini (Friuli Venezia Giulia)
17
Abbazia di Novacella (Alto Adige)
Ca' Rugate (Veneto)
Casanova di Neri (Tuscany)
Castellare di Castellina (Tuscany)
Conterno Fantino (Piedmont)
Lis Neris (Friuli Venezia Giulia)
Le Macchiole (Tuscany)
Montevertine (Tuscany)
Querciabella (Tuscany)

332

Le Vigne di Zamò (Friuli Venezia Giulia)
Fattoria Zerbina (Emilia Romagna)

16
Brancaia (Tuscany)
Luigi Cataldi Madonna (Abruzzo)
Aldo Conterno (Piedmont)
Romano Dal Forno (Veneto)
Donnafugata (Sicily)
Massolino (Piedmont)
Miani (Friuli Venezia Giulia)
Cantina Convento Muri-Gries (Alto Adige)
Palari (Sicily)
Giuseppe Quintarelli (Veneto)
Cantina di Santadi (Sardinia)
Sottimano (Piedmont)

15
Roberto Anselmi (Veneto)
Antoniolo (Piedmont)
Firriato (Sicily)
Kuenhof - Peter Pliger (Alto Adige)
Livon (Friuli Venezia Giulia)
Masi (Veneto)
Monsupello (Lombardy)
Fiorenzo Nada (Piedmont)
Fattoria Petrolo (Tuscany)
Albino Rocca (Piedmont)
Bruno Rocca (Piedmont)
Ronco dei Tassi (Friuli Venezia Giulia)
San Patrignano (Emilia Romagna)
Umani Ronchi (Marche)
Roberto Voerzio (Piedmont)

14
Avignonesi (Tuscany)
Lorenzo Begali (Veneto)
Bricco Rocche - Bricco Asili (Piedmont)
Bucci (Marche)
Coppo (Piedmont)
Franco M. Martinetti (Piedmont)
Doro Princic (Friuli Venezia Giulia)
Produttori del Barbaresco (Piedmont)
Ronco del Gelso (Friuli Venezia Giulia)
Uberti (Lombardy)
Velenosi (Marche)

13
Cav. G. B. Bertani (Veneto)
Biondi Santi - Tenuta Il Greppo (Tuscany)
Cavalleri (Lombardy)
Cavit (Alto Adige)
Le Due Terre (Friuli Venezia Giulia)
Poderi Luigi Einaudi (Piedmont)
Foradori (Trentino)
Tenuta di Ghizzano (Tuscany)
Edi Keber (Friuli Venezia Giulia)
Librandi (Calabria)
Maculan (Veneto)
Malvirà (Piedmont)
Bartolo Mascarello (Piedmont)
La Monacesca (Marche)
Oasi degli Angeli (Marche)
Pecchenino (Piedmont)
Tenuta Sant'Antonio (Veneto)
Viticoltori Speri (Veneto)
Suavia (Veneto)
Tormaresca (Puglia)
Tua Rita (Tuscany)
Tenuta Unterortl - Castel Juval (Alto Adige)
Vignalta (Veneto)
Viviani (Veneto)

12
Abbona (Piedmont)
Braida (Piedmont)

Piero Busso (Piedmont)
Castello dei Rampolla (Tuscany)
Tenute Cisa Asinari dei Marchesi di Grésy (Piedmont)
Tenuta Col d'Orcia (Tuscany)
Còlpetrone (Umbria)
Di Majo Norante (Molise)
Falkenstein - Franz Pratzner (Alto Adige)
Tenute Ambrogio e Giovanni Folonari (Tuscany)
Galardi (Campania)
Gini (Veneto)
Podere Grattamacco (Tuscany)
Dino Illuminati (Abruzzo)
Lungarotti (Umbria)
Pietracupa (Campania)
Graziano Prà (Veneto)
Dario Raccaro (Friuli Venezia Giulia)
Rocca di Frassinello (Tuscany)
Rocche dei Manzoni (Piedmont)
San Felice (Tuscany)

11
F.lli Alessandria (Piedmont)
Gianfranco Alessandria (Piedmont)
Azelia (Piedmont)
Benanti (Sicily)
Borgo San Daniele (Friuli Venezia Giulia)
Poderi Boscarelli (Tuscany)
La Cerbaiola (Tuscany)
Elvio Cogno (Piedmont)
F.lli Dorigati (Trentino)
Ferghettina (Lombardy)
Marchesi de' Frescobaldi (Tuscany)
Leone de Castris (Puglia)
Marchesi di Barolo (Piedmont)
La Massa (Tuscany)
Sergio Mottura (Lazio)
Piaggia (Tuscany)
Prunotto (Piedmont)
Fattoria Le Pupille (Tuscany)
Aldo Rainoldi (Lombardy)
Russiz Superiore (Friuli Venezia Giulia)
Tenuta di Valgiano (Tuscany)
Valle Reale (Abruzzo)
Vigneti Massa (Piedmont)
Villa Medoro (Abruzzo)
Villa Sparina (Piedmont)

10
Abate Nero (Trentino)
Giulio Accornero e Figli (Piedmont)
Brigaldara (Veneto)
Ca' del Baio (Piedmont)
Cavalchina (Veneto)
F.lli Cigliuti (Piedmont)
Eugenio Collavini (Friuli Venezia Giulia)
Cantina Produttori Cortaccia (Alto Adige)
Elena Fucci (Basilicata)
Ettore Germano (Piedmont)
Franz Haas (Alto Adige)
Hilberg - Pasquero (Piedmont)
Tenuta J. Hofstätter (Alto Adige)
Köfererhof - Günther Kerschbaumer (Alto Adige)
Mamete Prevostini (Lombardy)
Monchiero Carbone (Piedmont)
Monte Rossa (Lombardy)
Cantina Nals Margreid (Alto Adige)
Poggio Antico (Tuscany)
G. D. Vajra (Piedmont)
Villa Matilde (Campania)
Conti Zecca (Puglia)
Zenato (Veneto)

HOW TO USE THE GUIDE

WINERY INFORMATION
ANNUAL PRODUCTION
HECTARES UNDER VINE
VITICULTURE METHOD

SYMBOLS
O WHITE WINE
⊙ ROSÈ
● RED WINE

RATINGS

MODERATELY GOOD TO GOOD WINES IN THEIR RESPECTIVE CATEGORIES
VERY GOOD TO EXCELLENT WINES IN THEIR RESPECTIVE CATEGORIES
VERY GOOD TO EXCELLENT WINES THAT WENT FORWARD TO THE FINAL TASTINGS
EXCELLENT WINES IN THEIR RESPECTIVE CATEGORIES

WINES RATED IN PREVIOUS EDITIONS OF THE GUIDE ARE INDICATED BY WHITE GLASSES (Ⴤ, ႾჃ, ჃჃჃ),
PROVIDED THEY ARE STILL DRINKING AT THE LEVEL FOR WHICH THE ORIGINAL AWARD WAS MADE.

STAR ★
INDICATES WINERIES THAT HAVE WON TEN TRE BICCHIERI AWARDS FOR EACH STAR

PRICE RANGES

1 up to 5 euro	2 from € 5.01 to € 10.00
3 from € 10.01 to € 15.00	4 from € 15.01 to € 20.00
5 from € 20.01 to € 30.00	6 from € 30.01 to € 40.00
7 from € 40.01 to € 50.00	8 more than € 50.01

PRICES INDICATED REFER TO AVERAGE PRICES IN WINE STORES

ASTERISK *
INDICATES ESPECIALLY GOOD VALUE WINES

ABBREVIATIONS

A. A.	Alto Adige	P.R.	Peduncolo Rosso (red bunchstem)
C.	Colli		
Cl.	Classico	P.	Prosecco
C.S.	Cantina Sociale (co-operative winery)	Rif. Agr.	Riforma Agraria (agrarian reform)
CEV	Colli Etruschi Viterbesi	Ris.	Riserva
Cons.	Consorzio	Sel.	Selezione
Coop.Agr.	Cooperativa Agricola (farming co-operative)	Sup.	Superiore
		TdF	Terre di Franciacorta
C. B.	Colli Bolognesi	V.	Vigna (vineyard)
C. P.	Colli Piacentini	Vign.	Vigneto (vineyard)
Et.	Etichetta (label)	V. T.	Vendemmia Tardiva (late harvest)
FCO	Friuli Colli Orientali		
M.	Metodo (method)	V. V.	Vecchia Vigna/Vecchie Vigne (old vine /old vines)
M.to	Monferrato		
OP	Oltrepò Pavese		

VALLE D'AOSTA

Valle d'Aosta viticulture offers one of the most fascinating profiles in terms of landscape and native varieties. This year our tasting showed a significant growth among those producers who are not satisfied with just making a good and easily marketable product, but try to express through and through the power of these amazing high-altitude vineyards and native Aosta Valley vines. Best news first: this year Valle d'Aosta took home one of the special prizes, Sweet Wine of the Year, for a stellar 2013 Chambave Moscato Passito: Crotta di Vegneron's Prieuré. The number of awarded-winning wines has also grown, and there are now six, which is an all-time high for Aosta. The three whites are classics: Costantino Charrère's 2013 Cuvée Bois, in a textured, elegant performance; Elio Ottin's delicate, elegant 2014 Petite Arvine; and Marco Martin's Lo Triolet intense, well-balanced 2014 Pinot Gris. More good news comes from the red wine sector, with some distinguished Fumins, Cornalins, Mayolets and Vuillermins, as well as Nebbiolos from top winegrowers. At the end of the day, the best were judged to be two stunning reds: a 2013 Pinot Noir Semel Pater from Giorgio Anselmet, and a welcome new entry this year, Nicola Rosset's elegant, spicy, savoury 2013 Syrah. Two international vines, certainly, but in the sunny aspecting of this valley they have found an ideal habitat, allowing them to express their varietal character with finesse and without sacrificing their typical Alpine imprinting. Exceptionally positive signals that allow us to observe the future with great optimism. Young people are coming back to work the valiant mountain vineyards, determined to weave increasingly local products of great appeal, which must be accompanied by the unbelievable legacy of tradition and the wealth of native varieties. No other region of Italy, or in the world for that matter, grows vines at over 1,200 metres in altitude. No other terroir vaunts a tradition dating back thousands of years of mountain viticulture like that of the Aosta Valley. The magic of these old wines, which have truly challenged nature, offsets the only drawback in this lovely story, which is that they are very difficult to get hold of!

VALLE D'AOSTA

Maison Anselmet

FRAZ. VEREYTAZ, 30
11018 VILLENEUVE [AO]
TEL. 3484127121
www.maisonanselmet.it

CELLAR SALES
PRE-BOOKED VISITS
ANNUAL PRODUCTION 70,000 bottles
HECTARES UNDER VINE 8.00

Maison Anselmet is a regional icon for viticulture heading towards the future. Giorgio Anselmet's observant and innovative spirit forged the way for his wines, rooted in tradition and driven by modernization, winning over an increasingly demanding market. The winery operates in an area to the north of the region, in Villeneuve, on the road to Mont Blanc. Always on hand to explain the wines and the philosophy, Giorgio and his father Renato run a modern cellar that makes no secret of its traditional inspiration. Chardonnay Élevé en Fût de Chêne has always been the flagship here but this year Giorgio took our breath away with his Semel Pater 2013. The elegant, vibrant Pinot Nero, dedicated to his father, has spicy overtones, balance and irresistible well-defined wild strawberries and blackcurrants. The well-typed Fumin 2013 is untamed, harmonious and well-balanced. A Müller Thurgau 2014 is pleasantly fresh, with citrus notes.

Château Feuillet

LOC. CHÂTEAU FEUILLET, 12
11010 SAINT PIERRE
TEL. 3287673880
www.chateaufeuillet.vievini.it

CELLAR SALES
ACCOMMODATION AND RESTAURANT SERVICE
ANNUAL PRODUCTION 30,000 bottles
HECTARES UNDER VINE 5.00

Dynamic, resourceful and feisty are the perfect descriptors for Maurizio Fiorano, the driving force behind this pleasing cellar and its wines too. The winery works out of Saint Pierre, a sunny village north of Aosta, where climate and altitude guarantee elegant, quality wines that continue to improve with each passing year. We really liked the intense ruby Torrette Supérieur 2013, with a fruity nose of cherries and currant, ushering in a well-balanced, leisurely palate. The Petite Arvine 2014 is exceptionally true to type, showing mineral and floral, with hints of broom and white flowers, nuanced with citrus; the flavour is pleasantly balanced, fresh and clean. There are also mineral notes in the elegant, crisp Chardonnay 2014, with a generous nose which is fruit-rich as is the palate. A noteworthy Fumin offers an intense, inky colour and is rich and fruity in the mouth. Finally, the Syrah, with elegant tannins, recalls pepper notes that in no way overpower the fruit.

● Valle d'Aosta Pinot Noir Semel Pater '13	♟♟♟ 6
○ Valle d'Aosta Chardonnay Élevé en Fût de Chêne '14	♟♟ 5
● Valle d'Aosta Fumin Élevé en Fût de Chêne '13	♟♟ 4
○ Valle d'Aosta Chambave Muscat '14	♟♟ 3
○ Valle d'Aosta Chardonnay '14	♟♟ 3
○ Valle d'Aosta Müller Thurgau '14	♟♟ 3
○ Valle d'Aosta Petite Arvine '14	♟♟ 3
○ Valle d'Aosta Pinot Gris '14	♟♟ 3
○ Valle d'Aosta Chardonnay Élevé en Fût de Chêne '11	♟♟♟ 5
○ Valle d'Aosta Chardonnay Élevé en Fût de Chêne '10	♟♟♟ 5
○ Valle d'Aosta Chardonnay Élevé en Fût de Chêne '09	♟♟♟ 5

○ Valle d'Aosta Petite Arvine '14	♟♟ 3*
● Valle d'Aosta Torrette Sup. '13	♟♟ 3*
○ Valle d'Aosta Chardonnay '14	♟♟ 3
● Valle d'Aosta Fumin '14	♟♟ 4
● Valle d'Aosta Syrah '14	♟♟ 3
○ Valle d'Aosta Petite Arvine '12	♟♟♟ 3*
○ Valle d'Aosta Petite Arvine '11	♟♟♟ 3*
○ Valle d'Aosta Petite Arvine '10	♟♟♟ 3*
○ Valle d'Aosta Chardonnay '13	♟♟ 3*
● Valle d'Aosta Fumin '12	♟♟ 4
● Valle d'Aosta Fumin '09	♟♟ 4
○ Valle d'Aosta Petite Arvine '13	♟♟ 3*
● Valle d'Aosta Torrette Sup. '12	♟♟ 3*
● Valle d'Aosta Torrette Sup. '10	♟♟ 3*

★Les Crêtes

LOC. VILLETOS, 50
11010 AYMAVILLES [AO]
TEL. 0165902274
www.lescretes.it

CELLAR SALES
PRE-BOOKED VISITS
ANNUAL PRODUCTION 180,000 bottles
HECTARES UNDER VINE 20.00
SUSTAINABLE WINERY

Much has been written about Les Crêtes, but when it comes to Costantino Charrère and his family, there is still plenty to be said. The new cellar is now done and dusted although it lacks the finishing touch: the "multisensorial" tasting room to engage all five senses, next on Costantino's wish list, an authentic place of worship for wine aficionados. The new tasks for the near future include creation of a new vineyard but the variety to be planted is still a secret . . . A Tre Bicchieri goes to Chardonnay Cuvée Bois, a venerable Valle d'Aosta flagship in the wine world, where it holds its own against international competitors. The 2013 has lustrous colour, a nose which speaks of acacia flowers, showing unabashed fruit that ushers in cinnamon and vanilla spice; the tangy mouth is opulent but not oily, rich, fresh and leisurely. Both the floral Petite Arvine and the spicy Fumin are excellent.

○ Valle d'Aosta Chardonnay Cuvée Bois '13	▼▼▼	6
● Valle d'Aosta Fumin '12	▼▼	4
○ Valle d'Aosta Petite Arvine Fleur '14	▼▼	5
○ Valle d'Aosta Petite Arvine '14	▼▼	3
● Valle d'Aosta Syrah Coteau La Tour '13	▼▼	4
● Valle d'Aosta Torrette Sup. '14	▼▼	4
○ Valle d'Aosta Chardonnay Cuvée Bois '10	♀♀♀	6
○ Valle d'Aosta Chardonnay Cuvée Bois '09	♀♀♀	6
○ Valle d'Aosta Chardonnay Cuvée Bois '08	♀♀♀	6
○ Valle d'Aosta Chardonnay Cuvée Bois '07	♀♀♀	6
○ Valle d'Aosta Chardonnay Cuvée Bois '06	♀♀♀	6
○ Valle d'Aosta Chardonnay Cuvée Frissonnière Les Crêtes Cuvée Bois '05	♀♀♀	6
○ Valle d'Aosta Chardonnay Cuvée Frissonnière Les Crêtes Cuvée Bois '04	♀♀♀	5
○ Valle d'Aosta Petite Arvine '13	♀♀♀	3*

La Crotta di Vegneron

P.ZZA RONCAS, 2
11023 CHAMBAVE [AO]
TEL. 016646670
www.lacrotta.it

CELLAR SALES
PRE-BOOKED VISITS
RESTAURANT SERVICE
ANNUAL PRODUCTION 220,000 bottles
HECTARES UNDER VINE 34.00

Since ancient times bottles of Chambave have fuelled the souls of artists, writers and wine lovers. Today there are 120 growers in the cooperative, and their passion and commitment to tradition keep pace with the slow ripening of the grapes under the careful supervision of cellar technicians. A very extensive product range has led to an excellent market ranking and La Crotta's skill in raisining the grapes is a benchmark throughout the region. A Tre Bicchieri goes to Moscato Passito Prieuré 2013, one of the best of the year. It has a brilliant golden colour and an astonishing aromatic profile, opening on notes of apricot and peach that usher in floral nuances, followed by thyme, closing on dried fruit. The palate shows concentrated fruit, sweetness and, above all, freshness and elegance. Not to be missed. The Fumin Esprit Follet is typically untamed, with vegetal and fruit notes on the nose, and a rich and balanced structure. The Chambave Supérieur Quatre Vignobles 2013 is interesting, as is the dry version of the Chambave Muscat.

○ Valle d'Aosta Chambave Moscato Passito Prieuré '13	▼▼▼	5
● Valle d'Aosta Fumin Esprit Follet '13	▼▼	5
○ Valle d'Aosta Chambave Muscat '14	▼▼	3
● Valle d'Aosta Chambave Sup. Quatre Vignobles '13	▼▼	4
● Valle d'Aosta Pinot Noir '14	▼	3
○ Valle d'Aosta Chambave Moscato Passito Prieuré '12	♀♀♀	5
○ Valle d'Aosta Chambave Moscato Passito Prieuré '11	♀♀♀	5
○ Valle d'Aosta Chambave Moscato Passito Prieuré '08	♀♀♀	5
● Valle d'Aosta Fumin Esprit Follet '09	♀♀♀	3
● Valle d'Aosta Fumin Esprit Follet '07	♀♀♀	3*
● Valle d'Aosta Chambave Sup. Quatre Vignobles '12	♀♀	4

Di Barrò

Loc. Château Feuillet, 8
11010 Saint Pierre
Tel. 0165903671
www.dibarro.vievini.it

CELLAR SALES
PRE-BOOKED VISITS
ANNUAL PRODUCTION 20,000 bottles
HECTARES UNDER VINE 2.50

Torrette is the region's typical red from the petit rouge variety, and 11 municipalities are authorized for production. The wine takes its name from the zone and the Di Barrò winery lives in the heart of this terroir. The quality of the wines made by Elvira Rini and Andrea Barmaz has become a constant and a guarantee. The quest to ensure every label has varietal stamping is evident and while the production range is not huge the use of local clones alternated with several international cultivars takes these cellars to prominent market positions. This year we recommend the Torrette Supérieur Clos de Château Feuillet 2012, with an intriguing nose reminiscent of very ripe fruit and clear hints of cherry. The mouth also shows considerable complexity, with tannins still on the road to maturity. The well-structured Chardonnay is admirable, with an intense straw yellow colour and pleasant citrus notes rounded down by hints of honey. A mention also for the Torrette Supérieur Ostro 2009

Caves Cooperatives de Donnas

via Roma, 97
11020 Donnas [AO]
Tel. 0125807096
www.donnasvini.it

CELLAR SALES
PRE-BOOKED VISITS
ANNUAL PRODUCTION 150,000 bottles
HECTARES UNDER VINE 26.00

Terracing snatched from the mountain in sites almost impossible to access, reached by a monorail, is the birthplace of picotendro. This clone of the nebbiolo native to this area of the lower valley is trained on tall pergolas supported by small stone columns. Only the innate enthusiasm of the cooperative's vignerons keeps them committed to their work each year, and their offspring continues the work of their parents. Donnas is now a subdesignation of the Valle d'Aosta DOC, but in 1971 was the valley's first designation of origin. We liked the ruby red Donnas 2011, with it garnet nuances and hints of dried roses, ripe red berries and pleasantly delicate spicy notes; the palate is complex and leisurely. Napoléon 2012 is fresher, with more vibrant colour and lively hints of fruit on the palate. The Vieilles Vignes 2011 shows less finesse on the nose, with notes of very ripe red berries, salvaged only by the fresh, clean palate.

○ Valle d'Aosta Chardonnay '14	♥♥ 3
● Valle d'Aosta Fumin '11	♥♥ 4
● Valle d'Aosta Torrette Sup. Clos de Château Feuillet '12	♥♥ 3
● Valle d'Aosta Torrette Sup. Ostro '09	♥♥ 5
○ Lo Flapì	♥ 5
○ Valle d'Aosta Pinot Gris '13	♥ 3
○ Valle d'Aosta Chardonnay '12	♥♥♥ 3*
● Valle d'Aosta Torrette Sup. V. de Torrette '06	♥♥♥ 6
● Valle d'Aosta Fumin '09	♥♥ 4
● Valle d'Aosta Syrah V. de Conze '10	♥♥ 3
● Valle d'Aosta Torrette Sup. Clos de Château Feuillet '11	♥♥ 3*
● Valle d'Aosta Torrette Sup. Clos de Château Feuillet '10	♥♥ 3
● Valle d'Aosta Torrette Sup. Clos de Château Feuillet '09	♥♥ 3

● Valle d'Aosta Donnas '11	♥♥ 2*
● Valle d'Aosta Donnas Napoléon '12	♥ 2
● Valle d'Aosta Donnas Sup. V. V. '11	♥ 4
● Valle d'Aosta Donnas Napoléon '11	♥♥ 3
● Valle d'Aosta Donnas Napoléon '10	♥♥ 3
● Valle d'Aosta Donnas Napoléon '07	♥♥ 3
● Valle d'Aosta Donnas Napoléon '06	♥♥ 3
● Valle d'Aosta Donnas Napoléon '04	♥♥ 3
● Valle d'Aosta Donnas Sup. Napoleone '03	♥♥ 3
● Valle d'Aosta Donnas Sup. V. V. '07	♥♥ 4
● Valle d'Aosta Donnas Sup. V. V. Cavour '06	♥♥ 5
● Valle d'Aosta Donnas Sup. Vieilles Vignes '05	♥♥ 4
● Valle d'Aosta Donnas V. V. '09	♥♥ 4

Lo Triolet

LOC. JUNOD, 7
11010 INTROD [AO]
TEL. 016595437
www.lotriolet.vievini.it

CELLAR SALES
PRE-BOOKED VISITS
ANNUAL PRODUCTION 50,000 bottles
HECTARES UNDER VINE 5.00

Visitors heading to the Gran Paradiso Park pass right in front of Lo Triolet, Marco Martin's lovely Junod winery. So why not stop and enjoy local hospitality, with the excellent wines from the vineyards surrounding the winery? These are uncompromising, extreme wines and the Pinot Grigio is the best of them all. The Pinot Gris 2014 has a nice intense, bright straw-yellow colour and unleashes a feisty character with aromas of pear, flowers and smoky and pepper notes on the nose; the mouth shows backbone and harmony, with a champion's acidity and flesh, and a very long finish. This wine is still very young but is already well-orchestrated. The barriqued version acquires a vibrant, intense golden straw colour, and on the nose we find rich, slightly overdone notes of very ripe pears on a bed of spice and softwoods. This wine plays out on nose and palate complexity and intensity.

○ Valle d'Aosta Pinot Gris '14	🍷🍷🍷 3*
● Valle d'Aosta Fumin '13	🍷🍷 5
○ Valle d'Aosta Pinot Gris Élevé en Barriques '13	🍷🍷 5
○ Vallèe d'Aoste Muscat Petit Grain '14	🍷🍷 3
○ Valle d'Aosta Pinot Gris '13	🍷🍷🍷 3*
○ Valle d'Aosta Pinot Gris '12	🍷🍷🍷 3*
○ Valle d'Aosta Pinot Gris '09	🍷🍷🍷 3
○ Valle d'Aosta Pinot Gris '08	🍷🍷🍷 3*
○ Valle d'Aosta Pinot Gris '05	🍷🍷🍷 3*
○ Valle d'Aosta Pinot Gris Élevé en Barriques '10	🍷🍷🍷 5
● Valle d'Aosta Fumin '12	🍷🍷 5
● Valle d'Aosta Fumin '11	🍷🍷 3
○ Valle d'Aosta Pinot Gris Élevé en Barriques '12	🍷🍷 5
● Valle d'Aosta Rouge Coteau Barrage '12	🍷🍷 5

Cave du Mont Blanc de Morgex et La Salle

FRAZ. LA RUINE
CHEMIN DES ÎLES, 19
11017 MORGEX [AO]
TEL. 0165800331
www.cavemontblanc.com

CELLAR SALES
PRE-BOOKED VISITS
ANNUAL PRODUCTION 140,000 bottles
HECTARES UNDER VINE 19.00

Cave's production is centred around fresh, light wines echoing the aromas of the mountain. The priè blanc, still an ungrafted variety, has a very short growing season with late budding and early ripening, at incredible altitudes. When Horasse-Bénédict de Saussure, described the typical low Morgex pergola, which can only be tended by lying under it, he could not have imagined that one day the wine would become a regional flagship. The Piagne 2014 Blanc de Morgex was a pleasant surprise this year. The brilliant, lively greenish straw-yellow precedes an intense nose with pronounced notes of Granny Smith and mountain flowers, harmonized by rock mineral hints. It is subtle and appealing, with a well-defined mouth showing balanced acidity and flesh, signing off nice and long, with a hint of tartness in the finish. The Morgex 2014 is also interesting and the Metodo Classicos held their own. The sweet Chaudelune, made from later-harvest grapes, was as tempting as usual.

○ Valle d'Aosta Blanc de Morgex et de La Salle La Piagne '14	🍷 5
○ Valle d'Aosta Blanc de Morgex et de La Salle '14	🍷🍷 3
○ Valle d'Aosta Blanc de Morgex et de La Salle Chaudelune '12	🍷🍷 2*
○ Valle d'Aosta Blanc de Morgex et de La Salle Cuvée Gerbollier '11	🍷 8
○ Valle d'Aosta Blanc de Morgex et de La Salle Extra Brut '12	🍷 6
○ Valle d'Aosta Blanc de Morgex et de La Salle Rayon '13	🍷🍷 5
○ Valle d'Aosta Blanc de Morgex et de La Salle Vini Estremi '13	🍷🍷 5

Elio Ottin

FRAZ. POROSSAN NEYVES, 209
11100 AOSTA
TEL. 3474071331
www.ottinvini.it

CELLAR SALES
PRE-BOOKED VISITS
ANNUAL PRODUCTION 30,000 bottles
HECTARES UNDER VINE 4.50
SUSTAINABLE WINERY

Elio Ottin is an enthusiastic winemaker although his cellars have not been long on the market. We are certain that the quality of his wines, his courtesy and his attentive style will help him carve out a significant niche in the regional wine scenario. The winery can be found on the town's hill slope and the native vines are interspersed with some international varieties, but the result is always the same: cellarable, mouthfilling wines with the right attitude. The Petite Arvine is the quintessential expression of this typical Valle d'Aosta variety with a lively, bright straw-yellow colour, intense nose of elegant fruity and floral aromas with notes of citrus and vegetable nuances; the rich mouth is tangy and spirited. We also loved the Torrette Supérieur, with floral scents reminiscent of elderflower, notes of blackcurrant and hints of flint; the palate is rich, well-balanced and remarkably leisurely. The well-typed Fumin is austere and focused.

Ermes Pavese

S.DA PINETA, 26
11017 MORGEX [AO]
TEL. 0165800053
www.pavese.vievini.it

CELLAR SALES
PRE-BOOKED VISITS
ANNUAL PRODUCTION 35,000 bottles
HECTARES UNDER VINE 5.00

If vines are grown at 1,200 metres in altitude, with Mont Blanc looming overhead, it is no surprise that Valle d'Aosta viticulture is termed heroic. Ermes Pavese is a skilful traditional winemaker, a pioneering character who has been able to offer a new slant to priè blanc, a tricky variety on the physiological boundary of grape growing. The wines tasted from Ermes are the result of the work of an entire family, where young offspring are already out in the vineyard, breathing in the air of the vines and the cellar, absorbing tradition through their pores. Our favourite from the 2014 harvest is the base Blanc de Morgex et de La Salle, bright straw yellow with greenish reflections, bouquet of mountain herbs and white fruit, and with a layered, fresh palate. The Sette Scalinate 2013 is also admirable, with a complex nose expressing mineral notes woven with hints of white-fleshed fruit and touches of spice, and a long, fresh mouth. Marked spicy notes are also found in the fresh Nathan. Excellent sparklers here too.

○ Valle d'Aosta Petite Arvine '14	♟♟♟ 4*
● Valle d'Aosta Fumin '13	♟♟ 4
● Valle d'Aosta Torrette Sup. '13	♟♟ 4
● Valle d'Aosta Pinot Noir '13	♟♟ 4
○ Valle d'Aosta Petite Arvine Nuances '13	♟ 5
● Valle d'Aosta Fumin '12	♟♟♟ 3*
○ Valle d'Aosta Petite Arvine '12	♟♟♟ 3*
○ Valle d'Aosta Petite Arvine '11	♟♟♟ 3*
○ Valle d'Aosta Petite Arvine '10	♟♟♟ 3*
● Valle d'Aosta Fumin '11	♟♟ 3*
○ Valle d'Aosta Petite Arvine '13	♟♟ 3*
● Valle d'Aosta Pinot Noir '12	♟♟ 3
● Valle d'Aosta Pinot Noir '11	♟♟ 3
● Valle d'Aosta Torrette Sup. '12	♟♟ 4
● Valle d'Aosta Torrette Sup. '11	♟♟ 4

○ Valle d'Aosta Vin Blanc de Morgex et La Salle '14	♟♟ 2*
○ Valle d'Aosta Vin Blanc de Morgex et La Salle Le Sette Scalinate '13	♟♟ 8
○ Valle d'Aosta Vin Blanc de Morgex et La Salle Pavese Pas Dosé	♟♟ 3
○ Valle d'Aosta Vin Blanc de Morgex et La Salle Nathan '13	♟ 5
○ Valle d'Aosta Vin Blanc de Morgex et La Salle '13	♟♟ 2*
○ Valle d'Aosta Vin Blanc de Morgex et La Salle Le Sette Scalinate Carlo Pavese Ris. '11	♟♟ 6
○ Valle d'Aosta Vin Blanc de Morgex et La Salle Nathan '12	♟♟ 2*

Rosset Terroir

LOC. TORRENT DE MAILLOUD, 4
11020 QUART [AO]
TEL. 0165774111
www.rosseterroir.com

CELLAR SALES
PRE-BOOKED VISITS
ANNUAL PRODUCTION 15,000 bottles
HECTARES UNDER VINE 2.70

Rosset Terroir is a small, recently founded winery that has come to the fore in a short time for the authenticity of its products. Its strength is its link with the territory and particular attention to safeguarding the environment through careful application of sustainability protocols. In 2001, the Rosset family decided to plant a vineyard on land they own in the Senin district of Saint-Christophe. The three-hectare plot was initially planted with chardonnay, followed shortly thereafter by syrah and native cornalin, but the range is increasing. The Tre Bicchieri this year goes to the Syrah in well-deserved recognition of the passionate commitment of the Rossets and Matteo Moretto, the winery's agronomist and oenologist. The 2013 has typical hints of white pepper that open briskly to overtones of wild berries; the well-balanced palate is amazingly symmetrical and leisurely. The Cornalin has pervasive aromas; the Chardonnay is fresh and fruity.

● Valle d'Aosta Syrah '13	♛♛♛	4*
○ Valle d'Aosta Chardonnay '13	♛♛	4
● Valle d'Aosta Cornalin '13	♛♛	4
○ Valle d'Aosta Chardonnay '12	♛♛	4
○ Valle d'Aosta Chardonnay '07	♛♛	4
● Valle d'Aosta Syrah '12	♛♛	4
● Valle d'Aosta Syrah '07	♛♛	4
● Valle d'Aosta Syrah '06	♛♛	4

La Vrille

LOC. GRANGEON, 1
11020 VERRAYES [AO]
TEL. 0166543018
www.lavrille.it

CELLAR SALES
PRE-BOOKED VISITS
ACCOMMODATION AND RESTAURANT SERVICE
ANNUAL PRODUCTION 18,000 bottles
HECTARES UNDER VINE 2.30

La Vrille is on the road from Verrayes to Grangeon. This charming winery was set up 25 years ago by Hervé Deguillame and wife Luciana. Apart from the cellars, however, visitors can explore a wonderful landscape, staying a few days in the small hotel and eating in the restaurant where Luciana offers only what nature provides, served with the impeccable wines that Hervé brings to the table. Top of the range is the moscato bianco, but we also recommend fumin, cornalin and other natives that are part of the extensive production range made applying biodynamic procedures even though it is not officially certified. The Chambave Muscat Flétri 2013 has typical aromatic notes of flowers and fruit, harmonized by honey overtones; the mouth is balanced and pleasantly lingering. A very worthy typically untamed Fumin 2011 shows fruity aromas on the nose; the palate is well-orchestrated and well-structured. Always very pleasant, the Chambave Muscat shows not only the variety's classic aromas but also regales us with anise and cumin nuances.

○ Valle d'Aosta Chambave Muscat '13	♛♛	4
○ Valle d'Aosta Chambave Muscat Flétri '13	♛♛	7
● Valle d'Aosta Fumin '11	♛♛	5
○ Valle d'Aosta Chambave Muscat '12	♛♛♛	4*
○ Valle d'Aosta Chambave Muscat Flétri '11	♛♛♛	6
○ Valle d'Aosta Chambave Muscat Flétri '10	♛♛♛	5
○ Valle d'Aosta Chambave Muscat Flétri '07	♛♛♛	4*
○ Valle d'Aosta Chambave Muscat '11	♛♛	4
○ Valle d'Aosta Chambave Muscat Flétri '12	♛♛	7
● Valle d'Aosta Cornalin '13	♛♛	4
● Valle d'Aosta Fumin '10	♛♛	5

La Crotta de Tanteun e Marietta

VIA VEVEY, 23
11100 AOSTA
TEL. 3341822471
www.lacrottadetanteunemarietta.it

CELLAR SALES
PRE-BOOKED VISITS
ANNUAL PRODUCTION 10,000 bottles
HECTARES UNDER VINE 2.50

○ Valle d'Aosta Pinot Gris '13	♥♥	4
○ Valle d'Aosta Muscat Petit Grain '14	♥	5
● Valle d'Aosta Pinot Noir REM '13	♥	4

Feudo di San Maurizio

FRAZ. MAILLOD, 44
11010 SARRE [AO]
TEL. 3383186831
www.feudo.vievini.it

CELLAR SALES
PRE-BOOKED VISITS
ANNUAL PRODUCTION 40,000 bottles
HECTARES UNDER VINE 7.00

○ Valle d'Aosta Chardonnay '13	♥♥	3
● Valle d'Aosta Cornalin '13	♥	4
● Valle d'Aosta Fumin '13	♥	4

F.lli Grosjean

VILLAGGIO OLLIGNAN, 1
11020 QUART [AO]
TEL. 0165775791
www.grosjean.vievini.it

CELLAR SALES
PRE-BOOKED VISITS
ANNUAL PRODUCTION 90,000 bottles
HECTARES UNDER VINE 10.00
VITICULTURE METHOD Certified Organic

● Valle d'Aosta Pinot Noir '14	♥♥	4
○ Valle d'Aosta Chardonnay '14	♥	4
● Valle d'Aosta Fumin V. Rovettaz '11	♥	5
● Valle d'Aosta Pinot Noir V. Tzeriat '13	♥	4

Institut Agricole Régional

LOC. RÉGION LA ROCHÈRE, 1A
11100 AOSTA
TEL. 0165215811
www.iaraosta.it

CELLAR SALES
PRE-BOOKED VISITS
ANNUAL PRODUCTION 50,000 bottles
HECTARES UNDER VINE 7.30

○ Valle d'Aosta Nus Malvoisie '14	♥	2
○ Valle d'Aosta Petite Arvine '14	♥	3
● Valle d'Aosta Pinot Noir Sang des Salasses '13	♥	4

La Source

LOC. BUSSAN DESSOUS, 1
11010 SAINT PIERRE
TEL. 0165904038
www.lasource.it

CELLAR SALES
PRE-BOOKED VISITS
ANNUAL PRODUCTION 40,000 bottles
HECTARES UNDER VINE 7.00

○ Valle d'Aosta Chardonnay '14	♥♥	3*
● Valle d'Aosta Syrah '12	♥♥	3
○ Valle d'Aosta Petite Arvine '13	♥	3

Maison Albert Vevey

FRAZ. VILLAIR
S.DA DEL VILLAIR, 67
11017 MORGEX [AO]
TEL. 0165808930
www.vievini.it

CELLAR SALES
PRE-BOOKED VISITS
ANNUAL PRODUCTION 7,000 bottles
HECTARES UNDER VINE 1.50

○ Valle d'Aosta Blanc de Morgex et de La Salle '14	♥♥	4

PIEDMONT

On more than one occasion, when drafting the Piedmont regional introduction for the Guide, we have pointed out that alongside the platoon of different designations deriving from wonderful nebbiolo, there are wine districts of great interest and value. To hold on to this thought, for 2016 we would like to open by talking about the four Tre Bicchieri awards assigned to timorasso. In a world where people often claim they were they first to discover or promote an area, a producer or a wine, we can declare without fear of contradiction, that back in the mists of time we were the first to place our trust in the great potential of this grape. Moreover, we had faith in the entire group of producers, led by Walter Massa, who best expressed the varietal character, so we gave it visibility. Another important aspect of our work is our continuous search for new peaks of excellence and this year there were some significant new entries, many vaunting very affordable price tags: Rizzi, with a great 2010 Barbaresco Boito Riserva; Mazzoni, who presented a 2012 Ghemme dei Mazzoni that has earned its place among the great wines of northern Piedmont; Gaggino, with an Ovada Convivio 2013 that again testifies to the zone's dolcetto vocation; Gianni Doglia, who took his first Tre Bicchieri with a juicy, complex Barbera d'Asti Superiore Genio 201; Giovanni Corino, with a charming Barolo Giachini 2011, on the podium for the first time since his professional separation from brother Renato. These innovations, along with many deserving repeat performances, reveal Piedmont as a benchmark in domestic and world wine production. In this regard, as a fitting counterpart to the list of new awards, we should look at the regional map of some of the top awards taken home by brands known the world over, wineries that are gems in the Made-in-Italy crown: Giacomo Conterno, Gaja, Bruno Giacosa, Vietti, Pio Cesare, Elio Altare, to name just a few, all continuing to hold high the banner of their terroir around the world. Last, but not least, a tireless vigneron, Giulio Grasso of Ca' del Baio, is our Grower of the Year.

460 Casina Bric

Loc. Cascina Bricco
Fraz. Vergne
Via Sorello, 1a
12060 Barolo [CN]
Tel. 335283468
www.casinabric-barolo.com

CELLAR SALES
ANNUAL PRODUCTION 40,000 bottles
HECTARES UNDER VINE 8.00

Gianluca Viberti's first Barolo vintage was
the 2010, which was released in 2014, but
his wines have already made a name for
themselves among connoisseurs for their
elegance and balance. Most of the
vineyards are in the upper area of Barolo,
although the estate also has nebbiolo plots
in Alba, used for its Sparklers. Note the
unique bottle, which is not a quirky modern
design, but a faithful reproduction of the
classic "Poirinotta" used in the 18th
century. Barolo Bricco delle Viole 2011 has
repeated the brilliant result of its
predecessor, showing concentrated and
complex with attractive notes of dried
flowers, followed by a hint of liquorice on a
delicious fruity background. While not
overly powerful, the palate is very well
behaved, with fine-grained tannins and
alluring acidity ensuring vibrancy and
length. The basic Barolo of the same
vintage is less fresh and attractive on the
nose, but harmonious on the palate.

● Barolo Bricco delle Viole '11	♛♛♛ 7
● Barolo '11	♛♛ 6
☉ Gianluca Viberti Brut Rosè Collezione N°8 Prêt-à-Porter	♛ 4
● Ansj '11	♛♛ 4
● Barolo '10	♛♛ 6
● Barolo Bricco delle Viole '10	♛♛ 7

★Abbona

Loc. San Luigi
B.ta San Luigi, 40
12063 Dogliani [CN]
Tel. 0173721317
www.abbona.com

CELLAR SALES
PRE-BOOKED VISITS
ANNUAL PRODUCTION 250,000 bottles
HECTARES UNDER VINE 50.00

Abbona has always invested great
commitment in what it does. No sooner
was the handsome underground cellar
completed, than work was commenced
above its vaults on a large holiday farm,
which also promises to be spectacular.
However, the style of the estate's wines
remains the same, classically austere for
both the steel-aged Dogliani and the
Barolo, aged in large barrels. The wide
range features all the traditional Langhe
wines, as Marziano's estate now covers an
area of 50 hectares. Barolo Cerviano is a
true gem of complexity and harmony, which
deservedly won a Tre Bicchieri. Its nose
ranges from aniseed to tar and wild berries,
while the powerful palate is long, fresh and
full of character, making it one of the finest
products of the great 2010 vintage. The
2011 Barolos also did well, with the
Pressenda showing more austere and the
Terlo Ravera more linear and defined. The
2014 Doglianis were less exuberant.

● Barolo Cerviano '10	♛♛♛ 7
● Barolo Pressenda '11	♛♛ 7
● Barolo Terlo Ravera '11	♛♛ 7
● Barbera d'Alba Rinaldi '13	♛♛ 4
● Dogliani Papà Celso '14	♛♛ 4
● Dogliani San Luigi '14	♛♛ 2*
○ Langhe Bianco Cinerino '14	♛♛ 4
● Nebbiolo d'Alba Bricco Barone '13	♛♛ 4
● Barolo Terlo Ravera '08	♛♛♛ 6
● Barolo Terlo Ravera '06	♛♛♛ 6
● Dogliani Papà Celso '13	♛♛♛ 4*
● Dogliani Papà Celso '11	♛♛♛ 3*
● Dogliani Papà Celso '09	♛♛♛ 3
● Dogliani Papà Celso '07	♛♛♛ 3
● Dogliani Papà Celso '06	♛♛♛ 3
● Dogliani Papà Celso '05	♛♛♛ 3*

Anna Maria Abbona

FRAZ. MONCUCCO, 21
12060 FARIGLIANO [CN]
TEL. 0173797228
www.annamariaabbona.it

CELLAR SALES
PRE-BOOKED VISITS
ANNUAL PRODUCTION 75,000 bottles
HECTARES UNDER VINE 14.00

The success of Anna Maria Abbona's various Dolcettos has not stopped her intention to expand operations, and her decision to add Barolo to the range is already yielding very interesting results. It is fascinating and even moving to listen to her discuss her relationship with the terroir, her work, and the market, and her decision to change lifestyle in 1989, to dedicate herself totally to winegrowing. All the wines from dolcetto have very clean fruit, and vary in complexity according to their vineyard of origin and the fermentation and ageing methods used. Anyone who thinks Dolcetto is always just a simple, approachable wine should taste Dogliani San Bernardo 2012. Its complex nose of fruit and dark berries is accompanied by a powerful but supple palate, underpinned by alluringly dense, lively fruity flesh. The charming classic Barolo 2011 is as surprising as it is convincing.

● Dogliani Sup. San Bernardo '12	♥♥♥ 4*
● Barolo '11	♥♥ 6
● Barbera d'Alba '13	♥♥ 2*
● Dogliani Sup. Maioli '13	♥♥ 3
● Langhe Nebbiolo '12	♥♥ 3
● Dolcetto di Dogliani Sorì dij But '14	♥ 2
○ Langhe Nascetta Netta '14	♥ 3
○ Langhe Riesling L'Alman '13	♥ 3
● Dogliani Sup. San Bernardo '11	♀♀♀ 4*
● Barbera d'Alba '12	♀♀ 3
● Barolo '10	♀♀ 6
● Barolo '09	♀♀ 6
● Dogliani Sorì dij But '13	♀♀ 2*
● Dogliani Sup. Maioli '12	♀♀ 3
● Langhe Rosso Cadò '10	♀♀ 4
⊙ Rosà '13	♀♀ 2*

Orlando Abrigo

VIA CAPPELLETTO, 5
12050 TREISO [CN]
TEL. 0173630533
www.orlandoabrigo.it

CELLAR SALES
PRE-BOOKED VISITS
ACCOMMODATION AND RESTAURANT SERVICE
ANNUAL PRODUCTION 80,000 bottles
HECTARES UNDER VINE 20.00
SUSTAINABLE WINERY

Year after year, Giovanni Abrigo's winery has become one of the most important in the Barbaresco production zone. Its premises are very welcoming and include a beautiful guesthouse able to host its many Italian and foreign visitors. The first-rate vineyards yield a sizable production that allows Abrigo to distribute its wines in many countries, giving it increasing visibility as a top Piedmont producer. The 2012 vintage has shown itself to be a good one for the expressiveness of the two Barbarescos presented that, despite their varietal differences, both achieved impressive scores. Barbaresco Montersino is softer and more delineated, characterized by intriguing notes of liquorice and spice, and already well-resolved tannins, while Barbaresco Meruzzano is currently denser and more layered, with notes of dark berries and tobacco.

● Barbaresco Meruzzano '12	♥♥ 5
● Barbaresco Montersino '12	♥♥ 7
● Barbera d'Alba Mervisano '12	♥♥ 4
● Barbera d'Alba Roreto '13	♥♥ 3
● Langhe Nebbiolo Settevie '13	♥♥ 3
● Nebbiolo d'Alba Valmaggiore '12	♥♥ 5
● Dolcetto d'Alba dell'Erto '14	♥ 2
○ Langhe Très Plus '13	♥ 3
● Barbaresco Meruzzano '11	♀♀ 5
● Barbaresco Rocche Meruzzano '10	♀♀ 5
● Barbaresco Rongalio Ris. '06	♀♀ 6
● Barbera d'Alba Mervisano '10	♀♀ 3*
● Barbera d'Alba Roreto '12	♀♀ 2*
● Barbera d'Alba V. Roreto '11	♀♀ 2*
● Langhe Nebbiolo Settevie '12	♀♀ 3
● Langhe Rosso Livraie '11	♀♀ 4

★Giulio Accornero e Figli

Cascina Ca' Cima, 1
15049 Vignale Monferrato [AL]
Tel. 0142933317
www.accornerovini.it

CELLAR SALES
PRE-BOOKED VISITS
ACCOMMODATION
ANNUAL PRODUCTION 100,000 bottles
HECTARES UNDER VINE 22.00
SUSTAINABLE WINERY

This year Accornero has harnessed its full qualitative potential to reach its goal of the Star awarded for winning ten Tre Bicchieri, internationally synonymous with excellence, testifying to the hard work, sacrifices, and passion that are often drive winegrowers. Although Accornero is a big name today, Ermanno continues to tantalize the palates of wine lovers with intriguing novelties, like the vertical selection of Bricco Battista from the early years of this century, released a few months ago. The range of wines presented this year offers a fabulous snapshot of a terroir. Two Barberas reached our finals: Bricco Battista and Giulin. The first makes a big impression on the nose and palate, while the second is less firm, but delicate and elegant. Then there is Girotondo, a great Nebbiolo from the Casale zone, with a classic, varietal style, and Ermanno's baby, Grignolino Vigne Vecchie, which is simply unique.

● Barbera del M.to Sup. Bricco Battista '12	♟♟♟	5
● Barbera del M.to Giulin '13	♟♟	3*
● Grignolino del M.to Casalese Bricco del Bosco V. Vecchie '10	♟♟	6
● M.to Girotondo '12	♟♟	4
○ Fonsina '14	♟♟	2*
● Grignolino del M.to Casalese Bricco del Bosco '14	♟♟	2*
● M.to Freisa La Bernardina '14	♟♟	2*
● Piemonte Barbera Campomoro '13	♟	2
● Barbera del M.to Sup. Bricco Battista '11	♟♟♟	5
● Barbera del M.to Sup. Bricco Battista '09	♟♟♟	5
● Barbera del M.to Sup. Bricco Battista '07	♟♟♟	5
● Barbera del M.to Sup. Cima '07	♟♟♟	8
● M.to Rosso Centenario '06	♟♟♟	5

Marco e Vittorio Adriano

Fraz. San Rocco Seno d'Elvio, 13a
12051 Alba [CN]
Tel. 0173362294
www.adrianovini.it

CELLAR SALES
PRE-BOOKED VISITS
ANNUAL PRODUCTION 150,000 bottles
HECTARES UNDER VINE 23.00

Consistent high quality, stylistic clarity, and fair prices are the three principles on which brothers Marco and Vittorio Adriano have built their success. San Rocco Seno d'Elvio, the hamlet of Alba where the winery is located, has become a place of pilgrimage for the most intrepid explorers of Langhe, due to its fine range of wines from moscato, sauvignon, dolcetto, barbera, and freisa. However, the main attractions are its Barbarescos, aged in 3,500–5,000-litre Slavonian oak barrels, from the Bricco and Frati vineyards for the Sanadaive, and the Basarin cru in Neive, also used for the Riserva since 2004. It was the pair of Nebbiolos that gave the best performance again this year, with Sanadaive 2012 finishing a hair's breadth ahead of its sibling of the same vintage. Still a little reticent on the nose, it totally convinced us with its solid, taut structure, accompanied by a fine tannic weave. The Basarin is similar, but more predictable in its development.

● Barbaresco Sanadaive '12	♟♟	4
○ Ardi	♟♟	2*
● Barbaresco Basarin '12	♟♟	4
● Langhe Nebbiolo '13	♟♟	3
● Dolcetto d'Alba '14	♟	2
○ Langhe Sauvignon Basaricò '14	♟	2
● Barbaresco Basarin '11	♗♗	4
● Barbaresco Basarin Ris. '09	♗♗	5
● Barbaresco Sanadaive '11	♗♗	4
● Barbera d'Alba Sup. '11	♗♗	2*
● Dolcetto d'Alba '13	♗♗	2*
● Langhe Nebbiolo '12	♗♗	3
● Langhe Nebbiolo '11	♗♗	3
○ Langhe Sauvignon Basaricò '13	♗♗	2*
○ Langhe Sauvignon Basaricò '12	♗♗	2*
○ Moscato d'Asti '13	♗♗	2*

Claudio Alario

VIA SANTA CROCE, 23
12055 DIANO D'ALBA [CN]
TEL. 0173231808
www.alarioclaudio.it

CELLAR SALES
PRE-BOOKED VISITS
ANNUAL PRODUCTION 46,000 bottles
HECTARES UNDER VINE 10.00

Dolcetto di Diano has always struggled to make a name for itself, largely due to the more famous designations of Dogliani and Alba, but also because of the general confusion caused by a baffling system of designations that is difficult for the consumer to understand. However, there is no doubt that Claudio Alario's fruity, lively, drinkable Dolcetto can compete with many more famous names, as the foreign markets have quickly realized, buying up almost the entire production. The whole range is excellent, from the Barbera to the Nebbiolo, including the successful Barolo, whose production started 20 years ago. The fragrant Sorì Costa Fiore is one of the finest Dolcettos of the 2014 vintage, showing pleasantly fresh and nuanced. Sorì Pradurent 2013 is weightier with firmer structure, and faintly marked by ageing in oak. Nebbiolo d'Alba Cascinotto performed very well, with plenty of stuffing and an elegant nose. Both the Barolo vineyard selections have moderate structure and are nicely forthright.

● Barolo Riva Rocca '11	♥♥ 5
● Dolcetto di Diano d'Alba Sorì Costa Fiore '14	♥♥ 2*
● Barolo Sorano '11	♥♥ 6
● Dolcetto di Diano d'Alba Sorì Montagrillo '14	♥♥ 2*
● Dolcetto di Diano d'Alba Sup. Sorì Pradurent '13	♥♥ 3
● Nebbiolo d'Alba Cascinotto '13	♥♥ 4
● Barbera d'Alba Valletta '13	♥ 4
● Barolo Sorano '05	♥♥♥ 7
● Barolo Riva Rocca '10	♥♥ 6
● Barolo Sorano '09	♥♥ 6
● Dolcetto di Diano d'Alba Costa Fiore '12	♥♥ 2*
● Dolcetto di Diano d'Alba Sorì Costa Fiore '13	♥♥ 2*

★ F.lli Alessandria

VIA B. VALFRÉ, 59
12060 VERDUNO [CN]
TEL. 0172470113
www.fratellialessandria.it

CELLAR SALES
PRE-BOOKED VISITS
ANNUAL PRODUCTION 80,000 bottles
HECTARES UNDER VINE 14.00

Vittore Alessandria is one of the most talented and sensitive Langhe interpreters. For several years now he has been working full time alongside his father Gian Battista and his uncle Alessandro in their winery in Verduno. The estate vaunts around 15 hectares of vineyards planted with the main local grape varieties, with pelaverga and nebbiolo accounting for the lion's share in the most representative wines. Monvigliero and San Lorenzo (Verduno) and Gramolere (Monforte d'Alba) are the Barolo crus bottled separately. A fine contemporary style highlights their distinctive characteristics, with ageing in tonneaux and 2,000 and 3,000-litre oak barrels. We always enjoy the range presented by the Alessandria brothers, topped this time by the magnificent Barolo Gramolere 2011. It is concentrated, with layered notes of liquorice and white truffles, releasing its close-focused, ripe fruit on the palate, perfectly underpinned by a majestic tannic weave that is both dense and delicate.

● Barolo Gramolere '11	♥♥♥ 6
● Barolo Monvigliero '11	♥♥ 6
● Barbera d'Alba Sup. La Prìora '13	♥♥ 4
● Barolo '11	♥♥ 5
● Barolo San Lorenzo di Verduno '11	♥♥ 6
● Langhe Nebbiolo Prinsiot '13	♥♥ 3
● Verduno Pelaverga Speziale '14	♥ 3
● Barolo Gramolere '10	♀♀♀ 6
● Barolo Gramolere '05	♀♀♀ 6
● Barolo Monvigliero '09	♀♀♀ 6
● Barolo Monvigliero '06	♀♀♀ 6
● Barolo Monvigliero '00	♀♀♀ 6
● Barolo S. Lorenzo '08	♀♀♀ 6
● Barolo S. Lorenzo '04	♀♀♀ 6
● Barolo S. Lorenzo '01	♀♀♀ 6
● Barolo S. Lorenzo '97	♀♀♀ 6

★Gianfranco Alessandria

LOC. MANZONI, 13
12065 MONFORTE D'ALBA [CN]
TEL. 017378576
www.gianfrancoalessandria.com

CELLAR SALES
PRE-BOOKED VISITS
ANNUAL PRODUCTION 45,000 bottles
HECTARES UNDER VINE 7.00

Gianfranco has never wished to expand, preferring to carry out all the operations in his few hectares of vineyards and small cellar himself, with the help of his family, from pruning to bottling. He is thus certain of maintaining complete control over his wines, characterized by an elegant and never aggressive style, achieved with the aid of small French oak casks. The San Giovanni vineyard in Monforte has been yielding fantastic grapes for exactly 30 years, first and foremost Barolo nebbiolo and barbera. Barbera d'Alba Vittoria 2012 is fresh and lively, with medium structure and splendid dark berries. Barolo San Giovanni 2011 is tannic, with a close-knit palate needing further ageing and characterized by delicate hints of quinine and tar, while Langhe Nebbiolo 2013 is concentrated and full flavoured. Despite the difficult vintage, both the cherry-rich Dolcetto d'Alba and the acidulous Barbera d'Alba 2014 are well made.

● Barbera d'Alba Vittoria '12	▼▼ 5
● Barolo S. Giovanni '11	▼▼ 7
● Barbera d'Alba '14	▼▼ 3
● Barolo '11	▼▼ 6
● Dolcetto d'Alba '14	▼▼ 2*
● Langhe Nebbiolo '13	▼▼ 3
● Barbera d'Alba Vittoria '11	▼▼▼ 5
● Barbera d'Alba Vittoria '97	▼▼▼ 4*
● Barbera d'Alba Vittoria '96	▼▼▼ 6
● Barolo '93	▼▼▼ 6
● Barolo S. Giovanni '04	▼▼▼ 7
● Barolo S. Giovanni '01	▼▼▼ 7
● Barolo S. Giovanni '00	▼▼▼ 7
● Barolo S. Giovanni '99	▼▼▼ 8
● Barolo S. Giovanni '98	▼▼▼ 7
● Barolo S. Giovanni '97	▼▼▼ 7

Marchesi Alfieri

P.ZZA ALFIERI, 28
14010 SAN MARTINO ALFIERI [AT]
TEL. 0141976015
www.marchesialfieri.it

CELLAR SALES
PRE-BOOKED VISITS
ACCOMMODATION
ANNUAL PRODUCTION 100,000 bottles
HECTARES UNDER VINE 21.00

Marchesi Alfieri, owned by the San Martino di San Germano sisters, has been bottling some of the most interesting wines in the province of Asti for over quarter of a century. Production is dominated by Barbera, which accounts for over 75% of their vineyards and constitutes the heart of the original estate, with the Quaglia cru planted in 1937. The all-red range is completed by Grignolino, Nebbiolo and Pinot Nero, all complex and pleasant with a fruit-rich style. The two versions of Barbera d'Asti presented this year were both excellent. La Tota 2013 is fruit rich with still rather sharp acidity, but is long and enjoyable, while L'Alfiera 2012 has a classic nose of red berries, black pepper and forest floor, and a full, flavoursome palate. Piemonte Grignolino Sansoero 2014 is well made, with notes of aromatic herbs, as is Monferrato Rosso Sostegno 2013, a solid, characterful blend of barbera and pinot nero.

● Barbera d'Asti La Tota '13	▼▼ 3*
● Barbera d'Asti Sup. Alfiera '12	▼▼ 5
● M.to Rosso Sostegno '13	▼▼ 2*
● Piemonte Grignolino Sansoero '14	▼▼ 2*
● Barbera d'Asti Sup. Alfiera '07	▼▼▼ 5
● Barbera d'Asti Sup. Alfiera '05	▼▼▼ 5
● Barbera d'Asti Sup. Alfiera '01	▼▼▼ 5
● Barbera d'Asti Sup. Alfiera '00	▼▼▼ 5
● Barbera d'Asti Sup. Alfiera '99	▼▼▼ 5
● Barbera d'Asti La Tota '12	▼▼ 3*
● Barbera d'Asti La Tota '11	▼▼ 3
● Barbera d'Asti Sup. Alfiera '11	▼▼ 5
● Barbera d'Asti Sup. Alfiera '10	▼▼ 5
● M.to Rosso S. Germano '10	▼▼ 5
● M.to Rosso Sostegno '11	▼▼ 2*
● Piemonte Pinot Nero San Germano '11	▼▼ 4

Giovanni Almondo

VIA SAN ROCCO, 26
12046 MONTÀ [CN]
TEL. 0173975256
www.giovannialmondo.com

PRE-BOOKED VISITS
ANNUAL PRODUCTION 110,000 bottles
HECTARES UNDER VINE 16.00
SUSTAINABLE WINERY

The Almondo family, headed by Domenico, has been one of the leading names in Roero wine production for quarter of a century. All the vineyards lie within the municipal boundaries of Montà, at altitudes between 280 and 360 metres, and include veritable crus, like Bricco delle Ciliegie for arneis and Bric Valdiana for nebbiolo. Arneis, which accounts for over 60% of the estate's vineyards, is grown on the higher, sandier soils, while red grape varieties are planted on those with a higher percentage of clayey limestone. Roero Giovanni Almondo Riserva put up an excellent performance as usual. The mouthfilling 2012 vintage has good stuffing and notes of iodine and Mediterranean scrubland. Barbera d'Alba Valbianchéra 2013 is also very good, with rich fruit and a long finish nicely underpinned by acidity, as is the zesty Roero Arneis Bricco delle Ciliegie 2014, well behaved despite the difficult vintage, with a charming finish of citrus and white-fleshed fruit.

● Barbera d'Alba Valbianchèra '13	♟♟♟ 3*
○ Roero Arneis Bricco delle Ciliegie '14	♟♟♟ 3*
● Roero Giovanni Almondo Ris. '12	♟♟ 5
● Roero Bric Valdiana '13	♟♟ 5
○ Roero Arneis V. Sparse '14	♟ 2
● Roero Bric Valdiana '11	♟♟♟ 5
● Roero Bric Valdiana '07	♟♟♟ 5
● Roero Bric Valdiana '03	♟♟♟ 5
● Roero Bric Valdiana '01	♟♟♟ 4
● Roero Bric Valdiana '00	♟♟♟ 4*
● Roero Giovanni Almondo Ris. '11	♟♟♟ 5
● Roero Giovanni Almondo Ris. '09	♟♟♟ 5
● Barbera d'Alba Valbianchèra '12	♟♟ 3*
● Roero '12	♟♟ 3*
● Roero Bric Valdiana '12	♟♟ 5
● Roero Giovanni Almondo Ris. '10	♟♟ 5

★★★Elio Altare

FRAZ. ANNUNZIATA, 51
12064 LA MORRA [CN]
TEL. 017350835
www.elioaltare.com

CELLAR SALES
PRE-BOOKED VISITS
ANNUAL PRODUCTION 70,000 bottles
HECTARES UNDER VINE 11.00

Unstoppable in his 30-year battle to achieve increasingly elegant and well-defined wines, Elio Altare has been, and still is, an influential figure from whom many fine producers in Langhe and further afield have learned. His quest continues, also with the purchase of a few small plots in which to seek perfection. Following the splendid Bricco vineyard in the Ceretta cru in Serralunga, it is now the turn of a plot in Barolo's illustrious Cannubi cru, yielding just a few bottles destined exclusively for export. A Tre Bicchieri that manages to mask its weight in a rush of fresh, lively red fruit, particularly plums and cherries: this sums up the splendid Langhe Larigi 2013, from barbera. Barolo Cerretta Vigna Bricco 2009, among the best of its vintage, has been released after two further years of ageing in the cellar. It is long and juicy, with glossy tannins and a nose of medicinal herbs. The excellent Barolo 2011 offers exemplary roundness, while the elegant Langhe La Villa, from 60% barbera and 40% nebbiolo grapes, is modern and spicy, without being excessively full.

● Langhe Larigi '13	♟♟♟ 8
● Barolo '11	♟♟ 8
● Barolo Arborina '11	♟♟ 8
● Barolo Cerretta V. Bricco '09	♟♟ 8
● Barbera d'Alba '14	♟♟ 3
● Langhe Giàrborina '13	♟♟ 8
● Langhe La Villa '13	♟♟ 8
● Langhe Nebbiolo '14	♟♟ 4
● Dolcetto d'Alba '14	♟ 3
● Barolo Arborina '09	♟♟♟ 8
● Barolo Cerretta V. Bricco '06	♟♟♟ 8
● Barolo Cerretta V. Bricco '05	♟♟♟ 8
● Langhe Arborina '08	♟♟♟ 8
● Langhe La Villa '06	♟♟♟ 8
● Langhe Larigi '12	♟♟♟ 8
● Langhe Larigi '07	♟♟♟ 7

Antichi Vigneti di Cantalupo

VIA MICHELANGELO BUONARROTI, 5
28074 GHEMME [NO]
TEL. 0163840041
www.cantalupo.net

CELLAR SALES
PRE-BOOKED VISITS
ANNUAL PRODUCTION 200,000 bottles
HECTARES UNDER VINE 35.00

The Arlunno family own some of the most typical plots in the Colline Novaresi range of morainic hills formed by deposits left by the Monte Rosa glacier. Their vineyards cover an area of around 35 hectares, mainly dedicated to nebbiolo spanna, with the rest planted to vespolina, uva rara, erbaluce, arneis and chardonnay. There are four versions of Ghemme: a basic and three vineyard selections, from the legendary Breclema, Carella, Livelli, and Baraggiola crus. They do not share a single style but are interpreted according to the vintage, using a combination of large and small oak, always maintaining an austere, earthy profile. This year the winery's top two wines are very different. Signore di Bayard 2008 has roasted coffee beans and liquorice on the nose, accompanied by a dry, leisurely palate, while Anno Primo 2009 is more classic, with salty, rusty notes, and fuller flavour.

● Ghemme Cantalupo Anno Primo '09	💯💯 5
● Ghemme Signore di Bayard '08	💯💯 6
● Colline Novaresi Vespolina Villa Horta '12	💯💯 2*
● Ghemme Collis Carellae '09	💯💯 6
○ Carolus	💯 2
● Colline Novaresi Nebbiolo Abate di Cluny '09	💯 5
☉ Colline Novaresi Nebbiolo Il Mimo '14	💯 2
● Colline Novaresi Primigenia '12	💯 2
● Ghemme Collis Carellae '08	🏆🏆 6
● Ghemme Signore di Bayard '06	🏆🏆 6

Antico Borgo dei Cavalli

VIA DANTE, 54
28010 CAVALLIRIO [NO]
TEL. 016380115
www.vinibarbaglia.it

CELLAR SALES
PRE-BOOKED VISITS
ANNUAL PRODUCTION 25,000 bottles
HECTARES UNDER VINE 3.00

Founded in 1946 by Mario Barbaglio, Antico Borgo dei Cavalli is one of the oldest names in the Novara production zone. Today it is run by Mario's son Sergio and granddaughter Silvia, who plays an increasingly important role in production and stylistic choices. Her sensitive sunny personality can be discerned in the latest releases of Boca, now hailed as the estate's star wine by many connoisseurs, whose style is, in many respects, midway between classical and innovative. However, the entire range has come on by leaps and bounds, with the monovarietals from nebbiolo, uva rara, croatina, vespolina and erbaluce all worthy of note, along with the Curticella line of sparklers. This was confirmed by this year's tastings. The many excellent wines are once again topped by the Boca, whose 2011 vintage displays impressive fruity power, accompanied by good fullness and balance, in perfect agreement with its well-calibrated progression.

● Boca '11	💯💯 5
○ Colline Novaresi Bianco Biancaluce '14	💯💯 3
● Colline Novaresi Nebbiolo Il Silente '11	💯💯 3
○ Curticella Caballi Regis Brut M. Cl.	💯💯 5
● Boca '10	🏆🏆 5
● Boca '09	🏆🏆 5
● Boca '08	🏆🏆 5
● Boca '07	🏆🏆 5
○ Colline Novaresi Bianco Lucino '13	🏆🏆 3
○ Colline Novaresi Bianco Lucino '11	🏆🏆 3
○ Colline Novaresi Bianco Lucino '10	🏆🏆 3*
● Colline Novaresi Nebbiolo Il Silente '09	🏆🏆 3
○ Curticella Caballi Regis Brut M. Cl.	🏆🏆 5
○ Curticella Caballi Regis Dosaggio Zero M. Cl.	🏆🏆 5
● Passiolò	🏆🏆 5

★Antoniolo

C.SO VALSESIA, 277
13045 GATTINARA [VC]
TEL. 0163833612
antoniolovini@bmm.it

CELLAR SALES
PRE-BOOKED VISITS
ANNUAL PRODUCTION 60,000 bottles
HECTARES UNDER VINE 12.00

We use the term "transparent" in the broadest possible sense when discussing the unmistakable Nebbiolos the Antoniolo family have been offering for decades. It perfectly conjures up the clarity of their hue and nose, and above all their ability to describe in meticulous detail the terroir of majestic vineyards like San Francesco, Osso San Grato, and Castelle. These are the three crus that flank the basic version. Together, they form the most exciting range of Gattinaras, designed in the cellar with long ageing, mainly in large barrels. Lean, ferrous, and only apparently subtle, they are eminently cellarable, displaying their greatness from the moment of their release. The ratings below eloquently sum up the state of Antoniolo's range, represented by an impressive four wines in our finals. The expressiveness of Osso San Grato 2011 earned it our highest accolade, with a nose of roots, tobacco, and iodine, and a triumph of berry fruit on the palate, with majestic texture.

● Gattinara Osso S. Grato '11	♈♈♈ 8
● Gattinara '11	♈♈ 5
● Gattinara Le Castelle '10	♈♈ 7
● Gattinara S. Francesco '11	♈♈ 8
● Coste della Sesia Nebbiolo Juvenia '13	♈♈ 4
⊙ Bricco Lorella '14	♈ 3
● Gattinara Osso S. Grato '10	♉♉♉ 8
● Gattinara Osso S. Grato '09	♉♉♉ 8
● Gattinara S. Francesco '08	♉♉♉ 7
● Gattinara '10	♉♉ 5
● Gattinara '08	♉♉ 5
● Gattinara S. Francesco '10	♉♉ 8
● Gattinara S. Francesco '09	♉♉ 7

Odilio Antoniotti

V.LO ANTONIOTTI, 9
13868 SOSTEGNO [BI]
TEL. 0163860309
www.antoniotti.it

CELLAR SALES
PRE-BOOKED VISITS
ANNUAL PRODUCTION 10,500 bottles
HECTARES UNDER VINE 4.50

A small estate with plots in several classic vineyards and a cellar that is being modernized and now also vaunts a tasting room are the realm of Odilio Antoniotti and his young son Mattia, who is already determined to tread the path of quality wine production. He is following a tradition, born around 150 years ago, which has given great satisfaction to the generations of Antoniottis who have grown nebbiolo on this harsh, steep land. Although Bramaterra 2011 did not manage to repeat the result of the previous vintage, it is characterized by astonishing youthful exuberance, particularly considering the vintage. It has huge personality, with a nose of red and dark berry fruit, accompanied by a hint of smokiness derived from ageing in oak, and a long, compelling, powerful palate that undoubtedly requires more time in bottle to mellow out.

● Bramaterra '11	♈♈ 3*
● Bramaterra '10	♉♉♉ 3*
● Bramaterra '09	♉♉ 3*
● Bramaterra '08	♉♉ 3*
● Bramaterra '07	♉♉ 3*
● Pramartel	♉♉ 3

Arbiola

LOC. ARBIOLA
REG. SALINE, 67
14050 SAN MARZANO OLIVETO [AT]
TEL. 0141856194
www.arbiola.it

CELLAR SALES
PRE-BOOKED VISITS
ACCOMMODATION AND RESTAURANT SERVICE
ANNUAL PRODUCTION 250,000 bottles
HECTARES UNDER VINE 30.00
VITICULTURE METHOD Certified Organic

This legendary estate on the boundary between Monferrato and Langhe was managed by Saiagricola for a while, but is now back under the full control of the Terzano family. The vineyards, all in the municipality of San Marzano Oliveto, are on mainly marly soils. Over 60% are planted to barbera, with some vines more than 60 years old. The estate's wines are concentrated and fruit-rich, but also highly drinkable. Barbera d'Asti Superiore Nizza Romilda XVII 2012 stands out, reaching our finals with a very intense nose of dark berries and flowers, accompanied by hints of toasted oak and autumn leaves. On the palate it is complex, with good texture and staying power, and a finish with fine acidity and full flavour, which make it wonderfully drinkable. Barbera d'Asti Carlotta 2013 is vibrant and juicy, with attractive spicy and earthy notes.

L'Armangia

FRAZ. SAN GIOVANNI, 122
14053 CANELLI [AT]
TEL. 0141824947
www.armangia.it

CELLAR SALES
PRE-BOOKED VISITS
ANNUAL PRODUCTION 95,000 bottles
HECTARES UNDER VINE 11.00
SUSTAINABLE WINERY

Although the Giovine family have fermented their own grapes since 1850, the first two L'Armangia wines were not produced until 1993. Contrary to local tradition, they were both whites. Today the estate offers a wider range, featuring both reds and whites, from the fruit of several vineyards. The white grape varieties are grown on the medium-textured limestone soils of the Sant'Antonio hill, in Canelli, and the red on the heavier, more compact terrain of the vineyards in Moasca, San Marzano Oliveto and Castel Boglione. Barbera d'Asti Superiore Nizza Titon 2012 has a vibrant nose of red berries and quinine, followed by hints of tobacco and citrus, and a complex, full-bodied palate, with close-woven tannins, which is a little over the top but full of character. Barbera d'Asti Sopra Berruti 2014 is well made, with exuberant notes of plums and cherries underpinned by acidity, as is the fresh, aromatic Moscato d'Asti Canelli 2014.

● Barbera d'Asti Sup. Nizza Romilda XVII '12	♈♈ 4
● Barbera d'Asti Carlotta '13	♈♈ 3
● Barbera d'Asti '14	♈ 2
○ Moscato d'Asti '14	♈ 2
● Barbera d'Asti Sup. Nizza Romilda XIV '09	♈♈♈ 5
● Barbera d'Asti Carlotta '12	♈♈ 2*
● Barbera d'Asti Carlotta '11	♈♈ 2*
● Barbera d'Asti Sup. Nizza Romilda XIII '08	♈♈ 4
● Barbera d'Asti Sup. Nizza Romilda XV '10	♈♈ 5
● Barbera d'Asti Sup. Nizza Romilda XVI '11	♈♈ 5
☉ Nysus Brut M. Cl. '10	♈♈ 5

● Barbera d'Asti Sup. Nizza Titon '12	♈♈ 3*
● Barbera d'Asti Sopra Berruti '14	♈♈ 2*
○ Moscato d'Asti Canelli '14	♈♈ 2*
● Barbera d'Asti Sup. Nizza Vignali '10	♈ 5
○ Lorenzomariasole Extra Brut M. Cl.	♈ 4
● Monferrato Rosso Pacifico '10	♈ 3
● Barbera d'Asti Sopra Berruti '13	♈♈ 2*
● Barbera d'Asti Sopra Berruti '12	♈♈ 2*
● Barbera d'Asti Sup. Nizza Titon '11	♈♈ 3*
● Barbera d'Asti Sup. Nizza Titon '10	♈♈ 3*
● Barbera d'Asti Sup. Nizza Titon '09	♈♈ 3
● Barbera d'Asti Sup. Nizza Vignali '07	♈♈ 5
○ Moscato d'Asti Canelli '12	♈♈ 2*
○ Piemonte Chardonnay Robi & Robi '11	♈♈ 3

Paolo Avezza

REG. MONFORTE, 62
14053 CANELLI [AT]
TEL. 0141822296
www.paoloavezza.com

CELLAR SALES
PRE-BOOKED VISITS
ANNUAL PRODUCTION 25,000 bottles
HECTARES UNDER VINE 7.00

Flanked by his parents, wife and daughter, the talented and passionate Paolo Avezza has been at the helm of this family estate since 2001. Production ranges from a well–typed Barbera to a Metodo Classico sparkler. The still wines hail from four hectares of vineyards in Nizza Monferrato, while the sparklers, including the outstanding Alta Langa, are from three hectares in Canelli. In addition to barbera, the estate also grows moscato, nebbiolo, pinot nero, chardonnay and a little dolcetto. Moscato d'Asti La Commenda 2014 is among the best of the vintage for its type, offering a delicate nose of peaches and mint, with hints of lemon and orange peel, and a long, taut, rich palate with good acidity. Barbera d'Asti Superiore Nizza Sotto La Muda 2012 is also very good, with a nose of dark berry fruit and sweet spice, and a dense, close-knit palate with a rather austere finish. The vintage Barbera d'Asti is also well made, showing fresh, juicy, and approachable.

● Barbera d'Asti Sup. Nizza Sotto la Muda '12	♟♟ 4
○ Moscato d'Asti La Commenda '14	♟♟ 2*
● Barbera d'Asti '14	♟♟ 2*
● Barbera d'Asti Sup. Nizza Sotto la Muda '10	♟♟♟ 4*
● Barbera d'Asti Sup. Nizza Sotto la Muda '07	♟♟♟ 3*
○ Alta Langa Brut '10	♟♟ 4
● Barbera d'Asti '13	♟♟ 2*
● Barbera d'Asti Sup. Nizza Sotto la Muda '11	♟♟ 4
● Barbera d'Asti Sup. Nizza Sotto la Muda '09	♟♟ 4
○ Moscato d'Asti Canelli La Commenda '13	♟♟ 2*
○ Moscato d'Asti La Commenda '12	♟♟ 2*

★Azelia

FRAZ. GARBELLETTO
VIA ALBA-BAROLO, 53
12060 CASTIGLIONE FALLETTO [CN]
TEL. 017362859
www.azelia.it

CELLAR SALES
PRE-BOOKED VISITS
ANNUAL PRODUCTION 80,000 bottles
HECTARES UNDER VINE 16.00
SUSTAINABLE WINERY

Azelia was founded by Lorenzo Scavino in the 1920s. It owns about 16 hectares of vineyards, scattered between Castiglione Falletto, Serralunga d'Alba and Montelupo Albese. The various plots have long been assigned to the different wines of the range, topped by the Barolos: a basic of 30% Castiglione and 70% Serralunga, and the Bricco Fiasco, Margheria, San Rocco, and Bricco Voghera crus, with a Riserva made from the latter in the best vintages. They are fairly modern in style, made with the aid of roto-fermenters and aged in small casks (Bricco Fiasco and San Rocco) and large barrels (Margheria and Bricco Voghera). Azelia's Barolos fare extremely well, commencing with Bricco Voghera Riserva 2007, which is as supple and caressing as Bricco Fiasco 2011 is tight and spirited. However, the finest performance this year came from San Rocco 2011, its classic red berries and spice faithfully echoed on a well-behaved, luxuriant palate with solid backbone.

● Barolo S. Rocco '11	♟♟♟ 8
● Barolo Bricco Fiasco '11	♟♟ 8
● Barolo Bricco Voghera Ris. '07	♟♟ 8
● Barolo Margheria '11	♟♟ 8
● Barolo Bricco Fiasco '09	♟♟♟ 8
● Barolo Bricco Fiasco '01	♟♟♟ 7
● Barolo Margheria '06	♟♟♟ 7
● Barolo S. Rocco '08	♟♟♟ 8

Banfi - Vigne Regali

VIA VITTORIO VENETO, 76
15019 STREVI [AL]
TEL. 0144362600
www.castellobanfi.it

PRE-BOOKED VISITS
ANNUAL PRODUCTION 2,000,000 bottles
HECTARES UNDER VINE 76.00

The Mariani family's Piedmont winery is divided into two estates, both in the province of Alessandria. Principessa Gavia, in Novi Ligure, produces both still and semi-sparkling versions of Gavi, while the vineyards in Strevi yield the grapes for the rest of the production: the dessert wines, the basic Moscato d'Asti and Brachetto d'Acqui, and the two reds from dolcetto d'Acqui and albarossa. Finally, there is a wide range of Metodo Classico Brut sparklers, as well as the Rosé, made using the Charmat method. Vigne Regali's sparklers confirm their high quality, particularly Cuvée Aurora, in two equally alluring versions, Bianco and Rosé, with a lively hue and a fine, persistent bead. Banfi Brut Metodo Classico offers a sophisticated nose of wholemeal and fruit, reflected on a powerful, well-orchestrated palate with a long finish. Dolcetto d'Acqui L'Ardì 2014 and Albarossa LaLus 2012, from native grape varieties, also put up an excellent performance.

○ Alta Langa Cuvée Aurora '09	♟♟	5
☉ Alta Langa Cuvée Aurora Rosé '12	♟♟	6
○ Banfi Brut M. Cl.	♟♟	5
● Dolcetto d'Acqui L'Ardì '14	♟♟	3
● Piemonte Albarossa La Lus '12	♟♟	5
● Brachetto d'Acqui Rosa Regale '14	♟	4
○ Gavi Principessa Gavia '14	♟	3
○ Moscato d'Asti Sciandor '14	♟	3
○ Alta Langa Cuvée Aurora '08	♟♟	5
○ Alta Langa Cuvée Aurora '07	♟♟	5
○ Alta Langa Cuvée Aurora Rosé '10	♟♟	5
○ Banfi Brut M. Cl.	♟♟	3
● Dolcetto d'Acqui L'Ardì '12	♟♟	3
○ Gavi Principessa Gavia '13	♟♟	3
● Piemonte Albarossa La Lus '11	♟♟	5
● Piemonte Albarossa La Lus '10	♟♟	5

Osvaldo Barberis

B.TA VALDIBÀ, 42
12063 DOGLIANI [CN]
TEL. 017370054
www.osvaldobarberis.com

CELLAR SALES
PRE-BOOKED VISITS
ANNUAL PRODUCTION 20,000 bottles
HECTARES UNDER VINE 8.00
VITICULTURE METHOD Certified Organic

This small estate takes goes to great pains to ensure the sustainability of all its work, from the vineyard to the cellar, and is progressively improving the quality of its entire production. The wines are very focused and terroir true, without ever being predictable. Cellar operations are kept to a minimum, allowing all the traditional grape varieties of this corner of Langhe to be interpreted in an enviably authentic style. Dogliani Superiore Puncin 2013 is very convincing, with a well-defined nose and a fresh, juicy palate. Valdibà 2014, also from dolcetto, displays good structure in a difficult vintage, in which balance tends towards austerity. The potent, fragrant Nebbiolo Muntajà 2013 is just as good as the fine vintages of the past. Nascetta 2014, from the increasingly popular native grape variety, is uncomplicated and easy drinking, with slightly salty undertones.

● Dogliani Sup. Puncin '13	♟♟	3*
● Barbera d'Alba Cesca '13	♟♟	3
● Dogliani Valdibà '14	♟♟	2*
● Nebbiolo d'Alba Muntajà '13	♟♟	3
○ Langhe Nascetta Anì '14	♟	3
● Barbera d'Alba Castella '12	♟♟	3*
● Dogliani Avrì '12	♟♟	3
● Dogliani Sup. Puncin '12	♟♟	3
● Dogliani Sup. Puncin '11	♟♟	3*
● Dogliani Valdibà '13	♟♟	2*
● Dogliani Valdibà '12	♟♟	2*
● Dogliani Valdibà '11	♟♟	2*
● Nebbiolo d'Alba Muntajà '12	♟♟	3
● Nebbiolo d'Alba Muntajà '11	♟♟	3*
● Piemonte Barbera Brichat '13	♟♟	2*
● Piemonte Barbera Brichat '11	♟♟	2*

Batasiolo

FRAZ. ANNUNZIATA, 87
12064 LA MORRA [CN]
TEL. 017350130
www.batasiolo.com

PRE-BOOKED VISITS
ANNUAL PRODUCTION 2,500,000 bottles
HECTARES UNDER VINE 107.00

Cerequio and Brunate in La Morra,
Boscareto and Briccolina in Serralunga,
Bricco di Vergne in Barolo, Bussia Bofani in
Monforte: a glance at the list of farms
purchased by the Dogliani family in the
Barolo zone reveals the importance of
Batasiolo's estate. Over 100 hectares
under vine supply the grapes for its
extensive range focusing mainly on
traditional Langhe wines, with a few
concessions to international grape varieties,
without forgetting sparklers and passitos.
There are an impressive six Barolos, a
basic version and five crus, interpreted in
an accomplished, assertive style without
any technical intransigence. Briccolina and
Cerequio 2011 were among the best wines
tasted. Although the first is slightly vegetal
and the second a little too warm on the
palate, both have good stuffing and length.
Boscareto 2011 is more complete and
balanced; its apparently estery profile is
largely belied by its lively, juicy palate with
perfectly calibrated tannins.

● Barolo Boscareto '11	♟♟ 8
● Barolo Bussia Vign. Bofani '11	♟♟ 8
● Barbaresco '12	♟♟ 5
● Barolo Briccolina '11	♟♟ 8
● Barolo Brunate '11	♟♟ 8
● Barolo Cerequio '11	♟♟ 8
● Barolo '11	♟ 6
● Barolo Boscareto '05	♟♟♟ 7
● Barbaresco '11	♟♟ 5
● Barolo Boscareto '10	♟♟ 7
● Barolo Briccolina '10	♟♟ 8
● Barolo Cerequio '10	♟♟ 7
○ Gavi del Comune di Gavi Granée '13	♟♟ 3

Fabrizio Battaglino

LOC. BORGONUOVO
VIA MONTALDO ROERO, 44
12040 VEZZA D'ALBA [CN]
TEL. 0173658156
www.battaglino.com

CELLAR SALES
PRE-BOOKED VISITS
ANNUAL PRODUCTION 25,000 bottles
HECTARES UNDER VINE 5.00

This small family estate has been run by
Fabrizio Battaglino for almost 20 years,
following in the footsteps of Riccardo, who
already bottled his own wines in the 1960s.
Its range is made from the classic local
grape varieties: arneis, nebbiolo and
barbera. The arneis and nebbiolo vineyards
are situated at an altitude of 350 metres on
the Colla hill in Vezza d'Alba, not far from
the winery, while the barbera is grown on
the Montebello hill in Guarene. The two
versions of Nebbiolo d'Alba 2013 are
excellent: the Colla more complex, with
hints of tar, rain-soaked earth, and black
tea leaves on the nose, and a long, juicy
palate with good texture and fruit; the basic
one fresher and more approachable, with
notes of dark berry fruit and new-mown
grass. Barbera d'Alba Munbèl 2013 is also
very well made, with fruity notes and
earthy, vegetal hints, a little rustic but
pleasant, with plenty of pulp. We also liked
the mature, dense Roero Sergentin 2012.

● Nebbiolo d'Alba Colla '13	♟♟ 4
● Barbera d'Alba Munbèl '13	♟♟ 3
● Nebbiolo d'Alba '13	♟♟ 3
● Roero Sergentin '12	♟♟ 4
○ Roero Arneis '14	♟ 2
● Nebbiolo d'Alba V. Colla '07	♟♟♟ 3*
● Barbera d'Alba Munbèl '12	♟♟ 3*
● Barbera d'Alba V. Munbèl '11	♟♟ 3*
● Nebbiolo d'Alba Colla '12	♟♟ 4
● Nebbiolo d'Alba Colla '12	♟♟ 4
● Nebbiolo d'Alba V. Colla '11	♟♟ 4
● Roero '06	♟♟ 3*
○ Roero Arneis '09	♟♟ 2*
● Roero Sergentin '10	♟♟ 4
● Roero Sergentin '08	♟♟ 3*
● Roero Sergentin '07	♟♟ 3*

Battaglio

LOC. BORBORE
VIA SALERIO, 15
12040 VEZZA D'ALBA [CN]
TEL. 017365423
www.battaglio.com

CELLAR SALES
PRE-BOOKED VISITS
ANNUAL PRODUCTION 35,000 bottles
HECTARES UNDER VINE 5.00

The Battaglio family's winery was founded in 1981, although it did not begin bottling its wines until the late 1990s. Today the estate is divided between the Roero vineyards in Vezza d'Alba, and the Langhe plots in the hamlet of Serragrilli, in Neive. They are planted with the traditional local cultivars, from nebbiolo and barbera to dolcetto and arneis. Most of the wines presented were very good, commencing with Barbaresco Serragrilli 2012, offering a spicy nose of dark berry fruit and a dense, powerful, juicy palate, and the fruit-rich Barbera d'Alba Madunina 2013, vaunting notes of quinine and juniper berries, and great concentration balanced by acidity. The Barbaresco 2012 is equally good, with a nose of dried aromatic herbs and liquorice and a rather simple but pleasant and fairly long palate. Nebbiolo d'Alba Valmaggiore 2012 is full and concentrated, with rich fruit and sweet spicy hints.

● Barbaresco '12	▼▼ 6
● Barbaresco Serragrilli '12	▼▼ 6
● Barbera d'Alba Madunina '13	▼▼ 3
● Nebbiolo d'Alba Valmaggiore '12	▼▼ 3
○ Langhe Arneis Perlei '14	▼ 3
○ Roero Arneis Piasì '14	▼ 3
○ Amus	♈ 4
● Barbaresco '11	♈ 6
● Barbaresco '10	♈ 6
● Barbaresco Serragrilli '11	♈ 6
● Barbera d'Alba Madunina '11	♈ 3
● Barbera d'Alba Madunina '09	♈ 3
● Nebbiolo d'Alba Valmaggiore '11	♈ 3*
● Nebbiolo d'Alba Valmaggiore '10	♈ 3
● Nebbiolo d'Alba Valmaggiore '08	♈ 3
● Nebbiolo d'Alba Valmaggiore Sup. '11	♈ 5

Bava

S.DA MONFERRATO, 2
14023 COCCONATO [AT]
TEL. 0141907083
www.bava.com

CELLAR SALES
PRE-BOOKED VISITS
ACCOMMODATION
ANNUAL PRODUCTION 490,000 bottles
HECTARES UNDER VINE 55.00

The Bava family have lived in Cocconato since the 17th century and founded their winery over 100 years ago, in 1911. Today it vaunts estates in both Monferrato, where the vineyards in Cocconato, Cioccaro di Penango, and Agliano Terme are dominated by barbera, and Langhe, in Castiglione Falletto, which is also home to the cellar where Barolo and Dolcetto d'Alba are made. Since 1978 the family have also owned the Giulio Cocchi brand, which produces sparkling wines and aperitifs. Production of the former is becoming increasingly important, particularly the Alta Langa Pas Dosé Giulio Cocchi 2008, with a delicate nose of crusty bread, damsons, and white-fleshed fruit, and a complex palate underpinned by acidity, with a long, fresh finish. The other two versions of Alta Langa Brut are also well made, with great backbone and fullness. We also liked Barbera d'Asti Nizza Piano Alto 2011, with classic notes of dark berries and liquorice, and the pleasant, approachable Libera 2013.

○ Alta Langa Pas Dosé Giulio Cocchi '08	▼▼ 6
○ Alta Langa Brut Bianc 'd Bianc Giulio Cocchi '09	▼▼ 6
○ Alta Langa Brut Toto Corde Giulio Cocchi '10	▼▼ 5
● Barbera d'Asti Libera '13	▼▼ 3
● Barbera d'Asti Sup. Nizza Piano Alto '11	▼▼ 4
○ Alta Langa Brut Bianc 'd Bianc Giulio Cocchi '08	♈ 5
○ Alta Langa Brut Toto Corde Giulio Cocchi '09	♈ 4
● Barbera d'Asti Libera '11	♈ 3
● Barbera d'Asti Sup. Nizza Piano Alto '10	♈ 4
● Barolo Scarrone '10	♈ 7
○ Moscato d'Asti Bass Tuba '13	♈ 3

Bel Colle

Fraz. Castagni, 56
12060 Verduno [CN]
Tel. 0172470196
www.belcolle.it

CELLAR SALES
PRE-BOOKED VISITS
ANNUAL PRODUCTION 180,000 bottles
HECTARES UNDER VINE 10.00

This recently sold estate, which has rarely been the focus of media attention, has quietly managed to earn a place among the top Langhe producers over the years, due to the commitment and determination of the Pontiglione brothers and Giuseppe Priola. With the aid of Paolo Torchio, they have gradually made the most of the family vineyards, covering an area of around ten hectares concentrated mainly in Verduno and La Morra, with others lying between Asti, Roero, and Barbaresco. Initially known chiefly for Pelaverga, today it is its wines from nebbiolo that are in the spotlight. Despite the traditional style, the winery also experiments with more "modern" methods of maceration and ageing. This year Bel Colle presented a little vertical of Barbaresco Roncaglie and, contrary to our expectations, it was the 2011 that came out on top. It shows impressive fruity and spicy mobility, developing more in progression than in breadth and culminating in a long finish. The 2010 is also excellent, held back only by a few too many evolved notes.

● Barbaresco Roncaglie '11	🍷🍷	5
● Barolo Monvigliero '11	🍷🍷	5
● Barbaresco Roncaglie '10	🍷🍷	5
● Barbera d'Alba Sup. Le Masche '13	🍷🍷	3
● Verduno Pelaverga '14	🍷🍷	3
○ Roero Arnels '14	🍷	6
● Barbaresco Roncaglie Ris. '08	YYY	5
● Barolo Monvigliero '09	YYY	5
● Barolo Monvigliero '07	YYY	5
● Barolo Monvigliero '06	YYY	5
● Barbaresco Roncaglie '09	YY	5
● Barbera d'Alba Sup. Le Masche '11	YY	3
● Barolo '10	YY	5
● Barolo Boscato '09	YY	5
● Verduno Pelaverga '13	YY	3

Bera

via Castellero, 12
12050 Neviglie [CN]
Tel. 0173630500
www.bera.it

CELLAR SALES
PRE-BOOKED VISITS
RESTAURANT SERVICE
ANNUAL PRODUCTION 140,000 bottles
HECTARES UNDER VINE 26.00

The Bera family's winery is a well-established operation, known for its Moscato d'Asti and sparkling wines from Asti and Alta Langa. However, it also makes good still dry wines from native grape varieties, like barbera, dolcetto, and nebbiolo. The vineyards have an average age of around 40 years old and are situated on clayey-tufa hillsides, at altitudes between 320 and 380 metres. Moscato d'Asti Su Reimond 2014 is one of the finest of its kind. On the nose it is concentrated and very broad, with attractive notes of peaches, sage and candied lemon, while the palate has good backbone, well-balanced sugar and alcohol, and a long, refreshing finish. Barbera d'Alba Superiore La Lena 2012 is also very good, with a nose of ripe dark berries, tobacco and rain-soaked earth, and a full, complex palate with taut acidity ensuring balance, length, and character.

○ Moscato d'Asti Su Reimond '14	🍷🍷	3*
● Barbaresco '11	🍷🍷	5
● Barbera d'Alba '14	🍷🍷	2*
● Barbera d'Alba Sup. La Lena '12	🍷🍷	3
● Barbera d'Asti Sup. '12	🍷🍷	2*
○ Moscato d'Asti '14	🍷🍷	2*
○ Asti '14	🍷	3
○ Langhe Arneis '14	🍷	2
● Langhe Sassisto '12	🍷	3
● Barbaresco '10	YY	5
● Barbaresco '07	YY	5
● Barbaresco Ris. '09	YY	5
● Barbera d'Alba Sup. La Lena '11	YY	3
● Barbera d'Alba Sup. La Lena '04	YY	3*
● Barbera d'Asti Sup. '11	YY	2*
○ Moscato d'Asti Su Reimond '13	YY	2*

Cinzia Bergaglio

VIA GAVI, 29
15060 TASSAROLO [AL]
TEL. 01433422203
www.vinicinziabergaglio.it

CELLAR SALES
PRE-BOOKED VISITS
ANNUAL PRODUCTION 30,000 bottles
HECTARES UNDER VINE 9.00

Cinzia Bergaglio's vineyards cover an area of almost ten hectares, planted entirely to cortese. A sensitive, dedicated vigneronne, she personally crafts the small range of wines that fully reflect the different soils of the main vineyards where the grapes for the two classic whites are grown. Hailing from the prevalently calcareous clay Gavi hills, the fruit destined for the steel-aged Grifone delle Rovere undergoes brief cold soaking prior to fermentation. La Fornace is made from grapes from the Tassarolo vineyards, which lie on iron-rich tufa soils, fermented using the traditional off-the-skins method. The range is completed by Pulein, a Metodo Classico sparkler. Grifone delle Roveri made it into our finals with a very classic, varietal 2014 version. Showing straw yellow with pale green highlights, it offers a nose of fresh fruit with subtle herbaceous undertones, which are echoed on the fresh, balanced palate with a long finish. La Fornace is a little different in style, displaying a slightly more evolved nose and a firmly structured palate with less incisive acidity.

○ Gavi del Comune di Gavi Grifone delle Roveri '14	♟♟ 2*
○ Gavi La Fornace '14	♟♟ 2*
○ Gavi del Comune di Gavi Grifone delle Roveri '13	♟♟ 2*
○ Gavi del Comune di Gavi Grifone delle Roveri '12	♟♟ 2*
○ Gavi del Comune di Gavi Grifone delle Roveri '11	♟♟ 2*
○ Gavi La Fornace '13	♟♟ 2*
○ Gavi La Fornace '12	♟♟ 2*
○ Gavi La Fornace '10	♟♟ 2*
○ Gavi La Fornace '09	♟♟ 2*

Nicola Bergaglio

FRAZ. ROVERETO
LOC. PEDAGGERI, 59
15066 GAVI [AL]
TEL. 0143682195
nicolabergaglio@alice.it

CELLAR SALES
PRE-BOOKED VISITS
ANNUAL PRODUCTION 140,000 bottles
HECTARES UNDER VINE 17.00
SUSTAINABLE WINERY

If you think Cortese di Gavi is little more than a light summer white, for drinking up within a few months, Nicola Bergaglio's wines are guaranteed to make you change your mind. The small estate on the Pedaggeri hillsides was founded in 1945, but only started bottling its own wines in the early 1970s. Today it is run by Gianluigi, aided by his son Diego, and is a beacon for those seeking exciting, ageworthy Gavis, commencing with the stunning Minaia selection, fermented and aged in steel, which faithfully reflects the terroir of the Rovereto hill. Both of Nicola Bergaglio's Gavis reached our finals, despite the difficulties of the 2014 vintage. Minaia is delicate and complex, with a nose of white-fleshed fruit and flowers with mineral undertones, and a firmly structured palate. It opens up progressively and ends in a long, refreshing finish. The Gavi 2014 is very good, with a complex mineral tone.

○ Gavi del Comune di Gavi Minaia '14	♟♟♟ 4*
○ Gavi del Comune di Gavi Et. Bianca '14	♟♟ 3*
○ Gavi del Comune di Gavi Minaia '11	♟♟♟ 4*
○ Gavi del Comune di Gavi Minaia '10	♟♟♟ 4
○ Gavi del Comune di Gavi Minaia '09	♟♟♟ 4
○ Gavi del Comune di Gavi '13	♟♟ 2*
○ Gavi del Comune di Gavi '12	♟♟ 2*
○ Gavi del Comune di Gavi '11	♟♟ 3
○ Gavi del Comune di Gavi '10	♟♟ 2
○ Gavi del Comune di Gavi '09	♟♟ 3
○ Gavi del Comune di Gavi '08	♟♟ 2*
○ Gavi del Comune di Gavi '07	♟♟ 2*
○ Gavi del Comune di Gavi Minaia '13	♟♟ 4
○ Gavi del Comune di Gavi Minaia '12	♟♟ 3*
○ Gavi del Comune di Gavi Minaia '08	♟♟ 3*
○ Gavi del Comune di Gavi Minaia '07	♟♟ 2*

THE LOBSTER HAS PINCHED SOME IMPORTANT MEDALS.

Vermentino di Sardegna Aragosta.
Gold medal at Berliner Wein Trophy 2015,
Silver medal at Decanter 2015 and
Bronze medal at Wine Challenge 2015.

www.santamarialapalma.it

CANTINA SANTA MARIA LA PALMA

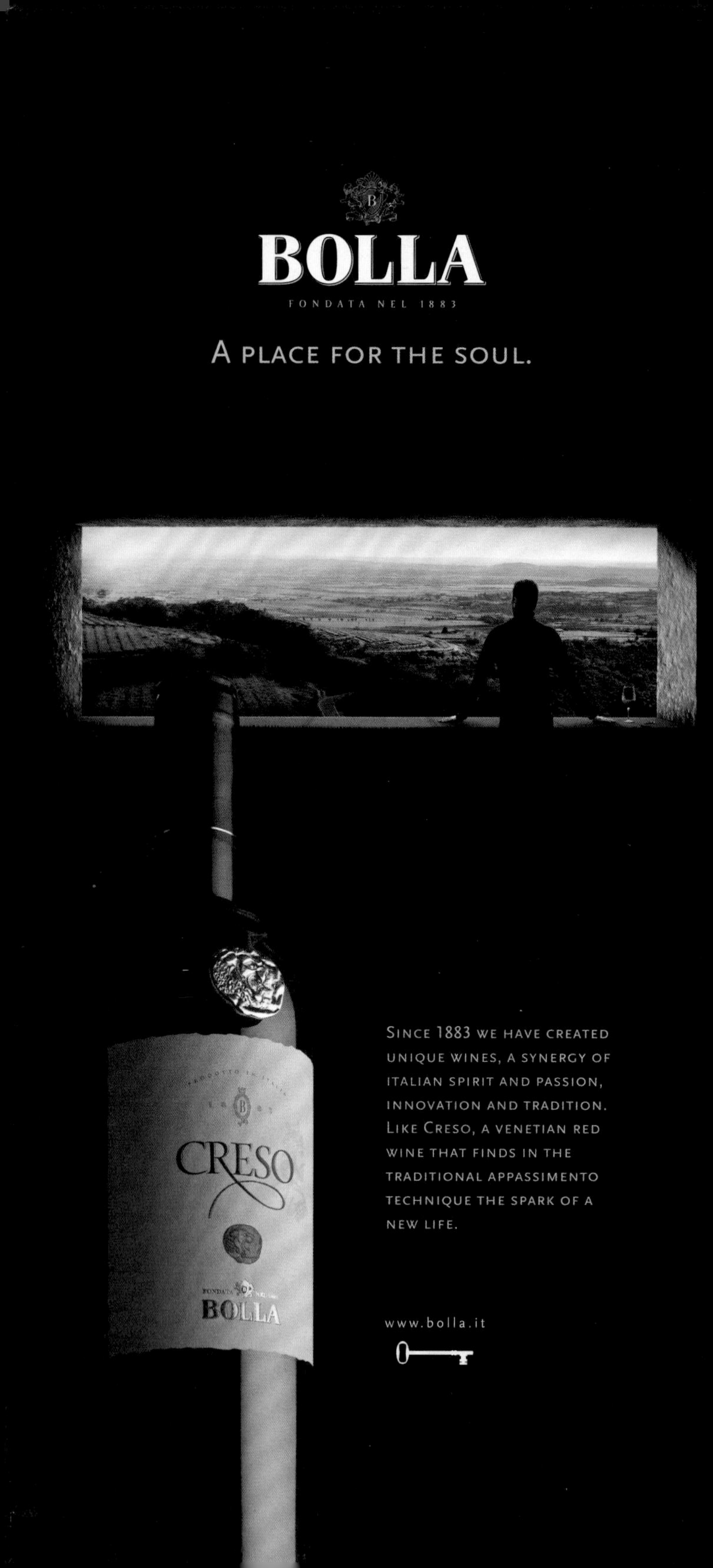

BOLLA

FONDATA NEL 1883

A PLACE FOR THE SOUL.

SINCE 1883 WE HAVE CREATED
UNIQUE WINES, A SYNERGY OF
ITALIAN SPIRIT AND PASSION,
INNOVATION AND TRADITION.
LIKE CRESO, A VENETIAN RED
WINE THAT FINDS IN THE
TRADITIONAL APPASSIMENTO
TECHNIQUE THE SPARK OF A
NEW LIFE.

www.bolla.it

Bersano

P.ZZA DANTE, 21
14049 NIZZA MONFERRATO [AT]
TEL. 0141720211
www.bersano.it

CELLAR SALES
PRE-BOOKED VISITS
ANNUAL PRODUCTION 1,800,000 bottles
HECTARES UNDER VINE 230.00

Ever since its foundation in 1935, Bersano's policy has been to purchase vineyards from which to make its own wine, as opposed to buying grapes from growers, as was customary at the time. This has made it the imposing winery it is today, with several estates in the Asti area, Monferrato and Langhe, planted with grapes ranging from barbera to Barolo nebbiolo, moscato, ruché, grignolino and brachetto. They yield a wide range of wines, including a Metodo Classico sparkler from pinot nero and chardonnay. Bersano gave a good all-round performance this year. We particularly liked the Barolo Riserva 2008, with a nicely balanced, concentrated nose of fresh fruit, tobacco and sweet spice, and a full, lively palate with finesse and exceptional length, and Barbera d'Asti Superiore Nizza Generala 2012, offering an earthy nose of dark berries with smoky hints, and a powerful, juicy palate.

Guido Berta

LOC. SALINE, 53
14050 SAN MARZANO OLIVETO [AT]
TEL. 0141856193
www.guidoberta.com

CELLAR SALES
PRE-BOOKED VISITS
ANNUAL PRODUCTION 3,000 bottles
HECTARES UNDER VINE 12.00

Guido Berta's winery was founded in 1997 in San Marzano Oliveto, where most of its vineyards are situated, with vines from 25 to over 50 years old, growing on calcareous clay soil. Barbera is the mainstay, but moscato and chardonnay are also grown in smaller amounts. This year the estate presented a very high-quality list of wines. We particularly liked the juicy, mineral Barbera d'Asti Superiore Nizza Canto di Luna 2012, with aromas of dark berry fruit, aromatic herbs, and Mediterranean scrubland, good stuffing, and long, gutsy finish. The delicate, balanced Moscato d'Asti 2014 is also very good, with fine notes of peaches and sage, good backbone for the vintage, and a very fresh, lingering finish. Barbera d'Asti Superiore 2013 is well made, with a classic nose of rain-soaked earth, tobacco, and ripe dark berry fruit, with hints of orange peel, and a full, close-knit palate.

● Barbera d'Asti Sup. Nizza Generala '12	❦❦❦5
● Barolo Ris. '08	❦❦❦7
○ Arturo Bersano Brut M. Cl. '11	❦❦4
⊙ Arturosè Brut Rosé M. Cl.	❦❦4
● Barbera d'Asti Sup. Cremosina '13	❦❦3
● Barolo Nirvasco '11	❦❦6
○ Moscato d'Asti Monteolivo '14	❦❦3
● Barbera d'Asti Sup. Generala '97	❦❦❦5
○ Arturo Bersano Brut M. Cl. '10	❦❦4
● Barbera d'Asti Costalunga '13	❦❦2*
● Barbera d'Asti Sup. Cremosina '12	❦❦3*
● Barbera d'Asti Sup. Nizza Generala '11	❦❦5
● Barolo Badarina '09	❦❦7
● Barolo Badarina '08	❦❦6
● Barolo Nirvasco '10	❦❦6
● Barolo Ris. '07	❦❦7

● Barbera d'Asti Sup. Nizza Canto di Luna '12	❦❦❦5
● Barbera d'Asti Sup. '13	❦❦3
○ Moscato d'Asti '14	❦❦3
● Barbera d'Asti Le Rondini '14	❦3
● Barbera d'Asti Sup. '12	❦❦4
● Barbera d'Asti Sup. '11	❦❦4
● Barbera d'Asti Sup. '09	❦❦4
● Barbera d'Asti Sup. '08	❦❦3
● Barbera d'Asti Sup. '07	❦❦3
● Barbera d'Asti Sup. Nizza Canto di Luna '11	❦❦5
● Barbera d'Asti Sup. Nizza Canto di Luna '10	❦❦5
● Barbera d'Asti Sup. Nizza Canto di Luna '09	❦❦5

Enzo Boglietti

VIA FONTANE, 18A
12064 LA MORRA [CN]
TEL. 017350330
www.enzoboglietti.com

CELLAR SALES
PRE-BOOKED VISITS
ACCOMMODATION
ANNUAL PRODUCTION 100,000 bottles
HECTARES UNDER VINE 22.50
VITICULTURE METHOD Certified Organic
SUSTAINABLE WINERY

The new winery is now ten years old. We recommend a visit to the handsome, practical cellar, partly to experience the warmth with which Enzo Boglietti (aided by his brother Gianni in the vineyard since 1996) welcomes visitors and lets them taste his elegant, toasty wines. The star attraction is Barolo, of which five different versions are produced, although the innovative Barbera d'Alba selections and the powerful Langhe Buio have always been a talking point. The vineyards are mainly in La Morra, with a few spilling over into Roddino and, particularly Serralunga d'Alba, from which the complex Barolo Arione hails. The Barolo 2011 vineyard selections are full and firmly structured, in keeping with the house style and aided, sometimes excessively, by the rather hot, sunny vintage. The Fossati is the most successful, with unexpected freshness that makes it youthful and juicily drinkable, despite its alcohol content. Although the Arione's nose of jam and brandied fruit is fading a little, it redeems itself with a beautifully balanced palate.

● Barolo Fossati '11	▼▼ 8
● Barbera d'Alba '13	▼▼ 3
● Barbera d'Alba Roscaleto '12	▼▼ 5
● Barbera d'Alba V. dei Romani '11	▼▼ 6
● Barolo Arione '11	▼▼ 8
● Barolo Case Nere '11	▼▼ 8
● Langhe Nebbiolo '13	▼▼ 3
● Barolo Boiolo '11	▼ 6
● Barolo Brunate '11	▼ 8
● Barolo Arione '06	▼▼▼ 8
● Barolo Arione '05	▼▼▼ 8
● Barolo Brunate '01	▼▼▼ 8
● Barolo Brunate '97	▼▼▼ 8
● Barolo Case Nere '04	▼▼▼ 8
● Barolo Case Nere '99	▼▼▼ 8
● Barolo V. Arione '07	▼▼▼ 8

Bondi - Cascina Banaia

S.DA CAPPELLETTE, 73
15076 OVADA [AL]
TEL. 0131299186
www.bondivini.it

CELLAR SALES
PRE-BOOKED VISITS
ANNUAL PRODUCTION 20,000 bottles
HECTARES UNDER VINE 5.00

The Bondi family founded their winery in 2000, with very clear ideas about the path they wished to take. Their vineyards are exceptionally well aspected, set on the fabled white marl-and-limestone soils that give the fruit an extra something, which is subsequently conveyed in the glass. This is particularly true of Dolcetto, a wine with huge potential, which is greatly underrated and the grape variety is still struggling to find its place on the international market, The path chosen by the Bondis is closely associated with quality and the meticulous passion of modern artisans, who know their future is in their own hands. Barbera Banaiotta is simply magnificent, offering aromas of cherries, plums, and blackberries enriched by spicy wood, which explodes on the rich, unctuous palate, underpinned by acidity, with a beautifully long finish. Ruvrin is even more austere, due to ageing in oak, but vaunts huge personality.

● Barbera del M.to Ruvrin '10	▼▼ 4
● Banaiotta	▼▼ 4
● M.to Rosso Ansensò '11	▼▼ 4
● Barbera del M.to Banaiotta '10	♀♀ 2*
● Barbera del M.to Banaiotta '06	♀♀ 4*
● Dolcetto di Ovada Nani '08	♀♀ 2*
● Dolcetto di Ovada Nani '07	♀♀ 2*
● Dolcetto di Ovada Sup. D'Uien '08	♀♀ 3
● Dolcetto di Ovada Sup. d'Uien '07	♀♀ 3
● Dolcetto di Ovada Sup. Du'ien '06	♀♀ 3
● M.to Barbera Banaiotta '09	♀♀ 4
● M.to Barbera Ruvrin '04	♀♀ 4
● M.to Barbera Ruvrin Sup. '07	♀♀ 4
● M.to Barbera Ruvrin Sup. '06	♀♀ 4
● M.to Rosso Ansensò '06	♀♀ 4
● Nani	♀♀ 2*

Bongiovanni

LOC. UCCELLACCIO
VIA ALBA BAROLO, 3
12060 CASTIGLIONE FALLETTO [CN]
TEL. 0173262184
www.cascinabongiovanni.com

CELLAR SALES
PRE-BOOKED VISITS
ANNUAL PRODUCTION 35,000 bottles
HECTARES UNDER VINE 7.20
SUSTAINABLE WINERY

Cascina Bongiovanni is a small family-run estate that is a fascinating and genuine expression of Langhe. Davide Mozzone continues a solid, deep-rooted tradition, interpreting the various grape varieties in a consistent and highly distinctive style. His vineyards are in Castiglione Falletto and a few particularly good locations in neighbouring municipalities, forming a first-rate estate. As has already happened several times in the past, Barolo Pernanno 2011 is still too young and not yet able to express its full potential. The nose proffers dark notes of liquorice and tar, before opening onto a powerful palate with still unresolved tannins. The basic Barolo is already more approachable and delicate, with rich fruity aromas. We very much liked the Barbera d'Alba, which focuses on juicy fruit, accompanied by a long, supple palate.

Gilberto Boniperti

VIA VITTORIO EMANUELE, 43/45
28010 BARENGO [NO]
TEL. 0321997123
www.bonipertivignaioli.com

CELLAR SALES
ANNUAL PRODUCTION 12,000 bottles
HECTARES UNDER VINE 3.50

Gilberto has chosen the motto "Sun, Terroir, Tradition" for his winery, but this does not mean great care is not lavished on the grapes and wines, both in the vineyard and in the cellar, where he is aided by oenologist Cristiano Garella. This is demonstrated by the ageing method used for the reds, which features French oak barrels of different sizes and ages. Focusing on the classic local grape varieties of nebbiolo, vespolina and barbera, the little winery enriches the increasingly lively and interesting world of North Piedmont wine production. Fara Bartön 2012 is still very youthful, with splendid fruit and a complex nose of soot and embers. On the palate it is tannic, but with dense fruit that ensures good development in bottle. The 2013 Vespolina tries to compensate for its lack of acidity with close-focused notes of white pepper, while the clean, flavoursome Rosadisera, from nebbiolo, confirms itself one of Piedmont's finest rosés.

● Barolo Pernanno '11	♟♟ 6
● Barbera d'Alba '13	♟♟ 3
● Barolo '11	♟♟ 5
● Dolcetto di Diano d'Alba '14	♟♟ 2*
● Langhe Rosso Faletto '13	♟♟ 4
● Dolcetto d'Alba '14	♟ 2
○ Langhe Arneis '14	♟ 2
● Barolo Pernanno '01	♟♟♟ 6
● Barbera d'Alba '11	♀♀ 3
● Barolo '10	♀♀ 5
● Barolo '09	♀♀ 5
● Barolo Pernanno '10	♀♀ 6
● Dolcetto di Diano d'Alba '13	♀♀ 2*
● Dolcetto di Diano d'Alba '12	♀♀ 2*
● Langhe Rosso Faletto '12	♀♀ 4

● Fara Bartön '12	♟♟ 4
● Colline Novaresi Nebbiolo Carlin '13	♟♟ 4
○ Rosadisera	♟♟ 3
● Colline Novaresi Vespolina Favolalunga '13	♟ 2
● Colline Novaresi Barbera Barblin '10	♀♀ 4
● Colline Novaresi Nebbiolo Bartön '10	♀♀ 4
● Colline Novaresi Nebbiolo Bartön '08	♀♀ 4
● Colline Novaresi Nebbiolo Carlin '12	♀♀ 4
● Colline Novaresi Nebbiolo Carlin '11	♀♀ 4
● Colline Novaresi Nebbiolo Carlin '10	♀♀ 4
● Colline Novaresi Vespolina Favolalunga '12	♀♀ 3

Borgo Isolabella

REG. CAFFI, 3
14051 LOAZZOLO [AT]
TEL. 014487166
www.isolabelladellacroce.it

CELLAR SALES
PRE-BOOKED VISITS
ANNUAL PRODUCTION 90,000 bottles
HECTARES UNDER VINE 14.00

The winery owned by the Isolabella della Croce family lies in a natural amphitheatre in the Upper Bormida Valley, over 500 metres above sea level, in one of Italy's smallest DOC zones. Here it produces a wide range of wines, from both native and international grape varieties. Indeed, in 2007 the moscato planted on the steeply sloping plots, surrounded by woodland, was joined by a pinot nero vineyard with 11,000 vines per hectare. It also owns three-hectare estate, entirely planted to barbera, in Calamandra, in the Nizza production zone. Borgo Isolabella's wines put up a good performance, although there were no pinnacles of excellence. We particularly liked the warm, caressing Barbera d'Asti Superiore Nizza Augusta 2011, with jammy fruit notes and a deliciously fresh finish, and Moscato d'Asti Valdiserre 2014, characterized by peach and mint, with hints of citrus, moderate structure, and a sweet finish.

Wine	Rating
● Barbera d'Asti Sup. Nizza Augusta '11	♟♟ 4
● Barbera d'Asti Sup. Serena '12	♟♟ 4
○ Moscato d'Asti Valdiserre '14	♟♟ 3
○ Piemonte Sauvignon Blanc '14	♟♟ 3
● Piemonte Pinot Nero Bricco del Falco '11	♟ 5
● Barbera d'Asti Sup. Nizza Augusta '09	♟♟ 4
● Barbera d'Asti Sup. Nizza Augusta '08	♟♟ 4
● Barbera d'Asti Sup. Serena '11	♟♟ 4
● Barbera d'Asti Sup. Serena '10	♟♟ 4
○ Loazzolo V. T. Solio '06	♟♟ 5
● M.to Rosso Bricco del Falco '09	♟♟ 5
○ Moscato d'Asti Valdiserre '12	♟♟ 3
● Piemonte Pinot Nero Bricco del Falco '10	♟♟ 5
○ Piemonte Sauvignon Blanc '13	♟♟ 3

Borgo Maragliano

VIA SAN SEBASTIANO, 2
14051 LOAZZOLO [AT]
TEL. 014487132
www.borgomaragliano.com

CELLAR SALES
PRE-BOOKED VISITS
ANNUAL PRODUCTION 285,000 bottles
HECTARES UNDER VINE 27.00
SUSTAINABLE WINERY

Although Carlo and Silvia Galliano's estate was founded in 1990, the family have been vignerons in Loazzolo, in the Upper Bormida Valley, since the mid 1800s. Over half their vineyards, lying on sandy, tufa and limestone soils, between 360 and 570 metres above sea level, are planted with moscato bianco di Canelli, which yields the estate's flagship wine, Loazzolo Vendemmia Tardiva. Moscato is flanked by chardonnay and pinot nero, used to make both still wines and sparklers, and brachetto is grown in a small vineyard in Bistagno, in the province of Alessandria. The finest of the range is Francesco Galliano Blanc de Blancs 2012, with a classic nose of wholemeal and crusty bread, accompanied by a faint note of quinine, and a delicate, well-orchestrated palate with attractive acidity ensuring freshness and staying power on the long finish. The rest of the range is good, particularly the citrussy, balsamic Moscato d'Asti La Caliera 2014, which is fresh and pleasant.

Wine	Rating
○ Francesco Galliano Blanc de Blancs Brut M. Cl. '12	♟♟ 4
⊙ Giovanni Galliano Brut Rosé M. Cl. '11	♟♟ 4
○ Giuseppe Galliano Brut M. Cl. Ris. '09	♟♟ 5
○ Moscato d'Asti La Caliera '14	♟♟ 2*
○ Chardonnay Brut	♟ 2
○ Monferrato Bianco PerFede '14	♟ 3
○ Giuseppe Galliano Ris. Brut M. Cl. '01	♟♟♟ 4*
○ Dogma Blanc de Noirs M. Cl. '10	♟♟ 5
○ El Calié '13	♟♟ 2*
○ El Calié '11	♟♟ 2*
○ Giovanni Galliano Brut Rosé M. Cl. '10	♟♟ 4
○ Giuseppe Galliano Brut M. Cl. '10	♟♟ 4
○ Giuseppe Galliano Brut M. Cl. '09	♟♟ 4
○ Giuseppe Galliano Ris. Brut M. Cl. '06	♟♟ 5
○ Loazzolo V. T. '10	♟♟ 5

Giacomo Borgogno & Figli

VIA GIOBERTI, 16
12060 BAROLO [CN]
TEL. 0173626108
www.borgogno.com

CELLAR SALES
PRE-BOOKED VISITS
ANNUAL PRODUCTION 150,000 bottles
HECTARES UNDER VINE 13.00
SUSTAINABLE WINERY

It is no accident that the production venture of Oscar Farinetti and his family commenced in Borgogno, a name that in Barolo conjures up a well-defined style, based on a tradition over 100 years old. Following its takeover in 2008, the winery's range has been expanded and the classic wines are now flanked by innovative lines (No Name, Le Teorie, I Colori del Barolo, Resistenza), which often reflect the latest trends. However, it is the estate's approximately 16 hectares of vineyards (over half of which planted to nebbiolo) in crus such as Cannubi, Cannubi San Lorenzo, Fossati, Liste, and San Pietro delle Viole that make the difference. As usual we were spoiled for choice with Borgogno's selection of Nebbiolos. The Barolo 2011 is already a gem of harmony and dynamism, exceeded only by Cannubi 2010 in terms of stuffing. However, the complex Liste 2010 is even better, with layered peppery and citrussy notes, and a palate that promises very well.

● Barolo Liste '10	▼▼▼ 8
● Barolo '11	▼▼ 7
● Barolo Cannubi '10	▼▼ 8
● Barolo Fossati '10	▼▼ 7
● Barolo Ris. '08	▼▼ 8
● Barolo Liste '08	♀♀♀ 8
● Barolo Liste '07	♀♀♀ 7
● Barolo Liste '05	♀♀♀ 7
● Barolo V. Liste '06	♀♀♀ 7

Francesco Boschis

FRAZ. SAN MARTINO DI PIANEZZO, 57
12063 DOGLIANI [CN]
TEL. 017370574
www.marcdegrazia.com

CELLAR SALES
PRE-BOOKED VISITS
ANNUAL PRODUCTION 40,000 bottles
HECTARES UNDER VINE 11.00

The estate's location, in a fairly high area of Dogliani, about 500 metres above sea level, means its wines, mainly from dolcetto, are pleasantly fresh. This is certainly welcome in a type (Dogliani) that tends towards tannin content rather than acidity. It is a small, family-run winery that pays great attention to the health of its vineyards and uses traditional cellar processes with appropriate technology, all accompanied by a passion for wine that has been handed down through the generations with excellent results. Sorì San Martino 2013 is exceptionally sound, with a nose of cocoa powder and bitter almonds, followed by a palate with remarkable backbone and slightly prominent tannins. Vigna dei Prey 2013 is a little more rustic, while the Pianezzo from the difficult 2014 vintage is small and slightly blurred. The Sauvignon confirms itself one of the zone's finest whites, with a nose of sage and tropical fruit and a long, fresh palate.

● Dogliani Sup. Sorì San Martino '13	▼▼ 3
● Dogliani Sup. V. dei Prey '13	▼▼ 3
○ Langhe Sauvignon V. dei Garisin '14	▼▼ 3
● Barbera d'Alba Sup. Le Masserie '12	▼ 3
● Dogliani Pianezzo '14	▼ 2
● Dogliani Pianezzo '13	♀♀ 2*
● Dogliani Pianezzo '12	♀♀ 2*
● Dogliani Sorì San Martino '10	♀♀ 2*
● Dogliani Sup. Sorì San Martino '12	♀♀ 3*
● Dogliani Sup. Sorì San Martino '11	♀♀ 3
● Dogliani Sup. V. dei Prey '12	♀♀ 3
● Dogliani Sup. V. dei Prey '11	♀♀ 3*
● Dogliani V. dei Prey '10	♀♀ 2*
● Langhe Rosso nei Sorì '10	♀♀ 4
○ Langhe Sauvignon V. dei Garisin '13	♀♀ 3
○ Langhe Sauvignon V. dei Garisin '12	♀♀ 3*

Agostino Bosco

VIA FONTANE, 24
12064 LA MORRA [CN]
TEL. 0173509466
www.barolobosco.com

CELLAR SALES
PRE-BOOKED VISITS
ANNUAL PRODUCTION 28,000 bottles
HECTARES UNDER VINE 5.50
SUSTAINABLE WINERY

This small winery is emblematic of the qualitative development of the Langhe wine world over the past 40 years. Grandfather Pietro concentrates more on work in the vineyards than on sales, while his son Agostino has developed the winemaking side and stopped selling the estate's grapes, and his grandson Andrea, a graduate of the Oenological School in Alba, has used his skills to further boost quality. The range is very narrow, with two Barolos, a Nebbiolo, a Barbera, and a Dolcetto, all painstakingly crafted in the small cellar, which is currently being expanded. The entire range is characterized by careful work in the cellar and drinkability. Barolo Neirane 2011 has traditional aromas and good tannic content, while the spicy La Serra vineyard selection has rather edgy tannins. Dolcetto d'Alba Vantrin 2014 is close focused and crisp, and Barbera d'Alba Superiore Volupta is sound and not overly challenging.

● Barbera d'Alba Sup. Volupta '13	♥♥ 3
● Barolo La Serra '11	♥♥ 6
● Barolo Neirane '11	♥♥ 5
● Dolcetto d'Alba Vantrin '14	♥♥ 2*
● Langhe Nebbiolo Rurem '13	♥ 3
● Barbera d'Alba Sup. Volupta '11	♀♀ 3
● Barbera d'Alba Volupta '11	♀♀ 3
● Barolo La Serra '10	♀♀ 6
● Barolo La Serra '09	♀♀ 6
● Barolo La Serra '08	♀♀ 5
● Barolo Neirane '10	♀♀ 5
● Barolo Neirane '09	♀♀ 5
● Dolcetto d'Alba Vantrin '13	♀♀ 2*
● Langhe Nebbiolo Rurem '12	♀♀ 3
● Langhe Nebbiolo Rurem '11	♀♀ 3
● Langhe Nebbiolo Rurem '10	♀♀ 2*

Luigi Boveri

LOC. MONTALE CELLI
VIA XX SETTEMBRE, 6
15050 COSTA VESCOVATO [AL]
TEL. 0131838165
www.boveriluigi.com

CELLAR SALES
PRE-BOOKED VISITS
ANNUAL PRODUCTION 80,000 bottles
HECTARES UNDER VINE 15.00

In the space of just over 20 years Luigi Boveri and his wife Germana have made the estate what it is today: an example of artisanal skill that respects rural traditions handed down for generations. Great attention is lavished on the entire production process, in both the cellar and the vineyard, where the average yield of around 5,000 kilograms per hectare is just the first stage in a virtuous cycle. The range features wines from Piedmont grape varieties: timorasso, cortese and moscato for the whites; barbera, croatina and bonarda piemontese for the reds. The sole exception is the rosé, from an equal blend of syrah and barbera. Luigi's wines are no longer a surprise. This year three of them made it into our finals: Filari di Timorasso, with a complex, vibrant nose and a rich, lingering palate; the elegant, approachable Derthona, with a nose of flowers and white-fleshed fruit against a mineral background and a fresh, well-behaved palate; and Vignalunga, a concentrated, stylish Barbera.

○ Colli Tortonesi Timorasso Filari di Timorasso '12	♥♥♥ 5
● Colli Tortonesi Barbera Vignalunga '12	♥♥ 5
○ Colli Tortonesi Timorasso Derthona '13	♥♥ 4
● Colli Tortonesi Barbera Poggio delle Amarene '13	♥♥ 4
● Colli Tortonesi Barbera Boccanera '14	♥ 2
○ Colli Tortonesi Cortese Terre del Prete '14	♥ 2
○ Ramasco	♥ 2
○ Colli Tortonesi Timorasso Derthona '11	♀♀♀ 4*
○ Colli Tortonesi Timorasso Filari di Timorasso '07	♀♀♀ 3
● Colli Tortonesi Barbera Boccanera '13	♀♀ 2*
● Colli Tortonesi Barbera Poggio delle Amarene '12	♀♀ 4
○ Colli Tortonesi Timorasso Filari di Timorasso '11	♀♀ 5

Gianfranco Bovio

FRAZ. ANNUNZIATA
B.TA CIOTTO, 63
12064 LA MORRA [CN]
TEL. 017350667
www.boviogianfranco.com

CELLAR SALES
PRE-BOOKED VISITS
ANNUAL PRODUCTION 75,000 bottles
HECTARES UNDER VINE 10.00

Gian Bovio has never needed to publicize his wines, for his client base is formed by the many thousands of tourists who dined in his renowned Belvedere restaurant in La Morra and who continue to visit Langhe, seeking pleasure at his welcoming Ristorante Bovio, whose wine list we recommend to everyone as educational online reading. The house style is very classic, with particular attention to the aromatic definition of Barolo, produced in four vineyard selections. La Morra's fine Gattera vineyard has produced a layered Barolo 2011 with remarkable stuffing and rugged character, derived from its huge tannins that will require long ageing to soften, accompanied by beautifully classic up-front aromas of roses and red berry fruit. Arborina 2011 is a little wilder and racier, with notes of citrus and brandied fruit on the nose and a tannic, austere palate due to the warm vintage.

★Braida

LOC. CIAPPELLETTE
S.DA PROVINCIALE 27, 9
14030 ROCCHETTA TANARO [AT]
TEL. 0141644113
www.braida.it

CELLAR SALES
PRE-BOOKED VISITS
ACCOMMODATION AND RESTAURANT SERVICE
ANNUAL PRODUCTION 650,000 bottles
HECTARES UNDER VINE 65.00
SUSTAINABLE WINERY

The Bologna family winery, now run by the third generation, Raffaella and Giuseppe, has been an important benchmark for production in Monferrato and beyond for half a century. Barbera is its speciality, yielding the estate's most renowned wines. Its vineyards are located in Rocchetta Tanaro, Costigliole d'Asti, Castelnuovo Calcea, Mango (where the moscato is grown) and Trezzo Tinella (from which the whites of the Serra dei Fiori hail). Barbera d'Asti Superiore Bricco dell'Uccellone is once again among the best of its type. The 2013 vintage has a concentrated nose of tobacco, quinine, and dark berries, followed by a compact, flavoursome, close-knit palate underpinned by acidity, with a very long, characterful finish. Barbera d'Asti Montebruna also continues to seduce us, showing fresh and fruity in the very well-typed, earthy, gutsy 2013 vintage. The rest of the list is worthy of its reputation.

● Barolo Gattera '11	♥♥♥ 6
● Barolo '11	♥♥ 6
● Barolo Arborina '11	♥♥ 6
● Langhe Nebbiolo '13	♥♥ 3
● Barbera d'Alba Il Ciotto '14	♥ 2
● Dolcetto d'Alba Dabbene '14	♥ 2
● Barolo Bricco Parussi Ris. '01	♥♥♥ 6
● Barolo Rocchettevino '06	♥♥♥ 5*
● Barolo V. Arborina '90	♥♥♥ 6
● Barbera d'Alba Il Ciotto '11	♥♥ 2*
● Barolo Arborina '10	♥♥ 6
● Barolo Arborina '09	♥♥ 6
● Barolo Gattera '10	♥♥ 6
● Barolo Gattera '09	♥♥ 6
● Barolo Rocchettevino '10	♥♥ 5
● Barolo Rocchettevino '09	♥♥ 5

● Barbera d'Asti Bricco dell'Uccellone '13	♥♥ 7
● Barbera d'Asti Montebruna '13	♥♥ 3*
● Barbera d'Asti Bricco della Bigotta '13	♥♥ 7
● Grignolino d'Asti Limonte '14	♥♥ 2*
○ Langhe Bianco Il Fiore '14	♥♥ 3
○ Langhe Chardonnay Asso di Fiori '13	♥♥ 5
○ Langhe Nascetta La Regina '14	♥♥ 3
○ Moscato d'Asti V. Senza Nome '14	♥♥ 3
● Barbera d'Asti Ai Suma '04	♥♥♥ 7
● Barbera d'Asti Bricco dell'Uccellone '12	♥♥♥ 7
● Barbera d'Asti Bricco dell'Uccellone '09	♥♥♥ 6
● Barbera d'Asti Bricco dell'Uccellone '05	♥♥♥ 6
● Barbera d'Asti Bricco dell'Uccellone '03	♥♥♥ 6
● Barbera d'Asti Bricco della Bigotta '07	♥♥♥ 6
● Barbera d'Asti Bricco della Bigotta '06	♥♥♥ 6
● Barbera d'Asti Montebruna '11	♥♥♥ 3*

Brandini

FRAZ. BRANDINI, 16
12064 LA MORRA [CN]
TEL. 017350266
www.agricolabrandini.it

CELLAR SALES
PRE-BOOKED VISITS
ACCOMMODATION AND RESTAURANT SERVICE
ANNUAL PRODUCTION 80,000 bottles
HECTARES UNDER VINE 15.50
VITICULTURE METHOD Certified Organic

Completion of the guest farm has made this estate has a veritable country resort, with the winery as its jewel and main attraction. The style of its wines is becoming ever clearer, and is highly original. The convincing Barolo selections are flanked by a range of wines with great balance and substance. Born in 2010 from a little plot in the Brandini vineyard, the 2011 vintage of Barolo Resa 56, focusing on delicate notes of violets, eucalyptus, and red berries, also took our top accolade, on the strength of impeccable balance and stuffing, confirming the path taken by this young and ambitious winery. All the wines performed very well, displaying character that made each of the tastings very interesting. The fresh, drinkable Langhe Nebbiolo Filari Corti 2013 is particularly good, showing complex and varietal.

● Barolo Resa 56 '11	▼▼▼ 7
● Barolo '11	▼▼ 5
● Barbera d'Alba Sup. Rocche del Santo '13	▼▼ 3
● Dolcetto d'Alba Filari Lunghi '14	▼▼ 3
○ Langhe Bianco Le Coccinelle '14	▼▼ 4
● Langhe Nebbiolo Filari Corti '13	▼▼ 3
● Barolo Resa 56 '10	♀♀♀ 7
● Barbera d'Alba Sup. Rocche del Santo '11	♀♀ 3
● Barbera d'Alba Sup. Rocche del Santo '10	♀♀ 3*
● Barolo '10	♀♀ 5
● Barolo '09	♀♀ 5
● Barolo '08	♀♀ 6
● Barolo Brandini '09	♀♀ 6
● Barolo Brandini '08	♀♀ 6
● Dolcetto d'Alba Filari Lunghi '13	♀♀ 3
● Langhe Nebbiolo Filari Corti '12	♀♀ 3

Brangero

VIA PROVINCIALE, 26
12055 DIANO D'ALBA [CN]
TEL. 017369423
www.brangero.com

PRE-BOOKED VISITS
ANNUAL PRODUCTION 50,000 bottles
HECTARES UNDER VINE 9.00

Marco Brangero has passionately run this lively Langhe estate for about 15 years. Most of the vineyards are in a splendid scenic location in Diano d'Alba, with a another important plot in La Morra's fine Monvigliero cru. The nebbiolo grapes are vinified in the DOCG zone, in Barolo, in accordance with the production protocol. Marco has always focused on elegant, well-calibrated wines, to the point of forgoing Dolcetto production in the 2014 vintage. Barolo Monvigliero 2011 has a remarkably delicate nose, with notes ranging from fruit to incense, and fairly restrained body. The Nebbiolo d'Alba is certainly pleasant, with a lovely fresh nose featuring notes of pennyroyal and raspberries, and a rather commanding, solidly built palate with good acidity and tannins. Marco's talent is confirmed by a fat, juicy Chardonnay in unmistakable Burgundy style.

● Barolo Monvigliero '11	▼▼ 6
● Barbera d'Alba La Soprana '12	▼▼ 3
○ Langhe Chardonnay Centofile '13	▼▼ 3
● Nebbiolo d'Alba Bricco Bertone '12	▼▼ 4
○ Langhe Arneis Centofile '14	▼ 3
● Langhe Rosso Tremarzo '12	▼ 4
● Barbera d'Alba La Soprana '11	♀♀ 3
● Barolo Monvigliero '10	♀♀ 6
● Dolcetto di Diano d'Alba Sörì Rabino Soprano '13	♀♀ 2*
● Dolcetto di Diano d'Alba Sörì Rabino Soprano '12	♀♀ 2*
● Dolcetto di Diano d'Alba Sörì Rabino Soprano '11	♀♀ 2*
● Langhe Rosso Tremarzo '11	♀♀ 4
● Langhe TreMarzo '10	♀♀ 4
● Nebbiolo d'Alba Bricco Bertone '10	♀♀ 4

Brema

VIA POZZOMAGNA, 9
14045 INCISA SCAPACCINO [AT]
TEL. 014174019
www.vinibrema.com

CELLAR SALES
PRE-BOOKED VISITS
ANNUAL PRODUCTION 150,000 bottles
HECTARES UNDER VINE 25.00
SUSTAINABLE WINERY

The Brema family settled in Incisa
Scapaccino to make quality wines back in
1887, five generations ago. The star of the
show is obviously Barbera, largely due to
the estate's vineyards in some of the finest
growing areas of Nizza Monferrato and
Fontanile d'Asti. In recent years the winery
has also purchased vineyards in several
municipalities of Monferrato, and barbera
has been joined by dolcetto, grignolino,
brachetto, moscato, cabernet sauvignon
and cortese. Barbera d'Asti Superiore Nizza
Dedicato a Luigi Veronelli is back on Tre
Bicchieri form with the 2012 vintage. It
offers a very complex nose, with top notes
of ripe red berries, and is very deep, dense
and full. The tannic weave is a little austere,
but nicely underpinned by fresh acidity,
resulting in a long, sound, taut finish.
Barbera d'Asti Ai Cruss 2013 is also well
made, with tight, juicy fruit.

● Barbera d'Asti Sup. Nizza A Luigi Veronelli '12	▼▼▼ 6
● Barbera d'Asti Ai Cruss '13	▼▼ 2*
● Barbera del M.to Frizzante Castagnei '14	▼▼ 2*
● Barbera d'Asti Sup. Volpettona '12	▼ 5
● Barbera d'Asti Sup. Nizza A Luigi Veronelli '06	♈♈♈ 6
● Barbera d'Asti Ai Cruss '12	♈♈ 2*
● Barbera d'Asti Ai Cruss '11	♈♈ 2*
● Barbera d'Asti Ai Cruss '10	♈♈ 2*
● Barbera d'Asti Sup. Nizza A Luigi Veronelli '11	♈♈ 6
● Barbera d'Asti Sup. Nizza A Luigi Veronelli '09	♈♈ 6
● Barbera d'Asti Sup. Volpettona '11	♈♈ 5
● Barbera del M.to Frizzante Castagnei '13	♈♈ 2*
○ Moscato d'Asti Mariasole '12	♈♈ 2*

Giacomo Brezza & Figli

VIA LOMONDO, 4
12060 BAROLO [CN]
TEL. 0173560921
www.brezza.it

CELLAR SALES
PRE-BOOKED VISITS
ACCOMMODATION AND RESTAURANT SERVICE
ANNUAL PRODUCTION 80,000 bottles
HECTARES UNDER VINE 17.50
VITICULTURE METHOD Certified Organic
SUSTAINABLE WINERY

The Brezza family's Barolos are textbook
wines, in the finest sense of the word,
traditional in form and contemporary in
substance, meticulously reflecting the
differences in vintage, and in the soil and
climate of important crus like Cannubi,
Castellero, and Sarmassa. It is worth
enjoying them in situ, perhaps stopping at
the cellar and guesthouse for a chat with
Oreste, a veritable repository of Langhe
history. The range has grown rapidly in
recent years in terms of consistency and
qualitative pinnacles, with wines made for
ageing, but also capable of satisfying the
impatient from the moment of release.
Brezza's Barolos showed their class for the
umpteenth time. The classic version is a
brilliant introduction to the hot 2011
vintage, which flaunts itself in the
Castellero with notes of tar and jam, and
conceals itself brilliantly in the Sarmassa.
The nose of currants, topsoil, and dried
herbs is followed by a palate enlivened and
amplified by a tangy, racy, linear vein that
accompanies it through to the long finish.

● Barolo Sarmassa '11	▼▼▼ 6
● Barolo Cannubi '11	▼▼ 6
● Barolo Castellero '11	▼▼ 6
● Barbera d'Alba Sup. '12	▼▼ 4
● Barolo '11	▼▼ 5
● Nebbiolo d'Alba V. Santa Rosalia '13	▼▼ 4
● Barbera d'Alba V. Santa Rosalia '13	▼ 3
○ Langhe Chardonnay '14	▼ 3
● Barolo Bricco Sarmassa '08	♈♈♈ 7
● Barolo Bricco Sarmassa '07	♈♈♈ 7
● Barolo Sarmassa '05	♈♈♈ 6
● Barolo Cannubi '10	♈♈ 6
● Barolo Castellero '10	♈♈ 6
● Barolo Sarmassa '10	♈♈ 6
● Barolo Sarmassa '09	♈♈ 6

Bric Cenciurio

VIA ROMA, 24
12060 BAROLO [CN]
TEL. 017356317
www.briccenciurio.com

CELLAR SALES
PRE-BOOKED VISITS
ANNUAL PRODUCTION 45,000 bottles
HECTARES UNDER VINE 15.00

This dynamic winery is confidently managed by Alessandro and Alberto Pittatore, the sons of its founder Franco, with the precious aid of their mother Fiorella Sacchetto and her brother Carlo. Its distinctive feature is its vineyards, divided between Roero and Langhe. This dual location, in neighbouring but very different zones, allows it to produce an original and complementary range of wines, capable of pleasing everyone. Our tastings witnessed an excellent general performance by the family of Barolos, topped by two versions of Costa di Rose. The 2011 is very sophisticated, with close-focused balsamic and spicy notes accompanied by hints of violets, and a well-integrated tannic weave. The Riserva 2009 is deep and solid, with dark notes of tar, dark berry fruit, and tobacco, and close-knit, layered tannins. We also liked Roero Arneis Sito dei Fossili, which is one of the finest interpretations of the grape variety.

● Barolo Coste di Rose '11	▼▼ 6
● Barolo Coste di Rose Ris. '09	▼▼ 7
● Barbera d'Alba Sup. Naunda '12	▼▼ 4
● Barolo '11	▼▼ 5
● Barolo Monrobiolo di Bussia '11	▼▼ 5
○ Langhe Riesling '13	▼▼ 3
○ Roero Arneis Sito dei Fossili '13	▼▼ 3
● Barbera d'Alba '13	▼ 2
● Langhe Nebbiolo '13	▼ 4
○ Roero Arneis '14	▼ 3
● Barbera d'Alba '12	♉ 2*
● Barbera d'Alba Sup. Naunda '11	♉ 4
● Barolo '10	♉ 5
● Barolo '09	♉ 5
● Barolo Costa di Rose '10	♉ 6
○ Roero Arneis Sito dei Fossili '12	♉ 3

Bricco del Cucù

LOC. BRICCO, 10
12060 BASTIA MONDOVÌ [CN]
TEL. 017460153
www.briccocucu.com

CELLAR SALES
PRE-BOOKED VISITS
ANNUAL PRODUCTION 50,000 bottles
HECTARES UNDER VINE 10.00

Dario Sciolla not only grows grapes, but also excellent hazelnuts on his estate, which is well worth a visit due to both the quality of all its products and the friendly, down-to-earth family who own it. This little corner, rarely shown on maps of the top wine areas of Langhe, has many very interesting surprises in store, due to its high altitude and temperature fluctuations capable of ensuring uniquely refreshing wines. Sciolla's wines are characterized by their indomitable spirit, which faithfully reflects their terroir. Dogliani Superiore Bricco San Bernardo 2012 is among the most vigorous and cellarable of its kind, and is still slightly introverted, showing closed but promising on the nose. It unfolds better on the palate, revealing notes of plum jam, leather and spice. Langhe Rosso Diavolisanti 2012 is juicy, with full-flavoured, fruity flesh.

● Dogliani Sup. Bricco S. Bernardo '12	▼▼ 2*
● Langhe Rosso Diavolisanti '12	▼▼ 2*
● Langhe Rosso Superboum '12	▼▼ 2*
● Dogliani '14	▼ 2
○ Langhe Bianco Livor '14	▼ 2
● Langhe Dolcetto '14	▼ 2
● Dogliani Sup. Bricco S. Bernardo '09	▼▼▼ 2*
● Dogliani '13	♉ 2*
● Dogliani Sup. Bricco S. Bernardo '11	♉ 2*
● Dogliani Sup. Bricco S. Bernardo '10	♉ 2*
○ Langhe Bianco Livor '13	♉ 2*
○ Langhe Bianco Livor '12	♉ 2*
● Langhe Dolcetto '13	♉ 2*
● Langhe Dolcetto '12	♉ 2*
● Langhe Rosso Diavolisanti '11	♉ 2*
● Langhe Rosso Diavolisanti '10	♉ 2*

Bricco Maiolica

FRAZ. RICCA
VIA BOLANGINO, 7
12055 DIANO D'ALBA [CN]
TEL. 0173612049
www.briccomaiolica.it

CELLAR SALES
PRE-BOOKED VISITS
ANNUAL PRODUCTION 110,000 bottles
HECTARES UNDER VINE 24.00

Just over 30 years have gone by since
Beppe Accomo started working on his
handsome estate. In this time he has
transformed it, concentrating solely on
viticulture and abandoning other crops.
Rightly famous for Dolcetto di Diano d'Alba,
Beppe also offers many other wines,
including the consistently first-rate
Nebbiolo and Barbera d'Alba. His passion
for wine has led him to make very
interesting small selections from French
grape varieties, ranging from pinot nero to
merlot, sauvignon and chardonnay. Lively
and packed with fruit and spice, the bright
Nebbiolo Cumot 2012 has an exuberant
personality that focuses not on power but
on a complex blend of countless
close-focused, forthright notes. The
balanced Barbera Vigna Vigia 2012 has a
concentrated, well-defined, but slightly less
layered nose, although its grace and
harmony make it irresistibly drinkable.
Chardonnay Pensiero Infinito is also very
good, among the very best of its kind in
Italy.

Bricco Mondalino

REG. MONDALINO, 5
15049 VIGNALE MONFERRATO [AL]
TEL. 0142933204
www.briccomondalino.it

CELLAR SALES
PRE-BOOKED VISITS
ANNUAL PRODUCTION 80,000 bottles
HECTARES UNDER VINE 14.00

The estate's 18 hectares of excellently
aspected vineyards are situated at altitudes
around 300 metres, on limestone-rich
marine sediment, ideal for viticulture. They
are planted with the classic Monferrato
grape varieties, two of which (barbera and
freisa) are also used to make semi-
sparkling monovarietals. The range is
composed of several different product lines,
all very well typed. In addition to barbera
and freisa, it also features grignolino,
cortese, and malvasia di Casorzo. These
top-quality wines reveal Marco Gaudio's
ability to interpret the native grape varieties.
Barbera and Grignolino gave peerless
performances, with a complex, intriguing
version of Zerolegno and a splendid
Grignolino made from selected bunches,
which is a model example of the great
classics of Monferrato Casalese.

● Barbera d'Alba Sup. V. Vigia '12	♟♟ 5
○ Langhe Bianco Pensiero Infinito '11	♟♟ 6
○ Langhe Sauvignon Castella '14	♟♟ 3*
● Nebbiolo d'Alba Sup. Cumot '12	♟♟ 5
● Barbera d'Alba '13	♟♟ 3
● Dolcetto di Diano d'Alba '14	♟♟ 3
● Langhe Merlot Filius '12	♟♟ 5
● Langhe Rosso Tris '13	♟♟ 3
○ Langhe Chardonnay Rolando '14	♟ 3
● Langhe Nebbiolo '13	♟ 3
● Langhe Pinot Nero Perlei '12	♟ 5
● Barbera d'Alba V. Vigia '98	♟♟♟ 4*
● Diano d'Alba Sup. Sörì	
Bricco Maiolica '07	♟♟♟ 3*
● Nebbiolo d'Alba Cumot '11	♟♟♟ 5
● Nebbiolo d'Alba Cumot '10	♟♟♟ 4*
● Nebbiolo d'Alba Cumot '09	♟♟♟ 4*

● Barbera d'Asti Zerolegno '13	♟♟ 4
● Grignolino del M.to Casalese	
Bricco Mondalino '13	♟♟ 2*
● Barbera d'Asti Il Bergantino '12	♟♟ 4
● Barbera del M.to Gaudium Magnum '11	♟♟ 6
● Barbera d'Asti Il Bergantino '10	♟♟ 3
● Barbera del M.to Zerolegno '09	♟♟ 2*
● Grignolino del M.to Casalese '12	♟♟ 2*
● Grignolino del M.to Casalese	
Bricco Mondalino '11	♟♟ 2*
● Grignolino del M.to Casalese	
Bricco Mondalino '10	♟♟ 2
● Malvasia di Casorzo Dolce Stil Novo '13	♟♟ 2*
● Malvasia di Casorzo Dolce Stil Novo '12	♟♟ 2*
● Malvasia di Casorzo Dolce Stil Novo '11	♟♟ 2*

PIEDMONT

Francesco Brigatti

VIA OLMI, 31
28019 SUNO [NO]
TEL. 032285037
www.vinibrigatti.it

CELLAR SALES
PRE-BOOKED VISITS
ANNUAL PRODUCTION 25,000 bottles
HECTARES UNDER VINE 6.50

Francesco Brigatti has been running the family estate for around 20 years, proving himself one of the most talented artisans of the Novara growing district. His vineyards cover an area of just over six hectares, on three hills in the Suno area: Ziflon (south-west facing, clay soils), Mötfrei (south-facing, iron-rich silt soils), and Campazzi (west-facing, sandy soils). The first two yield the top nebbiolo-based reds, made with slightly different procedures (3,000-litre Slavonian oak casks for the MötZiflon, and Allier tonneaux for the Mötfrei), which have been joined by Ghemme Oltre Il Bosco. Barbera, uva rara, vespolina, and erbaluce complete the array of grape varieties. This year it was Möt Ziflon 2012 that won the usual contest between Nebbiolos. It offers youthful notes of raspberries and fresh herbs, with spicy undertones, accompanied by a delicate palate with progressive tannins. The Mötfrei of the same vintage has a similar profile, but is more austere and drying.

● Colline Novaresi Nebbiolo MötZiflon '12	♛♛	3*
○ Colline Novaresi Bianco Mottobello '14	♛♛	2*
● Colline Novaresi Nebbiolo Mötfrei '12	♛♛	3
● Colline Novaresi Vespolina Maria '14	♛♛	2*
○ Costabella Passito	♛	5
● Colline Novaresi Barbera Campazzi '13	♕♕	3
● Colline Novaresi Nebbiolo Mötfrei '11	♕♕	3*
● Colline Novaresi Nebbiolo MötZiflon '11	♕♕	3
● Colline Novaresi Uva Rara Selvalunga '13	♕♕	2*
● Colline Novaresi Vespolina Maria '13	♕♕	2*
● Ghemme Oltre il Bosco '10	♕♕	4

Vitivinicola Broglia

LOC. LOMELLINA, 22
15066 GAVI [AL]
TEL. 0143642998
www.broglia.it

CELLAR SALES
PRE-BOOKED VISITS
ACCOMMODATION
ANNUAL PRODUCTION 480,000 bottles
HECTARES UNDER VINE 65.00

Founded by Bruno Broglia and now run by his sons Gian Piero and Paolo, La Meirana covers an area of around 100 hectares, planted chiefly to cortese. The Gavi grape variety is interpreted in an impressive four versions, all vinified in steel but each very different. Il Doge and La Meirana are the basic wines, released a few months after harvest and characterized by fresh fruit and linear verve. The Bruno Broglia selection, aged on the lees, generally offers more powerful stuffing and greater ageing potential. The range is completed by the two versions of Roverello Spumante, and the red Le Pernici, from dolcetto and barbera. The list presented this year was topped by Bruno Broglia, vaunting a deep straw yellow hue and a close-focused nose of resin and dried flowers, reflected on the powerful, continuous palate with a lingering finish. Meirana has more vegetal and fruity notes, on a mineral background, echoed on the long, complex palate.

○ Gavi del Comune di Gavi Bruno Broglia '13	♛♛	5
○ Gavi del Comune di Gavi La Meirana '14	♛♛	3
○ Gavi del Comune di Gavi Roverello Brut '13	♛	3
○ Gavi del Comune di Gavi Bruno Broglia '12	♕♕♕	5
○ Gavi del Comune di Gavi Bruno Broglia '08	♕♕♕	5
○ Gavi del Comune di Gavi Bruno Broglia '07	♕♕♕	5
○ Broglia Brut M. Cl.	♕♕	5
○ Gavi del Comune di Gavi La Meirana '13	♕♕	3

Brovia

VIA ALBA-BAROLO, 145
12060 CASTIGLIONE FALLETTO [CN]
TEL. 017362852
www.brovia.net

CELLAR SALES
PRE-BOOKED VISITS
ANNUAL PRODUCTION 60,000 bottles
HECTARES UNDER VINE 17.00
VITICULTURE METHOD Certified Organic

Villero, Rocche, and Garblèt Suè in Castiglione Falletto, and Cà Mia a Serralunga: it's hard to imagine a better assorted team than the Barolo crus mustered by Brovia. This is particularly true when they feature the unmistakable style to which we have been accustomed by sisters Cristina and Elena, with the aid of Alejandro Sanchez Solana. Fermented in concrete for 15–20 days and aged in large barrels for around three years, they are extremely vintage and terroir-true Nebbiolos, which always share an ethereal, almost feminine hint. If it's first and foremost fruity purity you're seeking, without excessive solidity and complexity, then these are the wines for you. Brovia's Barolos are among the best of the 2011 vintage. Ca' Mia has a sophisticated bouquet of roots, medicinal herbs, and yellow-fleshed fruit, slowed slightly on the palate by imposing tannins. Villero is unfaltering, a superior Nebbiolo in terms of texture and flavour. Last but not least, the elegant, aristocratic Rocche di Castiglione.

● Barolo Villero '11	♥♥♥ 8
● Barolo Brea V. Ca' Mia '11	♥♥ 8
● Barolo Rocche di Castiglione '11	♥♥ 8
● Barbera d'Alba Ciabot del Fi '12	♥♥ 4
● Barolo '11	♥♥ 6
● Barolo Garblèt Suè '11	♥♥ 8
● Barolo Brea V. Ca' Mia '10	♥♥♥ 8
● Barolo Ca' Mia '09	♥♥♥ 8
● Barolo Ca' Mia '00	♥♥♥ 8
● Barolo Rocche dei Brovia '06	♥♥♥ 7
● Barolo Villero '08	♥♥♥ 7
● Barolo Villero '06	♥♥♥ 7

G. B. Burlotto

VIA VITTORIO EMANUELE, 28
12060 VERDUNO [CN]
TEL. 0172470122
www.burlotto.com

CELLAR SALES
PRE-BOOKED VISITS
ACCOMMODATION
ANNUAL PRODUCTION 60,000 bottles
HECTARES UNDER VINE 15.00

In the mid-19th century Giovanni Battista Burlotto, universally remembered as "Il Commendatore", founded his little estate in Verduno, which subsequently became one of Langhe's most prestigious wineries. Today it is run by Fabio Alessandria, the son of Giuseppe and Marina, and covers an area of around 15 hectares, half of which planted to nebbiolo (Monvigliero, Neirane, Breri, and Rocche dell'Olmo in Verduno, and Cannubi in Barolo). They yield proudly traditional-style wines, aged in 3,500–5,000-litre barrels. The vineyard selections vie with the rare and unmistakable Pelaverga for the title of flagship, and are flanked by wines from barbera, dolcetto, sauvignon and freisa. The winery has given a series of impressive performances in recent years. Once again, the list is topped by the four Barolos. Acclivi, a selection exclusively from grapes grown in Verduno, took another Tre Bicchieri with its stunningly elegant tannic weave, which develops progressively and seamlessly, and its long, lingering nose of crisp raspberry notes, with complex undertones of liquorice and dried flowers.

● Barolo Acclivi '11	♥♥♥ 6
● Barolo Cannubi '11	♥♥ 7
● Barolo Vign. Monvigliero '11	♥♥ 7
● Barbera d'Alba Aves '13	♥♥ 4
● Barolo '11	♥♥ 6
● Langhe Nebbiolo '13	♥♥ 3
○ Langhe Sauvignon Dives '13	♥♥ 3
● Verduno Pelaverga '14	♥♥ 3
○ Langhe Sauvignon Viridis '14	♥ 3
● Barolo Acclivi '07	♥♥♥ 6
● Barolo Monvigliero '10	♥♥♥ 7
● Barbera d'Alba Aves '12	♥♥ 4
● Barolo Acclivi '10	♥♥ 6
● Barolo Acclivi '09	♥♥ 6
● Barolo Cannubi '10	♥♥ 7
○ Langhe Bianco Dives '12	♥♥ 3*

★Piero Busso

VIA ALBESANI, 8
12052 NEIVE [CN]
TEL. 017367156
www.bussopiero.com

CELLAR SALES
PRE-BOOKED VISITS
ANNUAL PRODUCTION 45,000 bottles
HECTARES UNDER VINE 10.00
SUSTAINABLE WINERY

Widely considered one of the most consistent and eclectic Langhe producers, Piero Busso must be credited for having maintained high interest in his work in the vineyard without allowing himself to be pigeonholed stylistically. Aided by his wife Lucia and their children Emanuela and Pierguido, he manages around ten hectares of estate-owned vineyards in Neive and Treiso, almost entirely planted with the traditional local grape varieties. Vinified separately, the four Barbaresco crus are Albesani Borgese, Gallina, Santo Stefanetto and Mondino (from the Balluri vineyard) and constitute the jewels of an extremely solid range, perfectly combining exuberant fruit and austerity. The two 2012 Barbarescos are equally good: the Mondino has the odd phenolic flaw, but what it lacks in supporting acidity it makes up for in florid sound fruit, while the San Stunet is deeper, with tobacco and citrus peel, but struggles to restrain its overpowering alcohol content. Gallina 2012 is exceptional, with powerful tannins and plenty of character, deservedly taking our highest accolade: a Barbaresco for laying down.

● Barbaresco Gallina '11	♙♙♙ 8
● Barbaresco Mondino '12	♙♙ 5
● Barbaresco S. Stunet '12	♙♙♙ 7
● Barbera d'Alba Majano '13	♙ 3
● Barbera d'Alba S. Stefanetto '12	♙♙ 5
● Langhe Nebbiolo '13	♙♙ 4
● Barbaresco Borgese '09	♕♕♕ 6
● Barbaresco Borgese '08	♕♕♕ 6
● Barbaresco Gallina '09	♕♕♕ 8
● Barbaresco Gallina '05	♕♕♕ 7
● Barbaresco S. Stefanetto '07	♕♕♕ 7
● Barbaresco S. Stefanetto '04	♕♕♕ 7
● Barbaresco S. Stefanetto '03	♕♕♕ 7
● Barbaresco S. Stefanetto '01	♕♕♕ 7
● Barbaresco S. Stunet '11	♕♕♕ 7

Ca' Bianca

REG. SPAGNA, 58
15010 ALICE BEL COLLE [AL]
TEL. 0144745420
www.cantinacabianca.it

CELLAR SALES
PRE-BOOKED VISITS
ANNUAL PRODUCTION 520,000 bottles
HECTARES UNDER VINE 24.00

Alice Bel Colle is located about six kilometres from Acqui Terme, in a scenic spot among the vast vineyards that extend over the hillsides, reaching altitudes of over 400 metres. This fine wine country is home to Ca' Bianca, the Piedmont winery owned by Gruppo Italian Vini, which uses the grapes from its 39 hectares of vineyards to make a range of wines representative of the region's leading designations. The battery of wines presented focuses on Barbera d'Asti, featured in three versions, with different vineyard yields and ageing times and methods. The top-of-the-range Chersì is made from grapes with a yield of less than 4,000 kilograms per hectare, and is aged for 12 months in new barriques. Antè is from slightly higher yields and is aged in once and twice-used oak, while Teis, the refreshing, youthful vintage Barbera, is aged exclusively in steel.

● Barbera d'Asti Sup. Antè '13	♙♙ 3
● Barbera d'Asti Sup. Chersì '12	♙♙ 3
● Barbera d'Asti Teis '14	♙♙ 2*
● Dolcetto d'Acqui '14	♙♙ 3
○ Gavi '14	♙ 3
○ Roero Arneis '14	♙ 3
● Barbera d'Asti Sup. Antè '12	♕♙ 3
● Barbera d'Asti Sup. Antè '11	♕♙ 3
● Barbera d'Asti Sup. Antè '10	♕♙ 3
● Barbera d'Asti Sup. Chersì '11	♕♙ 5
● Barbera d'Asti Sup. Chersì '10	♕♙ 5
● Barbera d'Asti Teis '13	♕♙ 2*
● Barbera d'Asti Teis '11	♕♙ 3
● Dolcetto d'Acqui '12	♕♙ 3
○ Gavi '12	♕♙ 3
○ Roero Arneis '10	♕♙ 2

Ca' d'Gal

FRAZ. VALDIVILLA
S.DA VECCHIA DI VALDIVILLA, 1
12058 SANTO STEFANO BELBO [CN]
TEL. 0141847103
www.cadgal.it

CELLAR SALES
PRE-BOOKED VISITS
ACCOMMODATION AND RESTAURANT SERVICE
ANNUAL PRODUCTION 95,000 bottles
HECTARES UNDER VINE 12.00

Alessandro Boido runs one of the most important estates in the moscato world, with over a century of history behind it. The majority of its vineyards lie on the hillsides of Santo Stefano Belbo, on sandy and calcareous clay soils. Production focuses chiefly on Moscato, and includes a Vigne Vecchie selection released after five years in bottle. We were bowled over by the delicate yet complex Moscato d'Asti Vite Vecchia 2009, very full and concentrated, with lovely notes of medicinal herbs and lemon peel, and still vibrant acidity. Moscato d'Asti Sant'Ilario 2014, also in our finals, hails from the Cassinasco plots, whose grapes were sold to Cantina di Canelli until a couple of years ago. Long ageing on the lees and the high altitude of the vineyards yield a fresh, elegant, long, and very pleasant wine, with notes of pears, white peaches, sage and rosemary.

○ Moscato d'Asti Sant'Ilario '14	🍷🍷 3*
○ Moscato d'Asti V. Vecchia '09	🍷🍷 7
● Barbera d'Asti '12	🍷🍷 3
○ Moscato d'Asti Lumine '14	🍷🍷 3
○ Moscato d'Asti V. Vecchia '14	🍷🍷 4
● Langhe Freisa Pian del Gaje '13	🍷 3
○ Moscato d'Asti V. V. '11	🍷🍷🍷 3*
○ Moscato d'Asti V. V. '12	🍷🍷 4
○ Moscato d'Asti V. V. '09	🍷🍷 3
○ Moscato d'Asti V. V. '07	🍷🍷 3*
○ Moscato d'Asti V. Vecchia '13	🍷🍷 4
○ Moscato d'Asti V. Vecchia '08	🍷🍷 3*
○ Moscato d'Asti V. Vecchia '07	🍷🍷 3
○ Moscato d'Asti V. Vecchia '06	🍷🍷 3
○ Moscato d'Asti V. Vecchia '05	🍷🍷 3

★Ca' del Baio

VIA FERRERE, 33
12050 TREISO [CN]
TEL. 0173638219
www.cadelbaio.com

CELLAR SALES
PRE-BOOKED VISITS
ANNUAL PRODUCTION 100,000 bottles
HECTARES UNDER VINE 25.00

The Grasso family, with daughters Paola, Valentina and Federica playing an increasingly active role in the general management of the estate, is consolidating its key role in the Barbaresco production zone. This year we applaud Giulio Grasso with our Grower of the Year award. The definition and character of the wines make the cellar's style highly recognizable, helping to expand the fan base both in Italy and abroad. The entire range, from the Riesling to the Barbaresco crus and the ever-convincing Moscato, offer an unbeatable quality-price ratio. We awarded a Tre Bicchieri to the elegant Barbaresco Asili 2012, with layered notes of tar, tobacco and eucalyptus. It heads a list that once again surprised us during our tastings with the exceptionally high quality of all the wines. Barbaresco Pora 2011 has a close-focused nose and silky, well-resolved tannins.

● Barbaresco Asili '12	🍷🍷🍷 6
● Barbaresco Pora '11	🍷🍷 6
● Barbaresco Vallegrande '12	🍷🍷 5
○ Langhe Riesling '13	🍷🍷 3*
● Barbaresco Marcarini '12	🍷🍷 5
○ Langhe Chardonnay Sermine '14	🍷🍷 3
● Langhe Nebbiolo '14	🍷🍷 2*
● Langhe Nebbiolo Bric del Baio '13	🍷🍷 3
○ Moscato d'Asti 101 '14	🍷🍷 2*
● Dolcetto d'Alba Lodoli '14	🍷 2
● Barbaresco Asili '10	🍷🍷🍷 6
● Barbaresco Asili '09	🍷🍷🍷 5
● Barbaresco Asili '06	🍷🍷🍷 5
● Barbaresco Pora '06	🍷🍷🍷 6
● Barbaresco Pora '04	🍷🍷🍷 6
● Barbaresco Valgrande '08	🍷🍷🍷 5

Ca' Nova

VIA SAN ISIDORO, 1
28010 BOGOGNO [NO]
TEL. 0322863406
www.cascinacanova.it

CELLAR SALES
PRE-BOOKED VISITS
ACCOMMODATION
ANNUAL PRODUCTION 35,000 bottles
HECTARES UNDER VINE 10.00

Giada Codecasa's entrepreneurial venture, launched almost 20 years ago, is a veritable paradise for the senses. The nature reserve in Bogogno is home not only to a golf club and the Relais Ca' Nova, but also a good proportion of the estate's ten hectares of vineyards. They are planted with the typical local grape varieties, first and foremost nebbiolo and erbaluce, which are also used for the sparklers of the Jad'Or line. However, the most impressive offerings are the two red flagship wines: the Ghemme and the Vigna San Quirico cru, from nebbiolo, which are rich and powerful, combining sweet fruit and a full-flavoured supporting structure. Ca' Nova's range is increasingly impressive, not only in terms of quality but also in its sheer number of wines. This year it is led by the Ghemme 2009, displaying top notes of close-focused fruit on a background of rust and blood that sets the pace on a nicely progressive palate, marked by rather insistent tannins.

Ca' Rome'

S.DA RABAJÀ, 86
12050 BARBARESCO [CN]
TEL. 0173635126
www.carome.com

CELLAR SALES
PRE-BOOKED VISITS
ANNUAL PRODUCTION 30,000 bottles
HECTARES UNDER VINE 5.00

This estate offers very clean wines, always with plenty of stuffing, and never overly delicate or lacking in personality, aged to eliminate any excessive oak aromas. The style is undeniably classic, and has enchanted a host of wine lovers all over the world, making the wines almost impossible to find in Italy. Romano Marengo has made a name for himself in particular for his Barbaresco Maria di Brun, but the Rapet and Cerretta Barolo vineyard selections from Serralunga d'Alba are consistently top notch. Barolo Rapet 2011 earned a Tre Bicchieri for its complex nose and well-orchestrated palate, which are both already so rich and balanced that the wine can only improve for many years to come. Barbaresco Maria di Brun 2011 also guarantees long and fine development, with a perfect, layered nose and a palate that is still slightly stiff. The other wines are all excellent.

● Ghemme '09	♥♥ 5
○ Colline Novaresi Bianco Rugiada '14	♥♥ 2*
⊙ Colline Novaresi Nebbiolo Aurora '14	♥♥ 2*
○ Jad'or Brut M. Cl.	♥♥ 4
● Colline Novaresi Nebbiolo Bocciòlo '14	♥ 2
● Colline Novaresi Nebbiolo V. San Quirico '08	♥ 4
● Colline Novaresi Vespolina '13	♥ 2
● Ghemme '08	♀♀ 4
● Ghemme '07	♀♀ 4
● Ghemme '06	♀♀ 4

● Barolo Rapet '11	♥♥♥ 7
● Barbaresco Chiaramanti '12	♥♥ 7
● Barbaresco Maria di Brun '11	♥♥ 8
● Barbaresco Rio Sordo '12	♥♥ 7
● Barolo Cerretta '11	♥♥ 7
● Barolo Rapet Ris. '09	♥♥ 8
● Barolo Rapet '08	♀♀♀ 7
● Barolo V. Cerretta '09	♀♀♀ 7
● Barbaresco Chiaramanti '11	♀♀ 6
● Barbaresco Chiaramanti '10	♀♀ 6
● Barbaresco Maria di Brun '10	♀♀ 6
● Barbaresco Rio Sordo '11	♀♀ 6
● Barbaresco Sorì Rio Sordo '10	♀♀ 6
● Barolo Cerretta '10	♀♀ 7
● Barolo Rapet '10	♀♀ 7
● Barolo Rapet '09	♀♀ 7

★Ca' Viola

B.TA SAN LUIGI, 11
12063 DOGLIANI [CN]
TEL. 017370547
www.caviola.com

CELLAR SALES
PRE-BOOKED VISITS
ACCOMMODATION AND RESTAURANT SERVICE
ANNUAL PRODUCTION 60,000 bottles
HECTARES UNDER VINE 12.00

Beppe Caviola's ongoing quest for excellent wines is very evident as he transforms his winery into a true Langhe gem. A prized plot in Novello, planted several years ago, has now joined the estate's vineyards in Montelupo Albese, allowing for a comprehensive range of wines. The style is well defined and classic, achieved using medium-sized barrels and shunning all forms of artifice. It is exemplified by Barolo Sottocastello di Novello 2010, the estate's first true great vintage, which offers an elegant austere nose of dark berry fruit and quinine, with hints of golden-leaf tobacco, and a wonderful assertive palate with very full structure, suitable for prolonged bottle ageing. Barbera d'Alba Bric du Luv, long the estate's star wine, together with the powerful Dolcetto d'Alba Barturot, is also splendid.

Ca.Vi.Mon. - Cantina Iuli

FRAZ. MONTALDO
VIA CENTRALE, 27
15020 CERRINA MONFERRATO [AL]
TEL. 0142946657
www.iuli.it

CELLAR SALES
PRE-BOOKED VISITS
ACCOMMODATION
ANNUAL PRODUCTION 50,000 bottles
HECTARES UNDER VINE 8.50
VITICULTURE METHOD Certified Organic

This winery has made a name for itself over the years, winning a series of awards. Today its entire production is vinified with a view to preserving the characteristics of the grapes, and consequently the long barrel ageing of the wines is not followed by clarifying or filtration. It thus comes as no surprise to find tiny tartrate crystals at the bottom of the bottle. However, they in no way detract from the quality of the product. On the contrary, they're a tangible sign of its soundness, denoting a genuine wine made like it used to be. Barabba is absent from the list, as for several years its grapes fell prey to the wild animals inhabiting the woods surrounding the vineyard. It will return to our tastings with the 2014 vintage. We consoled ourselves with the excellent performances offered by Barbera Rossore and Nebbiolo Malidea. Pinot Nero Nino is also very well made.

● Barolo Sottocastello di Novello '10	♛♛♛ 7
● Barbera d'Alba Bric du Luv '13	♛♛ 5
● Dolcetto d'Alba Barturot '13	♛♛ 4
● Langhe Nebbiolo '13	♛♛ 5
● Barbera d'Alba Brichet '13	♛♛ 4
● Dolcetto d'Alba Vilot '14	♛♛ 3
● Barbera d'Alba Bric du Luv '12	♛♛♛ 5
● Barbera d'Alba Bric du Luv '10	♛♛♛ 5
● Barbera d'Alba Bric du Luv '07	♛♛♛ 5
● Barolo Sottocastello '06	♛♛♛ 7
● Barolo Sottocastello di Novello '08	♛♛♛ 7
● Dolcetto d'Alba Barturot '07	♛♛♛ 3
● Dolcetto d'Alba Barturot '05	♛♛♛ 3
● Dolcetto d'Alba Barturot '01	♛♛♛ 3*
● Langhe Nebbiolo '08	♛♛♛ 5
● Langhe Rosso Bric du Luv '05	♛♛♛ 5

● Barbera del M.to Sup. Rossore '12	♛♛ 5
● M.to Rosso Malidea '11	♛♛ 5
● M.to Rosso Nino	♛♛ 5
● Barbera del M.to Sup. Barabba '10	♛♛♛ 6
● Barbera del M.to Sup. Barabba '04	♛♛♛ 5
● Barbera del M.to Sup. Barabba '07	♛♛ 5
● Barbera del M.to Sup. Barabba '06	♛♛ 5
● Barbera del M.to Sup. Barabba '01	♛♛ 5
● Barbera del M.to Sup. Barabba Magnum '04	♛♛ 5
● Barbera del M.to Sup. Rossore '10	♛♛ 3*
● Barbera del M.to Sup. Rossore '09	♛♛ 3*
● Barbera del M.to Sup. Rossore '07	♛♛ 3*
● M.to Rosso Malidea '10	♛♛ 5
● M.to Rosso Malidea '07	♛♛ 5
● M.to Rosso Nino '12	♛♛ 5
● M.to Rosso Nino '10	♛♛ 5

Cantina del Glicine

VIA GIULIO CESARE, 1
12052 NEIVE [CN]
TEL. 017367215
www.cantinadelglicine.it

CELLAR SALES
PRE-BOOKED VISITS
ANNUAL PRODUCTION 37,000 bottles
HECTARES UNDER VINE 6.00

A splendid 17th-century underground
cellar, hidden in the old town of Neive, is
where Adriana Marzi and Roberto Bruno,
the owners of Cantina del Glicine, make
their fine wines. The small family-run estate
uses the grapes from its five hectares of
vineyards, planted with the main Langhe
grape varieties. The range is very
convincing in terms of style, terroir trueness
and value for money, which is particularly
outstanding in the case of the Currà,
Marcorino, and Vigne Sparse Barbaresco
vineyard selections. La Sconsolata and La
Dormiosa are the two Barbera d'Alba
selections, with a solid, earthy character. It
is hard to choose between the two top
Nebbiolos produced in the controversial
2012 vintage. The Currà seems fairly
closed, but aeration reveals an austere,
thick profile, which promises very well for
the future. Despite its rugged tannins, the
Marcorino is far more expressive,
showing full with sophisticated notes of
blueberries, black pepper and tar, and so
elegant and well orchestrated as to have
earned a Tre Bicchieri.

● Barbaresco Marcorino '12	￼	5
● Barbaresco Currà '12	￼	5
● Barbaresco Vigne Sparse '12	￼	5
● Barbera d'Alba La Sconsolata '13	￼	2*
● Barbera d'Alba Sup. La Dormiosa '13	￼	3
● Nebbiolo d'Alba Calcabrume '13	￼	3
○ Roero Arneis Il Mandolo '14	￼	2
● Barbaresco Currà '10	￼	4*
● Barbaresco Currà '11	￼	5
● Barbaresco Marcorino '11	￼	5
● Barbaresco Vigne Sparse '11	￼	5
● Barbera d'Alba Sup. La Dormiosa '11	￼	3
● Nebbiolo d'Alba Calcabrume '12	￼	3

Cantina del Nebbiolo

VIA TORINO, 17
12050 VEZZA D'ALBA [CN]
TEL. 017365040
www.cantinadelnebbiolo.com

CELLAR SALES
PRE-BOOKED VISITS
ANNUAL PRODUCTION 300,000 bottles
HECTARES UNDER VINE 300.00
VITICULTURE METHOD Certified Organic

Cantina del Nebbiolo is one of Roero's
leading cooperative wineries. Founded in
1959 by 23 Roero vignerons on the ashes
of an earlier business, it now vaunts over
170 grower members. Roero provides 80%
of the grapes and the remainder from
Langhe. Production is not solely from
nebbiolo, but also other native grape
varieties, like barbera, bonarda, dolcetto,
freisa, brachetto, neretta cuneese, arneis,
favorita, nascetta and moscato. The
well-made Barolo Cannubi Boschis 2011
has a nose of citrus with hints of petrol,
and a medium-structured palate with
austere, close-knit tannins and a fairly long
finish. Barolo del Comune di Serralunga
d'Alba 2011 is just as good, showing
tannic, compact and long, as is Langhe
Nascetta Riveverse 2014, with a fresh,
concentrated nose of flowers and
white-fleshed fruit.

● Barolo Cannubi Boschis '11	￼	7
● Barolo del Comune di Serralunga d'Alba '11	￼	6
○ Langhe Nascetta Riveverse '14	￼	2*
● Barbaresco '12	￼	4
● Barbera D'Alba Sup. '12	￼	2
● Barolo '11	￼	5
● Nebbiolo d'Alba Valmaggiore '12	￼	2
● Barbaresco '11	￼	4
● Barbaresco '10	￼	4
● Barbaresco Meruzzano '10	￼	4*
● Barbera d'Alba '11	￼	2*
● Barolo '10	￼	5
● Barolo Cannubi Boschis '10	￼	7
● Langhe La Pranda '11	￼	2*
● Nebbiolo d'Alba Valmaggiore '11	￼	2*
● Roero '10	￼	2*

Cantina del Pino

S.DA OVELLO, 31
12050 BARBARESCO [CN]
TEL. 0173635147
www.cantinadelpino.com

ANNUAL PRODUCTION 35,000 bottles
HECTARES UNDER VINE 7.00

Fortunately the days in which the style of Langhe producers was based firmly on the size of the oak barrels used for ageing are long gone. Take, for example, Adriano and Renato Vacca's Nebbiolos, which are mainly aged in barriques, but certainly cannot be described as "modern" tout court. They resonate with the expressive awareness long cultivated during the partnership with Produttori del Barbaresco, but above all with the character of illustrious vineyards like Ovello and Albesani, along with painstaking attention to yields, the timing of harvests, and maceration times. We tasted the 2011 vintage of Cantina del Pino's two flagships at what is probably an interim stage. The Ovello has a classic nose of wild strawberries and balsamic notes, but is still rather simple on the palate, while the Albesani seems a little lacking in verve, with darker, leaner fruit, its nose dominated by spice and tar.

La Caplana

VIA CIRCONVALLAZIONE, 4
15060 BOSIO [AL]
TEL. 0143684182
www.lacaplana.com

CELLAR SALES
PRE-BOOKED VISITS
ANNUAL PRODUCTION 120,000 bottles
HECTARES UNDER VINE 5.00

The Bosio area is one of the farthest flung outposts of Piedmont, which is practically in Liguria from a sociolinguistic, cultural, and environmental point of view. It is home to La Caplana, a small family-run winery also known as Natalino Guido, which has always embodied this dual regional identity in its varied range, among the most competitive in terms of value for money. It is difficult to single out a single top wine from the Gavi whites and the Dolcetto d'Ovada reds, which are flanked by other wines from the Asti area, first and foremost Barbera, without forgetting the sparklers and Chardonnay. Two excellent terroir-true wines reached our finals. Dolcetto Narcys is a brilliant purple hue, with a complex nose of close-focused fruit that develops into notes of cocoa powder, heralding an elegant palate with a fine tannic weave and good length. Gavi di Gavi reveals great complexity and balance on the attack, which continue on the fresh, lively palate.

Wine	Rating
● Barbaresco '11	❨❨ 5
● Barbaresco Albesani '11	❨❨ 6
● Barbaresco Ovello '11	❨❨ 6
● Barbera d'Alba '13	❨❨ 4
● Barbaresco '04	❨❨❨ 5*
● Barbaresco '03	❨❨❨ 4*
● Barbaresco Albesani '05	❨❨❨ 6
● Barbaresco Ovello '07	❨❨❨ 6
● Barbaresco Ovello '99	❨❨❨ 5
● Barbaresco '10	❨❨ 5
● Barbaresco Albesani '10	❨❨ 6
● Barbaresco Albesani '08	❨❨ 6
● Barbaresco Ovello '10	❨❨ 6
● Barbaresco Ovello '08	❨❨ 6
● Barbera d'Alba '11	❨❨ 4
● Langhe Nebbiolo '13	❨❨ 3

Wine	Rating
● Dolcetto di Ovada Narcys '12	❨❨ 3*
○ Gavi del Comune di Gavi '14	❨❨ 2*
● Barbera d'Asti '13	❨❨ 2*
● Barbera d'Asti Rubis '11	❨❨ 3
○ Gavi '14	❨❨ 2*
○ Gavi Villa Vecchia '14	❨❨ 2*
● Dolcetto di Ovada '14	❨ 2
○ Piemonte Chardonnay '14	❨ 2
● Barbera d'Asti Rubis '10	❨❨ 3
● Barbera d'Asti Sup. '11	❨❨ 2*
● Dolcetto di Ovada Narciso '11	❨❨ 2*
○ Gavi Antico Podere di Vignavecchia '12	❨❨ 2*
○ Gavi del Comune di Gavi '13	❨❨ 2*
○ Gavi del Comune di Gavi '12	❨❨ 2*
○ Gavi Villavecchia '13	❨❨ 2*

Tenuta Carretta

LOC. CARRETTA, 2
12040 PIOBESI D'ALBA [CN]
TEL. 0173619119
www.tenutacarretta.it

CELLAR SALES
PRE-BOOKED VISITS
ACCOMMODATION AND RESTAURANT SERVICE
ANNUAL PRODUCTION 480,000 bottles
HECTARES UNDER VINE 70.00

Owned by the Miroglio family for 30 years,
Tenuta Carretta's 35 hectares of Roero
vineyards lie on the hills around the winery
and are planted mainly to arneis, barbera,
and nebbiolo. The winery also owns various
estates in Langhe, from Barolo to Treiso,
San Rocco Seno d'Elvio, and Madonna di
Como, as well as the Malgrà estate in the
Asti zone, for the production of Barolo,
Barbaresco, and Barbera d'Asti. Barbera
d'Asti Superiore Nizza Mora di Sassi 2012
stole the show, with spice and dark wild
berries on the nose, accompanied by a
fruit-rich palate underpinned by gutsy
acidity. Barbaresco Garassino 2012 has
impressive structure and acidity. Barbera
d'Alba Superiore Bric Quercia 2013 is also
good, with well-balanced fruit and acidity,
as is Roero Arneis Cayega 2014, showing
full-flavoured and almost tannic on the
palate.

La Casaccia

VIA D. BARBANO, 10
15034 CELLA MONTE [AL]
TEL. 0142489986
www.lacasaccia.biz

CELLAR SALES
PRE-BOOKED VISITS
ANNUAL PRODUCTION 25,000 bottles
HECTARES UNDER VINE 6.70
VITICULTURE METHOD Certified Organic

Elena and Giovanni Rava are a couple of
brilliant Monferrato vignerons. Both with
degrees in agriculture under their belt, they
have recommenced writing the history of
the family and viticulture in Cella Monte,
with a more modern approach that led
them to adopt organic farming methods 15
years ago. Their wines are made from
native grape varieties, such as barbera,
grignolino, and freisa, but they also grow
international varieties: chardonnay, vinified
as a monovarietal, and pinot nero, used
together with chardonnay in the very
elegant Spumante Metodo Classico. We
tasted a trio of native grape varieties, which
form a top-quality range of wines. Giuanìn
is a Barbera del Monferrato with an
explosive nose of quinine, tobacco, and
dark berry fruit, while Monfiorenza is a
Freisa vaunting a concentrated nose of wild
berries followed by spicy notes and
aromatic herbs. Last but not least, Poggeto
is a Grignolino in a classic, varietal style.

● Barbera d'Asti Sup. Nizza Mora dei Sassi '12	♥♥ 5
● Barbaresco Garassino '12	♥♥ 5
● Barbera d'Alba Sup. Bric Quercia '13	♥♥ 3
● Barbera d'Asti Sup. Fornace di Cerreto '12	♥♥ 2*
● Barbera d'Asti Sup. Gaiana '12	♥♥ 3
● Barolo Cascina Ferrero '11	♥♥ 6
○ Roero Arneis Cayega '14	♥♥ 3
● Barolo Vign. in Cannubi '00	♥♥♥ 7
● Barbera d'Alba Sup. Bric Quercia '12	♀♀ 3
● Barolo Cannubi '10	♀♀ 8
● Roero Bric Paradiso '10	♀♀ 4
● Roero Bric Paradiso '08	♀♀ 3
● Roero Sup. Bric Paradiso '03	♀♀ 4

● Barbera del M.to Giuanìn '13	♥♥ 3
● Grignolino del M.to Casalese Poggeto '14	♥♥ 2*
● M.to Freisa Monfiorenza '13	♥♥ 3
● Barbera d'Asti Sup. Calichè '09	♀♀ 3
● Barbera d'Asti Sup. Calichè '06	♀♀ 3*
● Barbera del M.to Bricco dei Boschi '11	♀♀ 3
● Barbera del M.to Calichè '10	♀♀ 3
● Barbera del M.to Giuanìn '12	♀♀ 2*
● Barbera del M.to Giuanìn '10	♀♀ 2*
● Barbera del M.to Sup. Bricco del Bosco '09	♀♀ 2
● Barbera del M.to Sup. Bricco del Bosco '07	♀♀ 2*
● Grignolino del M.to Casalese Poggeto '13	♀♀ 2*
○ La Casaccia Brut M.Cl. '10	♀♀ 4

Casalone

VIA MARCONI, 100
15040 LU [AL]
TEL. 0131741280
www.casalone.it

CELLAR SALES
PRE-BOOKED VISITS
ANNUAL PRODUCTION 50,000 bottles
HECTARES UNDER VINE 10.00

Lu is one of the finest terroirs in Monferrato Casalese, and the Casalone family have been among its worthy representatives for several generations. The estate's ten hectares of vineyards have different soils, from calcareous marl to medium-textured sandy terrain. Here the Casalones grow typical Monferrato grape varieties and international cultivars like pinot nero and merlot. Their wines from malvasia greca are excellent and available in several different versions, from still white to passito and sparklers. This year the Casalones only presented part of their range, and we were disappointed by the absence of the Metodo Classico sparkler that reached our finals last year. The estate's classics nonetheless fared well: Bricco Morlantino, with a very good nose; Rus, a Monferrato Rosso from barbera, merlot, and pinot nero, which is a tad rustic but with plenty of character; and Monemvasia, always on top form.

● Barbera del M.to Sup. Bricco Morlantino '11	♥♥ 2*
● M.to Rosso Rus '12	♥♥ 3
○ Monemvasia	♥♥ 2*
● Grignolino del M.to Casalese La Capletta '14	♥ 3
○ Monemvasia Affinato Barrique	♥ 4
○ Monemvasia Brut M. Cl.	♀♀ 4
● Barbera d'Asti Rubermillo '11	♀♀ 3*
● Barbera del M.to Sup. Bricco Morlantino '10	♀♀ 2*
● Barbera del M.to Sup. Bricco Morlantino '09	♀♀ 2*
● M.to Rosso Fandamat '10	♀♀ 3
● M.to Rosso Rus '10	♀♀ 3
○ Monemvasia Passito '10	♀♀ 3

Cascina Barisél

REG. SAN GIOVANNI, 30
14053 CANELLI [AT]
TEL. 0141824848
www.barisel.it

CELLAR SALES
PRE-BOOKED VISITS
ANNUAL PRODUCTION 35,000 bottles
HECTARES UNDER VINE 4.50

The Penna family's little estate is one of the most interesting in the Monferrato wine world. Its vineyards, which extend around the winery, in the municipality of Canelli, are on south-facing plots with limestone soils planted mainly to barbera, dolcetto, and moscato, with small amounts of chardonnay and pinot nero. The estate also has a little vineyard in San Marzano Oliveto where it grows favorita. Once again this year the range is topped by Barbera d'Asti Superiore La Cappelletta. The 2012 vintage is potent and complex, still marked by oak, but fruit rich with good acidic grip. Moscato d'Asti Canelli 2014 is well made, flavoursome, and very pleasant, showing supple with sappy notes and fresh, gutsy white-fleshed fruit. The other two versions of Barbera d'Asti are also very good, the Listoria 2013 offering notes of tobacco, quinine, and ripe red berries, and the easy-drinking 2014 approachable, fresh, and juicy.

● Barbera d'Asti Sup. La Cappelletta '12	♥♥ 4
● Barbera d'Asti '14	♥♥ 2*
● Barbera d'Asti Sup. Listoria '13	♥♥ 2*
○ Moscato d'Asti Canelli '14	♥♥ 2*
● Barbera d'Asti '12	♀♀ 2*
● Barbera d'Asti Sup. La Cappelletta '11	♀♀ 4
● Barbera d'Asti Sup. La Cappelletta '10	♀♀ 4
● Barbera d'Asti Sup. La Cappelletta '09	♀♀ 4
● Barbera d'Asti Sup. La Cappelletta '07	♀♀ 4
● Barbera d'Asti Sup. Listoria '12	♀♀ 2*
● Barbera d'Asti Sup. Listoria '11	♀♀ 2*
○ Moscato d'Asti '10	♀♀ 2*
○ Moscato d'Asti Canelli '13	♀♀ 2*
○ Moscato d'Asti Canelli '12	♀♀ 2*
○ Moscato d'Asti Canelli '11	♀♀ 2*

Cascina Ca' Rossa

LOC. CASCINA CA' ROSSA, 56
12043 CANALE [CN]
TEL. 017398348
www.cascinacarossa.com

CELLAR SALES
PRE-BOOKED VISITS
ANNUAL PRODUCTION 80,000 bottles
HECTARES UNDER VINE 13.00
VITICULTURE METHOD Certified Organic

The estate owned by Angelo Ferrio, now flanked by his son Stefano, has been among the leading producers in Roero for several years, due to the attentive and passionate work carried out in some of the region's most important and illustrious crus. For nebbiolo the finest are the Mompissano vineyard in Canale, a south-facing hill with clayey limestone, and the old, steeply sloping Audinaggio vineyard with sandy soil in Vezza d'Alba, in the legendary Valmaggiore area; while for barbera the Mulassa vineyard, also in Canale, deserves a mention. Angelo Ferrio is back on Tre Bicchieri form with a brilliant Roero Mompissano Riserva 2012, flaunting a floral nose with notes of red berries, and a long, full-flavoured, complex palate with evident but fine-grained tannins. Roero Audinaggio 2013 is elegant and delicate, yet full flavoured, with notes of aromatic herbs and raspberries, while the sturdy Barbera d'Alba Mulassa 2013 is packed with spicy fruit.

Cascina Chicco

VIA VALENTINO, 144
12043 CANALE [CN]
TEL. 0173979411
www.cascinachicco.com

CELLAR SALES
PRE-BOOKED VISITS
ANNUAL PRODUCTION 395,000 bottles
HECTARES UNDER VINE 45.00

In the space of just a few years brothers Enrico and Marco Faccenda have transformed Cascina Chicco with investments aimed at expanding and diversifying their area under vine and building suitable new premises. Their traditional Roero vineyards, in several municipalities and in some of the zone's most prestigious crus, such as Mompissano and Valmaggiore, are flanked by the Rocche di Castelletto estate in Monforte d'Alba, with five hectares under vine in the Ginestra cru for the production of Barolo. Cascina Chicco has won another Tre Bicchieri, thanks to Roero Valmaggiore Riserva 2012 and particularly to the restyling that has taken place in recent years, resulting in a highly recognizable, floral wine with hints of aromatic herbs, which is elegant, delicate and very enjoyable. The two Barolos are also first rate, with Rocche di Castelletto 2011 showing powerful and tannic, and Ginestra Riserva 2008 complex and spicy, as is the elegant Cuvée Zero Extra Brut.

● Roero Mompissano Ris. '12	🍷🍷🍷 5
● Barbera d'Alba Mulassa '13	🍷🍷 5
● Roero Audinaggio '13	🍷🍷 5
● Barbera d'Alba '14	🍷🍷 3
○ Roero Arneis Merica '14	🍷🍷 3
● Barbera d'Alba Mulassa '04	🍷🍷🍷 4*
● Roero Audinaggio '07	🍷🍷🍷 5
● Roero Audinaggio '06	🍷🍷🍷 5
● Roero Audinaggio '01	🍷🍷🍷 5
● Roero Mompissano Ris. '10	🍷🍷🍷 5
● Roero Mompissano Ris. '07	🍷🍷🍷 6
● Barbera d'Alba Mulassa '12	🍷🍷 5
● Roero Audinaggio '11	🍷🍷 5
● Roero Mompissano Ris. '11	🍷🍷 5

● Roero Valmaggiore Ris. '12	🍷🍷🍷 4*
● Barolo Ginestra Ris. '08	🍷🍷 7
● Barolo Rocche di Castelletto '11	🍷🍷 5
○ Cuvée Zero Extra Brut M. Cl.	🍷🍷 4
○ Arcass V.T.	🍷🍷 4
● Barbera d'Alba Bric Loira '13	🍷🍷 4
○ Cuvée Zero Rosé	🍷🍷 4
● Nebbiolo d'Alba Mompissano '13	🍷🍷 3
○ Roero Arneis Anterisio '14	🍷 2
● Roero Montespinato '13	🍷 3
○ Arcàss Passito '04	🍷🍷🍷 4
● Barbera d'Alba Bric Loira '98	🍷🍷🍷 4*
● Barbera d'Alba Bric Loira '97	🍷🍷🍷 4*
● Nebbiolo d'Alba Mompissano '99	🍷🍷🍷 3*
● Roero Montespinato '12	🍷🍷 3*
● Roero Valmaggiore Ris. '11	🍷🍷 4

Cascina Corte

FRAZ. SAN LUIGI
B.TA VALDIBERTI, 33
12063 DOGLIANI [CN]
TEL. 0173743539
www.cascinacorte.it

CELLAR SALES
PRE-BOOKED VISITS
ACCOMMODATION
ANNUAL PRODUCTION 30,000 bottles
HECTARES UNDER VINE 5.00
VITICULTURE METHOD Certified Organic
SUSTAINABLE WINERY

In an age in which the media hype surrounding wine, particularly organic products, sometimes reaches far beyond the actual value of the product and the work behind it, Sandro Barosi represents a very welcome professional example whose coherent choices are closely echoed in the linear style of all his wines. The organic concept becomes above all cultural, upon which to structure the various stages in the production process without invasive or unnecessary techniques. At the time of our tastings Dogliani Superiore Pirochetta Vecchie Vigne, which has become the symbol of the estate, was in a somewhat provisional phase, its nose still emerging and its palate characterized by juicy notes of red berry jam, spice, and well-integrated tannins. The Langhe Nebbiolo is vibrant and varietal, standing out for its fresh, stylish palate.

Cascina Cucco

LOC. CUCCO
VIA MAZZINI, 10
12050 SERRALUNGA D'ALBA [CN]
TEL. 0173613003
www.cascinacucco.com

CELLAR SALES
PRE-BOOKED VISITS
ANNUAL PRODUCTION 70,000 bottles
HECTARES UNDER VINE 12.50

The Stroppiana family have handed over the management of Cascina Cucco to the Rossi Cairo family, who are already active in the wine world with La Raia in Gavi. Their vocation for sustainability and aptitude for quality investments should ensure a rosy future for this leading Serralunga estate that, year after year, has carved itself out a special niche among the top Langhe producers. Another decisive factor will be the management of the first-rate vineyards, capable of yielding wines of character and elegance, whose ageing prospects are almost unrivalled. The range as a whole performed well, with the Barbera d'Alba Superiore revealing itself as one of the best of its kind, offering a complex, layered nose of fruit and spice, and a supple, juicy, full-flavoured palate with a refreshing finish with excellent length and acidity. Barolo Cerrati Vigna Cucco 2011 has a close tannic weave with considerable potential for development.

Wine	Rating
● Dogliani '14	♟♟ 3
● Dogliani Sup. Pirochetta V. V. '13	♟♟ 3
● Langhe Nebbiolo '13	♟♟ 4
● Barbetto	♟ 2
● Langhe Barbera '13	♟ 3
● Dogliani Vecchie V. Pirochetta '08	♟♟♟ 3*
● Barnedòl	♟♟ 4
● Dogliani '13	♟♟ 3
● Dogliani Pirochetta V. V. '10	♟♟ 3
● Dogliani Pirochetta V. V. '09	♟♟ 3*
● Dogliani Sup. Pirochetta V. V. '12	♟♟ 3*
● Dogliani Sup. Pirochetta V. V. '11	♟♟ 3*
● Langhe Barbera '11	♟♟ 3
● Langhe Nebbiolo '11	♟♟ 3
● Langhe Nebbiolo '10	♟♟ 3
● Piemonte Barbera '09	♟♟ 3

Wine	Rating
● Barolo Cerrati V. Cucco '11	♟♟ 6
● Barbera d'Alba Sup. '13	♟♟ 3
● Barolo Cerrati '11	♟♟ 6
● Barolo del Comune di Serralunga d'Alba '11	♟♟ 5
● Dolcetto d'Alba '14	♟ 2
● Langhe Nebbiolo '14	♟ 3
● Barbera d'Alba Sup. '12	♟♟ 4
● Barbera d'Alba Sup. '11	♟♟ 4
● Barolo Cerrati '10	♟♟ 6
● Barolo Cerrati '09	♟♟ 6
● Barolo Cerrati V. Cucco '10	♟♟ 7
● Barolo Cerrati V. Cucco '09	♟♟ 7
● Barolo del Comune di Serralunga d'Alba '10	♟♟ 5
● Barolo di Serralunga '09	♟♟ 5
● Langhe Rosso Mondo '12	♟♟ 4

Cascina del Monastero

FRAZ. ANNUNZIATA
CASCINA LUCIANI, 112A
12064 LA MORRA [CN]
TEL. 0173509245
www.cascinadelmonastero.it

CELLAR SALES
PRE-BOOKED VISITS
ACCOMMODATION
ANNUAL PRODUCTION 40,000 bottles
HECTARES UNDER VINE 12.00
VITICULTURE METHOD Certified Organic
SUSTAINABLE WINERY

This small estate, with an elegant guest farm, is becoming increasingly visible due to the efforts of the enthusiastic Giuseppe Grasso. Its wines are traditional in style, made from the classic local grape varieties, first and foremost nebbiolo, with tiny experiments with French cultivars, while white grapes are completely shunned. The grapes are mainly from vineyards in La Morra not far from the cellar, although the five hectares in the Perno hamlet of Monforte d'Alba make an important contribution to the estate's Barolo production. Our favourite Barolo selection was Riserva Bricco Rocca Riund, whose nose of herbs and fruit is enriched by a fabulous menthol note, followed by a medium-bodied palate that is fresh and lively, especially considering the hot 2009 vintage. The juicy Barbera d'Alba Superiore Perno 2012 has a nose of ripe cherries and sweet spice, accompanied by a complex, vivacious palate. We also enjoyed Barolo Perno 2011, whose winning cards are its delicacy and harmony.

● Barbera d'Alba Parroco '12	▼▼ 3
● Barbera d'Alba Sup. Perno '12	▼▼ 3
● Barolo Bricco Luciani '11	▼▼ 6
● Barolo Bricco Rocca Riund Ris. '09	▼▼ 6
● Barolo Perno '11	▼▼ 5
● Langhe Nebbiolo Monastero '11	▼ 3
● Barbera d'Alba Leprié '10	♀♀ 2*
● Barbera d'Alba Parroco '10	♀♀ 3
● Barolo Bricco Luciani '10	♀♀ 6
● Barolo Bricco Luciani '09	♀♀ 5
● Barolo Perno '10	♀♀ 5
● Barolo Perno '09	♀♀ 5
● Barolo Riund Ris. '08	♀♀ 7
● Barolo Riund Ris. '07	♀♀ 7

Cascina Fonda

VIA SPESSA, 29
12052 MANGO [CN]
TEL. 0173677877
www.cascinafonda.com

CELLAR SALES
PRE-BOOKED VISITS
ACCOMMODATION
ANNUAL PRODUCTION 110,000 bottles
HECTARES UNDER VINE 12.00

The little estate owned by brothers Marco and Massimo Barbero has several vineyards in Mango, where the winery is situated, and Neive. They are planted with vines up to 60 years old and are mainly south-east facing, at an altitude of around 450 metres. Moscato is undoubtedly the most important grape variety, but dolcetto, nebbiolo, arneis, and a few international cultivars are also grown. The Barbero brothers' wines are well made. Barbaresco Bertola 2012 offers red berry fruit and the sweet spiciness of oak on the nose, followed by a pleasing, balanced, medium-bodied palate without any rough edges, although a little lacking in grip. Moscato d'Asti Bel Piano 2014 has a sweet citrussy nose with spicy hints, accompanied by a supple, close-focused palate with good structure, especially considering the difficult vintage.

● Barbaresco Bertola '12	▼▼ 5
○ Moscato d'Asti Bel Piano '14	▼▼ 2*
○ Asti Bel Piasì '11	♀♀ 2*
○ Asti Spumante Bel Piasì '13	♀♀ 2*
○ Asti Spumante Bel Piasì '12	♀♀ 2*
● Barbaresco Bertola '10	♀♀ 5
○ Moscato d'Asti Bel Piano '13	♀♀ 2*
○ Moscato d'Asti Bel Piano '12	♀♀ 2*
○ Moscato d'Asti Bel Piano '11	♀♀ 2*
○ Moscato d'Asti Bel Piano '10	♀♀ 2
○ Moscato d'Asti Bel Piano '09	♀♀ 2*
○ Moscato d'Asti Bel Piano '08	♀♀ 2*
○ Moscato Spumante Tardivo '12	♀♀ 3*
○ Moscato Spumante Tardivo '11	♀♀ 3
○ Moscato Spumante Tardivo '10	♀♀ 3
○ Moscato Spumante Tardivo '09	♀♀ 3

Cascina Fontana

LOC. PERNO
VIA DELLA CHIESA, 2
12065 MONFORTE D'ALBA [CN]
TEL. 0173789005
www.cascinafontana.com

CELLAR SALES
PRE-BOOKED VISITS
ANNUAL PRODUCTION 25,000 bottles
HECTARES UNDER VINE 5.00
SUSTAINABLE WINERY

Mario Fontana is a poet of the earth, grapes and wine, and a glance at his website will reveal his passion, imbued with gratitude and respect for his predecessors. Consequently, he strives to vinify his grapes without adding or subtracting anything from the purity of the fruit and the magic of its transformation into wine. The Barolo vineyards are constituted by three small plots, including a very fine one in the Castiglione Falletto's Villero cru, whose grapes are combined in a single wine. The 2011 Barolo is classic and austere. Its aromas are still rather closed, with herbs in the sun on the nose, and the plush structure is still overwhelmed by tannins, but it promises very well. Langhe Nebbiolo 2013 is one of the very best of the vintage, with a complex, clean, alluring nose and a palate displaying exemplary softness and freshness. The Barbera d'Alba 2013 is very appealing.

● Barolo '11	▼▼	6
● Langhe Nebbiolo '13	▼▼	4
● Barbera d'Alba '13	▼▼	3
● Dolcetto d'Alba '14	▼	2
● Barolo '10	▽▽▽	7
● Barbera d'Alba '12	▽▽	5
● Barbera d'Alba '11	▽▽	5
● Barbera d'Alba '09	▽▽	3
● Barolo '09	▽▽	7
● Barolo '08	▽▽	7
● Barolo Villero e Valletta '07	▽▽	5
● Dolcetto d'Alba '11	▽▽	3
● Langhe Nebbiolo '10	▽▽	4
● Langhe Nebbiolo '09	▽▽	3

Cascina Gilli

VIA NEVISSANO, 36
14022 CASTELNUOVO DON BOSCO [AT]
TEL. 0119876984
www.cascinagilli.it

CELLAR SALES
PRE-BOOKED VISITS
ACCOMMODATION
ANNUAL PRODUCTION 120,000 bottles
HECTARES UNDER VINE 17.00

Gianni Vergnano has been THE benchmark for freisa and malvasia di Castelnuovo for 30 years. These two grape varieties are highly typical of the area but largely ignored by other producers. His vineyards lie around the farmstead and on the Cornareto hill in Castelnuovo Don Bosco, and on the Schierano hill in Passerano Marmorito. They are planted chiefly to freisa, which is used to make all the different versions, from semi-sparkling to still, from vintage to wine for laying down, and malvasia di Castelnuovo, along with smaller amounts of barbera, bonarda and chardonnay. Malvasia di Castelnuovo Don Bosco Gilli 2014 is exceptionally good, proffering fine varietal aromas of wild berries, well-balanced sugar and acidity, and a long, delicate finish. Freisa d'Asti Arvelé has a nose of black pepper, quinine, and tobacco, accompanied by an elegant, austere palate, while the refreshing, highly drinkable Barbera d'Asti Le More 2013 has earthy, mineral notes, with hints of ripe cherries.

● Barbera d'Asti Le More '13	▼▼	2*
● Freisa d'Asti Arvelé	▼▼	3
● Malvasia di Castelnuovo Don Bosco '14	▼▼	2*
● Malvasia di Castelnuovo Don Bosco Spumante Dolce	▼▼	2*
● Dlicà		▼ 3
● Barbera d'Asti Le More '12	▽▽	2*
● Barbera d'Asti Le More '11	▽▽	2*
● Barbera d'Asti V. delle More '10	▽▽	2*
● Barbera d'Asti V. delle More '04	▽▽	2*
● Freisa d'Asti Arvelé '07	▽▽	3
● Freisa d'Asti Frizzante Luna di Maggio '13	▽▽	2*
● Freisa d'Asti Il Forno '13	▽▽	2*
● Freisa d'Asti Il Forno '11	▽▽	2*
● Malvasia di Castelnuovo Don Bosco '13	▽▽	2*
● Piemonte Bonarda Sernù '11	▽▽	2*

Cascina Giovinale

S.DA SAN NICOLAO, 102
14049 NIZZA MONFERRATO [AT]
TEL. 0141793005
www.cascinagiovinale.com

CELLAR SALES
PRE-BOOKED VISITS
ANNUAL PRODUCTION 25,000 bottles
HECTARES UNDER VINE 7.00
SUSTAINABLE WINERY

Bruno Ciocca and Anna Maria Solaini have been enthusiastically running this interesting little estate since the beginning of the 1980s. It vaunts seven hectares of south-west-facing vineyards on the San Nicolao hill, in the Nizza zone, at an altitude of 260 metres. The main grape variety is barbera, which yields elegant, fruit-rich wines, although smaller amounts of moscato, cortese, dolcetto, and cabernet sauvignon are also grown. Barbera d'Asti Superiore Nizza AnssèmA is back in the spotlight, with the 2012 vintage making it into our finals. Its complex concentrated nose shows nice balance between the dominant notes of plums and morello cherries and spicy oak undertones, while the rich, potent palate has impressive but silky tannins and a finish underpinned by good acidity. Barbera d'Asti Superiore 2011 is also well made. It is lighter and less complex, with typical notes of dark berries and rain-soaked earth, but very pleasant.

● Barbera d'Asti Sup. Nizza Anssèma '12	♥♥	4
● Barbera d'Asti Sup. '11	♥♥	2*
● Barbera d'Asti '04	♀♀	2*
● Barbera d'Asti Sup. '10	♀♀	2*
● Barbera d'Asti Sup. '09	♀♀	2*
● Barbera d'Asti Sup. '07	♀♀	2*
● Barbera d'Asti Sup. '06	♀♀	2*
● Barbera d'Asti Sup. Nizza Anssèma '11	♀♀	3
● Barbera d'Asti Sup. Nizza Anssèma '10	♀♀	3*
● Barbera d'Asti Sup. Nizza Anssèma '09	♀♀	3*
● Barbera d'Asti Sup. Nizza Anssèma '08	♀♀	4
● Barbera d'Asti Sup. Nizza Anssèma '07	♀♀	4
● Barbera d'Asti Sup. Nizza Anssèma '06	♀♀	4*
● Barbera d'Asti Sup. Nizza Anssèma '05	♀♀	4
● Barbera d'Asti Sup. Nizza Anssèma '04	♀♀	4

★★Cascina La Barbatella

S.DA ANNUNZIATA, 55
14049 NIZZA MONFERRATO [AT]
TEL. 0141701434
www.labarbatella.com

CELLAR SALES
PRE-BOOKED VISITS
ANNUAL PRODUCTION 25,000 bottles
HECTARES UNDER VINE 4.00

The estate's few hectares of vineyards are arranged like an amphitheatre around the farmhouse above Nizza Monferrato. Its sandy limestone soils are planted mainly to barbera, including almost two hectares of old vines planted in 1945 and 1950, while the rest are divided between cabernet sauvignon, pinot nero, and less than half a hectare of white grapes: cortese and sauvignon. The wines are some of the finest contemporary interpretations of barbera, both as a monovarietal and in blends with international grape varieties. Monferrato Rosso Sonvico, an equal blend of barbera and cabernet sauvignon, is back in the limelight with the 2010 vintage, which offers a nose of spice, quinine, graphite, and blackcurrants, and a pleasant, juicy, fruit-rich palate with well-behaved tannins. Barbera d'Asti Superiore Nizza La Vigna dell'Angelo 2012 is also very good, with ripe dark berry fruit, cocoa powder and quinine on the nose, and a fleshy palate with good acidity, which is still seeking perfect balance.

● Barbera d'Asti Sup. Nizza V. dell'Angelo '12	♥♥	5
● M.to Rosso Sonvico '10	♥♥	6
● Barbera d'Asti La Barbatella '13	♥♥	3
● M.to Rosso Ruanera '12	♥♥	2*
● Barbera d'Asti Sup. Nizza V. dell'Angelo '11	♀♀♀	5
● Barbera d'Asti Sup. Nizza V. dell'Angelo '07	♀♀♀	5
● M.to Rosso Mystère '01	♀♀♀	6
● M.to Rosso Sonvico '09	♀♀♀	6
● M.to Rosso Sonvico '06	♀♀♀	5
● M.to Rosso Sonvico '04	♀♀♀	5
● M.to Rosso Sonvico '03	♀♀♀	5
● M.to Rosso Sonvico '00	♀♀♀	7
● M.to Rosso Sonvico '98	♀♀♀	5

Cascina La Maddalena

FRAZ. SAN GIACOMO
LOC. PIANI DEL PADRONE, 257
15078 ROCCA GRIMALDA [AL]
TEL. 0143876074
www.cascina-maddalena.com

CELLAR SALES
PRE-BOOKED VISITS
ACCOMMODATION
ANNUAL PRODUCTION 25,000 bottles
HECTARES UNDER VINE 4.00

Cascina La Maddalena has around 20 harvests under its belt and has been growing constantly since its foundation, in terms of both the quality of its wines and the methods chosen to convey the allure of the Ovada terroir. The flagship is Dolcetto d'Ovada, offered in three versions, produced with different fermentation and ageing techniques. The variety is also featured in a blend with barbera and merlot in Monferrato Rosso Bricco della Maddalena. Bricco del Bagatto vaunts a ruby hue tending to purple, and an appealing fruity nose with notes of cocoa powder and tobacco, echoed on a firmly structured palate with a fine tannic weave. The Dolcetto 2014 also fared well, offering attractive ripe fruit, and a concentrated, full-bodied palate with slightly rough-edged tannins on the finish. Rossa d'Ocra is intense and lingering on the nose and palate, displaying sophisticated notes of dark berry fruit and cocoa powder with the spicy undertones of well-calibrated oak.

Cascina Montagnola

S.DA MONTAGNOLA, 1
15058 VIGUZZOLO [AL]
TEL. 3480742701
www.cascinamontagnola.com

CELLAR SALES
PRE-BOOKED VISITS
ANNUAL PRODUCTION 30,000 bottles
HECTARES UNDER VINE 10.00

Eighteen vintages have passed since Donatella Giannotti and her husband decided to invest time and resources in their estate in Viguzzolo, a few kilometres from Tortona, on the right bank of the Grue river, near the point where it joins the Scrivia. They have made the most of this fine winegrowing country, producing wines from native grape varieties: timorasso, cortese, barbera and croatina, but at the same time targeting a wider market with products made from chardonnay, sauvignon blanc, and merlot. Morasso made it into our finals with an excellent performance. Showing straw yellow, with subtle golden highlights, its complex, delicate, mineral nose is followed by a rich, powerful palate underpinned by fine acidity, resulting in a very long finish. Barbera Amaranto and Cortese Dunin are also noteworthy.

● Dolcetto di Ovada Bricco del Bagatto '14	♟♟ 2*
● Dolcetto di Ovada '14	♟♟ 2*
● Rossa d'Ocra	♟♟ 2
● Bricco del Padrone	♟ 4
● Barbera del M.to '08	♟♟ 2*
● Barbera del M.to Rossa d'Ocra '11	♟♟ 2*
● Dolcetto di Ovada '13	♟♟ 2*
● Dolcetto di Ovada '12	♟♟ 2
● Dolcetto di Ovada '11	♟♟ 2
● Dolcetto di Ovada '10	♟♟ 2*
● Dolcetto di Ovada '09	♟♟ 2*
● Dolcetto di Ovada Bricco del Bagatto '13	♟♟ 2*
● Dolcetto di Ovada Bricco del Bagatto '12	♟♟ 3
● Dolcetto di Ovada Bricco del Bagatto '11	♟♟ 3
● Dolcetto di Ovada Migulle '09	♟♟ 4
● M.to Rosso Pian del Merlo '07	♟♟ 3

○ Colli Tortonesi Timorasso Morasso '13	♟♟ 4
● Colli Tortonesi Barbera Amaranto '12	♟ 2
○ Colli Tortonesi Cortese Dunin '14	♟ 2
● Colli Tortonesi Barbera Amaranto '11	♟♟ 2*
● Colli Tortonesi Barbera Rodeo '10	♟♟ 5
● Colli Tortonesi Barbera Rodeo '09	♟♟ 5
● Colli Tortonesi Barbera Rodeo '08	♟♟ 5
○ Colli Tortonesi Cortese Dunin '12	♟♟ 2*
○ Colli Tortonesi Cortese Dunin '10	♟♟ 2*
● Colli Tortonesi Croatina Donaldo '11	♟♟ 3
○ Colli Tortonesi Timorasso Derthona '10	♟♟ 3*
○ Colli Tortonesi Timorasso Morasso '12	♟♟ 4
○ Colli Tortonesi Timorasso Morasso '11	♟♟ 4
○ Colli Tortonesi Timorasso Morasso '09	♟♟ 4

Cascina Morassino

S.DA BERNINO, 10
12050 BARBARESCO [CN]
TEL. 0173635149
morassino@gmail.com

CELLAR SALES
PRE-BOOKED VISITS
ANNUAL PRODUCTION 20,000 bottles
HECTARES UNDER VINE 4.50

Roberto Bianco, aided by his father Mauro, firmly believes that small is beautiful and has made it his motto, ensuring that his estate is an entirely family-run affair, in both the vineyard and the cellar. He favours a traditional style in his production and in his relations with the outside world, refusing to be seduced by the notion of a website and preferring to be known exclusively through his wines, which are consistently sound. Barbaresco Ovello 2012, from one of the finest vineyards of the entire area, is very complex. The particularly concentrated, layered nose is highly alluring, with notes of fresh herbs, red berries and spice, followed by a rich, long palate subtly boosted by lively tannins. The Morassino of the same vintage is less exuberant but very classic.

Cascina Pellerino

LOC. SANT'ANNA, 93
12040 MONTEU ROERO [CN]
TEL. 0173978171
www.cascinapellerino.com

CELLAR SALES
PRE-BOOKED VISITS
ANNUAL PRODUCTION 50,000 bottles
HECTARES UNDER VINE 7.00

Cascina Pellerino was founded by the Bono family in 1980 and is now managed by Cristiano Bono and Enrica Cagliero. The estate's vineyards are situated in several municipalities, from Canale to Monteu Roero, Santo Stefano Roero, and Vezza d'Alba, and are planted with the typical local grape varieties (arneis, favorita, barbera and nebbiolo) and internationals like cabernet franc, chardonnay, and pinot nero, the latter two used for Metodo Classico sparklers. Barbera d'Alba Gran Madre is back at the forefront. The 2013 vintage has very well-typed earthy notes with hints of dark berries and autumn leaves, and a fruity palate with taut acidity. Vigna del Padre Riserva 2012 is also excellent, with notes of orange peel and ripe dark berries, and impressive stuffing and depth. Roero Vicot 2013 has rather rugged tannins, but is juicy with nice drive, while Roero Arneis Boneur 2014 is light with good fruit.

● Barbaresco Ovello '12	♟♟ 6
● Barbaresco Morassino '12	♟♟ 5
● Barbaresco Morassino '09	♟♟♟ 5
● Barbaresco Morassino '05	♟♟ 5
● Barbaresco Morassino '01	♟♟ 5*
● Barbaresco Ovello '11	♟♟ 6
● Barbaresco Ovello '10	♟♟ 6
● Barbaresco Ovello '09	♟♟ 6
● Barbaresco Ovello '08	♟♟ 6
● Barbaresco Ovello '07	♟♟ 6
● Barbaresco Ovello '06	♟♟ 6
● Barbaresco Ovello '05	♟♟ 6
● Barbaresco Ovello '04	♟♟ 6
● Barbaresco Ovello '03	♟♟ 6
● Barbaresco Ovello '02	♟♟ 6
● Barbera d'Alba Vignot '07	♟♟ 4*

● Barbera d'Alba Gran Madre '13	♟♟ 4
● Roero V. del Padre Ris. '12	♟♟ 5
○ Roero Arneis Boneur '14	♟♟ 3
● Roero Vicot '13	♟♟ 4
● Barbera d'Alba Eleonora '14	♟ 3
○ Poch ma Bon Passito	♟ 6
○ Roero Arneis Atipico '14	♟ 3
● Barbera d'Alba Sup. Gran Madre '11	♟♟ 5
● Barbera d'Alba Sup. Gran Madre '05	♟♟ 4
● Roero Leoni '04	♟♟ 5
● Roero Vicot '11	♟♟ 4
● Roero Vicot '08	♟♟ 5
● Roero Vicot '06	♟♟ 5
● Roero Vicot '05	♟♟ 4
● Roero Vigna del Padre '09	♟♟ 5
● Roero Vigna del Padre Ris. '11	♟♟ 5

Cascina Salicetti

VIA CASCINA SALICETTI, 2
15050 MONTEGIOCO [AL]
TEL. 0131875192
www.cascinasalicetti.it

CELLAR SALES
PRE-BOOKED VISITS
ANNUAL PRODUCTION 25,000 bottles
HECTARES UNDER VINE 16.00

Montegioco is a municipality in the Tortona area, lying on the hills to the left of the Grue river, and belongs to Mountain Community of the Curone, Grue and Ossona Valleys. This pleasant rural setting is home to the timorasso vines that have made brought great renown to the area, along with barbera, dolcetto, bonarda piemontese, and cortese. A skilled interpreter of timorasso, over the years Anselmo Franzosi's range has achieved very high quality, with peaks of excellence reached by the wines from dolcetto and Barbera Morganti. The 2012 vintage of DiMarzi still shows ruby tending to purple, and its vinous nose with notes of blackberries confirms its propensity for ageing. Its fine acidity is balanced by plenty of flesh on the very long palate. The Seguito, from cabernet sauvignon, has a nose of fresh herbs, currants and spice, accompanied by an elegant palate, with a well-orchestrated lingering finish.

○ Colli Tortonesi Cortese Montarlino '14	♥♥	4
● Colli Tortonesi Dolcetto Di Marzi '12	♥♥	2*
● Colli Tortonesi Rosso Il Seguito '12	♥♥	2*
● Colli Tortonesi Croatina Risulò '13	♥	4
● Colli Tortonesi Barbera Morganti '10	♀♀	2*
○ Colli Tortonesi Cortese Montarlino '12	♀♀	2*
○ Colli Tortonesi Timorasso Derthona '09	♀♀	3*
○ Colli Tortonesi Timorasso Ombra di Luna '12	♀♀	4
○ Colli Tortonesi Timorasso Ombra di Luna '11	♀♀	3*
○ Colli Tortonesi Timorasso Ombra di Luna '10	♀♀	3
○ Colli Tortonesi Timorasso Principio '10	♀♀	3

Cascina Val del Prete

S.DA SANTUARIO, 2
12040 PRIOCCA [CN]
TEL. 0173616534
www.valdelprete.com

CELLAR SALES
PRE-BOOKED VISITS
ANNUAL PRODUCTION 55,000 bottles
HECTARES UNDER VINE 11.00
VITICULTURE METHOD Certified Organic

Founded in 1977 by Bartolomeo and Carolina Roagna, Cascina Val del Prete has been managed by their son Mario Roagna for the past 20 years. In 2005 he converted both the vineyards and the cellar to biodynamic principles in order to produce wines that reflect the terroir as closely as possible. Surrounded by a splendid natural amphitheatre of estate-owned vineyards, at an altitude of approximately 200 metres, it offers the classic Roero wines from arneis, barbera and nebbiolo. The estate's top wine is again Roero Vigna di Lino, whose 2012 vintage offers notes of red berry fruit, tobacco and Mediterranean scrubland on the nose, and an elegant, fruit-rich palate, with solid, nicely tannic structure. The rest of the production is well made, particularly the other two Roeros: the well-balanced Riserva 2011, with notes of lavender and orange peel, and Bricco Medica 2012, which displays good fruit and fine tannins, but is a little short on body and thrust.

● Roero Vigna di Lino '12	♥♥	4
● Barbera d'Alba Serra de' Gatti '14	♥♥	3
● Roero Bricco Medica '12	♥♥	3
● Roero Ris. '11	♥♥	5
○ Roero Arneis Luèt '14	♥	2
● Nebbiolo d'Alba V. di Lino '00	♀♀♀	5
● Roero '04	♀♀♀	6
● Roero '03	♀♀♀	6
● Roero '01	♀♀♀	6
● Roero '00	♀♀♀	6
● Nebbiolo d'Alba V. di Lino '11	♀♀	4
● Roero '10	♀♀	6
● Roero '09	♀♀	6
● Roero '08	♀♀	6
● Roero '07	♀♀	6
● Roero Bricco Medica '09	♀♀	5

Francesca Castaldi

VIA NOVEMBRE, 6
28072 BRIONA [NO]
TEL. 0321826045
www.cantinacastaldi.it

CELLAR SALES
PRE-BOOKED VISITS
ANNUAL PRODUCTION 10,000 bottles
HECTARES UNDER VINE 6.30

It was a radical change of lifestyle that brought Francesca Castaldi and her brother Giuseppe to Briona, the southernmost reach of the famed morainic Novara hills, where the uplands start to slope down towards the first rice paddies. Here, between Pianazze, Val Ceresole and Belvedere, they renovated an area of over six hectares, planted to nebbiolo, vespolina, uva rara, and erbaluce, tended with environmentally friendly methods. The result is a small range, which has gradually been expanded in recent years with new wines, like Crepuscolo: a safe bet for fans of austere reds, with plenty of phenolic backbone. Fara 2011 fully respects this style, already vaunting close-focused tertiary notes of quinine and tobacco on the nose, partially belied by a palate with still stiff tannins. In this respect, Nebbiolo Bigin 2012 is more harmonious and luscious, albeit less complex.

● Fara '11	♟♟ 5	
● Colline Novaresi Nebbiolo Bigin '12	♟♟ 3	
○ Colline Novaresi Bianco Lucia '14	♟ 3	
○ Colline Novaresi Rosato Rosa Alba '14	♟ 3	
● Colline Novaresi Vespolina Nina '14	♟ 3	
● Colline Novaresi Barbera Martina '10	♟♟ 2*	
● Colline Novaresi Vespolina Nina '13	♟♟ 3	
● Crepuscolo	♟♟ 4	
● Fara '10	♟♟ 5	
● Fara '09	♟♟ 5	
● Fara '08	♟♟ 3*	

Castellari Bergaglio

FRAZ. ROVERETO, 136
15066 GAVI [AL]
TEL. 0143644000
www.castellaribergaglio.it

CELLAR SALES
PRE-BOOKED VISITS
ANNUAL PRODUCTION 90,000 bottles
HECTARES UNDER VINE 11.00

Each year Castellari Bergaglio presents an impressive seven versions of Cortese. Today the long-established estate is headed by Mario Bergaglio, active mainly in the vineyard, while his son Marco focuses on work in the cellar. Salluvii is the basic wine of the well-put-together range, while Fornaci and Rolona are the selections crafted from the hillside vineyards of the same name in the municipalities of Tassarolo and Gavi. The grapes from the old Rovereto vineyard undergo cold maceration on the skins. Then there are the late-harvest Pilin, aged in small oak casks, the Metodo Classico Ardé, and the Passito Gavium. This year it was the minor wines that shone, with the Salluvii and Fornaci giving excellent performances in the difficult 2014 vintage. The first has a fine fresh nose of herbs and flowers on a background of mineral notes and flint, followed by a fresh, taut palate with excellent length, while the Fornaci has well-defined mineral notes and fruit on a long, well-behaved palate.

○ Gavi del Comune di Tassarolo Fornaci '14	♟♟ 2*	
○ Gavi Salluvii '14	♟♟ 2*	
○ Gavi del Comune di Gavi Rolona '14	♟ 3	
○ Gavi del Comune di Gavi Rolona '13	♟♟ 3*	
○ Gavi del Comune di Gavi Rolona '12	♟♟ 3	
○ Gavi del Comune di Gavi Rolona '11	♟♟ 3*	
○ Gavi del Comune di Gavi Rovereto Vignavecchia '12	♟♟ 3*	
○ Gavi del Comune di Gavi Rovereto Vignavecchia '10	♟♟ 3	
○ Gavi del Comune di Tassarolo Fornaci '10	♟♟ 2	
○ Gavi Fornaci '13	♟♟ 2*	
○ Gavi Pilìn '12	♟♟ 5	
○ Gavi Pilìn '11	♟♟ 5	
○ Gavi Salluvii '13	♟♟ 2*	
○ Gavi Salluvii '12	♟♟ 2*	

Castello di Gabiano

VIA DEFENDENTE, 2
15020 GABIANO [AL]
TEL. 0142945004
www.castellodigabiano.com

CELLAR SALES
PRE-BOOKED VISITS
ACCOMMODATION AND RESTAURANT SERVICE
ANNUAL PRODUCTION 100,000 bottles
HECTARES UNDER VINE 21.00

The imposing castle that overlooks the Po Valley also houses the winery. In this breathtaking setting, with a medieval atmosphere, winemaking also contributes to Monferrato's history and age-old traditions, albeit with the aid of the necessary modern technologies. Vines have always been grown in this area, including difficult cultivars, like grignolino, wrongly considered capable of yielding only ready-drinking wines. In this case, history once again shows us the way, with bottles from the 1970s in perfect conditions offering astonishing and very classy tertiary aromas. History has given grignolino to this terroir and the grape is certainly capable of writing one all of its own. This year Monferrato Rosso Gavius, from barbera and pinot nero, gave an excellent performance. It offers intriguing aromas and flavours, with an elegant nose and a powerful, well-balanced palate. The rest of the production is on top form, although Il Ruvo reflects the difficult conditions of the 2014 vintage, despite being very well made.

● M.to Rosso Gavius '12	♟♟ 3*
○ M.to Bianco Corte '14	♟♟ 3
⊙ M.to Chiaretto Castelvere '14	♟♟ 2*
○ Piemonte Chardonnay Castello '13	♟♟ 5
● Rubino di Cantavenna '13	♟♟ 3
● Barbera d'Asti La Braja '13	♟ 2
● Grignolino del M.to Casalese Il Ruvo '14	♟ 2
● Barbera d'Asti La Braja '11	♟♟ 2*
● Barbera d'Asti Sup. Adornes '10	♟♟ 5
● Barbera d'Asti Sup. Adornes '09	♟♟ 5
● Gabiano Matilde Giustiniani Ris. '09	♟♟ 6
● Gabiano Matilde Giustiniani Ris. '08	♟♟ 6
● Grignolino del M.to Casalese Il Ruvo '13	♟♟ 2*
● Grignolino del M.to Casalese Il Ruvo '12	♟♟ 2*
● M.to Rosso Gavius '11	♟♟ 3
● Rubino di Cantavenna '12	♟♟ 3

Castello di Neive

VIA CASTELBORGO, 1
12052 NEIVE [CN]
TEL. 017367171
www.castellodineive.it

PRE-BOOKED VISITS
ANNUAL PRODUCTION 170,000 bottles
HECTARES UNDER VINE 27.00

The Stupino family own almost 30 hectares of vineyards, all in Neive. They include plots in universally renowned crus like Basarin, Gallina, Marcorino, and particularly Santo Stefano, from which the winery also produces a Barbaresco Riserva in the finest vintages. The castle after which the estate is named and that houses the ageing barrels is also in Neive. In 2012 it was joined by a second large cellar, ideal for fermenting nebbiolo, which is done in a traditional style. The Tre Bicchieri-winning Barbaresco Albesani Santo Stefano 2012 is exquisitely classic, offering a harmonious, multifaceted nose focusing on raspberries and wild strawberries, with hints of liquorice starting to emerge. Its exemplary palate is long, powerful and packed with juicy red berries. Barbera d'Alba Santo Stefano 2013 is a delectable mouthfilling wine, showing firm and layered, with a little oak still evident, dense and slightly tannic, with moderate acidity.

● Barbaresco Albesani S. Stefano '12	♟♟♟ 6
● Barbera d'Alba S. Stefano '13	♟♟ 3*
● Barbaresco '12	♟♟ 5
○ Langhe Arneis Montebertotto '14	♟♟ 3
● Langhe Pinot Nero I Cortini '14	♟♟ 4
○ Piemonte Pinot Nero M. Cl. '11	♟♟ 5
● Piemonte Albarossa '12	♟ 2
● Barbaresco S. Stefano Ris. '01	♟♟♟ 7
● Barbaresco S. Stefano Ris. '99	♟♟♟ 7
● Barbaresco '11	♟♟ 5
● Barbaresco Albesani S. Stefano '11	♟♟ 6
● Barbaresco Albesani S. Stefano Ris. '09	♟♟ 8
● Barbaresco Gallina '11	♟♟ 5
● Barbera d'Alba S. Stefano '11	♟♟ 3
● Barbera d'Alba Sup. '12	♟♟ 4
● Langhe Pinot Nero I Cortini '12	♟♟ 4

Tenuta Castello di Razzano

FRAZ. CASARELLO
VIA SAN CARLO, 2
15021 ALFIANO NATTA [AL]
TEL. 0141922124
www.castellodirazzano.it

CELLAR SALES
PRE-BOOKED VISITS
ACCOMMODATION
ANNUAL PRODUCTION 200,000 bottles
HECTARES UNDER VINE 30.00

The Olearo family are incredibly dynamic,
always busy developing new projects. Their
beautiful relais is housed in a castle with an
inner courtyard, which is also home to the
old cellars and wine museum. However, the
estate is also no stranger to innovative
agricultural technologies, which are
essential considering its statistics: an
annual production of around 200,000
bottles from over 40 hectares of vineyards,
and 60 hectares planted with other crops.
Our tastings highlighted Barbera d'Asti
Euganea, characterized by tertiary aromas
derived from ageing, and Il Beneficio, with
a complex, concentrated palate derived
from toasted oak. Cuntrà, a merlot
monovarietal, has a jammy nose with
leather notes, followed by a concentrated
palate underpinned by good acidity and a
very lingering finish.

Castello di Tassarolo

CASCINA ALBORINA, 1
15060 TASSAROLO [AL]
TEL. 0143342248
www.castelloditassarolo.it

CELLAR SALES
PRE-BOOKED VISITS
ANNUAL PRODUCTION 130,000 bottles
HECTARES UNDER VINE 20.00
VITICULTURE METHOD Certified Organic
SUSTAINABLE WINERY

Among the most original interpreters of
cortese di Gavi, Marchesi Massimilana and
Bonifacio Spinola are descendents of the
family that have owned Castello di
Tassarolo since 1300. Aided by Vincenzo
Munì and Henry Finzi-Constantine, they
recently converted the estate's 20 or so
hectares to biodynamic farming. However,
the most interesting and original wines
remain the whites: Spinola, Il Castello,
Titouan, Alborina, and most recently the
Sparkling. This year Gavi Alborina and Gavi
Il Castello reached our tasting finals.
Alborina 2013 (mistakenly written up last
year instead of the 2012) has a
concentrated, layered nose and an
extraordinarily full, dense palate with good
supporting acidity that guarantees its
cellarability. The classic-style Il Castello has
a fruity nose with mineral undertones,
accompanied by a rich palate and a
characterful finish.

● Barbera d'Asti Sup. Euganea '12	▼▼ 5
● Barbera d'Asti Sup. Il Beneficio '12	▼▼ 5
● M.to Rosso Cuntrà '11	▼▼ 3
● Barbera d'Asti Sup. Campasso '11	▼ 3
○ Costa al Sole '13	▼ 2
● Barbera d'Asti La Leona '11	♀♀ 2*
● Barbera d'Asti Sup. Campasso '09	♀♀ 2*
● Barbera d'Asti Sup. Campasso '07	♀♀ 2*
● Barbera d'Asti Sup. Del Beneficio '10	♀♀ 4
● Barbera d'Asti Sup. Del Beneficio '09	♀♀ 4
● Barbera d'Asti Sup. Euganea '11	♀♀ 4
● Barbera d'Asti Sup. Euganea '09	♀♀ 4
● Barbera d'Asti Sup. Il Beneficio '11	♀♀ 3
● Grignolino del M.to Casalese Pianaccio '13	♀♀ 2*

○ Gavi del Comune di Tassarolo Alborina '13	▼▼ 3*
○ Gavi del Comune di Tassarolo Il Castello '14	▼▼ 2*
● M.to Rosso Cuveè No Sulphites '14	▼ 3
○ Gavi del Comune di Tassarolo Alborina '13	♀♀ 3
○ Gavi del Comune di Tassarolo Alborina '12	♀♀ 3*
○ Gavi del Comune di Tassarolo Il Castello '13	♀♀ 2*
○ Gavi del Comune di Tassarolo Il Castello '12	♀♀ 2*
○ Gavi del Comune di Tassarolo Spinola '13	♀♀ 2*
○ Gavi del Comune di Tassarolo Spinola '12	♀♀ 2*
○ Gavi del Comune di Tassarolo Titouan '13	♀♀ 3

Castello di Uviglie

VIA CASTELLO DI UVIGLIE, 73
15030 ROSIGNANO MONFERRATO [AL]
TEL. 0142488132
www.castellodiuviglie.com

CELLAR SALES
PRE-BOOKED VISITS
ANNUAL PRODUCTION 90,000 bottles
HECTARES UNDER VINE 25.00

In the space of just a few years, Simone
Lupano has made Castello di Uviglie a
benchmark winery for Monferrato Casalese.
The historic premises, now also used as a
venue for events and ceremonies, vaunt a
cellar housing a series of top-quality wines.
They are made from both Monferrato grape
varieties and internationals, such as pinot
nero, chardonnay, and sauvignon,
sometimes blended to make veritable
gems, like the Brut Metodo Classico, aged
for 44 months on the lees in the castle's
tufa cellars, and the Passito, from half
chardonnay and half sauvignon grapes. The
wines presented this year were a splendid
bunch, with three of them reaching our
finals: a memorable version of Barbera Le
Cave, complex and elegant with an
exceptionally long finish, which won a fully
deserved Tre Bicchieri; Pico Gonzaga 2012;
and Grignolino San Sebastiano Terre
Bianche 2011, at its first release.

● Barbera del M.to Sup. Le Cave '13	▼▼▼ 3*
● Barbera del M.to Sup. Pico Gonzaga '12	▼▼ 5
● Grignolino del M.to Casalese San Bastiano Terre Bianche '11	▼▼ 5
● Barbera del M.to Bricco del Conte '14	▼▼ 2*
○ Bricco del Ciliegio Passito '11	▼▼ 5
○ Le Cave Extra Brut M. Cl. '11	▼▼ 5
● M.to Rosso 1491 '12	▼▼ 5
○ Piemonte Chardonnay Ninfea '14	▼▼ 2*
● Barbera del M.to Sup. Le Cave '09	♀♀♀ 3*
● Barbera del M.to Sup. Le Cave '07	♀♀♀ 3*
● Barbera del M.to Sup. Pico Gonzaga '07	♀♀♀ 4*
● Barbera del M.to Bricco del Conte '13	♀♀ 2*
● Grignolino del M.to Casalese San Bastiano '13	♀♀ 2*

Castello di Verduno

VIA UMBERTO I, 9
12060 VERDUNO [CN]
TEL. 0172470284
www.castellodiverduno.com

CELLAR SALES
PRE-BOOKED VISITS
ACCOMMODATION AND RESTAURANT SERVICE
ANNUAL PRODUCTION 68,000 bottles
HECTARES UNDER VINE 10.00
SUSTAINABLE WINERY

A family history deeply rooted in the culture
of Langhe wine production, a stunningly
beautiful cellar housed in a manor, and a
practically flawless range of traditional
wines underpin the international success
deservedly conquered by Castello di
Verduno. Gabriella Burlotto and her
husband Franco Bianco know how to
preserve and heighten the inimitable style
of austere, kaleidoscopic wines, usually
made even more alluring by patient bottle
ageing and prolonged aeration in the glass.
All aged in large barrels, the Barolo
vineyard selections are from the Massara
and Monvigliero crus in Verduno, while the
Barbarescos hail from Faset and Rabajà.
The house style and the sunny 2011
vintage are obviously highly compatible, as
exemplified by the complex, juicy Barolo
and the sharp, close-focused Barbaresco
Rabajà. However, the generous Monvigliero
Riserva 2009, with a kaleidoscopic nose of
jam and fresh citrus fruit, and an extremely
lively palate with flavoursome tannins,
demonstrates the estate's skill even with
this hot vintage.

● Barbaresco Rabajà '11	▼▼ 6
● Barolo Massara '11	▼▼ 6
● Barolo Monvigliero Ris. '09	▼▼ 7
● Barbaresco '12	▼▼ 5
● Barbaresco Rabajà Ris. '09	▼▼ 7
● Barbera d'Alba Bricco del Cuculo '13	▼▼ 4
● Verduno Pelaverga Basadone '14	▼▼ 3
● Barbaresco Rabajà '04	♀♀♀ 6
● Barolo Massara '08	♀♀♀ 6
● Barolo Massara '01	♀♀♀ 6
● Barolo Monvigliero Ris. '04	♀♀♀ 7
● Barbaresco Rabajà '10	♀♀ 6
● Barbera d'Alba Bricco del Cuculo '12	♀♀ 4
● Barolo Massara '09	♀♀ 6
● Barolo Monvigliero Ris. '08	♀♀ 7

La Caudrina

S.DA BROSIA, 21
12053 CASTIGLIONE TINELLA [CN]
TEL. 0141855126
www.caudrina.it

CELLAR SALES
PRE-BOOKED VISITS
ANNUAL PRODUCTION 200,000 bottles
HECTARES UNDER VINE 24.00

Romano Dogliotti's La Caudrina is a beacon of the Moscato wine world. Its moscato vineyards are in the municipality of Castiglione Tinella, on mainly limestone marl, and planted with vines aged from 35 to almost 50 years old. The winery also has an estate in Nizza Monferrato, where barbera, nebbiolo, and dolcetto are grown, and a chardonnay vineyard in Ottiglio Monferrato. The difficult 2014 vintage has prevented Romano Dogliotti from offering Moscatos of his usual high level. Moscato d'Asti La Galeisa is good, showing less complex and firmly structured than usual, but with sweet fruit finely balanced by taut acidity, while the basic Moscato d'Asti is simpler and suppler, focusing on notes of chlorophyll, aromatic herbs, and lemon peel. Barbera d'Asti La Solista 2013, on the other hand, is fruit-rich and flavoursome, with notes of rain-soaked earth and a long, characterful finish.

F.lli Cavallotto
Tenuta Bricco Boschis

LOC. BRICCO BOSCHIS
S.DA ALBA-MONFORTE
12060 CASTIGLIONE FALLETTO [CN]
TEL. 017362814
www.cavallotto.com

CELLAR SALES
PRE-BOOKED VISITS
ANNUAL PRODUCTION 110,000 bottles
HECTARES UNDER VINE 25.00
VITICULTURE METHOD Certified Organic

Every year Alfio and Giuseppe Cavallotto and their sister Laura are visited by a host of keen, loyal fans at Tenuta Bricco Boschis in Castiglione Falletto. Their monopoly cru covers an area of 25 hectares, on the geological boundary between the light marl of Diano d'Alba and the blue marl of La Morra, and is tended using natural methods. It is planted to barbera, dolcetto, freisa, grignolino, pinot nero and chardonnay, with the finest sites reserved for Barolo nebbiolo. Fermented in roto-macerator tanks and aged in large barrels, the fruit from the San Giuseppe and Vignolo vineyards is also used for the estate's Riservas in the finest vintages. On the subject of Barolo Riserva, the Cavallottos did not give it a miss in the controversial 2009 vintage, and our latest tastings would suggest they made the right decision. The Vignolo is placid and well behaved, retaining the typical earthy, smoky notes, while the development of the Vigna San Giuseppe seems more behind.

● Barbera d'Asti La Solista '13	♥♥ 2*
○ Moscato d'Asti La Galeisa '14	♥♥ 3
○ Moscato d'Asti La Caudrina '14	♥ 3
○ Asti La Selvatica '12	♀♀ 3
○ Asti La Selvatica '11	♀♀ 3
○ Asti La Selvatica	♀♀ 3
● Barbera d'Asti La Solista '12	♀♀ 2*
● Barbera d'Asti La Solista '11	♀♀ 2*
● Barbera d'Asti Sup. Monte Venere '10	♀♀ 3
○ Moscato d'Asti '13	♀♀ 3
○ Moscato d'Asti La Caudrina '12	♀♀ 3*
○ Moscato d'Asti La Caudrina '11	♀♀ 3
○ Moscato d'Asti La Galeisa '13	♀♀ 3
○ Moscato d'Asti La Galeisa '12	♀♀ 3
○ Moscato d'Asti La Galeisa '11	♀♀ 3*
○ Piemonte Moscato Passito Redento '11	♀♀ 4

● Barolo Bricco Boschis '11	♥♥ 7
● Barolo Bricco Boschis V. S. Giuseppe Ris. '09	♥♥ 8
● Barolo Vignolo Ris. '09	♥♥ 8
● Barbera d'Alba Sup. V. del Cuculo '12	♥♥ 5
● Langhe Nebbiolo '12	♥♥ 5
● Barolo Bricco Boschis '05	♀♀♀ 6
● Barolo Bricco Boschis '04	♀♀♀ 7
● Barolo Bricco Boschis V. S. Giuseppe Ris. '05	♀♀♀ 8
● Barolo Bricco Boschis V. S. Giuseppe Ris. '01	♀♀♀ 7
● Barolo Bricco Boschis V. S. Giuseppe Ris. '00	♀♀♀ 7
● Barolo Vignolo Ris. '06	♀♀♀ 8
● Barolo Vignolo Ris. '04	♀♀♀ 8

Ceretto

LOC. SAN CASSIANO, 34
12051 ALBA [CN]
TEL. 0173282582
www.ceretto.com

CELLAR SALES
PRE-BOOKED VISITS
RESTAURANT SERVICE
ANNUAL PRODUCTION 900,000 bottles
HECTARES UNDER VINE 105.00
VITICULTURE METHOD Certified Organic
SUSTAINABLE WINERY

We'd need a whole book to recount the details of all the projects developed over the years by the Ceretto family. Instead we'll concentrate on the jewels in the crown of this name that has played a leading role in the history of Piedmont wine, with vineyards extending from Bricco Rocche in Castiglione Falletto to Bricco Asili in Barbaresco, without forgetting the plots around the cellar in Alba, the I Vignaioli estate in Santo Stefano, the triple-Michelin-starred Piazza Duomo restaurant, the La Piola bistro, and much more besides. Traditional grape varieties and native cultivars mingle in the innovative wide range, whose leading Nebbiolo vineyard selections have been progressively reworked in a "neoclassical" style. The collective value of Ceretto's ranges continues to grow, particularly regarding its top Nebbiolos. The Asili 2012 proffers a magnificent nose of herbs and oriental spices, nicely echoed on a delicately juicy palate. The two 2001 Barolo crus are perfectly complementary: the cosseting Brunate and the beefy Bricco Rocche.

● Barolo Bricco Rocche '11	♥♥♥ 8
● Barbaresco Asili '12	♥♥ 8
● Barbaresco Bernardot '12	♥♥ 8
● Barolo Brunate '11	♥♥ 8
● Barolo Prapò '11	♥♥ 8
● Barbaresco '12	♥♥ 5
● Barolo '11	♥♥ 5
○ Langhe Arneis Blangé '14	♥♥ 5
○ Langhe Bianco Arbarei '14	♥♥ 5
● Langhe Rosso Monsordo '13	♥♥ 4
● Barolo Bricco Rocche '09	♥♥♥ 8
● Barolo Prapò '06	♥♥♥ 8
● Barolo Prapò '05	♥♥♥ 8
● Barolo Bricco Rocche '10	♥♥ 8
● Barolo Brunate '10	♥♥ 8
● Barolo Prapò '10	♥♥ 8

★★Michele Chiarlo

S.DA NIZZA-CANELLI, 99
14042 CALAMANDRANA [AT]
TEL. 0141769030
www.chiarlo.it

CELLAR SALES
PRE-BOOKED VISITS
ACCOMMODATION
ANNUAL PRODUCTION 1,100,000 bottles
HECTARES UNDER VINE 120.00
SUSTAINABLE WINERY

For over half a century the Chiarlo family winery has been a benchmark for Asti viticulture and one of the best-known and most highly regarded Piedmont producers in the world. Today it vaunts three separate sites, in Monferrato, Langhe and Gavi, made up of seven different estates, allowing it to produce a particularly wide range of wines representing the region's most important designations, from Barolo and Barbaresco to Nizza, Gavi and Moscato d'Asti. It is hard to say which is the estate's best wine, for the entire range is first class. A Tre Bicchieri went to Barbera d'Asti Superiore Nizza La Court 2012, with a concentrated, well-behaved nose of dark berry fruit, sweet spice, and cocoa powder, and a flavoursome, full-bodied palate with fine acid-tannin balance, and a long, fresh finish. Barolo Cerequio 2011 is almost as good, offering ripe fruit with balsamic hints on the nose, and good flesh on the powerful, juicy palate, with elegant fine-grained tannins.

● Barbera d'Asti Sup. Nizza La Court '12	♥♥♥ 5
● Barolo Cerequio '11	♥♥ 7
● Barolo Tortoniano '11	♥♥ 5
● Barbaresco Asili '12	♥♥ 6
● Barbera d'Asti Sup. Cipressi '13	♥♥ 3
● Barolo Cannubi '11	♥♥ 7
● Barolo Cerequio Ris. '07	♥♥ 8
○ Moscato d'Asti Nivole '14	♥♥ 2*
○ Gavi del Comune di Gavi Rovereto '14	♥ 3
● Barbera d'Asti Sup. Nizza La Court '09	♥♥♥ 5
● Barbera d'Asti Sup. Nizza La Court '06	♥♥♥ 5
● Barolo Cannubi '06	♥♥♥ 7
● Barolo Cannubi '04	♥♥♥ 7
● Barolo Cerequio '10	♥♥♥ 7
● Barolo Cerequio '09	♥♥♥ 7
● Barolo Cerequio '07	♥♥♥ 7

Quinto Chionetti

B.TA VALDIBERTI, 44
12063 DOGLIANI [CN]
TEL. 017371179
www.chionettiquinto.com

CELLAR SALES
PRE-BOOKED VISITS
ANNUAL PRODUCTION 88,000 bottles
HECTARES UNDER VINE 16.00
VITICULTURE METHOD Certified Organic

At the age of almost 90, the great Quinto has decided to leave the management of the winery that made him an internationally venerated producer to his grandson Nicola. His story is inextricably bound up with that of Dogliani and its Dolcetto, whose purity he has constantly upheld against all attempts to distort the cultivar's distinctive characteristics. Consequently, no cultured yeasts and no oak, only steel, allowing time and the experience of the cellarmaster to dictate the stages in the wine's development. Dolcetto Briccolero was still a little introverted at the time of our tastings, due to the complicated vintage. While it remains an archetype of its kind, struggles to unbend on the palate as in the past. Langhe Nebbiolo La Chiusa 2013 is very interesting, offering well-defined varietal notes, with hints of sweet liquorice and fresh menthol, which contribute to delineating a pleasant, stylish palate. Dogliani La Costa 2013 has a solid tannic weave and good stuffing.

● Langhe Nebbiolo La Chiusa '13	♟♟4
● Dogliani Briccolero '14	♟♟3
● Dogliani La Costa '13	♟4
● Dogliani San Luigi '14	♟3
● Dolcetto di Dogliani Briccolero '07	♟♟♟3*
● Dolcetto di Dogliani Briccolero '04	♟♟♟3*
● Dogliani Briccolero '13	♟♟3
● Dogliani Briccolero '12	♟♟3*
● Dogliani Briccolero '11	♟♟3*
● Dogliani S. Luigi '12	♟♟3
● Dogliani S. Luigi '11	♟♟3*
● Dogliani San Luigi '13	♟♟3
● Dolcetto di Dogliani Briccolero '09	♟♟3*
● Dolcetto di Dogliani Briccolero '08	♟♟3*
● Langhe Nebbiolo '13	♟♟3
● Langhe Nebbiolo '12	♟♟3

Cieck

FRAZ. SAN GRATO
CASCINA CASTAGNOLA, 2
10090 SAN GIORGIO CANAVESE [TO]
TEL. 0120330522
www.cieck.it

CELLAR SALES
PRE-BOOKED VISITS
ANNUAL PRODUCTION 80,000 bottles
HECTARES UNDER VINE 13.00

Remo Falconieri and Domenico Caretto's 13-hectare estate produces a range of wines centred on erbaluce, with two Metodo Classicos (the steel-aged San Giorgio and Calliope, aged in small oak casks), three still Calusos (the basic version, the vintage Misobolo, and the oak-aged T, released the following year), and Passito Alladium. Reds include Canavese Rosso and Neretto di San Giorgio, also in the Rosé Brut version. Nebbiolo, Freisa and Barbera complete the range. The estate confirms the vocation of the terroir and its personal meticulousness in the production of Alladium, an Erbaluce di Caluso Passito with enchanting top notes of dried apricots, followed by hints of walnut and coffee cream, which merge elegantly in its traditional profile. Erbaluce di Caluso T stands out among the still wines, aided by the 2013 vintage, which combines aniseed and fruit and offers a well-orchestrated palate with great character.

○ Erbaluce di Caluso Passito Alladium '08	♟♟5
○ Erbaluce di Caluso T '13	♟♟3*
○ Canavese Rosé Brut M.Cl.	♟♟3
○ Erbaluce di Caluso Calliope Brut '10	♟♟4
○ Erbaluce di Caluso Misobolo '14	♟♟2*
○ Erbaluce di Caluso '14	♟2
○ Erbaluce di Caluso S. Giorgio Brut M.Cl.	♟4
○ Erbaluce di Caluso Passito Alladium '06	♟♟♟5
○ Erbaluce di Caluso Misobolo '13	♟♟2*
○ Erbaluce di Caluso Misobolo '12	♟♟2*
○ Erbaluce di Caluso Misobolo '10	♟♟2*
○ Erbaluce di Caluso Passito Alladium '07	♟♟5
○ Erbaluce di Caluso Passito Alladium Ris. '04	♟♟5
○ Erbaluce di Caluso S. Giorgio Brut '09	♟♟4
○ Erbaluce di Caluso T '12	♟♟3

★F.lli Cigliuti

VIA SERRABOELLA, 17
12052 NEIVE [CN]
TEL. 0173677185
www.cigliuti.it

CELLAR SALES
PRE-BOOKED VISITS
ANNUAL PRODUCTION 30,000 bottles
HECTARES UNDER VINE 7.50

In the 1960s brothers Leone and Romualdo
Cigliuti gave their name to the little estate
they took over on the Neive hills. Renato has
proudly continued in their footsteps,
commencing work on the family estate as a
boy and subsequently flanked by his wife
Dina and their daughters Claudia and Silvia.
His wines reflect his intimate relationship with
the land, which is ultimately more important
than any cellar protocols. Distinguished by an
anarchical, sometimes even erratic profile,
they are made from the Serraboella vineyard
(Barbaresco, Dolcetto, and Barbera) and
Bricco di Neive cru (Barbaresco Via Erte and
Langhe Nebbiolo. If this is not the best
performance ever by the Cigliuti family's
wines, it must surely come close. Barbera
d'Alba Campass 2012 combines
uncommonly dense pulp with vibrant acidity,
and Barbaresco Vie Erte 2011 is equally
impressive, showing classic and vigorous.
The icing on the cake is the incredibly deep
Barbaresco Serraboella 2011, which holds
enormous promise for the future.

● Barbaresco Serraboella '11	��� 7
● Barbaresco Vie Erte '11	♕♕ 5
● Barbera d'Alba Campass '12	♕♕ 4
● Barbaresco Serraboella '10	♖♖♖ 7
● Barbaresco Serraboella '09	♖♖♖ 7
● Barbaresco Serraboella '01	♖♖♖ 6
● Barbaresco V. Erte '04	♖♖♖ 6

★Tenute Cisa Asinari dei Marchesi di Grésy

S.DA DELLA STAZIONE, 21
12050 BARBARESCO [CN]
TEL. 0173635222
www.marchesidigresy.com

CELLAR SALES
PRE-BOOKED VISITS
ANNUAL PRODUCTION 200,000 bottles
HECTARES UNDER VINE 35.00
SUSTAINABLE WINERY

Tenute Cisa Asinari, founded by Marchese
Alberto de Grésy in the 1970s, comprises
four distinct blocks of vineyards. Moscato is
grown at Cassine, in Monferrato; barbera
and merlot at the La Serra and Monte
Colombo estates; and dolcetto, chardonnay
and sauvignon at Monte Aribaldo, in Treiso.
However, the jewel in the crown remains the
Martinenga hill in Barbaresco, which is home
to the cellar and the almost 12-hectare
vineyard that yields Camp Gros and Gaiun.
These Nebbiolos are always strikingly
elegant and cellarable, modern in style more
than in substance, with relatively short
maceration times and at least partial ageing
in barrique. Once again, the estate
presented a well-assorted trio of
Barbarescos. Gaiun 2011 is currently
marked by oak, which is decidedly better
integrated in the weighty Martinenga 2012
with good grip. Camp Gros 2010 has greater
finesse and complexity, with a powerful,
close-knit structure showing admirable
balance.

● Barbaresco Camp Gros Martinenga Ris. '10	♕♕ 8
● Barbaresco Martinenga '12	♕♕ 7
● Barbaresco Martinenga Gaiun '11	♕♕ 8
● Barbera d'Asti '13	♕♕ 3
● Barbera d'Asti Monte Colombo '11	♕♕ 5
○ Langhe Chardonnay Grésy '13	♕♕ 5
○ Langhe Chardonnay '14	♕ 3
○ Langhe Sauvignon '14	♕ 3
● M.to Merlot da Solo '09	♕ 5
● Barbaresco Camp Gros '06	♖♖♖ 8
● Barbaresco Camp Gros '05	♖♖♖ 8
● Barbaresco Camp Gros '01	♖♖♖ 8
● Barbaresco Camp Gros Martinenga '09	♖♖♖ 8
● Barbaresco Camp Gros Martinenga '08	♖♖♖ 8
● Barbaresco Gaiun '04	♖♖♖ 8

★★Domenico Clerico

LOC. MANZONI, 67
12065 MONFORTE D'ALBA [CN]
TEL. 017378171
www.domenicoclerico.com

PRE-BOOKED VISITS
ANNUAL PRODUCTION 110,000 bottles
HECTARES UNDER VINE 21.00

Domenico Clerico has long been one of the big names behind the greatness of Barolo and Langhe. No wine lover or critic dares dispute his worth as a man of the vineyard and a driving force, due to his innate ability to transmit his affability and enthusiasm. He was among the first to focus on ageing in small oak casks, but in recent years the stylistic divide between his Barolos and those customarily described as "traditional" is becoming increasingly blurred. The range features an impressive five of them: Ciabot Mentin and Pajana, from the Ginestra cru in Monforte; Percristina from Mosconi, also in Monforte; Briccotto and Aeroplanservaj, from Serralunga. The very fine Barolo Percristina refutes all claims that the 2007 vintage was too hot to produce balanced wines. It shows bright and youthful commencing with its hue, which is followed by a nose of dark berry fruit and fresh spicy notes, and a vigorous, lively palate with a close-knit tannic weave and good acidic backbone. The austere Barolo 2011 is full bodied with notes of tar.

● Barolo '11	♥♥ 6
● Barolo Percristina '07	♥♥ 8
● Barolo Ciabot Mentin '08	♥♥♥ 8
● Barolo Ciabot Mentin Ginestra '05	♥♥♥ 8
● Barolo Ciabot Mentin Ginestra '04	♥♥♥ 8
● Barolo Ciabot Mentin Ginestra '01	♥♥♥ 7
● Barolo Ciabot Mentin Ginestra '99	♥♥♥ 8
● Barolo Ciabot Mentin Ginestra '92	♥♥♥ 8
● Barolo Ciabot Mentin Ginestra '86	♥♥♥ 8
● Barolo Pajana '95	♥♥♥ 8
● Barolo Percristina '01	♥♥♥ 8
● Barolo Percristina '99	♥♥♥ 8
● Barolo Percristina '98	♥♥♥ 8
● Barolo Percristina '97	♥♥♥ 8
● Barolo Percristina '96	♥♥♥ 8
● Barolo Percristina '95	♥♥♥ 8

★Elvio Cogno

VIA RAVERA, 2
12060 NOVELLO [CN]
TEL. 0173744006
www.elviocogno.com

CELLAR SALES
PRE-BOOKED VISITS
ANNUAL PRODUCTION 70,000 bottles
HECTARES UNDER VINE 13.00
VITICULTURE METHOD Certified Organic

The Ravera hill is one of the most famous sites of the Novello terroir. It is home to the estate founded by Elvio Cogno, today run by his daughter Nadia and her husband Valter Fissore. Its 13 hectares are planted to nebbiolo, barbera, dolcetto and nascetta, which yield a versatile and recognizable range, topped by the four Barolos: Vigna Elena, Ravera, Bricco Pernice, and Cascina Nuova. Each cru is interpreted with different fermentation and ageing methods, also taking into account the vintage. They're first and foremost Nebbiolos of great substance and power, and it makes little sense to describe them using outdated technical dichotomies. The superb Barolo Ravera 2011 offers notes of liquorice and violets, with hints of menthol, winning our highest award and topping the estate's range. Barolo Cascina 2011 is also very interesting, and eminently drinkable, due to its well-resolved tannins, while the varietal Barolo Bricco Pernice 2010 has impeccable texture and definition.

● Barolo Ravera '11	♥♥♥ 7
● Barolo Bricco Pernice '10	♥♥ 8
● Barolo Cascina Nuova '11	♥♥ 6
● Barbaresco Bordini '12	♥♥ 5
● Barbera d'Alba Bricco dei Merli '13	♥♥ 4
● Barolo V. Elena Ris. '09	♥♥ 8
○ Langhe Nascetta di Novello Anas-Cëtta '14	♥♥ 3
● Langhe Nebbiolo Montegrilli '14	♥♥ 3
● Dolcetto d'Alba Mandorlo '14	♥ 3
● Barolo Bricco Pernice '08	♥♥♥ 8
● Barolo Bricco Pernice '05	♥♥♥ 8
● Barolo Ravera '07	♥♥♥ 7
● Barolo Ravera '04	♥♥♥ 6
● Barolo V. Elena '04	♥♥♥ 8
● Barolo V. Elena Ris. '06	♥♥♥ 8

Poderi Colla

Loc. San Rocco Seno d'Elvio, 82
12051 Alba [CN]
Tel. 0173290148
www.podericolla.it

CELLAR SALES
PRE-BOOKED VISITS
ANNUAL PRODUCTION 150,000 bottles
HECTARES UNDER VINE 26.00

It is certainly no surprise that Beppe and Tino Colla's wines are celebrated and sought after the world over. We're talking of two leading figures in Langhe history, aided by their children Federica and Pietro, who have the rare talent of recounting the most austere yet welcoming side of vineyards like Roncaglie in Barbaresco, or Bussia Dardi Le Rose in Monforte d'Alba. Long aged in Slavonian oak, the Nebbiolo crus top a decidedly original range that also features the grapes grown on the 12-hectare Cascina Drago estate. It comprises monovarietals, blends, sparklers, and special wines, made from barbera, dolcetto, pinot nero, riesling, and moscato. The results of our latest tastings were rather ambivalent, particularly regarding Barolo Bussia Dardi Le Rose 2011, which is currently more austere than usual. However, Barbaresco Roncaglie 2012 is already more placid and resolved, with a powerful mid-palate and good overall fragrance.

● Barbaresco Roncaglie '12	♟♟ 6
● Langhe Bricco del Drago '10	♟♟ 4
● Barbera d'Alba Costa Bruna '13	♟♟ 3
● Barolo Bussia Dardi Le Rose '11	♟♟ 6
● Nebbiolo d'Alba '13	♟♟ 3
● Barolo Bussia Dardi Le Rose '09	♟♟♟ 6
● Barolo Bussia Dardi Le Rose '99	♟♟♟ 6
● Barbaresco Roncaglie '11	♟♟ 6
● Barbera d'Alba Costa Bruna '12	♟♟ 3
● Barolo Bussia Dardi Le Rose '10	♟♟ 6
● Langhe Pinot Nero Campo Romano '12	♟♟ 4
○ Langhe Riesling '13	♟♟ 3
● Nebbiolo d'Alba '12	♟♟ 3

Colle Manora

s.da Bozzola, 5
15044 Quargnento [AL]
Tel. 0131219252
www.collemanora.it

CELLAR SALES
PRE-BOOKED VISITS
ACCOMMODATION
ANNUAL PRODUCTION 90,000 bottles
HECTARES UNDER VINE 20.00

This internationally renowned estate offers fine wines from the native varieties barbera and albarossa, and the international cultivars cabernet sauvignon, merlot, sauvignon blanc, chardonnay, and viognier. High quality distinguishes every stage of the production chain, from the vineyard to the cellar, where fermentation and ageing are controlled and monitored by modern technologies. The cycle is completed by the meticulous use of oak, which is evident only in some vintages, and tends to be mitigated by the ageworthiness of the wines. The list of wines presented is very well made. It is headed by Barbera Manora, with elegant ripe cherries and spice on the nose, followed by a refined, well-orchestrated palate. Albarossa Ray and Pinot Nero Paloalto are also on top form, followed by Mila, the Monferrato Bianco from chardonnay and viognier, and finally the estate's classic Sauvignon Mimosa. Barbera Pais is also very nice.

● Barbera d'Asti Sup. Manora '13	♟♟ 3
○ M.to Bianco Mila '13	♟♟ 4
○ M.to Bianco Mimosa '14	♟♟ 2*
● M.to Rosso Paloalto '12	♟♟ 5
● Piemonte Albarossa Ray '13	♟♟ 3
● Barbera del M.to Pais '14	♟ 2
● Barbera d'Asti Sup. Manora '12	♟♟ 3
● Barbera d'Asti Sup. Manora '11	♟♟ 3
● Barbera del M.to Pais '13	♟♟ 2*
● Barbera del M.to Pais '11	♟♟ 2*
○ M.to Bianco Mila '12	♟♟ 4
○ M.to Bianco Mimosa '13	♟♟ 2*
○ M.to Bianco Mimosa '12	♟♟ 2*
● M.to Rosso Barchetta '11	♟♟ 3
● M.to Rosso Ray '12	♟♟ 3
● M.to Rosso Ray '11	♟♟ 3

La Colombera

S.DA COMUNALE PER VHO, 7
15057 TORTONA [AL]
TEL. 0131867795
www.lacolomberavini.it

CELLAR SALES
PRE-BOOKED VISITS
ANNUAL PRODUCTION 70,000 bottles
HECTARES UNDER VINE 20.00
SUSTAINABLE WINERY

The estate's eight wines exemplify the local production, where barbera, cortese, croatina, dolcetto, and timorasso are the most popular varieties. The latter is undoubtedly the star, producing wines that have conquered the international markets in recent years. However, the work lavished on improving quality has involved the entire production. The estate makes excellent Barberas, but also shows skill with peculiar grape varieties like croatina, which yields potent, tannic, ageworthy wines, and possesses great potential, not yet fully expressed. Il Montino and Derthona made it into our finals, due to their impressive sensory profiles. Il Montino still appears very young, with a delicate mineral nose and vegetal undertones, mirrored on the rich, powerful palate with an exceptionally long finish. We gave it a Tre Bicchieri. Derthona is more approachable, with a nose of dried herbs and white-fleshed fruit underpinned by tobacco notes, and a fresh palate that oozes personality.

○ Colli Tortonesi Timorasso Il Montino '13	🍷🍷🍷 5
○ Colli Tortonesi Timorasso Derthona '13	🍷🍷 3*
○ Colli Tortonesi Cortese Bricco Bartolomeo '14	🍷🍷 2*
● Colli Tortonesi Croatina La Romba '13	🍷🍷 3
● Colli Tortonesi Rosso Suciaja '13	🍷🍷 4
● Colli Tortonesi Rosso Vegia Rampana '14	🍷🍷 2*
● Colli Tortonesi Croatina Arché '12	🍷 4
● Colli Tortonesi Barbera Elisa '11	🍷🍷🍷 3*
○ Colli Tortonesi Timorasso Il Montino '09	🍷🍷🍷 5
○ Colli Tortonesi Timorasso Il Montino '06	🍷🍷🍷 4
○ Colli Tortonesi Timorasso Derthona '12	🍷🍷 4
○ Colli Tortonesi Timorasso Il Montino '12	🍷🍷 5
● Colli Tortonesi Barbera Elisa '10	🍷🍷 3*
● Colli Tortonesi Croatina La Romba '12	🍷🍷 3
● Colli Tortonesi Rosso Suciaja '12	🍷🍷 3
○ Colli Tortonesi Timorasso Il Montino '11	🍷🍷 5

Diego Conterno

VIA MONTÀ, 27
12065 MONFORTE D'ALBA [CN]
TEL. 0173789265
www.diegoconterno.it

CELLAR SALES
PRE-BOOKED VISITS
ANNUAL PRODUCTION 40,000 bottles
HECTARES UNDER VINE 7.50

After having worked for almost 20 years with his cousins Claudio Conterno and Guido Fantino, in 2000 Diego Conterno decided to strike out on his own, immediately showing himself to be one of Langhe's most talented interpreters. Aided by his son Stefano, he tends around seven hectares planted to barbera, dolcetto, nascetta, and of course nebbiolo for the Le Coste and Ginestra Monforte crus. They yield firmly structured Barolos that develop slowly, shaped in the cellar with a wide array of fermenting and ageing techniques, featuring concrete, steel, tonneaux, and larger barrels. Diego Conterno's most representative Barolo is as flawless as ever. The 2011 vintage also offers the typical menthol top notes of the Ginestra cru on the nose, accompanied by touches of roots and red berries, faithfully echoed on the lively, refreshing palate, with a slightly dusty finish.

● Barolo Ginestra '11	🍷🍷 6
● Barolo Le Coste '09	🍷🍷🍷 6
● Barbera d'Alba Ferrione '12	🍷🍷 3
● Barolo '10	🍷🍷 6
● Barolo Ginestra '10	🍷🍷 6
● Barolo Le Coste di Monforte '10	🍷🍷 6
● Nebbiolo d'Alba Baluma '12	🍷🍷 3

★★Giacomo Conterno

loc. Ornati, 2
12065 Monforte d'Alba [CN]
Tel. 017378221
www.conterno.it

Paolo Conterno

via Ginestra, 34
12065 Monforte d'Alba [CN]
Tel. 017378415
www.paoloconterno.com

PRE-BOOKED VISITS
ANNUAL PRODUCTION 60,000 bottles
HECTARES UNDER VINE 17.00

CELLAR SALES
PRE-BOOKED VISITS
ACCOMMODATION AND RESTAURANT SERVICE
ANNUAL PRODUCTION 72,000 bottles
HECTARES UNDER VINE 13.80
SUSTAINABLE WINERY

For many wine lovers and professionals, it is the finest Italian red in terms of consistent quality, incredible expressiveness, and cellarability. However, this definition appears increasingly limiting for Barolo Monfortino Riserva, which has become an international icon under the management of Roberto Conterno. His almost sartorial production sensibility is expressed in obsessive attention to detail and daily contact with the vineyard and the cellar. Everything continues to revolve around the Francia and Cerretta crus in Serralunga d'Alba, used for the eponymous Nebbiolos and Barberas. Barolo Monfortino Riserva 2008 is on top form again, in a version with impeccable expressivity on the nose and beautifully resolved tannins, making it a veritable archetype of its kind, managing to combine the nobility of the cultivar with stuffing and drinkability. Barbera d'Alba Francia 2013 is excellent, showing solid and vigorous, with notes of forest floor, tobacco, and red berries, underpinned by a refreshing swathe of acidity on the palate.

The handsome estate founded by Paolo Conterno in 1886 was initially known as Casa della Ginestra. These origins speak volumes about the indissoluble bond established from the outset with the famous Monforte cru. The finest plots, situated on steep slopes at altitudes between 300 and 350 metres, are used for Barolo Ginestra, which also comes in a Riserva version, and Riva del Bric. Giorgio and Marisa, the latest generation to run the winery, have developed an intentionally austere style, focusing chiefly on ageing in 3,500-litre French oak casks. Despite an impressive performance, Ginestra 2011 missed our top accolade by a hair's breadth. It offers a complex nose of raspberries and golden-leaf tobacco, refreshed by minty hints, and powerful tannins on the palate. Barolo Riva del Bric 2011 has a warm deep nose, centred on ripe raspberries, dried herbs and liquorice, and a powerful, almost imperious palate, slightly warmed by alcohol. The pleasant Barbera 2013 is clean, linear, and restrained.

● Barolo Monfortino Ris. '08	♥♥♥8
● Barbera d'Alba V. Francia '13	♥♥5
● Barbera d'Alba Cerretta '13	♥♥5
● Barolo Francia '11	♥♥8
● Barolo Cerretta '11	♥♥8
● Barolo Cascina Francia '06	♀♀♀8
● Barolo Cascina Francia '05	♀♀♀8
● Barolo Cascina Francia '04	♀♀♀8
● Barolo Francia '10	♀♀♀8
● Barolo Monfortino Ris. '06	♀♀♀8
● Barolo Monfortino Ris. '05	♀♀♀8
● Barolo Monfortino Ris. '04	♀♀♀8
● Barolo Monfortino Ris. '02	♀♀♀8
● Barolo Monfortino Ris. '01	♀♀♀8
● Barolo Monfortino Ris. '00	♀♀♀8
● Barolo Monfortino Ris. '99	♀♀♀8

● Barolo Ginestra '11	♥♥8
● Barolo Riva del Bric '11	♥♥6
● Barbera d'Alba Ginestra '13	♥♥3
● Langhe Nebbiolo A Mont '13	♥♥4
● Langhe Nebbiolo Bric Ginestra '11	♥♥5
● Dolcetto d'Alba L'Alto '14	♥3
● Barolo Ginestra '10	♀♀♀8
● Barolo Ginestra '06	♀♀♀8
● Barolo Ginestra '05	♀♀♀8
● Barolo Ginestra Ris. '06	♀♀♀8
● Barolo Ginestra Ris. '05	♀♀♀8
● Barolo Ginestra Ris. '01	♀♀♀8
● Barbera d'Alba Ginestra '12	♀♀3*
● Barolo Ginestra '09	♀♀8
● Barolo Riva del Bric '10	♀♀6
● Barolo Riva del Bric '09	♀♀6

★Conterno Fantino

VIA GINESTRA, 1
12065 MONFORTE D'ALBA [CN]
TEL. 017378204
www.conternofantino.it

PRE-BOOKED VISITS
ANNUAL PRODUCTION 150,000 bottles
HECTARES UNDER VINE 27.00
VITICULTURE METHOD Certified Organic

Langhe winemaking has consistently been able to count on the creations of Claudio Conterno and Guido Fantino for at least 30 years. Their Barolos easily adapted to the new style in the early 1990s while retaining their clear connection to the terroir of Monforte d'Alba, where the plots for Sorì Ginestra, Vigna del Gris, and Mosconi are situated. The winery's dynamic, constantly evolving approach is evident in the progressively lighter style of its latest releases, but also in its adoption of energy-saving protocols and the use of renewable sources in the recently extended and renovated cellar. We have nonetheless received ambivalent impressions in this respect while tasting the 2011 Barolos. The Mosconi appears a little held back by oak, in both its aromatic breadth and its drying finish, while Vigna del Gris has greater cohesion on the palate, but is almost dominated by spicy, estery notes.

Vigne Marina Coppi

VIA SANT'ANDREA, 5
15051 CASTELLANIA [AL]
TEL. 0131837089
www.vignemarinacoppi.com

CELLAR SALES
PRE-BOOKED VISITS
ANNUAL PRODUCTION 25,000 bottles
HECTARES UNDER VINE 4.50

Castellania is about 17 kilometres from Tortona, in a hilly area, on the right bank of the Scrivia. It has 90 inhabitants and its main attraction is Fausto Coppi's house, which was converted into a museum in 2000. Vigne Marina Coppi was founded by Francesco Bellocchio, the great cyclist's grandson, in 2003. In the space of a few years the range was expanded to feature several different wines, and was completed in 2009, with the release of the first vintage of Fausto, a Timorasso that soon became one of the finest of its kind. The 2013 vintage of the Fausto offers a mineral nose and a tangy palate, with up-front alcohol. I Grop 2011 is a very youthful Barbera in a modern style, with good fruit (cherries) and lingering tertiary notes of tobacco and spice. The concentrated, powerful palate is fresh and well orchestrated, with a long, juicy finish.

● Barolo Mosconi '11	▼▼ 8
● Barolo Sorì Ginestra '11	▼▼ 8
● Barolo V. del Gris '11	▼▼ 8
● Barbera d'Alba Vignota '13	▼▼ 3
○ Langhe Chardonnay Prinsipi '14	▼▼ 2*
● Langhe Nebbiolo Ginestrino '13	▼▼ 4
● Langhe Rosso Monprà '12	▼▼ 5
● Dolcetto d'Alba Bricco Bastia '14	▼ 2
○ Langhe Chardonnay Bastia '13	▼ 5
● Barolo Sorì Ginestra '10	▼▼▼ 8
● Barolo Sorì Ginestra '07	▼▼▼ 8
● Barolo Sorì Ginestra '00	▼▼▼ 7
● Barolo V. del Gris '09	▼▼▼ 8
● Barolo V. del Gris '04	▼▼▼ 8
● Barolo V. del Gris '01	▼▼▼ 8

● Colli Tortonesi Barbera Sup. I Grop '11	▼▼ 5
● Colli Tortonesi Timorasso '13	▼▼ 6
● Colli Tortonesi Barbera Sant'Andrea '14	▼▼ 3
● Colli Tortonesi Rosso Lindin '12	▼▼ 5
○ Colli Tortonesi Favorita Marine '13	▼ 5
○ Colli Tortonesi Timorasso Fausto '12	▼▼▼ 6
○ Colli Tortonesi Timorasso Fausto '11	▼▼▼ 6
○ Colli Tortonesi Timorasso Fausto '10	▼▼▼ 6
○ Colli Tortonesi Timorasso Fausto '09	▼▼▼ 6
● Colli Tortonesi Barbera Castellania '11	▼▼ 4
● Colli Tortonesi Barbera Castellania '10	▼▼ 4
● Colli Tortonesi Barbera Sant'Andrea '12	▼▼ 3*
● Colli Tortonesi Barbera Sup. I Grop '10	▼▼ 5
○ Colli Tortonesi Favorita Marine '11	▼▼ 5
● Colli Tortonesi Rosso Lindin '10	▼▼ 5
● Colli Tortonesi Rosso Lindin '11	▼▼ 5

★Coppo

VIA ALBA, 68
14053 CANELLI [AT]
TEL. 0141823146
www.coppo.it

CELLAR SALES
PRE-BOOKED VISITS
ANNUAL PRODUCTION 400,000 bottles
HECTARES UNDER VINE 22.00

The Coppo family have played a leading role in Asti winemaking since 1892. Today, the fourth generation vaunt vineyards extending from Canelli to Castelnuovo and Agliano Terme, which yield a range of wines featuring Barbera, Metodo Classico sparklers from chardonnay and pinot nero, Chardonnay, Moscato d'Asti, Barolo, and Gavi. It's worth pointing out the attention paid to the production of wines for laying down, both reds and whites. Once again, the range is extremely consistent. A Tre Bicchieri went to Barbera d'Asti Superiore Pomorosso 2012, with a pervasive nose of quinine, aniseed, plums, and rosemary, and a palate showing impressive structure and balance, accompanied by refreshing taut acidity and a long, juicy finish. The rich, full Piemonte Chardonnay Monteriolo 2011 has notes of damsons and acacia honey. It is still a little oak-heavy, but has a fine fresh finish, guaranteeing great cellarability.

Giovanni Corino

FRAZ. ANNUNZIATA, 25B
12064 LA MORRA [CN]
TEL. 0173509452
www.corino.it

CELLAR SALES
PRE-BOOKED VISITS
ANNUAL PRODUCTION 45,000 bottles
HECTARES UNDER VINE 8.00

The history of the Corino family is closely intertwined with that of Annunziata, the La Morra hamlet and hill that has always been listed among the finest Barolo crus. Former tenant farmer Giovanni founded the estate in the 1950s, and his sons Renato and Giulio accompanied it to the heights of the Langhe wine world before establishing separate wineries in 2005. The estate has around eight hectares of vineyards planted to nebbiolo, barbera, and dolcetto. Giachini, Arborina, and Vecchie Vigne, the three Barolo selections, are aged mainly in small, new oak casks, and stand out for their dense, juicy character, generally requiring further ageing in bottle to absorb the oak. This is not entirely true for Barolo Arborina 2011, whose fruity notes of blackberries and cherries are already fairly legible, further sweetened by spicy, toasty undertones, but countered by a powerful, full-flavoured profile. The austere Barolo Giachini 2011, on the other hand, appears overly modern.

● Barbera d'Asti Pomorosso '12	♀♀♀ 7
○ Piemonte Chardonnay Monteriolo '11	♀♀ 6
● Barbera d'Asti Cascina Gavelli '13	♀♀ 4
● Barbera d'Asti L'Avvocata '14	♀♀ 2*
⊙ Clelia Coppo Brut Rosé M. Cl. '10	♀♀ 5
○ Luigi Coppo Brut M. Cl.	♀♀ 4
○ Piemonte Chardonnay Costebianche '13	♀♀ 3
● Barbera d'Asti Pomorosso '11	♀♀♀ 7
● Barbera d'Asti Pomorosso '10	♀♀♀ 7
● Barbera d'Asti Pomorosso '08	♀♀♀ 6
● Barbera d'Asti Pomorosso '07	♀♀♀ 6
● Barbera d'Asti Pomorosso '05	♀♀♀ 6
● Barbera d'Asti Pomorosso '04	♀♀♀ 6
○ Piemonte Chardonnay Monteriolo '08	♀♀♀ 5
○ Piemonte Chardonnay Monteriolo '06	♀♀♀ 5
○ Piemonte Chardonnay Monteriolo '05	♀♀♀ 5

● Barolo Giachini '11	♀♀♀ 7
● Barolo Arborina '11	♀♀ 7
● Barolo Rocche '01	♀♀♀ 7
● Barolo V. V. '99	♀♀♀ 8
● Barolo '10	♀♀ 6
● Barolo '09	♀♀ 6
● Barolo Arborina '10	♀♀ 7
● Barolo Giachini '10	♀♀ 7
● Barolo V. Giachini '09	♀♀ 7
● Barolo V. V. '09	♀♀ 8

Renato Corino

FRAZ. ANNUNZIATA - B.TA POZZO, 49A
12064 LA MORRA [CN]
TEL. 0173500349
www.renatocorino.it

CELLAR SALES
PRE-BOOKED VISITS
ANNUAL PRODUCTION 50,000 bottles
HECTARES UNDER VINE 7.00

During his 30-year career Renato Corino
has proved himself an expert vigneron and
a talented cellar master, producing wines of
undisputed character, all with the same
sophisticated elegance. The Arborina
vineyard, on which the handsome little
cellar stands, is at the heart of the estate,
but it also comprises a portion of the
Rocche dell'Annunziata cru, one of the
finest sites in the entire Barolo zone.
Renato's son Stefano is playing an
increasingly active role in the cellar, which
also offers a Barolo Vecchie Vigne that is a
masterly blend of body and complexity. The
2011 vintage of Barolo Rocche
dell'Annunziata is in a class of its own. It
earned a Tre Bicchieri for its performance,
displaying rare finesse with a myriad of
kaleidoscopic notes characterized by fine
freshness and vitality, particularly
considering the hot vintage. The Arborina is
slightly more mature and oaky.

Cornarea

VIA VALENTINO, 150
12043 CANALE [CN]
TEL. 017365636
www.cornarea.com

CELLAR SALES
PRE-BOOKED VISITS
ACCOMMODATION
ANNUAL PRODUCTION 90,000 bottles
HECTARES UNDER VINE 14.00

The Bovone family have been running their
splendid estate on the Cornarea hill, just
outside Canale, for 40 years. It is no
exaggeration to describe it as one of the
birthplaces of Arneis as we know it today.
The vineyards, around 35 years old, form a
single plot surrounding the winery, and lie
on magnesium-rich clayey limestone soils.
Two-thirds are planted to arneis, and the
rest to nebbiolo. Cornarea has confirmed
its fine red production: the Roero 2012 has
a charming nose of flowers and forest floor,
with hints of red berry fruit, accompanied
by a long, nicely textured palate with tones
of fruit and spice. Roero Arneis 2014 is
also excellent, despite the vintage, showing
pleasant, taut, and floral, while Tarasco
Passito 2011, a monovarietal Arneis with
notes of dried figs, is very sweet and rich,
but not fully balanced.

● Barolo Rocche dell'Annunziata '11	♟♟♟ 8
● Barolo Arborina '11	♟♟ 7
● Barolo '11	♟♟ 5
● Barolo Rocche dell'Annunziata '10	♟♟♟ 7
● Barolo Rocche dell'Annunziata '09	♟♟♟ 7
● Barolo Vign. Rocche '06	♟♟♟ 7
● Barolo Vign. Rocche '04	♟♟♟ 8
● Barolo Vign. Rocche '03	♟♟♟ 8
● Barbera d'Alba V. Pozzo '10	♟♟ 5
● Barbera d'Alba V. Pozzo '09	♟♟ 5
● Barolo '10	♟♟ 5
● Barolo '09	♟♟ 5
● Barolo Arborina '10	♟♟ 7
● Barolo Arborina '09	♟♟ 7
● Barolo Arborina '08	♟♟ 7
● Barolo Ris. '07	♟♟ 8

● Roero '12	♟♟ 4
○ Roero Arneis '14	♟♟ 3*
○ Tarasco Passito '11	♟♟ 5
● Nebbiolo d'Alba '13	♟ 3
● Nebbiolo d'Alba '11	♟♟ 3
● Nebbiolo d'Alba '10	♟♟ 3
● Roero '11	♟♟ 4
● Roero '09	♟♟ 4
● Roero '08	♟♟ 4
● Roero '07	♟♟ 4
○ Roero Arneis '13	♟♟ 3
○ Roero Arneis '10	♟♟ 3*
○ Tarasco Passito '10	♟♟ 5
○ Tarasco Passito '09	♟♟ 5
○ Tarasco Passito '08	♟♟ 5
○ Tarasco Passito '07	♟♟ 5

93

★Matteo Correggia

LOC. GARBINETTO
VIA SANTO STEFANO ROERO, 124
12043 CANALE [CN]
TEL. 0173978009
www.matteocorreggia.com

CELLAR SALES
PRE-BOOKED VISITS
ANNUAL PRODUCTION 150,000 bottles
HECTARES UNDER VINE 20.00

The estate founded by Matteo Correggia in 1985 has been run by Ornella Costa Correggia since 2001. Today she is flanked by her son Giovanni and is able to count on several crus, from Val dei Preti to Ampsèj. Most of the vineyards are situated in the municipalities of Canale and Santo Stefano Roero on the fine-grained Astian sand soil typical of Roero, rich in fossils and mineral salts. The exception is Ampsèj, where the terrain is a mix of Astian and Tortonian soils. Matteo Correggia's production is of the usual high level. Roero Ròche d'Ampsèj Riserva 2011 is juicy with good fruit and stuffing, accompanied by hints of iodine, and notes of rosemary on the pleasant finish, while Roero La Val dei Preti 2013 is more floral and supple, with elegant mineral notes. Roero Arneis 2014 is also worthy of note and undoubtedly among the best of the vintage, showing spicy and full flavoured, with notes of white-fleshed fruit. The rest of the list is well made.

Giuseppe Cortese

S.DA RABAJÀ, 80
12050 BARBARESCO [CN]
TEL. 0173635131
www.cortesegiuseppe.it

CELLAR SALES
PRE-BOOKED VISITS
ACCOMMODATION
ANNUAL PRODUCTION 50,000 bottles
HECTARES UNDER VINE 8.00

While the painstaking work in the vineyard and cellar remains the same as ever, the change in direction that the Cortese family's range of wines has taken over the past few years is very evident. Giuseppe and Rossella, aided by their son Piercarlo, have given a qualitative boost to the entire range, from nebbiolo, dolcetto, and barbera, although it is Barbaresco Rabajà di Barbaresco, produced in vintage and Riserva versions, that has benefited most. Aged in oak of varying sizes and origin, it embodies the lighter, more luminous side of a cru usually associated with powerful wines with austere tannins. The product of an extraordinary terroir and a very classic vintage in terms of varietal profile, Barbaresco Rabajà Riserva 2008 expresses itself with hints of quinine, forest floor, tar, and tobacco, accompanied by austere but not invasive tannins. Barbaresco Rabajà 2012 is still rather closed on the nose, requiring further ageing to be at its best, but its excellent potential can already be glimpsed.

○ Roero Arneis '14	♟♟ 3*	
● Roero La Val dei Preti '13	♟♟ 5	
● Roero Ròche d'Ampsèj Ris. '11	♟♟ 6	
● Anthos	♟♟ 2	
● Barbera d'Alba '13	♟♟ 3	
● Barbera d'Alba Marun '13	♟♟ 5	
○ Langhe Sauvignon Matteo Correggia '13	♟♟ 5	
● Roero '13	♟♟ 3	
● Barbera d'Alba Bricco Marun '94	♟♟♟ 5	
● Barbera d'Alba Marun '04	♟♟♟ 5	
● Roero Ròche d'Ampsèj '04	♟♟♟ 6	
● Roero Ròche d'Ampsèj '01	♟♟♟ 6	
● Roero Ròche d'Ampsèj '00	♟♟♟ 6	
● Roero Ròche d'Ampsèj Ris. '09	♟♟♟ 6	
● Roero Ròche d'Ampsèj Ris. '07	♟♟♟ 6	
● Roero Ròche d'Ampsèj Ris. '06	♟♟♟ 6	

● Barbaresco Rabajà '12	♟♟ 5	
● Barbaresco Rabajà Ris. '08	♟♟ 8	
● Barbera d'Alba '14	♟♟ 3	
● Barbera d'Alba Morassina '13	♟♟ 3	
○ Langhe Chardonnay Scapulin '14	♟♟ 3	
● Langhe Nebbiolo '13	♟♟ 3	
● Dolcetto d'Alba '14	♟ 2	
○ Langhe Chardonnay '14	♟ 2	
● Barbaresco Rabajà '11	♟♟♟ 5	
● Barbaresco Rabajà '10	♟♟♟ 5	
● Barbaresco Rabajà Ris. '96	♟♟♟ 8	
● Barbaresco Rabajà '09	♟♟ 5	
● Barbaresco Rabajà '05	♟♟ 5	
● Barbaresco Rabajà Ris. '06	♟♟ 8	
● Barbaresco Rabajà Ris. '01	♟♟ 8	
● Langhe Nebbiolo '12	♟♟ 3	

Clemente Cossetti

VIA GUARDIE, 1
14043 CASTELNUOVO BELBO [AT]
TEL. 0141799803
www.cossetti.it

CELLAR SALES
PRE-BOOKED VISITS
ACCOMMODATION AND RESTAURANT SERVICE
ANNUAL PRODUCTION 500,000 bottles
HECTARES UNDER VINE 28.00

The Cossetti family's 100-year-old estate is a solid Monferrato operation that flanks its wine production with guest accommodation and fine dining at the Relais Ventitre. Its vineyards are in the municipality of Castelnuovo Belbo and are planted mainly to barbera, with smaller amounts of cortese, dolcetto and chardonnay, on mineral-rich soils. However, the winery also purchases grapes from growers in other zones of Piedmont for the production of various regional DOC and DOCG wines, such as Barolo, Barbaresco, Gavi, and Roero. The pleasant, very easy-drinking Grignolino d'Asti 2014 is particularly good, showing balanced and intensely fruity with typical peppery undertones and well-integrated tannins. The two versions of Barbera d'Asti presented are also well made: La Vigna Vecchia 2013 vaunts very dense extraction, but is also juicy and fruit rich, while Venti di Marzo 2014 is pleasant and fruity with good texture for the vintage.

Stefanino Costa

B.TA BENNA, 5
12046 MONTÀ [CN]
TEL. 0173976336
ninocostawine@gmail.com

CELLAR SALES
PRE-BOOKED VISITS
ANNUAL PRODUCTION 50,000 bottles
HECTARES UNDER VINE 9.50

Stefanino Costa's estate has vineyards in the municipalities of Canale, Montà, and Santo Stefano Roero. They include some of the most famous Roero crus, such as Bric del Medic for nebbiolo, which lie on the prevalently sandy soils typical of the region, mainly at altitudes between 350 and 400 metres, and are home to vines up to 40 years old. The classic local grape varieties are grown: arneis, barbera, brachetto, and nebbiolo. Nino Costa's estate has repeated last year's feat, taking a Tre Bicchieri for a truly magnificent Roero Gepin 2011, with a nose of dark berry fruit, iodine, and Mediterranean scrubland, with hints of orange peel, and an elegant, supple, well-behaved palate with silky tannins. The delightful Roero Medic 2012 is also well made, showing fresh and fluent, while the whites of the 2014 vintage appear a little under par, like those of most Roero producers.

● Barbera d'Asti La Vigna Vecchia '13	♟♟ 2*
● Barbera d'Asti Venti di Marzo '14	♟♟ 3
● Grignolino d'Asti '14	♟♟ 2*
● Barbera d'Asti La Vigna Vecchia '12	♟♟ 2*
● Barbera d'Asti La Vigna Vecchia '11	♟♟ 2*
● Barbera d'Asti Sup. Nizza '11	♟♟ 4
● Barbera d'Asti Sup. Nizza '10	♟♟ 4
● Barbera d'Asti Sup. Nizza '09	♟♟ 4
● Barbera d'Asti Sup. Nizza '08	♟♟ 4
● Barbera d'Asti Sup. Nizza '07	♟♟ 4
● Barbera d'Asti Venti di Marzo '13	♟♟ 3
● Barbera d'Asti Venti di Marzo '10	♟♟ 3
● Grignolino d'Asti '12	♟♟ 2*
● Piemonte Albarossa Amartè '10	♟♟ 3
● Ruchè di Castagnole Monferrato '13	♟♟ 3
● Ruchè di Castagnole Monferrato '10	♟♟ 3

● Roero Gepin '11	♟♟♟ 4*
● Roero Medic '12	♟♟ 3
○ Langhe Bianco Ricordi '14	♟ 3
○ Roero Arneis Sarun '14	♟ 3
● Roero Gepin '10	♟♟♟ 4*
● Barbera d'Alba '11	♟♟ 3
● Barbera d'Alba Cichin '12	♟♟ 2*
○ Langhe Bianco Ricordi '13	♟♟ 3
● Nebbiolo d'Alba '09	♟♟ 2*
● Roero '08	♟♟ 2*
○ Roero Arneis Sarun '13	♟♟ 3*
● Roero Bric del Medic '09	♟♟ 3*
● Roero Bric del Medic '07	♟♟ 3*
● Roero Medic '10	♟♟ 3*
● Roero V. V. '09	♟♟ 4
● Roero V. V. '08	♟♟ 4

Daniele Coutandin

B.TA CIABOT, 12
10063 PEROSA ARGENTINA [TO]
TEL. 0121803473
ramie.coutandin@alpimedia.it

CELLAR SALES
PRE-BOOKED VISITS
ANNUAL PRODUCTION 2,500 bottles
HECTARES UNDER VINE 0.80

This estate was founded without commotion or any commercial ambitions, as the demanding and laborious plaything that Laura and Giuliano Coutandin created to spend their retirement. However, their great love of nature and pride in their work soon came to the fore, and the plaything became a gruelling second job that gradually turned into a full-time one for their son Daniele. Today Daniele tends the steep terraced vineyards in Perosa Argentina and Pomaretto, in Val Chisone, as though they were ornamental vegetable plots, completely shunning the use of chemicals. These tiny plots of land yield a small production of high-quality wines. This year the estate did not present Barbichè, its simplest wine. Fortunately there is always the Ramiè, a blend that showcases the rich variety of local grape varieties, including avanà, avarengo, neretto, and bequet. The 2013 expresses its unadorned mountain soul, offering an untamed personality combining mineral and vegetal aromas with notes of black pepper.

Deltetto

C.SO ALBA, 43
12043 CANALE [CN]
TEL. 0173979383
www.deltetto.com

CELLAR SALES
PRE-BOOKED VISITS
ANNUAL PRODUCTION 170,000 bottles
HECTARES UNDER VINE 21.00
VITICULTURE METHOD Certified Organic
SUSTAINABLE WINERY

The family estate founded by Gualberto Deltetto in 1953 has been headed by his son Antonio since 1977. Under his guidance the cellar has expanded its production, which now comprises the classic Roero wines from traditional local cultivars like arneis, nebbiolo, favorita, nebbiolo, and barbera; sparklers mainly from chardonnay and pinot nero, but also from nebbiolo; Langhe wines such as Barolo and Dolcetto d'Alba; Gavi, and Moscato d'Asti. This year Deltetto presented a very consistent range of wines. Roero 2012 is excellent, showing close-focused and pleasant, with notes of dark berries, forest floor, and orange peel, as is the beautifully fresh Roero Arneis Daivej 2014, which is both complex and taut, with tones of aniseed and citrus. Deltetto Rosé Brut, the nicely complex Barolo Bussia 2010, and the fruity Roero Braja Riserva 2012 are also well made.

● Pinerolese Ramiè '13	▼▼ 5
● Barbichè '05	♈♈ 3*
● Barbichè '04	♈♈ 3*
● Barbichè '03	♈♈ 3*
● Pinerolese Ramiè '12	♈♈ 5
● Pinerolese Ramiè '11	♈♈ 4
● Pinerolese Ramiè '09	♈♈ 4
● Pinerolese Ramiè '08	♈♈ 4
● Pinerolese Ramiè '07	♈♈ 4
● Pinerolese Ramiè '06	♈♈ 4
● Pinerolese Ramiè '05	♈♈ 4
● Pinerolese Ramiè '04	♈♈ 4
● Pinerolese Ramiè '03	♈♈ 4

○ Roero '12	▼▼ 3*
○ Roero Arneis Daivej '14	▼▼ 2*
● Barolo Bussia '10	▼▼ 6
⊙ Deltetto Rosé Brut M. Cl.	▼▼ 5
● Roero Braja Ris. '12	▼▼ 4
● Barbera d'Alba Sup. Bramé '13	▼ 3
● Barbera d'Alba Sup. Rocca delle Marasche '12	▼ 5
○ Roero Arneis S. Michele '14	▼ 3
● Barbera d'Alba Sup. Rocca delle Marasche '04	♈♈♈ 5
● Roero Braja Ris. '09	♈♈♈ 4*
● Roero Braja Ris. '08	♈♈♈ 4
● Roero Braja Ris. '07	♈♈♈ 4

Gianni Doglia

VIA ANNUNZIATA, 56
14054 CASTAGNOLE DELLE LANZE [AT]
TEL. 0141878359
www.giannidoglia.it

CELLAR SALES
PRE-BOOKED VISITS
ANNUAL PRODUCTION 80,000 bottles
HECTARES UNDER VINE 8.00

This small winery in Castagnole delle Lanze offers first-rate selections of Moscato. In recent years its general quality has grown to the extent of making it one of the most reliable names in the area. It also offers several versions of Barbera, all very well made, displaying different and complementary characteristics. A small but extraordinary production of Merlot completes the very well-priced and absolutely unmissable range. After years of excellent performances, Gianni Doglia's estate has reached the highest pinnacle, taking our top award with Barbera d'Asti Superiore Genio 2012, a perfect synthesis of elegance and drinkability. Moscato Casa di Bianca 2012, at its second release, shows itself to be an excellent example of its type in terms of varietal definition and well-defined personality. We were also impressed by Monferrato Rosso !, from merlot, which always charms us with its texture and precise palate.

Dosio

REG. SERRADENARI, 6
12064 LA MORRA [CN]
TEL. 017350677
www.dosiovigneti.com

CELLAR SALES
PRE-BOOKED VISITS
ANNUAL PRODUCTION 65,000 bottles
HECTARES UNDER VINE 11.00

The winery founded by the wise and talented Beppe Dosio has recently been renovated by the Lanci family, who fully intend to continue to pursue quality and classic style. Indeed, they have expanded the team with the skilled Marco Dotta, one of the finest oenologists in the entire area. The winery is located in the upper part of La Morra, at an altitude of 500 metres, in a building with underground cellars that are well worth a visit. The Fossati vineyard, situated at an altitude of 350 metres in the municipality of Barolo, has yielded an excellent 2011 cru, with a close-focused nose and an impressively full-bodied, harmonious palate, which already displays nicely rounded tannins. Nebbiolo Barilà 2012 is among the very best of the vintage, aged for a full two years in used barrels and another in bottle before its release. Its finest qualities are its forthright fruit on the nose and its balanced palate.

● Barbera d'Asti Sup. Genio '12	♟♟♟4*
○ Moscato d'Asti Casa di Bianca '14	♟♟3*
● Barbera d'Asti Boscodonne '14	♟♟2*
● M.to Rosso ! '12	♟♟5
● Barbera d'Asti Boscodonne '13	♟♟2*
● Barbera d'Asti Boscodonne '12	♟♟2*
● Barbera d'Asti Boscodonne '11	♟♟2*
● Barbera d'Asti Sup. Genio '11	♟♟4
● M.to Rosso ! '11	♟♟5
● M.to Rosso ! '10	♟♟5
● M.to Rosso ! '09	♟♟5
○ Moscato d'Asti '13	♟♟2*
○ Moscato d'Asti '12	♟♟2*
○ Moscato d'Asti '11	♟♟2
○ Moscato d'Asti Casa di Bianca '13	♟♟3*
○ Moscato d'Asti Casa di Bianca '12	♟♟3*

● Barolo Fossati '11	♟♟5
● Langhe Nebbiolo Barilà '12	♟♟3*
● Barbera d'Alba '13	♟♟2*
● Barbera d'Alba Sant'Anna '97	♟♟2
● Barolo '10	♟♟5
● Barolo '09	♟♟4
● Barolo Fossati '09	♟♟5
● Barolo Fossati Ris. '08	♟♟8
● Dolcetto d'Alba '12	♟♟2*
● Langhe Rosso Momenti '11	♟♟5
● Nebbiolo d'Alba '09	♟♟2*

★Poderi Luigi Einaudi

B.ta Gombe, 31/32
12063 Dogliani [CN]
Tel. 017370191
www.poderieinaudi.com

CELLAR SALES
PRE-BOOKED VISITS
ACCOMMODATION
ANNUAL PRODUCTION 250,000 bottles
HECTARES UNDER VINE 52.00

The estate is rather large for the area, with over 50 hectares of vineyards and an annual production of 250–300,000 bottles. It is Dolcetto that has made it deservedly famous, particularly Dogliani Superiore Vigna Tecc, which is a fundamental benchmark for anyone wishing to get to know the type. The winery has two vineyards for the production of Barolo, both very prestigious and situated in the municipality of Barolo: the illustrious and balanced Cannubi, and the more structured Terlo, from which the Costa Grimaldi hails. The estate's wines performed very well in our tastings, particularly the 2011 vintage of Barolo Cannubi 2011, which we judged one of its finest ever. It displays classic varietal notes, with hints of eucalyptus, dried violets, and tobacco, and a supple, caressing palate, due to silky tannins that ensure a long, complex finish. Barolo Terlo Vigna Costa Grimaldi 2011 is very interesting.

Tenuta Il Falchetto

Fraz. Ciombi
via Valle Tinella, 16
12058 Santo Stefano Belbo [CN]
Tel. 0141840344
www.ilfalchetto.com

CELLAR SALES
PRE-BOOKED VISITS
ANNUAL PRODUCTION 280,000 bottles
HECTARES UNDER VINE 47.00

The Forno brothers head the family estate founded in 1940. The original vineyards, completely dedicated to moscato, are situated on the hills around Santo Stefano Belbo, but the operation now comprises estates in Castiglione Tinella, Calosso, and Agliano Terme. Moscato and barbera are the most important cultivars, together accounting for 80% of the area under vine, with the remainder consisting of small amounts of both native and international grape varieties. Despite the difficult 2014 vintage, Moscato d'Asti Tenuta del Fant confirms its high quality, offering apples and apricots, rosemary and sage on the nose, and a beautifully fresh, long palate. Barbera d'Asti Superiore Lurëi 2013 is similarly good, with a nose of plums, cocoa powder, and rain-soaked earth, and a palate whose close-knit tannic weave is balanced by fresh fruit and taut acidity. The juicy Piemonte Pinot Nero Solo 2012 is also well made, with notes of wild berries and spice.

● Barolo Cannubi '11	♟♟♟ 8
● Barolo Terlo '11	♟♟ 6
● Barolo Terlo V. Costa Grimaldi '11	♟♟ 7
● Dogliani '14	♟♟ 3
● Langhe Nebbiolo '13	♟♟ 3
● Langhe Rosso Luigi Einaudi '10	♟♟ 6
○ Langhe Bianco V. Meira '13	♟ 4
● Barolo Costa Grimaldi '05	♟♟♟ 8
● Barolo Costa Grimaldi '01	♟♟♟ 7
● Barolo nei Cannubi '00	♟♟♟ 8
● Barolo nei Cannubi '99	♟♟♟ 7
● Barolo nei Cannubi '98	♟♟♟ 7
● Dogliani Sup. V. Tecc '10	♟♟♟ 3*
● Dogliani V. Tecc '06	♟♟♟ 4
● Langhe Rosso Luigi Einaudi '04	♟♟♟ 5

● Barbera d'Asti Sup. Lurëi '13	♟♟ 3*
○ Moscato d'Asti Tenuta del Fant '14	♟♟ 2*
● Piemonte Pinot Nero Solo '12	♟♟ 3
● Barbera d'Asti Sup. Bricco Paradiso '13	♟ 3
● Barbera d'Asti Sup. Bricco Roche '11	♟ 3
● M.to Rosso La Mora '12	♟ 3
○ Moscato d'Asti Ciombo '14	♟ 2
○ Moscato d'Asti Tenuta del Fant '11	♟♟♟ 2*
○ Moscato d'Asti Tenuta del Fant '09	♟♟♟ 2*
● Barbera d'Asti Lurëi '11	♟♟ 3*
● Barbera d'Asti Sup. Bricco Paradiso '11	♟♟ 3*
● Barbera d'Asti Sup. Lurëi '12	♟♟ 3*
○ Moscato d'Asti Ciombo '13	♟♟ 2*
○ Moscato d'Asti Tenuta del Fant '13	♟♟ 2*
○ Moscato d'Asti Tenuta del Fant '12	♟♟ 2*
● Piemonte Pinot Nero Solo '11	♟♟ 3*

Favaro

s.da Chiusure, 1 bis
10010 Piverone [TO]
Tel. 012572606
www.cantinafavaro.it

CELLAR SALES
PRE-BOOKED VISITS
ANNUAL PRODUCTION 18,000 bottles
HECTARES UNDER VINE 3.00

Benito Favaro and his son Camillo are
deservedly reaping the fruits of the
meticulous work carried out in over 20
years at Le Chiusure. The three-hectare
estate is situated on the morainic hill of La
Serra, overlooking Lake Piverone. It
produces a highly original range, with
wines like F2, Basy, Rossomeraviglia, and
Rosacherosanonsei, classified as table
wines and made using syrah, freisa,
nebbiolo, and barbera. However, it is always
the erbaluce whites that steal the show
with their bright saltiness. The basic version
is vinified in steel, while the 13 Mesi is
fermented and partially aged in small oak
casks. After winning several Tre Bicchieri
awards in a row, this year the Favaro family
fell short of our highest accolade, despite
putting up a sound performance, partly due
to the particularly difficult 2014 vintage.
However, the estate's jewel remains
Erbaluce di Caluso Le Chiusure, whose
mineral personality is unaltered.

Giacomo Fenocchio

loc. Bussia, 72
78675 Monforte d'Alba [CN]
Tel. 017378675
www.giacomofenocchio.com

CELLAR SALES
PRE-BOOKED VISITS
ANNUAL PRODUCTION 90,000 bottles
HECTARES UNDER VINE 15.00
SUSTAINABLE WINERY

The Fenocchio brothers' wines have been
propelled into the limelight by a virtuous
circle created largely by word of mouth
between wine lovers. Their venerable estate
makes delicious Nebbiolos, Dolcettos,
Barberas, and Freisas at very friendly
prices, despite the world renown of crus
like Cannubi in Barolo, Villero in Castiglione
Falletto, and Bussia in Monforte. The
product of long maceration (up to 100 days
for some selections in the best vintages)
and patient ageing in Slavonian oak, these
are exemplary classic Barolos that are at
also highly ageworthy, approachable, and
enjoyable even shortly after release. The
high scores deservedly achieved by
Fenocchio's 2011 Barolos speak for
themselves. The soft, reassuring Castellero
and the austerely delicate Cannubi can be
trusted blindly, as can the thoroughbred
Bussia, with its aristocratic balsamic
suppleness.

○ Erbaluce di Caluso Le Chiusure '14	♟♟ 2*
○ Erbaluce di Caluso 13 Mesi '13	♟♟ 3
● Ros '13	♟♟ 4
● Rossomeraviglia '13	♟♟ 5
● F2	♟ 2
○ Erbaluce di Caluso Le Chiusure '13	♟♟♟ 2*
○ Erbaluce di Caluso Le Chiusure '12	♟♟♟ 2*
○ Erbaluce di Caluso Le Chiusure '11	♟♟♟ 2*
○ Erbaluce di Caluso Le Chiusure '10	♟♟♟ 2*
○ Erbaluce di Caluso 13 Mesi '12	♟♟ 3
○ Erbaluce di Caluso 13 Mesi '11	♟♟ 3*
○ Erbaluce di Caluso 13 Mesi '10	♟♟ 3*
○ Erbaluce di Caluso 13 Mesi '07	♟♟ 3
○ Erbaluce di Caluso Le Chiusure '09	♟♟ 2*
○ Erbaluce di Caluso Le Chiusure '08	♟♟ 2*
● Rossomeraviglia '12	♟♟ 5

● Barolo Bussia '11	♟♟♟ 6
● Barolo Cannubi '11	♟♟ 6
● Barolo Castellero '11	♟♟ 6
● Barolo Bussia Ris. '09	♟♟ 7
● Barolo Villero '11	♟♟ 6
● Barolo Bussia '09	♟♟♟ 6
● Barolo Bussia '10	♟♟ 6
● Barolo Bussia Ris. '08	♟♟ 7
● Barolo Cannubi '10	♟♟ 6
● Barolo Villero '10	♟♟ 6
● Langhe Nebbiolo '12	♟♟ 3

Ferrando

via Torino, 599
10015 Ivrea [TO]
Tel. 0125633550
www.ferrandovini.it

CELLAR SALES
PRE-BOOKED VISITS
ANNUAL PRODUCTION 50,000 bottles
HECTARES UNDER VINE 5.00

Carema's terraced vineyards, literally carved out of the rock, are the last frontier of Piedmont that is actually already Valle d'Aosta in terms of landscape, climate and geology. This micro-designation preserves the secrets of mountain nebbiolo, interpreted at its very finest by the legendary estate now headed by Roberto Ferrando. Etichetta Bianca is far more than a basic wine, while Etichetta Nera acts as a "riserva" in the best vintages. Although they undergo slightly different processes in the cellar, with small oak casks being used for the latter, they share the same austere, no-frills charm. In 2010 the estate produced a very small number of bottles of Carema Etichetta Nera, which sold out months ago, and so we tasted the 2011 vintage. Despite its recent bottling, it already displays enviable complexity, with a succession of delicate, layered aromas of gentian, iodine, tar, and liquorice.

Roberto Ferraris

fraz. Dogliano, 33
14041 Agliano Terme [AT]
Tel. 0141954234
www.robertoferraris.com

CELLAR SALES
PRE-BOOKED VISITS
ANNUAL PRODUCTION 50,000 bottles
HECTARES UNDER VINE 9.00
VITICULTURE METHOD Certified Organic

Roberto Ferraris's estate is situated in Agliano Terme, in the heart of the historic Barbera d'Asti zone. Its vineyards lie around the winery, and include some old vines on Vitis rupestris rootstocks. Barbera accounts for the lion's share, flanked by small amounts of nebbiolo and grignolino. The soils are mainly white limestone, with a high proportion of silt and little clay. This year Roberto presented a range of top-class wines. Our favourites were Barbera d'Asti Superiore La Cricca '12, with a nose of ripe plums, accompanied by notes of cocoa powder, juniper berries, and rain-soaked earth, and a palate combining great freshness, depth, and complexity, and Barbera d'Asti Nobbio 2013, with notes of black olives and pepper, and an extraordinarily dense, close-knit palate underpinned by a fine tannic weave and acidity. The gutsy Barbera d'Asti Superiore Bisavolo 2012 is also noteworthy for its rich fruit and character.

● Carema Et. Nera '11	♟♟♟ 7
● Carema Et. Bianca '11	♟♟ 5
○ Erbaluce di Caluso Brut La Torrazza '09	♟♟ 4
○ Erbaluce di Caluso Cariola '14	♟♟ 3
○ Erbaluce di Caluso La Torrazza '14	♟♟ 3
● Canavese Rosso La Torrazza '13	♟ 2
● Carema Et. Nera '09	♟♟♟ 6
● Carema Et. Nera '08	♟♟♟ 6
● Carema Et. Nera '07	♟♟♟ 6
● Carema Et. Nera '06	♟♟♟ 6
● Carema Et. Nera '05	♟♟♟ 6
● Carema Et. Nera '01	♟♟♟ 5
● Canavese Rosso La Torrazza '12	♟♟ 2*
● Carema Et. Bianca '10	♟♟ 5
○ Erbaluce di Caluso Cariola '12	♟♟ 3

● Barbera d'Asti Nobbio '13	♟♟ 2*
● Barbera d'Asti Sup. La Cricca '12	♟♟ 3*
● Barbera d'Asti '13	♟♟ 2*
● Barbera d'Asti Sup. Bisavolo '12	♟♟ 3
● M.to Rosso Grixa '12	♟♟ 3
● Barbera d'Asti '12	♟♟ 2*
● Barbera d'Asti '11	♟♟ 2*
● Barbera d'Asti '10	♟♟ 2*
● Barbera d'Asti '09	♟♟ 2*
● Barbera d'Asti Nobbio '12	♟♟ 2*
● Barbera d'Asti Nobbio '11	♟♟ 3*
● Barbera d'Asti Sup. Bisavolo '11	♟♟ 3*
● Barbera d'Asti Sup. La Cricca '11	♟♟ 3*
● Barbera d'Asti Sup. Riserva del Bisavolo '10	♟♟ 3*
● M.to Rosso Grixa '11	♟♟ 3

Carlo Ferro

FRAZ. SALERE 41
14041 AGLIANO TERME [AT]
TEL. 0141954000
www.ferrovini.com

CELLAR SALES
PRE-BOOKED VISITS
ANNUAL PRODUCTION 15,000 bottles
HECTARES UNDER VINE 12.00

The Ferro family have owned this little estate for three generations, enthusiastically tending their vineyards and focusing on the typical local grape varieties: mainly barbera, but also dolcetto, grignolino, and nebbiolo, flanked by the international cabernet sauvignon. However, they only started bottling their wines just over 20 years ago. Their south-aspected vineyards have 4–5,000 Guyot-trained vines per hectare. The range of wines presented is well made, particularly the various Barberas. Barbera d'Asti Superiore Notturno 2012 has rather toasty, vanillaed oaky top notes, which are soon covered by tones of fresh red berry fruit , and a long, supple palate that is complex and fruity. Barbera d'Asti Giulia 2013 focuses more on tones of quinine and rain-soaked earth, accompanied by impressive acidity and a rather austere finish, while Barbera d'Asti 2014 is pleasant and fruity.

Fontanabianca

VIA BORDINI, 15
12057 NEIVE [CN]
TEL. 017367195
www.fontanabianca.it

CELLAR SALES
PRE-BOOKED VISITS
ANNUAL PRODUCTION 60,000 bottles
HECTARES UNDER VINE 14.00

The changes that have been underway for several years in the darkness of the cellar are finally yielding their fruits in the wines created by Aldo Pola. Following the very well-interpreted phase of new oak and silky sensations, popular with both the press and the public, the wines are now returning to a balanced, restrained style, without completely denying their modern bent. Today the entire range is flawless, from the simplest to the noblest Barbaresco Bordini. Barbaresco Serraboella 2012, from one of the finest terroirs of the entire production zone, reveals its full elegance, distinguishing itself with a nose of menthol, wild berries, and tobacco, accompanied by a powerful, yet racy, full-flavoured palate. Barbaresco Bordini 2012 is slightly less legible at this stage of its development, as its impressive tannic structure is not yet fully integrated, but bodes very well for the future.

● Barbera d'Asti '14	▼▼ 2*
● Barbera d'Asti Giulia '13	▼▼ 2*
● Barbera d'Asti Sup. Notturno '12	▼▼ 2*
● Barbera d'Asti Sup. Roche '12	▼ 3
● Langhe Nebbiolo Tre Lune '13	▼ 2
● M.to Rosso Paolo '11	▼ 3
● Barbera d'Asti '13	▽▽ 1*
● Barbera d'Asti Giulia '11	▽▽ 2*
● Barbera d'Asti Giulia '10	▽▽ 2*
● Barbera d'Asti Sup. Notturno '11	▽▽ 2*
● Barbera d'Asti Sup. Roche '11	▽▽ 3
● Barbera d'Asti Superiore Notturno '10	▽▽ 2*
● Barbera d'Asti Superiore Notturno '09	▽▽ 2*
● Barbera d'Asti Superiore Notturno '07	▽▽ 2*
● M.to Rosso Paolo '09	▽▽ 3

● Barbaresco Bordini '12	▼▼ 6
● Barbaresco Serraboella '12	▼▼ 5
● Barbaresco '12	▼▼ 5
● Barbera d'Alba Sup. '13	▼ 3
● Langhe Nebbiolo '13	▼▼ 3
○ Langhe Arneis '14	▼ 2
● Barbaresco Serraboella '06	▽▽▽ 6
● Barbaresco Sorì Burdin '05	▽▽▽ 6
● Barbaresco Sorì Burdin '04	▽▽▽ 6
● Barbaresco Sorì Burdin '01	▽▽▽ 6
● Barbaresco Sorì Burdin '98	▽▽▽ 7
● Barbaresco '11	▽▽ 5
● Barbaresco Bordini '11	▽▽ 6
● Barbaresco Serraboella '11	▽▽ 5
● Barbaresco Serraboella '10	▽▽ 5
● Barbera d'Alba Sup. '11	▽▽ 3

Fontanafredda

VIA ALBA, 15
12050 SERRALUNGA D'ALBA [CN]
TEL. 0173626100
www.fontanafredda.it

CELLAR SALES
PRE-BOOKED VISITS
ACCOMMODATION AND RESTAURANT SERVICE
ANNUAL PRODUCTION 7,500,000 bottles
HECTARES UNDER VINE 100.00
SUSTAINABLE WINERY

The Fontanafredda project, with its
multitude of ramifications, is a veritable
entrepreneurial miracle. The brand evokes
centuries-old origins and contemporary
vision, with constant attention to the
challenges of today, from the sustainability
of everyday life to natural viticulture and
energy conservation. This dual soul is also
evident in the rich array of Piedmont wines,
which includes selections and crus made
with an "artisanal" approach. This is
particularly true of the Casa E. di Mirafiore
Barolos, which convey the essence of
renowned vineyards like Paiagallo and
Lazzarito in a sound, rigorous style.
Fontanafredda's usual impressive list of
wines deserves thorough perusal. We
particularly liked the 2011 Barolo crus: the
Paiagallo exudes youthfulness,
commencing with intense floral and fruity
sensations, while Vigna La Rosa is more
introverted and extracted, but shows
interesting potential for development.

● Barolo Fontanafredda V. La Rosa '11	♥♥ 7
● Barolo Paiagallo Mirafiore '11	♥♥ 7
● Barbera d'Alba Sup. Mirafiore '12	♥♥ 4
● Barolo Mirafiore '11	♥♥ 6
● Barolo del Comune di Serralunga d'Alba '11	♥ 6
● Barolo Casa E. di Mirafiore Ris. '04	♀♀♀ 8
● Barolo Fontanafredda V. La Rosa '07	♀♀♀ 7
● Barolo Lazzarito V. La Delizia '04	♀♀♀ 8
● Barolo Lazzarito V. La Delizia '01	♀♀♀ 7
● Barolo Lazzarito V. La Delizia '99	♀♀♀ 7
● Barolo V. La Rosa '04	♀♀♀ 7
● Barolo V. La Rosa '00	♀♀♀ 7
● Barolo V. La Rosa '98	♀♀♀ 7
● Barolo Mirafiore '10	♀♀ 6
● Barolo Paiagallo Mirafiore '10	♀♀ 6

Gabutti - Franco Boasso

B.TA GABUTTI, 3A
12050 SERRALUNGA D'ALBA [CN]
TEL. 0173613165
www.gabuttiboasso.com

CELLAR SALES
PRE-BOOKED VISITS
ACCOMMODATION
ANNUAL PRODUCTION 25,000 bottles
HECTARES UNDER VINE 7.00

The estate founded by the Boasso family in
the 1970s has about seven hectares of
vineyards in the Gabutti, Meriame and
Margheria crus, all in Serralunga d'Alba.
They are planted with the main Langhe
grape varieties, from barbera and dolcetto
to moscato and arneis, which make up a
very sound range that is also served at the
family's guest farm. However, it is the
Barolos that constantly head the list. Made
using the traditional method, with ageing
in medium-sized barrels, their fine
balance of austerity and natural
expressiveness makes them ever more
interesting. In some respects the hierarchy
of the range crafted by Franco Basso has
been reversed this year. The excellent
Margheria and Gabutti 2011 Barolos have
been overtaken in aromatic liveliness and
flavoursome power by the surprising
Barbera d'Alba 2012, with a nose of fresh
cherries, bouquet garni, and forest floor, and
a dense yet stylish, approachable palate.

● Barbera d'Alba '12	♥♥ 2*
● Barolo del Comune di Serralunga d'Alba '11	♥♥ 5
● Barolo Gabutti '11	♥♥ 6
● Barolo Margheria '11	♥♥ 6
● Barolo Margheria '05	♀♀♀ 5*
● Barbera d'Alba '11	♀♀ 2*
● Barolo del Comune di Serralunga d'Alba '10	♀♀ 5
● Barolo Gabutti '10	♀♀ 5
● Barolo Gabutti '09	♀♀ 5
● Barolo Margheria '10	♀♀ 5
● Barolo Margheria '09	♀♀ 5
● Barolo Serralunga '09	♀♀ 5
● Dolcetto d'Alba '13	♀♀ 2*

Gaggino

S.DA SANT'EVASIO, 29
15076 OVADA [AL]
TEL. 0143822345
www.gaggino.it

CELLAR SALES
PRE-BOOKED VISITS
ANNUAL PRODUCTION 150,000 bottles
HECTARES UNDER VINE 20.00

Few producers in the Ovada area are capable of bringing out the best in difficult grape varieties like dolcetto. Gabriele Gaggino is one of them. His wines have won important awards over and over again, often also for their excellent value. Proof that Gabriele will not compromise on quality can be found in the fact that even the most basic wines are underpinned by the elegance and cleanliness that give his products their sensory characteristics. The wide range is made up of reds and whites from native and international grape varieties. Gabriele has taken a Tre Bicchieri with a splendid version of Convivio. It shows a dense ruby, accompanied by a very complex nose with notes of dark berries followed by quinine and cocoa powder, echoed on a palate with exemplary finesse and harmony. Il Ticco, an explosive Barbera, in a modern style, also reached our finals, with a nose of plums and cherries foreshadowing a characterful palate with an endless finish.

● Ovada Convivio '13	♔♔♔ 2*
● Barbera del M.to Sup. Il Ticco '11	♔♔ 3*
● Barbera del M.to La Lazzarina '12	♔♔ 2*
○ Moscato d'Asti '14	♔♔ 2*
● Ovada S. Evasio '11	♔♔ 2*
○ Courtesia Brut	♔ 2
○ Piemonte Chardonnay La Pagliuzza '14	♔ 2
● Barbera del M.to La Lazzarina '10	♔♔ 2
○ Cortese dell'Alto M.to Madonna della Villa '10	♔♔ 4
● Dolcetto di Ovada Convivio '11	♔♔ 2*
● Dolcetto di Ovada Sup. Sant' Evasio '08	♔♔ 3
● Dolcetto di Ovada Un Rosso '10	♔♔ 2*
● M.to Rosso La Mora '11	♔♔ 1*
● Ovada S. Evasio '10	♔♔ 2*

★★★★★Gaja

VIA TORINO, 18
12050 BARBARESCO [CN]
TEL. 0173635158
www.gajawines.com

ANNUAL PRODUCTION 350,000 bottles
HECTARES UNDER VINE 92.00

Just one man is in control, and his labels are black and white. His name is Angelo Gaja. We hope fans of Fausto Coppi will not mind if we borrow the epithet that the radio commentator Mario Ferretti used when immortalizing his sporting achievements: the "campionissimo" of Italian wine lives in Barbaresco and continues to dominate our rankings, with over 50 Tre Bicchieri won in fewer than 30 editions of the Guide. Flanked by his wife Lucia and children Gaia, Rosanna, and Giovanni, he has never stopped travelling the world with his Lange Nebbiolos, reaping the glorious production legacy illuminated in very different times by his father Giovanni and his grandfather Angelo. This year the prestigious Barbaresco winery presented a reduced list. The 2012 vintage selections will not be released. Instead, we tasted a fantastic Sperss 2011, a compact, austere wine with a dark nose and a complex palate vaunting imposing but sweet tannins nicely integrated in its long body. Langhe Conteisa 2011 is also very good, while Barbaresco 2012 is as reliable as ever.

● Langhe Nebbiolo Sperss '11	♔♔♔ 8
● Barbaresco '12	♔♔ 8
● Langhe Nebbiolo Conteisa '11	♔♔ 8
● Barbaresco '09	♔♔♔ 8
● Barbaresco '08	♔♔♔ 8
● Barbaresco '04	♔♔♔ 8
● Langhe Nebbiolo Costa Russi '10	♔♔♔ 8
● Langhe Nebbiolo Costa Russi '08	♔♔♔ 8
● Langhe Nebbiolo Costa Russi '07	♔♔♔ 8
● Langhe Nebbiolo Costa Russi '05	♔♔♔ 8
● Langhe Nebbiolo Costa Russi '04	♔♔♔ 8
● Langhe Nebbiolo Sorì S. Lorenzo '06	♔♔♔ 8
● Langhe Nebbiolo Sorì Tildìn '11	♔♔♔ 8
● Langhe Nebbiolo Sorì Tildìn '07	♔♔♔ 8
● Langhe Nebbiolo Sorì Tildìn '06	♔♔♔ 8
● Langhe Nebbiolo Sperss '04	♔♔♔ 8

Filippo Gallino

FRAZ. MADONNA LORETO
VALLE DEL POZZO, 63
12043 CANALE [CN]
TEL. 017398112
www.filippogallino.com

CELLAR SALES
PRE-BOOKED VISITS
ANNUAL PRODUCTION 100,000 bottles
HECTARES UNDER VINE 14.00
SUSTAINABLE WINERY

The Gallino family's estate was among the first to believe in the potential of the Roero area and proclaim the quality of its wines. Its vineyards are in the municipality of Canale, lying on the clayey sandy soils of the Briccola, Renesio, and Mompissano hills around the winery, and are planted with the region's typical native grape varieties (arneis, barbera, and nebbiolo). They yield wines characterized by the combination of traditional vineyard techniques with a modern approach in the cellar. Roero Sorano Riserva is first rate, also in the 2011 version, with a nose of red berries and Mediterranean scrubland, and a flavoursome palate with well-calibrated tannins. The long, pleasantly fresh Roero Arneis 4 Luglio 2014 is among the best of the vintage, with pervasive citrus notes, while Roero Arneis 2014 is simpler but approachable and supple. Lastly, Seventy Brut Metodo Classico is well made this year, showing lively and gusty.

Tenuta Garetto

S.DA ASTI MARE, 30
14041 AGLIANO TERME [AT]
TEL. 0141954068
www.garetto.it

CELLAR SALES
PRE-BOOKED VISITS
ANNUAL PRODUCTION 110,000 bottles
HECTARES UNDER VINE 18.00

Alessandro Garetto's estate is almost entirely given over to barbera, which accounts for 80% of the area under vine, while the remaining 20% is divided between dolcetto, grignolino and chardonnay. Situated on the hills near Agliano Terme, mainly in a single plot surrounding the cellar, the vineyards lie on clayey soils with limestone and marl, and are home to vines up to 60 and 70 years old. Barbera d'Asti Superiore Nizza Favà confirms itself one of the finest wines of its type again this year. The 2012 vintage is very well typed, with a nose of dark berries, forest floor, and spice, while the palate has very close-knit tannins but is also juicy and fruit rich. Barbera d'Asti Superiore In Pectore 2013 is fresh and complex, with notes of blackberries and currants, while Barbera d'Asti Tra Neuit e Dì 2014 has plenty of flesh and is pleasantly approachable.

○ Roero Arneis 4 Luglio '14	♟♟ 2*	
● Roero Sorano Ris. '11	♟♟ 3*	
○ Roero Arneis '14	♟♟ 2*	
○ Seventy Brut M. Cl.	♟♟ 3	
● Barbera d'Alba Sup. '05	♟♟♟ 4*	
● Barbera d'Alba Sup. '04	♟♟♟ 4*	
● Roero '06	♟♟♟ 4*	
● Roero Sup. '03	♟♟♟ 3	
● Roero Sup. '01	♟♟♟ 5	
● Roero Sup. '99	♟♟♟ 5	
● Barbera d'Alba Sup. '11	♟♟ 4	
● Roero '09	♟♟ 4	
● Roero Sorano Ris. '10	♟♟ 3*	
● Roero Sorano Ris. '08	♟♟ 3*	

● Barbera d'Asti Sup. Nizza Favà '12	♟♟ 4	
● Barbera d'Asti Sup. In Pectore '13	♟♟ 5	
● Barbera d'Asti Tra Neuit e Dì '14	♟♟ 2*	
● Barbera d'Asti Sup. Nizza Favà '04	♟♟♟ 4	
● Barbera d'Asti Sup. In Pectore '12	♟♟ 5	
● Barbera d'Asti Sup. In Pectore '11	♟♟ 8	
● Barbera d'Asti Sup. In Pectore '10	♟♟ 8	
● Barbera d'Asti Sup. In Pectore '09	♟♟ 3	
● Barbera d'Asti Sup. Nizza Favà '11	♟♟ 4	
● Barbera d'Asti Sup. Nizza Favà '10	♟♟ 4	
● Barbera d'Asti Sup. Nizza Favà '09	♟♟ 5	
● Barbera d'Asti Sup. Nizza Favà '08	♟♟ 4	
● Barbera d'Asti Tra Neuit e Dì '13	♟♟ 2*	
● Barbera d'Asti Tra Neuit e Dì '12	♟♟ 2*	
● Barbera d'Asti Tra Neuit e Dì '10	♟♟ 2*	
○ M.to Bianco Il Biondo '13	♟♟ 3	

Generaj

B.TA TUCCI, 4
12046 MONTÀ [CN]
TEL. 0173976142
www.generaj.it

CELLAR SALES
PRE-BOOKED VISITS
ANNUAL PRODUCTION 50,000 bottles
HECTARES UNDER VINE 12.00
SUSTAINABLE WINERY

Giuseppe Viglione heads this family estate, founded by his grandfather in 1947. Its vineyards are entirely situated in the northernmost part of the municipality of Montà (and thus the entire Roero zone) on soil ranging from red sand to limestone, with some mixed gravelly areas. They're planted mainly with the typical Roero grape varieties: nebbiolo, barbera and arneis. Generaj has earned a full profile with a series of very good wines, topped by Roero Bric Aût 2012, with a delicate, close-focused nose offering notes of tobacco, raspberries, and spice, and a very long, complex fruity palate. Barbera d'Alba Superiore Ca' d'Pistola 2012 is well made, offering a concentrated nose of red berries and hints of spicy wood, accompanied by a dense, powerful palate with prominent acidity on the finish. The fruity, flavoursome Roero Arneis Quindicilune 2013 is equally sound, as is the Brut 2011, a pleasant, soft Metodo Classico.

● Roero Bric Aût '12	♟♟	4
● Barbera d'Alba Sup. Ca' d' Pistola '12	♟♟	3
○ Generaj Brut M. Cl. '11	♟♟	5
○ Roero Arneis Quindicilune '13	♟♟	3
● Roero Bric Aût Ris. '11	♟	5
○ Generaj Brut M. Cl. '10	♟♟	5
○ Roero Arneis Quindicilune '12	♟♟	3*
● Roero Bric Aût '11	♟♟	3

★Ettore Germano

LOC. CERRETTA, 1
12050 SERRALUNGA D'ALBA [CN]
TEL. 0173613528
www.germanoettore.com

CELLAR SALES
PRE-BOOKED VISITS
ACCOMMODATION
ANNUAL PRODUCTION 90,000 bottles
HECTARES UNDER VINE 16.00

Sergio Germano's tale has something of Hollywood about it, for his success is the result of years of hard toil, restyling, and gambles. An example is his investment in the Aglié estate in Alta Langa, where one of the region's finest ranges of white and sparkling wines from riesling, sauvignon, chardonnay, and pinot nero, has taken shape. At the same time he has found the way to make his Barolos, from first-rate plots in the Serralunga zone like Prapò, Cerretta, and Lazzarito, even more meticulously crafted and terroir true, displaying exponential growth in terms of extractive delicacy and expressive mobility. This was also confirmed by our most recent tastings, which were full of surprises, like the very lively Barolo Lazzarito Riserva 2009, with spicy personality, or the even more vibrant and progressive Cerretta 2011. However the pinnacle of the production is Prapò 2011, which is multidimensional and virile from start to finish.

● Barolo Prapò '11	♟♟♟	7
● Barolo Cerretta '11	♟♟	7
● Barolo Lazzarito Ris. '09	♟♟	8
○ Langhe Riesling Hérzu '13	♟♟	4
● Barbera d'Alba Sup. V. della Madre '12	♟♟	5
● Barolo del Comune di Serralunga d'Alba '11	♟♟	6
○ Langhe Nascetta '13	♟♟	3
● Barolo Cerretta '05	♟♟♟	8
● Barolo Cerretta '01	♟♟♟	6
● Barolo Lazzarito Ris. '08	♟♟♟	8
● Barolo Prapò '04	♟♟♟	6
○ Langhe Bianco Hérzu '11	♟♟♟	4*
○ Langhe Bianco Hérzu '10	♟♟♟	4*
○ Langhe Bianco Hérzu '09	♟♟♟	5
○ Langhe Bianco Hérzu '08	♟♟♟	5

La Ghibellina

FRAZ. MONTEROTONDO, 61
15066 GAVI [AL]
TEL. 0143686257
www.laghibellina.it

CELLAR SALES
PRE-BOOKED VISITS
RESTAURANT SERVICE
ANNUAL PRODUCTION 60,000 bottles
HECTARES UNDER VINE 7.90

This little winery was founded 15 years ago by Alberto and Maria Ghibellina. It vaunts just over seven hectares, planted with the traditional grapes of the Gavi production zone, with cortese obviously accounting for the lion's share. However, it is no ordinary cortese, but that vigorous variety with a sturdy mineral backbone grown in Monterondo, a hamlet of Gavi long hailed as particularly fine winegrowing country. It is used to produce six whites: two Metodo Classicos, two still dry versions, the steel-fermented Mainìn, and Altius, partially aged in small oak casks. The reds are dominated by barbera, alone in Chiaretto Sandrino and Nero del Montone, and blended with merlot in the Pituj. La Ghibellina presented a thoroughly decent list. Both Altius and Mainìn reached our finals, but they have very different personalities. The first has concentrated fruity aromas that rapidly develop into notes of almonds, tobacco and spice. Mainìn is younger and more approachable, with vegetal and fruity notes.

○ Gavi del Comune di Gavi Altius '13	♟♟ 3*
○ Gavi del Comune di Gavi Mainìn '14	♟♟ 3*
● M.to Rosso Pituj '13	♟♟ 3
○ Gavi del Comune di Gavi Brut M. Cl. '12	♟ 4
● M.to Rosso Nero del Montone '12	♟ 4
○ Gavi del Comune di Gavi Altius '11	♟♟ 3*
○ Gavi del Comune di Gavi Brut '08	♟♟ 4
○ Gavi del Comune di Gavi Brut M. Cl. '11	♟♟ 4
○ Gavi del Comune di Gavi M. Cl. Cuvée Marina	♟♟ 5
○ Gavi del Comune di Gavi Mainìn '13	♟♟ 3*
○ Gavi del Comune di Gavi Mainìn '12	♟♟ 3
● M.to Rosso Nero del Montone '10	♟♟ 4
● M.to Rosso Pituj '12	♟♟ 3
● M.to Rosso Pituj '10	♟♟ 3
● M.to Rosso Pituj '09	♟♟ 3

Attilio Ghisolfi

LOC. BUSSIA, 27
12065 MONFORTE D'ALBA [CN]
TEL. 017378345
www.ghisolfi.com

CELLAR SALES
PRE-BOOKED VISITS
ANNUAL PRODUCTION 45,000 bottles
HECTARES UNDER VINE 6.50

This small estate with highly consistent quality presents an interesting and convincing list of wines every year. Gianmarco Ghisolfi is able to count on an array of particularly fine plots for nebbiolo, and his several versions of Barolo offer a very fine interpretation of the true soul of Langhe, where balance, elegance, depth and original flavours merge in a unique and intriguing harmony. Over the years, Ghisolfi's wines have deservedly become available in many of the world's leading countries. Barolo Bricco Visette 2011 is still developing and will not be at its best for a few more years. At the moment it has a close-focused nose, with layered notes of violets and tobacco, and balsamic hints. The close-knit palate has impressive tannins that make it very powerful. The elegant, well-orchestrated Barolo Bussia 2011 unfolds with invigorating freshness, balanced by perfect structure.

● Barolo Bricco Visette '11	♟♟ 6
● Barolo Bussia '11	♟♟ 5
● Barbera d'Alba Maggiora '13	♟♟ 2*
○ Ghisolfi Extra Brut M. Cl. '11	♟♟ 5
● Barolo Bricco Visette '05	♟♟♟ 6
● Barolo Bricco Visette '01	♟♟♟ 6
● Barolo Bussia Bricco Visette '09	♟♟♟ 6
● Barolo Fantini Ris. '01	♟♟♟ 7
● Langhe Rosso Alta Bussia '01	♟♟♟ 5
● Langhe Rosso Alta Bussia '00	♟♟♟ 4
● Langhe Rosso Alta Bussia '99	♟♟♟ 5
● Barbera d'Alba Maggiora '10	♟♟ 2*
● Barolo Bricco Visette '10	♟♟ 6
● Barolo Bussia '10	♟♟ 5
● Barolo Fantini Ris. '08	♟♟ 7
○ Extra Brut M. Cl. '12	♟♟ 5

★★Bruno Giacosa

VIA XX SETTEMBRE, 52
12057 NEIVE [CN]
TEL. 017367027
www.brunogiacosa.it

ANNUAL PRODUCTION 300,000 bottles
HECTARES UNDER VINE 19.00
SUSTAINABLE WINERY

Bruno Giacosa is living legend for a huge
number of wine lovers and professionals.
His extraordinary knowledge of Langhe
vineyards enabled him to make some of the
best-ever Barolos and Barbarescos before
he founded his Falletto estate, which has
given its name to the wines that hail from
its vineyards today. He has long been
flanked by his daughter Bruna and, albeit
with a short break, oenologist Dante
Scaglione. However, the style is well
established: classic wines through and
through, which focus on details rather than
body. Although designed for decades of
ageing, their aristocratic stature is perfectly
legible from their youth. This time it was the
expressive details that led us to appoint
Barbaresco Asili 2012 captain of Giacosa's
legendary team. It displays a graceful
profile of tobacco, sweet spice, and red
berries, and bewitchingly elegant
progression, its velvety tannins ensuring a
crescendo finish.

● Barbaresco Asili '12	♔♔♔	8
● Barolo Falletto '11	♔♔	8
● Nebbiolo d'Alba Valmaggiore '13	♔♔	5
● Barbaresco Asili '05	♕♕♕	8
● Barbaresco Asili Ris. '07	♕♕♕	8
● Barbaresco Asili Ris. '04	♕♕♕	8
● Barbaresco Rabajà Ris. '01	♕♕♕	8
● Barbaresco Santo Stefano '01	♕♕♕	8
● Barolo Falletto '07	♕♕♕	8
● Barolo Falletto '04	♕♕♕	8
● Barolo Falletto '01	♕♕♕	8
● Barolo Le Rocche del Falletto '05	♕♕♕	8
● Barolo Le Rocche del Falletto '04	♕♕♕	8
● Barolo Le Rocche del Falletto Ris. '08	♕♕♕	8
● Barolo Le Rocche del Falletto Ris. '07	♕♕♕	8
● Barolo Le Rocche del Falletto Ris. '01	♕♕♕	8

Carlo Giacosa

S.DA OVELLO, 9
12050 BARBARESCO [CN]
TEL. 0173635116
www.carlogiacosa.it

CELLAR SALES
PRE-BOOKED VISITS
ANNUAL PRODUCTION 42,000 bottles
HECTARES UNDER VINE 5.50

Maria Grazia Giacosa runs the winery with
the same unwavering passion, but her
capable father Carlo keeps an eye on the
vineyards, and her son Luca is becoming
increasingly sure of himself in the cellar,
and is now able to monitor the entire
vinification process. The estate's great
vineyards, with plots not only in Montefico,
but also in the Asili, Ovello, and Cole crus
for its Barbaresco Narin, are accompanied
by small production figures, with
remarkably consistent, flawless quality
across the range. Barbaresco Luca
Riserva 2010 is exceptionally pleasant,
showing fully developed and ready to be
appreciated in all its nuances, which focus
more on dark berries and rhubarb than on
red fruit. The lively, no-nonsense
Barbaresco Montefico 2012 is youthful
with the rich tannic weave typical of this
prestigious cru, and Barbaresco Narin is
nicely balanced.

● Barbaresco Luca Ris. '10	♔♔	6
● Barbaresco Montefico '12	♔♔	5
● Barbaresco Narin '12	♔♔	5
● Barbera d'Alba Mucin '14	♔♔	3
● Langhe Nebbiolo Maria Grazia '13	♔♔	3
○ Langhe Arneis Sara '14	♔	3
⊙ Langhe Rosato Silvarosa '14	♔	3
● Barbaresco Montefico '08	♕♕♕	5*
● Barbaresco Luca Ris. '09	♕♕	6
● Barbaresco Luca Ris. '08	♕♕	6
● Barbaresco Montefico '11	♕♕	5
● Barbaresco Montefico '10	♕♕	5
● Barbaresco Narin '11	♕♕	5
● Barbaresco Narin '10	♕♕	5
● Barbera d'Alba Lina '12	♕♕	3
● Langhe Nebbiolo Maria Grazia '12	♕♕	3

F.lli Giacosa

VIA XX SETTEMBRE, 64
12057 NEIVE [CN]
TEL. 017367013
www.giacosa.it

CELLAR SALES
PRE-BOOKED VISITS
ANNUAL PRODUCTION 500,000 bottles
HECTARES UNDER VINE 50.00

The huge production of brothers Maurizio and Paolo Giacosa hails from many Langhe vineyards, centred on the impressive plots in the municipality of Neive, obviously largely dedicated to Barbaresco, and reaching as far as Castiglione Falletto and Monforte d'Alba for the production of Barolo, Alba for Dolcetto, and Trezzo Tinella for Chardonnay. The result is an impressive annual production in terms of both quantity and quality, for the most part destined for export. Barolo Vigna Mandorlo 2010 put up a good performance, vaunting a particularly deep hue, with a nose hinting at cocoa powder and quinine on a background of red berries that fade out nicely, and an impressive, slightly alcohol-rich palate that is long and convincing. Barolo Bussia 2011 offers an agreeable combination of fruit, oak and alcohol, with hints of liquorice.

● Barbaresco Basarin V. Gianmaté '12	♥♥ 6
● Barolo Scarrone V. Mandorlo '10	♥♥ 7
● Barbera d'Alba Maria Gioana '12	♥♥ 5
● Barolo Bussia '11	♥♥ 6
● Nebbiolo d'Alba '13	♥♥ 4
○ Langhe Chardonnay Ca' Lunga '13	♥ 5
● Barbaresco Basarin V. Gianmaté '11	♀♀ 6
● Barbaresco Basarin V. Gianmaté '10	♀♀ 6
● Barbera d'Alba Maria Gioana '11	♀♀ 4
● Barbera d'Alba Maria Gioana '10	♀♀ 4
● Barolo Bussia '10	♀♀ 6
● Barolo Bussia '09	♀♀ 6
● Barolo V. Mandorlo '09	♀♀ 7
● Barolo V. Mandorlo '08	♀♀ 7
○ Langhe Chardonnay Rorea '13	♀♀ 3
○ Langhe Chardonnay Rorea '12	♀♀ 3

Giovanni Battista Gillardi

CASCINA CORSALETTO, 69
12060 FARIGLIANO [CN]
TEL. 017376306
www.gillardi.it

CELLAR SALES
PRE-BOOKED VISITS
ANNUAL PRODUCTION 35,000 bottles
HECTARES UNDER VINE 7.00

Ever since he started working at his father's winery, Giacolino Gillardi has always strived to innovate, making small amounts of important wines from international grape varieties. However, he has also always sought to maximize the potential of the wines to which his father introduced him, particularly Dolcetto, and his Doglianis continue to be first rate. His Langhe roots led him to take the big decision: the purchase of a little cellar and a vineyard in Barolo, whose first bottles are about to be released. This year marked the first release of Gillardi's fine Barolo. Its nose of raspberries is underpinned by oak notes, while the palate is already fairly well behaved, with pleasant acidity. While the 2014 vintage was not a good one for dolcetto grapes, both versions of the monovarietal are pleasant and characterized by sun-dried herbs on the nose and tannins on the palate. Langhe Nebbiolo is exceptionally well orchestrated.

● Barolo del Comune di Barolo '11	♥♥ 3*
● Dogliani Cursalet '14	♥♥ 3
● Dogliani Maestra '14	♥♥ 2*
● Langhe Harys '13	♥♥ 6
● Langhe Nebbiolo '13	♥♥ 6
● Dogliani Cursalet '11	♀♀♀ 3*
● Harys '00	♀♀♀ 6
● Harys '99	♀♀♀ 6
● Harys '98	♀♀♀ 6
● Dogliani Cursalet '13	♀♀ 3*
● Dogliani Maestra '13	♀♀ 2*
● Granè '11	♀♀ 5
● Langhe Fiore di Harys '12	♀♀ 4
● Langhe Ilmerlò '12	♀♀ 6
● Langhe Rosso Harys '12	♀♀ 6
● Langhe Rosso Harys '11	♀♀ 6

La Giribaldina

REG. SAN VITO, 39
14042 CALAMANDRANA [AT]
TEL. 0141718043
www.giribaldina.com

CELLAR SALES
PRE-BOOKED VISITS
ACCOMMODATION
ANNUAL PRODUCTION 70,000 bottles
HECTARES UNDER VINE 11.00

The Colombo family's little winery is a
quality operation, founded in 1995 with the
renovation of the old Giribaldi farmstead.
Its most important barbera cru is Bricco
Castellaro, in the municipality of Vaglio
Serra. A further three hectares of barbera
are planted in the Val Sarmassa nature
reserve, while the estate has moscato,
sauvignon, and an old barbera vineyard in
San Vito, a hamlet of Calamandrana. The
firmly structured, fruit-rich Barbera d'Asti
Superiore Nizza Cala delle Mandrie 2012
made it into our finals with its impressively
balanced flesh, tannins and acidity, and a
long, easy-drinking finish. Barbera d'Asti
Superiore Vigneti della Val Sarmassa 2013
is well made, with notes of ripe plums; it's
not particularly elegant but full of
character. We also liked Grignolino d'Asti
Quercino 2014, with typical peppery notes
and less typical citrussy ones, and a
full-flavoured balanced palate that
makes it a pleasing, albeit not very
recognizable, wine.

● Barbera d'Asti Sup. Nizza Cala delle Mandrie '12	♟♟ 4
● Barbera d'Asti Sup. Vign. della Val Sarmassa '13	♟♟ 3
● Grignolino d'Asti Quercino '14	♟♟ 2*
● Barbera d'Asti Monte del Mare '14	♟ 2
○ Moscato d'Asti '14	♟ 2
● Barbera d'Asti Sup. Nizza Cala delle Mandrie '11	♟♟ 4
● Barbera d'Asti Sup. Nizza Cala delle Mandrie '10	♟♟ 4
● Barbera d'Asti Sup. Vign. della Val Sarmassa '12	♟♟ 3
● Barbera d'Asti Sup. Vign. della Val Sarmassa '11	♟♟ 3*
● Grignolino d'Asti Quercino '11	♟♟ 2*

La Gironda

S.DA BRICCO, 12
14049 NIZZA MONFERRATO [AT]
TEL. 0141701013
www.lagironda.com

CELLAR SALES
PRE-BOOKED VISITS
ANNUAL PRODUCTION 50,000 bottles
HECTARES UNDER VINE 9.00

Located in Bricco Cremosina, one of the
most interesting crus in Nizza Monferrato,
the first-rate estate run by Agostino
Galandrino with his daughter Susanna and
her husband Alberto Adamo focuses chiefly
on the star cultivar of the area, barbera,
with some vines over 50 years old. Smaller
amounts of moscato, cortese, dolcetto, and
nebbiolo are also grown, along with several
international cultivars. Barbera d'Asti
Superiore Nizza Le Nicchie 2012 has a very
fresh, concentrated nose, with rich fruit and
hints of roasted coffee beans and tobacco,
and a powerful palate with nice acidity,
ensuring a long, easy-drinking finish. The
other wines are well made, particularly
Barbera d'Asti La Lippa 2014, with crisp
fruit that is truly captivating for the vintage,
and Monferrato Rosso Soul 2012, a
Nebbiolo with notes of tobacco, raspberries,
and liquorice that is a little austere and
tannic, but has good flesh and length.

● Barbera d'Asti Sup. Nizza Le Nicchie '12	♟♟ 5
● Barbera d'Asti La Gena '13	♟♟ 3
● Barbera d'Asti La Lippa '14	♟♟ 2*
● M.to Rosso Soul '12	♟♟ 5
○ Moscato d'Asti '14	♟ 2
● Barbera d'Asti Sup. Nizza Le Nicchie '11	♟♟♟ 5
● Barbera d'Asti La Gena '12	♟♟ 3*
● Barbera d'AstiLa Gena '09	♟♟ 3*
● Barbera d'Asti Sup. Nizza Le Nicchie '10	♟♟ 5
● Barbera d'Asti Sup. Nizza Le Nicchie '09	♟♟ 4
● Barbera d'Asti Sup. Nizza Le Nicchie '07	♟♟ 4

La Giustiniana

FRAZ. ROVERETO, 5
15066 GAVI [AL]
TEL. 0143682132
www.lagiustiniana.it

CELLAR SALES
PRE-BOOKED VISITS
ANNUAL PRODUCTION 200,000 bottles
HECTARES UNDER VINE 39.00

The Lombardini family's magnificent La
Giustiniana estate is over 400 years old
and is located in the celebrated Rovereto
growing area, in the heart of the Gavi hills.
Managed with the aid of Enrico Tomalino,
its vineyards cover an area of around 40
hectares, almost entirely planted to cortese
and tended using methods with low
environmental impact. It was one of the
first wineries in the area to focus on the
personality of single vineyards, and its
range features two different crus: Lugara
(grey marl soil) and Montessora (iron-rich
clay soil). Both are vinified entirely in steel,
as is Nostro Gavi, a Rovereto selection that
is aged for longer on the lees. Montessora
reached our finals with a special version,
displaying a concentrated nose of
new-mown grass and white-fleshed fruit
with mineral undertones. On the palate it
develops good acidity, which underpins the
long, powerful attack. The Lugara is less
complex, but nonetheless shows good
varietal characteristics. Last but not least,
the semi-sparkling Roverì is uncomplicated
but easy drinking.

○ Gavi del Comune di Gavi Montessora '14	♟♟ 4
○ Gavi del Comune di Gavi Lugarara '14	♟♟ 3
○ Roverì Frizzante	♟ 4
○ Gavi del Comune di Gavi Il Nostro Gavi '07	♟♟♟ 4
○ Gavi del Comune di Gavi Il Nostro Gavi '10	♟♟ 4
○ Gavi del Comune di Gavi Lugarara '13	♟♟ 3*
○ Gavi del Comune di Gavi Lugarara '12	♟♟ 3*
○ Gavi del Comune di Gavi Lugarara '11	♟♟ 3
○ Gavi del Comune di Gavi Montessora '13	♟♟ 4
○ Gavi del Comune di Gavi Montessora '12	♟♟ 4
○ Gavi del Comune di Gavi Montessora '11	♟♟ 4
○ Gavi del Comune di Gavi Montessora '10	♟♟ 3
○ Giustiniana Brut M. Cl.	♟♟ 4

★Elio Grasso

LOC. GINESTRA, 40
12065 MONFORTE D'ALBA [CN]
TEL. 017378491
www.eliograsso.it

PRE-BOOKED VISITS
ANNUAL PRODUCTION 90,000 bottles
HECTARES UNDER VINE 18.00
SUSTAINABLE WINERY

The Nebbiolos crafted by Elio Grasso and
his family are rightly considered veritable
evergreens of the Langhe wine world. Their
well-deserved reputation is derived from
their consistent excellence, but above all
from their style that refused to be
pigeonholed, even at the height of the
polarization between traditional and
modern. The Vigna Casa Matè and Gavarini
Vigna Chiniera Barolo crus are generally
aged in 2,500-litre Slavonian oak barrels
and the Runcot Riserva in barriques, but
technical details suddenly seem
insignificant when faced with the distinctive
layered, close-woven texture of these three
magnificent Monforte vineyards. This year
our favourite wines tasted were the two
2011 Barolos, which are almost mirror
images in their expression. Gavarini
Chiniera opens with a slight spicy
sweetness derived from the oak in the stiff
tannins, while Ginestra Casa Maté is
undoubtedly more classic and harmonious
in style, but perhaps a little simple on the
finish.

● Barbera d'Alba V. Martina '12	♟♟ 5
● Barolo Gavarini Chiniera '11	♟♟ 8
● Barolo Ginestra Casa Maté '11	♟♟ 8
● Barolo Rüncot Ris. '08	♟ 8
● Langhe Nebbiolo Gavarini '14	♟ 3
● Barolo Gavarini Chiniera '09	♟♟♟ 8
● Barolo Gavarini V. Chiniera '06	♟♟♟ 8
● Barolo Gavarini V. Chiniera '01	♟♟♟ 7
● Barolo Gavarini V. Chiniera '00	♟♟♟ 7
● Barolo Ginestra Casa Maté '07	♟♟♟ 8
● Barolo Ginestra V. Casa Maté '05	♟♟♟ 8
● Barolo Ginestra V. Casa Maté '04	♟♟♟ 8
● Barolo Ginestra V. Casa Maté '03	♟♟♟ 7
● Barolo Rüncot '01	♟♟♟ 8
● Barolo Rüncot '00	♟♟♟ 8
● Barolo Rüncot '99	♟♟♟ 8

Silvio Grasso

FRAZ. ANNUNZIATA, 112
12064 LA MORRA [CN]
TEL. 017350322
www.silviograsso.com

CELLAR SALES
PRE-BOOKED VISITS
ANNUAL PRODUCTION 90,000 bottles
HECTARES UNDER VINE 14.00

Federico Grasso has entered the age-old traditional/innovative debate raging among Langhe producers without taking a single direction, preferring to offer a range with something for all wine lovers. And so he has flanked his two top wines, Bricco Luciani and Ciabot Manzoni, with their fairly modern style, with a Barolo called Turnè (meaning "return") to denote a version produced using classic fermentation and ageing methods. With its aromas of tobacco and liquorice, combined with notes of raspberries, and a tannic weave nicely balanced by fruity flesh, Turnè 2011 most definitely belongs to the traditional school. Bricco Luciani 2011 is a fairly deep ruby, with a concentrated nose showing an excellent balance of dark berry fruit and oak, and a firmly structured, velvety palate with impressive acidity that persists through to the very long, clean finish.

Bruna Grimaldi

VIA PAREA, 7
12060 GRINZANE CAVOUR [CN]
TEL. 0173262094
www.grimaldibruna.it

CELLAR SALES
PRE-BOOKED VISITS
ANNUAL PRODUCTION 70,000 bottles
HECTARES UNDER VINE 13.00

This 60-year-old estate started off quietly with the work of Bruna Grimaldi's grandfather in the vineyards of Grinzane Cavour, which was continued by her commercially minded father. Since 1999, Bruna herself and her husband Franco Schellino have been engaged in the family business, purchasing vineyards in different zones of Langhe, commencing with two prized hectares in Serralunga's Badarina cru. They yield the eponymous Barolo that is the estate's jewel, with firm structure and great finesse derived from meticulous ageing in large and small oak. Riserva Badarina 2009 is complex and balanced, with a complex nose of dried herbs and brandied cherries, accompanied by a touch of liquorice. Its classic palate is long and rounded, with smooth tannins. Barolo Badarina 2011 is more predictable, with hay on the nose and a palate rounded by alcohol, and Barolo Camilla of the same vintage is more evolved. The enjoyable Barbera d'Alba Scassa 2012 has attractive clean fruit.

● Barolo Bricco Luciani '11	♥♥ 7
● Barolo Bricco Manzoni '11	♥♥ 7
● Barolo '11	♥♥ 5
● Barolo Turné '11	♥♥ 7
● Barolo Bricco Luciani '04	♥♥♥ 7
● Barolo Bricco Luciani '01	♥♥♥ 6
● Barolo Bricco Luciani '96	♥♥♥ 6
● Barolo Bricco Luciani '95	♥♥♥ 6
● Barolo Bricco Luciani '90	♥♥♥ 6
● Barolo Bricco Manzoni '10	♥♥♥ 7
● Barolo Annunziata V. Plicotti '09	♀♀ 7
● Barolo Bricco Luciani '10	♀♀ 7
● Barolo Giachini '10	♀♀ 6
● Barolo Giachini '09	♀♀ 6
● Barolo Turné '10	♀♀ 7
● Barolo Turné '09	♀♀ 7

● Barolo Badarina '11	♥♥ 6
● Barolo Badarina Ris. '09	♥♥ 6
● Barbera d'Alba Sup. Scassa '12	♥♥ 3
● Barolo Bricco Ambrogio '11	♥♥ 5
● Barolo Camilla '11	♥♥ 5
○ Langhe Arneis '14	♀ 2
● Barbera d'Alba Sup. Scassa '11	♀♀ 3
● Barolo Badarina '10	♀♀ 6
● Barolo Badarina '09	♀♀ 6
● Barolo Bricco Ambrogio '10	♀♀ 5
● Barolo Bricco Ambrogio '09	♀♀ 5
● Barolo Bricco Ambrogio '08	♀♀ 5
● Barolo Camilla '10	♀♀ 5
● Dolcetto d'Alba S. Martino '11	♀♀ 2*
● Nebbiolo d'Alba Briccola '12	♀♀ 3
● Nebbiolo d'Alba Briccola '10	♀♀ 3

Giacomo Grimaldi

VIA LUIGI EINAUDI, 8
12060 BAROLO [CN]
TEL. 0173560536
www.giacomogrimaldi.com

CELLAR SALES
PRE-BOOKED VISITS
ANNUAL PRODUCTION 50,000 bottles
HECTARES UNDER VINE 13.00

Ferruccio Grimaldi, who heads the family
winery named after his father, continues
with determination and clear ideas. The
estate's prime vineyards allow the
production of a comprehensive range of
wines representing the district's finest
varieties. Our favourite is the Sotto Castello
di Novello cru, which is often still
overlooked on maps of the finest Barolo
vineyards, but is nonetheless capable of
offering truly unique and alluring elegance
and drinkability. The excellent 2011 vintage
fared very well in our tastings, combining
harmony and power, with dark notes of
tobacco and tar alternating with delicate
hints of violets and eucalyptus. The addition
of well-resolved tannins brought this Barolo
within a hair's breadth of our top accolade.
Barolo Le Coste has a less focused nose,
and requires further bottle ageing to reach
its best.

Sergio Grimaldi
Ca' du Sindic

LOC. SAN GRATO, 15
12058 SANTO STEFANO BELBO [CN]
TEL. 0141840341
www.cadusindic.it

CELLAR SALES
PRE-BOOKED VISITS
ANNUAL PRODUCTION 100,000 bottles
HECTARES UNDER VINE 16.50
SUSTAINABLE WINERY

Ca' du Sindic, owned by the Grimaldi
family, has been one of the best-known and
most important moscato producers for over
quarter of a century. Its vineyards lie on the
San Grato hill next to the winery, and on the
San Maurizio and Bauda hills, in the heart
of the Moscato d'Asti production zone, with
vines up to 60 years old. In addition to
moscato, they are also home to pinot nero
and chardonnay for the production of
sparkling wines, and dolcetto, barbera,
cortese, brachetto, and favorita. The
difficult 2014 vintage has certainly left its
mark on the estate's production. Its two
flagships, Moscato d'Asti Capsula Oro and
Moscato d'Asti Capsula Argento are well
made but less brilliant than in the past,
both lacking a little structure and fullness.
Capsula Oro has notes of saffron and nicely
balanced sugar and acidity on the palate,
whilethe easy-drinking Capsula Argento
offers a nose of white-fleshed and sweet
citrus fruit, and a supple palate.

● Barolo Sotto Castello di Novello '11	▼▼	6
● Barbera d'Alba Pistin '14	▼▼	3
● Barolo '11	▼▼	6
● Barolo Le Coste '11	▼▼	7
○ Dolcetto d'Alba '14	▼▼	2*
● Barolo Sotto Castello di Novello '05	▼▼▼	6
● Barbera d'Alba Fornaci '12	♀♀	4
● Barbera d'Alba Pistin '13	♀♀	3
● Barolo '10	♀♀	5
● Barolo '09	♀♀	5
● Barolo Le Coste '10	♀♀	6
● Barolo Le Coste '09	♀♀	6
● Barolo Sotto Castello di Novello '10	♀♀	6
● Barolo Sotto Castello di Novello '09	♀♀	6
● Barolo Sotto Castello di Novello '08	♀♀	6
● Nebbiolo d'Alba Valmaggiore '11	♀♀	3

○ Moscato d'Asti Capsula Argento '14	▼▼	2*
○ Moscato d'Asti Capsula Oro '14	▼▼	3
⊙ Ventuno Brut Rosé '13	▼	3
● Barbera d'Asti '12	♀♀	2*
● Barbera d'Asti '10	♀♀	2
● Barbera d'Asti San Grato '10	♀♀	2*
● Barbera d'Asti SanGrato '12	♀♀	2*
● Barbera d'Asti SanGrato '11	♀♀	2*
○ Moscato d'Asti Capsula Argento '13	♀♀	2*
○ Moscato d'Asti Capsula Argento '12	♀♀	2*
○ Moscato d'Asti Capsula Oro '13	♀♀	3
○ Moscato d'Asti Capsula Oro '12	♀♀	3
○ Moscato d'Asti Capsula Oro '11	♀♀	2*
○ Moscato d'Asti Capsula Oro '10	♀♀	2
⊙ Ventuno Brut Mill. '12	♀♀	3
⊙ Ventuno Brut Rosé '10	♀♀	3

La Guardia

POD. LA GUARDIA, 74
15010 MORSASCO [AL]
TEL. 014473076
www.laguardiavilladelfini.it

CELLAR SALES
PRE-BOOKED VISITS
ANNUAL PRODUCTION 100,000 bottles
HECTARES UNDER VINE 35.00

This year La Guardia is back to our full
profile after a short interlude. The Priarone
family's venerable Ovada estate has long
been a fine interpreter of Dolcetto di Ovada
and Barbera. A few years ago it also started
producing good wines from international
varieties like pinot nero, cabernet
sauvignon, merlot and chardonnay. It is
situated 350 metres above sea level in
Morsasco, a village with 700 inhabitants,
between Ovada and Acqui Terme. The
estate's wines are first rate. Sacro e
Profano, a blend of barbera and cabernet
sauvignon, has interesting nose-palate
symmetry, with sophisticated use of oak
and very smooth tannins, which emerge on
the finish, while Pinot Nero Leone is
delicate and elegant. Il Gamondino is a
Dolcetto di Ovada with great character,
showing close focused and varietal. Ornovo
is a fine Barbera, concentrated and
lingering.

● Barbera del M.to Ornovo '11	♥♥ 3
● M.to Rosso Leone '09	♥♥ 4
● M.to Rosso Sacro e Profano '09	♥♥ 4
● Ovada Il Gamondino Ris. '11	♥♥ 3
● L'Intrigante '10	♥ 3
● M.to Rosso Innominato '10	♥ 4
● Barbera del M.to Sup. La V. di Dante '08	♀♀ 4
● Barbera del M.to V. di Dante '07	♀♀ 4
● Doppio Rosso '08	♀♀ 4
● M.to Rosso Innominato '09	♀♀ 4
● M.to Rosso Innominato '07	♀♀ 4
● M.to Rosso Leone '08	♀♀ 4
● M.to Rosso Sacro e Profano '07	♀♀ 5
● M.to Rosso Sacroeprofano '06	♀♀ 5
● Ovada Il Gamondino Ris. '08	♀♀ 3
● Ovada Vign. Bricco Riccardo '10	♀♀ 3

Clemente Guasti

C.SO IV NOVEMBRE, 80
14049 NIZZA MONFERRATO [AT]
TEL. 0141721350
www.guasti.it

CELLAR SALES
PRE-BOOKED VISITS
ANNUAL PRODUCTION 120,000 bottles
HECTARES UNDER VINE 27.00

The family estate founded by Clemente
Guasti in 1946 is now run by his sons
Andrea and Alessandro. Its vineyards are
arranged in four farmsteads: Boschetto
Vecchio, Fonda San Nicolao, Santa Teresa,
and Gessara–San Vitale, three in the Nizza
area and one near Mombaruzzo. The first
two yield the eponymous Barolo selections,
devised for ageing that the estate usually
releases one or two years later than most
Asti wineries. This venerable operation
gave a very sound performance,
particularly with its Barolo crus. Barbera
d'Asti Superiore Boschetto Vecchio 2010
has a nose of red berries, tobacco, and
quinine, accompanied by a delicate but
austere palate, true to the house style.
However, it is also long and characterful,
as is often the case in cooler vintages.
Barbera d'Asti Superiore Severa 2010 is
powerful and spirited, with a long citrussy
finish, while Grignolino d'Asti 2014 is
peppery and very pleasant.

● Barbera d'Asti Sup. Boschetto Vecchio '10	♥♥ 4
● Barbera d'Asti Sup. Severa '10	♥♥ 3
● Grignolino d'Asti '14	♥♥ 3
● Barbera d'Asti Desideria '12	♥ 3
○ Moscato d'Asti Santa Teresa '14	♥ 3
● Barbera d'Asti Desideria '09	♀♀ 2*
● Barbera d'Asti Sup. Boschetto Vecchio '09	♀♀ 4
● Barbera d'Asti Sup. Boschetto Vecchio '07	♀♀ 4
● Barbera d'Asti Sup. Classica '07	♀♀ 3*
● Barbera d'Asti Sup. Fonda San Nicolao '09	♀♀ 4
● Barbera d'Asti Sup. Fonda San Nicolao '07	♀♀ 4
● Barbera d'Asti Sup. Nizza Barcarato '09	♀♀ 5
● Barbera d'Asti Sup. Nizza Barcarato '07	♀♀ 5
○ Moscato d'Asti Santa Teresa '13	♀♀ 3
○ Moscato d'Asti Santa Teresa '12	♀♀ 3

★Hilberg - Pasquero

VIA BRICCO GATTI, 16
12040 PRIOCCA [CN]
TEL. 0173616197
www.hilberg-pasquero.com

CELLAR SALES
PRE-BOOKED VISITS
ANNUAL PRODUCTION 24,000 bottles
HECTARES UNDER VINE 6.50
VITICULTURE METHOD Certified Organic

The estate owned by Michelangelo "Miclo" Pasquero and Anette Hillberg is at Bricco Gatti, on one of the hills overlooking Priocca. Its vineyards, in the Monteforche and Bricco Stella areas, and all around the winery, have white, silty and marly soils, with a higher clay content than the classic Roero terrain. They're planted mainly with the typical Roero red grape varieties: barbera, brachetto and nebbiolo, and work focuses chiefly on maximizing the potential of the terroir. Barbera d'Alba Superiore 2013 is excellent, offering a nose of fresh fruit and sweet spice, and a powerful but nicely balanced palate, with fresh acidity ensuring suppleness and length. Langhe Nebbiolo 2013 is well made, showing full flavoured and well orchestrated, with floral and fruity notes and hints of liquorice. Nebbiolo d'Alba 2013 is equally good, offering more austere tannins and remarkable gutsiness, as is the pleasant, approachable Barbera d'Alba 2014 that focuses on fruit.

Icardi

LOC. SAN LAZZARO
S.DA COMUNALE BALBI, 30
12053 CASTIGLIONE TINELLA [CN]
TEL. 0141855159
www.icardivini.it

CELLAR SALES
PRE-BOOKED VISITS
ANNUAL PRODUCTION 360,000 bottles
HECTARES UNDER VINE 75.00
VITICULTURE METHOD Certified Biodynamic

Claudio Icardi's estate, founded over a century ago, now vaunts a series of vineyards that range from the plots next to the cellar to Castiglione Tinella to the finest winegrowing areas of Monferrato and Langhe, commencing with the Barolo and Barbaresco designations. The vineyards are tended with biodynamic methods, and the wish to pursue this approach in greater depth has led Claudio to found Cascina San Lazzaro, a sort of experimental field in which to test the various processes. Barbaresco Montubert 2012 is truly first class, with a nose of raspberries followed by tobacco, aniseed and aromatic herbs, and a long, juicy palate with plenty of flesh and close-knit but very elegant tannins. The aromatic Piemonte Bianco Pafoj, a blend of 60% sauvignon and 40% chardonnay, is also well made, with notes of ripe fruit and good taut acidity, as is the spicy Barolo Parej 2011, with a fine balance of tannins and fruit, and good length.

● Barbera d'Alba Sup. '13	♥♥ 5
● Barbera d'Alba '14	♥♥ 3
● Langhe Nebbiolo '13	♥♥ 4
● Nebbiolo d'Alba '13	♥♥ 5
● Vareij '14	♥ 3
● Barbera d'Alba Sup. '09	♥♥♥ 5
● Barbera d'Alba Sup. '98	♥♥♥ 5
● Barbera d'Alba Sup. '97	♥♥♥ 5
● Nebbiolo d'Alba '06	♥♥♥ 5
● Nebbiolo d'Alba '05	♥♥♥ 5
● Nebbiolo d'Alba '04	♥♥♥ 5
● Nebbiolo d'Alba '03	♥♥♥ 5
● Nebbiolo d'Alba '01	♥♥♥ 5
● Nebbiolo d'Alba '00	♥♥♥ 4
● Nebbiolo d'Alba '99	♥♥♥ 4*
● Nebbiolo d'Alba '12	♥♥ 5

● Barbaresco Montubert '12	♥♥ 5
● Barolo Parej '11	♥♥ 8
○ Piemonte Bianco Pafoj '14	♥♥ 4
○ Dadelio Bianco '14	♥ 5
● Langhe Rosso Dadelio '12	♥ 5
● Barbaresco Montubert '11	♥♥ 5
● Barbera d'Alba Surì di Mù '12	♥♥ 5
● Barbera d'Asti Nuj Suj '12	♥♥ 5
● Barbera d'Asti Nuj Suj '11	♥♥ 5
● Barbera d'Asti Tabaren '12	♥♥ 2*
● Barolo Parej '10	♥♥ 8
● Langhe Rosso Dadelio Cascina San Lazzaro '11	♥♥ 5
● Langhe Rosso Pafoj '11	♥♥ 6
● Langhe Rosso Pafoj '10	♥♥ 6
○ M.to Bianco Pafoj '12	♥♥ 4
○ Piemonte Bianco Pafoj '13	♥♥ 4

Ioppa

FRAZ. MAULETTA
VIA DELLE PALLOTTE, 10
28078 ROMAGNANO SESIA [NO]
TEL. 0163833079
www.viniioppa.it

CELLAR SALES
PRE-BOOKED VISITS
ANNUAL PRODUCTION 140,000 bottles
HECTARES UNDER VINE 20.50

The winemaking adventure of brothers Giampiero and Giorgio Ioppa has had its ups and downs. Flanked by their sons Marco and Andrea, they tend around 20 hectares of vineyards divided between Romagnano Sesia and Ghemme, which yield three versions of Ghemme: a basic, the Bricco Balsina and the Santa Fè. While nebbiolo naturally accounts for the lion's share, well-aspected sites are also planted with erbaluce, uva rara, and vespolina, which is also used to make the Stransì passito. The style is decidedly more modern than the age-old history of the cellar might suggest: big reds, usually requiring patience to mellow their exuberant extract and toast. It is thus no coincidence that the top wines are released after prolonged ageing, like Ghemme Bricco Balsina 2008, which still displays heady fruity and smoky aromas, and particularly invigorating phenolic structure, made even edgier by its sharp citrus backbone. It is certainly worth monitoring in the coming years.

Tenuta Langasco

FRAZ. MADONNA DI COMO, 10
12051 ALBA [CN]
TEL. 0173286972
www.tenutalangasco.it

CELLAR SALES
PRE-BOOKED VISITS
ANNUAL PRODUCTION 60,000 bottles
HECTARES UNDER VINE 22.00

This estate with solid family roots has been active since 1979; a fairly long time in comparison to the more recent international success of Piedmont wine. Over the years it has carved itself out an excellent niche among the pinnacles of Langhe excellence. The setting of the cellar alone makes it worth a visit, along with the consistent quality of its wines, which showcase the traditional local grape varieties and are very reasonably priced. The estate's overall performance in our tastings this year was undoubtedly sound, with Dolcetto d'Alba Vigna Miclet 2014 showing as good as ever, despite the difficult vintage, with lively varietal notes packed with fruit and dark berries. Nebbiolo Sorì Coppa 2013 surprised us with its close-focused nose of ripe red berry fruit and hints of menthol and spice, accompanied by a finely balanced palate of carefully calibrated tannins and refreshing acidity.

● Ghemme Bricco Balsina '08	♔♔ 6
● Ghemme '08	♔♔ 4
● Ghemme Santa Fè '08	♔♔ 6
☉ Colline Novaresi Nebbiolo Rusin '14	♔ 2
○ San Grato Bianco	♔ 2
● Colline Novaresi Nebbiolo '11	♕♕ 2*
● Colline Novaresi Nebbiolo '09	♕♕ 2*
☉ Colline Novaresi Nebbiolo Rusin '13	♕♕ 2*
● Ghemme '07	♕♕ 4
● Ghemme Bricco Balsina '07	♕♕ 4
● Ghemme Santa Fè '07	♕♕ 6
● Ghemme Santa Fè '06	♕♕ 6

● Nebbiolo d'Alba Sorì Coppa '13	♔♔ 4
● Barbera d'Alba Sortì '13	♔♔ 3
● Barbera d'Alba V. Madonna di Como '13	♔♔ 2*
● Dolcetto d'Alba V. Madonna di Como '14	♔♔ 2*
● Dolcetto d'Alba V. Miclet '14	♔♔ 3
○ Moscato d'Asti '14	♔ 3
● Barbera d'Alba Madonna di Como '11	♕♕ 2*
● Barbera d'Alba Madonna di Como '10	♕♕ 3
● Barbera d'Alba Sorì '10	♕♕ 3*
● Barbera d'Alba V. Madonna di Como '12	♕♕ 2*
● Dolcetto d'Alba Madonna di Como V. Miclet '12	♕♕ 2*
● Dolcetto d'Alba V. Miclet '13	♕♕ 3*
● Nebbiolo d'Alba Sorì Coppa '12	♕♕ 4
● Nebbiolo d'Alba Sorì Coppa '11	♕♕ 4
● Nebbiolo d'Alba Sorì Coppa '10	♕♕ 3

Ugo Lequio

VIA DEL MOLINO, 10
12057 NEIVE [CN]
TEL. 0173677224
www.ugolequio.it

CELLAR SALES
PRE-BOOKED VISITS
ANNUAL PRODUCTION 30,000 bottles
HECTARES UNDER VINE

The atmosphere surrounding Ugo Lequio and his family is playful and relaxed. For over 30 years their winery has been a site of pilgrimage for those seeking forthright Barbarescos with reliable development, made from the grapes (purchased from the Marcorino family) of a special cru like the Gallina vineyard in Neive. The style can be considered classic, but not extreme, with medium-long maceration and ageing in mainly 2,500-litre French oak barrels. Carefully selected growers supply the grapes for the wines from barbera, dolcetto, and arneis, which offer equally distinctive expressiveness and firm structure, at very fair prices. On this occasion only the top note was missing from a range that is nonetheless very consistent overall. Barbaresco Gallina 2012 requires patient waiting, for its alcohol and tannins are not yet fully amalgamated, and the same strategy will probably also yield rewards with the rugged, territorial Gallina Riserva 2010.

● Barbaresco Gallina Ris. '10	♀♀6
● Barbaresco Gallina '12	♀♀5
● Barbera d'Alba Sup. Gallina '12	♀♀4
● Barbaresco Gallina '11	♀♀5
● Barbaresco Gallina '10	♀♀5
● Barbaresco Gallina '09	♀♀5
● Barbaresco Gallina '08	♀♀5
● Barbaresco Gallina '07	♀♀5
● Barbaresco Gallina Ris. '07	♀♀6
● Barbera d'Alba Sup. '11	♀♀4
● Barbera d'Alba Sup. Gallina '10	♀♀4
● Barbera d'Alba Sup. Gallina '09	♀♀3
● Barbera d'Alba Sup. Gallina '07	♀♀3
○ Langhe Arneis '13	♀♀3
○ Langhe Arneis '12	♀♀3
● Langhe Nebbiolo '09	♀♀3

Podere Macellio

VIA ROMA, 18
10014 CALUSO [TO]
TEL. 0119833511
www.erbaluce-bianco.it

CELLAR SALES
PRE-BOOKED VISITS
ANNUAL PRODUCTION 25,000 bottles
HECTARES UNDER VINE 3.50

The Bianco family's winery was named after the Caluso hill on which its three-and-a-half hectare estate, entirely planted to erbaluce, is located. Its winegrowing origins reach back to the second half of the 18th century, although it did not start to bottle its wines officially until the mid-1960s, under Renato Bianco, now flanked by his son Daniele. As always, their range features a still dry version, a Metodo Classico sparkler, and a passito, which undergoes long ageing in oak. They are very austere, linear interpretations, far removed from any notions of fancy fermentation, and with personalities to match their impressive ageing potential. Due to the variety of vintages presented, all strongly characterized by climate conditions, the results achieved by the Bianco family, able to compete in all categories, from still white to passito, appear livelier than usual. This year the Caluso Passito is excellent, the hot, sunny vintage fully exploited to express a wine with great balance and finesse.

○ Caluso Passito '09	♀♀5
○ Erbaluce di Caluso Brut M. Cl.	♀♀3
○ Erbaluce di Caluso '14	♀2
○ Caluso Passito '08	♀♀5
○ Caluso Passito '07	♀♀5
○ Caluso Passito '06	♀♀5
○ Caluso Passito '05	♀♀5
○ Caluso Passito '02	♀♀5
○ Erbaluce di Caluso '13	♀♀2*
○ Erbaluce di Caluso '12	♀♀2*
○ Erbaluce di Caluso '11	♀♀2*
○ Erbaluce di Caluso '10	♀♀2*
○ Erbaluce di Caluso '08	♀♀2*

PIEDMONT

Malabaila di Canale

VIA MADONNA DEI CAVALLI, 93
12043 CANALE [CN]
TEL. 017398381
www.malabaila.com

CELLAR SALES
PRE-BOOKED VISITS
ANNUAL PRODUCTION 100,000 bottles
HECTARES UNDER VINE 22.00
SUSTAINABLE WINERY

The estate owned by the Carrega Malabaila family and Valerio Falletti has revived and relaunched the legendary role of the house of Malabaila, associated with viticulture and the Roero wine trade since the 16th century. Its vineyards form a single 90-hectare plot on the typical loose soil of the area, with arid, steep slopes prone to erosion, some with gradients in excess of 50%. They are planted with the classic Roero grape varieties: arneis, nebbiolo, favorita, brachetto, and dolcetto. The estate's wines performed very well this year. Roero Bric Volta 2012 is floral and flavoursome, with big character, offering notes of forest floor and dark berries, while Roero Arneis Pradvaj 2014 is fresh, gutsy, and vibrant with citrus notes. The other wines are well made, particularly Roero Castelletto Riserva 2011, which is tannic with ripe notes, but long and fruit rich, and the full, flavoursome Roero Arneis 2014.

★Malvirà

LOC. CANOVA
VIA CASE SPARSE, 144
12043 CANALE [CN]
TEL. 0173978145
www.malvira.com

CELLAR SALES
PRE-BOOKED VISITS
ACCOMMODATION AND RESTAURANT SERVICE
ANNUAL PRODUCTION 300,000 bottles
HECTARES UNDER VINE 42.00

Malvirà, owned by the Damonte family, has been at the top of Roero production for several years now. Brothers Massimo and Roberto are responsible for the vineyard and the cellar respectively. The estate boasts vineyards in some of the most illustrious Roero crus, from Mombeltramo and Renesio to Saglietto, San Michele, and Trinità, as well as a small vineyard in La Morra for the production of Barolo. Its mission to maximize the area's potential also includes top-class welcoming guest accommodation, in the form of Villa Tiboldi. Roero Mombeltrano Riserva has taken another Tre Bicchieri with the 2011 vintage. It has a nose of red berries with hints of quinine and rhubarb, and a fresh, juicy, fruit-rich palate with good length and complexity. Roero Trinità Riserva 2011 is more evolved, but elegant, supple and long. Barbera d'Alba San Michele 2012 is also very good, showing well typed and varietal, with earthy, fruity notes, as is the fresh, floral Roero Arneis Trinità 2014.

○ Roero Arneis Pradvaj '14	▮▮ 3*
● Roero Bric Volta '12	▮▮ 3*
● Barbera d'Alba Giardino '13	▮▮ 2*
● Nebbiolo d'Alba Bric Merli '13	▮▮ 3
○ Roero Arneis '14	▮▮ 2*
● Roero Castelletto Ris. '11	▮▮ 4
● Barbera d'Alba Sup. Mezzavilla '12	▮ 3
● Barbera d'Alba Mezzavilla '11	♀♀ 3
● Barbera d'Alba Mezzavilla '10	♀♀ 3*
● Barbera d'Alba Mezzavilla '09	♀♀ 3*
● Barbera d'Alba Mezzavilla '07	♀♀ 3
○ Roero Arneis '10	♀♀ 2*
● Roero Bric Volta '11	♀♀ 3
● Roero Castelletto Ris. '10	♀♀ 5
● Roero Castelletto Ris. '09	♀♀ 4
● Roero Castelletto Ris. '08	♀♀ 4

● Roero Mombeltramo Ris. '11	▮▮▮ 5
● Barbera d'Alba S. Michele '12	▮▮ 3*
○ Roero Arneis Trinità '14	▮▮ 3*
● Roero Trinità Ris. '11	▮▮ 5
○ Langhe Bianco Treuve '13	▮▮ 3
○ Roero Arneis V. Renesio '14	▮▮ 3
● Roero '12	▮ 3
○ Roero Arneis '14	▮ 2
○ Roero Arneis Saglietto '13	▮ 3
● Roero Renesio Ris. '11	▮ 5
● Roero Mombeltramo Ris. '10	♀♀♀ 5
● Roero Mombeltramo Ris. '05	♀♀♀ 5
● Roero Renesio Ris. '05	♀♀♀ 5
● Roero Sup. Mombeltramo '04	♀♀♀ 5
● Roero Sup. Trinità '03	♀♀♀ 4
● Roero Trinità Ris. '07	♀♀♀ 5

Giovanni Manzone

VIA CASTELLETTO, 9
12065 MONFORTE D'ALBA [CN]
TEL. 017378114
www.manzonegiovanni.com

CELLAR SALES
PRE-BOOKED VISITS
ANNUAL PRODUCTION 45,000 bottles
HECTARES UNDER VINE 7.50

Giovanni Manzone has required no media hype to make a name for himself as one of the most scrupulous and consistent Langhe growers. Flanked by his son Mauro, it is a very familiar one to those seeking an authentic expression of the Monforte d'Alba terroir and its finest crus like Gramolere, Bricat, and Castelletto. The estate's Barolos are sometimes edgy and far from formal, but they are incisive and forthright in structure, and have nothing to do with standardized production. Among all this nebbiolo, we should also spare a word for the small production of Rosserto, which is very likely a white biotype of the Ligurian rossese grape. The Manzone family always have many strings to their bow and presented an excellent array of Barolos this year. Castelletto 2011 is very dynamic, albeit a tad short on balance on the palate, while the Gramolere of the same vintage compensates for what it lacks in weight with well-proportioned progression and nice backbone.

● Barolo Castelletto '11	♀♀ 6
● Barolo Gramolere '11	♀♀ 6
● Barolo Bricat '11	♀♀ 6
● Barolo Gramolere Ris. '08	♀♀ 8
● Barolo Bricat '05	♀♀♀ 6
● Barolo Castelletto '09	♀♀♀ 5
● Barolo Gramolere Ris. '05	♀♀♀ 7
● Barolo Le Gramolere '04	♀♀♀ 6
● Barolo Le Gramolere Ris. '01	♀♀♀ 7
● Barolo Le Gramolere Ris. '00	♀♀♀ 7
● Barolo Le Gramolere Ris. '99	♀♀♀ 7
● Barbera d'Alba Le Ciliegie '12	♀♀ 3
● Barolo Bricat '10	♀♀ 6
● Barolo Castelletto '10	♀♀ 5
● Barolo Gramolere '10	♀♀ 6
● Barolo Gramolere Ris. '07	♀♀ 7

Paolo Manzone

LOC. MERIAME, 1
12050 SERRALUNGA D'ALBA [CN]
TEL. 0173613113
www.barolomeriame.com

CELLAR SALES
PRE-BOOKED VISITS
ACCOMMODATION
ANNUAL PRODUCTION 85,000 bottles
HECTARES UNDER VINE 10.00
SUSTAINABLE WINERY

Until a few years ago the grapes from this vineyard were sold and blended with others; consequently the name Meriame did not appear on any label. Today four small producers have already staked interests in this cru, which has been officialized with a "Menzione Geografica Aggiuntiva" specification for Barolo. Paolo Manzone is a skilled oenologist, with experience at several estates, as demonstrated in his own wines, commencing with the Barolo produced from the vineyards surrounding the family's elegant guest farm. Barolo Meriame 2011 has a sophisticated concentrated nose offering fine notes of dried herbs and tobacco with undertones of red berries. While not particularly powerful on the palate, it is very well behaved and pleasant, with the rich fruit typical of its vintage. The Barolo Serralunga is only slightly less exuberant. Barbera d'Alba Superiore Fiorenza 2013 is very convincing, packed with plums, spice, and alcohol, while Nebbiolo Miriné is uncomplicated and slightly vegetal.

● Barolo Meriame '11	♀♀ 7
● Barbera d'Alba Sup. Fiorenza '13	♀♀ 3
● Barolo del Comune di Serralunga d'Alba '12	♀♀ 6
● Langhe Rosso Luvì '13	♀♀ 3
● Nebbiolo d'Alba Miriné '13	♀♀ 3
● Dolcetto d'Alba Magna '14	♀ 2
● Barolo del Comune di Serralunga d'Alba '10	♀♀ 3*
● Barolo Meriame '10	♀♀ 7
● Barolo Meriame '09	♀♀ 7
● Barolo Serralunga '09	♀♀ 6
● Dolcetto d'Alba Magna '12	♀♀ 2*
● Langhe Rosso Luvì '12	♀♀ 3
● Langhe Rosso Luvì '11	♀♀ 3
● Nebbiolo d'Alba Miriné '12	♀♀ 3

Marcalberto

VIA PORTA SOTTANA, 9
12058 SANTO STEFANO BELBO [CN]
TEL. 0141844022
www.marcalberto.it

CELLAR SALES
PRE-BOOKED VISITS
ANNUAL PRODUCTION 30,000 bottles
HECTARES UNDER VINE 5.00

Year after year this original family estate, entirely dedicated to Metodo Classico, tirelessly continues its path towards the loftiest pinnacles of Italian sparkling wine production. This year it has purchased new plots, with the aim of increasingly diversifying the fine agricultural land at its disposal. It should be noted that Marcalberto was among the first European producers to consistently offer a Metodo Classico without added sulphites. The complex Millesimato Extra Brut 2010 has a well-defined nose of croissants, rusks, and hedgerow, accompanied by an invigorating, caressing palate. The Nature without added sulphites is constantly changing, making it difficult to assess the characteristics of such an authentic, crystalline, vibrant wine with just one tasting. It is a wine conceived without intervention or compromises in terms of taste.

○ Marcalberto Extra Brut M. Cl. Millesimo2Mila10 '10	♀♀ 5
○ Marcalberto Brut M. Cl. Sansannée	♀♀ 4
⊙ Marcalberto Brut Rosé M. Cl.	♀♀ 4
○ Marcalberto Nature M. Cl. Senza Aggiunta di Solfiti	♀♀ 6
○ Marcalberto Brut M. Cl. Millesimo2Mila9 '09	♀ 5
○ Marcalberto Brut M. Cl. '08	♀ 5
○ Marcalberto Brut M. Cl. '07	♀ 5
○ Marcalberto Brut M. Cl. '06	♀ 5
○ Marcalberto Brut M. Cl. '05	♀ 5
○ Marcalberto Nature M. Cl.	♀ 6

Poderi Marcarini

P.ZZA MARTIRI, 2
12064 LA MORRA [CN]
TEL. 017350222
www.marcarini.it

CELLAR SALES
PRE-BOOKED VISITS
ACCOMMODATION
ANNUAL PRODUCTION 125,000 bottles
HECTARES UNDER VINE 20.00

As sensorially diverse as they are geographically close, La Morra's Brunate and La Serra vineyards are unanimously associated with the status of Grand Cru. Much of the credit for this is undeniably due to the work of the Marcarini family, who have managed to reveal their almost specular personalities with a long series of spectacular releases. Today the winery is headed by Anna Bava, with her daughter Luisa and son-in-law Manuel Marchetti. Its style is the same as ever, as immediately revealed by the bright, rarefied hue of the wines, achieved by long maceration and patient ageing in 2,000-4,000-litre oak barrels, ensuring intimately classic Nebbiolos that are eminently ageworthy. Barolo Brunate 2011 is vivid and complex on the nose, characterized by notes of spice, violets, and tobacco, with faint balsamic hints. It is more caressing on the palate than past versions, due to the generous fruit of the vintage.

● Barolo Brunate '11	♀♀ 6
● Barolo La Serra '11	♀♀ 6
● Barolo Brunate '05	♀♀♀ 6
● Barolo Brunate '03	♀♀♀ 6
● Barolo Brunate '01	♀♀♀ 6
● Barolo Brunate '99	♀♀♀ 6
● Barolo Brunate '96	♀♀♀ 6
● Barolo Brunate Ris. '85	♀♀♀ 6
● Dolcetto d'Alba Boschi di Berri '96	♀♀♀ 4*
● Barbera d'Alba Ciabot Camerano '12	♀♀ 3*
● Barbera d'Alba Ciabot Camerano '11	♀♀ 3
● Barolo Brunate '10	♀♀ 6
● Barolo Brunate '09	♀♀ 6
● Barolo La Serra '10	♀♀ 6
● Barolo La Serra '09	♀♀ 6

Marchese Luca Spinola

FRAZ. ROVERETO DI GAVI
LOC. CASCINA MASSIMILIANA, 97
15066 GAVI [AL]
TEL. 0143682514
www.marcheselucaspinola.it

CELLAR SALES
PRE-BOOKED VISITS
ANNUAL PRODUCTION 20,000 bottles
HECTARES UNDER VINE 15.00

The 15 hectares of vineyards managed by Marchese Luca Spinola have belonged to his family since time immemorial. Half are located in the Tassarolo area and half in Rovereto di Gavi, both classic growing zones for cortese. The range consists of three wines, distinguished by their different terroirs and vinification techniques. Most of the grapes go to make Gavi di Gavi, while just 3,000 bottles of Gavi del Comune di Tassarolo are produced. Production figures are not much higher for Tenuta Massimiliana, which undergoes slower fermentation at lower temperatures. The Rovereto di Gavi winery presented us with three versions of Gavi 2014. Tenuta Massimiliana vaunts a bright, lively hue and a concentrated nose, bursting with vegetal notes that fade into mineral tones. Its full-bodied palate is well behaved, with a fresh, tangy finish. Gavi del Comune di Gavi has plenty of character and personality, while Gavi Frizzante is more rustic with a firmly structured palate.

○ Gavi del Comune di Gavi Et. Blu '14	🍷🍷 2*
○ Gavi del Comune di Gavi Tenuta Massimiliana '14	🍷🍷 3
○ Gavi Frizzante '14	🍷 2
○ Gavi del Comune di Gavi '12	🍷🍷 2*
○ Gavi del Comune di Gavi '11	🍷🍷 2*
○ Gavi del Comune di Gavi '10	🍷🍷 2
○ Gavi del Comune di Gavi Tenuta Massimiliana '13	🍷🍷 3
○ Gavi del Comune di Gavi Tenuta Massimiliana '12	🍷🍷 3
○ Gavi del Comune di Gavi Tenuta Massimiliana '10	🍷🍷 2
○ Gavi del Comune di Tassarolo '13	🍷🍷 2*
○ Gavi del Comune di Tassarolo '10	🍷🍷 2*
○ Gavi del Comune di Tassarolo '09	🍷🍷 2*

★Marchesi di Barolo

VIA ALBA, 12
12060 BAROLO [CN]
TEL. 0173564400
www.marchesibarolo.com

CELLAR SALES
PRE-BOOKED VISITS
RESTAURANT SERVICE
ANNUAL PRODUCTION 1,500,000 bottles
HECTARES UNDER VINE 170.00

According to tradition, Langhe's "king of wines" was invented in the underground passages of Castello Falletti that house Marchesi di Barolo's old cellars. The Abbona family fell in love with this charming setting, purchasing it from the Agenzia della Tenuta Opera Pia in Barolo as their headquarters. Anna and Ernesto are the fifth generation to work in the winery and are responsible for its development , which manages to merge its deep historical roots with the challenges of the present. This is clearly reflected in the composition and style of the comprehensive range of wines made from the Langhe, Roero, and Monferrato estates. We were struck by the range as a whole during this year's tastings. Our favourite was the Barolo Cannubi, with a spicy, fruity, nose and an exceptionally well-orchestrated palate, which earned a well-deserved Tre Bicchieri. Barolo Coste di Rose 2011 has a concentrated, layered nose.

● Barolo Cannubi '11	🍷🍷🍷 8
● Barolo Coste di Rose '11	🍷🍷 7
● Barolo Sarmassa '11	🍷🍷 8
● Barbaresco Serragrilli '12	🍷🍷 6
● Barolo '10	🍷🍷 5
● Barolo del Comune di Barolo '11	🍷🍷 8
● Barolo Ris. '08	🍷🍷 8
● Barolo Cannubi '10	🍷🍷🍷 8
● Barolo Sarmassa '09	🍷🍷🍷 8
● Barolo Sarmassa '08	🍷🍷🍷 7
● Barolo Sarmassa '07	🍷🍷🍷 7
● Barolo Sarmassa '06	🍷🍷🍷 7
● Barolo Sarmassa '05	🍷🍷🍷 7

Marchesi Incisa della Rocchetta

VIA ROMA, 66
14030 ROCCHETTA TANARO [AT]
TEL. 0141644647
www.marchesiincisawines.com

CELLAR SALES
PRE-BOOKED VISITS
ACCOMMODATION AND RESTAURANT SERVICE
ANNUAL PRODUCTION 60,000 bottles
HECTARES UNDER VINE 17.00

Although officially founded in 1970, the Incisa della Rocchetta family estate was already a well-established winegrowing operation in Monferrato in the 19th century. Today Barbara Incisa della Rocchetta and her son Filiberto Massone run the 17 hectares under vine, part of which are in the Rocchetta Tanaro nature reserve. The vineyards lie on sandy clay soil and are planted mainly to barbera, with the addition of grignolino, pinot nero, grown here since the late 19th century, and merlot. This venerable winery's production is of the usual high level. The deep, close-knit Barbera d'Asti Superiore Sant'Emiliano 2012 has typical notes of tobacco and ripe cherries, and a fine balance of acidity and rich fruit. Piemonte Pinot Nero Marchese Leopoldo 2013 is fresh and agreeable, with notes of dark berries and earthy hints, while the easy-drinking Monferrato Rosso Colpo d'Ala 2013, an equal blend of barbera and merlot, is supple and caressing.

● Barbera d'Asti Sup. Sant'Emiliano '12	♥♥ 5
● M.to Rosso Colpo d'Ala '13	♥♥ 6
● Piemonte Pinot Nero Marchese Leopoldo '13	♥♥ 4
● Grignolino d'Asti '14	♥ 3
● Barbera d'Asti Sup. Sant'Emiliano '11	♀♀ 4
● Barbera d'Asti Sup. Sant'Emiliano '10	♀♀ 4
● Barbera d'Asti Sup. Sant'Emiliano '09	♀♀ 4
● Barbera d'Asti Sup. Sant'Emiliano '08	♀♀ 4
● Barbera d'Asti Valmorena '13	♀♀ 3
● Barbera d'Asti Valmorena '11	♀♀ 3
● Barbera d'Asti Valmorena '10	♀♀ 3*
● Grignolino d'Asti '13	♀♀ 3
● Grignolino d'Asti '12	♀♀ 3
● Grignolino d'Asti '11	♀♀ 3
● M.to Rosso Rollone '12	♀♀ 3
● M.to Rosso Rollone '11	♀♀ 3

Mario Marengo

VIA XX SETTEMBRE, 34
12064 LA MORRA [CN]
TEL. 017350115
marengo1964@libero.it

CELLAR SALES
PRE-BOOKED VISITS
ANNUAL PRODUCTION 35,000 bottles
HECTARES UNDER VINE 7.00

The history handed down through the generations of the Marengo family is proudly documented. It was 1899 when the first Barolo was bottled in the cellar in La Morra, whose annual production has remained only slightly higher than that of a garage winery, even following the purchase of plots in Castiglione Falletto and Barolo. The estate grows the traditional Langhe grapes (dolcetto, barbera, and nebbiolo), but its style is consciously innovative, achieved with brief fermentation in vertical roto-fermenters, intense extraction, and ageing in barrique. Although generally potent, the wines respect the unique characteristics of prestigious vineyards like Brunate and Bricco delle Viole. The Brunate cru regularly produces some of the most prized grapes of the entire production zone, which are particularly aromatic, never overly tannic, and always sugar rich. This year it has won Marco Marengo his umpteenth Tre Bicchieri, in the form of a powerful but already highly drinkable version, vaunting ripe fruit and aromas of violets, truffles, and tar.

● Barolo Brunate '11	♥♥♥ 7
● Barolo Bricco delle Viole '11	♥♥ 6
● Barbera d'Alba Vign. Pugnane '13	♥♥ 3
● Barolo '11	♥♥ 5
○ Dolcetto d'Alba '14	♥♥ 2*
● Nebbiolo d'Alba Valmaggiore '13	♥♥ 3
● Barolo Brunate '09	♀♀♀ 6
● Barolo Brunate '07	♀♀♀ 6
● Barolo Brunate '06	♀♀♀ 6
● Barolo Brunate '05	♀♀♀ 6
● Barolo Brunate '04	♀♀♀ 6
● Barolo Bricco Viole '05	♀♀ 5
● Barolo Bricco Viole '04	♀♀ 5
● Barolo Brunate '03	♀♀ 5
● Barolo Brunate '01	♀♀ 5*
● Barolo Brunate '00	♀♀ 5

Claudio Mariotto

S.DA PER SAREZZANO, 29
15057 TORTONA [AL]
TEL. 0131868500
www.claudiomariotto.it

CELLAR SALES
PRE-BOOKED VISITS
ANNUAL PRODUCTION 100,000 bottles
HECTARES UNDER VINE 32.00

Famous for the high quality of his
Timorasso, Claudio is also a dab hand with
red wines, especially Barbera. Tastings of
vintages of Vho and the basic Territorio at
least 10 years old have demonstrated their
ageworthiness and elegance. However, the
estate's Moscato is also excellent, with fine
acidity countering its high residual sugar. In
truth, Claudio's entire range is very sound,
for he lavishes the same meticulous care
and passion on his entire production. The
range of wines speaks for itself. Two
finalists and a Tre Bicchieri are the proof of
the estate's ability to achieve great things,
and not just with white wines. Pitasso and
Cavallina are two veritable Timorasso
flagships, very different from each other,
but complex and elegant like few others,
while Poggio del Rosso is a splendid,
potent Barbera with a never-ending finish.

Marsaglia

VIA MADAMA MUSSONE, 2
12050 CASTELLINALDO [CN]
TEL. 0173213048
www.cantinamarsaglia.it

CELLAR SALES
PRE-BOOKED VISITS
ANNUAL PRODUCTION 80,000 bottles
HECTARES UNDER VINE 15.00

The Marsaglia family, present in the area
since 1900, stared bottling their wines in
the 1980s. Today the estate is
enthusiastically run by Emilio and Marina
Marsaglia, with the help of their children
Enrico and Monica. Its vineyards, with vines
planted between the 1950s and 2000, are
all in the municipality of Castellinaldo, on
the sandy soils facing Canale, where their
most famous cru, Brich d'America, is
located, and on the more compact ones
towards Castagnito. The entire range is very
reliable. Roero Brich d'America 2011 has a
nose of red berries and sweet spice, and a
full, caressing palate. Roero Arneis
Serramiana 2014 is equally well made,
showing fruity, full bodied, and aromatic,
with a delicious long finish, as is the
fruit-rich Barbera d'Alba Castellinaldo 2011,
with notes of forest floor and good acidity.
Metodo Classico Accordo, with a nose of
yellow-fleshed fruit and crusty bread, and
the beefy Nebbiolo d'Alba 2012 are also
good.

○ Colli Tortonesi Timorasso Pitasso '13	♟♟♟ 6
● Colli Tortonesi Rosso Poggio del Rosso '12	♟♟ 5
○ Colli Tortonesi Timorasso Cavallina '13	♟♟ 5
● Colli Tortonesi Croatina Montemirano '13	♟♟ 4
○ Colli Tortonesi Timorasso Derthona '13	♟♟ 5
● Colli Tortonesi Vho '13	♟♟ 5
● Colli Tortonesi Barbera Territorio '14	♟ 3
● Colli Tortonesi Freisa Braghè '14	♟ 3
○ Colli Tortonesi Bianco Pitasso '06	♟♟♟ 5
○ Colli Tortonesi Bianco Pitasso '05	♟♟♟ 4
○ Colli Tortonesi Bianco Pitasso '04	♟♟♟ 4
○ Colli Tortonesi Timorasso Pitasso '12	♟♟♟ 6
○ Colli Tortonesi Timorasso Pitasso '08	♟♟♟ 5
○ Colli Tortonesi Timorasso Cavallina '12	♟♟ 5
○ Colli Tortonesi Timorasso Derthona '12	♟♟ 5
● Colli Tortonesi Vho '12	♟♟ 5

○ Accordo Brut M. Cl.	♟♟ 4
● Barbera d'Alba Castellinaldo '11	♟♟ 4
● Nebbiolo d'Alba '12	♟♟ 3
○ Roero Arneis Serramiana '14	♟♟ 3
● Roero Brich d'America '11	♟♟ 4
● Barbera d'Alba S. Cristoforo '13	♟ 3
● Barbera d'Alba Castellinaldo '10	♟♟ 4
● Barbera d'Alba S. Cristoforo '12	♟♟ 3
● Barbera d'Alba S. Cristoforo '11	♟♟ 3*
● Barbera d'Alba S. Cristoforo '10	♟♟ 3
● Nebbiolo d'Alba San Pietro '11	♟♟ 3
● Nebbiolo d'Alba San Pietro '10	♟♟ 3
○ Roero Arneis Serramiana '13	♟♟ 3
● Roero Brich d'America '10	♟♟ 4
● Roero Brich d'America '09	♟♟ 4
● Roero Brich d'America '08	♟♟ 4

★Franco M. Martinetti

C.SO TURATI, 14
10128 TORINO
TEL. 0118395937
www.francomartinetti.it

PRE-BOOKED VISITS
ANNUAL PRODUCTION 140,000 bottles
HECTARES UNDER VINE 5.00

Franco Martinetti, the great grape selector and expert in ageing Piedmont wines, is true to form and increases his renown as a white-wine specialist too. A tireless seeker of fine grapes, who pays meticulous attention to every detail of the vinification process, in 40 years he has become an unrivalled "vinIculturist", as he likes to call himself, with a particular predilection for Monferrato wines. The sole exception is his Quarantatré, an elegant Metodo Classico, from vineyards in Oltrepò Pavese, which is dosed with a few drops of 1943 Bas Armagnac. Gavi Minaia 2014 is already exceptionally drinkable, winning a Tre Bicchieri for its richness and complexity. Its fresh mineral notes will become more prominent over the coming decades, as the history of this wine has demonstrated. The Gavi del Comune di Gavi is more subtle, but alluring and close focused, while the famous Montruc, a veritable classic Barbera d'Asti, is pleasantly dry with notes of dark berries. The Martin is excellent, even though it did not manage to repeat last year's feat.

○ Gavi Minaia '14	♥♥♥ 5
● Barbera d'Asti Sup. Montruc '12	♥♥ 5
○ Colli Tortonesi Timorasso Martin '13	♥♥ 6
● Barolo Marasco '11	♥♥ 7
○ Colli Tortonesi Timorasso Biancofranco '14	♥♥ 5
○ Gavi del Comune di Gavi '14	♥♥ 3
○ Quarantatré Brut M. Cl. '07	♥♥ 6
● Sul Bric '12	♥ 6
● Barbera d'Asti Sup. Montruc '06	♥♥♥ 5
● Barbera d'Asti Sup. Montruc '01	♥♥♥ 5
● Barolo Marasco '01	♥♥♥ 7
● Barolo Marasco '00	♥♥♥ 7
○ Colli Tortonesi Timorasso Martin '12	♥♥♥ 6
● M.to Rosso Sul Bric '10	♥♥♥ 6
● M.to Rosso Sul Bric '09	♥♥♥ 6

★Bartolo Mascarello

VIA ROMA, 15
12060 BAROLO [CN]
TEL. 017356125

CELLAR SALES
PRE-BOOKED VISITS
ANNUAL PRODUCTION 30,000 bottles
HECTARES UNDER VINE 5.00

Those who knew Bartolo Mascarello are well aware how he shunned all attempts at consecration. Yet ten years after his death, the legend lives on of the partisan-vignernon who rallied himself to defend a well-defined notion of culture and tradition, above and beyond a stylistic model of Barolo. However, it would not have been possible without the work of his daughter Maria Teresa, who has made the family's Nebbiolos (and other wines) even more authoritative and significant in the Langhe wine world. Subjected to long maceration and ageing in large barrels, they are produced from the estate's plots in the Barolo crus of Canubbi, San Lorenzo, and Ruè, and the Rocche vineyard in La Morra. It is precisely in irregular vintages, such as the 2011 with a very hot summer, that the decision to combine the grapes from different vineyards in a single Barolo proves a winning one. The result is very fruity, with good acidity, an elegant close-focused nose, and a palate already showing fine harmony, earning a Tre Bicchieri for its eminently classical style.

● Barolo '11	♥♥♥ 8
● Barolo '10	♥♥♥ 8
● Barolo '09	♥♥♥ 8
● Barolo '07	♥♥♥ 8
● Barolo '06	♥♥♥ 8
● Barolo '05	♥♥♥ 8
● Barolo '01	♥♥♥ 8
● Barolo '99	♥♥♥ 8
● Barolo '98	♥♥♥ 8
● Barolo '89	♥♥♥ 8
● Barolo '85	♥♥♥ 8
● Barolo '84	♥♥♥ 8
● Barolo '83	♥♥♥ 8
● Barolo '08	♥♥ 8
● Barolo '04	♥♥ 8
● Barolo '03	♥♥ 8

Giuseppe Mascarello e Figlio

VIA BORGONUOVO, 108
12060 MONCHIERO [CN]
TEL. 0173792126
www.mascarello1881.com

CELLAR SALES
PRE-BOOKED VISITS
ANNUAL PRODUCTION 60,000 bottles
HECTARES UNDER VINE 13.50

Mauro and Giuseppe Mascarello represent the latest generation of an estate that recounts the most ancestral tradition of Langhe. Their wines are in many respects a journey back in time. Not only Nebbiolo, but also Barbera, Dolcetto, and Freisa, are subject to long maceration followed by extended ageing in large barrels. Apparently subtle and rarefied, commencing with their hue, sometimes with surprising aromatic profiles, the Barolo selections hail from such illustrious crus as Villero, Santo Stefano di Perno, and the Monprivato vineyard in Castiglione, which also yields Cà d'Morissio, exclusively from the michet clone, in great vintages. Our latest tastings of the estate's wines showed them entirely up to their reputation. Barolo Villero 2010 is classic through and through, offering a blaze of herbs, liquorice, and red berry fruit. However, Monprivato remains in a class of its own, and the 2010 vintage enraptured us with its close-knit transparency, packed with juice and flavour.

- Barolo Monprivato '10 — ♥♥♥ 8
- Barolo Villero '10 — ♥♥ 8
- Barolo Perno V. Santo Stefano '10 — ♥♥ 8
- Barolo Monprivato '09 — ♀♀♀ 8
- Barolo Monprivato '08 — ♀♀♀ 8
- Barolo Monprivato '01 — ♀♀♀ 8
- Barolo Monprivato '85 — ♀♀♀ 8
- Barolo S. Stefano di Perno '98 — ♀♀♀ 8
- Barolo Villero '96 — ♀♀♀ 8
- Barbera d'Alba Sup. S. Stefano di Perno '09 — ♀♀ 5
- Barolo S. Stefano di Perno '09 — ♀♀ 8
- Barolo S. Stefano di Perno '08 — ♀♀ 8
- Barolo Villero '09 — ♀♀ 8
- Barolo Villero '08 — ♀♀ 8
- Langhe Nebbiolo '11 — ♀♀ 6

★Massolino

P.ZZA CAPPELLANO, 8
12050 SERRALUNGA D'ALBA [CN]
TEL. 0173613138
www.massolino.it

CELLAR SALES
PRE-BOOKED VISITS
ANNUAL PRODUCTION 120,000 bottles
HECTARES UNDER VINE 24.00
SUSTAINABLE WINERY

If you go to Langhe seeking light, ethereal wines, be sure to give the estate owned by brothers Franco and Roberto Massolino a wide berth, as their ideal type of Nebbiolo (and other wines) has enormously powerful stuffing and tannic backbone. Its close-woven supporting structure appears biting when young, but acts as a sort of fuel for long ageing – as you'd expect from legendary vineyards like Parafada, Margheria, and Vigna Rionda (on the western slope of Serralunga) and Parussi (in Castiglione Falletto). The same style characterizes the rest of the range, from barbera, dolcetto, chardonnay, and moscato, which is among the most consistent and comprehensive of the entire zone. The estate's fine range has at least three flagships. Parafada stands out among the 2011 Barolos for its austere, restrained fullness, along with the sinuous Margheria, with a soft attack and a taut finish, while the 2009 version of Vigna Rionda Riserva is more approachable and caressing than usual.

- Barolo Parafada '11 — ♥♥♥ 8
- Barolo Margheria '11 — ♥♥ 8
- Barolo V. Rionda Ris. '09 — ♥♥ 8
- Barolo '11 — ♥♥ 5
- Barolo Parussi '11 — ♥♥ 8
- Langhe Nebbiolo '13 — ♥♥ 3
- Barolo Margheria '05 — ♀♀♀ 7
- Barolo Parafada '04 — ♀♀♀ 7
- Barolo V. Rionda Ris. '08 — ♀♀♀ 8
- Barolo V. Rionda Ris. '06 — ♀♀♀ 8
- Barolo V. Rionda Ris. '98 — ♀♀♀ 7
- Barolo V. Rionda Ris. '97 — ♀♀♀ 7
- Barolo Vigna Rionda Ris. '05 — ♀♀♀ 8
- Barolo Vigna Rionda Ris. '04 — ♀♀♀ 8
- Barolo Vigna Rionda Ris. '01 — ♀♀♀ 8
- Barolo Vigna Rionda Ris. '99 — ♀♀♀ 7

Tiziano Mazzoni

VIA ROMA, 73
28010 CAVAGLIO D'AGOGNA [NO]
TEL. 3488200635
www.vinimazzoni.it

CELLAR SALES
PRE-BOOKED VISITS
ANNUAL PRODUCTION 20,000 bottles
HECTARES UNDER VINE 4.50
SUSTAINABLE WINERY

Reborn in 1999 from its ashes documented as far back as the 16th century, this year the winery owned by Tiziano Mazzoni and his family boasts efficient new premises that are well worth a visit, together with the vineyards, in order to understand what it means to cultivate small plots under vine among the woods of this evocative area of northern Piedmont. The estate's delicate, well-orchestrated reds are highly representative of the zone. Ghemme dei Mazzoni 2012 is complex and concentrated with a layered nose of earth, roots, and red berries, and a fine palate with velvety stuffing underpinned by attractive tannins, resulting in a stimulating, balanced wine that thoroughly deserved our Tre Bicchieri. Ghemme ai Livelli is warmer, true to the 2011 vintage, while Vespolina Il Ricetto 2014 exudes vitality and freshness, with a nose of black pepper and golden-leaf tobacco, accompanied by an agreeably full-flavoured palate. Colline Novaresi Nebbiolo del Monteregio 2012 vaunts restrained structure and impressive harmony.

● Ghemme dei Mazzoni '12	♈♈♈ 5
● Colline Novaresi Nebbiolo del Monteregio '13	♈♈ 3
● Colline Novaresi Vespolina Il Ricetto '14	♈♈ 3
● Ghemme ai Livelli '11	♈♈ 6
○ Iris	♈ 3
● Colline Novaresi Nebbiolo Ai Franconi '11	♈♈ 3
● Colline Novaresi Nebbiolo del Monteregio '11	♈♈ 3
● Ghemme ai Livelli '10	♈♈ 6
● Ghemme ai Livelli '09	♈♈ 6
● Ghemme dei Mazzoni '11	♈♈ 5
● Ghemme dei Mazzoni '10	♈♈ 5
● Ghemme dei Mazzoni '09	♈♈ 5
● Ghemme dei Mazzoni '08	♈♈ 5
○ Passito Le Masche	♈♈ 4

Moccagatta

S.DA RABAJÀ, 46
12050 BARBARESCO [CN]
TEL. 0173635228
www.moccagatta.eu

CELLAR SALES
PRE-BOOKED VISITS
ANNUAL PRODUCTION 65,000 bottles
HECTARES UNDER VINE 12.00
SUSTAINABLE WINERY

Franco and Sergio Minuto are world-famous for being as traditional in the vineyard as they are modern in the cellar. You need only look at their hands and listen to their stories to realize the brothers' knowledge, sensitivity, and ability in the viticultural field. It is sufficient to taste their wines year after year to understand that their "Californian" style is forging ahead undaunted with the philosophy of great grapes and lots of new oak. The winery is well worth a visit. The Cole selection has generally stood out for its more classic style, but in the 2012 vintage it joins Basarin and Bric Balin in offering riper fruit, oak, and highly extracted tannins. While this style is certainly far removed from the canons of traditional Barbaresco, it will surely find many fans, particularly considering that these are wines capable of long bottle ageing.

● Barbaresco Bric Balin '12	♈♈ 6
● Barbaresco Cole '12	♈♈ 7
● Barbaresco Basarin '12	♈ 6
● Barbaresco Bric Balin '05	♈♈♈ 6
● Barbaresco Bric Balin '04	♈♈♈ 6
● Barbaresco Bric Balin '01	♈♈♈ 6
● Barbaresco Bric Balin '90	♈♈♈ 6
● Barbaresco Cole '97	♈♈♈ 6
● Barbaresco Basarin '11	♈♈ 6
● Barbaresco Basarin '10	♈♈ 6
● Barbaresco Bric Balin '11	♈♈ 6
● Barbaresco Bric Balin '10	♈♈ 6
● Barbaresco Cole '11	♈♈ 6
● Barbaresco Cole '10	♈♈ 6
○ Langhe Chardonnay '11	♈♈ 2*
○ Langhe Chardonnay Buschet '10	♈♈ 5

Mauro Molino

FRAZ. ANNUNZIATA GANCIA, 111A
12064 LA MORRA [CN]
TEL. 017350814
www.mauromolino.com

CELLAR SALES
PRE-BOOKED VISITS
ANNUAL PRODUCTION 95,000 bottles
HECTARES UNDER VINE 12.00
SUSTAINABLE WINERY

The founder Mauro and his children
Martina and Matteo are all graduates of
the Oenological School in Alba, testifying to
a family passion handed down through the
generations. Mauro's first Barolo was
bottled in 1982,and its style has remained
almost unchanged over the decades,
concentrating first and foremost on
elegance. All the vineyard selections focus
on delicacy rather than power, with the aid
of alluring notes of French oak that are
very evident during the early years in
bottle. The Molino family's handsome
winery is back on Tre Bicchieri form with
Barolo Gallinotto 2011. Fresh menthol
notes underlie pure close-focused aromas
of red berries, enlivened by spice on an
incredibly pleasing nose. The palate is
already almost silky and the wine flows
slow and juicy through to a finish with
notes of mint and sweet tobacco. Bricco
Luciani is equally sophisticated and
velvety, while the Conca is slightly oakier.
The basic Barolo is small but well
orchestrated.

● Barolo Gallinotto '11	♟♟♟	6
● Barolo Bricco Luciani '11	♟♟	6
● Barolo '11	♟♟	5
● Barolo Conca '11	♟♟	7
● Barolo La Serra '11	♟♟	7
● Barbera d'Alba V. Gattere '00	♟♟♟	5
● Barbera d'Alba V. Gattere '97	♟♟♟	7
● Barbera d'Alba V. Gattere '96	♟♟♟	7
● Barolo Gallinotto '03	♟♟♟	6
● Barolo Gallinotto '01	♟♟♟	6
● Barolo V. Conca '00	♟♟♟	7
● Barolo V. Conca '97	♟♟♟	7
● Barolo V. Conca '96	♟♟♟	7
● Barolo '10	♟♟	5
● Barolo Bricco Luciani '10	♟♟	6
● Barolo Gallinotto '10	♟♟	6

★Monchiero Carbone

VIA SANTO STEFANO ROERO, 2
12043 CANALE [CN]
TEL. 017395568
www.monchierocarbone.com

CELLAR SALES
PRE-BOOKED VISITS
ANNUAL PRODUCTION 180,000 bottles
HECTARES UNDER VINE 25.00
SUSTAINABLE WINERY

Francesco and Lucrezia Monchiero are one
of the closest and most dynamic couples
in the wine world, determined to maximize
Roero's potential and expand the family
winery. Their production, long centred in
Canale, uses the grapes from vineyards in
some of its finest crus, like Monbirone,
Renesio, and the Frailin hill, which yields
the Printi, but also from the estates in
Vezza d'Alba and Monteu Roero, planted
with white grapes, and Priocca, planted
mainly to barbera. Printi Riserva
confirms itself a touchstone for Roero
wines. The 2011 vintage is full, fruit rich,
and tannic but balanced, with a gutsy,
lip-smacking finish. Roero Srü 2012 is
almost as good, showing fresh and
pleasant, with a fruity, floral nose and a
taut palate with good length. The two
versions of Roero Arneis 2014 are also
among the best of their kind: the mineral
Cecu d'la Biunda with good acidity, and the
fresh, floral, tangy Recit.

● Roero Printi Ris. '11	♟♟♟	5
○ Roero Arneis Cecu d'la Biunda '14	♟♟	3*
○ Roero Arneis Recit '14	♟♟	2*
● Roero Srü '12	♟♟	4
● Barbera d'Alba Pelisa '13	♟♟	2*
● Barbera d'Alba MonBirone '10	♟♟♟	4*
● Roero Printi '04	♟♟♟	5
● Roero Printi '00	♟♟♟	5
● Roero Printi '99	♟♟♟	6
● Roero Printi Ris. '10	♟♟♟	5
● Roero Printi Ris. '09	♟♟♟	5
● Roero Printi Ris. '07	♟♟♟	5
● Roero Printi Ris. '06	♟♟♟	5
● Roero Srü '06	♟♟♟	3
○ Roero Arneis Cecu d'la Biunda '13	♟♟	3*
○ Roero Arneis Recit '13	♟♟	2*

Monfalletto
Cordero di Montezemolo
Fraz. Annunziata, 67
12064 La Morra [CN]
Tel. 017350344
www.corderodimontezemolo.com

CELLAR SALES
PRE-BOOKED VISITS
ANNUAL PRODUCTION 240,000 bottles
HECTARES UNDER VINE 35.00

The age-old cedar that dominates the legendary estate of the Cordero di Montezemolo family has become a veritable symbol of the Langhe landscape. It seems to watch over the single 30-hectare plot of the Monfalletto farmstead in La Morra, divided into several vineyards, each home to specific grape varieties, chiefly nebbiolo and dolcetto, followed by barbera, chardonnay, and arneis. It is the birthplace of the Monfalletto, Bricco Gattera, and Gorette Barolos, which are joined by the Enrico VI from the Villero cru in Castiglione Falletto. They are mainly made with brief maceration and ageing in French oak barrels, in a moderately modern style. This is reflected most closely by Barolo Bricco Gattera 2011, which has fruity pulp and spicy character, but is slightly clenched by oak and alcoholic warmth on the finish. The Enrico VI of the same vintage appears more "traditional", with layered notes of quinine and forest floor, and a supple finish despite its rugged tannins.

Il Mongetto
via Piave, 2
15049 Vignale Monferrato [AL]
Tel. 0142933442
www.mongetto.it

CELLAR SALES
PRE-BOOKED VISITS
ANNUAL PRODUCTION 40,000 bottles
HECTARES UNDER VINE 13.00

Vignale Monferrato is home to Il Mongetto's guest farm, which enjoys scenic views of the surrounding hills. It offers the chance to taste the farm's gourmet products teamed with its wines. All of them are characterized by a healthy artisanal spirit that allows visitors to taste all the facets of the regional tradition. The range of wines is composed of Barbera, Grignolino, and Cortese from native grape varieties, and Merlot, Cabernet Sauvignon (blended with Barbera in the Monferrato Rosso Telegro), and Chardonnay from international cultivars. Barbera d'Asti Guera is the estate's flagship. It shows an impenetrable ruby, with an explosion of fruit and juniper berries on the nose, accompanied by a caressing, velvety palate. The Barbera Superiore also fared very well, displaying its great potential, although it is currently still slightly dominated by oak.

● Barolo Bricco Gattera '11	♥♥ 8
● Barolo Enrico VI '11	♥♥ 8
● Barbera d'Alba Sup. Funtanì '12	♥♥ 5
● Barolo Monfalletto '11	♥♥ 6
● Barolo Enrico VI '04	♀♀♀ 7
● Barolo Enrico VI '03	♀♀♀ 7
● Barolo V. Enrico VI '00	♀♀♀ 7
● Barbera d'Alba '13	♀♀ 3
● Barbera d'Alba Sup. Funtanì '11	♀♀ 5
● Barolo Bricco Gattera '10	♀♀ 8
● Barolo Enrico VI '10	♀♀ 8
● Barolo Enrico VI '09	♀♀ 8
● Barolo Monfalletto '10	♀♀ 6
● Barolo Monfalletto '09	♀♀ 6
● Dolcetto d'Alba '13	♀♀ 3
○ Langhe Chardonnay Elioro '12	♀♀ 5

● Barbera d'Asti Vign. Guera '12	♥♥ 4
● Barbera del M.to Sup. '13	♥♥ 4
● Grignolino del M.to Casalese '14	♥ 3
● M.to Rosso Telegro '12	♥ 4
● Barbera d'Asti V. Guera '09	♀♀ 4
● Barbera d'Asti V. Guera '08	♀♀ 4
● Barbera d'Asti Vign. Guera '10	♀♀ 4
● Barbera del M.to Sup. '11	♀♀ 4
● Barbera del M.to Sup. V. Mongetto '09	♀♀ 2*
● Barbera del M.to Sup. V. Mongetto '08	♀♀ 2
● Barbera del M.to Sup. Vign. Mongetto '10	♀♀ 4
● Casorzo Vign. Rudifrà '11	♀♀ 2*
● Grignolino del M.to Casalese '13	♀♀ 3
● Grignolino del M.to Casalese '12	♀♀ 3
● M.to Rosso Telegro '11	♀♀ 4
● M.to Rosso Telegro '10	♀♀ 3

Montalbera

VIA MONTALBERA, 1
14030 CASTAGNOLE MONFERRATO [AT]
TEL. 0119433311
www.montalbera.it

CELLAR SALES
PRE-BOOKED VISITS
ANNUAL PRODUCTION 400,000 bottles
HECTARES UNDER VINE 162.00

Montalbera, owned by the Morando family, has become a benchmark producer for wines from ruché and grignolino, accounting for around 55% of the total production of Ruché di Castagnole Monferrato and about 12% of Grignolino d'Asti. The policy of expansion continues, and the estates in Castagnole di Monferrato (130 hectares of vineyards planted mainly to ruché) and Castiglione Tinella (15 hectares entirely dedicated to the production of Moscato) have now been joined by one in Castiglione Falletto, with three hectares of Barolo nebbiolo. Two of the estate's versions of Ruché di Castagnole Monferrato reached our finals. La Tradizione 2014 has a concentrated, varietal nose of roses, liquorice, and fresh red berries, accompanied by a balanced, fruit-rich palate with good structure and a long, enfolding finish, while the complex Laccento 2014 has more prominent tannins and remarkable character. The rest of the range is well made.

Tenuta Montemagno

VIA CASCINA VALFOSSATO, 9
14030 MONTEMAGNO [AT]
TEL. 014163624
www.tenutamontemagno.it

CELLAR SALES
PRE-BOOKED VISITS
ACCOMMODATION AND RESTAURANT SERVICE
ANNUAL PRODUCTION 96,000 bottles
HECTARES UNDER VINE 15.00

The quality of this estate's production is earning it increasing visibility on the Monferrato wine scene. Its vineyards extend for 15 hectares north-east from Montemagno, taking in Viarigi, Altavilla, and Casorzo. They yield around a dozen wines, focusing on reds from native grape varieties: Barbera, Ruché, Grignolino , and Malvasia di Casorzo. The whites include both monovarietals and blends of Timorasso and Sauvignon Blanc. There is also a Metodo Classico from barbera and grignolino, a sparkling rosé that is a relic from an unforgotten past . The list of wines tasted included a magnificent version of Barbera d'Asti Mysterium, which reached our finals. Its fruity aromas are so elegant and pronounced as to overshadow its ageing in oak, and are accompanied by a concentrated, palate with rich pulp and a very long finish. The grid below features most of the estate's production, a sure sign of high quality.

● Ruché di Castagnole M.to La Tradizione '14	♟♟ 3*
● Ruché di Castagnole M.to Laccento '14	♟♟ 3*
● Barbera d'Asti Sup. Nuda '12	♟♟ 7
● L'Accento Passito	♟♟ 4
● Ruché di Castagnole M.to Limpronta '13	♟♟ 5
● Ruché di Castagnole M.to Prima Decade '13	♟♟ 6
● Barbera d'Asti La Ribelle '14	♟ 2
● Grignolino d'Asti Grigné '14	♟ 2
⊙ Roseus Brut	♟ 2
● Ruché di Castagnole M.to La Tradizione '13	♟♟ 3
● Ruché di Castagnole M.to Laccento '13	♟♟ 3*

● Barbera d'Asti Sup. Mysterium '12	♟♟ 4
○ M.to Bianco Musae '13	♟♟ 2*
○ M.to Bianco Nymphae '14	♟♟ 2*
○ M.to Bianco Solis Vis '13	♟♟ 2*
○ TM Brut 24 M. Cl.	♟♟ 5
● Grignolino d'Asti Ruber '14	♟ 2
● M.to Rosso Violae '12	♟ 2
● Ruché di Castagnole M.to '14	♟ 3
● Barbera d'Asti Sup. Mysterium '11	♟♟ 4
● Grignolino d'Asti Ruber '12	♟♟ 2*
● Grignolino d'Asti Ruber '11	♟♟ 2*
○ M.to Bianco Nymphae '12	♟♟ 2*
○ M.to Bianco Nymphae '11	♟♟ 2*
● M.to Rosso Violae '11	♟♟ 2*
● M.to Rosso Violae '10	♟♟ 2*
○ TM Brut M. Cl.	♟♟ 5

Monti

FRAZ. CAMIE
LOC. SAN SEBASTIANO, 39
12065 MONFORTE D'ALBA [CN]
TEL. 017378391
www.paolomonti.com

CELLAR SALES
PRE-BOOKED VISITS
ANNUAL PRODUCTION 50,000 bottles
HECTARES UNDER VINE 16.00

In 20 years as a Barolo producer, Pier Paolo Monti has never ceased to innovate, in the quest for a personality that is expressed increasingly characteristically in each wine. This commitment has yielded its fruits not only with the traditional local grape varieties, but with international ones too, particularly in the form of a Merlot that has repeatedly made waves in international comparative tastings. However, Pier Paolo is true to his Langhe heart, producing an exceptional Barbera d'Alba in addition to his Barolos. The 2012 vintage has a concentrated, elegant nose with prominent red berries and fresh herbs, and a very rich, long palate with a savoury flavour bordering on saltiness, making it alluringly drinkable. The 2011 Barolo is complex and original, with a nose ranging from citrus fruit to rain-soaked earth. On the palate the tannins are still rather severe, advising further bottle ageing.

● Barbera d'Alba '12	♟♟ 5
● Barolo del Comune di Monforte d'Alba '11	♟♟ 7
● Langhe Dossi Rossi '11	♟♟ 5
● Nebbiolo d'Alba '12	♟♟ 4
● Barbera d'Alba '11	♀♀ 5
● Barbera d'Alba '09	♀♀ 5
● Barolo '09	♀♀ 7
● Barolo '08	♀♀ 7
● Barolo Bussia '09	♀♀ 8
● Barolo del Comune di Monforte d'Alba '10	♀♀ 7
● Langhe Dossi Rossi '09	♀♀ 5
● Nebbiolo d'Alba '11	♀♀ 4
● Nebbiolo d'Alba '10	♀♀ 4
● Nebbiolo d'Alba '09	♀♀ 4

Stefanino Morra

VIA CASTAGNITO, 50
12050 CASTELLINALDO [CN]
TEL. 0173213489
www.morravini.it

CELLAR SALES
PRE-BOOKED VISITS
ANNUAL PRODUCTION 65,000 bottles
HECTARES UNDER VINE 10.00

The Morra family's estate, founded in 1925, has been making wine for three generations and is now run by Stefanino. Its vineyards, planted with the traditional Roero grape varieties (arneis, nebbiolo, barbera, and favorita) are located in three municipalities (Canale, Castellinaldo, and Vezza d'Alba), all with the typical sandy calcareous soils of the area. This year we were struck more by the basic wines than the vineyard selections, commencing with Roero Arneis 2014, among the best of its vintage, with yellow-fleshed fruit and saffron on the nose, followed by a full-flavoured palate with good stuffing and acidic length, and Barbera d'Alba 2013, with a classic nose of dark berries and hints of spice, and an earthy palate with a lively acidic finish. The Roero 2012 has a nose of red berries, spice, and Mediterranean scrubland, and a fresh, fruit-rich palate, while Sräi Riserva 2011 is juicy and finely structured, but with rather aggressive tannins.

● Barbera d'Alba '13	♟♟ 3*
○ Roero Arneis '14	♟♟ 3*
● Barbera d'Alba Castellinaldo '12	♟♟ 4
● Roero '12	♟♟ 4
● Roero Srai Ris. '11	♟♟ 5
○ Roero Arneis Vign. S. Pietro '13	♟ 3
● Barbera d'Alba '11	♀♀ 3
● Barbera d'Alba '09	♀♀ 3*
● Barbera d'Alba Castellinaldo '11	♀♀ 4
● Barbera d'Alba Castellinaldo '09	♀♀ 4
● Barbera d'Alba Castlè '09	♀♀ 5
● Roero '11	♀♀ 4
● Roero '10	♀♀ 4
○ Roero Arneis '13	♀♀ 3
○ Roero Arneis M. Cl. Elena '10	♀♀ 4
● Roero Srai Ris. '09	♀♀ 5

F.lli Mossio

FRAZ. CASCINA CARAMELLI
VIA MONTÀ, 12
12050 RODELLO [CN]
TEL. 0173617149
www.mossio.com

CELLAR SALES
PRE-BOOKED VISITS
ACCOMMODATION
ANNUAL PRODUCTION 50,000 bottles
HECTARES UNDER VINE 10.00
SUSTAINABLE WINERY

The Mossio family are internationally
renowned as great interpreters of the
dolcetto grape, presented in different
versions. The most approachable and
drinkable, while still flavoursome and
fruit-rich, is Piano delli Perdoni. It is flanked
by the intense, caressing Bricco Caramelli,
and the more recent Gamus super-
selection, aged for a year in used oak,
which is one of the most interesting
expressions of Dolcetto d'Alba. The
powerful, tannic, alcohol-rich, Dolcetto
d'Alba Superiore Gamus 2013 will come as
a pleasant surprise to aficionados after
further bottle ageing. Bricco Caramelli 2014
is already more harmonious and delicate, its
agreeably fresh palate mirroring the vintage.
The Barbera d'Alba is pleasant and well
typed, with earthy and fruity aromatic
undertones. Langhe Rosso 2012 is
compelling, suitable for fans of a mature,
oaky style.

● Dolcetto d'Alba Bricco Caramelli '14	♟♟ 3*
● Dolcetto d'Alba Sup. Gamus '13	♟♟ 4
● Barbera d'Alba '13	♟♟ 4
● Dolcetto d'Alba Piano delli Perdoni '14	♟♟ 2*
● Langhe Nebbiolo '11	♟♟ 4
● Langhe Rosso '12	♟♟ 4
● Dolcetto d'Alba Bricco Caramelli '00	♟♟♟ 3*
● Barbera d'Alba '12	♟♟ 4
● Dolcetto d'Alba Bricco Caramelli '13	♟♟ 3*
● Dolcetto d'Alba Bricco Caramelli '12	♟♟ 3
● Dolcetto d'Alba Piano delli Perdoni '13	♟♟ 2*
● Dolcetto d'Alba Piano delli Perdoni '12	♟♟ 2*
● Dolcetto d'Alba Sup. Gamvs '12	♟♟ 4
● Dolcetto d'Alba Sup. Gamvs '11	♟♟ 4
● Langhe Nebbiolo '09	♟♟ 4

Ada Nada

LOC. ROMBONE
VIA AUSARIO, 12
12050 TREISO [CN]
TEL. 0173638127
www.adanada.it

CELLAR SALES
PRE-BOOKED VISITS
ACCOMMODATION AND RESTAURANT SERVICE
ANNUAL PRODUCTION 45,000 bottles
HECTARES UNDER VINE 9.00

While the premature loss of Gian Carlo
Nada in 2012 has left its mark, this
prominent Barbaresco estate has diligently
continued his precious legacy under Elvio
and Anna Lisa. All the wines are
noteworthy, characterized by reliable quality
and very reasonable prices, which places
them among the certainties of the zone. In
recent years we have noticed higher
definition on the palate and nose,
particularly in the various versions of
Barbaresco, hinting at the winery's
ceaseless work and its refusal to rest on its
laurels. The entire list performed
satisfactorily, topped by the complex
Barbaresco Cichin 2011, with a nose of
spice, forest floor, and tobacco heralding a
solid palate with well-integrated tannins.
Barbaresco Elisa 2012, from old vines in
the Rombone cru, is still a little reticent on
the nose, but possesses stuffing and
elegance that will be able to express
themselves to the full after further ageing.

● Barbaresco Cichin '11	♟♟ 6
● Barbaresco Rombone Elisa '12	♟♟ 5
● Barbaresco Valeirano '12	♟♟ 5
● Barbera d'Alba Pierin '13	♟♟ 3
● Dolcetto d'Alba Autinot '14	♟♟ 2*
○ Roero Arneis I Pairin '14	♟♟ 3
○ Langhe Bianco Neta '14	♟ 2
● Langhe Nebbiolo Serena '14	♟ 3
● Barbaresco Cichin '09	♟♟ 6
● Barbaresco Elisa '11	♟♟ 5
● Barbaresco Elisa '09	♟♟ 5
● Barbaresco Elisa '08	♟♟ 6
● Barbaresco Valeirano '11	♟♟ 5
● Barbaresco Valeirano '09	♟♟ 5
● Barbaresco Valeirano '08	♟♟ 5
● Langhe Rosso La Bisbetica '12	♟♟ 4

★Fiorenzo Nada

VIA AUSARIO, 12c
12050 TREISO [CN]
TEL. 0173638254
www.nada.it

CELLAR SALES
PRE-BOOKED VISITS
ANNUAL PRODUCTION 40,000 bottles
HECTARES UNDER VINE 8.00

Fiorenzo's store of country wisdom has
yielded its fruits, with both his son Bruno and
his young grandson Danilo following in his
footsteps. A thorough knowledge of grapes
has been flanked by decades of experience
with cellar techniques, in which Bruno has
become an undisputed master. Indeed, all
the wines, from Dolcetto d'Alba to
Barbaresco, are meticulously crafted,
unfailingly offering an elegant interpretation
of the grape and the vintage. However, the
ones that have won the estate international
renown are the beefy Barbaresco Rombone
and the alluring Langhe Seifile, from barbera
and nebbiolo. The mouthfilling Barbaresco
Rombone 2011 is still young and fruity, with
delicate notes of quinine and tobacco hinting
at rich development. The Manzola has a
beautifully defined nose but is slightly closed
and tannic. This vintage of the inky Seifile, a
classic Langhe blend, is particularly
concentrated and assertive on the palate.

● Barbaresco Manzola '11	▼▼ 6
● Barbaresco Rombone '11	▼▼ 7
● Langhe Rosso Seifile '11	▼▼ 7
● Langhe Nebbiolo '13	▼▼ 3
● Barbaresco '01	▽▽▽ 6
● Barbaresco Manzola '08	▽▽▽ 6
● Barbaresco Manzola '06	▽▽▽ 6
● Barbaresco Rombone '10	▽▽▽ 7
● Barbaresco Rombone '09	▽▽▽ 7
● Barbaresco Rombone '07	▽▽▽ 7
● Barbaresco Rombone '06	▽▽▽ 7
● Barbaresco Rombone '05	▽▽▽ 7
● Barbaresco Rombone '04	▽▽▽ 7
● Barbaresco Rombone '99	▽▽▽ 7
● Langhe Rosso Seifile '01	▽▽▽ 6
● Seifile '93	▽▽▽ 7

Cantina dei Produttori Nebbiolo di Carema

VIA NAZIONALE, 32
10010 CAREMA [TO]
TEL. 0125811160
www.caremadoc.it

CELLAR SALES
PRE-BOOKED VISITS
RESTAURANT SERVICE
ANNUAL PRODUCTION 65,000 bottles
HECTARES UNDER VINE

It's hard to say where the smallest and most
extreme designation in upper Piedmont
would be today without the social and
viticultural support of Cantina Produttori
Nebbiolo di Carema. This is "heroic
agriculture" in the truest sense of the word:
pergolas literally emerging between the
rocks, terraced slopes engulfed by the Alps,
and late harvests of the world's most linear,
austere nebbiolo. The 81 member-growers
are equally epic, the grapes from their 17 or
so hectares of vineyards going to make an
extremely good value range, where the colour
of the label distinguishes the vintage Carema
(black) from the Riserva (white), both aged in
large barrels for 24 to 36 months. Both the
versions of Carema we tasted are excellent.
Etichetta Bianca Riserva 2011 took a Tre
Bicchieri for its elegant freshness, with hints
of gentian on the nose. The dense, close-knit
palate is remarkably fruit rich and
mouthfilling, but accompanied by fine
supporting acidity through to the finish. The
long, well-calibrated Etichetta Nera 2012 is
harmonious and pleasantly fresh, with hints
of fruit and tar.

● Carema Et. Bianca Ris. '11	▼▼▼ 3*
● Carema Et. Nera '12	▼▼ 2*
● Carema Et. Bianca '07	▽▽▽ 3*
● Carema Et. Bianca Ris. '09	▽▽▽ 3*
● Carema Et. Bianca Ris. '08	▽▽▽ 3*
● Carema '05	▽▽ 2
● Carema '04	▽▽ 2
● Carema Et. Bianca '06	▽▽ 3*
● Carema Et. Bianca '05	▽▽ 3
● Carema Et. Bianca Ris. '10	▽▽ 3*
● Carema Et. Nera '11	▽▽ 2*
● Carema Et. Nera '10	▽▽ 2*
● Carema Et. Nera '08	▽▽ 2*
● Carema Et. Nera '06	▽▽ 2*
● Carema Ris. '04	▽▽ 3*
● Carema Ris. '02	▽▽ 3

Lorenzo Negro

FRAZ. SANT'ANNA, 55
12040 MONTEU ROERO [CN]
TEL. 017390645
www.negrolorenzo.com

CELLAR SALES
PRE-BOOKED VISITS
ANNUAL PRODUCTION 35,000 bottles
HECTARES UNDER VINE 8.00
SUSTAINABLE WINERY

Although his family has belonged to the
wine world for generations, Lorenzo Negro
founded his estate just ten years ago. The
winery lies on the Serra Lupini hill, about
300 metres above sea level, and is
surrounded by its vineyards on the classic
Roero soil composed of sand, silt, and clay.
They are planted with the typical local
grape varieties, from arneis to nebbiolo,
with the addition of a few rows of bonarda,
dolcetto, and albarossa. Roero San
Francesco Riserva has returned to our
finals with a 2011 vintage offering notes of
dark berries, toast, and Mediterranean
scrubland on the nose. The full, solid palate
has good depth, with notes of fruit and
iodine on a concentrated but still slightly
clenched finish. Roero Arneis 2014
manages the vintage well, showing fresh,
fruity, and gutsy. Lastly, the well-made
Barbera d'Alba 2013 is juicy with good
stuffing, accompanied by notes of red
berries and Mediterranean scrubland.

○ Roero Arneis '14	♟♟2*
● Roero San Francesco Ris. '11	♟♟3*
● Barbera d'Alba '13	♟♟2*
● Barbera d'Alba Sup. La Nanda '11	♟3
● Barbera d'Alba '12	♟♟2*
● Barbera d'Alba '11	♟♟2*
● Barbera d'Alba Sup. La Nanda '09	♟♟3
● Barbera d'Alba Sup. La Nanda '07	♟♟3
● Barbera d'Alba Sup. La Nanda '06	♟♟3
● Langhe Nebbiolo '12	♟♟2*
○ Roero Arneis '12	♟♟2*
○ Roero Arneis '11	♟♟2*
● Roero San Francesco Ris. '10	♟♟3
● Roero San Francesco Ris. '09	♟♟3
● Roero San Francesco Ris. '08	♟♟3*
● Roero San Francesco Ris. '07	♟♟3

Negro Angelo e Figli

FRAZ. SANT'ANNA, 1
12040 MONTEU ROERO [CN]
TEL. 017390252
www.negroangelo.it

CELLAR SALES
PRE-BOOKED VISITS
ANNUAL PRODUCTION 350,000 bottles
HECTARES UNDER VINE 60.00
SUSTAINABLE WINERY

The Negro family's estate is one of the
legendary wineries that act as a benchmark
for the Roero zone. Today it has a series of
vineyards in Canale, Magliano Alfieri, Monteu
Roero, and Santo Stefano Roero, along with a
Langhe estate in Neive, where it produces
Barbaresco and Dolcetto d'Alba. All the wines
are made using the traditional local grape
varieties (arneis, favorita, nebbiolo, barbera,
and brachetto), including the sparklers
(from arneis and nebbiolo). This year the
wines presented were of exceptionally high
quality, commencing with Roero Sudisfà
Riserva 2012, which took a Tre Bicchieri for
its long, flavoursome palate with rich fruit,
good stuffing and elegant tannins. Barbaresco
Basarin Riserva 2010 is taut and gutsy, with
impressively close-focused aromas. The spicy
Barbera d'Alba Bertu 2013 is very pleasant,
with notes of dark berries, as is the fresh
Roero Arneis Serra Lupini 2014, which
focuses on fruit.

● Roero Sudisfà Ris. '12	♟♟♟6
● Barbaresco Basarin Ris. '10	♟♟7
● Barbera d'Alba Bertu '13	♟♟5
○ Roero Arneis Serra Lupini '14	♟♟2*
● Barbaresco Basarin '12	♟♟5
● Barbera d'Alba Nicolon '13	♟♟3
○ Roero Arneis Brut Giovanni Negro M. Cl. '08	♟4
● Roero Sudisfà '04	♟♟♟5
● Roero Sudisfà Ris. '10	♟♟♟6
● Roero Sudisfà Ris. '09	♟♟♟5
● Roero Sudisfà Ris. '08	♟♟♟5
● Barbaresco Basarin Ris. '09	♟♟7
● Barbera d'Alba Bertu '12	♟♟4
○ Roero Arneis Serra Lupini '13	♟♟2*
● Roero Sudisfà Ris. '11	♟♟6

Nervi

c.so Vercelli, 117
13045 Gattinara [VC]
Tel. 0163833228
www.gattinara-nervi.it

CELLAR SALES
PRE-BOOKED VISITS
ANNUAL PRODUCTION 120,000 bottles
HECTARES UNDER VINE 24.00

Erling Astrup coordinates the winery owned by four Norwegian partners that has, over the past five years, shown admirable consistency in terms of quality and trueness to terroir and tradition. Now that the anxiety surrounding possible changes in its production line has been dispelled, Nervi presents itself with a very fine range of wines that we confidently recommend to fans of Northern Nebbiolos. The hot summer of 2009 has regaled Gattinara Molsino with a clean nose of ripe fruit and pleasant spicy hints of ginger, accompanied by a remarkably powerful, well-orchestrated palate with slightly evolved notes on the finish. The well-styled Valferana 2009 is a little more rugged due to its tannin content, while the basic Gattinara of the generous 2010 vintage is mature and astringent, and the Rosé Metodo Classico is razor sharp with plenty of character.

● Gattinara Molsino '09	♥♥ 5
● Gattinara Valferana '09	♥♥ 5
○ Erbaluce di Caluso Bianca '14	♥♥ 4
● Gattinara '10	♥♥ 4
⊙ Coste della Sesia Rosa '14	♥ 3
⊙ Jefferson 1787 Rosé Dosaggio Zero M. Cl.	♥ 5
● Gattinara Podere dei Ginepri '01	♥♥♥ 5
● Gattinara Vign. Molsino '00	♥♥♥ 5
● Gattinara '08	♥♥ 4
● Gattinara '06	♥♥ 4
● Gattinara Molsino '08	♥♥ 5
● Gattinara Podere dei Ginepri '04	♥♥ 5
● Gattinara Valferana '04	♥♥ 5
● Gattinara Vign. Molsino '06	♥♥ 5
● Gattinara Vign. Molsino '04	♥♥ 5

Andrea Oberto

b.ta Simane, 11
12064 La Morra [CN]
Tel. 017350104
www.andreaoberto.com

CELLAR SALES
PRE-BOOKED VISITS
ANNUAL PRODUCTION 100,000 bottles
HECTARES UNDER VINE 16.00

When your range boasts two crus of the stature of Rocche dell'Annunziata and Brunate, it automatically gains entry to Langhe's Mount Olympus. This family-run estate, which has progressively grown over the years, is increasingly making a name for itself, especially abroad, as a first-rate producer highly representative of its terroir. The style of its wines favours structure and texture, which may go a little against current trends, but is consistent with the estate's distinctive and unmistakable hallmark. Barolo Brunate 2011, from one of the finest crus of all, proffers a nose of dried flowers, tobacco, and violets, unbending on a solid, layered palate with a prominent tannic weave that requires further bottle ageing to integrate the oak. Barolo Albarella 2011 has a slightly more austere nose, with notes of red berries and tobacco alternating with darker hints of quinine and dried flowers.

● Barolo Albarella '11	♥♥ 7
● Barolo Brunate '11	♥♥ 6
● Barolo '11	♥♥ 6
● Barolo Rocche dell'Annunziata '11	♥♥ 7
● Barbera d'Alba Giada '00	♥♥♥ 5
● Barbera d'Alba Giada '97	♥♥♥ 5
● Barbera d'Alba Giada '96	♥♥♥ 5
● Barolo Vign. Albarella '01	♥♥♥ 7
● Barolo Vign. Brunate '05	♥♥♥ 8
● Barolo Vign. Rocche dell'Annunziata '96	♥♥♥ 8
● Barbera d'Alba Giada '11	♥♥ 5
● Barolo '10	♥♥ 6
● Barolo Albarella '10	♥♥ 7
● Barolo Brunate '10	♥♥ 6
● Barolo Rocche dell'Annunziata '10	♥♥ 7
● Langhe Rosso Fabio '09	♥♥ 7

Poderi e Cantine Oddero

FRAZ. SANTA MARIA
VIA TETTI, 28
12064 LA MORRA [CN]
TEL. 017350618
www.oddero.it

CELLAR SALES
PRE-BOOKED VISITS
ANNUAL PRODUCTION 150,000 bottles
HECTARES UNDER VINE 35.00
VITICULTURE METHOD Certified Organic

The Langhe estates able to compete with
the firepower of Poderi e Cantine Oddero's
vineyards can be counted on the fingers of
one hand. Its 35 hectares include an array
of incredibly prestigious vineyards like
Villero and Rocche in Castiglione Falletto,
Brunate in La Morra, Mondoca di Bussia
Superiore in Monforte, Vigna Rionda in
Serralunga, and Gallina in Barbaresco.
Today it is headed by sisters Mariacristina
and Mariavittoria that took over from their
father Giacomo and uncle Luigi, who left to
found his own winery in 2006. They
preserve the value of a range that has long
been admired for the elegant, lean style, not
just of its Barolos. It is practically impossible
to establish a linear hierarchy among
Oddero's famous crus. The Brunate 2011
has a unique vintage charm, which is
combined with sturdier, elegantly chiselled
phenolic structure in the Villero of the same
vintage. The Brunate 2010, on the other
hand, displays top notes of resin and
menthol and a finely balanced palate.

● Barolo Brunate '11	♟♟ 8
● Barolo Brunate '10	♟♟ 8
● Barolo Villero '11	♟♟ 8
● Barbaresco Gallina '12	♟♟ 6
● Barolo Bussia V. Mondoca Ris. '09	♟♟ 8
● Barolo Rocche di Castiglione '11	♟♟ 8
● Langhe Nebbiolo '12	♟♟ 4
● Barbera d'Alba Sup. '12	♟ 4
● Barbera d'Asti Sup. Vinchio '12	♟ 4
○ Langhe Bianco Collaretto '13	♟ 3
● Barbaresco Gallina '04	♟♟♟ 6
● Barolo Bussia V. Mondoca Ris. '08	♟♟♟ 8
● Barolo Mondoca di Bussia Soprana '04	♟♟♟ 7
● Barolo Rocche di Castiglione '09	♟♟♟ 7
● Barolo V. Rionda '01	♟♟♟ 8
● Barolo V. Rionda '00	♟♟♟ 8

Vigneti Luigi Oddero

FRAZ. SANTA MARIA
B.TA BETTOLOTTI, 95
12604 LA MORRA [CN]
TEL. 0173500386
www.vignetiluigioddero.it

CELLAR SALES
PRE-BOOKED VISITS
ANNUAL PRODUCTION 110,000 bottles
HECTARES UNDER VINE 35.00
SUSTAINABLE WINERY

In 2006, after having run Poderi e Cantine
Oddero with his brother Giacomo for almost
half a century, Luigi founded his own winery
with the aid of his wife Lena and their
children. Considered one of the standard-
bearers of the Langhe tradition, he has put
his experience at the service of prestigious
vineyards, such as Rive-Parà, Plaustra, and
Bettolotti in La Morra; Rocche dei Rivera in
Castiglione Falletto; and Vigna Rionda and
Baudana in Serralunga d'Alba The range is
completed by wines made from barbera,
dolcetto, freisa, and moscato (from Cascina
Fiori in Trezzo Tinella), interpreted in the
same proudly traditional style. This year the
focus was on two Barolos whose release
had been delayed: Vigna Rionda and
Rocche Rivera 2009. The first is
characterized by warm, evolved notes,
underpinned by lively tannic structure, while
the second appears more integrated and
complete, commencing with its nose of
white pepper and pencil lead, but
particularly in its racy full-flavoured
progression.

● Barolo Rocche Rivera '09	♟♟ 8
● Barbaresco '11	♟♟ 5
● Barolo Specola '09	♟♟ 7
● Barolo V. Rionda '09	♟♟ 8
● Langhe Nebbiolo '11	♟♟ 3
● Barbera d'Alba '12	♟ 3
● Barbaresco '10	♟♟ 5
● Barbaresco '08	♟♟ 5
● Barolo '09	♟♟ 6
● Barolo '08	♟♟ 5
● Barolo Rocche Rivera '08	♟♟ 8
● Barolo Rocche Rivera '06	♟♟ 6
● Barolo V. Rionda '08	♟♟ 8
● Barolo V. Rionda '07	♟♟ 8
● Langhe Nebbiolo '10	♟♟ 3
● Langhe Nebbiolo '08	♟♟ 3

Tenuta Olim Bauda

VIA PRATA, 50
14045 INCISA SCAPACCINO [AT]
TEL. 0141702171
www.tenutaolimbauda.it

CELLAR SALES
PRE-BOOKED VISITS
ANNUAL PRODUCTION 183,000 bottles
HECTARES UNDER VINE 30.00

Diana, Dino e Gianni Bertolino are the
fourth generation to run Tenuta Olim Bauda,
the family estate founded in 1961. Its
vineyards, located in the municipalities of
Nizza Monferrato, Isola d'Asti, Fontanile,
Castelnuovo Calcea and Gavi, are
characterized by different soils, ranging
from clay to sand. They were planted
between 1950 and 2003 and, apart from
those in Gavi that are obviously home to
cortese, consist mainly of barbera e
moscato, with some grignolino and
chardonnay. We awarded a Tre Bicchieri to
the Barbera d'Asti Superiore Nizza, which
has been at the top of its class for several
years now. While full and dense, the
fruit-rich 2012 vintage manages to remain
delicate and elegance, with acidity ensuring
a long finish. The succulent Monferrato
Rosso Trigo 2013 is an original blend of
40% barbera, 30% freisa, and 30%
nebbiolo, offering spicy notes of dark
berries, with good tannins, while
Barbera d'Asti La Villa 2014 is fresh and
very pleasant.

Orsolani

VIA MICHELE CHIESA, 12
10090 SAN GIORGIO CANAVESE [TO]
TEL. 012432386
www.orsolani.it

CELLAR SALES
PRE-BOOKED VISITS
ANNUAL PRODUCTION 140,000 bottles
HECTARES UNDER VINE 19.00

The winemaking venture of the Orsolani
family, who have played a leading role in
the promotion of erbaluce as a versatile
grape variety, can be summed up as a long
mingling of intuition and pioneering
choices. It was Gian Luigi's grandfather,
Gian Francesco, who made the first Caluso
sparkler, offered the first vineyard
selections for the still Vignot Sant'Antonio
and dry La Rustìa, and restyled the
passitos. The vineyards are divided
between Caluso, Mazzé, and San Giorgio. In
addition to erbaluce, they are also planted
with barbera and neretto, while carefully
selected growers supply the grapes for
Carema Le Tabbie. This year two wines
came within a hair's breadth of a Tre
Bicchieri: Erbaluce di Caluso La Rustia and the
former Cuvée Tradizione Gran Riserva
sparkler, now known as Cuvée Tradizione
1968. The former pays the price of the
2014 vintage, with a touch less depth on
the mid-palate than in better years, while
the latter is a Metodo Classico masterpiece.

● Barbera d'Asti Sup. Nizza '12	▼▼▼ 5
● Barbera d'Asti La Villa '14	▼▼ 3*
● M.to Rosso Trigo '13	▼▼ 2*
● Barbera d'Asti Sup. Le Rocchette '13	▼▼ 4
● Grignolino d'Asti Isolavilla '14	▼▼ 3
○ Moscato d'Asti Centive '14	▼ 2
● Nebbiolo d'Alba San Pietro '12	▼ 3
● Barbera d'Asti Sup. Nizza '11	♀♀♀ 5
● Barbera d'Asti Sup. Nizza '08	♀♀♀ 5
● Barbera d'Asti Sup. Nizza '07	♀♀♀ 5
● Barbera d'Asti Sup. Nizza '06	♀♀♀ 5
● Barbera d'Asti Sup. Le Rocchette '12	♀♀ 4
● Barbera d'Asti Sup. Le Rocchette '11	♀♀ 4
● Barbera d'Asti Sup. Le Rocchette '10	♀♀ 4
● Barbera d'Asti Sup. Nizza '10	♀♀ 5
● Grignolino d'Asti Isolavilla '12	♀♀ 2*

○ Caluso M. Cl. Cuvée Tradizione 1968 '09	▼▼ 5
○ Erbaluce di Caluso La Rustia '14	▼▼ 3*
○ Caluso Bianco Vignot S. Antonio '11	▼▼ 3
○ Caluso Passito Sulé '08	▼▼ 5
○ Caluso Passito Sulé '04	♀♀♀ 5
○ Caluso Passito Sulé '98	♀♀♀ 5
○ Erbaluce di Caluso La Rustia '13	♀♀♀ 3*
○ Erbaluce di Caluso La Rustia '12	♀♀♀ 3*
○ Erbaluce di Caluso La Rustia '11	♀♀♀ 3*
○ Erbaluce di Caluso La Rustia '10	♀♀♀ 2*
○ Erbaluce di Caluso La Rustia '09	♀♀♀ 2*
○ Caluso Brut Cuvée Tradizione '10	♀♀ 4
○ Caluso Passito Sulé '07	♀♀ 5
● Carema Le Tabbie '10	♀♀ 4
○ Erbaluce di Caluso '13	♀♀ 2*

I Paglieri - Roagna

LOC. PAJÉ
S.DA PAGLIERI, 7
12050 BARBARESCO [CN]
TEL. 0173635109
www.roagna.com

CELLAR SALES
PRE-BOOKED VISITS
ANNUAL PRODUCTION 50,000 bottles
HECTARES UNDER VINE 15.00

Luca Roagna often compares his estate's philosophy to a forest when explaining it to colleagues and wine lovers. A balanced environmental habitat, soil vitality, cover cropping, and biodiversity are the guidelines adopted for the management of illustrious crus like Pajé, Montefico, and Asili in Barbaresco; Pira, in Castiglione Falletto; and Vigna Rionda in Serralunga. The result is a comprehensive range of traditional Langhe wines, topped by Nebbiolos of undisputed expressive personality, the fruit of spontaneous fermentation, long maceration of up to 100 days when the vintage allows it, and patient ageing in large barrels. This prestigious Langhe estate put up an excellent performance, showing once again how the delayed release of vintages of big wines aids their complete and truest expression. Barbaresco Crichet Pajé 2006 shows vibrant and complex, focusing on balsamic notes alternating with darker hints of quinine and liquorice.

Paitin

LOC. BRICCO
VIA SERRA BOELLA, 20
12052 NEIVE [CN]
TEL. 017367343
www.paitin.it

CELLAR SALES
PRE-BOOKED VISITS
ACCOMMODATION
ANNUAL PRODUCTION 80,000 bottles
HECTARES UNDER VINE 17.00

The estate dates back to the very beginnings of Barbaresco, at the end of the 19th century and was among one of the first to bottle and export this "new" type of wine. Since then it has gradually expanded its interests, adding a comfortable guest farm 20 years ago. Its sound vineyard selections of Barbaresco include Sorì Paitin Vecchie Vigne Riserva, of which just 4,000 bottles are produced only in the best vintages. However, it is well worth hunting down for its complexity and firm structure accompanied by a fruitiness untainted by delicate ageing in Slavonian oak. The uncomplicated Barbaresco Sorì Paitin 2012 is fresh and deliciously drinkable, while the Barbaresco Serra of the same vintage is dry, spicy and tannic. The tannin-rich 2010 Riserva is still a little edgy, and the complex Barbera d'Alba Campolive 2012 is pleasantly spicy and even a little tannic from ageing in oak.

● Barbaresco Crichët Pajé '06	♟♟♟ 8
● Barbaresco Pajè V. V. '10	♟♟ 8
● Barolo Pira '10	♟♟ 8
● Barolo Pira V. V. '10	♟♟ 8
● Barbaresco Asili V. V. '10	♟♟ 8
● Barbaresco Montefico V. V. '10	♟♟ 8
● Barbaresco Pajè '10	♟♟ 6
● Barbaresco Asili V. V. '07	♟♟♟ 8
● Barbaresco Crichët Pajé '05	♟♟♟ 8
● Barbaresco Crichët Pajé '04	♟♟♟ 8
● Barbaresco Asili V. V. '09	♟♟ 8
● Barbaresco Asili V. V. '08	♟♟ 8
● Barbaresco Montefico V. V. '09	♟♟ 8
● Barbaresco Pajè '09	♟♟ 6
● Barbaresco Pajè V. V. '09	♟♟ 8
● Barolo Pira '09	♟♟ 8

● Barbaresco Sorì Paitin '12	♟♟ 6
● Barbaresco Serra '12	♟♟ 5
● Barbaresco Sorì Paitin V. V. Ris. '10	♟♟ 8
● Barbera d'Alba Sup. Campolive '12	♟♟ 5
● Nebbiolo d'Alba Ca Veja '12	♟♟ 4
○ Langhe Arneis Elisa '14	♟ 3
● Barbaresco Sorì Paitin '07	♟♟♟ 5
● Barbaresco Sorì Paitin '04	♟♟♟ 5
● Barbaresco Sorì Paitin '97	♟♟♟ 5
● Barbaresco Sorì Paitin '95	♟♟♟ 7
● Barbaresco Sorì Paitin V. V. '04	♟♟♟ 7
● Barbaresco Sorì Paitin V. V. '01	♟♟♟ 7
● Barbaresco Sorì Paitin V. V. '99	♟♟♟ 8
● Langhe Paitin '97	♟♟♟ 5
● Barbaresco Sorì Paitin '11	♟♟ 6

Palladino

P.ZZA CAPPELANO, 9
12050 SERRALUNGA D'ALBA [CN]
TEL. 0173613108
www.palladinovini.com

CELLAR SALES
ACCOMMODATION
ANNUAL PRODUCTION 230,000 bottles
HECTARES UNDER VINE 11.00

We're in the heart of Serralunga d'Alba, one of the most evocative places in Italy as far as fine wines are concerned. The terroirs available to this interesting Langhe operation are first class, yielding a range of wines with great depth and personality. Their style shuns excess, seeking instead balance and elegance as its defining characteristics. Brilliantly accompanied into the present by Maurilio Paladino, the arrival of the new generation has marked the estate's consecration as one of the élite producers of the Langhe wine world. Those who still think Serralunga Barolos always have stiff, aggressive tannins will be pleasantly surprised by this Parafalda 2011, which displays remarkable stuffing and welcome freshness, without any marked sensation of astringency or roughness. Its pervasive, elegant aromas of currants and cherries give it strong personality. The Ornato 2011 is slightly edgier, destined for long ageing.

● Barolo Ornato '11	▼▼ 6
● Barolo Parafada '11	▼▼ 6
● Barbera d'Alba Sup. Bricco delle Olive '12	▼▼ 2*
● Barolo del Comune di Serralunga d'Alba '11	▼▼ 5
● Barbera d'Alba Sup. Bricco delle Olive '10	♀▼ 2*
● Barolo del Comune di Serralunga d'Alba '10	♀▼ 5
● Barolo Ornato '10	♀▼ 6
● Barolo Parafada '10	♀▼ 6
● Barolo San Bernardo Ris. '08	♀▼ 6

Armando Parusso

LOC. BUSSIA, 55
12065 MONFORTE D'ALBA [CN]
TEL. 017378257
www.parusso.com

CELLAR SALES
PRE-BOOKED VISITS
ANNUAL PRODUCTION 125,000 bottles
HECTARES UNDER VINE 23.00

In 1986, freshly graduated from the Oenological School in Alba, Marco Parusso started to work full time on the family estate, which had started bottling its own production in 1971. Since then, in close agreement with his sister Tiziana, he has applied a philosophy aimed at respecting nature and the unique features of every single vineyard plot to the full. The result is an array of wines with great personality, sometimes difficult and other times more accessible, which faithfully mirror every single vintage. The two Barolo Riservas, called Oro and Argento like the colour of their labels, are produced only in rare particularly good vintages. All the 2011 Barolos are characterized by great concentration, maturity, and tannic weave. They are alcohol rich, with up-front oak, and good acid backbone to balance their impressive body. The 2006 Riserva is decidedly fresh and lively, with a particularly good vivid, layered palate with prominent acidity and tannins.

● Barolo Bussia Et. Oro Ris. '06	▼▼ 8
● Barolo Bussia '11	▼▼ 8
● Barolo Mariondino '11	▼▼ 7
○ Parusso Brut M. Cl. '11	▼▼ 6
● Barbera d'Alba Sup. '13	▼ 5
● Barolo '11	▼ 6
● Barolo Le Coste di Monforte '11	▼ 8
○ Langhe Bianco Rovella '12	▼ 5
● Barbera d'Alba Sup. '00	♀♀♀ 5
● Barolo Bussia V. Munie '99	♀♀♀ 8
● Barolo Bussia V. Munie '97	♀♀♀ 8
● Barolo Bussia V. Munie '96	♀♀♀ 8
● Barolo Le Coste Mosconi '03	♀♀♀ 7
● Barolo V. V. in Mariondino Ris. '99	♀♀♀ 8
● Langhe Rosso Bricco Rovella '96	♀♀♀ 8
● Barolo Mariondino '10	♀▼ 7

Massimo Pastura
Cascina La Ghersa

VIA CHIARINA, 2
14050 MOASCA [AT]
TEL. 0141856012
www.laghersa.it

CELLAR SALES
PRE-BOOKED VISITS
ANNUAL PRODUCTION 160,000 bottles
HECTARES UNDER VINE

During the last decade Massimo Pastura decided to expand production, adopting a policy of vineyard acquisitions in several of Piedmont's finest winegrowing areas, in order to widen the estate's range. Today it comprises 12 wines, divided into three lines: Vigneti Unici, I Classici and Piagè. Barbera remains the star of the show, in various versions, but it is flanked by Moscato d'Asti, Gavi, and Colli Tortonesi Timorasso, as well as several Monferratos, mainly from international grape varieties. The 2012 vintage was another excellent one for the estate's two Barbera d'Asti flagships: Muaschae and Vignassa. The first has a delicate but complex nose of dark berries and rain-soaked earth, accompanied by a nicely fleshy palate with soft, close-knit tannins, and good length, while the second is tannic, offering notes of blackberries and plums, followed by vanilla, roasted coffee beans and incense, with rich alcohol underpinned by fresh acidity.

● Barbera d'Asti Sup. Muaschae '12	▼▼ 6
● Barbera d'Asti Sup.Vignassa '12	▼▼ 5
● Barbera d'Asti Sup. Le Cave '12	▼▼ 3
● Barbera d'Asti Piagé '14	▼ 2
● Barbera d'Asti Sup. Camparò '13	▼ 2
○ Moscato d'Asti Giorgia '14	▼ 2
● Barbera d'Asti Piagé '13	♀♀ 2*
● Barbera d'Asti Sup. Camparò '12	♀♀ 2*
● Barbera d'Asti Sup. Camparò '11	♀♀ 2*
● Barbera d'Asti Sup. Le Cave '10	♀♀ 3*
● Barbera d'Asti Sup. Muaschae '11	♀♀ 6
● Barbera d'Asti Sup.Vignassa '11	♀♀ 5
● Barbera d'Asti Sup.Vignassa '10	♀♀ 5
○ Colli Tortonesi Timorasso Sivoy '12	♀♀ 4
○ Colli Tortonesi Timorasso Timian '11	♀♀ 4
○ Moscato d'Asti Giorgia '13	♀♀ 2*

Agostino Pavia e Figli

FRAZ. BOLOGNA, 33
14041 AGLIANO TERME [AT]
TEL. 0141954125
www.agostinopavia.it

CELLAR SALES
PRE-BOOKED VISITS
ACCOMMODATION
ANNUAL PRODUCTION 75,000 bottles
HECTARES UNDER VINE 9.00

This small but solid family-run winery has been active in the area for over half a century and is housed in Cascina La Marescialla, which has also been a guest farm since 2009. Planted almost exclusively to barbera, its vineyards lie mainly around the cellar on clayey soil, with some clayey marl terrain, and are home to some vines over 50 years old. After a pause of several years when it did not send its wines to our tastings, this venerable Asti estate has returned to the Guide with its Barbera d'Asti crus. La Marescialla 2012 has a nose of quinine, citrus and dark berry fruit, accompanied by a fairly tannic, austere palate with great character. Blina 2013 is fleshier, with plenty of fresh fruit, showing dense and close focused, with a long finish, while the Casareggio 2014 is extremely pleasant and drinkable, with elegant fruit and delicate acidity.

● Barbera d'Asti Blina '13	▼▼ 2*
● Barbera d'Asti Casareggio '14	▼▼ 2*
● Barbera d'Asti Sup. La Marescialla '12	▼▼ 4
● Barbera d'Asti Sup. Moliss '12	▼ 2
○ Grignolino d'Asti '14	▼ 2
● Barbera d'Asti Bricco Blina '09	♀♀ 2*
● Barbera d'Asti La Marescialla '08	♀♀ 4
● Barbera d'Asti La Marescialla '07	♀♀ 4
● Barbera d'Asti Sup. La Marescialla '06	♀♀ 4
● Barbera d'Asti Sup. La Marescialla '05	♀♀ 4
● Barbera d'Asti Sup. Moliss '07	♀♀ 2
● Barbera d'Asti Sup. Moliss '06	♀♀ 2
○ Grignolino d'Asti '09	♀♀ 2*
○ Grignolino d'Asti '08	♀♀ 2*
● M.to Rosso Talin '06	♀♀ 3
● Monferrato Rosso Talin '07	♀♀ 3

★Pecchenino

B.TA VALDIBERTI, 59
12063 DOGLIANI [CN]
TEL. 017370686
www.pecchenino.com

CELLAR SALES
PRE-BOOKED VISITS
ACCOMMODATION
ANNUAL PRODUCTION 130,000 bottles
HECTARES UNDER VINE 28.00
SUSTAINABLE WINERY

Its two centuries of history are certainly important, but the contribution that each generation has given the winery has been even more decisive. Today it vaunts 28 hectares of vineyards, tended with sustainable methods. The grape varieties have also changed over the years, not only with the addition of small amounts of white international cultivars for the complex Langhe Maestro, but above all through the repeated acquisition of Barolo nebbiolo crus in different positions in Monforte. The flagships are nonetheless still both from dolcetto and are aged in oak: two years for the exceptionally full Dogliani Bricco Botti, and one for the renowned, elegant Sirì d'Jermu. The valid Dogliani Superiore Bricco Botti 2012 stands out from the crowd with rare complexity and length for its type. It is a big, enjoyable wine, with sweet tannins and a hint of freshness on the palate. Of the two Barolos, we preferred the complex, fresh San Giuseppe. Barbera Quass 2013 has an interesting personality, with a caressing, close-woven palate.

● Barolo San Giuseppe '11	♥♥ 6
● Dogliani Sup. Bricco Botti '12	♥♥ 4
● Barbera d'Alba Quass '13	♥♥ 4
● Barolo Le Coste di Monforte '11	♥♥ 7
● Dogliani Sup. Sirì d'Jermu '13	♥♥ 4
● Dogliani San Luigi '14	♥ 3
● Barolo Le Coste '05	♥♥♥ 8
● Dogliani Bricco Botti '07	♥♥♥ 4
● Dogliani Sirì d'Jermu '09	♥♥♥ 3*
● Dogliani Sirì d'Jermu '06	♥♥♥ 4
● Dogliani Sup. Bricco Botti '10	♥♥♥ 4*
● Dolcetto di Dogliani S. Luigi '00	♥♥♥ 4*
● Dolcetto di Dogliani Sirì d'Jermu '03	♥♥♥ 3
● Dolcetto di Dogliani Sirì d'Jermu '01	♥♥♥ 3*
● Dolcetto di Dogliani Sup. Bricco Botti '04	♥♥♥ 4

Pelissero

FRAZ. FERRERE SOPRANA
VIA FERRERE, 10
12050 TREISO [CN]
TEL. 0173638430
www.pelissero.com

CELLAR SALES
PRE-BOOKED VISITS
ANNUAL PRODUCTION 250,000 bottles
HECTARES UNDER VINE 40.00

Giorgio Pelissero is a tireless traveller, convinced that Barbaresco should be esteemed and acknowledged throughout the world as one of its few great red wines. His estate has a well-equipped modern cellar able to transform the grapes of its five vineyards into approximately 250,000 bottles of wine each year. The finest cru is Vanotu, purchased and replanted by the Pelissero family in the 1970s, but a tour of the Tulin, Piani, Augenta, and Munfrina vineyards reveals how well aspected they all are, offering ideal growing conditions. The Vanotu selection is the most consistent on the palate and is marked by a sweet touch of new oak on the nose. The Nubiola offers a nose of spice rather than the classic red berries, and a balanced palate with good alcohol, while the Tulin has clean notes of oak and cocoa powder on the nose and powerful, dry tannins on the palate.

● Barbaresco Vanotu '12	♥♥ 8
● Barbaresco Nubiola '12	♥♥ 5
● Barbaresco Tulin '12	♥♥ 7
● Dolcetto d'Alba Augenta '14	♥♥ 3
● Langhe Long Now '12	♥♥ 5
● Langhe Nebbiolo '13	♥♥ 3
● Dolcetto d'Alba Munfrina '14	♥ 2
○ Langhe Favorita Le Nature '14	♥ 2
● Barbaresco Vanotu '08	♥♥♥ 8
● Barbaresco Vanotu '07	♥♥♥ 8
● Barbaresco Vanotu '06	♥♥♥ 8
● Barbaresco Vanotu '01	♥♥♥ 7
● Barbaresco Vanotu '99	♥♥♥ 7
● Barbaresco Vanotu '97	♥♥♥ 6
● Barbaresco Vanotu '95	♥♥♥ 6
● Barbaresco Vanotu '10	♥♥ 8

Elio Perrone

s.da San Martino, 3bis
12053 Castiglione Tinella [CN]
Tel. 0141855803
www.elioperrone.it

CELLAR SALES
PRE-BOOKED VISITS
ANNUAL PRODUCTION 200,000 bottles
HECTARES UNDER VINE 14.00
SUSTAINABLE WINERY

The Perrone family have been growing
moscato on the hills around Castiglione
Tinella since the end of the 19th century.
Stefano Perrone has run the estate since
1989, transforming it into one of the zone's
leading producers. Moscato, grown at an
average altitude of 360 metres, accounts
for the lion's share, but barbera,
chardonnay, and brachetto are also grown
in the municipality of Isola d'Asti, where the
winery purchased a barbera vineyard
planted in 1932 15 years ago. These old
vineyards yield Barbera d'Asti Superiore
Mongovone 2013, among the best
Barberas tasted this year, with notes of
plums and cherries on the nose,
accompanied by hints of spice and
rain-soaked earth, and a long, flavoursome,
fruit-rich palate with great freshness and
balance. Moscato d'Asti Sourgal 2014 is
also well made, showing finesse and rich
flesh, as is Barbera d'Asti Tasmorcan 2014,
with pleasant, approachable fruit, nicely
underpinned by acidity.

● Barbera d'Asti Sup. Mongovone '13	♥♥	5
● Barbera d'Asti Tasmorcan '14	♥♥	2*
○ Moscato d'Asti Sourgal '14	♥♥	2*
● Barbera d'Asti Grivò '06	♀♀	3*
● Barbera d'Asti Sup. Mongovone '12	♀♀	5
● Barbera d'Asti Sup. Mongovone '11	♀♀	5
● Barbera d'Asti Sup. Mongovone '08	♀♀	5
● Barbera d'Asti Sup. Mongovone '07	♀♀	5
● Barbera d'Asti Sup. Mongovone '06	♀♀	5
● Barbera d'Asti Tasmorcan '13	♀♀	2*
● Barbera d'Asti Tasmorcan '10	♀♀	2*
● Barbera d'Asti Tasmorcan '09	♀♀	2*
● Barbera d'Asti Tasmorcan '08	♀♀	2
○ Gi '13	♀♀	2*
○ Moscato d'Asti Sourgal '13	♀♀	2*
○ Moscato d'Asti Sourgal '10	♀♀	2*

Cantina Pertinace

loc. Pertinace, 2
12050 Treiso [CN]
Tel. 0173442238
www.pertinace.it

CELLAR SALES
PRE-BOOKED VISITS
ANNUAL PRODUCTION 500,000 bottles
HECTARES UNDER VINE 80.00

The quality of this important cooperative
winery, located in the celebrated town of
Treiso, has risen year after year, while its
prices have remained very reasonable in
relation to the quality of the various wines,
thus becoming an excellent benchmark in
the Barbaresco production zone for many
Italian and foreign wine lovers. Its
president Bruno Fiori and manager and
oenologist Cesare Barbero, the founder's
son, ensure a strict and professionally run
operation for all the growers involved. Our
tastings showed the very high average
level of the range, topped by Barbaresco
Castellizzano 2012, which is distinguished
by a very nicely layered nose of dried
violets, quinine, and tobacco, with
balsamic hints, and a palate underpinned
by solid but not invasive tannins.
Barbaresco Marcarini 2012 is slightly less
complex, still a little austere and
introverted, but with excellent potential for
the future. We were also impressed by
Dolcetto d'Alba 2014, which is fresh and
agreeable despite the difficult vintage.

● Barbaresco Castellizzano '12	♥♥	5
● Barbaresco '12	♥♥	5
● Barbaresco Marcarini '12	♥♥	5
● Barbaresco Nervo '12	♥♥	5
● Barbera d'Alba '13	♥♥	2*
● Dolcetto d'Alba '14	♥♥	2*
● Langhe Nebbiolo '13	♥♥	3
● Barbaresco '11	♀♀	5
● Barbaresco '08	♀♀	5
● Barbaresco Marcarini '11	♀♀	5
● Barbaresco Vign. Castellizzano '11	♀♀	5
● Barbaresco Vign. Castellizzano '08	♀♀	5
● Barbaresco Vign. Nervo '11	♀♀	5
● Barbera d'Alba '12	♀♀	2*
● Dolcetto d'Alba Vign. Castellizzano '13	♀♀	3
● Dolcetto d'Alba Vign. Nervo '13	♀♀	2*

Le Piane

VIA CERRI, 10
28010 BOCA [NO]
TEL. 3483354185
www.bocapiane.com

CELLAR SALES
PRE-BOOKED VISITS
ANNUAL PRODUCTION 45,000 bottles
HECTARES UNDER VINE 8.00

Cristoph Künzli's merits go far beyond aspects of production and quality. Indeed, fact that Boca is now a lively designation is largely due to the almost idealistic work carried out at Le Piane by the Swiss importer and grower, after having taken over the estate from Antonio Cerri in the early 1990s. Its few hectares of vineyards consist of dozens of little plots planted mainly with nebbiolo, croatina and vespolina, some of which trained with the traditional "maggiorina" system. In recent years the range has been expanded with new wines like Mimmo and Plinius I, although the style remains the same, focusing on citrussy structure and backbone. In recent years the estate brilliantly run by Christoph Künzli has accustomed us to rich, well-typed wines with lots of personality, from the simple Maggiorina to the complex Boca. However, unfortunately this year, for various reasons, we were unable to taste any new wines and had to console ourselves by retasting a few older ones.

● Boca '10	♀♀♀ 7
● Boca '08	♀♀♀ 7
● Boca '06	♀♀♀ 6
● Boca '05	♀♀♀ 6
● Boca '04	♀♀♀ 6
● Boca '03	♀♀♀ 6
● Boca '07	♀♀ 7
● Colline Novaresi La Maggiorina '09	♀♀ 3
● Colline Novaresi Le Piane '09	♀♀ 5
● Colline Novaresi Le Piane '08	♀♀ 5
● Colline Novaresi Le Piane '07	♀♀ 5
● La Maggiorina '11	♀♀ 3
● Maggiorina '12	♀♀ 3
● Mimmo '11	♀♀ 5
● Piane '11	♀♀ 5

Pico Maccario

VIA CORDARA, 87
14046 MOMBARUZZO [AT]
TEL. 0141774522
www.picomaccario.com

CELLAR SALES
PRE-BOOKED VISITS
ANNUAL PRODUCTION 650,000 bottles
HECTARES UNDER VINE 70.00

Brothers Pico and Vitaliano Maccario founded their estate in 1997 in Mombaruzzo, a single plot of 70 hectares of vineyards on the medium-textured clayey soils in the heart of the Barbera d'Asti designation. So approximately 60 hectares of vineyards are planted to barbera, accompanied by four hectares of merlot, two each of cabernet sauvignon, chardonnay, and sauvignon, one hectare of freisa, and another two of favorita. Pico Maccario makes its debut in our Guide this year thanks to two very well-made versions of Barbera d'Asti. Lavignone 2014 proffers a nose of fresh herbs, cherries, and liquorice, and a complex, layered palate with remarkable depth for the vintage, while Tre Roveri 2013 is rather dark on the nose due to spicy oak notes, but fresher on the dynamic, easy-drinking palate. Barbera d'Asti Superiore Epico 2012, one of the estate's top wines, is less spectacular, showing supple but rather evolved.

● Barbera d'Asti Lavignone '14	♀♀ 3
● Barbera d'Asti Sup. Tre Roveri '13	♀♀ 4
● Barbera d'Asti Sup. Epico '12	♀ 5

Pio Cesare

VIA CESARE BALBO, 6
12051 ALBA [CN]
TEL. 0173440386
www.piocesare.it

ANNUAL PRODUCTION 400,000 bottles
HECTARES UNDER VINE 70.00

One of the best-known names in Piedmont
wine was officially founded in 1881 by
Cesare Pio. It is synonymous with historical
awareness, international vision, and high
production figures by Langhe standards. Its
vineyards cover an area of 70 hectares,
both in the Barolo zone (the Ornato,
Colombaro, Gustava, Roncaglie, and Ravera
farmsteads) and the Barbaresco
designation (Il Bricco and Santo Stefanetto),
but it also purchases grapes from growers
selected by Pio Boffa and Cesare
Benvenuto. The estate's Nebbiolos display
a quietly innovative sensibility in respect to
its early years, but the quality of its range
has remained consistent and distinctive.
Once again this year Pio Cesare presented
a complementary range vaunting complete
stylistic and qualitative coherence.
Nebbiolo-based wines account for the lion's
share, headed by a Barolo Ornato 2011
that is at the same time powerful and
sophisticated, with rich fruity sensations.

● Barolo Ornato '11	▼▼▼ 8
● Barbaresco '11	▼▼ 8
● Barbaresco Bricco di Treiso '11	▼▼ 8
○ Langhe Chardonnay Piodilei '13	▼▼ 6
● Barbera d'Alba '13	▼▼ 4
○ Langhe Chardonnay L'Altro '14	▼▼ 6
○ Langhe Nebbiolo '12	▼▼ 5
● Langhe Rosso Il Nebbio '14	▼▼ 4
● Barbaresco Il Bricco '97	♀♀♀ 8
● Barolo Ornato '10	♀♀♀ 8
● Barolo Ornato '09	♀♀♀ 8
● Barolo Ornato '08	♀♀♀ 8
● Barolo Ornato '06	♀♀♀ 8
● Barolo Ornato '05	♀♀♀ 8
● Barolo Ornato '89	♀♀♀ 8
● Barolo Ornato '85	♀♀♀ 8

Luigi Pira

VIA XX SETTEMBRE, 9
12050 SERRALUNGA D'ALBA [CN]
TEL. 0173613106
pira.luigi@alice.it

CELLAR SALES
PRE-BOOKED VISITS
ANNUAL PRODUCTION 50,000 bottles
HECTARES UNDER VINE 12.00

Gianpaolo and Romolo Pira's wines closely
reflect the terroir of Serralunga d'Alba. The
brothers have taken over the winery from
their father Luigi, who founded it in the
1950s, initially selling its grapes and
subsequently deciding to make them into
wine and bottle it under his own name.
Although their Nebbiolos were originally
labelled as belonging to the "modernist"
school, over the years they have gradually
acquired a more contemporary sensitivity,
with cellar processes tailored to the
character of the individual crus. Generally
speaking, the "classic" Barolo and the
Margheria are aged in large barrels, while
barriques, tonneaux, and 2,500-litre
barrels are used for the Marenca and the
Vigna Rionda. Pira's entire range is on top
form, commencing with Barolo Vigna
Rionda 2011 which focuses on lightness
and harmony on the palate, and the
bigger, riper Margheria. However both
are eclipsed in depth and dynamism by
the Marenca 2011, which is slightly edgy
on the finish but holds great promise for
the future.

● Barolo Marenca '11	▼▼▼ 7
● Barolo Margheria '11	▼▼ 6
● Barolo V. Rionda '11	▼▼ 8
● Barbera d'Alba '13	▼▼ 3
● Barolo del Comune di Serralunga d'Alba '11	▼▼ 5
● Langhe Nebbiolo '13	▼▼ 3
● Barolo Marenca '09	♀♀♀ 7
● Barolo Marenca '08	♀♀♀ 7
● Barolo V. Marenca '01	♀♀♀ 7
● Barolo V. Marenca '97	♀♀♀ 8
● Barolo V. Rionda '06	♀♀♀ 8
● Barolo V. Rionda '04	♀♀♀ 8
● Barolo V. Rionda '00	♀♀♀ 8
● Barolo Marenca '10	♀♀ 7
● Barolo V. Rionda '10	♀♀ 8

E. Pira & Figli
Chiara Boschis

VIA VITTORIO VENETO, 1
12060 BAROLO [CN]
TEL. 017356247
www.pira-chiaraboschis.com

CELLAR SALES
PRE-BOOKED VISITS
ANNUAL PRODUCTION 35,000 bottles
HECTARES UNDER VINE 8.50
VITICULTURE METHOD Certified Organic

Chiara Boschis, who won her first Tre Bicchieri for her Barolo Riserva from the 1990 vintage, has remained the same young woman as back then: dynamic, full of plans, and a tireless worker. The estate's vineyards in the municipality of Barolo have recently been joined by a four-hectare plot in the Mosconi cru in Monforte, which is already yielding excellent results with the aid of Chiara's skilled brother Giorgio. The big, complex Barolo Cannubi 2011 is also an excellent interpretation of the vineyard, showing as elegant and balanced as ever but with fuller, juicier fruit than in cooler vintages, earning it a Tre Bicchieri. Barolo Mosconi has an elegant nose but is harsher and more incisive on the palate, in keeping with the Monforte terroir. However, it will mellow in the bottle. The Via Nova is more approachable and very alluring, already showing close focused and easy drinking.

Paolo Giuseppe Poggio

VIA ROMA, 67
15050 BRIGNANO FRASCATA [AL]
TEL. 0131784929
www.cantinapoggio.com

CELLAR SALES
PRE-BOOKED VISITS
ANNUAL PRODUCTION 18,000 bottles
HECTARES UNDER VINE 3.50

Paolo Poggio's little estate is located in Val Curone, a beautiful Apennine valley on the border between Piedmont and Lombardy, which has also been a route to the coast since ancient times. It is the perfect setting for Paolo's artisanal operation, which continues the work his family has carried out for generations. The three hectares of vineyards yield seven different wines, which faithfully reflect the terroir. They are planted with timorasso, cortese, and moscato for white wines, barbera and croatina for reds, and bonarda and freisa, blended with barbera in the Teo. Ronchetto 2013 is deep yellow, with a nose of sweet spice and fruit, and a long, concentrated palate with good supporting acidity. Derio is a Barbera with an impenetrable ruby hue and a spicy nose vaunting hints of plums and juniper, accompanied by a complex, potent palate with a long, alcohol-rich finish.

● Barolo Cannubi '11	🏆🏆🏆 8
● Barolo Mosconi '11	🏆🏆 8
● Barbera d'Alba Sup. '13	🏆🏆 4
● Barolo Via Nuova '11	🏆🏆 8
● Langhe Nebbiolo '13	🏆🏆 4
● Dolcetto d'Alba '14	🏆 2
● Barolo '94	🏆🏆🏆 7
● Barolo Cannubi '10	🏆🏆🏆 8
● Barolo Cannubi '05	🏆🏆🏆 8
● Barolo Cannubi '00	🏆🏆🏆 8
● Barolo Cannubi '97	🏆🏆🏆 8
● Barolo Cannubi '96	🏆🏆🏆 8
● Barolo Ris. '90	🏆🏆🏆 8
● Barolo Cannubi '09	🏆🏆 8
● Barolo Mosconi '10	🏆🏆 8
● Barolo Via Nuova '10	🏆🏆 8

● Colli Tortonesi Barbera Campo La Bà '13	🏆🏆 2*
● Colli Tortonesi Barbera Derio '11	🏆🏆 3
○ Colli Tortonesi Timorasso Ronchetto '13	🏆🏆 2*
● Colli Tortonesi Croatina Prosone '12	🏆 2
● Colli Tortonesi Barbera Campo La Bà '12	🏆🏆 2*
● Colli Tortonesi Barbera Campo La Bà '11	🏆🏆 2*
● Colli Tortonesi Barbera Campo La Bà '09	🏆🏆 2*
● Colli Tortonesi Barbera Campo La Bà '08	🏆🏆 2*
● Colli Tortonesi Barbera Derio '09	🏆🏆 3
○ Colli Tortonesi Cortese Campogallo '12	🏆🏆 1*
● Colli Tortonesi Croatina Prosone '10	🏆🏆 2*
● Colli Tortonesi Rosso Prosone '07	🏆🏆 1*
○ Colli Tortonesi Timorasso Ronchetto '12	🏆🏆 2*
○ Colli Tortonesi Timorasso Ronchetto '11	🏆🏆 3
○ Colli Tortonesi Timorasso Ronchetto '10	🏆🏆 2*
○ Colli Tortonesi Timorasso Ronchetto '09	🏆🏆 2*

Pomodolce

via IV Novembre, 7
15050 Montemarzino [AL]
Tel. 0131878135
www.pomodolce.it

CELLAR SALES
PRE-BOOKED VISITS
RESTAURANT SERVICE
ANNUAL PRODUCTION 14,000 bottles
HECTARES UNDER VINE 4.00
VITICULTURE METHOD Certified Organic

Pomodolce was founded in 2005, but is only the latest development in the history of the Davico family, who have been vignerons for generations. Their four hectares of vineyards are tended with organic methods and lie in three different zones – Fontanino, Pomodolce, and Barone – on well-aspected clayey limestone soils, at altitudes above 350 metres. They are home to the classic Tortona grape varieties of timorasso, barbera, and croatina, plus nebbiolo, which is little grown locally. The vines are Guyot-trained and planted with a density of 3,500–4,500 per hectare. Grue and Diletto are very different commencing from their colour, the former showing a more evolved pale gold, and the latter a vivid straw yellow. Grue offers a nose of dried herbs, tobacco, and spice, while Diletto has notes of candy floss, fruit, and spice. Last but not least, Grue has a rich, powerful palate with attractive freshness, while Diletto is softer.

○ Colli Tortonesi Timorasso Diletto '13	🍷🍷 3*
○ Colli Tortonesi Timorasso Grue '13	🍷🍷 5
● Colli Tortonesi Croatina Fontanino '12	🍷🍷 3
● Colli Tortonesi Monleale Marsen '12	🍷🍷 4
○ Colli Tortonesi Timorasso Derthona Grue '07	🍷🍷🍷 4
● Colli Tortonesi Barbera Cherubino '11	🍷🍷 2*
● Colli Tortonesi Barbera Marsèn '10	🍷🍷 4
● Colli Tortonesi Barbera Marsèn '09	🍷🍷 4
● Colli Tortonesi Croatina Fontanino '10	🍷🍷 3
● Colli Tortonesi Monleale Marsen '11	🍷🍷 4
○ Colli Tortonesi Timorasso Diletto '12	🍷🍷 3
○ Colli Tortonesi Timorasso Diletto '11	🍷🍷 3
○ Colli Tortonesi Timorasso Diletto '10	🍷🍷 3*
○ Colli Tortonesi Timorasso Grue '11	🍷🍷 5
○ Colli Tortonesi Timorasso Grue '10	🍷🍷 5
○ Petit Derthona '12	🍷🍷 4

Marco Porello

c.so Alba, 71
12043 Canale [CN]
Tel. 0173979324
www.porellovini.it

CELLAR SALES
PRE-BOOKED VISITS
ANNUAL PRODUCTION 130,000 bottles
HECTARES UNDER VINE 15.00

The Porello family's winery is split between two premises: a modern cellar for fermentation and bottling in Canale, which also comprises the headquarters, and an ageing cellar in Guarene, next to the castle. Its vineyards are in the municipalities of Canale and Vezza d'Alba, with prestigious crus like Mombirone, Bric Mommiano, and Tanone, on mainly sandy, mineral-rich soils, except for the barbera plots, on clayey limestone terrain. Roero Toretta is missing this year, replaced by Nebbiolo d'Alba 2013, with smoky, fruity notes and good fruit and length. The Roero Arneis 2014 stands out in this difficult vintage, showing fresh and citrussy, long and nicely underpinned by acidity, in contrast to the less lively Roero Arneis Camestrì, with rich yellow-fleshed fruit and a rather clenched finish. The complex, juicy Barbera d'Alba Filatura 2013 is also well made, as is the pleasant, full-flavoured Langhe Favorita 2014.

○ Roero Arneis '14	🍷🍷 2*
● Barbera d'Alba Filatura '13	🍷🍷 3
○ Langhe Favorita '14	🍷🍷 2*
● Nebbiolo d'Alba '13	🍷🍷 3
○ Roero Arneis Camestrì '14	🍷🍷 3
● Barbera d'Alba Mommiano '14	🍷 2
● Roero Torretta '06	🍷🍷🍷 3*
● Roero Torretta '04	🍷🍷🍷 3*
● Barbera d'Alba Filatura '12	🍷🍷 3
● Barbera d'Alba Filatura '11	🍷🍷 3
● Barbera d'Alba Mommiano '13	🍷🍷 2*
● Barbera d'Alba Mommiano '12	🍷🍷 2*
○ Roero Arneis '12	🍷🍷 2*
○ Roero Arneis Camestrì '12	🍷🍷 2*
● Roero Torretta '11	🍷🍷 3*
● Roero Torretta '10	🍷🍷 3*

Guido Porro

VIA ALBA, 1
12050 SERRALUNGA D'ALBA [CN]
TEL. 0173613306
www.guidoporro.com

CELLAR SALES
PRE-BOOKED VISITS
ACCOMMODATION
ANNUAL PRODUCTION 35,000 bottles
HECTARES UNDER VINE 8.00

The vineyards surrounding Guido Porro's winery in Serralunga d'Alba form practically a single plot. We're literally in the heart of Lazzarito, a veritable grand cru on the western slope, long associated with wines with balsamic energy and full-flavoured power. Nebbiolo is flanked by barbera and dolcetto in the two neighbouring plots, and yields Barolos with very different characters. The Lazzairasco is generally vigorous and tannic, while the Santa Caterina is decidedly lighter and more graceful. However, they evidently share the same style, also due to their classic fermentation in steel and concrete and their long ageing in 2,500-litre barrels. Barolo Lazzairasco 2011 took our top accolade for an impressive and very balanced performance, displaying fine-grained tannins and a lingering finish. Barolo Vigna Santa Caterina 2011 is also beautifully delineated, offering notes of medicinal herbs, accompanied by weighty but well-behaved tannins.

● Barolo V. Lazzairasco '11	♟♟♟ 5
● Barolo Gianetto '11	♟♟ 5
● Barolo V. Santa Caterina '11	♟♟ 5
● Barbera d'Alba V. Santa Caterina '14	♟♟ 3
● Dolcetto d'Alba '14	♟ 3
● Lange Nebbiolo Camilu '14	♟ 4
● Barolo V. Lazzairasco '09	♟♟♟ 5
● Barolo V. Lazzairasco '07	♟♟♟ 5
● Barbera d'Alba Santa Caterina '11	♀♀ 3
● Barbera d'Alba V. Santa Caterina '12	♀♀ 3
● Barolo Santa Caterina '09	♀♀ 5
● Barolo V. Lazzairasco '10	♀♀ 5
● Barolo V. Santa Caterina '10	♀♀ 5
● Barolo V. Santa Caterina '08	♀♀ 5*
● Barolo V. Santa Caterina '07	♀♀ 5
● Lange Nebbiolo Camilu '11	♀♀ 4

Post dal Vin
Terre del Barbera

FRAZ. POSSAVINA
VIA SALIE, 19
14030 ROCCHETTA TANARO [AT]
TEL. 0141644143
www.postdalvin.com

CELLAR SALES
PRE-BOOKED VISITS
ANNUAL PRODUCTION 80,000 bottles
HECTARES UNDER VINE 100.00

Post dal Vin – Terre del Barbera is a cooperative winery with around 100 member growers, whose vineyards lie mainly in the municipalities of Rocchetta Tanaro, Cortiglione, and Masio. True to tradition, barbera is king, yielding most of the wines, proposed in various versions. However, the winery also handles the other classic Monferrato grape varieties, like grignolino, dolcetto, freisa, and moscato. As always, Post dal Vin offers solid, well-made Barbera d'Asti. Bricco Fiore 2013 has a nose of medicinal herbs, spice, and dark berries, accompanied by a supple palate with up-front fruit. Castagnassa 2013 is denser and more concentrated, but slightly less well defined, with still prominent oak notes, while Maricca 2014 is smaller, in keeping with the vintage, but supple and easy drinking.

● Barbera d'Asti Castagnassa '13	♟♟ 2*
● Barbera d'Asti Maricca '14	♟♟ 2*
● Barbera d'Asti Sup. Bricco Fiore '13	♟♟ 2*
● Barbera d'Asti Maricca '12	♀♀ 2*
● Barbera d'Asti Maricca '11	♀♀ 2*
● Barbera d'Asti Maricca '10	♀♀ 2*
● Barbera d'Asti Sup. BriccoFiore '12	♀♀ 2*
● Barbera d'Asti Sup. BriccoFiore '11	♀♀ 2*
● Barbera d'Asti Sup. BriccoFiore '09	♀♀ 2*
● Barbera d'Asti Sup. Castagnassa '12	♀♀ 2*
● Barbera d'Asti Sup. Castagnassa '11	♀♀ 2*
● Barbera d'Asti Sup. Castagnassa '10	♀♀ 2*
● Barbera d'Asti Sup. Castagnassa '09	♀♀ 2
● Grignolino d'Asti '13	♀♀ 1*
● Grignolino d'Asti '12	♀♀ 1*
● Grignolino d'Asti '11	♀♀ 1*

Giovanni Prandi

FRAZ. CASCINA COLOMBÈ
VIA FARINETTI, 5
12055 DIANO D'ALBA [CN]
TEL. 017369248
www.prandigiovanni.it

CELLAR SALES
PRE-BOOKED VISITS
ANNUAL PRODUCTION 20,000 bottles
HECTARES UNDER VINE 5.00
SUSTAINABLE WINERY

Alessandro Prandi's range of wines is closely associated with tradition and varietal stamping, in both the choice of grape varieties and the vinification methods used. Consequently, the reds are almost entirely from dolcetto and barbera, and the whites from arneis, with the exception of a small amount of chardonnay. Steel reigns supreme in the cellar, in order to preserve the freshness and soundness of the fruit. A small but impressive winery. Despite the difficult summer of 2014, Alessandro Prandi managed to obtain vivid, fragrant, fresh-tasting grapes from his vineyards. Consequently, the Sörì Cristina is clean and elegant, offering a harmonious palate with discreet tannins and classic bitter almond notes on the finish. The sound Sörì Colombè is slightly more powerful and confident While the Arneis is not particularly fresh, it is still extremely drinkable, and the Barbera d'Alba is fruity and well orchestrated.

● Dolcetto di Diano d'Alba Sörì Cristina '14	🏆🏆 2*
● Barbera d'Alba '14	🏆🏆 2*
● Dolcetto di Diano d'Alba Sörì Colombè '14	🏆🏆 2*
○ Langhe Arneis '14	🏆 2
● Nebbiolo d'Alba '13	🏆 3
● Barbera d'Alba Santa Eurosia '12	🏆🏆 2*
● Dolcetto di Diano d'Alba Sörì Cristina '13	🏆🏆 2*
● Dolcetto di Diano d'Alba Sörì Cristina '12	🏆🏆 2*
● Dolcetto di Diano Sörì Colombè '13	🏆🏆 2*
● Dolcetto di Diano Sörì Colombè '12	🏆🏆 2*
● Dolcetto di Diano Sörì Colombè '11	🏆🏆 2*
● Dolcetto di Diano Sörì Colombè '10	🏆🏆 2*
● Dolcetto di Diano Sörì Colombè '09	🏆🏆 2*
● Dolcetto di Diano Sörì Cristina '10	🏆🏆 2*
● Nebbiolo d'Alba Colombè '12	🏆🏆 3*
● Nebbiolo d'Alba Colombè '10	🏆🏆 3

La Prevostura

CASCINA PREVOSTURA, 1
13853 LESSONA [BI]
TEL. 0158853188
www.laprevostura.it

CELLAR SALES
PRE-BOOKED VISITS
RESTAURANT SERVICE
ANNUAL PRODUCTION 15,000 bottles
HECTARES UNDER VINE 4.00

Brothers Marco and Davide Bellini's recently founded winery, named after the magnificent Prevostura vineyard, aims to become a benchmark for northern Piedmont, reviving a centuries-old winegrowing tradition that was in danger of dying out. It is doing so commencing with the well-established grape varieties of the area – nebbiolo, vespolina, and croatina – without so much as a nod at international cultivars. The traditional-style wines, aged in large barrels since 2012, are still settling. Bramaterra 2011 has a lively personality, with notes ranging from blood to quinine, herbs in the sun, and dark tobacco. The Lessona of the same vintage is more floral and slightly spicy, with a long palate showing more delicate tannic development, while the excellent Coste della Sesia Rosso Muntacc 2011 is full and layered. Coste della Sesia Rosato Corinna 2014, from nebbiolo and vespolina, is delicately fruity with well-defined acidity.

● Lessona '11	🏆🏆 5
● Bramaterra '11	🏆🏆 5
● Coste della Sesia Rosso Muntacc '11	🏆🏆 3
⊙ Coste della Sesia Rosato Corinna '14	🏆 3
● Coste della Sesia Rosso Garsun '13	🏆 3
● Coste della Sesia Rosso Muntacc '10	🏆🏆 3
● Lessona '10	🏆🏆 5
● Lessona '09	🏆🏆 5

★Produttori del Barbaresco

VIA TORINO, 54
12050 BARBARESCO [CN]
TEL. 0173635139
www.produttoridelbarbaresco.com

CELLAR SALES
PRE-BOOKED VISITS
ACCOMMODATION
ANNUAL PRODUCTION 450,000 bottles
HECTARES UNDER VINE 100.00

Produttori del Barbaresco has embodied
the best of Italy's cooperative winery
system for almost 60 years, particularly in
the relationship between quality and price.
This is thanks to its over 50 members, who
own around 100 hectares in Barbaresco,
accounting for just under 20% of the entire
area under vine. The result is a range
entirely dedicated to nebbiolo, enriched
with nine vineyard selections, produced
following traditional methods, in the finest
vintages. Their names are familiar to
aficionados: Montestefano, Montefico, Asili,
Pora, Moccagatta, Pajé, Rio Sordo, Ovello,
and Rabajà In the absence of the 2010
Riservas, which the winery decided not to
bottle separately, the only Barbaresco we
tasted was the 2011 vintage. It offers dried
herbs and red berries on a concentrated
nose somewhat lacking in focus, followed
by a palate still dominated by tannins and
alcohol. However, it has plenty of stuffing
and will achieve balance after sufficient
bottle ageing. The Nebbiolo is fresh and
beautifully drinkable.

● Barbaresco '11	♟♟ 5
● Langhe Nebbiolo '13	♟♟ 3
● Barbaresco Ovello Ris. '09	♟♟♟ 6
● Barbaresco Vign. in Montefico Ris. '00	♟♟♟ 5*
● Barbaresco Vign. in Montefico Ris. '99	♟♟♟ 5
● Barbaresco Vign. in Montestefano Ris. '05	♟♟♟ 6
● Barbaresco Vign. in Montestefano Ris. '04	♟♟♟ 6
● Barbaresco Vign. in Montestefano Ris. '01	♟♟♟ 5
● Barbaresco Vign. in Ovello Ris. '08	♟♟♟ 6
● Barbaresco Vign. in Pajé Ris. '01	♟♟♟ 5*
● Barbaresco Vign. in Pora Ris. '07	♟♟♟ 6
● Barbaresco Vign. in Rio Sordo Ris. '01	♟♟♟ 5

Cantina Produttori del Gavi

VIA CAVALIERI DI VITTORIO VENETO, 45
15066 GAVI [AL]
TEL. 0143642786
www.cantinaproduttoridelgavi.it

CELLAR SALES
PRE-BOOKED VISITS
ANNUAL PRODUCTION 300,000 bottles
HECTARES UNDER VINE 220.00

Cantina Produttori del Gavi has over 100
member growers, with more than 200
hectares of vineyards, making it one of the
leading cooperative wineries, and not just
in the province of Alessandria. Founded in
1951, and given its current name in 1974,
it produces a comprehensive range of
white wines from cortese, combining high
volume and reasonable prices with plenty
of personality. It includes an impressive
eight Gavis, almost all fermented and aged
in steel without malolactic fermentation,
with the exception of part of the Aureliana
selection, aged in small oak casks. The
skilled work of Cantina Produttori is evident
in an array of top-quality Gavis, which is
even more impressive considering the
difficult 2014 vintage. It is topped by the
Etichetta Nera and the G 2014, both of
which reached our finals with two versions
of the classic, varietal style. The first has
dense pulp and good backbone, while the
second shows a more austere palate, but
great personality.

○ Gavi del Comune di Gavi Et. Nera '14	♟♟ 2*
○ Gavi G '14	♟♟ 3*
○ Gavi Brut M. Cl.	♟♟ 4
○ Gavi GG '14	♟♟ 3
○ Gavi Il Forte '14	♟♟ 2*
○ Gavi Primi Grappoli '14	♟♟ 2*
○ Gavi del Comune di Gavi Maddalena '14	♟ 3
○ Gavi del Comune di Gavi Et. Nera '13	♟♟ 2*
○ Gavi del Comune di Gavi Et. Nera '12	♟♟ 2*
○ Gavi del Comune di Gavi GG '13	♟♟ 3*
○ Gavi del Comune di Gavi GG '12	♟♟ 3*
○ Gavi G '13	♟♟ 2*
○ Gavi G '12	♟♟ 3
○ Gavi La Maddalena '13	♟♟ 2*
○ Gavi Primi Grappoli '12	♟♟ 2*

★Prunotto

c.so Barolo, 14
12051 Alba [CN]
Tel. 0173280017
www.prunotto.it

PRE-BOOKED VISITS
ANNUAL PRODUCTION 850,000 bottles
HECTARES UNDER VINE 55.00

Alfredo Prunotto gave his name to one of the most familiar brands in the world, not only of Piedmont wine. Following the First World War, he took over the Ai Vini delle Langhe cooperative winery, before selling it to Beppe and Tino Colla in 1956, who in turn sold it to the Antinori family in the late 1980s. Under the latest management, the property has expanded to over 50 hectares, with the Bussia, Bric Turot, and Costamiole estates, and the range of wines has been extended and restyled accordingly. Steel has replaced concrete for the fermentation of the top Nebbiolos, which are now aged in barriques and medium-sized oak casks instead of the old 10,000-litre barrels. Barbaresco Bric Turot 11 does not have huge personality, but is pleasantly balanced, while the 2012 Barbaresco is subtle and well orchestrated. Barolo Bussia 2011 is small bodied with an attractive open nose of dried herbs, and Barolo Bussia Vigna Colonnello Riserva 2009 lacks the fresh vitality characteristic of that wonderful cru.

● Barbaresco Bric Turot '11	▼▼ 6
● Barbera d'Alba Pian Romualdo '12	▼▼ 4
● Barbera d'Asti Sup. Nizza Costamiòle '11	▼▼ 5
● Barolo Bussia '11	▼▼ 8
● Barbaresco '12	▼ 5
● Barolo '11	▼ 6
● Barolo Bussia V. Colonnello Ris. '09	▼ 8
● M.to Mompertone '12	▼ 3
● Nebbiolo d'Alba Occhetti '12	▼ 4
● Barbera d'Asti Costamiòle '99	▼▼▼ 4*
● Barbera d'Asti Costamiòle '96	▼▼▼ 6
● Barolo Bussia '01	▼▼▼ 8
● Barolo Bussia '99	▼▼▼ 8
● Barolo Bussia '98	▼▼▼ 8
● Barolo Bussia '96	▼▼▼ 8
● Barolo Bussia '85	▼▼▼ 8

Renato Ratti

fraz. Annunziata, 7
12064 La Morra [CN]
Tel. 017350185
www.renatoratti.com

CELLAR SALES
PRE-BOOKED VISITS
ACCOMMODATION
ANNUAL PRODUCTION 300,000 bottles
HECTARES UNDER VINE 40.00

This estate has deep, solid roots, and an array of fine vineyards, allowing it to offer a range truly representative of the region's main designations. Its consistent, distinctive style has allowed its products to win the favour of numerous Italian and particularly foreign wine lovers with their juicy fullness. Renato Ratti has conquered the world's leading markets and is a landmark of Piedmont and Italian winemaking. The result of our tastings is rather provisional, as we tried several wines that seemed too young and are consequently still marked by oak, concealing their full potential. Barolo Marcenasco 2011 offers notes of quinine, tobacco, and dried flowers, with well-calibrated oak, while Barolo Conca 2011 has a nose of red berries and tar, with subtle toast and balsamic hints, and discreet, mellow, tannins on the palate.

● Barolo Conca '11	▼▼ 8
● Barolo Marcenasco '11	▼▼ 6
● Barolo Rocche dell'Annunziata '11	▼▼ 8
● Dolcetto d'Alba Colombè '14	▼▼ 3
● Nebbiolo d'Alba Ochetti '13	▼▼ 4
● Barbera d'Alba Battaglione '14	▼ 3
● Barolo Rocche '06	▼▼▼ 8
● Barolo Rocche Marcenasco '84	▼▼▼ 6
● Barolo Rocche Marcenasco '83	▼▼▼ 6
● Barbera d'Asti '11	▼▼ 3
● Barolo Conca '10	▼▼ 8
● Barolo Marcenasco '10	▼▼ 6
● Barolo Marcenasco '09	▼▼ 6
● Barolo Rocche '09	▼▼ 8
● Barolo Rocche dell'Annunziata '10	▼▼ 8
● Nebbiolo d'Alba Ochetti '11	▼▼ 4

Ressia

Via Canova, 28
12052 Neive [CN]
Tel. 0173677305
www.ressia.com

CELLAR SALES
PRE-BOOKED VISITS
ANNUAL PRODUCTION 25,000 bottles
HECTARES UNDER VINE 5.50

Fabrizio Ressia confidently heads the family winery, which has many decades behind it. Over the years we have learned to appreciate the clarity on the palate of the various wines of the range, the distinctive personalities of the various grape varieties, and the competitive, fair prices. Based in the fabulous municipality of Neive, the estate's range is headed by the Barbaresco DOCG, which displays an authentic, very terroir-true style. We tasted two vintages of Barbaresco Canova: the 2011, whose release had been delayed, and the 2012. Both were very convincing, although we preferred the sensorial definition of the 2011, with a complex nose of balsamic notes and dark tones of quinine and juniper, underpinned by a beautifully textured tannic weave on the palate. Barbaresco Canova Riserva Oró 2010 is oaky and still not clearly legible, requiring more time to achieve clarity and full integration.

F.lli Revello

Fraz. Annunziata, 103
12064 La Morra [CN]
Tel. 017350276
www.revellofratelli.it

CELLAR SALES
PRE-BOOKED VISITS
ANNUAL PRODUCTION 85,000 bottles
HECTARES UNDER VINE 16.00
SUSTAINABLE WINERY

Brothers Carlo and Lorenzo Revello have been making wine for 25 years. There are at least three secrets to their success: they started out on the right foot, immediately winning recognition from connoisseurs and critics; their modern style, featuring the use of small French oak, has remained constant, ensuring splendid continuity in the glass; finally, their wines are eminently cellarable, with the vintages of the 1990s still in top form. In addition, they boast a handsome cellar, well worth a visit together with the guest farm, and excellent vineyards in the Annunziata cru of La Morra. Barolo Rocche dell'Annunziata 2011 has a beautifully layered, complex nose and attractive prominent acidity and tannins. The delicious, well-orchestrated Conca vaunts close-focused fruit and delicious precocious hints of tar, while the modern Giachini is spicy with good weight. Ciabot du Re 2013 is elegant in every detail, demonstrating the potential of Barbera d'Alba.

● Barbaresco Canova '11	♥♥ 5
● Barbaresco Canova '12	♥♥ 5
● Barbaresco Canova Ris. Oro '10	♥♥ 6
● Barbera d'Alba Sup. '12	♥♥ 5
● Dolcetto d'Alba Canova '14	♥ 2
○ Evien '14	♥ 2
● Barbaresco Canova '06	♥♥♥ 5*
● Barbaresco Canova '10	♥♥ 5
● Barbaresco Canova '09	♥♥ 5
● Barbaresco Canova Ris. Oro '09	♥♥ 6
● Barbaresco Oro Ris. '05	♥♥ 6
● Barbera d'Alba Sup. Canova '11	♥♥ 3
● Barbera d'Alba Sup. Canova '10	♥♥ 3
○ Evien '13	♥♥ 2*
○ Evien	♥♥ 2*
● Langhe Nebbiolo Gepù '11	♥♥ 3

● Barbera d'Alba Ciabot du Re '13	♥♥ 5
● Barolo Conca '11	♥♥ 7
● Barolo Rocche dell'Annunziata '11	♥♥ 8
● Barolo '11	♥♥ 5
● Barolo Gattera '11	♥♥ 6
● Barolo Giachini '11	♥♥ 7
● Langhe Nebbiolo '13	♥ 3
● Barbera d'Alba Ciabot du Re '05	♥♥♥ 5
● Barbera d'Alba Ciabot du Re '00	♥♥♥ 5
● Barolo '93	♥♥♥ 5
● Barolo Rocche dell'Annunziata '01	♥♥♥ 8
● Barolo Rocche dell'Annunziata '00	♥♥♥ 8
● Barolo Rocche dell'Annunziata '97	♥♥♥ 8
● Barolo V. Conca '99	♥♥♥ 7
● Barolo Rocche dell'Annunziata '08	♥♥ 8
● Barolo V. Conca '09	♥♥ 7

Michele Reverdito

FRAZ. RIVALTA
B.TA GARASSINI, 74B
12064 LA MORRA [CN]
TEL. 017350336
www.reverdito.it

CELLAR SALES
PRE-BOOKED VISITS
ANNUAL PRODUCTION 70,000 bottles
HECTARES UNDER VINE 16.00

In the space of just 15 years, the winery
owned by Michele Reverdito and his sister
Sonia has made a name for itself with its
focus on Barolo. Indeed, it has purchased
crus that now produce an impressive six
wines; work in the vineyard is carried out
with the utmost respect for the
environment, shunning all chemicals; and
the winemaking style strives for a clean
nose and drinkability without too much oak.
The vineyards are situated in La Morra,
Verduno, and Serralunga d'Alba. The three
vineyard selections of Barolo we tasted
were from three different vintages, but all
performed very well. Riva Rocca 2011 is
very classic, distinguished by its already
well-orchestrated palate, combined with
rather fresh aromas for the warm vintage.
The Riserva Dieci Anni is surprisingly firmly
structured and youthful, with still
perceptible oak.

Giuseppe Rinaldi

VIA MONFORTE, 5
12060 BAROLO [CN]
TEL. 017356156
carlotta.rinaldi@me.com

CELLAR SALES
PRE-BOOKED VISITS
ANNUAL PRODUCTION 35,000 bottles
HECTARES UNDER VINE 6.50

The generations are magnificently
intertwined at the Rinaldi family's winery.
Beppe "Citrico" remains its front man,
literally adored by fans scattered all over
the world, but it is a team that works in
unison, due to the talent of his daughters
Marta and Carlotta, who have long been
working full time in the small cellar in
Barolo. This is evident in the top vineyard
selections, some of which have changed
their name from the 2010 vintage onwards
(Brunate and Tre Tine), but not in their
terroir-true character or their style. The
Barolo Brunate took a Tre Bicchieri,
showing soft with rich pulp and a nose of
roses and dark berries. It is an alluring
combination, whose naturalness and
accessibility override the potential
ruggedness of the nebbiolo grapes, partly
thanks to the fine, ripe 2011 harvest.

● Barolo 10 Anni Ris. '05	♟♟ 8
● Barolo Riva Rocca '11	♟♟ 5
● Barolo Ascheri '11	♟♟ 5
● Barolo Badarina '11	♟♟ 5
● Barolo Bricco Cogni Ris. '09	♟♟ 6
● Langhe Nascetta '14	♟♟ 2*
● Barbera d'Alba Butti '13	♟ 2
● Verduno Pelaverga '14	♟ 2
● Barolo Bricco Cogni '04	♟♟♟ 6
● Barolo 10 Anni Ris. '04	♟♟ 8
● Barolo Ascheri '10	♟♟ 5
● Barolo Badarina '10	♟♟ 5
● Barolo Bricco Cogni Ris. '08	♟♟ 6
● Barolo Castagni '10	♟♟ 5
● Barolo Riva Rocca '10	♟♟ 5
● Langhe Nascetta '13	♟♟ 2*

● Barolo Brunate '11	♟♟♟ 7
● Barolo Tre Tine '11	♟♟ 7
● Langhe Nebbiolo '13	♟♟ 4
● Barolo Brunate-Le Coste '07	♟♟♟ 7
● Barolo Brunate-Le Coste '06	♟♟♟ 7
● Barolo Brunate-Le Coste '01	♟♟♟ 6
● Barolo Brunate-Le Coste '00	♟♟♟ 6
● Barolo Brunate-Le Coste '97	♟♟♟ 6
● Barolo Cannubi S. Lorenzo-Ravera '04	♟♟♟ 6
● Barolo Brunate '10	♟♟ 7
● Barolo Brunate-Le Coste '09	♟♟ 7
● Barolo Brunate-Le Coste '08	♟♟ 7
● Barolo Cannubi S. Lorenzo-Ravera '09	♟♟ 7
● Barolo Cannubi S. Lorenzo-Ravera '08	♟♟ 7
● Barolo Tre Tine '10	♟♟ 7
● Langhe Nebbiolo '11	♟♟ 4

Pietro Rinaldi

FRAZ. MADONNA DI COMO
12051 ALBA [CN]
TEL. 0173360090
www.pietrorinaldi.com

CELLAR SALES
PRE-BOOKED VISITS
ACCOMMODATION
ANNUAL PRODUCTION 70,000 bottles
HECTARES UNDER VINE 10.00

Monica Rinaldi and her husband Paolo
Tenino make no secret of their goals, which
aim to make the winery a benchmark for
connoisseurs of Langhe wines,
commencing of course with those from
nebbiolo. This has led them to seek out
only the finest vineyards, first and foremost
the Monvigliero cru in Verduno for Barolo.
They have also built an efficient,
well-equipped cellar, which is a joy to
behold, and draw on the expertise of
top-level consultant oenologists. The
well-made Barolo Monvigliero 2011
displays a very complex nose and a slightly
alcoholic palate, while the basic Barolo is
sound and only slightly less firmly
structured. Barbera d'Alba Cichetta is also
excellent, with a deep nose of cocoa
powder and plums, and plenty of flesh and
freshness on the palate. Barbaresco San
Cristoforo also fared well, still showing
slightly rugged tannins.

● Barbera d'Alba Sup. Bricco Cichetta '13	▼▼ 4
● Barolo Monvigliero '11	▼▼ 6
● Barbaresco San Cristoforo '12	▼▼ 5
● Barbera d'Alba Monpiano '13	▼▼ 3
● Barolo '11	▼▼ 6
● Dolcetto d'Alba Madonna di Como '14	▼ 2
○ Langhe Arneis Hortensia '14	▼ 2
● Barbaresco San Cristoforo '11	♈♈ 5
● Barbaresco San Cristoforo '09	♈♈ 5
● Barbaresco San Cristoforo '08	♈♈ 5
● Barbera d'Alba Sup. Bricco Cichetta '11	♈♈ 3
● Barolo '10	♈♈ 6
● Barolo '08	♈♈ 5
● Barolo Monvigliero '09	♈♈ 6
● Barolo Monvigliero '08	♈♈ 6
● Barolo Monvigliero '07	♈♈ 6

Rizzi

VIA RIZZI, 15
12050 TREISO [CN]
TEL. 0173638161
www.cantinarizzi.it

CELLAR SALES
PRE-BOOKED VISITS
ACCOMMODATION
ANNUAL PRODUCTION 50,000 bottles
HECTARES UNDER VINE 35.00

It may seem rather strange to talk of
surprises for an estate over 50 years old.
However, it is only relatively recently that
the wines produced by Rizzi, named after
the Treiso hamlet where the cellar and
most of the vineyards owned by the
Dellapiana family are situated, have shown
their full worth. The estate covers a total
area of approximately 35 hectares, planted
mainly with nebbiolo, dolcetto, and barbera,
which yield a flawless range. Nonetheless,
its top wines are Rizzi, Pajorè, Nervo, and
Boito Riserva, the four Barbarescos,
fermented traditionally and aged in large
Slavonian oak barrels, which consistently
share fabulously calibrated extract. The
splendid Boito Riserva 2010 marks the
definitive consecration of Rizzi's
Barbarescos. Its full nose of juniper,
tobacco, and liquorice is accompanied by
an elegant, progressive palate, with a
dazzling long finish. However, Pajoré 2011
is every bit as good in terms of terroir-true
character and expressiveness.

● Barbaresco Boito Ris. '10	▼▼▼ 6
● Barbaresco Pajorè '11	▼▼ 6
● Barbaresco Rizzi '12	▼▼ 5
● Barbaresco Rizzi '11	▼▼ 5
● Barbaresco Boito Ris. '09	♈♈ 6
● Barbaresco Nervo '11	♈♈ 5
● Barbaresco Nervo Fondetta '10	♈♈ 5
● Barbaresco Pajorè '10	♈♈ 6
● Barbaresco Rizzi '10	♈♈ 5

★Albino Rocca

S.DA RONCHI, 18
12050 BARBARESCO [CN]
TEL. 0173635145
www.albinorocca.com

CELLAR SALES
PRE-BOOKED VISITS
ANNUAL PRODUCTION 100,000 bottles
HECTARES UNDER VINE 18.00
SUSTAINABLE WINERY

Aided by Carlo Castellengo, sisters Paola, Monica, and Daniela Rocca continue the work commenced by their grandfather Albino and their father Angelo with extraordinary determination and pride. Their approximately 20-hectare estate is one of the finest in Langhe, due largely to the elegant, composed style of its Nebbiolos, crafted from the Montersino cru in San Rocco Seno d'Elvio and the Ovello and Ronchi vineyards in Barbaresco, and aged in 2,000-litre German and Austrian oak barrels. The remarkably consistent, reliable range is completed by Dolcetto, Barbera, Cabernet Franc, Cortese, Chardonnay, and Moscato. Barbaresco Ovello Vigna Loreto 2012 has a broad, complex nose of fresh fruit with hints of jam and liquorice, and a sound palate that is already well balanced and elegant. Barbaresco Ronchi 2012 is fresh and compact, but with a less close-focused nose than usual. Barbaresco Montersino is potent but husky, while the woody Duemiladodici is nicely spicy with fragrant raspberry notes.

● Barbaresco Ovello V. Loreto '12	♙♙ 6
● Barbaresco Ronchi '12	♙♙ 6
○ Piemonte Cortese La Rocca '14	♙♙ 4
● Barbaresco Duemiladodici '12	♙♙ 5
● Barbera d'Alba Gepin '13	♙♙ 5
○ Langhe Chardonnay da Bertü '14	♙♙ 3
● Nebbiolo d'Alba '13	♙♙ 3
● Barbaresco Montersino '12	♙ 6
● Barbera d'Alba '14	♙ 2
● Dolcetto d'Alba '14	♙ 2
● Barbaresco Ovello V. Loreto '11	♙♙♙ 6
● Barbaresco Ovello V. Loreto '09	♙♙♙ 6
● Barbaresco Ovello V. Loreto '07	♙♙♙ 6
● Barbaresco Ronchi '10	♙♙♙ 6
● Barbaresco Vign. Brich Ronchi Ris. '06	♙♙♙ 8
● Barbaresco Vign. Brich Ronchi Ris. '04	♙♙♙ 8

★Bruno Rocca

VIA RABAJÀ, 60
12050 BARBARESCO [CN]
TEL. 0173635112
www.brunorocca.it

CELLAR SALES
PRE-BOOKED VISITS
ANNUAL PRODUCTION 60,000 bottles
HECTARES UNDER VINE 15.00

The 15 hectares of vineyards personally tended by Bruno Rocca with the help of his children Francesco and Luisa are largely concentrated in Barbaresco's Rabajà cru. The impressive estate also includes plots in Treiso, Neive in the Currà area, and Vaglio Serra, where the Barbera d'Asti is made, with the remainder planted with dolcetto, cabernet, and chardonnay. In the absence of Rabajà 2012, this year we tasted three Barbarescos, characterized by a modern but constantly evolving style. The basic one and the Coparossa are aged exclusively in barriques, while the Maria Adelaide spends its second year in large barrels. Rocca's two latest Barbarescos are destined to satisfy different tastes. Coparossa 2012 is a "medium weight", with woody and balsamic notes on an already settled palate, while Maria Adelaide 2011 is more masculine, in terms of both aromatic profile and tannic vigour.

● Barbaresco Coparossa '12	♙♙ 8
● Barbaresco Maria Adelaide '11	♙♙ 8
● Barbera d'Asti '13	♙♙ 4
● Barbaresco '12	♙♙ 6
● Barbera d'Alba '13	♙♙ 4
● Langhe Nebbiolo Fralù '13	♙♙ 4
● Barbaresco Coparossa '04	♙♙♙ 8
● Barbaresco Maria Adelaide '07	♙♙♙ 8
● Barbaresco Maria Adelaide '04	♙♙♙ 8
● Barbaresco Maria Adelaide '01	♙♙♙ 8
● Barbaresco Rabajà '11	♙♙♙ 8
● Barbaresco Rabajà '10	♙♙♙ 8
● Barbaresco Rabajà '09	♙♙♙ 8
● Barbaresco Rabajà '01	♙♙♙ 8
● Barbaresco Rabajà '00	♙♙♙ 8
● Barbaresco Rabajà '98	♙♙♙ 8

Rocche Costamagna

Via Vittorio Emanuele, 8
12064 La Morra [CN]
Tel. 0173509225
www.rocchecostamagna.it

CELLAR SALES
PRE-BOOKED VISITS
ACCOMMODATION
ANNUAL PRODUCTION 95,000 bottles
HECTARES UNDER VINE 14.00
SUSTAINABLE WINERY

After more than 150 years of production, Rocche Costamagna seems to have achieved a well-articulated structure for its many components, with a handsome new cellar at Annunziata, as well as an elegant guest farm, and a shop. The woman behind this transformation is the charismatic, multitalented Claudia Ferraresi, aided by her dynamic son Alessandro Locatelli. Their wines have also benefited from the new cellar, appearing increasingly close focused in their classic style. Barolo Rocche dell'Annunziata 2011 is an excellent expression of a grand cru, displaying an alluring fresh nose with hints of liquorice, and a palate with powerful structure but discreet tannins. Riserva Bricco Francesco also shows sound structure, although it lacks a little freshness due to the hot 2009 vintage. The fine range is particularly interesting for its charming aromas, always clean and fruity.

● Barolo Rocche dell'Annunziata '11	♟♟	6
● Barbera d'Alba '13	♟♟	3
● Barolo '11	♟♟	5
● Barolo Bricco Francesco Ris. '09	♟♟	7
● Dolcetto d'Alba Murrae '14	♟♟	2*
● Langhe Nebbiolo Roccardo '13	♟♟	3
○ Langhe Arneis '14	♟	2
● Barolo Rocche dell'Annunziata '04	♟♟♟	5
● Barbera d'Alba Annunziata '11	♟♟	3
● Barbera d'Alba Sup. Rocche delle Rocche '11	♟♟	4
● Barbera d'Alba Sup. Rocche delle Rocche '10	♟♟	4
● Barolo Rocche dell'Annunziata '10	♟♟	5
● Barolo Rocche dell'Annunziata '09	♟♟	5
● Barolo Rocche dell'Annunziata Bricco Francesco Ris. '07	♟♟	6

★Rocche dei Manzoni

Loc. Manzoni Soprani, 3
12065 Monforte d'Alba [CN]
Tel. 017378421
www.rocchedeimanzoni.it

CELLAR SALES
PRE-BOOKED VISITS
ANNUAL PRODUCTION 250,000 bottles
HECTARES UNDER VINE 40.00

The impressive winery premises have gradually expanded, becoming a little hamlet, in whose artistic cellars tens of thousands of bottles, made from the estate's 50 hectares of vineyards, are aged for years. Its founder, Valentino Migliorini, focused on Barolo from the outset, always favouring a decidedly modern style. However, in far-off 1976, he also started producing a Metodo Classico sparkler, named after himself, which has constantly been acknowledged as one of the best of its kind in Italy. The style of all the Barolos, of which were able to taste just two this year, is distinguished by remarkable concentration, considerable amounts of new oak, and fullness on the palate, sometimes at the cost of freshness. Vigna Cappella di Santo Stefano, from one of the most evocative vineyards in the entire area, is characterized by vegetal and mineral hints on the nose, and monolithic close-woven tannins on the palate. The more delicate Barolo 2011 is also modern and still a little woody.

● Barolo Perno V. Cappella di S. Stefano '11	♟♟	8
○ Valentino Brut M. Cl. Riserva Elena '10	♟♟	5
● Barbera d'Alba La Cresta '10	♟	5
● Barolo '11	♟	6
○ Langhe Chardonnay L'Angelica '11	♟	7
● Barolo V. Big 'd Big '99	♟♟♟	8
● Barolo V. Cappella di S. Stefano '01	♟♟♟	8
● Barolo V. Cappella di S. Stefano '96	♟♟♟	8
● Barolo V. d'la Roul '07	♟♟♟	8
● Langhe Rosso Quatr Nas '99	♟♟♟	6
● Langhe Rosso Quatr Nas '96	♟♟♟	6
○ Valentino Brut Zero Ris. '98	♟♟♟	5
○ Valentino Brut Zero Ris. '93	♟♟♟	5
○ Valentino Brut Zerò Ris. '92	♟♟♟	5

Roccolo di Mezzomerico

CASCINA ROCCOLO BELLINI, 4
28040 MEZZOMERICO [NO]
TEL. 0321920407
www.ilroccolovini.it

CELLAR SALES
PRE-BOOKED VISITS
ANNUAL PRODUCTION 30,000 bottles
HECTARES UNDER VINE 7.00

Pietro Gelmini has just celebrated the 25th anniversary of his winery and sure-footedly continues along his path with the aid of all his family. The style of his wines, both reds and whites, is largely dictated by super-ripe grapes, sometimes partly dried on a specially built rack, and by assertive ageing in new oak that leaves its mark. Thanks to the aid of the skilled Claudio Introini, who vaunts long experience in Valpolicella and Valtellina, they naturally combine freshness and concentration. The range is topped by two passitos: Siduri Francesca and Gilgamesh Valentina. The first, from erbaluce and chardonnay, aged in small casks, has a dense, rich, complex palate, with alluring vibrant notes of dried fruit and candied citrus. The second is made from nebbiolo dried first on the vine and then on racks, and vaunts a complex nose and a well-orchestrated palate. The sound, slightly woody Colline Novaresi Nebbiolo Valentina 2010 is tannic and potent.

● Colline Novaresi Nebbiolo Valentina '10	♥♥ 3
● Colline Novaresi Nebbiolo Valentina V.T. '11	♥♥ 5
● Gilgamesh Valentina	♥♥ 5
○ Siduri Francesca	♥♥ 5
○ Colline Novaresi Bianco Francesca V.T. '13	♥ 3
○ Colline Novaresi Bianco Francesca '13	♀♀ 2*
● Colline Novaresi Nebbiolo La Cascinetta '09	♀♀ 2*
● Colline Novaresi Nebbiolo Valentina '08	♀♀ 3
● Colline Novaresi Nebbiolo Valentina '07	♀♀ 3*
● Colline Novaresi Nebbiolo Valentina '06	♀♀ 3*
● Colline Novaresi Nebbiolo Valentina V.T. Et. Oro '10	♀♀ 4
● Colline Novaresi Nebbiolo Valentina V.T. Et. Oro '09	♀♀ 4

Flavio Roddolo

FRAZ. BRICCO APPIANI
LOC. SANT'ANNA, 5
12065 MONFORTE D'ALBA [CN]
TEL. 017378535

CELLAR SALES
PRE-BOOKED VISITS
ANNUAL PRODUCTION 25,000 bottles
HECTARES UNDER VINE 6.00

The shy, retiring Flavio is a man of little words who lets the splendid bottles made at his Bricco Appiani estate in Monforte d'Alba do the talking. A keen supporter of natural viticulture, his work in the cellar focuses on long ageing, with the use of mainly used oak casks in small and medium sizes. He makes a single Barolo, from the Ravera cru, and two versions of Dolcetto d'Alba, including a Superiore. The range is completed by a Barbera, a Nebbiolo, and Bricco Appiani, a cabernet sauvignon monovarietal that is far more territorial than varietal in style. Although the estate has never stood out for its promptness in commercializing its wines, preferring to age them in the cellar for the necessary time, this year Roddolo astounded even us, presenting just two reds and a Barbera d'Alba 2008, older than the Barolo, albeit by just a year. However, what is truly strange is that the Barbera, showing attractive flesh and good structure, is more pleasant drinking than the austere Barolo.

● Barbera d'Alba '08	♥♥ 3
● Barolo Ravera '09	♥♥ 5
● Barolo Ravera '08	♀♀♀ 5
● Barolo Ravera '07	♀♀♀ 5
● Barolo Ravera '04	♀♀♀ 5
● Barolo Ravera '01	♀♀♀ 5
● Barolo Ravera '97	♀♀♀ 5
● Bricco Appiani '99	♀♀♀ 5
● Dolcetto d'Alba '11	♀♀ 2*
● Dolcetto d'Alba '10	♀♀ 2*
● Dolcetto d'Alba Sup. '11	♀♀ 3*
● Dolcetto d'Alba Sup. '10	♀♀ 3*
● Dolcetto d'Alba Sup. '09	♀♀ 3*
● Nebbiolo d'Alba '09	♀♀ 4
● Nebbiolo d'Alba '08	♀♀ 4
● Nebbiolo d'Alba '07	♀♀ 4

Ronchi

s.da Ronchi, 23
12050 Barbaresco [CN]
Tel. 0173635156
info@aziendaagricolaronchi.it

CELLAR SALES
PRE-BOOKED VISITS
ANNUAL PRODUCTION 30,000 bottles
HECTARES UNDER VINE 7.00

This family winery, meticulously and passionately run by Giancarlo Rocca, is set in a breathtaking corner of Langhe and boasts a first-rate array of vineyards, lying almost completely within the Ronchi "Menzione Geografica Aggiuntiva" specification. The profile of the wines is very focused and coherent with the types produced. Overall quality has risen across the range, and all the wines are characterized by very reasonable price tags in relation to their level of excellence. Both versions of Barbaresco 2011 have been released after a further year of ageing. The Ronchi is open and concentrated, with a nose focusing more on dried herbs and tar than red berries; the palate is nicely weighty, but suffers from an excess of oak and alcohol. The basic Barbaresco is fruitier and livelier, also marked by oak and austere tannins, which does not hinder the finish of currants and raspberries.

● Barbaresco '11	♟♟ 5
● Barbaresco Ronchi '11	♟♟ 5
○ Langhe Chardonnay '13	♟♟ 3
● Dolcetto d'Alba '14	♟ 2
○ Langhe Arneis '14	♟ 2
● Barbaresco Ronchi '04	♟♟♟ 6
● Barbaresco '10	♟♟ 5
● Barbaresco '09	♟♟ 5
● Barbaresco Et. Blu '08	♟♟ 5
● Barbaresco Et. Rossa '08	♟♟ 5
● Barbaresco Ronchi '10	♟♟ 5
● Barbera d'Alba Terlé '12	♟♟ 3
● Barbera d'Alba Terlé '11	♟♟ 3
● Dolcetto d'Alba '12	♟♟ 2*
○ Langhe Chardonnay Ronchi '12	♟♟ 3*
● Langhe Rosso '11	♟♟ 4

Giovanni Rosso

loc. Baudana, 6
12050 Serralunga d'Alba [CN]
Tel. 0173613340
www.giovannirosso.com

CELLAR SALES
PRE-BOOKED VISITS
ANNUAL PRODUCTION 130,000 bottles
HECTARES UNDER VINE 18.00

This splendid Langhe estate entirely dedicated to red wines has finally moved into its new premises. The new cellar may be less romantic, but it is decidedly more efficient. Barolo accounts for the majority of the production, with three versions, each more alluring than the last. However, the jewel in the crown is constituted by the tiny number of bottles of the Ester Canale Rosso selection, made from the grapes of one of the most magical vineyards of Barolo and the whole world: Vigna Rionda in Serralunga d'Alba. When personality, complexity, finesse, and structure merge completely in a wine, a masterpiece is born. Here it is represented by a new label (named after the active mother of the versatile Davide Rosso), currently only available at a few top wine bars and restaurants, but destined for wider distribution in a few years' time, when the vines just planted in Vigna Rionda will enter production. The complex Serra and Cerretta Barolos are both very sophisticated.

● Barolo V. Rionda Ester Canale Rosso '11	♟♟♟ 8
● Barolo Cerretta '11	♟♟ 8
● Barolo Serra '11	♟♟ 8
● Barolo del Comune di Serralunga d'Alba '11	♟♟ 5
● Langhe Nebbiolo '13	♟♟ 5
● Barbera d'Alba Donna Margherita '14	♟ 3
● Barolo Cerretta '06	♟♟♟ 7
● Barolo La Serra '09	♟♟♟ 7
● Barolo La Serra '08	♟♟♟ 7
● Barolo Serra '10	♟♟♟ 7
● Barbera d'Alba Donna Margherita '11	♟♟ 3
● Barolo Cerretta '10	♟♟ 7
● Barolo Cerretta '09	♟♟ 7
● Barolo del Comune di Serralunga d'Alba '10	♟♟ 5
● Barolo V. Rionda Tommaso Canale '09	♟♟ 8

Rovellotti

Interno Castello, 22
28074 Ghemme [NO]
Tel. 0163841781
www.rovellotti.it

CELLAR SALES
ANNUAL PRODUCTION 50,000 bottles
HECTARES UNDER VINE 17.00

Antonello and Paolo Rovellotti's winery is
undisputedly one of the most fascinating in
the entire upper Piedmont production zone,
almost hidden in the medieval Ricetto di
Ghemme. It naturally offers wines that
proudly follow the local winemaking
traditions, but with a few departures:
Nebbiolo, vespolina, uva rara and erbaluce
are the focus of the work in the vineyards,
but in the past the estate has also
experimented with international varieties
such as cabernet, merlot and pinot nero.
Despite the challenges of working in such
confined spaces, the top reds, like
Ghemme Chioso dei Pomi and Ghemme
Salmino Riserva, are bottled only after
prolonged oak-ageing. The Rovellotti
brothers presented fewer wines than usual
this year, but they all fared well. The best
performance was offered by the two wines
from the grape variety that cannot be
mentioned (erbaluce, due to the
regulations). Criccone Bianco 2014 still
shows primary notes, but has big structure,
while the Dosaggio Zero Spumante is taut
with good progression.

○ Colline Novaresi Bianco Vitigno Innominabile Il Criccone '14	♟♟ 2*
○ Vitigno Innominabile Dosaggio Zero M. Cl.	♟♟ 2*
● Ghemme Costa del Salmino Ris. '08	♟ 5
○ Valdenrico Passito '11	♟ 6
☉ Ghemme Chioso dei Pomi '07	♟♟♟ 4*
☉ Colline Novaresi Nebbiolo Rosato Valplazza '13	♟♟ 2*
● Colline Novaresi Nebbiolo Valplazza '10	♟♟ 2*
● Ghemme Chioso dei Pomi '08	♟♟ 4
● Ghemme Costa del Salmino Ris. '07	♟♟ 5
● Ghemme Costa del Salmino Ris. '05	♟♟ 5

Podere Ruggeri Corsini

loc. Bussia Corsini, 106
12065 Monforte d'Alba [CN]
Tel. 017378625
www.ruggericorsini.com

CELLAR SALES
PRE-BOOKED VISITS
ANNUAL PRODUCTION 75,000 bottles
HECTARES UNDER VINE 9.80
SUSTAINABLE WINERY

The interesting Monforte winery lovingly
and enthusiastically run by Loredana Addari
and Nicola Argamante, celebrates its 20th
anniversary this year. The goal of
associating the name of this recent arrival
on the Langhe scene with a series of
reliable, consistent wines has been
achieved and Ruggeri Corsini has managed
to carve itself out a satisfying niche on
several important international markets. Its
range of wines is balanced and expressive,
with the various versions displaying
increasingly precision on the palate. Barolo
Bricco San Pietro 2011 has attractive
raspberry top notes on an oaky
background. It is not powerfully structured,
but is very supple with fine acid-tannin
balance. The Bussia Corsini of the same
vintage is softer and more evolved, with
spice and cocoa powder already evident.
Barbera 2013 is easy drinking and
satisfying, despite being rather full bodied,
and the forthright Langhe Bianco 2014 is
also very drinkable.

● Barolo Bricco San Pietro '11	♟♟ 5
● Barbera d'Alba '13	♟♟ 2*
● Barolo Bussia Corsini '11	♟♟ 5
○ Langhe Bianco '14	♟ 2
● Barbera d'Alba Sup. Armujan '11	♟♟ 3
● Barbera d'Alba Sup. Armujan '10	♟♟ 3
● Barolo Bricco San Pietro '10	♟♟ 5
● Barolo Bussia Corsini '10	♟♟ 5
● Barolo Bussia Corsini '09	♟♟ 5
● Barolo San Pietro '09	♟♟ 5
● Barolo San Pietro '08	♟♟ 5
● Dolcetto d'Alba '12	♟♟ 2*
○ Langhe Bianco '12	♟♟ 2*
● Langhe Rosso Argamakow '11	♟♟ 4
● Langhe Rosso Autenzio '11	♟♟ 4
● Langhe Rosso Autenzio '09	♟♟ 4

Josetta Saffirio

LOC. CASTELLETTO, 39
12065 MONFORTE D'ALBA [CN]
TEL. 0173787278
www.josettasaffirio.com

CELLAR SALES
PRE-BOOKED VISITS
ANNUAL PRODUCTION 30,000 bottles
HECTARES UNDER VINE 5.00
SUSTAINABLE WINERY

Josetta Saffirio's bottles have a new look: the famous gnomes drawn by her daughter Sara, which have always been the estate's unmistakable hallmark, are still there but are now set in a more elegant, classical label. In the meantime, Sara has grown up and today she channels her passion and skill into the estate's various activities, commencing with the nebbiolo vineyards, which account for the lion's share of the area under vine. Josetta Saffirio's basic Barolo is one of the very finest of the 2011 vintage, showing very fruity on the nose, but already bursting with hints of liquorice and roses. On the palate it is vibrant and elegant, with attractive freshness, ensuring its future development. The Riserva 2009 is a touch more tannic and less graceful, while the white Rossese has big personality, a salty nose, and a pleasantly enfolding palate.

● Barolo '11	♟♟	5
● Barbera d'Alba '13	♟♟	3
● Barolo Millenovecento48 Ris. '09	♟♟	7
● Langhe Nebbiolo '13	♟♟	3
○ Langhe Rossese '12	♟♟	3
☉ Nebbiolo d'Alba Brut Rosé M. Cl. '13	♟	4
● Barolo '89	♟♟♟	6
● Barolo '88	♟♟♟	6
● Barbera d'Alba '11	♟♟	3*
● Barolo '10	♟♟	5
● Barolo '09	♟♟	5
● Barolo Millenovecento48 Ris. '08	♟♟	7
● Barolo Persiera '10	♟♟	7
● Langhe Nebbiolo '12	♟♟	3
● Langhe Nebbiolo '11	♟♟	3

San Bartolomeo

LOC. VALLEGGE
CASCINA SAN BARTOLOMEO, 26
15066 GAVI [AL]
TEL. 0143643180
www.sanbartolomeo-gavi.com

CELLAR SALES
PRE-BOOKED VISITS
ANNUAL PRODUCTION 50,000 bottles
HECTARES UNDER VINE 21.00

In the space of a few vintages Fulvio Bergaglio has proven himself one of the great interpreters of Gavi. It's a clear sign of the value of deep bonds with the area and family traditions in the professional as well as the personal sphere. His vineyards are planted solely to cortese, with 80-year-old vines still producing fruit: the proud legacy of a viticultural tradition that has not been undermined by modern winemaking techniques. Two excellent Gavis made it into our finals. Pelöia is delicate and complex, with top notes of herbs and flint on the nose, and a rich, full-flavoured palate that tapers elegantly into a long, full-flavoured finish. Quinto has a concentrated fruity nose, with floral and citrussy notes, and a full, complex, potent palate, with a lingering, characterful finish.

○ Gavi del Comune di Gavi Pelöia '14	♟♟	3*
○ Gavi Quinto '14	♟♟	2*
○ Gavi '09	♟♟	2*
○ Gavi del Comune di Gavi Pelöia '13	♟♟	3*
○ Gavi del Comune di Gavi Pelöia '12	♟♟	3
○ Gavi del Comune di Gavi Pelöia '11	♟♟	3*
○ Gavi del Comune di Gavi Pelöia '09	♟♟	3
○ Gavi Quinto '13	♟♟	3*
○ Gavi Quinto '12	♟♟	2*
○ Gavi Quinto '11	♟♟	2*
○ Gavi Quinto '10	♟♟	2*

Tenuta San Sebastiano

CASCINA SAN SEBASTIANO, 41
15040 LU [AL]
TEL. 0131741353
www.dealessi.it

CELLAR SALES
PRE-BOOKED VISITS
ANNUAL PRODUCTION 70,000 bottles
HECTARES UNDER VINE 9.00

We could call that something that drove
Roberto De Alessi to purchase Tenuta San
Sebastiano in the early 1990s the call of
the land or the lure of tradition. Both he and
his wines have come a long way since
then, following the traces of his family's
past. This strategy means no one leaves his
winery disappointed. His full-bodied, firmly
structured reds, his sparklers from pinot
meunier, which is another of his passions.
And the light in his eyes when he talks of
his work will make sure of that. The
flagship Barbera Mepari is back. The 2011
vintage is potent, commencing with its
deep, almost inky, ruby hue, and nose with
sophisticated notes of plums on a sweet
background of well-calibrated oak, echoed
on the palate through to the long, complex
finish. The other wines, from Monferrato
Bianco to the Passito, are on top form.

● Barbera del M.to Sup. Mepari '11	▼▼ 4
● Barbera del M.to '13	▼▼ 2*
○ LV Quinquagesimaquinta Mansio Passito '13	▼▼ 4
⊙ M.to Bianco '14	▼▼ 2*
⊙ Brut Rosè M. Cl.	▼ 3
● Piemonte Grignolino '14	▼ 2
● Barbera del M.to '12	♈♈ 2*
● Barbera del M.to '11	♈♈ 2*
● Barbera del M.to Sup. Mepari '10	♈♈ 4
● Barbera del M.to Sup. Mepari '08	♈♈ 4
● Barbera del M.to Sup. Mepari '07	♈♈ 4
● Barbera del M.to Sup. Mepari '06	♈♈ 4
⊙ Brut Rosè M. Cl. '10	♈♈ 3
○ LV Quinquagesimaquinta Mansio Passito '12	♈♈ 4

★Luciano Sandrone

VIA PUGNANE, 4
12060 BAROLO [CN]
TEL. 0173560023
www.sandroneluciano.com

PRE-BOOKED VISITS
ANNUAL PRODUCTION 100,000 bottles
HECTARES UNDER VINE 27.00

Luciano Sandrone has made a name for
himself as one of the first and most famous
cult garage wine producers. He literally
caused a commotion in Langhe's
well-established production tradition,
releasing about 1,500 bottles of the
legendary 1978 vintage of his stylistically
innovative Barolo, which is also shaped by
ageing in small oak casks. Today he is
flanked by his daughter Barbara and his
brother Luca, and his Nebbiolos are
considered veritable "new classics",
focusing above all on the personalities of
crus like Cannubi Boschis, Baudana,
Conterni, Merli, Vignane, and Villero. They
are aged mainly in partly new tonneaux,
following maceration for about two weeks.
The 2011 vintage of Barolo Cannubi
Boschis is a particularly convincing version
of one of the cornerstones of the Piedmont
and Italian wine scene. It offers a nose of
violets and tobacco, with fresh, vibrant
balsamic hints, accompanied by a powerful,
elegant palate with a long, caressing finish.
Barolo Le Vigne 2011 is simply excellent.

● Barolo Cannubi Boschis '11	▼▼▼ 8
● Barolo Le Vigne '11	▼▼ 8
● Barbera d'Alba '13	▼▼ 5
● Nebbiolo d'Alba Valmaggiore '13	▼▼ 5
● Barolo '84	♈♈♈ 8
● Barolo '83	♈♈♈ 7
● Barolo Cannubi Boschis '10	♈♈♈ 8
● Barolo Cannubi Boschis '08	♈♈♈ 8
● Barolo Cannubi Boschis '07	♈♈♈ 8
● Barolo Cannubi Boschis '06	♈♈♈ 8
● Barolo Cannubi Boschis '05	♈♈♈ 8
● Barolo Cannubi Boschis '04	♈♈♈ 8
● Barolo Cannubi Boschis '03	♈♈♈ 8
● Barolo Cannubi Boschis '01	♈♈♈ 8
● Barolo Cannubi Boschis '00	♈♈♈ 8
● Barolo Le Vigne '99	♈♈♈ 8

Cantine Sant'Agata

REG. MEZZENA, 19
14030 SCURZOLENGO [AT]
TEL. 0141203186
www.santagata.com

CELLAR SALES
PRE-BOOKED VISITS
RESTAURANT SERVICE
ANNUAL PRODUCTION 150,000 bottles
HECTARES UNDER VINE 12.00

The Cavallero family's century-old estate is run by brothers Claudio and Franco, who have greatly expanded it. Its vineyards are in Scurzolengo, Canelli, and Monforte d'Alba and are planted mainly with ruché, moscato, and nebbiolo. However, smaller amounts of barbera, grignolino, cortese, chardonnay, and pinot nero are also grown. Barbera d'Asti Superiore Cavalé 2012 is excellent, with a nose of plums, chocolate, and spice, and a juicy palate, with fine acidity and freshness, but as usual it's the various versions of Ruché di Castagnole Monferrato that account for the lion's share. 'Na Vota 2014 is concentrated and aromatic, with a typical nose of roses and red berries, and a long, balanced palate with good structure, while Il Cavaliere 2014 flanks notes of roses with hints of liquorice, and is supple and easy drinking. Genesis 2010 deserves a separate mention, showing full and tannic, without varietal notes, well made but far removed from the canons of its type.

● Ruché di Castagnole M.to 'Na Vota '14	♟♟	3*
● Barbera d'Asti Sup. Cavalé '12	♟♟	4
● Ruché di Castagnole M.to Genesi '10	♟♟	6
● Ruché di Castagnole M.to Il Cavaliere '14	♟♟	2*
○ Gavi di Gavi Ciarea '14	♟	3
● Ruché di Castagnole M.to Pro Nobis '12	♟	3
● Barbaresco La Fenice '10	♟♟	3
● Barbera d'Asti Sup. Altea '12	♟♟	3
● Barbera d'Asti Sup. Cavalé '11	♟♟	4
● Barolo Bussia '09	♟♟	7
● Barolo Bussia '08	♟♟	5
● M.to Rosso Monterovere '09	♟♟	4
● Ruché di Castagnole M.to 'Na Vota '13	♟♟	3
● Ruché di Castagnole M.to 'Na Vota '13	♟♟	3
● Ruché di Castagnole M.to Genesi '09	♟♟	6
● Ruché di Castagnole M.to Pro Nobis '11	♟♟	3

Paolo Saracco

VIA CIRCONVALLAZIONE, 6
12053 CASTIGLIONE TINELLA [CN]
TEL. 0141855113
www.paolosaracco.it

CELLAR SALES
PRE-BOOKED VISITS
ANNUAL PRODUCTION 600,000 bottles
HECTARES UNDER VINE 46.00

Founded in the early 20th century, Paolo Saracco's estate is one of the most important moscato producers. Today it vaunts 14 vineyards, covering a total area of 46 hectares, lying mainly on beds of sand, silt, and limestone at altitudes between 300 and 460 metres. They are planted to moscato, flanked by smaller amounts of pinot nero, riesling, and chardonnay. Piemonte Moscato d'Autunno is always at the forefront. Although the year was certainly not a good one for this type of wine, the 2014 version has a fresh nose of lime, with floral hints, sage, and honey, and a complex, full-flavoured palate with remarkable body for the vintage, nicely balanced sugar and acidity, and a long, pleasant finish. Moscato d'Asti 2014 is sound but far more influenced by the difficult vintage, while the well-made Piemonte Pinot Nero 2012 is complex, supple and expressive.

○ Piemonte Moscato d'Autunno '14	♟♟	3*
○ Moscato d'Asti '14	♟♟	3
● Piemonte Pinot Nero '12	♟♟	5
○ Langhe Chardonnay Prasuè '14	♟	3
○ Langhe Riesling '13	♟	3
○ Piemonte Moscato d'Autunno '09	♟♟♟	3*
● M.to Rosso Pinot Nero '08	♟♟	5
● M.to Rosso Pinot Nero '06	♟♟	5
● M.to Rosso Pinot Nero '05	♟♟	5
○ Piemonte Moscato d'Autunno '13	♟♟	3*
● Piemonte Pinot Nero '11	♟♟	5
● Piemonte Pinot Nero '10	♟♟	5
● Piemonte Pinot Nero '09	♟♟	5

Roberto Sarotto

VIA RONCONUOVO, 13
12050 NEVIGLIE [CN]
TEL. 0173630228
www.robertosarotto.com

CELLAR SALES
PRE-BOOKED VISITS
ANNUAL PRODUCTION 700,000 bottles
HECTARES UNDER VINE 84.00

Roberto Saracco's plots in several
designations, all very good and
representative of Piedmont's finest
production, from Barolo and Barbaresco to
Gavi and Moscato d'Asti, allow him to offer
a remarkable, diverse, and complementary
range of wines. All of them vaunt consistent
quality and are fairly and competitively
priced, making this important, dynamic
winery an attractive proposition on many
markets. Out of the comprehensive range
of wines we tasted, we were pleasantly
struck by Gavi Bric Sassi 2014, with a
pervasive floral nose accompanied by hints
of flint and aniseed, and a refreshing,
full-flavoured palate. Although Barolo
Audace 2011 still shows very youthful, it
has a layered nose with notes of sweet
tobacco and balsamic hints, before
unbending into a long finish. Barbaresco
Currà Riserva 2010 has an interesting nose
and a firmly structured, juicy palate.

Scagliola

VIA SAN SIRO, 42
14052 CALOSSO [AT]
TEL. 0141853183
www.scagliolavini.com

CELLAR SALES
PRE-BOOKED VISITS
ANNUAL PRODUCTION 200,000 bottles
HECTARES UNDER VINE 37.00

Moscato and barbera are the main grape
varieties grown on the Scagliola family's
estate, which vaunts vineyards in both
Calosso, around the winery, and Canelli, all
at altitudes between 350 and 400 metres.
Those in Calosso lie on medium-textured
clayey limestone soil and are planted
chiefly to barbera, while mainly moscato is
grown on the sandy marl soils in Canelli.
Small amounts of other cultivars, like
dolcetto and cortese, are also present. This
year we preferred Barbera d'Asti Superiore
Sansi 2013 to Sansi Antologia 2012
(formerly Selezione). The first offers a
splendid combination of spicy oak and dark
berries on the nose, and a very classic,
juicy palate, both fresh and powerful, while
the second also shows great structure and
compactness, with plenty of flesh, but has
not achieved the right balance with the acid
note. Foravia 2013 is more elegant and
less powerful than other Nizzas, among the
best of the DOCG zone.

● Barbaresco Currà Ris. '10	♟♟ 5
● Barolo Audace '11	♟♟ 6
○ Gavi del Comune di Gavi Bric Sassi Tenuta Manenti '14	♟♟ 2*
● Barbera d'Alba Elena La Luna '13	♟♟ 5
○ Gavi Aurora '14	♟♟ 2*
○ Piemonte Chardonnay Impuro '14	♟♟ 3
● Barbaresco Gaia Principe '12	♟ 6
● Barbera d'Alba Bricco Macchia '14	♟ 2
○ Langhe Arneis Runcneuv '14	♟ 2
○ Moscato d'Asti Solatio '14	♟ 2
● Barbaresco Currà Ris. '09	♟♟ 5
● Barbaresco Gaia Principe '11	♟♟ 6
○ Gavi del Comune di Gavi Bric Sassi Tenuta Manenti '13	♟♟ 2*

● Barbera d'Asti Sup. Nizza Foravia '13	♟♟ 5
● Barbera d'Asti Sup. SanSi '13	♟♟ 6
● Barbera d'Asti Sup. SanSì Antologia '12	♟♟ 8
● M.to Rosso Azörd '13	♟♟ 5
○ Moscato d'Asti Primo Bacio '14	♟♟ 3
○ Moscato d'Asti Volo di Farfalle '14	♟♟ 3
● Barbera d'Asti Sup. SanSì Sel. '01	♟♟♟ 6
● Barbera d'Asti Sup. SanSì Sel. '00	♟♟♟ 6
● Barbera d'Asti Sup. SanSì Sel. '99	♟♟♟ 5
● Barbera d'Asti Sup. SanSì '11	♟♟ 6
● Barbera d'Asti Sup. SanSì '07	♟♟ 6
● Barbera d'Asti Sup. SanSì '06	♟♟ 6
● Barbera d'Asti Sup. SanSì Sel. '10	♟♟ 7
● Barbera d'Asti Sup. SanSì Sel. '09	♟♟ 7
● Barbera d'Asti Sup. SanSì Sel. '07	♟♟ 7
● Barbera d'Asti Sup. SanSi Sel. '05	♟♟ 7

Giorgio Scarzello e Figli

VIA ALBA, 29
12060 BAROLO [CN]
TEL. 017356170
www.barolodibarolo.com

CELLAR SALES
PRE-BOOKED VISITS
ANNUAL PRODUCTION 25,000 bottles
HECTARES UNDER VINE 5.50

At a time in which tradition and authenticity are central themes in the world of wine and particularly Langhe wine, this solid little family-run Barolo estate embodies a contemporary revival. Its wines are austere to the core, without any frills, and consistent over time. They are understated, able to satisfy even the most demanding palates from the moment of their release, but also capable of ageing. Barolo Sarmassa Vigna Merenda 2009 is nicely styled, showing classic and typical of the rather warm vintage, with prominent notes of herbs in the sun. The Barolo del Comune di Barolo of the same vintage is more developed, and the 2013 Nebbiolo is very balanced and supple with delightful texture and clean, typical varietal aromas emerging, Barbera d'Alba Superiore 2011 lacks assertiveness.

★★Paolo Scavino

FRAZ. GARBELLETTO
VIA ALBA-BAROLO, 59
12060 CASTIGLIONE FALLETTO [CN]
TEL. 017362850
www.paoloscavino.com

CELLAR SALES
PRE-BOOKED VISITS
ANNUAL PRODUCTION 120,000 bottles
HECTARES UNDER VINE 25.00

This winery, founded in 1921, started to shine again among the great names of Langhe in the 1950s with the arrival of Enrico, now aided by his skilled daughters Enrica and Elisa. The magnificent premises are well worth a visit, and great care is lavished on work in the vineyard and the cellar, which is home to tanks specially designed for the optimal fermentation and maceration of nebbiolo grapes. Today eight versions of Barolo are offered, six from single vineyards plus two blends. The top wine remains Riserva Rocche dell'Annunziata, an inevitable touchstone for the Barolo zone, but the entire range is characterized by rare elegance and complexity. Bric dël Fiasc 2011 is exquisitely well behaved, earning a Tre Bicchieri not only for its perfect balance of tannins, alcohol and acidity on the palate, but also for the joyful undertones of raspberries that characterize its spicy, already slightly liquoricey notes. Carobric 2011 is particularly well made and the quality of the range in general is very high.

● Barolo del Comune di Barolo '09	♀♀ 5
● Barolo Sarmassa V. Merenda '09	♀♀ 6
● Langhe Nebbiolo '13	♀♀ 3
● Barbera d'Alba Sup. '11	♀ 4
● Barolo V. Merenda '99	♀♀♀ 5
● Barbera d'Alba Sup. '10	♀♀ 4
● Barbera d'Alba Sup. '07	♀♀ 4
● Barolo '07	♀♀ 5
● Barolo '06	♀♀ 5
● Barolo '05	♀♀ 5
● Barolo del Comune di Barolo '08	♀♀ 5
● Barolo Sarmassa V. Merenda '08	♀♀ 6
● Barolo Sarmassa V. Merenda '06	♀♀ 6
● Barolo V. Merenda '06	♀♀ 6
● Barolo V. Merenda '05	♀♀ 6
● Langhe Nebbiolo '12	♀♀ 3

● Barolo Bric dël Fiasc '11	♀♀♀ 8
● Barolo Carobric '11	♀♀ 8
● Barolo Monvigliero '11	♀♀ 8
● Barolo Rocche dell'Annunziata Ris. '09	♀♀ 8
● Barbera d'Alba Affinato in Carati '13	♀♀ 4
● Barolo Bricco Ambrogio '11	♀♀ 8
● Barolo Cannubi '11	♀♀ 8
● Barolo Enrico Scavino '11	♀♀ 7
○ Langhe Bianco Sorriso '14	♀♀ 3
● Langhe Nebbiolo '13	♀♀ 4
● Barbera d'Alba '14	♀ 3
● Dolcetto d'Alba '14	♀ 3
● Barolo Bric dël Fiasc '09	♀♀♀ 8
● Barolo Monvigliero '08	♀♀♀ 8
● Barolo Rocche dell'Annunziata Ris. '08	♀♀♀ 8
● Barolo Rocche dell'Annunziata Ris. '05	♀♀♀ 8

Schiavenza

VIA MAZZINI, 4
12050 SERRALUNGA D'ALBA [CN]
TEL. 0173613115
www.schiavenza.com

CELLAR SALES
PRE-BOOKED VISITS
RESTAURANT SERVICE
ANNUAL PRODUCTION 40,000 bottles
HECTARES UNDER VINE 9.50
SUSTAINABLE WINERY

The most untamed and spirited essence of nebbiolo can found at the Schiavenza winery and restaurant. Its Barolos are in many respects confusing if compared to the placid and welcoming nature of Luciano Pira and his family, expressing the already austere structure of vineyards such as Prapò, Bricco Cerretta, and Broglio in Serralunga, and Perno in Monforte with unusually powerful tannins. Very long ageing in medium-sized barrels is not usually sufficient to make them thoroughly accessible upon release, but it is often worth being patient in order to enjoy their purest and most vibrant features. It may not be everyone's style, but this is precisely what makes it unique and worth preserving at all costs. It is faithfully reproduced in the 2011 Barolos. It's worth starting with the Cerretta, which is the most astringent in this phase, followed by the Prapò with greater density and fruity sweetness. But the real star is the Broglio, with its spicy, earthy style, beautifully underpinned by rich structure.

● Barolo Broglio '11	♥♥♥ 5
● Barolo Prapò '11	♥♥ 6
● Barolo Bricco Cerretta '11	♥♥ 6
● Barolo Broglio '05	♀♀♀ 5
● Barolo Broglio '04	♀♀♀ 5
● Barolo Broglio Ris. '08	♀♀♀ 7
● Barolo Broglio Ris. '04	♀♀♀ 5
● Barolo Prapò '08	♀♀♀ 6
● Barolo Prapò '10	♀♀ 6

Mauro Sebaste

FRAZ. GALLO D'ALBA
VIA GARIBALDI, 222BIS
12051 ALBA [CN]
TEL. 0173262148
www.maurosebaste.it

CELLAR SALES
PRE-BOOKED VISITS
ANNUAL PRODUCTION 150,000 bottles
HECTARES UNDER VINE 30.00

Mauro Sebaste, the son of Sylla, an indomitable and unforgotten figure of Langhe winemaking, has built his own winery that uses both estate-grown grapes and fruit supplied by trusted growers, where he continues to produce a Freisa named after his mother. Mauro's renown is chiefly due to his elegant, classic Barolo. His sole concession to international grape varieties is represented by the pleasant Langhe Bianco Centobricchi, from viognier, which displays both vigour and finesse. Barolo Prapò 2011 is particularly sophisticated and effectively expresses the characteristics of the fine Serralunga cru from which it hails, particularly its power and freshness. The nose offers hints of tobacco and discreet oak, while the very subtle, close-knit tannins contribute lend richness and volume but without aggressiveness. The sound Ghè is more evolved, focusing on spices, while the Trèsüri is rather lacking in structure.

● Barolo Prapò '11	♥♥ 7
● Barbera d'Alba Sup. Centobricchi '13	♥♥ 5
● Barolo Ghé Ris. '09	♥♥ 8
● Barbera d'Alba '14	♥ 3
● Barolo Trèsüri '11	♥ 6
● Nebbiolo d'Alba Parigi '13	♥ 4
● Barbera d'Alba Sup. Centobricchi '12	♀♀ 4
● Barbera d'Alba Sup. Centobricchi '11	♀♀ 4
● Barbera d'Alba Sup. Centobricchi '10	♀♀ 4
● Barolo Ghé Ris. '08	♀♀ 8
● Barolo Monvigliero '07	♀♀ 6
● Barolo Prapò '09	♀♀ 7
● Barolo Prapò '08	♀♀ 7
○ Gavi '10	♀♀ 3
● Nebbiolo d'Alba Parigi '11	♀♀ 4
● Nebbiolo d'Alba Parigi '09	♀♀ 4

F.lli Seghesio

LOC. CASTELLETTO, 19
12065 MONFORTE D'ALBA [CN]
TEL. 017378108
www.fratelliseghesio.it

CELLAR SALES
PRE-BOOKED VISITS
ANNUAL PRODUCTION 55,000 bottles
HECTARES UNDER VINE 10.00

The Seghesio family own well-aspected vineyards not only for nebbiolo, with the La Villa cru, but also for barbera, with the La Chiesa cru in the Castelletto hamlet of Monforte, offering magnificent views over Serralunga d'Alba. The style of the wines is characterized by impressive cleanliness and finesse, sometimes with the aid of small French casks, although the oak is never too prominent. Barolo and Barbera d'Alba naturally top the range, but the entire production of exclusively red wines is distinguished by its great elegance and drinkability. The warm 2011 vintage made the Barolos fairly fruit-rich throughout the zone, but the Seghesio family have also added fine austerity and density. Indeed, the La Villa selection has a nose with prominent notes of quinine, followed by a decidedly solid, rich palate. The Barolo 2011 is concentrated and somewhat lacking in liveliness, but is destined to improve. Unfortunately, the new version of Barbera d'Alba La Chiesa was not ready for our tastings.

● Barolo La Villa '11	♥♥ 7
● Barolo '11	♥♥ 7
● Barbera d'Alba Vign. della Chiesa '00	♥♥♥ 4*
● Barbera d'Alba Vign. della Chiesa '97	♥♥♥ 4*
● Barolo Vign. La Villa '04	♥♥♥ 6
● Barolo Vign. La Villa '99	♥♥♥ 7
● Barolo Vign. La Villa '91	♥♥♥ 6
● Barbera d'Alba '13	♥♥ 3
● Barbera d'Alba '12	♥♥ 3
● Barbera d'Alba '10	♥♥ 2*
● Barbera d'Alba La Chiesa '12	♥♥ 4
● Barbera d'Alba Vign. della Chiesa '10	♥♥ 4
● Barolo La Villa '10	♥♥ 7
● Barolo La Villa '09	♥♥ 7
● Barolo Vign. La Villa '08	♥♥ 6
● Barolo Vign. La Villa '07	♥♥ 6

Tenute Sella

VIA IV NOVEMBRE, 130
13060 LESSONA [BI]
TEL. 01599455
www.tenutesella.it

CELLAR SALES
PRE-BOOKED VISITS
ANNUAL PRODUCTION 80,000 bottles
HECTARES UNDER VINE 22.00

Tenute Sella has been the hub of Biella wine production for over 300 years. It is a safe bet for lovers of the brightest and most ethereal type of nebbiolo, which plays the leading role in the blends with vespolina and croatina, making the winery a mecca for those wishing to taste the very different personalities of the sandy soils of Lessona and the porphyry of Bramaterra. The barrel cellar houses 2,500-litre Slavonian oak barrels and partly new barriques, but these technical variables have only a relative bearing on the definition of an authentically classic style, preserved even after a series of changes in cellar management. The estate's range put up a fine overall performance, commencing with Costa della Sesia Rosso Orbello 2013, perfect for the table with its exuberant fresh fruit. There is naturally greater depth and breadth in Bramaterra 2010, which offers an alluring bouquet of tobacco and dried herbs, marred only by a few rough edges on the finish.

● Bramaterra '10	♥♥ 5
⊙ Coste della Sesia Rosato Majoli '13	♥♥ 3
● Coste della Sesia Rosso Orbello '13	♥♥ 3
● Lessona S. Sebastiano allo Zoppo '09	♥♥ 6
○ Coste della Sesia Bianco Doranda '14	♥ 3
● Coste della Sesia Rosso Casteltorto '12	♥ 4
● Lessona Omaggio a Quintino Sella '06	♥♥♥ 7
● Bramaterra I Porfidi '09	♥♥ 5
○ Coste della Sesia Bianco Doranda '12	♥♥ 3
● Lessona Omaggio a Quintino Sella '08	♥♥ 7
● Lessona Omaggio a Quintino Sella '07	♥♥ 7
● Lessona S. Sebastiano allo Zoppo '07	♥♥ 6

Enrico Serafino

c.so Asti, 5
12043 Canale [CN]
Tel. 0173979485
www.enricoserafino.it

CELLAR SALES
PRE-BOOKED VISITS
ANNUAL PRODUCTION 500,000 bottles
HECTARES UNDER VINE 12.00

As announced in the trade press, Enrico Serafino no longer belongs to the Gruppo Campari's wine portfolio, following its official sale a few months ago. We are thus waiting to see the how the new owners fare and discover their intentions for an estate that, in recent years, has astonished us with its growth and consistent quality. And we hope that the close-knit team that has managed to put this venerable winery back in the spotlight in the space of less than a decade will continue its work. The wines presented this year, of good overall quality, belong to the old management. Alta Langa Brut Zero 2009 stands out from the list as one of Italy's finest sparklers. It has a nose of croissants, toasted bread, and hedgerow, followed by an extraordinary palate that is both solid and supple. Roero Pasiunà 2012 deserves a special mention for its well-defined varietal notes, which make it one of the benchmarks for the designation.

○ Alta Langa Brut Zero Cantina Maestra '09	▼▼▼ 6
○ Alta Langa Brut Cantina Maestra '09	▼▼ 4
● Barbera d'Alba Bacajé Cantina Maestra '14	▼▼ 3
● Barbera d'Alba Sup. Parduné Cantina Maestra '12	▼▼ 4
○ Roero Arneis Canteiò Cantina Maestra '14	▼▼ 3
● Roero Pasiunà Cantina Maestra '12	▼▼ 4
⊙ Alta Langa Brut Rosé Cantina Maestra '12	▼ 6
● Nebbiolo d'Alba Diauleri Cantina Maestra '13	▼ 3
○ Alta Langa Brut Zero Cantina Maestra '07	▼▼▼ 6
○ Alta Langa Brut Zero Sboccatura Tardiva Cantina Maestra '08	▼▼▼ 6

Aurelio Settimo

fraz. Annunziata, 30
12064 La Morra [CN]
Tel. 017350803
www.aureliosettimo.com

CELLAR SALES
PRE-BOOKED VISITS
ANNUAL PRODUCTION 40,000 bottles
HECTARES UNDER VINE 6.64

The nebbiolo grapes vinified in Tiziana Settimo's cellar are undisputedly pure. Whether they are used for the most straightforward Langhe, aged in fibreglass-lined concrete vats, the basic Barolo, or the Rocche dell'Annunziata cru, the estate always strives to preserve their personality and fruit. The same holds true for the rare Riserva, patiently aged in large Slavonian oak barrels for many years before release. The warm vintage led to rather evolved wines in 2011. Barolo Rocche dell'Annunziata has a nose of tobacco and herbs in the sun, followed by a rather tannic, incisive palate, with good length and overall structure. The basic Barolo of the same vintage has ripe red berry fruit and prominent alcohol, but is slightly short on freshness.

● Barolo '11	▼▼ 5
● Barolo Rocche dell' Annunziata '11	▼▼ 6
● Dolcetto d'Alba '14	▼ 2
● Barolo '10	♀♀ 5
● Barolo '09	♀♀ 5
● Barolo '08	♀♀ 5
● Barolo '07	♀♀ 5
● Barolo Rocche '06	♀♀ 5
● Barolo Rocche dell' Annunziata '10	♀♀ 6
● Barolo Rocche dell' Annunziata '09	♀♀ 6
● Barolo Rocche dell' Annunziata '08	♀♀ 6
● Barolo Rocche dell' Annunziata '07	♀♀ 5
● Barolo Rocche Ris. '04	♀♀ 7
● Dolcetto d'Alba '13	♀♀ 2*
● Langhe Nebbiolo '08	♀♀ 3
● Langhe Nebbiolo '06	♀♀ 3

PIEDMONT

Giovanni Silva

Cascine Rogge, 1b
10011 Agliè [TO]
Tel. 3473075648
www.silvavini.com

CELLAR SALES
PRE-BOOKED VISITS
ANNUAL PRODUCTION 50,000 bottles
HECTARES UNDER VINE 12.00

The Silva family have just celebrated 20 years in the sector, having started to bottle their own wines in 1995 after three generations as vignerons. As is fairly usual in the Canavese district, the winery focuses mainly on Erbaluce di Caluso, but its vineyards are also home to nebbiolo, barbera, freisa, and bonarda, which are used alone or in blends in its three red wines. The estate produces all the classic versions of Erbaluce: still, sparkling, and passito. Although they did not present the entire range as the spumantes, the passito and some of the reds were missing, one of the Silva family's wines reached our finals. It was Erbaluce Tre Ciochè 2014, which stands out in this difficult vintage for its elegant fruity notes of pears and vegetal hints of ferns and lichens, and a well-orchestrated palate distinguished by vibrant acidity and moderate body. The no-nonsense Dry Ice and the stiff Nebbiolo, which lacks a little warmth, come in behind.

○ Erbaluce di Caluso Tre Ciochè '14	♟♟	2*
○ Erbaluce di Caluso Dry Ice '14	♟♟	2*
● Canavese Nebbiolo '10	♟	4
○ Caluso Passito Poetica '03	♟♟	5
○ Caluso Passito Poetica '01	♟♟	5
○ Caluso Passito Poetica '00	♟♟	5
● Canavese Nebbiolo '08	♟♟	2*
● Canavese Rosso Tre Ciochè '03	♟♟	3
○ Erbaluce di Caluso Brut	♟♟	5
○ Erbaluce di Caluso Ca' Neuva '03	♟♟	3*
○ Erbaluce di Caluso Dry Silva '12	♟♟	2*
○ Erbaluce di Caluso Passito Poetica '04	♟♟	5
○ Erbaluce di Caluso Tre Ciochè '13	♟♟	2*
○ Erbaluce di Caluso Tre Ciochè '12	♟♟	2*
○ Erbaluce di Caluso Tre Ciochè '06	♟♟	2*
○ Erbaluce di Caluso Tre Ciochè '03	♟	2*

La Smilla

via Garibaldi, 7
15060 Bosio [AL]
Tel. 0143684245
www.lasmilla.it

CELLAR SALES
ANNUAL PRODUCTION 100,000 bottles
HECTARES UNDER VINE 5.00

La Smilla is the name of the Guido family's estate in Bosio, in the southern reaches of the province of Alessandria, where the Gavi and Dolcetto di Ovada designations overlap. It is a unique terroir in terms of soil and climate, almost suspended between the sea and the Apennines, which is faithfully reflected in the finest wines, prevalently from barbera, dolcetto and cortese. The entire range is steel aged, with the exception of Gavi I Bergi and Barbera Calicanto, aged in small French oak casks. Danilo's fantastic Dolcetto d'Ovada 2013 made it into our finals. It is very classic, with great personality and an elegant fruity nose echoed on the long, full, harmonious palate. The Gavi di Gavi is concentrated and sophisticated, with elegant citrus notes on a background of white-fleshed fruit and vegetal hints, followed by a rich, structured palate. The basic Gavi is fairly down to earth, but packed with power and character.

● Dolcetto di Ovada '13	♟♟	2*
○ Gavi '14	♟♟	2*
○ Gavi del Comune di Gavi '14	♟♟	2*
● Barbera del M.to '13	♟	2
● Dolcetto di Ovada '12	♟♟	2*
● Dolcetto di Ovada '10	♟♟	2*
● Dolcetto di Ovada '09	♟♟	2*
○ Gavi '13	♟♟	2*
○ Gavi '11	♟♟	2*
○ Gavi del Comune di Gavi '13	♟♟	2*
○ Gavi del Comune di Gavi '12	♟♟	2*
○ Gavi del Comune di Gavi '11	♟♟	2*
○ Gavi del Comune di Gavi '10	♟♟	2*
○ Gavi del Comune di Gavi I Bergi '11	♟♟	3
● M.to Rosso Calicanto '10	♟♟	3

Socré

S.DA TERZOLO, 7
12050 BARBARESCO [CN]
TEL. 3487121685
www.socre.it

PRE-BOOKED VISITS
ACCOMMODATION
ANNUAL PRODUCTION 30,000 bottles
HECTARES UNDER VINE 5.50

What might have seemed a weekend hobby has become a full-time job, which sees Marco Piacentino dividing his time between the handsome Roncaglie vineyard and his underground cellar, in between a wine fair in Germany and a tasting in Turin. His hard work has been accompanied by a steady rise in quality, and today Socré's range of wines is consistently sound, from the Barbera d'Alba to the Barbaresco. The well-made Barbaresco 2012 has a nose focusing more on layers than on elegance, with notes ranging from wet dog to currants, and excellent tannins on a full, fleshy palate with good structure. Barbera d'Alba Superiore 2013 is potent and laden with dark berries, enriched with hints of quinine and rain-soaked earth, which amplify its personality. We also liked the first release of Riserva di Barbaresco Roncaglie 2010, available in very limited quantities for now.

● Barbaresco '12	♟♟ 5
● Barbera d'Alba Sup. '13	♟♟ 3
● Cisterna d'Asti De Scapin '12	♟♟ 2*
● Barbera d'Asti '14	♟ 2
● Langhe Nebbiolo '13	♟ 3
● Barbaresco '11	♟♟ 5
● Barbaresco '10	♟♟ 5
● Barbaresco '08	♟♟ 5
● Barbaresco Roncaglie '11	♟♟ 6
● Barbaresco Roncaglie '10	♟♟ 7
● Barbaresco Roncaglie '09	♟♟ 7

★Sottimano

LOC. COTTÀ, 21
12052 NEIVE [CN]
TEL. 0173635186
www.sottimano.it

CELLAR SALES
PRE-BOOKED VISITS
ANNUAL PRODUCTION 85,000 bottles
HECTARES UNDER VINE 18.00

Currà, Cottà, Fausoni, and Pajoré are the tried-and-tested team of crus that Rino Sottimano can count on to craft his famous Barbarescos, with the aid of his wife Anna and children Andrea and Elena. They are modern-style Nebbiolos, due to ageing in barriques (only partly new), but they are widely appreciated for their austere texture and the quality of their fruity matière, the direct result of the meticulously tended vineyards in Neive. A Barbaresco Riserva is produced in the finest vintages from grapes of the Cottà and Pajorè crus. The range also includes Dolcetto Bric del Salto, Barbera Pairolero, and the dry Brachetto Maté. The Riserva di Barbaresco is the Sottimano family's best so far. Its perfect balance of potency and suppleness, oak and fruit, tannic weave and caressing palate earned it a Tre Bicchieri for finesse, harmony, and splendour in the same glass. Two other fantastic Barbarescos were very close behind: the austere, finely chiselled Currà 2011 and the restrained, elegant Pajoré 2012. Lastly, there is the long, progressive Cottà 2012.

● Barbaresco Ris. '10	♟♟♟ 8
● Barbaresco Cottà '12	♟♟ 7
● Barbaresco Currà '11	♟♟ 8
● Barbaresco Fausoni '12	♟♟ 7
● Barbera d'Alba Sup. Pairolero '13	♟♟ 4
● Langhe Nebbiolo '13	♟♟ 3
● Dolcetto d'Alba Bric del Salto '14	♟ 3
● Maté '14	♟ 3
● Barbaresco Cottà '05	♟♟ 7
● Barbaresco Currà '10	♟♟♟ 8
● Barbaresco Currà '08	♟♟♟ 7
● Barbaresco Pajoré '10	♟♟♟ 7
● Barbaresco Pajoré '08	♟♟♟ 7
● Barbaresco Ris. '05	♟♟♟ 8
● Barbaresco Ris. '04	♟♟♟ 8

PIEDMONT

Luigi Spertino

via Lea, 505
14047 Mombercelli [AT]
Tel. 0141959098
www.luigispertino.it

CELLAR SALES
PRE-BOOKED VISITS
ANNUAL PRODUCTION 40,000 bottles
HECTARES UNDER VINE 9.00

Mauro Spertino enthusiastically heads the family winery, which he has accompanied to the top of the Asti winemaking world, not only with the legendary Grignolino, which remains a veritable icon of its kind, but with the entire range, commencing with the Barbera. The choice to dry the grapes for the dry wines from the La Mandorla cru, and to ferment the sole white wine (from cortese) on the lees, has resulted in very personal, unique wines that successfully reflect the terroir. Barbera d'Asti Superiore La Mandorla took another Tre Bicchieri with the 2013 vintage. The nose has notes of dark berry fruit, juniper berries, and rain-soaked earth, while the juicy palate is underpinned by acidity, making it very pleasant drinking. No longer La Mandorla for bureaucratic reasons, Pinot Nero Monferrato Rosso 2012 has big character, with notes of currants and wild strawberries, while Barbera d'Asti 2013 is vibrant and fruit rich.

★★★La Spinetta

via Annunziata, 17
14054 Castagnole delle Lanze [AT]
Tel. 0141877396
www.la-spinetta.com

CELLAR SALES
PRE-BOOKED VISITS
ANNUAL PRODUCTION 500,000 bottles
HECTARES UNDER VINE 100.00
SUSTAINABLE WINERY

Year after year, Giorgio Rivetti's Piedmont winery has earned a fame that has made it a leading ambassador of Langhe wine throughout the world and the labels with the rhinoceros are present in the finest restaurants on all continents. Over the years the house style has changed considerably, without ever abandoning the precepts of modernity. Today the emphasis is no longer on rich extraction, but on the quest for ripe, close-focused fruit. The splendid, fresh Barbera Gallina 2012 is lively and complex, showing velvety and harmonious. Gallina 2012, a Barbaresco selection, is highly convincing, offering greater freshness and vitality due to a nose of raspberries and currants mingling with sweet tobacco and spice. The palate is pleasantly fresh and still tannic, with firm structure guaranteeing good development. The Valeirano has a pervasive nose of peach kernels and ripe red berries, accompanied by a very fresh palate.

● Barbera d'Asti Sup. La Mandorla '13	♟♟♟ 8
● Barbera d'Asti '13	♟♟ 4
● M.to Rosso Pinot Nero '12	♟♟ 7
● Grignolino d'Asti '14	♟♟ 3
● Barbera d'Asti Sup. La Mandorla '10	♟♟♟ 8
● Barbera d'Asti Sup. La Mandorla '09	♟♟♟ 8
● Barbera d'Asti Sup. La Mandorla '07	♟♟♟ 7
● Barbera d'Asti Sup. V. La Mandorla '12	♟♟♟ 8
● M.to Rosso La Mandorla '09	♟♟♟ 7
● M.to Rosso La Mandorla '07	♟♟♟ 5
● Barbera d'Asti '12	♟♟ 4
● Barbera d'Asti '10	♟♟ 4
● Grignolino d'Asti '13	♟♟ 3*
● Grignolino d'Asti '12	♟♟ 3
● Grignolino d'Asti '11	♟♟ 3*
○ Piemonte Cortese '11	♟♟ 7

● Barbaresco Gallina '12	♟♟ 8
● Barbaresco Valeirano '12	♟♟ 8
● Barbera d'Alba Gallina '12	♟♟ 6
● Barolo Campè '11	♟♟ 8
● Barbaresco Starderi '12	♟♟ 8
● Barbaresco Vign. Bordini '11	♟♟ 7
● Barbera d'Asti Ca' di Pian '12	♟♟ 4
● Barbera d'Asti Sup. Bionzo '12	♟♟ 6
● Barolo Vign. Garretti '11	♟♟ 7
● M.to Rosso Pin '12	♟♟ 6
○ Moscato d'Asti Biancospino '14	♟♟ 3
○ Moscato d'Asti Bricco Quaglia '14	♟♟ 3
● Barbaresco Gallina '11	♟♟♟ 8
● Barbaresco Vign. Starderi '07	♟♟♟ 8
● Barbera d'Asti Sup. Bionzo '09	♟♟♟ 6
● Barolo Campè '08	♟♟♟ 8

Sylla Sebaste

VIA SAN PIETRO, 4
12060 BAROLO [CN]
TEL. 017356266
www.syllasebaste.com

CELLAR SALES
PRE-BOOKED VISITS
RESTAURANT SERVICE
ANNUAL PRODUCTION 120,000 bottles
HECTARES UNDER VINE 10.00

This important Langhe cellar is over 30 years old. During this time it has shown itself capable of innovating and improving with the creation of a range of wines representative of some of the region's foremost designations. Its owner and current front man Fabrizio Merlo, aided by the skilled oenologist Luca Caramellino, is dynamically following a path that, year after year, is achieving ever greater success both in Italy and in many foreign countries. Barolo Bussia 2011 has a broad, layered nose with top notes of wild berries, followed by roots and forest floor. The palate focuses on balancing its still rather stark tannins with its full flesh, offering a pleasantly austere sensation. The basic Barolo offers short-term pleasure without any unnecessary ruggedness and the Barbera d'Alba 2013 is pleasantly vegetal, fresh, and lingering.

● Barolo Bussia '11	♟♟ 6
● Barbera d'Alba '13	♟♟ 3
● Barolo '11	♟♟ 6
● Nebbiolo d'Alba '12	♟♟ 3
● Barolo Bussia '85	♟♟♟ 6
● Barolo Bussia Ris. '84	♟♟♟ 6
● Barbera d'Alba '11	♟♟ 3
● Barolo '10	♟♟ 6
● Barolo '09	♟♟ 6
● Barolo '08	♟♟ 6
● Barolo Bussia '10	♟♟ 6
● Barolo Bussia '09	♟♟ 6
● Barolo Bussia '06	♟♟ 6
● Nebbiolo d'Alba '11	♟♟ 3
● Nebbiolo d'Alba '09	♟♟ 2*

Tacchino

VIA MARTIRI DELLA BENEDICTA, 26
15060 CASTELLETTO D'ORBA [AL]
TEL. 0143830115
www.luigitacchino.it

CELLAR SALES
PRE-BOOKED VISITS
ANNUAL PRODUCTION 12,000 bottles
HECTARES UNDER VINE 12.00

Romina and her brother Alessio confidently continue along the path they have trodden in recent years, among the hills of Dolcetto di Ovada. Dolcetto is a grape variety with great potential, which has finally found new interpreters capable of highlighting its power, elegance and ageing potential. There have been other great exponents of the cultivar in the past, like Pino Ratto, but today the team formed by the Tacchino family with oenologist Mario Ronco and agronomist Alberto Pansecchi, is capable of launching a new cycle, which could represent a turning point for this area. The worthy emblem of Dolcetto d'Ovada, Du Riva won its umpteenth Tre Bicchieri for the complex, concentrated 2012 vintage. On the nose, it is characterized by fruit that develops into notes of cocoa powder and liquorice, heralding a pulp-rich palate with a very long finish. The other labels are very well made: Albarola, which also made it into our finals, Dolcetto 2013, and Monferrato Rosso Di Fatto.

● Dolcetto di Ovada Sup. Du Riva '12	♟♟♟ 5
● Barbera del M.to Albarola '12	♟♟ 5
● Dolcetto di Ovada '13	♟♟ 2*
● M.to Rosso Di Fatto '12	♟♟ 4
○ Cortese dell'Alto M.to Marsenca '14	♟ 2
○ Gavi del Comune di Gavi '14	♟ 3
● Dolcetto di Ovada Sup. Du Riva '11	♟♟♟ 5
● Dolcetto di Ovada Sup. Du Riva '10	♟♟♟ 4*
● Dolcetto di Ovada Sup. Du Riva '09	♟♟♟ 4*
● Dolcetto di Ovada Sup. Du Riva '08	♟♟♟ 4*
● Barbera del M.to '13	♟♟ 2*
● Barbera del M.to '12	♟♟ 2*
○ Gavi del Comune di Gavi '13	♟♟ 3
○ Gavi del Comune di Gavi '12	♟♟ 3
● M.to Rosso Di Fatto '11	♟♟ 4
● M.to Rosso Di Fatto '10	♟♟ 5

Michele Taliano

c.so A. Manzoni, 24
12046 Montà [CN]
Tel. 0173975658
www.talianomichele.com

CELLAR SALES
PRE-BOOKED VISITS
ANNUAL PRODUCTION 60,000 bottles
HECTARES UNDER VINE 12.00

The estate owned by brothers Ezio and
Alberto Taliano has been bottling its own
wines since the mid-1990s. Today it has
vineyards in Roero and at San Rocco Seno
d'Elvio, in the Barbaresco DOCG zone. The
winery itself is in Montà, along with its
Roero vineyards, planted with arneis,
barbera, favorita, and nebbiolo, while the
Langhe plots are home to nebbiolo,
barbera, dolcetto and moscato. This year
Roero Ròche dra Bòssora Riserva is back
in the limelight. The 2011 vintage has a
nose of quinine, liquorice, and tobacco,
while the complex palate is fruit rich with
close-knit tannins and a long finish.
Nebbiolo d'Alba Blagheur 2013 is well
made with a layered nose of orange peel
and raspberries, and a dense palate with
good acidity and length. The Alba
production is less stunning than usual,
with Barbaresco Tera Mia Riserva 2008
showing very mature notes on both nose
and palate.

● Roero Ròche dra Bòssora Ris. '11		♟♟ 3*
● Nebbiolo d'Alba Blagheur '13		♟♟ 2*
● Barbaresco Tera Mia Ris. '08		♟ 5
○ Roero Arneis Sernì '14		♟ 2
● Barbaresco Ad Altiora '11		♟♟ 5
● Barbaresco Ad Altiora '09		♟♟ 5
● Barbaresco Ad Altiora '08		♟♟ 5
● Barbaresco Ad Altiora '07		♟♟ 5
● Barbaresco Ad Altiora '06		♟♟ 5
● Barbera d'Alba A Bon Rendre '13		♟♟ 2*
● Barbera d'Alba Laboriosa '11		♟♟ 3
● Barbera d'Alba Laboriosa '10		♟♟ 3
● Barbera d'Alba Laboriosa '06		♟♟ 3*
● Nebbiolo d'Alba Blagheur '08		♟♟ 3
● Nebbiolo d'Alba Blagheur '07		♟♟ 3
○ Roero Arneis Sernì '13		♟♟ 2*

Tenuta La Tenaglia

s.da Santuario di Crea, 5c
15020 Serralunga di Crea [AL]
Tel. 0142940252
www.latenaglia.com

CELLAR SALES
PRE-BOOKED VISITS
ACCOMMODATION
ANNUAL PRODUCTION 120,000 bottles
HECTARES UNDER VINE 30.00
SUSTAINABLE WINERY

Tenuta Tenaglia is among the gems of the
Monferrato wine world, the legacy of an
illustrious past whose unique features it
evokes. On these hills, the highest of
Monferrato Casalese, viticulture has been
practised for centuries and the area has
always been described as one of the very
finest. Today the Ehrmann family's estate
produces a wide range of wines from both
natives like barbera, grignolino, and
moscato d'Asti, and internationals like
chardonnay and syrah. It shows poetic
licence with timorasso, little used in the
Casalese area, blending it with chardonnay
in the Monferrato Bianco. The range is
headed by Barbera del Monferrato 1930, a
regular in our finals, which is fresh, well
orchestrated, and very long. It is followed
by the excellent Barbera d'Asti Emozioni,
which showed complex and concentrated
in every phase of tasting.

● Barbera del M.to Sup. 1930 Una Buona Annata '11		♟♟ 5
● Barbera d'Asti Briccolino '14		♟♟ 2*
● Barbera d'Asti Emozioni '09		♟♟ 4
● Barbera del M.to Cappella III '14		♟♟ 2*
● Grignolino del M.to Casalese '14		♟ 2
⊙ M.to Chiaretto Edenrose '14		♟ 2
○ Piemonte Chardonnay '14		♟ 2
● Barbera d'Asti Emozioni '99		♟♟♟ 4*
● Barbera d'Asti Bricco '13		♟♟ 2*
● Barbera d'Asti Giorgio Tenaglia '09		♟♟ 5
● Barbera del M.to Sup. 1930 Una Buona Annata '10		♟♟ 5
● Barbera del M.to Sup. 1930 Una Buona Annata '09		♟♟ 5
● Grignolino del M.to Casalese '13		♟♟ 2*

Terre del Barolo

VIA ALBA-BAROLO, 8
12060 CASTIGLIONE FALLETTO [CN]
TEL. 0173262053
www.terredelbarolo.com

CELLAR SALES
PRE-BOOKED VISITS
ANNUAL PRODUCTION 30,000,000 bottles
HECTARES UNDER VINE 650.00

In over 60 years of activity, this important cooperative winery has become a global beacon: from those picking up a bottle at a service station to visitors to the shop in Castiglione Falletto, and bottlers seeking a sound product, the range is wide and always interesting. Able to count on the 650 hectares of its member growers, this is the winery that enabled the continuation of large-scale viticulture in the Barolo area even during the dark years of the 1960s and '70s. The valid range of Barolos of different vintages is often released with a few extra years of ageing. Castello Riserva 2008 is well made, showing youthful and complex, and focusing more on freshness and complexity than on pure power, largely due to its impressive acidity. The Monvigliero 2009 and the Cannubi 2009 stand out among the other crus.

● Barolo Castello Ris. '08	🍷🍷 6
● Barolo Monvigliero '09	🍷🍷 6
● Barbera d'Alba Valdisera '12	🍷🍷 2*
● Barolo Cannubi '09	🍷🍷 7
● Barolo Ravera '09	🍷🍷 6
● Barolo Rocche di Castiglione Ris. '08	🍷🍷 7
● Barolo '11	🍷 5
● Diano d'Alba Sorì del Cascinotto '14	🍷 2
● Verduno Pelaverga '14	🍷 2
● Barolo Cannubi '08	🍷🍷 7
● Barolo Castello Ris. '07	🍷🍷 6
● Barolo Monvigliero '08	🍷🍷 6
● Barolo Ravera '08	🍷🍷 6
● Barolo Vinum Vita Est '10	🍷🍷 5

Torraccia del Piantavigna

VIA ROMAGNANO, 69A
28067 GHEMME [NO]
TEL. 0163840040
www.torracciadelpiantavigna.it

CELLAR SALES
PRE-BOOKED VISITS
ANNUAL PRODUCTION 150,000 bottles
HECTARES UNDER VINE 35.00
SUSTAINABLE WINERY

The destiny of the Francoli brothers' winegrowing project was in many respects written in its name. Piantavigna, meaning vine planter, was the surname of their maternal grandfather, while Torraccia is the name of the place in Ghemme where the first nebbiolo vineyard was planted in 1977. Bottling commenced in 1990, but the estate grew until reaching the current 40 hectares, in at least six different zones in the provinces of Novara and Vercelli, planted to typical local varieties. The resulting range is wide, headed by reds with weighty stuffing and sometimes extract, aged mainly in large oak, which generally require patience in order to reach their best. With the Gattinara not yet released, this year the task of heading the estate's small range fell to Ghemme Vigna Pelizzane 2010. It shows well-controlled development of dried flowers, rust, and salt, seeming to forgo fruit even on the palate, which is nonetheless vibrant due to its very full flavour and tannins, austere but not aggressive.

● Ghemme V. Pellizzane '10	🍷🍷🍷 6
● Colline Novaresi Nebbiolo Tre Confini '13	🍷🍷 3
● Colline Novaresi Vespolina La Mostella '13	🍷🍷 3
● Colline Novaresi Nebbiolo Ramale '11	🍷 4
● Gattinara '09	🍷🍷🍷 5
● Ghemme '10	🍷🍷🍷 5
● Ghemme Ris. '07	🍷🍷🍷 5
● Ghemme Ris. '07	🍷🍷🍷 5
● Gattinara '10	🍷🍷 5
● Gattinara '08	🍷🍷 5
● Gattinara '08	🍷🍷 5
● Ghemme '09	🍷🍷 5
● Ghemme Ris. '09	🍷🍷 6

Giancarlo Travaglini

VIA DELLE VIGNE, 36
13045 GATTINARA [VC]
TEL. 0163833588
www.travaglinigattinara.it

CELLAR SALES
PRE-BOOKED VISITS
ANNUAL PRODUCTION 250,000 bottles
HECTARES UNDER VINE 46.00
SUSTAINABLE WINERY

Owning more than half the vineyards of the designation, the Travaglini family are universally acknowledged as one of the leading custodians of the style of Gattinara nebbiolo. The iron-rich acidic soils, dry airy climate, and the influence of the nearby Alps are faithfully reflected in the basic version, the Tre Vigne selection, and the Riserva, all different types of wine from different vineyards and aged in oak for different lengths of time. They are flanked by Nebbiolo Il Sogno, from super-ripe grapes. Today the estate is run by Cinzia Travaglini, with the aid of her husband Massimo Collauto, who maintains a classic style in the finest sense of the word. This time the challenge between the two top Gattinaras, both from the 2010 vintage, was won by the Tre Vigne, which focuses as usual on richly extracted fruit, with notes of cherries and liquorice, while the Riserva expresses itself more subtly, with tertiary hints of iron filings and woodland.

● Gattinara Ris. '10	♟♟ 6
● Gattinara Tre Vigne '10	♟♟ 5
● Coste della Sesia Nebbiolo '13	♟♟ 3
● Gattinara '11	♟♟ 4
● Il Sogno '10	♟ 6
● Gattinara Ris. '06	♟♟♟ 6
● Gattinara Ris. '04	♟♟♟ 5
● Gattinara Ris. '01	♟♟♟ 5
● Gattinara Tre Vigne '04	♟♟♟ 5
● Gattinara '10	♟♟ 4
● Gattinara '09	♟♟ 4
● Gattinara Ris. '09	♟♟ 6
● Gattinara Ris. '08	♟♟ 6
● Gattinara Tre Vigne '09	♟♟ 5
● Gattinara Tre Vigne '08	♟♟ 5
● il Sogno '09	♟♟ 6

★G. D. Vajra

LOC. VERGNE
VIA DELLE VIOLE, 25
12060 BAROLO [CN]
TEL. 017356257
www.gdvajra.it

CELLAR SALES
PRE-BOOKED VISITS
ANNUAL PRODUCTION 220,000 bottles
HECTARES UNDER VINE 50.00

In many respects, Aldo and Milena Vajra's estate has a dual nature. On the one hand, it is strongly rooted to the Langhe winemaking tradition; on the other it is an authentic varietal and territorial test bench. These two sides merge harmoniously in a range featuring both classic wines and experiments with riesling renano or pinot nero, not to mention freisa and sparklers. The Nebbiolos are characterized by lightness and luminous fruit, and hail from Bricco delle Viole and Vergne in the upper part of Barolo, and the Serralunga plots acquired with the recent purchase of the Luigi Baudana estate. Vajra's 2011 vintages are sound, commencing with Barolo Cerretta that is still unyielding at this stage but holds great promise. The Ravera is dominated by the typical fruity generosity of the vintage, while Bricco delle Viole reaches greater heights of complexity and linear layering.

● Barbera d'Alba Sup. '12	♟♟ 5
● Barolo Bricco delle Viole '11	♟♟ 8
● Barolo Cerretta Luigi Baudana '11	♟♟ 6
● Barolo Ravera '11	♟♟ 7
● Barolo Albe '11	♟♟ 6
● Dolcetto d'Alba Coste & Fossati '14	♟♟ 4
● Langhe Nebbiolo '13	♟♟ 3
○ Langhe Riesling '14	♟♟ 5
● Barolo Baudana Luigi Baudana '09	♟♟♟ 6
● Barolo Bricco delle Viole '10	♟♟♟ 8
● Barolo Bricco delle Viole '05	♟♟♟ 8
● Barolo Cerretta Luigi Baudana '08	♟♟♟ 6
● Barolo Baudana Luigi Baudana '10	♟♟ 6
● Barolo Cerretta Luigi Baudana '10	♟♟ 6

Mauro Veglio

FRAZ. ANNUNZIATA
CASCINA NUOVA, 50
12064 LA MORRA [CN]
TEL. 0173509212
www.mauroveglio.com

CELLAR SALES
PRE-BOOKED VISITS
ANNUAL PRODUCTION 70,000 bottles
HECTARES UNDER VINE 14.00
SUSTAINABLE WINERY

The wineries of the Veglio and Altare families are situated just one door down from each other in the Annunziata hamlet of La Morra. However, this is not just a geographical curiosity, for Mauro's illustrious neighbour is the inspiration for his work, in which he has is aided by his wife Daniela and his brother Elio. His vineyards cover an area of around 12 hectares, divided between La Morra for the Arborina, Rocche, and Gattera Barolos, and Monforte d'Alba for Castelletto. While brief maceration in roto-fermenters, intense extraction, and ageing in French barriques are undoubtedly "modern" choices, they are not always evident in the end products, which are fresher and more classic than expected. This is particularly true for Mauro Veglio's 2011 Barolos. The Arborina has a fresh bouquet of wild berries and spring herbs, which nicely foreshadows the soft, balanced palate. The caressing, fruity character is even more evident in the Rocche dell'Annunziata.

● Barolo Arborina '11	♥♥	8
● Barolo Castelletto '11	♥♥	8
● Barolo Rocche dell'Annunziata '11	♥♥	8
● Barbera d'Alba Cascina Nuova '13	♥♥	7
● Barolo '11	♥♥	8
● Barolo Gattera '11	♥♥	8
● Langhe Nebbiolo Angelo '14	♥♥	5
● Barbera d'Alba '14	♥	4
● Dolcetto d'Alba '14	♥	4
● Barbera d'Alba Cascina Nuova '99	♥♥♥	6
● Barolo Arborina '10	♥♥♥	6
● Barolo Vign. Arborina '01	♥♥♥	6
● Barolo Vign. Arborina '00	♥♥♥	6
● Barolo Vign. Gattera '05	♥♥♥	6
● Barolo Castelletto '10	♥♥	6
● Barolo Rocche dell'Annunziata '10	♥♥	8

Vicara

VIA MADONNA DELLE GRAZIE, 5
15030 ROSIGNANO MONFERRATO [AL]
TEL. 0142488054
www.vicara.it

CELLAR SALES
PRE-BOOKED VISITS
ANNUAL PRODUCTION 200,000 bottles
HECTARES UNDER VINE 40.00
VITICULTURE METHOD Certified Biodynamic

One of the estate's missions – and we're talking of facts, not intentions – is to protect the terroir and its biodiversity. All work in the vineyard is carried out respecting the ecosystems, often even to the detriment of yields. The same attention is lavished in the cellar, where technology is at the service of a vision that does not neglect the rural traditions of an area for which viticulture holds few secrets. The range features a selection of strictly local specialities, along with international grape varieties used alone or in blends: cabernet sauvignon, pinot nero, chardonnay, and sauvignon. The contest between international grape varieties and native cultivars was won by the latter, with two brilliant versions of Barbera Superiore Vadmò and Barbera 33 Cascina Rocca. The first has a delicate, complex nose of red berries and quinine, while the second offers notes of plums and cocoa powder on the nose against a spicy background, echoed on the powerful, vibrant, concentrated palate.

● Barbera del M.to Cascina Rocca 33 '13	♥♥	3*
● Barbera del M.to Sup. Vadmò '11	♥♥	4
● Barbera del M.to Volpuva '14	♥♥	3
● Grignolino del M.to Casalese °G '14	♥♥	3
○ M.to Bianco Chardonnay Sarnì '09	♥♥	4
○ M.to Bianco Sauvignon Sarnì '09	♥♥	4
● Grignolino del M.to Casalese L'Uccelletta '11	♥	4
● Barbera del M.to Cascina Rocca '12	♥♥	3
● Barbera del M.to La Rocca '10	♥♥	3*
● Barbera del M.to Sup. Cantico della Crosia '10	♥♥	4
● Barbera del M.to Sup. Vadmò '10	♥♥	4
● Grignolino del M.to Casalese '12	♥♥	3*
● Grignolino del M.to Casalese '11	♥♥	3*
● Grignolino del M.to Casalese '10	♥♥	3*

PIEDMONT

Giacomo Vico

VIA TORINO, 80/82
12043 CANALE [CN]
TEL. 0173970984
www.giacomovico.it

CELLAR SALES
PRE-BOOKED VISITS
ANNUAL PRODUCTION 92,300 bottles
HECTARES UNDER VINE 18.00

Despite Giacomo Vico's recent death, the family continue to invest commitment and passion in running the winery, founded in the late 19th century and reopened about 20 years ago following its long closure. The estate's vineyards are mainly in Canale, Monticello d'Alba, and Vezza d'Alba, on the loose, sandy soil typical of Roero, and are planted with local grapes like arneis, barbera, brachetto, favorita, and nebbiolo, along with a small amount of chardonnay. As usual, all the wines presented were well made. Barolo 2010 has a spicy nose and a palate with prominent tannins and good acidity, while Roero Arneis 2014 has a nose of citrus and tropical fruit, and a pleasant palate that holds together well. Barbera d'Alba Superiore 2012 focuses on ripe fruit, while Nebbiolo d'Alba Valmaggiore has notes of dark berries and forest floor, and a well-behaved, flavoursome finish that's not particularly rich but pleasant.

★Vietti

P.ZZA VITTORIO VENETO, 5
12060 CASTIGLIONE FALLETTO [CN]
TEL. 017362825
www.vietti.com

CELLAR SALES
PRE-BOOKED VISITS
ANNUAL PRODUCTION 250,000 bottles
HECTARES UNDER VINE 37.00

The star of this important and well-coordinated estate shines brightly over Castiglione Falletto, for its string of worldwide successes, derived from a combination of great talent and hard work, has made it one of the top names in Italian wine. Its range features some of the region's key designations, guaranteeing astoundingly consistent quality, year after year. The comprehensive range of Barolo crus offers an unforgettable tasting tour of Langhe's finest terroirs. This year the Tre Bicchieri won by the famous Barolo Rocche di Castiglione 2011 coincides with its 50th anniversary. Its deep, complex nose, focusing on notes of quinine, tar, and violets, with balsamic hints, is accompanied by a palate underpinned by well-resolved tannins with a finish of rare length.

● Barbera d'Alba Sup. '12	♟♟ 4
● Barolo '10	♟♟ 5
● Nebbiolo D'Alba Valmaggiore '11	♟♟ 4
○ Roero Arneis '14	♟♟ 3
● Barbera d'Alba '12	♟♟ 3
● Barbera d'Alba '11	♟♟ 2*
● Barbera d'Alba Sup. '10	♟♟ 4
● Barolo '09	♟♟ 5
● Langhe Nebbiolo '12	♟♟ 3
● Langhe Rosso '10	♟♟ 2*
● Nebbiolo d'Alba '08	♟♟ 3
● Nebbiolo D'Alba Valmaggiore '10	♟♟ 4
● Roero '11	♟♟ 4
● Roero '09	♟♟ 4
○ Roero Arneis '12	♟♟ 2*
○ Roero Arneis '11	♟♟ 2*

● Barolo Rocche di Castiglione '11	♟♟♟ 8
● Barbaresco Masseria '11	♟♟ 8
● Barbera d'Asti Sup. Nizza La Crena '12	♟♟ 5
● Barolo Lazzarito '11	♟♟ 8
● Barolo Ravera '11	♟♟ 8
● Barbera d'Alba Scarrone V. Vecchia '13	♟♟ 6
● Barbera d'Alba Tre Vigne '13	♟♟ 3
● Barbera d'Alba V. Scarrone '13	♟♟ 5
● Barolo Brunate '11	♟♟ 8
● Barolo Castiglione '11	♟♟ 7
● Langhe Nebbiolo Perbacco '12	♟♟ 3
○ Roero Arneis '14	♟ 3
● Barbera d'Asti Sup. Nizza La Crena '09	♟♟♟ 5
● Barolo Rocche '08	♟♟♟ 8
● Barolo Villero Ris. '07	♟♟♟ 8
● Barolo Villero Ris. '06	♟♟♟ 8

I Vignaioli di Santo Stefano

LOC. MARINI, 26
12058 SANTO STEFANO BELBO [CN]
TEL. 0141840419
www.ivignaiolidisantostefano.it

CELLAR SALES
PRE-BOOKED VISITS
ANNUAL PRODUCTION 315,000 bottles
HECTARES UNDER VINE 35.00
SUSTAINABLE WINERY

Founded by the Ceretto, Santi, and Scavino families in 1976, I Vignaioli di Santo Stefano focuses exclusively on moscato. The estate's vineyards are mainly in the municipality of Santo Stefano Belbo, on the white soils of the southern slope of the hamlet of Valdivilla, along with a few small plots in Canelli and Calosso, all at altitudes between 320 and 450 metres. The Asti 2014 is certainly among the best of the vintage, with elegant, concentrated notes of sage and white-fleshed fruit on the nose, and a palate that is not particularly complex, but vaunts perfectly balanced residual sugar and prominent acidity, resulting in a fresh, elegant wine. The Moscato d'Asti 2014 is well made, offering riper notes of peaches in syrup and honey, and refreshing hints of Mediterranean scrubland on the nose, and a fairly complex palate for the vintage that is nonetheless pleasantly easy drinking.

○ Asti '14	♥♥ 3
○ Moscato d'Asti '14	♥♥ 5
○ Asti '13	♀♀ 3
○ Asti '12	♀♀ 3
○ Asti '11	♀♀ 3
○ Asti '10	♀♀ 3
○ Asti '07	♀♀ 3
○ Moscato d'Asti '13	♀♀ 4
○ Moscato d'Asti '12	♀♀ 4
○ Moscato d'Asti '11	♀♀ 3
○ Moscato d'Asti '10	♀♀ 3
○ Moscato d'Asti '09	♀♀ 4
○ Moscato d'Asti '08	♀♀ 4
○ Moscato d'Asti '07	♀♀ 3
○ Moscato d'Asti '06	♀♀ 2
○ Piemonte Moscato Passito IL '04	♀♀ 4

★Vigneti Massa

P.ZZA G. CAPSONI, 10
15059 MONLEALE [AL]
TEL. 013180302
vignetimassa@libero.it

CELLAR SALES
PRE-BOOKED VISITS
ANNUAL PRODUCTION 120,000 bottles
HECTARES UNDER VINE 25.00
SUSTAINABLE WINERY

After having dedicated 20 years to its project, this estate has become the mouthpiece for a terroir that is enjoying new-found fame. The decision to focus on Timorasso was underpinned by the local culture and winemaking traditions, as well as some fundamental strategic choices, not least that the winery would have had little chance of emerging from the crowd had it decided to concentrate on non-native or international grape varieties. It was a risky but winning choice, and native cultivars represent the challenge of the future for these lands, as there is no shortage of raw material. First up was a magnificent version of Sterpi, with a complex nose of white-fleshed fruit, almonds, and vegetal notes that develop into sensations of minerals and petrol on the potent, alcohol-rich palate. Montecitorio is complex and concentrated, although it has yet to reveal its full potential. Derthona is more approachable and ready to drink, but no less elegant and complex than its big sisters.

○ Sterpi '13	♥♥♥ 6
○ Derthona '13	♥♥ 5
○ Montecitorio '13	♥♥ 6
● Colli Tortonesi Monleale '11	♥♥ 5
● Colli Tortonesi Monleale Bigolla '09	♥♥ 6
● L'Avvelenata '11	♥ 4
● Pertichetta '11	♥ 4
● Sentieri '14	♥ 4
○ Colli Tortonesi Bianco Costa del Vento '05	♀♀♀ 7
○ Colli Tortonesi Timorasso Derthona '06	♀♀♀ 5
○ Colli Tortonesi Timorasso Sterpi '08	♀♀♀ 7
○ Colli Tortonesi Timorasso Sterpi '07	♀♀♀ 7
○ Costa del Vento '12	♀♀♀ 6
○ Derthona '09	♀♀♀ 5
○ Montecitorio '11	♀♀♀ 6
○ Montecitorio '10	♀♀♀ 6

Vigneti Valle Roncati

VIA NAZIONALE, 10A
28072 BRIONA [NO]
TEL. 3355732548
www.vignetivalleroncati.it

CELLAR SALES
PRE-BOOKED VISITS
ANNUAL PRODUCTION 40,000 bottles
HECTARES UNDER VINE 10.00

Corrado Fassa and Cecilia Bianchi have recently fermented their tenth harvest and have good reason to be satisfied with their work as vignerons, which has already received important recognition from the trade press and consumers alike. Their vineyards lie in the municipalities of Briona, Sizzano, Ghemme and are mainly densely planted with nebbiolo, ensuring low yields. Fara Ciada 2010 is decidedly open and ready, with the classic notes of roots and ferrous minerals of these red, pebbly soils; its tannins are still prominent but no longer aggressive. Although the pleasant, no-nonsense Vespolina 2013 has a less close-focused nose, it vaunts delicious peppery notes. The Barbera 2013 is agreeably drinkable, if not particularly complex, with a nose still characterized by fermenting must, while Uva Rara 2013 is uncomplicated and characterized by clear vegetal notes.

● Fara Ciada '10	♟♟ 3*
● Colline Novaresi Barbera V. di Mezzo '13	♟♟ 2*
● Colline Novaresi Uva Rara '13	♟♟ 2*
● Colline Novaresi Vespolina '13	♟♟ 2*
○ Colline Novaresi Bianco Particella 40 '14	♟ 2
● Pepin	♟ 4
● Colline Novaresi Nebbiolo V. di Sotto '09	♟♟ 2*
● Colline Novaresi Vespolina '12	♟♟ 2*
● Fara V. di Sopra '10	♟♟ 3
● Sizzano San Bartolomeo '11	♟♟ 3*

Villa Giada

REG. CEIROLE, 10
14053 CANELLI [AT]
TEL. 0141831100
www.andreafaccio.it

CELLAR SALES
PRE-BOOKED VISITS
ACCOMMODATION AND RESTAURANT SERVICE
ANNUAL PRODUCTION 180,000 bottles
HECTARES UNDER VINE 25.00

The old core of the Villa Giada winery, in Ceirole, dates from 1790, and the Faccio family have been a leading light in the Canelli district for three generations. Today they own three estates: the headquarters, with the cellar and seven acres of moscato vineyards, Dani in Agliano Terme, and Cascina del Parroco in Calosso, dedicated mainly to barbera. The wines presented this year are all good. Barbera d'Asti Superiore La Quercia 2013 has a nose of plums, cocoa powder and sweet spice, followed by a complex, full-bodied palate, with intentionally super-ripe fruit, and a long finish. Barbera d'Asti Superiore Nizza Bricco Dani 2013 is very dense on the palate, as usual, packed with dark berry jam, but nicely underpinned by taut acidity, while Moscato d'Asti Surì 2014 has a nose of candied peel and peaches, and a nicely balanced bittersweet palate with good length for the vintage.

● Barbera d'Asti Sup. La Quercia '13	♟♟ 3
● Barbera d'Asti Sup. Nizza Bricco Dani '13	♟♟ 4
○ Moscato d'Asti Surì '14	♟♟ 2*
● Barbera d'Asti Ajan '14	♟ 2
● Barbera d'Asti Surì '14	♟ 2
○ Moscato d'Asti Canelli '14	♟ 2
● Barbera d'Asti Ajan '10	♟♟ 2*
● Barbera d'Asti Sup. La Quercia '12	♟♟ 3*
● Barbera d'Asti Sup. Nizza Bricco Dani '11	♟♟ 4
● Barbera d'Asti Sup. Nizza Bricco Dani '10	♟♟ 4
● Barbera d'Asti Sup. Nizza Dedicato a... '10	♟♟ 5
● Barbera d'Asti Sup. Nizza Dedicato a... '08	♟♟ 5
● M.to Rosso Treponti '10	♟♟ 3
○ Moscato d'Asti '13	♟♟ 2*

★Villa Sparina

FRAZ. MONTEROTONDO, 56
15066 GAVI [AL]
TEL. 0143633835
www.villasparina.it

PRE-BOOKED VISITS
ACCOMMODATION AND RESTAURANT SERVICE
ANNUAL PRODUCTION 550,000 bottles
HECTARES UNDER VINE 65.00

The old estate, purchased by the
Moccagatta family in the 1970s, is now
home to the cellar, but also a splendid
resort with restaurant and spa. The
spectacular view does not distract from the
hub of activity, focused on the over 60
hectares of vineyards, planted mainly to
cortese, with sizable plots also in Cassinelle
in the Dolcetto d'Ovada production zone,
and Rivalta Bormida in Alto Monferrato for
barbera. It all converges in a flawless
range, which relentlessly conveys the
winery's intent to combine body and grip
with expressive fruit and cellarability.
Monterotondo 2013, one of the estate's
two great classics was missing at our
tastings this year, as it was not yet bottled,
so we have postponed our judgement until
next year. Barbera Superiore Rivalta shows
intriguing and complex at this stage of its
development, still slightly dominated by
oak, while Gavi Etichetta Gialla is mineral
and very ageworthy.

Cantina Sociale di Vinchio Vaglio Serra

REG. SAN PANCRAZIO, 1
14040 VINCHIO [AT]
TEL. 0141950903
www.vinchio.com

CELLAR SALES
PRE-BOOKED VISITS
ANNUAL PRODUCTION 1,640,000 bottles
HECTARES UNDER VINE 420.00

The long-standing Vinchio Vaglio Serra
cooperative has almost 200 member
growers and remains one of the leading
wineries in the province of Asti and the
whole of Piedmont. Most of its members'
vineyards, which include some over 60
years old, are situated on the Alto
Monferrato hills, characterized by mainly
chalky and sandy soils. The wide range is
highly diversified, but the focus remains on
the various types of Barbera. Barbera d'Asti
Superiore Nizza Laudana 2012 made it into
our finals with a nose of tobacco, dried
medicinal herbs, red berries, and black
pepper, accompanied by a pleasant, long,
supple palate with nice balance. Barbera
d'Asti Vigne Vecchie 50 2013 is fruity, with
good complexity and acidity, while Barbera
d'Asti Superiore I Tre Vescovi 2013 is more
potent but a little stiff. Lastly, I Tre Vescovi
Brut Rosé is well made, with good
complexity and acidity.

● Barbera del M.to Sup. Rivalta '12	♟♟ 6
○ Gavi del Comune di Gavi Et. Gialla '14	♟♟ 3*
○ M.to Bianco Montej '14	♟♟ 2*
● M.to Rosso Montej '13	♟♟ 2*
○ Villa Sparina Brut M. Cl.	♟♟ 3
⊙ M.to Chiaretto Montej Rosé '14	♟ 2
○ Gavi del Comune di Gavi Monterotondo '12	♟♟♟ 6
○ Gavi del Comune di Gavi Monterotondo '11	♟♟♟ 6
○ Gavi del Comune di Gavi Monterotondo '10	♟♟♟ 6
○ Gavi del Comune di Gavi Monterotondo '09	♟♟♟ 6
○ Gavi del Comune di Gavi Monterotondo '08	♟♟♟ 6

● Barbera d'Asti Sup. Nizza Laudana '12	♟♟ 3*
● Barbera d'Asti Sup. I Tre Vescovi '13	♟♟ 2*
● Barbera d'Asti Vigne Vecchie 50 '13	♟♟ 3
⊙ I Tre Vescovi Brut Rosé	♟♟ 4
● Barbera d'Asti Sorì dei Mori '14	♟ 2
● Barbera d'Asti Sup. Sei Vigne Insynthesis '01	♟♟♟ 6
● Barbera d'Asti Sorì dei Mori '12	♟♟ 2*
● Barbera d'Asti Sup. I Tre Vescovi '12	♟♟ 2*
● Barbera d'Asti Sup. I Tre Vescovi '11	♟♟ 2*
● Barbera d'Asti Sup. Nizza Laudana '11	♟♟ 3
● Barbera d'Asti Sup. Nizza Laudana '09	♟♟ 3*
● Barbera d'Asti Sup. Sei Vigne Insynthesis '07	♟♟ 6
● Barbera d'Asti Vigne Vecchie '12	♟♟ 3*
● Barbera d'Asti Vigne Vecchie 50 '11	♟♟ 3

Virna

via Alba, 24
12060 Barolo [CN]
Tel. 017356120
www.virnabarolo.it

CELLAR SALES
PRE-BOOKED VISITS
ANNUAL PRODUCTION 60,000 bottles
HECTARES UNDER VINE 12.00

This interesting estate boasts an array of truly remarkable vineyards comprising some of the finest terroirs in the whole of Langhe. Virna Borgogno, aided by her sister Ivana, is the vibrant chief of the winery that has recently joined the ranks of the designation's élite. The exhaustive range offers excellent versions of all types of Alba wines, topped by the harmonious, firmly structured Barolos that have managed to make a name for themselves on the most mature and demanding markets in the space of a few years. Barolo Cannubi Boschis 2011 has an alluring nose of tobacco, red berries, and eucalyptus, underpinned by a solid palate with good acid-tannin balance. Barolo Preda Sarmassa Limited Edition 2006 shows great texture and complexity. However, it is not easily legible, alternating dark notes of pencil lead and liquorice with a layered palate displaying unresolved tannins and a long, caressing finish.

● Barolo '11	♥♥ 5
● Barolo Cannubi Boschis '11	♥♥ 6
● Barolo del Comune di Barolo '11	♥♥ 6
● Barolo Preda Sarmassa Limited Edition 10 Anni '06	♥♥ 8
● Barolo Sarmassa '11	♥♥ 6
● Langhe Nebbiolo '13	♥♥ 3
● Barbera d'Alba '12	♥ 2
● Dolcetto d'Alba '14	♥ 2
○ Langhe Arneis Solouno '14	♥ 2
● Alba '11	♀♀ 3
● Barbera d'Alba San Giovanni '10	♀♀ 3
● Barolo '10	♀♀ 5
● Barolo Cannubi Boschis '10	♀♀ 6
● Barolo del Comune di Barolo '10	♀♀ 6
● Barolo Sarmassa '10	♀♀ 6

Vite Colte

via Bergesia, 6
12060 Barolo [CN]
Tel. 0173564611
www.vitecolte.it

CELLAR SALES
PRE-BOOKED VISITS
ANNUAL PRODUCTION 1,200,000 bottles
HECTARES UNDER VINE 300.00

Vite Colte is the new name chosen by Terre da Vino to present its new production philosophy. It will make little difference to us, for the wines are the same we have been tasting for years, but for Piero Quadrumolo and his team it is a watershed moment. Vite Colte is the flagship of a group of 180 selected growers with 300 hectares, some of the finest of the individual zones, getting up to speed with the sole objective of seeking absolute quality. The names of the most famous wines will remain the same under the new brand. Barolo Essenze put up an excellent performance as usual, but the real surprise was undoubtedly Barolo Paesi Tuoi and its close-focused nose of raspberries and liquorice, and its balanced palate, where fullness means power and strength, and never heaviness. The first release of a few bottles of Barbera La Luna and I Falò from the Nizza subzone was impressive, offering explosive fruit and a fresh yet velvety palate.

● Barbera d'Asti Sup. Nizza La Luna e I Falò '13	♥♥ 5
● Barolo del Comune di Barolo Essenze '11	♥♥ 6
● Barolo Paesi Tuoi '11	♥♥ 5
● Barbaresco La Casa in Collina '12	♥♥ 5
● Barbera d'Alba Sup. Croere '13	♥♥ 4
● Barbera d'Asti Sup. La Luna e I Falò '13	♥♥ 4
● Barbera d'Asti Sup. La Luna e I Falò '12	♀♀ 3
● Barbera d'Asti Sup. La Luna e I Falò '11	♀♀ 3*
● Barbera d'Asti Sup. La Luna e I Falò '10	♀♀ 3*
● Barbera d'Asti Sup. La Luna e I Falò '09	♀♀ 3*
● Barolo del Comune di Barolo Essenze '10	♀♀ 6
● Barolo del Comune di Barolo Essenze '09	♀♀ 6
● Barolo del Comune di Barolo Essenze '08	♀♀ 6

F.lli Abrigo
LOC. BERFI
VIA MOGLIA GERLOTTO, 2
12055 DIANO D'ALBA [CN]
TEL. 017369104
www.abrigofratelli.com

CELLAR SALES
PRE-BOOKED VISITS
ANNUAL PRODUCTION 100,000 bottles
HECTARES UNDER VINE 25.00

● Diano d'Alba Sörì dei Berfi '14	♟♟	2*
● Diano d'Alba Sup. Pietrin '13	♟♟	3
● Nebbiolo d'Alba Tardiss '13	♟♟	3
● Barbera d'Alba La Galùpa '13	♟	2

Alice Bel Colle
REG. STAZIONE, 9
15010 ALICE BEL COLLE [AL]
TEL. 014474413
www.cantinaalicebc.it

CELLAR SALES
PRE-BOOKED VISITS
ANNUAL PRODUCTION 80,000 bottles
HECTARES UNDER VINE 370.00

● Barbera d'Asti Sup. Alix '12	♟♟	3*
● Barbera d'Asti Al Casò '12	♟♟	2*
● Barbera d'Asti Filari Sociali '13	♟	2
○ Moscato d'Asti Paié '14	♟	2

Amalia Cascina in Langa
LOC. SANT' ANNA, 85
12065 CUNEO
TEL. 0173789013
www.cascinaamalia.it

CELLAR SALES
PRE-BOOKED VISITS
ANNUAL PRODUCTION 60,000 bottles
HECTARES UNDER VINE 14.00
SUSTAINABLE WINERY

● Barbera d'Alba '13	♟♟	4
● Barolo Le Coste di Monforte '10	♟♟	5
● Langhe Nebbiolo '13	♟	4

Antica Cascina Conti di Roero
LOC. VAL RUBIAGNO, 2
12040 VEZZA D'ALBA [CN]
TEL. 017365459
www.oliveropietro.it

CELLAR SALES
PRE-BOOKED VISITS
ANNUAL PRODUCTION 100,000 bottles
HECTARES UNDER VINE 13.50
SUSTAINABLE WINERY

● Barbera d'Alba '13	♟♟	2*
● Roero '12	♟♟	3
○ Roero Arneis '14	♟♟	2*
○ Brut M. Cl.	♟	4

Anzivino
C.SO VALSESIA, 162
13045 GATTINARA [VC]
TEL. 0163827172
www.anzivino.it

CELLAR SALES
PRE-BOOKED VISITS
ACCOMMODATION AND RESTAURANT SERVICE
ANNUAL PRODUCTION 40,000 bottles
HECTARES UNDER VINE 6.00

● Coste della Sesia Nebbiolo '12	♟♟	2*
● Gattinara Cesare 634 '11	♟♟	8
● Coste della Sesia Faticato '10	♟	5
● Gattinara '10	♟	4

F.lli Barale
VIA ROMA, 6
12060 BAROLO [CN]
TEL. 017356127
www.baralefratelli.it

CELLAR SALES
PRE-BOOKED VISITS
ANNUAL PRODUCTION 100,000 bottles
HECTARES UNDER VINE 20.00
SUSTAINABLE WINERY

● Barolo Cannubi '11	♟♟	8
● Barbaresco Serraboella '12	♟♟	7
● Barolo Bussia Ris. '09	♟♟	8
● Barolo Castellero '11	♟♟	7

OTHER WINERIES

Cantina Sociale Barbera dei Sei Castelli

REG. SALERE, 6
14041 AGLIANO TERME [AT]
TEL. 0141964004
www.barberaseicastelli.it

CELLAR SALES
PRE-BOOKED VISITS
ANNUAL PRODUCTION 80,000 bottles
HECTARES UNDER VINE 660.00

- Barbera d'Asti '13 ♟♟2*
- Barbera d'Asti 50 Anni di Barbera '13 ♟♟2*
- Barbera d'Asti Sup. Nizza '12 ♟4

Bea - Merenda con Corvi

S.DA SANTA CATERINA, 8
10064 PINEROLO [TO]
TEL. 0113402887
www.merendaconcorvi.it

CELLAR SALES
ACCOMMODATION
ANNUAL PRODUCTION 4,000 bottles
HECTARES UNDER VINE 1.00

- Pinerolese Barbera '12 ♟♟4
- Pinerolese Barbera Foravia '14 ♟♟3
- Merlot '12 ♟5

Antonio Bellicoso

FRAZ. MOLISSO, 5A
14048 MONTEGROSSO D'ASTI [AT]
TEL. 0141953233
antonio.bellicoso@alice.it

CELLAR SALES
PRE-BOOKED VISITS
ANNUAL PRODUCTION 10,000 bottles
HECTARES UNDER VINE 4.00
SUSTAINABLE WINERY

- Barbera d'Asti Merum '13 ♟♟4
- Freisa d'Asti '14 ♟♟2*
- Barbera d'Asti Amormio '14 ♟2

Massimo Bo

FRAZ. SANT'ANNA
VIA SANT'ANNA, 19
14055 COSTIGLIOLE D'ASTI [AT]
TEL. 0141961891
www.bomassimovini.it

CELLAR SALES
PRE-BOOKED VISITS
ANNUAL PRODUCTION 30,000 bottles
HECTARES UNDER VINE 6.00
SUSTAINABLE WINERY

- Barbera d'Asti Arbuc '13 ♟♟2*
- Barbera d'Asti Sup. Costiliolae '12 ♟♟3

Marco Bonfante

S.DA VAGLIO SERRA, 72
14049 NIZZA MONFERRATO [AT]
TEL. 0141725012
www.marcobonfante.com

CELLAR SALES
PRE-BOOKED VISITS
ANNUAL PRODUCTION 270,000 bottles
HECTARES UNDER VINE 20.00

- Barbera d'Asti Sup. Bricco Bonfante '12 ♟♟5
- Barbera d'Asti Sup. Stella Rossa '12 ♟♟2*
- Barolo Bussia '10 ♟♟6

Boroli

FRAZ. MADONNA DI COMO, 34
12051 ALBA [CN]
TEL. 0173365477
www.boroli.it

CELLAR SALES
PRE-BOOKED VISITS
ACCOMMODATION AND RESTAURANT SERVICE
ANNUAL PRODUCTION 200,000 bottles
HECTARES UNDER VINE 32.00
SUSTAINABLE WINERY

- Barolo Villero '11 ♟♟7
- Barolo '11 ♟♟6
- Barolo Villero Ris. '09 ♟♟8
- Dolcetto d'Alba '14 ♟2

Giacomo Boveri

VIA COSTA VESCOVATO, 15
15050 COSTA VESCOVATO [AL]
TEL. 0131838223
www.vignetiboveri.it

ANNUAL PRODUCTION 25,000 bottles
HECTARES UNDER VINE 10.00

○ Colli Tortonesi Timorasso
  Lacrime del Bricco '13 ▼▼5
○ Colli Tortonesi Timorasso
  Muntà L'è Ruma '13 ▼▼4

Gallino Domenico Bric Castelvej

MADONNA LORETO, 70
12043 CANALE [CN]
TEL. 017398108
www.gallinodomenico.com

CELLAR SALES
PRE-BOOKED VISITS
ANNUAL PRODUCTION 100,000 bottles
HECTARES UNDER VINE 12.40

● Roero '12 ▼▼4
● Roero Panera Alta Ris. '12 ▼▼6
● Barbera d'Alba '14 ▼2
○ Roero Arneis V. Bricco Novara '14 ▼3

Renato Buganza

LOC. CASCINA GARBINOTTO, 4
12040 PIOBESI D'ALBA [CN]
TEL. 0173619370
www.renatobuganza.it

CELLAR SALES
PRE-BOOKED VISITS
ANNUAL PRODUCTION 35,000 bottles
HECTARES UNDER VINE 11.00

● Barbera d'Alba Sup. V. Veja '12 ▼▼2*
○ Roero Arneis dla Trifula '14 ▼▼2*
● Roero Ris. '11 ▼▼3
○ Claudette Brut M. Cl. ▼3

Bussia Soprana

LOC. BUSSIA, 88A
12065 MONFORTE D'ALBA [CN]
TEL. 039305182
www.bussiasoprana.it

CELLAR SALES
PRE-BOOKED VISITS
ANNUAL PRODUCTION 60,000 bottles
HECTARES UNDER VINE 18.00

● Barolo V. Colonnello '11 ▼▼7
● Barolo Mosconi '11 ▼▼7

Marco Canato

FRAZ. FONS SALERA
LOC. CA' BALDEA, 18/2
15049 VIGNALE MONFERRATO [AL]
TEL. 0142933653
www.canatovini.it

CELLAR SALES
PRE-BOOKED VISITS
ANNUAL PRODUCTION 30,000 bottles
HECTARES UNDER VINE 11.00

● Grignolino del M.to Casalese Primo '10 ▼▼4
● Grignolino del M.to Casalese Celio '14 ▼▼3

Pierangelo Careglio

LOC. APRATO, 15
12040 BALDISSERO D'ALBA [CN]
TEL. 017240294
cantinacareglio@tiscali.it

CELLAR SALES
PRE-BOOKED VISITS
ANNUAL PRODUCTION 20,000 bottles
HECTARES UNDER VINE 6.00

○ Roero Arneis '14 ▼▼2*
○ Langhe Favorita '14 ▼2
● Roero '12 ▼2

Carussin

REG. MARIANO, 27
14050 SAN MARZANO OLIVETO [AT]
TEL. 0141831358
www.carussin.it

CELLAR SALES
PRE-BOOKED VISITS
RESTAURANT SERVICE
ANNUAL PRODUCTION 80,000 bottles
HECTARES UNDER VINE 15.00
VITICULTURE METHOD Certified Organic

○ Filari Corti '14	♟♟ 3
● Barbera d'Asti Asinoi '14	♟ 2
● Barbera d'Asti Lia Vi '14	♟ 3

Casavecchia

VIA ROMA, 2
12055 DIANO D'ALBA [CN]
TEL. 017369321
www.cantinacasavecchia.com

CELLAR SALES
PRE-BOOKED VISITS
ANNUAL PRODUCTION 40,000 bottles
HECTARES UNDER VINE 8.00

● Diano d'Alba Sörì Bruni '14	♟♟ 2*
● Diano d'Alba Sörì Richin '13	♟♟ 2*
● Nebbiolo d'Alba Piadvenza '11	♟♟ 3
● Langhe Rosso Pian del Lupo '10	♟ 3

Cascina Adelaide

VIA AIE SOTTANE, 14
12060 BAROLO [CN]
TEL. 0173560503
www.cascinaadelaide.com

CELLAR SALES
PRE-BOOKED VISITS
ANNUAL PRODUCTION 50,000 bottles
HECTARES UNDER VINE 9.50

● Barolo Baudana '11	♟♟ 7
● Barolo Cannubi '11	♟♟ 8

Cascina Castlet

S.DA CASTELLETTO, 6
14055 COSTIGLIOLE D'ASTI [AT]
TEL. 0141966651
www.cascinacastlet.com

CELLAR SALES
PRE-BOOKED VISITS
ANNUAL PRODUCTION 250,000 bottles
HECTARES UNDER VINE 30.00
SUSTAINABLE WINERY

● Barbera d'Asti '14	♟♟ 2*
● Barbera d'Asti Sup. Passum '11	♟♟ 5
● M.to Rosso Policalpo '12	♟♟ 4
○ Moscato d'Asti '14	♟ 2

Cascina Flino

VIA ABELLONI, 7
12055 DIANO D'ALBA [CN]
TEL. 017369231
cascinaflino@gmail.com

CELLAR SALES
PRE-BOOKED VISITS
ACCOMMODATION AND RESTAURANT SERVICE
ANNUAL PRODUCTION 10,000 bottles
HECTARES UNDER VINE 4.00

● Barolo San Lorenzo di Verduno '11	♟♟ 5
● Barbera d'Alba Sup. '12	♟ 3
● Diano di Diano d'Alba Sorì Cascina Flino '14	♟ 2

Cascina Galarin Giuseppe Carosso

VIA CAROSSI, 12
14054 CASTAGNOLE DELLE LANZE [AT]
TEL. 0141878586
www.galarin.it

CELLAR SALES
ANNUAL PRODUCTION 20,000 bottles
HECTARES UNDER VINE 5.00
VITICULTURE METHOD Certified Organic

● Barbera d'Asti Le Querce '13	♟♟ 2*
● Barbera d'Asti Superiore Tinella '12	♟♟ 5
○ Moscato d'Asti Prá Dône '14	♟ 2

Cascina Lana

c.so Acqui, 187
14049 Nizza Monferrato [AT]
Tel. 0141726734
www.cascinalana.com

CELLAR SALES
PRE-BOOKED VISITS
ANNUAL PRODUCTION 60,000 bottles
HECTARES UNDER VINE 20.00

● Barbera d'Asti Sup. Nizza '12	♟♟ 5	
● Barbera d'Asti La Cirimela '14	♟ 3	

Cascina Salerio

s.da Salerio, 16
14055 Costigliole d'Asti [AT]
Tel. 0141966294
casalerio@alice.it

CELLAR SALES
PRE-BOOKED VISITS
ANNUAL PRODUCTION 16,000 bottles
HECTARES UNDER VINE 12.00

● M.to Rosso Aqua '14	♟♟ 2*
● Barbera d'Asti Terra '14	♟ 2
● Grignolino d'Asti '14	♟ 2
● M.to Rosso Fuoco '13	♟ 3

Renzo Castella

via Alba, 15
12055 Diano d'Alba [CN]
Tel. 017369203
renzocastella@virgilio.it

CELLAR SALES
PRE-BOOKED VISITS
ANNUAL PRODUCTION 20,000 bottles
HECTARES UNDER VINE 8.00

● Dolcetto di Diano d'Alba Rivolia '14	♟♟ 2*
● Barbera d'Alba Piadvenza '13	♟♟ 2*
● Dolcetto di Diano d'Alba '14	♟♟ 2*
● Langhe Nebbiolo Madonnina '13	♟♟ 2*

Castello del Poggio

loc. Poggio, 9
14100 Portacomaro [AT]
Tel. 0141202543
www.poggio.it

CELLAR SALES
PRE-BOOKED VISITS
ANNUAL PRODUCTION 800,000 bottles
HECTARES UNDER VINE 158.00

● Barbera d'Asti Masaréj '12	♟♟ 4
○ Moscato d'Asti '14	♟♟ 2*
● Barbera d'Asti '13	♟ 2

Cavalier Bartolomeo

via Alba Barolo, 55
12060 Castiglione Falletto [CN]
Tel. 017362866
www.cavalierbartolomeo.com

ANNUAL PRODUCTION 15,000 bottles
HECTARES UNDER VINE 3.50

● Barolo Altenasso '11	♟♟ 4
● Barolo San Lorenzo '11	♟♟ 4

Le Cecche

via Moglia Gerlotto, 10
12055 Diano d'Alba [CN]
Tel. 017369323
www.lececche.com

CELLAR SALES
PRE-BOOKED VISITS
ANNUAL PRODUCTION 35,000 bottles
HECTARES UNDER VINE 5.00

● Barbera d'Alba '13	♟♟ 3
● Barolo Sorano '11	♟♟ 5
○ Langhe Riesling '13	♟♟ 3
● Langhe Rosso '14	♟♟ 3

Cerutti

VIA CANELLI, 205
14050 CASSINASCO [AT]
TEL. 0141851286
www.cascinacerutti.it

CELLAR SALES
PRE-BOOKED VISITS
ANNUAL PRODUCTION 20,000 bottles
HECTARES UNDER VINE 6.00
SUSTAINABLE WINERY

● Barbera d'Asti '14	♟♟ 2*
● Barbera d'Asti Sup. Föje Rùsse '11	♟♟ 3
○ Moscato d'Asti Canelli Surì Sandrinet '14	♟ 2

Franco e Pierguido Ceste

C.SO ALFIERI, 1
12040 GOVONE [CN]
TEL. 017358635
www.cestevini.com

CELLAR SALES
PRE-BOOKED VISITS
ANNUAL PRODUCTION 180,000 bottles
HECTARES UNDER VINE 20.00

● Barbaresco '12	♟♟ 3
● Barbera d'Alba Sup. '13	♟♟ 3
● Barolo '11	♟♟ 6

Il Chiosso

VIA LE GUGLIELMO MARCONI 45-47A
13045 GATTINARA [VC]
TEL. 0163826739
www.ilchiosso.it

CELLAR SALES
PRE-BOOKED VISITS
ANNUAL PRODUCTION 80,000 bottles
HECTARES UNDER VINE 12.00

● Colline Novaresi Nebbiolo '09	♟♟ 3
● Fara '10	♟♟ 3
● Gattinara '10	♟ 3
● Ghemme '09	♟ 3

Paride Chiovini

VIA GIUSEPPE GARIBALDI, 20
28070 SIZZANO [NO]
TEL. 3394304954
www.paridechiovini.it

CELLAR SALES
PRE-BOOKED VISITS
ANNUAL PRODUCTION 10,000 bottles
HECTARES UNDER VINE 3.00

● Ghemme '11	♟♟ 4
● Sizzano '10	♟♟ 4
● Colline Novaresi Uva Rara Briseide '14	♟ 3
● Colline Novaresi Vespolina Afrodite '14	♟ 2

Ciabot Berton

FRAZ. SANTA MARIA, 1
12064 LA MORRA [CN]
TEL. 017350217
www.ciabotberton.it

CELLAR SALES
PRE-BOOKED VISITS
ANNUAL PRODUCTION 50,000 bottles
HECTARES UNDER VINE 11.00

● Barolo del Comune di La Morra '11	♟♟ 5

Cantina Clavesana

FRAZ. MADONNA DELLA NEVE, 19
12060 CLAVESANA [CN]
TEL. 0173790451
www.inclavesana.it

CELLAR SALES
PRE-BOOKED VISITS
ANNUAL PRODUCTION 3,400,000 bottles
HECTARES UNDER VINE 520.00
SUSTAINABLE WINERY

● Barolo Olo '11	♟♟ 5
● Dogliani Sup. 587 '12	♟♟ 3
● Dogliani Sup. Il Clou di Clavesana '13	♟♟ 2*
● Dogliani '14	♟ 2

Aldo Clerico

Loc. Manzoni, 69
12065 Monforte d'Alba [CN]
Tel. 017378509
www.aldoclerico.it

CELLAR SALES
PRE-BOOKED VISITS
ANNUAL PRODUCTION 30,000 bottles
HECTARES UNDER VINE 6.00

● Barbera d'Alba '13	♟♟ 3
● Barolo '11	♟♟ 6
● Dolcetto d'Alba '14	♟ 2

Col dei Venti

Via La Serra, 38
14049 Vaglio Serra [AT]
Tel. 0141793071
www.coldeiventi.com

PRE-BOOKED VISITS
ANNUAL PRODUCTION 30,000 bottles
HECTARES UNDER VINE 10.00

● Barbaresco Túfoblu '12	♟♟ 6
● Barolo Debútto '11	♟♟ 6

Collina Serragrilli

Via Serragrilli, 30
12057 Neive [CN]
Tel. 0173677010
www.serragrilli.it

CELLAR SALES
PRE-BOOKED VISITS
ANNUAL PRODUCTION 100,000 bottles
HECTARES UNDER VINE 15.00

● Barbaresco Serragrilli '12	♟♟ 5
● Barbaresco Starderi '12	♟♟ 7
● Barbera d'Alba '13	♟♟ 2*

Colombera & Garella

Via Cascina Cottignano, 2
13866 Masserano [BI]
Tel. 01596967
colomberaegarella@gmail.com

CELLAR SALES
PRE-BOOKED VISITS
ANNUAL PRODUCTION 30,000 bottles
HECTARES UNDER VINE 9.00

● Bramaterra Cascina Cottignano '11	♟♟ 4
● Costa della Sesia Rosato Cascina Cottignano '14	♟♟ 4
● Costa della Sesia Rosso Cascina Cottignano '12	♟♟ 4

Colombo - Cascina Pastori

Reg. Cafra, 172/B
14051 Bubbio [AT]
Tel. 0144852807
www.colombovino.it

CELLAR SALES
PRE-BOOKED VISITS
ANNUAL PRODUCTION 40,000 bottles
HECTARES UNDER VINE 10.00
SUSTAINABLE WINERY

● Piemonte Pinot Nero Apertura Maxima Ris. '11	♟♟ 8
⊙ Alta Langa Brut Rosé Ris. '11	♟ 5
● Piemonte Pinot Nero Apertura '12	♟ 3

Contratto

Via G. B. Giuliani, 56
14053 Canelli [AT]
Tel. 0141823349
www.contratto.it

CELLAR SALES
PRE-BOOKED VISITS
ANNUAL PRODUCTION 140,000 bottles
HECTARES UNDER VINE 21.00

○ Asti De Miranda '12	♟♟ 5
○ Contratto Millesimato Extra Brut '10	♟♟ 5
⊙ For England Brut Rosé '10	♟♟ 6
○ For England Pas Dosé Blanc de Noirs '10	♟♟ 6

Cuvage

Stradale Alessandria, 90
15011 Acqui Terme [AL]
Tel. 0144371600
www.cuvage.com

ANNUAL PRODUCTION 80,000 bottles
HECTARES UNDER VINE 200.00

⊙ Brut Rosé M. Cl.	🍷🍷	3
○ Brut Blanc de Blancs M. Cl.	🍷	3
○ Pas Dosé Cuvage de Cuvage M. Cl.	🍷	3

Dacapo

s.da Asti Mare, 4
14040 Agliano Terme [AT]
Tel. 0141964921
www.dacapo.it

CELLAR SALES
PRE-BOOKED VISITS
ANNUAL PRODUCTION 50,000 bottles
HECTARES UNDER VINE 8.50
VITICULTURE METHOD Certified Organic

● Barbera d'Asti Sup. Nizza V. Dacapo '12	🍷🍷	5
● Barbera d'Asti Sanbastiàn '13	🍷🍷	2*
● Grignolino d'Asti '14	🍷	3
● Piemonte Pinot Nero Cantacucco '12	🍷	5

Giovanni Daglio

via Montale Celli, 10
15050 Costa Vescovato [AL]
Tel. 0131838262
www.vignetidaglio.com

CELLAR SALES
ANNUAL PRODUCTION 15,000 bottles
HECTARES UNDER VINE 10.00

● Colli Tortonesi Barbera Basinas '13	🍷🍷	4
● Colli Tortonesi Dolcetto Nibiö '13	🍷🍷	3
○ Colli Tortonesi Timorasso Cantico '13	🍷🍷	4
○ Vigna del Re	🍷	2

F.lli Facchino

loc. Val del Prato, 210
15078 Rocca Grimalda [AL]
Tel. 014385401
www.vinifacchino.it

CELLAR SALES
PRE-BOOKED VISITS
ANNUAL PRODUCTION 60,000 bottles
HECTARES UNDER VINE 17.00

● Dolcetto di Ovada Poggiobello '12	🍷🍷	2*
● Ovada Carasöi '13	🍷🍷	3
○ Cortese dell'Alto Monferrato Pacialan '14	🍷	2

Fabio Fidanza

via Rodotiglia, 55
14052 Calosso [AT]
Tel. 0141826921
a.a.fidanza@gmail.com

CELLAR SALES
PRE-BOOKED VISITS
ANNUAL PRODUCTION 20,000 bottles
HECTARES UNDER VINE 10.00

● Barbera d'Asti '13	🍷🍷	2*
● Barbera d'Asti Sup. Sterlino '12	🍷🍷	4
● M.to Rosso Que Duàn '13	🍷🍷	3
○ Moscato d'Asti '14	🍷🍷	2*

Forteto della Luja

reg. Candelette, 4
14051 Loazzolo [AT]
Tel. 014487197
www.fortetodellaluja.it

CELLAR SALES
PRE-BOOKED VISITS
ANNUAL PRODUCTION 50,000 bottles
HECTARES UNDER VINE 11.00
VITICULTURE METHOD Certified Organic

● Barbera d'Asti Mon Ross '14	🍷🍷	2*
○ Moscato d'Asti Piasa San Maurizio '14	🍷🍷	3
● M.to Rosso Le Grive '13	🍷	4

La Fusina

B.GO SANTA LUCIA, 33
12063 DOGLIANI [CN]
TEL. 017370488
www.lafusina.com

CELLAR SALES
PRE-BOOKED VISITS
ANNUAL PRODUCTION 80,000 bottles
HECTARES UNDER VINE 20.00

● Barbera d'Alba La Castella '11	♟♟ 3
● Barolo '11	♟♟ 5
○ Langhe Chardonnay '14	♟♟ 2*
● Dogliani Sup. Cavagnè '13	♟ 3

Garesio

LOC. SORDO, 1
12050 SERRALUNGA D'ALBA [CN]
TEL. 3667076775
www.garesiovini.it

ANNUAL PRODUCTION 11,000 bottles
HECTARES UNDER VINE 5.80

● Barbera d'Asti Superiore Nizza '12	♟♟ 4
● Barbera d'Asti Superiore Nizza '11	♟♟ 5
● Langhe Nebbiolo '13	♟ 3

Cantine Garrone

VIA SCAPACCIANO, 36
28845 DOMODOSSOLA [VB]
TEL. 0324242990
www.cantinegarrone.it

CELLAR SALES
PRE-BOOKED VISITS
ANNUAL PRODUCTION 50,000 bottles

● Munaloss	♟♟ 3
● Valli Ossolane Nebbiolo Sup. Prünent '12	♟♟ 4
● Valli Ossolane Rosso Tarlàp '13	♟♟ 2*

Tenuta L'Illuminata

LOC. SANT'ANNA, 30
12064 LA MORRA [CN]
TEL. 0302279601
www.lilluminata.it

CELLAR SALES
PRE-BOOKED VISITS
ACCOMMODATION
ANNUAL PRODUCTION 47,000 bottles
HECTARES UNDER VINE 11.00
SUSTAINABLE WINERY

● Barbera d'Alba Colbertina '11	♟♟ 3
● Barolo Tebavio '11	♟♟ 6

Incisiana

VIA SANT'AGATA, 10/12
14045 INCISA SCAPACCINO [AT]
TEL. 0141747113
www.incisiana.com

CELLAR SALES
PRE-BOOKED VISITS
ACCOMMODATION
ANNUAL PRODUCTION 20,000 bottles
HECTARES UNDER VINE 5.00

● Barbera d'Asti '12	♟♟ 4
● Barbera d'Asti Sup. Zerosso '11	♟♟ 5

Marenco

P.ZZA VITTORIO EMANUELE II, 10
15019 STREVI [AL]
TEL. 0144363133
www.marencovini.com

CELLAR SALES
PRE-BOOKED VISITS
ANNUAL PRODUCTION 300,000 bottles
HECTARES UNDER VINE 80.00

● Dolcetto d'Acqui Marchesa '14	♟♟ 3
○ Moscato d'Asti Scrapona '14	♟♟ 3
● Barbera d'Asti Bassina '14	♟ 2
● Brachetto d'Acqui Pineto '14	♟ 4

Le Marie

VIA SAN DEFENDENTE, 6
12032 BARGE [CN]
TEL. 0175345159
www.lemarievini.eu

CELLAR SALES
PRE-BOOKED VISITS
RESTAURANT SERVICE
ANNUAL PRODUCTION 24,000 bottles
HECTARES UNDER VINE 8.00

○ Blanc de Lissart	♥♥ 2
● Pinerolese Rosso Debargès '12	♥♥ 3
⊙ Le Marie Pas Dosé Rosato M. Cl.	♥ 3
○ Sant'Agostino	♥ 3

La Masera

S.DA SAN PIETRO, 32
10010 PIVERONE [TO]
TEL. 0113164161
www.lamasera.it

CELLAR SALES
PRE-BOOKED VISITS
ANNUAL PRODUCTION 18,000 bottles
HECTARES UNDER VINE 4.20
SUSTAINABLE WINERY

● Canavese Nebbiolo '12	♥♥ 3
⊙ Canavese Rosato Bolle Brut M. Cl.	♥♥ 3
○ Erbaluce di Caluso Anima '14	♥ 2
○ Erbaluce di Caluso Passito Venanzia '10	♥ 4

Tenuta La Meridiana

VIA TANA BASSA, 5
14048 MONTEGROSSO D'ASTI [AT]
TEL. 0141956172
www.tenutalameridiana.com

CELLAR SALES
PRE-BOOKED VISITS
ANNUAL PRODUCTION 80,000 bottles
HECTARES UNDER VINE 10.00
VITICULTURE METHOD Certified Organic
SUSTAINABLE WINERY

● Barbera d'Asti Le Gagie '13	♥♥ 2*
● Barbera d'Asti Vitis '13	♥♥ 2*
● Barbera d'Asti Sup. Tra La Terra e Il Cielo '11	♥ 4

La Mesma

FRAZ. MONTEROTONDO, 7
15066 GAVI [AL]
TEL. 0143342012
www.lamesma.it

CELLAR SALES
PRE-BOOKED VISITS
ANNUAL PRODUCTION 52,000 bottles
HECTARES UNDER VINE 25.00

○ Gavi Brut M. Cl. '09	♥♥ 4
○ Gavi del Comune di Gavi Et. Gialla '14	♥♥ 2*
○ Gavi V. della Rovere Verde Ris. '13	♥♥ 3

F.lli Monchiero

VIA ALBA-MONFORTE, 58
12060 CASTIGLIONE FALLETTO [CN]
TEL. 017362820
www.monchierovini.it

CELLAR SALES
PRE-BOOKED VISITS
ANNUAL PRODUCTION 40,000 bottles
HECTARES UNDER VINE 12.00

● Barolo Rocche di Castiglione Falletto '12	♥♥ 5
● Barolo Rocche di Castiglione Falletto Ris. '09	♥♥ 5

Franco Mondo

REG. MARIANO, 33
14050 SAN MARZANO OLIVETO [AT]
TEL. 0141834096
www.francomondo.net

CELLAR SALES
PRE-BOOKED VISITS
ANNUAL PRODUCTION 75,000 bottles
HECTARES UNDER VINE 13.00

● Barbera d'Asti '13	♥♥ 2*
● Barbera d'Asti V. del Salice '11	♥♥ 3
● Barbera d'Asti Sup. Nizza V. delle Rose '10	♥ 5

Diego Morra

VIA CASCINA MOSCA, 37
12060 VERDUNO [CN]
TEL. 3284623209
www.verdunopelaverga.it

CELLAR SALES
PRE-BOOKED VISITS
ANNUAL PRODUCTION 15,000 bottles
HECTARES UNDER VINE 30.00

● Barolo Monvigliero '11	♟♟	4
● Verduno Pelaverga '14	♟♟	4

Giuseppe Negro

VIA GALLINA, 22
12052 NEIVE [CN]
TEL. 0173677468
www.negrogiuseppe.com

CELLAR SALES
PRE-BOOKED VISITS
ANNUAL PRODUCTION 55,000 bottles
HECTARES UNDER VINE 9.00

● Barbaresco Gallina '12	♟♟	6
● Barbaresco Pian Cavallo '12	♟♟	6
● Dolcetto d'Alba Pian Cavallo '14	♟	3

Cantina Sociale di Nizza

S.DA ALESSANDRIA, 57
14049 NIZZA MONFERRATO [AT]
TEL. 0141721348
www.nizza.it

CELLAR SALES
PRE-BOOKED VISITS
ANNUAL PRODUCTION 200,000 bottles
HECTARES UNDER VINE 560.00
VITICULTURE METHOD Certified Organic

● Barbera d'Asti Sup. 50 Vendemmie '12	♟♟	4
● Barbera d'Asti Sup. Magister '12	♟♟	2*
● Barbera d'Asti Sup. Nizza Ceppi Vecchi '12	♟♟	4
● Piemonte Barbera Progetto in Origine '14	♟♟	2*

Silvano Nizza

FRAZ. BALLA LORA 29A
12040 SANTO STEFANO ROERO [CN]
TEL. 017390516
www.nizzasilvano.com

CELLAR SALES
PRE-BOOKED VISITS
ANNUAL PRODUCTION 65,000 bottles
HECTARES UNDER VINE 8.00

● Roero '12	♟♟	5
○ Roero Arneis '14	♟♟	3
● Roero Ca' Boscarone Ris. '12	♟♟	6

Pace

FRAZ. MADONNA DI LORETO
CASCINA PACE, 52
12043 CANALE [CN]
TEL. 0173979544
dinonegropace@gmail.com

CELLAR SALES
PRE-BOOKED VISITS
ANNUAL PRODUCTION 60,000 bottles
HECTARES UNDER VINE 22.00

● Barbera d'Alba '13	♟♟	2*
○ Roero Arneis '14	♟♟	2*
● Langhe Nebbiolo '13	♟	2
● Roero Ris. '11	♟	5

Pelassa

B.GO TUCCI, 43
12046 MONTÀ [CN]
TEL. 0173971312
www.pelassa.com

CELLAR SALES
ANNUAL PRODUCTION 80,000 bottles
HECTARES UNDER VINE 14.00

● Barbera d'Alba Sup. San Pancrazio '13	♟♟	3
● Nebbiolo d'Alba Sot '12	♟♟	3
○ Roero Arneis San Vito '14	♟♟	2*
● Roero Antaniolo Ris. '11	♟	4

Pasquale Pelissero

Cascina Crosa, 2
12052 Neive [CN]
Tel. 017367376
www.pasqualepelissero.com

CELLAR SALES
PRE-BOOKED VISITS
ANNUAL PRODUCTION 35,000 bottles
HECTARES UNDER VINE 8.00

● Barbaresco Bricco San Giuliano '12	♥♥ 5
● Barbaresco Ciabot Ris. '10	♥♥ 4

Pescaja

via San Matteo, 59
14010 Cisterna d'Asti [AT]
Tel. 0141979711
www.pescaja.com

PRE-BOOKED VISITS
ANNUAL PRODUCTION 150,000 bottles
HECTARES UNDER VINE 19.00

● Barbera d'Asti Soliter '14	♥♥ 2*
● Barbera d'Asti Sup. Nizza Solneri '12	♥♥ 4
○ Terre Alfieri Arneis '14	♥♥ 2*
● Terre Alfieri Nebbiolo Tuké '13	♥♥ 3

Le Pianelle

s.da Forte, 24
13862 Brusnengo [BI]
www.lepianelle.com

HECTARES UNDER VINE 3.00

● Bramaterra '12	♥♥ 8
⊙ Coste della Sesia Rosato Al Posto dei Fiori '14	♥♥ 3

Pianpolvere Soprano Bussia

loc. Bussia, 32
12065 Monforte d'Alba [CN]
Tel. 017378421
www.pianpolveresoprano.it

CELLAR SALES
PRE-BOOKED VISITS
ANNUAL PRODUCTION 10,000 bottles
HECTARES UNDER VINE 7.00

● Barolo Bussia Ris. '08	♥♥ 8

Pier

via Giacosa, 22
12050 Treiso [CN]
Tel. 0173638041
www.piervini.it

CELLAR SALES
PRE-BOOKED VISITS
ANNUAL PRODUCTION 130,000 bottles
HECTARES UNDER VINE 40.00

● Barbaresco Rio Sordo Ris. '10	♥♥ 6
● Barbaresco Vila Ris. '09	♥♥ 6
● Barbera d'Alba Sup. Pajun '11	♥♥ 3

Platinetti

via Roma, 60
28074 Ghemme [NO]
Tel. 01119567820
platinettiguido@libero.it

CELLAR SALES
PRE-BOOKED VISITS
ANNUAL PRODUCTION 10,000 bottles
HECTARES UNDER VINE 5.00

● Colline Novaresi Vespolina '14	♥♥ 2*
● Ghemme V. Ronco Maso '10	♥♥ 4
● Colline Novaresi Barbera Pieleo '12	♥ 3
● Colline Novaresi Nebbiolo '13	♥ 3

I Pola

VIA ALBA, 6
15010 CREMOLINO [AL]
TEL. 3356133283
www.ipola.it

CELLAR SALES
ACCOMMODATION
ANNUAL PRODUCTION 60,000 bottles
HECTARES UNDER VINE 18.00
VITICULTURE METHOD Certified Organic

● Barbaresco '12	♀♀ 5
● Barbera d'Alba '13	♀♀ 3
● Ovada Orchestra '13	♀♀ 4
● Dolcetto di Ovada '12	♀ 3

Prinsi

VIA GAIA, 5
12052 NEIVE [CN]
TEL. 017367192
www.prinsi.it

CELLAR SALES
PRE-BOOKED VISITS
ANNUAL PRODUCTION 60,000 bottles
HECTARES UNDER VINE 14.50

● Barbaresco Gallina '12	♀♀ 5
● Barbaresco Fausoni Ris. '10	♀♀ 5
● Barbaresco Gaia Principe '10	♀ 5

La Raia

S.DA MONTEROTONDO, 79
15067 NOVI LIGURE [AL]
TEL. 0143743685
www.la-raia.it

CELLAR SALES
PRE-BOOKED VISITS
ACCOMMODATION
ANNUAL PRODUCTION 150,000 bottles
HECTARES UNDER VINE 42.00
VITICULTURE METHOD Certified Organic

○ Gavi V. della Madonnina Ris. '13	♀♀ 3*
● Piemonte Barbera '13	♀♀ 3
○ Gavi '14	♀ 3

F.lli Raineri

VIA TORINO, 2
12060 FARIGLIANO [CN]
TEL. 017376223
www.rainerivini.com

CELLAR SALES
PRE-BOOKED VISITS
ANNUAL PRODUCTION 20,000 bottles
HECTARES UNDER VINE 3.30

● Barbera d'Alba Sagrin '13	♀♀ 5
● Barolo Monserra '11	♀♀ 6
● Barolo '11	♀ 5
● Langhe Nebbiolo Snart '13	♀ 3

Rattalino

S.DA GIRO DEL MONDO, 4
12050 BARBARESCO [CN]
TEL. 3492155012
www.massimorattalino.it

CELLAR SALES
PRE-BOOKED VISITS
ANNUAL PRODUCTION 30,000 bottles
HECTARES UNDER VINE 5.80
SUSTAINABLE WINERY

● Barbaresco Ronchi Quarantacinque45 '11	♀♀ 6
● Barbaresco Quarantadue42 '11	♀♀ 5
● Barolo Trentacinque35 '10	♀♀ 5
● Barolo Trentaquattro34 '10	♀♀ 5

Carlo Daniele Ricci

VIA MONTALE CELLI, 9
15050 COSTA VESCOVATO [AL]
TEL. 0131838115
www.aziendaagricolaricci.com

CELLAR SALES
PRE-BOOKED VISITS
ACCOMMODATION AND RESTAURANT SERVICE
ANNUAL PRODUCTION 40,000 bottles
HECTARES UNDER VINE 8.00

○ Colli Tortonesi Timorasso San Leto '11	♀♀ 5
○ Colli Tortonesi Timorasso Terre del Timorasso '13	♀ 3
○ Il Giallo di Costa '11	♀ 4

Francesco Rinaldi & Figli

VIA CROSIA, 30
12051 BAROLO [CN]
TEL. 0173440484
www.rinaldifrancesco.it

CELLAR SALES
PRE-BOOKED VISITS
ANNUAL PRODUCTION 70,000 bottles
HECTARES UNDER VINE 11.00

● Barbera d'Alba '13	♥♥ 3
● Barolo Brunate '11	♥♥ 6
● Barolo Cannubi '11	♥♥ 7
● Nebbiolo d'Alba '13	♥ 3

Silvia Rivella

LOC. MONTESTEFANO, 17
12050 BARBARESCO [CN]
TEL. 0173635040
www.agriturismorivella.it

CELLAR SALES
ACCOMMODATION AND RESTAURANT SERVICE
ANNUAL PRODUCTION 7,000 bottles
HECTARES UNDER VINE 1.50

● Barbaresco Montestefano '11	♥♥ 7
● Barbaresco '12	♥♥ 6

Massimo Rivetti

VIA RIVETTI, 22
12052 NEIVE [CN]
TEL. 017367505
www.rivettimassimo.it

PRE-BOOKED VISITS
ANNUAL PRODUCTION 50,000 bottles
HECTARES UNDER VINE 25.00
VITICULTURE METHOD Certified Organic

● Barbera d'Alba Sup. V. Serraboella '12	♥♥ 4
● Barbaresco Froi '12	♥♥ 5
● Barbaresco Serraboella '12	♥♥ 5
● Barbera d'Alba Sup. Froi '13	♥ 2

Rivetto

LOC. LIRANO, 2
12050 SINIO [CN]
TEL. 0173613380
www.rivetto.it

CELLAR SALES
PRE-BOOKED VISITS
ACCOMMODATION
ANNUAL PRODUCTION 100,000 bottles
HECTARES UNDER VINE 20.00

● Barolo Leon Ris. '09	♥♥ 8
● Barolo Briccolina '10	♥♥ 7
● Barolo del Comune di Serralunga D'Alba '11	♥♥ 6

Il Rocchin

LOC. VALLEMME, 39
15066 GAVI [AL]
TEL. 0143642228
www.ilrocchin.it

CELLAR SALES
PRE-BOOKED VISITS
ANNUAL PRODUCTION 50,000 bottles
HECTARES UNDER VINE 20.00

○ Gavi del Comune di Gavi '14	♥♥ 2*
● Dolcetto di Ovada '14	♥ 2
○ Gavi del Comune di Gavi Il Bosco '14	♥ 3

Rocco di Carpeneto

S.DA CASCINA ROCCO, 500
15071 CARPENETO [AL]
TEL. 01431870034
www.roccodicarpeneto.it

CELLAR SALES
ACCOMMODATION
ANNUAL PRODUCTION 21,000 bottles
HECTARES UNDER VINE 5.00
VITICULTURE METHOD Certified Organic

● Barbera del M.to Sup. Rapp '12	♥♥ 3
● Barbera del M.to Sup. Rataraura '12	♥♥ 3
● Ovada Losna '13	♥♥ 3
● M.to Dolcetto Aur-Oura '13	♥ 2

Rossi Contini

s.da San Lorenzo, 20
15076 Ovada [AL]
Tel. 0143822530
www.rossicontini.com

CELLAR SALES
PRE-BOOKED VISITS
ANNUAL PRODUCTION 17,000 bottles
HECTARES UNDER VINE 4.50
SUSTAINABLE WINERY

● Dolcetto di Ovada Vign. Ninan '12	♟♟ 4
○ Cortese dell'Alto M.to Cortesia '14	♟ 2
● Dolcetto di Ovada San Lorenzo '13	♟ 2

Poderi Rosso Giovanni

p.zza Roma, 1
14041 Agliano Terme [AT]
Tel. 0141954006
www.poderirossogiovanni.it

CELLAR SALES
PRE-BOOKED VISITS
ANNUAL PRODUCTION 45,000 bottles
HECTARES UNDER VINE 12.00

● Barbera d'Asti Podere San Bastian '14	♟♟ 2*
● Barbera d'Asti Sup. Cascina Perno '13	♟♟ 3
● Barbera d'Asti Sup. Gioco dell'Oca '12	♟♟ 6
○ Quattro Brut	♟ 4

San Fereolo

loc. San Fereolo
b.ta Valdibà, 59
12063 Dogliani [CN]
Tel. 0173742075
www.sanfereolo.com

PRE-BOOKED VISITS
ANNUAL PRODUCTION 46,000 bottles
HECTARES UNDER VINE 12.00

● Langhe Rosso Il Provinciale '10	♟♟ 4
● Dogliani '09	♟♟ 3
○ Langhe Bianco Coste di Riavolo '11	♟♟ 3

Tenuta San Pietro

loc. San Pietro, 2
15060 Tassarolo [AL]
Tel. 0143342422
www.tenutasanpietro.it

CELLAR SALES
PRE-BOOKED VISITS
ANNUAL PRODUCTION 250,000 bottles
HECTARES UNDER VINE 30.00
VITICULTURE METHOD Certified Organic
SUSTAINABLE WINERY

○ Gavi del Comune di Tassarolo Gorrina '12	♟♟ 6
○ Gavi del Comune di Tassarolo Il Mandorlo '14	♟♟ 5
○ Gavi del Comune di Tassarolo San Pietro '14	♟♟ 3

Tenuta Santa Caterina

via Guglielmo Marconi, 17
14035 Grazzano Badoglio [AT]
Tel. 0141925108
www.tenuta-santa-caterina.it

ANNUAL PRODUCTION 50,000 bottles
HECTARES UNDER VINE 23.00

● Barbera d'Asti Sup. Setecàpita '11	♟♟ 3
● Barbera d'Asti Sup. V. Lina '12	♟♟ 3
● Freisa d'Asti Sorì di Giul '11	♟♟ 3
● Grignolino d'Asti '13	♟ 2

Giacomo Scagliola

reg. Santa Libera, 20
14053 Canelli [AT]
Tel. 0141831146
www.scagliola-canelli.it

CELLAR SALES
ANNUAL PRODUCTION 80,000 bottles
HECTARES UNDER VINE 15.00

● Barbera d'Asti Sup. La Faia '13	♟♟ 2*
○ Moscato d'Asti Sifasol '14	♟♟ 2*

Simone Scaletta
LOC. MANZONI, 61
12065 MONFORTE D'ALBA [CN]
TEL. 3484912733
www.simonescaletta.it

CELLAR SALES
PRE-BOOKED VISITS
ACCOMMODATION
ANNUAL PRODUCTION 20,000 bottles
HECTARES UNDER VINE 4.75

- Barolo Chirlet '11 ▼▼ 6
- Langhe Nebbiolo Autin 'd Madama '13 ▼▼ 3
- Barbera d'Alba Sup. Sarsera '13 ▼ 3

Segni di Langa
LOC. RAVINALI, 25
12060 RODDI [CN]
TEL. 3803945151
www.segnidilanga.it

CELLAR SALES
PRE-BOOKED VISITS
ACCOMMODATION
ANNUAL PRODUCTION 6,000 bottles
HECTARES UNDER VINE 0.90
SUSTAINABLE WINERY

- Langhe Pinot Nero '14 ▼▼ 4
- Barbera d'Alba Sup. Greta '14 ▼▼ 4

Poderi Sinaglio
FRAZ. RICCA
VIA SINAGLIO, 5
12055 DIANO D'ALBA [CN]
TEL. 0173612209
www.poderisinaglio.it

CELLAR SALES
PRE-BOOKED VISITS
ACCOMMODATION AND RESTAURANT SERVICE
ANNUAL PRODUCTION 44,000 bottles
HECTARES UNDER VINE 13.00

- Barbera d'Alba Erta '13 ▼▼ 3
- Dolcetto di Diano d'Alba Sorì Bricco Maiolica '14 ▼▼ 2*
- Langhe Rosso Sinaij '12 ▼▼ 3

Sobrero Francesco e Figli
VIA PUGNANE, 5
12060 CASTIGLIONE FALLETTO [CN]
TEL. 017362864
www.sobrerofrancesco.it

CELLAR SALES
PRE-BOOKED VISITS
ACCOMMODATION
ANNUAL PRODUCTION 90,000 bottles
HECTARES UNDER VINE 16.00

- Barbera d'Alba Selectio '13 ▼▼ 3
- Barolo Ciabot Tanasio '11 ▼▼ 6
- Barolo Pernanno Ris. '09 ▼▼ 7
- Langhe Nebbiolo '13 ▼ 4

La Spinosa Alta
CASCINA SPINOSA ALTA, 5
15038 OTTIGLIO [AL]
TEL. 0142921372
www.laspinosaalta.it

CELLAR SALES
PRE-BOOKED VISITS
ACCOMMODATION
ANNUAL PRODUCTION 12,000 bottles
HECTARES UNDER VINE 2.50

- Barbera del M.to Sup. La Punta '10 ▼▼ 3
- M.to Rosso Tenebroso '10 ▼▼ 3
- Piemonte Barbera '12 ▼▼ 2*
- ⊙ M.to Chiaretto '14 ▼ 2

Giuseppe Stella
S.DA BOSSOLA, 8
14055 COSTIGLIOLE D'ASTI [AT]
TEL. 0141966142
www.stellavini.it

CELLAR SALES
PRE-BOOKED VISITS
ANNUAL PRODUCTION 45,000 bottles
HECTARES UNDER VINE 11.00

- Barbera d'Asti Sup. Il Maestro '12 ▼▼ 4
- Grignolino d'Asti Sufragio '14 ▼▼ 3
- Freisa d'Asti Convento '13 ▼ 3

Oreste Stroppiana

FRAZ. RIVALTA SAN GIACOMO, 6
12064 LA MORRA [CN]
TEL. 0173509419
www.cantinastroppiana.com

CELLAR SALES
PRE-BOOKED VISITS
ANNUAL PRODUCTION 35,000 bottles
HECTARES UNDER VINE 5.00

● Barolo Bussia '11	♟♟ 6
● Barolo Leonardo '11	♟♟ 5
● Barolo San Giacomo '11	♟♟ 6
● Barbera d'Alba Sup. Altea '13	♟ 3

Cantine Terre Astesane

VIA MARCONI, 2
14042 MOMBERCELLI [AT]
TEL. 0141959155
www.terreastesane.it

CELLAR SALES
PRE-BOOKED VISITS
ANNUAL PRODUCTION 100,000 bottles
HECTARES UNDER VINE 230.00

● Barbera d'Asti Sup. '12	♟♟ 2*
● Barbera d'Asti Sup. Mumbersè '11	♟♟ 3
● Barbera d'Asti La '14	♟ 2
● Grignolino d'Asti '14	♟ 2

La Toledana

LOC. SERMOIRA,5
15066 GAVI [AL]
TEL. 0141837287
www.latoledana.it

CELLAR SALES
PRE-BOOKED VISITS
ANNUAL PRODUCTION 145,000 bottles
HECTARES UNDER VINE 28.00

● Barolo Ravera Lo Zoccolaio '10	♟♟ 7
○ Gavi del Comune di Gavi La Toledana '14	♟♟ 5
● Barolo Lo Zoccolaio '10	♟ 6
○ Gavi La Doria '14	♟ 3

Trediberri

B.TA TORRIGLIONE, 4
12064 LA MORRA [CN]
TEL. 3391605470
www.trediberri.com

CELLAR SALES
PRE-BOOKED VISITS
ANNUAL PRODUCTION 25,000 bottles
HECTARES UNDER VINE 8.00
VITICULTURE METHOD Certified Organic

● Barolo Rocche dell'Annunziata '11	♟♟ 7
● Barolo '11	♟♟ 5

F.lli Trinchero

VIA GORRA, 49
14048 MONTEGROSSO D'ASTI [AT]
TEL. 0141956167
www.fllitrincherovino.com

CELLAR SALES
PRE-BOOKED VISITS
ANNUAL PRODUCTION 50,000 bottles
HECTARES UNDER VINE 12.00

● Barbera d'Asti Sup. Rico '11	♟♟ 3*
● Barbera d'Asti La Trincherina '13	♟♟ 2*

Laura Valditerra

S.DA MONTEROTONDO, 75
15067 NOVI LIGURE [AL]
TEL. 0143381247
www.valditerra.it

CELLAR SALES
PRE-BOOKED VISITS
ACCOMMODATION
ANNUAL PRODUCTION 20,000 bottles
HECTARES UNDER VINE 5.00
SUSTAINABLE WINERY

○ Gavi '14	♟♟ 2*

Valfaccenda

FRAZ. MADONNA LORETO
LOC. VALFACCENDA 43
12043 CANALE [CN]
TEL. 3397303837
www.valfaccenda.it

CELLAR SALES
PRE-BOOKED VISITS
ANNUAL PRODUCTION 14,000 bottles
HECTARES UNDER VINE 2.00
SUSTAINABLE WINERY

● Roero '13	♟♟ 4
○ Roero Arneis '14	♟ 3

La Vecchia Posta

VIA MONTEBELLO, 2
15050 AVOLASCA [AL]
TEL. 0131876254
lavecchiaposta@virgilio.it

CELLAR SALES
PRE-BOOKED VISITS
ACCOMMODATION AND RESTAURANT SERVICE
ANNUAL PRODUCTION 10,000 bottles
HECTARES UNDER VINE 2.70
VITICULTURE METHOD Certified Organic

● Colli Tortonesi Rosso Rebelot '14	♟♟ 4
○ Colli Tortonesi Timorasso Il Selvaggio '13	♟♟ 3*
● Colli Tortonesi Barbera Languia '12	♟♟ 3

Alessandro Veglio

FRAZ. ANNUNZIATA, 53
12064 LA MORRA [CN]
TEL. 3385699102
www.risveglioinlanga.it

ANNUAL PRODUCTION 10,000 bottles
HECTARES UNDER VINE 3.00

● Barolo '11	♟♟ 5
● Barolo Gattera '11	♟♟ 7
● Langhe Nebbiolo '13	♟♟ 3

Eraldo Viberti

FRAZ. SANTA MARIA
B.TA TETTI, 53
12064 LA MORRA [CN]
TEL. 017350308
www.eraldoviberti.com

CELLAR SALES
PRE-BOOKED VISITS
ANNUAL PRODUCTION 27,000 bottles
HECTARES UNDER VINE 5.00

● Barolo Rocchettevino '11	♟♟ 7
● Barolo Roncaglie '11	♟♟ 7
● Langhe Nebbiolo '12	♟ 3

Giovanni Viberti

VIA DELLE VIOLE 30
12060 BAROLO [CN]
TEL. 017356192
www.viberti-barolo.com

CELLAR SALES
PRE-BOOKED VISITS
RESTAURANT SERVICE
ANNUAL PRODUCTION 80,000 bottles
HECTARES UNDER VINE 18.00

● Barolo Buon Padre '11	♟♟ 6
● Barbera d'Alba Sup. Bricco Airoli '11	♟♟ 4
● Langhe Nebbiolo '13	♟♟ 3
● Barbera d'Alba La Gemella '13	♟ 3

Alberto Voerzio

FRAZ. ANNUNZIATA, 103A
12064 LA MORRA [CN]
TEL. 3333927654
www.albertovoerzio.com

CELLAR SALES
PRE-BOOKED VISITS
ANNUAL PRODUCTION 12,000 bottles
HECTARES UNDER VINE 5.00

● Barolo '11	♟♟ 6
● Barolo La Serra '11	♟♟ 6

LIGURIA

It was a bit of a funny year, 2014. The far
western coast was excellent; other areas scraped
in on the tail-end of summer with some gentle
warmth that brought the grapes to ripeness.
The Riviera di Ponente microclimate saved the
land from the abundant summer rains. Here we are in
the home not only of Pigato and Vermentino, but also Dolceacqua, Liguria's top
red wine, which romped home this year. Only one wine, Maccario Dringenberg
2013 Posaù made the podium, but the designation overall was noteworthy for
its general quality. These are wines that tell the story of an area unique not
least of all for its fascinating regional landscape of small terraced vineyards
carved from the mountainside, outright balconies overlooking the sea. We
should be aware that in the last decade, the unity and determination of these
vignerons has produced a collective result of extraordinary importance. On the
far east side, however, growers had to intervene several times in the rows to
protect the grapes threatened by persistent rains. A mild, dry September saved
anyone with strong nerves who waited it out and reaped the rewards. La Spezia
province took home three Tre Bicchieri awards. Two were old hands: Lunae
Bosoni with a 2014 Vermentino Etichetta Nera and Ottaviano Lambruschi with a
2014 Il Maggiore; and another 2014 Vermèntino from Conte Picedi Benettini, a
producer who deserves all our attention. Imperia showed two excellent Pigatos:
Bruna's classic U Baccan 2013 and Poggio dei Gorleri's Albium 2014. Last up,
recent innovations in the region includes a growing trend for sparkling wines,
still seeking the right direction to follow to guarantee a quality product with its
own identity. In conclusion, we are in no doubt that this year Liguria has seen
widespread growth in the quality of its production, despite 2014 certainly not
being a stroll. The result is down to commitment and dedication to the vine
that really does winegrowers of Liguria proud, and in many cases deserve an
accolade not only for the quality of their wines but also for the great and heroic
land conservation they have always performed.

LIGURIA

Massimo Alessandri

VIA COSTA PARROCCHIA, 42
18020 RANZO [IM]
TEL. 018253458
www.massimoalessandri.it

CELLAR SALES
PRE-BOOKED VISITS
RESTAURANT SERVICE
ANNUAL PRODUCTION 35,000 bottles
HECTARES UNDER VINE 7.00

There was a good harvest in 2014, with
white varieties picked late, in early October,
but with yields up by 30%. The first to
ripen was vermentino, grown on Canata's
sandy soils at an elevation of 150 metres,
then came pigato, planted along the coast
up to elevations of 350 metres on clay
and limestone soils with ferrous minerals.
Massimo is the factotum of this young
winery, established in 1996 in the small
town of Ranzo. Production is set to increase
next year, with a new vineyard planted to
rossese. The piquant, full-bodied Vigne
Vegie 2014 boasts great elegance and
balance. Mediterranean notes of aniseed,
almond and dried flowers further enrich the
harmonious, elegant body, with a pleasing,
long, tangy finish. The fresh, vibrant, bright
straw-yellow Viorus 2013 shows notes
of apricots and peach, and a generous,
complex body.

Laura Aschero

P.ZZA VITTORIO EMANUELE, 7
18027 PONTEDASSIO [IM]
TEL. 0183710307
www.lauraaschero.it

CELLAR SALES
PRE-BOOKED VISITS
ANNUAL PRODUCTION 60,000 bottles
HECTARES UNDER VINE 50.00

The production of native varieties continues
at Laura Aschero's winery, and the quality
of the last harvest was mainly down to the
month of September, which brought the
grapes to ripeness, albeit with lower sugar
levels. Overall, this was a good harvest,
with only a slight drop in production figures
of the Riviera Ligure di Ponente Pigato.
Marco Rizzo, his wife Carla, and their
daughter Bianca, have invested in the
winery, building a large new tasting room
to welcome the many tourists who visit
every day. We liked the brilliant, lustrous,
lively Pigato 2014, with classic notes of
medicinal herbs and white-fleshed fruit
over salty aromas. On the palate, it shows
a tight-knit, mineral structure, with intense
flavour, a rounded body and good harmony.
The Vermentino 2014 offers distinctive
aromas of broom, dandelion, and ripe
pineapple, over a full-flavoured, pleasant
palate with intense, harmonious notes.

○ Riviera Ligure di Ponente Pigato Vigne Vegie '14	♟♟ 4
● Riviera Ligure di Ponente Granaccia '13	♟♟ 4
○ Riviera Ligure di Ponente Pigato Costa de Vigne '14	♟♟ 3
○ Viorus '13	♟♟ 5
● Ligustico '12	♟ 6
○ Riviera Ligure di Ponente Vermentino Costa de Vigne '14	♟ 3
○ Riviera Ligure di Ponente Pigato Costa de Vigne '13	♟♟ 3*
○ Riviera Ligure di Ponente Pigato Costa de Vigne '12	♟♟ 3*
○ Riviera Ligure di Ponente Pigato Vigne Vëggie '12	♟♟ 4

○ Riviera Ligure di Ponente Pigato '14	♟♟ 3
○ Riviera Ligure di Ponente Vermentino '14	♟♟ 3
○ Riviera Ligure di Ponente Vermentino '10	♟♟♟ 3*
○ Riviera Ligure di Ponente Pigato '13	♟♟ 3*
○ Riviera Ligure di Ponente Pigato '12	♟♟ 3
○ Riviera Ligure di Ponente Pigato '11	♟♟ 3*
○ Riviera Ligure di Ponente Pigato '08	♟♟ 3*
○ Riviera Ligure di Ponente Pigato '06	♟♟ 3
● Riviera Ligure di Ponente Rossese '07	♟♟ 3
○ Riviera Ligure di Ponente Vermentino '12	♟♟ 3*
○ Riviera Ligure di Ponente Vermentino '11	♟♟ 3
○ Riviera Ligure di Ponente Vermentino '09	♟♟ 3
○ Riviera Ligure di Ponente Vermentino '08	♟♟ 3*
○ Riviera Ligure di Ponente Vermentino '07	♟♟ 3
○ Riviera Ligure di Ponente Vermentino '06	♟♟ 3
○ Riviera Ligure di Ponente Vermentino '05	♟♟ 3*

La Baia del Sole

FRAZ. LUNI ANTICA
VIA FORLINO, 3
19034 ORTONOVO [SP]
TEL. 0187661821
www.cantinefederici.com

CELLAR SALES
PRE-BOOKED VISITS
ANNUAL PRODUCTION 150,000 bottles
HECTARES UNDER VINE 25.00

Winds of change are blowing through the winery, starting with the purchase of a three-hectare plot of land, which is fairly big for Liguria, to add to existing holdings. So far, one hectare of the new land has been planted to vermentino, while the remaining work has been put off until next season. The new cellar has been operational since December, and has already produced its first wines. The winery avails itself of around 60 growers, who provide selected grapes for production, which is directly supervised by the Federici family. The 2014 harvest was difficult as grapes ripened late and were not ready until mid-September. Despite the difficulties, the Solaris 2014 made our finals. This exciting wine shows attractive notes of medicinal and dried herbs, acacia blossom and elderflower on the palate, in a profile of great finesse and elegance, with a long, classy finish. The characterful, fresh Sarticola 2014 opens to grassy, salty notes over pineapple and melon, and ends with impressive personality.

○ Colli di Luni Vermentino Sarticola '14	♟♟	4
○ Colli di Luni Vermentino Solaris '14	♟♟	3*
○ Colli di Luni Gladius '14	♟♟	2*
● Colli di Luni Terre d'Oriente Ris. '09	♟♟	5
● Colli di Luni Eutichiano '14	♟	3
○ Colli di Luni Vermentino Oro d'Isèe '14	♟	4
○ Muri Grandi '14	♟	2
● Colli di Luni Eutichiano '12	♟♟	3*
● Colli di Luni Eutichiano '11	♟♟	3
○ Colli di Luni Vermentino Oro d'Isèe '13	♟♟	3
○ Colli di Luni Vermentino Oro d'Isèe '12	♟♟	4
○ Colli di Luni Vermentino Oro d'Isèe '11	♟♟	4
○ Colli di Luni Vermentino Sarticola '12	♟♟	5
○ Colli di Luni Vermentino Solaris '13	♟♟	2*
○ Colli di Luni Vermentino Solaris '12	♟♟	3
○ Muri Grandi '13	♟♟	2*

Maria Donata Bianchi

VIA MEREA, 101
18013 DIANO ARENTINO [IM]
TEL. 0183498233
www.aziendaagricolabianchi.it

CELLAR SALES
PRE-BOOKED VISITS
ACCOMMODATION
ANNUAL PRODUCTION 30,000 bottles
HECTARES UNDER VINE 4.00

This operation has been producing wines of great quality and elegance since 1977. Last year, Marta, daughter of Maria Donata and Emanuele Trevia, joined the team, and deals with the harvest. Her university studies in oenology will soon allow her to take over the helm of the company, which over the years has grown not only in quality but also in terms of production figures, and can also boast an elegant agriturismo. The last harvest was acceptable overall, despite a wet July, resulting in good fixed acidity, softened by late picking in the second week of September. Notes of sea salt, rosemary, apples and pears, and intense, ripe peach, distinguish the Pigato 2014, whose great personality is expressed in a potent, elegant body, rich in mineral notes and extract. Intensely fresh with clear mineral notes, the Vermentino 2014 is redolent of its homeland, with fresh Mediterranean herbs, and boasts an elegantly-contoured, solid structure.

○ Riviera Ligure di Ponente Pigato '14	♟♟	3*
○ Riviera Ligure di Ponente Vermentino '14	♟♟	3
● Bormano '12	♟	4
○ Riviera Ligure di Ponente Pigato '12	♟♟♟	3*
○ Riviera Ligure di Ponente Vermentino '09	♟♟♟	3
○ Riviera Ligure di Ponente Vermentino '07	♟♟♟	3*
○ Antico Sfizio '12	♟♟	4
● Bormano '07	♟♟	4
● La Mattana '06	♟♟	5
○ Riviera Ligure di Ponente Pigato '13	♟♟	3*
○ Riviera Ligure di Ponente Pigato '11	♟♟	4
○ Riviera Ligure di Ponente Pigato '09	♟♟	3
○ Riviera Ligure di Ponente Vermentino '13	♟♟	3
○ Riviera Ligure di Ponente Vermentino '11	♟♟	4
○ Riviera Ligure di Ponente Vermentino '10	♟♟	3
○ Riviera Ligure di Ponente Vermentino '08	♟♟	4

BioVio

FRAZ. BASTIA
VIA CROCIATA, 24
17031 ALBENGA [SV]
TEL. 018220776
www.biovio.it

CELLAR SALES
PRE-BOOKED VISITS
ANNUAL PRODUCTION 40,000 bottles
HECTARES UNDER VINE 6.00
VITICULTURE METHOD Certified Organic

The Vio family continue to produce certified organic wines. Their time-honoured vineyards have now been joined by new plantings of pigato from Ponterotto and Resie at Ranzo, in the province of Imperia, which will soon become new crus. The winery is in constant growth, also thanks to the extension of the production facility and agriturismo, but above all thanks to the arrival of new blood: Caterina, with a degree in oenology, works alongside her father Aimone in the cellar, while Carolina loves tending the rows, and mother Chiara takes care of the agriturismo. Camilla still has to complete her studies, but will soon join the team. The bright straw-yellow Vermentino Aimone 2014 has classic Mediterranean notes and citrus, over a backdrop of medicinal herbs, leading into a silky, velvety palate of great finesse. Equally good is the Bon in da Bon 2014, whose great harmony on the nose shows iodine and mineral notes, followed by delicate hints of dried herbs. This is a complex, attractively elegant wine.

○ Riviera Ligure di Ponente		
Pigato Albenganese Bon in da Bon '14	♟♟	2*
○ Riviera Ligure di Ponente		
Pigato Albenganese Ma René '14	♟♟	2*
○ Riviera Ligure di Ponente		
Vermentino Albenganese Aimone '14	♟♟	2*
● Granaccia Gigò '14	♟♟	3
● Riviera Ligure di Ponente		
Rossese U Bastiò '14	♟♟	2*
○ Grand Pere '13	♟	2
○ Riviera Ligure di Ponente		
Vermentino Aimone '11	♟♟♟	2*
○ Riviera Ligure di Ponente		
Pigato Albenganese Bon in da Bon '13	♟♟	3*

Samuele Heydi Bonanini

VIA SAN ANTONIO, 72
19017 RIOMAGGIORE [SP]
TEL. 0187920959
www.possa.it

CELLAR SALES
PRE-BOOKED VISITS
ANNUAL PRODUCTION 7,000 bottles
HECTARES UNDER VINE 1.50

Samuele is continuing to do impressive work among the rugged hills of Riomaggiore, one of the pearls of the Cinque Terre. It is impossible to appreciate the wines of this territory unless we are aware of the difficulties and care involved in their production, and the 2014 harvest was particularly challenging, with heavy rain keeping sugar levels low, and the harvest spread over two picking sessions. The first began on 6 September, and a second at the end of the month, to allow the grapes to ripen to the full. The increased yield benefitted production of the Cinque Terre, to the detriment of the more select, elegant Sciacchetrà. Inviting with its attractive golden straw hue, the highly characterful Cinque Terre 2014 shows attractive sea salt, citrus zest and mature fruit, with spicy notes of white pepper, followed by generous structure on the richly extracted palate. We also saw great personality and elegance in the intense, velvety, sweet Sciacchetrà Riserva 2010, an unforgettable wine.

○ Cinque Terre '14	♟♟	5
○ Cinque Terre Sciacchetrà Ris. '10	♟♟	8
● U Neigru '14	♟	5
○ Cinque Terre '13	♟♟♟	5
○ Cinque Terre '12	♟♟♟	5
○ Cinque Terre '11	♟♟	5
○ Cinque Terre '10	♟♟	6
○ Cinque Terre Sciacchetrà '12	♟♟	8
○ Cinque Terre Sciacchetrà '11	♟♟	8
○ Cinque Terre Sciacchetrà '10	♟♟	8
○ Cinque Terre Sciacchetrà Ris. '09	♟♟	8
○ Cinque Terre Vetua '11	♟♟	5
● Passito '10	♟♟	8
● Passito La Rinascita '11	♟♟	8
● Passito La Rinascita '10	♟♟	8
○ Vin dei Vecci	♟♟	2*

Cantina Bregante

VIA UNITÀ D'ITALIA, 47
16039 SESTRI LEVANTE [GE]
TEL. 018541388
www.cantinebregante.it

CELLAR SALES
PRE-BOOKED VISITS
ANNUAL PRODUCTION 900,000 bottles
HECTARES UNDER VINE 1.50

Sergio and Simona continue to pursue quality in a difficult and often ungenerous territory. Their main variety is bianchetta genovese, joined by vermentino, ciliegiolo and moscato. This year saw the new San Bernardo vineyard at Sestri Levante started production. The grapes, planted on terraces at elevations of around 150 metres, were harvested in late August. The mixed soil, with good levels of minerals, and the slightly early harvest, which helped preserve acidity, resulted in minimum production figures, of around 700 bottles of Metodo Classico Dosaggio Zero. The Moscato 2014 boasts an attractive mousse, along with intense flavours and fresh, aromatic notes of spring flowers and pineapple, with a hint of candied orange peel. The generous, complex palate offers intense, attractive plushness and an elegant finish. We were won over by the Rosso Ca' du Diau 2014, with its seductive red berry fruit and spice. In the mouth, it plays on attractive harmony and elegance rather than intensity.

● Golfo del Tigullio Ca' du Diau '14	♟♟	3
○ Portofino Moscato '14	♟♟	3
○ Bianchetta Genovese Segesta Tigullorium '14	♟	2
○ Golfo del Tigullio Baia delle Favole M. Cl. '14	♟	5
● Golfo del Tigullio Ciliegiolo '14	♟	2
○ Portofino Vermentino '14	♟	2
○ Golfo del Tigullio Bianchetta Genovese Segesta Tigullorium '12	♟♟	2*
○ Golfo del Tigullio Vermentino Segesta Tigullorium '12	♟♟	2*
○ Portofino Bianchetta Genovese Segesta Tigullorium '13	♟♟	2*
● Portofino Ca' du Diau '13	♟♟	2*
○ Portofino Moscato '13	♟♟	3
○ Portofino Moscato '12	♟♟	3
○ Portofino Passito Sole della Costa '12	♟♟	5

Bruna

FRAZ. BORGO
VIA UMBERTO I, 81
18020 RANZO [IM]
TEL. 0183318082
www.brunapigato.it

CELLAR SALES
PRE-BOOKED VISITS
ANNUAL PRODUCTION 30,000 bottles
HECTARES UNDER VINE 7.50

The growing year was not one of the best, which is why Francesca and Roberto had to reduce quantity in order to maintain quality. The harvest was challenging, and was postponed to 20 September, with the rows also hit by two hailstorms on 8–9 July, forcing the owners of this fine Ligurian winery to make a drastic reduction of 40% in production. Their uncompromising approach led them to sacrifice quantity, producing only 30,000 bottles, setting aside production of Riviera Ligure di Ponente Pigato U Baccan 2014, whose grapes were used for Le Russeghine. We consoled ourselves with the outstanding U Baccan 2013, with its lively, youthful bright straw hue. Notes of medicinal herbs, eucalyptus and iodine pave the way for a leisurely, attractive, well-managed palate, with an intense finish of real finesse. The youthful Le Russeghine 2014 shows notes of elderflower, aromatic herbs and summer flowers, and although delicate does not lack character.

○ Riviera Ligure di Ponente Pigato U Baccan '13	♟♟♟	5
○ Riviera Ligure di Ponente Pigato Le Russeghine '14	♟♟	3*
○ Riviera Ligure di Ponente Pigato Majé '14	♟♟	3*
● Bansigu '14	♟	2
● Rosso Pulin '13	♟	4
○ Riviera Ligure di Ponente Pigato U Baccan '12	♟♟♟	5
○ Riviera Ligure di Ponente Pigato U Baccan '11	♟♟♟	5
○ Riviera Ligure di Ponente Pigato U Baccan '07	♟♟♟	5
○ Riviera Ligure di Ponente Pigato U Baccan '06	♟♟♟	4
○ Riviera Ligure di Ponente Pigato U Baccan '05	♟♟♟	4

LIGURIA

Cheo

via Brigate Partigiane, 1
19018 Vernazza [SP]
Tel. 0187821189
bartolocheo@gmail.com

CELLAR SALES
PRE-BOOKED VISITS
ANNUAL PRODUCTION 8,000 bottles
HECTARES UNDER VINE 2.00
SUSTAINABLE WINERY

Lise Bertram and Bartolomeo Lercari
work tirelessly year after year to improve
quality and fight natural adversities.
Having renovated the vineyards after the
2011 floods, they now have to deal with
invasions of wild boar that destroy the
harvest and devastate the terraces. In
2014 they purchased 5,000 square metres
of vineyards, an enormous plot for this
territory, on terraces between Vernazza
and Monterosso, at elevations of 40–80
metres, planted to bosco, vermentino and
albarola. Set alongside the path linking the
two small towns, the rows make a fantastic
sight. The superb Sciacchetrà 2012, with
its bright, lively amber hue, opens to a nose
of summer flowers, dandelion and broom,
with notes of cocoa powder and pepper,
against a backdrop of sultanas and dates.
The impressive palate finishes with great
harmony, underpinned by serious tannins.
We also loved the Perciò 2014, in which
intense aromas of acacia blossom and
jasmine lead into a fresh, elegant palate
with a lingering finish.

○ Cinque Terre Perciò '14	♀♀ 4
○ Cinque Terre Sciacchetrà '12	♀♀ 8
○ Cinque Terre Cheo '14	♀♀ 3
● Cheo Rosso '13	♀ 4
○ Cinque Terre '12	♀♀ 4
○ Cinque Terre Cheo '13	♀♀ 3*
○ Cinque Terre Cheo '09	♀♀ 3
○ Cinque Terre Perciò '13	♀♀ 4
○ Cinque Terre Perciò '12	♀♀ 4
○ Cinque Terre Perciò '11	♀♀ 4
○ Cinque Terre Perciò '10	♀♀ 4
○ Cinque Terre Sciacchetrà '11	♀♀ 8
○ Cinque Terre Sciacchetrà '10	♀♀ 7
○ Cinque Terre Sciacchetrà '09	♀♀ 7
○ Cinque Terre Sciacchetrà '07	♀♀ 7
● Riviera di Levante '11	♀♀ 4

Cantina Cinque Terre

fraz. Manarola
loc. Groppo
19010 Riomaggiore [SP]
Tel. 0187920435
www.cantinacinqueterre.com

PRE-BOOKED VISITS
ANNUAL PRODUCTION 200,000 bottles
HECTARES UNDER VINE 45.00
VITICULTURE METHOD Certified Organic

To appreciate the wines of Cinque Terre
to the full, tasting them is not enough; a
visit is required to the almost inaccessible
vineyards, perched on their terraces, as
beautiful to look at as they are difficult to
work, surviving only thanks to the great
passion of the local growers. Cantina
delle Cinque Terre plays a crucial role in
preserving this ancient tradition, with 200
member-growers tending 45 hectares
spread over the steep coastal hills. The
traditional pergola bassa training system
is used here, and helps protect clusters
from the hot summer sun, but above all
from the sea breezes that risk burning the
berries. The inviting Sciacchetrà 2012 won
us over with its bright, vibrant old gold hue,
and a nose of acacia blossom and candied
papaya, caramel and currant, with notes of
pink pepper and oriental spice. The palate
is buttressed by attractive acidity and
despite its alcoholic warmth, avoids being
cloying. This wonderfully complex, balanced
wine shows well-judged sweetness offset
by an understated tannic weave.

○ Cinque Terre Sciacchetrà '12	♀♀ 6
○ Cinque Terre Costa da Posa '14	♀♀ 3
○ Cinque Terre Costa de Sèra '14	♀♀ 3
○ Cinque Terre '14	♀ 2
○ Cinque Terre Pergole Sparse '14	♀ 4
○ Cinque Terre Vigne Alte '14	♀ 2
○ Cinque Terre '13	♀♀ 2*
○ Cinque Terre Costa da' Posa '13	♀♀ 3
○ Cinque Terre Costa da' Posa '11	♀♀ 3
○ Cinque Terre Costa da' Posa di Volastra '10	♀♀ 3
○ Cinque Terre Costa de Sèra '12	♀♀ 3
○ Cinque Terre Costa du Campu '10	♀♀ 3
○ Cinque Terre Pergole Sparse '13	♀♀ 4
○ Cinque Terre Sciacchetrà '11	♀♀ 6
○ Cinqueterre Sciacchetrà Un Paesaggio Un Vino '10	♀♀ 6

Fontanacota

FRAZ. PONTI
VIA PROVINCIALE, 137
18100 PORNASSIO [IM]
TEL. 3339807442
www.fontanacota.it

CELLAR SALES
PRE-BOOKED VISITS
ANNUAL PRODUCTION 40,000 bottles
HECTARES UNDER VINE 6.00

Marina and Fabio Berta's vineyards are situated in the province of Imperia, but in different zones, with the white grape varieties, vermentino and pigato, planted near Dolcedo, and the red ormeasco at Pornassio. On the high ground, the harvest was on schedule, on 10 October, with the grapes perfectly ripe, while the Fontanacota vineyard, in Val Prino, suffered hail in the summer months which compromised some of the production and forced the harvest to be moved back to 15 September. Good weather in September however ensured that quality did not suffer. Rosemary, broom and hawthorn dominate the nose of the satisfying Pigato 2014, with its fresh, tangy palate, playing on mineral notes and impressive length. The intense straw-yellow Vermentino 2014 opens to Mediterranean aromas of sage and rosemary, with notes of dried herbs and ripe fruit, followed by velvety smoothness in the mouth and a pleasing, leisurely finish.

○ Riviera Ligure di Ponente Pigato '14	♥♥ 3*
○ Riviera Ligure di Ponente Vermentino '14	♥♥ 3
● Pornassio '14	♥ 3
● Riviera Ligure di Ponente Rossese '14	♥ 3
○ Riviera Ligure di Ponente Pigato '11	♥♥♥ 3*
● Ormeasco di Pornassio '07	♥♥ 2
● Ormeasco di Pornassio Sup. '11	♥♥ 3
● Ormeasco di Pornassio Sup. '10	♥♥ 3
● Ormeasco di Pornassio Sup. '06	♥♥ 3
● Pornassio Sup. '12	♥♥ 3
○ Riviera Ligure di Ponente Pigato '13	♥♥ 3*
○ Riviera Ligure di Ponente Pigato '12	♥♥ 3
○ Riviera Ligure di Ponente Pigato '10	♥♥ 2*
○ Riviera Ligure di Ponente Pigato '09	♥♥ 2*
○ Riviera Ligure di Ponente Pigato '07	♥♥ 2
○ Riviera Ligure di Ponente Vermentino '12	♥♥ 3*

Giacomelli

VIA PALVOTRISIA, 134
19030 CASTELNUOVO MAGRA [SP]
TEL. 0187674155

CELLAR SALES
PRE-BOOKED VISITS
ANNUAL PRODUCTION 50,000 bottles
HECTARES UNDER VINE 12.00
SUSTAINABLE WINERY

Roberto Petacchi, who heads the winery, has started important replanting work at Boboli, one of the historic crus of Castelnuovo Magra. Lying behind the medieval castle, in this century-old vineyard, he has preserved old plants, which are still perfectly healthy and productive. The winery also has plots at Ortonovo and on the coast, totalling around 12 hectares, farmed using organic methods with integrated pest management. In the cellar, in addition to the use of nitrogen to keep sulphites in check, he uses corks made from sugarcane polymers as an environmentally sustainable option. We were impressed with the intensely straw-hued Boboli 2013, displaying a warm, cushiony body. Well-extracted, with aromas of acacia blossom and elderflower, it is brimming with ripe fruit and dried lemon zest, which provide harmony in a complex body with a long finish. Salty notes, aromatic herbs, and appley scents, over an intensely mineral, tangy palate are the hallmarks of the Pianacce 2014.

○ Colli di Luni Vermentino Boboli '13	♥♥ 4
○ Colli di Luni Vermentino Pianacce '14	♥♥ 2*
○ Paduletti '14	♥ 2
● Colli di Luni Rosso Canal di Bocco '11	♥♥ 4
○ Colli di Luni Vermentino '04	♥♥ 3*
○ Colli di Luni Vermentino Boboli '11	♥♥ 4
○ Colli di Luni Vermentino Boboli '08	♥♥ 4
○ Colli di Luni Vermentino Boboli '05	♥♥ 4
○ Colli di Luni Vermentino Pianacce '12	♥♥ 2*

LIGURIA

La Ginestraia

VIA STERIA
18100 CERVO [IM]
TEL. 3272683692
www.laginestraia.com

ANNUAL PRODUCTION 50,000 bottles
HECTARES UNDER VINE 7.00

This adventure originated with Marco Brangero's enthusiasm and his love for the white wines of Liguria. In 2007, with his friends Lupi and Leporieri, he rented a cellar in the town of Cervo, which he still uses for vinification and bottling. In the imminent future, the new, cutting-edge cellar will begin processing grapes from the vermentino vineyard, covering around one hectare near the town, and of pigato, from around six hectares at Ortovero. The 2014 growing year was difficult, and Marco wisely decided to limit quantity in favour of quality. We were convinced by the warm, intense Via Maestra 2014, with its notes of eucalyptus, attractive tanginess, and complex body, leading to a seemingly endless finish. Hot on its heels was the bright-hued Vermentino 2014, regaling fresh Mediterranean damson sustained by a warm, yet incisively fresh body. The purple-tinged Rossese 2014 offers focused blackberry and plum on a rounded, velvet-smooth palate.

○ Riviera Ligure di Ponente Pigato Via Maestra '14	♥♥ 3*
● Riviera Ligure di Ponente Rossese '14	♥♥ 3
○ Riviera Ligure di Ponente Vermentino '14	♥♥ 3
○ Riviera Ligure di Ponente Pigato '14	♥ 3
○ Riviera Ligure di Ponente Pigato Biancodamare '11	♀♥ 3
○ Riviera Ligure di Ponente Pigato Via Maestra '12	♀♥ 3
○ Riviera Ligure di Ponente Pigato Via Maestra '11	♀♥ 3

Ka' Manciné

FRAZ. SAN MARTINO
VIA MACIURINA, 7
18036 SOLDANO [IM]
TEL. 0184289089
www.kamancine.it

CELLAR SALES
PRE-BOOKED VISITS
ANNUAL PRODUCTION 20,000 bottles
HECTARES UNDER VINE 3.00

We are on the western tip of the province of Imperia, where for years producers have been focusing above all on quality, with Maurizio Anfosso being one of the leading examples. The vineyards are situated in two different zones at Soldano; east- and north-facing Beragna at an elevation of 350 metres; and Galeae with a south-east aspect, at elevations of 300–390 metres. In the latter vineyard, on a more south-facing plot around 200 metres above sea level, with crumbly, marly, limestone soil and lower yields, selected grapes are used to produce Angè, vinified in stainless steel and aged in used barriques. The Beragna 2014 charmed us with its great personality and individuality, starting with its youthful ruby hue, and a complex, attractive nose of blackberry and raspberry. This pleasing, characterful wine shows great power on the full-flavoured palate, with serious tannins and a warm finish. Persistent scents of berry fruit in the Galeae Riserva Angè 2013 pave the way for an elegant body and attractive length.

● Dolceacqua Beragna '14	♥♥ 3*
● Dolceacqua Galeae Angè Ris. '13	♥♥ 3*
● Dolceacqua Galeae '14	♥♥ 3
☉ Sciakk '14	♥ 3
● Dolceacqua Galeae '13	♥♥♥ 3*
● Dolceacqua Beragna '13	♀♥ 3
● Dolceacqua Galeae Angè Ris. '12	♀♥ 3*
● Rossese di Dolceacqua Beragna '12	♀♥ 3
● Rossese di Dolceacqua Beragna '11	♀♥ 3*
● Rossese di Dolceacqua Beragna '10	♀♥ 3
● Rossese di Dolceacqua Beragna '09	♀♥ 3
● Rossese di Dolceacqua Beragna '08	♀♥ 3*
● Rossese di Dolceacqua Beragna '07	♀♥ 3
● Rossese di Dolceacqua Galeae '12	♀♥ 3*

Ottaviano Lambruschi

VIA OLMARELLO, 28
19030 CASTELNUOVO MAGRA [SP]
TEL. 0187674261
www.ottavianolambruschi.com

CELLAR SALES
PRE-BOOKED VISITS
ANNUAL PRODUCTION 36,000 bottles
HECTARES UNDER VINE 10.00

A new face at the winery is that of Fabio's young daughter Ylenia, who helps her father in sales and communication. In the rows, the ever-present Ottaviano has ensured quality, despite the somewhat unsettled growing season, with rain until late July, followed by better weather in September. The harvest, postponed to 15 September, took place in two phases, to allow picking at optimum ripeness, and ended with the highest vineyard, Il Maggiore, at around 240 metres, where the harvest was moved back until 5 October. The wait has been worthwhile: this year Il Maggiore 2014 is back for another Tre Bicchieri. Its bright, intense colour accompanies a palate of medicinal herbs and fresh fruit, supported by a complex, fresh body, with incredible length and harmony on the finish. The inviting Vermentino 2014 boasts a powerful, firmly structured body.

○ Colli di Luni Vermentino Il Maggiore '14	♟♟♟ 5
○ Colli di Luni Vermentino '14	♟♟ 3*
○ Colli di Luni Vermentino Costa Marina '14	♟♟ 4
● Colli di Luni Rosso Maniero '14	♟ 2
○ Colli di Luni Vermentino Costa Marina '11	♟♟♟ 4*
○ Colli di Luni Vermentino Costa Marina '09	♟♟♟ 3
○ Colli di Luni Vermentino Il Maggiore '13	♟♟♟ 5
○ Colli di Luni Vermentino Il Maggiore '12	♟♟♟ 4*
○ Colli di Luni Vermentino Sarticola '08	♟♟♟ 3*
○ Colli di Luni Vermentino Costa Marina '12	♟♟ 4
○ Colli di Luni Vermentino Costa Marina '10	♟♟ 3
○ Colli di Luni Vermentino Costa Marina '08	♟♟ 3
○ Colli di Luni Vermentino Il Maggiore '11	♟♟ 4
○ Colli di Luni Vermentino Sarticola '10	♟♟ 3
○ Colli di Luni Vermentino Sarticola '09	♟♟ 3
● Maniero '12	♟♟ 3

Cantine Lunae Bosoni

FRAZ. ISOLA DI ORTONOVO
VIA BOZZI, 63
19034 ORTONOVO [SP]
TEL. 0187669222
www.cantinelunae.com

CELLAR SALES
PRE-BOOKED VISITS
ACCOMMODATION
ANNUAL PRODUCTION 450,000 bottles
HECTARES UNDER VINE 65.00

The Bosoni family's operation continues to grow, both in quality, already high, and in size, with the addition of a new one-hectare vineyard planted to albarola, at Ortonovo. As usual, grapes from the winery's own holdings are supplemented by those from 100-plus local growers, under the supervision of the winery's technical staff. The growers have agreed to abolish the use of herbicides completely, introducing organic fertilizers and integrated pest management, and to harvest the grapes by hand, using crates. Summer 2015 also saw the commencement of work on the new vinification facility, a major project that is bound to bring benefits in terms of quality. Once again, the Vermentino Etichetta Nera 2014 took top honours. Its intriguing bright greenish hue combines with a pleasing body, offering hints of basil, intense aromas of wild rose and marked notes of ripe fruit. We loved its mouthfilling structure, persistent intensity and soft finish. Focused notes of apricot and ripe peach distinguish the Cavagino 2013.

○ Colli di Luni Vermentino Et. Nera '14	♟♟♟ 4*
○ Colli di Luni Vermentino Cavagino '13	♟♟ 5
○ Colli di Luni Vermentino Et. Grigia '14	♟♟ 3*
○ Colli di Luni Bianco Fior di Luna '14	♟ 3
○ Colli di Luni Vermentino Et. Nera '13	♟♟♟ 4*
○ Colli di Luni Vermentino Et. Nera '12	♟♟♟ 4*
○ Colli di Luni Vermentino Et. Nera '11	♟♟♟ 4*
○ Colli di Luni Vermentino Et. Nera '10	♟♟♟ 4
○ Colli di Luni Vermentino Lunae Et. Nera '09	♟♟♟ 4
○ Colli di Luni Vermentino Lunae Et. Nera '08	♟♟♟ 4*
○ Colli di Luni Albarola '12	♟♟ 4
○ Colli di Luni Bianco Fior di Luna '13	♟♟ 3
○ Colli di Luni Vermentino Cavagino '12	♟♟ 5
○ Colli di Luni Vermentino Cavagino '11	♟♟ 5
○ Colli di Luni Vermentino Et. Grigia '13	♟♟ 3*

Maccario Dringenberg

VIA TORRE, 3
18036 SAN BIAGIO DELLA CIMA [IM]
TEL. 0184289947
maccariodringenberg@yahoo.it

CELLAR SALES
PRE-BOOKED VISITS
ANNUAL PRODUCTION 23,000 bottles
HECTARES UNDER VINE 4.00

This small, serious winery is the result of untiring dedication and a commitment to quality. Giovanna and her husband Goetz decided not to present the Dolceacqua Luvaira 2013, due to the difficult growing year, while the 2014 achieved good quality thanks to optimal, gradual ripening of the grapes. The first vineyard to be harvested was Posaù at San Biagio della Cima, at elevations of 250–350 metres, on 10 September, while the last was Brae, in the municipality of Perinaldo. Due to its north-facing aspect and altitude up to 480 metres, grapes ripen more slowly here, for fresher, more delicate wines. Harvesting takes place solely in the morning, while in the afternoon work focuses on the cellar and fermentation. The superlative Dolceacqua Posaù 2013 vaunts a captivating ruby hue, leading to explosive, irresistible intensity in the mouth, delicate harmony and unique character. The layered body displays freshness, serious tannins and great power, following through for a finish of impressive impact. Nor should we forget the characterful Brae and San Biagio della Cima.

● Dolceacqua Sup. Vign. Posaù '13	▼▼▼	3*
● Dolceacqua Brae '14	▼▼	3
● Dolceacqua San Biagio della Cima '14	▼▼	3
● Rossese di Dolceacqua Sup. Vign. Posaù '10	♀♀♀	3*
● Dolceacqua Sup. '13	♀♀	3*
● Dolceacqua Sup. Vign. Luvaira '12	♀♀	4
● Dolceacqua Sup. Vign. Posaù '12	♀♀	3*
● Rossese di Dolceacqua '12	♀♀	3*
● Rossese di Dolceacqua '11	♀♀	3*
● Rossese di Dolceacqua Brae '12	♀♀	3
● Rossese di Dolceacqua Sup. Vign. Luvaira '10	♀♀	4

Maixei

LOC. PORTO
18035 DOLCEACQUA [IM]
TEL. 0184205015
www.maixei.it

CELLAR SALES
PRE-BOOKED VISITS
ANNUAL PRODUCTION 35,000 bottles
HECTARES UNDER VINE

Great things are happening at the Maixei winery, thanks to Fabio Corradi, oenologist and manager-factotum, and to Pasquale Restuccio, agronomist and vice-chairman of the winery. And, of course, the growers, who in line with the enhanced quality of Liguria's important red, Dolceacqua, are following the good example by producing grapes of the highest standard. Around 20 member-growers provide rossese, accounting for around 70% of raw materials, while the remaining 30% is made up of the white grape varieties, vermentino and pigato. It is the Dolceacqua, however, that brings the winery its greatest satisfaction. The spectacular Superiore 2013 won us over with its attractive fruit, notes of cocoa powder and leaf tobacco, great complexity, and beautifully lingering finish. The 2014, with intense, forthright notes of ripe fruit, offers an elegant, rounded body, enlivened by close-knit tannins and good acidity, with a pleasing, leisurely finish.

● Dolceacqua '14	▼▼	3*
● Dolceacqua Sup. '13	▼▼	4
● Dolceacqua Sup. Barbadirame '13	▼	4
● Dolceacqua '12	♀♀	3
● Dolceacqua Rossese Sup. '10	♀♀	4
○ Dolceacqua Rossese Sup. '09	♀♀	4
○ Dolceacqua Rossese Sup. '08	♀♀	4
● Dolceacqua Sup. '12	♀♀	4
● Dolceacqua Sup. Barbadirame '12	♀♀	4

Il Monticello

VIA GROPPOLO, 7
19038 SARZANA [SP]
TEL. 0187621432
www.ilmonticello.it

CELLAR SALES
PRE-BOOKED VISITS
ACCOMMODATION
ANNUAL PRODUCTION 68,000 bottles
HECTARES UNDER VINE 10.00

This was a difficult year for eastern
Levante Ligure. Neri, where they have
been practising organic and biodynamic
methods for years, was no exception,
and had to deal with a challenging
harvest. They were helped by the latest
technology in the rows, which allowed
the constant, scientific monitoring of
the grapes up until the beginning of the
harvest, which was late, in around mid-
September. Here, grapes are picked not
by vineyard but on the basis of selection,
and are vinified separately using ambient
yeasts. Production figures are up thanks
to investments in the rows and the
continued purchase of new vineyards.
The Vermentino Groppolo 2014 shows a
beautiful, intensely bright straw hue, and
a pleasing, fresh flavour, brimming with
Mediterranean notes, white-fleshed fruit
and damson. The well-managed, velvet-
soft palate perfectly combines freshness
with breadth, and finishes warm, and
incredibly long.

○ Colli di Luni Vermentino Groppolo '14	♟♟♟ 3*
● Colli di Luni Rosso Rupestro '14	♟ 2
● Colli di Luni Rosso Serasuolo '14	♟ 2
● Colli di Luni Rosso Poggio dei Magni Ris. '11	♟♟ 3
● Colli di Luni Rosso Rupestro '12	♟♟ 2*
○ Colli di Luni Vermentino '12	♟♟ 3*
○ Colli di Luni Vermentino '08	♟♟ 2*
○ Colli di Luni Vermentino Poggio Paterno '10	♟♟ 3*
○ Colli di Luni Vermentino Poggio Paterno '09	♟♟ 3
○ Colli di Luni Vermentino Poggio Paterno '08	♟♟ 3
○ Passito dei Neri '12	♟♟ 4
○ Poggio Paterno Il Bocciato '11	♟♟ 3*

Conte Picedi Benettini

VIA MAZZINI, 57
19038 SARZANA [SP]
TEL. 0187625147
www.picedibenettini.it

CELLAR SALES
PRE-BOOKED VISITS
ACCOMMODATION
ANNUAL PRODUCTION 30,000 bottles
HECTARES UNDER VINE 7.00

Over the years, this venerable, age-old
winery in the Luni area, on the Baccano
di Arcola hillside, has established a
reputation for quality and elegance. The
poet D'Annunzio wrote " ... Land of Luni,
like an Etruscan vase ...", and like a
precious treasure, this winery is imbued
with the spirit of its owner, Papirio Picedi
Benettini. Despite having already made
a mark with his production figures and
quality, he continues to look ahead and
plan new plantings for the future. This
great, undisputed quality is confirmed
in the Vermentino Il Chioso 2014, which
achieves the accolade of a Tre Bicchieri.
Its bright, lively hue heralds perfect
harmony between the classic notes of
Mediterranean scrub and intense fruit. In
the mouth, it shows stunning complexity
and elegance, attractive freshness and a
long, leisurely finish.

○ Colli di Luni Vermentino Il Chioso '14	♟♟♟ 2*
○ Colli di Luni Vermentino Stemma '14	♟♟ 3
○ Colli di Luni Vermentino '14	♟ 2
⊙ Ciliegiolo '10	♟♟ 2*
○ Colli di Luni Bianco Villa Il Chioso '09	♟♟ 2*
● Colli di Luni Rosso Gran Baccano '08	♟♟ 2*
○ Colli di Luni Vermentino '12	♟♟ 2*
○ Colli di Luni Vermentino Il Chioso '13	♟♟ 2*
○ Colli di Luni Vermentino Il Chioso '12	♟♟ 2*
○ Colli di Luni Vermentino Il Chioso '11	♟♟ 2*
○ Colli di Luni Vermentino Il Chioso '09	♟♟ 2*
○ Colli di Luni Vermentino Stemma '13	♟♟ 3
○ Colli di Luni Vermentino Stemma '12	♟♟ 3
○ Colli di Luni Vermentino Stemma '11	♟♟ 3*
○ Colli di Luni Vermentino Stemma '10	♟♟ 3
○ Passito del Chioso '08	♟♟ 3

La Pietra del Focolare

FRAZ. ISOLA DI ORTONOVO
VIA ISOLA, 76
19034 ORTONOVO [SP]
TEL. 0187662129
www.lapietradelfocolare.it

CELLAR SALES
PRE-BOOKED VISITS
ANNUAL PRODUCTION 30,000 bottles
HECTARES UNDER VINE 6.00
SUSTAINABLE WINERY

Stefano Salvetti and Laura Angelini tend
their vineyards with care, and in the future
aim to produce a certified organic wine. Not
an easy goal, however, and although they
are extremely attentive, using only sulphur
and copper, the fragmented distribution
of the vineyards makes it difficult to cope
with the peculiarities of the weather, as
in 2014, when the winery was forced to
monitor the rows constantly and reduce
volumes. A new vineyard near Sarzana of
2,000 square metres, planted solely to
vermentino, has now come into production,
and joins the winery's 12 other tiny plots
spread over the territory. Attractive aromas
of rosemary and Mediterranean scrub,
followed by tobacco, distinguish the Villa
Linda 2014. The superlative, complex
palate shows great finesse and a long
finish of real character. A straw-yellow hue
with golden highlights is the hallmark of the
intense, buttery L'Aura di Sarticola 2014,
which vaunts impressive character and a
leisurely finish.

Poggi dell'Elmo

C.SO VERBONE, 135
18036 SOLDANO [IM]
TEL. 0184289148
www.poggidellelmo.com

CELLAR SALES
PRE-BOOKED VISITS
ACCOMMODATION AND RESTAURANT SERVICE
ANNUAL PRODUCTION 15,000 bottles
HECTARES UNDER VINE 2.50
SUSTAINABLE WINERY

The Guglielmi winery can also vaunt a
decent 2014 harvest and this will be
reflected in next year's Riservas. Among
its vineyards, all in the municipality of
Soldano, we find Pini in Val Verbone, with
aspects ranging from south to north-
east, at elevations of 150–400 metres,
producing all the grapes vinified in the
cellar, including vermentino. The small
operation counts on the constant work of
the family: Gianni, his wife Maria, and his
mother, also called Maria. They are soon
to be joined by his daughter Valentina,
who will deal with communication and
marketing. Intense, pleasant, ripe red
berry fruit follows the attractive lively
garnet hue of the inviting, characterful
Pini Soldano 2013, and leads into a warm
palate with a powerful body and abundant
tannins. The Dolceacqua 2014, meanwhile,
shows ripe blackberry and plum, with good
body, pleasing harmony and admirable
balance.

○ Colli di Luni Vermentino Villa Linda '14	▼▼ 3*
○ Colli di Luni Vermentino L'Aura di Sarticola '14	▼▼ 6
● Colli di Luni Rosso La Merla dal Becco '12	♀♀ 5
○ Colli di Luni Vermentino Augusto '08	♀♀ 2*
○ Colli di Luni Vermentino Augusto '06	♀♀ 2
○ Colli di Luni Vermentino Solarancio '11	♀♀ 5
○ Colli di Luni Vermentino Solarancio '10	♀♀ 4
○ Colli di Luni Vermentino Solarancio '09	♀♀ 5
○ Colli di Luni Vermentino Solarancio '08	♀♀ 4
○ Colli di Luni Vermentino Solarancio '07	♀♀ 4
○ Colli di Luni Vermentino Solarancio '06	♀♀ 3
○ Colli di Luni Vermentino Sup. Augusto '13	♀♀ 3*
○ Colli di Luni Vermentino Villa Linda '11	♀♀ 3
○ Colli di Luni Vermentino Villa Linda '05	♀♀ 3*
○ Colli di Luni Vermentino Viva Luce '05	♀♀ 1*
○ Solarancio '13	♀♀ 3

● Dolceacqua Sup. Pini Soldano '13	▼▼ 3*
● Dolceacqua '14	▼▼ 3
● Roseto '14	▼ 3
● Dolceacqua '13	♀♀ 3*
● Dolceacqua Elmo Primo '11	♀♀ 3
● Dolceacqua Sup. Pini Soldano '12	♀♀ 3*
● Rossese di Dolceacqua '11	♀♀ 3
● Rossese di Dolceacqua '09	♀♀ 3
● Rossese di Dolceacqua '07	♀♀ 3
● Rossese di Dolceacqua '06	♀♀ 2*
● Rossese di Dolceacqua Elmo '09	♀♀ 3
● Rossese di Dolceacqua Sup. '10	♀♀ 4
● Rossese di Dolceacqua Sup. '06	♀♀ 3
● Rossese di Dolceacqua Sup. Pini Soldano '11	♀♀ 3*
● Rossese di Dolceacqua Vigneto dei Pini '09	♀♀ 3

Poggio dei Gorleri

FRAZ. DIANO GORLERI
VIA SAN LEONARDO
18013 DIANO MARINA [IM]
TEL. 0183495207
www.poggiodeigorleri.com

CELLAR SALES
PRE-BOOKED VISITS
ACCOMMODATION
ANNUAL PRODUCTION 80,000 bottles
HECTARES UNDER VINE 10.50

Poggio dei Gorleri is an important young winery on the Ligurian scene, and has expanded with the addition of two new vineyards: one at Andora covering 2.3 hectares, planted to vermentino and pigato, and the other at Arnasco, in the province of Savona, producing solely pigato. This change will mean that the Merano family can use almost exclusively its own grapes. The two brothers, Davide who deals with the cellar and sales, and Matteo in the rows, have given a great boost to quality, with extraordinary results again this time round, despite the difficult growing year. This approach has earned them another place in the finals, but this time for the Albium 2013, thanks to its attractively youthful bright straw hue, and its intense aromas of fresh herbs and white-fleshed fruit. On the mouthfilling palate, attractive acidity combines with a velvet-smooth body, unfolding in a leisurely finish. Cycnus and Vigna Sorì, both 2014s, are close behind and show impressive quality, considering the vintage.

○ Riviera Ligure di Ponente Pigato Albium '13	▼▼▼ 5
○ Riviera Ligure di Ponente Pigato Cycnus '14	▼▼ 3*
○ Riviera Ligure di Ponente Vermentino V. Sorì '14	▼▼ 3*
○ Riviera Ligure di Ponente Vermentino '14	▼▼ 3
● Riviera Ligure di Ponente Granaccia Shalok '13	▼ 5
○ Riviera Ligure di Ponente Pigato Albium '10	▽▽▽ 5
○ Riviera Ligure di Ponente Pigato Cycnus '13	▽▽▽ 3*
○ Riviera Ligure di Ponente Pigato Cycnus '12	▽▽▽ 3*
○ Riviera Ligure di Ponente Pigato Cycnus '10	▽▽▽ 3

Natale Sassarini

LOC. PIAN DEL CORSO 1
19016 MONTEROSSO AL MARE [SP]
TEL. 0187818063
www.sassarini5terre.it

This winery in the Levante Ligure area is new to the Guide this year. It is situated at Monterosso where, in addition to its own vineyards, it vinifies the grapes of growers spread over this territory, which is as difficult as it is beautiful. The winery selects the grapes for production: firstly for Schiacchetrà, then for the Cian du Corsu, with grapes picked from an excellent south-facing, early-ripening vineyard at Monterosso. The winery continues to invest in improvements, despite the difficulties in pursuing high quality in such a difficult, fragmented territory. An attractive old gold hue ushers in the fresh, intense Sciacchetrà 2011, with elegant notes of ripe apricot and a complex nose ranging from sweet spice to oak. Equally good was the warm Cian Irti 2014, with its tangy, mineral swathe and a palate dominated by white-fleshed fruit, underpinned by impressive body and refreshing acidity. The complex, velvety Bucce 2013 shows notes of dandelion.

○ Cinque Terre Cian Irti '14	▼▼ 4
○ Cinque Terre Sciacchetrà '11	▼▼ 5
○ Cinque Terre '14	▼▼ 4
○ Cinque Terre Bucce '13	▼▼ 3
○ Cinque Terre Cian du Corsu '14	▼▼ 4
○ Cinque Terre Campo al Sole '13	▼ 3

Terenzuola

VIA VERCALDA, 14
54035 FOSDINOVO [MS]
TEL. 0187670387
www.terenzuola.it

ANNUAL PRODUCTION 137,000 bottles
HECTARES UNDER VINE 21.00

Lunigiana is a beautiful area, snaking between Liguria and Tuscany, where the Colli di Luni DOC straddles the regional borders, unifying the production area under a single appellation. Ivan Giuliani has preserved this identity with vineyards at Castelnuovo Magra and Sarzana in Liguria and Fosdinovo and Carrara in Tuscany. Of the 21 or so hectares, ten of which are owned by the estate and about 11 rented, some are situated on the hills of Riomaggiore, Volastra and Corniglia growing albarola, bosco and vermentino in recovered modified bush-trained vineyards to produce Cinque Terre wine as well as Sciacchetrà, the feather in the estate's cap. The Riserva 2010 has bags of personality: pleasant hints of dried fruit, plums and apricots evolving into white chocolate, and a fresh, tangy palate with a very long finish. The Fosso di Corsano 2014 offers Mediterranean, salty hints of eucalyptus and maritime pines. A complex wine in which the alcohol strength blends nicely in the lingering palate.

Terre Bianche

LOC. ARCAGNA
18035 DOLCEACQUA [IM]
TEL. 018431426
www.terrebianche.com

CELLAR SALES
PRE-BOOKED VISITS
ACCOMMODATION
ANNUAL PRODUCTION 55,000 bottles
HECTARES UNDER VINE 8.50
SUSTAINABLE WINERY

The Terre Bianche winery is today run by Filippo Rondelli, one of the growers behind the territory's geographical recognition, and Franco Laconi. Their Arcagna vineyard in Val Nervia provides the majority of their grapes and brings them their most satisfying results. The west-facing vineyard, at elevations of 300–400 metres, is farmed according to the dictates of organic viticulture, with the use of copper and sulphur, and without herbicides. Vermentino, meanwhile, is grown at Scartozzoni, also in Val Nervia, with its characteristic red soil. The superlative Dolceacqua 2014 boasts a fine, intense garnet ruby hue, with a nose of berries, liquorice, leaf tobacco and quinine. Elegance and harmony on the palate pave the way for a long, powerful finish. The well-structured, characterful Bricco Arcagna 2013 offers charred oak and abundant fruit. Elderflower, sage, hawthorn and citrus fruit distinguish the elegant Pigato 2014.

○ Cinqueterre Sciacchetrà Ris. '10	🍷🍷 4
○ Colli di Luni Vermentino Sup. Fosso di Corsano '14	🍷🍷 3
● Merla della Miniera '12	🍷🍷 4
○ Colli di Luni Vermentino V. Basse '14	🍷 3
● Vermentino Nero '14	🍷 3
○ Cinque Terre '11	🍷🍷 3
○ Colli di Luni Vermentino Fosso di Corsano '08	🍷🍷 3
○ Colli di Luni Vermentino Sup. Fosso di Corsano '13	🍷🍷 3*
○ Colli di Luni Vermentino Sup. Fosso di Corsano '12	🍷🍷 3*
○ Colli di Luni Vermentino Sup. Fosso di Corsano '11	🍷🍷 3*
● Merla della Miniera '11	🍷🍷 3

● Dolceacqua '14	🍷🍷 3*
● Dolceacqua Bricco Arcagna '13	🍷🍷 5
○ Riviera Ligure di Ponente Pigato '14	🍷🍷 3
○ Riviera Ligure di Ponente Vermentino '14	🍷 3
● Dolceacqua Bricco Arcagna '12	🍷🍷🍷 5
● Rossese di Dolceacqua '12	🍷🍷🍷 3*
● Rossese di Dolceacqua Bricco Arcagna '09	🍷🍷🍷 4
● Rossese di Dolceacqua Bricco Arcagna '08	🍷🍷🍷 5
● Dolceacqua '13	🍷🍷 3*
○ Riviera Ligure di Ponente Pigato '13	🍷🍷 3
○ Riviera Ligure di Ponente Vermentino '13	🍷🍷 3
○ Riviera Ligure di Ponente Vermentino '12	🍷🍷 3*
● Rossese di Dolceacqua Bricco Arcagna '11	🍷🍷 5

Il Torchio

VIA DELLE COLLINE, 24
19033 CASTELNUOVO MAGRA [SP]
TEL. 3318585633
gildamusetti@gmail.com

CELLAR SALES
PRE-BOOKED VISITS
ACCOMMODATION AND RESTAURANT SERVICE
ANNUAL PRODUCTION 60,000 bottles
HECTARES UNDER VINE 12.00

This year, the young Edoardo, still an
oenology student, took over vinification, and
the results are rather satisfying. With the
supervision of his uncle Claudio in the rows
and the support of his sister Gilda in sales,
the operation continues to achieve important
successes, such as increased exports.
The vineyards are situated with a south,
south-east aspect, at low elevations, and
vinification is based on selections of grapes
rather than by vineyard. We were won over
by the attractively intense straw yellow
hue of the Vermentino 2014, with notes of
medicinal herbs and Mediterranean scrub,
evolving towards blossom and white fruit.
On the tangy, well-balanced palate, intensity
joins forces with a long, faintly bitterish
finish. The incisive, warm Il Bianco 2014
shows notes of dried herbs and rosemary,
honey and damson, and is complex, buttery
and full-flavoured.

○ Colli di Luni Vermentino '14	♥♥ 3*
○ Colli di Luni Il Bianco '14	♥♥ 3
● Il Nero '14	♥ 4
● Colli di Luni Rosso Il Torchio '13	♀♀ 4
○ Colli di Luni Vermentino '07	♀♀ 3*
○ Colli di Luni Vermentino '06	♀♀ 3
○ Colli di Luni Vermentino Il Bianco '13	♀♀ 3
○ Colli di Luni Vermentino Il Torchio '13	♀♀ 3*

Vis Amoris

LOC. CARAMAGNA
S.DA MOLINO JAVÈ, 23
18100 IMPERIA
TEL. 3483959569
www.visamoris.it

CELLAR SALES
PRE-BOOKED VISITS
ANNUAL PRODUCTION 24,000 bottles
HECTARES UNDER VINE 3.50
SUSTAINABLE WINERY

The 2014 growing year was undoubtedly
a difficult one, compensated for by a
postponed harvest which allowed the
grapes to ripen fully at the cost of lower
yields. Despite the vicinity to the sea
and the elevations of the vineyards, at
50–100 metres, harvesting began on 20
September, except for the grapes used
for sparklers. The vineyards are situated
on two different soils: clayey for the
spumante and the Domè; rocky for the
Verum. Meanwhile the Regis is a product
unto itself, with grapes selected to ensure
a balanced wine. We adored the Pigato Vis
Domè 2014, with its intense straw yellow
colour and youthful highlights, followed on
the palate by fresh Mediterranean flavours,
sea salt and fruit notes of citrus and
damson, for an enjoyable, complex wine of
great length and elegance. The intriguing
Pigato Sogno 2013, with marked notes of
aniseed and tobacco, displays an elegant
profile and a lingering finish.

○ Riviera Ligure di Ponente Pigato Vis Domè '14	♥♥ 3*
○ Riviera Ligure di Ponente Pigato Sogno '13	♥♥ 4
○ Verum '14	♥♥ 5
○ Vis Amoris Brut M. Cl. '12	♥ 5
○ Dulcis in Fundo '11	♀♀ 5
○ Riviera Ligure di Ponente Pigato Domè '13	♀♀ 3*
○ Riviera Ligure di Ponente Pigato Sogno '12	♀♀ 4
○ Riviera Ligure di Ponente Pigato Sogno '11	♀♀ 4
○ Riviera Ligure di Ponente Pigato Sogno '10	♀♀ 4
○ Riviera Ligure di Ponente Pigato Verum '13	♀♀ 3

Carlo Alessandri

VIA UMBERTO I, 15
18020 RANZO [IM]
TEL. 0183318114
az.alessandricarlo@libero.it

CELLAR SALES
PRE-BOOKED VISITS
ANNUAL PRODUCTION 19,100 bottles
HECTARES UNDER VINE 2.13

○ Vermentino '14	♟♟	3
● Ormeasco di Pornassio '14	♟	3
● Ormeasco di Pornassio Sciac-Trà '14	♟	3
○ Pigato '14	♟	2

Tenuta Anfosso

C.SO VERBONE, 175
18036 SOLDANO [IM]
TEL. 0184289906
www.tenutaanfosso.it

CELLAR SALES
ACCOMMODATION
ANNUAL PRODUCTION 20,000 bottles
HECTARES UNDER VINE 4.00

● Dolceacqua Sup. '13	♟♟	4
● Dolceacqua Sup. Foulavin '13	♟♟	4
● Dolceacqua Sup. Luvaira '13	♟♟	4
● Dolceacqua Sup. Poggio Pini '13	♟	4

Bisson

C.SO GIANELLI, 28
16043 CHIAVARI [GE]
TEL. 0185314462
www.bissonvini.it

CELLAR SALES
PRE-BOOKED VISITS
ANNUAL PRODUCTION 80,000 bottles
HECTARES UNDER VINE 12.00

○ Portofino Bianchetta Genovese Ü Pastine '14	♟	2
○ Portofino Cimixià L'Antico '14	♟	3
○ Portofino Passito '11	♟	6
○ Portofino Vermentino Intrigoso '14	♟	3

Cantine Calleri

LOC. SALEA
REG. FRATTI, 2
17031 ALBENGA [SV]
TEL. 018220085
www.cantinecalleri.com

ANNUAL PRODUCTION 55,000 bottles
HECTARES UNDER VINE 6.00

○ Riviera Ligure di Ponente Pigato di Albenga '14	♟♟	3*
○ Riviera Ligure di Ponente Vermentino I Müzazzi '14	♟♟	3

Luigi Calvini

VIA SOLARO, 76-78A
18038 SANREMO [IM]
TEL. 0184660242
www.luigicalvini.com

CELLAR SALES
PRE-BOOKED VISITS
ANNUAL PRODUCTION 50,000 bottles
HECTARES UNDER VINE 3.50

○ Riviera Ligure di Ponente Pigato '14	♟♟	3
○ Riviera Ligure di Ponente Vermentino '14	♟♟	3

Altare Bonanni De Grazia Campogrande

VIA DI LOCA, 189
19017 RIOMAGGIORE [SP]
TEL. 017350835
www.cinqueterre-campogrande.com

PRE-BOOKED VISITS
ANNUAL PRODUCTION 6,000 bottles
HECTARES UNDER VINE 2.00

○ Telemaco '13	♟♟	7
○ Vino Bianco	♟	2
● Vino Rosso	♟	4

Cascina delle Terre Rosse

VIA MANIE, 3
17024 FINALE LIGURE [SV]
TEL. 019698782

CELLAR SALES
PRE-BOOKED VISITS
ANNUAL PRODUCTION 30,000 bottles
HECTARES UNDER VINE 4.50

○ Riviera Ligure di Ponente Pigato '14	♥♥ 4
○ Riviera Ligure di Ponente Vermentino '14	♥♥ 4
● Solitario '13	♥♥ 7
○ Apogeo '14	♥ 4

Azienda Agricola Durin

LOC. ORTOVERO
VIA ROMA, 202
17037 ORTOVERO [SV]
TEL. 0182547007
www.durin.it

CELLAR SALES
PRE-BOOKED VISITS
ACCOMMODATION AND RESTAURANT SERVICE
ANNUAL PRODUCTION 130,000 bottles
HECTARES UNDER VINE 16.50
SUSTAINABLE WINERY

● Alicante '12	♥ 3
● Granaccia '14	♥ 3
○ Riviera Ligure di Ponente Pigato Braie '14	♥ 3

Podere Grecale

LOC. BUSSANA
VIA DUCA D'AOSTA, 52E
18038 SANREMO [IM]
TEL. 01841956107
www.poderegrecale.it

CELLAR SALES
PRE-BOOKED VISITS
ANNUAL PRODUCTION 18,000 bottles
HECTARES UNDER VINE 2.50
VITICULTURE METHOD Certified Organic

○ Riviera Ligure di Ponente Vermentino '14	♥♥ 3
○ Riviera Ligure di Ponente Pigato '14	♥ 3

Guglierame

FRAZ. VILLA
VIA CASTELLO, 10
18024 PORNASSIO [IM]
TEL. 018333037
www.ormeasco-guglierame.it

CELLAR SALES
PRE-BOOKED VISITS
ANNUAL PRODUCTION 18,000 bottles
HECTARES UNDER VINE 2.50

● Ormeasco di Pornassio Sciac-trà '13	♥♥ 3
● Ormeasco di Pornassio '13	♥ 3

Viticoltori Ingauni

VIA ROMA, 3
17037 ORTOVERO [SV]
TEL. 0182547127
www.viticoltoriingauni.it

ANNUAL PRODUCTION 300,000 bottles
HECTARES UNDER VINE 84.50

○ Riviera Ligure di Ponente Vermentino '14	♥♥ 2*
● Ormeasco di Pornassio Sup. '12	♥ 2
○ Riviera Ligure di Ponente Pigato Antigu '13	♥ 3

Podere Lavandaro

VIA CASTIGLIONE
54035 FOSDINOVO [MS]
TEL. 018768202
www.poderelavandaro.it

CELLAR SALES
PRE-BOOKED VISITS
ANNUAL PRODUCTION 22,000 bottles
HECTARES UNDER VINE 4.00

○ Colli di Luni Vermentino '14	♥♥ 3*
○ Maséro '13	♥ 4
⊙ Merla Rosa '14	♥ 3
● Vignanera '13	♥ 3

Gino Pino

FRAZ. MISSANO
VIA PODESTÀ, 31
16030 CASTIGLIONE CHIAVARESE [GE]
TEL. 0185408036
pinogino.az.agricola@tin.it

ANNUAL PRODUCTION 25,000 bottles
HECTARES UNDER VINE 3.50

○ Portofino Moscato '14	♟♟ 3
○ Portofino Bianchetta Genovese '14	♟ 2
● Portofino Ciliegiolo '14	♟ 3

Roberto Rondelli

FRAZ. BRUNETTI, 1
18033 CAMPOROSSO [IM]
TEL. 3280348055
rondellivini@gmail.com

CELLAR SALES
PRE-BOOKED VISITS
ACCOMMODATION AND RESTAURANT SERVICE
ANNUAL PRODUCTION 22,000 bottles
HECTARES UNDER VINE 3.50

○ Riviera Ligure di Ponente Pigato V. Ciotti '14	♟♟ 3*
● Dolceacqua Migliarina '12	♟♟ 3
○ Riviera Ligure di Ponente Vermentino '14	♟♟ 3

Valdiscalve

LOC. REGGIMONTI
S.DA PROV.LE 42
19011 BONASSOLA [SP]
TEL. 0187818178
www.vermenting.com

CELLAR SALES
ANNUAL PRODUCTION 5,000 bottles
HECTARES UNDER VINE 1.00

○ Colline di Levanto Terre del Salice '14	♟♟ 3
○ Colline di Levanto Bianco Costa di Macinara '14	♟ 2
○ Colline di Levanto Terre di Reggimonti '14	♟ 3

La Vecchia Cantina

FRAZ. SALEA
VIA CORTA, 3
17031 ALBENGA [SV]
TEL. 0182586256
www.lavecchiacantinacalleri.it

CELLAR SALES
PRE-BOOKED VISITS
ANNUAL PRODUCTION 15,000 bottles
HECTARES UNDER VINE 3.00

○ Riviera Ligure di Ponente Albenganese Pigato '14	♟♟ 3*
○ Riviera Ligure di Ponente Albenganese Vermentino '14	♟♟ 3

Claudio Vio

FRAZ. CROSA, 16
17032 VENDONE [SV]
TEL. 018276338
claudio.vio@libero.it

CELLAR SALES
PRE-BOOKED VISITS
ANNUAL PRODUCTION 13,000 bottles
HECTARES UNDER VINE 2.00

○ Riviera Ligure di Ponente Pigato Albenganese '14	♟♟ 3
○ Riviera Ligure di Ponente Vermentino Albenganese '14	♟ 3

Zangani

LOC. PONZANO SUPERIORE
VIA GRAMSCI, 46
19037 SANTO STEFANO DI MAGRA [SP]
TEL. 0187632406
www.zangani.it

CELLAR SALES
PRE-BOOKED VISITS
ACCOMMODATION AND RESTAURANT SERVICE
ANNUAL PRODUCTION 40,000 bottles
HECTARES UNDER VINE 5.00

○ Colli di Luni Vermentino Boceda '14	♟♟ 3
● Colli di Luni Montale '14	♟ 3
○ Marfi Bianco '14	♟ 2
● Marfi Rosso '14	♟ 2

LOMBARDY

As the curtain fell on our tastings, the overall picture of Lombardy appears as complex and as rich as ever. The region hosting Expo Milano 2015 is the heartland of fine Italian food and wine, confirmed as one of the most interesting in northern Italy and surely true vineyard country for production of sparkling wine. An impressive 14 of the 22 award-winning wines this year are Metodo Classico cuvées, from the region's two acknowledged terroirs: Franciacorta and Oltrepò Pavese. Franciacorta really took the lion's share, as was to be expected. The surprises came in the form of the sheer variety of Franciacorta styles and vintages achieving a level of excellence. Where the area was once considered a stronghold of chardonnay, today we see that some of the most interesting cuvées come from monovarietal pinot noir or with the cultivar taking the lead in the blend. And in the case of the Sparkler of the Year, Ca' del Bosco's spectacular Vintage Collection Dosage Zèro Noir 2006 is perfect for celebrating a milestone as important as the fourth star, 40 Tre Bicchieri awards in its career. Equally satisfying is the Guido Berlucchi Palazzo Lana Extrême Reserve with 2007, and a long series of excellent labels ranging from mature vintages like 2004, like Castello Bonomi's stunning Cru Perdu, to a 2011 Naturae from Barone Pizzini. Oltrepò Pavese is in search of its true identity. A territory where a number of terroirs, cultivars and traditions live side by side, ranging from carefree Bonarda to structured reds and stellar Metodo Classicos. Precisely these cuvées are the underpinning for the designation's modern identity, based on pinot noir as the cultivar of excellence, vinified both as sparkling and red wines. And if Ballabio, Monsupello, Castello di Cigognola, and Calatroni spotlight the brand more than the designation, Giorgi is proud to exhibit it on the label, as are Frecciarossa and Tenuta Mazzolino with their fine reds. Even so, the district still has great potential to be tapped and we do hope a satisfactory agreement is reached in the near future. Lombardy, however, does not stop here. There is Valtellina with its heroic vineyards clutching at the Alps to give us another five memorable wines, from Nino Negri, Dirupi, Ar.Pe.Pe., Rainoldi, and Mamete Prevostini. The 2014 vintage has been very generous with Lugana, but Ca' Maiol still swoops to capture the Tre Bicchieri, even though the whole area deserves praise for commitment and for technical and agricultural growth in recent years. But the region abounds with good to very good and always affordable labels from Botticino to San Colombano, Valcalepio to Mantua.

LOMBARDY

Marchese Adorno

VIA GARLASSOLO, 30
27050 RETORBIDO [PV]
TEL. 0383374404
www.marcheseadorno-wines.it

CELLAR SALES
PRE-BOOKED VISITS
ANNUAL PRODUCTION 250,000 bottles
HECTARES UNDER VINE 85.00

This winery is worth watching carefully.
Marchese Marcello Cattaneo Adorno has
invested heavily in it, building a new cellar
and renovating the entire estate. The
guidelines were defined by oenologist
Francesco Cervetti, focusing chiefly on
riesling, pinot nero and barbera, and the
quest for quality, also achieved by
lowering yields, is giving impressive
results. All that remains to be done now is
to maximize the potential of the available
resources. Pinot Nero Rile Nero Riserva
Privata 2010 is a classy wine with elegant
tertiary notes and nice backbone, while
the coherent, zesty Riesling Arcolaio 2013
has a fine balance of fruity and floral
notes, with hints of minerals. Barbera
Vigna del Re 2012 is less exuberant than
last year, with fruit still struggling a little to
emerge. Cliviano is a Merlot expressly
desired by the Marchese. It is well made
and easy drinking, showing typical and
varietal. Pinot Nero Querciolo 2013 has
great potential but needs more time to
develop.

● OP Pinot Nero Rile Nero Riserva Privata '10	♟♟ 5
○ OP Riesling Sup. Arcolaio '13	♟♟ 3*
● Cliviano '13	♟♟ 3
● OP Barbera V. del Re '12	♟♟ 4
● OP Pinot Nero Rile Nero '13	♟♟ 5
● OP Bonarda Costa del Sole '14	♟ 3
○ OP Pinot Grigio Dama d'Oro '14	♟ 3
● OP Barbera V. del Re '11	♟♟ 4
● OP Barbera V. del Re '10	♟♟ 4
● OP Barbera Poggio Marino '11	♟♟ 2*
● OP Bonarda Costa del Sole '13	♟♟ 2*
○ OP Pinot Grigio Dama D'Oro '13	♟♟ 2*
● OP Pinot Nero Rile Nero '11	♟♟ 5
● OP Pinot Nero Rile Nero '09	♟♟ 5
○ OP Riesling Sup. Arcolaio '12	♟♟ 3*
○ OP Riesling Sup. Arcolaio '11	♟♟ 3

F.lli Agnes

VIA CAMPO DEL MONTE, 1
27040 ROVESCALA [PV]
TEL. 038575206
www.fratelliagnes.it

CELLAR SALES
PRE-BOOKED VISITS
ANNUAL PRODUCTION 120,000 bottles
HECTARES UNDER VINE 21.00

Sergio and Cristiano Agnes have a deep
knowledge of pignola (a variety of croatina
with small, closely packed bunches, locally
known as bonarda), the soil, and the terroir
that is home to Bonarda, namely
Rovescala. Although the 2014 harvest was
under par for vintage wines, the average
level of the entire range remains a
benchmark for the area, from the young
semi-sparklers to the still, oak-aged wines
for cellaring. Millennium 2011, a Bonarda
aged in oak barrels, is complex, with notes
of dark berries, liquorice and cloves, and
very lively, chafing tannins, requiring
further time in bottle. The two versions of
Bonarda Vivace 2012, Campo del Monte
and Cresta del Ghiffi 2014, usually among
the best in Oltrepò, are a little under par.
Indeed, it was a difficult vintage for
croatina, with vegetal notes emerging to
interfere with the fruit. The first is better,
more open. Loghetto 2014 is sound and
well made, both fruity and floral.

● Loghetto '14	♟♟ 3
● OP Bonarda Millennium '11	♟♟ 4
● OP Bonarda Vivace Campo del Monte '14	♟ 2
● OP Bonarda Vivace Cresta del Ghiffi '14	♟ 2
● Loghetto '13	♟♟ 3
● OP Bonarda Campo del Monte '13	♟♟ 2*
● OP Bonarda Cresta del Ghiffi '13	♟♟ 2*
● OP Bonarda Millennium '10	♟♟ 4
● OP Possessione del Console '13	♟♟ 3
● Poculum '12	♟♟ 4
● Poculum '11	♟♟ 4

Annibale Alziati

VIA SCAZZOLINO, 55
27040 ROVESCALA [PV]
TEL. 038575261
www.gaggiarone.it

CELLAR SALES
PRE-BOOKED VISITS
ANNUAL PRODUCTION 100,000 bottles
HECTARES UNDER VINE 19.00
VITICULTURE METHOD Certified Organic
SUSTAINABLE WINERY

Rovescala is the home of Bonarda. It is here, in the Scazzolino hamlet, defined a cru by Luigi Veronelli in his time, that Annibale Alziati tends around 19 hectares of vineyards with organic farming techniques. The majority are planted with old vines, which yield an array of different, largely still, croatina-based wines, rigorously aged in concrete tanks. They are austere, earthy wines that evoke the terroir and generally reach their best after several years. Gaggiarone Riserva 2005 is dark in hue and nose, with notes of coffee, liquorice, pencil lead, and dark berries. On the palate it is lively, with good pulp and a long, typically almondy finish. The pleasantly rustic Gaggiarone Vigne Vecchie 2010 has top notes of leather, followed by fruit, and a dynamic finish with smoky hints. Dispensator de' Triboli 2011 is an intriguing off-dry wine, with aromas of wild cherries, plums, and cocoa powder.

Anteo

LOC. CHIESA
27040 ROCCA DE' GIORGI [PV]
TEL. 038599073
www.anteovini.it

CELLAR SALES
PRE-BOOKED VISITS
ANNUAL PRODUCTION 200,000 bottles
HECTARES UNDER VINE 27.00

The handsome winery, founded by Trento Cribellati and now run by his children Ettore Piero and Antonella, is in the heart of the finest sparkling winegrowing country of Oltrepò Pavese, where the Versa and Scuropasso valleys commence. Here, almost 400 metres above sea level, the bottles are still hand-riddled on the racks in the large vaulted underground cellar, where the temperature remains constant all year round. Brut Tradition, from Pinot Nero blended with a small amount of Chardonnay, performed well this year, earning a place in our finals with its complex nose and long, harmonious, full-flavoured palate of aromatic herbs and honey. Riserva del Poeta 2007, dedicated to Trento Cribellati, also fared well, showing fresh and zesty, despite long ageing on the lees. The other Metodo Classicos presented were simpler yet pleasant.

● OP Gaggiarone Ris. '05	♈♈ 5
● OP Gaggiarone V. V. '10	♈♈ 4
● Dispensator de' Triboli '11	♈ 4
● Gaggiarone '07	♈♈ 5
● Gaggiarone '04	♈♈ 5
● Gaggiarone Vitigni Giovani '06	♈♈ 3*
● OP Bonarda Gaggiarone '09	♈♈ 4
● OP Bonarda Gaggiarone '07	♈♈ 4
● OP Bonarda Gaggiarone '05	♈♈ 5
● OP Bonarda Gaggiarone Vitigni Giovani '10	♈♈ 3
● OP Bonarda Gaggiarone Vitigni Giovani '09	♈♈ 3
● OP Bonarda Vivace Garzoncello Scherzoso '09	♈♈ 3

○ OP Spumante Brut Tradition '09	♈♈ 4
○ OP Pinot Nero Brut Riserva del Poeta '07	♈♈ 6
○ Brut Sabrage	♈ 3
● OP Bonarda Vivace Staffolo '14	♈ 2
○ OP Cruasé	♈ 4
● OP Pinot Nero Coste del Roccolo '14	♈ 2
○ OP Riesling Quadro di Mezzo '14	♈ 2
● OP Bonarda Staffolo '13	♈♈ 2*
○ OP Moscato La Volpe e L'Uva '13	♈♈ 2*
○ OP Pinot Nero Nature Écru '09	♈♈ 5

LOMBARDY

Antica Fratta

VIA FONTANA, 11
25040 MONTICELLI BRUSATI [BS]
TEL. 030652068
www.anticafratta.it

CELLAR SALES
PRE-BOOKED VISITS
ANNUAL PRODUCTION 300,000 bottles
HECTARES UNDER VINE 4.00

Antica Fratta is housed in a handsome
19th-century palazzo, perfectly restored by
the Ziliani family at the end of the 1970s,
which now hosts events and receptions. Its
stunning vaulted cellar laid out in the
shape of a cross is known locally as the
"Cantinon", for the palazzo was once the
home of a rich wine merchant, Cavalier
Rossetti. The winery operates
independently from Guido Berlucchi, using
grapes from its own vineyards and from
trusted suppliers. Essence Satèn 2011 put
up a good show in our finals, and remains
one of the most convincing interpretations
of this type of Franciacorta Blanc de
Blancs. Delicate and creamy, it has a nose
of candied citrus fruit and vanilla, and a
fresh, zesty palate with aromatic herbs on
a long, satisfying, complex finish. Essence
Rosé displays an attractive onionskin hue,
a nose of red berries, and good
progression on the palate.

Antica Tesa

LOC. MATTINA
VIA MERANO, 28
25080 BOTTICINO [BS]
TEL. 0302691500

CELLAR SALES
PRE-BOOKED VISITS
ANNUAL PRODUCTION 40,000 bottles
HECTARES UNDER VINE 10.00

Botticino is a small designation in a valley
and the upper foothills of the Rhaetian
Prealps. This corner of Lombardy is famous
for its prized marble, but the red wines
made from its handsome south-facing
vineyards, caressed by breezes and planted
with sangiovese, barbera, marzemino, and
schiava gentile, are particularly distinctive
and characterful. Pierangelo Noventa and
his estate are a benchmark for the DOC
zone. The vineyards, 450 metres above sea
level, are tended with organic methods.
This year Botticino Vigna Gobbio 2011
performed well in our finals. It is made from
grapes slightly dried in small wooden
crates. Its garnet hue is accompanied by a
nose of ripe red and dark berries, spices,
and cocoa powder, and a palate with
impressive structure and balance.
Botticino Già de la Tesa 2011 is also good,
showing elegant and lingering, while Colle
degli Ulivi 2011 is more easy drinking.

○ Franciacorta Satèn Essence '11	♥♥ 5
○ Franciacorta Brut	♥♥ 4
○ Franciacorta Rosé Essence '10	♥♥ 5
○ Franciacorta Brut Essence '08	♀♀ 5
○ Franciacorta Brut Essence '07	♀♀ 6
○ Franciacorta Brut Essence '06	♀♀ 5
○ Franciacorta Essence Nature '09	♀♀ 5
○ Franciacorta Extra Brut Quintessence Ris. '07	♀♀ 7
○ Franciacorta Extra Brut Quintessence Ris. '06	♀♀ 7
⊙ Franciacorta Rosé	♀♀ 5
⊙ Franciacorta Rosé Essence '09	♀♀ 5
⊙ Franciacorta Rosé Essence '08	♀♀ 5
○ Franciacorta Satèn Essence '10	♀♀ 5
○ Franciacorta Satèn Essence '09	♀♀ 5
○ Franciacorta Satèn Essence '08	♀♀ 5

● Botticino V. del Gobbio '11	♥♥ 5
● Botticino Pià de la Tesa '11	♥♥ 3
● Botticino Colle degli Ulivi '11	♥ 2
● Botticino Colle degli Ulivi	♀♀ 2*
● Botticino Pià de la Tesa '10	♀♀ 3
● Botticino Pià de la Tesa '09	♀♀ 3
● Botticino Pià de la Tesa '08	♀♀ 3*
● Botticino Pià de la Tesa '07	♀♀ 3*
● Botticino Pià de la Tesa '06	♀♀ 3
● Botticino V. degli Ulivi '07	♀♀ 2*
● Botticino V. del Gobbio '10	♀♀ 5
● Botticino V. del Gobbio '09	♀♀ 5
● Botticino V. del Gobbio '08	♀♀ 5
● Botticino V. del Gobbio '06	♀♀ 5
● Botticino V. del Gobbio '05	♀♀ 5
● Botticino V. del Gobbio '04	♀♀ 5

Ar.Pe.Pe.

VIA DEL BUON CONSIGLIO, 4
23100 SONDRIO
TEL. 0342214120
www.arpepe.com

CELLAR SALES
PRE-BOOKED VISITS
ANNUAL PRODUCTION 80,000 bottles
HECTARES UNDER VINE 13.00

This winery produces one of the finest alpine Nebbiolos. Currently run by the fifth generation of the Pelizzatti Perego family, it has always been in the cross-sights of the most demanding wine drinkers, in Italy as in the United States and Australia. Long maceration on the skins, prolonged ageing in large barrels, and very slow bottle ageing are the secret to an impressive four selections of Sassella, two of Grumello, an Inferno, and an excellent Rosso di Valtellina. They are subtle and penetrating, rather than big-bodied wines, simultaneously light and very flavoursome. The magnificent Sassella Riserva Rocce Rosse 2005 is an example of what time can do. It is a deep, even youthful, wine, proffering a nose of leather and tobacco, with hints of gentian, iodine and rust. On the palate it is full and austere, its tannins nicely supported by plenty of fleshy extracted fruit. Sassella Ultimi Raggi 2007 is concentrated and fruity, with notes of gentian and dried flowers, and a powerful, progressive palate, with a very long, well-orchestrated finish.

● Valtellina Sup.	
Sassella Rocce Rosse Ris. '05	▼▼▼ 7
● Rosso di Valtellina '13	▼▼ 4
● Valtellina Sup.	
Sassella Ultimi Raggi Ris. '07	▼▼ 8
● Valtellina Sup.	
Sassella Stella Retica Ris. '10	♈♈♈ 5
● Valtellina Sup.	
Sassella Stella Retica Ris. '06	♈♈♈ 4*
● Rosso di Valtellina '12	♈♈ 3
● Valtellina Sup.	
Grumello Rocca de Piro Ris. '10	♈♈ 5
● Valtellina Sup.	
Inferno Fiamme Antiche Ris. '10	♈♈ 5
● Valtellina Sup.	
Sassella Rocce Rosse Ris. '02	♈♈ 6

Ballabio

VIA SAN BIAGIO, 32
27045 CASTEGGIO [PV]
TEL. 0383805728
www.ballabio.net

CELLAR SALES
PRE-BOOKED VISITS
ANNUAL PRODUCTION 100,000 bottles
HECTARES UNDER VINE 60.00

This longstanding Casteggio winery, founded by Angelo Ballabio in 1905, is now run by Filippo Nevelli who aims to revive its old glory, focusing in particular on sparklers. The exceptionally well-equipped cellar vaunts modern systems with vats for microvinification and impressive storage capacity. Consultant oenologists of the calibre of Francesco Cervetti and Carlo Casavecchia are proof of its ambitions. After reaching our finals last year, the excellent Brut Farfalla had no trouble taking a Tre Bicchieri this year for the creaminess, verve, and fullness derived from long ageing on the lees, which detracts not in the least from its backbone. A classy finish completes the picture of excellence. The elegant Rosé is also good, as is the fragrant Clastidium 2013, dedicated to the founder, from Pinot Grigio with a little Pinot Bianco.

○ Brut Farfalla	▼▼▼ 4*
○ Brut Rosé Farfalla	▼▼ 4
○ OP Pinot Grigio Clastidium '13	▼▼ 2*
● OP Bonarda V. delle Cento Pertiche '13	♈♈ 3

Barone Pizzini

VIA SAN CARLO, 14
25050 PROVAGLIO D'ISEO [BS]
TEL. 0309848311
www.baronepizzini.it

CELLAR SALES
PRE-BOOKED VISITS
ACCOMMODATION
ANNUAL PRODUCTION 380,000 bottles
HECTARES UNDER VINE 47.00
VITICULTURE METHOD Certified Organic
SUSTAINABLE WINERY

The estate headed by Silvano Brescianini not only makes top-end products, but has made a name for itself over the years as one of the most advanced in terms of sustainability and low environmental impact. You only need visit the modern cellar, inspired by bioarchitecture, and the vineyards, tended with organic and biodynamic methods to realize the depth of this commitment. The Franciacorta estate is now flanked by two others: Ghiaccioforte in Maremma, Tuscany, and Pievalta in Marche, all of which use natural methods. Brut Naturae won a Tre Bicchieri for the fourth year running, this time with the 2011 vintage, with its bright straw green hue, a very fine bead, and an elegant, complex nose of citrus and white-fleshed fruit, and delicate hints of aromatic herbs. The palate is fleshy and satisfying, sustained by a lively vein of acidity and mineral notes on the long finish. The Satèn 2011 is also excellent.

○ Franciacorta Brut Naturae '11	♟♟♟ 5
○ Franciacorta Satèn '11	♟♟ 5
○ Curtefranca Polzina Bianco '14	♟♟ 3
● Curtefranca Rosso '13	♟♟ 3
○ Franciacorta Animante Brut	♟♟ 5
● San Carlo '12	♟♟ 5
⊙ Franciacorta Rosé Brut '11	♟ 5
○ Franciacorta Brut Nature '10	♟♟♟ 5
○ Franciacorta Brut Nature '09	♟♟♟ 5
○ Franciacorta Brut Nature '08	♟♟♟ 5
○ Franciacorta Brut Bagnadore Ris. '08	♟♟ 5
○ Franciacorta Brut Nature Bagnadore '04	♟♟ 5
⊙ Franciacorta Rosé Brut '08	♟♟ 5
○ Franciacorta Satèn '08	♟♟ 5
○ Franciacorta Satèn '07	♟♟ 5
○ Franciacorta Satèn '07	♟♟ 5

★★Bellavista

VIA BELLAVISTA, 5
25030 ERBUSCO [BS]
TEL. 0307762000
www.bellavistawine.it

CELLAR SALES
PRE-BOOKED VISITS
ANNUAL PRODUCTION 1,300,000 bottles
HECTARES UNDER VINE 190.00
SUSTAINABLE WINERY

Vittorio Moretti has managed to make all his dreams come true. In the 1970s, this businessman with a love of the countryside founded a series of estates that went to form the Terra Moretti group, alongside his many other enterprises. Bellavista was the first, and its international prestige makes it one of the most important names not just in Franciacorta but in the entire Italian wine world. Today Bellavista boasts 190 hectares of splendidly aspected vineyards and a series of prestigious labels that represent the best of Italian sparkling wine production. The Bellavista style, developed over the years with the aid of oenologist Mattia Vezzola, is an unmistakable blend of elegance and complexity. In order to understand it fully, just taste Riserva Vittorio Moretti 2008, an extraordinarily elegant, complex Extra Brut. We were enchanted by the nose of jasmine, the creamy, caressing effervescence, the sound fruit, the lively backbone, and the lingering aromas, which earned it a Tre Bicchieri.

○ Franciacorta Extra Brut Vittorio Moretti Ris. '08	♟♟♟ 8
○ Franciacorta Pas Operé '08	♟♟ 7
○ Curtefranca Alma Terra '14	♟♟ 4
○ Curtefranca Convento SS. Annunciata '12	♟♟ 6
○ Curtefranca Uccellanda '12	♟♟ 6
○ Franciacorta Brut '10	♟♟ 6
○ Franciacorta Brut Cuvée Alma	♟♟ 5
⊙ Franciacorta Brut Rosé '10	♟♟ 7
○ Franciacorta Satèn '10	♟♟ 7
○ Franciacorta Brut Gran Cuvée '04	♟♟♟ 6
○ Franciacorta Extra Brut Vittorio Moretti Ris. '06	♟♟♟ 8
○ Franciacorta Gran Cuvée Pas Operé '06	♟♟♟ 8
○ Franciacorta Gran Cuvée Pas Operé '05	♟♟♟ 7
○ Franciacorta Gran Cuvée Pas Operé '04	♟♟♟ 7

Guido Berlucchi & C.

LOC. BORGONATO
P.ZZA DURANTI, 4
25040 CORTE FRANCA [BS]
TEL. 0309984381
www.berlucchi.it

CELLAR SALES
PRE-BOOKED VISITS
ACCOMMODATION
ANNUAL PRODUCTION 4,300,000 bottles
HECTARES UNDER VINE 520.00
VITICULTURE METHOD Certified Organic
SUSTAINABLE WINERY

Franco Ziliani founded this famous winery
over 50 years ago, in 1961, together with
Guido Berlucchi, marking the start of
Franciacorta's recent history. He is still
chairman today, flanked by his children
Paolo, Cristina and oenologist Arturo.
Together, the family, who have returned to
using only Franciacorta grapes for their
cuvées, have earned the winery the title of
Italian sparkling wine leader, with an annual
production of over four million bottles, and
constantly growing exports. Brut Extrême
2007 confirms itself as one of the best
cuvées of the designation. It is made from
the pinot nero grapes of two vineyards in
Borgonato, Quindicipiò and Brolo, next to
the iconic Palazzo Lana, where the winery
is housed. After ageing on the lees for over
six years, it is fresh, stylish and spirited,
characterized by elegant hints of red
berries, citrus fruit, and aromatic herbs,
and a well-defined zestiness on the finish.
The rest of the list is excellent.

○ Franciacorta Extra Brut Extrême Palazzo Lana Ris. '07	♟♟♟ 7
○ Franciacorta Cuvée Imperiale Vintage '11	♟♟ 5
⊙ Franciacorta Brut 61	♟♟ 5
⊙ Franciacorta Brut Rosé Cellarius '10	♟♟ 5
○ Franciacorta Cellarius Brut '10	♟♟ 5
○ Franciacorta Cuvée Imperiale Brut	♟♟ 5
⊙ Franciacorta Cuvée Imperiale Max Rosé	♟♟ 5
○ Franciacorta Demi Sec Cuvée Imperiale	♟♟ 5
⊙ Franciacorta Rosé 61	♟♟ 5
○ Franciacorta Satèn 61	♟♟ 5
○ Franciacorta Brut Cellarius '07	♟♟♟ 5
○ Franciacorta Brut Extrême Palazzo Lana Ris. '06	♟♟♟ 6
○ Franciacorta Cellarius Brut '08	♟♟♟ 5
○ Franciacorta Satèn Palazzo Lana '06	♟♟♟ 6

Cantina Bersi Serlini

LOC. CERETO
VIA CERETO, 7
25050 PROVAGLIO D'ISEO [BS]
TEL. 0309823338
www.bersiserlini.it

CELLAR SALES
PRE-BOOKED VISITS
ACCOMMODATION AND RESTAURANT SERVICE
ANNUAL PRODUCTION 200,000 bottles
HECTARES UNDER VINE 30.00
VITICULTURE METHOD Certified Organic

In 1886, the Bersi Serlini family purchased
this handsome estate in Provaglio, on the
shores of Lake Iseo, which was once the
grange of the nearby Benedictine
monastery of San Pietro in Lamosa.
Following extensive renovation and
extension work, today the complex is a
charming blend of old and new. The
30-hectare estate is headed by sisters
Maddalena and Chiara Bersi Serlini and
uses only its own grapes. The winery has a
special talent for Extra Brut and the elegant
2011 vintage confirms itself a
thoroughbred, distinguished by
extraordinary freshness. It is complex,
zesty, and well-orchestrated, characterized
by elegant notes of white peaches and pink
grapefruit, offering finesse and expressive
depth. The 2008 is equally alluring, with
notes of alpine herbs and white-fleshed
fruit, and the rest of the range is also
exceptionally good.

○ Franciacorta Extra Brut '11	♟♟ 6
○ Franciacorta Brut '11	♟♟ 6
○ Franciacorta Brut Anniversario	♟♟ 6
○ Franciacorta Brut Anteprima	♟♟ 5
⊙ Franciacorta Brut Rosé Rosa Rosae	♟♟ 5
○ Franciacorta Extra Brut '08	♟♟ 6
○ Franciacorta Satèn	♟♟ 5
○ Franciacorta Demi Sec Nuvola	♟ 4
○ Franciacorta Brut Cuvée n. 4 '08	♟♟ 5
○ Franciacorta Brut Cuvée n. 4 '06	♟♟ 4*
○ Franciacorta Brut Vintage Ris. '06	♟♟ 7
○ Franciacorta Brut Vintage Ris. '04	♟♟ 7
○ Franciacorta Extra Brut '10	♟♟ 6
○ Franciacorta Extra Brut '02	♟♟ 5
○ Franciacorta Extra Brut '01	♟♟ 5

Bertagna

LOC. BANDE
S.DA MADONNA DELLA PORTA, 14
46040 CAVRIANA [MN]
TEL. 037682211
www.cantinabertagna.it

CELLAR SALES
PRE-BOOKED VISITS
ANNUAL PRODUCTION 120,000 bottles
HECTARES UNDER VINE 13.00

The winery run by Gianfranco Bertagna, the latest of four generations of growers active in the Colli Morenici Mantovani del Garda designation, performed well again this year. The elegant Lugana showed well paced, with golden highlights, hints of citrus and tropical fruit, and a nice finish. Rosso del Barone 2012 is a blend of Cabernet Sauvignon and Cabernet Franc, with typically vegetal, spicy notes and a lively finish. Montevolpe Rosso 2011, from cabernet, merlot and corvina grapes, is more complex, and this vintage appears one of the best ever. The style is super-ripe, but not cloying, with warm, concentrated, weighty fruit, and a very intriguing spicy note. The rest of the list is good, particularly the delicate, fragrant Chardonnay Montevolpe Bianco 2014, which is balanced and pleasant.

F.lli Bettini

LOC. SAN GIACOMO
VIA NAZIONALE, 4A
23036 TEGLIO [SO]
TEL. 0342786068
bettvini@tin.it

CELLAR SALES
PRE-BOOKED VISITS
ANNUAL PRODUCTION 200,000 bottles
HECTARES UNDER VINE 15.00

Pietro Bettini's estate is an historic name in Valtellina winemaking since 1881. It is situated in San Giacomo di Teglio, in the heart of Valgella, at an altitude of 900 metres on the slopes of the Bergamasque Alps. The vineyards cover an area of about 15 hectares, scattered over the main Valtellina subzones. The range is consistently excellent, managing to reconcile quality with quantity. The 2010 vintage of Vigneti di Spina is classic and original, offering a characteristic austere nose of quinine and tobacco, with hints of cocoa powder and brandied fruit. The palate is rounded, with good structure, noble tannins, and a long, lingering finish Valgella Vigna La Cornella 2010 is complex, with notes of iron filings and rain-soaked earth. On the palate it is full and juicy, with a very long finish.

○ Lugana '14	♥♥ 2*
● Montevolpe Rosso '11	♥♥ 3
● Rosso del Barone '12	♥♥ 2*
○ Montevolpe Bianco '14	♥ 2
● Rosso del Chino '12	♥ 2
○ Lugana '13	♥♥ 2*
○ Montevolpe Bianco '11	♥♥ 3
● Montevolpe Rosso '10	♥♥ 3
● Rosso del Barone '10	♥♥ 3
● Rosso del Barone '09	♥♥ 3
● Rosso del Chino '10	♥♥ 3
● Rosso del Chino '09	♥♥ 3
● Rosso del Chino '08	♥♥ 3

● Sforzato di Valtellina V. di Spina '10	♥♥ 6
● Valtellina Sup. Inferno Prodigio '10	♥♥ 4
● Valtellina Sup. Sassella Reale '10	♥♥ 4
● Valtellina Sup. Valgella V. La Cornella '10	♥♥ 4
● Valtellina Sfursat '11	♥♥ 5
● Valtellina Sfursat '10	♥♥ 5
● Valtellina Sfursat '09	♥♥ 5
● Valtellina Sfursat '07	♥♥ 5
● Valtellina Sup. Inferno Prodigio '09	♥♥ 3
● Valtellina Sup. Inferno Prodigio '08	♥♥ 3
● Valtellina Sup. Sant'Andrea '10	♥♥ 4
● Valtellina Sup. Sant'Andrea '09	♥♥ 4
● Valtellina Sup. Sassella Reale '09	♥♥ 3
● Valtellina Sup. Valgella V. La Cornella '09	♥♥ 3
● Valtellina Sup. Valgella V. La Cornella '08	♥♥ 3

Bisi

LOC. CASCINA SAN MICHELE
FRAZ. VILLA MARONE, 70
27040 SAN DAMIANO AL COLLE [PV]
TEL. 038575037
www.aziendagricolabisi.it

CELLAR SALES
PRE-BOOKED VISITS
ANNUAL PRODUCTION 90,000 bottles
HECTARES UNDER VINE 30.00

In Bisi's case, it is true to say that wine reflects the characteristics and personality of its producer. Claudio is reserved but determined, solid, and generous, as are his wines, commencing with Barbera Roncolongo. They are never commonplace or predictable, and do not yield too easily, but once they reveal themselves they display breadth, depth, confidence, and emotion. They are wines that inspire passion, to be understood slowly, over time. In our tastings Roncolongo 2011 came out on top, with very high average scores: a wine that never disappoints, with plenty of texture, accompanied by spicy notes of cherry and wild berry jam, and good backbone and depth. Riesling LaGrà 2014, a monovarietal riesling renano, is fairly evolved despite its young age, proffering a concentrated nose with petrol already discernible among the floral notes. Pinot Nero Calonga 2012 is well made, varietal and spicy, although the best of the entire difficult 2014 vintage is perhaps Bonarda La Peccatrice. The bottle-fermented Ultrapadum, a succulent blend of barbera and croatina, is well worth trying.

● Roncolongo '11	♥♥	4
● Calonga '12	♥♥	5
○ LaGrà '14	♥♥	3
● OP Bonarda Vivace La Peccatrice '14	♥♥	2*
● Pramattone '13	♥♥	3
● Ultrapadum '13	♥♥	3
○ Pezzabianca '13	♥	3
● OP Bonarda Vivace La Peccatrice '13	♀♀	2*
○ Bianco Passito Villa Marone '11	♀♀	4
○ LaGrà '13	♀♀	3*
● Pramattone '12	♀♀	3
● Roncolongo '10	♀♀	4

Castello Bonomi

VIA SAN PIETRO, 46
25030 COCCAGLIO [BS]
TEL. 0307721015
www.castellobonomi.it

CELLAR SALES
PRE-BOOKED VISITS
ANNUAL PRODUCTION 100,000 bottles
HECTARES UNDER VINE 20.00

This longstanding Franciacorta winery vaunts 20 hectares of mainly terraced vineyards at the foot of Mount Orfano, on the designation's oldest soils, in its far south. A few years ago it joined the group owned by the Paladin family from Veneto, which also comprises the Paladin and Bosco del Merlo estates, as well as Vescine in Radda, in Chianti Classico. Roberto and Lucia Paladin have given new energy to the winery, which produces unique and extraordinarily cellarable cuvées. The 2004 vintage has earned the winery its second Tre Bicchieri and this time we gave the top accolade to the Brut Cru Perdu 2004. The Chardonnay and 30% Pinot Nero cuvée, aged almost ten years on the lees, is extraordinarily fresh and lively, with still sound fruit and a caressing mineral vein underpinning the long, satisfying finish. Its hints of white-fleshed fruit, hazelnuts and aromatic herbs are intensified by an extraordinarily fine bead and a caressing effervescence.

○ Franciacorta Brut Cru Perdu '04	♥♥♥	7
● Curtefranca Rosso Cordelio '10	♥♥	7
○ Franciacorta Brut Cru Perdù	♥♥	6
○ Franciacorta Gran Cuvée	♥♥	6
⊙ Franciacorta Rosé	♥♥	7
⊙ Franciacorta Rosé Lucrezia Ris. '06	♥♥	8
○ Franciacorta Satèn	♥♥	7
○ Franciacorta Extra Brut Lucrezia Et. Nera '04	♀♀♀	8
● Curtefranca Rosso Cordelio '09	♀♀	7
● Curtefranca Rosso Cordelio '07	♀♀	5
○ Franciacorta Brut '06	♀♀	6
○ Franciacorta Dosage Zero '07	♀♀	8
○ Franciacorta Extra Brut Lucrezia '04	♀♀	8

Tenuta Il Bosco

LOC. IL BOSCO
27049 ZENEVREDO [PV]
TEL. 0385245326
www.ilbosco.com

CELLAR SALES
PRE-BOOKED VISITS
ANNUAL PRODUCTION 1,000,000 bottles
HECTARES UNDER VINE 152.00

With over 150 hectares under vine, the Zonin family's Oltrepò estate, run by Piernicola Olmo, could not fail to become a benchmark for the typical wines of the area, without detracting in any way from the many good local vignerons. In the recent past, it played a fundamental role in redefining the concept of Bonarda Frizzante, also commercially, and it is currently focusing on Metodo Classico. It is no coincidence that last year the first, and so far only, Cruasé to have won a Tre Bicchieri came from this winery. Although it missed repeating the feat by a hair's breadth this year, it is nonetheless an excellent and very elegant sparkler, with a nose of wild berries and blood oranges, a beautiful onionskin hue, and good stuffing. Its white sister is also very good, deep and alluring. The new and recently disgorged Nature 2010, has a very layered nose, but the palate still needs to settle.

Bosio

LOC. TIMOLINE
VIA MARIO GATTI
25040 CORTE FRANCA [BS]
TEL. 030984398
www.bosiofranciacorta.it

CELLAR SALES
PRE-BOOKED VISITS
ANNUAL PRODUCTION 100,000 bottles
HECTARES UNDER VINE 30.00

La Bosio is the classic family business, founded around 15 years ago by oenologist and agronomist Cesare Bosio and his economics graduate sister Laura, who pooled their knowhow to extend the family estate, bringing it up to 30 hectares under vine, and built a modern cellar in Corte Franca. The level of their Franciacortas and wines is excellent, due to the fine vineyards tended with Cesare's skill and the utmost respect for the environment. Nature 2010 gave an excellent performance this year, faring well in our finals. It is an elegant bright straw yellow, with a very fine bead and a nose with top notes of flowers mingling with white-fleshed and citrus fruit. On the palate it is full and zesty, with plenty of fruit supported by vibrant acidity, which accompanies the long, flavoursome finish. The Rosé 2011 has good acidic grip and exceptionally clean fruit.

● OP Bonarda Vivace '14	♟♟ 2*
☉ OP Cruasé Oltrenero	♟♟ 5
○ OP Pinot Nero Brut Cl. Oltrenero	♟♟ 5
○ OP Pinot Nero Brut Nature Oltrenero '10	♟♟ 6
☉ Philèo Rosé Martinotti Extra Dry	♟♟ 2
○ Malvasia Vivace '14	♟ 3
○ OP Pinot Nero Brut Martinotti Philéo	♟ 3
○ Brera '11	♟♟ 3
● OP Bonarda '13	♟♟ 2*
● OP Bonarda Vivace '12	♟♟ 2*
● OP Bonarda Vivace '11	♟♟ 2*
○ OP Brut Oltrenero	♟♟ 5
● OP Pinot Nero Poggio Pelato '11	♟♟ 3
● OP Pinot Nero Poggio Pelato '10	♟♟ 3

○ Franciacorta Nature '10	♟♟ 5
☉ Franciacorta Brut Rosé '11	♟♟ 5
○ Franciacorta Extra Brut Boschedòr '10	♟♟ 5
○ Franciacorta Satèn	♟♟ 5
● Curtefranca Rosso Zenighe '11	♟ 4
○ Franciacorta Brut	♟ 5
○ Franciacorta Brut '08	♟♟ 5
○ Franciacorta Brut Rosé '09	♟♟ 5
○ Franciacorta Extra Brut Boschedòr '09	♟♟ 5
○ Franciacorta Extra Brut Boschedòr '08	♟♟ 5
○ Franciacorta Extra Brut Boschedòr '07	♟♟ 5
○ Franciacorta Extra Brut Boschedòr '05	♟♟ 5
○ Franciacorta Pas Dosé Girolamo Bosio Ris. '07	♟♟ 5
○ Franciacorta Pas Dosé Girolamo Bosio Ris. '06	♟♟ 5

Alessio Brandolini

FRAZ. BOFFALORA, 68
27040 SAN DAMIANO AL COLLE [PV]
TEL. 038575232
www.alessiobrandolini.com

ANNUAL PRODUCTION 50,000 bottles
HECTARES UNDER VINE 9.00

Alessio Brandolini belongs to the Oltrepò in Fermento group of young Oltrepò growers, founded with the ambitious intention of improving the conditions of the area that does not always take as much care of itself as it deserves. We have been following his progress for years, ever since he took the helm of the family estate after graduating from Milan University, and soon found himself having to do without the precious support of his father Costante in the vineyard, following his premature death. After having witnessed the growth of his wines and his ambition, this year we have decided to award him a full profile. The red Beneficio 2011 is already full, broad, and chewy, showing excellent restrained use of pre-used oak and good ageing prospects. Malvasia Secca Il Bardughino 2014 is as fragrant as ever, with notes of lychees and passion fruit. Metodo Classico Luogo D'Agosto 2010 is soft and complex, more elegant than the very fruity Rosé 2009, while Bonarda Vivace Il Cassino 2014 is among the best of the vintage.

● Il Beneficio '11	♟♟ 2*	
○ Brut M. Cl. Luogo D'Agosto '10	♟♟ 3	
● Il Bardughino '14	♟♟ 2*	
● OP Bonarda Vivace Il Cassino '14	♟♟ 2*	
⊙ Brut M. Cl. Rosé Note D'Agosto '09	♟ 3	
● Il Negrese '12	♟ 2	
● OP Bonarda Il Soffio '13	♟ 2	
○ Il Bardughino '13	♟♟ 2*	
● OP Bonarda Il Soffio '11	♟♟ 2*	
● OP Bonarda Vivace Il Cassino '13	♟♟ 2*	
● OP Bonarda Vivace Il Cassino '12	♟♟ 2*	

La Brugherata

FRAZ. ROSCIATE
VIA G. MEDOLAGO, 47
24020 SCANZOROSCIATE [BG]
TEL. 035655202
www.labrugherata.it

CELLAR SALES
PRE-BOOKED VISITS
ANNUAL PRODUCTION 40,000 bottles
HECTARES UNDER VINE 7.00

Among the most reliable in the entire Bergamo district, La Brugherata is one of the wineries that focus on the moscato di Scanzo grape variety, the true local speciality, still little-known elsewhere, producing both the classic passito and a dry version. This year the Valcalepio DOC and IGT wines from Bordeaux grape varieties were not presented as they were not yet ready. Doge 2012 appeared less ready than in previous years, with more aggressive tannins. However, the familiar nose of spice, raisins, Californian prunes, and incense portends the warm fruity stuffing that lies beneath this somewhat brusque initial impact. It just requires a little patience while it continues to rest in the bottle. The fresh, fruity Vermiglio di Roxia 2013 is a pleasant dry red from moscato di Scanzo grapes, while Vescovado del Feuto 2014 is a white from chardonnay, with aromas of citrus and tropical fruit.

● Moscato di Scanzo Doge '12	♟♟ 7	
● Moscato Rosso Vermiglio di Roxia '13	♟♟ 3	
○ Vescovado del Feudo '14	♟♟ 2*	
● Moscato di Scanzo Doge '11	♟♟ 7	
● Moscato di Scanzo Doge '10	♟♟ 7	
● Moscato di Scanzo Doge '09	♟♟ 7	
● Moscato di Scanzo Doge '08	♟♟ 7	
● Priore '12	♟♟ 5	
● Priore '09	♟♟ 3	
○ Valcalepio Bianco Vescovado del Feudo '11	♟♟ 2*	
● Valcalepio Rosso Doglio Ris. '10	♟♟ 4	
● Valcalepio Rosso Doglio Ris. '07	♟♟ 3	
● Valcalepio Rosso Vescovado '11	♟♟ 2*	
○ Vescovado del Feudo '12	♟♟ 2*	

Cà Maiol

VIA DEI COLLI STORICI
25015 DESENZANO DEL GARDA [BS]
TEL. 0309910006
www.provenzacantine.it

CELLAR SALES
PRE-BOOKED VISITS
ANNUAL PRODUCTION 1,500,000 bottles
HECTARES UNDER VINE 155.00

Fabio Contato runs the handsome family estate outside Sirmione, which vaunts many hectares in the Lugana and neighbouring Valtenesi production zones. He is flanked by his sister Patrizia, and their production focuses on the wines of the designations, interpreted trying to combine tradition with modern knowledge. The wide range of top-notch products is topped by the excellent Garda whites. Lugana Molin is made from a careful selection of the estate's finest grapes, vinified exclusively in steel. The resulting wine gets better with each year that passes, standing out for its fragrant nose, uncorrupted by non-traditional grape varieties, and its very long, approachable, crisp palate, earning it a well-deserved Tre Bicchieri. Brut 60 Mesi, a solid Metodo Classico, is very interesting, with deep aromas and a gutsy palate.

○ Lugana Molin '14	♥♥♥	3*
● Garda Cl. Groppello Joel '13	♥♥	3
● Garda Rosso Cl. Sel. Fabio Contato '10	♥♥	5
○ Lugana Brut M. Cl.	♥♥	4
○ Lugana Brut M. Cl. Fabio Contato 60 Mesi	♥♥	5
○ Lugana Prestige '14	♥♥	3
⊙ Valtènesi Chiaretto Roseri '14	♥♥	3
○ Lugana Molin '13	♥♥♥	3*
○ Lugana Molin '12	♥♥♥	3*
○ Lugana Sup. Sel. Fabio Contato '11	♥♥♥	5
○ Lugana Sup. Sel. Fabio Contato '10	♥♥♥	5
○ Lugana Sup. Sel. Fabio Contato '09	♥♥♥	5

Ca' dei Frati

FRAZ. LUGANA
VIA FRATI, 22
25019 SIRMIONE [BS]
TEL. 030919468
www.cadeifrati.it

CELLAR SALES
PRE-BOOKED VISITS
ACCOMMODATION AND RESTAURANT SERVICE
ANNUAL PRODUCTION 1,800,000 bottles
HECTARES UNDER VINE 150.00

Brothers Igino and Gian Franco Dal Cero and their sister Anna Maria are among the producers that made Lugana one of the most sought-after Italian white wines in the world. Their vineyards cover many hectares, particularly in the southern Garda production zone, but in recent years in Valpolicella too. The high production figures of a small number of labels testify to the estate's close ties to its roots that have made designer wines a rarity here. This year our favourite wine was again a Lugana: Brolettina, a fruity white from the fine 2013 vintage, aged in small oak casks for about 10 months. The nose offers clearly defined notes of ripe apples and pears, with an emerging mineral note, while the complex palate is underpinned by a zesty acidity that lengthens the finish. The 2014 vintage was far more complicated, resulting in a spirited, racy Lugana I Frati. The Amarone is full and powerful, with impressive fruity extract.

● Amarone della Valpolicella Pietro Dal Cero '09	♥♥	8
○ Lugana Brolettino '13	♥♥	3*
○ Lugana I Frati '14	♥♥	2*
○ Cuvée dei Frati Brut '11	♥♥	3
⊙ Cuvée dei Frati Brut M. Cl. Rosé '11	♥♥	4
○ Lugana Brolettino Affinato 5 anni in bottiglia '09	♥♥	5
○ Lugana I Frati Affinato 5 anni in bottiglia '09	♥♥	4
○ Tre Filer Passito '11	♥♥	3
⊙ Riviera del Garda Bresciano Rosa dei Frati '14	♥	3
● Ronchedone '12	♥	3
○ Lugana Brolettino '12	♥♥♥	3*
○ Lugana Brolettino '11	♥♥♥	3*
○ Lugana Brolettino '10	♥♥♥	3*

★★★★Ca' del Bosco

VIA ALBANO ZANELLA, 13
25030 ERBUSCO [BS]
TEL. 0307766111
www.cadelbosco.com

CELLAR SALES
PRE-BOOKED VISITS
ANNUAL PRODUCTION 1,470,000 bottles
HECTARES UNDER VINE 184.50
SUSTAINABLE WINERY

Few wineries are as worth a visit as Ca' del Bosco. Set among the woods and its beautiful vineyards, the welcoming, modern premises are full of artworks and equipped with the most sophisticated cellar technologies. Ca' Bosco's founder and chairman Maurizio Zanelli has headed the winery since the very outset, in the early 1970s. His extraordinary passion for quality wines has propelled the estate into the exclusive realm of the world's top producers. The extraordinary Dosage Zéro Noir 2006 of the Vintage Collection range has earned Ca' del Bosco its 40th Tre Bicchieri and its fourth star. Ageing for over eight years on the lees has given this Blanc de Noirs exceptional depth and complexity, making it a benchmark for absolute quality. Its masterful performance earned it our Sparkler of the Year award and risks overshadowing the splendid and truly elegant 2006 Annamaria Clementi.

Ca' del Gè

FRAZ. CA' DEL GÈ, 3
27040 MONTALTO PAVESE [PV]
TEL. 0383870179
www.cadelge.it

CELLAR SALES
PRE-BOOKED VISITS
ANNUAL PRODUCTION 180,000 bottles
HECTARES UNDER VINE 40.00

Stefania, Sara and Carlo Padroggi run the family estate, following in the footsteps of their late father Enzo. It boasts 40 hectares of excellently aspected vineyards on the hills of Montalto Pavese, dominated by chalky soils ideal for growing riesling and pinot nero. Like many family-run Oltrepò estates, its wide range offers excellent value for money and includes some real gems. One of these is the rich, ripe Brut 2010, which offers a beautiful golden hue, with a nose of red berries and aromatic herbs, and a creamy palate that is full, yet taught and spirited, showing exemplary progression and cleanliness on the finish. The brand new Riesling Brinà 2014, from 100% riesling italico, has a fragrant nose of flowers, white peaches and bay leaf, and a fine zesty palate. The rest of the list is also good.

○ Franciacorta Dosage Zéro Noir Vintage Collection Ris. '06	♀♀♀ 8
● Carmenero '08	♀♀ 8
○ Franciacorta Cuvée Annamaria Clementi Ris. '06	♀♀ 8
● Pinèro '11	♀♀ 8
○ Curtefranca Bianco '14	♀♀ 5
○ Curtefranca Chardonnay '11	♀♀ 8
● Curtefranca Rosso '11	♀♀ 5
○ Franciacorta Brut Cuvée Prestige	♀♀ 5
○ Franciacorta Brut Vintage Collection '10	♀♀ 8
○ Franciacorta Dosage Zéro Vintage Collection '10	♀♀ 8
⊙ Franciacorta Rosé Cuvée Prestige	♀♀ 6
○ Franciacorta Satén Vintage Collection '10	♀♀ 8
● Maurizio Zanella '09	♀♀ 8

○ OP Pinot Nero Brut M. Cl. '10	♀♀ 3*
○ OP Riesling Brinà '14	♀♀ 2*
● OP Bonarda Vivace Bricco del Prete '14	♀ 2
● OP Buttafuoco Fajro '11	♀ 4
○ OP Moscato Frizzante '14	♀ 2
● OP Bonarda Vivace '13	♀♀ 2*
● OP Bonarda Vivace '12	♀♀ 2*
○ OP Moscato Frizzante '13	♀♀ 2*
○ OP Pinot Nero Brut '09	♀♀ 3

LOMBARDY

Ca' di Frara

VIA CASA FERRARI, 1
27040 MORNICO LOSANA [PV]
TEL. 0383892299
www.cadifrara.com

CELLAR SALES
PRE-BOOKED VISITS
ANNUAL PRODUCTION 400,000 bottles
HECTARES UNDER VINE 46.00

The Bellani family's estate was among the first to perceive the need for a sort of wine Renaissance in Oltrepò Pavese, implementing strict selections in the vineyard, and adopting modern cellar techniques and new ideas, but without rejecting tradition. While everything has not always gone smoothly, there have been pinnacles of excellence alongside less successful wines, and we have full confidence in Luca's ability, particularly regarding his long-term Metodo Classico project, despite the fact that it is not always easy to navigate the various types and vintages presented. This year, for example, we tasted two Riservas: a Nature 2004 and a Rosé 2008. Both are undeniably interesting, the first with spice and white chocolate, still showing good vigour and effervescence; the second with wild berries and dried herbs. However neither managed the master stroke needed to reach the finals. The pleasant non-vintage Nature is more simple, while the still wines were disappointing, particularly in view of the excellent versions of a few years ago.

○ OP Pinot Nero Brut	
Oltre il Classico Nature Ris. '04	♟♟5
⊙ OP Pinot Nero Brut	
Oltre il Classico Rosé Ris. '08	♟♟5
○ OP Pinot Grigio	
Selezione dei Vent'Anni '14	♟4
○ OP Pinot Nero Brut	
Oltre il Classico Nature	♟4
● OP Pinot Nero Ris. '10	♟5
○ OP Riesling Oliva '13	♟4
● OP Rosso Il Frater Ris. '11	♟5
○ OP Pinot Grigio Raccolta Tardiva '13	♟♟3
● OP Pinot Nero '12	♟♟3
○ OP Riesling Oliva '12	♟♟3
○ OP Riesling Renano Apogeo	
Raccolta Tardiva '12	♟♟3

Ca' Lojera

LOC. ROVIZZA
VIA 1886, 19
25019 SIRMIONE [BS]
TEL. 0457551901
www.calojera.com

CELLAR SALES
PRE-BOOKED VISITS
RESTAURANT SERVICE
ANNUAL PRODUCTION 120,000 bottles
HECTARES UNDER VINE 20.00

Ambra Tiraboschi has expanded Ca' Lojera, the estate founded with her husband Franco on the southern shore of Lake Garda, where the clay-rich soil is perfect for ripening turbiana grapes. The closer to the lake, the higher the percentage of clay in the soil, while it is lower moving inland, towards the morainic hills, making the vineyards there better suited to other cultivars. Lugana del Lupo is a Riserva from super-ripe grapes, which is slowly aged in steel vats. The result is a wine with a concentrated nose of white-fleshed fruit and flowers, and a slight hint of botrytis that adds complexity. On the palate zesty acidity keeps the fullness in check, ensuring lightness and grip. The fruity Superiore is more approachable, while fresh vegetal and floral notes prevail over the fruit in the fragrant, refreshing Lugana 2014.

○ Lugana '14	♟♟3
○ Lugana Riserva del Lupo '13	♟♟5
○ Lugana Sup. '13	♟♟3
⊙ Rosato Monte della Guardia '14	♟2
○ Lugana del Lupo '10	♟♟4
○ Lugana Riserva del Lupo '12	♟♟5
○ Lugana Riserva del Lupo '11	♟♟4
○ Lugana Sup. '12	♟♟3
○ Lugana Sup. '10	♟♟3
○ Lugana Sup. '09	♟♟3
● Merlot Monte della Guardia '09	♟♟2*

Ca' Tessitori

VIA MATTEOTTI, 15
27043 BRONI [PV]
TEL. 038551495
www.catessitori.it

CELLAR SALES
PRE-BOOKED VISITS
ANNUAL PRODUCTION 120,000 bottles
HECTARES UNDER VINE 40.00

It is worth keeping a careful eye on the
wines of the estate run by Luigi Giorgio
with his sons Giovanni and Francesco.
Fermentation takes place in concrete vats,
although a few tonneaux have appeared
after the decision to abandon barriques.
The hillside vineyards in Montecalvo
Versiggia and Finigeto yield characterful
wines that reflect both the terroir and the
vintage. Now that a suitable cellar, called
La Sala, is available again, the move
towards Metodo Classico will gain even
more momentum. Indeed, the Brut M.V.
(the intials stand for Montecalvo
Versiggia) reached our finals already this year, with a
fulness and opulence that do not detract
from its freshness. It is an impressive wine,
commencing with its deep golden hue,
offering top notes of cakes, followed by
fruit and aromatic herbs, good backbone,
and a long finish of candied peel in a
unique and intriguing style. The rest of the
production is also very good, with the
fragrant white Agòlo 2014, from 80%
sauvignon, worthy of special mention.

○ OP Pinot Nero Brut Cl. M. V. '10	♟♟ 4
○ Agòlo '14	♟♟ 2*
● OP Bonarda Avita '14	♟♟ 2*
○ OP Pinot Nero Brut Cl. '11	♟♟ 4
● OP Bonarda Vivace '14	♟ 2
⊙ OP Cruasé '11	♟ 3
● OP Rosso Borghesa '14	♟ 2
○ Agòlo '13	♟♟ 2*
● Gnese '11	♟♟ 3
● OP Bonarda Avita '13	♟♟ 2*
● OP Bonarda Vivace '13	♟♟ 2*

Calatroni

LOC. CASA GRANDE, 7
27040 MONTECALVO VERSIGGIA [PV]
TEL. 038599013
www.calatronivini.it

CELLAR SALES
PRE-BOOKED VISITS
RESTAURANT SERVICE
ANNUAL PRODUCTION 80,000 bottles
HECTARES UNDER VINE 15.00
SUSTAINABLE WINERY

We were quite right last year when we
decided to award our full profile to the
winery run by young Christian and Stefano
Calatroni, the fourth generation of growers
since its foundation in 1964. Indeed, the
wines show increasingly more personality,
as well as steadily higher quality. Not
surprisingly, considering the location of the
vineyards and the soil, the grape varieties
that yield the best results are riesling
renano and pinot nero. Talking of Riesling,
after the excellent 2010 and the surprising
2007 vintages presented last year, this year
the 2009 positions itself midway between
the two, with a handsome hue and
attractive typical notes of saffron and bay
leaf on the nose, accompanied by fruit,
flowers and petrol. The young 2014, with
fresher notes, is also very good, while the
Brut 64 is excellent, earning a Tre Bicchieri
with its fullness, complexity, well-typed
notes of red fruit and aromatic herbs, fine
bead, and crescendo finish.

○ Pinot Nero Brut 64 '11	♟♟♟ 5
○ OP Riesling '09	♟♟ 2*
● OP Pinot Nero '13	♟♟ 2*
○ OP Riesling '14	♟♟ 2*
● OP Bonarda Vivace Vigiö '14	♟ 2
⊙ OP Cruasé Norema '11	♟ 3
● OP Rosso Perorossino '12	♟ 3
● OP Rosso Perorossino '10	♟ 4
● OP Bonarda Vivace Unico '13	♟♟ 2*
⊙ OP Cruasé '10	♟♟ 3
○ OP Riesling '07	♟♟ 2*
○ Pinot Nero Brut 64	♟♟ 4

Il Calepino

VIA SURRIPE, 1
24060 CASTELLI CALEPIO [BG]
TEL. 035847178
www.ilcalepino.it

CELLAR SALES
PRE-BOOKED VISITS
ANNUAL PRODUCTION 230,000 bottles
HECTARES UNDER VINE 15.00

While Il Calepino also makes still red wines, which are sometimes very interesting, and white wines, there is no doubt that the real strength of the estate owned by the Plebani brothers lies in its Metodo Classico sparklers. Over the years we have seen how they always stand out, not only in terms of quality, but particularly for their unmistakable style, which we also find in the new products, such as the uncomplicated, early-drinking BDB, bearing the new Terre del Colleoni designation. The flagship remains Fra'Ambrogio Riserva, whose 2008 vintage again shows its greatness, commencing with its golden hue and tactile sensation of the very fine bead, with notes of butter, vanilla and crusty bread, and a lively finish. The Non Dosato 2009 is very good, with an elegant, razor-sharp mineral vein; the Brut 2010 is stylish, with a long finish; and the Rosé is rather muscular, with prominent notes of wild berries.

○ Brut Cl. Fra' Ambrogio Ris. '08	♟♟	4
○ Brut Cl. Il Calepino '10	♟♟	3
○ Brut Cl. Non Dosato '09	♟♟	4
⊙ Brut Cl. Rosé	♟♟	3
● Kalòs '10	♟♟	5
○ TdC Brut Cl. BDB	♟	4
● Valcalepio Rosso Surìe Ris. '11	♟	3
○ Brut Cl. Fra' Ambrogio '07	♟♟	4
○ Brut Cl. Fra' Ambrogio Ris. '06	♟♟	4
○ Brut Cl. Non Dosato '07	♟♟	4
⊙ Brut Cl. Rosé '08	♟♟	3
⊙ Brut Cl. Rosé (Cuvée '04/'05)	♟♟	3
● MAS '08	♟♟	5

Cantrina

VIA COLOMBERA, 7
25081 BEDIZZOLE [BS]
TEL. 0306871052
www.cantrina.it

CELLAR SALES
ANNUAL PRODUCTION 35,000 bottles
HECTARES UNDER VINE 7.90

Cristina Inganni's estate is in the little hamlet of Borgo di Cantrina, in the municipality of Bedizzole, and the Valtenesi zone, the inland area to the west of Lake Garda, characterized by morainic hills that make it ideal for viticulture. The vineyards cover just a few hectares, dedicated partly to international grape varieties and partly to native cultivars, such as groppello and rebo, a hybrid of merlot and teroldego, which is widely grown in the area. Nepomuceno is a blend of Merlot, Marzemino and Rebo that undergoes long ageing in the cellar. It has a nose of red berries and spice, accompanied by a crisp, lively palate that is still astonishingly youthful, showing long and elegant, with discreet oak. Rosanoire, a monovarietal pinot nero rosé, put up an excellent performance, with an enviably clean nose of berry fruit and flowers, and a dry, satisfying palate.

● Nepomuceno '09	♟♟	5
⊙ Rosanoire '14	♟♟	2*
○ Rinè '13	♟	3
● Zerdì '12	♟	3
● Garda Cl. Groppello '12	♟♟	2*
● Garda Cl. Groppello '10	♟♟	2*
● Garda Cl. Groppello Libero Esercizio di Stile '11	♟♟	2*
○ Rinè '12	♟♟	3
⊙ Rosanoire '13	♟♟	2*
○ Sole di Dario '09	♟♟	5
● Valtenesi '13	♟♟	3

CastelFaglia - Monogram

FRAZ. CALINO
LOC. BOSCHI, 3
25046 CAZZAGO SAN MARTINO [BS]
TEL. 0307751042
www.cavicchioli.it

CELLAR SALES
PRE-BOOKED VISITS
ANNUAL PRODUCTION 350,000 bottles
HECTARES UNDER VINE 22.00

The Cavicchioli family from Modena have been making wine since 1928. Today they own two top sparkling wine brands: Bellei in Bomporto, in Emilia, and CastelFaglia in Cazzago San Martino, in Franciacorta. There, in the hamlet of Calino, Sandro Cavicchioli crafts elegant Franciacorta cuvées for the CastelFaglia and Monogram product lines from the estate's 22 hectares of partially terraced vineyards bellow the old Faglia Castle. Two of the estate's cuvées reached our finals. Dosage Zero 2011 from the Monogram range is admirably complex, with a fine bead, an alluring nose of tropical fruit and aromatic herbs, and an elegant, zesty finish. The Brut 2007 from the same line offers juicy fruit, and clean, fresh structure.

Castello di Cigognola

P.ZZA CASTELLO, 1
27040 CIGOGNOLA [PV]
TEL. 0385284828
www.castellodicigognola.com

CELLAR SALES
PRE-BOOKED VISITS
ANNUAL PRODUCTION 75,000 bottles
HECTARES UNDER VINE 30.00

Castello di Cigognola, founded in 1212 in a strategic position overlooking the plain and the access to the Scuropasso valley, is now owned by Gianmarco and Letizia Moratti. It is not just a producer of fine wines, but also a research centre associated with Milan University, whose projects include the experimental vinification of old local grape varieties. Barbera and pinot nero are the main cultivars used. The latter, fermented off the skins, yields Brut 'More 2011, which took a Tre Bicchieri award for the second year running, with its citrussy, floral nose, and full, creamy palate with a fine bead and gutsy vigour. La Maga 2012 is a compact Barbera, with notes of liquorice and dark berries, the big sister of the more fragrant, easy-drinking Barbera Dodicidodici 2013. The intriguing La Bianca 2014 is a very floral wine made by fermenting barbera grapes off the skins, while 'More Rosé 2012 is delicate with pleasant fruit.

○ Franciacorta Dosage Zero Monogram '11	♈♈♈ 5
○ Franciacorta Monogram Brut '07	♈♈ 5
○ Franciacorta Brut Blanc de Blancs Monogram	♈♈ 5
○ Franciacorta Satèn Cuvée Monogram	♈♈ 5
⊙ Franciacorta Rosé Cuvée Monogram	♈ 5
○ Franciacorta Brut Monogram '02	♈♈ 7
○ Franciacorta Brut Monogram '07	♈♈ 5
○ Franciacorta Brut Monogram Cuvée Giunone '07	♈♈ 6
○ Franciacorta Dosage Zéro '09	♈♈ 5

○ Brut 'More '11	♈♈♈ 4*
● OP Barbera La Maga '12	♈♈ 4
○ La Bianca '14	♈♈ 3
● OP Barbera Dodicidodici '13	♈♈ 3
⊙ Brut 'More Rosé '12	♈ 4
○ Brut 'More '10	♈♈♈ 4*
● OP Barbera Castello di Cigognola '07	♈♈♈ 6
● OP Barbera Castello di Cigognola '06	♈♈♈ 6
● OP Barbera Dodicidodici '11	♈♈♈ 3*
● OP Barbera Poggio Della Maga '05	♈♈♈ 7
○ OP Pinot Nero Brut 'More '08	♈♈♈ 4*
⊙ Brut 'More Rosé '11	♈♈ 4
⊙ Brut 'More Rosé '10	♈♈ 4
● OP Barbera Dodicidodici '12	♈♈ 3
● OP Barbera La Maga '11	♈♈ 4
○ OP Pinot Nero Brut 'More '09	♈♈ 4

★Cavalleri

VIA PROVINCIALE, 96
25030 ERBUSCO [BS]
TEL. 0307760217
www.cavalleri.it

CELLAR SALES
PRE-BOOKED VISITS
ANNUAL PRODUCTION 250,000 bottles
HECTARES UNDER VINE 45.00
VITICULTURE METHOD Certified Organic

The Cavalleri family of Erbusco own one of
Franciacorta's oldest estates. Indeed, they
were mentioned as landowners as early as
1450, although it was "only" in 1968 that
Gian Paolo and his son Giovanni started
producing wine and Franciacortas. Today
the estate is run by Giovanni's daughters
Maria and Giulia, and grandchildren
Francesco and Diletta, flanked by a
competent staff. It vaunts an impressive 45
hectares of handsome vineyards on the
best-aspected sites in Erbusco. Two of the
estate's wines reached our finals this year.
Pas Dosé 2010 is a Blanc de Blancs aged
on the skins for 44 months, with a bright
straw green, impressive fruit and mineral
notes, and a satisfying, zesty palate. Pas
Dosé Riserva Au Contraire 2008, a cuvée
with 20% Pinot Nero, is rich and complex,
with a beautiful coppery straw colour and a
spicy finish of dried fruit.

○ Franciacorta Pas Dosé '10	♟♟ 6
○ Franciacorta Pas Dosé Au Contraire Ris. '08	♟♟ 8
○ Curtefranca Bianco V. Rampaneto '13	♟♟ 5
● Curtefranca Rosso '12	♟♟ 4
○ Franciacorta Brut Blanc de Blancs	♟♟ 5
○ Franciacorta Collezione Grandi Cru '09	♟♟ 7
○ Franciacorta Satèn	♟♟ 5
○ Franciacorta Brut Collezione '05	♟♟♟ 6
○ Franciacorta Brut Collezione Esclusiva Giovanni Cavalleri '05	♟♟♟ 8
○ Franciacorta Brut Collezione Esclusiva Giovanni Cavalleri '04	♟♟♟ 7
○ Franciacorta Collezione Grandi Cru '08	♟♟♟ 6
○ Franciacorta Pas Dosé '07	♟♟♟ 5
○ Franciacorta Pas Dosé Au Contraire '01	♟♟♟ 7
○ Franciacorta Pas Dosé R. D. '06	♟♟♟ 6

Battista Cola

VIA INDIPENDENZA, 3
25030 ADRO [BS]
TEL. 0307356195
www.colabattista.it

CELLAR SALES
PRE-BOOKED VISITS
ANNUAL PRODUCTION 70,000 bottles
HECTARES UNDER VINE 10.00
SUSTAINABLE WINERY

The Colas are an old farming family, but
their estate was founded in 1985, when
Battista started to make wine and
Franciacortas from his little vineyard on
Monte Alto, in Adro. Over the years,
production has risen, particularly with the
arrival of his son Stefano, who runs the
estate today. The vineyards now cover an
area of ten hectares, and annual
production is around 70,000 bottles, but
the wines and Franciacortas still have the
authentic character of "grower" production,
where work in the vineyard and cellar is
prevalently manual and artisanal, and as
environmentally sustainable as ever. Once
again this year Stefano Cola presented a
sound range of Franciacortas. Our
favourite was the Brut 2010, which is a
lovely bright straw yellow hue and has a
complex nose of ripe white-fleshed fruit,
with hints of wholemeal, aromatic herbs,
and citron peel. On the palate it is full,
juicy and satisfying, with creamy
effervescence and an intriguing soft, lively
finish. The Extra Brut is good too, with a
more spirited, mineral style.

○ Franciacorta Brut '10	♟♟ 5
○ Franciacorta Brut	♟♟ 4
○ Franciacorta Extra Brut	♟♟ 4
○ Franciacorta Non Dosato '10	♟♟ 5
⊙ Franciacorta Rosé Brut Athena	♟♟ 5
○ Franciacorta Satèn '10	♟♟ 5
○ Franciacorta Brut '07	♟♟ 5
○ Franciacorta Brut Ris. '07	♟♟ 5
○ Franciacorta Dosage Zéro Etichetta Storica '06	♟♟ 5
○ Franciacorta Dosage Zéro Etichetta Storica '05	♟♟ 4
○ Franciacorta Non Dosato '09	♟♟ 5
○ Franciacorta Non Dosato '07	♟♟ 5
○ Franciacorta Satèn '09	♟♟ 5
○ Franciacorta Satèn '08	♟♟ 5
○ Franciacorta Satèn '07	♟♟ 5

Contadi Castaldi

LOC. FORNACE BIASCA
VIA COLZANO, 32
25030 ADRO [BS]
TEL. 0307450126
www.contadicastaldi.it

CELLAR SALES
PRE-BOOKED VISITS
ANNUAL PRODUCTION 900,000 bottles
HECTARES UNDER VINE 130.00
SUSTAINABLE WINERY

Contadi Castaldi in Adro belongs to the Terra Moretti group, which also owns the Bellavista estate, but operates independently and has its own vineyards. The cellar is housed in Adro's ancient brick kilns and receives the fruit from an impressive array of estate-owned, leased and growers' vineyards, allowing an annual production approaching a million high-quality bottles. It is enthusiastically headed by talented oenologist Gian Luca Uccelli, who honed his craft during years spent at the parent company. Two of the estate's wines reached our finals this year. The first is Franciacorta Zero Pinonero 2009, a Blanc de Noirs that won us over with its notes of tobacco and medicinal and aromatic herbs, firm structure, full body, and balanced palate. Zero 2011 has a smoky, toasty nose, accompanied by a full-bodied palate with plenty of fruit and zestiness, and notes of coffee and spice on the finish. The elegant Brut is fresh and citrussy.

○ Franciacorta Zero '11	♟♟ 5
○ Franciacorta Zero Pinònero Ris. '09	♟♟ 6
○ Curtefranca Bianco '14	♟♟ 3
○ Franciacorta Brut	♟♟ 4
⊙ Franciacorta Rosé	♟♟ 5
○ Franciacorta Satèn '10	♟♟ 5
○ Franciacorta Soul Satèn '08	♟♟ 6
● Pinodisé	♟♟ 5
○ Franciacorta Satèn Soul '05	♟♟♟ 6
○ Franciacorta Soul Satèn '06	♟♟♟ 6
○ Franciacorta Zero '09	♟♟♟ 5
○ Franciacorta Soul Satèn '07	♟♟ 6
○ Franciacorta Soul Satèn '01	♟♟ 6
○ Franciacorta Zero '10	♟♟ 5
○ Franciacorta Zero '07	♟♟ 5
○ Franciacorta Zero '06	♟♟ 5

Conte Vistarino

FRAZ. SCORZOLETTA, 82/84
27040 PIETRA DE' GIORGI [PV]
TEL. 038585117
www.contevistarino.it

CELLAR SALES
PRE-BOOKED VISITS
ANNUAL PRODUCTION 400,000 bottles
HECTARES UNDER VINE 200.00

In the second half of the 19th century, Conte Vistarino and Conte Gancia decided to plant French pinot nero clones, having pinpointed the Scuropasso valley as the ideal terroir for the production of Metodo Classico sparklers. And indeed, the great Piedmontese wineries did just this. Today with young Ottavia at the helm, Conte Vistarino, with its large family estate (800 hectares, of which 200 under vine and the rest mainly woodland) is determined to make a name for itself once and for all. The 2009 vintage of Brut 1865 reached our final but, unlike last year, missed our top accolade by a hair's breadth, showing a fine bead, the coppery highlights typical of pinot nero, hints of ripe fruit and crusty bread, verve, and almost earthy mineral notes. It is a very territorial sparkler, in the best possible sense. Pinot Nero Pernice 2012 also performed well, showing spicy earthy with fragrant wild berries; it too is earthy and promises well. The trio of Pinot Neros is completed by the well-crafted, Cruasé, which also offers citrus notes.

○ OP Pinot Nero Brut 1865 '09	♟♟ 5
● OP Pinot Nero Pernice '12	♟♟ 5
⊙ OP Cruasé Saignée della Rocca	♟♟ 5
● OP Sangue di Giuda Costiolo '14	♟♟ 2*
○ Brut Cl. Cépage	♟ 4
○ OP Pinot Nero Brut Conti Vistarino 1865 '08	♟♟♟ 4*
● OP Pinot Nero Pernice '06	♟♟♟ 4*
○ OP Pinot Nero Brut Conte Vistarino 1865 '06	♟♟ 4
● OP Pinot Nero Pernice '11	♟♟ 5
● OP Pinot Nero Pernice '10	♟♟ 5
○ OP Riesling 7 Giugno '12	♟♟ 3

Conti Ducco

LOC. CAMIGNONE
VIA DEGLI EROI, 70
25040 PASSIRANO [BS]
TEL. 0306850566
www.contiducco.it

PRE-BOOKED VISITS
ANNUAL PRODUCTION 720,000 bottles
HECTARES UNDER VINE 90.00

Catturich Ducco is one of the leading
names in the history of Franciacorta. In
1967 Piero Catturich founded the winery
that is now run by his son Giorgio. It covers
an area of 125 hectares, with 90 under
vine, in Monticelli Brusati and Camignone
di Passirano, divided into crus that are
fermented separately. Today the old hamlet
of Camignone, where wine has been made
since Roman times, is home to Conti
Catturich Ducco's well-equipped
modern cellars. The estate's range is
extremely interesting. Extra Brut Reserve
Collection 2005 is a thoroughbred
Franciacorta that made it into our finals. It
is evolved and complex, but surprisingly
dynamic and well orchestrated,
characterized by a creamy mousse,
pervasive fruit, and solid, balanced
structure, with a lingering finish of
aromatic herbs. Pas Dosé 2008 is also
excellent, with carefully calibrated oak.

○ Franciacorta Extra Brut Reserve Collection Ris. '05	♥♥ 5
○ Franciacorta Brut '10	♥♥ 5
○ Franciacorta Pas Dosé '08	♥♥ 4
○ Franciacorta Brut Ouverture	♥ 5
⊙ Franciacorta Rosé de Noirs	♥ 4
○ Franciacorta Satèn	♥ 5
○ Franciacorta Brut '10	♥♥ 5
○ Franciacorta Pas Dosé '08	♥♥ 4

La Costa

FRAZ. COSTA
VIA CURONE, 15
23888 PEREGO [LC]
TEL. 0395312218
www.la-costa.it

CELLAR SALES
PRE-BOOKED VISITS
ACCOMMODATION AND RESTAURANT SERVICE
ANNUAL PRODUCTION 40,000 bottles
HECTARES UNDER VINE 12.00
VITICULTURE METHOD Certified Organic

The Crippa family have managed to drive
Brianza viticulture towards new qualitative
horizons. Their winery is situated in the
Montevecchia and Val Curone Regional
Park, not far from Lake Como. They use
only the grapes from their organically
farmed 12-hectare estate, which focuses in
particular on riesling renano, merlot and
pinot nero. Claudia Crippa confirms her
ability to interpret the characteristics of the
terroir and translate them into subtle,
nuanced wines that echo the mineral-rich
limestone soil. Pinot Nero San Giobbe 2013
has surprisingly big personality, showing
elegant and complex, with aromas that
range from peppery and earthy to currants
and blueberries. Its nicely calibrated acidity
and tannins are balanced by fleshy fruit
and completed by very classy finale.
Solesta 2013 has a nose of citrus fruit and
spring flowers, with mineral notes
reminiscent of petrol, typical of Riesling. It
is elegant and complex, very taut, and
refreshingly acidic.

● San Giobbe '13	♥♥ 4
● Solesta '13	♥♥ 4
● Seriz '12	♥♥ 3
○ Brigante Bianco '14	♥ 3
● Brigante Rosso '13	♥ 3
● San Giobbe '12	♥♥ 4
● San Giobbe '11	♥♥ 4
● San Giobbe '10	♥♥ 4
● Seriz '11	♥♥ 3
● Seriz '10	♥♥ 3
● Seriz '09	♥♥ 3
○ Solesta '12	♥♥ 3*
○ Solesta '11	♥♥ 3*
○ Solesta '10	♥♥ 3*

Costaripa

VIA COSTA, 1A
25080 MONIGA DEL GARDA [BS]
TEL. 0365502010
www.costaripa.it

CELLAR SALES
PRE-BOOKED VISITS
ANNUAL PRODUCTION 400,000 bottles
HECTARES UNDER VINE 40.00

Mattia Vezzola is one of the biggest names in the Italian sparkling wine world. He not only works for a prestigious Franciacorta estate, but also runs the family winery, Costaripa, which vaunts 40 hectares of fine vineyards in the Valtenesi production zone, on the southern shores of Lake Garda. His mission is to produce cellarable rosés, or more precisely Chiaretto, and to revive the area's native grape variety, groppello. The sparklers of the new Mattia Vezzola range were the exciting new discovery in this year's tastings. The elegance and great stylistic purity of the two 2010 vintages, Brut and Rosé, and their perfect balance and fine bead are absolutely seductive. The non-vintage Cremant and Rosé versions are almost as alluring, and Rosé Rosamara 2014 is a benchmark for the entire designation.

○ Lugana Pievecroce '14	♟♟ 2*
○ Mattia Vezzola Brut '10	♟♟ 5
○ Mattia Vezzola Cremant	♟♟ 5
⊙ Mattia Vezzola Rosé '10	♟♟ 5
⊙ Mattia Vezzola Rosé	♟♟ 5
⊙ Valtenesi Chiaretto Rosamara '14	♟♟ 2*
● Valtènesi Maim '11	♟♟ 3
○ Costaripa Brut '08	♟ 5
○ Costaripa Brut Ris. '04	♟ 4
⊙ Garda Cl. Chiaretto Molmenti '11	♟ 4
● Garda Cl. Groppello Maim '09	♟ 4
○ Lugana Pievecroce '12	♟ 2*
⊙ Valtenesi Chiaretto Rosamara '13	♟ 2*
● Valtènesi Le Castelline '12	♟ 3

Derbusco Cives

VIA PROVINCIALE, 83
25030 ERBUSCO [BS]
TEL. 0307731164
www.derbuscocives.com

CELLAR SALES
PRE-BOOKED VISITS
RESTAURANT SERVICE
ANNUAL PRODUCTION 60,000 bottles
HECTARES UNDER VINE 12.00

Derbusco Cives is a group of five friends – all proud Erbusco citizens – headed by Giuseppe Vezzoli, who in 2004 decided to found a new winery, naming it simply "citizens of Erbusco", to underscore the uniqueness of its terroir. Ten years later, the winery has earned itself an impressive reputation and the performance of its Franciacortas, made using innovative techniques, make it one of the most interesting names in the production zone. The grapes for Derbusco's cuvées come from the estate's 12 hectares of vineyards, tended using methods with low environmental impact. Doppio Erre Dì (delayed disgorgement-recently disgorged) is a Brut from chardonnay grapes that undergoes long ageing on the lees and is disgorged immediately before delivery to the client. Once again this year it was our favourite of the estate's wines. It made it into our finals with its concentrated, refreshing, citrus nose, and its dense, creamy palate with crisp freshness and notes of liquorice and iodine on the finish.

○ Franciacorta Brut '09	♟♟ 6
○ Franciacorta Brut Doppio Erre Di	♟♟ 5
○ Franciacorta Extra Brut '10	♟♟ 8
⊙ Franciacorta Rosé '10	♟ 6
○ Franciacorta Brut '08	♟ 6
○ Franciacorta Brut '07	♟ 6
○ Franciacorta Brut '05	♟ 6
○ Franciacorta Brut Doppio Erre Di '05	♟ 5
○ Franciacorta Extra Brut '09	♟ 7
○ Franciacorta Extra Brut '08	♟ 7
○ Franciacorta Extra Brut '07	♟ 6
○ Franciacorta Extra Brut '06	♟ 7
⊙ Franciacorta Extra Brut Rosé '09	♟ 6

Dirupi

LOC. MADONNA DI CAMPAGNA
VIA GRUMELLO, 1
23020 MONTAGNA IN VALTELLINA [SO]
TEL. 3472909779
www.dirupi.com

CELLAR SALES
PRE-BOOKED VISITS
ANNUAL PRODUCTION 15,000 bottles
HECTARES UNDER VINE 4.50

Davide Fasolini and Pierpaolo di Franco, known to everyone as "Birba" and "Faso", are the Blues Brothers of Valtellina wine: two carefree young men with boundless energy and talent. In the space of just a few years they have renovated the old vineyards on the steep mountainsides, while also developing a sales network. Their wines are brilliant both in hue and profile, with uncommon fragrance, tautness, and complexity. The wines embody the essence of the terroir, interpreted in a precise, rhythmic style. The Riserva 2012 is particularly striking, offering a sophisticated nose of raspberries and wild strawberries, with hints of tobacco and liquorice. On the palate it is exceptionally fine, crisp and juicy, with a very long finish. The vibrant Dirupi 2013 is well defined and layered, with a fine nose of red berries and aromatic herbs, and a fresh, even gutsy palate, whose fine-grained tannins are nicely balanced by fruit and acidity.

F.lli Berlucchi

FRAZ. BORGONATO
VIA BROLETTO, 2
25040 CORTE FRANCA [BS]
TEL. 030984451
www.fratelliberlucchi.it

CELLAR SALES
PRE-BOOKED VISITS
ANNUAL PRODUCTION 400,000 bottles
HECTARES UNDER VINE 70.00

The Berlucchis are one of Franciacorta's oldest families. Today the siblings' winery, headed by the dynamic Pia Donata and her daughter Tilli Rizzo, uses only grapes from its 70-hectare estate to create an excellent range of cuvées and wines. The cellars are part of the complex of the family's 16th-century villa, Casa delle Colonne, in Borgonato, and their range is divided into two product lines: Casa delle Colonne and Freccia Nera. The basic Brut 25 is the only non-vintage wine. This year the elegant, spirited Freccianera Nature 2010 made it into our finals with its firm structure and long, complex finish of vanilla, white-fleshed fruit, and citron. Riserva Casa delle Colonne Zero 2008 vaunts deep mineral notes and alluring tones of chamomile and medicinal herbs, while Freccianera Rosé 2011 is among the finest of the designation.

● Valtellina Sup. Dirupi Ris. '12	♔♔♔	6
● Valtellina Sup. Dirupi '13	♔♔	4
● Rosso di Valtellina Olè '14	♔♔	3
● Valtellina Sup. Dirupi Ris. '11	♕♕♕	6
● Valtellina Sup. Dirupi Ris. '09	♕♕♕	6
● Sforzato di Valtellina Vino Sbagliato '12	♕♕	6
● Valtellina Sup. Dirupi '12	♕♕	4
● Valtellina Sup. Dirupi '11	♕♕	4
● Valtellina Sup. Dirupi '10	♕♕	4
● Valtellina Sup. Dirupi '09	♕♕	4
● Valtellina Sup. Dirupi Ris. '10	♕♕	6
● Valtellina Sup. Ris. '07	♕♕	5

○ Franciacorta Nature Freccianera '10	♔♔	7
○ Curtefranca Bianco Dossi delle Querce '13	♔♔	3
○ Franciacorta Brut Freccianera '10	♔♔	6
○ Franciacorta Casa delle Colonne Brut Ris. '08	♔♔	7
○ Franciacorta Casa delle Colonne Zero Ris. '08	♔♔	8
⊙ Franciacorta Freccianera Rosa '11	♔♔	6
○ Franciacorta Satèn Freccianera '11	♔♔	7
○ Curtefranca Bianco Ca' Brusade '14	♔	3
○ Franciacorta Brut 25	♔	4
○ Franciacorta Brut '06	♕♕	4*
○ Franciacorta Casa delle Colonne Zero Ris. '07	♕♕	8
○ Franciacorta Casa delle Colonne Zero Ris. '06	♕♕	7
○ Franciacorta Pas Dosé '07	♕♕	5

Sandro Fay

LOC. SAN GIACOMO DI TEGLIO
VIA PILA CASELLI, 1
23030 TEGLIO [SO]
TEL. 0342786071
elefay@tin.it

CELLAR SALES
PRE-BOOKED VISITS
ANNUAL PRODUCTION 38,000 bottles
HECTARES UNDER VINE 13.00

Valgella is one of Valtellina's most
interesting subzones, covering an area of
137 hectares around the municipality of
Teglio. Here, in 1973, Sandro Fay decided
to boost the family winery by founding the
estate now capably run by his son Marco.
His aim was three-fold: to maximize the
potential of the old vineyards, to preserve
the terroir with sustainable viticulture, and
to shift production to higher altitudes to
obtain exceptionally fresh, fragrant wines.
They turned out to be brilliant, far-sighted
choices. Cà Moréi 2012 is simply delicious
and skillfully crafted with a view to the
future. It is concentrated and very elegant,
offering a nose of red berries and flowers,
with hints of black pepper, tobacco, and
salt. The very fresh, powerful palate has
rigid tannins and a long, velvety finish.
Sforzato Ronco del Picchio 2011 is
concentrated, with ripe fruit and dried
flowers on the nose, accompanied by hints
of tobacco and prominent liquorice. The
elegant palate is very well orchestrated,
with exceptionally fine-grained, silky
tannins, and a long, austere finish.

★Ferghettina

VIA SALINE, 11
25030 ADRO [BS]
TEL. 0307451212
www.ferghettina.it

CELLAR SALES
PRE-BOOKED VISITS
ANNUAL PRODUCTION 400,000 bottles
HECTARES UNDER VINE 160.00
SUSTAINABLE WINERY

Just over 20 years ago Roberto Gatti rented
a vineyard and premises equipped as a
cellar, commencing his adventure as a
producer. Today Ferghettina is one of the
leading wineries in the area, also due to the
efforts of Roberto's wife Andreina and their
children, Laura and Matteo, now both
oenology graduates. The estate boasts 160
hectares of vineyards and a handsome,
well-equipped cellar, enabling an annual
production of over 400,000 bottles. This
year our top accolade went to the Extra
Brut 2009 as one of the finest expressions
of the production zone. A Chardonnay with
20% Pinot Nero, it was aged for six long
years on the lees before disgorgement. On
the nose it is rich and elegant, with tones of
white-fleshed fruit and tropical hints
followed by aromatic herbs. The
concentrated, dense palate is assertive,
elegant and very easy drinking, with notes
of candied peel on the attractive finish.

● Valtellina Sforzato Ronco del Picchio '11	♟♟ 6
● Valtellina Sup. Valgella Cà Moréi '12	♟♟ 5
● La Faya '12	♟♟ 5
● Valtellina Sup. Costa Bassa '12	♟♟ 4
● Valtellina Sup. Sassella Il Glicine '12	♟♟ 4
● Valtellina Sup. Valgella Carterìa '12	♟♟ 5
● Valtellina Sforzato Ronco del Picchio '10	♟♟♟ 6
● Valtellina Sforzato Ronco del Picchio '09	♟♟♟ 6
● Valtellina Sforzato Ronco del Picchio '02	♟♟♟ 6
● La Faya '11	♟♟ 4
● La Faya '10	♟♟ 4
● Valtellina Sup. Costa Bassa '11	♟♟ 3
● Valtellina Sup. Sassella Il Glicine '11	♟♟ 4
● Valtellina Sup. Sassella Il Glicine '10	♟♟ 4
● Valtellina Sup. Valgella Cà Moréi '11	♟♟ 4
● Valtellina Sup. Valgella Carterìa '11	♟♟ 4

○ Franciacorta Extra Brut '09	♟♟♟ 5
○ Franciacorta Brut Milledì '11	♟♟ 5
○ Curtefranca Bianco '14	♟♟ 2*
○ Franciacorta Brut	♟♟ 4
⊙ Franciacorta Rosé Milledì '11	♟♟ 5
○ Franciacorta Satèn '11	♟♟ 5
● Merlot Baladello '11	♟♟ 5
○ Franciacorta Extra Brut '06	♟♟♟ 5
○ Franciacorta Extra Brut '05	♟♟♟ 5
○ Franciacorta Extra Brut '04	♟♟♟ 5
○ Franciacorta Extra Brut '02	♟♟♟ 5
○ Franciacorta Extra Brut '98	♟♟♟ 5
○ Franciacorta Pas Dosé 33 Ris. '07	♟♟♟ 5
○ Franciacorta Pas Dosé 33 Ris. '06	♟♟♟ 6
○ Franciacorta Satèn '04	♟♟♟ 5
○ Franciacorta Satèn '99	♟♟♟ 5

Fiamberti

VIA CHIESA, 17
27044 CANNETO PAVESE [PV]
TEL. 038588019
www.fiambertivini.it

CELLAR SALES
PRE-BOOKED VISITS
ANNUAL PRODUCTION 140,000 bottles
HECTARES UNDER VINE 18.00

Each year, step after step, we have the pleasure of seeing that Ambrogio Fiamberti and his son Giulio have not lost sight of their goal to strive to improve the overall quality of their production. The estate's tradition and its fine vineyards allow it to make wines of all types, and it offers the classic wide range of labels typical of Oltrepò producers. However, we feel it is now legitimate to expect the emergence of a few pinnacles of genuine excellence from this historic winery, which still continue to elude it. The Brut, for example, hinges on oxidized tones, with notes of tropical fruit. It is fairly evolved and complex, but somewhat lacking in verve and, above all, in elegance. Buttafuoco Storico Vigna Sacca del Prete 2009 is a wine of substance and depth, with solid stuffing supported by good acidity, and Sangue di Giuda Lella 2014 is well made, considering the difficult vintage. The Cruasé is very fruity with an exceptionally deep colour.

● OP Buttafuoco Storico V. Sacca del Prete '09	♟♟ 4
○ OP Pinot Nero Brut Fiamberti	♟♟ 4
● OP Sangue di Giuda Lella '14	♟♟ 3
⊙ OP Cruasé	♟ 4
● OP Bonarda Vivace La Briccona '14	♟ 2
● OP Bonarda Vivace Bricco della Sacca '13	♟♟ 2*
○ OP Riesling Italico V. Croce Monteveneroso '13	♟♟ 2*
● OP Sangue di Giuda V. Costa Paradiso '13	♟♟ 2*

Le Fracce

FRAZ. MAIRANO
VIA CASTEL DEL LUPO, 5
27045 CASTEGGIO [PV]
TEL. 038382526
www.lefracce.com

CELLAR SALES
PRE-BOOKED VISITS
ANNUAL PRODUCTION 180,000 bottles
HECTARES UNDER VINE 40.00

This handsome estate, long owned by the Fondazione Bussolera-Branca, is worth a visit not only for its wine, but also for its beautiful Italian gardens and vintage car and carriage collections. It is splendidly situated on the hillsides of Mairano, above Casteggio, where the white soils ideal for riesling, pinot grigio and pinot nero are flanked by clay well suited to the local red grape varieties. Roberto Gerbino, the estate's oenologist has always sought elegance rather than power in his wines. After having offered the excellent long Charmat method Cuvée Bussolera for many years, Le Fracce presented a Metodo Classico for the first time in its history this year. It is the lovely Bussolera Grand Rosé, a non-vintage rosé Pinot Nero, which seduced us with its pale coppery hue, sound fruit, zestiness, freshness, and drinkability. We also appreciated La Rubiosa and Landò, considering the difficult vintage for Bonarda and Riesling.

⊙ Bussolera Grand Rosè Brut	♟♟ 5
● OP Bonarda Vivace La Rubiosa '14	♟♟ 3
○ OP Riesling Landò '14	♟♟ 3
○ OP Pinot Grigio Levriere '14	♟ 3
● OP Pinot Nero '11	♟ 5
● Garboso '11	♟♟ 3
● OP Bohemi '07	♟♟ 6
● OP Bonarda Vivace La Rubiosa '13	♟♟ 3
● OP Bonarda Vivace La Rubiosa '12	♟♟ 3
○ OP Cirgà '06	♟♟ 3
○ OP Pinot Grigio Levriere '12	♟♟ 3
○ OP Riesling Landò '13	♟♟ 3
● OP Rosso Bohemi '08	♟♟ 6
● OP Rosso Bohemi '06	♟♟ 6
● OP Rosso Bohemi '01	♟♟ 5

Frecciarossa

VIA VIGORELLI, 141
27045 CASTEGGIO [PV]
TEL. 0383804465
www.frecciarossa.com

CELLAR SALES
PRE-BOOKED VISITS
ANNUAL PRODUCTION 120,000 bottles
HECTARES UNDER VINE 34.00

This handsome estate remains one of
Oltrepò's finest producers, offering new
wines crafted with the guidance of
oenologist Gianluca Scaglione aided by
newcomer Cristiano Garella. Pinot nero and
riesling are still the main grape varieties,
while the new versions of Metodo Classico
appear more convincing than the first
releases. Once again, the estate's star is
Pinot Nero Giorgio Odero, which wins its
sixth Tre Bicchieri. It has now found its own
dimension and unmistakable style, showing
well orchestrated, deep and as elegant as
ever, with an enviable balance of wild
berries, aromatic herbs, coffee and
tertiary notes. The full, flavoursome Riesling
Gli Orti 2013 is also very good, showing
balsamic, fresh, and very long. Carillo 2013
is a new Pinot Nero that is young and spicy
with plenty of personality. The two Bruts, in
very different styles, are both good,
although we have a slight preference for
the zesty, mineral I Moschettieri Pas Dosé,
from pinot nero grapes, over the softer
Frecciarossa, a cuvée of Pinot Nero,
Chardonnay and Riesling.

● OP Pinot Nero Giorgio Odero '12	♛♛♛ 5	
○ OP Riesling Gli Orti '13	♛♛ 2*	
○ OP Brut M. Cl. Frecciarossa '09	♛♛ 6	
● OP Pinot Nero Carillo '13	♛♛ 3	
○ Pas Dosé I Moschettieri '11	♛♛ 4	
○ OP Pinot Nero in bianco Sillery '14	♛ 2	
● Uva Rara '14	♛ 2	
● OP Pinot Nero Giorgio Odero '11	♛♛♛ 5	
● OP Pinot Nero Giorgio Odero '10	♛♛♛ 5	
● OP Pinot Nero Giorgio Odero '08	♛♛♛ 5	
● OP Pinot Nero Giorgio Odero '07	♛♛♛ 5	
● OP Bonarda Vivace Dardo '13	♛♛ 2*	
● OP Bonarda Vivace Dardo '12	♛♛ 2*	
○ OP Riesling Gli Orti '11	♛♛ 2*	
○ OP Riesling Renano Gli Orti '12	♛♛ 2*	
● Uva Rara '13	♛♛ 2*	

Enrico Gatti

VIA METELLI, 9
25030 ERBUSCO [BS]
TEL. 0307267999
www.enricogatti.it

CELLAR SALES
PRE-BOOKED VISITS
ANNUAL PRODUCTION 120,000 bottles
HECTARES UNDER VINE 17.00

This year the winery founded by Enrico
Gatti celebrated its 40th anniversary.
Enrico's children Lorenzo and Paola, along
with his son-in-law Enzo Balzarini, have
turned it into a little gem, a veritable
boutique winery that uses only the grapes
from its 17-hectare estate. Its
Franciacortas are held in high esteem and
display their own personal style that
reflects the characteristics of the Erbusco
terroir, focusing on structure, opulent fruit,
acid backbone and mineral notes. However,
this in no way detracts from their elegance
and appeal. Nature is the wine that
embodies all the characteristics of
Franciacorta according to Gatti. Indeed, it
vaunts a handsome bright straw yellow
colour, a fine bead, and creamy mousse.
The nose has top notes of white peaches
and hawthorn, fading into citrussy tones,
while the palate is solid and linear,
sometimes austere, before unfolding fresh
and fruity, with notes of tropical fruit, mint
and liquorice. We gave it a Tre Bicchieri.

○ Franciacorta Nature	♛♛♛ 5	
○ Franciacorta Brut	♛♛ 4	
○ Franciacorta Brut Millesimo '09	♛♛ 6	
⊙ Franciacorta Rosé	♛♛ 5	
○ Franciacorta Satèn '11	♛♛ 5	
○ Franciacorta Brut '05	♛♛♛ 6	
○ Franciacorta Nature '07	♛♛♛ 5	
○ Franciacorta Satèn '05	♛♛♛ 5	
○ Franciacorta Satèn '03	♛♛♛ 5	
○ Franciacorta Satèn '02	♛♛♛ 4	
○ Franciacorta Satèn '01	♛♛♛ 4	
○ Franciacorta Satèn '00	♛♛♛ 5	
○ Franciacorta Brut Millesimo '08	♛♛ 6	
○ Franciacorta Satèn '04	♛♛ 5	

I Gessi - Fabbio Defilippi

FRAZ. FOSSA, 8
27050 OLIVA GESSI [PV]
TEL. 0383896606
www.cantineigessi.it

CELLAR SALES
PRE-BOOKED VISITS
ACCOMMODATION
ANNUAL PRODUCTION 160,000 bottles
HECTARES UNDER VINE 41.00

We continue to confide in Fabbio Defilippi's little estate: a family-run organic winery with adjoining guest farm, around 40 hectares of vineyards on mainly white soil, and the guidance of an expert oenologist like his brother Emilio. A few interesting wines always emerge at our blind tastings, such as the pleasant, well-made Brut Maria Cristina, which for the third year running showed fragrant and well-orchestrated, with notes of tropical and citrus fruit, a fine bead, good backbone and stuffing, and an attractively racy finish. The Cruasé is also well made, with a nose of wild berries, an attractive pale coppery onionskin hue, and good fruit and backbone. Barbera 2013 is good, with evolved but not tired notes, super-ripe fruit, nice flesh, and a fine vein of acidity. The Riesling 2014 is not quite as good as last year, with a fragrant nose of medicinal herbs and bay leaf, but a bit less body.

● OP Barbera '13	♟♟ 2*
⊙ OP Cruasé Maria Cristina	♟♟ 3
○ OP Pinot Nero Brut M. Cl. Maria Cristina	♟♟ 3
○ OP Pinot Grigio Crocetta '14	♟ 2
○ OP Riesling '14	♟ 1*
○ OP Pinot Nero Brut M. Cl. Maria Cristina '10	♟♟ 3
○ OP Riesling '13	♟♟ 1*
○ OP Riesling '12	♟♟ 1*
○ OP Riesling I Gessi '11	♟♟ 1*

F.lli Giorgi

FRAZ. CAMPONOCE, 39A
27044 CANNETO PAVESE [PV]
TEL. 0385262151
www.giorgi-wines.it

CELLAR SALES
PRE-BOOKED VISITS
ANNUAL PRODUCTION 1,600,000 bottles
HECTARES UNDER VINE 30.00

The winery run by Antonio Giorgi and his dynamic son Fabiano has always managed to keep up with the times and reconcile its two different sides: the more commercial one, albeit with consistently high quality, symbolized by Pinot Frizzante, whose production runs to hundreds of thousands of bottles each year, and the top range, made from the finest grapes and produced in limited amounts, focusing chiefly on Metodo Classico. In this sector too, Fabiano does not fail to present new products, the latest being the very pleasant undosed Top Zero, available with labels in six different colours. However, the true flagship remains the 1870, whose 2011 vintage took a Tre Bicchieri for its distinctive familiar mineral notes, zestiness, grip, backbone, harmony and elegance. The Gianfranco Giorgi and the Cruasé are also good, although we'd prefer the latter a little paler. Other noteworthy wines from the wide range are Riesling Il Bandito 2014 and a very good version of Vigalòn, although the Buttafuoco Storico seemed a little under par.

○ OP Pinot Nero Brut 1870 '11	♟♟♟ 5
⊙ OP Cruasé '12	♟♟ 4
○ OP Pinot Nero Brut Gianfranco Giorgi '12	♟♟ 5
● OP Pinot Nero Monteroso '13	♟♟ 3
○ OP Riesling Il Bandito '14	♟♟ 4
● Vigalòn '14	♟♟ 2*
○ Brut Cl. Top Zero	♟ 4
● OP Buttafuoco Storico V. Casa del Corno '11	♟ 3
○ OP Pinot Nero Brut 1870 '10	♟♟♟ 5
○ OP Pinot Nero Brut 1870 '09	♟♟♟ 5
○ OP Pinot Nero Brut 1870 '08	♟♟♟ 5
○ OP Pinot Nero Brut 1870 '07	♟♟♟ 5
○ OP Pinot Nero Brut 1870 '06	♟♟♟ 5

Isimbarda

FRAZ. CASTELLO
CASCINA ISIMBARDA
27046 SANTA GIULETTA [PV]
TEL. 0383899256
www.tenutaisimbarda.it

CELLAR SALES
PRE-BOOKED VISITS
ANNUAL PRODUCTION 130,000 bottles
HECTARES UNDER VINE 40.00

This fine estate is one of the oldest in Oltrepò, for wine production by the Marchesi Isimbardi in the hills of Santa Giulietta is documented as far back as the 17th century. The estate covers an area of almost 40 hectares, with some clay soil, but mainly limestone and marl, which are well suited to white grape varieties and pinot nero. Owned by Luigi Meroni and managed by Daniele Zangelmi, several years ago the estate started flanking its traditional red and white wines (above all Riesling), with the production of sparklers. This year it was Riesling Vigna Martina 2014 that scored highest, despite the difficult vintage. Its primary aromas are the same as ever, with meadow flowers, chamomile, and hints of tropical fruit, and the palate has good breadth, fullness, and balance, awaiting the mineral notes that will appear in time. The two Metodo Classicos are good, although we leaned more to the white, with its nice palate progression, while the nose is the main attraction of the Cruasé. Rosso Monplò 2013 has attractive sound, clean-tasting fruit.

⊙ OP Cruasé	🍷🍷	4
○ OP Pinot Nero Brut	🍷🍷	3
○ OP Riesling Renano V. Martina '14	🍷🍷	2*
● OP Rosso Monplò '13	🍷🍷	3
○ Brut Martinotti Riserva degli Isimbardi	🍷	3
● OP Bonarda Vivace V. delle More '14	🍷	2
● OP Bonarda Vivace V. delle More '13	🍷🍷	2*
● OP Bonarda Vivace V. delle More '12	🍷🍷	2*
● OP Bonarda Vivace V. delle More '11	🍷🍷	2
● OP Pinot Nero V. del Cardinale '11	🍷🍷	4
○ OP Riesling Renano V. Martina '13	🍷🍷	2*
○ OP Riesling Renano V. Martina '12	🍷🍷	2*
○ OP Riesling Renano V. Martina '11	🍷🍷	2*
● OP Rosso Monplò '10	🍷🍷	3
○ Varméi '11	🍷🍷	2*

Lantieri de Paratico

LOC. COLZANO
VIA VIDETTI
25031 CAPRIOLO [BS]
TEL. 030736151
www.lantierideparatico.it

CELLAR SALES
PRE-BOOKED VISITS
ACCOMMODATION AND RESTAURANT SERVICE
ANNUAL PRODUCTION 140,000 bottles
HECTARES UNDER VINE 18.00
VITICULTURE METHOD Certified Organic

The noble Lantieri de Paratico family already made excellent wine in the 16th century, which was popular with the European aristocracy of the day. Today Fabio Lantieri keeps the tradition alive and has created a well-equipped modern cellar in the old family home, where he makes his excellent cuvées from the grapes of his 18 hectares of handsome organic vineyards. This year we really liked Riserva Origines 2009, a non-dosed Franciacorta cuvée of Chardonnay and 25% Pinot Nero, aged for five long years on the lees. It has a very fine bead and a complex, alluring nose of aromatic herbs with Mediterranean hints. On the palate it is complex, full and creamy, with a long citrussy finish.

○ Franciacorta Extra Brut Origines Ris. '09	🍷🍷	7
○ Franciacorta Brut	🍷🍷	4
○ Franciacorta Brut Arcadia '11	🍷🍷	5
⊙ Franciacorta Brut Rosé	🍷🍷	5
○ Franciacorta Extra Brut	🍷🍷	4
● Curtefranca Rosso Colzano '12	🍷	4
○ Franciacorta Satèn	🍷	5
○ Franciacorta Brut Arcadia '10	🍷🍷	5
○ Franciacorta Brut Arcadia '09	🍷🍷	5
○ Franciacorta Brut Arcadia '08	🍷🍷	5
○ Franciacorta Brut Arcadia '07	🍷🍷	5
○ Franciacorta Brut Arcadia '05	🍷🍷	5
○ Franciacorta Brut Arcadia '04	🍷🍷	5
○ Franciacorta Brut Arcadia '02	🍷🍷	5
○ Franciacorta Brut Arcadia '01	🍷🍷	5

Majolini

LOC. VALLE
VIA MANZONI, 3
25050 OME [BS]
TEL. 0306527378
www.majolini.it

CELLAR SALES
PRE-BOOKED VISITS
ANNUAL PRODUCTION 150,000 bottles
HECTARES UNDER VINE 24.00
SUSTAINABLE WINERY

Based in Ome, on the eastern side of
Franciacorta, the Majolini are a family of
industrialists with agricultural origins
reaching back to the 15th century. In 1981
they founded this magnificent estate
specializing in Franciacorta production,
entrusting it to the management of Ezio.
Today his work is continued by the young
and highly motivated Simone. The estate
vaunts 24 hectares of well-aspected partly
terraced vineyards in the Ome district,
which are tended with organic methods.
The Frenchman oenologist Jean-Pierre
Valade is on hand. Majolini's Satèn is
undoubtedly among the best tasted this
year. It is made from a selection of the
estate's finest chardonnay grapes, and is
aged partly in small casks before bottle
fermentation for at least three years. The
resulting wine is a lovely bright straw
yellow with green highlights, a tiny bead,
and an exuberant nose brimming with
white-fleshed fruit, especially peaches,
accompanied by vanilla and aromatic
herbs; on the palate it is supple, velvety
and satisfying.

○ Franciacorta Satèn '10	♈♈	5
○ Franciacorta Brut	♈♈	5
○ Franciacorta Brut Blanc de Noirs	♈♈	6
⊙ Franciacorta Demi Sec Rosé	♈♈	5
○ Franciacorta Pas Dosé Aligi Sassu '07	♈♈	5
⊙ Franciacorta Rosé Altera	♈♈	5
○ Franciacorta Brut Electo '00	♈♈♈	6
○ Franciacorta Brut Electo '99	♈♈♈	5
○ Franciacorta Brut Electo '97	♈♈♈	5
○ Franciacorta Aligi Sassu Pas Dosé '03	♈♈	7
○ Franciacorta Brut Electo '06	♈♈	5
○ Franciacorta Brut Electo '05	♈♈	8
○ Franciacorta Electo Brut '01	♈♈	6
○ Franciacorta Pas Dosé Aligi Sassu '06	♈♈	8
○ Franciacorta Pas Dosé Aligi Sassu '05	♈♈	7
○ Franciacorta Satèn Ante Omnia '03	♈♈	7

★Mamete Prevostini

LOC. MESE
VIA DON PRIMO LUCCHINETTI, 63
23020 MESE [SO]
TEL. 034341522
www.mameteprevostini.com

CELLAR SALES
PRE-BOOKED VISITS
RESTAURANT SERVICE
ANNUAL PRODUCTION 180,000 bottles
HECTARES UNDER VINE 20.00
SUSTAINABLE WINERY

For several years now there has been a
very lively, close-knit atmosphere among
Valtellina producers. Growers are unified
and display an unusual singularity of
purpose, particularly in the Italian wine
world. Much of the merit for this must be
attributed to the work of Mamete Prevostini,
producer and chairman of the Consorzio
Vini di Valtellina, who has managed to unite
the many small wineries of the region to
promote its production. His estate in
Valchiavenna produces complex, vibrant,
fruit-rich wines. The magnificent Sassella
Sommarovina 2013 seduced us with its
combination of elegance and unique alpine
Nebbiolo character. Its concentrated nose
offers top notes of tobacco, jam, roasted
coffee beans and spices, and the powerful
palate is enlivened by a long, fresh finish
with good acidity and tannins. Sforzato
Corte di Cama 2012 displays exceptional
finesse, making it a classic. It vaunts a
nose of brandied fruit with spicy notes and
typical balsamic hints, and a warm, full,
wonderfully behaved palate, with a fine
balance of noble tannins and acidity.

● Valtellina Sup. Sassella Sommarovina '13	♈♈♈	5
● Valtellina Sforzato Corte di Cama '12	♈♈	6
● Valtellina Sup. Sassella San Lorenzo '12	♈♈	6
● Valtellina Sup. Sassella '13	♈♈	3
● Rosso di Valtellina Santarita '14	♈	3
● Valtellina Sforzato Albareda '09	♈♈♈	6
● Valtellina Sforzato Albareda '08	♈♈♈	6
● Valtellina Sforzato Albareda '06	♈♈♈	6
● Valtellina Sforzato Albareda '05	♈♈♈	6
● Valtellina Sforzato Albareda '04	♈♈♈	6
● Valtellina Sup. Ris. '09	♈♈♈	5
● Valtellina Sup. Sassella San Lorenzo '10	♈♈♈	5
● Valtellina Sforzato Albareda '12	♈♈	6
● Valtellina Sup. Sassella Sommarovina '12	♈♈	4

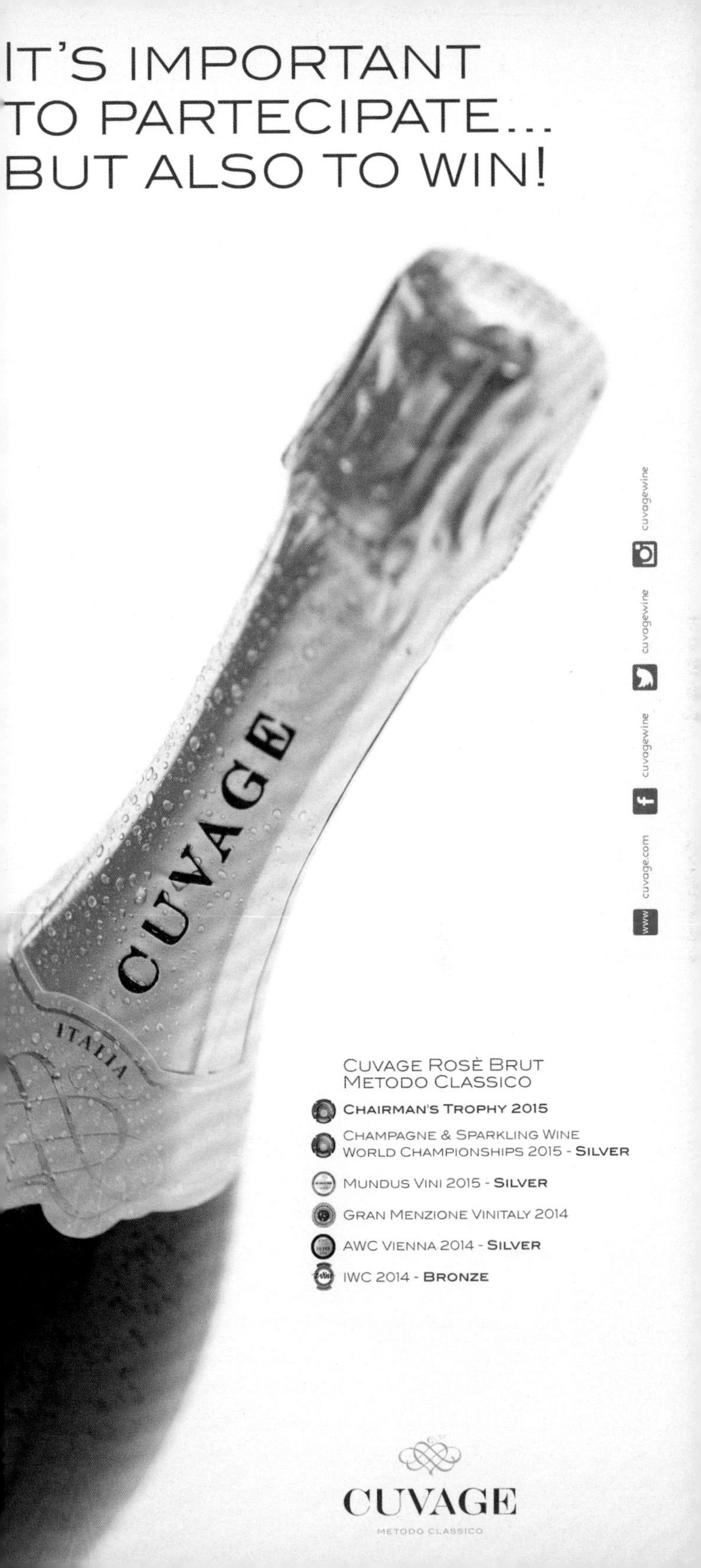

IT'S IMPORTANT TO PARTECIPATE... BUT ALSO TO WIN!

Cuvage Rosè Brut
Metodo Classico

CHAIRMAN'S TROPHY 2015

CHAMPAGNE & SPARKLING WINE
WORLD CHAMPIONSHIPS 2015 - SILVER

MUNDUS VINI 2015 - SILVER

GRAN MENZIONE VINITALY 2014

AWC VIENNA 2014 - SILVER

IWC 2014 - BRONZE

CUVAGE

METODO CLASSICO

VALLONE

350 military infrastructure dedicated to the defense of the Adriatic coast; 1789 transformed into a fortified Masseria; nowadays it's a modern family owned winery who's scope is to diffuse on global markets a piece of authentic taste through unique century-old indigenous varieties. Tenuta Castel Serranova wines, entirely produced and estate bottled by the family.

40°41'42.8"N 17°45'32.8"E"

TENUTA SERRANOVA FIANO

40°42'22.9"N 17°46'49.1"E

VIGNACASTELLO

40°42'32.39"N 17°46'30.04"E

STEFANO PRAMM

CATCH THE WIND OF RENEWALS

Visit our new proposals 2016
and start dreaming
your next unforgettable summer holiday.

EARLY
BOOKING
BONUS

10% Discount by reserving
your next holiday before March 31s

Golfo del Sole
reka:ɔ
Hotel & Holiday Resort in Tuscany

YOUR FAMILY, YOUR WELLNESS, YOUR HOLIDAY

www.golfodelsole.com

Le Marchesine

VIA VALLOSA, 31
25050 PASSIRANO [BS]
TEL. 030657005
www.lemarchesine.it

CELLAR SALES
PRE-BOOKED VISITS
ANNUAL PRODUCTION 450,000 bottles
HECTARES UNDER VINE 47.00

Although the Biattas have ancient roots in the Brescian viticultural world, it was not until the mid-1980s that Giovanni Biatta founded the family estate. Today Loris and his children Alice and Andrea enthusiastically pursue the quality that has always characterized Le Marchesine's production. The estate now boasts 47 hectares of fine vineyards, and an annual production of around half a million bottles. French oenologist Jean-Pierre Valade, an international Metodo Classico expert, acts as consultant. The 2008 vintage of Secolo Novo Riserva is one of the best in recent years and had no trouble earning a Tre Bicchieri. It is a Blanc de Blancs from the finest grapes from the Colle della Santissima vineyard in Gussago, whose unique temperature fluctuations enhance the character of chardonnay. It is a bright straw green, with a complex nose of fruit, hazelnuts, toasted oak and yeast. However, it is on the palate that it reveals its great structure, complexity, balance, and extraordinarily expressive freshness.

○ Franciacorta Dosage Zero Secolo Novo Ris. '08	♔♔♔ 8
○ Franciacorta Brut Blanc de Noir '11	♔♔ 6
○ Franciacorta Blanc de Blancs '11	♔♔ 6
○ Franciacorta Brut	♔♔ 4
⊙ Franciacorta Brut Rosé '10	♔♔ 5
○ Franciacorta Extra Brut	♔♔ 5
○ Franciacorta Satèn '11	♔♔ 5
○ Franciacorta Brut '04	♕♕♕ 5
○ Franciacorta Brut Blanc de Noir '09	♕♕♕ 5
○ Franciacorta Brut Secolo Novo '05	♕♕♕ 7
○ Franciacorta Brut Blanc de Noir '10	♕♕ 5
○ Franciacorta Brut Nature Secolo Novo Giovanni Biatta '07	♕♕ 5
○ Franciacorta Dosage Zero Secolo Novo Ris. '07	♕♕ 7
○ Franciacorta Satèn '08	♕♕ 5

Tenuta Mazzolino

VIA MAZZOLINO, 34
27050 CORVINO SAN QUIRICO [PV]
TEL. 0383876122
www.tenuta-mazzolino.com

CELLAR SALES
PRE-BOOKED VISITS
ANNUAL PRODUCTION 130,000 bottles
HECTARES UNDER VINE 22.00

Following the departure last year of Jean-François Coquard, this year the Oltrepò agronomist Claudio Giorgi also took his leave. The longstanding Greek-born French consultant oenologist Kyriakos Kinigopoulos remains, while the new manager, Stefano Ruini, has arrived from Bordeaux following extensive experience in France. We will see in future how these changes will influence the wines of Sandra Braggiotti's estate, where French remains the main language and pinot nero and chardonnay the star grape varieties. Pinot Nero Noir 2012 promptly reconquered the Tre Bicchieri that it missed by a hair's breadth last year. It has a well-typed, open, complex nose of wild berries and spice, and a full, well-orchestrated palate, with noble tannins and fine racy finish. Our favourite of the two sparklers was the creamy, harmonious Blanc de Blancs, with a beautifully lively fine bead, while the Cruasé, although pleasant, has a faint note of bruised fruit. The Blanc 2013 is impeccable, with aromas of pineapple and grapefruit, accompanied by the vanilla notes of new oak.

● OP Pinot Nero Noir '12	♔♔♔ 5
○ Brut Mazzolino Blanc de Blancs	♔♔ 4
○ OP Chardonnay Blanc '13	♔♔ 3
○ Camarà '14	♔ 2
● OP Bonarda Mazzolino '14	♔ 2
⊙ OP Cruasé Mazzolino	♔ 4
● Pinot Nero Terrazze '14	♔ 3
● OP Pinot Nero Noir '10	♕♕♕ 5
● OP Pinot Nero Noir '09	♕♕♕ 5
● OP Pinot Nero Noir '08	♕♕♕ 5
● OP Pinot Nero Noir '07	♕♕♕ 5
● OP Pinot Nero Noir '06	♕♕♕ 5
○ OP Chardonnay Blanc '10	♕♕ 3*
● OP Pinot Nero Noir '11	♕♕ 5
● OP Pinot Nero Noir '05	♕♕ 5
● OP Pinot Nero Noir '00	♕♕ 5

Mirabella

VIA CANTARANE, 2
25050 RODENGO SAIANO [BS]
TEL. 030611197
www.mirabellafranciacorta.it

CELLAR SALES
PRE-BOOKED VISITS
ANNUAL PRODUCTION 450,000 bottles
HECTARES UNDER VINE 50.00

In 1979 Teresio Schiavi and a group of friends with small vineyards in Franciacorta founded a new winery to pool their properties and create a shared brand. Today it is safe to say that they have come a long way. The estate boasts a handsome headquarters, 50 hectares of vineyards and a well-equipped modern cellar. Mirabella's great success is also due to the commitment of managing director Francesco Bracchi, and Teresio's sons, oenologist Alessandro and sales director Alberto. The level of production is excellent (almost half a million bottles) and shows particular sensitivity to sustainable development and salubrious products. Mirabella presented a very sound range this year. The fresh, full-flavoured Extra Brut Élite, from chardonnay grapes without the addition of sulphites, is particularly good, with attractive top notes of white-fleshed fruit, followed by pleasant tones of Mediterranean scrubland. We also liked the lively citrus notes of the Brut, and the soft drinkability of the Satèn.

○ Franciacorta Brut	♟♟ 4
☉ Franciacorta Brut Rosé	♟♟ 4
○ Franciacorta Extra Brut Élite	♟♟ 7
○ Franciacorta Satèn	♟♟ 5
○ Franciacorta Brut Cuvée Demetra	♟♟ 5
○ Franciacorta Dosaggio Zero Dom '04	♟♟ 6
● Nero d'Ombra '04	♟♟ 5
● Nero d'Ombra '01	♟♟ 5
○ Passito Incanto '04	♟♟ 5
● TdF Rosso Maniero '04	♟♟ 2*

★ Monsupello

VIA SAN LAZZARO, 5
27050 TORRICELLA VERZATE [PV]
TEL. 0383896043
www.monsupello.it

CELLAR SALES
PRE-BOOKED VISITS
ANNUAL PRODUCTION 260,000 bottles
HECTARES UNDER VINE 50.00

What can we say about this winery that has not already been said? Pierangelo and Laura Boatti, aided by their mother Carla and oenologist Marco Bertelegni, continue in the tradition of their father Carlo, and Monsupello undoubtedly remains Oltrepò's finest estate, particularly for sparkling wine production. The only criticism we could make is that it offers too many different labels for a family-run winery. However, the Nature, Sparkler of the year in last year's edition of the Guide, confirms its unbeatable status, in terms of both its sheer excellence, which unfailing emerges at our blind tastings, and extraordinary good value. It is a complex, full wine, showing fresh and linear, due to an exemplary vein of acidity. Headily fragrant with wild berries as only a Pinot Nero can be, it offers an exceptionally clean finish. The 2010 vintage is also very good, displaying a broader, more layered style. Ca' del Tava is more opulent, while the Brut is simpler but very pleasant, and the Rosé is as alluring as ever.

○ Brut Nature	♟♟♟ 4
○ Brut '10	♟♟ 5
○ Brut	♟♟ 5
○ Brut Cuvée Ca' del Tava	♟♟ 6
☉ Brut Rosé	♟♟ 4
● Calcacabio '13	♟♟ 2*
● Cipperi Merlot '07	♟♟ 5
● Riesling '14	♟♟ 2
● OP Bonarda Vivace Vaiolet '14	♟ 2
○ Brut '08	♟♟♟ 5
☉ Brut Rosé	♟♟♟ 4*
○ OP Brut Classese '06	♟♟♟ 5
○ OP Brut Classese '04	♟♟♟ 5

Francesco Montagna

VIA CAIROLI, 67
27043 BRONI [PV]
TEL. 038551028
www.cantinemontagna.it

CELLAR SALES
PRE-BOOKED VISITS
RESTAURANT SERVICE
ANNUAL PRODUCTION 800,000 bottles
HECTARES UNDER VINE 18.00

Owned by the Bertè and Cordini families for over 40 years, one of this estate's distinctive features is its endless list of wines, divided into various product lines that sometimes make it rather complicated to navigate. Nonetheless, the division between the estate's purely commercial soul and its side focusing on the quest for quality, embodied by Natale Bertè's oenologist son Matteo, is bearing increasingly interesting fruits. This year, for example, the Cuvée Tradizione 2010 won a place in our finals with a complex nose of fruit and flowers, and a compelling palate showing good progression and a delightful long finish. We also liked the full-flavoured Cuvée Nero d'Oro, from Pinot Nero, with aromas of wild berries, and the chewy Cruasé, offering a fine balance of flesh and acidity The Spumante Metodo Martinotti and Sangue di Giuda 2014 are also well made, while Sauvignon Masaria 2014 is very varietal.

○ OP Pinot Nero Brut Cuvée Tradizione '10	🍷🍷 4
○ OP Cruasé Bertè & Cordini	🍷🍷 5
○ OP Pinot Nero Brut M. Cl. Cuvée Nero d'Oro	🍷🍷 4
○ OP Pinot Nero Brut Martinotti Bertè & Cordini	🍷🍷 4
● OP Sangue di Giuda Bertè & Cordini '14	🍷🍷 2*
○ OP Pinot Nero Brut Cl. Cuvée della Casa	🍷 5
○ OP Sauvignon Masaria '14	🍷 2
○ OP Pinot Nero Brut Cl. Cuvée della Casa Bertè & Cordini	🍷🍷 5
○ OP Pinot Nero Brut Cl. Cuvée Tradizione Bertè & Cordini	🍷🍷 5
⊙ OP Pinot Nero Brut Rosé Cl.	🍷🍷 4

★Monte Rossa

FRAZ. BORNATO
VIA MONTE ROSSA, 1
25040 CAZZAGO SAN MARTINO [BS]
TEL. 030725066
www.monterossa.com

CELLAR SALES
PRE-BOOKED VISITS
ANNUAL PRODUCTION 500,000 bottles
HECTARES UNDER VINE 70.00

Today it is Emanuele Rabotti, in partnership with Oscar Farinetti, who runs the family estate with passion, painstaking care and creativity, producing around 500,000 bottles of excellent wine each year from its 70 hectares of vineyards. Monte Rosa is deservedly one of Franciacorta's most representative longstanding wineries, founded by Paolo Rabotti and his wife Paola in the early 1970s, and soon attaining iconic status. While awaiting the new vintage of the estate's prestigious Brut Cabochon, this year we saw a good performance in the finals from the delicious Non Dosato Coupé, a cuvée of Chardonnay with a touch of Pinot Nero, aged on the lees for over two years before disgorgement. It has a complex, alluring nose with top notes of fruit that fade nicely into vanilla and then aromatic herbs. The broad, zesty palate is spirited, with plenty of soft flesh and elegant notes of white chocolate and vanilla on the finish.

○ Franciacorta Non Dosato Coupé	🍷🍷 5
○ Franciacorta Brut Rosé Flamingo	🍷🍷 6
○ Franciacorta Brut Satèn Sansevé	🍷🍷 5
○ Franciacorta Extra Brut Salvàdek '10	🍷🍷 6
○ Franciacorta Brut P. R.	🍷 5
○ Franciacorta Brut Prima Cuvée	🍷 4
○ Franciacorta Brut Cabochon '05	🍷🍷🍷 6
○ Franciacorta Brut Cabochon '04	🍷🍷🍷 6
○ Franciacorta Brut Cabochon '03	🍷🍷🍷 6
○ Franciacorta Brut Cabochon '01	🍷🍷🍷 6
○ Franciacorta Brut Cabochon '99	🍷🍷🍷 7
○ Franciacorta Brut Cabochon '98	🍷🍷🍷 6
○ Franciacorta Brut Cabochon '97	🍷🍷🍷 6

Tenuta Montenisa

loc. Cazzago San Martino
fraz. Calino
via Paolo VI, 62
25046 Cazzago San Martino [BS]
Tel. 0307750838
www.montenisa.it

PRE-BOOKED VISITS
ANNUAL PRODUCTION 300,000 bottles
HECTARES UNDER VINE 60.00

In 1999 the Florentine Antinori family made a business agreement with the Maggi family for the management of their handsome Calino estate. Montenisa has been lovingly supervised by the Antinori sisters Albiera, Alessia and Allegra, who have renovated the estate, with its 60 hectares of vineyards, and its old buildings, which now house the well-equipped modern cellars. The complex is dominated by the palazzo of the Conti Maggi, a fine 16th-century structure between two large colonnaded courtyards. This year is quiet for Montenisa, as it awaits the release of its more important vintages. However, it is often said that the validity of an estate should be judged from its basic product, rather than its flagships. In that case, we give a thumbs up for the excellent Rosé Brut, among the best of the designation, with notes of red berries and wholemeal, and fine expressive depth. We can say the same for the excellent Brut, which is full flavoured, juicy and well orchestrated. The slightly more evolved Conte Aimo Brut 2007 is also interesting.

○ Franciacorta Brut	▼▼ 5
● Franciacorta Brut Conte Aimo '07	▼▼ 8
⊙ Franciacorta Brut Rosé	▼▼ 5
○ Franciacorta Brut Contessa Camilla Maggi '02	▽▽ 7
○ Franciacorta Brut Contessa Camilla Maggi '01	▽▽ 6
○ Franciacorta Brut Contessa Camilla Maggi '00	▽▽ 6
○ Franciacorta Brut Contessa Maggi '06	▽▽ 7
○ Franciacorta Satèn '09	▽▽ 6
○ Franciacorta Satèn '06	▽▽ 6
○ Franciacorta Satèn '04	▽▽ 6
○ Franciacorta Satèn '04	▽▽ 6
○ Franciacorta Satèn '03	▽▽ 6

Il Mosnel

loc. Camignone
via Barboglio, 14
25040 Passirano [BS]
Tel. 030653117
www.ilmosnel.com

CELLAR SALES
PRE-BOOKED VISITS
RESTAURANT SERVICE
ANNUAL PRODUCTION 250,000 bottles
HECTARES UNDER VINE 40.00

Il Mosnel is one of Franciacorta's most handsome wineries. It was founded by Emanuela Barboglio, who as early as the 1960s converted the family estate to wine production. Today it is lovingly and competently run by her children Lucia and Giulio Barzanò, who have perfectly restored the winery's headquarters, the 16th-century hamlet of Camignone di Passirano, set among the estate's impressive 40 hectares of vineyards in a single plot. This year it was the Satèn 2011 that reached our finals. It is undoubtedly one of the most representative wines of its type, showing a bright straw yellow, with greenish highlights, a creamy mousse and a fine bead. The alluring nose has complex, elegant notes of ripe yellow and white-fleshed fruit, vanilla, and aromatic herbs. On the palate it is complex and velvety, supported by a fresh swathe of acidity, which accompanies the very long vanilla finish.

○ Franciacorta Satèn '11	▼▼ 5
○ Curtefranca Bianco Campolarga '14	▼▼ 2*
○ Franciacorta Brut	▼▼ 4
⊙ Franciacorta Brut Rosé	▼▼ 5
○ Franciacorta Extra Brut EBB '10	▼▼ 5
○ Franciacorta Pas Dosé	▼▼ 4
● Curtefranca Rosso Fontecolo '13	▼ 2
○ Franciacorta Extra Brut EBB '09	▽▽▽ 5
○ Franciacorta Pas Dosé QdE Ris. '04	▽▽▽ 6
○ Franciacorta Satèn '05	▽▽▽ 5
○ Franciacorta Extra Brut EBB '08	▽▽ 5
⊙ Franciacorta Pas Dosé Parosé '07	▽▽ 5
⊙ Franciacorta Pas Dosé Parosé '05	▽▽ 5
⊙ Franciacorta Pas Dosé Parosé '04	▽▽ 5
○ Franciacorta Pas Dosé QdE Ris. '06	▽▽ 6
○ Franciacorta Satèn '06	▽▽ 5

★★Nino Negri

VIA GHIBELLINI
23030 CHIURO [SO]
TEL. 0342485211
www.ninonegri.it

CELLAR SALES
PRE-BOOKED VISITS
RESTAURANT SERVICE
ANNUAL PRODUCTION 800,000 bottles
HECTARES UNDER VINE 36.00
SUSTAINABLE WINERY

This historic Valtellina winery is almost 120 years old and is the jewel in the crown of the Gruppo Italiano Vini. With its 36 hectares of vineyards, Nino Negri is a beacon for the whole of Valtellina. It is a constantly developing winery increasingly attentive to the environmental sustainability of its production, which is founded on some of the best-aspected vineyards in the entire region and a technical team at the cutting edge of Italian winemaking. We have had the chance to test the cellar lifespan of the estate's wines several times and know to expect surprising and very prolonged development in bottle. Sforzato Carlo Negri 2012 is elegant and classically modern, with a nose of ripe fruit, spice, plums, and cocoa powder, and faint notes of tobacco. The complex palate has well-balanced flesh, fine-grained tannins and a very long finish. Vigneto Fracia 2013 surprised us, offering top notes of raspberries on the nose, with hints of black pepper, rusty iron, and dried flowers.. The dense, velvety palate is sustained by close-woven tannins and good acidity.

● Valtellina Sfursat 5 Stelle '11	♟♟♟	8
● Valtellina Sfursat Carlo Negri '12	♟♟	6
● Valtellina Sup. Mazer '12	♟♟	4
● Valtellina Sup. Vign. Fracia '13	♟♟	5
● Valtellina Sup. Grumello V. Sassorosso '12	♟♟	4
● Valtellina Sup. Inferno Carlo Negri '12	♟♟	5
● Valtellina Sup. Sassella Le Tense '12	♟♟	4
● Valtellina Sup. Sciur '12	♟♟	4
● Valtellina Sfursat '05	♟♟♟	8
● Valtellina Sfursat '04	♟♟♟	6
● Valtellina Sfursat 5 Stelle '10	♟♟♟	7
● Valtellina Sfursat 5 Stelle '09	♟♟♟	7
● Valtellina Sfursat 5 Stelle '07	♟♟♟	7
● Valtellina Sfursat 5 Stelle '06	♟♟♟	7
● Valtellina Sfursat Carlo Negri '11	♟♟♟	8
● Valtellina Sup. Vign. Fracia '08	♟♟♟	6

Pasini - San Giovanni

FRAZ. RAFFA
VIA VIDELLE, 2
25080 PUEGNAGO SUL GARDA [BS]
TEL. 0365651419
www.pasiniproduttori.it

CELLAR SALES
PRE-BOOKED VISITS
RESTAURANT SERVICE
ANNUAL PRODUCTION 300,000 bottles
HECTARES UNDER VINE 36.00

Cousins Paolo, Luca, Laura and Sara Pasini are the third generation to run the family winery. San Giovanni is a fascinating wine project, with 36 hectares of organic vineyards in the Valtenesi and Lugana production zones. The estate is committed to sustainability and is equipped with modern cellars powered by renewable energy. The level of production is already good and rising. Valtènesi Arzane 2012 is a Groppello from the eponymous vineyard, with admirable balance, rich fruity notes, and delicate spiciness. San Gioan i Carati 2010, the estate's historic selection, is a red from cabernet sauvignon and groppello that ages very elegantly. Brut Centopercento is a fragrant, full-flavoured Blanc de Noir from groppello. The other wines are also very interesting.

○ Brut M. Cl. Centopercento	♟♟	4
○ Lugana Brut	♟♟	2
● San Gioan Rosso i Carati '10	♟♟	4
● Valtènesi Arzane '12	♟♟	3
○ Garda Cl. Bianco Il Renano '14	♟	2
○ Il Lugana Bio '14	♟	3
○ San Gioan Brinat '12	♟	4
⊙ Valtènesi Il Chiaretto '14	♟	3
⊙ Valtènesi Il Chiaretto Rosagreen '14	♟	3
⊙ Valtènesi Il Chiaretto Il Vino di una Notte '13	♟♟	3
● Valtènesi Il Valtenesi '12	♟♟	2*
● Valtènesi Picedo '12	♟♟	2*

Andrea Picchioni

FRAZ. CAMPONOCE, 8
27044 CANNETO PAVESE [PV]
TEL. 0385262139
www.picchioniandrea.it

CELLAR SALES
PRE-BOOKED VISITS
ACCOMMODATION
ANNUAL PRODUCTION 70,000 bottles
HECTARES UNDER VINE 10.00
VITICULTURE METHOD Certified Organic
SUSTAINABLE WINERY

The determined and single-minded Andrea Picchioni long ago managed to bring the wines of his small estate and his production philosophy to the attention of the wine world. On the inaccessible ridges of Val Solinga, where most of the estate's vineyards are situated, he grows mainly croatina, barbera and ughetta di Canneto, which yield both young, early-drinking wines and others that reach their best after long ageing. His two flagships, Buttafuoco Bricco Riva Bianca and Rosso d'Asia (90% croatina, 10% ughetta di Canneto), which compete for our favour, are of the latter type. Last year Buttafuoco 2010 reached our finals; this time it's the turn of Rosso d'Asia 2011, which appeared more mature, with silky tannins, fine fleshy pulp, and good length and depth. It should age very well (as shown by the spectacular 1999 magnum we tasted last winter), like the austere Bricco Riva Bianca 2011 with sound fruit. Buttafuoco Luogo della Cerasa 2014 is very fragrant.

● Rosso d'Asia '11	♥♥	4
● OP Buttafuoco Bricco Riva Bianca '11	♥♥	4
● OP Buttafuoco Luogo della Cerasa '14	♥♥	2*
● OP Bonarda Vivace Luogo dei Ronchi '14	♥	2
● OP Pinot Nero Arfena '13	♥	3
● OP Sangue di Giuda Fior del Vento '14	♥	2
● OP Bonarda Vivace Luogo dei Ronchi '13	♥♥	2*
● OP Buttafuoco Bricco Riva Bianca '10	♥♥	4
○ OP Profilo Brut Nature M. Cl. '00	♥♥	5
○ OP Profilo Brut Nature M. Cl. '98	♥♥	5
○ OP Profilo Brut Nature M. Cl. '97	♥♥	5
○ OP Profilo Brut Nature M. Cl. '96	♥♥	5
○ OP Profilo Brut Nature M. Cl. '94	♥♥	6
● OP Sangue di Giuda Fior del Vento '13	♥♥	2*
● Rosso d'Asia '10	♥♥	4
● Rosso d'Asia '05	♥♥	3

Plozza

VIA CAPPUCCINI, 26
23037 TIRANO [SO]
TEL. 0342701297
www.plozza.com

CELLAR SALES
PRE-BOOKED VISITS
ANNUAL PRODUCTION 450,000 bottles
HECTARES UNDER VINE 25.00

Andrea Zanolari runs the winery founded by Pietro Plozza in 1919. It has two cellars, one in Tirano and the other in Brusio, in Switzerland, and vineyards covering an area of 25 hectares in the main zones of Valtellina, at altitudes between 400 and 700 metres. The wines are characterized by a quietly modern, extractive style, which in recent years has led to a series of labels increasingly associated with projects focusing on the terroir, and featuring more dynamic, racy palates. The 2012 vintage of Numero 1 can only be described as luxuriant. It is a monovarietal Nebbiolo from grapes that have been dried for about three months. The concentrated nose offers notes of caramel and chestnut, dried flowers and cocoa powder, while the palate is opulent yet harmonious, with a pleasant balance of close-woven tannins and refreshing acidity. Inferno 2011 is good and very classic, showing deep, with a nose of tobacco, mint and liquorice, and an impressive palate with austere tannins, and a very long finish.

● Sforzato di Valtellina Black Edition '11	♥♥	6
● Valtellina Numero 1 '12	♥♥	7
● Valtellina Sup. Inferno Red Edition '11	♥♥	5
● Valtellina Sup. Sassella Red Edition '11	♥♥	5
● Valtellina Numero Uno '01	♥♥♥	7
● Valtellina Numero Uno '11	♥♥	7
● Valtellina Numero Uno '10	♥♥	7
● Valtellina Numero Uno '09	♥♥	7
● Valtellina Numero Uno '07	♥♥	7
● Valtellina Sforzato Vin da Ca' '10	♥♥	5
● Valtellina Sforzato Vin da Ca' '09	♥♥	5
● Valtellina Sforzato Vin da Ca' '08	♥♥	5
● Valtellina Sup. Inferno Ris. '10	♥♥	3
● Valtellina Sup. Sassella La Scala Ris. '10	♥♥	3*

Pratello

VIA PRATELLO, 26
25080 PADENGHE SUL GARDA [BS]
TEL. 0309907005
www.pratello.com

CELLAR SALES
ACCOMMODATION AND RESTAURANT SERVICE
ANNUAL PRODUCTION 300,000 bottles
HECTARES UNDER VINE 31.00
VITICULTURE METHOD Certified Organic

Vincenzo Bertola passionately runs his
winery, whose history spans more than
150 years. Its handsome headquarters lie
behind Padenghe Castle, on a breathtaking
hilltop site overlooking Lake Garda and
Valtenesi. The estate covers over 70
hectares, planted with vines and olive
trees, tended with organic methods. Most
of the 31 hectares of vineyards are high
density plantings (6,250–8,500 vines per
hectare), designed for high-quality
production. This year we liked Valtènesi
Torrazzo 2013, from groppello, which is
remarkably elegant and pleasant. The
close-focused Lugana Catulliano 2014 is
fruity and full flavoured, convincing us
more than the oak-aged Il Rivale, of the
same vintage. The Riesling 2014 is
excellent, as is the refreshing, juicy,
fruit-rich Valtènesi Chiaretto
Sant'Emiliano 2014, with a beautiful
pale hue.

Quadra

VIA SANT'EUSEBIO, 1
25033 COLOGNE [BS]
TEL. 0307157314
www.quadrafranciacorta.it

CELLAR SALES
PRE-BOOKED VISITS
RESTAURANT SERVICE
ANNUAL PRODUCTION 140,000 bottles
HECTARES UNDER VINE 32.00
SUSTAINABLE WINERY

Quadra was founded in 2003 by Ugo
Ghezzi, an entrepreneur in the renewable
energy sector. Together with his children
Cristina and Marco, he decided to buy a
small winery, which he renovated entirely.
Today the estate has 32 hectares of
vineyards. Alongside chardonnay, the main
grape variety of the area and the
designation, the winery is working on
valorizing pinot bianco, for which three
highly complementary sites have been
identified, and pinot nero, for which several
plots on the morainic hillsides have been
destined. The estate is managed by Mario
Falcetti, an oenologist with a long career as
a researcher behind him. Mario Falcetti's
hunch regarding the role of pinot bianco in
Franciacorta is proving to be a very fertile
one, as shown by EretiQ 2010, the second
vintage of this equal blend of Pinot Bianco
and Pinot Nero, aged on the lees for almost
three years. It is fresh and lively, with good
fruit and backbone, and a wonderfully
satisfying, balanced palate. It will be
interesting to see how the concept
develops.

○ Lugana Catulliano '14		♥♥ 3
○ Lugana Il Rivale '14		♥♥ 5
● Mille 1 '13		♥♥ 3
○ Riesling '14		♥♥ 3
⊙ Valtènesi Chiaretto Sant'Emiliano '14		♥♥ 3
● Valtènesi Torrazzo '13		♥♥ 3
○ Lieti Conversari '13		♥ 4
⊙ Garda Cl. Chiaretto '11		♀♀ 3
● Garda Marzemino Poderi Ogaria '10		♀♀ 3
● Lieti Conversari '10		♀♀ 3
○ Lugana Il Rivale '12		♀♀ 5
● Nero per Sempre '12		♀♀ 5
○ Pratello Brut Rosé '09		♀♀ 3
● Rebo '08		♀♀ 4
⊙ Valtènesi Chiaretto Sant'Emiliano '12		♀♀ 3

○ Franciacorta Brut QBlack		♥♥ 4
○ Franciacorta Dosaggio Zero EretiQ '10		♥♥ 6
○ Franciacorta QSatèn '10		♥♥ 5
○ Franciacorta Quvée 46 '09		♥♥ 5
⊙ Franciacorta QRosé		♥ 5
○ Franciacorta Brut Q39 '08		♀♀ 5
○ Franciacorta Brut '06		♀♀ 4
○ Franciacorta Dosaggio Zero EretiQ '10		♀♀ 6
○ Franciacorta Extra Brut Q Zero '08		♀♀ 5
○ Franciacorta Extra Brut QZero '09		♀♀ 5
○ Franciacorta QSatèn '09		♀♀ 5
○ Franciacorta QSatèn '08		♀♀ 5
○ Franciacorta Satèn '07		♀♀ 5
● TdF Curtefranca Rosso Dosso Oriane '05		♀♀ 4
● TdF Curtefranca Rosso Dosso Oriane '04		♀♀ 4

Francesco Quaquarini

LOC. MONTEVENEROSO
VIA CASA ZAMBIANCHI, 26
27044 CANNETO PAVESE [PV]
TEL. 038560152
www.quaquarinifrancesco.it

CELLAR SALES
PRE-BOOKED VISITS
ANNUAL PRODUCTION 650,000 bottles
HECTARES UNDER VINE 60.00
VITICULTURE METHOD Certified Organic

Francesco Quaquarini, along with his son Umberto and daughter Maria Teresa, manage this classic family-run Oltrepò estate. It offers the traditional local wines, an extensive range, good value for money, a line of more commercial products and one of higher quality, and a very good average level. However, so far there have been none of those pinnacles of absolute excellence that were are sure it is capable of achieving. Rather than criticism, this is intended as an incentive, particularly in relation to the estate's ageworthy reds and its Metodo Classico. Our favourite wine was once again Barbera Poggio Anna, whose 2012 vintage is concentrated and fruity, simultaneously powerful and very drinkable due to good supporting acidity. Buttafuoco Storico Vigna Pregana 2009 is warm and sound, with notes of plums and spices, and a flawless finish. Buttafuoco Vigna La Guasca 2011 is fresher and more approachable, while Classese 2008 has a pleasant citrussy nose, but is a little short on the palate.

● OP Barbera Poggio Anna '12	♛♛	3
● OP Buttafuoco Storico V. Pregana '09	♛♛	5
● OP Bonarda Vivace '14	♛	2
● OP Buttafuoco V. La Guasca '11	♛	3
○ OP Pinot Nero Brut Classese '08	♛	2
● OP Sangue di Giuda Acqua Calda '14	♛	3
● OP Barbera Poggio Anna '11	♛♛	3
● OP Barbera Poggio Anna '10	♛♛	3
● OP Bonarda Vivace '13	♛♛	2*
● OP Bonarda Vivace '12	♛♛	2*
● OP Buttafuoco V. Pregana '07	♛♛	5
● OP Pinot Nero Blau '10	♛♛	3
● OP Pinot Nero Blau '05	♛♛	2*
● OP Sangue di Giuda '13	♛♛	2*
● OP Sangue di Giuda '12	♛♛	2*
● OP Sangue di Giuda V. Acqua Calda '13	♛♛	3

★Aldo Rainoldi

LOC. CASACCE DI CHIURO
VIA STELVIO, 128
23030 CHIURO [SO]
TEL. 0342482225
www.rainoldi.com

CELLAR SALES
PRE-BOOKED VISITS
ANNUAL PRODUCTION 180,000 bottles
HECTARES UNDER VINE 9.60

The consistent high quality of the Chiuro winery run by Aldo Rainoldi is rock solid. Over the past 20 years Aldo has managed to accelerate the expansion of his business. On the one hand, he has doubled his promotional efforts on the foreign markets, and on the other he has acquired vineyards in the finest growing areas and reappraised relations with his grower members. He has also gradually honed the style of the wines, and today they increasingly reflect their terroir, interpreted with an original and expressive touch, which enables them to age well. Fruttaio Ca' Rizzieri 2011 is exceptionally complex and well behaved. It is a "old-fashioned" class act, proffering an excellent nose of nicely balanced fruit and cocoa powder, with medicinal herbs and fresh end notes. The palate is both taut and velvety, with very fine-grained tannins and an exceedingly long finish. Crespino 2010 put up an excellent show, with a concentrated, harmonious nose of fresh raspberries, tobacco and spice. The lively, elegant palate is juicy with a long, layered finish.

● Valtellina Sfursat Fruttaio Ca' Rizzieri '11	♛♛♛	6
● Valtellina Sup. Crespino '10	♛♛	5
○ Ghibellino '14	♛♛	3
● Valtellina Sup. Grumello '11	♛♛	4
● Valtellina Sup. Inferno '11	♛♛	3
● Valtellina Sfursat '08	♛♛♛	5
● Valtellina Sfursat Fruttaio Ca' Rizzieri '10	♛♛♛	6
● Valtellina Sfursat Fruttaio Ca' Rizzieri '09	♛♛♛	6
● Valtellina Sfursat Fruttaio Ca' Rizzieri '06	♛♛♛	6
● Valtellina Sfursat Fruttaio Ca' Rizzieri '02	♛♛♛	6
● Valtellina Sfursat Fruttaio Ca' Rizzieri '00	♛♛♛	6
● Valtellina Sfursat Fruttaio Ca' Rizzieri '98	♛♛♛	6
● Valtellina Sfursat Fruttaio Ca' Rizzieri '97	♛♛♛	6
● Valtellina Sfursat Fruttaio Ca' Rizzieri '95	♛♛♛	6
● Valtellina Sup. Sassella Ris. '06	♛♛♛	5

Ricci Curbastro

via Adro, 37
25031 Capriolo [BS]
Tel. 030736094
www.riccicurbastro.it

CELLAR SALES
PRE-BOOKED VISITS
ACCOMMODATION
ANNUAL PRODUCTION 200,000 bottles
HECTARES UNDER VINE 27.00
SUSTAINABLE WINERY

An agronomist and oenologist, Riccardo Ricci Curbastro is also chairman of the European Federation of Origin Wines or EFOW, and its Italian counterpart FederDoc. He has given a strong boost to the estate founded by his father Gualberto in 1967, which now vaunts 27 hectares of vineyards on the finest sites in the production zone, and successfully exports its cuvées all over the world. The winery produces a comprehensive range of Franciacortas and local wines. The Extra Brut style obviously comes naturally to the estate, as once again shown by the 2011 vintage, which put up a fine performance in our finals. It is an equal blend of Chardonnay and Pinot Nero, aged for 42 months on the lees before disgorgement. The result is a lovely coppery straw colour, with a complex nose of red berries and flowers, followed by wholemeal and oriental spices, and an elegant, close-focused, linear palate. The other wines are all good.

○ Franciacorta Extra Brut '11	TT	5
● Curtefranca Rosso V. Santella del Gröm '11	TT	3
○ Franciacorta Brut	TT	4
○ Franciacorta Brut Museum Release '06	TT	5
⊙ Franciacorta Brut Rosé	TT	5
○ Franciacorta Dosaggio Zero Gualberto '08	TT	6
○ Franciacorta Satèn '11	TT	5
○ Franciacorta Dosaggio Zero Gualberto '06	YYY	6
○ Franciacorta Extra Brut '07	YYY	5
○ Franciacorta Dosaggio Zero Gualberto '05	YY	5
○ Franciacorta Extra Brut '10	YY	5
○ Franciacorta Extra Brut '09	YY	5
○ Franciacorta Satèn Brut '09	YY	5

Ronco Calino

fraz. Torbiato
via Fenice, 45
25030 Adro [BS]
Tel. 0307451073
www.roncocalino.it

CELLAR SALES
PRE-BOOKED VISITS
ANNUAL PRODUCTION 70,000 bottles
HECTARES UNDER VINE 10.00
VITICULTURE METHOD Certified Organic
SUSTAINABLE WINERY

In 1996 Paolo Radici decided to purchase as his country retreat the estate in Torbiato di Adro, which once belonged to the famous pianist Arturo Benedetti Michelangeli. The villa is surrounded by ten hectares of vineyards in a spectacular morainic amphitheatre, and the modern new cellar produces a carefully crafted range of local wines and Franciacortas with the aid of consultant oenologist Leonardo Valenti. Today Paolo is assisted in the management of the estate by his daughter Lara Imberti Radici. This year it was the Satèn that most impressed us. Its style is both complex and enjoyable, with the complexity of the balsamic notes melding with a soft, creamy swathe of fruit with end notes of citrus and aromatic herbs. Extra Brut Centoventi 2004 is also very interesting. After ageing on the lees for ten years, it is now deep and complex, with rich tertiary and balsamic notes, making it satsifying and exceptionally pleasant.

○ Curtefranca Bianco Lèant '14	TT	3
● Curtefranca Rosso Ponènt '11	TT	4
○ Franciacorta Brut	TT	4
○ Franciacorta Extra Brut Centoventi '04	TT	8
○ Franciacorta Satèn	TT	5
○ Curtefranca Bianco '10	YY	3
○ Curtefranca Bianco Lèant '11	YY	3
● Curtefranca Rosso '08	YY	4
● Curtefranca Rosso Ponènt '10	YY	4
● Curtefranca Rosso Ponènt '09	YY	4
○ Franciacorta Brut '08	YY	5
○ Franciacorta Brut Centoventi '01	YY	8
○ Franciacorta Nature '09	YY	5
○ Franciacorta Nature '08	YY	5
○ Franciacorta Nature '07	YY	5
● Pinot Nero L'Arturo '11	YY	5

Tenuta Roveglia

LOC. ROVEGLIA, 1
25010 POZZOLENGO [BS]
TEL. 030918663
www.tenutaroveglia.it

CELLAR SALES
PRE-BOOKED VISITS
ANNUAL PRODUCTION 250,000 bottles
HECTARES UNDER VINE 70.00

The Azzone family run the family winery on the southern shores of Lake Garda, which focuses mainly on Lugana. The estate's extensive area under vine supplies all the grapes required for production. The style is forthright and easy drinking, although there are also wines with great character, like Vendemmia Tardiva Filo di Arianna, the progenitor of its type and a benchmark for the entire designation. It is the estate's most interesting wine, managing to combine the vintage's super-ripe fruit with an innate freshness revealing the grape variety. Its broad nose ranges from candied citrus fruit to meadow flowers, with subtle undertones of botrytis, while the concentrated, powerful palate is almost unctuous, but with an unexpected, spirited acidic backbone that assures tautness and length. The mature, complex Vigne di Catullo is full and nicely rounded.

○ Lugana V. T. Filo di Arianna '12	♥♥ 3*
○ Lugana Limne '14	♥♥ 2*
○ Lugana Brut	♥ 3
○ Lugana Sup. Vigne di Catullo Ris. '12	♥ 3
● Garda Merlot '11	♀♀ 2*
○ Lugana Limne '13	♀♀ 2*
○ Lugana Limne '10	♀♀ 2
○ Lugana Limne '09	♀♀ 2*
○ Lugana Sup. Filo di Arianna '08	♀♀ 3
○ Lugana Sup. Vigne di Catullo '08	♀♀ 3
○ Lugana Sup. Vigne di Catullo '07	♀♀ 3*
○ Lugana Sup. Vigne di Catullo Ris. '11	♀♀ 3
○ Lugana V. T. Filo di Arianna '11	♀♀ 3*

Ruiz de Cardenas

LOC. MAIRANO
VIA MOLLIE, 35
27045 CASTEGGIO [PV]
TEL. 038382301
www.ruizdecardenas.it

CELLAR SALES
PRE-BOOKED VISITS
ANNUAL PRODUCTION 25,000 bottles
HECTARES UNDER VINE 5.00

Gianluca Ruiz de Cardenas is a gentleman from a bygone age. He runs his tiny "garagiste" winery with savoir-faire and a touch of humour, as is evident from the introduction on his website: "Being a sort of amateur producer – my main business is air conditioning – the wine making is a not-for-profit activity, and has proven to be quite successful at achieving this goal." The estate's small plots are planted to pinot nero and chardonnay, used to make still wines and Metodo Classico sparklers. This year Gianluca decided to send us samples, and the range was convincing enough to earn its first full profile in our Guide. Brumano 2010, for example, is an impressive Pinot Nero, with well-expressed, evolved fruit. It is full and elegant, with a firm, balsamic palate. Our favourite of the Metodo Classicos was the copper-hued Galanta Rosé, which is fruity and mineral. The Reserve 2006 is also good, showing full and opulent, with pervasive bready aromas and a concentrated finish.

● Pinot Nero Brumano '10	♥♥ 4
○ Galanta Brut M. Cl. Reserve '06	♥♥ 5
⊙ OP Pinot Nero Brut Rosé Galanta	♥♥ 4
○ Blanc de Blanc Extra Brut Cuvée Armonia	♥ 4
● Pinot Nero Miraggi '13	♥ 3

Cantine Selva Capuzza

FRAZ. SAN MARTINO DELLA BATTAGLIA
LOC. SELVA CAPUZZA
25010 DESENZANO DEL GARDA [BS]
TEL. 0309910381
www.selvacapuzza.it

CELLAR SALES
PRE-BOOKED VISITS
ACCOMMODATION AND RESTAURANT SERVICE
ANNUAL PRODUCTION 300,000 bottles
HECTARES UNDER VINE 25.00

Selva Capuzza is a large estate covering 50
or so hectares in the southern area inland
from Lake Garda, south of San Martino
della Battaglia. It is entirely dedicated to the
traditional local grape varieties, interpreted
to enhance their close relationship with the
terroir. The wide range also includes
sparkling wines, produced with both the
Charmat and classic methods. Despite the
difficult 2014 vintage, Lugana Selva is
among the most interesting of the
production zone, vaunting a nose of fresh
flowers and white-fleshed fruit, with subtle
vegetal undertones. On the palate, it
manages to be full without forgoing either
elegance or tautness. The San Virgilio of
the same vintage has a more closed nose
that needs more time to develop, and a
zesty, satisfying palate.

Lo Sparviere

VIA COSTA, 2
25040 MONTICELLI BRUSATI [BS]
TEL. 030652382
www.losparviere.com

CELLAR SALES
PRE-BOOKED VISITS
ANNUAL PRODUCTION 120,000 bottles
HECTARES UNDER VINE 30.00

Ugo Gussalli Beretta, the descendent of one
of the world's oldest industrial dynasties,
documented from 1526, and his wife
Monique have a great passion for wine and
the countryside. Over the years it led them
to found the Agricole Gussalli Beretta
group, which also includes Castello di
Radda in Chianti Classico, Orlandi Contucci
Ponno in Abruzzo, and Cascina Pressenda
in Castelletto di Monforte d'Alba. The
Franciacorta estate covers an area of 150
hectares, including 30 under vine. Its
beautiful winery is housed in a perfectly
restored 16th-century villa with
outbuildings. Dosaggio Zero Riserva 2008
is one of the most interesting Franciacortas
we tasted this year, showing a handsome
bright straw yellow, with a tiny, fine,
continuous bead. The nose has complex
and sometimes austere mineral and smoky
top notes, which do not cover the sound,
lively fruit. On the palate it is firm, taut, rich
and full, with notes of fruit and citrus peel
on a satisfying long finish. The rest of the
range is very sound.

Wine	Rating
⊙ Garda Cl. Chiaretto San Donino '14	♟♟ 2*
● Garda Cl. Groppello San Biagio '14	♟♟ 3
○ Lugana Dosaggio Zero M. Cl.	♟♟ 3
○ Lugana San Vigilio '14	♟♟ 2*
○ Lugana Selva '14	♟♟ 2*
● Garda Cl. Rosso Dunant '13	♟ 3
● Garda Cl. Sup. Rosso Madèr '12	♟ 3
○ Lugana Brut M. Cl.	♟ 3
○ Lugana Menasasso Ris. '11	♟ 3
○ Lume	♟ 4
○ San Martino della Battaglia Campo del Soglio '14	♟ 3
⊙ Garda Cl. Chiaretto San Donino '13	♟♟ 2*
○ Lugana Menasasso Ris. '09	♟♟ 3
○ Lugana Selva '12	♟♟ 2*
○ Lume '11	♟♟ 3

Wine	Rating
○ Franciacorta Dosaggio Zero Ris. '08	♟♟♟ 6
○ Franciacorta Extra Brut	♟♟ 5
○ Franciacorta Rosé Monique	♟♟ 5
○ Franciacorta Brut Cuvée N. 7	♟ 4
○ Franciacorta Satèn	♟ 6
○ Franciacorta Extra Brut '08	♟♟♟ 5
○ Franciacorta Extra Brut '07	♟♟♟ 5
○ Franciacorta Brut '09	♟♟ 5
○ Franciacorta Brut '05	♟♟ 4
○ Franciacorta Brut '04	♟♟ 4
○ Franciacorta Brut	♟♟ 5
○ Franciacorta Dosaggio Zero Ris. '07	♟♟ 6
○ Franciacorta Dosaggio Zero Ris. '06	♟♟ 8
○ Franciacorta Extra Brut '05	♟♟ 5
○ Franciacorta Extra Brut '01	♟♟ 5
○ Franciacorta Extra Brut '98	♟♟ 4*

Travaglino

LOC. TRAVAGLINO, 6A
27040 CALVIGNANO [PV]
TEL. 0383872222
www.travaglino.it

CELLAR SALES
PRE-BOOKED VISITS
ACCOMMODATION AND RESTAURANT SERVICE
ANNUAL PRODUCTION 220,000 bottles
HECTARES UNDER VINE 80.00

The Travaglino estate has a long history, and was purchased at auction by the Comi family in 1868. Its current owner, Vincenzo Comi, was responsible for its zoning, subdividing it into individual vineyards according to soil type in 1965. Today it is being completely overhauled, commencing with its technical management, entrusted to the highly capable and experienced oenologist Carlo Casavecchia, and the results are already showing, although we are sure that we will be in for real some treats in the coming years. In the meantime, we enjoyed the balanced, well-orchestrated Riesling Campo della Fojada 2014, which has returned to its former glory, with upfront aromas of flowers and aromatic herbs. The range of Metodo Classicos is also good: Cruasé Montecersino 2011, with sound fruit and intriguing notes of black pepper and pennyroyal; the taut, vigorous Cuvée 59 2012, with unfaltering minerality; and the Grand Cuvée 2009, which has nice flesh and stuffing but is a little more staid.

⊙ OP Pinot Nero Brut Cruasé Montecersimo '11	♟♟ 4
○ OP Pinot Nero Brut Cuvée 59 '12	♟♟ 3
○ OP Riesling Campo della Fojada '14	♟♟ 3
● OP Bonarda La Moranda '14	♟ 2
○ OP Gran Cuvée Brut	♟ 4
○ OP Pinot Nero Grand Cuvée '09	♟ 4
● OP Pinot Nero Poggio della Buttinera '12	♟ 4
○ OP Brut Classese '09	♟♟ 5
○ OP Brut Cuvée 59 '10	♟♟ 5
⊙ OP Cruasé Montecersimo '08	♟♟ 4
⊙ OP Pinot Nero Brut Cruasé Montecersimo '07	♟♟ 3
○ OP Pinot Nero Brut Cuvée 59 '08	♟♟ 3
○ OP Riesling Campo della Fojada '12	♟♟ 3
○ OP Riesling Campo della Fojada '11	♟♟ 3
○ OP Riesling Campo della Fojada '09	♟♟ 3*

★Uberti

LOC. SALEM
VIA E. FERMI, 2
25030 ERBUSCO [BS]
TEL. 0307267476
www.ubertivini.it

PRE-BOOKED VISITS
ANNUAL PRODUCTION 180,000 bottles
HECTARES UNDER VINE 25.00

In 1980 Agostino and his wife Eleonora decided to continue the family tradition that has seen the Ubertis in the vineyards of the province of Brescia since 1739. Aided by their daughters, Francesca and oenologist Silvia, they practise organic viticulture with minimal cellar intervention, which tends to showcase the unique features of their 25 hectares of excellent vineyards in prime positions. The distinctive Francesco I, Magnificentia, Comarì del Salem, and Sublimis are all from different vineyards. However, Quinque, the latest addition to the range, represents the distinctive features of several plots and from five vintages. Comarì del Salem 2009, from the old vineyard next to the winery, made it into our finals. It is a flavoursome, saline Extra Brut from chardonnay, with nice backbone and soft, juicy fruit that has developed nicely, after six years ageing on the lees. The elegant finish is complex, with notes of vanilla and attractive oak. Magnificentia 2011 is plush and floral, while Extra Brut Francesco I is more austere and linear.

○ Curtefranca Bianco Maria Medici '12	♟♟ 4
○ Franciacorta Extra Brut Comarì del Salem '09	♟♟ 6
○ Franciacorta Extra Brut Francesco I	♟♟ 5
○ Franciacorta Non Dosato Sublimis '08	♟♟ 6
○ Franciacorta Satèn Magnificentia '11	♟♟ 6
● Rosso dei Frati Priori	♟♟ 5
○ Franciacorta Brut Francesco I	♟ 5
○ Franciacorta Extra Brut Quinque	♟ 8
○ Franciacorta Rosé Francesco I	♟ 5
○ Franciacorta Brut Comarì del Salem '00	♟♟♟ 6
○ Franciacorta Extra Brut Comarì del Salem '03	♟♟♟ 6
○ Franciacorta Extra Brut Comarì del Salem '02	♟♟♟ 6
○ Franciacorta Extra Brut Comarì del Salem '01	♟♟♟ 6

Vanzini

FRAZ. BARBALEONE, 7
27040 SAN DAMIANO AL COLLE [PV]
TEL. 038575019
www.vanzini-wine.com

CELLAR SALES
PRE-BOOKED VISITS
ANNUAL PRODUCTION 600,000 bottles
HECTARES UNDER VINE 27.00

As always, the winery owned by brothers
Antonio and Pierpaolo Vanzini and their
sister Michela is among the best in Oltrepò
for traditional wines, with second
fermentation in pressure tanks, whether they
be semi-sparkling or long Charmat method
sparklers. The tradition is well established,
and Pierpaolo, the oenologist, has such a
sure hand in the cellar that even the wines
from the difficult 2014 vintage, while
inevitably below the estate's usual level in
terms of structure, are nonetheless among
the best of the entire production zone. The
three versions of Spumante Extra Dry remain
the winery's stars. The Rosé is very fruity
with scented wild berries; the white is
fragrant and easy drinking, with a fine
mousse and more floral notes; while the
Aedo is richer and more complex, floral and
fruity, with full flavour. Hard work in the
vineyard has managed to save the good
Bonarda and the even better Sangue di
Giuda 2014 from vegetal notes, making
them fragrant with nicely sound fruit.
Moscato Spumante 2014 is also well made,
with elegant citrussy aromas.

○ Moscato Spumante '14	♟♟ 3
● OP Bonarda Vivace '14	♟♟ 2*
● OP Sangue di Giuda '14	♟♟ 3
○ Pinot Nero Extra Dry Martinotti	♟♟ 3
○ Pinot Nero Extra Dry Martinotti Aedo	♟♟ 3
⊙ Pinot Nero Extra Dry Martinotti Rosé	♟♟ 3
● Barbera '14	♟ 3
○ Pinot Grigio '14	♟ 4
○ Riesling Renano '14	♟ 2
● OP Barbera Frizzante '13	♟♟ 2*
● OP Bonarda V. Guardia '13	♟♟ 3
● OP Bonarda Vivace '12	♟♟ 2*
● OP Bonarda Vivace '11	♟♟ 2*
● OP Bonarda Vivace '10	♟♟ 2*
● OP Bonarda Vivace '09	♟♟ 2*
● OP Sangue di Giuda '13	♟♟ 3

Bruno Verdi

VIA VERGOMBERRA, 5
27044 CANNETO PAVESE [PV]
TEL. 038588023
www.brunoverdi.it

CELLAR SALES
PRE-BOOKED VISITS
ANNUAL PRODUCTION 900,000 bottles
HECTARES UNDER VINE 9.00

Paolo Verdi took the helm of the estate at
just 20 years old, due to the premature
loss of his father Bruno, after whom it is
named. Although he has not yet managed
to achieve our highest accolade, for many
years now one, or often two, of his wines
have been making it into our finals. This is
no mean feat, considering the number of
wines bottled, and the fact that he does
almost everything himself, although he has
now been joined by his son Jacopo, a
fresh graduate of the famous Gallini
agricultural college in Voghera. This year
our favourite red was the concentrated
Barbera Campo del Marrone 2012, with
sound, fragrant, fruity flesh and the
estate's characteristic note of pennyroyal.
Extra Brut Vergomberra 2010 also reached
our finals. It too proffers notes of aromatic
herbs, along with pervasive tones of
tropical fruit and wild berries, and is
characterized by a fine bead and an
alluring softness. The Cavariola is as good
as ever, although the 2011 vintage may
need more time to develop.

● OP Barbera Campo del Marrone '12	♟♟ 3*
○ OP Pinot Nero Extra Brut Vorgomberra '10	♟♟ 4
● OP Bonarda Vivace Possessione di Vergombera '14	♟♟ 2*
○ OP Cruasé '12	♟♟ 4
● OP Rosso Cavariola Ris. '11	♟♟ 5
● OP Buttafuoco '14	♟ 2
○ OP Pinot Grigio '14	♟ 2
○ OP Riesling Renano V. Costa '14	♟ 2
● OP Rosso Cavariola Ris. '10	♟♟♟ 5
● OP Rosso Cavariola Ris. '07	♟♟♟ 4
● OP Barbera Campo del Marrone '11	♟♟ 3*
● OP Barbera Campo del Marrone '09	♟♟ 3*
● OP Bonarda Vivace Possessione di Vergombera '09	♟♟ 2*

Giuseppe Vezzoli

VIA COSTA SOPRA, 22
25030 ERBUSCO [BS]
TEL. 0307267579
www.vezzolivini.it

CELLAR SALES
PRE-BOOKED VISITS
ANNUAL PRODUCTION 130,000 bottles
HECTARES UNDER VINE 60.00

Keen grower and experimenter Giuseppe Vezzoli founded his winery in 1994, commencing with the small family vineyard. Today his estate has an impressive annual production of 130,000 bottles, made from the grapes of around 60 hectares of vineyards, mainly in Erbusco and both estate-owned and leased. Giuseppe's children Jessica and Dario also contribute enthusiastically to the family business and have founded Sullali, an innovative little estate of their own. The elegant, full Brut 2011 was our favourite of the top-notch wines presented by the estate this year. It offers concentrated fruit on the nose and palate, supported by a very elegant acidic note that fades into a pleasant finish of peaches and mineral notes. The Dosaggio Zero is more austere and linear, while the newcomer Vendemmia Zero has more complex, citrussy notes.

○ Franciacorta Brut '11	♥♥ 5
○ Franciacorta Brut	♥♥ 4
○ Franciacorta Dosaggio Zero	♥♥ 6
○ Franciacorta Extra Brut Nefertiti Dizeta '09	♥♥ 6
○ Franciacorta Extra Brut Vendemmia Zero	♥♥ 6
○ Franciacorta Satèn	♥♥ 5
○ Franciacorta Brut '09	♀♀ 5
○ Franciacorta Extra Brut Nefertiti Dizeta '08	♀♀ 6
○ Franciacorta Extra Brut Nefertiti Dizeta '07	♀♀ 6
○ Franciacorta Extra Brut Nefertiti Dizeta '06	♀♀ 6

Villa Crespia

LOC. ADRO
VIA VALLI, 31
25030 ADRO [BS]
TEL. 0307451051
www.arcipelagomuratori.com

CELLAR SALES
PRE-BOOKED VISITS
ANNUAL PRODUCTION 350,000 bottles
HECTARES UNDER VINE 60.00
SUSTAINABLE WINERY

The Muratori family are entrepreneurs with solid roots in agriculture. Over the years they have put together a group of first-rate estates in various regions, known as Arcipelago Muratori. In addition to Villa Crespia in Franciacorta, it includes Rubbia al Colle in Maremma, Oppida Aminea in Sannio, and Giardini Arimei on the island of Ischia. Villa Crespia is one of the most important estates in Franciacorta, with 60 hectares of vineyards capable of ensuring both quantity and quality in production. Operations are entrusted to oenologist Francesco Iacono, who crafts a series of Franciacortas expressing the estate's different terroirs. The 2007 vintage of the estate's flagship Franciacorta Riserva Francesco Iacono made it into our finals again. It is a Dosaggio Zero, almost exclusively pinot nero from the Fornaci vineyard, which undergoes long ageing on the lees. Its fruity notes and fresh, alluring style belie its age. On the palate it is firm and deep, with hazelnut and citrus notes on a velvety finish.

○ Franciacorta Dosaggio Zero Francesco Iacono Ris. '07	♥♥ 7
○ Franciacorta Brut Millè '07	♥♥ 5
○ Franciacorta Dosaggio Zero Cisiolo	♥♥ 5
○ Franciacorta Extra Brut Rosé Brolese	♥♥ 5
○ Franciacorta Brut Novalia	♥ 4
○ Franciacorta Brut Simbiotico	♥ 5
○ Franciacorta Dosaggio Zero Numerozero	♥ 5
○ Franciacorta Satèn Cesonato	♥ 5
○ Franciacorta Dosaggio Zero Francesco Iacono Ris. '04	♀♀♀ 7
○ Franciacorta Dosaggio Zero Francesco Iacono Ris. '06	♀♀ 7
○ Franciacorta Dosaggio Zero Francesco Iacono Ris. '05	♀♀ 7

Villa Franciacorta

via Villa, 12
25040 Monticelli Brusati [BS]
Tel. 030652329
www.villafranciacorta.it

PRE-BOOKED VISITS
ACCOMMODATION AND RESTAURANT SERVICE
ANNUAL PRODUCTION 300,000 bottles
HECTARES UNDER VINE 37.00

The 16th-century hamlet of Villa di Monticelli Brusati truly deserves a visit. It was purchased, with the 100 hectares of surrounding land, in the 1960s by Alessandro Bianchi, and today, after long and meticulous restoration, it is one of the most prestigious names in Franciacorta, with an elegant relais. Its vineyards, covering an area of almost 40 hectares, some on the terraced slopes of Monte della Madonna della Rosa, supply the top-quality grapes used for its wines. Today the estate is run by Alessandra Bianchi and her husband Paolo Piziol. Brut Cuvette 2007, a special edition dedicated to Expo 2015, exemplifies the style of Villa's Franciacortas. It is a clean, limpid wine, with a fine bead, and a fine, elegant nose of white-fleshed fruit, flowers and vanilla. The delicately structured palate shows good progression and a long, silky finish with notes of white-fleshed fruit and aromatic herbs. Rosé Bokè 2011 has a handsome onionskin hue and great expressive finesse, making it among the finest tasted this year.

○ Franciacorta Brut Cuvette Limited Edition Expo 2015 '07	♥♥ 7
● Barbera Bianchi Roncalli '11	♥♥ 6
● Curtefranca Gradoni '11	♥♥ 4
○ Franciacorta Brut Emozione '11	♥♥ 5
⊙ Franciacorta Brut Rosé Bokè '11	♥♥ 5
○ Franciacorta Extra Brut Extra Blu '09	♥♥ 5
○ Franciacorta Pas Dosé Diamant '08	♥♥ 5
○ Franciacorta Satèn '11	♥♥ 5
○ Franciacorta Brut Emozione '09	♥♥♥ 5
○ Franciacorta Extra Brut '98	♥♥♥ 4*
⊙ Franciacorta Brut Rosé '09	♥♥ 5
○ Franciacorta Brut Sel. '05	♥♥ 6
○ Franciacorta Pas Dosé Diamant '07	♥♥ 5
○ Franciacorta Satèn '10	♥♥ 5
○ Franciacorta Satèn '09	♥♥ 5
○ Franciacorta Satèn '07	♥♥ 5

Chiara Ziliani

via Franciacorta, 7
25050 Provaglio d'Iseo [BS]
Tel. 030981661
www.cantinazilianichiara.it

PRE-BOOKED VISITS
ANNUAL PRODUCTION 280,000 bottles
HECTARES UNDER VINE 18.00

With her enthusiasm and dynamism, Chiara exemplifies the new generation of Franciacorta growers in the spotlight today. Her modern, well-equipped cellar is on a hilltop in Provaglio d'Iseo, surrounded by 18 hectares of densely planted vineyards, with over 7,000 plants per hectare, and tended using methods with low environmental impact. The ideal location of the south and south-east-facing vineyards, 250 metres above sea level, and the care lavished on work in the cellar ensure the growing popularity of the estate's wide range, divided into three lines. Our pick of the many wines presented this year include the excellent Rosé Brut, pale hued with delicate aromas of berry fruit; the Brut 2010, opulent and buttery yet fresh and balanced; the non-vintage Brut, with refreshing notes of apples, mint, and vanilla; and the round, juicy Satèn 2010, all from the Ziliani C line. Brut Duca d'Iseo is complex and firmly structured, while Rosé Conte di Provaglio is full flavoured and invigorating.

○ Franciacorta Brut Conte di Provaglio	♥♥ 3
○ Franciacorta Brut Duca d'Iseo	♥♥ 5
⊙ Franciacorta Brut Rosé Ziliani C	♥♥ 4
○ Franciacorta Brut Ziliani C	♥♥ 3
○ Franciacorta Extra Brut Ziliani C '10	♥♥ 4
⊙ Franciacorta Rosé Conte di Provaglio	♥♥ 3
○ Franciacorta Satèn Conte di Provaglio	♥♥ 3
○ Franciacorta Satèn Maria Maddalena Cavalieri Ris. '10	♥♥ 6
○ Franciacorta Satèn Ziliani C '10	♥♥ 4
○ Franciacorta Brut Italo Ziliani C '09	♀♀ 5
○ Franciacorta Extra Brut Ziliani C '09	♀♀ 4
○ Franciacorta Pas Dosé Ziliani C '09	♀♀ 4
○ Franciacorta Satèn Ziliani C '09	♀♀ 4
○ Franciacorta Satèn Ziliani Maria Maddalena Cavalieri Ris. '07	♀♀ 5

1701

P.ZZA MARCONI, 6
25046 CAZZAGO SAN MARTINO [BS]
TEL. 030775 0875
www.1701franciacorta.it

CELLAR SALES
PRE-BOOKED VISITS
ANNUAL PRODUCTION 70,000 bottles
HECTARES UNDER VINE 11.00
VITICULTURE METHOD Certified Organic

○ Franciacorta Satèn	♟♟ 4
○ Franciacorta Brut	♟ 4
⊙ Franciacorta Brut Rosé	♟ 4

Elisabetta Abrami

S.DA VICINALE DELLE FOSCHE
25050 PROVAGLIO D'ISEO [BS]
TEL. 0306857185
www.vinielisabettaabrami.it

CELLAR SALES
ACCOMMODATION
ANNUAL PRODUCTION 60,000 bottles
HECTARES UNDER VINE 15.00
VITICULTURE METHOD Certified Organic

⊙ Franciacorta Brut Rosé	♟♟ 5
○ Franciacorta Extra Brut Blanc de Noirs '11	♟♟ 5
○ Franciacorta Pas Dosé '11	♟♟ 6

Al Rocol

VIA PROVINCIALE, 79
25050 OME [BS]
TEL. 0306852542
www.alrocol.com

CELLAR SALES
PRE-BOOKED VISITS
ACCOMMODATION AND RESTAURANT SERVICE
ANNUAL PRODUCTION 60,000 bottles
HECTARES UNDER VINE 13.00

○ Franciacorta Brut Ca' del Luf	♟♟ 5
○ Franciacorta Dosaggio Zero Castellini '10	♟♟ 5
○ Franciacorta Satèn Martignac '11	♟ 4

Avanzi

VIA TREVISAGO, 19
25080 MANERBA DEL GARDA [BS]
TEL. 0365551013
www.avanzi.net

CELLAR SALES
PRE-BOOKED VISITS
ANNUAL PRODUCTION 500,000 bottles
HECTARES UNDER VINE 77.00

○ Lugana Sirmione '14	♟♟ 2*
○ Lugana Borghetta '12	♟ 3
⊙ Valtènesi Chiaretto '14	♟ 2

La Basia

LOC. LA BASIA
VIA PREDEFITTE, 31
25080 PUEGNAGO SUL GARDA [BS]
TEL. 0365555958
www.labasia.it

CELLAR SALES
PRE-BOOKED VISITS
ANNUAL PRODUCTION 17,000 bottles
HECTARES UNDER VINE 4.00

● Predefitte '10	♟♟ 3
● Valtenesi Estate di San Martino '11	♟ 2

Cantina Sociale Bergamasca

VIA BERGAMO, 10
24060 SAN PAOLO D'ARGON [BG]
TEL. 035951098
www.cantinabergamasca.it

CELLAR SALES
PRE-BOOKED VISITS
ANNUAL PRODUCTION 650,000 bottles
HECTARES UNDER VINE 90.00

○ Terre del Colleoni Brut Colleoni '11	♟♟ 5
○ Terre del Colleoni Incrocio Manzoni '14	♟♟ 5
⊙ Terre del Colleoni Schiava '14	♟ 2

Podere Bignolino

LOC. BIGNOLINO
S.DA PROV.LE 44
27040 BRONI [PV]
TEL. 0383870160
www.poderebignolino.it

ANNUAL PRODUCTION 80,000 bottles
HECTARES UNDER VINE 40.00

| ● OP Barbera Costa Bercé '13 | ♟ 3 |
| ○ Pinot Grigio '14 | ♟ 2 |

Biondelli

LOC. BORNATO
VIA BASSO CASTELLO, 2
25046 CAZZAGO SAN MARTINO [BS]
TEL. 0307759896
www.biondelli.com

CELLAR SALES
PRE-BOOKED VISITS
ANNUAL PRODUCTION 40,000 bottles
HECTARES UNDER VINE 10.00
VITICULTURE METHOD Certified Organic

| ○ Franciacorta Brut | ♟♟ 4 |
| ○ Franciacorta Brut Première Dame '10 | ♟♟ 5 |

Bonaldi - Cascina del Bosco

LOC. PETOSINO
VIA GASPAROTTO, 96
24010 SORISOLE [BG]
TEL. 035571701
www.cascinadelbosco.it

CELLAR SALES
PRE-BOOKED VISITS
ANNUAL PRODUCTION 25,000 bottles
HECTARES UNDER VINE 4.00

| ○ Valcalepio Bianco '14 | ♟ 3 |
| ● Valcalepio Rosso '13 | ♟ 4 |

Bonfadini Franciacorta

VIA L. DI BERNARDO, 85
25049 ISEO [BS]
TEL. 0309826721
www.bonfadini.it

CELLAR SALES
PRE-BOOKED VISITS
ANNUAL PRODUCTION 50,000 bottles
HECTARES UNDER VINE 10.00

○ Franciacorta Dosaggio Zero Veritas	♟♟ 4
⊙ Franciacorta Rosé Opera	♟♟ 4
○ Franciacorta Satèn Carpe Diem	♟♟ 4
○ Franciacorta Brut Nobilium	♟ 4

La Boscaiola

VIA RICCAFANA, 19
25033 COLOGNE [BS]
TEL. 0307156386
www.laboscaiola.com

CELLAR SALES
PRE-BOOKED VISITS
ANNUAL PRODUCTION 50,000 bottles
HECTARES UNDER VINE 7.00

○ Franciacorta Brut Sessanta '07	♟♟ 6
○ Franciacorta Zero	♟♟ 4
○ Franciacorta Satèn	♟ 5

Luciano Brega

FRAZ. BERGAMASCO, 7
27040 MONTÙ BECCARIA [PV]
TEL. 038560237
www.lucianobrega.it

CELLAR SALES
PRE-BOOKED VISITS
ANNUAL PRODUCTION 150,000 bottles
HECTARES UNDER VINE 70.00

| ○ Brut M. Cl. Gran Montù '11 | ♟♟ 4 |
| ● OP Bonarda Casapaia '14 | ♟ 2 |

Ca d'Or

VIA L. GUSSALLI, 15
25125 BRESCIA
TEL. 0303583079
www.cadorwine.it

PRE-BOOKED VISITS
ACCOMMODATION AND RESTAURANT SERVICE
ANNUAL PRODUCTION 200,000 bottles
HECTARES UNDER VINE 28.00

○ Franciacorta Pas Dosé '08	🍷🍷 6
○ Franciacorta Brut Noble Cuvée	🍷 5
⊙ Franciacorta Brut Noble Rosé	🍷 5

Ca' del Santo

LOC. CAMPOLUNGO, 4
27040 MONTALTO PAVESE [PV]
TEL. 0383870545
www.cadelsanto.it

CELLAR SALES
PRE-BOOKED VISITS
ANNUAL PRODUCTION 25,000 bottles
HECTARES UNDER VINE 6.00

● OP Rosso Carolo Ris. '12	🍷🍷 3
● 50 + 50 '13	🍷 3

Valter Calvi

FRAZ. PALAZZINA, 24
27040 CASTANA [PV]
TEL. 038582136
www.vinicalvi.it

CELLAR SALES
PRE-BOOKED VISITS
ANNUAL PRODUCTION 45,000 bottles
HECTARES UNDER VINE 8.00

● OP Pinot Nero Marion '12	🍷🍷 3
● OP Bonarda Vivace '14	🍷 2

Caminella

VIA DANTE ALIGHIERI, 13
24069 CENATE SOTTO [BG]
TEL. 035941828
www.caminella.it

CELLAR SALES
PRE-BOOKED VISITS
ACCOMMODATION
ANNUAL PRODUCTION 40,000 bottles
HECTARES UNDER VINE 5.50

○ Verde Luna '14	🍷🍷 2*
● Goccio di Sole '12	🍷 5
● Luna Rossa '12	🍷 4
○ Ripa di Luna Brut '12	🍷 4

Camossi

VIA METELLI, 5
25030 ERBUSCO [BS]
TEL. 0307268022
www.camossi.it

CELLAR SALES
PRE-BOOKED VISITS
ANNUAL PRODUCTION 60,000 bottles
HECTARES UNDER VINE 30.00

⊙ Franciacorta Brut Rosé	🍷🍷 5
○ Franciacorta Extra Brut '08	🍷🍷 6
○ Franciacorta Extra Brut Pietro Camossi Ris. '07	🍷🍷 8

Cantina di Canneto

FRAZ. CAMPONOCE, 27
27044 CANNETO PAVESE [PV]
TEL. 038560078
www.cantinacanneto.it

ANNUAL PRODUCTION 2,000,000 bottles
HECTARES UNDER VINE 335.00

● OP Pinot Nero I Gioielli Brut M. Cl. '10	🍷🍷 4
● OP Buttafuoco Collegheppio '12	🍷 3

Le Cantorìe

FRAZ. CASAGLIO
VIA CASTELLO DI CASAGLIO, 24/25
25064 GUSSAGO [BS]
TEL. 0302523723
www.lecantorie.it

ANNUAL PRODUCTION 75,000 bottles
HECTARES UNDER VINE 12.00

⊙ Franciacorta Rosé Rosi delle Margherite	♥♥	7
○ Franciacorta Satèn Armonia	♥♥	4
○ Franciacorta Pas Dosé Armonia Ris. '08	♥	6

Cascina Belmonte

FRAZ. MONIGA DEL BOSCO
LOC. TOPPE
25080 MUSCOLINE [BS]
TEL. 3335051606
www.cascinabelmonte.it

PRE-BOOKED VISITS
ANNUAL PRODUCTION 15,000 bottles
HECTARES UNDER VINE 6.00

● Stramonia '13	♥♥	3
● Rebo Singia '14	♥	3
○ Serése '14	♥	3

Castello di Gussago

VIA MANICA, 9
25064 GUSSAGO [BS]
TEL. 0302525267
www.castellodigussago.it

CELLAR SALES
PRE-BOOKED VISITS
ANNUAL PRODUCTION 120,000 bottles
HECTARES UNDER VINE 15.00

⊙ Franciacorta Brut Rosé	♥♥	5
○ Franciacorta Pas Dosé '11	♥♥	5
○ Franciacorta Brut '10	♥	4

Castello di Luzzano

LOC. LUZZANO, 5
27040 ROVESCALA [PV]
TEL. 0523863277
www.castelloluzzano.it

CELLAR SALES
PRE-BOOKED VISITS
ACCOMMODATION AND RESTAURANT SERVICE
ANNUAL PRODUCTION 120,000 bottles
HECTARES UNDER VINE 76.00

● OP Bonarda Vivace Sommossa '14	♥	2
● OP Pinot Nero Umore Nero '14	♥	2

Castello di Stefanago

LOC. CASTELLO DI STEFANAGO
27040 BORGO PRIOLO [PV]
TEL. 0383875227
www.baruffaldivini.it

CELLAR SALES
PRE-BOOKED VISITS
HECTARES UNDER VINE 20.00
VITICULTURE METHOD Certified Organic

● Pinot Nero Campo Castagna '11	♥	4
⊙ Stefanago Ancestrale Rosé '11	♥	4

Castelveder

VIA BELVEDERE, 4
25040 MONTICELLI BRUSATI [BS]
TEL. 030652308
www.castelveder.it

CELLAR SALES
PRE-BOOKED VISITS
ANNUAL PRODUCTION 90,000 bottles
HECTARES UNDER VINE 11.00

○ Franciacorta Brut '09	♥♥	5
○ Franciacorta Extra Brut	♥♥	4
○ Franciacorta Satèn	♥♥	5
○ Franciacorta Pas Dosé	♥	5

Cantine Cavallotti

VIA EUROPA, 9A
20080 BUBBIANO [MI]
TEL. 0290848829
www.cantinecavallotti.it

CELLAR SALES
ANNUAL PRODUCTION 120,000 bottles
HECTARES UNDER VINE 14.00

● OP Cruasé Nero Puro '10	♟♟ 4
● OP Buttafuoco BB '12	♟ 4

Le Chiusure

FRAZ. PORTESE
VIA BOSCHETTE, 2
25010 SAN FELICE DEL BENACO [BS]
TEL. 0365626243
www.lechiusure.net

CELLAR SALES
PRE-BOOKED VISITS
ACCOMMODATION
ANNUAL PRODUCTION 22,000 bottles
HECTARES UNDER VINE 4.00

● Malborghetto '11	♟♟ 5
● Valtènesi Campei '12	♟♟ 2*
⊙ Valtènesi Chiaretto '14	♟ 3

Citari

FRAZ. SAN MARTINO DELLA BATTAGLIA
LOC. CITARI, 2
25015 DESENZANO DEL GARDA [BS]
TEL. 0309910310
www.citari.it

CELLAR SALES
PRE-BOOKED VISITS
ANNUAL PRODUCTION 150,000 bottles
HECTARES UNDER VINE 22.00
SUSTAINABLE WINERY

○ Lugana Sorgente '14	♟♟ 3
○ Mimi' '14	♟♟ 2*
○ San Martino della Battaglia Il Vecchio Vigneto '13	♟♟ 3

Civielle

VIA PERGOLA, 21
25080 MONIGA DEL GARDA [BS]
TEL. 0365502002
www.civielle.com

CELLAR SALES
ANNUAL PRODUCTION 500,000 bottles
HECTARES UNDER VINE 72.00
VITICULTURE METHOD Certified Organic

○ Lugana Biocòra '14	♟♟ 2*
○ Lugana Pergola '14	♟♟ 3
⊙ Valtènesi Chiaretto Pergola '14	♟ 4

Colline della Stella

VIA FORCELLA,70
25064 GUSSAGO [BS]
TEL. 3478039339
www.collinedellastella.com

CELLAR SALES
PRE-BOOKED VISITS
ANNUAL PRODUCTION 50,000 bottles
HECTARES UNDER VINE 10.00

○ Franciacorta Dosaggio Zero '09	♟♟ 4
○ Franciacorta Dosaggio Zero	♟♟ 4
⊙ Franciacorta Dosaggio Zero Rosé	♟♟ 4

Corte Aura

VIA COLZANO, 13
25030 ADRO [BS]
TEL. 030 7357281
www.corteaura.it

CELLAR SALES
PRE-BOOKED VISITS
ANNUAL PRODUCTION 170,000 bottles
HECTARES UNDER VINE 5.00

○ Franciacorta Brut	♟♟ 4
○ Franciacorta Pas Dosé Armonia Ris.	♟♟ 5
⊙ Franciacorta Rosé	♟♟ 4
○ Franciacorta Satèn	♟ 4

Corte Bianca

LOC. SERGNANA
VIA CADUTO ANTONINI, 1
25050 PROVAGLIO D'ISEO [BS]
TEL. 030983293
www.cortebianca.it

CELLAR SALES
PRE-BOOKED VISITS
ANNUAL PRODUCTION 12,000 bottles
HECTARES UNDER VINE 5.00
VITICULTURE METHOD Certified Organic

○ Franciacorta Dosaggio Zero Bianca Ris. '08	♥♥ 6
○ Franciacorta Satèn '09	♥♥ 5
○ Franciacorta Extra Brut	♥ 5
⊙ Franciacorta Rosé '11	♥ 6

Tenuta La Costa

FRAZ. COSTA, 68
27040 CASTANA [PV]
TEL. 0385241527
tenutalacosta@libero.it

PRE-BOOKED VISITS
ANNUAL PRODUCTION 50,000 bottles
HECTARES UNDER VINE 12.00

⊙ OP Cruasé Campo del Prete '11	♥♥ 3
○ OP Pinot Nero Extra Brut '08	♥♥ 4
○ OP Riesling Vigna del Mattino '14	♥ 3

La Costaiola

FRAZ. COSTAIOLA
VIA COSTAIOLA, 25
27054 MONTEBELLO DELLA BATTAGLIA [PV]
TEL. 038383169
www.lacostaiola.it

CELLAR SALES
ACCOMMODATION
ANNUAL PRODUCTION 80,000 bottles
HECTARES UNDER VINE 13.00

○ OP Pinot Nero Brut M. Cl. Rossetti & Scrivani	♥♥ 3
● Bricca '14	♥ 2
○ Nové Brut M. Cl.	♥ 3

De Toma

VIA BATTISTI, 7
24020 SCANZOROSCIATE [BG]
TEL. 035657329

CELLAR SALES
PRE-BOOKED VISITS
ANNUAL PRODUCTION 5,000 bottles
HECTARES UNDER VINE 2,5

● Moscato di Scanzo '12	♥♥ 7

Delai

VIA MORO, 1
25080 PUEGNAGO SUL GARDA [BS]
TEL. 0365555527

ANNUAL PRODUCTION 80,000 bottles
HECTARES UNDER VINE 8.00

● Merzemino Sovenigo '11	♥♥ 3
⊙ Garda Bresciano Chiaretto Notte Rosa '14	♥ 3

Diana

VIA ROMA 63
27040 CASTANA [PV]
TEL. 0385249618
www.dianawine.it

CELLAR SALES
PRE-BOOKED VISITS
ANNUAL PRODUCTION 35,000 bottles
HECTARES UNDER VINE 9.00

● OP Barbera Sentiero della Guerra '12	♥♥ 3
● OP Pinot Nero Valle del Portico '11	♥ 3

Luca Faccinelli

VIA CESURE, 19
23030 CHIURO [SO]
TEL. 3470807011
www.lucafaccinelli.it

CELLAR SALES
ANNUAL PRODUCTION 8,500 bottles
HECTARES UNDER VINE 1.50

● Valtellina Sup. Ortensio Lando '10   ♟♟ 5

Finigeto

LOC. CELLA, 27
27040 MONTALTO PAVESE [PV]
TEL. 328 7095347
www.finigeto.com

CELLAR SALES
PRE-BOOKED VISITS
ACCOMMODATION
ANNUAL PRODUCTION 70,000 bottles
HECTARES UNDER VINE 33.00

● OP Barbera Il Ribaldo '13   ♟♟ 3
○ Riesling Lo Spavaldo '14   ♟♟ 2*
○ Moscato '14   ♟ 3

La Fiòca

FRAZ. NIGOLINE
VIA VILLA, 13B
25040 CORTE FRANCA [BS]
TEL. 0309826313
www.lafioca.com

CELLAR SALES
PRE-BOOKED VISITS
ACCOMMODATION
ANNUAL PRODUCTION 40,000 bottles
HECTARES UNDER VINE 4.00

⊙ Franciacorta Brut Rosé   ♟♟ 5
○ Franciacorta Dosaggio Zero '08   ♟♟ 5
○ Franciacorta Extra Brut Ris. '07   ♟♟ 8

La Fiorita

VIA MAGLIO, 14
25020 OME [BS]
TEL. 030652279
www.lafiorita.bs.it

CELLAR SALES
PRE-BOOKED VISITS
ANNUAL PRODUCTION 60,000 bottles
HECTARES UNDER VINE 7.00

○ Franciacorta Brut   ♟♟ 4
⊙ Franciacorta Brut Rosé   ♟♟ 4
○ Franciacorta Dosaggio Zero   ♟♟ 4
○ Franciacorta Satèn   ♟♟ 4

Giorgio Gianatti

VIA DEI PORTICI, 82
23020 MONTAGNA IN VALTELLINA [SO]
TEL. 0342380033
gianatti.giorgio@alice.it

CELLAR SALES
PRE-BOOKED VISITS
ANNUAL PRODUCTION 8,000 bottles
HECTARES UNDER VINE 2.00

● Valtellina Sup. Grumello '09   ♟♟ 3*

Giubertoni

LOC. BAGNOLO SAN VITO
FRAZ. SAN NICOLÒ PO
VIA PAPA GIOVANNI XXIII
46031 BAGNOLO SAN VITO [MN]
TEL. 0376252762
www.cantinegiubertoni.it

ANNUAL PRODUCTION 100,000 bottles

● Lambrusco Mantovano G '14   ♟♟ 2*
⊙ Lambrusco Rosato '14   ♟ 2

Lazzari

VIA MELLA, 49
25020 CAPRIANO DEL COLLE [BS]
TEL. 0309747387
www.lazzarivini.it

CELLAR SALES
PRE-BOOKED VISITS
ANNUAL PRODUCTION 35,000 bottles
HECTARES UNDER VINE 7.20
SUSTAINABLE WINERY

● Capriano del Colle Adagio '13	♛♛ 3
● Capriano del Colle Riserva degli Angeli '12	♛♛ 5
● Capriano del Colle Berzamì '14	♛ 3

Cantine Lebovitz

LOC. GOVERNOLO
V.LE RIMEMBRANZE, 4
46037 RONCOFERRARO [MN]
TEL. 0376668115
www.cantinelebovitz.it

CELLAR SALES
PRE-BOOKED VISITS
ANNUAL PRODUCTION 50,000 bottles

● Lambrusco Mantovano Rosso dei Concari '14	♛♛ 2*
● Lambrusco Mantovano al Scagarün '14	♛ 1
● Lambrusco Mantovano Sedamat '14	♛ 1*

Lovera

VIA LOVERA, 14A
25030 ERBUSCO [BS]
TEL. 0307760491
www.cantinalovera.it

CELLAR SALES
PRE-BOOKED VISITS
ANNUAL PRODUCTION 150,000 bottles
HECTARES UNDER VINE 24.00

○ Franciacorta Brut	♛♛ 5
○ Franciacorta Brut Ris. '08	♛♛ 5
○ Franciacorta Satèn	♛ 5

Lurani Cernuschi

VIA CONVENTO, 3
24031 ALMENNO SAN SALVATORE [BG]
TEL. 035642576
www.luranicernuschi.it

CELLAR SALES
PRE-BOOKED VISITS
RESTAURANT SERVICE
ANNUAL PRODUCTION 80,000 bottles
HECTARES UNDER VINE 13.00

○ Valcalepio Bianco Armisa '14	♛♛ 3
● Umbriana '11	♛ 3

Tenuta Maddalena

S.DA TIBASSI
46049 VOLTA MANTOVANA [MN]
TEL. 037683323
www.tenutamaddalena.it

CELLAR SALES
PRE-BOOKED VISITS
ANNUAL PRODUCTION 40,000 bottles
HECTARES UNDER VINE 9.00

○ D'Alloro '14	♛♛ 2*
● Val di Pietra '12	♛♛ 3
● Monte Cervo '13	♛ 3

Eligio Magri

VIA COLLE DEI PASTA, 8A
24060 TORRE DE' ROVERI [BG]
TEL. 0354528868
www.eligiomagri.it

CELLAR SALES
PRE-BOOKED VISITS
ANNUAL PRODUCTION 80,000 bottles
HECTARES UNDER VINE 15.00

● Patrizio '11	♛♛ 4
● Elogio '09	♛ 3
○ Moscato Giallo Lucelio '14	♛ 3

Manuelina

FRAZ. RUINELLO DI SOTTO, 3A
27047 SANTA MARIA DELLA VERSA [PV]
TEL. 0385278247
www.manuelina.com

CELLAR SALES
PRE-BOOKED VISITS
ANNUAL PRODUCTION 230,000 bottles
HECTARES UNDER VINE 22.00

○ Brut 137 '11	♈♈ 3
⊙ OP Cruasé 145 '11	♈ 3

Marangona

LOC. MARANGONA 1
25010 POZZOLENGO [BS]
TEL. 030919379
www.marangona.com

CELLAR SALES
PRE-BOOKED VISITS
ANNUAL PRODUCTION 30,000 bottles
HECTARES UNDER VINE 27.00

○ Lugana '14	♈♈ 2*
○ Lugana Rabbiosa '14	♈ 3
○ Lugana Trecampane '14	♈ 2

Marsadri

LOC. RAFFA DI PUEGNAGO
VIA NAZIONALE, 26
25080 PUEGNAGO SUL GARDA [BS]
TEL. 0365651005
www.cantinemarsadri.com

ANNUAL PRODUCTION 200,000 bottles
HECTARES UNDER VINE 15.00

● Garda Cl. Groppello Brolo '14	♈♈ 3
● Garda Cl. Rosso Brolo '14	♈ 4
● Garda Marzemino Brolo '14	♈ 2

Alberto Marsetti

VIA SCARPATETTI, 15
23100 SONDRIO
TEL. 0342216329
www.marsetti.it

ANNUAL PRODUCTION 20,000 bottles
HECTARES UNDER VINE 5.00

● Valtellina Sup. Grumello '11	♈♈ 5
● Valtellina Sup. Le Prudenze '11	♈♈ 5
● Sforzato di Valtellina '10	♈ 6

Martilde

FRAZ. CROCE, 4A1
27040 ROVESCALA [PV]
TEL. 0385756280
www.martilde.it

CELLAR SALES
PRE-BOOKED VISITS
ANNUAL PRODUCTION 30,000 bottles
HECTARES UNDER VINE 15.00

○ OP Malvasia Piume '14	♈♈ 2*

Monte Cicogna

VIA DELLE VIGNE, 6
25080 MONIGA DEL GARDA [BS]
TEL. 0365503200
www.montecicogna.it

CELLAR SALES
PRE-BOOKED VISITS
ANNUAL PRODUCTION 150,000 bottles
HECTARES UNDER VINE 30.00

● Garda Cl. Rosso Groppello Beana '13	♈♈ 2*
⊙ Garda Cl. Chiaretto Sicli '14	♈ 2
○ Garda Cl. Il Torrione '12	♈ 2

Montelio

via D. Mazza, 1
27050 Codevilla [PV]
Tel. 0383373090
montelio.gio@alice.it

CELLAR SALES
PRE-BOOKED VISITS
ACCOMMODATION AND RESTAURANT SERVICE
ANNUAL PRODUCTION 130,000 bottles
HECTARES UNDER VINE 27.00

● OP Barbera '13	♟♟ 2*
● OP Rosso Solarolo Ris. '11	♟♟ 4
○ Noblerot '12	♟ 4

Montenato Griffini

via Sparano, 13/14
27040 Bosnasco [PV]
Tel. 0385272904
www.montenatogriffini.it

CELLAR SALES
PRE-BOOKED VISITS
ANNUAL PRODUCTION 15,000 bottles
HECTARES UNDER VINE 10.40

● OP Bonarda Puntofermo '06	♟ 3
● OP Rosso Bariola '10	♟ 3

Monterucco

Valle Cima, 38
27040 Cigognola [PV]
Tel. 038585151
www.monterucco.it

CELLAR SALES
PRE-BOOKED VISITS
ANNUAL PRODUCTION 100,000 bottles
HECTARES UNDER VINE 20.00

○ Malvasia Valentina '14	♟♟ 2*
○ OP Pinot Nero Brut '09	♟♟ 3
● OP Buttafuoco Sanluigi '12	♟ 3

Il Montù

via Marconi, 10
27040 Montù Beccaria [PV]
Tel. 0385262252
www.ilmontu.com

CELLAR SALES
PRE-BOOKED VISITS
ANNUAL PRODUCTION 600,000 bottles
HECTARES UNDER VINE 85.00

○ Brut Il Millesimato '07	♟♟ 4
○ Extra Dry L'Extra '08	♟ 3

Alfio Mozzi

via Ca' Bianca, 19
23012 Castione Andevenno [SO]
Tel. 3393707018
www.alfiomozzi.com

CELLAR SALES
PRE-BOOKED VISITS
ANNUAL PRODUCTION 15,000 bottles
HECTARES UNDER VINE 3.50

● Sforzato di Valtellina '12	♟♟ 7
● Valtellina Sup. Sassella Grisone Ris. '11	♟♟ 6

Angelo Pecis

via San Pietro delle Passere, 12
24060 San Paolo d'Argon [BG]
Tel. 035959104
www.pecis.it

CELLAR SALES
PRE-BOOKED VISITS
ANNUAL PRODUCTION 25,000 bottles
HECTARES UNDER VINE 5.00

● Valcalepio Rosso della Pezia Ris. '09	♟♟ 3
○ Brut Maximus '07	♟ 4
⊙ Quadrifoglio Brut Rosé '12	♟ 4

Peri Bigogno

VIA GARIBALDI, 64
25014 CASTENEDOLO [BS]
TEL. 0302731572
www.bigogno.com

CELLAR SALES
PRE-BOOKED VISITS
ANNUAL PRODUCTION 50,000 bottles
HECTARES UNDER VINE 9.00

○ Talento Peri 46 '10	♥♥ 5
● Rosso Gobbo '08	♥ 3
☉ Talento Peri Rosé '11	♥ 4

La Perla

LOC. TRESENDA
VIA VALGELLA, 29B
23036 TEGLIO [SO]
TEL. 3462878894
www.vini-laperla.com

CELLAR SALES
PRE-BOOKED VISITS
ANNUAL PRODUCTION 20,000 bottles
HECTARES UNDER VINE 3.30

● Sforzato di Valtellina Quattro Soli '11	♥♥ 7
● Valtellina Sup. La Mossa '11	♥♥ 4

Piccolo Bacco dei Quaroni

FRAZ. COSTAMONTEFEDELE
27040 MONTÙ BECCARIA [PV]
TEL. 038560521
www.piccolobaccodeiquaroni.it

CELLAR SALES
PRE-BOOKED VISITS
ANNUAL PRODUCTION 35,000 bottles
HECTARES UNDER VINE 11.50

● OP Pinot Nero Vign. La Fiocca '14	♥ 2
● OP Buttafuoco Vign. Ca' Padroni '11	♥ 3
○ OP Riesling Vign. del Pozzo '14	♥ 2

Pilandro

FRAZ. SAN MARTINO DELLA BATTAGLIA
LOC. PILANDRO, 1
25010 DESENZANO DEL GARDA [BS]
TEL. 0309910363
www.pilandro.it

CELLAR SALES
PRE-BOOKED VISITS
ANNUAL PRODUCTION 200,000 bottles
HECTARES UNDER VINE 20.00

○ Lugana '14	♥♥ 2*
○ Lugana Terecrea '14	♥♥ 2*

Plozza di Ome

VIA LIZZANA, 13
25050 OME [BS]
TEL. 0306527775
www.plozzaome.it

CELLAR SALES
PRE-BOOKED VISITS
ANNUAL PRODUCTION 40,000 bottles
HECTARES UNDER VINE 4.00

○ Franciacorta Brut	♥♥ 5
☉ Franciacorta Rosé	♥♥ 5
○ Franciacorta Satèn	♥♥ 5

Prime Alture

VIA MADONNA, 109
27045 CASTEGGIO [PV]
TEL. 038383214
www.primealture.it

CELLAR SALES
PRE-BOOKED VISITS
ACCOMMODATION AND RESTAURANT SERVICE
ANNUAL PRODUCTION 40,000 bottles
HECTARES UNDER VINE 8.00

● Pinot Noir Centopercento '13	♥♥ 5
● Il Rosso 60 & 40 '14	♥ 3
○ Io per Te Blanc de Noir	♥ 4

Le Quattro Terre

FRAZ. BORGONATO
VIA RISORGIMENTO, 11
25040 CORTE FRANCA [BS]
TEL. 030984312
www.quattroterre.it

CELLAR SALES
PRE-BOOKED VISITS
ACCOMMODATION AND RESTAURANT SERVICE
ANNUAL PRODUCTION 45,000 bottles
HECTARES UNDER VINE 7.00

○ Franciacorta Brut		♟♟ 5
○ Franciacorta Dosaggio Zero '09		♟♟ 5
○ Franciacorta Brut '11		♟ 5
○ Franciacorta Extra Brut		♟ 5

Riccafana - Fratus

VIA F.LLI FACCHETTI, 91
25033 COLOGNE [BS]
TEL. 0307156797
www.riccafana.com

CELLAR SALES
ANNUAL PRODUCTION 100,000 bottles
HECTARES UNDER VINE 12.00
VITICULTURE METHOD Certified Organic

○ Franciacorta Brut		♟♟ 5
○ Franciacorta Satèn		♟♟ 5
☉ Franciacorta Rosé Territori '11		♟ 5

Ricchi

FRAZ. RICCHI
VIA FESTONI, 13D
46040 MONZAMBANO [MN]
TEL. 0376800238
www.cantinaricchi.it

CELLAR SALES
PRE-BOOKED VISITS
ANNUAL PRODUCTION 300,000 bottles
HECTARES UNDER VINE 40.00

○ Garda Chardonnay Meridiano '13		♟♟ 3
● Garda Merlot Carpino '11		♟ 5

Riva di Franciacorta

LOC. FANTECOLO
VIA CARLO ALBERTO, 19
25050 PROVAGLIO D'ISEO [BS]
TEL. 0309823701
www.rivadifranciacorta.it

CELLAR SALES
PRE-BOOKED VISITS
ANNUAL PRODUCTION 200,000 bottles
HECTARES UNDER VINE 31.00
SUSTAINABLE WINERY

☉ Franciacorta Brut Rosé		♟♟ 5
○ Franciacorta Pas Dosé Rivalto 75		♟♟ 5
○ Franciacorta Satèn		♟♟ 5
○ Franciacorta Brut		♟ 5

Romantica

VIA VALLOSA, 29
25050 PASSIRANO [BS]
TEL. 03042059
www.romanticafranciacorta.com

PRE-BOOKED VISITS
ACCOMMODATION
ANNUAL PRODUCTION 30,000 bottles
HECTARES UNDER VINE 10.00

○ Franciacorta Brut		♟♟ 5
○ Franciacorta Satèn		♟♟ 5

La Rotonda

LOC. CALINO
FRAZ. 25046
VIA BOSCHI, 1
25046 CAZZAGO SAN MARTINO [BS]
TEL. 0307750909
www.larotondafranciacorta.it

PRE-BOOKED VISITS
ANNUAL PRODUCTION 80,000 bottles
HECTARES UNDER VINE 12.72
VITICULTURE METHOD Certified Organic

○ Franciacorta Brut EsseA		♟♟ 3
○ Franciacorta Dosaggio Zero DiZeta '09		♟♟ 5
☉ Franciacorta Rosé EsseA		♟ 4

San Cristoforo

VIA VILLANUOVA, 2
25030 ERBUSCO [BS]
TEL. 0307760482
www.sancristoforo.eu

CELLAR SALES
PRE-BOOKED VISITS
ANNUAL PRODUCTION 80,000 bottles
HECTARES UNDER VINE 10.00
SUSTAINABLE WINERY

○ Franciacorta Brut	♔♔ 4
○ Franciacorta Pas Dosé '10	♔♔ 6
○ Franciacorta Brut '10	♔ 6
⊙ Franciacorta Rosé	♔ 4

San Michele

VIA PARROCCHIA, 57
25020 CAPRIANO DEL COLLE [BS]
TEL. 0309444091
www.sanmichelevini.it

CELLAR SALES
PRE-BOOKED VISITS
ANNUAL PRODUCTION 100,000 bottles
HECTARES UNDER VINE 16.00
VITICULTURE METHOD Certified Organic

○ Capriano del Colle Bianco Otten '12	♔♔ 3
● Capriano del Colle Rosso Canto '13	♔♔ 2*
● Merlot Nubes '13	♔ 2

Sant'Egidio

VIA FONTANELLA, 13C
24039 SOTTO IL MONTE GIOVANNI XXIII [BG]
TEL. 035794732
www.sant-egidio.it

ACCOMMODATION AND RESTAURANT SERVICE
ANNUAL PRODUCTION 15,000 bottles
HECTARES UNDER VINE 3.00
VITICULTURE METHOD Certified Organic

● Tessere '12	♔♔ 3
● Turano '12	♔ 3

Santus

VIA BADIA, 68
25038 ROVATO [BS]
TEL. 0308367074
www.santus.it

PRE-BOOKED VISITS
ANNUAL PRODUCTION 50,000 bottles
HECTARES UNDER VINE 9.00

○ Francacorta Brut	♔♔ 4
○ Francacorta Satèn	♔♔ 4
⊙ Franciacorta Extra Brut Rosé	♔ 4

Le Sincette

LOC. PICEDO DI POLPENAZZE DEL GARDA
VIA ROSARIO, 44
25080 POLPENAZZE DEL GARDA [BS]
TEL. 0365651471
www.lesincette.it

CELLAR SALES
PRE-BOOKED VISITS
ANNUAL PRODUCTION 30,000 bottles
HECTARES UNDER VINE 11.00
VITICULTURE METHOD Certified
OrganicCertified Biodynamic

● Garda Cl. Groppello '14	♔♔ 2*
● Ronco del Garda '13	♔♔ 2*
○ Garda Chardonnay '14	♔ 2
⊙ Valtenesi Chiaretto '14	♔ 2

Tenimenti Castelrotto - Torti

FRAZ. CASTELROTTO, 6
27047 MONTECALVO VERSIGGIA [PV]
TEL. 0385951000
www.tortiwinepinotnero.com

CELLAR SALES
PRE-BOOKED VISITS
ACCOMMODATION AND RESTAURANT SERVICE
ANNUAL PRODUCTION 250,000 bottles
HECTARES UNDER VINE 35.00

● OP Barbera '10	♔♔ 3
● OP Pinot Nero '09	♔♔ 4
○ Brut Martinotti Casaleggio	♔ 3

Benedetto Tognazzi

FRAZ. CAIONVICO
VIA SANT'ORSOLA, 161
25135 BRESCIA
TEL. 0302692695
www.tognazzivini.it

CELLAR SALES
PRE-BOOKED VISITS
ANNUAL PRODUCTION 65,000 bottles
HECTARES UNDER VINE 12.00

○ Lugana Cascina Ardea '14	♥♥ 2*

Torrevilla

VIA EMILIA, 4
27050 TORRAZZA COSTE [PV]
TEL. 038377003
www.torrevilla.it

CELLAR SALES
PRE-BOOKED VISITS
ANNUAL PRODUCTION 3,000,000 bottles
HECTARES UNDER VINE 650.00

○ OP Pinot Grigio La Genisia '14	♥♥ 2*
○ OP Novemesi La Genisia	♥ 2

Pietro Torti

FRAZ. CASTELROTTO, 9
27047 MONTECALVO VERSIGGIA [PV]
TEL. 038599763
www.pietrotorti.it

CELLAR SALES
PRE-BOOKED VISITS
ACCOMMODATION
ANNUAL PRODUCTION 30,000 bottles
HECTARES UNDER VINE 12.50

○ OP Riesling Moglialunga '14	♥ 2
● OP Bonarda Vivace '14	♥ 2
⊙ OP Cruasé '12	♥ 4

Triacca

VIA NAZIONALE, 121
23030 VILLA DI TIRANO [SO]
TEL. 0342701352
www.triacca.eu

CELLAR SALES
PRE-BOOKED VISITS
RESTAURANT SERVICE
ANNUAL PRODUCTION 450,000 bottles
HECTARES UNDER VINE 40.00

● Valtellina Sforzato San Domenico '11	♥♥ 6
● Valtellina Sup. Prestigio '12	♥♥ 6
● Valtellina Sup. La Gatta Ris. '11	♥ 5

F.lli Turina

VIA PERGOLA, 68
25080 MONIGA DEL GARDA [BS]
TEL. 0365502103
www.turinavini.it

CELLAR SALES
PRE-BOOKED VISITS
ANNUAL PRODUCTION 300,000 bottles
HECTARES UNDER VINE 20,000.00

○ Lugana '14	♥♥ 2*
○ Lugana V. Fenil Boi '14	♥♥ 2*

La Valle

VIA SANT'ANTONIO, 4
25050 RODENGO SAIANO [BS]
TEL. 0307722045
www.vinilavalle.it

CELLAR SALES
PRE-BOOKED VISITS
ANNUAL PRODUCTION 50,000 bottles
HECTARES UNDER VINE 6.00

○ Franciacorta Extra Brut Blanc de Noir '11	♥♥ 5
○ Franciacorta Extra Brut Naturalis '09	♥♥ 6
○ Franciacorta Satèn	♥♥ 5

Tenuta La Vigna

CASCINA LA VIGNA
25020 CAPRIANO DEL COLLE [BS]
TEL. 0309748061
www.tenutalavigna.it

CELLAR SALES
PRE-BOOKED VISITS
ANNUAL PRODUCTION 35,000 bottles
HECTARES UNDER VINE 7.00

○ Capriano del Colle Bianco Torrazza '14	♥♥ 3
● Capriano del Colle Rosso Monte Bruciato Ris. '11	♥ 4

Vigna Dorata

FRAZ. CALINO
VIA SALA, 80
25046 CAZZAGO SAN MARTINO [BS]
TEL. 0307254275
www.vignadorata.it

CELLAR SALES
PRE-BOOKED VISITS
ANNUAL PRODUCTION 70,000 bottles
HECTARES UNDER VINE 6.00

○ Franciacorta Brut	♥♥ 4
○ Franciacorta Extra Brut	♥♥ 5
○ Franciacorta Satèn	♥♥ 5
○ Franciacorta Rosé	♥ 5

Vigne Olcru

VIA BUCA, 26
27047 SANTA MARIA DELLA VERSA [PV]
TEL. 0385799958
vigneolcru.com

PRE-BOOKED VISITS
ANNUAL PRODUCTION 100,000 bottles
HECTARES UNDER VINE 29.00

○ OP Pinot Nero Extra Brut Verve '09	♥♥ 4
○ OP Brut Virtus '09	♥ 4
● OP Pinot Nero Coppiere Nero '12	♥ 4

Visconti

FRAZ. SAN MARTINO DELLA BATTAGLIA
VIA SELVA CAPUZZA, 1
25010 DESENZANO DEL GARDA [BS]
TEL. 0309910381
www.viscontiwines.it

CELLAR SALES
PRE-BOOKED VISITS
ANNUAL PRODUCTION 250,000 bottles
HECTARES UNDER VINE 20.00

○ Lugana '14	♥♥ 2*
○ Lugana Collo Lungo '14	♥♥ 2*
○ Lugana Franco Visconti '14	♥♥ 3

Zamichele

VIA ROVEGLIA PALAZZINA, 2
25010 POZZOLENGO [BS]
TEL. 030918631
cantinazamichele@alice.it

CELLAR SALES
PRE-BOOKED VISITS
ANNUAL PRODUCTION 45,000 bottles
HECTARES UNDER VINE 8.00

○ Lugana Gardè '13	♥♥ 2*
○ Lugana '14	♥ 2

Carlo Zenegaglia

VIA LONGARONE 27
25010 POZZOLENGO [BS]
TEL. 030918622
www.carlozenegaglia.com

CELLAR SALES
HECTARES UNDER VINE 12.00

○ Lugana Tre Grazie '14	♥♥ 4
○ Lugana Montefluno '14	♥ 4

TRENTINO

TrentoDoc continues to fly the Trentino winegrowing
flag in Italy and worldwide. There are now over 40
(41 to be exact, but the number increases in the
blink of an eye) wineries ranging in size from giants
like Ferrari, Mezzacorona or Cavit, to artisanal
boutique cellars. This year we tasted well over 100 labels
and there is a very interesting aspect: over 20 reached our final tastings, with seven
wines taking the top Tre Bicchieri spot on the podium. A major achievement, the
result of years of hard work across the entire Trentino wine industry. If this region
ferries over one million quintals of grapes to cellars annually, there can be no doubt
that chardonnay grapes, and increasing amounts of pinot noir, for sparkling wine
production are tended with meticulous care by these passionate winegrowers. These
are the wines "reborn" during second fermentation, which have generated their own
particular style, that of mountain (Dolomite to be precise) sparklers. Wines rich in
acid backbone, clean and smooth, with huge minerality. Wines that can mature for
years and years on the lees, intensifying depth and elegance with time. And all this
in the absence of some prestigious labels like Riserva del Fondatore Giulio Ferrari
or Rotari's Flavio, still ageing on the yeasts and awaiting disgorgement. As we
mentioned, seven awards were given, with a welcome new entry, Opera, a dynamic
young Valle di Cembra winery which stands proud alongside champions like Ferrari,
Cavit, Letrari, Abate Nero, Balter and the unfailingly excellent Methius. If Trentino
has sparkling success with its sparklers, the same cannot be said of the still wines.
Only Marchese Guerrieri Gonzaga's San Leonardo held its own, saving fame and
traditional elegance. There were mixed reviews for Teroldego. The fault of the vintage
and some due to forcing the hand in the cellar, which penalized results, but there
were also several versions missing, still maturing. While the reds failed to impress,
the whites were only marginally better. The thrill was missing even though several
labels reached our finals. So this year the banner for mountain whites was carried
by Vigna delle Forche, La Vis' Müller Thurgau, garnering a much-deserved award
for Cembra vignerons, who are not only vineyard artisans but also custodians of this
difficult territory. Last but not least, a sweet wine, a great Trentino product: the Vino
Santo Arèle, from Pravis, whose name pays homage to the drying mats where Valle
dei Laghi nosiola grapes are left until Easter week.

★Abate Nero

FRAZ. GARDOLO
S.DA TRENTINA, 45
38121 TRENTO
TEL. 0461246566
www.abatenero.it

CELLAR SALES
PRE-BOOKED VISITS
ANNUAL PRODUCTION 65,000 bottles
HECTARES UNDER VINE 65.00

Abate Nero is a TrentoDoc stalwart and the result of almost half a century of constant attention to winemaking processes and meticulous grape selection. Luciano Lau is the soul of the winery, assisted in a solid partnership by his Castel Terlago family. Once again winery production shines for its standard and consistent quality. All very evident starting with the winery's latest arrival Domini Nero 2010, a vintage with a clear style: taut and very persuasive, vibrant floral impact, overtones of pinot nero and great length. Tre Bicchieri. As always an excellent performance from the Riserva Cuvée dell'Abate 2008, with golden nuances and intense, tangy palate: a Brut to sip slowly. The other traditionals are equally racy, from the classic Brut to the seductive Rosé, with a well-deserved special mention for the Extra Brut and the Domini, both pure chardonnay.

○ Trento Brut Domini Nero '10	♟♟♟	5
○ Trento Brut Cuvée dell'Abate Ris. '08	♟♟	6
○ Trento Brut	♟♟	4
○ Trento Brut Domini '09	♟♟	5
⊙ Trento Brut Rosé	♟♟	4
○ Trento Extra Brut	♟♟	4
○ Trento Brut Cuvée dell'Abate Ris. '04	♟♟♟	6
○ Trento Brut Cuvée dell'Abate Ris. '03	♟♟♟	5
○ Trento Brut Cuvée dell'Abate Ris. '02	♟♟♟	5
○ Trento Brut Cuvée dell'Abate Ris. '01	♟♟♟	5
○ Trento Brut Domini '07	♟♟♟	5
○ Trento Brut Domini '05	♟♟♟	5
○ Trento Brut Domini Nero '08	♟♟♟	5
○ Trento Domìni Nero '09	♟♟♟	5

Cantina Aldeno

VIA ROMA, 76
38060 ALDENO [TN]
TEL. 0461842511
www.cantina-aldeno.it

CELLAR SALES
PRE-BOOKED VISITS
ANNUAL PRODUCTION 240,000 bottles
HECTARES UNDER VINE 340.00

A rural tradition is renewed in the quest for new ways of interpreting wines, starting with growing techniques all inspired by a natural approach, and vinification without animal content to make vegan products. This is the mission of this longstanding winery found in a hamlet along the banks of the River Adige, between Trento and Rovereto. A choice backed by the cooperative's chairman, Alessandro Bertagnolli, a radical vegan winegrower, and by the Consorzio Vini del Trentino. This has always been merlot country, even hosting an annual competition dedicated to the variety. all natural things at the service of wine, with Aldeno offering about ten certified vegan wines and some Trentino classics. The San Zeno 2010, a champion Bordeaux blend, is full-bodied and developing nicely. The Merlot Enopere is of excellent quality. We also saw a good performance from the Trento Altinum Extra Brut. Among the vegans we can report a tempting Moscato Giallo.

● Trentino San Zeno Ris. '10	♟♟	4
● Trentino Merlot Enopere '11	♟♟	2*
○ Trento Extra Brut Altinum Ris. '09	♟♟	4
● Trentino Lagrein Vegan '14	♟	3
○ Trentino Moscato Giallo Vegan '14	♟	3
● Vallagarina Cabernet Sauvignon Vegan '14	♟	3
○ Trentino Chardonnay Enopere '10	♟♟	2*
● Trentino Merlot Enopere '10	♟♟	2*
● Trentino Merlot Enopere '09	♟♟	2*
○ Trentino Moscato Giallo Flumen '10	♟♟	2*
● Trentino Pinot Nero '12	♟♟	6
● Trentino Rosso San Zeno '09	♟♟	5
● Trentino Rosso San Zeno '07	♟♟	3
○ Trentino Traminer Bio-Vegan '13	♟♟	2*

Nicola Balter

VIA VALLUNGA II, 24
38068 ROVERETO [TN]
TEL. 0464430101
www.balter.it

CELLAR SALES
PRE-BOOKED VISITS
ANNUAL PRODUCTION 80,000 bottles
HECTARES UNDER VINE 10.00

The Balter estate sits snug on the plateau overlooking the oak town, as Rovereto is known. The tidy vineyards are aligned among oaks and tall trees, showing that vines and mountains can live side by side. The winery is entirely underground so there is no environmental impact, only a pretty rural archetype. Nicola Balter has passed his passion on to his young daughter Clementina, today in the forefront of winery management and in the higher echelons of the Consorzio Vignaioli del Trentino. Wines are genuine and engaging. Top of the list is Dosaggio Zero Riserva 2010, a haughty Trento with exquisite balance and finesse, tangy and elegant. We gave it a Tre Bicchieri without a second thought. The other Trentos, Brut and Rosé, are all noteworthy, as are the still wines, both the properly tangy Sauvignon with feisty vegetable notes and acid verve, and the traditional Cabernet Sauvignon 2013, intense and plush.

Bellaveder

LOC. MASO BELVEDERE
38010 FAEDO [TN]
TEL. 0461650171
www.bellaveder.it

CELLAR SALES
PRE-BOOKED VISITS
ANNUAL PRODUCTION 70,000 bottles
HECTARES UNDER VINE 12.00
SUSTAINABLE WINERY

Bellaveder reconciles two different viticultural situations, one integrating the other: first the cellar, on the Faedo alluvial fan, above the renowned Istituto Agrario di San Michele; secondly, the estate vineyards, on the thickets dominating Lake Cavedine, in Valle dei Laghi. The winery keeps a careful eye on the grapes for Müller Thurgau, especially for the Trento, processed with masterly skill by Tranquillo Lucchetta, assisted by Luca Gasperinatti. Sustainable methods are applied in the vineyards and vinification takes place in a fascinating cellar, underneath the vineyards. Trento Nature Riserva 2010 and Lagrein Mansum 2012 are both outstanding this year. The fresh, supple sparkler flew to the finals, showing itself to be as promising as it is elegant, a potpourri of exotic fruit with hints of vanilla and mountain herbs. The Mansum is mighty, a rarity for Trentino. Cracking both the Müller Thurgau, at the top of its class, and the elegant Pinot Nero.

○ Trento Dosaggio Zero Ris. '10	♥♥♥ 7
● Cabernet Sauvignon '13	♥♥ 3*
○ Sauvignon '14	♥♥ 3
○ Trento Brut	♥♥ 4
⊙ Trento Brut Rosé	♥♥ 5
○ Barbanico '97	♥♥♥ 4*
○ Trento Balter Ris. '06	♥♥♥ 5
○ Trento Balter Ris. '05	♥♥♥ 5
○ Trento Balter Ris. '04	♥♥♥ 5
○ Trento Balter Ris. '01	♥♥♥ 5
○ Trento Pas Dosé Balter Ris. '09	♥♥♥ 5
● Cabernet Sauvignon '10	♥♥ 3*
○ Sauvignon Vallagarina '13	♥♥ 3
○ Trento Brut Ris. '08	♥♥ 5

● Trentino Lagrein Mansum '12	♥♥ 4
○ Trento Brut Nature Ris. '10	♥♥ 5
○ Trentino Müller Thurgau San Lorenz '14	♥♥ 3
● Trentino Pinot Nero Faedi Ris. '12	♥♥ 5
○ Trentino Sauvignon '14	♥♥ 2*
○ Pinot Bianco Faedi '13	♥♥ 2*
○ Sauvignon Faedi '13	♥♥ 4
○ Sauvignon Faedi '12	♥♥ 4
● Trentino Lagrein Mansum '11	♥♥ 4
○ Trentino Müller Thurgau San Lorenz '13	♥♥ 2*
○ Trentino Müller Thurgau San Lorenz '12	♥♥ 2*
● Trentino Pinot Nero '11	♥♥ 5
○ Trentino Traminer '13	♥♥ 3
○ Trento Brut Nature '09	♥♥ 5
○ Trento Brut Nature '08	♥♥ 5
○ Trento Brut Ris. '08	♥♥ 5

Bolognani

VIA STAZIONE, 19
38015 LAVIS [TN]
TEL. 0461246354
www.bolognani.com

CELLAR SALES
PRE-BOOKED VISITS
ANNUAL PRODUCTION 70,000 bottles
HECTARES UNDER VINE 4.40

There are four siblings in the Baldacchino dynasty of winegrowers: Diego, Sergio, Renzo, and Lucia, all working in the business. The cellar is set amid the Lavis vineyards and it processes a number of grape varieties. At the moment the grapes are largely provided by trusted growers in the area, since the five hectares of Baldacchino estate are not yet in full production but results from the first harvests are very encouraging. Red grapes come from Gabàn, an archaeological site of the city of Trento, while the Vigolana side, above Trento, provides traminer. Not a bad word to be said on the wines presented for tasting. The Gabàn blend of Cabernet Sauvignon and Merlot is juicy, savoury and full, with fat, ripe tannins, this crunchy red, with a fine Trentino touch, gives the wine its due. The Sanròc is another typical Dolomite wine, a fragrant, dynamic Traminer with palate verve. All the other wines are well-made early-drinkers, especially the Teroldego Armìlo.

● Gabàn '11	♥♥	5
○ Müller Thurgau '14	♥♥	2*
○ Sauvignon '14	♥♥	3
● Teroldego Armìlo '13	♥♥	3
○ Trentino Gewürztraminer Sanròc '13	♥♥	3
○ Nosìola '14	♥	2
● Teroldego Armìlo '06	♥♥♥	2*
● Gabàn '09	♀♀	5
○ Moscato Giallo '13	♀♀	2*
○ Moscato Giallo '11	♀♀	2*
● Teroldego Armìlo '12	♀♀	3
● Teroldego Armìlo '11	♀♀	3
● Teroldego Armìlo '10	♀♀	3
○ Trentino Traminer Aromatico Sanròc '12	♀♀	3

Borgo dei Posseri

LOC. POZZO BASSO, 1
38061 ALA [TN]
TEL. 0464671899
www.borgodeiposseri.com

CELLAR SALES
PRE-BOOKED VISITS
ANNUAL PRODUCTION 60,000 bottles
HECTARES UNDER VINE 21.00
VITICULTURE METHOD Certified Organic
SUSTAINABLE WINERY

Borgo dei Posseri is an eyrie perched on the slopes of the Piccole Dolomiti, the impressive mountains which rise from the lower Vallagarina, on the border between Trentino and Veneto, an unspoiled enclave of woods and pastures that the de Pilati-Mainenti family recovered for wine cultivation some years ago, tended with organic methods. The high hill position encourages mainly white varieties but both pinot nero and merlot are present. The family's flagship wine is its tangy Tananai, a resolutely mountain-style Trento, with offbeat aromatic approach, tons of character, hints of wild strawberries, overtones of elderberry, and a crisp finale. Quaron is a Müller Thurgau sailing happily alongside the best of the bunch, assertive and aroma-rich, with nice acidity. As always the Rocol from merlot and the Paradis from pinot nero are sound. The Furiel, from sauvignon, has some way to go.

● Merlot Rocol '13	♥♥	3
○ Müller Thurgau Quaron '14	♥♥	3
● Pinot Nero Paradis '13	♥♥	3
○ Trento Brut Tananai '11	♥♥	5
○ Sauvignon Furiel '14	♥	3
● Merlot Rocol '09	♀♀	3
● Merlot Rocòl '08	♀♀	3
○ Müller Thurgau Quaron '13	♀♀	3
○ Müller Thurgau Quaron '12	♀♀	3
○ Müller Thurgau Quaron '11	♀♀	3
○ Müller Thurgau Quaron '09	♀♀	3
● Pinot Nero Paradis '11	♀♀	3
○ Sauvignon Furiel '13	♀♀	3
○ Tananai Brut '08	♀♀	5
○ Traminer Arliz '13	♀♀	3
○ Trento Brut Tananai '10	♀♀	5

Cantina Sociale di Trento

VIA DEI VITICOLTORI, 2-4
38123 VOLANO [TN]
TEL. 0461920186
www.cantinasocialetrento.it

CELLAR SALES
PRE-BOOKED VISITS
ANNUAL PRODUCTION 250,000 bottles
HECTARES UNDER VINE 50.00
SUSTAINABLE WINERY

The Cantina di Trento cooperative has moulded the evolution of fine drinking in this region, always in the vanguard for engaging the members who tend each miniscule hill plot in an exciting interaction between urban and country processes. The cellar has been fully renovated, including headquarters and management, in a fusion of rural expertise and managerial skills underpinned by winemaking partnerships like that with Concilio Vini for the overseas market. Zell is a classy TrentoDoc, a pure Chardonnay with a lovely golden robe, crystalline reflections, mountain apples on the palate and delightful progression showing quince compote and stewed citron. Of the wines tasted we recommend the silky elegance of the Merlot Novaline, a cellar cert. Then a very approachable but feisty Heredia Bordeaux blend. The traditional 2014s, a tangy Linea 1399 Nosiola and a Traminer, are both very fruity and balanced, especially the former.

★Cavit

VIA DEL PONTE, 31
38040 TRENTO
TEL. 0461381711
www.cavit.it

CELLAR SALES
PRE-BOOKED VISITS
ANNUAL PRODUCTION 70,000,000 bottles
HECTARES UNDER VINE 5500.00

Cavit, a wine-producing colossus competing on the international market, relies on quality production thanks to the efforts of the amazing 5,000 Trentino winegrowers. Today it is a fast-growing brand thanks to effective marketing strategies and the standard of its vast range of products. It is no easy task to sum up the extent of its range in a few lines, but the Trento Altemasi Riserva Graal 2008 deserved its Tre Bicchieri. A lustrous colour and persuasive aromatic profile, with notes of orange blossom, despite being a mountain wine, cadenced by the leisurely, captivating progression, not to mention the nose-palate symmetry. Another Cavit flagship is the Maso Cervara, a mighty Teroldego rich in tannins albeit austere, clean and persuasive. Look out for some exciting new wines like Altemasi Pas Dosé, the Bordeaux blend Quattro Vicariati, and the fragrant Zeveri, a versatile Müller Thurgau produced in large numbers.

● Trentino Heredia '12	♟♟ 3
● Trentino Merlot Novaline Ris. '12	♟♟ 4
○ Trentino Nosiola 1339 '14	♟♟ 2*
○ Trento Brut Zell '11	♟♟ 5
○ Trentino Traminer 1339 '14	♟ 2
○ Trentino Bianco Heredia '10	♟♟ 2*
● Trentino Lagrein Heredia '09	♟♟ 3
○ Trentino Pinot Grigio Heredia '12	♟♟ 2*
● Trentino Pinot Nero Heredia '11	♟♟ 3
● Trentino Rosso Heredia '11	♟♟ 3
● Trentino Rosso Heredia '08	♟♟ 3

○ Trento Brut Altemasi Graal Ris. '08	♟♟♟ 6
● Teroldego Rotaliano Maso Cervara '11	♟♟ 4
○ Trentino Chardonnay Sup. Maso Toresella '13	♟♟ 4
○ Trentino Sup. Müller Thurgau Zeveri '14	♟♟ 3
○ Trento Altemasi Pas Dosé '07	♟♟ 5
● Teroldego Rotaliano Maso Cervara '07	♟♟♟ 4
○ Trento Altemasi Graal Brut Ris. '03	♟♟♟ 6
○ Trento Altemasi Graal Brut Ris. '02	♟♟♟ 6
○ Trento Brut Altemasi Graal Ris. '06	♟♟♟ 6
○ Trento Brut Altemasi Graal Ris. '05	♟♟♟ 7
○ Trento Brut Altemasi Graal Ris. '04	♟♟♟ 7

Cesarini Sforza

FRAZ. RAVINA
VIA STELLA, 9
38123 TRENTO
TEL. 0461382200
www.cesarinisforza.com

CELLAR SALES
PRE-BOOKED VISITS
ANNUAL PRODUCTION 1,300,000 bottles
HECTARES UNDER VINE 800.00

The eagle icon of this respected Trentino cellar flies high, austere and tenacious. The sparkling wines are confirmed as some of the most influential in the TrentoDoc scenario, thanks to a parent company, La Vis, that leaves management plenty of leeway to run the winery on its own terms and to guarantee quality. There are six sparklers on the shelves, one a Charmat method, ensuring a range of wines to satisfy every palate. The flagship is Aquila Reale, Riserva di Trento, a 2008 that missed our highest accolade by a whisker. Every nuance of this floral, layered sparkler is intense, with its creamy mousse and well-paced lingering palate. Another nice performance for Tridentum Dosaggio Zero, crisp and racy, oozing vitality from every pore. Far more mature and to be tasted with care, the very worthy vintage Tridentum Brut Extra. The Brut, the Rosé, and last but not least the Cuvée Brut Riserva are all charming and memorable.

○ Trento Aquila Reale Ris. '08	♟♟ 6
○ Trento Brut Rosé Tridentum '09	♟♟ 4
○ Trento Brut Tridentum '11	♟♟ 4
○ Trento Dosaggio Zero Tridentum '11	♟♟ 5
○ Trento Extra Brut Tridentum Ris. '08	♟♟ 5
○ Cuvée Brut Ris.	♟ 4
○ Trento Aquila Reale Ris. '05	♟♟♟ 7
○ Trento Aquila Reale Ris. '02	♟♟♟ 7
⊙ Trento Brut Rosé '07	♟♟ 4
⊙ Trento Brut Rosé Tridentum '08	♟♟ 4
○ Trento Brut Tridentum	♟♟ 4
○ Trento Extra Brut Tridentum '07	♟♟ 4
○ Trento Extra Brut Tridentum Ris. '07	♟♟ 5
○ Trento Pinot Nero Dosaggio Zero Tridentum '09	♟♟ 5
⊙ Trento Tridentum	♟♟ 4
○ Trento Tridentum Aquila Reale Ris. '07	♟♟ 6

De Vescovi Ulzbach

P.ZZA GARIBALDI, 12
38016 MEZZOCORONA [TN]
TEL. 0461605648
www.devescoviulzbach.it

CELLAR SALES
PRE-BOOKED VISITS
ANNUAL PRODUCTION 20,000 bottles
HECTARES UNDER VINE 3.50

Giulio De Vescovi is an innovator, but with a family tradition dating back to the 1700s, and an expert winegrower with a degree in agricultural studies. His mission is to rethink the local Teroldego Rotaliano, and in his sparkling clean, uncomplicated winery he tries out vinification methods. He is also growing white varieties to blend in a Sauvignon and has plans for a couple of stunning sparklers in the near future: just a few thousand bottles, from grapes grown at almost 1,000 metres on the mountain above Mezzocorona. Meanwhile, the mighty 2013 Vigilius Teroldego Rotaliano is confirmed at its top spot, a must in its class, a perfect blend of fullness and weight with the momentum of jovial elegance, modern temperament and behaviour. Similar traits are also seen in the 2013 Teroldego, more easy-drinking but no less exciting. A badge of honour for the new wine, a fruity Sauvignon Blanc of perfect acidity, very varietal overtones, nicely untamed and slightly tart.

● Teroldego Rotaliano Vigilius '13	♟♟ 5
● Teroldego Rotaliano '13	♟♟ 3
● Teroldego Rotaliano Vigilius '12	♟♟♟ 5
● Teroldego Rotaliano '12	♟♟ 3*
● Teroldego Rotaliano '11	♟♟ 3
● Teroldego Rotaliano '10	♟♟ 3
● Teroldego Rotaliano '07	♟♟ 3
● Teroldego Rotaliano '05	♟♟ 3
● Teroldego Rotaliano Vigilius '11	♟♟ 5
● Teroldego Rotaliano Vigilius '09	♟♟ 5
● Teroldego Rotaliano Vigilius Ris. '04	♟♟ 5

★F.lli Dorigati

VIA DANTE, 5
38016 MEZZOCORONA [TN]
TEL. 0461605313
www.dorigati.it

CELLAR SALES
PRE-BOOKED VISITS
ANNUAL PRODUCTION 100,000 bottles
HECTARES UNDER VINE 13.00
SUSTAINABLE WINERY

A farming family involved in winemaking since 1858 and one that would probably never have imagined it would become a leading player in the best Italian sparkling wine tradition. The Dorigatis started life as cellar folk, making Teroldego wine, and began to focus on Classic Methods only a few decades ago. The fifth generation of the dynasty is now at the helm: young cousins Paolo and Michele, armed with youthful enthusiasm but also with oenology studies, hands-on experience, and the teaching of their fathers. The Methius Riserva 2009 rides the crest of very positive vintage and was awarded our Tre Bicchieri for the creaminess on the nose enhanced by scents of wild apples and a vanilla note nuanced with pine resin, returning on the palate, where the caressing flavour is supported by lively acidity. Among the reds we noted the Teroldego Diedri for smooth tannins that are a true rarity. Excellent fruit in the basic and very pleasant version of Rebo, always a vaunt for Dorigati.

○ Trento Brut Methius Ris. '09	♥♥♥	6
● Teroldego Rotaliano '13	♥♥	3
● Teroldego Rotaliano Diedri '12	♥♥	5
⊙ Trentino Lagrein Kretzer '14	♥	2
○ Trentino Pinot Grigio '14	♥	3
● Trentino Rebo '13	♥	3
○ Trento Brut Methius Ris. '08	♀♀♀	6
○ Trento Brut Methius Ris. '06	♀♀♀	6
○ Trento Brut Methius Ris. '05	♀♀♀	6
○ Trento Brut Methius Ris. '04	♀♀♀	6
○ Trento Brut Methius Ris. '03	♀♀♀	6
○ Trento Brut Methius Ris. '02	♀♀♀	6
○ Trento Brut Methius Ris. '00	♀♀♀	6
○ Trento Brut Methius Ris. '98	♀♀♀	6
○ Trento Methius Ris. '95	♀♀♀	4
○ Trento Methius Ris. '92	♀♀♀	4*

Endrizzi

LOC. MASETTO, 2
38010 SAN MICHELE ALL'ADIGE [TN]
TEL. 0461650129
www.endrizzi.it

CELLAR SALES
PRE-BOOKED VISITS
ANNUAL PRODUCTION 600,000 bottles
HECTARES UNDER VINE 55.00
SUSTAINABLE WINERY

The Endrici family has a solid winemaking past and has been a leading player on local and far-off wine markets for over 130 years. Indeed the Endrizzi Endrici also have estates in Tuscany, although the parent winery, where technology is in full harmony with the natural qualities of the surrounding vineyards, is on the border between Trentino and Alto Adige. A point where the trails for enjoyable excursions among the vines are marked by the nests woven by flocks of birds among the eco-friendly rows. Paolo and Christine Endrici, assisted by their young family, offer a range of unbeatable wines including all the region's classics, with a sparkling Trento Riserva at the top of the list. This elegant, perky wine is right on form and so is the winery's other flagship, Gran Masetto, a sterling Teroldego from slightly over-ripe grapes that make for a plush, powerful red. The traditional labels include a good Teroldego, the Chardonnay and two versions of Masetto, Nero and Bianco.

● Gran Masetto '11	♥♥	7
○ Trento Brut Pian di Castello Ris. '10	♥♥	4
○ Masetto Bianco '13	♥♥	3
● Masetto Nero '12	♥♥	3
● Teroldego Rotaliano '13	♥♥	2*
○ Trentino Chardonnay '14	♥	2
● Gran Masetto '10	♀♀	2*
● Gran Masetto '09	♀♀	7
○ Masetto Bianco '12	♀♀	3
○ Masetto Bianco '11	♀♀	3
● Masetto Nero '11	♀♀	3
● Teroldego Rotaliano '11	♀♀	3
● Teroldego Rotaliano Tradizione '11	♀♀	2*
● Trentino Pinot Nero Pian di Castello '10	♀♀	3
○ Trento Brut Pian di Castello '09	♀♀	4
○ Trento Brut Pian di Castello '08	♀♀	4

★★Ferrari

VIA PONTE DI RAVINA, 15
38123 TRENTO
TEL. 0461972311
www.ferraritrento.it

CELLAR SALES
PRE-BOOKED VISITS
RESTAURANT SERVICE
ANNUAL PRODUCTION 4,450,000 bottles
HECTARES UNDER VINE 120.00
SUSTAINABLE WINERY

Ferrari, spumante, Trento. A trio rooted in time, impossible to separate, even if the Lunelli family continues to invest in estates away from the parent company, aiming to diversify its wine offering and meet the market's new quality challenges. So Ferrari is still in pole position, even if we were unable to sample the legendary Riserva del Fondatore this year. The Lunellis nonetheless turned in two champion wines: the delightful Perlé, of which half a million bottles were produced, pipped at the Tre Bicchieri post by the captivating Riserva di Famiglia, whose aromatic profile was just a tad silkier and brisker, woven with citrus overtones and the fragrance of freshly-baked bread. Technically impeccable the other Trentos, the Perlé Rosé, and the more versatile Maximum, prototypes of elegance, all showing a masterly touch, in no small measure thanks to the cellar's winemaker, the talented Ruben Larentis.

○ Trento Extra Brut Lunelli Ris. '07	♟♟♟ 7
○ Trento Brut Perlé '09	♟♟ 6
○ Trentino Chardonnay Villa Margon '13	♟♟ 4
● Trentino Pinot Nero Maso Montalto '12	♟♟ 5
○ Trento Brut Maximum	♟♟ 5
⊙ Trento Brut Perlé Rosé '09	♟♟ 7
○ Trento Brut Giulio Ferrari Riserva del Fondatore '04	♟♟♟ 8
○ Trento Brut Giulio Ferrari Riserva del Fondatore '01	♟♟♟ 8
○ Trento Brut Giulio Ferrari Riserva del Fondatore '00	♟♟♟ 8
○ Trento Brut Perlé '02	♟♟♟ 5
○ Trento Extra Brut Perlé Nero '07	♟♟♟ 8
○ Trento Extra Brut Perlé Nero '06	♟♟♟ 8
○ Trento Extra Brut Perlé Nero '05	♟♟♟ 8
○ Trento Extra Brut Perlé Nero '04	♟♟♟ 8

Fondazione Mach

VIA EDMONDO MACH, 1
38010 SAN MICHELE ALL'ADIGE [TN]
TEL. 0461615252
www.ismaa.it

CELLAR SALES
PRE-BOOKED VISITS
ANNUAL PRODUCTION 250,000 bottles
HECTARES UNDER VINE 60.00
VITICULTURE METHOD Certified Organic

Over the last 150 years or so the school has forged ranks of winegrowers and a myriad of fruitmakers, experts in every cultivation sector, although the curriculum priority is the vine. A school that has taught many a lesson and pursues genetic research, experimenting with advanced farming techniques, exploring the seasons and methods of biodynamics. It is difficult to sum up FEM's many activities as research projects are defined and wines offered. Creamy but feisty, the Trento dedicated to Edmund Mach, is a remarkably elegant version. Then there is the textbook Pinot Bianco, definitely the best of the Trentinos, a fusion of winemaking skill and respect for the variety's spontaneous vigour, for a savoury, racy and well-structured wine. Monastero is also full-bodied and well-orchestrated, from cabernet franc grapes, with the unfailing seal of crunchy bell peppers and berries.

○ Trentino Pinot Bianco '14	♟♟ 2*
○ Trento Mach Riserva del Fondatore '10	♟♟ 5
● Trentino Cabernet Franc Monastero '13	♟♟ 3
● Trentino Moscato Rosa '13	♟♟ 4
○ Trentino Nosiola '14	♟♟ 3
○ Castel San Michele Bianco '14	♟ 3
○ Trento Mach Riserva del Fondatore '09	♟♟♟ 5
○ Trento Mach Riserva del Fondatore '07	♟♟♟ 5
○ Trento Mach Riserva del Fondatore '04	♟♟♟ 5
○ Manzoni Bianco '13	♟♟ 4
● Trentino Cabernet Franc Monastero '11	♟♟ 3
● Trentino Cabernet Franc Monastero '10	♟♟ 3
○ Trentino Pinot Bianco Monastero '13	♟♟ 3*
● Trentino Pinot Nero Monastero '10	♟♟ 6
○ Trentino Riesling '13	♟♟ 2*
○ Trento Mach Riserva del Fondatore '08	♟♟ 5

Francesco Moser

FRAZ. MEANO
VIA CASTEL DI GARDOLO, 5
38121 TRENTO
TEL. 0461990786
www.cantinemoser.com

CELLAR SALES
PRE-BOOKED VISITS
ACCOMMODATION
ANNUAL PRODUCTION 100,000 bottles
HECTARES UNDER VINE 15.00

The vineyards are found on extensive terraces on a steep hillside overlooking the Trento hamlet of Gardolo, towards Valle di Cembra. The area has marvellous aspecting and is reached by a steep ascent from the valley floor. A milestone of sorts for cyclists with plenty of puff. Francesco Moser, a world legend and holder of the hour record, has not thrown his bike away: he still uses it to get quickly to the vineyards surrounding his winery at Maso Warth, a 1300s' village. His team includes son Carlo, daughter Francesca, and nephew Matteo, oenologist and an expert in sparkling wines. The Trento sparkler is named after the 51.151 kilometres of the hour record. Decidedly racy, lingering and with a nice pace in the prickle with the tanginess... pedalling well. The traditional wines are always led by the dry Moscato Giallo, a pleasant early-drinker.

Grigoletti

VIA GARIBALDI, 12
38060 NOMI [TN]
TEL. 0464834215
www.grigoletti.com

CELLAR SALES
PRE-BOOKED VISITS
ANNUAL PRODUCTION 60,000 bottles
HECTARES UNDER VINE 10.00

The Grigolettis are a typical forthright farming family from Nomi, a village on the right bank of the River Adige. They make wine only from grapes grown on estates they manage in person and this involves the whole family, from the most senior Bruno to Carmelo, the winery's driving force, and even the youngest of them all, Federico and Marina. They are a fine example of true winegrowers and have turned the cellar into a small wine temple, hosting fun food and wine events. This year the Merlot Antica Vigna 2012 is on form, after slow barrel maturation, and confirming at each vintage that it is a reliable cellarable wine. Another endorsement for Gonzalier, a Cabernet and Merlot blend that applies a calendar of rural vinification methods for a bracing meditation wine, intense in its own way. The Chardonnay L'Opera selection is also pleasant and uncomplicated, as is the traditional Marzemino.

○ Moscato Giallo '14	♟♟	3
○ Trento Brut 51,151	♟♟	5
○ Müller Thurgau '14	♟	2
○ Riesling '13	♟	3
○ Traminer '13	♟	3
○ 51,151 '10	♟♟	5
● Lagrein Dea Mater '09	♟♟	3
● Lagrein Deamater '05	♟♟	3
○ Riesling '12	♟♟	3
○ Riesling '10	♟♟	2*
○ Trento 51,151 '09	♟♟	5

● Gonzalier '12	♟♟	5
○ Trentino Chardonnay L'Opera '14	♟♟	3
● Trentino Merlot Antica Vigna '12	♟♟	4
○ San Martim V.T. '13	♟	4
● Trentino Marzemino '14	♟	2
● Gonzalier '11	♟♟	5
○ Retiko '13	♟♟	3
○ Retiko '11	♟♟	3
○ Retiko '10	♟♟	3
● Speciale 30° '09	♟♟	6
○ Trentino Chardonnay L'Opera '13	♟♟	3
○ Trentino Chardonnay L'Opera '12	♟♟	3
○ Trentino Chardonnay L'Opera '11	♟♟	3
● Trentino Marzemino '13	♟♟	2*
● Trentino Marzemino '12	♟♟	2*

La Vis/Valle di Cembra

VIA CARMINE, 7
38034 LAVIS [TN]
TEL. 0461440111
www.la-vis.com

CELLAR SALES
PRE-BOOKED VISITS
ACCOMMODATION AND RESTAURANT SERVICE
ANNUAL PRODUCTION 1,000,000 bottles
HECTARES UNDER VINE 850.00
VITICULTURE METHOD Certified Organic
SUSTAINABLE WINERY

Spurred on by over 1,000 vigneron
members, La Vis is confirmed as one of the
best makers of Trentino wine. Thanks to the
obstinacy of those who preferred to target
quality to meet demands for a wider
market. All wines we tasted this year are
valid not only for type and technique, but
also their decidedly Dolomitic style. They
speak the language of local viticulture and
the varieties grown at altitude, on the
terraces of the Cembra Valley and the
unusual vineyards set along the River
Adige. Müller Thurgau Vigna delle Forche,
from a high-altitude vineyard in the upper
Avisio Valley, surrounded by woods and
porphyry, set against the Dolomites, is a
deserving Tre Bicchieri for its healthy fruit
and finely balanced acidity. The most
striking wines included an excellent
Chardonnay Simboli, of which several
hundred thousand bottles are produced,
selling at a very affordable price. L'Altro
Manzoni, Teroldego Rover and Trento Oro
Rosso are all worthy of mention for their
indisputable value.

○ V. delle Forche '14	♟♟♟ 3*
○ Trentino Chardonnay Simboli '14	♟♟ 2*
○ L'Altro Manzoni '14	♟♟ 4
● Teroldego Rover '13	♟♟ 3
● Trentino Pinot Nero V. di Saosent '13	♟♟ 5
○ Trento Oro Rosso Extra Brut '09	♟♟ 5
○ Trentino Gewürztraminer Ai Padri '14	♟ 4
○ Ritratto Bianco '07	♟♟♟ 4
● Ritratto Rosso '03	♟♟♟ 4
○ Trentino Müller Thurgau V. delle Forche '13	♟♟♟ 3*
○ Trentino Müller Thurgau Vigna delle Forche '12	♟♟♟ 3*
○ Trento Oro Rosso Brut 60 Mesi	♟♟ 5
○ Trentino Traminer Aromatico Ai Padri '13	♟♟ 4

Letrari

VIA MONTE BALDO, 13/15
38068 ROVERETO [TN]
TEL. 0464480200
www.letrari.it

CELLAR SALES
PRE-BOOKED VISITS
ANNUAL PRODUCTION 160,000 bottles
HECTARES UNDER VINE 23.00

Leonello "Nello" Letrari is a wine patriarch,
not only for Trentino, and in the 1960s was
among the first in Italy to use small oak
barrels and the Classic Method. Despite
being in his eighties, he is attentive and
curious, and his legacy of expertise has
been handed over along with the family
business to daughter Lucia, also an
oenologist and always ready to take up new
challenges. Sparklers are always close to
the cellar heart but neither does it neglect
traditional wines. Pending the patient
cellaring of some of the aristocratic Trentos,
needing more time, we gave the Tre
Bicchieri to the Riserva 2005, dedicated to
the winery founder. Wine of rare, intense
brilliance, the texture as fine as the palate
is close-knit, the sensorial profile is layered
with candied citrus and delicious notes of
roasted coffee. Equally elegant and
powerful, Quore, and then the classic
Rosé, dedicated to the four ladies of the
house of Letrari, and a tangy, well-defined
Dosaggio Zero.

○ Trento Riserva del Fondatore 976 '05	♟♟♟ 8
○ Trento Letrari Quore Ris. '09	♟♟ 5
● Ballistarius '10	♟♟ 5
● Trentino Cabernet Franc '10	♟♟ 5
● Trentino Moscato Rosa '11	♟♟ 6
⊙ Trento Brut Rosé +4 '11	♟♟ 6
○ Trento Dosaggio Zero Letrari '12	♟♟ 5
○ Trento Brut Letrari Ris. '09	♟♟♟ 5
○ Trento Brut Letrari Ris. '08	♟♟♟ 5
○ Trento Brut Letrari Ris. '07	♟♟♟ 5
○ Trento Brut Letrari Ris. '05	♟♟♟ 5
○ Trento Brut Ris. '06	♟♟♟ 5
● Ballistarius '09	♟♟ 5
○ Trento Brut Letrari	♟♟ 5
⊙ Trento Brut Rosé +4 '09	♟♟ 6
○ Trento Dosaggio Zero Letrari '11	♟♟ 5

Maso Martis

LOC. MARTIGNANO
VIA DELL'ALBERA, 52
38121 TRENTO
TEL. 0461821057
www.masomartis.it

CELLAR SALES
PRE-BOOKED VISITS
ANNUAL PRODUCTION 65,000 bottles
HECTARES UNDER VINE 12.00
VITICULTURE METHOD Certified Organic

The vineyards are nestled among the villas of the Trento hill, towards the slopes of Calisio, a mountain always kissed by the sun. The family of Roberta and Antonio Stelzer has just celebrated its 25th harvest in the 12 hectares surrounding the winery. A magical place and not surprisingly once dedicated to the god Mars. The cellar was founded with the specific aim of saving this hilly area from urban expansion and converting it into a small temple to TrentoDoc. Mission accomplished. The enchanting Madame Martis 2005, a special cuvée, is a true champion whose only defect may be the small number of bottles produced, just 1,000. We definitely enjoyed the other three house Trentos. One in particular, a Rosé from pinot nero, is well-robed with very rich berry fruit notes. Dosaggio Zero, what we might term a vertical wine, also performed well and offered the right drinkability for a traditional Brut.

○ Trento Madame Martis Ris. '05	🍷🍷	6
⊙ Trento Brut Rosé '11	🍷🍷	5
○ Trento Maso Martis Dosaggio Zero Ris. '10	🍷🍷	5
○ Trento Maso Martis Brut	🍷	4
○ Trento Brut '09	🍷🍷	4
○ Trento Brut Ris. '07	🍷🍷	5
○ Trento Brut Ris. '06	🍷🍷	5
○ Trento Brut Ris. '04	🍷🍷	5
○ Trento Brut Ris. '03	🍷🍷	5
⊙ Trento Brut Rosé	🍷🍷	5
○ Trento Dosaggio Zero '10	🍷🍷	5
○ Trento Dosaggio Zero '09	🍷🍷	5
○ Trento Dosaggio Zero Maso Martis '09	🍷🍷	5
○ Trento Madame Martis Ris. '04	🍷🍷	6
○ Trento Maso Martis Ris. '08	🍷🍷	5
○ Trento Maso Martis Ris. '05	🍷🍷	5

MezzaCorona

VIA DEL TEROLDEGO, 1
38016 MEZZOCORONA [TN]
TEL. 0461616399
www.mezzacorona.it

CELLAR SALES
PRE-BOOKED VISITS
ANNUAL PRODUCTION 30,000,000 bottles
HECTARES UNDER VINE 2800.00

Mezzacorona was founded in 1904 and is now a large international company operating in diversified territories and decidedly far from home, like Sicily. Its roots, however, are firmly planted in Teroldego and in Pinot Grigio, a white wine that Mezzacorona was one of the first to launch on the world market. A meticulous selection of specific varieties, cutting-edge technology and effective interactive communication are critical to the success of a range boasting several prestige labels. Like Nos, this is a "super Teroldego", available only in the best vintages. It was up there with our highest scorers and has all the poise of a true leader: compact, intense and deep. As pleasant and versatile as ever, the Teroldego Riserva from the Castel Firmian line, 100,000 bottles of sheer wine delight. Great Trentos.

● Teroldego Rotaliano Nos '09	🍷🍷	5
● Teroldego Rotaliano Castel Firmian Ris. '12	🍷🍷	2*
○ Trento Talento Cuvée 28°	🍷🍷	4
⊙ Trento Talento Rotari Rosé	🍷	4
● Teroldego Rotaliano Nos Ris. '04	🍷🍷🍷	5
○ Trento Rotari Flavio Ris. '07	🍷🍷🍷	5
○ Trento Rotari Flavio Ris. '06	🍷🍷🍷	5
● Teroldego Rotaliano Ris. '10	🍷🍷	4
○ Trentino Chardonnay Castel Firmian '12	🍷🍷	3
○ Trentino Pinot Grigio Castel Firmian '13	🍷🍷	3
● Trentino Pinot Nero Castel Firmian '12	🍷🍷	3
○ Trentino Traminer Castel Firmian '12	🍷🍷	3
○ Trento Extra Brut AlpeRegis '09	🍷🍷	5
○ Trento Extra Brut AlpeRegis '07	🍷🍷	5

Casata Monfort

VIA CARLO SETTE, 21
38015 LAVIS [TN]
TEL. 0461246353
www.cantinemonfort.it

CELLAR SALES
PRE-BOOKED VISITS
ANNUAL PRODUCTION 170,000 bottles
HECTARES UNDER VINE 40.00
SUSTAINABLE WINERY

The company has vineyards at two sites, one at Lavis and another at Civezzano, remaining loyal to the identity of its wines. The Simonis have focused on varietal typing, emphasizing the nature of the vineyard sites. The wines on offer are well-typed and very drinkable. Lavis is home to the main cellar while the picturesque Civezzano Austro-Hungarian fort processes only grapes harvested in the area. Federico Simoni heads up the winery and is a committed, expert vigneron. He sent us a Trento Reserve Monfort with the finest of perlage, brilliant in colour, a floral nose of broom notes, well-orchestrated for a smooth flow. Among the many wines tasted, the Trento Rosé and the intriguing Blanc de Sers, a blend of ancient local varieties like vanderbara. And also the San Lorenzo, from saint laurent Habsburg variety, closing with a good Pinot Nero and a scented Traminer.

Opera Vitivinicola in Valdicembra

FRAZ. VERLA
VIA TRE NOVEMBRE, 8
38030 GIOVO [TN]
TEL. 0461684302
www.operavaldicembra.it

CELLAR SALES
PRE-BOOKED VISITS
ANNUAL PRODUCTION 60,000 bottles
HECTARES UNDER VINE 15.00

Red porphyry cadences the Val di Cembra landscape, but from Lavis to Valle di Fiemme the vine defines the territory. To take advantage of the beautiful valley and especially the peculiarities of mountain grapes, two friends created this upcoming boutique cellar for sparkling wine, managed first-hand by Alfio Garzetti with oenological support from Paolo. Each year the tens of thousands of bottles produced are unarguable proof of success. The four versions of their Trento all have character, made with textbook technique to achieve a pleasing sensorial profile. The 2008 Dosaggio Zero took a Tre Bicchieri, showing remarkable quality, admirable aromatic backbone, porphyry in the structure, lively acidity, a real new leader in Trento. Also worthy of note the Noir from pinot nero, and a classic, coppery Brut Rosé.

○ Blanc de Sers '13	♈♈ 3
● Pinot Nero '13	♈♈ 3
● San Lorenzo '14	♈♈ 2*
○ Trentino Gewürztraminer '14	♈♈ 3
○ Trento Brut Ris. '09	♈♈ 5
⊙ Trento Rosé	♈♈ 4
● Trentino Lagrein '11	♀♀ 3
● Trentino Pinot Nero Forte di Mezzo '11	♀♀ 3*
● Trentino Pinot Nero Maso Cantanghel '08	♀♀ 3
○ Trentino Traminer Aromatico V. Caselle '12	♀♀ 3
○ Trento Brut Ris. '08	♀♀ 5

○ Trento Brut Dosaggio Zero Opera Ris. '08	♈♈♈ 7
⊙ Trento Brut Noir Opera	♈♈ 5
⊙ Trento Brut Opera	♈♈ 5
⊙ Trento Brut Rosé Opera	♈♈ 5
⊙ Trento Brut Opera '09	♀♀ 5
⊙ Trento Brut Rosé Noir '09	♀♀ 5
○ Trento Nature '08	♀♀ 4
○ Trento Nature Opera '09	♀♀ 5

Pisoni

LOC. SARCHE
FRAZ. PERGOLESE DI LASINO
VIA SAN SIRO, 7A
38076 LASINO [TN]
TEL. 0461564106
www.pisoni.net

CELLAR SALES
PRE-BOOKED VISITS
ANNUAL PRODUCTION 23,500 bottles
HECTARES UNDER VINE 16.00

On the Trentino wine scene the Pisonis are
known for their dedication to the entire
winegrowing chain. They are vignerons,
sparkling winegrowers and distillers. Each
branch of the family has a specific role to
achieve efficient management of the various
business sectors. Stefano in the vineyard
also conducts biodynamic trials; Marco runs
the cellar with Francesco, who manages the
sparkling wines, while Elio is in charge of
grappa. With their management approach,
the four cousins continue a dynasty founded
on centuries of rural pride. Their Trentos
are kept in a deep, breath-taking tunnel
dug from the rock. The standard is as
excellent as ever with an Extra Brut 80 Mesi
Riserva 2007 of golden undertones, hints of
plum, crunchy, nicely salty, and with lively
progression. The Nature is fresh, engaging,
approachable. Among the others we noted
the Vino Santo 2001, a raisined wine of
great elegance, and a supple, perky Pinot
Nero. Offbeat spiced balsamic overtones for
the syrah blend Sarica.

Pojer & Sandri

LOC. MOLINI, 4
38010 FAEDO [TN]
TEL. 0461650342
www.pojeresandri.it

CELLAR SALES
PRE-BOOKED VISITS
ACCOMMODATION
ANNUAL PRODUCTION 200,000 bottles
HECTARES UNDER VINE 32.00
VITICULTURE METHOD Certified Organic

Mario Pojer and Fiorentino Sandri can now
vaunt 41 vintages together, and a lifetime
of work for promoting high-hill grapes from
Faedo and the nearby Valle di Cembra.
Today their offspring have joined these
authentic winegrowers who are
experimenters, at times rebellious, always
authoritative, and whose wines are nigh-on
perfect. They were the first to propose a
schiava rosé, and they also wagered on
Müller Thurgau, on late harvests and,
recently, on wines from interspecific grapes
for total zero impact sustainable cultivation.
There were two wines that made the finals:
Palai, Müller Thurgau with a well-
orchestrated timbre whose acidity defies
time; the Pinot Nero Rodel Pianezzi, a
flawless expression of vigneron devotion for
a wine of gentle elegance. Intense and
feisty, the Faye red from cabernet and
lagrein. The drinkable Besler Biank juggles
riesling and kerner. Last, but not least, the
classic sparkling wines and the unusual,
low-alcohol white Filii.

○ Trento Extra Brut 80 Mesi Ris. '07	♼♼ 5
○ Trento Extra Brut Ris. '08	♼♼ 5
● Sarica Rosso '11	♼♼ 4
○ Trentino Vino Santo '01	♼♼ 6
○ Trento Brut Nature '11	♼♼ 4
○ Nosiola '14	♼ 2
● Pinot Nero '12	♼ 4
● Pinot Nero '11	♼♼ 4
● Sarica Rosso '10	♼♼ 4
● Sarica Rosso '08	♼♼ 4
○ Trentino Vino Santo '00	♼♼ 6
○ Trento Brut '10	♼♼ 4
○ Trento Brut '09	♼♼ 4
⊙ Trento Brut Rosé '10	♼♼ 5
○ Trento Extra Brut '10	♼♼ 5
○ Trento Extra Brut Ris. '07	♼♼ 5

○ Palai '14	♼♼ 3*
● Pinot Nero Rodel Pianezzi '11	♼♼ 5
● Rosso Faye '11	♼♼ 6
○ Besler Biank '11	♼♼ 3
○ Extra Brut	♼♼ 5
○ Filii '14	♼♼ 2*
⊙ Spumante Brut Rosé	♼♼ 5
○ Bianco Faye '08	♼♼♼ 5
○ Bianco Faye '01	♼♼♼ 5
● Pinot Nero Rodel Pianezzi '09	♼♼♼ 5
● Rosso Faye '05	♼♼♼ 5
● Rosso Faye '00	♼♼♼ 5
○ Besler Biank '10	♼♼ 3
○ Bianco Faye '11	♼♼ 5

Pravis

LOC. LE BIOLCHE, 1
38076 LASINO [TN]
TEL. 0461564305
www.pravis.it

CELLAR SALES
PRE-BOOKED VISITS
ANNUAL PRODUCTION 200,000 bottles
HECTARES UNDER VINE 32.00

1975–2015, the years of the growth of
Pravis, a Valle dei Laghi winery, its
vineyards set against the Brenta Dolomites,
scattered across terraces that seem to
hang in the sky over the blue lakes. The
cellar grows international vines flanked by
interspecific varieties like solaris, to name
but one, and others saved from oblivion,
like negrara and groppello di Revò. The
best interpretation is of the nosiola grape,
true to local custom but with some
innovative touches. Oenologist Erika Pedrini
and vineyard manager Alessio Chistè have
a solid legacy inherited from their fathers,
making wines that stand out for their
elegant simplicity. Pravis is also
synonymous with attention to raisining of
specific white grapes, mainly kerner and
Riesling, used to make a singular Stravino
di Stravino; Ora from nosiola; and above all
Arèle, a truly powerful Vino Santo that took
our Tre Bicchieri, an elegant sipping wine
that will withstand the test of time.

○ Vino Santo Arèle '06	♟♟♟	6
○ Stravino di Stravino '12	♟♟	4
○ l'Ora '12	♟♟	4
● Madruzzo '12	♟♟	3
● Syrae '12	♟♟	4
○ Kerner '14	♟	2
○ Nosiola Le Frate '14	♟	2
● Fratagranda '10	♟♟♟	4*
● Fratagranda '09	♟♟♟	4*
● Fratagranda '07	♟♟♟	4
○ Stravino di Stravino '99	♟♟♟	4*
● Fratagranda '11	♟♟	4
○ l'Ora '11	♟♟	4
● Madruzzo '11	♟♟	3
○ Stravino di Stravino '11	♟♟	4

Cantina Rotaliana

VIA TRENTO, 65B
38017 MEZZOLOMBARDO [TN]
TEL. 0461601010
www.cantinarotaliana.it

CELLAR SALES
PRE-BOOKED VISITS
ANNUAL PRODUCTION 1,200,000 bottles
HECTARES UNDER VINE 330.00
SUSTAINABLE WINERY

Teroldego is in its blood but the winery has
no issues with white grapes, used for its
Metodo Classico. The main priority is still
the native Campo Rotaliano vineyard,
hundreds of hectares of alluvial land at the
confluence of the Noce and Adige rivers.
Rotaliana is a lively cooperative that has
ties with Cavit, and is deeply involved with
TrentoDoc. Merit of Leonardo Pilati,
manager and oenologist, a big fan of
sparklers, although he admits his first love
is Teroldego. Their selection, Clesurae, has
powerful extract and relaxed tannins for
fleshy, satisfying stuffing. The Teroldego
Etichetta Rossa is also beefy and enjoyable.
To the fore of wines presented this year we
noted the Lagrein and a mature Pinot
Grigio with a satisfactory follow-through,
while the Trento Redor Brut was the most
persuasive, with its spirited elegance and
finesse.

● Teroldego Rotaliano Clesurae '12	♟♟	6
● Teroldego Rotaliano Et. Rossa '14	♟♟	2*
○ Trento Brut Redor	♟♟	4
● Trentino Lagrein '14	♟	2
○ Trentino Müller Thurgau '14	♟	2
○ Trentino Pinot Grigio '14	♟	2
● Teroldego Rotaliano Clesurae '06	♟♟♟	5
● Teroldego Rotaliano Clesurae '02	♟♟♟	5
● Teroldego Rotaliano Clesurae '99	♟♟♟	5
● Teroldego Rotaliano Ris. '04	♟♟♟	3
● Teroldego Rotaliano Clesurae '11	♟♟	6
● Teroldego Rotaliano Clesurae '10	♟♟	6
● Teroldego Rotaliano Clesurae '09	♟♟	5
● Teroldego Rotaliano Ris. '11	♟♟	4
○ Trentino Pinot Bianco '12	♟♟	2*
○ Trento Brut Redor Ris. '07	♟♟	5

★Tenuta San Leonardo

FRAZ. BORGHETTO ALL'ADIGE
LOC. SAN LEONARDO
38060 AVIO [TN]
TEL. 0464689004
www.sanleonardo.it

CELLAR SALES
PRE-BOOKED VISITS
ANNUAL PRODUCTION 250,000 bottles
HECTARES UNDER VINE 34.00
SUSTAINABLE WINERY

The Guerrieri Gonzaga can vaunt critical and market acclaim that few others in the Dolomites enjoy. Their beautiful estate has manicured vineyards and within the space of a few harvests, when new plantings become productive, the entire winery will be under biodynamic management. And another wine, Riesling, will soon flank the house white of Sauvignon Blanc. Meanwhile, we tasted an amazing 2010 San Leonardo, with elegant cassis and pepper notes, showing a fresh balsamic overtone. Palate attack is silky, expanding gradually to close leisurely on hints of spice and fruit. No Tre Bicchieri was more well-deserved. The Villa Gresti, a persuasive blend of Merlot and Carmenère, is very similar, while Terre is worthy of the crest it wears and a most approachable wine.

Toblino

FRAZ. SARCHE
VIA LONGA, 1
38070 CALAVINO [TN]
TEL. 0461564168
www.toblino.it

CELLAR SALES
PRE-BOOKED VISITS
RESTAURANT SERVICE
ANNUAL PRODUCTION 400,000 bottles
HECTARES UNDER VINE 700.00

In the administrative reorganization of Trentino municipalities, this enclave of territory between the Santa Massenza, Toblino and Cavedine lakes, will become part of Madruzzo, with its eponymous castle dominating the cellar's vineyards. Here management is geared to organic, as part of the green district being implemented. Perfect vineyard country for sparklers. Not surprisingly, Toblino works hand-in-hand with Cavit, an iconic Italian sparkling wine producer. Specialities do include Vino Santo and Nosiola, however. Toblino uses these grapes for a persuasive Vino Santo, and the Largiller, an old-style Nosiola, a 2007 vintage left to age in large barrels. With its amazing length and vibrant acidity, the wine is outright addictive. The 2001 Vino Santo is delicious. Other worthy wines in the range include L'Ora, an acacia barrel Nosiola, then an organic Moscato Giallo, a ready-to-drink red Rebo, and the well-made Antares, a Trento named after a star as it shines in the Trentino sparkler firmament.

● San Leonardo '10	♥♥♥ 7
● Villa Gresti '10	♥♥ 5
● Terre di San Leonardo '12	♥♥ 3
○ Vette di San Leonardo '14	♥♥ 3
● Carmenère '07	♥♥♥ 8
● San Leonardo '08	♥♥♥ 7
● San Leonardo '07	♥♥♥ 7
● San Leonardo '06	♥♥♥ 7
● San Leonardo '05	♥♥♥ 7
● San Leonardo '04	♥♥♥ 7
● San Leonardo '03	♥♥♥ 7
● San Leonardo '01	♥♥♥ 7
● San Leonardo '00	♥♥♥ 7
● San Leonardo '99	♥♥♥ 7
● San Leonardo '97	♥♥♥ 7
● Villa Gresti '03	♥♥♥ 6

○ Trentino Vino Santo '01	♥♥ 6
○ L'Ora '11	♥♥ 3
○ Largiller '07	♥♥ 3
○ Moscato Giallo Bio '14	♥♥ 2*
○ Trento Brut Antares '10	♥♥ 3
● Trentino Rebo '13	♥ 2
● Elimarò '09	♥♥ 3
○ L'Ora '09	♥♥ 3
○ Manzoni Bianco '13	♥♥ 2*
○ Trentino Chardonnay '13	♥♥ 2*
○ Trentino Müller Thurgau '13	♥♥ 2*
○ Trentino Nosiola '13	♥♥ 2*
○ Trentino Traminer Aromatico '11	♥♥ 2*
○ Trentino Vino Santo '00	♥♥ 5
○ Trento Brut Antares '09	♥♥ 3

Vallarom

FRAZ. MASI, 21
38063 AVIO [TN]
TEL. 0464684297
www.vallarom.it

CELLAR SALES
PRE-BOOKED VISITS
ACCOMMODATION AND RESTAURANT SERVICE
ANNUAL PRODUCTION 45,000 bottles
HECTARES UNDER VINE 7.00
VITICULTURE METHOD Certified Organic
SUSTAINABLE WINERY

The vineyards surround the Scienza family
farm, a rural residence recently renovated to
give the cellar a charming reception area.
Barbara and Filippo Scienza work across the
board, from the vines to the winemaking,
including sales of the end product. They
focus on Metodo Classico sparklers and
Fufluns, a red named after the Etruscan god
of the grape, which has replaced their Campi
Sarni. The austere 2011 has deep garnet
hues, and a silky body, not overly close-knit,
while the shiraz, cabernet and merlot
content adds a brisk note of spice; the finale
is magic. Last but not least, the easy-
drinking Marzemino is vibrant with good
fruit, some youthful vigour, and conjures up
the violets of Alpine meadows not only in the
colour. Another definite thumbs-up for the
Cabernet Sauvignon and the Pinot Nero,
which may benefit from a few more years in
the cellar. There are two classic sparkling
wines, a Dosaggio Zero and an intentionally
deep-hued Rosé.

Roberto Zeni

FRAZ. GRUMO
VIA STRETTA, 2
38010 SAN MICHELE ALL'ADIGE [TN]
TEL. 0461650456
www.zeni.tn.it

CELLAR SALES
PRE-BOOKED VISITS
ANNUAL PRODUCTION 160,000 bottles
HECTARES UNDER VINE 16.00
VITICULTURE METHOD Certified Organic

The Zenis never seek to impress. Expert
winegrowers, they know that time is a key
quality factor, so some of their wines were
not presented. A number of different labels
are still spending time in the cellar. The two
brothers, Andrea and Roberto, have over 40
vintages to their name now and are happy to
accommodate the innovative drive brought
by their offspring, who are continuing the
family business. Winegrowers, certainly, but
also expert master distillers and increasingly
authoritative makers of sparkling wines. And
a Trento bounces them straight into our
finals. Maso Nero is a very tempting and
sunny sparkler, with notes of toasted bread
nuanced with pine resin, and honeyed hints.
Leaving the Teroldego Ternet to mature, we
tasted the traditional Lealbere 2013,
well-defined, well-orchestrated, palate
depth, and certainly progressing nicely. An
enjoyable Rossara 2014 is a fresh wine from
an ancient local variety. The Lecroci 2014 is
a good early-drinking Müller Thurgau.

● Fufluns '11	♟♟ 4
● Trentino Marzemino '14	♟♟ 3
● Vallagarina Pinot Nero '13	♟♟ 4
○ Vo' Dosaggio Zero '12	♟♟ 4
● Vallagarina Cabernet Sauvignon '13	♟ 4
⊙ Vo' Rosé '12	♟ 4
● Cabernet Sauvignon '10	♟♟ 3
● Campi Sarni Rosso '10	♟♟ 4
● Lambrusco a Foglia Frastagliata Enantio '11	♟♟ 3
● Pinot Nero '10	♟♟ 4
● Trentino Marzemino '13	♟♟ 3
● Trentino Marzemino '12	♟♟ 3
● Trentino Marzemino '12	♟♟ 3
● Vallagarina Campi Sarni '11	♟♟ 4
● Vallagarina Pinot Nero '11	♟♟ 4
○ Vo' Dosaggio Zero '10	♟♟ 4

○ Trento Brut Nero Maso Ris. '09	♟♟ 5
○ Müller Thurgau Lecroci '14	♟♟ 2*
● Rossara Legiare '14	♟♟ 2*
● Teroldego Rotaliano Lealbere '13	♟♟ 3
○ Trentino Pinot Bianco Seipergole '14	♟♟ 2*
⊙ Pinot Grigio Ramato Fontane '14	♟ 3
● Ternet Schwarzhof '10	♟♟♟ 5
● Teroldego Rotaliano Pini '09	♟♟♟ 6
● Rossara '13	♟♟ 2*
○ Sorti '11	♟♟ 4
● Ternet Schwarzhof '11	♟♟ 5
● Teroldego Rotaliano Le Albere '11	♟♟ 3*
● Teroldego Rotaliano Pini '10	♟♟ 6
● Teroldego Ternet Schwarzhof '12	♟♟ 5
○ Trentino Chardonnay Vign. Zaraosti '13	♟♟ 2*
○ Trentino Traminer Schwarzhof '13	♟♟ 2*

Agraria Riva del Garda

LOC. SAN NAZZARO, 4
38066 RIVA DEL GARDA [TN]
TEL. 0464552133
www.agririva.it

CELLAR SALES
PRE-BOOKED VISITS
ANNUAL PRODUCTION 250,000 bottles
HECTARES UNDER VINE 280.00

● Rosso Gère '13	♟♟ 3
○ Trento Brut Brezza Riva	♟♟ 3
● Pinot Nero Elesi '13	♟ 3

Barone de Cles

VIA G. MAZZINI, 18
38017 MEZZOLOMBARDO [TN]
TEL. 0461601081
www.baronedecles.it

CELLAR SALES
PRE-BOOKED VISITS
ANNUAL PRODUCTION 80,000 bottles
HECTARES UNDER VINE 39.00

● Teroldego Rotaliano Sup. Riserva del Cardinale '11	♟♟ 5
● Teroldego Rotaliano Maso Scari '12	♟♟ 3

Bossi Fedrigotti

VIA UNIONE, 43
38068 ROVERETO [TN]
TEL. 0456832511
masi@masi.it

CELLAR SALES
PRE-BOOKED VISITS
ANNUAL PRODUCTION 160,000 bottles
HECTARES UNDER VINE 40.00

● Fojaneghe Rosso '11	♟♟ 5
● Mas'est '13	♟♟ 3
○ Trento Brut Conte Federico '11	♟♟ 5
○ Vign'Asmara '13	♟♟ 4

Cembranidoc

VIA IV NOVEMBRE, 52
38034 CEMBRA [TN]
TEL. 0461090906

CELLAR SALES
PRE-BOOKED VISITS
ANNUAL PRODUCTION 10,000 bottles

● Teroldego Rotaliano Petramontis Villa Corniole '13	♟♟ 4
○ Trentino Riesling Le Strope Zanotelli '12	♟♟ 3

Cobelli

FRAZ. SORNI
LOC. MASO DI SOPRA, 22
38015 LAVIS [TN]
TEL. 3495259503
www.cobelli.it

CELLAR SALES
PRE-BOOKED VISITS
ANNUAL PRODUCTION 90,000 bottles
HECTARES UNDER VINE 6.00

○ Chardonnay Arlevo '13	♟♟ 4
● Teroldego Grill '12	♟♟ 5
○ Traminer Gess '13	♟♟ 5

Concilio

ZONA IND. 2
38060 VOLANO [TN]
TEL. 0464411000
www.concilio.it

CELLAR SALES
PRE-BOOKED VISITS
ANNUAL PRODUCTION 6,000,000 bottles
HECTARES UNDER VINE 640.00
SUSTAINABLE WINERY

● Trentino Rosso Mori Vecio '11	♟♟ 3
○ Trentino Sauvignon Arjent '14	♟♟ 3
○ Trento Brut 600Uno	♟♟ 4

De Tarczal

FRAZ. MARANO D'ISERA
VIA G. B. MIORI, 4
38060 ISERA [TN]
TEL. 0464409134
www.detarczal.com

CELLAR SALES
PRE-BOOKED VISITS
RESTAURANT SERVICE
ANNUAL PRODUCTION 120,000 bottles
HECTARES UNDER VINE 17.00

- Trentino Sup. Marzemino Husar '12   ♟♟ 3
- ○ Belvedere '11   ♟ 3

Marco Donati

VIA CESARE BATTISTI, 41
38016 MEZZOCORONA [TN]
TEL. 0461604141
www.cantinadonatimarco.it

CELLAR SALES
PRE-BOOKED VISITS
ANNUAL PRODUCTION 100,000 bottles
HECTARES UNDER VINE 20.00
SUSTAINABLE WINERY

- Teroldego Rotaliano Bagolari '13   ♟♟ 4
- Trentino Marzemino Orme '14   ♟♟ 3
- ○ Vendemmia Tardiva Traminer '13   ♟ 5

Donatoni

LOC. MASI, 6
38063 AVIO [TN]
TEL. 3316320238
www.donatoniwines.it

HECTARES UNDER VINE 10.00

- Corvina '14   ♟♟ 4
- Massenà '13   ♟♟ 3
- Terradeiforti Enantio La Guglia '11   ♟♟ 5
- Valdadige Enantio Coletto '11   ♟♟ 5

Cipriano Fedrizzi

VIA 4 NOVEMBRE, 1
38017 MEZZOLOMBARDO [TN]
TEL. 0461602328
fedrizzicipriano@alice.it

CELLAR SALES
PRE-BOOKED VISITS
ANNUAL PRODUCTION 32,000 bottles
HECTARES UNDER VINE 6.50

- Teroldego Rotaliano Due Vigneti '13   ♟♟ 5
- Teroldego Rotaliano Teroldigo '13   ♟♟ 3

Bruno Grigolli

VIA SAN BERNARDINO,10
38065 MORI [TN]
TEL. 0464917368
www.grigollibruno.it

CELLAR SALES
ANNUAL PRODUCTION 13,000 bottles
HECTARES UNDER VINE 5.00

- Trentino Merlot Sup. Noal '09   ♟♟ 6
- Trentino Rosso Trilogia '09   ♟♟ 6
- ○ Traminer '13   ♟ 5

Maso Cantanghel

VIA CARLO SETTE, 21
38015 LAVIS [TN]
TEL. 0461246353
www.masocantanghel.eu

CELLAR SALES
PRE-BOOKED VISITS
ANNUAL PRODUCTION 20,000 bottles
HECTARES UNDER VINE 8.50
VITICULTURE METHOD Certified Organic
SUSTAINABLE WINERY

- Trentino Pinot Nero V. Cantanghel '12   ♟♟ 5
- ○ Sot Sàs Cuvée '12   ♟♟ 3
- ○ Pinot Grigio MasoPapa '13   ♟ 3
- ○ Trentino Sauvignon V. Cantanghel '14   ♟ 3

Tenuta Maso Corno

LOC. VALBONA
38061 ALA [TN]
TEL. 0464421130
www.tenutamasocorno.it

PRE-BOOKED VISITS
ANNUAL PRODUCTION 10,000 bottles
HECTARES UNDER VINE 5.00

● Santa Maria Maso Corno Ris. '12	♼♼ 4	

Maso Grener

LOC. MASI DI PRESSANO

38015 LAVIS [TN]
TEL. 0461871514
www.masogrener.it

CELLAR SALES
PRE-BOOKED VISITS
ANNUAL PRODUCTION 18,000 bottles
HECTARES UNDER VINE 3.00

○ Trentino Chardonnay V. Tratta '13	♼♼ 3
● Trentino Pinot Nero V. Bindesi '13	♼♼ 3
○ Trentino Sauvignon '14	♼ 2

Maso Poli

LOC. MASI DI PRESSANO, 33
38015 LAVIS [TN]
TEL. 0461871519
www.masopoli.com

CELLAR SALES
PRE-BOOKED VISITS
ACCOMMODATION
ANNUAL PRODUCTION 80,000 bottles
HECTARES UNDER VINE 13.00

● Trentino Pinot Nero '12	♼♼ 3
● Trentino Sorni Rosso Marmoram '11	♼♼ 3
○ Trentino Nosiola '14	♼ 3
○ Trentino Riesling '14	♼ 3

Giuliano Micheletti

VIA E. CONCI, 74
38123 TRENTO
TEL. 3493306929
gm.limina@gmail.com

ANNUAL PRODUCTION 3,000 bottles
HECTARES UNDER VINE 3.00

● Merlot Limen '10	♼♼ 5
○ Riesling Limen '13	♼♼ 4

Mori - Colli Zugna

VIA DEL GARDA, 35
38065 MORI [TN]
TEL. 0464918154
www.cantinamoricollizugna.it

CELLAR SALES
PRE-BOOKED VISITS
ANNUAL PRODUCTION 220,000 bottles
HECTARES UNDER VINE 600.00

● Trentino Rosso Vicarius '10	♼♼ 4
● Trentino Sup. Marzemino d'Isera '13	♼♼ 3
○ Trentino Chardonnay '13	♼ 2
● Trentino Pinot Nero '11	♼ 3

Pedrotti Spumanti

VIA ROMA, 2A
38060 NOMI [TN]
TEL. 0464835111
www.predottispumanti.it

CELLAR SALES
ANNUAL PRODUCTION 30,000 bottles
HECTARES UNDER VINE 3.00
SUSTAINABLE WINERY

○ Trento Brut Pedrotti '10	♼♼ 5
○ Trento Pas Dosé Ris. 111 '08	♼♼ 6
○ Trento Brut Pedrotti Rosé '11	♼ 5

Revì
VIA FLORIDA, 10
38060 ALDENO [TN]
TEL. 0461843155
www.revispumanti.com

CELLAR SALES
PRE-BOOKED VISITS
ANNUAL PRODUCTION 20,000 bottles
HECTARES UNDER VINE 1.70
VITICULTURE METHOD Certified Organic

○ Trento Extra Brut Paladino '10	▼▼ 7
○ Trento Brut Revì '11	▼▼ 4
⊙ Trento Rosé Revì '11	▼▼ 5

Arcangelo Sandri
VIA VANEGGE, 4A
38010 FAEDO [TN]
TEL. 0461650935
www.arcangelosandri.it

CELLAR SALES
PRE-BOOKED VISITS
ANNUAL PRODUCTION 22,000 bottles
HECTARES UNDER VINE 3.00

○ Trentino Müller Thurgau Cosler '14	▼▼ 2*
○ Trentino Chardonnay I Canopi '14	▼ 2
○ Trentino Traminer Razer '14	▼ 2

Armando Simoncelli
VIA NAVICELLO, 7
38068 ROVERETO [TN]
TEL. 0464432373
www.simoncelli.it

CELLAR SALES
PRE-BOOKED VISITS
ANNUAL PRODUCTION 90,000 bottles
HECTARES UNDER VINE 10.50

● Trentino Marzemino '14	▼▼ 3
● Trentino Rosso Navesèl '12	▼▼ 4
○ Trentino Pinot Bianco '14	▼ 3

Enrico Spagnolli
VIA G. B. ROSINA, 4A
38060 ISERA [TN]
TEL. 0464409054
www.vinispagnolli.it

CELLAR SALES
PRE-BOOKED VISITS
ANNUAL PRODUCTION 100,000 bottles
HECTARES UNDER VINE 16.00

● Trentino Marzemino Don Giovanni '12	▼▼ 3
● Lagrein '13	▼ 2
● Trentino Marzemino '13	▼ 2
○ Trentino Moscato Giallo '14	▼ 2

Marco Tonini
LOC. FOLASO
VIA ROSMINI, 8
38060 ISERA [TN]
TEL. 3404991043

CELLAR SALES
PRE-BOOKED VISITS
ANNUAL PRODUCTION 8,000 bottles
HECTARES UNDER VINE 4.00

● Trentino Marzemino d'Isera '14	▼▼ 3
○ Trento Nature Marco Tonini	▼▼ 4

Rudi Windimian
VIA ZAMBANA, 40
38064 LAVIS [TN]
TEL. 0461240373
www.windimian.it

CELLAR SALES
PRE-BOOKED VISITS
RESTAURANT SERVICE
ANNUAL PRODUCTION 15,000 bottles
HECTARES UNDER VINE 3.00

○ Fuori Standard '13	▼▼ 4
○ Kerner '13	▼▼ 4
○ Manzoni Bianco '13	▼ 4
● Teroldego '13	▼ 4

ALTO ADIGE

Quality. That is the first thing that comes to mind today when the province of Bolzano is mentioned in connection with wine. Little more than 5,000 hectares under vine garnered a respectable 27 Tre Bicchieri accolades, which means one for every 200 hectares of vineyard, more than in any other area of Italy, except for Valle d'Aosta. Although the region vaunts such a variety of soils, mesoclimates and varietals, and is the only region where it is usual to find vines growing from 250 to 1,000 metres in altitude, these objective factors are not enough to explain its success. Moreover, just 30 years ago, the reality was quite the reverse, with a scenario of one- or two-litre bottles, and bulk wine. The climate has not become tropical virtually overnight, nor has a steppe evolved in place of mountains so easy on the eye and so tempting to explore. So the secret must be a subjective factor, a human factor. The quality seed must have been sown in the minds of winegrowers, of the great families of wine, and the kellermeisters of the cooperatives, driven by instincts as diverse as they are convergent: personal pride, competition or pressing requests from major commercial partners, or even more simply, to keep pace with the times. The result is now before our eyes, with a large number of labels earning a place alongside top international products. And this is just another salient point in Alto Adige's virtuous cycle: the desire to emerge even abroad after reaching some success in our country. Perhaps this is why the new wines with superlative profiles emerging are produced in such small numbers. After Cantina Terlano's Alto Adige Terlano I Grande Cuvée, Cantina Produttori Colterenzio's Alto Adige Bianco LR Reserve, and Cantina Produttori San Michele Appiano's Alto Adige Bianco Appius, the 2012 vintage made us rejoice for a terrific red from Cantina Girlan: Alto Adige Pinot Nero Mazon Ganger Riserva. A handful of exceptional bottles which represent just the tip of an iceberg composed of hundreds of labels comparable with the best international offering. As tangible proof of the region's recent inspired production of white wines, we picked out 17 for a Tre Bicchieri, as opposed to nine for reds, and just one for a raisined wine. It is no coincidence that the Sustainable Viticulture Award goes to Alto Adige's Manincor winery, acknowledging the region's sensitivity to this issue.

★Abbazia di Novacella

FRAZ. NOVACELLA
VIA DELL'ABBAZIA, 1
39040 VARNA/VAHRN [BZ]
TEL. 0472836189
www.abbazianovacella.it

CELLAR SALES
PRE-BOOKED VISITS
RESTAURANT SERVICE
ANNUAL PRODUCTION 650,000 bottles
HECTARES UNDER VINE 20.00

Novacella Abbey lies at the heart of the Isarco Valley, Italy's northernmost winegrowing area. The cellar is inside the Augustinian Friary itself, whereas the vines are spread out over most of the valley, though there are also some lagrein and schiava plots further south, on the Bolzano plain, and sauvignon and moscato rosa in the Appiano area. Urban von Klebelsberg, the director, and kellermeister Celestino Lucin, run the cellar with great care and attention. The stunning Riesling Praepositus 2013 makes the best of the cool growing year and 12 months in the cellar. Initially rather closed, it opens into smoky notes interwoven with juicy, ripe exotic fruitiness, with a benzene edge emerging from the background. In the mouth it handles the impressive acidity successfully thanks to its tangy palate and full texture. Also exceptional are the gutsy Veltliner 2014 and the nicely-balanced Moscato Rosa Praepositus 2013.

Tenuta Baron Di Pauli

VIA CANTINE, 12
39052 CALDARO/KALTERN [BZ]
TEL. 0471963696
www.barondipauli.com

CELLAR SALES
PRE-BOOKED VISITS
ANNUAL PRODUCTION 46,000 bottles
HECTARES UNDER VINE 15.00

The Baroni Di Pauli's longstanding relationship with Alto Adige winegrowing began 300 years ago, and the estate is fast regaining its historical role as a regional leader. The estate has two main centres, Arzenhof in Caldaro, and Höfl unterm Stein in Söll, near Termeno. Sun-drenched areas in which the grapes ripen gradually, while cellar processes are based on long ageing times, both for the reds and for the whites. This adds up to a spectacular return to the fold for the Baron Di Pauli winery, with a Lago di Caldaro Kalkofen showing a highly-refined aromatic profile of sweet ripe fruitiness, paving the way for hints of fines herbes and soft minerality. The piquant mouth shows an expansive flavour buttressed by perfectly smooth tannins. Enosi is a blend of riesling, sauvignon and pinot bianco, combining tangy aromatic notes with exotic fruit, while the mouth reveals harmony and a lingering finish.

○ A. A. Valle Isarco Riesling Praepositus '13	♥♥♥	4*
● A. A. Moscato Rosa Praepositus '13	♥♥	5
○ A. A. Valle Isarco Veltliner '14	♥♥	3*
● A. A. Lagrein Praepositus Ris. '12	♥♥	5
○ A. A. Valle Isarco Gewürztraminer Praepositus '14	♥♥	4
○ A. A. Valle Isarco Kerner '14	♥♥	3
○ A. A. Valle Isarco Kerner Praepositus '14	♥♥	4
○ A. A. Valle Isarco Müller Thurgau '14	♥♥	3
○ A. A. Valle Isarco Pinot Grigio '14	♥♥	3
○ A. A. Valle Isarco Sylvaner '14	♥♥	3
○ A. A. Valle Isarco Sylvaner Praepositus '14	♥♥	4
○ A. A. Valle Isarco Veltliner Praepositus '13	♥♥	3
○ A. A. Valle Isarco Sylvaner Praepositus '12	♀♀♀	4*
○ A. A. Valle Isarco Veltliner Praepositus '12	♀♀♀	3

● A. A. Lago di Caldaro Cl. Sup. Kalkofen '13	♥♥	3*
● A. A. Arzio Merlot Cabernet '11	♥♥	6
● A. A. Carano Lagrein Ris. '12	♥♥	5
○ A. A. Gewürztraminer Exilissi '11	♥♥	6
○ Enosi '13	♥♥	3
● A. A. Arzio Merlot Cabernet '05	♀♀	6
○ A. A. Enosi '04	♀♀	3
○ A. A. Gewürztraminer Exilissi '09	♀♀	6
○ A. A. Gewürztraminer Exilissi '08	♀♀	6
○ A. A. Gewürztraminer Exilissi '07	♀♀	6
○ A. A. Gewürztraminer Exilissi '03	♀♀	6
● A. A. Lago di Caldaro Cl. Sup. Kalkofen '07	♀♀	3*
● A. A. Lago di Caldaro Cl. Sup. Kalkofen '06	♀♀	3*
○ Enosi '08	♀♀	3*
○ Enosi '06	♀♀	3*

Baron Widmann

Endergasse, 3
39040 Cortaccia/Kurtatsch [BZ]
Tel. 0471880092
www.baron-widmann.it

CELLAR SALES
PRE-BOOKED VISITS
ANNUAL PRODUCTION 35,000 bottles
HECTARES UNDER VINE 15.00

The Widmann family have been making
wine for two centuries, in Cortaccia, one of
the last outposts of Alto Adige on the
provincial boundary between Bolzano and
Trentino. Now it is Andreas' turn to run the
15 hectares of vineyards at elevations of
200 to 600 metres, growing mainly
classical Alto Adige varietals but also the
odd international intruder. The Weiss is
once again Widmann's most impressive
wine, a blend predominantly of chardonnay
and pinot bianco aged in oak. Its aromas
are still rather youthful, dominated by
white-fleshed fruit, with a hint of oak in the
background. The palate reveals good
fullness, with a fragrance which finds its
best expression in a lip-smacking flavour
with good length. The Gewürztraminer
focuses more on ripeness and a caressing
mouthfeel.

○ A. A. Gewürztraminer '13	♊♊ 3
● A. A. Schiava '14	♊♊ 3
○ Weiss '14	♊♊ 3
● Rot '13	♊ 5
○ Weiss '11	♊♊♊ 5
○ Weiss '10	♊♊ 5
○ A. A. Gewürztraminer '12	♊♊ 3
○ A. A. Sauvignon '12	♊♊ 3
○ A. A. Sauvignon '10	♊♊ 3*
● A. A. Schiava '12	♊♊ 3
● A. A. Schiava '11	♊♊ 2*
● A. A. Schiava '10	♊♊ 2*
● Vigneto delle Dolomiti Rosso Rot '10	♊♊ 4
● Vigneto delle Dolomiti Rosso Rot '09	♊♊ 3
○ Weiss '13	♊♊ 3*
○ Weiss '12	♊♊ 5

★★Cantina Bolzano

Via Brennero, 15
39100 Bolzano/Bozen
Tel. 0471270909
www.cantinabolzano.com

CELLAR SALES
PRE-BOOKED VISITS
ANNUAL PRODUCTION 1,100,000 bottles
HECTARES UNDER VINE 320.00

Cantina di Bolzano is one of the province's
leading lights, bringing together two
apparently very diverse winegrowing
cultures in one cellar, namely the majestic
generosity of Lagrein and the lightness of
Santa Maddalena. The origins of this winery
go back some 15 years, to the merger
between the Gries and Santa Maddalena
cellars. Stephan Filippi is still the oenologist
and he also runs the operation, governing
two seemingly irreconcilable worlds that
have somehow found perfect harmony in
Bolzano's central Piazza Gries. The Lagrein
Taber Riserva was the obvious choice for
yet another Tre Bicchieri. One of the
keystones of this school, which has so far
always made its class count, with intense
aromas of black berry fruit, cocoa powder
and spices, its real power lying in gutsy
background minerality. In the mouth, its
firm structure is well balanced by acidity
and a close-woven but sweet tannic
complexity. Also very impressive is the
younger sibling in the Prestige line, while
the Vinalia is the usual stylish passito.

● A. A. Lagrein Taber Ris. '13	♊♊♊ 6
● A. A. Lagrein Prestige Line Ris. '13	♊♊ 4
○ A. A. Moscato Giallo Passito Vinalia '13	♊♊ 3*
● A. A. Cabernet Mumelter Ris. '13	♊♊ 6
● A. A. Gewürztraminer Kleinstein '14	♊♊ 5
● A. A. Merlot Siebeneich Ris. '13	♊♊ 5
○ A. A. Pinot Bianco Dellago '14	♊♊ 4
● A. A. Pinot Nero Ris. '13	♊♊ 5
● A. A. Santa Maddalena Cl. Huck am Bach '14	♊♊ 2*
○ A. A. Chardonnay Kleinstein '14	♊ 4
● A. A. Lagrein - Merlot Mauritius '13	♊ 5
○ A. A. Sauvignon Mock '14	♊ 4
● A. A. Lagrein Taber Ris. '12	♊♊♊ 6
● A. A. Lagrein Taber Ris. '11	♊♊♊ 6
● A. A. Lagrein Taber Ris. '10	♊♊♊ 6
● A. A. Lagrein Taber Ris. '09	♊♊♊ 6

Josef Brigl

LOC. SAN MICHELE
VIA MADONNA DEL RIPOSO, 3
39057 APPIANO/EPPAN [BZ]
TEL. 0471662419
www.brigl.com

CELLAR SALES
PRE-BOOKED VISITS
RESTAURANT SERVICE
ANNUAL PRODUCTION 1,200,000 bottles
HECTARES UNDER VINE 50.00

Brigl has been one of Alto Adige's renowned winegrowing surnames since time immemorial, faithful interpreters of the region's longstanding varieties. Its vineyards cover about 50 hectares, on some of the best-exposed hillsides in the region, their huge production being ensured by an army of grower-suppliers for whom the winery provides assistance throughout the course of the year. The Merlot Windegg is a finely-crafted red, with an intense bouquet of red berries and spices, with subtle vegetal notes underpinned by a hint of oak. In the mouth, the excellent follow-through on the palate paves the way for smooth, lingering tannins. The problematic 2014 harvest gave a Pinot Bianco Haselhof that plays on its immediate accessibility, dominated by fruity sensations on the nose and a full, juicy palate with a rather racy freshness. The Pinot Nero Briglhof is subtle and spirited.

Brunnenhof
Kurt Rottensteiner

LOC. MAZZON
VIA DEGLI ALPINI, 5
39044 EGNA/NEUMARKT [BZ]
TEL. 0471820687
www.brunnenhof-mazzon.it

CELLAR SALES
PRE-BOOKED VISITS
ANNUAL PRODUCTION 25,000 bottles
HECTARES UNDER VINE 7.00

Kurt and Johanna Rottensteiner's winery is in Mazzon, at the heart of what is now regarded as Italy's prime subzone for pinot nero. Most of their few hectares are found here, at around 400 metres above sea level, sheltered to the east by Prato del Re, which keeps mornings in the vineyards fresh and cool. There is also a small plot on the valley floor, with an ancient vineyard planted to lagrein, which needs more heat to ripen its fruits. The interesting Lagrein, a red whose nose expresses intensely fruity, spicy notes, with a firm palate offset by a fresh acidity which makes it crisp and juicy. The Pinot Nero Riserva, in contrast, expresses all the warmth of the 2012 vintage, mature and enfolding from the bouquet onwards. The curious, partially cask-aged Gewürztraminer, with its concentrated and distinctive aromatic profile, offers full-flavoured drinkability.

● A. A. Merlot Windegg '12	▼▼ 3
○ A. A. Pinot Bianco Haselhof '14	▼▼ 2*
● A. A. Pinot Nero Briglhof '12	▼▼ 3
● A. A. Schiava Grigia Kaltenburg '14	▼ 3
○ A. A. Gewürztraminer Windegg '14	▼ 3
● A. A. Lago di Caldaro Cl. Windegg '14	▼ 3
● A. A. Lagrein Briglhof Ris. '12	▼ 5
○ A. A. Pinot Grigio Windegg '14	▼ 3
○ A. A. Riesling '14	▼ 3
● A. A. Santa Maddalena Rielerhof '14	▼ 3
● A. A. Schiava Haselhof '14	▼ 2
○ A. A. Pinot Grigio Windegg '11	▼▼▼ 3*
● A. A. Lagrein Briglhof '11	♀♀ 5
● A. A. Lagrein Briglhof Ris. '10	♀♀ 5
○ A. A. Terlano Drei König Hof '10	♀♀ 2*

○ A. A. Gewürztraminer '14	▼▼ 4
● A. A. Pinot Nero Ris. '12	▼▼ 5
● A.A. Lagrein '13	▼▼ 5
○ Eva '14	▼▼ 4
○ A. A. Gewürztraminer '11	♀♀ 4
○ A. A. Gewürztraminer '10	♀♀ 4
○ A. A. Gewürztraminer '09	♀♀ 4
○ A. A. Gewürztraminer '08	♀♀ 4
○ A. A. Gewürztraminer '07	♀♀ 4
○ A. A. Gewürztraminer '06	♀♀ 4
● A. A. Lagrein V. V. '12	♀♀ 5
● A. A. Pinot Nero Ris. '11	♀♀ 5
● A. A. Pinot Nero Ris. '09	♀♀ 5
● A. A. Pinot Nero Ris. '07	♀♀ 5
● A. A. Pinot Nero Ris. '06	♀♀ 5
● A. A. Pinot Nero Ris. '05	♀♀ 5

★Cantina di Caldaro

VIA CANTINE, 12
39052 CALDARO/KALTERN [BZ]
TEL. 0471963149
www.kellereikaltern.com

CELLAR SALES
PRE-BOOKED VISITS
ANNUAL PRODUCTION 2,000,000 bottles
HECTARES UNDER VINE 300.00

Cantina di Caldaro is one of the largest cooperatives in the province, with 300 hectares under vine painstakingly tended by a legion of over 400 growers. The main focus is on schiava, for Lago di Caldaro, but over recent decades there has been a shift towards all of the other varietals grown in the province, with the exception of the typical Isarco Valley grapes. Production is rounded off by a series of wines from highly prestigious estates such as Castel Giovanelli or Pfarrhof and the biodynamic Solos range. Hard to choose the best from such a quality array of wines, but Cabernet Pfarrhof, Sauvignon Castel Giovanelli and Serenade are a whisper ahead of the field. The Cabernet has a classy aromatic profile, dominated by forest fruits and balsamic herbs, with lively flavours and a lingering finish. The Sauvignon expresses the aromatic exuberance of this refined variety in an understated way, making for a full-flavoured finish. And finally the Serenade plays on its harmonious, elegant flavours.

○ A. A. Moscato Giallo Passito Serenade '12	♟♟♟ 6
● A. A. Cabernet Sauvignon Pfarrhof Ris. '12	♟♟ 6
○ A. A. Sauvignon Castel Giovanelli '13	♟♟ 5
○ A. A. Chardonnay Wadleith '14	♟♟ 3
○ A. A. Kerner Carned '14	♟♟ 3
● A. A. Lago di Caldaro Scelto Cl. Sup. Pfarrhof '14	♟♟ 3
● A. A. Lagrein Solos Ris. '12	♟♟ 6
○ A. A. Pinot Bianco Vial '14	♟♟ 3
● A. A. Pinot Nero Pfarrhof Ris. '12	♟♟ 6
○ A. A. Sauvignon Premstaler '14	♟♟ 3
● A. A. Lago di Caldaro Scelto Cl. Sup. Pfarrhof '13	♟♟♟ 3*
○ A. A. Moscato Giallo Passito Serenade '10	♟♟♟ 6

Castel Sallegg

V.LO DI SOTTO, 15
39052 CALDARO/KALTERN [BZ]
TEL. 0471963132
www.castelsallegg.it

CELLAR SALES
PRE-BOOKED VISITS
ANNUAL PRODUCTION 120,000 bottles
HECTARES UNDER VINE 30.00

The Kuenburg family's Castel Sallegg winery dominates the centre of Caldaro and is one of the most delightful properties in the area. Their 30-plus hectares under vine stand at an altitude of between 200 and 600 metres, mostly around the lake itself. The cellar inside the castle is where all the vinification takes place, producing wines characterized by clear definition and easily-identifiable cultivars. An exceptional performance from the Pinot Bianco Pratum, made entirely from grapes grown at the Preyhof estate, located over 500 metres above sea level. Its nose beguiles with an extremely peachy clarity, backed up by hints of oak and sweet spice. On the palate, the wine unbends with a taut grace, paving the way for a lengthy, persistent finish. As ever, the Moscato Rosa is one of the province's finest, dominated by the aromatic profile of the varietal, mirrored in its full-bodied, distinctively sweet palate.

○ A. A. Moscato Rosa Passito '12	♟♟ 6
○ A. A. Terlano Pinot Bianco Pratum '13	♟♟ 3*
○ A. A. Bianco Ars Lyrica '13	♟♟ 3
● A. A. Cabernet Sauvignon Ris. '11	♟♟ 3
● A. A. Gewürztraminer Lotterbrunnen '14	♟♟ 3
● A. A. Lago di Caldaro Scelto Bischofsleiten '14	♟♟ 2*
● A. A. Merlot Nussleiten '11	♟♟ 6
○ A. A. Moscato Giallo Steinleiten '14	♟♟ 3
○ A. A. Pinot Bianco Prey '14	♟ 2
○ A. A. Pinot Grigio Pulvernai '14	♟ 3
● A. A. Pinot Nero '13	♟ 3
○ A. A. Sauvignon Leisen '14	♟ 2
● A. A. Lago di Caldaro Scelto Bischofsleiten '13	♟♟ 2*
● A. A. Pinot Nero Ris. '11	♟♟ 3*

Castelfeder

VIA PORTICI, 11
39040 EGNA/NEUMARKT [BZ]
TEL. 0471820420
www.castelfeder.it

CELLAR SALES
PRE-BOOKED VISITS
ANNUAL PRODUCTION 400,000 bottles
HECTARES UNDER VINE 20.00

The history of the Giovannet family winery began over 40 years ago, but it was not until Günther took over at the helm some 20 years later, transferring the cellar to the Cortina site on the Strada del Vino trail, that it really took off. Today, help for Günther and his wife Alessandra comes increasingly from their children Ivan, on the production side, and Ines, who handles marketing. Around 20 hectares of their own under vine are the basis for their production, integrated by grapes from growers in the Lower Adige Valley. This year's production makes a similarly excellent impression to its predecessor, with the Chardonnay Burgum Novum and Pinot Bianco Tecum vying for top spot. The Chardonnay has a bouquet ranging from white-fleshed fruit to toasty oak, with a gradually-emerging insistent minerality. The rich palate has a crisp, succulent flavour. By contrast, the Tecum has a rather closed nose, opening up to display finesse and a crisp, sophisticated and rounded palate.

★Cantina Produttori Colterenzio

LOC. CORNAIANO/GIRLAN
S.DA DEL VINO, 8
39057 APPIANO/EPPAN [BZ]
TEL. 0471664246
www.colterenzio.it

CELLAR SALES
PRE-BOOKED VISITS
ANNUAL PRODUCTION 1,600,000 bottles
HECTARES UNDER VINE 300.00
SUSTAINABLE WINERY

Though Luis Raifer's spirit still pervades the interiors of this beautiful building in Cornaiano, his son Wolfgang has now taken over at the helm of Cantina Produttori di Colterenzio, alongside chairman Max Niedermayr and kellermeister Martin Lemayr. This winery's strength lies in the passion of its 300 members tending the same number of hectares under vine, mainly in the Oltradige and Lower Adige Valley. A great performance from the Cabernet Lafòa, one of the finest expressions of this variety in Alto Adige and probably in Italy. From a hot growing year, it shows ripe plum to medicinal herbs on the nose, paving the way for a full-bodied palate backed up by sweet tannins and richness of flavour to provide length and suppleness. Not far behind, the Sauvignon of the same name has a very youthful aromatic profile still, though the palate promises an outstanding future. Also excellent is the Pinot Nero St. Daniel, true to type on the nose with a well-balanced flavour. The Bianco LR 2012 should not be missed, though not many bottles were produced.

○ A. A. Chardonnay Burgum Novum Ris. '12	♟♟	4
○ A. A. Pinot Bianco Tecum '13	♟♟	3*
● A. A. Cabernet Burgum Novum Ris. '12	♟♟	4
○ A. A. Gewürztraminer Vom Lehm '14	♟♟	3
● A. A. Lagrein Burgum Novum Ris. '12	♟♟	4
○ A. A. Pinot Bianco Vom Stein '14	♟♟	2*
○ A. A. Pinot Grigio 15 '14	♟♟	2*
● A. A. Pinot Nero Burgum Novum Ris. '12	♟♟	5
● A. A. Schiava Breitbacher '14	♟♟	2*
○ Sauvignon Raif '14	♟♟	3
○ A. A. Chardonnay Doss '14	♟	3
● A. A. Pinot Nero Glener '13	♟	3
○ A. A. Pinot Bianco Tecum '10	♟♟♟	3*
● A. A. Lagrein Burgum Novum Ris. '11	♟♟	4

● A. A. Cabernet Sauvignon Lafòa '12	♟♟♟	7
● A. A. Pinot Nero St. Daniel Ris. '12	♟♟	4
○ A. A. Sauvignon Lafòa '13	♟♟	5
○ A. A. Bianco LR '12	♟♟	8
○ A. A. Chardonnay Formigar '13	♟♟	5
○ A. A. Gewürztraminer Atisis '13	♟♟	5
⊙ A. A. Lagrein Sigis Mundus '11	♟♟	5
● A. A. Merlot Siebeneich Ris. '12	♟♟	4
○ A. A. Pinot Bianco Thurner '14	♟♟	3
○ A. A. Sauvignon Prail '14	♟♟	3
○ A. A. Chardonnay Altkirch '14	♟	2
○ A. A. Moscato Giallo Sand '14	♟	3
● A. A. Cabernet Sauvignon Lafòa '11	♟♟♟	7
● A. A. Cabernet Sauvignon Lafòa '10	♟♟♟	7

★Cantina Produttori Cortaccia

S.DA DEL VINO, 23
39040 CORTACCIA/KURTATSCH [BZ]
TEL. 0471880115
www.cantina-cortaccia.it

CELLAR SALES
PRE-BOOKED VISITS
ANNUAL PRODUCTION 1,100,000 bottles
HECTARES UNDER VINE 170.00

Founded in 1900, Cantina Cortaccia now has over 250 members, each cultivating an average of under a hectare, turning the vineyards into a sort of jigsaw puzzle surrounding the village, from 200 all the way up to 900 metres above sea level. Andreas Kofler, the recently-elected young chairman, has brought in a decided change of pace, which is leading to some excellent reviews and improved sales, by focusing on the varieties most suited to member vineyards. Peerless performance from the Gewürztraminer Brentall Riserva, a white unlike any other from this aromatic Alto Adige varietal. Long ageing in the cellar has led to a wine of great complexity and depth on the nose, giving the palate a fullness offset nicely by a marked richness of flavour, for a long and alluring finish. Also spellbinding was the Aruna, a late-harvest moscato giallo and gewürztraminer displaying a sophisticated bouquet and a supple, leisurely palate. The Merlot Brenntal is complex, muscular and juicy.

Hartmann Donà

VIA RAFFEIN, 8
39010 CERMES/TSCHERMS [BZ]
TEL. 3292610628
hartmann.dona@rolmail.net

ANNUAL PRODUCTION 35,000 bottles
HECTARES UNDER VINE 4.65

Vigneron Hartmann Donà is a complex chap and profound connoisseur of his region, but also a great craftsman of a series of wines true to the territory of origin. Today, he divides his attention between the family business and consultancy work for other wineries, focusing not only on his expertise but also on his personal vision of wine. Delicacy and style underscore both his cellarwork and his winegrowing, reducing impact in the vineyard to a minimum and often allowing nature simply to take its course. The Donà Noir is a Pinot Nero with a deeply sophisticated personality, dominated by suggestions of forest fruits and rain-soaked earth, its aromatic profile refreshed by medicinal herbs. In the mouth, the excellent follow-through allows the wine to unbend with elegance and length. The Donà Rouge from schiava embellished by a dash of lagrein and pinot nero, softens out in the cellar to become mature and beguilingly drinkable.

○ A. A. Gewürztraminer Brenntal Ris. '12	♥♥♥	5
● A. A. Merlot Brenntal '12	♥♥	5
○ Aruna V. T. '13	♥♥	6
● A. A. Cabernet Kirchhügel Ris. '12	♥♥	4
● A. A. Merlot Cabernet Soma '12	♥♥	5
● A. A. Moscato Rosa Ushas '13	♥♥	6
○ A. A. Müller Thurgau Graun '14	♥♥	3
○ A. A. Pinot Bianco Hoftatt '14	♥♥	3
○ A. A. Sauvignon Kofl '14	♥♥	4
● A. A. Schiava Grigia Sonntaler '14	♥♥	3
○ A. A. Chardonnay Pichl '14	♥	3
○ A. A. Pinot Grigio Penòner '14	♥	3
○ A. A. Gewürztraminer Brenntal '02	♥♥♥	5
● A. A. Lagrein Scuro Fohrhof '00	♥♥♥	5

● A.A. Pinot Nero Donà Noir '11	♥♥	3*
● A. A. Lagrein '13	♥♥	3
○ A.A. Sauvignon '14	♥♥	3
○ Donà Blanc '11	♥♥	3
● Donà Rouge '10	♥♥	3
○ A. A. Chardonnay '14	♥	3
○ A. A. Gewürztraminer '14	♥	3
○ A.A. Pinot Bianco '14	♥	3
○ A.A. Gewürztraminer '13	♀♀	3
● A. A. Lagrein '12	♀♀	3
● A.A. Pinot Nero Donà Noir '10	♀♀	3
● A.A. Pinot Nero Donà Noir '09	♀♀	3*
● Donà Noir '08	♀♀	3*
● Donà Rouge '09	♀♀	3
● Donà Rouge '08	♀♀	3*
● Donà Rouge '07	♀♀	3*

Tenuta Ebner
Florian Unterthiner

FRAZ. CAMPODAZZO, 18
39054 RENON/RITTEN [BZ]
TEL. 0471353386
www.weingutebner.it

CELLAR SALES
PRE-BOOKED VISITS
RESTAURANT SERVICE
HECTARES UNDER VINE 4.50

On the Alto Adige wine scene, the Isarco
Valley keeps pumping out new talent,
young winegrowers who choose to develop
their parents' holdings, following a virtuous
path of total respect for the environment
and for traditions, while also improving the
quality of their wines and extending their
markets beyond the confines of the
province to encompass the whole world.
Florian and Brigitte Unterthiner have
developed the Ebner estate, five hectares
of south- and southeast-facing vineyards at
about 500 metres above sea level,
overlooking the Isarco Valley. The Pinot
Bianco, with a sophisticated nose,
characterized by the perfect of ripe
fruitiness and fresh floral aromas, performs
commendably. The mouth is well-rounded,
with a nicely balanced flavour. Also of note
is the Sauvignon, which steps away from
tangy, vegetable notes and displays a
delightfully variegated spectrum with exotic
fruit in the foreground backed up by flowers
and spices.

● A. A. Schiava '14	♟♟ 2*
○ A.A. Pinot Bianco '14	♟♟ 3
○ A.A. Sauvignon '14	♟♟ 3
○ A.A. Valle Isarco Gewürztraminer '14	♟♟ 4
○ A.A. Valle Isarco Veltliner '14	♟♟ 3
● Zweigelt '13	♟♟ 3
○ A.A. Pinot Bianco '12	♟♟ 3
○ A.A. Sauvignon '13	♟♟ 3

Erbhof Unterganzner
Josephus Mayr

FRAZ. CARDANO
VIA CAMPIGLIO, 15
39053 BOLZANO/BOZEN
TEL. 0471365582
www.tirolensisarsvini.it

CELLAR SALES
PRE-BOOKED VISITS
ANNUAL PRODUCTION 65,000 bottles
HECTARES UNDER VINE 9.00

Josephus Mayr has earned himself a
special place on the Santa Maddalena wine
scene. With the help of his wife Barbara, he
runs the family estate, less than ten
hectares on ancient volcanic soils around
Cardano, where the cool breezes from the
Rio Ega which flows into the Isarco meet
the heat of the Bolzano basin. The grapes
ripen with consistency and balance, tended
with great enthusiasm and expertise by
Josephus, who uses no chemical
compounds. The Mayr winery's Lagrein is
always strikingly firm. With its dark,
brooding robe, its initially closed, almost
coy aromas open up slowly to tones of
forest fruits, pencil lead and spices, with a
subtle smokiness expressed peerlessly in
the mouth, where the wine manages to
unbend despite its formidable structure,
paving the way for a long, crisp finish. The
Santa Maddalena Classico is complex and
mature, showing perfect generosity. The
Cabernet Riserva is complex and
close-knit.

● A. A. Cabernet Ris. '12	♟♟ 5
● A. A. Lagrein Ris. '12	♟♟ 5
● A. A. Santa Maddalena Cl. '13	♟♟ 3*
○ A. A. Lagrein Rosato V. T. '14	♟ 3
○ A. A. Sauvignon Platt & Pignat '14	♟♟ 3
● Composition Reif '13	♟♟ 6
○ A. A. Kerner '14	♟ 3
○ Passito Marie Josephine '13	♟ 7
● A. A. Lagrein Ris. '11	♟♟♟ 5
● A. A. Lagrein Scuro Ris. '05	♟♟♟ 4
● Lamarein '05	♟♟♟ 6
● A. A. Cabernet Kampill Ris. '11	♟♟ 5
○ A. A. Lagrein Rosato V. T. '13	♟♟ 3
● A. A. Santa Maddalena Cl. '12	♟♟ 3*
○ A. A. Sauvignon Platt & Pignat '13	♟♟ 3
● Composition Reif '12	♟♟ 6
● Lamarein '12	♟♟ 6

Erste+Neue

VIA DELLE CANTINE, 5/10
39052 CALDARO/KALTERN [BZ]
TEL. 0471963122
www.erste-neue.it

CELLAR SALES
PRE-BOOKED VISITS
ANNUAL PRODUCTION 1,400,000 bottles
HECTARES UNDER VINE 250.00

Prima e Nuova is a long-established Alto
Adige winery, with 200 hectares under
vine, from the warm sunny slopes
overlooking Lake Caldaro to the cool
breezes crossing the tableland below the
Mendola, offering soils, exposures and
diurnal temperature ranges that enable the
native Alto Adige varietals to express their
personality to the full. Manfred Schullian's
guiding hand and kellermeister Gerhard
Sanin's precision in the cellar ensure
high-profile production. This year no other
wine came close to the Leuchtenburg, a
Lago di Caldaro which exploits the
freshness of the 2014 vintage to show
sophisticated aromas of forest fruits and
spices, enhanced by a palate that
combines lightness, richness of flavour and
personality. A splendid way to drink light. By
contrast, the Sauvignon Puntay displays a
nose of gooseberry and exotic fruit, for a
piquant, yet balanced finish of good length;
one of the best in the province.

★Falkenstein
Franz Pratzner

VIA CASTELLO, 15
39025 NATURNO/NATURNS [BZ]
TEL. 0473666054
www.falkenstein.bz

CELLAR SALES
PRE-BOOKED VISITS
ANNUAL PRODUCTION 45,000 bottles
HECTARES UNDER VINE 7.00

Valle Venosta is one of Alto Adige's
warmest and driest valleys, crowned by the
presence of some top-quality small
winegrowing estates. One of these belongs
to Franz Pratzner, whose Falkenstein has a
great sense of place, reflecting the quality
of this splendid territory. Just a handful of
hectares, often clinging to breathtakingly
steep slopes, provide the grapes for wines
characterized by clear-cut aromas and
outstanding grip. Franz's efforts are not
limited to the agricultural side though, as
this time around he decided to put off
presenting his whites until next year,
delaying bottling to enable his wines to
reach maturity unhurriedly. So, with its
bouquet of wild berries intertwining with
oaky, spicy notes, paving the way for a
palate of excellent grip and suppleness, it is
the Pinot Nero that expresses the very best
of this estate,

● A. A. Lago di Caldaro Cl. Sup. Leuchtenburg '14	♛♛♛ 2*
○ A. A. Sauvignon Puntay '13	♛♛ 5
○ A. A. Chardonnay Salt '14	♛♛ 3
○ A. A. Gewürztraminer Puntay '13	♛♛ 5
● A. A. Lagrein Lareith '13	♛♛ 3
○ A. A. Pinot Bianco Prunar '14	♛♛ 3
● A. A. Santa Maddalena Gröbnerhof '14	♛♛ 3
○ A. A. Sauvignon Stern '14	♛♛ 3
○ Anthos Bianco Passito '12	♛♛ 5
○ A. A. Gewürztraminer Puntay '01	♛♛♛ 3
● A. A. Lago di Caldaro Cl. Sup. Leuchtenburg '12	♛♛♛ 2*
● A. A. Lago di Caldaro Cl. Sup. Puntay '10	♛♛♛ 3*
○ A. A. Sauvignon Puntay '06	♛♛♛ 4
○ Anthos Bianco Passito '10	♛♛♛ 5

● A. A. Val Venosta Pinot Nero '12	♛♛ 5
○ A. A. Val Venosta Pinot Bianco '07	♛♛♛ 4
○ A. A. Val Venosta Riesling '12	♛♛♛ 5
○ A. A. Val Venosta Riesling '11	♛♛♛ 5
○ A. A. Val Venosta Riesling '10	♛♛♛ 5
○ A. A. Val Venosta Riesling '09	♛♛♛ 5
○ A. A. Val Venosta Riesling '08	♛♛♛ 5
○ A. A. Val Venosta Riesling '07	♛♛♛ 5
○ A. A. Val Venosta Riesling '06	♛♛♛ 5
○ A. A. Val Venosta Riesling '05	♛♛♛ 5
○ A. A. Val Venosta Riesling '00	♛♛♛ 3
○ A. A. Valle Venosta Riesling '13	♛♛♛ 5
A. A. Valle Venosta Riesling '98	♛♛♛ 3*

Garlider
Christian Kerschbaumer

VIA UNTRUM, 20
39040 VELTURNO/FELDTHURNS [BZ]
TEL. 0472847296
www.garlider.it

CELLAR SALES
PRE-BOOKED VISITS
ANNUAL PRODUCTION 26,000 bottles
HECTARES UNDER VINE 4.20
VITICULTURE METHOD Certified Organic

Valle Isarco winds sinuously up into the
Bolzano mountains towards the Austrian
border, and the slopes it has cut between
the mountains provide excellent inclines
and exposures for winegrowing. This is
where Christian Kerschbaumer plies his
trade, on a handful of organically-tended
hectares, partnered by wife Veronika. Their
production has been welcomed for its great
character and for its firm, dry palate. The
decision to delay bottling and to present the
whole range a year later is paying off
splendidly. Tidy and well-orchestrated, his
wines show outstanding character. The
Sylvaner has distinctive smoky and sulphur
notes over a firm, full-flavoured palate.
Lively fruitiness distinguishes the Pinot
Grigio, revealing a mouth of full texture and
a fine acid grip. Finally, the striking Veltliner
shows off a complex array of aromas, with
notes of exotic fruit, Mediterranean scrub
and sulphur, developing nicely on the
palate.

Cantina Girlan

LOC. CORNAIANO/GIRLAN
VIA SAN MARTINO, 24
39057 APPIANO/EPPAN [BZ]
TEL. 0471662403
www.girlan.it

CELLAR SALES
PRE-BOOKED VISITS
ANNUAL PRODUCTION 1,300,000 bottles
HECTARES UNDER VINE 220.00

The Girlan winery's greatest heritage is
over 200 hectares under vine, mostly on
the hills to the south-west of Bolzano, at
elevations of 450–550 metres above sea
level, on mineral-rich sand or clay soils. Not
forgetting, of course, the team of over 200
grower-members who work closely
alongside kellermeister Gerhard Kofler, with
great love and passion for the territory. The
intense partnership with sales director
Oscar Lorandi has led to top-quality wines
with no chinks in the armour. This year's
range is once again impressive, with the
Pinot Nero Trattmann taking the lion's share
of the plaudits. Grapes from the Mazzon
subzone give this wine its sophisticated
bouquet, where the role of forest fruits is
well contrasted by spices and by an
oakiness waiting to be fully absorbed. On
the palate, the wine is firm and
underpinned by refined tannins. Schiava
Gschleier, Gewürztraminer Flora and Pinot
Bianco Sandbichler from the Lun winery
are superb examples of their types. Don't
miss the wonderful Trattmann selection, the
Riserva Ganger 2012.

○ A. A. Valle Isarco Sylvaner '13	♥♥♥	3*
○ A. A. Valle Isarco Veltliner '13	♥♥	4
○ Pinot Grigio '13	♥♥	4
○ A. A. Valle Isarco Sylvaner '09	♀♀♀	3*
○ A. A. Valle Isarco Veltliner '08	♀♀♀	3*
○ A. A. Valle Isarco Veltliner '07	♀♀♀	3
○ A. A. Valle Isarco Veltliner '05	♀♀♀	3*
● A. A. Pinot Nero '12	♀♀	4
○ A. A. Valle Isarco Grüner Veltliner '12	♀♀	4
○ A. A. Valle Isarco Müller Thurgau '13	♀♀	3
● A. A. Valle Isarco Pinot Nero '10	♀♀	3
○ A. A. Valle Isarco Sylvaner '12	♀♀	3*
○ A. A. Valle Isarco Sylvaner '11	♀♀	3
○ A. A. Valle Isarco Veltliner '11	♀♀	3*

● A. A. Pinot Nero Trattmann Mazon Ris. '12	♥♥♥	5
○ A. A. Gewürztraminer Flora '14	♥♥	6
○ A. A. Pinot Bianco Sandbichler H. Lun '14	♥♥	3*
● A. A. Schiava Gschleier Alte Reben '13	♥♥	3*
○ A. A. Bianco Cuvée Flora Ris. '12	♥♥	5
○ A. A. Chardonnay Flora '13	♥♥	5
○ A. A. Gewürztraminer Sandbichler H. Lun '14	♥♥	4
○ A. A. Gewürztraminer V.T. Pasithea Oro '14	♥♥	6
● A. A. Lagrein Sandbichler Ris. Lun '12	♥♥	4
○ A. A. Pinot Bianco H. Lun '14	♥♥	3
○ A. A. Pinot Bianco Plattenriegl '14	♥♥	3
● A. A. Pinot Nero Patricia '13	♥♥	3
○ A. A. Riesling H. Lun '14	♥♥	3
● A. A. Schiava Faß N° 9 '14	♥♥	2*

Glögglhof - Franz Gojer

FRAZ. SANTA MADDALENA
VIA RIVELLONE, 1
39100 BOLZANO/BOZEN
TEL. 0471978775
www.gojer.it

CELLAR SALES
PRE-BOOKED VISITS
ANNUAL PRODUCTION 55,000 bottles
HECTARES UNDER VINE 7.40

Franz Gojer's estate sits atop the Santa
Maddalena hill, a mere handful of hectares
on sun-drenched limestone and porphyry
soils, which enjoy both the warm sunshine
of the Bolzano basin and the cool breezes
blowing down the Valle Isarco. Over the
years, they have added the Rencio, Gries
and Ora estates, especially for lagrein, and
the Cornedo all'Isarco vineyards, at higher
altitudes, so more suitable for white
varieties. The Lagrein Riserva and the
Santa Maddalena Rondell both put in good
performances. After an initially rather
closed nose, the Lagrein shows generous
and full of fruit-fuelled, smoky notes with a
hint of medicinal herbs, completed by a
lively palate, handling the imposing
structure in a carefree fashion. The Rondell
is always one of the most convincing Santa
Maddalenas, displaying aromas of spices
and wild berries, with a juicy, very supple
mouth. Among the whites, the sophisticated
Pinot Bianco stood out.

Griesbauerhof
Georg Mumelter

VIA RENCIO, 66
39100 BOLZANO/BOZEN
TEL. 0471973090
www.griesbauerhof.it

CELLAR SALES
PRE-BOOKED VISITS
ANNUAL PRODUCTION 30,000 bottles
HECTARES UNDER VINE 3.80

Georg Mumelter runs the family winery just
outside Bolzano, at the foot of the Santa
Maddalena and Santa Giustina hills, where
the heat of the Bolzano basin is rapidly
cooled by the breezes blowing in from the
nearby Isarco Valley. With just a few
hectares to its name, run with great
expertise by Georg, this winery's selection
of labels is centred mainly around Santa
Maddalena and Lagrein, with white grapes
playing a decidedly supporting role. Of the
winery's two Lagreins, we preferred the
2013 for its fruit-laden aromatic profile of
spicy, smoky notes. In the mouth, it reveals
a firm body, walking a tightrope between
power and drinkability. Within a whisker of
the finals came the Cabernet Sauvignon
Riserva, with its intense, rather forthright
bouquet of medicinal herbs and sweet
fruitiness, showing smooth tannins and a
crisp, polished mouth.

● A. A. Lagrein Ris. '12	♥♥ 4
● A. A. Santa Maddalena Cl. Rondell '14	♥♥ 3*
○ A. A. Pinot Bianco Karneid '14	♥♥ 3
● A. A. Santa Maddalena Cl. '14	♥♥ 2*
● A. A. Vernatsch Alte Reben '14	♥♥ 2*
○ A. A. Kerner Karneid '14	♥ 3
○ A. A. Sauvignon Karneid '14	♥ 3
○ A. A. Kerner Karneid '13	♀♀ 3
● A. A. Lagrein Ris. '11	♀♀ 4
● A. A. Santa Maddalena Cl. '13	♀♀ 2*
● A. A. Santa Maddalena Rondell '13	♀♀ 3*
● A. A. Vernatsch Alte Reben '13	♀♀ 2*

● A. A. Lagrein '13	♥♥ 3*
● A. A. Cabernet Sauvignon Ris. '12	♥♥ 3
● A. A. Lagrein Ris. '12	♥♥ 5
○ A. A. Pinot Bianco '14	♥♥ 3
● A. A. Santa Maddalena Cl. '14	♥♥ 2*
● Schiava Isarcus '13	♥♥ 3
● A. A. Merlot Spitz '13	♥ 3
○ A. A. Pinot Grigio '14	♥ 3
● A. A. Lagrein Ris. '09	♀♀♀ 5
● A. A. Lagrein '12	♀♀ 3
● A. A. Lagrein Ris. '11	♀♀ 5
● A. A. Merlot Spitz '12	♀♀ 3

Gummerhof - Malojer

VIA WEGGESTEIN, 36
39100 BOLZANO/BOZEN
TEL. 0471972885
www.malojer.it

CELLAR SALES
PRE-BOOKED VISITS
ANNUAL PRODUCTION 100,000 bottles
HECTARES UNDER VINE 18.00

The Malojer family has owned this estate for over half a century, with 20 hectares under vine, supplying grapes for part of the winery's production. Over the years, Alfred Malojer and his father Urban have built up a strong relationship with local growers, assisting them throughout the year, thus enabling them to supply the rest of the grapes needed for production. While schiava and lagrein may be the heart of their long-established business, white grapes are expanding their share thanks to a series of top-quality wines. Once again, the Lagrein Riserva is first in line at the Malojer winery. Its bouquet gradually wins us over, beginning with the red berry notes, followed up by the smoky quinine, giving way to an attractively spicy edge, which finds perfect expression in a crisp palate with nice pressure. Also impressive are the Riserva di Cabernet and Pinot Nero, with their well-defined aromatic profiles and elegantly lean palates.

● A. A. Lagrein Ris. '12	♟♟ 4
● A. A. Cabernet Lagrein Bautzanum Cuvée Ris. '12	♟♟ 4
● A. A. Cabernet Ris. '12	♟♟ 4
○ A. A. Müller Thurgau Kreiter '14	♟♟ 2*
○ A. A. Pinot Bianco Kreiter '14	♟♟ 3
○ A. A. Pinot Grigio Gur zu Sand '14	♟♟ 3
● A. A. Pinot Nero Ris. '12	♟♟ 4
● A. A. Santa Maddalena Cl. Loamer '14	♟♟ 2*
○ A. A. Chardonnay '14	♟ 3
○ A. A. Gewürztraminer Kui '14	♟ 3
● A. A. Lagrein Scuro Gummer zu Gries '13	♟ 3
○ A. A. Sauvignon Gur zu Sand '14	♟ 3
● A. A. Lagrein Gries '09	♟♟♟ 2*
○ A. A. Pinot Grigio Gur zu Sand '13	♟♟ 3*

Gumphof
Markus Prackwieser

LOC. NOVALE DI PRESULE, 8
39050 FIÈ ALLO SCILIAR/VÖLS AM SCHLERN [BZ]
TEL. 0471601190
www.gumphof.it

CELLAR SALES
PRE-BOOKED VISITS
ANNUAL PRODUCTION 45,000 bottles
HECTARES UNDER VINE 5.00

Markus Prackwieser winery is in Fiè allo Sciliar. Just a handful of hectares under vine, mainly given over to white varieties, which enjoy the huge contrasts in climate caused by the heat of the Bolzano basin meeting the cool breezes flowing down the Isarco Valley from the Alps. The soils reveal the complex origins of this area, the porphyry dating back to ancient volcanic formations which blends in with the alluvial deposits on the valley floor. The quality of this year's range from Markus meant that several of his wines either reached our finals or only just missed out. All three versions of Pinot Bianco performed admirably, led by the new oak-aged Riserva Aventuere. The fruity aromas delicately intertwine with spicy oak notes for a sophisticated aromatic profile promising better to come; supple on the palate, succulent and with great ageing potential. The Praesulis, however, seems rather more uncomplicated and gutsy, while the eponymous Sauvignon has a rosy future ahead.

○ A. A. Pinot Bianco Praesulis '14	♟♟♟ 3*
○ A. A. Pinot Bianco Aventuere Ris. '12	♟♟ 3*
○ A. A. Sauvignon Praesulis '14	♟♟ 4
○ A. A. Gewürztraminer '14	♟♟ 4
○ A. A. Pinot Bianco '14	♟♟ 3
● A. A. Schiava '14	♟♟ 3
○ A. A. Pinot Bianco Praesulis '06	♟♟♟ 3*
○ A. A. Sauvignon Praesulis '13	♟♟♟ 4*
○ A. A. Sauvignon Praesulis '09	♟♟♟ 3*
○ A. A. Sauvignon Praesulis '07	♟♟♟ 3*
○ A. A. Sauvignon Praesulis '04	♟♟♟ 3*
○ A. A. Pinot Bianco '13	♟♟ 3
○ A. A. Pinot Bianco '12	♟♟ 3*
○ A. A. Pinot Bianco Praesulis '13	♟♟ 3*
○ A. A. Pinot Bianco Praesulis '12	♟♟ 3*
● A. A. Schiava '13	♟♟ 3

★Franz Haas

VIA VILLA, 6
39040 MONTAGNA/MONTAN [BZ]
TEL. 0471812280
www.franz-haas.it

CELLAR SALES
PRE-BOOKED VISITS
ANNUAL PRODUCTION 300,000 bottles
HECTARES UNDER VINE 50.00
SUSTAINABLE WINERY

Franz Haas is a tireless, dynamic
winegrower, always on the lookout for ways
to improve his wines, for a vineyard that
might give something extra, or for a vine
variety that will enjoy specific soil and
climatic conditions. All of this commitment
has enabled him to put together a large
estate, ranging from vineyards at elevations
of just a few hundred metres to others way
above the 1000-metre mark. Pinot Nero,
Franz's true passion, and the Haas winery's
Moscato Rosa are the biggest attractions
for wine lovers. This year, though, alongside
the Moscato Rosa, the Sauvignon puts in a
shining performance; with its bouquet of
white peach and flowers, its mouth
focusing on elegance and charm, it places
the aromatic exuberance of the vine type
very much centre-stage. The Moscato Rosa
shows an aromatic framework dominated
by hints of super-ripe strawberry, medicinal
herbs and trifle. In the mouth, its
overwhelming sweetness is kept at bay by
a full-flavoured grip which regales the
palate with lightness and drinkability.

○ A. A. Sauvignon '13	♟♟♟	5
● A. A. Moscato Rosa '13	♟♟	5
○ A. A. Gewürztraminer '14	♟♟	4
○ A. A. Pinot Bianco Lepus '14	♟♟	3
● A. A. Pinot Nero '13	♟♟	5
● A. A. Pinot Nero Schweizer '12	♟♟	6
○ Manna '13	♟♟	5
● A. A. Moscato Rosa '12	♟♟♟	5
● A. A. Moscato Rosa '11	♟♟♟	5
● A. A. Moscato Rosa Schweizer '00	♟♟♟	4
● A. A. Moscato Rosa Schweizer '99	♟♟♟	
● A. A. Pinot Nero Schweizer '02	♟♟♟	5
● A. A. Pinot Nero Schweizer '01	♟♟♟	5
○ Manna '07	♟♟♟	4
○ Manna '05	♟♟♟	4
○ Manna '04	♟♟♟	4

Haderburg

FRAZ. BUCHOLZ
LOC. POCHI, 30
39040 SALORNO/SALURN [BZ]
TEL. 0471889097
www.haderburg.it

CELLAR SALES
PRE-BOOKED VISITS
ANNUAL PRODUCTION 100,000 bottles
HECTARES UNDER VINE 12.00
VITICULTURE METHOD Certified Biodynamic

The fact that Alto Adige is discovering its
propensity for Metodo Classico wines is
due in no small part to cellars like Alois
Ochsenreiter's, one of the pioneers of Alto
Adige sparklers. The property covers a
dozen or so hectares, tended
biodynamically, on two main plots, the
historical Hausmannhof in Pochi and the
more recent Obermairlhof in the Isarco
Valley, where the typical grape varieties can
be found. Excellent results both in the still
and sparkling wine sectors, with our
favourite being the Pas Dosé 2011, a
chardonnay-based sparkler topped up with
pinot nero which partially softens the oak
flavours. The aromas are reminiscent of
yellow-fleshed fruit, grilled bread and dried
flowers, while the mouth highlights the
perfect fusion with the fizz, giving it a long
and savoury finish. The most impressive
stills, meanwhile, are the two Pinot Neros,
both displaying more of a balanced palate
than any expressive range of aromas.

● A. A. Merlot - Cabernet Sauvignon Erah Hausmannhof '11	♟♟	5
● A. A. Pinot Nero Hausmannhof '13	♟♟	5
● A. A. Pinot Nero Hausmannhof Ris. '12	♟♟	6
○ A. A. Sauvignon Hausmannhof '14	♟♟	4
○ A. A. Spumante Brut	♟♟	5
○ A. A. Spumante Pas Dosé '11	♟♟	5
○ A. A. Spumante Brut Rosé	♟	5
○ A. A. Spumante Ris. '97	♟♟♟	6
○ A. A. Valle Isarco Sylvaner Obermairlhof '05	♟♟♟	3*
● A. A. Pinot Nero Hausmannhof '11	♟♟	5
● A. A. Pinot Nero Hausmannhof Ris. '10	♟♟	6
○ A. A. Sauvignon Hausmannhof Ris. '05	♟♟	4
○ A. A. Spumante Pas Dosé '10	♟♟	5

Kettmeir

VIA DELLE CANTINE, 4
39052 CALDARO/KALTERN [BZ]
TEL. 0471963135
www.kettmeir.com

CELLAR SALES
PRE-BOOKED VISITS
ANNUAL PRODUCTION 330,000 bottles
HECTARES UNDER VINE 36.00

Kettmeir may be part of Gruppo Santa Margherita, but the winery's soul remains distinctly Alto Adige. Joseph Romen has been running the estate for over 30 years. Born in Caldaro, he enjoys an indissoluble link with the wines of his terroir. Around 30 hectares under vine, owned wither by the winery or its growers, with some of the best-exposed slopes in the province, at Pochi, Caldaro and Soprabolzano. Various soils, aspects and altitudes for a range producing increasingly impressive wines year on year. Making the most of the excellent 2013 vintage is the Chardonnay Maso Reiner, with a performance to write home about. The nose encapsulates the perfect fusion between fruit and oak, lengthening on the palate with grip and elegance, resulting in a long, juicy finish. The whole Metodo Classico range is excellent, with our preference going to the Brut Rosé, from hilltop pinot nero. With a nose of berries and croissant, its mouth develops generosity as well as richness of flavour and elegance.

○ A. A. Chardonnay Maso Reiner '13	♟♟ 3*
○ A. A. Chardonnay '14	♟♟ 3
○ A. A. Gewürztraminer '14	♟♟ 3
● A. A. Lagrein Athesis Ris. '12	♟♟ 5
○ A. A. Müller Thurgau Athesis '14	♟♟ 4
○ A. A. Pinot Bianco '14	♟♟ 3
● A. A. Pinot Nero Maso Reiner '12	♟♟ 4
○ A. A. Spumante Brut	♟♟ 3
⊙ A. A. Spumante Brut Rosé	♟♟ 4
⊙ A. A. Lagrein Rosato '14	♟ 2
○ A. A. Müller Thurgau '14	♟ 3
○ A. A. Sauvignon '14	♟ 3
○ A. A. Müller Thurgau Athesis '13	♟♟ 4
○ A. A. Müller Thurgau Athesis '12	♟♟ 3*

Tenuta Klosterhof Oskar Andergassen

LOC. CLAVENZ, 40
39052 CALDARO/KALTERN [BZ]
TEL. 0471961046
www.garni-klosterhof.com

CELLAR SALES
PRE-BOOKED VISITS
ACCOMMODATION AND RESTAURANT SERVICE
ANNUAL PRODUCTION 20,000 bottles
HECTARES UNDER VINE 3.50

The Andergassen family divide their time between caring for the vineyard and looking after their guest facilities in Caldaro, but each year the winegrowing takes a stronger hold. They have very few hectares under vine but that is enough for the winery's production, which Oskar and son Hannes oversee in person from start to finish, from vineyard management through to bottling. They even go so far as to commission a famous local cooper to make acacia casks from estate-owned trees in the Montiggl area. There are no dizzying heights among this year's Andergassen range, but no weaknesses either. The Pinot Bianco Trifall shows an aromatic framework dominated by notes of yellow-fleshed fruit, with a hint of vegetal in the background refreshing the aromas, then encoring perfectly on the palate, where the wine displays firmness and grip. The Pinot Nero Panigl hinges around spicy fruitiness, while the mouth is full and juicy.

● A. A. Merlot Ris. '12	♟♟ 4
○ A. A. Moscato Giallo Birnbaum '14	♟♟ 3
○ A. A. Pinot Bianco Trifall '14	♟♟ 3
● A. A. Pinot Nero Panigl '12	♟♟ 5
⊙ A. A. Pinot Nero Rosé Summer '14	♟♟ 4
● A. A. Lago di Caldaro Cl. Sup. Plantaditsch '14	♟♟ 2*
● A. A. Lago di Caldaro Cl. Sup. Plantaditsch '12	♟♟ 2*
● A. A. Lago di Caldaro Cl. Sup. Plantaditsch R '13	♟♟ 3
● A. A. Lago di Caldaro Cl. Sup. Plantaditsch R '12	♟♟ 3*
○ A. A. Moscato Giallo Birnbaum '13	♟♟ 3
○ A. A. Pinot Bianco Trifall '13	♟♟ 3*
● A. A. Pinot Nero Panigl '13	♟♟ 5

★Köfererhof
Günther Kerschbaumer

FRAZ. NOVACELLA
VIA PUSTERIA, 3
39040 VARNA/VAHRN [BZ]
TEL. 3474778009
www.koefererhof.it

CELLAR SALES
PRE-BOOKED VISITS
RESTAURANT SERVICE
ANNUAL PRODUCTION 80,000 bottles
HECTARES UNDER VINE 10.00

Günther Kerschbaumer's wines made their debut halfway through the 1990s, and over the next couple of decades the winery has become a benchmark for lovers of Alto Adige wines. A dozen or so hectares under vine at the heart of the Isarco Valley, at elevations of 800–900 metres, where the strong diurnal temperature range ensures healthy grapes with an expressive aromatic profile. The winery style is all firmness and grip. Günther's range this year is breathtaking, starting with a stunning Sylvaner R, showing a rather sulphurous nose with hints of crisp white-fleshed fruit. The mouth is a no contest, with a palate that lacks nothing: full texture, grip, personality and length. The Pinot Grigio has a nose of pear and dried flowers, while the palate is pervasive and generous but racy at one and the same time. The Veltliner is more closed and unfathomable on the nose but comes into its own on the palate.

Tenuta Kornell

FRAZ. SETTEQUERCE
VIA BOLZANO, 23
39018 TERLANO/TERLAN [BZ]
TEL. 0471917507
www.kornell.it

CELLAR SALES
PRE-BOOKED VISITS
ANNUAL PRODUCTION 100,000 bottles
HECTARES UNDER VINE 15.00

Florian Brigl runs the family winery in the Settequerce district of Terlano, with its 15 hectares of vines stretching east almost as far as the outskirts of Bolzano. Over its 15-year history, the cellar has managed to make wines that are totally true to the territory, where the loose, sandy porphyry soils enjoy a sunny and rather warm climate, giving wines a bright, open disposition. An outstanding performance from the Lagrein Staves, a Riserva with intense aromas of black berry fruit and spices, a hint of garden vegetables refreshing the profile. The mouth reveals an outstandingly firm body, handled with precision and even suppleness, for a juicy, satisfying finish. Also very good is the eponymous Cabernet Sauvignon, showing a sophisticated bouquet of fruit and medicinal herbs, which on the palate highlights a particularly smooth and glossy tannin.

○ A. A. Valle Isarco Sylvaner R '13	♥♥♥ 5
○ A. A. Valle Isarco Pinot Grigio '14	♥♥ 3*
○ A. A. Valle Isarco Veltliner '13	♥♥ 4
○ A. A. Valle Isarco Gewürztraminer '14	♥♥ 4
○ A. A. Valle Isarco Kerner '14	♥♥ 3
○ A. A. Valle Isarco Müller Thurgau '14	♥♥ 3
○ A. A. Valle Isarco Riesling '13	♥♥ 5
○ A. A. Valle Isarco Sylvaner '14	♥♥ 3
○ A. A. Valle Isarco Pinot Grigio '13	♀♀♀ 3*
○ A. A. Valle Isarco Pinot Grigio '12	♀♀♀ 3*
○ A. A. Valle Isarco Pinot Grigio '11	♀♀♀ 3*
○ A. A. Valle Isarco Pinot Grigio '09	♀♀♀ 3*
○ A. A. Valle Isarco Riesling '10	♀♀♀ 4
○ A. A. Valle Isarco Sylvaner R '09	♀♀♀ 4
○ A. A. Valle Isarco Sylvaner R '08	♀♀♀ 4
○ A. A. Valle Isarco Sylvaner R '07	♀♀♀ 4

● A. A. Lagrein Staves Ris. '12	♥♥♥ 5
● A. A. Cabernet Sauvignon Staves Ris. '12	♥♥ 5
● A. A. Lagrein Greif '14	♥♥ 3
○ A. A. Sauvignon Oberberg '14	♥♥ 3
● Zeder '13	♥♥ 3
○ A. A. Gewürztraminer Damian '14	♥ 3
● A. A. Merlot Staves Ris. '12	♥ 5
○ A. A. Pinot Bianco Eich '14	♥ 3
○ A. A. Sauvignon Cosmas '14	♥ 3
● A. A. Merlot Staves Ris. '11	♀♀ 5
● A. A. Pinot Nero Marit '12	♀♀ 6

Tenuta Kränzelhof
Graf Franz Pfeil

VIA PALADE, 1
39010 CERMES/TSCHERMS [BZ]
TEL. 0473564549
www.labyrinth.bz

CELLAR SALES
PRE-BOOKED VISITS
ANNUAL PRODUCTION 35,000 bottles
HECTARES UNDER VINE 6.00

Most Alto Adige estates are based on intensive viticulture, though in some cases winegrowing can be the main task in a farming world still focused on fruit-growing. Conte Franz Pfeil, by contrast, runs his family estate in a different way: he seeks to bring out the beauty in everything around, from his maze garden to his Gothic-style mansion, from his art collection to his wines. Just a few hectares under vine at an altitude of between 300 and 600 metres, for reliable top-quality production. Rather than displaying an outstandingly intense aromatic profile, the Sauvignon Blanc goes for subtlety, with a delicate flowery bouquet on a backdrop of white-fleshed fruit. In the mouth, balance reigns supreme, ushering in a long, full-flavoured finish. In the Merlot, the fruit is still rather overshadowed by the oak, whereas the palate is somewhat more mature, showing suppleness and smooth tannins.

★Kuenhof - Peter Pliger

LOC. MARA, 110
39042 BRESSANONE/BRIXEN [BZ]
TEL. 0472850546
pliger.kuenhof@rolmail.net

CELLAR SALES
PRE-BOOKED VISITS
ANNUAL PRODUCTION 40,000 bottles
HECTARES UNDER VINE 6.00
SUSTAINABLE WINERY

Peter Pliger and his wife Brigitte are among Valle Isarco's most popular producers, with their outstanding interpretations of riesling and especially sylvaner. Just a few of hectares of terraces tended with sustainable practices, on incredibly steep southeast-facing slopes where white grapes enjoy the huge diurnal temperature range that fixes the aromas we find expressed in Pliger wines. The Sylvaner 2014 has surprisingly focused aromas, dominated by a crisp, approachable fruitiness, attractively offset by a delicate flowery expressiveness. However, the mouth is where this wine moves up a notch, with full texture, thrust and grip banishing the simplicity, for a palate characterized by a strong personality. Not far behind is the Veltliner, with a more complex nose and, like the Sylvaner, with good firmness and length. Flowers and citrus for the racy Kaiton.

● A. A. Meranese '13	♥♥	3
○ Corona '14	♥♥	4
● Merlot '13	♥♥	3
● Pinot Nero '12	♥♥	6
○ Sauvignon Blanc '14	♥♥	3
○ Pinot Bianco '13	♥	4
● A. A. Meranese Baslan '12	♀♀	3*
● A. A. Meranese Meraner Hügel '11	♀♀	3
○ Dorado Passito '12	♀♀	5
○ Pinot Bianco Helios '13	♀♀	4
○ Pinot Bianco Mitterberg '12	♀♀	4
● Pinot Nero '11	♀♀	6
● Pinot Nero Graf Pfeil '09	♀♀	3
● Schiava Baslan '10	♀♀	3*

○ A. A. Valle Isarco Sylvaner '14	♥♥♥	3*
○ A. A. Valle Isarco Veltliner '14	♥♥	3*
○ A. A. Valle Isarco Riesling Kaiton '14	♥♥	3
○ A. A. Valle Isarco Gewürztraminer '14	♥	3
○ A. A. Valle Isarco Riesling Kaiton '12	♀♀♀	4*
○ A. A. Valle Isarco Riesling Kaiton '11	♀♀♀	4*
○ A. A. Valle Isarco Riesling Kaiton '10	♀♀♀	4
○ A. A. Valle Isarco Riesling Kaiton '07	♀♀♀	3*
○ A. A. Valle Isarco Sylvaner '13	♀♀♀	3*
○ A. A. Valle Isarco Sylvaner '08	♀♀♀	3
○ A. A. Valle Isarco Sylvaner '06	♀♀♀	3*
○ A. A. Valle Isarco Veltliner '09	♀♀♀	3*
○ A. A. Valle Isarco Riesling Kaiton '13	♀♀	3*
○ A. A. Valle Isarco Sylvaner '12	♀♀	3
○ A. A. Valle Isarco Veltliner '13	♀♀	3*
○ A. A. Valle Isarco Veltliner '12	♀♀	3*

Laimburg

LOC. LAIMBURG, 6
39040 VADENA/PFATTEN [BZ]
TEL. 0471969700
www.laimburg.bz.it

CELLAR SALES
PRE-BOOKED VISITS
ANNUAL PRODUCTION 160,000 bottles
HECTARES UNDER VINE 41.00

Laimburg is much more than just a winery: it is an experimental facility belonging to Bolzano's provincial Centro di Sperimentazione Agraria e Forestale, an estate that not only works on production but also tests the interaction between various cultivars and soil types in the area, at different altitudes and exposures. Around 40 hectares, producing wines that remain faithful to the most typical expression of the vine variety, it also comes up with very characterful wines. We were impressed by the Cabernet Sauvignon Sass Roà, its bouquet dominated by sweet, juicy red berries, with a vein of bitter chocolate and aromatic herbs. It youthfulness is revealed in the mouth, resulting in a gutsy wine with good prospects. The Lagrein Barbagòl hinges totally on full flavour, while the Pinot Nero has an attack dominated by oak, paving the way for ripe juicy forest fruit.

Loacker Schwarhof

LOC. SANTA JIUSTINA, 3
39100 BOLZANO/BOZEN
TEL. 0471365125
www.loacker.net

CELLAR SALES
PRE-BOOKED VISITS
ANNUAL PRODUCTION 60,000 bottles
HECTARES UNDER VINE 7.00
VITICULTURE METHOD Certified Organic
SUSTAINABLE WINERY

The Loacker family have been running the Schwarhof estate since the late 1970s. Rainer handed over the reins to Hayo and Franz Josef, who have followed in their father's footsteps, continuing with a biodynamic approach using homeopathic remedies to tend their south-facing three and a half hectares of vineyard on Santa Maddalena hill, almost overlooking the Isarco River. Their other two estates cover a total area of seven hectares. The Lagrein Gran Lareyn shows a deep nose gradually showing black berry fruit, then notes of medicinal herbs, followed by spice, and subtle minerality still evolving. The palate is very rich with gutsy flavours and great character. The Kastlet is a blend of cabernet sauvignon and lagrein with a nose of forest fruits and aniseed, while the palate is full, revealing a tannic bite of great precision.

● A. A. Cabernet Sauvignon Sass Roà Ris. '12	♟♟5
● A. A. Lagrein Barbagòl Ris. '12	♟♟5
○ A. A. Gewürztraminer Elyònd Ris. '13	♟♟4
● A. A. Pinot Nero Ris. '13	♟♟4
○ A. A. Sauvignon Oyèll '14	♟♟4
○ A. A. Sauvignon Passito Saphir '13	♟♟6
○ A. A. Pinot Bianco '14	♟2
○ A. A. Riesling '14	♟4
● Col de Réy '10	♟6
● A. A. Cabernet Sauvignon Sass Roà Ris. '11	♟♟5
○ A. A. Gewürztraminer Elyònd '12	♟♟4
● A. A. Merlot Ris. '12	♟♟3

● A. A. Lagrein Gran Lareyn '13	♟♟4
○ Gewürztraminer Atagis '14	♟♟5
● Kastlet '12	♟♟5
○ Chardonnay Ateyon '13	♟4
○ Sauvignon Blanc Tasnim '14	♟4
● A. A. Merlot Ywain '04	♟♟♟4*
● A. A. Lagrein Gran Lareyn Ris. '10	♟♟4
● A. A. Lagrein Ris. '10	♟♟4
● A. A. Santa Maddalena Morit '11	♟♟3
● Cabernet Sauvignon - Lagrein '10	♟♟4
○ Gewürztraminer '12	♟♟4
○ Gewürztraminer Atagis '11	♟♟5
● Kastlet '11	♟♟5
● Lagrein '11	♟♟4
● Merlot '11	♟♟4
● Merlot Ywain '12	♟♟4

Manincor

loc. San Giuseppe al Lago, 4
39052 Caldaro/Kaltern [BZ]
Tel. 0471960230
www.manincor.com

CELLAR SALES
PRE-BOOKED VISITS
ANNUAL PRODUCTION 300,000 bottles
HECTARES UNDER VINE 50.00
VITICULTURE METHOD Certified Biodynamic
SUSTAINABLE WINERY

Sophie and Michael Goëss-Enzenberg run
the family winery in Caldaro. The 50
hectares of estate-owned vineyards,
divided into five plots, are farmed entirely
with biodynamic methods, under the
watchful eye of Helmut Zozin. Everything
revolves around the concept of quality, not
just in terms of the organoleptic profile of
the wines, which in any case is flawless,
but also in terms of sustainability, both in
the vineyards and in the lovely winery set
below the vines themselves. That's why we
have awarded the prize for sustainable
growing to Manincor. Tannenberg is a
Sauvignon with intense notes of
white-fleshed fruit and flowers. The wine
opens out with savory flavor and tension,
and of great length. The Chardonnay
Sophie still has oak to the fore then
explodes into a luscious fruitiness shot
through with minerally notes for a
full-bodied and sophisticated mouthfeel.
The Réserve della Contessa is also
excellent.

K. Martini & Sohn

loc. Cornaiano
via Lamm, 28
39057 Appiano/Eppan [BZ]
Tel. 0471663156
www.martini-sohn.it

CELLAR SALES
PRE-BOOKED VISITS
ANNUAL PRODUCTION 230,000 bottles
HECTARES UNDER VINE 28.00

This Cornaiano winery has been working
with great expertise on the Alto Adige wine
scene for over 30 years, all stemming from
Gabriel Martini and his son Lukas's passion
for their work, and their close partnerships
with the many local growers who bring in
grapes from over 30 hectares of vineyards.
Vinification at the Via Lamm cellar is
designed to bring out the varietal stamping
and underline the quality of the soils,
through a delicate balance between
technology and tradition. The Martini family
have come up with a broad range of wines
with the Sauvignon Palladium topping our
list of preferences. Although the nose is still
rather youthful and predictable, the palate
has an attractive ability to combine fullness
of flavour and suppleness, making for a
racy finish with good length. The Pinot
Bianco from the same range expresses a
ripe fruitiness developing into a full and
gutsy palate. The spirited and adaptable
Schiava Rueslhof Gurnzan is well-made.

○ A. A. Terlano Sauvignon Tannenberg '13	♼♼♼ 5
○ A. A. Terlano Chardonnay Sophie '13	♼♼ 5
○ A. A. Terlano Réserve della Contessa '14	♼♼ 3*
● A. A. Pinot Nero Mason '13	♼♼ 5
● A. A. Pinot Nero Mason di Mason '12	♼♼ 7
○ A. A. Terlano Pinot Bianco Eichhorn '14	♼♼ 5
○ A. A. Terlano Sauvignon Lieben Aich '13	♼♼ 7
○ Le Petit '13	♼♼ 6
○ A. A. Terlano Pinot Bianco Eichhorn '13	♼♼♼ 5
○ A. A. Terlano Pinot Bianco Eichhorn '12	♼♼♼ 5
○ A. A. Terlano Pinot Bianco Eichhorn '10	♼♼♼ 4
○ A. A. Terlano Pinot Bianco Eichhorn '09	♼♼♼ 4
● A. A. Pinot Nero Mason '12	♼♼ 5
○ A. A. Terlano Réserve della Contessa '13	♼♼ 3
○ A. A. Terlano Sauvignon Lieben Aich '12	♼♼ 5
○ Le Petit '12	♼♼ 6

○ A. A. Gewürztraminer Palladium '14	♼♼ 4
● A. A. Lagrein Maturum '12	♼♼ 5
● A. A. Lagrein Scuro Rueslhof Gurnzan '14	♼♼ 2*
○ A. A. Pinot Bianco Palladium '14	♼♼ 2*
○ A. A. Sauvignon Palladium '14	♼♼ 3
● A. A. Schiava Palladium '14	♼♼ 2*
● Coldirus Palladium '13	♼♼ 3
○ A. A. Chardonnay Maturum '13	♼ 4
○ A. A. Kerner Palladium '14	♼ 2
● A. A. Pinot Nero Palladium '13	♼ 3
● A. A. Schiava Kellermeistertrunk '14	♼ 2
○ A. A. Sauvignon Palladium '04	♼♼♼ 2*
○ A. A. Gewürztraminer Palladium '13	♼♼ 4
● A. A. Lago di Caldaro Cl. Felton '12	♼♼ 2*
● A. A. Lagrein Maturum '11	♼♼ 5
○ A. A. Pinot Bianco Palladium '13	♼♼ 2*

Cantina Meran Burggräfler

VIA CANTINA, 9
39020 MARLENGO/MARLING [BZ]
TEL. 0473447137
www.cantinamerano.it

CELLAR SALES
PRE-BOOKED VISITS
ANNUAL PRODUCTION 1,000,000 bottles
HECTARES UNDER VINE 250.00

The merger between Vini Merano and
Burggräfler created the biggest winery in
the Burgraviato, the winegrowing area
comprising Merano and the surrounding
villages, with no less than 380 members
cultivating some 250 hectares. In the
cellar, kellermeister Stefan Kapfinger has
set up production of four different ranges,
the best of which are the Selection, the
Graf von Meran and the Sonnenberg,
wholly devoted to the wines of Val Venosta.
The splendid Pinot Bianco Tyrol makes the
most of the excellent 2013 vintage to
create a highly-sophisticated aromatic
profile, showing white-fleshed fruit shot
through with flowery, spicy nuances. The
mouth is both light and firm, giving it
length and a sweeping finish. The
Meranese Schickenburg is a red that will
send schiava enthusiasts into ecstasy,
thanks to its fresh aromatic framework and
essential mouth.

★Cantina Convento Muri-Gries

FRAZ. GRIES
P.ZZA GRIES, 21
39100 BOLZANO/BOZEN
TEL. 0471282287
www.muri-gries.com

CELLAR SALES
ANNUAL PRODUCTION 700,000 bottles
HECTARES UNDER VINE 50.00

Christian Werth has been the oenologist at
Cantina Muri-Gries for nearly 30 years, the
main driving force behind the development
of lagrein, one of Bolzano province's two
native grape varieties, the other being
schiava. The winery is located inside the
Benedictine monastery itself and vinifies
grapes from its 50 hectares under vine,
mostly lagrein from Gries and the Bolzano
basin, as well as smaller amounts of white
Appiano Monte and San Michele grapes.
The winery champion is again the Lagrein
Abtei Muri, one of the labels that has won
most awards from us. The sunny 2012
vintage led to a red with a compact colour,
fragrance concentrated dominated by a
chewy, sweet black berries, shot through by
notes of smokiness, spices and aromatic
herbs. In the mouth the oak initially
prevails, paving the way for fruitiness,
which runs right through to the full-bodied,
muscular palate. Also very good are the
Abtei Muri Bianco and the Pinot Nero, that
play on finesse and elegance.

○ A. A. Pinot Bianco Tyrol '13	▼▼▼ 4*
● A. A. Meranese Schickenburg Graf von Meran '14	▼▼ 3*
○ A. A. Moscato Giallo Passito Sissi '12	▼▼ 6
○ A. A. Sauvignon Mervin '13	▼▼ 4
● A. A. Cabernet Graf von Meran Ris. '12	▼▼ 4
○ A. A. Gewürztraminer Labers '13	▼▼ 4
○ A. A. Moscato Giallo Graf von Meran '14	▼▼ 3
○ A. A. Pinot Bianco Ris. '10	▼▼ 2*
○ A. A. Pinot Grigio Festival '14	▼▼ 2*
○ A. A. Sauvignon Graf von Meran '14	▼▼ 4
○ A. A. Val Venosta Pinot Bianco Sonnenberg '14	▼▼ 3
● A. A. Pinot Nero Zeno Ris. '12	▼ 4
○ A. A. Valle Venosta Pinot Bianco Sonnenberg '13	♈♈♈ 3*

● A. A. Lagrein Abtei Muri Ris. '12	▼▼▼ 5
○ A. A. Bianco Abtei Muri '13	▼▼ 3*
● A. A. Pinot Nero Abtei Muri Ris. '12	▼▼ 5
● A. A. Lagrein '14	▼▼ 2*
⊙ A. A. Lagrein Rosato '14	▼▼ 2*
○ A. A. Moscato Rosa V. T. Abtei Muri '13	▼▼ 5
○ A. A. Pinot Grigio '14	▼▼ 2*
○ A. A. Terlano Pinot Bianco '14	▼▼ 2*
● A. A. Pinot Nero '14	▼ 3
● A. A. Lagrein Abtei Muri Ris. '11	♈♈♈ 5
● A. A. Lagrein Abtei Muri Ris. '10	♈♈♈ 5
● A. A. Lagrein Abtei Muri Ris. '09	♈♈♈ 5
● A. A. Lagrein Abtei Ris. '07	♈♈♈ 5
● A. A. Lagrein Abtei Ris. '06	♈♈♈ 4
● A. A. Lagrein Abtei Ris. '05	♈♈♈ 4
● A. A. Lagrein Abtei Ris. '04	♈♈♈ 4

★Cantina Nals Margreid

VIA HEILIGENBERG, 2
39010 NALLES/NALS [BZ]
TEL. 0471678626
www.kellerei.it

CELLAR SALES
PRE-BOOKED VISITS
ANNUAL PRODUCTION 950,000 bottles
HECTARES UNDER VINE 150.00
SUSTAINABLE WINERY

Cantina Nals Margreid may be one of the smallest cooperatives in the province, but is also one of its best-known, with the hard-working, expert staff under the guidance of kellermeister Harald Schraffl. Its 150 hectares under vine are located in two main areas, i.e. Nalles close to Merano, and Magrè, further south close to the Trentino border. In addition to these two large areas are lagrein and schiava vineyards in Bolzano, as well as the Mazzon area for pinot nero. Plenty of impressive wines this year, headed by a gutsy and almost essential version of Sirmian, the Pinot Bianco that has often topped our preferences, with its fresh, compact and penetrating aromas. In the mouth, the cool 2014 vintage gave a palate of great depth and length. The Mantele, meanwhile, is a Sauvignon which steps away from vegetable notes to display a profile of good breadth, with a full-flavoured, balanced mouth. The Pinot Grigio Punggl expresses its pleasantly rustic, troubled soul.

Ignaz Niedrist

LOC. CORNAIANO/GIRLAN
VIA RONCO, 5
39050 APPIANO/EPPAN [BZ]
TEL. 0471664494
www.ignazniedrist.com

CELLAR SALES
PRE-BOOKED VISITS
ANNUAL PRODUCTION 45,000 bottles
HECTARES UNDER VINE 10.00
SUSTAINABLE WINERY

Ignaz Niedrist's winery gets its grapes from three different estates, each with its own soil and climate conditions, which helps bring out the best in each grape variety grown there. The Cornaiano area specializes mainly in red grape varieties, whereas Appiano Monte is much more of a white area. Last but not least, at the Berger Gei family farmstead in Gries, Elizabeth Niedrist tends the lagrein vineyard, in the area regarded as the variety's birthplace. The Trias is a largely chardonnay-based blend which has less striking aromatics this year and more emphasis on its rounded palate. Its initial impact is delicate, ushering in richness of flavour, balance and length, making it one of Alto Adige's finest whites. The Lagrein has a profound nose of fruitiness with notes of steak tartare and spices, developing into a full-bodied mouth, buttressed by an elegant tannic weave and taut acidity.

○ A. A. Pinot Bianco Sirmian '14	▼▼▼ 5
○ A. A. Pinot Grigio Punggl '14	▼▼ 4
○ A. A. Sauvignon Mantele '14	▼▼ 5
○ A. A. Chardonnay Baron Salvadori Ris. '13	▼▼ 6
○ A. A. Chardonnay Magré '14	▼▼ 4
○ A. A. Gewürztraminer Lyra '14	▼▼ 4
● A. A. Lagrein Gries Ris. '12	▼▼ 5
● A. A. Merlot-Cabernet Anticus Baron Salvadori Ris. '12	▼▼ 6
○ A. A. Moscato Giallo Passito Baronesse Baron Salvadori '12	▼▼ 6
○ A. A. Sauvignon Gennen '14	▼▼ 3
● A. A. Schiava Galea '14	▼▼ 3
○ A. A. Pinot Bianco Penon '14	▼ 3
○ A. A. Pinot Bianco Sirmian '13	♀♀♀ 4*

○ Trias '14	▼▼▼ 4*
● A. A. Lagrein Berger Gei '12	▼▼ 4
● A. A. Pinot Nero Vom Kalk '12	▼▼ 6
○ A. A. Terlano Sauvignon '14	▼▼ 4
○ A. A. Riesling Berg '14	▼ 4
○ A. A. Terlano Pinot Bianco Berg '14	▼ 4
○ A. A. Riesling Berg '11	♀♀♀ 4*
○ A. A. Terlano Pinot Bianco '12	♀♀♀ 3*
○ A. A. Terlano Sauvignon '10	♀♀♀ 3
● A. A. Lagrein Berger Gei '11	♀♀ 4
● A. A. Pinot Nero '12	♀♀ 5
○ A. A. Riesling Berg '13	♀♀ 4
○ A. A. Riesling Berg '12	♀♀ 4
○ A. A. Terlano '14	♀♀ 4
○ A. A. Terlano Pinot Bianco Berg '13	♀♀ 4
○ A. A. Terlano Sauvignon '12	♀♀ 4

Niklaserhof - Josef Sölva

LOC. SAN NICOLÒ
VIA DELLE FONTANE, 31A
39052 CALDARO/KALTERN [BZ]
TEL. 0471963434
www.niklaserhof.it

CELLAR SALES
PRE-BOOKED VISITS
ANNUAL PRODUCTION 50,000 bottles
HECTARES UNDER VINE 6.00

The Sölva family winery lies in Caldaro, a small village which owes its fame to the nearby lake, and especially to the fragrant red produced on its banks. Josef and his son Dieter work the six hectares under vine in a highly sustainable fashion, aiming to minimize their impact on the soil and air, though without leaving their vineyards at the mercy of events. Alongside the farmstay facilities, this family-run wine cellar is a fascinating blend of tradition and technology. The Pinot Bianco, from the complicated 2014 vintage, is one of the best we tasted, intensely fruit-forward with offbeat vegetal nuances making the aromatics fresh and almost pungent, while the richness of flavour provides length and personality. The Klaser, a Riserva di Pinot Bianco, displays a more mature and layered profile, the wine merging perfectly with the oak. The Lago di Caldaro Classico is fresh, racy and highly drinkable.

Pacherhof - Andreas Huber

FRAZ. NOVACELLA
V.LO PACHER, 1
39040 VARNA/VAHRN [BZ]
TEL. 0472835717
www.pacherhof.com

CELLAR SALES
PRE-BOOKED VISITS
ACCOMMODATION AND RESTAURANT SERVICE
ANNUAL PRODUCTION 30,000 bottles
HECTARES UNDER VINE 8.00

Andreas Huber runs the family business, without doubt one of the first to bring Valle Isarco to the attention of the wider world. Its eight hectares under vine enjoy some of the finest aspects anywhere in the valley. Just above Bressanone, in Novacella, the vines not only benefit from the outstanding hours of sunlight and diurnal temperature range of these areas but also the poor yet mineral-rich soils. Tended carefully and wherever possible with a biodynamic approach, the terrain gives the grapes enhanced fragrance and character as they ripen. This year's range from Huber was only missing a star, as all the wines lived up to their reputation. The Sylvaner Alte Reben shows intense aromas reminiscent of flowers and citrus fruit, expanding in the mouth with strong acidity and a subtle softness which refines its progression. The Riesling is even more knife-edged, showing particularly pungent aromas with shades of green apple and once again citrus fruit.

○ A. A. Pinot Bianco '14	♼♼ 2*
○ A. A. Bianco Mondevinum Ris. '12	♼♼ 4
○ A. A. Kerner '14	♼♼ 2*
○ A. A. Kerner Mondevinum Ris. '12	♼♼ 4
● A. A. Lago di Caldaro Cl. '14	♼♼ 2*
● A. A. Lago di Caldaro Scelto Cl. '14	♼♼ 2*
● A. A. Lagrein '13	♼♼ 2*
● A. A. Lagrein Mondevinum Ris. '12	♼♼ 4
● A. A. Lagrein-Cabernet Klaser Ris. '12	♼♼ 4
○ A. A. Pinot Bianco Klaser Ris. '12	♼♼ 3
○ A. A. Sauvignon '14	♼ 3
● A. A. Lagrein-Cabernet Klaser Ris. '11	♼♼ 4
○ A. A. Pinot Bianco Klaser Ris. '11	♼♼ 3*

○ A. A. Valle Isarco Riesling '14	♼♼ 4
○ A. A. Valle Isarco Sylvaner Alte Reben '14	♼♼ 5
○ A. A. Valle Isarco Kerner '14	♼♼ 3
○ A. A. Valle Isarco Müller Thurgau '14	♼♼ 3
○ A. A. Valle Isarco Pinot Grigio '14	♼♼ 3
○ A. A. Valle Isarco Sylvaner '14	♼♼ 3
○ A. A. Valle Isarco Veltliner '14	♼♼ 4
○ Bianco '14	♼♼ 4
○ A. A. Valle Isarco Gewürztraminer '14	♼ 4
○ A. A. Valle Isarco Riesling '04	♼♼♼ 3
○ A. A. Valle Isarco Sylvaner '13	♼♼♼ 3*
○ A. A. Valle Isarco Sylvaner Alte Reben '05	♼♼♼ 4
○ A. A. Valle Isarco Pinot Grigio '13	♼♼ 4
○ A. A. Valle Isarco Riesling '13	♼♼ 4

Pfannenstielhof
Johannes Pfeifer

VIA PFANNESTIEL, 9
39100 BOLZANO/BOZEN
TEL. 0471970884
www.pfannenstielhof.it

CELLAR SALES
PRE-BOOKED VISITS
ANNUAL PRODUCTION 43,000 bottles
HECTARES UNDER VINE 4.00

Johannes Pfeifer and his wife Margareth's
winery nestles among vineyards on the
eastern outskirts of Bolzano, where the
factories of the industrial estate suddenly
give way to agricultural concerns, lending
the landscape an altogether more natural
appearance. Here they tend a handful of
hectares under vine with great care and in
environmentally-sustainable fashion, with
the traditional schiava in the vineyards
above the winery, and lagrein elsewhere.
They also have a smallholding in the
Caldaro area where they focus on pinot
nero. The Santa Maddalena from the 2014
harvest is one of the DOC zone's finest,
with a refined bouquet reminiscent of wild
berries and medicinal herbs, paving the
way for a lively, balanced, and lingering
palate. The warm 2012 vintage helped
make a Lagrein Riserva featuring a sweet,
chewy fruitiness interwoven with
concentrated notes of mint and thyme. The
palate is generous and firm, and yet also
supple and taut.

Tenuta Ritterhof

S.DA DEL VINO, 1
39052 CALDARO/KALTERN [BZ]
TEL. 0471963298
www.ritterhof.it

CELLAR SALES
PRE-BOOKED VISITS
RESTAURANT SERVICE
ANNUAL PRODUCTION 300,000 bottles
HECTARES UNDER VINE 7.50

Ludwig Kaneppele has been at the helm of
the Roner family winery for years, with
results that have made Tenuta Ritterhof a
beacon on the Alto Adige wine scene,
especially for Gewürztraminer. Given that
their seven hectares under vine would not
produce enough wine, Ludwig and
oenologist Berhard Hannes have turned to
around 40 local growers for help, and they
supply the winery with their own grapes.
The Roner winery champion is
unquestionably the unrivalled
Gewürztraminer Aureus, which in a difficult
harvest year such as 2014 was able to
throw all of its considerable weight into the
ring. The bouquet shows intense notes of
candied citrus, rose petals and spices,
amplified in a rich, mouthfilling palate
which manages to be both juicy and
polished. Also excellent is the Pinot Grigio
Opes, dominated by yellow-fleshed fruit
with flowery and smoky nuances. The full
palate has a lip-smacking, balanced
flavour.

● A. A. Santa Maddalena Cl. '14	♟♟♟ 3*
● A. A. Lagrein Ris. '12	♟♟ 5
● A. A. Lagrein vom Boden '14	♟♟ 5
● A. A. Pinot Nero '12	♟♟ 4
● A. A. Santa Maddalena Cl. '09	♟♟♟ 2*
● A. A. Lagrein Ris. '11	♟♟ 5
● A. A. Lagrein Ris. '09	♟♟ 5
● A. A. Lagrein vom Boden '13	♟♟ 3
● A. A. Lagrein vom Boden '11	♟♟ 3
● A. A. Lagrein vom Boden '10	♟♟ 3*
● A. A. Pinot Nero '10	♟♟ 4
● A. A. Santa Maddalena Cl. '13	♟♟ 3*
● A. A. Santa Maddalena Cl. '11	♟♟ 3
● A. A. Santa Maddalena Cl. '10	♟♟ 3*

○ A. A. Gewürztraminer Auratus Crescendo '14	♟♟♟ 5
○ A. A. Pinot Grigio Opes Crescendo '13	♟♟ 4
○ A. A. Gewürztraminer '14	♟♟ 3
○ A. A. Gewürztraminer Passito Sonus '12	♟♟ 5
● A. A. Lago di Caldaro Cl. Sup. Novis '14	♟♟ 3
● A. A. Lagrein Latus Crescendo '12	♟♟ 5
● A. A. Lagrein Manus '11	♟♟ 4
● A. A. Pinot Nero Dignus Crescendo '11	♟♟ 5
● A. A. Santa Maddalena '14	♟♟ 3
○ A. A. Sauvignon '14	♟♟ 2*
○ A. A. Pinot Bianco Verus '14	♟ 3
● A. A. Pinot Nero Jansen '13	♟ 2
○ A. A. Gewürztraminer Auratus Crescendo '13	♟♟♟ 4*
○ A. A. Gewürztraminer Auratus Crescendo '12	♟♟♟ 4*

Röckhof - Konrad Augschöll

VIA SAN VALENTINO, 22
39040 VILLANDRO/VILLANDERS [BZ]
TEL. 0472847130
roeck@rolmail.net

CELLAR SALES
PRE-BOOKED VISITS
RESTAURANT SERVICE
ANNUAL PRODUCTION 20,000 bottles
HECTARES UNDER VINE 3.50

Konrad Augschöll is an enthusiastic
producer with a passion for his territory,
Valle Isarco. Here, just north of Villandro, he
tends a couple of hectares mostly devoted
to local white grape varieties, as well as a
few rows of now unfashionable varietals,
such as zweigelt, Saint Laurent, or the
hard-to-find furner hottler. The San
Valentino farmstead is a fascinating blend
of the old and the new, with the
400-year-old main structure being closely
connected to the ultra-modern cellar by
underground passageways, like a mother
and her child. An excellent performance
from the Riesling Viel Anders, a white with
a rather closed profile which needs time to
express itself. In the mouth, apples, citrus
fruit and flowery notes show rounded,
complemented by a progression of great
firmness and grip. The same goes for the
Caruess, a blend of gewürztraminer,
sylvaner and pinot grigio, with a richer,
more caressing palate.

Hans Rottensteiner

FRAZ. GRIES
VIA SARENTINO, 1A
39100 BOLZANO/BOZEN
TEL. 0471282015
www.rottensteiner-weine.com

CELLAR SALES
PRE-BOOKED VISITS
ANNUAL PRODUCTION 450,000 bottles
HECTARES UNDER VINE 10.00

The winery founded by Hans Rottensteiner
has now been handed down to his son Toni
and grandson Hannes. The estate-owned
vineyards only cover a dozen or so
hectares, supplemented by grapes from
around 60 local grower-producers who
bring their production to the winery. Most of
the cellar's sizeable production is made up
of typical Bolzano basin wines, such as
Lagrein and Santa Maddalena, although
they also make classical Alto Adige versions
too. There were two Rottensteiner Riservas
in the finals, Lagrein Grieser and Cabernet,
both from the Select range. The Lagrein
features a close-knit, brooding robe,
unleashing aromatics reminiscent of black
berry fruit, autumn leaves and spices. In
the mouth it shows great forcefulness, but
the close-woven tannins give a crisp
mouthfeel. The Cabernet is more mature
and pervasive, with red berries ushering in
notes of oak and grilled vegetables. In the
mouth it reveals excellent consistency and
a well-balanced progression.

Wine	Rating
○ A. A. Valle Isarco Riesling Viel Anders '14	🍷🍷 3*
○ A. A. Valle Isarco Müller Thurgau '14	🍷🍷 3
○ A. A. Valle Isarco Veltliner Gail Fuass '14	🍷🍷 3
○ Caruess Weiß '14	🍷🍷 3
○ A. A. Valle Isarco Riesling Viel Anders '08	🍷🍷🍷 3*
○ A. A. Valle Isarco Veltliner '11	🍷🍷🍷 3*
○ A. A. Valle Isarco Müller Thurgau '13	🍷🍷 3
○ A. A. Valle Isarco Müller Thurgau '11	🍷🍷 3
○ A. A. Valle Isarco Müller Thurgau '10	🍷🍷 3*
○ A. A. Valle Isarco Riesling Viel Anders '13	🍷🍷 3
○ A. A. Valle Isarco Riesling Viel Anders '10	🍷🍷 3*
○ A. A. Valle Isarco Veltliner Gail Fuass '13	🍷🍷 3
○ A. A. Valle Isarco Veltliner Gail Fuass '12	🍷🍷 3*
○ Caruess '12	🍷🍷 3*
○ Caruess '11	🍷🍷 3*
○ Caruess Weiß '13	🍷🍷 3

Wine	Rating
● A. A. Cabernet Select Ris. '12	🍷🍷 5
● A. A. Lagrein Grieser Select Ris. '12	🍷🍷 5
○ A. A. Gewürztraminer Passito Cresta '13	🍷🍷 6
○ A. A. Pinot Grigio '14	🍷🍷 2*
● A. A. Santa Maddalena Cl. Premstallerhof '14	🍷🍷 2*
○ A. A. Gewürztraminer Cancenai '14	🍷 4
● A. A. Lagrein Rosato '14	🍷 2
○ A. A. Müller Thurgau '14	🍷 2
○ A. A. Pinot Bianco Carnol '14	🍷 3
● A. A. Pinot Nero Select '12	🍷 5
○ A. A. Sauvignon '14	🍷 3
● Prem '13	🍷 3
● A. A. Lagrein Ris. '02	🍷🍷🍷 2*
● A. A. Cabernet Select Ris. '11	🍷🍷 4
● A. A. Lagrein Grieser Select Ris. '11	🍷🍷 4
● A. A. Lagrein Grieser Select Ris. '10	🍷🍷 4

ALTO ADIGE

★★Cantina Produttori San Michele Appiano

VIA CIRCONVALLAZIONE, 17/19
39057 APPIANO/EPPAN [BZ]
TEL. 0471664466
www.stmichael.it

CELLAR SALES
PRE-BOOKED VISITS
ANNUAL PRODUCTION 2,000,000 bottles
HECTARES UNDER VINE 370.00

It is hard to distinguish the San Michele Appiano winery from its long-serving kellermeister, Hans Terzer, because it is mostly his work that has made it one of the region's best-known producers. Even though he retired last year, he is still the driving force behind the winery, with a keen eye both for market trends and for the potential of various different vineyards, varietals and growers. With its over 400 hectares, this is the largest estate in the province, and Hans knows it like the back of his hand, with an instinctive understanding of nature's generosity. From the Sanct Valentin flagship line comes a scintillating Pinot Bianco, with aromas of apples and pears, flowers and spices, merging perfectly with the oak. The rich, fresh palate ushers in a lively progression of great finesse which easily wins our Tre Bicchieri. The whole line is full of impressive wines, from the timeless Sauvignon to the Chardonnay, not forgetting the charmingly sophisticated Gewürztraminer Passito Comtess.

○ A. A. Pinot Bianco St. Valentin '13	▼▼▼ 5
○ A. A. Bianco Passito Comtess St. Valentin '11	▼▼ 5
○ A. A. Chardonnay St. Valentin '13	▼▼ 5
○ A. A. Sauvignon St. Valentin '14	▼▼ 5
○ A. A. Gewürztraminer St. Valentin '14	▼▼ 5
● A. A. Lagrein St. Valentin '11	▼▼ 7
● A. A. Merlot Cabernet De Piano '12	▼▼ 5
○ A. A. Pinot Bianco Schulthauser '14	▼▼ 3
○ A. A. Pinot Grigio Anger '14	▼▼ 3
○ A. A. Pinot Grigio St. Valentin '13	▼▼ 5
● A. A. Pinot Nero St. Valentin '12	▼▼ 5
○ A. A. Riesling Montiggl '14	▼▼ 3
○ A. A. Pinot Bianco St. Valentin '11	▼▼▼ 5
○ A. A. Pinot Grigio Anger '11	▼▼▼ 3*
○ A. A. Sauvignon St. Valentin '13	▼▼▼ 5
○ A. A. Sauvignon St. Valentin '10	▼▼▼ 5

Cantina Produttori San Paolo

LOC. SAN PAOLO
VIA CASTEL GUARDIA, 21
39050 APPIANO/EPPAN [BZ]
TEL. 0471662183
www.cantinasanpaolo.com

CELLAR SALES
PRE-BOOKED VISITS
ANNUAL PRODUCTION 1,200,000 bottles
HECTARES UNDER VINE 175.00
SUSTAINABLE WINERY

Cantina Produttori San Paolo is in the southern part of Bolzano province, at the heart of wine country, with over 200 members cultivating some 170 hectares of vineyards. Of course, with so much land under vine, the soil and climate conditions can vary hugely from one vineyard holding to another. Kellermeister Wolfgang Tratter has the task of co-ordinating the growers in such a way as not only to ensure excellent quality but also to express the specific conditions to the full. The Pinot Bianco Passion is a Riserva that softens out in large casks and expresses aromas of great finesse, bewitching the drinker with its nose of mature fruit and flowers. On the palate, its richness of flavour and grip won us over, as did its long, balanced finish. The Sauvignon Gfill charms with the breadth of its aromatic profile and its well-defined progression, while the Kössler line has an appealing Gewürztraminer, winning us over not so much through its opulence as the elegance of its palate.

○ A. A. Gewürztraminer Kössler '13	▼▼ 3*
○ A. A. Pinot Bianco Passion Ris. '13	▼▼ 4
○ A. A. Sauvignon Gfill '14	▼▼ 3*
○ A. A. Gewürztraminer Passion '14	▼▼ 5
○ A. A. Gewürztraminer Sel. Kössler '14	▼▼ 3
● A. A. Lagrein Passion Ris. '13	▼▼ 5
● A. A. Merlot Passion Ris. '13	▼▼ 3
○ A. A. Pinot Bianco Kössler '14	▼▼ 2*
● A. A. Pinot Nero Passion Ris. '13	▼▼ 5
○ A. A. Praeclarus Cuvée St. Paulus M. Cl.	▼▼ 5
● A. A. Schiava Missianer '14	▼▼ 2*
● A. A. Schiava Passion '14	▼▼ 3
○ A. A. Pinot Bianco Plotzner '14	▼ 2
○ A. A. Pinot Bianco Passion '09	▼▼▼ 4
○ A. A. Pinot Bianco Passion Ris. '11	▼▼▼ 4*

Peter Sölva & Söhne

VIA DELL'ORO, 33
39052 CALDARO/KALTERN [BZ]
TEL. 0471964650
www.soelva.com

CELLAR SALES
PRE-BOOKED VISITS
ANNUAL PRODUCTION 75,000 bottles
HECTARES UNDER VINE 12.00

The Sölva family history goes back several
centuries, and their close connection with
winegrowing has been a constant
throughout. So much so that today yet
another Sölva, this time Stephen, is at the
helm of the winery. The vineyards stretch
across the Oltradige and Lower Adige
Valley, growing the grapes for a production
based on three different ranges: Vigneti, De
Silva and Amistar. The first, as its name
suggests, covers the province's typical
monovarietals; the second expresses the
property's finest vines; while the third
represents the family's winegrowing
tradition, based entirely on late-harvest
wines. Once again the Pinot Bianco DeSilva
impresses the most. Made from two
different hillside varietals, one from Caldaro
and the other from Pochi, its aromas are
reminiscent of ripe yellow-fleshed fruit and
dried flowers, while palate expands with
good alcohol and length. We were
impressed by the Lago di Caldaro
Peterleiten red, with its approachable
fragrance of wild berries and flowers.

○ A. A. Pinot Bianco DeSilva '14	♈♈ 4
● A. A. Lago di Caldaro Scelto Cl. Sup. Peterleiten '14	♈♈ 2*
○ A. A. Sauvignon DeSilva '14	♈ 5
○ Amistar Bianco '13	♈ 6
● Amistar Edizione Rosso '11	♈ 8
○ A. A. Terlano Pinot Bianco DeSilva '10	♈♈♈ 3
○ A. A. Terlano Pinot Bianco DeSilva '09	♈♈♈ 3
● A. A. Lago di Caldaro Cl. Sup. '12	♔♔ 2*
● A. A. Lagrein Ris. '11	♔♔ 3
○ A. A. Pinot Bianco DeSilva '13	♔♔ 4
○ A. A. Pinot Bianco DeSilva '12	♔♔ 4
● A. A. Pinot Nero '11	♔♔ 4
● A.A. Lago di Caldaro Cl. Sup. Peterleiten DeSilva '13	♔♔ 2*
○ Amistar Bianco '12	♔♔ 4
● Amistar Rosso '12	♔♔ 5

Stachlburg
Baron von Kripp

VIA MITTERHOFER, 2
39020 PARCINES/PARTSCHINS [BZ]
TEL. 0473968014
www.stachlburg.com

CELLAR SALES
PRE-BOOKED VISITS
ANNUAL PRODUCTION 30,000 bottles
HECTARES UNDER VINE 7.00
VITICULTURE METHOD Certified Organic

Barone Sigmund von Kripp has been
running the family estate since 1990, and
he introduced winegrowing to the property,
converting just a few years later to organic.
There are just a few hectares under vine,
mainly around Parcines Castle which
houses the wine cellar, in the Naturno
area, and finally in Andriano, where the
lower altitude allows him to grow varieties
which need more warmth, such as merlot.
And the Merlot is the Stachlburg winery's
finest wine this year, a red aged in
Hungarian oak barriques. The clean fruity
nose notes are echoed by nuances of
medicinal herbs and spices. On the palate,
there is more focus on elegance than on
firm structure, for a long close and
well-balanced tannins. The Terlano
Sauvignon shows well-developed yet
delicate aromas progressing into a
full-flavoured palate of great harmony. We
also enjoyed the crisp, stylish Chardonnay,
whose character reflects the cool 2014
vintage.

● A. A. Merlot '12	♈♈ 4
● A. A. Lagrein '13	♈♈ 3
○ A. A. Terlano Sauvignon '14	♈♈ 4
○ A. A. Valle Venosta Chardonnay '14	♈♈ 3
○ A. A. Valle Venosta Gewürztraminer '12	♈♈ 3
○ A. A. Valle Venosta Pinot Bianco '14	♈♈ 3
⊙ A. A. Lagrein Rosato '14	♈ 3
○ A. A. Pinot Grigio '14	♈ 2
● A. A. Valle Venosta Pinot Nero '12	♈ 3
○ A. A. Valle Venosta Pinot Bianco '13	♈♈♈ 3*
○ A. A. Valle Venosta Pinot Bianco '10	♈♈♈ 3*
● A. A. Merlot Wolfsthurn '11	♔♔ 4
○ A. A. Pinot Grigio '12	♔♔ 2*
○ A. A. Terlano Sauvignon Wolfsthurn '13	♔♔ 4
○ A. A. Valle Venosta Chardonnay '13	♔♔ 3
● A. A. Valle Venosta Pinot Nero '11	♔♔ 3

Strasserhof
Hannes Baumgartner

FRAZ. NOVACELLA
LOC. UNTERRAIN, 8
39040 VARNA/VAHRN [BZ]
TEL. 0472830804
www.strasserhof.info

CELLAR SALES
PRE-BOOKED VISITS
ACCOMMODATION
ANNUAL PRODUCTION 45,000 bottles
HECTARES UNDER VINE 5.50

It may be only just over a decade since
Hannes Baumgartner took over the family
farm in Novacella, but the winery has
already become a benchmark for all
aficionados of Valle Isarco's lean wines.
There are five hectares of hilltop vineyards
dedicated to the valley's classical white
grape types, together with a dash of the
traditional though little-known zweigelt. A
cool year like 2014 brought out the
knife-edge profiles of Hannes' wines.
Indeed, we were struck by the Riesling's
intense citrussy aromas, showing flowers
and spices which emerge after slight
aeration and come together splendidly in
the taut, spirited mouth. The Sylvaner's
aromatic profile is better developed,
dominated by notes of exotic fruit paving
the way for flinty hints of minerality which
will improve drinkability with time. The
palate requires no help from the sugars,
resulting in a spirited, lean-edged wine with
an attractive length.

Stroblhof

LOC. SAN MICHELE
VIA PIGANÒ, 25
39057 APPIANO/EPPAN [BZ]
TEL. 0471662250
www.stroblhof.it

CELLAR SALES
PRE-BOOKED VISITS
ANNUAL PRODUCTION 40,000 bottles
HECTARES UNDER VINE 5.20

Rosmarie Hanny and her husband Andreas
Nicolussi-Leck run Stroblhof, a lovely estate
in Appiano where they divide their time
between their hotel guests and their wine
production. They have just a handful of
hectares, farmed in an environmentally
sustainable fashion, with a nod and a wink
to the organic world. The finest exposures,
together with a qualitative overhaul of the
vinestock carried out many years ago have
ushered in the production of excellent
wines. Top of our list of favourites this
year is the Pinot Bianco Strahler, whose
attractively clean aromatics are dominated
by white-fleshed fruit with floral and
almond nuances. On the palate its structure
is not assertive, giving the wine a lightness
of touch and suppleness, for a crisp, rather
long finish. The Pinot Nero Riserva, one of
the winery's mainstays, pulls out the stops
again with the 2012 vintage, which is well
balanced and highly drinkable.

○ A. A. Valle Isarco Riesling '14	🍷🍷 4	
○ A. A. Valle Isarco Sylvaner '14	🍷🍷 3*	
○ A. A. Valle Isarco Kerner '14	🍷🍷 3	
○ A. A. Valle Isarco Müller Thurgau '14	🍷🍷 3	
○ A. A. Valle Isarco Sylvaner Anjo '14	🍷🍷 4	
○ A. A. Valle Isarco Veltliner '14	🍷🍷 3	
○ A. A. Valle Isarco Gewürztraminer '14	🍷 4	
○ A. A. Valle Isarco Riesling '12	🍷🍷🍷 3*	
○ A. A. Valle Isarco Riesling '11	🍷🍷🍷 3*	
○ A. A. Valle Isarco Veltliner '10	🍷🍷🍷 3*	
○ A. A. Valle Isarco Veltliner '09	🍷🍷🍷 3*	
○ A. A. Valle Isarco Kerner '13	🍷🍷 3	
○ A. A. Valle Isarco Müller Thurgau '13	🍷🍷 3	
○ A. A. Valle Isarco Riesling '13	🍷🍷 3*	
○ A. A. Valle Isarco Sylvaner '13	🍷🍷 3*	
○ A. A. Valle Isarco Veltliner '13	🍷🍷 3	

○ A. A. Pinot Bianco Strahler '14	🍷🍷 3	
● Pinot Nero Ris. '12	🍷🍷 6	
○ A. A. Chardonnay Schwarzhaus '14	🍷 3	
○ A. A. Sauvignon Nico '14	🍷 4	
○ A. A. Pinot Bianco Strahler '09	🍷🍷🍷 3*	
● A. A. Pinot Nero Ris. '05	🍷🍷🍷 5	
○ A. A. Chardonnay Schwarzhaus '13	🍷🍷 3	
○ A. A. Chardonnay Schwarzhaus '11	🍷🍷 3*	
○ A. A. Pinot Bianco Strahler '13	🍷🍷 3	
○ A. A. Pinot Bianco Strahler '11	🍷🍷 3*	
● A. A. Pinot Nero Pigeno '12	🍷🍷 5	
● A. A. Pinot Nero Pigeno '09	🍷🍷 4	
● A. A. Pinot Nero Ris. '11	🍷🍷 6	
⊙ A. A. Pinot Nero Rosato Pinot Rosé '13	🍷🍷 3	

Taschlerhof - Peter Wachtler

LOC. MARA, 107
39042 BRESSANONE/BRIXEN [BZ]
TEL. 0472851091
www.taschlerhof.com

CELLAR SALES
PRE-BOOKED VISITS
ANNUAL PRODUCTION 30,000 bottles
HECTARES UNDER VINE 4.20

Peter Wachtler is the driving force behind Taschlerhof, one of the Isarco Valley's finest wineries. A few hectares on the outskirts of Bressanone, on some of the designation's steepest slopes, which over the centuries were terraced to make them easier to tend. Fantastic exposures, a huge diurnal temperature range and a sunny but not hot climate all help create wines which bring out all the expressive range of aromas that native cultivars provide, as well as the minerality which the grapes take from the soils. One of the characteristic features of Peter's wines is their slow ageing, as can be seen in the Riesling 2014, whose aromas are still rather predictable, centred around white-fleshed fruit, citrus and flowers. The palate, though, reveals its personality, displaying a generosity kept perfectly in check by acidity and sea salt, for a long finish that wins it our Tre Bicchieri but the fresh, fruity Sylvaner missed out by a whisker.

○ A. A. Valle Isarco Riesling '14	♟♟♟	4*
○ A. A. Valle Isarco Sylvaner '14	♟♟	3*
○ A. A. Valle Isarco Veltliner '14	♟♟	3*
○ A. A. Valle Isarco Kerner '14	♟♟	4
○ A. A. Valle Isarco Gewürztraminer '14	♟	4
○ A. A. Valle Isarco Kerner '13	♟♟	3
○ A. A. Valle Isarco Kerner '12	♟♟	3*
○ A. A. Valle Isarco Kerner '10	♟♟	3
○ A. A. Valle Isarco Riesling '13	♟♟	4
○ A. A. Valle Isarco Sylvaner '13	♟♟	3*
○ A. A. Valle Isarco Sylvaner '12	♟♟	3
○ A. A. Valle Isarco Sylvaner Lahner '13	♟♟	4
○ A. A. Valle Isarco Sylvaner Lahner '12	♟♟	4
○ A. A. Valle Isarco Sylvaner Lahner '09	♟♟	4
○ A. A. Valle Isarco Sylvaner Lahner '08	♟♟	5

Alois Tenutae Lageder

LOC. TÒR LÖWENGANG
V.LO DEI CONTI, 9
39040 MAGRÈ/MARGREID [BZ]
TEL. 0471809500
www.aloislageder.eu

CELLAR SALES
PRE-BOOKED VISITS
RESTAURANT SERVICE
ANNUAL PRODUCTION 1,500,000 bottles
HECTARES UNDER VINE 160.00
VITICULTURE METHOD Certified Biodynamic
SUSTAINABLE WINERY

Alois Lageder, the dynamic producer of Magrè, is increasingly convinced that the future lies in a sustainable, non-invasive approach to the environment. While his 50 hectares have been tended biodynamically for years, many of the growers who supply his winery with grapes are being won over by his vision, with a quarter of their production now meeting such requirements. His vast production is very much true to the various grape types he grows. Once again Lageder's winners are the Cabernets, with the Cor Römigberg putting in a performance to write home about. The fruit on the nose gradually emerges from behind notes of medicinal herbs and spices, opening up into a complex, balanced palate with an excellent tannic weave. The Löwengang, by contrast, features a more approachable aromatic profile and a highly-refined palate. The Lagrein Lindenburg's intense nose ushers in a juicy, rounded palate.

● A. A. Cabernet Sauvignon Cor Römigberg '11	♟♟♟	7
● A. A. Cabernet Löwengang '11	♟♟	7
○ A. A. Chardonnay Löwengang '12	♟♟	6
● A. A. Lago di Caldaro Römigberg '14	♟♟	3
● A. A. Lagrein Lindenburg '11	♟♟	5
● A. A. Pinot Nero Krafuss '11	♟♟	6
○ A. A. Riesling Rain '14	♟♟	4
● Casòn '11	♟♟	6
○ A. A. Chardonnay Guan '14	♟	4
○ A. A. Pinot Bianco Haberle '14	♟	4
○ A. A. Pinot Grigio Porer '14	♟	4
○ A. A. Sauvignon Lehen '13	♟	5
● A. A. Cabernet Löwengang '10	♟♟♟	7
● A. A. Cabernet Sauvignon Cor Römigberg '08	♟♟♟	7

★★Cantina Terlano

VIA SILBERLEITEN, 7
39018 TERLANO/TERLAN [BZ]
TEL. 0471257135
www.cantina-terlano.com

CELLAR SALES
PRE-BOOKED VISITS
ANNUAL PRODUCTION 1,000,000 bottles
HECTARES UNDER VINE 165.00

It is hard to talk about Cantina di Terlano without slipping into rhetoric. Today, quite simply, this winery embodies the image of Alto Adige around the world. With 143 partners working 165 hectares of vineyard, annual production exceeds a million bottles. Such production, though, also has a few labels designed to be sold only after lengthy ageing, providing a truly complete overview of what the region is capable of expressing. The class of the Terlano Nova Domus emerged in great abundance once again this year. Kellermeister Rudi Kofler crafted its quality around a crisp, mature white grape, giving it a firm, stylish mouth and a spectacularly long finish. The Chardonnay Rarità 2003 is surprisingly fresh, while the Gewürztraminer Passito Juvelo is intense, beguiling and sophisticated. The Vorberg lives up to its reputation as a firm, complex thoroughbred, while true aficionados may still be able find one of the few bottles of Terlaner I Grande Cuvée 2012. Although we have not reviewed it, we guarantee the effort will be well repaid by the tasting.

○ A. A. Terlano Nova Domus Ris. '12	♟♟♟6
○ A. A. Chardonnay Rarità '03	♟♟4
○ A. A. Gewürztraminer Passito Juvelo Andriano '13	♟♟5
● A. A. Lagrein Riserva Andriano Tor di Lupo '12	♟♟4
○ A. A. Pinot Bianco Vorberg Ris. '12	♟♟3*
○ A. A. Gewürztraminer Lunare '13	♟♟6
● A. A. Lagrein Porphyr Ris. '12	♟♟6
● A. A. Merlot Gant Adriano Ris. '12	♟♟4
○ A. A. Pinot Bianco '14	♟♟2*
● A. A. Pinot Nero Montigl Ris. '12	♟♟5
○ A. A. Sauvignon Andrius Andriano '13	♟♟5
○ A. A. Sauvignon Quarz '13	♟♟3
○ A. A. Sauvignon Winkl '14	♟♟3
○ A. A. Terlano Chardonnay Kreuth '13	♟♟4
○ A. A. Terlano Cl. '14	♟♟2*

Tiefenbrunner

FRAZ. NICLARA
VIA CASTELLO, 4
39040 CORTACCIA/KURTATSCH [BZ]
TEL. 0471880122
www.tiefenbrunner.com

CELLAR SALES
PRE-BOOKED VISITS
RESTAURANT SERVICE
ANNUAL PRODUCTION 800,000 bottles
HECTARES UNDER VINE 25.00

The relationship between the Tiefenbrunner family and the Turmhof estate dates back to the 17th century and continues to this day. Christof has been running the 25-hectare estate with his wife Sabine for around 30 years, interacting with an army of grower-producers who supply the winery with grapes, for annual production figures of some 800,000 bottles. Each vineyard is tended according to its specific soil and climate conditions, in a sustainable way, sometimes even organically. The Hofstatt vineyard, at an elevation of 1,000 metres on Mount Favogna, brings forth super-ripe grapes dedicated to the Feldmarschall, for a Müller Thurgau which once again fends off all comers. With its intense of apples and pears, spices and flowers, it shows a latent minerality pushing into the foreground. The palate is lively, taut and has a spectacularly long finish. Also worthy was the Pinot Nero Linticlarus, a Riserva with a generous nose and refined palate.

○ A. A. Müller Thurgau Feldmarschall von Fenner zu Fennberg '13	♟♟♟5
● A. A. Pinot Nero Linticlarus Ris. '12	♟♟5
● A. A. Cabernet - Merlot Linticlarus '12	♟♟6
● A. A. Cabernet Sauvignon Linticlarus Ris. '11	♟♟6
○ A. A. Gewürztraminer Turmhof '14	♟♟4
● A. A. Lagrein Linticlarus Ris. '12	♟♟5
○ A. A. Pinot Grigio Turmhof '14	♟♟3
○ A. A. Sauvignon Turmhof '14	♟♟4
○ A. A. Chardonnay Linticlarus '12	♟5
○ A. A. Chardonnay Turmhof '14	♟3
○ A. A. Pinot Bianco Anna Turmhof '14	♟3
○ A. A. Müller Thurgau Feldmarschall von Fenner zu Fennberg '13	♡♡♡5
○ A. A. Müller Thurgau Feldmarschall von Fenner zu Fennberg '11	♡♡♡4*

★★Cantina Tramin

S.DA DEL VINO, 144
39040 TERMENO/TRAMIN [BZ]
TEL. 0471096633
www.cantinatramin.it

CELLAR SALES
PRE-BOOKED VISITS
ANNUAL PRODUCTION 1,500,000 bottles
HECTARES UNDER VINE 250.00

Interesting developments at the Cantina in
Termeno, where kellermeister Willy Sturz,
with full approval from chairman Leo
Tiefenthaler, decided to leave the white
selections to age in the cellar for another
year, delaying bottling and allowing the wine
to spend longer in the bottle before it goes to
market. We congratulate them on taking
such a courageous leap, which looks like
being a winning move for such top-quality
wines. Once again there are some
high-profile wines with one of the best-ever
versions of Pinot Nero Maglen. The 2012
vintage gave this wine an exceptionally
alluring profile, in which the more classic
varietal aromas of wild berries and peony
are enhanced by sweet spicy nuances. So
too on the palate, where its most pleasingly
captivating aspects of sweet juicy fruit are
harmoniously balanced by an acidic
freshness. We also enjoyed the Roen,
younger sibling of the Terminum which we
will also be tasting next year.

★Tenuta Unterortl
Castel Juval

LOC. JUVAL, 1B
39020 CASTELBELLO CIARDES/KASTELBELL TSCHARS [BZ]
TEL. 0473667580
www.unterortl.it

CELLAR SALES
PRE-BOOKED VISITS
ANNUAL PRODUCTION 33,000 bottles
HECTARES UNDER VINE 4.00

Reinhold Messner is the owner of the
Unterortl estate, more commonly known as
Castel Juval, but Martin and Gisela Aurich do
the actual running of this lovely property at
the mouth of Val Venosta. Just a few
hectares on Juval's dizzying slopes, with a
vine density of up to 8,000 plants per
hectare, and wines which bring out the best
of the soil and climate conditions of this
corner of Alto Adige. The combination of
southeast-facing vineyards and gneiss-rich
soils traps the heat and warms up the vines,
in stark contrast to the cold winds blowing
down from nearby Val Senales every night,
making the grapes ripen healthy, aromatic
and mineral-rich. The Riesling 2014 is a
simple yet polished wine with a fresh nose of
citrus and flowers, paving the way for a stiff,
full-flavoured palate and almost knife-edged
acidity. Deeper and slower to open up, the
Windbichel has a layered bouquet and a
complex, harmonious mouthfeel.

● A. A. Pinot Nero Maglen '12	♟♟ 5
● A. A. Cabernet Merlot Loam '12	♟♟ 5
○ A. A. Gewürztraminer '14	♟♟ 2*
○ A. A. Gewürztraminer Roen V. T. '13	♟♟ 5
○ A. A. Pinot Bianco Moriz '14	♟♟ 2*
○ A. A. Sauvignon '14	♟♟ 3
○ A. A. Sauvignon Pepi '14	♟♟ 4
● A. A. Schiava Freisinger '14	♟♟ 3
○ T Bianco '14	♟♟ 2*
○ A. A. Chardonnay '14	♟ 2
○ A. A. Gewürztraminer Nussbaumer '13	♟♟♟ 5
○ A. A. Gewürztraminer Nussbaumer '12	♟♟♟ 5
○ A. A. Gewürztraminer Nussbaumer '11	♟♟♟ 5
○ A. A. Gewürztraminer Nussbaumer '10	♟♟♟ 5
○ A. A. Gewürztraminer Nussbaumer '09	♟♟♟ 5

○ A. A. Valle Venosta Riesling '14	♟♟♟ 4*
○ A. A. Valle Venosta Riesling Windbichel '13	♟♟ 5
○ A. A. Valle Venosta Müller Thurgau '14	♟♟ 3
○ A. A. Valle Venosta Pinot Bianco '14	♟♟ 3
○ A. A. Val Venosta Pinot Bianco Castel Juval '12	♟♟♟ 3*
○ A. A. Val Venosta Riesling Castel Juval '11	♟♟♟ 4*
○ A. A. Val Venosta Pinot Bianco Castel Juval '13	♟♟♟ 3*
○ A. A. Val Venosta Riesling Windbichel '11	♟♟ 5
○ A. A. Valle Venosta Pinot Bianco Castel Juval '11	♟♟ 3*
○ A. A. Valle Venosta Riesling Castel Juval '13	♟♟ 4
○ A. A. Valle Venosta Riesling Windbichel '12	♟♟ 5
○ A. A. Valle Venosta Riesling Windbichel '10	♟♟ 5

Cantina Produttori Valle Isarco

VIA COSTE, 50
39043 CHIUSA/KLAUSEN [BZ]
TEL. 0472847553
www.cantinavalleisarco.it

CELLAR SALES
PRE-BOOKED VISITS
ANNUAL PRODUCTION 750,000 bottles
HECTARES UNDER VINE 140.00

Travelling up the Isarco Valley, winegrowing thins out, with vineyards becoming smaller, steeper and more terraced. Growers often cultivate tiny plots, and though production may be limited in terms of quantity, the quality is excellent. This is home to Cantina Produttori Valle Isarco, the smallest cooperative winery in the province, made up of 130 enthusiastic and committed growers working in the valley. The most prestigious vineyard is without doubt Sabiona, owned by the Benedictine Abbey which seems to dominate the whole valley. These vineyards produce the grapes for the eponymous Sylvaner, with its aromas reminiscent of apples, black pepper and dried flowers; expansive on the palate, sophisticated and with great length. The Aristos line is perfectly represented by the Veltliner, with aromas of great personality, sulphurous with fruit only in the background, and a generous, full, expressive palate.

Vivaldi - Arunda

VIA JOSEF-SCHWARZ, 18
39010 MELTINA/MÖLTEN [BZ]
TEL. 0471668033
www.arundavivaldi.it

CELLAR SALES
PRE-BOOKED VISITS
ANNUAL PRODUCTION 90,000 bottles
HECTARES UNDER VINE 12.00

Josef "Sepp" and Marianne Reiterer own Vivaldi Arunda, the main sparkler winery in Alto Adige. It is located in Meltina, at a staggering 1,200 metres above sea level because, as Sepp says, that is the perfect elevation for ageing sparkling wines. The grapes come from a close network of selected growers in various production areas, especially Oltradige for pinot bianco, Terlano for chardonnay and Salorno for pinot nero. In the cellar, vinification is performed under optimal conditions, to create wines that not only tell a story of quality but also have a marked sense of place. The Cuvée Marianna is an Extra Brut which bases its firmness on pinot nero, with the addition of 20% barrique-aged Chardonnay. The nose shows a bouquet of hazelnut and biscuit, while the sparkle on the palate gives the wine a generous, nicely taut style. The Extra Brut Riserva uses the same varietals but inverts the percentages, for a racy sparkler with good length.

○ A. A. Valle Isarco Sylvaner Sabiona '13	♟♟ 5
○ A. A. Valle Isarco Veltliner Aristos '14	♟♟ 3*
○ A. A. Valle Isarco Gewürztraminer Aristos '14	♟♟ 4
○ A. A. Valle Isarco Gewürztraminer Passito Nectaris '13	♟♟ 6
○ A. A. Valle Isarco Kerner Passito Nectaris '13	♟♟ 6
○ A. A. Valle Isarco Pinot Grigio Aristos '14	♟♟ 4
○ A. A. Valle Isarco Riesling Aristos '14	♟♟ 4
○ A. A. Valle Isarco Sauvignon Aristos '14	♟♟ 4
○ A. A. Valle Isarco Sylvaner Aristos '14	♟♟ 4
○ A. A. Valle Isarco Kerner Aristos '14	♟ 4
○ A. A. Valle Isarco Kerner Sabiona '13	♟ 5
○ A. A. Valle Isarco Müller Thurgau Aristos '14	♟ 3
○ A. A. Valle Isarco Kerner Aristos '05	♟♟♟ 3*

○ A. A. Spumante Extra Brut Arunda Ris. '09	♟♟ 5
○ A. A. Spumante Extra Brut Cuvée Marianna	♟♟ 5
○ A. A. Spumante Blanc de Blancs Arunda	♟ 5
○ A. A. Spumante Brut Arunda	♟ 5
⊙ A. A. Spumante Brut Rosé Arunda	♟ 5
○ A. A. Spumante Extra Brut Arunda	♟ 5
○ A. A. Spumante Arunda Ris. '08	♀♀ 5
○ A. A. Spumante Arunda Ris. '07	♀♀ 5
⊙ A. A. Spumante Brut Rosé Arunda	♀♀ 5
○ A. A. Spumante Cuvée Marianna Arunda	♀♀ 5
○ A. A. Spumante Extra Brut Cuvée Marianna	♀♀ 5
○ A. A. Spumante Extra Brut Ris. '08	♀♀ 5
○ A. A. Spumante Rosé Talento Arunda	♀♀ 3*
⊙ Spumante Excellor Rosé	♀♀ 5

★★Elena Walch

VIA A. HOFER, 1
39040 TERMENO/TRAMIN [BZ]
TEL. 0471860172
www.elenawalch.com

CELLAR SALES
PRE-BOOKED VISITS
RESTAURANT SERVICE
ANNUAL PRODUCTION 500,000 bottles
HECTARES UNDER VINE 33.00

One of the most esteemed winemakers in the region, having come up with some of the labels that have relaunched Bolzano's image on the international wine scene, Elena Walch is now accompanied on a permanent basis by her daughters Julia and Karoline. Her vineyards cover a total area of over 30 hectares, the most prestigious of which are the Castel Ringberg estate in Caldaro and Kastelaz in Termeno. Production would not be possible without the help of a select group of local grower-producers who supply the winery with grapes. The Castel Ringberg Lagrein is a pedigree red. Not content with focusing on the typical exuberance of the varietal, it explores the crisper nuances, marrying firm structure, suppleness and length. The Cabernet Sauvignon from the same line follows in its footsteps, playing on the ripeness of its fruit and fullness on its palate. We did enjoy the Cashmere, a raisined gewürztraminer aiming more for finesse and balance.

● A. A. Lagrein Castel Ringberg Ris. '11	▼▼▼	5
● A. A. Cabernet Sauvignon Castel Ringberg Ris. '11	▼▼	8
○ A. A. Bianco Beyond the Clouds '13	▼▼	6
○ A. A. Gewürztraminer Kastelaz '14	▼▼	5
○ A. A. Gewürztraminer Passito Cashmere '13	▼▼	8
● A. A. Merlot Kastelaz Ris. '12	▼▼	6
○ A. A. Pinot Bianco '14	▼▼	2*
○ A. A. Resling Castel Ringberg '14	▼▼	4
● Kermesse '11	▼▼	6
○ A. A. Pinot Grigio Castel Ringberg '14	▼	4
● A. A. Pinot Nero Ludwig '12	▼	5
○ A. A. Sauvignon Castel Ringberg '14	▼	4
○ A. A. Gewürztraminer Kastelaz '13	▼▼▼	5
○ A. A. Gewürztraminer Kastelaz '12	▼▼▼	5
○ A. A. Gewürztraminer Kastelaz '11	▼▼▼	5

Tenuta Waldgries

LOC. SANTA GIUSTINA, 2
39100 BOLZANO/BOZEN
TEL. 0471323603
www.waldgries.it

CELLAR SALES
PRE-BOOKED VISITS
ANNUAL PRODUCTION 65,000 bottles
HECTARES UNDER VINE 8.20

Christian Plattner is the driving force behind Tenuta Waldgries, an almost ten-hectare estate in the Santa Maddalena subzone on the outskirts of Bolzano. Christian's outstanding respect for his land and its traditions ensure that Waldgries wines are anything but banal, expressing that special connection between land, varietal and tradition. Alongside the classic Alto Adige cultivars, Christian focuses on producing Moscato Rosa, a small-scale yet invaluable gem on the Bolzano wine scene. Indeed, this was our favourite Plattner, with dog rose, strawberry and spice on the nose, ushering a palate of complex progression, sweetness to the fore, reined in thanks to its tanginess and balanced acidity. The Pinot Bianco Isos, from grapes grown in Schwarzhaus and Appiano, partially aged in tonneaux, is equally mature and fresh, with a long, crisp finish. Also very good is the Santa Maddalena Classico, full of fruity sensations and with a lively profile.

○ A. A. Moscato Rosa '12	▼▼	6
○ A. A. Pinot Bianco Isos '13	▼▼	4
● A. A. Santa Maddalena Cl. '14	▼▼	3*
● A. A. Santa Maddalena Cl. Antheos '14	▼▼	5
○ A. A. Sauvignon Myra '14	▼▼	4
● A. A. Lagrein Mirell '09	▼▼▼	6
● A. A. Lagrein Scuro Mirell '08	▼▼▼	6
● A. A. Lagrein Scuro Mirell '07	▼▼▼	6
● A. A. Santa Maddalena Cl. Antheos '13	▼▼▼	4*
● A. A. Santa Maddalena Cl. Antheos '12	▼▼▼	4*
● A. A. Santa Maddalena Cl. Antheos '11	▼▼▼	4*
● A. A. Lagrein Mirell '12	▼▼	6
● A. A. Lagrein Ris. '11	▼▼	5
● A. A. Moscato Rosa Passito '10	▼▼	5
● A. A. Santa Maddalena Cl. '13	▼▼	3*

Josef Weger

LOC. CORNAIANO
VIA CASA DEL GESÙ, 17
39050 APPIANO/EPPAN [BZ]
TEL. 0471662416
www.wegerhof.it

CELLAR SALES
PRE-BOOKED VISITS
ACCOMMODATION AND RESTAURANT SERVICE
ANNUAL PRODUCTION 80,000 bottles
HECTARES UNDER VINE 8.00

Josef Weger's long-established winery has its roots deep in history. The family name has been closely associated with Alto Adige wines for over two centuries, and today it is a member of the sixth generation, Johannes, who runs the winery. The cellar in Cornaiano is made up of several underground rooms, some of which even reach underneath the main road. The vineyards cover around ten hectares, enough to provide the grapes needed for two lines. The simplest, Tenuta Josef Weger, is destined to become one of the classic spirited Bolzano wines providing excellent value for money, whereas Maso delle Rose stands out among the more ambitious cask-aged wines. On the nose the Pinot Bianco Lithos offers fresh-cut flowers and kiwi fruit, with subtle hints of green apple in the background. The stylish, racy palate ushers in a long, juicy drinkability. The Chardonnay Leite shows sweeter and more mature aromatics, while the palate maintains a subtle, fresh profile.

Peter Zemmer

S.DA DEL VINO, 24
39040 CORTINA SULLA STRADA DEL VINO/KURTINIG [BZ]
TEL. 0471817143
www.peterzemmer.com

CELLAR SALES
PRE-BOOKED VISITS
ANNUAL PRODUCTION 500,000 bottles
HECTARES UNDER VINE 65.00

Now close to celebrating its centenary, the Zemmer family estate lies on the Strada del Vino trail around Cortina, the smallest municipality in Alto Adige, near the border with Trentino. Most of the Zemmer vineyards are located in this morainic area, but the best are on the nearby slopes. Peter focuses on production that brings out the uniqueness of this territory, with its hot days and its nights cooled by the Ora wind that every evening blows north from Lake Garda. The Lagrein Selection R displays a well-defined, approachable aromatic profile, with fruit in the foreground, medicinal herbs, spices and smoky hints. On the palate, the wine is supple, making for satisfyingly succulent drinkability. By contrast, the Chardonnay from the same line has riper, more caressing aromatics, with just a hint of oak in the background, and a highly elegant, mouthfilling palate.

○ A. A. Müller Thurgau Pursgla '14	♥♥	3
○ A. A. Chardonnay Leite '14	♥♥	3
● A. A. Lagrein Stoa '13	♥♥	3
○ A. A. Pinot Bianco Lithos '14	♥♥	3
● A. A. Pinot Nero Johann '13	♥♥	3
● A. A. Schiava '14	♥	2
○ Rodon Passito Maso delle Rose '14	♥	5
○ A. A. Gewürztraminer Maso delle Rose '09	♥♥	3
○ A. A. Pinot Bianco '13	♥♥	3
○ A. A. Pinot Bianco Maso delle Rose '10	♥♥	4
○ A. A. Pinot Bianco Maso delle Rose '09	♥♥	4
○ A. A. Sauvignon Maso delle Rose '13	♥♥	4
● Joanni Maso delle Rose '11	♥♥	4
● Joanni Maso delle Rose '06	♥♥	4
○ Rodon '06	♥♥	5
○ Rodon '04	♥♥	5

● A. A. Lagrein Selection R '13	♥♥	3*
○ A. A. Chardonnay Selection R '13	♥♥	4
○ A. A. Gewürztraminer Selection R '14	♥♥	4
● A. A. Pinot Nero Rollhütt '14	♥♥	4
○ Cortinie Bianco '14	♥♥	3
● Cortinie Rosso '13	♥♥	3
○ A. A. Chardonnay Peter Zemmer '14	♥	3
● A. A. Lagrein Raut '14	♥	3
● A. A. Müller Thurgau Gfrill '14	♥	3
○ A. A. Pinot Bianco Punggl '14	♥	3
○ A. A. Pinot Grigio Peter Zemmer '14	♥	2
○ A. A. Riesling Peter Zemmer '14	♥	3
○ A. A. Chardonnay Reserve '12	♥♥	4
○ A. A. Gewürztraminer Reserve '12	♥♥	4
● A. A. Lagrein Reserve '12	♥♥	4
○ A. A. Pinot Grigio Peter Zemmer '12	♥♥	3*

Bergmannhof

LOC. SAN PAOLO
RIVA DI SOTTO, 46
39050 APPIANO/EPPAN [BZ]
TEL. 0471637082
www.bergmannhof.it

CELLAR SALES
PRE-BOOKED VISITS
ANNUAL PRODUCTION 13,000 bottles
HECTARES UNDER VINE 2.20

○ A.A. Chardonnay Der Bergmann Ris. '13	🏆🏆	4
● A.A. Lagrein Der Bergmann Ris. '12	🏆🏆	4

Bessererhof - Otmar Mair

LOC. NOVALE DI PRESULE, 10
39050 FIÈ ALLO SCILIAR/VÖLS AM SCHLERN [BZ]
TEL. 0471601011
www.bessererhof.it

CELLAR SALES
PRE-BOOKED VISITS
ANNUAL PRODUCTION 35,000 bottles
HECTARES UNDER VINE 1.50

○ A. A. Valle Isarco Kerner '14	🏆🏆	4
○ A. A. Chardonnay Ris. '12	🏆	3
○ A. A. Gewurztraminer '14	🏆	4
○ A. A. Moscato Giallo '14	🏆	4

Castello Rametz

LOC. MAIA ALTA
VIA LABERS, 4
39012 MERANO/MERAN [BZ]
TEL. 0473211011
www.rametz.com

CELLAR SALES
PRE-BOOKED VISITS
RESTAURANT SERVICE
ANNUAL PRODUCTION 400,000 bottles
HECTARES UNDER VINE 8.00

○ A. A. Pinot Grigio '14	🏆	2
○ Chardonnay Césuret '12	🏆	2

Tenuta Donà

LOC. RIVA DI SOTTO, 73
39057 APPIANO/EPPAN [BZ]
TEL. 0473221866
www.weingut-dona.com

CELLAR SALES
PRE-BOOKED VISITS
ACCOMMODATION
ANNUAL PRODUCTION 30,000 bottles
HECTARES UNDER VINE 6.00

● A. A. Schiava '14	🏆🏆	2*
○ A. A. Terlano Chardonnay '14	🏆🏆	3
● A.A. Lagrein '13	🏆🏆	4
○ A.A. Sauvignon '14	🏆	3

Egger-Ramer

VIA GUNCINA, 5
39100 BOLZANO/BOZEN
TEL. 0471280541
www.egger-ramer.com

CELLAR SALES
PRE-BOOKED VISITS
ANNUAL PRODUCTION 120,000 bottles
HECTARES UNDER VINE 14.00

● A. A. Lagrein Kristan '13	🏆🏆	3
● A. A. Lagrein Kristan Ris. '12	🏆🏆	3
● A. A. Santa Maddalena Cl. Reisegger '14	🏆🏆	2*
○ A.A. Valle Isarco Müller Thurgau Sabbiolino '14	🏆	2

Glassierhof - Stefan Vaja

VIA VILLA, 13
39044 EGNA/NEUMARKT [BZ]
TEL. 3351031673
glassierhof@tin.it

CELLAR SALES
PRE-BOOKED VISITS
ANNUAL PRODUCTION 17,500 bottles
HECTARES UNDER VINE 3.40
VITICULTURE METHOD Certified Organic

● A. A. Cabernet Sauvignon Merlot Learn '12	🏆🏆	4
● A. A. Lagrein Glassier Ris. '12	🏆🏆	4
○ A.A. Sauvignon Geboch '13	🏆	4

Haidenhof

VIA MONTELEONE, 17
39010 CERMES/TSCHERMS [BZ]
TEL. 0473562392
www.haidenhof.it

CELLAR SALES
PRE-BOOKED VISITS
RESTAURANT SERVICE
ANNUAL PRODUCTION 30,000 bottles
HECTARES UNDER VINE 3.50

○ A.A. Pinot Bianco Cermes '14		▼▼ 2*
○ A.A. Sauvignon Cermes '14		▼ 2

Lieselehof
Werner Morandell

VIA KARDATSCH, 6
39052 CALDARO/KALTERN [BZ]
TEL. 3299011593
www.lieselehof.com

CELLAR SALES
PRE-BOOKED VISITS
ACCOMMODATION
ANNUAL PRODUCTION 20,000 bottles
HECTARES UNDER VINE 3.00
VITICULTURE METHOD Certified Organic

● A. A. Pinot Nero Bachgart '13		▼▼ 3
● Maximilian '10		▼▼ 5
○ Sweet Claire '13		▼▼ 6
○ Pinot Bianco '13		▼ 3

Marinushof - Heinrich Pohl

LOC. MARAGNO
S.DA VECCHIA, 9B
39020 CASTELBELLO CIARDES/KASTELBELL TSCHARS [BZ]
TEL. 0473624717
www.marinushof.it

CELLAR SALES
PRE-BOOKED VISITS
ACCOMMODATION
ANNUAL PRODUCTION 8,000 bottles
HECTARES UNDER VINE 1.20

● A.A. Valle Venosta Pinot Nero '13		▼▼ 5
○ A.A. Valle Venosta Riesling '14		▼▼ 3
○ A.A. Valle Venosta Pinot Grigio '14		▼ 4

Lorenz Martini

LOC. CORNAIANO/GIRLAN
VIA PRANZOL, 2D
39057 APPIANO/EPPAN [BZ]
TEL. 0471664136
www.lorenz-martini.it

CELLAR SALES
PRE-BOOKED VISITS
ANNUAL PRODUCTION 15,000 bottles
HECTARES UNDER VINE 2.00

○ A. A. Brut Comitissa Ris. '10		▼▼ 5

Maso Hemberg
Klaus Lentsch

S.DA REINSPERG, 18A
39057 APPIANO/EPPAN [BZ]
TEL. 0471967263
www.klauslentsch.eu

CELLAR SALES
PRE-BOOKED VISITS
ANNUAL PRODUCTION 50,000 bottles
HECTARES UNDER VINE 6.00

○ A. A. Moscato Giallo '14		▼▼ 2*
● A. A. Pinot Nero Bachgart '12		▼▼ 2*
○ A. A. Pinot Bianco Amperg '14		▼ 2
○ A. A. Valle Isarco Veltliner Eichberg '13		▼ 2

Messnerhof
Bernhard Pichler

LOC. SAN PIETRO, 7
39100 BOLZANO/BOZEN
TEL. 0471977162
www.messnerhof.net

CELLAR SALES
PRE-BOOKED VISITS
ANNUAL PRODUCTION 15,000 bottles
HECTARES UNDER VINE 2.90

○ A. A. Terlano Sauvignon '14		▼▼ 3
● Mos Maiorum '12		▼▼ 3
● A. A. Lagrein Ris. '12		▼ 4
● Belleus '12		▼ 4

Obermoser
H. & T. Rottensteiner

FRAZ. RENCIO
VIA SANTA MADDALENA, 35
39100 BOLZANO/BOZEN
TEL. 0471973549
www.obermoser.it

CELLAR SALES
PRE-BOOKED VISITS
ANNUAL PRODUCTION 30,000 bottles
HECTARES UNDER VINE 3.80

● A. A. Lagrein Grafenleiten Ris. '13	♟♟ 5
● A. A. Santa Maddalena Cl. '14	♟♟ 2*
● A. A. Lagrein '14	♟ 3
○ A. A. Sauvignon '14	♟ 3

Tenuta Pfitscherhof
Klaus Pfitscher

VIA DOLOMITI, 17
39040 MONTAGNA/MONTAN [BZ]
TEL. 0471819773
www.pfitscher.it

CELLAR SALES
PRE-BOOKED VISITS
ANNUAL PRODUCTION 60,000 bottles
HECTARES UNDER VINE 7.00

○ A. A. Müller Thurgau Dola '14	♟♟ 4
○ A. A. Pinot Bianco Langenfeld '14	♟♟ 3
● A. A. Pinot Nero Fuchsleiten '13	♟♟ 4
○ A. A. Chardonnay Arvum '14	♟ 3

Thomas Pichler

VIA DELLE VIGNE, 4
39052 CALDARO/KALTERN [BZ]
TEL. 0471963094
www.thomas-pichler.it

CELLAR SALES
PRE-BOOKED VISITS
ANNUAL PRODUCTION 15,000 bottles
HECTARES UNDER VINE 1.50

● A. A. Lago di Caldaro Scelto Cl. Sup. Olte Reben '14	♟♟ 3
● A. A. Lagrein Sond Ris. '13	♟ 5
○ A. A. Sauvignon Puiten '14	♟ 4

Prälatenhof
Roland Rohregger

PIANIZZA DI SOTTO, 15A
39052 CALDARO/KALTERN [BZ]
TEL. 0471962541
www.paelatenhof.it

CELLAR SALES
PRE-BOOKED VISITS
ACCOMMODATION
ANNUAL PRODUCTION 15,000 bottles
HECTARES UNDER VINE 2.50

● A. A. Lago Di Caldaro Cl. Sup. '14	♟♟ 3
○ A. A. Sauvignon '13	♟♟ 3
○ A. A. Pinot Bianco '14	♟ 3
○ A. A. Pinot Grigio '13	♟ 3

St. Quirinus - Robert Sinn

VIA PIANIZZA DI SOPRA, 4B
39052 CALDARO/KALTERN [BZ]
TEL. 329 8085003
www.st-quirinus.it

CELLAR SALES
PRE-BOOKED VISITS
ACCOMMODATION
ANNUAL PRODUCTION 12,000 bottles
HECTARES UNDER VINE 2.50
VITICULTURE METHOD Certified Organic

● A. A. Lago di Caldaro Cl. Sup. '14	♟♟ 3
○ A. A. Sauvignon '14	♟♟ 3
⊙ Planties Rosé '14	♟♟ 3
○ Planties Bianco '14	♟ 3

Thurnhof - Andreas Berger

LOC. ASLAGO
VIA CASTEL FLAVON, 7
39100 BOLZANO/BOZEN
TEL. 0471288460
www.thurnhof.com

CELLAR SALES
PRE-BOOKED VISITS
ANNUAL PRODUCTION 25,000 bottles
HECTARES UNDER VINE 3.50

● A. A. Lagrein Ris. '12	♟♟ 4
○ A. A. Moscato Giallo '14	♟♟ 3
○ A. A. Sauvignon 800 '14	♟♟ 3

Thomas Unterhofer

Loc. Pianizza di Sopra, 5
39052 Caldaro/Kaltern [BZ]
Tel. 0471669133
www.weingut-unterhofer.com

CELLAR SALES
PRE-BOOKED VISITS
ANNUAL PRODUCTION 10,000 bottles
HECTARES UNDER VINE 3.00

○ A. A. Chardonnay '14	♥♥ 3
○ A. A. Sauvignon '13	♥♥ 3
○ Reitl '14	♥ 2
● Santa Maddalena '14	♥ 3

Untermoserhof Georg Ramoser

via Santa Maddalena, 36
39100 Bolzano/Bozen
Tel. 0471975481
untermoserhof@rolmail.net

CELLAR SALES
PRE-BOOKED VISITS
ACCOMMODATION
ANNUAL PRODUCTION 30,000 bottles
HECTARES UNDER VINE 3.70

● A. A. Lagrein Ris. '12	♥♥ 5
● A. A. Santa Maddalena Cl. '14	♥♥ 3
● A. A. Merlot Ris. '12	♥ 5

Villscheiderhof Florian Hilpold

Pian di Sotto, 13
39042 Bressanone/Brixen [BZ]
Tel. 0472832037
villscheider@akfree.it

CELLAR SALES
PRE-BOOKED VISITS
ANNUAL PRODUCTION 4,500 bottles
HECTARES UNDER VINE 1.50

○ A. A. Valle Isarco Kerner '14	♥♥ 3
○ A. A. Valle Isarco Sylvaner '14	♥ 3

Von Blumen

via Nazionale, 9/1
39040 Salorno/Salurn [BZ]
Tel. 0457230110
www.vonblumenwine.com

CELLAR SALES
PRE-BOOKED VISITS
ANNUAL PRODUCTION 380,000 bottles
HECTARES UNDER VINE 40.00

○ A.A. Gewurztraminer '14	♥♥ 3
● A.A. Lagrein '13	♥♥ 3
● A.A. Pinot Nero '13	♥♥ 3
○ A.A. Sauvignon '14	♥ 3

Wassererhof

Loc. Novale di Fiè, 21
39050 Fiè allo Sciliar/Völs am Schlern [BZ]
Tel. 0471724114
www.wassererhof.com

CELLAR SALES
PRE-BOOKED VISITS
RESTAURANT SERVICE
ANNUAL PRODUCTION 35,000 bottles
HECTARES UNDER VINE 4.00

● A.A. Santa Maddalena Cl. '14	♥♥ 3
○ A.A. Sauvignon '14	♥♥ 3
○ A.A. Pinot Bianco '14	♥ 3

Weinberghof

In der Au, 4a
39040 Termeno/Tramin [BZ]
Tel. 0471863224
www.weinberg-hof.com

CELLAR SALES
PRE-BOOKED VISITS
ACCOMMODATION
ANNUAL PRODUCTION 20,000 bottles
HECTARES UNDER VINE 2.80

● A. A. Lagrein Ris. '12	♥♥ 5
○ A.A. Pinot Grigio Drau '14	♥♥ 3
○ A. A. Gewürztraminer Plon '14	♥ 3
● A. A. Lagrein Unterstoan '14	♥ 3

VENETO

The Veneto region continues to be a leader in the production of quality wine, buttressed by designations always on the crest of the wave, like Prosecco or Amarone della Valpolicella, and many small and large designations whose producers set very high standards. From east to west, the vineyards and grape varieties roll seamlessly, with glera occupying most of the eastern vineyards then giving way gradually to Bordeaux varieties, which have been at home in much of central Veneto for centuries. Lastly, Verona, where there is no lack of traditional grapes, from garganega to Soave and Gambellara, corvina, and cortese on the shores of Lake Garda, and further enhancements are almost always in the pipeline. The endless energy of Prosecco is still driving the entire sector, with excellent wines to be found within the DOCG, with admirable long-standing cellars concentrating on Bordeaux varieties and quality. Serafini & Vidotto on Montello, Piovene Porto Godi on the Euganean Hills, and the Zonta cousins in Breganze, all offering an idea of how well merlot and cabernet blend in this part of the region. The great 2013 growing year gave us high standards in Soave, whose distinguished wineries were joined for the first time by Marcato. In Valpolicella there is always something new to see, with cellars missing from top accolades over recent years but now back on top. Alongside there is the reassuring arrival of debutantes Tre Bicchieri winners like the small Villa Spinosa, or I Campi, certainly not new to the podium but garnering the first award for a red. Finally, great results from less weighty names: Monte del Frà's Custoza Ca' del Magro, and a Bardolino de Le Vigne from San Pietro. Not to mention the small but stunning world of sweet wines, with repeatedly outstanding performances from Roeno's Cristina and Vignalta's Alpianae. Finally it is worth mentioning that our 2016 Winery of the Year went to Allegrini, a Veneto operation whose entrepreneurial skills and quality were the underpinning to each project, flying the Made-in-Italy flag worldwide.

Stefano Accordini

FRAZ. CAVALO
LOC. CAMPAROL, 10
37022 FUMANE [VR]
TEL. 0457760138
www.accordinistefano.it

CELLAR SALES
PRE-BOOKED VISITS
ANNUAL PRODUCTION 120,000 bottles
HECTARES UNDER VINE 13.00

Over the last decade, Tiziano Accordini first invested in vineyards high in the hills, giving new life blood to his production, and subsequently made the dream of a lifetime come true, with a modern, functional winery beautifully set in the Cavalo hills. Here, surrounded by vineyards, the new facility allows him to work to his high standards while respecting the environment, resulting in wines distinguished by rich fruit and a firm palate. Two wines made it through to our finals, the Amarone il Fornetto 2007 and the Recioto della Valpolicella Acinatico 2012. The former offers dried fruit and aromatic herbs against an intense mineral backdrop, leading into a solid palate with clenched tannins. The latter, meanwhile, is brimming with fruit, set off by notes of truffle and crushed flowers, over a dense, succulent palate.

● Amarone della Valpolicella Cl. Vign. il Fornetto '07	♟♟ 8
● Recioto della Valpolicella Cl. Acinatico '12	♟♟ 5
● Amarone della Valpolicella Cl. Acinatico '11	♟♟ 7
○ Bricco della Terrazza Passito '11	♟♟ 5
● Paxxo '13	♟♟ 4
● Valpolicella Cl. '14	♟♟ 2*
● Valpolicella Cl. Sup. Ripasso Acinatico '13	♟♟ 3
● Amarone della Valpolicella Cl. Acinatico '95	♟♟♟ 5
● Amarone della Valpolicella Cl. Vign. il Fornetto '93	♟♟♟ 5
● Recioto della Valpolicella Cl. Acinatico '04	♟♟♟ 6
● Recioto della Valpolicella Cl. Acinatico '00	♟♟♟ 8

Adami

FRAZ. COLBERTALDO
VIA ROVEDE, 27
31020 VIDOR [TV]
TEL. 0423982110
www.adamispumanti.it

CELLAR SALES
PRE-BOOKED VISITS
ANNUAL PRODUCTION 700,000 bottles
HECTARES UNDER VINE 12.00

The worth of a winery can obviously be seen in the quality and consistency of its products, but when we are faced with a vintage like 2014, ruined by difficult weather at harvest and during the growing season, that put producers' nerves to the test, any assessment must also take into account how winegrowers dealt with the problem. Infinite patience, respect for the territory and confidence in their work once again allowed Franco and Armando Adami to achieve an excellent vintage. Meticulous care resulted in a splendid version of Col Credas, a Prosecco with extremely low residual sugars, from the vineyard at Torri di Credazzo, which seems to hang in the sky. On the nose we find attractive white-fleshed fruit and blossom, paving the way for a zesty, gutsy palate with impressive length. Diametrically opposed is the Vigneto Giardino, a Dry with an open, inviting nose and a harmonious, charming palate.

○ Valdobbiadene Rive di Colbertaldo Dry Vign. Giardino '14	♟♟ 3*
○ Valdobbiadene Rive di Farra di Soligo Brut Col Credas '14	♟♟ 3*
○ Cartizze	♟♟ 5
○ Valdobbiadene Brut Bosco di Gica	♟♟ 3
○ Valdobbiadene Extra Dry Dei Casel	♟ 3
○ Valdobbiadene Frizzante Sui Lieviti	♟ 3
○ Valdobbiadene Rive di Farra di Soligo Brut Col Credas '13	♟♟♟ 3*
○ Valdobbiadene Rive di Farra di Soligo Brut Col Credas '12	♟♟♟ 3*
○ Valdobbiadene Rive di Colbertaldo Dry Vign. Giardino '13	♟♟ 4
○ Valdobbiadene Rive di Colbertaldo Dry Vign. Giardino '12	♟♟ 4

Ida Agnoletti

LOC. SELVA DEL MONTELLO
VIA SACCARDO, 55
31040 VOLPAGO DEL MONTELLO [TV]
TEL. 0423621555
www.agnoletti.it

CELLAR SALES
PRE-BOOKED VISITS
ANNUAL PRODUCTION 50,000 bottles
HECTARES UNDER VINE 7.00

Ida Agnoletti's winery is on the southern slopes of Montello, on high ground stretching out to the north of Treviso, on the way to the Prealps. Here, on karst, clayey soils, the vineyards of around seven hectares are mainly planted to glera and Bordeaux varieties, with a small yet important presence of Manzoni bianco. The wide range on offer shows Ida's desire to take risks and explore the potential of this territory. We saw a good performance from the Manzoni Bianco Follia, which is released after long cellar ageing, and shows a complex nose with fruit swathed in intense sulphur and smoky notes, leading into a rich, full-flavoured, beautifully taut palate. Vita is a Bordeaux blend showing a delicate nose of wild berries and aromatic herbs, with smooth tannins and an attractively long, dry finish. The two Merlots display wonderfully intense fruit.

★★★Allegrini

VIA GIARE, 5
37022 FUMANE [VR]
TEL. 0456832011
www.allegrini.it

CELLAR SALES
PRE-BOOKED VISITS
ACCOMMODATION AND RESTAURANT SERVICE
ANNUAL PRODUCTION 900,000 bottles
HECTARES UNDER VINE 110.00
SUSTAINABLE WINERY

Marilisa and Franco Allegrini have managed to turn the winery established by their father Giovanni into one of Italy's winemaking treasures, which has developed well beyond regional confines while remaining deeply bound to its homeland. This is why it earned the accolade of Winery of the Year. It now has over 100 hectares of vineyards in Valpolicella, distributed over the best-aspected slopes of the DOC zone, shunning the valley floor in pursuit of the freshness that only the hills can give, for a solid, authentic range of wines. The sumptuous Amarone is always one of the most convincing in its class. On the nose, simple, fresh aromas are dominated by crisp, succulent red berry fruit. There is a change of gear on the palate, however, with smooth tannins and extraordinary length. This was a performance that rightly earned a Tre Bicchieri.

○ Manzoni Bianco Follia '13	♟♟ 2*
● Montello e Colli Asolani Merlot '13	♟♟ 2*
● Montello e Colli Asolani Merlot La Ida '13	♟♟ 2*
● Seneca '12	♟♟ 3
● Vita Life is Red '13	♟♟ 3
○ Glera Frizzante PSL Always	♟ 2
○ Manzoni 6.0.13 '13	♟ 2
● Montello e Colli Asolani Cabernet Sauvignon '13	♟ 2
○ Prosecco di Treviso Frizzante Selva n. 55	♟ 2
○ Prosecco di Treviso Il Tranquillo '14	♟ 2
● Recantina '13	♟ 2
● Rosso di Selva	♟ 3
○ Manzoni Bianco Follia '12	♟♟ 2*
● Montello e Colli Asolani Cabernet Sauvignon '12	♟♟ 2*
● Vita Life is Red '11	♟♟ 3

● Amarone della Valpolicella Cl. '11	♟♟♟ 8
● La Poja '11	♟♟ 8
● Recioto della Valpolicella Cl. Giovanni Allegrini '12	♟♟ 6
● La Grola '12	♟♟ 4
● Palazzo della Torre '12	♟♟ 4
○ Soave '14	♟♟ 2*
● Valpolicella Cl. '14	♟♟ 2*
● Amarone della Valpolicella Cl. '10	♟♟♟ 8
● Amarone della Valpolicella Cl. '09	♟♟♟ 8
● Amarone della Valpolicella Cl. '08	♟♟♟ 8
● Amarone della Valpolicella Cl. '07	♟♟♟ 8
● Amarone della Valpolicella Cl. '06	♟♟♟ 8
● Amarone della Valpolicella Cl. '05	♟♟♟ 7
● Amarone della Valpolicella Cl. '04	♟♟♟ 7
● Amarone della Valpolicella Cl. '03	♟♟♟ 7

Andreola

VIA CAVRE,19
31010 FARRA DI SOLIGO [TV]
TEL. 0438989379
www.andreola.eu

CELLAR SALES
PRE-BOOKED VISITS
ANNUAL PRODUCTION 900,000 bottles
HECTARES UNDER VINE 47.00

In recent years, Stefano Pola's winery has made important progress. While in previous decades he had extended his vineyards significantly, today the most important development is the completion of the cellar at Farra di Soligo, where all phases of production take place, and the showroom and offices are to be found. A wide range of sparklers is available, focusing entirely on glera, and differing from each other on the basis of residual sugar levels and the vineyards of provenance. Stefano presented an excellent range this year, led by the Brut 26esimo 1°. The difficult 2014 harvest did not stop him from producing a superb sparkler, with aromas ranging from traditional apple and pear to citrus and wild flowers. On the palate, acid tautness is attractively underpinned by full flavour and a long finish. With a fruity nose and creamy palate, the Extra Dry Mas de Fer is succulent and satisfying in the mouth.

Antolini

VIA PROGNOL, 22
37020 MARANO DI VALPOLICELLA [VR]
TEL. 0457755351
www.antolinivini.it

CELLAR SALES
PRE-BOOKED VISITS
ACCOMMODATION
ANNUAL PRODUCTION 50,000 bottles
HECTARES UNDER VINE 9.00

Brothers Pier Paolo and Stefano Antolini are based in the Marano Valley, the part of the Valpolicella Classica zone which more than any other seems to have remained dedicated to traditional farming. Narrow and carpeted with vineyards, the valley slopes rise steeply for a few hundred metres, and offer views of vines and dry stone walls. In addition to five hectares here, the Antolini brothers also farm a hectare at Semonte and a further two at Ca' Coato, in the municipality of Marano. We saw an excellent performance from the Valpolicella Superiore Ripasso, with ripe fruit aromas joined by spice and crushed flowers. The full palate is nicely underpinned by acidity and crisp tannins. Two Amarones were presented: Moròpio, from the vineyards of Marano, offers a ripe, complex nose, over an exuberant palate kept in check by stiff tannins; and Ca' Coato, from the vineyards at Negrar, shows a softer profile.

○ Cartizze '14	♟♟ 5
○ Valdobbiadene Brut Vign. Dirupo	♟♟ 3
○ Valdobbiadene Extra Dry Vign. Dirupo	♟♟ 2*
○ Valdobbiadene Rive di Col San Martino Brut 26esimo 1° '14	♟♟ 3
○ Valdobbiadene Rive di Soligo Extra Dry Mas de Fer '14	♟♟ 2*
○ Pensieri Passito	♟ 5
○ Valdobbiadene Dry '14	♟ 3
○ Valdobbiadene Dry 6° Senso	♟ 3
○ Cartizze '13	♟♟ 4
○ Valdobbiadene Brut Vign. Dirupo '13	♟♟ 2*
○ Valdobbiadene Rive di Soligo Extra Dry Mas de Fer '13	♟♟ 2*
○ Valdobbiadene Vign. Dirupo Extra Dry '13	♟♟ 2*

● Valpolicella Cl. Sup. Ripasso '13	♟♟ 4
● Amarone della Valpolicella Cl. Ca' Coato '11	♟ 6
● Amarone della Valpolicella Cl. Moròpio '11	♟♟ 6
● Recioto della Valpolicella Cl. '11	♟♟ 5
● Theobroma '11	♟♟ 4
● Valpolicella Cl. '14	♟ 2
● Amarone della Valpolicella Cl. Ca' Coato '10	♟♟ 6
● Amarone della Valpolicella Cl. Ca' Coato '09	♟♟ 6
● Amarone della Valpolicella Cl. Ca' Coato '08	♟♟ 6
● Amarone della Valpolicella Cl. Ca' Coato '07	♟♟ 6
● Amarone della Valpolicella Cl. Moròpio '06	♟♟ 5

Albino Armani

VIA CERADELLO, 401
37020 DOLCÈ [VR]
TEL. 0457290033
www.albinoarmani.com

CELLAR SALES
PRE-BOOKED VISITS
ANNUAL PRODUCTION 900,000 bottles
HECTARES UNDER VINE 220.00
SUSTAINABLE WINERY

Albino Armani has created an operation that can now rely on extremely extensive vineyards, with over 200 hectares in various parts of the north-east. The oldest are located in Valdadige, straddling the provinces of Verona and Trento. In addition to these, there are estates in Valpolicella, in the province of Treviso, where attention is given to glera, and lastly in the Grave DOC zone in Friuli. The style of the large range focuses on well-typed expressions of the various varieties. The superb Amarone shows intense jammy aromas, against a backdrop of medicinal herbs and spices. Its power on the palate is evident, but well governed by close-knit tannins and succulent acidity, with a warm, caressing finish. Among the whites, we should mention the impressive, copper-hued Pinot Grigio Colle Ara, with yellow-fleshed fruit and blossom on the nose, paving the way for a full, creamy palate and a delicately tannic finish.

Balestri Valda

VIA MONTI, 44
37038 SOAVE [VR]
TEL. 0457675393
www.vinibalestrivalda.com

CELLAR SALES
PRE-BOOKED VISITS
ANNUAL PRODUCTION 60,000 bottles
HECTARES UNDER VINE 13.00

The area behind the towns of Soave and Monteforte d'Alpione is characterized by a dense network of volcanic hills. Here, depending on aspect and position, the soils vary from black basalt to yellow tufa, allowing garganega, the real prima donna in this corner of Veneto, to express its great character. The Rizzotto family winery is behind Soave, on the slopes leading to the small town of Castelcerino, and covers a dozen hectares. The Soave from the Sengialta vineyard is the champion at Rizzotto, and is aged in large oak, to be released only after sufficient time in the cellar. Its aromas of white-fleshed fruit, vegetal and floral notes emerge slowly, leading into a medium-bodied palate, with good flavour and grip. The simpler Soave Classico, also as a result of the difficult harvest, shows a more approachable nose and a lean, spirited palate.

● Amarone della Valpolicella Cl. Cuslanus '09	♥♥ 6
○ Trentino Chardonnay Capitel '14	♥♥ 2*
○ Trento Brut '10	♥♥ 4
○ Valdadige Pinot Grigio Corvara '14	♥♥ 2*
○ Valdadige Terra dei Forti Pinot Grigio Colle Ara '14	♥♥ 2*
○ Friuli Grave Sauvignon Claps '14	♥ 2
○ Lugana '14	♥ 3
○ Sauvignon Campo Napoleone '14	♥ 2
● Valpolicella Ripasso '12	♥ 3
● Amarone della Valpolicella '08	♥♥ 5
● Recioto della Valpolicella '12	♥♥ 5
○ Sauvignon Campo Napoleone '13	♥♥ 2*

○ Soave Cl. Vign. Sengialta '13	♥♥ 2*
○ Soave Cl. '14	♥ 2
○ Soave Cl. Lunalonga '13	♥ 3
○ Recioto di Soave Cl. '08	♥♥ 5
○ Soave Cl. '12	♥♥ 2*
○ Soave Cl. '11	♥♥ 2*
○ Soave Cl. '09	♥♥ 2
○ Soave Cl. '08	♥♥ 2*
○ Soave Cl. Lunalonga '12	♥♥ 3*
○ Soave Cl. Lunalonga '11	♥♥ 3*
○ Soave Cl. Lunalonga '08	♥♥ 3*
○ Soave Cl. Sengialta '11	♥♥ 2*
○ Soave Cl. Sengialta '10	♥♥ 2*
○ Soave Cl. Sengialta '09	♥♥ 2*
○ Soave Cl. Sengialta '08	♥♥ 2*
○ Soave Cl. Vign. Sengialta '12	♥♥ 2*

Barollo

VIA RIO SERVA, 4B
35123 PREGANZIOL [TV]
TEL. 0422633014
www.barollo.com

CELLAR SALES
PRE-BOOKED VISITS
ANNUAL PRODUCTION 57,000 bottles
HECTARES UNDER VINE 45.00

The plain of Treviso offers views that clearly bear witness to its traditional, widespread farming activity, with an ordered succession of fields interrupted by sinuous rivers and stately homes. It is here that we find the winery of Marco and Nicola Barollo, covering over 40 hectares dedicated to producing reliable wines that express individual varieties to the full. Great attention is paid to international cultivars, but also classic glera and Manzoni bianco. The outstanding Frank! has never been closer to top honours. It opens to focused notes of ripe red berry fruit, pepper, and the delicate vegetal hints typical of the cabernet franc on which the wine is based. On the palate, it shows suppleness, but also the weight of its class, and a long, dry finish. We were also intrigued by the Chardonnay 2013, with a nose of fruit and spice, and a rich, zesty palate.

● Frank! '13	♟♟ 4
○ Alfredo Barollo Brut M. Cl. Ris. '10	♟♟ 4
○ Piave Chardonnay '13	♟♟ 4
○ Pinot Bianco '14	♟♟ 3
○ Manzoni Bianco '14	♟ 3
○ Piave Chardonnay Frater '14	♟ 2
● Piave Merlot Frater '14	♟ 2
○ Prosecco di Treviso Extra Dry '14	♟ 2
○ Sauvignon '14	♟ 3
● Frank '09	♟♟ 3
● Frank! '12	♟♟ 4
● Frank! '11	♟♟ 4
● Frank! '10	♟♟ 3*

★Lorenzo Begali

VIA CENGIA, 10
37020 SAN PIETRO IN CARIANO [VR]
TEL. 0457725148
www.begaliwine.it

CELLAR SALES
PRE-BOOKED VISITS
ANNUAL PRODUCTION 90,000 bottles
HECTARES UNDER VINE 12.00

The Begali family has managed to earn a solid reputation on the wine scene of Valpolicella, thanks to products that remain faithful to tradition while offering a focused, rich style that avoids excessive raisiny notes. The vineyards are located almost entirely near the cellar, at Cengia, partly on the valley floor and partly in the hills, covering a few hectares with a splendid south-east aspect, and provide grapes for the more ambitious labels. The cool, sunny 2010 harvest provided perfect grapes for the production of the Amarone Monte Ca' Bianca, with elegant fruit aromas slowly making way for medicinal herbs, spices and crushed flowers, for a nose of great depth. On the palate, it shows its thoroughbred status, with power balanced by tannins and acidity, and a seductive finish. More approachable is the succulent Amarone Classico, while the harmonious Recioto shows intact, crunchy fruit.

● Amarone della Valpolicella Cl. Monte Ca' Bianca '10	♟♟♟ 8
● Amarone della Valpolicella Cl. '11	♟♟ 6
● Recioto della Valpolicella Cl. '11	♟♟ 6
● Tigiolo '11	♟♟ 5
● Valpolicella Cl. Sup. Ripasso La Cengia '13	♟♟ 3
● Valpolicella Cl. '14	♟ 2
● Amarone della Valpolicella Cl. Vign. Monte Ca' Bianca '09	♟♟♟ 8
● Amarone della Valpolicella Cl. Vign. Monte Ca' Bianca '08	♟♟♟ 8
● Amarone della Valpolicella Cl. Vign. Monte Ca' Bianca '07	♟♟♟ 8
● Amarone della Valpolicella Cl. Vign. Monte Ca' Bianca '06	♟♟♟ 8

★Cav. G. B. Bertani

VIA ASIAGO, 1
37023 GREZZANA [VR]
TEL. 0458658444
www.bertani.net

CELLAR SALES
PRE-BOOKED VISITS
ANNUAL PRODUCTION 2,100,000 bottles
HECTARES UNDER VINE 200.00
SUSTAINABLE WINERY

This major winery at Grezzana joined the holdings of the Angelini family as a major player, and was soon at the forefront of the Bertani Domains project, which brings together all the estates. The change in ownership in no way compromised the classic style of the winery, however, and it is still faithful to its traditional products, and to an image that makes it one of the icons of Italian wine worldwide. The vineyards cover 200 hectares, providing grapes for wines with unmistakable character. Thanks also to an extra year in the cellar, the Amarone Classico 2007 trounced the competition. Faced with an array of wines designed to stun, Bertani's won us over with its class, and its delicate aromas of super-ripe fruit swathed in fines herbes and spice. On the palate, it is even more delicate, managing to govern impressive body with lightness and full flavour, and leading to an elegant, unforgettable finish. The Ognisanti is fresher and racier.

● Amarone della Valpolicella Cl. '07	♟♟♟	8
● Valpolicella Cl. Sup. Ognisanti '13	♟♟	4
● Amarone della Valpolicella Valpantena Villa Arvedi '12	♟♟	6
● Secco Bertani Vintage Edition '12	♟♟	4
○ Soave Giovan Battista Bertani '13	♟♟	3
● Valpolicella Cl. Villa Novare '14	♟♟	2*
● Valpolicella Ripasso '12	♟♟	3
● Amarone della Valpolicella Cl. '06	♟♟♟	8
● Amarone della Valpolicella Cl. '05	♟♟♟	8
● Amarone della Valpolicella Cl. '04	♟♟♟	8
● Amarone della Valpolicella Cl. '03	♟♟♟	8
● Amarone della Valpolicella Cl. '01	♟♟♟	8
● Amarone della Valpolicella Cl. '00	♟♟♟	8
● Valpolicella Cl. Sup. Vign. Ognisanti '06	♟♟♟	4*

BiancaVigna

VIA CREVADA, 9/1
31020 SAN PIETRO DI FELETTO [TV]
TEL. 0438801098
www.biancavigna.it

PRE-BOOKED VISITS
ACCOMMODATION
ANNUAL PRODUCTION 400,000 bottles
HECTARES UNDER VINE 18.00
SUSTAINABLE WINERY

In only a few years, Elena Moschetta and her brother Enrico have created an operation that is now a benchmark for the DOC zone, not so much in terms of volume, which is still limited considering the extent of the Prosecco phenomenon, but in terms of quality across the board. Around 20 hectares, mainly in the eastern area of the historic DOC zone, have now been joined by a brand-new cellar perfectly integrated into the surrounding farmland. Enrico has produced a superb Rive di Soligo Brut that relies little on sweetness, which missed out on our finals by a hair's breadth. Thanks also to a difficult growing year, which produced interesting wines, he managed to exploit the characteristics of the vintage to provide an introverted wine, almost reticent in its vegetal and white-fleshed fruit aromas, which unfolds in a palate of great grip and tautness. The Brut and Extra Dry, meanwhile, showed a more aromatic nose and harmonious profile.

○ Conegliano Valdobbiadene Brut '14	♟♟	3
○ Conegliano Valdobbiadene Brut Rive di Soligo '14	♟♟	3
○ Conegliano Valdobbiadene Extra Dry '14	♟♟	3
○ Prosecco Brut	♟♟	2
○ Prosecco Extra Dry	♟	2
○ Prosecco Tranquillo '14	♟	2
☉ Spumante Rosa Brut	♟	2
○ Conegliano Valdobbiadene Brut '13	♟♟	3
○ Conegliano Valdobbiadene Brut '12	♟♟	3
○ Conegliano Valdobbiadene Extra Dry '13	♟♟	3
○ Conegliano Valdobbiadene Extra Dry '12	♟♟	3

VENETO

Desiderio Bisol & Figli

FRAZ. SANTO STEFANO
VIA FOLLO, 33
31049 VALDOBBIADENE [TV]
TEL. 0423900138
www.bisol.it

CELLAR SALES
PRE-BOOKED VISITS
ANNUAL PRODUCTION 1,800,000 bottles
HECTARES UNDER VINE 126.00

One of the main wineries to have elevated Prosecco to the role of phenomenon that we know today, must surely be that of the Bisol family. For decades they have worked to make this white sparkler from Treviso world famous. Even now that the DOC zone has been extended as far as the border with Slovenia, Gianluca and Desiderio are still firmly attached to the old winery at Valdobbiadene. Production is based both on the winery's holdings and on long-standing partnerships with local growers. Once again, the Vigneti del Fol is the most interesting wine from Bisol. By now an iconic label in the DOC zone, it is always an important benchmark for lovers of Valdobbiadene sparklers. Its aromas of pear, cut flowers and sugared almonds are followed on the palate by a perfect fusion with the fizz, giving harmony, length and elegance. There is also a limited but interesting production of Metodo Classico sparklers, in particular the Cuvée del Fondatore Eliseo Bisol.

○ Valdobbiadene Extra Dry Vign. del Fol '14	♥♥	4
○ Cartizze '14	♥♥	5
○ Cuvée del Fondatore Eliseo Bisol Brut M. Cl '04	♥♥	5
○ Valdobbiadene Brut Garnei '13	♥♥	3
○ Valdobbiadene Extra Dry Colmei	♥♥	2
○ Valdobbiadene Extra Dry Molera '14	♥♥	3
○ Pas Dosé M. Cl. '04	♥	3
○ Prosecco Extra Dry Belstar	♥	3
○ Cartizze '13	♀♀	5
○ Cartizze Private Non Dosato '12	♀♀	5
○ Pas Dosé M. Cl. '02	♀♀	3
○ Valdobbiadene Brut Crede '13	♀♀	4
○ Valdobbiadene Extra Dry Vign. del Fol '13	♀♀	4

F.lli Bolla

FRAZ. PEDEMONTE
VIA ALBERTO BOLLA, 3
37029 SAN PIETRO IN CARIANO [VR]
TEL. 0456836555
www.bolla.it

CELLAR SALES
PRE-BOOKED VISITS
ANNUAL PRODUCTION 12,000,000 bottles
HECTARES UNDER VINE 188.00

In recent years, this consolidated Pedemonte winery has managed to become a benchmark for the entire Valpolicella DOC zone, thanks to meticulous work on reviewing production methods and the range of wines. The attention of Cristian Scrinzi and his staff focus on tradition, and each of the wines produced express this, in a style that brings together the fullness and roundness sought by the market with the depth and elegance typical of this DOC zone. The Amarone Le Origini, thanks also to long cellar ageing, boasts a complex nose dominated by fleshy, summery fruit, interlaced with delicate notes of crushed flowers and spice, which then explode on the rich, voluptuous palate. Subtler but equally complex is the Ripasso Le Poiane, with ripe cherry and dried flowers, showing a taut palate and attractive tannic weave.

● Amarone della Valpolicella Cl. Le Origini Ris. '10	♀♀	6
● Valpolicella Cl. Sup. Ripasso Le Pojane '13	♥♥	4
● Amarone della Valpolicella Cl. Rhetico '10	♥♥	6
● Creso '12	♥♥	4
○ Custoza La Real Casa '14	♥♥	2*
○ Soave Cl. Sup. Tufaie '13	♥♥	3
● Valpolicella Cl. Sup. Colforte '13	♥♥	3
⊙ Bardolino Chiaretto Cl. La Canestraia '14	♥	2
○ Soave Cl. Retrò '14	♥	2
● Valpolicella Cl. Il Calice '14	♥	2
● Amarone della Valpolicella Cl. Le Origini '09	♀♀	7
● Amarone della Valpolicella Cl. Le Origini '08	♀♀	7

Borgo Stajnbech

VIA BELFIORE, 109
30020 PRAMAGGIORE [VE]
TEL. 0421799929
www.borgostajnbech.com

CELLAR SALES
PRE-BOOKED VISITS
ANNUAL PRODUCTION 90,000 bottles
HECTARES UNDER VINE 15.00

The province of Venice lies along the shores of the Adriatic, and from Chioggia to Bibione beaches roll seamlessly along the coast, behind them an area of intense farming activity. It is here that the Valent family winery occupied 15 hectares between the sea and the Prealps, with clayey soils that bring to the fore characteristics of certain varieties, tai in particular. The wide range of wines is reliable and extremely drinkable. It was precisely Valent's Lison Classico 150 that convinced us most, a white released after well-judged ageing. Opening to smoky aromas and yellow-fleshed fruit, it offers a relaxed, graceful palate, revealing a firm body and attractive acidic grip. We also loved the Refosco, initially closed on the nose, but slowly opening to blossom and wild berries, while the harmonious palate is in no hurry to sign off.

Borgoluce

LOC. MUSILE, 2
31058 SUSEGANA [TV]
TEL. 0438435287
www.borgoluce.it

CELLAR SALES
PRE-BOOKED VISITS
ACCOMMODATION AND RESTAURANT SERVICE
ANNUAL PRODUCTION 250,000 bottles
HECTARES UNDER VINE 70.00

The Collalto family winery has managed in only a few years to become a leading name in the world of Prosecco, thanks to vineyard holdings in the rolling hills around Conegliano and long experience in the sector. The estate actually covers over 1,000 hectares, dedicated to a wide range of farming activities, including arable crops and livestock breeding, all with the utmost respect for the environment, and providing jobs for many young people in the area. We saw a solid performance from the two Rive di Collalto labels. The operation's best vineyards gave superb grapes for a brace of wines that manage to bring out the more elegant side of this type. The Rive Brut offers an essential aromatic profile, with white-fleshed fruit and flowers, and a perfect fusion of sparkle, flavour and acidity on the palate. The Rive Extra Dry shows a more open, summery nose, while maintaining a dry palate of good length.

○ Lison-Pramaggiore Cl. 150 '13	🏆🏆 3
● Lison-Pramaggiore Refosco P.R. '13	🏆🏆 2*
● Stajnbech Rosso '11	🏆🏆 3
● Malbech '13	🏆 2
● Pinot Nero '13	🏆 2
○ Sauvignon Bosco della Donna '14	🏆 3
● Lison – Pramaggiore Refosco P.R. '12	🏆🏆 2*
○ Lison-Pramaggiore Chardonnay Stajnbech Bianco '11	🏆🏆 3
○ Lison-Pramaggiore Chardonnay Stajnbech Bianco '10	🏆🏆 4
○ Lison-Pramaggiore Cl. 150 '12	🏆🏆 3
● Lison-Pramaggiore Merlot '12	🏆🏆 2*
● Malbech '12	🏆🏆 2*
● Rosso '09	🏆🏆 3

○ Valdobbiadene Brut	🏆🏆 3
○ Valdobbiadene Rive di Collalto Brut '14	🏆🏆 2*
○ Valdobbiadene Rive di Collalto Extra Dry '14	🏆🏆 2*
○ Valdobbiadene Extra Dry	🏆 3
○ Valdobbiadene Dry Mill. '10	🏆🏆 3
○ Valdobbiadene Rive di Collalto Brut '13	🏆🏆 2*
○ Valdobbiadene Rive di Collalto Extra Dry '13	🏆🏆 2*
○ Valdobbiadene Rive di Collalto Extra Dry '12	🏆🏆 2*
○ Valdobbiadene Rive di Collalto Extra Dry '11	🏆🏆 2*

Borin Vini & Vigne

FRAZ. MONTICELLI
VIA DEI COLLI, 5
35043 MONSELICE [PD]
TEL. 042974384
www.viniborin.it

CELLAR SALES
PRE-BOOKED VISITS
ANNUAL PRODUCTION 105,000 bottles
HECTARES UNDER VINE 28.00

Entering the Parco dei Colli Euganei from the east, heading for Arquà Petrarca, at the end of a long straight road, we find the winery of the Borin family, who have been farming here for over 50 years. The vineyards cover around 30 hectares on both the flat land around the winery and in some of the best-aspected hillside sites that Arquà can offer. Production is entirely dedicated to the traditional varieties of the zone, interpreted with an eye to intact fruit and drinkability. As always, the Fiore di Gaia was a great success, opening to aromas of citrus, jasmine and white pepper, over a hefty palate with good grip and length. The Zuan meanwhile shows the warmer, sunnier side of Colli Euganei, with a nose of ripe plum, Mediterranean scrub and spice, leading into a full, rounded palate. The Corte Borin is a firm, drinkable white.

Bortolomiol

VIA GARIBALDI, 142
31049 VALDOBBIADENE [TV]
TEL. 04239749
www.bortolomiol.com

CELLAR SALES
PRE-BOOKED VISITS
RESTAURANT SERVICE
ANNUAL PRODUCTION 1,800,000 bottles
HECTARES UNDER VINE 5.00
VITICULTURE METHOD Certified Organic
SUSTAINABLE WINERY

The historic winery in Valdobbiadene's Via Garibaldi bases its solid performance on a close-knit network of growers, who have been providing the grapes for its impressive production numbers for generations. While in the past, the innovation of Giuliano Bortolomiol, the founder of the company, focused on the birth of Prosecco Brut, today attention is on sustainable farming, and the operation is committed to achieving a better approach to viticulture, which is echoed in the cellar with the utmost respect for the raw materials. The Brut Prior shows an attractive bright hue with fine sparkle, and elegant appley aromas, alongside flowers and sugared almonds, developed on the consistent, elegant palate. The Motus Vitae, dedicated to the founder Giuliano Bortolomiol, shows a more mature, complex nose, with fruit swathed in dried flowers and Mediterranean scrub, followed through on the palate and perfectly integrated with the fizz.

● Colli Euganei Cabernet Sauvignon Mons Silicis Ris. '11	♟♟ 4
○ Colli Euganei Fior d'Arancio Fiore di Gaia '14	♟♟ 2*
○ Colli Euganei Manzoni Bianco Corte Borin '13	♟♟ 3
● Colli Euganei Rosso Zuan '13	♟♟ 3
● Coldivalle Syrah '12	♟ 3
● Colli Euganei Cabernet Sauvignon V. Costa '13	♟ 3
○ Colli Euganei Chardonnay V. Bianca '13	♟ 3
○ Colli Euganei Fior d'Arancio Spumante '14	♟ 2
○ Colli Euganei Pinot Bianco Monte Archino '14	♟ 2
○ Colli Euganei Fior d'Arancio Fiore di Gaia '13	♟♟ 2*
● Colli Euganei Rosso Zuan '12	♟♟ 3*

○ Valdobbiadene Brut Prior '14	♟♟♟ 3*
○ Cartizze	♟♟ 5
○ Valdobbiadene Brut Rive San Pietro di Barbozza Motus Vitae '13	♟♟ 5
○ Valdobbiadene Dry Maior '14	♟♟ 3
○ Valdobbiadene Extra Dry Banda Rossa '14	♟♟ 3
⊙ Filanda Rosé Brut '14	♟ 3
○ Riserva del Governatore Extra Brut	♟ 3
○ Valdobbiadene Brut Ius Naturae '14	♟ 4
○ Valdobbiadene Demi Sec Suavis	♟ 3
○ Valdobbiadene Extra Dry Senior '14	♟ 3
○ Valdobbiadene Brut Ius Naturae '13	♟♟ 4
○ Valdobbiadene Brut Ius Naturae '12	♟♟ 4

Carlo Boscaini

VIA SENGIA, 15
37010 SANT'AMBROGIO DI VALPOLICELLA [VR]
TEL. 0457731412
www.boscainicarlo.it

CELLAR SALES
PRE-BOOKED VISITS
ACCOMMODATION
ANNUAL PRODUCTION 60,000 bottles
HECTARES UNDER VINE 14.00

Of all the valleys of Valpolicella, that of Sant'Ambrogio is perhaps the least known, partly because it opens up into Valdadige, which makes it seem less of an enclosed valley, partly because a few major wineries have monopolized holdings here. There are, however, some hidden treasures, such as the winery owned by brothers Carlo and Mario Boscaini, whose dozen-or-so hectares are entirely dedicated to the varieties of Valpolicella, giving wines with firm palates and well-typed noses. The 2012 harvest made it possible to produce an excellent Valpolicella Superiore La Preosa, with a nose of wild berries over aromatic herbs and white pepper. On the rounded palate, it shows full flavour and attractively rugged tannins. The Ripasso Zane meanwhile is more mature and caressing, both on the nose and in the mouth. The Amarone shows a profile that plays on its fullness of flavour.

Bosco del Merlo

VIA POSTUMIA, 12
30020 ANNONE VENETO [VE]
TEL. 0422768167
www.boscodelmerlo.it

CELLAR SALES
PRE-BOOKED VISITS
ANNUAL PRODUCTION 240,000 bottles
HECTARES UNDER VINE 84.00
SUSTAINABLE WINERY

In the extensive panorama of Venetian viticulture, a prime place goes to the winery of the Paladin brothers, with vineyards of over 80 hectares between the Adriatic coast to the south and the hills to the north, and over half a century of tradition. Great care is taken in tending the rows and utmost respect given to the raw materials at the cellar, resulting in wines with focused fruit and elegance on the palate. These are precisely the finest qualities of the 360 Ruber Capite, a Bordeaux blend topped up with a splash of malbech that offers fruit on the nose, rapidly making way for medicinal herbs, blossom and pepper. This is echoed on the taut, elegant palate, for a result that missed our top honours by a whisker. A mature nose and harmonious palate distinguish the Refosco Roggio dei Roveri.

● Amarone della Valpolicella Cl. San Giorgio '11	♟♟ 5
● Valpolicella Cl. Sup. La Preosa '12	♟♟ 3
● Valpolicella Cl. Sup. Ripasso Zane '11	♟♟ 4
● Valpolicella Cl. Ca' Bussin '13	♟ 2
● Amarone della Valpolicella Cl. San Giorgio '10	♟♟ 5
● Amarone della Valpolicella Cl. San Giorgio '09	♟♟ 5
● Amarone della Valpolicella Cl. San Giorgio '08	♟♟ 5
● Recioto della Valpolicella Cl. La Sengia '12	♟♟ 4
● Valpolicella Cl. Ca' Bussin '12	♟♟ 2*
● Valpolicella Cl. Sup. La Preosa '11	♟♟ 3
● Valpolicella Cl. Sup. Ripasso Zane '09	♟♟ 3

● 360 Ruber Capite '12	♟♟ 5
● Lison-Pramaggiore Refosco P.R. Roggio dei Roveri '12	♟♟ 5
○ Lison-Pramaggiore Sauvignon Turriano '14	♟♟ 4
● Malbech Gli Aceri Paladin '12	♟♟ 6
○ Lison-Pramaggiore Lison Cl. Juti '14	♟ 4
● Lison-Pramaggiore Merlot Campo Camino '12	♟ 4
○ Prosecco Brut Mill. '14	♟ 3
● Lison-Pramaggiore Refosco P. R. Roggio dei Roveri Ris. '11	♟♟ 5
○ Lison-Pramaggiore Sauvignon Turriano '13	♟♟ 4
○ Lison-Pramaggiore Sauvignon Turriano '12	♟♟ 4
○ Lison-Pramaggiore Sauvignon Turranio '11	♟♟ 6

★Brigaldara

FRAZ. SAN FLORIANO
VIA BRIGALDARA, 20
37029 SAN PIETRO IN CARIANO [VR]
TEL. 0457701055
www.brigaldara.it

CELLAR SALES
PRE-BOOKED VISITS
ANNUAL PRODUCTION 300,000 bottles
HECTARES UNDER VINE 50.00

Stefano Cesari is the heart and soul of
Brigaldara, a family winery that has around
50 hectares, partly in the classic zone and
partly in the more eastern area, at a range
of altitudes, exploiting a variety of aspects
and staggered harvesting so as to get the
best out of each vintage. In the summer,
the grapes are dried with care, and Stefano
uses them to produce wines of great
aromatic intensity, which are supple, never
overpowering. The entire range is dedicated
to the classic wines of the territory. The
Ripasso Il Vegro shows a traditional nose
and beautifully firm palate, showing how
Ripasso can have an identity of its own
without simply copying Amarone. It is
however the latter type that provides the
winery's two champions: the Case Vecie,
from eastern vineyards, shows a ripe, juicy
nose of red berry fruit swathed in medicinal
herbs and toasty notes, leading into a rich,
succulent palate. The Classico shows
cherry jam and a dynamic palate.

● Amarone della Valpolicella Case Vecie '10	▼▼ 6
● Amarone della Valpolicella Cl. '11	▼▼ 6
● Valpolicella Cl. '14	▼▼ 3
● Valpolicella Cl. Sup. Ripasso Il Vegro '13	▼▼ 4
○ Soave '14	▼ 3
● Amarone della Valpolicella Case Vecie '07	▽▽▽ 7
● Amarone della Valpolicella Case Vecie '03	▽▽▽ 7
● Amarone della Valpolicella Case Vecie '00	▽▽▽ 6
● Amarone della Valpolicella Cl. '10	▽▽▽ 7
● Amarone della Valpolicella Cl. '06	▽▽▽ 6
● Amarone della Valpolicella Cl. '05	▽▽▽ 6
● Amarone della Valpolicella Ris. '07	▽▽▽ 8

Sorelle Bronca

FRAZ. COLBERTALDO
VIA MARTIRI, 20
31020 VIDOR [TV]
TEL. 0423987201
www.sorellebronca.com

CELLAR SALES
PRE-BOOKED VISITS
ACCOMMODATION
ANNUAL PRODUCTION 300,000 bottles
HECTARES UNDER VINE 22.00
VITICULTURE METHOD Certified Organic

There are few wineries in Valdobbiadene
territory that can count on large vineyard
holdings; they usually rely on a network of
growers to provide the cellar with grapes.
Ersiliana and her daughter Elisa, Antonella
and her husband Piero, meanwhile, tend
around 20 hectares on hillside plots, mainly
planted to glera, for overall production of
300,000 bottles per year. The range of still
wines, while marginal in terms of volume, is
excellent. Also this year, the Particella 68 is
Bronca's most convincing wine. This
Valdobbiadene is produced solely using
grapes from the vineyard lying in land
registry map parcel 68, and is refermented
directly from the must. Its nose of tropical
fruit and lime blossom is followed by a
beautifully harmonious, elegant palate. The
Ser Bele is, as always, a red of great
presence and maturity, with a dynamic
palate and excellent length.

● Colli di Conegliano Rosso Ser Bele '12	▼▼ 5
○ Valdobbiadene Brut Particella 68 '14	▼▼ 4
○ Valdobbiadene Brut	▼▼ 3
○ Valdobbiadene Extra Dry	▼▼ 3
● Colli di Conegliano Rosso Ser Bele '09	▽▽▽ 5
● Colli di Conegliano Rosso Ser Bele '05	▽▽▽ 5
○ Valdobbiadene Brut Particella 68 '13	▽▽▽ 4*
○ Colli di Conegliano Bianco Delico '12	▽▽ 3
● Colli di Conegliano Rosso Ser Bele '11	▽▽ 5
● Colli di Conegliano Rosso Ser Bele '10	▽▽ 5
● Colli di Conegliano Rosso Ser Bele '08	▽▽ 5
○ Valdobbiadene Brut Particella 68 '12	▽▽ 4
○ Valdobbiadene Brut Particella 68 '11	▽▽ 4

Luigi Brunelli

VIA CARIANO, 10
37029 SAN PIETRO IN CARIANO [VR]
TEL. 0457701118
www.brunelliwine.com

CELLAR SALES
PRE-BOOKED VISITS
ACCOMMODATION
ANNUAL PRODUCTION 90,000 bottles
HECTARES UNDER VINE 12.00

The Brunelli family's winery owns around ten hectares in the Valpolicella Classica DOC zone, plus a few vineyards in nearby Custoza. Luigi and his son Alberto supervise all the phases of work, from the rows to the bottle, producing under 100,000 bottles per year. Alongside the classic wines of the territory, they offer a range of fragrant, drinkable inventive wines from native varieties. This year's selection was entirely dedicated to the wines of the DOC zone, with the Amarone Campo del Titari missing top honours by a whisker. Intense aromas of red berry fruit, spice and medicinal herbs are exalted on a firm, potent palate. The Campo Inferi is more closed on the nose, but shows dynamic on the palate, with stiff tannins which still need time to soften. The Pa' Riondo is fragrant and pleasurably harmonious.

Buglioni

FRAZ. CORRUBIO
VIA CAMPAGNOLE, 55
37029 SAN PIETRO IN CARIANO [VR]
TEL. 0456760681
www.buglioni.it

CELLAR SALES
PRE-BOOKED VISITS
ANNUAL PRODUCTION 70,000 bottles
HECTARES UNDER VINE 48.00

Mariano Buglioni's winery covers almost 40 hectares in the Valpolicella Classica zone, with around 15 hectares at Corrubbio, around the lovely cellar, and the rest situated in dotted around the valleys of San Pietro in Cariano and Sant'Ambrogio. The winery produces more grapes than it needs, which allows Mariano and the oenologist Diego Bertoni to select the best batches for partial drying or immediate vinification. The Amarone shows intense aromas of super-ripe fruit, with attractive mineral nuances peeping through. Attack on the palate is warm and velvety, but the wine progresses with decisiveness, recovering focus and length. We saw a convincing performance from Il Ruffiano, a Valpolicella Superiore from partially dried grapes, giving a nose of ripe fruit and spice, over a taut, linear palate. Sunnier and more approachable, the Bugiardo is a firm, juicy Ripasso.

● Amarone della Valpolicella Cl. Campo del Titari Ris. '10	▼▼ 8
● Amarone della Valpolicella Cl. Campo Inferi Ris. '10	▼▼ 8
● Amarone della Valpolicella Cl. '11	▼▼ 8
● Valpolicella Cl. Ripasso Pa' Riondo '13	▼▼ 3
● Recioto della Valpolicella Cl. '13	▼ 5
● Valpolicella Cl. '14	▼ 2
● Amarone della Valpolicella Cl. Campo del Titari '97	▼▼▼ 8
● Amarone della Valpolicella Cl. Campo del Titari '96	▼▼▼ 8
● Amarone della Valpolicella Cl. Campo del Titari Ris. '09	♀♀ 8
● Amarone della Valpolicella Cl. Campo Inferi Ris '06	♀♀ 8
● Amarone della Valpolicella Cl. Campo Inferi Ris. '07	♀♀ 8

● Amarone della Valpolicella Cl. L'Amarone '10	▼▼ 6
● Valpolicella Cl. Sup. Il Ruffiano '13	▼▼ 3
● Valpolicella Cl. Sup. Ripasso Il Bugiardo '12	▼▼ 4
● Amarone della Valpolicella Cl. L'Amarone '04	♀♀ 6
● Recioto della Valpolicella Cl. '03	♀♀ 5
● Recioto della Valpolicella Cl. Il Recioto '05	♀♀ 5
● Valpolicella Cl. Sup. Il Ruffiano '04	♀♀ 3*
● Valpolicella Cl. Sup. Il Ruffiano '02	♀♀ *
● Valpolicella Cl. Sup. Ripasso Il Bugiardo '05	♀♀ 4
● Valpolicella Cl. Sup. Ripasso Il Bugiardo '04	♀♀ 4
● Valpolicella Cl. Sup. Ripasso Il Bugiardo '03	♀♀ 4

Ca' Ferri

VIA CA' FERRI, 43
35020 CASALSERUGO [PD]
TEL. 049655518
www.vinicaferri.com

CELLAR SALES
PRE-BOOKED VISITS
ANNUAL PRODUCTION 10,000 bottles
HECTARES UNDER VINE 8.00

Ca' Ferri is the brainchild of Gian Paolo
Prandstraller, and was set up around 15
years ago. It is now one of the most
interesting wineries in the Colli Euganei.
The vineyards are spread over two distinct
territories, the Parco Regionale dei Colli
Euganei and the plains around
Casalserugo. The former provides the
outfit's top wine, the Taurilio, and the latter
a convincing line of products imprinted with
aromatic fragrance and drinkability. Taurilio
is the star at Ca' Ferri, with an outstanding
performance. The aromatic profile ranges
from ripe red berry fruit to spice, taking in
fresh-cut flowers and medicinal herbs on
the way. The wine shows marvellous
nose-palate consistency, and offers a firm
body perfectly buttressed by acidity and
smooth tannins. In the Ser Ugo line we
appreciated the fresh, approachable
Cabernet, with its nose of fresh fruit and
pepper.

● Colli Euganei Rosso Taurilio '13	♥♥	2*
● Corti Benedettine Cabernet Ser Ugo '13	♥	1*
● Corti Benedettine Merlot Ser Ugo '13	♥	1*
○ Manzoni Bianco Ser Ugo '13	♥	1*
● Raboso Ser Ugo '13	♥	1*
● Colli Euganei Rosso Taurilio '12	♥♥	3
● Colli Euganei Rosso Taurilio '11	♥♥	3
● Corti Benedettine Cabernet Ser Ugo '12	♥♥	3
● Corti Benedettine Cabernet Ser Ugo '11	♥♥	3

Ca' La Bionda

FRAZ. VALGATARA
VIA BIONDA, 4
37020 MARANO DI VALPOLICELLA [VR]
TEL. 0456801198
www.calabionda.it

CELLAR SALES
PRE-BOOKED VISITS
ANNUAL PRODUCTION 150,000 bottles
HECTARES UNDER VINE 29.00
VITICULTURE METHOD Certified Organic

Brothers Alessandro and Nicola Castellani
manage the family business in great
harmony with their father Pietro. The
vineyards cover around 30 hectares within
the classic zone, mainly in the Marano
Valley, at elevations of 150–300 metres,
which give the grapes great finesse and
aromatic freshness. Production is entirely
dedicated to the traditional types of the
area, interpreted without excessive drying
of the grapes, for elegant results with great
ageing potential. In the duel between
Ravazzol and Campo Casal Vegri, the
Amarone wins by a whisker. A bright ruby
hue is followed by a nose of cherry, thyme
and pepper, exalted on the palate, where
exuberance is reined in by fresh, tangy
acidity, underpinned by glossy tannins. The
Valpolicella Superiore, meanwhile, is a
sunnier character, with fruit aromas
accompanied by mineral nuances and
Mediterranean scrub, over a savoury,
relaxed, leisurely palate.

● Amarone della Valpolicella Cl. Vign. di Ravazzol '11	♥♥♥	8
● Valpolicella Cl. Sup. Campo Casal Vegri '13	♥♥	5
● Valpolicella Cl. '14	♥♥	2*
● Valpolicella Cl. Sup. Ripasso Malavoglia '12	♥♥	4
● Amarone della Valpolicella Cl. Vign. di Ravazzol '07	♥♥♥	6
● Valpolicella Cl. Sup. Campo Casal Vegri '11	♥♥♥	5
● Amarone della Valpolicella Cl. Vign. di Ravazzol '09	♥♥	8
● Amarone della Valpolicella Cl. Vign. di Ravazzol Ris. '05	♥♥	6
● Valpolicella Cl. Sup. Campo Casal Vegri '12	♥♥	5

Ca' Lustra - Zanovello

LOC. FAEDO
VIA SAN PIETRO, 50
35030 CINTO EUGANEO [PD]
TEL. 042994128
www.calustra.it

CELLAR SALES
PRE-BOOKED VISITS
ANNUAL PRODUCTION 170,000 bottles
HECTARES UNDER VINE 25.50
VITICULTURE METHOD Certified Organic
SUSTAINABLE WINERY

Franco Zanovello and his son Marco run the family winery according to organic principles. Over 20 hectares within the Parco Regionale dei Colli Euganei constitute a viticultural asset of great value, whose plots are worked and vinified separately, to allow each one to express itself to the full. Production is divided into two lines, one dedicated to entry-level wines, and the Zanovello for more ambitious labels. Natio is a Bordeaux blend from long maceration and three years' oak ageing. The hot 2009 harvest endowed it with deep, ripe aromas, which come to the fore on a full, luscious palate of great elegance. The more tropical, summery Fior d'Arancio Passito shows a nose of candied peel and liquorice, whose irrepressible sweetness is perfectly offset by full flavour. The Nero Musqué is a splendid curiosity, a late-harvest Moscato Nero from Parenzo which the producer himself calls a "migrant" wine.

Ca' Orologio

VIA CA' OROLOGIO, 7A
35030 BAONE [PD]
TEL. 042950099
www.caorologio.com

CELLAR SALES
PRE-BOOKED VISITS
ACCOMMODATION
ANNUAL PRODUCTION 24,000 bottles
HECTARES UNDER VINE 12.00
VITICULTURE METHOD Certified Organic

Ca' Orologio, found right in the south of the Colli Euganei, covers a dozen hectares along the slopes of Mount Cecilia, where the vineyards alternate with small patches of woodland. Here, in an organic set-up, Mariagioia Rosellini grows mainly traditional red grape varieties: merlot, cabernet sauvignon and carmenere, which have been planted in this area for over a century. Her elegant range of wines have a superb sense of place. The hot 2012 harvest gave the Calaóne an even sunnier, more Mediterranean character than usual, with red berry fruit interlaced with swathes of Mediterranean scrub, spice and dried flowers. On the palate this abundance is judiciously managed, and thanks to glossy tannins and tangy acidity, the wine benefits in terms of length and grip. Salaróla is instead a blend of moscato and pinot bianco, showing a fresh, crisper nose over a long, succulent palate.

○ Colli Euganei Fior d'Arancio Passito '10	🍷🍷 4
● Colli Euganei Rosso Natio '09	🍷🍷 5
● Colli Euganei Cabernet '12	🍷🍷 2*
○ Colli Euganei Manzoni Bianco Pedevenda '13	🍷🍷 3
● Colli Euganei Rosso Moro Polo '12	🍷🍷 3
○ Moscato Secco 'A Cengia '13	🍷🍷 3
● Nero Musqué '12	🍷🍷 4
○ Colli Euganei Bianco Olivetani '13	🍷 2
○ Colli Euganei Fior d'Arancio Spumante '14	🍷 3
● Marzemino Belvedere '12	🍷 2
● Colli Euganei Cabernet Girapoggio '05	🍷🍷🍷 3
○ Colli Euganei Fior d'Arancio Passito '07	🍷🍷🍷 4
● Colli Euganei Merlot Sassonero Villa Alessi '05	🍷🍷🍷 3

● Colli Euganei Rosso Calaóne '12	🍷🍷 4
○ Salaróla '14	🍷🍷 3
● Colli Euganei Rosso Calaóne '05	🍷🍷🍷 3*
● Relógio '09	🍷🍷🍷 4*
● Relógio '07	🍷🍷🍷 4
● Relógio '06	🍷🍷🍷 4
● Relógio '04	🍷🍷🍷 4*
● Colli Euganei Rosso Calaóne '11	🍷🍷 4
● Colli Euganei Rosso Calaóne '10	🍷🍷 4
● Relógio '11	🍷🍷 5
● Relógio '10	🍷🍷 5

VENETO

★Ca' Rugate

VIA PERGOLA, 36
37030 MONTECCHIA DI CROSARA [VR]
TEL. 0456176328
www.carugate.it

CELLAR SALES
PRE-BOOKED VISITS
ANNUAL PRODUCTION 600,000 bottles
HECTARES UNDER VINE 72.00

Today, the most popular Italian white wine internationally is Pinot Grigio, but if we just go back a few years, Soave was the worldwide favourite. Today, Michele Tessari at Ca' Rugate represents the bond with that tradition, producing wines which manage to be classic and innovative at the same time, interpreting changing times but firmly rooted in values such as the territory, heritage varieties and a respect for tradition. Once again we saw a range of wines from Tessari without any weak points. Our favourite was, not for the first time, the Soave Monte Alto, a white from garganega that shows a perfect fusion of varietal aromas and oak, with an elegant nose and good progression on the palate. It fully deserved a Tre Bicchieri. Studio and Monte Fiorentine show fresh aromas and a crisp palate. We should also mention an impressive leap in quality for the Amarone and Valpolicella Campo Lavei.

○ Soave Cl. Monte Alto '13	♟♟♟ 3*
● Amarone della Valpolicella '11	♟♟ 7
○ Recioto di Soave La Perlara '12	♟♟ 5
○ Soave Cl. Monte Fiorentine '14	♟♟ 3*
○ Studio '13	♟♟ 4
● Valpolicella Sup. Campo Lavei '13	♟♟ 4
○ Lessini Durello Pas Dosé Amedeo M. Cl. '10	♟♟ 5
○ Soave Cl. San Michele '14	♟♟ 2*
● Valpolicella Rio Albo '14	♟♟ 2*
○ Soave Cl. Monte Alto '11	♟♟♟ 3*
○ Soave Cl. Monte Alto '10	♟♟♟ 3*
○ Soave Cl. Monte Alto '09	♟♟♟ 3*
○ Soave Cl. Monte Fiorentine '13	♟♟♟ 3*
○ Studio '10	♟♟♟ 4*

Giuseppe Campagnola

FRAZ. VALGATARA
VIA AGNELLA, 9
37020 MARANO DI VALPOLICELLA [VR]
TEL. 0457703900
www.campagnola.com

CELLAR SALES
PRE-BOOKED VISITS
ANNUAL PRODUCTION 4,800,000 bottles
HECTARES UNDER VINE 130.00

Situated in the northern part of the Marano Valley, Giuseppe Campagnola's winery has managed to grow while retaining a deep bond with this land and its traditions. Looking at the numbers, we might imagine a large-scale industry, but in fact all of the production in the Verona area is based on long-standing agreements with local growers, that together with the undisputed skills of the technical staff result in solid, traditional wines. We saw a fine performance from the winery's two flagship labels, the Amarone and Valpolicella Superiore Caterina Zardini. The former shows ripe, sweet aromas of red berry fruit, with depth provided by spice and cocoa powder, leading into a full palate with good stuffing and a leisurely finish. The Valpolicella offers a more elegant nose, with fresh fruit swathed in fines herbes and pepper, while on the palate, its greater freshness is evident in its dynamic progression and satisfying grip.

● Amarone della Valpolicella Cl. Caterina Zardini Ris. '10	♟♟ 6
● Valpolicella Cl. Sup. Caterina Zardini '13	♟♟ 3*
● Amarone della Valpolicella Cl. Vign. Vallata di Marano '12	♟♟ 5
● Valpolicella Cl. Sup. Ripasso '13	♟♟ 3
⊙ Bardolino Cl. Chiaretto Roccolo del Lago '14	♟ 2
● Bardolino Cl. Roccolo del Lago '14	♟ 2
⊙ Pinot Grigio Vign. Campo dei Gelsi Arnaces '14	♟ 2
● Recioto della Valpolicella Cl. Casotto del Merlo '12	♟ 5
○ Soave Cl. Monte Foscarino Le Bine '14	♟ 2
● Valpolicella Cl. Le Bine '14	♟ 2
● Amarone della Valpolicella Cl. Caterina Zardini '04	♟♟♟ 6

I Campi

LOC. ALLODOLA
FRAZ. CELLORE D'ILLASI
VIA DELLE PEZZOLE, 3
37032 ILLASI [VR]
TEL. 0456175915
www.icampi.it

CELLAR SALES
PRE-BOOKED VISITS
ANNUAL PRODUCTION 60,000 bottles
HECTARES UNDER VINE 14.00

Flavio Prà has finally managed to transfer the entire production process to the new, intimate winery at Cellore di Illasi, in eastern Valpolicella, both for the Soave and local classic reds. Alongside innovations in the cellar there are also those in the rows, with important acquisitions of land in northern Valpolicella, where Flavio, rising to the challenge of altitude and wide temperature ranges, aims to pursue even greater elegance in his wines. Elegance is the distinctive trait of a great version of Campo Ciotoli, a Ripasso that plays on aromatic finesse and grip rather than fullness. Long, dense and fragrant, it had no trouble taking a Tre Bicchieri. The Soave Campo Vulcano, meanwhile, boasts fresh, almost pungent aromas, over a dry, linear palate. Bursting with ripe aromas, the Amarone Campo Marna offers a dry, leisurely palate.

● Valpolicella Sup. Ripasso Campo Ciotoli '13	♟♟♟ 3*
○ Soave Cl. Campo Vulcano '14	♟♟ 3*
● Amarone della Valpolicella Campi Lunghi '12	♟♟ 6
● Amarone della Valpolicella Campo Marna 500 '09	♟♟ 8
● Campo Prognare '10	♟♟ 8
○ Soave Campo Base '14	♟ 2
○ Soave Cl. Campo Vulcano '13	♟♟♟ 3*
○ Soave Cl. Campo Vulcano '12	♟♟♟ 3*
○ Soave Cl. Campo Vulcano '11	♟♟♟ 5
○ Soave Cl. Campo Vulcano '10	♟♟♟ 3*
○ Soave Cl. Campo Vulcano '09	♟♟♟ 3*
○ Soave Cl. Campo Vulcano '08	♟♟♟ 3*

Canevel Spumanti

LOC. SACCOL
VIA ROCCAT E FERRARI, 17
31049 VALDOBBIADENE [TV]
TEL. 0423975940
www.canevel.it

PRE-BOOKED VISITS
ANNUAL PRODUCTION 700,000 bottles
HECTARES UNDER VINE 12.00
VITICULTURE METHOD Certified Organic

The Saccol winery is a chapter in the modern history of Prosecco, with extensive vineyards and the precious contributions of around 60 growers, assisted throughout the year, who provide the cellar with grapes. Today, the operation is run by Tatiana and Carlo, wife and son of the founder, Carlo Caramel, together with trusty oenologist Roberto De Lucchi and with Roberto Covre, who deals with sales. Although production has increased significantly over the last 30 years, it has remained faithful to the traditional types, interpreted with precision and skill. The Millesimato is an Extra Dry with intense aromas of apple and pear, and delicate floral nuances which encore on the dynamic, zesty palate. The Cartizze shows a riper, sunnier nose, over a harmonious palate in which sweetness, acidity and sparkle are perfectly balanced. The Vigneto del Faè has impressive grip.

○ Cartizze '14	♟♟ 5
○ Valdobbiadene Brut '14	♟♟ 4
○ Valdobbiadene Dosaggio Zero Vign. del Faè '14	♟♟ 4
○ Valdobbiadene Extra Dry Il Millesimato '14	♟♟ 5
○ Valdobbiadene Extra Dry '14	♟ 4

Cantina del Castello

CORTE PITTORA, 5
37038 SOAVE [VR]
TEL. 0457680093
www.cantinacastello.it

CELLAR SALES
PRE-BOOKED VISITS
ANNUAL PRODUCTION 130,000 bottles
HECTARES UNDER VINE 12.00

After a few years in which the wines of
Arturo Stocchetti failed to convince us
completely, the winery is back on excellent
form. Merit obviously goes to Arturo's skill,
but also to the extraordinary terroir of his
vineyards, covering a dozen hectares in the
heart of the Soave Classico DOC zone,
which over the years have been replanted
and are now finally reaching maturity. The
products embody a supple, drinkable style
of wine. The Soave Carniga is released
after extremely long cellar ageing, and
shows its excellence already on the nose.
Harking from a west-facing vineyard at an
elevation of around 150 metres, it shows
intense notes of dried flowers and
yellow-fleshed fruit, perfectly echoed on the
palate, which progresses with grip and
good length, leading into a dry, elegant
finish. The more approachable, fresh
Pressoni plays on its aromatic fragrance
and drinkability.

La Cappuccina

FRAZ. COSTALUNGA
VIA SAN BRIZIO, 125
37032 MONTEFORTE D'ALPONE [VR]
TEL. 0456175036
www.lacappuccina.it

CELLAR SALES
PRE-BOOKED VISITS
RESTAURANT SERVICE
ANNUAL PRODUCTION 300,000 bottles
HECTARES UNDER VINE 42.00
VITICULTURE METHOD Certified Organic

Elena, Sisto and Pietro Tessari head up a
winery that converted to organic long
before it was fashionable. The fine estate
covers around 40 hectares on the eastern
side of the Soave DOC zone. Right from the
outset, they chose a row training system,
which allowed less invasive vineyard
management, a decision that turned out to
be especially useful in difficult harvests
such as 2014. Tessari's range was entirely
dedicated to Soave this year, with a tour de
force Recioto Arzimo. On the nose, aromas
of candied peel and blossom join forces
with attractive tropical nuances, paving the
way for liquorice and ginger. On the palate,
sweetness comes to the fore, but is kept in
line by tangy thrust. We loved the Soave,
which, despite the difficult 2014 harvest,
gave an impressive performance. The
Fontégo vineyard gives its name to an
elegant, succulent white.

Wine	Rating
○ Soave Cl. Carniga '11	♀♀ 3*
○ Soave Cl. Pressoni '14	♀♀ 3
○ Soave Cl. Castello '14	♀ 2
○ Soave Cl. Sup. Monte Pressoni '01	♀♀♀ 3
○ Recioto di Soave Cl. Ardens '08	♀♀ 5
○ Soave Cl. Carniga '10	♀♀ 3
○ Soave Cl. Carniga '08	♀♀ 3
○ Soave Cl. Carniga '07	♀♀ 3
○ Soave Cl. Castello '12	♀♀ 2*
○ Soave Cl. Castello '08	♀♀ 2
○ Soave Cl. Castello '07	♀♀ 2*
○ Soave Cl. Pressoni '13	♀♀ 3
○ Soave Cl. Pressoni '08	♀♀ 3*
○ Soave Cl. Pressoni '07	♀♀ 3

Wine	Rating
○ Recioto di Soave Arzimo '12	♀♀ 5
○ Soave '14	♀♀ 2*
○ Soave Fontégo '14	♀♀ 2*
○ Soave San Brizio '13	♀ 3
● Campo Buri '10	♀♀ 4
● Campo Buri '09	♀♀ 4
● Carmenos Passito '11	♀♀ 4
○ Recioto di Soave Arzimo '11	♀♀ 4
○ Recioto di Soave Arzimo '10	♀♀ 4
○ Recioto di Soave Arzimo '08	♀♀ 4
○ Soave '11	♀♀ 2*
○ Soave Fontégo '13	♀♀ 2*
○ Soave Fontégo '12	♀♀ 2*
○ Soave Monte Stelle '13	♀♀ 3
○ Soave San Brizio '11	♀♀ 3
○ Soave San Brizio '10	♀♀ 3

Le Carline

VIA CARLINE, 24
30020 PRAMAGGIORE [VE]
TEL. 0421799741
www.lecarline.com

CELLAR SALES
PRE-BOOKED VISITS
ANNUAL PRODUCTION 400,000 bottles
HECTARES UNDER VINE 18.00
VITICULTURE METHOD Certified Organic

Le Carline was established in the late 1950s, as a livestock farm also producing grapes, but with the arrival of Daniele Piccini, the current owner and heart and soul of the operation, Pramaggiore became what we know today. Around 20 hectares of vineyards cultivated with organic methods and enjoying the particular conditions of this DOC zone, characterized by closeness to the Adriatic and clayey soil, which gives the grapes unique character. Dogale is a late-harvest wine from verduzzo grapes which are dried at length, vinified, then aged in barriques for nine months. The result is a wine with complex aromas, showing notes of dates, caramel and spice, followed through on the palate, where sweetness never steals the limelight, but is part of a full-flavoured, elegantly harmonious whole. The Carline Rosso is a sunny, fragrant Bordeaux blend with a splash of refosco.

● Carline Rosso '12		♟♟ 3
○ Dogale Passito		♟♟ 3
○ Lison Cl. '14		♟ 2
● Lison-Pramaggiore Cabernet '14		♟ 2
○ Spumante Brut		♟ 2
○ Venezia Pinot Grigio '14		♟ 2
● Carline Rosso '11		♀♀ 3
● Carline Rosso '10		♀♀ 3
● Carline Rosso '07		♀♀ 4
● Carline Rosso '07		♀♀ 4
○ Lison Cl. '12		♀♀ 2*
○ Lison-Pramaggiore Lison '09		♀♀ 2*
● Lison-Pramaggiore Refosco P.R. senza solfiti aggiunti '13		♀♀ 2*

Carpenè Malvolti

VIA ANTONIO CARPENÉ, 1
31015 CONEGLIANO [TV]
TEL. 0438364611
www.carpene-malvolti.com

PRE-BOOKED VISITS
ANNUAL PRODUCTION 5,300,000 bottles
HECTARES UNDER VINE 26.00

Carpenè Malvolti is not just a winery; it is an institution. Due to its role within the Prosecco DOC zone, it cannot be compared to any other operation in the area and, more than any other, it is the winery that took Treviso sparklers to the forefront of the international scenario. Despite its size, it displays an unchanged love for this land and an ability to produce focused, fragrant white sparkling wines, thanks also to grapes from a close-knit network of hill growerss. If it were possible, production now focuses even more on Prosecco, and to support this, the owners have decided to go back to marketing the wines themselves. A new wine, the PVXINVM, debuted with an excellent performance. This Extra Dry offers an intense nose and fresh fruit, followed by harmonious progression on the palate, nicely supported by fine sparkle. The Extra Dry 1868 is firm and juicy.

○ Cartizze 1868		♟♟ 5
○ Conegliano Valdobbiadene Extra Dry 1868		♟♟ 3
○ Conegliano Valdobbiadene Extra Dry PVXINVM '14		♟♟ 5
○ Conegliano Valdobbiadene Brut 1868		♟ 3
○ Conegliano Valdobbiadene Dry 1868		♟ 3

Casa Cecchin

VIA AGUGLIANA, 11
36075 MONTEBELLO VICENTINO [VI]
TEL. 0444649610
www.casacecchin.it

PRE-BOOKED VISITS
ANNUAL PRODUCTION 25,000 bottles
HECTARES UNDER VINE 7.00

Gambellara territory, which covers around 1,000 hectares at the foot of the hills, seems to usher in that of Lessinia, which is infinitely larger but has much less land planted to vine. Renato and Roberta Cecchin's work here focuses on the traditional varieties garganega and durella, interpreted without frills and pursuing territorial character and good varietal typing. Garganella is used only for still wines, while durella also ends up in classic method sparklers. The wines proposed by the Cecchin family this year were all impeccable, but our favourite was the Durello San Nicolò, opening to a delicate nose of flowers and white-fleshed fruit. On the palate, this incredibly drinkable wine changes gear, and shows dry, gutsy and beautifully long, with surprising character. The Nostrum is a sparkler that spends three years on the lees, and offers a fragrant nose perfectly buttressed by acidity and fizz in the mouth.

○ Lessini Durello Extra Brut Nostrum M. Cl '10	♈♈ 4
○ Lessini Durello Il Durello '14	♈♈ 2*
○ Lessini Durello Non Dosato M. Cl. Ris. '09	♈♈ 5
○ Lessini Durello San Nicolò '14	♈♈ 2*
○ Lessini Durello Brut M. Cl. Ris. '08	♈♈ 3
○ Lessini Durello Brut M. Cl. Ris. '07	♈♈ 3
○ Lessini Durello Il Durello '13	♈♈ 2*
○ Lessini Durello Sup. '09	♈♈ 2*
○ Lessini Il Durello '12	♈♈ 2*

Casa Roma

VIA ORMELLE, 19
31020 SAN POLO DI PIAVE [TV]
TEL. 0422855339
www.casaroma.com

CELLAR SALES
PRE-BOOKED VISITS
ANNUAL PRODUCTION 250,000 bottles
HECTARES UNDER VINE 17.00

Luigi Peruzzetto, a persevering grower who works along the banks of the Piave, has managed to build up Casa Roma while remaining faithful to this wine country. Around 20 hectares, characterized by alternating gravel and clay, are dedicated to a style of viticulture in which each variety exploits the soil most congenial to it. Alongside international varieties, which have been in this area for over a century, great importance is given to native varieties, in particular raboso. It is no easy task to endow elegance and lightness to a wine whose production protocol envisages the use of partially-dried raboso, not a variety known for its finesse. Gigi Peruzzetto has managed to do the impossible, and his wine boasts mature, sweet aromas without sacrificing freshness and floral charm, while on the palate the wine combines potency and finesse, ending long and captivating. This was a superb performance. We also liked the stiffer, tauter Raboso Piave, and the Nesio, which gets better every year.

● Piave Malanotte '09	♈♈ 6
⊙ Nesio Brut M. Cl. '10	♈♈ 5
● Piave Raboso '10	♈♈ 4
● Raboso Passito Callarghe '09	♈♈ 5
○ Marzemina Bianca '14	♈ 3
● Piave Carmenère '14	♈ 2
○ Piave Manzoni Bianco '14	♈ 2
● Venezia Cabernet Sauvignon '14	♈ 2
● Venezia Merlot '14	♈ 2
⊙ Nesio Brut M. Cl. '09	♈♈ 5
● Piave Raboso '09	♈♈ 4
● Piave Raboso '06	♈♈ 4
● Pro Fondo Rosso Frizzante '13	♈♈ 2*
○ San Dordi '13	♈♈ 2*

Case Paolin

VIA MADONNA MERCEDE, 53
31040 VOLPAGO DEL MONTELLO [TV]
TEL. 0423871433
www.casepaolin.it

CELLAR SALES
PRE-BOOKED VISITS
ANNUAL PRODUCTION 75,000 bottles
HECTARES UNDER VINE 12.00
VITICULTURE METHOD Certified Organic
SUSTAINABLE WINERY

Going from Treviso towards the foothills, the plateau of Montello stands in isolation almost halfway along the journey, with one side facing the plains and the other the Piave riverbanks, looking towards the Prosecco hills. The Pozzobon brothers operate in this area, with vineyards that extend for a dozen hectares between the plains and the slopes of Montello itself, using organic methods to grow Bordeaux varieties along with Manzoni bianco and, naturally, glera. The Pozzobon brothers have proposed an excellent version of their Asolo Brut, a Prosecco opening to floral and white-fleshed fruit aromas on the nose. On the palate, it shows the originality of this territory, which gives the grapes good acid backbone and full flavour, perfectly supported by the caressing fizz. The Rosso del Milio is a Bordeaux blend showing a mature nose of fruit and spice, over a supple, juicy palate. We were won over by the Costa degli Angeli, a complex, crisp Manzoni Bianco.

○ Asolo Brut	♟♟ 2
○ Manzoni Bianco Costa degli Angeli '13	♟♟ 3
● Rosso del Milio '12	♟♟ 3
● Cabernet '14	♟ 2
○ Prosecco di Treviso Extra Dry	♟ 2
○ Manzoni Bianco Santi Angeli '12	♟♟ 2*
● Montello e Colli Asolani Rosso del Milio '11	♟♟ 3
● Montello e Colli Asolani Rosso del Milio '10	♟♟ 3
● Montello e Colli Asolani Rosso del Milio '09	♟♟ 3*
● Montello e Colli Asolani Sup. San Carlo '11	♟♟ 4
○ Soér Passito '11	♟♟ 4

Michele Castellani

FRAZ. VALGATARA
VIA GRANDA, 1
37020 MARANO DI VALPOLICELLA [VR]
TEL. 0457701253
www.castellanimichele.it

CELLAR SALES
PRE-BOOKED VISITS
ANNUAL PRODUCTION 300,000 bottles
HECTARES UNDER VINE 50.00

Sergio Castellani has been at the head of the family business since the 1990s, and now has plots covering around 50 hectares, some his own and some rented vineyards. He is supported with skill and passion by his children Michele, Mara and Martina. In the cellar at Valgatara the batches of grapes are divided on the basis of provenance and quality, to be used for the two lines that represent the winery, the Ca' del Pipa and the Castei. Sergio's aim is to bring out the fullness that partial drying confers on the wines of this area. The excellent Recioto was once again this year one of the most interesting from the DOC zone. The Monte Fasenara offers a nose dominated by sweet, juicy red berry fruit, over subtle hints of medicinal herbs and spice. On the palate, its evident sweetness is offset by attractive acidic thrust. Among the Amarones presented, we appreciated the rich nose and taut, full-flavoured palate of the Cinquestelle.

● Recioto della Valpolicella Cl. Monte Fasenara I Castei '12	♟♟ 5
● Amarone della Valpolicella Cl. Campo Casalin I Castei '11	♟♟ 6
● Amarone della Valpolicella Cl. Cinquestelle Collezione Ca' del Pipa '11	♟♟ 7
● Amarone della Valpolicella Cl. Italia I Castei '12	♟♟ 5
● Valpolicella Cl. Sup. Ripasso Costamaran I Castei '13	♟♟ 3
● Italia I Castei '13	♟ 4
● Valpolicella Cl. Campo del Biotto I Castei '14	♟ 2
● Amarone della Valpolicella Cl. Cinquestelle Collezione Ca' del Pipa '10	♟♟ 7
● Recioto della Valpolicella Cl. Monte Fasenara I Castei '10	♟♟ 5

★Cavalchina

LOC. CAVALCHINA
FRAZ. CUSTOZA
VIA SOMMACAMPAGNA, 7
37066 SOMMACAMPAGNA [VR]
TEL. 045516002
www.cavalchina.com

CELLAR SALES
PRE-BOOKED VISITS
ANNUAL PRODUCTION 445,000 bottles
HECTARES UNDER VINE 50.00

Established in the heart of the Custoza DOC
zone, the winery of the Piona brothers has
developed towards the Mincio and
Valpolicella, so now covers around 50
hectares. This means three areas and their
products for Luciano and Franco: the
fragrant wines of the Veronese banks of
Lake Garda; the solid wines of Tenuta
Prendina; and lastly, the exuberance of
reds from part-dried grapes. Great attention
is given to viticulture and an approach at
the winery aimed at preserving to the
utmost the characteristics of the grapes.
Once again, the winery from Custoza
presented an impressive range, led by the
superb Custoza Amedeo. Its fresh, elegant
nose shows tropical fruit, making way for
fresh-cut flowers and mineral hints, leading
into the palate that manages to be rich, yet
supple and fresh. We were extremely
impressed with the Amarone, which, thanks
to the hot harvest, shows a full, summery
nose, over a powerful, warm palate.

○ Custoza Sup. Amedeo '13	♉♉♉ 3*
● Amarone della Valpolicella Torre d'Orti '11	♉♉ 6
● Bardolino Sup. S. Lucia '13	♉♉ 3
○ Custoza '14	♉♉ 2*
● Garda Cabernet Sauvignon Falcone Prendina '12	♉♉ 4
○ Garda Garganega Paroni Prendina '13	♉♉ 3
● Garda Merlot Faial Prendina '12	♉♉ 5
○ Garda Sauvignon Valbruna Prendina '13	♉♉ 2*
⊙ La Rosa Passito '14	♉♉ 3
● Bardolino '14	♉ 2
⊙ Bardolino Chiaretto '14	♉ 2
○ Garda Pinot Bianco Prendina '14	♉ 3
○ Pinot Grigio Prendina '14	♉ 2
● Valpolicella Ripasso Torre d'Orti '12	♉ 3
● Valpolicella Sup. Morari Torre d'Orti '12	♉ 4

Cavazza

C.DA SELVA, 22
36054 MONTEBELLO VICENTINO [VI]
TEL. 0444649166
www.cavazzawine.com

CELLAR SALES
PRE-BOOKED VISITS
ACCOMMODATION
ANNUAL PRODUCTION 860,000 bottles
HECTARES UNDER VINE 150.00

The family farms no fewer than 150
hectares between the Gambellara and Colli
Berici DOC zones. Established between the
wars, the winery has grown from what was
once a small farm to become a benchmark
in both the districts. Today, production is
mainly dedicated to garganega at
Gambellara and to red Bordeaux varieties in
the Colli Berici, where they are also joined
by the traditional tai rosso variety. We saw
a good performance from the wines from
the estate in the Colli Berici, with the
Cabernet showing aromas of ripe red berry
fruit, pepper and medicinal herbs, paving
the way for a full, taut palate, buttressed by
attractively rugged, crisp tannins. The more
summery, open Merlot shows seductive
notes of autumn leaves and more delicate,
glossy tannins. The Corallo, meanwhile,
shows the gentler side of tai rosso, offering
elegant aromas over a full-flavoured,
supple palate.

● Colli Berici Cabernet Cicogna '12	♉♉ 4
● Colli Berici Merlot Cicogna '12	♉♉ 4
● Colli Berici Tai Rosso Corallo '13	♉♉ 3
● Fornetto '12	♉ 3
○ Gambellara Cl. La Bocara '14	♉ 2
○ Recioto di Gambellara Cl. Capitel S. Libera '11	♉ 4
● Colli Berici Cabernet Cicogna '11	♉♉ 4
● Colli Berici Cabernet Cicogna '10	♉♉ 4
● Colli Berici Merlot Cicogna '11	♉♉ 4
● Colli Berici Merlot Cicogna '10	♉♉ 4
○ Gambellara Cl. Creari '12	♉♉ 3
○ Gambellara Cl. Creari '10	♉♉ 3
○ Gambellara Cl. La Bocara '12	♉♉ 2*
○ Recioto di Gambellara Cl. Capitel S. Libera '10	♉♉ 4
● Syrah Cicogna '11	♉♉ 4

Giorgio Cecchetto

FRAZ. TEZZE DI PIAVE
VIA PIAVE, 67
31028 VAZZOLA [TV]
TEL. 043828598
www.rabosopiave.com

CELLAR SALES
PRE-BOOKED VISITS
ANNUAL PRODUCTION 200,000 bottles
HECTARES UNDER VINE 73.00
SUSTAINABLE WINERY

Year after year, Giorgio Cecchetto and his wife Cristina develop the family winery, which now extends to over 70 hectares. They work on three plots: the original land at Tezze di Piave around the cellar, distributed on the gravelly plains of the Piave, at Motta di Livenza with its more clayey soils, and lastly at Cornuda, the only one near the hills, in which attention focuses entirely on the production of glera. Giorgio and Cristina's dedication to the production of Raboso resulted in a 2011 version that expressed intense notes of fresh fruit, with a touch of refreshing lightness provided by vegetal hints. In the mouth, the typically rustic nature of the variety is offset by smooth tannins, for taut, elegant progression. The Sante Rosso is a Merlot that offers super-ripe red berry fruit on the nose and a full, juicy, approachable palate.

Gerardo Cesari

LOC. SORSEI, 3
37010 CAVAION VERONESE [VR]
TEL. 0456260928
www.cesariverona.it

CELLAR SALES
PRE-BOOKED VISITS
ANNUAL PRODUCTION 1,600,000 bottles
HECTARES UNDER VINE 109.00
SUSTAINABLE WINERY

This winery at Cavaion has interests in various DOC zones, but the heart of its activity is linked to Valpolicella. Its entry into the Caviro group did not lead to changes in management, and once again this year the wines of the Cesari winery convinced our tasters. The most important vineyards are in the heart of Valpolicella Classica, at Sant'Ambrogio, Castelrotto and Corrubbio, supported by the Centofilari estate at Lugana, whose wines benefit from long ageing in the cellar. The Amarone Il Bosco comes from a single vineyard on the slopes of Castelrotto, at an elevation of around 150 metres. The grapes from the hot 2009 harvest were dried at length, and give the wine a mature, sunny character, dominated by red berry jam, over a full palate with incredibly delicate tannins. The fresher, more floral, citrusy Lugana Cento Filari shows a lean, juicy profile.

● Piave Raboso '11	♟♟ 3
⊙ Rosa Bruna Cuvée 21 Brut M.Cl. '11	♟♟ 3
● Sante Rosso '12	♟♟ 3
● Cabernet Sauvignon '14	♟ 2
● Carmenère '14	♟ 2
○ Manzoni Bianco '14	♟ 2
● Malanotte Gelsaia '11	♟♟ 5
● Merlot Sante Rosso '11	♟♟ 3
● Merlot Sante Rosso '10	♟♟ 3
● Merlot Sante Rosso '09	♟♟ 3*
⊙ Rosa Bruna Cuvée 21 Brut M.Cl. '10	♟♟ 3

● Amarone della Valpolicella Cl. Il Bosco '09	♟♟ 7
○ Lugana Cento Filari '14	♟♟ 3
● Amarone della Valpolicella Cl. '11	♟ 6
● Jèma Corvina Veronese '11	♟ 5
● Valpolicella Sup. Ripasso Mara '13	♟ 3
● Amarone della Valpolicella Bosan '06	♟♟ 8
● Amarone della Valpolicella Bosan '05	♟♟ 8
● Amarone della Valpolicella Cl. Il Bosco '08	♟♟ 7
● Amarone della Valpolicella Cl. Il Bosco '07	♟♟ 7
● Valpolicella Sup. Ripasso Bosan '11	♟♟ 5
● Valpolicella Sup. Ripasso Mara '10	♟♟ 3

Italo Cescon

FRAZ. RONCADELLE
P.ZZA DEI CADUTI, 3
31024 ORMELLE [TV]
TEL. 0422851033
www.cesconitalo.it

CELLAR SALES
PRE-BOOKED VISITS
ANNUAL PRODUCTION 800,000 bottles
HECTARES UNDER VINE 115.00
VITICULTURE METHOD Certified Organic

Italo Cescon's winery, with its great
tradition, in recent years has managed to
find new energy and ambition in the work
of the siblings Gloria, Graziella and
Domenico, who have taken over from their
parents and radically transformed the
family business, remaining strongly linked
to their roots but also investing in the
future. Compared to the past, the cellar
now has larger vineyard holdings, and the
traditional range with the hallmark cane
cutting tied to the bottle has now been
joined by a high-profile line. If there is a
winery in Veneto that is exploring the
enormous potential of Manzoni bianco, it is
without doubt that of the Cescon brothers.
The unfiltered version, aged in oak, offers
mature, deep aromas of yellow-fleshed
fruit, gradually making way for citrus and
flint. The full-bodied, taut palate shows
great flavour and length. The Bordeaux
blend Chieto shows a complex nose and
harmonious palate.

● Amaranto 72 '12	♟♟	5
● Chieto '12	♟♟	4
○ Manzoni Bianco Non Filtrato '13	♟♟	5
○ Manzoni Bianco Svejo '14	♟♟	3
● Piave Raboso Rabià '10	♟	5
○ Sauvignon Mejo '14	♟	3
● Amaranto 72 '11	♟♟	5
● Chieto '11	♟♟	3
● Chieto '10	♟♟	3
○ Manzoni Bianco Non Filtrato '12	♟♟	3
○ Manzoni Bianco Non Filtrato '11	♟♟	3
○ Manzoni Bianco Svejo '11	♟♟	2*

Coffele

VIA ROMA, 5
37038 SOAVE [VR]
TEL. 0457680007
www.coffele.it

CELLAR SALES
PRE-BOOKED VISITS
ANNUAL PRODUCTION 120,000 bottles
HECTARES UNDER VINE 25.00
VITICULTURE METHOD Certified Organic

Alberto and Chiara Coffele have managed
to give continuity to the winery created by
their father Giuseppe and mother Giovanna,
and today run a fine operation covering 25
hectares in a single plot at Castelcerino,
where the altitude and temperature ranges
allow garganega and trebbiano grapes to
ripen while maintaining enviable freshness
and lightness. Grape-drying takes place in
the first-rate facility at Castecerino;
vinification and ageing in the heart of
Soave. Alberto and Chiara give of their best
in difficult harvests, and their 2014 is a
textbook performance. The Ca' Visco, from
vineyards high in the hills, shows no signs
of suffering from the difficult year, and
offers intense layers of white-fleshed fruit
and blossom, swathed in persistent mineral
notes, over a surprisingly firm, taut, gutsy
palate. As always, we were captivated by
the harmonious, caressing Recioto Le
Sponde.

○ Soave Cl. Ca' Visco '14	♟♟♟	3*
○ Recioto di Soave Cl. Le Sponde '13	♟♟	5
○ Soave Cl. Alzari '13	♟♟	3
○ Soave Cl. '14	♟	2
○ Recioto di Soave Cl. Le Sponde '09	♟♟♟	5
○ Soave Cl. Ca' Visco '05	♟♟♟	3*
○ Soave Cl. Ca' Visco '04	♟♟♟	2
○ Soave Cl. Ca' Visco '03	♟♟♟	2
○ Soave Cl. Alzari '11	♟♟	3*
○ Soave Cl. Ca' Visco '13	♟♟	3*
○ Soave Cl. Ca' Visco '12	♟♟	3*
○ Terra Crea Passito '06	♟♟	8

Col Vetoraz

FRAZ. SANTO STEFANO
S.DA DELLE TRESIESE, 1
31040 VALDOBBIADENE [TV]
TEL. 0423975291
www.colvetoraz.it

CELLAR SALES
PRE-BOOKED VISITS
ANNUAL PRODUCTION 800,000 bottles
HECTARES UNDER VINE 12.00

The Col Vetoraz winery and headquarters
are on the hill of the same name,
overlooking the small Cartizze zone,
surrounded by extremely steep vineyards.
Francesco Miotto, Paolo De Bortoli and
Loris Dall'Acqua have managed to turn this
operation into one of the most respected in
the entire DOC zone, with an appealing
style that has attracted fans from all over
the world. The sparklers of Col Vetoraz are
fragrant, fresh and wonderfully supple. We
saw an excellent performance from the
Cartizze, a sparkler from the most
important vineyard in the DOC zone with
intense fruit and citrus on the nose
swathed in delicate floral notes. The palate
surprises with its perfect fusion of
sweetness, acidity and fizz, for a satisfying,
juicy result. Diametrically opposed is the
style of the Zero, a Valdobbiadene which,
as its name suggests, is a pas dosé,
offering a floral nose followed by a gutsy,
unforgettable palate.

○ Cartizze '14	♏♏ 4
○ Valdobbiadene Brut Zero '14	♏♏ 3
○ Valdobbiadene Dry Mill. '14	♏♏ 3
○ Valdobbiadene Brut '14	♏ 3
○ Valdobbiadene Extra Dry '14	♏ 3
○ Valdobbiadene Dry '13	♍♍ 3
○ Valdobbiadene Dry '12	♍♍ 3*

Le Colture

FRAZ. SANTO STEFANO
VIA FOLLO, 5
31049 VALDOBBIADENE [TV]
TEL. 0423900192
www.lecolture.it

CELLAR SALES
PRE-BOOKED VISITS
ACCOMMODATION
ANNUAL PRODUCTION 700,000 bottles
HECTARES UNDER VINE 35.00

Cesare Ruggeri, today helped by his
children Silvia, Veronica and Alberto, has
managed to develop the family business by
maintaining important relations with local
growers and at the same time developing
large vineyard holdings of his own. The
rows lie mainly in the heart of
Valdobbiadene, although there are also
vineyards in the nearby zone of Montello.
The most interesting wine from the Ruggeri
family comes from the most famous
subzone in the DOC zone, Cartizze. The
nose opens to intense notes of apple, pear
and wisteria, while on the palate, the wine
unfolds with grace and fullness, perfectly
offset by fizz. The Gerardo, from the nearby
Rive di Santo Stefano, expresses a more
floral character, and a gutsy, taut palate.
We also loved the caressing Cruner, with its
delicate residual sweetness.

○ Cartizze	♏♏ 3
○ Valdobbiadene Brut Fagher	♏♏ 3
○ Valdobbiadene Dry Cruner	♏♏ 3
○ Valdobbiadene Extra Dry Pianer	♏♏ 3
○ Valdobbiadene Sup. Rive di Santo Stefano Brut Gerardo '14	♏♏ 3
○ Rosé Brut	♏ 2
○ Valdobbiadene Extra Dry Prime Gemme '14	♏ 3
○ Valdobbiadene Sup. Rive di Santo Stefano Brut Gerardo '13	♍♍ 3

VENETO

Vignaioli Contrà Soarda

S.DA SOARDA, 26
36061 BASSANO DEL GRAPPA [VI]
TEL. 0424505562
www.contrasoarda.it

CELLAR SALES
PRE-BOOKED VISITS
RESTAURANT SERVICE
ANNUAL PRODUCTION 80,000 bottles
HECTARES UNDER VINE 20.00
VITICULTURE METHOD Certified Organic

Mirco Gottardi came to viticulture a little late, but has taken on this new challenge with enthusiasm and great commitment. Today, helped by his wife Gloria and son Marcello, he farms around 20 hectares in Breganze, where the volcanic nature of the soil offers an interesting basis for viticulture. His passion for wine, together with an interpretation of the territory which is still evolving, has led Mirco to produce a range of innovative labels that explore the zone's great potential. The range proposed by the Gottardi family continues to expand, with interest also shown in experiments on alternative vinification methods. The Vignacorejo remains the most important wine, a Pinot Nero that impresses with the depth of its aromas, with wild berries increasingly making way for medicinal herbs and spices, over a firm, lingering palate. The Torcolato Sarson shows well-balanced sweetness and a nose of apricot and tropical fruit.

● Breganze Pinot Nero Vignacorejo '12	♥♥ 7
○ Breganze Torcolato Sarson Ris. '12	♥♥ 5
● Musso Serafino '10	♥♥ 3
● 121 b.C. Carmenere '12	♥ 5
○ 121 b.C. Vespaiolo '13	♥ 5
● Breganze Rosso Terre di Lava Ris. '10	♥ 4
○ Breganze Vespaiolo Soarda '14	♥ 3
○ Breganze Vespaiolo Vignasilan '12	♥ 4
● Marzemino Nero Gaggion '12	♥ 3
● Rosso '11	♥ 4
● Breganze Rosso Terre di Lava Ris. '05	♀♀ 5
● Contrà Soarda '09	♀♀ 3
● Marzemino Nero Gaggion '11	♀♀ 3
● Vigna Correjo '10	♀♀ 7

Corte Gardoni

LOC. GARDONI, 5
37067 VALEGGIO SUL MINCIO [VR]
TEL. 0457950382
www.cortegardoni.it

CELLAR SALES
PRE-BOOKED VISITS
ANNUAL PRODUCTION 200,000 bottles
HECTARES UNDER VINE 25.00

The Corte Gardoni estate covers over 50 hectares in the morainic hills to the south of Lake Garda. In reality, only half of this area is under vine, while the remaining land bears witness to the origins of this operation, which has been growing fruit since the 1980s. The founder, Gianni Piccoli, has gradually made way for his sons, Mattia, Andrea and Stefano, while he continues to supervise and give advice. The Custoza Mael is always one of the most interesting in the DOC zone, also this year swathed in elegant aromas led by blossom, against a backdrop of white-fleshed fruit and notes of flint, which will come to the fore with ageing. The character of the 2014 vintage is evident on the palate, showing leanness and good length. The Pradicà opens to a complex, spicy nose, sustained on the elegant, juicy palate.

● Bardolino Sup. Pradicà '13	♥♥ 3*
○ Custoza Mael '14	♥♥ 3*
● Bardolino Le Fontane '14	♥♥ 2*
⊙ Becco Rosso '13	♥♥ 3
⊙ Bardolino Chiaretto '14	♥ 2
○ Custoza '14	♥ 2
⊙ Bianco di Custoza Mael '09	♀♀♀ 2*
⊙ Bianco di Custoza Mael '08	♀♀♀ 2*
○ Custoza Mael '13	♀♀♀ 3*
○ Custoza Mael '11	♀♀♀ 3*
● Bardolino Sup. Pradicà '11	♀♀ 3*
○ Custoza Mael '12	♀♀ 3*

Corte Moschina

VIA MOSCHINA, 1
37030 RONCÀ [VR]
TEL. 0457460788
www.cortemoschina.it

CELLAR SALES
PRE-BOOKED VISITS
ANNUAL PRODUCTION 75,000 bottles
HECTARES UNDER VINE 28.00
SUSTAINABLE WINERY

The zone of Roncà, at the eastern end of the Soave DOC zone, is turning out to be one of the new frontiers for this Veronese white, with a large number of wineries on the way up. These include Corte Moschina, a family-run operation covering around 30 hectares, only in part providing grapes for bottled wines. Great attention is dedicated to the production of Soave, but Classic Method sparklers are also rapidly gaining importance. In the space of a few years, Corte Moschina has made a few well judged adjustments, and today the range proposed by the winery at Roncà has few weak points. Our favourite was I Tarai, a Soave from a late harvest that shows an intense nose of ripe peach and apricot, with a hint of oak that amplifies its warmth. On the palate, meanwhile, richness is offset by racy energy, making this one of the most interesting new wines in the DOC zone.

Corte Rugolin

FRAZ. VALGATARA
LOC. RUGOLIN, 1
37020 MARANO DI VALPOLICELLA [VR]
TEL. 0457702153
www.corterugolin.it

CELLAR SALES
PRE-BOOKED VISITS
ANNUAL PRODUCTION 80,000 bottles
HECTARES UNDER VINE 12.00

In the chaos of Valpolicella, where some wineries have grown out of all proportion in recent years, it is a pleasure to see an operation such as that of the Coati siblings, Elena and Federico, who step-by-step have developed the family business, concentrating on quality rather than volume. A dozen hectares under vine produce fewer than 100,000 bottles, entirely dedicated to the classic types of Valpolicella, interpreted in a focused, fragrant style. This was a year to remember for the Coati brothers, with all the wines proving to be perfect examples of their types, and two, namely the Amarone Monte Danieli and Valpolicella Superiore San Giorgio, making our finals. We were particularly impressed with the latter, which on its debut immediately won us over with its focused, elegant nose and dynamic, refined palate, expressing all the potential of this territory. The Monte Danieli, meanwhile, is a mature, gutsy red.

○ Raise '12	♥♥ 5
○ Recioto di Soave Incanto '11	♥♥ 4
○ Soave Evaos '14	♥♥ 2*
○ Soave I Tarai '13	♥♥ 3
○ Soave Roncathe '14	♥♥ 2*
● Cabernet Colle Alto '13	♥ 3
○ Lessini Durello Extra Brut M. Cl. '10	♀♀ 4
○ Recioto di Soave Incanto '10	♀♀ 4
○ Recioto di Soave Incanto '08	♀♀ 4
○ Soave Evaos '13	♀♀ 2*
○ Soave I Tarai '12	♀♀ 3*
○ Soave I Tarai '11	♀♀ 3
○ Soave I Tarai '10	♀♀ 3*
○ Soave Roncathe '13	♀♀ 2*

● Amarone della Valpolicella Cl. Monte Danieli '10	♥♥ 7
● Valpolicella Cl. Sup. San Giorgio '13	♥♥ 5
● Amarone della Valpolicella Cl. Crosara de le Strie '10	♥♥ 6
● Recioto della Valpolicella Cl. '13	♥♥ 5
● Valpolicella Cl. '14	♥♥ 2*
● Valpolicella Cl. Sup. Ripasso '12	♥♥ 4
● Amarone della Valpolicella Cl. Monte Danieli '09	♀♀ 6
● Amarone della Valpolicella Cl. Monte Danieli '04	♀♀ 7
● Amarone della Valpolicella Cl. Monte Danieli '03	♀♀ 6
● Valpolicella Cl. Sup. Ripasso '11	♀♀ 4
● Valpolicella Cl. Sup. Ripasso '10	♀♀ 4
● Valpolicella Cl. Sup. Ripasso '04	♀♀ 3

Corte Sant'Alda

LOC. FIOI
VIA CAPOVILLA, 28
37030 MEZZANE DI SOTTO [VR]
TEL. 0458880006
www.cortesantalda.it

CELLAR SALES
PRE-BOOKED VISITS
ACCOMMODATION
ANNUAL PRODUCTION 90,000 bottles
HECTARES UNDER VINE 19.00
VITICULTURE METHOD Certified Biodynamic

Corte Sant'Alda was one of the first
wineries in Valpolicella to convert its
production process in line with the ideas of
Rudolf Steiner, achieving biodynamic
certification that it does not see simply as
something to mention on the labels but
which reflects a more respectful and less
invasive approach to the environment. The
20-or-so hectares in the hills surrounding
the house-cellar give wines that respect
tradition and have a sense of place. The hot
2011 harvest gave the Amarone
Valmezzane a mature, juicy profile, with a
fruit-driven nose that somewhat subdued
the aromas of medicinal herbs and spice.
On the palate, the wine is approachable
and juicy, and plays on its fullness of
flavour. The intriguing Ripasso Campi Magri
shows a nose of forest floor and damp
leaves against a backdrop of cherry and
blackberry, leading into a captivating palate
which manages to be both rich and supple.

● Amarone della Valpolicella	
Valmezzane '11	♥♥ 8
● Valpolicella Sup. Ripasso	
Campi Magri '12	♥♥ 4
○ Agathe '14	♥♥ 4
○ Soave '14	♥♥ 3
● Valpolicella Ca' Fiui '14	♥♥ 3
● Amarone della Valpolicella '10	♥♥♥ 8
● Amarone della Valpolicella '06	♥♥♥ 7
● Amarone della Valpolicella '00	♥♥♥ 7
● Amarone della Valpolicella '98	♥♥♥ 7
● Valpolicella Sup. '03	♥♥♥ 3*
● Valpolicella Sup. Mithas '04	♥♥♥ 6

Dal Cero
Tenuta di Corte Giacobbe

VIA MOSCHINA, 11
37030 RONCÀ [VR]
TEL. 0457460110
www.vinidalcero.com

CELLAR SALES
PRE-BOOKED VISITS
ANNUAL PRODUCTION 300,000 bottles
HECTARES UNDER VINE 38.00

In recent decades, the Dal Cero family has
managed to develop its winery in Soave
and also a Tuscan estate near Cortona. The
heart and soul, however, remain faithfully
rooted in the Verona area and in the
capable hands of Francesca, Davide,
Alberto, and Nico, winning an excellent
reputation. The vineyards are planted on
volcanic soils in the hills, where garganega
rules the roost, with pinot grigio playing a
supporting role. Every year the Runcata
becomes more interesting, with well-dosed
oak and judicious ageing, which gives the
wines complex aromas of white-fleshed
fruit and spice, with subtle hints of dried
flowers providing depth. On the firm, gutsy
palate, oak is evident, but does nothing to
hinder progression, leading to a long, dry
finish. We also loved the fresh, juicy Soave
2014, while among the sparklers we
appreciated the class of the Augusto.

○ Soave Sup. Vign. Runcata '13	♥♥ 2*
○ Brut M. Cl.	♥♥ 3
○ Dosaggio Zero M. Cl. Cuvée Augusto '10	♥♥ 5
○ Soave '14	♥♥ 2*
○ Pinot Grigio '14	♥ 2
○ Pinot Grigio Ramato '14	♥ 2
○ Soave Runcata '10	♥♥ 2*
○ Soave Runcata '09	♥♥ 2*
○ Soave Sup. Runcata '12	♥♥ 2*
○ Soave Sup. Runcata '11	♥♥ 2*

Luigino Dal Maso

c.da Selva, 62
36054 Montebello Vicentino [VI]
Tel. 0444649104
www.dalmasovini.com

CELLAR SALES
PRE-BOOKED VISITS
ANNUAL PRODUCTION 450,000 bottles
HECTARES UNDER VINE 30.00

The 30 hectares of vineyards distributed in the Gambellara and Colli Berici DOC zones are the most important assets of Dal Maso, in addition to the important legacy left by its founder Luigino: a passion for this land and for wine. Today, Anna, Silvia and Nicola Dal Maso run the family business with the same passion, and it is a benchmark both for Gambellara and the Colli Berici DOC zone. The solid, reliable range is dedicated to the classic wines of the territory. We saw an impressive debut for the winery's Vin Santo di Gambellara di casa, a passito from garganega grapes aged for over ten years before bottling. Its brown hue is indicative of its nose, brimming with dried figs, hazelnuts and aromatic herbs, while on the palate it is even more irrepressible, with a sweetness of rare concentration and a seemingly endless finish. The Colpizzarda, meanwhile, is the usual champion of finesse and aromatic freshness, and shows a dense, elegant palate.

● Colli Berici Tai Rosso Colpizzarda '13	♥♥ 4
○ Gambellara Cl. Vin Santo '03	♥♥ 8
● Cabernet Casara Roveri '13	♥♥ 4
● Colli Berici Merlot Casara Roveri '12	♥♥ 4
○ Gambellara Cl. Ca' Fischele '14	♥♥ 2*
● Montebelvedere '13	♥♥ 3
○ Serafino '14	♥♥ 2*
● Terra dei Rovi Rosso '13	♥♥ 5
○ Gambellara Cl. Riva del Molino '07	♥♥♥ 2*
● Colli Berici Merlot Casara Roveri '11	♀♀ 4
● Colli Berici Tai Rosso Colpizzarda '12	♀♀ 2*
● Colli Berici Tai Rosso Colpizzarda '12	♀♀ 3*
● Colli Berici Tai Rosso Colpizzarda '10	♀♀ 3*
○ Gambellara Cl. Riva del Molino '11	♀♀ 3*
○ Recioto di Gambellara Cl. Riva dei Perari '11	♀♀ 5
● Terra dei Rovi Rosso '12	♀♀ 5

De Stefani

via Cadorna, 92
30020 Fossalta di Piave [VE]
Tel. 042167502
www.de-stefani.it

CELLAR SALES
PRE-BOOKED VISITS
ANNUAL PRODUCTION 300,000 bottles
HECTARES UNDER VINE 40.00
SUSTAINABLE WINERY

Alessandro De Stefani, with the precious assistance of his father Tiziano, has turned the family winery into a small treasure dedicated to a solid, consistently convincing range of wines. The vineyards are distributed in three areas: Fossalta di Piave and Monastier, in which clay soils show their influence, and Refrontolo, where alongside glera we find extensive plantings of marzemino, used for the winery's top label. Fossalta presented a wide range of convincing wines this year, starting with Olmera, a blend of tai and sauvignon that sacrifices some of its former richness to give a more interesting result, with a fresher, more elegant nose over a long, supple palate. Among the reds, we saw a similar approach in the Soler, a Bordeaux blend with a splash of marzemino and refosco, showing fresh, variegated aromas, echoed on the fruity, satisfying palate.

● Colli di Conegliano Refrontolo Passito '12	♥♥ 6
● Kreda Refosco '12	♥♥ 5
○ Olmera '14	♥♥ 5
● Plavis '13	♥♥ 4
● Soler '13	♥♥ 4
○ Vitalys '14	♥♥ 2*
○ Pinot Grigio '14	♥ 3
○ Venis '14	♥ 3
● Kreda '11	♀♀ 5
○ Olmera '13	♀♀ 5
● Soler '11	♀♀ 5
○ Vitalys '12	♀♀ 3

Conte Emo Capodilista La Montecchia

VIA SALAROLA
35030 BAONE [PD]
TEL. 049637294
www.lamontecchia.it

CELLAR SALES
PRE-BOOKED VISITS
ACCOMMODATION
ANNUAL PRODUCTION 130,000 bottles
HECTARES UNDER VINE 30.00

Giordano Capodilista is one of the most attentive growers in Colli Euganei, a land of volcanic origin that allows red grapes to ripen perfectly, and particularly Bordeaux varieties, which have been planted here for almost two centuries. The vineyards are distributed among various estates, the first around the cellar in the area to the north of the hills, and the second at the other end, where the winery manages to produce grapes of extraordinary richness. It is precisely the vineyards further south, on Mount Castello, that provide the grapes for the Ireneo, a Cabernet Sauvignon with mature, spicy aromas, followed by fruit, coming to the fore only afterwards, and almost concealing the notes of Mediterranean scrub. The rich, succulent palate shows focused, gentle tannins. The Donna Daria is the usual thoroughbred, with an intense nose of apricot and orange blossom over an approachable, caressing palate of great harmony.

Farina

LOC. PEDEMONTE
VIA BOLLA, 11
37029 SAN PIETRO IN CARIANO [VR]
TEL. 0457701349
www.farinawines.com

CELLAR SALES
PRE-BOOKED VISITS
ANNUAL PRODUCTION 650,000 bottles
HECTARES UNDER VINE 10.00

The winery of the Farina family is today solidly led by a trio of young entrepreneurs: Claudio, Elena and Davide, who have managed to give a new lease of life to an operation that started out a century ago. The vineyards cover around ten hectares at Castelrotto and Masua, in addition to a further 35 hectares owned by growers who have been working with the winery for many years. Production is dedicated to the reds of Valpolicella, and partly to the wines of Lake Garda. The Amarone Montefante is a Riserva that boasts complexity on the nose, although the fruit is held back by spice and oak, and takes time to emerge. The palate is more approachable and juicy, and perfectly buttressed by acidity and tannins. Of the two Valpolicella di Ripassos, we preferred the Montecorna for its mature aromas, dominated by sweet, appealing red berry fruit, echoed on the long palate.

● Colli Euganei Cabernet Sauvignon Ireneo '12	▼▼▼ 4*
○ Colli Euganei Fior d'Arancio Passito Donna Daria '13	▼▼ 5
● Baon '12	▼▼ 5
● Ca' Emo '13	▼▼ 2*
● Colli Euganei Merlot '13	▼▼ 5
● Colli Euganei Villa Capodilista '12	▼▼ 5
○ Colli Euganei Fior d'Arancio Spumante '14	▼ 2
○ Colli Euganei Pinot Bianco '14	▼ 2
● Godimondo '14	▼ 2
○ Piùchebello '14	▼ 2
● Progetto Recupero '12	▼ 3
○ Colli Euganei Fior d'Arancio Passito Donna Daria '06	▼▼▼ 5
● Baon '06	♀♀ 5
○ Colli Euganei Fior d'Arancio Passito Donna Daria '07	♀♀ 5

● Amarone della Valpolicella Cl. '12	▼▼ 5
● Amarone della Valpolicella Cl. Montefante Ris. '10	▼▼ 8
● Recioto della Valpolicella Cl. '13	▼▼ 5
● Valpolicella Cl. Sup. Ripasso Montecorna '13	▼▼ 3
● Valpolicella Cl. Sup. Ripasso Remo Farina '13	▼▼ 2*
● Corte Conti Cavalli '13	▼ 4
● Amarone della Valpolicella Cl. Montefante Ris. '09	♀♀ 8
● Amarone della Valpolicella Cl. Montefante Ris. '07	♀♀ 8
● Valpolicella Cl. Sup. Ripasso Montecorna '12	♀♀ 3
● Valpolicella Cl. Sup. Ripasso Remo Farina '12	♀♀ 2*

Fattori

FRAZ. TERROSSA
VIA OLMO, 6
37030 RONCÀ [VR]
TEL. 0457460041
www.fattoriwines.com

CELLAR SALES
PRE-BOOKED VISITS
ANNUAL PRODUCTION 242,000 bottles
HECTARES UNDER VINE 57.00
SUSTAINABLE WINERY

Antonio Fattori, an experienced producer in the Soave area, has managed to change gear over the last decade. Today, alongside important production dedicated to bianco scaligero, he is also making the reds of Valpolicella, the result of an important investment in Col de la Bastia, where the 12 hectares of vineyards are dominated by the new cellar, surrounded by dense woodland that frames for this splendid location. The most interesting results however come from Soave, with a natural version of Recioto Motto Piane. On the nose, intense notes of apricot and tropical fruits combine with hazelnut, leading into irrepressible sweetness on the palate, offset by full flavour and attractive acidity. We also enjoyed the fruity, floral Soave, showing a delicate, taut palate. Among the reds, the Amarone expresses powerful maturity on the nose, over a rounded, velvety palate.

● Amarone della Valpolicella '10	♟♟	8
○ Recioto di Soave Motto Piane '13	♟♟	5
○ Soave Cl. Danieli '14	♟♟	2*
○ Soave Cl. Runcaris '14	♟♟	2*
○ Soave Motto Piane '13	♟♟	3
● Valpolicella Ripasso Col de la Bastia '12	♟♟	5
○ Lessini Durello Brut I Singhe	♟	3
○ Lessini Durello Brut Roncà M. Cl. '11	♟	4
○ Pinot Grigio Valparadiso '14	♟	3
○ Roncha '13	♟	3
○ Sauvignon Vecchie Scuole '14	♟	3
● Valpolicella Col de la Bastia '13	♟	3
○ Recioto di Soave Motto Piane '12	♟♟	4
○ Sauvignon Vecchie Scuole '13	♟♟	3
○ Soave Motto Piane '12	♟♟	3

Filippi

LOC. CASTELCERINO
VIA LIBERTÀ, 55
37038 SOAVE [VR]
TEL. 0457675005
www.cantinafilippi.it

CELLAR SALES
PRE-BOOKED VISITS
ANNUAL PRODUCTION 60,000 bottles
HECTARES UNDER VINE 20.00
VITICULTURE METHOD Certified Organic

Filippo Filippi is the heart and soul of the family winery, located high in the hills of Castelcerino, an historic property dedicated almost entirely to garganega and trebbiano di Soave. At an elevation of 400 metres these are probably the highest vineyards in the Soave DOC zone. The operation started out providing grapes for a cooperative, and subsequently started to bottle its own wine a decade ago, when it also took steps to introduce methods that limited environmental impact. Today, Filippo works to organic and eco-friendly methods, and in spring the vineyards are covered with wild flowers. Intervention in the cellar is also kept to a minimum. The excellent Soave Castelcerino is a Garganega that opens to intense notes of sulphur over white fleshed fruit and flowers, leading into a relaxed, tangy palate with good grip. We found the Monteseroni to be attractively rustic and gutsy.

○ Soave Castelcerino '13	♟♟	2*
○ Soave Colli Scaligeri Monteseroni '13	♟♟	2*
○ Soave Colli Scaligeri Vigna della Brà '13	♟	2
○ Susinaro '13	♟	3
○ Turbiana '13	♟	2
○ Recioto di Soave Calprea '06	♟♟	5
○ Recioto di Soave Calprea '05	♟♟	5
○ Recioto di Soave Calprea '04	♟♟	5
○ Soave Colli Scaligeri Castelcerino '06	♟♟	2*
○ Soave Colli Scaligeri Castelcerino '05	♟♟	2*
○ Soave Colli Scaligeri Monteseroni '06	♟♟	2

Il Filò delle Vigne

VIA TERRALBA, 14
35030 BAONE [PD]
TEL. 042956243
www.ilfilodellevigne.it

CELLAR SALES
PRE-BOOKED VISITS
ANNUAL PRODUCTION 50,000 bottles
HECTARES UNDER VINE 20.00

Il Filò delle Vigne is one of the most interesting wineries in the Colli Euganei DOC zone, lying at the southern end of the Parco Regionale dei Colli and covering around 20 hectares. Carlo Giordani and Niccolò Voltan have found in Matteo Zanaica a precious assistant, able to manage all of the winery's activities with care and expertise, resulting in a limited range but one of great quality. Alongside the Bordeaux varieties, the winery focuses on those of tradition, which are transformed into an original red. The peerless Cabernet Borgo delle Casette is a Riserva that offers an intense, fruit-driven nose with hints of spice, Mediterranean scrub and pencil lead, that perfectly express the sunny character of this red. On the palate, the wine shows full and juicy, backed up by vibrant, attractively rugged tannins. We enjoyed the Cecilia di Baone, aged entirely in concrete, for its approachable aromas and firm palate. The Terralba di Baone is mineral and succulent.

Silvano Follador

LOC. FOLLO
FRAZ. SANTO STEFANO
VIA CALLONGA, 11
31040 VALDOBBIADENE [TV]
TEL. 0423900295
www.silvanofollador.it

CELLAR SALES
PRE-BOOKED VISITS
ANNUAL PRODUCTION 20,000 bottles
HECTARES UNDER VINE 3.50

If there is a winery that reserves respect and passion for Prosecco, without pursuing commercial success at all costs, it is without doubt that of Silvano and Alberta Follador. A few hectares tended with the utmost deference to the environment, without turning to outside growers, allow the siblings from Santo Stefano to produce wines with a marked sense of place, in the pursuit of the best expression of the variety-vineyard combination, without the crutch of sweetness or aromatic excess. The characterful Valdobbiadene Brut Nature presents an attractive bright straw yellow, and is more deeply hued than we would expect from this type of Prosecco. On the nose, it shows white-fleshed fruit and flowers with a deep mineral swathe. The palate, whose richness is not a result of sweetness, but of the expressive power of the fruit, shows good grip and length, perfectly sustained by fizz. The Dosaggio Zero meanwhile shows more complex aromas and a delicate palate.

● Colli Euganei Cabernet Borgo delle Casette Ris. '11	🍷🍷 5
● Colli Euganei Cabernet Cecilia di Baone Ris. '12	🍷🍷 4
○ Terralba di Baone '13	🍷🍷 3
● Colli Euganei Cabernet Borgo delle Casette Ris. '10	🍷🍷🍷 5
● Colli Euganei Cabernet Borgo delle Casette Ris. '09	🍷🍷 5
● Colli Euganei Cabernet Borgo delle Casette Ris. '08	🍷🍷 5
● Colli Euganei Cabernet Borgo delle Casette Ris. '07	🍷🍷 5
● Colli Euganei Cabernet V. Cecilia di Baone Ris. '11	🍷🍷 4
● Io di Baone '11	🍷🍷 3*
● Io di Baone '08	🍷🍷 3

○ Valdobbiadene Brut Nature '14	🍷🍷 4
○ Valdobbiadene Sup. Brut Dosaggio Zero M. Cl. '12	🍷🍷 3
○ Cartizze Brut '08	🍷🍷🍷 4
○ Cartizze Brut '10	🍷🍷 4
○ Cartizze Brut Nature '13	🍷🍷 4
○ Cartizze Brut Nature '11	🍷🍷 4
○ Cartizze Nature '12	🍷🍷 4
○ Valdobbiadene Brut Dosaggio Zero M. Cl. '10	🍷🍷 3
○ Valdobbiadene Brut Nature '13	🍷🍷 4
○ Valdobbiadene Brut Nature '12	🍷🍷 3*

Le Fraghe

LOC. COLOMBARA, 3
37010 CAVAION VERONESE [VR]
TEL. 0457236832
www.fraghe.it

CELLAR SALES
PRE-BOOKED VISITS
ACCOMMODATION
ANNUAL PRODUCTION 120,000 bottles
HECTARES UNDER VINE 28.00
VITICULTURE METHOD Certified Organic

Matilde Poggi has been a grower for 30 years, yet chatting with her, time seems to have stood still. She has the same enthusiasm as always, the same passion, but greater awareness of her role as a custodian of the land, and of the way in which a territory can express its character in wine. She farms under 30 hectares using organic methods in superb wine country, with gravelly soils and a climate that benefits from alternating breezes from Lake Garda and Valdadige. The Brol Grande comes from the homonymous south-facing vineyard at Affi, at an elevation of 190 metres, and is aged in large oak. A year after harvest, the wine displays an attractive pale ruby hue, followed by a nose of forest fruits and spice, echoed on the taut, savoury palate. The Bardolino 2014, meanwhile, exploits the cool harvest to highlight its racy, spirited character. The classy Quaiare shows great depth.

★Gini

VIA MATTEOTTI, 42
37032 MONTEFORTE D'ALPONE [VR]
TEL. 0457611908
www.ginivini.com

CELLAR SALES
PRE-BOOKED VISITS
ANNUAL PRODUCTION 200,000 bottles
HECTARES UNDER VINE 56.00

Among the Soave wineries, a leading place goes to that of the Gini siblings, who have developed their father Olinto's legacy with great ability. They now have over 50 hectares of vineyards, mainly in the heart of the Soave Classico DOC zone, but also at Campiano, where they have been producing wines from international varieties since the 1990s, and where they are preparing for a future production of Valpolicella reds. Claudio and Sandro decided to delay the release of the Salvarenza, and allow the wine to mature further in the cellar. We saw an excellent performance from La Froscà, an approachable, refreshing white offering an intense nose of fruit and flowers, over a supple, long, satisfying palate. The Recioto Col Foscarin, meanwhile, shows a more exotic, sunnier nose, leading into a sweetly harmonious and richly-flavoured palate.

● Bardolino Cl. Brol Grande '13	⟡⟡ 3*
● Bardolino '14	⟡⟡ 2*
⊙ Bardolino Chiaretto Ròdon '14	⟡⟡ 2*
○ Garganega Camporengo '14	⟡⟡ 2*
● Quaiare '12	⟡⟡ 4
● Chelidon '10	⟡ 2
● Bardolino Cl. Brol Grande '12	⟡⟡⟡ 3*
● Bardolino Cl. Brol Grande '11	⟡⟡⟡ 3*
● Bardolino '12	⟡⟡ 2*
● Bardolino '11	⟡⟡ 2*
● Bardolino '10	⟡⟡ 2*
○ Garganega Camporengo '11	⟡⟡ 2*

○ Recioto di Soave Cl. Col Foscarin '10	⟡⟡ 4
○ Soave Cl. La Froscà '14	⟡⟡ 4
● Campo alle More '11	⟡⟡ 5
○ Lessini Sorai '13	⟡⟡ 4
○ Maciete Fumé '13	⟡⟡ 4
○ Soave Cl. '14	⟡⟡ 3
○ Soave Cl. Contrada Salvarenza V. V. '09	⟡⟡⟡ 5
○ Soave Cl. Contrada Salvarenza V. V. '08	⟡⟡⟡ 5
○ Soave Cl. Contrada Salvarenza V. V. '07	⟡⟡⟡ 5
○ Soave Cl. La Froscà '11	⟡⟡⟡ 4*
○ Soave Cl. La Froscà '06	⟡⟡⟡ 4*
○ Soave Cl. La Froscà '05	⟡⟡⟡ 4*
○ Soave Cl. Sup. Contrada Salvarenza V. V. '00	⟡⟡⟡ 5

Giusti Wine

VIA DEL VOLANTE, 4
31040 NERVESA DELLA BATTAGLIA [TV]
TEL. 0422720198
www.giustiwine.com

CELLAR SALES
PRE-BOOKED VISITS
ACCOMMODATION
ANNUAL PRODUCTION 200,000 bottles
HECTARES UNDER VINE 75.00
SUSTAINABLE WINERY

Even though it has only been around for a few years, it is difficult to summarize the story of Giusti Wine in a few words. This is not just a winery, it is a man's act of love for the land of his birth: Montello. Ermenegildo Giusti made his fortune in Canada in the construction sector, and in the early 2000s decided to come back to Italy and invest in his homeland. The operation soon had 70 hectares under vine, partly on hillside sites and partly at the foot of Montello, where the new cellar is planned. Ermenegildo now dedicates his energies to producing the typical wines of this area, both Prosecco and still wines. The spectacular Umberto I, a Bordeaux blend with an intense nose of fruit and spice, offers a rich, harmonious palate. The well-managed Pinot Grigio Longheri opens to a nose of pear, and shows a tangy palate, while among the sparklers we preferred the creamy Asolo Extra Dry, a succulent, extremely pleasurable Prosecco.

● Amarone della Valpolicella Cl. '11	♥♥ 8
○ Asolo Extra Dry	♥♥ 2
○ Pinot Grigio Longheri '14	♥♥ 2*
● Umberto I '09	♥♥ 8
○ Asolo Brut	♥ 2
○ Chardonnay Dei Carni '14	♥ 2
○ Cuvée Giusti Extra Brut	♥ 3
● Valpolicella Sup. Ripasso '12	♥ 4
● Umberto I '08	♥♥ 2*

Gregoletto

FRAZ. PREMAOR
VIA SAN MARTINO, 83
31050 MIANE [TV]
TEL. 0438970463
www.gregoletto.com

CELLAR SALES
PRE-BOOKED VISITS
ANNUAL PRODUCTION 200,000 bottles
HECTARES UNDER VINE 18.00

In a territory in which Prosecco has strongly conditioned the development of wineries, resulting in a frenetic pace ill-adapted to the slower rhythms of country life, it is a pleasure to find an operation such as that of Luigi Gregoletto, a grower who has never lost sight of his mission. He has around 20 hectares of vineyards between Conegliano and Valdobbiadene, dedicated only partly to glera, along with international varieties and traditionals such as verdiso. As happens every year, the DOC zone's best still Prosecco of the year was Luigi Gregoletto's. This is a wine type widely abandoned in favour of the sparkling version, but here at the winery at Miane it is still the star of the show, maybe not in terms of production figures but definitely in terms of product quality. Delicate aromas dominated by apples and pears are developed on a dry, light yet full-flavoured, leisurely palate. We were also convinced by the drinkable Merlot, which alternates fruit and pepper on the nose and shows great harmony on the palate.

○ Chardonnay Zhopai '14	♥♥ 3
○ Colli di Conegliano Bianco Albio '14	♥♥ 3
○ Conegliano Valdobbiadene Prosecco Tranquillo '14	♥♥ 2*
○ Manzoni Bianco '14	♥♥ 3
● Merlot '13	♥♥ 3
○ Verdiso Frizzante Sui Lieviti	♥♥ 3
● Cabernet '13	♥ 3
○ Conegliano Valdobbiadene Extra Dry	♥ 3
⊙ Le Rosé Frizzante sui Lieviti	♥ 2
● P. di Treviso Frizzante sui Lieviti	♥ 4
○ Pinot Bianco '14	♥ 3
● Cabernet '12	♥♥ 3
○ Chardonnay Zhopai '13	♥♥ 3
○ Colli di Conegliano Bianco Albio '13	♥♥ 3
● Colli di Conegliano Rosso '09	♥♥ 5
● Merlot '12	♥♥ 3

Guerrieri Rizzardi

S.DA CAMPAZZI, 2
37011 BARDOLINO [VR]
TEL. 0457210028
www.guerrieri-rizzardi.it

CELLAR SALES
PRE-BOOKED VISITS
ANNUAL PRODUCTION 700,000 bottles
HECTARES UNDER VINE 100.00
SUSTAINABLE WINERY

Guerrieri Rizzardi is one of the historic
wineries in the area around Verona, with
vineyards covering around 100 hectares in
all the most important DOC zones of the
province. Today at the helm of the winery
we find Giuseppe and his brother Agostino,
who contribute in different ways to giving a
new lease of life to the operation. While the
vineyards have mostly been reorganized
according to more stringent quality needs,
the most important change has been the
new cellar at Campazzi. Giuseppe Rizzardi's
great sensitivity is evident in his Ripasso
Pojega, which eschews potency to achieve
success via another route, pursuing depth
on the nose and grip on the palate. The
leisurely, captivating result earned a Tre
Bicchieri. We saw the usual consistent
performance of the Amarone Villa Rizzardi,
while the Calcarole Edizione del Centenario
spent longer in oak to give a profile of great
complexity and finesse.

Inama

LOC. BIACCHE, 50
37047 SAN BONIFACIO [VR]
TEL. 0456104343
www.inamaaziendaagricola.it

CELLAR SALES
PRE-BOOKED VISITS
ANNUAL PRODUCTION 450,000 bottles
HECTARES UNDER VINE 62.00
VITICULTURE METHOD Certified Organic

Stefano Inama's winery has been active for
just over 20 years, yet it has made an
indelible mark on the development of
modern Soave. Today he is flanked by son
Matteo and even if the growing interest in
the nearby Colli Berici area has turned this
into an operation that produces both whites
and reds, its heart remains strongly rooted
in Soave, where the winery farms some of
the finest vineyards in the DOC zone. The
style has always focused on rich, elegant
wines. The Soave Vigneti di Foscarino is
always one of the most interesting wines in
the area, and harks from vineyards on the
most famous hill in the DOC zone. Oak
ageing provides aromatic depth and finesse
on the savoury, long palate. A hot 2011
harvest instead gave the Oratorio di San
Lorenzo aromatic ripeness and impressive
fullness on the palate, rounded off with a
warm, velvety finish. The Vin Soave is
succulent and drinkable.

● Valpolicella Cl. Sup. Ripasso Pojega '13	♟♟♟	3*
● Amarone della Valpolicella Cl. Calcarole Edizione del Centenario '06	♟♟	8
● Amarone della Valpolicella Cl. Villa Rizzardi '11	♟♟	7
● Bardolino Cl. Sup. Munus '13	♟♟	3
● Bardolino Cl. Tacchetto '14	♟♟	2*
● Clos Roareti '11	♟♟	5
○ Vignaunica '14	♟♟	8
⊙ Bardolino Chiaretto Cl. '14	♟	2
● Bardolino Cl. '14	♟	2
⊙ Rosa Rosae '14	♟	2
○ Soave Cl. Costeggiola '14	♟	2
○ Soave Cl. Rocca '13	♟	2
● Amarone della Valpolicella Cl. Calcarole '09	♟♟♟	8
● Valpolicella Cl. Sup. Ripasso Poiega '07	♟♟♟	3*

● Colli Berici Carmenère Oratorio di San Lorenzo Ris. '11	♟♟	6
○ Soave Cl. Vign. di Foscarino '13	♟♟	4
○ Soave Cl. Vign. Du Lot '13	♟♟	4
○ Soave Cl. Vin Soave '14	♟♟	3
○ Vulcaia Sauvignon '14	♟♟	3
○ Chardonnay '14	♟	3
● Bradisismo '08	♟♟♟	5
● Colli Berici Carmenère Oratorio di San Lorenzo Ris. '09	♟♟♟	6
○ Soave Cl. Vign. di Foscarino '08	♟♟♟	4
○ Soave Cl. Vign. Du Lot '05	♟♟♟	2*
○ Soave Cl. Vign. Du Lot '01	♟♟♟	4

Conte Loredan Gasparini

FRAZ. VENEGAZZÙ
VIA MARTIGNAGO ALTO, 23
31040 VOLPAGO DEL MONTELLO [TV]
TEL. 0423870024
www.loredangasparini.it

CELLAR SALES
ACCOMMODATION
ANNUAL PRODUCTION 450,000 bottles
HECTARES UNDER VINE 60.00

Lorenzo Palla runs the family winery on the southern slopes of Montello, covering around 60 hectares in the foothills, planted mainly to Bordeaux varieties and glera. The two most important estates are those at Venegazzù, which surrounds the cellar and covers around 40 hectares planted almost entirely to red grapes, and Giavera, with over 20 hectares dedicated to glera. All of Pallas' most important wines are missing this year, left to age in the cellar, but the limited selection presented was excellent. The extremely drinkable Cabernet Sauvignon shows aromas of ripe red berry fruit and medicinal herbs, over a crunchy, succulent palate. The winery is doing interesting work with Prosecco, so much so that both the wines are from the 2013 vintage. The summery, caressing Cuvée Indigene is the result of spontaneous fermentation, while the Vigna Monti undergoes bottle re-fermentation and offers a dense, gutsy palate.

○ Asolo Extra Brut V. Monti '13	♟♟ 3
○ Asolo Extra Dry Cuvée Indigene '13	♟♟ 3
● Montello e Colli Asolani Cabernet Sauvignon '13	♟♟ 3
○ Asolo Extra Brut V. Monti '12	♟♟ 3
○ Asolo Extra Dry Cuvée Indigene '12	♟♟ 3
● Capo di Stato '08	♟♟ 6
● Capo di Stato '07	♟♟ 6
● Montello e Colli Asolani Cabernet Sauvignon '12	♟♟ 2*
● Montello e Colli Asolani Venegazzù Sup. Capo di Stato '09	♟♟ 5

★Maculan

VIA CASTELLETTO, 3
36042 BREGANZE [VI]
TEL. 0445873733
www.maculan.net

CELLAR SALES
PRE-BOOKED VISITS
ANNUAL PRODUCTION 750,000 bottles
HECTARES UNDER VINE 50.00

The territory of Breganze lies in the rolling foothills between Thiene and Bassano. The plots are mainly south-facing, and display a limited but significant presence of volcanic soils. Here, Fausto Maculan's winery has around 40 hectares, and production also relies on the precious collaboration of numerous local growers. Fausto is helped by his daughters Angela and Maria Vittoria, who are taking on increasingly important duties. The range proposed by the winery in Breganze is impressively wide, led as always by Fratta and Torcolato. The former is a blend of cabernet sauvignon and merlot showing an intense nose of red berry fruit, spice and cocoa powder, leading into a firm palate with rugged, gutsy tannins. The latter, meanwhile, from vespaiola grapes dried at length, and aged in barriques, shows a nose of tropical fruit and spice, echoed on the seductive, elegant palate.

○ Breganze Torcolato '11	♟♟ 6
● Fratta '12	♟♟ 8
● Breganze Cabernet Sauvignon Palazzotto '12	♟♟ 4
○ Breganze Chardonnay Ferrata '13	♟♟ 5
● Breganze Pinot Nero '12	♟♟ 3
● Crosara '12	♟♟ 8
● Dindarello '14	♟♟ 4
● Speaia '12	♟♟ 3
○ Bidibi '14	♟ 2
○ Breganze Vespaiolo '14	♟ 2
● Brentino '13	♟ 3
● Cabernet '13	♟ 2
⊙ Costadolio '14	♟ 2
● Madoro '13	♟ 3
○ Pino & Toi '14	♟ 2
○ Tre Volti Brut M. Cl.	♟ 5

Manara

FRAZ. SAN FLORIANO
VIA DON CESARE BIASI, 53
37029 SAN PIETRO IN CARIANO [VR]
TEL. 0457701086
www.manaravini.it

CELLAR SALES
PRE-BOOKED VISITS
ANNUAL PRODUCTION 130,000 bottles
HECTARES UNDER VINE 11.00
SUSTAINABLE WINERY

The brothers Lorenzo, Fabio and Giovanni Manara are at the helm of this winery established over 60 years ago at San Floriano. Despite the great success of Valpolicella reds, they have not been tempted to enlarge out of proportion, and today they farm just over ten hectares of hillside vineyards, for wines with a distinctive traditional style. The small cellar in Via Don Cesare Biasi allows them to deal with the entire production process, from drying of the grapes to bottling. The Amarone Postera boasts a deep, complex nose, with notes of dried red berry fruit interlaced with spice and dry aromatic herbs, over a full, harmonious palate whose power is well managed, with its rough edges tamed by long cellar ageing. Huskier and edgier, the Ripasso Le Morete offers a succulent palate that brings its vegetal and dried fruit notes to the fore.

● Amarone della Valpolicella Cl. Postera '09	♛♛ 6
● Valpolicella Cl. Sup. Le Morete Ripasso '12	♛♛ 3
● Guido Manara '10	♛ 6
● Recioto della Valpolicella Cl. Moronalto '12	♛ 5
● Valpolicella Cl. Sup. Vecio Belo '12	♛ 2
● Amarone della Valpolicella Cl. Corte Manara '10	♛♛ 5
● Amarone della Valpolicella Cl. Corte Manara '09	♛♛ 5
● Recioto della Valpolicella Cl. El Rocolo '11	♛♛ 5
● Recioto della Valpolicella Cl. Moronalto '11	♛♛ 5
● Valpolicella Cl. Sup. Vecio Belo '10	♛♛ 2*

Marcato

VIA PRANDI, 10
37030 RONCÀ [VR]
TEL. 0457460070
www.marcatovini.it

CELLAR SALES
PRE-BOOKED VISITS
ANNUAL PRODUCTION 450,000 bottles
HECTARES UNDER VINE 40.00

Gianni Tessari has quite simply revolutionized the winery at Roncà, imposing order on the entire production, both in the rows and at the cellar. The operation works on three fronts, starting with Lessinia. Here, the winery plays a leading role in the production of Metodo Classico, with a solid range of excellent quality. In Soave, the figures are lower, but the leap in quality achieved is impressive. Lastly, there is the estate in Colli Berici, dedicated almost entirely to Bordeaux varieties. The most interesting wine, however, comes from the territory of Soave, namely the Soave Pigno, a monovarietal garganega that harks from the vineyard of the same name, at an elevation of 120 metres. The wine ages in barrels and offers intense yellow-fleshed fruit and flowers on the nose, against a backdrop of citrus and spice, while the full, taut palate completes what is a textbook performance. The Brut 60 Mesi offers dried flowers and toast on the nose, over a dynamic palate with well integrated fizz.

○ Soave Cl. Pigno '13	♛♛♛ 3*
● Colli Berici Pian Alto Ris. '11	♛♛ 5
○ Lessini Durello Brut 36 Mesi M. Cl.	♛♛ 3
○ Lessini Durello Brut 60 Mesi '08	♛♛ 5
○ Soave Cl. Monte Tenda '14	♛♛ 3
● Colli Berici Merlot Baraldo '12	♛ 4
● Colli Berici Merlot Baraldo La Giareta '09	♛♛ 4
● Colli Berici Pian Alto Ris. '10	♛♛ 5
○ Lessini Durello Brut 60 Mesi '07	♛♛ 5
○ Soave Cl. Monte Tenda '12	♛♛ 3
○ Soave Cl. Pigno '12	♛♛ 3*

Marion

FRAZ. MARCELLISE
VIA BORGO MARCELLISE, 2
37036 SAN MARTINO BUON ALBERGO [VR]
TEL. 0458740021
www.marionvini.it

PRE-BOOKED VISITS
ANNUAL PRODUCTION 40,000 bottles
HECTARES UNDER VINE 14.00

The estate of Stefano Campedelli and his
wife Nicoletta is in the Marcellise Valley,
and comprises just over a dozen hectares
dedicated mainly to traditional varieties
Valpolicella, with small plantings of varieties
from elsewhere but often found in this area,
even if in reduced quantities, such as
teroldego. Production is equally traditional,
with long ageing, and wines that show
elegance and restraint. We have often
complimented the winery for its Valpolicella
Superiore, but this year it was the Amarone
2010 that most convinced our tasting
panels. It opens to intense notes of
super-ripe fruit, gradually making way for
fines herbes and spice. On the palate, it
unfolds with finesse and density, elegantly
managing the impressive body. The
Valpolicella Superiore, from a hot harvest,
is mature and pervasive on the nose, and
ends warm.

● Amarone della Valpolicella '10	♈♈♈ 7
● Valpolicella Sup. '11	♈♈ 4
● Cabernet Sauvignon '11	♈♈ 4
● Calto '09	♈♈ 4
○ Passito Bianco '07	♈♈ 5
● Teroldego '12	♈♈ 5
● Valpolicella Borgomarcellise '13	♈ 3
● Valpolicella Sup. '10	♉♉♉ 4*
● Valpolicella Sup. '09	♉♉♉ 4*
● Amarone della Valpolicella '09	♉♉ 7
● Amarone della Valpolicella '08	♉♉ 7
● Valpolicella Sup. '08	♉♉ 4

Masari

LOC. MAGLIO DI SOPRA
VIA BEVILACQUA, 2A
36078 VALDAGNO [VI]
TEL. 0445410780
www.masari.it

CELLAR SALES
PRE-BOOKED VISITS
ANNUAL PRODUCTION 30,000 bottles
HECTARES UNDER VINE 4.00

The Agno Valley lies to the north of Vicenza,
in a hillside area of volcanic origin
protected to the north by the Piccole
Dolomiti. Here, Massimo Dal Lago and his
wife Arianna Tessari set up Masari, a
first-rate winery that has restored farming
to its traditional importance in this territory.
It has just a few hectares under vine on the
two sides of the valley, volcanic soil on one
plot, limestone on the other, for elegant
wines with great ageing potential. Masari's
best wine this year comes from afar. The
Antico Pasquale, a raisin wine from durella
grapes that have undergone long drying,
and which spends years ageing in oak, is
only released after eight years. Opening to
a bright amber hue, it shows a deep,
complex nose of dates and hazelnuts,
Mediterranean scrub and spices. The
surprise comes on the palate, with
unexpected but superb acid tautness,
providing lightness and length. The
Bordeaux blend Masari is summery and
harmonious.

○ Antico Pasquale Passito Bianco '07	♈♈ 8
○ AgnoBianco '13	♈♈ 2*
○ Doro Passito Bianco '11	♈♈ 5
○ Leon Durello Dosaggio Zero M. Cl.	♈♈ 4
● Masari '12	♈♈ 5
● Vicenza Rosso San Martino '12	♈♈ 3
○ Antico Pasquale Passito Bianco '06	♉♉ 8
○ Doro Passito Bianco '08	♉♉ 5
● Masari '09	♉♉ 5
● Vicenza Rosso San Martino '11	♉♉ 3*
● Vicenza Rosso San Martino '10	♉♉ 3*

★Masi

FRAZ. GARGAGNAGO
VIA MONTELEONE, 26
37015 SANT'AMBROGIO DI VALPOLICELLA [VR]
TEL. 0456832511
www.masi.it

CELLAR SALES
PRE-BOOKED VISITS
ACCOMMODATION
ANNUAL PRODUCTION 4,200,000 bottles
HECTARES UNDER VINE 640.00

The Boscaini family winery is one of the best known in the world, with a deep-rooted viticultural tradition and production distributed in the four corners of the globe. Sandro Boscaini has now been joined by his children Alessandra and Raffaele, who continue with equal determination and skill the work begun many years ago, which still revolves around Valpolicella, although the family now also has an estate to the north east and a major operation in Argentina. The peerless Amarone Campolongo di Torbe, from vineyards high in the hills, reflects the 2009 vintage, with its nose of intense super-ripe fruit against a backdrop of light oak. Significant power in the mouth is offset by the tautness and focus provided by acidity and the tannins. The Vaio Armaron, meanwhile, shows a more approachable nose, leading to a rounded palate with attractively rugged tannins. We were intrigued by the firm, crunchy Valpolicella Superiore Toar.

● Amarone della Valpolicella Cl. Campolongo di Torbe '09	▼▼▼ 8
● Amarone della Valpolicella Cl. Vaio Armaron Serègo Alighieri '09	▼▼ 8
● Amarone della Valpolicella Cl. Costasera '10	▼▼ 7
● Recioto della Valpolicella Cl. Mezzanella Amandorlato '09	▼▼ 8
● Valpolicella Cl. Sup Toar '11	▼▼ 4
● Recioto della Valpolicella Cl. Casal dei Ronchi Serègo Alighieri '11	▼ 6
● Amarone della Valpolicella Cl. Campolongo di Torbe '07	♀♀♀ 8
● Amarone della Valpolicella Cl. Costasera Ris. '09	♀♀♀ 8
● Amarone della Valpolicella Cl. Mazzano '06	♀♀♀ 8

Masottina

LOC. CASTELLO ROGANZUOLO
VIA BRADOLINI, 54
31020 SAN FIOR [TV]
TEL. 0438400775
www.masottina.it

CELLAR SALES
PRE-BOOKED VISITS
ANNUAL PRODUCTION 1,000,000 bottles
HECTARES UNDER VINE 50.00
SUSTAINABLE WINERY

The Dal Bianco family winery is at San Fior, a few kilometres to the east of Conegliano Veneto, one of the two capitals of Prosecco. The surface under vine exceeds 50 hectares, and to achieve production figures which are now at around a million bottles a year, Masottina avails itself of a series of growers that it supervises all year round. The planetary success of Prosecco means that today production is mainly dedicated to Treviso sparklers, in a light, elegant style. Ogliano's best vineyards, at the eastern end of the DOC zone, give the grapes for the fragrant Extra Dry Rive di Ogliano, a sparkler with an unmistakable aroma of white-fleshed fruit and flowers, whose subtle citrus hints confer lightness and freshness. On the full-flavoured palate, we find a perfect fusion of acidity, sweetness and fizz. We were also won over by the two simpler Proseccos, the gutsy Brut and the more approachable, creamy Extra Dry.

○ Conegliano Valdobbiadene Brut	▼▼ 6
○ Conegliano Valdobbiadene Extra Dry	▼▼ 6
○ Conegliano Valdobbiadene Extra Dry Rive di Ogliano '14	▼▼ 7
○ Manzoni Bianco '14	▼ 2
○ Conegliano Valdobbiadene Extra Dry	♀♀ 6
○ Conegliano Valdobbiadene Rive di Ogliano Contrada Granda Brut '13	♀♀ 7
● Piave Cabernet Sauvignon Vign. ai Palazzi Ris. '09	♀♀ 4
● Piave Cabernet Sauvignon Vign. ai Palazzi Ris. '08	♀♀ 4
● Piave Cabernet Sauvignon Vign. ai Palazzi Ris. '07	♀♀ 4
● Piave Merlot Vign. Ai Palazzi Ris. '08	♀♀ 6
● Piave Merlot Vign. ai Palazzi Ris. '07	♀♀ 3

Massimago

VIA GIARE, 21
37030 MEZZANE DI SOTTO [VR]
TEL. 0458880143
www.massimago.com

ANNUAL PRODUCTION 45,000 bottles
HECTARES UNDER VINE 12.00

Massimago is found at Mezzane di Sotto, in the heart of eastern Valpolicella, where a dozen hectares produce grapes for the facility in Via Giare, an old stately home set in a splendid estate. Here, Camilla Rossi Chauvenet runs the family business with enthusiasm and care, availing herself of the help of Guido Busatto, who accompanies her in the pursuit of the elegance and tautness typical of the grapes of Valpolicella. The winery at Mezzane offered only one wine, but it was a perfect expression of what the territory, varieties and traditions of Valpolicella can offer. The excellent Amarone 2011 boasts slightly raisined red berry fruit and spice and a refreshing light vegetal swathe that enlivens the powerful palate, offset by gentle, glossy tannins.

Roberto Mazzi

LOC. SAN PERETTO
VIA CROSETTA, 8
37024 NEGRAR [VR]
TEL. 0457502072
www.robertomazzi.it

CELLAR SALES
PRE-BOOKED VISITS
ACCOMMODATION AND RESTAURANT SERVICE
ANNUAL PRODUCTION 45,000 bottles
HECTARES UNDER VINE 8.00

Antonio and Stefano Mazzi run the family winery at San Peretto, a small town in Valpolicella that has maintained its rural nature despite the planetary success that Amarone has brought to the area. Under ten hectares of vineyards are farmed with the utmost respect for the environment, allowing the two brothers to work with grapes of great quality, that are processed in the small, functional cellar in Via Crosetta, for a range entirely dedicated to Valpolicella. The Amarone Vigneto Castel offers an intense fruit nose, refreshed by pungent pepper and delicate medicinal herbs. Acidic thrust and full flavour on the rich, juicy palate join forces to give good length. We were also convinced by the Valpolicella Poiega, which shows greater tautness and integrity than in the past. A nose of autumn leaves and mint leads into a crisp, satisfying palate.

● Amarone della Valpolicella '11	♟♟ 8
● Amarone della Valpolicella '10	♟♟ 8
● Amarone della Valpolicella '09	♟♟ 8
● Valpolicella Sup. Profasio '12	♟♟ 5
● Valpolicella Sup. Profasio '11	♟♟ 5

● Amarone della Valpolicella Cl. Vign. Castel '10	♟♟ 7
● Valpolicella Cl. Sup. Vign. Poiega '12	♟♟ 4
● Amarone della Valpolicella Cl. Punta di Villa '10	♟♟ 7
● Valpolicella Cl. '14	♟♟ 2*
● Valpolicella Cl. Sup. Sanperetto '13	♟♟ 3
● Valpolicella Cl. Sup. Sanperetto '11	♟♟♟ 3*
● Amarone della Valpolicella Cl. Punta di Villa '09	♟♟ 7
● Amarone della Valpolicella Cl. Punta di Villa '08	♟♟ 7
● Recioto della Valpolicella Cl. Le Calcarole '09	♟♟ 5
● Recioto della Valpolicella Cl. Le Calcarole '07	♟♟ 5
● Valpolicella Cl. Sup. Sanperetto '10	♟♟ 3*
● Valpolicella Cl. Sup. Vign. Poiega '11	♟♟ 4

Merotto

LOC. COL SAN MARTINO
VIA SCANDOLERA, 21
31010 FARRA DI SOLIGO [TV]
TEL. 0438989000
www.merotto.it

CELLAR SALES
PRE-BOOKED VISITS
ANNUAL PRODUCTION 550,000 bottles
HECTARES UNDER VINE 21.00

With a life dedicated to Prosecco, Graziano Merotto had the clear-sightedness and force of will to review his whole operation a few years back, and started to look for people to help him turn around the business. In the space of a few years, the winery at Col San Martino became a benchmark for the DOC zone tanks to important estates and production that focuses on the best expression of variety from each vineyard, eschewing soft, commercial interpretations in the pursuit of excellence. It is precisely its elegance that distinguishes the Graziano Merotto, a Brut with a fresh, inviting nose of blossom and spring flowers. The change of gear comes on the palate, where the wine reveals a spirited, racy soul, showing good length, elegance and grip, without the help of added sugar. There was also an excellent performance from the La Primavera di Barbara, a Dry which instead relies on its velvety softness to bring out notes of tropical fruit and sugared almond, over a full-flavoured, harmonious palate.

○ Valdobbiadene Brut Rive di Col San Martino Cuvée del Fondatore Graziano Merotto '14	♛♛♛ 4*
○ Cartizze	♛♛ 5
○ Le Fare Extra Brut	♛♛ 2*
○ Prosecco di Treviso Dry Colmolina Mill. '14	♛♛ 3
○ Valdobbiadene Brut Bareta	♛♛ 3
○ Valdobbiadene Dry La Primavera di Barbara '14	♛♛ 3
⊙ Grani Rosa di Nero Brut	♛ 3
○ Valdobbiadene Extra Dry Colbelo	♛ 3
○ Valdobbiadene Brut Rive di Col San Martino Cuvée del Fondatore Graziano Merotto '13	♛♛♛ 4*

Monte dall'Ora

LOC. CASTELROTTO
VIA MONTE DALL'ORA, 5
37029 SAN PIETRO IN CARIANO [VR]
TEL. 0457704462
www.montedallora.com

CELLAR SALES
PRE-BOOKED VISITS
ANNUAL PRODUCTION 35,000 bottles
HECTARES UNDER VINE 6.00
VITICULTURE METHOD Certified Organic

Found on the small Castelrotto hill, the winery owned by Carlo Venturini and his wife Alessandra covers a few hectares farmed without chemicals. They encourage the presence of insects in the rows and pursue an approach to viticulture that aims to work in harmony with nature rather than against it. The entire production process takes place in the small cellar, and displays respect for tradition and each wine's natural development. No fewer than three of Venturini's wines made our finals, with the Valpolicella Superiore Camporenzo leading the pack. Its deep nose shows super-ripe red berry fruit and spice, over a rounded, elegant palate. The Ripasso Saustò shows a more mature nose and silky palate. Lastly, the Amarone Stropa offers wonderfully complex aromas and a full, flavoursome palate with well-managed tannins. Although released eight years after harvest, it still shows youthful character and warmth.

● Amarone della Valpolicella Cl. Stropa '07	♛♛ 8
● Valpolicella Cl. Sup. Camporenzo '12	♛♛ 4
● Valpolicella Cl. Sup. Ripasso Saustò '11	♛♛ 5
● Valpolicella Cl. Saseti '14	♛♛ 2*
● Valpolicella Cl. Sup. Camporenzo '11	♛♛♛ 4*
● Valpolicella Cl. Sup. Camporenzo '10	♛♛♛ 4*
● Valpolicella Cl. Sup. Ripasso Saustò '07	♛♛♛ 5
● Amarone della Valpolicella Cl. '08	♛♛ 6
● Amarone della Valpolicella Cl. '06	♛♛ 6
● Amarone della Valpolicella Cl. '09	♛♛ 6
● Recioto della Valpolicella Cl. Sant' Ulderico '09	♛♛ 6
● Recioto della Valpolicella Cl. Sant' Ulderico '07	♛♛ 6
● Recioto della Valpolicella Cl. Sant' Ulderico '06	♛♛ 6
● Valpolicella Cl. Sup. Camporenzo '09	♛♛ 4

Monte del Frà

S.DA PER CUSTOZA, 35
37066 SOMMACAMPAGNA [VR]
TEL. 045510490
www.montedelfra.it

CELLAR SALES
PRE-BOOKED VISITS
ANNUAL PRODUCTION 1,000,000 bottles
HECTARES UNDER VINE 177.00

In the space of around ten years, the
Bonomo family winery has radically
changed its production methods. The
vineyards, already fairly extensive, have
expanded to cover almost 200 hectares
thanks to the purchase of important plots,
above all in Valpolicella. In the cellar,
meanwhile, attention has been given above
all to improving quality, resulting in
products of undisputed worth, with wines
that show a real sense of place. Once
again, the Custoza Ca' del Magro was the
champion at Bonomo. This white, aged in
stainless steel, boasts an intense nose of
tropical fruit and saffron, with attractive
notes of blossom and gunflint gradually
emerging. The rich, fruity palate shows
good flavour and incisive acidity. The
Colombara is a late-harvest wine from
garganega with a dynamic, racy palate,
while the Valpolicella Superiore Lena di
Mezzo plays on its aromatic finesse and
elegant palate.

○ Custoza Sup. Ca' del Magro '13	♟♟♟	3*
○ Colombara '12	♟♟	3*
● Valpolicella Cl. Sup. Lena di Mezzo '13	♟♟	3*
● Amarone della Valpolicella Cl. Lena di Mezzo '11	♟♟	6
● Bardolino '14	♟♟	2*
◐ Bardolino Chiaretto '14	♟♟	2*
○ Custoza '14	♟♟	2*
● Valpolicella Cl. Sup. Ripasso Lena di Mezzo '13	♟♟	3
● Valpolicella Cl. Lena di Mezzo '14	♟	3
○ Custoza Sup. Ca' del Magro '12	♕♕♕	2*
○ Custoza Sup. Ca' del Magro '11	♕♕♕	2*
○ Custoza Sup. Ca' del Magro '10	♕♕♕	2*
○ Custoza Sup. Ca' del Magro '09	♕♕♕	2*
○ Custoza Sup. Ca' del Magro '08	♕♕♕	2*

Monte Faustino

VIA BURE ALTO
37029 SAN PIETRO IN CARIANO [VR]
TEL. 0457701651
www.fornaser.com

CELLAR SALES
PRE-BOOKED VISITS
ANNUAL PRODUCTION 70,000 bottles
HECTARES UNDER VINE 6.00

That of the Fornaser family is a
consolidated winery, but it was with the
arrival of son Paolo, in the mid-1980s, and
subsequently of his brothers, Giorgio,
Fabiano and Massimiliano, that the
operation grew to its present size. The
vineyards cover three different plots, the
historic Monte Faustino vineyard, nearby
Traversagna, and the most recent
purchase, Costalunga, entirely dedicated to
the traditional Valpolicella grapes, with
small amounts of garganega and malvasia.
They have a real feeling for Amarone at
Fornaser, as was evident when tasting both
the Classico 2010 and the Riserva
dedicated to their father, "junior school
teacher and teacher of life" as his children
call him. The former expresses intact fruit
with perfectly integrated notes of oak, while
on the palate, fullness and warmth are
evident. The latter is more complex and
deeper, with a nose on which fines herbes
and mineral notes also appear. On the
palate, it is rich but full flavoured, and
shows great elegance.

● Amarone della Valpolicella Cl. '10	♟♟	7
● Amarone della Valpolicella Cl. Maestro Fornaser Ris. '08	♟♟	8
● Valpolicella Cl. Sup. La Traversagna '11	♟♟	4
● Valpolicella Cl. '14	♟	2
● Amarone della Valpolicella Cl. '09	♕♕	7
● Amarone della Valpolicella Cl. '07	♕♕	7
● Amarone della Valpolicella Cl. '05	♕♕	7
● Amarone della Valpolicella Cl. '01	♕♕	7
● Amarone della Valpolicella Cl. Maestro Fornaser Ris. '07	♕♕	8
● Pelara '11	♕♕	3*
● Recioto della Valpolicella Cl. '06	♕♕	5
● Valpolicella Cl. Sup. Ripasso La Traversagna '07	♕♕	4
● Valpolicella Cl. Sup. Ripasso La Traversagna '05	♕♕	4

Monte Tondo

LOC. MONTE TONDO
VIA SAN LORENZO, 89
37038 SOAVE [VR]
TEL. 0457680347
www.montetondo.it

CELLAR SALES
PRE-BOOKED VISITS
ACCOMMODATION
ANNUAL PRODUCTION 200,000 bottles
HECTARES UNDER VINE 32.00

The Magnabosco family winery was literally built by Gino who managed not only to work as a grower, but also lent a hand with the actual construction of the winery, combining his skills as a mason and wine merchant. Today, his children Stefania, Marta and Luca are helping him, dealing with the various tasks involved in the management of an operation that now has over 30 hectares in the DOC zones of Soave and Valpolicella, giving a reliable, approachable range of wines. The Soave Casette Foscarin, aged in small oak, comes from the best-known hill in the DOC zone, Foscarino. Garganega brings fruits and fullness on the palate, while the small percentage of trebbiano di Soave confers floral notes and an attractive touch of acidity. Opening on the nose to intense notes of tropical fruit and spice, the wine presents a rich, velvety, harmonious palate. The Foscarin Slavinus is slower to express its aromas and shows a drier palate.

Cantina Sociale di Monteforte d'Alpone

VIA XX SETTEMBRE, 24
37032 MONTEFORTE D'ALPONE [VR]
TEL. 0457610110
www.cantinadimonteforte.it

CELLAR SALES
PRE-BOOKED VISITS
ANNUAL PRODUCTION 2,000,000 bottles
HECTARES UNDER VINE

The Cantina Sociale di Monteforte relies on 600 growers and over 1,000 hectares of vineyards, mainly on hillside plots, dedicated to the traditional grapes of the territory, garganega and trebbiano di Soave, with small amounts of Valpolicella. Over recent years, the winery has concentrated on making the most of the best-suited vineyards, today resulting in a range of labels that perfectly represents the value of Soave. We saw an excellent performance from the Soave Castellaro, the result of a painstaking selection of the best grapes from the classic zone, subsequently aged in barriques and large oak. The nose ranges from yellow-fresh fruit to notes of gunflint, citrus and blossom, all held together by delicate oak. On the palate, it boasts elegance and harmony, proving supple and extremely long. We were also convinced by the fresh, racy Soave Clivus.

Wine	Rating
○ Soave Cl. Casette Foscarin '13	♛♛ 3*
● Amarone della Valpolicella '11	♛♛ 6
○ Soave Cl. '14	♛♛ 2*
○ Soave Cl. Sup. Foscarin Slavinus '13	♛♛ 4
● Valpolicella Ripasso Campo Grande '12	♛ 4
● Valpolicella San Pietro '13	♛ 2
○ Soave Cl. Casette Foscarin '12	♛♛ 3
○ Soave Cl. Monte Tondo '13	♛♛ 2*
○ Soave Cl. Monte Tondo '11	♛♛ 2*
○ Soave Cl. Sup. Foscarin Slavinus '12	♛♛ 4
○ Soave Cl. Sup. Foscarin Slavinus '11	♛♛ 4
○ Soave Cl. Sup. Foscarin Slavinus '10	♛♛ 4

Wine	Rating
○ Soave Cl. Sup. Vign. di Castellaro '13	♛♛ 2*
● Amarone della Valpolicella Re Teodorico '11	♛♛ 5
○ Soave Cl. Clivus '14	♛♛ 1*
● Valpolicella Ripasso '13	♛♛ 2*
● Cabernet Sauvignon Cavaliere '14	♛ 2
○ Lessini Durello Brut le Terre dei Cimbri '13	♛ 3
○ Lessini Durello Brut M. Cl.	♛ 3
○ Recioto di Soave Il Sigillo '12	♛ 3
○ Soave Cl. Il Vicario '14	♛ 2
● Versante '13	♛ 1*
○ Soave Cl. Clivus '13	♛♛ 1*
○ Soave Cl. Clivus '11	♛♛ 1*
○ Soave Cl. Il Vicario '13	♛♛ 2*
○ Soave Cl. Sup. Vign. di Castellaro '12	♛♛ 2*
○ Soave Cl. Sup. Vign. di Castellaro '10	♛♛ 2*
○ Soave Cl. Sup. Vign. di Castellaro '09	♛♛ 2*

Montegrande

VIA TORRE, 2
35030 ROVOLON [PD]
TEL. 0495226276
www.vinimontegrande.it

CELLAR SALES
PRE-BOOKED VISITS
ANNUAL PRODUCTION 250,000 bottles
HECTARES UNDER VINE 30.00

Raffaele Cristofanon runs the family winery in the heart of the Parco Regionale dei Colli Euganei, a hillside area in the Po Valley to the south of Padua, of volcanic origin with a long tradition of viticulture. The vineyards cover around 30 hectares and provide all the grapes necessary for production, dedicated, as always in this area, above all to merlot and cabernet, interpreted in pursuit of aromatic fragrance and drinkability. Among the wines presented by Raffaele, the quality of the Cabernet Sereo stands out. From the vineyards at Rovolon, this Cabernet Sauvignon with a nose of red berry fruit and spice is slow to reveal its aromas. On the palate, the wine unfolds gracefully, revealing a body in which richness is balanced by acidic thrust and tannins. The Fior d'Arancio Passito shows a complex nose of tropical fruit and candied citrus, echoed on the long, juicy palate.

● Colli Euganei Cabernet Sereo '12	♥♥ 3
○ Colli Euganei Fior d'Arancio Passito '12	♥♥ 3
○ Castearo '14	♥ 2
○ Colli Euganei Bianco Erto '14	♥ 2
● Colli Euganei Cabernet '14	♥ 2
○ Colli Euganei Extra Dry Serprino	♥ 2
○ Colli Euganei Fior d'Arancio Spumante '14	♥ 2
● Colli Euganei Merlot '14	♥ 2
○ Colli Euganei Pinot Bianco '14	♥ 2
● Colli Euganei Rosso V. delle Roche '12	♥ 3
● Colli Euganei Cabernet Sereo '11	♀♀ 3
○ Colli Euganei Fior d'Arancio Passito '11	♀♀ 3

Monteversa

VIA MONTE VERSA, 1024
35030 VÒ [PD]
TEL. 0499941092
www.monteversa.it

CELLAR SALES
PRE-BOOKED VISITS
ANNUAL PRODUCTION 23,000 bottles
HECTARES UNDER VINE 17.00
VITICULTURE METHOD Certified Organic

The Colli Euganei area is composed of a group of hills of volcanic origin, in the middle of the Po Valley. The Monteversa winery is located on the west-facing slopes of the hill from which it takes its name, and covers just under 20 hectares, planted above all to Bordeaux varieties. The Voltazza family took over the helm just a few years ago, but the results are already more than encouraging. The hot 2012 harvest allowed the production of a fantastic Animaversa, a wine whose composition may change from year to year. The version we tasted was a Cabernet, opening to a nose of forest floor and damp leaves with dark berry fruit, swathed in fresh mineral notes and aromatic herbs. On the palate, the wine shows a full, juicy body, buttressed by smooth tannins and finishing long. The rich, succulent Rosso Versacinto is wonderfully drinkable.

● Colli Euganei Cabernet Animaversa '12	♥♥ 4
● Colli Euganei Rosso Versacinto '13	♥♥ 3
○ Versavò '14	♥♥ 2*
○ Colli Euganei Bianco Animaversa '12	♀♀ 3
○ Colli Euganei Bianco Versavò '13	♀♀ 2*
○ Colli Euganei Bianco Versavò '11	♀♀ 2*
● Colli Euganei Rosso Animaversa '11	♀♀ 4
● Colli Euganei Rosso Animaversa '10	♀♀ 4
● Colli Euganei Rosso Versacinto '12	♀♀ 2*
● Colli Euganei Rosso Versacinto '11	♀♀ 2*

Le Morette

v.le INDIPENDENZA
37019 PESCHIERA DEL GARDA [VR]
TEL. 0457552724
www.lemorette.it

CELLAR SALES
ANNUAL PRODUCTION 280,000 bottles
HECTARES UNDER VINE 31.00

Fabio and Paolo Zenato manage the family winery on the border between the provinces of Verona and Brescia, along the southern shores of Lake Garda, where the significant presence of clay in the soil allows turbiana to give of its best. The vineyards extend for around 30 hectares in two zones, the first around the new cellar, the other slightly more to the west, at Palazzo di Sirmione. Only Lugana for the Zenato family this year, with two excellent versions of Mandolara and Benedictus, both from the difficult 2014 vintage. The first is a refreshing white with flowers and white-fleshed fruit on the nose, perfectly echoed on the dry, linear palate. The second is the result of a selection of particularly ripe grapes, and is partially aged in oak. Opening to a sweet, ripe, sunny nose, on the palate the wine shows firm body and good harmony.

○ Lugana Benedictus '14	♀♀	3
○ Lugana Mandolara '14	♀♀	2*
○ Lugana Benedictus '11	♀♀	3
○ Lugana Benedictus '07	♀♀	3
○ Lugana Mandolara '13	♀♀	2*
○ Lugana Ris. '11	♀♀	3
○ Lugana Vigna La Mandolara '08	♀♀	2*

Marco Mosconi

VIA PARADISO, 5
37031 ILLASI [VR]
TEL. 0456529109
www.marcomosconi.it

CELLAR SALES
PRE-BOOKED VISITS
ANNUAL PRODUCTION 25,000 bottles
HECTARES UNDER VINE 10.00

In only a few years in the business, Marco Mosconi quickly realized that wines do not need to be powerful just for the sake of it, but that it is nevertheless a fundamental feature for wines of Valpolicella, as important as depth and elegance. His reliable and increasingly convincing wines come from ten hectares of vineyards in Val d'Illasi, where the Soave and Valpolicella DOC zones fight over the best aspects. The Valpolicella Superiore 2011 in fact made a great impression, and despite the hot harvest, imposed its class, showing grip and finesse. While the nose is dominated by super-ripe, warm fruit, on the palate the wine changes gear, unfolding with elegance and grip towards a long, stylish finish. The oak is still evident, but will soften with time. The Amarone from the same vintage is spicy and crisp, and we were impressed with the Recioto della Valpolicella.

● Valpolicella Sup. '11	♀♀	5
● Amarone della Valpolicella '11	♀♀	8
● Recioto della Valpolicella '11	♀♀	6
○ Recioto di Soave '13	♀♀	5
○ Soave Corte Paradiso '14	♀♀	2*
● Valpolicella Montecurto '14	♀♀	3
● Amarone della Valpolicella '09	♀♀	8
○ Soave Rosetta '13	♀♀	3
○ Soave Sup. Corte Paradiso '13	♀♀	2*
● Turan Cabernet Sauvignon '11	♀♀	3
● Valpolicella Sup. '10	♀♀	5

Mosole

LOC. CORBOLONE
VIA ANNONE VENETO, 60
30029 SANTO STINO DI LIVENZA [VE]
TEL. 0421310404
www.mosole.com

CELLAR SALES
PRE-BOOKED VISITS
ANNUAL PRODUCTION 220,000 bottles
HECTARES UNDER VINE 30.00

The Mosole family winery is at Annone
Veneto, just a few kilometres north of the
Adriatic, on clay soils influenced by the sea,
which also conditions the climate and the
breezes. Production focuses on Bordeaux
varieties, which have been planted in this
area for many years. The collaboration with
Gianni Menotti has allowed Lucio to
improve his wines further so they are
increasingly representative of the territory.
The Cabernet Hora Sexta is a shining
example of what a Cabernet from the
Veneto plains can be, with an intense nose
of red berry fruit and spice, accompanied
by delicate vegetal hints providing
character and freshness. On the rich, juicy
palate, good grip combines with impressive
length, for smooth progression. We were
also convinced by the Passito Ad Nonam,
whose irrepressible sweetness is offset by
acidic thrust and full flavour, resulting in a
harmonious palate.

○ Ad Nonam Passito '13	♟♟ 4
● Lison-Pramaggiore Cabernet Hora Sexta '12	♟♟ 3*
○ Hora Prima '13	♟♟ 4
○ Lison Eleo '14	♟♟ 3
● Lison-Pramaggiore Merlot Ad Nonam '12	♟♟ 5
● Lison-Pramaggiore Merlot '14	♟ 2
○ Pinot Grigio '14	♟ 2
○ Tai '14	♟ 2
● Venezia Cabernet Franc '14	♟ 2
○ Venezia Chardonnay '14	♟ 2
○ Lison-Pramaggiore Eleo '13	♟♟ 3*
● Lison-Pramaggiore Merlot Ad Nonam '11	♟♟ 4

Il Mottolo

LOC. LE CONTARINE
VIA COMEZZARE
35030 BAONE [PD]
TEL. 3479456155
www.ilmottolo.it

CELLAR SALES
PRE-BOOKED VISITS
ANNUAL PRODUCTION 20,000 bottles
HECTARES UNDER VINE 6.00

Little by little, the winery based in Via
Comezzare has extended its vineyards, thus
allowing production to continue with the
same quality but slightly higher volume,
above all for the simpler products, some of
the best to be found in the Colli Euganei
area. The vineyards, situated in the
southern area of the hills, enjoy perfect
exposure to sunlight, allowing red grapes to
ripen perfectly every year, and giving wines
that manage to combine richness and
elegance. The absence of top honours at
Fortin should not lead us astray; if anything,
the range proposed was even more
convincing than in previous years, the
result of meticulous work in all the
production phases. The Serro expresses
summery aromas of fruit and spice,
reflecting the hot harvest, against a
backdrop of aromatic herbs, which are
echoed on the juicy, elegant palate. The
Vignànima is more powerful and warmer,
while we should mention the textbook
performance from the simpler wines.

● Colli Euganei Rosso Serro '12	♟♟ 3*
● Vignànima '12	♟♟ 3*
● Colli Euganei Cabernet V. Marè '13	♟♟ 2*
● Colli Euganei Merlot Comezzara '13	♟♟ 2*
● Colli Euganei Rosso Serro '11	♟♟♟ 3*
● Colli Euganei Rosso Serro '10	♟♟♟ 3*
● Colli Euganei Rosso Serro '09	♟♟♟ 3*
○ Colli Euganei Fior d'Arancio Passito V. del Pozzo '12	♟♟ 3
○ Colli Euganei Fior d'Arancio Passito V. del Pozzo '10	♟♟ 3*
● Colli Euganei Merlot Comezzara '12	♟♟ 2*
● Colli Euganei Rosso Serro '08	♟♟ 3
● Colli Euganei Rosso Serro '07	♟♟ 3*
● Vingnànima '11	♟♟ 3*
● Vingnànima '10	♟♟ 3*
● Vingnànima '08	♟♟ 3*

Musella

loc. Ferrazze
via Ferrazzette, 2
37036 San Martino Buon Albergo [VR]
Tel. 045973385
www.musella.it

CELLAR SALES
PRE-BOOKED VISITS
ACCOMMODATION
ANNUAL PRODUCTION 260,000 bottles
HECTARES UNDER VINE 50.00
VITICULTURE METHOD Certified Biodynamic

Maddalena Pasqua's winery is part of the
Musella estate, a corner of unspoiled
countryside a stone's throw from Verona.
The vineyards, tended with biodynamic
farming methods, cover 50 hectares
surrounded by woods and olive groves at
elevations of just over 100 metres. Here,
the plots are given over almost entirely to
traditional grapes of the province of Verona,
leaving just a few rows for international
varieties. The winery has a real feeling for
Valpolicella, as the tastings of both the
Superiore and Ripasso show. The former
offers an intense, elegant nose of wild
berries, aromatic herbs and flowers,
leading into a stylish, long palate, earning it
a Tre Bicchieri. The latter shows riper, more
summery fruit, notes of balsam and
Mediterranean scrub, and a flavoursome,
relaxed palate, with perfectly integrated
tannins.

● Valpolicella Sup. '13	▼▼▼ 3*
● Valpolicella Sup. Ripasso '12	▼▼ 4
● Amarone della Valpolicella '10	▼▼ 6
○ Drago Bianco '14	▼ 3
☉ Drago Rosé '14	▼ 3
● Amarone della Valpolicella Ris. '07	▽▽▽ 6
● Valpolicella Sup. '12	▽▽▽ 2*
● Amarone della Valpolicella '09	▽▽ 6
● Amarone della Valpolicella Ris. '09	▽▽ 6
● Amarone della Valpolicella Ris. '08	▽▽ 7
● Amarone della Valpolicella Ris. '06	▽▽ 6
○ Bianco del Drago '13	▽▽ 3
● Valpolicella Sup. Ripasso '11	▽▽ 4
● Valpolicella Sup. Ripasso '10	▽▽ 3
● Valpolicella Sup. Ripasso '07	▽▽ 3*

Daniele Nardello

via IV novembre, 56
37032 Monteforte d'Alpone [VR]
Tel. 0457612116
www.nardellovini.it

CELLAR SALES
PRE-BOOKED VISITS
ANNUAL PRODUCTION 50,000 bottles
HECTARES UNDER VINE 16.00

The Soave district is scattered with small
cellars that produce grapes for cooperative
wineries but there are also a large number
of other operations that have decided to
strike out on their own and deal with the
entire production process. Some of them
produce the most important wines in the
DOC zone. Daniele Nardello and his sister
Federica farm over 15 hectares of their
own vineyards in the classic zone, using
the grapes from the best plots for their
extremely elegant wines. This elegance is
also pursued in the most important wine,
the Soave Monte Zoppega, which embodies
the unmistakable hallmark that this hill
gives its grapes. The position of the
vineyard at the bottom of the hill, and the
south-facing aspect, sheltered from the
cooler breezes, endows the wine with a
sunny nature, seen in its aromas of
yellow-fleshed fruit and the creamy,
full-flavoured palate, exalted by partial
ageing in oak. The Vigna Turbian meanwhile
seeks greater freshness and grip, and
displays a dry, linear, juicy palate.

○ Soave Cl. Monte Zoppega '13	▼▼ 3*
○ Blanc De Fè '14	▼▼ 2*
○ Soave Cl. Meridies '14	▼▼ 2*
○ Soave Cl. V. Turbian '14	▼▼ 2*
○ Soave Cl. Meridies '13	▽▽ 2*
○ Soave Cl. Meridies '12	▽▽ 2*
○ Soave Cl. Monte Zoppega '12	▽▽ 3
○ Soave Cl. Monte Zoppega '11	▽▽ 3*
○ Soave Cl. V. Turbian '13	▽▽ 2*
○ Soave Cl. V. Turbian '12	▽▽ 2*

Angelo Nicolis e Figli

VIA VILLA GIRARDI, 29
37029 SAN PIETRO IN CARIANO [VR]
TEL. 0457701261
www.vininicolis.com

CELLAR SALES
PRE-BOOKED VISITS
ANNUAL PRODUCTION 220,000 bottles
HECTARES UNDER VINE 42.00

The winery owned by the Nicolis brothers is one of the best known and most appreciated in Valpolicella, with decades of experience in this territory and a vineyard that covers over 40 hectares, providing the grapes for production dedicated almost entirely to the DOC zone's typical wines. The cellar in Via Villa Girardi Giuseppe is dedicated to the production of classic-style wines, which combine tradition and the unique potential that Giancarlo manages to extract from his grapes. The Amarone boasts an original aromatic profile of dried red berry fruit over smoky and mineral aromas, swathed in notes of Mediterranean scrub and pepper. In the mouth, power is not sought as an end in itself, but to support the succulent, caressing palate, which finishes long. The Valpolicella Seccal avails itself of the ripasso technique to offer complex, articulated aromas, that come to the fore on a firm, crisp palate.

● Amarone della Valpolicella Cl. '09	♟♟	6
● Testal '12	♟♟	4
● Valpolicella Cl. Sup. Ripasso Seccal '12	♟♟	3
● Valpolicella Cl. '14	♟	2
● Amarone della Valpolicella Cl. Ambrosan '06	♟♟♟	7
● Amarone della Valpolicella Cl. '08	♟♟	6
● Amarone della Valpolicella Cl. '07	♟♟	6
● Amarone della Valpolicella Cl. Ambrosan '07	♟♟	7
● Recioto della Valpolicella Cl. '10	♟♟	5
● Valpolicella Cl. Sup. '11	♟♟	3
● Valpolicella Cl. Sup. '10	♟♟	3

Nino Franco

VIA GARIBALDI, 147
31049 VALDOBBIADENE [TV]
TEL. 0423972051
www.ninofranco.it

CELLAR SALES
PRE-BOOKED VISITS
ACCOMMODATION AND RESTAURANT SERVICE
ANNUAL PRODUCTION 1,000,000 bottles
HECTARES UNDER VINE 3.50

With nearly a century in business, the Franco family winery is reaping the rewards of its development, which probably made it the best-known brand of Prosecco abroad in the 1970s, when the young Primo took over the reins of the company. Today, half a century later, he is still the winery's heart and soul, assisted by his daughter Silvia who increasingly lends a hand in both marketing and management. Production is based on a dense network of growers, who are supervised throughout the production process. The Grave di Stecca was left to rest in the cellar, but the Riva di San Floriano made up for it. On the nose, white-fleshed fruit and jasmine pave the way for an even more convincing palate, with the fizz elegantly accompanying dynamic progression and gutsy acidic grip. The Primo Franco is as always a thoroughbred, boasting summery fruit aromas and a creamy palate. Already excellent, it will hold wonderful surprises for those prepared to wait a few years.

○ Valdobbiadene Brut V. della Riva di S. Floriano '14	♟♟	3*
○ Valdobbiadene Dry Primo Franco '14	♟♟	3*
○ Cartizze	♟♟	4
○ Valdobbiadene Brut	♟♟	3
○ P. di Treviso Brut Rustico	♟	2
○ Brut Grave di Stecca '11	♟♟♟	5
○ Brut Grave di Stecca '09	♟♟♟	5
○ Valdobbiadene Brut Grave di Stecca '08	♟♟♟	5
○ Valdobbiadene Brut V. della Riva di S. Floriano '11	♟♟♟	3*
○ Brut Grave di Stecca '10	♟♟	5
○ P. di Valdobbiadene Dry Primo Franco '07	♟♟	3
○ Valdobbiadene Brut V. della Riva di S. Floriano '12	♟♟	3*
○ Valdobbiadene Dry Primo Franco '13	♟♟	3*

Novaia

via Novaia, 1
37020 Marano di Valpolicella [VR]
Tel. 0457755129
www.novaia.it

CELLAR SALES
PRE-BOOKED VISITS
ANNUAL PRODUCTION 45,000 bottles
HECTARES UNDER VINE 7.00
VITICULTURE METHOD Certified Organic
SUSTAINABLE WINERY

Giampaolo and Marcello Vaona farm seven hectares of their own vineyards in the Marano Valley using organic farming methods. They seek a balance between the desire to produce quality wines and environmental and economic sustainability. There are two lines dedicated entirely to the wines of the territory, with the most ambitious indicating the vineyard of provenance, while the other, more traditional line offers wines of great charm. As always, the products of the Vaona family focus on finesse, with the Amarone Corte Vaona showing an impressively composed nose of crushed fruit swathed in spice and dried flowers, followed by silky tannins underpinning the subtle, long palate. The Valpolicella I Cantoni offers a more expressive nose of chewy fruit framed in oak, over powerful thrust on the palate and a warm finish.

● Amarone della Valpolicella Cl. Corte Vaona '11	▼▼ 5
● Recioto della Valpolicella Cl. Le Novaje '13	▼▼ 4
● Valpolicella Cl. Sup. I Cantoni '12	▼▼ 4
● Valpolicella Cl. Sup. Ripasso '12	▼▼ 3
⊙ Rosé '14	▼ 2
● Valpolicella Cl. '14	▼ 2
● Amarone della Valpolicella Cl. '08	▽▽ 5
● Amarone della Valpolicella Cl. Corte Vaona '09	▽▽ 5
● Amarone della Valpolicella Cl. Le Balze '01	▽▽ 6
● Valpolicella Cl. '13	▽▽ 2*
● Valpolicella Cl. Sup. I Cantoni '11	▽▽ 4
● Valpolicella Cl. Sup. I Cantoni '07	▽▽ 3
● Valpolicella Cl. Sup. Ripasso '11	▽▽ 3

Ottella

fraz. San Benedetto di Lugana
loc. Ottella
37019 Peschiera del Garda [VR]
Tel. 0457551950
www.ottella.it

CELLAR SALES
PRE-BOOKED VISITS
ANNUAL PRODUCTION 350,000 bottles
HECTARES UNDER VINE 40.00

Francesco and Michele Montresor are among the most attentive and appreciated growers in the Lake Garda area, and are at the forefront of promoting Lugana all over the world. Today, their vineyards cover around 40 hectares, mostly in southern Garda, in addition to an estate at Ponti sul Mincio, where they focus instead on red grape varieties. The style exalts the fragrance of turbiana in extremely drinkable wines. Over the years, the Molceo has offered a style of aromatic fragrance and grip, and the 2013 version deservedly took home a Tre Bicchieri. Le Creete shows even more forthright aromas, dominated by tropical fruit and blossom, with persistent vegetal thrust, leading into a full-flavoured, dry palate with good progression. We were also convinced by the simpler Lugana, with its highly pleasurable palate.

○ Lugana Molceo Ris. '13	▼▼▼ 4*
● Campo Sireso '12	▼▼ 4
○ Lugana '14	▼▼ 2*
○ Lugana Le Creete '14	▼▼ 3
⊙ Roses Roses '14	▼▼ 2*
○ Vignenuove '14	▼▼ 2*
● Gemei Rosso '14	▼ 2
○ Lugana Molceo Ris. '12	▽▽▽ 4*
○ Lugana Sup. Molceo '11	▽▽▽ 4*
○ Lugana Sup. Molceo '10	▽▽▽ 4*
○ Lugana Sup. Molceo '09	▽▽▽ 4
○ Lugana Sup. Molceo '08	▽▽▽ 4
○ Lugana Sup. Molceo '07	▽▽▽ 4
○ Lugana Le Creete '12	▽▽ 3*
○ Prima Luce Passito '09	▽▽ 5
○ Prima Luce Passito '08	▽▽ 5

VENETO

Pasqua - Cecilia Beretta

LOC. SAN FELICE EXTRA
VIA BELVEDERE, 135
37131 VERONA
TEL. 0458432111
www.pasqua.it

CELLAR SALES
PRE-BOOKED VISITS
ANNUAL PRODUCTION 13,000,000 bottles
HECTARES UNDER VINE 139.00

The Pasqua family winery is one of Italy's great producers, present all over the world and at the same time deeply rooted in its land of origin, Valpolicella. The entire production process takes place in the cellar at San Felice, using grapes from the 100-plus hectares of the cellar's own vineyards and from a large number of local growers, resulting in a range that shows consistent quality year after year. The operation has its own farm, Cecilia Beretta, which is its crowning glory. The range proposed by this major winery from Verona has no weak points, with two Amarones just a whisker off top honours. The Terre di Cariano, a fine Riserva version, shows elegant aromas of black berry fruit, quinine and pepper, over a dry, firm palate of impressive length. The more Mediterranean, complex Famiglia Pasqua shows exuberant fruit with hints of crushed flowers, hemmed in by oak. Although full and lustrous, the palate loses nothing in harmony and drinkability.

★★Leonildo Pieropan

VIA CAMUZZONI, 3
37038 SOAVE [VR]
TEL. 0456190171
www.pieropan.it

CELLAR SALES
PRE-BOOKED VISITS
ANNUAL PRODUCTION 380,000 bottles
HECTARES UNDER VINE 62.00
VITICULTURE METHOD Certified Organic

The Pieropan family winery should be taken as an example not only for the impeccable quality of its wines, but for the way in which it has managed to develop over the years, increasing its vineyard holdings without rushing, choosing the best-aspected sites and remaining focused on traditional types, without pandering to a market that wants something new every year. Nino and Teresita are gradually handing over to sons Andrea and Dario, who work to the style established by their parents. The tasting of the Calvarino 2013 confirms this vision. The wine gradually releases its aromas on the nose, first white-fleshed fruit, then fresh-cut flowers, and lastly mineral notes, which will come to the fore with ageing. The subtle palate perfectly echoes the nose, and is long and captivating. La Rocca, from soils with higher levels of limestone and barrel aged, shows sweet, ripe fruit, while maintaining grip and length on the palate. The Amarone is firm, supple and linear.

● Amarone della Valpolicella Cl. Terre di Cariano Cecilia Beretta Ris. '10	▼▼ 8
● Amarone della Valpolicella Famiglia Pasqua '06	▼▼ 6
● Amarone della Valpolicella Cecilia Beretta '11	▼▼ 6
● Amarone della Valpolicella Cl. Villa Borghetti Pasqua '11	▼▼ 6
● Picàie Cecilia Beretta '11	▼▼ 5
● Valpolicella Cl. Sup. Terre di Cariano Cecilia Beretta '12	▼▼ 2*
● Valpolicella Sup. Mizzole Cecilia Beretta '12	▼▼ 3
● Valpolicella Sup. Ripasso Cecilia Beretta '13	▼▼ 3
● Valpolicella Sup. Ripasso Famiglia Pasqua '13	▼▼ 4
○ Soave Cl. Brognoligo Cecilia Beretta '14	▼ 1*

○ Soave Cl. Calvarino '13	▼▼▼ 4*
○ Soave Cl. La Rocca '13	▼▼ 5
● Amarone della Valpolicella '11	▼▼ 6
○ Recioto di Soave Le Colombare '11	▼▼ 5
○ Soave Cl. '14	▼▼ 3
● Valpolicella Sup. Ruberpan V. Garzon '12	▼▼ 4
○ Soave Cl. Calvarino '09	▼▼▼ 4*
○ Soave Cl. Calvarino '08	▼▼▼ 4
○ Soave Cl. Calvarino '07	▼▼▼ 4
○ Soave Cl. Calvarino '06	▼▼▼ 4
○ Soave Cl. Calvarino '05	▼▼▼ 3
○ Soave Cl. Calvarino '04	▼▼▼ 3
○ Soave Cl. La Rocca '12	▼▼▼ 5
○ Soave Cl. La Rocca '11	▼▼▼ 5
○ Soave Cl. La Rocca '10	▼▼▼ 5

Albino Piona

FRAZ. CUSTOZA
VIA BELLAVISTA, 48
37060 SOMMACAMPAGNA [VR]
TEL. 045516055
www.albinopiona.it

CELLAR SALES
PRE-BOOKED VISITS
ANNUAL PRODUCTION 200,000 bottles
HECTARES UNDER VINE 77.00

The operation the Piona brothers inherited from their father Albino is dedicated to the production of reliable, pleasurable wines, and they have turned it into a winery that pursues the highest quality in the DOC zones of Lake Garda: Bardolino and Custoza. The chance to work with an extremely large vineyard, while significantly limiting production, allows Silvio, Monica, Alessandro, and Massimo to make uncompromising choices both in the rows and in the cellar, for products that show great personality while remaining light and drinkable. In the absence of the SP selections, left to rest in the cellar for another year, we concentrated on the Custoza, a wine which, despite the complicated 2014 harvest, shows an aromatic profile of great complexity, dominated by white-fleshed fruit, but also showing elegant nuances of fresh-cut flowers and saffron. On the palate, impressive grip is buttressed by full flavour, leading to a long finish. The Bardolino meanwhile plays on its spice, and shows a taut, gutsy palate with satisfying progression.

○ Custoza '14	♛♛	2*
● Bardolino '14	♛♛	2*
● Campo Massimo Corvina Veronese '12	♛♛	2*
⊙ Bardolino Chiaretto '14	♛	2
● Campo Massimo Merlot '09	♛	3
○ Estro di Piona Brut	♛	4
○ Verde Piona Frizzante	♛	2
● Bardolino '13	♛♛	2*
● Bardolino SP '12	♛♛	2*
● Bardolino SP '11	♛♛	2*
● Campo Massimo Corvina Veronese '11	♛♛	2*
○ Custoza '13	♛♛	2*
○ Custoza '12	♛♛	2*
○ Custoza SP '13	♛♛	2*
○ Custoza SP '12	♛♛	2*
○ Custoza Sup. Campo del Selese '12	♛♛	2*

Piovene Porto Godi

FRAZ. TOARA
VIA VILLA, 14
36020 VILLAGA [VI]
TEL. 0444885142
www.piovene.com

CELLAR SALES
PRE-BOOKED VISITS
ANNUAL PRODUCTION 100,000 bottles
HECTARES UNDER VINE 36.00

The winery of Tommaso Piovene Porto Godi is based in the southern part of the Colli Berici, and covers over 200 hectares, of which over 30 are under vine. This southern strip of Veneto enjoys an extremely sunny, dry climate, which allows the grapes to ripen perfectly every year, exploiting the cooler aspects and elevations of up to 250 metres, which give the grapes freshness and finesse. The main focus is on the traditional variety of the zone, tai rosso, as well as on Bordeaux varieties, interpreted in rich, summery wines. The Cabernet del Vigneto Pozzare embodies a perfect fusion of warmth, Mediterranean character and grip. Dominant aromas of fruit on the nose increasingly make way for aromatic herbs and cloves, to then encore powerfully on the rich, juicy, long palate. The Tai Rosso Thovara shows greater complexity on the nose, but still overly evident oak on the palate. Time will do justice to this splendid wine.

● Colli Berici Cabernet Vign. Pozzare '12	♛♛♛	4*
● Colli Berici Tai Rosso Thovara '12	♛♛	5
○ Colli Berici Garganega Vign. Riveselle '14	♛♛	2*
○ Colli Berici Pinot Bianco Polveriera '14	♛♛	4
○ Thovara Passito '12	♛♛	4
○ Colli Berici Sauvignon Vign. Fostine '14	♛	2
● Colli Berici Tai Rosso Vign. Riveselle '14	♛	2
● Colli Berici Cabernet Vign. Pozzare '07	♛♛♛	3
● Colli Berici Cabernet Vign. Pozzare '08	♛♛	3
● Colli Berici Merlot Fra i Broli '12	♛♛	4
● Colli Berici Merlot Fra i Broli '11	♛♛	4
● Colli Berici Merlot Fra i Broli '09	♛♛	5
● Colli Berici Merlot Fra i Broli '08	♛♛	5
● Colli Berici Merlot Fra i Broli '07	♛♛	5
● Colli Berici Tai Rosso Thovara '11	♛♛	5
● Colli Berici Tai Rosso Thovara '09	♛♛	5

★Graziano Prà

VIA DELLA FONTANA, 31
37032 MONTEFORTE D'ALPONE [VR]
TEL. 0457612125
www.vinipra.it

CELLAR SALES
PRE-BOOKED VISITS
ACCOMMODATION
ANNUAL PRODUCTION 250,000 bottles
HECTARES UNDER VINE 35.00
VITICULTURE METHOD Certified Organic

Among the companies that best represent Soave in the world, a leading role surely goes to Graziano Prà's winery, which has been working for decades here. Alongside the production of Soave, for the last ten years it has also been producing Valpolicella, from the Morandina estate, a vineyard high in the hills of bright white marl and limestone soil, producing grapes with an aromatic, spirited character. Production, dedicated to focused, elegant Soaves, takes place in the cellar at Monteforte. The Soave Staforte, a monovarietal garganega from basalt soils at Monteforte, made an excellent impression. Long ageing in stainless steel provides aromatic depth, with fruit over a backdrop of fresh-cut flowers and flint, followed by a full, grippy palate. The Monte Grande, aged in oak barrels, exploits the 2014 vintage to show greater freshness and dynamism.

○ Soave Cl. Staforte '13	♥♥♥ 4*
○ Soave Cl. Monte Grande '14	♥♥ 4
● Valpolicella Sup. Rip. Morandina '13	♥♥ 4
○ Soave Cl. Otto '14	♥ 2
● Valpolicella Morandina '14	♥ 2
○ Soave Cl. Monte Grande '11	♥♥♥ 4*
○ Soave Cl. Monte Grande '08	♥♥♥ 4
○ Soave Cl. Monte Grande '06	♥♥♥ 4
○ Soave Cl. Monte Grande '05	♥♥♥ 3
○ Soave Cl. Monte Grande '04	♥♥♥ 3
○ Soave Cl. Monte Grande '03	♥♥♥ 2*
○ Soave Cl. Staforte '11	♥♥♥ 4*
○ Soave Cl. Staforte '08	♥♥♥ 4
○ Soave Cl. Staforte '06	♥♥♥ 4*

★Giuseppe Quintarelli

VIA CERÈ, 1
37024 NEGRAR [VR]
TEL. 0457500016
giuseppe.quintarelli@tin.it

CELLAR SALES
PRE-BOOKED VISITS
ANNUAL PRODUCTION 60,000 bottles
HECTARES UNDER VINE 10.00

Many things have changed in recent years at Quintarelli, but now as before the wine remains perfectly true to an approach in which tradition, respect for the type, modernity and charm converge, earning this winery iconic status in Valpolicella. The vineyards, planted on a bare ten hectares in the heart of the classic zone, are dedicated to the traditional grapes of the territory, while at the cellar in Via Cerè the wines mature for long periods until considered ready for the market. The Amarone 2006 presents intense sensations of super-ripe fruit on the nose, with deep meaty aromas and dried flowers, leading into medicinal herbs that refresh and provide thrust. Hefty power on the palate is governed with grace and precision, and the wine shows glossy tannins and dynamic, elegant progression. The Valpolicella, from the following vintage, shows attractive notes of dried fruit and spice over a warm, caressing palate.

● Amarone della Valpolicella Cl. '06	♥♥♥ 8
● Valpolicella Cl. Sup. '07	♥♥ 7
● Amarone della Valpolicella Cl. '03	♥♥♥ 8
● Amarone della Valpolicella Cl. '98	♥♥♥ 8
● Amarone della Valpolicella Cl. '97	♥♥♥ 8
● Amarone della Valpolicella Cl. Sup. Monte Cà Paletta '00	♥♥♥ 8
● Amarone della Valpolicella Cl. Sup. Monte Cà Paletta '93	♥♥♥ 8
● Amarone della Valpolicella Cl. Sup. Ris. '85	♥♥♥ 8
● Recioto della Valpolicella Cl. '01	♥♥♥ 8
● Recioto della Valpolicella Cl. '95	♥♥♥ 5
● Recioto della Valpolicella Cl. Monte Ca' Paletta '97	♥♥♥ 8
● Rosso del Bepi '96	♥♥♥ 8
● Valpolicella Cl. Sup. '99	♥♥♥ 7

Le Ragose

FRAZ. ARBIZZANO
VIA LE RAGOSE, 1
37024 NEGRAR [VR]
TEL. 0457513241
www.leragose.com

CELLAR SALES
PRE-BOOKED VISITS
ANNUAL PRODUCTION 120,000 bottles
HECTARES UNDER VINE 18.00

Paolo and Marco Galli are faithful
interpreters of Valpolicella, the guardians of
a territory and tradition that they do not
want to forget or distort. The estate covers
around 20 hectares in the hills on the edge
of the DOC zone, where the heat of the
summer days promptly cools when night
falls. Their viticultural methods respect
environment and tradition, and are echoed
in equally judicious cellar practices, which
allow the wines to evolve naturally. The
Amarone Marta Galli is in fact not released
until eight years after the harvest. This red
shows a nose of dried fruit, with original
animal and mineral notes, followed by a
rich, enfolding palate in which a certain
sweetness is offset by acidity and tannins.
The Cabernet Sauvignon shows a nose
dominated by vegetal aromas and a dense,
leisurely palate.

F.lli Recchia

LOC. JAGO
VIA CA' BERTOLDI, 30
37024 NEGRAR [VR]
TEL. 0457500584
www.recchiavini.it

CELLAR SALES
PRE-BOOKED VISITS
ANNUAL PRODUCTION 250,000 bottles
HECTARES UNDER VINE 100.00

The Recchia family has managed to
increase production significantly but has
never compromised the winery style or
purchased grapes from outside. The
vineyards, which cover around 100
hectares, allow the winery to make
judicious decisions on the batches to use
for its wines, subdividing the range into two
lines: the Masua di Jago for the more
traditional labels, and a series of more
ambitious wines from the best plots. We
saw a good performance from the Ripasso
Masua di Jago, offering a nose of
super-ripe fruit and spice against an
intensely smoky backdrop. Good length on
the palate is accompanied by captivating
flavour and grip. The Amarone Ca' Bertoldi
instead shows upfront aromas of dried fruit
on the nose, with swathes of bitter
chocolate and tobacco, leading into a
powerful palate. The Ripasso Le Muraie
boasts a potent, exuberant character, with
oaky notes still evident.

● Amarone della Valpolicella Cl. Marta Galli '07	♥♥ 7
● Cabernet Sauvignon '10	♥♥ 3
● Valpolicella Cl. Sup. Ripasso Le Sassine '11	♥♥ 3
● Valpolicella Cl. '14	♥ 2
● Amarone della Valpolicella Cl. Caloetto '06	♥♥♥ 7
● Amarone della Valpolicella Cl. Marta Galli '05	♥♥♥ 8
● Amarone della Valpolicella Marta Galli '01	♥♥ 7
● Valpolicella Cl. Ripasso '09	♥♥ 3*
● Valpolicella Cl. Sup. Le Sassine '05	♥♥ 3
● Valpolicella Cl. Sup. Le Sassine '03	♥♥ 3
● Valpolicella Cl. Sup. Ripasso Le Sassine '07	♥♥ 3

● Amarone della Valpolicella Cl. Ca' Bertoldi '09	♥♥ 5
● Recioto della Valpolicella Cl. La Guardia '11	♥♥ 4
● Valpolicella Cl. Sup. Ripasso Le Muraie '13	♥♥ 3
● Valpolicella Cl. Sup. Ripasso Masua di Jago '13	♥♥ 2*
● Amarone della Valpolicella Cl. Masua di Jago '12	♥ 5
● Recioto della Valpolicella Cl. Masua di Jago '13	♥ 4
● Valpolicella Cl. Masua di Jago '14	♥ 2
● Amarone della Valpolicella Cl. Masua di Jago '11	♥♥ 5
● Valpolicella Cl. Sup. Ripasso Masua di Jago '12	♥♥ 2*

Roccolo Grassi

VIA SAN GIOVANNI DI DIO, 19
37030 MEZZANE DI SOTTO [VR]
TEL. 0458880089
www.roccolograssi.it

PRE-BOOKED VISITS
ANNUAL PRODUCTION 49,000 bottles
HECTARES UNDER VINE 14.00
SUSTAINABLE WINERY

Marco and Francesca Sartori have
managed to manage the success of their
winery with great composure, without
bowing down to the pressing requests of
the market, but instead developing their
wines the way they see fit. Great attention
is given to the vineyards, strictly used for
one type rather than another on the basis
of their individual characteristics, while at
the cellar there has been continuous
experimentation, initially with small oak,
then larger barrels and now concrete. The
Amarone 2011 offers intense aromas of
intact, ripe red berry fruit, with a certain
oakiness that just needs time to soften.
Notes of white pepper and thyme slowly
emerge to once more make way for fruit on
the palate, where the wine's power is
managed admirably. We find a similar style,
albeit scaled down, in the Valpolicella,
which is fresher and more elegant, but
equally harmonious. We should lastly note
an excellent version of Soave La Broia, a
white of substance and finesse.

● Amarone della Valpolicella '11	♥♥	8
● Valpolicella Sup. '12	♥♥	5
○ Soave Sup. La Broia '13	♥♥	3
● Amarone della Valpolicella
Roccolo Grassi '07	♥♥♥	8
● Amarone della Valpolicella
Roccolo Grassi '00	♥♥♥	7
● Amarone della Valpolicella
Roccolo Grassi '99	♥♥♥	7
● Valpolicella Sup. '11	♥♥♥	5
● Valpolicella Sup. Roccolo Grassi '09	♥♥♥	5
● Valpolicella Sup. Roccolo Grassi '07	♥♥♥	5
● Valpolicella Sup. Roccolo Grassi '04	♥♥♥	5
● Amarone della Valpolicella '09	♥♥	8
● Recioto della Valpolicella
Roccolo Grassi '09	♥♥	5

Roeno

VIA MAMA, 5
37020 BRENTINO BELLUNO [VR]
TEL. 0457230110
www.cantinaroeno.com

CELLAR SALES
PRE-BOOKED VISITS
ACCOMMODATION AND RESTAURANT SERVICE
ANNUAL PRODUCTION 340,000 bottles
HECTARES UNDER VINE 60.00
SUSTAINABLE WINERY

The Fugatti brothers' operation grows year
by year, with vineyards now found all over
Valdadige. They have a clear mission,
aimed at developing and promoting this
borderland, lying between the two giants of
Alto Adige to the north, and the Veronese
DOC zones to the south. Alongside the
typical international varieties of the zone,
great attention is given to enantio, the
cultivar that more than any other is
characteristic of this area. Once again this
year, our praises go to the Cristina, a
late-harvest wine from pinot grigio,
chardonnay, gewürztraminer and
sauvignon, with a kaleidoscopic nose of
citrus, tropical fruit and liquorice. On the
palate, the sweetness is elegantly kept in
check by the acidity. We were impressed
with the new wine from Roeno, the Riesling
Collezione di Famiglia, a white which
undergoes long cellar ageing and shows a
German style, with a penetrating nose and
spirited palate, well sustained by acidity
and residual sugar.

○ Cristina V. T. '12	♥♥♥	5
○ Riesling Renano
Collezione di Famiglia '14	♥♥	5
● La Rua Marzemino '14	♥♥	2*
○ Praecipuus '13	♥♥	4
● Roeno '11	♥♥	4
○ Valdadige Pinot Grigio Tera Alta '14	♥♥	2*
● Valdadige Terra dei Forti Enantio '11	♥♥	4
☉ Bardolino Chiaretto Brut Matì Rosé	♥	3
☉ Teroldego I Dossi '13	♥	2
○ Valdadige Chardonnay Le Fratte '14	♥	2
○ Cristina V. T. '11	♥♥♥	5
○ Cristina V. T. '08	♥♥♥	5
○ Cristina V. T. '10	♥♥	5
○ Cristina V. T. '09	♥♥	5
○ Cristina V. T. '07	♥♥	5
● Valdadige Terra dei Forti Enantio Ris. '08	♥♥	4

Rubinelli Vajol

LOC. SAN FLORIANO
VIA PALADON, 31
37029 SAN PIETRO IN CARIANO [VR]
TEL. 0456839277
www.rubinellivajol.it

CELLAR SALES
PRE-BOOKED VISITS
ACCOMMODATION
ANNUAL PRODUCTION 50,000 bottles
HECTARES UNDER VINE 10.00

The Rubinelli family, who have a long history in Valpolicella, established this winery just a few years ago and today farm around ten hectares within a south-facing amphitheatre in the area known as Vajol. The entire production process, from partial drying to bottling, takes place in the cellar in Via Paladon. Production figures are still limited, but year after year the wines win over critics for their ability to interpret tradition with lightness and elegance. The Ripasso was emblematic; this is a type which is generally interpreted to exalt richness and sweetness, but at Rubinelli it pursues aromatic complexity and grip. Super-ripe fruit and Mediterranean scrub on the nose are followed on the palate by peppery nuances, and the wine progresses supple and long. The more straightforward Amarone offers intense fruit on the nose over a full, juicy palate.

● Valpolicella Cl. Sup. Ripasso '12	♥♥	5
● Amarone della Valpolicella Cl. '11	♥♥	7
● Valpolicella Cl. Sup. '11	♥♥	4
● Valpolicella Cl. '14	♥	3
● Amarone della Valpolicella Cl. '10	♀♀	6
● Amarone della Valpolicella Cl. '07	♀♀	6
● Recioto della Valpolicella Cl. '11	♀♀	6
● Valpolicella Cl. '13	♀♀	2*
● Valpolicella Cl. Sup. '10	♀♀	4
● Valpolicella Cl. Sup. Ripasso '11	♀♀	4

Ruggeri & C.

VIA PRÀ FONTANA, 4
31049 VALDOBBIADENE [TV]
TEL. 04239092
www.ruggeri.it

CELLAR SALES
PRE-BOOKED VISITS
ANNUAL PRODUCTION 1,000,000 bottles
HECTARES UNDER VINE 17.00

Things have been happening at the Ruggeri winery, with the acquisition of a small vineyard in the heart of Cartizze, resting on an unbelievably steep slope that offers a view over the vineyards which is to say the least breath-taking. It has become part of the small Prosecco holdings of the Bisol family, who rely on consolidated partnerships with many local growers for the rest of their raw materials, supervising throughout the year. In a difficult growing year such as 2014, the skill of those working in the rows and at the cellar was crucial, but we should also remember that the oldest vineyards were better able to cope with difficulties. It is no surprise that the Vecchie Viti gave a textbook performance, with aromas of blossom and white-fleshed fruit, over an exceptionally gutsy, taut palate. The Giustino B., Celebrating its first 20 years of production, offers an elegant nose and harmonious palate, and is an outstanding example of the Extra Dry type.

○ Valdobbiadene Brut V. V. '14	♥♥♥	4*
○ Valdobbiadene Extra Dry Giustino B. '14	♥♥	4
○ Cartizze	♥♥	5
○ Valdobbiadene Brut Quartese	♥♥	3
○ Valdobbiadene Dry S. Stefano	♥♥	3
○ Valdobbiadene Extra Dry Giall'Oro	♥♥	3
○ Valdobbiadene Extra Dry Vigne Alte	♥♥	4
○ Valdobbiadene Brut Vecchie Viti '13	♀♀♀	4*
○ Valdobbiadene Extra Dry Giustino B. '12	♀♀♀	3*
○ Valdobbiadene Extra Dry Giustino B. '11	♀♀♀	3*
○ Valdobbiadene Extra Dry Giustino B. '10	♀♀♀	3
○ Valdobbiadene Extra Dry Giustino B. '09	♀♀♀	3
○ Valdobbiadene Extra Dry Giustino B. '13	♀♀	4

Le Salette

VIA PIO BRUGNOLI, 11c
37022 FUMANE [VR]
TEL. 0457701027
www.lesalette.it

CELLAR SALES
PRE-BOOKED VISITS
ANNUAL PRODUCTION 130,000 bottles
HECTARES UNDER VINE 20.00

Franco Scamperle has turned the family
farm into a benchmark for lovers of
Amarone, with a vineyard located in some
of the area's best wine country. At Fumane,
Sant'Ambrogio and San Floriano he tends
vineyards in which pergola and Guyot
training systems alternate according to the
age of the vineyard. Plantings are entirely
dedicated to traditional varieties, and
grapes are selected specifically at harvest
for the most important labels. The two
Pergole Vece wines, an Amarone and a
Recioto, were excellent. The former boasts
an approachable, captivating nose of
sweet, juicy red berry fruit, slowly making
way for notes of pepper and medicinal
herbs, followed by a full, succulent palate.
The latter, if possible, shows even more
approachable, abundant fruit, while the
irrepressible sweetness on the palate is
counterpointed by good acidity and tannins,
for well-managed yet exuberant
progression. The Amarone La Marega is
velvety and racy.

● Amarone della Valpolicella Cl. Pergole Vece '11	▼▼ 8
● Recioto della Valpolicella Cl. Pergole Vece '12	▼▼ 6
● Amarone della Valpolicella Cl. La Marega '11	▼▼ 6
● Ca' Carnocchio '12	▼▼ 4
● Valpolicella Cl. Sup. Ripasso I Progni '13	▼▼ 3
● Valpolicella Cl. '14	▼ 2
● Amarone della Valpolicella Cl. Pergole Vece '05	♀♀♀ 8
● Amarone della Valpolicella Cl. Pergole Vece '10	♀♀ 8
● Amarone della Valpolicella Cl. Pergole Vece '07	♀♀ 8
● Recioto della Valpolicella Cl. Pergole Vece '09	♀♀ 6

SalvaTerra

LOC. NEGARINE
VIA NEGARINE, 14
37029 SAN PIETRO IN CARIANO [VR]
TEL. 0456801833
www.salvaterrawine.it

CELLAR SALES
PRE-BOOKED VISITS
ANNUAL PRODUCTION 80,000 bottles
HECTARES UNDER VINE 16.00

Although the SalvaTerra winery is extremely
new on the scene, the brothers behind this
adventure have a much deeper and longer
bond with wine, and with Valpolicella in
particular. The Furia brothers, together with
a group of investors, also with experience
in other winegrowing zones, have
established this new winery with extensive
vineyard holdings covering an area that
ranges from Lake Garda to eastern Veneto,
although the Valpolicella estates in the
SalvaTerra project number four: Prun, in the
northern part of the Valpolicella Classica
zone; Villa Giona, a beautiful farm at
Cengia; and Mezzane and Cazzano di
Tramigna in eastern Valpolicella. It was
precisely the vineyard at Prun that gave us
an Amarone Riserva of great aromatic
depth, with an elegant, supple, linear
palate. The Amarone Classico, meanwhile,
expresses greater freshness on the nose
and a dry, dynamic palate. The grapes for
the production of Prosecco and Pinot Grigio
instead come from the Vescovana estate,
on the edge of the Colli Euganei.

● Amarone della Valpolicella Cl. '08	▼▼ 8
● Amarone della Valpolicella Cl. Cave di Prun Ris. '04	▼▼ 5
● Valpolicella Cl. Sup. Ripasso '12	▼▼ 5
● Lazzarone '10	▼ 5
○ Pinot Grigio '14	▼ 5
○ Prosecco Extra Dry	▼ 4
● Valpolicella Cl. '13	▼ 3

Marco Sambin

LOC. VALNOGAREDO
VIA FATTORELLE, 20A
35030 CINTO EUGANEO [PD]
TEL. 3456812050
www.vinimarcus.com

CELLAR SALES
PRE-BOOKED VISITS
RESTAURANT SERVICE
ANNUAL PRODUCTION 7,700 bottles
HECTARES UNDER VINE 3.00
SUSTAINABLE WINERY

Marco Sambin is not a typical entrepreneur, since he is also a professor of psychology at the University of Padua. At the beginning of the new millennium, he decided to start something new, and establish a farm in the heart of Colli Euganei, an area he had always visited and loved. Here, he now produces wine and teaches the young psychotherapists who come to stay. He owns a few hectares in Valnogaredo, on the south-western slopes of Monte Versa, on dry limestone soil, where the vines grow in ideal conditions. Although not producing any wines that fall within the Colli Euganei DOC zone, Sambin's style is deeply rooted in this territory, as we see when tasting its top label, the Marcus, a Bordeaux blend with a splash of syrah that struck us with its ripe, caressing, sunny Mediterranean aromas, which come back with force on the full, juicy, beautifully long palate. Its little brother, Alter, from younger vineyards, shows greater freshness and self-confidence on the palate.

● Alter '13	▼▼ 4
● Marcus '12	▼▼ 5
○ Martha.due '14	▼▼ 3
⊙ Isabel '14	▼ 3
● Marcus '11	♀♀ 5
● Marcus '10	♀♀ 5
● Marcus '09	♀♀ 4
● Marcus '08	♀♀ 4
● Micael '11	♀♀ 5

San Rustico

FRAZ. VALGATARA DI VALPOLICELLA
VIA POZZO, 2
37020 MARANO DI VALPOLICELLA [VR]
TEL. 0457703348
www.sanrustico.it

CELLAR SALES
PRE-BOOKED VISITS
ANNUAL PRODUCTION 250,000 bottles
HECTARES UNDER VINE 22.00

The great success sweeping over Valpolicella in recent decades has not found the Campagnola brothers unprepared, and they have responded to the pressing needs of the market without sacrificing a traditional yet modern interpretation of the wines of this territory. Their 20-plus hectares of vineyards lie between the valleys of Marano and Fumane, for production entirely dedicated to the reds of Valpolicella, interpreted with care in a seductive style. Our favourite wine was the Ripasso Gaso, a red strongly linked to local tradition, with a nose of super-ripe fruit and crushed flowers, against a backdrop of intense vegetal notes and spice. On the palate, its richness is never excessive, and is accompanied by soft, caressing tannins. The Amarone is richer and more potent, but shows similar progression on the nose, indicative of its great ageing potential.

● Amarone della Valpolicella Cl. '10	▼▼ 6
● Amarone della Valpolicella Cl. Gaso '09	▼▼ 8
● Valpolicella Cl. Sup. Ripasso Gaso '11	▼▼ 4
● Corte Porta '10	▼ 3
● Valpolicella Cl. '14	▼ 2
● Amarone della Valpolicella Cl. '09	♀♀ 6
● Amarone della Valpolicella Cl. '08	♀♀ 5
● Amarone della Valpolicella Cl. Gaso '08	♀♀ 7
● Amarone della Valpolicella Cl. Gaso '07	♀♀ 6
● Amarone della Valpolicella Cl. Gaso '06	♀♀ 6
● Recioto della Valpolicella Cl. '09	♀♀ 5
● Recioto della Valpolicella Cl. Gaso '13	♀♀ 5
● Valpolicella Cl. Sup. '12	♀♀ 2*
● Valpolicella Cl. Sup. Ripasso Gaso '10	♀♀ 3

Tenuta Sant'Anna

LOC. LONCON
VIA MONSIGNOR P. L. ZOVATTO, 71
30020 ANNONE VENETO [VE]
TEL. 0422864511
www.tenutasantanna.it

CELLAR SALES
PRE-BOOKED VISITS
ANNUAL PRODUCTION 2,500,000 bottles
HECTARES UNDER VINE 140.00

Lison-Pramaggiore is set between the
Adriatic and the Veneto Prealps, with clayey
soils that have not yet expressed their full
potential. Tenuta Sant'Anna, which is part
of the Genagricola group, has been working
for decades here, dedicating its attention
above all to vintage wines that express the
character of the variety perfectly. In recent
years, however, efforts have focused on
quality, with increasing attention given to
Prosecco. We saw a good performance
from the Pinot Grigio of the Goccia line, a
white aged in stainless steel that offers a
broad aromatic profile, with notes of pear
and blossom over barely perceptible garden
vegetables. On the palate, the creaminess
typical of this variety is nicely offset by
good acidity, a consequence of the cool
2014 harvest. The Refosco is also
interesting, and plays on freshness,
aromatic fragrance, and approachability.

● Lison-Pramaggiore Refosco P. R. Poderi '14	♥♥ 2*
○ Venezia Pinot Grigio Goccia '14	♥♥ 2*
○ Cartizze	♥ 5
○ Lison-Pramaggiore Cl. Goccia '14	♥ 2
● Lison-Pramaggiore Merlot Poderi '14	♥ 2
○ Lison-Pramaggiore Sauvignon Goccia '14	♥ 2
○ Prosecco Extra Dry	♥ 2
● Venezia Cabernet Sauvignon Poderi '14	♥ 2
● Lison-Pramaggiore Cabernet Sauvignon P 47 '09	♥♥ 3
● Lison-Pramaggiore Cabernet Sauvignon Podere 47 Ris. '07	♥♥ 4
○ Lison-Pramaggiore Cl. Goccia '11	♥♥ 2*
● Lison-Pramaggiore Refosco P. R. '08	♥♥ 2
● Venezia Cabernet Sauvignon P 22 '13	♥♥ 2*
● Venezia Cabernet Sauvignon Pod. 47 '09	♥♥ 3

★Tenuta Sant'Antonio

LOC. SAN ZENO
VIA CERIANI, 23
37030 COLOGNOLA AI COLLI [VR]
TEL. 0457650383
www.tenutasantantonio.it

CELLAR SALES
PRE-BOOKED VISITS
ANNUAL PRODUCTION 700,000 bottles
HECTARES UNDER VINE 100.00

If greater interest is shown in eastern
Valpolicella today, much of the merit goes
to the winery of the Castagnedi brothers,
who have managed, in the space of 20
years, to bring to the limelight an area
which is largely unknown but has great
potential. Today, Armando, Tiziano, Paolo,
and Massimo run an impressive operation,
with convincing interpretation of tradition
with a style that will satisfy even the most
demanding. The large holdings under vine
provide reliable, solid wines. The hot 2011
harvest gave the Amarone Campo dei Gigli
a sunny, ripe character, with fruit perfectly
expressed in a profile in which smoky
nuances and autumn leaves also appear.
On the palate, the wine shows its usual
character, offering not only fullness and
roundness but also rich flavour. The
Valpolicella La Bandina shows a fresher,
more intriguing nose, over a juicy, taut
palate. There was an excellent debut from
the Amarone Télos, produced without
added sulphites.

● Amarone della Valpolicella Campo dei Gigli '11	♥♥♥ 8
● Valpolicella Sup. La Bandina '11	♥♥ 5
● Amarone della Valpolicella Sel. Antonio Castagnedi '12	♥♥ 6
● Amarone della Valpolicella Télos '11	♥♥ 6
○ Soave Monte Ceriani '13	♥♥ 3
○ Soave Monte Ceriani V. V. '12	♥♥ 3
● Valpolicella Sup. Ripasso Monti Garbi '13	♥♥ 3
● Valpolicella Nanfré '13	♥ 3
● Amarone della Valpolicella Campo dei Gigli '08	♥♥♥ 8
● Amarone della Valpolicella Campo dei Gigli '07	♥♥♥ 8
● Amarone della Valpolicella Campo dei Gigli '06	♥♥♥ 8
● Amarone della Valpolicella Campo dei Gigli '05	♥♥♥ 8

LE TENUTE
DI GENAGRICOLA

Discover Our World
www.letenute.it

TENUTA DI
LILLIANO

www.lilliano.it

Santa Margherita

VIA ITA MARZOTTO, 8
30025 FOSSALTA DI PORTOGRUARO [VE]
TEL. 0421246111
www.santamargherita.com

CELLAR SALES
PRE-BOOKED VISITS
ANNUAL PRODUCTION 13,500,000 bottles
HECTARES UNDER VINE 50.00

Santa Margherita is one of the Italian wineries best known worldwide, with production hinging on Pinot Grigio. The vineyards are found mainly on the plains of Veneto heading towards Friuli, but it is thanks to its agreements with important operations in Alto Adige that the winery receives the grapes for the production of its most important white. Increasing attention is given to the production of its Prosecco, distinguished by firmness on the palate. It was precisely from Alto Adige that the most interesting wines came, led by a Pinot Grigio which over the years has become a benchmark for excellence. Smoky nuances and pear aromas are followed on the palate by admirable harmony and length. We also appreciated the new version of the Luna dei Feldi, an original blend from chardonnay, müller thurgau, gewürztraminer and pinot bianco, offering elegant aromas of citrus and flowers over a succulent, taut palate.

Santa Sofia

FRAZ. PEDEMONTE DI VALPOLICELLA
VIA CA' DEDÉ, 61
37020 SAN PIETRO IN CARIANO [VR]
TEL. 0457701074
www.santasofia.com

CELLAR SALES
PRE-BOOKED VISITS
ANNUAL PRODUCTION 550,000 bottles
HECTARES UNDER VINE 38.00

For decades the Begnoni family has been one of the leading names in Valpolicella, a consolidated brand that has taken the image of Verona's wines all over the world. Luciano Begnoni is the current ambassador, assisted by his father Giancarlo, whose experience is always at hand. Production focuses on the Valpolicella wines, interpreted with great attention to tradition and long cellar ageing. The hot 2009 growing year gave Santa Sofia's Amarone a ripe, sunny nature, with jammy red fruit on the nose over a warm, alcoholic, yet silky and caressing palate. Even more interesting was the Montegradella, a Valpolicella Superiore whose fruit aromas are nicely counterpointed by fresh aromatic herbs and pepper, leading into a graceful, taut palate with good harmony and length. The Ripasso boasts a deep nose and firm palate.

○ A. A. Luna dei Feldi '14	♥♥ 3
○ A. A. Pinot Grigio Brut M.Cl. '11	♥♥ 2*
○ A. A. Pinot Grigio Impronta del Fondatore '14	♥♥ 2*
○ Cartizze	♥♥ 4
○ Valdobbiadene Brut	♥♥ 2
○ Valdobbiadene Extra Dry 52 '14	♥♥ 2*
○ Valdobbiadene Rive di Refrontolo Brut 52 '14	♥♥ 3
● Lison-Pramaggiore Malbech Impronta del Fondatore '13	♥ 2
● Lison-Pramaggiore Refosco P.R. Impronta del Fondatore '13	♥ 2
○ Valdadige Pinot Grigio '14	♥ 2
○ Valdobbiadene Extra Dry	♥ 2
● Venezia Cabernet Franc Impronta del Fondatore '13	♥ 2

● Amarone della Valpolicella Cl. '09	♥♥ 7
● Valpolicella Cl. Sup. Montegradella '11	♥♥ 4
● Valpolicella Sup. Ripasso '12	♥♥ 4
● Arleo Rosso '07	♥ 5
● Valpolicella Cl. '13	♥ 2
● Amarone della Valpolicella Cl. '08	♀♀ 6
● Amarone della Valpolicella Cl. '07	♀♀ 6
● Amarone della Valpolicella Cl. '06	♀♀ 6
● Amarone della Valpolicella Cl. '05	♀♀ 6
● Amarone della Valpolicella Cl. Gioé '07	♀♀ 7
○ Lugana '12	♀♀ 2*
● Recioto della Valpolicella Cl. '06	♀♀ 5
● Valpolicella Cl. Sup. Montegradella '08	♀♀ 4
● Valpolicella Cl. Sup. Montegradella '06	♀♀ 4
● Valpolicella Sup. Ripasso '10	♀♀ 4
● Valpolicella Sup. Ripasso '07	♀♀ 4

Santi

VIA UNGHERIA, 33
37031 ILLASI [VR]
TEL. 0456269600
www.carlosanti.it

CELLAR SALES
PRE-BOOKED VISITS
ANNUAL PRODUCTION 1,400,000 bottles
HECTARES UNDER VINE 50.00

Santi is one of the major wineries within Gruppo Italiano Vini, and the first, many years ago, to invest in its estates and the quality of its wines. Today, it can rely on 50 hectares of vineyards, and only the local expertise of its technicians makes it possible to achieve increasing characterization of its products, dedicating to each label only the grapes from the most suitable vineyards. The result is there for the whole world to see. The Amarone Proemio is once again the winery's benchmark, and one of the most interesting in the DOC zone by virtue of its aromatic profile, which unfolds slowly to reveal intriguing mineral nuances and pepper alongside the fruit, leading into a dense, austere, memorable palate. The Ripasso Solane, which plays on finesse rather than power, shows a more immediate nose and delicate palate.

Casa Vinicola Sartori

FRAZ. SANTA MARIA
VIA CASETTE, 4
37024 NEGRAR [VR]
TEL. 0456028011
www.sartorinet.com

PRE-BOOKED VISITS
ANNUAL PRODUCTION 15,600,000 bottles
HECTARES UNDER VINE 120.00

The Sartori family has been engaged for generations in the production of the wines of the province of Verona, and the lion's share obviously goes to the reds of Valpolicella. The grapes for the winery's significant production figures come from its own vineyards, from a close-knit network of local growers and from other major operations in the area. The style is aimed at highlighting the traditional characteristics of the types without forgoing drinkability. The winery's most interesting label, the Valpolicella Superiore I Saltari, comes from eastern Valpolicella. Initially somewhat closed on the nose, vegetal notes gradually make way for ripe, juicy red berry fruit, swathed in spice and pepper. On the palate, it shows good stuffing, underpinned by smooth tannins and tangy acidity. The Montegradella is also excellent, with a balsamic nose and a racier palate with a leisurely finish.

● Amarone della Valpolicella Cl. Proemio '10	🏆🏆 7
● Amarone della Valpolicella Cl. '10	🏆🏆 6
● Bardolino Cl. Ca' Bordenis '14	🏆🏆 2*
○ Lugana Melibeo '14	🏆🏆 2*
● Valpolicella Cl. Sup. Ripasso Solane '13	🏆🏆 4
● Amarone della Valpolicella Proemio '05	🏆🏆🏆 6
● Amarone della Valpolicella Proemio '03	🏆🏆🏆 6
● Amarone della Valpolicella Proemio '00	🏆🏆🏆 5
● Valpolicella Cl. Sup. Ripasso Solane '09	🏆🏆🏆 3*
● Amarone della Valpolicella Cl. '09	🏆🏆 6
● Amarone della Valpolicella Proemio '08	🏆🏆 7
● Bardolino Cl. Vign. Ca' Bordenis '12	🏆🏆 2*
● Valpolicella Cl. Le Caleselle '13	🏆🏆 2*
● Valpolicella Cl. Le Caleselle '12	🏆🏆 2*
● Valpolicella Cl. Sup. Ripasso Solane '12	🏆🏆 4
● Valpolicella Cl. Sup. Ripasso Solane '11	🏆🏆 4

● Valpolicella Sup. I Saltari '11	🏆🏆 4
● Amarone della Valpolicella Cl. Reius '10	🏆🏆 7
● Valpolicella Cl. Sup. Montegradella '12	🏆🏆 3
● Valpolicella Sup. Ripasso Regolo '12	🏆🏆 3
● Cent'Anni '11	🏆 4
○ Lugana La Musina '14	🏆 3
○ Recioto di Soave Vernus '13	🏆 5
○ Soave Cl. Sella '14	🏆 2
● Amarone della Valpolicella Cl. Corte Brà '08	🏆🏆 7
● Amarone della Valpolicella Cl. Reius '09	🏆🏆 7
● Amarone della Valpolicella Cl. Reius '08	🏆🏆 7
● Recioto della Valpolicella Cl. Rerum '11	🏆🏆 6
● Valpolicella Cl. Sup. Vign. di Montegradella '11	🏆🏆 3
● Valpolicella Sup. I Saltari '10	🏆🏆 4
● Valpolicella Sup. Ripasso Regolo '11	🏆🏆 3

Secondo Marco

V.LE CAMPOLONGO, 9
37022 FUMANE [VR]
TEL. 0456800954
www.secondomarco.it

PRE-BOOKED VISITS
ANNUAL PRODUCTION 50,000 bottles
HECTARES UNDER VINE 15.00

Marco Speri is rapidly earning a reputation both on the market and with critics, thanks to progress in quality in the quest for wine that manages to express the value of tradition without forgoing varietal expression and elegance. Around 15 hectares of vineyards provide the grapes for wines that are produced with sensitivity. Great attention is also given to the ageing of the wines, which are only released after long cellaring. The excellent Amarone 2010 show an extremely complex nose of intense super-ripe fruit and spice against a backdrop of forest floor, rain-soaked earth and autumn leaves. On the palate, it charms with its dynamism rather than upfront power, and boasts a long, satisfying finish. We were also impressed with the fresher Ripasso, with aromas of medicinal herbs and an even more spirited, linear palate swathed in white pepper.

★Serafini & Vidotto

VIA LUIGI CARRER, 8
31040 NERVESA DELLA BATTAGLIA [TV]
TEL. 0422773281
www.serafinividotto.it

CELLAR SALES
PRE-BOOKED VISITS
ANNUAL PRODUCTION 250,000 bottles
HECTARES UNDER VINE 23.00

Set up around 30 years ago, the winery of Francesco Serafini and Antonello Vidotto soon managed to earn a place of honour among Italian Bordeaux-style wines. The vineyards lie on the southern side of the Montello plateau, to the north of Treviso overlooking the River Piave. This land rich in iron gives the grapes good acid backbone and low sugar levels. The entire range embodies the pursuit of elegance. The sunny warmth of the 2012 harvest gave the winery's champion, the Rosso dell'Abbazia, more intense aromas of fruit and fines herbes, over a rich, juicy palate, perfectly buttressed by fine-woven, attractively rugged tannins, earning it our top rating. The Phigaia meanwhile offers a nose of wild berries and flowers, over a taut, succulent, supple palate. We also found the Asolo Extra Dry interesting, with its complex nose and harmonious palate.

● Amarone della Valpolicella Cl. '10	♟♟ 7
● Recioto della Valpolicella Cl. '12	♟♟ 6
● Valpolicella Cl. '13	♟♟ 3
● Valpolicella Cl. Sup. Ripasso '12	♟♟ 5
● Amarone della Valpolicella Cl. '09	♟♟ 7
● Amarone della Valpolicella Cl. '08	♟♟ 7
● Amarone della Valpolicella Cl. '07	♟♟ 7
● Recioto della Valpolicella Cl. '11	♟♟ 6
● Recioto della Valpolicella Cl. '10	♟♟ 6
● Recioto della Valpolicella Cl. '09	♟♟ 6
● Recioto della Valpolicella Cl. '08	♟♟ 6
● Valpolicella Cl. '12	♟♟ 2*
● Valpolicella Cl. '11	♟♟ 3
● Valpolicella Cl. Ripasso Sup. '08	♟♟ 6
● Valpolicella Cl. Sup. Ripasso '11	♟♟ 4
● Valpolicella Cl. Sup. Ripasso '10	♟♟ 4

● Montello e Colli Asolani Il Rosso dell'Abbazia '12	♟♟♟ 5
○ Asolo Extra Dry Bollicine di Prosecco	♟♟ 3
○ Il Bianco '14	♟♟ 3
○ Montello e Colli Asolani Manzoni Bianco '14	♟♟ 2*
● Montello e Colli Asolani Phigaia '12	♟♟ 4
● Pinot Nero '12	♟♟ 6
⊙ Bollicine Rosé Brut	♟ 3
● Montello e Colli Asolani Recantina '14	♟ 3
○ P. di Treviso Extra Dry Bollicine di Prosecco	♟ 2
● Montello e Colli Asolani Il Rosso dell'Abbazia '11	♟♟♟ 6
● Montello e Colli Asolani Il Rosso dell'Abbazia '10	♟♟♟ 5
● Montello e Colli Asolani Il Rosso dell'Abbazia '08	♟♟♟ 5

Cantina di Soave

FRAZ. SOAVE
V.LE VITTORIA, 100
37038 SOAVE [VR]
TEL. 0456191250
www.cantinasoave.it

CELLAR SALES
PRE-BOOKED VISITS
ANNUAL PRODUCTION 30,000,000 bottles
HECTARES UNDER VINE 6000.00

A large percentage of the vineyards in the DOC zone of Soave is farmed by the grower-members of Cantina di Soave, a major cooperative winery set up over a century ago. Over the last decade, alongside the production of this Veronese white, it is focusing increasingly on drinkable Valpolicella reds. The significant production is spread over a number of lines, led by Rocca Sveva, whose wines are often based on grapes from individual vineyards. We saw an excellent performance from the Amarone Riserva 2006, presented after long ageing. On the nose, it shows deep aromas of super-ripe fruit and aromatic herbs, with subtle swathes of spice. On the palate, its potency is counterpointed by racy acidity. As for the Soaves, the Castelcerino displayed all the class of its homeland, offering elegant, floral aromas and a dry, dynamic palate with good length.

★Viticoltori Speri

LOC. PEDEMONTE
VIA FONTANA, 14
37029 SAN PIETRO IN CARIANO [VR]
TEL. 0457701154
www.speri.com

CELLAR SALES
PRE-BOOKED VISITS
ANNUAL PRODUCTION 350,000 bottles
HECTARES UNDER VINE 60.00
VITICULTURE METHOD Certified Organic
SUSTAINABLE WINERY

After many years spent investing in vineyards, both new and replanted, this year the Speri family has turned its attention to the cellar, beginning renovation work to extend and optimize the premises required for the various phases of vinification. Production is dedicated entirely to the wines of the DOC zone and remains firmly rooted in tradition. This benchmark for Valpolicella offers wines that interpret the various types with precision and focus. The Amarone Sant'Urbano returns to its usual spectacular form, expressing all the warmth of the 2011 vintage, with up-front super-ripe fruit gradually making way for black pepper and crushed flowers. On the palate, its incredible power is perfectly managed in a long, elegant finish. The Valpolicella Sant'Urbano also impressed, with wild berries echoed on the juicy, taut palate. La Roggia is always one of the classiest examples of Recioto della Valpolicella.

● Amarone della Valpolicella Rocca Sveva '10	♟♟ 8
● Amarone della Valpolicella Rocca Sveva Ris. '06	♟♟ 8
○ Recioto di Soave Cl. Rocca Sveva '10	♟♟ 5
○ Soave Cl. Sup. Castelcerino Rocca Sveva '13	♟♟ 3
○ Équipe 5 Brut M. Cl. '10	♟ 5
○ Lessini Durello Brut Settecento 33	♟ 3
○ Maximilian I Brut	♟ 2
○ Maximilian I Müller Thurgau Perlit Brut	♟ 2
○ Soave Cl. Duca del Frassino '14	♟ 2
○ Soave Cl. Rocca Sveva '14	♟ 2
○ Soave Cl. Sup. Castelcerino Rocca Sveva '07	♟♟ 3
● Valpolicella Sup. Ripasso Rocca Sveva '10	♟♟ 4
● Valpolicella Sup. Rocca Sveva '11	♟♟ 3

● Amarone della Valpolicella Cl. Vign. Sant'Urbano '11	♟♟♟ 7
● Recioto della Valpolicella Cl. La Roggia '12	♟♟ 6
● Valpolicella Cl. Sup. Sant'Urbano '12	♟♟ 4
● Valpolicella Cl. Sup. Ripasso '13	♟♟ 4
● Valpolicella Cl. '14	♟ 2
● Amarone della Valpolicella Cl. Vign. Monte Sant'Urbano '09	♟♟♟ 7
● Amarone della Valpolicella Cl. Vign. Monte Sant'Urbano '08	♟♟♟ 7
● Amarone della Valpolicella Cl. Vign. Monte Sant'Urbano '07	♟♟♟ 7
● Amarone della Valpolicella Cl. Vign. Monte Sant'Urbano '06	♟♟♟ 7
● Amarone della Valpolicella Cl. Vign. Monte Sant'Urbano '04	♟♟♟ 7

I Stefanini

VIA CROSARA, 21
37032 MONTEFORTE D'ALPONE [VR]
TEL. 0456175249
www.istefanini.it

CELLAR SALES
PRE-BOOKED VISITS
ANNUAL PRODUCTION 100,000 bottles
HECTARES UNDER VINE 17.00

Francesco Tessari managed to establish the I Stefanini winery in the space of only a few years, and now, just over a decade after his passing, it is one of the most interesting in the area, thanks to its ability to interpret garganega by combining character and modernity. The vineyards lie in the classic zone, in particular on Mount Tenda, and in the main DOC zone, which provides the grapes for the basic wine. The few labels offer character, great firmness and grip. The firm, gutsy Monte de Toni, a Soave from basalt-rich soils, shows a nose of tropical fruit, Mediterranean scrub and an original touch of grape skin. The close-knit, dynamic palate shows full flavour and good grip. The Monte di Fice is more reticent on the nose, but juicy and ripe on the palate. Lastly, we should mention the excellent Selese, a characterful white offered at an attractive price.

David Sterza

VIA CASTERNA, 37
37022 FUMANE [VR]
TEL. 0457704201
www.davidsterza.it

CELLAR SALES
PRE-BOOKED VISITS
ANNUAL PRODUCTION 30,000 bottles
HECTARES UNDER VINE 4.50

This small winery at Casterna is run by two cousins, David Sterza and Paolo Mascanzoni. The limited area under vine, covering only a few hectares, has not stopped the two of them from experimenting and finding an original stylistic approach which at the same time is faithful to tradition. They only work with the grapes of the territory, and display great care in both the rows and the cellar, for products that show firm body and intact fruit without forgoing elegance and tautness. Sterza's wines are increasingly convincing, with the Amarone and Ripasso both reaching our finals. The former shows aromas of ripe, intact fruit, with intense medicinal herbs and autumn leaves, developed on the rich, dry, gutsy palate. The Ripasso meanwhile has a nose in the same style but fresher, with spice to the fore, over a crisp, supple palate with a long finish.

○ Soave Cl. Monte de Toni '14	♟♟ 2*
○ Soave Cl. Monte di Fice '14	♟♟ 3
○ Soave Il Selese '14	♟♟ 1*
○ Soave Cl. Monte de Toni '12	♟♟♟ 2*
○ Soave Cl. Sup. Monte di Fice '07	♟♟♟ 2*
○ Soave Cl. Monte de Toni '13	♟♟ 2*
○ Soave Cl. Monte de Toni '11	♟♟ 2*
○ Soave Cl. Monte de Toni '08	♟♟ 2*
○ Soave Cl. Monte de Toni '07	♟♟ 2*
○ Soave Cl. Monte de Toni '06	♟♟ 2*
○ Soave Cl. Monte di Fice '10	♟♟ 2*
○ Soave Cl. Sup. Monte di Fice '13	♟♟ 3*
○ Soave Cl. Sup. Monte di Fice '12	♟♟ 3*
○ Soave Cl. Sup. Monte di Fice '08	♟♟ 2*
○ Soave Cl. Sup. Monte di Fice '06	♟♟ 2*

● Amarone della Valpolicella Cl. '11	♟♟ 6
● Valpolicella Cl. Sup. Ripasso '13	♟♟ 3*
● Recioto della Valpolicella Cl. '13	♟♟ 5
● Valpolicella Cl. '14	♟♟ 2*
● Amarone della Valpolicella Cl. '10	♟♟ 6
● Amarone della Valpolicella Cl. '09	♟♟ 6
● Amarone della Valpolicella Cl. '08	♟♟ 6
● Amarone della Valpolicella Cl. '07	♟♟ 6
● Corvina Veronese '09	♟♟ 4
● Recioto della Valpolicella Cl. '12	♟♟ 5
● Valpolicella Cl. '13	♟♟ 2*
● Valpolicella Cl. '12	♟♟ 2*
● Valpolicella Cl. Sup. Ripasso '12	♟♟ 3
● Valpolicella Cl. Sup. Ripasso '11	♟♟ 3
● Valpolicella Cl. Sup. Ripasso '10	♟♟ 3
● Valpolicella Cl. Sup. Ripasso '09	♟♟ 3

★Suavia

FRAZ. FITTÀ DI SOAVE
VIA CENTRO, 14
37038 SOAVE [VR]
TEL. 0457675089
www.suavia.it

CELLAR SALES
PRE-BOOKED VISITS
ANNUAL PRODUCTION 100,000 bottles
HECTARES UNDER VINE 12.00

This winery at Fittà is a women-only operation: the four sisters Arianna, Meri, Valentina, and Alessandra, each with different duties, deal with every aspect of the production and marketing of their wines. Especially in the rows, they can count on the advice of their parents, whose experience helped them tackle a difficult harvest such as 2014 without losing their cool. Production is entirely dedicated to the traditional garganega and trebbiano di Soave, and alternates classic Soaves with more original interpretations. There are no weak points at Tessari, with the Soave Monte Carbonare leading an impressive range of wines. On the nose, it offers ripe yellow-fleshed fruit, with attractive dried flowers and a touch of gunflint. On the palate, it has sacrificed some of its usual grip to pursue finesse and style. The Massifitti, a monovarietal trebbiano di Soave, shows an elegant nose of blossom and peach, leading into a long, stylish and supple palate.

Sutto

LOC. CAMPO DI PIETRA
VIA ARZERI, 34/1
31040 SALGAREDA [TV]
TEL. 0422744063
www.sutto.it

CELLAR SALES
PRE-BOOKED VISITS
ACCOMMODATION AND RESTAURANT SERVICE
ANNUAL PRODUCTION 153,000 bottles
HECTARES UNDER VINE 75.00

The operation established recently by Stefano and Luigi Sutto produces wines which are more convincing with every passing year. The winery focuses above all on Prosecco, in a style that emphasizes the fragrance and flavour of the base variety. But it is in the still wines that we have seen the most interesting improvements. Since they have large vineyard holdings, the Sutto brothers can choose the best batches to dedicate to their products, resulting in a range of rich wines with a sense of place. We saw greater expressiveness in the Campo Sella, a Merlot which reached our finals with the 2012 vintage, thanks to a nose of great depth and complexity, with plum counterpointed by subtle, refreshing aromatic herbs and spice, over a palate which manages to be rich without sacrificing grip and suppleness. We also saw improvements from the Proseccos, such as the Valdobbiadene Extra Dry, which charms with its fruit-driven nose and harmonious palate.

○ Massifitti '12	♟♟ 3*
○ Soave Cl. Monte Carbonare '13	♟♟ 3*
○ Le Rive '11	♟♟ 4
○ Recioto di Soave Acinatium '09	♟♟ 5
○ Soave Cl. '14	♟♟ 2*
○ Opera Semplice Dosaggio Zero M. Cl.	♟ 4
○ Soave Cl. Le Rive '02	♟♟♟ 4
○ Soave Cl. Monte Carbonare '12	♟♟♟ 3*
○ Soave Cl. Monte Carbonare '11	♟♟♟ 3*
○ Soave Cl. Monte Carbonare '10	♟♟♟ 3*
○ Soave Cl. Monte Carbonare '09	♟♟♟ 3*
○ Soave Cl. Monte Carbonare '08	♟♟♟ 3*
○ Soave Cl. Monte Carbonare '07	♟♟♟ 3*
○ Soave Cl. Monte Carbonare '06	♟♟♟ 3*
○ Soave Cl. Monte Carbonare '05	♟♟♟ 3*
○ Soave Cl. Monte Carbonare '04	♟♟♟ 3

● Campo Sella '12	♟♟ 5
● Cabernet '14	♟♟ 2*
○ Chardonnay '14	♟♟ 2*
○ Pinot Grigio '14	♟♟ 2*
○ Ultimo '13	♟♟ 3
○ Valdobbiadene Extra Dry Batiso '13	♟♟ 2
○ Manzoni Bianco '14	♟ 2
● Merlot '14	♟ 2
○ Prosecco Brut Batiso	♟ 2
○ Prosecco Extra Dry Batiso	♟ 2
● Campo Sella '11	♟♟ 5
● Dogma Rosso '12	♟♟ 4
● Dogma Rosso '11	♟♟ 4
○ Pinot Grigio '13	♟♟ 2*
○ Ultimo '12	♟♟ 3
○ Ultimo '11	♟♟ 3
○ Valdobbiadene Extra Dry Batiso '13	♟♟ 2*

T.E.S.S.A.R.I.

LOC. BROGNOLIGO
VIA FONTANA NUOVA, 86
37032 MONTEFORTE D'ALPONE [VR]
TEL. 0456176041
www.cantinatessari.com

CELLAR SALES
PRE-BOOKED VISITS
ANNUAL PRODUCTION 40,000 bottles
HECTARES UNDER VINE 17.00

Antonio, Germano and Cornelia Tessari run the family winery at Brognoligo, with just under 20 hectares dedicated almost entirely to garganega, the real queen of this territory, tended with the passion that their parents Aldo and Bianca, and before them grandfather Antonio, managed to instil in their children. All the phases of production take place in the modern cellar in Via Fontana Nuova, and focus entirely on the wines of tradition. We saw good performance from the Soave Grisela, a monovarietal garganega which reflects the cool 2014 harvest, with a nose of white-fleshed fruit and flowers. On the palate, it shows attractive acidity, counterpointed by soft, creamy mouthfeel. The Recioto Tre Colli, meanwhile, plays on ripe fruit, swathed in charred oak and dried flowers, developed on a palate with measured sweetness, which continues through to the finish.

Tamellini

FRAZ. COSTEGGIOLA
VIA TAMELLINI, 4
37038 SOAVE [VR]
TEL. 0457675328
piofrancesco.tamellini@tin.it

CELLAR SALES
PRE-BOOKED VISITS
ANNUAL PRODUCTION 250,000 bottles
HECTARES UNDER VINE 27.00

In recent years the Tamellini brothers have managed to consolidate the production figures of their range, limited to three labels from garganega, and a fourth, Recioto, that is only produced when the growing year is right. The vineyards lie on the western tip of the classic zone of Soave, where basalt soils gradually make way for tufa and limestone. Just under 30 hectares give firm-bodied wines with a real sense of place. The winery's most important label, the Soave Le Bine de Costiola, comes from the vineyards at Costeggiola, covering three hectares on a south-facing plot, planted solely to garganega. Tasted two years after harvest, it shows intense notes of ripe apricots, peaches and tropical fruit, followed by blossom and mineral nuances. On the palate, its fullness is well governed by savoury thrust. We were also convinced by the younger Soave, a spirited, racy wine.

○ Soave Cl. Grisela '14	�♛ 2*
○ Garganega Brut	♛ 3
○ Recioto di Soave Tre Colli '12	♛ 5
○ Soave Cl. Grisela '13	♛♛ 2*
○ Soave Cl. Grisela '12	♛♛ 2*
○ Soave Cl. Grisela '11	♛♛ 2*
○ Soave Cl. Grisela '08	♛♛ 2*
○ Soave Cl. Grisela '07	♛♛ 2*
○ Soave Cl. Le Bine Longhe '10	♛♛ 5*
○ Soave Cl. Le Bine Longhe di Costalta '12	♛♛ 3
○ Soave Cl. Le Bine Longhe di Costalta '11	♛♛ 3

○ Soave Cl. Le Bine de Costiola '13	♛♛♛ 3*
○ Soave '14	♛♛ 2*
○ Soave Cl. Le Bine '04	♛♛♛ 3*
○ Soave Cl. Le Bine de Costiola '11	♛♛♛ 3*
○ Soave Cl. Le Bine de Costiola '06	♛♛♛ 3*
○ Soave Cl. Le Bine de Costiola '05	♛♛♛ 3*
○ Extra Brut M. Cl. '09	♛♛ 4
○ Extra Brut M. Cl. 36 mesi '09	♛♛ 4
○ Soave '11	♛♛ 2*
○ Soave '10	♛♛ 2*
○ Soave Cl. '13	♛♛ 2*
○ Soave Cl. '12	♛♛ 2*
○ Soave Cl. Le Bine de Costiola '12	♛♛ 3*
○ Soave Cl. Le Bine de Costiola '10	♛♛ 3*
○ Soave Cl. Le Bine de Costiola '09	♛♛ 3*
○ Soave Cl. Le Bine de Costiola '08	♛♛ 3*

VENETO

F.lli Tedeschi

FRAZ. PEDEMONTE
VIA G. VERDI, 4
37029 SAN PIETRO IN CARIANO [VR]
TEL. 0457701487
www.tedeschiwines.com

CELLAR SALES
PRE-BOOKED VISITS
ANNUAL PRODUCTION 550,000 bottles
HECTARES UNDER VINE 46.00
SUSTAINABLE WINERY

The Tedeschi winery lacks a champion, but this absence, once again, shows the attention that Antonietta, Sabrina and Riccardo also pay to the ageing of their wines, aware that their products need time to express themselves to the full. This is especially true now, with the new vineyards only just starting to mature and provide excellent raw materials, which means that the wines take time to achieve harmony and eloquence. The style of the wines is rich yet faithful to tradition. With a great sense of responsibility, the brothers from Pedemonte decided to delay the release of all the more important wines, to allow them to age further in the cellar, rather than rush to bottle and market them. The Amarone 2011 gave a fine performance, showing an approachable nose dominated by raisined red berry fruit, over a full palate well counterpointed by rugged, lively tannins.

● Amarone della Valpolicella Cl. '11	▼▼ 6
● Valpolicella Cl. Sup. Capitel dei Nicalò '13	▼▼ 3
● Valpolicella Sup. San Rocco Ripasso '13	▼▼ 4
● Amarone della Valpolicella Cl. Capitel Monte Olmi '07	▼▼▼ 8
● Amarone della Valpolicella Cl. Capitel Monte Olmi '01	▼▼▼ 7
● Amarone della Valpolicella Cl. Capitel Monte Olmi '99	▼▼▼ 7
● Amarone della Valpolicella Cl. Capitel Monte Olmi '97	▼▼▼ 8
● Amarone della Valpolicella Cl. Capitel Monte Olmi '95	▼▼▼ 8
● Valpolicella Sup. Maternigo '11	▼▼▼ 4*
● Amarone della Valpolicella Cl. '10	♈♈ 6

Le Tende

FRAZ. COLÀ DI LAZISE
VIA TENDE, 35
37017 LAZISE [VR]
TEL. 0457590748
www.letende.it

CELLAR SALES
PRE-BOOKED VISITS
ANNUAL PRODUCTION 100,000 bottles
HECTARES UNDER VINE 10.00
VITICULTURE METHOD Certified Organic

Le Tende covers around dozen hectares near the eastern shores of Lake Garda, between Colà di Lazise and Cavaion, resting on the morainic hills that have always been used for viticulture. Set up by the Fortuna and Lucillini families, it is run by the capable Mauro Fortuna, an attentive interpreter of the Lakeside types who allows himself the occasional experiment with international varieties, while remaining true to the "Lake Garda style", hinging on fragrance and drinkability. We saw a convincing performance from the Custoza, a white that despite the complicated 2014 harvest shows intense aromas of white-fleshed fruit and blossom, and unfolds on the palate with lightness and grip. The Cicisbeo is a Cabernet Sauvignon with a nose of plum and spice, over a supple, long palate. Lastly, we should mention the straightforward, highly pleasurable Bardolino, with its intense nose of forest fruits and pepper, encored on the lean, full-flavoured palate.

● Bardolino Cl. '14	▼▼ 2*
● Cicisbeo '12	▼▼ 3
○ Custoza '14	▼▼ 2*
⊙ Bardolino Chiaretto Brut Voluttà	▼ 2
⊙ Bardolino Chiaretto Cl. '14	▼ 2
● Bardolino Cl. Sup. '13	▼ 2
○ Lucillini '13	▼ 2
● Bardolino Cl. '13	♈♈ 2*
● Bardolino Cl. '11	♈♈ 2*
● Bardolino Cl. '08	♈♈ 2*
● Bardolino Cl. Sup. '12	♈♈ 2*
● Bardolino Cl. Sup. '11	♈♈ 2*
● Bardolino Cl. Sup. '10	♈♈ 2*
● Bardolino Cl. Sup. '08	♈♈ 2
○ Bianco di Custoza Lucillini '12	♈♈ 2*
● Garda Cabernet Sauvignon Cicisbeo '07	♈♈ 3

Viticoltori Tommasi

LOC. PEDEMONTE
VIA RONCHETTO, 2
37020 SAN PIETRO IN CARIANO [VR]
TEL. 0457701266
www.tommasiwine.it

CELLAR SALES
PRE-BOOKED VISITS
ANNUAL PRODUCTION 1,000,000 bottles
HECTARES UNDER VINE 162.00

In recent years, the Tommasi family have developed their viticultural activity intensively, purchasing important operations in many regions of Italy, from Puglia to Oltrepò, Maremma and Montalcino. The heart of their business, however, remains firmly in Valpolicella, their homeland, where their efforts focus on bringing the best out of traditional types. The large vineyard, alternating areas on the valley floor with splendid, well-aspected hillside plots, allows significant production figures and respect for tradition. Even if its name is part of the winery's history, the Amarone Ca' Florian 2008 is actually a new product, the result of a reviewed approach to the production process of this great red. The long period of ageing, first in medium oak and subsequently in large barrels, gives great depth on the nose, where fruit joins forces with spice and fines herbes. On the palate, its power is well managed, for a compact, taut, youthful profile.

● Amarone della Valpolicella Cl. Ca' Florian Ris. '08	�································· 7
○ Lugana Il Sestante '14	�································· 2*
○ Lugana Le Fornaci '14	�································· 2*
● Valpolicella Cl. Sup. Rafael '13	�································· 4
● Valpolicella Cl. Sup. Ripasso '13	�································· 4
● Alicante Poggio al Tufo '11	�································· 4
● Amarone della Valpolicella Cl. '10	�································· 7
● Amarone della Valpolicella Cl. '09	�································· 7
● Amarone della Valpolicella Cl. '08	�································· 7
● Crearo della Conca d'Oro '11	�································· 4
○ Lugana Vign. San Martino Il Sestante '13	�································· 2*
● Valpolicella Cl. Sup. Rafael '12	�································· 3
● Valpolicella Cl. Sup. Rafael '11	�································· 3
● Valpolicella Cl. Sup. Ripasso '12	�································· 4
● Valpolicella Cl. Sup. Ripasso '11	�································· 4

Trabucchi d'Illasi

LOC. MONTE TENDA
37031 ILLASI [VR]
TEL. 0457833233
www.trabucchidillasi.it

CELLAR SALES
PRE-BOOKED VISITS
ANNUAL PRODUCTION 120,000 bottles
HECTARES UNDER VINE 25.00
VITICULTURE METHOD Certified Organic

Among the many wineries that are in some way representative of Valpolicella, that of Giuseppe Trabucchi and his wife Raffaella clearly deserves a place of honour. Straddling the valleys of Tramigna and Illasi, the property covers around 25 hectares, and is farmed using organic methods. The winery aims to combine sustainability in the vineyard with respect for the natural ageing times of the wines, which are released on the market only when they are considered ready. The whole range is composed of the typical wines of the area. The long ageing of the Amarone 2008 gave the wine an aromatic profile of great complexity, with fruit taking centre stage, supported by fines herbes, then spice, and lastly mineral notes, which will develop over time. On the palate, it shows impressive richness, nicely counterpointed by acidity and tannins. We were also convinced by the Terra del Cereolo, an elegant, full-bodied Valpolicella.

● Amarone della Valpolicella '08	�································· 8
● Valpolicella Sup. Terre del Cereolo '08	�································· 5
● Valpolicella Un Anno '14	�································· 2*
○ Margherita '14	�································· 4
● Amarone della Valpolicella '06	�································· 8
● Amarone della Valpolicella '04	�································· 8
● Recioto della Valpolicella Cereolo '05	�································· 8
● Valpolicella Sup. Terre di S. Colombano '03	�································· 4*
● Amarone della Valpolicella Alberto Trabucchi Ris. '06	�································· 8
● Valpolicella Sup. La Gardellina '12	�································· 4
● Valpolicella Sup. Terre di S. Colombano '08	�································· 3
● Valpolicella Un Anno '13	�································· 2*
● Valpolicella Un Anno '12	�································· 2*
● Valpolicella Un Anno '11	�································· 2*

VENETO

Spumanti Valdo

VIA FORO BOARIO, 20
31049 VALDOBBIADENE [TV]
TEL. 04239090
www.valdo.com

CELLAR SALES
PRE-BOOKED VISITS
ANNUAL PRODUCTION 9,000,000 bottles
HECTARES UNDER VINE 155.00

The Valdobbiadene zone is characterized by a large number of growers, often working extremely small plots, who sell their grapes to the large sparkling wine producers. Valdo is one of the most important of these, with significant production figures of DOC Prosecco, now at almost ten million bottles a year, sold all over the world. The wines show an approachable style that highlights the fragrance of the base variety. The Cuvée di Boj is a Valdobbiadene Brut showing attractive aromatic expression, with focused white-fleshed fruit on the nose, swathed in blossom. On the palate, the wine reveals the typical acid grip of the year, showing long and racy. The Cartizze Cuvée Viviana offers riper, sunnier aromas, dominated by apricots, peach and tropical fruit, supported in the mouth by elegant fizz. The range shows reliability across the board, even in the simpler wines.

○ Cartizze Cuvée Viviana	♔♔	5
○ Valdobbiadene Brut Cuvée di Boj	♔♔	2
○ Valdobbiadene Cuvée del Fondatore '13	♔♔	3
○ Valdobbiadene Extra Dry Cuvée 1926	♔♔	2
○ Numero 10 Brut M. Cl.	♔	4
○ Prosecco di Treviso Extra Dry	♔	2
○ Numero 10 Brut M. Cl. '10	♔♔	4

Cantina Valpantena Verona

LOC. QUINTO
VIA COLONIA ORFANI DI GUERRA, 5B
37142 VERONA
TEL. 045550032
www.cantinavalpantena.it

CELLAR SALES
PRE-BOOKED VISITS
ANNUAL PRODUCTION 8,000,000 bottles
HECTARES UNDER VINE 750.00

Over 60 years after being set up, Cantina della Valpantena now has around 250 grower-members, who tend 750 hectares of vineyards. Production obviously focuses on Valpolicella and its wines, but also covers the other wines of the province, which contribute to a balanced range of approachable, well-typed wines, albeit in smaller quantities. The Quinto estate is also involved in olive production, to which 150 growers contribute. The Ripasso Torre del Falasco offers intensely ripe fruit on the nose, echoed on the full, well-structured palate, buttressed by attractively rugged tannins. Raisined aromas are obviously more evident in the Amarone Torre del Falasco, with jammy fruit and white chocolate, for a velvety, caressing palate. The Valpantena Ritocco, meanwhile, pursues greater aromatic freshness and shows a leaner, more supple palate.

● Amarone della Valpolicella '12	♔♔	5
● Amarone della Valpolicella Torre del Falasco '11	♔♔	6
● Valpolicella Sup. Ripasso Torre del Falasco '13	♔♔	3
● Valpolicella Valpantena Ritocco '13	♔♔	3
○ Chardonnay Baroncino '14	♔	2
● Corvina Torre del Falasco '14	♔	1*
○ Garganega Torre del Falasco '14	♔	1*
○ Lugana Torre del Falasco '14	♔	2
● Recioto della Valpolicella '13	♔	5
● Valpolicella Sup. Torre del Falasco '13	♔	2
● Valpolicella Sup. Ripasso Torre del Falasco '11	♔♔	3
● Valpolicella Sup. Ripasso Torre del Falasco '09	♔♔	3*
● Valpolicella Valpantena Ritocco '12	♔♔	2*

Cantina Valpolicella Negrar

VIA CA' SALGARI, 2
37024 NEGRAR [VR]
TEL. 0456014300
www.cantinanegrar.it

CELLAR SALES
PRE-BOOKED VISITS
RESTAURANT SERVICE
ANNUAL PRODUCTION 7,000,000 bottles
HECTARES UNDER VINE 700.00

Cantina di Negrar was set up between the wars and now has over 200 grower-members who tend vineyards covering 700 hectares, mainly in the Valpolicella Classica DOC zone. Obviously, the production of so many grapes means wines with different characters, subdivided according to the quality of the raw materials and target market. The Domini Veneti line leads the range, with wines firmly linked to their provenance, produced with care and the utmost respect for tradition. We saw an excellent range presented by Cantina di Negrar, with the Amarone Mater pulling off a wonderful performance. It opens to a nose of raisined red berry fruit, swathed in minerals and thyme, followed by great power on the mouth, reined in by close-knit tannins. The Recioto Vigneti di Moron, meanwhile, is brimming with fruit, and boasts incredible sweetness on the palate. The operation's organic wines are increasingly convincing.

Odino Vaona

LOC. VALGATARA
VIA PAVERNO, 41
37020 MARANO DI VALPOLICELLA [VR]
TEL. 0457703710
www.vaona.it

CELLAR SALES
PRE-BOOKED VISITS
ANNUAL PRODUCTION 70,000 bottles
HECTARES UNDER VINE 10.00
SUSTAINABLE WINERY

Today the Vaona family winery is run by Alberto, and can count on vineyard holdings of around ten hectares in the heart of Valpolicella Classica. All the vineyards lie on generally west-facing hillside plots at elevations of between 200 and 250 metres, and over the years have been gradually replanted, substituting the traditional pergola with a row-based training system that allows better exposure to sunlight and keeps yields low. We saw some superb wines presented this year by the winery at Marano, with the approachable Amarone Pegrandi standing out for its focused nose with super-ripe fruit shot through with balsam and pepper, over a rich, supple palate with good grip and length. We saw a similar style in the Ripasso Pegrandi, which shows a velvety, approachable palate. Concentration is instead the leitmotif of the chamois-soft Amarone Pegrandi Riserva.

● Amarone della Valpolicella Cl. Mater Domini Veneti Ris. '08	♟♟ 8
● Recioto della Valpolicella Cl. Vign. di Moron Domini Veneti '11	♟♟ 4
● Amarone della Valpolicella Cl. Biologico Domini Veneti '08	♟♟ 6
● Amarone della Valpolicella Cl. Vign. di Jago Domini Veneti '08	♟♟ 7
● Valpolicella Cl. Sup. Ripasso La Casetta Domini Veneti '12	♟♟ 4
● Valpolicella Cl. Sup. Ripasso Vign. di Jago Domini Veneti '13	♟♟ 3
● Valpolicella Cl. Sup. Verjago Domini Veneti '10	♟♟ 4
○ Raudii Bianco Domini Veneti '14	♟ 2
● Raudii Rosso Domini Veneti '13	♟ 2
● Valpolicella Cl. Biologico Domini Veneti '14	♟ 2
● Valpolicella Cl. Sup. Domini Veneti '13	♟ 2

● Amarone della Valpolicella Cl. Pegrandi '11	♟♟ 5
● Amarone della Valpolicella Cl. Paverno '12	♟♟ 5
● Amarone della Valpolicella Cl. Pegrandi Ris. '09	♟♟ 8
● Valpolicella Cl. Sup. Ripasso Pegrandi '13	♟♟ 3
● Valpolicella Sup. '13	♟♟ 2*
● Amarone della Valpolicella Cl. Pegrandi '09	♟♟♟ 5
● Amarone della Valpolicella Cl. Pegrandi '08	♟♟♟ 5
● Recioto della Valpolicella Le Peagnà '11	♟♟ 4
● Valpolicella Cl. Sup. Ripasso Pegrandi '12	♟♟ 3
● Valpolicella Cl. Sup. Ripasso Pegrandi '11	♟♟ 3
● Valpolicella Sup. '12	♟♟ 2*

Massimino Venturini

FRAZ. SAN FLORIANO
VIA SEMONTE, 20
37020 SAN PIETRO IN CARIANO [VR]
TEL. 0457701331
www.viniventurini.com

CELLAR SALES
PRE-BOOKED VISITS
ANNUAL PRODUCTION 100,000 bottles
HECTARES UNDER VINE 12.00

Mirco and Daniele Venturini run the family winery established over 50 years ago by their father Massimino. A dozen hectares entirely set in the Valpolicella Classica zone provide the grapes for wines with a classic style that require long ageing. Today, as then, the vineyards are farmed using the traditional pergola system, which allows the grapes destined for drying to be protected from the excessive heat of the sun. The rest is down to great sensitivity in the cellar, where the grapes are worked with care and a light hand. This year the Venturini Bros presented a new Riserva of Amarone, released ten years after the harvest. The deep, complex aromas of dried fruit are perfectly fused with notes of Mediterranean scrub and spice. This perfect harmony is also found in the mouth, with an exceptional balance of alcohol, sweetness, tannins and acidity. There was also a convincing performance from the Semonte Alto, a ripe, summery Ripasso, which reveals unexpected freshness on the palate.

● Amarone della Valpolicella Cl. Ris. '05	♟ 5
● Valpolicella Cl. Sup. Ripasso Semonte Alto '11	♟ 3*
● Recioto della Valpolicella Cl. '11	♟ 5
● Valpolicella Cl. Sup. '12	♟♟ 2*
● Valpolicella Cl. '14	♟ 2
● Amarone della Valpolicella Cl. Campomasua '07	♟♟♟ 6
● Amarone della Valpolicella Cl. Campomasua '05	♟♟♟ 6
● Recioto della Valpolicella Cl. Le Brugnine '97	♟♟♟ 5
● Amarone della Valpolicella Cl. '10	♟♟ 5
● Amarone della Valpolicella Cl. '09	♟♟ 5
● Recioto della Valpolicella Cl. Le Brugnine '11	♟♟ 5
● Valpolicella Cl. '13	♟♟ 2*

Agostino Vicentini

FRAZ. SAN ZENO
VIA C. BATTISTI, 62C
37030 COLOGNOLA AI COLLI [VR]
TEL. 0457650539
www.vinivicentini.com

CELLAR SALES
PRE-BOOKED VISITS
ANNUAL PRODUCTION 100,000 bottles
HECTARES UNDER VINE 20.00

Agostino Vicentini's winery is at the mouth of the Val d'Illasi, an area known for its viticultural qualities, in which the two most important DOC wines of the area around Verona, Soave and Valpolicella, fight for the best aspects. Alongside him, his wife Teresa and children Manuele and Francesca are increasingly involved in the running of the operation. The vineyards cover around 20 hectares and are mainly dedicated to garganega, with growing interest in the grapes of Valpolicella. Soave is however at the centre of attention this year, with a spectacular version of Il Casale, the Superiore that Agostino produces from garganega on limestone soil, limiting yields as far as possible and ageing wine solely in stainless steel. On the nose, the aromas are still reticent, with white-fleshed fruit glimpsed among blossom and vegetal nuances. In the mouth, however, the wine shows its true colours, showing fullness and firmness at the same time, for a dynamic, full-flavoured palate of great length.

○ Soave Sup. Il Casale '14	♟♟♟ 3*
○ Soave Vign. Terre Lunghe '14	♟♟ 2*
● Valpolicella Vign. Boccascalucce '14	♟♟ 2*
○ Soave Sup. Il Casale '13	♟♟♟ 3*
○ Soave Sup. Il Casale '12	♟♟♟ 3*
○ Soave Sup. Il Casale '09	♟♟♟ 3*
○ Soave Sup. Il Casale '08	♟♟♟ 3*
○ Soave Sup. Il Casale '07	♟♟♟ 3*
○ Soave Vign. Terre Lunghe '13	♟♟ 2*
○ Soave Vign. Terre Lunghe '12	♟♟ 2*
● Valpolicella Sup. '12	♟♟ 3
● Valpolicella Sup. '10	♟♟ 3
● Valpolicella Sup. Idea Bacco '11	♟♟ 5
● Valpolicella Sup. Idea Bacco '10	♟♟ 5
● Valpolicella Sup. Palazzo di Campiano '11	♟♟ 5
● Valpolicella Vign. Boccascalucce '10	♟♟ 2*

Vigna Roda

LOC. CORTELÀ
VIA MONTE VERSA, 1569
35030 VÒ [PD]
TEL. 0499940228
www.vignaroda.com

CELLAR SALES
PRE-BOOKED VISITS
ANNUAL PRODUCTION 52,000 bottles
HECTARES UNDER VINE 17.00

In the last two decades the Colli Euganei area has witnessed a generational turnover, with young growers starting to run family wineries and committed to promoting the undisputed qualities of this beautiful territory. Gianni Strazzacappa, alongside his wife Elena, tends almost 20 hectares of vineyards in the western part of the DOC zone, pursuing richness and elegance in his wines, mainly dedicated to red Bordeaux varieties. The champion at Strazzacappa, the Scarlatto, is a merlot-heavy Bordeaux blend proffering wild berries, autumn leaves and thyme on the nose, followed by firm body without excessive concentration, and a full-flavoured, caressing finish. The cool 2014 growing year gave the Cabernet Espero an even more restless character than usual, but the wine charms with its consistency and suppleness. We also liked the aromatic thrust of the Fior d'Arancio Spumante.

● Colli Euganei Rosso Scarlatto '12	♥♥ 3*
● Colli Euganei Cabernet Espero '14	♥♥ 2*
○ Colli Euganei Fior d'Arancio Spumante '14	♥♥ 2*
○ Colli Euganei Bianco '14	♥ 2
○ Colli Euganei Chardonnay Ca' Zamira '14	♥ 2
○ Colli Euganei Extra Dry Serprino	♥ 2
● Colli Euganei Rosso '14	♥ 2
○ Colli Euganei Serprino Frizzante '14	♥ 2
● Colli Euganei Cabernet Espero '13	♥♥ 2*
○ Colli Euganei Fior d'Arancio Passito Petali d'Ambra '10	♥♥ 4
● Colli Euganei Rosso '13	♥♥ 2*
● Colli Euganei Rosso '12	♥♥ 2*
● Colli Euganei Rosso Scarlatto '11	♥♥ 3
● Colli Euganei Rosso Scarlatto '10	♥♥ 3

Vignale di Cecilia

LOC. FORNACI
VIA CROCI, 14
35030 BAONE [PD]
TEL. 042951420
www.vignaledicecilia.it

PRE-BOOKED VISITS
ANNUAL PRODUCTION 20,000 bottles
HECTARES UNDER VINE 8.00
VITICULTURE METHOD Certified Organic

The area of Baone, in the southern part of Colli Euganei, has one of the hottest climates in Veneto, albeit mitigated by the extensive woodlands, and it is here that merlot and cabernet ripen perfectly and consistently. Paolo Brunello started farming here over a decade ago, and gave a new lease of life to the family business. Today, his vineyards are organically farmed, and production focuses on rich, hearty, characterful wines. Paolo Brunello presented an outstanding version of his Passacaglia, a merlot-heavy Bordeaux blend that shows ripe, deep aromas, with fruit well sustained by intense pepper and balsamic herbs, against a backdrop of mineral notes that will come through with time. The rounded palate is offset by attractive acid thrust, providing good length. The Covolo, a well-managed red at an attractive price, is spot-on.

● Colli Euganei Rosso Passacaglia '12	♥♥ 4
● Colli Euganei Rosso Covolo '13	♥♥ 3
○ Val di Spin Frizzante	♥♥ 2*
○ Benavides '13	♥ 2
○ Benavides '11	♥♥ 2*
○ Cocài '12	♥♥ 3
○ Cocài '11	♥♥ 3
○ Cocài '10	♥♥ 3
● Colli Euganei Rosso Covolo '10	♥♥ 3
● Colli Euganei Rosso Passacaglia '11	♥♥ 4
● Colli Euganei Rosso Passacaglia '09	♥♥ 4
● Colli Euganei Rosso Passacaglia '08	♥♥ 4
● El Moro '10	♥♥ 3
● El Moro '08	♥♥ 3*
● L'Otto	♥♥ 3

★Vignalta

VIA SCALETTE, 23
35032 ARQUÀ PETRARCA [PD]
TEL. 0429777305
www.vignalta.it

CELLAR SALES
PRE-BOOKED VISITS
ANNUAL PRODUCTION 240,000 bottles
HECTARES UNDER VINE 50.00

If Colli Euganei is today known internationally as one of the most interesting zones in Italy for the production of Merlot and Cabernet, this is thanks to Lucio Gomiero and his Vignalta, the first winery that showed the world the quality of its vineyards. They extend for many hectares over the slopes of these volcanic hills, with elevations of around 200 metres, mainly dedicated to Bordeaux varieties, but also large plantings of moscato fior d'arancio. In the year in which Vignalta's champion reds are absent, the Alpianae gave a brilliant performance. The Passito Fior d'Arancio shows a bright, luminous hue, followed by intense candied citrus peel, blossom and spice in a seemingly endless whirlwind of aromas. On the captivating palate, the wine shows sweetness well governed by acidity, for good length. The mature, complex Cabernet Riserva offers a juicy palate with glossy tannins.

○ Colli Euganei Fior d'Arancio Passito Alpianae '12	♀♀♀	5
● Colli Euganei Cabernet Ris. '07	♀♀	8
● Agno Tinto '09	♀♀	5
○ Colli Euganei Pinot Bianco '14	♀♀	3
⊙ Extra Brut Rosé	♀♀	4
● Pinot Nero '13	♀♀	5
○ Colli Euganei Moscato Secco Sirio '14	♀	3
● Colli Euganei Rosso Venda '11	♀	3
● Colli Euganei Rosso Gemola '09	♀♀♀	5
● Colli Euganei Rosso Gemola '08	♀♀♀	5
○ Colli Euganei Fior d'Arancio Passito Alpianae '11	♀♀	4
● Colli Euganei Rosso Arquà '10	♀♀	6
● Colli Euganei Rosso Ris. '10	♀♀	3
● Pinot Nero '10	♀♀	2*

Le Vigne di San Pietro

VIA SAN PIETRO, 23
37066 SOMMACAMPAGNA [VR]
TEL. 045510016
www.levignedisanpietro.it

CELLAR SALES
PRE-BOOKED VISITS
ANNUAL PRODUCTION 70,000 bottles
HECTARES UNDER VINE 10.00

Carlo Nerozzi has always been an original grower, constantly torn between his many activities, but with his heart firmly rooted in the soil and his homeland. In the hills of Sommacampagna, he tends about ten hectares using natural methods, dedicated mainly to the grapes that form the base of the wines of tradition, Bardolino and Custoza. His style aims at giving richness and depth to these two types without sacrificing lightness and elegance. In a harvest such as that of 2014, Carlo pulled the rabbit out of the hat, with one of the best ever versions of his Bardolino. It opens to intense forest fruits, followed by nuances of pepper and thyme, perfectly echoed on the palate, which is rich, deep, and at the same time linear. Closed and reticent on the nose, the Custoza boasts a dynamic, full-flavoured, grippy palate.

● Bardolino '14	♀♀♀	2*
⊙ Bardolino Chiaretto CorDeRosa '14	♀♀	2*
○ Custoza '14	♀♀	2*
● Bardolino '11	♀♀♀	2*
● Amarone della Valpolicella Cl. '09	♀♀	7
● Amarone della Valpolicella Cl. '07	♀♀	6
● Bardolino '13	♀♀	2*
● Bardolino '12	♀♀	2*
● Bardolino '10	♀♀	2*
⊙ CorDeRosa '13	♀♀	2*
○ Custoza '13	♀♀	2*
○ Custoza '12	♀♀	2*
○ Custoza '11	♀♀	2*
○ Custoza '10	♀♀	2*
● Refolà '09	♀♀	6

Vigneto Due Santi

V.LE ASIAGO, 174
36061 BASSANO DEL GRAPPA [VI]
TEL. 0424502074
www.vignetoduesanti.it

CELLAR SALES
PRE-BOOKED VISITS
ANNUAL PRODUCTION 100,000 bottles
HECTARES UNDER VINE 18.00
SUSTAINABLE WINERY

The Breganze zone extends along the hills
leading to the Prealps, from Thiene to
Bassano, where the Po Valley is cooled by
the currents from Valsugana to the north,
resulting in a wide range of temperatures
and low humidity. Stefano and Adriano
Zonta run the family winery, today covering
around 20 hectares, and mainly dedicated
to merlot and cabernet. The wines show
well-typed aromas and tautness on the
palate. The cousins from Bassano are back
on Tre Bicchieri form, with a splendid
version of their Cabernet Due Santi. The
result of a selection which is meticulous to
say the least, the wine shows a bright ruby
hue, followed on the nose by intense dark
berry fruit and forest floor, spice and damp
leaves. The rich, succulent palate is
underpinned by smooth tannins, giving
excellent length. The Cavallare, a
merlot-rich Bordeaux blend, offers red
berry fruit and flowers on the nose, over a
savoury, elegant palate.

Villa Bellini

LOC. CASTELROTTO DI NEGARINE
VIA DEI FRACCAROLI, 6
37020 SAN PIETRO IN CARIANO [VR]
TEL. 0457725630
www.villabellini.com

CELLAR SALES
PRE-BOOKED VISITS
ANNUAL PRODUCTION 10,000 bottles
HECTARES UNDER VINE 3.50
VITICULTURE METHOD Certified Organic

Cecilia Trucchi's small winery is a
benchmark for lovers of wines that play on
finesse and character. In the estates around
the villa, the vineyards are set amidst
cypresses and cover just under five
hectares, partly planted to bush vines and
partly pergola-trained. Cecilia decided to
stop producing Amarone some time ago, so
as to dedicate her full attention and best
grapes solely to Taso, her Valpolicella
Superiore. It is precisely the Taso which is
the most ambitious wine from Trucchi, a
red that undergoes partial drying of its
grapes, with spontaneous fermentation and
a couple of years' ageing in oak. On the
nose, the warmth of the harvest is evident,
with dense, sweet fruit, swathed in notes of
balsam and Mediterranean scrub, over a
rounded, elegant palate. The intriguing
Sotto le Fresche Frasche, a vintage
Valpolicella, is, as its melodious name
suggests, a dynamic, drinkable red.

● Breganze Cabernet Vign. Due Santi '12	🍷🍷🍷 4*
● Breganze Rosso Cavallare '12	🍷🍷 4
● Breganze Cabernet '12	🍷🍷 2*
● Breganze Merlot '12	🍷🍷 2*
○ Breganze Sauvignon '14	🍷🍷 3
○ Malvasia Campo di Fiori '14	🍷🍷 2*
○ Breganze Bianco Rivana '14	🍷 2
○ Breganze Torcolato '11	🍷 5
○ Prosecco Extra Dry	🍷 2
● Breganze Cabernet Vign. Due Santi '08	🍷🍷🍷 4*
● Breganze Cabernet Vign. Due Santi '07	🍷🍷🍷 4
● Breganze Cabernet Vign. Due Santi '05	🍷🍷🍷 4
● Breganze Cabernet '11	🍷🍷 2*
● Breganze Cabernet Vign. Due Santi '11	🍷🍷 4
● Breganze Merlot '11	🍷🍷 2*

● Valpolicella Cl. Sup. Il Taso '12	🍷🍷 5
● Valpolicella Cl. Sotto le Fresche Frasche '14	🍷🍷 3
● Recioto della Valpolicella Cl. Uva Passa '11	🍷🍷🍷 7
● Valpolicella Cl. Sotto le Fresche Frasche '13	🍷🍷 3
● Valpolicella Cl. Sotto le Fresche Frasche '12	🍷🍷 3
● Valpolicella Cl. Sotto le Fresche Frasche '11	🍷🍷 3*
● Valpolicella Cl. Sup. Il Taso '11	🍷🍷 5
● Valpolicella Cl. Sup. Il Taso '10	🍷🍷 5
● Valpolicella Cl. Sup. Il Taso '09	🍷🍷 5
● Valpolicella Cl. Sup. Il Taso '08	🍷🍷 5
● Valpolicella Cl. Sup. Il Taso '07	🍷🍷 5

Villa Sandi

VIA ERIZZO, 112
31035 CROCETTA DEL MONTELLO [TV]
TEL. 0423665033
www.villasandi.it

CELLAR SALES
PRE-BOOKED VISITS
ACCOMMODATION AND RESTAURANT SERVICE
ANNUAL PRODUCTION 4,800,000 bottles
HECTARES UNDER VINE 480.50
SUSTAINABLE WINERY

The pride and joy of the Moretti Polegato family, for generations committed to producing wine in the area to the north of Treviso, is Villa Sandi, a Palladian house dating back to the mid-1600s. The large holdings are distributed between the slopes of Montello and the hills of Valdobbiadene, and the pride and joy is Vigna La Rivetta, in the heart of Cartizze. Prosecco accounts for the lion's share of impressive production figures, but there are also still wines and the important Opere Trevigiane line of Metodo Classico sparklers. Once again this year, the Cartizze Vigna La Rivetta is the star of the show at Polegato, showing a nose of fresh-cut flowers, apples and pears, developed on the elegant palate, perfectly sustained by creamy, caressing sparkle. We saw an interesting debut from the new Serenissima, a Metodo Classico conceived with a focus on freshness and fragrance. The Corpore is rich, crisp and harmonious.

Villa Spinosa

VIA JAGO DALL'ORA, 16
37024 NEGRAR [VR]
TEL. 0457500093
www.villaspinosa.it

CELLAR SALES
PRE-BOOKED VISITS
ACCOMMODATION
ANNUAL PRODUCTION 45,000 bottles
HECTARES UNDER VINE 20.00

Enrico Cascella's winery covers around 20 hectares along the ridge that separates the Negrar from the Marano Valley. Here, vineyards of varying ages show the progressive abandonment of pergola veronese in favour of a more modern overhead vine-training system. Great care is taken in the cellar, where the wines age for much longer than elsewhere, since Enrico is aware that traditional interpretations of the wines of this area need time to express themselves fully. A perfect example of this philosophy is the Ripasso Jago, from a vineyard that has always given austere wines, as we see here with deep, complex aromas of morello cherry and autumn leaves, accompanied by pepper and thyme, followed by a full, grippy, savoury palate, and a beautifully harmonious finish. A Tre Bicchieri was never in doubt. The Amarone is somewhat reticent on the nose, but shows a captivating, supple palate.

○ Cartizze Brut V. La Rivetta	♔♔♔ 6
● Còrpore '12	♔♔ 5
○ Opere Trevigiane Brut Ris. '10	♔♔ 5
○ Serenissima Opere Trevigiane Brut	♔♔ 5
○ Valdobbiadene Dry Cuvée Oris	♔♔ 3
○ Valdobbiadene Extra Dry	♔♔ 3
● Filio '13	♔ 4
○ Marinali Manzoni Bianco '14	♔ 3
● Marinali Rosso Raboso '11	♔ 3
○ Opere Trevigiane Brut	♔ 4
○ Prosecco di Treviso Il Fresco Brut	♔ 2
○ Valdobbiadene Brut '14	♔ 3
○ Opere Trevigiane Brut Ris. '09	♔♔ 5

● Valpolicella Cl. Sup. Ripasso Jago '11	♔♔♔ 3*
● Amarone della Valpolicella Cl. '06	♔♔ 7
● Valpolicella Cl. '13	♔♔ 2*
● Amarone della Valpolicella Cl. '04	♔♔ 7
● Amarone della Valpolicella Cl. Guglielmi di Jago '01	♔♔ 7
● Amarone della Valpolicella Cl. Guglielmi di Jago 10 Anni '04	♔♔ 8
● Recioto della Valpolicella Cl. Francesca Finato Spinosa '08	♔♔ 5
● Valpolicella Cl. '12	♔♔ 2*
● Valpolicella Cl. Sup. Figari '11	♔♔ 3
● Valpolicella Cl. Sup. Figari '08	♔♔ 3*
● Valpolicella Cl. Sup. Figari '07	♔♔ 2*
● Valpolicella Cl. Sup. Ripasso Jago '10	♔♔ 3
● Valpolicella Cl. Sup. Ripasso Jago '08	♔♔ 3
● Valpolicella Cl. Sup. Ripasso Jago '06	♔♔ 3

Vigneti Villabella

FRAZ. CALMASINO DI BARDOLINO
LOC. CANOVA, 2
37011 BARDOLINO [VR]
TEL. 0457236448
www.vignetivillabella.com

CELLAR SALES
PRE-BOOKED VISITS
ACCOMMODATION
ANNUAL PRODUCTION 500,000 bottles
HECTARES UNDER VINE 220.00

Villabella was established by the
Cristoforetti and Delibori families, and
works vineyards of around 100 hectares,
mainly in thc Lake Garda DOC zone of
Bardolino, although it also makes forays
into adjacent DOCs. The cellar's pride and
joy is Villa Cordevigo, the splendid
18th-century stately home which has been
turned into a country hotel, and is
surrounded by vineyards tended with the
utmost respect for the environment, which
provide the grapes for the more aspirational
labels. We were bowled over by the
Bardolino Vigna Morlongo Anniversario, a
red aged for a year, which shows all the
elegance this type can offer. On the nose,
notes of forest floor, dark berry fruit and
pepper, lead into a supple, elegant palate.
Diametrically opposed is the Villa Cordevigo
Rosso, a blend of traditional varieties and
lightly dried Bordeaux grapes which plays
on its full body and ripe aromas.

● Bardolino Cl. V. Morlongo Anniversario '13	♥♥ 2*
● Villa Cordevigo Rosso '09	♥♥ 5
● Amarone della Valpolicella Cl. '09	♥♥ 5
● Amarone della Valpolicella Cl. Fracastoro Ris. '08	♥♥ 6
● Valpolicella Cl. Sup. Ripasso '13	♥♥ 3
☉ Bardolino Chiaretto Brut	♥ 2
☉ Bardolino Chiaretto Cl. '14	♥ 2
☉ Bardolino Chiaretto Cl. Villa Cordevigo '14	♥ 2
○ Chardonnay Biologico Villa Cordevigo '14	♥ 2
○ Custoza '14	♥ 2
○ Lugana Ca' del Lago '14	♥ 3
○ Pinot Grigio '14	♥ 2
● Amarone della Valpolicella Cl. '08	♀♀ 5
● Bardolino Cl. V. Morlongo '13	♀♀ 2*
○ Lugana Ca' del Lago '13	♀♀ 2*

★Viviani

VIA MAZZANO, 8
37020 NEGRAR [VR]
TEL. 0457500286
www.cantinaviviani.com

CELLAR SALES
PRE-BOOKED VISITS
ANNUAL PRODUCTION 80,000 bottles
HECTARES UNDER VINE 10.00
SUSTAINABLE WINERY

The northern part of the Negrar Valley is a
viticultural environment of great interest.
Here the grapes ripen later than those on
the valley floor, but above all they mature
with less heat, a greater temperature range
and stronger sunlight. Claudio Viviani
knows the land around the winery like the
back of his hand, and for years has been
one of the few producers able to combine
the potency given by drying with the
lightness and finesse typical of grapes
grown in these hills. We saw an impressive
range presented by Claudio this year, both
in terms of quality and character, with a
memorable version of the Amarone Casa
dei Bepi. On the nose, super-ripe red berry
fruit takes centre stage, but gradually
makes way for fines herbes, freshly ground
coffee and spice, to then come back to the
fore, sweet and juicy, on the firm, taut,
almost austere palate. The Campo Morar
offers greater freshness and excellent
length, while the Amarone 2011 shows a
dry style and great suppleness.

● Amarone della Valpolicella Cl. Casa dei Bepi '10	♥♥♥ 8
● Amarone della Valpolicella Cl. '11	♥♥ 6
● Recioto della Valpolicella Cl. '10	♥♥ 6
● Valpolicella Cl. Sup. Campo Morar '12	♥♥ 5
● Valpolicella Cl. '14	♥ 2
● Amarone della Valpolicella Cl. Casa dei Bepi '09	♀♀♀ 8
● Amarone della Valpolicella Cl. Casa dei Bepi '05	♀♀♀ 8
● Amarone della Valpolicella Cl. Casa dei Bepi '04	♀♀♀ 8
● Amarone della Valpolicella Cl. Casa dei Bepi '01	♀♀♀ 8
● Valpolicella Cl. Sup. Campo Morar '05	♀♀♀ 5
● Valpolicella Cl. Sup. Campo Morar '10	♀♀ 5

Pietro Zanoni

LOC. QUINZANO
VIA ARE ZOVO, 16D
37125 VERONA
TEL. 0458343977
www.pietrozanoni.it

CELLAR SALES
PRE-BOOKED VISITS
ANNUAL PRODUCTION 20,000 bottles
HECTARES UNDER VINE 6.50

Pietro Zanoni has managed to take over the helm of the family winery and transform it completely. At the end of the last century, what ahd been a business dedicated to producing grapes for others developed into a winery, while remaining strongly committed to wines of tradition. Zanoni only use the classic grapes of the DOC zone, shunning the solely commercial approach seen in Valpolicella over the years. The vineyards cover around seven hectares in the southern part of the DOC, almost at the gates of Verona, on three different plots: Avesa, Parona and Quinzano. We were incredibly impressed with the Amarone Zovo, from the oldest vines situated around the cellar, which shows a deep nose of red berry fruit and spice, over a powerful yet dry, grippy palate. The Valpolicella Superiore Campo Denari, whose grapes are lightly dried, shows intense notes of super-ripe fruit followed by a caressing, succulent palate.

Pietro Zardini

VIA DON P. FANTONI, 3
37029 SAN PIETRO IN CARIANO [VR]
TEL. 0456800989
www.pietrozardini.it

CELLAR SALES
PRE-BOOKED VISITS
ANNUAL PRODUCTION 20,000 bottles
HECTARES UNDER VINE 7.00

Giampietro Zardini has developed the family winery, which now has a new, functional cellar at San Pietro in Cariano. Production is mainly dedicated to the wines of Valpolicella, with the occasional foray towards Lake Garda, not to mention a couple of creative wines from traditional varieties. Giampietro's style is the result of many years working with wineries in the area, which have given him the vision required to reinterpret tradition. We were bowled over by the Amarone, with its nose of ripe, juicy red fruit, and fresh, attractive notes of medicinal herbs, paving the way for a firm, crisp palate with impressive length. The aromatic profile of the Ripasso Austero is similar to that of the Amarone, accompanied by a dry, powerful palate. A partnership with the former footballer Damiano Tommasi, a native of Valpolicella, resulted in a Ripasso with an intense nose and beautifully rounded palate.

● Amarone della Valpolicella Zovo '10	♥♥ 6
● Recioto della Valpolicella '09	♥♥ 4
● Valpolicella Sup. '13	♥♥ 2*
● Valpolicella Sup. Campo Denari '11	♥♥ 4
● Amarone della Valpolicella Zovo '09	♀♀ 6
● Amarone della Valpolicella Zovo '07	♀♀ 6
● Amarone della Valpolicella Zovo '04	♀♀ 6
● Valpolicella Sup. '08	♀♀ 4
● Valpolicella Sup. Campo Denari '10	♀♀ 4

● Amarone della Valpolicella '10	♥♥ 6
● Valpolicella Cl. Sup. Ripasso 17	♥♥ 3
● Valpolicella Sup. Ripasso Austero '11	♥♥ 4
⊙ Bardolino Chiaretto Rosignol Brut	♥ 6
○ Lugana '14	♥ 2
● Rosignol	♥ 4
● Amarone della Valpolicella '05	♀♀ 6
● Amarone della Valpolicella '04	♀♀ 6
● Amarone della Valpolicella Cl. '07	♀♀ 6
● Amarone della Valpolicella Cl. '03	♀♀ 6
● Amarone della Valpolicella Cl. Leone Zardini '05	♀♀ 6
● Amarone della Valpolicella Cl. Leone Zardini Ris. '08	♀♀ 6
○ Lugana '07	♀♀ 2
○ Lugana '06	♀♀ 2
● Valpolicella Sup. Ripasso Austero '07	♀♀ 4

★Zenato

FRAZ. SAN BENEDETTO DI LUGANA
VIA SAN BENEDETTO, 8
37019 PESCHIERA DEL GARDA [VR]
TEL. 0457550300
www.zenato.it

CELLAR SALES
PRE-BOOKED VISITS
ANNUAL PRODUCTION 2,000,000 bottles
HECTARES UNDER VINE 75.00

Nadia and Alberto Zenato capably run the operation established by their father Sergio many years ago, and which operates in all the most important DOC zones of the area to the west of Verona. Since the beginning, their main focus has been on the territory of Lugana, of course, but the importance of Valpolicella has also increased. The vineyards now cover over 70 hectares, and local growers contribute to the production figures. After a few years' absence, the winery at Peschiera once more takes home a Tre Bicchieri with an outstanding Amarone Sergio Zenato. The aromas are dominated by sweet, juicy red berry fruit, inebriating in its intensity and focus, against a backdrop of pepper and chocolate, paving the way for an incredibly full, harmonious palate. We also loved the Lugana of the same name, a white released after long oak ageing, which shows a ripe nose and a firm, fruity palate.

- Amarone della Valpolicella Cl. Sergio Zenato Ris. '09 — ▼▼▼ 8
- ○ Lugana Sergio Zenato Ris. '12 — ▼▼ 5
- Amarone della Valpolicella Cl. '10 — ▼▼ 6
- Cresasso '09 — ▼▼ 5
- ○ Lugana Massoni Santa Cristina '14 — ▼▼ 3
- Valpolicella Cl. Sup. '12 — ▼▼ 3
- ○ Lugana S. Benedetto '14 — ▼ 2
- Amarone della Valpolicella Cl. '05 — ♀♀♀ 6
- Amarone della Valpolicella Cl. Sergio Zenato '05 — ♀♀♀ 6
- Amarone della Valpolicella Cl. Sergio Zenato '03 — ♀♀♀ 6
- ○ Lugana Sergio Zenato '08 — ♀♀♀ 4
- Amarone della Valpolicella Cl. Sergio Zenato Ris. '08 — ♀♀ 8
- ○ Lugana Sergio Zenato Ris. '11 — ♀♀ 5
- Valpolicella Cl. Sup. '11 — ♀♀ 3

Zeni 1870

VIA COSTABELLA, 9
37011 BARDOLINO [VR]
TEL. 0457210022
www.zeni.it

CELLAR SALES
PRE-BOOKED VISITS
ANNUAL PRODUCTION 1,000,000 bottles
HECTARES UNDER VINE 25.00

It is the children of Gaetano Zeni to run the family winery, and continue the work started by Nino in the 1970s, always in tune with what is happening in the world of wine today. The winery's estate is not particularly big, so it also relies on a large network of growers who have been providing grapes for decades, and who are supervised throughout the year to give Fausto, Elena and Federica the best grapes possible. Zeni's best wine harks from Valpolicella: a 2005 Amarone dedicated to the founder. On the nose, the ten years of ageing have brought complexity, with the fruit now fused with notes of dried flowers and spice, while on the palate it shows great power and velvety, caressing progression. We also found the Bardolino Vigne Alte interesting. This red relies on its aromatic fragrance and taut palate. Among the whites, we were impressed with the Lugana Vigne Alte.

- Amarone della Valpolicella Cl. Nino Zeni '05 — ▼▼ 8
- Amarone della Valpolicella Cl. Barrique '10 — ▼▼ 7
- Amarone della Valpolicella Cl. Vigne Alte '11 — ▼▼ 6
- Bardolino Cl. Vigne Alte '14 — ▼▼ 2*
- ○ Lugana Marogne '14 — ▼▼ 3
- ○ Lugana Vigne Alte '14 — ▼▼ 2*
- Valpolicella Cl. Sup. Ripasso Marogne '13 — ▼▼ 3
- Valpolicella Sup. Vigne Alte '13 — ▼▼ 2*
- Bardolino Chiaretto Cl. Marogne '13 — ▼ 3
- ☉ Bardolino Chiaretto Cl. Vigne Alte '14 — ▼ 2
- Bardolino Cl. Filari del Nino '14 — ▼ 5
- Costalago Rosso '13 — ▼ 3
- Cruino Rosso '11 — ▼ 6
- Recioto della Valpolicella Cl. '13 — ▼ 4

Zonin 1821

VIA BORGOLECCO, 9
36053 GAMBELLARA [VI]
TEL. 0444640111
www.zonin.it

CELLAR SALES
PRE-BOOKED VISITS
ANNUAL PRODUCTION 38,000,000 bottles
HECTARES UNDER VINE 2000.00

With 2,000 hectares of vineyards and production of almost 40 million bottles, the Zonin family group is one of the most important privately owned wine producers in Italy. Based in Gambellara, this family has been in the wine trade since 1821, and now has nine estates in Italy's best wine country, as well as the historic estate at Barboursville in Virginia, which once belonged to the President Jefferson. Gambellara is also the location of Podere Il Giangio, dedicated to the classic Vicenza white. Zonin's wines are appreciated for their focused, supple style and drinkability. These are qualities are the key to the brand's success along with their excellent value for money. The Amarone 2012 is rich, succulent and warm, with chocolate and aromatic herbs in the finale. The well-balanced Valpolicella Superiore Ripasso 2013 shows flavoursome morello cherries and coffee. The Gambellara Classico Il Giangio is focused and enjoyable, but pays the price of a difficult growing year, as does the sweet Recioto di Gambellara Spumante. The Prosecco Brut Cuvée 1821 has grown in quality.

● Amarone della Valpolicella '12	♟♟ 5
● Valpolicella Sup. Ripasso '13	♟♟ 3
○ Gambellara Cl. Il Giangio '14	♟ 2
○ Prosecco Brut Cuvée 1821	♟ 3
○ Recioto di Gambellara Spumante	♟ 3
● Amarone della Valpolicella '10	♟♟ 6
● Amarone della Valpolicella '09	♟♟ 6
● Berengario '09	♟♟ 4
○ Gambellara Cl. Podere Il Giangio '13	♟♟ 2*
● Valpolicella Sup. Ripasso '12	♟♟ 3
● Valpolicella Sup. Ripasso '11	♟♟ 3

Zymè

LOC. SAN FLORIANO
VIA CA' DEL PIPA, 1
37029 SAN PIETRO IN CARIANO [VR]
TEL. 0457701108
www.zyme.it

CELLAR SALES
PRE-BOOKED VISITS
ANNUAL PRODUCTION 80,000 bottles
HECTARES UNDER VINE 30.00
SUSTAINABLE WINERY

This year Celestino Gaspari has opened the new cellar, a fine facility that fits perfectly into the territory, flanked by the old sandstone quarry and built for the most part under ground level, recycling the stone extracted to construct the walls. The vineyards lie on around 30 hectares distributed mainly in Valpolicella, an area that also provides grapes for most of the wines without DOC status. Celestino's great sensitivity in the production of Valpolicella is once more showcased in the 2008 vintage. On the nose, the fruit is swathed in pepper and autumn leaves, with original vegetal nuances, leading into a caressing palate that just goes on and on. The Valpolicella Superiore shows the same complexity, but a fresher, racier palate.

● Amarone della Valpolicella Cl. '08	♟♟ 8
● Valpolicella Cl. Sup. '11	♟♟ 5
● 60 20 20 '10	♟♟ 5
● Harlequin '08	♟♟ 8
○ Il Bianco From Black to White	♟♟ 3
● Kairos '10	♟♟ 7
● Oseleta '09	♟♟ 6
○ Dosaggio Zero M. Cl.	♟ 5
● Valpolicella Reverie '14	♟ 2
● Amarone della Valpolicella Cl. '06	♟♟♟ 8
● Amarone della Valpolicella Cl. La Mattonara Ris. '03	♟♟♟ 8
● Valpolicella Cl. Sup. '10	♟♟ 5
● Valpolicella Cl. Sup. '09	♟♟ 6
● Valpolicella Revirie '13	♟♟ 2*
● Valpolicella Revirie '12	♟♟ 2*

Aldo Adami

LOC. CUSTOZA
VIA VALBUSA, 29
37066 SOMMACAMPAGNA [VR]
TEL. 045516105
www.cantinaaldoadami.com

CELLAR SALES
PRE-BOOKED VISITS
ANNUAL PRODUCTION 130,000 bottles
HECTARES UNDER VINE 10.00

○ Custoza '14	♟♟ 2*
● Bardolino '14	♟ 2
⊙ Bardolino Chiaretto '14	♟ 2
○ Custoza Sup. Ciampani '13	♟ 3

Aldegheri

VIA A. VOLTA, 9
37010 SANT'AMBROGIO DI VALPOLICELLA [VR]
TEL. 0456861356
www.cantinealdegheri.it

CELLAR SALES
PRE-BOOKED VISITS
ANNUAL PRODUCTION 800,000 bottles
HECTARES UNDER VINE 52.00

● Amarone della Valpolicella Cl. '10	♟♟ 6
● Amarone della Valpolicella Cl. Ris. '06	♟♟ 8
● Amarone della Valpolicella Cl. Santambrogio '10	♟ 6

Astoria Vini

VIA CREVADA, 44
31020 REFRONTOLO [TV]
TEL. 04236699
www.astoria.it

CELLAR SALES
PRE-BOOKED VISITS
ANNUAL PRODUCTION 15,000,000 bottles
HECTARES UNDER VINE 40.00
SUSTAINABLE WINERY

● Colli di Conegliano Croder Rosso '12	♟♟ 4
○ Valdobbiadene Extra Dry	♟♟ 4
○ Valdobbiadene Brut Rive di Refrontolo Casa di Vittorino '14	♟ 4

Beato Bartolomeo

VIA ROMA, 100
36042 BREGANZE [VI]
TEL. 0445873112
www.cantinabreganze.it

CELLAR SALES
ANNUAL PRODUCTION 2,500,000 bottles
HECTARES UNDER VINE 700.00

● Breganze Cabernet Kilò Ris. '12	♟♟ 4
● Breganze Cabernet Bosco Grande '12	♟ 3
● Breganze Merlot Bosco Grande '12	♟ 3
○ Breganze Vespaiolo Sup. Savardo '14	♟ 2

Bellenda

FRAZ. CARPESICA
VIA GIARDINO, 90
31029 VITTORIO VENETO [TV]
TEL. 0438920025
www.bellenda.it

CELLAR SALES
PRE-BOOKED VISITS
ACCOMMODATION
ANNUAL PRODUCTION 1,000,000 bottles
HECTARES UNDER VINE 38.00

○ Conegliano Valdobbiadene Brut M. Cl. Sei Uno	♟♟ 4
○ Saiph Brut M. Cl.	♟♟ 4

Bellussi Spumanti

VIA ERIZZO, 215
31049 VALDOBBIADENE [TV]
TEL. 0423983411
www.bellussi.com

CELLAR SALES
PRE-BOOKED VISITS
ANNUAL PRODUCTION 1,300,000 bottles

○ Brut Belcanto	♟♟ 3
○ Valdobbiadene Extra Dry Belcanto	♟♟ 3
○ Valdobbiadene Dry	♟ 3

Bergamini

LOC. COLÀ
VIA CÀ NOVA, 2
37010 LAZISE [VR]
TEL. 0456490407
www.bergaminivini.it

CELLAR SALES
PRE-BOOKED VISITS
ANNUAL PRODUCTION 45,000 bottles
HECTARES UNDER VINE 11.50

○ Custoza '14	🏆🏆	1*
○ Custoza Sup. '14	🏆🏆	3
● Bardolino '14	🏆	2
○ Garda Cortese '14	🏆	2

Le Bertole

VIA EUROPA, 20
31049 VALDOBBIADENE [TV]
TEL. 0423975332
www.lebertole.com

CELLAR SALES
PRE-BOOKED VISITS
ANNUAL PRODUCTION 250,000 bottles
HECTARES UNDER VINE 16.00

○ Cartizze	🏆🏆	4
○ Valdobbiadene Brut	🏆🏆	3
○ Valdobbiadene Extra Dry	🏆🏆	3
○ Valdobbiadene Dry Supreme	🏆	3

Bonotto delle Tezze

FRAZ. TEZZE DI PIAVE
VIA DUCA D'AOSTA, 16
31020 VAZZOLA [TV]
TEL. 0438488323
www.bonottodelletezze.it

CELLAR SALES
PRE-BOOKED VISITS
ANNUAL PRODUCTION 120,000 bottles
HECTARES UNDER VINE 44.00

● Piave Malanotte '11	🏆🏆	6
● Piave Carmenere Barabane '13	🏆	3
● Piave Merlot Spezza '13	🏆	3
● Piave Raboso Potestà '11	🏆	3

F.lli Bortolin

FRAZ. SANTO STEFANO
VIA MENEGAZZI, 5
31049 VALDOBBIADENE [TV]
TEL. 0423900135
www.bortolin.com

CELLAR SALES
PRE-BOOKED VISITS
ANNUAL PRODUCTION 300,000 bottles
HECTARES UNDER VINE 20.00

○ Valdobbiadene Dry	🏆🏆	2*
○ Valdobbiadene Extra Dry Rù '14	🏆🏆	3
○ Cartizze Dry	🏆	4
○ Valdobbiadene Extra Dry	🏆	2

Castello di Lispida

VIA IV NOVEMBRE, 4
35043 MONSELICE [PD]
TEL. 0429780530
www.lispida.com

CELLAR SALES
PRE-BOOKED VISITS
ANNUAL PRODUCTION 18,000 bottles
HECTARES UNDER VINE 8.00

● Terraforte '11	🏆🏆	5
○ H Frizzante '13	🏆	4

Tenuta Chiccheri

LOC. CHICCHERI, 1
37039 TREGNAGO [VR]
TEL. 0458774333
www.tenutachiccheri.it

ANNUAL PRODUCTION 20,000 bottles
HECTARES UNDER VINE 10.00
SUSTAINABLE WINERY

● Amarone della Valpolicella '10	🏆🏆	6
● Valpolicella Sup. '10	🏆🏆	4
○ Monte Belloca Brut M. Cl.	🏆	4
● Valpolicella '13	🏆	2

OTHER WINERIES

Conte Collalto

VIA 24 MAGGIO, 1
31058 SUSEGANA [TV]
TEL. 0438435811
www.cantine-collalto.it

CELLAR SALES
PRE-BOOKED VISITS
ANNUAL PRODUCTION 850,000 bottles
HECTARES UNDER VINE 150.00
SUSTAINABLE WINERY

○ Conegliano Valdobbiadene Extra Dry	🍷🍷	3
● Piave Cabernet Torrai Ris. '09	🍷🍷	5
○ Conegliano Valdobbiadene Brut	🍷	3
○ Conegliano Valdobbiadene Dry '14	🍷	3

Corte Adami

VIA CIRCONVALLAZIONE ALDO MORO, 32
37038 SOAVE [VR]
TEL. 0457680423
www.corteadami.it

CELLAR SALES
PRE-BOOKED VISITS
ANNUAL PRODUCTION 100,000 bottles
HECTARES UNDER VINE 38.00
SUSTAINABLE WINERY

● Amarone della Valpolicella '11	🍷🍷	6
○ Soave V. della Corte '13	🍷🍷	3
○ Soave '14	🍷	2
○ Soave Cl. Cimalta '14	🍷	2

Alla Costiera

VIA NINA, 900
35030 VO [PD]
TEL. 0499940492
www.allacostiera.it

ANNUAL PRODUCTION 30,000 bottles
HECTARES UNDER VINE 7.00

○ Colli Euganei Bianco Terreni Bianchi '14	🍷🍷	2*
● Colli Euganei Merlot Vò Vecchio '12	🍷🍷	3

Paolo Cottini

LOC. CASTELROTTO DI SAN PIETRO IN CARIANO
VIA BELVEDERE, 29
37029 VERONA
TEL. 0456837293
www.paolocottini.it

CELLAR SALES
PRE-BOOKED VISITS
ANNUAL PRODUCTION 30,000 bottles
HECTARES UNDER VINE 3.50

● Amarone della Valpolicella '11	🍷🍷	3
● Valpolicella Cl. Sup. Ripasso '11	🍷🍷	3
● Castrum '14	🍷	2
● Valpolicella Cl. '14	🍷	3

Giulietta Dal Bosco
Le Guaite

VIA CAPOVILLA , 10A
37030 MEZZANE DI SOTTO [VR]
TEL. 045 8880396
www.sisure.it

CELLAR SALES
PRE-BOOKED VISITS
ANNUAL PRODUCTION 25,000 bottles
HECTARES UNDER VINE 2.00

● Amarone della Valpolicella		
Le Guaite di Giulietta '08	🍷🍷	7
● Recioto della Valpolicella		
Le Guaite di Noemi '08	🍷🍷	5

Fongaro

VIA MOTTO PIANE, 12
37030 RONCÀ [VR]
TEL. 0457460240
www.fongarospumanti.it

CELLAR SALES
PRE-BOOKED VISITS
ANNUAL PRODUCTION 68,000 bottles
HECTARES UNDER VINE 7.00
VITICULTURE METHOD Certified Organic

○ Lessini Durello Pas Dosé M. Cl. '10	🍷🍷	5
○ Lessini Durello Brut M. Cl. '10	🍷	4

Gorgo

FRAZ. CUSTOZA
LOC. GORGO
37066 SOMMACAMPAGNA [VR]
TEL. 045516063
www.cantinagorgo.com

ANNUAL PRODUCTION 350,000 bottles
HECTARES UNDER VINE 50.00

○ Custoza San Michelin '14	🍷🍷 2*
○ Custoza Sup. Summa '14	🍷🍷 2*
● Bardolino Sup. Monte Maggiore '13	🍷 3
● Ca' Nova '12	🍷 2

La Giuva

VIA TREZZOLANO, 20C
37141 VERONA
TEL. 3421117089
www.lagiuva.com

CELLAR SALES
PRE-BOOKED VISITS
ANNUAL PRODUCTION 20,000 bottles
HECTARES UNDER VINE 9.50
VITICULTURE METHOD Certified Organic

● Recioto della Valpolicella '13	🍷🍷 3
● Valpolicella Sup. Il Rientro '12	🍷🍷 3
● Valpolicella Il Valpo '14	🍷 2

Latium

LOC. LEON
37030 MEZZANE DI SOTTO [VR]
TEL. 0457834037
www.latiummorini.it

CELLAR SALES
PRE-BOOKED VISITS
ANNUAL PRODUCTION 130,000 bottles
HECTARES UNDER VINE 39.00

● Amarone della Valpolicella Due Mori Ris. '08	🍷🍷 8
● Valpolicella Sup. Campo Prognai '11	🍷🍷 4
○ Soave Campo Le Calle '14	🍷 3

Lenotti

VIA SANTA CRISTINA, 1
37011 BARDOLINO [VR]
TEL. 0457210484
www.lenotti.com

CELLAR SALES
PRE-BOOKED VISITS
ANNUAL PRODUCTION 1,400,000 bottles
HECTARES UNDER VINE 105.00

● Amarone della Valpolicella Cl. '10	🍷🍷 6
○ Custoza '14	🍷🍷 2*
● Bardolino Sup. Le Olle '13	🍷 3
○ Lugana Decus '14	🍷 3

Giuseppe Lonardi

VIA DELLE POSTE, 2
37020 MARANO DI VALPOLICELLA [VR]
TEL. 0457755154
www.lonardivini.it

CELLAR SALES
PRE-BOOKED VISITS
ACCOMMODATION
ANNUAL PRODUCTION 51,000 bottles
HECTARES UNDER VINE 7.00

● Amarone della Valpolicella Cl. '11	🍷🍷 8
● Recioto della Valpolicella Cl. Le Arele '12	🍷🍷 6
● Privilegia Rosso '11	🍷 5
● Valpolicella Cl. '14	🍷 2

Maccari

VIA GENERALE CANTORE, 55
31020 TREVISO
TEL. 0438441248
www.maccarivini.it

ANNUAL PRODUCTION 1,400,000 bottles
HECTARES UNDER VINE 10.00

○ Valdobbiadene Extra Dry '14	🍷🍷 2*
● Piave Raboso Templaris '05	🍷 3
⊙ Rosé Dry	🍷 2
○ Valdobbiadene Dry '14	🍷 2

Le Mandolare

Loc. Brognoligo
via Sambuco, 180
37032 Monteforte d'Alpone [VR]
Tel. 0456175083
www.cantinalemandolare.com

CELLAR SALES
PRE-BOOKED VISITS
ANNUAL PRODUCTION 60,000 bottles
HECTARES UNDER VINE 20.00

○ Il Vignale Passito '11	🍷🍷 4
○ Soave Cl. Monte Sella '12	🍷🍷 3
○ Soave Cl. Corte Menini '14	🍷 2
○ Soave Cl. Il Roccolo '14	🍷 2

Marsuret

Loc. Guia
via Spinade, 41
31040 Valdobbiadene [TV]
Tel. 0423900139
www.marsuret.it

CELLAR SALES
PRE-BOOKED VISITS
ANNUAL PRODUCTION 450,000 bottles
HECTARES UNDER VINE 45.00

○ Valdobbiadene Dry Agostino '14	🍷🍷 3
○ Valdobbiadene Extra Dry Il Soller '14	🍷🍷 3
○ Valdobbiadene Brut Rive di Guia '14	🍷 2
○ Valdobbiadene Brut San Boldo '14	🍷 3

Menegotti

Loc. Acquaroli, 7
37069 Villafranca di Verona [VR]
Tel. 0457902611
www.menegotticantina.com

CELLAR SALES
PRE-BOOKED VISITS
ANNUAL PRODUCTION 180,000 bottles
HECTARES UNDER VINE 22.00

○ Custoza Sup. Elianto '13	🍷🍷 2*
● Mezzacosta '12	🍷🍷 2*
○ Brut M. Cl. '08	🍷 3
○ Custoza '14	🍷 2

Ornella Molon Traverso

fraz. Campo di Pietra
via Risorgimento, 40
31040 Salgareda [TV]
Tel. 0422804807
www.ornellamolon.it

CELLAR SALES
PRE-BOOKED VISITS
RESTAURANT SERVICE
ANNUAL PRODUCTION 450,000 bottles
HECTARES UNDER VINE 42.00
SUSTAINABLE WINERY

○ Bianco di Ornella '11	🍷🍷 4
● Vite Rossa '11	🍷🍷 4
● Piave Malanotte Raboso '09	🍷 5
○ Traminer '14	🍷 3

Monte Santoccio

Loc. Santoccio, 6
37022 Fumane [VR]
Tel. 3496461223
www.montesantoccio.it

ANNUAL PRODUCTION 14,000 bottles
HECTARES UNDER VINE 3.00

● Amarone della Valpolicella Cl. '11	🍷🍷 7
● Valpolicella Cl. Sup. Ripasso '12	🍷🍷 4
● Valpolicella Cl. Sup. '13	🍷 2

Monte Zovo

Loc. Zovo, 23a
37013 Caprino Veronese [VR]
Tel. 0457281301
www.montezovo.com

CELLAR SALES
PRE-BOOKED VISITS
ACCOMMODATION AND RESTAURANT SERVICE
ANNUAL PRODUCTION 1,000,000 bottles
HECTARES UNDER VINE 100.00

● Amarone della Valpolicella Ris. '09	🍷🍷 8
● Valpolicella Sup. Ripasso '12	🍷🍷 4
● Valpolicella '14	🍷 2

Montecariano

VIA VALENA, 3
37029 SAN PIETRO IN CARIANO [VR]
TEL. 0456838335
www.montecariano.it

CELLAR SALES
PRE-BOOKED VISITS
ANNUAL PRODUCTION 20,000 bottles
HECTARES UNDER VINE 21.00

● Valpolicella Cl. Sup. Corte Monte '12	🍷🍷 3
● Amarone della Valpolicella Cl. '09	🍷 7
● Valpolicella Cl. '14	🍷 2
● Valpolicella Cl. Sup. Ripasso '11	🍷 4

Montelvini

VIA CAL TREVIGIANA, 51
31040 VOLPAGO DEL MONTELLO [TV]
TEL. 04238777
www.montelvini.it

CELLAR SALES
ANNUAL PRODUCTION 1,200,000 bottles
HECTARES UNDER VINE 35.00
VITICULTURE METHOD Certified Organic

○ Asolo Brut	🍷🍷 2*
○ Asolo Extra Dry	🍷🍷 2*
○ Asolo Prosecco Frizzante	🍷 3
○ Luna Storta	🍷 4

Walter Nardin

LOC. RONCADELLE
VIA FONTANE, 5
31024 ORMELLE [TV]
TEL. 0422851622
www.vinwalternardin.it

PRE-BOOKED VISITS
ANNUAL PRODUCTION 350,000 bottles
HECTARES UNDER VINE 30.00

● Rosso del Nane La Zerbaia '13	🍷🍷 2*
● Rosso della Ghiaia La Zerbaia '11	🍷🍷 4
● Refosco P. R. La Zerbaia '12	🍷 3
○ Tai La Zerbaia '13	🍷 2

Tenuta Polvaro

VIA POLVARO, 35
30020 ANNONE VENETO [VE]
TEL. 0421281023
www.tenutapolvaro.it

CELLAR SALES
PRE-BOOKED VISITS
ANNUAL PRODUCTION 300,000 bottles
HECTARES UNDER VINE 60.00

● Venezia Polvaro Nero '13	🍷🍷 2*
○ Polvaro Oro '13	🍷 2
● Venezia Cabernet Sauvignon '13	🍷 1
● Venezia Merlot '11	🍷 1

Provolo

VIA SAN CASSIANO, 2
37030 MEZZANE DI SOTTO [VR]
TEL. 0458880106
www.viniprovolo.com

CELLAR SALES
PRE-BOOKED VISITS
ANNUAL PRODUCTION 100,000 bottles
HECTARES UNDER VINE 20.00

● Amarone della Valpolicella Cl. '10	🍷🍷 6
● Recioto della Valpolicella '09	🍷🍷 6
● Valpolicella Cl. '14	🍷 3
● Valpolicella Sup. Campotorbian Ripasso '11	🍷 5

Punto Zero

GALLERIA EZZELLINO, 5
35139 PADOVA
TEL. 0457701108
www.puntozerowine.it

CELLAR SALES
PRE-BOOKED VISITS
ANNUAL PRODUCTION 15,000 bottles
HECTARES UNDER VINE
SUSTAINABLE WINERY

● Idea '12	🍷🍷 3
● Punto '11	🍷🍷 8
● Dimezzo '10	🍷 5
○ Trasparenza '14	🍷 3

Azienda Agricola Rebuli

LOC. SACCOL
VIA STRADA DI SACCOL, 40
31030 VALDOBBIADENE [TV]
TEL. 0423973307
www.rebuli.it

CELLAR SALES
PRE-BOOKED VISITS
ANNUAL PRODUCTION 700,000 bottles
HECTARES UNDER VINE 42.00

○ Valdobbiadene Brut Angelo Rebuli '13	🍷🍷 3
○ Valdobbiadene Rive di San Pietro di Barbozza Brut La Riva '14	🍷🍷 3
○ Cartizze	🍷 3

Ettore Righetti

VIA SAN MARTINO, 8
37024 NEGRAR [VR]
TEL. 0457500062

CELLAR SALES
ANNUAL PRODUCTION 45,000 bottles
HECTARES UNDER VINE 5.00

● Amarone della Valpolicella Cl. '11	🍷🍷 5
● Arsi '13	🍷 4
● Valpolicella Cl. Sup. Ripasso '12	🍷 4

San Cassiano

VIA SAN CASSIANO, 17
37030 MEZZANE DI SOTTO [VR]
TEL. 0458880665
www.cantinasancassiano.it

ANNUAL PRODUCTION 50,000 bottles
HECTARES UNDER VINE 11.00

● Amarone della Valpolicella '11	🍷🍷 6
● Valpolicella Sup. Ripasso '12	🍷🍷 2*
● Valpolicella '13	🍷 2

San Nazario

LOC. CORTELÀ
VIA MONTE VERSA, 1519
35030 VÒ [PD]
TEL. 0499940194
www.vinisannazario.it

CELLAR SALES
PRE-BOOKED VISITS
ANNUAL PRODUCTION 50,000 bottles
HECTARES UNDER VINE 10.00
VITICULTURE METHOD Certified Organic

● Colli Euganei Cabernet '12	🍷🍷 2*
● Colli Euganei Merlot Ruzante '13	🍷🍷 2*
○ Colli Euganei Bianco Dulcamara '14	🍷 2
● Colli Euganei Rosso Brolo delle Femmine '10	🍷 2

La Sansonina

LOC. SANSONINA
37019 PESCHIERA DEL GARDA [VR]
TEL. 0457551905
www.sansonina.it

CELLAR SALES
ANNUAL PRODUCTION 21,000 bottles
HECTARES UNDER VINE 12.00

● Sansonina '13	🍷🍷 6

Giovanna Tantini

FRAZ. OLIOSI
LOC. I MISCHI
37014 CASTELNUOVO DEL GARDA [VR]
TEL. 0457575070
www.giovannatantini.it

CELLAR SALES
PRE-BOOKED VISITS
ACCOMMODATION
ANNUAL PRODUCTION 30,000 bottles
HECTARES UNDER VINE 11.50

● Bardolino '13	🍷 2
⊙ Bardolino Chiaretto '14	🍷 2
○ Custoza '14	🍷 2

Terre di Leone

LOC. PORTA
37020 MARANO DI VALPOLICELLA [VR]
TEL. 0456895040
www.terredileone.it

CELLAR SALES
PRE-BOOKED VISITS
ANNUAL PRODUCTION 36,000 bottles
HECTARES UNDER VINE 10.00

- Amarone della Valpolicella Re Pazzo '11 ♥♥ 3
- Valpolicella Re Pazzo '13 ♥♥ 3
- Valpolicella Sup. Ripasso Re Pazzo '11 ♥♥ 4
- Mapple 108 '10 ♥ 2

Terre di Pietra

LOC. MARCELLISE
VIA ARCANDOLA, 4
37036 SAN MARTINO BUON ALBERGO [VR]
TEL. 0458740684
www.terredipietra.it

CELLAR SALES
PRE-BOOKED VISITS
ANNUAL PRODUCTION 18,000 bottles
HECTARES UNDER VINE 4.50
SUSTAINABLE WINERY

- Amarone della Valpolicella Cl. Rosson '09 ♥♥ 7
- Valpolicella Cl. Sup. Mesal '10 ♥♥ 4
- Valpolicella Sup. V. del Peste '12 ♥♥ 3
- Valpolicella Cl. Stelar '14 ♥ 2

Tezza

FRAZ. POIANO DI VALPANTENA
STRADELLA MAIOLI, 4
37142 VERONA
TEL. 045550267
www.tezzawines.it

CELLAR SALES
PRE-BOOKED VISITS
ANNUAL PRODUCTION 200,000 bottles
HECTARES UNDER VINE 27.00

- Recioto della Valpolicella Valpantena '09 ♥♥ 5
- Valpolicella Valpantena Ripasso
  Brolo delle Giare '09 ♥♥ 4
- Amarone della Valpolicella Corte Majoli '11 ♥ 5

Villa Medici

VIA CAMPAGNOL, 11
37066 SOMMACAMPAGNA [VR]
TEL. 045515147
www.cantinavillamedici.it

ANNUAL PRODUCTION 220,000 bottles
HECTARES UNDER VINE 32.00

- ○ Bianco di Custoza Passito
  La Valle del Re '09 ♥♥ 3
- ○ Custoza Sup. '13 ♥♥ 2*
- ● Bardolino '14 ♥ 2

Villa Minelli

VIA VILLA MINELLI, 1
31050 PONZANO VENETO [TV]
TEL. 0422912355
www.villaminelli.it

CELLAR SALES
PRE-BOOKED VISITS
ANNUAL PRODUCTION 40,000 bottles
HECTARES UNDER VINE 9.50

- ● Rosso Villa Minelli '13 ♥♥ 2*
- ○ Bianco Villa Minelli '14 ♥ 2
- ○ Malvasia Villa Minelli '13 ♥ 2
- ● Merlot Villa Minelli '12 ♥ 2

Zardetto Spumanti

VIA MARTIRI DELLE FOIBE, 18
31015 CONEGLIANO [TV]
TEL. 0438394969
www.zardettoprosecco.com

CELLAR SALES
PRE-BOOKED VISITS
ANNUAL PRODUCTION 2,000,000 bottles
HECTARES UNDER VINE 40.00
VITICULTURE METHOD Certified Organic

- ○ Conegliano Valdobbiadene Brut
  Rive di Ogliano Tre Venti '14 ♥♥ 3
- ○ Conegliano Valdobbiadene Sup. Brut
  Viti di San Mor '14 ♥♥ 5

FRIULI VENEZIA GIULIA

The lead-up to this year's tastings was ripe with curiosity to test the wines of the 2014 growing year, a season with decidedly unusual weather that cast producers afloat without a compass, leaving them to their own devices, so each winery gave free rein to personal ability in negotiating both vineyard and cellar. In the end, tastings gave really positive outcomes if we think that Friuli Venezia Giulia took home 24 Tre Bicchieri awards, and over half went to 2014 wines, confirming the unquestionable talent of regional vintners. The only red was a 2013 Sacrisassi from Le Due Terre, a marvellous voice of its area, based on equal parts of two native varieties: refosco dal peduncolo rosso and schioppettino. All the others are whites that stand as the ultimate expression of different types of vinification. Friulano 2014 is the best wine for illustrating territorial potential and on the podium we find a Russiz Superiore, a prestigious Collio brand, together with Schiopetto which – hear ye! hear ye! – is also White of the Year. A double award that pays homage to the great Mario, undisputed pioneer of quality winemaking in this region, and celebrating the 50th anniversary of his first bottle labels. Jermann, Livon, Collavini, and Ronchi di Manzano fly the flag for the reputation of the blends category, always a regional preserve. Confirming last year's trend, five Tre Bicchieri were attributed to Pinot Blanc 2014, two for Collio (Toros and Castello di Spessa), two for Colli Orientali (Torre Rosazza and new entry Zorzettig), and one for Grave, to Le Monde, for the third consecutive year. Malvasia Istriana also garnered unanimous approval both for the freshness of the Collio di Doro Princic and the Ronco dei Tassi, both 2014s, and for the fragrance of the more elaborate versions from earlier vintages of Kante and Il Carpino. Chardonnay was to the fore with Vie di Romans' 2013 Ciampagnis Vieris and Angoris' Spìule 2014, another great new entry. Volpe Pasini was our choice for Sauvignon 2014, while for Pinot Grigio the aristocratic Gris 2013 by Lis Neris was joined by Branko's 2014. Oslavia Ribolla Gialla, known for its skin contact, was best interpreted by Primosic and Gravner, respectively with a Riserva 2011 and a 2007. Last but not least, we bow to the most noble grape, with a Picolit 2008, in Adriano Gigante's beautiful rendering. The jury is out on the Sauvignons from several of the region's wineries, currently under investigation by the competent authorities. We are confident the investigations will conclude to everyone's satisfaction.

Tenuta di Angoris

LOC. ANGORIS, 7
34071 CORMÒNS [GO]
TEL. 048160923
www.angoris.it

CELLAR SALES
PRE-BOOKED VISITS
RESTAURANT SERVICE
ANNUAL PRODUCTION 650,000 bottles
HECTARES UNDER VINE 110.00
SUSTAINABLE WINERY

Established in 1648 Tenuta di Agoris holds its rightful place alongside other historic estates. Managed by various owners over three centuries it was purchased in 1968 by Luciano Locatelli. Of the estate's 630 hectares scattered over some of the region's best winegrowing areas, 110 are under vine, many surrounding the magnificent villa at Cormòns. Members of the Locatelli family have taken turns at the helm, and now Marta confidently guides the estate towards peaks of excellence with enthusiasm, energy and great spirit. The choices in the vineyards and the cellar are entrusted to estate winemaker Alessandro Dal Zovo. Gratifying results have not been slow in coming thanks to the Chardonnay Spìule 2013, which wins the cellar its first Tre Bicchieri this year. Generous, coherent and flavoursome, this trailblazer of a wine won over our palates with the harmonious blend of fruity and vanilla flavour sensations.

Antonutti

FRAZ. COLLOREDO DI PRATO
VIA D'ANTONI, 21
33037 PASIAN DI PRATO [UD]
TEL. 0432662001
www.antonuttivini.it

CELLAR SALES
PRE-BOOKED VISITS
ANNUAL PRODUCTION 780,000 bottles
HECTARES UNDER VINE 51.00
SUSTAINABLE WINERY

With skill and determination Adriana Antonutti runs one of the best-known wineries in the region, established back in 1921 by her grandfather Ignazio, at Colloredo di Prato, not far from Udine. Her husband Lino also owns vineyards, at Barbeano in the municipality of Spilimbergo. Both estates cover lean, stony ground in Grave di Friuli, which has always been considered an excellent growing area. With their children Caterina and Nicola they form a close-knit team which takes pride in family tradition. Pleasing, well-typed basic wines are flanked by the Vis Terrae products which are the best expression of the terroir's potential. The 2013 Cabernet Sauvignon shows very fruity and fragrant on both nose and palate, with a satisfying palate closing on promising balsam sensations. The Sauvignon stood out for its fresh flavour while the 2013 Lindul, from dried traminer aromatico, is sweetly lingering.

○ FCO Chardonnay Spìule '13	♛♛♛ 4*
⊙ 1648 Brut Rosé '11	♛♛ 6
○ Collio Bianco '13	♛♛ 3
○ FCO Friulano '14	♛♛ 3
○ FCO Picolit '10	♛♛ 6
● FCO Schioppettino '12	♛♛ 3
● COF Merlot Ravost '12	♛ 4
○ Friuli Isonzo Pinot Bianco '14	♛ 2
○ COF Friulano '13	♛♛ 3
○ COF Friulano '11	♛♛ 3*
● COF Pignolo '08	♛♛ 5
○ COF Sauvignon Blanc '12	♛♛ 3
● COF Schioppettino '11	♛♛ 3
○ Collio Bianco '12	♛♛ 3*
○ Collio Pinot Grigio '13	♛♛ 3
○ Friuli Isonzo Pinot Bianco '13	♛♛ 2*
○ Friuli Isonzo Sauvignon Blanc '13	♛♛ 3

○ Brut M. Cl. Ant '10	♛♛ 5
● Friuli Grave Cabernet Sauvignon '13	♛♛ 2*
○ Friuli Grave Sauvignon '14	♛♛ 2*
○ Lindul '13	♛♛ 6
● Friuli Grave Merlot '13	♛ 2
○ Friuli Grave Pinot Grigio '14	♛ 2
○ Friuli Grave Traminer Aromatico '14	♛ 2
● Poppone '13	♛ 5
● Friuli Grave Cabernet Sauvignon Vis. Terrae '10	♛♛ 3
○ Friuli Grave Chardonnay '13	♛♛ 2*
○ Friuli Grave Friulano '13	♛♛ 2*
○ Friuli Grave Sauvignon '13	♛♛ 2*
○ Lindul '11	♛♛ 6
○ Lindul '10	♛♛ 6
● Ros di Murì Vis Terrae '09	♛♛ 6

Aquila del Torre

FRAZ. SAVORGNANO DEL TORRE
VIA ATTIMIS, 25
33040 POVOLETTO [UD]
TEL. 0432666428
www.aquiladeltorre.it

CELLAR SALES
PRE-BOOKED VISITS
ACCOMMODATION
ANNUAL PRODUCTION 50,000 bottles
HECTARES UNDER VINE 18.00
VITICULTURE METHOD Certified Organic

With enviable synergy, Michele and
Francesca Ciani run the Aquila del Torre
farm, purchased in 1996. From the
beginning their father Claudio started an
ambitious reconversion plan in order to
preserve the existing valuable native
varietal biotypes. The vineyards are divided
into 16 distinct plots according to aspect,
soil and weather conditions, in magnificent,
often steep and arduous, natural
amphitheatres. Here in the extreme north of
Friuli, the Colli Orientali's luxurious natural
vegetation occupies the land not under
vine, surrounded by dense woods of oak,
chestnut, and hornbeam completing this
beautiful landscape. Only a few wines were
presented for tasting this year. The one we
enjoyed most was the promising At Refosco
dal Penduncolo Rosso 2012 with its
generous aromas of fruit and liquorice
reflected on the palate. Also very good, the
At Friulano 2014 emphasizes the freshness
of that year and closes on a pleasantly
bitterish note.

○ FCO At Friulano '14	♟♟	3
● FCO At Refosco P. R. '12	♟♟	3
○ FCO Sauvignon Vit dai Maz '13	♟	5
○ COF At Friulano '13	♟♟	3
○ COF At Friulano '11	♟♟	3
○ COF At Picolit '12	♟♟	6
● COF At Refosco P. R. '11	♟♟	3
○ COF At Riesling '12	♟♟	3
○ COF At Sauvignon Blanc '13	♟♟	3
● COF Friulano Ronc di Miez '12	♟♟	5
● COF Friulano Ronc di Miez '11	♟♟	5
○ COF Sauvignon Vit dai Maz '12	♟♟	5
○ Oasi '12	♟♟	6

Bastianich

LOC. GAGLIANO
VIA DARNAZZACCO, 44/2
33043 CIVIDALE DEL FRIULI [UD]
TEL. 0432700943
www.bastianich.com

CELLAR SALES
PRE-BOOKED VISITS
ACCOMMODATION AND RESTAURANT SERVICE
ANNUAL PRODUCTION 270,000 bottles
HECTARES UNDER VINE 35.00

Celebrities Joe and Lidia Bastianich own
numerous restaurants in the US, where
they still export Italian culinary delicacies
and wine, especially regional products.
Friuli's potential for producing
internationally renowned white wines led
Joe to set up a winery here in 1997, which
he still manages personally with frequent
visits to the Gagliano cellar near Cividale
del Friuli. Joe set himself the goal of
absolute excellence from the very
beginning, and draws on the proven
winemaking experience of Emilio Del
Medico and the invaluable advice of
consultant Maurizio Castelli. The estate's
most typical wine is Vespa Bianco 2013, a
blend of chardonnay and sauvignon
enriched with a small but important
addition of picolit. The enjoyable and
flawless blend of aromas create a pleasing
effect on the nose and, above all, a
flavoursome palate.

○ Vespa Bianco '13	♟♟	5
● Calabrone '11	♟♟	8
○ Plus '12	♟♟	6
○ Vespa Bianco '04	♟♟♟	4
○ Vespa Bianco '03	♟♟♟	4
○ Vespa Bianco '01	♟♟♟	4
○ Vespa Bianco '00	♟♟♟	3
○ COF Friulano V. Orsone '13	♟♟	3
○ COF Sauvignon V. Orsone '13	♟♟	3
○ Plus '09	♟♟	6
○ Plus '08	♟♟	4
○ Vespa Bianco '12	♟♟	5
● Vespa Rosso '11	♟♟	5
● Vespa Rosso '10	♟♟	5

Tenuta Beltrame

FRAZ. PRIVANO
LOC. ANTONINI, 4
33050 BAGNARIA ARSA [UD]
TEL. 0432923670
www.beltramewine.com

CELLAR SALES
PRE-BOOKED VISITS
ANNUAL PRODUCTION 80,000 bottles
HECTARES UNDER VINE 25.00

In 1991, the Beltrame family bought the old estate formerly owned by the Conti Antonini, consisting of 40 hectares, with 25 under vine, on the Friuli plains. Cristian Beltrame, then very young, managed the estate and, with the invaluable help of oenologist Bepi Gollino, proceeded to reorganize and replant the vineyards, focusing on native local varieties, building a cellar and renovating the 15th-century country house, which would become the winery's headquarters. The vineyards are now mature and Cristian is reaping the rewards of his early choices. The land is mainly clay-based and particularly well-suited to red wine production. The flattering results obtained by the whole range of wines, even more appreciable if compared to the prices, reflect the estate's philosophy to preserve varietal features. The wines are never too lively but well-balanced, approachable and very drinkable.

Borgo delle Oche

VIA BORGO ALPI, 5
33098 VALVASONE ARZENE [PN]
TEL. 0434840640
www.borgodelleoche.it

CELLAR SALES
PRE-BOOKED VISITS
ACCOMMODATION
ANNUAL PRODUCTION 35,000 bottles
HECTARES UNDER VINE 7.00
SUSTAINABLE WINERY

Borgo delle Oche was established very recently, in 2004 and is named after the village where it is situated, in the beautiful medieval Valvasone, in the province of Pordenone. Owner Luisa Menini holds a degree in food technology and works closely with her husband, agronomist and oenologist Nicola Pittina. The couple are firm supporters of the potential of this terroir and succeed in highlighting the specific features of each individual variety. Their wines prove that even in quite underrated terroirs like Friuli's Grave, top quality results can be achieved using selective and focused techniques. Amber colour hues characterize the Traminer Aromatico Alba 2013 made from dried grapes. Marrons glacés and almond brittle on the nose, while the palate is richly extracted, flavoursome and sweet but not cloying. The other wines are excellent, mouthwatering and full of flavour.

● Friuli Aquileia Cabernet Franc '13	♟♟ 2*
● Friuli Aquileia Cabernet Sauvignon Ris. '12	♟♟ 3
○ Friuli Aquileia Chardonnay Pribus '12	♟♟ 3
● Friuli Aquileia Merlot Ris. '12	♟♟ 3
● Friuli Aquileia Refosco P. R. '13	♟♟ 2*
● Pinot Nero '12	♟♟ 2*
● Friuli Aquileia Cabernet Sauvignon '13	♟ 2
○ Friuli Aquileia Chardonnay '14	♟ 2
○ Friuli Aquileia Sauvignon '14	♟ 2
○ Friuli Aquileia Verduzzo Friulano '11	♟ 2
○ Pinot Grigio '14	♟ 2
● Tazzelenghe '10	♟ 3
● Friuli Aquileia Cabernet Franc '12	♟♟ 2*
● Friuli Aquileia Merlot Ris. '08	♟♟ 3*
● Friuli Aquileia Merlot Ris. '05	♟♟ 3*
○ Pinot Grigio '13	♟♟ 2*

○ Lupi Terrae '13	♟♟ 3
● Merlot '12	♟♟ 2*
○ Terra & Cielo Brut '11	♟♟ 3
○ Traminer Aromatico Alba '13	♟♟ 5
○ Sauvignon '14	♟ 2
○ Lupi Terrae '12	♟♟ 2*
● Merlot '11	♟♟ 2*
● Merlot '10	♟♟ 2*
○ Pinot Grigio '13	♟♟ 2*
○ Pinot Grigio '12	♟♟ 2*
● Refosco P. R. '12	♟♟ 2*
● Rosso Svual '10	♟♟ 3
● Rosso Svual '09	♟♟ 3
○ Traminer Aromatico '13	♟♟ 2*
○ Traminer Aromatico '12	♟♟ 2*
○ Traminer Aromatico Alba '11	♟♟ 5

Borgo Judrio

VIA AQUILEIA, 79
33040 CORNO DI ROSAZZO [UD]
TEL. 0432755896
www.viniborgojudrio.it

CELLAR SALES
PRE-BOOKED VISITS
ANNUAL PRODUCTION 20,000 bottles
HECTARES UNDER VINE 12.00

At Corno di Rosazzo the Gigante family has long been synonymous with fine quality wines. In 2007 brothers Alberto and Ariedo decided to assert their identity by creating their own winery. Their choice of name was inspired by the River Judrio, which traces the border between Colli Orientali del Friuli and Collio, a strip of land that has become increasingly famous over the centuries for the special quality of the wines produced on both sides of the river. Inspired by a shared passion for the land and the vineyards, the brothers immediately set the course for consistent quality and pleasing features throughout the range at more than competitive prices. In a problematic year like 2014 it is important to note that the white wines stand out for their edgy and pleasing features, with subtle but strongly varietal aromas and fragrant, generous flavour. An honourable mention also goes to the reds from the previous year for their subtle spicing and lively vigour.

★Borgo San Daniele

VIA SAN DANIELE, 16
34071 CORMÒNS [GO]
TEL. 048160552
www.borgosandaniele.it

CELLAR SALES
PRE-BOOKED VISITS
ACCOMMODATION
ANNUAL PRODUCTION 56,000 bottles
HECTARES UNDER VINE 19.00
SUSTAINABLE WINERY

Courteous, refined siblings Mauro and Alessandra Mauri are also very sensitive, with good taste. A few years ago, when still young, they inherited some vineyards from their grandfather and with slightly reckless entrepreneurial spirit, decided to try to manage them. So they founded their estate and chose to name it after the little Cormòns village where the cellar is located. Mauro's winegrowing recipe traces that of all great wines: high planting density, low vigour, grassing and summer thinning out, late harvesting, lengthy maceration also for white wines, malolactic fermentation, long periods on the yeasts, unfiltered bottling. Although it does not say so on the label, Arbis Ros 2009 is a monovarietal Pignolo. It is amazingly fragrant and complex on the nose with a close-knit, mouthfilling and flavoursome palate. The very stylish Friulano 2103 and Pinot Grigio 2013 both deservedly made the finals, with sophisticated tropical aromas.

● FCO Cabernet Franc '13	♀♀ 2*
○ FCO Friulano '14	♀♀ 2*
○ FCO Sauvignon '14	♀♀ 2*
● Merlot '13	♀♀ 2*
○ Ribolla Gialla '14	♀♀ 2*
● FCO Refosco P. R. '13	♀ 2
○ FCO Verduzzo Friulano '13	♀ 2
● COF Cabernet Franc '12	♀♀ 2*
● COF Cabernet Sauvignon '12	♀♀ 2*
● COF Cabernet Sauvignon '10	♀♀ 2*
○ COF Friulano '13	♀♀ 2*
○ COF Friulano '12	♀♀ 2*
○ COF Ribolla Gialla '12	♀♀ 2*

● Arbis Ros '09	♀♀ 5
○ Friuli Isonzo Friulano '13	♀♀ 4
○ Friuli Isonzo Pinot Grigio '13	♀♀ 4
○ Arbis Blanc '13	♀♀ 5
○ Friuli Isonzo Malvasia '13	♀♀ 4
○ Arbis Blanc '10	♀♀♀ 4*
○ Arbis Blanc '09	♀♀♀ 4
○ Arbis Blanc '05	♀♀♀ 4
○ Friuli Isonzo Friulano '08	♀♀♀ 4*
○ Friuli Isonzo Friulano '07	♀♀♀ 4*
● Arbis Ros '08	♀♀ 5
○ Friuli Isonzo Friulano '12	♀♀ 4
○ Friuli Isonzo Malvasia '12	♀♀ 4
○ Friuli Isonzo Pinot Grigio '12	♀♀ 4

Borgo Savaian

VIA SAVAIAN, 36
34071 CORMÒNS [GO]
TEL. 048160725
stefanobastiani@libero.it

CELLAR SALES
PRE-BOOKED VISITS
ANNUAL PRODUCTION 100,000 bottles
HECTARES UNDER VINE 18.00

In the Mount Quarin foothills at Cormòns, in the village from which it takes its name, the Bastiani winery is a classic family affair. Since 2001 it has been run by youngsters Stefano and Rosanna who have brought a dose of fresh energy and innovation. The recent cellar extension enables Stefano to work more easily and put the experience inherited from family tradition, and supported by enological studies, into practice. Fair prices and consistent quality have consolidated the range of products which reveals appreciable attention to preserving the organoleptic features of each individual variety. The very well-typed Malvasia 2014 presents confident, enthralling aromas and an equally determined flavour: hints of bay leaves, toasted almonds and freshly harvested wheat. The Ribolla Gialla 2014 stood out for its fresh-tasting palate and fragrant floral and citrus aromas.

Cav. Emiro Bortolusso

VIA OLTREGORGO, 10
33050 CARLINO [UD]
TEL. 043167596
www.bortolusso.it

CELLAR SALES
PRE-BOOKED VISITS
ACCOMMODATION
ANNUAL PRODUCTION 120,000 bottles
HECTARES UNDER VINE 40.00

Cavaliere Emiro Bortolusso is credited with being the greatest promoter of the Friuli Annia DOC, and his two children, Sergio and Clara, have been running a flourishing winery for some time now. The estate overlooks the Adriatic Riviera, enjoying the benefits of the nearby sea, which enriches the wines with tangy organoleptic features. The wines are made solely from the estate's own grapes, applying the teachings of Emiro, who left a great legacy of knowledge, and a modern technological approach to guarantee consistent quality development. The cellar offers a vast range of excellent quality wines at competitive prices. Both the vibrant, sunny Malvasia and the fragrant, citrus-rich Sauvignon from 2014 present marked organoleptic features. Also worth a mention is the 2014 Pinot Grigio, with light coppery hues, ripe pear aromas and a very soft palate. Honeyed sensations characterize the Friulano 2014.

○ Collio Ribolla Gialla '14	♥♥ 3
● Friuli Isonzo Cabernet Franc '13	♥♥ 3
○ Friuli Isonzo Malvasia '14	♥♥ 3
○ Collio Friulano '14	♥ 3
● Collio Merlot '13	♥ 3
○ Collio Pinot Grigio '14	♥ 3
○ Collio Friulano '13	♀♀ 3
● Collio Merlot Tolrem '09	♀♀ 3
○ Collio Pinot Bianco '12	♀♀ 3
○ Collio Ribolla Gialla '13	♀♀ 3
○ Collio Sauvignon '12	♀♀ 3
○ Collio Sauvignon '11	♀♀ 3
● Friuli Isonzo Cabernet Franc '12	♀♀ 3*
○ Friuli Isonzo Malvasia '12	♀♀ 3
○ Collio Sauvignon '13	♀ 3
○ Friuli Isonzo Malvasia '13	♀ 3

○ Friuli Annia Friulano '14	♥♥ 2*
○ Malvasia '14	♥♥ 2*
○ Pinot Grigio '14	♥♥ 2*
○ Sauvignon '14	♥♥ 2*
○ Traminer Aromatico '14	♥♥ 2*
○ Verduzzo Friulano '14	♥♥ 3
○ Chardonnay '13	♀♀ 2*
○ Friulano '13	♀♀ 2*
○ Friuli Annia Friulano '12	♀♀ 2*
○ Friuli Annia Malvasia '12	♀♀ 2*
○ Friuli Annia Sauvignon '12	♀♀ 2*
○ Sauvignon '13	♀♀ 2*
○ Traminer Aromatico '13	♀♀ 2*

Branko

Loc. Zegla, 20
34071 Cormòns [GO]
Tel. 0481639826
www.brankowines.com

CELLAR SALES
PRE-BOOKED VISITS
ANNUAL PRODUCTION 45,000 bottles
HECTARES UNDER VINE 9.00

Branko is a small but extremely well-tended and functional estate, situated in one of the best winegrowing areas: Zegla, in the heart of Collio, close to the Slovenian border. Igor Erzetic runs the estate named after its founder, his father Branko. Most of the vineyards surround the cellar while the others cover the hills around Plessiva and Novali: gentle slopes, excellent aspect, significant temperature variation and light breezes. The small size of the estate enables Igor to look after it with loving care reflected in the typing and marked personality of his wines. Here is the Pinot Grigio, back on form in 2014 after a few years of limbo, to win our Tre Bicchieri again. This is without doubt the estate's most typical wine, and it is certainly no coincidence that even in an unusual vintage year it succeeds in offering the best possible expression of the grape's potential.

Livio e Claudio Buiatti

via Lippe, 25
33042 Buttrio [UD]
Tel. 0432674317
www.buiattivini.it

CELLAR SALES
PRE-BOOKED VISITS
ANNUAL PRODUCTION 35,000 bottles
HECTARES UNDER VINE 8.00

Claudio Buiatti manages the family estate inherited from father Livio. The cellar is in the centre of Buttrio while the eight hectares of vineyards cover the gentle, sunny slopes of the Eocenic hills extending from the town to Premariacco, on the wonderful landscape known as "in Mont e Poanis". The generations of the Buiatti family have respected local traditions while remaining open to innovation, and Claudio inherited the innate passion for tending vineyards that has enabled him to establish his winery among the best in the region. Forthright, well-made and fragrant wines at reasonable prices are his recipe for success. Aromas of spring flowers, apples, pears, citrus fruit and green tea characterize the Pinot Grigio 2014, with a fresh, tangy flavour. The 2014 Malvasia presents hints of summer hay and golden-leaf tobacco on the nose, followed by an impressively gutsy palate. The Friulano 2014 and Merlot 2013 are both good with pleasing flavour.

○ Collio Pinot Grigio '14	♀♀♀ 4*
○ Capobranco '14	♀♀ 4
○ Collio Chardonnay '14	♀♀ 4
○ Collio Friulano '14	♀♀ 4
○ Collio Sauvignon '14	♀♀ 4
● Red Branko '12	♀♀ 4
○ Collio Pinot Grigio '08	♀♀♀ 3*
○ Collio Pinot Grigio '07	♀♀♀ 3
○ Collio Pinot Grigio '06	♀♀♀ 3
○ Collio Pinot Grigio '05	♀♀♀ 3
○ Capobranco '13	♀♀ 4
○ Collio Chardonnay '13	♀♀ 4
○ Collio Pinot Grigio '13	♀♀ 4
○ Collio Sauvignon '13	♀♀ 4
○ Collio Sauvignon '12	♀♀ 4

○ FCO Friulano '14	♀♀ 3
○ FCO Malvasia '14	♀♀ 3
● FCO Merlot '13	♀♀ 3
○ FCO Pinot Grigio '14	♀♀ 3
● FCO Refosco P. R. '13	♀ 3
○ FCO Sauvignon '14	♀ 3
● COF Cabernet Franc '12	♀♀ 3
○ COF Friulano '12	♀♀ 3
● COF Merlot '12	♀♀ 3
● COF Merlot '11	♀♀ 3
● COF Momon Ros Ris. '10	♀♀ 4
● COF Momon Ros Ris. '09	♀♀ 4
○ COF Pinot Grigio '13	♀♀ 3
○ COF Sauvignon '13	♀♀ 3
○ COF Sauvignon '11	♀♀ 3*

La Buse dal Lôf

VIA RONCHI, 90
33040 PREPOTTO [UD]
TEL. 0432701523
www.labusedallof.com

CELLAR SALES
PRE-BOOKED VISITS
ANNUAL PRODUCTION 100,000 bottles
HECTARES UNDER VINE 25.00

In 1972 Giuseppe Pavan founded this lovely Prepotto estate and named it after the location: "La Buse dal Lôf" means "the wolf's den" in Friuli dialect. It is now run with excellent results by his son Michele, in true Friuli winegrowing style, both in the vine-training system and in vinification methods, which fully respects the varietal features of the grapes. The vineyards cover Friuli's Colli Orientali on sloping land of Eocenic origin, consisting essentially of marl and sandstone, protected by the Julian Alps and exposed to the breezes of the nearby Adriatic. It is important to note that every year the most complimentary comments are always directed at the Schioppettino di Prepotto, the most typical wine of this terroir. The 2011 vintage presents aromas of forest floor, tobacco and black pepper with a soft, coherent, balanced and harmonious palate.

○ COF Pinot Bianco In Bocca al Lupo '13	♥♥ 3
● COF Refosco P. R. '11	♥♥ 3
● COF Schioppettino di Prepotto '11	♥♥ 4
○ FCO Friulano '14	♥♥ 3
○ FCO Sauvignon '14	♥♥ 3
● COF Cabernet Sauvignon '12	♥ 3
○ FCO Chardonnay '14	♥ 3
○ COF Chardonnay '13	♡♡ 3
○ COF Chardonnay '12	♡♡ 3
○ COF Friulano '13	♡♡ 3
○ COF Friulano '12	♡♡ 3
○ COF Pinot Bianco In Bocca al Lupo '12	♡♡ 3
○ COF Pinot Grigio '13	♡♡ 3
● COF Schioppettino '07	♡♡ 4
● COF Schioppettino di Prepotto '10	♡♡ 4
● COF Schioppettino di Prepotto '09	♡♡ 4

Valentino Butussi

VIA PRÀ DI CORTE, 1
33040 CORNO DI ROSAZZO [UD]
TEL. 0432759194
www.butussi.it

CELLAR SALES
PRE-BOOKED VISITS
ACCOMMODATION
ANNUAL PRODUCTION 120,000 bottles
HECTARES UNDER VINE 18.00
VITICULTURE METHOD Certified Organic
SUSTAINABLE WINERY

The Butussi family's winemaking history is rooted in the marly sandstone lands of Prà di Corte at Corno di Rosazzo in Friuli's Colli Orientali. Experience, knowledge and little secrets have been handed down through the generations since Valentino Butussi began the journey in the early 20th century. His son Angelo carried it forward with perseverance and determination, establishing the estate as one of the best in the region, and leading the way for the new generation: Tobia, Filippo, Mattia and Erika. This high-level family management system is based on preserving values, team spirit, careful task sharing and a sense of responsibility. An excellent 2012 Refosco dal Peduncolo Rosso drew unanimous approval, bringing it into the final selections. The nose presents hints of crushed black berries alongside liquorice and coffee sensations, perfectly reflected on the palate which closes on a pleasant note of balsam.

● FCO Refosco P. R. '12	♥♥ 3*
● FCO Cabernet Franc '13	♥♥ 3
● FCO Cabernet Sauvignon '12	♥♥ 3
○ FCO Chardonnay '14	♥♥ 2*
○ FCO Ribolla Gialla '14	♥♥ 2*
● FCO Rosso di Corte '11	♥♥ 4
○ FCO Friulano '14	♥ 2
○ FCO Pinot Grigio '14	♥ 2
○ COF Chardonnay '13	♡♡ 2*
○ COF Friulano '13	♡♡ 2*
○ COF Picolit '08	♡♡ 6
● COF Pignolo '09	♡♡ 5
○ COF Sauvignon '13	♡♡ 2*

Maurizio Buzzinelli

LOC. PRADIS, 20
34071 CORMÒNS [GO]
TEL. 048160902
www.buzzinelli.it

CELLAR SALES
PRE-BOOKED VISITS
ACCOMMODATION
ANNUAL PRODUCTION 120,000 bottles
HECTARES UNDER VINE 35.00

For three generations, in Pradis, near
Cormòns, the Buzzinelli family have handed
down knowledge and experience from one
harvest to the next. Now it is Maurizio's
turn to take care of the vineyards covering
the Collio Goriziano area, renowned for
white wine production. The hills enjoy a
local microclimate and splendid exposure
to the sun's rays. Looking down from the
gentle slopes, the plain below stretches to
the nearby Adriatic. The estate's other
vineyards belong to the Friuli Isonzo DOC
and are mainly planted with black grape
varieties, which benefit from the subsoil
rich in iron and mineral salts. Once again
this year the wines earned excellent
approval but the Sauvignon 2014 was
really outstanding, so much so that it made
a worthy appearance in the finals. Its
distinctively fragrant aromas blend hints of
citrus with melon and kiwi fruit, with
balanced freshness and softness on the
palate.

○ Collio Sauvignon '14	♀♀	3*
○ Collio Chardonnay '14	♀♀	3
○ Collio Friulano '14	♀♀	3
○ Collio Ribolla Gialla '14	♀♀	3
○ Collio Friulano '12	♀♀	3*
○ Collio Friulano '11	♀♀	3
○ Collio Malvasia '13	♀♀	2*
○ Collio Malvasia '12	♀♀	2*
○ Collio Malvasia '11	♀♀	2*
○ Collio Pinot Grigio '13	♀♀	3*
○ Collio Pinot Grigio '11	♀♀	3*
○ Collio Ribolla Gialla '13	♀♀	3
○ Collio Sauvignon '13	♀♀	2*

Ca' Bolani

VIA CA' BOLANI, 2
33052 CERVIGNANO DEL FRIULI [UD]
TEL. 043132670
www.cabolani.it

CELLAR SALES
PRE-BOOKED VISITS
ANNUAL PRODUCTION 2,700,000 bottles
HECTARES UNDER VINE 550.00

Tenuta Ca' Bolani, in the heart of the Friuli
Aquileia DOC zone, extends over three
different estates: Ca' Bolani, Molin del
Ponte, and Ca' Vescovo. Of the 800
hectares, 550 are under vine, making this
the largest vineyard area in northern Italy,
and the first winegrowing estate outside
Veneto to be purchased by the Zonin family.
There followed renovation of winery
headquarters, restoring its original
splendour, and building a cellar equipped
with advanced technology. For many years
the staff have been led in loco by expert
oenologist Marco Rabino. This is one of the
most prestigious wineries in Friuli and its
wines are enjoyed worldwide. These wines
respect the features of the grape varieties
and the natural pace of the vintage year:
the aromas are sometimes subtle but the
flavour is always satisfying. The Sauvignon
Aquilis 2014 stands out with delightful
hints of grapefruit and limes to perk up and
enhance the pleasant flavour.

○ Friuli Aquileia Sauvignon Aquilis '14	♀♀	2*
○ Friuli Aquileia Pinot Bianco Sup. '14	♀♀	3
● Friuli Aquileia Refosco P. R. Sup. '13	♀♀	3
○ Friuli Aquileia		
Traminer Aromatico Sup. '14	♀♀	3
● Friuli Aquileia Cabernet Franc '13	♀	3
○ Friuli Aquileia Friulano Sup. '14	♀	3
○ Friuli Aquileia Pinot Grigio Sup. '14	♀	3
○ Friuli Aquileia Sauvignon Sup. '14	♀	3
○ Prosecco Brut	♀	3
○ Friuli Aquileia Pinot Bianco '09	♀♀♀	2*
● Friuli Aquileia Merlot '10	♀♀	2*
● Friuli Aquileia Refosco P. R. '08	♀♀	2*
○ Friuli Aquileia Sauvignon Aquilis '11	♀♀	2*
○ Friuli Aquileia Sauvignon Aquilis '10	♀♀	2*

Ca' Tullio

VIA BELIGNA, 41
33051 AQUILEIA [UD]
TEL. 0431919700
www.catullio.it

CELLAR SALES
PRE-BOOKED VISITS
ANNUAL PRODUCTION 200,000 bottles
HECTARES UNDER VINE 100.00

The magnificent building built in the early
20th century, and formerly used for
tobacco drying, houses the Ca' Tullio
winery. Meticulous renovations in 1994
restored its former beauty while preserving
the architectural structure. This is where
the grapes from Ca' Tullio's vineyards in the
Friuli Aquileia DOC zone are processed
along with those from Sdricca di Manzano
on the Colli Orientali del Friuli. Both lines
are entrusted to experienced estate
oenologist Francesco Visintin who has
proved able to enhance the potential of the
sandy soils at Viola: in this particular
location it is still possible to grow ungrafted
traminer. The two different producing
estates make the range of wines more
varied and interesting, providing
confirmation of the individual features of
each terroir. The intriguing Pignolo 2011
presents hints of bottled plums, dark
chocolate and black olives on a salty
background on the nose, enhancing the
flavour with perky vitality.

● Cabernet Franc '13	♥♥ 2*
● FCO Pignolo Sdricca di Manzano '11	♥♥ 3
○ FCO Ribolla Gialla Sdricca di Manzano '14	♥♥ 3
○ FCO Sauvignon Sdricca di Manzano '14	♥♥ 3
● Merlot '13	♥♥ 2*
○ FCO Friulano Sdricca di Manzano '14	♥ 3
○ Friuli Aquileia Chardonnay '14	♥ 2
○ Friuli Aquileia Pinot Grigio '14	♥ 2
● Friuli Aquileia Refosco P. R. '12	♥ 2
○ Friuli Aquileia Traminer Viola '14	♥ 2
○ Prosecco Extra Dry '14	♥ 2
○ COF Friulano Sdricca '09	♥♥ 3*
● COF Pignolo Sdricca '06	♥♥ 3
○ Friuli Aquileia Chardonnay '13	♥♥ 2*
○ Friuli Aquileia Friulano '13	♥♥ 2*
○ Friuli Aquileia Pinot Grigio '13	♥♥ 2*

Cadibon

VIA CASALI GALLO, 1
33040 CORNO DI ROSAZZO [UD]
TEL. 0432759316
www.cadibon.com

CELLAR SALES
PRE-BOOKED VISITS
RESTAURANT SERVICE
ANNUAL PRODUCTION 55,000 bottles
HECTARES UNDER VINE 14.00
VITICULTURE METHOD Certified Organic

In 1977, when Gianni Bon set up his
estate, called it Cadibon, meaning "here at
the Bon estate" in local dialect, and it was
an open invitation to visit. It is now
managed by his two children Luca and
Francesca, who enjoy the generous spaces
and avant-garde technology with which the
cellar is equipped. The new energy they
have brought has led to an increase in
quality we have been pointing out for some
years now. The recent restyling of the
bottles and labels of the whole range of
whites demonstrates their desire to offer
the market a new, sophisticated and
elegant image which mirrors the freshness
and fragrance of the wines. The many
wines presented for tasting provided an
overview of the whole range, and
reconfirmed the flattering results obtained
in previous editions. Both whites and reds
stood out for their clean aromas and
faithful expression of the grape varieties
and, above all, for pleasant, coherent
flavours.

○ Collio Sauvignon '14	♥♥ 3
○ FCO Friulano Bontaj '14	♥♥ 3
● FCO Refosco P. R. '13	♥♥ 3
● FCO Schioppettino '13	♥♥ 3
○ Ronco del Nonno '14	♥♥ 3
○ Collio Chardonnay '14	♥ 3
● FCO Cabernet Franc '13	♥ 3
● FCO Merlot '13	♥ 3
○ FCO Pinot Grigio '14	♥ 3
○ FCO Ribolla Gialla '14	♥ 3
○ FCO Verduzzo Friulano '14	♥ 3
● COF Cabernet Franc '12	♥♥ 3
● COF Merlot '12	♥♥ 3
○ COF Pinot Grigio '13	♥♥ 3
● COF Schioppettino '12	♥♥ 3
○ Ronco del Nonno '13	♥♥ 3

Canus

Loc. Casali Gallo
via Gramogliano, 21
33040 Corno di Rosazzo [UD]
Tel. 0432759427
www.canus.it

CELLAR SALES
PRE-BOOKED VISITS
ANNUAL PRODUCTION 50,000 bottles
HECTARES UNDER VINE 9.00
VITICULTURE METHOD Certified Organic

At Gramogliano, on the Corno di Rosazzo hills, there has always been a flourishing winegrowing estate. Following purchase by Pordenone entrepreneur Ugo Rossetto in 2004, it was named Canus, which means white-haired man, a reference to the Rossetto family nickname of "grison". It is now managed by his enterprising children Dario and Lara, to whom credit is due for placing the estate at the peaks of quality in the crowded regional overview. Alongside the well-established Canus line, which has been pursuing an organic direction for some time, the more recent Ronco del Gris offers fresher wines with a lower alcohol content. The more mature wines from previous vintages had the edge and were top of our list of preferences, although the young wines fought their corner well, especially the fragrantly aromatic Malvasia and Chardonnay, both 2014, from the Ronco del Gris line.

○ Chardonnay Ronco del Gris '14	♥♥ 2*
○ FCO Chardonnay '13	♥♥ 3
● FCO Refosco P. R. '10	♥♥ 4
○ Malvasia Ronco del Gris '14	♥♥ 2*
○ Bianco Flor di Cuar Ronco del Gris '14	♥ 2
○ FCO Friulano '14	♥ 3
● FCO Merlot '10	♥ 4
○ FCO Ribolla Gialla di Rosazzo '14	♥ 3
○ FCO Sauvignon '13	♥ 3
○ Pinot Grigio Ronco del Gris '14	♥ 2
○ Ribolla Gialla Ronco del Gris '14	♥ 2
○ Sauvignon Ronco del Gris '14	♥ 2
○ Bianco Flor di Cuar Ronco del Gris '13	♀♀ 2*
○ COF Friulano '12	♀♀ 3*
○ Malvasia Ronco del Gris '13	♀♀ 2*
○ Ribolla Gialla '13	♀♀ 2*

Fernanda Cappello

s.da di Sequals, 15
33090 Sequals [PN]
Tel. 042793291
www.fernandacappello.it

CELLAR SALES
PRE-BOOKED VISITS
ANNUAL PRODUCTION 60,000 bottles
HECTARES UNDER VINE 126.00
SUSTAINABLE WINERY

In 1988, architect Fernanda Cappello made the life choice to abandon her previous career and embark on what she describes as an exciting adventure, running the wine estate purchased by her father in the late 1960s. Fernanda Cappello's estate covers 135 hectares, of which 126 are under vine, on alluvial land with dolomitic limestone, set between the Cellina and Meduna rivers, just under the Sequals hills in the Pordenone area. Fernanda admires the combination of beauty and good flavour so, helped by oenologist Fabio Coser, she has always tried to obtain the best from these famously arid lands, rich in delightful aromatic qualities. The excellent 2014 Sauvignon delighted on the nose with pleasant hints of hay meadow flowers, ripe grapefruit and limes, and a balanced, rounded, richly extracted and aromatic palate. The 2013 Cabernet Franc is very varietal with freshly mown grass and green peppers on the nose and a fragrant, succulent flavour.

● Friuli Grave Cabernet Franc '13	♥♥ 2*
○ Friuli Grave Chardonnay '14	♥♥ 2*
○ Friuli Grave Friulano '14	♥♥ 2*
○ Friuli Grave Sauvignon '14	♥♥ 2*
● Friuli Grave Merlot '13	♥ 2
○ Friuli Grave Pinot Grigio '14	♥ 2
○ Friuli Grave Traminer Aromatico '14	♥ 2
○ Prosecco	♥ 2
○ Friuli Grave Friulano '13	♀♀ 2*
● Friuli Grave Merlot '11	♀♀ 2*
○ Friuli Grave Pinot Grigio '13	♀♀ 2*
○ Friuli Grave Sauvignon '13	♀♀ 2*
○ Friuli Grave Sauvignon '12	♀♀ 2*
○ Friuli Grave Traminer Aromatico '12	♀♀ 2*
● Primo Rosso '11	♀♀ 3

Carlo di Pradis

LOC. PRADIS, 22B
34071 CORMÒNS [GO]
TEL. 048162272
www.carlodipradis.it

CELLAR SALES
PRE-BOOKED VISITS
ANNUAL PRODUCTION 70,000 bottles
HECTARES UNDER VINE 15.00

Pradis is a flourishing hillside location in the Collio Goriziano area, home to many of the region's outstanding wine estates, with magnificent aspect and an ideal microclimate. The winery owned by brothers Boris and Daved Buzzinelli is named after their father Carlo, from whom they have inherited a passion for the land and above all the valuable vineyards, now managed by the third generation of the family. Seven of the estate's 15 hectares surround the winery buildings while the other eight extend over the plains in the Friuli Isonzo DOC. The estate philosophy seeks pleasing qualities as well as structure with fruity, vibrant and varietal aromas even in the versions fermented or matured in oak. This year the white wines are remarkably fresh-tasting especially the 2104 Friulano del Collio which made it to the finals thanks to sophisticated floral, fruity aromas enhanced with fascinating hints of liquorice and mint. The 2014 Sauvignons from both DOCs are also excellent.

○ Collio Friulano '14	♟♟	3*
○ Collio Sauvignon '14	♟♟	3
○ Friuli Isonzo Sauvignon '14	♟♟	2*
○ Friuli Isonzo Chardonnay '14	♟	3
○ Friuli Isonzo Friulano '14	♟	2
● Friuli Isonzo Merlot '13	♟	3
○ Collio Friulano '13	♟♟	3
○ Collio Friulano '12	♟♟	3
○ Collio Pinot Grigio '13	♟♟	3
○ Collio Sauvignon '12	♟♟	3*
○ Friuli Isonzo Chardonnay '13	♟♟	3
○ Friuli Isonzo Chardonnay '12	♟♟	3
○ Friuli Isonzo Sauvignon '12	♟♟	2*

Il Carpino

LOC. SOVENZA, 14A
34070 SAN FLORIANO DEL COLLIO [GO]
TEL. 0481884097
www.ilcarpino.com

CELLAR SALES
PRE-BOOKED VISITS
ANNUAL PRODUCTION 70,000 bottles
HECTARES UNDER VINE 16.00

In 1987, Anna and Franco Sosol established their own estate and as often happens, named it after its location. Borgo del Carpino is near Sovenza on the road from Oslavia to San Floriano del Collio. They are now assisted by their children, Naike and Manuel, and the family nature of the business enables and enforces monitoring of all the stages of the production process from the vineyards to vinification and ageing. The grapes from the younger vineyards are fermented in stainless steel but the trend hereabouts is to go back to the old ways, so 15- and 20-hectolitre barrels are gradually replacing barriques. This year we awarded Tre Bicchieri to the Malvasia 2011 which earned our approval with its intoxicating aromas of toasted hazelnuts, summer hay, dried flowers and petit fours. But what impressed us most was the crisp flavour and lingering, mouthfilling palate.

○ Malvasia '11	♟♟♟	5
○ Collio Malvasia V. Runc '14	♟♟	3*
● Rubrum Carpino '07	♟♟	8
○ Exordium '11	♟♟	5
○ Vis Uvae '11	♟♟	5
○ Collio Bianco V. Runc '10	♟♟♟	2*
○ Collio Malvasia V. Runc '11	♟♟♟	3*
● Rubrum '99	♟♟♟	3*
○ Bianco Carpino '09	♟♟	4
○ Bianco Runc '11	♟♟	3*
○ Collio Sauvignon V. Runc '13	♟♟	2*
○ Exordium '09	♟♟	5
○ Malvasia '10	♟♟	5
○ Vis Uvae '10	♟♟	5

Castello di Buttrio

VIA DEL POZZO, 5
33042 BUTTRIO [UD]
TEL. 0432673015
www.castellodibuttrio.it

CELLAR SALES
PRE-BOOKED VISITS
ACCOMMODATION AND RESTAURANT SERVICE
ANNUAL PRODUCTION 60,000 bottles
HECTARES UNDER VINE 25.00

The ancient origins of the little town of
Buttrio date back to the 11th century, and
certainly the main pages of its history refer
to the castle, destroyed and rebuilt a
number of times. In 1994 the estate was
purchased by Marco Felluga who began
turning it into a winegrowing estate. Thanks
to his daughter Alessandra, these
extraordinary walls have regained the
splendour of the past and the purchase of
a nearby cellar with adjacent vineyards
have further reinforced the property. When
Trentino oenologist Hartman Donà joined
the business, the result was a striking
change in style throughout the range of
wines, prioritizing coherent and pleasing
features. The excellent Bianco Torre Butria
Riserva 2011, a blend of chardonnay,
friulano and sauvignon, was our favourite,
with stylish, sophisticated aromas and,
above all, a very pleasing flavour. The
obvious strength of the Pignolo 2010 is
assuaged by soft hints of ripe fruit and
sweet spice.

○ FCO Friulano '14	♟♟	3
● FCO Pignolo '10	♟♟	5
○ FCO Sauvignon '14	♟♟	3
○ FCO Torre Butria Ris. '11	♟♟	5
○ FCO Verduzzo Friulano Mille e una Botte '12	♟♟	5
○ FCO Chardonnay '14	♟	3
● FCO Refosco P. R. '13	♟	3
○ FCO Ribolla Gialla '14	♟	3
○ COF Friulano '11	♟♟	3*
○ COF Friulano '12	♟♟	3*
● COF Merlot '11	♟♟	3
● COF Merlot '09	♟♟	3*
● COF Rosso Mon Rouge '11	♟♟	3
○ COF Sauvignon '13	♟♟	3
○ COF Torre Butria Chardonnay Ris. '09	♟♟	5
● COF Uve Carate Merlot Ris. '09	♟♟	3

Castello di Spessa

VIA SPESSA, 1
34070 CAPRIVA DEL FRIULI [GO]
TEL. 048160445
www.paliwines.com

CELLAR SALES
PRE-BOOKED VISITS
ACCOMMODATION AND RESTAURANT SERVICE
ANNUAL PRODUCTION 300,000 bottles
HECTARES UNDER VINE 83.00

In 1987 Castello di Spessa was purchased
by Loretto Pali along with the surrounding
vineyards. It stands in the heart of Collio, on
a gently sloping hillside, elegantly
immersed in the greenery of a beautiful
Italian garden. Its origins date back to the
13th century and for centuries the castle
was the home of Friuli noble families. The
bunker connecting the castle and the cellar,
created in 1939 and used by occupying
troops during World War II, houses wines
ageing in natural, constant temperature
and humidity conditions. Winemaking is
entrusted to Gianni Menotti, and the wines
are typically sophisticated with strong
personality. The 2014 Pinot Bianco earns
another well-deserved Tre Bicchieri but the
other wines are not far behind, especially
the Merlot Torriani 2009, well-structured
yet extremely soft and flavoursome, and the
2011 Pinot Nero Casanova with distinctive
elegant spice and soft, smooth tannins.

○ Collio Pinot Bianco '14	♟♟♟	3*
● Collio Merlot Torriani '09	♟♟	5
○ Collio Friulano '14	♟♟	3
● Collio Merlot V. Rosaris '12	♟♟	5
○ Collio Pinot Grigio '14	♟♟	3
● Collio Pinot Nero Casanova '11	♟♟	5
○ Collio Sauvignon '14	♟♟	3
○ Collio Ribolla Gialla '14	♟	3
○ Collio Pinot Bianco '13	♟♟♟	3*
○ Collio Pinot Bianco '11	♟♟♟	3*
○ Collio Pinot Bianco '06	♟♟♟	3*
○ Collio Tocai Friulano '05	♟♟♟	3*
○ Collio Friulano '13	♟♟	3*
● Collio Merlot V. Rosaris '09	♟♟	5
● Collio Rosso Conte di Spessa '03	♟♟	5
○ Collio Sauvignon Segrè '13	♟♟	5

Castello Sant'Anna

LOC. SPESSA
VIA SANT'ANNA, 9
33043 CIVIDALE DEL FRIULI [UD]
TEL. 0432716289
centasantanna@libero.it

CELLAR SALES
PRE-BOOKED VISITS
ANNUAL PRODUCTION 25,000 bottles
HECTARES UNDER VINE 7.00
VITICULTURE METHOD Certified Organic

Once the summer home of noble Cividale families, Castello Sant'Anna is surrounded by vineyards. It was purchased in 1966 by Giuseppe Gaiotti who decided to abandon his industrial career and return to the countryside to which he felt strongly connected. The castle's surrounding walls contain 18th-century buildings and are marked by two cylindrical towers about ten metres high, restored in the 17th century, with 13th- or 14th-century foundations. The estate is managed by Andrea Gaiotti, representing the third generation. The small size of the estate and limited production numbers enable him to focus meticulous personal attention on the whole production cycle. The whole range is excellent, but we particularly enjoyed two of the red wines: the 2011 Schioppettino and the 2012 Cabernet Franc. The former has sweet spices, golden tobacco and ginger on the nose with a richly extracted, soft palate. The Franc is extremely pleasant and well-balanced.

● FCO Cabernet Franc '12	♟♟ 4
● FCO Schioppettino '11	♟♟ 5
○ FCO Friulano '13	♟♟ 3
○ FCO Pinot Grigio '13	♟♟ 3
● FCO Refosco P. R. '11	♟♟ 4
○ FCO Sauvignon '13	♟♟ 3
● FCO Pinot Nero '11	♟ 4
○ COF Friulano '12	♟♟ 3
● COF Merlot '11	♟♟ 4
● COF Merlot Ris. '08	♟♟ 4
○ COF Pinot Grigio '12	♟♟ 3*
○ COF Pinot Grigio '11	♟♟ 3*
○ COF Ribolla Gialla '12	♟♟ 3*

Castelvecchio

VIA CASTELNUOVO, 2
34078 SAGRADO [GO]
TEL. 048199742
www.castelvecchio.com

CELLAR SALES
PRE-BOOKED VISITS
ACCOMMODATION AND RESTAURANT SERVICE
ANNUAL PRODUCTION 150,000 bottles
HECTARES UNDER VINE 35.00
SUSTAINABLE WINERY

The history of the Gorizia Carso land is marked by magnificence and ruin, and the patches of beautiful unspoilt nature still contend today with harsh, arid, rocky terrain, capable of unexpected alliances with mankind. Here, just above Sagrado, is the location of the Castelvecchio estate, owned by the Terraneo family. The rocks, the sparse red iron-rich and limestone topsoil, the particularly windy climate and late harvesting all imprint the grapes with unique aromatic features. These are judiciously preserved in the wines by oenologist Saverio Di Giacomo who has enjoyed the invaluable decision-making advice of Gianni Menotti for some time. It is always very gratifying to have a wine in the finals, as confirmation of the excellent standard of quality achieved and maintained. This year our attention focused on the Malvasia Dileo 2014: taut, fragrant, tangy, accomplished, with delightful aromas of dried herbs, bay leaves and cinnamon.

○ Carso Malvasia Dileo '14	♟♟ 4
○ Carso Cabernet Franc '12	♟♟ 3
● Carso Cabernet Sauvignon '12	♟♟ 3
● Carso Cabernet Sauvignon Dileo '11	♟♟ 5
○ Carso Malvasia '14	♟♟ 3
● Carso Merlot Dileo '09	♟♟ 5
○ Carso Traminer Aromatico '14	♟♟ 3
☉ Terrano Rosé Brut	♟♟ 4
○ Brut Masia	♟ 4
○ Carso Pinot Grigio '14	♟ 3
● Carso Refosco P. R. '12	♟ 3
○ Carso Sauvignon '143 '14	♟ 3
● Carso Terrano '14	♟ 3
● Carso Cabernet Franc '11	♟♟ 4
● Carso Merlot '06	♟♟ 5
○ Carso Sauvignon '12	♟♟ 3*

Marco Cecchini

LOC. CASALI DE LUCA
VIA COLOMBANI
33040 FAEDIS [UD]
TEL. 0432720563
www.cecchinimarco.com

CELLAR SALES
PRE-BOOKED VISITS
ACCOMMODATION
ANNUAL PRODUCTION 35,000 bottles
HECTARES UNDER VINE 8.00

A one-hectare vineyard inherited from his
grandfather. A harvest. A bolt of lightning.
This was the creation of Marco Cecchini's
estate in 1998. With a degree in economics
and a free, outdoor spirit, he took the first
steps towards an unbreakable connection
with nature. Of the eight or so hectares of
vineyards, half are now planted with vines
that on average are 40 years old. Marco
likes to call himself a wine artisan, but he is
perhaps more like an artist able to interpret
the terroir. The vineyards cover the Faedis
hills, in the northernmost part of the Colli
Orientali Friulani. Marco gives all his wines
equal importance and therefore sells them
all at the same price. Marco's range of
wines consists of just a few labels, and this
year we were only able to taste three. The
2013 Friulano Tovè 1867 presents
wildflowers, yellow peaches and broom
flowers on the nose with a soft, velvety
palate. The Rosso Malatesta 2013 is clear
and transparent with raspberry aromas and
a nicely drinkable flavour.

★Eugenio Collavini

LOC. GRAMOGLIANO
VIA DELLA RIBOLLA GIALLA, 2
33040 CORNO DI ROSAZZO [UD]
TEL. 0432753222
www.collavini.it

CELLAR SALES
PRE-BOOKED VISITS
ANNUAL PRODUCTION 1,500,000 bottles
HECTARES UNDER VINE 173.50
SUSTAINABLE WINERY

Helped by his sons Luigi and Giovanni,
Manlio Collavini still manages the estate
set up in 1896 by his ancestor Eugenio. In
the 1970s Manlio purchased a 16th-
century manor house which would become
the family home and winery headquarters.
At the same time, he started a gradual
process of development, although the real
quality turning point came in 1996 with a
global modernization programme in the
vineyards and a grower loyalty scheme
monitored by an estate agronomist. The
vast range of wines covers all possible
market demands and the large numbers
include niche products and excellent
sparkling wines. This year the estate
flagship, Collio Bianco Broy 2014, made it
to the finals along with two great reds:
Pignolo 2006 and Forresco 2008. Both
present aromas of cocoa powder, red berry
jam, coffee and dark spices, with a very
lingering palate and nicely balsamic finish.

○ FCO Friulano Tovè 1867 '13	♟♟ 3
● Malatesta '13	♟♟ 3
○ Pinot Grigio '14	♟♟ 3
○ COF Bianco Tovè '10	♟♟ 3*
○ COF Bianco Tovè '08	♟♟ 3*
○ COF Friulano '12	♟♟ 3
● COF Refosco P. R. '11	♟♟ 3
● COF Refosco P. R. '09	♟♟ 3
○ COF Verduzzo Friulano Verlit '08	♟♟ 3*
○ Pinot Grigio '13	♟♟ 3
○ Pinot Grigio '12	♟♟ 3
○ Riesling '11	♟♟ 5

○ Collio Bianco Broy '14	♟♟♟ 5
● FCO Pignolo '06	♟♟ 6
● FCO Rosso Forresco '08	♟♟ 5
○ Collio Pinot Grigio '14	♟♟ 3
○ Collio Sauvignon Blanc Fumât '14	♟♟ 3
○ FCO Ribolla Gialla Turian '14	♟♟ 4
○ Collio Bianco Broy '13	♟♟♟ 5
○ Collio Bianco Broy '11	♟♟♟ 4*
○ Collio Bianco Broy '10	♟♟♟ 4
○ Collio Bianco Broy '09	♟♟♟ 4*
○ Collio Bianco Broy '08	♟♟♟ 4*
● COF Rosso Forresco '06	♟♟ 5
● COF Rosso Forresco '05	♟♟ 5
● Collio Merlot dal Pic '06	♟♟ 5
○ Collio Pinot Grigio '13	♟♟ 3*

Colle Duga

loc. Zegla, 10
34071 Cormòns [GO]
Tel. 048161177
www.colleduga.com

CELLAR SALES
PRE-BOOKED VISITS
ANNUAL PRODUCTION 50,000 bottles
HECTARES UNDER VINE 9.00

Colle Duga has been run by Damijan Princic, the third generation of the family, since 1991. He is helped by his wife Monica and father Luciano, still active in the vineyards, while the future is guaranteed by his children Karin and Patrik, who already play an active role. The estate is named after the Colle Duga cru, which appears on local toponymical maps, where the vineyards are situated. This is near Cormòns, at Zegla, in the heart of the Collio area, shoulder to shoulder with the Slovenian hills of Goriska Brda. Great and meticulous attention is paid to the few wines, all excellent, with essentially typical and mineral features. The 2014 Collio Bianco made its mark in the final selections for a lovely smoky sensation enhancing the fruity aromas, and opening out on the palate with velvety sensations. The 2014 Chardonnay is also excellent, with white peaches and citron on the nose and a fresh, fragrant, dynamic palate.

○ Collio Bianco '14	🍷🍷 4
○ Collio Chardonnay '14	🍷🍷 3*
○ Collio Friulano '14	🍷🍷 3
● Collio Merlot '13	🍷🍷 4
○ Collio Pinot Grigio '14	🍷🍷 3
○ Collio Sauvignon '14	🍷🍷 3
○ Collio Bianco '11	🥂🥂🥂 4*
○ Collio Bianco '08	🥂🥂🥂 3*
○ Collio Bianco '07	🥂🥂🥂 3
○ Collio Friulano '09	🥂🥂🥂 3*
○ Collio Tocai Friulano '06	🥂🥂🥂 3*
○ Collio Tocai Friulano '05	🥂🥂🥂 3*
○ Collio Bianco '12	🥂🥂 4
○ Collio Chardonnay '13	🥂🥂 3*
○ Collio Friulano '13	🥂🥂 3*
○ Collio Sauvignon '12	🥂🥂 3*

Colmello di Grotta

loc. Grotta
via Gorizia, 133
34072 Farra d'Isonzo [GO]
Tel. 0481888445
www.colmello.it

CELLAR SALES
PRE-BOOKED VISITS
ANNUAL PRODUCTION 75,000 bottles
HECTARES UNDER VINE 15.00

In 1965 Luciana Bennati transformed a crumbling and abandoned old hamlet into a functional wine estate. This was the start of Colmello di Grotta, now managed with passion and innate entrepreneurial skill by her daughter Francesca Bortolotto. The vineyards cover the River Isonzo plain and the slopes of the Collio area, on completely different types of land and soil and climate features. Fabio Coser, who knows the morphology of the area well, is entrusted with the task of highlighting its particular features. The results have not been long in coming, and this beautiful estate has taken its rightful place at the crowded peak of regional production. The wines from both DOCs obtained our unanimous approval and there was no discrepancy between the plains and the hills, an indication of solid agronomical choices. The reds are well-structured with pleasing flavour while the whites are fresh, dynamic and rich in aromas.

○ Collio Pinot Grigio '14	🍷🍷 3
● Friuli Isonzo Cabernet Franc '14	🍷🍷 3
○ Friuli Isonzo Chardonnay '14	🍷🍷 2*
● Friuli Isonzo Merlot '12	🍷🍷 3
○ Friuli Isonzo Pinot Grigio '14	🍷🍷 2*
○ Collio Chardonnay '14	🍷 3
○ Collio Ribolla Gialla '14	🍷 3
● Friuli Isonzo Cabernet Sauvignon '12	🍷 3
○ Friuli Isonzo Sauvignon '14	🍷 2
○ Collio Chardonnay '13	🥂🥂 3*
○ Collio Pinot Grigio '13	🥂🥂 3
○ Collio Ribolla Gialla '10	🥂🥂 3*
○ Collio Sauvignon '11	🥂🥂 3*
● Rondon Rosso '10	🥂🥂 5

Gianpaolo Colutta

VIA ORSARIA, 32A
33044 MANZANO [UD]
TEL. 0432510654
www.coluttagianpaolo.com

CELLAR SALES
PRE-BOOKED VISITS
ANNUAL PRODUCTION 150,000 bottles
HECTARES UNDER VINE 30.00

As the descendent of a noble family with farming experience documented in the Manzano area over a thousand years ago, in 1999 Gianpaolo Colutta set up his own estate which he runs today with his daughter, Elisabetta. The vineyards cover about 30 hectares on the gentle slopes of the Friuli Colli Orientali DOC zone. These are the lower north-east hills, the most exposed to breezes from the nearby Adriatic sea, and form a natural amphitheatre, the pride of regional winegrowing. During replanting of some vineyards the estate decided to make the most of the terroir using clones of old and almost totally neglected local varieties. And indeed the most typical native black grape is used to make the Refosco dal Peduncolo Rosso 2011, a dynamic wine with ripe cherries and blackberries on the nose followed by liquorice and spice. The palate is mouthfilling and flavoursome. The Chardonnay 2014 and Pinot Grigio, also 2014, are both excellent.

○ FCO Chardonnay '14	♥♥ 3
○ FCO Pinot Grigio '14	♥♥ 3
● FCO Refosco P. R. '11	♥♥ 3
● FCO Pinot Nero '12	♥ 4
○ FCO Ribolla Gialla '14	♥ 4
○ COF Bianco Prarion '13	♥♥ 4
○ COF Bianco Prarion '12	♥♥ 4
○ COF Friulano '13	♥♥ 3
● COF Merlot '09	♥♥ 3
● COF Rosso Frassinolo '07	♥♥ 5
● COF Schioppettino '12	♥♥ 5
● COF Tazzelenghe '07	♥♥ 6
○ COF Verduzzo Friulano '11	♥♥ 4

Giorgio Colutta - Bandut

VIA ORSARIA, 32
33044 MANZANO [UD]
TEL. 0432740315
www.colutta.it

CELLAR SALES
PRE-BOOKED VISITS
ACCOMMODATION
ANNUAL PRODUCTION 140,000 bottles
HECTARES UNDER VINE 21.00

An 18th-century manor house purchased by Antonio Colutta in the early 20th century, is the home of the winery run by current owner Giorgio Colutta. In the past the winery was better known as Bandut, from an old place-name on the property. The vineyards extend over the prestigious Parco della Vite e del Vino included in the Friuli Colli Orientali DOC, and are managed by expert Antonio Maggio. The range of typically traditional, beautifully typed and coherent wines has been enriched with fascinating sparklers and, in the best years, wines made from grapes grown in particularly prestigious crus. The standard label whites proved well-made with bags of personality. The Friulano 2014 presents sunny hints of wildflowers and ripe fruit while the palate is both fresh and creamy. The Ribolla Gialla 2014 reveals hints of Mediterranean vegetation and is beautifully fragrant.

○ FCO Friulano '14	♥♥ 3
○ FCO Pinot Grigio '14	♥♥ 3
● FCO Refosco P. R. '13	♥♥ 3
○ FCO Ribolla Gialla '14	♥♥ 4
○ FCO Sauvignon '14	♥ 3
○ Prosecco Brut	♥ 2
○ COF Friulano '13	♥♥ 3
○ COF Friulano '12	♥♥ 3
● COF Pignolo '07	♥♥ 7
○ COF Pinot Grigio '13	♥♥ 3
○ COF Pinot Grigio '12	♥♥ 3
● COF Refosco P. R. '12	♥♥ 3
● COF Refosco P. R. '11	♥♥ 3
○ COF Sauvignon '13	♥♥ 3
● COF Schioppettino '11	♥♥ 5

Paolino Comelli

FRAZ. COLLOREDO DI SUFFUMBERGO
CASE COLLOREDO, 8
33040 FAEDIS [UD]
TEL. 0432711226
www.comelli.it

CELLAR SALES
PRE-BOOKED VISITS
ACCOMMODATION AND RESTAURANT SERVICE
ANNUAL PRODUCTION 60,000 bottles
HECTARES UNDER VINE 12.50
SUSTAINABLE WINERY

After the First World War Paolino Comelli
purchased an old hamlet of abandoned
crumbling farmhouses, in the hills near
Colloredo di Soffumbergo, in the
municipality of Faedis. With admirable
forward thinking he decided turn it into a
farm and began renovations. It is now a
model estate run by Pierluigi Comelli,
helped by his wife Daniela and their sons
Nicola and Filippo. Pierluigi, locally known
as Pigi, has succeeded in further enhancing
local traits to preserve varietal
characteristics, surrounding himself with a
close-knit and competent team, and relying
on the technical advice of Emilio Del
Medico. The Comelli brand is considered a
guarantee of quality in the region and this
is confirmed once again this year with
flattering results throughout the range of
wines. Both the whites and the reds
performed well in typing, elegance, balance
and enjoyable flavour.

Dario Coos

VIA RAMANDOLO, 5
33045 NIMIS [UD]
TEL. 0432790320
www.dariocoos.it

CELLAR SALES
PRE-BOOKED VISITS
ANNUAL PRODUCTION 65,000 bottles
HECTARES UNDER VINE 10.00

For at least 500 years, grapes have been
grown here at Ramandolo, in the
northernmost part of the Friuli Colli Orientali
DOC zone where the hills are almost
mountains. For five generations the Coos
family have tended vineyards on the steep
slopes, almost tearing them out of the land.
Dario set up the estate in 1986 and still
does all the cellar work. Here, where the
nights are cold and the days are hot and
rainy, they grow verduzzo giallo, a variety
which produces small bunches with thick,
durable skin, ideal for super-ripening. This
grape is used for Ramandolo, a wine which
has won over the most demanding palates
and made this terroir famous. And indeed,
a very sweet Ramandolo 2012 impressed
us most, alongside the Malvasia 2014 with
its enjoyable aromas of quince, chamomile
and wisteria and tangy, flavoursome palate.
The Refosco dal Peduncolo Rosso 2012 is
also excellent with generous aromas and a
mouthfilling, velvety flavour.

● Esprimo Red '13	♥♥ 2*
○ Esprimo White '13	♥♥ 2*
○ FCO Malvasia Locum Nostrum '13	♥♥ 3
○ FCO Picolit Eoos '12	♥♥ 6
○ FCO Pinot Grigio Amplius '14	♥♥ 3
○ FCO Friulano '14	♥ 3
○ FCO Sauvignon '14	♥ 3
● Rosso Soffumbergo '12	♥ 4
○ Bianco Soffumbergo '12	♥♥ 4
● COF Pignolo '07	♥♥ 5
○ COF Sauvignon '13	♥♥ 3*
○ Esprimo White '12	♥♥ 2*
● Rosso Soffumbergo '11	♥♥ 4
● Rosso Soffumbergo '08	♥♥ 4
● Rosso Soffumbergo '07	♥♥ 4

○ FCO Picolit '12	♥♥ 6
○ Malvasia '14	♥♥ 3
○ Ramandolo V.T. '12	♥♥ 4
● Refosco P.R. '12	♥♥ 4
○ Ribolla Gialla '14	♥♥ 3
○ Sauvignon '14	♥♥ 3
○ FCO Friulano '14	♥ 3
○ Pinot Grigio '14	♥ 3
● Schioppettino '13	♥ 4
○ COF Friulano '13	♥♥ 3
○ COF Picolit '06	♥♥ 6
● COF Pignolo '10	♥♥ 4
● Pignolo '07	♥♥ 4
○ Ramandolo '10	♥♥ 4
○ Ribolla Gialla '13	♥♥ 3
○ Vindos '12	♥♥ 3

Cantina Produttori di Cormòns

VIA VINO DELLA PACE, 31
34071 CORMÒNS [GO]
TEL. 048162471
www.cormons.com

CELLAR SALES
PRE-BOOKED VISITS
ACCOMMODATION AND RESTAURANT SERVICE
ANNUAL PRODUCTION 2,250,000 bottles
HECTARES UNDER VINE 471.00
SUSTAINABLE WINERY

In the late 1960s some Cormòns winegrowers decided to join forces, in shared conviction that the future of grapes and wine was not linked to passing trends but to determined promotion of the terroir. They drew up a statute, supported by an agricultural register, a detailed code of practice which all members still comply with. This flourishing winery, with a large number of products, is managed today by Rodolfo Rizzi. The vineyards belonging to over 200 member-growers, scattered over the best winegrowing DOCs in the region, are monitored by experienced agronomists. The positive results obtained by the wines we tasted show that a well-stocked range and large quantities are not always incompatible with quality. The best grapes are carefully selected for use in wines that are beautifully typed and very enjoyable, enhancing the prestige of the winery.

○ Collio Bianco Collio & Collio '14	♟♟	3
○ Collio Pinot Bianco '14	♟♟	3
○ Collio Friuliano '14	♟	3
○ Friuli Isonzo Chardonnay '14	♟	2
○ Friuli Isonzo Malvasia '14	♟	2
○ Collio Friuliano '12	♟♟	2*
○ Collio Friuliano '11	♟♟	2*
○ Collio Pinot Bianco '13	♟♟	3
○ Collio Pinot Bianco '12	♟♟	2*
○ Collio Pinot Grigio '13	♟♟	3
○ Collio Pinot Grigio '11	♟♟	3
○ Vino della Pace '09	♟♟	5

Crastin

LOC. RUTTARS, 33
34070 DOLEGNA DEL COLLIO [GO]
TEL. 0481630310
www.vinicrastin.it

CELLAR SALES
PRE-BOOKED VISITS
ANNUAL PRODUCTION 35,000 bottles
HECTARES UNDER VINE 6.00

Crastin is the name of a beautiful location overlooking Slovenia from the Ruttars hills. Here, in the early 1950s, sharecroppers Olivo and Cornelia Collarig set up a mixed farm. In 1980 their son Sergio took over management and, understanding the potential of the land, devoted more attention to the two-and-a-half hectares of vineyards. He began producing wines of indisputable quality which he offered to visitors to the agritourism complex he had opened in the meantime with his sister, Vilma. With the newly planted vineyards the estate now boasts six hectares, mainly planted with white grape varieties. For several years now, all the wines presented have obtained flattering results, and the Friulano 2014 made it to the final tastings once again this year, thanks to stylish aromas and a fragrant flavour. The dynamic Ribolla Gialla 2014 was also distinctively fresh and crisp.

○ Collio Friulano '14	♟♟	2*
● Collio Cabernet Franc '13	♟♟	3
● Collio Merlot '12	♟♟	2*
○ Collio Pinot Grigio '14	♟♟	3
○ Collio Ribolla Gialla '14	♟♟	2*
○ Collio Sauvignon '14	♟♟	3
○ Collio Friulano '12	♟♟	2*
○ Collio Friulano '11	♟♟	2*
○ Collio Pinot Grigio '13	♟♟	3
○ Collio Pinot Grigio '11	♟♟	3*
○ Collio Ribolla Gialla '13	♟♟	2*
○ Collio Ribolla Gialla '12	♟♟	2*
○ Collio Sauvignon '13	♟♟	3

di Lenardo

FRAZ. ONTAGNANO
P.ZZA BATTISTI, 1
33050 GONARS [UD]
TEL. 0432928633
www.dilenardo.it

CELLAR SALES
PRE-BOOKED VISITS
ANNUAL PRODUCTION 700,000 bottles
HECTARES UNDER VINE 50.00
SUSTAINABLE WINERY

The di Lenardo vineyard estate stretches over the sunny Friuli plain while the cellar is in the small town of Ontagnano, a few kilometres from the famous bastions of Palmanova, a town whose original layout is a nine-pointed star. The winery boasts a 200-year history and is run today by Massimo di Lenardo who has proved that plains winegrowing can yield more than gratifying results if conducted with intelligence and a contemporary spirit. The vineyards are scattered over various areas with different subsoils and microclimates, but Massimo labels all the wines only with the geographical indication to assign them equal importance. The whole range lived up to the high standard and excellent results achieved in previous Guides, but the Pinot Grigio 2014 was particularly distinctive, and deserved another tasting in the finals: vibrant aromas of ripe fruit and dried herbs, and a soft, flavoursome palate.

○ Pinot Grigio '14	▼▼ 2*
○ Chardonnay '14	▼▼ 2*
○ Friulano Toh! '14	▼▼ 2*
● Merlot Just Me '12	▼▼ 4
○ Pinot Grigio Ramato Gossip '14	▼▼ 2*
○ Comemivuoi '14	▼ 2
○ Father's Eyes '14	▼ 3
○ Pass the Cookies '14	▼ 3
● Ronco Nolè Rosso '13	▼ 2
○ Sarà Brut	▼ 3
○ Sauvignon '14	▼ 2
○ Chardonnay '13	♀♀ 2*
○ Pinot Grigio '13	♀♀ 2*
○ Pinot Grigio Ramato Gossip '12	♀♀ 2*
● Ronco Nolè Rosso '12	♀♀ 2*

★★Dorigo

LOC. BELLAZOIA
VIA SUBIDA, 16
33040 POVOLETTO [UD]
TEL. 0432634161
www.dorigowines.com

CELLAR SALES
PRE-BOOKED VISITS
ANNUAL PRODUCTION 120,000 bottles
HECTARES UNDER VINE 20.00

The lovely new winery created by Alessio Dorigo keeps the standard of appreciation high for a brand that continues to be one of the cornerstones of regional winegrowing. The recent handover of generations from Girolamo to Alessio coincided with many changes, not least the move from the historical location at Buttrio to the new cellar at Bellazoia. It also brought a breath of fresh air to the whole range of products, especially the Classic Method sparkling wines. Back in the day Dorigo contributed to the promotion of native local varieties, especially Ribolla Gialla, which is now enjoying huge popularity on the international market. The positive results obtained by the Blanc de Noir Dosage Zéro and Blanc de Blancs Pas Dosé sparklers confirm the estate's particular talent for this type of wine. However it was the Sauvignon Ronc di Juri 2013 that made the finals this year, with yellow peaches and lemon cream on the nose and buttery, flavoursome palate.

○ COF Sauvignon Ronc di Juri '13	▼▼ 5
○ Blanc de Blancs Pas Dosé	▼▼ 5
○ Blanc de Noir Dosage Zéro	▼▼ 5
● COF Cabernet Franc '13	▼▼ 3
○ COF Chardonnay Ronc di Juri '13	▼▼ 5
● COF Merlot '13	▼▼ 3
● COF Pignolo '12	▼▼ 8
● COF Rosso Montsclapade '12	▼▼ 6
● COF Schioppettino '13	▼▼ 3
○ Dorigo Brut Cuvée	▼▼ 4
○ FCO Pinot Grigio '14	▼▼ 3
● COF Pignolo di Buttrio '03	♀♀♀ 8
● COF Pignolo di Buttrio '02	♀♀♀ 8
● COF Pignolo di Buttrio '01	♀♀♀ 8
● COF Rosso Montsclapade '06	♀♀♀ 6
● COF Rosso Montsclapade '04	♀♀♀ 6

GIUSTI

A collection of 8.767 bottles

GIUSTI

UMBERTO I

Tenuta Abazia

ROSSO VENETO
ITALIA

www.giustiwine.com

FROM ETNA, SINCE FIVE GENERATIONS

Vulkà Etna Rosso
DOC 2013

Vulkà Etna Bianco
DOC 2014

OSCAR QUALITÀ-PREZZO
BEREBENE 2016

Sosta Tre Santi
Nerello Mascalese
Rosso IGT Sicilia 2010

Sosta Tre Santi
Nero D'Avola
Rosso IGT Sicilia 2009

Fondo Filara Etna Rosso
DOC 2012

Fondo Filara
Nerello Mascalese
Rosso DOC Sicilia 2013

NICOSIA

www.cantinenicosia.it

ph. +39 095 7806767 | info@cantinenicosia.it | f cantinenicosia | nicosiawinery

Draga

LOC. SCEDINA, 8
34070 SAN FLORIANO DEL COLLIO [GO]
TEL. 0481884182
www.draga.it

CELLAR SALES
PRE-BOOKED VISITS
ANNUAL PRODUCTION 40,000 bottles
HECTARES UNDER VINE 15.00
SUSTAINABLE WINERY

San Floriano del Collio is the birthplace of dozens of wine estates, all family-run, feathers in the cap of the regional winegrowing business. For three generations the Miklus family have lovingly tended their vineyards, clinging to the steep slopes that benefit from sunshine but mean that only manual work is possible. The Draga estate, named after a nearby locality, is currently run by Milan Miklus, his wife Anna and their children, Denis and Mitja. The Draga brand identifies the basic line of wines, fresh-tasting with generous aromas, while the Miklus line includes traditional, impressive wines with frank personality. Through to the finals for the Malvasia Miklus 2012, thanks to candied fruit and dried herbs on the nose and a full, rounded flavour. The Ribolla Gialla Miklus 2009 is also excellent with hints of sultana, almond and marron glacé on the nose and a caressing, memorable palate.

Drius

VIA FILANDA, 100
34071 CORMÒNS [GO]
TEL. 048160998
www.drius.it

CELLAR SALES
PRE-BOOKED VISITS
ANNUAL PRODUCTION 50,000 bottles
HECTARES UNDER VINE 15.00
SUSTAINABLE WINERY

The Drius family history is lost in the mists of time but they have lived in Cormòns forever, or at least for many generations, and have always been farmers. Family unity is the added value that has enabled Mauro to fulfil his abilities. Originally a firm supporter of cattle breeding, he is now a dynamic and meticulous full-time vigneron. Aided by rural pride, calloused hands, stout shoes and love for the land, Mauro has made sure his wines celebrate the potential of the terroir and above all, his own excellent vineyards covering the upper Isonzo plain and the slopes of Mount Quarin, in the heart of Collio. All the wines are flawlessly made, fresh, fruity and fragrant with nicely drinkable flavour. Standing out in the crowd is the Friulano 2014 del Collio, as in previous editions of the Guide: always a step ahead and making its mark in the finals too, just falling short of the highest accolade.

○ Collio Malvasia Miklus '12	♟♟ 4
○ Collio Friulano '14	♟♟ 3
○ Collio Pinot Grigio '14	♟♟ 3
● Collio Rosso Miklus Negro di Collina '12	♟♟ 4
○ Collio Sauvignon '14	♟♟ 3
○ Miklus Pas Dosé M. Cl. '12	♟♟ 5
○ Ribolla Gialla Miklus '09	♟♟ 5
○ Collio Ribolla Gialla '14	♟ 3
○ Collio Malvasia Miklus '10	♟♟♟ 7
○ Collio Malvasia Draga '10	♟♟ 3*
● Collio Merlot Miklus '09	♟♟ 5
○ Collio Ribolla Gialla Miklus '08	♟♟ 5
○ Collio Ribolla Gialla Miklus '07	♟♟ 5
○ Sauvignon Miklus '10	♟♟ 5

○ Collio Friulano '14	♟♟ 3*
○ Collio Sauvignon '14	♟♟ 3
○ Friuli Isonzo Friulano '14	♟♟ 3
○ Friuli Isonzo Malvasia '14	♟♟ 3
○ Friuli Isonzo Pinot Bianco '14	♟♟ 3
○ Friuli Isonzo Pinot Grigio '14	♟♟ 3
● Friuli Isonzo Cabernet Sauvignon '11	♟ 4
○ Collio Tocai Friulano '05	♟♟♟ 3*
○ Collio Tocai Friulano '02	♟♟♟ 2*
○ Friuli Isonzo Bianco Vignis di Siris '02	♟♟♟ 3*
○ Friuli Isonzo Friulano '07	♟♟♟ 3
○ Friuli Isonzo Malvasia '08	♟♟♟ 3*
○ Friuli Isonzo Pinot Bianco '09	♟♟♟ 3*
○ Friuli Isonzo Pinot Bianco '00	♟♟♟ 3*
○ Collio Friulano '13	♟♟ 3*
○ Collio Sauvignon '13	♟♟ 3

★Le Due Terre

VIA ROMA, 68B
33040 PREPOTTO [UD]
TEL. 0432713189
fortesilvana@libero.it

CELLAR SALES
PRE-BOOKED VISITS
ANNUAL PRODUCTION 18,000 bottles
HECTARES UNDER VINE 5.00

Just five hectares of vineyards and four wines, but a good deal of passion and courage, and undeniable winemaking skills enabled Flavio Basilicata and Silvana Forte to create and run this estate over the years, making it a jewel in the regional winegrowing crown. The Le Due Terre brand owes its name to the estate's position on a hill in the well-known area of Prepotto, one slope of which consists of marly sandstone terrain and the other mainly red clayey soil. During the excavations to build the cellar, stones were found which appeared to belong to an old church, and inspired the name of the estate's blends: Sacrisassi. Once again, this year the Rosso Sacrisassi 2013 deserved our Tre Bicchieri, as it has in the last six editions of the Guide, proving itself as the most typical red wine in the region, made from two native local varieties, schioppettino and refosco dal peduncolo rosso.

Ermacora

FRAZ. IPPLIS
VIA SOLZAREDO, 9
33040 PREMARIACCO [UD]
TEL. 0432716250
www.ermacora.it

CELLAR SALES
PRE-BOOKED VISITS
ANNUAL PRODUCTION 165,000 bottles
HECTARES UNDER VINE 47.00
SUSTAINABLE WINERY

Brothers Dario and Luciano Ermacora own an avant-garde estate with a simple philosophy: respect nature's own pace, avoid forcing even if using innovative technology, to obtain straightforward wines with bags of personality that reflect the features of the grape variety. In the early 20th century the Ermacora family chose to plant their vineyards, with flawless forward thinking, on the Ipplis hill, aware that the Eocene limestone-clay subsoil, quite infertile but rich in minerals, was particularly suitable for producing very prestigious wines. The family business has since been handed down through the generations. A really remarkable performance from the wines of the latest vintage, particularly the Friulano 2014 with outstandingly sophisticated aromas of apple and pear fruit, enhanced by a subtle, balsamic, minty sensation. The palate is coherent, taut, supple and enjoyably fresh and symmetrical.

● FCO Rosso Sacrisassi '13	♟♟♟	5
● FCO Merlot '13	♟♟	5
○ FCO Bianco Sacrisassi '13	♟♟	5
● FCO Pinot Nero '13	♟♟	5
○ COF Bianco Sacrisassi '05	♟♟♟	5
● COF Merlot '03	♟♟♟	5
● COF Merlot '02	♟♟♟	5
● COF Merlot '00	♟♟♟	5
● COF Rosso Sacrisassi '12	♟♟♟	5
● COF Rosso Sacrisassi '11	♟♟♟	5
● COF Rosso Sacrisassi '10	♟♟♟	5
● COF Rosso Sacrisassi '09	♟♟♟	5
● COF Rosso Sacrisassi '08	♟♟♟	5
● COF Rosso Sacrisassi '07	♟♟♟	5

○ FCO Friulano '14	♟♟	3*
○ FCO Picolit '12	♟♟	6
○ FCO Pinot Bianco '14	♟♟	3
○ FCO Pinot Grigio '14	♟♟	3
○ FCO Ribolla Gialla '14	♟♟	3
○ FCO Sauvignon '14	♟♟	3
● FCO Schioppettino '13	♟♟	3
● FCO Merlot '13	♟	3
● COF Pignolo '00	♟♟♟	5
○ COF Friulano '13	♟♟	3
○ COF Friulano '12	♟♟	3
● COF Pignolo '09	♟♟	5
○ COF Pinot Bianco '13	♟♟	3
○ COF Pinot Bianco '12	♟♟	3
○ COF Pinot Grigio '13	♟♟	3
○ COF Ribolla Gialla '13	♟♟	3
● COF Schioppettino '12	♟♟	3

Fantinel

FRAZ. TAURIANO
VIA TESIS, 8
33097 SPILIMBERGO [PN]
TEL. 0427591511
www.fantinel.com

CELLAR SALES
PRE-BOOKED VISITS
RESTAURANT SERVICE
ANNUAL PRODUCTION 4,500,000 bottles
HECTARES UNDER VINE 300.00
SUSTAINABLE WINERY

In 1969 Mario Fantinel bought some vineyards at Dolegna del Collio to produce wines destined to fulfil the demands of customers in the hotel-restaurant he managed at Carnia. A few years later his children decided to increase the family estate by purchasing more vineyards in the Collio, Friuli Grave and Friuli Colli Orientali DOC zones. These 16 hectares quickly expanded to 300, now run by the third generation, Marco, Stefano and Mariaelena. The estate headquarters at Tauriano di Spilimbergo is a model of winegrowing and hospitality. Fantinel offers a vast range of wines which stand out on the huge worldwide overview. This year, too, the Collio Bianco Frontiere San'Helena 2013 was our favourite. Hints of magnolia flowers and dried herbs enhance the pleasant nose and are reflected on the palate, closing on a nicely aromatic note. The other wines are also good, flavoursome and coherent on the palate.

★★Livio Felluga

FRAZ. BRAZZANO
VIA RISORGIMENTO, 1
34071 CORMÒNS [GO]
TEL. 048160203
www.liviofelluga.it

PRE-BOOKED VISITS
ANNUAL PRODUCTION 800,000 bottles
HECTARES UNDER VINE 160.00
SUSTAINABLE WINERY

On 1st September 2014, patriarch of Friuli winemaking Livio Felluga turned 100. To celebrate this event his four children, Maurizlo, Elda, Andrea, and Filippo, dedicated the Vigne Museum to him: an impressive work of art standing on a hill overlooking Rosazzo Abbey, a joint art-architecture project by Yona Friedman and Jean-Baptiste Decavèle. The success of Livio's wines is proved by the famous historical label he designed in 1956, visible and recognized all over the world, showing the map of his hills. This brand has been and is still a driving force for regional winemaking, a guarantee of professionalism and absolute quality. The Rosazzo Bianco Terre Alte 2013 never fails to make it into the final selection. Sophisticated and complex on the nose, opening out on the palate with memorable, lingering aromas. The Rosazzo Rosso Sossò 2011 is excellent too, with generous aromas and a mouthfilling, soft, balanced and harmonious flavour.

○ Collio Bianco Frontiere Sant'Helena '13	♙♙ 4
○ Collio Pinot Grigio Sant'Helena '14	♙♙ 3
● Collio Rosso Venko Sant'Helena '09	♙♙ 4
○ Collio Sauvignon Sant'Helena '14	♙♙ 3
○ Ribolla Gialla Sant'Helena '14	♙♙ 3
○ Prosecco Brut One & Only '14	♙ 3
○ Ribolla Gialla Brut	♙ 3
○ Collio Bianco Frontiere Sant'Helena '12	♟♟ 3
○ Collio Bianco Frontiere Vigneti Sant'Helena '11	♟♟ 3*
○ Collio Chardonnay Sant'Helena '11	♟♟ 3*
○ Collio Pinot Grigio Sant'Helena '13	♟♟ 3
○ Collio Sauvignon Sant'Helena '13	♟♟ 3
● Friuli Grave Refosco P. R. Sant'Helena '06	♟♟ 3
○ Ribolla Gialla Sant'Helena '13	♟♟ 3

● COF Rosazzo Rosso Sossò Ris. '11	♙♙ 7
○ Rosazzo Terre Alte '13	♙♙ 7
○ COF Bianco Illivio '13	♙♙ 5
○ FCO Chardonnay '14	♙♙ 3
○ FCO Friulano '14	♙♙ 4
○ FCO Pinot Grigio '14	♙♙ 4
○ FCO Sauvignon '14	♙♙ 4
○ COF Bianco Illivio '10	♟♟♟ 5
○ COF Rosazzo Bianco Terre Alte '09	♟♟♟ 7
○ COF Rosazzo Bianco Terre Alte '08	♟♟♟ 7
○ COF Rosazzo Bianco Terre Alte '07	♟♟♟ 7
○ COF Rosazzo Bianco Terre Alte '06	♟♟♟ 6
○ COF Rosazzo Bianco Terre Alte '04	♟♟♟ 6
● COF Rosazzo Sossò Ris. '01	♟♟♟ 6
○ Rosazzo Terre Alte '12	♟♟♟ 7
○ Rosazzo Terre Alte '11	♟♟♟ 7

Marco Felluga

VIA GORIZIA, 121
34072 GRADISCA D'ISONZO [GO]
TEL. 048199164
www.marcofelluga.it

CELLAR SALES
PRE-BOOKED VISITS
RESTAURANT SERVICE
ANNUAL PRODUCTION 600,000 bottles
HECTARES UNDER VINE 100.00

Marco Felluga, who trained in Conegliano's prestigious winemaking school in the 1950s, is credited with having driven a significant acceleration in regional winegrowing production by making his own estate a benchmark for the whole area. He has been a great innovator for the Collio DOC and the same can be said of his son Roberto who, in recent years, has applied farsighted determination in setting up a courageous project to promote ageable white wines through the selection of riservas released to the market several years after harvest. An example to be followed if wines are to be left to express their potential to the full. This decision has proved to be the right one. For the third year running, the Pinot Grigio Mongris Riserva has appeared in the final selection. Delightful citrus aromas of orange and mandarin are enhanced by blasts of dried fruit and vanilla, while the palate is buttery, rounded, flavoursome and lingering.

Fiegl

FRAZ. OSLAVIA
LOC. LENZUOLO BIANCO, 1
34070 GORIZIA
TEL. 0481547103
www.fieglvini.com

CELLAR SALES
PRE-BOOKED VISITS
ANNUAL PRODUCTION 150,000 bottles
HECTARES UNDER VINE 30.00

The Fiegl family are a close-knit, hardworking group that has brought to fruition the experience handed down through many generations of dedicated winegrowers. A purchase agreement dated 1782 testifies that Valentino Fiegl purchased a vineyard in Oslavia, on the steep slopes of the Collio Settentrionale, close to Slovenia, where many prestigious estates are situated. Today the estate is run by brothers Alessio, Giuseppe and Rinaldo, who can count on the active support of the new generation: in perfect synergy, Martin, Robert and Matej have shared out the roles, so as to make their contribution to progressive improvement of quality. This year we were only able to taste white wines from the last vintage except for the Collio Bianco Cuvée Blanc 2013, which benefited from the particular features of a favourable year. The other wines were all flawlessly made with fresh aromas and nicely balanced flavour.

○ Collio Pinot Grigio Mongris Ris. '12	♥♥ 5
○ Collio Bianco Molamatta '13	♥♥ 5
○ Collio Friulano '14	♥♥ 3
● Collio Merlot '12	♥♥ 3
○ Collio Pinot Grigio '14	♥♥ 5
○ Collio Ribolla Gialla '14	♥♥ 3
○ Collio Sauvignon '14	♥ 3
● Collio Cabernet Sauvignon '11	♀♀ 5
● Collio Merlot Varneri '06	♀♀ 3*
○ Collio Pinot Grigio Mongris Ris. '11	♀♀ 6
○ Collio Pinot Grigio Mongris Ris. '10	♀♀ 6
○ Collio Pinot Grigio Mongris Ris. '08	♀♀ 4
○ Collio Pinot Grigio Mongris Ris. '07	♀♀ 4
○ Collio Sauvignon '13	♀♀ 5

○ Collio Bianco Cuvée Blanc '13	♥♥ 4
○ Collio Chardonnay '14	♥♥ 3
○ Collio Friulano '14	♥♥ 3
○ Collio Sauvignon '14	♥♥ 3
○ Collio Malvasia '14	♥ 3
○ Collio Pinot Grigio '14	♥ 3
○ Collio Ribolla Gialla '14	♥ 3
○ Collio Friulano '13	♀♀ 3
● Collio Merlot Leopold '08	♀♀ 4
○ Collio Pinot Grigio '13	♀♀ 3
○ Collio Ribolla Gialla '13	♀♀ 3
● Collio Rosso Leopold Cuvée Rouge '06	♀♀ 5
○ Meja '01 '11	♀♀ 5

Adriano Gigante

VIA ROCCA BERNARDA, 3
33040 CORNO DI ROSAZZO [UD]
TEL. 0432755835
www.adrianogigante.it

CELLAR SALES
PRE-BOOKED VISITS
ANNUAL PRODUCTION 60,000 bottles
HECTARES UNDER VINE 25.00

Adriano Gigante's estate is a consolidated benchmark which honours the unique territorial features of the Friuli Colli Orientali DOC. It is well known that in 1957 his grandfather Ferruccio abandoned his business as a miller to devote full-time care to his Storico tocai friuliano vineyard, whose potential was clear to him and which is still in operation. Today the estate's 25 hectares of vineyards extend over the slopes of Rocca Bernarda. Assisted by his wife Giuliana in running the winery and by his cousin Ariedo in the vineyard and cellar procedures, Adriano carries forward the family tradition with a very high quality range of wines. An excellent performance from all the wines but the Picolit 2008 delighted the palate, deservedly receiving a Tre Bicchieri. It is fragrant and crisp on the nose with intriguing puffs of saffron, pollen and catmint, while the palate is sheer poetry. The Merlot Riserva 2009 is also excellent: creamy, mouthfilling and unforgettable.

○ FCO Picolit '08	▼▼▼	6
● FCO Merlot Ris. '09	▼▼	5
● FCO Cabernet Franc '13	▼▼	3
○ FCO Chardonnay '13	▼▼	3
○ FCO Friulano '14	▼▼	3
○ FCO Friulano Vign. Storico '14	▼▼	4
● FCO Merlot '12	▼▼	3
● FCO Pignolo '07	▼▼	5
● FCO Refosco P. R. Ris. '12	▼▼	3
● FCO Schioppettino '11	▼▼	3
⊙ Prima Nera Brut Rosé	▼▼	3
○ FCO Verduzzo Friulano '10	▼	3
⊙ Prima Gialla Brut	▼	3
○ COF Tocai Friulano Vign. Storico '06	▼▼▼	4
○ COF Tocai Friulano Vign. Storico '05	▼▼▼	4

Gori

VIA G.B. GORI, 14
33045 NIMIS [UD]
TEL. 0432878475
www.goriagricola.com

HECTARES UNDER VINE 18.00

This winery was established recently, in 2009, by Giampiero Gori at Nimis in the westernmost and coldest part of Friuli's Colli Orientali zone. The winery building soars at the top of a hill, its modern, polished architectural design standing above the three underground levels of the cellar, designed to make full use of the gravitational factor in the vinification process. The estate's 12 hectares of vineyards are entrusted to the care of expert consultant agronomist Giovanni Bigot, while the cellar procedures are managed by Natale Favretto. The red wines are matured in Alliers oak tonneaux and large barrels. A very high scoring and really promising debut in the Guide considering the young age of many of the vineyards. This is mostly due to a magnificent performance from the Refosco dal Peduncolo Rosso Redelbosco 2012, with winning aromas of vibrant tobacco, leather and chocolate and a firm, mouthfilling palate.

● Refosco P. R. Redelbosco '12	▼▼	4
● Chardonnay Giugiù '13	▼▼	4
● Merlot Toni Vasùt '13	▼▼	4
● Rosso Meni Vasùt '12	▼▼	4
● Pinot Nero Nemas I '13	▼	4
○ Verduzzo Friulano OrodiNemas '12	▼	3

Gradis'ciutta

LOC. GIASBANA, 10
34070 SAN FLORIANO DEL COLLIO [GO]
TEL. 0481390237
www.gradisciutta.eu

CELLAR SALES
PRE-BOOKED VISITS
ANNUAL PRODUCTION 100,000 bottles
HECTARES UNDER VINE 20.00

Princic is a surname shared by many vignerons who have worked for generations on the slope of the Collio Goriziano. Robert Princic is one of these. Practically born in the vineyard, he set up the winery in 1997 after graduating in oenology, and began to work full-time alongside his father Isidoro. He chose the name Gradis'ciutta in honour of the country village near San Floriano del Collio around which his venerable vineyards are situated. Other vineyards are scattered over various and sometimes distant areas, with distinct subsoils and microclimates, making clonal selection possible to enhance the potential of every single grape variety. All the wines from the last vintage are very fragrant and rich in flavour but the Collio Bianco Bratinis 2013 once again earned a place in our final selections. Made from nicely blended chardonnay, sauvignon and ribolla gialla, it offers vibrant floral and fruity aromas, and a richly mineral palate.

○ Collio Bianco Bratinis '13	♥♥	3*
○ Collio Chardonnay '14	♥♥	3
○ Collio Pinot Grigio '14	♥♥	3
○ Collio Ribolla Gialla '14	♥♥	3
○ Collio Sauvignon '14	♥♥	3
○ Collio Bianco Bratinis '12	♀♀	3*
○ Collio Bianco Bratinis '11	♀♀	3
○ Collio Bianco Bratinis '10	♀♀	3*
○ Collio Chardonnay '13	♀♀	3*
○ Collio Chardonnay '12	♀♀	2*
○ Collio Friulano '13	♀♀	3
○ Collio Friulano '12	♀♀	2*
○ Collio Malvasia '13	♀♀	3
○ Collio Malvasia '12	♀♀	2*
○ Collio Pinot Grigio '13	♀♀	3
○ Collio Ribolla Gialla '12	♀♀	2*

★★Gravner

FRAZ. OSLAVIA
LOC. LENZUOLO BIANCO, 9
34070 GORIZIA
TEL. 048130882
www.gravner.it

CELLAR SALES
PRE-BOOKED VISITS
ANNUAL PRODUCTION 30,000 bottles
HECTARES UNDER VINE 18.00

We have always thought Josko Gravner's wines exciting, whatever the vinification procedure, the result of an uncompromising production philosophy. Josko is a great winegrower, researcher, and true countryman, one of those who really love the land and understand the way it breathes. Stainless steel is gone from the cellar, replaced by magnificent Caucasus amphoras where white grapes are also macerated, sometimes for over six months. In the large Slavonian oak barrels wines mature for many years. The golden, amber-toned white wines made from healthy grapes and ancient techniques are released after at least seven years. The reds age even longer. It is almost taken for granted that all the wines presented by Josko will reach the final. We know that seven years is the minimum waiting period to taste them, but it is worth the wait. The Ribolla Gialla 2007 earns a Tre Bicchieri: complex, lively but not excessive on the nose, and dynamic and memorable on the palate.

○ Ribolla Gialla '07	♥♥♥	5
○ Bianco Breg '07	♥♥	7
● Rosso Breg '04	♥♥	7
○ Breg '00	♀♀♀	8
○ Breg '99	♀♀♀	7
○ Breg '98	♀♀♀	7
○ Breg Anfora '06	♀♀♀	7
○ Breg Anfora '03	♀♀♀	7
○ Breg Anfora '02	♀♀♀	7
○ Collio Chardonnay Ris. '91	♀♀♀	7
○ Ribolla Anfora '05	♀♀♀	7
○ Ribolla Anfora '04	♀♀♀	7
○ Ribolla Anfora '02	♀♀♀	7
○ Ribolla Anfora '01	♀♀♀	7
● Rosso Gravner '04	♀♀♀	7

Iole Grillo

VIA ALBANA, 60
33040 PREPOTTO [UD]
TEL. 0432713201
www.vinigrillo.it

CELLAR SALES
PRE-BOOKED VISITS
ACCOMMODATION
ANNUAL PRODUCTION 40,000 bottles
HECTARES UNDER VINE 9.00

In the little town of Albana di Prepotto, at
the mouth of a beautiful valley in the
northern part of the Friuli Colli Orientali
DOC zone, the beautiful gate to an
18th-century villa, with its Santa Justina
votive chapel, marks the entrance to the
estate. Anna Muzzolini, assisted by her
husband Andrea, runs the winery with
determination and undeniable
entrepreneurial skill, having taken up the
inheritance left by her father Sergio, who
set up the estate in the 1970s and named
it after his wife, Iole Grillo. Painstaking
renovations revealed the villa's original
stone walls and underground areas which
still house the cellar where the wines
mature in oak barrels. We are postponing
our review of the Sauvignon 2014 and the
Sauvignon 2013. Instead we tasted an
excellent Merlot Riserva 2011, with a
pleasant, coherent flavour rich in small
berry fruit and subtle vegetal sensations,
smooth tannins and a lingering finish. The
Merlot 2013 is also good.

● FCO Merlot Ris. '11	♥♥ 3
○ FCO Friulano '14	♥ 3
● FCO Merlot '13	♥ 3
○ COF Friulano '11	♀♀ 3
○ COF Il Sauvignon '12	♀♀ 4
● COF Merlot Ris. '09	♀♀ 3
● COF Refosco P. R. '11	♀♀ 3
● COF Rosso Guardafuoco '11	♀♀ 3
○ COF Sauvignon '12	♀♀ 3
● COF Schioppettino di Prepotto '11	♀♀ 3
● COF Schioppettino di Prepotto '09	♀♀ 3

Jacùss

FRAZ. MONTINA
V.LE KENNEDY, 35A
33040 TORREANO [UD]
TEL. 0432715147
www.jacuss.it

CELLAR SALES
PRE-BOOKED VISITS
ANNUAL PRODUCTION 50,000 bottles
HECTARES UNDER VINE 11.00

Jacùss is the local dialect version of
Iacuzzi, the surname of brothers Sandro
and Andrea, who decided to forsake their
practice of mixed farming in 1990, to focus
more on their own vineyards and wine
production. Their steady work and
dedication brought about modernization of
the training systems, and consequently a
tangible improvement in quality which
allowed their small estate to stand out in
the crowded Cividale DOC area. With roots
firmly anchored in the precepts observed
by their ancestors they have preserved the
values of rural tradition, impressing their
wines with their simple, honest personality.
The red wines from previous years have
proved to be a step ahead of the whites
from the last vintage which however gave
an excellent performance. The Merlot 2011
is lovely and mature on the nose with
generous flavour while the Refosco dal
Peduncolo Rosso 2012 is still rather tannic
but pleasant and promising.

● FCO Merlot '11	♥♥ 3
○ FCO Pinot Bianco '14	♥♥ 3
● FCO Refosco P. R. '12	♥♥ 3
● FCO Schioppettino Fucs e Flamis '13	♥♥ 3
● FCO Tazzelenghe '10	♥♥ 3
○ FCO Sauvignon '14	♥ 3
● COF Cabernet Sauvignon '10	♀♀ 3
● COF Cabernet Sauvignon '09	♀♀ 3
○ COF Friulano '13	♀♀ 3
● COF Merlot '09	♀♀ 3
○ COF Picolit '09	♀♀ 6
○ COF Pinot Bianco '13	♀♀ 3
○ COF Pinot Bianco '12	♀♀ 3
○ COF Verduzzo Friulano '09	♀♀ 3

★★Jermann

FRAZ. RUTTARS
VIA MONTE FORTINO, 21
34072 FARRA D'ISONZO [GO]
TEL. 0481888080
www.jermann.it

CELLAR SALES
PRE-BOOKED VISITS
ANNUAL PRODUCTION 900,000 bottles
HECTARES UNDER VINE 160.00

In this region, the Jermann brand is synonymous with absolute quality, tradition and promotion of the area. In the 1970s, Silvio Jermann used his genius and imagination to create Vintage Tunina, an exceptional wine able to win over the most demanding palates, which shot the winery to the heights of national and then international winemaking. Silvio's surname demonstrates his family's Germanic roots and this explains his particular devotion to grapes originating from the land of his ancestors. The historical centre at Villanova di Farra is still active, while the more prestigious wines mature in the magical atmosphere of the splendid Ruttars cellar. A new accolade for the Vintage Tunina 2013 which adds this Tre Bicchieri to its already well-stocked collection. Stylish, complex, with aromas of bud flowers and fragrant fruit followed by subtle, spicy and tropical sensations. Generous, persistent, flavoursome and very lingering on the palate.

○ Vintage Tunina '13	♟♟♟ 6
○ Capo Martino '13	♟♟ 4
○ W.... Dreams.... '13	♟♟ 8
○ Chardonnay '14	♟♟ 4
○ Pinot Bianco '14	♟♟ 4
○ Pinot Grigio '14	♟♟ 4
○ Ribolla Gialla Vinnae '14	♟♟ 4
○ Capo Martino '10	♟♟♟ 8
○ Vintage Tunina '12	♟♟♟ 6
○ Vintage Tunina '11	♟♟♟ 6
○ Vintage Tunina '08	♟♟♟ 7
○ Vintage Tunina '07	♟♟♟ 7
○ W.... Dreams... '09	♟♟♟ 6
○ W.... Dreams... '06	♟♟♟ 6
○ W.... Dreams.... '12	♟♟♟ 8

Kante

FRAZ. SAN PELAGIO
LOC. PREPOTTO, 1A
34011 DUINO AURISINA [TS]
TEL. 040200255
www.kante.it

ANNUAL PRODUCTION 45,000 bottles
HECTARES UNDER VINE 13.00

In Trieste's Carso district, Edi Kante is generally considered a forefather and forerunner, the man who brought winegrowing to the headlines in an area where everyone believed it to be objectively hard, if not impossible, to plant vines and make wine. Edi is a child of this land, always non-conformist, an obstinate, curious but sensitive soul. His wines are the fruit of a long journey, a challenge to the rocks, the wind and the drought. Frank and authentic, interpreting the terroir in exemplary fashion, they mature for many months at constant temperatures and humidity, on the three floors above the cellar carved from the karst with the indispensable help of dynamite. Edi's wines are the children of his own character and personality: audacious, vigorous, tenacious and sometimes lively like the Malvasia 2012, which very deservedly receives our Tre Bicchieri. This is a generous, complex wine with aromas of bay leaves, aniseed, fine spice and fresh almonds. Simply superlative.

○ Malvasia '12	♟♟♟ 4*
○ Chardonnay '12	♟♟ 4
○ Sauvignon '12	♟♟ 4
○ Sauvignon '09	♟♟ 5
○ Vitovska '12	♟♟ 4
○ Carso Malvasia '07	♟♟♟ 5
○ Carso Malvasia '06	♟♟♟ 5
○ Carso Malvasia '05	♟♟♟ 5
○ Carso Sauvignon '91	♟♟♟ 5
○ Carso Vitovska Sel. '04	♟♟ 5
○ Chardonnay '11	♟♟ 4
○ Malvasia '10	♟♟ 4
○ Vitovska '11	♟♟ 4

★Edi Keber

LOC. ZEGLA, 17
34071 CORMÒNS [GO]
TEL. 048161184
www.edikeber.it

CELLAR SALES
PRE-BOOKED VISITS
ACCOMMODATION
ANNUAL PRODUCTION 50,000 bottles
HECTARES UNDER VINE 12.00

Edi Keber's winery is at Zegla, not far from
Cormòns, in the heart of Collio. The Keber
family is originally from Medana, just a few
hundred metres away. Zegla and Medana
are border towns which have flown
different flags, either by choice or by force.
Those who lived here found themselves in
Austria, then Italy, then Yugoslavia and
again in Italy without ever moving. The
estate produces just one wine, Collio, a
white wine of superior quality consisting
solely of native grape varieties: tocai
friulano, malvasia istriana and ribolla gialla.
A courageous choice that has traced a
journey now shared by Edi's son Kristian.
Edi's Collio 2014 is a little different this
time but that is as it should be, every
vintage year should express its own
features depending on the weather. This is,
in any case, a great wine: gutsy, stylish and
fresh, playing on creamy, fruity sensations
like a good fruit salad.

○ Collio '14	♥♥ 3*
○ Collio Bianco '10	♥♥♥ 3*
○ Collio Bianco '09	♥♥♥ 3
○ Collio Bianco '08	♥♥♥ 3*
○ Collio Bianco '04	♥♥♥ 3*
○ Collio Bianco '02	♥♥♥ 3
○ Collio Tocai Friulano '07	♥♥♥ 3
○ Collio Tocai Friulano '06	♥♥♥ 3
○ Collio Tocai Friulano '05	♥♥♥ 3
○ Collio Tocai Friulano '03	♥♥♥ 3*
○ Collio Tocai Friulano '01	♥♥♥ 3
○ Collio Tocai Friulano '99	♥♥♥ 3*

Renato Keber

LOC. ZEGLA, 15
34071 CORMÒNS [GO]
TEL. 0481639844
www.renatokeber.com

CELLAR SALES
PRE-BOOKED VISITS
ACCOMMODATION
ANNUAL PRODUCTION 60,000 bottles
HECTARES UNDER VINE 15.00

Vigneron Renato Keber lives in symbiosis
with nature's own pace. He maintains that
wine must come from the traditions
established by preceding generations and
therefore tries to work in the most natural
way possible, without going to extremes:
no hurrying, respecting the pace and
unique features of the grapes. These
characteristics have led to his reputation
as a benchmark winegrower in the region.
The Kebers settled in Zegla in the
late-19th century and, having understood
the potential of the terroir, immediately
planted vines. Now the fourth generation,
Renato, is in charge of these precious
vineyards which enjoy enviable lands and
aspect. We only managed to taste a few of
Renato's wines but they are always
intriguing and exciting. The Friulano Zio
Romi Riserva 2012 has extremely pleasant
aromas, deep, invigorating, with generous
flavour. The Pinot Bianco Riserva 2009 has
tropical fruit and petit fours on the nose
and a soft, flavoursome palate.

○ Collio Friulano Zio Romi Ris. '12	♥♥ 5
○ Collio Pinot Bianco Ris. '09	♥♥ 5
○ Collio Friulano Zegla '05	♥♥♥ 5
○ Collio Friulano Zegla Ris. '08	♥♥♥ 5
○ Collio Friulano Zegla Ris. '09	♥♥ 5
○ Collio Friulano Zio Romi Ris. '11	♥♥ 5
○ Collio Bianco Beli Grici '10	♥♥ 4
○ Collio Chardonnay Grici '06	♥♥ 5
● Collio Merlot Grici Ris. '06	♥♥ 5
○ Collio Sauvignon Grici '05	♥♥ 5
○ Collio Sauvignon Grici Ris. '08	♥♥ 5
○ Ribolla Gialla Extreme '09	♥♥ 5

Albino Kurtin

LOC. NOVALI, 9
34071 CORMÒNS [GO]
TEL. 048160685
www.winekurtin.it

CELLAR SALES
PRE-BOOKED VISITS
ANNUAL PRODUCTION 60,000 bottles
HECTARES UNDER VINE 10.00

Young Alessio Kurtin is the fourth
generation of winegrowers since 1906 to
work in Novali, near Cormòns, in the heart
of Collio. The untimely passing of his father
Albino forced him to shoulder the
responsibilities of the estate, drawing on
his previous work experience acquired in
various parts of Italy. Naturally he follows
the path carved by his father who, firmly
supporting tradition but open to innovation,
had to adapt to changes in expression of
the grape varieties, and succeeded. His
wines speak a different language around
the world thanks to the pursuit of a middle
way between specific territorial features
and international tastes. It is certainly no
easy matter to maintain a high standard of
quality in an unusual year like 2014, but
Alessio has managed it beautifully. The
Sauvignon 2014 and the Opera Prima
Bianco 2014 met with our general approval
for their freshness and fragrance, and
supple palates.

Le Monde

LOC. LE MONDE
VIA GARIBALDI, 2
33080 PRATA DI PORDENONE [PN]
TEL. 0434622087
www.lemondewine.com

CELLAR SALES
PRE-BOOKED VISITS
ANNUAL PRODUCTION 220,000 bottles
HECTARES UNDER VINE 50.00
SUSTAINABLE WINERY

Le Monde is a flourishing business situated
between the Livenza and Meduna rivers on
the border with Veneto. The area once part
of the Austro-Hungarian empire and takes
its name from the Germanic term Mundio,
indicating the protection given by the
Emperor of Austria to some areas. The
estate was set up in 1970 and taken over
in 2008 by dynamic young entrepreneur
Alex Maccan. Le Monde is considered to be
a real cru, with very low yields per hectare
and an average vine age of well over 30
years. The vineyards grow on limestone-
clayey soil, which differs greatly from the
usual gravelly soil of the Friuli plain. For the
third year running, the Pinot Grigio 2014
obtained our unanimous approval in the
selections, made it to the finals, and was
awarded our Tre Bicchieri. A very gratifying
result for the estate and for the region, and
confirmation that this grape variety is
winning back the popularity denied it by the
market in the past.

○ Collio Sauvignon '14	♈♈ 3
○ Opera Prima Bianco '14	♈♈ 3
○ Collio Chardonnay '14	♈ 3
○ Collio Friulano '14	♈ 3
○ Collio Chardonnay '13	♈♈ 3
○ Collio Friulano '12	♈♈ 3
○ Collio Friulano '11	♈♈ 3
○ Collio Malvasia '11	♈♈ 3
● Collio Rosso '08	♈♈ 4
○ Collio Sauvignon '11	♈♈ 3
○ Opera Prima Bianco '13	♈♈ 4
○ Opera Prima Bianco '12	♈♈ 3
○ Opera Prima Bianco '11	♈♈ 3*
○ Opera Prima Bianco '10	♈♈ 3

○ Friuli Grave Pinot Bianco '14	♈♈♈ 2*
○ Friuli Grave Pinot Grigio '14	♈♈ 2*
● Friuli Grave Cabernet Franc '13	♈♈ 2*
● Friuli Grave Cabernet Sauvignon '13	♈♈ 2*
● Friuli Grave Refosco P. R. '13	♈♈ 2*
○ Friuli Grave Sauvignon '14	♈♈ 2*
○ Ribolla Gialla '14	♈♈ 3
○ Friuli Grave Chardonnay '14	♈ 2
○ Friuli Grave Friulano '14	♈ 2
○ Ribolla Gialla Brut	♈ 3
○ Friuli Grave Pinot Bianco '13	♈♈♈ 2*
○ Friuli Grave Pinot Bianco '12	♈♈♈ 2*
○ Friuli Grave Pinot Bianco '01	♈♈♈ 2
● Friuli Grave Cabernet Sauvignon '12	♈♈ 2*
○ Friuli Grave Friulano '13	♈♈ 2*
● Friuli Grave Refosco P. R. '12	♈♈ 2*

★Lis Neris

VIA GAVINANA, 5
34070 SAN LORENZO ISONTINO [GO]
TEL. 048180105
www.lisneris.it

CELLAR SALES
PRE-BOOKED VISITS
ACCOMMODATION
ANNUAL PRODUCTION 400,000 bottles
HECTARES UNDER VINE 70.00

Since 1879 four generations of the Pecorari family have poured hard work and passion into creating one of the region's most representative wine-producing estates here at San Lorenzo Isontino. Since Alvaro took over management in 1981, the estate has grown exponentially. He has created such an unmistakeably personal vinification approach that it is known as Lis Neris style, characterized by softness, fragrant aromas and complexity. The vineyards grow close to the estate headquarters on a small upland of deep gravel dragged into the valley by meltwater from the glaciers of the Alpi Orientali, between the border with Slovenia and the right bank of the River Isonzo. The umpteenth validation for the Pinot Grigio Gris 2013 which earns Tre Bicchieri again this year, adding another trophy to its well-stocked collection. The complex, vibrant aromas recall dried flowers, russet pears and ripe tropical fruit, while the palate is balanced and symmetrical.

○ Friuli Isonzo Pinot Grigio Gris '13	♟♟♟	4*
○ Tal Lùc '09	♟♟	8
○ Friuli Isonzo Chardonnay Jurosa '13	♟♟	4
○ Friuli Isonzo Friulano La Vila '13	♟♟	4
○ Friuli Isonzo Sauvignon Picòl '13	♟♟	4
○ Lis '12	♟♟	5
○ Fiore di Campo '06	♟♟♟	3
○ Friuli Isonzo Pinot Grigio Gris '12	♟♟♟	4*
○ Friuli Isonzo Pinot Grigio Gris '11	♟♟♟	4*
○ Friuli Isonzo Pinot Grigio Gris '10	♟♟♟	4*
○ Friuli Isonzo Pinot Grigio Gris '09	♟♟♟	4*
○ Lis '03	♟♟♟	5
○ Pinot Grigio Gris '08	♟♟♟	4*
○ Pinot Grigio Gris '04	♟♟♟	4*
○ Sauvignon Picòl '06	♟♟♟	3*
○ Tal Lùc '02	♟♟♟	8

★Livon

FRAZ. DOLEGNANO
VIA MONTAREZZA, 33
33048 SAN GIOVANNI AL NATISONE [UD]
TEL. 0432757173
www.livon.it

CELLAR SALES
PRE-BOOKED VISITS
ACCOMMODATION
ANNUAL PRODUCTION 750,000 bottles
HECTARES UNDER VINE 180.00

For some years Valneo and Tonino Livon have been running the estate established by their father Dorino in 1964. With excellent entrepreneurial skill they have expanded outside the region, so that their own prestigious brand has been joined by Borgo Salcetino at Radda in Chianti and Colsanto in Umbria. The estate's longstanding oenologist Rinaldo Stocco works alongside them, supervising all the production estates, and the range of wines is varied and well-organized, highlighting the particular features of each place of origin. Now the brothers' respective children, Matteo and Francesca, have joined the business bringing enthusiasm, and engaging, innovative ideas. With the wonderful Malvasia Soluna 2013 close on its heels with gooseberry and vanilla aromas, the Braide Alte 2013 takes back the sceptre for the estate with a Tre Bicchieri. Confident and fragrant on the nose with tropical fruit and crusty bread aromas, the palate reveals intriguing aromatic sensations.

○ Braide Alte '13	♟♟♟	5
○ Collio Malvasia Soluna '13	♟♟	3*
○ Collio Friulano Manditocai '13	♟♟	5
○ Collio Pinot Grigio Braide Grande '14	♟♟	3
○ Collio Ribolla Gialla RoncAlto '14	♟♟	3
● TiareBlù '12	♟♟	5
○ Braide Alte '11	♟♟♟	5
○ Braide Alte '09	♟♟♟	5
○ Braide Alte '07	♟♟♟	5
○ Braide Alte '00	♟♟♟	5
○ Braide Alte '98	♟♟♟	5
● COF Refosco P. R. Riul '02	♟♟♟	3
○ Collio Braide Alte '08	♟♟♟	3
○ Collio Friulano Manditocai '12	♟♟♟	5
○ Collio Friulano Manditocai '10	♟♟♟	5
● TiareBlù '00	♟♟♟	5

Tenuta Luisa

FRAZ. CORONA
VIA CAMPO SPORTIVO , 13
34070 MARIANO DEL FRIULI [GO]
TEL. 048169680
www.tenutaluisa.com

CELLAR SALES
PRE-BOOKED VISITS
ANNUAL PRODUCTION 350,000 bottles
HECTARES UNDER VINE 79.00

Eddi Luisa, wife Nella and sons Michele and
Davide, work In the beautiful winery at
Corona, Mariano del Friuli, part of the Friuli
Isonzo DOC. The two generations work in
perfect harmony in a swirl of enthusiasm,
courage and forward thinking that has
brought Tenuta Luisa steady expansion over
the years. Meticulous care over every single
detail demonstrates the family's passionate
devotion to their work. The vineyards cover
the sunny expanse of the Isonzo plain with
typical subsoil that is particularly rich in
minerals, especially iron. This red soil
inspired the name of the I Ferretti selection.
The white wines of the last vintage met with
unanimous approval but the brilliant scores
obtained by the Cabernet Sauvignon
Selezione I Ferretti 2011 brought it rightfully
into the finals. Vibrant aromas of
blackberries, morello cherries, aniseed,
cardamom and quinine, with a tangy,
mouthfilling flavour.

● Friuli Isonzo Cabernet Sauvignon I Ferretti '11	🍷🍷 4
○ Friuli Isonzo Chardonnay '14	🍷🍷 3
○ Friuli Isonzo Friulano '14	🍷🍷 3
○ Friuli Isonzo Pinot Bianco '14	🍷🍷 3
○ Ribolla Gialla '14	🍷🍷 3
● Rol I Ferretti '11	🍷🍷 4
○ Friuli Isonzo Pinot Grigio '14	🍷 3
○ Desiderium Sel. I Ferretti '09	🍷🍷🍷 4*
○ Friuli Isonzo Tocai Friulano '03	🍷🍷🍷 2*
○ Chardonnay I Ferretti '07	🏆🏆 4
● Friuli Isonzo Cabernet I Ferretti '07	🏆🏆 4
○ Friuli Isonzo Friulano I Ferretti '12	🏆🏆 3*
● Friuli Isonzo Refosco P. R. '08	🏆🏆 3*

Magnàs

LOC. BOATINA
VIA CORONA, 47
34071 CORMÒNS [GO]
TEL. 048160991
www.magnas.it

CELLAR SALES
PRE-BOOKED VISITS
ACCOMMODATION AND RESTAURANT SERVICE
ANNUAL PRODUCTION 25,000 bottles
HECTARES UNDER VINE 10.00

In the early 1970s Luciano Visintin decided
to reshape the estate moulded by a century
of experience accumulated by a family
always linked to farming, and thus Magnàs
was established. The name was inspired by
the nickname with which his branch of the
family was usually identified locally. The
responsibility for managing the estate and
especially the vinification process was
handed on to his son Andrea some time
ago. The Cellar is situated in Boatina in the
Cormòns DOC zone, and the vineyards are
planted in the Friuli Isonzo DOC, with its
notorious lean, dry, stony soil, ideal for
growing vines. In the last edition of the
Guide we mentioned a new wine made with
grapes grown in the Gorizia Collio area.
This year the Collio Bianco 2013 won our
favour and made it to the finals. Complex
and nicely integrated aromas, with an
enthralling, soft, flavoursome palate.

○ Collio Bianco '13	🍷🍷 3*
○ Friuli Isonzo Friulano '14	🍷🍷 3
○ Malvasia '14	🍷🍷 3
○ Pinot Grigio '14	🍷🍷 3
○ Chardonnay '14	🍷 3
○ Friuli Isonzo Chardonnay '13	🏆🏆 3
○ Friuli Isonzo Friulano '13	🏆🏆 3
○ Friuli Isonzo Friulano '12	🏆🏆 3
○ Friuli Isonzo Friulano '11	🏆🏆 3
○ Friuli Isonzo Friulano '09	🏆🏆 3*
○ Friuli Isonzo Pinot Grigio '11	🏆🏆 3
○ Friuli Isonzo Sauvignon '13	🏆🏆 3
○ Malvasia '12	🏆🏆 3

Valerio Marinig

VIA BROLO, 41
33040 PREPOTTO [UD]
TEL. 0432713012
www.marinig.it

CELLAR SALES
PRE-BOOKED VISITS
ANNUAL PRODUCTION 25,000 bottles
HECTARES UNDER VINE 8.00

Valerio Marinig is the fourth generation to
run the family estate, almost a century old.
Back in 1921 his great-grandfather Luigi,
owner of a small farm, bought another and
invested in it all his skill and experience as
a winegrower. Today Valerio, with his father
Sergio alongside him in the vineyard,
manages the farm with the same passion
and professionalism handed down by his
ancestors, following their agronomical and
oenological methods. The vineyards extend
over the Prepotto hills whose unusual
morphology and climate have laid the
foundations for quality winegrowing,
reflected in the fragrance and typical
features of the wines. This year the Refosco
dal Peduncolo Rosso 2012 adds to the
estate's many accolades by reaching the
finals: fragrant, fruity aromas both on the
nose and palate, with hints of cherry jam,
dark chocolate, quinine and sweet spice.
The Schioppettino di Prepotto 2011 is also
excellent: balanced, supple and
flavoursome.

● FCO Refosco P. R. '12		♟♟ 3*
○ FCO Pinot Bianco '14		♟♟ 2*
● FCO Schioppettino di Prepotto '11		♟♟ 4
○ FCO Friulano '14		♟ 2
○ FCO Verduzzo Friulano '14		♟ 3
○ COF Friulano '13		♟♟ 2*
○ COF Friulano '12		♟♟ 2*
○ COF Friulano '08		♟♟ 2*
● COF Pignolo '08		♟♟ 4
○ COF Pinot Bianco '13		♟♟ 2*
○ COF Pinot Bianco '12		♟♟ 2*
○ COF Sauvignon '13		♟♟ 3
○ COF Sauvignon '12		♟♟ 3
○ COF Sauvignon '09		♟♟ 2*
○ COF Sauvignon '06		♟♟ 2

Masùt da Rive

VIA MANZONI, 82
34070 MARIANO DEL FRIULI [GO]
TEL. 048169200
www.masutdarive.com

CELLAR SALES
PRE-BOOKED VISITS
ANNUAL PRODUCTION 80,000 bottles
HECTARES UNDER VINE 20.00
SUSTAINABLE WINERY

The Gallo family has lived in Marino del
Friuli since the early 20th century. They
have always been winegrowers on the
northern bank of the River Isonzo and the
various branches of the family have
established estates with different names.
Silvano Gallo chose to call his Masùt da
Rive, which is the nickname of his branch.
Credit is due to him for always having
believed in the potential of pinot noir,
considered by many to be impossible to
grow here, and for stubbornly continuing to
grow it. His sons Fabrizio and Marco
treasured his belief and improved on them
every day so that it can now be considered
the estate's flagship wine. It is certainly no
coincidence that both versions of the Pinot
Nero presented for tasting were the most
popular. In particular, the Pinot Nero
Maurus 2012 made it through to the final
selections this year with aromas of
raspberry liqueur and sweet spice, and a
soft, lingering palate.

● Friuli Isonzo Pinot Nero Maurus '12		♟♟ 6
○ Friuli Isonzo Chardonnay Rive Alte '14		♟♟ 3
● Friuli Isonzo Pinot Nero '13		♟♟ 4
○ Friuli Isonzo Sauvignon Rive Alte '14		♟♟ 3
● Friuli Isonzo Cabernet Franc '13		♟ 3
● Friuli Isonzo Cabernet Sauvignon '13		♟ 3
○ Friuli Isonzo Tocai Friulano '04		♟♟♟ 3*
● Friuli Isonzo Cabernet Franc '12		♟♟ 3*
○ Friuli Isonzo Pinot Bianco '09		♟♟ 3*
○ Friuli Isonzo Pinot Grigio '08		♟♟ 3*
● Friuli Isonzo Pinot Nero Maurus '11		♟♟ 6
● Friuli Isonzo Refosco P. R. '12		♟♟ 3
○ Friuli Isonzo Sauvignon Rive Alte '13		♟♟ 3

Davino Meroi

via Stretta, 7b
33042 Buttrio [UD]
Tel. 0432673369
www.meroidavino.it

CELLAR SALES
PRE-BOOKED VISITS
RESTAURANT SERVICE
ANNUAL PRODUCTION 35,000 bottles
HECTARES UNDER VINE 19.00
SUSTAINABLE WINERY

Meroi is named after its founder, Davino, but his son Paolo has been in charge for many years. The vineyards covering the sunny slopes of the Buttrio hills, the closest to the Adriatic, are considered historic as they were planted with the old-style skill of grandfather Domenico. Old vines producing healthy, perfectly ripe and richly aromatic grapes, enabling Paolo to imprint his wines with a distinctively unique, sophisticated and personal style. The wines are firmly structured, richly extracted, flavoursome, ageworthy: the fruit of tested experience and undeniable skill in no-frills, moderate vinification in oak. This year two wines competed for the top prize and made a lovely couple in the finals. The enthralling Malvasia Zitelle Durì 2013 is new to our tasting panel, presenting a sophisticated nose and satisfying palate. Also excellent, the Merlot Vigna Dominin 2012 is sumptuous, powerful and rounded.

○ FCO Malvasia Zitelle Durì '13	**YY**	6
● FCO Merlot V. Dominin '12	**YY**	8
○ COF Chardonnay '13	**YY**	5
○ COF Friulano '13	**YY**	5
● COF Merlot Ros di Buri '12	**YY**	5
○ FCO Picolit '13	**YY**	6
○ FCO Sauvignon '13	**YY**	4
○ FCO Verduzzo Friulano '12	**YY**	5
○ COF Friulano '11	YYY	5
○ COF Friulano '10	YYY	5
○ COF Verduzzo Friulano '08	YYY	5
○ COF Chardonnay '11	YY	5
○ COF Chardonnay '10	YY	5
● COF Merlot V. Dominin '11	YY	8

Moschioni

loc. Gagliano
via Doria, 30
33043 Cividale del Friuli [UD]
Tel. 0432730210
www.michelemoschioni.it

CELLAR SALES
PRE-BOOKED VISITS
ANNUAL PRODUCTION 38,000 bottles
HECTARES UNDER VINE 14.00
SUSTAINABLE WINERY

Michele Moschioni never fails to amaze us. In the last edition we remarked on his decision to delay the release of his wines, obliging us to wait another year to taste the 2009 vintage, while 2010 has some news. Since it was an unusual year, with low temperatures and less than ideal weather conditions, Michele decided to produce just one wine, Rosso Bisest, linking it to the negative aspects of Leap Years, consisting of a blend of all his wines: Pignolo, Schioppettino, Refosco dal Peduncolo Rosso, Rosso Celtico and Rosso Real. Just one wine then: but what a wine! The Rosso Bisest 2010 astonished our palates with its majestic qualities: bright ruby red colour with a dark, inky centre; hints of wild black berries, wood tar and black truffles delighting the nose; and a sturdy, mouthfilling, memorable palate.

● FCO Rosso Bisest '10	**YY**	5
● COF Rosso Celtico '04	YYY	5
● COF Schioppettino '06	YYY	6
● COF Pignolo '07	YY	6
● COF Refosco P. R. '06	YY	4
● COF Rosso Celtico '09	YY	5
● COF Rosso Celtico '06	YY	5
● COF Rosso Reâl '09	YY	5
● Rosso Pit Franc '08	YY	6

Muzic

LOC. BIVIO, 4
34070 SAN FLORIANO DEL COLLIO [GO]
TEL. 0481884201
www.cantinamuzic.it

CELLAR SALES
PRE-BOOKED VISITS
ANNUAL PRODUCTION 90,000 bottles
HECTARES UNDER VINE 21.00
SUSTAINABLE WINERY

The Muzic estate can be reached from the
"wine and cherries road" leading from
Gorizia up to San Floriano, and the
vineyards are situated in the Collio DOC
zone. Elija and Fabijan are the new
generation who, on completion of their
studies, will run the estate. The current
owner is their father Giovanni, locally known
as Ivan: a free spirit who loves to be among
the vines, a true artisan of wine. His wife
Orieta is the beating heart of the estate,
busying herself with welcoming guests to
the lovely 16th-century underground cellar
with exposed stone walls and vaulted
ceilings, where the red wines mature in
barriques. Once again our favourite was the
Friulano Vigna Valeris 2014, consolidating
its role as the estate's most typical wine:
satisfyingly sophisticated and creamy on
both nose and palate. We liked the fragrant
flavour of the Chardonnay 2014 very much,
while the Malvasia 2014 has aromas of
sagebrush and aniseed.

○ Collio Friulano V. Valeris '14	♥♥	3*
○ Collio Bianco '14	♥♥	3
● Collio Cabernet Sauvignon '13	♥♥	3
○ Collio Chardonnay '14	♥♥	3
○ Collio Malvasia '14	♥♥	3
○ Collio Pinot Grigio '14	♥♥	3
○ Collio Sauvignon V. Pàjze '14	♥♥	3
○ Collio Bianco Bric '11	♀♀	3*
○ Collio Friulano V. Valeris '13	♀♀	3*
○ Collio Friulano V. Valeris '12	♀♀	3*
○ Collio Friulano V. Valeris '11	♀♀	3*
○ Collio Pinot Grigio '12	♀♀	3*
○ Collio Pinot Grigio '11	♀♀	3*
○ Collio Sauvignon V. Pàjze '13	♀♀	3*

Paraschos

LOC. BUCUIE, 13A
34070 SAN FLORIANO DEL COLLIO [GO]
TEL. 0481884154
www.paraschos.it

CELLAR SALES
PRE-BOOKED VISITS
ANNUAL PRODUCTION 14,000 bottles
HECTARES UNDER VINE 6.00

Bibliographic sources dating back to the
18th century establish that in Collio and the
Vipacco valley the practice of fermenting
grape must on the skins for a few days in
vats, before pressing, had been adopted to
improve the flavour, aroma and longevity of
the wine. Evangelos Paraschos, obviously
of Greek origin, settled in San Floriano del
Collio in 1979 and embraced this way of
interpreting winegrowing. In 1998 he
established his estate. His wines are
neither filtered, nor clarified, nor stabilized,
and they are bottled after at least two
years. Their colour is rich, sometimes
veiled, but they are always fascinating and
enthralling. This year only two wines were
presented but were enough to confirm the
excellent standards recorded in previous
editions. The Merlot 2010 was tasted again
in the final selections and praised for its
beautiful development with spicy hints of
star anise and black pepper.

● Merlot '10	♥♥	3*
○ Kaj '11	♥♥	5
○ Amphoreus Bianco '09	♀♀	5
○ Amphoreus Malvasia '10	♀♀	6
○ Malvasia Amphoreus '11	♀♀	6
● Merlot '09	♀♀	4
○ Pinot Grigio Not '11	♀♀	5
● Ponka '10	♀♀	5
○ Ribolla Gialla '09	♀♀	5
○ Ribolla Gialla '08	♀♀	5
○ Ribolla Gialla Amphoreus '11	♀♀	5
● Skala '07	♀♀	5

Alessandro Pascolo

LOC. RUTTARS, 1
34070 DOLEGNA DEL COLLIO [GO]
TEL. 048161144
www.vinipascolo.com

CELLAR SALES
PRE-BOOKED VISITS
ANNUAL PRODUCTION 25,000 bottles
HECTARES UNDER VINE 7.00
SUSTAINABLE WINERY

Young agronomist, oenologist and sommelier Alessandro Pascolo personally manages the prestigious seven hectares of vineyards purchased by his grandfather in the 1970s on a lucky hunch. The property includes a farmhouse, now a cellar, on the sunny slopes of the Ruttàrs hill, the jewel in the Dolegna del Collio area's crown. Alessandro embraces a production philosophy which aims at wines with a marked varietal identity. His attention focuses on the vineyard, obtaining generous fruit to guarantee structure. The white wines are fermented in stainless steel while very fine-grained tonneaux are used for the red wines to avoid altering their varietal features. The Rosso Pascal 2011, made from cabernet sauvignon and merlot, has aromas of prunes, tobacco and forest floor, with a firm, sturdy palate. The Merlot Selezione 2012 reveals clear toasty hints and lively but smooth tannins. The Bianco Agnul 2013 is well-structured and very fruity with generous aromas.

○ Bolla Gialla Brut	♙♙ 3
○ Collio Bianco Agnul '13	♙♙ 4
● Collio Merlot Sel. '12	♙♙ 5
● Pascal '11	♙♙ 3
○ Collio Bianco Agnul '10	♙♙ 3
○ Collio Friulano '12	♙♙ 3
○ Collio Friulano '11	♙♙ 3*
○ Collio Malvasia '13	♙♙ 3
○ Collio Malvasia '12	♙♙ 3
○ Collio Pinot Bianco '12	♙♙ 3
○ Collio Pinot Grigio '11	♙♙ 3*
○ Riesling Briach '07	♙♙ 4

Perusini

LOC. GRAMOGLIANO
VIA TORRIONE, 13
33040 CORNO DI ROSAZZO [UD]
TEL. 0432675018
www.perusini.com

CELLAR SALES
PRE-BOOKED VISITS
ACCOMMODATION AND RESTAURANT SERVICE
ANNUAL PRODUCTION 70,000 bottles
HECTARES UNDER VINE 13.00

At the end of the 19th century when the fashion for French wines prevailed, Giacomo Perusini began his selection of native regional grape varieties, reviving the noble picolit and closely linking his name to that of the estate. His successors have written important pages in the history of local winemaking, down to current owner Teresa Perusini. An enthusiastic winegrower with a passion for art history, she runs the winery and prestigious vineyards on the hillsides of Gramogliano, Rosazzo and Rocca Bernarda in the Colli Orientali del Friuli with severe training systems and dense planting, enjoying the magnificent, sunny aspects. An excellent performance from the whole range demonstrates the sheer quality achieved and maintained for all the types of wine. The standard label whites and 2012 reds won unanimous approval, with a special mention for the Picolit 2012 and its wonderfully enjoyable palate.

● COF Merlot '12	♙♙ 3
● COF Picolit '12	♙♙ 8
● COF Refosco P.R. '12	♙♙ 3
● COF Rosso del Postiglione '12	♙♙ 3
○ FCO Pinot Grigio '14	♙♙ 3
○ FCO Ribolla Gialla '14	♙♙ 3
○ FCO Sauvignon '14	♙♙ 3
● COF Cabernet Franc '09	♙♙ 3
● COF Cabernet Sauvignon '09	♙♙ 3
● COF Merlot '09	♙♙ 3
○ COF Pinot Grigio '12	♙♙ 3
● COF Refosco P.R. '09	♙♙ 3
○ COF Ribolla Gialla '11	♙♙ 3
● COF Rosso del Postiglione '09	♙♙ 3
○ COF Sauvignon '11	♙♙ 3
○ COF Sauvignon '08	♙♙ 3*

Petrucco

VIA MORPURGO, 12
33042 BUTTRIO [UD]
TEL. 0432674387
www.vinipetrucco.it

CELLAR SALES
PRE-BOOKED VISITS
ANNUAL PRODUCTION 80,000 bottles
HECTARES UNDER VINE 25.00

Italo Balbo's wartime exploits fill many
pages of history books concerning the two
world wars of the 20th century, but
perhaps few people know that before his
plane was shot down over Libya in 1940,
he planted some vineyards on the Buttrio
hills at Buttrio di Monte, where the
beautiful natural amphitheatre of the Colli
Orientali del Friuli begins. The winery was
taken over in 1981 by Paolo Petrucco and
his wife Lina who, helped by excellent
oenologist Flavio Cabas, tend with
meticulous care the old vineyards that still
yield prestigious grapes, carefully selected
to produce the Ronco del Balbo line of
wines. The Pinot Bianco 2014 was our
favourite, reaching the finals thanks to its
sophisticated aromas of spring flowers and
fragrant fruit, as well as a very pleasing
palate. The Merlot Ronco del Balbo 2012
is also excellent, with hints of bottled
cherries and dark chocolate and a
powerful, vigorous palate.

● COF Merlot Ronco del Balbo '12	♀♀ 4
○ FCO Pinot Bianco '14	♀♀ 3*
● COF Refosco P. R. Ronco del Balbo '12	♀♀ 4
○ FCO Chardonnay '14	♀♀ 3
○ FCO Friulano '14	♀♀ 3
○ FCO Pinot Grigio '14	♀♀ 3
○ FCO Ribolla Gialla '14	♀ 3
○ COF Chardonnay '13	♀♀ 3
● COF Merlot Ronco del Balbo '11	♀♀ 3*
● COF Merlot Ronco del Balbo '10	♀♀ 3*
● COF Pignolo Ronco del Balbo '10	♀♀ 5
○ COF Pinot Grigio '13	♀♀ 3
○ COF Pinot Grigio '09	♀♀ 2*
● COF Refosco P. R. Ronco del Balbo '11	♀♀ 4
● COF Refosco P. R. Ronco del Balbo '08	♀♀ 3
○ COF Sauvignon '13	♀♀ 3

Petrussa

VIA ALBANA, 49
33040 PREPOTTO [UD]
TEL. 0432713192
www.petrussa.it

CELLAR SALES
PRE-BOOKED VISITS
ACCOMMODATION
ANNUAL PRODUCTION 40,000 bottles
HECTARES UNDER VINE 10.00

In 1986 Gianni and Paolo Petrussa decided
to devote themselves to the family estate,
leaving their steady jobs. This caused a
certain amount of anxiety for their parents
who were aware that this choice would
force them to face a future of uncertain
finances and definite hard, tiring work. But,
convinced of the potential of the Prepotto
terroir and driven by their iron will to
enhance its typical features, they drew on
the thousand-year rural history of their
ancestors and imprinted their wines with
their own frank personality. Special care is
taken over the Schioppettino, made from
ribolla nera, a native local grape with
strong local features. And indeed the
Schioppettino di Prepotto 2012 topped the
estate's ranking list, making a
well-deserved appearance in the
finals. Blackberries, tobacco and coffee on
the nose with a lively, well-paced palate.
The Rosso Petrussa 2012, a
monovarietal merlot, confirmed the praise
earned last year.

○ COF Schioppettino di Prepotto '12	♀♀ 5
○ COF Chardonnay S. Elena '13	♀♀ 4
● COF Merlot Rosso Petrussa '12	♀♀ 5
○ FCO Friulano '14	♀♀ 3
○ FCO Pinot Bianco '14	♀♀ 3
○ Pensiero '12	♀♀ 5
● Cabernet Sauvignon Collezione Personale '10	♀ 8
○ FCO Sauvignon '14	♀ 3
○ COF Chardonnay S. Elena '12	♀♀ 4
○ COF Friulano '13	♀♀ 3
○ COF Friulano '12	♀♀ 3
○ COF Pinot Bianco '13	♀♀ 3
○ COF Pinot Bianco '12	♀♀ 3*
● COF Rosso Petrussa '11	♀♀ 5
○ COF Sauvignon '13	♀♀ 3

FRIULI VENEZIA GIULIA

Roberto Picéch

LOC. PRADIS, 11
34071 CORMÒNS [GO]
TEL. 048160347
www.picech.it

CELLAR SALES
PRE-BOOKED VISITS
ACCOMMODATION
ANNUAL PRODUCTION 30,000 bottles
HECTARES UNDER VINE 7.00
SUSTAINABLE WINERY

Roberto Picéch is a well-established leader in regional winegrowing. Although he scaled the heights of excellence long ago, he is still open to innovation in his ongoing pursuit of new stimuli. With increasingly sustained maceration periods and the courage to shun current trends and techniques, he endows his wines with distinctive features in an increasingly personal and identifiable style. His frankness and stubbornness are inherited from his father Egidio, known locally as "the rebel", a determined forward-thinker who, in 1963, managed to purchase the property containing the vineyards he had worked for many years in the Gorizia Collio area, at Pradis. The whole range is excellent, but the Malvasia 2014 stands out for stylish aromas with clear fruity hints of peaches and pineapple. But it performs best on the palate, showing freshness and softness in perfect harmony with the other components.

Vigneti Pittaro

VIA UDINE, 67
33033 CODROIPO [UD]
TEL. 0432904726
www.vignetipittaro.com

CELLAR SALES
PRE-BOOKED VISITS
ACCOMMODATION
ANNUAL PRODUCTION 400,000 bottles
HECTARES UNDER VINE 90.00

Piero Pittaro's winery is a benchmark for regional winegrowing. It covers 90 hectares in the Codroipo area on the dry, stony land of Grave del Friuli, renowned vineyard country, and another five hectares on the beautiful Ramandolo hills in the Friuli Colli Orientali DOC zone. The cellar is a harmonious blend of technology and architecture surrounded by vineyards and therefore perfectly immersed in its surroundings. Cellar manager Stefano Trinco has proven experience in the production of Classic Method sparkling wines, the feather in the estate's cap and vaunt of the whole region. The Pittaro Brut Etichetta Oro 2008 lives up to its reputation and the tasting is more impressive and satisfying every year. However the whole range consolidates the excellent standard achieved and maintained, offering a varied series of products to satisfy all possible demands.

○ Collio Malvasia '14	♟♟ 3*
○ Collio Bianco Athena Magnum '12	♟♟ 7
○ Collio Bianco Jelka '13	♟♟ 4
○ Collio Pinot Bianco '14	♟♟ 3
● Collio Rosso '13	♟♟ 3
● Collio Rosso Ruben Ris. '12	♟♟ 6
○ Collio Bianco Athena '05	♟♟♟ 7
○ Collio Bianco Jelka '99	♟♟♟ 7
○ Collio Pinot Bianco '13	♟♟♟ 3*
○ Collio Bianco Athena '07	♟♟ 7
○ Collio Bianco Jelka '11	♟♟ 4
○ Collio Bianco Jelka '09	♟♟ 4
○ Collio Friulano '10	♟♟ 3
○ Collio Pinot Bianco '11	♟♟ 3*
● Collio Rosso Ruben Ris. '11	♟♟ 6

○ Pittaro Brut Et. Oro '08	♟♟ 5
○ FCO Friulano Ronco Vieri '14	♟♟ 3
○ Friuli Grave Cabernet '12	♟♟ 4
● Friuli Grave Rosso Agresto '10	♟♟ 4
○ Picolit Ronco Vieri '12	♟♟ 6
○ Pittaro Brut Et. Argento	♟♟ 4
○ Ramandolo Ronco Vieri '13	♟♟ 3
○ Ribolla Gialla Brut	♟♟ 3
⊙ Apicio	♟ 3
● FCO Refosco Ronco Vieri '13	♟ 3
○ Friuli Grave Chardonnay Mousqué '14	♟ 3
○ Friuli Grave Sauvignon Blanc '14	♟ 3
● Moscato Rosa Valzer in Rosa '14	♟ 3
⊙ Pittaro Brut Pink	♟ 5

Denis Pizzulin

VIA BROLO, 43
33040 PREPOTTO [UD]
TEL. 0432713425
www.pizzulin.com

Renata Pizzulin

VIA CELSO MACOR, 1
34070 MORARO [GO]
TEL. 0432713027
www.renatapizzulin.it

CELLAR SALES
PRE-BOOKED VISITS
ANNUAL PRODUCTION 25,000 bottles
HECTARES UNDER VINE 11.00

CELLAR SALES
ANNUAL PRODUCTION 9,000 bottles
HECTARES UNDER VINE 3.00
SUSTAINABLE WINERY

Denis Pizzulin's small estate has just 11 hectares of vineyards divided into various plots on the Prepotto hills. Here, winegrowing has a thousand-year history. The area has an unusual microclimate owed to its sunny position, protected from the wind, and soil based on a mixture of sandstone and marl ideal for growing vines. The small size makes it possible to supervise the whole production process with meticulous care. Denis has achieved a high standard of quality, has clear ideas and above all, shows great determination and skill. The Schioppettino di Prepotto 2012 has blackberries, black pepper, forest floor, damp earth and woodfires on the nose, with a palate still juggling lively tannins, though it promises to develop and age well. The Rosso Rarisolchi 2009 is complex, spicy and balsamic with a generous flavour supported by good vigorous acidity.

From the very beginning Alberto Pelos and Renata Pizzulin set up their small estate to produce fine quality wines. Despite his youth, Alberto has already accumulated experience in the sector and he felt ready to face a personal journey. The vineyards are planted in four different locations in the municipal areas of Moraro and Mariano del Friuli, and belong to the Friuli Isonzo DOC. Each location was chosen to make the very best of the features of each variety, and each wine is identified with the place name of the vineyard where the grapes are grown. The estate's small size makes it possible to choose sustainable agronomical practices. Last year we tasted Renata Pizzulin's wines for the first time, and were delighted. This year we confirmed that it was not just chance: there are only four wines but all of a very high standard, as sophisticated and complex on the nose as they are confident and persistent on the palate.

● COF Refosco P. R. '12	♟♟ 4	○ Friuli Isonzo Bianco Teolis '13	♟♟ 3
● COF Rosso Rarisolchi Ris. '09	♟♟ 4	○ Friuli Isonzo Chardonnay Paladis '13	♟♟ 3
● COF Schioppettino di Prepotto '12	♟♟ 3	○ Friuli Isonzo Malvasia Melaris '13	♟♟ 3
○ FCO Pinot Grigio '14	♟ 3	● Friuli Isonzo Refosco P. R. Murellis '12	♟♟ 3
○ COF Friulano '13	♟♟ 3*	○ Friuli Isonzo Bianco Teolis '12	♟♟ 3
○ COF Friulano '11	♟♟ 2*	○ Friuli Isonzo Chardonnay Paladis '12	♟♟ 3
● COF Merlot '12	♟♟ 3	○ Friuli Isonzo Malvasia Melaris '12	♟♟ 3
○ COF Pinot Bianco '13	♟♟ 3	● Murellis '12	♟♟ 3
○ COF Pinot Bianco '12	♟♟ 3		
○ COF Sauvignon '13	♟♟ 3		
● COF Schioppettino di Prepotto '11	♟♟ 3		
● COF Schioppettino di Prepotto '10	♟♟ 3		

Damijan Podversic

VIA BRIGATA PAVIA, 61
34170 GORIZIA
TEL. 048178217
www.damijanpodversic.com

CELLAR SALES
PRE-BOOKED VISITS
ANNUAL PRODUCTION 28,000 bottles
HECTARES UNDER VINE 10.00
VITICULTURE METHOD Certified Organic

Damijan Podversic lives in Doberdò del
Lago on the Gorizia Carso, but his
vineyards cover the beautiful slopes of
Mount Calvario on the right bank of the
River Isonzo. Although he has to travel quite
a way every day, he says he feels very
fortunate to be doing what he has dreamed
of since childhood. Motivated by the
teachings of Josko Gravner, with whom he
shares friendship and admiration, and
aware that the mistakes made along the
way have matured and perfected his skills,
he began with courageous choices: long
maceration on the skins and total exclusion
of selected yeasts, clarification, filtration or
controlled temperatures. Having three
wines in the finals is by now the norm for
Damijan, and all of them came close to the
top accolade. The magnificent Nekaj 2011
is warm and sunny with sun-dried hay
aromas and a tangy palate. The Ribolla
Gialla 2011 offers crisp, salty hints of
sesame seeds.

○ Kaplja '11	♥♥	6
○ Nekaj '11	♥♥	6
○ Ribolla Gialla '11	♥♥	6
○ Malvasia '11	♥♥	6
● Rosso Prelit '11	♥♥	6
○ Kaplja '08	♥♥♥	6
○ Malvasia '10	♥♥♥	6
○ Malvasia '09	♥♥♥	6
○ Kaplja '10	♥♥	6
○ Kaplja '09	♥♥	6
○ Nekaj '10	♥♥	6
○ Ribolla Giall '10	♥♥	6
○ Ribolla Gialla '09	♥♥	6
● Rosso Prelit '10	♥♥	6

Isidoro Polencic

LOC. PLESSIVA, 12
34071 CORMÒNS [GO]
TEL. 048160655
www.polencic.com

CELLAR SALES
PRE-BOOKED VISITS
ACCOMMODATION
ANNUAL PRODUCTION 120,000 bottles
HECTARES UNDER VINE 28.00

Elisabetta, Michele and Alex Polencic run
the estate created in 1968 by their father
Isidoro, carrying forward the family tradition
which is documented back to the late
1800s. Despite their youth the three
siblings are unusually at ease with running
the estate and have maintained the
standard of quality achieved when they
were still able to benefit from their father's
assistance. The winery headquarters is at
Plessiva, near Cormòns. Some vineyards
surround it while others are planted in
neighbouring areas on different types of
land with varying microclimates, allowing
them to present a full picture of the Collio
potential. The Friulano Fisc 2013 is always
at the top of our list of favourites. Aromas
of confectioner's cream and marron glacé
under a veil of sweet spice, and a creamy
and enjoyable palate, despite a slightly
woody note weighing it down. The wines of
the latest vintage are all excellent, supple
and drinkable.

○ Collio Chardonnay '14	♥♥	3
○ Collio Friulano '14	♥♥	3
○ Collio Friulano Fisc '13	♥♥	4
○ Collio Pinot Grigio '14	♥♥	3
○ Oblin Blanc '12	♥♥	4
○ Collio Pinot Bianco '14	♥	3
○ Collio Chardonnay '13	♥♥	3*
○ Collio Friulano '13	♥♥	3
○ Collio Friulano Fisc '12	♥♥	4
○ Collio Pinot Bianco '13	♥♥	3
○ Collio Pinot Grigio '13	♥♥	3
○ Oblin Blanc '11	♥♥	5

Primosic

FRAZ. OSLAVIA
LOC. MADONNINA DI OSLAVIA, 3
34070 GORIZIA
TEL. 0481535153
www.primosic.com

CELLAR SALES
PRE-BOOKED VISITS
ANNUAL PRODUCTION 200,000 bottles
HECTARES UNDER VINE 30.00

The Oslavia hill, a stronghold of Collio on the border with Slovenia, enjoys a unique and particularly suitable microclimate for winegrowing. The Primosic family settled there in the late 19th century and now Marko and Boris run the estate founded by their father Silvestro in 1956. An extensive zoning project for recognition of the crus has effectively made it possible to identify the best zones for each grape variety and the names of the wines often include the vineyard of origin. Ancient techniques are adopted such as maceration, even of white grapes, to produce riservas that inspire the emotions of times past, even years later. And the Ribolla Gialla di Oslavia Riserva 2011 is the one to sweep away the competition with Tre Bicchieri. Aromas of orange zest, golden tobacco, rum, and apricot tart, and a very dry, warm, mouthfilling palate. All the other wines are beautifully made including the standard label versions.

○ Collio Ribolla Gialla di Oslavia Ris. '11	♒♒♒	5
○ Collio Bianco Klin Ris. '10	♒♒	5
○ Collio Friulano Belvedere '14	♒♒	3
● Collio Merlot Murno '11	♒♒	3
○ Collio Sauvignon Gmajne '14	♒♒	4
○ Collio Pinot Grigio Murno '14	♒	3
○ Ribolla Gialla '14	♒	3
○ Collio Chardonnay Gmajne '11	♈♈♈	4*
○ Collio Bianco Klin Platinum '09	♈♈	5
○ Collio Pinot Grigio Murno '13	♈♈	3
○ Collio Sauvignon Gmajne '12	♈♈	4
○ Pinot Grigio '12	♈♈	2*
○ Ribolla Gialla '13	♈♈	3

★Doro Princic

LOC. PRADIS, 5
34071 CORMÒNS [GO]
TEL. 048160723
doroprincic@virgilio.it

CELLAR SALES
PRE-BOOKED VISITS
ANNUAL PRODUCTION 60,000 bottles
HECTARES UNDER VINE 10.00

Everyone in the Gorizia Collio zone remembers Doro Princic as an emblematic and charismatic figure to turn to in times of trouble. Now, the estate he set up at Pradis in 1950 is run by Alessandro and wife Mariagrazia. This dyed-in-the-wool vigneron has upgraded the estate further with the help of young winemaker Carlo, who works alongside Alessandro both in the vineyards and the cellar. The wines stand out for the imprinting of territorial features in every variety. Practices exclude blending, forcing or manipulative methods. Instead they aim to obtain the best from each grape variety, by extracting what nature created, and they succeed. The Pinot Bianco 2014 made it to our finals, meeting the standard of the wines that received our highest accolade a few years ago. However, it was the Malvasia 2014 that received Tre Bicchieri, for the seventh year running, thanks to its complex aromas and faithful representation of the variety.

○ Collio Malvasia '14	♒♒♒	5
○ Collio Pinot Bianco '14	♒♒	5
○ Collio Friulano '14	♒♒	5
○ Collio Pinot Grigio '14	♒♒	5
○ Collio Ribolla Gialla '14	♒♒	5
○ Collio Sauvignon '14	♒	5
○ Collio Malvasia '13	♈♈♈	5
○ Collio Malvasia '12	♈♈♈	5
○ Collio Friulano '13	♈♈	5
○ Collio Pinot Bianco '13	♈♈	5
○ Collio Pinot Bianco '12	♈♈	5
○ Collio Pinot Bianco '11	♈♈	5

Puiatti - Tenimenti Angelini

LOC. ZUCCOLE, 4
34076 ROMANS D'ISONZO [GO]
TEL. 0481909608
www.puiatti.com

CELLAR SALES
PRE-BOOKED VISITS
ANNUAL PRODUCTION 400,000 bottles
HECTARES UNDER VINE 50.00
SUSTAINABLE WINERY

Vittorio Puiatti has written many pages of
the recent history of regional winegrowing.
In 1967 he established the winery as a
pioneer of technology largely unknown at
that time. As a staunch avoider of oak, he
has imprinted his wines with an
unmistakeable style that respects the
original and natural features of every
individual variety, with a limited alcohol
content to make them more drinkable. This
philosophy has not altered with the recent
change in ownership. Since the estate
became part of Tenimenti Angelini, special
attention has been focused on native local
varieties, especially ribolla gialla produced
using innovative techniques. Just like the
last edition of the Guide, the Archetipi was
considered the best wine overall. A nicely
measured brew of whole grapes makes it
generous and creamy with hints of yellow
peaches and apricots. The Ribolla Gialla
Lus 2014 is fresher, supple and coherent,
like the rest of the wines.

★Dario Raccaro

FRAZ. RÒLAT
VIA SAN GIOVANNI, 87
34071 CORMÒNS [GO]
TEL. 048161425
az.agr.raccaro@alice.it

CELLAR SALES
PRE-BOOKED VISITS
ANNUAL PRODUCTION 30,000 bottles
HECTARES UNDER VINE 6.00

This small estate dates back to 1928 but
Dario Raccaro only decided to focus on
winegrowing in the 1980s. As well as the
estate's own vineyards, which surround the
winery on the slopes of Mount Quarin in the
heart of Collio, he managed to rent an old
vineyard planted with tocai friulano: Vigna
del Rolàt. This longstanding vineyard was
planted in the early 20th century and later
replanted using the scions of the original
vines. This perfectly acclimatized vineyard
yields a wine that is unanimously
acknowledged to be one of the best. And
once again this year the Friulano Vigna del
Rolat 2014 takes the leading role in our
finals, coming close to the highest
accolade. Very generous aromas with hints
of apple and pear fruit and dried medicinal
herbs; soft and symmetrical on the palate
perfectly balanced by fragrant freshness.

○ Friuli Isonzo Friulano Vuj '14	▼▼ 3
○ Ribolla Gialla Archetipi '13	▼▼ 5
○ Ribolla Gialla Lus '14	▼▼ 3
○ Sauvignon Fun '14	▼ 3
○ Blanc de Blancs Extra Brut	♀♀ 3
○ Collio Chardonnay Archetipi '04	♀♀ 4
● Collio Pinot Nero Ruttars '08	♀♀ 3
○ Collio Ribolla Gialla '08	♀♀ 3
○ Friuli Isonzo Friulano Vuj '13	♀♀ 3
○ Friuli Isonzo Ribolla Gialla Archetipi '12	♀♀ 3
○ Friuli Isonzo Ribolla Gialla Lus '13	♀♀ 4
○ Oltre il Metodo Extra Brut '06	♀♀ 5
⊙ Rosé de Noir Extra Brut	♀♀ 5

○ Collio Friulano V. del Rolat '14	▼▼ 4
○ Collio Bianco '14	▼▼ 4
○ Collio Malvasia '14	▼▼ 5
● Collio Merlot '13	▼ 5
○ Collio Bianco '03	♀♀♀ 3
○ Collio Friulano V. del Rolat '09	♀♀♀ 4
○ Collio Friulano V. del Rolat '08	♀♀♀ 4
○ Collio Friulano V. del Rolat '07	♀♀♀ 4
○ Collio Malvasia '12	♀♀♀ 5
○ Collio Malvasia '11	♀♀♀ 4*
○ Collio Tocai Friulano '05	♀♀♀ 4
○ Collio Tocai Friulano V. del Rolat '06	♀♀♀ 4
○ Collio Friulano V. del Rolat '13	♀♀ 4
● Collio Merlot '08	♀♀ 5

La Rajade

LOC. PETRUS, 2
34070 DOLEGNA DEL COLLIO [GO]
TEL. 0481639273
www.larajade.it

CELLAR SALES
PRE-BOOKED VISITS
ANNUAL PRODUCTION 50,000 bottles
HECTARES UNDER VINE 6.50

In local dialect La Rajade means a ray of sunshine. The estate is situated on the eastern foothills of Friuli, in the River Judrior valley, along the Slovenian border, the northernmost part of Collio where nature has the upper hand and dictates the rhythm of time. The owner is Sergio Campeotto but Diego Zanin manages the estate: despite his youth he can boast significant winemaking experience and is supported in his decisions by consultant Andrea Romano Rossi. The unusual microclimate of this valley and the contours of the hills create the conditions for good temperature variation, in turn ideal for moulding the aromas that characterize the wines. Unanimous approval for the whole range, especially the more mature, defined reds. The Cabernet Sauvignon 2012, in particular, deserved its place in the finals for its pleasant aromas with hints of morello cherries, dark spice, cocoa powder and damp earth. The palate is confident, mouthfilling and flavoursome.

● Collio Cabernet Sauvignon Ris. '12	♟♟ 4
○ Collio Bianco '14	♟♟ 3
● Collio Merlot Ris. '12	♟♟ 4
○ Collio Pinot Grigio '14	♟♟ 3
○ Collio Ribolla Gialla '14	♟♟ 3
○ Collio Sauvignon '14	♟♟ 3
○ Collio Friulano '14	♟ 3
○ Collio Bianco '13	♟♟ 3
● Collio Cabernet Sauvignon Ris. '11	♟♟ 4
● Collio Cabernet Sauvignon Ris. '08	♟♟ 4
● Collio Merlot Ris. '11	♟♟ 4
● Collio Merlot Ris. '09	♟♟ 4
○ Collio Pinot Grigio '13	♟♟ 3
○ Collio Sauvignon '09	♟♟ 3*
○ Collio Sauvignon '08	♟♟ 3*

Rocca Bernarda

FRAZ. IPPLIS
VIA ROCCA BERNARDA, 27
33040 PREMARIACCO [UD]
TEL. 0432716914
www.sagrivit.it

CELLAR SALES
PRE-BOOKED VISITS
ANNUAL PRODUCTION 190,000 bottles
HECTARES UNDER VINE 36.00

Rocca Bernarda is situated on the hillside of the same name, overlooked by a magnificent building with four round corner towers. It may look like a castle but was actually a noble country residence built by the Conti Valvason Maniago family back in 1567. A plaque in the old walls shows that the cellars were built before the villa. The winemaking tradition has been maintained over the centuries especially thanks to the Conti Perusini who donated the property to the Sovereign Military Order of Malta in 1977. Since 2006 the estate has been managed by the Società Agricola Vitivinicola Italiana, who have entrusted Maurilio Chioccia with winemaking. This year we were not offered whites from the last vintage, so our favourite was the Merlot Centis 2009: pleasantly mature on the nose with aromas of tobacco, coffee and cocoa powder, and a well-structured, mouthfilling, flavoursome palate. The Bianco Novecento 1113–2013 is also excellent, fragrant and dynamic.

● COF Merlot Centis '09	♟♟ 4
● COF Refosco P. R. '13	♟♟ 3
○ Novecento 1113-2013 '13	♟♟ 3
● COF Cabernet Franc '13	♟ 3
● COF Merlot Centis '99	♟♟♟ 7
○ COF Picolit '03	♟♟♟ 7
○ COF Picolit '98	♟♟♟ 7
○ COF Picolit '97	♟♟♟ 7
○ COF Friulano '08	♟♟ 3*
○ COF Friulano '07	♟♟ 3
○ COF Picolit '05	♟♟ 7
● COF Pignolo '07	♟♟ 5
● COF Pignolo '06	♟♟ 5
○ COF Pinot Grigio '06	♟♟ 3
○ COF Tocai Friulano '06	♟♟ 3

Paolo Rodaro

LOC. SPESSA
VIA CORMONS, 60
33043 CIVIDALE DEL FRIULI [UD]
TEL. 0432716066
www.rodaropaolo.it

CELLAR SALES
PRE-BOOKED VISITS
ANNUAL PRODUCTION 200,000 bottles
HECTARES UNDER VINE 50.00
SUSTAINABLE WINERY

This is a long-established regional
winegrowing estate and manager Paolo
Rodaro shares his name with its founder.
Credit goes to the last three generations for
transforming a small country inn into a
highly prestigious and precious business,
culminating with the purchase of the
marvellous Conte Romano estate and
quality vineyards which yield the grapes for
winery's flagship Romain line. Paolo likes to
call himself a farmer, in the noblest sense
of the word, rather than a winegrower, and
is proud to be a descendent of a family that
has always practiced this profession with
dignity, simplicity and discretion. The whole
range of wines tasted obtained very high
scores, especially the Schioppettino
Romain 2010: hints of tobacco and nutmeg
on the nose, and a sweet caress of tannin
on the palate. A special mention goes to
the sparkling Rosé Pas Dosé 2011, made
from pinot noir grapes.

● COF Refosco P. R. Romain '08	♥♥ 6
● COF Schioppettino Romain '10	♥♥ 5
○ COF Verduzzo Friulano Pra Zenâr '12	♥♥ 5
○ FCO Ribolla Gialla '14	♥♥ 3
⊙ Rosé Pas Dosé M.Cl. '11	♥♥ 5
● COF Pignolo Romain '06	♥ 6
● COF Refosco P. R. Romain '03	♥♥♥ 6
○ COF Sauvignon Bosc Romain '96	♥♥♥ 4*
○ Ronc '00	♥♥♥ 3
● COF Merlot Romain '09	♥♥ 5
○ COF Picolit '08	♥♥ 6
● COF Schioppettino Romain '08	♥♥ 4
○ COF Verduzzo Passito Pra Zenâr '09	♥♥ 5
○ COF Verduzzo Passito Pra Zenâr '07	♥♥ 5

Ronc di Vico

FRAZ. BELLAZOIA
VIA CENTRALE, 5
33040 POVOLETTO [UD]
TEL. 3208822002
roncdivicobellazoia@libero.it

CELLAR SALES
PRE-BOOKED VISITS
ANNUAL PRODUCTION 12,000 bottles
HECTARES UNDER VINE 7.00

The Ronc di Vico headquarters is at
Bellazoia in the municipality of Povoletto,
near Udine. Back in 2004 Gianni del
Fabbro, then involved in a completely
different business, found himself with a few
hectares of vineyards to manage on the
Faedis hills, inherited from his father. After
seeking advice from a professional
vigneron friend he decided to undertake a
programme of reconversion of the
vineyards, and rented some others,
knowing that he would be helped by his
young son Lodovico, named after his
grandfather and to whom the brand is
dedicated. The decision to focus on just a
few vineyards has proved to be the right
one. Only a few wines but all very
prestigious. Both the Vicorosso 2012 and
the Titut Ros 2012 are made from merlot
grapes, and both earned the unanimous
approval of the tasting panel for their
complex aromas, with spicy, balsamic hints,
and above all, for their well-structured,
pleasing palate.

● FCO Titut Ros '12	♥♥ 6
● FCO Vicorosso '12	♥♥ 4
○ FCO Sauvignon '13	♥ 4
○ COF Il Friulano '09	♥♥♥ 4
○ COF Il Friulano '08	♥♥♥ 4*
○ COF Il Friulano '12	♥♥ 4
○ COF Il Friulano '10	♥♥ 4
○ COF Picolit '11	♥♥ 7
● COF Refosco P. R. '07	♥♥ 6
○ COF Sauvignon '12	♥♥ 4
● COF Titut Ros '07	♥♥ 5
● COF Vicorosso '11	♥♥ 4
● COF Vicorosso '09	♥♥ 4

Ronc Soreli

LOC. NOVACUZZO, 46
33040 PREPOTTO [UD]
TEL. 0432713005
www.roncsoreli.com

CELLAR SALES
ANNUAL PRODUCTION 100,000 bottles
HECTARES UNDER VINE 42.00

At the turn of this century Flavio Schiratti took over an estate, already active for some time, in the old village of Borgo di Novacuzzo, near Prepotto. His choice of name was inspired by the shape of the hillside on which his vineyards are planted, constantly exposed to the sun. Aided by the oenological experience of Emilio Del Medico, the estate was soon established among the best in the region. The vineyards skirt the Bosco Romagno nature reserve down as far as the right bank of the River Judrio, a natural border with Collio. The estate has embraced an environmental sustainability project to safeguard the whole production area. This year the Friulano Vigna delle Robinie 2013 stood out in the finals and came very close to our highest accolade, which it had won with the 2011 vintage, proving to be the estate flagship. Vibrant, complex aromas with nicely forward hints of fruit, and a fragrant, pleasing palate.

La Roncaia

FRAZ. CERGNEU
VIA VERDI, 26
33045 NIMIS [UD]
TEL. 0432790280
www.fantinel.com

CELLAR SALES
PRE-BOOKED VISITS
ANNUAL PRODUCTION 50,000 bottles
HECTARES UNDER VINE 22.00

La Roncaia was established in 1998 when the Fantinel group, winegrowers for three generations, decided to expand their property in the region, including Tenuta Sant'Helena in Collio and Borgo Tesis in Grave del Friuli, by adding an already consolidated winery at Cergneu, near Nimis in the extreme north of the Colli Orientali del Friuli, the birthplace of Ramandolo. This was the missing link that enabled the winery to fulfil its objective to provide the best possible representation of the features of every single DOC zone, with a range of interesting products able to satisfy every type of market demand. The wines tasted this year are all of a very high standard. The Friulano 2013 has vibrant aromas of tinned peaches and caramel, while balance is maintained on the creamy palate by the significant acidity. The Merlot 2012 reveals complex aromas and a well-structured, confident, taut and dynamic palate.

○ FCo Friulano V. delle Robinie '13	♥♥ 3*
○ FCO Pinot Grigio V. dei Melograni '13	♥♥ 3
○ FCO Ribolla Gialla V. dei Nespoli '13	♥♥ 3
○ FCO Sauvignon V. dei Peschi '13	♥♥ 3
● FCO Ribolla Nera V. delle Marasche '12	♥ 3
○ COF Friulano V. delle Robinie '11	♥♥♥ 3*
○ COF Friulano '09	♀♀ 3*
○ COF Friulano Otto Lustri '09	♀♀ 3*
○ COF Friulano V. delle Robinie '12	♀♀ 3
○ COF Picolit '08	♀♀ 5
○ COF Pinot Grigio '09	♀♀ 3*
● COF Schioppettino di Prepotto Ris. '09	♀♀ 5
● COF Schioppettino di Prepotto Ris. '08	♀♀ 5

○ FCO Friulano '13	♥♥ 4
● FCO Merlot '12	♥♥ 5
○ FCO Picolit '11	♥♥ 5
○ Ramandolo '11	♥♥ 5
○ Eclisse '12	♀♀♀ 4*
○ COF Bianco Eclisse '13	♀♀ 4
○ COF Friulano '12	♀♀ 4
○ COF Friulano '10	♀♀ 3*
● COF Refosco P.R. '07	♀♀ 5
○ Eclisse '10	♀♀ 4
○ Eclisse '09	♀♀ 4
○ Ramandolo '10	♀♀ 5
○ Ramandolo '08	♀♀ 5

Il Roncal

FRAZ. COLLE MONTEBELLO
VIA FORNALIS, 148
33043 CIVIDALE DEL FRIULI [UD]
TEL. 0432730138
www.ilroncal.it

CELLAR SALES
PRE-BOOKED VISITS
ACCOMMODATION AND RESTAURANT SERVICE
ANNUAL PRODUCTION 130,000 bottles
HECTARES UNDER VINE 20.00

Roncal was opened in 1986 by Roberto Zorzettig, who started a project to create a model estate where technology and tradition could coexist smoothly. He then decided to renew and improve the vineyards on the Montebello hills in the heart of Colli Orientali del Friuli, designed the new cellar himself, attentive to every detail, and began construction. After his untimely passing in 2006, his wife Martina Moreale completed the work. A woman of considerable personality and unquestionable business skills, Martina succeeded in this task and her wines immediately stood out for their frank, typical character and specific territorial features. A wonderful Sauvignon 2014 dominates the rest of the range and earns a place in the final selections. Very sophisticated, clean, with sunny aromas but the palate is where all its most pleasing qualities emerge: symmetrical, soft, creamy, yet fresh, fragrant and perfectly balanced.

○ FCO Sauvignon '14	♥♥ 3*
○ FCO Bianco Ploe di Stelis '13	♥♥ 4
● FCO Pignolo '09	♥♥ 5
○ FCO Ribolla Gialla '14	♥♥ 3
● FCO Schioppettino '12	♥♥ 4
● FCO Rosso Civon '10	♥ 5
○ COF Bianco Ploe di Stelis '11	♥♥ 4
● COF Merlot '10	♥♥ 3
● COF Pignolo '08	♥♥ 5
○ COF Pinot Grigio '12	♥♥ 3
● COF Refosco P.R. '11	♥♥ 4
○ COF Sauvignon '12	♥♥ 3

Il Roncat - Giovanni Dri

LOC. RAMANDOLO
VIA PESCIA, 7
33045 NIMIS [UD]
TEL. 0432790260
www.drironcat.com

CELLAR SALES
PRE-BOOKED VISITS
ANNUAL PRODUCTION 40,000 bottles
HECTARES UNDER VINE 10.00

Giovanni Dri is a byword for Ramandolo. He may not have invented it but he has certainly had a hand in making it famous. He proudly defines himself as a rocky character, born in Ramandolo among the rocks, below Mount Bernadia. Here he built the cellar he had designed, bringing a longstanding dream to fruition, naming it La Capanna, "the shed", because it is a simple, though spacious, structure, welcoming and functional, made from vintage natural materials. His ongoing pursuit of new stimuli includes producing grappa, naturally using his own marc. His daughter Stefania, an oenological science graduate, is in charge of vinification. And once again, this year, the Schioppettino Monte dei Carpini 2011 earns its place in the finals thanks to excellent and consistent quality. Cherries, flowering hay, cocoa powder and spices on the nose with a dry, deep palate. Acidic backbone and vibrant tannins liven up the flavour.

● COF Schioppettino Monte dei Carpini '11	♥♥ 4
● COF Merlot '11	♥♥ 3
● COF Refosco P.R. '11	♥♥ 3
○ Picolit Il Roncat '11	♥♥ 7
○ Ramandolo Uve Decembrine '10	♥♥ 5
● COF Rosso Il Roncat '08	♥ 4
○ Ramandolo '11	♥ 4
● COF Cabernet '11	♥♥ 3
○ COF Picolit '10	♥♥ 7
○ COF Picolit '08	♥♥ 7
● COF Refosco P.R. '10	♥♥ 3
● COF Schioppettino Monte dei Carpini '10	♥♥ 4
○ Ramandolo '09	♥♥ 5
○ Ramandolo Uve Decembrine '09	♥♥ 6

Ronchi di Cialla

FRAZ. CIALLA
VIA CIALLA, 47
33040 PREPOTTO [UD]
TEL. 0432731679
www.ronchidicialla.it

CELLAR SALES
PRE-BOOKED VISITS
ANNUAL PRODUCTION 100,000 bottles
HECTARES UNDER VINE 26.00

When we present Ronchi di Cialla we
always refer to the passion that drove Paolo
and Dina Rapuzzi to abandon their existing
profession back in 1970 and begin a new
adventure at Cialla. Having fallen in love
with this little valley surrounded by woods
of chestnut, oak and wild cherry, they
renovated an old farmhouse and began a
family-run estate aiming to promote native
Friuli varieties, and to this end they
managed to get Cialla officially recognized
as a subzone, particularly well-suited to
winegrowing. Now Pierpaolo and Ivan
continue the path marked out by their
father with his same passion and
determination. The estate chooses to
release the Schioppettino di Cialla five
years after the harvest, so we tasted the
2011. Captivating spices, hints of bottled
cherries and liquorice root on the nose, and
a coherent, salty palate.

Ronchi di Manzano

VIA ORSARIA, 42
33044 MANZANO [UD]
TEL. 0432740718
www.ronchidimanzano.com

CELLAR SALES
PRE-BOOKED VISITS
ANNUAL PRODUCTION 200,000 bottles
HECTARES UNDER VINE 60.00

Thanks to Roberta Borghese, Ronchi di
Manzano is now one of the most
representative estates for the potential of
the Friuli Colli Orientali DOC to produce
quality wines. Roberta is an active doyenne
of the wine community, an entrepreneur
with the heart of an artisan and an innate
touch of elegance. She supervises the
whole production process from the vineyard
to the cellar, assisted by her daughters Lisa
and Nicole. The 60-odd hectares of
vineyards are divided into several production
areas: Ronc di Scossai and Roc di Subule
surround the cellar at Manzano while Ronc
di Rosazzo is further east in the subzone
where the white grapes have long been the
pride of the DOCG. And indeed, the Rosazzo
Bianco 2013 was awarded our Tre Bicchieri.
Along with the Bianco Ellegri 2014, it went
to the finals and stood out by a head over
the standard label blend. A generous,
complex nose with harmonious aromas is
reflected on the palate in perfectly blended
aromas and flavours.

● FCO Schioppettino di Cialla '11	♟♟ 6
○ FCO Ribolla Gialla '14	♟♟ 3
● COF Schioppettino di Cialla '05	♟♟♟ 6
○ COF Picolit di Cialla '07	♟♟ 6
○ COF Picolit di Cialla '06	♟♟ 8
● COF Refosco P.R. di Cialla '06	♟♟ 6
● COF Schioppettino di Cialla '10	♟♟ 6
● COF Schioppettino di Cialla '08	♟♟ 6
● COF Schioppettino di Cialla '07	♟♟ 6
● COF Schioppettino di Cialla '06	♟♟ 6

○ Rosazzo Bianco '13	♟♟♟ 3*
○ FCO Bianco Ellégri '14	♟♟ 3*
● FCO Cabernet Franc '12	♟♟ 3
● FCO Merlot '12	♟♟ 3
● FCO Rosazzo Rosso Braûros '11	♟♟ 3
○ FCO Sauvignon '14	♟♟ 3
○ FCO Friulano '14	♟ 3
○ FCO Picolit '13	♟ 5
○ COF Ellegri '13	♟♟♟ 3*
○ COF Friulano '10	♟♟♟ 3
○ COF Friulano '09	♟♟♟ 3*
● COF Merlot Ronc di Subule '99	♟♟♟ 3*
● COF Merlot Ronc di Subule '96	♟♟♟ 3*
○ COF Rosazzo Bianco Ellégri '11	♟♟♟ 3*

Ronchi San Giuseppe

VIA STRADA DI SPESSA, 8
33043 CIVIDALE DEL FRIULI [UD]
TEL. 0432716172
www.ronchisangiuseppe.com

PRE-BOOKED VISITS
ANNUAL PRODUCTION 300,000 bottles
HECTARES UNDER VINE 70.00
SUSTAINABLE WINERY

Zorzettig has always been synonymous with quality winegrowing in the region. Pietro was the founding father of this and many other estates across the Colli Orientali del Friuli. The mother winery at Spessa di Cividale is called Ronchi San Giuseppe, after the little white church built in 1522, which overlooks the estate's vineyards from a hill. The winery is managed today by Franco Zorzettig and his son Fulvio, in a perfect blend of tradition and innovation, and they have skilfully guided it to the heights of regional excellence with the simplicity and authenticity endowed by the pace and variations of nature, always avoiding excess. This year, too, the tasting confirmed the high standard achieved with wines that respect the features of the grape: sometimes accessible but always coherent and flavoursome, and very drinkable, as the current market demands. Not to be underestimated, the very reasonable price.

○ FCO Friulano '14	▼▼ 2*
○ FCO Pinot Grigio '14	▼▼ 2*
● FCO Refosco P. R. '13	▼▼ 2*
○ FCO Sauvignon '14	▼▼ 2*
● FCO Schioppettino '13	▼▼ 2*
● FCO Pinot Nero '14	▼ 2
○ FCO Ribolla Gialla '14	▼ 2
○ COF Friulano '13	▼▼ 2*
○ COF Friulano '12	▼▼ 2*
○ COF Pinot Grigio '13	▼▼ 2*
○ COF Pinot Grigio '12	▼▼ 2*
○ COF Sauvignon '13	▼▼ 2*
● COF Schioppettino '12	▼▼ 2*

Ronco Blanchis

VIA BLANCHIS, 70
34070 MOSSA [GO]
TEL. 048180519
www.roncoblanchis.it

PRE-BOOKED VISITS
ANNUAL PRODUCTION 35,000 bottles
HECTARES UNDER VINE 12.00
SUSTAINABLE WINERY

On the sunny slopes of the Blanchis hill, a backdrop to the rural hamlet of Mossa, close to Gorizia, Giancarlo Palla and his sons Alberto and Lorenzo produce prestigious white wines assisted by consultant oenologist Gianni Menotti. The marly, clayey Collio hillsides, sheltered by the Alpi Giulie and refreshed by the cool breeze from the nearby Adriatic sea, are the secret ingredient in the unmistakeable character of these wines. In the valley bottom, morning mists encourage Botrytis cinerea, which whitens the grapes in the natural phenomenon that gave its name to the hill and in certain years endows the wines with prestigious aromas. Due to the unusual weather during the last vintage year some wines had to be excluded from the range but the few labels produced lived up to previous years. The Friulano 2014 made it to the finals: delightful fruity and tropical aromas with a sophisticated, pleasing palate.

○ Collio Friulano '14	▼▼ 3*
○ Collio Blanc de Blanchis '14	▼▼ 3
○ Collio Pinot Grigio '14	▼▼ 3
○ Collio '13	▼▼▼ 3*
○ Collio '12	▼▼▼ 3*
○ Collio '10	▼▼ 3
○ Collio Friulano '11	▼▼ 3*
○ Collio Friulano '09	▼▼ 3
○ Collio Pinot Grigio '11	▼▼ 3*
○ Collio Sauvignon '12	▼▼ 3*

★Ronco dei Tassi

LOC. MONTONA, 19
34071 CORMÒNS [GO]
TEL. 048160155
www.roncodeitassi.it

CELLAR SALES
PRE-BOOKED VISITS
ANNUAL PRODUCTION 110,000 bottles
HECTARES UNDER VINE 18.00

In 1989 Fabio Coser and his wife Daniela decided to purchase an estate and set up a winery at Montona, Cormòns, on the slope of Mount Quarin that overlooks Slovenia. Their choice of name was inspired by the colonies of badgers living in the woods surrounding the vineyards, greedy consumers of the sweetest bunches of ripe grapes. Fabio's sons Matteo and Enrico are an integral part of the estate and, as is usual for family businesses, they do a bit of everything. Fabio also owns another estate, Vigna del Lauro, created to offer the market uncomplicated, very drinkable wines with typical features at a reasonable price. We were expecting confirmation and that is what we got. The Malvasia 2014 earns Tre Bicchieri for the fourth year in a row. This is the most highly appreciated wine, while we wait to taste the next version of the Fosarin, and it is an elegant delight for nose and palate.

○ Collio Malvasia '14	♛♛♛ 3*
○ Collio Picolit '11	♛♛ 6
● Collio Rosso Cjarandon Ris. '11	♛♛ 5
○ Collio Sauvignon '14	♛♛ 3
○ Collio Friulano '14	♛ 3
○ Collio Pinot Grigio '14	♛ 3
○ Collio Ribolla Gialla '14	♛ 3
○ Collio Bianco Fosarin '10	♛♛♛ 3
○ Collio Bianco Fosarin '09	♛♛♛ 3*
○ Collio Bianco Fosarin '08	♛♛♛ 3*
○ Collio Malvasia '13	♛♛♛ 3*
○ Collio Malvasia '12	♛♛♛ 3*
○ Collio Malvasia '11	♛♛♛ 3*

★Ronco del Gelso

VIA ISONZO, 117
34071 CORMÒNS [GO]
TEL. 048161310
www.roncodelgelso.com

CELLAR SALES
PRE-BOOKED VISITS
ANNUAL PRODUCTION 150,000 bottles
HECTARES UNDER VINE 25.00

The little town of Cormòns is linked to Collio wines but the area also includes some very high profile estates belonging to the Friuli Isonzo DOC. Ronco del Gelso is undoubtedly one of the noblest of these. Giorgio Badin manages 25 hectares of vineyards covering the plains to the right of the River Isonzo on lean, stony, dry soil, brought by landslides caused by crumbling of the marly and sandstone hills nearby. The area also enjoys a special microclimate, with hot days and cool nights, ideal for the production of well-structured white wines and some weighty, well-typed reds. Unanimous approval for the whole range provides further confirmation of the excellent standard achieved and maintained for many years. The Pinot Bianco 2014, in particular, stood out in the finals for its sophisticated hints of spring flowers and citrus, and gutsy flavour.

○ Friuli Isonzo Pinot Bianco '14	♛♛ 3*
○ Friuli Isonzo Friulano Toc Bas '13	♛♛ 3
○ Friuli Isonzo Malvasia V. della Permuta '14	♛♛ 3
○ Friuli Isonzo Pinot Grigio Sot Lis Rivis '14	♛♛ 3
○ Friuli Isonzo Sauvignon Sottomonte '14	♛♛ 3
○ Friuli Isonzo Chardonnay Siet Vignis '13	♛ 3
⊙ Friuli Isonzo Rosato Rosimi '13	♛ 3
○ Schulz Riesling '13	♛ 4
○ Friuli Isonzo Malvasia '10	♛♛♛ 3*
● Friuli Isonzo Merlot '01	♛♛♛ 4
○ Friuli Isonzo Tocai Friulano '06	♛♛♛ 3*
○ Friuli Isonzo Tocai Friulano '05	♛♛♛ 3
○ Friuli Isonzo Tocai Friulano '04	♛♛♛ 3*
○ Friuli Isonzo Tocai Friulano '03	♛♛♛ 3*
○ Friuli Isonzo Tocai Friulano '01	♛♛♛ 2

Ronco delle Betulle

LOC. ROSAZZO
VIA ABATE COLONNA, 24
33044 MANZANO [UD]
TEL. 0432740547
www.roncodellebetulle.it

CELLAR SALES
PRE-BOOKED VISITS
ANNUAL PRODUCTION 60,000 bottles
HECTARES UNDER VINE 12.00
SUSTAINABLE WINERY

The Ronco delle Betulle estate enjoys a consolidated position at the peak of regional wine production thanks to Ivana Abami's stubbornness and female entrepreneurship. Her father Giovanbattista played a lucky hunch in 1967 on the potential of the Rosazzo hills, where vineyards have always surrounded the famous 11th-century abbey and this has always been a place where vines are protected. In 1990 it was Ivana's turn to take over, embracing a simple philosophy focused on producing high quality wines, and she involved her son Simone who now helps run the estate. Our unanimous approval of all the wines offers recognition of consistent quality, while the fact that the leading wines alternate confirms the attention lavished on each individual variety. This year the leader of the pack is the Cabernet Franc 2011, with incisive hints of liquorice and roasted coffee beans.

Ronco Severo

VIA RONCHI, 93
33040 PREPOTTO [UD]
TEL. 04337133440
www.roncosevero.it

CELLAR SALES
PRE-BOOKED VISITS
ANNUAL PRODUCTION 22,000 bottles
HECTARES UNDER VINE 8.00
VITICULTURE METHOD Certified Organic

In 1968 Severo Novello had the chance to purchase a few hectares of land at Prepotto, in the Colli Orientali del Friuli, and rebuilt a ruined farmhouse, transforming it into a winery and home. The estate named after him is now managed by his son Stefano, a staunch supporter of organic and biodynamic farming. This practice consists mainly of following old vinification methods, without using chemical products, selected yeasts, enzymes or even sulphur dioxide. The must stays on the skins, even for the white wines, for several weeks and sometimes for months. After ageing, the wines are bottled when the moon is waning, without filtering or clarification. The previous edition's Severo Bianco earned the highest accolade and this year the 2013 made it to the finals. Enthralling aromas and a captivating flavour highlight the specific features of the grape varieties used: friulano, chardonnay, sauvignon and picolit.

● FCO Cabernet Franc '11	♼♼ 3*
○ FCO Bianco Vanessa '13	♼♼ 3
○ FCO Friulano '14	♼♼ 3
● FCO Merlot '12	♼♼ 3
● FCO Refosco P. R. '12	♼♼ 3
● Franconia '11	♼♼ 3
○ FCO Pinot Grigio '14	♼ 3
○ FCO Sauvignon '14	♼ 3
● Narciso Rosso '94	♼♼♼ 4*
○ COF Picolit '07	♼♼ 4
○ COF Rosazzo Bianco Vanessa '09	♼♼ 3
○ COF Rosazzo Bianco Vanessa '08	♼♼ 3
● COF Rosazzo Pignolo '05	♼♼ 6
○ Rosazzo Bianco '12	♼♼ 4

○ Severo Bianco '13	♼♼ 4
○ FCO Friulano Ris '13	♼♼ 4
● FCO Merlot Artiûl Ris. '12	♼♼ 5
● FCO Schioppettino di Prepotto '12	♼♼ 4
○ Pinot Grigio '13	♼♼ 4
○ Ribolla Gialla '13	♼♼ 4
○ Severo Bianco '12	♼♼♼ 4*
○ COF Friulano '11	♼♼ 3*
● COF Merlot Artiûl '08	♼♼ 5
● COF Merlot Artiûl Ris. '09	♼♼ 5
○ COF Pinot Grigio '11	♼♼ 4
○ Severo Bianco '09	♼♼ 3*

Roncùs

VIA MAZZINI, 26
34076 CAPRIVA DEL FRIULI [GO]
TEL. 0481809349
www.roncus.it

CELLAR SALES
PRE-BOOKED VISITS
ACCOMMODATION
ANNUAL PRODUCTION 40,000 bottles
HECTARES UNDER VINE 10.00

Roncùs is owned by Marco Perco, a painstaking winegrower who is carrying forward his production philosophy, including concentration of varietal aromas obtained through an extensive period on the fine lees. This means the wines need longer to mature, but in the end they will age well. His very personal, almost Alsatian, style is suited to the potential of Collio. The vineyards are scattered over many different plots on the terraced hillsides of Capriva del Friuli, in the heart of Collio, many of which are over 50 years old. The old vines are a real heritage, producing just a few bunches of excellent quality. All the positive comments about the wines tasted remarked on their pleasing, complex and original aromas and the follow-through on the very clean palates. The Friulano 2013 stood out in particular for its generous aromas, mouthfilling flavour and typical hints of fresh almonds in the finish.

○ Collio Friulano '13	🍷🍷	4
○ Pinot Bianco '13	🍷🍷	4
○ Ribolla Gialla '14	🍷🍷	3
● Val di Miez '12	🍷🍷	5
○ Collio Bianco '13	🍷	3
○ Roncùs Bianco V. V. '01	🍷🍷🍷	5
○ Collio Bianco V. V. '10	🍷🍷	5
○ Collio Bianco V. V. '09	🍷🍷	5
○ Collio Bianco V. V. '08	🍷🍷	5
○ Collio Friulano '10	🍷🍷	4
○ Pinot Bianco '12	🍷🍷	4
● Val di Miez '06	🍷🍷	5

★Russiz Superiore

VIA RUSSIZ, 7
34070 CAPRIVA DEL FRIULI [GO]
TEL. 048180328
www.marcofelluga.it

CELLAR SALES
PRE-BOOKED VISITS
ACCOMMODATION
ANNUAL PRODUCTION 180,000 bottles
HECTARES UNDER VINE 50.00
SUSTAINABLE WINERY

On the Capriva del Friuli hills in the heart of Collio, the village of Russiz Superiore lent its name to the estate established in 1966 by Marco Felluga. Generally considered to be a pioneer in the winegrowing sector, he has proved to be an innovator par excellence with an innate skill for looking ahead that has enabled him to make the very best of the area's potential, creating a brand that guarantees absolute quality throughout the range of wines. This has always been a model farm, the pride of Friuli winemaking, scaling the heights of regional excellence. Today it is run by Marco's son Roberto with entrepreneurial skill and passion inherited from his father. The indisputably sound quality of the whole range is always represented in the finals by one or two wines. This time the Sauvignon Riserva 2011 rewarded Roberto's project to offer the markets mature white wines, while the Friulano 2014, with generous aromas and a satisfying palate, obtained a well-deserved Tre Bicchieri.

○ Collio Friulano '14	🍷🍷🍷	4*
○ Collio Sauvignon Ris. '11	🍷🍷	5
○ Collio Bianco Col Disôre '12	🍷🍷	5
● Collio Cabernet Franc '12	🍷🍷	4
○ Collio Pinot Bianco '14	🍷🍷	4
○ Collio Pinot Grigio '14	🍷🍷	4
○ Collio Sauvignon '14	🍷🍷	4
○ Verduzzo Friulano '14	🍷🍷	4
○ Collio Bianco Russiz Disôre '01	🍷🍷🍷	4
○ Collio Bianco Russiz Disôre '00	🍷🍷🍷	4
○ Collio Pinot Bianco '07	🍷🍷🍷	4
○ Collio Pinot Grigio '11	🍷🍷🍷	4*
○ Collio Sauvignon '05	🍷🍷🍷	3
○ Collio Sauvignon '04	🍷🍷🍷	5
○ Collio Sauvignon '98	🍷🍷🍷	4*
○ Collio Tocai Friulano '99	🍷🍷🍷	3*

FRIULI VENEZIA GIULIA

Sant'Elena

VIA GASPARINI, 1
34072 GRADISCA D'ISONZO [GO]
TEL. 048192388
www.sant-elena.com

CELLAR SALES
PRE-BOOKED VISITS
ANNUAL PRODUCTION 130,000 bottles
HECTARES UNDER VINE 30.00

The Sant'Elena estate was created in the 19th century by the Klodic family and purchased in 1997 by Dominic Nocerino, a well-known importer of Italian wines to the US, with a strong belief in the potential of the Isonzo DOC zone. This notoriously flat area, consists of a superficial layer of red soil rich in iron oxide, of alluvial origin, resting on land poor in limestone and organic content. Aware that very high quality grapes could be obtained here, rich in aromas and minerals, able to endow the wines with unique and inimitable features, Dominic built a cellar immediately and entrusted the winemaking practices to the experienced Maurizio Drascek. This year only red wines from 2011 were presented for tasting and they are all richly extracted, backed up by acidity with vibrant tannins. The Pignolo Quantum 2011 is particularly well-structured with fragrant aromas of morello cherries and liquorice.

Marco Sara

VIA DEI MONTI, 3A
33040 POVOLETTO [UD]
TEL. 0432666066
www.marcosara.com

CELLAR SALES
PRE-BOOKED VISITS
ANNUAL PRODUCTION 18,000 bottles
HECTARES UNDER VINE 8.00
VITICULTURE METHOD Certified Organic

Along with his wife Sandra, Marco Sara has run this new jewel in the regional winemaking crown since 2000. The winery is situated at Savorgnano del Torre in the westernmost and coolest part of the Colli Orientali del Friuli. The estate's vineyards consist of about ten small plots in various areas, which permit a richer range of expression and strongly territorial features. Since 2005 the vineyard and cellar practices have been entirely organic, with certification arriving in 2011. An old cabernet franc vineyard has been preserved but all the other grapes grown on the estate are local native varieties. We tasted the whole range of wines from the 2013 vintage, one after the other, in an extraordinary performance. With great satisfaction we welcomed the Picolit 2103 into the finals: hints of apricots, crème brûlée and strawberry-tree honey on the nose, opening out on the palate with unforgettably sweet sensations.

● Cabernet Franc '11	♟♟ 3	
● Friuli Isonzo Pignolo Quantum '11	♟♟ 7	
● Merlot '11	♟♟ 4	
● Cabernet Sauvignon '11	♟ 4	
● Friuli Isonzo Pignolo Quantum '10	♟♟ 7	
● Friuli Isonzo Pignolo Quantum '09	♟♟ 7	
○ Friuli Isonzo Pinot Grigio Rive Alte '13	♟♟ 3	
○ Friuli Isonzo Sauvignon Blanc Rive Alte '13	♟♟ 4	
● Merlot '10	♟♟ 4	
● Merlot '09	♟♟ 3	
● Merlot Ròs di Rôl '10	♟♟ 5	
● Merlot Ròs di Rôl '09	♟♟ 6	
○ Sauvignon '12	♟♟ 3	
● Tato '10	♟♟ 5	
● Tato '09	♟♟ 5	

○ COF Picolit '13	♟♟ 5	
● COF Cabernet Franc Frank '13	♟♟ 3	
○ COF Erba Alta '13	♟♟ 4	
○ COF Friulano '13	♟♟ 2*	
● COF Refosco P. R. El Re '13	♟♟ 3	
● COF Schioppettino '13	♟♟ 3	
○ COF Bianco '12	♟♟ 3	
● COF Cabernet Franc '12	♟♟ 3	
● COF Schioppettino '12	♟♟ 3*	
○ Picolit un Picolit dal Dòdis '12	♟♟ 5	

Sara & Sara

LOC. SAVORGNANO DEL TORRE
VIA DEI MONTI, 5
33040 POVOLETTO [UD]
TEL. 04323859042
www.saraesara.com

CELLAR SALES
PRE-BOOKED VISITS
ANNUAL PRODUCTION 25,000 bottles
HECTARES UNDER VINE 7.50

Sara is the surname of brothers Alessandro and Manuele who, along with their mother Oriana, manage this little estate at Savorgnano del Torre in the extreme west of the Colli Orientali del Friuli DOC. The area is rich in rivers, evergreen woods, and hills with marly and clayey sandstone soil. The cold north wines guarantee significant night–day temperature variation which establishes the aromas. The drying verduzzo and picolit grapes enjoy an unusual local microclimate which facilitates the natural formation of botrytis on the bunches. The brothers apply ancient techniques and the wines are never filtered, to preserve the integrity of their features. In the last edition of the Guide we mentioned that late bottling prevented us from tasting the Verduzzo Friulano Crei 2012. This year, this was the only wine presented. It is a delight. Aromas of honey, dried figs, orange zest and liquorice, and memorable sweetness caressing the palate.

★★Schiopetto

VIA PALAZZO ARCIVESCOVILE, 1
34070 CAPRIVA DEL FRIULI [GO]
TEL. 048180332
www.schiopetto.it

CELLAR SALES
PRE-BOOKED VISITS
ANNUAL PRODUCTION 165,000 bottles
HECTARES UNDER VINE 30.00
SUSTAINABLE WINERY

Back in 1965 Mario Schiopetto bottled his first monovarietal Tocai Friulano. Since then, nothing has been the same. The true founding father of Friuli white winemaking and more, he is a communicator, innovator, visionary: in a word, the leader of Friuli's winemaking renaissance. Several leading lights in Friuli's contemporary winemaking overview learned the basics of the craft in his "workshop". Today, 50 years on, Emilio Rotolo and his sons Francesco and Alessandro follow his footsteps and philosophy daily, helped by Lorenzo Landi, while vinification is entrusted to Mauro Simeoni. Another admirable performance from the whole range, but above all the Friulano 2014, which earns itself another Tre Bicchieri thanks to unanimous approval in both selection sessions. Generous, complex and harmonious on both nose and palate, with hints of ripe fruit, clear honey and flowering hay. White Wine of the Year for us.

○ FCO Verduzzo Friulano Crei '12	♥♥ 5
○ COF Verduzzo Friulano Crei '10	♥♥♥ 5
○ COF Friulano '12	♥♥ 3
○ COF Picolit '10	♥♥ 5
○ COF Picolit '09	♥♥ 5
○ COF Picolit '07	♥♥ 5
○ COF Verduzzo Friulano Crei '11	♥♥ 5
○ COF Verduzzo Friulano Crei '09	♥♥ 5
○ COF Verduzzo Friulano Crei '08	♥♥ 5
● Il Rio Falcone	♥♥ 3
○ Sauvignon '12	♥♥ 2*

○ Collio Friulano '14	♥♥♥ 4*
○ Collio Malvasia '14	♥♥ 4
○ Collio Pinot Bianco '14	♥♥ 4
○ Collio Sauvignon '14	♥♥ 4
○ Blanc des Rosis '14	♥♥ 4
○ Collio Pinot Grigio '14	♥♥ 4
● Poderi dei Blumeri Rosso '11	♥♥ 5
● Rivarossa '12	♥♥ 4
○ Blanc des Rosis '07	♥♥♥ 4
○ Blanc des Rosis '06	♥♥♥ 4
○ Collio Friulano '13	♥♥♥ 4*
○ Collio Tocai Friulano '00	♥♥♥ 4
○ Mario Schiopetto Bianco '08	♥♥♥ 5
○ Mario Schiopetto Bianco '07	♥♥♥ 5
○ Mario Schiopetto Bianco '03	♥♥♥ 5
○ Mario Schiopetto Bianco '02	♥♥♥ 5

La Sclusa

LOC. SPESSA
VIA STRADA DI SANT'ANNA, 7/2
33043 CIVIDALE DEL FRIULI [UD]
TEL. 0432716259
www.lasclusa.it

CELLAR SALES
PRE-BOOKED VISITS
ACCOMMODATION
ANNUAL PRODUCTION 160,000 bottles
HECTARES UNDER VINE 30.00

Giobatta Zorzettig was the father of a
generation of winegrowers working since
1963 in Spessa di Cividale, in the heart of
the Colli Orientali del Friuli. His
descendants have formed various family
groups, all dedicated winegrowers. One of
the most numerous of these is headed by
Gino, who has managed his estate for over
40 years. A section of the Corno river called
La Sclusa, which crosses the vineyards,
gave the winery its name and a clearly
defined identity. Now his sons Germano,
Maurizio and Luciano run the estate and
their own children are active in the
well-organized family business, each with a
specific role but turning their hand to all
that is necessary. Very flattering results for
the whole range in a vintage year with such
unusual weather conditions. All the wines
are fresh, supple and very drinkable, but
we particularly liked the Ribolla Gialla 2014
for its delightful aromas and palate.

○ FCO Chardonnay '14	♟♟ 3
○ FCO Friulano '14	♟♟ 3
○ FCO Picolit '11	♟♟ 6
○ FCO Pinot Grigio '14	♟♟ 2*
○ FCO Ribolla Gialla '14	♟♟ 3
● FCO Merlot '14	♟ 3
● FCO Refosco P. R. '14	♟ 3
○ COF Friulano '12	♟♟ 2*
● COF Merlot '12	♟♟ 3
○ COF Picolit '10	♟♟ 6
○ COF Pinot Grigio '13	♟♟ 2*
○ COF Ribolla Gialla '13	♟♟ 3
○ COF Sauvignon '12	♟♟ 3

Roberto Scubla

FRAZ. IPPLIS
VIA ROCCA BERNARDA, 22
33040 PREMARIACCO [UD]
TEL. 0432716258
www.scubla.com

CELLAR SALES
PRE-BOOKED VISITS
ANNUAL PRODUCTION 60,000 bottles
HECTARES UNDER VINE 12.00

In 1991 Roberto Scubla chose to leave the
bank where he worked and purchase a few
hectares of vineyards adjacent to a
crumbling old house on the slopes of Rocca
Bernarda. Today that ruin is a prestigious
home of architectural value with welcoming
interiors and a bucolic atmosphere. With
limited production quantities meticulous
care is possible in the vineyards, and close
friend Gianni Menotti offers valuable
support in the cellar decisions. We like to
recall that Bianco Pomèdes is named after
the alpine shelter where the two invented
this wine while trapped during a storm,
deciding to use mainly pinot bianco
blended with friulano and a touch of
riesling renano. Once again, three wines
made it to the finals, demonstrating the
high standard throughout the range. One of
these was, of course, the Verduzzo Friulano
Cràtis 2012, which just fell short of the
highest accolade, like the Pomèdes 2013.
An excellent performance also from the
Refosco dal Peduncolo Rosso 2013.

○ FCO Bianco Pomèdes '13	♟♟ 5
● FCO Refosco P. R. '13	♟♟ 4
○ FCO Verduzzo Friulano Cràtis '12	♟♟ 5
● FCO Cabernet Franc '13	♟♟ 3
● FCO Cabernet Sauvignon '13	♟♟ 3
○ FCO Friulano '14	♟♟ 3
○ FCO Malvasia Lo Speziale '14	♟♟ 3
○ FCO Pinot Bianco '14	♟♟ 3
● FCO Rosso Scuro '12	♟♟ 4
○ FCO Sauvignon '14	♟♟ 3
○ COF Bianco Pomèdes '12	♟♟ 5
○ COF Verduzzo Friulano Cràtis '11	♟♟ 5
○ Riesling Passito '10	♟♟ 5

Renzo Sgubin

VIA FAET, 15/1
34071 CORMÒNS [GO]
TEL. 0481630297
www.renzosgubin.it

CELLAR SALES
PRE-BOOKED VISITS
ANNUAL PRODUCTION 28,000 bottles
HECTARES UNDER VINE 12.00
SUSTAINABLE WINERY

Renzo Sgubin's labels bear the unmistakeable outline of Mount Quarin, which rises behind Cormòns, as a tribute to his roots. Both his parents were born at the foot of the castle looming on the hilltop and then settled down in the town, and later in Pradis, between the Collio and Friuli Isonzo DOC zones. They worked as sharecroppers until they had the opportunity in the 1970s to purchase their first vineyards. In 1997 Renzo decided to establish the estate and in 2003 he began to bottle his wines. He is proud to call himself a countryman. Less talk and more action is the best way to stand out. In recent editions we have remarked on the constant improvement throughout the range, and this year, again, two wines made the finals. The Pinot Grigio 2014 is subtly elegant, beautifully fresh with an enthralling flavour. The 3,4,3. 2013 is an excellent wine, created to mark the birth of Renzo's firstborn son.

○ 3, 4, 3 '13	♟♟ 3*
○ Friuli Isonzo Pinot Grigio '14	♟♟ 3*
● Collio Merlot '12	♟♟ 3
○ Friuli Isonzo Chardonnay '14	♟♟ 3
○ Friuli Isonzo Friulano '14	♟♟ 3
○ Friuli Isonzo Malvasia '14	♟♟ 3
○ 3, 4, 3 '12	♟♟ 3
○ Friuli Isonzo Chardonnay '13	♟♟ 3
○ Friuli Isonzo Friulano '13	♟♟ 3
○ Friuli Isonzo Malvasia '13	♟♟ 3
○ Friuli Isonzo Sauvignon '13	♟♟ 3

Sirch

VIA FORNALIS, 277/1
33043 CIVIDALE DEL FRIULI [UD]
TEL. 0432709835
www.sirchwine.com

CELLAR SALES
PRE-BOOKED VISITS
ANNUAL PRODUCTION 150,000 bottles
HECTARES UNDER VINE 25.00

In 2002 Luca Sirch started a journey to produce simple, approachable wines: classic monovarietal products, standing apart from fashions and trends, made in clean, modern style. This estate philosophy actually masks the ambition to achieve subtle complexity and increasingly elegant and richly nuanced wines. His 25 hectares of vineyards are mostly subdivided into small plots in various parts of Cividale, in the municipal areas of Albana and Prepotto on the Colli Orientali del Friuli. For some time now his wines have been distributed exclusively by Feudi San Gregorio at a very competitive price. A lovely array of wines, faithful to the varietal features of every single grape and corresponding to the weather conditions of the vintage year. Freshness is the common denominator in the white wines, strongly aromatic with minerally, salty hints, while the reds are pleasant and coherent.

○ FCO Bianco Cladrecis '13	♟♟ 3
○ FCO Chardonnay '14	♟♟ 3
○ FCO Friulano '14	♟♟ 3
● FCO Merlot '13	♟♟ 3
○ FCO Pinot Grigio '14	♟♟ 3
○ FCO Ribolla Gialla '14	♟♟ 3
○ FCO Sauvignon '14	♟♟ 3
● FCO Schioppettino '13	♟♟ 3
● FCO Cabernet '13	♟ 3
● FCO Refosco P.R. '13	♟ 3
○ COF Friulano '13	♟♟ 3
○ COF Sauvignon '13	♟♟ 3

Skerk

FRAZ. SAN PELAGIO
LOC. PREPOTTO, 20
34011 DUINO AURISINA [TS]
TEL. 040200156
www.skerk.com

CELLAR SALES
PRE-BOOKED VISITS
RESTAURANT SERVICE
ANNUAL PRODUCTION 22,000 bottles
HECTARES UNDER VINE 7.00
VITICULTURE METHOD Certified Organic

Sandi Skerk's well-established winery is in the Trieste Carso area and to understand what heroic winegrowing means, a visit to this area is instructive, with vigneron and rock in daily conflict. Everything is done by hand, in limited space, on sparse, dry red soil, barren and stony but rich in limestone and iron. Here and there, in sunny loops overlooking the sea, vineyards are tended like gardens. The cellar carved from the karst rock is a true masterpiece, with constant temperature and humidity throughout the year. The wines follow natural processes, never clarified or filtered, lengthy maceration on the skins, and racking only as the moon begins to wane. Sandi's decision to delay bottling the 2013 wines prevented us from tasting them but to make up for it, we were able to enjoy two different versions of the Terrano, both extraordinary. The Terrano Selezione 2011, made from selected grapes, is astonishing, richly extracted and powerful.

Skerlj

VIA SALES, 44
34010 SGONICO [TS]
TEL. 040229253
www.agriturismoskerlj.com

CELLAR SALES
PRE-BOOKED VISITS
ACCOMMODATION AND RESTAURANT SERVICE
ANNUAL PRODUCTION 5,000 bottles
HECTARES UNDER VINE 2.00
VITICULTURE METHOD Certified Organic

For the Trieste Carso area a winegrowing overview shows many small estates some tiny, but real gems. Matej and Kristina Skerlj are an example of this, with their two hectares of vineyards inherited from their grandparents. They producs just 4,400 bottles for three label ranges: Malvasia, Vitovska and Terrano, from three quintessential native varieties, rich in charm and personality. Vinification is traditional, with two or three weeks of maceration even for white grapes, without temperature control. The wines mature in oak barrels for at least two years and are bottled without filtration. In the last edition the best wine was the Malvasia, while this year it is the Vitovska 2102: a magnificent interpretation of a generally little-known grape variety of great significance for the Carso area. It is resistant to drought and theBora wind, does not lose its leaves, and guarantees the harvest.

● Terrano Sel. '11	♥♥ 5
● Terrano Ris. '06	♥♥ 5
○ Carso Malvasia '08	♥♥♥ 4
○ Ograde '12	♥♥♥ 5
○ Ograde '11	♥♥♥ 5
○ Ograde '10	♥♥♥ 4
○ Ograde '09	♥♥♥ 4*
○ Malvasia '12	♥♥ 5
○ Malvasia '11	♥♥ 5
● Terrano '12	♥♥ 5
○ Vitovska '12	♥♥ 5
○ Vitovska '11	♥♥ 5

○ Vitovska '12	♥♥ 5
○ Malvasia '12	♥♥ 5
● Terrano '12	♥♥ 5
○ Malvasia '11	♥♥ 5
○ Malvasia '10	♥♥ 5
○ Malvasia '09	♥♥ 4
○ Malvasia '08	♥♥ 4
○ Malvasia '07	♥♥ 4
○ Malvasia '06	♥♥ 4
● Terrano '07	♥♥ 4
○ Vitovska '11	♥♥ 5
○ Vitovska '10	♥♥ 5
○ Vitovska '09	♥♥ 4
○ Vitovska '08	♥♥ 4
○ Vitovska '07	♥♥ 4
○ Vitovska '06	♥♥ 4

Edi Skok

loc. Giasbana, 15
34070 San Floriano del Collio [GO]
Tel. 0481390280
www.skok.it

CELLAR SALES
PRE-BOOKED VISITS
ANNUAL PRODUCTION 38,000 bottles
HECTARES UNDER VINE 11.00

The Skok family has ancient farming roots
and deep connections to tradition and the
Collio area. They live close to the Slovenian
border in a 16th-century villa nestling on
the slopes of Giasbana, near San Floriano
del Collio. The estate is managed by Edi
and Orietta Skok and since the last harvest
they have been working in a new cellar, of
beautiful architectural design, blending
perfectly with the environment. To prove
their respect for nature they feel morally
obliged to make great wines in scrupulous
observance of the famously strict Collio
regulations applicable to training systems,
production process and bottling. All the
wines we tasted obtained unanimous
approval, but this year the honour of
reaching the final selections was reserved
for the Merlot Villa Jasbinae 2009. It is
well-structured, complex and deep with
dark spices and damson jam on the nose
and a soft, mouthfilling palate.

● Collio Merlot Villa Jasbinae '09	♥♥ 3*
○ Collio Bianco Pe Ar '13	♥♥ 3
○ Collio Chardonnay '14	♥♥ 2*
○ Collio Friulano Zabura '14	♥♥ 3
● Collio Merlot '13	♥♥ 3
○ Collio Pinot Grigio '14	♥♥ 3
○ Collio Sauvignon '14	♥ 3
○ Collio Bianco Pe Ar '12	♀♀ 3
○ Collio Chardonnay '13	♀♀ 2*
○ Collio Friulano Zabura '13	♀♀ 3*
○ Collio Friulano Zabura '12	♀♀ 3*
○ Collio Friulano Zabura '11	♀♀ 3*
○ Collio Pinot Grigio '13	♀♀ 3
○ Collio Pinot Grigio '09	♀♀ 3*
○ Collio Sauvignon '13	♀♀ 3
○ Collio Sauvignon '08	♀♀ 3*

Leonardo Specogna

via Rocca Bernarda, 4
33040 Corno di Rosazzo [UD]
Tel. 0432755840
www.specogna.it

CELLAR SALES
PRE-BOOKED VISITS
ANNUAL PRODUCTION 120,000 bottles
HECTARES UNDER VINE 18.00
VITICULTURE METHOD Certified Organic

Young oenologists Michele and Cristian run
the Specogna estate, set up in 1963 by
their grandfather Leonardo, with the
support and active help of the whole
family. This beautiful winery has made its
name due to a vast range of products, with
Cristian's innate communication skills
launching its on international markets. The
vineyards cover the sunny slopes of Rocca
Bernarda, judiciously terraced by
generations of winegrowers, enjoying an
ideal microclimate protected by the Alps
and exposed to the breezes from the
nearby Adriatic. A series of richly extracted
and mouthwatering wines are offered
alongside the well-known traditional line.
The red Oltre 2011 is made from selected
merlot grapes grown in a vineyard over 50
years old. Satisfying on the nose, with
vibrant hints of crushed morello cherries,
wild berries, quinine and spices; soft and
well-structured on the palate with
generous flavour and aromas enhanced by
vibrant tannins.

● COF Merlot '13	♥♥ 4
● COF Oltre '11	♥♥ 6
● COF Pignolo '10	♥♥ 6
● COF Refosco P. R. '13	♥♥ 3
○ COF Identità '12	♥ 6
○ FCO Friulano '14	♥ 3
○ FCO Pinot Grigio '14	♥ 3
○ FCO Ribolla Gialla '14	♥ 3
○ COF Chardonnay '07	♀♀ 3*
○ COF Friulano '13	♀♀ 3
● COF Pignolo '07	♀♀ 5
○ COF Sauvignon '09	♀♀ 3
○ Pinot Grigio '13	♀♀ 3
● Rosso Oltre '09	♀♀ 5
○ Sauvignon Duality '09	♀♀ 3*

Tenuta Stella

FRAZ. SCRIÒ
VIA SOENCINA, 1
34070 DOLEGNA DEL COLLIO [GO]
TEL. 0499318135
www.tenutastellacollio.it

CELLAR SALES
PRE-BOOKED VISITS
ANNUAL PRODUCTION 24,000 bottles
HECTARES UNDER VINE 12.00
VITICULTURE METHOD Certified Organic
SUSTAINABLE WINERY

Recently established, Tenuta Stella embraces the philosophy of growing only native white varieties like friulano, ribolla gialla and malvasia istriana. The estate has been fortunate enough to find the perfect terroir to express them at Scriò. The 12 hectares of vineyards are situated at Dolegna del Collio, the highest part of the Collio DOC zone, where the steeply sloping hills are as harsh and tiring to work on as they are generous in offering unique and inimitable qualities. The vineyards are terraced following the natural slope of the land, which means most procedures have to be carried out by hand. In the last edition we complimented this new jewel in the crown of regional winemaking on its entry in the Guide. This year we received confirmation of its validity. The Ribolla Gialla 2103 earned a place in the finals for its complex aromas, and above all, the full-bodied, lively flavour.

○ Collio Ribolla Gialla '13	▼▼	4
○ Collio Friulano Scriò '13	▼▼	3
○ Collio Malvasia '13	▼▼	4
○ Cuvée Tanni Brut	▼▼	5
○ Ribolla Gialla Brut	▼▼	4
○ Collio Bianco '12	♀♀	3
○ Collio Friulano Scriò '12	♀♀	3*
○ Collio Malvasia '12	♀♀	4
○ Collio Ribolla Gialla '12	♀♀	4

Subida di Monte

LOC. SUBIDA
VIA SUBIDA, 6
34071 CORMÒNS [GO]
TEL. 048161011
www.subidadimonte.it

CELLAR SALES
PRE-BOOKED VISITS
ACCOMMODATION
ANNUAL PRODUCTION 45,000 bottles
HECTARES UNDER VINE 9.00

Luigi Antonutti is a forward-thinker and lover of beauty, with an open mind as far as innovation is concerned. In 1972 he fulfilled his dream of becoming a winegrower, moving to Subida, in Cormòns, where he built a lovely cellar overlooking a steep slope of the Gorizia Collio between the Isonzo and Judrio rivers where the vineyards are bathed in sunshine and protected by the embrace of the Alps, while enjoying the briny Adriatic breezes. This was the birthplace of Subida di Monte and its development enthusiastically continues with Luigi's sons Cristian and Andrea, who have gladly embraced the sustainable farming philosophy of natural organic fertilizers and minimal anti-parasite treatments. All the standard-label white wines confirmed the consolidated standard, but we also liked the Rosso Poncaia 2012, made from merlot with a little cabernet franc. The nose hints at bottled cherries and chocolate while the palate is soft and mouthfilling.

○ Collio Friulano '14	▼▼	3
○ Collio Malvasia '14	▼▼	3
● Collio Merlot '13	▼▼	3
● Collio Rosso Poncaia '12	▼▼	4
○ Collio Sauvignon '14	▼▼	3
● Collio Cabernet Franc '13	▼	3
○ Collio Pinot Grigio '14	▼	3
● Collio Cabernet Franc '12	♀♀	3
○ Collio Friulano '13	♀♀	3
○ Collio Friulano '12	♀♀	3
○ Collio Friulano '11	♀♀	3*
○ Collio Malvasia '13	♀♀	3*
○ Collio Malvasia '12	♀♀	3*
○ Collio Pinot Grigio '13	♀♀	3
○ Collio Sauvignon '13	♀♀	3
○ Collio Tocai Friulano '05	♀	2*

Matijaz Tercic

LOC. BUCUIE, 4
34070 SAN FLORIANO DEL COLLIO [GO]
TEL. 0481884920
www.tercic.com

CELLAR SALES
PRE-BOOKED VISITS
ANNUAL PRODUCTION 30,000 bottles
HECTARES UNDER VINE 9.50

The steep San Floriano del Collio hill slopes
are considered one of the best-suited
microclimates for winegrowing, thanks to
the special contours of the land and above
all to the joint effect of the Bora wind that
snakes through the Vipacco Valley, with sea
breezes which provide an ideal ventilation
to set the aromas and dry the grapes. The
Ter?i? family estate is no exception.
Generations of the family have produced
wine here but the real turning point came
in 1994 when Matijaz bottled the first
wines, and the winery grew steadily to
consolidate its position at the heights of
regional excellence. This year only three
wines from the 2013 vintage were
presented, obtaining very respectable
scores. The Pinot Grigio 2013 confirmed
the results of previous editions with aromas
of russet pears and flowering hay, and a
fragrant, supple palate closing on a
pleasantly bitterish sensation.

Tiare - Roberto Snidarcig

FRAZ. VENCÒ
LOC. SANT'ELENA, 3A
34070 DOLEGNA DEL COLLIO [GO]
TEL. 048162491
www.tiaredoc.com

CELLAR SALES
PRE-BOOKED VISITS
RESTAURANT SERVICE
ANNUAL PRODUCTION 90,000 bottles
HECTARES UNDER VINE 10.00
SUSTAINABLE WINERY

In 1985 a one-hectare vineyard on the
slopes of Mount Quarin, which shields
Cormòns from the cold east winds, was
sufficient to make Roberto Snidarcig fall
deeply in love with the land. In subsequent
years the vineyards grew exponentially in
number and working with his wife Sandra,
he moved to Dolegna del Collio in 1991.
Here he built a new cellar, a few hundred
metres from the border with Slovenia and
chose an emblematic name for his winery:
Tiare, which means land in local dialect.
Roberto's wines are all top notch and his
Sauvignons are the most striking. These
strongly aromatic wines always lead to
discussions. This year we decided to
postpone our review, but this takes nothing
away from a high profile range. The vibrant
Malvasia 2014 stands out for judicious use
of new oak barrels. We also liked the
Friulano 2014, Ribolla Gialla 2014 and the
excellent Pinot Nero from the same year.

○ Collio Pinot Grigio '13	♟♟ 3
○ Collio Sauvignon '13	♟♟ 3
○ Collio Ribolla Gialla '13	♟ 3
○ Collio Pinot Grigio '07	♟♟♟ 3*
○ Collio Bianco Planta '11	♟♟ 4
○ Collio Bianco Planta '08	♟♟ 3
○ Collio Chardonnay '12	♟♟ 3*
○ Collio Pinot Grigio '12	♟♟ 3*
○ Collio Pinot Grigio '11	♟♟ 3*
○ Collio Sauvignon '12	♟♟ 3
○ Collio Sauvignon '11	♟♟ 3*
○ Collio Sauvignon Scemen '09	♟♟ 4
○ Collio Sauvignon Scemen '08	♟♟ 3
○ Vino degli Orti '12	♟♟ 3
○ Vino degli Orti '11	♟♟ 3

○ Collio Malvasia '14	♟♟ 3*
○ Collio Friulano '14	♟♟ 4
● Collio Pinot Nero '14	♟♟ 2*
○ Collio Ribolla Gialla '14	♟♟ 4
○ Collio Sauvignon '13	♟♟♟ 3*
○ Collio Friulano '12	♟♟ 3*
○ Collio Malvasia '13	♟♟ 3
○ Collio Pinot Grigio '13	♟♟ 3
● Collio Pinot Nero '12	♟♟ 2*
○ Collio Ribolla Gialla '13	♟♟ 3*
○ Collio Rosemblanc '10	♟♟ 5
○ Collio Sauvignon '11	♟♟ 3*
○ Collio Sauvignon Empire '11	♟♟ 3*
● Friuli Isonzo Cabernet Franc '10	♟♟ 3

FRIULI VENEZIA GIULIA

★Franco Toros

LOC. NOVALI, 12
34071 CORMÒNS [GO]
TEL. 048161327
www.vinitoros.com

CELLAR SALES
PRE-BOOKED VISITS
ANNUAL PRODUCTION 60,000 bottles
HECTARES UNDER VINE 11.00

Franco Toros descends from a family of countrymen who settled at Novali, near Cormòns, at the beginning of the last century. It did not take long to realize that the land was ideal for winegrowing and they immediately became meticulous vignerons. Like all great winegrowers, Franco gives Mother Nature the credit for the quality of his wines but we all know that without the right skill, the results would not be the same. His wines stand out for their linear, frank qualities, great respect for varietal features and, above all, their pleasant, drinkable flavour. These flawless, terroir-faithful wines are true ambassadors of the unique features of Collio. The Pinot Bianco repeats last year's performance, earning another Tre Bicchieri. It delights the nose with fragrant citrus hints of oranges, mandarins and limes, followed by white peaches, grass and plant sap. The stylish palate is soaked in velvety, aromatic sensations.

Torre Rosazza

FRAZ. OLEIS
LOC. POGGIOBELLO, 12
33044 MANZANO [UD]
TEL. 0422864511
www.torrerosazza.com

CELLAR SALES
PRE-BOOKED VISITS
ANNUAL PRODUCTION 220,000 bottles
HECTARES UNDER VINE 110.00
SUSTAINABLE WINERY

Torre Rosazza is the top winery of Le Tenute di Genagricola, whose Friuli estates include Poggiobello, Borgo Magredo and Tenuta Sant'Anna. The group, which also owns properties in Veneto, Piedmont, Romagna and Lazio, bought this estate in 1979 and immediately began studying and zoning the 110 hectares of vineyards in order to understand the soil and climate features of each area, and thus identify the plots best suited to expressing the varietal characteristics of each grape according to aspect and geological properties. Two magnificent natural amphitheatre terraces surround the 18th-century Palazzo De Marchi where the offices and cellar are located. Unanimous appreciation of the whole range confirms the sound quality of this estate's wines which include all types of vinification. This year, the favourite was the Pinot Bianco 2014 which earns Tre Bicchieri for its elegant aromas and soft palate.

○ Collio Pinot Bianco '14	♥♥♥ 4*
○ Collio Pinot Grigio '14	♥♥ 4
○ Collio Chardonnay '14	♥♥ 4
○ Collio Friulano '14	♥♥ 4
● Collio Merlot '11	♥♥ 4
○ Collio Sauvignon '14	♥♥ 4
○ Collio Friulano '12	♥♥♥ 4*
○ Collio Friulano '11	♥♥♥ 4*
○ Collio Friulano '10	♥♥♥ 4
○ Collio Friulano '09	♥♥♥ 4*
○ Collio Friulano '08	♥♥♥ 4*
○ Collio Pinot Bianco '13	♥♥♥ 4*
○ Collio Pinot Bianco '08	♥♥♥ 4*
○ Collio Pinot Bianco '07	♥♥♥ 4
○ Collio Pinot Bianco '05	♥♥♥ 4
○ Collio Tocai Friulano '06	♥♥♥ 4

○ FCO Pinot Bianco '14	♥♥♥ 3*
○ Blanc di Neri Brut	♥♥ 5
● COF Cabernet Sauvignon '13	♥♥ 3
● COF Merlot L'Altromerlot '11	♥♥ 5
○ COF Picolit '13	♥♥ 5
● COF Pignolo '11	♥♥ 5
● COF Refosco P. R. '13	♥♥ 3
○ FCO Sauvignon '14	♥♥ 3
○ FCO Friulano '14	♥ 3
○ FCO Ribolla Gialla '14	♥ 3
○ COF Pinot Grigio '13	♥♥♥ 3*
○ COF Pinot Grigio '12	♥♥♥ 3*
○ COF Bianco Ronco del Masiero '10	♥♥ 3*
○ COF Bianco Ronco del Masiero '09	♥♥ 3*
○ COF Ribolla Gialla '12	♥♥ 3*
○ COF Sauvignon '11	♥♥ 3*

La Tunella

FRAZ. IPPLIS
VIA DEL COLLIO, 14
33040 PREMARIACCO [UD]
TEL. 0432716030
www.latunella.it

CELLAR SALES
PRE-BOOKED VISITS
ANNUAL PRODUCTION 390,000 bottles
HECTARES UNDER VINE 70.00
SUSTAINABLE WINERY

La Tunella is a model estate with 70 hectares of vineyards on the Colli Orientali del Friuli, with high production quantities. Young brothers Massimo and Mauro Zorzettig run the winery, drawing on the accumulated experience of three generations of winegrowers. With the help of expert oenologist Luigino Zamparo and a dynamic, close-knit team, they work in an avant-garde winery both in architectural design and advanced technology, with generous cellar space and well-ventilated, temperature-controlled drying rooms. The youth, determination and energy of this estate are reflected in the wines which are approachable both on the nose and the palate. This year three wines reached the finals, coming close to the highest accolade. In particular, the BiancoSesto 2013, made from equal quantities of friulano and ribolla gialla, offers satisfying, vibrant fruity aromas while the supple, flavoursome palate is velvety and mouthfilling.

○ COF BiancoSesto '13	**YY**	4
○ COF Friulano Col Livius '13	**YY**	4
● COF Schioppettino '11	**YY**	4
○ COF Bianco La Linda '13	**YY**	5
● COF Pignolo '09	**YY**	5
○ COF Ribolla Gialla Col de Bliss '13	**YY**	4
● COF Rosso L'Arcione '10	**YY**	5
○ COF Sauvignon Col Matìss '13	**YY**	4
○ COF BiancoSesto '11	YYY	4*
○ COF BiancoSesto '07	YYY	3
○ COF BiancoSesto '06	YYY	3*
○ Noans '12	YYY	5
○ COF BiancoSesto '12	YY	4
○ COF Friulano Col Livius '12	YY	4
○ COF Friulano Col Livius '11	YY	4
○ COF Noans '10	YY	5

Valchiarò

FRAZ. TOGLIANO
VIA DEI LAGHI, 4C
33040 TORREANO [UD]
TEL. 0432715502
www.valchiaro.it

CELLAR SALES
PRE-BOOKED VISITS
ANNUAL PRODUCTION 45,000 bottles
HECTARES UNDER VINE 14.00
SUSTAINABLE WINERY

The Chiarò river runs through the municipal area of Torreano di Cividale, between the foothills and the Julian Prealps, and the river valley lent its name to the winery, set up in 1991 by six partners who decided to join forces in one estate. This is a story of passion and friendship which encouraged Armando, Doris, Galliano, Lauro, Luigi, and Stefano to create a partnership, each contributing their own grapes and fermenting them together. What initially seemed to be a slightly ingenuous decision actually proved to be a well-founded reality. With the invaluable help of Gianni Menotti, Valchiarò has now become a benchmark brand and guarantee of quality. In the selections, all the wines obtained really excellent scores which confirmed the quality of the whole range. The standard-label whites stood out for coherent features, freshness and fragrance while the Riserva reds showed complex aromas and mouthfilling palates. The sweet wines are also excellent, creamy but not cloying.

● COF Cabernet '11	**YY**	3
● COF Merlot Ris. '11	**YY**	3
○ COF Picolit '10	**YY**	6
○ COF Verduzzo Friulano '11	**YY**	4
○ FCO Friulano '14	**YY**	3
○ FCO Pinot Grigio '14	**YY**	3
○ FCO Sauvignon '14	**YY**	3
○ COF Friulano '13	YY	3
○ COF Friulano Nexus '13	YY	3
○ COF Friulano Nexus '12	YY	3
○ COF Pinot Grigio '13	YY	3
● COF Refosco P. R. '06	YY	3*
○ COF Verduzzo Friulano '10	YY	4
○ COF Verduzzo Friulano '09	YY	4*
○ COF Verduzzo Friulano '08	YY	3*
○ COF Verduzzo Friulano '07	YY	3*

FRIULI VENEZIA GIULIA

Valpanera

VIA TRIESTE, 5A
33059 VILLA VICENTINA [UD]
TEL. 0431970395
www.valpanera.it

CELLAR SALES
PRE-BOOKED VISITS
ANNUAL PRODUCTION 450,000 bottles
HECTARES UNDER VINE 55.00

The Casa del Refosco sign looms large over the entrance, endorsing the estate's philosophy: promoting the region's most widespread native black grape variety. In the vast world of refosco, the red-stemmed cultivar has found its ideal habitat in the Aquileia DOC area, on sandy but clay-rich soil, with constant ventilation thanks to the Bora wind, while the cool breezes from the nearby Adriatic help ripen the healthy, flavoursome grapes. Valpanera was created by Giampietro Dal Vecchio and his son Giovanni who, with courage and determination, focus almost solely on this grape in significant quantities. This year, again, we tasted various expressions of refosco dal peduncolo rosso grapes, used alongside cabernet sauvignon and merlot in the blend for the Rosso Alma 2008. Many versions, all sharing the same common denominator: black berry jam, spice, tobacco, complex tannins and strong flavour.

★Venica & Venica

LOC. CERÒ, 8
34070 DOLEGNA DEL COLLIO [GO]
TEL. 048161264
www.venica.it

CELLAR SALES
PRE-BOOKED VISITS
ACCOMMODATION
ANNUAL PRODUCTION 250,000 bottles
HECTARES UNDER VINE 39.00
SUSTAINABLE WINERY

Gianni and Giorgio Venica's artisan and entrepreneurial skills have launched the estate to the peaks of regional excellence, making it a benchmark winery worthy of imitation. The Venica & Venica brand guarantees reliable and excellent quality. They also play an important role internationally as ambassadors for the potential of Collio. The close-knit family, Ornella's drive and Giampaolo's energy are the added value in this beautiful winery which, with true country spirit, has capitalized on the products of the over 80-year-old vineyards purchased by grandfather Daniele on the Cerò hillside. The umpteenth demonstration of superiority by the Sauvignon Ronco delle Mele 2014, although it missed out on Tre Bicchieri by a hair's breadth. We have to acknowledge the attenuating circumstances of a particularly difficult year, but the varietal features have been perfectly preserved.

● Friuli Aquileia Refosco P. R. '13	♟♟ 2*
● Friuli Aquileia Refosco P. R. Ris. '11	♟♟ 5
● Friuli Aquileia Refosco P. R. Sup. '12	♟♟ 3
● Friuli Aquileia Rosso Alma '08	♟♟ 5
● Friuli Aquileia Refosco P. R. '12	♟♟ 2*
● Friuli Aquileia Refosco P. R. Ris. '08	♟♟ 5
● Friuli Aquileia Refosco P. R. Ris. '07	♟♟ 5
● Friuli Aquileia Refosco P. R. Ris. '06	♟♟ 4
● Friuli Aquileia Refosco P. R. Ris. '05	♟♟ 4
● Friuli Aquileia Refosco P. R. Sup. '10	♟♟ 3
● Friuli Aquileia Refosco P. R. Sup. '09	♟♟ 3*
● Friuli Aquileia Refosco P. R. Sup. '07	♟♟ 2*
● Friuli Aquileia Rosso Alma '06	♟♟ 3*
● Rosso di Valpanera '12	♟♟ 2*
● Rosso di Valpanera '10	♟♟ 2*

○ Collio Sauvignon Ronco delle Mele '14	♟♟ 6
○ Collio Friulano Ronco delle Cime '14	♟♟ 4
○ Collio Malvasia Pètris '14	♟♟ 4
● Collio Merlot Perilla '11	♟♟ 5
○ Collio Pinot Bianco Tàlis '14	♟♟ 4
○ Collio Sauvignon Ronco del Cerò '14	♟♟ 4
○ Collio Traminer Aromatico '14	♟♟ 4
○ Collio Sauvignon Ronco delle Mele '13	♟♟♟ 6
○ Collio Sauvignon Ronco delle Mele '12	♟♟♟ 6
○ Collio Sauvignon Ronco delle Mele '11	♟♟♟ 6
○ Collio Sauvignon Ronco delle Mele '10	♟♟♟ 5
○ Collio Sauvignon Ronco delle Mele '09	♟♟♟ 5
○ Collio Sauvignon Ronco delle Mele '08	♟♟♟ 5
○ Collio Sauvignon Ronco delle Mele '07	♟♟♟ 5
○ Collio Tocai Friulano Ronco delle Cime '06	♟♟♟ 4

La Viarte

via Novacuzzo, 51
33040 Prepotto [UD]
Tel. 0432759458
www.laviarte.it

CELLAR SALES
PRE-BOOKED VISITS
ACCOMMODATION
ANNUAL PRODUCTION 100,000 bottles
HECTARES UNDER VINE 27.00
SUSTAINABLE WINERY

In 1973 Giuseppe and Carla Ceschin's purchase of a plot among the magnificent hills stretching from Corno di Rosazzo to Prepotto, was the origin of La Viarte, meaning "springtime" in local dialect. The first bottles were released in 1984 because it took many years to shape the terraces, plant the vineyards and build the cellar. The estate was recently purchased by Alberto Piovan, but the change in ownership has not affected the setup of the winery; instead the intention was to consolidate the still untapped potential. This desire to grow was further enriched by the recent acquisition of Gianni Menotti as consultant oenologist. The recent reorganization of the estate prevented us from giving a full report on the potential of the whole range, but the signs are very promising. The standard-label whites are youthful, fresh, succulent and fragrant, while the Sauvignon Liende 2013 presents flawless nose-palate coherence.

● COF Merlot '11	♟♟	4
○ COF Sauvignon Liende '13	♟♟	5
○ FCO Chardonnay '14	♟♟	3
○ FCO Friulano '14	♟♟	3
○ FCO Pinot Bianco '14	♟♟	3
● COF Merlot '09	♟♟	4
● COF Merlot '03	♟♟	3
○ COF Sauvignon '13	♟♟	3*
○ COF Sauvignon '05	♟♟	3
● COF Schioppettino '06	♟♟	4
● COF Schioppettino '02	♟♟	4
● COF Tazzelenghe '08	♟♟	5
○ Siùm '07	♟♟	5
○ Siùm '06	♟♟	5
○ Siùm '05	♟♟	5
○ Siùm '04	♟♟	5

Vidussi

via Spessa, 18
34071 Capriva del Friuli [GO]
Tel. 048180072
www.vinimontresor.it

CELLAR SALES
PRE-BOOKED VISITS
ANNUAL PRODUCTION 500,000 bottles
HECTARES UNDER VINE 30.00

Vidussi, situated at Capriva del Friuli, was taken over in 2000 by the Montresor group of Verona. To increase the range of wines and cover all aspects of the market, including the USA, the estate's existing vineyards on the hills towards Cormòns, in the heart of Collio, have been joined by other plots in the neighbouring Friuli Colli Orientali and Friuli Isonzo DOC zones. Considerable technological investments in the cellar have enabled longstanding cellar manager Gigi Spessot to work more easily and efficiently. Technical management and responsibility for the entire production process is entrusted to the proven experience of wine technician Luigino di Giuseppe. The excellent scores awarded to the whole, vast range presented this year, all from the latest vintage, prove that even in a year with unusual weather conditions, shrewd winegrowing practice will lead to prestigious results that respect the features of the grape variety.

○ Collio Chardonnay '14	♟♟	2*
○ Collio Friulano '14	♟♟	3
○ Collio Malvasia '14	♟♟	2*
○ Collio Pinot Bianco '14	♟♟	3
○ Collio Pinot Grigio '14	♟♟	2*
○ Collio Ribolla Gialla '14	♟♟	2*
○ Collio Sauvignon '14	♟♟	2*
○ Collio Traminer Aromatico '14	♟♟	2*
● Ribolla Nera o Schioppettino '14	♟♟	3
● Collio Merlot '14	♟	3
● Collio Refosco P. R. '14	♟	3
○ COF Picolit Soreli a Mont '09	♟♟	5
○ Collio Pinot Bianco '13	♟♟	3*
○ Collio Pinot Bianco '06	♟♟	3

★★Vie di Romans

LOC. VIE DI ROMANS, 1
34070 MARIANO DEL FRIULI [GO]
TEL. 048169600
www.viediromans.it

CELLAR SALES
PRE-BOOKED VISITS
ANNUAL PRODUCTION 250,000 bottles
HECTARES UNDER VINE 53.00

The headquarters of Vie de Romans, created in 1978 by Gianfranco Gallo, is in the prestigious cellar at Mariano del Friuli. Countless barriques containing mainly white wines fill the underground floors, which will be released at least two years after the harvest. This winery is a real jewel in the region's winegrowing crown. The Gallo family's journey in growing and producing wine has taken a century but the best parts of the story are undoubtedly those offered today by Gianfranco. His complex and fragrant wines enhance the particular features of the Friuli Isonzo DOC, protected by the Alps and refreshed by the breezes from the nearby Adriatic. Four wines in the finals, often alternating, confirm the potential of the whole range, and in the end at least one earns the highest accolade. This year the Tre Bicchieri goes to the Chardonnay Ciampagnis Vieris 2013 which pipped the Malvasia Dis Cumieris 2013 at the post.

Vigna del Lauro

LOC. MONTONA, 19
34071 CORMÒNS [GO]
TEL. 0481629549
www.vignadellauro.it

CELLAR SALES
PRE-BOOKED VISITS
ANNUAL PRODUCTION 60,000 bottles
HECTARES UNDER VINE 10.00

Vigna di Lauro was established in 1994 by the partnership between Fabio Coser, former owner of Ronco dei Tassi, and German importer of Italian wines, Eberhard Spangenberg, in response to the need to vary production to satisfy the demands of the German market, which wanted simple, easy-drinking wines with typical features at affordable prices. To this end a first vineyard was identified, surrounded by the old laurel trees that give the estate its name. Other plots were added subsequently, some the estate's own and others rented, and there are now ten hectares near Cormòns: some on Collio and some in the Friuli Isonzo DOC zone. In the last edition we observed no significant differences between the two production zones, but this year the Collio wines are definitely a step ahead. They stand out for their vibrant, pleasing aromas but above all, for their fragrance and faithful expression of the grape.

○ Friuli Isonzo Chardonnay Ciampagnis Vieris '13	♟♟♟ 4*
○ Friuli Isonzo Friulano Dolée '13	♟♟ 5
○ Friuli Isonzo Malvasia Dis Cumieris '13	♟♟ 5
○ Friuli Isonzo Sauvignon Vieris '13	♟♟ 5
○ Dut'Un '12	♟♟ 6
○ Friuli Isonzo Bianco Flors di Uis '13	♟♟ 4
○ Friuli Isonzo Chardonnay Vie di Romans '13	♟♟ 5
○ Friuli Isonzo Pinot Grigio Dessimis '13	♟♟ 5
○ Friuli Isonzo Sauvignon Piere '13	♟♟ 5
○ Friuli Isonzo Bianco Flors di Uis '09	♟♟♟ 4*
○ Friuli Isonzo Friulano Dolée '12	♟♟♟ 5
○ Friuli Isonzo Friulano Dolée '11	♟♟♟ 4*
○ Friuli Isonzo Sauvignon Piere '10	♟♟♟ 4*
○ Friuli Isonzo Sauvignon Piere '08	♟♟♟ 4*

○ Collio Friulano '14	♟♟ 3
○ Collio Pinot Grigio '14	♟♟ 3
○ Collio Ribolla Gialla '14	♟♟ 3
○ Collio Sauvignon '14	♟♟ 3
● Friuli Isonzo Cabernet Franc '14	♟ 2
○ Friuli Isonzo Chardonnay '14	♟ 2
● Friuli Isonzo Merlot '13	♟ 2
○ Friuli Isonzo Traminer Aromatico '14	♟ 2
● Collio Sauvignon '99	♟♟♟ 2*
○ Collio Friulano '10	♟♟ 2*
○ Collio Pinot Grigio '13	♟♟ 3*
○ Collio Ribolla Gialla '06	♟♟ 3*
○ Collio Sauvignon '13	♟♟ 3
○ Collio Sauvignon '07	♟♟ 2*
● Friuli Isonzo Merlot '12	♟♟ 2*
● Friuli Isonzo Merlot '07	♟♟ 2*

Vigna Petrussa

VIA ALBANA, 47
33040 PREPOTTO [UD]
TEL. 0432713021
www.vignapetrussa.it

CELLAR SALES
PRE-BOOKED VISITS
ANNUAL PRODUCTION 30,000 bottles
HECTARES UNDER VINE 6.50

Hilde Petrussa is a doyenne, no . . . a
grand dame of the wine sector. In 1995
she remarried and retired to Albana di
Prepotto, and found herself looking after
the family estate established back in 1890,
flourishing in the early 20th century before
being abandoned. She tackled the problem
with determination, entrusting the vineyard
and cellar management to experts with
proven experience. When the vineyards
had to be converted she chose native
varieties, preferring ribolla nera which is
used to make Schioppettino. This wine has
always been linked to the Prepotto valley,
where the River Judrio marks the border
between Collio and Colli Orientali del Friuli.
The best feedback was awarded to the
Sauvignon 2014, with satisfying aromas of
varietal sensations blending with a
tropical hint, and a succulent, pleasing
palate. Also excellent, the Schioppettino di
Prepotto 2011 presents aromas of cherry
jam and green pepper, with a smoky hint,
and a soft, lively palate.

● COF Cabernet Franc '12	♟♟	3
● COF Schioppettino di Prepotto '11	♟♟	4
○ FCO Sauvignon '14	♟♟	3
○ Richenza '12	♟♟	4
○ FCO Friulano '14	♟	3
○ COF Bianco Richenza '10	♟♟	4
○ COF Bianco Richenza '09	♟♟	4
● COF Cabernet Franc '10	♟♟	3
● COF Cabernet Franc '08	♟♟	3*
○ COF Friulano '13	♟♟	3
○ COF Picolit '09	♟♟	5
● COF Refosco P. R. '06	♟♟	3*
● COF Schioppettino '07	♟♟	4
● COF Schioppettino di Prepotto '10	♟♟	4
○ Richenza '11	♟♟	4

Vigna Traverso

VIA RONCHI, 73
33040 PREPOTTO [UD]
TEL. 0422804807
www.vignatraverso.it

CELLAR SALES
PRE-BOOKED VISITS
RESTAURANT SERVICE
ANNUAL PRODUCTION 80,000 bottles
HECTARES UNDER VINE 22.00

Vigna Traverso dates back to 1998 when
Giancarlo Traverso and his wife Ornella
Molon, owners of the estate of the same
name in nearby Veneto, decided to
purchase 22 hectares of vineyards at
Ronco di Castagneto on the Prepotto hills in
the Colli Orientali del Friuli zone. They
entrusted their son Stefano with the
running of the estate: although very young
he was an oenologist with extensive
experience in the winegrowing sector.
Helped by vine physiologist Stefano
Zaninotti, he immediately set about
recovering old vineyards and then building
a new cellar equipped with modern
technology, while reintroducing the
traditional concrete vats. The Bianco
Sottocastello 2012, mainly chardonnay with
the addition of sauvignon, reveals
enthralling aromas of crème caramel,
vanilla and powder puff, while the
flavoursome palate closes with pleasing
aromatic sensations. The Schioppettino
Prepotto 2011 is lush, very spicy, soft,
mouthfilling and satisfying.

○ COF Bianco Sottocastello '12	♟♟	4
● COF Merlot '11	♟♟	3
● COF Schioppettino di Prepotto '11	♟♟	4
○ FCO Friulano '14	♟♟	3
○ FCO Sauvignon '14	♟♟	3
○ FCO Pinot Grigio '14	♟	3
○ FCO Ribolla Gialla '14	♟	3
● COF Cabernet Franc '11	♟♟	3*
○ COF Friulano '13	♟♟	3
○ COF Pinot Grigio '13	♟♟	3
○ COF Pinot Grigio '10	♟♟	3*
● COF Refosco P. R. '11	♟♟	3
● COF Rosso Sottocastello '04	♟♟	6
● COF Rosso Troj '11	♟♟	3
○ COF Sauvignon '09	♟♟	3*
● COF Schioppettino '11	♟♟	4

Vigne del Malina

FRAZ. ORZANO
VIA PASINI VIANELLI, 9
33047 REMANZACCO [UD]
TEL. 0432649258
www.vignedelmalina.com

CELLAR SALES
PRE-BOOKED VISITS
ANNUAL PRODUCTION 45,000 bottles
HECTARES UNDER VINE 10.00

In 1967 the Bacchetti family purchased an estate at Orzano di Remanzacco, in the Friuli Grave DOC zone, along with the prestigious 19th-century Villa Pasini Vianelli. The 150-hectare property included vineyards and in 2007 Roberto Bacchetti and Maria Luisa Trevisan decided to start producing wine. The two rivers running through the property, the Malina and the Ellero, trace the shape of a wineglass and inspired the name of the winery: Vigne del Malina. The vineyards and cellar are supervised by estate expert Omar Pantarotto and consultant oenologist Natale Favretto. This was the first estate in the region to obtain certification for vegan wines. The winery chooses to release the wines only when they have matured perfectly, after long months of bottle ageing. The Chardonnay 2012 has aromas of yellow peaches and broom flowers, and a supple, stylish palate. The Cabernet Franc 2011 has hints of red roses and tobacco, with a very succulent palate.

● Cabernet Franc '11	▼▼	3
○ Chardonnay '12	▼▼	3
○ Pinot Grigio '12	▼▼	3
○ Sauvignon '12	▼▼	3
● Cabernet Franc '09	♀♀	3
○ Friuli Grave Chardonnay '07	♀♀	4
● Friuli Grave Refosco P.R. '07	♀♀	4
○ Friuli Grave Sauvignon '09	♀♀	3
○ Friuli Grave Sauvignon '08	♀♀	2*
○ Pinot Grigio '11	♀♀	3
○ Pinot Grigio '10	♀♀	3
● Refosco P.R. '09	♀♀	4
○ Sauvignon '11	♀♀	3

★Le Vigne di Zamò

LOC. ROSAZZO
VIA ABATE CORRADO, 4
33044 MANZANO [UD]
TEL. 0432759693
www.levignedizamo.com

CELLAR SALES
PRE-BOOKED VISITS
ANNUAL PRODUCTION 280,000 bottles
HECTARES UNDER VINE 67.00
SUSTAINABLE WINERY

This famous winery dates back to 1996, the result of a project undertaken by Tullio Zamò, the unforgettable pioneer of quality Friuli wine production. In 1978 he created Vigne dal Leon on the slopes of Rocca Bernarda and a few years later introduced the Abbazia di Rosazzo brand. Following the purchase of another 15 hectares of vineyards opposite the abbey, he opened Le Vigne di Zamò with his sons Pierluigi and Silvano. Today the Zamò family's path has crossed and merged with that of the Farinetti group, aka Eataly. By joining forces they have been able to consolidate the winery and guarantee considerable international visibility. The Pinot Bianco Tullio Zamò 2102 reveals vibrant aromas of vanilla, dried fruit and incense, caressing and soaking the palate with delightfully silky sensations. The Friulano Vigna Cinquant'Anni 2013 repeats the performance seen in previous editions: generous, creamy, well-structured and harmonious as ever.

○ COF Friulano V. Cinquant'Anni '13	▼▼	5
○ COF Pinot Bianco Tullio Zamò '12	▼▼	5
● COF Refosco P. R. Re Fosco '09	▼▼	5
○ COF Ronco delle Acacie '12	▼▼	4
○ COF Rosazzo Bianco '12	▼▼	5
● COF Rosazzo Pignolo '08	▼▼	6
● COF Schioppettino '09	▼▼	5
○ FCO Ribolla Gialla di Rosazzo '14	▼	3
○ FCO Sauvignon '14	▼	3
○ COF Friulano V. Cinquant'Anni '09	♀♀♀	5
○ COF Friulano V. Cinquant'Anni '08	♀♀♀	5
● COF Merlot V. Cinquant'Anni '09	♀♀♀	5
● COF Merlot V. Cinquant'Anni '06	♀♀♀	5
○ COF Tocai Friulano V. Cinquant'Anni '06	♀♀♀	5

Villa de Puppi

VIA ROMA, 5
33040 MOIMACCO [UD]
TEL. 0432722461
www.depuppi.it

CELLAR SALES
PRE-BOOKED VISITS
ANNUAL PRODUCTION 70,000 bottles
HECTARES UNDER VINE 25.00
SUSTAINABLE WINERY

The winery created in 1991 by Conte Luigi de Puppi is found in the Moimacco villa, surrounded by its vineyards. Another ten hectares cover the beautiful hillsides of Rosazzo in the Colli Orientali del Friuli DOC. Originally from Tuscany the family descends from the famous Conti Guidi, prominent landowners and mercenaries who settled at Cividale del Friuli in the 13th century, enjoying distinguished careers in politics, law and the church. Today the estate is run by Luigi's children Caterina and Valfredo, and has expanded to incorporate the prestigious Rosa Bosco brand, made from selected grapes are aged in oak. All the wines are released as IGTs. An excellent performance from both product lines, and a particular mention for the Refosco dal Peduncolo Rosso Cate 2010 which received our unanimous approval and was ushered into the final selections. Vibrant aromas with hints of ripe morello cherries and dark chocolate, and a generous, succulent palate.

● Refosco P.R. Cate '10	♥♥ 5
● Cabernet '12	♥♥ 2*
● Merlot Il Boscorosso di Rosa Bosco '10	♥♥ 4
● Refosco P. R. '12	♥♥ 3
○ Ribolla Gialla di Rosa Bosco '13	♥♥ 4
○ Sauvignon '13	♥♥ 2*
○ Sauvignon Blanc di Rosa Bosco '12	♥♥ 4
○ Taj Blanc '13	♥♥ 2*
● Merlot '12	♥ 2
○ Chardonnay '12	♀♀ 2*
○ Chardonnay Cate '07	♀♀ 3*
● Merlot Il Boscorosso di Rosa Bosco '09	♀♀ 4
○ Sauvignon '12	♀♀ 3
○ Taj Blanc '12	♀♀ 2*
○ Taj Blanc '08	♀♀ 2*

★★Villa Russiz

VIA RUSSIZ, 6
34070 CAPRIVA DEL FRIULI [GO]
TEL. 048180047
www.villarussiz.it

CELLAR SALES
PRE-BOOKED VISITS
ANNUAL PRODUCTION 220,000 bottles
HECTARES UNDER VINE 45.00
SUSTAINABLE WINERY

Villa Russiz has a history of insights and generosity. In 1869 French count Teodoro de La Tour had the greatest vision, when he saw the sunny Collio hills as an ideal place to live with his Austrian wife Elvine Ritter and, especially, to grow vines. He is credited with introducing not only French grape varieties to Collio, where they have become the pride of the region, but also hitherto unknown winemaking techniques. Since they had no heirs, they decided to leave the estate and all their lands to the region as a charitable institution for disadvantaged children. This was the genesis of the Casa Famiglia, still running on the estate today. We usually find this prestigious estate's wines in the finals. This year it was the turn of the Merlot Gräf de La Tour 201, firm and flavoursome on the palate following the hints of crushed morello cherries, liquorice and coffee on the nose, and the fragrant, citrus-rich Pinot Bianco 2014, supple and well-balanced.

○ Collio Merlot Gräf de La Tour '11	♥♥ 6
○ Collio Pinot Bianco '14	♥♥ 4
○ Collio Friulano '14	♥♥ 4
○ Collio Malvasia '14	♥♥ 4
● Collio Merlot '12	♥♥ 4
○ Collio Pinot Grigio '14	♥♥ 4
○ Collio Sauvignon Bleu '13	♥♥ 7
○ Collio Sauvignon de La Tour '14	♥♥ 6
○ Collio Chardonnay Gräfin de La Tour '02	♀♀♀ 5
○ Collio Friulano '09	♀♀♀ 4*
● Collio Merlot Gräf de La Tour '02	♀♀♀ 6
○ Collio Pinot Bianco '07	♀♀♀ 3
○ Collio Sauvignon de La Tour '08	♀♀♀ 5
○ Collio Sauvignon de La Tour '05	♀♀♀ 5
○ Collio Sauvignon de La Tour '02	♀♀♀ 5
○ Collio Tocai Friulano '04	♀♀♀ 3

Tenuta Villanova

LOC. VILLANOVA
VIA CONTESSA BERETTA, 29
34072 FARRA D'ISONZO [GO]
TEL. 0481889311
www.tenutavillanova.com

CELLAR SALES
PRE-BOOKED VISITS
ANNUAL PRODUCTION 600,000 bottles
HECTARES UNDER VINE 105.00

Giuseppina Grossi Bennati and her nephew Alberto Grossi still run the estate purchased by her husband Arnaldo, a forward-thinking entrepreneur, back in 1932. Tenuta Villanova dates back to 1499 and its walls are custodians of over five centuries of history. The estate's natural meadows and dense woodlands surround 105 hectares under vine on the Collio hills, and on the equally excellent Isonzo plain wine country. These are cared for by technician Emanuele Mian who relies on expert consultant Giovanni Bigot. In the cellar, Sara Nadalutti takes care of vinification, with grapes from different areas enabling the winery to satisfy all market demands. A lovely performance from the whole range, proving that a large number of wines does not always compromise quality. The Refosco dal Peduncolo Rosso 2012 shows aromas of black cherries, blackberries, liquorice and spice, while the palate is soft and fragrant. The white wines are lovely and fresh, with coherent, supple palates.

○ Collio Pinot Grigio Ronco Cucco '14	♥♥ 3
○ Collio Ribolla Gialla Ronco Cucco '14	♥♥ 3
● Friuli Isonzo Refosco P. R. '12	♥♥ 2*
○ Friuli Isonzo Sauvignon '14	♥♥ 2*
○ Villanova Brut	♥♥ 3
○ Friuli Isonzo Chardonnay '14	♥ 2
○ Collio Chardonnay Ronco Cucco '07	♥♥ 3
● Collio Merlot Ronco Cucco '10	♥♥ 3
○ Collio Picolit Ronco Cucco '10	♥♥ 5
○ Collio Pinot Grigio Ronco Cucco '13	♥♥ 3
○ Friuli Isonzo Malvasia '13	♥♥ 2*
○ Friuli Isonzo Pinot Grigio '13	♥♥ 2*

Andrea Visintini

VIA GRAMOGLIANO, 27
33040 CORNO DI ROSAZZO [UD]
TEL. 0432755813
www.vinivisintini.com

CELLAR SALES
PRE-BOOKED VISITS
ANNUAL PRODUCTION 110,000 bottles
HECTARES UNDER VINE 20.00
VITICULTURE METHOD Certified Organic
SUSTAINABLE WINERY

The lovely watchtower built in 1560 that soars on the Corno di Rosazzo hillsides is part of the old feudal castle of Gramogliano, on whose ruins the Visintini winery is built. Of course, over the centuries there were many owners, until 1884 when it passed from the Conti Zucco di Cuccagna to the Visintini family. After being handed down through the generations, Andrea Visintini took over in 1973 and now his son Oliviero, with twins Cinzia and Palmira, continue the family business with renewed enthusiasm. Out of respect for family tradition, Oliviero practices simple winegrowing that respects the environment and keeps treatments to a minimum. Comparing scores obtained by the whole range of wines with their prices, we were impressed by what a good buy they are. All the standard-label wines are well-made and enjoyable, and the Refosco dal Peduncolo Rosso 2013 reached the finals for its complex aromas and balanced flavour.

● COF Refosco P. R. '13	♥♥ 2*
○ FCO Bianco '14	♥♥ 2*
○ FCO Sauvignon '14	♥♥ 2*
○ Malvasia '14	♥♥ 2*
○ FCO Friulano '14	♥ 2
○ FCO Pinot Bianco '14	♥ 2
○ FCO Pinot Grigio '14	♥ 2
○ FCO Ribolla Gialla '14	♥ 2
○ COF Bianco '13	♥♥ 2*
● COF Merlot '12	♥♥ 2*
○ COF Ribolla Gialla '13	♥♥ 2*
○ COF Sauvignon '13	♥♥ 2*
○ COF Sauvignon '11	♥♥ 2*
○ COF Sauvignon '09	♥♥ 2*

Oltrepò Pavese,
Pinot noir hills of Lombardy

Oltrepò Pavese, the agricultural soul of Lombardy

What is Oltrepò Pavese? It is the extreme point of the region of Lombardy, in the Province of Pavia, lying south of the river Po. It is roughly triangular in shape, like a kind of compact grape bunch attached to a cane, represented by the great river. The 13,500 hectares of vineyards make Oltrepò Pavese one of the most Italy's largest appellation. In this infinite sea of vineyards there are several different varieties but the unquestioned prince is Pinot Noir: with a surface area of about 3,000 hectares it is the largest area in Italy dedicated to this variety.

Over a century of traditional method white wine making

Already at the start of the twentieth century in Oltrepò, Pinot Noir was being made into large quantities of sparkling white wine, the most common wine type in the world using the traditional method. The result was a product that stood out from the spectrum of bubblies for the backbone and austerity of the variety, much appreciated by connoisseurs and more or less intensely softened by the contribution of yeasts during the long years of lees contact (vintage wines).

Cruasé, the flagship brand of the region

The creation of the Oltrepò Pavese Metodo Clasicco DOCG led to a debate which identified rosé as a real strong point. This wine is emblematic of the region, the grape variety and the noblest sparkling wine making method, all at the same time. The decision to make a rosé united the very individual nature of this bubbly together with the value of naturalness (lightly crushing Pinot Noir naturally generated a pinkish-coloured must), therefore the Consorzio Tutela Vini Oltrepò Pavese decided to reinforce it by endowing it with an immediately recognisable brand for the consumer, 'Cruasé'. 'Cruasé', (from 'cru' and rosé) defines the traditional method rosé made from Pinot Noir grapes in Oltrepò Pavese and today this product distinguishes the area from other traditional method sparkling wine-making areas, both in Italy and abroad. It is made as 'Brut', 'Extrabrut' and 'Brut Nature' and rests on the lees for at least 18 months; ideal with all courses of a meal, excellent with appetisers and finger food or as an original and seductive aperitif.

Pinot Noir as a red, a noble but difficult choice

Optimising the fermentation of Pinot Noir on the skins, done by some wineries at the start of the 1950s, led to the creation of the 'Pinot nero dell'Oltrepò pavese' DOC in 2010, wholly dedicated to this still wine. Vinification of Pinot Noir with skin contact, as winemakers all over the world know well, is beset with tensions and often disappointment, but heralds the most amazing successes when all the elements of the suitability of the winemaking area are expressed. A difficult challenge that allows Oltrepò to compete with areas of the world where bottles epitomise the legend of the wine itself.

Discover
Oltrepò Pavese

www.vinoltrepo.it / info@vinoltrepo.it

CAMPAGNA FINANZIATA AI SENSI DEL REG. CE. N. 1308/2013
CAMPAIGN FUNDED UNDER EC REG. N. 1308/2013

Vitas 1907

LOC. STRASSOLDO
VIA SAN MARCO, 5
33050 CERVIGNANO DEL FRIULI [UD]
TEL. 043193083
www.vitas.it

CELLAR SALES
PRE-BOOKED VISITS
ACCOMMODATION
ANNUAL PRODUCTION 70,000 bottles
HECTARES UNDER VINE 15.00
SUSTAINABLE WINERY

Villa Vitas was created in the early 20th
century by Romano Vitas, and since 1993
has been managed by the fourth
generation, Roberto Vitas. The headquarters
are at Strassoldo, in the historic
18th-century residence immersed in an
ancient park and surrounded by vineyards.
The 15 hectares of vineyards fall within the
Friuli Aquileia DOC zone, where the subsoil
is alluvial in origin, clayey and rich in
mineral debris. Proximity to the sea creates
an ideal microclimate that softens the
winter temperatures and reduces humidity
with constant breezes. Roberto's dynamic
energy and ongoing renewal, are supported
by consultant oenologist Andrea Pittana.
This year, again, the wines obtained
excellent scores, demonstrating continuity
of their high quality, especially considering
the reasonable prices. The Vigneto
Romano 2010, a blend of merlot, cabernet
and refosco, was particularly good, earning
the same appreciative feedback as in last
year's edition.

● Friuli Aquileia Refosco P. R. '13	♥♥	2*
○ Friuli Aquileia Sauvignon '14	♥♥	2*
○ Marlet '13	♥♥	3
○ Traminer Aromatico '14	♥♥	2*
● Vign. Romano '10	♥♥	3
○ Friuli Aquileia Friulano '14	♥	2
● Friuli Aquileia Cabernet Franc '13	♥	2
● Malvasia Villa Vitas '14	♥	2
● Friuli Aquileia Cabernet Franc '12	♀♀	2*
● Friuli Aquileia Refosco dal P. R. '12	♀♀	3
○ Friuli Aquileia Sauvignon '11	♀♀	3
○ Marlet '12	♀♀	4
● Vign. Romano '09	♀♀	3
● Vign. Romano '07	♀♀	3

★Volpe Pasini

FRAZ. TOGLIANO
VIA CIVIDALE, 16
33040 TORREANO [UD]
TEL. 0432715151
www.volpepasini.it

CELLAR SALES
PRE-BOOKED VISITS
ACCOMMODATION
ANNUAL PRODUCTION 400,000 bottles
HECTARES UNDER VINE 52.00
SUSTAINABLE WINERY

A visit to Volpe Pasini is an engaging and
enthralling experience for any wine buff. Its
sheer history, dating back to 1596,
vineyard-gardens, cellars steeped in
tradition with an eye to the future, and
above all the passion of the men and
women united in pursuit of the best
possible quality while respecting the
balance of nature. This is the wonderful
recipe that over the last 20 years has led
to an incredible standard of excellence,
achieved immediately and increased year
after year. Emilio Rotolo and his sons
Francesco and Alessandro, with Lorenzo
Landi, continue to aim for the best,
always. Expert John Turato is tasked with
the cellarwork. The Sauvignon Zuc di
Volpe 2014 is by now established at the
top of the heap, earning Tre Bicchieri for
the sixth year running. A complex,
well-organized nose with fragrant hints of
bud flowers, citrus fruit and white melon,
while the palate is dynamic, sophisticated
and enjoyable.

○ FCO Sauvignon Zuc di Volpe '14	♥♥♥	5
● COF Merlot Focus '11	♥♥	5
○ FCO Pinot Bianco Zuc di Volpe '14	♥♥	5
○ FCO Pinot Grigio Zuc di Volpe '14	♥♥	4
● COF Refosco P. R. Volpe Pasini '11	♥♥	3
● COF Refosco P. R. Zuc di Volpe '11	♥♥	5
○ FCO Friulano Volpe Pasini '14	♥♥	3
○ FCO Pinot Grigio Grivò Volpe Pasini '14	♥♥	3
○ FCO Ribolla Gialla Zuc di Volpe '14	♥♥	4
○ FCO Sauvignon Volpe Pasini '14	♥♥	3
○ COF Pinot Bianco Zuc di Volpe '12	♀♀♀	4*
○ COF Pinot Bianco Zuc di Volpe '10	♀♀♀	4
○ COF Sauvignon Zuc di Volpe '13	♀♀♀	4*
○ COF Sauvignon Zuc di Volpe '12	♀♀♀	4*
○ COF Sauvignon Zuc di Volpe '11	♀♀♀	4*

Francesco Vosca

FRAZ. BRAZZANO
VIA SOTTOMONTE, 19
34071 CORMÒNS [GO]
TEL. 048162135
www.voscavini.it

CELLAR SALES
PRE-BOOKED VISITS
ANNUAL PRODUCTION 50,000 bottles
HECTARES UNDER VINE 8.50

Today we associate the name of Collio with great wines, flourishing nature and general wellbeing, but Francesco Vosca likes to remember that in the 1970s poverty reigned and many were forced to emigrate. As a child, he himself was forced to go and dig the fields. His small estate at Brazzano, in the Cormòns district, has proudly humble origins. The lay of the land planted with vineyards, on the Collio hills and the Isonzo plain, makes manual procedures necessary and Francesco's wife Anita has no qualms about joining in the work. Son Gabriele is in charge of vinification and Elisabetta looks after accounts and public relations. The whole range is very coherent, showing that there is practically no difference between the wines produced from plains-grown or hill-grown grapes. The Malvasia 2014 was praised for its nose-palate consistency with varietal features of dried herbs and bay leaves, and its perfectly balanced flavour.

○ Collio Friulano '14	♟♟	3
○ Collio Malvasia '14	♟♟	3
○ Collio Ribolla Gialla '14	♟♟	3
○ Friuli Isonzo Pinot Grigio '14	♟♟	3
○ Friuli Isonzo Sauvignon '14	♟♟	3
○ Friuli Isonzo Chardonnay '14	♟	3
○ Collio Friulano '13	♟♟	3
○ Collio Friulano '12	♟♟	3*
○ Collio Malvasia '13	♟♟	3
○ Collio Malvasia '11	♟♟	3*
○ Collio Malvasia '09	♟♟	2*
● Collio Merlot '11	♟♟	4
○ Collio Ribolla Gialla '13	♟♟	3
○ Friuli Isonzo Pinot Grigio '13	♟♟	3
○ Friuli Isonzo Pinot Grigio '12	♟♟	3

Zidarich

LOC. PREPOTTO, 23
34011 DUINO AURISINA [TS]
TEL. 040201223
www.zidarich.it

CELLAR SALES
PRE-BOOKED VISITS
ANNUAL PRODUCTION 28,000 bottles
HECTARES UNDER VINE 8.00

In 1988 Beniamino Zidarich revolutionized his father's estate at Duino Aurisina, Prepotto, in the heart of the Trieste Carso. The property then had just half a hectare of vineyards but progressive development and expansion, though fragmented, has been very successful, especially considering the morphological composition of the lands with plenty of rock and little red soil. The cellar was carved out of the rock, as typically happens hereabouts, and keeps the wines at cool subsoil temperatures, while from above it enjoys a magnificent view of the gulf of Trieste. The no-frills wines are hardy, richly extracted, mouthwatering and uncompromising. Beniamino decided to delay bottling the 2013 vintage so we will have to wait till next year's Guide to review them. This year we just tasted the Ruje 2010, a monovarietal Merlot aged in barriques for 48 months, and the Vitovska Kamen 2013, fermented in karst stone vats.

● Ruje '10	♟♟	7
○ Vitovska Kamen '13	♟♟	7
○ Carso Malvasia '09	♟♟♟	5
○ Carso Malvasia '06	♟♟♟	5
○ Carso Vitovska V. Collezione '09	♟♟♟	8
○ Prulke '10	♟♟♟	5
○ Prulke '08	♟♟♟	5
○ Malvasia '12	♟♟	5
○ Prulke '12	♟♟	5
● Terrano '12	♟♟	5
○ Vitovska '12	♟♟	5

Zorzettig

FRAZ. SPESSA
S.DA SANT'ANNA, 37
33043 CIVIDALE DEL FRIULI [UD]
TEL. 0432716156
www.zorzettigvini.it

CELLAR SALES
PRE-BOOKED VISITS
ACCOMMODATION AND RESTAURANT SERVICE
ANNUAL PRODUCTION 800,000 bottles
HECTARES UNDER VINE 110.00
SUSTAINABLE WINERY

The estate established in 1986 by Cavalier
Giuseppe Zorzettig has maintained the
family name, shared by many generations
of winegrowers at Spessa di Cividale. It is
now managed with innate entrepreneurial
skill by Annalisa Zorzettig, while her brother
Alessandro is in charge of the 110 hectares
of vineyards in the Colli Orientali del Friuli
zone. The pursuit of new stimuli and the
desire to distinguish itself have motivated
the family to launch an ambitious project
now in the hands of Fabio Coser, which
consists of selecting the best grapes for a
new production line named Myò. The
constant improvement in quality we noted
in previous editions of the Guide has now
been consolidated with two wines in the
finals, and the Pinot Bianco Myò 2014
earning its first Tre Bicchieri. Delightfully
fragrant, fruity aromas reflected on the
tangy, soft, delicious palate.

○ FCO Pinot Bianco Myò '14	♥♥♥ 4*
● COF Refosco P.R. Myò '12	♥♥ 4
● COF Pignolo Myò '11	♥♥ 6
● COF Schioppettino Myò '12	♥♥ 5
○ FCO Chardonnay '14	♥♥ 3
○ FCO Friulano '14	♥♥ 3
○ FCO Friulano Myò '14	♥♥ 4
○ FCO Malvasia Myò '14	♥♥ 4
○ FCO Pinot Grigio '14	♥ 3
○ FCO Ribolla Gialla '14	♥ 3
○ Spumante Brut Optimum '14	♥ 3
○ COF Friulano Myò '13	♀♀ 4
○ COF Pinot Bianco Myò '13	♀♀ 4
○ COF Sauvignon Myò '13	♀♀ 4

Zuani

LOC. GIASBANA, 12
34070 SAN FLORIANO DEL COLLIO [GO]
TEL. 0481391432
www.zuanivini.it

CELLAR SALES
PRE-BOOKED VISITS
ACCOMMODATION
ANNUAL PRODUCTION 75,000 bottles
HECTARES UNDER VINE 15.00

In 2001 Patrizia Felluga followed in the
footsteps of her renowned father Marco,
and moved to San Floriano del Collio,
setting up the Zuani estate in a pleasant
location called Giasbana. She purchased
15 hectares of vineyards planted with four
white grape varieties: friulano, chardonnay,
sauvignon, and pinot grigio, in practically
equal parts. She and children Antonio and
Caterina took on the challenge of producing
a single wine: Collio, an authentic
expression of the terroir. This courageous
choice derived from their belief that these
vineyards could fulfil a longstanding dream
and that wine now comes in two versions:
Zuani Vigne, fermented in stainless steel,
and Zuani Riserva, aged in oak. In past
editions, the Zuani Vigne almost always
obtained the best scores, while this year
the two versions were of the same
standard. The steel-fermented version is
naturally fresh, subtle and floral on the
nose with a supple palate, while the
oak-aged version is more sumptuous,
structured and creamy.

○ Collio Bianco Zuani Ris. '12	♥♥ 5
○ Collio Bianco Zuani Vigne '14	♥♥ 4
○ Collio Bianco Zuani Vigne '10	♀♀♀ 3
○ Collio Bianco Zuani Vigne '07	♀♀♀ 3
○ Collio Bianco Zuani '08	♀♀ 5
○ Collio Bianco Zuani '07	♀♀ 5
○ Collio Bianco Zuani Ris. '11	♀♀ 5
○ Collio Bianco Zuani Ris. '10	♀♀ 5
○ Collio Bianco Zuani Ris. '09	♀♀ 5
○ Collio Bianco Zuani Vigne '13	♀♀ 4
○ Collio Bianco Zuani Vigne '12	♀♀ 3*
○ Collio Bianco Zuani Vigne '11	♀♀ 3
○ Collio Bianco Zuani Vigne '09	♀♀ 3
○ Collio Bianco Zuani Vigne '08	♀♀ 3*

Giuseppe e Luigi Anselmi

VIA BASSI, 16
33050 POCENIA [UD]
TEL. 0432779157
www.giuseppeeluigivini.it

CELLAR SALES
PRE-BOOKED VISITS
ANNUAL PRODUCTION 1,800,000 bottles
HECTARES UNDER VINE 217.30

● Collio Cabernet Franc La Reguta '13	♟♟ 3
○ Collio Friulano La Reguta '14	♟♟ 3
○ Collio Pinot Grigio La Reguta '14	♟♟ 3
○ Collio Ribolla Gialla La Reguta '14	♟♟ 3

Anzelin

VIA PLESSIVA, 4
34071 CORMÒNS [GO]
TEL. 0481639821
www.anzelin.it

CELLAR SALES
PRE-BOOKED VISITS
ANNUAL PRODUCTION 24,000 bottles
HECTARES UNDER VINE 9.00

○ Collio Friulano '14	♟♟ 3
○ Collio Pinot Grigio '14	♟♟ 3
○ Collio Sauvignon '14	♟♟ 3
○ Collio Pinot Bianco '14	♟ 3

Maurizio Arzenton

FRAZ. SPESSA
VIA CORMONS, 221
33043 CIVIDALE DEL FRIULI [UD]
TEL. 0432716139
www.arzentonvini.it

CELLAR SALES
PRE-BOOKED VISITS
ANNUAL PRODUCTION 30,000 bottles
HECTARES UNDER VINE 10.00

○ FCO Friulano '14	♟♟ 2*
○ FCO Pinot Grigio '14	♟♟ 2*
○ FCO Sauvignon '14	♟♟ 3
● COF Schioppettino '12	♟ 3

Attems

FRAZ. CAPRIVA DEL FRIULI
VIA AQUILEIA, 30
34070 GORIZIA
TEL. 0481806098
www.attems.it

CELLAR SALES
PRE-BOOKED VISITS
ANNUAL PRODUCTION 365,000 bottles
HECTARES UNDER VINE 62.00

○ Collio Friulano '14	♟♟ 2*
○ Collio Sauvignon Blanc Cicinis '13	♟♟ 4
○ Pinot Grigio '14	♟♟ 2*
○ Sauvignon Blanc '14	♟ 3

Bajta

VIA SALES, 108
34010 SGONICO [TS]
TEL. 0402296090
www.bajta.it

ANNUAL PRODUCTION 18,000 bottles
HECTARES UNDER VINE 4.00

○ Malvasia '13	♟♟ 3
○ Vitovska '14	♟♟ 3
● Terrano '14	♟ 3

La Bellanotte

S.DA DELLA BELLANOTTE, 3
34072 FARRA D'ISONZO [GO]
TEL. 0481888020
www.labellanotte.it

CELLAR SALES
PRE-BOOKED VISITS
ANNUAL PRODUCTION 100,000 bottles
HECTARES UNDER VINE 12.00
SUSTAINABLE WINERY

⊙ Pinot Grigio Ramato Conte Lucio '13	♟♟ 3
○ Collio Pinot Grigio '14	♟ 3
● Friuli Isonzo Merlot Roja de Isonzo '12	♟ 4
○ Vento dell'Est '14	♟ 8

Benincasa

LOC. SPESSA DI CIVIDALE
S.DA RONCHI SAN GIUSEPPE, 5
33043 CIVIDALE DEL FRIULI [UD]
TEL. 0432716419
vinibenincasa@libero.it

ANNUAL PRODUCTION 25,000 bottles
HECTARES UNDER VINE 10.00

○ COF Chardonnay '13	♥♥ 4
○ COF Sauvignon '13	♥♥ 4
○ COF Pinot Grigio '13	♥ 4

Bidoli

FRAZ. ARCANO SUPERIORE
VIA FORNACE, 19
33030 RIVE D'ARCANO [UD]
TEL. 0432810796
www.bidolivini.com

CELLAR SALES
PRE-BOOKED VISITS
ANNUAL PRODUCTION 1,000,000 bottles
HECTARES UNDER VINE

○ Friuli Grave Pinot Grigio '14	♥♥ 2*
○ Friuli Grave Sauvignon Blanc Le Alte '14	♥ 2
○ Friuli Grave Traminer Aromatico Le Alte '14	♥ 2

Blason

VIA ROMA, 32
34072 GRADISCA D'ISONZO [GO]
TEL. 048192414
www.blasonwines.com

CELLAR SALES
PRE-BOOKED VISITS
ANNUAL PRODUCTION 60,000 bottles
HECTARES UNDER VINE 18.00

○ Friuli Isonzo Bruma Bianco '13	♥♥ 3
○ Friuli Isonzo Pinot Grigio '14	♥♥ 3
○ Malvasia '14	♥♥ 3
● Friuli Isonzo Cabernet Sauvignon '13	♥ 2

Blazic

LOC. ZEGLA, 16
34071 CORMÒNS [GO]
TEL. 048161720
www.blazic.it

CELLAR SALES
PRE-BOOKED VISITS
ANNUAL PRODUCTION 15,000 bottles
HECTARES UNDER VINE 6.50

○ Collio Sauvignon '14	♥♥ 3
○ Collio Ribolla Gialla '14	♥ 3

Tenuta Borgo Conventi

S.DA DELLA COLOMBARA, 13
24070 FARRA D'ISONZO [GO]
TEL. 0481888004
www.borgoconventi.it

CELLAR SALES
PRE-BOOKED VISITS
ANNUAL PRODUCTION 350,000 bottles
HECTARES UNDER VINE 40.00

○ Collio Ribolla Gialla '14	♥♥ 3
○ Collio Sauvignon '14	♥♥ 3
○ Friuli Isonzo Friulano '14	♥♥ 2*
○ Collio Chardonnay '14	♥ 3

Borgo Magredo

LOC. TAURIANO
VIA BASALDELLA, 5
33090 SPILIMBERGO [PN]
TEL. 0422864511
www.borgomagredo.it

CELLAR SALES
PRE-BOOKED VISITS
ANNUAL PRODUCTION 480,000 bottles
HECTARES UNDER VINE 98.00
SUSTAINABLE WINERY

○ Friuli Grave Chardonnay '14	♥ 2
● Friuli Grave Merlot '14	♥ 2
● Friuli Grave Refosco P. R. '14	♥ 2
○ Friuli Grave Sauvignon '14	♥ 2

Braidot

LOC. VERSA
VIA PALMANOVA, 20 B
34076 ROMANS D'ISONZO [GO]
TEL. 0481908970
www.braidotwines.it

CELLAR SALES
PRE-BOOKED VISITS
ANNUAL PRODUCTION 400,000 bottles
HECTARES UNDER VINE 60.00

○ Bianco 1870 Ris. '13	♥♥	2*
○ Ribolla Gialla '14	♥♥	2*
○ Sauvignon Blanc '14	♥♥	2*
○ Traminer Aromatico '14	♥	2

Ca' Ronesca

FRAZ. LONZANO
VIA CASALI ZORUTTI, 2
34070 DOLEGNA DEL COLLIO [GO]
TEL. 048160034
www.caronesca.it

CELLAR SALES
PRE-BOOKED VISITS
ANNUAL PRODUCTION 250,000 bottles
HECTARES UNDER VINE 55.00

○ Collio Pinot Bianco '14	♥♥	3
○ Collio Sauvignon '14	♥♥	3
○ Collio Marnà '13	♥	4
○ Collio Pinot Grigio '14	♥	3

Ca' Selva

S.DA DI SEQUALS, 11A
33090 SEQUALS [PN]
TEL. 0434630216
www.caselva.it

CELLAR SALES
PRE-BOOKED VISITS
ANNUAL PRODUCTION 900,000 bottles
HECTARES UNDER VINE 22.00
VITICULTURE METHOD Certified Organic

● Rosso 55 '13	♥♥	3
○ Prosecco Brut '14	♥	2
○ Ribolla Gialla '14	♥	2
○ Sauvignon '14	♥	2

Cantarutti

VIA RONCHI, 9
33048 SAN GIOVANNI AL NATISONE [UD]
TEL. 0432756317
www.cantaruttialfieri.it

CELLAR SALES
PRE-BOOKED VISITS
ACCOMMODATION AND RESTAURANT SERVICE
ANNUAL PRODUCTION 110,000 bottles
HECTARES UNDER VINE 54.00

○ FCO Pinot Grigio '14	♥♥	2*
○ FCO Ribolla Gialla '14	♥♥	3
○ FCO Friulano '14	♥	2

Colli di Poianls

VIA POIANIS, 34A
33040 PREPOTTO [UD]
TEL. 0432713185
www.collidipoianis.it

CELLAR SALES
ACCOMMODATION
ANNUAL PRODUCTION 50,000 bottles
HECTARES UNDER VINE 11.00
SUSTAINABLE WINERY

○ COF Chardonnay '13	♥♥	3
● COF Rosso Ronco della Poiana '11	♥♥	4
○ FCO Pinot Grigio '14	♥♥	3
○ FCO Friulano '14	♥	3

Conti Formentini

VIA OSLAVIA, 5
34070 SAN FLORIANO DEL COLLIO [GO]
TEL. 0481884131
www.contiformentini.it

CELLAR SALES
PRE-BOOKED VISITS
ANNUAL PRODUCTION 200,000 bottles
HECTARES UNDER VINE 85.00

○ Collio Chardonnay '14	♥♥	3
○ Collio Ribolla Gialla Rajande '14	♥♥	3
○ Collio Friulano Furlanà '14	♥	3
○ Collio Pinot Grigio '14	♥	3

Le Due Torri

LOC. VICINALE DEL JUDRIO
VIA SAN MARTINO, 19
33040 CORNO DI ROSAZZO [UD]
TEL. 0432759150
www.le2torri.com

CELLAR SALES
PRE-BOOKED VISITS
ANNUAL PRODUCTION 36,000 bottles
HECTARES UNDER VINE 7.60

○ Friuli Grave Friulano '14	🍷🍷 2*
● Friuli Grave Refosco P.R. '11	🍷🍷 3
○ Ribolla Gialla '14	🍷🍷 2*
○ Friuli Grave Sauvignon '14	🍷 2

Le Favole

LOC. TERRA ROSSA
VIA DIETRO CASTELLO, 7
33077 CANEVA [PN]
TEL. 0434735604
www.lefavole.com

CELLAR SALES
PRE-BOOKED VISITS
ACCOMMODATION
ANNUAL PRODUCTION 60,000 bottles
HECTARES UNDER VINE 20.00

○ Friuli Annia Malvasia Istriana '14	🍷🍷 2*
● Friuli Annia Noglar '11	🍷🍷 3
● Friuli Annia Refosco P. R. Storiis '12	🍷🍷 3
○ Giallo di Roccia Brut	🍷🍷 4

I Feudi di Romans

LOC. PIERIS
VIA CA DEL BOSCO, 16
34075 SAN CANZIAN D'ISONZO [GO]
TEL. 048176445
www.ifeudidiromans.it

CELLAR SALES
ANNUAL PRODUCTION 500,000 bottles
HECTARES UNDER VINE 90.00

○ Friuli Isonzo Chardonnay '14	🍷🍷 2*
○ Friuli Isonzo Pinot Bianco '14	🍷🍷 2*
○ Malvasia Istriana '14	🍷🍷 2*
○ Friuli Isonzo Sauvignon Blanc '14	🍷 3

Flaibani

VIA CASALI COSTA, 7
33043 CIVIDALE DEL FRIULI [UD]
TEL. 0432730943
www.flaibani.it

CELLAR SALES
PRE-BOOKED VISITS
ANNUAL PRODUCTION 12,000 bottles
HECTARES UNDER VINE 3.50
VITICULTURE METHOD Certified Organic

● COF Merlot '12	🍷🍷 4
● Refosco P.R. '13	🍷🍷 4
○ Riviere Bianco '14	🍷🍷 3
○ FCO Pinot Grigio Ramato '14	🍷 3

Foffani

FRAZ. CLAUIANO
P.ZZA GIULIA, 13
33050 TRIVIGNANO UDINESE [UD]
TEL. 0432999584
www.foffani.it

CELLAR SALES
PRE-BOOKED VISITS
ACCOMMODATION
ANNUAL PRODUCTION 80,000 bottles
HECTARES UNDER VINE 10.00

○ Friuli Aquileia Pinot Grigio Sup. '14	🍷🍷 2*
○ Friuli Aquileia Sauvignon '14	🍷 3
○ Merlot Bianco '14	🍷 3
⊙ Moscato Rosa '13	🍷 3

Forchir

LOC. CASALI BIANCHINI, 1
33030 CAMINO AL TAGLIAMENTO [UD]
TEL. 042796037
www.forchir.it

CELLAR SALES
PRE-BOOKED VISITS
ANNUAL PRODUCTION 1,200,000 bottles
HECTARES UNDER VINE 230.00
VITICULTURE METHOD Certified Organic

○ Friuli Grave Sauvignon Soresere '14	🍷🍷 2*
○ Friuli Grave Traminer Aromatico Glère '14	🍷🍷 2*
○ Friuli Grave Pinot Grigio Lamis '14	🍷 2
● Friuli Grave Pinot Nero '13	🍷 3

Fossa Mala

VIA BASSI, 81
33080 FIUME VENETO [PN]
TEL. 0434957997
www.fossamala.it

CELLAR SALES
PRE-BOOKED VISITS
ACCOMMODATION AND RESTAURANT SERVICE
ANNUAL PRODUCTION 100,000 bottles
HECTARES UNDER VINE 37.00

○ Friuli Grave Chardonnay '14	🍷🍷 2*
● Friuli Grave Refosco P. R. Re Fossa Ris. '11	🍷🍷 4
○ Friuli Grave Friulano '14	🍷 2
○ Friuli Grave Traminer Aromatico '14	🍷 2

Humar

LOC. VALERISCE, 20
34070 SAN FLORIANO DEL COLLIO [GO]
TEL. 0481884197
www.humar.it

CELLAR SALES
PRE-BOOKED VISITS
ANNUAL PRODUCTION 60,000 bottles
HECTARES UNDER VINE 12.00

○ Collio Ribolla Gialla '14	🍷🍷 3
● Collio Merlot '13	🍷 3
○ Collio Pinot Grigio '14	🍷 3

Rado Kocjancic

FRAZ. DOLINA
VIA CROGOLE, 11
34018 SAN DORLIGO DELLA VALLE [TS]
TEL. 3483063298
www.radokocjancic.eu

CELLAR SALES
PRE-BOOKED VISITS
ANNUAL PRODUCTION 15,000 bottles
HECTARES UNDER VINE 5.00

○ Carso Malvasia '13	🍷🍷 2*
● Carso Refosco P. R. '13	🍷 5

Albano Guerra

LOC. MONTINA
V.LE KENNEDY, 39A
33040 TORREANO [UD]
TEL. 0432715479
www.guerraalbano.it

CELLAR SALES
PRE-BOOKED VISITS
ANNUAL PRODUCTION 60,000 bottles
HECTARES UNDER VINE 10.00

● COF Merlot '10	🍷🍷 2*
○ COF Passion Bianco Guerra Albano '12	🍷🍷 2*
○ FCO Malvasia Istriana '14	🍷🍷 2*
○ Giuliet Brut	🍷 3

Isola Augusta

CASALI ISOLA AUGUSTA, 4
33056 PALAZZOLO DELLO STELLA [UD]
TEL. 043158046
www.isolaugusta.com

CELLAR SALES
PRE-BOOKED VISITS
ACCOMMODATION AND RESTAURANT SERVICE
ANNUAL PRODUCTION 270,000 bottles
HECTARES UNDER VINE 65.00
SUSTAINABLE WINERY

● Friuli Latisana Augusteo '10	🍷🍷 4
○ Friuli Latisana Chardonnay '14	🍷 2
● Friuli Latisana Refosco P. R. '12	🍷 2
○ Ribolla Gialla '14	🍷 2

Komjanc

LOC. GIASBANA, 35
34070 SAN FLORIANO DEL COLLIO [GO]
TEL. 0481391228
www.komjancalessio.com

CELLAR SALES
PRE-BOOKED VISITS
ANNUAL PRODUCTION 70,000 bottles
HECTARES UNDER VINE 23.00
SUSTAINABLE WINERY

○ Collio Friulano '14	🍷🍷 2*
○ Malvasia Istriana '14	🍷🍷 2*
○ Collio Pinot Grigio '14	🍷 2
○ Collio Ribolla Gialla '14	🍷 2

Obiz

B.GO GORTANI, 2
33052 CERVIGNANO DEL FRIULI [UD]
TEL. 043131900
www.obiz.it

CELLAR SALES
ANNUAL PRODUCTION 100,000 bottles
HECTARES UNDER VINE 25.00

○ Friuli Aquileia Friulano Tampia '14	♛♛ 2*
● Friuli Aquileia Merlot Popone '14	♛♛ 2*
● Friuli Aquileia Refosco P.R. Teodoro '13	♛♛ 2*
● Natissa '13	♛♛ 2*

Parovel

LOC. CARESANA, 81
34018 SAN DORLIGO DELLA VALLE [TS]
TEL. 040227050
www.parovel.com

ANNUAL PRODUCTION 35,000 bottles
HECTARES UNDER VINE 11.00
SUSTAINABLE WINERY

○ Carso Malvasia Istriana Poje '13	♛♛ 5
○ Carso Vitovska Onavè '12	♛♛ 5
○ Matos Nonet '11	♛♛ 6
● Terrano Hodì '13	♛♛ 4

Norina Pez

VIA ZORUTTI, 4
34070 DOLEGNA DEL COLLIO [GO]
TEL. 0481639951
www.norinapez.it

CELLAR SALES
PRE-BOOKED VISITS
ANNUAL PRODUCTION 40,000 bottles
HECTARES UNDER VINE 7.00

● Collio Cabernet Franc '13	♛♛ 2*
● Rosso El Neri di Norina '11	♛♛ 5
○ Collio Friulano '14	♛ 2
○ Collio Sauvignon '14	♛ 2

Pighin

FRAZ. RISANO
V.LE GRADO, 11/1
33050 PAVIA DI UDINE [UD]
TEL. 0432675444
www.pighin.com

CELLAR SALES
PRE-BOOKED VISITS
ANNUAL PRODUCTION 1,000,000 bottles
HECTARES UNDER VINE 180.00

● Collio Merlot '12	♛♛ 5
○ Collio Picolit '13	♛♛ 5
○ Collio Sauvignon '14	♛♛ 5
● Friuli Grave Refosco P. R. '12	♛♛ 4

Tenuta Pinni

VIA SAN OSVALDO, 3
33098 SAN MARTINO AL TAGLIAMENTO [PN]
TEL. 0434899464
www.tenutapinni.com

CELLAR SALES
PRE-BOOKED VISITS
ANNUAL PRODUCTION 30,000 bottles
HECTARES UNDER VINE 23.55
SUSTAINABLE WINERY

○ Chardonnay '14	♛♛ 3
○ Sauvignon '14	♛♛ 3
○ Friuli Grave Friulano '13	♛ 2
○ Traminer Aromatico '13	♛ 2

Pitars

VIA TONELLO, 10
33098 SAN MARTINO AL TAGLIAMENTO [PN]
TEL. 043488078
www.pitars.it

CELLAR SALES
PRE-BOOKED VISITS
ANNUAL PRODUCTION 250,000 bottles
HECTARES UNDER VINE 125.00

● Friuli Grave Brumal '12	♛♛ 3
○ Friuli Grave Friulano '14	♛♛ 2*
○ Friuli Grave Pinot Grigio '14	♛♛ 2*
○ Tureis '12	♛♛ 3

Polje

loc. Novali, 11
34071 Cormòns [GO]
Tel. 047160660
www.polje.com

CELLAR SALES
PRE-BOOKED VISITS
ANNUAL PRODUCTION 25,000 bottles
HECTARES UNDER VINE 12.00

○ Collio Sauvignon '14 🍷🍷 3
○ Collio Friulano '14 🍷🍷 3
○ Collio Ribolla Gialla '14 🍷 3

Pradio

loc. Felettis
via Udine, 17
33050 Bicinicco [UD]
Tel. 0432990123
www.pradio.it

CELLAR SALES
PRE-BOOKED VISITS
ANNUAL PRODUCTION 400,000 bottles
HECTARES UNDER VINE 33.00

● Friuli Grave Cabernet Sauvignon Crearo '12 🍷🍷 2*
○ Friuli Grave Chardonnay Teraje '14 🍷🍷 2*
○ Friuli Grave Pinot Grigio Priara '14 🍷🍷 2*
○ Friuli Grave Sauvignon Sobaja '14 🍷🍷 2*

Ronco dei Pini

via Ronchi, 93
33040 Prepotto [UD]
Tel. 0432713239
www.roncodeipini.it

CELLAR SALES
PRE-BOOKED VISITS
ANNUAL PRODUCTION 90,000 bottles
HECTARES UNDER VINE 15.00

● COF Schioppettino di Prepotto '11 🍷🍷 5
○ FCO Friulano '14 🍷🍷 3
○ FCO Sauvignon '14 🍷🍷 5
● Limes Rosso '11 🍷🍷 5

Ronco Margherita

via Udine, 40
33044 Manzano [UD]
Tel. 0427949809
www.roncomargherita.it

CELLAR SALES
PRE-BOOKED VISITS
ANNUAL PRODUCTION 100,000 bottles
HECTARES UNDER VINE 40.00

○ Bianco '12 🍷🍷 3
● COF Cabernet Franc '11 🍷🍷 3
● COF Refosco P. R. '12 🍷🍷 3
○ FCO Pinot Grigio '14 🍷 3

Russolo

via San Rocco, 58a
33080 San Quirino [PN]
Tel. 0434919577
www.russolo.it

CELLAR SALES
PRE-BOOKED VISITS
ANNUAL PRODUCTION 165,000 bottles
HECTARES UNDER VINE 16.00
SUSTAINABLE WINERY

● Borgo di Peuma '11 🍷🍷 5
○ Chardonnay Ronco Calaj '14 🍷🍷 3
○ Doi Raps '13 🍷🍷 3
○ Sauvignon Ronco Calaj '14 🍷🍷 3

San Simone

loc. Rondover
via Prata, 30
33080 Porcia [PN]
Tel. 0434578633
www.sansimone.it

CELLAR SALES
PRE-BOOKED VISITS
ANNUAL PRODUCTION 900,000 bottles
HECTARES UNDER VINE 85.00
SUSTAINABLE WINERY

● Friuli Grave Cabernet Franc Sugano '12 🍷🍷 2*
● Friuli Grave Merlot Evante Ris. '12 🍷 3
○ Friuli Grave Pinot Grigio '14 🍷 2
○ Friuli Grave Sauvignon '14 🍷 2

Scarbolo

FRAZ. LAUZACCO
V.LE GRADO, 4
33050 PAVIA DI UDINE [UD]
TEL. 0432675612
www.scarbolo.com

CELLAR SALES
PRE-BOOKED VISITS
RESTAURANT SERVICE
ANNUAL PRODUCTION 160,000 bottles
HECTARES UNDER VINE 30.00

○ Bianco My Time '12	♛♛ 4
● Campo del Viotto Merlot '12	♛♛ 4
○ Pinot Grigio Ramato XL '12	♛♛ 3
● Cabernet '13	♛ 3

Scolaris

VIA BOSCHETTO, 4
34070 SAN LORENZO ISONTINO [GO]
TEL. 0481809920
www.scolaris.it

CELLAR SALES
PRE-BOOKED VISITS
ANNUAL PRODUCTION 600,000 bottles
HECTARES UNDER VINE 20.00
SUSTAINABLE WINERY

○ Collio Chardonnay '14	♛♛ 3
○ Collio Pinot Grigio '14	♛♛ 3
● Collio Cabernet Franc '14	♛ 3
○ Collio Ribolla Gialla '14	♛ 3

Ferruccio Sgubin

VIA MERNICO, 8
34070 DOLEGNA DEL COLLIO [GO]
TEL. 048160452
www.ferrucciosgubin.it

CELLAR SALES
PRE-BOOKED VISITS
ANNUAL PRODUCTION 100,000 bottles
HECTARES UNDER VINE 20.00

○ Collio Ribolla Gialla Petruss '13	♛♛ 3

F.lli Stanig

VIA ALBANA, 44
33040 PREPOTTO [UD]
TEL. 0432713234
www.stanig.it

CELLAR SALES
ACCOMMODATION AND RESTAURANT SERVICE
ANNUAL PRODUCTION 45,000 bottles
HECTARES UNDER VINE 9.00

● COF Schioppettino di Prepotto '12	♛♛ 3
○ FCO Malvasia '14	♛♛ 3
● FCO Cabernet '14	♛ 3

Stocco

VIA CASALI STOCCO, 12
33050 BICINICCO [UD]
TEL. 0432934906
www.vinistocco.it

CELLAR SALES
PRE-BOOKED VISITS
RESTAURANT SERVICE
ANNUAL PRODUCTION 150,000 bottles
HECTARES UNDER VINE 44.20

● Cabernet Franc '13	♛♛ 2*
○ Sauvignon '14	♛♛ 2*
○ Sericus '13	♛♛ 3
● Merlot '11	♛ 4

Tarlao

VIA S. ZILI, 41
33051 AQUILEIA [UD]
TEL. 043191417
www.tarlao.eu

CELLAR SALES
PRE-BOOKED VISITS
ANNUAL PRODUCTION 18,000 bottles
HECTARES UNDER VINE 5.00

○ Friuli Aquileia Malvasia '14	♛♛ 3
○ Friuli Aquileia Pinot Bianco Poc ma Bon '14	♛♛ 3
○ Mosaic Blanc '14	♛♛ 3

Tenuta Conte Romano

VIA DELLE PRIMULE, 12
33044 MANZANO [UD]
TEL. 0432755339

PRE-BOOKED VISITS
ANNUAL PRODUCTION 40,000 bottles
HECTARES UNDER VINE 10.00

○ COF Sauvignon '13	♟♟	3
○ FCO Sauvignon '14	♟♟	3
○ FCO Friulano '14	♟	3
○ FCO Malvasia '14	♟	3

Terre del Faet

V.LE ROMA, 82
34071 CORMÒNS [GO]
TEL. 3470103325
andreadrius.vino@hotmail.it

PRE-BOOKED VISITS
ANNUAL PRODUCTION 10,000 bottles
HECTARES UNDER VINE 3.00

○ Collio Friulano '14	♟♟	3
○ Collio Friulano Sel. '13	♟♟	3
○ Collio Malvasia '14	♟	3
○ Collio Pinot Bianco '14	♟	3

Terre di Ger

FRAZ. FRATTINA
S.DA DELLA MEDUNA, 17
33076 PRAVISDOMINI [PN]
TEL. 0434644452
www.terrediger.it

CELLAR SALES
PRE-BOOKED VISITS
ANNUAL PRODUCTION 100,000 bottles
HECTARES UNDER VINE 50.00

○ Sauvignon Blanc '14	♟♟	3*
● Friuli Grave Cabernet Franc '13	♟♟	2*
○ Limine '12	♟♟	3
○ Friuli Grave Chardonnay '14	♟	2

Toblâr

LOC. RAMANDOLO, 17
33045 NIMIS [UD]
TEL. 0432755840
www.specogna.it

CELLAR SALES
ANNUAL PRODUCTION 130,000 bottles
HECTARES UNDER VINE 5.00

● Friuli Isonzo Schioppettino '12	♟♟	3
○ Ramandolo '09	♟♟	3
○ Sauvignon '14	♟♟	3
● Uve Rosse '10	♟♟	3

Paolo Venturini

VIA ISONZO, 135
34071 CORMÒNS [GO]
TEL. 048160446
www.venturinivini.it

CELLAR SALES
PRE-BOOKED VISITS
ANNUAL PRODUCTION 70,000 bottles
HECTARES UNDER VINE 17.00
SUSTAINABLE WINERY

○ Collio Malvasia '14	♟♟	3
● Collio Merlot '13	♟♟	3
○ Collio Pinot Grigio '14	♟♟	3
○ Collio Friulano '14	♟	3

Vistorta

VIA VISTORTA, 82
33077 SACILE [PN]
TEL. 0434782490
www.vistorta.it

CELLAR SALES
PRE-BOOKED VISITS
ANNUAL PRODUCTION 250,000 bottles
HECTARES UNDER VINE 36.00
VITICULTURE METHOD Certified Organic

● Friuli Grave Merlot Vistorta '11	♟♟	4
○ Friuli Grave Pinot Grigio '14	♟♟	2*
○ Friuli Grave Sauvignon '14	♟♟	2*
○ Friuli Grave Friulano '14	♟	2

EMILIA ROMAGNA

Emilia Romagna is a patchwork of territories, a journey along Via Emilia, surprising for its richness and diversity, with 300 kilometres of tradition and amazing communities. Setting off from the north, the first zone in the region is Colli Piacentini, comprising four parallel valleys that converge at Piacenza. Today, the artisans are the stars of the district, while the two cooperatives and more structured, longstanding wineries struggle to decipher territorial identity. Continuing the journey, we arrive in the world of Lambrusco, wine country that is becoming more populated with new players each year. The area is brimming with energy and is changing the philosophy of its production model: Lambrusco has stopped being a wine brand and is slowly acquiring a territorial identity. This new chapter is being written by artisans, cooperatives and large private cellars, namely the entire supply chain. Each plays their own role in raising the quality of the wines, but above all in building a clearer narrative, comprehensible to the outside world. Sorbara is the driving force in this revolution and once again Bomporto is in lead position for the community. The Colli Bolognesi district is involved in the Pignoletto DOC project and has raised the stakes in the gamble. Right now we see small signals, but we believe that a real renaissance is upon us. The last leg of our trip is around Romagna, for 150 kilometres of valleys and diversity, a legacy well described by the subzones classified in the Romagna Sangiovese DOC over the last few years. Here, too, today's generation is expressing the most interesting things and the new interpretation of the territory developed by small artisans is now the area's most valuable heritage. The oldest wineries strive to adapt their established vinification style to modern wine production and some of Romagna's big names were literally crushed in the comparison with the purest local expressions. On the other hand, the cooperatives have really taken this new approach on board and are producing simple, popular wines of great quality and sense of place. In this regard, one point should be considered: Romagna's future probably lies in Sangiovese Superiore and a better knowledge of terroirs, with producers specializing, has highlighted the boundaries of the districts less suited to the Riserva. This is good news as it means the territory has evolved and it was needed for further growth. The white wines from albana, a variety finally beginning to express its great potential, are increasingly compelling.

Ancarani

VIA SAN BIAGIO ANTICO, 14
48018 FAENZA [RA]
TEL. 0546642162
www.viniancarani.it

CELLAR SALES
PRE-BOOKED VISITS
RESTAURANT SERVICE
ANNUAL PRODUCTION 30,000 bottles
HECTARES UNDER VINE 14.00

Claudio Ancarani's wines show rustic character, and are perfect examples of tradition. They may not always be easy, but they are always genuine. The winery's top label remains the Albana Santa Lusa, which brings together power, acidity and the tannins that distinguish this white grape variety. Ancarani's vineyards lie near Torre di Oriolo, a small area that is earning a reputation as perfect wine country for albana. He has also done interesting work on centesimino, a native aromatic red grape variety typical of the countryside near Faenza. The Santa Lusa 2013 is full of surprises. Rustic, dense and flavoursome, it also shows a supple palate, thanks to cutting acidity on the finish and warmth on the attack. This is a wine that changes from glass to glass, as if it had a multiple personality, and each one had its own story to tell.

○ Romagna Albana Secco Santa Lusa '13	♥♥ 3
● Uvappesa '11	♥♥ 4
○ Albana di Romagna Santa Lusa '12	♀♀ 3*
○ Albana di Romagna Santa Lusa '11	♀♀ 3
○ Albana di Romagna Santa Lusa '06	♀♀ 3*
● Sangiovese di Romagna Oriolo '12	♀♀ 2*
● Sangiovese di Romagna Oriolo '11	♀♀ 2
● Sangiovese di Romagna Sup. Biagio Antico '11	♀♀ 2*
● Sâvignon Rosso Centesimino '12	♀♀ 3
● Uvappesa '10	♀♀ 4
● Uvappesa '09	♀♀ 4
● Uvappesa '07	♀♀ 4

Balìa di Zola

VIA CASALE, 11
47015 MODIGLIANA [FC]
TEL. 0546940577
www.baliadizola.com

CELLAR SALES
PRE-BOOKED VISITS
ANNUAL PRODUCTION 30,000 bottles
HECTARES UNDER VINE 5.00

Veruska Eluci and her husband Claudio Fiore arrived in Romagna from Tuscany in 1999 to run the Fiore Castelluccio family cellar. They fell in love with the area, and in 2003 bought their own winery, starting to invest first of all in vineyards, and later in a small cellar, set up in a converted stable. Today, this is one of the operations taking the reputation of Modigliana and its terroir of lean marl and sandstone soils to new heights. The Redinoce 2012 is a deep, savoury Sangiovese with an elegant vegetal soul and mineral hints that will come through with time. The fruit is austere, and the tannins from the oak slightly heavy, but acidity provides rhythm and grip. The firm, peppery Balitore 2014 reflects the vintage and shows focused floral aromas over a supple, relaxed palate.

● Romagna Sangiovese Modigliana Redinoce Ris. '12	♥♥ 4
● Romagna Sangiovese Sup. Balitore '14	♥♥ 2*
● Sangiovese di Romagna Redinoce Ris. '09	♀♀♀ 4*
● Sangiovese di Romagna Redinoce Ris. '08	♀♀♀ 4*
● Sangiovese di Romagna Balitore '10	♀♀ 2*
● Sangiovese di Romagna Redinoce Ris. '11	♀♀ 4
● Sangiovese di Romagna Redinoce Ris. '10	♀♀ 4

Le Barbaterre

LOC. BERGONZANO
VIA CAVOUR, 2A
42020 QUATTRO CASTELLA [RE]
TEL. 0522247573
www.barbaterre.it

CELLAR SALES
PRE-BOOKED VISITS
ACCOMMODATION AND RESTAURANT SERVICE
ANNUAL PRODUCTION 30,000 bottles
HECTARES UNDER VINE 8.00
VITICULTURE METHOD Certified Organic
SUSTAINABLE WINERY

Second fermentation in the bottle without disgorgement is a traditional Emilia winemaking procedure, a practice that is part of the region's culture of sparkling wine. Today, wines produced using this method are sought after once more, and Le Barbaterre is one of the most important names behind its renaissance. Erika Tagliavini farms eight hectares of vineyards on loose soils of silt, clay and marl at an elevation of 350 metres near Val d'Enza, in the hills near Quattro Castella, in the heart of the territory that Matilda of Canossa defended with a series of castles at Pianello, Rossena, Canossa, Sarzano and Carpineti. The good overall quality of the wines is a sign of the stylistic maturity achieved. The Sauvignon Frizzante 2013, which undergoes secondary fermentation in the bottle without disgorgement, expresses a classic citrus repertoire of citron, grapefruit, and lemon, alongside savoury capers, oregano, pink pepper, on a nose of great complexity, over a fresh palate with good stuffing.

○ CSC Pinot Nero Spumante L'Orlando Bianco '11	🍷🍷 5
○ Oro di Collina '10	🍷🍷 5
○ Sauvignon Frizzante '13	🍷🍷 3
● Pinot Nero '12	🍷 3
⊙ Besmein Capoleg Marzemino Frizzante Rosé '12	🍷🍷 2*
⊙ L'Angelica Brut Nature Rosé '11	🍷🍷 3
● Lambrusco dell'Emilia '13	🍷🍷 2*
● Lambrusco dell'Emilia '12	🍷🍷 2*
○ Sauvignon Brut M. Cl. '11	🍷🍷 3

Francesco Bellei

FRAZ. CRISTO DI SORBARA
VIA NAZIONALE, 132
41030 BOMPORTO [MO]
TEL. 059902009
www.francescobellei.it

CELLAR SALES
PRE-BOOKED VISITS
ANNUAL PRODUCTION 70,000 bottles
HECTARES UNDER VINE 5.00

There is an exciting plot to this long story of wine which spans families and generations, and it also has a happy ending, with Francesco Bellei still enjoying an excellent reputation today. The first bottles were released in 1920 and the operation continued for three generations until Sandro Cavicchioli took up the legacy of the Bellei family, with his vision and intuition that Metodo Classico sparklers had a tradition, a home and a possible future in Modena. Sandro has also shown extreme sensitivity in developing his line of wines based on "ancestral" fermentation, namely in the bottle without disgorgement, a classic technique in this territory. A case in point is the 2014, an incredibly complex monovarietal sorbara with a nose that ranges from spicy notes of cloves and mace to delicate aromas of bitter orange and tangerine. The lean, savoury palate is taut and spirited, and shows great elegance.

● Lambrusco di Modena Rifermentazione Ancestrale '14	🍷🍷 3*
● Cuvée Brut Rosso M.Cl. '13	🍷🍷 3
● Modena Pignoletto Rifermentazione Ancestrale '14	🍷🍷 3
● Lambrusco di Modena Rifermentazione Ancestrale '13	🍷🍷 2*
● Lambrusco di Modena Rifermentazione Ancestrale '12	🍷🍷 2*
● Lambrusco di Modena Rifermentazione Ancestrale '11	🍷🍷 2*
● Lambrusco di Modena Rifermentazione Ancestrale '10	🍷🍷 2*
● Modena Pignoletto Rifermentazione Ancestrale '13	🍷🍷 2*
● Modena Pignoletto Rifermentazione Ancestrale '11	🍷🍷 2*

Braschi

VIA ROMA, 37
47025 MERCATO SARACENO [FC]
TEL. 054791061
www.cantinabraschi.com

CELLAR SALES
PRE-BOOKED VISITS
ANNUAL PRODUCTION 125,000 bottles
HECTARES UNDER VINE 11.50

This consolidated Romagna winery in the Savio Valley was established in 1949 and taken over by oenologist Vincenzo Vernocchi and Davide Moky Castagnoli in 2011. In the space of only a few years, their dynamic approach has given a new lease of life to a cellar whose reputation is quickly growing, and which produces increasingly convincing wines. The concept behind the range is clear: two base wines, a white and a red, and a series of labels linked to the winery's various vineyards. These are classic, traditional, well-crafted wines which clearly express their various terroirs of provenance, from Bertinoro to the valley of Savio. Monte Sasso 2013 is a classic Sangiovese, vinified in large oak using grapes from what can only be defined as a cru. It plays on its "hardness", showing austere and stiff, vibrant and nuanced, and requires time and understanding. This is a Sangiovese with rigid, tidy tannins, showing a nose of focused fruit and a supple, flavoursome palate.

● Romagna Sangiovese San Vicinio Monte Sasso '13		♔♔ 3*
● Romagna Sangiovese Bertinoro Il Costone Ris. '12		♔♔ 4
● Sangiovese di Romagna San Vicinio Monte Sasso '12		♔♔♔ 3*
● Sangiovese di Romagna Sup. Il Costone '11		♔♔ 3
● Sangiovese di Romagna Sup. Il Costone '10		♔♔ 3

Cantina della Volta

VIA PER MODENA, 82
41030 BOMPORTO [MO]
TEL. 0597473312
www.cantinadellavolta.com

CELLAR SALES
PRE-BOOKED VISITS
ANNUAL PRODUCTION 120,000 bottles
HECTARES UNDER VINE 14.00

Cantina della Volta has become a leading name in its territory and a benchmark in Italy for classic method wines. Christian Bellei has brought his personal and family experience to bear in a series of inspired choices, translating into a range which is impressive both in terms of reliability and overall quality across the board. He works with sorbara in the hills around Modena, where eight hectares of pinot nero and chardonnay have also been planted on the dark soils of Riccò di Serramazzoni, a small area that over the years has shown itself to be well-suited for the production of reliable base wines for Metodo Classico. The Rimosso 2014 boasts aromas of the sea, followed by fresh, fragrant fruit, with wild strawberries, cherries and a touch of spice providing complexity. On the palate it shows the stuffing given by the lees and good progression provided by attractive acidity. The Rosato 2011 is delicate and full of character.

○ Lambrusco di Modena Brut Rosé M. Cl. '11		♔♔ 5
● Lambrusco di Sorbara Secco Rimosso '14		♔♔ 3*
○ Il Mattaglio Blanc de Blancs '10		♔♔ 6
○ Il Mattaglio Blanc de Noirs '10		♔♔ 6
● Lambrusco di Sorbara Rimosso '13		♔♔♔ 3*
● Lambrusco di Sorbara Rimosso '12		♔♔♔ 3*
○ Brut M. Cl. La Svolta Rosato '10		♔♔ 7
○ Il Mattaglio Brut D.Z. '11		♔♔ 5
○ Il Mattaglio Brut M. Cl '11		♔♔ 5
○ La Base Chardonnay Fermo '13		♔♔ 3
● Lambrusco di Modena Brut M. Cl. Trentasei '10		♔♔ 4

Cantina Sociale di Carpi e Sorbara

VIA CAVATA
41012 CARPI [MO]
TEL. 059 643071
www.cantinadicarpiesorbara.it

HECTARES UNDER VINE 2,300.00

The cooperative wineries in the province of Modena are some of the oldest in Italy, initiated in the early 20th century by Gino Friedmann, a great pioneer in the field. Today, the two wineries, Carpi, established in 1903, and Sorbara, established in 1923, have become a single operation, in which 1,600 grower-members farm 2,300 hectares of vineyards. Only a small amount of the wine produced is bottled, and this allows rigorous selection of the batches of grapes, so that perfect wines can be produced even in difficult growing years such as 2014. The non-disgorged version of Omaggio a Gino Friedmann Fermentazione in Bottiglia 2014 is an icy, linear wine, with extremely delicate fruit over an austere, lean palate, where body is provided by the lees in suspension, and it offers a salty, citrussy finish. The dynamic, focused Omaggio a Gino Friedmann 2014 is thrusting, mineral and crisp, with a nose of blossom, red berry fruit and apples.

Cavicchioli U. & Figli

VIA CANALETTO, 52
41030 SAN PROSPERO [MO]
TEL. 059812411
www.cavicchioli.it

CELLAR SALES
PRE-BOOKED VISITS
ANNUAL PRODUCTION 10,000,000 bottles
HECTARES UNDER VINE 90.00

The symbiosis between the brothers Sandro and Claudio, and Gruppo Italiano Vini, which took over the winery in 2010, is now consolidated, and the winery is in full swing. Its selections of sorbara are always some of the best in the DOC zone, and the winery's classic products of more popular brands, such as those in the Tre Medaglie line, are increasingly reliable and convincing. It is no mean feat to maintain this level of quality with such large production figures, and this operation is increasingly seen as a classic in its territory. The extremely delicate, elegant Vigna del Cristo 2014 is a salty, aromatic wine with original hints of tangerine and rose over a lean, grippy palate, with interesting notes of spice on the finish, bringing complexity. The Rosé del Cristo 2011 is a whirlwind of energy, enveloping the nose in a cloud of blossom and citrus, red berry fruit and spice. It shows a delicate style and incredible complexity.

- Lambrusco di Sorbara Secco
  Omaggio a Gino Friedmann FB '14 ▼▼▼ 3*
- Lambrusco di Sorbara Secco
  Omaggio a Gino Friedmann '14 ▼▼ 3*
- Lambrusco di Sorbara Amabile
  Emma '14 ▼▼ 2*
- Lambrusco di Sorbara Secco
  Le Bolle '14 ▼▼ 2*
- Lambrusco Salamino di S. Croce Secco
  Novecento03 '14 ▼▼ 2*
- Lambrusco di Sorbara Secco
  Omaggio a Gino Friedmann '13 ♀♀♀ 3*
- Lambrusco di Sorbara Secco
  Omaggio a Gino Friedmann FB '13 ♀♀ 3*

- Lambrusco di Sorbara V. del Cristo '14 ▼▼▼ 2*
- ☉ Lambrusco di Sorbara Brut
  Rosé del Cristo '11 ▼▼ 5
- Lambrusco di Modena 1928 '14 ▼▼ 2*
- Lambrusco di Sorbara Tre Medaglie '14 ▼▼ 2*
- Lambrusco di Sorbara V. del Cristo '13 ♀♀♀ 2*
- Lambrusco di Sorbara V. del Cristo '12 ♀♀♀ 2*
- Lambrusco di Sorbara V. del Cristo '11 ♀♀♀ 2*
- Lambrusco di Modena 1928 '12 ♀♀ 2*
- Lambrusco di Sorbara Secco
  Marchio Storico '13 ♀♀ 2*
- Lambrusco di Sorbara Secco
  Marchio Storico '12 ♀♀ 2*
- Lambrusco di Sorbara Tre Medaglie '13 ♀♀ 2*
- Lambrusco Grasparossa di Castelvetro
  Amabile Tre Medaglie '13 ♀♀ 2*
- ☉ Rosé del Cristo Brut Rosé '10 ♀♀ 5

Caviro

VIA CONVERTITE, 12
48018 FAENZA [RA]
TEL. 0546629111
www.caviro.it

CELLAR SALES
ANNUAL PRODUCTION 25,000,000 bottles
HECTARES UNDER VINE 31.00

This cooperative group is one of Italy's wine giants, bringing together 32 cooperative wineries in eight different regions, vinifying grapes from a total of 12,000 growers, and managing a certified production chain which is unique in terms of size and coverage. Alongside everyday reliable labels such as Tavernello, which is produced using wines from all over Italy, there are products linked specifically to Romagna, which remains the homeland of this colossus. And it is precisely when we go back to these regional roots that we find its more interesting wines. The range of wines shows overall reliability, even if we were unable to try the Romagna Sangiovese 2014, not yet bottled at the moment of our tastings. The Riserva Terragens 2012 boasts an extremely modern, international style, with upfront fruit over a palate where fine acidity governs progression. The Albana Romio 2014 shows notes of summer flowers and citrus over a tangy, fresh palate.

○ Romagna Albana Secco Romio '14	♟♟ 2*
● Romagna Sangiovese Sup. Terragens Ris. '12	♟♟ 4
● Romagna Sangiovese Sup. Romio '13	♟ 3
○ Romagna Trebbiano Terre Forti '14	♟ 1*
● Sangiovese di Romagna Brumale '13	♟♟ 2*
● Sangiovese di Romagna Brumale '12	♟♟ 2*
● Sangiovese di Romagna Terre Forti '13	♟♟ 2*
● Sangiovese di Romagna Terre Forti '12	♟♟ 2*

Celli

V.LE CARDUCCI, 5
47032 BERTINORO [FC]
TEL. 0543445183
www.celli-vini.com

CELLAR SALES
PRE-BOOKED VISITS
ANNUAL PRODUCTION 280,000 bottles
HECTARES UNDER VINE 30.00

The wines of the Sirri and Casadei families are classics in their territory, universally seen as expressions of the true soul of Romagna. The 30 hectares of vineyards, partly owned and partly rented, are all in the territory of Bertinoro, on its typical limestone soils rich in local spungone rock. The winery is famous for its traditional, well-crafted Albanas, but its Sangioveses are also good examples of the dense, weighty style typical of this subzone. Thanks to a difficult yet cool growing year, I Croppi 2014 is a wine of great expressiveness and depth. Albana's warm beeswax, salt, summer flowers, apricot, and oregano soul is offset by acidity, giving the wine rhythm and length. Despite mouth-drying tannins, it ends vibrant and tangy. Le Grillaie 2014 is richly flavoured and balanced. Le Querce 2014 is an Albana with a dry palate and well-calibrated sweetness.

○ Romagna Albana Secco I Croppi '14	♟♟ 2*
○ Romagna Albana Dolce Le Querce '14	♟♟ 2*
○ Romagna Pagadebit Campi di Fratta '14	♟♟ 2*
● Romagna Sangiovese Sup. Le Grillaie '14	♟♟ 2*
○ Albana di Romagna Dolce Le Querce '12	♟♟ 2*
○ Albana di Romagna Passito Solara '11	♟♟ 4
○ Albana di Romagna Secco I Croppi '13	♟♟ 2*
○ Albana di Romagna Secco I Croppi '12	♟♟ 2*
● Bron & Rusèval Sangiovese '11	♟♟ 3
● Sangiovese di Romagna Sup. Le Grillaie '12	♟♟ 2*

Umberto Cesari

VIA STANZANO, 1120
40024 CASTEL SAN PIETRO TERME [BO]
TEL. 0516947811
www.umbertocesari.it

Cleto Chiarli Tenute Agricole

VIA BELVEDERE, 4
41104 CASTELVETRO DI MODENA [MO]
TEL. 0593163311
www.chiarli.it

CELLAR SALES
PRE-BOOKED VISITS
ANNUAL PRODUCTION 3,000,000 bottles
HECTARES UNDER VINE 280.00
VITICULTURE METHOD Certified Organic

CELLAR SALES
PRE-BOOKED VISITS
ANNUAL PRODUCTION 900,000 bottles
HECTARES UNDER VINE 100.00

In 2014 Umberto Cesari celebrated 50 harvests, and a long series of successes, to the point that for many foreign markets this is Romagna's best known operation, and an ambassador for its territory. This is a role it fully deserves, and is the result of years of investments in travel and promoting its homeland, and of the realization, many years ago, that if you want to be a successful farmer you also need to be a businessman. The winery is now led by Gianmaria who inherited his father's vision and desire to look to the future. Umberto Cesari's wines have always been an expression of Romagna, also appreciated abroad, although the winery has realized that the time is ripe to focus on more territorial expressions. Liano 2012 is richly spiced and fruited, with a fresh, vibrant palate and a tannic finish. The Riserva 2012 shows Mediterranean aromas, and is focused, full and clenched.

A century of history and a knowledge of the territory which has few equals are the distinctive traits of a family whose brand of Lambrusco di Modena is known worldwide. Alongside the historic operation, Chiarli 1860, Anselmo and Mauro Chiarli have built up this farm that only vinifies grapes from its own vineyards. The idea was to revolutionize the world of quality Lambrusco with a new experience that could exploit modern technology and a strict production philosophy. Their success is today one of the keystones of Lambrusco's renaissance. Fondatore 2014 is a complex wine that expresses the various souls of Sorbara in the glass. We first perceive the cutting, vibrant soul of its typical, attractively salty acidity, then its floral, austere soul of cold, focused aromas, and finally its spicy, earthy side, the result of second fermentation in bottle. This is a multifaceted, elegant, well-articulated wine.

● Liano '12	♥♥ 4
● Romagna Sangiovese Sup. Ris. '12	♥♥ 3
○ Liano Bianco '13	♥ 4
● Romagna Sangiovese Sup. Ca' Grande '14	♥ 2
● Liano '09	♥♥ 5
● Sangiovese di Romagna Laurento Ris. '10	♥♥ 3
● Sangiovese di Romagna Laurento Ris. '09	♥♥ 3

● Lambrusco di Sorbara del Fondatore '14	♥♥♥ 3*
● Lambrusco di Sorbara Vecchia Modena Premium '14	♥♥ 2*
● Lambrusco Grasparossa di Castelvetro Nivola '14	♥♥ 2*
● Lambrusco Grasparossa di Castelvetro Villa Cialdini '14	♥♥ 2*
● Lambrusco di Sorbara del Fondatore '12	♥♥♥ 3*
● Lambrusco di Sorbara del Fondatore '11	♥♥♥ 2*
● Lambrusco di Sorbara Vecchia Modena Premium '13	♥♥♥ 2*
● Lambrusco di Sorbara Vecchia Modena Premium '10	♥♥♥ 2*

Condé

VIA LUCCHINA, 27
47016 PREDAPPIO [FC]
TEL. 0543940860
www.conde.it

CELLAR SALES
RESTAURANT SERVICE
ANNUAL PRODUCTION 250,000 bottles
HECTARES UNDER VINE 77.00

For some time now, Chiara Condello has been working alongside her father on this visionary, ambitious project, with almost 80 hectares of vineyards tended with commitment and care, and an idea of hospitality that has few equals in Romagna. The operation has been given a new lease of life, partly thanks to the new cellar inaugurated with the 2014 harvest, and partly thanks to Chiara's dedication and the new style, both classic and territorial, she has brought to the winery. The Tuscan oenologist Federico Staderini, the undisputed master of sangiovese, joined the operation this year to follow vinification. The Romagna Sangiovese Predappio Riserva 2011 is obtained from east-aspected vineyards in the highest part of the estate, where the soils are leaner and show outcrops of local spungone rock. This mineral, elegant, austere wine shows an earthy, delicate character. Alongside the Sangioveses, the winery produces extremely limited quantities of Massera, an exceptional monovarietal Merlot, now released in the 2012 version.

● Massera Merlot '12	♟♟ 3
● Romagna Sangiovese Predappio '12	♟♟ 3
● Romagna Sangiovese Predappio Ris. '11	♟♟ 2*
● Sangiovese di Romagna '09	♟♟ 2
● Sangiovese di Romagna Capsula Nera '10	♟♟ 2*
● Sangiovese di Romagna Sup. '11	♟♟ 2*
● Sangiovese di Romagna Sup. '09	♟♟ 2*
● Sangiovese di Romagna Sup. Condè Capsula Blu Ris. '09	♟♟ 5
● Sangiovese di Romagna Sup. Condè Capsula Rossa '10	♟♟ 3
● Sangiovese di Romagna Sup. Ris. '10	♟♟ 2*
● Sangiovese di Romagna Sup. Ris. '08	♟♟ 2*

Leone Conti

LOC. SANTA LUCIA
VIA POZZO, 1
48018 FAENZA [RA]
TEL. 0546642149
www.leoneconti.it

CELLAR SALES
PRE-BOOKED VISITS
ANNUAL PRODUCTION 80,000 bottles
HECTARES UNDER VINE 17.00

Leone Conti is an intelligent, highly sensitive man who thinks about wine in an original, creative way, leading him to experiment like few others. Over the years, he has focused above all on minor native varieties: albana, centesimino, uva ruggine, famoso, and longanesi. His extraordinary work is now pursued by new lifeblood, in the shape of his young nephew Francesco Conti, who has become a permanent presence at the winery. There is no doubt that Albana is the leading light in the range of this small winery from Faenza. The 2014 La mia Albana Progetto 1 shows captivating freshness and a dry palate thanks to the tannins typical of this white variety. Its attractive aromatic profile boasts sage, honey, apricot, and saltiness on the finish. Le Betulle 2012 is a classic, gracefully contoured Sangiovese with a fruit-infused, supple palate and balanced tannins. Impressioni di Settembre 2012, from syrah, is an aromatic, crisp rosé.

⊙ Impressioni di Settembre '14	♟♟ 2*
○ Romagna Albana Passito Nontiscordardime '11	♟♟ 6
○ Romagna Albana Secco La mia Albana Progetto 1 '14	♟♟ 3
● Romagna Sangiovese Sup. Le Betulle '12	♟♟ 3
● Romagna Sangiovese Sup. Never Walk Alone '14	♟ 2
○ Albana di Romagna Secco Progetto 1 '13	♟♟ 3
○ Oro et Laboro	♟♟ 5
● Sangiovese di Romagna Sup. Contiriserva Ris. '09	♟♟ 4
● Sangiovese di Romagna Sup. Never Walk Alone '13	♟♟ 2*
● Sangiovese di Romagna Sup. Never Walk Alone '12	♟♟ 2*

Costa Archi

LOC. SERRA
VIA RINFOSCO, 1690
48014 CASTEL BOLOGNESE [RA]
TEL. 3384818346
www.costaarchi.wordpress.com

CELLAR SALES
PRE-BOOKED VISITS
ANNUAL PRODUCTION 15,000 bottles
HECTARES UNDER VINE 13.00

If the subzone of Serra today has its own clear identity, we owe this to passionate grower Gabriele Succi and his desire to produce territorial wines. He has released monovarietal Sangioveses with increasingly interesting results, thanks to exceptional work in the rows and great respect for grapes during vinification. The operation's 13 hectares are located in two distinct plots in the hills of Castel Bolognese: Podere Beneficio at an elevation of around 80 metres and the higher Podere Monte Brullo, at around 160 metres. The savoury, somewhat tannic Assiolo 2013 is emblematic of the Serra style. It shows excellent overall balance and suppleness on the palate with admirable freshness, preceded by a nose with austere fruit and a touch of herbs and earthiness. GS 2012 comes from a hot growing year but is elegant and full of energy. On the nose, it shows floral aromas and hints of tangerine, leading to attractive vegetal notes and full flavour in the mouth.

Tenuta Croci

LOC. MONTEROSSO, 8
29014 CASTELL'ARQUATO [PC]
TEL. 0523803321
www.vinicroci.com

CELLAR SALES
PRE-BOOKED VISITS
ACCOMMODATION
ANNUAL PRODUCTION 30,000 bottles
HECTARES UNDER VINE 8.50
VITICULTURE METHOD Certified Organic

Massimiliano Croci and his father Ermanno run the family winery established in 1935. We are a stone's throw from Castell'Arquato on the Monterosso hill in Val d'Arda. The farming and vinification methods are all informed by an artisanal, "natural" philosophy, and the results are ever-more interesting. The wines are produced by spontaneous fermentation and show a marked sense of place. Emozioni di Ghiaccio 2008, from malvasia di Candia aromatica topped up with moscato, is a raisin wine obtained from grapes left to dry on the vine before a staggered harvest between late December and January. This complex wine boasts a nose of spring flowers, apricot, figs and candied citrus peel, followed by interesting salty notes of capers, herbs and horehound, over a rich, yet taut, dry palate. The mineral Gutturnio 2013 shows elegant vegetal notes and focused austere fruit over a dry, crisp palate, ending to citrus notes of orange zest.

● Romagna Sangiovese Sup. Assiolo '13	♛♛♛ 3*
● GS Sangiovese '12	♛♛ 5
● Colli di Faenza Prima Luce '09	♛♛ 2*
● Colli di Faenza Prima Luce '07	♛♛ 2*
● GS Sangiovese '11	♛♛ 3*
● Il Beneficio '08	♛♛ 2*
● Sangiovese di Romagna Sup. Assiolo '12	♛♛ 2*
● Sangiovese di Romagna Sup. Assiolo '11	♛♛ 2*
● Sangiovese di Romagna Sup. Assiolo '10	♛♛ 2*
● Sangiovese di Romagna Sup. Monte Brullo Ris. '10	♛♛ 2*
● Sangiovese di Romagna Sup. Monte Brullo Ris. '09	♛♛ 2*
● Sangiovese di Romagna Sup. Monte Brullo Ris. '08	♛♛ 2*

○ Emozioni di Ghiaccio Passito '08	♛♛ 6
● Gutturnio Sur Lie '13	♛♛ 2*
○ Lubigo Bianco Frizzante '13	♛♛ 2*
● C.P. Monterosso Val d'Arda '13	♛ 2
○ Colli Piacentini Monterosso Val d'Arda '12	♛♛ 2*
○ Emozioni di Ghiaccio Passito '07	♛♛ 6
● Gutturnio Sur Lie '12	♛♛ 2*

Denavolo

LOC. GATTAVERA
FRAZ. DENAVOLO

29020 TRAVO [PC]
TEL. 3356480766
denavolo@gmail.com

CELLAR SALES
ANNUAL PRODUCTION 15,000 bottles
HECTARES UNDER VINE 3.00
SUSTAINABLE WINERY

This small, family-run winery has a few hectares of white grapes, tended and vinified by Giulio Armani and his son Jacopo. The landscape is that of the northern part of Val Trebbia, with its traditional heritage of white grape varieties: ortrugo, malvasia di Candia aromatica, trebbiano romagnolo, and marsanne. Giulio interprets his grapes in his own way, with the long macerations of which he is an undisputed master. The result is a range of complex, multifaceted, nuanced wines with extremely fresh, dry, vibrant palates. These wines show original, surprising balance, and are always highly drinkable. The Dinavolino 2014 is dry and complex, showing the tannins that come from maceration on the skins, and offers a citrus finish, with original hints of spring flowers and mountain herbs. The crisp Catavela 2014 shows citron and dried apricot over a dry, lean palate.

Donelli

VIA CARLO SIGONIO, 54
41100 MODENA
TEL. 0522908715
www.donellivini.it

CELLAR SALES
ANNUAL PRODUCTION 30,000,000 bottles
HECTARES UNDER VINE 120.00

Antonio Giacobazzi, today assisted by three of his four children, has deep knowledge of the territories of Lambrusco, and his experience enables him to select grapes and wines reliably. This translates into a high overall standard for the 30 million bottles the winery exports all over the world. With grapes from the 120 hectares of his own vineyards, he produces the Sergio Scaglietti line, named after the famous Ferrari coachbuilder who designed the bottle. This dedication shows the family's relationship with Ferrari and the world of Formula 1. The family that owned this brand for a time post-1992, in 2015 regained possession. The Reggiano Sergio Scaglietti 2014 is an elegant wine and a faithful reflection of the vintage, with delicate tannins and a lean palate that plays on freshness rather than weight, showing attractive citrussy hints of lemon zest.

○ Catavela '14	♟♟ 2*
○ Dinavolino '14	♟♟ 5
○ Catavela '13	♟♟ 2*
○ Catavela '12	♟♟ 2*
○ Catavela '11	♟♟ 2*
○ Dinavolino '12	♟♟ 5
○ Dinavolino '10	♟♟ 2*
○ Dinavolo '10	♟♟ 4
○ Dinavolo '09	♟♟ 4
○ Dinavolo '08	♟♟ 4

● Lambrusco di Sorbara Secco Sergio Scaglietti '14	♟♟ 2*
● Reggiano Lambrusco Secco Sergio Scaglietti '14	♟♟ 2*
● Lambrusco di Sorbara Secco Sergio Scaglietti '13	♟♟ 2*
● Lambrusco di Sorbara Secco Sergio Scaglietti '12	♟♟ 2*
● Lambrusco Reggiano Secco Sergio Scaglietti '13	♟♟ 2*
● Lambrusco Reggiano Secco Sergio Scaglietti '12	♟♟ 2*

Drei Donà Tenuta La Palazza

LOC. MASSA DI VECCHIAZZANO
VIA DEL TESORO, 23
47100 FORLÌ
TEL. 0543769371
www.dreidona.it

CELLAR SALES
PRE-BOOKED VISITS
ANNUAL PRODUCTION 130,000 bottles
HECTARES UNDER VINE 27.00

The Drei Donà family's winery is one of the oldest operations in Romagna, and can boast vineyards of rare maturity for this area. In the early 1980s Claudio Drei Donà dedicated himself to improving quality in the family's estates near Forlì, making them a benchmark for the entire region. The winery is today headed by his son Enrico Carmona, who was the brains behind the winery's international development. The winery has one of the most interesting historic cellars in the region. As usual, the wines showed good quality across the board, although characterized by an oakiness which often prevents them from fully expressing the territorial traits on which the winery built its reputation. Pruno 2012 boasts attractive acidity and close-knit, mature tannins. Cuvée Palazza 2012, fermented in concrete and aged in large oak, shows a clenched, dense palate.

○ Il Tornese '14	♟♟ 3
● Notturno Sangiovese '13	♟♟ 2*
● Romagna Sangiovese Sup. Cuvée Palazza Ris. '12	♟♟ 5
● Romagna Sangiovese Sup. Pruno Ris. '12	♟♟ 5
● Le Vigne Nuove '12	♟♟ 2*
● Sangiovese di Romagna Sup. Cuvée Palazza Ris. '11	♟♟ 5
● Sangiovese di Romagna Sup. Pruno Ris. '11	♟♟ 5
● Sangiovese di Romagna Sup. Pruno Ris. '10	♟♟ 5

Emilia Wine

VIA 11 SETTEMBRE 2001, 3
42019 SCANDIANO [RE]
TEL. 0522989107
www.emiliawine.eu

ANNUAL PRODUCTION 300,000 bottles
HECTARES UNDER VINE 1900.00

Emilia Wine was established in 2014 as the result of a merger of three cooperatives, Arceto, Correggio and Prato, in the area around Reggio Emilia. Together, the growers in this new operation process grapes from around 1,900 hectares of vineyards, for a total of 35 million litres of wine. This is a great community, but above all an extraordinary production system, composed of a mosaic of vineyards in this land of Lambrusco. The foresight of the chairman Davide Frascari and the technical expertise of oenologist Luca Tognoli have resulted in an operation of the highest order. The bottled production is released under the Cantina di Arceto brand. Cardinale Pighini 2014 shows austere and supple, with complex aromas and interesting, characterful tannins, accompanied by attractive acidity that provides progression on the palate. Fascia Blu 2014 is a good interpretation of the vintage, and shows peppery fruit over a subtle, fresh palate. The Rossospino 2014 shows fruit aromas of cherry and white peach over a vibrant palate.

● Colli di Scandiano e di Canossa Grasparossa Cardinale Pighini Cantina di Arceto '14	♟♟ 1*
● Colli di Scandiano e di Canossa Lambrusco Rossospino Cantina di Arceto '14	♟♟ 2*
● Reggiano Lambrusco Secco Fascia Blu Cantina di Arceto '14	♟♟ 2*
○ Colli di Scandiano e di Canossa Brut La Spergola Cantina di Arceto '13	♟ 3
● Colli di Scandiano e di Canossa Lambrusco Rossospino Cantina di Arceto '13	♟♟ 2*
● Migliolungo Lambrusco '08	♟♟ 2*
● Reggiano Lambrusco Secco Fascia Blu Cantina di Arceto '13	♟♟ 2*

Stefano Ferrucci

VIA CASOLANA, 3045/2
48014 CASTEL BOLOGNESE [RA]
TEL. 0546651068
www.stefanoferrucci.it

CELLAR SALES
PRE-BOOKED VISITS
ANNUAL PRODUCTION 95,000 bottles
HECTARES UNDER VINE 16.00

Ilaria and Serena Ferrucci manage this small winery founded by their father Stefano in the hills above Castel Bolognese. Vineyards lie in the Serra subzone on 16 hectares of clay at an altitude of 200–250 metres, an area renowned over the years for its production of albana. Nonetheless, the flagship here is a Sangiovese, the Domus Caia from slightly raisined grapes, moulded into a fresher, more elegant wine thanks to the suggestions of oenologists Federico Giotto and Andrea Ruggeri, which halved drying times. Domus Caia 2012 opens with a typical raisining repertoire then slowly expresses its characteristic fruit and spice overtones. In the mouth it has a certain elegance and is delicate despite its richness. Nice balance overall. Domus Aurea 2013 is rich, savoury, crisp, and tannic, with nice fruity aromas of dried apricots and figs.

Fiorini

LOC. GANACETO
VIA NAZIONALE PER CARPI, 1534
41010 MODENA
TEL. 059386028
www.fiorini1919.com

CELLAR SALES
PRE-BOOKED VISITS
ANNUAL PRODUCTION 100,000 bottles
HECTARES UNDER VINE 9.00

Fiorini, active from 1919, is an historic Modena label for Lambrusco, founded in Sorbara territory and still a brilliant performer. The cellar is managed by Alberto Fiorini and his sister Cristina, and the plots are dotted across the estate: the grasparossa vineyards are at Riccò, at 450 metres , Savignano sul Panaro (Torre dei Nanni), and the old sorbara vineyard is between Secchia and Villanova, where there are nine hectares of loose sand and silt terrain. Corte degli Attimi 2014 is a pure, savoury, complex, classic Sorbara, with a sense of place. The nose has a nice repertoire of mineral and earthy aromas; the full-flavoured mouth is knife-edged and the tannins give a nice, very natural and balanced touch. Terra al Sole 2014 is an open, expressive wine with echoes of bitter aromas but also of fruit; the palate is creamy and tight-knit. Vigna del Caso will be ageing for a year, vinified in 2014 for the first time as a pure Sorbara.

○ Romagna Albana Passito Domus Aurea '13	♀♀ 5	
● Romagna Sangiovese Sup. Centurione '14	♀♀ 2*	
● Romagna Sangiovese Sup. Domus Caia Ris. '12	♀♀ 5	
○ Colli di Faenza Bianco Chiaro della Serra '14	♀ 2	
● Romagna Sangiovese Auriga '14	♀ 2	
○ Romagna Trebbiano Mattinale '14	♀ 1*	
○ Albana di Romagna Passito Domus Aurea '12	♀♀ 5	
○ Albana di Romagna Passito Domus Aurea '11	♀♀ 5	
● Sangiovese di Romagna Sup. Domus Caia Ris. '11	♀♀ 5	
● Sangiovese di Romagna Sup. Domus Caia Ris. '10	♀♀ 5	

● Lambrusco di Sorbara Corte degli Attimi '14	♀♀ 2*	
● Lambrusco Grasparossa di Castelvetro Terre al Sole '14	♀♀ 2*	
● Lambrusco di Sorbara Corte degli Attimi '13	♀♀ 2*	
● Lambrusco di Sorbara Corte degli Attimi '12	♀♀ 2*	
● Lambrusco di Sorbara Corte degli Attimi '10	♀♀ 2*	
● Lambrusco Grasparossa di Castelvetro Becco Rosso '10	♀♀ 3	
● Lambrusco Grasparossa di Castelvetro Becco Rosso '09	♀♀ 3*	
● Lambrusco Grasparossa di Castelvetro Terre al Sole '13	♀♀ 2*	
● Lambrusco V. del Caso '12	♀♀ 2*	
● Lambrusco V. del Caso '11	♀♀ 2*	

Paolo Francesconi

LOC. SARNA
VIA TULIERO, 154
48018 FAENZA [RA]
TEL. 054643213
www.francesconipaolo.it

CELLAR SALES
PRE-BOOKED VISITS
RESTAURANT SERVICE
ANNUAL PRODUCTION 20,000 bottles
HECTARES UNDER VINE 8.00
VITICULTURE METHOD Certified Organic

Winegrower Paolo Francesconi has cut
down his vineyards on evolved red clay
soils in the very first Faenza hill strip to
eight hectares, and now uses biodynamic
methods. His expertise with sangiovese has
reached perfection and he has now begun
some interesting work on albana, with
lengthy macerations on the skins. The
Riserva di Sangiovese Le ladi takes its
name from wood nymphs, springs and
marshes. Earthy and austere, as
Sangiovese so often is, this wine is savoury
and deep, with ripe tannins and a real
sense of place. Limbecca 2013 has energy
and character, fruit, acidity, and a
flavoursome mouth.

Maria Galassi

LOC. PADERNO DI CESENA
VIA CASETTE, 688
47023 CESENA [FC]
TEL. 054721177
www.galassimaria.it

CELLAR SALES
PRE-BOOKED VISITS
ANNUAL PRODUCTION 18,000 bottles
HECTARES UNDER VINE 18.00
VITICULTURE METHOD Certified Organic

Maria Galassi's winery is located between
the Savio Valley and Bertinoro, in a position
that is, however, fully part of the latter for
soil characteristics, with active lime and the
presence of local spungone rock.
Oenologist Francesco Bordini works with
the best grapes from the 18 hectares
under vine, farmed organically for over 20
years. Thanks to very natural vinification
and ageing in large wood, the cellar has
perfected an elegant style that exalts the
minerality of bertinorese, handling the
abundant tannins with grace. natoRe 2013
is a pure Sangiovese partly aged in large
wood. It is a taut, elegant wine, lip-
smacking and full of flavour, with tight-knit
tannic weave. The 2013 Paternus is a
sangiovese blend topped up with merlot
and cabernet sauvignon, with well-defined
fruit and great mineral notes, and a
pleasing progression that closes delicately.

● Romagna Sangiovese Sup. Le ladi Ris. '11	♥♥ 5
○ Arcaica '14	♥♥ 3
● Romagna Sangiovese Sup. Limbecca '13	♥♥ 3
● Sangiovese di Romagna Sup. Limbecca '11	♥♥♥ 3*
● Sangiovese di Romagna Sup. Limbecca '10	♥♥♥ 3*
○ Antiqua Albana '13	♥♥ 3
○ Arcaica '13	♥♥ 3*
● Sangiovese di Romagna Sup. Limbecca '12	♥♥ 3*
● Sangiovese di Romagna Sup. Limbecca '09	♥♥ 3*

● Romagna Sangiovese Sup. natoRe '13	♥♥ 2*
● Romagna Sangiovese Sup. Paternus '13	♥♥ 2*
● Sangiovese di Romagna Sup. natoRe '10	♥♥♥ 2*
● Sangiovese di Romagna Sup. natoRe Ris. '11	♥♥ 2*
● Sangiovese di Romagna Sup. natoRe Ris. '09	♥♥ 2*
● Sangiovese di Romagna Sup. natoRe Ris. '08	♥♥ 2*
● Sangiovese di Romagna Sup. Paternus '11	♥♥ 2*
● Sangiovese di Romagna Sup. Paternus '10	♥♥ 2*
● Sangiovese di Romagna Sup. Paternus '09	♥♥ 2*
● Sangiovese di Romagna Sup. Smembar '13	♥♥ 5

Gallegati

VIA LUGO, 182
48018 FAENZA [RA]
TEL. 0546621149
www.aziendaagricolagallegati.it

CELLAR SALES
PRE-BOOKED VISITS
ACCOMMODATION
ANNUAL PRODUCTION 15,000 bottles
HECTARES UNDER VINE 6.00

Cesare and Antonio Gallegati are true artisans who work six hectares of sangiovese on the lower Faenza hill strip of clay, formerly part of the municipal area of Brisighella. These are the purest clay soils of the Faenza area, a terroir that endows muscle and succulent fruit. The Gallegati brothers have developed excellent skills in balancing these traits and the wines are always austere, fresh and elegant. Cesare is the winemaker and Antonio takes care of the rows. The deep, elegant Corallo Nero 2011 acquires its complexity and earthy tones with bottle ageing, and also showing fruit that is still well-defined and fresh. The savoury, spirited mouth has tight-knit tannins. The taut acidity upholds the character and the rough edges that time will smooth away, and which are part and parcel of its sense of place.

● Romagna Sangiovese Sup. Brisighella Corallo Nero Ris. '11	♀♀ 4
○ Albana di Romagna Passito Regina di Cuori Ris. '10	♀♀♀ 4*
○ Albana di Romagna Passito Regina di Cuori Ris. '09	♀♀♀ 4*
● Sangiovese di Romagna Sup. Corallo Nero Ris. '06	♀♀♀ 3
○ Albana di Romagna Passito Regina di Cuori Ris. '11	♀♀ 4
● Sangiovese di Romagna Brisighella Corallo Rosso '13	♀♀ 2*
● Sangiovese di Romagna Sup. Corallo Nero Ris. '10	♀♀ 4
● Sangiovese di Romagna Sup. Corallo Nero Ris. '09	♀♀ 4
● Sangiovese di Romagna Sup. Corallo Nero Ris. '07	♀♀ 4

Gruppo Cevico

VIA FIUMAZZO, 72
48022 LUGO [RA]
TEL. 0545284711
www.gruppocevico.com

CELLAR SALES
PRE-BOOKED VISITS
ANNUAL PRODUCTION 20,000,000 bottles
HECTARES UNDER VINE 6700.00

The community of 4,500 growers and 6,700 hectares under vine make up Cevico, one of Italy's leading wine players. The cooperative's deep attachment its roots translates into a constant commitment to promoting the Romagna designation and communication that places the territory at the heart of every message. Its wines are popular, reliable and tasty, representing the soul of the entire offering and quality growth of recent years, which has been oriented to reflecting the terroir. The main brands are Terre Cevico, Vigneti Galassi, Sancrispino, Ronco, Romandiola, and Bernardi. The cooperative's production is generally quite reliable and it shows an ability for combining large volumes and quality. Across the range, the brand that shows most sense of place is Terre Cevico, while the most modern in style is Galassi. Good work has also been done on the Pignoletto, a wine the region is promoting heavily.

● Bosco Eliceo Merlot Terre Cevico '14	♀♀ 1*
○ Colli di Imola Pignoletto Frizzante Romandiola '14	♀♀ 2*
● Romagna Sangiovese Sup. Romandiola Novilunio '14	♀♀ 2*
● Romagna Sangiovese Sup. Terre Cevico '14	♀♀ 2*
● Romagna Sangiovese Sup. Vign. Galassi '14	♀♀ 2*
● Romagna Sangiovese Terre Cevico '14	♀♀ 2*
● Romagna Sangiovese Sup. Romandiola Il Malatesta '14	♀ 2
● Sangiovese di Romagna Sup. Romandiola Novilunio '13	♀♀ 2*
● Sangiovese di Romagna Sup. Vign. Galassi '13	♀♀ 2*
● Sangiovese di Romagna Terre Cevico '13	♀♀ 2*

Lini 910

LOC. CANOLO DI CORREGGIO
VIA VECCHIA CANOLO, 7
42015 CORREGGIO [RE]
TEL. 0522690162
www.lini910.it

CELLAR SALES
PRE-BOOKED VISITS
ANNUAL PRODUCTION 400,000 bottles
HECTARES UNDER VINE 25.00

More than 100 years of history and a story that spans four generations, now travelling the world with an increasingly terroir-true wine concept. Cousins Alicia and Alberto are committed to consolidating the reputation of a brand that has always focused on quality, even when the universe of Lambrusco was based on a completely different approach. Fabio and Massimo Lini have always been passionate about Classic Method and were among the first in Emilia to gain experience in this technique. Their intensive consultant work gives this small family winery a great opportunity to select quality base wines for its Metodo Classico production. Gran Cuvée 2012 is spicy and complex, with dogwood, mace, rose, hazelnut, and earthy notes; the dynamic palate is creamy and balanced. Lambrusco Scuro 2014 is compact and elegant, relaxed and fresh.

● Gran Cuvée di Lambrusco M. Cl. '12	🍷🍷	4
● In Correggio Lambrusco Scuro '14	🍷🍷	2*
○ In Correggio Brut M. Cl. '07	🍷🍷	4
○ In Correggio Brut M. Cl. '04	🍷🍷	4
○ In Correggio Brut M. Cl. Bianco '09	🍷🍷	4
● In Correggio Brut M. Cl. Gran Cuvée	🍷🍷	4
⊙ In Correggio Brut Rosé M. Cl. '09	🍷🍷	2*
● In Correggio Brut Rosso M. Cl. '08	🍷🍷	4
● In Correggio Brut Rosso M. Cl. '05	🍷🍷	3*
● In Correggio Brut Rosso M. Cl. '03	🍷🍷	3*
⊙ In Correggio Lambrusco Rosato '12	🍷🍷	2*
● In Correggio Lambrusco Scuro '13	🍷🍷	2*
○ In Correggio Moscato Spumante '12	🍷🍷	2*
○ In Correggio Pas Dosé M. Cl '09	🍷🍷	4

Giovanna Madonia

LOC. VILLA MADONIA
VIA DE' CAPPUCCINI, 130
47032 BERTINORO [FC]
TEL. 0543444361
www.giovannamadonia.it

CELLAR SALES
PRE-BOOKED VISITS
RESTAURANT SERVICE
ANNUAL PRODUCTION 60,000 bottles
HECTARES UNDER VINE 12.00

Giovanna Madonia has been making wine in Bertinoro since the 1990s. Her vineyards are on Mount Maggio, on the typical soils rich in active limestone and local spungone rock found in large quantities everywhere, but with a cooler microclimate compared to the sea slope, and ripening times that take 20 more days. Madonia wines take time and Giovanna continues bottle ageing until she is sure all the hard edges have been rounded off the dense, close-knit but always ripe tannins. Neblina 2014 is an exciting and feisty Albana. The nose is austere and linear, almost razor sharp, with a textured, minerally mouth. Nice taut acidity drives the palate to a savoury finale, brimful of references to herbs and the variety's typical scents, beeswax and apricot. Ombroso 2011 is earthy and feral, gradually opening up to reveal very austere fruit; the mouth is elegant and especially subtle.

○ Romagna Albana Secco Neblina '14	🍷🍷🍷	2*
● Romagna Sangiovese Bertinoro Ombroso Ris. '11	🍷🍷	5
● Sangiovese di Romagna Sup. Fermavento '10	🍷🍷	3
● Sangiovese di Romagna Sup. Fermavento '09	🍷🍷	3
● Sangiovese di Romagna Sup. Ombroso Ris. '09	🍷🍷	5
● Sangiovese di Romagna Sup. Ombroso Ris. '08	🍷🍷	5
● Sterpigno Merlot '07	🍷🍷	5
● Tenentino '12	🍷🍷	2*

Ermete Medici & Figli

LOC. GAIDA
VIA NEWTON, 13A
42040 REGGIO EMILIA
TEL. 0522942135
www.medici.it

CELLAR SALES
PRE-BOOKED VISITS
ANNUAL PRODUCTION 800,000 bottles
HECTARES UNDER VINE 75.00
SUSTAINABLE WINERY

With the arrival of the Cevico group, flanking the Medici family in the winery, this company is now in an ideal condition to develop the fantastic work for promoting quality Lambrusco around the world, which Alberto Medici made his mission 30 years ago. Concerto, the Medici flagship, is proof of the reliable work undertaken across the cellar range. Medici also produces an excellent traditional Reggio Emilia balsamic vinegar. Concerto 2014 has the usual impeccable quality we are familiar with, but showing a drier, more convincing and elegant style than before. It is creamy, fruity, rounded and well-paced, austere with currant and cherry notes, tasty all the way to a long finale. A well-defined, deep wine. Gran Concerto 2012 is earthy and multifaceted, iridescent and minerally, with citrus and spice. A windy, rainy wine. Unique 2012 is subtle and knife-edged, with great complexity. Lemon zest, hazelnut, a hint of sea salt, and spices typical of Metodo Classico.

● Reggiano Lambrusco Concerto '14	▼▼▼	2*
⊙ Brut Rosé M. Cl. Unique '12	▼▼	3
● Gran Concerto Brut M. Cl. '12	▼▼	3
● Reggiano Lambrusco Assolo '14	▼▼	2*
● Reggiano Lambrusco I Classici '14	▼▼	2*
● Reggiano Lambrusco I Quercioli '14	▼▼	2*
● Colli di Scandiano e di Canossa Grasparossa Bocciolo '14	▼	2
● Reggiano Lambrusco Concerto '13	▽▽▽	2*
● Reggiano Lambrusco Concerto '12	▽▽▽	2*
● Reggiano Lambrusco Concerto '11	▽▽▽	2*
● Reggiano Lambrusco Concerto '10	▽▽▽	2*
● Reggiano Lambrusco Concerto '09	▽▽▽	2*
● Reggiano Lambrusco Concerto '08	▽▽▽	2*
● Reggiano Assolo '09	▽▽	2
● Reggiano Lambrusco Assolo '11	▽▽	2*

Monte delle Vigne

LOC. OZZANO TARO
VIA MONTICELLO, 13
43046 COLLECCHIO [PR]
TEL. 0521309704
www.montedellevigne.it

CELLAR SALES
PRE-BOOKED VISITS
ACCOMMODATION
ANNUAL PRODUCTION 350,000 bottles
HECTARES UNDER VINE 60.00

Monte delle Vigne represents a real opportunity for Parma, fielding excellent resources like a new, state-of-the-art cellar, 60 hectares of vines, and expert consultants. The vineyards are all on hilly terrain characterized by calcareous clay and are farmed with organic methods. Andrea Ferrari and Paolo Pizzarotti have installed a photovoltaic system so are almost autonomous for energy consumption, and are awaiting Carbon 0 certification. The wines tend to lean to an international style but always show quality that can only derive from good grapes and well-tended vintages. It is perhaps for this reason that the simplest labels are the most interesting, with less impact from wood ageing, which is too forward in the more ambitious wines. Poem 2014 is austere and complex, with an elegant varietal and a fresh, tasty mouth. Lambrusco 2014 is rich and charming, as Parma now prefers.

○ Colli di Parma Malvasia Frizzante '14	▼▼	2*
○ Colli di Parma Malvasia Poem '14	▼▼	2*
● Lambrusco Emilia '14	▼▼	2*
● Argille Malvasia '08	▽▽	5
○ Callas Malvasia '12	▽▽	2*
○ Callas Malvasia '11	▽▽	4
○ Callas Malvasia '07	▽▽	3
● Colli di Parma Malvasia Poem '12	▽▽	2*
● Colli di Parma Malvasia Poem '11	▽▽	2*
○ Colli di Parma Sauvignon '13	▽▽	2*
● Lambrusco '08	▽▽	2*
● Lambrusco '07	▽▽	2*
○ Malvasia Frizzante Dolce '12	▽▽	2*
● Nabucco '06	▽▽	4
● Nabucco '03	▽▽	4
⊙ Rubina Brut Rosé '13	▽▽	4

Fattoria Monticino Rosso

VIA MONTECATONE, 7
40026 IMOLA [BO]
TEL. 054240577
www.fattoriadelmonticinorosso.it

CELLAR SALES
PRE-BOOKED VISITS
ANNUAL PRODUCTION 70,000 bottles
HECTARES UNDER VINE 18.00

Gianni and Luciano Zeoli are tireless
workers and testify to the fabulous and
passionate work done in the rows and in
the cellar. They have worked non-stop over
recent years, expanding the winery and
always experimenting with something new,
or making improvements. Their consultant
oenologist is Giancarlo Soverchia, a great
human being and outright supporter of their
curiosity and their dreams. A philosophy of
continuous research, observation and risks
taken together, and of patience to wait
respectfully as the wines mature. A 2014 is
a knife-edged, deep Albana, and is fresh
enough to support an aromatic profile
ranging from "hot" beeswax and
Mediterranean herbs to "cool" citrus and
apricot. Complexity comes from an
breath-taking richness of flavour.
Sangiovese S 2014 expresses the lightness
of its vintage and develops delicate fruit
themes, with peppery vegetal notes and a
hard but supple mouth. Codronchio 2013
deploys its usual complexity.

○ Colli d'Imola Pignoletto P '14	♀♀ 2*
○ Romagna Albana Passito '10	♀♀ 4
○ Romagna Albana Secco A '14	♀♀ 2*
○ Romagna Albana Secco Codronchio '13	♀♀ 3
● Romagna Sangiovese Sup. Le Morine '11	♀♀ 3
● Romagna Sangiovese Sup. S '14	♀♀ 2*
● Romagna Sangiovese Sup. Le Morine Ris. '11	♀ 4
○ Albana di Romagna Secco A '13	♀♀ 2*
○ Albana di Romagna Secco A '12	♀♀ 2*
○ Albana di Romagna Secco A Special Edition '11	♀♀ 3*
○ Albana di Romagna Secco Codronchio '12	♀♀ 3
○ Albana di Romagna Secco Codronchio '10	♀♀ 3*

Fattoria Moretto

VIA TIBERIA, 13B
41014 CASTELVETRO DI MODENA [MO]
TEL. 059790183
www.fattoriamoretto.it

CELLAR SALES
PRE-BOOKED VISITS
ANNUAL PRODUCTION 60,000 bottles
HECTARES UNDER VINE 10.00
VITICULTURE METHOD Certified Organic
SUSTAINABLE WINERY

Fausto and Fabio Altariva are grasparossa
artisans and their authentic wines are
increasingly reliable, country classics, true
to the terroir. Moreover, they were among
the first to vinify each vineyard separately,
applying a concept of soil analysis rare in
the world of Lambrusco. Their vineyards
are at 200 metres of altitude, all facing
south and south-east on clay soils, in an
ideal microclimatic situation for organic
methods. The winemaking processes are
loyal to this philosophy and are based on
long maceration, allowing the wine to take
its time. Canova 2014 is a classic wine of
great personality, a must-drink for anyone
who wants to understand the deepest soul
of this variety. As always, this wine skilfully
combines the two aspects: a fruity, mainly
cherry register, and the rustic, earthy but
also citrussy notes of the tannins. Nice
savoury shades complete the picture with
caper, mace, and oregano.

● Lambrusco Grasparossa di Castelvetro Secco Canova '14	♀♀ 3*
● Lambrusco Grasparossa di Castelvetro Secco Monovitigno '14	♀♀ 3
● Lambrusco Grasparossa di Castelvetro Amabile Semprebon '13	♀♀ 2*
⊙ Lambrusco Grasparossa di Castelvetro Rosato '13	♀♀ 2*
● Lambrusco Grasparossa di Castelvetro Secco Canova '13	♀♀ 3*
● Lambrusco Grasparossa di Castelvetro Secco Canova '12	♀♀ 3*
● Lambrusco Grasparossa di Castelvetro Secco Monovitigno '13	♀♀ 3
● Lambrusco Grasparossa di Castelvetro Secco Monovitigno '12	♀♀ 3
● Lambrusco Grasparossa di Castelvetro Secco Tasso '13	♀♀ 2*

EMILIA ROMAGNA

Poderi Morini

LOC. ORIOLO DEI FICHI
VIA GESUITA
48018 FAENZA [RA]
TEL. 0546634257
www.poderimorini.com

ANNUAL PRODUCTION 100,000 bottles
HECTARES UNDER VINE 26.00
SUSTAINABLE WINERY

Alessandro Morini is a Faenza artisan who makes wine from the grapes of his 26 hectares of vineyards, all in Oriolo dei Fichi, a small terroir of the lower hill strip that vaunts a remarkable network of small producers. This group, including Alessandro, dedicated some time to minor old vines and revived the ancient centesimino aromatic red varietal along with a few other minor natives. The area is also very interesting for its albana, which grows flavoursome and textured here. Morale 2014 is an easy, well-made Sangiovese that handles the cold vintage in a masterly way. Peppery, austere, well-defined, with persuasively clean fruit, a taut, dry mouth, and a supple, delicate tannic weave. The Savignone 2013 has well-balanced and austere aromatics, gradually revealing the nuances that give it some complexity: rose, a hint of cinnamon, tangerine, petunia, white pepper. The mouth is full-flavoured and spicy, dry and fresh.

Fattoria Nicolucci

LOC. PREDAPPIO ALTA
VIA UMBERTO I, 21
47010 PREDAPPIO [FC]
TEL. 0543922361
www.vini-nicolucci.it

CELLAR SALES
PRE-BOOKED VISITS
ANNUAL PRODUCTION 70,000 bottles
HECTARES UNDER VINE 10.00
SUSTAINABLE WINERY

Alessandro Nicolucci is heir to two traditions: that of his family, with its four generations of growers preceding him, and that of a territory that has a unique history in Romagna for the cultivation of the vine, and indeed has a clone with an elliptical berry named Predappio. For Romagna, Predappio Alta is a symbol of regional viticulture and as early as the 1800s there is documentation of 7,000 bush vines planted per hectare. Alessandro vinifies in the classic style and ages his Sangiovese in large wood, as his family has always done, drawing forth the elegant vegetal and mineral notes inherited from a rare terroir whose vineyards are interspersed with sulphur outcrops. Vigna del Generale 2012 is an elegant, deep, complex and multifaceted wine, with earthy but well-defined fruit and a vibrant, well-balanced mouth. It will need a little time to be read properly and for the "green note" to shift into pencil lead and refined mineral hints.

● Sangiovese di Romagna Sup. Morale '14	♥♥ 3
● Savignone Centesimo '13	♥♥ 2*
○ Albana di Romagna Secco Sette Note '14	♥ 2
● Sangiovese di Romagna Sup. Morale '10	♀♀ 3
● Sangiovese di Romagna Sup. Nonno Rico Ris. '10	♀♀ 2*
● Sangiovese di Romagna Sup. Nonno Rico Ris. '09	♀♀ 2*
● Sangiovese di Romagna Sup. Torre di Oriolo '11	♀♀ 3
● Sangiovese di Romagna Sup. Torre di Oriolo '10	♀♀ 3
● Savignone '11	♀♀ 2*

● Romagna Sangiovese Sup. V. del Generale Ris. '12	♥♥♥ 5
● Romagna Sangiovese Sup. Tre Rocche '14	♥ 3
● Sangiovese di Romagna Predappio di Predappio V. del Generale '11	♀♀♀ 5
● Sangiovese di Romagna Sup. V. del Generale Ris. '10	♀♀♀ 5
● Sangiovese di Romagna Sup. V. del Generale Ris. '08	♀♀♀ 5
● Sangiovese di Romagna V. del Generale Ris. '09	♀♀♀ 5
● Sangiovese di Romagna V. del Generale Ris. '05	♀♀♀ 4
● Sangiovese di Romagna Sup. Tre Rocche '13	♀♀ 3*

Enio Ottaviani

VIA PANORAMICA, 199
47842 SAN GIOVANNI IN MARIGNANO [RN]
TEL. 0541952608
www.enioottaviani.it

CELLAR SALES
PRE-BOOKED VISITS
ANNUAL PRODUCTION 130,000 bottles
HECTARES UNDER VINE 12.00

Davide and Massimo Lorenzi have added an agricultural dimension to their grandfather's venerable vintner trade, and are working with good results both on reds and whites. The 12 hectares of vineyards are located in the south of Romagna, in the hills behind Cattolica, at the foot of the Conca Valley. The wines are brisk and well-defined thanks to Davide's meticulous cellar work, and are now focusing on an increasingly precise sense of place. Primalba 2014 is a pure Sangiovese that opens slowly in the glass to show well-defined, tidy fruit. The nose has peppery hints that ageing in concrete has endowed with complexity; the palate is taut and dry. A nice gentle touch of tannins. Caciara 2014 is open and Mediterranean on the nose, its strength lying in the supple palate. Nicely savoury. Clemente Primo is a textured, salty sauvignon blanc, riesling and pagadebit blend.

○ Clemente Primo '14	🍷🍷 2*
● Romagna Sangiovese Primalba '14	🍷🍷 2*
● Romagna Sangiovese Sup. Caciara '14	🍷🍷 2*
○ Romagna Trebbiano Tre Soli '14	🍷 2
● Romagna Sangiovese Sup. Primalba '13	🍷🍷 2*
● Romagna Sangiovese Sup. Sole Rosso Ris. '11	🍷🍷 3

Gianfranco Paltrinieri

FRAZ. SORBARA
VIA CRISTO, 49
41030 BOMPORTO [MO]
TEL. 059902047
www.cantinapaltrinieri.it

CELLAR SALES
PRE-BOOKED VISITS
ANNUAL PRODUCTION 90,000 bottles
HECTARES UNDER VINE 15.00

Paltrinieri is the quintessence of artisanal Lambrusco, proof that this wine is ousting brand preconceptions to start a completely new territorial concept that Alberto has pursued to the most extreme idea of cru. The loose soils on this strip of land between the Secchia and the Panaro are the great terroir of sorbara and the 15 hectares at the heart of this designation. Paltrinieri wines, peasant in spirit and refined in expression, are among the great wines made from sorbara: lean and knife-edged, delicate and brimming with energy. Radice 2014 is a lean, soulful wine, with a story to tell. It is savoury, brisk, briny, and austere, knife-edged and clean, flying so fast across the palate there is a risk of missing it. Only a few bottles were produced, with a crown cap, sought after by fans, but sold as Modena Lambrusco. Textured and balanced, Leclisse 2014 is a rustic, peasant wine in the best sense.

● Lambrusco di Sorbara Radice '14	🍷🍷 2*
● Lambrusco di Modena M. Cl. Grosso '12	🍷🍷 2*
● Lambrusco di Sorbara Leclisse '14	🍷🍷 2*
● Lambrusco di Sorbara Leclisse '10	🍷🍷🍷 3*
● Lambrusco di Sorbara Radice '13	🍷🍷🍷 2*
● Lambrusco di Modena Greto '13	🍷🍷 2*
● Lambrusco di Modena M. Cl. Grosso '11	🍷🍷 2*
● Lambrusco di Sorbara Leclisse '08	🍷🍷 2*
● Lambrusco di Sorbara La Piria '13	🍷🍷 2*
● Lambrusco di Sorbara La Piria '12	🍷🍷 2*
● Lambrusco di Sorbara Leclisse '13	🍷🍷 2*
● Lambrusco di Sorbara Leclisse '12	🍷🍷 2*
● Lambrusco di Sorbara Leclisse '11	🍷🍷 3*
● Lambrusco di Sorbara Radice '11	🍷🍷 3*
● Lambrusco di Sorbara Radice '10	🍷🍷 2*

Tenuta Pertinello

S.DA ARPINETO PERTINELLO, 2
47010 GALEATA [FC]
TEL. 0543983156
www.tenutapertinello.it

CELLAR SALES
ANNUAL PRODUCTION 50,000 bottles
HECTARES UNDER VINE 12.00

The Bidente Valley climbs up from Forlì to the beech woods of the Parco Nazionale delle Foreste Casentinesi. Tenuta Pertinello's 12 hectares under vine are the highest and the marly sandstone stretching from 350 to 430) are ideal for imprinting the wines with freshness, cellarability and a lot of character. In recent years the wines have shown they do enjoy a good lifespan. Pertinello 2012 has a beautiful mouth: elegant, minerally, savoury but sadly a tad dried out by its time in the wood. The nose is austere and the fruit has nice nuances that will offer complexity with time. Il Bosco 2014 is well-defined, flavoursome, with a vibrant, supple, well-paced mouth. Crisp fruit, taut palate. Il Sasso 2010 has great stuffing, flavour and freshness, but is hampered by a heavy hand in the wood, which is mouth-drying and simplifies its expressions.

● Colli Romagna Centrale Sangiovese Il Bosco '14	♥♥ 2*
● Colli Romagna Centrale Sangiovese Il Sasso Ris. '10	♥♥ 5
● Colli Romagna Centrale Sangiovese Pertinello '12	♥♥ 3
● Colli Romagna Centrale Sangiovese Pertinello '08	♥♥♥ 3
● Colli Romagna Centrale Sangiovese Il Bosco '12	♀♀ 2*
● Colli Romagna Centrale Sangiovese Il Sasso Ris. '09	♀♀ 5
● Colli Romagna Centrale Sangiovese Pertinello '11	♀♀ 3
● Colli Romagna Centrale Sangiovese Pertinello '10	♀♀ 3

Poderi dal Nespoli

LOC. NESPOLI
VILLA ROSSI, 50
47012 CIVITELLA DI ROMAGNA [FC]
TEL. 0543989911
www.poderidalnespoli.com

CELLAR SALES
PRE-BOOKED VISITS
ANNUAL PRODUCTION 900,000 bottles
HECTARES UNDER VINE 30.00

Poderi dal Nespoli is one of the most important brands in Romagna and shows the successful combination of the business skills of Alfeo and Marco Martini (MGM mondo del vino) and the experience of the Ravaioli family, active in the Bidente Valley since 1929, now represented by Fabio and Celita. Today Poderi dal Nespoli has resources and vision, and the winery has indeed grown in recent years, with 30 hectares of its own grapes flanked by those purchased locally with experience and skill, often from the same growers who have guaranteed quality over the years. The Nespoli 2012 is an expressive, open Sangiovese which offers fruit generously. The palate is clean, harmonious and fresh, meaty and spicy. Prugneto 2014 is well-defined and charming, with crisp fruit and a flavoursome mouth. Borgo dei Guidi 2012, from sangiovese topped up with cabernet sauvignon and merlot, has an international stamp and the spiced nuances come from ageing in wood.

● Sangiovese di Romagna Sup. Il Nespoli Ris. '12	♥♥ 4
● Borgo dei Guidi '12	♥♥ 5
● Sangiovese di Romagna Sup. Il Prugneto '14	♥♥ 2*
● Sangiovese di Romagna Sup. Il Nespoli Ris. '07	♥♥♥ 4*
● Sangiovese di Romagna Sup. Il Nespoli Ris. '06	♥♥♥ 4*
● Borgo dei Guidi '11	♀♀ 5
● Sangiovese di Romagna Sup. Il Nespoli Ris. '11	♀♀ 4
● Sangiovese di Romagna Sup. Il Nespoli Ris. '10	♀♀ 4
● Sangiovese di Romagna Sup. Il Prugneto '13	♀♀ 2*

Il Pratello

VIA MORANA, 14
47015 MODIGLIANA [FC]
TEL. 0546942038
www.ilpratello.net

CELLAR SALES
PRE-BOOKED VISITS
ANNUAL PRODUCTION 20,000 bottles
HECTARES UNDER VINE 5.50
VITICULTURE METHOD Certified Organic

Modigliana territory is definitely the most
suitable in Romagna for producing
time-defying wines, partly due to the
altitude and partly due to the loose marl
and sandstone soils. The Ibola Valley, one of
the three above Modigliana, is the most
extreme example of these features and the
wines produced here are savoury and
linear, powered by the energy of their deep
mineral freshness. Opening old vintages of
Sangiovese de Il Pratello is always a
surprise for their magical staying power
and the complexity developed over the
years. Campore 2013, from chardonnay
and sauvignon blanc, shows mineral with
the austere character of this area. The deep
nose ushers in a mouth combining texture
and tautness. No doubt about its usual
amazing cellarability. Castagnara 2011,
from pinot nero, is delicate and hard, with
complex Mediterranean aromas and a
knife-edged mouth. A tempting vegetal
core of earth, pencil lead and damp chalk
plaster will find its elegance with time.

● Castagnara '11	❑❑ 4
○ Le Campore '13	❑❑ 2*
● Colli di Faenza Sangiovese Mantignano V. V. Ris. '04	❑❑❑ 3*
● Mantignano V. V. '08	❑❑❑ 3*
● Badia Raustignolo '08	❑❑ 5
○ Le Campore '10	❑❑ 2*
○ Le Campore '08	❑❑ 2*
● Mantignano V. V. '09	❑❑ 3
● Mantignano Vecchie Vigne '07	❑❑ 2*

Quarticello

VIA MATILDE DI CANOSSA, 1A
42027 MONTECCHIO EMILIA [RE]
TEL. 0522866220
www.quarticello.it

ANNUAL PRODUCTION 25,000 bottles
HECTARES UNDER VINE 5.00

Roberto Maestri has been running this
hillside winery on the Reggio side of the
River Enza since 2001, obtaining
increasingly high-quality results. He is one
of the few artisans in the world of
Lambrusco, a grower who tends his five
hectares of vineyards personally and deals
with all the vinification. He always relies on
natural second fermentation in the bottle,
as tradition demands, and adopts natural
techniques in the cellar. The result is
reliable, extremely classic, focused,
austere wines with a real sense of place.
The energetic Ferrando 2014 speaks in
sophisticated terms drawing on new
nuances. Earthy notes, followed by orange
zest, roses, palate grip, delicate spices.
The mouthfeel is dry, lively and elegant.
Despina 2014 is savoury and minerally,
with the citrus overtones of grapefruit and
citron, closing with a nice complexity.
Attractively reminiscent of hazelnut,
alternating with crisp flint in the finish.

○ Despina '14	❑❑ 2*
⊙ Ferrando '14	❑❑ 2*
○ Despina '13	❑❑ 2*
○ Despina '12	❑❑ 2*
⊙ Ferrando '13	❑❑ 2*
⊙ Ferrando '11	❑❑ 2*
⊙ Ferrando '11	❑❑ 2*
○ Stradora '13	❑❑ 3*

EMILIA ROMAGNA

Noelia Ricci

VIA PANDOLFA, 35
47016 PREDAPPIO [FC]
TEL. 0543940073
info@noeliaricci.it

PRE-BOOKED VISITS
ACCOMMODATION
ANNUAL PRODUCTION 200,000 bottles
HECTARES UNDER VINE 9.00
SUSTAINABLE WINERY

Marco Cirese has revolutionized his well-established family winery, Tenuta Pandolfa, changing its philosophy so radically that he needed a new name to underline the novelty of his initiative. So, while the estate continues to work to the full, he has "invented" a project that brings together the best of the old family heritage and motivated, well-trained staff: Francesco Bordini handles the agronomic side, while Francesco Guazzugli Marini runs the commercial operations. Sangiovese 2014 Vespa, with its wasp-design label, is a red of austere, well-defined fruitiness, flowery notes and almost imperceptible delicate orange zest. In the mouth it is all energy and thrust, with moderate tannins that stay stylish right through to the finish. A full-flavoured wine, hinging on suppleness, skilfully pared down. An excellent example of how Romagna can express great quality in simple yet sophisticated vintage wines.

● Romagna Sangiovese Sup. Il Sangiovese '14	♥♥♥ 2*
○ Bro '14	♥♥ 3
● Romagna Sangiovese Sup. '13	♀♀ 2*
● Romagna Sangiovese Sup. Godenza '13	♀♀ 2*

Cantine Riunite & Civ

VIA G. BRODOLINI, 24
42040 CAMPEGINE [RE]
TEL. 0522905711
www.riuniteciv.it

CELLAR SALES
ANNUAL PRODUCTION 130,000,000 bottles
HECTARES UNDER VINE 3500.00
SUSTAINABLE WINERY

This huge cooperative comprises 2,600 grower-members making wines from their 3,500 hectares of vineyard. These incredible figures, combined with sales by GIV Gruppo Italiano Vini make this Italy's largest producer of wine. Despite its bulk, however, its soul and values remain those of a local farmer, as well as its spirit of solidarity; this guiding philosophy is the fruit too of the personal histories of Riunite's managers, starting with President Corrado Casoli. Its bond with the growing area and its growers has led Riunite to invest in the small Albinea Canali cooperative and make it a true workshop for high quality. Vanni Lusetti has come up with a range of highly reliable wines, reflecting the improvements in Emilia Romagna cooperative production. FB 2014 is a no-nonsense, ice-cool, taut wine, with delicate aromas and a vibrant mouth. Grasparossa Gaetano Righi 2014 is brisk and fragrant, with a polished, chewy fruitiness, close-woven tannins and lots of flavour .

● Lambrusco Emilia FB Metodo Ancestrale Albinea Canali '14	♥♥ 2*
● Lambrusco Grasparossa di Castelvetro Secco Gaetano Righi '14	♥♥ 2*
● Lambrusco di Sorbara Gaetano Righi '14	♥♥ 2*
● Lambrusco di Sorbara Secco Righi '14	♥♥ 2*
○ Pignoletto Spumante Righi '14	♥♥ 2*
● Reggiano Lambrusco Albinea Canali '14	♥♥ 2*
● Reggiano Lambrusco Albinea Canali Foglie Rosse '14	♥♥ 2*
● Reggiano Lambrusco Secco 1950 '14	♥♥ 2*
● Lambrusco Reggiano Albinea Canali '13	♀♀ 2*
● Lambrusco Emilia FB Metodo Ancestrale Albinea Canali '13	♀♀ 2*
● Reggiano Lambrusco Albinea Canali Foglie Rosse '13	♀♀ 2*
● Reggiano Lambrusco Secco dell'Olma '13	♀♀ 2*

Cantine Romagnoli

LOC. VILLÒ
VIA GENOVA, 20
29020 VIGOLZONE [PC]
TEL. 0523870904
www.cantineromagnoli.it

CELLAR SALES
PRE-BOOKED VISITS
ANNUAL PRODUCTION 300,000 bottles
HECTARES UNDER VINE 45.00
SUSTAINABLE WINERY

This long-standing Piacenza winery was recently taken over by the Perini family. Oenologist Luciana Biondo is in charge of winemaking, and she has brought with her a wind of change to help conquer the challenges that lie ahead. Here, in one of the prime territories of the Piacenza area, Val Nure, regarded as the cradle of viticulture around Piacenza, the valley is brimming with established, very well-known wineries. Cantine Romagnoli own 45 hectares under vine on ancient red clay soils, which owe their colour to the iron sediments they contain. Colto Vitato 2014, from barbera, is a brisk wine, full of personality. Displaying an austere, fragrant fruitiness, in the mouth it is knife-edged with a citrus nuance in the finale. A delicious interpretation of the vintage. Caravaggio 2012, from bonarda, barbera and pinot nero, displays nice flesh and expression, great elegance and a grip which speeds up the pace on the palate with good development.

● Caravaggio '12	▼▼ 5
● Colto Vitato del Cicotto '14	▼▼ 2*
○ Sasso Nero del Nure Bianco '14	▼▼ 2*
○ Sasso Nero del Nure Malvasia '14	▼▼ 2*
● Gutturnio Frizzante Sasso Nero '13	♀♀ 3
○ Ortrugo Frizzante Sasso Nero Tappo a Corona '13	♀♀ 2*
● V. del Ciccotto Barbera '13	♀♀ 3

San Biagio Vecchio

VIA SALITA DI ORIOLO, 13
48018 FAENZA [RA]
TEL. 3393523168
www.cantinasanbiagiovecchio.com

CELLAR SALES
PRE-BOOKED VISITS
ANNUAL PRODUCTION 8,000 bottles
HECTARES UNDER VINE 5.50

Andrea Balducci has inherited the extraordinary experience of Don Antonio Baldassari, the parish priest of San Biagio, but above all a great specialist in rustic, marvellous, sweet expressions of Albana. Starting from that experience, Andrea and his wife Lucia Ziniti have continued to work, managing to get a dry wine to express the difficult but wonderful identity of this white vine variety made up of acidity, plenty of power, and tannins. The winery is located near Torre di Oriolo, in what we could call the grand cru of albana, a corner of Romagna in the foothills between Faenza and the small district of Santa Lucia. Sabbiagialla 2014 is the result of three staggered harvests, the last of which features grapes attacked by noble rot. Vinified in steel after two days of maceration on the skins, the nose is complex and multifaceted with bay leaf, curry plant, saffron, a touch of oregano, acacia honey. In mouth it is savoury and knife-edged, full-flavoured yet stylish and with citrus note in the finale.

○ Sabbiagialla '14	▼▼ 2*
● Romagna Sangiovese Oriolo 2013 '13	▼ 2
○ Ambrosia Albana Passito '07	♀♀ 3
● Centesimino Passito '12	♀♀ 4
○ Quintessenza Albana Passito '12	♀♀ 3
○ Sabbiagialla '13	♀♀ 2*
○ Sabbiagialla '12	♀♀ 2*
○ Sabbiagialla '11	♀♀ 3
● Sangiovese di Romagna Sup. Barbatello '12	♀♀ 3
● Sangiovese di Romagna Sup. Serraglio '10	♀♀ 3
● Sangiovese di Romagna Sup. Serraglio '09	♀♀ 2*

EMILIA ROMAGNA

★San Patrignano

VIA SAN PATRIGNANO, 53
47853 CORIANO [RN]
TEL. 0541362111
www.sanpatrignano.org

PRE-BOOKED VISITS
RESTAURANT SERVICE
ANNUAL PRODUCTION 500,000 bottles
HECTARES UNDER VINE 110.00
VITICULTURE METHOD Certified Organic

With 110 hectares of fully-productive vines as well as a spacious modern cellar, the Community of San Patrignano provides work and tools for of the young people working in the vineyards and in the cellar, overseen by Riccardo Cotarella. The estate is situated in the foothills near Rimini, where the mild climate provided by the sea gives its wines both expressive fruit and appealing tannins, even in sangiovese. It is the ideal climate for Bordeaux varieties, which in Rimini can develop complexity and elegance. Avi 2011 opens a new season for this long-standing Riserva di Sangiovese, a season where ageing in large barrels and a more delicate hand in its vinification express the sense of place. Indeed, the overall impression is that this wine is elegant, with both its flavour and its light tannic weave developing in the mouth, as is typical of this terroir. Montepirolo 2011 has the personality of a true Bordeaux, spicy and close-woven.

● Romagna Sangiovese Sup. Avi Ris. '11	▼▼▼	5
● Colli di Rimini Cabernet Montepirolo '11	▼▼	4
● Romagna Sangiovese Sup. Ora '14	▼▼	3
○ Vie '14	▼▼	3
○ Aulente Bianco '14	▼	2
● Aulente Rosso '14	▼	2
● Colli di Rimini Cabernet Montepirolo '06	♈♈♈	5
● Colli di Rimini Cabernet Montepirolo '04	♈♈♈	5
● Colli di Rimini Rosso Noi '04	♈♈♈	4
● Sangiovese di Romagna Sup. Avi Ris. '08	♈♈♈	5
● Sangiovese di Romagna Sup. Avi Ris. '07	♈♈♈	5
● Sangiovese di Romagna Sup. Avi Ris. '06	♈♈♈	5
● Sangiovese di Romagna Sup. Avi Ris. '05	♈♈♈	5
● Sangiovese di Romagna Sup. Ora '12	♈♈♈	3*
● Sangiovese di Romagna Sup. Ora '11	♈♈♈	3*

Cantina Sociale Santa Croce

S.S. 468 DI CORREGGIO, 35
41012 CARPI [MO]
TEL. 059664007
www.cantinasantacroce.it

CELLAR SALES
PRE-BOOKED VISITS
ANNUAL PRODUCTION 400,000 bottles
HECTARES UNDER VINE 500.00

This historical operation, dating back to 1907, is located in Santa Croce, near Carpi, in the heart of the zone that gives its name to lambrusco salamino. Its 250 member-growers farm more than 500 hectares of vineyard in the plains south of Modena. Some members are in the province of Reggio Emilia, just north of the loose-textured soils ideal for growing sorbara, at Limidi and Sozzigalli, on the left bank of the Secchia. These richer, clayey terrains are perfect for salamino, which here displays outstanding elegance. The original cellar still serves as the centre of production. The soul of the great winemaker Villiam Friggeri who died recently lives on, and we wish Maurizio Boni, who has just put his name to his first vintage, all the very best as winery director. Salamino Tradizione 2014 displays very clear fruit, reminiscent of Vignola cherries. It is close-woven, creamy, full di flavour and freshness. A hint of dogwood in the close, with a dry, elegant finish. As always very well-typed with a strong local identity.

○ 100 Vendemmie Rosé Brut '14	▼▼	2*
● Lambrusco Grasparossa di Castelvetro secco '14	▼▼	2*
● Lambrusco Salamino di S. Croce Tradizione '14	▼▼	1*
● Lambrusco di Sorbara Secco '14	▼	2
● Lambrusco Salamino di S. Croce '14	▼	1*
● Lambrusco di Sorbara Secco '12	♈♈	2*
● Lambrusco Grasparossa di Castelvetro '12	♈♈	2*
● Lambrusco Salamino di S. Croce Enoteca '13	♈♈	1*
● Lambrusco Salamino di S. Croce Enoteca '12	♈♈	1*
● Lambrusco Salamino di S. Croce Tradizione '13	♈♈	1*
● Lambrusco Salamino di S. Croce Tradizione '12	♈♈	1*

Matteo Serraglio - De Pietri

FRAZ. SALICETO BUZZALINO
VIA VECCHIA, 28
41100 CAMPOGALLIANO [MO]
TEL. 3356534069
www.lambruscoilserraglio.it

CELLAR SALES
PRE-BOOKED VISITS
ANNUAL PRODUCTION 16,500 bottles
HECTARES UNDER VINE 10.00

The De Pietri Matteo farm is divided into three plots around the village of Campogalliano on the left bank of the Secchia. One of them, Serraglio, which gives its name to the wine, lies on alluvial soils in the Saliceto Buzzalino area, at the heart of the Lambrusco di Sorbara production district. The De Pietri family have been producing top-quality sorbara grapes for three generations, which they have always sold on to prestigious local labels, but in 2014 they decided to produce their own brand, vinified in conjunction with the Vezzelli winery. Serraglio 2014 is well-defined and austere, drawing on Sorbara's cool fruity repertoire of white peach, hawthorn, herbs, lemon and citron zest, damson and a hint of mint leaf with great elegance; the mouth is knife-edged and lean. Compared to its sibling fermented in a pressurized vat, Serraglio Fermentazione in Bottiglia 2014 is spicier, with an earthy soul. The two wines have labels signed by Modenese artist Giuliano Della Casa.

● Lambrusco di Sorbara Il Serraglio '14	ΨΨ 3*
● Lambrusco di Sorbara Il Serraglio Fermentazione in Bottiglia '14	ΨΨ 3

La Stoppa

LOC. ANCARANO
29029 RIVERGARO [PC]
TEL. 0523958159
www.lastoppa.it

CELLAR SALES
PRE-BOOKED VISITS
RESTAURANT SERVICE
ANNUAL PRODUCTION 160,000 bottles
HECTARES UNDER VINE 32.00
VITICULTURE METHOD Certified Organic

The red clay soils of La Stoppa have played a leading role in quality viticulture for over a century. In fact, as far back as the early 1900s, the Genoese lawyer Ageno experimented here with some French varieties, in what was an extremely modern project for the time. In 1973, the Pantaleoni family purchased the winery, and since then La Stoppa has channelled its experience into producing multifaceted, pure wines with incredible depth and austerity, that challenge time with their extraordinary longevity. A continuous pursuit for style has made this operation one of the most important Italian producers of natural wine. Barbera 2010 is one of the deepest, most territorial wines to have been produced in the Piacentino. The cool growing year helped to give rhythm and austerity to the earthy, fruity repertoire of this great classic. Flint, tangerine zest, cherry, a range of leaves and mosses, with an animal hint: its complexity is never-ending.

● Barbera della Stoppa '10	ΨΨ 4
○ Ageno '11	ΨΨ 4
● Macchiona '11	ΨΨ 4
● Trebbiolo '13	ΨΨ 2*
○ Vigna del Volta '08	ΨΨΨ 5
● Barbera della Stoppa '09	ΨΨ 4
● Barbera della Stoppa '07	ΨΨ 4
● Macchiona '09	ΨΨ 4
● Macchiona '07	ΨΨ 4
● Macchiona '02	ΨΨ 5
● Trebbiolo '12	ΨΨ 2*
● Trebbiolo '11	ΨΨ 2*
○ Vigna del Volta '09	ΨΨ 5

Terre della Pieve

FRAZ. DIEGARO
VIA EMILIA PONENTE, 2412
47023 CESENA [FC]
TEL. 0547611535
www.terredellapieve.com

PRE-BOOKED VISITS
ANNUAL PRODUCTION 25,000 bottles
HECTARES UNDER VINE 5.00

Sergio Lucchi is a craftsman who tends five hectares under vine around Bertinoro, alongside the Pieve di Polenta featured in the winery name. Here at an altitude of 300 metres, on the active lime soils typical of this corner of Romagna. The Sangioveses made here are close-woven with mature tannins, never rough in character, with good ageing potential and admirable richness of flavour. We were fascinated by their work with albana, which Lucchi partially dries in the old house next to the vineyard. Stil Novo 2012, from raisined albana, is a sweet, down-to-earth wine anticipating sea salt and tannins from the nose. The aromatics are brimful of apricot, mint, caper, candied lemon peel, dates, dried figs and summer flowers; the rich, fleshy palate is flavoursome and textured. A gorgeous acidity keeps everything taut, the life and soul underpinning all this generosity. The offbeat tannins, the characteristic challenge offered by this complex white varietal, are handled well.

Torre San Martino

VIA SAN MARTINO IN MONTE
47015 MODIGLIANA [FC]
TEL. 3351891992
www.torre1922.it

CELLAR SALES
PRE-BOOKED VISITS
ANNUAL PRODUCTION 38,000 bottles
HECTARES UNDER VINE 7.50

The Modigliana area displays unique characteristics giving its Sangioveses a delightfully savoury mouth, elegant tannins and good acidity. This makes their style quite unmistakable, as well as giving them excellent ageing potential. Maurizio Costa has strengthened the family roots in Romagna with a project that over the years has become a real passion. The winery also owns the oldest vineyard in Romagna, dating back to 1922, a bush-trained plot patiently restored by the winery's agronomist and oenologist, Francesco Bordini. Gemme 2014 is a wine of great austerity, tangy and knife-edged, flowery and well-paced. It grabs the palate with its incredible freshness, offering a surefooted progression with pepper and green notes. The 2012 vintage of Vigna 1922 unfolds vibrant on the palate, with a delicate nose combining the sweetness of oak ageing with a warm growing year. We enjoyed the repertoire of balsamic, Mediterranean aromas.

○ Stil Novo '12	♟♟ 4
● Romagna Sangiovese Sup. A Virgilio '13	♟ 2
● Sangiovese di Romagna Sup. A Virgilio '10	♟♟ 2*
● Sangiovese di Romagna Sup. Nobis Ris. '11	♟♟ 3
● Sangiovese di Romagna Sup. Nobis Ris. '10	♟♟ 3
● Sangiovese di Romagna Sup. Nobis Ris. '09	♟♟ 3*
○ Stil Novo '09	♟♟ 4

● Romagna Sangiovese Sup. Gemme '14	♟♟♟ 3*
● Romagna Sangiovese Sup. V. 1922 Ris. '12	♟♟ 6
● Colli di Faenza V. Claudia Ris. '12	♟♟ 3
● Sangiovese di Romagna V. 1922 Ris. '11	♟♟♟ 6
○ Colli di Faenza Torre '12	♟♟ 2*
○ Colli di Faenza V. della Signora '13	♟♟ 2*
● Sangiovese di Romagna Sup. Gemme '11	♟♟ 6
● Sangiovese di Romagna Sup. V. 1922 Ris. '10	♟♟ 6
● Sangiovese di Romagna V. 1922 '08	♟♟ 6
● Vigna alle Querce '08	♟♟ 5

Venturini Baldini

FRAZ. RONCOLO
VIA TURATI, 42
42020 QUATTRO CASTELLA [RE]
TEL. 0522249011
www.venturinibaldini.it

CELLAR SALES
PRE-BOOKED VISITS
RESTAURANT SERVICE
ANNUAL PRODUCTION 300,000 bottles
HECTARES UNDER VINE 35.00
VITICULTURE METHOD Certified Organic

Venturini Baldini was founded in 1975, but its roots go back much further, being set around an estate villa dating back to 1670. Here in the closest hills to Reggio are its 35 hectares under vine, organically tended for 20 years, surrounded by 150 hectares of woodland and meadow. This property has recently been bought up by a large Italian wine holding owned by the Iverna investment company. The winery is now run by Giuseppe Prestia, who has worked hard together with Lorenzo Tersi and Monica Franceschetti to bring this established brand into the group portfolio, with a steadfast belief in the potential both of the area and of top-quality Lambrusco. Carlo Ferrini is behind the first vinifications in this new season for the cellar, and the 2014 array of wines submitted is good overall, which is good news and underlines the potential of their vineyards. Reggiano 2014 is creamy and tight-knit, well-fruited and charming. Tenuta Roncola 2014 is delicate and elegant.

○ Colli di Scandiano e di Canossa Malvasia Frizzante Tenuta Roncola '14		�杯♡ 2*
⊙ Reggiano Lambrusco Rosato Secco '14		♡♡ 2*
● Reggiano Lambrusco Secco '14		♡♡ 2*
● Rubino del Cerro Mater Spumante '14		♡♡ 2*

Francesco Vezzelli

FRAZ. SAN MATTEO
VIA CANALETTO NORD, 878A
41122 MODENA
TEL. 059318695
aavezzelli@gmail.com

CELLAR SALES
PRE-BOOKED VISITS
ANNUAL PRODUCTION 120,000 bottles
HECTARES UNDER VINE 15.00

Vezzelli is a small family operation founded in 1958, with the third generation now on board. The cellar is located in San Matteo, close to Modena, while the vineyards are in Sozzigalli, in the floodplains between in lowest river levees and the main levee, at the Secchia. These loose, nutrient-poor soils do extraordinary favours for lambrusco sorbara, bringing out lovely floral and mineral qualities. The Grasparossas are vinified here with grapes bought in from Levizzano Rangone. Rifermentazione Ancestrale 2014 is a subtle, razor-sharp wine, with an essential tannic weave, brimming with surprising expressiveness. It displays mace, orange and tangerine zest, rose, petunia, and the minerally motifs of sorbara, tanginess in particular. Rive dei Ciliegi 2014 is an extremely elegant, down-to-earth and refined Grasparossa, with balanced tannins, mature and tight-knit, earthy but also fruity.

● Lambrusco di Sorbara Rifermentazione Ancestrale '14		♡♡ 2*
● Lambrusco Grasparossa di Castelvetro Rive dei Ciliegi '14		♡♡ 2*
● Lambrusco di Sorbara Il Selezione '14		♡♡ 2*
⊙ Lambrusco di Sorbara Rosé MoRosa '14		♡♡ 2*
● Lambrusco di Sorbara Il Selezione '13		♡♡ 2*
● Lambrusco di Sorbara Il Selezione '12		♡♡ 2*
● Lambrusco di Sorbara Il Selezione '11		♡♡ 2*
⊙ Lambrusco di Sorbara Rosé MoRosa '13		♡♡ 2*
⊙ Lambrusco di Sorbara Rosé MoRosa '12		♡♡ 2*
⊙ Lambrusco di Sorbara Rosé MoRosa '11		♡♡ 2*
● Lambrusco Grasparossa di Castelvetro Rive dei Ciliegi '11		♡♡ 2*
● Lambrusco Il Bricco di Checco '11		♡♡ 2*

Vigne dei Boschi

LOC. VALPIANA
VIA TURA, 7A
48013 BRISIGHELLA [RA]
TEL. 054651648
www.vignedeiboschi.it

CELLAR SALES
PRE-BOOKED VISITS
ANNUAL PRODUCTION 15,000 bottles
HECTARES UNDER VINE 6.50
VITICULTURE METHOD Certified Biodynamic

We were enlightened by Paolo Babini's experience of winegrowing in a new area such as the upper Lamone Valley, with its marly sandstone, where woodland and vineyard contend the soils. He brings with him great sensitivity and an outstanding ability to interpret the vintage. His flagship project is the Sangiovese Poggio Tura, from a vineyard produced by collecting grafts from century-old plants in the valley. The vines are mainly cultivated according to biodynamic principles. Poggio Tura 2011 is unusually tannin-heavy and fruit-rich. The palate is marked by a sharp acidity, leading into a finish full of surprises. Indeed, it closes with a sophisticated repertoire of citrus and delicate spice. The 2013 vintage of 16 Anime maintains a fine balance between linear acidity and expansive flowers and fruits.

Villa di Corlo

LOC. BAGGIOVARA
S.DA CAVEZZO, 200
41126 MODENA
TEL. 059510736
www.villadicorlo.com

CELLAR SALES
PRE-BOOKED VISITS
ANNUAL PRODUCTION 85,000 bottles
HECTARES UNDER VINE 26.50

Maria Antonietta Munari has built up this winery with passion and commitment, making the most of the family land and estate villa where one of Modena's most venerable vinegar cellars is located. Here, above Via Emilia, on soils beloved by grasparossa, the winery ferments its main product exclusively from estate-owned grapes. The quality of the wines is reliable, the Grasparossa style aims for a very appealing, fruity register, quite unlike the more characteristic expressions of the terroir. Primevo 2014 is lean and taut, with expressive fruitiness of wild strawberry, some hedgerow flowers, plus a dash of minerality. A wine of great simplicity. Corleto 2014 shows exuberant fruit and a rich, tempting mouth with crisp tannins. Its progression is enhanced by a plethora of residual sugars.

○ "16" Anime '13	♟♟ 3*
● Poggio Tura '11	♟♟ 4
○ Persefone '13	♟♟ 3
● Poggio Tura '10	♟♟♟ 4*
● Poggio Tura '05	♟♟♟ 5
○ "16" Anime '12	♟♟ 3
○ "16" Anime '11	♟♟ 3
○ "16" Anime '10	♟♟ 3
○ MonteRè '11	♟♟ 6
○ Monteré '06	♟♟ 6
● Poggio Tura '09	♟♟ 4
● Poggio Tura '08	♟♟ 4
● Poggio Tura '07	♟♟ 4
○ Sedici Anime '09	♟♟ 3

● Lambrusco di Sorbara Primevo '14	♟♟ 2*
● Lambrusco Grasparossa di Castelvetro Corleto '14	♟ 2
● Lambrusco Grasparossa di Castelvetro Secco '14	♟ 2
○ Fraeli Brut Blanc de Blancs '11	♟♟ 3
○ Fraeli Brut Blanc de Blancs '10	♟♟ 3
● Lambrusco di Sorbara Primevo '13	♟♟ 2*
● Lambrusco di Sorbara Primevo '12	♟♟ 2*
● Lambrusco Grasparossa di Castelvetro '12	♟♟ 2*
● Lambrusco Grasparossa di Castelvetro Amabile '13	♟♟ 2*
● Lambrusco Grasparossa di Castelvetro Corleto '13	♟♟ 2*

Villa Papiano

VIA IBOLA, 24
47015 MODIGLIANA [FC]
TEL. 0546941790
www.villapapiano.it

CELLAR SALES
PRE-BOOKED VISITS
ANNUAL PRODUCTION 50,000 bottles
HECTARES UNDER VINE 10.00

Modigliana is a hilltop terroir with marly sandstone soils which gives the wines their inimitable style. Sangiovese di Modiglianas are savoury and knife-edged, with austere yet light tannins, unbeatable in terms of ageability. Villa Papiano lies in the Ibola Valley, on the southern slopes of Mount Chioda at an elevation of 500 metres, in rather extreme environmental conditions. Francesco Bordini makes classic wine with a sense of place, achieving focused results with a pure mineral expression. I Probi 2012 is graceful and the high elevations of its vineyards freed it from the limitations of a hot growing year. On the nose it is austere and flowery, with a delicate fruitiness, while the palate is spirited and minerally, complex and linear. The tannins are in pure Modigliana style, with polished, muscular tannins, good for laying down. Le Papesse 2014 is a peppery, spicy, well-focused, savoury and knife-edged, with citrus at the back of the palate.

Villa Venti

LOC. VILLAVENTI DI RONCOFREDDO
VIA DOCCIA, 1442
47020 FORLÌ
TEL. 0541949532
www.villaventi.it

CELLAR SALES
PRE-BOOKED VISITS
ACCOMMODATION
ANNUAL PRODUCTION 27,500 bottles
HECTARES UNDER VINE 7.00
VITICULTURE METHOD Certified Organic

Mauro Giardini and Davide Castellucci's seven hectares under vine stand on a mosaic of soils including sands, red clays and sandy yellow clays. Understanding and prising out the diversity of the terroir takes meticulous precision, as well as the confidence that comes from spending long days among the vines. Organic farming, classic natural fermentations, and the ability to interpret the vintage are the tools of the trade for these two winemakers who have shown what territory truly means and what it means to be craftsmen, risks included. This winery's flagship was not in the tastings: the Sangiovese Primo Segno 2013 has been given more time to age in the bottle. Riserva 2012, produced in a hot difficult year, displays warm, almost balsamic, Mediterranean fragrances. On the palate it is tight-knit, but finds unexpected polish through its stunning acidity and well-balanced tannins.

● Romagna Sangiovese I Probi di Papiano Ris. '12	♟♟♟ 3*
● Romagna Sangiovese Sup. Le Papesse di Papiano '14	♟♟ 2*
○ Terra! '14	♟♟ 3
○ Tregenda Albana Passita Ris. '13	♟♟ 3
● Sangiovese di Romagna I Probi di Papiano Ris. '11	♀♀♀ 3*
● Sangiovese di Romagna I Probi di Papiano Ris. '10	♀♀♀ 3*
● Sangiovese di Romagna I Probi di Papiano Ris. '09	♀♀♀ 3*
○ Le Tresche di Papiano '12	♀♀ 3
● Sangiovese di Romagna Sup. Le Papesse di Papiano '11	♀♀ 2*
○ Tregenda Albana Passita '13	♀♀ 3
○ Tregenda Albana Passita '11	♀♀ 3
○ Tregenda Albana Passita Ris. '12	♀♀ 3*

● Romagna Sangiovese Longiano Ris. '12	♟♟ 4
● Sangiovese di Romagna Longiano Primo Segno '11	♀♀♀ 3*
● Sangiovese di Romagna Sup. Primo Segno '09	♀♀♀ 3*
● Sangiovese di Romagna Sup. Primo Segno '08	♀♀♀ 3*
○ Felis Leo '09	♀♀ 3
● Sangiovese di Romagna Longiano Ris '11	♀♀ 4
● Sangiovese di Romagna Sup. Maggese '10	♀♀ 3*
● Sangiovese di Romagna Sup. Primo Segno '12	♀♀ 3
○ Serenaro Famoso '12	♀♀ 3

EMILIA ROMAGNA

★Fattoria Zerbina

FRAZ. MARZENO
VIA VICCHIO, 11
48018 FAENZA [RA]
TEL. 054640022
www.zerbina.com

CELLAR SALES
PRE-BOOKED VISITS
ANNUAL PRODUCTION 220,000 bottles
HECTARES UNDER VINE 33.00

Cristina Geminiani has taken on a few new partners, and runs this long-standing Romagna winery with a passion and an ability to ferment her grapes with charming consistency and a very territorial register. The winery has 33 hectares under vine, all on the red clay which characterizes the Marzeno subzone. It is a precious heritage of mature vines, mostly bush-trained. The overall reliability of their wines is very impressive, and alongside their Sangiovese they are now also doing some excellent work with Albana, including dry versions. Scacco Matto 2012 is an extraordinarily complex wine, capable of maintaining tautness thanks to its gorgeous acidity. Complex, almost oily, brimming over with fruity notes of apricot, dried figs, lychees, passion fruit, enlivened by a savoury vein across the palate. Only a few bottles of the outstanding AR 2010 were produced, an extreme wine, complex and deep, smoky and citrussy.

Zucchi

VIA VIAZZA, 64
41030 SAN PROSPERO [MO]
TEL. 059908934
www.vinizucchi.it

CELLAR SALES
PRE-BOOKED VISITS
ANNUAL PRODUCTION 130,000 bottles
HECTARES UNDER VINE 10.00

Zucchi is a small artisanal winery that has been producing quality wines since 1950, all sold in the courtyard with trade and private customers coming and going, with the feel of a bygone era. Wine-bottling began with Bruno Zucchi before passing to his son Davide and wife, Maura. Today, the winery can count on the fresh energies of the youngest daughter, Silvia, who decided to dedicate herself full-time to the family business after she completed studies in oenology. This is the heart of the production zone of sorbara, the estate's speciality. Rito 2014 is a lean, subtle wine, thrusting and energetic, austere yet savoury. A stylish, minerally Sorbara, with the depth this wine is capable of displaying when stuffing and tannins are properly handled. Sorbara Secco 2014 is a classic, a peasant wine in the best and most poetic sense of the term. Marascone 2014, a monovarietal Salamino, has well-defined fruitiness and a creamy, well-paced mouth.

○ Albana di Romagna Passito AR '10	♀♀ 8
○ Romagna Albana Passito Scacco Matto '12	♀♀ 6
● Marzieno '09	♀♀ 4
○ Romagna Albana Passito Arrocco '11	♀♀ 5
○ Romagna Albana Secco Ceparano '14	♀♀ 2*
● Romagna Sangiovese Sup. Ceregio '14	♀♀ 2*
● Romagna Sangiovese Sup. Torre di Ceparano Ris. '11	♀♀ 3
○ Romagna Trebbiano Dalbiere '14	♀♀ 2*
● Sangiovese di Romagna Sup. Pietramora Ris. '11	♀♀♀ 5
○ Albana di Romagna Passito Scacco Matto '09	♀♀ 3*
● Sangiovese di Romagna Sup. Pietramora Ris. '09	♀♀ 6
● Sangiovese di Romagna Sup. Torre di Ceparano Ris. '10	♀♀ 3

● Lambrusco di Sorbara Rito '14	♀♀♀ 2*
● Lambrusco di Sorbara Secco '14	♀♀ 2*
● Modena Lambrusco Marascone '14	♀♀ 2*
● Lambrusco di Sorbara Secco '13	♀♀ 2*
● Lambrusco di Sorbara Secco Rito '13	♀♀ 2*

Agrintesa

VIA G. GALILEI, 15
48018 FAENZA [RA]
TEL. 059952511
www.agrintesa.it

ANNUAL PRODUCTION 350,000 bottles
HECTARES UNDER VINE 44.00

○ Albana di Romagna Secco	
I Calanchi Loveria '12	🍷🍷 2*
○ Albana di Romagna Secco	
I Calanchi Spighea '14	🍷🍷 2*

Ariola Vigne e Vini

LOC. CALICELLA DI PILASTRO
FRAZ. PILASTRO
S.DA DELLA BUCA, 5A
43010 LANGHIRANO [PR]
TEL. 0521637678
www.viniariola.it

CELLAR SALES
PRE-BOOKED VISITS
RESTAURANT SERVICE
ANNUAL PRODUCTION 800,000 bottles
HECTARES UNDER VINE 48.00

○ Forte Rigoni Malvasia Nature '14	🍷🍷 3
● Marcello Nature '14	🍷🍷 3

Barbolini

LOC. CASINALBO
VIA FIORI, 40
41043 FORMIGINE [MO]
TEL. 059550154
www.barbolinicantina.it

CELLAR SALES
PRE-BOOKED VISITS
ANNUAL PRODUCTION 350,000 bottles
HECTARES UNDER VINE 15.00
VITICULTURE METHOD Certified Organic

● Lambrusco Grasparossa di Castelvetro	
Nero di Nero '14	🍷🍷 2*
● Lambrusco Grasparossa di Castelvetro	
Trimalcione '14	🍷🍷 2*

La Berta

VIA BERTA, 13
48013 BRISIGHELLA [RA]
TEL. 054684998
www.poderelaberta.com

CELLAR SALES
PRE-BOOKED VISITS
ANNUAL PRODUCTION 55,000 bottles
HECTARES UNDER VINE 20.00

● Sangiovese di Romagna	
Olmatello Ris. '12	🍷🍷 4
● Sangiovese di Romagna Sup. Solano '13	🍷🍷 2*
● Sangiovese di Romagna '14	🍷 2

Raffaella Alessandra Bissoni

LOC. CASTICCIANO
VIA COLECCHIO, 280
47032 BERTINORO [FC]
TEL. 0543460382
www.vinibissoni.com

CELLAR SALES
PRE-BOOKED VISITS
ANNUAL PRODUCTION 25,000 bottles
HECTARES UNDER VINE 5.00
SUSTAINABLE WINERY

○ Albana di Romagna Passito '10	🍷🍷 5
● Sangiovese di Romagna Sup.	
Bertinoro Ris. '11	🍷 4

Ca' di Sopra

LOC. MARZENO
VIA FELIGARA, 15
48013 BRISIGHELLA [RA]
TEL. 0544521209
www.cadisopra.com

CELLAR SALES
PRE-BOOKED VISITS
ANNUAL PRODUCTION 24,000 bottles
HECTARES UNDER VINE 28.00
SUSTAINABLE WINERY

● Sangiovese di Romagna	
Marzeno Cadisopra Ris. '11	🍷🍷 4
● Remel '12	🍷 3

Calonga

LOC. CASTIGLIONE
VIA CASTEL LEONE, 8
47100 FORLÌ
TEL. 0543753044
www.calonga.it

CELLAR SALES
PRE-BOOKED VISITS
ANNUAL PRODUCTION 30,000 bottles
HECTARES UNDER VINE 8.00

● Ordelaffo '14	♥♥ 2*
● Sangiovese di Romagna Sup. Leggiolo '13	♥ 4

Campodelsole

VIA CELLAIMO, 850
47032 BERTINORO [FC]
TEL. 0543444562
www.campodelsole.it

CELLAR SALES
PRE-BOOKED VISITS
ANNUAL PRODUCTION 60,000 bottles
HECTARES UNDER VINE 75.00

● Sangiovese di Romagna Durano '14	♥♥ 2*
○ Albana di Romagna Selva '14	♥ 2

Tenuta Carbognano

VIA CARBOGNANO, 3
47855 GEMMANO [RN]
TEL. 0541984507
www.tenutacarbognano.it

CELLAR SALES
PRE-BOOKED VISITS
ACCOMMODATION
ANNUAL PRODUCTION 10,000 bottles
HECTARES UNDER VINE 3.00
VITICULTURE METHOD Certified Organic

● Ali '12	♥♥ 3
● Sangiovese di Romagna Sup. Amen Ris. '12	♥♥ 3

Cardinali

POD. MONTEPASCOLO
29014 CASTELL'ARQUATO [PC]
TEL. 0523803502
www.cardinalidoc.it

CELLAR SALES
PRE-BOOKED VISITS
ANNUAL PRODUCTION 30,000 bottles
HECTARES UNDER VINE 5.50

● C. P. Gutturnio Sup. '13	♥♥ 3

Carra di Casatico

LOC. CASATICO
S.DA LA NAVE, 10B
43013 LANGHIRANO [PR]
TEL. 0521863510
www.carradicasatico.com

CELLAR SALES
PRE-BOOKED VISITS
ANNUAL PRODUCTION 120,000 bottles
HECTARES UNDER VINE 25.00

○ Colli di Parma Malvasia Frizzante '14	♥♥ 2*
● Torcularia Lambrusco Emilia '14	♥♥ 2*

Casali Viticultori

FRAZ. PRATISSOLO
VIA DELLE SCUOLE, 7
42019 SCANDIANO [RE]
TEL. 0522855441
www.casalivini.it

CELLAR SALES
PRE-BOOKED VISITS
ANNUAL PRODUCTION 1,500,000 bottles
HECTARES UNDER VINE 48.00

● Reggiano Lambrusco Pra di Bosso '14	♥♥ 2*
● Lambruscone '14	♥ 2
⊙ Reggiano Lambrusco Rosato Secco '14	♥ 3

Casè

LOC. CASAL POZZINO
29020 TRAVO [PC]
TEL. 3472590551
www.naturallywine.com

CELLAR SALES
PRE-BOOKED VISITS
ANNUAL PRODUCTION 20,000 bottles
HECTARES UNDER VINE 4.00
VITICULTURE METHOD Certified Organic

○ Casè Bianco '14	🍷🍷	2*
● Casè Riva del Ciliegio '12	🍷🍷	3
● Casè Rosso '14	🍷🍷	2*

Castelli del Duca

LOC. MORETTA, 58
42124 BORGONOVO VAL TIDONE [PC]
TEL. 0522942135
www.medici.it

CELLAR SALES
PRE-BOOKED VISITS
ANNUAL PRODUCTION 400,000 bottles
HECTARES UNDER VINE 1200.00
VITICULTURE METHOD Certified Organic

● C. P. Barbera Ranuccio '13	🍷🍷	2*
● Gutturnio Alessandro Ris. '12	🍷🍷	2*
○ C. P. Malvasia Secco Isabella '14	🍷	2

Andrea Cervini

LOC. POGGIO SUPERIORE, 1
29020 TRAVO [PC]
TEL. 3357597119
andreacervini.ilpoggio@gmail.com

CELLAR SALES
PRE-BOOKED VISITS
ACCOMMODATION AND RESTAURANT SERVICE
ANNUAL PRODUCTION 20,000 bottles
HECTARES UNDER VINE 4.00
VITICULTURE METHOD Certified Organic

○ Vino del Poggio Bianco '11	🍷🍷	3
● Vino del Poggio Navel '10	🍷🍷	3

Tenuta Diavoletto

VIA TOMBETTA, 2541
47032 BERTINORO [FC]
TEL. 3344286558
www.tenutadiavoletto.com

CELLAR SALES
PRE-BOOKED VISITS
ANNUAL PRODUCTION 20,000 bottles
HECTARES UNDER VINE 10.00

○ Albana di Romagna Secco Cinquecento '14	🍷🍷	2*
● Satirello '12	🍷	3

Cantina Sociale Formigine Pedemontana

VIA RADICI IN PIANO, 228
41043 FORMIGINE [MO]
TEL. 059558122
www.lambruscodoc.it

CELLAR SALES
PRE-BOOKED VISITS
ANNUAL PRODUCTION 960,000 bottles
HECTARES UNDER VINE 580.00
VITICULTURE METHOD Certified Organic

● Lambrusco Grasparossa di Castelvetro Passione '14	🍷🍷	1*

Gavioli

VIA PROVINCIALE OVEST
41015 NONANTOLA [MO]
TEL. 059545462
www.gaviolivini.com

CELLAR SALES
PRE-BOOKED VISITS
ANNUAL PRODUCTION 250,000 bottles
HECTARES UNDER VINE 60.00

● Lambrusco Emilia M. Cl. Pas Dosé '11	🍷🍷	4
● Lambrusco Emilia M. Cl. 30 Mesi '11	🍷	4

La Grotta

LOC. SAIANO
VIA CIMADORI, 621
47023 CESENA [FC]
TEL. 0547326368
www.lagrottavini.it

CELLAR SALES
PRE-BOOKED VISITS
ANNUAL PRODUCTION 24,000 bottles
HECTARES UNDER VINE 12.00

○ Albana di Romagna Damadora '14   ♥♥ 2*
● Sangiovese di Romagna
   Conte Dursano Sup. Ris. '13   ♥♥ 3
● Sangiovese di Romagna Sup. Sallius '13 ♥♥ 2*

Guido Guarini Matteucci

FRAZ. SAN TOMÈ
VIA MINARDA, 2
47122 FORLÌ
TEL. 0543476147
www.viniguarini.it

CELLAR SALES
PRE-BOOKED VISITS
ANNUAL PRODUCTION 40,000 bottles
HECTARES UNDER VINE 15.00
SUSTAINABLE WINERY

● Sangiovese di Romagna Sup. Rubbio '13 ♥♥ 2*
● Sangiovese di Romagna Sup. Ebe '12   ♥ 2

Lamoretti

LOC. CASATICO
S.DA DELLA NAVE, 6
43013 LANGHIRANO [PR]
TEL. 0521863590
www.lamorettivini.com

CELLAR SALES
PRE-BOOKED VISITS
ANNUAL PRODUCTION 100,000 bottles
HECTARES UNDER VINE 25.00

○ Colli di Parma Malvasia Frizzante '14   ♥♥ 2*

Lusenti

LOC. CASA PICCIONI, 57
29010 ZIANO PIACENTINO [PC]
TEL. 0523868479
www.lusentivini.it

CELLAR SALES
PRE-BOOKED VISITS
ANNUAL PRODUCTION 100,000 bottles
HECTARES UNDER VINE 17.00
VITICULTURE METHOD Certified Organic

○ C. P. Malvasia Frizzante Emiliana '14   ♥♥ 2*
● Gutturnio Frizzante Tournesol '12   ♥♥ 2*

Alberto Lusignani

LOC. VIGOLENO
VIA CASE ORSI, 9
29010 VERNASCA [PC]
TEL. 0523895178
lusignani@agonet.it

CELLAR SALES
PRE-BOOKED VISITS
ANNUAL PRODUCTION 3,000 bottles
HECTARES UNDER VINE 10.00

○ C. P. Vin Santo di Vigoleno '05   ♥♥ 8
○ C. P. Ortrugo Frizzante '14   ♥♥ 2*

Lusvardi

LOC. MOLINO DI GAZZATA
VIA CANALE PER REGGIO, 2
42018 SAN MARTINO IN RIO [RE]
TEL. 0522646516
www.lusvardi.it

● Grato '13   ♥♥ 2
⊙ Lambrusco Emilia Brut Rosé '14   ♥♥ 2*
● Reggiano Lambrusco '14   ♥♥ 2*

La Mancina

FRAZ. MONTEBUDELLO
VIA MOTTA, 8
40050 MONTEVEGLIO [BO]
TEL. 051832691
www.lamancina.it

CELLAR SALES
PRE-BOOKED VISITS
ANNUAL PRODUCTION 110,000 bottles
HECTARES UNDER VINE 25.00

○ C. B. Pignoletto
   Terre di Montebudello '14   ♛♛ 2*
● C. B. Cabernet Sauvignon
   Comandante della Guardia '12   ♛ 4

Tenuta Mara

VIA CA' BACCHINO, 1665
47832 SAN CLEMENTE [RN]
TEL. 0541988870
www.tenutamara.com

CELLAR SALES
PRE-BOOKED VISITS
ANNUAL PRODUCTION 20,000 bottles
HECTARES UNDER VINE 6.50
VITICULTURE METHOD Certified
OrganicCertified Biodynamic

● Maramia Sangiovese '13   ♛♛ 7

Tenuta Masselina

LOC. SERRÀ
VIA POZZE, 1030
48014 CASTEL BOLOGNESE [RA]
TEL. 0545651004
www.masselina.it

CELLAR SALES
ANNUAL PRODUCTION 35,000 bottles
HECTARES UNDER VINE 16.00

○ Anfora Albana '13   ♛♛ 7
● Anfora Sangiovese '12   ♛♛ 7
● Sangiovese di Romagna Ris. '12   ♛ 4

Fattoria Paradiso

LOC. CAPOCOLLE
VIA PALMEGGIANA, 285
47032 BERTINORO [FC]
TEL. 0543445044
www.fattoriaparadiso.com

CELLAR SALES
PRE-BOOKED VISITS
ANNUAL PRODUCTION 500,000 bottles
HECTARES UNDER VINE 100.00

● Sangiovese di Romagna Sup.
   V. delle Lepri Ris. '12   ♛♛ 3
○ Albana di Romagna Secco '14   ♛ 2
● Sangiovese di Romagna Sup. '14   ♛ 2

Pezzuoli

VIA VIGNOLA, 136
41053 MARANELLO [MO]
TEL. 0536948800
www.pezzuoli.it

CELLAR SALES
PRE-BOOKED VISITS
ANNUAL PRODUCTION 400,000 bottles
HECTARES UNDER VINE 120.00

● Lambrusco di Sorbara Pietrarossa '14   ♛♛ 2*
● Lambrusco Grasparossa di Castelvetro
   Pietrascura '14   ♛♛ 2*
○ Pignoletto Pietragialla '14   ♛ 2

Quinto Passo

LOC. SOZZIGALLI DI SOLIERA
VIA CANALE, 267
410109 MODENA
TEL. 0593163311
www.quintopasso.it

CELLAR SALES
ANNUAL PRODUCTION 40,000 bottles
HECTARES UNDER VINE 12.00

⊙ Modena Rosé Brut M. Cl. '12   ♛♛ 4

Podere Riosto

VIA DI RIOSTO, 12
40065 PIANORO [BO]
TEL. 051777109
www.podereriosto.it

CELLAR SALES
PRE-BOOKED VISITS
ACCOMMODATION
ANNUAL PRODUCTION 80,000 bottles
HECTARES UNDER VINE 15.80
SUSTAINABLE WINERY

○ C. B. Pignoletto Frizzante '14	♥♥ 2*
● Vecchio Riosto Vite del Fantini '14	♥♥ 3
○ C. B. Pignoletto Sup. Fermo '14	♥ 2

Le Rocche Malatestiane

VIA EMILIA, 104
47900 RIMINI
TEL. 0541743079
www.lerocchemalatestiane.it

CELLAR SALES
PRE-BOOKED VISITS
ANNUAL PRODUCTION 800,000 bottles
HECTARES UNDER VINE 800.00

● Romagna Sangiovese Sup. I Diavoli '14	♥♥ 2*
● Romagna Sangiovese Sup. I Tre Miracoli '14	♥♥ 3

I Sabbioni

LOC. SABBIONI
VIA DEI SABBIONI, 22
47121 FORLÌ
TEL. 0543755711
www.isabbioni.it

CELLAR SALES
ANNUAL PRODUCTION 46,000 bottles
HECTARES UNDER VINE 7.00

● Romagna Sangiovese Sup. Rubrarosa Bonadea '14	♥♥ 2*
● Romagna Sangiovese Sup. Rubrarosa Elaide Ris. '13	♥♥ 4

Tenuta Saiano

VIA CASONE, 30
47825 TORRIANA [RN]
TEL. 3667862921
www.tenutasaiano.it

CELLAR SALES
PRE-BOOKED VISITS
ACCOMMODATION
ANNUAL PRODUCTION 10,000 bottles
HECTARES UNDER VINE 10.00
VITICULTURE METHOD Certified Organic

● Romagna Sangiovese Sup. Gianciotto '14	♥♥ 2*
● Saiano Rosso '14	♥♥ 2*

Vigne di San Lorenzo

VIA CAMPIUME, 6
48013 BRISIGHELLA [RA]
TEL. 3391137070
www.vignedisanlorenzo.it

CELLAR SALES
PRE-BOOKED VISITS
ACCOMMODATION AND RESTAURANT SERVICE
ANNUAL PRODUCTION 10,000 bottles
HECTARES UNDER VINE 3.00
VITICULTURE METHOD Certified Organic

● Campiume '11	♥♥ 4
● San Lorenzo '11	♥♥ 4

San Valentino

FRAZ. SAN MARTINO IN VENTI
VIA TOMASETTA, 13
47900 RIMINI
TEL. 0541752231
www.vinisanvalentino.com

CELLAR SALES
PRE-BOOKED VISITS
ACCOMMODATION
ANNUAL PRODUCTION 120,000 bottles
HECTARES UNDER VINE 20.00
VITICULTURE METHOD Certified Biodynamic

● Sangiovese di Romagna Sup. Scabi '13	♥♥ 2*
○ Vin Santo Contesse Muschietti '03	♥♥ 3

Tenuta Santa Lucia

VIA GIARDINO, 1400
47025 MERCATO SARACENO [FC]
TEL. 054790441
www.santaluciavinery.it

CELLAR SALES
PRE-BOOKED VISITS
ACCOMMODATION
ANNUAL PRODUCTION 90,000 bottles
HECTARES UNDER VINE 16.00
VITICULTURE METHOD Certified Organic
SUSTAINABLE WINERY

○ Albana di Romagna Secco Albarara '13	♥♥ 2*
● Centuplo Centesimino '13	♥♥
● Sangiovese di Romagna Sup. Taibo '13	♥ 2

Tenuta Santini

FRAZ. PASSANO
VIA CAMPO, 33
47853 CORIANO [RN]
TEL. 0541656527
www.tenutasantini.com

CELLAR SALES
PRE-BOOKED VISITS
ANNUAL PRODUCTION 40,000 bottles
HECTARES UNDER VINE 22.00

● Sangiovese di Romagna Sup. Cornelianum Ris. '12	♥♥ 4
● Sangiovese di Romagna Sup. Beato Enrico '14	♥ 2

Santodeno

VIA VILLA ROSSI, 50
47012 CIVITELLA DI ROMAGNA [FC]
TEL. 3356556747
fabio.ravaioli@santodeno.it

CELLAR SALES
PRE-BOOKED VISITS
ACCOMMODATION
ANNUAL PRODUCTION 400,000 bottles
HECTARES UNDER VINE 70.00

● Romagna Sangiovese Sup. '14	♥♥ 2*

Cantina Sociale Settecani

VIA MODENA, 184
41014 CASTELVETRO DI MODENA [MO]
TEL. 059702505
www.cantinasettecani.it

CELLAR SALES
ANNUAL PRODUCTION 1,000,000 bottles
HECTARES UNDER VINE 530.00

● Lambrusco Grasparossa di Castelvetro Amabile '14	♥♥ 1*
● Lambrusco Grasparossa di Castelvetro Secco '14	♥♥ 1*

TerraQuilia

VIA CALDANA
41052 GUIGLIA [MO]
TEL. 059931023
www.terraquilia.it

CELLAR SALES
PRE-BOOKED VISITS
ANNUAL PRODUCTION 40,000 bottles
HECTARES UNDER VINE 6.00
VITICULTURE METHOD Certified Organic

● Falconero Zero '14	♥♥ 2*
○ Terrebianche '14	♥♥ 2*

Trerè

LOC. MONTICORALLI
VIA CASALE, 19
48018 FAENZA [RA]
TEL. 054647034
www.trere.com

CELLAR SALES
PRE-BOOKED VISITS
ACCOMMODATION AND RESTAURANT SERVICE
ANNUAL PRODUCTION 150,000 bottles
HECTARES UNDER VINE 30.00

● Colli di Faenza Rosso Montecorallo Ris. '12	♥♥ 3
● Sangiovese di Romagna Amarcord d'un Ross Ris. '12	♥♥ 3

Valla

VIA MONTECUCCO, 229c
29010 ZIANO PIACENTINO [PC]
TEL. 0523868115
www.vinivalla.it

PRE-BOOKED VISITS
ANNUAL PRODUCTION 10,000 bottles
HECTARES UNDER VINE 4.70

● C. P. Gutturnio Frizzante '13		♥♥ 2*
● C. P. Gutturnio Sup. Merum '13		♥♥ 2*
○ C. P. Ortrugo Frizzante '14		♥♥ 2*

Vallona

LOC. FAGNANO
40050 CASTELLO DI SERRAVALLE [BO]
TEL. 0516703333
www.fattorievallona.it

CELLAR SALES
PRE-BOOKED VISITS
ANNUAL PRODUCTION 100,000 bottles
HECTARES UNDER VINE 31.00

○ C. B. Pignoletto Cl. Amestesso '10		♥♥ 4
○ C. B. Bologna Bianco '14		♥ 2

Marta Valpiani

LOC. CASTROCARO TERME
VIA BAGNOLO, 156/158
47011 FORLÌ
TEL. 0543769598
www.vinimartavalpiani.it

CELLAR SALES
PRE-BOOKED VISITS
ANNUAL PRODUCTION 20,000 bottles
HECTARES UNDER VINE 8.00

● Castrum Castrocari Et. Bianca '11		♥♥ 2*
● Marta Valpiani '12		♥♥ 2*
● Castrum Castrocari Et. Viola '11		♥ 3

Podere Vecciano

VIA VECCIANO, 23
47852 CORIANO [RN]
TEL. 0541658388
www.poderevecciano.it

CELLAR SALES
PRE-BOOKED VISITS
ANNUAL PRODUCTION 100,000 bottles
HECTARES UNDER VINE 15.00
VITICULTURE METHOD Certified Organic
SUSTAINABLE WINERY

● C. di Rimini Sangiovese Montetauro '14		♥♥ 2*
● Sangiovese di Romagna Sup. D'Enio Ris. '11		♥♥ 4
● Vignalavolta '12		♥♥ 2*

Consorzio Vini Tipici di San Marino

LOC. BORGO MAGGIORE
STRADA SERRABOLINO, 89
47893 SAN MARINO
TEL. 0549903124
www.consorziovini.sm

CELLAR SALES
ANNUAL PRODUCTION 900,000 bottles
HECTARES UNDER VINE 120.00

● Brugneto di San Marino Ris. '12		♥♥ 2*
○ Roncale di San Marino '14		♥ 2
● Sangiovese di San Marino '14		♥ 2

Tenuta La Viola

VIA COLOMBARONE, 888
47032 BERTINORO [FC]
TEL. 0543445496
www.tenutalaviola.it

CELLAR SALES
PRE-BOOKED VISITS
ANNUAL PRODUCTION 42,500 bottles
HECTARES UNDER VINE 7.00
VITICULTURE METHOD Certified Organic

● Sangiovese di Romagna Sup. Oddone '14		♥♥ 2*
● Particella 25 '12		♥ 5
● Sangiovese di Romagna Sup. Il Colombarone '13		♥ 3

TUSCANY

With this year's 79 Tre Bicchieri awards, Tuscany is the Guide's top scorer and this is certainly the merit of the region as a whole, able to rely on stunning territories and an army of top-notch winegrowers who construct a production mosaic of large – sometimes huge – operations but also of small-scale businesses. Confirming that quality is not a direct reflection of the scale of production. We should also consider the wonder of the 2010 vintage in Montalcino, ensuring a significant number of wines the Tre Bicchieri podium. There are 18 winners this year, from the most solidly built of the warmer areas to the light-bodied products of the north; from the most traditional to the most modern. But all delicious. Chianti Classico continues to hold its own and its 2013 vintage wines, initially off the radar, are now coming into their own and will bring great satisfaction. We await the Riserva and the Gran Selezione with bated breath. This year 19 DOCs won awards, from vintages ranging from the aforementioned 2013, to 2010, and there were also 6 IGTs whose standard would make them worthy of a DOC label. A special mention also for the Nobile di Montepulciano area, out of the doldrums after several static seasons, seeming to have come to a better understanding of the interaction between sangiovese and the clay soils typical of the zone. Thank goodness. The coast arrived with many confirmations and only a few new names, but all very interesting. The three newbie award winners, Podere San Cristoforo, Bruni and Guado al Melo – also voted Up-and-Coming Winery of 2016 – are all from the seaside. They speak of a zone that is on the move, seeking to interpret its wine in contemporary terms, flanking body usually guaranteed by soil and climate, with vibrancy and elegance. Finally, heartfelt thanks to the consortiums and many private outfits that were by our side for this long process of organizing and collecting wine samples. Tuscany is a region with an immense scale of production, with many local businesses – some consortiums, others not – but all, starting with the producers themselves (all of them, even the most renowned) invariably sending us their wine for rating, supporting our work to create the kind of synergy that elevates the Made-in-Italy wine industry.

Abbadia Ardenga

FRAZ. TORRENIERI
VIA ROMANA, 139
53028 MONTALCINO [SI]
TEL. 0577834150
www.abbadiardengapoggio.it

CELLAR SALES
PRE-BOOKED VISITS
ANNUAL PRODUCTION 40,000 bottles
HECTARES UNDER VINE 10.00

Abbadia Ardenga's history is closely linked to the fortunes of the Castello della Torre Nera, owned by the Società di Esecutori di Pie Disposizioni di Siena. Having served as a Benedictine monastery, hostelry and coaching inn on Via Francigena in the Middle Ages, today it has been transformed into a cellar and museum. Here, at the north-eastern tip of Torrenieri di Montalcino, the ten or so hectares of vineyards are mainly planted with sangiovese grapes. The Brunello could hardly be anything but traditional in style, with about three weeks' maceration and ageing in Slavonian oak for about 36 months. Once again the best signals come from the Vigna Piaggia cru from which we expected a little more grace and energy, bearing in mind a favourable 2010. This interpretation is warm and buttery, with austere, close-knit tannins slightly holding back the tangy flavour development. The 2010 Brunello is even more closed.

● Brunello di Montalcino V. Piaggia '10	♥♥	5
● Brunello di Montalcino '10	♥	5
● Rosso di Montalcino '13	♥	3
● Brunello di Montalcino '08	♀♀	5
● Brunello di Montalcino '07	♀♀	5
● Brunello di Montalcino '06	♀♀	5
● Brunello di Montalcino V. Piaggia '09	♀♀	5
● Brunello di Montalcino V. Piaggia '08	♀♀	5
● Brunello di Montalcino V. Piaggia '07	♀♀	5
● Rosso di Montalcino '10	♀♀	3

Acquabona

LOC. ACQUABONA
57037 PORTOFERRAIO [LI]
TEL. 0565933013
www.acquabonaelba.it

CELLAR SALES
PRE-BOOKED VISITS
ANNUAL PRODUCTION 90,000 bottles
HECTARES UNDER VINE 18.00

The name reflects the importance of water on an island. A spring still on the estate was well-known for the quality of the water and a farm was built around it in the early 18th century. The modern farm dates back to the late 1950s, organized as was usual then for different crops including fodder and cereals, and livestock, now abandoned in favour of vineyards. The current owners, three agronomist friends, joined forces in the 1980s to relaunch the estate and with success now offer a range of products showing a recognizable stylistic identity and very reliable quality. The 2014 Vermentino is interesting and very vibrant on the nose with floral hints, apricot and pineapple fruit, and a mouthfilling, weighty, close-knit and flavoursome palate. The Benvenuto 2013, a monovarietal Merlot, presents lovely spicy aromas with a soft, silky body, and enjoyable, lingering flavour.

● Benvenuto '13	♥♥	2*
● Elba Rosso Ris. '11	♥♥	4
○ Elba Vermentino '14	♥♥	3
● Voltraio '11	♥♥	4
○ Elba Ansonica '14	♥	3
○ Elba Bianco '14	♥	2
⊙ Elba Rosato '14	♥	2
● Elba Rosso '13	♥	2
● Benvenuto '11	♀♀	2*
● Benvenuto '09	♀♀	3
○ Elba Ansonica '13	♀♀	3
○ Elba Bianco '13	♀♀	2*
● Elba Rosso '09	♀♀	2*
● Elba Rosso Ris. '07	♀♀	4
● Voltraio '10	♀♀	4
● Voltraio '09	♀♀	4

Altesino

LOC. ALTESINO, 54
53028 MONTALCINO [SI]
TEL. 0577806208
www.altesino.it

CELLAR SALES
PRE-BOOKED VISITS
ANNUAL PRODUCTION 230,000 bottles
HECTARES UNDER VINE 41.00

The Altesino brand was created in the
Seventies by the Consonno family and
taken over by Elisabetta Gnudi Angelini in
2002. Today 25 of its 40 hectares under
vine are registered as Brunello. The main
winegrowing locations are at Montosoli in
the northern district; the estate near
Castello di Velona on the south-eastern
slope; and one at Pianezzine, in the south,
not far from Sesta. Simone Giunti
supervises the rows while Guido Orzalesi is
the technical manager. Other varieties
grown alongside sangiovese include merlot,
cabernet, chardonnay, vermentino, viognier,
trebbiano, and malvasia. The Brunellos are
the leaders of the pack as usual, often
described as traditional due to their long
ageing in 50-hectolitre Slavonian oak. In
the glass things are slightly different: both
the standard label and the Montosoli cru
from 2010 reveal powerful, rich texture
which will probably smooth out over time.

Fattoria Ambra

VIA LOMBARDA, 85
59015 PRATO
TEL. 3358282552
www.fattoriaambra.it

CELLAR SALES
PRE-BOOKED VISITS
ANNUAL PRODUCTION 80,000 bottles
HECTARES UNDER VINE 20.00

The estate managed by Beppe Rigoli and
owned by his family since the mid-1950s
maintains a steady pace. The range
produced has always been rooted in criteria
that shun fashionable trends and respect
the production philosophy of the owner,
who was the first to introduce the idea of
crus in the Carmignano area, bottling wines
according to their terroir of origin. So by
tasting all the products it is possible to
grasp the different typical features of this
zone, the potential of each vineyard being
fully exploited. The Riserva Elzana 2011 is
fresh and lively on the nose with hints of
cherries and pipe tobacco, lovely juicy fruit
and smooth, slightly mature tannin. The
Montefortini 2012 has dark fruit aromas,
like damson, and a generous, rich, tangy
palate with plenty of texture. The Riserva
Montalbiolo 2011 has a fruity, vegetal nose
with a creamy palate and very slightly
rushed finish.

● Brunello di Montalcino '10	🍷🍷 6
● Brunello di Montalcino Montosoli '10	🍷🍷 8
● Rosso di Montalcino '13	🍷 3
● Brunello di Montalcino '00	🍷🍷 6

● Carmignano Elzana Ris. '11	🍷🍷 5
● Carmignano Montalbiolo Ris. '11	🍷🍷 5
● Carmignano Montefortini '12	🍷🍷 3
● Barco Reale '14	🍷 2
● Carmignano V. S. Cristina in Pilli '12	🍷 3
⊙ Rosato di Carmignano Vin Ruspo '14	🍷 2
○ Trebbiano '14	🍷 2
● Barco Reale '13	🍷🍷 2*
● Carmignano Le Vigne Alte di Montalbiolo Ris. '09	🍷🍷 4
● Carmignano S. Cristina in Pilli '11	🍷🍷 3
● Carmignano V. di Montefortini '11	🍷🍷 3
○ Trebbiano '13	🍷🍷 2*
○ Vin Santo di Carmignano '07	🍷🍷 5
○ Vin Santo di Carmignano '06	🍷🍷 5

Stefano Amerighi

FRAZ. FARNETA
VIA DI POGGIOBELLO
52044 CORTONA [AR]
TEL. 0575649241
www.stefanoamerighi.it

CELLAR SALES
PRE-BOOKED VISITS
ANNUAL PRODUCTION 25,000 bottles
HECTARES UNDER VINE 8.50
VITICULTURE METHOD Certified Biodynamic

Stefano Amerighi began working as a winegrower with a clear idea in his head and a project that he managed to bring to fruition: to produce a fine quality wine in harmony with his chosen environment. Great care was taken at the start: selection of the most suitable land, syrah as the only grape variety which would express its greatest potential, and then the decision to use biodynamic methods from the start. Thanks to a team of colleagues in tune with the guidelines, his idea became reality and now the goal is to extend the system to other crops, in a fully eco-sustainable project. The Syrah Apice 2011 has a generous array of aromas with recognizable hints of damp earth and leather, light, spicy pepper and cloves, and lively, ripe cherry fruit. The palate opens with taut, vibrant body, nicely blended tannins and a very agreeable tanginess in the finish. The Syrah 2012 is fruitier with lighter flavour.

● Cortona Syrah Apice '11	♥♥ 6
● Cortona Syrah '12	♥♥ 5
● Cortona Syrah '11	♥♥♥ 5
● Cortona Syrah '10	♥♥♥ 5
● Cortona Syrah '09	♥♥♥ 5
● Cortona Syrah '08	♥♥ 5
● Cortona Syrah '07	♥♥ 5
● Cortona Syrah Apice '10	♥♥ 6
● Cortona Syrah Apice '09	♥♥ 5

Ampeleia

FRAZ. ROCCATEDERIGHI
LOC. MELETA
58028 ROCCASTRADA [GR]
TEL. 0564567155
www.ampeleia.it

CELLAR SALES
PRE-BOOKED VISITS
ANNUAL PRODUCTION 135,000 bottles
HECTARES UNDER VINE 35.00
VITICULTURE METHOD Certified Organic
SUSTAINABLE WINERY

In the early 2000s, a clear vision of the future of wine, or at least their own wines, enabled three friends to start up a winegrowing project that unquestionably differed from the classic style. Elisabetta Foradori, Giacomo Pondini and, at the beginning of the adventure, Thomas Widmann, set themselves specific objectives: to use non-native grape varieties that adapted well to their chosen terroir, to enrich their wine with prestigious nuances that made it unique, and to apply natural methods in the vineyards and the cellar. Thus, in 2009, the conversion to biodynamic processes began which will gradually involve the three different vineyard plots divided. A place in the finals for Ampeleia 2012, mainly cabernet franc with sangiovese and other complementary grapes: clean, assertive, fruity aromas with hints of ink and a striking rounded palate on a taut, vibrant body, for a lingering succulent finish. The Kepos 2013 blend of various grapes is also good, with an enthralling nose and close-knit body.

● Ampeleia '12	♥♥ 5
● Kepos '13	♥♥ 4
● Alicante '14	♥ 5
● Cabernet Franc '14	♥ 5
● Unlitro '14	♥ 3
● Kepos '06	♥♥♥ 3*
● Ampeleia '11	♥♥ 5
● Ampeleia '10	♥♥ 5
● Ampeleia '09	♥♥ 5
● Ampeleia '08	♥♥ 5
● Empatia '07	♥♥ 4
● Kepos '12	♥♥ 4
● Kepos '11	♥♥ 3*
● Kepos '10	♥♥ 3*
● Kepos '09	♥♥ 3
● Unlitro '12	♥♥ 2*

★★Marchesi Antinori

p.zza degli Antinori, 3
50123 Firenze
Tel. 0552937501
www.antinori.it

PRE-BOOKED VISITS
ACCOMMODATION AND RESTAURANT SERVICE
ANNUAL PRODUCTION 2,000,000 bottles
HECTARES UNDER VINE 2350.00

Over 2,000 hectares of property scattered over the best growing areas in the peninsula make Antinori the winegrowing family with the most land under vine anywhere in Europe. And it is apparently still developing, given the Florentine brand's recent purchase of Castello di San Sano in Gaiole in Chianti, with 80 hectares of vineyards. It is here in Chianti Classico that Antinori wines reach their most significant peaks of excellence. These technically flawless wines in a modern style have shaped the oenological history of this region, and beyond. A good 2012 version of Tignanello, the classic Supertuscan made from sangiovese, cabernet sauvignon and cabernet franc: multifaceted, clean aromas and a mouthwatering palate. Chianti Classico Villa Antinori Riserva 2012 has lovely texture, dark fruit aromas and a deep palate. Solaia 2012 is nicely made, generous and well-defined. Chianti Classico Péppoli 2013 is very enjoyable.

● Chianti Cl. Villa Antinori Ris. '12	▼▼ 4
● Nobile di Montepulciano Santa Pia Ris. La Braccesca '11	▼▼ 5
● Tignanello '12	▼▼ 8
● Chianti Cl. Marchese Antinori Ris. '12	▼▼ 5
● Chianti Cl. Pèppoli '13	▼▼ 3
● Cortona Syrah Achelo La Braccesca '12	▼▼ 5
● Solaia '12	▼▼ 8
● Nobile di Montepulciano La Braccesca '12	▼ 4
● Rosso di Montepulciano Sabazio La Braccesca '13	▼ 2
● Santa Cristina '14	▼ 2
● Vie Cave Fattoria Aldobrandesca '12	▼ 4
● Villa Antinori Rosso '12	▼ 4
● Solaia '07	▽▽▽ 8

Tenuta di Arceno - Arcanum

loc. Arceno
fraz. San Gusmé
53010 Castelnuovo Berardenga [SI]
Tel. 0577359346
www.tenutadiarceno.com

CELLAR SALES
PRE-BOOKED VISITS
ANNUAL PRODUCTION 250,000 bottles
HECTARES UNDER VINE 92.00

Since 1994 Tenuta di Arceno has belonged to Jess Jackson and Barbara Banke, owners of the American winegrowing colossus Kendall-Jackson. The style of the wines produced in this Castelnuovo Berardenga winery is evidently influenced by the best Californian methods: ripe fruit in the forefront and considerable support from the oak used for ageing. The overall impact of the wines therefore tends to be powerful and intense, softened by the pedoclimatic features of their area of origin, the southernmost strip of Chianti Classico. Vibrant, concentrated aromas for the Chianti Classico Riserva 2012, and a firm, flavoursome palate. The Chianti Classico 2013 is more approachable but equally delicious with toasty aromas and a soft, lip-smacking flavour. The fruit is slightly penalized by oak in the Chianti Classico Strada al Sasso Riserva 2011, but the texture is good and the palate mouthfilling.

● Chianti Cl. Ris. '12	▼▼ 5
● Chianti Cl. '13	▼▼ 3
● Arcanum '10	▼ 8
● Chianti Cl. Strada al Sasso Ris. '11	▼ 5
● Il Fauno '10	▼ 4
● Arcanum '08	▽▽ 8
● Arcanum I '07	▽▽ 8
● Arcanum I '03	▽▽ 7
● Chianti Cl. '12	▽▽ 3
● Chianti Cl. '11	▽▽ 3
● Chianti Cl. '09	▽▽ 3
● Chianti Cl. Ris. '08	▽▽ 5
● Chianti Cl. Ris. '04	▽▽ 5
● Chianti Cl. Strada al Sasso Ris. '10	▽▽ 5
● Fauno '07	▽▽ 5
● Il Fauno '08	▽▽ 4
● Valadorna '08	▽▽ 7

Tenuta Argentiera

LOC. PIANALI
FRAZ. DONORATICO
VIA AURELIA, 412A
57022 CASTAGNETO CARDUCCI [LI]
TEL. 0565773176
www.argentiera.eu

CELLAR SALES
PRE-BOOKED VISITS
ANNUAL PRODUCTION 450,000 bottles
HECTARES UNDER VINE 75.00

Tenuta Argentiera stands out among the other Bolgheri wineries as the benchmark for the DOC zone. This is a real gem, with over 70 hectares of vineyards in some of the area's best plots. The owners are Corrado and Marcello Fratini. The vineyards are planted on clayey, stony soil, ideal for classic Bolgheri grape varieties: cabernet sauvignon and franc, merlot syrah. The wines are among the best-made in the DOC zone, with a modern style. The excellent Giorgio Bartholomaus 2012 is mature and fruity with confident hints of the oak used for ageing. The palate is succulent, firm, nicely edgy with a long, clenched finish. The Bolgheri Superiore 2012 is good but falls slightly short of our expectations. The well-typed Poggio ai Ginerpi 2012 has cocoa powder and smoky aromas, and a succulent, taut palate with a pleasing tannic finish.

★Avignonesi

FRAZ. VALIANO DI MONTEPULCIANO
VIA COLONICA, 1
53040 MONTEPULCIANO [SI]
TEL. 0578724304
www.avignonesi.it

CELLAR SALES
PRE-BOOKED VISITS
ANNUAL PRODUCTION 700,000 bottles
HECTARES UNDER VINE 200.00

The name derives from the family who established the estate now owned by Virginie Saverys, a Belgian businesswoman who decided to move to Tuscany in 2007 after a successful legal career. In 2009 she bought the estate and began work according to a specific programme. Her aims were very clear: to produce wholesome wines while respecting the environment. So it was a natural step to convert the estate to organic methods, despite the difficulties involved. The 200 hectares of vineyards are divided over eight plots in Montepulciano and two in Cortona, and the results obtained have made it worth the wait. Another Tre Bicchieri, several years on, for the Nobile 2012 thanks to a complex array of aromas including medicinal herbs, tobacco and spice, and a racy, well-paced palate with lip-smacking, pervasive acidity and a flavoursome finish. The Rosso 2013 is surprisingly fresh on the nose and lively on the palate, while the two versions of Vin Santo are very impressive again.

● Bolgheri Rosso Poggio ai Ginepri '13	♀♀	3
● Bolgheri Sup. '12	♀♀	8
● Giorgio Bartholomaus '12	♀♀	8
⊙ Bolgheri Rosato Poggio ai Ginepri '14	♀	2
● Bolgheri Rosso Villa Donoratico '12	♀	5
● Bolgheri Sup. '11	♀♀♀	8
● Bolgheri Sup. Argentiera '10	♀♀♀	7
● Bolgheri Sup. Argentiera '09	♀♀	7
● Giorgio Bartholomaus '11	♀♀	8
● Lavinia Maria '11	♀♀	8
⊙ Poggio ai Ginepri '12	♀♀	3

● Nobile di Montepulciano '12	♀♀♀	4*
● Rosso di Montepulciano '13	♀♀	2*
○ Vin Santo di Montepulciano '00	♀♀	8
● Vin Santo Occhio di Pernice '00	♀♀	8
● 50 & 50 '10	♀	8
○ Il Marzocco '14	♀	3
● Merlot Desiderio '12	♀	6
● Nobile di Montepulciano Grandi Annate '11	♀	7
● 50 & 50 Avignonesi e Capannelle '99	♀♀♀	8
○ Vin Santo '98	♀♀♀	8
○ Vin Santo '96	♀♀♀	8
○ Vin Santo '95	♀♀♀	8
○ Vin Santo '93	♀♀♀	8
● Vin Santo Occhio di Pernice '97	♀♀♀	8
● Vin Santo Occhio di Pernice '93	♀♀♀	8
○ Vin Santo Occhio di Pernice '90	♀♀♀	8

Badia a Coltibuono

LOC. BADIA A COLTIBUONO
53013 GAIOLE IN CHIANTI [SI]
TEL. 0577746110
www.coltibuono.com

CELLAR SALES
PRE-BOOKED VISITS
ACCOMMODATION AND RESTAURANT SERVICE
ANNUAL PRODUCTION 240,000 bottles
HECTARES UNDER VINE 62.00
VITICULTURE METHOD Certified Organic
SUSTAINABLE WINERY

Organic vineyards; good growing land in Gaiole and Monti in Chianti, two of Chianti Classico's top subzones; stable, well-established and consistent quality: these are some of the strongpoints of the Stucchi Prinetti family estate, now a benchmark in the DOC. We said some of the strongpoints, because the most significant is probably the style of Badia a Coltibuono wines, which expresses finesse and absolute personality in harmony with the DOC's most authentic character. The Chianti Classico 2013 displays sunny aromas and a tangy, well-organized palate, making it much more drinkable than others of this type. The Chianti Classico RS 2013 is just as good: subtle, clean aromas but the ace up its sleeve is a supple, well-paced flavour. Warmer aromas and a slightly more ruffled palate for the Chianti Classico Cultus Boni 2011; the same applies to the Chianti Classico Riserva 2011 and Sangioveto 2011.

Badia di Morrona

VIA DEL CHIANTI, 6
56030 TERRICCIOLA [PI]
TEL. 0587658505
www.badiadimorrona.it

CELLAR SALES
PRE-BOOKED VISITS
ACCOMMODATION AND RESTAURANT SERVICE
ANNUAL PRODUCTION 350,000 bottles
HECTARES UNDER VINE 110.00

An extraordinary place of outstanding historical importance, Badia di Morrona dates back to around the year 1000, as a Benedictine monastery. In the late 1930s Italo and Mario Gaslini purchased the property in the municipal area of Terricciola between Pisa and Volterra. Of the overall 600 hectares, over 100 are under vine. The wines seem to be growing confidently and hold a secure position among the best in the zone. Mostly syrah in the very good Taneto 2012: vibrant aromas and firm tannic backbone. The Felciaio 2014 is citrussy and racy, not bad at all. The Vin Santo del Chianti 2009 is on top form with classic oxidized aromas. The N'Antia 2102 has lovely ripe fruit and a vibrant nose but the tannin is slightly held back.

● Chianti Cl. '13	♈♈♈ 3*
● Chianti Cl. RS '13	♈♈ 2*
● Chianti Cl. Cultus Boni '11	♈ 4
● Chianti Cl. Ris. '11	♈ 5
● Sangioveto '11	♈ 6
● Chianti Cl. '12	♈♈♈ 3*
● Chianti Cl. '06	♈♈♈ 3*
● Chianti Cl. Cultus Boni '09	♈♈♈ 4*
● Chianti Cl. Ris. '09	♈♈♈ 5
● Chianti Cl. Ris. '07	♈♈♈ 5
● Chianti Cl. Ris. '04	♈♈♈ 5
● Sangioveto '95	♈♈♈ 6

○ Felciaio '14	♈♈ 2*
● Taneto '12	♈♈ 3
○ Vin Santo del Chianti '09	♈♈ 4
● Chianti I Sodi del Paretaio '14	♈ 2
○ La Suvera '13	♈ 3
● N'Antia '12	♈ 5
● N'Antia '10	♈♈ 5
● N'Antia '09	♈♈ 4
● Taneto '11	♈♈ 3*
● VignAalta '10	♈♈ 5
● VignAalta '09	♈♈ 5

Fattoria di Bagnolo

VIA IMPRUNETANA PER TAVARNUZZE, 36
50023 IMPRUNETA [FI]
TEL. 0552313403
www.bartolinibaldelli.it

CELLAR SALES
PRE-BOOKED VISITS
ANNUAL PRODUCTION 25,000 bottles
HECTARES UNDER VINE 10.00

The Bartolini Baldelli family have three farming headquarters: Montozzi castle at Pergine Valdarno, in the province of Arezzo; Fattoria Scaletta at San Miniato, in the province of Pisa; and the Bagnolo farm at Impruneta, which is the best suited to winegrowing. The farm's origins date back to the 11th century and since the heyday of the Medici court it has enjoyed a series of acknowledgements up to the present day. Current owner, Marco Bartolini Baldelli is still committed to wine and olive production and, more recently, to the agritourism business. The Chianti Colli Fiorentini Riserva 2012 made it to the finals with a vibrant bouquet of wild berries, hints of spice and aromatic herbs. The structure is coherent and nicely organized with a tangy, lingering finish. The good Chianti Colli Fiorentini 2013 has excellent flavour and a lean body. The powerful Capro Rosso 2012 is a sangiovese and colorino blend.

● Chianti Colli Fiorentini Ris. '12	♥♥ 4
● Capro Rosso '12	♥♥ 5
● Chianti Colli Fiorentini '13	♥♥ 2*
● Capro Rosso '11	♀♀ 5
● Capro Rosso '10	♀♀ 5
● Capro Rosso '09	♀♀ 5
● Capro Rosso '08	♀♀ 5
● Capro Rosso '07	♀♀ 4
● Chianti Colli Fiorentini '08	♀♀ 2
● Chianti Colli Fiorentini Ris. '11	♀♀ 4
● Chianti Colli Fiorentini Ris. '10	♀♀ 4
● Chianti Colli Fiorentini Ris. '08	♀♀ 3
○ Vin Santo del Chianti Ris. '04	♀♀ 5

I Balzini

LOC. PASTINE, 19
50021 BARBERINO VAL D'ELSA [FI]
TEL. 0558075503
www.ibalzini.it

PRE-BOOKED VISITS
ANNUAL PRODUCTION 70,000 bottles
HECTARES UNDER VINE 12.00

It all began in 1980 when accountant Vincenzo d'Isanto found some land suitable for planting vines and began working as a winegrower. His choice of land fell outside the classic Tuscan districts, and this made it possible to experiment with varieties that were new at the time. In the years that followed, his wife Antonella became so involved that she left her job as a work consultant to supervise the vineyards and cellar personally, as she still does today alongside their daughter Deiana. Over the years the project has developed in a positive direction, as we can see from the gradual increase in the number of wines. The Black Label 2014, from cabernet sauvignon and merlot, present good aromas of spice, vanilla and cloves on a base of wild berries. The palate opens generous, well-rounded and nicely textured with a lingered, flavoursome finish. The White Label 2012 is an appetizing, pleasant blend of sangiovese and cabernet sauvignon.

● I Balzini Black Label '12	♥♥ 6
● I Balzini White Label '12	♥♥ 5
● I Balzini Green Label '14	♥ 3
⊙ I Balzini Pink Label '14	♥ 2
● I Balzini Red Label '14	♥ 3
● I Balzini Black Label '11	♀♀ 6
● I Balzini Black Label '10	♀♀ 6
● I Balzini Black Label '09	♀♀ 6
● I Balzini Black Label '08	♀♀ 5
● I Balzini Black Label '07	♀♀ 5
● I Balzini Green Label '12	♀♀ 2*
● I Balzini Green Label '11	♀♀ 2*
● I Balzini Red Label '11	♀♀ 3
● I Balzini White Label '11	♀♀ 5
● I Balzini White Label '08	♀♀ 5
● I Balzini White Label '07	♀♀ 5

Bandini - Villa Pomona

LOC. POMONA, 39

53011 CASTELLINA IN CHIANTI [SI]
TEL. 0577740473
www.fattoriapomona.it

CELLAR SALES
PRE-BOOKED VISITS
ACCOMMODATION
ANNUAL PRODUCTION 16,000 bottles
HECTARES UNDER VINE 4.70
VITICULTURE METHOD Certified Organic

This estate in Castellina in Chianti might be considered a good example of Italian artisan winemaking that has indelibly influenced traditional production. The strongpoints of Villa Pomona wines are their classic style, starting with ageing in large wood, which leaves no room for convenient shortcuts in the cellar and relies, above all, on the work done in the organic vineyards. The result is wines that are always original and extremely enjoyable, able to express marked character and one of the strongest links to the terroir in the whole of Chianti. The Chianti Classico 2013 is undoubtedly one of the best-typed in the DOC. Very fresh aromas with a distinctive hint of clear-cut, vibrant cherry fruit; racy, well-organized and delicious on the palate. The Chianti Classico Riserva 2012 is equally interesting with clearly defined aromas heralding the lip-smacking, crisp flavour.

Baracchi

LOC. CEGLIOLO, 21
52044 CORTONA [AR]
TEL. 0575612679
www.baracchiwinery.com

CELLAR SALES
PRE-BOOKED VISITS
ACCOMMODATION AND RESTAURANT SERVICE
ANNUAL PRODUCTION 140,000 bottles
HECTARES UNDER VINE 30.00
SUSTAINABLE WINERY

Riccardo Baracchi continues the family wine-producing business established in 1860. Brilliant and proactive, he transformed a country property into a charming resort surrounded by the vineyards. Today he is helped by his son Benedetto in a clearly defined project: the practice of modern winegrowing, with a careful eye to the local area, favouring a grape like syrah, which has found its ideal habitat here, without neglecting other traditional varieties, processed in a different way, like sparkling wines made on the estate from grapes like trebbiano and sangiovese. The aromas expressed in the Syrah Riserva 2012 focus on cherry and plum fruit, softened by spicy hints of pepper and pleasant vegetal nuances of medicinal herbs. The palate opens softly with nicely measured tannins and a relaxed, deliciously drinkable finish.

● Chianti Cl. '13	♟♟♟ 3*
● Chianti Cl. Ris. '12	♟♟ 4
● Chianti Cl. '12	♟♟♟ 3*
● Chianti Cl. '11	♟♟ 3
● Chianti Cl. '09	♟♟ 3
● Chianti Cl. Ris. '11	♟♟ 4
● Chianti Cl. Ris. '10	♟♟ 4
● Chianti Cl. Ris. '09	♟♟ 4
● Chianti Cl. Ris. '08	♟♟ 4

● Cortona Syrah Ris. '12	♟♟ 6
● Ardito '12	♟♟ 6
● Cortona Merlot Smeriglio '13	♟♟ 4
● Cortona Sangiovese Smeriglio '13	♟♟ 4
● Cortona Syrah Smeriglio '13	♟♟ 4
● O'Lillo '14	♟♟ 2*
● Pinot Nero '12	♟♟ 6
○ Astore '14	♟ 3
⊙ Brut Sangiovese Rosé M. Cl. '13	♟ 5
○ Brut Trebbiano M. Cl. '12	♟ 5
● Ardito '11	♟♟ 6
● Ardito '10	♟♟ 6
○ Astore '13	♟♟ 3
● Cortona Sangiovese Smeriglio '11	♟♟ 4
● Cortona Syrah Smeriglio '12	♟♟ 4
● Pinot Nero '11	♟♟ 6

Fattoria dei Barbi

LOC. PODERNOVI, 170
53024 MONTALCINO [SI]
TEL. 0577841111
www.fattoriadeibarbi.it

CELLAR SALES
PRE-BOOKED VISITS
ACCOMMODATION AND RESTAURANT SERVICE
ANNUAL PRODUCTION 600,000 bottles
HECTARES UNDER VINE 66.00

Without the legendary Barbi bottles with their shield emblem, Montalcino would be missing a crucial piece of history. This is a popular brand in the best sense of the word, proudly embodying the centuries-long tradition, repeatedly defended and relaunched by Stefano Cinelli Colombini. The cellar and museum is situated at the famously well-suited growing zone of Podernovi along with most of the 100-odd hectares planted with sangiovese. The estate makes three Brunellos: as well as the standard version, the best vintage years produce the Vigna del Fiore cru and the Riserva, the fruit of long maceration and patient ageing in large wood. And the auspicious 2010 season shaped a very nicely matched pair. The Brunello shows the pace of a great classic, with herbs and tobacco on the nose, while the Vigna del Fiore displays riper fruit on the nose and weightier extract, if curbed in this phase by stiff tannins.

Baricci

LOC. COLOMBAIO DI MONTOSOLI, 13
53024 MONTALCINO [SI]
TEL. 0577848109
www.baricci.it

CELLAR SALES
PRE-BOOKED VISITS
ANNUAL PRODUCTION 30,000 bottles
HECTARES UNDER VINE 5.00

Nello Baricci, universally remembered as the pioneer of small independent Brunello growers, has definitively passed the baton to the second and third generations working at the Colombaio farm. His whole family, comprising children Graziano and Graziella, son-in-law Piero Buffi, and grandsons Federico and Francesco, are involved in the farm work which revolves around their five hectares of vineyards in the eastern part of the Montosoli hill, a real grand cru of northern Montalcino. The six adjoining plots are harvested separately and undergo classic vinification in steel, long maceration and ageing in 20- and 40-hectolitre Slavonian oak. 2010 is a vintage year to remember chez Baricci. For the first time in 60 years a Brunello Riserva will be released but the classic version is already a lively champion in the making, with tangy texture. Damp earth, roots, spices: surgical consistency with the terroir alongside surprisingly authentic flavour.

● Brunello di Montalcino '10	▼▼ 5
● Brunello di Montalcino V. del Fiore '10	▼▼ 7
● Morellino di Scansano '13	▼ 3
● Rosso di Montalcino '13	▼ 3
● Brunello di Montalcino '09	♈♈ 5
● Brunello di Montalcino '08	♈♈ 5
● Brunello di Montalcino '07	♈♈ 5
● Brunello di Montalcino '06	♈♈ 5
● Brunello di Montalcino '04	♈♈ 5
● Brunello di Montalcino Ris. '08	♈♈ 7
● Brunello di Montalcino Ris. '07	♈♈ 7
● Brunello di Montalcino Ris. '04	♈♈ 7
● Brunello di Montalcino V. del Fiore '08	♈♈ 7
● Brunello di Montalcino V. del Fiore '07	♈♈ 7
● Brunello di Montalcino V. del Fiore '06	♈♈ 7
● Rosso di Montalcino '12	♈♈ 3

● Brunello di Montalcino '10	▼▼▼ 6
● Rosso di Montalcino '13	▼▼ 4
● Brunello di Montalcino '09	♈♈♈ 5
● Brunello di Montalcino '07	♈♈♈ 5
● Brunello di Montalcino '08	♈♈ 5
● Brunello di Montalcino '00	♈♈ 5
● Rosso di Montalcino '11	♈♈ 3*
● Rosso di Montalcino '10	♈♈ 3
● Rosso di Montalcino '03	♈♈ 3

★★Barone Ricasoli

LOC. CASTELLO DI BROLIO
53013 GAIOLE IN CHIANTI [SI]
TEL. 05777301
www.ricasoli.it

CELLAR SALES
PRE-BOOKED VISITS
ACCOMMODATION
ANNUAL PRODUCTION 2,000,000 bottles
HECTARES UNDER VINE 235.00
SUSTAINABLE WINERY

The Barone Ricasoli is historic in the truest sense, and an unwavering presence in Chianti Classico. The wines are among the best known in Italy and beyond, and have been successful thanks to their modern style, which in the recent past has been less focused on rich fruit and generous use of oak. The entire range has been polished and stands out today for its elegance and finesse. This is one of the most extensive Chianti estates in the DOC zone, and has selected its own sangiovese clone, named Brolio. The Chianti Classico Rocca Guicciarda Riserva 2012 is well-focused with clearly defined aromas and a succulent, satisfying flavour. The basic qualities of the Chianti Classico 2013 are approachability and drinkable flavour plus very fruity aromas, while the Chianti Classico Castello di Brolio Gran Selezione 2012 is a generous wine with firm, close-knit structure and a slightly rough finish, though it will probably reveal its usual class with time.

● Chianti Cl. Rocca Guicciarda Ris. '12	♟♟♟	5
● Bolgheri '13	♟♟	6
● Bolgheri Sup. Astuto '12	♟♟	8
● Brunello dei Montalcino Torre della Trappola '10	♟♟	8
● Chianti Cl. '13	♟♟	3
● Chianti Cl. Castello di Brolio Gran Sel. '12	♟♟	8
○ Vin Santo del Chianti Cl. Castello di Brolio '07	♟	6
● Casalferro '08	♟♟♟	8
● Casalferro '05	♟♟♟	8
● Chianti Cl. Castello di Brolio '07	♟♟♟	8
● Chianti Cl. Castello di Brolio '06	♟♟♟	8
● Chianti Cl. Castello di Brolio '04	♟♟♟	7
● Chianti Cl. Colledilà '10	♟♟♟	7
● Chianti Cl. Colledilà Gran Sel. '11	♟♟♟	8

Fattoria di Basciano

V.LE DUCA DELLA VITTORIA, 159
50068 RUFINA [FI]
TEL. 0558397034
www.renzomasibasciano.it

CELLAR SALES
PRE-BOOKED VISITS
ANNUAL PRODUCTION 200,000 bottles
HECTARES UNDER VINE 35.00

The ancient heart of the farm is the 13th-century tower and little hamlet that is now an agritourism structure. The Masi family still run the whole estate, established by Renzo in 1925. In charge of the winegrowing and production sector today is Renzo's son Paolo Masi, the owner, while his wife Anna Rita looks after international sales. The estate's products are divided into two lines: Fattoria di Basciano, made from grapes grown on the estate, and the Renzo Masi brand, for which the family are négociants for wines made from purchased grapes. An excellent overall performance from the wines presented: they may not seem fully true to terroir but they offer a consistently interesting impression. The very pleasing Chianti Rufina 2013 is spicy and fruity on the nose with smooth tannins and a nicely tangy finish, while the 2012 Riserva shows more generous and mouthfilling flavour.

● Chianti Rufina '13	♟♟	2*
● Chianti Rufina Ris. '12	♟♟	3
● Erta e China '13	♟♟	2*
● I Pini '13	♟♟	4
○ Vin Santo Chianti Rufina '08	♟♟	3
● Chianti Ris. '12	♟	2
● Chianti Rufina Ris. '11	♀♀	3
● Chianti Rufina Ris. '10	♀♀	3
● Erta e China '12	♀♀	2*
● Erta e China '10	♀♀	2*
● I Pini '12	♀♀	4
● I Pini '11	♀♀	4
● Il Corto '10	♀♀	3
○ Vin Santo Chianti Rufina Ris. '07	♀♀	3
○ Vin Santo Chianti Rufina Ris. '06	♀♀	3
○ Vin Santo Rufina '06	♀♀	3

Basile

POD. MONTE MARIO
58044 CINIGIANO [GR]
TEL. 0564993227
www.basilessa.it

CELLAR SALES
PRE-BOOKED VISITS
ANNUAL PRODUCTION 50,000 bottles
HECTARES UNDER VINE 8.00
VITICULTURE METHOD Certified Organic
SUSTAINABLE WINERY

Giovan Battista Basile knew what he
wanted when he moved from Campania to
Tuscany: to make wine in full respect of the
local area. From the start, he decided to
farm the vineyards according to organic
principles, an easy choice in this area
because the land had been uncultivated
for decades, and was suited to modern
vineyard planting criteria. With constant
work and steady growth, he made his
estate a success, above all through his
belief in the Montecucco area, for which
he became an ambassador, and is now
the deputy chairman of the Consortium.
The Montecucco Sangiovese Ad Agio
Riserva 2011 made it to the finals with an
array of fresh aromas, hints of mint and
minerals alternating with fruit. The palate is
succulent and nicely complex with
fine-grained tannins and a tangy finish. The
Comandante 2012, mainly sangiovese with
some merlot, is enjoyable with a subtle,
alluring nose, harmonious structure and
lingering finish.

● Montecucco Sangiovese Ad Agio Ris. '11	♥♥ 5
● Maremma Comandante '12	♥♥ 3
● Montecucco Sangiovese Cartacanta '12	♥♥ 3
○ Artéteca '14	♥ 2
● Montecucco Ad Agio Ris. '08	♀♀ 3
● Montecucco Cartacanta '11	♀♀ 3
● Montecucco Cartacanta '08	♀♀ 2*
● Montecucco Sangiovese Ad Agio Ris. '09	♀♀ 3

Podere Le Berne

LOC. CERVOGNANO
VIA POGGIO GOLO, 7
53040 MONTEPULCIANO [SI]
TEL. 0578767328
www.leberne.it

CELLAR SALES
ANNUAL PRODUCTION 25,000 bottles
HECTARES UNDER VINE 6.00

The Natalini family estate marches
confidently on with owner Andrea also
covering the post of chairman of the
Consorzio di Montepulciano. The production
zone is Cervognano, with arable land and
olive groves on the estate as well as
vineyards. Its name is a word dating back
to the Etruscan period: "verna" or "verena"
meant a hill giving shelter during winter,
with the best position for sunlight. Naturally
it follows that this is the best place to grow
vines. Interesting work has been done to
maintain the native grape varieties, now
almost abandoned but typical of the area,
including the pulcinculo used for Vin Santo.
The 2012 Nobile displays generous
minerally and fruity hints with an edgy, firm
and beautifully powerful palate, well-judged
tannin and a satisfying, lingering flavour.
The 2011 Riserva shows more austere,
oxidized aromas with hints of leather and
coffee. The palate is broad, well-blended,
even and very lingering.

● Nobile di Montepulciano '12	♥♥ 3*
● Nobile di Montepulciano Ris. '11	♥♥ 5
○ Vin Santo di Montepulciano Ada '07	♥♥ 5
● Rosso di Montepulciano '14	♥ 2
● Nobile di Montepulciano '11	♀♀♀ 3*
● Nobile di Montepulciano '06	♀♀♀ 3
● L'Affronto '11	♀♀ 2*
● Nobile di Montepulciano '09	♀♀ 3
● Nobile di Montepulciano '07	♀♀ 3
● Nobile di Montepulciano Ris. '10	♀♀ 5
● Nobile di Montepulciano Ris. '09	♀♀ 5
● Nobile di Montepulciano Ris. '08	♀♀ 5
● Nobile di Montepulciano Ris. '07	♀♀ 5
● Nobile di Montepulciano Ris. '01	♀♀ 5
● Rosso di Montepulciano '11	♀♀ 2*
○ Vin Santo di Montepulciano Ada '06	♀♀ 5

Tenuta di Bibbiano

VIA BIBBIANO, 76
53011 CASTELLINA IN CHIANTI [SI]
TEL. 0577743065
www.tenutadibibbiano.com

CELLAR SALES
PRE-BOOKED VISITS
ACCOMMODATION
ANNUAL PRODUCTION 100,000 bottles
HECTARES UNDER VINE 25.00
VITICULTURE METHOD Certified Organic
SUSTAINABLE WINERY

With vineyards in the southern part of the Castellina in Chianti subzone, bordering with the municipal area of Poggibonsi, Tenuta di Bibbiano has been owned by the Marrocchesi Marzi family since 1865, and has bottled its Chianti Classico since 1970. The style of the wines keeps an eye on the character of sangiovese, without chasing after passing trends. The wine is aged in large oak and the final result is a range of traditional, characterful wines, sometimes a little austere, not always immediately accessible. Good vibrations from the glass of Chianti Classico 2013, with distinctive lush fruity aromas and a tangy flavour with plenty of pace. Forward toasty aromas in the Chianti Classico Montornello Riserva 2012 but the strong point is its racy flavour. The Chianti Classico Vigna del Capannino Gran Selezione 2011 is, once again, a little too marked by the oak ageing vessels. The Vin Santo del Chianti Classico 2010 is austere.

Bindella

FRAZ. ACQUAVIVA
VIA DELLE TRE BERTE, 10A
53045 MONTEPULCIANO [SI]
TEL. 0578767777
www.bindella.it

CELLAR SALES
PRE-BOOKED VISITS
ANNUAL PRODUCTION 160,000 bottles
HECTARES UNDER VINE 36.50

30 years ago the Bindella family decided to invest their energy, money and commitment in the Montepulciano area. They chose Vallocaia for its beautifully positioned vineyards and the lovely natural setting. The owners, originally from Switzerland, worked there in production for many years, and then in the catering industry, running restaurants, which were the driving force to promote their Italian products. They then returned to Italy and the general appreciation voiced by customers persuaded them to continue and intensify their efforts, generating excellent results. The Nobile 2012 displays well-defined spicy aromas over clear cherry fruit, while the palate is soft, nicely powerful and generous with a deliciously moreish finish. We also liked the Nobile I Quadri 2012: a fresh, fruity nose and full-bodied, fleshy palate.

● Chianti Cl. '13	♥♥♥ 3*
● Chianti Cl. Montornello Ris. '12	♥♥ 4
● Chianti Cl. V. del Capannino Gran Sel. '11	♥ 5
○ Vin Santo del Chianti Cl. San Lorenzo a Bibbiano '10	♥ 5
● Chianti Cl. '11	♥♥ 3*
● Chianti Cl. '10	♥♥ 3
● Chianti Cl. Montornello '11	♥♥ 3
● Chianti Cl. Montornello '10	♥♥ 3
● Chianti Cl. Montornello '09	♥♥ 3
● Chianti Cl. Montornello '08	♥♥ 3
● Chianti Cl. V. del Capannino Gran Sel. '10	♥♥ 5
● Chianti Cl. V. del Capannino Ris. '10	♥♥ 5

● Nobile di Montepulciano I Quadri '12	♥♥♥ 5
● Nobile di Montepulciano '12	♥♥ 4
○ Vin Santo di Montepulciano Dolce Sinfonia '11	♥♥ 5
● Nobile di Montepulciano I Quadri '09	♥♥ 5
● Nobile di Montepulciano I Quadri '08	♥♥ 4
● Nobile di Montepulciano I Quadri '07	♥♥ 4
● Nobile di Montepulciano I Quadri '06	♥♥ 4
● Nobile di Montepulciano I Quadri '05	♥♥ 4
● Nobile di Montepulciano I Quadri '04	♥♥ 4
● Nobile di Montepulciano I Quadri '03	♥♥ 4
● Nobile di Montepulciano Ris. '06	♥♥ 4
● Vallocaia '04	♥♥ 5
○ Vin Santo Dolce Sinfonia '06	♥♥ 5

TUSCANY

★Biondi Santi
Tenuta Il Greppo

LOC. VILLA GREPPO, 183
53024 MONTALCINO [SI]
TEL. 0577848087
www.biondisanti.it

CELLAR SALES
PRE-BOOKED VISITS
ACCOMMODATION
ANNUAL PRODUCTION 80,000 bottles
HECTARES UNDER VINE 25.00

There is surely no need to underline the role played by the Biondi Santi brand on the chessboard of worldwide production. It is and always has been the Montalcino flagship winery, the one that has best expressed the ageing and emotional potential of Brunello, which was literally invented at the Greppo estate in the late 1800s. Jacopo stands at the helm today, determined to pursue the work begun by his father Franco. Above all, he respects the stylistic concept based on patience, with lengthy ageing in large wood and biting acidity. User instructions which serve up to a point with the Brunello 2010: this is a very young wine, probably destined to develop in the bottles for many years, but its champion status is already fully evident. The airy, deep aromas are traced by beautiful nuances of flowers and eau de Cologne, while the palate is even more enthralling, thanks to a delightful contrast of fruity sweetness and citrus edge, flavour and silky tannin.

● Brunello di Montalcino '10	♥♥♥ 8
● Brunello di Montalcino '09	♥♥♥ 8
● Brunello di Montalcino '06	♥♥♥ 7
● Brunello di Montalcino '04	♥♥♥ 8
● Brunello di Montalcino '03	♥♥♥ 8
● Brunello di Montalcino '01	♥♥♥ 8
● Brunello di Montalcino Ris. '07	♥♥♥ 8
● Brunello di Montalcino Ris. '06	♥♥♥ 8
● Brunello di Montalcino Ris. '04	♥♥♥ 8
● Brunello di Montalcino Ris. '01	♥♥♥ 8
● Brunello di Montalcino '08	♥♥ 8
● Brunello di Montalcino '07	♥♥ 8
● Brunello di Montalcino '05	♥♥ 8
● Brunello di Montalcino Ris. '08	♥♥ 8

Tenuta di Biserno

LOC. PALAZZO GARDINI
P.ZZA GRAMSCI, 9
57020 BIBBONA [LI]
TEL. 0586671099
www.biserno.it

ANNUAL PRODUCTION 160,000 bottles
HECTARES UNDER VINE 99.00

Biserno represents a gamble taken by brothers Lodovico and Piero Antinori, along with Umberto Mannori, when they decided to focus on Bibbona as a terroir for producing great wines. The landscape is breathtaking, with the Tirreno sea nearby, and beautifully trained vineyards surrounded by Mediterranean vegetation. The wines are modern in style and made from the typical varieties for this area, aged in French oak barriques. Of the wines presented the 2011 Biserno impressed us the most. A Bordeaux blend of mainly merlot and cabernet sauvignon with a vibrant, mature, concentrated nose alternating aromas of black berries, vegetal hints and vibrant spice. The palate is clenched and compact with plenty of tannins and a broad, well-coordinated finish. The Insoglio 2013, a little clenched and dark, still needs to find more balanced expression.

● Biserno '11	♥♥ 8
● Insoglio del Cinghiale Campo del Sasso '13	♥ 4
● Biserno '10	♥♥♥ 8
● Biserno '08	♥♥♥ 6
● Il Pino di Biserno '09	♥♥♥ 6
● Biserno '09	♥♥ 3
● Il Pino di Biserno '11	♥♥ 6
● Il Pino di Biserno '10	♥♥ 6
● Il Pino di Biserno '08	♥♥ 6
● Insoglio del Cinghiale '09	♥♥ 4*
● Insoglio del Cinghiale Campo del Sasso '11	♥♥ 4

Borgo Salcetino

LOC. LUCARELLI
53017 RADDA IN CHIANTI [SI]
TEL. 0577733541
www.livon.it

PRE-BOOKED VISITS
ANNUAL PRODUCTION 95,000 bottles
HECTARES UNDER VINE 15.00

The famous wine-producing Livon family of Friuli, with strong links to white wine, has branched out and purchased two red wine estates, Col Santo in Umbria and Borgo Salcetino in Tuscany. The latter, situated at Radda in Chianti, was bought in the mid-1990s and is yielding very impressive results. The estate's style is strongly loyal to the traditional principles of Chianti Classico, starting with ageing in large oak. The wines show elegant style and dynamic flavour, standing out increasingly often among the best in the DOC zone. No beating about the bush: the Chianti Classico 2013 is a delightful wine. Clean, airy aromas, gutsy and nuanced flavour on the fluent, assertive palate. The Chianti Classico Lucarello Riserva 2012 reveals a slightly hesitant nose but the palate is lovely, fresh and well-coordinated. The Rossole 2013, mainly sangiovese, is uncomplicated.

● Chianti Cl. '13	▼▼▼ 3*
● Chianti Cl. Lucarello Ris. '12	▼▼ 4
● Rossole '13	▼ 3
● Chianti Cl. '11	▽▽▽ 3*
● Rossole '12	▽▽▽ 3*
● Chianti Cl. '09	▽▽ 3
● Chianti Cl. '01	▽▽ 3
● Chianti Cl. Lucarello Ris. '06	▽▽ 4
● Chianti Cl. Lucarello Ris. '99	▽▽ 4
● Rossole '00	▽▽ 3

Borgo Scopeto

LOC. VAGLIAGLI
53010 CASTELNUOVO BERARDENGA [SI]
TEL. 0577322729
www.borgoscopeto.com

CELLAR SALES
PRE-BOOKED VISITS
ACCOMMODATION
ANNUAL PRODUCTION 350,000 bottles
HECTARES UNDER VINE 70.00

Elisabetta Gnudi is not only the owner of Caparzo at Montalcino: her little winegrowing empire includes 60 hectares of vineyards at Magliano in Toscana, forming the Doga delle Clavule estate, and these 40 hectares producing Chianti Classico wines of impressive quality. A shrewd blend of traditional and modern styles, the wines are aged in small and large oak, and often their expression of the terroir and pleasing flavour place Borgo Scopeto wines among the most interesting in the DOC zone, particularly in the recent past. The Chianti Classico Vigna Misciano Riserva 2011 is fragrant, succulent and well-paced with nicely integrated oak. The delicious Morellino di Scansano 2014 Doga delle Clavule is fresh and flavoursome while the Chianti Classico 2013 is approachable. The lovely sweet Borgonero 2011 is made from sangiovese, syrah and cabernet sauvignon. The Vermentino 2014 Doga delle Clavule is a tangy little wine.

● Chianti Cl. V. Misciano Ris. '11	▼▼ 4
● Morellino di Scansano Doga delle Clavule '14	▼▼ 3
● Borgonero '11	▼ 5
● Chianti Cl. '13	▼ 3
○ Vermentino Doga delle Clavule '14	▼ 2
○ Vin Santo del Chianti Cl. '06	▼ 5
● Chianti Cl. '03	▽▽ 3
● Chianti Cl. Misciano Ris. '06	▽▽ 4
○ Vermentino Doga delle Clavule '07	▽▽ 2*

Il Borro

FRAZ. SAN GIUSTINO VALDARNO
LOC. IL BORRO, 1
52020 LORO CIUFFENNA [AR]
TEL. 055977053
www.ilborro.it

CELLAR SALES
PRE-BOOKED VISITS
ACCOMMODATION AND RESTAURANT SERVICE
ANNUAL PRODUCTION 160,000 bottles
HECTARES UNDER VINE 45.00

The Ferragamo family estate is rich in ancient history, dating back to the year 1000. Named for the Borri family who bought it in the 16th century, Borro Borri's grandson Alessandro brought the estate to the size we see today. Successive families owned the property over the centuries, until Ferruccio Ferragamo bought it in 1993 and restored it to its former splendour. The first vintage produced was 1999, since the early years were spent identifying the most suitable areas for the varieties selected. In later years the new cellar was equipped and the vineyards became productive; today, the focus is on converting the land to biodynamic farming methods. The Borro 2102 is a blend of mainly merlot and cabernet sauvignon with a little syrah and petit verdot. The nose is subtle and complex with hints of wild berries, spice and medicinal herbs. The palate is smooth, nicely powerful with a fresh and very lingering finish.

● Il Borro '12	♥♥ 7
● Vin Santo del Chianti	
Occhio di Pernice '09	♥♥ 7
● Polissena '11	♥♥ 5
● Pian di Nova '12	♥ 3
● Il Borro '09	♀♀ 4
● Il Borro '08	♀♀ 6
● Il Borro '07	♀♀ 6
● Il Borro '06	♀♀ 6
● Il Borro '05	♀♀ 6
● Pian di Nova '09	♀♀ 3
● Pian di Nova '06	♀♀ 3*
● Polissena '07	♀♀ 5*
● Polissena '06	♀♀ 5
● Polissena '05	♀♀ 5

★Poderi Boscarelli

FRAZ. CERVOGNANO
VIA DI MONTENERO, 28
53045 MONTEPULCIANO [SI]
TEL. 0578767277
www.poderiboscarelli.com

CELLAR SALES
PRE-BOOKED VISITS
ANNUAL PRODUCTION 100,000 bottles
HECTARES UNDER VINE 14.00

Roots count and have to be respected: this explains estate founder Egisto Corradi's love for this area. Having left to pursue a career in Genoa and Milan, he decided to return to his childhood home to purchase the land where he would build a haven. The choice fell on two partly-abandoned estates which until then had been farmed using the classic crop rotation method. Egisto's daughter Paola, and her husband Ippolito De Ferrari, began the winegrowing activity, planting the first vineyards. Today the work is continued by Paola's sons: Luca, who is in charge of sales, and Nicolò, more involved with supervising the vineyards and cellar. The Nocio 2011 reveals complex, seductive aromas of aromatic herbs, like mint and bay, complex fruit ranging from damsons to blackberries, and subtle spices like nutmeg. The broad, silky palate makes a good, compelling impact, with a long and deliciously lingering finish.

● Nobile di Montepulciano Il Nocio '11	♥♥♥ 8
● Nobile di Montepulciano	
Et. Nera Ris. '10	♥♥ 6
● De Ferrari '14	♥♥ 3
● Nobile di Montepulciano '12	♥♥ 5
● Nobile di Montepulciano	
Et. Bianca Ris. '11	♥♥ 6
● Rosso di Montepulciano Prugnolo '14	♥ 3
○ Vin Santo di Montepulciano Familiae '03	♥ 7
● Nobile di Montepulciano	
Nocio dei Boscarelli '10	♀♀♀ 8
● Nobile di Montepulciano	
Nocio dei Boscarelli '09	♀♀♀ 8
● Nobile di Montepulciano	
Nocio dei Boscarelli '08	♀♀♀ 8
● Nobile di Montepulciano	
Nocio dei Boscarelli '07	♀♀♀ 8
● Nobile di Montepulciano Ris. '06	♀♀♀ 5

★Brancaia

LOC. POPPI, 42
53017 RADDA IN CHIANTI [SI]
TEL. 0577742007
www.brancaia.com

CELLAR SALES
PRE-BOOKED VISITS
ACCOMMODATION
ANNUAL PRODUCTION 700,000 bottles
HECTARES UNDER VINE 80.00
SUSTAINABLE WINERY

With vineyards in the subzone of Radda in Chianti, Brancaia has proved able to build up a solid reputation over time thanks to products of consistently high quality, well above average, with well-defined and coherent stylistic features. The wines have a modern touch, enhanced by the extensive use of barriques, articulated with balance and elegance, not to mention dynamic energy and freshness. A judicious combination which places the Chianti wines from the estate owned by the Widmer family among the benchmark products in the DOC zone. The polished, delightful Chianti Classico 2013 has slightly balsamic aromas enriched with beautifully fragrant hints of currants. The palate displays tangy, acidic freshness blending with crisp, lively tannins. The very moreish Chianti Classico Riserva 2012 is ruffled by slightly excessive vegetal hints. The Tre 2013, from sangiovese, cabernet and merlot, is well made and the Il Bianco 2014, sauvignon, gewürztraminer, sémillon e viognier, is really delicious.

● Chianti Cl. Brancaia '13	♟♟♟	4*
● Chianti Cl. Brancaia Ris. '12	♟♟	5
○ Brancaia Il Bianco '14	♟	2
● Brancaia Tre '13	♟	3
● Brancaia Il Blu '08	♟♟♟	8
● Brancaia Il Blu '07	♟♟♟	7
● Brancaia Il Blu '06	♟♟♟	6
● Brancaia Il Blu '05	♟♟♟	6
● Brancaia Il Blu '04	♟♟♟	6
● Brancaia Il Blu '03	♟♟♟	6
● Chianti Cl. Ris. '11	♟♟♟	5
● Chianti Cl. Ris. '10	♟♟♟	4*
● Chianti Cl. Ris. '09	♟♟♟	7

Brancatelli

LOC. RIOTORTO
CASA ROSSA, 2
57020 PIOMBINO [LI]
TEL. 056520655
www.brancatelli.eu

CELLAR SALES
PRE-BOOKED VISITS
ACCOMMODATION AND RESTAURANT SERVICE
ANNUAL PRODUCTION 75,000 bottles
HECTARES UNDER VINE 15.00
VITICULTURE METHOD Certified Organic

It is often hard to resist the call of the homeland. This is what happened to Giuseppe Brancatelli, originally from Messina, who decided to leave his country and seek his fortune in Holland. Business prospered, the job worked out well, but his childhood memories returned and his family vineyard was more than a sweet memory: the desire to go back to working the land as a farmer began to overwhelm him. So he started looking for an estate in Italy where he could fulfil his dream, and he found it in Val di Cornia. The Splendente 2014 is a very interesting monovarietal ansonica with fruity and vegetal sensations: pleasant pear and apricot fruit in the background on a weighty, succulent body with a lovely finish. The enthralling Giuseppe Brancatelli 2012, made from syrah, has spicy hints of pepper and leather on the nose with a powerful structure leading to a relaxed, pleasing finish.

○ Ansonica Splendente '14	♟♟	3
● Cabernet Sauvignon Segreto '11	♟♟	7
● Giuseppe Brancatelli '12	♟♟	4
● Valle del Sogno '12	♟♟	4
● Valle delle Stelle '13	♟♟	3
● Questo Dedicato A '13	♟	2

Brunelli - Le Chiuse di Sotto

LOC. PODERNOVONE, 154
53024 MONTALCINO [SI]
TEL. 0577849337
www.giannibrunelli.it

CELLAR SALES
PRE-BOOKED VISITS
ACCOMMODATION AND RESTAURANT SERVICE
ANNUAL PRODUCTION 30,000 bottles
HECTARES UNDER VINE 6.50

Two profoundly different terroirs determine the production of this estate created by Gianni Brunelli and run by his wife Maria Laura after his death. Le Chiuse di Sotto is the name of the location on the north-eastern slope of Montalcino, not far from I Canalicchi, home to the time-honoured vineyards planted by Dino Brunelli in the post-Second World War period. Podernovone, in the south-east strip, is the location of the main body of vineyards and the cellar. These places are expertly narrated in superlative Brunellos, anything but ingratiating while young, developed though medium-long maceration and ageing in 20- and 30-hectolitre oak. No gambling with time is required however to grasp the qualities of this great jewel of a wine, the Brunello 2010. A seductive impact of wild berries and Mediterranean scrubland, citrus fruit and bath salts reinforces the thermal hints on a clearly linear palate, not without acidity and flavour. Another richly deserved Tre Bicchieri.

● Brunello di Montalcino '10	♀♀♀	6
● Rosso di Montalcino '13	♀♀	4
● Amor Costante '05	♀♀♀	5
● Amor Costante '10	♀♀	5
● Amor Costante '06	♀♀	5
● Brunello di Montalcino '09	♀♀	6
● Brunello di Montalcino '08	♀♀	6
● Brunello di Montalcino '07	♀♀	6
● Brunello di Montalcino '06	♀♀	6
● Brunello di Montalcino Ris. '07	♀♀	8
● Brunello di Montalcino Ris. '06	♀♀	8
● Brunello di Montalcino Ris. '04	♀♀	8
● Rosso di Montalcino '12	♀♀	4

Bruni

FRAZ. FONTEBLANDA
LOC. LA MARTA, 6
58010 ORBETELLO [GR]
TEL. 0564885445
www.aziendabruni.it

CELLAR SALES
PRE-BOOKED VISITS
ANNUAL PRODUCTION 400,000 bottles
HECTARES UNDER VINE 36.00

In 1955 the Bruni family's winemaking story began, when Leonardo Bruni and his son Paolo bought their first farm in Maremma, still uncharted territory from a farming point of view. The following year the estate was established and the early years were needed to start up the crops after reclaiming the land. In 1973 they began bottling wine and from the next year, winegrowing became the farm's main activity. Since 1995 the estate has been managed by twins Marco and Moreno Bruni, the current owners, who poured passion and commitment into the work, increased the vineyards and modernized the cellar, making it more functional. The pleasing Morellino Laire Riserva 2012 has complex aromas with recognizable fruit, damsons and blackberries, and spice, on a firm-bodied, nicely blended palate with a generous, lingering flavour. The monovarietal grenache, Oltreconfine 2013, is also impressive with clean, defined aromas and a firm, but not massive body with a fresh streak of acidity.

● Grenache Oltreconfine '13	♀♀♀	2*
● Morellino di Scansano Laire Ris. '12	♀♀	4
● Morellino di Scansano Marteto '14	♀	2
○ Perlaia V. T. '14	♀	3
○ Plinio '14	♀	2
○ Vermentino Perlaia '14	♀	3
● Capalbio Sangiovese Moresco '04	♀♀	2*
○ Dolce Muffato Perlaia '13	♀♀	5
● Morellino di Scansano Laire Ris. '10	♀♀	4
● Morellino di Scansano Laire Ris. '09	♀♀	4
● Morellino di Scansano Marteto '13	♀♀	2*
● Morellino di Scansano Marteto '12	♀♀	2*
● Syrah Perlaia '13	♀♀	3
● Syrah Perlaia '11	♀♀	3
○ Vermentino Perlaia '11	♀♀	3
○ Vermentino Plinio '11	♀♀	3

Bulichella

LOC. BULICHELLA, 131
57028 SUVERETO [LI]
TEL. 0565829892
www.bulichella.it

CELLAR SALES
PRE-BOOKED VISITS
ACCOMMODATION AND RESTAURANT SERVICE
ANNUAL PRODUCTION 60,000 bottles
HECTARES UNDER VINE 17.00
VITICULTURE METHOD Certified Organic

The story of Hideyuki Miyakawa and his wife Maria Luisa Bassano is one of love and of exemplary service to others. When they decided to live in the Suvereto area in 1983, with three other families, the area was not as famous as it is now. They had to get down to work and put things in order, starting from scratch and becoming the estate owners in 1999. The predominant source of inspiration in the fields was nature: they chose organic farming methods from the start, at a time when it was an unusual path to follow. After Maria Luisa passed away, Hideyuki continued alone with his children, renovating the cellar and increasing the number of hectares with newly planted vineyards. The interesting Maria Shizuko 2012, a monovarietal merlot, has sweet cherry aromas enhanced by spices and vegetal hints. Smooth and mouthfilling flavour with subtle, fine-grained tannins. The Coldipietrerosse 2012, cabernet franc and sauvignon with a little petit verdot, has a generous nose and lovely juicy fruit.

Tenuta del Buonamico

LOC. CERCATOIA
VIA PROVINCIALE DI MONTECARLO, 43
55015 MONTECARLO [LU]
TEL. 058322038
www.buonamico.it

CELLAR SALES
PRE-BOOKED VISITS
ACCOMMODATION
ANNUAL PRODUCTION 140,000 bottles
HECTARES UNDER VINE 33.00

Tenuta del Buonamico at Cercatoia, south-west of Montecarlo, is an unusual estate, belonging to the oldest pages of local history but it is also one of its most modern wineries. Established in the early 1960s, it has been run for some years now by the Fontana family, who are responsible for the new direction and significant modernization work. The many wines produced reveal a real passion for sparklers. We liked the Il Fortino 2012 best: a herby, spicy Syrah that opens in the glass with dark hints that gradually become clearer. The Vasario 2012 is very original with vibrant aromas and a smooth-textured palate. The best among the sparklers was the Particolare Inedito, but the Particolare Rosé is just as good, with fragrant wild strawberries and wisteria on the nose and a fresh, tangy palate.

● Val di Cornia Suvereto Merlot Maria Shizuko '12	🍷🍷 5
● Syrah Hide '12	🍷🍷 5
● Val di Cornia Suvereto Coldipietrerosse '12	🍷🍷 5
● Val di Cornia Suvereto Tuscanio '12	🍷🍷 5
⊙ Rosé Afrodite '14	🍷 2
● Rubino '13	🍷 2
○ Vermentino Tuscanio '14	🍷 3
● Aleatico Sfiziale '13	🍷🍷 4
● Hide '10	🍷🍷 5
● Suvereto Cabernet Sauvignon Coldipietrerosse '12	🍷🍷 5
● Suvereto Sangiovese Tuscanio '11	🍷🍷 5
● Val di Cornia Coldipietrerosse '10	🍷🍷 5
● Val di Cornia Merlot Maria Shizuko '10	🍷🍷 6
● Val di Cornia Suvereto Tuscanio '10	🍷🍷 5

● Il Fortino '12	🍷🍷 6
○ Vasario '12	🍷🍷 4
○ Particolare Brut Inedito	🍷 3
⊙ Particolare Brut Rosé	🍷 3
⊙ Rosé '14	🍷 3
○ Vermentino '14	🍷 2
○ Viognier '14	🍷 2
● Cercatoja Rosso '11	🍷🍷 5
● Cercatoja Rosso '10	🍷🍷 5
● Cercatoja Rosso '09	🍷🍷 5
● Cercatoja Rosso '08	🍷🍷 4
● Cercatoja Rosso '07	🍷🍷 4
● Il Fortino Syrah '10	🍷🍷 6
● Il Fortino Syrah '09	🍷🍷 6
● Il Fortino Syrah '07	🍷🍷 6
● Il Fortino Syrah '06	🍷🍷 5

Ca' Marcanda

Loc. Santa Teresa, 272
57022 Castagneto Carducci [LI]
Tel. 0565763809
info@camarcanda.com

CELLAR SALES
PRE-BOOKED VISITS
ANNUAL PRODUCTION 450,000 bottles
HECTARES UNDER VINE 120.00

The Gaja family's Bolgheri estate remains
one of the healthiest in the DOC zone,
seemingly unstoppable in the race to
purchase land in neighbouring areas.
Currently there are over 100 hectares of
vineyards, planted with varieties that find
their best expression in this corner of
Tuscany: cabernet sauvignon and franc,
merlot and syrah, all of which are included
in the three blends on offer today, in
varying percentages. The wines are aged in
barriques, each for different amounts of
time also according to the characteristic
features of the wine. The estate's leading
wine, Camarcanda, is flawless as usual.
The 2012 version offers generous,
concentrated aromas of blackberry jam and
balsamic, almost resinous sensations. A
well-sustained, tannic, richly extracted
palate in classic Bolgherese style. Magari
and Promis, both 2013, benefit from the
good year with grip and mouthfilling flavour,
and a touch more texture in the former.

● Bolgheri Camarcanda '12	▼▼ 8
● Bogheri Magari '13	▼▼ 8
● Promis '13	▼▼ 7
● Bolgheri Camarcanda '07	▼▼▼ 8
● Bolgheri Camarcanda '01	▼▼▼ 8
● Bolgheri Camarcanda '11	♀♀ 8
● Bolgheri Camarcanda '10	♀♀ 8
● Bolgheri Camarcanda '09	♀♀ 8
● Bolgheri Camarcanda '08	♀♀ 8
● Bolgheri Camarcanda '06	♀♀ 8
● Bolgheri Camarcanda '05	♀♀ 8
● Bolgheri Camarcanda '04	♀♀ 8
● Magari '12	♀♀ 8
● Magari '11	♀♀ 8
● Magari '10	♀♀ 8
● Magari '09	♀♀ 8

Cacciagrande

Fraz. Tirli
Loc. Ampio
58040 Castiglione della Pescaia [GR]
Tel. 0564944168
www.cacciagrande.com

CELLAR SALES
PRE-BOOKED VISITS
ANNUAL PRODUCTION 100,000 bottles
HECTARES UNDER VINE 20.00
SUSTAINABLE WINERY

The Tuccio family has poured commitment
and passion into the estate, firstly to
reorganize the land and then to bring their
winegrowing experience to fruition. They
made the decision to keep sangiovese as
the most traditional grape, and enhance it
with different clones but better suited to
this area, with excellent results. They later
increased the selection of grapes planted,
adding many international varieties. As well
as wine, the main product, the estate
produces extra virgin olive oil and grappa,
and offers agritourism facilities. A good
2013 version of the Castiglione, a blend of
syrah, merlot and petit verdot with minty
nuances on the fresh nose alongside grilled
peppers and assorted spices; the palate is
well-rounded, lively, full-bodied and
succulent with a lovely tangy, lingering
finish. The pleasant Viognier 2014 has
fragrant hints of flowers and apricots, a
smooth, mouthfilling palate and nicely
developed finish.

● Maremma Tosscana Castiglione '13	▼▼ 4
○ Viognier '14	▼▼ 3
● Cacciagrande '14	▼ 2
● Cortigliano '13	▼ 3
● Castiglione '11	♀♀ 4
● Cortigliano '09	♀♀ 3
● Monteregio di Massa Marittima Rosso '09	♀♀ 2*

Camigliano

LOC. CAMIGLIANO
VIA D'INGRESSO, 2
53024 MONTALCINO [SI]
TEL. 0577844068
www.camigliano.it

CELLAR SALES
PRE-BOOKED VISITS
ACCOMMODATION AND RESTAURANT SERVICE
ANNUAL PRODUCTION 320,000 bottles
HECTARES UNDER VINE 90.00

Nestling on the western tip of the vast Montalcino area, Camigliano is a village with an ancient history. Immersed in unspoilt Mediterranean nature, it vaunts a magnificent view of Alta Maremma and the Colline Metallifere. The Ghezzi family took it over in the late Fifties, making a deliberate decision to keep alive the beating heart of production, revolving around 100-odd hectares of vineyards. The main portion is planted with sangiovese, expressed here with a powerful, sunny voice in Brunellos that tend to be warmer and more mature than those originating from the slopes further from the sea. These features are skilfully interpreted in a fairly fresh year like 2010: despite some raw tannins, the standard Brunello combines verve and drinkable flavour, focusing on prestigious aromas of raspberries, flowers and herbs. A similar profile for the Rosso 2013, even more impressively delicious with racy citrus sensations.

● Brunello di Montalcino '10	🍷🍷 6
● Brunello di Montalcino Gualto Ris. '09	🍷🍷 7
● Rosso di Montalcino '13	🍷🍷 3
○ Gamal '14	🍷 2
● Brunello di Montalcino '09	🍷🍷 6
● Brunello di Montalcino '08	🍷🍷 6
● Brunello di Montalcino '08	🍷🍷 6
● Brunello di Montalcino '06	🍷🍷 6
● Brunello di Montalcino '05	🍷🍷 5
● Brunello di Montalcino '04	🍷🍷 5
● Brunello di Montalcino Gualto Ris. '07	🍷🍷 7
● Brunello di Montalcino Gualto Ris. '06	🍷🍷 7
● Brunello di Montalcino Gualto Ris. '05	🍷🍷 7
● Brunello di Montalcino Gualto Ris. '04	🍷🍷 7
○ Moscadello di Montalcino L'Aura '10	🍷🍷 5

Antonio Camillo

FRAZ. ALBERESE
S.DA BANDITELLA, 2
58100 GROSSETO
TEL. 0564405099
www.poggioargentiera.com

CELLAR SALES
PRE-BOOKED VISITS
ANNUAL PRODUCTION 20,000 bottles
HECTARES UNDER VINE 5.00
VITICULTURE METHOD Certified Organic

Antonio Camillo's story is exemplary: after years as Gianpaolo Paglia's right-hand man in the Poggio Argentiera estate, he decided to fulfil his dream of producing a ciliegiolo-based wine under his own name. With Gianpaolo's agreement he started to look around the area for old plants, hoping to distinguish this variety that was considered pleasant but rustic. He found a property owned by three brothers, Corrado, Aristeo and Alessandro, with the features he sought: varied soils that can offer different expressions of the grapes. Through to the finals for the Vallerana Alta 2013 with hints of cherries and wild berries alongside vegetal hints of Mediterranean scrubland. The palate opens light and soft with barely perceptible tannin, delicious flavour and a lip-smacking finish. The Principio 2014, a monovarietal ciliegiolo, is also enjoyable: strong ripe fruit sensations, appetizing spices like pepper, a light texture and nice relaxed finish.

● Vallerana Alta '13	🍷🍷 3*
● Principio '14	🍷🍷 2*
● Morellino Cotozzino '14	🍷 2
○ Alture '11	🍷🍷 3
● Principio '13	🍷🍷 2*
● Principio '11	🍷🍷 2*
● Vallerana Alta '12	🍷🍷 3*
● Vallerana Alta '11	🍷🍷 3*
● Vallerana Alta '10	🍷🍷 3*

Campo al Pero

FRAZ. DONORATICO
VIA DEL CASONE UGOLINO, 12
57022 CASTAGNETO CARDUCCI [LI]
TEL. 0565774329
www.campoalpero.it

CELLAR SALES
PRE-BOOKED VISITS
ANNUAL PRODUCTION 30,000 bottles
HECTARES UNDER VINE 8.00

Next year will mark the ten-year anniversary of the start of Maurizio Piccoli's wine-producing adventure. Although his professional career was not without gratification, the desire to explore a different pace of life was pressing, so he and his wife Doriana, who works alongside him on the estate, began looking for the right place to explore his passion. They chose a newly renovated farmstead with vineyards planted between the late 1990s and 2003. Attention to detail, absolute dedication to the vineyards and the desire to work well in the cellar are the ingredients that enabled them to grow steadily in quality. The Dorianae 2012 has generous aromas with marked hints of cloves, wild berries, and forest floor blended on a smooth and moderate body with tannins nicely integrated with the alcohol and a light, flavoursome finish. Also interesting is the Campo al Pero 2013: a seductive nose and mouthfilling palate.

● Bolgheri Sup. Campo al Pero '13	▼▼ 3
● Bolgheri Sup. Dorianae '12	▼▼ 5
● Bolgheri Sup. Zephyro '13	▼▼ 2*
⊙ Bolgheri Rosato di Campo al Pero '14	▼ 2
○ Bolgheri Vermentino Mistral '14	▼ 2

Canalicchio
Franco Pacenti

LOC. CANALICCHIO DI SOPRA, 6
53024 MONTALCINO [SI]
TEL. 0577849277
www.canalicchiofrancopacenti.it

CELLAR SALES
PRE-BOOKED VISITS
RESTAURANT SERVICE
ANNUAL PRODUCTION 40,000 bottles
HECTARES UNDER VINE 10.00

The ten hectares planted entirely to sangiovese are tended by Franco Pacenti, his wife Carla and children Lisa, Serena and Lorenzo. The estate takes its name from the long-standing Canalicchi production area, in the northern district of Montalcino: typical medium-textured soil, richer in clay than stones, at about 300 metres altitude. The pedoclimatic features are evident in the austere Brunellos which usually benefit from adequate aerating. These versions are in some ways reminiscent of Nebbiolo with their hints of truffles and roots, also due to strongly traditional vinification procedures. As fond admirers of Franco Pacenti's Sangioveses, we might as well state our slight disappointment at the performance offered by the 2010 Brunello. Make no mistake, this is an excellent wine, solid and coherent, but the flavour profile is overly simple and the tannins are hard enough to be severe. These limitations are more forgivable in the light Rosso 2013.

● Brunello di Montalcino '10	▼▼ 5
● Rosso di Montalcino '13	▼▼ 3
● Brunello di Montalcino '04	▽▽▽ 5
● Brunello di Montalcino '09	▽▽ 5
● Brunello di Montalcino '08	▽▽ 5
● Brunello di Montalcino '07	▽▽ 5
● Brunello di Montalcino '06	▽▽ 5
● Brunello di Montalcino '05	▽▽ 5
● Brunello di Montalcino Ris. '07	▽▽ 7
● Brunello di Montalcino Ris. '04	▽▽ 7
● Rosso di Montalcino '10	▽▽ 3

Canalicchio di Sopra

Loc. Casaccia, 73
53024 Montalcino [SI]
Tel. 0577848316
www.canalicchiodisopra.com

CELLAR SALES
PRE-BOOKED VISITS
ACCOMMODATION
ANNUAL PRODUCTION 55,000 bottles
HECTARES UNDER VINE 15.00

Steadfastness, recognizable features, stylistic personality are the basic pillars on which Canalicchio di Sopra has built its across-the-board success. Here is the meeting point for the experience and resources of two great Montalcino wine-producing families: the Pacenti branch which started up the Canalicchi estate in 1962, where the cellar is situated; and, in the Eighties, the vineyards planted at Montosoli by the Ripaccioli family, made available to the farm. A few hundred metres away on the northern slope, there are two very different but complementary crus, the perfect foundation for a genuinely contemporary style of Brunello. The 2010 version has to be tasted to be believed: despite its extreme youth, it already reveals polished hints of currants, quinine, black pepper and balsamic herbs. These are faithfully reproduced on a palate weighty with energy and flavour, with vibrant, lingering aromas. Also worth watching is the Rosso 2013, a real gem of fruity grip.

● Brunello di Montalcino '10	♟♟♟	6
● Rosso di Montalcino '13	♟♟	3
● Brunello di Montalcino '07	♟♟♟	6
● Brunello di Montalcino '06	♟♟♟	6
● Brunello di Montalcino '04	♟♟♟	6
● Brunello di Montalcino Ris. '07	♟♟♟	8
● Brunello di Montalcino Ris. '04	♟♟♟	7
● Brunello di Montalcino Ris. '01	♟♟♟	7
● Brunello di Montalcino '09	♟♟	6
● Brunello di Montalcino '08	♟♟	6
● Brunello di Montalcino '05	♟♟	5
● Brunello di Montalcino Ris. '06	♟♟	8

Capanna

Loc. Capanna, 333
53024 Montalcino [SI]
Tel. 0577848298
www.capannamontalcino.com

CELLAR SALES
PRE-BOOKED VISITS
ANNUAL PRODUCTION 70,000 bottles
HECTARES UNDER VINE 20.00

A hardworking man of few words, Patrizio Cencioni is what we might term a true vigneron. His headquarters are at the Capanna farm, purchased by the family in 1957: a small hillock overlooking the Montosoli hill in the heart of northern Montalcino, at about 300 metres' altitude on marl-rich soil. The 20-odd hectares of vineyards are almost all planted to sangiovese, producing proud, rigorous wines, not suited to less attentive, hurried drinkers. The wine is also aged in 10- and 30-hectolitre barrels which often makes them difficult to read when young, due to the apparent contrast between the impact of tertiary aromas and the spare tannic structure. Particularly useful information when approaching a 2010 Brunello that clams up initially, but becomes clearer with every tasting. Slightly evolved veiling takes nothing away from the vibrant earthy and spicy hints, perfectly reflected on a close-knit, flavoursome palate, and enhanced by the powerful but mature tannins.

● Brunello di Montalcino '10	♟♟	6
○ Moscadello di Montalcino '14	♟♟	3
● Rosso di Montalcino '13	♟♟	3
● Brunello di Montalcino Ris. '06	♟♟♟	7
● Brunello di Montalcino Ris. '04	♟♟♟	7
● Brunello di Montalcino '09	♟♟	6
● Brunello di Montalcino '08	♟♟	6
● Brunello di Montalcino '07	♟♟	5
● Brunello di Montalcino '06	♟♟	5
● Brunello di Montalcino '05	♟♟	5
● Brunello di Montalcino '04	♟♟	5
● Brunello di Montalcino Ris. '07	♟♟	7
● Brunello di Montalcino Ris. '01	♟♟	7

Tenuta Caparzo

LOC. CAPARZO
S.DA PROV.LE DEL BRUNELLO KM 1,700
53024 MONTALCINO [SI]
TEL. 0577848390
www.caparzo.com

CELLAR SALES
PRE-BOOKED VISITS
ACCOMMODATION
ANNUAL PRODUCTION 900,000 bottles
HECTARES UNDER VINE 90.00

Named after the Ca' del Pazzo building, the Caparzo brand took shape in the 1960s and has been owned by Elisabetta Gnudi Angelini since 1998, following a long series of changes in company structure. Today it is a large farm, with almost 100 hectares of vineyards scattered over many strategic areas of Montalcino. The varieties grown include chardonnay, sauvignon blanc, traminer, and cabernet sauvignon, but the leading wines are the classic sangiovese-based products. In the best years, basic, Riserva and Vigna La Casa Brunellos are produced, which often undergo mixed ageing in barriques and large barrels. This is undoubtedly one of the best-orchestrated performances in recent years from Caparzo wines. The Brunello Vigna La Casa 2010 stands out with airy, breathable fruit that develops further on a mouthfilling, creamy palate, nicely backed up by tannic structure and only held back by slightly drying alcohol.

● Brunello di Montalcino V. La Casa '10	▼▼ 8
● Brunello di Montalcino '10	▼▼ 6
● Brunello di Montalcino Ris. '09	▼▼ 7
● Morellino di Scansano '13	▼▼ 3
● Rosso di Montalcino '13	▼▼ 3
○ Le Grance '11	▼ 3
● Rosso di Montalcino La Caduta '12	▼ 4
○ Vermentino '14	▼ 2
● Brunello di Montalcino '09	♀♀ 6
● Brunello di Montalcino '07	♀♀ 6
● Brunello di Montalcino La Casa '07	♀♀ 8
● Brunello di Montalcino La Casa '06	♀♀ 8
● Brunello di Montalcino Ris. '07	♀♀ 7
● Brunello di Montalcino V. La Casa '08	♀♀ 8
● Brunello di Montalcino V. La Casa Ris. '06	♀♀ 8
● Rosso di Montalcino La Caduta '07	♀♀ 4

Tenuta di Capezzana

LOC. SEANO
VIA CAPEZZANA, 100
59015 CARMIGNANO [PO]
TEL. 0558706005
www.capezzana.it

CELLAR SALES
PRE-BOOKED VISITS
ACCOMMODATION AND RESTAURANT SERVICE
ANNUAL PRODUCTION 450,000 bottles
HECTARES UNDER VINE 80.00

Capezzana has a fascinating history. Wine has been produced here since the 19th century but it was only when the Contini Bonacossi family took over as owners that its importance in the winegrowing sector began to increase. When Alessandro Contini Bonacossi returned to Italy from Spain in the 1920s he decided to purchase the estate and expanded it with another two farms, Il Poggetto and Trefiano. Since the post-war period, the real protagonist has been his grandson Ugo, who engineered a definitive quantum leap. Today Ugo's children run the business, which also relies on good extra virgin olive oil production and agritourism facilities. The 2008 Vin Santo is legendary: apricots, smoky hints, bay leaves and almonds on the nose and a complex, sweet, creamy, velvety and extraordinarily lingering palate. The Carmignano 2011 displays vibrant currant and blueberry aromas with smooth tannins on the juicy palate, very close-knit but invigorating, with a succulent, lingering finish.

○ Vin Santo di Carmignano Ris. '08	▼▼▼ 6
● Barco Reale '13	▼▼ 2*
● Carmignano Villa di Capezzana '11	▼▼ 4
○ Trebbiano '13	▼▼ 4
● Ghiaie della Furba '10	▼ 5
● Carmignano Villa di Capezzana '07	♀♀♀ 4
● Carmignano Villa di Capezzana '05	♀♀♀ 4
● Ghiaie della Furba '01	♀♀♀ 5
○ Vin Santo di Carmignano Ris. '07	♀♀♀ 6
○ Vin Santo di Carmignano Ris. '05	♀♀♀ 5
● Barco Reale '12	♀♀ 2*
● Carmignano Villa di Capezzana '10	♀♀ 4
● Ghiaie della Furba '09	♀♀ 5
○ Trebbiano '11	♀♀ 4

Caprili

FRAZ. TAVERNELLE
POD. CAPRILI, 268
53024 MONTALCINO [SI]
TEL. 0577848566
www.caprili.it

CELLAR SALES
PRE-BOOKED VISITS
ACCOMMODATION
ANNUAL PRODUCTION 70,000 bottles
HECTARES UNDER VINE 21.00

Half a century has passed since the Bartolommei family purchased the Caprili farm in the area of Montalcino overlooking the Orcia and Ombrone rivers. The first Brunello was bottled back in 1978 but in the last five years, in particular, the winery has carved itself a firm foothold among the top estates in the DOC zone. This is thanks to a clearly defined style which often succeeds in combining powerful texture with rigorous linearity, just as we might expect from an area that is warm, but steep and airy with very stony soil. Sangiovese vineyards occupy the vast majority of the 15-hectare estate, divided into plots and vinified separately, to be blended after lengthy ageing in large oak. The outstanding Brunello 2010 confirms the currently brilliant form of the Caprili range. Clear-cut fruit, seaside vegetation, smoky sensations and a winning palate in continual progression: paced more like a mid-distance runner than a short, sharp sprinter. We predict a radiant future.

● Brunello di Montalcino '10	♟♟♟ 6
● Rosso di Montalcino '13	♟♟ 3
● Brunello di Montalcino '06	♟♟♟ 7
● Brunello di Montalcino Ris. '08	♟♟♟ 7
● Brunello di Montalcino Ris. '06	♟♟♟ 7
● Brunello di Montalcino Ris. '04	♟♟♟ 5
● Brunello di Montalcino '09	♟♟ 5
● Brunello di Montalcino '08	♟♟ 5
● Brunello di Montalcino '07	♟♟ 5
● Brunello di Montalcino '05	♟♟ 5

Fattoria Carpineta Fontalpino

FRAZ. MONTAPERTI
LOC. CARPINETA
53019 CASTELNUOVO BERARDENGA [SI]
TEL. 0577369219
www.carpinetafontalpino.it

CELLAR SALES
PRE-BOOKED VISITS
ACCOMMODATION
ANNUAL PRODUCTION 100,000 bottles
HECTARES UNDER VINE 23.00
VITICULTURE METHOD Certified Organic

Gioia and Filippo Cresti's winemaking project took off in 1994, so it is a relatively young winery. It has, however, proved capable of rapidly achieving significant results. The vineyards are situated in the subzone of Castelnuovo Berardenga, in the southern part of Chianti Classico, close to Montaperti in the Sienese countryside. The wines are modern in style, starting with the fact that they are aged mainly in barriques, but not without balance and character which reflect the soil and weather features of this area. The Do ut des 2012 displays vibrant, fruity and well-defined aromas while the palate shows confident texture, still young but already clearly paced and progressive. The Chianti Classico 2013 is taut and gutsy with a nice tangy character enhancing the drinkable flavour. The Montaperto 2013, from sangiovese, gamay and Alicante, is clean and approachable. The Chianti Classico Riserva 2012 is slightly penalized by imprecise aromas but the structure is dense and compact.

● Do ut des '12	♟♟♟ 5
● Chianti Cl. Fontalpino '13	♟♟ 3
● Chianti Cl. Fontalpino Ris. '12	♟ 5
● Montaperto '13	♟ 3
● Do ut des '11	♟♟♟ 5
● Do ut des '10	♟♟♟ 5
● Do ut des '09	♟♟♟ 5
● Do ut des '07	♟♟♟ 5
● Dofana '10	♟♟♟ 7
● Dofana '07	♟♟♟ 8
● Chianti Cl. Fontalpino '12	♟♟ 3
● Chianti Cl. Fontalpino '11	♟♟ 3*
● Chianti Cl. Fontalpino Ris. '11	♟♟ 5
● Chianti Cl. Fontalpino Ris. '10	♟♟ 5
● Do ut des '08	♟♟ 5
● Dofana '06	♟♟ 8

Casa alle Vacche

FRAZ. PANCOLE
LOC. LUCIGNANO, 73A
53037 SAN GIMIGNANO [SI]
TEL. 0577955103
www.casaallevacche.it

CELLAR SALES
PRE-BOOKED VISITS
ACCOMMODATION AND RESTAURANT SERVICE
ANNUAL PRODUCTION 115,000 bottles
HECTARES UNDER VINE 28.00

The Ciappi family is healthily anchored to
tradition and the name they chose for their
estate is intended to be a proof of the hard,
tiring work that led to the construction of a
modern and dynamic winery. The oldest
building used to be a barn for ivestock used
to work in the fields. The wine and oil
production was later joined by an
agritourism centre. In the vineyards the
owners have chosen to apply integrated
farming techniques in order to care for the
environment in which they work. The estate
produces many different types of wine due
to rediscovery and separate fermentation of
native local varieties. The Aglieno 2012 is a
blend of merlot, cabernet sauvignon and
syrah with vibrant aromas of wild berries
and spices like cloves and cinnamon. The
palate is soft and nicely defined with
smooth tannins and a lingering, pleasant
finish. The Vernaccia I Macchioni is also
good, with a fresh, edgy flavour.

● Aglieno '12	♟♟ 2*
○ Vernaccia di S. Gimignano I Macchioni '14	♟♟ 2*
● Canaiolo '14	♟ 2
● Chianti Colli Senesi '14	♟ 2
● Chianti Colli Senesi Cinabro '12	♟ 3
● Ciliegiolo '14	♟ 2
● Merlot '12	♟ 2
○ Vernaccia di S. Gimignano '14	♟ 2
○ Vernaccia di S. Gimignano Crocus Ris. '11	♟♟ 2*
○ Vernaccia di S. Gimignano '11	♟♟ 2*
○ Vernaccia di S. Gimignano Crocus Ris. '10	♟♟ 2*
○ Vernaccia di S. Gimignano Crocus Ris. '09	♟♟ 3
○ Vernaccia di S. Gimignano Crocus Ris. '08	♟♟ 2*
○ Vernaccia di S. Gimignano I Macchioni '11	♟♟ 2*
○ Vernaccia di S. Gimignano I Macchioni '10	♟♟ 2*

Casa Dei

LOC. SAN ROCCO
57028 SUVERETO [LI]
TEL. 0558300800
www.tenutacasadei.it

PRE-BOOKED VISITS
ANNUAL PRODUCTION 80,000 bottles
HECTARES UNDER VINE 16.00
VITICULTURE METHOD Certified Organic

Stefano Casadei has always been
committed to farming, both supervising the
vineyards of others, and as the owner of
this estate purchased in 1996, fulfilling his
dream to become a winegrower. The
business has grown over the years and
includes Castello di Trebbio, owned by his
wife Anna, and the Olianas estate in
Sardinia. He chose Suvereto for the
excellent climate conditions and the
possibility of enjoying regular harvests
with great results, a theory which has
proved correct. Research is currently
underway to convert the vineyards to
biodynamic farming methods. The Syrah
Le Anfore 2014 is intriguing: gamy aromas
soften into lively fruit and tobacco, while
the palate is nicely fruity, firm and
succulent with forward but nicely managed
tannins and a long, appetizing finish. The
Filare 18 is a monovarietal cabernet franc
with enjoyable vegetal hints on the nose
and a relaxed, supple palate with a very
lingering flavour.

● Filare 18 '13	♟♟ 6
● Filare 41 '13	♟♟ 6
● Sogno Mediterraneo '13	♟♟ 4
● Syrah Le Anfore '14	♟♟ 5
● Armonia '14	♟ 2
● Filare 41 '11	♟♟ 5
● Filare 41 '09	♟♟ 5

Casa Emma

LOC. CORTINE
S.DA PROV.LE DI CASTELLINA IN CHIANTI, 3
50021 BARBERINO VAL D'ELSA [FI]
TEL. 0558072239
www.casaemma.com

CELLAR SALES
PRE-BOOKED VISITS
RESTAURANT SERVICE
ANNUAL PRODUCTION 90,000 bottles
HECTARES UNDER VINE 25.00

The Bucalossi family purchased the estate in the early 1970s. The vineyards are mostly situated in San Donato in Poggio, the Florentine part of Chianti Classico, also flanking the Sienese area of Castellina in Chianti. The wines are nicely defined in a style that typically seeks6 the ripeness of the fruit, and aged mainly in small wood; however, the modern style of the products is articulated with balance and without pointless forcing. The results are technically flawless wines that often express close links to the terroir of origin. A blend of fruity and spicy aromas for the Chianti Classico 2013, and a generally harmonious and nicely fluent palate; the Chianti Classico Vignalparco 2012 is flavoursome and well-coordinated with nuanced aromas. The Chianti Classico Gran Selezione '10 is still slightly marked by the oak ageing vessels.

● Chianti Cl. '13	♟♟	3
● Chianti Cl. Vignalparco '12	♟♟	3
● Chianti Cl. Gran Sel. '10	♟	5
● Chianti Cl. Ris. '95	♟♟♟	4*
● Chianti Cl. Ris. '93	♟♟♟	5
● Sololo '94	♟♟♟	4*
● Chianti Cl. '11	♟♟	3*
● Chianti Cl. '10	♟♟	3
● Chianti Cl. '08	♟♟	3
● Chianti Cl. '07	♟♟	3
● Chianti Cl. Ris. '11	♟♟	5
● Chianti Cl. Ris. '09	♟♟	5
● Chianti Cl. Ris. '08	♟♟	5
● Chianti Cl. Ris. '07	♟♟	5
● Chianti Cl. Ris. '05	♟♟	5
● Chianti Cl. Vignalparco '11	♟♟	3

Fattoria Le Casalte

FRAZ. SANT'ALBINO
VIA DEL TERMINE, 2
53045 MONTEPULCIANO [SI]
TEL. 0578798246
www.lecasalte.com

CELLAR SALES
PRE-BOOKED VISITS
ANNUAL PRODUCTION 50,000 bottles
HECTARES UNDER VINE 13.00

The history of Le Casalte began with Guido Barioffi, father of current owner Chiara. He fell in love with the area and decided to invest in the purchase of a partly-abandoned farmstead in the Montepulciano area, to begin working as a winegrower. He was so committed to the idea that he started to study agricultural science and winegrowing in order to understand the best methods to obtain good products. His daughter nurtured the same passion and became a full-time wine producer. After careful consideration, the conversion to organic methods has obtained encouraging results in the wines. The Nobile Quercetonda 2012 is a very good selection with fresh aromas of wild berries and hints of cinnamon and medicinal herbs. The palate is vigorous, appetizing, with well-designed tannins, and a fresh flavour in the tangy finish. The Rosso 2013 has a compelling nose and dynamic, succulent palate.

● Nobile di Montepulciano Quercetonda '12	♟♟	5
● Rosso di Montepulciano '13	♟♟	2*
● Nobile di Montepulciano '12	♟	3
● Nobile di Montepulciano Quercetonda '06	♟♟♟	5
● Nobile di Montepulciano Quercetonda '07	♟♟	5
● Nobile di Montepulciano Quercetonda '04	♟♟	5
● Nobile di Montepulciano Quercetonda '03	♟♟	5
● Nobile di Montepulciano '08	♟♟	3
● Nobile di Montepulciano '06	♟♟	3
● Rosso di Montepulciano '10	♟♟	2*
● Rosso Toscano '08	♟♟	2*
● Rosso Toscano '06	♟♟	1*
○ Vin Santo di Montepulciano '03	♟♟	7
○ Vin Santo di Montepulciano '00	♟♟	7
○ Vin Santo di Montepulciano '99	♟♟	7

★Casanova di Neri

POD. FIESOLE
53024 MONTALCINO [SI]
TEL. 0577834455
www.casanovadineri.com

PRE-BOOKED VISITS
ACCOMMODATION
ANNUAL PRODUCTION 225,000 bottles
HECTARES UNDER VINE 63.00

One of the best-known brand names in
Montalcino, Casanova dei Neri was founded
by Giovanni Neri in 1971 and is managed
today by his son Giacomo. The 60-plus
hectares of vineyards include plots in Fiesole
and Poderuccio at Torrenieri, near the
winery; Podernuovo, Cerretalto and Spereta,
in the eastern district; Le Cetine and
Pietradonice on the south side. The estate
covers a total of 60 hectares, and includes
non-native grape varieties. The top products
are still the sangiovese-based reds: the
Tenuta Nuova and Cerretalto selections tend
to flaunt ripe, opulent fruit, while the basic
Brunello is more classic in style. This year
the Casanova di Neri team presents a partly
reworked line-up. The Brunello Cerretalto
was not produced in 2009 so the role of
leader of the pack is taken by the 2010
Tenuta Nuova, which is all about ripe fruit
and a flavour that is broad rather than deep.
The basic Brunello 2010 is excellent.

Castell'in Villa

LOC. CASTELL'IN VILLA
53019 CASTELNUOVO BERARDENGA [SI]
TEL. 0577359074
www.castellinvilla.com

CELLAR SALES
PRE-BOOKED VISITS
ANNUAL PRODUCTION 100,000 bottles
HECTARES UNDER VINE 54.00

Journalist and editor Paolo Panerai's
Chianti-based winemaking project took off
almost 40 years ago when he decided to put
four farm estates to use in the subzone of
Castellina in Chianti. From the very
beginning, with the release in 1979 of the
first bottles of I Sodi di S. Niccolò, the
estate's stylistic approach was clear,
favouring classic features over adventurous
fashionable choices. This strategy has never
wavered and characterizes today's products,
making this Chianti Classico estate a
benchmark for the whole area. Tre Bicchieri
for the delicious Chianti Classico 2011:
subtle red fruit like strawberries and morello
cherries on the nose with medicinal herbs
and dried leaves, while the palate shows grip
and length and a sharp, clean finish with an
endless, tangy back-palate. The Riserva is a
little less lively, with dark sensations of
tobacco and blood-rich meat, held back in
the finish by slightly harsh tannin.

● Brunello di Montalcino Tenuta Nuova '10	♥♥ 8
● Brunello di Montalcino '10	♥♥ 6
● Rosso di Montalcino '13	♥ 5
● Brunello di Montalcino '09	♀♀♀ 6
● Brunello di Montalcino Cerretalto '07	♀♀♀ 8
● Brunello di Montalcino Cerretalto '06	♀♀♀ 8
● Brunello di Montalcino Cerretalto '04	♀♀♀ 8
● Brunello di Montalcino Cerretalto '01	♀♀♀ 8
● Brunello di Montalcino Tenuta Nuova '06	♀♀♀ 8
● Brunello di Montalcino Tenuta Nuova '05	♀♀♀ 7
● Brunello di Montalcino Tenuta Nuova '01	♀♀♀ 6
● Pietradonice '05	♀♀♀ 8

● Chianti Cl. '11	♥♥♥ 5
● Chianti Cl. Poggio delle Rose Ris. '10	♥♥ 6
● Chianti Cl. '09	♀♀♀ 5
● Chianti Cl. '08	♀♀♀ 5
● Chianti Cl. Ris. '85	♀♀♀ 6
● Chianti Cl. '10	♀♀ 5
● Chianti Cl. Ris. '09	♀♀ 6
● Chianti Cl. Ris. '08	♀♀ 6
● Santa Croce '07	♀♀ 6
○ Vin Santo del Chianti Cl. '95	♀♀ 8

★Castellare di Castellina

LOC. CASTELLARE
53011 CASTELLINA IN CHIANTI [SI]
TEL. 0577742903
www.castellare.it

CELLAR SALES
PRE-BOOKED VISITS
ACCOMMODATION
ANNUAL PRODUCTION 200,000 bottles
HECTARES UNDER VINE 28.00

Castell'in Villa has come a long way: established in 1967, the estate produced its first Chianti Classico in 1971. This is a story built primarily on stylistic coherence and rigorous production, that has kept this Castelnuovo Berardenga estate away from passing oenological trends while respecting the greatest Chianti tradition. Coralia Pignatelli's style is uncompromising: pale, subtle colour, austere and multi-shaded flavour development, complex and nuanced aromas, elegance and balance keeping the upper hand. The 2011 version also stands out thanks to is contrasting nuances and dynamic flavour. The Chianti Classico Il Poggiale Riserva 2012 is impressively aromatic. The sunny Chianti Classico 2013 is very well-focused and the Chianti Classico Riserva 2101 is firm and austere.

★Castello Banfi

LOC. SANT'ANGELO SCALO
CASTELLO DI POGGIO ALLE MURA
53024 MONTALCINO [SI]
TEL. 0577840111
www.castellobanfi.com

CELLAR SALES
PRE-BOOKED VISITS
ACCOMMODATION AND RESTAURANT SERVICE
ANNUAL PRODUCTION 10,500,000 bottles
HECTARES UNDER VINE 850.00

At the risk of sounding repetitive, it is impossible to present a complete account of the global success of Brunello without mentioning the role played by the Mariani family. They purchased Castello Banfi in the Seventies but many things have changed in the interim period: over 800 hectares of vineyards just in Montalcino. They produce about ten million bottles per year, when Vigne Reali in Piedmont and the Banfi Toscana line are included. It is impossible to list all the wines produced by this real farming colossus managed by Enrico Viglierchio and Remo Grassi, but it is worth mentioning the classic reds, showing their usual recognizable soft, juicy character. This is skilfully summed up in the 2009 Brunello Poggio alle Mura Riserva: despite the tricky year, this is a joyous, well-proportioned wine with prestigious floral nuances and nicely blended tannins. But this is just the diamond-head of a range that always shows a high standard.

● I Sodi di S. Niccolò '11	♟♟♟	8
● Chianti Cl. '13	♟♟	3*
● Chianti Cl. Il Poggiale Ris. '12	♟♟	5
● Chianti Cl. Ris. '12	♟	4
● I Sodi di S. Niccolò '10	♟♟♟	8
● I Sodi di S. Niccolò '09	♟♟♟	8
● I Sodi di S. Niccolò '08	♟♟♟	7
● I Sodi di S. Niccolò '07	♟♟♟	7
● I Sodi di S. Niccolò '06	♟♟♟	7
● I Sodi di S. Niccolò '05	♟♟♟	7
● I Sodi di S. Niccolò '04	♟♟♟	7
● I Sodi di S. Niccolò '03	♟♟♟	7

● Brunello di Montalcino Poggio alle Mura Ris. '09	♟♟	8
● Brunello di Montalcino '10	♟♟	6
● Brunello di Montalcino Poggio alle Mura '10	♟♟	7
○ La Pettegola '14	♟♟	2*
● Rosso di Montalcino '13	♟♟	3
● Belnero '12	♟	4
● Centine Rosso '13	♟	2
● Cum Laude '12	♟	3
● Rosso di Montalcino Poggio alle Mura '13	♟	4
● Brunello di Montalcino Poggio all'Oro Ris. '04	♟♟♟	8
● Sant'Antimo Mandrielle '04	♟♟♟	3
● Summus '88	♟♟♟	7

Castello d'Albola

LOC. PIAN D'ALBOLA, 31
53017 RADDA IN CHIANTI [SI]
TEL. 0577738019
www.albola.it

CELLAR SALES
PRE-BOOKED VISITS
ANNUAL PRODUCTION 800,000 bottles
HECTARES UNDER VINE 157.00

This is one of the most interesting estates in the subzone of Radda in Chianti, not only for its size but also because it includes some of the best vineyards in the area, at altitudes between 400 and 600 metres, like Ellere and Madonnino. Castello d'Albola has belonged to the Zonin group, one of the biggest wine-producing names in Italy, since the 1970s. The winery's style highlights the fresh features of the area with impeccable technical skill and considerable personality. The wines are aged in large and small wood. The Chianti Classico Il Solatio Gran Selezione 2011 is slender, edgy, with clear, subtle aromas, with exemplary finesse and elegance. Equally well-typed is the Chianti Classico Le Ellere 2012, with iron-like character and confidently tangy flavour. The Chianti Classico 2012 is approachable and delicious, while the sweet Chianti Classico Riserva 2011 is slightly less relaxed. The chardonnay Poggio alle Fate 2014 is simple but well made.

★Castello del Terriccio

LOC. TERRICCIO
VIA BAGNOLI, 16
56040 CASTELLINA MARITTIMA [PI]
TEL. 050699709
www.terriccio.com

CELLAR SALES
PRE-BOOKED VISITS
ANNUAL PRODUCTION 150,000 bottles
HECTARES UNDER VINE 60.00

Gian Annibale Rossi di Medelana is an eclectic character with plenty of initiative: his latest idea was to set up a literary prize named for the estate and dedicated to historical romance. The castle has a thousand-year history, and was put to agricultural use in the 19th century by the Poniatowski family. The current owner's family took over after the First World War and carried out a great deal of work to make the estate modern and functional. Known for many years for its production of cereals, Il Terriccio became famous for winegrowing when Gian Annibale joined the business, considerably expanding the vineyards. Tre Bicchieri for the Lupicaia, from cabernet sauvignon with a small amount of petit verdot: an alluring nose with hints of eucalyptus, ripe black berries and spicy notes of juniper. The palate makes a subtle impact with tannins shy to come forward, well-dosed acidity and a lively, tangy finish.

● Chianti Cl. Il Solatio Gran Sel. '11	▼▼▼ 5
● Chianti Cl. Le Ellere '12	▼▼ 3*
● Chianti Cl. '12	▼▼ 3
● Chianti Cl. Ris. '11	▼ 4
○ Poggio alle Fate '14	▼ 3
● Acciaiolo '06	♈♈♈ 6
● Acciaiolo '04	♈♈♈ 6
● Acciaiolo '01	♈♈♈ 6
● Acciaiolo '95	♈♈♈ 5
● Chianti Cl. Il Solatio Gran Sel. '10	♈♈♈ 5
● Chianti Cl. Le Ellere '08	♈♈♈ 3
● Chianti Cl. Ris. '09	♈♈♈ 4*
● Chianti Cl. Ris. '08	♈♈♈ 4*

● Lupicaia '11	▼▼▼ 8
● Castello del Terriccio '10	▼▼ 8
● Tassinaia '11	▼▼ 6
● Castello del Terriccio '07	♈♈♈ 8
● Castello del Terriccio '04	♈♈♈ 8
● Castello del Terriccio '03	♈♈♈ 8
● Castello del Terriccio '01	♈♈♈ 8
● Castello del Terriccio '00	♈♈♈ 8
● Lupicaia '10	♈♈♈ 8
● Lupicaia '07	♈♈♈ 8
● Lupicaia '06	♈♈♈ 8
● Lupicaia '05	♈♈♈ 8
● Lupicaia '04	♈♈♈ 8
● Lupicaia '01	♈♈♈ 8
● Lupicaia '00	♈♈♈ 8
● Lupicaia '99	♈♈♈ 8

Castello del Trebbio

VIA SANTA BRIGIDA, 9
50060 PONTASSIEVE [FI]
TEL. 0558304900
www.vinoturismo.it

CELLAR SALES
PRE-BOOKED VISITS
ANNUAL PRODUCTION 300,000 bottles
HECTARES UNDER VINE 52.00

The castle has ancient origins: the first building dates back to 1184 and was owned by the de' Pazzi family. The original venerable charm is preserved in the old cellars, which can still be visited. A remarkable series of commercial tourism activities have developed around it, from the agritourism facilities to wine tourism, weddings, and olive oil and saffron production. In 1968 the estate changed hands and the Castle became the property of the Baj Macario family. Anna, the owner, and her husband Stefano Casadei supervise the wine production business. Their passion led them to start making wine in Val di Cornia and outside of Tuscany, in Sardinia. A memorable result for the winery and the Rufina area, with the first ever Tre Bicchieri for a Chianti Rufina: the Riserva Lastricato 2011. A striking nose with fresh, clean aromas, hints of balsam and lively fruit, and a well-balanced body with nicely blended tannins and a minerally, lingering, flavoursome aftertaste with aromatic herbs.

● Chianti Rufina Lastricato Ris. '11	▼▼▼ 4*
○ Bianco della Congiura '14	▼▼ 3
● De' Pazzi '11	▼▼ 4
● Sangiovese '13	▼▼ 5
○ Vin Santo del Chianti '07	▼▼ 4
● Chianti '14	▼ 2
● Pazzesco '10	▼ 5
● Cabernet Franc Casa Dei '12	▽▽ 5
● Chianti Rufina Lastricato Ris. '10	▽▽ 4
● Pazzesco '11	▽▽ 5
● Petit Verdot Casa Dei '12	▽▽ 5
● Vigneti Trebbio '11	▽▽ 4
○ Viognier Casa Dei '13	▽▽ 4

★★Castello di Ama

LOC. AMA
53013 GAIOLE IN CHIANTI [SI]
TEL. 0577746031
www.castellodiama.com

CELLAR SALES
PRE-BOOKED VISITS
ANNUAL PRODUCTION 300,000 bottles
HECTARES UNDER VINE 90.00

The estate was established in 1972 in the small village of Ama, not far from Gaiole in Chianti, and released its first bottles on the market in the late 1970s. This was the beginning of a journey marked by success, as well as a project that has never lost sight of the central role of the land and the DOC zone. Today, Castello di Ama is firmly established in a prominent position among the crowded overview of Chianti production, and Lorenza Sebasti and Marco Pallanti have never stopped offering wines in a flawless style, expressing a rare sense of authenticity. The Chianti Classico San Lorenzo Gran Selezione 2011 has clearly defined aromas and a confident, succulent flavour. The Chianti Classico 2013 is really delicious: wild berries and damp earth on the nose and a tangy, well-paced palate. The Chianti Classico Vigneto La Casuccia Gran Selezione 2011 is sunny and generous, while the Chianti Classico Vigneto Bellavista Gran Selezione 2011 is juicy but with unripe aromas.

● Chianti Cl. Ama '13	▼▼ 4
● Chianti Cl. San Lorenzo Gran Sel. '11	▼▼ 6
● Chianti Cl. Vign. La Casuccia Gran Sel. '11	▼▼ 8
● Chianti Cl. Vign. Bellavista Gran Sel. '11	▼ 8
● Chianti Cl. Ama '11	▽▽▽ 4*
● Chianti Cl. Bellavista '01	▽▽▽ 8
● Chianti Cl. Castello di Ama '05	▽▽▽ 5
● Chianti Cl. Castello di Ama '03	▽▽▽ 5
● Chianti Cl. Castello di Ama '01	▽▽▽ 5
● Chianti Cl. Castello di Ama '00	▽▽▽ 5
● Chianti Cl. La Casuccia '04	▽▽▽ 8
● Chianti Cl. La Casuccia '01	▽▽▽ 8
● l'Apparita Merlot '01	▽▽▽ 8
● l'Apparita Merlot '00	▽▽▽ 8

Castello di Bolgheri

LOC. BOLGHERI
S.DA LAURETTA, 7
57020 CASTAGNETO CARDUCCI [LI]
TEL. 0565762110
www.castellodibolgheri.eu

CELLAR SALES
PRE-BOOKED VISITS
ACCOMMODATION
ANNUAL PRODUCTION 80,000 bottles
HECTARES UNDER VINE 50.00

This estate has distant historical roots: it was once part of the huge property owned by the Conti della Gherardesca and dates back to the 1500s. Today, proudly anchored to its roots, Castello di Bolgheri is a modern estate skilfully managed by the owners, the Zileri dal Verme family. Of the estate's lovely 130 hectares, there are 50 under vine, planted on sandy and clayey soil rich in stony limestone material. The wines produced in the beautiful cellar are stylish and complex, nicely balanced and judiciously extracted. The Bolgheri Superiore Castello di Bolgheri is a wonderful wine, as usual, certainly one of the best in the DOC zone. The 2012 vintage shows bags of personality, dominated by ripe, but not heavy fruit sensations nicely blended with the seductively spicy texture. The palate is both weighty and succulent, with very lingering echoes of delicious dark fruit.

Castello di Bossi

LOC. BOSSI IN CHIANTI
53019 CASTELNUOVO BERARDENGA [SI]
TEL. 0577359330
www.bacciwines.it

CELLAR SALES
PRE-BOOKED VISITS
ACCOMMODATION
ANNUAL PRODUCTION 687,700 bottles
HECTARES UNDER VINE 124.00

The Bacci family owns estates in Montalcino, Maremma and Chianti Classico. The style favours ripe fruit and powerful structure, while the wines are aged mainly in barriques and are often very complex, sometimes suffering due to a lack of change in pace. The monovarietal merlot Grido Tenuta di Renieri 2011 is nicely typed with mature, clean aromas and a firm but well-paced flavour. The Morellino Riserva Tempo 2011, made at the Talmo estate, shows good structure with a generous, mouthfilling flavour. The Vin San Laurentino 2006, from sangiovese, malvasia and trebbiano is sweet but never cloying. The Mega Tenuta di Renieri 2011, a blend of sangiovese and cabernet sauvignon, is held back slightly by the oak used for ageing, as is the Chianti Classico Tenuta di Renieri Riserva 2011. The Maremma whites, Vento Vermentino e Vento Teso Viognier, both 2014, are fresh and delicious.

● Bolgheri Sup. Rosso Castello di Bolgheri '12	♔♔♔ 6
● Bolgheri Varvàra '13	♔♔ 4
● Bolgheri Sup. Castello di Bolgheri '10	♔♔♔ 6
● Bolgheri Sup. Castello di Bolgheri '09	♔♔♔ 6
● Bolgheri Sup. Castello di Bolgheri '07	♔♔♔ 6
● Bolgheri Sup. Castello di Bolgheri '11	♔♔ 6
● Bolgheri Sup. Castello di Bolgheri '08	♔♔ 6
● Bolgheri Sup. Castello di Bolgheri '06	♔♔ 7
● Bolgheri Varvàra '12	♔♔ 4

● Grido Tenuta Renieri '11	♔♔ 6
● Morellino Tempo Terre di Talamo Ris. '11	♔♔ 6
○ Vin San Laurentino '06	♔♔ 8
● Chianti Cl. Tenuta Renieri Ris. '11	♔ 5
● Mega Tenuta Renieri '11	♔ 6
○ Vermentino Vento Terre di Talamo '14	♔ 5
○ Viogner Vento Teso Terre di Talamo '14	♔ 4
● Corbaia '03	♔♔♔ 6
● Corbaia '99	♔♔♔ 5
● Corbaia '11	♔♔ 8
● Girolamo '04	♔♔ 6
● Morellino Tempo Terre di Talamo '12	♔♔ 5
● PerCecco Terre di Talamo '11	♔♔ 5
○ San Laurentino '01	♔♔ 7
○ Vin San Laurentino '99	♔♔ 7

★★★Castello di Fonterutoli

LOC. FONTERUTOLI
VIA OTTONE III DI SASSONIA, 5
53011 CASTELLINA IN CHIANTI [SI]
TEL. 057773571
www.mazzei.it

CELLAR SALES
PRE-BOOKED VISITS
ACCOMMODATION AND RESTAURANT SERVICE
ANNUAL PRODUCTION 800,000 bottles
HECTARES UNDER VINE 117.00
SUSTAINABLE WINERY

The Mazzei family has worked in the wine sector for centuries, and is an emblematic element of Chianti Classico, Tuscan winemaking, and much more. Their success is rooted in powerful, vigorous red wines in a style that has recently become more polished thanks, among other things, to separate fermentation of the grapes from the 120 plots in Castellina and Radda in Chianti. The Mix36 2011 is a monovarietal sangiovese with clear-cut aromas and a firm, flavoursome palate, with some extension and a fragrant, lingering finish. The Philip 2011 is a Cabernet Sauvignon with lovely aromatic expression and a focused, stylish, flavoursome palate. The impressive Chianti Classico Ser Lapo Riserva Privata 2011 is polished and pleasantly paced with the vaguely faded flavour we like so much.

Castello di Gabbiano

FRAZ. MERCATALE VAL DI PESA
VIA GABBIANO, 22
50020 SAN CASCIANO IN VAL DI PESA [FI]
TEL. 055821053
www.castellogabbiano.it

CELLAR SALES
PRE-BOOKED VISITS
ACCOMMODATION AND RESTAURANT SERVICE
ANNUAL PRODUCTION 1,000,000 bottles
HECTARES UNDER VINE 145.00

Castello di Gabbiano produces large quantities from its modern estate with almost 150 hectares under vine in the San Casciano area. The wines are international in style but without excessive ripening or too much oak, adapting to the taste of the target market. The most widely grown grape is Sangiovese, alongside inevitable international varieties and some white cultivars. Castello di Gabbiano also has a hospitality structure and as a location is well worth a visit. The Chianti Classico Riserva 2012 is firm and not without personality, showing vibrant, mature aromas and a succulent, nicely paced palate. The Alleanza 2012, a blend of sangiovese, merlot and cabernet sauvignon, is nicely made and just a little stiff in the finish. The well-styled Chianti Classico 2012 just lacks a little depth.

● Mix36 '11	♥♥♥ 8
● Chianti Cl. Ser Lapo Riserva Privata '11	♥♥ 5
● Philip '11	♥♥ 6
● Chianti Cl. Fonterutoli '13	♥♥ 5
● Serrata di Belguardo Tenuta di Belguardo '13	♥♥ 4
● Siepi '12	♥♥ 8
○ Vermentino Codice V Tenuta di Belguardo '14	♥♥ 5
● Chianti Cl. Ser Lapo Ris. '12	♥ 5
● Morellino di Scansano Bronzone Ris. Tenuta di Belguardo '12	♥ 4
⊙ Rosato Tenuta di Belguardo '14	♥ 4
○ Vermentino di Toscana Tenuta di Belguardo '14	♥ 4
● Siepi '11	♀♀♀ 8

● Chianti Cl. Ris. '12	♥♥ 5
● Alleanza '12	♥ 5
● Chianti Cl. '12	♥ 3
● Alleanza '08	♀♀ 5
● Bellezza '06	♀♀ 5
● Chianti Cl. '11	♀♀ 3
● Chianti Cl. Bellezza Gran Sel. '11	♀♀ 5
● Chianti Cl. Ris. '09	♀♀ 5
● Chianti Cl. Ris. '07	♀♀ 5
● Chianti Cl. Ris. '06	♀♀ 4

Castello di Meleto

LOC. MELETO
53013 GAIOLE IN CHIANTI [SI]
TEL. 0577749217
www.castellomeleto.it

CELLAR SALES
PRE-BOOKED VISITS
ACCOMMODATION AND RESTAURANT SERVICE
ANNUAL PRODUCTION 600,000 bottles
HECTARES UNDER VINE 125.00

Castello di Meleto in the Gaiole in Chianti
subzone is a leading estate for this DOC,
both in the size of its vineyards and the
particularly well-suited locations. The
wines have settled, especially recently, into
a style that pays close attention to
preserving the most intimate Chianti
features and the current results place
Meleto among the most interesting
wineries in the Chianti Classico DOC. The
Vigna Casi Riserva 2012 has a subtle
array of aromas with hints of strawberries,
light minty sensations and an elegant, firm
flavour with a sharp finish. Fragrant
aromas and a flavoursome palate
characterize the monovarietal Merlot
Fiore 2010, with a streamlined finish. The
Chianti Classico 2013 is focused and
delicious, while the well-typed Vin Santo
del Chianti Classico 2008 displays lovely
hints of dried figs, dates and orange zest.

Castello di Monsanto

VIA MONSANTO, 8
50021 BARBERINO VAL D'ELSA [FI]
TEL. 0558059000
www.castellodimonsanto.it

CELLAR SALES
PRE-BOOKED VISITS
ANNUAL PRODUCTION 450,000 bottles
HECTARES UNDER VINE 72.00

Monsanto is one of the most charming
estates in Chianti Classico, representing
traditional and classic features in one of
the area's most coherent and rigorous
expressions. The wines, mainly aged in
large wood, are truly cellarable, polished
and elegant, at times a little austere and
not always immediately accessible. This
can only increase the charm of wines that
offer a good interpretation of the terroir,
Barberino
Val d'Elsa. The Chianti Classico Il Poggio
Riserva 2010 is a really great wine, with
subtle aromas and lovely flavour,
freshness and pace on the palate, polished
up with characterful tannic hardness. The
equally good Chianti Classico 2013 is
fragrant and tangy while the Chianti
Classico Riserva '12 is firm and austere.

● Chianti Cl. V. Casi Ris. '12	▼▼ 5
● Chianti Cl. '13	▼▼ 3
● Fiore '10	▼▼ 5
○ Vin Santo del Chianti Cl. '08	▼▼ 5
○ Vermentino '14	▼ 3
● Chianti Cl. Ris. '03	▼▼▼ 4
● Chianti Cl. V. Casi Ris. '11	▼▼▼ 5
● Borgaio '11	▼▼ 3
● Chianti Cl. '09	▼▼ 3
● Chianti Cl. Gran Sel. '10	▼▼ 6
● Chianti Cl. Pieve di Spaltenna '07	▼▼ 3
● Chianti Cl. V. Casi Ris. '07	▼▼ 5
● Chianti Cl. V. Casi Ris. '06	▼▼ 5
● Chianti Cl. V. Poggiarso Ris. '06	▼▼ 5
● Fiore '09	▼▼ 5
● Meletino '07	▼▼ 2*

● Chianti Cl. Il Poggio Ris. '10	▼▼▼ 8
● Chianti Cl. '13	▼▼ 3*
● Chianti Cl. Ris. '12	▼▼ 5
● Nemo '10	▼▼ 6
● Chianti Cl. 50 Vendemmie Ris. '12	▼ 6
● Chianti Cl. '11	▼▼▼ 3*
● Chianti Cl. Cinquantenario Ris. '08	▼▼▼ 6
● Chianti Cl. Il Poggio Ris. '06	▼▼▼ 6
● Chianti Cl. Il Poggio Ris. '88	▼▼▼ 5
● Chianti Cl. Ris. '11	▼▼▼ 5
● Nemo '01	▼▼▼ 6
● Chianti Cl. '12	▼▼ 3*
● Chianti Cl. Ris. '09	▼▼ 5

Castello di Poppiano

Fraz. Poppiano
Via Fezzana, 45
50025 Montespertoli [FI]
Tel. 05582315
www.guicciardini1199.it

CELLAR SALES
PRE-BOOKED VISITS
ANNUAL PRODUCTION 270,000 bottles
HECTARES UNDER VINE 130.00

"For me, inheriting Castello di Poppiano in the Chianti Colli Fiorentini area, represents the heritage of the Guicciardini family since the 11th century," says current owner Francesco Guicciardini for whom the production of wine, olive oil and other crops has been in the family's DNA for generations. The castle, a powerful Medieval construction with three rings of walls, is a symbol of the strength shown in care for the vineyards and the use of new production techniques, while preserving the oldest parts of the estate intact. The family's wine-related dreams are also coming true in the area of Morellino di Scansano. Through to the finals for the Chianti Colli Fiorentini Riserva 2012 with complex aromas, nicely varied fruit softened by hints of cinnamon and cloves and a pleasing flavour and marked lingering fragrance. The rest of the range is good, and La Historia 2012, a Merlot, stands out for its complexity.

Castello di Potentino

Loc. Potentino, 6
58038 Seggiano [GR]
Tel. 0564950014
www.potentino.com

CELLAR SALES
PRE-BOOKED VISITS
ACCOMMODATION
ANNUAL PRODUCTION 20,000 bottles
HECTARES UNDER VINE 4.00

Castello di Potentino is a remarkable location, splendid and inaccessible, and above all identifies Charlotte Horton's highly original winegrowing project. About 30 kilometres from Montalcino, the general conditions are, however, very different from those in Brunello itself. Potentino is as agreeable as it is unspoilt, a fantastic landscape, its climate influenced by Mount Amiata. The vineyards are planted on steep land and the wines are coherent, mineral and vibrant. The excellent Sacromonte 2011, a monovarietal Sangiovese, is fermented and matured for two years in 50-hectolitre French oak barrels. This generous wine has lovely mature aromas of leather, tobacco and red berries. This is a bony, minimal wine capable of positive vibrations and food-friendly.

● Chianti Colli Fiorentini Ris. '12	♥♥ 4
● Chianti Colli Fiorentini Il Cortile '13	♥♥ 2*
● La Historia '12	♥♥ 5
● Syrah '13	♥♥ 3
● Toscoforte '13	♥♥ 3
● Tricorno '12	♥♥ 6
○ Vin Santo della Torre Grande del Chianti '07	♥♥ 5
⊙ Campo Segreto '14	♥ 2
● Morellino di Scansano I Massi '13	♥ 3
● Morellino di Scansano Massi di Mandorlaia Ris. '12	♥ 4
⊙ Rosato della Costa '14	♥ 2
○ Vermentino Massi di Mandorlaia '14	♥ 2
● Chianti Colli Fiorentini Il Cortile '12	♥♥ 2*
● Chianti Colli Fiorentini Ris. '11	♥♥ 4

● Sacromonte '11	♥♥ 3*
● Piropo '11	♥♥ 4
⊙ Jaspidem '12	♥ 2
● Balaxus '08	♥♥ 3
● Piropo '10	♥♥ 4
● Sacromonte '10	♥♥ 3*

Castello di Querceto

LOC. QUERCETO
VIA A. FRANÇOIS, 2
50020 GREVE IN CHIANTI [FI]
TEL. 05585921
www.castellodiquerceto.it

CELLAR SALES
PRE-BOOKED VISITS
ACCOMMODATION
ANNUAL PRODUCTION 600,000 bottles
HECTARES UNDER VINE 60.00

Castello di Querceto is in the subzone of Greve in Chianti. The 60 hectares of vineyards are planted at altitudes of up to 500 metres. Since 1978 the estate has been in the hands of Alessandro and Maria Antonietta François. Meticulous care is applied in the vineyards, avoiding forcing. The style pursues ripeness of the fruit and the considerable support of oak, with small or large barrels depending on the type of wine, which sometimes penalizes the personality of the wines although they never fail to display flawless technique. The Chianti Classico Riserva 2012 is really well-made with lush fruit and spicy aromas, and a succulent, dynamic palate. The Chianti Classico Il Picchio Gran Selezione 2012 has a few hard edges that need softening in the flavour, but the palate is sweet and generous. Black berries rule the nose of the Chianti Classico 2013, a full-bodied and relaxed wine.

● Chianti Cl. Ris. '12	♟♟ 4
● Chianti Cl. '13	♟♟ 3
● Chianti Cl. Il Picchio Gran Sel. '12	♟♟ 6
● Cignale '11	♟ 7
● La Corte '11	♟ 5
● Chianti Cl. Il Picchio Ris. '07	♟♟ 5
● Chianti Cl. Il Picchio Ris. '06	♟♟ 5
● Chianti Cl. Il Picchio Ris. '03	♟♟ 5
● Chianti Cl. Ris. '06	♟♟ 4
● Chianti Cl. Ris. '05	♟♟ 4
● Chianti Cl. Ris. '04	♟♟ 4
● Chianti Cl. Ris. '03	♟♟ 4
● Chianti Cl. Ris. '01	♟♟ 4
■ Il Sole di Alessandro '04	♟♟ 7
● La Corte '98	♟♟ 6

Castello di Radda

LOC. IL BECCO
53017 RADDA IN CHIANTI [SI]
TEL. 0577738992
www.castellodiradda.it

CELLAR SALES
PRE-BOOKED VISITS
ANNUAL PRODUCTION 100,000 bottles
HECTARES UNDER VINE 32.50

The Gussalli Beretta group is a farming business headed by the Beretta family, and includes Lo Sparviere in Franciacorta, Orlando Contucci Ponnio in Abruzzo, and Castello di Radda, which has already attracted attention with its very interesting wines. A combination of vineyards planted at different times and minimal interventions in the cellar where ageing is measured with care, are the main features of a traditional winery style that produces subtle, elegant wines that reflect the terroir accurately. The 2012 Chianti Classico Riserva is probably among the very best of its type: a clearly defined, vibrant nose and a fluent, nicely progressive and nuanced palate. The aromas in the Chianti Classico Gran Selezione 2011 are slightly hidden by the oak, and the flavour is sweet and lively. The Granbruno 2014 is accessibly delicious, made from sangiovese from the younger vineyards.

● Chianti Cl. Ris. '12	♟♟♟ 5
● Chianti Cl. Gran Sel. '11	♟♟ 3
● Granbruno '14	♟ 3
● Chianti Cl. Ris. '11	♟♟ 6
● Chianti Cl. Ris. '07	♟♟ 5
● Chianti Cl. Gran Sel. '10	♟♟ 3
● Chianti Cl. Poggio Selvale Ris. '09	♟♟ 4
● Chianti Cl. Ris. '10	♟♟ 6
● Guss '11	♟♟ 6

Castello di Sonnino

VIA VOLTERRANA NORD, 6A
50025 MONTESPERTOLI [FI]
TEL. 0571609198
www.castellosonnino.it

CELLAR SALES
PRE-BOOKED VISITS
ACCOMMODATION
ANNUAL PRODUCTION 250,000 bottles
HECTARES UNDER VINE 40.00

Castello di Sonnino has belonged to the De Renzis family since the early 19th century, but Alessandro and Caterina can take the credit for having restarted the winegrowing business at a high level of quality as well as for the recovery of the property, through lengthy and meticulous restoration work, making it possible to continue using the old cellars and beautiful vin santo barrel cellar, which is certainly worth a visit. This is a very important estate for the Chianti Montespertoli area, producing classic, traditional wines with just a few concessions to international grape varieties. The deliciously fragrant Chianti Montespertoli Sonnino 2014 exactly meets our expectations for a wine from this DOC zone. Red berry aromas with subtle hints of medicinal herbs and freshly mown grass, and a succulent, relaxed, flavoursome palate with pungent tannin in the finish. The Leone Rosso 2014 shows good structure and a nice mouthfilling finish.

Castello di Vicchiomaggio

LOC. LE BOLLE
VIA VICCHIOMAGGIO, 4
50022 GREVE IN CHIANTI [FI]
TEL. 055854079
www.vicchiomaggio.it

CELLAR SALES
PRE-BOOKED VISITS
ACCOMMODATION AND RESTAURANT SERVICE
ANNUAL PRODUCTION 300,000 bottles
HECTARES UNDER VINE 38.00
SUSTAINABLE WINERY

Castello di Vicchiomaggio, owned by the Matta family since 1964, steered towards fine quality winegrowing back in 1982 and has gradually become one of the leading wine estates in the Greve in Chianti area with increasingly impressive wines. Today, they show promisingly consistent and reliable quality, with no lack of character. Flawlessly well-made with lovely texture, they are aged in large oak or barriques, according to their type. The Chianti Classico Vigna La Prima Gran Selezione 2011 is beautifully stylish with accomplished aromas and a measured palate with some extension and nuancing. The delicious Chianti Classico San Jacopo 2013 has lively flavour and fragrant aromas. The Chianti Classico Agostina Pieri Riserva 2012 is a little too harsh while the Ripa delle More 2012, from sangiovese, cabernet sauvignon and merlot, is still marked by the oak.

● Chianti Montespertoli Sonnino '14	♥♥ 2*
● Leone Rosso '14	♥♥ 2*
● Chianti Montespertoli C astello di Montespertoli Ris. '11	♥ 3
○ Virginio '14	♥ 2
● Cantinino '09	♥♥ 4
● Cantinino '08	♥♥ 5
● Chianti Montespertoli '13	♥♥ 2*
● Leone Rosso '10	♥♥ 2

● Chianti Cl. La Prima Gran Sel. '11	♥♥ 5
● Chianti Cl. San Jacopo da Vicchiomaggio '13	♥♥ 3
● Chianti Cl. Agostino Petri da Vicchiomaggio Ris. '12	♥ 5
● Maremma Toscana Colle Alto Villa Vallemaggiore '13	♥ 3
● Ripa delle More '12	♥ 5
● Chianti Cl. Vigna La Prima Gran Sel. '10	♥♥♥ 7
● FSM '07	♥♥♥ 8
● FSM '04	♥♥♥ 5
● Ripa delle More '97	♥♥♥ 6
● Ripa delle More '94	♥♥♥ 7
● Chianti Cl. Agostino Petri da Vicchiomaggio Ris. '10	♥♥ 5

Castello di Volpaia

LOC. VOLPAIA
53017 RADDA IN CHIANTI [SI]
TEL. 0577738066
www.volpaia.com

CELLAR SALES
PRE-BOOKED VISITS
ACCOMMODATION AND RESTAURANT SERVICE
ANNUAL PRODUCTION 200,000 bottles
HECTARES UNDER VINE 46.00
VITICULTURE METHOD Certified Organic
SUSTAINABLE WINERY

The Mascheroni Stianti family not only deserves credit for preserving one of the most beautiful corners of Chianti Classico but also, and above all, for moulding their wine production in the image and likeness of that village. These are flawlessly made wines with a modern style, able to express both marked personality and the typical features of the huskiest Chianti Classicos, with very judicious use of oak and a fresh flavour that does not disguise the origins of the grapes, even those planted at 500 metres. Fresh, nuanced aromas characterize the Chianti Classico 2013 which shows light, tangy and contrasting flavour. Some over-mature hints on the nose of the Chianti Classico Il Puro Vigneto Casanova Gran Selezione 2010, while the palate is deep and progressive. The Chianti Classico Coltassala Riserva 2011 is firm and nicely coordinated while the Chianti Classico Riserva 2012 is generous, soft and fragrant.

Castello Romitorio

LOC. ROMITORIO, 279
53024 MONTALCINO [SI]
TEL. 0577847212
www.castelloromitorio.com

CELLAR SALES
PRE-BOOKED VISITS
ACCOMMODATION
ANNUAL PRODUCTION 150,000 bottles
HECTARES UNDER VINE 15.00

Castello Romitorio wines are considered to be among Sandro Chia's best recent works of art. This artist-producer, often referred to as one of the greatest exponents of the Transavantgarde, has embraced Montalcino wine production with great intelligence, at every vintage adding another layer of consistency and stylistic identity. It all revolves around a plot of about 15 hectares in the western part of the DOC zone, with other plots in the Chianti Senese and Morellino di Scansano areas. The winemaking choices place his Brunellos among those in a more modernist style but in the glass they express a somewhat less schematic nature. Just try the surprising 2010 version: roots, beet tops, a hint of blood-rich meat, and oaky sensations nicely integrated in the harmonious, edgy, flavoursome palate, with fine-grained tannins. This is contemporary Brunello in the best possible sense, deserving Tre Bicchieri.

Wine	Rating
● Chianti Cl. '13	♈♈♈ 3*
● Chianti Cl. Coltassala Ris. '11	♈♈ 7
● Chianti Cl. Il Puro Vign. Casanova Gran Sel. '10	♈♈ 8
● Chianti Cl. Ris. '12	♈♈ 5
● Balifico '00	♉♉♉ 6
● Chianti Cl. Coltassala Ris. '04	♉♉♉ 6
● Chianti Cl. Coltassala Ris. '01	♉♉♉ 6
● Chianti Cl. Il Puro Vign. Casanova Ris. '08	♉♉♉ 8
● Chianti Cl. Il Puro Vign. Casanova Ris. '06	♉♉♉ 8
● Chianti Cl. Ris. '10	♉♉♉ 5
● Chianti Cl. Ris. '08	♉♉♉ 5
● Chianti Cl. Ris. '07	♉♉♉ 5
● Balifico '06	♉♉ 6

Wine	Rating
● Brunello di Montalcino '10	♈♈♈ 8
● Brunello di Montalcino Filo di Seta '10	♈♈ 8
○ Costanza '14	♈ 3
● Il Toro '11	♈ 3
● Morellino di Scansano Blu Label '14	♈ 3
● Rosso di Montalcino '13	♈ 5
● Sant'Antimo Rosso Romito del Romitorio '11	♈ 4
● Brunello di Montalcino '05	♉♉♉ 8
● Brunello di Montalcino Ris. '97	♉♉♉ 8
● Brunello di Montalcino '09	♉♉ 8
● Brunello di Montalcino '07	♉♉ 7
● Brunello di Montalcino XXV Vendemmia '06	♉♉ 8
● Rosso di Montalcino '12	♉♉ 5
● Rosso di Montalcino '10	♉♉ 4

Castelvecchi

LOC. CASTELVECCHI
53017 RADDA IN CHIANTI [SI]
TEL. 0577735612
www.chianticastelvecchi.it

CELLAR SALES
PRE-BOOKED VISITS
ACCOMMODATION AND RESTAURANT SERVICE
ANNUAL PRODUCTION 70,000 bottles
HECTARES UNDER VINE 18.00
SUSTAINABLE WINERY

The estate owned by the Paladin family from Veneto is at Radda in Chianti, with vineyards in two separate areas: one near the village of Vescine, in the south, by the border with Castellina in Chianti; the other, Tenuta Castelvecchi, is to the north, in the heart of this unique Chianti Classico subzone. The wines reveal a stylistic identity that favours balance above all, consistently faithful to the terroir. Both large and small oak is used with judicious care for ageing although sometimes it does make a marked impact the lovely fruit. The interesting Chianti Classico Madonnino della Pieve Gran Selezione 2011 has subtly fruity aromas and a firm, well-paced flavour. The Chianti Lodolaio Riserva 2011 is more austere with mature red fruit aromas and a rounded, soft flavour. The Chianti Classico Capotondo 2012 is supple on the palate.

Castelvecchio

LOC. SAN PANCRAZIO
VIA CERTALDESE, 30
50026 SAN CASCIANO IN VAL DI PESA [FI]
TEL. 0558248032
www.castelvecchio.it

CELLAR SALES
PRE-BOOKED VISITS
ACCOMMODATION
ANNUAL PRODUCTION 120,000 bottles
HECTARES UNDER VINE 22.00
VITICULTURE METHOD Certified Organic
SUSTAINABLE WINERY

An estate with venerable origins, known to be a farm in the 12th century, part of Cavalcanti family heritage. Current owners, the Rocchi family, bought it in the 1960s and Renzo restored the farmhouse to its former splendour, making it the heart of the estate, planted the vineyards, and built a cellar to start up wine production. In 1993 his grandchildren Filippo and Stefania joined the business, marking the definitive move towards fine quality wine production. Filippo spends his time between the vineyards and the cellar while Stefania is in charge of the commercial side. The same passion and attention to detail is applied to the agritourism facility. Back to the finals for Il Brecciolino 2012, a blend of sangiovese, merlot and petit verdot with enthralling aromas of spices and aromatic herbs, and a fluent, nicely lively body. The very interesting Numero Otto 2013, from canaiolo, shows unusual aromas and a compelling structure.

● Chianti Cl. Lodolaio Ris. '11	♟♟ 6
● Chianti Cl. Madonnino della Pieve Gran Sel. Tenute di Castelvecchi '12	♟♟ 5
● Chianti Cl. Capotondo '12	♟ 5
● Chianti Cl. '07	♟♟ 3
● Chianti Cl. Capotondo '11	♟♟ 3
● Chianti Cl. Lodolaio Ris. '10	♟♟ 5
● Chianti Cl. Lodolaio Ris. '09	♟♟ 5
● Chianti Cl. Lodolaio Ris. '08	♟♟ 6
● Chianti Cl. Lodolaio Ris. '07	♟♟ 6
● Chianti Cl. Madonnino della Pieve Gran Sel. Tenute di Castelvecchi '10	♟♟ 5
● Chianti Cl. Tenuta Castelvecchi Ris. '09	♟♟ 4
● Chianti Cl. Tenute di Castelvecchi '10	♟♟ 5
● Chianti Cl. Tenute di Castelvecchi '09	♟♟ 6
● Chianti Cl. Tenute di Castelvecchi '08	♟♟ 6

● Il Brecciolino '12	♟♟ 5
○ Vin Santo del Chianti Chiacchierata Notturna '04	♟♟ 6
● Chianti Colli Fiorentini Il Castelvecchio '13	♟♟ 2*
● Numero Otto '13	♟♟ 3
● Chianti Santa Caterina '13	♟ 2
● Il Brecciolino '11	♟♟♟ 5
● Il Brecciolino '09	♟♟ 5
● Il Brecciolino '08	♟♟ 5
● Il Brecciolino '07	♟♟ 5
● Il Brecciolino '04	♟♟ 5
● Numero Otto '07	♟♟ 3
● Vin Santo del Chianti Chiacchierata Notturna '03	♟♟ 6

Famiglia Cecchi

LOC. CASINA DEI PONTI, 56
53011 CASTELLINA IN CHIANTI [SI]
TEL. 057754311
www.cecchi.net

PRE-BOOKED VISITS
ANNUAL PRODUCTION 8,000,000 bottles
HECTARES UNDER VINE 330.00
SUSTAINABLE WINERY

Since 1893 the Cecchi family has played a
leading role in the Tuscan and national
winemaking sector: first as wine merchants
and later, with increasing commitment,
following the path of quality with the
gradual acquisition of vineyards and
estates. These include, in Tuscany, Castello
di Montauto at San Gimignano and Val dele
Rose in Maremma. Of course, the
quantities are those of a large-scale winery
but it is possible to identify with reassuring
continuity wines with considerable
personality and expression in the
well-stocked range. The firm and succulent
Chianti Classico Villa Cerna Riserva 2012
has well-coordinated, clear-cut aromas.
The beautifully drinkable Chianti Classico
Storia di Famiglia 2012 has clean aromas
and a slender, vigorous palate. The Merlot
La Mora 2013 produced in Maremma is
vibrant and fragrant. The Chianti Classico
Villa Cerna 2013 is delicious and
well-made while the Chianti Classico
Riserva di Famiglia 2012 is generous and
nuanced.

● Chianti Cl. Villa Cerna Ris. '12	♙♙♙	5
● Chianti Cl. Storia di Famiglia '12	♙♙	3*
● Merlot La Mora '13	♙♙	4
● Chianti Cl. Riserva di Famiglia '12	♙♙	5
● Chianti Cl. Villa Cerna '13	♙♙	3
○ Litorale '14	♙♙	3
● Morellino di Scansano Val delle Rose '13	♙♙	3
○ Vernaccia di S. Gimignano Castello di Montauto '14	♙♙	3
● Chianti Castello di Montauto '13	♙	2
● Morellino di Scansano Poggio al Leone Val delle Rose Ris. '11	♙	4
● Chianti Cl. Riserva di Famiglia '07	♙♙♙	5
● Chianti Cl. Villa Cerna Ris. '08	♙♙♙	5
● Coevo '11	♙♙♙	8
● Coevo '10	♙♙♙	7
● Coevo '06	♙♙♙	7

Centolani

LOC. FRIGGIALI
S.DA MAREMMANA
53024 MONTALCINO [SI]
TEL. 0577849454
www.tenutafriggialiepietranera.it

CELLAR SALES
PRE-BOOKED VISITS
ACCOMMODATION
ANNUAL PRODUCTION 260,000 bottles
HECTARES UNDER VINE 70.00

Two farms with fundamentally
complementary features form the backdrop
for the Peluso-Centolani family's wine
production. Tenuta Friggiali, in the western
part of the DOC zone, consists of three
large plots situated at 250–450 metres in
altitude on mostly loose-textured soil. A
short distance from the abbey of
Sant'Antimo, Tenuta Pietranera is the basis
of weightier Brunellos due to the combined
effect of lower altitudes and more compact
soil, in which marl combines with veins of
silt and clay. Differences in terrain which,
however, share a clear stylistic feature in
the cellar, mostly based on ageing in 30-
and 50-hectolitre oak. This round of
tastings lacked a top note but the overall
performance was very impressive. The
Brunello Tenuta Friggiali 2010 is the most
exuberant and scrumptious, with hints of
blueberries and flowers, while the
Pietranera from the same year is a perfect
alter ego, with confident spice and a more
forward toasty sensation.

● Brunello di Montalcino Pietranera '10	♙♙	5
● Brunello di Montalcino Poggiotondo '10	♙♙	5
● Brunello di Montalcino Tenuta Friggiali '10	♙♙	5
● Rosso di Montalcino Pietranera '13	♙	3
● Brunello di Montalcino Tenuta Friggiali '04	♙♙♙	5
● Brunello di Montalcino Tenuta Friggiali Ris. '99	♙♙♙	7
● Brunello di Montalcino Poggiotondo '09	♙♙	5
● Brunello di Montalcino Tenuta Friggiali '09	♙♙	5
● Brunello di Montalcino Tenuta Friggiali '08	♙♙	5
● Brunello di Montalcino Tenuta Friggiali Ris. '07	♙♙	6

Ceralti

VIA DEI CERALTI, 77
57022 CASTAGNETO CARDUCCI [LI]
TEL. 0565763989
www.ceralti.com

CELLAR SALES
PRE-BOOKED VISITS
ACCOMMODATION
ANNUAL PRODUCTION 50,000 bottles
HECTARES UNDER VINE 9.00
VITICULTURE METHOD Certified Organic

The small Bolgheri estates keep pace easily
with the large brand names filling the DOC
zone. Ceralti, in our opinion, offers one of
the clearest and most brilliant examples of
this. The Rutili family is at the helm,
involved in every phase of the productive
and commercial process. The basis of the
range of products consists of lush
vineyards on the hills between Castagneto
Carducci and Bolgheri. Once again, we
found the wines to be prestigiously made
with good personality. The best of the
bunch is the Bolgheri Alfeo 2012, with its
fresh, youthful sensations. Almost heady,
nicely vibrant aromas that find some
complexity in the subtle grassy sensations.
The palate shows nicely weighty, dark fruity
texture with a distinctive long and slightly
alcoholic finish. To us, Scirè 2013 seemed
to be a developing wine, with forward
sensations of blood-rich meat, still pursuing
full definition.

● Bolgheri Scirè '13	♥♥	3
● Bolgheri Sup. Alfeo '12	♥♥	5
○ Bolgheri Vermentino '14	♥♥	3
● Bolgheri Rosso Alfeo '03	♀♀	4
● Bolgheri Scirè '11	♀♀	3
● Bolgheri Sup. Alfeo '11	♀♀	5
● Bolgheri Sup. Alfeo '10	♀♀	5
● Bolgheri Sup. Sonoro '11	♀♀	7
○ Bolgheri Vermentino Ceralti '04	♀♀	2

★La Cerbaiola

P.ZZA CAVOUR, 19
53024 MONTALCINO [SI]
TEL. 0577848499
www.aziendasalvioni.com

PRE-BOOKED VISITS
RESTAURANT SERVICE
ANNUAL PRODUCTION 15,000 bottles
HECTARES UNDER VINE 4.00

A single plot of four hectares located at an
altitude of about 400 metres at Cerbaie
Alte in the north-eastern part of Montalcino.
Here, in less than 30 years, Giulio Salvioni
has become one of the best-known and
best-loved exponents of Brunello, helped by
his wife Mirella and more recently by his
children David and Alessia. The tough,
marly consistency of the soil helps define
the dour, restless character of his
sangioveses but technical details alone are
not sufficient to explain the truly inimitable
style. These are classic yet anarchic wines,
the result of spontaneous fermentation and
ageing in 20-hectolitre Slavonian oak. In
many ways, a cautious assessment of the
Salvioni Brunello 2010, which has given
fluctuating performances in the various
stages of tasting. But the best bottles win
us over with their brilliance and balsamic
strength, as well as the invigorating,
austere flavour, livened up by the
boisterous tanginess.

● Brunello di Montalcino '10	♥♥	8
● Brunello di Montalcino '09	♀♀♀	8
● Brunello di Montalcino '06	♀♀♀	8
● Brunello di Montalcino '04	♀♀♀	8
● Brunello di Montalcino '00	♀♀♀	8
● Brunello di Montalcino '99	♀♀♀	8
● Brunello di Montalcino '97	♀♀♀	8
● Brunello di Montalcino '08	♀♀	8
● Brunello di Montalcino '07	♀♀	8
● Brunello di Montalcino '05	♀♀	8
● Brunello di Montalcino '03	♀♀	8
● Brunello di Montalcino '01	♀♀	8
● Brunello di Montalcino '98	♀♀	8

Vincenzo Cesani

Loc. Pancole, 82d
53037 San Gimignano [SI]
Tel. 0577955084
www.cesani.it

CELLAR SALES
PRE-BOOKED VISITS
ACCOMMODATION
ANNUAL PRODUCTION 100,000 bottles
HECTARES UNDER VINE 21.00
VITICULTURE METHOD Certified Organic

The Cesani family, originally from the
Marche region, moved to Tuscany in the
1950s. The post-war period was one of
great change and it was common for
people to seek new places and
inspirations. Vincenzo Cesani was the one
who believed deeply in the potential of the
land and tried to farm vineyards respecting
the environment while producing quality
wines. This long journey did bear fruit:
today, the whole family is involved in the
farming business and agritourism, with
daughter Letizia in the frontline, currently
covering the role of Chair of the Consorzio
della Vernaccia. The Vernaccia Sanice
Riserva 2012 is through to the finals with
fragrant pot-pourri aromas alongside ripe
white peach fruit and light hints of
aromatic herbs. The palate is appetizing
and mouthfilling with fresh sensations
adding verve and a well-paced finish with
measured tanginess.

Giovanni Chiappini

Loc. Felciaino
via Bolgherese, 189c
57020 Bolgheri [LI]
Tel. 0565765201
www.giovannichiappini.it

CELLAR SALES
PRE-BOOKED VISITS
ANNUAL PRODUCTION 70,000 bottles
HECTARES UNDER VINE 23.00
VITICULTURE METHOD Certified Organic
SUSTAINABLE WINERY

This small model winery is certainly one of
the most fascinating in the Bolgheri area. It
all began very simply thanks to Giovanni
Chiappini, the son of country folk from the
Marche region who moved to Bolgheri in
the 1950s, and the work is continued
brilliantly today with the help of his
daughters Martina and Lisa. The 23-odd
hectares of vineyards are divided into farms
which often produce separate wines. The
leading varieties are cabernet sauvignon
and franc, merlot, petit verdot and, to a
lesser extent, sangiovese and vermentino.
Since 2010 the vineyards have been
organically farmed. The Bolgheri Superiore
Guado de' Gemoli 2012 is really very good.
It opens on sweet, subtle ripe cherry
sensations, enfolded in herbal hints of bay
leaves and verbena: a beautifully complex,
balanced and lingering red wine with a
piquant, strikingly original finish. The Lienà
Cabernet Franc is as well-typed as ever
with lovely grassy sensations.

○ Vernaccia di S. Gimignano Sanice Ris. '12	▼▼ 3*
● Luenzo '11	▼▼ 4
● San Gimignano Rosso Cellori '09	▼▼ 4
● Serisè '12	▼ 3
● Chianti Colli Senesi '14	▼ 2
⊙ Serarosa '14	▼ 2
○ Vernaccia di S. Gimignano '14	▼ 2
● Chianti Colli Senesi '13	♀♀ 2*
● Luenzo '02	♀♀ 5
● Luenzo '01	♀♀ 5
● San Gimignano Rosso Cellori '04	♀♀ 4
○ Vernaccia di S. Gimignano '12	♀♀ 2*
○ Vernaccia di S. Gimignano Sanice '11	♀♀ 2*
○ Vernaccia di S. Gimignano Sanice '09	♀♀ 3*
○ Vernaccia di S. Gimignano Sanice '08	♀♀ 3*

● Bolgheri Sup. Guado de' Gemoli '12	▼▼ 8
● Bolgheri Felciaino '13	▼▼ 4
● Lienà Cabernet Franc '12	▼▼ 8
● Bolgheri Rosso Felciaino '12	♀♀ 3
● Bolgheri Rosso Felciaino '09	♀♀ 2*
● Bolgheri Rosso Ferrugini '11	♀♀ 3
● Bolgheri Sup. Gaudo de' Gemoli '09	♀♀ 6
● Bolgheri Sup. Gaudo de' Gemoli '08	♀♀ 6
● Bolgheri Sup. Gaudo de' Gemoli '07	♀♀ 6
● Lienà Cabernet Franc '11	♀♀ 7
● Lienà Cabernet Franc '10	♀♀ 7
● Lienà Cabernet Franc '09	♀♀ 7
● Lienà Cabernet Franc '08	♀♀ 7
● Lienà Cabernet Sauvignon '11	♀♀ 7
● Lienà Cabernet Sauvignon '10	♀♀ 7
● Lienà Cabernet Sauvignon '09	♀♀ 7
● Lienà Cabernet Sauvignon '08	♀♀ 7

Le Chiuse

LOC. PULLERA, 228
53024 MONTALCINO [SI]
TEL. 055597052
www.lechiuse.com

CELLAR SALES
PRE-BOOKED VISITS
ACCOMMODATION
ANNUAL PRODUCTION 30,000 bottles
HECTARES UNDER VINE 8.00
VITICULTURE METHOD Certified Organic

Although it has yet to celebrate 30 bottled harvests, the estate run by Simonetta Valiani and Nicolà Magnelli has long been considered one of the brightest stars on the Montalcino production scene. The true "Le Chiuse style" highlights the long-standing vocation of this estate, inherited on the passing of Fiorella Biondi Santi and used for a long time to make the Il Greppo Riservas. The six or so hectares are all located in the northern area opposite the Montosoli hill, organically farmed and planted with sangiovese. In the cellar, spontaneous fermentation, lengthy maceration and ageing in 20-, 30- and 50-hectolitre oak. Complex and multifaceted despite the odd reductive flaw, Le Chiuse's 2010 Brunello has everything we could wish for in a champ. Fragrant fruit, prestigious hints of damp earth and iodine, and accomplished on the palate with acidity and flavour, hinting above all at significant ageing potential.

Cigliano

VIA CIGLIANO, 17
50026 SAN CASCIANO IN VAL DI PESA [FI]
TEL. 055820033
www.villadelcigliano.it

CELLAR SALES
PRE-BOOKED VISITS
ANNUAL PRODUCTION 40,000 bottles
HECTARES UNDER VINE 25.00

The Maccaferri Montecchi family, who descend from a branch of the Antinori family, own this estate in San Casciano Val di Pesa on the nearest Chianti Classico slopes to Florence. The estate aims to produces wines with a clear connection to the terroir, despite some slight blips in consistent quality. The wines tend to be lean and very classic in style, thanks to good work in the vineyard and measured procedures in the cellar, where the wines are aged in concrete vats and large oak. The Chianti Classico Cigliano 2012 has clear, defined aromas and a slender, tangy, well-paced palate, nicely polished with pleasant hardness. The Chianti Classico Riserva 2011 does not disappoint either: a subtly fragrant noise and particularly fresh acidic verve which extends the depth and length of the flavour. The Suganella 2011, a blend of sangiovese, cabernet sauvignon and merlot, is more cropped.

● Brunello di Montalcino '10	♟♟♟ 7
● Brunello di Montalcino Ris. '09	♟♟ 8
● Rosso di Montalcino '13	♟♟ 4
● Brunello di Montalcino '07	♟♟♟ 7
● Brunello di Montalcino Ris. '07	♟♟♟ 8
● Brunello di Montalcino '09	♟♟ 7
● Brunello di Montalcino '08	♟♟ 7
● Brunello di Montalcino '06	♟♟ 6
● Brunello di Montalcino Ris. '06	♟♟ 8
● Rosso di Montalcino '12	♟♟ 4
● Rosso di Montalcino '11	♟♟ 4
● Rosso di Montalcino '10	♟♟ 3

● Chianti Cl. Cigliano '12	♟♟ 3*
● Chianti Cl. Villa Cigliano Ris. '11	♟♟ 4
● Suganella '11	♟ 4
● Chianti Cl. '10	♟♟ 2*
● Chianti Cl. '07	♟♟ 2*
● Chianti Cl. Cigliano '11	♟♟ 3
● Chianti Cl. Ris. '99	♟♟ 3
● Chianti Cl. Villa Cigliano Ris. '09	♟♟ 4
● Suganella '06	♟♟ 4

Fattoria di Cinciano

LOC. CINCIANO, 2
53036 POGGIBONSI [SI]
TEL. 0577936588
www.cinciano.it

ANNUAL PRODUCTION 70,000 bottles
HECTARES UNDER VINE 25.00

Fattoria di Cinciano is situated in the Chianti Classico DOC zone, near Poggibonsi. Thanks also to renewal of the vineyards and more judicious use of mainly small oak casks to age the wines, the winery style seems more defined today, showing personality and coherent links to the wines' terroir of origin. There is probably still work to be done on continuity of quality, which needs to be consolidated, but the estate seems to be on the right path and the wines do not lack pleasing, drinkable qualities and elegant style. The Chianti Classico Riserva 2012 has a nuanced flavour, good pace and a lovely tang, while the aromas are well-defined and fragrant. Those in the Chianti Classico Gran Selezione 2011 are more concealed but the wine opens out rounded and nuanced on the palate. The well-made Chianti Classico 2013 has floral, damp earth aromas and a subtle, fluent palate.

Le Cinciole

VIA CASE SPARSE, 83
50020 PANZANO [FI]
TEL. 055852636
www.lecinciole.it

CELLAR SALES
PRE-BOOKED VISITS
ANNUAL PRODUCTION 45,000 bottles
HECTARES UNDER VINE 11.00
VITICULTURE METHOD Certified Organic

Organically farmed vineyards planted at high altitudes, some over 400 metres, and ageing in large and small oak. This is the basic picture of this small but interesting estate run by Luca and Valeria Orsini, with the not insignificant support of Panzano, one of the most enchanting terroirs and subzones of Chianti Classico. The estate's style is clearly defined by fresh-tasting and ageable wines, often with pleasantly hard features. The Chianti Classico 2012 certainly shines among the best of its year. The complex aromas hint at flowers, herbs and even stony sensations. The palate moves along at a good pace, with nuancing and plenty of freshness enhancing the enjoyable flavour. Delicious, to say the least. The well-coordinated, fragrant and very tangy Cinciorosso 2012 is a blend of sangiovese, cabernet sauvignon, syrah and merlot, while the monovarietal Sangiovese Petresco 2010 is succulent and vigorous.

● Chianti Cl. Gran Sel. '11	♟♟ 5
● Chianti Cl. Ris. '12	♟♟ 3*
● Chianti Cl. '13	♟ 3
● Chianti Cl. '12	♟♟ 3
● Chianti Cl. '11	♟♟ 3
● Chianti Cl. '06	♟♟ 3
● Chianti Cl. Ris. '11	♟♟ 3
● Chianti Cl. Ris. '10	♟♟ 3*
● Chianti Cl. Ris. '06	♟♟ 4
● Chianti Cl. Ris. '05	♟♟ 4
● Pietraforte '11	♟♟ 2*
● Pietraforte '07	♟♟ 4

● Chianti Cl. '12	♟♟♟ 3*
● Cinciorosso '12	♟♟ 3
● Petresco '10	♟♟ 5
● Camalaione '04	♟♟♟ 7
● Chianti Cl. Petresco Ris. '01	♟♟♟ 5
● Camalaione '06	♟♟ 7
● Camalaione '03	♟♟ 6
● Chianti Cl. '11	♟♟ 3
● Chianti Cl. '10	♟♟ 3
● Chianti Cl. '04	♟♟ 3
● Chianti Cl. '01	♟♟ 3
● Chianti Cl. Petresco Ris. '08	♟♟ 5
● Chianti Cl. Petresco Ris. '07	♟♟ 5
● Chianti Cl. Petresco Ris. '05	♟♟ 5
● Chianti Cl. Petresco Ris. '04	♟♟ 5
⊙ Rosato '13	♟♟ 2*

Donatella Cinelli Colombini

LOC. CASATO, 17
53024 MONTALCINO [SI]
TEL. 0577662108
www.cinellicolombini.it

CELLAR SALES
PRE-BOOKED VISITS
ACCOMMODATION AND RESTAURANT SERVICE
ANNUAL PRODUCTION 120,000 bottles
HECTARES UNDER VINE 34.00

Donatella Cinelli Colombini is an emblematic figure in female winemaking. Founder of the Wine Tourism Movement, creator of Cantine Aperte, and university professor specializing in wine marketing, she left the family estate in 1998 to set up her own Fattoria del Colle at Trequanda and Casato Prime Donne at Montalcino, one of the first estates to be run entirely by women. Her Brunellos are shaped by the vineyards in the northern part of the DOC zone, revealing a sober, modern element in the ripe fruit and smoky, spicy qualities from the oak used for ageing, of different sizes and origins. These stylistic impressions are confirmed by the latest tastings which bring the apparently simpler range into the spotlight, starting with the remarkably solid Rosso 2012. The basic version wins the challenge against the 2010 Brunellos thanks to its fresh, mouthfilling profile, slightly penalized in the more mature Prime Donne.

● Brunello di Montalcino '10	♈♈ 5
● Rosso di Montalcino '12	♈♈ 3
● Brunello di Montalcino Prime Donne '10	♈ 6
● Brunello di Montalcino Prime Donne '01	♈♈♈ 6
● Brunello di Montalcino '09	♈♈ 5
● Brunello di Montalcino Prime Donne '08	♈♈ 6
● Brunello di Montalcino Prime Donne '07	♈♈ 6
● Brunello di Montalcino Ris. '07	♈♈ 8
● Brunello di Montalcino Ris. '06	♈♈ 7

La Cipriana

LOC. CAMPASTRELLO, 176B
57022 CASTAGNETO CARDUCCI [LI]
TEL. 0565775568
www.lacipriana.com

CELLAR SALES
PRE-BOOKED VISITS
ACCOMMODATION AND RESTAURANT SERVICE
ANNUAL PRODUCTION 30,000 bottles
HECTARES UNDER VINE 8.00

Cipriana is a longstanding estate in the Bolgheri DOC zone, one of the first to produce fine quality wine and olive oil in the area. The vineyards occupy about eight hectares divided over two different areas, one next to the winery and the other on the famous Via Bolgherese. They are planted with the typical varieties: cabernet sauvignon, merlot, petit verdot and syrah. The wines are moderately modern in style, fermented in concrete vats, and only estate-grown grapes are used. The Cipriana wines we tasted were excellent with the really praiseworthy Bolgheri 2013 circled in red: a wine that offers a very good reading of the year, with fine spicy aromas, lovely hints of sandalwood, and a spectacular, salty palate, with wonderful depth and finesse. The San Martino 2012 is good, if slightly affected by the uneven vintage year, with slightly clenched tannin.

● Bolgheri Rosso Cipriana '13	♈♈ 3*
● Bolgheri Rosso Sup. San Martino '12	♈♈ 6
○ Bolgheri Vermentino Paguro '14	♈♈ 2*
● Bolgheri Rosso Scopaio '13	♈ 4
● Lunatico Aleatico Passito '13	♈ 3
● Bolgheri Rosso '08	♈♈ 4
● Bolgheri Rosso Sup. San Martino '07	♈♈ 6
● Bolgheri Rosso Sup. Scopaio '08	♈♈ 4

Citille di Sopra

FRAZ. TORRENIERI
LOC. CITILLE DI SOPRA, 46
53024 MONTALCINO [SI]
TEL. 0577832749
www.citille.com

CELLAR SALES
PRE-BOOKED VISITS
ANNUAL PRODUCTION 35,000 bottles
HECTARES UNDER VINE 6.00

The Citille di Sopra estate, set up by Fabio Innocenti in 1957 and run today by his son Fabio, is named after the location in Torrenieri in the north-easternmost part of the vast Montalcino DOC zone. The land is situated at an altitude of around 300 metres and is rich in clay and iron with streaks of tuff. This leads us to expect weighty and sometimes austere Sangioveses, and we are not disappointed. The features of the six or so hectares of land are explored in the three Brunellos (classic, Riserva and Poggio Ronconi cru), for which the winemaking choices often vary in terms of ageing, based on the aspects of the individual vintage. The umpteenth excellent pairing from Citille di Sopra's 2010 Brunellos. The standard version just lacks a change in pace in the airy, spontaneous flavour while the Poggio Ronconi shows greater breadth and volume on the nose with hints of cherries, balsam, spices. At the moment the gallic tannin holds it back but it is worth keeping an eye on for a few years.

● Brunello di Montalcino V. Poggio Ronconi '10	♟♟ 5
● Brunello di Montalcino '10	♟♟ 5
● Brunello di Montalcino V. Poggio Ronconi '07	♟♟♟ 5
● Brunello di Montalcino '08	♟♟ 5
● Brunello di Montalcino Ris. '06	♟♟ 7
● Brunello di Montalcino V. Poggio Ronconi '09	♟♟ 5
● Brunello di Montalcino V. Poggio Ronconi '08	♟♟ 5
● Rosso di Montalcino '12	♟♟ 3

★Tenuta Col d'Orcia

VIA GIUNCHETTI
53020 MONTALCINO [SI]
TEL. 057780891
www.coldorcia.it

CELLAR SALES
PRE-BOOKED VISITS
ANNUAL PRODUCTION 800,000 bottles
HECTARES UNDER VINE 142.00
VITICULTURE METHOD Certified Organic

A passion for wine is probably linked to one's birthplace: Alberto Carnasciali and Franca Buzzegoli, both originally from Chianti, chose to become winegrowers in Maremma. They fell in love with the still-wild area and in 1997 bought the land to set up their estate. Their goals were clear: firstly, Morellino di Scansano wine, since they were in the heart of the DOC zone, and then international grape varieties like cabernet sauvignon and merlot that adapted well to the area. Commitment and passion for their work were never lacking, and it continues today also thanks to their son who has joined the business. The results have always been consistently positive. Without devaluing the house champ, in this round of tastings we preferred the Brunello 2010. A memorable version also in view of the quantities, anything but limited at 250,000 bottles, and the price which is fair, to say the least. Classic, sunny style, opening out with skilful fluency in an invigorating, well-supported flavour.

● Brunello di Montalcino '10	♟♟ 7
● Brunello di Montalcino Poggio al Vento Ris. '08	♟♟ 8
● Rosso di Montalcino Banditella '12	♟♟ 5
● Rosso di Montalcino '13	♟ 4
● Sant'Antimo Nearco '11	♟ 4
● Spezieri '14	♟ 2
● Brunello di Montalcino Poggio al Vento Ris. '06	♟♟♟ 8
● Brunello di Montalcino Poggio al Vento Ris. '04	♟♟♟ 8
● Brunello di Montalcino Poggio al Vento Ris. '99	♟♟♟ 8
● Brunello di Montalcino Poggio al Vento Ris. '97	♟♟♟ 7

Col di Bacche

FRAZ. MONTIANO
S.DA DI CUPI
58010 MAGLIANO IN TOSCANA [GR]
TEL. 0564589538
www.coldibacche.com

CELLAR SALES
PRE-BOOKED VISITS
ANNUAL PRODUCTION 80,000 bottles
HECTARES UNDER VINE 13.50

Col d'Orcia is without doubt one of Montalcino's top estates in terms of history, consistency and statistics. Owned since 1973 by the Marone Cinzano family and run today by Conte Francesco, it consists of a large vineyard-covered hillside of about 150 of the winery's total 500-plus hectares, overlooking the Orcia river and close to Mount Amiata which stabilizes the temperature. Different grape varieties are planted here, but sangiovese takes the lion's share in the leading wines. These include Poggio al Vento, first produced in 1982 and one of the first real Brunello crus, aged for almost four years in 25- and 75-litre Allier and Slavonian oak. The interesting Morellino Rovente Riserva 2012 has complex aromas with hints of blackberry jam, spices like ginger and pepper, a nicely weighty body and smooth tannins, closing on a nice crescendo. The Cupinero 2012 is vibrant on the nose with coffee, spices and ripe fruit. The generous palate is just slightly cropped.

● Cupinero '12	♥♥5
● Morellino di Scansano Rovente Ris. '12	♥♥5
● Morellino di Scansano '14	♥3
○ Vermentino '14	♥2
● Cupinero '09	♥♥♥5
● Morellino di Scansano Rovente '05	♥♥♥4
● Cupinero '11	♥♥5
● Cupinero '08	♥♥5
● Cupinero '07	♥♥5
● Cupinero '06	♥♥5
● Maremma Toscana Cupinero '10	♥♥5
● Morellino di Scansano '11	♥♥3
● Morellino di Scansano Ris. '09	♥♥4*
● Morellino di Scansano Rovente '08	♥♥5
● Morellino di Scansano Rovente '07	♥♥5
● Morellino di Scansano Rovente Ris. '11	♥♥5

Fattoria Collazzi

LOC. TAVARNUZZE
VIA COLLERAMOLE, 101
50029 IMPRUNETA [FI]
TEL. 0552374902
www.collazzi.it

CELLAR SALES
PRE-BOOKED VISITS
ANNUAL PRODUCTION 80,000 bottles
HECTARES UNDER VINE 32.00

Bona Marchi owns the estate purchased by the family in 1933, with over 700 hectares at the gates of the city of Florence. The villa at their centre is one of the most prestigious buildings in the area, its design attributed to Michelangelo Buonarroti. A large part of the land is planted with olive groves, but wine is given fundamental importance, especially since the 1990s when the vineyards were completely reorganized, new varieties planted, the cellars modernized and more attentive agronomical and oenological management entrusted to Lamberto Frescobaldi, Bona's son. The Colazzi 2011, a blend of merlot, cabernet sauvignon and cabernet franc, has a striking nose with hints of vanilla and cloves alongside spice like juniper and nutmeg. The palate opens smoothly with silky tannins, soft texture, and a lingering, delicious finish. The Ferro 2012, a monovarietal Petit Verdot, has powerful aromas and a lovely structure.

● Collazzi '11	♥♥6
● Ferro '12	♥♥5
● Libertà '12	♥♥2*
○ Otto Muri '14	♥♥3
● Chianti Cl. I Bastioni '13	♥3
● Chianti Cl. I Bastioni '11	♥♥3
● Collazzi '10	♥♥6
● Collazzi '09	♥♥6
● Collazzi '08	♥♥6
● Collazzi '07	♥♥6
● Collazzi '04	♥♥6
● Collazzi '03	♥♥5
● Libertà '11	♥♥2*
● Libertà '10	♥♥2*
● Libertà '09	♥♥2*
○ Otto Muri '12	♥♥3

Colle di Bordocheo

LOC. SEGROMIGNO IN MONTE
VIA DI PIAGGIORI BASSO, 123
55012 CAPANNORI [LU]
TEL. 0583929821
www.colledibordocheo.com

CELLAR SALES
PRE-BOOKED VISITS
ACCOMMODATION
ANNUAL PRODUCTION 30,000 bottles
HECTARES UNDER VINE 10.00

Colle di Bordocheo is immersed in the extraordinary natural and, to say the least, scenic landscape of the Colline Lucchesi. It is owned by the Chelini family who began making purchases in 1950, starting with a farmhouse that is now the cellar. The vineyards are planted on clayey soil rich in stony material with southern exposure. The grapes are mainly sangiovese, ciliegiolo, chardonnay, merlot, vermentino and trebbiano. The wines impressed us favourably. The Picchio Rosso 2012 has forward toasty sensations, nicely blended into the fruit, with seductive hints of plums. The palate is chewy with lively, evident tannins and good extract. The Bordocheo Bianco 2014 is good, its green aromas hinting at elderflower and a fresh-tasting finish.

○ Colline Lucchesi Bordocheo Bianco '14	♥♥ 2*
● Colline Lucchesi Rosso Picchio '12	♥♥ 3
○ Bianco dell'Oca '14	♥ 3
● Colline Lucchesi Bordocheo Rosso '13	♥ 2
○ Bianco dell'Oca '13	♥♥ 3
● Colline Lucchesi Picchio Rosso '11	♥♥ 3

Colle Massari

LOC. POGGI DEL SASSO
58044 CINIGIANO [GR]
TEL. 0564990496
www.collemassari.it

CELLAR SALES
PRE-BOOKED VISITS
ACCOMMODATION
ANNUAL PRODUCTION 500,000 bottles
HECTARES UNDER VINE 110.00
VITICULTURE METHOD Certified Organic
SUSTAINABLE WINERY

When he came to this area in the late 1990s, with his sister Maria Iris, Claudio Tipa had in mind a business project that might seem ambitious but proved absolutely solid: to build a sort of French-style Domaine in Tuscany, with estates in the region's best growing areas. The choice to begin farming in a virgin area like Montecucco, with olive groves and arable land as well as vineyards, was a positive one. The attention attracted by the quality of these wines has enabled a generally unknown DOC zone, which saw little reward and gratification for the work, to grow. Two wines in the finals and an excellent standard throughout the rest of the range, while the Montecucco Sangiovese Poggio Lombrone Riserva 2011 earns Tre Bicchieri thanks to its subtle, complex aromas. Fresh sensations of mint and bay leaves alternate with fruity hints of cherries and currants, and a racy, well-balanced palate with an intensely vibrant finish.

● Montecucco Sangiovese Lombrone Ris. '11	♥♥♥ 6
● Montecucco Rosso Ris. '12	♥♥ 3*
● Montecucco Rosso Rigoleto '13	♥♥ 2*
● Montecucco Sangiovese Rigomoro '12	♥♥ 5
● Canaiolo Tenuta di Montecucco '14	♥ 2
⊙ Montecucco Grottolo '14	♥ 2
○ Montecucco Vermentino Irisse '13	♥ 3
○ Montecucco Vermentino Le Melacce '14	♥ 3
● Montecucco Rosso Colle Massari Ris. '08	♥♥♥ 3
● Montecucco Sangiovese Lombrone Ris. '10	♥♥♥ 6
● Montecucco Sangiovese Lombrone Ris. '09	♥♥♥ 6

Colle Santa Mustiola

VIA DELLE TORRI, 86A
53043 CHIUSI [SI]
TEL. 057820525
www.poggioaichiari.it

CELLAR SALES
PRE-BOOKED VISITS
ANNUAL PRODUCTION 18,000 bottles
HECTARES UNDER VINE 5.00
SUSTAINABLE WINERY

An outstanding area between Tuscany and Umbria in the Chiusi area, where it has become an absolute benchmark for fine wines. This is where Fabio Cenni inherited family lands, where vineyards had always played a leading role, and set up an extraordinary project to promote the sangiovese grape. The wines are wonderful, detailed, very tangy and linear: ideal for those who love the type or who want to taste an original version of the leading, classic Tuscan grape. The cellar is worth visiting, partly carved from an ancient Etruscan tomb. 2008 was not an easy year. The Possgio ai Chiari remains in the annals with its usual land-rooted charm, perhaps less vigorous and vibrant and slightly hesitant on the nose. But it's still a really delicious wine capable of surprises. The moreish Vigna Flavia 2011 is very good.

Fattoria Colle Verde

FRAZ. MATRAIA
LOC. CASTELLO
55010 LUCCA
TEL. 0583402310
www.colleverde.it

CELLAR SALES
PRE-BOOKED VISITS
ANNUAL PRODUCTION 30,000 bottles
HECTARES UNDER VINE 7.00

Fattoria di Colle Verde belongs to Piero Tartagni and Francesca Pardini who, having left the city, planted their vineyards on the beautiful hills of Matraia, now firmly anchored in biodynamic farming principles. It is not just the production philosophy that is charming: the wines, too, seem to follow a seductive direction, as artisanal as it is well-focused and accessible. An excellent performance from the whole range of wines tasted. Brania delle Ghiandaie 2012 is wonderful: ripe cherry aromas and a crisp, flavoursome, mature yet fluent palate with a lovely finish. The Terre di Matraja 2013 is very good: hints of wild plums and very drinkable flavour. The Nero della Spinosa is a bit woody: we'll see if bottle ageing sorts out the excessive toastiness.

● Poggio ai Chiari '08	♥♥ 6
● Vigna Flavia '11	♥♥ 5
● Poggio ai Chiari '07	♥♥♥ 6
● Poggio ai Chiari '06	♥♥♥ 6
● Poggio ai Chiari '05	♀♀ 6
● Poggio ai Chiari '04	♀♀ 6
● Poggio ai Chiari '00	♀♀ 6
● Vigna Flavia '10	♀♀ 5
● Vigna Flavia '09	♀♀ 5

● Colline Lucchesi Rosso Brania delle Ghiandaie '12	♥♥ 5
● Colline Lucchesi Rosso Terre di Matraja '12	♥♥ 2*
● Nero della Spinosa '12	♥ 5
● Colline Lucchesi Rosso Brania delle Ghiandaie '11	♀♀ 5
● Colline Lucchesi Rosso Brania delle Ghiandaie '09	♀♀ 4
● Colline Lucchesi Rosso Brania delle Ghiandaie '08	♀♀ 5
● Colline Lucchesi Rosso Terre di Matraja '11	♀♀ 2*
● Colline Lucchesi Rosso Terre di Matraja '09	♀♀ 2*
● Nero della Spinosa '11	♀♀ 5
● Nero della Spinosa '08	♀♀ 5

Collelceto

LOC. CAMIGLIANO
POD. LA PISANA
53024 MONTALCINO [SI]
TEL. 0577816606
www.collelceto.it

CELLAR SALES
PRE-BOOKED VISITS
ANNUAL PRODUCTION 22,000 bottles
HECTARES UNDER VINE 6.00

This small, family-run estate managed by Elia Palazzesi is one of the hottest names in the Montalcino DOC. Literally named Colle dei Lecci, the estate is situated in the south-westernmost area which has a very unusual microclimate. This is a canyon on the Ombrone river at an altitude of close to 200 metres, with typical clay loam soil. These conditions are evident in the markedly Mediterranean features of the sangiovese wines, which are also taut and racy thanks to the tempering effect of the sea currents. This double nature is underlined with ageing procedures based on the aspects of the vintage, using barriques and medium-sized oak. Another Tre Bicchieri for Collelceto thanks to a stylish, multifaceted Brunello 2010, heralded by fresh, balsamic aromas with veins of eau de Cologne completing the picture. The ideal prelude to a slender palate, not without support and counterpoints, and almost stony minerality in the finish.

● Brunello di Montalcino '10	▼▼▼ 5
● Rosso di Montalcino '13	▼▼ 3
● Brunello di Montalcino '06	♔♔♔ 5
● Brunello di Montalcino '09	♔♔ 5
● Brunello di Montalcino '08	♔♔ 5
● Brunello di Montalcino Elia Ris. '07	♔♔ 6
● Brunello di Montalcino Elia Ris. '06	♔♔ 6
● Rosso di Montalcino '12	♔♔ 3
● Rosso di Montalcino '10	♔♔ 3*

Le Colline di Sopra

VIA DELLE COLLINE 17
56040 MONTESCUDAIO [PI]
TEL. 0586650377
www.collinedisopra.com

CELLAR SALES
PRE-BOOKED VISITS
ANNUAL PRODUCTION 27,000 bottles
HECTARES UNDER VINE 5.10
VITICULTURE METHOD Certified Organic
SUSTAINABLE WINERY

It is unusual for two Piedmontese to decide to leave their birthplace and go to make wine in Tuscany, but this is what Luisa Salvestrini and her husband Paolo did in 2005 when they decided to start a new business. The work that awaited them was no mean feat because the vineyards had to be planted ex novo and the rest had to be built. From the beginning, organic methods were used with renewable energy and careful usage of water. This was challenging but very gratifying work, and the first wines showed that the direction taken was the right one. The Ramanto 2013, cabernet franc and merlot, has vibrant mint and bell peppers on the nose alongside forest floor and aromatic herbs, with a hint of cloves. The palate opens smoothly with a fresh vein of acidity, well-blended tannins and a lingering, flavoursome finish. The Larà 2013, a blend of merlot and syrah, is deliciously graceful and drinkable.

● Ramanto '13	▼▼ 4
● Larà '13	▼▼ 3
● Montescusaio Sangiovese Sopra '12	▼▼ 5
○ Tredici '14	▼▼ 3
● Eola '13	▼ 2
● Eola '11	♔♔ 2*
● Larà '11	♔♔ 2*
○ Moscato Passito Lùis '11	♔♔ 3
● Ramanto '11	♔♔ 4

Colognole

LOC. COLOGNOLE
VIA DEL PALAGIO, 15
50068 RUFINA [FI]
TEL. 0558319870
www.colognole.it

CELLAR SALES
PRE-BOOKED VISITS
ACCOMMODATION AND RESTAURANT SERVICE
ANNUAL PRODUCTION 90,000 bottles
HECTARES UNDER VINE 27.00

The Conti Spalletti family has owned the
estate since the late 1800s. Its traditional
charm is preserved today in the main
nucleus of buildings surrounding the
ancient residence that speaks of the
owners' devotion to their vineyards. A
passion for this location is evident in the
whole area: a charming village with villas,
apartments, farmhouses with swimming
pools, and gardens linked to the
agritourism and bed-and-breakfast
business. Brothers Cesare and Mario Coda
Nunziante, the sons of Gabriella Spalletti
Trivelli, manage the winemaking and
commercial sides today, preserving the
strongly local imprint on the style of their
wines. An excellent performance from the
Riserva del Don 2011, opening with
distinctive minty, balsamic elements that
give way to fruity sensations. The palate is
succulent, powerful, generous with a
crescendo finish. The 2012 version is also
good: more minerally on the nose with a
subtle, stylish structure and pleasing,
lingering tangy sensation in the finish.

● Chianti Rufina '12	♥♥ 2*
● Chianti Rufina Riserva del Don '11	♥♥ 5
● Chianti Sinopie '14	♥ 2
○ Sinopie '14	♥ 2
● Chianti Rufina '09	♥♥ 2*
● Chianti Rufina '08	♥♥ 2*
● Chianti Rufina '06	♥♥ 2*
● Chianti Rufina '02	♥♥ 2
● Chianti Rufina '01	♥♥ 2
● Chianti Rufina Ris. del Don '09	♥♥ 5
● Chianti Rufina Ris. del Don '08	♥♥ 5
● Chianti Rufina Ris. del Don '04	♥♥ 4
● Chianti Rufina Ris. del Don '03	♥♥ 4

Il Colombaio di Santa Chiara

LOC. RACCIANO
VIA SAN DONATO, 1
53037 SAN GIMIGNANO [SI]
TEL. 0577942004
www.colombaiosantachiara.it

CELLAR SALES
PRE-BOOKED VISITS
ACCOMMODATION
ANNUAL PRODUCTION 90,000 bottles
HECTARES UNDER VINE 12.00
VITICULTURE METHOD Certified Organic

When Alessio Logi decided to undertake a
career as a winegrower he had the
teachings of his father Mario clear in his
mind: the conviction that the most
important work is done in the vineyards,
allowing the cellar practices to bring to
fruition what nature has provided, without ill
effects. Hence the choice not to use
insecticides in the vineyards and to respect
the local area. The estate grows native local
varieties that express the San Gimignano
area. As well as wine production the estate
has agritourism facilities and there is a
Romanesque church on the property dating
back to the 12th century. Tre Bicchieri for
the 2013 Vernaccia l'Albereta Riserva
thanks to a complex nose with fragrant
floral hints alongside minerally sensations
and alternating citrus and apple fruit. The
palate is nicely weighty with a lively vein of
acidity nicely blended with the other
components and a pleasant, lingering
finish.

○ Vernaccia di S. Gimignano l'Albereta Ris. '12	♥♥♥ 5
● Chianti Colli Senesi Campale '13	♥ 2
⊙ Rosato Cremisi '14	♥ 2
○ Vernaccia di S. Gimignano Campo della Pieve '13	♥ 4
○ Vernaccia di San Gimignano Selvabianca '14	♥ 3
○ Vernaccia di S. Gimignano Campo della Pieve '11	♥♥♥ 3*
○ Vernaccia di S. Gimignano l'Albereta Ris. '11	♥♥♥ 4*
○ Vernaccia di S. Gimignano Selvabianca '12	♥♥ 2*
○ Vernaccia di San Gimignano Selvabianca '13	♥♥ 2*
○ Vernaccia di San Gimignano Selvabianca '11	♥♥ 2*

Contucci

VIA DEL TEATRO, 1
53045 MONTEPULCIANO [SI]
TEL. 0578757006
www.contucci.it

CELLAR SALES
PRE-BOOKED VISITS
ACCOMMODATION
ANNUAL PRODUCTION 100,000 bottles
HECTARES UNDER VINE 21.00

The Contucci family, long-established in
Montepulciano with the family home and
old cellars in the town centre, near the
cathedral, can boast a very long history of
winegrowing. During the Renaissance,
grapes were grown and sold, and
18th-century documents show the quality
of the wines produced, with certifications of
merit throughout the following centuries.
The cellars date back even earlier, probably
of 13th-century origin. In the vineyard only
native grape varieties are grown, with
strong local links, like mammolo. The older
vineyards are currently being replanted.
The enjoyable Nobile Mulinvecchio 2012
has varied aromas of forest floor and ferns,
with rounded, confident fruit like cherries
and strawberries. The palate is juicy, with
excellent texture and tannins blended with
the alcohol, and works up to a remarkable
crescendo finish. The Rosso 2014 is
austere and volatile.

● Nobile di Montepulciano Mulinvecchio '12	♥♥ 5
● Rosso di Montepulciano '14	♥♥ 2*
● Nobile di Montepulciano '12	♥ 3
● Nobile di Montepulciano Pietra Rossa '12	♥ 4
● Nobile di Montepulciano Ris. '11	♥ 5
● Nobile di Montepulciano Mulinvecchio '08	♀♀ 5
● Nobile di Montepulciano Mulinvecchio '07	♀♀ 5
● Nobile di Montepulciano Pietra Rossa '10	♀♀ 4
● Nobile di Montepulciano Pietra Rossa '08	♀♀ 4
● Nobile di Montepulciano Pietra Rossa '07	♀♀ 4
● Nobile di Montepulciano Pietra Rossa '03	♀♀ 4
● Nobile di Montepulciano Ris. '06	♀♀ 5
○ Santo '07	♀♀ 6

Il Conventino

FRAZ. GRACCIANO
VIA DELLA CIARLIANA, 25B
53040 MONTEPULCIANO [SI]
TEL. 0578715371
www.ilconventino.it

CELLAR SALES
PRE-BOOKED VISITS
ANNUAL PRODUCTION 55,000 bottles
HECTARES UNDER VINE 12.00
VITICULTURE METHOD Certified Organic

There must be a close connection linking
the professions of lawyer and winegrower,
considering the large number of
professionals who devote passion and
commitment to the wine sector. This is true
of the Brini brothers, who decided to
establish a winery back in 2003, in
Montepulciano where wine can be an
expression of the local area without forcing
nature and the habitat where the vines
grow. This is why it was one of the first
wineries in the area to introduce organic
grape growing, and the results are easy to
see in the wines. As well as wine
production, the estate offers a small
agritourism accommodation facility. A good
range of aromas in the Nobile Riserva 2011:
blackberry jam, spicy hints of pepper and
cinnamon, refreshing minty sensations. The
palate is firm, broad and smooth with nicely
measured texture and evenly dosed
fine-grained tannins, and a beautifully
drinkable, lingering finish. The Nobile 2012
is supple, dynamic and succulent.

● Nobile di Montepulciano Ris. '11	♥♥ 5
● Nobile di Montepulciano '12	♥♥ 4
● Nobile di Montepulciano '10	♀♀♀ 4*
● Il Cambio '04	♀♀ 4
● Nobile di Montepulciano '11	♀♀ 4
● Nobile di Montepulciano '09	♀♀ 4
● Nobile di Montepulciano Ris. '10	♀♀ 5
● Nobile di Montepulciano Ris. '09	♀♀ 5
● Nobile di Montepulciano Ris. '08	♀♀ 5
● Nobile di Montepulciano Ris. '06	♀♀ 5
● Nobile di Montepulciano Ris. '04	♀♀ 5
● Nobile di Montepulciano Ris. '03	♀♀ 5
● Nobile di Montepulciano Ris. '01	♀♀ 5
● Rosso di Montepulciano '12	♀♀ 2*

Villa Le Corti

LOC. LE CORTI
VIA SAN PIERO DI SOTTO, 1
50026 SAN CASCIANO IN VAL DI PESA [FI]
TEL. 055829301
www.principecorsini.com

CELLAR SALES
PRE-BOOKED VISITS
ACCOMMODATION
ANNUAL PRODUCTION 150,000 bottles
HECTARES UNDER VINE 50.00
VITICULTURE METHOD Certified Organic

Duccio Corsini runs one of the oldest estates in the Chianti Classico DOC, in its Florentine sector, at San Casciano Val di Pesa. The Corsini family also makes wine in Maremma at Tenuta Marsiliana. The production style typically shows an intelligent reference to Chianti tradition, with lively, drinkable wines. The work in the vineyard is meticulous and the cellar makes alternate use of concrete vats, large oak and barriques: a well-focused mixture that guarantees quality and personality in the wines produced by this estate today. The Chianti Classico 2012 displays charming aromas with hints of mint and fresh cherries, ushering in an equally impressive, flavoursome and succulent palate. The Chianti Classico Don Tommaso Gran Selezione 2011 is generous, while the Chianti Classico Cortevecchia Riserva 2011 has firm structure. The lively, sunny Birillo 2011 is a blend of cabernet sauvignon and merlot.

Fattoria Corzano e Paterno

VIA SAN VITO DI SOPRA
50020 SAN CASCIANO IN VAL DI PESA [FI]
TEL. 0558248179
www.corzanoepaterno.com

CELLAR SALES
PRE-BOOKED VISITS
ACCOMMODATION
ANNUAL PRODUCTION 85,000 bottles
HECTARES UNDER VINE 19.00
VITICULTURE METHOD Certified Organic

The story of this estate is the sort you tell in the evening, in front of the fire, with a glass of wine. It is exciting to retrace the route that led to today's modern and functional estate, producing high quality wine, oil and cheese. It took a courageous, visionary man with a plan to transform two semi-abandoned farms into a complex like the one we see today, practising organic farming and imprinting the work with respect for the environment. Architect Wendelin Gelpke began the adventure in 1969, gradually involving the whole family who carry on his dream today. The Chianti I Tre Borri Riserva 2012 reveals itself on the nose with lively sensations of ripe fruit like cherries, small vegetal nuances and light hints of spice. The palate shows full-bodied, generous structure, with nicely coordinated tannins and a fresh hint of acidity, with a lively, pulsating finish.

● Chianti Cl. '12	♟♟♟ 3*
● Chianti Cl. Cortevecchia Ris. '11	♟♟ 4
● Chianti Cl. Don Tommaso Gran Sel. '11	♟♟ 5
● Birillo Tenuta Marsiliana '12	♟ 3
● Chianti Cl. Cortevecchia Ris. '05	♟♟♟ 4
● Chianti Cl. Don Tommaso '99	♟♟♟ 4*
● Chianti Cl. Le Corti '10	♟♟♟ 3*
● Chianti Cl. A-101 Ris. '06	♟♟ 3*
● Chianti Cl. Cortevecchia Ris. '09	♟♟ 4
● Chianti Cl. Cortevecchia Ris. '07	♟♟ 4
● Chianti Cl. Cortevecchia Ris. '06	♟♟ 4
● Chianti Cl. Don Tommaso '05	♟♟ 5
● Chianti Cl. Don Tommaso '04	♟♟ 5
● Chianti Cl. Don Tommaso Gran Sel. '10	♟♟ 5
● Marsiliana '04	♟♟ 6
○ Vin Santo del Chianti Cl. Sant'Andrea '99	♟♟ 6

● Chianti I Tre Borri Ris. '12	♟♟ 5
○ Il Corzanello '14	♟♟ 2*
○ Passito di Corzano '02	♟♟ 6
● Chianti Terre di Corzano '13	♟ 3
● Il Corzano '12	♟ 5
● Chianti I Tre Borri Ris. '07	♟♟♟ 5
● Il Corzano '05	♟♟♟ 5
● Il Corzano '97	♟♟♟ 6
● Chianti I Tre Borri Ris. '11	♟♟ 5
● Chianti I Tre Borri Ris. '09	♟♟ 5
● Chianti I Tre Borri Ris. '08	♟♟ 5
● Il Corzano '11	♟♟ 5
● Il Corzano '10	♟♟ 5
● Il Corzano '09	♟♟ 5
○ Passito di Corzano '11	♟♟ 6
○ Passito di Corzano '00	♟♟ 5

Andrea Costanti

LOC. COLLE AL MATRICHESE
53024 MONTALCINO [SI]
TEL. 0577848195
www.costanti.it

CELLAR SALES
PRE-BOOKED VISITS
ANNUAL PRODUCTION 60,000 bottles
HECTARES UNDER VINE 12.00

The Brunellos which take shape at Colle al Matrichese, a historic location in the eastern area of Montalcino, are to all intents and purposes noble wines. Not only because of the Costanti family's ancestors, but mainly due to the aristocratic expressive features evident for over 30 years in the sangioveses nurtured by Andrea. About ten hectares of vineyards scattered at altitudes of 300 to 450 metres on mainly marl-based soil are the foundation of wines which usually present earthy tones and a strongly tangy, tannic structure. In the cellar the wines undergo lengthy maceration and are matured in tonneaux and in 30-hectolitre oak, and almost always benefit from patient bottle ageing too. And the 2010 Brunello will probably be worth the wait. We tasted it at several points with divided impressions, one of the main limitations being a slightly evolved profile. But it's hard not to be charmed by the vibrant, spicy flavour, with a salty note mid-palate.

● Brunello di Montalcino '10	♟♟ 6
● Brunello di Montalcino '06	♟♟♟ 6
● Brunello di Montalcino '09	♟♟ 6
● Brunello di Montalcino '08	♟♟ 6
● Brunello di Montalcino '07	♟♟ 6
● Brunello di Montalcino '99	♟♟ 6
● Brunello di Montalcino Calbello '00	♟♟ 6
● Brunello di Montalcino Calbello '99	♟♟ 6
● Rosso di Montalcino '11	♟♟ 4

La Cura

LOC. CURA NUOVA, 12
58024 MASSA MARITTIMA [GR]
TEL. 0566918094
www.cantinalacura.it

CELLAR SALES
PRE-BOOKED VISITS
ANNUAL PRODUCTION 30,000 bottles
HECTARES UNDER VINE 12.00

Cereals and vegetables were once grown here, but then in 1968, an auspicious year for changes, Andrea Corsi purchased the estate and the first thing he did was plant two hectares of vineyards, thanks to his passion for wine. At the beginning he sold his wine unbottled, but in the late 1990s he began to bottle first the whites and then the Monteregio. Andrea's son Enrico is now at the helm, and a selection of grape varieties have been planted on the estate in an agreement with the University of Pisa, including a large number of international grapes. The 2013 Breccerosse, from sangiovese with some cabernet sauvignon and merlot, reveals a vibrant, fruity nose with blackberries and plums, fresh, spicy ginger and a firm, nicely paced palate with s lingering, succulent finish. The fresh, appetizing Trinus 2014 is a blend of vermentino, malvasia and chardonnay.

● Monteregio di Massa Marittima Rosso Breccerosse '13	♟♟ 3
○ Trinus '14	♟♟ 2*
● Vedetta '13	♟♟ 4
⊙ Rosato '14	♟ 2
○ Valdemàr '14	♟ 2
● Maremma Merlot La Cura '12	♟♟ 5
● Maremma Podere di Monte Muro Vedetta '11	♟♟ 3
● Merlot '11	♟♟ 5
● Monteregio di Massa Marittima Rosso Breccerosse '11	♟♟ 3
● Monteregio di Massa Marittima Rosso Breccerosse '10	♟♟ 3
● Predicatore '13	♟♟ 3
● Predicatore '11	♟♟ 3
● Predicatore '10	♟♟ 3

Dal Cero
Tenuta Montecchiesi

LOC. MONTECCHIO DI CORTONA
CASE SPARSE, 403
52044 CORTONA [AR]
TEL. 0575618503
www.vinidalcero.com

CELLAR SALES
PRE-BOOKED VISITS
ANNUAL PRODUCTION 300,000 bottles
HECTARES UNDER VINE 65.00

The Dal Cero brothers' Tuscan adventure dates back to 1980. Giuseppe and Dario, sons of the founder of the wine-producing estate in Cortona, Veneto, were struck by the beautiful landscape and, grasping its potential, decided to invest their passion and resources here. The original ten or so hectares of vineyards are now 65, planted at altitudes between 260 and 350 metres. As well as the quintessentially Tuscan sangiovese grape, there is also syrah, a variety that has proved to acclimatize perfectly in this corner of Tuscany. The Cortona Syrah Klanis 2012 from the vineyard of the same name has vibrant, fruity aromas with fresh vegetal hints and a firm palate with nicely lingering flavour. The Sangiovese 2013 is equally good, making the most of the good year with fresh red berries and hints of Alpine herbs.

● Cortona Syrah Klanis '12	♥♥	5
○ Podere Bianchino '14	♥♥	2*
● Preziosaterra '13	♥♥	3
● Sangiovese '13	♥♥	2*
● Cortona Syrah Selverello '13	♥	3
● Cortona Syrah '13	♀♀	5
● Cortona Syrah Klanis '11	♀♀	5
● Cortona Syrah Klanis '08	♀♀	5

Maria Caterina Dei

VIA DI MARTIENA, 35
53045 MONTEPULCIANO [SI]
TEL. 0578716878
www.cantinedei.com

CELLAR SALES
PRE-BOOKED VISITS
ACCOMMODATION
ANNUAL PRODUCTION 230,000 bottles
HECTARES UNDER VINE 55.00

Driven by his great passion for winegrowing Alibrando Dei purchased land in the Montepulciano area for this purpose. As a businessman in a different sector, this was a dream come true. The area he chose, Bossona, yielded such impressive results that he later also purchased the Martiena property, with its villa. The first bottles were produced in 1989 with the construction of the new cellar. After devoting her time to her passion for singing and acting, Maria Caterina Dei moved to Montepulciano in the early 1990s and now carries on the work begun by her grandfather with expertise. The Nobile Bossona Riserva 2010 has a striking nose with vibrant minty and balsamic sensations followed by blackcurrants and blueberries, and subtle spices like cloves and cinnamon. The sturdy, powerful palate opens out evenly with a taut, vibrant finish.

● Nobile di Montepulciano Bossona Ris. '10	♥♥	6
● Nobile di Montepulciano '12	♥	4
● Rosso di Montepulciano '13	♥	2
○ Vin Santo di Montepulciano '09	♥	5
● Nobile di Montepulciano Bossona Ris. '04	♀♀♀	5
● Nobile di Montepulciano '10	♀♀	4
● Nobile di Montepulciano '08	♀♀	4
● Nobile di Montepulciano '01	♀♀	3
● Nobile di Montepulciano Bossona Ris. '08	♀♀	5
● Nobile di Montepulciano Bossona Ris. '06	♀♀	5
● Nobile di Montepulciano Bossona Ris. '03	♀♀	5
● Nobile di Montepulciano Bossona Ris. '01	♀♀	5
● Nobile di Montepulciano Bossona Ris. '99	♀♀	5

Fabrizio Dionisio

FRAZ. OSSAIA
LOC. IL CASTAGNO
52040 CORTONA [AR]
TEL. 063223541
www.fabriziodionisio.it

PRE-BOOKED VISITS
ANNUAL PRODUCTION 30,000 bottles
HECTARES UNDER VINE 15.00

A love of Tuscany and a desire to leave behind the chaos of Rome, played a part in the decision of Sergio Dionisio, father of current owner Fabrizio, to find a place in the country to spend his free time and he chose as his pleasant retreat a farmstead at Cortona, with vineyards and olive groves. In the 1990s he bought another plot of land which brought the estate to its current size, and laid the foundations for a traditional winegrowing business. The first wine was produced in 2003 and not be anything but a Syrah because this was the only choice of grape since it finds good favourable expression in this area. The 2012 Castagno displays a lovely variety of aromas: wild berries softened by spicy hints of pepper and nutmeg and little minty nuances. A light entry on the palate which gathers strength slowly, revealing nicely blended tannins and a flavoursome, relaxed finish. The Castagnino 2014 is more subtle and approachably drinkable.

● Cortona Syrah Il Castagno '12	♟♟♟	5
● Cortona Syrah Castagnino '14	♟♟	3
⊙ Rosa del Castagno '14	♟	3
● Cortona Syrah Il Castagno '11	♟♟♟	5
● Cortona Syrah Il Castagno '10	♟♟♟	5
● Cortona Syrah '07	♟♟	4
● Cortona Syrah '06	♟♟	4
● Cortona Syrah '05	♟♟	4
● Cortona Syrah '04	♟♟	4
● Cortona Syrah '03	♟♟	4
● Cortona Syrah Castagnino '09	♟♟	3*
● Cortona Syrah Cuculaia '10	♟♟	7
● Cortona Syrah Cuculaia '09	♟♟	6
● Cortona Syrah Cuculaia '08	♟♟	6
● Cortona Syrah Il Castagno '09	♟♟	5
● Cortona Syrah Il Castagno '08	♟♟	5

Donna Olga

LOC. FRIGGIALI
S.DA MAREMMANA
53024 MONTALCINO [SI]
TEL. 0577849454
www.tenutedonnaolga.it

CELLAR SALES
PRE-BOOKED VISITS
ACCOMMODATION
ANNUAL PRODUCTION 25,000 bottles
HECTARES UNDER VINE 11.00

Olga Peluso Centolani runs her personal project here, to which she has dedicated all her passion and energy, and continues to do so. Just over ten hectares of vineyards are planted on two different slopes with different soil and weather features. To the south-west a high flint content, and galestro to the south-east at higher altitudes. The combination produces sound, flavoursome, modern Brunellos which are the fruit of lengthy fermentation and ageing in 30-hectolitre barrels. 2010 produced a very well-focused Brunello with classic red berry sensations interwoven with spices and medicinal herbs. No lack of structure and extract on the palate, which faithfully expresses the more southern character of these wines. The Rosso 2012 is also very good, tidy and compact with lively fruit accompanying the flavour in the mouthfilling finish.

● Brunello di Montalcino '10	♟♟	7
● Brunello di Montalcino Favorito Collezione Arte '09	♟♟	7
⊙ Lady '0	♟	4
● Brunello di Montalcino '09	♟♟♟	7
● Brunello di Montalcino '06	♟♟♟	7
● Brunello di Montalcino '01	♟♟♟	6
● Brunello di Montalcino Collezione Arte '06	♟♟♟	7
● Brunello di Montalcino Ris. '01	♟♟♟	6
● Brunello di Montalcino '08	♟♟	7
● Brunello di Montalcino '07	♟♟	7

Donna Olimpia 1898

FRAZ. BOLGHERI
LOC. MIGLIARINI, 142
57020 CASTAGNETO CARDUCCI [LI]
TEL. 0302279601
www.donnaolimpia1898.it

CELLAR SALES
ACCOMMODATION AND RESTAURANT SERVICE
ANNUAL PRODUCTION 150,000 bottles
HECTARES UNDER VINE 45.00
SUSTAINABLE WINERY

The Donna Olimpia estate belongs to Guido Folonari, a leading figure in the Tuscan and Italian wine-producing overview. It was named in 1898 after Olimpia Alliata, Lady of Biserno and wife of the famous Gherardo della Gherardesca. The 45 hectares of vineyards are the result of a partnership with Professor Scienza of the University of Milan, regarding cloning. The chosen varieties are cabernet sauvignon, cabernet franc, merlot, syrah and petit verdot for the reds; vermentino, viognier and petit manseng for the whites. The Bolgheri Rosso Superiore Millepassi is excellent. 2012 endowed it with vibrant grassy aromas and perfectly ripe, fruity aromas. Mouthfilling, silky fruit on the palate with good balance and seductive tannic texture. The Bolgheri Rosso 2012 is well-typed despite very toasty sensations.

Duemani

LOC. ORTACAVOLI
56046 RIPARBELLA [PI]
TEL. 0583975048
www.duemani.eu

ANNUAL PRODUCTION 40,000 bottles
HECTARES UNDER VINE 10.00
VITICULTURE METHOD Certified Biodynamic
SUSTAINABLE WINERY

Perhaps many consultant winemakers dream of owning their own estate. Luca D'Attoma has succeeded in doing so with his wife, Elena Celli, and he chose to work in the province of Pisa, according to a very specific philosophy: finding a place where his favourite grape varieties – cabernet franc, syrah and merlot – would find their ideal habitat. In 2000 his search was successful and he began replanting the vineyards, following the principles of biodynamic farming. The resulting wines show bags of personality, offering a clearly defined expression of the terroir while enhancing the features of the grape. The Duemani 2012, a monovarietal Cabernet Franc, displays lively fruit on the nose like bilberries and blackberries, softened by sage and rosemary with hints of juniper. A dynamic entry on the palate with juicy fruit and good texture, evident but well-blended tannins and a lovely final thrust into a really delicious, lingering finish.

Wine	Rating
● Bolgheri Rosso '12	♥♥ 5
● Bolgheri Rosso Sup. Millepassi '12	♥♥ 6
○ Obizzo '14	♥ 2
● Bolgheri Rosso Sup. Millepassi '11	♥♥♥ 8
● Bolgheri '05	♥♥ 4
● Bolgheri Rosso '10	♥♥ 5
● Bolgheri Rosso '09	♥♥ 5
● Bolgheri Rosso '08	♥♥ 4
● Bolgheri Rosso Sup. Millepassi '09	♥♥ 8
● Bolgheri Rosso Sup. Millepassi '08	♥♥ 6
● Tageto '09	♥♥ 2

Wine	Rating
● Duemani '12	♥♥♥ 8
● Cifra '13	♥♥ 5
● Altrovino '13	♥♥ 5
● Suisassi '12	♥♥ 8
⊙ Sì '14	♥ 5
● Duemani '09	♥♥♥ 8
● Suisassi '10	♥♥♥ 8
● Altrovino '11	♥♥ 5
● Altrovino '10	♥♥ 5
● Cifra '11	♥♥ 4
● Cifra '10	♥♥ 4
● Duemani '11	♥♥ 8
● Duemani '10	♥♥ 8
● Duemani '08	♥♥ 8
● Suisassi '11	♥♥ 8
● Suisassi '09	♥♥ 8

Eucaliptus

VIA BOLGHERESE, 275A
57022 LIVORNO
TEL. 0565763511
www.agriturismoeucaliptus.com

PRE-BOOKED VISITS
ACCOMMODATION AND RESTAURANT SERVICE
ANNUAL PRODUCTION 20,000 bottles
HECTARES UNDER VINE 5.00

This is a small winery with a long tradition.
It has existed since the 1960s when the
wine was still sold unbottled. At the helm is
vigneron Pasqualino Di Vaira, and the
varieties grown are: black grapes, merlot,
cabernet sauvignon, petit verdot, syrah and
sangiovese; white grapes, vermentino and
chardonnay. Once again in the last tasting,
the wines performed well, showing juicy
fruit, good structure and excellent maturity.
We can start with the Bolgheri Superiore
Ville Rustiche 2012: harmonious and nicely
blended, the fruit enclosed in toasty
sensations. We thoroughly recommend this
red, which is not the most complex in its
category but is definitely good and
flavoursome. The Clarice 2013 is darker,
also in the hints of oak, but with beautiful
definition and texture.

I Fabbri

LOC. LAMOLE
VIA CASOLE, 52
50022 GREVE IN CHIANTI [FI]
TEL. 339412622
www.agricolaifabbri.it

CELLAR SALES
PRE-BOOKED VISITS
ANNUAL PRODUCTION 35,000 bottles
HECTARES UNDER VINE 11.00
VITICULTURE METHOD Certified Organic

The name of the I Fabbri farm recalls the
blacksmith's forge in the old village that
overlooks the farmsteads. The estate has
made wine since 2000 thanks to the hard
work of sisters Susanna and Maddalena
Grassi. Situated in the Lamole subzone, the
vineyards are currently converting to
organic farming methods. Very basic work
in the cellar and ageing in tonneaux, steel
and concrete vats produce wines with a
clearly defined, subtle style. While not
immediately accessible they are coherent
with the features of this particular Chianti
Classico terroir. The Chianti Classico 2013
is very fresh, with lovely hints of wild
berries. Some slightly excessive oakiness
appears alongside the lush fruit in the
Chianti Classico Olinto 2012, with rounded,
tangy flavour while the strong point of the
more austere Chianti Classico Podere
Sestilio Riserva 2012 is its dynamic flavour.
The Chianti Classico Terra di Lamole 2012
is linear with very dry flavour.

● Bolgheri Clarice '13	▼▼ 3
● Bolgheri Sup. Ville Rustiche '12	▼▼ 5
● Bolgheri Clarice '12	♀♀ 3
● Bolgheri Don Clarice '11	♀♀ 3
● Bolgheri Sup. Ville Rustiche '11	♀♀ 5
● Bolgheri Sup. Ville Rustiche '10	♀♀ 5

● Chianti Cl. '13	▼▼ 4
● Chianti Cl. Olinto '12	▼▼ 4
● Chianti Cl. Podere Sestilio Ris. '12	▼ 4
● Chianti Cl. Terra di Lamole '12	▼ 3
● Chianti Cl. '12	♀♀ 4
● Chianti Cl. '10	♀♀ 4
● Chianti Cl. '06	♀♀ 3*
● Chianti Cl. Gran Sel. '11	♀♀ 6
● Chianti Cl. Lamole '11	♀♀ 2*
● Chianti Cl. Olinto '10	♀♀ 4
● Chianti Cl. Olinto '08	♀♀ 4
● Chianti Cl. Ris. '11	♀♀ 4
● Chianti Cl. Ris. '10	♀♀ 4
● Chianti Cl. Ris. '07	♀♀ 4
● Chianti Cl. Terra di Lamole '10	♀♀ 2*
● Chianti Cl. Terra di Lamole '06	♀♀ 2*

Il Falcone

LOC. FALCONE, 186
57028 SUVERETO [LI]
TEL. 0565829331
www.ilfalcone.net

CELLAR SALES
PRE-BOOKED VISITS
ANNUAL PRODUCTION 40,000 bottles
HECTARES UNDER VINE 10.00

The Petri family has owned the estate since 1911. It is currently managed by sisters Paola and Rosa, who carry forward with care and commitment a business handed down through the generations, making this one of the oldest estates in Val di Cornia. Back in 1821 the farm was marked on the cadastral maps of the Grand Duchy of Tuscany. The estate grows olives as well as vineyards and also has a significant agritourism business, divided over two farms. A good performance from the Vallin dei Ghiri 2013, a monovarietal Syrah with complex, pleasant aromas of cherries and strawberries, light hints of aromatic herbs and mixed spice, from ginger to rhubarb. A generous entry on the palate with lovely structure, balanced acidity and a succulent finish. The Boccalupo 2012, an unusual blend of sangiovese, giacomino, merlot and cabernet sauvignon, has a complex nose and nicely weighty palate.

● Falcorosso '13	▼▼ 2*
● Valdicornia Suvereto Boccalupo '12	▼▼ 4
● Vallin dei Ghiri '13	▼▼ 5
○ Vermentino Falcobianco '14	▼ 2
● Vallin dei Ghiri '12	♈♈ 5

Fanti

FRAZ. CASTELNUOVO DELL'ABATE
POD. PALAZZO, 14
53020 MONTALCINO [SI]
TEL. 0577835795
www.fantisanfilippo.com

CELLAR SALES
PRE-BOOKED VISITS
ANNUAL PRODUCTION 200,000 bottles
HECTARES UNDER VINE 50.00

No one can claim to know all about the recent history of Montalcino wine without having chatted face-to-face with the pleasant and enthusiastic Filippo Fanti. A leading protagonist in the golden years of Brunello, he runs the estate alongside his daughter Elisa, with almost 50 hectares of vineyards all in the Castelnuovo dell'Abate area. This sunny spot is ideal to bring out the most engaging, Mediterranean features of sangiovese, a style which reflects the personality of its creators but has been progressively redesigned in recent years to express aromas of greater elegance and sobriety. Excellent signs of this come from the recently released Brunellos. The most relaxed and harmonious is certainly the standard 2010, while the Vallocchio of the same year presents more toasty sensations from the oak used for ageing. A good performance also from the Vigna Le Macchiarelle Riserva 2009 with charming balsamic aromas.

● Brunello di Montalcino '10	▼▼ 6
● Brunello di Montalcino V. Le Macchiarelle Ris. '09	▼▼ 6
● Brunello di Montalcino Vallocchio '10	▼▼ 6
● Rosso di Montalcino '13	▼ 3
● Brunello di Montalcino '07	♈♈♈ 5
● Brunello di Montalcino '00	♈♈♈ 6
● Brunello di Montalcino '09	♈♈ 6
● Brunello di Montalcino '08	♈♈ 6
● Brunello di Montalcino '06	♈♈ 5
● Brunello di Montalcino '05	♈♈ 5
● Brunello di Montalcino '04	♈♈ 6
● Brunello di Montalcino Ris. '07	♈♈ 8

Fattoi

LOC. SANTA RESTITUTA
POD. CAPANNA, 101
53024 MONTALCINO [SI]
TEL. 0577848613
www.fattoi.it

CELLAR SALES
PRE-BOOKED VISITS
ANNUAL PRODUCTION 50,000 bottles
HECTARES UNDER VINE 9.00

The Fattoi family have been bottling their Brunello for over 30 years, grown on the estate's ten or so hectares in the prestigious Pieve Santa Restituta growing zone. This quiet work has met with increasing approval and recognition in recent years thanks above all to the original, recognizable style which is traditional but by no means stuck in the past. The austere, mouthwatering Sangioveses aged in 33- and 45-hectolitre Slavonian oak are ideal table wines, and the odd reductive note and youthful phenolic huskiness are easily forgiven. The first honour for Ofelio Fattoi and his family was on the cards, and is won by the sumptuous 2010 Brunello. Aeration is a valuable ally in releasing the lush fruit, initially concealed behind the resinous and spicy sensations. Time will help relax the close-knit tannic texture which already counterbalances the engaging tangy, authentic flavour. The multifaceted Rosso 2013 is also of a high standard.

● Brunello di Montalcino '10	♥♥♥	5
● Rosso di Montalcino '13	♥♥	3
● Brunello di Montalcino '09	♀♀	5
● Brunello di Montalcino '07	♀♀	6
● Brunello di Montalcino '06	♀♀	6
● Brunello di Montalcino Ris. '08	♀♀	7
● Brunello di Montalcino Ris. '07	♀♀	7
● Rosso di Montalcino '12	♀♀	3
● Rosso di Montalcino '10	♀♀	3

★★Fattoria di Felsina

VIA DEL CHIANTI, 101
53019 CASTELNUOVO BERARDENGA [SI]
TEL. 0577355117
www.felsina.it

CELLAR SALES
PRE-BOOKED VISITS
ANNUAL PRODUCTION 480,000 bottles
HECTARES UNDER VINE 94.00

Felsina is an iconic Tuscan estate, with its rigorous wines that steer clear of short-lived winemaking trends and stand out instead for their elegance and personality. Domenico Poggiali, a businessman from Ravenna, purchased the original nucleus of the estate in 1966 and laid the foundations for the Felsina wine-producing project. In 1981 came the purchase of the Castello di Farnetella in Sinalunga, followed in 1995 by Pagliarese in Castelnuovo Berardenga. A long, intense history that has brought this estate and its production style to the absolute heights of Italian winemaking. The 2012 Fontalloro, from sangiovese grapes, displays a well-defined nose with lush fruit ushering in the deep, well-coordinated palate. The Chianti Classico Riserva 2012 is marked by edgy tannin and slightly excessive hardness, but the aromas are fresh and the flavour pleasing. The Maestro Raro 2012 is a satisfying monovarietal Cabernet Sauvignon: fragrant with lovely firm structure.

● Fontalloro '12	♥♥	6
● Chianti Cl. Berardenga Ris. '12	♥♥	5
● Maestro Raro '12	♥♥	6
● Chianti Cl. Berardenga '13	♥	4
● Chianti Cl. Colonia Gran Sel. '10	♥	8
● Chianti Cl. Rancia Ris. '12	♥	6
○ I Sistri '13	♥	4
○ Vin Santo del Chianti Cl. Berardenga '06	♥	5
● Chianti Cl. Rancia Ris. '07	♀♀♀	6
● Chianti Cl. Rancia Ris. '05	♀♀♀	5
● Chianti Cl. Rancia Ris. '04	♀♀♀	5
● Fontalloro '10	♀♀♀	6
● Fontalloro '07	♀♀♀	6
● Fontalloro '06	♀♀♀	6
● Fontalloro '05	♀♀♀	6
● Maestro Raro '08	♀♀♀	6

Fattoria di Fiano

LOC. FIANO
VIA FIRENZE, 11
50050 CERTALDO [FI]
TEL. 0571669048
www.fattoriadifiano.it

CELLAR SALES
PRE-BOOKED VISITS
ANNUAL PRODUCTION 150,000 bottles
HECTARES UNDER VINE 22.00

The Bing family has owned the farm since 1940. It is named after the village and derives from the Alfani family to whom a street is dedicated in Florence. The property extends over two basic areas and current owner Ugo spent a great deal of time understanding in depth the behavior of grape varieties in the various plots of land, which enabled him to find the perfect blend of native varieties like sangiovese, colorino and canaiolo, with modern planting and farming techniques. He is helped today by his son Francesco, to whom he has passed on his passion and meticulous attention to detail. A lovely overall performance from the Chianti Colli Fiorentini wines, which impressed us particularly with their clean aromas dominated by fruit. The basic 2013 is nicely vigorous without harshness, with well-judged acidity, while the tannins and alcohol are in step in the 2012 Riserva, on a pleasing palate with a very lingering finish.

● Chianti Colli Fiorentini '13	▼▼ 2*
● Chianti Colli Fiorentini Ugo Bing Ris. '12	▼▼ 2*
● Fianesco '12	▼▼ 5
● Chianti Ris. '12	▼ 2
● Fianesco '11	♀♀ 5
● Fianesco '10	♀♀ 5
● Fianesco '06	♀♀ 5

Poderi Firenze

LOC. L'ABBANDONATO
58031 ARCIDOSSO [GR]
TEL. 0564967271
www.poderifirenze.it

PRE-BOOKED VISITS
ACCOMMODATION
ANNUAL PRODUCTION 80,000 bottles
HECTARES UNDER VINE 18.00

Flavia Tagliabue's farm is situated at l'Abbandonato, a name which explains the family's motivation for starting this adventure in the area. In 2003 the winegrowing activity began, along with the agritourism which is still an important element, in a charming and still unspoilt area. Once a Roman settlement, the abandoned for many years, the location was part of a latifundium owned by the Marchesi Della Greca which enabled it to remain free from intensively grown crops. Sangiovese is the main grape variety grown, along with ciliegiolo and syrah, both of which have adapted to the terroir with excellent results. The intriguing Sciresa 2013, a monovarietal Ciliegiolo, has blackberry and cherry aromas supported by hints of Mediterranean scrubland, and a rich, lively, rounded palate with a fresh streak of acidity and remarkable crescendo finish. The enjoyable Montecucco Sangiovese Sottocasa 2011 has generous fruit aromas and a crisp palate.

● Maremma Toscana Sciresa '13	▼▼ 2*
● Montecucco Sangiovese Sottocasa '11	▼▼ 2*
● Montecucco Sangiovese Sottocasa '10	♀♀ 3
● Scireza '11	♀♀ 2*

★Tenute Ambrogio e Giovanni Folonari

LOC. PASSO DEI PECORAI
VIA DI NOZZOLE, 12
50022 GREVE IN CHIANTI [FI]
TEL. 055859811
www.tenutefolonari.com

CELLAR SALES
PRE-BOOKED VISITS
ACCOMMODATION
ANNUAL PRODUCTION 1,400,000 bottles
HECTARES UNDER VINE 200.00

Ambrogio and Giovanni Folonari are part of one of the leading Italian wine dynasties. In 2000 they set off on an independent path in this sector, where they had always taken a leading role, starting in Tuscany where their main estates are situated: Nozzole at Greve in Chianti, Campo al Mare at Bolgheri, La Fuga at Montalcino, Torcalvano at Montepulciano and Vigne a Porrona in Maremma. The wines are technically flawless with a modern style and aged in small oak, with focus on colour, structure and fruit. The Chianti Classico La Forra Gran Selezione 2012 displays spicy and beautifully sweet aromas and a well-coordinated, generous palate with a soft, satisfying flavour. The Cabreo Il Borgo 2012, a blend of sangiovese and cabernet sauvignon, offers vibrant ripe fruit aromas alongside hints of coffee powder and vanilla. The flavour is succulent on a well-structured, nicely textured palate.

● Chianti Cl. La Forra Gran Sel. '12	▼▼ 5
● Cabreo Il Borgo '12	▼▼ 6
○ Cabreo La Pietra '13	▼ 6
● Chianti Cl. '12	▼ 4
● Il Pareto '13	▼ 8
● Nobile di Montepulciano Torcalvano '12	▼ 3
● Cabreo Il Borgo '06	▼▼▼ 5
● Chianti Cl. La Forra Ris. '90	▼▼▼ 4*
● Il Pareto '09	▼▼▼ 7
● Il Pareto '07	▼▼▼ 7
● Il Pareto '04	▼▼▼ 7
● Il Pareto '01	▼▼▼ 7
● Il Pareto '00	▼▼▼ 7
● Il Pareto '98	▼▼▼ 7
● Il Pareto '97	▼▼▼ 7
● Il Pareto '93	▼▼▼ 7

Le Fonti

LOC. PANZANO IN CHIANTI
50020 GREVE IN CHIANTI [FI]
TEL. 055852194
www.fattorialefonti.it

CELLAR SALES
PRE-BOOKED VISITS
ANNUAL PRODUCTION 45,000 bottles
HECTARES UNDER VINE 8.60
VITICULTURE METHOD Certified Organic

Le Fonti has been owned by the Schmitt-Vitali family since 1994, and is situated in the subzone of Panzano. The fairly small size of this estate makes it possible to devote accurate care to the vineyards and cellar, and this has brought their wines into the limelight, especially in the recent past, even with some inconsistencies. Small wood is preferred for ageing but the oak is judiciously measured and the wines show a nicely defined style with no lack of freshness, personality and coherence with the features of the terroir of origin. The delightful Chianti Classico 2012 has complex aromas alternating floral hints with tobacco and leather, as a prologue to the fluent, flavoursome palate, tangy with fresh acidity. The Chianti Classico Riserva 2011 is also interesting with nuaced aromas and a close-knit but well-paced palate. La Lepre delle Fonti 2012 is a more closed and cropped blend of sangiovese and merlot.

● Chianti Cl. '12	▼▼ 3*
● Chianti Cl. Ris. '11	▼▼ 4
● La Lepre delle Fonti '12	▼ 2
● Chianti Cl. Ris. '07	▼▼▼ 4
● Fontissimo '06	▼▼▼ 5
● Chianti Cl. '11	▼▼ 3
● Chianti Cl. '08	▼▼ 3
● Chianti Cl. '07	▼▼ 3
● Chianti Cl. Ris. '09	▼▼ 4
● Chianti Cl. Ris. '08	▼▼ 4
● Chianti Cl. Ris. '07	▼▼ 4
● Chianti Cl. Ris. '04	▼▼ 4
● Fontissimo '04	▼▼ 5
● Fontissimo '01	▼▼ 5
● V. della Lepre '07	▼▼ 2

★★Fontodi

FRAZ. PANZANO IN CHIANTI
VIA SAN LEOLINO, 89
50020 GREVE IN CHIANTI [FI]
TEL. 055852005
www.fontodi.com

CELLAR SALES
PRE-BOOKED VISITS
ACCOMMODATION
ANNUAL PRODUCTION 300,000 bottles
HECTARES UNDER VINE 80.00
VITICULTURE METHOD Certified Organic

The unanimous acknowledgement of the very famous Conca d'Oro of Panzano as one of the best Chianti Classico subzones is certainly due mostly to the estate owned by the Manetti family since 1968, which has presented an absolutely authentic interpretation of sangiovese grapes grown in this area. Today Fontodi's quality is enriched by organic farming methods in the vineyards, indicating an increasingly marked pursuit of the character and personality of their wines. Flaccianello della Pieve 2012 displays powerful aromas and a close-knit, well-coordinated palate, with rounded fruity, fresh sensations alongside the deep, succulent, well-paced flavour. The Chianti Classico 2013 is accessibly delicious, with fine spice on the nose and a fragrant, fluent palate. The Chianti Classico Vigna del Sorbo Gran Selezione 2012 is austere while the Pinot Nero Case Via 2013 has enjoyable relaxed flavour.

Fornacelle

LOC. FORNACELLE, 232A
57022 CASTAGNETO CARDUCCI [LI]
TEL. 0565775575
www.fornacelle.it

CELLAR SALES
PRE-BOOKED VISITS
ANNUAL PRODUCTION 35,000 bottles
HECTARES UNDER VINE 15.00

The family-run Fornacelle estate has ancient roots but a perfectly focused current approach with a steady pace. This is one of most reliable Bolgheri estates, run by the Billi Batistoni family, covering about 15 hectares. The turning point towards quality came in the late 1990s and resulted in beautifully made wines with accomplished expression. A lovely example for this DOC. The very good Bolgheri Rosso Zizzolo 2013 provides its own reading of a more than interesting vintage year that yielded crisp, succulent wines. The aromas are immediately impressive: fruity, slightly grassy, with a subtly salty background, and the palate is flavoursome and astute. The Bolgheri Riserva Guarda Boschi proves less focused, at least on the nose, while the palate shows good extract with a detailed and clear-cut palate. The Zizzolo Vermentino 2014 is taut and minerally.

● Flaccianello della Pieve '12	♛♛♛ 8
● Chianti Cl. '12	♛♛ 4
● Chianti Cl. V. del Sorbo Gran Sel. '12	♛ 6
● Pinot Nero Case Via '13	♛ 5
● Syrah Case Via '12	♛ 6
● Chianti Cl. '10	♛♛♛ 4*
● Chianti Cl. V. del Sorbo Ris. '01	♛♛♛ 6
● Flaccianello della Pieve '09	♛♛♛ 8
● Flaccianello della Pieve '08	♛♛♛ 8
● Flaccianello della Pieve '07	♛♛♛ 6
● Flaccianello della Pieve '05	♛♛♛ 6
● Flaccianello della Pieve '03	♛♛♛ 6
● Flaccianello della Pieve '01	♛♛♛ 6
● Flaccianello della Pieve '00	♛♛♛ 6
● Flaccianello della Pieve '85	♛♛♛ 8
● Flaccianello della Pieve '83	♛♛♛ 8

● Bolgheri Rosso Zizzolo '13	♛♛ 3
● Bolgheri Sup. Guarda Boschi '12	♛♛ 6
○ Bolgheri Vermentino Zizzolo '14	♛♛ 3
● Bolgheri Rosso Zizzolo '12	♛♛ 3
● Bolgheri Sup. Guarda Boschi '11	♛♛ 6
● Bolgheri Sup. Guarda Boschi '08	♛♛ 6
● Foglio 38 '11	♛♛ 6

Podere Forte

LOC. PETRUCCI, 13
53023 CASTIGLIONE D'ORCIA [SI]
TEL. 05778885100
www.podereforte.it

CELLAR SALES
PRE-BOOKED VISITS
ANNUAL PRODUCTION 12,000 bottles
HECTARES UNDER VINE 15.00
VITICULTURE METHOD Certified Biodynamic
SUSTAINABLE WINERY

Pasquale Forte's estate has staked its claim as one of the benchmarks of innovative winegrowing, not only in Tuscany, thanks to uncompromising hard work that began in the late 1990s. The work was strongly oriented towards the pursuit of absolute excellence, alongside unceasing experimentation which has led to the adoption of biodynamic production procedures as well as organic. The Guardavinga 2012 is a blend of cabernet franc, petit verdot and merlot with rounded, well-defined aromas and a weighty palate that is also fresh and lingering. The fragrant Orcia Petruccino 2013 is really delicious. The Orcia Petrucci 2012 is harder work on the palate with an oakiness still striving to blend.

● Guardiavigna '12		🍷🍷 8
● Orcia Petruccino '13		🍷🍷 0
● Orcia Petrucci '12		🍷 8
● Orcia Guardiavigna '01		🍷🍷🍷 8
● Guardiavigna '11		🍷🍷 8
● Guardiavigna '10		🍷🍷 8
● Guardiavigna '09		🍷🍷 8
● Guardiavigna '05		🍷🍷 8
● Orcia Petrucci '10		🍷🍷 8
● Orcia Petruccino '06		🍷🍷 5

Fortulla - Agrilandia

LOC. CASTIGLIONCELLO
S.DA VICINALE DELLE SPIANATE
57016 ROSIGNANO MARITTIMO [LI]
TEL. 3404524453
www.fortulla.it

ACCOMMODATION
ANNUAL PRODUCTION 50,000 bottles
HECTARES UNDER VINE 7.00
VITICULTURE METHOD Certified Organic

It has been 20 years since the Agrilandia project took shape at the behest of owner Fulvio Martini. Its aim was to bring back to life beautiful natural areas that had been abandoned over time, through crops suited to the land in that area. Just like many other stories of Tuscan wine, in this case, too, the work started with the reconstruction of a ruined old house, now transformed into a quality hotel, planting of vineyards and olive groves and later, honey production and a riding stables. The surrounding area inspired the name of the leading wine, dedicated to the movie filmed in the area by Dino Risi. The Sorpasso 2011 is an excellent blend of cabernet franc and merlot with hints of chocolate, coffee, and ripe fruit on the nose, followed by spicy cinnamon notes. The palate is mouthfilling, soft and nicely weighty with a lingering finish. The enthralling Bianco 2014, from vermentino with a little viognier, is fragrant, lively and nicely stylish.

● Sorpasso '11		🍷🍷 5
○ Bianco Fortulla '14		🍷🍷 4
● Fortulla Rosso '13		🍷🍷 4
⊙ Fortulla Rosé '14		🍷 3
● Fortulla Rosso '12		🍷🍷 4
● Sorpasso '10		🍷🍷 5

Podere Fortuna

via San Giusto a Fortuna, 7
50038 Scarperia e San Piero [FI]
Tel. 0558487214
www.poderefortuna.com

CELLAR SALES
PRE-BOOKED VISITS
ACCOMMODATION
ANNUAL PRODUCTION 25,000 bottles
HECTARES UNDER VINE 6.00

The place chosen by Alessandro Brogi to make wine is rich in traces of history: next to the castle of Cafaggiolo, at Mugello, built by the Medici family and inherited by Lorenzo il Magnifico. A document dating back to 1465 records the production of wine in this place even then. Over the centuries, however, farming trends shaped the area for cereal crops. In the late 1990s, then the owner decided to start up the winegrowing activity again, he also decided to study the land and the climate, and planted pinot nero grapes. This is certainly not a commonly grown variety in Tuscany, but the results prove him right. The Fortuni 2012 made the finals with subtle aromas of wild berries and aromatic herbs like mint and sage. A light, delicate entry on the slender-bodied palate with pleasing acidity and a really satisfying, lingering flavour.

Tenuta La Fortuna

loc. La Fortuna, 83
53024 Montalcino [SI]
Tel. 0577848308
www.tenutalafortuna.it

CELLAR SALES
PRE-BOOKED VISITS
ANNUAL PRODUCTION 60,000 bottles
HECTARES UNDER VINE 18.00

It was easy for us to predict a prompt return to the main section of the Guide for the lovely estate owned by husband and wife Gioberto and Felicetta Zannoni, who work alongside their children Angelo and Romina. This is the sixth generation to work the La Fortuna farm, with just under 20 hectares divided over two main plots in the north-eastern part of Montalcino and in Castelnuovo dell'Abate. Apart from a few rows of cabernet sauvignon, sangiovese grapes reign in the vineyards with vibrant, generous features. The wine is aged in medium-sized oak and in barriques for the Riserva. The two excellent Brunellos from the glorious 2010 vintage fit the stylistic profile perfectly. The standard version is warm and jolly with hints of boiled sweets and piquant spice, while the Giobi selection focuses mainly on mature aromas and more confident phenolic extract, without compromising the overall balance.

● Fortuni '12	♟♟ 5
● Coldaia '12	♟♟ 5
● 1465 MCDLXV '10	♟♟♟ 8
● 1465 MCDLXV '09	♟♟ 8
● Ardito del Mugello '10	♟♟ 3
○ Campo de' Tre Filari '07	♟♟ 6
● Coldaia '11	♟♟ 5
● Coldaia '09	♟♟ 5
● Coldaia '07	♟♟ 5
● Fortuni '10	♟♟ 6
● Fortuni '09	♟♟ 6
○ Greto alla Macchia '12	♟♟ 5
○ Greto alla Macchia '10	♟♟ 5
● MCDLXV (1465) '07	♟♟ 8
● Pinot Nero Coldaia '06	♟♟ 5
● Pinot Nero Coldaia '05	♟♟ 5

● Brunello di Montalcino '10	♟♟ 6
● Brunello di Montalcino Giobi '10	♟♟ 6
● Rosso di Montalcino '13	♟ 3
● Brunello di Montalcino '01	♟♟♟ 5
● Brunello di Montalcino '08	♟♟ 6
● Brunello di Montalcino Ris. '07	♟♟ 7
● Rosso di Montalcino '11	♟♟ 3

TUSCANY

La Fralluca

LOC. BARBICONI, 153
57028 SUVERETO [LI]
TEL. 0565829076
www.lafralluca.com

CELLAR SALES
PRE-BOOKED VISITS
ANNUAL PRODUCTION 40,000 bottles
HECTARES UNDER VINE 10.00
SUSTAINABLE WINERY

The estate is named after its two owners, Luca Recine and Francesca Bellini, who fell in love with the area and decided to begin the journey to become wine producers. Driven by a deep passion and the desire to radically change their lives, leaving behind the fashion sector where they originally worked, they left Milan for Francesca's birthplace, to work the land. Luca is directly responsible for the vineyards while Francesca has always been in charge of the commercial side. The first vineyards were planted in 2005 and the varieties were chosen after careful evaluation of the soil, which is mainly limestone and stony material. The Cabernet Franc 2012 has a fresh, lively nose with hints of ferns and lemon verbena, followed by bilberries and currants. The palate is soft, delicate and beautifully complex with a fresh, flavoursome finish. The impressive Viognier Bauci 2013 has mature aromas of peach and apricot and a nicely blended palate, lively and fresh with appetizing tangy flavour.

● Cabernet Franc '12	♥♥ 5
● Fillide '12	♥♥ 3
● Syrah Pitis '12	♥♥ 5
○ Viognier Bauci '13	♥♥ 3
○ Val di Cornia Vermentino Filemone '14	♥ 3
● Cabernet Franc '11	♥♥ 6
● Syrah Pitis '10	♥♥ 3
○ Viognier '11	♥♥ 2*
○ Viognier Bauci '12	♥♥ 3

Frank & Serafico

FRAZ. ALBERESE
S.DA SPERGOLAIA
58100 GROSSETO
TEL. 0564418491
www.frankeserafico.com

CELLAR SALES
PRE-BOOKED VISITS
RESTAURANT SERVICE
ANNUAL PRODUCTION 30,000 bottles
HECTARES UNDER VINE 25.00

There were once two friends who had followed different paths but then met again and to walk together along the same route: Maremma. Fabrizio is Frank, who first travelled around Italy and then moved to California, returning later to Maremma. He met Pier Paolo, or Serafico, who had lived on the family estate in Maremma since he was seven. Their first meeting was not exactly all hearts and flowers but their relationship became stronger and in 2010 they set up their estate. The land is scattered over various parts of Maremma, and the vinification techniques aim to preserve the natural features of the grapes as much as possible. The Morellino Mr 2013 is interesting: aromatic hints of sage and bay leaves, ripe fruit and a well-organized palate with fresh, lively sensations and a tangy, succulent finish. We also liked the Sangiovese 2011: mature aromas, cherry fruit on a nicely blended, full-bodied palate and crescendo finish.

● Morellino di Scansano Mr '13	♥♥ 2*
● Sangiovese '11	♥♥ 4
● Frank '13	♥ 3
○ Maremma Toscana Redola Bianco '14	♥ 2
● Maremma Toscana Redola Rosso '14	♥ 2
○ Serafico '12	♥ 4
○ Vermentino VR '14	♥ 2
● Frank '09	♥♥ 6
● Morellino di Scansano Mr '12	♥♥ 2*
○ Vermentino '10	♥♥ 4

Frascole

LOC. FRASCOLE, 27A
50062 DICOMANO [FI]
TEL. 0558386340
www.frascole.it

CELLAR SALES
PRE-BOOKED VISITS
ACCOMMODATION
ANNUAL PRODUCTION 65,000 bottles
HECTARES UNDER VINE 16.00
VITICULTURE METHOD Certified Organic

The small village at the heart of the estate originates from Etruscan and Roman ruins. Near the winery the traces of an Etruscan fortification can be visited. The owners, the Lippi and Santoni families, live on the site which includes another five medieval constructions immersed in the vineyards and olive groves, and offers accommodation. The farming and cellar procedures and commercial side are entrusted to owner Enrico Lippi, who has always believed in using virgin land for winegrowing. The unusual position of the vineyards, which are quite high compared to the surrounding production area, endows the wines with a particular fresh and minerally quality. The Riserva 2012 made the finals with subtle, delicate, minerally aromas backed up by black berries and hints of cinnamon. The palate makes a frank, lively entry with evident but measured tannin and a long, stylish finish. Also interesting, the experimental InAlbis 2011, a monovarietal Trebbiano matured on the skins.

● Chianti Rufina Ris. '12	♥♥	3*
○ Bianco InAlbis '13	♥♥	2*
○ Bianco InAlbis Sulle Bucce '11	♥♥	2*
● Chianti Rufina '13	♥♥	2*
● Limine '10	♥♥	2*
● Bitornino '13	♥	2
● Rosso Limine '09	♀♀	2*
○ Vin Santo del Chianti Rufina '05	♀♀	7
○ Vin Santo del Chianti Rufina '04	♀♀	7
○ Vin Santo del Chianti Rufina '03	♀♀	7
○ Vin Santo del Chianti Rufina '02	♀♀	7
○ Vin Santo del Chianti Rufina '01	♀♀	7
○ Vin Santo del Chianti Rufina '99	♀♀	7
○ Vin Santo del Chianti Rufina '97	♀♀	7
○ Vin Santo del Chianti Rufina '96	♀♀	7
○ Vin Santo del Chianti Rufina '95	♀♀	7

★Marchesi de' Frescobaldi

VIA SANTO SPIRITO, 11
50125 FIRENZE
TEL. 05527141
www.frescobaldi.it

CELLAR SALES
PRE-BOOKED VISITS
ANNUAL PRODUCTION 10,000,000 bottles
HECTARES UNDER VINE 1200.00

Respect for tradition and the ongoing search for new projects are innate characteristics of the Frescobaldi family, passionate about wine since the 14th century. The estate extends throughout Tuscany, starting with the winery at Rufina and on to Maremma, the Montalcino area and even reaching Friuli. Worth mentioning is the family's social commitment to the Gorgona Island detention centre where, since 2012, inmates have had the opportunity to try winegrowing at a professional level supervised by the winery's team. Once Lamberto Frescobaldi took over the running of the estate, he pushed on with renewal of the property which is evident in the style of the wines. The Riserva Vecchie Viti 2012 stands out for subtle, stylish aromas of wild berries softened by minerally sensations, and a slender, supple palate with excellent, lingering flavour. The Mormoreto 2012 is also good, with opulent aromas of ripe fruit and various spices and a lovely well-coordinated structure.

● Chianti Rufina V. V. Ris. '12	♥♥	6
● Mormoreto '12	♥♥	8
● Chianti Rufina Nipozzano Ris. '12	♥♥	5
● Giramonte Rosso '12	♥♥	8
○ Gorgona '14	♥♥	4
● Maremma Toscana Cabernet Sauvignon Terre More '13	♥♥	3
● Montesodi '12	♥♥	6
○ Pomino Il Benefizio '13	♥♥	3
● Tenuta di Castiglioni '12	♥♥	4
⊙ Alie '14	♥	3
● Ammiraglia '11	♥	7
○ Massovivo '14	♥	2
● Morellino di Scansano Pietraregia dell'Ammiraglia Ris. '11	♥	5
○ Pomino '14	♥	3
● Rèmole '14	♥	2

Fuligni

VIA SALONI, 33
53024 MONTALCINO [SI]
TEL. 0577848710
www.fuligni.it

CELLAR SALES
PRE-BOOKED VISITS
ANNUAL PRODUCTION 52,000 bottles
HECTARES UNDER VINE 12.00

The estate run by Maria Flora Fuligni has
been operative for over a century and is
constantly mentioned among the reliable
names for those who love a neoclassic
Brunello, aged in 30-hectolitre oak after a
brief passage in tonneaux. When young the
wines can be edgy and constricted but in
their best version they bring together the
good texture and lightness we expect from
Sangioveses originating from the
north-eastern part of Montalcino. The
estate's ten or so hectares of vineyards are
at I Cottimelli, one of the highest locations in
the DOC zone at altitudes between 380 and
450 metres, on marly, stony soil. It was easy
to predict another Tre Bicchieri in the near
future for Fuligni, but the Brunello 2010
gave a performance beyond our
expectations. From the first impact it is
lustrous and deep, with aromas from
medicinal herbs to orange zest, tobacco and
roots, while texture is polished to say the
least with tangy flow and silky tannins. One
of the very best.

● Brunello di Montalcino '10	♟♟♟	6
● Rosso di Montalcino Ginestreto '13	♟♟	4
● Brunello di Montalcino Ris. '01	♀♀♀	8
● Brunello di Montalcino Ris. '97	♀♀♀	8
● Brunello di Montalcino '09	♀♀	6
● Brunello di Montalcino '08	♀♀	6
● Brunello di Montalcino '07	♀♀	6
● Brunello di Montalcino '06	♀♀	6
● Brunello di Montalcino Ris. '07	♀♀	8
● Brunello di Montalcino Ris. '06	♀♀	8
● Brunello di Montalcino Ris. '04	♀♀	8
● S. J. '12	♀♀	3

Gattavecchi

LOC. SANTA MARIA
PIAZZA GRANDE, 12
53045 MONTEPULCIANO [SI]
TEL. 0578757110
www.gattavecchi.it

CELLAR SALES
PRE-BOOKED VISITS
RESTAURANT SERVICE
ANNUAL PRODUCTION 280,000 bottles
HECTARES UNDER VINE 40.00

Over a century of tradition accompanies the
Gattavecchi family in the wine sector. The
various generations that have run the
estate have all contributed something new
that enabled it to keep pace with the times.
Today's owners are siblings Luca, Gionata
and Daniela, who have different roles to
play alongside their mother in managing
the business. The vineyards are found in
various parts of the Montepulciano area, to
make the most of the different soil and
weather features. All the grapes are
matured in the old cellars that formerly
belonged to the 13th-century Padri Serviti
convent, recently equipped with a tasting
area for wines and typical dishes. The
Nobile Parceto 2012 has blackberry jam
aromas alongside roasted coffee beans and
spicy hints of cinnamon. The palate opens
generous and mouthfilling with fine-
grained, well-dosed tannins and a long,
tangy finish.

● Nobile di Montepulciano Parceto Poggio alla Sala '12	♟♟	5
● Nobile di Montepulciano '12	♟	4
● Nobile di Montepulciano Poggio alla Sala '12	♟	5
● Nobile di Montepulciano Poggio alla Sala Ris. '11	♟	5
● Nobile di Montepulciano Riserva dei Padri Serviti '11	♟	5
● Chianti Colli Senesi '13	♀♀	2*
● Nobile di Montepulciano Poggio alla Sala '10	♀♀	5
● Nobile di Montepulciano Poggio alla Sala Ris. '10	♀♀	5
● Nobile di Montepulciano Riserva dei Padri Serviti '10	♀♀	4
● Rosso di Montepulciano Poggio alla Sala '11	♀♀	2*

★Tenuta di Ghizzano

FRAZ. GHIZZANO
VIA DELLA CHIESA, 4
56037 PECCIOLI [PI]
TEL. 0587630096
www.tenutadighizzano.com

CELLAR SALES
PRE-BOOKED VISITS
ACCOMMODATION
ANNUAL PRODUCTION 80,000 bottles
HECTARES UNDER VINE 20.00
VITICULTURE METHOD Certified Organic

Tenuta di Ghizzano is eye-bogglingly beautiful and well looked-after. On this estate of over 350 hectares, the vineyards share the space with the surrounding natural environment. The sandy, clayey soil is of marine origin with plenty of fossil material. One of the best known women in the wine sector runs the estate: Ginevra Venerosi Pesciolini, who was responsible for the decision to adopt first organic and now biodynamic farming methods. A great version of the Nambrot. The 2012 version of this classic blend of merlot, cabernet franc and petit verdot is very appealing thanks to wild black and red berry fruit and a subtle spicy sensation. The palate shows pace and grip, again with ripe, satisfying fruit and sweet, beautifully extracted tannin.

Marchesi Ginori Lisci

FRAZ. PONTEGINORI
LOC. QUERCETO
56040 MONTECATINI VAL DI CECINA [PI]
TEL. 058837443
www.marchesiginorilisci.it

CELLAR SALES
ACCOMMODATION AND RESTAURANT SERVICE
ANNUAL PRODUCTION 35,000 bottles
HECTARES UNDER VINE 17.00
VITICULTURE METHOD Certified Organic

The Ginori Lisci family history is among those written in school textbooks. Many descendents of the owners of Castello di Querceto, in Val di Cecina, hold important public positions in Florence and elsewhere in Italy. As far as wine is concerned, the turning point came in the late 1980s when Lionardo Ginori and his nephew Luigi Malenchini started to make changes to the estate, planting new vineyards and finding new spaces on the property to build a more modern and functional cellar. The hamlet where the estate is located dates back to the year 1000 and has been fully renovated with spaces for office use and holiday apartments. Into the finals for the Macchion del Lupo 2011, a monovarietal Cabernet Sauvignon, with lovely fresh hints of aromatic herbs, like bay and rosemary, and wild berries and plums. Tannins in step with the alcohol on a lively, intriguing palate with delicious flavour thanks to the well-measured freshness.

● Terre di Pisa Nambrot '12	♟♟♟ 6
● Terre di Pisa Veneroso '12	♟♟ 5
● il Ghizzano '13	♟ 3
● Nambrot '09	♟♟♟ 6
● Nambrot '08	♟♟♟ 6
● Nambrot '06	♟♟♟ 6
● Nambrot '05	♟♟♟ 6
● Nambrot '04	♟♟♟ 6
● Nambrot '03	♟♟♟ 6
● Veneroso '10	♟♟♟ 5
● Veneroso '07	♟♟♟ 5
● Veneroso '04	♟♟♟ 5
● Veneroso '01	♟♟♟ 5

● Montescudaio Cabernet Macchion del Lupo '11	♟♟ 3*
● Montescudaio Merlot Campordigno '12	♟♟ 2*
● Montescudaio Merlot Castello Ginori '11	♟♟ 2*
○ Vermentino Virgola '14	♟ 2
● Castello Ginori '07	♟♟ 4
● Castello Ginori '06	♟♟ 4
● Montescudaio Cabernet Macchion del Lupo '09	♟♟ 3
● Montescudaio Cabernet Macchion del Lupo '08	♟♟ 3*
● Montescudaio Macchion del Lupo '07	♟♟ 3*
● Montescudaio Merlot '08	♟♟ 2*
● Montescudaio Merlot Castello Ginori '09	♟♟ 4
● Montescudaio Rosso Campordigno '10	♟♟ 2*
● Montescudaio Rosso Campordigno '08	♟♟ 3*

I Giusti e Zanza

VIA DEI PUNTONI, 9
56043 FAUGLIA [PI]
TEL. 058544354
www.igiustiezanza.it

CELLAR SALES
PRE-BOOKED VISITS
ANNUAL PRODUCTION 100,000 bottles
HECTARES UNDER VINE 17.00
VITICULTURE METHOD Certified Organic

Paolo Giusti's wine-producing estate has operated on the Fauglia hills since the early 1990s. The land hereabouts is sandy and clayey, with plenty of gravel that helps with drainage. For several years the estate has been pursuing greater awareness and respect for the local area, embracing first organic farming and then changing over in recent years to biodynamic methods. The wines can be defined as modern in style but without any kind of excess or forcing, both in terms of ripeness of the fruit and the use of wood. The grapes are predominantly black varieties: cabernet sauvignon and franc, merlot, petit verdot. The Dulcamara 2012, mostly cabernet, has a charming nose with jammy hints of cherries and blackberries, and a vibrant, tannic, still-clenched palate. The Belcore 2013 is lighter while the monovarietal Syrah PerBruno 2013 is vibrant and spicy, tangy and succulent despite the still rather stiff tannin.

● Dulcamara '12	♟♟ 5
● Belcore '13	♟♟ 3
● PerBruno '13	♟♟ 4
○ Nemorino Bianco '14	♟ 2
● Nemorino Rosso '14	♟ 2
● Dulcamara '11	♟♟ 5
● Dulcamara '10	♟♟ 5
● Dulcamara '09	♟♟ 5
● Dulcamara '08	♟♟ 5
● Dulcamara '07	♟♟ 5
● Dulcamara '06	♟♟ 5
● Dulcamara '05	♟♟ 5
● PerBruno '12	♟♟ 4

★Podere Grattamacco

LOC. LUNGAGNANO
57022 CASTAGNETO CARDUCCI [LI]
TEL. 0565765069
www.collemassari.it

CELLAR SALES
PRE-BOOKED VISITS
ANNUAL PRODUCTION 120,000 bottles
HECTARES UNDER VINE 16.00
VITICULTURE METHOD Certified Organic
SUSTAINABLE WINERY

Grattamacco was established in the 1970s and rapidly became one of Bolgheri's success stories. Today it is run by the Tipa brothers and a few recent purchases have increased the estate's winegrowing capacity. Production rests on solid foundations with a high standard of quality. The vineyards share the landscape with woodlands and are planted on different types of soil, from sandy to marly limestone. The wines scale the heights of the DOC thanks to their complexity and finesse. The Bolgheri Superiore Grattamacco 2012 is on top form: dark colour, very vibrant aromas, as mature as they are complex, with hints of wild berries and marzipan. The palate is weighty and racy as usual, with very fine texture. The L'Alberello of the same year is harmonious and approachably pleasing.

● Bolgheri Rosso Sup. Grattamacco '12	♟♟♟ 8
● Bolgheri Sup. L'Alberello '12	♟♟ 6
○ Bolgheri Vermentino Grattamacco '13	♟♟ 5
● Bolgheri Rosso '13	♟ 4
● Bolgheri Rosso Sup. Grattamacco '10	♟♟♟ 7
● Bolgheri Rosso Sup. Grattamacco '09	♟♟♟ 7
● Bolgheri Rosso Sup. Grattamacco '07	♟♟♟ 7
● Bolgheri Rosso Sup. Grattamacco '06	♟♟♟ 7
● Bolgheri Rosso Sup. Grattamacco '05	♟♟♟ 7
● Bolgheri Rosso Sup. Grattamacco '04	♟♟♟ 7
● Bolgheri Rosso Sup. Grattamacco '03	♟♟♟ 7
● Bolgheri Rosso Sup. Grattamacco '01	♟♟♟ 8
● Bolgheri Sup. L'Alberello '11	♟♟♟ 6

Fattoria di Grignano

via di Grignano, 22
50065 Pontassieve [FI]
Tel. 0558398490
www.fattoriadigrignano.com

CELLAR SALES
PRE-BOOKED VISITS
ANNUAL PRODUCTION 200,000 bottles
HECTARES UNDER VINE 53.00
VITICULTURE METHOD Certified Organic
SUSTAINABLE WINERY

Where the Sieve river meets the Arno, and the first hints of the Appennines are visible, stands Fattoria di Grignano. The estate has 600 hectares in the Rufina area, divided into 47 farms with various crops. The nucleus of the estate is the 15th-century villa built by the Marchesi Gondi and modified in the 18th century, and which still houses the cellar. Since 1999 the Pievecchia has also been part of the estate: another farm which takes its name from the old church on the property. The Inghirami family has owned the estate since 1972, pouring passion and commitment into the production of wine and olive oil, above all. Through to the finals for the Chianti Rufina Riserva Poggio Gualtieri 2011: excellent, complex aromas with marked fragrant hints of dried flowers, clear-cut fruit, and spicy cloves. The palate is beautifully balanced, generous and flavoursome. The 2012 is also enjoyable, with a delicate nose and fresh, delicious flavour.

● Chianti Rufina Poggio Gualtieri Ris. '11	▼▼	4
● Chianti Rufina '12	▼▼	2*
○ Vin Santo del Chianti Rufina '08	▼▼	4
○ 0575 '14	▼	2
○ Spumante Brut	▼	4
● Chianti Rufina '09	▽▽	2
● Chianti Rufina '08	▽▽	2*
● Chianti Rufina Poggio Gualtieri Ris. '09	▽▽	3
● Chianti Rufina Poggio Gualtieri Ris. '08	▽▽	3
● Chianti Rufina Poggio Gualtieri Ris. '07	▽▽	3
● Chianti Rufina Ris. '06	▽▽	3*
● Salicaria '09	▽▽	4
● Salicaria '05	▽▽	4
○ Vin Santo del Chianti Rufina '04	▽▽	4
○ Vin Santo del Chianti Rufina '03	▽▽	4

Guado al Melo

loc. Murrotto, 130a
57022 Castagneto Carducci [LI]
Tel. 0565763238
www.guadoalmelo.it

CELLAR SALES
PRE-BOOKED VISITS
ANNUAL PRODUCTION 150,000 bottles
HECTARES UNDER VINE 25.00
VITICULTURE METHOD Certified Organic
SUSTAINABLE WINERY

Michele Scienza's winery was the revelation of the year for Bolgheri, with a range of wines that were all very good to excellent. The 17 hectares of vineyards are farmed with maniacal care for quality and sustainability while the cellarwork is mainly artisanal and non-invasive. The several grape varieties grown here represent Mediterranean and Caucasian tradition: a kind of collection, dominated however by the classic Bolgheri varieties. In addition to the first Tre Bicchieri, Guado al Melo earns the Up-and-Coming Winery award. The Bolgheri Superiore Atis 2012 makes a magnificent impression: richly complex, subtle aromas in which ripe fruit blends perfectly with grassy and balsamic sensations. These aromas are faithfully reflected on the palate, leading the flavour into a long, appetizing finish. Just a nose behind is the Bolgheri Rosso Rute 2013: crisp, with almost smoky sensations.

● Bolgheri Rosso Sup. Atis '12	▼▼▼	6
● Bolgheri Rosso Rute '13	▼▼	5
○ Guado al Melo Bianco '13	▼	5

TUSCANY

Tenuta Guado al Tasso

LOC. BELVEDERE, 140
57020 BOLGHERI [LI]
TEL. 0565749735
www.antinori.it

CELLAR SALES
PRE-BOOKED VISITS
ANNUAL PRODUCTION 800,000 bottles
HECTARES UNDER VINE 300.00

Guado al Tasso is a Bolgheri project belonging to the venerable Italian wine house of Antinori, of worldwide fame. This is a very large property: about 300 hectares under vine but 1000 overall, with plenty of woodlands and Mediterranean scrubland. The grapes grown here represent the most widespread local red wine varieties, including merlot, cabernet sauvignon and petit verdot as well as sangiovese. For white wines, vermentino is the predominant variety. All the wines are modern in style and beautifully made. The Bolgheri Superiore Guado al Tasso 2012 is still weighed down by larked toasty sensations, and needs to relax in the bottles to express all its potential. The Il Bruciato 2013 is more readable and succulent while the Vermentino 2014 is very good, with enthralling floral aromas and a lovely tangy flavour.

Gualdo del Re

LOC. NOTRI, 77
57028 SUVERETO [LI]
TEL. 0565829888
www.gualdodelre.it

CELLAR SALES
PRE-BOOKED VISITS
ACCOMMODATION AND RESTAURANT SERVICE
ANNUAL PRODUCTION 100,000 bottles
HECTARES UNDER VINE 20.00
VITICULTURE METHOD Certified Organic

The Rossi family is committed to running this estate which has, over time, become an increasingly important business both in winemaking terms and as a hospitality structure, with a resort and restaurant that attract many tourists. In the 1960s the concept of making fine quality wine in this area was a gamble, but current owner Nico nurtured the dream from his childhood and, with his wife Teresa, made it come true. Thus in the 1990s an adventure began that would never stop providing gratification. The Cabraia 2012, from cabernet franc with a small amount of cabernet sauvignon, makes an intriguing aromatic impact with hints of spice, leather and tobacco combined with minty sensations. Generous and soft on the palate, nicely lively, with well-blended tannins and a long, pleasantly lingering finish.

● Bolgheri Rosso Il Bruciato '13	♟♟ 5
● Bolgheri Rosso Sup. Guado al Tasso '12	♟♟ 8
○ Bolgheri Vermentino '14	♟♟ 3
⊙ Bolgheri Rosato Scalabrone '14	♟ 3
● Bolgheri Rosso Sup. Guado al Tasso '01	♟♟♟ 8
● Bolgheri Rosso Sup. Guado al Tasso '90	♟♟♟ 8
● Bolgheri Rosso Il Bruciato '12	♟♟ 4
● Bolgheri Rosso Sup. Guado al Tasso '10	♟♟ 8
● Bolgheri Rosso Sup. Guado al Tasso '09	♟♟ 8
● Bolgheri Rosso Sup. Guado al Tasso '08	♟♟ 8
○ Bolgheri Vermentino '13	♟♟ 3

● Cabraia '12	♟♟ 6
● Federico Primo '12	♟♟ 5
● Val di Cornia Rosso I'Rennero '12	♟♟ 7
● Val di Cornia Sangiovese Gualdo del Re '12	♟♟ 5
○ Vermentino Valentina '14	♟♟ 3
○ Eliseo Bianco '14	♟ 2
⊙ Shiny '14	♟ 2
● Val di Cornia Rosso I'Rennero '05	♟♟♟ 6
● Val di Cornia Rosso I'Rennero '01	♟♟♟ 7
● Cabraia '11	♟♟ 6
○ Eliseo Bianco '11	♟♟ 2*
● Eliseo Rosso '12	♟♟ 2*
● Federico Primo '11	♟♟ 5
● Gualdo del Re '11	♟♟ 5
● Val di Cornia Rosso I'Rennero '11	♟♟ 7
● Val di Cornia Sangiovese Suvereto '11	♟♟ 5

Tenute Guicciardini Strozzi

LOC. CUSONA, 5
53037 SAN GIMIGNANO [SI]
TEL. 0577950028
www.guicciardinistrozzi.it

CELLAR SALES
PRE-BOOKED VISITS
ANNUAL PRODUCTION 800,000 bottles
HECTARES UNDER VINE 115.00

Describing the Guicciardini Strozzi family's
San Gimignano estate at Cusona is a bit
like writing a historical essay, considering
the important role this family has played in
the events of Italy's past. For example, their
ancestors include the very Monna Lisa
painted by painted by Leonardo da Vinci.
Returning to this area, the first Vernaccia
produced here dates back to the 13th
century, while many centuries later
Francesco Guicciardini, minister for
agriculture and later mayor of Florence,
made the property into a model estate. The
father of the current owner, Girolamo
Strozzi, first bottled Vernaccia in Bordeaux
bottles in 1933. The enjoyable Vernaccia
Riserva 2012 has vibrant aromas of
almonds and apple and pear fruit alongside
refreshing vegetal hints. The palate opens
lively and fresh with slender, edgy body, not
too lingering but impressively tangy. We
liked all the other wines too.

○ Vernaccia di S. Gimignano Ris. '12	♟♟	3
○ Arabesque '14	♟	2
● Chianti Colli Senesi Titolato Strozzi '14	♟	2
● Momi '14	♟	3
● Morellino di Scansano Titolato Strozzi '14	♟	2
○ Vernaccia di S. Gimignano Cusona 1933 '13	♟	3
○ Vernaccia di S. Gimignano Titolato Strozzi '14	♟	2
● Morellino di Scansano Titolato Strozzi '12	♟♟	2*
○ Vernaccia di S. Gimignano Cusona 1933 '12	♟♟	3
○ Vernaccia di S. Gimignano Titolato Strozzi '12	♟♟	2*
○ Vernaccia di S. Gimignano Titolato Strozzi '11	♟♟	2*

★★Isole e Olena

LOC. ISOLE, 1
50021 BARBERINO VAL D'ELSA [FI]
TEL. 0558072763
www.isoleolena.it

CELLAR SALES
PRE-BOOKED VISITS
ANNUAL PRODUCTION 200,000 bottles
HECTARES UNDER VINE 56.00

Paolo De Marchi has over 35 years of work
in the Chianti Classico area. Originally from
Piedmontese he is by now a fully fledged
Chiantigiano and probably one of the most
rigorous vignerons the Gallo Nero DOC
zone can boast of. His work is based on
consistency and professionalism in pursuit
of the most profound expression of the
local area, helping considerably to
relaunch it. Alongside more traditional
wines the range of Isole e Olena products
includes an intentional digression into the
so-called international types, which stand
outside any kind of schematic definition.
The Cepparello 2012 is a really well-typed
version: fresh, fruity aromas and very
stylish hints of iron filings, followed by a
succulent, well-balanced palate. The
Chianti Classico 2013 is equally good with
floral, earthy aromas as a prologue to a
nuanced, very flavoursome palate. The Vin
Santo del Chianti Classico 2006 has a
creamy palate with aromas of dried fruit
and candied orange peel.

● Cepparello '12	♟♟♟	8
● Chianti Cl. '13	♟♟	5
○ Vin Santo del Chianti Classico '06	♟♟	7
● Cabernet Sauvignon Collezione De Marchi '11	♟	8
● Cabernet Sauvignon '97	♟♟♟	8
● Cepparello '09	♟♟♟	8
● Cepparello '07	♟♟♟	8
● Cepparello '05	♟♟♟	8
● Cepparello '03	♟♟♟	7
● Cepparello '01	♟♟♟	6
● Cepparello '00	♟♟♟	6
● Cepparello '99	♟♟♟	6
● Cepparello '98	♟♟♟	6
● Cepparello '97	♟♟♟	6
● Syrah '99	♟♟♟	5

Istine

VIA ROMA, 11
53017 RADDA IN CHIANTI [SI]
TEL. 0577733684
www.istine.it

ANNUAL PRODUCTION 20,000 bottles
HECTARES UNDER VINE 34.00

Istine is a recently emerging estate on the
Chianti Classico overview, so recent in fact
that its first bottles are from the 2009
vintage. Since 2012 the sangiovese has
been fermented separately according to the
vineyard of origin. So this is the birthplace
of the Chianti Classico Vigna Istine
(between Radda and Castellina), Vigna
Casanova (Radda) and, since 2013, the
Chianti Classico Vigna Cavarchione (Gaiole).
At the helm is Angela Fronti, with a clear
oenological plan, confirmed by the wines
themselves which are all aged in large oak
and show a clearly defined style featuring
supple flavour and elegance. The Chianti
Classico Le Vigne Riserva 2012 has
well-coordinated aromas and a pleasantly
vigorous, nicely fluent palate. The delicious
Chianti Classico Vigna Casanova 2013 has
crystal-clear aromas and a well-paced,
succulent and very flavoursome palate. The
same fresh, balanced sensations appear in
the other wines in the range.

● Chianti Cl. Le Vigne Ris. '12	♟♟ 3*
● Chianti Cl. V. Casanova '13	♟♟ 3*
● Chianti Cl. '13	♟♟ 3
● Chianti Cl. V. Istine '13	♟♟ 3
● Chianti Cl. V. Cavarchione '13	♟ 3
● Chianti Cl. '11	♟♟ 3
● Chianti Cl. '10	♟♟ 3*
● Chianti Cl. V. Casanova '12	♟♟ 3
● Chianti Cl. V. Istine '12	♟♟ 3

Maurizio Lambardi

LOC. CANALICCHIO DI SOTTO, 8
53024 MONTALCINO [SI]
TEL. 0577848476
www.lambardimontalcino.it

CELLAR SALES
PRE-BOOKED VISITS
ANNUAL PRODUCTION 17,000 bottles
HECTARES UNDER VINE 6.50

Also known as Canalicchio di Sotto, the
Lambardi family's farm is one of
Montalcino's veteran bottling estates with
over 40 harvests under its belt. The small
range is closely linked to the features of the
north-eastern slope where the over six
hectares belonging to the farm are almost
all planted with sangiovese. They yield
wines of classic texture shaped by lengthy
maceration and ageing in medium-sized
oak: deceptively uncomplicated Brunellos
which combine apparently light body with a
vigorous linear structure that can be biting
when young. And the hesitancy we note in
the Brunello 2010 should probably be
interpreted in this light. Reductive and
slightly dark aromas of plums, cocoa
powder and hints of blood-rich meat and a
palate currently dominated by the very dry
tannin, and dusty texture. These hard
qualities are also present in the balsamic
Rosso 2013.

● Brunello di Montalcino '10	♟♟ 5
● Rosso di Montalcino '13	♟ 3
● Brunello di Montalcino '09	♟♟ 5
● Brunello di Montalcino '08	♟♟ 5
● Brunello di Montalcino '07	♟♟ 5
● Brunello di Montalcino '06	♟♟ 5
● Brunello di Montalcino '05	♟♟ 5

Lamole di Lamole

LOC. LAMOLE
50022 GREVE IN CHIANTI [FI]
TEL. 0559331411
www.lamole.com

CELLAR SALES
PRE-BOOKED VISITS
RESTAURANT SERVICE
ANNUAL PRODUCTION 242,000 bottles
HECTARES UNDER VINE 57.00

The Veneto Santa Margherita group represents one of the leading winegrowing businesses in Italy, with property in many areas of the country. Turning to Tuscany, there are two productive estates in the Chianti Classico zone: Lamole di Lamole at Greve in Chianti and Villa Vistarenni at Gaiole. Despite the quantities, the Chianti products, particularly those from Lamole, show a typical style based on strong personality and marked territorial features, tending to be sober and anything but commonplace. They are aged in both large and small oak. This could be the best 2012 Chianti Classico, a Tre Bicchieri with no ifs and buts. The Etichetta Blu shows clearly defined aromas of wild berries and fresh cherries which herald the succulent, very tangy flavour supported by a lively, fluent acidity. The Chianti Classico Etichetta Bianca is also good, with vibrant aromas and a tangy palate, though the oak is slightly less integrated in the flavour.

● Chianti Cl. Lamole di Lamole Et. Blu '12	ŸŸŸ	3*
● Chianti Cl. Lamole di Lamole Et. Bianca '12	ŸŸ	3
● Chianti Cl. Vign. di Campolungo Gran Sel. '11	ŸŸ	5
● Chianti Cl. Ris. '11	Ÿ	3
● Chianti Cl. Villa Vistarenni '12	Ÿ	4
● Chianti Cl. Vign. di Campolungo Gran Sel. '10	♀♀♀	5
● Chianti Cl. Vign. di Campolungo Ris. '09	♀♀♀	5
● Chianti Cl. Lamole di Lamole '10	♀♀	3
● Chianti Cl. Lamole di Lamole Et. Blu '11	♀♀	3
● Chianti Cl. Lamole di Lamole Et. Blu '09	♀♀	4
● Chianti Cl. Lamole di Lamole Ris. '10	♀♀	4
● Chianti Cl. Lamole di Lamole Ris. '09	♀♀	4
● Chianti Cl. Villa Vistarenni Ris. '08	♀♀	4

Lanciola

LOC. POZZOLATICO
VIA IMPRUNETANA, 210
50023 IMPRUNETA [FI]
TEL. 055208324
www.lanciola.it

CELLAR SALES
PRE-BOOKED VISITS
ANNUAL PRODUCTION 250,000 bottles
HECTARES UNDER VINE 40.00

The Impruneta area is a relatively recent discovery for quality wine production, but the first farming and winemaking organization in the area dates back to the noble Ricci family who were contemporaries of the Medici, and contributed towards promoting the area, while also making room for olive groves. Current owners the Guarneri family have carried on this mission, digressing into various business sectors such as hotels and restaurants. Heading the group is Carlo, helped by his son Giancarlo, who is in charge of the commercial side. One part of the estate produces Chianti Classico wine in the heart of that Doc, at Greve. Through to the finals is Ricciotto 2013, an unusual blend of sangiovese and pinot nero, with lightly dried grapes: vibrant aromas of wild berries ennobled by spicy hints and a pleasing, mouthfilling and smooth palate with a fresh finish. The Terricci 2011, also interesting, is an austere and compact blend of sangiovese with cabernet franc and sauvignon.

● Ricciotto '13	ŸŸ	4
● Chianti Cl. Le Masse di Greve Ris. '12	ŸŸ	4
● Riccionero '12	ŸŸ	3
● Terricci '11	ŸŸ	5
● Chianti Colli Fiorentini '13	Ÿ	2
○ Ricciobianco '14	Ÿ	4
⊙ Ricciorosa '14	Ÿ	3
● Chianti Cl. Le Masse di Greve Gran Sel. '11	♀♀	5
○ Ricciobianco '08	♀♀	4
● Terricci '09	♀♀	5

La Lastra

fraz. Santa Lucia
via R. De Grada, 9
53037 San Gimignano [SI]
Tel. 0577941781
www.lalastra.it

CELLAR SALES
PRE-BOOKED VISITS
ANNUAL PRODUCTION 58,000 bottles
HECTARES UNDER VINE 7.00
SUSTAINABLE WINERY

La Lastra's story is that of a group of
friends united by a passion for wine that
led them to Tuscany after studying
oenological science at San Michele
all'Adige. Following work experience as
consultant winemakers, they decided to
establish a winery in 1994, under the
particular care of Nadia Betti and her
husband Renato Spanu, and also involving
Nadia's brother Enrico, Valerio Zorzi and
Enrico Paternoster. In 2000 came the
addition of a small estate near Siena
where they set up an agritourism and
practised organic farming in the vineyards
from the start. The production philosophy is
simple and open: environment before
business, people before brand, substance
before form. The Vernaccia Riserva 2012
shows a vibrant, minerally nose with fresh
hints of herbs like lemon verbena and
rounded, clear-cut fruity sensations on a
fluent palate that releases freshness and
texture. The finish is tangy and intriguing.

○ Vernaccia di S. Gimignano Ris. '12	♥♥ 3*
● Cabernet Franc '10	♥ 3
● Canaiolo '14	♥ 3
● Chianti Colli Senesi '13	♥ 2
○ Vernaccia di S. Gimignano '14	♥ 2
○ Vernaccia di S. Gimignano Ris. '09	♥♥♥ 3*
● Rovaio '09	♀♀ 4
● Rovaio '05	♀♀ 4
○ Vernaccia di S. Gimignano '13	♀♀ 2*
○ Vernaccia di S. Gimignano '12	♀♀ 2*
○ Vernaccia di S. Gimignano '11	♀♀ 2*
○ Vernaccia di S. Gimignano '10	♀♀ 2*
○ Vernaccia di S. Gimignano Ris. '11	♀♀ 3*
○ Vernaccia di S. Gimignano Ris. '10	♀♀ 3*
○ Vernaccia di S. Gimignano Ris. '05	♀♀ 3*

Lavacchio

via di Montefiesole, 55
50065 Pontassieve [FI]
Tel. 0558317472
www.fattorialavacchio.com

CELLAR SALES
PRE-BOOKED VISITS
ACCOMMODATION AND RESTAURANT SERVICE
ANNUAL PRODUCTION 100,000 bottles
HECTARES UNDER VINE 22.00
VITICULTURE METHOD Certified Organic

"True organic estate" is the winery's motto,
which speaks volumes about the passion
and respect for the local area, and a deep
conviction about the farming methods to
adopt for the best results. Nestling between
hills of olive groves and vineyards the farm
has a long history: passing from family to
family since the 18th century, starting with
the Peruzzi and ending up with the Lottero.
Faye is now at the helm, pouring plenty of
enthusiasm into the numerous activities on
offer: agritourism, restaurant, shop, a
windmill that still grinds wheat… The
estate has many different branches and its
emblem is an ancient cedar of Lebanon, an
immediate statement of their longstanding
passion for the land. A good overall
performance with most of the wines
presented on excellent form, especially
those closely expressing the terroir: the
2012, thanks to a relaxed, efficient palate;
the Riserva Cedro 2010 for its nicely
judged strength; the Ludié 2010 for its
overall elegance and finesse.

● Chianti Rufina Cedro '12	♥♥ 2*
● Chianti Rufina Cedro Ris. '10	♥♥ 4
● Chianti Rufina Ludié Ris. '10	♥♥ 5
○ Pachar '13	♥♥ 4
○ Vin Santo del Chianti Rufina Ris. '09	♥♥ 5
● Chianti Puro '14	♥ 2
● Fontegalli '09	♥ 5
○ Oro del Cedro V. T. '13	♥ 5
● Chianti Rufina Cedro Ris. '09	♀♀ 4
● Fontegalli '08	♀♀ 5
○ Oro del Cedro V. T. '12	♀♀ 5
○ Pachar '12	♀♀ 4
○ Vin Santo del Chianti Rufina '01	♀♀ 4
○ Vin Santo del Chianti Rufina Ris. '08	♀♀ 5
○ Vin Santo del Chianti Rufina Ris. '07	♀♀ 5

La Lecciaia

LOC. VALLAFRICO
53024 MONTALCINO [SI]
TEL. 0583928366
www.lecciaia.it

PRE-BOOKED VISITS
ANNUAL PRODUCTION 200,000 bottles
HECTARES UNDER VINE 16.00

It was back in 1983 when Mauro Pacini managed to buy the La Lecciaia farm in the south-eastern area of Montalcino and gradually transformed it into one of the DOC's best-established estates. The farm covers 60 hectares, 15 of which are planted to vines, situated at about 450 metres altitude on medium-textured sandy and clayey soil with good stony content. These conditions help understand the sometimes dry and austere tone of the four Brunellos when young. The basic Brunello and Vigna Manapetra cru are available in vintage and Riserva versions, undergo lengthy maceration and are matured in 50-hectolitre oak. The La Lecciaia range always has a few aces up its sleeve, starting with the flourishing Brunello 2010 and precise Riserva 2009. Leader of the pack is the Vigna Manapetra 2010, which just lacks a touch more definition and softness in the tannins, but it is a very good vibrant, multilayered Brunello.

● Brunello di Montalcino V. Manapetra '10	♟♟ 6
● Brunello di Montalcino '10	♟♟ 5
● Brunello di Montalcino Ris. '09	♟♟ 6
● Rosso di Montalcino '13	♟ 3
● Brunello di Montalcino V. Manapetra '09	♟♟♟ 6
● Brunello di Montalcino Ris. '08	♟♟ 6
● Brunello di Montalcino V. Manapetra '08	♟♟ 5
● Brunello di Montalcino V. Manapetra Ris. '08	♟♟ 6

Cantine Leonardo da Vinci

VIA PROVINCIALE MERCATALE, 291
50059 VINCI [FI]
TEL. 0571902444
www.cantineleonardo.it

CELLAR SALES
PRE-BOOKED VISITS
ACCOMMODATION AND RESTAURANT SERVICE
ANNUAL PRODUCTION 4,500,000 bottles
HECTARES UNDER VINE 650.00

It began in 1961 when 30 small producers in Vinci, with a total of 70 hectares, decided to join forces and start producing fine quality wines. The business grew steadily with other growers deciding to join, convinced by the possibilities and the quality of the wines. In 1990 came the important step of purchasing the Cantina di Montalcino enabling work to begin also in the Siena area. Today the cooperative numbers 200 members and has grown a great deal, both in organization and in image, proving to be a modern and up-to-date winery. In 2012 the estate passed to the Caviro group. The Chianti Da Vinci Riserva 2012 presents an array of red berry aromas with light spicy hints of cinnamon and cloves. The palate is understated and weighty with nicely blended tannins and fresh vein of acidity, and a relaxed, flavoursome finish. The Vin Santo 2008 is charming and sweet.

● Chianti Da Vinci Ris. '12	♟♟ 3*
○ Bianco dell'Empolese Vin Santo Da Vinci '08	♟♟ 5
● Brunello di Montalcino Cantina di Montalcino '10	♟♟ 5
● Rosso di Montalcino Cantina di Montalcino '13	♟♟ 2*
● Chianti '14	♟ 2
● Leonardo '13	♟ 2
○ Vermentino Poggio del Sasso Cantina di Montalcino '14	♟ 2
● Chianti Da Vinci '09	♟♟ 2*
● Chianti Da Vinci Ris. '11	♟♟ 3*
● Chianti Da Vinci Ris. '10	♟♟ 3
● Chianti Leonardo '13	♟♟ 2*
● Chianti Leonardo '12	♟♟ 2*
● Rosso di Montalcino Leonardo '11	♟♟ 3

Tenuta di Lilliano

LOC. LILLIANO, 8
53011 CASTELLINA IN CHIANTI [SI]
TEL. 0577743070
www.lilliano.com

CELLAR SALES
PRE-BOOKED VISITS
ACCOMMODATION
ANNUAL PRODUCTION 150,000 bottles
HECTARES UNDER VINE 35.00

Tenuta di Lilliano might well represent the best expression of wines from the subzone of Castellina in Chianti. The Ruspoli family, who have owned it since 1920, have lived through much of Chianti Classico's history, preserving a traditional style in their wines despite an overall, more contemporary reinterpretation of the range. This process has produced wines with enhanced and unspoilt classic features, with increasingly evident nuancing alongside the elegance and finesse. The Chianti Classico Gran Selezione 2011 is one of the best of its type. The aromas are slightly closed but a few minutes in the glass release hints of iron filings, red berries and some citrus sensations. The palate makes a sweet entry, developing creamy, well-paced and deep. The Chianti Classico 2013 has a beautifully supple and pleasing flavour with fresh fruity and floral aromas.

Lisini

FRAZ. SANT'ANGELO IN COLLE
POD. CASANOVA
53024 MONTALCINO [SI]
TEL. 0577844040
www.lisini.com

CELLAR SALES
PRE-BOOKED VISITS
ANNUAL PRODUCTION 90,000 bottles
HECTARES UNDER VINE 21.00

The Lisini family name always comes up when talking about classic Brunellos which present a consistent blend of the Mediterranean atmosphere of southern Montalcino and the taut austerity of Sangioveses designed to last over time. Most of the estate's vineyards are situated around the winery in the highly suitable growing area of Sesta, with its typical cool, mineral-rich lands. The location which brings the Ugolaia cru to life is tangibly different, with its recognizable red tufaceous soil. After a few years the Riserva has rejoined the line-up, aged in medium-sized Slavonian oak like the other Brunellos. As usual a nicely combined threesome from Lisini. The 2010 Brunello reveals a sober, basic profile, articulated in the 2009 Riserva but with greater layering and roundness. As usual the Ugolaia is more "masculine": the 2009 is a little too held back by evolved sensations and severe tannin.

● Chianti Cl. Gran Sel. '11	♜♜♜ 5
● Chianti Cl. '13	♜♜ 3
● Chianti Cl. '10	♛♛♛ 3*
● Chianti Cl. '09	♛♛♛ 3
● Chianti Cl. E. Ruspoli Berlingieri Ris. '85	♛♛♛ 8
● Chianti Cl. Ris. Gran Sel. '10	♛♛♛ 6
● Anagallis '11	♛♛ 5
● Anagallis '10	♛♛ 5
● Chianti Cl. '11	♛♛ 3
● Chianti Cl. '06	♛♛ 2*
● Chianti Cl. Ris '08	♛♛ 5
● Chianti Cl. Ris. '10	♛♛ 5
● Chianti Cl. Ris. '09	♛♛ 5
● Chianti Cl. Ris. '07	♛♛ 5
● Chianti Cl. Ris. '06	♛♛ 5
● Vignacatena '10	♛♛ 5

● Brunello di Montalcino '10	♜♜ 6
● Brunello di Montalcino Ris. '09	♜♜ 7
● Brunello di Montalcino Ugolaia '09	♜♜ 8
● Rosso di Montalcino '13	♜ 4
● Brunello di Montalcino '90	♛♛♛ 5
● Brunello di Montalcino '88	♛♛♛ 5
● Brunello di Montalcino Ugolaia '06	♛♛♛ 8
● Brunello di Montalcino Ugolaia '04	♛♛♛ 8
● Brunello di Montalcino Ugolaia '01	♛♛♛ 8
● Brunello di Montalcino Ugolaia '00	♛♛♛ 7
● Brunello di Montalcino Ugolaia '91	♛♛♛ 7
● Brunello di Montalcino Ris. '08	♛♛ 7
● Brunello di Montalcino Ris. '07	♛♛ 7
● Brunello di Montalcino Ugolaia '08	♛♛ 8
● Brunello di Montalcino Ugolaia '07	♛♛ 8
● Rosso di Montalcino '11	♛♛ 4

Livernano

LOC. LIVERNANO, 67A
53017 RADDA IN CHIANTI [SI]
TEL. 0577738353
www.livernano.it

CELLAR SALES
PRE-BOOKED VISITS
ACCOMMODATION AND RESTAURANT SERVICE
ANNUAL PRODUCTION 150,000 bottles
HECTARES UNDER VINE 27.00

Livernano is in the Sienese Chianti Classico subzone of Radda in Chianti. The vineyards are very strictly managed, starting with the type of training system, which is almost exclusively bush-trained, and oriented towards maximum respect for the environment. Barriques only in the cellar, following the style chosen by the estate which aims for generous, fruity wines as well as that fundamental element of oakiness which seems to be more balanced in recent years. The well-made Chianti Classico 2012 reveals fragrant, clean aromas as a prologue to a vigorous, succulent, well-coordinated palate. The Chianti Classico Gran Selezione 2011 has slightly evolved aromas and the palate is its strongpoint, with a lovely tangy sensation characterizing the flavour. A blend of chardonnay, sauvignon, viognier and traminer, L'Anima 2014 is very fresh-tasting with a beautifully paced flavour.

● Chianti Cl. '12	▼▼	3*
● Chianti Cl. Gran Selezione '11	▼▼	7
○ L'Anima '14	▼▼	3
● Chianti Cl. Ris. '04	▼▼▼	4
● Livernano '05	▼▼▼	6
● Livernano '03	▼▼▼	6
● Livernano '99	▼▼▼	7
● Livernano '98	▼▼▼	6
● Livernano '97	▼▼▼	6
● Chianti Cl. '08	▼▼	3*
● Chianti Cl. '06	▼▼	3*
● Chianti Cl. Ris. '11	▼▼	4
● Livernano '07	▼▼	6

Lunadoro

FRAZ. VALIANO
LOC. TERRAROSSA PAGLIARETO
53040 MONTEPULCIANO [SI]
TEL. 0578748154
www.lunadoro.com

CELLAR SALES
PRE-BOOKED VISITS
ACCOMMODATION
ANNUAL PRODUCTION 45,000 bottles
HECTARES UNDER VINE 12.00
VITICULTURE METHOD Certified Organic
SUSTAINABLE WINERY

Husband and wife team the Cappellis didn't come far to fulfil their dream of growing wine on the Pagliareto estate: from Val d'Orcia, or Pienza to be exact. In 2002 they made the leap, with the purchase of land and patient, meticulous care over the vineyards, and the construction of the new cellar. The name was chosen from among the farms where the vineyards are planted. Mindful of their hometown, they set up an agritourism centre at Pienza along with cereal crops for the production of artisan pasta, named after the estate. The Nobile Quercione 2011 has a beautifully complex nose with alternating delicious fruit, softened by Mediterranean herbs, with hints of nutmeg. The palate makes a soft entry and then gains vigour, closing in a very satisfying finish. The Nobile Pagliareto 2012 has approachable wild berries on the nose and a relaxed palate.

● Nobile di Montepulciano Quercione '11	▼▼	4
● Nobile di Montepulciano Pagliareto '12	▼▼	4
● Rosso di Montepulciano Prugnanello '13	▼	3
● Nobile di Montepulciano '11	♀♀	4
● Nobile di Montepulciano '09	♀♀	4
● Nobile di Montepulciano '08	♀♀	3
● Nobile di Montepulciano Quercione '10	♀♀	4
● Nobile di Montepulciano Quercione '06	♀♀	4
● Nobile di Montepulciano Quercione '05	♀♀	4
● Nobile di Montepulciano Quercione '04	♀♀	4
● Nobile di Montepulciano Quercione Ris. '09	♀♀	5
● Nobile di Montepulciano Quercione Ris. '07	♀♀	4
● Orcia Eclisse '11	♀♀	2*
● Rosso di Montepulciano '08	♀♀	2*
● Rosso di Montepulciano Primo Senso '11	♀♀	3

I Luoghi

Loc. Campo al Capriolo, 201
57022 Castagneto Carducci [LI]
Tel. 0565777379
www.iluoghi.it

CELLAR SALES
ANNUAL PRODUCTION 15,000 bottles
HECTARES UNDER VINE 3.80
VITICULTURE METHOD Certified Organic

This very original estate in the Bolgheri
overview represents an intimate
relationship between the young owners, the
vineyards (divided into two separate plots)
and the cellar. Stefano Granata and his wife
Paola have based their farm and project on
solid foundations of great authenticity. That
said, the style of the wines and their
absolute high quality are the reason I
Luoghi is so admired and keep it amongst
the most respected estates in the DOC
zone. This year we liked the Bolgheri Rosso
Podere Ritorti 2012 best. Certainly a red
with prospects, it still has to come to terms
with the cumbersome yet elegant toasty
aromas, which the fruit will handle after a
while in the bottles. But it is an
extraordinarily generous wine, almost
subtle and airy in texture, the flavour
closing with intriguing hints of coffee
beans. Less impressive, to be honest, is the
Campo al Fico: open and a bit loose in
tannins.

● Bolgheri Sup. Podere Ritorti '12	♥♥ 5
● Bolgheri Sup. Campo al Fico '12	♥ 7
● Bolgheri Sup. Campo al Fico '10	♥♥♥ 7
● Bolgheri Sup. Campo al Fico '09	♥♥♥ 7
● Bolgheri Sup. Campo al Fico '08	♥♥♥ 7
● Bolgheri Sup. Campo al Fico '07	♥♥ 7
● Bolgheri Sup. Podere Ritorti '11	♥♥ 5
● Bolgheri Sup. Podere Ritorti '09	♥♥ 5
● Bolgheri Sup. Podere Ritorti '08	♥♥ 5

★Le Macchiole

via Bolgherese, 189a
57022 Castagneto Carducci [LI]
Tel. 0565766092
www.lemacchiole.it

PRE-BOOKED VISITS
ANNUAL PRODUCTION 150,000 bottles
HECTARES UNDER VINE 24.00

This beautiful and very successful business
was one of the first and most important to
bring prestige to the Bolgheri terroir. Le
Macchiole is a model winery able to
produce wines that enjoy worldwide fame.
But it is by no means resting on its laurels,
quite the contrary: an air of great activity in
the cellar, no lack of brilliant projects and
new little events mark the dynamic
continuity of this prestigious estate's
history. The central figure is Cinzia Merli,
the dazzling, capable and considerate
hostess. The wines are spectacular, as
usual. Let's start with the winery's
emblematic Paleo, created in the early
1990s. The 2012 has forward grassy and
spicy aromas, nicely put-together on a
prestigious fruity background. The palate is
the same, fleshy and racy, lively and
brilliant, extraordinarily deep. We also liked
the Messorio 2012, with dark, toasty
sensations, perfectly harmonious overall.

● Paleo Rosso '12	♥♥♥ 8
● Messorio '12	♥♥ 8
○ Paleo Bianco '13	♥♥ 5
● Scrio '12	♥♥ 8
● Bolgheri Rosso '13	♥ 4
● Messorio '07	♥♥♥ 8
● Messorio '06	♥♥♥ 8
● Messorio '01	♥♥♥ 8
● Messorio '99	♥♥♥ 8
● Paleo Rosso '11	♥♥♥ 8
● Paleo Rosso '10	♥♥♥ 8
● Paleo Rosso '09	♥♥♥ 8
● Paleo Rosso '03	♥♥♥ 8
● Paleo Rosso '01	♥♥♥ 8
● Scrio '08	♥♥♥ 8
● Scrio '01	♥♥♥ 8

Le Maimache

s.da prov.le 55 di Sant'Antimo km 4,85
53024 Montalcino [SI]
Tel. 0577849168
www.lemacioche.it

Le Macioche

CELLAR SALES
PRE-BOOKED VISITS
ACCOMMODATION
ANNUAL PRODUCTION 18,000 bottles
HECTARES UNDER VINE 3.00

Riccardo Caliari, Stefano Brunetto and
Massimo Bronzato are the three young
friends and entrepreneurs from Veneto who
now own the Le Macioche estate, set up by
Matilde Zecca and Achille Mazzocchi in
1985. The small estate, with three hectares
of vineyards, is familiar to enthusiasts in
the know for its subtle, minimalist
Brunellos, linked to the moods of the
Sant'Antimo slopes: altitudes above 400
metres and limestone, marl-rich soil. We'll
see in the next few years whether and how
the interpretation changes. Until now it is
based on bare bones cellarwork,
spontaneous fermentation in oak vats and
lengthy ageing in 40-hectolitre barrels. In
the meantime the 2010 Brunello fully
expresses the style we have come to
expect from Le Macioche. Red berry fruit,
orange pastilles, bouquet garni: a charming
array of aromas which is not fully reflected
on the palate, supple but with slightly raw
texture and chilly flavour.

● Brunello di Montalcino '10	♟♟ 7
● Rosso di Montalcino '13	♟♟ 4
● Brunello di Montalcino '09	♟♟ 7
● Brunello di Montalcino '08	♟♟ 7
● Brunello di Montalcino '07	♟♟ 7
● Brunello di Montalcino '06	♟♟ 6
● Brunello di Montalcino Ris. '06	♟♟ 8
● Rosso di Montalcino '11	♟♟ 4
● Rosso di Montalcino '10	♟♟ 4
● Rosso di Montalcino '09	♟♟ 4

La Mannella

loc. La Mannella, 322
53024 Montalcino [SI]
Tel. 0577848268
www.lamannella.it

PRE-BOOKED VISITS
ANNUAL PRODUCTION 35,000 bottles
HECTARES UNDER VINE 8.00

There are at least two valid reasons to
make a diversion to La Mannella in
Montalcino: Marco Cortonesi's patient
kindness, and the barrel tastings which are,
to say the least, educational. The various
plots are kept separate until the final blend
and you can clearly recognize the
complementary features of the two main
vineyards: those situated around the winery
(northern slope, 250 metres altitude, clayey
soil) and those in the south-eastern district
(400 metres, marly soil). The differences
are respected in the cellar with specific
vinification and maturation procedures for
the three Brunellos (vintage, I Poggiarelli
cru and Riserva in the best years). The
umpteenth brilliant team effort for the La
Mannella Sangioveses. The Rosso 2103 is
subtle and nuanced with a remarkably
efficient flavour while the Brunello 2010
challenge ends in a tie: the basic version is
slightly too light and raw in texture while
the I Poggiarelli lacks a little flavour and
energy.

● Brunello di Montalcino '10	♟♟ 5
● Brunello di Montalcino I Poggiarelli '10	♟♟ 5
● Rosso di Montalcino '13	♟♟ 3
● Brunello di Montalcino '09	♟♟ 5
● Brunello di Montalcino '08	♟♟ 5
● Brunello di Montalcino '07	♟♟ 5
● Brunello di Montalcino '06	♟♟ 5
● Brunello di Montalcino Ris. '06	♟♟ 6

Fattoria Mantellassi

LOC. BANDITACCIA, 26
58051 MAGLIANO IN TOSCANA [GR]
TEL. 0564592037
www.fattoriamantellassi.it

CELLAR SALES
PRE-BOOKED VISITS
ANNUAL PRODUCTION 900,000 bottles
HECTARES UNDER VINE 72.00

The Mantelassi family, originally from
Pistoia, moved to Maremma in 1860 to
work as pruners and grafters for other
estates. Over the years they acquired
property and land without being involved in
wine. The vineyards did not come along
until 1960 with the ploughing of the first
four hectares and the planting of the main
nucleus of vineyards. The number of
hectares under vine has gradually
increased over the years, focusing mainly
on sangiovese for Morellino di Scansano.
The estate is managed today by brothers
Giuseppe and Aleardo who personally
surpervise every productive phase, sales
and public relations. The interesting
Morellino Mentore 2014 has classic
aromas of cherries alongside aromatic
herbs and hints of spice. The rich palate
opens confidently with evident but not
burred tannins, an interesting flavour and
tangy finish. The other wines maintain a
consistently good standard of quality.

Marchesi Gondi
Tenuta Bossi

LOC. BOSSI
VIA DELLO STRACCHINO, 32
50065 PONTASSIEVE [FI]
TEL. 0558317830
www.tenutabossi.com

CELLAR SALES
PRE-BOOKED VISITS
ACCOMMODATION
ANNUAL PRODUCTION 50,000 bottles
HECTARES UNDER VINE 19.00

Since the late 16th century, many
generations of the Gondi family have kept a
tight hold on this estate, to preserve the
integrity and beauty of the environment.
Wine producers for over 500 years, current
owners Bernardo, his sons Gerardo and
Lapo, and his sister Donatella, focus on
diversifying the farming activity on the
300-plus hectares: agritourism facilities,
visits and tasting, olive oil, cereals, woods
extending as far as Pontassieve, on the
Volmiano farm at Calenzano, on the slopes
of Monte Morello. Giuliano Gondi began
renewal work on the estate after the
Second World War, transforming the old
sharecropping farm into one managed
directly by the farmer. An excellent
performance from the three Chianti Rufina
wines: the San Giuliano 2012 with supple,
fresh flavour, the Riserva Villa Bossi 2010
with austere but not angular structure and
the Riserva Pian dei Sorbi 2011 with
fragrant aromas and a rounded, dynamic
palate.

● Morellino di Scansano Mentore '14	▼▼ 2*
○ Lucumone '14	▼ 2
⊙ Maestrale '14	▼ 2
● Morellino di Scansano Le Sentinelle Ris. '11	▼ 4
● Morellino di Scansano San Giuseppe '14	▼ 3
● Querciolaia '10	▼ 4
○ Scalandrino '14	▼ 2
● Morellino di Scansano Le Sentinelle Ris. '10	♈ 4
● Morellino di Scansano Le Sentinelle Ris. '09	♈ 4
● Morellino di Scansano Le Sentinelle Ris. '06	♈ 4
● Morellino di Scansano Mentore '11	♈ 2*
● Querciolaia '07	♈ 4
● Querciolaia '05	♈ 4

● Chianti Rufina Pian dei Sorbi Ris. '11	▼▼ 3
● Chianti Rufina San Giuliano '12	▼▼ 2*
● Chianti Rufina Villa di Bossi Ris. '10	▼▼ 3
● Mazzaferrata '09	▼▼ 4
○ Vin Santo del Chianti Rufina Cardinal de Retz Ris. '04	▼▼ 5
○ Colli dell'Etruria Centrale Sassobianco '14	▼ 2
● Ser Amerigo '09	▼ 4
● Chianti Rufina Pian dei Sorbi Ris. '05	♈ 2*
● Chianti Rufina San Giuliano '06	♈ 2*
● Chianti Rufina San Giuliano '04	♈ 2
● Chianti Rufina Villa di Bossi Ris. '07	♈ 3
○ Vin Santo del Chianti Rufina Cardinal de Retz Ris. '03	♈ 5
○ Vin Santo del Chianti Rufina Cardinal de Retz Ris. '01	♈ 5

Il Marroneto

LOC. MADONNA DELLE GRAZIE, 307
53024 MONTALCINO [SI]
TEL. 0577849382
www.ilmarroneto.com

CELLAR SALES
PRE-BOOKED VISITS
ANNUAL PRODUCTION 30,000 bottles
HECTARES UNDER VINE 6.00
SUSTAINABLE WINERY

The emotional and, above all, stylistic impact of the wines produced at Marroneto by Alessandro Mori is no longer a secret. It was set up by his father Giuseppe in the Seventies as one of the first "garage" wineries in the Montalcino zone: an old drying space for chestnuts (hence the name) which has become almost a place of worship for lovers of austere, bare-bones Brunellos, Nordic in the best possible sense of the word. It can be found a few dozen metres outside the town centre, in the heart of the Madonna delle Grazie cru, a small vineyard overlooking the Montosoli hill which is interpreted through lengthy ageing in various ages and sizes of Slavonian oak. The winery's global fame is boosted by a wonderful pair of 2010 Brunellos. The basic version is irresistible with bright, feminine colour, only surpassed in prospect and intensity by the Madonna delle Grazie. Heart-rending aromas of incense, forest floor and pencil lead, opening into multiple layers in the majestic tannic architrave.

● Brunello di Montalcino Madonna delle Grazie '10	▼▼▼ 8
● Brunello di Montalcino '10	▼▼ 7
● Rosso di Montalcino Ignaccio '13	▼▼ 3
● Brunello di Montalcino Madonna delle Grazie '08	♀♀♀ 8
● Brunello di Montalcino '09	♀♀ 7
● Brunello di Montalcino '08	♀♀ 7
● Brunello di Montalcino '07	♀♀ 6
● Brunello di Montalcino '06	♀♀ 6
● Brunello di Montalcino Madonna delle Grazie '09	♀♀ 8
● Brunello di Montalcino Madonna delle Grazie '07	♀♀ 8
● Brunello di Montalcino Madonna delle Grazie '06	♀♀ 8

Mastrojanni

FRAZ. CASTELNUOVO DELL'ABATE
POD. LORETO SAN PIO
53024 MONTALCINO [SI]
TEL. 0577835681
www.mastrojanni.com

CELLAR SALES
PRE-BOOKED VISITS
ANNUAL PRODUCTION 100,000 bottles
HECTARES UNDER VINE 24.00

Several long-standing estates in Montalcino have changed hands in recent years but none has perhaps made such a smooth transformation with confident planning and style as Mastrojanni. It was purchased by the Illy group in 2008, who wisely chose to keep Andrea Machetti on as the technical manager and continue to promote the classic, rigorous nature of sangiovese grown at Castelnuovo dell'Abate. Oak of various sizes are used in the cellar, larger ones for the Vigna Loreto cru and smaller for the other house champ, Vigna Schiena d'Asino. The umpteenth show of strength from the Brunello Vigna Loreto: the 2010 version is penalized by slightly hesitant aromas, gradually replaced by the usual hints of citrus and medicinal herbs. Time will probably help soften the sharp edges of acidity and tannins thanks to the lush, close-knit texture. Excellent results too from the 2010 Brunello and delicious Rosso 2013.

● Brunello di Montalcino V. Loreto '10	▼▼▼ 7
● Brunello di Montalcino '10	▼▼ 5
● Rosso di Montalcino '13	▼▼ 3
● Brunello di Montalcino '97	♀♀♀ 7
● Brunello di Montalcino '90	♀♀♀ 7
● Brunello di Montalcino Ris. '88	♀♀♀ 6
● Brunello di Montalcino Schiena d'Asino '08	♀♀♀ 8
● Brunello di Montalcino Schiena d'Asino '93	♀♀♀ 7
● Brunello di Montalcino Schiena d'Asino '90	♀♀♀ 7
● Brunello di Montalcino V. Loreto '09	♀♀♀ 7
● Brunello di Montalcino '09	♀♀ 5
● Rosso di Montalcino '12	♀♀ 3

Giorgio Meletti Cavallari

VIA CASONE UGOLINO, 12
57022 CASTAGNETO CARDUCCI [LI]
TEL. 0565775620
www.giorgiomeletticavallari.it

CELLAR SALES
PRE-BOOKED VISITS
ACCOMMODATION
ANNUAL PRODUCTION 40,000 bottles
HECTARES UNDER VINE 10.00

A famous name in the Italian wine sector, the Meletti Cavallari family have written important pages of the development of Bolgheri wine. Giorgio represents the family's new generation of vignerons taking his first steps in the early part of this century. The estate's two emblematic vineyards are Piastraia on top of the Castagneto hill, and Vallone, lower down, around the estate's agritourism structure. The soil is rich in stony material and galestro, producing racy, flavoursome wines. The Bolgheri Superiore Impronte 2012 is fantastic: charming from the aromas onwards, blending fresh but ripe fruit with very elegant spicy, toasty hints enfolded by a vegetal note that is never intrusive. A fine quality red wines, very original, with seductive flavour and excellent balance. The Borgeri 2013 is not bad and the Borgeri Bianco 2014 is really well-typed, floral and tangy, with a long finish.

Melini

LOC. GAGGIANO
53036 POGGIBONSI [SI]
TEL. 0577998511
www.cantinemelini.it

CELLAR SALES
PRE-BOOKED VISITS
ANNUAL PRODUCTION 3,300,000 bottles
HECTARES UNDER VINE 136.00

Melini of Poggibonsi and Macchiavelli of San Casciano Val di Pesa are the GIV wine-producing estates in Chianti Classico, representing an important part of the DOC's history. These are probably among the most widespread and best-known Chianti brands worldwide, and the range of products offers well-established, coherent quality. Typically flawlessly made and aged mainly in large oak, these wines do not lack personality and prioritize stylish, drinkable qualities over strength. Beautifully fresh aromas characterize the Chianti Classico Granaio 2013, but its strongpoint is the palate, with tangy, progressive flavour. The Chianti Classico La Selvanella Riserva 2012 has dark sensations on the nose with a well-coordinated and quite lingering palate. The Chianti Classico Solatìo del Tani 2012 has clean, clear-cut aromas and a soft, nicely fluent palate.

● Bolgheri Sup. Impronte '12	🍷🍷 5
○ Bolgheri Bianco Borgeri '14	🍷🍷 3
● Bolgheri Rosso Borgeri '13	🍷🍷 3
⊙ Bolgheri Rosato '14	🍷 3
● Bolgheri Rosso Borgeri '12	🍷🍷 3
● Bolgheri Rosso Borgeri '06	🍷🍷 3
● Bolgheri Rosso Impronte '04	🍷🍷 5
● Bolgheri Sup. Impronte '11	🍷🍷 5

● Chianti Cl. Granaio '13	🍷🍷 3
● Chianti Cl. La Selvanella Ris. '12	🍷🍷 5
● Chianti Cl. Solatìo del Tani Fattoria Machiavelli '13	🍷🍷 3
● Chianti Governo all'uso Toscano '12	🍷 2
● Chianti San Lorenzo '14	🍷 2
● I Coltri '14	🍷 2
● Il Principe Fattoria Machiavelli '12	🍷 5
○ Vernaccia di S. Gimignano Le Grillaie '14	🍷 2
● Chianti Cl. La Selvanella Ris. '06	🍷🍷🍷 5
● Chianti Cl. La Selvanella Ris. '03	🍷🍷🍷 4
● Chianti Cl. La Selvanella Ris. '01	🍷🍷🍷 4
● Chianti Cl. La Selvanella Ris. '00	🍷🍷🍷 4
● Chianti Cl. La Selvanella Ris. '99	🍷🍷🍷 5

Mocali

LOC. MOCALI
53024 MONTALCINO [SI]
TEL. 0577849485
azmocali@tiscali.it

CELLAR SALES
PRE-BOOKED VISITS
ANNUAL PRODUCTION 120,000 bottles
HECTARES UNDER VINE 9.00

Dino Ciacci is remembered by many as one of the 25 winegrowers who brought to life the first nucleus of the Consorzio del Brunello di Montalcino, back in the Fifties. His grandson Tiziano has fully taken up the inherited reins and brought Mocali firmly into the DOC's hit parade, thanks to eclectic, sturdy yet linear sangioveses aged in small casks and Slavonian oak, depending on the cru or vintage year. All this is based on about ten hectares of vineyards in the south-westernmost corner, at altitudes between 350 and 400 metres, where the tough soils are enriched with marl and alberese. Once again the edgy strength of the Brunello Vigna delle Raunate stands out in the lovely range of Mocali wines. The favourable 2010 vintage adds extra spicy, smoky strength, directed into richly textured but well-proportioned flavour, a little too much extract in the finish but still progressive thanks to the considerable salty element.

Fattoria Montellori

VIA PISTOIESE, 1
50054 FUCECCHIO [FI]
TEL. 0571260641
www.fattoriamontellori.it

CELLAR SALES
PRE-BOOKED VISITS
RESTAURANT SERVICE
ANNUAL PRODUCTION 250,000 bottles
HECTARES UNDER VINE 50.00
VITICULTURE METHOD Certified Organic

Alessandro Nieri is carrying forward a family tradition that dates back to 1895, when leather merchant Giuseppe Nieri purchased the villa and lands forming the old central part of the estate, to dedicate some of his time to farming. Subsequent generations brought on the original project, planted vineyards and equipped the cellar as required, but it was in the mid-1980s that the buildings took on their current identity, with a definitive step into the world of modern winemaking. As well as wine the estate stands out for its involvement in the contemporary art world, setting up exhibitions in the garden of the villa. The Metodo Classico Pas Dosé 2011 is intriguing with fragrant hints of spring flowers and crusty bread, a nicely structured palate with well-blended fizz and a long, relaxed finish. The Vin Santo 2009 has seductive ripe fruit on the nose and a sweet, mouthfilling palate.

● Brunello di Montalcino V. delle Raunate '10	♟♟ 6
● Brunello di Montalcino '10	♟♟ 5
● Maremma Toscana Alpan '14	♟ 2
● Maremma Toscana Mirus '12	♟ 4
● Morellino di Scansano Suberli '13	♟ 3
● Morellino di Scansano Suberli Ris. '12	♟ 3
● Rosso di Montalcino '13	♟ 2
● Brunello di Montalcino V. delle Raunate '08	♟♟♟ 6
● Brunello di Montalcino '09	♟♟ 5
● Brunello di Montalcino '08	♟♟ 5
● Brunello di Montalcino Ris. '07	♟♟ 7
● Brunello di Montalcino V. delle Raunate '09	♟♟ 6
● Brunello di Montalcino V. delle Raunate '07	♟♟ 6

○ Bianco dell'Empolese Vin Santo '09	♟♟ 5
○ Montellori Pas Dosé '11	♟♟ 5
● Moro '12	♟♟ 3
● Salamartano '12	♟♟ 6
● Chianti '13	♟ 2
● Chianti Sup. Caselle '13	♟ 2
● Dicatum '12	♟ 5
○ Mandorlo '14	♟ 2
○ Bianco dell'Empolese Vin Santo '07	♟♟ 5
○ Bianco dell'Empolese Vin Santo '06	♟♟ 5
○ Bianco dell'Empolese Vin Santo '05	♟♟ 5
○ Blanc des Blancs Pas Dosé '09	♟♟ 4
● Moro '09	♟♟ 3
● Salamartano '11	♟♟ 5
● Salamartano '09	♟♟ 6
● Tuttosole '09	♟♟ 4

Montenidoli

LOC. MONTENIDOLI
53037 SAN GIMIGNANO [SI]
TEL. 0577941565
www.montenidoli.com

CELLAR SALES
ACCOMMODATION
ANNUAL PRODUCTION 100,000 bottles
HECTARES UNDER VINE 24.00
VITICULTURE METHOD Certified Organic

50 years ago Elisabetta Fagiuoli moved to San Gimignano with Sergio, in love with a place that was still wild. These were years in which the countryside was being abandoned and its residents moving into the city, so it was six years before the first wine was produced, following restoration of the vineyards and olive groves. Since then the productive philosophy has not changed: only native local grapes, biodynamic farming always, even before certification, the greatest respect for the environment, which leads to increasingly positive results. An agritourism facility is available to visitors, and is also used for groups studying education and winegrowing. This year the Tre Bicchierie go to the Vernaccia Carato 2011, with vibrant citrus aromas alongside peach and apricot fruit and a firm, mouthfilling palate with well-defined freshness and an appetizing, lingering finish.

Montepeloso

LOC. MONTEPELOSO, 82
57028 SUVERETO [LI]
TEL. 0565828180
www.montepeloso.it

ANNUAL PRODUCTION 22,000 bottles
HECTARES UNDER VINE 7.00
SUSTAINABLE WINERY

This estate, purchased in 1999 by Fabio Chiarelotto, has never courted fame, despite its continuous, fast-paced and steady march forward, with consistent results from the products. It could not have been otherwise, with an owner so certain of his choices in the vineyards and cellar. The desire to change his life and become a wine producer was sparked by the tasting of wine produced by the farm's previous management, convincing him of the potential for quality in an area like this. The Nardo 2012 made the finals: a blend of sangiovese, montepulciano and cabernet sauvignon with subtle aromas of ripe cherries and spicy hints of cloves and medicinal herbs. The palate makes a light entry, mouthfilling but not excessively, with delicate tannin and a tangy, well-judged, very lingering finish. The intriguing Gabbro 2012 is a blend of cabernet franc and sauvignon with petit verdot.

○ Vernaccia di S. Gimignano Carato '11	♟♟♟	4*
○ Vernaccia di S. Gimignano Fiore '13	♟♟	3
○ Vernaccia di S. Gimignano Tradizionale '13	♟♟	2*
☉ Canaiuolo '14	♟	3
○ Templare '11	♟	3
○ Vernaccia di S. Gimignano Carato '05	♟♟♟	5
○ Vernaccia di S. Gimignano Carato '02	♟♟♟	5
○ Vernaccia di S. Gimignano Tradizionale '12	♟♟♟	2*
☉ Canaiuolo '13	♟♟	3
☉ Canaiuolo '12	♟♟	3
○ Vernaccia di S. Gimignano Carato '09	♟♟	4
○ Vernaccia di S. Gimignano Fiore '11	♟♟	3*
○ Vernaccia di S. Gimignano Tradizionale '11	♟♟	2*

● Nardo '12	♟♟	8
● A Quo '13	♟♟	5
● Eneo '12	♟♟	5
● Gabbro '12	♟♟	8
● Sangiovese '12	♟	8
● Gabbro '02	♟♟♟	8
● Nardo '01	♟♟♟	8
● Nardo '00	♟♟♟	8
● Eneo '02	♟♟	4
● Gabbro '08	♟♟	8
● Gabbro '06	♟♟	8
● Gabbro '03	♟♟	8
● Gabbro '01	♟♟	8
● Nardo '08	♟♟	8
● Nardo '02	♟♟	8
● Sangiovese '02	♟♟	8

Monteraponi

LOC. MONTERAPONI
53017 RADDA IN CHIANTI [SI]
TEL. 0577738280
www.monteraponi.it

CELLAR SALES
PRE-BOOKED VISITS
ACCOMMODATION
ANNUAL PRODUCTION 30,000 bottles
HECTARES UNDER VINE 10.00
VITICULTURE METHOD Certified Organic

The estate owned by Michele Braganti has
become a benchmark for the Chianti
Classico winemaking overview, thanks to
the strongly traditional style of these
wines, a sort of journey back in time with
irresistible charm. The strongpoint of these
wines is their pursuit of the best possible
expression of sangiovese grown in the
Radda subzone, and no digression from
this objective is allowed. Their typical
feature is the alternation of aromas
between more vibrant and more nuanced
hints, while the flavour develops taut,
tangy and very dynamic. Once again the
Chianti Classico Baron'Ugo Riserva, in the
2011 version, stands out in our tastings
with enfolding, expressive aromas while
the very succulent palate moves at a firm
pace. The subtle but really delicious
Chianti Classico 2013 has a light, tangy
flavour while the Chianti Classico II
Campitello Riserva 2012 is more rugged
but pleasantly edgy.

Montesalario

FRAZ. MONTENERO D'ORCIA
LOC. MONTESALARIO, 27
58040 CASTEL DEL PIANO [GR]
TEL. 0564954173
www.aziendamontesalario.it

CELLAR SALES
PRE-BOOKED VISITS
ANNUAL PRODUCTION 15,000 bottles
HECTARES UNDER VINE 4.80

An estate that manages to maintain a
constant level of quality in its wines,
thanks to the work of the owners, the
Pasqui brothers, who are totally committed
to caring for the vineyards and olive
groves. The vineyards are situated below
Mount Amiata, which particularly
influences the features of the sangiovese
grape grown in Montecucco. This variety
receives most of the brothers' attention,
with low yields per plan and enhancement
of the natural features in the cellar.
Alongside wine, the estate grows olive,
using typical local cultivars. Through to the
finals for the Montecucco Sangiovese
Riserva 2012: excellent, varied aromas
with recognizable vibrant hints of cherry
and raspberry fruit, spicy cinnamon and
fresh aromatic herbs. The flavour is fluent
thanks to the well-measured, beautifully
lingering tannin. We also enjoyed the
Montecucco Rosso 2013, with stylish
mineral aromas and an appetizing flavour.

● Chianti Cl. Baron'Ugo Ris. '11	♟♟ 7
● Chianti Cl. '13	♟♟ 3
● Chianti Cl. Il Campitello Ris. '12	♟♟ 5
● Chianti Cl. Baron'Ugo Ris. '10	♟♟♟ 7
● Chianti Cl. Baron'Ugo Ris. '09	♟♟♟ 7
● Chianti Cl. Baron'Ugo Ris. '07	♟♟♟ 5
● Chianti Cl. '12	♟♟ 3
● Chianti Cl. '11	♟♟ 3
● Chianti Cl. '10	♟♟ 4
● Chianti Cl. '09	♟♟ 3
● Chianti Cl. '03	♟♟ 3*
● Chianti Cl. Il Campitello Ris. '11	♟♟ 5
● Chianti Cl. Il Campitello Ris. '10	♟♟ 5
● Chianti Cl. Il Campitello Ris. '09	♟♟ 5
● Chianti Cl. Ris. Il Campitello '04	♟♟ 5
● Vin Santo del Chianti Cl. '05	♟♟ 6

● Montecucco Sangiovese Ris. '12	♟♟ 4
● Montecucco Rosso '13	♟♟ 2*
● Montecucco Sangiovese '12	♟ 3
● Montecucco Sangiovese '10	♟♟♟ 3*
● Montecucco Rosso '11	♟♟ 2*
● Montecucco Sangiovese '11	♟♟ 3
● Montecucco Sangiovese Ris. '09	♟♟ 4
● Montecucco Sangiovese Ris. '08	♟♟ 4

Tenuta Monteti

VIA DELLA SGRILLA, 6
58011 CAPALBIO [GR]
TEL. 0564896160
www.tenutamonteti.it

CELLAR SALES
PRE-BOOKED VISITS
ANNUAL PRODUCTION 120,000 bottles
HECTARES UNDER VINE 28.00

Paolo Baratta had a childhood dream: although his profession took him around the world, he sought a place where he could recharge his batteries and experience the emotions of the childhood he spent among the vineyards of Oltrepò Pavese. He fell in love with Tuscany and decided to focus his efforts on Maremma, at Capalbio, where his dream finally came true. In 1998 work began to plough up and plant the vineyards with international grape varieties, and then in 2001 the cellar was built in full respect for the surrounding environment. The first wines were produced in 2004. His daughter Eva and her husband Javier now manage the estate. Tenuta Monteti 2011 is a blend of petit verdot, cabernet franc and cabernet sauvignon with fresh vegetal hints of green peppers and medicinal herbs, blackcurrant jam and cinnamon. The palate is full-bodied, mouthfilling, with tannins and alcohol in step and a long, lively finish.

● Monteti '11	♥♥	5
● Caburnio '11	♥♥	3
⊙ TM Rosé '14	♥♥	3
● Caburnio '06	♀♀	3
● Caburnio '05	♀♀	3
● Caburnio '04	♀♀	3
● Monteti '07	♀♀	5
● Monteti '05	♀♀	5
● Monteti '04	♀♀	5

Monteverro

S.DA AURELIA CAPALBIO, 11
58011 CAPALBIO [GR]
TEL. 0564890721
www.monteverro.com

CELLAR SALES
ANNUAL PRODUCTION 120,000 bottles
HECTARES UNDER VINE 27.00

Julia and Georg Weber own this estate in the Capalbio area, a part of Tuscany which struck them with its beauty and untapped potential for winegrowing which could both be exploited. They made their choice after viewing land in various parts of the world. Georg is an avid collector with a deep knowledge of wine, so when he changed from consumer to producer he wanted to make a rational, wholehearted choice. Aided by an international team the owners have created products suited to worldwide consumers, with a modern style that still betrays its Mediterranean origins. The Monteverro 2012, a blend of cabernet franc and sauvignon, petit verdot and merlot, has strikingly vibrant aromas of spices like cinnamon and cloves, and balsamic hints, as well as rich fruity sensations of currants and blueberries. The palate is broad, mouthfilling and nicely weighty with a delicious, lingering finish.

● Monteverro '12	♥♥	8
● Terra di Monteverro '12	♥♥	7
● Tinata '12	♥♥	8
○ Chardonnay '12	♥	8
● Monteverro '08	♀♀	8
● Terra di Monteverro '09	♀♀	5
● Tinata '08	♀♀	8
○ Vermentino '13	♀♀	3

★Montevertine

LOC. MONTEVERTINE
53017 RADDA IN CHIANTI [SI]
TEL. 0577738009
www.montevertine.it

PRE-BOOKED VISITS
ANNUAL PRODUCTION 85,000 bottles
HECTARES UNDER VINE 15.00

Montevertine has been and continues to be,
with enviable continuity, the birthplace of
what are probably the most accomplished
and representative wines of the Chianti
Classico, even though the estate produces
no wines under the Gallo Nero brand. These
wines have long represented a sort of
stylistic model for many producers: subtle
aromas, slightly austere and complex, the
pace of the palate dominated by the great
contrast between absolute freshness and
stylish flavour. Martino Manetti's estate is on
the hills of Radda in Chianti. The wines are
mainly aged in large oak. The inevitable
umpteenth Tre Bicchieri for Le Pergole Torte,
in the 2012 version. Despite one of the less
stylish recent vintage years, it reflects
skilful, delicate yet deep extraction,
expressing all the potential of the local area.
Red berries soon give way to leaves and
medicinal herbs on the nose, while the
crisp, tangy palate is almost endless,
reminding us in the finish that this is a
Sangiovese. The tannin attracts our
attention and perks us up physically and
mentally.

● Le Pergole Torte '12	▼▼▼	8
● Montevertine '12	▼▼	6
● Pian del Ciampolo '13	▼▼	4
● Le Pergole Torte '11	♀♀♀	8
● Le Pergole Torte '10	♀♀♀	8
● Le Pergole Torte '09	♀♀♀	8
● Le Pergole Torte '07	♀♀♀	8
● Le Pergole Torte '04	♀♀♀	8
● Le Pergole Torte '03	♀♀♀	7
● Le Pergole Torte '01	♀♀♀	8
● Le Pergole Torte '99	♀♀♀	8
● Montevertine '04	♀♀♀	5
● Montevertine '01	♀♀♀	5

Cantina Vignaioli del Morellino di Scansano

LOC. SARAGIOLO
58054 SCANSANO [GR]
TEL. 0564507288
www.cantinadelmorellino.it

CELLAR SALES
PRE-BOOKED VISITS
ANNUAL PRODUCTION 2,000,000 bottles
HECTARES UNDER VINE 470.00

An example of a cooperative winery that
has reinvented itself to keep pace with the
times. Established in 1972, its 152
members have estates throughout the main
DOC zone, Scansano, as well as more
peripheral areas like Pitigliano. The winery's
development has been agreed by growers,
applying stricter and more meticulous
regulations to improve the quality of the
grapes transported to the cellar. Some
belong to families with traditional links to
the sector while others are younger and
more recently involved in farming. Attention
to protecting the local area is demonstrated
by the winery's adherence to the national
environmental programme prescribed by
the Ministry for the Environment. The
pleasing Morellino Roggiano 2014 has
fresh aromas of blueberries and
blackberries, fragrant dried flowers and a
racy, dynamic, succulent palate with a
tangy, powerful finish. The Morellino
Riserva 2012 is more austere on the nose
with mature tobacco aromas and a firm
palate with a clean-cut finish.

● Morellino di Scansano Roggiano '14	▼▼	2*
● Morellino di Scansano Roggiano Ris. '12	▼▼	3
● Maremma Toscana Ciliegiolo Capoccia '14	▼	2
● Morellino di Scansano Roggiano Bio '14	▼	2
● Morellino di Scansano Sicomoro Ris. '11	▼	3
● Morellino di Scansano Vigna Benefizio '14	▼	2
⊙ Rosato Scantianum '14	▼	2
● Sangiovese Scantianum '14	▼	1*
○ Vermentino Scantianum '14	▼	2
○ Viognier '14	▼	2
● Maremma Toscana Rosso Capoccia '12	♀♀	2*
● Morellino di Scansano Cantina del Morellino '11	♀♀	2*
● Morellino di Scansano Roggiano Bio '13	♀♀	2*
● Morellino di Scansano Roggiano Ris. '10	♀♀	3
● Morellino di Scansano Vignabenefizio '13	♀♀	2*
● Scantianum '12	♀♀	1*

Morisfarms

Loc. Cura Nuova
Fattoria Poggetti
58024 Massa Marittima [GR]
Tel. 0566919135
www.morisfarms.it

CELLAR SALES
PRE-BOOKED VISITS
ACCOMMODATION
ANNUAL PRODUCTION 300,000 bottles
HECTARES UNDER VINE 71.00

The history of the Moris family has ancient origins: 200 year ago they arrived from Spain and settled in an ideal place as a habitat and as a place to nurture their passion for wine. Today the estate is divided into two main bodies: Fattoria Poggetti in the Monteregio area of Massa Marittima, and the other at Poggio alla Mozza, in the Morellino di Scansano DOC. Very important work was done in replanting all the vineyards, starting in 1990 and continuing throughout the following years until the productive base was completely renewed. The estate produces olive oil and grappa as well as wine. The 2102 Avvoltore, a blend of sangiovese, cabernet sauvignon and syrah, displays mature aromas of blackberries and blueberries softened by spicy hints and aromatic herbs like sage. The palate is generous with evident tannin nicely blended in the structure and a firm body with a flavoursome, lingering finish.

● Avvoltore '12	♥♥ 6
○ Vermentino '14	♥♥ 2*
● Maremma Toscana Mandriolo '14	♥ 2
☉ Maremma Toscana Rosato Mandriolo '14	♥ 2
● Monteregio di Massa Marittima Barbaspinosa '12	♥ 3
○ Monteregio di Massa Marittima Bianco Santa Chiara '14	♥ 2
● Morellino di Scansano '14	♥ 2
● Morellino di Scansano Ris. '12	♥ 4
● Avvoltore '06	♥♥♥ 5
● Avvoltore '04	♥♥♥ 5
● Avvoltore '01	♥♥♥ 5
● Avvoltore '00	♥♥♥ 5
● Avvoltore '99	♥♥♥ 5
● Avvoltore '11	♥♥ 6
● Avvoltore '10	♥♥ 6

Tenute Silvio Nardi

Loc. Casale del Bosco
53024 Montalcino [SI]
Tel. 0577808269
www.tenutenardi.com

CELLAR SALES
PRE-BOOKED VISITS
ANNUAL PRODUCTION 250,000 bottles
HECTARES UNDER VINE 80.00

Silvio Nardi is remembered by many as one of the first "non-native" producers to invest in Montalcino in 1950, in many ways an antithetic period for winegrowing and marketing, compared to the Brunello boom a few decades later. Emilia is at the helm today, leading an estate of over 50 hectares divided into more than 30 different plots on the farms of Casale del Bosco, in the north-west, and Manachiara, on the eastern slope. Sangiovese is the unchallenged protagonist of the varied range, in which the leading wines undergo mixed maturation in large barrels and tonneaux. The long-established Nardi family winery reclaims its place in the main section of the Guide thanks to the brilliant 2010 Brunellos. The standard version is very approachable while the crus show more character: the Vigneto Manachiara is more modern and rich in extract while the Vigneto Poggio Doria is slender and linear.

● Brunello di Montalcino '10	♥♥ 5
● Brunello di Montalcino Vign. Manachiara '10	♥♥ 8
● Brunello di Montalcino Vign. Poggio Doria '10	♥♥ 8
● Brunello di Montalcino Manachiara '99	♥♥♥ 7
● Brunello di Montalcino Manachiara '06	♥♥ 8
● Brunello di Montalcino Manachiara '04	♥♥ 8
● Rosso di Montalcino '07	♥♥ 3
○ Vin Santo del Chianti '99	♥♥ 5

Tenute Niccolai - Palagetto

Via Monteoliveto, 46
53037 San Gimignano [SI]
Tel. 0577943090
www.tenuteniccolai.it

CELLAR SALES
PRE-BOOKED VISITS
ACCOMMODATION
ANNUAL PRODUCTION 250,000 bottles
HECTARES UNDER VINE 44.00

This is the nerve centre of the chain of
Tenute Niccolai estates, where Sabrina
Niccolai continues the work begun by her
father Luano, an industrialist with a passion
for the countryside, inherited from his
father and father-in-law, both cellarmen. As
well as the farm in San Gimignano there is
Podere Bellarina in Montalcino and Pian de'
Cerri in the Montecucco area. The main
work is done at San Gimignano, in the
modern, functional cellar where most of the
wine from the other estates is produced.
They are committed to working well with
respect for the land, giving great
importance to the leading grape variety,
considering the different versions of
Vernaccia on offer. I'Niccolò 2014 is a
blend of vermentino, chardonnay and
sauvignon, with charming fruity and spicy
aromas, a soft, nicely weighty body and a
fresh, lingering finish. We laos liked the
Vernaccia Riserva 2012, with ripe apples
and fresh flowers on the nose and a deep,
contoured palate with a long, dynamic
finish.

○ I'Niccolò '14	♟♟ 3
● San Gimignano Sangiovese Merlot	
Uno di Quattro '10	♟♟ 6
○ Vernaccia di S. Gimignano Ris. '12	♟♟ 3
○ Vernaccia di S. Gimignano	
V. Santa Chiara '13	♟♟ 2*
● Chianti Colli Senesi '13	♟ 2
● Chianti Colli Senesi Ris. '10	♟ 3
● San Gimignano Sottobosco '10	♟ 4
○ Sauvignon Esse '14	♟ 3
● Solleone '11	♟ 5
○ Vernaccia di S. Gimignano '14	♟ 2
○ Vernaccia di S. Gimignano Ventanni '13	♟ 2
○ I'Niccolò '12	♟♟ 3
○ Vernaccia di S. Gimignano Ris. '10	♟♟ 3*
○ Vernaccia di S. Gimignano Ris. '09	♟♟ 3
○ Vernaccia di S. Gimignano Ventanni '12	♟♟ 2*

Fattoria Nittardi

Loc. Nittardi
53011 Castellina in Chianti [SI]
Tel. 0577740269
www.nittardi.com

CELLAR SALES
PRE-BOOKED VISITS
ANNUAL PRODUCTION 94,000 bottles
HECTARES UNDER VINE 29.00

Fattoria Nittardi, owned by the Femfert
Canali family since 1982, is situated not far
from Castellina in Chianti and includes an
annex in Maremma of 37 hectares,
purchased in 1999. The wines are modern
in style: aged in small oak, pursuing the
greatest possible ripeness, weighty
structure, full body and sweet flavour. All
this is expressed with grace and elegance,
allowing the wines to maintain their depth
and a good dose of typicality. The Nectar
Dei 2013 is a stylish and really well-made
blend of cabernet sauvignon, merlot, petit
verdot and syrah grown in Maremma:
crystal-clear aromas and a succulent,
well-coordinated palate. The delicious
Chianti Classico Belcanto 2013 is fragrant
and flavoursome while the Chianti Classico
Riserva 2012 has fluent, well-paced flavour
with sweet spice and fresh cherries on the
nose. The Ad Astra 2013, a Maremma
blend of sangiovese, cabernet, merlot and
syrah, is pleasantly approachable.

● Nectar Dei '13	♟♟ 7
● Ad Astra '13	♟♟ 3
● Chianti Cl. Belcanto '13	♟♟ 4
● Chianti Cl. Ris. '12	♟♟ 6
● Chianti Cl. Casanuova di Nittardi '13	♟ 4
● Ad Astra '08	♟♟♟ 3
● Chianti Cl. Ris. '11	♟♟♟ 6
● Chianti Cl. Ris. '98	♟♟♟ 6
● Chianti Cl. Casanuova di Nittardi '12	♟♟ 4
● Chianti Cl. Casanuova di Nittardi '11	♟♟ 4
● Chianti Cl. Ris. '04	♟♟ 6
● Chianti Cl. Ris. '00	♟♟ 6
● Nectar Dei '09	♟♟ 7
● Nectar Dei '06	♟♟ 6
● Nectar Dei '05	♟♟ 6
● Nectar Dei '03	♟♟ 6

Podere Orma

via Bolgherese
57022 Castagneto Carducci [LI]
Tel. 0575477857
www.ormabolgheri.com

ANNUAL PRODUCTION 30,000 bottles
HECTARES UNDER VINE 5.50
SUSTAINABLE WINERY

Although this wine is not part of the leading
Bolgheri DOCs, we can say that it bears an
unmistakeable imprint of the area. Orma is
the brainchild of Antonio Moretti, a
successful businessman in love with wine,
well-known for having launched estates like
Tenuta Sette Ponti in the province of Arezzo
and Feudo Maccari in Sicily. Orma is a little
gem with just five hectares of vineyards on
clayey soil rich in stony material. Just one
wine, charming, complex and elegant. And
that's how the Orma 2012 is. A tricky year
has produced a red free from inflection or
concession: it shows character and
strength as well as the usual finesse, and
the aromas, darker than usual on hints of
ripe wild berries and spices, are flawlessly
clear and defined in expression. The palate
sustains magical balance between all the
components, with outstanding length.

★★Ornellaia

fraz. Bolgheri
loc. Ornellaia, 191
57022 Castagneto Carducci [LI]
Tel. 056571811
www.ornellaia.it

PRE-BOOKED VISITS
ANNUAL PRODUCTION 930,000 bottles
HECTARES UNDER VINE 112.00

Ornellaia is one of the most prestigious
brands of Italian wine in the world,
established in the early 1980s. After
changing hands various times, this splendid
estate now belongs to the Frescobaldi
family, the famous Tuscan wine-producing
house with many interests in the wine
sector. Ornellaia is a single plot within the
farm of the same name, except for the
Bellaria lands in the northern part of the
DOC zone. The wines have extraordinary
features and some have long-since entered
international winemaking legend. While last
year we crowned a very elegant Masseto,
this year our preference goes to Ornellaia
with a sumptuous 2012 version, really
impressive in stylistic precision, detailed
oaky component and wonderful fruity
extract. This wine is already readable, with
body worthy of its name, unfolding in a
flavour as complex as it is deep. We're very
curious about the white version of
Ornellaia, which we preview tasted and will
soon be released.

● Orma '12	▼▼▼ 8
● Orma '11	♈♈♈ 8
● Orma '10	♈♈♈ 7
● Orma '09	♈♈♈ 6
● Orma '08	♈♈♈ 6
● Orma '07	♈♈♈ 5
● Orma '06	♈♈♈ 6
● Orma '05	♈♈ 6

● Bolgheri Sup. Ornellaia '12	▼▼▼ 8
● Masseto '12	▼▼ 8
● Bolgheri Rosso Le Serre Nuove '13	▼▼ 6
● Bolgheri Rosso Le Volte '13	▼ 3
○ Poggio alle Gazze '13	▼ 5
● Bolgheri Sup. Ornellaia '10	♈♈♈ 8
● Bolgheri Sup. Ornellaia '07	♈♈♈ 8
● Bolgheri Sup. Ornellaia '05	♈♈♈ 8
● Bolgheri Sup. Ornellaia '04	♈♈♈ 8
● Bolgheri Sup. Ornellaia '02	♈♈♈ 8
● Bolgheri Sup. Ornellaia '01	♈♈♈ 8
● Masseto '11	♈♈♈ 8
● Masseto '09	♈♈♈ 8
● Masseto '06	♈♈♈ 8
● Masseto '04	♈♈♈ 8
● Masseto '01	♈♈♈ 8

Siro Pacenti

LOC. PELAGRILLI, 1
53024 MONTALCINO [SI]
TEL. 0577848662
www.siropacenti.it

CELLAR SALES
PRE-BOOKED VISITS
ANNUAL PRODUCTION 60,000 bottles
HECTARES UNDER VINE 22.00

The estate run by Giancarlo dates back to
1971 and was one of the many farms
owned by the Pacenti family, absolute
rulers of the northern slope of Montalcino.
The venerable vineyards of Pelagrilli,
situated at about 350 metres on typically
clayey, silty soil, are mainly used for the
Brunello of the same name and the Ps
Riserva. Later additions include plots in the
southern area of Piancornello, a warmer
area dominated by stony soil with a high
iron content, used in the Vecchie Vigne and
the Rosso. The wines share a certain
powerful texture, achieved also through
barrique ageing, and increasingly
harmonious in recent years. One of the
best partnerships ever is formed by
Giancarlo Pacenti and his 2010 Brunellos.
The Pelagrilli is impressively soft and
classic in expression, with violets, yellow
peaches and nutmeg; the Vecchie Vigne is
more masculine and earthy but also
complex and deep.

Il Palagione

VIA PER CASTEL SAN GIMIGNANO, 36
53037 SAN GIMIGNANO [SI]
TEL. 0577953134
www.ilpalagione.com

CELLAR SALES
PRE-BOOKED VISITS
ACCOMMODATION
ANNUAL PRODUCTION 40,000 bottles
HECTARES UNDER VINE 16.00
VITICULTURE METHOD Certified Organic

Monica Rota's estate is located on the
road to Volterra in a village called Castel
San Gimignano, built in the 14th century to
defend the main city. Documents in the
Episcopal archive of Colle Val d'Elsa
confirm the existence of the farm, where
grapes are grown today, in 1594. Today it
is a well-organized estate: the principal
crop is grapes, as well as extra virgin olive
oil, and there are also orchards with
walnuts and cherries as well as arable
land. The winery chooses natural
conservation techniques for the wines, so
the barrels are kept in an underground
area carved into the tufaceous rock. A
good performance from the Vernaccia Ori
Riserva 2013 with sweet, buttery hints of
vanilla alongside peach and banana fruit.
Creamy on the palate with considerable
edgy acidity and a flavoursome finish. The
Sangiovese Antajr 2009 is austere but with
beautiful flavour.

● Brunello di Montalcino V. V. '10	♟♟♟ 8
● Brunello di Montalcino Pelagrilli '10	♟♟ 6
● Rosso di Montalcino '13	♟ 5
● Brunello di Montalcino '97	♟♟♟ 7
● Brunello di Montalcino '96	♟♟♟ 7
● Brunello di Montalcino '95	♟♟♟ 7
● Brunello di Montalcino '88	♟♟♟ 7
● Brunello di Montalcino PS Ris. '07	♟♟♟ 8
● Brunello di Montalcino '09	♟♟ 8
● Brunello di Montalcino '07	♟♟ 8
● Brunello di Montalcino Pelagrilli '09	♟♟ 6
● Brunello di Montalcino Pelagrilli '08	♟♟ 6
● Rosso di Montalcino PS '11	♟♟ 5

● Antajr '09	♟♟ 4
● Chianti Colli Senesi Caelum '13	♟♟ 2*
○ Vernaccia di S. Gimignano Ori Ris. '13	♟♟ 3
● Chianti Colli Senesi Drago Ris. '12	♟ 3
○ Vernaccia di S. Gimignano Hydra '14	♟ 2
● Antajr '06	♟♟ 5
● Antajr '05	♟♟ 5
● Chianti Colli Senesi Draco Ris. '11	♟♟ 3
○ Vernaccia di S. Gimignano Hydra '11	♟♟ 2*
○ Vernaccia di S. Gimignano Hydra '09	♟♟ 2
○ Vernaccia di S. Gimignano Hydra '07	♟♟ 2*
○ Vernaccia di S. Gimignano Ori '10	♟♟ 3
○ Vernaccia di S. Gimignano Ori Ris. '11	♟♟ 3
○ Vernaccia di S. Gimignano Ori Ris. '05	♟♟ 3
○ Vernaccia di S. Gimignano Ori Ris. '04	♟♟ 3

Tenuta Il Palazzo

LOC. ANTRIA
52100 AREZZO
TEL. 0575 361338
www.tenutailpalazzo.it

CELLAR SALES
PRE-BOOKED VISITS
ANNUAL PRODUCTION 300,000 bottles
HECTARES UNDER VINE 40.00

In the 1970s Anna Maria and Primo Banelli began conservation work to restore the pre-existent hamlet to the former charm it had displayed over the decades, as a thoroughfare on the salt route joining Rome and Rimini. Since 2005 the cellar has completed the work invested in the vineyards, planted on the typical Chianti land: clay, sand, limestone, and especially, galestro. Sangiovese is mainly grown here, alongside canaiolo, cabernet, merlot, syrah, trebbiano and malvasia. The wines are modern in style without excessive extraction or maturation. The Chianti Riserva 2012 is particularly impressive with fragrant red berries, hints of balsam and a fresh, captivating flavour, nicely balancing acidity and tannin. Moro is a Sangiovese topped up with syrah and merlot. The 2012 has spicy, lively aromas with a palate ruffled by tannin, but it is only a matter of time.

● Chianti Ris. '12	♟♟ 3
● Moro '12	♟♟ 4
○ Vin Santo del Chianti Ris. '06	♟♟ 4

Panizzi

LOC. SANTA MARGHERITA, 34
53037 SAN GIMIGNANO [SI]
TEL. 0577941576
www.panizzi.it

CELLAR SALES
PRE-BOOKED VISITS
ACCOMMODATION
ANNUAL PRODUCTION 210,000 bottles
HECTARES UNDER VINE 50.00

Simone Niccolai is at the helm of the winery established by Giovanni Panizzi in 1979. A native Lombard with a passion for Tuscany, he chose San Gimignano as his winegrowing home, convinced that Vernaccia was not given the consideration it deserved. Credit goes to Giovanni for helping the public at large to understand the real potential of a complex, interesting grape. In 2005 Simone's father, Luano, purchased the estate where Panizzi continued to work until he passed away in 2010. It has developed since then with an increase in the hectares of vineyards and the range of wines, and the production of olive oil is also promoted. The Vernaccia Riserva 2012 makes it to the final with varied aromas, stylish fruity hints of apricot and peach alongside fresh citrus sensations of mandarins and spice. The palate is well-coordinated, nicely weighty, deep with vibrant acidity and a flavoursome, lingering finish with a good aftertaste.

○ Vernaccia di S. Gimignano Ris. '12	♟♟♟ 5
○ Rosato Cremisi '14	♟ 3
● San Gimignano Pinot Nero '13	♟ 2
○ Vernaccia di S. Gimignano '14	♟ 2
○ Vernaccia di S. Gimignano Ris. '07	♟♟♟ 5
○ Vernaccia di S. Gimignano Ris. '05	♟♟♟ 5
○ Vernaccia di S. Gimignano Ris. '98	♟♟♟ 4*
○ Vernaccia di S. Gimignano '13	♟♟ 2*
○ Vernaccia di S. Gimignano '11	♟♟ 2*
○ Vernaccia di S. Gimignano Ris. '11	♟♟ 5
○ Vernaccia di S. Gimignano Ris. '10	♟♟ 5
○ Vernaccia di San Gimignano V. Santa Margherita '13	♟♟ 3
○ Vernaccia di San Gimignano V. Santa Margherita '11	♟♟ 3*
○ Vernaccia di San Gimignano V. Santa Margherita '10	♟♟ 3

Tenuta La Parrina

FRAZ. ALBINIA
S.DA DELLA PARRINA
58010 ORBETELLO [GR]
TEL. 0564862636
www.parrina.it

CELLAR SALES
PRE-BOOKED VISITS
ACCOMMODATION AND RESTAURANT SERVICE
ANNUAL PRODUCTION 200,000 bottles
HECTARES UNDER VINE 57.00
VITICULTURE METHOD Certified Organic

This is the only example of a DOC that
physically coincides with just one estate.
Franca Spinola's farm is very old yet
avant-garde in its respect for local
biodiversity and organization of the estate.
It was established by banker Michele
Giuntini in 1830 and was one of the
earliest examples of investment in an
impoverished area. Determination and
clear-sightedness won the day and the
working model applied on the estate served
as a benchmark for the whole Maremma
area. Wine production began in the 19th
century, and the cellars date back to that
time, but Parrina DOC wines have only
existed since 1971. The pleasant Ansonica
Costa dell'Argentario 2014 has vibrant ripe
apple and pear fruit, a substantial,
generous body and a tangy, compelling
finish. The interesting Radaia 2013 is a
monovarietal Merlot with hints of red
berries and spicy pepper and cinnamon on
the nose and a smooth body with a lovely
long finish.

● Parrina Radaia '13	▼▼6
○ Ansonica Costa dell'Argentario '14	▼▼3
● Parrina Rosso Muraccio '13	▼▼3
● Parrina Sangiovese Ris. '12	▼▼5
○ Parrina Bianco '14	▼2
● Parrina Sangiovese '14	▼2
○ Poggio della Fata '14	▼3
● Parrina Rosso Muraccio '12	♀♀3
● Parrina Rosso Muraccio '11	♀♀3
● Parrina Sangiovese '10	♀♀4

Petra

LOC. SAN LORENZO ALTO, 131
57028 SUVERETO [LI]
TEL. 0565845308
www.petrawine.it

CELLAR SALES
PRE-BOOKED VISITS
ANNUAL PRODUCTION 350,000 bottles
HECTARES UNDER VINE 94.00
SUSTAINABLE WINERY

When the estate was established it became
a talking point for its futuristic cellar,
undoubtedly still avant-garde today,
designed by Mario Botta. Today, the Moretti
family lets the wines speak for themselves,
of their terroir of origin. Today Francesca
Moretti manages the estate. Her father
Vittorio had decided to invest in a little
known area, after having consolidated his
passion for winegrowing in Franciacorta,
producing sparkling wines. Tre Bicchieri for
the Petra 2012, from merlot and cabernet
sauvignon, with fresh black berry fruit like
blueberries and currants, and vibrant spice,
ginger followed by liquorice, on a palate
with light tannins balanced by the alcohol
and a long, mouthwatering finish. All the
other wines are excellent, proving the
extraordinary standard of work thus far.

● Petra Rosso '12	▼▼▼8
● Alto '11	▼▼6
● Ebo '12	▼▼3
● Potenti '12	▼▼6
● Quercegobbe '12	▼▼6
● Petra Rosso '11	♀♀♀8
● Petra Rosso '04	♀♀♀7
● Alto '09	♀♀6
● Ebo '11	♀♀3
● Petra Rosso '06	♀♀7
● Potenti '11	♀♀6
● Potenti '10	♀♀6
● Potenti '09	♀♀6
● Quercegobbe '11	♀♀6
● Quercegobbe '10	♀♀6
● Val di Cornia Ebo '10	♀♀3

Fattoria di Petroio

LOC. QUERCEGROSSA
VIA DI MOCENNI, 7
53019 CASTELNUOVO BERARDENGA [SI]
TEL. 0577328045
www.fattoriapetroio.it

CELLAR SALES
PRE-BOOKED VISITS
ANNUAL PRODUCTION 40,000 bottles
HECTARES UNDER VINE 15.00

Fattoria di Petroio at Castelnuovo
Berardenga is a jewel in the Chianti
Classico crown owned by the Lenzi family
since 1961. The wines a gracefully modern
in style offering a faithful expression of the
generous, charming land of origin: the
southernmost part of the Chianti Classico
area, in Sienese territory. The direction
taken in the vineyards is all about balance,
in terms of yields, which are never too low
in pursuit of forced extract, and also of
maturation. In the cellar, oak of various
sizes are used. This year, again, the Poggio
al Mandorlo impressed us the most. The
2012 is a monovarietal Sangiovese
focusing on fruity, earthy aromas with
smoky hints. The palate shows good texture
and linear structure, not without some
hardness that makes the flavour more
assertive. The Chianti Classico 2012 is
delightfully drinkable.

● Chianti Cl. '12	♥♥ 2*
● Poggio al Mandorlo '12	♥♥ 5
● Chianti Cl. '10	♥♥ 2*
● Chianti Cl. '08	♥♥ 2
● Chianti Cl. Ris. '10	♥♥ 4
● Chianti Cl. Ris. '07	♥♥ 4
● Chianti Cl. Ris. '05	♥♥ 4
● Chianti Cl. Ris. '04	♥♥ 4
● Chianti Cl. Ris. '03	♥♥ 4
● Chianti Cl. Ris. '01	♥♥ 4
● Poggio al Mandorlo '11	♥♥ 5
● Poggio al Mandorlo '10	♥♥ 2*

★Fattoria Petrolo

FRAZ. MERCATALE VALDARNO
VIA PETROLO, 30
52021 BUCINE [AR]
TEL. 0559911322
www.petrolo.it

ACCOMMODATION
ANNUAL PRODUCTION 70,000 bottles
HECTARES UNDER VINE 27.00

This is an estate with ancient roots:
certainly Roman as the name suggests,
indicating a noble villa, and probably earlier,
from the Etruscan period, from the local
place names. Luca Sanjust is the current
owner along with his mother, Lucia
Bazzocchi, whose family purchased the
property in the Second World War period.
The change to winegrowing came in the
mid-1980s with renewal of the vineyards,
more densely planted, and modernization
of the cellar. Since then meticulous
attention is paid to every wine and success
has not been slow in coming, even for
experimentation, like ageing the wines in
amphoras. Another Tre Bicchieri for the
Galatrona 2012, with generous, complex
aromas ranging from ripe berries to light
hints of spice like juniper and cinnamon.
The palate opens soft and mouthfilling with
tannins in step with the alcohol and fresh
acidity enlivening and enhancing the
lingering finish.

● Galatrona '12	♥♥♥ 8
● Valdarno di Sopra Bogginanfora '12	♥♥ 6
○ San Petrolo '05	♥♥ 8
● Valdarno di Sopra Boggina '12	♥♥ 6
● Valdarno di Sopra Torrione '13	♥♥ 5
● Galatrona '11	♥♥♥ 8
● Galatrona '10	♥♥♥ 8
● Galatrona '09	♥♥♥ 8
● Galatrona '08	♥♥♥ 8
● Galatrona '07	♥♥♥ 8
● Galatrona '06	♥♥♥ 8
● Galatrona '05	♥♥♥ 8
● Galatrona '04	♥♥♥ 7
● Galatrona '01	♥♥♥ 8
● Galatrona '00	♥♥♥ 7
● Torrione '11	♥♥♥ 5

★Piaggia

LOC. POGGETTO
VIA CEGOLI, 47
59016 POGGIO A CAIANO [PO]
TEL. 0558705401
www.piaggia.com

CELLAR SALES
PRE-BOOKED VISITS
ANNUAL PRODUCTION 75,000 bottles
HECTARES UNDER VINE 15.00

Mauro Vannucci created this estate in the mid-1970s. While working in the textiles industry he developed a passion for the countryside and decided to put it into practice, by buying land. The decision to make wine on a regular basis came later, with the gradual planting of the vineyards, and production began in 1991. Also in those years, more land was purchased, bringing the estate to its current size. Today Mauro's daughter Silvia manages the estate, continuing her father's work with meticulous care in the vineyards and subsequently in the cellar, which enables her to maintain a constant level of quality. Once again Tre Bicchieri go to the Carmignano Riserva 2012, with aromas of black berries softened by spicy hints. The palate is nicely full-bodied with close-knit, blended, tangy tannins and a long, harmonious finish. The Cabernet Franc Poggio de' Colli 2013 is very good, creamy and rich in extract, while the Carmignano Il Sasso 2013 is vibrant and rounded.

● Carmignano Ris. '12	▼▼▼ 6
● Carmignano Il Sasso '13	▼▼ 5
● Poggio de' Colli '13	▼▼ 7
● Carmignano Ris. '11	▽▽▽ 6
● Carmignano Ris. '08	▽▽▽ 5
● Carmignano Ris. '07	▽▽▽ 5
● Carmignano Sasso '07	▽▽▽ 4
● Il Sasso '01	▽▽▽ 4
● Poggio de' Colli '11	▽▽▽ 7
● Poggio de' Colli '10	▽▽▽ 6
● Carmignano Il Sasso '12	▽▽ 5
● Carmignano Il Sasso '11	▽▽ 5
● Carmignano Ris. '10	▽▽ 6
● Carmignano Ris. '09	▽▽ 5
● Carmignano Ris. '06	▽▽ 5
● Poggio de' Colli '12	▽▽ 7

Piancornello

LOC. PIANCORNELLO
53024 MONTALCINO [SI]
TEL. 0577844105
piancornello@libero.it

CELLAR SALES
PRE-BOOKED VISITS
ANNUAL PRODUCTION 50,000 bottles
HECTARES UNDER VINE 10.00

An upland overlooking the Orcia river, with Amiata on the horizon: this is Piancornello, one of the most distinctive estates on the southern slope of Montalcino. Set up in 1991, the estate is run today by Silvana Pieri and Claudio Monaci and covers about ten hectares, standing out for its typical Mediterranean microclimate and very steep, drainable land rich in stones and rocks. These conditions favour early and complete maturation of the sangiovese grapes, producing a warmer, more generous wine than the average without necessarily becoming too accessible or ingratiating. The wines are often quite tannic, also due to the ageing in barriques and tonneaux. This identikit is less successful than on other occasions when describing the splendid 2010 Brunello. This is an incredibly charming version, rich in herby freshness and light, airy flavour, with almost fluvial mineral notes in the background. Well-paced and flowing it is a perfect blend of sinew and sunny Mediterranean warmth.

● Brunello di Montalcino '10	▼▼▼ 6
● Rosso di Montalcino '13	▼ 3
● Brunello di Montalcino '06	▽▽▽ 6
● Brunello di Montalcino '99	▽▽▽ 6
● Brunello di Montalcino '09	▽▽ 6
● Brunello di Montalcino '08	▽▽ 6
● Brunello di Montalcino '07	▽▽ 6
● Brunello di Montalcino '04	▽▽ 6
● Brunello di Montalcino '03	▽▽ 6
● Brunello di Montalcino Ris. '06	▽▽ 6
● Brunello di Montalcino Ris. '04	▽▽ 6
● Brunello di Montalcino Ris. '01	▽▽ 6
● Rosso di Montalcino '11	▽▽ 3
● Rosso di Montalcino '08	▽▽ 3*

Piandaccoli

via di Piandaccoli, 7
50055 Lastra a Signa [FI]
Tel. 0550750005
www.piandaccoli.it

CELLAR SALES
PRE-BOOKED VISITS
ACCOMMODATION
ANNUAL PRODUCTION 80,000 bottles
HECTARES UNDER VINE 20.00

Giampaolo Bruni is a man of rational mind who knows what he wants. When he wanted to start up fine winegrowing activity on the family estate he carried out market research to understand the new trends in taste among worldwide consumers. The results expressed a demand for wines with greater balance and finesse, confirming his intentions, which were to promote the native grape varieties at risk of being abandoned. This is why his vineyards contain less common grapes like barsaglina or mammolo, not to mention foglia tonda and pugnitello, although the lion's share is taken by sangiovese. This has proved to be a positive and forward-thinking choice. The Foglia Tonda 2012 offers vegetal hints on the nose of roasted peppers and grassy sensations of medicinal herbs. A light entry on the palate with acidity in balance with the alcohol and subtle tannins, and a delicate, lingering finish.

● Foglia Tonda del Rinascimento '12	▼▼ 6
● Maiorem '12	▼▼ 5
● Chianti Cosmus Ris. '12	▼▼ 2*
● In Primis '12	▼ 3
● Chianti Cosmus '11	♀♀ 2*
● Maiorem '11	♀♀ 5
● Maiorem '10	♀♀ 5

Pianirossi

loc. Porrona
pod. Santa Genoveffa, 1
58044 Cinigiano [GR]
Tel. 0564990573
www.pianirossi.it

CELLAR SALES
PRE-BOOKED VISITS
ACCOMMODATION AND RESTAURANT SERVICE
ANNUAL PRODUCTION 50,000 bottles
HECTARES UNDER VINE 14.00

Not everyone can manage to fulfil a dream that might, in too many cases, become a regret: Stefano Sincini has succeeded. His main business is fashion but has always had a passion for wine and the countryside in general that is now bearing fruit. In over 20 years the owner has managed to create a farm which follows his way of thinking: the farmhouses were renovated according to ecosustainable principles, in harmony with the surrounding environment, and the care for the vineyards and work in the cellar are carried out with the greatest attention to detail, with very high quality results An excellent performance from the Pinairossi 2012, a blend of montepulciano, petit verdot and cabernet sauvignon: a stylish bouquet with hints of chocolate, pepper and cloves, a mouthfilling palate with silky tannins and a long, compelling finish. The Montecucco Rosso Sidus 2013 is fresh and delicious.

● Montecucco Sidus '13	▼▼ 2*
● Pianirossi '12	▼▼ 6
● Solus '12	▼▼ 3
● Montecucco Sidus '11	♀♀ 4
● Pianirossi '11	♀♀ 6
● Pianirossi '09	♀♀ 6
● Pianirossi '08	♀♀ 6
● Solus '11	♀♀ 4
● Solus '10	♀♀ 4

Enrico Pierazzuoli

VIA VALICARDA, 35
50056 CAPRAIA E LIMITE [FI]
TEL. 0571910078
www.enricopierazzuoli.com

CELLAR SALES
PRE-BOOKED VISITS
ACCOMMODATION
ANNUAL PRODUCTION 156,000 bottles
HECTARES UNDER VINE 32.00

All the Pierazzuoli family is involved in the work on the two estates, in very good growing areas: Tenuta Cantagallo in the Montalbano area and Le Farnete at Carmignano. Since 1970 there has been no lack of passion and commitment and this has led to the construction of an agritourism facility with a restaurant which serves vegetables grown on the property. Olive production is also carefully tended. Enrico Pierazzuoli is personally involved in the vineyard and cellar procedures, fulfilling his clear and simple motto: "a bottle of wine for each plant", which sums up his thoughts on wine without too many explanations.
Through to the finals for the Carmignano Riserva 2012: vibrant blackberry and plum aromas softened by spices with a clearly defined flavour on an elegant, succulent palate with a harmonious, lingering finish. The Gioveto 2012, from merlot, syrah and sangiovese, is also good, with hints of turmeric and pomegranate on the nose, and a harmonious, excellent flavour.

● Carmignano Le Farnete Ris. '12	♥♥ 4
● Carmignano Le Farnete '13	♥♥ 3
● Chianti Montalbano Ris. '12	♥♥ 3
● Gioveto '12	♥♥ 4
○ Vin Santo del Chianti Montalbano Millarium Ris. '09	♥♥ 5
● Barco Reale Le Farnete '14	♥ 2
● Chianti Montalbano '14	♥ 2
● Barco Reale Le Farnete '13	♥♥ 2*
● Carmignano Le Farnete '12	♥♥ 3
● Carmignano Le Farnete '11	♥♥ 3*
● Carmignano Le Farnete Ris. '11	♥♥ 4
● Carmignano Le Farnete Ris. '10	♥♥ 4
○ Vin Santo del Chianti Montalbano Millarium Ris. '08	♥♥ 5
○ Vin Santo del Chianti Montalbano Millarium Ris. '07	♥♥ 5

La Pierotta

LOC. LA PIEROTTA, 19
58020 SCARLINO [GR]
TEL. 056637218
www.@lapierotta.it

CELLAR SALES
PRE-BOOKED VISITS
ANNUAL PRODUCTION 50,000 bottles
HECTARES UNDER VINE 11.00

The Rustici family's history is that of the Italy that once was. They have owned the estate since 1957, a time when Maremma was very different from the area we know today. A few hectares available for growing cereals, enough vineyards for family consumption, a stable situation up until the 1970s when Alberto and his wife Floriana decided to increase the area of land planted with vineyards. At the same time farming was being abandoned and the countryside deserted. When their children joined the business in the 1990s this coincided with the first bottled wines, updating of the cellar equipment, and an increase in sales, also abroad. The very intriguing Ciliegiolo 2013 has vibrant aromas of cherries and red plums, hints of forest floor, tobacco and leather, and a well-coordinated, succulent and lively palate with a tangy, fresh flavour. The Scarilius 2012 is a good Sangiovese with fresh hints of ripe cherries and minerals, and a smooth flavour.

● Maremma Toscana Ciliegiolo '13	♥♥ 3
● Monteregio di Massa Marittima Scarilius '12	♥♥ 3
⊙ Monteregio di Massa Marittima Rosato '14	♥ 2
● Monteregio di Massa Marittima Rosso Selvaneta '13	♥ 2
● Terra Solare '13	♥ 3
● Monteregio di Massa Marittima Rosso Selvaneta '12	♥♥ 2*
● Terra Solare '11	♥♥ 3*

Pietroso

LOC. PIETROSO, 257
53024 MONTALCINO [SI]
TEL. 0577848573
www.pietroso.it

CELLAR SALES
PRE-BOOKED VISITS
ANNUAL PRODUCTION 30,000 bottles
HECTARES UNDER VINE 5.00

Pietroso was opened in the Seventies by Domenico Berni and is one of the Montalcino estates to have grown most exponentially in terms of stylistic consistency and character. Today it is run by his grandson Gianni Pignattai with a small production originating from about four hectares of vineyards all planted to sangiovese and divided into three main areas: Fornello (northern sector, 350 metres altitude, marly soil), Colombaiolo (southern slope, near the abbey of Sant'Antimo, 400 metres altitude, clay, tuff and marl) and Pietroso (500 metres, poor soil with plenty of stones and rocks). The plots are fermented separately and each follows its own ageing procedure, mainly in 30-hectolitre oak, before the final blend. The Brunello di Pietroso doesn't repeat last year's fantastic performance but the 2010 is still an original reading. An anarchic profile of nectarines, wild herbs, and coffee beans on a palate as soft on entry as it is edgy in development, with severe tannins.

● Brunello di Montalcino '10	♀♀	6
● Rosso di Montalcino '13	♀♀	4
● Villa Montosoli '11	♀	7
● Brunello di Montalcino '09	♀♀♀	6
● Brunello di Montalcino '08	♀♀	6
● Rosso di Montalcino '12	♀♀	4
● Rosso di Montalcino '11	♀♀	3*

Podere 414

LOC. MAIANO LAVACCHIO, 10
58051 MAGLIANO IN TOSCANA [GR]
TEL. 0564507818
www.podere414.it

CELLAR SALES
PRE-BOOKED VISITS
ANNUAL PRODUCTION 150,000 bottles
HECTARES UNDER VINE 22.00
VITICULTURE METHOD Certified Organic

Simone Castelli was born into the wine sector, but while his father Maurizio, is an oenologist renowned for his consultant work, not only in Italy, Simone decided to follow a different path after graduating in agricultural science, that of a vigneron. With an interest in the Maremma area, in the late 1990s he decided alongside his father and grandfather to find a suitable place to express his idea of wine. Their choice fell on a farm which still maintains its name, or rather the number it was assigned by the land reform authority appointed in the 1960s to break up the estates and redistribute them to the families. It was an untamed place ready for an adventure. Varied aromas in the Morellino 2013, alternating wild berries, pepper and cinnamon and hints of autumn leaves, and a pleasant, non-aggressive palate with a fresh, lingering finish. The charming Aleatico Passito 2014 reveals blackberry and cherry jam on the nose with cloves and fresh minty sensations. The palate is mouthfilling and creamy, sweet and lingering.

● Aleatico Passito '14	♀♀	7
● Morellino di Scansano '13	♀♀	3
○ Rosato Flower Power '14	♀	2
● Aleatico Passito '13	♀♀	7
● Morellino di Scansano '12	♀♀	3
● Morellino di Scansano '10	♀♀	3

Poderi del Paradiso

LOC. STRADA, 21A
53037 SAN GIMIGNANO [SI]
TEL. 0577941500
www.poderidelparadiso.it

CELLAR SALES
PRE-BOOKED VISITS
ACCOMMODATION
ANNUAL PRODUCTION 130,000 bottles
HECTARES UNDER VINE 27.00

The Cetti family of San Gimignano have a long history. Indeed, the first known ancestor was a certain Puccio di Cetto who came from Val di Pesa, back in the year 1000. The estate's origins also date back to the distant past, because the Paradiso area is documented back in the 13th century, although the family only purchased it in 1973. Since then a great deal of work has been done to bring the estate up to date, with renewal of the vineyards, planted with many international grape varieties. Olive oil is also particularly important and meticulously supervised and there are agritourism facilities for tourists. A good performance from the Sangiovese Bottaccio 2011, with sweet, balsamic aromas of wild berries and vanilla. The palate is firm-bodied but smooth and mouthfilling with a pleasant, lingering, flavour. The Chianti Colli Senesi Riserva 2012 is also enjoyable with fresh fruity aromas, and a tidy, beautifully lively palate.

Fattoria Poggerino

LOC. POGGERINO, 6
53017 RADDA IN CHIANTI [SI]
TEL. 0577738958
www.poggerino.com

CELLAR SALES
PRE-BOOKED VISITS
ACCOMMODATION
ANNUAL PRODUCTION 60,000 bottles
HECTARES UNDER VINE 11.30
VITICULTURE METHOD Certified Organic

Il Poggerino has been a Chianti Classico producer since the Eighties, and is one of the many examples of artisanal winemaking typical of the DOC's production network. The winery is managed by Piero and Benedetta Lanza who have applied organic growing methods in their vineyards for over ten years. Technological interventions are kept to an absolute minimum in the cellar. This is the birthplace of wines in which the sangiovese grape finds its very best expression although the estate's style is typically based on almost extreme pursuit of ripeness in the fruit, which does not diminish the character and personality of the wines. 2012 brings an extraordinary version of the Chianti Classico Bugialla: fragrant aromas, with very stylish forward citrus sensations The palate is very dynamic and flavoursome with a deep, fruity finish. The Chianti Classico 2012 is equally well-typed with clear cherry aromas and a tangy, succulent palate.

● Chianti Colli Senesi Ris. '12	♥♥ 3
● San Gimignano Sangiovese Bottaccio '11	♥♥ 4
● Chianti Colli Senesi '13	♥ 2
○ Vernaccia di S. Gimignano '14	♥ 1*
○ Vernaccia di S. Gimignano Biscondola '13	♥ 3
● A Filippo '02	♥♥♥ 4
● Saxa Calida '00	♥♥♥ 5
● Saxa Calida '99	♥♥♥ 4
● Mangiafoco '04	♥♥ 5
● San Gimignano Sangiovese Bottaccio '10	♥♥ 5
○ San Gimignano Vin Santo '07	♥♥ 5
● Saxa Calida '04	♥♥ 6
○ Vernaccia di S. Gimignano '12	♥♥ 3
○ Vernaccia di S. Gimignano '10	♥♥ 2
○ Vernaccia di S. Gimignano Biscondola '11	♥♥ 3
○ Vernaccia di S. Gimignano Biscondola '10	♥♥ 3

● Chianti Cl. Bugialla Ris. '12	♥♥♥ 5
● Chianti Cl. '12	♥♥ 3*
● Chianti Cl. Bugialla Ris. '09	♥♥♥ 5
● Chianti Cl. Bugialla Ris. '08	♥♥♥ 5
● Chianti Cl. Ris. '90	♥♥♥ 4*
● Primamateria '01	♥♥♥ 5
● Chianti Cl. '08	♥♥ 3
● Chianti Cl. '06	♥♥ 3*
● Chianti Cl. '04	♥♥ 3
● Chianti Cl. '01	♥♥ 3
● Chianti Cl. Bugialla Ris. '10	♥♥ 5
● Chianti Cl. Bugialla Ris. '04	♥♥ 5
● Chianti Cl. Bugialla Ris. '99	♥♥ 4
● Primamateria '10	♥♥ 5
● Primamateria '00	♥♥ 5
● Primamateria '99	♥♥ 5

Poggio al Gello

FRAZ. PAGANICO
LOC. GELLO, 66
58045 CIVITELLA PAGANICO [GR]
TEL. 0564906025
www.poggioalgello.it

CELLAR SALES
PRE-BOOKED VISITS
ANNUAL PRODUCTION 20,000 bottles
HECTARES UNDER VINE 4.00
VITICULTURE METHOD Certified Organic
SUSTAINABLE WINERY

Business and life partners Alda and Giorgio
decided to build their life's work in Tuscany,
in harmony with their chosen environmental
surroundings. The decision to produce wine
and olive oil according to organic farming
principles was taken immediately and with
great conviction, out of respect owing to an
area that had enchanted them. So the
production process is never intensive or
stimulated, and attention is focused on
lesser known native varieties like foglia
tonda and pugnitello, so as to preserve a
heritage still able to offer pleasant surprises
in the bottles. Also worth mentioning is the
special care lavished on the olive groves.
The Montecucco Sangiovese 2011 makes
the finals with a varied array of aromas,
hints of bay leaves and sage alternating
with blackberries and plums. The palate
shows good, firm structure and a vibrant,
lingering finish. The Montecucco
Sangiovese Riserva 2011 is also pleasant,
with a nice assortment of mature aromas.

● Montecucco Sangiovese Rosso del Gello '11	♔♔ 3*
● Montecucco Sangiovese Rosso del Gello Ris. '11	♔♔ 4
● Agellus '13	♔ 4

Poggio al Tesoro

LOC. FELCIAINO
VIA BOLGHERESE, 189B
57022 BOLGHERI [LI]
TEL. 0565773051
www.poggioaltesoro.it

CELLAR SALES
PRE-BOOKED VISITS
ANNUAL PRODUCTION 283,000 bottles
HECTARES UNDER VINE 60.50

Poggio al Tesoro owned by the Allegrini
family wins Winery of the Year this year, as
it establishes its position as a benchmark
for the Bolgheri area. The grape varieties
are those typical of the area, planted on
variable lands ranging from those rich in
stones and clay to heavier, and sometimes
extremely sandy soils. The wines seem to
be growing in maturity and stylistic identity,
with lush aromas that are a kind of
trademark. A really great 2012 version of
the Dedicato a Walter, one of the best
Bolgheri Superiore we tasted. The aromatic
profile is citrus and grassy, very fresh and
original. Traces left by time in oak are
evident but the fruit keeps them at bay:
redcurrants and citrus over rather
compelling balsamic hints are in the
foreground. The grassy sensation also runs
through the palate which is stylish and racy
rather than weighty and robust.

● Dedicato a Walter '12	♔♔♔ 7
● Bolgheri Sup. Sondraia '12	♔♔ 5
● Mediterra '13	♔♔ 3
☉ Bolgheri Rosato Cassiopea '14	♔ 2
○ Bolgheri Vermentino Solosole '14	♔ 3
● Bolgheri Sup. Sondraia '11	♔♔♔ 5
● Bolgheri Sup. Sondraia '10	♔♔♔ 5
● Dedicato a Walter '09	♔♔♔ 7
● Dedicato a Walter '08	♔♔ 7
● Dedicato a Walter '07	♔♔ 5
● Dedicato a Walter '06	♔♔ 5

★Poggio Antico

LOC. POGGIO ANTICO
53024 MONTALCINO [SI]
TEL. 0577848044
www.poggioantico.com

CELLAR SALES
PRE-BOOKED VISITS
RESTAURANT SERVICE
ANNUAL PRODUCTION 120,000 bottles
HECTARES UNDER VINE 32.00

The wines of Poggio Antico seem to be undergoing a kind of second youth. The more recent vintages have restored the estate owned by Paola Godler and Alberto Montefiori to the glories of the 1980s when their Brunellos were firmly established among the most exciting interpretations of the type. The particular location of the vineyards, south of the village but in a high, airy position, represents an ideal starting point for a pedigree sangiovese focusing on mouthwatering juiciness and verve rather than muscle. The cellar's choices, far-sighted in this case, include the use of 37- and 55-hectolitre oak for the vintage version while barriques and tonneaux are used for the Riserva and the Altero. Poggio Antico always presents a remarkable range, just missing the cherry on the cake. Leader of the pack once again is the Brunello Altero: the 2010 version shows more extract and toastiness than expected but the usual sound, succulent aromas of blackberries, pepper and cocoa powder.

● Brunello di Montalcino Altero '10	♥♥ 7
● Brunello di Montalcino '10	♥♥ 6
● Rosso di Montalcino '13	♥♥ 4
● Lemartine '13	♥ 5
● Brunello di Montalcino '05	♥♥♥ 7
● Brunello di Montalcino Altero '09	♥♥♥ 7
● Brunello di Montalcino Altero '07	♥♥♥ 8
● Brunello di Montalcino Altero '06	♥♥♥ 8
● Brunello di Montalcino Altero '04	♥♥♥ 8

Poggio Argentiera

LOC. ALBERESE
S.DA BANDITELLA, 2
58010 GROSSETO
TEL. 3484952767
www.poggioargentiera.com

CELLAR SALES
PRE-BOOKED VISITS
ANNUAL PRODUCTION 200,000 bottles
HECTARES UNDER VINE 22.00
VITICULTURE METHOD Certified Organic

The estate was established in 1997 when Gianpaolo Paglia bought the Adua farm, dating back to the reclamation of the Maremma area, and began planting vineyards and perfecting the cellar. In 2001 the new purchase in the Scansano area brought the estate to its current size, along with the construction of a new cellar. In February of this year the estate was rented out to a company formed by the owners of the Tua Rita estate in Suvereto. The new owners aim to maintain the quality standard achieved over the year and further penetrate the international market. The interesting Morellino Capatosta 2012 has a nose dominated by ripe fruit, a well-textured palate with nicely blended acidity and a crescendo finish.

● Morellino di Scansano Capatosta '12	♥♥ 5
○ Maremma Toscana Bucce '13	♥ 3
○ Maremma Toscana Vermentino Guazza '14	♥ 2
● Finisterre '07	♥♥♥ 6
● Morellino di Scansano Capatosta '00	♥♥♥ 5*
○ Fonte_40 '10	♥♥ 3
○ Guazza '13	♥♥ 2*
● Maremmante '09	♥♥ 2
● Morellino di Scansano Bellamarsilia '13	♥♥ 3*
● Morellino di Scansano Bellamarsilia '12	♥♥ 2*
● Morellino di Scansano Bellamarsilia '11	♥♥ 2*
● Morellino di Scansano Capatosta '11	♥♥ 5
● Morellino di Scansano Capatosta '10	♥♥ 5
● Morellino di Scansano Capatosta '07	♥♥ 5
● Morellino di Scansano Capatosta '06	♥♥ 5

Poggio Bonelli

VIA DELL'ARBIA, 2
53019 CASTELNUOVO BERARDENGA [SI]
TEL. 057756661
www.poggiobonelli.it

CELLAR SALES
PRE-BOOKED VISITS
ACCOMMODATION AND RESTAURANT SERVICE
ANNUAL PRODUCTION 125,000 bottles
HECTARES UNDER VINE 83.00

The estate is part of MPS Tenimenti,
owned by the Montepaschi di Siena group,
who own another winegrowing estate, also
in the Castelnuovo Berardenga area: Villa
Chigi Saracini. The vineyards are therefore
situated in the southern part of Chianti
Classico, an area in which the wines
acquire particular strength and fullness.
These features are faithfully expressed by
the winery style despite the considerable
use of mainly small oak. The well-made
Chianti Classico 2013 has vibrant,
clear-cut aromas with hints of fresh wild
berries and a slender, focused palate,
progressive and flavoursome. The light,
succulent and very drinkable Chianti Villa
Chigi Saracini 2014 has cherries on the
nose and a well-paced, tangy flavour. The
Chianti Classico Riserva 2010 is less
focused on the nose, but the palate is its
strongpoint, with flavour, fresh acidity and
lovely depth.

Poggio di Sotto

FRAZ. CASTELNUOVO DELL'ABATE
LOC. POGGIO DI SOTTO
53024 MONTALCINO [SI]
TEL. 0577835502
www.poggiodisotto.com

CELLAR SALES
PRE-BOOKED VISITS
ACCOMMODATION
ANNUAL PRODUCTION 35,000 bottles
HECTARES UNDER VINE 12.00
VITICULTURE METHOD Certified Organic
SUSTAINABLE WINERY

The Tipa family have built up a real dream
team of farms in Tuscany. Collemassari at
Montecucco and Grattamacco at Bolgheri
were joined in 2011 by Poggio di Sotto, set
up by Piero Palmucci, which has quickly
become one of the best-loved names in
Montalcino. Everything revolves around a
single plot of ten hectares on the hills at
Castelnuovo dell'Abate, in the south-
eastern part of the DOC zone. This is an
extraordinarily beautiful area, set between
Monte Amiata and the Orcia river, with the
Tirreno coast a distant influence on the
microclimate. This is the birthplace of only
apparently light sangioveses, mainly aged
in 30-hectolitre Slavonian oak. The 2010
vintage in interpreted in true Poggio di
Sotto style: berry jam, dried herbs, etheral
hints on the nose but the best comes with
the flavoursome, racy palate which holds
back biting tannins with invigorating,
spontaneous flavour. Tre Bicchieri.

● Tramonto d'Oca '10	♟♟♟ 5
● Chianti Cl. '13	♟♟ 3
● Chianti Villa Chigi Saracini '14	♟♟ 3
● Chianti Cl. Ris. '10	♟ 5
● Poggiassai '11	♟♟♟ 6
● Poggiassai '10	♟♟♟ 6
● Poggiassai '08	♟♟♟ 5
● Poggiassai '07	♟♟♟ 5
● Poggiassai '06	♟♟♟ 5
● Chianti Villa Chigi Saracini '13	♟♟ 3
● Chianti Villa Chigi Saracini '12	♟♟ 3
● Tramonto d'Oca '04	♟♟ 5
● Tramonto d'Oca '03	♟♟ 5
○ Vin Santo del Chianti Cl. Occhio di Pernice '06	♟♟ 8

● Brunello di Montalcino '10	♟♟♟ 8
● Rosso di Montalcino '12	♟♟ 8
● Brunello di Montalcino '07	♟♟♟ 8
● Brunello di Montalcino '04	♟♟♟ 8
● Brunello di Montalcino '99	♟♟♟ 8
● Brunello di Montalcino Ris. '07	♟♟♟ 8
● Brunello di Montalcino Ris. '99	♟♟♟ 8
● Brunello di Montalcino Ris. '95	♟♟♟ 8
● Rosso di Montalcino '07	♟♟♟ 6
● Brunello di Montalcino '08	♟♟ 8
● Brunello di Montalcino '06	♟♟ 8
● Brunello di Montalcino Ris. '08	♟♟ 8
● Brunello di Montalcino Ris. '06	♟♟ 8
● Rosso di Montalcino '11	♟♟ 7
● Rosso di Montalcino '10	♟♟ 7
● Rosso di Montalcino '09	♟♟ 7

635

TUSCANY

Poggio Rubino

LOC. LA SORGENTE, 62
S.DA PROVINCIALE CASTIGLION DEL BOSCO
53024 MONTALCINO [SI]
TEL. 05771698133

CELLAR SALES
PRE-BOOKED VISITS
ACCOMMODATION AND RESTAURANT SERVICE
ANNUAL PRODUCTION 32,000 bottles
HECTARES UNDER VINE 7.00

Situated on the central western slope of Montalcino, at about 450 metres altitude, Poggio Rubino is a small estate with seven hectares of vineyards, run by Edward Corsi and Alessandra Marzocchi. The plots, scattered over several areas of the DOC zone, are mainly planted to sangiovese and farmed using biosustainable methods. This winegrowing approach is reflected in the traditional cellar choices, with lengthy maceration and ageing in 25- and 30-hectolitre oak. The result is a pair of Brunellos in a classic but certainly not nostalgic style: they are weighty, densely tannic wines which are worth the patient wait. The latest tests traced a rather open-ended profile, but in any case coherent with the stylistic concept of Poggio Rubino. The 2010 Brunello is penalized by excessive oakiness and brusque tannins, but broadens out just the same thanks to really lively tanginess. The Rosso 2013 is not bad.

Poggio Trevvalle

LOC. ARCILLE
58042 CAMPAGNATICO [GR]
TEL. 0564998142

CELLAR SALES
PRE-BOOKED VISITS
ANNUAL PRODUCTION 80,000 bottles
HECTARES UNDER VINE 13.35
VITICULTURE METHOD Certified Organic
SUSTAINABLE WINERY

Bernardo and Umberto Valle chose Maremma to put their passion for wine into practice in the late 1990s, starting at once with organic methods in the conviction that this was a good method to obtain excellent results in terms of quality. They were proved right: some areas of the vineyards were completely replanted but some still have the old vines. Most of them are planted with sangiovese, but there are also international varieties. Some of the production area includes the Montecucco zone, although most falls within the Morellino DOC. An interesting Morellino Pàssera 2014 with intriguing aromas of cherries and blackberries alongside hints of forest floor. The palate is fresh, lively and delicious. The more austere Riserva 2012 has evolved tobacco and leather aromas, a powerful and well-coordinated structure and a lingering, mouthwatering finish.

Wine	Rating
● Brunello di Montalcino '10	▼▼ 6
● Rosso di Montalcino '13	▼ 3
● Brunello di Montalcino '09	♀♀ 6
● Brunello di Montalcino '08	♀♀ 6
● Brunello di Montalcino '07	♀♀ 6
● Brunello di Montalcino '06	♀♀ 6
● Brunello di Montalcino Ris. '07	♀♀ 7
● Brunello di Montalcino Ris. '06	♀♀ 6

Wine	Rating
● Morellino di Scansano Larcille Ris. '12	▼▼ 4
● Morellino di Scansano Pàssera '14	▼▼ 3
● Montecucco Rosso '12	▼ 3
● Morellino di Scansano '13	▼ 3
● Morellino di Scansano '12	♀♀♀ 2*
● Morellino di Scansano '11	♀♀ 2*
● Morellino di Scansano Fròndina '04	♀♀ 2
● Morellino di Scansano Larcille '03	♀♀ 4
● Morellino di Scansano Larcille '00	♀♀ 3
● Morellino di Scansano Pàssera '13	♀♀ 2*
● Morellino di Scansano Pàssera '12	♀♀ 2*
● Rafele '08	♀♀ 2

Tenuta Il Poggione

FRAZ. SANT'ANGELO IN COLLE
LOC. MONTEANO
53024 MONTALCINO [SI]
TEL. 0577844029
www.tenutailpoggione.it

CELLAR SALES
PRE-BOOKED VISITS
ACCOMMODATION
ANNUAL PRODUCTION 600,000 bottles
HECTARES UNDER VINE 127.00

Fabrizio Bindocci has devoted his whole career to serving what is actually one of the most significant farms in Montalcino, with over 100 hectares of vineyards. Owned by the Franceschini family for five generations, the Il Poggione properties are situated in the southern zone of Sant'Angelo in Colle with small quantities of merlot, vermentino and chardonnay alongside the sangiovese. A broad, varied range is led by Brunellos in a proudly traditional style (vintage and Vigna Paganelli Riserva) which includes maceration of about 20 days and ageing in 30- and 50-hectolitre French oak. The positive impressions of recent years are fully confirmed by the latest tastings. The delicate, pragmatic Rosso 2013 deserves a look, and it will probably be worth waiting for the 2010 Brunello, already impressive with enfolding, dynamic aromas but able to develop complexity with bottle ageing.

● Brunello di Montalcino '10	♥♥ 7
● Rosso di Montalcino '13	♥♥ 4
○ Bianco di Toscana Vermentino Chardonnay '14	♥ 3
● Il Poggione '12	♥ 2
⊙ Lo Sbrancato '14	♥ 3
● Brunello di Montalcino Ris. '97	♥♥♥ 7
● Brunello di Montalcino '09	♥♥ 6
● Brunello di Montalcino '08	♥♥ 6
● Brunello di Montalcino '07	♥♥ 6
● Brunello di Montalcino V. Paganelli Ris. '07	♥♥ 7
● Brunello di Montalcino V. Paganelli Ris. '06	♥♥ 7
● Rosso di Montalcino '12	♥♥ 3
● Rosso di Montalcino '11	♥♥ 3

★★Poliziano

LOC. MONTEPULCIANO STAZIONE
VIA FONTAGO, 1
53045 MONTEPULCIANO [SI]
TEL. 0578738171
www.carlettipoliziano.com

CELLAR SALES
PRE-BOOKED VISITS
ANNUAL PRODUCTION 650,000 bottles
HECTARES UNDER VINE 160.00

Owner Federico Carletti has brought the estate to its important international role. His father Dino purchased the first 22 hectares in the Montepulciano area where he began planting the first vineyards. This choice was inspired by a desire to maintain a link with his area of origin rather than by a real passion for winegrowing, which was what convinced Federico to leave his job and become a full-time vigneron. Over the years, many other purchases have led to the current size of the estate: in the meantime, there has always been a constant desire to grow and experiment in the vineyard with experimentation with organic and biodynamic agricultural methods. The Nobile Asinone 2012 has a majestic nose with vibrant hints of juniper, bay leaves, and vanilla softening the fruity cherry sensations. The palate is warm, full-bodied and succulent with a lingering, exciting finish. The Nobile 2012 has stylish aromas and a subtle, well-balanced palate.

● Nobile di Montepulciano Asinone '12	♥♥♥ 7
● Nobile di Montepulciano '12	♥♥ 5
● Morellino di Scansano Lhosa '13	♥ 2
● Rosso di Montepulciano '13	♥ 3
● Le Stanze '03	♥♥♥ 6
● Le Stanze '00	♥♥♥ 6
● Nobile di Montepulciano '09	♥♥♥ 4*
● Nobile di Montepulciano Asinone '11	♥♥♥ 7
● Nobile di Montepulciano Asinone '07	♥♥♥ 6
● Nobile di Montepulciano Asinone '06	♥♥♥ 6
● Nobile di Montepulciano Asinone '05	♥♥♥ 6
● Nobile di Montepulciano Asinone '04	♥♥♥ 6
● Nobile di Montepulciano Asinone '03	♥♥♥ 6
● Nobile di Montepulciano Asinone '01	♥♥♥ 6
● Nobile di Montepulciano Asinone '00	♥♥♥ 6
● Nobile di Montepulciano Asinone '99	♥♥♥ 5

Tenuta Le Potazzine

LOC. LE PRATA, 262
53024 MONTALCINO [SI]
TEL. 0577846168
www.lepotazzine.it

CELLAR SALES
PRE-BOOKED VISITS
RESTAURANT SERVICE
ANNUAL PRODUCTION 50,000 bottles
HECTARES UNDER VINE 4.70

The great tits featured on the colourful labels of Le Potazzine wines gave the estate, set up by Giuseppe Gorelli and Gigliola Giannetti, its name, the Tuscan name for this bird and an affectionate nickname for their daughters when children. Viola and Sofia's births in 1993 and 1996 marked the most important stages in the estate's winegrowing development. Three and a half hectares are situated in Le Prata, in the western part of Montalcino, an area unique in many ways for the altitude (about 500 metres), considerable temperature variation and iron-rich soil. Another 1.2 hectares are at Torre, the area linking Sesta and Sant'Angelo in Colle. The almost feminine character often displayed by Le Potazzine Brunellos is perfectly embodied in the 2010 version. Fresh, sunny fruit, enriched with balsamic, spicy hints when aerated in the glass, counterbalancing the slight lack of acidity and expansion with sweetness and flavour.

● Brunello di Montalcino '10	♟♟♟ 6
● Rosso di Montalcino '13	♟♟ 4
● Parus '13	♟ 3
● Brunello di Montalcino '08	♀♀♀ 6
● Brunello di Montalcino '09	♀♀ 6
● Brunello di Montalcino '07	♀♀ 6
● Brunello di Montalcino '04	♀♀ 7
● Brunello di Montalcino Ris. '06	♀♀ 7
● Brunello di Montalcino Ris. '04	♀♀ 7
● Rosso di Montalcino '12	♀♀ 4
● Rosso di Montalcino '10	♀♀ 4

Pratesi

LOC. SEANO
VIA RIZZELLI, 10
59011 CARMIGNANO [PO]
TEL. 0558704108
www.pratesivini.it

CELLAR SALES
PRE-BOOKED VISITS
RESTAURANT SERVICE
ANNUAL PRODUCTION 60,000 bottles
HECTARES UNDER VINE 12.00

Back in 1875 Pietro Pratesi, an ancestor of the current owner, decided to purchase land in the Lolocco area where wine and olive oil were already being produced on a regular basis. Today Fabrizio Pratesi runs the winery, expressing clear ideas from the start about the type of wine he wanted to make: high planting density, and modern cellar techniques aiming to obtain wines with great ageing potential. What might have initially been a secondary activity later proved to be a real passion. Fabrizio is now Chairman of the Consorzio dei Vini di Carmignano, which places him in the frontline, promoting the potential of an area he has always loved. The Barche di Bacchareto 2012 has a generous, varied and spicy nose with a close-knit, creamy palate finishing on lovely lingering fruity hints. The Riserva Il Circo Rosso 2012 has ripe fruity aromas, a slender structure with well-organized tannins and a flavoursome finish.

● Carmignano '13	♟♟ 4
● Carmignano Il Circo Rosso Ris. '12	♟♟ 6
● Merlot Barche di Bacchereto '12	♟♟ 3
● Barco Reale '14	♟ 2
● Carmignano '12	♀♀ 3
● Carmignano '08	♀♀ 4
● Carmignano '01	♀♀ 5
● Carmignano Circo Rosso Ris. '11	♀♀ 5
● Carmignano Circo Rosso Ris. '10	♀♀ 4
● Carmignano Circo Rosso Ris. '08	♀♀ 5
● Carmignano V. di Carmio Ris. '07	♀♀ 5
● Carmione '10	♀♀ 4
● Carmione '08	♀♀ 5
● Carmione '07	♀♀ 5
● Merlot Barche di Barchereto '10	♀♀ 3

★Fattoria Le Pupille

S.DA PIAGGE DEL MAIANO
58100 GROSSETO
TEL. 0564409517
www.fattorialepupille.it

CELLAR SALES
PRE-BOOKED VISITS
ACCOMMODATION
ANNUAL PRODUCTION 450,000 bottles
HECTARES UNDER VINE 80.00

Elisabetta Geppetti is one of the top
ambassadors of Morellino thanks to her
exciting personal history, ahead of her time,
making choices that later demonstrated the
potential of the area. The farm originated
from a central nucleus that has been
enlarged over the years and was
transformed into an excellent winegrowing
estate from 1985 onwards, with a project
consolidated over time, the purchase of
new vineyards and the creation of wines
that would become famous worldwide.
Running the estate alongside her today is
her elder daughter Clara, as a new
generation steps in respecting the
experience gathered over time. The
Saffredi 2012 is a blend of cabernet
sauvignon, merlot and petit verdot with
vibrant aromas of autumn leaves, tobacco
and leather alongside spicy hints of
liquorice over a jammy background. The
palate is warm, harmonious and broad with
subtle tannins and an intriguing, very
lingering flavour.

● Maremma Toscana Saffredi '12	▼▼8
○ Maremma Toscana SolAlto '08	▼▼3
● Morellino di Scansano '13	▼2
● Morellino di Scansano Poggio Valente Ris. '11	▼5
● Pelofino '14	▼2
○ Poggio Argentato '14	▼2
⊙ Rosa Mati '14	▼2
● Morellino di Scansano Poggio Valente '04	♈♈♈5
● Saffredi '05	♈♈♈8
● Saffredi '04	♈♈♈8
● Saffredi '03	♈♈♈8
● Saffredi '02	♈♈♈7
● Saffredi '01	♈♈♈7

La Querce

VIA IMPRUNETANA PER TAVARNUZZE, 41
50023 IMPRUNETA [FI]
TEL. 0552011380
www.laquerce.com

CELLAR SALES
PRE-BOOKED VISITS
ACCOMMODATION
ANNUAL PRODUCTION 35,000 bottles
HECTARES UNDER VINE 8.00

A large oak tree shaded the villa and cellar
until the Second World War. Since then,
although the tree was cut down by the
Germans, it has remained as the emblem
of the estate. We have to jump forward to
the 1960s to meet owner Gino Marchi who,
driven by a passion for wine, brought the
winery to international fame in just ten
years. His son Massimo continues to care
for the vineyards and cellar, rendered
modern and functional by manager Marco
Ferretti. The Marchi family with Donatella,
Benedetta and Giulio, has also successfully
focused on the hospitality sector in the old
villa. The La Querce 2012, from sangiovese
and colorino, makes the finals again with a
pleasant bouquet of red berries and fine
spices like pepper and cinnamon. The
palate is smooth, stylish and nicely weighty
with a pleasant, lingering finish. The Chianti
Colli Fiorentini La Torretta 2013 also
performs well with fresh, pleasant aromas
and a supple, dynamic structure with a
lovely lingering flavour.

● La Querce '12	▼▼5
● Chianti Colli Fiorentini La Torretta '13	▼▼2*
● Chianti Sorrettole '14	▼2
⊙ Rosa di Maggio '14	▼2
● La Querce '11	♈♈♈5
● La Querce '10	♈♈5
● La Querce '09	♈♈5
● La Querce '07	♈♈4
● La Querce '06	♈♈4
● La Querce '05	♈♈4

Querce Bettina

LOC. LA CASINA DI MOCALI, 275
53024 MONTALCINO [SI]
TEL. 0577848588
www.quercebettina.it

CELLAR SALES
PRE-BOOKED VISITS
ANNUAL PRODUCTION 15,000 bottles
HECTARES UNDER VINE 2.35

Truly unique environmental conditions have inspired the work of the Morettis at Querce Bettina since the late Nineties. Here, in the extreme south-west of Montalcino, is an area immersed in the woods and practically intact, where over two hectares are planted to sangiovese at over 400 metres altitude on soil rich in clay and silty marl mixed with stones. The resulting wines are lively and often unpredictable in expression, impossible to define within technical schematic terms, and it is no coincidence that flexible solutions are applied for maceration and ageing, preferably in 25-hectolitre Austrian oak. These user instructions are effective in reading the 2010 Brunello, the only wine tasted this time round. It is developing well in the bottles and it may be worth waiting for the generous salty structure to blend further with the angular tannins and slightly overripe fruit.

● Brunello di Montalcino '10	♀♀ 7
● Brunello di Montalcino '06	♀♀♀ 7
● Brunello di Montalcino '09	♀♀ 7
● Brunello di Montalcino '08	♀♀ 6
● Brunello di Montalcino '07	♀♀ 7
● Brunello di Montalcino Ris. '07	♀♀ 8
● Brunello di Montalcino Ris. '06	♀♀ 8
● Rosso di Montalcino '08	♀♀ 3

Le Ragnaie

LOC. LE RAGNAIE
53024 MONTALCINO [SI]
TEL. 0577848639
www.leragnaie.com

CELLAR SALES
PRE-BOOKED VISITS
ACCOMMODATION
ANNUAL PRODUCTION 80,000 bottles
HECTARES UNDER VINE 15.00
VITICULTURE METHOD Certified Organic

Riccardo Campinoti is in charge of one of the most successful Montalcino estates in the last generation. Le Ragnaie was taken over in 2002 and soon became synonymous with "pinot-like" Brunellos, with a fresh, fruity bouquet, nicely proportioned profile, and expressive variety articulated through the crus. Since 2007 the Vigna Vecchia (at Lume Spento pass, about 600 metres altitude) and Fornace (Loreto, at Castelnuovo dell'Abate) plots have been processed separately but the winegrowing overview is more complex thanks to the Pietroso vineyards. Various ageing options are applied in the cellar according to the vintage, mainly 25-hectolitre oak following lengthy maceration. A simply exciting range of 2010 wines presented by Le Ragnaie: the basic Brunello is already a little wonder with delicate, salty verve and the Fornace shows its most classic and mouthfilling aspects. However the Vigne Vecchie towers over them with depth and finesse, in the running for the best ever wine from this young winery.

● Brunello di Montalcino V. V. '10	♀♀♀ 8
● Brunello di Montalcino Fornace '10	♀♀ 8
● Brunello di Montalcino '10	♀♀ 6
● Chianti Colli Senesi '13	♀♀ 2*
● Rosso di Montalcino '12	♀ 4
● Brunello di Montalcino Fornace '08	♀♀♀ 8
○ Bianco '11	♀♀ 4
● Brunello di Montalcino '09	♀♀ 6
● Brunello di Montalcino '08	♀♀ 6
● Brunello di Montalcino V. V. '09	♀♀ 8
● Brunello di Montalcino V. V. '08	♀♀ 8

Rampa di Fugnano

LOC. FUGNANO, 55
53037 SAN GIMIGNANO [SI]
TEL. 0577941655
www.rampadifugnano.com

CELLAR SALES
PRE-BOOKED VISITS
ACCOMMODATION
ANNUAL PRODUCTION 70,000 bottles
HECTARES UNDER VINE 9.00

Business and life partners Gisela Traxler
and Herbert Ehrenold chose San Gimignano
back in the day as the place to create their
ideal job: immersed in the Tuscan
countryside, with a wine-producing estate
that respects the local environment,
producing characterful wines suited to an
international audience without betraying
their roots. The project has been
consolidated over the years with the
creation of an organic vegetable garden
and an agritourism structure. From 2010 to
2013 the estate was rented, while since
2014 the owners have started direct
production again. The interesting Vi ogni è
2014 is a monovarietal Viognier with stylish
fruity aromas, apricots and peaches in the
foreground with captivating spice like
mustard and vanilla. The palate makes a
smooth, velvety entry before livening up
with well-judged acidity and a lingering,
flavoursome finish. The late harvested
Topazio 2014 is sweet, alluring and
intriguing.

○ Bianco Topazio V. T. '14	♟♟ 4
○ Vernaccia di S. Gimignano Privato '13	♟♟ 3
○ Vi ogni è '14	♟♟ 3
● Bombereto '11	♟ 4
○ Vernaccia di S. Gimignano Alata '14	♟ 2
● Gisèle '01	♟♟♟ 5
● Gisèle '04	♟♟ 5
● Gisèle '03	♟♟ 5
● Gisèle '02	♟♟ 6
○ Vernaccia di S. Gimignano Privato '11	♟♟ 3
○ Vi ogni è '07	♟♟ 3*
○ Vi ogni è '01	♟♟ 3

Podere La Regola

LOC. SAN MARTINO
56046 RIPARBELLA [PI]
TEL. 0586698145
www.laregola.com

CELLAR SALES
PRE-BOOKED VISITS
ANNUAL PRODUCTION 90,000 bottles
HECTARES UNDER VINE 20.00

The Nuti family owns this estate which
stands on the site of a former Etruscan
village, selected for the fertile land and the
climate and very well-suited to
winegrowing and production, as
demonstrated by the many amphoras
discovered in the area. Luca has promoted
the development of the family farm where
wine was produced mainly for family
consumption, consolidating his idea after
graduating in agricultural science. His
brother Flavio, a professional lawyer, is
involved in sales and communications.
Some excellent work has been done, with
new vineyards planted with international
varieties, and the recovery of existing plots.
Into the finals for the La Regola 2012,
mainly cabernet franc with petit verdot and
merlot: complex aromas with wild berries
blending with balsamic hints and spicy
juniper. The palate is smooth, nicely
weighty and flavoursome with a remarkable
crescendo finish.

● La Regola '12	♟♟ 6
● Strido '11	♟♟ 8
● Syrah '13	♟♟ 3
● Vallino '11	♟♟ 5
● Beloro '08	♟ 6
○ Lauro Bianco '11	♟ 4
○ Spumante Brut M. Cl.	♟ 4
● Beloro '09	♟♟ 6
● La Regola '11	♟♟ 6
● La Regola '09	♟♟ 6
○ Sondrete '05	♟♟ 6
● Strido '09	♟♟ 8
● Syrah La Regola '12	♟♟ 3
● Vallino '09	♟♟ 5

Rocca delle Macìe

LOC. LE MACÌE, 45
53011 CASTELLINA IN CHIANTI [SI]
TEL. 05777321
www.roccadellemacie.com

CELLAR SALES
PRE-BOOKED VISITS
ACCOMMODATION AND RESTAURANT SERVICE
ANNUAL PRODUCTION 3,700,000 bottles
HECTARES UNDER VINE 210.00
SUSTAINABLE WINERY

The estate owned by Sergio Zingarelli, reconfirmed as Chairman of the Consorzio del Chianti Classico, is a long-established presence in the subzone of Castellina. The style has developed and the wines present a skilful blend of modern and traditional features, perfectly clean and approachable on one hand, and on the other balanced with uncommon character. The estate does not only produce Chianti Classico, and has another two farms in Maremma, Campomaccione and Casamaria. The Chianti Classico Sergio Zingarelli Gran Selezione 2011 is probably one of the best versions of its type. Aromas rich in fruity and floral hints with barely perceptible smokiness which will soften with time. The palate is balanced and dynamic rather than weighty and voluminous. The same stylistic tone applies to the Chianti Classico Riserva di Fizzano Gran Selezione 2012 which is nice and tangy but more delicate and less complex.

Rocca di Castagnoli

LOC. CASTAGNOLI
53013 GAIOLE IN CHIANTI [SI]
TEL. 0577731004
www.roccadicastagnoli.com

CELLAR SALES
PRE-BOOKED VISITS
ACCOMMODATION AND RESTAURANT SERVICE
ANNUAL PRODUCTION 500,000 bottles
HECTARES UNDER VINE 132.00

Back in 1981, lawyer Calogero Calì became the owner of this long-established Chianti Classico estate, and followed it up with the purchase of Tenuta di Capraia, Poggio Maestrino-Spiaggiole in Maremma, and Poggio Graffetta in Sicily, all united today in the Alimenta Spa company. The quality of these wines is among the most solid in the area. Their style grasps nuances from the different areas, pursuing the most typical features of Chianti wines, balance and elegance, without pointless forcing. Fresh flavour, clear and approachable aromas are the basic features of Rocco di Castagnoli's 2013 Chianti Classico. The Chianti Classico Stielle Gran Selezione 2011 shows the pace of a leading wine with close-knit, well-coordinated structure and complex aromas. The Chianti Classico 2013 from Tenuta Capraia is well-paced while the Riserva 2012 from the same estate has tangy flavour and markedly floral aromas.

Wine	Rating
● Chianti Cl. Sergio Zingarelli Gran Sel. '11	♛♛♛ 8
● Chianti Cl. Famiglia Zingarelli '13	♛♛ 3*
● Chianti Cl. Riserva di Fizzano Gran Sel. '12	♛♛ 6
● Chianti Cl. Famiglia Zingarelli Ris. '12	♛♛ 4
● Morellino di Scansano Campomaccione '14	♛♛ 3
○ Moonlite '14	♛ 2
● Roccato '12	♛ 6
○ Vermentino Occhio a Vento '14	♛ 2
● Chianti Cl. Famiglia Zingarelli Ris. '09	♟♟♟ 3*
● Chianti Cl. Fizzano Ris. '10	♟♟♟ 5
● Roccato '00	♟♟♟ 6
● Roccato '99	♟♟♟ 6
● Chianti Cl. Famiglia Zingarelli Ris. '10	♟♟ 4
● Chianti Cl. Famiglia Zingarelli Ris. '08	♟♟ 3
● Chianti Cl. Fizzano Ris. '06	♟♟ 5
● Chianti Cl. Sergio Zingarelli Gran Sel. '10	♟♟ 6

Wine	Rating
● Chianti Cl. Stielle Gran Sel. '11	♛♛ 6
● Chianti Cl. Rocca di Castagnoli '13	♛♛ 3
● Chianti Cl. Tenuta di Capraia '13	♛♛ 4
● Chianti Cl. Tenuta di Capraia Ris. '12	♛♛ 5
● Buriano '11	♛ 6
● Chianti Cl. Poggio ai Frati Ris. '12	♛ 4
○ Molino delle Balze '13	♛ 3
● Vin Santo del Chianti Cl. '09	♛ 7
● Chianti Cl. Capraia Ris. '07	♟♟♟ 4
● Chianti Cl. Poggio ai Frati Ris. '08	♟♟♟ 4
● Chianti Cl. Poggio ai Frati Ris. '06	♟♟♟ 4*
● Chianti Cl. Poggio ai Frati Ris. '04	♟♟♟ 4
● Chianti Cl. Tenuta di Capraia Ris. '06	♟♟♟ 4*
● Chianti Cl. Tenuta di Capraia Ris. '05	♟♟♟ 4
● Stielle '00	♟♟♟ 7
● Chianti Cl. Poggio ai Frati Ris. '11	♟♟ 4

★Rocca di Frassinello

loc. Giuncarico
58023 Gavorrano [GR]
Tel. 056688400
www.roccadifrassinello.it

CELLAR SALES
PRE-BOOKED VISITS
ACCOMMODATION
ANNUAL PRODUCTION 350,000 bottles
HECTARES UNDER VINE 70.00

Rocca di Frassinello is owned by editor
Paolo Panerai, already a wine producer in
the Chianti Classico DOC with Castellare di
Castellina and in Sicily with Feudo del
Pisciotto. About 350,000 bottles per year of
wines in a Mediterranean yet also
international style, faithfully expressing the
features of this part of Maremma, a stone's
throw from the sea. The productive
vineyards are planted with non-native
grapes like cabernet, franc and sauvignon,
merlot, petit verdot, syrah, which is
particularly suited to the climate, but native
varieties sangiovese and vermentino are
also present. Also this year Rocca di
Frassinello doesn't miss the Tre Bicchieri
achievement. The Merlot Baffo Nero 2013
is vibrant and mouthfilling with blackberry
and blueberry jam, balsamic and minty
hints, tight-knit tannins and extraordinary
extract. The Rocca di Frassinello, also
2013, is a blend of sangiovese with merlot
and cabernet sauvignon: mature,
well-structured, confidently Mediterranean.

● Maremma Toscana Baffo Nero '13	♙♙♙	8
● Maremma Toscana Rocca di Frassinello '13	♙♙	6
● Maremma Toscana Le Sughere di Frassinello '13	♙♙	4
● Maremma Toscana Ornello '13	♙	3
● Maremma Toscana Vermentino '14	♙	3
● Poggio alla Guardia '13	♙	3
● Baffo Nero '12	♙♙♙	8
● Baffo Nero '11	♙♙♙	8
● Baffo Nero '10	♙♙♙	8
● Baffo Nero '09	♙♙♙	8
● Baffo Nero '07	♙♙♙	8
● Rocca di Frassinello '12	♙♙♙	6
● Rocca di Frassinello '11	♙♙♙	6
● Rocca di Frassinello '08	♙♙♙	5
● Rocca di Frassinello '06	♙♙♙	5

Rocca di Montegrossi

fraz. Monti in Chianti
53010 Gaiole in Chianti [SI]
Tel. 0577747977
www.roccadimontegrossi.it

CELLAR SALES
PRE-BOOKED VISITS
ANNUAL PRODUCTION 80,000 bottles
HECTARES UNDER VINE 18.00
VITICULTURE METHOD Certified Organic

The estate owned by Marco Ricasoli
Firidolfi definitely favours authentic wines
that reveal their Chianti character. The
stylistic journey took off in the early 1980s
and, after necessary technical revision,
continues to characterize the products of
Monti in Chianti today. Of course the
leading role is played by the longstanding
native grapes: sangiovese, colorino and, in
the future, pugnitello, while white trebbiano
and malvasia grapes are used for the
excellent Vin Santo. In the cellar both large
oak and barriques are used. Distinctive,
lovely complex aromas for the Chianti
Classico Vigneto San Marcellino 2011 with
lush fruit blending with sweet spice and
hints of freshly mown grass. The palate
shows well-organized texture, still
greatly supported by the oak. The Chianti
Classico 2013 is absolutely delicious with
fluent, mouthwatering, nicely paced flavour.
The Vin Santo Chianti Classico 2006 is
traditional in style.

● Chianti Cl. Vign. S. Marcellino '11	♙♙	5
● Chianti Cl. '13	♙♙	3
○ Vin Santo del Chianti Cl. '06	♙♙	5
● Chianti Cl. Vign. S. Marcellino '07	♙♙♙	6
● Chianti Cl. Vign. S. Marcellino Ris. '99	♙♙♙	4
● Chianti Cl. '12	♙♙	3
● Chianti Cl. '11	♙♙	3*
● Chianti Cl. Vign. S. Marcellino '10	♙♙	5
● Chianti Cl. Vign. S. Marcellino '09	♙♙	5
● Chianti Cl. Vign. S. Marcellino Ris. '04	♙♙	5
● Geremia '03	♙♙	5

Rocca di Montemassi

FRAZ. MONTEMASSI
VIA SANT'ANNA
58027 ROCCASTRADA [GR]
TEL. 0564579700
www.roccadimontemassi.it

CELLAR SALES
PRE-BOOKED VISITS
ANNUAL PRODUCTION 200,000 bottles
HECTARES UNDER VINE 165.00

Gianni Zonin decided to purchase the estate in the late 1990s to increase his presence in Tuscany. Looking at the Maremma area he realized the landscape and surrounding environment were exciting places inspiring emotions he could weave into the winegrowing process. After he bought the estate he renovated it according to one specific principle: no buildings that would leave a harsh impact on surroundings. Instead, he created a habitat that harmonized with the local area. Thus the complex we see today blends nicely into the environmental context. There is also a museum on the estate dedicated to local rural civilization. The remarkable Rocca di Montemassi 2013, from petit verdot with some merlot and syrah, has a nicely varied bouquet of aromas alternating fresh, aromatic hints of Mediterranean scrubland with pure fruity sensations of blueberries and currants, and hints of pepper. The palate opens smooth and mouthfilling with nicely blended freshness and a lip-smacking finish.

● Maremma Toscana Rocca di Montemassi '13	♥♥♥ 5
○ Maremma Toscana Astraio '14	♥ 4
● Maremma Toscana Le Focaie '14	♥ 3
● Maremma Toscana Sassabruna '13	♥ 3
○ Maremma Toscana Vermentino '14	♥ 3
● Rocca di Montemassi '10	♥♥♥ 5
● Rocca di Montemassi '09	♥♥♥ 5
○ Calasole '11	♥♥ 3
○ Calasole '10	♥♥ 3
● Maremma Rocca di Montemassi '12	♥♥ 5
● Monteregio di Massa Marittima Sassabruna '11	♥♥ 3
● Monteregio di Massa Marittima Sassabruna '09	♥♥ 3
● Rocca di Montemassi '11	♥♥ 5

Roccapesta

LOC. MACERETO 9
50854 SCANSANO [GR]
TEL. 0564599252
www.roccapesta.it

CELLAR SALES
PRE-BOOKED VISITS
ANNUAL PRODUCTION 100,000 bottles
HECTARES UNDER VINE 18.50

The estate's history began in 1974 at a time when talk of winegrowing in Maremma was futuristic. They started with sangiovese and ciliegiolo, in the vineyard after which the leading wine is named. In 2003 Leonardo and Alberto Tanzini purchased the estate and the production philosophy changed, with a more decisive direction towards quality, starting with spasmodic attention to the land and cellar. Sangiovese remains the main variety grown but other varieties, both international and native, have gradually been introduced with respect for the features of the growing zone. The well-organized process has allowed the product range to grow constantly and steadily. The Morellino Calestaia Riserva 2011 presents powerful aromas of ripe fruit like cherries and blackberries, opening out into refreshing minty, balsamic sensations. A light entry on the palate growing steadily, tannins blending with the alcohol and a lingering finish.

● Morellino di Scansano Calestaia Ris. '11	♥♥♥ 5
● Morellino di Scansano '13	♥♥ 3*
● Masca '13	♥♥ 2*
● Morellino di Scansano Ribeo '13	♥♥ 3
● Morellino di Scansano Ris. '12	♥♥ 4
● Pugnitello '12	♥♥ 5
● Morellino di Scansano Calestaia Ris. '10	♥♥ 5
● Morellino di Scansano Calestaia Ris. '09	♥♥ 5
● Masca '12	♥♥ 2*
● Masca '11	♥♥ 2*
● Morellino di Scansano '11	♥♥ 3
● Morellino di Scansano '10	♥♥ 3*
● Morellino di Scansano Ribeo '11	♥♥ 3*
● Morellino di Scansano Ris. '11	♥♥ 4
● Morellino di Scansano Ris. '10	♥♥ 4
● Pugnitello '11	♥♥ 5

★Ruffino

P.LE RUFFINO, 1
50065 PONTASSIEVE [FI]
TEL. 05583605
www.ruffino.it

CELLAR SALES
PRE-BOOKED VISITS
ANNUAL PRODUCTION 18,000,000 bottles
HECTARES UNDER VINE 550.00

A leading Italian wine estate, for its history and production tradition, owned by the American colossus, Constellation Brands which also owns other very important high profile wine-producing estates in Tuscany: Greppone Mazzi at Montalcino, Lodola Nuova at Montepulciano, Santedame, Gretolaio, Montemasso and Poggio Casciano in Chianti Classico, and La Solatia at Monteriggioni, in the province of Siena. The wines show constant high The Chianti Classico Riserva Ducale Oro Gran Selezione 2011 has clearly defined, clean and complex aromas as a worthy prologue to the creamy, succulent palate. The Modus 2012, a blend of cabernet sauvignon, merlot and sangiovese, has tangy, deep flavour despite the marked oakiness in aromas and flavour.

Salcheto

LOC. SANT'ALBINO
VIA DI VILLA BIANCA, 15
53045 MONTEPULCIANO [SI]
TEL. 0578799031
www.salcheto.it

CELLAR SALES
PRE-BOOKED VISITS
ACCOMMODATION AND RESTAURANT SERVICE
ANNUAL PRODUCTION 300,000 bottles
HECTARES UNDER VINE 50.00
VITICULTURE METHOD Certified Organic
SUSTAINABLE WINERY

The name chosen for the estate is linked to the history of wine and this area: the river that runs nearby has the same name, deriving from Salco, or willow, a tree whose branches were used to tie vines. Michele Manelli came here with the desire to become a winegrower, following experience gained in other sectors, and over the years he has developed a very personal concept of winegrowing and winemaking, outside conventional models. He chooses sustainability, applied to all aspects of the work: biodynamic growing methods in the vineyard, autonomous energy in the cellar, and self-produced fertilizers are just a few examples. The result is extremely clean, land-rooted wines. The Nobile Salco 2011 has fresh aromas of medicinal herbs, minty sensations and clearly defined blueberry fruit. A light, non-aggressive entry on the palate with lip-smacking flavour and a compelling crescendo finish.

● Chianti Cl. Riserva Ducale Oro Gran Sel. '11	♟♟ 6
● Modus '12	♟♟ 5
● Brunello di Montalcino Greppone Mazzi '05	♟♟♟ 6
● Chianti Cl. Riserva Ducale Oro '04	♟♟♟ 5
● Chianti Cl. Riserva Ducale Oro '01	♟♟♟ 5
● Chianti Cl. Riserva Ducale Oro '00	♟♟♟ 5
● Modus '04	♟♟♟ 5
● Romitorio di Santedame '00	♟♟♟ 7
● Romitorio di Santedame '99	♟♟♟ 7
● Romitorio di Santedame '98	♟♟♟ 7
● Romitorio di Santedame '97	♟♟♟ 7

● Nobile di Montepulciano Salco '11	♟♟♟ 6
● Rosso di Montepulciano '14	♟♟ 2*
● Chianti Colli Senesi '14	♟ 2
● Nobile di Montepulciano '12	♟ 4
● Nobile di Montepulciano Ris. '11	♟ 5
⊙ Rosato Obvius '14	♟ 3
● Nobile di Montepulciano '10	♟♟♟ 4*
● Nobile di Montepulciano Salco '10	♟♟♟ 5
● Nobile di Montepulciano Salco Evoluzione '06	♟♟♟ 6
● Nobile di Montepulciano Salco Evoluzione '01	♟♟♟ 6
● Nobile di Montepulciano '09	♟♟ 4
● Nobile di Montepulciano Ris. '10	♟♟ 4
● Nobile di Montepulciano Salco Evoluzione Ris. '07	♟♟ 6

Podere San Cristoforo

LOC. BAGNO
VIA FORNI
58023 GAVORRANO [GR]
TEL. 3358212413
www.poderesancristoforo.it

CELLAR SALES
PRE-BOOKED VISITS
ACCOMMODATION
ANNUAL PRODUCTION 50,000 bottles
HECTARES UNDER VINE 16.00
VITICULTURE METHOD Certified Organic

Lorenzo Zonin put his idea of winegrowing into practice in this strip of Tuscan land, chosen to best express his personal interpretation of wine. The vineyards are biodynamically farmed, a choice made immediately and with conviction, in the knowledge that the best way to obtain quality is to make the land fertile and the vines productive without any kind of forcing. So what he looks for in his wines is a style that respects the terroir, of course, but is also easy to read and to drink. The other crops on the estate, like olives, cereals and sunflowers, are subjected to the same productive philosophy. The estate includes a farmhouse used as an agritourism structure. The Podere San Cristoforo 2013, a monovarietal Petit Verdot, offers fresh aromas of rosemary and bay leaves, blackberries and bilberries, and balsamic hints. A soft palate with smooth tannins and a fresh, flavoursome acidity, and nicely progressive finish.

● Maremma Toscana Podere San Cristoforo '13	▼▼▼ 3*
● Maremma Toscana Sangiovese Amaranto '14	▼▼ 2*
● Carandelle '14	▼ 3
○ Luminoso '11	♀♀ 3
○ Luminoso '10	♀♀ 3
● Podere San Cristoforo '12	♀♀ 5
● San Cristoforo '10	♀♀ 5
● San Cristoforo '09	♀♀ 4

Fattoria San Donato

LOC. SAN DONATO, 6
53037 SAN GIMIGNANO [SI]
TEL. 0577941616
www.sandonato.it

CELLAR SALES
PRE-BOOKED VISITS
ACCOMMODATION AND RESTAURANT SERVICE
ANNUAL PRODUCTION 70,000 bottles
HECTARES UNDER VINE 20.00
VITICULTURE METHOD Certified Organic

In 1932 Umberto Lenzi, grandfather and namesake of the current owner, decided to purchase the San Donato farm and start a winegrowing business. Later, management of the estate passed on to his daughter, while the current owner took over in 2001: since then it has been a family-run business, with his wife particularly focused on the agritourism side and his mother-in-law cooking for the guests. The vineyards are organically farmed, a choice the owners explain in simple terms: it has to be a means to achieve the highest possible quality in their wines without ruining their typical features. As well as wine, they produce extra virgin olive oil and saffron. Into the finals for the Vernaccia Benedetta Riserva 2013, with complex aromas of dried flowers, aromatic herbs like star anise, and citrus fruit. The palate makes a confident, mouthfilling start with fresh sensations, well-judged texture and a nice crescendo finish. We also liked the fragrant and appetizing Vernaccia Angelica 2012.

○ Vernaccia di S. Gimignano Benedetta Ris. '13	▼▼ 3*
● Chianti Colli Senesi '12	▼▼ 2*
○ Vernaccia di S. Gimignano Angelica '12	▼▼ 3
● Chianti Colli Senesi Fede Ris. '11	▼ 3
● Chianti Colli Senesi Fiamma '11	▼ 3
○ Vernaccia di S. Gimignano '14	▼ 2
● Chianti Colli Senesi Fede Ris. '10	♀♀ 3
● Chianti Colli Senesi Fiamma '10	♀♀ 3
○ Vernaccia di S. Gimignano '11	♀♀ 1*
○ Vernaccia di S. Gimignano Angelica '07	♀♀ 2*
○ Vernaccia di S. Gimignano Benedetta Ris. '10	♀♀ 3*
○ Vernaccia di S. Gimignano Benedetta Ris. '07	♀♀ 3

★San Felice

LOC. SAN FELICE
53019 CASTELNUOVO BERARDENGA [SI]
TEL. 05773991
www.agricolasanfelice.it

CELLAR SALES
PRE-BOOKED VISITS
ACCOMMODATION AND RESTAURANT SERVICE
ANNUAL PRODUCTION 900,000 bottles
HECTARES UNDER VINE 140.00

San Felice, owned by the Allianz group, has made its mark on the history of Tuscan wine production, starting with the Supertuscan phenomenon launched by the Castelnuovo Berardenga estate with its 1968 Vigorello. The estate has done pioneering research, particularly in the conservation of the genetic heritage of grape varieties grown in the past. Today San Felice has been active in the Chianti Classico DOC for over 40 years, offering a range of solid, reliable wines which sometimes scales the heights of excellence. The Chianti Classico Il Grigio da San Felice 2011 has a fragrant, complex nose with a tangy, well-coordinated palate, deep and succulent. The Chianti Classico Poggio Rosso Riserva 2011 is equally impressive but for slightly excessive oakiness: sunny, mature aromas and a fruity, progressive flavour. Forward oak characterizes the Chianti Classico Il Grigio da San Felice Riserva 2011.

● Chianti Cl. Il Grigio da San Felice Gran Sel. '11	♟♟♟ 5
● Chianti Cl. Il Grigio da San Felice Ris. '11	♟♟ 4
● Chianti Cl. Poggio Rosso Ris. '11	♟♟ 6
● Chianti Cl. '12	♟ 3
● Vigorello '11	♟ 6
● Chianti Cl. Il Grigio da San Felice Gran Sel. '10	♟♟♟ 5
● Chianti Cl. Poggio Rosso Ris. '03	♟♟♟ 5
● Chianti Cl. Poggio Rosso Ris. '00	♟♟♟ 5
● Pugnitello '07	♟♟♟ 6
● Pugnitello '06	♟♟♟ 6
● Vigorello '10	♟♟♟ 6
● Vigorello '08	♟♟♟ 6

San Gervasio

LOC. SAN GERVASIO
VIA PALAIESE
56036 PALAIA [PI]
TEL. 0587483360
www.sangervasio.com

CELLAR SALES
PRE-BOOKED VISITS
ACCOMMODATION AND RESTAURANT SERVICE
ANNUAL PRODUCTION 100,000 bottles
HECTARES UNDER VINE 22.00
VITICULTURE METHOD Certified Organic

Luca Tommasini has effected a profound change in the family estate since the mid-Nineties: what was formerly a classic wine producing business has changed direction and now follows a high quality regime. During these years the old cellars were rebuilt and renovated, and new land purchased and planted with avant-garde vineyards. The old vines were regrafted in a real revolution of the vineyards, with absolutely impressive results. Organic farming methods were adopted demonstrating that excellent grapes must form the basis of fine quality products. The Merlot Renai 2009 offers ripe fruit on the nose, wild berries alongside spices and toasty hints. The palate is assertive, smooth and mouthfilling with perceptible tannins and a long, appetizing finish. The Sangervasio Rosso 2009 displays minty, balsam sensations and a powerful, harmonious structure.

○ Colli Etruria Vin Santo Recinaio '04	♟♟ 5
● I Renai '09	♟♟ 5
● Sangervasio Rosso '09	♟♟ 2*
● Terre di Pisa Sangervasio '11	♟♟ 4
● A Sirio '09	♟ 5
● Chianti '13	♟ 2
● A Sirio '00	♟♟ 5
○ Chardonnay '04	♟♟ 4
● I Renai '03	♟♟ 5
● I Renai '01	♟♟ 6
● I Renai '00	♟♟ 6
○ Sangervasio Bianco '06	♟♟ 2
○ Sangervasio Bianco '05	♟♟ 2
● Sangervasio Rosso '05	♟♟ 2

San Giusto a Rentennano

LOC. SAN GIUSTO A RENTENNANO, 20
53013 GAIOLE IN CHIANTI [SI]
TEL. 0577747121
www.fattoriasangiusto.it

CELLAR SALES
PRE-BOOKED VISITS
ANNUAL PRODUCTION 80,000 bottles
HECTARES UNDER VINE 27.00
VITICULTURE METHOD Certified Organic
SUSTAINABLE WINERY

The estate owned by the Martini di Cigala family started to distinguish itself with its wines in the mid-1970s. Today San Giusto a Rentennano is still one of the most prestigious names in Chianti Classico but, especially in recent times, it seems to have partly lost its legendary style, with dynamic wines offering a very faithful expression of the Monti subzone, often reaching peaks of absolute excellence. The estate's wines currently seem to be suffering, above all, from excessive use of oak for ageing, which smothers the expressive qualities of potentially first-class fruit. The Chianti Classico 2013 has good acidic verve supporting the flavour on a pleasing palate, despite the excessively forward spicy sensations from the oak ageing vessels. This element is also noticeable in the aromas, in which the fruit is almost invisible, penalizing fragrance and freshness.

● Chianti Cl. '13	▼▼	4
● Chianti Cl. Le Baroncole Ris. '12	▼	5
● Percarlo '11	▼	8
● Chianti Cl. '10	▼▼▼	4*
● Percarlo '07	▼▼▼	7
● Percarlo '99	▼▼▼	7
● Chianti Cl. '09	▼▼	3
● Chianti Cl. Le Baroncole Ris. '11	▼▼	5
● Chianti Cl. Le Baroncole Ris. '10	▼▼	5
● Chianti Cl. Le Baroncole Ris. '09	▼▼	5
● Chianti Cl. Le Baroncole Ris. '07	▼▼	5
● Chianti Cl. Le Baroncole Ris. '06	▼▼	5
● Chianti Cl. Le Baroncole Ris. '05	▼▼	5
● La Ricolma '04	▼▼	6
● Percarlo '05	▼▼	7
● Percarlo '04	▼▼	7

★★Tenuta San Guido

FRAZ. BOLGHERI
LOC. LE CAPANNE, 27
57022 CASTAGNETO CARDUCCI [LI]
TEL. 0565762003
www.sassicaia.com

PRE-BOOKED VISITS
RESTAURANT SERVICE
ANNUAL PRODUCTION 780,000 bottles
HECTARES UNDER VINE 90.00

In all probability Sassicaia is the most famous Italian wine in its own country and abroad. Tenuta San Guido, who make it, was set up by the Marchesi Incisa della Rocchetta: they created the legend and they were the architects of the Bolgheri area in winemaking terms. The property extends from the Tirreno sea to the hills of Castiglioncello: this is where some long-established plots of vineyards combine with a perfect vinification process to reproduce the magic that is Sassicaia, every year. 2012 was not the easiest year in our opinion and it gave us a more enigmatic Sassicaia than usual. Of course, this is a great wine, very complex with classic finesse. However it was less relaxed when we tasted it, with tannic resolution still underway. A bottle for the cellar, to be fully enjoyed when time has done its work. In any case, don't forget this is a red wine with outstanding ageing potential: It would be a mistake to demand everything at once.

● Bolgheri Sassicaia '12	▼▼▼	8
● Le Difese '13	▼▼	4
● Bolgheri Sassicaia '11	▼▼▼	8
● Bolgheri Sassicaia '10	▼▼▼	8
● Bolgheri Sassicaia '09	▼▼▼	8
● Bolgheri Sassicaia '08	▼▼▼	8
● Bolgheri Sassicaia '07	▼▼▼	8
● Bolgheri Sassicaia '06	▼▼▼	8
● Bolgheri Sassicaia '05	▼▼▼	8
● Bolgheri Sassicaia '04	▼▼▼	8
● Bolgheri Sassicaia '03	▼▼▼	8
● Bolgheri Sassicaia '02	▼▼▼	8
● Bolgheri Sassicaia '01	▼▼▼	8
● Bolgheri Sassicaia '00	▼▼▼	8
● Guidalberto '08	▼▼▼	6
● Guidalberto '04	▼▼▼	6

San Michele a Torri

VIA SAN MICHELE, 36
50020 SCANDICCI [FI]
TEL. 055769111
www.fattoriasanmichele.it

CELLAR SALES
PRE-BOOKED VISITS
ANNUAL PRODUCTION 200,000 bottles
HECTARES UNDER VINE 55.00
VITICULTURE METHOD Certified Organic

The farm's location enjoys a pleasant climate, in an area that crosses the Chianti zone including Chianti Classico and Colli Fiorentini. Owner Paolo Nocentini, an entrepreneur in the transport sector, drove hard towards fine quality winegrowing, renewing the vineyards and maintaining the olive groves and arable land. Wheat cultivation is based on the selection of ancient varieties according to the idea that the consumer needs to be reached directly, at a local level, so the estate has opened a restaurant, patisserie and wine shops in various parts of Florence, to put into practice the concept of zero miles products. A good performance from the two Chianti Colli Fiorentini. The 2013 standard version stands out for its fresh, balsamic aromas and supple structure with very drinkable acidity. The Riserva 2012 has more massive structure and a good balance of tannin and alcohol, generous and flavoursome. The intriguing, velvety Vin Santo 2011 has a clean nose.

● Chianti Colli Fiorentini '13	♟♟ 2*
● Chianti Colli Fiorentini S. Giovanni Novantasette Ris. '12	♟♟ 4
○ Colli dell'Etruria Centrale Vin Santo '11	♟♟
● Chicchirossi '13	♟ 3
● Chianti Cl. '11	♟♟ 3
● Chianti Cl. Tenuta La Gabbiola '07	♟♟ 3*
○ Chianti Colli Fiorentini Vin Santo '07	♟♟ 3
● Murtas '11	♟♟ 5
● Murtas '09	♟♟ 5
○ Vin Santo '08	♟♟ 6

San Polo

LOC. PODERNOVI, 161
53024 MONTALCINO [SI]
TEL. 0577835101
www.poggiosanpolo.com

CELLAR SALES
PRE-BOOKED VISITS
ANNUAL PRODUCTION 150,000 bottles
HECTARES UNDER VINE 17.00

17 hectares at Podernovi on the south-eastern slope of Montalcino, a true natural balcony overlooking the valley of Sant'Antimo at over 400 metres altitude. This is the backdrop against which the San Polo project takes place, officially set up in 2007 when the Allegrini family, a revered name in Valpolicella, purchased the estate. At the helm is Nicola Biasi, his technical management aiming towards moderately innovative Sangioveses fermented in concrete vats and aged in barriques and Slavonian oak and medium-sized Allier oak for the Brunellos. The latest tastings confirm the impressions often underlined over the years, to the millimetre: San Polo wines leave nothing to be desired in terms of form, but we expected a bit more personality. This is the only limitation to the Brunello 2010: open, accomplished, perhaps surpassed in firm, compact structure by the excellent Rosso 2013.

● Brunello di Montalcino '10	♟♟ 6
● Rosso di Montalcino '13	♟♟ 3
● Brunello di Montalcino '09	♟♟ 6
● Brunello di Montalcino '08	♟♟ 6
● Brunello di Montalcino '07	♟♟ 6
● Brunello di Montalcino '06	♟♟ 6
● Brunello di Montalcino Ris. '06	♟♟ 7
● Rosso di Montalcino '12	♟♟ 3
● Rosso di Montalcino '11	♟♟ 3
● Rubio '10	♟♟ 2*

Podere Sanlorenzo

POD. SANLORENZO, 280
53024 MONTALCINO [SI]
TEL. 3396070930
www.poderesanlorenzo.net

CELLAR SALES
PRE-BOOKED VISITS
ANNUAL PRODUCTION 18,000 bottles
HECTARES UNDER VINE 4.50

First of all there is an unbreakable
generation connection behind the success
of Sanlorenzo, one of the most widely
explored and appreciated brands on
Montalcino's productive scene today.
Founder Bramante Ferretti has recently
turned 100 years old and his grandson
Lorenzo Ciolfi has worked alongside him for
some time. In 2003 he decided to take the
step of transforming most of the estate's
grapes. The four or so hectares situated at
almost 500 metres at Le Prata, on the
south-west slope, with its typical clayey soil
mixed with sand and marl, is an ideal
backdrop for producing Sangioveses as
forceful as they are sinuous. The wines
undergo lengthy maceration and ageing in
30-hectolitre Slavonian oak. Sanlorenzo
Brunellos are an obligatory benchmark for
the DOC zone and further proof comes
from the Bramante 2010. It seems a little
behind in development, but the blood-rich
and balsamic sensations are already there,
alongside a very raw and austere structure.

● Brunello di Montalcino Bramante '10	♀♀ 6
● Rosso di Montalcino '13	♀♀ 3
● Brunello di Montalcino Bramante '07	♀♀♀ 6
● Brunello di Montalcino Bramante Ris. '07	♀♀♀ 8
● Brunello di Montalcino Bramante '09	♀♀ 6
● Brunello di Montalcino Bramante '08	♀♀ 6
● Rosso di Montalcino '11	♀♀ 3
● Rosso di Montalcino '10	♀♀ 3
● Rosso di Montalcino '09	♀♀ 3

Sant'Agnese

LOC. CAMPO ALLE FAVE, 1
57025 PIOMBINO [LI]
TEL. 0565277069
www.santagnesefarm.it

CELLAR SALES
PRE-BOOKED VISITS
ANNUAL PRODUCTION 25,000 bottles
HECTARES UNDER VINE 6.00
SUSTAINABLE WINERY

Retirement can play strange tricks on
destiny: in 1994 Paolo Gigli, father of the
current owner, decided to take part in the
auction of a farm, which had been a dream
he nurtured during his years working in
management, a job which often took him
away from home. So he found himself with
an estate to rebuild: abandoned land and
buildings to renovate. However, his
enthusiasm and passion overcame the rest
of the problems, and today Paolo is at the
helm of a very respectable wine estate,
small but well-organized, where traditional
Tuscan grape varieties grow alongside
others which have found an ideal habitat in
the area. Through to the finals, the Merlot
Rubido 2012 has a nose rich in vibrant fruit
like strawberries, cherries and raspberries
with spicy hints of cloves and cinnamon.
The palate makes a delicate impact with
mouthfilling structure and a fresh, nicely
paced finish.

● Rubido '12	♀♀ 2*
● Spirto '09	♀♀ 5
○ Kalendamaia '14	♀ 2
● Libatio '09	♀ 4
● I Fiori Blu '08	♀♀ 6
● I Fiori Blu '07	♀♀ 4
● Libatio '08	♀♀ 4
● Merlot I Fiori Blu '09	♀♀ 6
● Paleatico '04	♀♀ 3
● Rubido '11	♀♀ 2*
● Spirto '08	♀♀ 5
● Spirto '06	♀♀ 5
● Spirto '01	♀♀ 5
○ Val di Cornia Kalendamaia '11	♀♀ 2*
● Val di Cornia Rubido '09	♀♀ 2*
● Val di Cornia Rubido '08	♀♀ 2*

Podere Sapaio

LOC. LO SCOPAIO, 212
57022 CASTAGNETO CARDUCCI [LI]
TEL. 0565765187
www.sapaio.it

PRE-BOOKED VISITS
ANNUAL PRODUCTION 75,000 bottles
HECTARES UNDER VINE 25.00

Massimo Piccini's winery is fairly young but
has made its presence known in just a
short time among the Bolgheri estates. Of
the estate's overall 40 hectares, 25 are
under vine, with classic local varieties
planted on sandy, limestone soil. The
winery style is quite modern, with lovely
extract and ageing in new oak. When young
these wines are slightly boisterous but
show good potential for ageing in the
bottles. The Bolgheri Rosso Superiore 2012
has toasty, full-bodied structure. This is a
leading wine in a well-established style,
able to astonish with its close-knit fruity
texture. It is also a work in progress, slightly
behind in development with tannins still
tight-knit, working on the slow, progressive
expansion.

Fattoria Sardi

LOC. MONTE SAN QUIRICO
VIA DELLA MAULINA, 747
55100 LUCCA
TEL. 0583341230
www.sardigiustiniani.com

CELLAR SALES
PRE-BOOKED VISITS
ACCOMMODATION
ANNUAL PRODUCTION 100,000 bottles
HECTARES UNDER VINE 14.00
VITICULTURE METHOD Certified Organic

In the early 2000s Jacopo and Matteo
Giustiniani took over this lovely estate and
brought the winegrowing project several
steps further on. This is a 45-hectare
property with 18 under vine, certified
organic grape cultivation since 2011 and
more than one nod to biodynamic farming.
The wines are authentic and personal in
style, corresponding to the best this
zone can offer. The Colline Lucchesi
Sebastiano 2012 lives up to our
expectations. It isn't a big wine, all texture
and maturity, but a light, fluent red, even
hard in some ways. Highly recommended
to lovers of this type. The Colline Lucchesi
Vermentino is one of the best in its
category, with a fruity nose and citrus fruit
in a lovely flavour.

● Bolgheri Rosso Sup. '12	♟♟♟	7
● Bolgheri Volpolo '13	♟♟	5
● Bolgheri Rosso Sup. '11	♟♟♟	7
● Bolgheri Sup. Sapaio '10	♟♟♟	6
● Bolgheri Sup. Sapaio '09	♟♟♟	6
● Bolgheri Sup. Sapaio '08	♟♟♟	6
● Bolgheri Sup. Sapaio '07	♟♟♟	6
● Bolgheri Sup. Sapaio '06	♟♟♟	6
● Bolgheri Sup. Sapaio '05	♟♟	6
● Bolgheri Sup. Sapaio '04	♟♟	6
● Bolgheri Volpolo '12	♟♟	4
● Bolgheri Volpolo '11	♟♟	4
● Bolgheri Volpolo '08	♟♟	4
● Bolgheri Volpolo '07	♟♟	4
● Bolgheri Volpolo '06	♟♟	4

● Colline Lucchesi Merlot Sebastiano '12	♟♟	3
○ Colline Lucchesi Vermentino '14	♟♟	3
● Colline Lucchesi Rosso Vallebuia '14	♟♟	3
● Le Cicale '14	♟	2
⊙ Rosato '14	♟	2
○ Colline Lucchesi Bianco Fattoria Sardi '13	♟♟	1*
● Colline Lucchesi Merlot Sebastiano '11	♟♟	3
○ Colline Lucchesi Sauvignon Fattoria Sardi '13	♟♟	3
○ Colline Lucchesi Vermentino Fattoria Sardi '13	♟♟	2*
● Fattoria Sardi Rosso '12	♟♟	3

Sassotondo

LOC. PIAN DI CONATI, 52
58010 SOVANA [GR]
TEL. 0564614218
www.sassotondo.it

CELLAR SALES
PRE-BOOKED VISITS
ANNUAL PRODUCTION 50,000 bottles
HECTARES UNDER VINE 12.00
VITICULTURE METHOD Certified Organic

We could describe Carla Benini and
Edoardo Ventimiglia's story as one of love
and passion: she, an agronomist from
Trento, tired of the frenetic pace travelling
and working in an uninteresting sector; he,
a Roman producer of documentaries for his
family's business; together they decided to
move to Sovana in 1990. On this virgin
land, ready to be shaped, they had to
rebuild the cellar, plant vineyards and
recreate a modern, functional structure.
Success came in 1997 when at last the
first harvest took place. Fulfilled objectives
include promotion of the ciliegiolo grape
variety that had, at the time, almost fallen
into disuse but has now come back into
fashion. The San Lorenzo 2012 offers clear,
vibrant, minerally aromas with well-defined
cherry and plum fruit. The palate is firm
and broad with clear-cut tannins blending
with the alcohol and a flavoursome finish
with a remarkable crescendo.

● Maremma Toscana San Lorenzo '12	♥♥ 6
○ Numero Dieci '11	♥♥ 6
● Maremma Toscana Ciliegiolo '14	♥ 3
○ Tufo Bianco '14	♥ 2
● Tufo Rosso '14	♥ 2
● Ciliegiolo '12	♥♥ 2*
● Ciliegiolo '11	♥♥ 2*
● San Lorenzo '08	♥♥ 6
● San Lorenzo '07	♥♥ 6
● San Lorenzo '06	♥♥ 6
● San Lorenzo '05	♥♥ 6
● San Lorenzo '04	♥♥ 5
● San Lorenzo '03	♥♥ 5
● San Lorenzo '02	♥♥ 5
● Sovana Rosso Sup. Sassotondo '09	♥♥ 3

Michele Satta

LOC. VIGNA AL CAVALIERE, 61B
57022 CASTAGNETO CARDUCCI [LI]
TEL. 0565773041
www.michelesatta.com

CELLAR SALES
PRE-BOOKED VISITS
ANNUAL PRODUCTION 150,000 bottles
HECTARES UNDER VINE 20.00

An overall glance at the wineries of
Bolgheri immediately highlights the original
nature of Michele Satta's project. This is a
winery with a lot of experience behind it,
established in the late 1980s, certainly not
among the latecomers. The producer's
ideas include stylistic itineraries and grape
preferences that follow unique directions,
at least for this area. As well as the usual
cabernet and merlot, for example, Satta
believes strongly in sangiovese. This year
the wines seemed well-focused, following
the format to which their creator has made
us accustomed. The Bolgheri Rosso
Piastraia 2012 made an excellent
impression: vibrant but fragrant aromas,
quietly charming and full of woodland,
damp earth sensations. The Syrah 2012 is
also very good, with grassy and spicy
nuances gradually becoming clearer and
more elegant. The Bolgheri Rosso 2013 is
fresh and succulent.

● Bolgheri Rosso '13	♥♥ 3
● Bolgheri Rosso Piastraia '12	♥♥ 5
● Syrah '12	♥♥ 5
○ Giovin Re '14	♥ 6
● Bolgheri Rosso Piastraia '02	♥♥♥ 6
● Bolgheri Rosso Piastraia '01	♥♥♥ 6
⊙ Bolgheri Rosato '13	♥♥ 2*
● Bolgheri Rosso '12	♥♥ 3
● Bolgheri Rosso '11	♥♥ 3
● Bolgheri Rosso Piastraia '11	♥♥ 5
● Bolgheri Rosso Piastraia '10	♥♥ 5
● Bolgheri Rosso Piastraia '09	♥♥ 6
● Bolgheri Rosso Piastraia '08	♥♥ 6
● Bolgheri Rosso Sup. I Castagni '09	♥♥ 6
● Bolgheri Rosso Sup. I Castagni '08	♥♥ 8
○ Costa di Giulia '11	♥♥ 5

La Selva

Loc. Fonte Blanda
s.da prov.le 81 Osa, 7
58010 Orbetello [GR]
Tel. 0564885669
www.cantinalaselva-bio.eu

CELLAR SALES
PRE-BOOKED VISITS
ACCOMMODATION
ANNUAL PRODUCTION 200,000 bottles
HECTARES UNDER VINE 32.00
VITICULTURE METHOD Certified Organic

One of the first estates to practise large-scale organic farming in Tuscany, La Selva was established in the 1980s with the decision to work in a huge area where cereal crops, vegetables and fruit were grown and focus on wine, in a still unspoilt area like Scansano. The methods applied to the other crops were also used for the vineyards: aiming to preserve the natural features of the products and to promote and render productive the native grape varieties without excluding some experimentation with international grapes that adapt well to the local soil and weather features. The Ciliegiolo 2012 presents raspberries and strawberries on the nose softened by rhubarb and pepper, and a meaty, firm palate with forward but nicely blended tannins and an appetizing, rounded finish. The Bianco 2014 is fragrant and fruity with fresh acidity.

Fattoria Selvapiana

Loc. Selvapiana, 43
50068 Rufina [FI]
Tel. 0558369848
www.selvapiana.it

CELLAR SALES
PRE-BOOKED VISITS
ANNUAL PRODUCTION 220,000 bottles
HECTARES UNDER VINE 60.00

The villa with annexed farm was once a refuge for bishops fleeing the heat of the city; over the centuries it later passed into the hands of rich merchants, to be purchased by Michele Giuntini in 1827. During the post-war period, another Michele in the family was one of the greatest champions of the distinction between Rufina and the rest of Chianti, thanks to its soil and weather features and altitude. Today management is in the hands of Silvia and Federico Giuntini Masseti, who is currently chairman of the Consortium. Together they carry forward the challenge of promoting this area recognized by Cosimo de' Medici as a fine quality winegrowing location. Into the finals for the La Riserva Bucerchiale 2012: vibrant evolved aromas of tobacco and leather giving way to blackberry jam. Powerful, well-coordinated structure on the palate with nicely placed tannins. The very appealing Vin Santo 2007 has a seductive nose with hints of citrus fruit, hazelnuts and butter, and a velvety, mouthfilling palate, creamy and very lingering.

○ Bianco Toscano '14	♟♟ 2*
● Maremma Toscana Ciliegiolo '12	♟♟ 3
● Avorio '14	♟ 2
● Maremma Toscana Privo '14	♟ 2
○ Maremma Toscana Vermentino '14	♟ 2
● Morellino di Scansano '14	♟ 2
● Morellino di Scansano Colli dell'Uccellina '12	♟ 3
● Prima Causa '12	♟ 5
⊙ Rosato '14	♟ 2
● Sangiovese '14	♟ 2
● Morellino di Scansano '12	♟♟ 2*
● Morellino di Scansano '11	♟♟ 2*
● Morellino di Scansano '10	♟♟ 2*
● Prima Causa '11	♟♟ 5
● Prima Causa '08	♟♟ 5
● Pugnitello '11	♟♟ 5

● Chianti Rufina Bucerchiale Ris. '12	♟♟ 5
○ Vin Santo del Chianti Rufina '07	♟♟ 2*
● Chianti Rufina '13	♟♟ 2*
● Pomino Villa Petrognano '12	♟♟ 2*
● Chianti Rufina '12	♟♟ 2*
● Chianti Rufina '11	♟♟ 2*
● Chianti Rufina '10	♟♟ 2*
● Chianti Rufina Bucerchiale '04	♟♟ 5
● Chianti Rufina Bucerchiale Ris. '11	♟♟ 5
● Chianti Rufina Bucerchiale Ris. '10	♟♟ 5
● Chianti Rufina Bucerchiale Ris. '09	♟♟ 5
● Chianti Rufina Bucerchiale Ris. '03	♟♟ 5
● Fornace '11	♟♟ 5
● Fornace '09	♟♟ 5
● La Fornace '00	♟♟ 5

Sensi

VIA CERBAIA, 107
51035 LAMPORECCHIO [PT]
TEL. 057382910
www.sensivini.com

CELLAR SALES
PRE-BOOKED VISITS
ANNUAL PRODUCTION 2,000,000 bottles
HECTARES UNDER VINE 80.00

The Sensi family has a long history, dating back to 1895 when Pietro Sensi began his career as a merchant selling wine from his vineyards in the district markets. During the post-Second World War period the activity grew under Pietro's grandchildren until it reached a national level. Current owners Massimo and Roberta Sensi joined the business in 1987 and make a considerable contribution towards the estate's definitive leap onto the international market. The family estates are Tenuta del Poggio and Fattoria di Calappiano in the Chianti Fiorentino zone, with 80 hectares of vineyards distributed between the two properties. The Chianti Vinciano Riserva 2012 offers hints of ripe fruit like blackberries and cherries supported by sensations of spices and forest floor. The palate is flavoursome with well-blended, non-aggressive tannins, fresh acidity and a succulent, flavoursome finish. The Lungarno 2013 is an austere but balanced blend of sangiovese and colorino.

Serpaia

LOC. FONTEBLANDA
VIA GOLDONI, 15
58100 GROSSETO
TEL. 0461650129
www.serpaiamaremma.it

ANNUAL PRODUCTION 134,500 bottles
HECTARES UNDER VINE 30.00

15 years have passed since Paolo and Christine Endrici, owners of a winegrowing estate at San Michele dell'Adige, decided to start a new wine adventure in Tuscany with Christine's brother Thomas. They fell in love with a hillside area which they decided was the best place to plant a vineyard and it is farmed today using integrated farming methods without chemical treatments and following the concept of ecosustainability. The experience they gained in Trentino has been useful in winegrowing that focuses mainly on sangiovese and other international black grapes, which have yielded excellent results locally. The pleasant Morellino 2013 has vibrant fruity aromas of wild berries, and spices like cloves and pepper. The generous palate expands to become mouthfilling and closes with a flavoursome, graceful finish. The Morellino Dino Riserva 2011 offers evolved aromas of chocolate, coffee and toasty oak, with a firm body and lingering flavour.

● Chianti Vinciano Fattoria di Calappiano Ris. '12	♥♥ 6
● Chianti Dalcampo Ris. '12	♥♥ 3
● Lungarno Fattoria Calappiano '13	♥♥ 7
● Mantello '13	♥♥ 4
● Chianti Campoluce '14	♥ 2
● Chianti Sup. Vagante '13	♥ 3
● Ninfato '14	♥ 4
● Testardo '13	♥ 4
○ Vernaccia di S. Gimignano Collegiata '14	♥ 2
● Bolgheri Sabbiato '11	♥♥ 5
● Brunello di Montalcino Boscoselvo '08	♥♥ 7
● Chianti Campoluce '12	♥♥ 2*
● Chianti Fattoria Calappiano Ris. '11	♥♥ 3
● Lungarno Fattoria Calappiano '12	♥♥ 7
● Lungarno Fattoria Calappiano '11	♥♥ 3
● Testardo '12	♥♥ 4

● Morellino di Scansano '13	♥♥ 2*
● Morellino di Scansano Dono Ris. '11	♥♥ 3
● Mèria '11	♥ 3
● Serpaiolo '13	♥ 2
● Morellino di Scansano '12	♥♥ 2*
● Morellino di Scansano Dono Ris. '08	♥♥ 3

Serraiola

FRAZ. FRASSINE
LOC. SERRAIOLA
58025 MONTEROTONDO MARITTIMO [GR]
TEL. 0566910026
www.serraiola.it

CELLAR SALES
PRE-BOOKED VISITS
ANNUAL PRODUCTION 40,000 bottles
HECTARES UNDER VINE 12.00

Current owner Fiorella Lanzi was one of the first wine producers to believe in the potential of the Maremma area. The family had owned the estate since the late 1960s but once Fiorella joined the business it was modernized and brought up to date. The vineyards planted in the 1960s have already been replanted with grape varieties and clones better suited to the area, and the existing cellar equipment and structures have been modernized. The result is very well-typed products that nicely express their origins while not always using native grape varieties. The Cmapo Montecristo 2013, a monovarietal merlot, has a generous array of fruity aromas with hints of cinnamon and cloves with a firm, smooth body, mouthfilling with smooth tannins and a nice finish. The pleasant Sangiovese Lentisco 2013 has vibrant cherry and plum fruit, a well-defined palate and a succulent, generous finish.

● Campo Montecristo '13	♟♟ 5
● Monteregio Massa Marittima Lentisco '13	♟♟ 3
● Shiraz '13	♟♟ 3
○ Maremma Toscana Violina '14	♟ 3
● Sassonero '14	♟ 2
○ Serrabacio '14	♟ 3
○ Vermentino '14	♟ 2
● Campo Montecristo '08	♟♟ 5
● Campo Montecristo '07	♟♟ 5
● Campo Montecristo '06	♟♟ 5
● Campo Montecristo '05	♟♟ 5
● Monteregio di Massa Marittima Lentisco '11	♟♟ 3
● Shiraz '07	♟♟ 3
● Shiraz '06	♟♟ 3
● Shiraz '05	♟♟ 3
○ Vermentino '13	♟♟ 2*

Tenuta di Sesta

FRAZ. CASTELNUOVO DELL'ABATE
LOC. SESTA
53024 MONTALCINO [SI]
TEL. 0577835612
www.tenutadisesta.it

CELLAR SALES
PRE-BOOKED VISITS
ANNUAL PRODUCTION 150,000 bottles
HECTARES UNDER VINE 30.00

Sesta is one of the few areas in Montalcino which truly deserves to be described as a cru, for its history and suitable conditions: an ideal meeting of soil and weather and expressive qualities between the terroirs of Sant'Angelo in Colle and Castelnuovo dell'Abate. Here in the southern part of the DOC is an enclave at altitudes between 200 and 400 metres with distinctive generally lean soil, rich in limestone with tufaceous streaks. The Ciacci family have produced Brunellos here since 1966, even before the DOC was recognized, respecting their rangy, airy character with bare-bones cellarwork featuring lengthy maturation in medium-sized oak. The coherent style overarches the individual scores, expressed at its best in the 2009 Riserva: delicious and fragrant, free and easy on the palate and making up for a lack of weight and drive with judicious measure. A similar profile for the Brunello 2010, with a simpler, more raw texture.

● Brunello di Montalcino Ris. '09	♟♟ 7
● Brunello di Montalcino '10	♟♟ 5
● Rosso di Montalcino '13	♟♟ 3
● Poggio d'Arna '13	♟ 2
● Brunello di Montalcino '09	♟♟ 5
● Brunello di Montalcino '08	♟♟ 5
● Brunello di Montalcino '07	♟♟ 5
● Brunello di Montalcino '06	♟♟ 5
● Brunello di Montalcino '05	♟♟ 5
● Brunello di Montalcino Ris. '07	♟♟ 7
● Brunello di Montalcino Ris. '06	♟♟ 7
● Poggio d'Arna '11	♟♟ 2*
● Poggio d'Arna '10	♟♟ 2*
● Rosso di Montalcino '11	♟♟ 3
● Rosso di Montalcino '10	♟♟ 3*

Sesti - Castello di Argiano

FRAZ. SANT'ANGELO IN COLLE
LOC. CASTELLO DI ARGIANO
53024 MONTALCINO [SI]
TEL. 0577843921
www.sestiwine.com

CELLAR SALES
PRE-BOOKED VISITS
ANNUAL PRODUCTION 61,000 bottles
HECTARES UNDER VINE 9.00

It is no exaggeration to say that Castello di Argiano is one of the most enchanting places in the world, and not only for its wine. The Sesti family headquarters belnds into the woodland and Mediterranean scrubland in the south-western corner of Montalcino, an area influenced by sea breezes and tufaceous, sandy soil. A harmonious environment, energy flow, cosmic breaks: these are the key concepts behind all the production, in the final analysis more meaningful than strictly technical data. Inspiration finds its mooring in Sangioveses that are, in many aspects, dreamlike, as if suspended between warmth and backbone, weight and lightness. This is exactly the model of expression we find in the 2010 Brunello. Aromas of mandarins, thyme, pink pepper and, for once, a good opportunity to use the term "Burgundyesque" due to its delicious linear character, although it might be a touch of expansion short of being a great wine. The Rosso 2013 is also multifaceted and engaging.

● Brunello di Montalcino '10	♟♟ 6
☉ Rosato '14	♟♟ 2*
● Rosso di Montalcino '13	♟♟ 4
● Grangiovese '13	♟ 2
○ Sauvignon '14	♟ 3
● Brunello di Montalcino '06	♟♟♟ 6
● Brunello di Montalcino Phenomena Ris. '07	♟♟♟ 8
● Brunello di Montalcino Phenomena Ris. '01	♟♟♟ 8
● Brunello di Montalcino Ris. '04	♟♟♟ 8
● Brunello di Montalcino '09	♟♟ 6
● Brunello di Montalcino '08	♟♟ 6
● Brunello di Montalcino '07	♟♟ 6
● Brunello di Montalcino Phenomena '08	♟♟ 8
● Brunello di Montalcino Phenomena Ris. '06	♟♟ 8

Tenuta Sette Ponti

VIA SETTE PONTI, 71
52029 CASTIGLION FIBOCCHI [AR]
TEL. 0575477857
www.tenutasetteponti.it

CELLAR SALES
PRE-BOOKED VISITS
ACCOMMODATION
ANNUAL PRODUCTION 225,000 bottles
HECTARES UNDER VINE 55.00
SUSTAINABLE WINERY

The Moretti family purchased the estate in the 1950s from sisters Margherita and Maria Cristina di Savoia. Initially used as a country residence, it was fared using conventional methods, including the vineyard. When current owner Antonio Moretti took over, a fashion entrepreneur with a passion for wine, things changed drastically with transformation of the vineyards, modernization of the cellar and expansion into other areas with the purchase of estates in Bolgheri, Maremma and Sicily. He is also responsible for the name of the winery, which honours the road running through it, emphasizing a connection with the terroir. The Oreno 2012, merlot, cabernet sauvignon and petit verdot, offers fresh grassy hints with eucalyptus, spices like juniper and cloves, and a cherry fruit base. The palate opens smooth and silky with nicely expansive tannins, a relaxed body and a long, delicious finish.

● Oreno '12	♟♟♟ 7
● Crognolo '13	♟♟ 4
● Chianti V. di Pallino '14	♟♟ 2*
● Poggio al Lupo '13	♟♟ 5
● Morellino di Scansano Poggio al Lupo '13	♟ 2
● Oreno '11	♟♟♟ 7
● Oreno '10	♟♟♟ 7
● Oreno '09	♟♟♟ 7
● Oreno '05	♟♟♟ 7
● Oreno '00	♟♟♟ 5
● Crognolo '12	♟♟ 4
● Crognolo '11	♟♟ 4
● Morellino di Scansano Poggio al Lupo '12	♟♟ 5
● Poggio al Lupo '12	♟♟ 5

Signano

LOC. SANTA MARGHERITA, 36
53037 SAN GIMIGNANO [SI]
TEL. 0577941085
www.casolaredibucciano.com

CELLAR SALES
PRE-BOOKED VISITS
ANNUAL PRODUCTION 80,000 bottles
HECTARES UNDER VINE 25.00

Next year the estate will celebrate the 25th
anniversary of the first vineyards planted
with vernaccia and sangiovese by founding
owner, Ascanio Biagini. In 1961 he bought
two hectares of land in an interesting area,
and started up the business from its central
building. There are now 25 hectares of
vineyards. The responsibility has passed on
to Ascanio's son Manrico, aided today by
his son Pietro, who has adopted new
processing techniques in the cellar and
extended the range of wines produced. As
well as wine, the estate produces extra
virgin olive oil and breeds pigs for the
production of cold cuts served in the
agritourism in the village of Bucciano. The
good Vernaccia La Ginestra Riserva 2103
has complex aromas of apples and hay
alongside almonds. The palate appears
generous, juicy, fresh with hints of citrus
fruit and saffron in the aftertaste. We also
liked the Ginepro 2011, sangiovese with
some merlot: stylish and spicy on the nose,
with a fleshy, persistent palate.

● S. Gimignano Rosso Il Ginepro '11	▼▼ 3
○ Vernaccia di S. Gimignano La Ginestra Ris. '13	▼▼ 3
● Chianti Colli Senesi Poggiarelli '13	▼ 3
○ Vernaccia di S. Gimignano '14	▼ 2
○ Vernaccia di S. Gimignano Poggiarelli '14	▼ 2
● Chianti Colli Senesi '11	♀♀ 2*
● Chianti Colli Senesi '09	♀♀ 2
● Chianti Colli Senesi Poggiarelli '06	♀♀ 3
○ San Gimignano Vin Santo '06	♀♀ 5
○ Vernaccia di S. Gimignano '12	♀♀ 2*
○ Vernaccia di S. Gimignano '11	♀♀ 2*
○ Vernaccia di S. Gimignano '10	♀♀ 2
○ Vernaccia di S. Gimignano La Ginestra Ris. '11	♀♀ 3
○ Vernaccia di S. Gimignano Ris. '07	♀♀ 2*

Fattoria Sorbaiano

LOC. SORBAIANO
56040 MONTECATINI VAL DI CECINA [PI]
TEL. 058830243
www.fattoriasorbaiano.it

CELLAR SALES
PRE-BOOKED VISITS
ACCOMMODATION
ANNUAL PRODUCTION 80,000 bottles
HECTARES UNDER VINE 27.00
VITICULTURE METHOD Certified Organic

Maria Grazia Picciolini owns the estate that
has been in her family since the 1950s. It
once belonged to the Inghirami family and
the site is a former Roman agricultural
settlement, showing that even then the
area was considered suitable and efficient
for farming. Maria Grazia's work has been
significant in making the estate modern
and functional: she has renovated the old
houses, adapting them for use as holiday
accommodation, and made extensive
changes in the vineyards, embracing
organic growing methods, certified in 2013.
Her aim is to bring the main characteristic
features, passed on from the land to the
grapes, straight into the bottles. The Rosso
delle Miniere 2012 is a blend of sangiovese,
malvasia nera and cabernet franc: fresh,
minty aromas with liquorice and ripe plum
and cherry fruit. The palate is meek to begin
with, acquiring sinew and liveliness, good
grip with succulent flavour and a steady
crescendo to the extended finish.

● Montescudaio Rosso delle Miniere '12	▼▼ 5
○ Montescudaio Bianco '14	▼▼ 2*
● Montescudaio Rosso '13	▼▼ 2*
○ Montescudaio Vin Santo '08	▼▼ 5
● Pian del Conte '12	▼ 3
⊙ Rosato '14	▼ 2
● Cabernet Franc '07	♀♀ 5
○ Montescudaio Bianco '12	♀♀ 2*
○ Montescudaio Bianco Lucestraia '13	♀♀ 3
○ Montescudaio Bianco Lucestraia '11	♀♀ 3
● Montescudaio Rosso delle Miniere '10	♀♀ 4
● Montescudaio Rosso delle Miniere '09	♀♀ 4
● Velathri '11	♀♀ 3
● Velathri '10	♀♀ 3
● Velathri '09	♀♀ 3
○ Vin Santo di Montescudaio '07	♀♀ 4

Tenimenti Luigi d'Alessandro

VIA MANZANO, 15
52042 CORTONA [AR]
TEL. 0575618667
www.tenimentidalessandro.it

CELLAR SALES
PRE-BOOKED VISITS
ACCOMMODATION AND RESTAURANT SERVICE
ANNUAL PRODUCTION 130,000 bottles
HECTARES UNDER VINE 37.00

The winery's history began in the 18th century and it has been owned by a succession of families. Only in 1967 when the d'Alessandro family bought the property did the area's potential for wine production become clear. The desire to experiment with new winegrowing solutions led to the first syrah vineyards, a decision that would influence the character of the whole Cortona area, as estates decided to convert production to this new variety, giving birth to a DOC zone. Today Tenimenti d'Alessandro is owned by Giuseppe Calabresi, who has not failed to involve his children in the project that includes a splendid hotel. The Borgo 2013 has a captivating nose with spicy aromas of pepper and cinnamon, redcurrants and cherries and hints of tobacco. The palate is fleshy, generous and nicely juicy with a delicious relaxed finish.

Tenuta Tre Rose
Bertani Domains

FRAZ. VALIANO DI MONTEPULCIANO
VIA DELLA STELLA, 3
53040 MONTEPULCIANO [SI]
TEL. 0577804101
www.tenimentiangelini.it

CELLAR SALES
PRE-BOOKED VISITS
ANNUAL PRODUCTION 650,000 bottles
HECTARES UNDER VINE 75.00

This is one of the Tuscan Bertani Domains properties: the estate, purchased in 1994, belongs to the group that also controls the Val di Suga estate in Montalcino and San Leonino in Castellina in Chianti, as well as other wine-producing estates in Friuli and Marche. Over the years a real village has developed around the 16th-century villa that houses the headquarters, including a hotel and restaurant. About a third of the estate is under vine, mostly for the production of Nobile di Montepulciano. The style of the wines is meant to appeal to international consumers but in recent years it has attempted to express more local, territorial features. The nobile Santa Caterina 2012 has spicy aromas of juniper and ginger with a cherry fruit base, and a bold, nicely lively palate, well-structured with succulent, light tannins and a crescendo finish. The Noble Simposio 2010 is austere and nicely put-together.

● Cortona Syrah Borgo '13	♀♀ 3*
○ Fontarca '13	♀♀ 5
● Cortona Il Bosco '09	♀♀♀ 6
● Cortona Il Bosco '06	♀♀♀ 6
● Cortona Il Bosco '04	♀♀♀ 5
● Cortona Il Bosco '03	♀♀♀ 5
● Cortona Il Bosco '01	♀♀♀ 6
● Cortona Syrah Migliara '08	♀♀♀ 8
● Cortona Syrah Migliara '07	♀♀♀ 8
○ Bianco del Borgo '13	♀♀ 3
● Cortona Syrah Borgo '12	♀♀ 3
● Cortona Syrah Borgo '11	♀♀ 3
● Cortona Syrah Borgo V. V. '11	♀♀ 5
● Cortona Syrah Migliara '10	♀♀ 8

● Nobile di Montepulciano Santa Caterina '12	♀♀ 4
● Nobile di Montepulciano Simposio '10	♀♀ 6
● Rosso Salterio '14	♀ 2
● Nobile di Montepulciano Simposio '97	♀♀♀ 5

Tenute del Cerro

FRAZ. ACQUAVIVA DI MONTEPULCIANO
VIA GRAZIANELLA, 5
53045 MONTEPULCIANO [SI]
TEL. 0578767722
www.tenutedelcerro.it

CELLAR SALES
PRE-BOOKED VISITS
ACCOMMODATION AND RESTAURANT SERVICE
ANNUAL PRODUCTION 1,500,000 bottles
HECTARES UNDER VINE 180.00

The estates are part of the Unipol insurance group, which inherited them from former owners and decided to continue to invest in the agricultural sector. There are other wine-producing estates in Tuscany, at Montalcino and Val di Cornia, while another two are situated in Umbria. The Montepulciano property is one of the largest and best developed, and is the largest private estate in Montepulciano. It includes an agritourism business and restaurant, with production of olive oil and grappa as well as wine. Vino Nobile is the main interest and accounts for the largest number of bottles, and attention has increasingly focused in this direction in recent years. The vibrant, mature Nobile Riserva 2011 has fruity, nicely managed aromas of redcurrants and wildflowers. The palate is smooth, silky with nice tannic texture and a flavoursome, nicely calibrated finish. The Nobile Antica Chiusina 2012 has light vegetal aromas with a relaxed but flavoursome and lively palate.

Terenzi

LOC. MONTEDONICO
58054 SCANSANO [GR]
TEL. 0564599601
www.terenzi.eu

CELLAR SALES
PRE-BOOKED VISITS
ACCOMMODATION AND RESTAURANT SERVICE
ANNUAL PRODUCTION 350,000 bottles
HECTARES UNDER VINE 60.00

The Terenzi family decided to begin their winegrowing adventure in Maremma, enchanted by the place and the potential it could express. They chose the land carefully, carrying out research into the grape varieties to use, which led to the selection of eight varieties, including two different clones of sangiovese. The functional, practical cellar meets the criteria of modern winegrowing. Respect for the local area is one of the goals pursued through the use of integrated farming. As well as wine the estate produces extra virgin olive oil and grappa, and the Locanda named after the family offers hospitality. The Morellino Madrechiesa Riserva 2012 has a fresh nose with minty sensations on a fruity base of strawberries and cherries. The palate is stylish, clean and pleasantly balanced with a juicy, powerful finish. The Morellino 2014 has a fragrant nose and rounded, delicious palate.

● Nobile di Montepulciano Ris. '11	♟♟♟ 4*
● Nobile di Montepulciano Antica Chiusina '12	♟♟ 6
○ Cerrus Brut M. Cl.	♟ 5
● Chianti Colli Senesi '14	♟ 2
● Manero Rosso '13	♟ 2
● Nobile di Montepulciano '12	♟ 3
● Rosso di Montepulciano '14	♟ 2
○ Spumante Extra Dry La Grazianella	♟ 2
● Nobile di Montepulciano '11	♟♟♟ 3*
● Nobile di Montepulciano '10	♟♟♟ 3*
● Nobile di Montepulciano Ris. '06	♟♟♟ 4
● Nobile di Montepulciano Vign. Antica Chiusina '00	♟♟♟ 6
● Nobile di Montepulciano Vign. Antica Chiusina '99	♟♟♟ 6

● Morellino di Scansano Madrechiesa Ris. '12	♟♟♟ 5
● Morellino di Scansano '14	♟♟ 3*
● Morellino di Scansano Ris. '12	♟♟ 3*
● Francesca Romana '11	♟♟ 5
○ Maremma Toscana Viognier Montedonico '14	♟♟ 3
● Maremma Toscana Bramaluce '13	♟ 3
○ Maremma Toscana Vermentino Balbino '14	♟ 3
○ Petit Manseng Passito '12	♟ 5
● Morellino di Scansano Madrechiesa Ris. '11	♟♟♟ 5
● Morellino di Scansano Madrechiesa Ris. '10	♟♟♟ 5
● Morellino di Scansano Madrechiesa Ris. '09	♟♟♟ 5

Terre del Marchesato

FRAZ. BOLGHERI
LOC. SANT'UBERTO, 164
57020 CASTAGNETO CARDUCCI [LI]
TEL. 0565749752
www.fattoriaterredelmarchesato.it

CELLAR SALES
PRE-BOOKED VISITS
ACCOMMODATION
ANNUAL PRODUCTION 60,000 bottles
HECTARES UNDER VINE 9.50

This winery's history began in the early 1950s with the purchase of land belonging to the Marchesi d'Incisa della Rocchetta by Emilio Fuselli, from Marche, who had decided to move to Tuscany. Today Maurizio carries on his grandfather's project and is responsible for the change to a modern style, starting with investments in the vineyards and cellar. For a few years the wines have been among the best in Bolgheri. Another wonderful performance from this winery with a little line-up of wines of enviable quality. The Marchesale 2912 stands out for its well-coordinated aromas of black berries, balsamic hints and well-made, firm palate. Next in line is the Tarabuso of the same year, and among the others, the Bianco Papeo 2013, with hawthorn aromas, and the sweet Nobilis 2011. All very good.

● Marchesale '12	♟♟ 7
● Bolgheri Rosso Emilio I '13	♟♟ 3
○ Nobilis '11	♟♟ 5
○ Papeo '13	♟♟ 6
● Tarabuso '12	♟♟ 6
○ Emilio I '14	♟ 2
● Inedito '14	♟ 2
● Bolgheri Rosso Emilio I '12	♟♟ 3
○ Emilio I '13	♟♟ 5
● Inedito '13	♟♟ 2*
● Marchesale '08	♟♟ 7
● Tarabuso '11	♟♟ 6

Teruzzi & Puthod

LOC. CASALE, 19
53037 SAN GIMIGNANO [SI]
TEL. 0577940143
www.teruzzieputhod.it

CELLAR SALES
PRE-BOOKED VISITS
ANNUAL PRODUCTION 1,000,000 bottles
HECTARES UNDER VINE 94.00

Back in 1974 Enrico Teruzzi and his wife Carmen Puthod decided to leave Milan and move to San Gimignano to become winegrowers. With a passion for the place and tradition, and skill as an innovator in the winegrowing sector, Enrico made his name on the market for the quality of his products and for his ability to use unconventional methods to promote his image, also through his labels. In 2013 the estate was bought by the Campari group who invested heavily in remodernization of the vineyards and new purchases, making it the private estate with the largest area of vernaccia vineyards. The 2014 Vernaccia di San Gimignano gives an excellent performance, the best ever, with hints of flowers and hay, fresh sensations of mint and lemon and ripe fruit like peaches and apples. The palate is well-judged, lively, nicely tangy with perfectly lingering flavour. The Peperino 2012, sangiovese and merlot, is fun, spicy, fresh and enjoyable.

○ Vernaccia di S. Gimignano '14	♟♟ 2*
● Peperino '12	♟♟ 2*
○ Terre di Tufi '13	♟ 4
● Arcidiavolo '08	♟♟ 5
● Arcidiavolo '07	♟♟ 5
● Peperino '08	♟♟ 2*
● Peperino '07	♟♟ 2*
○ Terre di Tufi '09	♟♟ 4
○ Terre di Tufi '08	♟♟ 4
○ Terre di Tufi '07	♟♟ 4
○ Vernaccia di S. Gimignano '13	♟♟ 2*
○ Vernaccia di S. Gimignano '12	♟♟ 2*
○ Vernaccia di S. Gimignano '11	♟♟ 2*
○ Vernaccia di S. Gimignano '09	♟♟ 2*
○ Vernaccia di S. Gimignano Ris. '11	♟♟ 4
○ Vernaccia di S. Gimignano Ris. '10	♟♟ 4

Testamatta

VIA DI VINCIGLIATA, 19
50014 FIESOLE [FI]
TEL. 055597289
www.bibigraetz.com

PRE-BOOKED VISITS
ANNUAL PRODUCTION 500,000 bottles
HECTARES UNDER VINE 10.00

Bibi Graetz is undoubtedly an extreme
character. He decided to be a winegrower
after starting as an artist (a painter) like his
father, an internationally renowned sculptor.
The project developed outside the canonical
models, aiming to promote grapes that had
almost been set aside and bring them back
in a form that appealed to international
consumers. Proof of this is the wine made
from ansonica del Giglio, with grapes
selected on the island, by convincing the
country people to care for the vines instead
of abandoning them. In addition the labels
show beautiful images drawn from Bibi's
own artwork. The Colore 2010 is a blend of
colorino, sangiovese and canaiolo with
vibrant aromas of autumn leaves alongside
hints of tobacco and leather on a fruity
cherry base. The palate is rounded with
subtle tannins and a lovely crescendo finish.

● Colore '10	▼▼ 8
○ Bugia '14	▼▼ 6
● Soffocone di Vincigliata '13	▼▼ 5
● Testamatta '12	▼▼ 8
○ Casamatta Bianco '14	▼ 2
● Chianti Le Cicale di Vincigliata '13	▼ 2
○ Bugia '13	♀♀ 6
○ Casamatta Bianco '11	♀♀ 2*
○ Gigliese '11	♀♀ 3
● Grilli del Testamatta '10	♀♀ 5
● Grilli del Testamatta '09	♀♀ 5
● It's a Game '10	♀♀ 2*
● Soffocone di Vincigliata '12	♀♀ 5
● Soffocone di Vincigliata '11	♀♀ 5
● Soffocone di Vincigliata '09	♀♀ 5
● Testamatta '09	♀♀ 8

Tiezzi

LOC. PODERE SOCCORSO
53024 MONTALCINO [SI]
TEL. 0577848187
www.tiezzivini.it

CELLAR SALES
PRE-BOOKED VISITS
ACCOMMODATION
ANNUAL PRODUCTION 23,000 bottles
HECTARES UNDER VINE 5.50

The Tiezzi family's work is nourished by
proud claims to productive roots. The
Soccorso farm, where the winery is
situated, may be where the first Brunello in
history was bottled, and today it is the only
Montalcino cru to use the bush-training
system, situated at about 500 metres
altitude, on sandy, silty soil rich in stony
material. Before buying it the estate owned
the Cerrino and Cigaleta farms in the
eastern area of the DOC, planted on clayey,
silty land. These differences in terroir are
synthesized in "naked" Sangioveses,
sometimes capricious in the early phases,
aged in 10- and 40-hectolitre Slavonian
oak. These expressive dynamics help us to
be patient with the two 2010 Brunellos,
probably encountered at a complicated
phase. The Poggio Cerrino seems affected
by very mature aromas while the Vigna
Soccorso is already more dynamic and
weighty, despite the chestnut overtone to
the tannins.

● Brunello di Montalcino V. Soccorso '10	▼▼ 6
● Brunello di Montalcino Poggio Cerrino '10	▼ 5
● Brunello di Montalcino '07	♀♀ 5
● Brunello di Montalcino Poggio Cerrino '09	♀♀ 5
● Brunello di Montalcino V. del Soccorso '08	♀♀ 6
● Brunello di Montalcino V. del Soccorso '07	♀♀ 6
● Brunello di Montalcino V. del Soccorso '06	♀♀ 6
● Brunello di Montalcino V. del Soccorso Ris. '07	♀♀ 6
● Brunello di Montalcino V. Soccorso '09	♀♀ 6
● Brunello di Montalcino V. Soccorso Ris. '08	♀♀ 6
● Rosso di Montalcino Poggio Cerrino '11	♀♀ 3*

Tolaini

LOC. VALLENUOVA
S.DA PROV.LE 9 DI PIEVASCIATA, 28
53019 CASTELNUOVO BERARDENGA [SI]
TEL. 0577356972
www.tolaini.it

CELLAR SALES
PRE-BOOKED VISITS
ANNUAL PRODUCTION 250,000 bottles
HECTARES UNDER VINE 50.00
VITICULTURE METHOD Certified Organic

Pierluigi Tolaini's winemaking project made his fortune as an emigrant to Canada. It all began in 1998 with the purchase of the San Giovanni and Montebello farms between Pianella and Vagliagli. The first vinification procedures took place in 2002 and since adapting its approach to a complex area like Chianti, the estate has produced definitely well-made wines. This is the result of a winegrowing process that leaves nothing to chance and rigorous work in the cellar, starting with the judiciously measured use of mainly small oak. A weighty palate and deep aromas characterize the Valdisanti 2011, a blend of sangiovese, cabernet sauvignon and cabernet franc, an elegant wine confirming its solid quality. The interesting Chianti Classico Gran Selezione 2011 is strongest on fruity, crystal-clear aromas. The palate also shows the pace of a great wine, especially in the succulent flavour, but some slightly excessive oak breaks up the rhythm.

● Valdisanti '11	♟♟ 5
● Chianti Cl. Gran Sel. '11	♟♟ 5
● Al Passo '11	♟ 4
● Picconero '10	♟♟♟ 8
● Picconero '09	♟♟♟ 8
● Valdisanti '08	♟♟♟ 8
● Al Passo '09	♟♟ 4
● Al Passo '07	♟♟ 4
● Chianti Cl. Montebello Vign. n.7 Ris. '10	♟♟ 6
● Chianti Cl. Ris. '10	♟♟ 5
● Chianti Cl. Ris. '08	♟♟ 5
● Picconero '08	♟♟ 8
● Picconero '07	♟♟ 8
● Picconero '06	♟♟ 8
● Picconero '04	♟♟ 7
● Valdisanti '09	♟♟ 8

Fattoria Torre a Cona

LOC. SAN DONATO IN COLLINA
50010 RIGNANO SULL'ARNO [FI]
TEL. 055699000
www.villatorreacona.com

CELLAR SALES
PRE-BOOKED VISITS
ACCOMMODATION
ANNUAL PRODUCTION 30,000 bottles
HECTARES UNDER VINE 14.00

Torre a Cona in the Colli Fiorentini, one of the most beautiful estates in Tuscany, has belonged to the Conti Rossi di Montelera for almost a century. Over the years the new generations have carried out extraordinary restorations in the vineyards and cellar, and more recently in the building as a whole, making it one of the loveliest reception structures in the region. The vineyards are planted with the classic typical, local varieties, especially sangiovese, with some merlot for the monovarietal wine. The Sangiovese Riserva Badia a Corte is always outstanding with delicate hints of strawberries and medicinal herbs, slightly minty sensations and a succulent, well-defined palate with a very flavoursome, biting finish. Another Sangiovese, the Terre di Cino 2012, maintains its airy character. An honourable mention for the 2012 Merlot, well-defined and structured on nose and palate alike.

● Chianti Colli Fiorentini Badia a Corte Ris. '12	♟♟ 4
● Merlot '12	♟♟ 3*
● Chianti Colli Fiorentini Conti Rossi di Montelera '13	♟♟ 3
● Terre di Cino '12	♟♟ 3
○ Vin Santo del Chianti Merlaia '08	♟♟ 3
● Chianti Colli Fiorentini '10	♟♟ 3
● Chianti Colli Fiorentini '09	♟♟ 3
● Chianti Colli Fiorentini Badia a Corte Ris. '11	♟♟ 4
● Chianti Colli Fiorentini Badia a Corte Ris. '10	♟♟ 4
● R09 '09	♟♟ 4
● Terre di Cino '11	♟♟ 3
● Terre di Cino '09	♟♟ 3
○ Vin Santo del Chianti Merlaia '06	♟♟ 3

Le Torri

VIA SAN LORENZO A VIGLIANO, 31
50021 BARBERINO VAL D'ELSA [FI]
TEL. 0558076161
www.letorri.net

CELLAR SALES
PRE-BOOKED VISITS
ACCOMMODATION AND RESTAURANT SERVICE
ANNUAL PRODUCTION 150,000 bottles
HECTARES UNDER VINE 28.00

A passion for Tuscany, combined with the love of a good wine drove a group of friends to invest in this strip of land bordering Chianti Classico in the 1980s, and build a farm with annexed agritourism structure, a highly innovative activity back in the day. Over the years the hospitality facilities have grown and improved, with careful attention to catering, while the leap in quality for the wines came with Beatrice Mozzi, daughter of one of the partners, who turned production around and renewed the style of the wines with different ageing approaches to those used in the past and also special attention to olive cultivation. The Chianti Colli Fiorentini Riserva 2012 made the finals with intriguing aromas, a lovely blend of fruit and spice enhanced by hints of aromatic herbs. An impressive, soft impact with light, well-measured tannin and an appetizing, lingering finish. We also liked the San Lorenzo 2012, a Sangiovese, less austere than it used to be, fresh and well-structured.

● Chianti Colli Fiorentini Ris. '12	♀♀ 3*
● Magliano '12	♀♀ 5
● Meridius '13	♀♀ 2*
● San Lorenzo '12	♀♀ 5
● Chianti Colli Fiorentini '13	♀ 2
○ Soleluna '14	♀ 2
⊙ Spumante Brut Rosé	♀ 4
● Chianti Colli Fiorentini Ris. '11	♀♀ 3
● Chianti Colli Fiorentini Ris. '10	♀♀ 3
● Magliano '10	♀♀ 5
● Magliano '09	♀♀ 5

Travignoli

VIA TRAVIGNOLI, 78
50060 PELAGO [FI]
TEL. 0558361098
www.travignoli.com

CELLAR SALES
PRE-BOOKED VISITS
ANNUAL PRODUCTION 250,000 bottles
HECTARES UNDER VINE 70.00

Here you can breathe history, the history of ancient Etruscan civilizations, with the discovery of a stele dating back to 500 BC, demonstrating that banquets were held at which wine was served. In the late 15th century the boundaries of the property were defined and by the 17th it had acquired prestige that brought recognition for the owners. The estate was purchased by the Busi family and in 1924 Clemente Busi established the Chianti Putto consortium, and received a medal for producing excellent wine. Since then the successes have notched up and the estate is now in the hands of owner, and chairman of the Chianti consortium, Giovanni Busi. A good performance from the Riserva Tegolaia 2012: lovely varied aromas, hints of jam and ripe fruit and a rounded, nicely weighty palate with stylish tannin and a tangy vigorous finish. The old-style Vin Santo 2009 has dried fruit like dates and figs alternating with hints of almonds and aromatic herbs. The palate is mouthfilling but not cloying, well balanced in a delicious finish.

● Chianti Rufina Tegolaia Ris. '12	♀♀ 3
○ Vin Santo Chianti Rufina '09	♀♀ 4
● Chianti Rufina '13	♀ 2
○ Gavignano '14	♀ 2
● Calice del Conte '08	♀♀ 5
● Calice del Conte '04	♀♀ 5
● Chianti Rufina '12	♀♀ 2*
● Chianti Rufina Ris. '05	♀♀ 3
● Chianti Rufina Tegolaia Ris. '11	♀♀ 3
● Chianti Rufina Tegolaia Ris. '10	♀♀ 3
● Chianti Rufina Tegolaia Ris. '09	♀♀ 3
● Chianti Rufina Tegolaia Ris. '08	♀♀ 3
● Chianti Rufina Tegolaia Ris. '07	♀♀ 3
● Tegolaia '06	♀♀ 4
○ Vin Santo Chianti Rufina '01	♀♀ 4
○ Vin Santo Chianti Rufina '00	♀♀ 4

Tenuta di Trinoro

VIA VAL D'ORCIA, 15
53047 SARTEANO [SI]
TEL. 0578267110
www.trinoro.it

CELLAR SALES
PRE-BOOKED VISITS
ANNUAL PRODUCTION 80,000 bottles
HECTARES UNDER VINE 20.00

From the distribution of prestigious wines in America in the 1980s, via oenological studies in Bordeaux, Andrea Franchetti at last dropped anchor in the 1990s in Val d'Orcia, near the town of Sarteano, where he breathed life into a rigorously designed winemaking project. The first experimental harvest came in 1995 and even then the estate's aims were clearly defined: to achieve an absolute high standard of excellence. An uncompromising journey which is consolidated in concrete terms today. The Tenuta di Trinoro 2013 is a blend of sangiovese, cabernet sauvignon and cabernet franc: complex aromas with a smooth yet lively flavour, showing very classy detailing. The Cabernet Franc Magnacosta is firm-bodied and not without pleasant hardness, while the Merlot Palazzi 2013 is mouthfilling and very richly extracted. The Le Cupole 2013 is a more approachable, sometimes more relaxed blend of grapes from the estate's younger vineyards.

● Tenuta di Trinoro '13	♥♥	8
● Magnacosta '13	♥♥	8
● Palazzi '13	♥♥	8
● Le Cupole di Trinoro '13	♥	5
● Tenuta di Trinoro '08	♥♥♥	8
● Tenuta di Trinoro '04	♥♥♥	8
● Tenuta di Trinoro '03	♥♥♥	8
● Le Cupole di Trinoro '11	♥♥	5
● Magnacosta '12	♥♥	8
● Palazzi '12	♥♥	8
● Palazzi '11	♥♥	8
● Palazzi '10	♥♥	8
● Tenuta di Trinoro '12	♥♥	8
● Tenuta di Trinoro '11	♥♥	8
● Tenuta di Trinoro '10	♥♥	8
● Tenuta di Trinoro '09	♥♥	8

★Tua Rita

LOC. NOTRI, 81
57028 SUVERETO [LI]
TEL. 0565829237
www.tuarita.it

PRE-BOOKED VISITS
ANNUAL PRODUCTION 250,000 bottles
HECTARES UNDER VINE 35.00
VITICULTURE METHOD Certified Organic

A love story, between Virgilio Bisti, who passed away prematurely, and Rita Tua, which was consolidated in the things they did together. Despite being involved in other jobs, in 1984 they decided to buy some land in Val di Cornia, at that time far from becoming famous for wine production. The two hectares were sufficient to ignite their passion for wine which led them, step by step, to build an increasingly efficient and organized estate, also thanks to Stefano Frascolla, husband of their daughter Simona, who works in promotion and marketing. Important news from the last year is that they have rented the Poggio Argentiera estate in the Morellino zone. The Giusto di Notri 2011 is a blend of cabernet sauvignon with merlot and cabernet franc, with a powerful, fresh, grassy nose on a clean, clear fruity base. The palate is juicy and lively, stylish and complex with a crescendo finish. The Per Sempre 2012 is a Syrah with intriguing aromas, spicy and generous with a firm, dynamic palate.

● Giusto di Notri '11	♥♥	8
● Rosso dei Notri '14	♥♥	4
● Syrah Per Sempre '12	♥♥	8
● Perlato del Bosco Rosso '13	♥	5
● Redigaffi '08	♥♥♥	8
● Redigaffi '07	♥♥♥	8
● Redigaffi '06	♥♥♥	8
● Redigaffi '04	♥♥♥	8
● Redigaffi '03	♥♥♥	8
● Redigaffi '02	♥♥♥	8
● Redigaffi '01	♥♥♥	8
● Redigaffi '00	♥♥♥	7

Uccelliera

FRAZ. CASTELNUOVO DELL'ABATE
POD. UCCELLIERA, 45
53020 MONTALCINO [SI]
TEL. 0577835729
www.uccelliera-montalcino.it

CELLAR SALES
PRE-BOOKED VISITS
ANNUAL PRODUCTION 60,000 bottles
HECTARES UNDER VINE 6.00

Andrea Cortonesi's Brunellos are very distinctive. His style is openly southern, often dividing opinions of critics and enthusiasts, but he is generally respected for the way in which he blends the features of the terroir with the expressive sensitivity of a true vigneron. The Uccelliera estate covers about six hectares at Castelnuovo dell'Abate in the extreme south-east of the Montalcino DOC zone, where medium-textured clayey, sandy soil prevails at altitudes around 250 metres. The vinification procedures are adapted to suit each plot and the specific features of each harvest, sometimes using barriques alongside untoasted Slavonian oak. Bearing in mind the warm area and basically cool year, we expected great things from Uccelliera's 2010 Brunello. But we could not have imagined such an astounding performance: incense, balsam, piquant spice, hugely powerful fruit moving with surgical balance towards the long, invigorating, thirst-quenching finish.

● Brunello di Montalcino '10	♥♥♥ 6
● Rosso di Montalcino '13	♥ 4
● Brunello di Montalcino '08	♥♥♥ 7
● Brunello di Montalcino Ris. '97	♥♥♥ 8
● Brunello di Montalcino '09	♥♥ 6
● Brunello di Montalcino '07	♥♥ 7
● Brunello di Montalcino Ris. '08	♥♥ 8
● Brunello di Montalcino Ris. '07	♥♥ 8
● Rosso di Montalcino '11	♥♥ 4

F.lli Vagnoni

LOC. PANCOLE, 82
53037 SAN GIMIGNANO [SI]
TEL. 0577955077
www.fratellivagnoni.com

CELLAR SALES
PRE-BOOKED VISITS
ACCOMMODATION
ANNUAL PRODUCTION 120,000 bottles
HECTARES UNDER VINE 17.00
VITICULTURE METHOD Certified Organic

The Vagnoni brothers own the winery that this year celebrates 60 years of business in the San Gimignano area. Thus the family tradition continues, with the development over the years of a consolidated winery through the gradual increase of the surface area of vineyards without abandoning any of the land used for orchards and arable crops. In 2007 the new cellar was inaugurated, increasing the available space as it was placed alongside the old one. As well as wine, the estate produces extra virgin olive oil and grappa and has an agritourism facility. The Vernaccia Riserva I Mocali 2012 made a good impression with a fresh, lively style, hints of grapefruit and melon and vegetal sensations with medicinal herbs. The palate is juicy, intriguing, and complex with a well-sustained finish. We also liked the Sodi Lunghi 2011, sangiovese with colorino: hints of pepper and autumn leaves on the nose with a supple, well-coordinated palate and vibrant finish.

● Chianti Colli Senesi Capanneto Ris. '11	♥♥ 3
● Sodi Lunghi '11	♥♥ 3
○ Vernaccia di S. Gimignano I Mocali Ris. '12	♥♥ 3
● Chianti Colli Senesi '13	♥ 2
⊙ San Gimignano Rosato Pancolino '14	♥ 2
● Toscana Rosso '14	♥ 1*
○ Vernaccia di S. Gimignano '14	♥ 2
○ Vernaccia di S. Gimignano '12	♥♥ 2*
○ Vernaccia di S. Gimignano Fontabuccio '13	♥♥ 2*
○ Vernaccia di S. Gimignano I Mocali Ris. '11	♥♥ 3*
○ Vernaccia di S. Gimignano I Mocali Ris. '10	♥♥ 3*
○ Vernaccia di S. Gimignano I Mocali Ris. '09	♥♥ 3*

Podere Val delle Corti

LOC. LA CROCE, 141
53017 RADDA IN CHIANTI [SI]
TEL. 0577738215
www.valdellecorti.it

CELLAR SALES
PRE-BOOKED VISITS
ACCOMMODATION
ANNUAL PRODUCTION 30,000 bottles
HECTARES UNDER VINE 6.00
VITICULTURE METHOD Certified Organic

Vineyards farmed organically for years and now attaining biodynamic status; deliberately minimal winemaking procedures, and ageing mainly in large oak. These are the secrets of Giorgio Bianchi's estate, along with the important fact that it is located in one of the best and most attractive growing areas in Chianti Classico, Radda in Chianti. The result is products of an excellent standard: very characterful and completely consistent wines with an authentic land-rooted quality that is almost unparalleled in the DOC. The 2012 Chianti Classico is really a delight, a kind of compendium of Chianti wine. Crystal-clear aromas alternating lovely fresh citrus fruit, floral hints and stony, earthy sensations. The palate is well-coordinated, nicely paced and assertive with good grip and a tangy, deep flavour. The same tangy quality appears in the simpler Rosé Scuro 2014, from sangiovese grapes.

Val di Suga
Bertani Domains

LOC. VAL DI CAVA
53024 MONTALCINO [SI]
TEL. 0577804101
www.tenimentiangelini.it

CELLAR SALES
PRE-BOOKED VISITS
ANNUAL PRODUCTION 270,000 bottles
HECTARES UNDER VINE 55.00

The mapping work started in recent years by Bertani Domains (formerly Tenimenti Angelini) on its Montalcino estates continues without respite. The Val di Suga brand, purchased in 1994, brings together about 60 hectares of vineyards managed according to biosustainable methods and divided according to their geographical location and soil composition, under the supervision of David Landini and Andrea Lonardi. For now, the three Brunello crus are bottled separately: Vigna Spuntali (south-western slope), Vigna del Lago (northern area) and Poggio al Granchio (an upland in the south-east of the zone, rich in marl). The tasting of the Val di Suga 2010 selections is postponed till next year's Guide. In the meantime we'll make do, so to speak, with the standard Brunello, reassuringly fruity and spicy and further enhanced by the delicate flavour, with focused tannic extract. Juicy flavour also appears in the authoritative Rosso 2013.

● Chianti Cl. '12	♟♟♟ 4*
⊙ Rosé Scuro '14	♟ 2
● Chianti Cl. '11	♟♟♟ 3*
● Chianti Cl. '10	♟♟♟ 3*
● Chianti Cl. '09	♟♟♟ 2*
● Chianti Cl. '06	♟♟ 2*
● Chianti Cl. '05	♟♟ 2*
● Chianti Cl. '04	♟♟ 2*
● Chianti Cl. '03	♟♟ 2
● Chianti Cl. Ris. '11	♟♟ 5
● Chianti Cl. Ris. '09	♟♟ 5
● Chianti Cl. Ris. '07	♟♟ 4
● Chianti Cl. Ris. '00	♟♟ 4
● Il Campino	♟♟ 2*

● Brunello di Montalcino Val di Suga '10	♟♟ 5
● Rosso di Montalcino '13	♟♟ 3
● Brunello di Montalcino V. Spuntali '95	♟♟♟ 8
● Brunello di Montalcino Val di Suga '07	♟♟♟ 5
● Brunello di Montalcino Poggio al Granchio '09	♟♟ 7
● Brunello di Montalcino V. del Lago '09	♟♟ 8
● Brunello di Montalcino V. Spuntali '09	♟♟ 8
● Brunello di Montalcino V. Spuntali Val di Suga '07	♟♟ 8
● Brunello di Montalcino Val di Suga '08	♟♟ 5
● Brunello di Montalcino Val di Suga Ris. '07	♟♟ 5

Tenuta Valdipiatta

VIA DELLA CIARLIANA, 25A
53040 MONTEPULCIANO [SI]
TEL. 0578757930
www.valdipiatta.it

CELLAR SALES
PRE-BOOKED VISITS
ACCOMMODATION
ANNUAL PRODUCTION 80,000 bottles
HECTARES UNDER VINE 23.00

Giulio Caporali might be defined as a leader of the past who, having fought a thousand battles, is resting today and meditating on his surroundings. Formerly a manager in the public sector, in the late 1980s he decided to get involved in farming and bought an estate at Montepulciano, charmed by the place and its history. He did some excellent work, enabling his wines to be known and enjoyed abroad, before handing over management to his daughter, Miriam. For years she has been responsible for the winegrowing and commercial sides of the business and has shown skill in developing and consolidating the estate's image abroad. The Nobile Vigna d'Alfiero 2012 has subtle aromas of aromatic herbs, red berries and spices, while the palate is confident, generous with relaxed tannins that enliven the overall profile. The finish is long and well-managed. The Nobile 2012 is fresh with lovely flavour.

● Nobile di Montepulciano '12	♛♛ 4
● Nobile di Montepulciano V. d'Alfiero '12	♛♛ 6
● Chianti Colli Senesi Tosca '13	♛ 2
● Rosso di Montepulciano '13	♛ 3
● Nobile di Montepulciano Ris. '90	♛♛♛ 5
● Nobile di Montepulciano V. d'Alfiero '99	♛♛♛ 5
● Nobile di Montepulciano '11	♛♛ 4
● Nobile di Montepulciano '10	♛♛ 4
● Nobile di Montepulciano '09	♛♛ 4
● Nobile di Montepulciano '08	♛♛ 4
● Nobile di Montepulciano Ris. '07	♛♛ 6
● Nobile di Montepulciano V. d'Alfiero '10	♛♛ 6
● Nobile di Montepulciano V. d'Alfiero '08	♛♛ 6
● Nobile di Montepulciano V. d'Alfiero '06	♛♛ 6
● Nobile di Montepulciano V. d'Alfiero '05	♛♛ 6
● Rosso di Montepulciano '10	♛♛ 3

Valentini

LOC. VALPIANA
POD. FIORDALISO, 69
58024 MASSA MARITTIMA [GR]
TEL. 0566918058
www.agricolavalentini.it

CELLAR SALES
PRE-BOOKED VISITS
ACCOMMODATION
ANNUAL PRODUCTION 40,000 bottles
HECTARES UNDER VINE 5.50

A classic family-run estate with the fifth generation working the land now that Giovanni has been joined by his children Chiara and Luca, and a lovely development in quality compared to the past. Today the main crops are grapes and olives, and special care is taken over the renewal of the vineyards since the estate decided to really pursue fine quality winegrowing. The addition of international grape varieties has yielded some excellent results and the agritourism sector also plays an important role. The Vivoli 2013 has fresh aromas of cherries with hints of tobacco and spice, while the palate is warm and well-structured with a clean, juicy finish. The Merlot Atunis 2012 is also pleasant with appetizing aromas of wild berries, hints of coffee and liquorice, a soft body with smooth tannins and a long, mouthfilling finish.

● Atunis '12	♛♛ 5
● Monteregio di Massa Marittima Vivoli '13	♛♛ 4
● Aule '12	♛ 4
● Crebesco '12	♛ 5
○ Maremma Toscana Vermentino '14	♛ 2
● Monteregio di Massa Marittima Monteregio '13	♛ 2
● Sangiovese '14	♛ 2
● Atunis '11	♛♛ 5
● Atunis '09	♛♛ 5
● Crebesco '07	♛♛ 5
● Monteregio di Massa Marittima Vivoli '11	♛♛ 4

★Tenuta di Valgiano

VIA DI VALGIANO, 7
55015 LUCCA
TEL. 0583402271
www.valgiano.it

CELLAR SALES
PRE-BOOKED VISITS
ANNUAL PRODUCTION 70,000 bottles
HECTARES UNDER VINE 20.00
VITICULTURE METHOD Certified Biodynamic

Not only is this a beautiful place, with magnetic charm, and an estate in harmony with nature, capable of producing richly vibrant wines: Tenuta di Valgiano is above all a master here in the Colline Lucchesi. This winery wrote the beginning of the collective story and was the architect of an area that is becoming a talking point. This is thanks to Moreno Petrini and Laura di Collobiano, as well as the technical input and sensitivity of Saverio Patrilli, a reference point in Italy when the subject is biodynamic farming. The Tenuta di Valgiano is the top wine in Colline Lucchesi and one of the best-known in Tuscany. 2012 endowed it with great charm and complexity: slightly foxy sensations soon give way to spicy, almost smoky hints and the palate is mouthfilling, flavoursome and deep. The Palistorti is also splendid with intriguing hints of sandalwood and other oriental woods.

Varramista

LOC. VARRAMISTA
VIA RICAVO
56020 MONTOPOLI IN VAL D'ARNO [PI]
TEL. 057144711
www.varramista.it

CELLAR SALES
PRE-BOOKED VISITS
ACCOMMODATION
ANNUAL PRODUCTION 65,000 bottles
HECTARES UNDER VINE 14.20

The history of Varramista is paved with extraordinary characters and famous families. In the 1950s, the Piaggio and Agnelli families chose this as their personal country residence. Giovanni Alberto Agnelli even made it his home, and started up some projects for the vineyard. During that period, in the 1990s, the estate began to promote the syrah grape and the winegrowing activity as a whole. The Sterpato 2012, a blend of sangiovese, merlot and cabernet sauvignon, made an excellent impression: pleasant, nuanced aromas of red berries with non-intrusive grassy and spicy hints. The toastiness is present but generally discreet. The surprising Chianti Monsonaccio 2012 is delicious, all focused on raspberries and wild berries.

● Colline Lucchesi Tenuta di Valgiano '12	♛♛♛	6
● Colline Lucchesi Palistorti di Valgiano '12	♛♛	4
● Colline Lucchesi Tenuta di Valgiano '11	♛♛♛	6
● Colline Lucchesi Tenuta di Valgiano '10	♛♛♛	6
● Colline Lucchesi Tenuta di Valgiano '09	♛♛♛	6
● Colline Lucchesi Tenuta di Valgiano '08	♛♛♛	6
● Colline Lucchesi Tenuta di Valgiano '07	♛♛♛	6
● Colline Lucchesi Tenuta di Valgiano '06	♛♛♛	6
● Colline Lucchesi Tenuta di Valgiano '05	♛♛♛	6
○ Colline Lucchesi Palistorti Bianco '13	♛♛	5
○ Colline Lucchesi Palistorti Bianco '11	♛♛	5
● Colline Lucchesi Palistorti Rosso '11	♛♛	4
● Colline Lucchesi Palistorti Rosso '10	♛♛	4
● Colline Lucchesi Palistorti Rosso '09	♛♛	4
● Colline Lucchesi Rosso dei Palistorti '08	♛♛	4

● Chianti Monsonaccio '12	♛♛	2*
● Sterpato '12	♛♛	2*
● Varramista '00	♛♛♛	6
● Frasca Rosso '11	♛♛	3
● Sterpato '11	♛♛	2*

TUSCANY

Vecchia Cantina di Montepulciano

VIA PROVINCIALE, 7
53045 MONTEPULCIANO [SI]
TEL. 0578716092
www.vecchiacantina.com

CELLAR SALES
PRE-BOOKED VISITS
ANNUAL PRODUCTION 3,500,000 bottles
HECTARES UNDER VINE 1000.00

The cooperative winery in the Nobile di Montepulciano area was established in 1937 and is therefore the oldest functional winery of its type in Tuscany. It was particularly effective in developing and consolidating the union of winegrowers after the Second World War and when the countryside was being abandoned, in the late 1960s. It took on a more contemporary and functional role over the years, while keeping pace with the times. In order to improve its position on the market and identify the various marketing areas, three product lines are offered to consumers: Vecchia Cantina, Cantina del Redi and Poggio Stella. The Nobile Riserva 2012 has a strikingly varied fruity base with recognizable hints of redcurrants, raspberries and cherries as well as spicy cloves. The palate is soft with subtle tannins, good texture and a succulent, lingering finish. The two versions of Vin Santo are stylish and engaging.

● Nobile di Montepulciano Briareo Cantine del Redi Ris. '09	♟♟ 5
● Nobile di Montepulciano Ris. '12	♟♟ 4
○ Vin Santo di Montepulciano Cantina del Redi '09	♟♟ 6
○ Vin Santo di Montepulciano Poggio Stella '10	♟♟ 6
● Chianti dei Colli Senesi '13	♟ 2
● Rosso di Montepulciano Poggio Stella '14	♟ 2
● Nobile di Montepulciano '11	♟♟ 3
● Nobile di Montepulciano Poggio Stella '10	♟♟ 3
● Nobile di Montepulciano Redi '10	♟♟ 4
● Nobile di Montepulciano Vecchia Cantina '10	♟♟ 3
● Rosso di Montepulciano Poggio Stella '13	♟♟ 2*
● Rosso di Montepulciano Redi '13	♟♟ 2*

I Veroni

LOC. I VERONI
VIA TIFARITI, 5
50065 PONTASSIEVE [FI]
TEL. 0558368886
www.iveroni.it

CELLAR SALES
PRE-BOOKED VISITS
ACCOMMODATION
ANNUAL PRODUCTION 100,000 bottles
HECTARES UNDER VINE 15.00

The estate is one of many owned by the Conti Guidi, who used to control the area between the Sieve and Arno rivers with their watchtowers. One of these towers was on the Veroni estate, demonstrating the ancient history of the area. The tower has now been incorporated on the farm which is managed with passion and enthusiasm by Lorenzo Mariani, son of the owner. Thanks to him there has been extensive renewal of the vineyards, and attention to new techniques while respecting the typical features of the terroir, which are never disturbed. Alongside wine the estate produces olive oil and runs an agritourism business. Back into the finals for the Riserva: the 2012 version is nicely vibrant on the nose with alternating hints of plums and cherries and delicious spicy notes. The palate is rich and harmonious with subtle tannins and an expansive finish. The standard version is also pleasant with fresh aromas of Mediterranean scrubland and a slender palate with a tangy, enjoyable flavour.

● Chianti Rufina Ris. '12	♟♟ 4
● Chianti Rufina '13	♟♟ 2*
● Rosso di Toscana '13	♟♟ 2*
○ Vin Santo del Chianti Rufina '06	♟♟ 5
● I Veroni '14	♟ 2
● Chianti Rufina '12	♟♟ 2*
● Chianti Rufina '11	♟♟ 2*
● Chianti Rufina Ris. '11	♟♟ 4
● Chianti Rufina Ris. '10	♟♟ 4
● Chianti Rufina Ris. '09	♟♟ 4
● Chianti Rufina Ris. '08	♟♟ 4
● Chianti Rufina Ris. '04	♟♟ 3
○ Vin Santo del Chianti Rufina '05	♟♟ 5
○ Vin Santo del Chianti Rufina '04	♟♟ 5
○ Vin Santo del Chianti Rufina '03	♟♟ 5
○ Vin Santo del Chianti Rufina '99	♟♟ 4

Vignamaggio

VIA DI PETRIOLO, 5
50022 GREVE IN CHIANTI [FI]
TEL. 055854661
www.vignamaggio.com

CELLAR SALES
PRE-BOOKED VISITS
ACCOMMODATION AND RESTAURANT SERVICE
ANNUAL PRODUCTION 350,000 bottles
HECTARES UNDER VINE 62.50
VITICULTURE METHOD Certified Organic

Villa Vignamaggio, run today by French
lawyer Patrice Taravella, who recently took
it over from the former owners, is one of
the leading wineries in the Greve in Chianti
subzone. The winery style pursues good
structure and generous fruit in the wines,
alongside a good dose of both large and
small oak. This choice is applied with grace
and measure, so that the wines never lack
elegance and the leading products have
often scaled the heights of absolute
excellence, also in the recent past. The
Chianti Classico Terre di Prenzano 2013 is
lean and vigorous with clear-cut aromas
and a delicious flavour. The Chianti Classico
Gherardino 2013 has earthy, floral aromas
and a juicy palate livened up by pleasant
hardness. The Chianti Classico Castello di
Monnalisa Gran Selezione 2012 is austere
with some oakiness still not completely
absorbed.

Villa Pillo

VIA VOLTERRANA, 24
50050 GAMBASSI TERME [FI]
TEL. 0571680212
www.villapillo.com

CELLAR SALES
PRE-BOOKED VISITS
ANNUAL PRODUCTION 350,000 bottles
HECTARES UNDER VINE 40.00

Many historical documents demonstrate
this estate's Medieval origins, as proof that
the land and climate have always been
ideal for farming in general and vines in
particular. In 1989 American couple Kathe
and John Dyson bought the estate and
began a process of modernization,
renovating the buildings and replanting the
vineyards, that involved almost the whole
area under vine. It was a shrewd choice to
grow international grapes known and
enjoyed in California alongside the classic
sangiovese. The Borgoforte 2013,
sangiovese with merlot and cabernet
sauvignon, has nice spicy aromas
alongside ripe wild berries and spices. The
palate opens warm and soft, broad with
lingering flavour. The Vivaldaia 2013, a
monovarietal cabernet franc, has enjoyable
vegetal and balsamic hints, fluent body and
a delicious, lingering flavour.

● Chianti Cl. Gherardino '13	♟♟ 3
● Chianti Cl. Terre di Prenzano '13	♟♟ 3
● Chianti Cl. Castello di Monnalisa Gran Sel. '12	♟ 5
○ Vin Santo del Chianti Cl. '09	♟ 6
● Chianti Cl. Monna Lisa Ris. '99	♟♟♟ 5
● Chianti Cl. Monna Lisa Ris. '95	♟♟♟ 5
● Vignamaggio '06	♟♟♟ 7
● Vignamaggio '05	♟♟♟ 7
● Vignamaggio '04	♟♟♟ 6
● Vignamaggio '01	♟♟♟ 6
● Vignamaggio '00	♟♟♟ 6
● Chianti Cl. Gherardino '10	♟♟ 4
● Chianti Cl. Monna Lisa Ris. '10	♟♟ 5
● Vignamaggio '10	♟♟ 7
● Vignamaggio '08	♟♟ 7
● Vignamaggio '03	♟♟ 6

● Borgoforte '13	♟♟ 3
● Sant'Adele '13	♟♟ 5
○ Sauvignon Blanc '14	♟♟ 2*
● Vivaldaia '13	♟♟ 4
● Castagnino '14	♟ 5
● Syrah '13	♟ 5
● Syrah '97	♟♟♟ 5
● Borgoforte '12	♟♟ 3
● Cypresses '12	♟♟ 3
● Cypresses '11	♟♟ 3
● Cypresses '10	♟♟ 3
● Merlot Sant'Adele '12	♟♟ 5
● Merlot Sant'Adele '11	♟♟ 5
● Syrah '12	♟♟ 5
○ Vin Santo del Chianti '10	♟♟ 5
● Vivaldaia '11	♟♟ 4

Tenuta Vitanza

FRAZ. TORRENIERI
POD. BELVEDERE, 145
52024 MONTALCINO [SI]
TEL. 0577832882
www.tenutavitanza.it

CELLAR SALES
PRE-BOOKED VISITS
ANNUAL PRODUCTION 200,000 bottles
HECTARES UNDER VINE 26.00

Tenuta Vitanza has recently celebrated its first 20 harvests but many think of it as a classic voice in the Brunello world. The estate set up by Rosalba Vitanza and Guido Andretta covers four locations: the first property was bought in 1994, at the Renaione farm, but today most of the vineyards are situated at Belvedere di Torrenieri, in the north-easternmost corner of Montalcino where the winery is also located. The lands at Caselle and San Polino complete the full 25 hectares, used to produce robust, austere Sangioveses which are aged in both small and large oak. A double whammy for Tenuta Vitanza, back in the main section of the Guide and a well-deserved appearance in the finals for the Brunello Tradizione 2010. Wonderful old-style character in the hints of resin and smoky undergrowth, as well as the powerful tannin, juicy and flavoursome. The Rosso 2013 is also firm and fragrant.

Fattoria Viticcio

VIA SAN CRESCI, 12A
50022 GREVE IN CHIANTI [FI]
TEL. 055854210
www.fattoriaviticcio.com

CELLAR SALES
PRE-BOOKED VISITS
ACCOMMODATION
ANNUAL PRODUCTION 250,000 bottles
HECTARES UNDER VINE 36.00
SUSTAINABLE WINERY

Fattoria Viticcio has a long past in the Chianti Classico DOC zone, dating back to 1964 when the first wines were released. The winery style aims for well-structured wines with plenty of texture, supported by a fairly marked presence of oak, judiciously measured thanks to the alternation of small and large oak. The result is a range of wines showing very reliable quality which can stand alongside the best with reassuring continuity. The Chianti Classico Riserva 2012 is definitely pleasing, with lovely fresh aromas and a soft, flavoursome palate. The Vin Santo del Chianti Classico Dolce Arianna 2007 also has lovely aromas, creamy and never cloying. The Chianti Classico Beatrice Gran Selezione 2012 offers mature aromas, slightly held in check by the oak from the ageing vessels, like the Prunaio 2012, a monovarietal sangiovese, and the Monile 2012, from cabernet sauvignon and merlot. The Chianti Classico 2013 has a slightly dark overall feel.

● Brunello di Montalcino Tradizione '10	♥♥ 5
● Rosso di Montalcino '13	♥♥ 3
● Brunello di Montalcino Firma Ris. '09	♥ 6
● Brunello di Montalcino Ris. '09	♥ 6
● Brunello di Montalcino '00	♥♥♥ 6
● Brunello di Montalcino Tradizione '04	♥♥♥ 5
● Brunello di Montalcino '06	♥♥ 6
● Brunello di Montalcino '05	♥♥ 6
● Brunello di Montalcino Andreatta '07	♥♥ 7
● Brunello di Montalcino Firma Ris. '08	♥♥ 6
● Brunello di Montalcino Tradizione '09	♥♥ 5
● Brunello di Montalcino Tradizione '08	♥♥ 5
● Brunello di Montalcino Tradizione '07	♥♥ 6
● Brunello di Montalcino Tradizione '06	♥♥ 5
● Rosso di Montalcino '11	♥♥ 3
● Rosso di Montalcino '08	♥♥ 3

● Chianti Cl. Ris. '12	♥♥ 4
○ Vinsanto del Chianti Cl. Dolce Arianna '07	♥♥ 4
● Chianti Cl. '13	♥ 3
● Chianti Cl. Beatrice Gran Sel. '12	♥ 5
● Monile '12	♥ 6
● Prunaio '12	♥ 6
● Chianti Cl. '11	♥♥ 3*
● Chianti Cl. '10	♥♥ 3*
● Chianti Cl. Beatrice Gran Sel. '11	♥♥ 5
● Chianti Cl. Beatrice Ris. '00	♥♥ 5
● Chianti Cl. Ris. '11	♥♥ 4
● Chianti Cl. Ris. '99	♥♥ 5
● Monile '11	♥♥ 6
● Prunaio '11	♥♥ 6
● Prunaio '01	♥♥ 7

Podere Allocco

LOC. SEANO
VIA CAPEZZANA, 19
59015 CARMIGNANO [PO]
TEL. 0574622462
www.podereallocco.it

CELLAR SALES
PRE-BOOKED VISITS
ANNUAL PRODUCTION 9,000 bottles
HECTARES UNDER VINE 1.50

● Carmignano '12	▼▼ 4
○ Bacano '14	▼ 3
● Barco Reale '13	▼ 3
☉ Rosato di Carmignano Vin Ruspo '14	▼ 2

Altura

LOC. MULINACCIO
58012 GIGLIO
TEL. 0564806041
www.vignetoaltura.it

CELLAR SALES
PRE-BOOKED VISITS
RESTAURANT SERVICE
ANNUAL PRODUCTION 9,000 bottles
HECTARES UNDER VINE 3.50

○ Ansonaco '13	▼▼ 6

Amantis

LOC. COLOMBAIO LE BIBE
58033 CASTEL DEL PIANO [GR]
TEL. 057785440
www.agricolaamantis.com

CELLAR SALES
PRE-BOOKED VISITS
ANNUAL PRODUCTION 40,000 bottles
HECTARES UNDER VINE 5.17
SUSTAINABLE WINERY

● Iperione '10	▼▼ 6
● Montecucco Rosso Birbanera '11	▼▼ 3
● Montecucco Sangiovese Ris. '07	▼▼ 5
● Montecucco Sangiovese '09	▼ 4

Argiano

FRAZ. SANT'ANGELO IN COLLE
53024 MONTALCINO [SI]
TEL. 0577844037
www.argiano.net

PRE-BOOKED VISITS
ACCOMMODATION
ANNUAL PRODUCTION 350,000 bottles
HECTARES UNDER VINE 51.00

● Non Confunditur '13	▼▼ 3
● Brunello di Montalcino '10	▼ 6
● Rosso di Montalcino '13	▼ 3

Arrighi

LOC. PIAN DEL MONTE, 1
57036 PORTO AZZURRO [LI]
TEL. 3356641793
www.arrighivigneolivi.it

CELLAR SALES
PRE-BOOKED VISITS
ANNUAL PRODUCTION 30,000 bottles
HECTARES UNDER VINE 6.00

○ Era Ora '14	▼▼ 4
○ V.I.P '14	▼▼ 4
○ Elba Ansonica Mattanto '14	▼ 3

Artimino

FRAZ. ARTIMINO
V.LE PAPA GIOVANNI XXIII, 1
59015 CARMIGNANO [PO]
TEL. 0558751423
www.artimino.com

CELLAR SALES
PRE-BOOKED VISITS
ACCOMMODATION AND RESTAURANT SERVICE
ANNUAL PRODUCTION 420,000 bottles
HECTARES UNDER VINE 88.00

● Carmignano '11	▼▼ 3
● Carmignano V. Grumarello Ris. '10	▼▼ 4
● Barco Reale '14	▼ 2
● Chianti '13	▼ 2

Assolati

FRAZ. MONTENERO
POD. ASSOLATI, 47
58040 CASTEL DEL PIANO [GR]
TEL. 0564954146
www.assolati.it

CELLAR SALES
PRE-BOOKED VISITS
ACCOMMODATION
ANNUAL PRODUCTION 18,000 bottles
HECTARES UNDER VINE 4.00

● Montecucco Sangiovese Ris. '12	🏆🏆 3
○ Dionysos '14	🏆 2
● Montecucco Rosso '13	🏆 2
● Montecucco Sangiovese '11	🏆 2

Tenuta La Badiola

LOC. BADIOLA
58043 CASTIGLIONE DELLA PESCAIA [GR]
TEL. 0564944919
www.tenutalabadiola.it

CELLAR SALES
ACCOMMODATION AND RESTAURANT SERVICE
ANNUAL PRODUCTION 150,000 bottles
HECTARES UNDER VINE 30.00

● Acquagiusta Rosso '12	🏆🏆 3*
○ Acquadoro '13	🏆 4
⊙ Acquagiusta Rosato '14	🏆 3
○ Acquagiusta Vermentino '14	🏆 3

Pietro Beconcini

FRAZ. LA SCALA
VIA MONTORZO, 13A
56020 SAN MINIATO [PI]
TEL. 0571464570
www.pietrobeconcini.com

CELLAR SALES
PRE-BOOKED VISITS
ANNUAL PRODUCTION 100,000 bottles
HECTARES UNDER VINE 12.00

● Ixe '13	🏆🏆 3
● Maurleo '13	🏆🏆 2*
● Vigna alle Nicchie '11	🏆🏆 6
○ Vin Santo del Chianti Caratello '07	🏆🏆 5

Begnardi

LOC. MONTEANTICO
POD. CAMPOROSSO, 34
58030 CIVITELLA PAGANICO [GR]
TEL. 0564991030
www.begnardi.com

CELLAR SALES
PRE-BOOKED VISITS
ACCOMMODATION AND RESTAURANT SERVICE
ANNUAL PRODUCTION 20,000 bottles
HECTARES UNDER VINE 5.00

● Montecucco Sangiovese Ceneo '13	🏆🏆 3
● Montecucco Rosso '13	🏆 3

Cantine Bellini

VIA PIAVE, 1
50068 RUFINA [FI]
TEL. 0558396025
www.bellinicantine.it

CELLAR SALES
ANNUAL PRODUCTION 900,000 bottles
HECTARES UNDER VINE 15.00

● Chianti Rufina Ris. '12	🏆🏆 2*
● Chianti '14	🏆 1*
● Comedia '11	🏆 2
● Le Lodole '11	🏆 2

Belpoggio - Bellussi

FRAZ. CASTELNUOVO DELL'ABATE
LOC. BELLARIA
53024 MONTALCINO [SI]
TEL. 0423982147
www.belpoggio.it

PRE-BOOKED VISITS
ANNUAL PRODUCTION 25,000 bottles
HECTARES UNDER VINE 5.00

● Brunello di Montalcino '10	🏆🏆 6
● Rosso di Montalcino '13	🏆 4

Le Bertille

VIA DELLE COLOMBELLE, 7
53045 MONTEPULCIANO [SI]
TEL. 0578758330
www.lebertille.com

CELLAR SALES
PRE-BOOKED VISITS
ANNUAL PRODUCTION 65,000 bottles
HECTARES UNDER VINE 14.00
SUSTAINABLE WINERY

● Nobile di Montepulciano '11		♟♟ 3*

La Biagiola

LOC. PIANETTI C.S. CASALE
58010 SOVANA [GR]
TEL. 0564614032
www.labiagiola.it

PRE-BOOKED VISITS
ANNUAL PRODUCTION 60,000 bottles
HECTARES UNDER VINE 8.50

● Maremma Toscana Alideo '12		♟♟ 3
○ Maremma Toscana Matan '14		♟ 3
● Maremma Toscana Tesan '13		♟ 3

Ca' del Vispo

VIA DI FUGNANO, 31
53037 SAN GIMIGNANO [SI]
TEL. 0577943053
www.cadelvispo.it

CELLAR SALES
PRE-BOOKED VISITS
ANNUAL PRODUCTION 60,000 bottles
HECTARES UNDER VINE 7.00

○ Segumo '13		♟♟ 3
⊙ Ra Fa Tù '14		♟ 3
○ Vernaccia di S. Gimignano '14		♟ 2
○ Vernaccia di S. Gimignano V. in Fiore '14		♟ 3

Tenuta Campo al Mare

FRAZ. VALLONE DEI MESSI
VIA BOLGHERESE
57024 CASTAGNETO CARDUCCI [LI]
TEL. 055859811
www.tenutefolonari.com

PRE-BOOKED VISITS
ANNUAL PRODUCTION 100,000 bottles
HECTARES UNDER VINE 30.00

● Bolgheri Rosso '13		♟♟ 4

Campo alla Sughera

LOC. CACCIA AL PIANO, 280
57020 BOLGHERI [LI]
TEL. 0565766936
www.campoallasughera.com

CELLAR SALES
PRE-BOOKED VISITS
ANNUAL PRODUCTION 110,000 bottles
HECTARES UNDER VINE 16.50

○ Bolgheri Bianco Achenio '14		♟♟ 5
● Bolgheri Sup. Arnione '12		♟♟ 6
● Bolgheri Adeo '13		♟ 4

Candialle

VIA CHIANTIGIANA, KM 34, IV
50020 PANZANO [FI]
TEL. 055852201
www.candialle.com

CELLAR SALES
PRE-BOOKED VISITS
ANNUAL PRODUCTION 35,000 bottles
HECTARES UNDER VINE 11.30
SUSTAINABLE WINERY

● Chianti Cl. '12		♟♟ 4
● Chianti Cl. La Misse di Candialle '13		♟ 3

Canneta

LOC. SANTA LUCIA, 27
53037 SAN GIMIGNANO [SI]
TEL. 0577941540
www.poderecanneta.it

CELLAR SALES
PRE-BOOKED VISITS
ANNUAL PRODUCTION 36,000 bottles
HECTARES UNDER VINE 5.50
VITICULTURE METHOD Certified Organic

○ Vernaccia di S. Gimignano
   La Luna e le Torri '13   ♛♛ 2*
● Merlot di Canneta '13   ♛ 2
○ Vernaccia di S. Gimignano '14   ♛ 2

Canneto

VIA DEI CANNETI, 14
53045 MONTEPULCIANO [SI]
TEL. 0578757737
www.canneto.com

CELLAR SALES
PRE-BOOKED VISITS
ACCOMMODATION
ANNUAL PRODUCTION 100,000 bottles
HECTARES UNDER VINE 30.00
VITICULTURE METHOD Certified Organic

● Nobile di Montepulciano Ris. '11   ♛♛ 5
○ Calamus '14   ♛ 2
● Filippone '11   ♛ 6
● Nobile di Montepulciano '12   ♛ 3

Fattoria il Capitano

VIA SAN MARTINO A QUONA, 2B
50065 PONTASSIEVE [FI]
TEL. 0558315600
www.fattoriailcapitano.com

ANNUAL PRODUCTION 10,000 bottles
HECTARES UNDER VINE 10.00

○ Vin Santo del Chianti '07   ♛♛ 3*
● Chianti Rufina Ris. '11   ♛ 2
○ Fanticchio '14   ♛ 1*
● Il Poggio '13   ♛ 2

Cappella Sant'Andrea

LOC. CASALE, 26
53037 SAN GIMIGNANO [SI]
TEL. 0577940456
www.cappellasantandrea.it

CELLAR SALES
PRE-BOOKED VISITS
RESTAURANT SERVICE
ANNUAL PRODUCTION 45,000 bottles
HECTARES UNDER VINE 9.00
VITICULTURE METHOD Certified Organic
SUSTAINABLE WINERY

○ Vernaccia di S. Gimignano Rialto '13   ♛♛ 3
● Tinano '13   ♛ 2
○ Vernaccia di S. Gimignano '14   ♛ 2

Capua Winery

FRAZ. SATURNIA
LOC. PIAN D'ARTINO 21
58014 MANCIANO [GR]
TEL. 3287456174
www.capuawinery.com

CELLAR SALES
PRE-BOOKED VISITS
ANNUAL PRODUCTION 18,000 bottles
HECTARES UNDER VINE 6.00

○ DolceAmore '14   ♛♛ 4
● Fiammante '13   ♛♛ 4
● MioSogno '13   ♛ 5
● TuttoCuore '13   ♛ 4

Podere Il Carnasciale

POD. IL CARNASCIALE
52020 MERCATALE VALDARNO [AR]
TEL. 0559911142
www.caberlot.eu

PRE-BOOKED VISITS
ANNUAL PRODUCTION 10,000 bottles
HECTARES UNDER VINE 4.50

● Caberlot '12   ♛♛ 8

Fattoria Casa di Terra

FRAZ. BOLGHERI
LOC. LE FERRUGGINI, 162A
57022 CASTAGNETO CARDUCCI [LI]
TEL. 0565749810
www.fattoriacasaditerra.com

CELLAR SALES
PRE-BOOKED VISITS
ACCOMMODATION
ANNUAL PRODUCTION 180,000 bottles
HECTARES UNDER VINE 44.50

● Bolgheri Mosaico '12	♥♥ 5
○ Bolgheri Vermentino '14	♥♥ 3
● Bolgheri Moreccio '13	♥ 3
● Poggio Querciolo '12	♥ 5

Casa Sola

S.DA DI CORTINE, 5
50021 BARBERINO VAL D'ELSA [FI]
TEL. 0558075028
www.fattoriacasasola.it

CELLAR SALES
PRE-BOOKED VISITS
ACCOMMODATION
ANNUAL PRODUCTION 100,000 bottles
HECTARES UNDER VINE 26.00

● Chianti Cl. Gran Sel. '11	♥♥ 7
● Chianti Cl. '13	♥ 4

Casavyc

POD. CAMPOROMANO, 43
58054 SCANSANO [GR]
TEL. 3356880673
www.casavyc.it

CELLAR SALES
PRE-BOOKED VISITS
ANNUAL PRODUCTION 40,000 bottles
HECTARES UNDER VINE 14.00

● Morellino di Scansano 070707 Ris. '12	♥♥ 6
● Up&Down '10	♥♥ 3
○ Piano Piano Poco Poco '14	♥ 6
● Temerario '12	♥ 6

Castelsina

FRAZ. SINALUNGA
LOC. OSTERIA 54A
53011 SINALUNGA [SI]
TEL. 0577663595
www.castelsina.it

CELLAR SALES
PRE-BOOKED VISITS
ANNUAL PRODUCTION 2,000,000 bottles
HECTARES UNDER VINE 400.00

● Chianti '14	♥♥ 2*
● Chianti Ris. '10	♥♥ 2*
● Orcia '14	♥♥ 3
● Sangiovese '14	♥ 2

Castelvecchio

LOC. SEANO
VIA DELLE MANNELLE, 19
59011 CARMIGNANO [PO]
TEL. 0558705451
www.castelvecchio.net

CELLAR SALES
PRE-BOOKED VISITS
ANNUAL PRODUCTION 40,000 bottles
HECTARES UNDER VINE 10.00

● Carmignano '11	♥♥ 3
○ Vin Santo di Carmignano '11	♥♥ 4
● Barco Reale '13	♥ 2
⊙ Carmignano Rosato Vin Ruspo '14	♥ 2

Castiglion del Bosco

LOC. CASTIGLION DEL BOSCO
53024 MONTALCINO [SI]
TEL. 05771913750
www.castigliondelbosco.com

CELLAR SALES
PRE-BOOKED VISITS
ACCOMMODATION AND RESTAURANT SERVICE
ANNUAL PRODUCTION 20,000 bottles
HECTARES UNDER VINE 67.00

● Brunello di Montalcino Campo del Drago '10	♥♥ 8
● Brunello di Montalcino '10	♥ 6
● Rosso di Montalcino '13	♥ 3

Simona Ceccherini

LOC. POGGIO CURZIO
58024 MASSA MARITTIMA [GR]
TEL. 0566904230
www.simonaceccherini.it

CELLAR SALES
PRE-BOOKED VISITS
ACCOMMODATION AND RESTAURANT SERVICE
ANNUAL PRODUCTION 15,000 bottles
HECTARES UNDER VINE 5.00
VITICULTURE METHOD Certified Organic

● Fontefossoli '13	♟♟ 2*
● Confiente '12	♟ 4
● Maremma Toscana Ciliegiolo Poggio Curzio '12	♟ 4

Celler del Gat

VIA VALMARINA, 24
58011 CAPALBIO [GR]
TEL. 3477589508
www.cellerdelgat.com

CELLAR SALES
ANNUAL PRODUCTION 3,500 bottles
HECTARES UNDER VINE 1.50
SUSTAINABLE WINERY

● Malakai '13	♟♟ 3
● Cinquevite '12	♟ 4

Il Cerchio

VIA VALAMRINA, 24
58011 CAPALBIO [GR]
TEL. 0564898856
www.ilcerchiobio.it

CELLAR SALES
PRE-BOOKED VISITS
HECTARES UNDER VINE 5.00
VITICULTURE METHOD Certified Organic
SUSTAINABLE WINERY

○ Ansonica Passito l'Altro '13	♟♟ 3
● Maremma Toscana Alicante Tinto '12	♟♟ 4
○ Ansonica Costa dell'Argentario '14	♟ 2
○ Maremma Toscana l'Altro Bianco '14	♟ 5

Il Civettaio

LOC. CIVETTAIO
58048 CIVITELLA PAGANICO [GR]
TEL. 3487029229
www.civettaio.it

CELLAR SALES
PRE-BOOKED VISITS
ACCOMMODATION AND RESTAURANT SERVICE
ANNUAL PRODUCTION 30,000 bottles
HECTARES UNDER VINE 7.50
VITICULTURE METHOD Certified Organic
SUSTAINABLE WINERY

● Montecucco Poggio al Commessario '12	♟♟ 2*
⊙ Montecucco Rosato Chiù '14	♟ 2
○ Montecucco Vermentino '14	♟ 2

Podere della Civettaja

VIA DI CASINA ROSSA, 5A
52100 AREZZO
TEL. 3397098418

CELLAR SALES
PRE-BOOKED VISITS
ANNUAL PRODUCTION 7,000 bottles
HECTARES UNDER VINE 3.00
VITICULTURE METHOD Certified Organic

● Pinot Nero '12	♟♟ 3

Collemattoni

LOC. SANT'ANGELO IN COLLE
POD. COLLEMATTONI, 100
53020 MONTALCINO [SI]
TEL. 0577844127
www.collemattoni.it

CELLAR SALES
PRE-BOOKED VISITS
ANNUAL PRODUCTION 35,000 bottles
HECTARES UNDER VINE 6.70

● Rosso di Montalcino '13	♟♟ 3*
● Brunello di Montalcino '10	♟♟ 6

Colline San Biagio

LOC. BACCHERETO
VIA SAN BIAGIO 6/8
59015 CARMIGNANO [PO]
TEL. 0558717143
www.collinesanbiagio.it

CELLAR SALES
PRE-BOOKED VISITS
ACCOMMODATION
ANNUAL PRODUCTION 35,000 bottles
HECTARES UNDER VINE 7.00
SUSTAINABLE WINERY

● Donna Mingarda '10	♟♟ 4
● Carmignano Sancti Blasii '09	♟♟ 4

Tenuta di Collosorbo

FRAZ. CASTELNUOVO DELL'ABATE
LOC. VILLA A SESTA, 25
53024 MONTALCINO [SI]
TEL. 0577835534
www.collosorbo.com

CELLAR SALES
PRE-BOOKED VISITS
ANNUAL PRODUCTION 100,000 bottles
HECTARES UNDER VINE 27.00

● Brunello di Montalcino '10	♟♟ 6
● Rosso di Montalcino '13	♟ 4

Podere Concori

LOC. FIATTONE
VIA PROVINCIALE, 1
55027 GALLICANO [LU]
TEL. 0583766039
www.podereconcori.com

CELLAR SALES
PRE-BOOKED VISITS
ANNUAL PRODUCTION 1,000 bottles
HECTARES UNDER VINE 4.00

● Pinot Nero '13	♟♟ 4
● Melograno Rosso '13	♟ 4

Corbucci

VIA SANT'ANDREA A GAVIGNALLA, 25A
50050 GAMBASSI TERME [FI]
TEL. 0571638201
www.corbuccichianti.com

ANNUAL PRODUCTION 40,000 bottles
HECTARES UNDER VINE 22.00

● 17Rè '12	♟♟ 6
● Corba Nero '12	♟♟ 6
● Chianti Ris. '12	♟ 5

Tenuta Il Corno

FRAZ. SAN PANCRAZIO
VIA MALAFRASCA, 64
50026 SAN CASCIANO IN VAL DI PESA [FI]
TEL. 0558248009
www.tenutailcorno.com

CELLAR SALES
PRE-BOOKED VISITS
ANNUAL PRODUCTION 200,000 bottles
HECTARES UNDER VINE 67.00

● Chianti Colli Fiorentini Foss'a Spina '12	♟♟ 2*
● Chianti Colli Fiorentini San Camillo Ris. '12	♟♟ 2*
○ Albios '14	♟ 2
● Chianti '13	♟ 3

La Corsa

S.DA VIVINALE DEL PRATACCIONE, 19
58015 ORBETELLO [GR]
TEL. 0564880007
www.lacorsawine.it

CELLAR SALES
PRE-BOOKED VISITS
ANNUAL PRODUCTION 25,000 bottles
HECTARES UNDER VINE 14.00

○ Dueluglio '14	♟♟ 3
● Petit Verdot '14	♟♟ 4
● Aghiloro '14	♟ 3
⊙ Macchiatonda '14	♟ 3

Corte alla Flora

FRAZ. ACQUAVIVA
VIA DI CERVOGNANO, 23
53040 MONTEPULCIANO [SI]
TEL. 0578766003
www.corteallaflora.it

PRE-BOOKED VISITS
ANNUAL PRODUCTION 200,000 bottles
HECTARES UNDER VINE 35.00

● Nobile di Montepulciano '12	▼▼ 3
● Rosso di Montepulciano '14	▼ 2

Croce di Febo

LOC. SANT'ALBINO
VIA DI FONTELLERA, 19A
53045 MONTEPULCIANO [SI]
TEL. 0578799337
www.crocedifebo.com

CELLAR SALES
PRE-BOOKED VISITS
ACCOMMODATION
ANNUAL PRODUCTION 15,000 bottles
HECTARES UNDER VINE 9.19
VITICULTURE METHOD Certified Organic

● Nobile di Montepulciano Amore Mio Ris. '11	▼▼ 6
● Nobile di Montepulciano '12	▼ 4

Ivana Cupelli

V.LE MARCONI, 203
56028 SAN MINIATO [PI]
TEL. 0571400413
www.cupellivini.com

CELLAR SALES
PRE-BOOKED VISITS
RESTAURANT SERVICE
ANNUAL PRODUCTION 39,000 bottles
HECTARES UNDER VINE 7.50

○ L'Erede	▼▼ 4
○ L'Erede Limited Edition '10	▼▼ 4

Casale Daviddi

VIA NOTTOLA, 9
53045 MONTEPULCIANO [SI]
TEL. 0578738257
www.casaledaviddi.it

ANNUAL PRODUCTION 100,000 bottles
HECTARES UNDER VINE 20.00

● Nobile di Montepulciano '12	▼▼ 4
● Rosso di Montepulciano '13	▼ 2

Fattoria Dianella

VIA DIANELLA, 48
50059 VINCI [FI]
TEL. 0571508166
www.fattoriadianella.it

CELLAR SALES
PRE-BOOKED VISITS
ACCOMMODATION
ANNUAL PRODUCTION 70,000 bottles
HECTARES UNDER VINE 25.00
SUSTAINABLE WINERY

○ Dolci Ricordi '09	▼▼ 5
● Il Matto delle Giuncaie '13	▼▼ 2*
● Chianti '14	▼ 2
● Le Veglie di Neri '13	▼ 3

Dievole

FRAZ. VAGLIAGLI
VIA DIEVOLE, 6
53010 CASTELNUOVO BERARDENGA [SI]
TEL. 0577322613
www.dievole.it

CELLAR SALES
PRE-BOOKED VISITS
ACCOMMODATION AND RESTAURANT SERVICE
ANNUAL PRODUCTION 350,000 bottles
HECTARES UNDER VINE 80.00

● Chianti Cl. '13	▼▼ 4

Donne Fittipaldi

LOC. BOLGHERI
VIA BOLGHERESE, 198
57022 CASTAGNETO CARDUCCI [LI]
TEL. 0565762175
www.donnefittipaldi.it

ANNUAL PRODUCTION 60,000 bottles
HECTARES UNDER VINE 9.50

● Malaroja '12	♥♥ 8
● Bolgheri Rosso '13	♥ 4
● Bolgheri Rosso Superiore '12	♥ 6
○ Sauvignon Bianco '14	♥ 4

Fattoria Fibbiano

FRAZ. TERRICCIOLA
VIA VIA FIBBIANO
56030 TERRICCIOLA [PI]
TEL. 0587635677
www.fattoria-fibbiano.it

CELLAR SALES
PRE-BOOKED VISITS
ACCOMMODATION AND RESTAURANT SERVICE
ANNUAL PRODUCTION 129,000 bottles
HECTARES UNDER VINE 16.00

○ Fonte delle Donne '14	♥♥ 2*
● Ceppatella '11	♥ 6
● L'Aspetto '12	♥ 5
● Le Pianette '13	♥ 2

La Fornace

POD. FORNACE, 154A
53024 MONTALCINO [SI]
TEL. 0577848465
www.agricola-lafornace.it

CELLAR SALES
PRE-BOOKED VISITS
ANNUAL PRODUCTION 15,000 bottles
HECTARES UNDER VINE 4.50

● Brunello di Montalcino '10	♥♥ 6
● Rosso di Montalcino '13	♥ 3

Fattoria di Fubbiano

LOC. SAN GENNARO
VIA DI TOFORI FUBBIANO
55010 CAPANNORI [LU]
TEL. 0583978011
www.fattoriadifubbiano.it

CELLAR SALES
PRE-BOOKED VISITS
ACCOMMODATION
ANNUAL PRODUCTION 100,000 bottles
HECTARES UNDER VINE 20.00

○ Colline Lucchesi Bianco '14	♥♥ 2*
● Colline Lucchesi Rosso '13	♥ 2
○ Colline Lucchesi Vermentino '14	♥ 2
● Schiller '14	♥ 3

La Gerla

LOC. CANALICCHIO
POD. COLOMBAIO, 5
53024 MONTALCINO [SI]
TEL. 0577848599
www.lagerla.it

CELLAR SALES
PRE-BOOKED VISITS
ANNUAL PRODUCTION 80,000 bottles
HECTARES UNDER VINE 11.50

● Brunello di Montalcino '10	♥♥ 5
● Rosso di Montalcino '13	♥♥ 3

Giannoni Fabbri

LOC. SAN MARCO IN VILLA, 2
52044 CORTONA [AR]
TEL. 3475883939
www.giannonifabbri.it

CELLAR SALES
PRE-BOOKED VISITS
ANNUAL PRODUCTION 10,000 bottles
HECTARES UNDER VINE 14.00

● Cortona Syrah Amato '12	♥♥ 3
○ Cortona Vin Santo '06	♥♥ 6

Giomi Zannoni

VIA AURELIA NORD, 63
57029 CAMPIGLIA MARITTIMA [LI]
TEL. 0565846416
www.giomi-zannoni.com

ANNUAL PRODUCTION 18,000 bottles
HECTARES UNDER VINE 7.00

○ Val di Cornia Bianco Corniola '14	♟♟	3
○ Vermentino Ninà 910 '14	♟♟	3
● Cabernet Sauvignon Aldò 917 '13	♟	5
● Val di Cornia Sangiovese Rodantonio '12	♟	5

Guidi 1929

VIA LIGURIA
53036 POGGIBONSI [SI]
TEL. 0577936356
www.guidisrl1929.com

CELLAR SALES
PRE-BOOKED VISITS
ANNUAL PRODUCTION 100,000 bottles
HECTARES UNDER VINE 14.00
SUSTAINABLE WINERY

○ Vernaccia di San Gimignano '14	♟♟	2*
● Chianti '14	♟	2
○ Prima Luce Chardonnay '14	♟	2
○ Vernaccia di San Gimignano Aurea Ris. '12	♟	2

Icario

VIA DELLE PIETROSE, 2
53045 MONTEPULCIANO [SI]
TEL. 0578758845
www.icario.it

CELLAR SALES
PRE-BOOKED VISITS
ANNUAL PRODUCTION 110,000 bottles
HECTARES UNDER VINE 20.00

● Nobile di Montepulciano '12	♟♟	4
● Nobile di Montepulciano Vitaroccia Ris. '10	♟	5
● Rosso di Montepulciano '14	♟	2

Fattoria Kappa

LOC. LE BADIE
VIA ROMA, 118
56040 CASTELLINA MARITTIMA [PI]
TEL. 3346619711
a.dimaio74@virgilio.it

CELLAR SALES
PRE-BOOKED VISITS
ANNUAL PRODUCTION 20,000 bottles
HECTARES UNDER VINE 6.00

● Kappa '13	♟♟	5
● Lambda '13	♟♟	3
● Syrah '12	♟♟	5

Tenuta Lenzini

FRAZ. GRAGNANO
VIA DELLA CHIESA, 44
55012 CAPANNORI [LU]
TEL. 0583974037
www.tenutalenzini.it

CELLAR SALES
PRE-BOOKED VISITS
ACCOMMODATION
ANNUAL PRODUCTION 60,000 bottles
HECTARES UNDER VINE 14.00
VITICULTURE METHOD Certified Organic

● Syrah '12	♟♟	5
○ Vermignon '14	♟♟	3
● Colline Lucchesi Casa e Chiesa '13	♟	2

Luiano

LOC. MERCATALE VAL DI PESA
VIA DI LUIANO, 32
50024 SAN CASCIANO IN VAL DI PESA [FI]
TEL. 055821039
www.luiano.it

CELLAR SALES
PRE-BOOKED VISITS
ACCOMMODATION
ANNUAL PRODUCTION 160,000 bottles
HECTARES UNDER VINE 20.00

● Chianti Cl. Ottantuno Gran Sel. '12	♟♟	6
● Chianti Cl. '13	♟	3
● Chianti Cl. Ris. '12	♟	5
● Lui '12	♟	6

La Magia

LOC. LA MAGIA
53024 MONTALCINO [SI]
TEL. 0577835667
fattorialamagia@tiscali.it

ANNUAL PRODUCTION 80,000 bottles
HECTARES UNDER VINE 15.00

● Brunello di Montalcino '10		♟♟ 5

Malenchini

LOC. GRASSINA
VIA LILLIANO E MEOLI, 82
50015 BAGNO A RIPOLI [FI]
TEL. 055642602
www.malenchini.it

CELLAR SALES
PRE-BOOKED VISITS
ANNUAL PRODUCTION 120,000 bottles
HECTARES UNDER VINE 17.00

● Chianti Colli Fiorentini '13		♟♟ 2*
○ Vin Santo Colli Fiorentini '10		♟♟ 4
● Bruzzico '12		♟ 4

Maté

LOC. SANTA RESTITUTA
53024 MONTALCINO [SI]
TEL. 0577847215
www.matewine.com

CELLAR SALES
ANNUAL PRODUCTION 28,000 bottles
HECTARES UNDER VINE 7.00

● Brunello di Montalcino '10		♟♟ 6

Le Miccine

LOC. LE MICCINE
S.S. TRAVERSA CHIANTIGIANA, 44
53013 GAIOLE IN CHIANTI [SI]
TEL. 0577749526
www.lemiccine.com

CELLAR SALES
PRE-BOOKED VISITS
ACCOMMODATION
ANNUAL PRODUCTION 30,000 bottles
HECTARES UNDER VINE 7.00
VITICULTURE METHOD Certified Organic

● Chianti Cl. Ris. '12		♟♟ 5
● Chianti Cl. '13		♟ 2

Mola

LOC. GELSARELLO, 2
57031 PORTO AZZURRO [LI]
TEL. 0565958151
www.tenutepavoletti.it

CELLAR SALES
PRE-BOOKED VISITS
ANNUAL PRODUCTION 47,000 bottles
HECTARES UNDER VINE 12.00

● Elba Aleatico Passito '11		♟♟ 4
○ Cuvée Brut A '13		♟ 3
○ Elba Vermentino '14		♟ 2

Podere Monastero

LOC. MONASTERO
53011 CASTELLINA IN CHIANTI [SI]
TEL. 0577740436
www.poderemonastero.com

CELLAR SALES
PRE-BOOKED VISITS
ACCOMMODATION
ANNUAL PRODUCTION 7,000 bottles
HECTARES UNDER VINE 3.00

● Campanaio '13		♟♟ 6
● La Pineta '13		♟♟ 6

Montemercurio

VIA DI TOTONA, 25A
53045 MONTEPULCIANO [SI]
TEL. 0578716610
www.montemercurio.com

CELLAR SALES
PRE-BOOKED VISITS
ANNUAL PRODUCTION 40,000 bottles
HECTARES UNDER VINE 10.00

● Nobile di Montepulciano Messaggero '10		🏆🏆 4

Montepepe

VIA SFORZA, 76
54038 MONTIGNOSO [MS]
TEL. 0585831042
www.montepepe.com

CELLAR SALES
PRE-BOOKED VISITS
ANNUAL PRODUCTION 20,000 bottles
HECTARES UNDER VINE 5.40

○ Degeres '12		🏆🏆 6
○ Montepepe Bianco '13		🏆🏆 4
○ Montepepe Bianco Vintage '10		🏆🏆 5
● Montepepe Rosso '12		🏆 5

La Mormoraia

LOC. SANT'ANDREA, 15
53037 SAN GIMIGNANO [SI]
TEL. 0577940096
www.mormoraia.it

CELLAR SALES
PRE-BOOKED VISITS
ACCOMMODATION
ANNUAL PRODUCTION 230,000 bottles
HECTARES UNDER VINE 40.00

○ Vernaccia di S. Gimignano '14		🏆🏆 2*
● Chianti Colli Senesi '13		🏆 2

Mulini di Segalari

LOC. FELCIAINO, 115A
57022 CASTAGNETO CARDUCCI [LI]
TEL. 0565765202
www.mulinidisegalari.it

ANNUAL PRODUCTION 10,000 bottles
HECTARES UNDER VINE 2.50
VITICULTURE METHOD Certified Organic
SUSTAINABLE WINERY

● Bolgheri Rosso Ai Confini del Bosco '12		🏆🏆 4
● Soloterra '13		🏆 4

Muralia

VIA DEL SUGHERETO
58036 ROCCASTRADA [GR]
TEL. 0564577223
www.muralia.it

CELLAR SALES
PRE-BOOKED VISITS
ACCOMMODATION AND RESTAURANT SERVICE
ANNUAL PRODUCTION 65,000 bottles
HECTARES UNDER VINE 14.00
SUSTAINABLE WINERY

● Manolibera '13		🏆🏆 2*
● Babione '11		🏆 2
● Monteregio di Massa Marittima Altana '12		🏆 2
● Muralia '12		🏆 4

Pakravan-Papi

LOC. ORTACAVOLI NUOVA
VIA DEL COMMERCIO
56046 RIPARBELLA [PI]
TEL. 0586786076
www.pakravan-papi.it

CELLAR SALES
PRE-BOOKED VISITS
ANNUAL PRODUCTION 40,000 bottles
HECTARES UNDER VINE 15.00

● Campo del Pari '13		🏆🏆 6
● Cancellaia '13		🏆🏆 5
○ Serra dei Cocci '14		🏆🏆 3
○ Valdimare Bianco '14		🏆🏆 3

Fattoria Il Palagio

FRAZ. CASTEL SAN GIMIGNANO
LOC. IL PALAGIO
53030 COLLE DI VAL D'ELSA [SI]
TEL. 0577953004
www.ilpalagio.it

CELLAR SALES
PRE-BOOKED VISITS
ANNUAL PRODUCTION 800,000 bottles
HECTARES UNDER VINE 79.00

○ Melaia '13	♥♥ 3
● Chianti Cellini '13	♥ 3
● L'Eremo '13	♥ 3
○ Vermentino '14	♥ 3

La Palazzetta

FRAZ. CASTELNUOVO DELL'ABATE
VIA BORGO DI SOTTO, 40
53024 MONTALCINO [SI]
TEL. 0577835531
palazzettafanti@gmail.com

CELLAR SALES
PRE-BOOKED VISITS
ACCOMMODATION
ANNUAL PRODUCTION 70,000 bottles
HECTARES UNDER VINE 20.00

● Brunello di Montalcino '10	♥♥ 5
● Rosso di Montalcino '13	♥ 3

Palazzo

LOC. PALAZZO, 144
53024 MONTALCINO [SI]
TEL. 0577849226
www.aziendapalazzo.it

CELLAR SALES
PRE-BOOKED VISITS
ANNUAL PRODUCTION 20,000 bottles
HECTARES UNDER VINE 4.00
VITICULTURE METHOD Certified Biodynamic

● Brunello di Montalcino '10	♥♥ 6
● Brunello di Montalcino Ris. '09	♥ 7
● Rosso di Montalcino '13	♥ 3

Palazzo Vecchio

FRAZ. VALIANO
VIA TERRAROSSA, 5
53040 MONTEPULCIANO [SI]
TEL. 0578724170
www.vinonobile.it

CELLAR SALES
PRE-BOOKED VISITS
RESTAURANT SERVICE
ANNUAL PRODUCTION 45,000 bottles
HECTARES UNDER VINE 25.00

● Nobile di Montepulciano Maestro '12	♥♥ 4
○ Vin Santo di Montepulciano '07	♥♥ 7

Fattoria Pancole

LOC. PANCOLE
53037 SAN GIMIGNANO [SI]
TEL. 0577955078
www.fattoriadipancole.it

CELLAR SALES
PRE-BOOKED VISITS
ANNUAL PRODUCTION 150,000 bottles
HECTARES UNDER VINE 17.00
VITICULTURE METHOD Certified Organic

● Baracca 1903 '11	♥♥ 3
● Chianti dei Colli Senesi '14	♥ 2
● Dogato '11	♥ 4
○ Vernaccia di S. Gimignano '14	♥ 2

Il Paradiso di Manfredi

VIA CANALICCHIO, 305
53024 MONTALCINO [SI]
TEL. 0577848478
www.ilparadisodimanfredi.com

HECTARES UNDER VINE

● Brunello di Montalcino '10	♥♥ 5

Parmoleto

LOC. MONTENERO D'ORCIA
POD. PARMOLETONE, 44
58040 CASTEL DEL PIANO [GR]
TEL. 0564954131
www.parmoleto.it

CELLAR SALES
PRE-BOOKED VISITS
ACCOMMODATION AND RESTAURANT SERVICE
ANNUAL PRODUCTION 23,000 bottles
HECTARES UNDER VINE 6.00

● Montecucco Sangiovese '11	♛♛	3
● Montecucco Sangiovese Ris. '10	♛♛	3
○ Inciucio	♛	2
● Montecucco Rosso '11	♛	2

Perazzeta

LOC. MONTENERO D'ORCIA
VIA DELL'AIA, 14
58040 CASTEL DEL PIANO [GR]
TEL. 0564954158
www.perazzeta.it

CELLAR SALES
PRE-BOOKED VISITS
ANNUAL PRODUCTION 40,000 bottles
HECTARES UNDER VINE 7.50

● Montecucco Sangiovese Licurgo Ris. '11	♛♛	4
● Maremma Terre dei Bocci '12	♛	3
● Montecucco Rosso Alfeno '13	♛	2

Peteglia

POD. PETEGLIA
58033 CASTEL DEL PIANO [GR]
TEL. 0564954108
www.peteglia.com

CELLAR SALES
PRE-BOOKED VISITS
ACCOMMODATION AND RESTAURANT SERVICE
ANNUAL PRODUCTION 25,000 bottles
HECTARES UNDER VINE 6.00

● Montecucco Sangiovese Ris. '10	♛♛	4
● Montecucco Sangiovese '11	♛	3
○ Montecucco Vermentino '14	♛	2

Petricci e Del Pianta

LOC. SAN LORENZO, 20
57028 SUVERETO [LI]
TEL. 0565845140
www.petriccidelpianta.it

CELLAR SALES
PRE-BOOKED VISITS
ANNUAL PRODUCTION 40,000 bottles
HECTARES UNDER VINE 11.00

● Cerosecco '12	♛♛	3
○ Val di Cornia Aleatico Passito Stillo '13	♛♛	5
○ Fabula '14	♛	2
○ Liseo	♛	3

Piandibugnano

LOC. PIAN DI BUGNANO
58038 SEGGIANO [GR]
TEL. 0564950773
www.piandibugnano.com

CELLAR SALES
PRE-BOOKED VISITS
ANNUAL PRODUCTION 27,800 bottles
HECTARES UNDER VINE 3.80

● Nanerone '13	♛♛	4
● Montecucco Cuccaia '12	♛	3
● Montecucco Cuccallegro '14	♛	2
● Montecucco Sangiovese L'Erpico '12	♛	5

Agostina Pieri

FRAZ. SANT'ANGELO SCALO
LOC. PIANCORNELLO
53026 MONTALCINO [SI]
TEL. 0577844163
www.pieriagostina.it

ANNUAL PRODUCTION 45,000 bottles
HECTARES UNDER VINE 10.78

● Brunello di Montalcino '10	♛♛	6
● Rosso di Montalcino '13	♛	3

Pieve de' Pitti

LOC. PIEVE DE' PITTI, 7BIS
56030 TERRICCIOLA [PI]
TEL. 0587635724
www.pievedepitti.it

CELLAR SALES
PRE-BOOKED VISITS
ANNUAL PRODUCTION 50,000 bottles
HECTARES UNDER VINE 32.00

○ Aprilante '14	🍷🍷 2*
● Scopaiolo '11	🍷🍷 3
● Chianti Sup. Cerretello '11	🍷 2
● Moro di Pava '08	🍷 4

Pieve Santo Stefano

LOC. SARDINI
55060 LUCCA
TEL. 0583394115
www.pievedisantostefano.com

CELLAR SALES
PRE-BOOKED VISITS
ACCOMMODATION
ANNUAL PRODUCTION 45,000 bottles
HECTARES UNDER VINE 10.68
SUSTAINABLE WINERY

● Ludovico Sardini '12	🍷🍷 3
● Colline Lucchesi Villa Sardini '14	🍷 2

Pinino

LOC. PININO, 327
53024 MONTALCINO [SI]
TEL. 0577849381
www.pinino.com

CELLAR SALES
PRE-BOOKED VISITS
ANNUAL PRODUCTION 90,000 bottles
HECTARES UNDER VINE 16.00

● Brunello di Montalcino '10	🍷🍷 6
● Rosso di Montalcino '13	🍷 3

Poggio al Sole

LOC. BADIA A PASSIGNANO
S.DA RIGNANA, 2
50028 TAVARNELLE VAL DI PESA [FI]
TEL. 0558071850
www.poggioalsole.com

CELLAR SALES
PRE-BOOKED VISITS
ACCOMMODATION
ANNUAL PRODUCTION 100,000 bottles
HECTARES UNDER VINE 22.00
SUSTAINABLE WINERY

● Chianti Cl. '12	🍷🍷 3
● Chianti Cl. Casasilia Gran Sel. '12	🍷 6

Poggio al Tufo

LOC. POGGIO CAVALLUCCIO
58017 PITIGLIANO [GR]
TEL. 0457701266
www.tommasiwine.it

CELLAR SALES
ANNUAL PRODUCTION 165,000 bottles
HECTARES UNDER VINE 66.00

○ Vermentino '14	🍷🍷 3
● Alicante '12	🍷 3
● Cabernet Sauvignon '13	🍷 2
● Rompicollo '13	🍷 2

Poggio Alloro

LOC. SANT'ANDREA
53037 SAN GIMIGNANO [SI]
TEL. 0577950276
www. fattoriapoggioalloro.com

ANNUAL PRODUCTION 200,000 bottles
HECTARES UNDER VINE 25.00

○ Vernaccia San Gimignano '14	🍷🍷 2*
○ Vernaccia San Gimignano Le Mandorle Ris. '13	🍷🍷 3
○ Vernaccia San Gimignano Nicchiaio '14	🍷 2

Poggio Capponi

LOC. SAN DONATO A LIVIZZANO
VIA MONTELUPO, 184
50025 MONTESPERTOLI [FI]
TEL. 0571671914
www.poggiocapponi.it

CELLAR SALES
PRE-BOOKED VISITS
ACCOMMODATION
ANNUAL PRODUCTION 200,000 bottles
HECTARES UNDER VINE 32.00

○ Bianco di Binto '14	♟♟ 2*
● Tinorso '11	♟♟ 3
● Chianti '14	♟ 2
● Chianti Montespertoli Petriccio '12	♟ 3

Il Poggiolo

LOC. POGGIOLO, 259
53024 MONTALCINO [SI]
TEL. 0577848412
www.ilpoggiolomontalcino.com

CELLAR SALES
PRE-BOOKED VISITS
ANNUAL PRODUCTION 40,000 bottles
HECTARES UNDER VINE 7.00

● Brunello di Montalcino '10	♟♟ 6

Tenuta Poggiorosso

FRAZ. POPULONIA
LOC. POGGIO ROSSO, 1
57025 PIOMBINO [LI]
TEL. 056529553
www.tenutapoggiorosso.it

CELLAR SALES
PRE-BOOKED VISITS
ANNUAL PRODUCTION 35,000 bottles
HECTARES UNDER VINE 6.00

● Tages '13	♟♟ 3*
○ Feronia '14	♟♟ 4
● Fufluna '14	♟ 3
○ Phylika '14	♟ 3

Poggiotondo

LOC. POGGIOTONDO
52010 SUBBIANO [AR]
TEL. 057548182
www.poggiotondo.it

CELLAR SALES
PRE-BOOKED VISITS
ANNUAL PRODUCTION 10,000 bottles
HECTARES UNDER VINE 4.20

● C66 Cinzia '12	♟♟ 5
○ Vin Santo del Chianti Colle Fresco '07	♟♟ 6
● Chianti Le Rancole '12	♟ 3
● Poggiotondo '12	♟ 4

Poggiotondo

VIA TORRIBINA, 83
50050 CERRETO GUIDI [FI]
TEL. 0571559167
www.poggiotondowines.com

PRE-BOOKED VISITS
ACCOMMODATION
ANNUAL PRODUCTION 300,000 bottles
HECTARES UNDER VINE 20.00

● Chianti Vigna del 28 Ris. '11	♟♟ 6
● Marmoreccia '11	♟♟ 7
○ Vermentino '13	♟♟ 2*
● Chianti V. delle Conchiglie Ris. '11	♟ 6

Poggioventoso

S.DA DI TERENZANA, 5
56046 RIPARBELLA [PI]
TEL. 3938973677
www.poggioventoso.com

CELLAR SALES
PRE-BOOKED VISITS
ANNUAL PRODUCTION 20,000 bottles
HECTARES UNDER VINE 6.00

● Fuochi '12	♟♟ 6
● Assurdino '14	♟ 4
○ Poetico '14	♟ 5
⊙ Rosato di Poggioventoso '14	♟ 4

Il Ponte

S.DA CARIGE ALTA, 15
58010 CAPALBIO [GR]
TEL. 068547928
www.agricolailponte.it

CELLAR SALES
PRE-BOOKED VISITS
ANNUAL PRODUCTION 25,000 bottles
HECTARES UNDER VINE 14.00

○ Ansonica Costa dell'Argentario T - Lex '14		♥♥ 4
● Balto '11		♥♥ 4
● Capalbio T - Lex '13		♥♥ 4

Provveditore

LOC. SALAIOLO, 174
58054 SCANSANO [GR]
TEL. 3487018670
www.provveditore.net

CELLAR SALES
PRE-BOOKED VISITS
RESTAURANT SERVICE
ANNUAL PRODUCTION 15,000 bottles
HECTARES UNDER VINE 30.00

● Morellino di Scansano '13		♥♥ 3
○ Appassitodifufo '07		♥ 3
● Morellino di Scansano Irio '14		♥ 2

La Rasina

LOC. RASINA, 132
53024 MONTALCINO [SI]
TEL. 0577848536
www.larasina.it

CELLAR SALES
PRE-BOOKED VISITS
ACCOMMODATION
ANNUAL PRODUCTION 60,000 bottles
HECTARES UNDER VINE 11.00

● Brunello di Montalcino '10		♥♥ 6
● Rosso di Montalcino '13		♥ 3

Renicci

VIA DON MINZONI, 94
57028 SUVERETO [LI]
TEL. 0565828110
www.renicci.it

CELLAR SALES
PRE-BOOKED VISITS
ANNUAL PRODUCTION 20,000 bottles
HECTARES UNDER VINE 7.00

● Diorè '11		♥♥ 6
● Renicci '11		♥♥ 8
● Spirasole '11		♥♥ 8

Massimo Romeo

FRAZ. GRACCIANO
LOC. NOTTOLA, SS 326, 25
53040 MONTEPULCIANO [SI]
TEL. 0578708599
www.massimoromeo.it

CELLAR SALES
PRE-BOOKED VISITS
ANNUAL PRODUCTION 20,000 bottles
HECTARES UNDER VINE 6.00

● Nobile di Montepulciano '12		♥♥ 3

Rubicini

LOC. SAN BENEDETTO, 17C
53037 SAN GIMIGNANO [SI]
TEL. 0577944816
www.rubicini.com

CELLAR SALES
PRE-BOOKED VISITS
ANNUAL PRODUCTION 60,000 bottles
HECTARES UNDER VINE 10.00

● San Gimignano Rosso Pepe Nero '10		♥♥ 3
○ Vernaccia di S. Gimignano Etherea '12		♥♥ 2*
○ Vernaccia di S. Gimignano '14		♥ 2

Sada

s.da prov.le dei 3 Comuni
56040 Casale Marittimo [PI]
Tel. 0586650180
www.agricolasada.com

CELLAR SALES
PRE-BOOKED VISITS
ANNUAL PRODUCTION 60,000 bottles
HECTARES UNDER VINE 11.50
VITICULTURE METHOD Certified Organic

● Bolgheri Sup. '12	♟♟ 6
● Baldoro '13	♟♟ 5
● Integolo '12	♟ 6
○ Vendemmia Tardiva '11	♟ 3

Salustri

fraz. Poggi del Sasso
loc. La Cava
58040 Cinigiano [GR]
Tel. 0564990529
www.salustri.it

CELLAR SALES
PRE-BOOKED VISITS
ACCOMMODATION
ANNUAL PRODUCTION 80,000 bottles
HECTARES UNDER VINE 25.00
VITICULTURE METHOD Certified Organic
SUSTAINABLE WINERY

● Montecucco Santa Marta '12	♟♟ 4

San Benedetto

loc. San Benedetto 4a
53037 San Gimignano [SI]
Tel. 3386958705
www.agrisanbenedetto.com

CELLAR SALES
ANNUAL PRODUCTION 40,000 bottles
HECTARES UNDER VINE 25.00

● Japigo '12	♟♟ 4
○ Vernaccia di San Gimignano '14	♟ 2

Conti di San Bonifacio

loc. Casteani, 1
58023 Gavorrano [GR]
Tel. 056680006
www.contidisanbonifacio.com

CELLAR SALES
ACCOMMODATION AND RESTAURANT SERVICE
ANNUAL PRODUCTION 18,400 bottles
HECTARES UNDER VINE 7.00
VITICULTURE METHOD Certified Organic

● Monteregio di Massa Marittima '12	♟♟ 3
● Docet '12	♟ 5
● Sustinet '12	♟ 6

Fattoria San Felo

loc. Pagliatelli
58051 Magliano in Toscana [GR]
Tel. 05641856727
www.fattoriasanfelo.it

PRE-BOOKED VISITS
ANNUAL PRODUCTION 100,000 bottles
HECTARES UNDER VINE 25.00

● Morellino di Scansano Lampo '12	♟♟ 3
● Aulus '12	♟ 4
○ Maremma Toscana Viognier '14	♟ 2
● Morellino di Scansano San Felo '13	♟ 2

Tenuta San Jacopo

loc. Castiglioncello, 151
52022 Cavriglia [AR]
Tel. 055966003
www.tenutasanjacopo.it

CELLAR SALES
PRE-BOOKED VISITS
ACCOMMODATION
ANNUAL PRODUCTION 25,000 bottles
HECTARES UNDER VINE 40.00
VITICULTURE METHOD Certified Organic

● Orma del Diavolo '11	♟♟ 3
○ Quarto di Luna '14	♟♟ 2*
● Chianti Cl. Poggio ai Grilli '12	♟ 2
● Chianti Classico Poggio ai Grilli Ris. '11	♟ 3

San Luciano

LOC. SAN LUCIANO, 90
52048 MONTE SAN SAVINO [AR]
TEL. 0575848518
www.sanlucianovini.it

CELLAR SALES
PRE-BOOKED VISITS
ANNUAL PRODUCTION 113,300 bottles
HECTARES UNDER VINE 63.00

● Boschi Salviati '12	♟♟ 3
● Colle Carpito '12	♟ 2
● D'Ovidio '10	♟ 5
○ Resico '14	♟ 2

Fabbrica di San Martino

VIA PIEVE SANTO STEFANO, 2511
55100 LUCCA
TEL. 3476247497
www.fabbricadisanmartino.it

CELLAR SALES
PRE-BOOKED VISITS
ACCOMMODATION
ANNUAL PRODUCTION 13,000 bottles
HECTARES UNDER VINE 2.0
VITICULTURE METHOD Certified Organic

● Arcipressi '14	♟♟ 3

SanCarlo

FRAZ. TAVERNELLE
LOC. SAN CARLO
53024 MONTALCINO [SI]
TEL. 0577 848616
www.sancarlomontalcino.it

CELLAR SALES
PRE-BOOKED VISITS
ANNUAL PRODUCTION 10,000 bottles
HECTARES UNDER VINE 3.00

● Rosso di Montalcino '12	♟♟ 3
● Brunello di Montalcino '10	♟ 5

Santa Lucia

FRAZ. FONTEBLANDA
VIA AURELIA, 264
58010 ORBETELLO [GR]
TEL. 0564885474
www.azsantalucia.com

CELLAR SALES
PRE-BOOKED VISITS
ACCOMMODATION
ANNUAL PRODUCTION 150,000 bottles
HECTARES UNDER VINE 30.00
SUSTAINABLE WINERY

● Morellino di Scansano A Luciano '14	♟♟ 2*
○ Capalbio Vin Santo Graticcio	♟ 4
○ Maremma Toscana Vermentino Brigante '14	♟ 2

Fattoria Santa Vittoria

LOC. POZZO
VIA PIANA, 43
52045 FOIANO DELLA CHIANA [AR]
TEL. 057566807
www.fattoriasantavittoria.com

CELLAR SALES
PRE-BOOKED VISITS
ACCOMMODATION AND RESTAURANT SERVICE
ANNUAL PRODUCTION 37,000 bottles
HECTARES UNDER VINE 35.00
SUSTAINABLE WINERY

○ Conforta '13	♟♟ 4
○ Valdichiana Vin Santo '10	♟♟ 5
● Leopoldo '12	♟ 4
● Poggio del Tempio '12	♟ 2

Sapereta

LOC. MOLA
VIA PROVINCIALE OVEST, 73
57036 PORTO AZZURRO [LI]
TEL. 056595033
www.sapereta.it

CELLAR SALES
PRE-BOOKED VISITS
ANNUAL PRODUCTION 90,000 bottles
HECTARES UNDER VINE 14.00

● Aleatico Don Foscardo '14	♟♟ 3
● Elba Aleatico Passito Dalidiè '14	♟♟ 5
○ Elba Bianco V. Thea '14	♟ 2

SassodiSole

LOC. SANTA GIULIA I, 48A
FRAZ. TORRENIERI
LOC. SASSODISOLE, 85
53024 MONTALCINO [SI]
TEL. 0577834303
www.sassodisole.it

CELLAR SALES
PRE-BOOKED VISITS
ANNUAL PRODUCTION 30,000 bottles
HECTARES UNDER VINE 5.00
SUSTAINABLE WINERY

● Brunello di Montalcino '10	♟♟ 5

Il Sassolo

VIA CITERNA, 5
59015 CARMIGNANO [PO]
TEL. 0558706488
www.ilsassolo.it

ANNUAL PRODUCTION 9,000 bottles
HECTARES UNDER VINE 5.50

● Carmignano '12	♟♟ 3
● Barco Reale '13	♟ 1*
⊙ Carmignano Rosato Vin Ruspo '14	♟ 2

Savignola Paolina

VIA PETRIOLO, 58
50022 GREVE IN CHIANTI [FI]
TEL. 0558546036
www.savignolapaolina.it

CELLAR SALES
PRE-BOOKED VISITS
ACCOMMODATION
ANNUAL PRODUCTION 35,000 bottles
HECTARES UNDER VINE 6.00

● Chianti Cl. Ris. '11	♟♟ 4
● Chianti Cl. '13	♟ 3

Fulvio Luigi Serni

LOC. LE LAME, 237
57022 CASTAGNETO CARDUCCI [LI]
TEL. 0565763585
www.sernifulvioluigi.it

CELLAR SALES
PRE-BOOKED VISITS
ANNUAL PRODUCTION 18,500 bottles
HECTARES UNDER VINE 3.00

● Bolgheri Rosso Acciderba '12	♟♟ 4
● Bolgheri Rosso Tegoleto '13	♟♟ 3
○ Bolgheri Vermentino Radius '14	♟♟ 2*
○ Campofitto '14	♟♟ 2*

Solaria - Cencioni Patrizia

POD. CAPANNA, 102
53024 MONTALCINO [SI]
TEL. 0577849426
www.solariacencioni.com

CELLAR SALES
PRE-BOOKED VISITS
RESTAURANT SERVICE
ANNUAL PRODUCTION 30,000 bottles
HECTARES UNDER VINE 9.00

● Brunello di Montalcino '10	♟♟ 5
● Rosso di Montalcino '13	♟ 4

Borgo La Stella

LOC. VAGLIAGLI
B.GO LA STELLA, 60
53017 RADDA IN CHIANTI [SI]
TEL. 0577740699
www.borgolastella.com

ANNUAL PRODUCTION 21,000 bottles
HECTARES UNDER VINE 4.50

● Chianti Cl. '13	♟♟ 3
● Cronos '12	♟♟ 5

Tenuta di Sticciano

VIA DI STICCIANO, 207
50052 CERTALDO [FI]
TEL. 0571669191
www.tenutadisticciano.it

CELLAR SALES
PRE-BOOKED VISITS
ACCOMMODATION
ANNUAL PRODUCTION 65,000 bottles
HECTARES UNDER VINE 25.00
VITICULTURE METHOD Certified Organic

● Attimo '11	🍷🍷 3
○ Vin Santo del Chianti Ris. '06	🍷🍷 7
● Cantastorie '09	🍷 4
● Chianti Maggiano '13	🍷 2

Stomennano

LOC. STOMENNANO
53035 MONTERIGGIONI [SI]
TEL. 0577304033
www.stomennano.it

PRE-BOOKED VISITS
ACCOMMODATION
ANNUAL PRODUCTION 50,000 bottles
HECTARES UNDER VINE 15.00

● Chianti Cl. Ris. '10	🍷🍷 4

Talenti

FRAZ. SANT'ANGELO IN COLLE
LOC. PIAN DI CONTE
53020 MONTALCINO [SI]
TEL. 0577844064
www.talentimontalcino.it

CELLAR SALES
PRE-BOOKED VISITS
ANNUAL PRODUCTION 100,000 bottles
HECTARES UNDER VINE 21.00

● Brunello di Montalcino '10	🍷🍷 6
● Rosso di Montalcino '13	🍷 3

Fattoria della Talosa

VIA PIETROSE, 15A
53045 MONTEPULCIANO [SI]
TEL. 0578758277
www.talosa.it

CELLAR SALES
PRE-BOOKED VISITS
ANNUAL PRODUCTION 100,000 bottles
HECTARES UNDER VINE 35.00

○ Vin Santo di Montepulciano Ris. '95	🍷🍷 8
● Nobile di Montepulciano '12	🍷 4
● Nobile di Montepulciano Ris. '11	🍷 4

Tassi

V.LE P. STROZZI, 1/3
53024 MONTALCINO [SI]
TEL. 0577848025
www.tassimontalcino.com

HECTARES UNDER VINE

● Brunello di Montalcino Franci '10	🍷🍷 5
● Brunello di Montalcino Tassi '10	🍷🍷 4
● Rosso di Montalcino '12	🍷🍷 4
● Brunello di Montalcino Franci Ris. '09	🍷 6

Tenuta degli Dei

VIA SAN LEOLINO, 56
50022 GREVE IN CHIANTI [FI]
TEL. 055852593
www.deglidei.it

PRE-BOOKED VISITS
ANNUAL PRODUCTION 65,000 bottles
HECTARES UNDER VINE 9.00

● Chianti Cl. '13	🍷🍷 3
● Cavalli '12	🍷 6

Tenuta La Chiusa

LOC. MAGAZZINI, 93
57037 PORTOFERRAIO [LI]
TEL. 0565933046
lachiusa@elbalink.it

CELLAR SALES
PRE-BOOKED VISITS
ACCOMMODATION
ANNUAL PRODUCTION 25,000 bottles
HECTARES UNDER VINE 7.50

○ Elba Bianco '14	♟♟ 2*
○ Elba Vermentino '14	♟♟ 2*
⊙ Elba Rosato '14	♟ 3
● Elba Rosso '14	♟ 2

Terradonnà

LOC. NOTRI, 78
57028 SUVERETO [LI]
TEL. 0565838702
www.terradonna.it

CELLAR SALES
PRE-BOOKED VISITS
ANNUAL PRODUCTION 26,000 bottles
HECTARES UNDER VINE 6.00

● Giaietto '12	♟♟ 2*
● Spato '12	♟♟ 3
○ Faden '14	♟ 2
○ Kalsi '14	♟ 3

Terre di Fiori - Tenute Costa

S.DA GRILLESE UNO
58100 GROSSETO
TEL. 0564405457
www.tenutecosta.it

CELLAR SALES
PRE-BOOKED VISITS
ANNUAL PRODUCTION 120,000 bottles
HECTARES UNDER VINE 32.00

● Morellino di Scansano '13	♟♟ 2*
○ Maremma Toscana Vermentino '14	♟ 3
● Monteregio di Massa Marittima '13	♟ 3
● Morellino di Scansano Ventaio '13	♟ 5

Terre Nere

LOC. CASTELNUOVO DELL'ABATE
53024 MONTALCINO [SI]
TEL. 3358107743
www.terreneremontalcino.com

CELLAR SALES
PRE-BOOKED VISITS
ACCOMMODATION
ANNUAL PRODUCTION 50,000 bottles
HECTARES UNDER VINE 10.00

● Brunello di Montalcino '10	♟♟ 5
● Brunello di Montalcino Ris. '09	♟ 6

Tollena

VIA SAN GIOVANNI, 69
53037 SAN GIMIGNANO [SI]
TEL. 0577907178
www.tollena.it

CELLAR SALES
ANNUAL PRODUCTION 50,000 bottles
HECTARES UNDER VINE 22.00

○ Vernaccia di San Gimignano Signorina Vittoria Ris. '12	♟♟ 3
● Barbacane '11	♟ 2

Marchesi Torrigiani

LOC. VICO D'ELSA
P.ZZA TORRIGIANI, 15
50021 BARBERINO VAL D'ELSA [FI]
TEL. 0558073001
www.marchesitorrigiani.it

CELLAR SALES
PRE-BOOKED VISITS
ANNUAL PRODUCTION 140,000 bottles
HECTARES UNDER VINE 33.00

● Guidaccio '11	♟♟ 5
● Torre di Ciardo '12	♟♟ 3
● Chianti '13	♟ 2

Antonino Tringali - Casanuova

LOC. CASA AL PIANO, 68
57022 CASTAGNETO CARDUCCI [LI]
TEL. 0565774101
www.tringalipro.it

CELLAR SALES
PRE-BOOKED VISITS
ACCOMMODATION
ANNUAL PRODUCTION 35,000 bottles
HECTARES UNDER VINE 4.00

● Bolgheri 1698 '13	♥♥ 4

Fattoria Uccelliera

VIA PONTITA, 26
56043 FAUGLIA [PI]
TEL. 050662747
www.uccelliera.com

CELLAR SALES
PRE-BOOKED VISITS
ACCOMMODATION
ANNUAL PRODUCTION 90,500 bottles
HECTARES UNDER VINE 15.00

● Chianti '13	♥♥ 2*
● Ginepraia '14	♥♥ 2*
○ Ficaia '14	♥ 2
○ Ginepraia '14	♥ 2

Urlari

LOC. URLARI
56046 RIPARBELLA [PI]
TEL. 335215031
www.urlari.com

CELLAR SALES
PRE-BOOKED VISITS
ANNUAL PRODUCTION 30,000 bottles
HECTARES UNDER VINE 6.00

● L'Urlo '12	♥♥ 5
● Ritasso '12	♥♥ 3
● Pervale '12	♥ 3

Val di Toro

LOC. POGGIO LA MOZZA
S.DA DELLE CAMPORE, 18
58100 GROSSETO
TEL. 0564409600
www.valditoro.it

CELLAR SALES
PRE-BOOKED VISITS
ANNUAL PRODUCTION 70,000 bottles
HECTARES UNDER VINE 10.00

● Maremma Toscana Val di Toro '11	♥♥ 3
○ Maremma Toscana Auramaris '14	♥ 2
⊙ Maremma Toscana Rosato Anna's Secret '14	♥ 3

Valdonica

FRAZ. SASSOFORTINO
LOC. CASALONE DELL'EBREO
58036 ROCCASTRADA [GR]
TEL. 0564567251
www.valdonica.com

CELLAR SALES
PRE-BOOKED VISITS
ANNUAL PRODUCTION 35,000 bottles
HECTARES UNDER VINE 10.00
VITICULTURE METHOD Certified Organic

● Arnaio '11	♥♥ 3
○ Maremma Vermentino Ballarino '13	♥♥ 3
● Monteregio Saragio '10	♥♥ 5

Ventolaio

LOC. VENTOLAIO, 51
53024 MONTALCINO [SI]
TEL. 0577835779

ANNUAL PRODUCTION 70,000 bottles
HECTARES UNDER VINE 13.00

● Brunello di Montalcino '10	♥♥ 5
● Rosso di Montalcino '12	♥♥ 2*

Villa Corliano

LOC. BRUCIANESI
VIA DI CORLIANO, 4
50058 LASTRA A SIGNA [FI]
TEL. 0558734542
www.villacorliano.com

CELLAR SALES
PRE-BOOKED VISITS
ANNUAL PRODUCTION 35,000 bottles
HECTARES UNDER VINE 6.78

● Chianti Colli Fiorentini Briccole '13	▼▼ 2*
○ Colli dell'Etruria Centrale Vin Santo Dedicato '05	▼▼ 5
● Chianti Colli Fiorentini Briccole Ris. '11	▼ 3

Villa La Ripa

LOC. ANTRIA, 38
52100 AREZZO
TEL. 057523330
www.villalaripa.it

CELLAR SALES
PRE-BOOKED VISITS
ANNUAL PRODUCTION 10,000 bottles
HECTARES UNDER VINE 5.00
SUSTAINABLE WINERY

● Peconio '12	▼▼ 3
● Psyco '12	▼▼ 5
⊙ Rosato Spazio Libero '14	▼ 2
● Tiratari '12	▼ 5

Villa Loggio

FRAZ. CIGNANO
LOC. IL LOGGIO, 24
52044 CORTONA [AR]
TEL. 0575618306
www.villaloggio.com

PRE-BOOKED VISITS
ANNUAL PRODUCTION 150,000 bottles
HECTARES UNDER VINE 70.00

● Cortona Syrah Tinia '13	▼▼ 3
● Curtun '10	▼ 8
● Lucius '10	▼ 5
○ Vermentino '13	▼ 3

Villa Pinciana

S.DA VILLA PINCIANA, 2
58011 CAPALBIO [GR]
TEL. 0564896598
www.villapinciana.com

CELLAR SALES
PRE-BOOKED VISITS
ANNUAL PRODUCTION 40,000 bottles
HECTARES UNDER VINE 9.00

● Tilaria '12	▼▼ 3
○ Maremma Toscana Airali '14	▼ 3

Villa Sant'Anna

LOC. ABBADIA DI MONTEPULCIANO
VIA DELLA RESISTENZA, 143
53045 MONTEPULCIANO [SI]
TEL. 0578708017
www.villasantanna.it

CELLAR SALES
PRE-BOOKED VISITS
ANNUAL PRODUCTION 80,000 bottles
HECTARES UNDER VINE 18.00

○ Vin Santo di Montepulciano '06	▼▼ 8
● Nobile di Montepulciano '12	▼ 4

Tenuta Vitereta

VIA CASANUOVA, 108/1
52020 LATERINA [AR]
TEL. 057589058
www.tenutavitereta.com

CELLAR SALES
PRE-BOOKED VISITS
ACCOMMODATION
ANNUAL PRODUCTION 45,000 bottles
HECTARES UNDER VINE 45.00
VITICULTURE METHOD Certified Organic

● Merlot '13	▼▼ 3
○ Trebbiano di Toscana '13	▼▼ 4
● Chianti Lo Sterpo '13	▼ 2
● Ripa della Mozza '12	▼ 3

MARCHE

Consortia representatives who hosted Marche tastings received samples from 175 different wineries and covered up almost 1,000 wine labels. These numbers would have been unthinkable a decade ago, testifying to how viticulture is now seen as a profession to be pursued, a sector in which to believe. The subsequent samplings confirmed a healthy region, with average quality developing comfortably. The Tre Bicchieri ranking, as usual, was headed up by the Verdicchio dei Castelli di Jesi. It strolled in also thanks to the 2013 vintage, which gave excellent grapes. Venerable brands like Bucci, Umani Ronchi, Garofoli, and Santa Barbara were not struggling to turn them into memorable wines. Similarly the Sparapani family made sure it encored last year's success. Not quite the same for talented vintner Roberto Venturi, who received his well-deserved induction to the Tre Bicchieri hall of fame thanks to an astonishing Qudì. Leo Felici and Tenuta di Tavignano take yet another top award win with their most representative wines. Their performance in more complicated growing years places them among the most inspired and consistent protagonists of the designation. Matelica's share has decreased among the leaders, but the district is lively and its wines have an innate ability to reflect a strong territorial identity. In this respect, Belisario and Collestefano gave two contrasting but complementary interpretations. Nice try from Piceno, witnessing the unstoppable rise of its white wine identity thanks to Pecorino di Offida. Two awards were taken home: one went to the now well-established Tenuta Spinelli, while a newcomer in the ranks was Fiorano, which has always been in the vanguard for defending the interests of small growers and organic farming. The reds, however, did not shirk, with montepulciano and sangiovese united in the Piceno designation to give life to three contemporary wines, adept at fusing pleasurableness, fine tannic weave and complexity. Great stuff from Le Caniette, Velenosi and Moncaro. Oasi degli Angeli was also back on top form, with its majestic Kupra. Macerata doubled up and while Pollenza makes no secret of its focus on international varieties, La Murola hit the spot with its elegant Montepulciano, particularly interesting as it arrived from a site not in the variety's classic terroir.

Aurora

LOC. SANTA MARIA IN CARRO
C.DA CIAFONE, 98
63073 OFFIDA [AP]
TEL. 0736810007
www.viniaurora.it

CELLAR SALES
PRE-BOOKED VISITS
ACCOMMODATION
ANNUAL PRODUCTION 53,300 bottles
HECTARES UNDER VINE 9.50
VITICULTURE METHOD Certified Organic

It was 36 years ago that a group of youngsters met in an ancient farmhouse, armed with plenty of good intentions, solid ideals of shared aims, and hopes for what tomorrow would bring. Around them the unspoiled beauty of one of Piceno's most extensive vineyard districts. Time has in no way sapped their spirit and their steadfast faith in organic farming is now upheld by personal experience and biodynamic methods: constant presence in the vineyard, minimal use of sulphites and no selected yeasts, old wood for maturation of top wines, artisanal production methods in the strictest sense. Their wines reflect the vintage, with a restless nose that needs to open up a few minutes in the glass, but with a palate displaying proud character. Barricadiero 2012 has an earthy, blood-rich nose, with rather edgy tannins, but is a resolute proponent of the most authentic Montepulciano identity. The Piceno Superiore is decidedly good, with its hints of spices and fruit, occasionally briny.

● Barricadiero '12	♥♥ 4
● Rosso Piceno Sup. '12	♥♥ 2*
○ Offida Pecorino Fiobbo '13	♥ 3
● Rosso Piceno '14	♥ 2
● Barricadiero '10	♥♥♥ 4*
● Barricadiero '09	♥♥♥ 4
● Barricadiero '06	♥♥♥ 4
● Barricadiero '04	♥♥♥ 3
● Barricadiero '03	♥♥♥ 3*
● Barricadiero '02	♥♥♥ 3
● Barricadiero '01	♥♥♥ 3*
● Offida Rosso Barricadiero '11	♥♥♥ 4*

Belisario

VIA ARISTIDE MERLONI, 12
62024 MATELICA [MC]
TEL. 0737787247
www.belisario.it

CELLAR SALES
PRE-BOOKED VISITS
ANNUAL PRODUCTION 1,000,000 bottles
HECTARES UNDER VINE 300.00

If Matelica and Cerreto d'Esi have retained their vineyard heritage intact, each one with its respective diversities and traits, we can thank the four decades of work put in by Belisario. The cooperative has encouraged and supported financially the technical work in the vines of many small growers. The large cellars have allowed development of wines that could interpret the versatility of the verdicchio grape, forging a modern, pleasing and approachable style for the seaon's wines, and elegant complexity for aged versions. The Cambrugiano celebrates its 25th vintage in fine style with a 2012 showing aromas of candied citrus peel and almond on a lively palate contrasting with the placid typically matelica richness of flavour, with a satisfyingly intense, deep finish. Of the early drinkers, the complexity of the Vigneti B. 2014, with its hints of aniseed, and the polished vigour of the flowery Del Cerro 2014 with its dynamic flavours.

○ Verdicchio di Matelica Cambrugiano Ris. '12	♥♥♥ 3*
○ Verdicchio di Matelica Vign. B. '14	♥♥ 3*
○ Verdicchio di Matelica Del Cerro '14	♥♥ 2*
○ Verdicchio di Matelica L'Anfora '14	♥♥ 2*
○ Verdicchio di Matelica Meridia '12	♥♥ 3
○ Verdicchio di Matelica Terre di Valbona '14	♥♥ 2*
● Colli Maceratesi Rosso Coll'Amato '14	♥ 2
○ Esino Bianco '14	♥ 1*
○ Verdicchio di Matelica Brut Cuvée Nadir	♥ 2
○ Verdicchio di Matelica Cambrugiano Ris. '08	♥♥♥ 3*
○ Verdicchio di Matelica Cambrugiano Ris. '06	♥♥♥ 3*
○ Verdicchio di Matelica Meridia '10	♥♥♥ 3*
○ Verdicchio di Matelica Meridia '07	♥♥♥ 3*

Bisci

VIA FOGLIANO, 120
62024 MATELICA [MC]
TEL. 0737787490
www.bisciwines.it

CELLAR SALES
PRE-BOOKED VISITS
ANNUAL PRODUCTION 120,000 bottles
HECTARES UNDER VINE 19.00
VITICULTURE METHOD Certified Organic

The vineyards planted at the foot of Mount San Vicino's western slope have ideal aspecting and make the most of the unique Camerino syncline microclimate. For this reason wines made by the Bisci family, active in the area since 1980, are the most typical and austere that the Matelica terroir has to offer. Produced without use of wood or special techniques, they are still able to withstand the test of time thanks to their sheer mettle and a sturdy acid backbone that provides bright tanginess at a young age and captivating minerality a few years down the line. A cool vintage like 2014 brings out the adamantine brilliance of Verdicchios in white-fleshed fruit, rain-washed pebbles, the true-to-type flavours of bitter almond and lemon zest to mark out a full, vibrant mouth. And if you are looking for cellarability, what better than the Senex 2009, softened out for six years, with its contrasting notes of minerality and sweet apricot on an impressively mature, complex palate?

○ Verdicchio di Matelica '14	♟♟ 2*
○ Verdicchio di Matelica Senex '09	♟♟ 4
○ Verdicchio di Matelica Vign. Fogliano '10	♟♟♟ 3*
○ Verdicchio di Matelica Vign. Fogliano '08	♟♟♟ 3*
● Piangifame '07	♟♟ 4
● Rosso Fogliano '10	♟♟ 3
○ Verdicchio di Matelica '13	♟♟ 3
○ Verdicchio di Matelica '12	♟♟ 2*
○ Verdicchio di Matelica '11	♟♟ 3
○ Verdicchio di Matelica '10	♟♟ 2*
○ Verdicchio di Matelica '09	♟♟ 2*
○ Verdicchio di Matelica Vign. Fogliano '11	♟♟ 3*
○ Verdicchio di Matelica Vign. Fogliano '07	♟♟ 3*

Boccadigabbia

LOC. FONTESPINA
C.DA CASTELLETTA, 56
62012 CIVITANOVA MARCHE [MC]
TEL. 073370728
www.boccadigabbia.com

CELLAR SALES
PRE-BOOKED VISITS
ANNUAL PRODUCTION 100,000 bottles
HECTARES UNDER VINE 25.00

Boccadigabbia was a leading regional winery in the golden years at the turn of the century. Elvio Alessandri, a well-known Civitanova businessman, drew inspiration from the Napoleonic name of his estate to create a cellar based on French varietals, interpreting them in a Mediterranean key. He travelled to France and went with the spirit of the times: small wood, deep hues, powerful yet elegant wines that would charm foreign buyers. Changes in consumer tastes wrong-footed the winery but that was not enough to stop it pursuing its mission, adjusting excesses. The solidly-built Akronte 2010, from cabernet sauvignon, has a dark fruit and robe, with sweet tannins and an attractive oak finish. Pix 2010, from merlot, is an outpouring of red berries and balsamic hints on a tactile, soft, exuberant palate. Of the local denominations, always held in high esteem, the maceratino grape holds sway with an extraordinarily flowery Le Grane 2014 that is a pleasure to drink.

● Akronte '10	♟♟ 8
○ Colli Maceratesi Ribona Le Grane '14	♟♟ 3
● Pix '10	♟♟ 6
○ Falerio Pecorino '14	♟ 3
● Rosso Piceno '12	♟ 3
● Saltapicchio '10	♟ 4
● Akronte '98	♟♟♟ 7
● Akronte '97	♟♟♟ 7
● Akronte '95	♟♟♟ 7
● Akronte '94	♟♟♟ 7
● Akronte '93	♟♟♟ 7
● Akronte Cabernet '92	♟♟♟ 7
● Akronte '08	♟♟ 7
○ La Castelletta Pinot Grigio '12	♟♟ 3
☉ Roseo '12	♟♟ 2*
● Saltapicchio Sangiovese '07	♟♟ 4

Borgo Paglianetto

LOC. PAGLIANO, 393
62024 MATELICA [MC]
TEL. 073785465
www.borgopaglianetto.it

CELLAR SALES
PRE-BOOKED VISITS
ANNUAL PRODUCTION 60,000 bottles
HECTARES UNDER VINE 25.00
VITICULTURE METHOD Certified Organic

Although Mario Bassilissi is both the brains and brawn of the winery, the Borgo Paglianetto project was conceived with the active collaboration of the Roversi family, renowned agricultural entrepreneurs. They combined forces to created one of the finest wine businesses in the Matelica area, which vaunts outstanding and consistent quality. The merits of the strict farming tenets applied by Mario and the work of oenologist Aroldo Bellelli, who uses only steel and different stages of grape ripeness, result in some very well-typed Verdicchios. Jera 2011 will fit the bill for those looking for the elegance, detailed richness of flavour and cellarability of the best Matelicas, while Vertis 2013 is more powerful and juicy with unique terroir-true flavours. The fruity, flavoursome Terravignata 2014 and the Petrara 2014, whose delicate progression and good long salty finish we liked, are both simpler, focusing on immediate drinkability.

Brunori

V.LE DELLA VITTORIA, 103
60035 JESI [AN]
TEL. 0731207213
www.brunori.it

CELLAR SALES
PRE-BOOKED VISITS
ANNUAL PRODUCTION 60,000 bottles
HECTARES UNDER VINE 7.00

A hypothetical hall of fame with the names of the acknowledged fathers of Verdicchio di Jesi would be incomplete without that of vigneron and oenologist Giorgio Brunori. To understand his significance as a vine specialist, suffice to say that in 2016 his business will celebrate its 60th anniversary, started when he converted from bulk to bottled wine. In later years Brunori wines have not changed physiognomy and remain stalwart classics, aged in steel and concrete to enhance the briny tanginess of the River Esino's right bank. Also well-known is the ability to glide through time, acquiring nuanced charm and subtleties less evident in the young wine. An exception to this is San Nicolò Riserva 2013, a far better expression of the more intimate descriptors of verdicchio, such as almond, lime blossom and fines herbes, on a lean, tidy palate. The eponymous Classico Superiore 2014 is full-flavoured, slightly vegetal and mouthfilling.

○ Verdicchio di Matelica Jera Ris. '11	♟♟ 4
○ Verdicchio di Matelica Vertis '13	♟♟ 3*
○ Verdicchio di Matelica Petrara '14	♟♟ 2*
○ Verdicchio di Matelica Terravignata '14	♟♟ 2*
○ Verdicchio di Matelica Jera Ris. '10	♟♟♟ 4*
○ Verdicchio di Matelica Vertis '09	♟♟♟ 3*
○ Verdicchio di Matelica Aja Lunga '05	♟♟ 2*
○ Verdicchio di Matelica Jera Ris. '09	♟♟ 4
○ Verdicchio di Matelica Petrara '13	♟♟ 2*
○ Verdicchio di Matelica Petrara '09	♟♟ 2*
○ Verdicchio di Matelica Petrara '08	♟♟ 2*
○ Verdicchio di Matelica Terravignata '13	♟♟ 2*
○ Verdicchio di Matelica Terravignata '11	♟♟ 2*
○ Verdicchio di Matelica Vertis '12	♟♟ 3*
○ Verdicchio di Matelica Vertis '10	♟♟ 3*
○ Verdicchio di Matelica Vertis '08	♟♟ 3*

○ Verdicchio dei Castelli di Jesi Cl. § San Nicolò Ris. '13	♟♟ 3*
○ Verdicchio dei Castelli di Jesi Cl. Sup. San Nicolò '14	♟♟ 2*
○ Verdicchio dei Castelli di Jesi Cl. Le Gemme '14	♟ 2
○ Castelli di Jesi Verdicchio Cl. San Nicolò Ris. '12	♟♟ 3
○ Verdicchio dei Castelli di Jesi Cl. Le Gemme '13	♟♟ 2*
○ Verdicchio dei Castelli di Jesi Cl. Le Gemme '10	♟♟ 2*
○ Verdicchio dei Castelli di Jesi Cl. Sup. San Nicolò '10	♟♟ 2*
○ Verdicchio dei Castelli di Jesi Cl. Sup. San Nicolò Ris. '09	♟♟ 3

★Bucci

fraz. Pongelli
via Cona, 30
60010 Ostra Vetere [AN]
Tel. 071964179
www.villabucci.com

CELLAR SALES
PRE-BOOKED VISITS
ANNUAL PRODUCTION 120,000 bottles
HECTARES UNDER VINE 31.00
VITICULTURE METHOD Certified Organic

Not a blind tasting in the world could actually conceal Ampelio Bucci's unique touch of style, forged with the help of Giorgio Grai, his trusty consultant oenologist. An indelible mark of poise and austerity is ferried in by old vines and patient maturation in large wooden barrels for Villa Bucci and more suitable steel tanks for baby brother Bucci Classico. Pursuing the winery's established tradition, all wines are not the result of a particular cru but blends of several vineyards scattered around the Montecarotto, Serra de' Conti and Barbara hills. The Villa Bucci 2013 is magnificent. Though still very youthful, it already offers a sumptuous body with a voice that whispers rather than shouts: aromatic herbs, almond and a touch of aniseed for a nose of great finesse, mirrored in a highly-balanced palate, not lacking taut saltiness. Not far behind comes the dynamic Classico Superiore 2013, with an almond twist and irresistible drinkability.

La Calcinara

fraz. Candia
via Calcinara, 102a
60131 Ancona
Tel. 3285552643
www.lacalcinara.it

CELLAR SALES
PRE-BOOKED VISITS
ANNUAL PRODUCTION 26,000 bottles
HECTARES UNDER VINE 13.00
SUSTAINABLE WINERY

We imagine Mario Berluti, long-time vigneron, must have been very satisfied when both his children, Paolo and Eleonora, graduated in oenology. After some time spent abroad, they came home and carved out their own space, not in their father's bulk and large-scale sales business. Precisely to define their territory, they built a small cellar where they prepare an expert range of artisanal wines based only the montepulciano grape. The Folle 2010 ages in small wood, picking up notes of marasca cherry, spices, and a slightly smoky nuance, while the mouth combines intensity, energy and unusual poise. The Terra Calcinara 2012, aged in large barrels, displays moody tannins. Ageing in steel softens out Il Cacciatore 2013: a stylish, well-balanced mouth and clean, fruit-driven vigour. The Mun 2014 is a Provençal-type rosé: aromas of fines herbes and white-fleshed fruit so drinkable you will shake out every last drop.

○ Castelli di Jesi Verdicchio Cl. Villa Bucci Ris. '13	♟♟♟ 6
○ Verdicchio dei Castelli di Jesi Cl. Sup. '13	♟♟ 3*
● Rosso Piceno Tenuta Pongelli '13	♟ 3
○ Castelli di Jesi Verdicchio Cl. Villa Bucci Ris. '12	♟♟♟ 6
○ Castelli di Jesi Verdicchio Cl. Villa Bucci Ris. '10	♟♟♟ 6
○ Verdicchio dei Castelli di Jesi Cl. V illa Bucci Ris. '09	♟♟♟ 6
○ Verdicchio dei Castelli di Jesi Cl. Villa Bucci Ris. '07	♟♟♟ 6
○ Verdicchio dei Castelli di Jesi Cl. Villa Bucci Ris. '06	♟♟♟ 6
○ Verdicchio dei Castelli di Jesi Cl. Villa Bucci Ris. '05	♟♟♟ 5

● Conero Folle Ris. '10	♟♟ 5
⊙ Mun '14	♟♟ 2*
● Rosso Conero Il Cacciatore di Sogni '13	♟♟ 2*
● Conero Terra Calcinara Ris. '12	♟ 3
● Conero Folle Ris. '07	♟♟ 5
● Rosso Conero Il Cacciatore di Sogni '12	♟♟ 2*
● Rosso Conero Terra Calcinara '09	♟♟ 3
● Rosso Conero Terra Calcinara '08	♟♟ 3

Le Caniette

C.DA CANALI, 23
63065 RIPATRANSONE [AP]
TEL. 07359200
www.lecaniette.it

CELLAR SALES
PRE-BOOKED VISITS
ANNUAL PRODUCTION 60,000 bottles
HECTARES UNDER VINE 16.00
VITICULTURE METHOD Certified Organic

With adjustments to stylistic register, the Vagnoni brothers regularly get their cellar's wines to the top of their respective designations. The well-aspected vineyards have always been tended in the fullest respect of organic farming. The ten-year-old cellars are not only eye-catching but very efficient. The style was revised by rightly aiming for a less frantic concentration of grapes and a more judicious use of small wood. A breath of fresh air that has brought evident results. Morellone 2010 is once again one of the area's most elegant reds: a nose of flowers and charming spiciness, and the mouth embellished by a sophisticated tannic weave and a masterful balance. Cinabro 2011, from grenache, is stylish and layered, with a reverberating nose of Mediterranean scrub. Iosonogaia 2013 is reminiscent of grapefruit zest and white chocolate on a delicately salty palate.

● Piceno Morellone '10	♟♟♟ 4*
● Cinabro '11	♟♟ 8
○ Offida Pecorino Iosonogaia non sono Lucrezia '13	♟♟ 4
● Piceno Nero di Vite '07	♟♟ 6
○ Offida Pecorino Veronica Non Filtrato '14	♟♟ 3
● Piceno Rosso Bello '12	♟♟ 2*
○ Lucrezia '14	♟ 2
● Piceno Morellone '08	♟♟♟ 4*
● Cinabro '10	♟♟ 8
● Cinabro '09	♟♟ 8
○ Offida Pecorino Iosonogaia non sono Lucrezia '12	♟♟ 4
● Rosso Piceno Morellone '07	♟♟ 4
● Rosso Piceno Morellone '06	♟♟ 4
● Rosso Piceno Nero di Vite '05	♟♟ 6

La Cantina dei Colli Ripani

C.DA TOSCIANO, 28
63065 RIPATRANSONE [AP]
TEL. 07359505
www.colliripani.it

CELLAR SALES
PRE-BOOKED VISITS
ANNUAL PRODUCTION 1,500,000 bottles
HECTARES UNDER VINE 650.00

If there are still striking hills cloaked in vineyards making up the typical patchwork of Piceno's landscape, it is due to the work of coordination and support that Colli Ripani has offered its 350 members in Ripatransone, Offida and neighbouring municipalities. The large Contrada Tosciano cellar is a lighthouse in the stormy sea of these difficult times. Here the best grapes are brought to fruition for wines that are a pleasure to drink and at the right price. Whites in steel and wood of various sizes accommodate the natural evolutionary process of winemaking, taking care not to disperse the aromatic bounty of the grapes in the most traditional. The talented Pecorino leads the whites: the refreshing, citrussy Rugaro 2014 slips down well, while the Rugaro Gold 2014 is softer and more solidly built, with a better aromatic profile, as well as more decisive flavour in the finish. Khorakhanè 2009, from montepulciano with a touch of cabernet is a resolute, placid and complex wine.

○ Falerio Pecorino Rugaro '14	♟♟ 2*
○ Khorakhanè '09	♟♟ 5
○ Offida Pecorino Rugaro Gold '14	♟♟ 2*
○ Offida Passerina Ninfa Ripana Gold '14	♟ 2
● Rosso Piceno Biologico '14	♟ 2
● Rosso Piceno Rupe Nero Gold '14	♟ 2
● Rosso Piceno Sup. Castellano '11	♟ 2
○ Falerio Brezzolino '13	♟♟ 1*
○ Falerio Brezzolino '12	♟♟ 2*
○ Falerio Pecorino Rugaro '13	♟♟ 2*
○ Offida Passerina Passito Anima Mundi '08	♟♟ 4
○ Offida Passerina Passito Anima Mundi '07	♟♟ 5
○ Offida Pecorino Rugaro Gold '13	♟♟ 2*

Carminucci

VIA SAN LEONARDO, 39
63013 GROTTAMMARE [AP]
TEL. 0735735869
www.carminucci.com

CELLAR SALES
ANNUAL PRODUCTION 200,000 bottles
HECTARES UNDER VINE 52.00
VITICULTURE METHOD Certified Organic

Just a year before the 1929 Wall Street
Crash, the Carminucci family started in the
wine trade. Over the years, many
generations have played their roles in the
supply chain: not only vignerons, but bulk
sellers, contractors, merchants. Undoubtedly
they know the system inside out. The current
manager is Giovanni Carminucci, who was
wise enough to convert all the hectares he
could to organic methods, while making
true-to-terroir contemporary wines, rich in
fruity sensations that accentuate the
pleasurableness. The Pecorino Belato 2014
is the best demonstration, finely blending
citrus fruits with hints of wild herbs, mirrored
on an incisive, refreshing and dynamic
palate. The Falerio Naumachos 2014 has
less backbone but shares its smoothness
and drinkability. Plenty of personality, with
moodier swings, for the Piceno Superiore
Naumachos 2012: oregano, black olives and
slightly salty notes combine on a decent
palate with balanced tannins.

○ Offida Pecorino Belato '14	♀♀ 2*
○ Casta '14	♀♀ 2*
○ Falerio Naumachos '14	♀♀ 2*
● Rosso Piceno Sup. Naumachos '12	♀♀ 2*
○ Falerio Grotte sul Mare '14	♀ 1*
● Paccaosso '11	♀ 7
● Rosso Piceno Grotte sul Mare '14	♀ 1*
○ Casta '12	♀♀ 2*
○ Falerio Naumachos '13	♀♀ 2*
○ Falerio Naumachos '12	♀♀ 2*
○ Offida Pecorino Belato '13	♀♀ 2*
○ Offida Pecorino Belato '12	♀♀ 2*
● Paccaosso '09	♀♀ 7
● Rosso Piceno Sup. Naumachos '11	♀♀ 2*
● Rosso Piceno Sup. Naumachos '10	♀♀ 2*

CasalFarneto

VIA FARNETO, 12
60030 SERRA DE' CONTI [AN]
TEL. 0731889001
www.casalfarneto.it

CELLAR SALES
PRE-BOOKED VISITS
ANNUAL PRODUCTION 580,000 bottles
HECTARES UNDER VINE 32.00

When the Togni family decided to purchase
CasalFarneto they were thinking of
spearheading their own production. They
were already well established in large-scale
sparkling wine production and in mineral
water, then deciding to grapple with quality
but in small numbers. Togni vines are in
true wine country, with top-notch staff led
by the experienced Danilo Solustri, plus an
avant-garde cellar, all contributing to
production characterized by Verdicchios
that tend more to finesse that to power, to
drinkability rather than too much structure.
In the absence of the refined Crisio, still
ageing in glass, the range is led by one of
the finest Grancasales we ever tasted: the
nose combines apple, aniseed and almond
ushering in a full-flavoured, racy finish.
Honeyed and saffron notes add a touch of
magic to the Cimaio 2012, a deep and
minerally late-harvest Verdicchio. The
Fontevecchia 2014 is exceptionally citrussy
and lean.

○ Verdicchio dei Castelli di Jesi Cl. Sup. Grancasale '13	♀♀♀ 3*
○ Cimaio '12	♀♀ 4
○ Verdicchio dei Castelli di Jesi Cl. Sup. Fontevecchia '14	♀♀ 2*
○ Verdicchio dei Castelli di Jesi Passito Ikòn '10	♀♀ 5
● Merago '11	♀ 3
○ Verdicchio dei Castelli di Jesi Cl. '14	♀ 2
○ Castelli di Jesi Verdicchio Cl. Crisio Ris. '12	♀♀♀ 3*
○ Castelli di Jesi Verdicchio Cl. Crisio Ris. '11	♀♀♀ 3*
○ Verdicchio dei Castelli di Jesi Cl. Crisio Ris. '10	♀♀♀ 3*

MARCHE

Maria Pia Castelli

c.da Sant'Isidoro, 22
63015 Monte Urano [FM]
Tel. 0734841774
www.mariapiacastelli.it

CELLAR SALES
PRE-BOOKED VISITS
ANNUAL PRODUCTION 20,000 bottles
HECTARES UNDER VINE 8.00

At the beginning of the century, when Enrico Bartoletti and Maria Pia Castelli decided to plant only native cultivars in their vineyards, and build their cosy winery on two floors, with the ground floor for steel barrels and tapered wooden fermentation vats, below for the cellar, their two children were mere tots. Today they offer their precious contribution, flanking exceptional and trusted co-workers. This artisanal winery produces bottles of extreme originality, aged at length, not exactly approachable on first impact but surrendering slowly in the glass. This is especially true for the Erasmo Castelli 2011, a monovarietal Montepulciano with hints of iron and woodland, black berry fruit and burnt embers, accompanied by a spontaneous, energetic and sanguine palate. The slightly buttery Stella Flora 2012 displays ginger and apricots, ushering in a soft, diffuse palate and an alluring finish of aromatic herbs.

● Erasmo Castelli '11	♔♔ 5
☉ Sant'Isidoro '13	♔♔ 2*
○ Stella Flora '12	♔♔ 5
● Orano '12	♔ 4
● Erasmo Castelli '06	♔♔♔ 5
● Erasmo Castelli '10	♔♔ 5
● Erasmo Castelli '09	♔♔ 5
● Erasmo Castelli '07	♔♔ 5
● Orano '11	♔♔ 4
● Orano '10	♔♔ 3
● Orano '09	♔♔ 3
○ Stella Flora '11	♔♔ 5
○ Stella Flora '10	♔♔ 5
○ Stella Flora '09	♔♔ 5
○ Stella Flora '08	♔♔ 5
○ Stella Flora '07	♔♔ 5

Giacomo Centanni

c.da Aso, 159
63062 Montefiore dell'Aso [AP]
Tel. 0734938530
www.vinicentanni.it

CELLAR SALES
ACCOMMODATION
ANNUAL PRODUCTION 100,000 bottles
HECTARES UNDER VINE 30.00
VITICULTURE METHOD Certified Organic

The Aso River valley, with its rolling hills near the Adriatic, makes its presence felt with constant ventilation even in the hottest summers. This is farmland with a true vocation, known above all for its fruit trees. The young Giacomo Centanni, a graduate in oenology, has given his family's wine business a major boost in developing quality. Working with oenologist Vittorio Festa, the cellar produces wines with a pleasing slant, applying the rulebook but in the right growing years giving typical Piceno vines free rein. Both the Pecorino and the Passerina 2014s are a success, the former all power and aromatic intensity, while the other focuses more on citrus verve and flowing palate. In its chic bottles with glass stoppers, we came across the Monte Floris 2013, from montepulciano, with its fleshy palate, chamois-soft tannins, and intact fruit.

● Monte Floris '13	♔♔ 2*
○ Offida Passerina '14	♔♔ 2*
○ Offida Pecorino '14	♔♔ 2*
○ Falerio Il Borgo '14	♔ 2
☉ Profumo di Rosa '14	♔ 2
○ Terre di Offida Passerina Brut M. Cl. '12	♔ 4
● Monte Floris '12	♔♔ 2*
● Monte Floris '11	♔♔ 2*
○ Offida Passerina '13	♔♔ 2*
○ Offida Passerina '12	♔♔ 2*
○ Offida Pecorino '12	♔♔ 2*
○ Offida Pecorino '11	♔♔ 2*

Cherri d'Acquaviva

VIA ROMA, 40
63075 ACQUAVIVA PICENA [AP]
TEL. 0735764416
www.vinicherri.it

CELLAR SALES
PRE-BOOKED VISITS
ANNUAL PRODUCTION 160,000 bottles
HECTARES UNDER VINE 32.00

The Cherri family's hilly estate in Acquaviva Picena is a snapshot of the Piceno countryside: a patchwork of plots where sunflowers, cereals, olive groves and vineyards cohabit, located on land where a significant amount of clay gives rise to the badlands visible nearby. Paolo Cherri opened his new cellar here in 2003, and works with the important oenological support of Franco Bernabei, making judiciously modern wines without cutting ties to the varietal character of local cultivars. When montepulciano is married with sangiovese, red wines become interesting: the latest Rosso Piceno is fragrant and juicy while a genuine Piceno Superiore 2013 shows a full-flavoured meaty palate that makes it very food-friendly. This year's derby among the whites was a no contest, with the soft Offida Pecorino Altissimo 2014, displaying full fruity vitality. Also much appreciated, the Pecorino Brut, a Charmat with delicate tanginess.

● Rosso Piceno Sup. '13	♀♀	2*
○ Offida Pecorino Altissimo '14	♀♀	3
● Rosso Piceno '14	♀♀	2*
⊙ Ancella '14	♀	2
○ Falerio '14	♀	2
○ Offida Passerina Radiosa '14	♀	3
● Offida Rosso Tumbulus '11	♀	4
○ Pecorino Brut	♀	3
● Rosso Piceno Sup. Laudi '12	♀	4
○ Offida Pecorino Altissimo '13	♀♀	3*
● Offida Rosso Tumbulus '09	♀♀	4
● Offida Tumbulus '07	♀♀	4
● Offida Tumbulus '06	♀♀	4
● Rosso Piceno '13	♀♀	2*
● Rosso Piceno Sup. '12	♀♀	2*

Ciù Ciù

LOC. SANTA MARIA IN CARRO
C.DA CIAFONE, 106
63035 OFFIDA [AP]
TEL. 0736810001
www.ciuciuvini.it

CELLAR SALES
PRE-BOOKED VISITS
ACCOMMODATION AND RESTAURANT SERVICE
ANNUAL PRODUCTION 800,000 bottles
HECTARES UNDER VINE 180.00
VITICULTURE METHOD Certified Organic

The Bartolomei brothers have worked hard in recent years to bring their winery up to its current speed. Massimiliano is the vine man, all organic methods to ensure only top quality enters the cellars. Walter is the connection between the winery and intensive sales network. The wines are made keeping a close eye on the moods of the market: impeccably tailored, pleasant and approachable, velvety palates for the season's wines and textured structure for the more prestigious bottles. Despite their tactile juicy palate, ripe fruitiness rather thwarts the ambitions of both Offida Esperanto 2009 and Piceno Superiore Gotico 2012, lacking a deft touch of freshness that would give them more complexity and balance. This is even more marked in the case of Oppidum 2011, a dense, alcoholic Montepulciano. The flowery Pecorino Le Merlettaie 2014 is more even, focusing on a pleasant drinkability. Both native grape Charmat Bruts are equally pleasant.

○ Offida Pecorino Le Merlettaie '14	♀♀	2*
● Offida Rosso Esperanto '09	♀♀	5
● Rosso Piceno Sup. Gotico '12	♀♀	2*
○ Altamarea Brut	♀	2
○ Evoé '14	♀	2
○ Falerio Oris '14	♀	2
○ Merlettaie Brut	♀	3
● Oppidum '11	♀	4
● Rosso Piceno Bacchus '14	♀	2
● Saggio '13	♀	3
○ Offida Pecorino Le Merlettaie '13	♀♀	2*
○ Offida Pecorino Le Merlettaie '12	♀♀	2*
● Oppidum '08	♀♀	4
● Oppidum '07	♀♀	4
● Rosso Piceno Sup. Gotico '11	♀♀	2*

MARCHE

Tenuta Cocci Grifoni

LOC. SAN SAVINO
C.DA MESSIERI, 12
63038 RIPATRANSONE [AP]
TEL. 073590143
www.tenutacoccigrifoni.it

CELLAR SALES
PRE-BOOKED VISITS
ACCOMMODATION
ANNUAL PRODUCTION 330,000 bottles
HECTARES UNDER VINE 50.00

Cocci Grifoni means memory, the most entrenched tradition of Piceno viticulture. All thanks to the talent of Guido, acknowledged father of Marche winegrowing and defender of local varietals. We will never tire of repeating that he was the first to rediscover the pecorino grape and save it from oblivion in the foothills where it was confined. We recall his undisguised irritation towards small wood, preferring large oak. His wife Diana, daughters Marilena and Paola continue to follow his path, never forgetting the past, looking to the future, starting with the complete makeover of the cellar into an elegant and lively meeting place. The démodé charm of Vigna Messieri 2010, a Piceno Superiore, was outclassed by the gutsy character of Le Torri 2011, displaying a bouquet of steak tartare, tar and black olives, and a lively yet relaxed mouth and progression. Good performance too from the Colle Vecchio 2014, a touch vegetal, austere, and slightly shallow.

Collestefano

LOC. COLLE STEFANO, 3
62022 CASTELRAIMONDO [MC]
TEL. 0737640439
www.collestefano.com

CELLAR SALES
PRE-BOOKED VISITS
ACCOMMODATION
ANNUAL PRODUCTION 110,000 bottles
HECTARES UNDER VINE 17.50
VITICULTURE METHOD Certified Organic

Temperature ranges in the upper Esino Valley, on the border with Umbria, the mountains set behind the vineyards to protect them from the sea, a continental climate that makes Matelica unique in the region. Fabio Marchionni created his small oeno-socio-economic miracle here, among vines surrounded by woods at 400 metres in altitude, under organic management since 1998. His Verdicchio is a wine for all, he likes to say, even his vineyard workers, who will be drinking very well judging by results achieved in recent years. Despite the unpromising vintage, the Collestefano 2014 hit the bullseye, on a slightly more readable version with a touch less grip than usual: almond and white-fleshed fruit, grapefruit and briny aromas, accompanied by a classic tangy, racy palate. The intriguing Extra Brut 2012 impressed with its peppery fizz and admirably contained dosage. Though Rosa di Elena was originally made just for fun, it has now become a winery stalwart.

● Rosso Piceno Sup. Le Torri '11	♟♟	2*
○ Offida Pecorino Colle Vecchio '14	♟♟	3
● Rosso Piceno Sup. V. Messieri '10	♟♟	4
○ Adamantea '14	♟	2
○ Passerina Brut Gaudio Magno '14	♟	3
○ Offida Pecorino Colle Vecchio '13	♟♟	3
○ Offida Pecorino Podere Colle Vecchio '12	♟♟	3
○ Offida Pecorino Podere Colle Vecchio '10	♟♟	3*
● Rosso Piceno Sup. Le Torri '10	♟♟	3
● Rosso Piceno Sup. Le Torri '08	♟♟	3
● Rosso Piceno Sup. Tenute Messieri '10	♟♟	4

○ Verdicchio di Matelica Collestefano '14	♟♟♟	2*
○ Collestefano Extra Brut M. Cl. '12	♟♟	3
⊙ Rosa di Elena '14	♟♟	2*
○ Verdicchio di Matelica Collestefano '13	♟♟♟	2*
○ Verdicchio di Matelica Collestefano '12	♟♟♟	2*
○ Verdicchio di Matelica Collestefano '07	♟♟♟	2*
○ Verdicchio di Matelica Collestefano '06	♟♟♟	2*
○ Verdicchio di Matelica Collestefano '11	♟♟	2*
○ Verdicchio di Matelica Collestefano '10	♟♟	2*
○ Verdicchio di Matelica Collestefano '09	♟♟	2*
○ Verdicchio di Matelica Collestefano '08	♟♟	2*
○ Verdicchio di Matelica Collestefano '05	♟♟	2*
○ Verdicchio di Matelica Collestefano '04	♟♟	2*
○ Verdicchio di Matelica Collestefano '03	♟♟	2*
○ Verdicchio di Matelica Collestefano '02	♟♟	2
○ Verdicchio di Matelica Collestefano '01	♟♟	2

Cantina Cològnola Tenuta Musone

LOC. COLOGNOLA, 22A/BIS
62011 CINGOLI [MC]
TEL. 0733616438
www.tenutamusone.it

CELLAR SALES
PRE-BOOKED VISITS
ANNUAL PRODUCTION 150,000 bottles
HECTARES UNDER VINE 25.00

Once he purchased Cològnola, Walter Darini spared no expense to upgrade the vineyards, build a brand-new cellar, and reshape the wines. To make no secret of his attachment to the territory, he included the name of the Musone, the river lapping his estate, and the stylized outline of Mount San Vicino. Only grapes from his own property enter the modern building that houses the winemaking processes, all geared to respecting the classic style tenets for Verdicchio, available in several versions. Particular attention is paid to producing sparkling wine, which exploits the versatility of the grape. Both sparklers hit the mark: the Darini 2012 has elegant, yeasty notes of camphor, while Musa 2013 is fresh and balsamic, with a relaxed drinkability. The best of the still Verdicchios is Ghiffa 2013, whose appley notes are underscored by greener hints of celery and wild herbs, while the palate is enjoyably zesty.

● Cantamaggio '13	♥♥ 3
○ Verdicchio dei Castelli di Jesi Brut Darini M. Cl. '12	♥♥ 5
○ Verdicchio dei Castelli di Jesi Brut Musa '13	♥♥ 3
○ Verdicchio dei Castelli di Jesi Cl. Sup. Ghiffa '13	♥♥ 3
○ Castelli di Jesi Verdicchio Cl. Labieno Ris. '13	♥ 3
○ Verdicchio dei Castelli di Jesi Cl. Sup. Via Condotto '14	♥ 2
● Buraco '11	♀♀ 4
○ Castelli di Jesi Verdicchio Cl. Labieno Ris. '12	♀♀ 3*
○ Verdicchio dei Castelli di Jesi Cl. Via Condotto '13	♀♀ 2*

Il Conte Villa Prandone

C.DA COLLE NAVICCHIO, 28
63033 MONTEPRANDONE [AP]
TEL. 073562593
www.ilcontevini.it

CELLAR SALES
PRE-BOOKED VISITS
ANNUAL PRODUCTION 200,000 bottles
HECTARES UNDER VINE 50.00

A family of winegrowers. The cellar motto expresses the spirit of the four De Angelis siblings perfectly. Led by Emmanuel, they are winemakers who apply a family approach while producing significant numbers: fathers, offspring and various spouses are employed in the different departments. The heart of production is the extensive Colle Navicchio vineyard, at Monteprandone, whose sunny, fertile terrains are provided with irrigation during the hottest growing years. The spacious, well-equipped cellar receives grapes that are always in perfect health and properly ripe. The style seeks an international feel without crushing the character of Piceno's typical montepulciano and pecorino varietals. And it is the LuKont 2012 which sets out the montepulciano grape's generosity of spirit and rich extraction. The Zipolo 2012, from a blend of montepulciano topped up with 15% merlot and 15% sangiovese, is even more solid.

● Donello '14	♥♥ 2*
● LuKont '12	♥♥ 6
○ Offida Pecorino Navicchio '14	♥♥ 3
● Zipolo '12	♥♥ 5
○ Cavaceppo '14	♥ 2
○ Emmanuel Maria Extra Dry	♥ 3
○ Falerio Aurato '14	♥ 2
● Rosso Piceno Conte Rosso '14	♥ 2
● Rosso Piceno Sup. Marinus '13	♥ 3
● Donello '13	♀♀ 2*
● Donello '11	♀♀ 2*
● LuKont '11	♀♀ 6
○ Offida Pecorino Navicchio '13	♀♀ 3
● Rosso Piceno Conte Rosso '11	♀♀ 2*
● Zipolo '11	♀♀ 5

Fattoria Coroncino

C.DA CORONCINO, 7
60039 STAFFOLO [AN]
TEL. 0731779494
www.coroncino.it

CELLAR SALES
PRE-BOOKED VISITS
ANNUAL PRODUCTION 45,000 bottles
HECTARES UNDER VINE 9.50

"We are solitary, independent, artisan winegrowers." In their own words, this just about sums up the philosophy of Lucio and Fiorella Cai, who moved here from Rome 30 years ago, enamoured of the peace of the Staffolo hills and of Verdicchio. Lucio is a key figure in this designation and his powerful, velvety, cellarable whites are landmarks. Flying in the face of style trends for more subtle wines, he sticks to his guns, bottling after lengthy maturation in small wood, toil in the vineyard and no shortcuts in the cellar. The wines are the epitome of the "creaminess" verdicchio grapes offer when late-harvested. Coroncino 2013 is stunning, its candied orange zest and twirl of candyfloss enveloping a pervasive, lengthy, hypnotic mouth. The Gaiospino Fumé 2012 draws smokiness from the tonneaux in which it ages, marrying it with strong alcohols suitably tangy underpinning.

Tenuta De Angelis

VIA SAN FRANCESCO, 10
63030 CASTEL DI LAMA [AP]
TEL. 073687429
www.tenutadeangelis.it

CELLAR SALES
PRE-BOOKED VISITS
ANNUAL PRODUCTION 500,000 bottles
HECTARES UNDER VINE 50.00

At a first glance the large De Angelis–Fausti family winery in Castel di Lama may mislead into thinking it only handles large numbers. Actually, Quinto Fausti has been pushing in the quality direction for many years. Certainly not by pursuing rare, go-getting garagiste-style bottling, but by seeking to make the most of the vines and their local designations. Value-for-money pricing means everyone can enjoy well-crafted, territorial wines every day. The Pecorino is very good at this, with its nose of herbs, cereals and ripe apples, on a very pleasant palate. No less so are the two Picenos: the Superiore Oro 2011 (mistakenly shown in last year's Guide, when in fact we had tasted the 2010) better expressed montepulciano's fruity energy and power, while the Superiore 2013 is more delicate and flowery, as if the cool growing year allowed the character of the sangiovese to prevail. The Anghelos 2012 is mature, spicy and has good length.

○ Verdicchio dei Castelli di Jesi Cl. Sup. Il Coroncino '13	♥♥ 2*
○ Verdicchio dei Castelli di Jesi Cl. Sup. Gaiospino '13	♥♥ 4
○ Verdicchio dei Castelli di Jesi Cl. Sup. Gaiospino Fumé '12	♥♥ 5
● Ganzerello '13	♥ 4
○ Verdicchio dei Castelli di Jesi Cl. Sup. Il Bacco '13	♥ 2
○ Verdicchio dei Castelli di Jesi Passito Bambulè '11	♥ 3
○ Verdicchio dei Castelli di Jesi Cl. Sup. Gaiospino '03	♥♥♥ 4
○ Verdicchio dei Castelli di Jesi Cl. Sup. Gaiospino '97	♥♥♥ 4*
○ Verdicchio dei Castelli di Jesi Cl. Sup. Il Coroncino '11	♥♥ 2*

● Anghelos '12	♥♥ 3
○ Offida Pecorino '14	♥♥ 2*
● Rosso Piceno Sup. '13	♥♥ 2*
● Rosso Piceno Sup. Oro '11	♥♥ 3
○ Offida Passerina '14	♥ 2
● Rosso Piceno '14	♥ 1*
● Anghelos '01	♥♥♥ 4
● Anghelos '99	♥♥♥ 4*
● Anghelos '11	♥♥ 3
● Anghelos '10	♥♥ 3
○ Offida Pecorino '13	♥♥ 2*
○ Offida Pecorino '12	♥♥ 2*
● Rosso Piceno '12	♥♥ 1*
● Rosso Piceno Sup. '12	♥♥ 2*
● Rosso Piceno Sup. '11	♥♥ 2*
● Rosso Piceno Sup. '10	♥♥ 2*

Fattoria Dezi

c.da Fontemaggio, 14
63029 Servigliano [FM]
Tel. 0734710090
fattoriadezi@hotmail.com

CELLAR SALES
PRE-BOOKED VISITS
ACCOMMODATION
ANNUAL PRODUCTION 45,000 bottles
HECTARES UNDER VINE 15.00

From the terrace above the Dezi wine cellar
there is a view of most of the vineyards
managed by Davide. At any time of year
even the less expert eye will see the order,
care and harmony screening the intense
work on the traditional cultivars that brother
Stefano transforms into powerful wines,
exuberant when young but blessed with the
ability to age slowly and round off any rough
edges, whether an excess of oak or a
hiccough in the aromatics. Complexity is also
intentional in the whites, one obtained from
pecorino, the other a blend of verdicchio and
malvasia, both aged a year in total, in
concrete and steel. The listings are
dominated by the chewy fibre of Regina del
Bosco 2011, with a nose of marasca cherry,
steak tartare and iron filings. A close-knit
tannic weave typifies the Dezio 2013, from
montepulciano with a dash of sangiovese,
without overpowering its flavour and fruity
vitality. The Solo 2013 is dark, blood-rich
and tannin-heavy.

Emanuele Dianetti

loc. Carassai
c.da Vallerosa, 25
63063 Carassai [AP]
Tel. 3383928439
www.dianettivini.it

CELLAR SALES
PRE-BOOKED VISITS
ANNUAL PRODUCTION 6,600 bottles
HECTARES UNDER VINE 2.00

The work of Emanuele Dianetti may inspire
anyone thinking that large amounts of
capital and skilled personnel are needed to
become a winegrower. In reality, what you
need is wine country with perfectly
acclimatized vines, along with passion, a hint
of technical skill, perfect awareness of being
in the hands of nature. And you need to be
ready for the unexpected. Emanuele would
like to spend more time in his winery but as
he works full time in a bank, his mother
Giuliana is there to lend a helping hand.
From this Lilliputian cellar come two shining
gems, a fresh-tasting Pecorino 2014 with a
nose of bitter orange, white peach and
herbs, with outstanding drinkability, and an
Offida Rosso 2012, where the impulsive
character of montepulciano is tamed by
suitable ageing on the vine and in small oak
casks. The result is a wine of intact
fruitiness, with a close-woven, sweet tannic
weave perfectly integrated with the alcohol.

● Dezio '13	♥♥ 3
● Regina del Bosco '11	♥♥ 6
○ Falerio Pecorino Servigliano P. '13	♥ 3
○ Solagne '13	♥ 3
● Solo '13	♥ 6
● Regina del Bosco '06	♥♥♥ 6
● Regina del Bosco '05	♥♥♥ 6
● Regina del Bosco '03	♥♥♥ 6
● Solo Sangiovese '05	♥♥♥ 6
● Solo Sangiovese '01	♥♥♥ 5
● Solo Sangiovese '00	♥♥♥ 6
● Dezio '12	♥♥ 3
● Dezio '11	♥♥ 3
● Regina del Bosco '10	♥♥ 6
● Solo '12	♥♥ 6

○ Offida Pecorino Vignagiulia '14	♥♥ 3*
● Offida Rosso Vignagiulia '12	♥♥ 4
○ Offida Pecorino Vignagiulia '13	♥♥ 3
● Offida Rosso Vignagiulia '11	♥♥ 4

MARCHE

Fazi Battaglia

VIA ROMA, 117
60031 CASTELPLANIO [AN]
TEL. 073181591
www.fazibattaglia.it

CELLAR SALES
PRE-BOOKED VISITS
ANNUAL PRODUCTION 1,600,000 bottles
HECTARES UNDER VINE 200.00

Many things have changed at Fazi Battaglia. The Sparaco–Giannotti family, key players in the Verdicchio story, take their leave and hand over the property to the Angelini family of Bertani Domains fame. The transition will be made one a step at a time but important decisions have already been taken by Emilio Pedron, the group's guiding light. The most important is the decision to leave technical management to Lorenzo Landi who will thus be able to consolidate the good work of recent years. A graphic restyling is involved all labels while, for now, we tasted all the flagships of the old management team. The San Sisto 2013 is brimming over with elegance and personality, its imperceptible ageing in oak bringing complexity and magnetic charm. But do not underestimate the personality of the Massaccio 2013, faithfully reflecting the varietal characteristics and bursting with flavour in the finish. Arkezia 2012 is a sophisticated Verdicchio with balanced sweetness and hints of candied orange.

○ Arkezia '12	🍷🍷 5
○ Castelli di Jesi Verdicchio Cl. San Sisto Ris. '13	🍷🍷 4
○ Verdicchio dei Castelli di Jesi Cl. Sup. Massaccio '13	🍷🍷 3*
○ Verdicchio dei Castelli di Jesi Cl. Sup. Le Moie '14	🍷🍷 2*
○ Verdicchio dei Castelli di Jesi Cl. Titulus '14	🍷 2
○ Castelli di Jesi Verdicchio Cl. San Sisto Ris. '10	🍷🍷🍷 4*
○ Verdicchio dei Castelli di Jesi Cl. San Sisto Ris. '09	🍷🍷🍷 4*
○ Verdicchio dei Castelli di Jesi Cl. San Sisto Ris. '07	🍷🍷🍷 4
○ Verdicchio dei Castelli di Jesi Cl. San Sisto Ris. '05	🍷🍷🍷 4

Andrea Felici

VIA SANT'ISIDORO, 28
62021 APIRO [MC]
TEL. 0733611431
www.andreafelici.it

CELLAR SALES
PRE-BOOKED VISITS
ANNUAL PRODUCTION 53,000 bottles
HECTARES UNDER VINE 9.00
VITICULTURE METHOD Certified Organic

Leopardo Felici is a young man who started from scratch to build his dream of becoming a vigneron in Apiro, first shaping taste and empathy with Gordon Ramsay and Enoteca Pinchiorri, the Italian temple of wine. He has had a leg up from an exceptional terroir, which produces various expressions of Verdicchio: on one hand Mediterranean might in Jesi, on the other hand, the influence of Mount San Vicino on the border with Matelica. At the centre, a vineyard with a pool, innovative choices like screw caps for the whole line, and the pursuit of maximum territorial expression. Mission accomplished for the Cantico 2012, a slow-ageing Riserva, a marathon runner whose citrus fruit, particularly grapefruit and citron, with mountain herb and flower hints are the harbingers of future success, mirrored in a powerful, richly-flavoured, progressive palate. And the winery calling card is equally distinguished: the Andrea Felici 2014 is a masterful interpretation of the vintage.

○ Castelli di Jesi Verdicchio Cl. Il Cantico della Figura Ris. '12	🍷🍷🍷 4*
○ Verdicchio dei Castelli di Jesi Cl. Sup. Andrea Felici '14	🍷🍷 3*
○ Castelli di Jesi Verdicchio Cl. Il Cantico della Figura Ris. '11	🍷🍷🍷 4*
○ Castelli di Jesi Verdicchio Cl. Il Cantico della Figura Ris. '10	🍷🍷🍷 4*
○ Verdicchio dei Castelli di Jesi Cl. Il Cantico della Figura Ris. '09	🍷🍷🍷 4*
○ Verdicchio dei Castelli di Jesi Cl. Sup. Andrea Felici '13	🍷🍷 2*
○ Verdicchio dei Castelli di Jesi Cl. Sup. Andrea Felici '12	🍷🍷 2*
○ Verdicchio dei Castelli di Jesi Cl. Sup. Andrea Felici '11	🍷🍷 2*
○ Verdicchio dei Castelli di Jesi Cl. Sup. Andrea Felici '10	🍷🍷 2*

Fiorano

C.DA FIORANO, 19
63067 COSSIGNANO [AP]
TEL. 073598446
www.agrifiorano.it

CELLAR SALES
PRE-BOOKED VISITS
ACCOMMODATION
ANNUAL PRODUCTION 30,000 bottles
HECTARES UNDER VINE 6.00
VITICULTURE METHOD Certified Organic

Paolo Beretta left his work as a dental technician to pursue his dream of becoming an skilled winegrower. Even his Milanese speech is now coloured with local expressions. All thanks to Cossignano, which dazzled him with the peaceful beauty of its unspoiled countryside. He and wife Paola turned the old holiday farmhouse into a magical place, set above the amphitheatre of vineyards and underground cellar. They are supporters of organic farming and the Italian federation of independent vintners, making crystalline, territorial wines of well-defined character. For years, Donna Orgilla has been one of the best Pecorinos in the region. The 2014 is outstanding, with its fresh nose of citrus fruit and aromatic herbs, extremely lively mouthfeel and lengthy saline trail. It brings home its first well-deserved Tre Bicchieri. Fragrance, marked flowery notes and drinkability characterize the Sangiovese Fiorano 2014, whereas Terre di Giobbe 2012 has a nose of juicy marasca cherries and cocoa powder on a rich mouth.

Cantine Fontezoppa

C.DA SAN DOMENICO, 38
62012 CIVITANOVA MARCHE [MC]
TEL. 0733790504
www.cantinefontezoppa.it

CELLAR SALES
PRE-BOOKED VISITS
ACCOMMODATION AND RESTAURANT SERVICE
ANNUAL PRODUCTION 290,000 bottles
HECTARES UNDER VINE 38.00

Fontezoppa activities are divided between the production sites of Civitanova, home of the winery, and vineyards of varieties other than vernaccia and pinot nero. The latter come from the property at Serrapetrona, a unique foothill terroir. All the vineyards are undergoing organic conversion. The cellar's spacious rooms allow for a wide range of products covering most of the Macerata designations. The Carapetto 2011, a monovarietal cabernet sauvignon, makes a great impression, with dark balsamic aromas; lean and austere on the palate, it has a very bright future. As the Morò was missing, we tasted a good Falcotto 2012: the typically spicy tones of vernaccia combine with a resolute character and progressive palate. The Cascina 2007, a mahogany brown passito of great complexity displaying notes of coffee cream, cola and pomegranate, on a palate overflowing with counterpoints and nuances.

○ Offida Pecorino Donna Orgilla '14	♟♟♟ 3*
● Fiorano '14	♟♟ 2*
● Rosso Piceno Sup. Terre di Giobbe '12	♟♟ 3
○ Giulia Erminia '13	♟ 2
● Fiorano Sangiovese '10	♟♟ 2*
○ Offida Pecorino Donna Orgilla '13	♟♟ 3*
○ Offida Pecorino Donna Orgilla '12	♟♟ 3
○ Offida Pecorino Donna Orgilla '11	♟♟ 3
○ Offida Pecorino Donna Orgilla '10	♟♟ 3*
○ Offida Pecorino Donna Orgilla '08	♟♟ 3*
● Rosso Piceno Sup. Terre di Giobbe '11	♟♟ 3
● Rosso Piceno Sup. Terre di Giobbe '10	♟♟ 3
● Rosso Piceno Sup. Terre di Giobbe '09	♟♟ 2*
● Rosso Piceno Sup. Terre di Giobbe '08	♟♟ 2*
● Rosso Piceno Sup. Terre di Giobbe '07	♟♟ 2*
● Sangiovese '11	♟♟ 2*

● Carapetto '11	♟♟ 5
● I Terreni di San Severino	
Cascià Passito '07	♟♟ 4
● Serrapetrona Falcotto '12	♟♟ 4
○ Citanò '14	♟ 2
● Colli Maceratesi Rosso Catò '12	♟ 3
⊙ Extra Brut Rosé M. Cl.	♟ 5
⊙ Frapiccì '14	♟ 2
● Serrapetrona Carpignano '12	♟ 2
● Vernaccia di Serrapetrona Dolce Fabrini	♟ 2
● Vernaccia di Serrapetrona Secco Fabrini	♟ 2
○ Colli Maceratesi Ribona '11	♟♟ 3
● Dedicato a Piero '09	♟♟ 5
● Serrapetrona Carpignano '09	♟♟ 2*
● Serrapetrona Falcotto '09	♟♟ 4
● Serrapetrona Morò '09	♟♟ 5

★Gioacchino Garofoli

VIA CARLO MARX, 123
60022 CASTELFIDARDO [AN]
TEL. 0717820162
www.garofolivini.it

CELLAR SALES
PRE-BOOKED VISITS
ANNUAL PRODUCTION 2,000,000 bottles
HECTARES UNDER VINE 42.00

Gianfranco and Carlo Garofoli are two key figures in the Marche wine scenario. They own one of the best-known companies for history, professional standards, size and distribution network, and their commitment extends far beyond the boundaries of their business. Gianfranco is chairman of the super consortium IMT; Carlo is dedicated to pursuing a refined wine style applied not only to the famous Verdicchios but also to Conero montepulciano and the tricky field of sparklers. The hospitable Castelfidardo cellar produces wines for all pockets, and always aiming for the heights of quality. Just when we thought that Podium would fail to amaze us ever again, along came the 2013: almond, aniseed, pollen and flowery hints usher in balsamic shades; the palate is pure and extremely detailed, closing with a bewitching salinity. The others include a perky Macrina 2014, the mouthfilling smack of the Grosso Agontano 2011 and the silky Dorato 2013, with its strong hints of botrytis.

Marco Gatti

VIA LAGUA E SAN MARTINO, 2
60043 CERRETO D'ESI [AN]
TEL. 0732677012
www.gattiagri.it

CELLAR SALES
PRE-BOOKED VISITS
ANNUAL PRODUCTION 10,000 bottles
HECTARES UNDER VINE 7.00

On more than one occasion new wineries have turned up with stunning products we had to take into account. One of these was Marco Gatti, a winegrower who is one of the myriad artisan vintners that are the soul of the Verdicchio di Matelica viticulture district. Well, not only has Marco confirmed last year's exploit, he has also raised the quality bar. This agronomist and nurseryman manages his estates under vine in person. In his small Cerreto d'Esi cellars he produces Verdicchio with significant alcohol and extract, underpinned by typical matelica terroir vigour. The counterpoints between a massive structure and high acidity give balance to the palate of the Millo 2013, while the nose bathes in a whirl of aniseed, rain-washed pebbles, and slightly peaty, balsamic hints. The Villa Marilla 2014 shows a nose of acerbic apple and a juicy, linear palate with a leisurely salty finish.

○ Verdicchio dei Castelli di Jesi Cl. Sup. Podium '13	♟♟♟ 4*
○ Dorato '13	♟♟ 3*
● Camerlano '09	♟♟ 4
○ Castelli di Jesi Verdicchio Cl. Serra Fiorese Ris. '10	♟♟ 4
● Conero Grosso Agontano Ris. '11	♟♟ 5
☉ Kòmaros '14	♟♟ 2*
● Rosso Conero Piancarda '12	♟♟ 3
● Rosso Piceno Colle Ambro '12	♟♟ 2*
○ Verdicchio dei Castelli di Jesi Brut M. Cl. Delis '11	♟♟ 4
○ Verdicchio dei Castelli di Jesi Cl. Sup. Macrina '14	♟♟ 2*
○ Verdicchio dei Castelli di Jesi Passito Brumato '07	♟♟ 4
○ Verdicchio dei Castelli di Jesi Cl. Sup. Podium '12	♟♟♟ 4*

○ Verdicchio di Matelica Millo Ris. '13	♟♟ 3*
○ Verdicchio di Matelica Villa Marilla '14	♟♟ 2*
○ Verdicchio di Matelica '14	♟♟ 2*
○ Verdicchio di Matelica '13	♟♟ 2*
○ Verdicchio di Matelica Millo Ris. '12	♟♟ 3
○ Verdicchio di Matelica Villa Marilla '13	♟♟ 2*

Luciano Landi

VIA GAVIGLIANO, 16
60030 BELVEDERE OSTRENSE [AN]
TEL. 073162353
www.aziendalandi.it

CELLAR SALES
PRE-BOOKED VISITS
ACCOMMODATION AND RESTAURANT SERVICE
ANNUAL PRODUCTION 80,000 bottles
HECTARES UNDER VINE 20.00

Luciano Landi is a name that cannot be
overlooked when listing the winegrowers
who elevated Lacrima di Morro d'Alba to its
rightful position. He has never gone over
the top, preferring to stay within the
confines of what has been family winery
style since the 1950s. With Sergio
Paolucci, the oenologist who has worked
with him since the beginning, he has
promoted a plush, richly extracted style
made possible by long ripening on the vine
and patient ageing in small wood for this
more aspirational labels. One quirk: his
vines are not limited to lacrima or
verdicchio, as he also grows montepulciano
and some international cultivars. And it is
these three varietals, with small quantities
of merlot and cabernet sauvignon, that
yield the Goliardo 2010, with its still
fresh-tasting fruit, vivid red and chocolatey
shades, and warm smooth palate. The
Lacrimas are among the best in the district,
with the suitably complex Gavigliano 2013
having well-defined fruit-forward tones.

● Goliardo '10	♟♟ 4
● Lacrima di Morro d'Alba '14	♟♟ 2*
● Lacrima di Morro d'Alba Sup. Gavigliano '13	♟♟ 3
○ Verdicchio dei Castelli di Jesi Cl. '14	♟ 2
● Goliardo '09	♟♟ 4
● Kore '09	♟♟ 3
● Lacrima di Morro d'Alba '10	♟♟ 2*
● Lacrima di Morro d'Alba Sup. Gavigliano '11	♟♟ 3
● Nobilnero '09	♟♟ 6
● Ragosto '11	♟♟ 2*
● Ragosto '10	♟♟ 2*
☉ Syla '13	♟♟ 2*
☉ Syla '11	♟♟ 2*

Conte Leopardi Dittajuti

VIA MARINA II, 24
60026 NUMANA [AN]
TEL. 0717390116
www.conteleopardi.it

CELLAR SALES
PRE-BOOKED VISITS
ANNUAL PRODUCTION 350,000 bottles
HECTARES UNDER VINE 49.00

Piervittorio Leopardi Dittajuti has taken a
clearly modern approach for his winery,
pursued in the Numana cellars with
attentive styling. He uses various sizes of
wood, typically small, for maturation of the
reds; the aromatic freshness of his whites
is achieved using steel and vinification at
controlled temperatures. Montepulciano,
merlot and syrah, as well as sauvignon,
grow in Sirolo and Numana, in vineyards
that enjoy the influence of the nearby
Adriatic. His verdicchio comes from
vineyards out in Staffolo. Once again we
were impressed by the Conero Riserva
Pigmento 2012: an original hint of
rosemary elbows through notes of red
berry, giving complexity to a piquant,
fragrant palate of sound character. The
Casirano 2013 has fruity energy while the
Villa Marina 2013 offers a soft palate and
notes of sour cherry. Among the whites, we
highlight the elegant almond twist of the
Castelverde 2014, with its supple dainty
body.

● Conero Pigmento Ris. '12	♟♟ 5
● Rose del Coppo '14	♟♟ 2*
● Rosso Conero Casirano '13	♟♟ 4
● Rosso Conero Villa Marina '13	♟♟ 3
○ Verdicchio dei Castelli di Jesi Cl. Castelverde '14	♟♟ 2*
○ Bianco del Coppo Sauvignon '14	♟ 2
○ Calcare '14	♟ 3
● Rosso Conero Fructus '14	♟ 2
● Rosso Conero Fructus '12	♟♟ 2*
● Rosso Conero Villa Marina '11	♟♟ 3
● Rosso Conero Villa Marina '10	♟♟ 3*
○ Verdicchio dei Castelli di Jesi Cl. Artemano '11	♟♟ 2*
○ Verdicchio dei Castelli di Jesi Cl. Castelverde '12	♟♟ 2*

Stefano Mancinelli

VIA ROMA, 62
60030 MORRO D'ALBA [AN]
TEL. 073163021
www.mancinellivini.it

CELLAR SALES
PRE-BOOKED VISITS
ACCOMMODATION
ANNUAL PRODUCTION 150,000 bottles
HECTARES UNDER VINE 25.00

Unlike the Sun King, to whom the cellar devotes a great raisined wine, after Stefano Mancinelli there will not be floods! His untiring work of recovery, study and diffusion of lacrima nera, Morro d'Alba's native, semi-aromatic black grape has brought results in the small territory multiplying through dozens of wineries now in business. Mancinelli continues to be a benchmark for consistency and precision, with crisp, modern wines, with generous aromas, wide selections, and eminently cellarable. The Lacrima Superiore 2013 shows the most admirable side of the varietal: concentrated notes of cloves, cherry and dried roses lead to a fruit-driven, full and consistent mouth, backed up by beautifully mature tannins. These sensations are even more apparent in the creamy Passito Re Sole 2010. The Lacrima 2013 has markedly floral notes and a crisp, spicy, beautifully typed palate. Two fruity, subtle wines with a good acid backbone make the most of Verdicchio's tendency to flow across the palate.

● Lacrima di Morro d'Alba Passito Re Sole '10	♥♥ 5
● Lacrima di Morro d'Alba Sup. '13	♥♥ 3*
● Lacrima di Morro d'Alba '13	♥♥ 2*
● Terre dei Goti '10	♥♥ 5
○ Verdicchio dei Castelli di Jesi Cl. '14	♥ 2
○ Verdicchio dei Castelli di Jesi Cl. Sup. '14	♥ 2
● Lacrima di Morro d'Alba Passito Re Sole '07	♀♀ 5
● Lacrima di Morro d'Alba Santa Maria del Fiore '12	♀♀ 2*
● Lacrima di Morro d'Alba Santa Maria del Fiore '11	♀♀ 2*
● Lacrima di Morro d'Alba Sensazioni di Frutto '13	♀♀ 2*
● Lacrima di Morro d'Alba Sup. '12	♀♀ 3
● Lacrima di Morro d'Alba Sup. '11	♀♀ 3

Maurizio Marchetti

FRAZ. PINOCCHIO
VIA DI PONTELUNGO, 166
60131 ANCONA
TEL. 071897386
www.marchettiwines.it

CELLAR SALES
PRE-BOOKED VISITS
ANNUAL PRODUCTION 60,000 bottles
HECTARES UNDER VINE 20.00

Maurizio Marchetti, son of vignerons, embodies the story of Conero, bringing his winery into modern times by renovating vineyards surrounding Villa Bonomi, his old family manor house. The different plots start down on valley floors towards Candia, a hilly Ancona hamlet with extensive vineyards. The best-aspected are dedicated to montepulciano and this is true wine country for the variety, which ripens without concern here. Remaining plots are for sangiovese and a few international cultivars. The cellar adjacent to the villa is minimal and houses the wood used for ageing the Riserva Villa Bonomi, whose 2012 has intense aromas of morello cherry and chocolate, encoring on the palate where the alcohol harmonizes well with the close-knit, chewy tannins. Fragrant aromatics and an appealingly soft, wide palate characterize the Tenuta del Cavaliere 2014. The Castro di San Silvestro has a nose of fresh-tasting cherry and drinkability.

● Conero Villa Bonomi Ris. '12	♥♥ 5
○ Verdicchio dei Castelli di Jesi Cl. Sup. Tenuta del Cavaliere '14	♥♥ 3
● Rosso Conero Castro di San Silvestro '14	♥ 2
○ Verdicchio dei Castelli di Jesi Cl. '14	♥ 2
● Rosso Conero Villa Bonomi Ris. '02	♀♀♀ 4
● Conero Villa Bonomi Ris. '11	♀♀ 5
● Conero Villa Bonomi Ris. '10	♀♀ 4
● Rosso Conero Villa Bonomi Ris. '08	♀♀ 4
○ Verdicchio dei Castelli di Jesi Cl. '13	♀♀ 2*
○ Verdicchio dei Castelli di Jesi Cl. Sup. Tenuta del Cavaliere '13	♀♀ 3
○ Verdicchio dei Castelli di Jesi Cl. Sup. Tenuta del Cavaliere '11	♀♀ 3
○ Verdicchio dei Castelli di Jesi Cl. Sup. Tenuta del Cavaliere '10	♀♀ 3

Marotti Campi

VIA SANT'AMICO, 14
60030 MORRO D'ALBA [AN]
TEL. 0731618027
www.marotticampi.it

CELLAR SALES
PRE-BOOKED VISITS
ACCOMMODATION
ANNUAL PRODUCTION 220,000 bottles
HECTARES UNDER VINE 68.00

The walls of the beautiful manor house testify to a long history that was brought into the modern era only in 1991, when it was decided to upgrade the area under vine. The cellar was built in 1999, fitting into the group of buildings that dominate a landscape of vineyards, to process the grapes of numerous plots, the best of which are located in Contrada Sant'Amico. Vinification is mindful of the varietal character of lacrima and verdicchio. Small wood is reserved for the benefit of only the most important wines, and the rest are managed in steel. Orgiolo 2013 remains our first choice: flowery, spicy, with a firm backbone for an impressive Lacrima, one of the best in the district. Rùbico 2014 displays vigour and a tenaciously aromatic finish. Salmariano 2012 is creamy, very flavoursome, slightly weighed down by its soft progression. Donderè 2011 is an unusual mix of petit verdot, montepulciano and cabernet: black pepper and rose petals on an elegantly sinuous palate.

Valter Mattoni

VIA PESCOLLA, 1
63030 CASTORANO [AP]
TEL. 073687329
www.valtermattoni.it

CELLAR SALES
PRE-BOOKED VISITS
ANNUAL PRODUCTION 6,000 bottles
HECTARES UNDER VINE 3.50

In the Noughties, if a fortune-teller had predicted that Valter Mattoni would become a champion vigneron, with a new winery, overwhelming sales success, and a number of wines among Piceno's best, we are sure he would have mocked the idea with one of his colourful dialect quips. He was happy enough with what he was producing in his grandfather's vineyard. Things changed when he was persuaded by the encouragement and advice of Marco Casolanetti and our hypothetical prediction has come to pass. Arshura 2013 is one of the most successful pure Montepulcianos in the district: an iridescent, multifaceted nose combining the fruitiness of marasca cherry, burnt embers and the vivid pungency of spices, leading into a palate of sweeping energy, varietal to its core, untamed. A delicate flurry of roots, raspberry, and minerally phrases breathe life into a Rossobordò 2012 displaying a rarefied, démodé palate, at first sight rather fragile but capable of unimagined depth.

○ Castelli di Jesi Verdicchio Cl. Salmariano Ris. '12	♟♟ 3
● Donderè '11	♟♟ 3
● Lacrima di Morro d'Alba Rùbico '14	♟♟ 2*
● Lacrima di Morro d'Alba Sup. Orgiolo '13	♟♟ 3
○ Verdicchio dei Castelli di Jesi Cl. Sup. Luzano '14	♟♟ 2*
⊙ Brut Rosé	♟ 3
⊙ Rosato '14	♟ 2
○ Verdicchio dei Castelli di Jesi Cl. Albiano '14	♟ 1*
○ Verdicchio dei Castelli di Jesi Cl. Salmariano Ris. '08	♟♟♟ 3*
○ Verdicchio dei Castelli di Jesi Cl. Salmariano Ris. '07	♟♟♟ 2*

● Arshura '13	♟♟ 5
● Rossobordò '12	♟♟ 8
● Arshura '11	♟♟♟ 3*
● Arshura '12	♟♟ 5
● Arshura '10	♟♟ 3*
● Arshura '09	♟♟ 3
● Arshura '08	♟♟ 3
⊙ Cose Cose '13	♟♟ 3
⊙ Cose Cose '12	♟♟ 2*
⊙ Cose Cose '11	♟♟ 2*
● Rosso Bordò '10	♟♟ 8
● Rossobordò '11	♟♟ 8
⊙ Trebbien '13	♟♟ 3
⊙ Trebbien '12	♟♟ 2*

★La Monacesca

C.DA MONACESCA
62024 MATELICA [MC]
TEL. 0733672641
www.monacesca.it

CELLAR SALES
PRE-BOOKED VISITS
ANNUAL PRODUCTION 180,000 bottles
HECTARES UNDER VINE 30.00

If Matelica can stand up to be counted with other great Italian and international white wine terroirs, it is mainly thanks to Aldo Cifola's magnificent versions of Verdicchio. For 35 years he has travelled the world with wines made from the grapes picked near the ancient convent and Farfa church after which the small renovated hamlet is named. The complex includes the vinification cellar with steel tanks used to make the Chardonnays and Verdicchio Ecclesias, and the barrel cellar for maturation of his Camerte, a sangiovese grosso with 30% merlot, the red sneaking in among the many whites. Mirum 2013 did not make the listings: occasionally bottling times are out of kilter with our tasting calendar. Its younger brother proffers a fruity nose and mouthfilling palate while still maintaining its salinity typical of matelica. Ecclesia 2013 is reminiscent of white-fleshed fruit salad with a juicy, truly leisurely palate. Camerte 2011 is redolent of flowers, offering a gutsy and vibrant mouthfeel.

○ Verdicchio di Matelica La Monacesca '13	♟♟ 2*
● Camerte '11	♟♟ 4
● Ecclesia '13	♟♟ 3
● Camerte '99	♟♟♟ 5
○ Mirum '94	♟♟♟ 3*
○ Verdicchio di Matelica '94	♟♟♟ 3
○ Verdicchio di Matelica Mirum Ris. '12	♟♟♟ 5
○ Verdicchio di Matelica Mirum Ris. '11	♟♟♟ 5
○ Verdicchio di Matelica Mirum Ris. '10	♟♟♟ 4*
○ Verdicchio di Matelica Mirum Ris. '09	♟♟♟ 4
○ Verdicchio di Matelica Mirum Ris. '08	♟♟♟ 4
○ Verdicchio di Matelica Mirum Ris. '07	♟♟♟ 4*
○ Verdicchio di Matelica Mirum Ris. '06	♟♟♟ 4
○ Verdicchio di Matelica Mirum Ris. '04	♟♟♟ 4
○ Verdicchio di Matelica Mirum Ris. '02	♟♟♟ 3

Monte Schiavo

FRAZ. MONTESCHIAVO
VIA VIVAIO
60030 MAIOLATI SPONTINI [AN]
TEL. 0731700385
www.monteschiavo.it

CELLAR SALES
PRE-BOOKED VISITS
ANNUAL PRODUCTION 1,500,000 bottles
HECTARES UNDER VINE 115.00

The Rosora Tassanare and Poggio San Marcello Coste del Molino crus have little to envy the best Verdicchio vineyards, and Monteschiavo harnesses their features to perfection. Red grapes, mostly montepulciano, sangiovese and some international varieties are grown in the rows around the spacious, efficient Scorcelletti cellar. Recently the Pieralisi family proceeded to make radical changes in the technical management of the winery and now works with Carlo Ferrini and Simone Schiaffino, both oenologists. While awaiting the handover getting up to speed, we tasted a selection bereft of many flagships. Rosso Conero Serenelli 2011 can still display intact fruit and an admirably mineral vein providing complexity without any loss of smoothness on the palate. Also rather vibrant is the Pallio 2014, a fruity, floral white with a dynamic drinkability. Decidedly sound, the Sassaiolo 2012, displaying a tenacious, well-profiled structure.

● Rosso Conero Serenelli '11	♟♟ 3*
● Lacrima di Morro d'Alba Marzaiola '14	♟♟ 2*
● Rosso Piceno Sassaiolo '12	♟♟ 2*
○ Verdicchio Castelli di Jesi Cl. Passito Arché '09	♟♟ 4
○ Verdicchio dei Castelli di Jesi Cl. Sup. Pallio di S. Floriano '14	♟♟ 3
● Rosso Conero Adeodato '00	♟♟♟ 5
○ Verdicchio dei Castelli di Jesi Cl. Sup. Pallio di S. Floriano '11	♟♟♟ 2*
○ Verdicchio dei Castelli di Jesi Cl. Sup. Pallio di S. Floriano '10	♟♟♟ 2*
○ Verdicchio dei Castelli di Jesi Cl. Sup. Pallio di S. Floriano '09	♟♟♟ 2*
○ Castelli di Jesi Verdicchio Cl. Le Giuncare Ris. '11	♟♟ 3*

Montecappone

VIA COLLE OLIVO, 2
60035 JESI [AN]
TEL. 0731205761
www.montecappone.com

CELLAR SALES
PRE-BOOKED VISITS
ANNUAL PRODUCTION 150,000 bottles
HECTARES UNDER VINE 70.00

Gianluca Mirizzi has a clear vision of his wines: scented, pleasing, vigorous, and intensely aromatic. Anyone who purchases a bottle should never leave half unconsumed on the table. He was guided in the right direction by Lorenzo Landi and his "defensive" winemaking, which suggests early harvest for whites, not for reds where it is always important to taste the grape seed; total protection of aromatic precursors from oxidation, to be implemented with accurate temperature control: use of reductive winemaking environments and methodologies. For reds only, small, used wood. Utopia Riserva shows its stylish silhouette despite the hot 2012 growing year, with a peerless piquant grip and a dynamically citrus finish. The Federico II 2014 is subtly complex, while the Tabano Rosso 2013 is juicy and fruit-driven. The pleasant new arrival, a scented Sauvignon Extra Dry 2014, makes an irresistible aperitif.

○ Castelli di Jesi Verdicchio Cl. Utopia Ris. '12	♟♟ 4
○ Akinos	♟♟ 3
○ Sauvignon Extra Dry '14	♟♟ 3
● Tabano Rosso '13	♟♟ 4
○ Verdicchio dei Castelli di Jesi Cl. Sup. Federico II a.D. 1194 '14	♟♟ 3
○ La Breccia '14	♟ 3
● Rosso Piceno '14	♟ 2
○ Tabano Bianco '14	♟ 4
● Utopia '12	♟ 6
○ Verdicchio dei Castelli di Jesi Cl. Utopia Ris. '08	♟♟♟ 4
○ Verdicchio dei Castelli di Jesi Cl. Utopia Ris. '07	♟♟♟ 4*

Muròla

C.DA VILLAMAGNA, 9
62010 URBISAGLIA [MC]
TEL. 0733506843
www.murola.it

CELLAR SALES
PRE-BOOKED VISITS
ANNUAL PRODUCTION 700,000 bottles
HECTARES UNDER VINE 60.00

Jerzy Mosiewicz is the heir of an ancient family active in Macerata's agricultural sector since 1724. The impressive estates are located in a sheltered valley that winds through the Riserva Naturale dell'Abbadia di Fiastra and the municipality of Mogliano. The vineyards that host regional winegrowing classics like montepulciano, sangiovese and maceratino but also international varieties, were planted in more recent times. Vinification takes place in a state-of-the-art winery set among the vines and this is where the wines are made: contemporary, with a cosmopolitan feel and true to the territory. And it was the Teodoro 2012, a pure Montepulciano aged 24 months in barrique and glass, that most impressed the tasting panel, with its nose of elegant spice and morello cherry notes and a mouth of intact fruit, fragrant and complex at the same time. The same finesse characterized the Camà 2012 from sangiovese, with its expressive flowery nose and smooth palate.

● Teodoro '12	♟♟♟ 3*
● Camà '12	♟♟ 2*
○ Jurek Brut M.Cl. '12	♟♟ 4
● Sangiovese '14	♟♟ 2*
○ Colli Maceratesi Ribona '14	♟ 2
○ Colli Maceratesi Ribona Andrea Baccius '14	♟ 3
○ Grechetto '14	♟ 2
⊙ Jole Brut '13	♟ 3
○ Passerina '14	♟ 2
● Camà '11	♟♟ 3*
● Camà '10	♟♟ 4
○ Colli Maceratesi Ribona '12	♟♟ 2*
○ Colli Maceratesi Ribona '11	♟♟ 2*
○ Jurek M.Cl. '11	♟♟ 4
● Teodoro '11	♟♟ 3
● Teodoro '10	♟♟ 3

★Oasi degli Angeli

c.da Sant'Egidio, 50
63012 Cupra Marittima [AP]
Tel. 0735778569
www.kurni.it

CELLAR SALES
PRE-BOOKED VISITS
ANNUAL PRODUCTION 5,000 bottles
HECTARES UNDER VINE 16.00

It is above all a cultural process that allows Marco Casolanetti and Eleonora Rossi to go beyond the theoretical limits of the varietal and create unforgettable wines. Everything is meticulously studied and evaluated. Then the decisive collaboration with nature is defined. This is the only way to explain the dense plantings of montepulciano, the choice of fine woods for maturing the wines, the use of farming methods very close to biodynamics. Or the desire to resurrect an ancient clone of grenache on the brink of extinction for its low productivity when Piceno farmers had given it a vineyard haven and a name: bordò. Kupra 2012 is its modern version, showing a beguiling nose of Oriental spices, solidly sophisticated character, and firecracker-like finish. The Kurni 2013 makes the most of the cool growing year to display a more supple body, without sacrificing its impressively solid structure and overwhelming fruit-driven intensity.

● Kupra '12	♥♥♥	8
● Kurni '13	♥♥	8
● Kupra '10	♀♀♀	8
● Kurni '10	♀♀♀	8
● Kurni '09	♀♀♀	8
● Kurni '08	♀♀♀	8
● Kurni '07	♀♀♀	8
● Kurni '04	♀♀♀	8
● Kurni '03	♀♀♀	8
● Kurni '02	♀♀♀	8
● Kurni '01	♀♀♀	8
● Kurni '00	♀♀♀	8
● Kurni '98	♀♀♀	8
● Kurni '97	♀♀♀	8

Pantaleone

via Colonnata Alta, 118
63100 Ascoli Piceno
Tel. 3478757476
www.pantaleonewine.com

PRE-BOOKED VISITS
ANNUAL PRODUCTION 60,000 bottles
HECTARES UNDER VINE 13.00
VITICULTURE METHOD Certified Organic

Pantaleone is a small, dynamic winery managed by two young owners: Francesca and Federica Pantaloni. What was almost a hobby for the father of the two girls was given the drive to become a business by Giuseppe Infriccioli, who had grown up in a family that had always been in wine and today is Francesca's husband. The vineyards lie outside the classic Piceno zone, between Ascoli and Mount Ascensione, well-aspected, breezy, little human presence. In the cellar Pantaleone seeks "northern" freshness for its whites, vinified in reduction, while reds go for more intense fruitiness and concentration, aged in small wood. Heading the field once again is the fresh-tasting Onirocep 2014, with its nose of grapefruit and sage on a lean, refreshing palate. Boccascena 2012 marries the fruity character of montepulciano with the spiciness of cabernet sauvignon on a palate of consistent, abundant tannins.

● Boccascena '12	♥♥	3
○ Falerio Pecorino Onirocep '14	♥♥	2*
○ Chicca '14	♥	2
● Atto I '10	♀♀	2*
● Atto I '09	♀♀	2*
○ Chicca '13	♀♀	2*
○ Falerio Pecorino Onirocep '13	♀♀	2*
● Io Boccascena '06	♀♀	3
● La Ribalta '10	♀♀	8
○ Onirocep '11	♀♀	2*
○ Onirocep '10	♀♀	3
● Sipario '09	♀♀	2*
● Sipario '06	♀♀	2*

Pievalta

VIA MONTESCHIAVO, 18
60030 MAIOLATI SPONTINI [AN]
TEL. 0731705199
www.baronepizzini.it

CELLAR SALES
PRE-BOOKED VISITS
ANNUAL PRODUCTION 110,500 bottles
HECTARES UNDER VINE 26.50
VITICULTURE METHOD Certified Biodynamic

Barone Pizzini is a leading Franciacorta
operation that arrived in the Marche in
2002, purchasing two plots of land. One is
adjacent to an old, solitary country church
that inspired the name of the winery; the
other is in Follonica, in San Paolo di Jesi, a
cru already known for its grape quality.
Upgrading of the vineyards, building of the
cellar and reception areas took the best
part of a decade. Today Pievalta is one of
the most influential labels in the area,
thanks to the work of Lombardy-born
Alessandro Fenino who developed his
professional skills in Verdicchio. His
biodynamic approach, hands-on
management, the understated attention to
the wine as it evolves achieve vibrant,
well-structured versions that reflect in full
the performance of the growing year. Thus
razor-sharp sinew underpins the sensations
of both wines submitted: while the Dominè
is more solidly-built and salty, the Pievalta
is more essential, with hints of medicinal
herbs and ripe apple.

○ Verdicchio dei Castelli di Jesi Cl. Sup. Dominè '14	♙♙ 2*
○ Verdicchio dei Castelli di Jesi Cl. Sup. Pievalta '14	♙♙ 2*
○ Castelli di Jesi Verdicchio Cl. San Paolo Ris. '10	♙♙♙ 3*
○ Verdicchio dei Castelli di Jesi Cl. Sup. Pievalta '09	♙♙♙ 2*
○ Verdicchio dei Castelli di Jesi Cl. Sup. Dominè '13	♙♙ 2*
○ Verdicchio dei Castelli di Jesi Cl. Sup. Pievalta '13	♙♙ 2*
○ Verdicchio dei Castelli di Jesi Passito Curina '12	♙♙ 4

Podere sul Lago

LOC. BORGIANO
VIA CASTELLO, 20
62020 SERRAPETRONA [MC]
TEL. 3333017380
www.poderesullago.it

CELLAR SALES
PRE-BOOKED VISITS
ANNUAL PRODUCTION 10,000 bottles
HECTARES UNDER VINE 4.00
SUSTAINABLE WINERY

Sandrino Quadraroli has served
Serrapetrona wine for years in his popular
eatery. The dream of becoming a producer
came true when he crossed paths with
Giancarlo and David Soverchia, agronomist
and oenologist. One step at a time, feet
firmly on the ground and caution to the fore,
they moulded their plan: a vineyard estate
overlooking the scenic shore location on
Lake Caccamo, a small cellar for the
vinification of vernaccia nera and merlot, a
miniscule barrel cellar and they were on
their way. Serrapetrona is a mountain terroir
producing feisty wines. Torcular 2013 is a
pure steel-aged Vernaccia with peppery
aromas and a smooth, powerful mouth, with
a strong local identity. The Ruggero 2013,
from merlot, combines red berries, slightly
charred oak and subtle strokes of
greenness on a persistent, full palate. Spicy,
taut and almost bony, the Cercis 2013, an
equal blend of vernaccia and merlot, aged
without oak.

● Cercis '13	♙♙ 3
● Il Ruggero '13	♙♙ 5
● Serrapetrona Torcular '13	♙♙ 2*
● Serrapetrona Lacus '13	♙ 5

Il Pollenza

LOC. TOLENTINO
C.DA CASONE, 4
62029 TOLENTINO [MC]
TEL. 0733961989
www.ilpollenza.it

PRE-BOOKED VISITS
ANNUAL PRODUCTION 200,000 bottles
HECTARES UNDER VINE 60.00

Sometimes lots of money is not the key to making an unknown spot on the national viticultural map into the location for the vinification of wines to be reckoned with. There has to be planning, a pool of experts, a pinch of patience and business skills. This was where Aldo Brachetti Peretti succeeded: his spectacular state-of-the-art cellar, set in a jewel of 16th-century architecture designed by Sangallo, consistently produces wines of remarkable, clean style, speaking an impeccable international language, rendered possible by sophisticated use of international varieties. The Pollenza 2012 is very Bordeaux-like, a sophisticated kaleidoscope of dark fruit, balsamic and cedarwood hints, and a confident, close-knit, almost stiff palate. A wine of great charm. The Cosmino 2012 mirrors its qualities, though without the same depth of movement. Seductive notes of honey, lavender, candied lemon peel intertwine on the Pius IX 2013's not oversweet palate.

● Il Pollenza '12	▼▼▼ 8
● Cosmino '12	▼▼ 5
○ Pius IX '13	▼▼ 6
○ Colli Maceratesi Ribona Angera '14	▼▼ 3
⊙ Extra Brut M.Cl. Il Pollenza ABP '11	▼▼ 7
● Porpora '12	▼▼ 3
⊙ Didi '14	▼ 3
● Il Pollenza '11	▼▼▼ 7
● Il Pollenza '10	▼▼▼ 7
● Il Pollenza '09	▼▼▼ 7
● Il Pollenza '07	▼▼▼ 7
● Cosmino '11	▼▼ 5
● Cosmino '10	▼▼ 5
⊙ Il Pollenza M. Cl. '10	▼▼ 5
○ Pius IX Mastai '12	▼▼ 6

Saladini Pilastri

VIA SALADINI, 5
63078 SPINETOLI [AP]
TEL. 0736899534
www.saladinipilastri.it

CELLAR SALES
PRE-BOOKED VISITS
ANNUAL PRODUCTION 1,000,000 bottles
HECTARES UNDER VINE 150.00
VITICULTURE METHOD Certified Organic
SUSTAINABLE WINERY

The Saladini Pilastri family roots lie deep the history of Piceno territory. Suffice it to say that the cellar is located in a 1400s farmhouse behind the imposing stately home. Conte Saladino Saladini Pilastri has invested significantly in the agricultural side of the 300-hectare estate. Half of the land is under vine, and for many years has been farmed by organic methods. The vineyards wind smoothly among the hills behind San Benedetto del Tronto, through the towns of Spinetoli and Monteprandone. Warm, sunny terrains where the montepulciano and sangiovese grapes do not struggle to ripen. The cooler slopes are given over to pecorino, trebbiano and passerina to maintain their acidity and aromatic precursors. Vigna Monteprandone 2013 has a fine nose of spices, red berry fruit and burnt firewood, with a correctly textured palate. Meadow herbs and flowers characterize a bright and varietal Pecorino 2014.

○ Offida Pecorino '14	▼▼ 3
● Rosso Piceno Sup. Montetinello '13	▼▼ 3
● Rosso Piceno Sup. V. Monteprandone '13	▼▼ 5
○ Offida Passerina '14	▼ 3
● Pregio del Conte '13	▼ 4
● Rosso Piceno Piediprato '13	▼ 3
● Rosso Piceno Sup. V. Monteprandone '00	▼▼▼ 3
● Pregio del Conte Rosso '10	▼▼ 4
● Rosso Piceno Piediprato '09	▼▼ 2*
● Rosso Piceno Sup. V. Monteprandone '10	▼▼ 4
● Rosso Piceno Sup. V. Monteprandone '09	▼▼ 4
● Rosso Piceno Sup. V. Monteprandone '08	▼▼ 4
● Rosso Piceno Sup. V. Montetinello '10	▼▼ 2*
● Rosso Piceno V. Piediprato '11	▼▼ 3

Poderi San Lazzaro

FRAZ. BORGO MIRIAM
C.DA SAN LAZZARO, 88
63073 OFFIDA [AP]
TEL. 0736889189
www.poderisanlazzaro.it

CELLAR SALES
PRE-BOOKED VISITS
ANNUAL PRODUCTION 45,000 bottles
HECTARES UNDER VINE 7.50
VITICULTURE METHOD Certified Organic

In Paolo Capriotti the group of Piceno winegrowers has one of the most respected vignerons of his generation. A tireless worker, a believer in a hands-on approach: from the farming of the land to the vinification carried out in the new, spacious cellar. He is attached to tradition and is involved in an articulate defence of territory that led him onto the organic path long since. His wines are admirably crafted in the artisanal manner and any puckering in the aromas is smoothed out in a few minutes when left to breathe and the revitalizing oxygen draws forth enthralling energy. Thus the Grifola 2012, slightly pungent with a cornucopia of marasca cherry, steak tartare and black olives, offers an austere, layered, lingering body. A wine of great character. The 2012 version of the Podere 72 is also slow and purposeful, but the coarse-grained tannins hold back its fruity succulence. The floral Sangiovese Polesio 2014 shows supple and easy-drinking.

● Offida Rosso Grifola '12	♟♟ 4
● Piceno Sup. Podere 72 '12	♟♟ 2*
● Polesio '14	♟♟ 2*
⊙ Elisetta '14	♟ 2
○ Offida Passerina '14	♟ 2
○ Offida Pecorino Pistillo '13	♟ 2
● Offida Rosso Grifola '11	♟♟♟ 4*
● Bordò '11	♟♟ 7
● Grifola '10	♟♟ 4
○ Offida Passerina '12	♟♟ 2*
○ Offida Passerina '11	♟♟ 2*
● Piceno Sup. Podere 72 '11	♟♟ 2*
● Polesio '13	♟♟ 2*
● Polesio '11	♟♟ 2*
● Rosso Piceno Sup. Podere 72 '10	♟♟ 2*
● Rosso Piceno Sup. Podere 72 '09	♟♟ 2*

Fattoria San Lorenzo

VIA SAN LORENZO, 6
60036 MONTECAROTTO [AN]
TEL. 073189656
az-crognaletti@libero.it

CELLAR SALES
PRE-BOOKED VISITS
ACCOMMODATION AND RESTAURANT SERVICE
ANNUAL PRODUCTION 100,000 bottles
HECTARES UNDER VINE 30.00
VITICULTURE METHOD Certified Organic

These are not streamlined, textbook wines by any means, and Natalino Crognaletti has constructed a style that goes in the opposite direction: organic vineyards, lengthy ageing maturation, minimal cellar intervention, native yeasts, low sulphites; time, concrete and old wood are his only allies for maturation of the wine. With the exception of the Di Gino vintage wines with their deceptively simple drinkability, production is characterized by interpretations of mouthfilling, glycerine-rich native varietals, with the lingering palate pepped up by feisty volatile acidity. Beautifully crafted artisan wines to be respected for their stubborn defence of an alternative but equally credible approach. The Paradiso 2010 displays great charm, with the most original Lacrima bouquet we have come across. Equally attractive is the mature, subtle San Lorenzo 2002, capable of pastel hints on the nose and a more decisive and complex palate.

● Paradiso '10	♟♟ 4
○ Il San Lorenzo '02	♟♟ 6
● Rosso Piceno Di Gino '13	♟♟ 2*
○ Verdicchio dei Castelli di Jesi Cl. Sup. Campo delle Oche '12	♟♟ 4
● Rosso Piceno Burello '11	♟ 3
○ Verdicchio dei Castelli di Jesi Di Gino '14	♟ 2
○ Verdicchio dei Castelli di Jesi Cl. Vign. delle Oche Ris. '01	♟♟♟ 3
● Paradiso '09	♟♟ 4
○ Verdicchio dei Castelli di Jesi Cl. Sup. Campo delle Oche '11	♟♟ 4
○ Verdicchio dei Castelli di Jesi Cl. Sup. Campo delle Oche '10	♟♟ 4
● Vigna Paradiso '08	♟♟ 4

San Savino - Poderi Capecci

loc. San Savino
via Santa Maria in Carro, 13
63065 Ripatransone [AP]
Tel. 073590107
www.sansavino.com

CELLAR SALES
PRE-BOOKED VISITS
ANNUAL PRODUCTION 120,000 bottles
HECTARES UNDER VINE 22.00
VITICULTURE METHOD Certified Organic

Simone Capecci was among the first to go to Guido Cocci Grifoni and inquire about the vine he had just recovered after years of oblivion. He went home with scions to plant in cooler spots near his cellar. Others did the same and each travelled their own path. Simone chose to work with cold maceration, extracting the sharpest, most citrussy nuances, creating Pecorino Ciprea, whose style is now widely replicated. Before this, Simone had been known for his reds focusing on the generous, intense fruit of sangiovese and montepulciano. Their marriage has produced Picus. The 2013 has an authentic character and juicy mouth, reminiscent of ripe cherries. Ciprea 2014 has graceful scents of bitter orange blossom and peel, and a lively mouth with deep, tidy, slightly salty flavours. Quinta Regio 2011 needs to be laid down in the bottle a while longer to reconcile the weighty tannic texture with the vigorous alcohols into an integrated structure.

○ Offida Pecorino Ciprea '14	♥♥ 3*
● Rosso Piceno Sup. Picus '13	♥♥ 2*
● Fedus '13	♥♥ 4
● Quinta Regio '11	♥♥ 5
● Rosso Piceno Collemura '14	♥ 2
○ Tufilla '14	♥ 2
● Fedus Sangiovese '06	♥♥♥ 4
● Moggio Sangiovese '98	♥♥♥
○ Offida Pecorino Ciprea '10	♥♥♥ 3*
○ Offida Pecorino Ciprea '09	♥♥♥ 3*
○ Offida Pecorino Ciprea '08	♥♥♥ 3*
● Quinta Regio '01	♥♥♥ 5
● Quinta Regio '00	♥♥♥ 5
○ Offida Pecorino Ciprea '13	♥♥ 3
● Rosso Piceno Sup. Picus '12	♥♥ 2*

Santa Barbara

b.go Mazzini, 35
60010 Barbara [AN]
Tel. 0719674249
www.vinisantabarbara.it

CELLAR SALES
PRE-BOOKED VISITS
ANNUAL PRODUCTION 650,000 bottles
HECTARES UNDER VINE 45.00

Stefano Antonucci always has surprises in store. His decades of experience, skill in capturing the mood of the market, and tireless sales drive are the devastating weapons of mass communication that he uses with unsurpassed skill. Over the years he has managed to put together a range that includes the region's main designations and every possible type, made possible by his own vineyards or those of his trusted grower. A top-notch team ensures flexibility and attention to the winemaking process, all based on modern technology and the assistance of small wood for the most ambitious wines. Another rabbit out of the hat for the Verdicchio macerated on skins, with its aromas of white tea and citrus peel, and deep, salty palate. Our favourite is still the Verdicchio Stefano Antonucci 2013 with its fine, fruity, balanced aromas. The heavenly Pathos 2013 is elegant and vibrant despite its heavy backbone.

○ Verdicchio dei Castelli di Jesi Cl. Sup. Stefano Antonucci '13	♥♥♥ 3*
● Pathos '13	♥♥ 6
○ Verdicchio dei Castelli di Jesi Back to Basics '13	♥♥ 5
○ Animale Celeste '14	♥♥ 3
● Colleravara '13	♥♥ 3
● Mossi '13	♥♥ 5
● Rosso Piceno Il Maschio da Monte '13	♥♥ 5
● Stefano Antonucci Rosso '13	♥♥ 3
○ Verdicchio dei Castelli di Jesi Cl. Le Vaglie '14	♥♥ 3
○ Verdicchio dei Castelli di Jesi Passito Lina '12	♥♥ 5
● Mossone '12	♥ 7
○ Stefano Antonucci Brut	♥ 5
○ Verdicchio dei Castelli di Jesi Cl. Tardivo ma non Tardo Ris. '13	♥ 5

Sartarelli

VIA COSTE DEL MOLINO, 24
60030 POGGIO SAN MARCELLO [AN]
TEL. 073189732
www.sartarelli.it

CELLAR SALES
PRE-BOOKED VISITS
ANNUAL PRODUCTION 280,000 bottles
HECTARES UNDER VINE 55.00

Donatella Sartarelli and Patrizio Chiacchiarini have dedicated a lifetime to the Jesi grape. A nice specialization that has led to some of the finest expressions in the history of Verdicchio, and the best of which is linked to the famous Balciana, a legendary wine for those who seek aromatic stratification and the creaminess of the vine when slightly raisined. The different labels have distinct styles and satisfy every palate, refined only in stainless steel: the ripeness of the grapes makes the difference. The Classico 2014 is firmly true-to-type, fluid and food-friendly, making it an ideal everyday wine offering great value for money. Tralivio 2013 is a good choice for those looking for backbone and complexity, flavour and intact fruit. The Balciana 2013 displays overwhelming power on the palate, and over-the-top alcohol, offset by an extraordinarily fine nose featuring thyme, candied orange peel and toasted almond.

○ Verdicchio dei Castelli di Jesi Cl. Sup. Tralivio '13	▼▼ 3*
○ Brut '14	▼▼ 3
○ Verdicchio dei Castelli di Jesi Cl. '14	▼▼ 2*
○ Verdicchio dei Castelli di Jesi Cl. Sup. Balciana '13	▼▼ 5
○ Verdicchio dei Castelli di Jesi Cl. Sup. Balciana '09	♀♀♀ 5
○ Verdicchio dei Castelli di Jesi Cl. Sup. Balciana '04	♀♀♀ 5
○ Verdicchio dei Castelli di Jesi Cl. Sup. Contrada Balciana '98	♀♀♀ 5
○ Verdicchio dei Castelli di Jesi Cl. Sup. Contrada Balciana '97	♀♀♀ 5
○ Verdicchio dei Castelli di Jesi Cl. Sup. Contrada Balciana '95	♀♀♀ 5

Sparapani - Frati Bianchi

VIA BARCHIO, 12
60034 CUPRAMONTANA [AN]
TEL. 0731781216
www.fratibianchi.it

CELLAR SALES
PRE-BOOKED VISITS
RESTAURANT SERVICE
ANNUAL PRODUCTION 40,000 bottles
HECTARES UNDER VINE 14.00

Sparapani is an iconic family that lives its territory completely, from catering to wine production, in Cupramontana, the true, great Castelli di Jesi cru, the heart of the business. The adventure started in the back of their restaurant in the early 1980s and led to the creation of a modern winery, retaining family management and the artisan soul of wines in perfect harmony with their habitat. Even the name of the winery makes clear reference to the nearby hermitage. Tre Bicchieri for the Il Priore 2013, a Verdicchio selection which uses the cool growing year to add a touch of briny freshness, with a balsamic vegetal hint embellishing the classic no-nonsense profile which distinguishes it. Tanginess and backbone achieve admirable balance for a very cellarable wine. We were also impressed by the Salerna 2014, which responded well to the rigours of a tough growing year, with a vibrant, persuasive mouth.

○ Verdicchio dei Castelli di Jesi Cl. Sup. Il Priore '13	▼▼▼ 2*
○ Verdicchio dei Castelli di Jesi Cl. Salerna '14	▼▼ 2*
○ Verdicchio dei Castelli di Jesi Cl. Sup. Il Priore '12	♀♀♀ 2*
○ Verdicchio dei Castelli di Jesi Cl. Sup. Il Priore '06	♀♀♀ 2*
○ Verdicchio dei Castelli di Jesi Cl. Salerna '08	♀♀ 2*
○ Verdicchio dei Castelli di Jesi Cl. Sup. Il Priore '10	♀♀ 3
○ Verdicchio dei Castelli di Jesi Cl. Sup. Il Priore '09	♀♀ 3
○ Verdicchio dei Castelli di Jesi Cl. Sup. Il Priore '08	♀♀ 3*

MARCHE

Tenuta Spinelli

VIA LAGO, 2
63032 CASTIGNANO [AP]
TEL. 0736821489
www.tenutaspinelli.it

CELLAR SALES
PRE-BOOKED VISITS
ACCOMMODATION
ANNUAL PRODUCTION 30,000 bottles
HECTARES UNDER VINE 7.00

Enthusiasm and a dash of youthful exuberance led Simone Spinelli to plant pecorino on a stony plot at 600 metres above sea level on Mount Ascensione. A challenging territory and in some ways its potential was unexplored. The tenacity and experience of winemaker Pierluigi Lorenzetti turned Artemisia into a budding cult. In the same spirit as last year, he has planted pinot nero, the world's most difficult and capricious variety. For now, his small cellar only handles white grapes vinified in steel and a few riddling racks for a limited amount of Mèroe, a Classic Method Pecorino. While the cool, rainy 2014 growing season slightly dulled the profile it did not affect the dauntless personality of Artemisia, a white with a mountain temperament, all penetrating acidity, with grapefruit and wild herbs at the finish. Eden 2014 is an approachable, citrussy Passerina which flows deliciously across the palate. Mèroe 2012 is prickly, with a mature profile and tart finish.

○ Offida Pecorino Artemisia '14	♟♟♟	2*
○ Mèroe Pecorino M. Cl. '12	♟	4
○ Offida Passerina Eden '14	♟	2
○ Offida Pecorino Artemisia '13	♟♟♟	2*
○ Offida Pecorino Artemisia '12	♟♟♟	2*
○ Eden '13	♟♟	2*
○ Eden '11	♟♟	2*
○ Mèroe Pecorino M. Cl. '09	♟♟	3
○ Offida Pecorino Artemisia '11	♟♟	2*

La Staffa

VIA CASTELLARETTA, 19
60039 STAFFOLO [AN]
TEL. 0731779810
www.vinilastaffa.it

CELLAR SALES
PRE-BOOKED VISITS
ANNUAL PRODUCTION 30,000 bottles
HECTARES UNDER VINE 8.00
VITICULTURE METHOD Certified Organic

Figures such as Riccardo Baldi inspire trust and raise awareness for the entire area. He is young, enthusiastic, and media savvy, yet his feet are firmly on the ground and he has taken up the reins of what was a pastime for his family, making it his profession. He has protected and extended the old clones he inherited and did not hesitate to do away with the inadequate old cellar, replacing it with a massive and almost completely underground construction, overlooking the valley formed by the Castellaretta and Salmagina crus. Inside there is plenty of room for the steel vats where the Verdicchio softens out, and a few barriques for the limited production of Rubinia, a monovarietal Montepulciano whose invigorating 2011 version displays varietal stamping, juiciness and richness of flavour. A touch of greenness takes the edge off the Classico Superiore 2014's aromas of apple, straw and almond, unbending into a tasty, rhythmic, food-friendly palate.

● Rubinia '11	♟♟	4
○ Verdicchio dei Castelli di Jesi Cl. Sup. La Staffa '14	♟♟	3
○ Verdicchio dei Castelli di Jesi Cl. Sup. Rincrocca '13	♟	3
● Rubinia '06	♟♟	3
○ Verdicchio dei Castelli di Jesi Cl. '13	♟♟	2*
○ Verdicchio dei Castelli di Jesi Cl. '12	♟♟	2*
○ Verdicchio dei Castelli di Jesi Cl. Sup. La Rincrocca '10	♟♟	3
○ Verdicchio dei Castelli di Jesi Cl. Sup. La Rincrocca '06	♟♟	2*
○ Verdicchio dei Castelli di Jesi Cl. Sup. Rincrocca '08	♟♟	2*

Tenuta di Tavignano

Loc. Tavignano
62011 Cingoli [MC]
Tel. 0733617303
www.tenutaditavignano.it

CELLAR SALES
PRE-BOOKED VISITS
ANNUAL PRODUCTION 100,000 bottles
HECTARES UNDER VINE 30.00
SUSTAINABLE WINERY

The gate to Stefano Aymerich's place should declare "Kalòs kai agathòs". Beauty and virtue are here. The beauty is in the green farmlands, a castle-like farm dominating the hill between the River Esino and the River Musone. All around, manicured vineyards, airy, well-aspected, on calcareous clay soils. And the virtue? We find it in the bounty of the bottle and this winery has been spoiling us for years in that respect. The 2014 Misco selection is again on the podium with crystalline aromatics, notes of pennyroyal, almond and white-fleshed fruit, and a full-flavoured mouth with a perky acidity so typical of cool growing years. The Misco Riserva is always approachable for its good flesh and matière, even from a cool year like 2013, but currently suffering its extreme youth, it will recover in the bottle. Last but not least, the new-born Pestifero, a fresh and lively Classic Method with a good finale.

○ Verdicchio dei Castelli di Jesi Cl. Sup. Misco '14	♟♟♟	3*
○ Castelli di Jesi Verdicchio Cl. Misco Ris. '13	♟♟	4
○ Offida Pecorino '14	♟♟	2*
● Rosso Piceno Libenter '12	♟♟	3
○ Il Pestifero Pas Dosè '14	♟	2
● Rosso Piceno Cervidoni '13	♟	2
○ Verdicchio dei Castelli di Jesi Cl. Sup. Villa Torre '14	♟	2
○ Verdicchio dei Castelli di Jesi Cl. Misco Ris. '06	♟♟♟	3*
○ Verdicchio dei Castelli di Jesi Cl. Sup. Misco '13	♟♟♟	3*
○ Verdicchio dei Castelli di Jesi Cl. Sup. Misco '10	♟♟♟	3*

Fattoria Le Terrazze

Via Musone, 4
60026 Numana [AN]
Tel. 0717390352
www.fattorialeterrazze.it

CELLAR SALES
PRE-BOOKED VISITS
ANNUAL PRODUCTION 100,000 bottles
HECTARES UNDER VINE 20.00

Antonio Terni's winery is one of the best-known names in Conero thanks to centuries of history, a magnificent estate whose architecture resembles a French château, and a legacy of vineyards that exploit the warmer areas for red grape varieties and the cooler aspecting for chardonnay. The international style, meticulous vinification and Antonio's propensity to travel the world are what brought the brand to the attention of more developed markets in the 1990s, giving drive and visibility to the entire territory. Chaos is a montepulciano, merlot and syrah blend that is just being presented. The 2011 is elegant, delicately smoky amidst copious notes of bell pepper and red fruits, and a relaxed palate of tamed tannins. The Rosso Conero 2013 is another good performer with healthy fruit making a feisty palate, acidity and flavour blending for a tempting progression. The Sassi Neri 2011 is a little too forceful.

● Chaos '11	♟♟	5
● Rosso Conero Le Terrazze '13	♟♟	2*
● Conero Sassi Neri Ris. '11	♟	5
○ Le Cave Chardonnay '14	♟	2
⊙ Pink Fluid '14	♟	2
● Rosso Conero Praeludium '14	♟	2
● Chaos '04	♟♟♟	5
● Chaos '01	♟♟♟	6
● Conero Sassi Neri Ris. '04	♟♟♟	5
● Rosso Conero Sassi Neri '02	♟♟♟	5
● Rosso Conero Sassi Neri '99	♟♟♟	5
● Rosso Conero Sassi Neri '98	♟♟♟	5
● Rosso Conero Visions of J '01	♟♟♟	7

MARCHE

Terre Cortesi Moncaro

VIA PIANOLE, 7A
63036 MONTECAROTTO [AN]
TEL. 073189245
www.moncaro.com

CELLAR SALES
PRE-BOOKED VISITS
RESTAURANT SERVICE
ANNUAL PRODUCTION 7,500,000 bottles
HECTARES UNDER VINE 1200.00

Moncaro's enormous estate under vine makes it the largest winery in the Marche and allows selection of the best grapes. From the hills of Verdicchio to the Conero promontory and the southernmost edge of the Marche, there are superb plots available to the cellar team, captained by Riccardo Cotarella and Giuliano D'Ignazi. Doriano Marchetti is an experienced chairman who knows how to reconcile the demands of members scattered across half the region, ensuring each territory is properly represented with modern wines that focus on varietal characteristics. A surprise from the Piceno area was the Superiore Roccaviva 2012, showing top montepulciano credentials, yielding fleshy fruit woven with velvety tannins, engaging progression and leisurely pace. Equally pleasant, the citrus verve in the Ofithe Pecorino 2014. Among the Jesi labels, it was no surprise to find Vigna Novali Riserva 2012 leading the field, counterpointed with velvety tones and a long tangy finale.

● Rosso Piceno Sup. Roccaviva '12	♟♟♟	2*
● Conero Montescuro Ris. '12	♟♟	3
○ Offida Pecorino Ofithe '14	♟♟	3
○ Verdicchio dei Castelli di Jesi Cl. Le Vele '14	♟♟	2*
○ Verdicchio dei Castelli di Jesi Cl. Sup. Fondiglie '14	♟♟	3
○ Verdicchio dei Castelli di Jesi Cl. V. Novali Ris. '12	♟♟	3
● Conero Cimerio Ris. '12	♟	3
○ Verdicchio dei Castelli di Jesi Cl. Sup. Verde Ca' Ruptae '14	♟	3
○ Castelli di Jesi Verdicchio Cl. V. Novali Ris. '10	♟♟♟	3*
○ Castelli di Jesi Verdicchio Cl. V. Novali Ris. '09	♟♟♟	3*
○ Verdicchio dei Castelli di Jesi Cl. V. Novali Ris. '08	♟♟♟	3*

★Umani Ronchi

VIA ADRIATICA, 12
60027 OSIMO [AN]
TEL. 0717108019
www.umanironchi.com

CELLAR SALES
PRE-BOOKED VISITS
ANNUAL PRODUCTION 2,800,000 bottles
HECTARES UNDER VINE 230.00
VITICULTURE METHOD Certified Organic
SUSTAINABLE WINERY

Massimo and Michele Bernetti have gradually built a business model and for many years everything has been running like clockwork in Osimo. An unstoppable ascent taking them to the top of the private cellar ranks for hectares and bottles produced. What convinces is primarily the tenacious determination for hands-on management of many hectares located around the Cupramontana and Montecarotto areas of the Jesi district, of Conero, and the Abruzzo estates. Here the best grapes are used to create a refined style, in no way heavy-handed, a risk when using large amounts of local cultivars. The flagships are increasingly complex and well-designed each year, with vintage wines aligned to an easy-drinking philosophy without a hint of cliché. A fusion of the subtlest overtones of anise, balsam and white-fleshed fruit gives the Vecchie Vigne 2013 nuances of masterful harmony, cadenced in the long finish. The airy, elegant San Giorgio 2010 has a mature, relaxed palate.

○ Verdicchio dei Castelli di Jesi Cl. Sup. Vecchie Vigne '13	♟♟♟	4*
● Conero Campo San Giorgio Ris. '10	♟♟	7
● Conero Cùmaro Ris. '11	♟♟	4
● Pelago '11	♟♟	5
○ Castelli di Jesi Verdicchio Cl. Plenio Ris. '12	♟♟	4
○ Maximo '12	♟♟	4
● Rosso Conero San Lorenzo '13	♟♟	3
○ Sans Anné Extra Brut M. Cl.	♟♟	4
○ Vellodoro '14	♟♟	2*
○ Verdicchio dei Castelli di Jesi Cl. Sup. Casal di Serra '14	♟♟	3
○ Verdicchio dei Castelli di Jesi Cl. Villa Bianchi '14	♟♟	2*
● Montepulciano d'Abruzzo Jorio '13	♟	3
● Rosso Conero Serrano '14	♟	2

Vallerosa Bonci

VIA TORRE, 15
60034 CUPRAMONTANA [AN]
TEL. 0731789129
www.vallerosa-bonci.com

Valturio

VIA DEI PELASGI, 10
61023 MACERATA FELTRIA [PU]
TEL. 0722728049
www.valturio.com

CELLAR SALES
PRE-BOOKED VISITS
ANNUAL PRODUCTION 250,000 bottles
HECTARES UNDER VINE 26.00

CELLAR SALES
PRE-BOOKED VISITS
ACCOMMODATION
ANNUAL PRODUCTION 40,000 bottles
HECTARES UNDER VINE 10.00

Peppe Bonci and his family have dedicated more than 50 years to Cupramontana, the town at the heart of the Verdicchio district. Of course they have majestic vineyards: Pietrone, Viatorre, Manciano and, especially, San Michele, showing how the Boncis have always believed in the potential of Cupramontana Verdicchio. Their unfaltering rich, powerful style, often with the glycerine-rich touch from the generous aspecting and drawn-out ageing, has led to the best results over the years. The 2010 Brut Metodo Classico made our finals and just missed a Tre Bicchieri for a sparkling wine of great class and varietal stamping, all almond, pear, ginger and white flowers. The mousse caresses the palate and the dosage is perfect, proving that Classic Methods are a house special. The San Michele just missed the finals, confirming our sparkling wine theory: the 2013 showed mentholated and balsamic, zesty and mighty in the mouth, supported by a vibrant acid backbone.

Only the doggedness of Adriano Galli could conceive planting a vineyard there, in Montefeltro, among woods, dizzying slopes, panoramas of incomparable beauty over raw, unspoiled nature. But he enjoys a tough challenge and equipping his cellar as best he could in that setting, planting dense vineyards of bush vines, today he brings to life wines of enchanting personality, steeped in the uniqueness of the terroir. The brightest star is the Sangiovese named after the wine. The 2011 is an austere, elegant version with the mountain imprint expressed in cool nose notes and inflexible palate. Still very young, so it will improve with time. We found the Solco 2012 to be in the same mould. This rebo with a hint of merlot, has a nose of peony and red fruits, with balsamic puffs encoring in the sinuous, dancing palate. For wines outside the box, we say the 1759, a 2011 Classic Method pinot nero blend, and the 2012 Chiù Bordeaux blend, close-knit but capable of unexpected lightness.

○ Verdicchio dei Castelli di Jesi Cl. Brut M. Cl. '10	♀♀ 5
○ Verdicchio dei Castelli di Jesi Cl. Sup. S. Michele '13	♀♀ 3
○ Verdicchio dei Castelli di Jesi Cl. Brut	♀ 3
○ Verdicchio dei Castelli di Jesi Cl. Manciano '14	♀ 2
○ Verdicchio dei Castelli di Jesi Cl. Pietrone Ris. '04	♀♀♀ 3
○ Verdicchio dei Castelli di Jesi Cl. Sup. Le Case '04	♀♀♀ 3*
○ Verdicchio dei Castelli di Jesi Cl. Sup. S. Michele '10	♀♀♀ 3*
○ Verdicchio dei Castelli di Jesi Cl. Sup. S. Michele '06	♀♀♀ 3

● Solco '12	♀♀ 5
● Valturio '11	♀♀ 4
● Chiù '12	♀♀ 6
⊘ Extra Brut Rosé 1759 M. Cl. '11	♀♀ 5
● Olmo '13	♀ 2
● Valturio '09	♀♀♀ 4
● Valturio '08	♀♀♀ 4
● Valturio '07	♀♀♀ 4
● Chiù '10	♀♀ 6
● Chiù '09	♀♀ 2*
● Solco '09	♀♀ 4
● Valturio '10	♀♀ 4
● Valturio '06	♀♀ 4

★Velenosi

LOC. MONTICELLI
VIA DEI BIANCOSPINI, 11
63100 ASCOLI PICENO
TEL. 0736341218
www.velenosivini.com

CELLAR SALES
PRE-BOOKED VISITS
ANNUAL PRODUCTION 2,500,000 bottles
HECTARES UNDER VINE 192.00

The untiring Angela Velenosi scales
increasingly higher mountains. If she had
time to stop and look down at the origins of
the small family business, she would feel
dizzy. But she is too busy, with all her
commitments, meetings at the winery,
worrying about the next plane to catch to
promote her wines all over the world, or in
her role as chairman of the Consorzio dei
Vini Piceni. Her tried-and-tested staff
prepares pleasantly fruity wines with
well-defined aromas, perfect early-drinkers.
The more aspirational wines guarantee
structure, complexity and cellarability. As
usual the Roggio 2012 boldly unveiled its
fruit-rich soul, expressed on the palate with
well-attuned energy buoyed by subtle
tannin extraction. A textbook tasting from
the 2013 Rêve, with stunning hints of
grapefruit that encore at length in the
finale. We also recommend the fresh
Falerio Pecorino 2014 and the refined The
Rose 2010.

Roberto Venturi

VIA CASE NUOVE, 1A
60010 CASTELLEONE DI SUASA [AN]
TEL. 3381855566
www.viniventuri.it

CELLAR SALES
PRE-BOOKED VISITS
ANNUAL PRODUCTION 60,000 bottles
HECTARES UNDER VINE 8.00

Roberto Venturi was a child when he took
his first steps in the vineyards,
accompanying his father and following in
his grandfather's footsteps. The Venturis
were small winegrowers, active in the bulk
sector but Roberto decided to make the
quantum leap and began bottling. He
oversees everything in person, from the
vineyard to the cellar, and in the
Castelleone di Suasa plots he grows
verdicchio, moscato and an aleatico clone
that old farmers call balsamino for its
aroma. In 2009 he began renting an old
vineyard of half a hectare at Busche of
Montecarotto, a true grand cru of the River
Esino's left bank, producing grapes for
Qudì. From the stunning 2013 harvest, the
wine took this small artisan outfit straight to
its first Tre Bicchieri. A Verdicchio with
acacia blossom, almond, and hints of anise
and mixed herbs at the core, and a vibrant,
dynamic, lean palate with thrusting
tanginess. Desiderio 2014 has an intense
nose of grapefruit zest ushering in a
refreshing palate.

● Rosso Piceno Sup. Roggio del Filare '12	♛♛♛ 7
○ Offida Pecorino Rêve '13	♛♛ 5
○ Falerio Pecorino Villa Angela '14	♛♛ 4
● Lacrima di Morro d'Alba Sup. Querciantica '14	♛♛ 5
● Offida Rosso Ludi '12	♛♛ 7
● Rosso Piceno Sup. Il Brecciarolo Gold '13	♛♛ 5
○ The Rose M. Cl. '10	♛♛ 7
○ Chardonnay Villa Angela '14	♛ 4
○ Falerio V. Solaria '14	♛ 3
○ Offida Pecorino Villa Angela '14	♛ 4
○ Passerina Brut	♛ 3
○ Passerina Villa Angela '14	♛ 4
● Rosso Piceno Sup. Brecciarolo '13	♛ 4
○ Velenosi Gran Cuvée Brut M. Cl. '10	♛ 6
○ Verdicchio dei Castelli di Jesi Cl. '14	♛ 4
● Rosso Piceno Sup. Roggio del Filare '11	♛♛♛ 7

○ Verdicchio dei Castelli di Jesi Cl. Sup. Qudì '13	♛♛♛ 2*
○ Desiderio '14	♛♛ 2*
● Balsamino '14	♛ 2
○ Desiderio '13	♛♛ 2*
○ Verdicchio dei Castelli di Jesi Cl. Sup. Qudì '12	♛♛ 2*

Vicari

VIA POZZO BUONO, 3
60030 MORRO D'ALBA [AN]
TEL. 073163164
www.vicarivini.it

CELLAR SALES
PRE-BOOKED VISITS
ANNUAL PRODUCTION 95,000 bottles
HECTARES UNDER VINE 21.00

Nazzareno Vicari's family is exemplary for its commitment to safeguarding local varieties. They are artisans who craft wines with a proud rural soul given a modern lustre. We can thank Vico and Valentina, the second generation and embodiment of the open arms and smiling faces that welcome the world. In their cellar, Lacrima is narrated in every style: Essenza, whose seductive olfactory intensity is accomplished thanks to the use of carbonic maceration; Dacanay retains the more traditional character of the variety; Lacrima is a complex, structured voice. Then there is Amaranto, a sweet Passito ringing with persuasive mulberry and candied rose petal notes. For the Verdicchio, production is simply split down the middle for a citrussy Classico and a well-structured and incredibly tasty Superiore with a lingering finish. The tail end of each wine's name pays homage to Pozzo Buono, the district where they have put down roots, like most of their vines.

● Lacrima di Morro d'Alba Passito Amaranto del Pozzo Buono '12	⚕⚕ 4
● Lacrima di Morro d'Alba Sup. del Pozzo Buono '13	⚕⚕ 3
● Rosso Piceno del Pozzo Buono '13	⚕⚕ 2*
○ Verdicchio dei Castelli di Jesi Cl. Sup. Insolito del Pozzo Buono '13	⚕⚕ 3
● Lacrima di Morro d'Alba Dasempre del Pozzo Buono '14	⚕ 2
● Lacrima di Morro d'Alba Essenza del Pozzo Buono '14	⚕ 3
○ Verdicchio dei Castelli di Jesi Cl. del Pozzo Buono '14	⚕ 2
● Lacrima di Morro d'Alba Dasempre del Pozzo Buono '12	⚖ 2*
● Lacrima di Morro d'Alba Sup. del Pozzo Buono '12	⚖ 3*

Vignamato

VIA BATTINEBBIA, 4
60038 SAN PAOLO DI JESI [AN]
TEL. 0731779197
www.vignamato.com

CELLAR SALES
PRE-BOOKED VISITS
ANNUAL PRODUCTION 100,000 bottles
HECTARES UNDER VINE 27.00

The new partnership between Andrea Ceci, son of Maurizio and grandson of Amato, after whom the winery is named, and oenologist Pierluigi Lorenzetti is getting up to speed. The wines have toned down from their past exuberant alcohol and extract, to embrace a more refreshing, rakish feel, with clean aromas, balanced alcohol thanks to the particularly generous sugar content of the vineyards between Staffolo and San Paolo di Jesi, and cadenced progression that means the bottle is soon empty. Next they need a quantum leap to the top of the podium, but the cellar is heading in the right direction. Our favourite wines for the vintage are the perky and agile Eos, the tasty flavour and tangy grip of the Valle delle Lame, and a Versiano with an evident fruit imprint, with the structure an improvement on to the other two. Ambrosia is a 2011 Riserva still embracing the concept of richness and concentration, with plush mouthfeel and a lingering aromatic finale.

● Rosso Piceno Campalliano '11	⚕⚕ 3
○ Verdicchio dei Castelli di Jesi Cl. Ambrosia Ris. '11	⚕⚕ 3
○ Verdicchio dei Castelli di Jesi Cl. Sup. Eos '14	⚕⚕ 2*
○ Verdicchio dei Castelli di Jesi Cl. Sup. Versiano '14	⚕⚕ 3
○ Verdicchio dei Castelli di Jesi Cl. Valle delle Lame '14	⚕⚕ 2*
● Esino Rosso Rosolaccio '13	⚕ 2
○ Verdicchio dei Castelli di Jesi Cl. Eos '13	⚖ 2*
○ Verdicchio dei Castelli di Jesi Cl. Sup. Versiano '13	⚖ 2*
○ Verdicchio dei Castelli di Jesi Cl. Valle delle Lame '13	⚖ 2*

MARCHE

Vignedileo - Tre Castelli

VIA SAN FRANCESCO, 2A
60039 STAFFOLO [AN]
TEL. 0731779283
www.vignedileo.it

CELLAR SALES
PRE-BOOKED VISITS
ANNUAL PRODUCTION 100,000 bottles
HECTARES UNDER VINE 28.00

The "Leo" on the shingle is Leonardo,
father of Emanuele and Pierfilippo
Palpacelli, who died far too young but his
legacy to his sons was the proper love for
local varietals, the importance of hard work,
and skill in managing the vineyard by
applying strict quality criteria, belief in
tradition. For 15 years now the two tireless
brothers have been stalwarts in Staffolo
wine country. The big, renovated cellar
allows them to manage harvests to
perfection and assemble a range distinctive
for its excellent value for money. Verdicchio
is the core product: Frocco 2013 has
magnetic aromas of orange peel, botrytis
and aromatic herbs; the lean, subtle mouth
has lingering aromas. We also like
Classico 2014's vibrant sinew and almondy
sensations, and the fragrant Brut 2013, a
Charmat whose pace and consistency
would do honour to a Classic Method. The
Sangiovese 2013 has pretty floral tones
and a simple but well-orchestrated palate.

● Sangiovese '13	♟♟	1*
○ Spumante Brut '13	♟♟	2*
○ Verdicchio di Castelli di Jesi Cl. '14	♟♟	1*
○ Verdicchio di Castelli di Jesi Cl. Sup. Frocco '13	♟♟	2*
● Esino Rosso '12	♟	1*
● Lalocco '07	♟♟	2*
○ Verdicchio di Castelli di Jesi Cl. '11	♟♟	1*
○ Verdicchio di Castelli di Jesi Cl. Sup. Frocco '10	♟♟	2*

Fattoria Villa Ligi

LOC. PERGOLA
VIA ZOCCOLANTI, 25A
61045 PERGOLA [PU]
TEL. 0721734351
www.villaligi.it

CELLAR SALES
PRE-BOOKED VISITS
ANNUAL PRODUCTION 50,000 bottles
HECTARES UNDER VINE 23.00

The unusual grapes that grow so well on
the Pergola hills inland of Pesaro are called
"vernaccia" by local farmers, but it is
simply an aleatico clone that has
acclimatized well and spread here. Stefano
Tonelli took it under his wing in 1985 and
now his son Francesco continues to
develop it with the support of talented
oenologist Marco Gozzi. Together they
create increasingly compelling wines. In
addition to bringing to the fore aleatico's
aromatic character, the cellar also
embraces international vines and
montepulciano grapes, growing at one of
its northernmost boundaries. This is the
birthplace of Parlengo, still a tad toasty on
the nose but with oodles of juicy fruit on
the palate. The two Pergolas are
interesting, but the Grifoglietto 2013 has an
extra spark, pale colour, obvious bitter
orange in the appealing aromas; the
consistent, tasty mouth shows a salty
counterpoint in the finale. The sleek, light
Vernaculum 2014 has raspberry notes and
closes with a hint of citrus.

● Parlengo '12	♟♟	3
● Pergola Aleatico Sup. Grifoglietto '13	♟♟	2*
● Rubicondo '10	♟♟	3
● Pergola Aleatico Vernaculum '14	♟	2
○ Seralta '12	♟	2

Campo di Maggio

LOC. PAGLIARE DEL TRONTO
VIA FORMALE, 24
63036 SPINETOLI [AP]
TEL. 3493110296
www.cantinacampodimaggio.it

CELLAR SALES
PRE-BOOKED VISITS
ANNUAL PRODUCTION 22,000 bottles
HECTARES UNDER VINE 4.00

○ Offida Pecorino '14	♟♟ 2*
● Rosso Piceno Sup. '12	♟♟ 2*

La Canosa

C.DA SAN PIETRO, 6
63030 ROTELLA [AP]
TEL. 0736374556
www.lacanosaagricola.it

CELLAR SALES
PRE-BOOKED VISITS
ANNUAL PRODUCTION 150,000 bottles
HECTARES UNDER VINE 28.00

● Musé '13	♟ 3
● Nullius '13	♟ 3
○ Offida Pecorino Pekò '14	♟ 2
● Rosso Piceno Sup. Nummaria '13	♟ 2

Casaleta

LOC. OSTERIA
VIA FORNACE, 1
60030 SERRA DE' CONTI [AN]
TEL. 0731879185
www.casaleta.it

CELLAR SALES
PRE-BOOKED VISITS
ANNUAL PRODUCTION 13,000 bottles
HECTARES UNDER VINE 11.00

○ Verdicchio dei Castelli di Jesi Cl. Castijo '13	♟♟ 2*
○ Verdicchio dei Castelli di Jesi Cl. Sup. La Posta '13	♟♟ 3

Cantine di Castignano

C.DA SAN VENANZO, 31
63032 CASTIGNANO [AP]
TEL. 0736822216
www.cantinedicastignano.com

CELLAR SALES
PRE-BOOKED VISITS
ANNUAL PRODUCTION 450,000 bottles
HECTARES UNDER VINE 520.00
VITICULTURE METHOD Certified Organic

○ Offida Pecorino Montemisio '14	♟♟ 2*
○ Falerio dei Colli Ascolani Pecorino Destriero '14	♟♟ 1*
○ Gramelot '13	♟ 2

Cavalieri

VIA RAFFAELLO, 1
62024 MATELICA [MC]
TEL. 073784859
www.cantinacavalieri.it

PRE-BOOKED VISITS
ANNUAL PRODUCTION 15,000 bottles
HECTARES UNDER VINE 8.24

○ Verdicchio di Matelica Gegè d'Antan '13	♟ 3
○ Verdicchio di Matelica Cavalieri '14	♟ 2
○ Verdicchio di Matelica Gegè '13	♟ 3

Enrico Ceci

VIA SANTA MARIA D'ARCO, 7
60038 SAN PAOLO DI JESI [AN]
TEL. 0731779033
www.cecienrico.it

CELLAR SALES
PRE-BOOKED VISITS
ANNUAL PRODUCTION 10,000 bottles
HECTARES UNDER VINE 8.00

○ Verdicchio dei Castelli di Jesi Cl. Sup. Santa Maria d'Arco '13	♟♟ 2*
● Rosso Piceno Santa Maria d'Arco '13	♟♟ 2*

Col di Corte

VIA SAN PIETRO, 19A
60036 MONTECAROTTO [AN]
TEL. 073189435
www.coldicorte.it

CELLAR SALES
PRE-BOOKED VISITS
ANNUAL PRODUCTION 40,000 bottles
HECTARES UNDER VINE 11.50
VITICULTURE METHOD Certified Organic
SUSTAINABLE WINERY

● Sant'Ansovino '12		♥♥ 5
○ Verdicchio dei Castelli di Jesi Cl. Anno I '14		♥♥ 2*

Colonnara

VIA MANDRIOLE, 6
60034 CUPRAMONTANA [AN]
TEL. 0731780273
www.colonnara.it

CELLAR SALES
PRE-BOOKED VISITS
ANNUAL PRODUCTION 1,000,000 bottles
HECTARES UNDER VINE 120.00

○ Verdicchio dei Castelli di Jesi Cl. Sup. Cuprese '14		♥♥ 2*
○ Verdicchio dei Castelli di Jesi Cuvée Tradition Brut '14		♥ 3

Costadoro

VIA MONTE AQUILINO, 2
63039 SAN BENEDETTO DEL TRONTO [AP]
TEL. 073581781
www.vinicostadoro.com

CELLAR SALES
PRE-BOOKED VISITS
ANNUAL PRODUCTION 1,500,000 bottles
HECTARES UNDER VINE 87.00

○ Offida Pecorino '14		♥♥ 2*
● Rosso Piceno Sup. Il Cardinale '11		♥♥ 3
○ Offida Pecorino Danù '14		♥ 2

Colli di Serrapetrona

VIA COLLI, 7/8
62020 SERRAPETRONA [MC]
TEL. 0733908329
www.collidiserrapetrona.it

CELLAR SALES
PRE-BOOKED VISITS
ACCOMMODATION AND RESTAURANT SERVICE
ANNUAL PRODUCTION 60,000 bottles
HECTARES UNDER VINE 19.00

● Serrapetrona Robbione '10		♥♥ 5
● Serrapetrona Collequanto '13		♥ 3

Conti degli Azzoni

VIA DON MINZONI, 26
62010 MONTEFANO [MC]
TEL. 0733850219
www.degliazzoni.it

CELLAR SALES
PRE-BOOKED VISITS
ACCOMMODATION AND RESTAURANT SERVICE
ANNUAL PRODUCTION 100,000 bottles
HECTARES UNDER VINE 130.00

● Il Galantuomo '12		♥♥ 3
● Passatempo '12		♥♥ 5
● Rosso Piceno '12		♥ 2
○ Sultano		♥ 4

Viticoltori Finocchi

VIA DONATORI DEL SANGUE, 6
60039 STAFFOLO [AN]
TEL. 0731779573
www.viticoltorifinocchi.it

CELLAR SALES
PRE-BOOKED VISITS
ANNUAL PRODUCTION 25,000 bottles
HECTARES UNDER VINE 7.50

○ Verdicchio dei Castelli di Jesi Cl.Sup. Il Pojo '13		♥♥ 2*
● Visciole		♥♥ 3
○ Verdicchio dei Castelli di Jesi Cl. '14		♥ 2

Fiorini

VIA GIARDINO CAMPIOLI, 5
61040 BARCHI [PU]
TEL. 072197151
www.fioriniwines.it

CELLAR SALES
PRE-BOOKED VISITS
ACCOMMODATION AND RESTAURANT SERVICE
ANNUAL PRODUCTION 200,000 bottles
HECTARES UNDER VINE 45.00

○ Bianchello del Metauro Sup. Tenuta Campioli '14	♙♙ 2*
● Colli Pesaresi Sangiovese Sirio '14	♙♙ 2*
○ Monsavium Passito	♙ 3

Esther Hauser

C.DA CORONCINO, 1A
60039 STAFFOLO [AN]
TEL. 0731770203
www.estherhauser.it

CELLAR SALES
PRE-BOOKED VISITS
ANNUAL PRODUCTION 6,000 bottles
HECTARES UNDER VINE 1.00

● Il Ceppo '12	♙♙ 4
● Il Cupo '12	♙♙ 5

Roberto Lucarelli

LOC. RIPALTA
VIA PIANA, 20
61030 CARTOCETO [PU]
TEL. 0721893019
www.laripe.com

CELLAR SALES
PRE-BOOKED VISITS
ANNUAL PRODUCTION 200,000 bottles
HECTARES UNDER VINE 32.00

● Colli Pesaresi Sangiovese Goccione '11	♙♙ 3
○ Bianchello del Metauro La Ripe '14	♙ 2
○ Bianchello del Metauro Sup. Rocho '13	♙ 2
● Colli Pesaresi Sangiovese La Ripe '13	♙ 2

Filippo Maraviglia

LOC. PIANNÉ, 584
62024 MATELICA [MC]
TEL. 0737786340
www.vinimaraviglia.com

CELLAR SALES
PRE-BOOKED VISITS
ANNUAL PRODUCTION 30,000 bottles
HECTARES UNDER VINE 27.00

○ Verdicchio di Matelica Alarico '14	♙♙ 2*
○ Verdicchio di Matelica Grappoli d'Oro Ris. '12	♙♙ 3
● Colli Maceratesi Rosso Onorio '11	♙ 2

La Marca di San Michele

VIA TORRE, 13
60034 CUPRAMONTANA [AN]
TEL. 0731781183
www.lamarcadisanmichele.com

CELLAR SALES
PRE-BOOKED VISITS
ACCOMMODATION
ANNUAL PRODUCTION 25,000 bottles
HECTARES UNDER VINE 6.00
VITICULTURE METHOD Certified Organic

○ Verdicchio dei Castelli di Jesi Cl. Sup. Capovolto '14	♙♙ 3

Clara Marcelli

VIA FONTE VECCHIA, 8
63030 CASTORANO [AP]
TEL. 073687289
www.claramarcelli.it

PRE-BOOKED VISITS
ANNUAL PRODUCTION 40,000 bottles
HECTARES UNDER VINE 14.00
VITICULTURE METHOD Certified Organic

● K'un '12	♙♙ 3
● Corbù '13	♙ 2
● Rosso Piceno Sup. '12	♙ 3

Poderi Mattioli

VIA FARNETO, 17A
60030 SERRA DE' CONTI [AN]
TEL. 0731878676
www.poderimattioli.it

PRE-BOOKED VISITS
ANNUAL PRODUCTION 13,500 bottles
HECTARES UNDER VINE 5.00
VITICULTURE METHOD Certified Organic

○ Verdicchio dei Castelli di Jesi Cl. Sup. Ylice '14	♟♟ 3
○ Castelli di Jesi Verdicchio Cl. Lauro Ris. '12	♟ 3

Federico Mencaroni

VIA OLMIGRANDI, 72
60013 CORINALDO [AN]
TEL. 0717975625
www.mencaroni.eu

PRE-BOOKED VISITS
ANNUAL PRODUCTION 30,000 bottles
HECTARES UNDER VINE 7.50

○ Verdicchio dei castelli di Jesi Brut Nature Apollonia '10	♟♟ 5
● Urbano '13	♟ 3
○ Verdicchio dei Castelli di Jesi Isola '12	♟ 3

Claudio Morelli

V.LE ROMAGNA, 47B
61032 FANO [PU]
TEL. 0721823352
www.claudiomorelli.it

CELLAR SALES
PRE-BOOKED VISITS
ANNUAL PRODUCTION 110,000 bottles
HECTARES UNDER VINE 40.00

○ Bianchello del Metauro Borgo Torre '14	♟♟ 2*
○ Bianchello del Metauro Brut M. Cl. Mòrell '12	♟♟ 5
○ Bianchello del Metauro San Cesareo '14	♟ 2

Alessandro Moroder

VIA MONTACUTO, 121
60029 ANCONA
TEL. 071898232
www.moroder-vini.it

CELLAR SALES
PRE-BOOKED VISITS
ANNUAL PRODUCTION 130,000 bottles
HECTARES UNDER VINE 18.00
VITICULTURE METHOD Certified Organic
SUSTAINABLE WINERY

○ Bianconero	♟♟ 2*
● Rosso Conero Aiòn '13	♟♟ 2*
⊙ Rosa '14	♟ 2
● Rosso Conero '12	♟ 2

Cantina Offida

VIA DELLA REPUBBLICA , 70
63073 OFFIDA [AP]
TEL. 0736880104
www.cantinaoffida.com

CELLAR SALES
ANNUAL PRODUCTION 300,000 bottles
HECTARES UNDER VINE 300.00
VITICULTURE METHOD Certified Organic

● Rosso Piceno Sup. Il Podestà '11	♟♟ 3

Piersanti

B.GO SANTA MARIA, 60
60038 SAN PAOLO DI JESI [AN]
TEL. 0731703214
www.piersantivini.com

CELLAR SALES
PRE-BOOKED VISITS
ANNUAL PRODUCTION 4,000,000 bottles
HECTARES UNDER VINE 23.50

● Rosso Conero Rubjo Ris. '11	♟♟ 3
○ Verdicchio dei Castelli di Jesi Cl. Sup. Bachero '14	♟♟ 2*

Ripa Marchetti

VIA FONDE SANTA LIBERATA
60030 MAIOLATI SPONTINI [AN]
TEL. 3337376888
www.ripamarchetti.it

ANNUAL PRODUCTION 18,000 bottles
HECTARES UNDER VINE 6.00

○ Castelli di Jesi Verdicchio Cl. V. Roncone Ris. '12	♛♛ 3
○ Verdicchio dei Castelli di Jesi Cl. Sup. Apicus '13	♛♛ 2*

Sabbionare

VIA SABBIONARE, 10
60036 MONTECAROTTO [AN]
TEL. 0731889004
www.sabbionare.it

CELLAR SALES
PRE-BOOKED VISITS
ANNUAL PRODUCTION 35,000 bottles
HECTARES UNDER VINE 15.00

○ Verdicchio dei Castelli di Jesi Cl. Sup. Sabbionare '13	♛♛ 2*
○ Verdicchio dei Castelli di Jesi Cl. I Pratelli '14	♛ 1*

San Giovanni

C.DA CIAFONE, 41
63035 OFFIDA [AP]
TEL. 0736889032
www.vinisangiovanni.it

PRE-BOOKED VISITS
ANNUAL PRODUCTION 180,000 bottles
HECTARES UNDER VINE 35.00
VITICULTURE METHOD Certified Organic

○ Falerio Pecorino Gyo '14	♛♛ 2*
○ Offida Pecorino Kiara '14	♛ 3
○ Offida Pecorino Zagros '14	♛ 4
● Offida Rosso Zeii '11	♛ 3

Le Senate

C.DA BARBOLANO, 14
63827 ALTIDONA [FM]
TEL. 3487807017
www.lesenate.it

PRE-BOOKED VISITS
ANNUAL PRODUCTION 9,000 bottles
HECTARES UNDER VINE 7.00

● Cacinello '12	♛♛ 3
● Barbula '13	♛ 2

Alberto Serenelli

LOC. PIETRALACROCE
VIA BARTOLINI, 2
60129 ANCONA
TEL. 07135505
www.albertoserenelli.com

CELLAR SALES
PRE-BOOKED VISITS
ANNUAL PRODUCTION 30,000 bottles
HECTARES UNDER VINE 7.00

● Rosso Conero Varano '12	♛♛ 6
○ Verdicchio dei Castelli di Jesi Cl. Sora Elvira '13	♛♛ 3
● Boranico '11	♛ 5

Fattoria Serra San Martino

VIA SAN MARTINO, 1
60030 SERRA DE' CONTI [AN]
TEL. 0731878025
www.serrasanmartino.com

CELLAR SALES
PRE-BOOKED VISITS
ANNUAL PRODUCTION 13,000 bottles
HECTARES UNDER VINE 3.00
VITICULTURE METHOD Certified Organic

● Il Paonazzo '12	♛♛ 5
● Lysipp '11	♛♛ 5
● Roccuccio '12	♛♛ 3
● Costa dei Zoppi '11	♛ 4

Silvano Strologo

VIA OSIMANA, 89
60021 CAMERANO [AN]
TEL. 071731104
www.vinorossoconero.com

CELLAR SALES
PRE-BOOKED VISITS
ANNUAL PRODUCTION 70,000 bottles
HECTARES UNDER VINE 14.00

● Conero Decebalo Ris. '11	♟♟ 4
⊙ Spumante Brut Pink	♟♟ 2*
● Rosso Conero Julius '13	♟ 2
● Rosso Conero Traiano '09	♟ 4

Terracruda

VIA SERRE, 28
61040 FRATTE ROSA [PU]
TEL. 0721777412
www.terracruda.it

CELLAR SALES
PRE-BOOKED VISITS
ACCOMMODATION
ANNUAL PRODUCTION 60,000 bottles
HECTARES UNDER VINE 11.00

○ Ara Murata	♟♟ 5
● Colli Pesaresi Sangiovese Olpe Ris. '12	♟♟ 5
○ Bianchello del Metauro Boccalino '14	♟ 2
● Pergola Rosso Vettina '14	♟ 3

Tenuta dell' Ugolino

LOC. CASTELPLANIO
VIA COPPARONI, 32
60031 CASTELPLANIO [AN]
TEL. 07310731 812569
www.tenutaugolino.it

CELLAR SALES
PRE-BOOKED VISITS
ANNUAL PRODUCTION 40,000 bottles
HECTARES UNDER VINE 6.00

○ Verdicchio dei Castelli di Jesi Cl. Sup. Vign. del Balluccio '14	♟♟ 3

Le Vigne di Franca

C.DA SANTA PETRONILLA, 69
63900 FERMO
TEL. 3356512938
www.levignedifranca.it

ANNUAL PRODUCTION 30,000 bottles
HECTARES UNDER VINE 4.50

● Crismon '12	♟♟ 3
○ Lumes '14	♟ 2
● Rubrum '13	♟ 2

Casale Vitali

VIA CELESTIALE, 15
63853 MONTELPARO [FM]
TEL. 0734 789083
www.casalevitali.it

CELLAR SALES
PRE-BOOKED VISITS
ANNUAL PRODUCTION 25,000 bottles
HECTARES UNDER VINE 20.00

○ Falerio Pecorino Celestiale '14	♟♟ 2*
○ Brut M. Cl. Mont'illi '13	♟ 3
○ Montelpare '14	♟ 2

Zaccagnini

VIA SALMAGINA, 9/10
60039 STAFFOLO [AN]
TEL. 0731779892
www.zaccagnini.it

CELLAR SALES
PRE-BOOKED VISITS
ACCOMMODATION AND RESTAURANT SERVICE
ANNUAL PRODUCTION 250,000 bottles
HECTARES UNDER VINE 35.00

○ Verdicchio dei Castelli di Jesi Cl. Sup. Cima Signoria '14	♟♟ 2*
○ Verdicchio dei Castelli di Jesi Cl. Sup. Salmàgina '14	♟♟ 2*

UMBRIA

A consideration of Umbria's winemaking pyramid must go beyond its Tre Bicchieri, and it would be misleading to look only at the peaks of excellence. They are only a partial snapshot of the region, however flattering, based on goals achieved by producer decisions and the effect of growing years. Beneath the excellent of the ten Tre Bicchieri there is an ocean of wine and many cellars worth exploring, and several established and emerging districts all worth a visit. That said, a shallow reading, so to speak, would suggest that this year was almost entirely dominated by the Montefalco district. And nothing could be further from the truth. We are, of course, talking about one of the region's most prestigious areas and perhaps the only one able to guarantee a significant critical mass, binding terroir to variety indivisibly. Fortunately, the map of the best regional wines is much more complex and diverse, speaking very different languages. First of all, the wines are not only red. In recent years there has been a new-found awareness of the potential of whites, beginning with an iconic terroir like Orvieto and albeit limited, there are encouraging signals of a revival in progress. This year, perhaps coincidentally due to the vintages, the area did not deliver memorable wines except for the usual Cervaro della Sala. Nonetheless, the area is heading in the right direction and in recent editions we have offered ample proof. Another fascinating "white story" is that of Trebbiano Spoletino, hitting the bullseye this year with a superlative Trebium 2014 from Filippo Antonelli. We can now turn to the reds. Except for Lungarotti's sumptuous Torgiano Rubesco Riserva Vigna Monticchio 2010, a real year of grace, there was a string of Sagrantino stars. The zone shows us its increasing maturity and character, as well as a diversification of style that paints a fascinating, multifaceted scenario. We think that is good news, typical of a region that is discovering more interpretations than in the past and which it would be unfair to assess just on the basis of its award-winning wines.

UMBRIA

Adanti

LOC. ARQUATA
VIA BELVEDERE, 2
06031 BEVAGNA [PG]
TEL. 0742360295
www.cantineadanti.com

CELLAR SALES
PRE-BOOKED VISITS
ANNUAL PRODUCTION 160,000 bottles
HECTARES UNDER VINE 30.00
SUSTAINABLE WINERY

A classic is a classic, and Adanti clearly
belongs to this category, at least among the
wineries producing Sagrantino. The reason
is simple: this is one of the historic
operations in the DOC zone, uninterested in
being a slave to fashion, and preferring a
decidedly traditional style. The stately home
that houses the winery is near Bevagna,
while the vineyards, partly around the
house, are divided into various plots.
Vinification envisages solely native yeasts,
extraction is moderate, and barrel ageing
used with a judicious hand. The Montefalco
Sagrantino 2009 spellbound us with its full,
mature aromas, typical of the vintage,
alongside iodine and salty notes. Despite a
silky attack, the succulent palate closes to
stiff tannins and slight alcoholic warmth.
The peerless Montefalco Rosso 2011 offers
a juicy plum palate. Even better is the
Rosso Riserva 2010, with its appealing
salty and quinine notes.

Antonelli - San Marco

LOC. SAN MARCO, 60
06036 MONTEFALCO [PG]
TEL. 0742379158
www.antonellisanmarco.it

CELLAR SALES
PRE-BOOKED VISITS
ACCOMMODATION
ANNUAL PRODUCTION 350,000 bottles
HECTARES UNDER VINE 50.00
VITICULTURE METHOD Certified Organic
SUSTAINABLE WINERY

Filippo Antonelli's wines resemble their
maker: elegant, complex, and with an
intriguing personality. The wines never
display excessive extract, but good balance
with the oak in which they age, and
interesting development over time. The
producer's style and technique prove to be
decisive, despite this being one of the best
terroirs in the DOC zone: the subzone of
San Marco. The products of this area have
been famous since time immemorial, and
the Antonelli family boasts experience
dating back to 1881. We were curious to
try the new reds, but ended up being
bowled over by an extraordinary white, the
Trebium 2014, a Trebbiano Spoletino with a
brief passage in oak. This epitome of
flavour and tautness is one of the best
interpretations of the vintage to be found
among the whites of central Italy. Sweet
and full-flavoured, savoury and deep, it
plays on contrasts yet achieves great
harmony, closing to mineral nuances, citrus
and Alpine butter.

● Montefalco Rosso Ris. '10	♟♟ 4
● Montefalco Sagrantino '09	♟♟ 5
○ Montefalco Bianco '14	♟♟ 2*
● Montefalco Rosso '11	♟♟ 2*
⊙ Amanter '14	♟ 2
● Montefalco Sagrantino Arquata '08	♟♟♟ 6
○ Colli Martani Grechetto '12	♟♟ 2*
● Montefalco Rosso '10	♟♟ 2*
● Montefalco Rosso Ris. '09	♟♟ 3*
● Montefalco Rosso Ris. '08	♟♟ 3
● Montefalco Sagrantino Arquata '07	♟♟ 5
● Montefalco Sagrantino Il Domenico '08	♟♟ 6
● Montefalco Sagrantino Il Domenico '07	♟♟ 6

○ Spoleto Trebbiano Spoletino Trebium '14	♟♟♟ 3*
● Montefalco Sagrantino Chiusa di Pannone '08	♟♟ 6
○ Colli Martani Grechetto '14	♟♟ 2*
● Montefalco Rosso '12	♟♟ 3
● Montefalco Sagrantino '10	♟♟ 5
● Montefalco Sagrantino '09	♟♟♟ 5
● Montefalco Sagrantino '08	♟♟♟ 5
○ Colli Martani Grechetto '13	♟♟ 2*
● Montefalco Rosso '11	♟♟ 3
● Montefalco Rosso '10	♟♟ 3
● Montefalco Rosso Ris. '08	♟♟ 4
● Montefalco Sagrantino Chiusa di Pannone '07	♟♟ 6
● Montefalco Sagrantino Passito '11	♟♟ 5
○ Trebbiano Spoletino Trebium '12	♟♟ 3

Barberani

LOC. CERRETO
05023 BASCHI [TR]
TEL. 0763341820
www.barberani.it

CELLAR SALES
PRE-BOOKED VISITS
ACCOMMODATION
ANNUAL PRODUCTION 350,000 bottles
HECTARES UNDER VINE 55.00
VITICULTURE METHOD Certified Organic

This is not only an historic winery, which has just celebrated its 50th anniversary; Barberani is above all a benchmark for those looking for the best expressions of the wines of Orvieto. It has made convincing progress over the last decade, in terms of both quality and style. The latest generation of the family, comprising the two brothers Bernardo and Niccolò, assisted by their parents Luigi and Giovanna, is taking its reputation to new heights, with wines that show an increasing sense of place and reliability, in both everyday drinkers and premium labels. Two wines made our finals this year. The Orvieto Classico Superiore Luigi e Giovanna never disappoints, and continues to raise the bar for the DOC zone, while the Calcaia needs no introduction, and for some time has been a benchmark in the world of Italian sweet wines. This is a winery on top form, with high average quality across the board.

Tenuta Bellafonte

LOC. TORRE DEL COLLE
VIA COLLE NOTTOLO, 2
06031 BEVAGNA [PG]
TEL. 0742710019
www.tenutabellafonte.it

CELLAR SALES
PRE-BOOKED VISITS
ACCOMMODATION
ANNUAL PRODUCTION 5,500 bottles
HECTARES UNDER VINE 7.00
SUSTAINABLE WINERY

Although new on the scene, this winery is already a point of reference for the territory. Bellafonte and its owner, Peter Heilbron, have created an extremely important, and in some ways innovative operation in the variegated landscape of Sagrantino. The estate's wines show crystal-clear focus and purity, extreme finesse and natural expression. Aged in large oak, and vinified with a light hand, they display textbook extraction, not to mention rare character for this DOC zone. Here, excellent wine country joins forces with painstaking work in the rows and natural vinification techniques. After a subdued 2010, with graceful, nuanced tones, the 2011 is equally faithful to the vintage. It shows a broodier nose than its predecessor, with notes of black cherry, liqueur cherries and spice, but its charm remains unchanged thanks to all-round finesse. This outstanding wine differs from many other Sagrantinos on the palate, displaying a graceful, elegant weave, full flavour and depth.

○ Orvieto Cl. Sup. Luigi e Giovanna Villa Monticelli '12	♟♟ 5	
○ Orvieto Cl. Sup. Muffa Nobile Calcaia '12	♟♟ 5	
● Aleatico Passito Villa Monticelli '08	♟♟ 6	
● Foresco '13	♟♟ 3	
○ Moscato Passito Villa Monticelli '12	♟♟ 6	
● Polago '13	♟♟ 3	
○ Orvieto Cl. Sup. Luigi e Giovanna Villa Monticelli '11	♟♟♟ 5	
○ Orvieto Cl. Sup. Muffa Nobile Calcaia '10	♟♟♟ 5	
● Lago di Corbara Rosso Polvento Villa Monticelli '09	♟♟ 5	
● Lago di Corbara Rosso Polvento Villa Monticelli '08	♟♟ 5	
○ Moscato Passito Villa Monticelli '09	♟♟ 6	
○ Orvieto Cl. Sup. Castagnolo '13	♟♟ 3*	

● Montefalco Sagrantino Collenottolo '11	♟♟♟ 6
● Montefalco Sagrantino '09	♟♟♟ 6
● Montefalco Sagrantino Collenottolo '10	♟♟♟ 6
● Montefalco Sagrantino '08	♟♟ 5

Bigi

loc. Ponte Giulio
05018 Orvieto [TR]
Tel. 0763315888
www.cantinebigi.it

PRE-BOOKED VISITS
ANNUAL PRODUCTION 4,000,000 bottles
HECTARES UNDER VINE 196.00

Bigi boasts a long history in the production of the typical wines of Orvieto with good results. The winery now belongs to Gruppo Italiano Vini, which has managed over time to maintain its reputation and develop the business from many points of view. Bigi's wines show great consistency, and all the labels hit home, offering reliability and excellent quality at the right price. This was another good all-round performance, especially as far as regards the whites in the portfolio. We tried two good interpretations of Orvieto Classico. The 2014 shows clean aromas of white peach, grapefruit and citrus, leading to a fresh, supple palette. The Torricella from the same vintage shows greater staffing, apple and peach, as well as good length. We also enjoyed an excellent Est Est Est 2014, a type not usually found in this region.

○ Est Est Est di Montefiascone '14	▼▼ 2*
○ Orvieto Cl. Secco '14	▼▼ 2*
○ Orvieto Cl. Torricella '14	▼▼ 2*
○ Grechetto Strozzavolpe '14	▼ 2
○ Vipra Bianca '14	▼ 2
● Vipra Rossa '14	▼ 2
○ Grechetto Strozzavolpe '13	▽▽ 2*
○ Orvieto Cl. Torricella '11	▽▽ 3
● Sartiano '12	▽▽ 3
● Sartiano '11	▽▽ 3
○ Strozzavolpe '12	▽▽ 2*
○ Strozzavolpe '11	▽▽ 2*
⊙ Vipra Rosa '12	▽▽ 2*
● Vipra Rossa '12	▽▽ 2*

Bocale

loc. Madonna della Stella
via Fratta Alzatura
06036 Montefalco [PG]
Tel. 0742399233
www.bocale.it

CELLAR SALES
PRE-BOOKED VISITS
ANNUAL PRODUCTION 24,000 bottles
HECTARES UNDER VINE 4.20

An historic territory, an ancient farming tradition, and a small, young winery combine to give us Bocale, run by the Valentini family, which in a short time has earned a reputation as one of the best in the DOC zone. Despite limited production figures, its stylistic development is increasingly clear and focused. Ever since the very first vintages, the reds have been making a name for their originality and sense of place. Maceration on the skins is fairly long and, since 2009, large oak has replaced barriques for the ageing of the Sagrantino. The results are evident, as in the masterful Montefalco Sagrantino 2012, with a superlative nose dominated by fresh cherry, wild berries and fine spice, leading into a relaxed, rounded palate with a consistent aromatic framework, showing youthful and full-bloodied. The tannins are still young, but have great potential. We were also impressed with the Montefalco Rosso 2013.

● Montefalco Sagrantino '12	▼▼ 5
● Montefalco Rosso '13	▼▼ 3
● Montefalco Rosso '12	▽▽ 2*
● Montefalco Rosso '09	▽▽ 4
● Montefalco Rosso '08	▽▽ 4
● Montefalco Sagrantino '11	▽▽ 5
● Montefalco Sagrantino '10	▽▽ 5
● Montefalco Sagrantino '09	▽▽ 5
● Montefalco Sagrantino '07	▽▽ 5
● Montefalco Sagrantino '06	▽▽ 5
● Montefalco Sagrantino Passito '09	▽▽ 5

Leonardo Bussoletti

S.DA DELLE PRETARE, 62
05035 NARNI [TR]
TEL. 0744715687
www.leonardobussoletti.it

PRE-BOOKED VISITS
ANNUAL PRODUCTION 20,000 bottles
HECTARES UNDER VINE 7.00
VITICULTURE METHOD Certified Organic

Leonardo Bussoletti's small estate has been one of the revelations in Umbria in recent years. The vins de garde of this passionate producer rest on a solid basis: long experience in the world of wine, a terroir that is proving to be up to the challenge, with both new vines and old plantings, and an original style, increasingly convincing and constantly improving. His love for traditional varieties has led him to concentrate above all on the traditional varieties of the Narni area, starting with his beloved ciliegiolo. 2013 is a vintage that marks a turning point, in particular for the wines based on ciliegiolo, which clearly changed gear to achieve finesse and expressiveness, free from the restraints of charred oak seen in the past. A demonstration of this is the oh-so-drinkable Il Brecciaro 2013, boasting a suffused, full pleasurable style, over a backdrop of forest fruits, Mediterranean herbs and black pepper.

● Brecciaro '13	♥♥ 3*
● 05035 Narni Rosso '14	♥♥ 2*
● Ciliegiolo di Narni Vigna Vecchia '12	♥♥ 7
○ Narni Bianco '14	♥ 2
○ Colle Ozio Grechetto '12	♥♥♥ 3*
● Brecciaro '12	♥♥ 3
● Brecciaro '11	♥♥ 3
● Brecciaro '10	♥♥ 3
● Ciliegiolo di Narni V. V. '11	♥♥ 7
● Ciliegiolo di Narni V. V. '10	♥♥ 7
○ Colle Ozio '12	♥♥ 3

★★Arnaldo Caprai

LOC. TORRE
06036 MONTEFALCO [PG]
TEL. 0742378802
www.arnaldocaprai.it

CELLAR SALES
PRE-BOOKED VISITS
ANNUAL PRODUCTION 750,000 bottles
HECTARES UNDER VINE 136.00

Caprai and Sagrantino form an indissoluble bond, without which the wine of Montefalco would probably have not achieved its current fame. This has been a difficult journey, and is the result of imagination, expertise, research and business development. Above all, the project revolves around a precise idea of wine with an unmistakable identity. Caprai's wines express this, and are continually developing, yet always modern and dynamic. Whatever your opinion of them, they never leave you indifferent. The hot growing year gave a 25 Anni of exceptional power, with quintessentially Mediterranean mature aromas, leading into hefty structure and tannins on the palate. We were only partly convinced, however, and preferred the splendid Collepiano 2011, which shows much more balance and a lean, almost delicate texture of wild berries, including blackcurrant, over a supple palate. We loved the Montefalco Rosso 2013.

● Montefalco Sagrantino Collepiano '11	♥♥♥ 7
● Montefalco Sagrantino 25 Anni '11	♥♥ 8
○ Montefalco Bianco '14	♥♥ 3
● Montefalco Rosso '13	♥♥ 4
○ Colli Martani Grechetto Grecante '14	♥ 4
● Montefalco Rosso V. Flaminia Maremmana '13	♥ 4
● Montefalco Sagrantino 25 Anni '10	♥♥♥ 8
● Montefalco Sagrantino 25 Anni '09	♥♥♥ 8
● Montefalco Sagrantino 25 Anni '08	♥♥♥ 8
● Montefalco Sagrantino 25 Anni '07	♥♥♥ 8
● Montefalco Sagrantino 25 Anni '06	♥♥♥ 8
● Montefalco Sagrantino 25 Anni '05	♥♥♥ 8
● Montefalco Sagrantino 25 Anni '04	♥♥♥ 8
● Montefalco Sagrantino Collepiano '08	♥♥♥ 6
● Montefalco Sagrantino Collepiano '03	♥♥♥ 6
● Rosso Outsider '03	♥♥♥ 8

Carini

LOC. CANNETO
FRAZ. COLLE UMBERTO
S.DA DEL TEGOLARO, 3
06133 PERUGIA
TEL. 0756059495
www.agrariacarini.it

CELLAR SALES
PRE-BOOKED VISITS
ANNUAL PRODUCTION 40,000 bottles
HECTARES UNDER VINE 10.00

The wines of the Carini brothers are no longer a source of surprise. The extremely attractive winery is set in breathtaking landscape, halfway between Perugia and Lake Trasimeno, where everything seems to be in great harmony: the woodland, the olive groves, the small lakes, the attractive farm buildings, the farm breeding cinta senese pigs, and of course the vineyard. The wines pursue a modern style, not without the use of international varieties but also those of the territory. The consistently reliable labels now display a consolidated style. Their plush, generous wines offer interesting contrasts, such as Il Tegolaro 2012: enjoyable but with slightly overripe fruit, and toasty aromas that accentuate its sweetness. The Òscano shows well-rounded, impeccable Mediterranean character, while the Poggio Canneto is slightly oaky yet very drinkable.

La Carraia

LOC. TORDIMONTE, 56
05018 ORVIETO [TR]
TEL. 0763304013
www.lacarraia.it

CELLAR SALES
PRE-BOOKED VISITS
ANNUAL PRODUCTION 580,000 bottles
HECTARES UNDER VINE 119.00

This historic winery in the Orvieto area is known as much for its typical whites as for its reds, which are among the most interesting in the area. At the helm are two prestigious families that need few introductions, Gialletti and Cotarella, and the vineyards are home to both international and native varieties. The modern-styled wines cover various types, both red and white. Once again this year all the labels proved to be extremely reliable. The good 2014 version of Poggio Calvelli is an Orvieto Classico Superiore that manages to stand out from the indistinct masses of the DOC zone. The growing year gives notes of chalk and melon, with slightly aromatic and floral hints, over a well-managed, tidy, focused palate with good progression and freshness.

○ Poggio Canneto '13	♟♟ 3
● Tegolaro '12	♟♟ 5
● C. del Trasimeno Òscano '14	♟ 2
● C. del Trasimeno Òscano '12	♟♟ 2*
○ C. del Trasimeno Rile '12	♟♟ 2*
○ C. del Trasimeno Rile '11	♟♟ 2*
● Òscano '09	♟♟ 2
● Poggio Canneto '12	♟♟ 3*
○ Poggio Canneto '09	♟♟ 3
○ Poggio Canneto '08	♟♟ 3*
● Rile '13	♟♟ 7
● Tegolaro '11	♟♟ 5
● Tegolaro '08	♟♟ 5
● Tegolaro '07	♟♟ 5
● Tegolaro Selezione Armando '08	♟♟ 5

○ Orvieto Cl. Sup. Poggio Calvelli '14	♟♟ 2*
● Fobiano '12	♟♟ 5
● Cabernet Sauvignon La Carraia '14	♟ 2
● Sangiovese La Carraia '14	♟ 2
● Solcato '13	♟ 3
● Tizzonero '13	♟ 3
● Fobiano '03	♟♟♟ 4
● Cabernet Sauvignon '12	♟♟ 2*
● Fobiano '11	♟♟ 5
● Fobiano '10	♟♟ 4
○ Orvieto Cl. Sup. Poggio Calvelli '13	♟♟ 2*
○ Orvieto Cl. Sup. Poggio Calvelli '12	♟♟ 2*
● Sangiovese '12	♟♟ 2*
● Tizzonero '12	♟♟ 3

Tenuta Castelbuono

LOC. BEVAGNA
VOC. CASTELLACCIO, 9
06031 PERUGIA
TEL. 0742361670
www.tenutacastelbuono.it

ANNUAL PRODUCTION 123,000 bottles
HECTARES UNDER VINE 32.00

This splendid estate and project, topped off by a winery that is a work of art, and one of Italy's finest, is part of the Tenute Lunelli project. Castelbuono, near Bevagna, rests on a hill with breathtaking views and a perfect position. Some of the vineyards lie in this magical setting, others in the municipality of Montefalco. The winery's reds, aiming for increasingly measured extraction, still lack a distinctive identity, and are aged in a mix of medium and large oak. Our favourite was a captivating Montefalco Rosso Riserva Lampante 2010, perhaps the best of the vintage in its category. This wine of great territorial charm offers a nose of red berry fruit, rain-soaked earth and forest floor, with an elegant tertiary tobacco swathe. The perfectly-managed palate is lean, showing blood-rich meat and a good acid backbone.

★★Castello della Sala

LOC. SALA
05016 FICULLE [TR]
TEL. 076386127
www.antinori.it

PRE-BOOKED VISITS
ANNUAL PRODUCTION 750,000 bottles
HECTARES UNDER VINE 140.00

The land around Orvieto has been famous since time immemorial for the production of great white wines. It is thus no surprise that the Antinori family decided some years ago to establish its white-wine making project here. The splendid vineyards and winery are set in an extraordinary position, in outstanding wine country. The expertise of the family and their staff do the rest, producing labels of the highest quality, with pride of place going to the Cervaro della Sala. The Cervaro 2013 plays on its elegance and finesse, sacrificing a little flesh and stuffing to display a linear, caressing style of great dynamism. A similar style can be detected on the nose, with delicate, complex, yet not overpowering aromas and subtle toasty notes. This is a fine version, as is the Muffato della Sala 2010.

● Montefalco Rosso Lampante Ris. '10	♟♟ 5
● Montefalco Rosso Ziggurat '11	♟♟ 3
● Montefalco Sagrantino '10	♟♟ 5
● Montefalco Rosso '10	♀♀ 3
● Montefalco Rosso '09	♀♀ 3
● Montefalco Rosso Ris. '09	♀♀ 5
● Montefalco Rosso Ris. '08	♀♀ 5
● Montefalco Sagrantino '08	♀♀ 5
● Montefalco Sagrantino '07	♀♀ 5
● Montefalco Sagrantino '06	♀♀ 5
● Montefalco Sagrantino Carapace '09	♀♀ 5
● Montefalco Sagrantino Passito '10	♀♀ 5

○ Cervaro della Sala '13	♟♟♟ 6
○ Muffato della Sala '10	♟♟ 6
○ Bramito del Cervo '14	♟♟ 3
○ Orvieto Cl. Sup. San Giovanni della Sala '14	♟♟ 3
○ Conte della Vipera '14	♟ 5
● Pinot Nero '13	♟ 6
○ Cervaro della Sala '12	♀♀♀ 6
○ Cervaro della Sala '11	♀♀♀ 6
○ Cervaro della Sala '10	♀♀♀ 6
○ Cervaro della Sala '09	♀♀♀ 6
○ Cervaro della Sala '08	♀♀♀ 6
○ Cervaro della Sala '07	♀♀♀ 6
○ Cervaro della Sala '06	♀♀♀ 6
○ Cervaro della Sala '05	♀♀♀ 6
○ Cervaro della Sala '04	♀♀♀ 6

Cantina Castello Monte Vibiano Vecchio

LOC. MONTE VIBIANO VECCHIO DI MERCATELLO
VOC. PALOMBARO, 22
06072 MARSCIANO [PG]
TEL. 0758783386
www.montevibiano.it

CELLAR SALES
PRE-BOOKED VISITS
ANNUAL PRODUCTION 300,000 bottles
HECTARES UNDER VINE 35.00
SUSTAINABLE WINERY

This magnificent, ambitious project was one of the first in the world to achieve zero CO_2 emissions. Although this has always been a centre for viticulture, there are few wineries of any importance here, which makes this operation all the more special. Monte Vibiano deserves attention for various reasons. Not least, of course, is the standard achieved in recent years by the wines, which boast a modern style yet great character, good structure and focus, and are based on an attractive mix of native and international varieties. The superb Monvì 2012, a seductive red with aromas of ripe cherry and a refreshing grassy swathe, ushering in a plush, succulent palate and slightly sandy tannins on the finish. The surprise came with the whites. The Maria Camilla, for example, offers a floral nose, together with attractive vanilla and buttery notes, followed by a soft attack on the palate, offset by a citrus finish and good acidity, making it tangy and dynamic.

● Colli Perugini Rosso Monvì '12	♟♟	2*
○ Maria Camilla '14	♟♟	3
○ Villa Monte Vibiano Bianco '14	♟♟	2*
● Colli Perugini Rosso L'Andrea '08	♟♟♟	5
● Colli Perugini Rosso L'Andrea '10	♟♟	5
● Colli Perugini Rosso L'Andrea '09	♟♟	5
● Colli Perugini Rosso Monvì '10	♟♟	2*
● Colli Perugini Rosso Monvì '09	♟♟	2*
○ Maria Camilla '13	♟♟	3
⊙ Maryam '12	♟♟	3

Cantina Cenci

FRAZ. SAN BIAGIO DELLA VALLE
VOC. ANTICELLO, 1
06072 MARSCIANO [PG]
TEL. 3805198980
www.cantinacenci.it

CELLAR SALES
PRE-BOOKED VISITS
ANNUAL PRODUCTION 20,000 bottles
HECTARES UNDER VINE 5.00
SUSTAINABLE WINERY

Giovanni Cenci's arrival on the Umbrian wine scene was nothing short of a revolution. Young, volcanic, and attentive to the sustainability and territorial identity of his wines, Giovanni is an agronomist and oenologist with extensive experience. The winery is based in an old rural settlement that once belonged to the Olivetan monks, near the vineyard that forms a splendid natural amphitheatre. The hillside plots are on clay, silt and limestone soils, with a beneficial presence of travertine. The natural, authentic wines display a pure style and a light hand. We were bowled over by the Grechetto Anticello 2014, a wine that pays homage to a traditional Umbrian white grape and raises it to heights of absolute hedonism. The full nose offers notes of grape skin without compromising balance and finesse, and is followed by a fleshy, leisurely palate underpinned by wild flowers. We were also impressed by the Sangiovese Piantata 2013, as pale as it is full-flavoured, with blood-rich meat on the caressing palate.

○ Anticello '14	♟♟	2*
● Piantata '13	♟♟	4
○ Giole '14	♟♟	2*
● Ascheria '13	♟	4
● Sanbiagio '13	♟	3
○ Alago '12	♟♟	3
○ Anticello '12	♟♟	2*
● Piantata '12	♟♟	2*

Fattoria Colleallodole

LOC. COLLE ALLODOLE
06031 BEVAGNA [PG]
TEL. 0742361897
www.fattoriacolleallodole.it

CELLAR SALES
PRE-BOOKED VISITS
ANNUAL PRODUCTION 60,000 bottles
HECTARES UNDER VINE 15.00

If you are looking for authentic wines, which are artisanal in the noblest sense of the term, supervised at every stage of the production process by a family that has played an important role in the development of its territory, visit the Fattoria Colleallodole. Here, near Bevagna, you will find a passionate, dedicated family, as attentive in the rows as they are in the cellar, whose charming wines are the result of a clear philosophy. The reds show excellence across the board and give unforgettable emotions. We saw a brace of unbeatable Sagrantinos, proving that the 2012 wines of the Antano family are a precious resource for the wine scene of Montefalco and Umbria in general. The Colleallodole selection is splendid, but we were even more impressed with the vintage version, matured solely in large oak. This flavourful, authentic red boasts pervasive earthy aromas of dried leaves and wild berries over an elegant weave and mineral hints, as well as extraordinary length.

● Montefalco Sagrantino '12	♥♥♥ 6
● Montefalco Sagrantino Colleallodole '12	♥♥ 8
● Montefalco Rosso Ris. '12	♥♥ 5
● Montefalco Sagrantino Passito '12	♥♥ 7
● Montefalco Rosso '13	♥ 3
● Montefalco Sagrantino Colleallodole '10	♀♀♀ 8
● Montefalco Sagrantino Colleallodole '09	♀♀♀ 8
● Montefalco Rosso '12	♀♀ 3
● Montefalco Rosso Ris. '11	♀♀ 5
● Montefalco Sagrantino '10	♀♀ 5
● Montefalco Sagrantino '09	♀♀ 5
● Montefalco Sagrantino Colleallodole '11	♀♀ 8

Fattoria Colsanto

LOC. MONTARONE
06031 BEVAGNA [PG]
TEL. 0742360412
www.livon.it

CELLAR SALES
PRE-BOOKED VISITS
ACCOMMODATION
ANNUAL PRODUCTION 50,000 bottles
HECTARES UNDER VINE 15.00

The project failed to take off at first, and seemed to be beset by a crisis of identity. Luckily, it was not difficult to turn things around, and today Colsanto's wines are among the best in the area. The operation is based near Bevagna, and is the work of the Livon family. The estate's reds are not only outstanding, but also display an original, lean, relaxed style. Ageing takes place in the large barrels of Italian tradition. More mature and concentrated, both on the nose and palate, the Montefalco Sagrantino 2011 is representative of the vintage, offering aromas of fruit, also liqueur fruits, and a generous, velvety palate. The Ruris 2013 continues to impress, above all because of its value for money. We also liked the Montefalco Rosso 2012.

● Montefalco Sagrantino '11	♥♥ 5
● Ruris Rosso '13	♥♥ 2*
● Montefalco Rosso '12	♥ 3
● Montefalco Rosso '10	♀♀ 3
● Montefalco Rosso '09	♀♀ 3*
● Montefalco Sagrantino '10	♀♀ 5
● Montefalco Sagrantino '09	♀♀ 5
● Montefalco Sagrantino '08	♀♀ 5
● Montefalco Sagrantino '07	♀♀ 5
● Montefalco Sagrantino '03	♀♀ 5
● Ruris Rosso '12	♀♀ 2*

Decugnano dei Barbi

LOC. FOSSATELLO, 50
05019 ORVIETO [TR]
TEL. 0763308255
www.decugnano.it

CELLAR SALES
PRE-BOOKED VISITS
ANNUAL PRODUCTION 120,000 bottles
HECTARES UNDER VINE 32.00

Decugnano dei Barbi is an honoured member of the small club of Orvieto's best wineries, and an example of all-round excellence. The marvellous cellar is imbued with history, starting with the Etruscan grottoes in which some of the wines are aged, and is also graced with excellent soils, rich in fossils. The winery is set in the hills overlooking Lake Corbara, with a breath-taking view, and its splendid wines include clean, vibrantly mineral whites and elegant, mature reds. Il Bianco is one of Orvieto's most authoritative wines. The 2014 growing year was far from easy, but the results are in any case impressive. The attractive nose of pear, peach and blossom paves the way for a lean, fresh and satisfying body. The outstanding Il Rosso shows succulent, full flavoured and pleasurable. The Pourriture Noble 2013 is complex, and the Villa Barbi Rosso 2013 intriguing.

Di Filippo

VOC. CONVERSINO, 153
06033 CANNARA [PG]
TEL. 0742731242
www.vinidifilippo.com

CELLAR SALES
PRE-BOOKED VISITS
ANNUAL PRODUCTION 215,000 bottles
HECTARES UNDER VINE 30.00
VITICULTURE METHOD Certified Organic
SUSTAINABLE WINERY

The Di Filippo family produces a large number of wines, often from native varieties and good wine country. They do so with passion and professionalism, eschewing any shortcuts, following a tradition which has become, over time, an example of convinced modernity. Organic for years, and one of the first in Umbria to be so, the Di Filippo operation is now fully mature, both qualitatively and stylistically, but no stranger to innovation. This profile also covers the biodynamic Planiarche wines. A wide range of labels was presented, and we were excited by the great character of the Montefalco Sagrantino 2011, with clarity on the nose and good extract, lively but well-crafted tannins, and clear notes of balsam. From the Planiarche line, the Sagrantino Brown Label shows a fine weave and delicate nose, playing on raspberry and forest fruits. The Colli Martani Grechetto is concentrated and full flavoured.

○ Orvieto Cl. Sup. Il Bianco '14	♟♟ 3*
● Il Rosso '13	♟♟ 3
○ Orvieto Cl. Sup. Pourriture Noble '13	♟♟ 5
● Villa Barbi Rosso '13	♟♟ 2*
○ Orvieto Cl. Sup. Villa Barbi Bianco '14	♟ 2
● "IL" Rosso '98	♟♟♟ 5
○ Orvieto Cl. Sup. "IL" '11	♟♟♟ 3*
○ Orvieto Cl. Sup. Il Bianco '12	♟♟♟ 3*
○ Orvieto Cl. Sup. Il Bianco '10	♟♟♟ 3
○ Orvieto Cl. Sup. Il Bianco '09	♟♟♟ 4
● Il Rosso '12	♟♟ 4
● Lago di Corbara "IL" '02	♟♟ 5
● Lago di Corbara "IL" '01	♟♟ 5
○ Orvieto Cl. Sup. "IL" '01	♟♟ 3
○ Orvieto Cl. Sup. Il Bianco '13	♟♟ 3*

● Montefalco Sagrantino '11	♟♟ 5
○ Colli Martani Grechetto Planiarche '14	♟♟ 2*
● Colli Martani Vernaccia di Cannara '14	♟♟ 4
● Montefalco Rosso '13	♟♟ 2*
● Montefalco Rosso Sallustio '12	♟♟ 3
● Montefalco Sagrantino Planiarche Black Label '09	♟♟ 5
● Montefalco Sagrantino Planiarche Brown Label '10	♟♟ 5
○ Trebbiano Spoletino Farandola '14	♟♟ 2*
○ Colli Martani Grechetto '14	♟ 2
● Colli Martani Sangiovese '13	♟ 2
● Colli Martani Sangiovese Properzio Ris. '12	♟ 3
● Montefalco Sagrantino Etnico '11	♟ 4
○ Villa Conversino Bianco '14	♟ 2

Duca della Corgna

VIA ROMA, 236
06061 CASTIGLIONE DEL LAGO [PG]
TEL. 0759652493
www.ducadellacorgna.it

CELLAR SALES
PRE-BOOKED VISITS
ANNUAL PRODUCTION 280,000 bottles
HECTARES UNDER VINE 55.00

A benchmark for the wines of Lake
Trasimeno, Duca della Corgna is the most
ambitious project of a well-organized
cooperative winery, today presided over by
Carlo Corbacella. The state-of-the-art
production facility is based in the
municipality of Castiglione del Lago, as is
the shop. In the heart of Città della Pieve,
meanwhile, the winery boasts a beautiful
historic cellar. The vines lie on a limestone
outcrop, with subzones of various
geological origin. Among the varieties used,
special mention should be made of
Trasimeno gamay, a species of grenache
planted for some time now in the hills of
the zone. Difficult to choose the best wine
when all the labels are noteworthy. Two
reds were, however, impressive and
unbelievably from the 2014 vintage! On
one hand there was an incredibly good
value Baccio del Rosso, a juicy wine with
red berry fruit aromas, with a delicate,
caressing grassy swathe of ivy and
verbena. On the other, the usual peppery,
easy-drinking Divina Villa Etichetta Bianca,
a Trasimeno Gamay.

● C. del Trasimeno Baccio del Rosso '14	♥♥ 2*
● C. del Trasimeno Gamay Divina Villa Et. Bianca '14	♥♥ 2*
● C. del Trasimeno Rosso Corniolo Ris. '12	♥♥ 4
○ C. del Trasimeno Baccio del Bianco '14	♥ 2
○ C. del Trasimeno Grechetto Nuricante '14	♥ 2
☉ Martavello Rosato '14	♥ 2
● C. del Trasimeno Baccio del Bianco '13	♥♥ 2*
● C. del Trasimeno Baccio del Rosso '13	♥♥ 2*
● C. del Trasimeno Gamay Divina Villa Et. Bianca '13	♥♥ 2*
● C. del Trasimeno Gamay Divina Villa Ris. '12	♥♥ 3
● C. del Trasimeno Rosso Corniolo Ris. '11	♥♥ 4
● C. del Trasimeno Rosso Corniolo Ris. '09	♥♥ 4

Podere Fontesecca

VOC. FONTESECCA, 30
06062 CITTÀ DELLA PIEVE [PG]
TEL. 0763835008
www.fontesecca.it

CELLAR SALES
PRE-BOOKED VISITS
ACCOMMODATION
ANNUAL PRODUCTION 10,000 bottles
HECTARES UNDER VINE 3.80
VITICULTURE METHOD Certified Organic

Among the small wineries in the region,
that of Paolo Bolla struck us as one of the
most interesting. Harking from outside
Umbria, this grower chose a territory full of
promise but little known, and decided to
invest in small plots of old vines, starting
with traditional varieties. We are near Città
della Pieve, on the border between Umbria,
Lazio and Tuscany, where the soils clearly
show their marine origin. The family aims to
produce authentic wines, based on an
approach seeking symbiosis with the
environment and "natural" vinification
methods. With a growing year like 2013,
the Ciliegiolo Fontesecca was bound to be
delicious, and it lived up to expectations,
proving to be a pleasurable easy-drinker,
with a nose of ripe red berry fruit and
abundant peppery notes. The chewy,
succulent palate is a paean to drinkability
without ever sacrificing complexity. Equally
impressive is the tangy, fragrant Canaiolo
Rosato 2014.

☉ Canaiolo '14	♥♥ 3
● Ciliegiolo '13	♥♥ 3
○ Bianco Fontesecca '09	♥♥ 3
☉ Canaiolo '13	♥♥ 3
☉ Canaiolo '12	♥♥ 3
☉ Canaiolo '10	♥♥ 3
● Ciliegiolo '12	♥♥ 3
● Ciliegiolo '11	♥♥ 3
● Ciliegiolo '10	♥♥ 3*
○ Elso '13	♥♥ 2*
○ Elso '12	♥♥ 2*
● Pino Sangiovese '09	♥♥ 3*

Goretti

LOC. PILA
S.DA DEL PINO, 4
06132 PERUGIA
TEL. 075607316
www.vinigoretti.com

PRE-BOOKED VISITS
ANNUAL PRODUCTION 300,000 bottles
HECTARES UNDER VINE 50.00

The Goretti winery is one of the region's oldest operations, and one of the few in the past to produce the wines of Colli Perugini. Located at Pila, with a beautiful, recently renovated historic tower, it is popular with wine lovers looking for a wide range and value for money. Some years ago the family also invested in the Montefalco area, with a vineyard and new cellar, where they immediately began to achieve impressive results. We can start with Le Mura Saracene and a stunning Sagrantino 2011, one of the best of this vintage. It has a light, delicate, fine character imbued with red berry fruit, sandalwood and spice, ash and topsoil. In the mouth, it is even more convincing, with a graceful weave and full-flavoured tannins. From the Perugia area we liked the Grechetto Il Moggio, showing chamomile, vanilla and citrus.

Cantina La Spina

FRAZ. SPINA
VIA EMILIO ALESSANDRINI, 1
06055 MARSCIANO [PG]
TEL. 0758738120
www.cantinalaspina.it

CELLAR SALES
PRE-BOOKED VISITS
ANNUAL PRODUCTION 14,000 bottles
HECTARES UNDER VINE 2.20

Moreno Peccia is one of Umbria's most respected growers. The few hectares of his La Spina winery lie in the rolling hills between Perugia and Marsciano, and what is attractive, apart from its small size, is the balance he achieves in his wines, which, in an age of disputes and firmly-held views, elude any attempt at classification and dogma. The classic yet modern wines are impeccable but full of authentic character, and based on native varieties as well as those from further afield. The whole range confirmed its worth. The Rosso Spina 2013 is a spectacle, proffering an elegant nose of dark berry fruit and sandalwood over hints of black pepper. The succulent, fragrant palate shows a touch of charred oak that needs to be absorbed, but is already perfectly enjoyable. Among the whites, we loved the Eburneo and the Filare Maiore, both from the 2014 vintage.

● Montefalco Sagrantino Le Mure Saracene '11	▼▼ 3*
○ Il Moggio '14	▼▼ 3
○ Colli Perugini Grechetto '14	▼ 2
● Colli Perugini Rosso L'Arringatore '11	▼ 5
● Montefalco Rosso '12	▼ 3
● Colli Perugini Rosso L'Arringatore '08	♀♀ 3
● Colli Perugini Rosso L'Arringatore '07	♀♀ 3
● Fontanella Rosso '12	♀♀ 2*
● Montefalco Sagrantino Le Mure Saracene '10	♀♀ 3
● Montefalco Sagrantino Le Mure Saracene '07	♀♀ 5
● Montefalco Sagrantino Le Mure Saracene '06	♀♀ 5

○ Eburneo '14	▼▼ 2*
○ Filare Maiore '14	▼▼ 2*
● Rosso Spina '13	▼▼ 3
● Cimaàlta '14	▼ 2
● Polimante della Spina '13	▼ 4
○ Eburneo '13	♀♀ 2*
● Merlato '09	♀♀ 2
● Polimante della Spina '11	♀♀ 3
● Polimante della Spina '10	♀♀ 3
● Rosso Spina '12	♀♀ 3
● Rosso Spina '11	♀♀ 3
● Rosso Spina '10	♀♀ 3
● Rosso Spina '09	♀♀ 3
● Rosso Spina '08	♀♀ 3
○ V. Maiore '13	♀♀ 2*
○ V. Maiore '12	♀♀ 2*

★Lungarotti

v.le Giorgio Lungarotti, 2
06089 Torgiano [PG]
Tel. 075988661
www.lungarotti.it

Moretti Omero

loc. San Sabino, 19
06030 Giano dell'Umbria [PG]
Tel. 0742290426
www.morettiomero.it

CELLAR SALES
PRE-BOOKED VISITS
ACCOMMODATION AND RESTAURANT SERVICE
ANNUAL PRODUCTION 2,400,000 bottles
HECTARES UNDER VINE 250.00
VITICULTURE METHOD Certified Organic
SUSTAINABLE WINERY

It cannot have been easy for the Lungarotti
family to ensure continuity for its prestigious
past while giving a new lease of life to the
operation, when the need emerged in the
late 1990s. When the winery at Torgiano was
left bereft of its founder, it was forced to start
afresh, finding a way to "speak the same
language as always, but with new words," as
they love to put it. The winery's strategy
means taking this important operation into
the future, whilst ensuring its previous
reputation remains intact. We were taken
with many of the wines tasted so we will at
the top, obviously, which can only mean the
Riserva Vigna Monticchio 2010. This
sensational wine is the result of a journey of
stylistic growth and of a vintage that will go
down in history: in short, a great classic in
the making. Also splendid is the deceptively
simple, quintessentially Mediterranean
Torgiano Rosso Rubesco 2012.

CELLAR SALES
PRE-BOOKED VISITS
ACCOMMODATION AND RESTAURANT SERVICE
ANNUAL PRODUCTION 75,000 bottles
HECTARES UNDER VINE 13.00
VITICULTURE METHOD Certified Organic
SUSTAINABLE WINERY

Moretti Omero is above all an Umbrian
farmer of the old school, not just a grower.
He began by using the tried-and-tested
approach of tradition, and has always
adopted organic farming methods,
eschewing fashion with great conviction. The
winery is at Giano dell'Umbria, one of the
less-planted Sagrantino growing areas, at
the foot of the Martani hills. Moretti's wines
are genuine and artisanal, albeit at the cost
of some small imperfections. Starting with
the whites we see that the 2014 vintage has
freshness and flavour, grip and drinkability
like few others. The Grechetto is vibrant,
while the delicately aromatic Nessuno shows
sensations of gentian root. We also liked the
Sagrantino 2011, even if the reds seemed a
touch more oaked than usual.

● Torgiano Rosso V. Monticchio Ris. '10	♟♟♟ 6
● Torgiano Rosso Rubesco '12	♟♟ 2*
○ Torre di Giano '14	♟♟ 2*
○ Torgiano Bianco Torre di Giano V. il Pino '12	♟ 5
○ Torgiano Bianco Torre di Giano V. il Pino Ris. '08	♟♟♟ 3*
● Torgiano Rosso Rubesco V. Monticchio Ris. '07	♟♟♟ 6
● Torgiano Rosso V. Monticchio Ris. '09	♟♟♟ 6
● Torgiano Rosso V. Monticchio Ris. '08	♟♟♟ 6
● Torgiano Rosso V. Monticchio Ris. '06	♟♟♟ 5
● Torgiano Rosso V. Monticchio Ris. '05	♟♟♟ 5*
● Torgiano Rosso V. Monticchio Ris. '04	♟♟♟ 5
● Torgiano Rosso Vigna Monticchio Ris. '03	♟♟♟ 5
● Torgiano Rosso Vigna Monticchio Ris. '01	♟♟♟ 5

○ Grechetto '14	♟♟ 2*
● Montefalco Sagrantino '11	♟♟ 5
○ Nessuno '14	♟♟ 2*
● Montefalco Rosso '13	♟ 3
● Montefalco Sagrantino Vignalunga '08	♟ 7
○ Grechetto '12	♟♟ 2*
○ Grechetto dell'Umbria '10	♟♟ 2
● Montefalco Rosso '10	♟♟ 3
● Montefalco Rosso '09	♟♟ 5
● Montefalco Sagrantino '09	♟♟ 5
● Montefalco Sagrantino '08	♟♟ 5
● Montefalco Sagrantino '07	♟♟ 5
○ Nessuno '13	♟♟ 2*
○ Nessuno '12	♟♟ 2*

UMBRIA

La Palazzola

LOC. VASCIGLIANO
05039 STRONCONE [TR]
TEL. 0744609091
www.lapalazzola.it

ANNUAL PRODUCTION 150,000 bottles
HECTARES UNDER VINE 28.00

La Palazzola is undeniably an original operation. Although this is one of Umbria's historic wineries, it is also highly innovative and full of surprises. The merit goes to Stefano Grilli, a true-bred grower, his estate at Vascigliano, near Terni, and his volcanic passion. The range is not limited to reds and whites, but covers a wide variety of labels, with excellent results in sweet wines and above all sparklers. Grilli has been producing the latter with excellent results since long before the market for fizz became as crowded as it now is. The captivating Amelia Vin Santo 2011 has some stunning traditional charm, with a nose of aniseed, oriental wood and spice, over hints of macaroon and a refreshing balsamic backdrop that provides balance, great harmony and drinkability. It goes without saying that the Metodo Ancestrale sparklers are on their usual excellent form, headed by the Riesling Brut.

Palazzone

LOC. ROCCA RIPESENA, 68
05019 ORVIETO [TR]
TEL. 0763344921
www.palazzone.com

CELLAR SALES
PRE-BOOKED VISITS
ACCOMMODATION AND RESTAURANT SERVICE
ANNUAL PRODUCTION 130,000 bottles
HECTARES UNDER VINE 24.00

Giovanni Dubini is a tenacious, skilled and sensitive grower. People are once again beginning to talk about Orvieto and its white wines, albeit shyly, but for many years he was one of the very few to keep the zone's flag flying high. Palazzone thus plays a vital role, not only because of its project and wines, but above all because of its example. The splendid whites produced on this small plot of excellent wine country show a real sense of place, and can stand the test of time like few others. The Campo del Guardiano is a benchmark of incredible longevity. The 2013 vintage gave us a still developing, austere, stony, and at times harsh white, with typical Mediterranean tones but leaner and more dynamic than usual. It will no doubt live up to expectations, and could have wonderful surprises in store for us in the future. We appreciated the Terre Vineate 2014 and the Piviere 2013.

○ Amelia Vin Santo '11	♟♟ 4
○ Extra Dry '11	♟♟ 4
○ Riesling Brut Metodo Ancestrale '11	♟♟ 3
⊙ Rosé Brut '10	♟♟ 4
○ Brut '10	♟ 4
○ Gran Cuvée Brut '11	♟♟ 4
○ Riesling Brut Metodo Ancestrale '10	♟♟ 3*
● Rubino '09	♟♟ 5
● Syrah '11	♟♟ 3
● Umbria Passito '09	♟♟ 4
● Umbria Passito '08	♟♟ 4

○ Orvieto Cl. Sup. Campo del Guardiano '13	♟♟ 3*
○ Orvieto Cl. Sup. Terre Vineate '14	♟♟ 2*
○ Grek '14	♟♟ 2*
● Piviere '13	♟♟ 3
○ Viognier '14	♟ 3
● Armaleo '00	♟♟♟ 5
● Armaleo '98	♟♟♟ 5
● Armaleo '97	♟♟♟ 5
● Armaleo '95	♟♟♟ 5
○ Orvieto Cl. Sup. Campo del Guardiano '11	♟♟♟ 2*
○ Orvieto Cl. Sup. Campo del Guardiano '09	♟♟♟ 3
○ Orvieto Cl. Sup. Campo del Guardiano '07	♟♟♟ 3
○ Orvieto Cl. Sup. Terre Vineate '11	♟♟♟ 2*

F.lli Pardi

VIA GIOVANNI PASCOLI, 7/9
06036 MONTEFALCO [PG]
TEL. 0742379023
www.cantinapardi.it

CELLAR SALES
PRE-BOOKED VISITS
ANNUAL PRODUCTION 55,000 bottles
HECTARES UNDER VINE 11.00

The fine Pardi winery is modern and traditional at the same time, and the family boasts a prestigious past in various fields of local craftsmanship, including wine. The operation as we know it today is however fairly recent, and is based a stone's throw from the walls of Montefalco. Some of the vines are planted here, even though the vineyards are distributed over various small plots. The wines, meanwhile, share a common denominator in their finesse and ability to reflect the family's idea of wine. The hot growing year made itself felt, and the well-rounded Sagrantino 2011 shows maturity and sweet fruit. This dense, well-balanced wine lacks just a touch of grip found in more classic vintages. Moreover, we are talking of an artisanal winery, and this confirms the authenticity of the project. Among the whites, the Trebbiano Spoletino is once again splendid.

● Montefalco Sagrantino '11	♟♟ 5
○ Spoleto Trebbiano Spoletino '14	♟♟ 2*
○ Montefalco Bianco Colle di Giove '14	♟ 2
● Montefalco Rosso '13	♟ 3
○ Colli Martani Grechetto '13	♟♟ 2*
○ Colli Martani Grechetto '12	♟♟ 2*
● Montefalco Rosso '12	♟♟ 3
● Montefalco Rosso '11	♟♟ 2*
● Montefalco Rosso '10	♟♟ 2*
● Montefalco Sagrantino '10	♟♟ 5
● Montefalco Sagrantino '09	♟♟ 5
● Montefalco Sagrantino Sacrantino '10	♟♟ 6
● Montefalco Sagrantino Sacrantino '08	♟♟ 6
○ Spoleto Trebbiano Spoletino '13	♟♟ 2*

Domenico Pennacchi

FRAZ. MARCELLANO
VIA SANT'ANGELO, 10
06035 GUALDO CATTANEO [PG]
TEL. 0742920069
pennacchidomenico@tiscalinet.it

CELLAR SALES
PRE-BOOKED VISITS
ANNUAL PRODUCTION 12,000 bottles
HECTARES UNDER VINE 6.00

Domenico Pennacchi's small winery is firmly rooted in its territory and traditional values, and is highly appreciated in the area. The marketing methods and style that we know today, however, only date back to the early 1990s. We are at Marcellano, Gualdo Cattaneo, one of the most important areas for the production of Sagrantino, whose unique soils are characterized by the presence of lignite. The vineyards lie in the hills, reaching elevations of up to 400 metres. Vinification methods are simple and fairly traditional, and envisage long maceration on the skins. The best of the bunch this year, surprise surprise, were two Sagrantinos. The elegant 2009 shows a silky weave. Full-bodied and leisurely, it is however just a touch too tannin-heavy for its age. The classic Sagrantino Passito 2010, of which this grower is a master, shows seductive, traditional character: not overly sweet, its slender body makes it extremely drinkable.

○ Colli di Fontivecchie Grechetto '14	♟♟ 2*
● Montefalco Sagrantino '09	♟♟ 5
● Montefalco Sagrantino Passito '10	♟ 5
● Colli di Fontivecchie Rosso '10	♟♟ 2*
● Montefalco Rosso '08	♟♟ 3
● Montefalco Rosso Ris. '08	♟♟ 4
● Montefalco Rosso Ris. '07	♟♟ 4
● Montefalco Sagrantino '08	♟♟ 5
● Montefalco Sagrantino '07	♟♟ 5
● Montefalco Sagrantino Terre dei Capitani '05	♟♟ 5

UMBRIA

Cantina Peppucci

LOC. SANT'ANTIMO
FRAZ. PETRORO, 4
06059 TODI [PG]
TEL. 0758947439
www.cantinapeppucci.com

CELLAR SALES
PRE-BOOKED VISITS
ACCOMMODATION
ANNUAL PRODUCTION 70,000 bottles
HECTARES UNDER VINE 12.50

This cellar has been on the way up for some years now, and has earned an excellent reputation in the region. We are in the beautiful rolling hills across the valley from Todi, with the border of the Sagrantino DOC zone a stone's throw away. It is no coincidence, then, that one of its top reds comes from this excellent local variety. Among the whites, meanwhile, pride of place goes to the Grechetto. Peppucci deserves a visit, not only for the quality of his wines but also for the beauty of the setting. L'Altro lo 2011, practically a monovarietal Sagrantino, is exceptional, and has nothing to fear from a comparison with similar blends in the area. This wine shows complex aromas with a clear Mediterranean character, against a backdrop of ripe fruit and tar, leading to a dense yet supple palate, and a leisurely finish with notes of aromatic herbs and roots. We loved the Grechetto 2014.

● Altro lo '11	▼▼▼ 5
○ Todi Grechetto Montorsolo '14	▼▼ 2*
● Todi Rosso Petroro 4 '14	▼▼ 2*
● Giovanni '11	▼ 4
● Altro lo '10	♀♀ 5
● Giovanni '10	♀♀ 4
● Giovanni '09	♀♀ 4
● Petroro 4 '11	♀♀ 2*
● Petroro 4 '09	♀♀ 3*
○ Todi Grechetto Montorsolo '13	♀♀ 2*
○ Todi Grechetto Montorsolo '12	♀♀ 2*
○ Todi Grechetto Montorsolo '11	♀♀ 2*
○ Todi Petroro 4 '12	♀♀ 2*
● Todi Rosso Petroro 4 '13	♀♀ 2*

Perticaia

LOC. CASALE
06036 MONTEFALCO [PG]
TEL. 0742379014
www.perticaia.it

CELLAR SALES
PRE-BOOKED VISITS
ANNUAL PRODUCTION 110,000 bottles
HECTARES UNDER VINE 15.50

The winery is located at Casale, a subzone with beautiful landscapes in the municipality of Montefalco. It is here that the new winery and vineyards are located, on various plots of good wine country. Perticaia, from an idea of Guido Guardigli, has become in a short time one of the most interesting operations in Umbria, offering wines of high quality and impressive style. The reds represent the productive and commercial foundation of the project, but forays into Trebbiano Spoletino have also rapidly borne fruit. We were very impressed with the Montefalco Sagrantino 2011, both in terms of its absolute quality and increasingly personal, convincing style. Considering the type, it is delicate, with nuanced, seductive red fruit, swathed in balsam, followed by a palate in which flavour holds sway over power. The tannins, although youthful, are perfectly extracted. The Trebbiano Spoletino is impeccable.

● Montefalco Sagrantino '11	▼▼▼ 5
○ Spoleto Trebbiano Spoletino '14	▼▼ 2*
● Montefalco Rosso '12	▼ 3
● Umbria Rosso '14	▼ 2
● Montefalco Sagrantino '10	♀♀♀ 5
● Montefalco Sagrantino '09	♀♀♀ 5
● Montefalco Sagrantino '07	♀♀♀ 5
● Montefalco Sagrantino '06	♀♀♀ 5
● Montefalco Sagrantino '05	♀♀♀ 5
● Montefalco Sagrantino '04	♀♀♀ 5
● Montefalco Rosso Ris. '11	♀♀ 4
● Montefalco Rosso Ris. '09	♀♀ 4
● Montefalco Rosso Ris. '08	♀♀ 4
● Montefalco Sagrantino '08	♀♀ 5
● Montefalco Sagrantino '03	♀♀ 5
● Montefalco Sagrantino '01	♀♀ 5

Pucciarella

LOC. VILLA DI MAGIONE
VIA CASE SPARSE, 39
06063 MAGIONE [PG]
TEL. 0758409147
www.pucciarella.it

CELLAR SALES
PRE-BOOKED VISITS
ACCOMMODATION
ANNUAL PRODUCTION 250,000 bottles
HECTARES UNDER VINE 58.50
SUSTAINABLE WINERY

In recent years, Pucciarella has moved up a gear, showing admirable consistency across the range, as well as some high points of extreme charm and excellence. This is an important project with a modern style, that endows prestige on the somewhat inconsistent wine zone of Trasimeno. The soils and winery are set in the DOC zone of the lake area, between Magione and Corciano. The breathtaking landscape, where the typical hills of Umbria meet a mild climate, are excellent for viticulture. The vineyards, at elevations of over 300 metres, are on medium-textured stony soils. The spectacular Colli del Trasimeno Rosso Berlingero 2013 is a modern-styled wine of great finesse, that explodes on the nose with blueberry and elegant grassy balsamic notes, with clear hints of bay leaf, leading into a concentrated, dynamic palate, with good depth and aromatic consistency. We should also mention the excellent Cabernet 2013, produced without the addition of sulphites.

● C. del Trasimeno Rosso Berlingero '13	♥♥ 2*
● C. del Trasimeno Cabernet '13	♥♥ 5
○ Arsiccio '14	♥ 3
● C. del Trasimeno Rosso Sant'Anna di Pucciarella Ris. '12	♥ 3
○ Arsiccio '13	♥♥ 3
○ Arsiccio '11	♥♥ 3
● Buggea Trequanda '10	♥♥ 1*
● C. del Trasimeno Rosso Sant'Anna Ris. '10	♥♥ 2*
● C. del Trasimeno Rosso Sant'Anna Ris. '09	♥♥ 2*
○ C. del Trasimeno Vin Santo '10	♥♥ 3*
○ C. del Trasimeno Vin Santo '09	♥♥ 3
○ C. del Trasimeno Vin Santo '08	♥♥ 3
● Empireo '10	♥♥ 3

Raina

LOC. TURRI
VIA CASE SPARSE, 42
06036 MONTEFALCO [PG]
TEL. 0742621356
www.raina.it

CELLAR SALES
PRE-BOOKED VISITS
RESTAURANT SERVICE
ANNUAL PRODUCTION 50,000 bottles
HECTARES UNDER VINE 10.00
VITICULTURE METHOD Certified Organic

Francesco Mariani began like many, in a conventional way and with the services of a consultant oenologist. After a few years, however, he decidedly changed course, putting himself in charge of the technical side of his small operation. The vines are grown here, first according to organic, and now biodynamic methods. The wines are delicately extracted, at least by the standards of the area, and barriques are making way for large barrels. In the same way, the Raina wines are abandoning their role as second-leads to increasingly take centre-stage. The new Sagrantino, the selection Le Pretelle 2010, goes straight to the top, showing an intriguing nose of forest fruit and autumn leaves. Still youthful with lively tannins and some rough edges from oak ageing, this wine is to be seen in terms of future development. We should underline the masterful touch of this grower with whites, and the authentic, natural versions of Grechetto and Trebbiano Spoletino.

● Montefalco Sagrantino Le Pretelle '10	♥♥ 5
○ Grechetto '14	♥♥ 2*
● Rosso della Gobba '13	♥♥ 2*
○ Spoleto Trebbiano Spoletino '14	♥♥ 3
● Montefalco Rosso '12	♀♀ 2*
● Montefalco Rosso '11	♀♀ 2*
● Montefalco Sagrantino '08	♀♀ 5
● Montefalco Sagrantino Campo di Raina '10	♀♀ 4
● Montefalco Sagrantino Campo di Raina '09	♀♀ 4
● Rosso della Gobba '12	♀♀ 2*
○ Trebbiano Spoletino '12	♀♀ 2*

Roccafiore

FRAZ. CHIOANO
VOC. COLLINA, 110A
06059 TODI [PG]
TEL. 0758942416
www.roccafiorewines.com

CELLAR SALES
PRE-BOOKED VISITS
ACCOMMODATION AND RESTAURANT SERVICE
ANNUAL PRODUCTION 90,000 bottles
HECTARES UNDER VINE 11.00
VITICULTURE METHOD Certified Organic

The Baccarelli family has been working in wine for a relatively short time, but has managed to create a project of great value and personality. Of course, the territory, in the rolling hills around Todi, is an important factor in their success, but their approach and philosophy also play a decisive role. Roccafiore enjoys a "dynamic balance", in which strategies, decisions and also changes always seem to be part of a harmonious whole. The varieties planted speak the local language, while the viticultural approach is in harmony with nature, and vinification always light-handed. The Fiorfiore is a decidedly original Grechetto, the result of a careful selection of grapes from old vines and ageing in large oak. After last year's rounded, mature version, we have a much slicker, more linear 2013. Opening to beeswax, pollen, blossom and fruit, with a delicate hint of butter on the nose, it shows succulent and harmonious on the palate. If it finds a touch more raciness and verve it will be excellent.

○ Todi Grechetto Sup. Fiorfiore '13	♟♟♟ 3*
● Prova d'Autore '12	♟♟ 4
● Todi Sangiovese Sup. Il Roccafiore '12	♟♟ 3
○ Collina d'Oro Passito '14	♟ 5
○ Fiordalis '14	♟ 2
● Todi Rosso Melograno '13	♟ 2
○ Fiordaliso '12	♟♟ 2*
● Roccafiore Rosso '09	♟♟ 2*
○ Todi Bianco Fiordaliso '13	♟♟ 2*
○ Todi Grechetto Sup. Fiordaliso '10	♟♟ 3
○ Todi Grechetto Sup. Fiorfiore '12	♟♟ 3*
○ Todi Grechetto Sup. Fiorfiore '11	♟♟ 3*
● Todi Rosso Melograno '12	♟♟ 2*
● Todi Rosso Melograno '11	♟♟ 2*
● Todi Sangiovese Rosso '10	♟♟ 2*
● Todi Sangiovese Sup. Il Roccafiore '11	♟♟ 3*

Romanelli

LOC. COLLE SAN CLEMENTE, 129A
06036 MONTEFALCO [PG]
TEL. 0742371245
www.romanelli.se

CELLAR SALES
PRE-BOOKED VISITS
ANNUAL PRODUCTION 40,000 bottles
HECTARES UNDER VINE 7.50

All the members of the family that gives its name to the winery work here, but there is no doubt that the young Davis Romanelli is the key figure. We are at Colle San Clemente, near Montefalco, where the clay and silt soils lie at elevations of up to 350 metres. Farming is organic and vinification techniques keep intervention to a minimum. The Sagrantino undergoes long maceration, and barrel ageing envisages small and large oak, ranging from 225 to 2,500 litres. The wines of recent years reflect the interesting style found in this area. After the extraordinary 2010, Romanelli repeats the performance with a superlative Sagrantino 2011. Rather than being an explosive red, this delightful wine is all whispers and caresses, unusual for this DOC zone. Its aromas are immediately enfolding, and display particularly Mediterranean traits in addition to elegant spice. On the palate, it shows slender and linear, with richly flavoured tannins.

● Montefalco Sagrantino '11	♟♟♟ 5
● Montefalco Rosso '11	♟♟ 3
○ Colli Martani Grechetto '14	♟ 2
● Montefalco Rosso Molinetta Ris. '10	♟ 5
● Montefalco Sagrantino '10	♟♟♟ 5
○ Colli Martani Grechetto '13	♟♟ 2*
○ Colli Martani Grechetto '12	♟♟ 2*
○ Colli Martani Grechetto '11	♟♟ 2*
○ Colli Martani Grechetto '08	♟♟ 2
● Montefalco Rosso '10	♟♟ 2*
● Montefalco Rosso '09	♟♟ 2*
● Montefalco Rosso '08	♟♟ 3
● Montefalco Rosso '07	♟♟ 3
● Montefalco Rosso Ris. '09	♟♟ 3
● Montefalco Sagrantino Passito '08	♟♟ 5

Scacciadiavoli

LOC. CANTINONE, 31
06036 MONTEFALCO [PG]
TEL. 0742371210
www.scacciadiavoli.it

CELLAR SALES
PRE-BOOKED VISITS
ANNUAL PRODUCTION 200,000 bottles
HECTARES UNDER VINE 32.00

Not only a winery of great historical value, now adapted to the needs of a modern operation, Scacciadiavoli is also a project of contemporary importance, which underwent significant change in the early 2000s, thanks to the Pambuffetti family. The wines are the direct consequence of these investments, which obviously also regarded the significant vineyard holdings. The reds have been achieving high standards for some years now, and show increasing stylistic focus. Sagrantino Scacciadiavoli 2010 is a good vintage, a modern wine, undoubtedly, but with charming character. It opens to red berry fruit, followed hard on by cigar box aromas and spice, paving the way for elegant, caressing texture in the mouth. The deep finish shows perfectly extracted lively tannins.

● Montefalco Sagrantino '10	♟♟♟ 5
○ Montefalco Bianco '13	♟♟ 3
● Montefalco Rosso '12	♟♟ 3
○ Spumante Brut	♟ 2
● Montefalco Rosso '11	♟♟ 3
● Montefalco Rosso '10	♟♟ 3
● Montefalco Rosso '09	♟♟ 3*
● Montefalco Sagrantino '09	♟♟ 5
● Montefalco Sagrantino '08	♟♟ 5
● Montefalco Sagrantino '07	♟♟ 5
● Montefalco Sagrantino Passito '07	♟♟ 5

Sportoletti

VIA LOMBARDIA, 1
06038 SPELLO [PG]
TEL. 0742651461
www.sportoletti.com

CELLAR SALES
PRE-BOOKED VISITS
ANNUAL PRODUCTION 230,000 bottles
HECTARES UNDER VINE 30.00

The whole of the Sportoletti family is committed to the winery's success, now that the young generations have become a permanent part of the business. The winery is set in the hills of Spello, in a perfect position of unmatchable beauty. The family's farming origins are well known, but the operation in its current form dates back to the 1990s. Native varieties rub shoulders with the major international cultivars, for modern-style, focused wines that show extreme cleanness and approachable drinkability. The Villa Fidelia Rosso 2013 is a wine of great maturity and extraction, offering toasty, spicy notes, over a harmonious, rounded palate with a good finish and attractive tannins. The fantastic Assisi Rosso 2014, as usual, showed outstanding value for money. Also peerless, the Villa Fidelia Bianco 2013 with its spicy, silky palate.

● Villa Fidelia Rosso '13	♟♟ 4
● Assisi Rosso '14	♟♟ 2*
○ Villa Fidelia Bianco '13	♟♟ 3
○ Assisi Grechetto '14	♟ 1*
○ Assisi Grechetto '13	♟♟ 1*
○ Assisi Grechetto '12	♟♟ 1*
● Assisi Rosso '13	♟♟ 2*
● Assisi Rosso '12	♟♟ 2*
○ Villa Fidelia Bianco '12	♟♟ 3
○ Villa Fidelia Bianco '11	♟♟ 3
○ Villa Fidelia Passito '11	♟♟ 4
● Villa Fidelia Rosso '12	♟♟ 4
● Villa Fidelia Rosso '11	♟♟ 4
● Villa Fidelia Rosso '10	♟♟ 4

UMBRIA

Giampaolo Tabarrini

FRAZ. TURRITA
06036 MONTEFALCO [PG]
TEL. 0742379351
www.tabarrini.com

CELLAR SALES
PRE-BOOKED VISITS
ANNUAL PRODUCTION 70,000 bottles
HECTARES UNDER VINE 18.00

If everyone is writing about the definitive consecration of Giampaolo Tabarrini, he throws himself into an unbelievable futuristic project to extend the winery. If his wines attract universal approval and enjoy a certain economic success, he decides that the time has come for a further change in style, abandoning barriques and medium-sized oak in favour of the classic large barrels of tradition. This is typical of his character, never standing still and full of ideas. The wines seem to listen to his desires, and inevitably end up resembling him. Our favourite is the Montefalco Sagrantino Campo alla Cerqua 2011, the result of a selection that manages to temper the variety's natural exuberance with elegance. Opening to a nuanced nose, this is a red rich in contrasts, offering elegant spice and a deep, dynamic palate with good body. Its slight alcoholic warmth does not affect its drinkability and tangy finish.

● Montefalco Sagrantino Campo alla Cerqua '11	♔♔♔ 6
○ Adarmando '13	♔♔ 3*
● Montefalco Sagrantino Colle alle Macchie '11	♔♔ 6
● Montefalco Rosso '12	♔♔ 3
● Montefalco Sagrantino Colle Grimaldesco '11	♔♔ 5
● Montefalco Sagrantino Campo alla Cerqua '10	♔♔♔ 6
● Montefalco Sagrantino Campo alla Cerqua '08	♔♔♔ 6
● Montefalco Sagrantino Campo alla Cerqua '07	♔♔♔ 6
● Montefalco Sagrantino Colle alle Macchie '09	♔♔♔ 6
● Montefalco Sagrantino Colle Grimaldesco '06	♔♔♔ 5

Terre de La Custodia

LOC. PALOMBARA
06035 GUALDO CATTANEO [PG]
TEL. 0742929586
www.terredelacustodia.it

CELLAR SALES
PRE-BOOKED VISITS
ANNUAL PRODUCTION 1,000,000 bottles
HECTARES UNDER VINE 128.00

The Farchioni family have built their business success on exclusive farming products, from olive oil to wine, not to mention their recent passion for beer, using barley grown in Umbria. These have all been successful projects, conceived and interpreted according to a precise production and commercial philosophy. Their forays into the world of wine started with a fine winery, set in the rolling hills of Gualdo Cattaneo. All the labels, divided by line and commercial expectations, are well made, displaying aromatic intensity and rounded palates. The winery's products gave a good overall performance, including an excellent Colli Martani Grechetto 2014, a brilliant, personal and lively easy-drinker with a long citrus finish. We loved the Montefalco Sagrantino Passito Melanto and the succulent, extremely enjoyable Colli Martani Rosso Collezione.

○ Colli Martani Grechetto '14	♔♔ 2*
● Colli Martani Rosso Collezione '14	♔♔ 2*
○ Colli Martani Spumante Gladius Sublimis '10	♔♔ 4
● Montefalco Rosso '12	♔♔ 4
● Montefalco Sagrantino Passito Melanto '11	♔♔ 5
● Montefalco Sagrantino '11	♔ 6
● Colli Martani Collezione '12	♔♔ 2*
○ Colli Martani Grechetto '13	♔♔ 2*
○ Colli Martani Grechetto Plentis '12	♔♔ 3
○ Colli Martani Spumante Sublimis Gladius '09	♔♔ 4
● Montefalco Sagrantino '10	♔♔ 6
● Montefalco Sagrantino '09	♔♔ 6
● Montefalco Sagrantino '06	♔♔ 5

Todini

FRAZ. ROSCETO
VIA COLLINA, 29
06059 TODI [PG]
TEL. 075887122
www.cantinafrancotodini.com

CELLAR SALES
PRE-BOOKED VISITS
ACCOMMODATION AND RESTAURANT SERVICE
ANNUAL PRODUCTION 300,000 bottles
HECTARES UNDER VINE 20.00

An important family of entrepreneurs, the
Todinis made their dream come true with
this excellent winery, a stone's throw from
Todi, in a spectacular natural setting. It is
here that the operation started out in the
1970s and subsequently grew to its
current size of 120 hectares, of which 20
or so are planted to vine, with a brand new
winery and a country hotel. The modern
wines are based on both native and
international varieties. This style is
reflected in the admirably crafted Merlot
2013. Although not particularly original, it
perfectly combines ripe dark berry fruit
and toasty notes of oak, followed by a
dense, dynamic palate with notes of citrus
that provide sweet, fresh, succulent
progression. Simpler yet well-managed is
the Marte 2014, with pervasive blueberry
and grassy notes. The Bianco del Cavaliere
is compromised by an overpowering nose.

Tudernum

LOC. PIAN DI PORTO, 146
06059 TODI [PG]
TEL. 0758989403
www.tudernum.it

CELLAR SALES
PRE-BOOKED VISITS
ACCOMMODATION AND RESTAURANT SERVICE
ANNUAL PRODUCTION 2,000,000 bottles
HECTARES UNDER VINE 350.00

The cooperative model can work, be
modern and attractive, and result in quality,
territorial wines. Among the most superb
demonstrations of these simple truths,
Tudernum represents an added value for
Umbria and the areas where its members
work the rows. These include Todi, above
all, where Grechetto is standard bearer, but
classic or more internationally-styed reds
are also produced, and Montefalco, where
it is easy to imagine the varieties grown.
Tudernum produces good, well-managed,
competitively-priced wines. It comes as no
surprise, then, that the winery's best label
this year is the Montefalco Sagrantino
Fidenzio 2010, a great vintage and a great
wine, the likes of which we have not seen
since perhaps the 2004. This graceful yet
fleshy red offers a delicate but full body
with toothsome, well-extracted tannins.

● Marte '14	♥♥ 2*
● Merlot '13	♥♥ 2*
○ Todi Bianco del Cavaliere '14	♥ 2
● Todi Rubro '13	♥ 4
● Colli Martani Sangiovese Rubro '11	♀♀ 4
○ Grechetto di Todi Bianco del Cavaliere '10	♀♀ 3
○ Grechetto di Todi Bianco del Cavaliere Sup. '11	♀♀ 3
○ Grechetto Riesling '12	♀♀ 2*
● Nero della Cervara '08	♀♀ 5
● Nero della Cervara '07	♀♀ 5
● Nero della Cervara '05	♀♀ 5
● Relais Rosso '13	♀♀ 3
● Relais Rosso '12	♀♀ 2*
○ Todi Bianco del Cavaliere '12	♀♀ 2*
● Todi Rubro '12	♀♀ 4

● Montefalco Sagrantino Fidenzio '10	♥♥ 4
○ Todi Grechetto '14	♥♥ 2*
● Todi Rosso '14	♥♥ 2*
● Todi Rosso Sup. Rojano '12	♥♥ 3
○ Todi Grechetto Sup. Colle Nobile '14	♥ 2
● Todi Merlot '13	♥ 2
● Todi Sangiovese '13	♥ 2
● Merlot '07	♀♀ 2*
● Merlot '05	♀♀ 2*
● Montefalco Rosso '09	♀♀ 3
● Montefalco Sagrantino '07	♀♀ 5
● Montefalco Sagrantino Tudernum '04	♀♀ 5
● Montefalco Sagrantino Tudernum '01	♀♀ 4
● Rojano '03	♀♀ 2*
○ Todi Grechetto Sup. Colle Nobile '13	♀♀ 2*
● Todi Rosso Sup. Rojano '11	♀♀ 3*

Tenuta Le Velette

FRAZ. CANALE DI ORVIETO
LOC. LE VELETTE, 23
05019 ORVIETO [TR]
TEL. 076329090
www.levelette.it

CELLAR SALES
PRE-BOOKED VISITS
ANNUAL PRODUCTION 320,000 bottles
HECTARES UNDER VINE 119.00

This marvellous estate breathes history from every pore. Here, in the 1950s, the Bottai family decided to invest in their lifetime's ambition. We are in a zone of volcanic origin, different from the classic "marine soils" of Orvieto, and it is here that the 100-plus hectares of vineyards are located. Such a large area clearly means a certain variation in terms of soils, aspects and microclimates, and each zone has a distinctive character, with different varieties and different results. What they share is the style of the wines, judiciously modern and equally impressive, in both the reds and classic whites of Orvieto. These were the wines that most impressed us in our final tastings, in particular the Lunato 2014, from the oldest vineyards with the lowest yields. Aromas of peach and a beautiful salty swathe are echoed on the palate in this racy, tangy and highly pleasurable wine. Hot on its heels is the succulent, lip-smacking, firmly-structured Berganorio 2014.

○ Orvieto Cl. Sup. Lunato '14	▼▼	2*
○ Orvieto Cl. Berganorio '14	▼▼	2*
● Rosso Orvietano Rosso di Spicca '13	▼▼	2*
○ Sole Uve '13	▼▼	3
● Calanco '03	▽▽▽	4
● Gaudio '03	▽▽▽	4
● Accordo '10	▽▽	4
● Calanco '08	▽▽	4
● Calanco '07	▽▽	4
● Gaudio '10	▽▽	4
● Gaudio '08	▽▽	4
○ Orvieto Cl. Berganorio '13	▽▽	2*
○ Orvieto Cl. Berganorio '11	▽▽	2*
○ Orvieto Cl. Sup. Lunato '10	▽▽	2*

Villa Mongalli

VIA DELLA CIMA, 52
06031 BEVAGNA [PG]
TEL. 0742360703
www.villamongalli.com

CELLAR SALES
ACCOMMODATION
ANNUAL PRODUCTION 70,000 bottles
HECTARES UNDER VINE 15.00

In our opinion, Villa Mongalli is one of the most convincing new operations in the growing area of Sagrantino in recent years. We strongly recommend a visit to the winery: the natural setting is breathtaking, and dotted with excellent vineyards. The cellar is modern, but vinification and ageing methods are aimed at exalting the fruits of the earth and keeping intervention to a minimum. At the heart of the project is the Menghini family, with Pierpaolo increasingly at ease in his role as a vigneron. Vinification does not envisage the addition of cultured yeasts, while extraction is judicious and oak ageing well managed. The Montefalco Sagrantino Colcimino is a delightful wine of extreme finesse, boasting a nose that is at once delicate yet layered, intense yet relaxed. Opening to Mediterranean scrub, with notes of bark enveloping beautifully ripe, refreshing fruit, on the palate it offers unintegrated, never intrusive tannins, combined with a long, consistent finish.

● Montefalco Sagrantino Colcimino '12	▼▼	8
○ Trebbiano Spoletino Calicanto '14	▼▼	5
● Montefalco Sagrantino Della Cima '11	▼▼	8
● Montefalco Sagrantino Pozzo del Curato '11	▼▼	7
● Montefalco Rosso Le Grazie '13	▼	5
● Montefalco Sagrantino Colcimino '08	▽▽▽	3*
● Montefalco Sagrantino Della Cima '10	▽▽▽	8
● Montefalco Sagrantino Della Cima '06	▽▽▽	6
● Montefalco Sagrantino Pozzo del Curato '09	▽▽▽	6
○ Calicanto Trebbiano Spoletino '13	▽▽	5
● Montefalco Rosso Le Grazie '12	▽▽	5
● Montefalco Rosso Le Grazie '11	▽▽	5
● Montefalco Sagrantino Colcimino '11	▽▽	8
● Montefalco Sagrantino Colcimino '10	▽▽	3*
● Montefalco Sagrantino Della Cima '08	▽▽	3*

Tenuta Alzatura

LOC. FRATTA ALZATURA, 108
06036 MONTEFALCO [PG]
TEL. 0742399435
www.tenuta-alzatura.it

PRE-BOOKED VISITS
ANNUAL PRODUCTION 22,600 bottles
HECTARES UNDER VINE 29.00

● Montefalco Rosso '13	♟♟ 3
● Montefalco Sagrantino '11	♟♟ 5

Argillae

VOC. POMARRO, 45
05010 ALLERONA [TR]
TEL. 0763624604
www.argillae.eu

CELLAR SALES
PRE-BOOKED VISITS
ANNUAL PRODUCTION 65,000 bottles
HECTARES UNDER VINE 70.00

○ Grechetto '14	♟♟ 2*
○ Orvieto Cl. Panata '14	♟♟ 2*
○ Orvieto '14	♟ 2

Berioli

LOC. CASE SPARSE, 21
06063 MAGIONE [PG]
TEL. 3355498173
www.cantinaberioli.it

ANNUAL PRODUCTION 15,000 bottles
HECTARES UNDER VINE 12.00

○ Colli del Trasimeno Grechetto Vercanto '14	♟♟ 3
● Topporosso '11	♟ 3

Briziarelli

VIA COLLE ALLODOLE, 10
06031 BEVAGNA [PG]
TEL. 07587461
www.cantinebriziarelli.it

CELLAR SALES
PRE-BOOKED VISITS
ACCOMMODATION AND RESTAURANT SERVICE
ANNUAL PRODUCTION 70,000 bottles
HECTARES UNDER VINE 18.50

● Montefalco Rosso '11	♟♟ 2*
● Montefalco Rosso Mattone '11	♟♟ 3
● Montefalco Sagrantino Vitruvio '09	♟♟ 4

Brogal Vini

LOC. BASTIA UMBRA
VIA DEGLI OLMI, 9
06083 PERUGIA
TEL. 0758001501
www.brogalvini.com

CELLAR SALES
PRE-BOOKED VISITS
ACCOMMODATION AND RESTAURANT SERVICE
ANNUAL PRODUCTION 3,000,000 bottles
HECTARES UNDER VINE 75.00

● Montefalco Sagrantino Preda del Falco '08	♟♟ 7
● Ru '12	♟♟ 4
○ Montefalco Bianco Nido del Falco '14	♟ 4

Brunozzi

LOC. COLLE ARFUSO, 2
06036 MONTEFALCO [PG]
TEL. 0742379673
www.aziendagrariabrunozzi.it

CELLAR SALES
PRE-BOOKED VISITS
ANNUAL PRODUCTION 10,000 bottles
HECTARES UNDER VINE 2.00

● Montefalco Sagrantino Carlotto '11	♟♟ 4
● Montefalco Rosso '12	♟♟ 3
● Stradaviola '14	♟ 2

Castello di Corbara

Loc. Corbara, 7
05018 Orvieto [TR]
Tel. 0763304035
www.castellodicorbara.it

CELLAR SALES
PRE-BOOKED VISITS
ANNUAL PRODUCTION 200,000 bottles
HECTARES UNDER VINE 100.00

● Lago di Corbara '13	♟♟ 3
● Lago di Corbara Sangiovese Calistri '12	♟♟ 4
● Lago di Corbara Merlot De Coronis '12	♟ 4

Castello di Magione

Via dei Cavalieri di Malta, 31
06063 Magione [PG]
Tel. 0755057319
www.sagrivit.it

CELLAR SALES
PRE-BOOKED VISITS
ANNUAL PRODUCTION 200,000 bottles
HECTARES UNDER VINE 41.00

○ C. del Trasimeno Grechetto Monterone '14	♟♟ 2*
○ Colli del Trasimeno Grechetto '14	♟♟ 2*
● Sangiovese '14	♟ 2

Chiorri

Loc. Sant'Enea
Via Todi, 100
06132 Perugia
Tel. 075607141
www.chiorri.it

CELLAR SALES
PRE-BOOKED VISITS
ACCOMMODATION AND RESTAURANT SERVICE
ANNUAL PRODUCTION 100,000 bottles
HECTARES UNDER VINE 25.00

○ Grechetto '14	♟♟ 2*
● Sangiovese '13	♟♟ 2*
● Merlot Sel. Antonio Chiorri '11	♟ 4

Le Cimate

Loc. Cecapecore, 41
06036 Montefalco [PG]
Tel. 0742290136
www.lecimate.it

CELLAR SALES
PRE-BOOKED VISITS
ANNUAL PRODUCTION 800,000 bottles
HECTARES UNDER VINE 20.00

● Macchieto '10	♟♟ 2*
● Montefalco Rosso '12	♟♟ 3
● Montefalco Sagrantino '11	♟ 5

Cantina Colle Ciocco

Via Petrauta
06036 Montefalco [PG]
Tel. 0742379859
www.colleciocco.it

CELLAR SALES
PRE-BOOKED VISITS
ANNUAL PRODUCTION 45,000 bottles
HECTARES UNDER VINE 15.00

● Montefalco Sagrantino '09	♟♟ 5
● Montefalco Rosso '11	♟ 3
○ Spoleto Trebbiano Spoletino Tempestivo '14	♟ 3

Custodi

Loc. Canale
V.le Venere
05018 Orvieto [TR]
Tel. 076329053
www.cantinacustodi.com

CELLAR SALES
PRE-BOOKED VISITS
ANNUAL PRODUCTION 65,000 bottles
HECTARES UNDER VINE 40.00

● Austero '13	♟♟ 3
○ Orvieto Cl. Belloro '14	♟ 1*

Cantina Dionigi

VOC. MADONNA DELLA PIA, 92
06031 BEVAGNA [PG]
TEL. 0742360395
www.cantinadionigi.it

CELLAR SALES
PRE-BOOKED VISITS
ACCOMMODATION
ANNUAL PRODUCTION 40,000 bottles
HECTARES UNDER VINE 6.00

● Montefalco Rosso '12	♥♥ 3
● Montefalco Rosso Ris. '11	♥♥ 3
○ Passo Greco '11	♥♥ 3
○ Scialo '11	♥♥ 3

Fattoria Giro di Vento

LOC. SCHIFANOIA
S.DA COLLESPINO, 39
05035 NARNI [TR]
TEL. 3356136353
www.fattoriagirodivento.it

CELLAR SALES
ANNUAL PRODUCTION 30,000 bottles
HECTARES UNDER VINE 10.50
SUSTAINABLE WINERY

● Ciliegiolo di Narni Spiffero '14	♥♥ 2*
○ Lunaria '14	♥♥ 2*

La Madeleine

S.DA MONTINI, 38
05035 NARNI [TR]
TEL. 3453208914
www.cantinalamadeleine.it

PRE-BOOKED VISITS
ANNUAL PRODUCTION 42,000 bottles
HECTARES UNDER VINE 6.50

● Sfide '13	♥♥ 3*
● NarnOt '12	♥ 6
⊙ Nerosé	♥ 5

Madrevite

LOC. VAIANO
VIA CIMBANO, 36
06061 CASTIGLIONE DEL LAGO [PG]
TEL. 0759527220
www.madrevite.com

CELLAR SALES
PRE-BOOKED VISITS
RESTAURANT SERVICE
ANNUAL PRODUCTION 45,000 bottles
HECTARES UNDER VINE 10.00

○ Il Reminore '14	♥♥ 3
● Colli del Trasimeno Glanio '13	♥ 3

Morami

FRAZ. PANICAROLA
VOC. MORAMI
06060 CASTIGLIONE DEL LAGO [PG]
TEL. 0759589107
www.morami.it

CELLAR SALES
PRE-BOOKED VISITS
ACCOMMODATION
ANNUAL PRODUCTION 16,000 bottles
HECTARES UNDER VINE 11.00

○ Cardissa Chardonnay '13	♥ 3
● Podicerri '12	♥ 4

Cantina Ninni

FRAZ. TERRAIA
06049 SPOLETO [PG]
TEL. 3355450523
www.cantinaninnispoleto.com

CELLAR SALES
PRE-BOOKED VISITS
ANNUAL PRODUCTION 15,000 bottles
HECTARES UNDER VINE 3.00

● Poggiolaccio Merlot '13	♥♥ 3
○ Spoleto Trebbiano Spoletino Poggio del Vescovo '14	♥♥ 2*
● Diavolacciu '12	♥ 3

Pomario

LOC. POMARIO
06066 PIEGARO [PG]
TEL. 064818418
www.pomario.it

CELLAR SALES
PRE-BOOKED VISITS
ANNUAL PRODUCTION 8,000 bottles
HECTARES UNDER VINE 6.00
VITICULTURE METHOD Certified Organic

○ Arale '14	♼♼ 4
● Sariano '12	♼♼ 3

Rocca di Fabbri

LOC. FABBRI
06036 MONTEFALCO [PG]
TEL. 0742399379
www.roccadifabbri.com

CELLAR SALES
PRE-BOOKED VISITS
ACCOMMODATION
ANNUAL PRODUCTION 250,000 bottles
HECTARES UNDER VINE 64.50

● Montefalco Rosso '12	♼♼ 2*
○ Chardonnay '14	♼ 2

Sandonna

LOC. SELVE
05024 GIOVE [TR]
TEL. 0744992274
www.cantinasandonna.it

CELLAR SALES
PRE-BOOKED VISITS
ANNUAL PRODUCTION 28,000 bottles
HECTARES UNDER VINE 5.50

● Ciliegiolo di Narni '14	♼♼ 2*
○ Grechetto '14	♼♼ 2*
● Jovio '12	♼ 2

Terre Margaritelli

FRAZ. CHIUSACCIA
LOC. MIRALDUOLO
06089 TORGIANO [PG]
TEL. 0757824668
www.terremargaritelli.com

CELLAR SALES
PRE-BOOKED VISITS
ANNUAL PRODUCTION 120,000 bottles
HECTARES UNDER VINE 52.00
VITICULTURE METHOD Certified Organic

○ Torgiano Bianco Costellato '14	♼♼ 2*
○ Greco di Renabianca '13	♼ 3
● Torgiano Rosso Mirantico '13	♼ 2

Tenuta di Titignano

LOC. CIVITELLA DEL LAGO
VOC. SALVIANO, 11
05020 BASCHI [TR]
TEL. 0744950459
info@titignano.it

CELLAR SALES
PRE-BOOKED VISITS
ANNUAL PRODUCTION 150,000 bottles
HECTARES UNDER VINE 70.00

○ Orvieto Cl. Sup. Salviano '14	♼♼ 2*
○ Salviano di Salviano '14	♼♼ 2*
● Lago di Corbara Rosso Solideo '12	♼ 2

Zanchi

VIA ORTANA, 122
05022 AMELIA [TR]
TEL. 0744970011
www.cantinezanchi.it

CELLAR SALES
PRE-BOOKED VISITS
ANNUAL PRODUCTION 80,000 bottles
HECTARES UNDER VINE 31.00

○ Amelia Grechetto Arvore '14	♼♼ 2*
● Amelia Ciliegiolo Carmìno '14	♼ 2
● Amelia Rosso Armané '12	♼ 2

LAZIO

Over the last couple of years, with some satisfaction we have watched a number of positive signals coming from the Lazio wine scene. The impression is that many producers finally decided to shatter the aura of mediocrity enveloping regional production. Small and large wineries, new and venerable names, have all come up with some truly appealing proposals that are stirring attention at national and international level. Last year hailed the excellence of Ponza viticulture, the expansion of Grechetto near Viterbo, and the first Tre Bicchieri garnered by two benchmark makers like Principe Pallavicini and Casale del Giglio. This year we can include two more debuts in the Tre Bicchieri club, to Trappolini and Valle Vermiglia, and mention the spotlight turning to a zone and a grape, Anzio and bellone, rarely seen outside the area of origin in the past. The first Tre Bicchieri to the Trappolini family winery is for its Grechetto 2014, a challenging year that nonetheless held some pleasant surprises in store, above all in Viterbo. The award acknowledges a cellar that has been a local star for years, but it also pays homage to a territory, Tuscia, whose native grechetto has given it a stable position in Italy's leading white wine production zones. For Mario Masini's Valle Vermiglia and his 2013 Frascati Superiore Eremo Tuscolano, however, we are seeing the first rewards for a project that began 15 years ago with the stated goal of developing a Frascati wine of the finest standard. A unique wine given the conditions of production, but also a success that can only drive attempts to restore the name Frascati to its leading nationwide ranking. Last but not least, Antonio Santarelli is back with another striking debut, his Antium Bellone 2014, a wine we hope will give new impetus to an area and a vine that seem to have dropped out of sight. Alongside these innovations, we ought to remember the compelling confirmation of Tenuta di Fiorano, with its splendid Fiorano Bianco 2013, and the constant commanding presence of wineries like Sergio Mottura, with his now classic Grechetto Poggio della Costa; Falesco, with its timeless Montiano; and Poggio Le Volpi with Baccarossa, a fine expression of nero buono di Cori, another native variety.

Antiche Cantine Migliaccio

VIA PIZZICATO
04027 PONZA [LT]
TEL. 3392822252
lucianasabino@libero.it

CELLAR SALES
PRE-BOOKED VISITS
ANNUAL PRODUCTION 10,000 bottles
HECTARES UNDER VINE 2.50

Unspoilt vines accessible along a mule-track eked out of the Mediterranean scrub, passable only on foot or by donkey. Emanuele Vittorio and his wife Luciana are winemaking heroes: in 2000, they founded their estate in Punta Fieno, one of the still-intact parts of Ponza island, respecting its character to the full. Assisted by oenologist Vincenzo Mercurio, they have been successful in bringing out the potential of priceless native vines such as biancolella, forastera, guarnaccia, aglianico and piedirosso, many ungrafted. The excellent Biancolella 2014, truly a daughter of the sea: salty and spirited, with a deeply textured body, this fresh-tasting wine has plenty of depth. We also liked the Fieno, both in the white and red: the Bianco 2014 is floral and citrusy, showing nice freshness, clean and pleasant, while the Rosso 2013 is slightly vegetal, with a nose of bramble and cherry, and a mouthfeel that is initially rather muscular, opening out to a full fruitiness and a good structure.

○ Biancolella di Ponza '14	♟♟	5
○ Fieno di Ponza Bianco '14	♟♟	4
● Fieno di Ponza Rosso '13	♟♟	4
○ Biancolella di Ponza '13	♟♟	5
○ Biancolella di Ponza '12	♟♟	5
○ Biancolella di Ponza '11	♟♟	3

Marco Carpineti

LOC. CAPO LE MOLE
S.DA PROV.LE VELLETRI-ANZIO, KM 14,300
04010 CORI [LT]
TEL. 069679860
www.marcocarpineti.com

CELLAR SALES
PRE-BOOKED VISITS
ANNUAL PRODUCTION 270,000 bottles
HECTARES UNDER VINE 52.00
VITICULTURE METHOD Certified Organic

In this area Marco Carpineti was a pioneer of organic viticulture, and is also a rather impressive artisan in his architectural jewel of a cellar. This year, two of his historic top labels have once again come to the fore: the Moro 2013, a simultaneous explosion of exotic fruits and minerally notes which make it both layered and intriguing, as well as highly drinkable. Not far behind is the Dithyrambus 2010, an equal blend of montepulciano and nero buono whose long ageing, and the quality of the grapes, of course, has lent it spicy tertiary notes, outstandingly soft tannins and a broad harmonious structure. A new name is the Kius 2012, a sparkler made from bellone grapes, with the same quality and drinkability as before. The same qualities can be found in the Capolemole Bianco 2014, with its pleasant, persistent palate. Sadly, the Apolide 2010, a monovarietal Nero Buono, lacks balance, with rather too jammy notes.

● Dithyrambus '10	♟♟	5
● Moro '13	♟♟	3*
● Capolemole Bianco '14	♟♟	2*
○ Kius Brut '12	♟	3
● Apolide '10	♟	5
● Tufaliccio '14	♟	2
● Apolide '09	♟♟	5
○ Capolemole Bianco '13	♟♟	2*
○ Capolemole Bianco '12	♟♟	2*
● Capolemole Rosso '12	♟♟	3*
● Dithyrambus '09	♟♟	5
○ Marco Carpineti Brut '11	♟♟	3
○ Moro '12	♟♟	3*
○ Moro '11	♟♟	3
⊙ Os Rosae '13	♟♟	2*
● Tufaliccio '13	♟♟	2*

Casale del Giglio

LOC. LE FERRIERE
S.DA CISTERNA-NETTUNO KM 13
04100 LATINA
TEL. 0692902530
www.casaledelgiglio.it

CELLAR SALES
PRE-BOOKED VISITS
ANNUAL PRODUCTION 1,276,600 bottles
HECTARES UNDER VINE 164.00
SUSTAINABLE WINERY

Proof of Antonio Santarelli and oenologist
Paolo Tiefenthaler's commitment to native
varieties can be seen in their purchase of
one of Ponza's venerable cellars, where
they vinify the biancolella from nearby
vineyards, as well as the bellone from sites
planted decades ago in Anzio's prime wine
areas, achieving quite excellent results.
The full-flavoured and gutsy Faro della
Guardia 2014 only got as far as the final,
but in itself this was an achievement. The
debutant Antium 2014 sailed into top spot,
impressing with its minerality, length and
nose-palate harmony. Given that the Mater
Matuta was not produced in 2012, the
international cultivar flag is flown by the
Tempranijo 2013, a perfect balance of
elegance and weight, and even more so
by the Antinoo 2013, from viognier and
a touch of chardonnay, perhaps the best
version yet. The rest of their range stands
up well, being sound and technically
pristine.

Casale della Ioria

P.ZZA REGINA MARGHERITA, 1
03010 ACUTO [FR]
TEL. 077556031
www.casaledellaioria.com

CELLAR SALES
PRE-BOOKED VISITS
ANNUAL PRODUCTION 65,000 bottles
HECTARES UNDER VINE 38.00

After a year off, the estate flagship
Cesanese Torre del Piano 2012 has come
up with a quality version that deservedly
reached the final: a berry fruit nose with
tertiary notes and a warm, generous,
well-developed mouth, with just the right
tannins. For its part, the youthful in terms of
inception and vintage Campo Novo 2014
now has its own well-defined and
distinctive identity: very drinkable, it flows
across the palate, but is far from banal in
its immediacy. We are more than happy to
spread the word about the Olivella 2011,
the best version yet, to encourage Paolo
Perinelli's excellent work. Perhaps the only
true believer in this rare Frosinone vine, his
faith paid off after long maturing with a
version displaying breadth and good
nose-palate symmetry. Both Passerinas,
still and sparkling, were less dazzling than
in previous years, marked by aggressive
citrus overtones, but 2014 was not a very
good year for whites here.

○ Antium Bellone '14	♟♟♟ 4*
○ Antinoo '13	♟♟ 5
○ Biancolella Faro della Guardia '14	♟♟ 5
○ Aphrodisium '14	♟♟ 6
○ Sauvignon '14	♟♟ 3
● Tempranijo '13	♟♟ 5
⊙ Albiola Rosato '14	♟ 3
● Cabernet Sauvignon '12	♟ 5
● Madreselva '12	♟ 5
● Merlot '13	♟ 3
○ Petit Manseng '14	♟ 4
○ Satrico '14	♟ 3
● Shiraz '13	♟ 4
○ Biancolella Faro della Guardia '13	♟♟♟ 5
● Mater Matuta '11	♟♟ 7
● Mater Matuta '10	♟♟ 6

● Cesanese del Piglio Sup. Torre del Piano Ris. '12	♟♟ 4
● Cesanese del Piglio Campo Novo '14	♟♟ 2*
● Olivella '11	♟♟ 2*
● Cesanese del Piglio Sup. Tenuta della Ioria '13	♟ 3
○ Passerina Colle Bianco '14	♟ 2
○ Passerina Extra Dry	♟ 2
● Cesanese del Piglio Campo Novo '11	♟♟ 2*
● Cesanese del Piglio Campo Novo '10	♟♟ 2*
● Cesanese del Piglio Campo Nuovo '13	♟♟ 2*
● Cesanese del Piglio Sup. Torre del Piano Ris. '11	♟♟ 4
● Cesanese del Piglio Torre del Piano '10	♟♟ 4
● Cesanese del Piglio Torre del Piano '09	♟♟ 4
● Cesanese del Piglio Torre del Piano '08	♟♟ 4
● Cesanese del Piglio Torre del Piano '03	♟♟ 4

Cincinnato

VIA CORI-CISTERNA KM 2
04010 CORI [LT]
TEL. 069679380
www.cincinnato.it

CELLAR SALES
PRE-BOOKED VISITS
ANNUAL PRODUCTION 4,500,000 bottles
HECTARES UNDER VINE 400.00

It may sound a tad repetitive to keep singing the praises of this cooperative winery, but it is well deserved because it achieves such great results and because it is a quite unique business concern in the area. Nazareno Milita and Carlo Morettini will be delighted to have introduced two new products: farmstay accommodation and a tasting room. This year's cream of the crop were the whites, with a classic like the Castore 2014, a Bellone combining balance, drinkability and complexity, and the Pantaleo 2014, a Greco which after just a few short years has carved out its own identity, made up of varietal notes, freshness and a nice full flavour. Not far behind are the aggressive Pozzodorico Bellone 2013 and the ever-pleasing Illirio 2014. Among the reds, the Ercole Nero Buono 2013 performed much as it has in the past, while the excellently interpreted Arcatura 2013, a Cesanese with remarkably clean aromas, has at long last fulfilled its promise.

○ Castore '14	♟♟ 2*
○ Pantaleo '14	♟♟ 2*
● Arcatura '13	♟♟ 2*
● Ercole Nero Buono '12	♟♟ 3
○ Cori Bianco Illirio '14	♟ 2
● Cori Rosso Raverosse '12	♟ 2
● Pollùce '13	♟ 2
○ Pozzodorico Bellone '13	♟ 2
○ Castore '13	♟♟ 2*
○ Castore '12	♟♟ 1*
○ Cori Bianco Illirio '13	♟♟ 2*
● Cori Rosso Raverosse '11	♟♟ 2*
● Cori Rosso Raverosse '09	♟♟ 2
● Ercole Nero Buono '11	♟♟ 3
○ Pantaleo '13	♟♟ 2*
○ Pozzodorico Bellone '12	♟♟ 2*

Damiano Ciolli

VIA DEL CORSO
00035 OLEVANO ROMANO [RM]
TEL. 069563334
www.damianociolli.it

CELLAR SALES
PRE-BOOKED VISITS
ANNUAL PRODUCTION 25,000 bottles
HECTARES UNDER VINE 5.00
SUSTAINABLE WINERY

Damiano Ciolli remains one of a small group of Cesanese wizards, being the benchmark producer in the Olevano Romano denomination. Damiano has been bottling since 2001, but his family has been working the vine for four generations. His cesanese di Affile vines have been growing on red volcanic soils at an altitude of around 450 metres for between 15 and 35 years. He also has about a hectare of 60-year-old plants, for making his Olevano Romano Cesanese Cirsium, whose 2011 version is back at the top of the DOC heap. Its complex aromas of chocolate, black berry fruit and spices give way to a rich juicy palate, with a long finale with cloves to the fore. Also nicely crafted is the Olevano Romano Cesanese Superiore Silene 2013, a pleasing fruit-rich wine.

● Cesanese di Olevano Romano Cirsium '11	♟♟ 5
● Cesanese di Olevano Romano Sup. Silene '13	♟♟ 3
● Cesanese di Olevano Cirsium '08	♟♟ 5
● Cesanese di Olevano Cirsium '07	♟♟ 4
● Cesanese di Olevano Cirsium '06	♟♟ 4
● Cesanese di Olevano Cirsium '04	♟♟ 4
● Cesanese di Olevano Cirsium '03	♟♟ 4
● Cesanese di Olevano Cirsium '01	♟♟ 5
● Cesanese di Olevano Romano Sup. Cirsium '09	♟♟ 5
● Cesanese di Olevano Romano Sup. Cirsium Ris. '10	♟♟ 5
● Cesanese di Olevano Romano Sup. Silene '12	♟♟ 3
● Cesanese di Olevano Silene '11	♟♟ 2*

Antonello Coletti Conti

VIA VITTORIO EMANUELE, 116
03012 ANAGNI [FR]
TEL. 0775728610
www.coletticonti.it

CELLAR SALES
PRE-BOOKED VISITS
ANNUAL PRODUCTION 20,000 bottles
HECTARES UNDER VINE 20.00

Antonello Coletti Conti can count on several popes among his ancestors, and runs both vines and cellar without making concessions to anyone, least of all himself. That explains why every year any wine which fails to live up to his exacting standards is left out (this time it was his Cosmato and Arcadia), but he is also his own fiercest critic of his bottlings. So while it has to be said that his two Cesanese 2013s have not quite reached the peaks of recent years, they are nevertheless on excellent form, as our grading shows. As always, the Romanico 2013 makes the final; slightly less solidly built than usual, but fruit-rich, with a nicely concentrated nose and excellent tannic weave. Hernicus 2013, usually quicker to reach balanced maturity, seemed to be lagging behind and rather undefined but is well worth waiting a few years for. Make no mistake, the Passerina del Frusinate Hernicus 2014 is the best of its type, confirming Antonello's talent for whites.

Paolo e Noemia D'Amico

FRAZ. VAIANO
LOC. PALOMBARO
01024 CASTIGLIONE IN TEVERINA [VT]
TEL. 0761948034
www.paoloenoemiadamico.it

CELLAR SALES
PRE-BOOKED VISITS
ANNUAL PRODUCTION 150,000 bottles
HECTARES UNDER VINE 25.00
SUSTAINABLE WINERY

Paolo and Noemia D'Amico's estate is celebrating its 30th anniversary. Paolo is the third generation of a ship-owning dynasty, growing up in the family vineyards, while Noemia, of Portuguese origin, has put heart and soul into building up their estate in the badlands of the upper Tiber valley. Their vines grow on volcanic soils in the heart of the Tuscia, dominated by international varietals. Another finalist was the Calanchi di Vaiano 2014, a pure Chardonnay combining summer flowers, white-fleshed fruit and fresh citrus, with full-flavoured overtones in a lingering finish. We also liked the Notturno dei Calanchi 2012, a Pinot Nero with overtones of Mediterranean scrub, elegant tannins making way for a close-focused redcurrant palate and a lovely acid finish. Lastly, the Cabernet Franc Atlante 2012 was a pleasant surprise with its well-gauged tannins and acid staying power, a marked improvement on last year.

● Cesanese del Piglio Sup. Romanico '13	♟♟ 5
● Cesanese del Piglio Sup. Hernicus '13	♟♟ 3
○ Passerina del Frusinate Hernicus '14	♟♟ 3
● Cesanese del Piglio Romanico '11	♟♟♟ 5
● Cesanese del Piglio Romanico '07	♟♟♟ 5
● Cesanese del Piglio Sup. Hernicus '12	♟♟♟ 3*
○ Arcadia '10	♟♟ 3
● Cesanese del Piglio Hernicus '11	♟♟ 3*
● Cesanese del Piglio Hernicus '10	♟♟ 3
● Cesanese del Piglio Hernicus '09	♟♟ 3
● Cesanese del Piglio Romanico '12	♟♟ 5
● Cesanese del Piglio Romanico '10	♟♟ 5
● Cesanese del Piglio Romanico '09	♟♟ 5
● Cesanese del Piglio Romanico '08	♟♟ 5
● Cosmato '12	♟♟ 5
○ Passerina del Frusinate Hernicus '12	♟♟ 3*

○ Calanchi di Vaiano '14	♟♟ 3*
● Atlante '12	♟♟ 5
● Notturno dei Calanchi '12	♟♟ 5
○ Orvieto Noe dei Calanchi '14	♟ 2
○ Terre di Ala '14	♟ 3
● Villa Tirrena '11	♟ 3
○ Calanchi di Vaiano '12	♟♟ 3
○ Calanchi di Vaiano '11	♟♟ 3*
○ Calanchi di Vaiano '10	♟♟ 3
○ Falesia '11	♟♟ 4
○ Falesia '10	♟♟ 4
○ Falesia '09	♟♟ 4
● Notturno dei Calanchi '11	♟♟ 5
○ Seiano Bianco '11	♟♟ 2*
● Seiano Rosso '11	♟♟ 2*
○ Terre di Ala '13	♟♟ 3

★★Falesco

LOC. SAN PIETRO
05020 MONTECCHIO [TR]
TEL. 07449556
www.falesco.it

CELLAR SALES
PRE-BOOKED VISITS
ACCOMMODATION
ANNUAL PRODUCTION 2.600.000 bottiglie
HECTARES UNDER VINE 370,00

At Falesco, Renzo and Riccardo Cotarella are now flanked by an all-female generation, completing a family deeply rooted in this land between Lazio and Umbria. The winery's august vineyards are located in the province of Viterbo, in the part between Montefiascone and Lake Bolsena, where both native and international varieties are grown on the volcanic soil. On the hills south of Orvieto we find merlot, cabernet, sangiovese, verdicchio, and vermentino, with some experimental varieties. The Montiano confirms its excellence for 2013, showing lots of matière and spicy, toasty notes of tobacco, aromatic herbs, and red fruits, above all cherries. Of the reds the Tellus Syrah was good, with red fruit and pepper on the nose, and a consistent palate with crisp fruit. The stellar Est Est Est Poggio dei Gelsi 2014 should not go unnoticed, fresh and pleasant with hints of sage, medlar and white peach.

● Montiano '13	♟♟♟	6
● Tellus Syrah '14	♟♟	3*
● Appunto '14	♟♟	2*
○ Est Est Est di Montefiascone Accenno '14	♟♟	2*
○ Est Est Est di Montefiascone Poggio dei Gelsi '14	♟♟	2*
● Marciliano '12	♟♟	7
● Messidoro '14	♟♟	2*
● Montefalco Sagrantino 2R '12	♟♟	6
● Trentanni '13	♟♟	4
☉ Falesco Brut Rosé M. Cl.	♟	4
● Pomele '14	♟	3
○ Vitiano Bianco '14	♟	2
● Vitiano Rosso '13	♟	2
● Montiano '12	♟♟♟	6

Fontana Candida

VIA FONTANA CANDIDA, 11
00040 MONTE PORZIO CATONE [RM]
TEL. 069401881
www.fontanacandida.it

CELLAR SALES
PRE-BOOKED VISITS
RESTAURANT SERVICE
ANNUAL PRODUCTION 3,700,000 bottles
HECTARES UNDER VINE 97.00

Part of Gruppo Italiano Vini, Fontana Candida processes around 50,000 quintals of grapes, from vineyards in Frascati, Grottaferrata, Monte Porzio Catone, Rome, and Montecompatri, brought here by over 190 growers. Their iconic wine is the Frascati, from grapes grown on sandy pozzolan soils of volcanic origin in the Agro Tuscolano area, rich in potassium, phosphorus, calcium, magnesium, iron and trace elements, but poor in nitrogen. Absent from last year's competition, but now a finalist, the Frascati Superiore Luna Mater Riserva, from old vineyards planted to malvasia di Candia, malvasia del Lazio, greco and bombino. The 2014 vintage has a very rich nose, with peach and apricot aromas, a balanced mouth, caressing with fine minerally notes. We liked the Siroe 2014, a leisurely spicy blend of cesanese and syrah, and the other 2014 Frascatis, Vigneto Santa Teresa, fruit-driven with vegetal aromas, Terre dei Grifi, fresh and fragrant, and the base wine, forthright and supple.

○ Frascati Secco '14	♟♟	2*
○ Frascati Sup. Luna Mater Ris. '14	♟♟	4
○ Frascati Sup. Terre dei Grifi '14	♟♟	2*
○ Frascati Sup. Vign. Santa Teresa '14	♟♟	2*
● Siroe '14	♟♟	3
○ Frascati Sup. Luna Mater '11	♟♟	3*
○ Frascati Sup. Luna Mater '10	♟♟	3
○ Frascati Sup. Luna Mater Ris. '12	♟♟	3*
○ Frascati Sup. Santa Teresa '12	♟♟	2*
○ Frascati Sup. Santa Teresa '11	♟♟	2*
○ Frascati Sup. Terre dei Grifi '13	♟♟	2*
○ Frascati Sup. Terre dei Grifi '12	♟♟	2*
○ Frascati Sup. Vign. Santa Teresa '13	♟♟	2*
● Kron '10	♟♟	4
○ Malvasia Puntinata '13	♟♟	3
● Sesto 21 Syrah '10	♟♟	4

Casale Marchese

VIA DI VERMICINO, 68
00044 FRASCATI [RM]
TEL. 069408932
www.casalemarchese.it

CELLAR SALES
PRE-BOOKED VISITS
ANNUAL PRODUCTION 150,000 bottles
HECTARES UNDER VINE 40.00

The Carletti family has owned their 50
hectares under vine at the heart of Frascati
country for two centuries. The seventh
generation is now at the helm: Alessandro
runs the business and Ferdinando is the
estate agronomist. For years they have
been developing local native grape varieties
such as malvasia puntinata, malvasia di
Candia, trebbiano toscano, greco, bombino
and bellone, alongside international
classics including chardonnay, merlot and
cabernet sauvignon. The farmhouse,
erstwhile residence of Marchese Emilio de'
Cavalieri, is where all of the estate's
operations take place, including olive oil
production. The Frascati Superiore 2014
remains a benchmark for the DOC zone:
typical tones reminiscent of apple and
almond, all wrapped up in aromatic herbs.
The balanced, gutsy palate holds together
well, and has good length. Also good is the
spicy, lingering Clemens 2013, but the
overtones of vanilla and sweet citrus are a
little cloying.

★Sergio Mottura

LOC. POGGIO DELLA COSTA, 1
01020 CIVITELLA D'AGLIANO [VT]
TEL. 0761914533
www.motturasergio.it

CELLAR SALES
PRE-BOOKED VISITS
ACCOMMODATION AND RESTAURANT SERVICE
ANNUAL PRODUCTION 97,000 bottles
HECTARES UNDER VINE 37.00
VITICULTURE METHOD Certified Organic

Sergio Mottura, undoubtedly the pioneer of
the grechetto renaissance, is continuing his
search for varietal stamping, helped by the
quality of the product and by his concern
for the environment. His estate is set
among the clay gullies of Civitella d'Agliano
and the Tiber valley: 37 organically-grown
hectares under vine, as the porcupine on
the labels reminds us. In the absence of the
Latour a Civitella, pride of place went to the
Grechetto Poggio della Costa 2014, taking
a Tre Bicchieri with its hints of citrus and
sage on the bouquet, while the palate has
apricot, white melon and a dazzling
richness of flavour, making the mouth
leisurely and taut. Also excellent were the
Orvieto Tragugnano 2014, among the best
in the DOC zone, fresh-tasting and
minerally, reminiscent of apple and
aromatic herbs, and the champagne
method Mottura Brut 2009, Blanc de
Blancs from chardonnay, full and caressing,
with bready, peach and apricot hints.

○ Frascati Sup. '14	♟♟ 2*
○ Clemens '13	♟♟ 3
● Marchese de' Cavalieri '13	♟ 4
● Novum '14	♟ 3
○ Clemens '09	♟♟♟ 3
○ Clemens '12	♟♟ 4
○ Clemens '11	♟♟ 4
○ Clemens '10	♟♟ 3
○ Frascati Sup. '13	♟♟ 2*
○ Frascati Sup. '12	♟♟ 2*
○ Frascati Sup. '11	♟♟ 2*
○ Frascati Sup. '10	♟♟ 2*
○ Frascati Sup. '09	♟♟ 2
○ Frascati Sup. '08	♟♟ 2*
● Novum '13	♟♟ 3

○ Grechetto Poggio della Costa '14	♟♟♟ 3*
○ Mottura Brut M. Cl. '09	♟♟ 5
○ Orvieto Tragugnano '14	♟♟ 3*
○ Orvieto '14	♟♟ 3
⊙ Civitella Rosato '14	♟ 3
● Civitella Rosso '13	♟ 3
○ Grechetto Latour a Civitella '11	♟♟♟ 4*
○ Grechetto Latour a Civitella '06	♟♟♟ 4*
○ Grechetto Latour a Civitella '05	♟♟♟ 4*
○ Grechetto Latour a Civitella '04	♟♟♟ 4*
○ Grechetto Latour a Civitella '01	♟♟♟ 3
○ Grechetto Poggio della Costa '10	♟♟♟ 3*
○ Grechetto Poggio della Costa '09	♟♟♟ 3*
○ Grechetto Poggio della Costa '08	♟♟♟ 3*
○ Poggio della Costa '12	♟♟♟ 3*
○ Poggio della Costa '11	♟♟♟ 3*

LAZIO

Omina Romana

VIA FONTANA PARATA, 75
00049 VELLETRI [RM]
TEL. 0696430193
www.ominaromana.com

CELLAR SALES
PRE-BOOKED VISITS
ANNUAL PRODUCTION 120,000 bottles
HECTARES UNDER VINE 76.00

It was in 2004 that German entrepreneur Anton F. Börner decided to invest in an 80-hectare estate in Velletri, in the Colli Albani, around 40 kilometres from Rome. With his phoenix on his labels and a talismanic local dialect name for his wines, Börner focused on the reds, flying in the face of local wine-growing tradition. Oenologist Claudio Gori and agronomist Paula Pacheco use twelve different native and international red grape types and seven varieties of white grape to make a series of good quality wines. But the finest was the 2012 Diana Nemorensis I, a classic Bordeaux blend of merlot, cabernet sauvignon and cabernet franc, of which it has all the hallmarks: a black berry fruit, bell pepper and dried spice bouquet, with a fresh, focused palate given great character by the soft tannins. Also excellent was the Merlot 2012 with its marked overtones of cherry and a fruit-rich, soft and mouthfilling palate.

Principe Pallavicini

VIA ROMA, 121
00030 COLONNA [RM]
TEL. 069438816
www.vinipallavicini.com

CELLAR SALES
PRE-BOOKED VISITS
RESTAURANT SERVICE
ANNUAL PRODUCTION 600,000 bottles
HECTARES UNDER VINE 65.00

The Pallavicinis have been an important family in Lazio since the 17th century, with an array of princes, cardinals, popes and wine: 345 year of vitivinicultural history, based at the ancient Colonna complex in the Castelli Romani. This is still where the estate headquarters is located, now run by Maria Camilla Pallavicini, with its 80 hectares under vine, 54 of which given over to white grapes for Frascati wines, making it the largest privately-owned vineyard in the area. The excellent Frascati Superiore Poggio Verde 2014, with a lightly spiced nose of peach, apricot and almond, and a leisurely yet gutsy mouthfeel, hinges around its Mediterranean scrub flavours, and the classic Stillato 2013, a late-harvest Malvasia with hints of dried fruit, honey and candied apricot. We also liked the Casa Romana 2012, a blend of petit verdot and cabernet, with good thrust, and balsamic and black berry fruit notes.

● Diana Nemorensis I '12	♥♥ 6
● Merlot '12	♥♥ 7
○ Bellone Brut '13	♥ 4
● Cabernet Sauvignon '12	♥ 6
☉ Rosato Merlot '14	♥ 3
● Cabernet Sauvignon '11	♀♀ 7

○ Frascati Sup. Poggio Verde '14	♥♥ 2*
○ Stillato '13	♥♥ 3*
● Casa Romana '12	♥♥ 5
● Amarasco '13	♥ 3
● Syrah '13	♥ 2
○ Frascati Sup. Poggio Verde '13	♥♥♥ 2*
○ 1670 '09	♀♀ 3
● Amarasco '11	♀♀ 3
○ Frascati '13	♀♀ 2*
○ Frascati Sup. Poggio Verde '12	♀♀ 2*
○ Frascati Sup. Poggio Verde '09	♀♀ 2*
● Soleggio '10	♀♀ 3
● Soleggio '08	♀♀ 3
○ Stillato '12	♀♀ 3
○ Stillato '10	♀♀ 3

Tenuta La Pazzaglia

S.DA DI BAGNOREGIO, 4
01024 CASTIGLIONE IN TEVERINA [VT]
TEL. 0761947114
www.tenutalapazzaglia.it

CELLAR SALES
PRE-BOOKED VISITS
ACCOMMODATION
ANNUAL PRODUCTION 56,000 bottles
HECTARES UNDER VINE 12.00

Since 1990, the Verdecchia family have been successfully running a viticultural project based from the start on bringing together tradition and innovation. The winery is run by Maria Teresa and brother Pierfrancesco, the offspring of Randolfo and Agnese. The cellar has undergone several refurbishments to help boost production over recent years, and now is almost all stainless steel. Grechetto and merlot are the commonest cultivars, alongside native and international varietals, for a range of pleasing, drinkable wines. The full-flavoured, fresh Grechetto 109 2014, with aromas of lemon and thyme, and pleasant mouthfeel, is still a winner. Il Corno 2014, a blend of grechetto with touches of chardonnay and pinot bianco, is also good, with its aromatic citrussy hints and great supporting acidity, while the pleasantly fresh Rosé Marie 2014, from aleatico and pinot nero, has overtones of cherries and red berries.

Pietra Pinta

VIA LE PASTINE KM 20,200
04010 CORI [LT]
TEL. 069678001
www.pietrapinta.com

CELLAR SALES
PRE-BOOKED VISITS
ACCOMMODATION AND RESTAURANT SERVICE
ANNUAL PRODUCTION 300,000 bottles
HECTARES UNDER VINE 33.00
VITICULTURE METHOD Certified Organic
SUSTAINABLE WINERY

Consolidated quality over the years has earned Cesare Ferretti's estate a full-length profile once again. In addition to the winery in the countryside near Cori, he also offers excellent farmstay accommodation and interesting olive oil, also used in the cosmetics sector. Nevertheless, pride of place still goes to the grape. Cesare works alongside his brother Francesco and his children, Bruno and Anna Laura, together with expert advice from Lorenzo Costantini, to achieve production balance between local and international grape types. As shown by the Costa Vecchia Rosso 2013, a highly successful blend of syrah, petit verdot and nero buono; and by the Costa Vecchia Bianco 2014, where chardonnay and sauvignon mingle perfectly with aromatic malvasia puntinata. Similarly, the varietal Sauvignon 2014, the fruity aromatic Malvasia Puntinata 2014 and the Nero Buono 2013, with hints of autumn leaves and a good matière. The rest of their range also stands up well.

○ Grechetto 109 '14	♟♟ 3
○ Il Corno '14	♟♟ 2*
⊙ Rosé Marie '14	♟♟ 2*
○ Orvieto '14	♟ 2
● Palagio '14	♟ 2
○ Poggio Triale '13	♟ 3
○ Grechetto 109 '13	♛ 3*
○ Il Corno '12	♛ 2*
○ Il Corno '10	♛ 2
○ Il Corno '09	♛ 2*
● Montijone '12	♛ 3
● Montijone '10	♛ 4
○ Orvieto '12	♛ 2*
○ Orvieto '11	♛ 2*
○ Poggio Triale '12	♛ 3
⊙ Rosé Marie '13	♛ 2*

○ Costa Vecchia Bianco '14	♟♟ 2*
● Costa Vecchia Rosso '13	♟♟ 2*
○ Malvasia Puntinata '14	♟♟ 2*
● Nero Buono '13	♟♟ 2*
○ Sauvignon '14	♟♟ 2*
○ Chardonnay '14	♟ 2
● Colle Amato '11	♟ 4
● Petit Verdot '13	♟ 2
● Shiraz '13	♟ 2
○ Viognier '14	♟ 2
○ Carinthia '12	♛ 2*
○ Chardonnay '13	♛ 2*
● Colle Amato '10	♛ 4
○ Costa Vecchia Bianco '13	♛ 2*
● Costa Vecchia Rosso '11	♛ 2*
● Shiraz '11	♛ 2*

LAZIO

Poggio Le Volpi

VIA COLLE PISANO, 27
00040 MONTE PORZIO CATONE [RM]
TEL. 069426980
www.poggiolevolpi.it

CELLAR SALES
PRE-BOOKED VISITS
ANNUAL PRODUCTION 230,000 bottles
HECTARES UNDER VINE 35.00

Felice Mergè is the third generation of a vigneron family, continuing the work of his father Armando and grandfather Manlio. He has inherited the legacy of passion and memory combining it with technological innovation in vinification processes. The estate's vineyards are planted mainly to native cultivars on volcanic clay soils, at an altitude of 400 metres on the slopes of Monte Porzio Catone. The Baccarossa 2013 takes a Tre Bicchieri: this monovarietal Nero Buono, with its fresh bouquet of autumn leaves and hints of mature black berry fruit, has a palate of cherry and liquorice, with rather marked initial tannins giving way to a lingeringly crispy fruity finish. By contrast, despite its fine body, sweet spice and banana tones and good drinkability, the Frascati Superiore Epos 2014 is not very well-typed. The Donnaluce 2014, with its notes of melon and Mediterranean scrub, is correct.

Sant'Andrea

LOC. BORGO VODICE
VIA RENIBBIO, 1720
04019 TERRACINA [LT]
TEL. 0773755028
www.cantinasantandrea.it

CELLAR SALES
PRE-BOOKED VISITS
ANNUAL PRODUCTION 1,000,000 bottles
HECTARES UNDER VINE 85.00

Our tastings provided confirmation that Gabriele and Andrea Pandolfo's estate is going in different directions: while the Circeo denomination wines are maintaining their more-than-solid reputation, even at the lower end, the winery's Moscato range, once a delight for the palate, now appears to be stuck in the doldrums. Hum 2014 seems to have improved this year, but both the dry Oppidum 2014 and the Oppidum 2014 sparkler, the latter and the Templum no longer in the Moscato di Terracina denomination, express the aromatic qualities of the vine without the balance and elegance that once made them such gems. The positive notes are thus sounded by the Riflessi range, especially the intense, full-bodied Circeo Rosso 2014, and the pleasantly fresh-tasting Circeo Rosato 2014 (one of the province's best). Also well-crafted are the Moscato di Terracina Passito Capitolium 2013, nicely balanced notes of dried fig and candied fruit. The Templum Spumante Dolce 2014 is uncomplicated yet pleasant.

● Baccarossa '13	▼▼▼ 4*
○ Frascati Sup. Epos '14	▼▼ 2*
○ Donnaluce '14	▼ 3
● Baccarossa '11	▼▼▼ 4*
○ Frascati Sup. Epos '13	▼▼▼ 2*
○ Frascati Sup. Epos '11	▼▼▼ 2*
○ Frascati Sup. Epos '10	▼▼▼ 2*
○ Frascati Sup. Epos '09	▼▼▼ 2*
● Baccarossa '12	▽▽ 4
● Baccarossa '10	▽▽ 4
● Baccarossa '09	▽▽ 4
● Baccarossa '08	▽▽ 4
○ Donnaluce '13	▽▽ 3
○ Donnaluce '12	▽▽ 3
○ Donnaluce '10	▽▽ 3
○ Frascati Cannellino	▽▽ 3*

○ Circeo Rosato Riflessi '14	▼▼ 2*
● Circeo Rosso Riflessi '14	▼▼ 2*
○ Moscato di Terracina Passito Capitolium '13	▼▼ 4
○ Spumante Dolce Templum '14	▼▼ 2*
○ Circeo Bianco Dune '13	▼ 2
○ Circeo Bianco Riflessi '14	▼ 2
○ Moscato di Terracina Amabile Templum '14	▼ 2
○ Moscato di Terracina Hum '14	▼ 2
○ Moscato di Terracina Secco Oppidum '14	▼ 2
○ Oppidum Brut '14	▼ 2
○ Riflessi Extra Dry	▼ 2
○ Riflessi Rosé Extra Dry	▼ 2
● Circeo Rosso Riflessi '13	▽▽ 2*
○ Moscato di Terracina Amabile Templum '13	▽▽ 2*

Tenuta di Fiorano

VIA DI FIORANELLO, 19-31
00134 ROMA
TEL. 0679340093
www.tenutadifiorano.it

CELLAR SALES
PRE-BOOKED VISITS
RESTAURANT SERVICE
ANNUAL PRODUCTION 18,000 bottles
HECTARES UNDER VINE 6.00

Alessandrojacopo Boncompagni Ludovisi,
initially with the guidance of his uncle
Alberico, who discreetly oversaw the choice
of plots, clones and plantings, has revived
Tenuta di Fiorano, on the Appia Antica. With
a return to its roots, from organic
management in its vineyards to vinification,
the whole production line remains based on
excellence. A Tre Bicchieri for the Fiorano
Bianco 2013, a rich, layered blend of 50%
grechetto and 50% viognier, with its nose
of almond, summer flowers and white
peach, while the mouthfeel, adorned by a
tangy and minerally acidity, offers a
complex, balanced backbone. Both the
complex and deep Fiorano Rosso 2010,
with its notes of cassis and blueberry,
liquorice and coffee, full of great length and
charm, and the Fiorano Rosso 2009, a little
less gutsy but mature and expansive, were
splendid. The Fioranello Bianco 2014,
fragrant and fresh, and the Fioranello
Rosso 2013, fruit-driven and pleasant,
were both well-crafted.

○ Fiorano Bianco '13	♟♟♟ 5
● Fiorano Rosso '10	♟♟ 7
● Fiorano Rosso '09	♟♟ 7
○ Fioranello Bianco '14	♟♟ 3
● Fioranello Rosso '13	♟♟ 4
○ Fiorano Bianco '12	♟♟♟ 4*
○ Fiorano Bianco '10	♟♟♟ 5
○ Fioranello Bianco '12	♟♟ 3
● Fioranello Rosso '12	♟♟ 3
○ Fiorano Bianco '11	♟♟ 4
● Fiorano Rosso '08	♟♟ 4
● Fiorano Rosso '07	♟♟ 4
● Fiorano Rosso '06	♟♟ 6

Giovanni Terenzi

LOC. LA FORMA
VIA FORESE, 13
03010 SERRONE [FR]
TEL. 0775594286
www.viniterenzi.com

CELLAR SALES
PRE-BOOKED VISITS
ANNUAL PRODUCTION 200,000 bottles
HECTARES UNDER VINE 12.00

The lovely Terenzi estate's wines are the
result of a family passion and love for the
land which we cannot praise too highly. The
two Cesaneses are again noteworthy.
Though apparently worlds apart, even in
price, they encapsulate a very versatile
terroir and grape type. The Vajoscuro 2012
has a weighty structure, spicy tertiary notes
on the nose and a full mouth with
remarkable length. By contrast, the
Velobra 2013 might seem light-bodied, but
a second tasting reveals elegance and
balance, making it one of the more
interesting wines of the denomination,
especially as it is also excellent value for
money. The winery has also made
successful forays into the neighbouring
denomination of Cesanese di Olevano
Romano, its most authentic expression
being the Colle San Quirico 2013 which
nevertheless remains very drinkable. The
well-managed Passerina Villa Santa 2014
is slightly off-dry, but may well be attractive
for a number of consumers.

● Cesanese del Piglio Sup. Vajoscuro Ris. '12	♟♟ 4
● Cesanese del Piglio Velobra '13	♟♟ 2*
● Cesanese di Olevano Romano Colle S. Quirico '13	♟♟ 2*
○ Passerina Villa Santa '14	♟ 2
● Cesanese del Piglio Sup. Colle Forma '11	♟♟ 4
● Cesanese del Piglio Sup. Colle Forma '10	♟♟ 4
● Cesanese del Piglio Sup. Vajoscuro Ris. '11	♟♟ 4
● Cesanese del Piglio Sup. Vajoscuro Ris. '09	♟♟ 4
● Cesanese del Piglio Vajoscuro '10	♟♟ 5
● Cesanese del Piglio Velobra '12	♟♟ 2*
● Cesanese del Piglio Velobra '11	♟♟ 2*
● Cesanese del Piglio Velobra '08	♟♟ 2*
○ Passerina Villa Santa '12	♟♟ 2*

Trappolini

VIA DEL RIVELLINO, 65
01024 CASTIGLIONE IN TEVERINA [VT]
TEL. 0761948381
www.trappolini.com

CELLAR SALES
PRE-BOOKED VISITS
ANNUAL PRODUCTION 150,000 bottles
HECTARES UNDER VINE 30.00

In the early 1960s, Mario Trappolini started up his winery selling bulk wine from his own vineyards on the Lazio-Umbria border. Over half a century has passed since then, with three successive generations taking over at the helm, making Trappolini one of upper Tuscia's major estates. Now run by Roberto and Paolo, winery production is still based on its heritage of native grapes, from grechetto to procanico, from aleatico to sangiovese, which thrive both on the volcanic soils lending them minerality and rich flavour, and on the clayey alluvial soils which give the wines a firm structure. This is shown by the quality of the whole range submitted, and especially by the first Tre Bicchieri for the Grechetto 2014, with its concentrated and layered bouquet, notes of almond and apple, and a complex and full-flavoured mouthfeel. The intense and well-textured Procanico 2014 is in the same league, while the best of the reds is the Paterno 2013, fruit-driven, balsamic and spicy.

Valle Vermiglia

VIA ANTONIO GRAMSCI, 7
00197 ROMA
TEL. 3487221073
www.vallevermiglia.it

CELLAR SALES
ANNUAL PRODUCTION 30,000 bottles
HECTARES UNDER VINE 8.00

The Monte Porzio Catone slopes of Mount Tuscolo are home to the Valle Vermiglia wine estate. Back in 2000, with a view to creating a quality Frascati, Mario Masini planted up a vineyard in the eight hectares of on very loose volcanic soils at 600 metres in altitude, around the cloistered Benedictine abbey of Monte Corona, whose severe rules forbid women from entering. Strictly hand-picked native cultivars like malvasia di Candia and malvasia del Lazio, trebbiano giallo, trebbiano toscano and bombino bianco, are used for the Frascati Superiore Eremo Tuscolano 2013, the only label produced, faithful to a long vitivinicultural tradition. A deserving Tre Bicchieri for its elegance and varietal stamping: the well-defined bouquet of citrus and almond and consistent palate, containing white-fleshed fruit and hints of chalk and aromatic herbs; the palate is cool and full-flavoured.

○ Grechetto '14	♥♥♥	2*
○ Procanico '14	♥♥	2*
○ Brecceto '14	♥♥	3
● Cabernet Franc '13	♥♥	3
● Canaiolo Nero '14	♥♥	3
● Paterno '13	♥♥	4
○ Brecceto '13	♀♀	3*
● Cenereto '13	♀♀	2*
○ Est! Est!! Est!!! di Montefiascone '12	♀♀	2*
○ Grechetto '13	♀♀	2*
○ Orvieto '12	♀♀	2*
● Paterno '12	♀♀	4
● Paterno '11	♀♀	3*
○ Procanico '13	♀♀	2*
○ Sartei '11	♀♀	1*

○ Frascati Sup. Eremo Tuscolano '13	♥♥♥	3*
○ Frascati Sup. Eremo Tuscolano '12	♀♀	3*

Castel de Paolis

VIA VAL DE PAOLIS
00046 GROTTAFERRATA [RM]
TEL. 069413648
www.casteldepaolis.it

CELLAR SALES
PRE-BOOKED VISITS
RESTAURANT SERVICE
ANNUAL PRODUCTION 80,000 bottles
HECTARES UNDER VINE 12.00

○ Frascati Campo Vecchio '14	♀♀ 2*
● I Quattro Mori '11	♀♀ 5
● Campo Vecchio Rosso '13	♀ 3
○ Donna Adriana '14	♀ 4

Cantina Sociale Cesanese del Piglio

VIA PRENESTINA, KM 42
03010 PIGLIO [FR]
TEL. 0775502356
www.cesanesedelpiglio.it

CELLAR SALES
PRE-BOOKED VISITS
ANNUAL PRODUCTION 450,000 bottles
HECTARES UNDER VINE 18.00

● Cesanese del Piglio Cerciole '14	♀♀ 2*
○ Passerina Elcini '14	♀ 1*
○ Passerina Ilia '14	♀ 1*

Cominium

VIA RITINTO
03041 ALVITO [FR]
TEL. 0776510683
www.cantinacominium.it

CELLAR SALES
ANNUAL PRODUCTION 70,000 bottles
HECTARES UNDER VINE 18.00

● Atina Cabernet Ris. '12	♀♀ 5
○ Maturano '14	♀♀ 2*

Cordeschi

LOC. ACQUAPENDENTE
VIA CASSIA KM 137,400
00121 ACQUAPENDENTE [VT]
TEL. 3356953547
www.cantinacordeschi.it

CELLAR SALES
PRE-BOOKED VISITS
ANNUAL PRODUCTION 35,000 bottles
HECTARES UNDER VINE 8.50

● Ost '13	♀♀ 3*
● Saino '12	♀♀ 3
○ Palea '14	♀ 2
⊙ Siele '14	♀ 2

Corte dei Papi

LOC. COLLETONNO
03012 ANAGNI [FR]
TEL. 0775769271
www.cortedeipapi.it

CELLAR SALES
PRE-BOOKED VISITS
ANNUAL PRODUCTION 40,000 bottles
HECTARES UNDER VINE 25.00

● Cesanese del Piglio Colle Ticchio '14	♀♀ 2*
● Cesanese del Piglio San Magno '13	♀ 4
○ Passerina '14	♀ 2

Agricola Emme

VIA MAGGIORE, 126
03010 PIGLIO [FR]
TEL. 0775769859
www.agricolaemme.com

ANNUAL PRODUCTION 25,000 bottles
HECTARES UNDER VINE 25.70

● Cesanese del Piglio Sup. Casal Cervino '12	♀♀ 3
○ Passerina Casal Cervino '14	♀♀ 2*
● Cesanese del Piglio Hyperius '14	♀ 2

La Ferriera

VIA FERRIERA, 723
03042 ATINA [FR]
TEL. 0776691226
www.laferriera.it

CELLAR SALES
PRE-BOOKED VISITS
ANNUAL PRODUCTION 50,000 bottles
HECTARES UNDER VINE 15.00

● Atina Cabernet Real Magona '11	♟♟	3
● Atina Cabernet Real Magona Ris. '11	♟	5
○ Dorato '13	♟	2

Fontana Lottola

VIA COLLE BUONO, SNC
03041 ALVITO [FR]
TEL. 3929779332
www.fontanalottola.it

PRE-BOOKED VISITS
ANNUAL PRODUCTION 9,000 bottles
HECTARES UNDER VINE 2.00

● Atina Cabernet Il Magistrato Ris. '11	♟♟	5
● Il Magistrato Merlot '12	♟	4
⊙ Il Magistrato Rosato '14	♟	3

Alberto Giacobbe

C.DA SAN GIOVENALE
03018 PALIANO [FR]
TEL. 0775579198
www.vinigiacobbe.it

PRE-BOOKED VISITS
ANNUAL PRODUCTION 25,000 bottles
HECTARES UNDER VINE 9.00

● Cesanese di Olevano Romano Sup. '13	♟♟	3
● Cesanese del Piglio Sup. Lepanto Ris. '11	♟	4
○ Passerina Juvenalis '14	♟	2

Donato Giangirolami

LOC. BORGO MONTELLO
VIA DEL CAVALIERE, 1414
04100 LATINA
TEL. 3358394890
www.donatogiangirolami.it

CELLAR SALES
PRE-BOOKED VISITS
ANNUAL PRODUCTION 70,000 bottles
HECTARES UNDER VINE 38.00
VITICULTURE METHOD Certified Organic

○ Cardito '14	♟♟	2*
● Pancarpo '12	♟♟	3
● Prodigo '14	♟	2
○ Regius '14	♟	2

Podere Grecchi

S.DA SAMMARTINESE, 8
01100 VITERBO
TEL. 0761305671
www.poderegrecchi.com

CELLAR SALES
PRE-BOOKED VISITS
ANNUAL PRODUCTION 70,000 bottles
HECTARES UNDER VINE 10.50
SUSTAINABLE WINERY

○ Chardonnay '14	♟♟	2*
○ Eliandré '14	♟♟	2*
○ San Silvestro '14	♟	2

Antica Cantina Leonardi

VIA DEL PINO, 12
01027 MONTEFIASCONE [VT]
TEL. 0761826028
www.cantinaleonardi.it

CELLAR SALES
PRE-BOOKED VISITS
ACCOMMODATION
ANNUAL PRODUCTION 100,000 bottles
HECTARES UNDER VINE 37.00
VITICULTURE METHOD Certified Organic

○ Est! Est!! Est!!! di Montefiascone Poggio del Cardinale '14	♟♟	2*
○ Pensiero '14	♟♟	2*
○ Vivi '14	♟	2

Occhipinti

LOC. MONTEMAGGIORE
S.DA COMUNALE MONTEMAGGIORE
01010 GRADOLI [VT]
TEL. 3355789773
www.occhipintiagricola.it

CELLAR SALES
PRE-BOOKED VISITS
ANNUAL PRODUCTION 15,000 bottles
HECTARES UNDER VINE 3.00
VITICULTURE METHOD Certified Organic

● LaCaldera '13	♥♥ 3
● Rosso Arcaico	♥♥ 3
● Alea Viva '13	♥ 3

Tenuta Ronci di Nepi

LOC. VALLE RONCI
01036 NEPI [VT]
TEL. 0761555125
www.roncidinepi.it

CELLAR SALES
PRE-BOOKED VISITS
ANNUAL PRODUCTION 130,000 bottles
HECTARES UNDER VINE 30.00

○ Grechetto '14	♥♥ 2*
○ Oro di Nè '14	♥♥ 2*
● Veste Porpora '12	♥♥ 2*
● Ronci '12	♥ 4

San Giovenale

LOC. LA MACCIA
01010 BLERA [VT]
TEL. 066877877
www.sangiovenale.it

CELLAR SALES
PRE-BOOKED VISITS
ANNUAL PRODUCTION 7,000 bottles
HECTARES UNDER VINE 10.00
VITICULTURE METHOD Certified Organic
SUSTAINABLE WINERY

● Habemus '13	♥♥ 7

Cantine San Marco

LOC. VERMICINO
VIA DI MOLA CAVONA, 26/28
00044 FRASCATI [RM]
TEL. 069409403
www.sanmarcofrascati.it

CELLAR SALES
PRE-BOOKED VISITS
ANNUAL PRODUCTION 1,500,000 bottles
HECTARES UNDER VINE 32.00

○ Frascati Sup. Crio 8 '14	♥♥ 2*
● Solomerlot '13	♥♥ 2*
● Cesanese De Notari '13	♥ 2
○ Malvasia De Notari '14	♥ 2

Tenuta Santa Lucia

LOC. SANTA LUCIA
02047 POGGIO MIRTETO [RI]
TEL. 076524616
www.tenutasantalucia.com

CELLAR SALES
PRE-BOOKED VISITS
RESTAURANT SERVICE
ANNUAL PRODUCTION 180,000 bottles
HECTARES UNDER VINE 43.00

○ Pecorino '14	♥♥ 2*
● Colli della Sabina Domina Sabina '12	♥ 2
○ Falanghina '14	♥ 2
○ Miooo '14	♥ 2

Tenuta Le Quinte

VIA DELLE MARMORELLE, 71
00040 MONTECOMPATRI [RM]
TEL. 069438756
www.tenutalequinte.it

CELLAR SALES
PRE-BOOKED VISITS
ANNUAL PRODUCTION 250,000 bottles
HECTARES UNDER VINE 20.00

○ Malvasia Orchidea '14	♥♥ 3
● Rasa di Marmorata '13	♥♥ 2*
○ Montecompatri Colonna Sup. Virtù Romane '14	♥ 2

Terra delle Ginestre

S.S. 630 AUSONIA, 59
04020 SPIGNO SATURNIA [LT]
TEL. 3495617153
www.terradelleginestre.it

CELLAR SALES
PRE-BOOKED VISITS
ANNUAL PRODUCTION 15,000 bottles
HECTARES UNDER VINE 4.00

● Il Generale '13	♟♟	3
○ Invito Senza Solfiti Aggiunti '14	♟♟	4
● Ricordi Rosso '13	♟♟	2*
○ Letizia '14	♟	2

Tre Botti

S.DA DELLA POGGETTA, 10
01024 CASTIGLIONE IN TEVERINA [VT]
TEL. 0761948930
www.trebotti.it

CELLAR SALES
ACCOMMODATION
ANNUAL PRODUCTION 50,000 bottles
HECTARES UNDER VINE 10.00
VITICULTURE METHOD Certified Organic

● Gocce '12	♟♟	4
● Tusco '14	♟♟	2*
○ 3S L'Incrocio '14	♟	3
○ Orvieto Sup. Incanthus '14	♟	2

Villa Caviciana

LOC. TOJENA CAVICIANA
01025 GROTTE DI CASTRO [VT]
TEL. 0763798212
www.villacaviciana.com

CELLAR SALES
PRE-BOOKED VISITS
ANNUAL PRODUCTION 25,000 bottles
HECTARES UNDER VINE 16.00
VITICULTURE METHOD Certified
OrganicCertified Biodynamic

● Faustina '12	♟♟	6
● Letizia '12	♟♟	5
● Eleonora '13	♟	3
○ Filippo '14	♟	3

Villa Gianna

FRAZ. B.GO SAN DONATO
S.DA MAREMMANA
04010 SABAUDIA [LT]
TEL. 0773250034
www.villagianna.it

CELLAR SALES
PRE-BOOKED VISITS
ANNUAL PRODUCTION 100,000 bottles
HECTARES UNDER VINE 65.00
VITICULTURE METHOD Certified Organic

○ Circeo Bianco Innato '14	♟♟	2*
○ Vigne del Borgo Sauvignon '14	♟♟	2*
● Barriano '12	♟	3
○ Moscato di Terracina Secco '14	♟	1*

Villa Simone

VIA FRASCATI COLONNA, 29
00040 MONTE PORZIO CATONE [RM]
TEL. 069449717
www.villasimone.com

CELLAR SALES
PRE-BOOKED VISITS
ANNUAL PRODUCTION 200,000 bottles
HECTARES UNDER VINE 21.00
SUSTAINABLE WINERY

○ Frascati Sup. Vign. Filonardi '14	♟♟	3
○ Frascati Sup. Villa dei Preti '14	♟♟	3
○ Frascati Secco '14	♟	2
● Syrah '12	♟	2

La Visciola

C.DA CARCASSANO
03010 PIGLIO [FR]
TEL. 0775501950
maccioccapiero@libero.it

PRE-BOOKED VISITS
ANNUAL PRODUCTION 6,000 bottles
HECTARES UNDER VINE 2.00
VITICULTURE METHOD Certified Organic

● Cesanese del Piglio Priore Ju Quarto '13	♟♟	5
● Cesanese del Piglio Priore Mozzatta '13	♟♟	5
● Cesanese del Piglio Priore Vicinale '13	♟♟	5
● Cesanese del Piglio Priore Vignali '13	♟	5

ABRUZZO

Year after year we proceed with the hard work of tasting of wines from Abruzzo and after we are done, a question mark lingers. More cellars are assessed (we now receive samples from a hundred or so) and the wines are better defined and of higher quality, from the solid Montepulciano d'Abruzzos to the poetic Trebbianos, and the impetuous native whites. We see an ever more convincing rediscovery of roots and traditional techniques, with spontaneous fermentation, and organic or even biodynamic agriculture now quite commonplace. This year we again noted that quality overall is increasingly solid, for wines that travel successfully to every corner of the globe. And this is as true for the mega wineries bottling millions of litres as it is for the boutique-scale colleagues. Sounds like an idyllic setting, but there are unexplained grey areas. The market still fails to see Italy's fourth biggest region for wine production as a significant wine district. Maybe we should not be surprised: the story of Abruzzo wines sometimes stumbles because there is too much production and too little ambition. To the south of the River Tronto there is no community effort, the bold step that would get the green region the acknowledgment it deserves as a truly great terroir. Then there is the fact that 80% of product continues to be bottled outside the region and this is the story of Abruzzo wine. Local vignerons must realize they have to take control of production and stop the downward bidding process that is throttling the industry. It is no longer enough just to make good wines: someone has to make sure the Italians and the competitive international markets, seeking more than ever identifiable, terroir-true bottles, are aware of it. The Abruzzo wine system seems to be stuck in a solipsistic, self-indulgent isolation, keeping it all in the family: Montepulciano is among the top-selling wines in Italy, with steady percentage increases, but this is offset by constant drops in the average price per bottle. With 15 award-winning wines saying all that needs to be said about this variety, which takes us on a guided tour from the Adriatic coast to the Apennine glaciers. A line-up of wines with dissimilar origin, but similar quality. Venerable wineries and large cooperatives, alongside artisan cellars, drafting a great folk tale of everyday quality that deserves to be better known and appreciated.

Agriverde

LOC. CALDARI
VIA STORTINI, 32A
66020 ORTONA [CH]
TEL. 0859032101
www.agriverde.it

CELLAR SALES
PRE-BOOKED VISITS
ACCOMMODATION AND RESTAURANT SERVICE
ANNUAL PRODUCTION 900,000 bottles
HECTARES UNDER VINE 65.00
VITICULTURE METHOD Certified Organic

Ortona, with blazing sunshine and fat lands, the Adriatic before us and Majella behind, is a unique place, usually ruled by large-scale wine production. But years ago, Giannicola de Carlo chose a different path and was one of the first in the region to opt for organic farming; contemporary, ambitious wines; a lovely boutique hotel for wine tourism; a cutting-edge cellar run by the precepts of bioarchitecture. The wines made in this setting are well-typed, modern, often very well-made and pleasing to competitive international markets. Remarkable numbers for the items presented, from the simpler, fragrant, good value wines to the leading crus. The Plateo is still maturing, but the "unpretentious" Riseis 2013 makes up for its absence: a well-typed, fragrant Montepulciano with husky varietal aromas of soot and cherries, and a generous, powerful, very dynamic flavour over clear-cut tannins. The 2014 Natum, a certified vegan-organic wine, is fragrant and approachable with an authentic, impulsive Montepulciano character.

● Montepulciano d'Abruzzo Riseis '13	♟♟ 3*
⊙ Cuvée Prestige 830	♟♟ 5
● Montepulciano d'Abruzzo Natum Bio '14	♟♟ 2*
○ Passerina Riseis '14	♟♟ 3
○ Pecorino Riseis '14	♟♟ 3
○ Trebbiano d'Abruzzo Natum Bio '14	♟♟ 2*
⊙ Montepulciano d'Abruzzo Cerasuolo Natum '14	♟ 3
⊙ Montepulciano d'Abruzzo Cerasuolo Solàrea '14	♟ 3
○ Pecorino Natum Bio '14	♟ 3
● Montepulciano d'Abruzzo Plateo Ris. '09	♟♟ 6
● Montepulciano d'Abruzzo Solàrea Ris. '10	♟♟ 4
○ Pecorino Natum Bio '13	♟♟ 3
○ Trebbiano d'Abruzzo Piane di Maggio '13	♟♟ 2*

F.lli Barba

LOC. SCERNE DI PINETO
S.DA ROTABILE PER CASOLI
64020 PINETO [TE]
TEL. 0859461020
www.fratellibarba.it

CELLAR SALES
PRE-BOOKED VISITS
ACCOMMODATION
ANNUAL PRODUCTION 350,000 bottles
HECTARES UNDER VINE 68.00

The Teramo hills are a top Abruzzo terroir: a gentle chain of hills overlooking the sea, with Gran Sasso behind. This has always been the home of the Barba winery, with two estates between Scerne and Pineto: 70 hectares under vine and a cellar big on substance but very low key. The wines are the fruit of Giovanni's passion, old vinification techniques and new insights, from the spontaneous fermentation of the powerful Montepulciano crus to recent experiments with trebbiano fermented in amphoras. The wines are always interesting and recognizable. A slightly below par tasting performance from this Roseto winery this year, with its interesting and ambitious wines. The Collemorino 2013 Etichetta Bianca is a natural, mouthwatering Montepulciano with nice husky, fruity contrasts. Vasari 2012, also Montepulciano, has consistent, raw meat aromas and a fascinating floral hint while the flavour is well-rounded with citrus and cherry fruit.

● Montepulciano d'Abruzzo Colle Morino Et. Bianca '13	♟♟ 2*
● Montepulciano d'Abruzzo I Vasari '12	♟♟ 5
⊙ Montepulciano d'Abruzzo Cerasuolo Vignafranca '14	♟♟ 2*
● Montepulciano d'Abruzzo Colle Morino '14	♟♟ 2*
● Montepulciano d'Abruzzo Vignafranca '12	♟♟ 3
○ Trebbiano d'Abruzzo '12	♟♟ 4
○ Trebbiano d'Abruzzo Colle Morino '14	♟♟ 1*
○ Vignafranca Bianco '13	♟♟ 3
⊙ Montepulciano d'Abruzzo Cerasuolo Colle Morino '14	♟ 1*
○ Pecorino '14	♟ 3
● Montepulciano d'Abruzzo I Vasari '10	♟♟♟ 5
● Montepulciano d'Abruzzo I Vasari '09	♟♟♟ 5
● Montepulciano d'Abruzzo I Vasari '08	♟♟♟ 5
● Montepulciano d'Abruzzo Vignafranca '07	♟♟♟ 3*

Barone Cornacchia

C.DA TORRI, 20
64010 TORANO NUOVO [TE]
TEL. 0861887412
www.baronecornacchia.it

CELLAR SALES
PRE-BOOKED VISITS
ACCOMMODATION
ANNUAL PRODUCTION 300,000 bottles
HECTARES UNDER VINE 42.00
VITICULTURE METHOD Certified Organic

A venerable winery in the competitive Colline Teramane scenario, the only Abruzzo DOCG and the zone responsible for the new drive behind this unique terroir. The estate, a single 30-hectare plot, forms a natural amphitheatre between the Adriatic and Gran Sasso, organically farmed, shaping amazing grapes thanks to the presence of both sunshine and sea. The Controguerra cellar works in a grounded, classic style, recently showing the more modern, graceful touch of newer generations taking up the reins of the estate. The well-made wines tread a path between the contemporary and the traditional. A compact line-up, solid and classic through to the ambitious Montepulciano crus. The Vigna Le Coste 2012 is generous, ripe and sunny, with perky clear-cut fruit aromas. Although still very young and a little stiff on the nose, it will open out well as the close-knit, well-paced palate testifies. The Passerina Villa Torri demonstrates the potential of this grape in this area: well-defined floral and medlar aromas, and a dynamic, food-friendly flavour.

● Montepulciano d'Abruzzo V. Le Coste '12	❦❦ 3*
○ Controguerra Passerina Villa Torri '14	❦❦ 2*
● Montepulciano d'Abruzzo '13	❦❦ 2*
● Montepulciano d'Abruzzo Colline Teramane Vizzarro '11	❦❦ 5
● Montepulciano d'Abruzzo Poggio Varano '12	❦❦ 3
○ Pecorino Villa Torri '14	❦❦ 2*
● Controguerra Rosso Villa Torri '14	❦ 3
○ Trebbiano d'Abruzzo Sup. '14	❦ 2
● Montepulciano d'Abruzzo '12	♉♉ 2*
● Montepulciano d'Abruzzo '11	♉♉ 2*
● Montepulciano d'Abruzzo Colline Teramane Vizzarro '10	♉♉ 5
● Montepulciano d'Abruzzo Poggio Varano '11	♉♉ 3
● Montepulciano d'Abruzzo V. Le Coste '11	♉♉ 3

Tenute Barone di Valforte

C.DA PIOMBA, 11
64029 SILVI MARINA [TE]
TEL. 0859353432
www.baronedivalforte.it

CELLAR SALES
PRE-BOOKED VISITS
ANNUAL PRODUCTION 280,000 bottles
HECTARES UNDER VINE 50.00

The 50 hectares under vine at Silvi Marina are set on the gently rolling hills overlooking the sea. There are two estates with very different land and weather features. Recently the brand name, already known in Abruzzo and beyond, has expanded. The Sorricchio brothers come from a traditional, venerable winegrowing background, but they only began bottling products a few years ago. The wines have proved very popular generally: fresh, drinkable whites and high-flying reds, a pleasing dialogue between tradition and innovation. The wines tasted are interesting, very well-made and modern in style. The fresh-tasting whites impressed us with their confident, boisterous aromas, and easy-going, well-paced palates: for example, the Trebbiano Villa Chiara 2014 with its nice toasty and grassy aromas, and tangy flavour. The Colle Sale 2013 is an ambitious Montepulciano with a warm, sunny, lively nose and powerful, mouthwatering palate, on which the dense texture is backed up by typical varietal acidity.

● Montepulciano d'Abruzzo Colline Teramane Colle Sale '13	❦❦ 3*
⊙ Montepulciano d'Abruzzo Cerasuolo Valforte Rosé '14	❦❦ 2*
○ Passerina '14	❦❦ 2*
○ Pecorino '14	❦❦ 2*
○ Trebbiano d'Abruzzo Villa Chiara '14	❦❦ 2*
● Montepulciano d'Abruzzo '14	❦ 2
● Montepulciano d'Abruzzo '13	♉♉ 2*
● Montepulciano d'Abruzzo '12	♉♉ 2*
⊙ Montepulciano d'Abruzzo Cerasuolo '13	♉♉ 2*
● Montepulciano d'Abruzzo Colline Teramane Colle Sale '10	♉♉ 3*
● Montepulciano d'Abruzzo Ris. '10	♉♉ 3*
○ Passerina '13	♉♉ 2*
○ Pecorino '13	♉♉ 2*

Nestore Bosco

C.DA CASALI, 147
65010 NOCCIANO [PE]
TEL. 085847345
www.nestorebosco.com

CELLAR SALES
PRE-BOOKED VISITS
ANNUAL PRODUCTION 600,000 bottles
HECTARES UNDER VINE 75.00

For over a century Bosco has been in the spotlight on the Pescara winegrowing scene, opening the international market to Abruzzo wines. The beautiful old ageing cellar alone is worth a visit for the bottles on display. The 70 hectares are divided into two estates: Nocciano, on the gentle Pescara hills overlooking the sea; and the more recent acquisition in the Subequana valley in the heart of Majella, on harsher land with typically significant temperature variation. Good, solid wines with classic features, local varieties in a more modern key. The well-stocked and sometimes ambitious range is better established every year, with impressive classic lines. The Donna Bosco 2012 is a dark and brooding Montepulciano with fruity aromas and a close-knit, pleasantly tannic palate. The Montepulciano 2012 reveals vibrant fruit aromas and strikingly intense acidity, and a food-friendly palate.

● Montepulciano d'Abruzzo '12	▼▼ 2*
● Montepulciano d'Abruzzo 110 Ris. '10	▼▼ 6
● Montepulciano d'Abruzzo Don Bosco Ris. '11	▼▼ 4
● Montepulciano d'Abruzzo Donna Bosco '12	▼▼ 4
○ Pecorino '14	▼▼ 2*
○ Pecorino Donna Bosco '14	▼▼ 3
● Montepulciano d'Abruzzo Pan Ris. '11	▼ 4
○ Passerina '14	▼ 2
● Linfa '10	▽▽ 2*
● Montepulciano d'Abruzzo '11	▽▽ 2*
⊙ Montepulciano d'Abruzzo Cerasuolo '13	▽▽ 2*
● Montepulciano d'Abruzzo Donna Bosco '11	▽▽ 4
● Montepulciano d'Abruzzo Pan '09	▽▽ 4
● Montepulciano d'Abruzzo Pan Ris. '10	▽▽ 4

Castorani

LOC. C.DA ORATORIO
VIA CASTORANI, 5
65020 ALANNO [PE]
TEL. 3466355635
www.castorani.it

CELLAR SALES
PRE-BOOKED VISITS
ANNUAL PRODUCTION 1,000,000 bottles
HECTARES UNDER VINE 72.00

This winery aims to combine an artisan's care with large-scale quantities. Jarno Trulli's estate impresses us every year with interesting wines that are true children of the lovely Colline Pescaresi terroir. Between Majella and the Adriatic, over 100 hectares of vineyards on the Alanno hills are constantly pounded by the breeze blowing from sea to mountains and back again, producing extraordinary grapes. These are fermented in the new cellar in concrete vats and using the drying technique in the very modern drying room. Due to a tricky year the range presented was a little less impressive than usual. Podere Castorani 2013, a Montepulciano shaped by concrete vats and daring maturation, earns another Tre Bicchieri. Fruity sweetness and Mediterranean herbs on the nose, and a rounded, close-knit palate with typical sooty hints. The Passerina Rocco 2014 shows impressive floral aromas and a well-paced, tangy palate.

● Montepulciano d'Abruzzo Podere Castorani Ris. '10	▼▼▼ 5
● Montepulciano d'Abruzzo Cadetto '13	▼▼ 2*
⊙ Montepulciano d'Abruzzo Cerasuolo Costa delle Plaie '14	▼▼ 3
○ Passerina Le Paranze '14	▼▼ 2*
○ Passerina Rocco '14	▼▼ 4
○ Pecorino Amorino '14	▼▼ 3
● Rocco '12	▼▼ 4
○ Trebbiano d'Abruzzo Cadetto '14	▼▼ 2*
○ Pecorino Le Paranze '14	▼ 2
● Montepulciano d'Abruzzo Amorino '10	▽▽▽ 3*
● Montepulciano d'Abruzzo Amorino '07	▽▽▽ 3*
● Montepulciano d'Abruzzo Podere Castorani '08	▽▽▽ 5
● Montepulciano d'Abruzzo Ris. '09	▽▽▽ 5
● Montepulciano d'Abruzzo Costa delle Plaie '11	▽▽ 2*

★Luigi Cataldi Madonna

Loc. Piano
67025 Ofena [AQ]
Tel. 0862954252
www.cataldimadonna.com

CELLAR SALES
PRE-BOOKED VISITS
ANNUAL PRODUCTION 240,000 bottles
HECTARES UNDER VINE 31.00
SUSTAINABLE WINERY

Situated on a small upland entirely
surrounded by mountains, Cataldi Madonna
turns out wines that are famous beyond
this region, sculpted by the rugged,
mountainous terroir with typical extreme
temperature variation. Ofena is in the
province of L'Aquila, immediately below
the Calderone Apennine glacier in a
charming landscape interpreted over four
generations in this artisan winery in wines
with recognizable identity: the aromas
and high levels of acidity are preserved
during vinification producing edgy, dynamic
wines. The "Professor's" wines are once
again among the best in the region, and
artisan products really come up trumps
in tricky years like this one. I Malandrini,
a Montepulciano, is all about a drinkable
palate with universal appeal. The rounded,
well-paced, fruity flavour is supported by
lovely varietal acidity. The Tonì is quite
simply still young and undeveloped, but will
open out given time. Giulia is a fragrant,
gutsy Pecorino.

● Montepulciano d'Abruzzo Malandrino '13	♥♥♥ 3*
● Montepulciano d'Abruzzo Tonì '12	♥♥ 6
⊙ Cataldino '14	♥♥ 2*
○ Pecorino Giulia '14	♥♥ 3
⊙ Montepulciano d'Abruzzo Cerasuolo '14	♥ 2
○ Trebbiano d'Abruzzo '14	♥ 2
● Montepulciano d'Abruzzo Malandrino '12	♥♥♥ 3*
● Montepulciano d'Abruzzo Tonì '07	♥♥♥ 5
● Montepulciano d'Abruzzo Tonì '06	♥♥♥ 5
○ Pecorino '11	♥♥♥ 5
○ Pecorino '10	♥♥♥ 5
○ Pecorino '09	♥♥♥ 5
○ Pecorino '08	♥♥♥ 5
○ Pecorino '07	♥♥♥ 5
○ Pecorino '06	♥♥♥ 5

Cirelli

Loc. Treciminiere
via Colle San Giovanni, 1
64032 Atri [TE]
Tel. 0858700106
www.agricolacirelli.com

CELLAR SALES
PRE-BOOKED VISITS
ACCOMMODATION AND RESTAURANT SERVICE
ANNUAL PRODUCTION 26,000 bottles
HECTARES UNDER VINE 5.00
VITICULTURE METHOD Certified Organic

22 hectares of certified organic hillside
vineyards at Atri, the noble heart of Teramo,
in a fully functioning farm on the lovely hills
tumbling down towards the sea. Cirelli has
won us over with breezy, artisan wines.
The fragrant classic line with its cheerful
screwtop bottles impressed us with its
suitability as a table wine and its simple,
but never commonplace character, while
recent fermentations in amphoras offer a
new interpretation with agreeable ancestral
hints of Abruzzo varieties. The 2014 harvest
was a tough and tricky, and it shows in
this year's line-up from this small, artisan
winery in Atri. The wines are impressive,
as ever, but slightly less resplendent than
usual. The Cerasuolo 2014 fermented in
amphoras has impressively husky, vivacious
aromas, with a gamy hint, but the flavour
is fresh and well-paced. The two versions
of Montepulciano, fermented in amphoras
and stainless steel, are impressive and
food-friendly, with varietal acidity and perky,
lively fruit.

⊙ Montepulciano d'Abruzzo Cerasuolo Amphora '14	♥♥ 5
● Montepulciano d'Abruzzo '14	♥♥ 2*
● Montepulciano d'Abruzzo Amphora '14	♥♥ 5
⊙ Montepulciano d'Abruzzo Cerasuolo '14	♥♥ 2*
⊙ Trebbiano d'Abruzzo Amphora '14	♥♥ 5
○ Trebbiano d'Abruzzo '14	♥ 2
● Montepulciano d'Abruzzo '13	♥♥ 2*
● Montepulciano d'Abruzzo '12	♥♥ 2*
● Montepulciano d'Abruzzo Amphora '13	♥♥ 5
● Montepulciano d'Abruzzo Amphora '12	♥♥ 5
⊙ Montepulciano d'Abruzzo Cerasuolo '13	♥♥ 2*
⊙ Montepulciano d'Abruzzo Cerasuolo Amphora '13	♥♥ 5
⊙ Montepulciano d'Abruzzo Cerasuolo Amphora '12	♥♥ 5
○ Trebbiano d'Abruzzo '13	♥♥ 2*

ABRUZZO

Codice Citra

C.DA CUCULLO
66026 ORTONA [CH]
TEL. 0859031342
www.citra.it

CELLAR SALES
PRE-BOOKED VISITS
ANNUAL PRODUCTION 18,000,000 bottles
HECTARES UNDER VINE 6,000.00

A second-tier cooperative winery which brings together the work of many cooperatives scattered across the Chieti area. In recent years Citra has bravely undertaken a process of protecting and expressing the specific features of this province, one of the leaders in Italian wine production. The area displays variable geographical and soil and climate conditions, from the Majella foothills to the sunny slopes facing the Adriatic, and such a rich landscape breeds modern, well-made wines, champions on competitive international markets, and a successful combination of quality and quantity. A remarkable tasting here, confirming the significant achievement in raising the quality of the wines. The Aulicus 2012 is an ambitious Montepulciano of international appeal, with very good, typical contrasting of acidity and fragrance. The Volpe all'Uva 2012 astonished us all. This is a very good sulphite-free Pecorino, which does justice to the splendid variety and its natural ageing capacity.

○ La Volpe all'Uva Pecorino '12	♟♟	3*
● Montepulciano d'Abruzzo Aulicus '12	♟♟	3*
○ Aer '14	♟♟	3
⊙ Montepulciano d'Abruzzo Cerasuolo Omen '14	♟♟	3
⊙ Montepulciano d'Abruzzo Cerasuolo Palio '14	♟♟	2*
○ Pecorino Palio '14	♟♟	2*
○ Trebbiano d'Abruzzo Palio '14	♟♟	2*
● Montepulciano d'Abruzzo Laus Vitae '09	♟	5
● Montepulciano d'Abruzzo Palio '13	♟	2
○ Passerina Tibi '14	♟	3
○ Trebbiano d'Abruzzo Laus Vitae '11	♟	5
● Montepulciano d'Abruzzo Aulicus '11	♟♟	3
● Montepulciano d'Abruzzo Caroso Ris. '10	♟♟	4
● Montepulciano d'Abruzzo Palio '12	♟♟	2*
○ Pecorino Quoque '13	♟♟	3

Collebello - Tenuta Terraviva

VIA DEL LAGO, 19
64081 TORTORETO [TE]
TEL. 0861786056
www.tenutaterraviva.it

CELLAR SALES
PRE-BOOKED VISITS
ANNUAL PRODUCTION 65,000 bottles
HECTARES UNDER VINE 18.00
VITICULTURE METHOD Certified Organic

At Tortoreto, in the competitive Colline Teramane zone, this winery has reinvented itself in just a few years. Almost 20 hectares on the gentle hills between the Adriatic and Gran Sasso are now fully organic and use spontaneous fermentation to make wines in a solid, classic style using traditional, minimal winemaking techniques. The wines are cleaner and more focused every year, in a natural style which is increasingly appealing. The Montepulciano 2013 is fragrant and easy-going, with clear-cut citrussy fruit on the nose as well as stylish floral hints, and a rounded, well-paced flavour. The Luì 2012 is a charming, old-school Montepulciano with husky aromas of blood-rich meat and ashes, and a close-knit, mouthwatering palate. The Passerina is clear-cut and fragrant with wildflowers and herbs.

● Montepulciano d'Abruzzo '13	♟♟	2*
● Montepulciano d'Abruzzo Luì '12	♟♟	3*
○ Abruzzo Pecorino Ekwo '14	♟♟	3
⊙ Montepulciano d'Abruzzo Cerasuolo Giusi '14	♟♟	2*
○ Passerina 12.1 '14	♟♟	2*
○ Trebbiano d'Abruzzo '14	♟♟	2*
○ Trebbiano d'Abruzzo Mario's 41 '13	♟♟	3
● Polifemus '09	♟	2
○ Ekwo '13	♟♟	3
○ Ekwo Terraviva '12	♟♟	2*
● Montepulciano d'Abruzzo Luì '11	♟♟	3*
○ Passerina 12.1 '13	♟♟	2*
○ Solobianco '13	♟♟	2*
○ Trebbiano d'Abruzzo '13	♟♟	2*
○ Trebbiano d'Abruzzo Mario's 40 '12	♟♟	3

Collefrisio

LOC. PIANE DI MAGGIO
66030 FRISA [CH]
TEL. 0859039074
www.collefrisio.it

CELLAR SALES
PRE-BOOKED VISITS
ANNUAL PRODUCTION 230,000 bottles
HECTARES UNDER VINE 36.00
VITICULTURE METHOD Certified Organic
SUSTAINABLE WINERY

A solid Abruzzo winery that exports its
modern, carefully made wines all over
the world. There are two estates: one
facing the Adriatic, the other on the
Colline Teatine at the foot of Majella. Both
are long-standing winegrowing terroirs,
moulding wines that reveal a harmonious
blend of modern and traditional features.
From the tidy and affordable basic line to
the go-getting Montepulciano reds, all the
wines have the gift of pleasing consumers.
An interesting tasting with a range of
well-made, compelling wines in a modern,
intriguing style. The Morrecine 2013 is
a close-knit, ambitious Montepulciano
with old-fashioned smoky aromas and a
fresh-tasting, dynamic flavour, with clearly
defined, clean hints of fruit. The Pecorino
Vignaquadra 2014 is interesting: boisterous
aromas of catmint and juniper, with a
tangy, balsamic palate. The uncomplicated
Trebbiano d'Abruzzo Filarè 2014 is a
perfect white for serving with food, with
fresh flavour and aromas of freshly mown
grass.

● Montepulciano d'Abruzzo Morrecine '13	♟♟	2*
● Montepulciano d'Abruzzo '11	♟♟	2*
⊙ Montepulciano d'Abruzzo Cerasuolo '14	♟♟	2*
○ Passerina Vignaquadra '14	♟♟	2*
○ Pecorino Vignaquadra '14	♟♟	2*
○ Trebbiano d'Abruzzo Filarè '14	♟♟	2*
○ Falanghina Vignaquadra '14	♟	2
● Montepulciano d'Abruzzo '13	♟	2
● Montepulciano d'Abruzzo Vignaquadra '11	♟	3
○ Trebbiano d'Abruzzo Vignaquadra '13	♟	3
⊙ Montepulciano d'Abruzzo Cerasuolo '13	♟♟	2*
● Montepulciano d'Abruzzo Morrecine '12	♟♟	2*
● Montepulciano d'Abruzzo Vignaquadra '10	♟♟ 3	
○ Pecorino Vignaquadra '13	♟♟	2*
○ Trebbiano d'Abruzzo Filarè '13	♟♟	2*
○ Trebbiano d'Abruzzo Vignaquadra '11	♟♟	3*

Contesa

S.DA DELLE VIGNE, 28
65010 COLLECORVINO [PE]
TEL. 0858205078
www.contesa.it

CELLAR SALES
PRE-BOOKED VISITS
RESTAURANT SERVICE
ANNUAL PRODUCTION 260,000 bottles
HECTARES UNDER VINE 39.00

This beautiful estate of over 40 hectares
is on the sunny Collecorvino hills near
Pescara, between Majella and the sea.
It has always produced quality grapes
and the lovely, hi-tech cellar is now firmly
in place. Here Rocco Pasetti turns out
wines in an interesting combination of
modern and traditional features. The new
generation brought a breath of fresh air
and curiosity about more traditional, less
invasive procedures, making it possible to
mould wines that are always impressive
and appeal to an increasingly diverse
consumer base. This year's tasting bears
witness to the changes that have taken
place in this lovely Collecorvino winery. The
wines are tidy and well-made, sometimes
seeking more freedom: the S'ha Fatte
da Se 2014 Trebbiano undergoes
spontaneous fermentation, doing justice
to the varietal aromas: it is still a little stiff
but will unbend over time on typical hints
of hazelnuts and aromatic herbs. The
Montepulciano Riserva 2010 is densely
textured with a warm, sunny flavour.

○ Trebbiano d'Abruzzo Fermentazione Spontanea S'ha fatt' da sole '14	♟♟	3*
● Montepulciano d'Abruzzo Ris. '10	♟♟	4
○ Passerina Vigna Corvino '14	♟♟	2*
○ Pecorino '14	♟♟	3
● Montepulciano d'Abruzzo '13	♟	3
⊙ Montepulciano d'Abruzzo Cerasuolo '14	♟	2
● Montepulciano d'Abruzzo V. Corvino '14	♟	2
● Montepulciano d'Abruzzo Ris. '08	♟♟♟	3*
● Montepulciano d'Abruzzo '12	♟♟	3
⊙ Montepulciano d'Abruzzo Cerasuolo '13	♟♟	2*
● Montepulciano d'Abruzzo Ris. '09	♟♟	4
○ Pecorino '13	♟♟	3
○ Trebbiano d'Abruzzo '13	♟♟	2*

De Angelis Corvi

C.DA PIGNOTTO
64010 CONTROGUERRA [TE]
TEL. 086189475
www.deangeliscorvi.it

CELLAR SALES
PRE-BOOKED VISITS
ANNUAL PRODUCTION 40,000 bottles
HECTARES UNDER VINE 8.00
VITICULTURE METHOD Certified Organic

The 13 hectares of certified organic vineyards are in Controguerra, at the heart of the Colline Teramane terroir, between the mountains and the sea. The winery is in a transitional phase: a few years ago Corrado decided to set aside the classic, conventional regime for a more traditional but complex route, and the wines are developing every year. The choices of organic farming, spontaneous fermentation and minimalist, old-style vinification are paying off and bringing the first tangible results. The wines presented for tasting this year are all good with recognizable identity. The Fonte Ravagliano 2014 is a deceptively simple, food-friendly Trebbiano with subtle floral aromas and typical hints of hazelnuts. The expansive flavour develops over hints of juicy apples and pears. The Cerasuolo 2014 is dark and brooding with hints of almonds and wild strawberries and a linear, acidic sensation, fresh and well-paced. The Elevito 2010 is a lively, thrusting Colline Teramane.

⊙ Montepulciano d'Abruzzo Cerasuolo Sup. '14	♟♟ 2*
○ Trebbiano d'Abruzzo Sup. Fonte Raviliano '14	♟♟ 2*
● Montepulciano d'Abruzzo Colline Teramane Elevito Ris. '10	♟♟ 5
● Montepulciano d'Abruzzo Fonte Raviliano '12	♟♟ 3
● Montepulciano d'Abruzzo '06	♟♟ 3*
⊙ Montepulciano d'Abruzzo Cerasuolo Sup. '11	♟♟ 3
⊙ Montepulciano d'Abruzzo Cerasuolo Sup. '10	♟♟ 3
● Montepulciano d'Abruzzo Colline Teramane Elevito Ris. '09	♟♟ 5
● Montepulciano d'Abruzzo Fonte Raviliano '08	♟♟ 3

Nicoletta De Fermo

C.DA CORDANO
65014 LORETO APRUTINO [PE]
TEL. 0858289136
www.defermo.it

PRE-BOOKED VISITS
ANNUAL PRODUCTION 16,000 bottles
HECTARES UNDER VINE 17.00
VITICULTURE METHOD Certified Organic

This is one of the artisan wineries changing the face of Abruzzo wine. The wines are traditional and carefully made, drawing in equal measure from old teachings and more up-to-date focus and generosity. The few bottles produced are the children of this lovely estate at Loreto Aprutino, in the heart of Abruzzo, between the Adriatic and Majella. The rest is up to the biodynamic care, never flaunted, maniacal attention in the old cellar and the use of concrete and used oak barrels during vinification. Only a few wines offered for tasting from this little artisan winery in Loreto Aprutino, but all sturdy and very impressive. The Cerasuolo Le Cince 2014 does the type justice, earning Tre Bicchieri. As tradition dictates this is a perfect wine to serve with food, with complex aromas of bitter almonds and medicinal herbs, and a vibrant, well-paced flavour, ever-changing on the palate in a succession of sweet and acidic sensations. The Prologo is a very robust and boisterous Montepulciano, still rather youthful.

⊙ Montepulciano d'Abruzzo Cerasuolo Le Cince '14	♟♟♟ 4*
● Montepulciano d'Abruzzo Prologo '13	♟♟ 5
○ Don Carlino Pecorino '14	♟♟ 4
○ Launegild '13	♟♟ 5
● Montepulciano d'Abruzzo Prologo '12	♟♟♟ 5
○ Don Carlino '13	♟♟ 4
○ Launegild '12	♟♟ 5
⊙ Montepulciano d'Abruzzo Cerasuolo Le Cince '13	♟♟ 4
⊙ Montepulciano d'Abruzzo Cerasuolo Le Cince '12	♟♟ 4
● Montepulciano d'Abruzzo Prologo '11	♟♟ 5
● Montepulciano d'Abruzzo Prologo '10	♟♟ 2*
○ Piè Tancredi '11	♟♟ 4

Eredi Legonziano

C.DA NASUTI, 169
66034 LANCIANO [CH]
TEL. 087245210
www.eredilegonziano.it

Faraone

VIA NAZIONALE PER TERAMO, 290
64020 GIULIANOVA [TE]
TEL. 0858071804
www.faraonevini.it

CELLAR SALES
PRE-BOOKED VISITS
ANNUAL PRODUCTION 50,000 bottles
HECTARES UNDER VINE 9.00

The lower Chieti area is all about large quantities, with a significant history of cooperative wineries, and has changed the face of Abruzzo winegrowing. This is one of the leading provinces in Italy in terms of production, but times change and the need to work on quality has prevailed. This must have been the thought process here in this venerable Lanciano cooperative, where the courage and passion of country folk now look to a new season. The increasingly impressive wines offer a glimpse of further development in the future. The sturdy Metodo Classicos are masterful, following the recognizable path of native varieties without dosage. The 36 is a surprising sparkler, balancing grip, salty tang and fruity vigour. Very good. The Carmine Festa is the most ambitious, with 48 months on the yeasts and sweet, subtle floral aromas. We also liked the sinewy Pecorino with lovely salty aromas.

Faraone is a venerable Colline Teramane winery on the Giulianova hills, opened in the early Seventies. Just nine hectares of vineyards are farmed with rural passion and hard graft, producing grapes of legendary quality. Giovanni, helped by his children, runs the winery with a classic and traditional hand, making artisan wines strongly imprinted with the terroir, pleasingly husky and with unexpected ageing potential. Santa Maria dell'Arco is a Colline Teramane released almost ten years after the harvest. Perky aromas on the nose with clear-cut, appealing fruit and floral hints, while the flavour is sound and easy-going with a lovely fresh hint of blood oranges driving the palate. The Le Vigne di Faraone 2013 is a charming Trebbiano with salty, grassy aromas and a still-vigorous palate which hints at excellent ageing potential.

○ Abruzzo Spumante	♀♀ 3
○ Brut M. Cl. 36	♀♀ 4
○ Carmine Festa M. Cl.	♀♀ 4
○ Pecorino Methys '13	♀♀ 2*
⊙ Abruzzo Rosé	♀ 3
● Montepulciano d'Abruzzo Diocleziano '11	♀ 2
○ Spumante Brut	♀ 3
○ Brut Legonziano	♀♀ 3
○ Brut M. Cl. 36	♀♀ 4
● Montepulciano d'Abruzzo Diocleziano '10	♀♀ 2*
○ Pecorino Anxanum '13	♀♀ 2*

⊙ Montepulciano d'Abruzzo Cerasuolo Le Vigne di Faraone '14	♀♀ 2*
● Montepulciano d'Abruzzo Colline Teramane Santa Maria dell'Arco Ris. '06	♀♀ 4
● Montepulciano d'Abruzzo Le Vigne di Faraone '11	♀♀ 2*
○ Trebbiano d'Abruzzo Le Vigne di Faraone '13	♀♀ 2*
⊙ Montepulciano d'Abruzzo Cerasuolo Le Vigne '13	♀♀ 2*
⊙ Montepulciano d'Abruzzo Cerasuolo Le Vigne '11	♀♀ 2*
● Montepulciano d'Abruzzo Le Vigne '09	♀♀ 2*
○ Passerina Colle Pietro '12	♀♀ 2*
○ Trebbiano d'Abruzzo Le Vigne '12	♀♀ 2*
○ Trebbiano d'Abruzzo Le Vigne '10	♀♀ 2*

ABRUZZO

Tenuta I Fauri

S.DA CORTA, 9
66100 CHIETI
TEL. 0871332627
www.tenutaifauri.it

CELLAR SALES
PRE-BOOKED VISITS
ANNUAL PRODUCTION 150,000 bottles
HECTARES UNDER VINE 35.00

These are crucial years for this lovely artisan winery in the Colline Teatine, years of growth and consolidation, after easy initial success. The wines produced by Valentina and Luigi Di Camillo are no longer a surprise: straightforward and impactful, excellent table wines, and never commonplace or predictable. The splendid grapes are moulded by the variable character of the 30 or so hectares near Chieti, scattered between the Adriatic and Majella's slopes, and the legendary care of the winegrowers themselves. The harvest is processed in the understated Ari cellars with meticulous care and respect for tradition. A memorable tasting this year from this cellar. The carefree wines mainly impressed us with their precise interpretation of a tricky year like 2014. The Pecorino walks away with another Tre Bicchieri, thanks to herb and citrus aromas, and a generous, close-knit flavour. The 2014 version of the Ottobre Rosso, a Montepulciano with a very pleasing palate, is particularly well-focused.

○ Abruzzo Pecorino '14	♟♟♟	2*
● Montepulciano d'Abruzzo		
Ottobre Rosso '14	♟♟	2*
○ Passerina '14	♟♟	2*
● Montepulciano d'Abruzzo Baldovino '14	♟♟	2*
⊙ Montepulciano d'Abruzzo Cerasuolo		
Baldovino '14	♟♟	2*
○ Spumante Brut	♟♟	2*
○ Trebbiano d'Abruzzo Baldovino '14	♟♟	2*
⊙ Alba Rosa '14	♟	2
● Graffionero '14	♟	2
○ Abruzzo Pecorino '13	♟♟♟	2*
⊙ Alba Rosa Frizzante '13	♟♟	2*
○ Genio '12	♟♟	2*
● Montepulciano d'Abruzzo Baldovino '13	♟♟	2*
● Montepulciano d'Abruzzo		
Santa Cecilia '11	♟♟	4

Gentile

VIA DEL GIARDINO, 7
67025 OFENA [AQ]
TEL. 0862956618
www.gentilevini.it

CELLAR SALES
PRE-BOOKED VISITS
ANNUAL PRODUCTION 90,000 bottles
HECTARES UNDER VINE 12.00

This small artisan winery, with only a few hectares of vineyards, impresses us more every year. This is the mountainous part of Abruzzo, a plateau below Gran Sasso, entirely surrounded by mountains with unusual soil and climate conditions: harsh land; significant temperature variation; unrelenting sunshine by day, and by night-time cold due to the wind from the mountains, which stabilizes the aromas. The rest is down to a countryman's care in the vineyards and artisan skill in the cellar. A pared-down array of wines presented for tasting bears witness to a cellar working towards increasingly focused products. The Pecorino Piè delle Grotte 2014 manages to impress even in a difficult year, with lively aromas of Seville oranges and tropical fruit, with a lovely well-paced flavour backed up by lively acidity, making it a good table wine. The Montepulciano 2014 is gutsy and mouthwatering with varietal aromas and a challenging tannic texture.

○ Pecorino Piè della Grotta '14	♟♟	2*
⊙ Montepulciano d'Abruzzo Cerasuolo		
Pié della Grotta '14	♟♟	3
● Montepulciano d'Abruzzo		
Pié della Grotta '13	♟♟	2*
○ Trebbiano d'Abruzzo Pié della Grotta '14	♟♟	1*
● Montepulciano d'Abruzzo		
Vecchie Vigne Ris. '11	♟	4
⊙ Montepulciano d'Abruzzo Cerasuolo		
Pié della Grotta '13	♟♟	3
● Montepulciano d'Abruzzo		
Pié della Grotta '12	♟♟	2*
● Montepulciano d'Abruzzo V. di Ofena '11	♟♟	4
● Montepulciano d'Abruzzo V. V. Ris. '09	♟♟	4
○ Pecorino Piè della Grotta '13	♟♟	2*
○ Trebbiano d'Abruzzo Pié della Grotta '13	♟♟	1*
○ Trebbiano d'Abruzzo V. di Ofena '12	♟♟	2*

★Dino Illuminati

C.DA SAN BIAGIO, 18
64010 CONTROGUERRA [TE]
TEL. 0861808008
www.illuminativini.it

CELLAR SALES
PRE-BOOKED VISITS
ANNUAL PRODUCTION 1,150,000 bottles
HECTARES UNDER VINE 130.00

All over the world, Illuminati means Montepulciano d'Abruzzo. Cavalier Dino was a pioneer who brought this DOC to wine shops across the globe. Without his pride and confidence in the quality of these gentle hills overlooking the sea, the Colline Teramane would not exist. These Mediterranean-style wines are the offspring of generous soils, blazing sunshine, sea breezes, embracing the challenging extract and staggering strength. Dino's children are an increasingly present in the cellar, bravely refusing to make too many changes to their lovely Controguerra winery. Like every year, the line-up presented by this Teramo winery is valid and extensive. The Pieluni is an ambitious Montepulciano Colline Teramane, powerful and sunny, which impressed us all with its close-knit, alluring texture and tangy, generous flavour. Tre Bicchieri. The "simple" Riparosso 2014, a very pleasant Montepulciano produced in large quantities, is excellent as usual.

● Montepulciano d'Abruzzo Colline Teramane Pieluni Ris. '10	♥♥♥	6
○ Brut M. Cl. '11	♥♥	4
○ Controguerra Bianco Costalupo '14	♥♥	2*
● Controguerra Rosso Lumen Ris. '10	♥♥	5
⊙ Montepulciano d'Abruzzo Cerasuolo Campirosa '14	♥♥	2*
● Montepulciano d'Abruzzo Ilico '13	♥♥	2*
● Montepulciano d'Abruzzo Riparosso '14	♥♥	2*
● Montepulciano d'Abruzzo Spiano '14	♥♥	2*
○ Controguerra Bianco Pligia '14	♥	2
○ Controguerra Pecorino '14	♥	2
● Montepulciano d'Abruzzo Colline Teramane Pieluni Ris. '07	♥♥♥	6
● Montepulciano d'Abruzzo Colline Teramane Zanna Ris. '10	♥♥♥	5
● Montepulciano d'Abruzzo Colline Teramane Zanna Ris. '08	♥♥♥	4*

★★Masciarelli

VIA GAMBERALE, 1
66010 SAN MARTINO SULLA MARRUCINA [CH]
TEL. 087185241
www.masciarelli.it

CELLAR SALES
PRE-BOOKED VISITS
ACCOMMODATION
ANNUAL PRODUCTION 2,500,000 bottles
HECTARES UNDER VINE 300.00
SUSTAINABLE WINERY

This winery is famous worldwide for its stylish Mediterranean-type wines, synonymous with Abruzzo. The numbers are impressive for an estate with an artisan soul: 400 hectares under vine in all four Abruzzo provinces; a variety of landscapes and a wealth of different soil and climate, terroirs and aspects; over four million bottles produced per year. The wines are always well-typed with recognizable identity, in perfect Masciarelli style: an impressive interpretation combining modern and traditional features. The array of labels presented for tasting this year is very impressive: lots of wines, all well-made and interesting. The Montepulciano Marina Cvetic 2013 is excellent with complex aromas ranging from ashes to clear-cut, lively fruit, and a close-knit, rounded palate with prominent, expansive, varietal tannins. The flavour is tangy and dynamic despite the powerful structure. The Montepulciano 2013 is very pleasing with typical, boisterous aromas.

● Montepulciano d'Abruzzo Marina Cvetic '13	♥♥♥	4*
○ Chardonnay Marina Cvetic '13	♥♥	5
● Montepulciano d'Abruzzo '13	♥♥	2*
⊙ Montepulciano d'Abruzzo Cerasuolo Villa Gemma '14	♥♥	3
● Montepulciano d'Abruzzo Colline Teramane Iskra '09	♥♥	5
● Montepulciano d'Abruzzo Gianni Masciarelli '13	♥♥	2*
○ Pecorino Castello di Semivicoli '14	♥♥	3
⊙ Rosé '14	♥♥	2*
○ Trebbiano d'Abruzzo Castello di Semivicoli '13	♥♥	5
○ Trebbiano d'Abruzzo Gianni Masciarelli '14	♥♥	2*
○ Trebbiano d'Abruzzo Marina Cvetic Ris. '13	♥♥	5

Camillo Montori

Loc. Piane Tronto, 80
64010 Controguerra [TE]
Tel. 0861809900
www.montorivini.it

CELLAR SALES
PRE-BOOKED VISITS
ACCOMMODATION AND RESTAURANT SERVICE
ANNUAL PRODUCTION 600,000 bottles
HECTARES UNDER VINE 50.00

This venerable Teramo winery is owned by Camillo Montori, one of the founding fathers of the Colline Teramane DOC, persuaded of the unique features of this slice of land between the Adriatic and Gran Sasso. The lovely Controguerra estate has 40 hectares under vine, with generous soil and intense sunshine to grow weighty, extract-rich grapes. The cellar, as always, works with large oak and lengthy maceration to create powerful, Mediterranean-style Montepulcianos that withstand the test of time. A somewhat below par tasting this year with tidy, well-focused wines just lacking that spark of recognizable identity that we have come to expect. The 2014 version of the Pecorino Fonte Cupa is less dynamic than usual due to the tricky year: lively aromatic herbs and citrus fruit on the nose, with a sweet, vibrant flavour. The Montepulciano Fontecupa 2011 has sunny, warm, complex aromas with hints of soot and red berries, and coffee and juicy fruit sensations on the palate.

⊙ Montepulciano d'Abruzzo Cerasuolo Fonte Cupa '14	🍷🍷 2*
● Montepulciano d'Abruzzo Colline Teramane Casa Montori '10	🍷🍷 2*
● Montepulciano d'Abruzzo Fonte Cupa '11	🍷🍷 2*
○ Pecorino Fonte Cupa '14	🍷🍷 3
○ Controguerra Passerina Fonte Cupa '14	🍷 2
○ Trebbiano d'Abruzzo Fonte Cupa '14	🍷 2
○ Controguerra Passerina Trend '13	🍷🍷 2*
● Montepulciano d'Abruzzo '10	🍷🍷 2*
● Montepulciano d'Abruzzo Colline Teramane Casa Montori '09	🍷🍷 2*
● Montepulciano d'Abruzzo Fonte Cupa '07	🍷🍷 2*
● Montepulciano d'Abruzzo Fonte Cupa Ris. '07	🍷🍷 2*
○ Pecorino Fonte Cupa '13	🍷🍷 3*
○ Pecorino Trend '13	🍷🍷 2*
○ Trebbiano d'Abruzzo Fonte Cupa '12	🍷🍷 2*

Bruno Nicodemi

C.da Veniglio
64024 Notaresco [TE]
Tel. 085895493
www.nicodemi.com

CELLAR SALES
PRE-BOOKED VISITS
ANNUAL PRODUCTION 250,000 bottles
HECTARES UNDER VINE 30.00

On this 30-hectare estate lying on the sunny Notaresco plain, this artisan winery is capably run by sister and brother Elena and Alessandro Nicodemi, the family's second generation of Teramo winegrowers. This estate is one of the leaders in the Colline Teramane zone, with its intense sunshine and generous soils offering mighty wines in a winning Mediterranean style, shaped by a terroir between mountains and sea. The line-up is as impressive as ever, from the solid and affordable classic line to the Montepulciano and Trebbiano crus. Nicodemi presents a pared-down list of: just a few wines but all impressive, from the incisive classic labels all the way up to the ambitious crus. The Notari 2012 earns Tre Bicchieri this year: a densely textured, powerful Montepulciano Colline Teramane with typical aromas of cherries and Mediterranean herbs, and confident but complex tannins with a lovely hint of ripe fruit. The Neromoro 2011 is powerful and still very young, but will open out well in the bottle.

● Montepulciano d'Abruzzo Colline Teramane Neromoro Ris. '11	🍷🍷 5
● Montepulciano d'Abruzzo Colline Teramane Notàri '12	🍷🍷 3*
● Montepulciano d'Abruzzo '13	🍷🍷 2*
⊙ Montepulciano d'Abruzzo Cerasuolo '14	🍷🍷 4
○ Trebbiano d'Abruzzo '14	🍷 2
● Montepulciano d'Abruzzo Colline Teramane Neromoro Ris. '09	🍷🍷🍷 5
● Montepulciano d'Abruzzo Colline Teramane Neromoro Ris. '03	🍷🍷🍷 5
● Montepulciano d'Abruzzo '12	🍷🍷 2*
⊙ Montepulciano d'Abruzzo Cerasuolo '13	🍷🍷 4
● Montepulciano d'Abruzzo Colline Teramane Notàri '11	🍷🍷 3*
● Montepulciano d'Abruzzo Colline Teramane Notàri '10	🍷🍷 3*
○ Trebbiano d'Abruzzo Notàri '13	🍷🍷 2*

Orlandi Contucci Ponno

LOC. PIANA DEGLI ULIVI, 1
64026 ROSETO DEGLI ABRUZZI [TE]
TEL. 0858944049
www.orlandicontucci.com

CELLAR SALES
PRE-BOOKED VISITS
ANNUAL PRODUCTION 180,000 bottles
HECTARES UNDER VINE 31.00

This winery shaped the history of the
Colline Teramane as one of the first to
work on quality and spread its wings.
Here in Roseto degli Abruzzi, overlooking
the Adriatic sea, with Gran Sasso behind,
the tumbling hills have always been
suited to winegrowing. The mountains
are just a few kilometres away so a cool
breeze constantly refreshes the vineyards,
producing high-flying wines. Alongside
the solid Montepulcianos are wines made
from non-native grapes, aiming for an
international elegance. A compact line-up
of red wines only, all interesting and
showing development. The Regia Specula
is a rounded, close-knit Colline Teramane
with vibrant aromas of Mediterranean
scrub and ripe fruit, and a dense flavour
over the supple, velvety tannins. The
Collefunaro 2011 is an expressive
Cabernet with freshly mown grass and
vibrant fruit on the nose and a smooth,
fragrant flavour despite the considerable
ageing.

● Colle Funaro '11	♟♟ 3
● Montepulciano d'Abruzzo Colline Teramane Podere La Regia Specula '12	♟♟ 3
● Montepulciano d'Abruzzo Colline Teramane Ris. '11	♟♟ 5
● Montepulciano d'Abruzzo Rubiolo '14	♟♟ 2*
● Liburnio '11	♟ 5
● Montepulciano d'Abruzzo Colline Teramane Podere La Regia Specula '10	♕♕ 3
● Montepulciano d'Abruzzo Colline Teramane Podere La Regia Specula '09	♕♕ 3
● Montepulciano d'Abruzzo Colline Teramane Ris. '10	♕♕ 5
● Montepulciano d'Abruzzo Colline Teramane Ris. '09	♕♕ 5

Pasetti

LOC. C.DA PRETARO
VIA SAN PAOLO, 21
66023 FRANCAVILLA AL MARE [CH]
TEL. 08561875
www.pasettivini.it

CELLAR SALES
PRE-BOOKED VISITS
ACCOMMODATION AND RESTAURANT SERVICE
ANNUAL PRODUCTION 600,000 bottles
HECTARES UNDER VINE 70.00

Two estates in the mountains: one
on the Pescara side of Majella, at
Pescosansonesco, and the other beneath
Gran Sasso at Capestrano. Overall, 70
rugged hectares under vine yielding grapes
moulded by the temperature variations and
rocky terrain. Vinification, as always, takes
place in the family cellar at Francavilla al
Mare, shaping popular wines with a modern
feel and contemporary style. Husband and
wife Mimmo and Laura Pasetti manage the
winery with their children, now the third
generation of winegrowers. A good tasting
with very well-made and pleasing wines.
The Testarossa 2011 is a nicely worked,
ambitious Montepulciano, distinctively
typical and varietal, with subtle, stylish oaky
aromas, and a bright flavour with clear-cut
fruit and varietal acidity. The Pecorino is a
classic and the 2014 version is perky and
fresh with citrus fruit and herbs.

● Montepulciano d'Abruzzo Testarossa '11	♟♟ 4
○ Abruzzo Pecorino '14	♟♟ 2*
● Montepulciano d'Abruzzo '12	♟♟ 2*
⊙ Testarossa Rosato '14	♟♟ 2*
○ Trebbiano d'Abruzzo Zarachè '14	♟♟ 2*
● Diecicoppe '14	♟ 2
○ Passerina Testarossa '14	♟ 2
○ Abruzzo Pecorino Colle Civetta '13	♕♕ 3
○ Gesmino '10	♕♕ 4
● Montepulciano d'Abruzzo '11	♕♕ 2*
● Montepulciano d'Abruzzo '10	♕♕ 2*
● Montepulciano d'Abruzzo Testarossa '10	♕♕ 4
○ Passerina Testarossa '13	♕♕ 2*
○ Trebbiano d'Abruzzo Zarachè '13	♕♕ 2*

Emidio Pepe

VIA CHIESI, 10
64010 TORANO NUOVO [TE]
TEL. 0861856493
www.emidiopepe.com

CELLAR SALES
PRE-BOOKED VISITS
ACCOMMODATION AND RESTAURANT SERVICE
ANNUAL PRODUCTION 80,000 bottles
HECTARES UNDER VINE 15.00
VITICULTURE METHOD Certified Biodynamic

This artisan winery is a slice of Italian history, beautifully described by Mario Soldati. Little or nothing has changed since then in this lovely Torano Nuova estate. The generations continue, the wines have become legendary worldwide. The 15 hectares under vine lie on a gentle series of hills in a dazzling landscape, a few kilometres from the sea with Gran Sasso behind. The old Abruzzo pergola vines are tended with a countryman's passion and organic or biodynamic methods. In the cellar the recipe remains the same: vinification in concrete and lengthy ageing. A bare-bones line-up as usual with a very good Trebbiano 2013 showing a multifaceted nose with hints of freshly mown grass and typical toasty hints, and a rounded, fragrant flavour supported by apple and pear fruit. The Montepulciano 2012 is still very young but already promising, with consistent sooty aromas, a typical husky note and bubbly fruit. The Cerasuolo is a dark and very approachable table wine.

Pietrantonj

VIA SAN SEBASTIANO, 38
67030 VITTORITO [AQ]
TEL. 0864727102
www.vinipietrantonj.it

CELLAR SALES
PRE-BOOKED VISITS
ANNUAL PRODUCTION 650,000 bottles
HECTARES UNDER VINE 60.00

This venerable winery is in inland, at Vittorito, on the Majella slopes near L'Aquila, where land is unforgiving and hard to farm. This is a traditional growing area for montepulciano grapes. Over the years, many have moved to the more fertile coastal plains, but Pietrantonj remains, growing grapes with artisan skill and transforming them in a classic style, with lengthy maceration and ageing in large oak. The functional, multi-layered cellar is a splendid feat of winemaking architecture, with an old glass-tiled tank. An array of well-focused wines often plays up acidity and aromas moulded by local temperature variation. The Cerano 2014 is the usual high-altitude Montepulciano, with vibrant fruit and mountain herbs on the nose and a dense, rounded flavour with ripe cherries giving way to rosemary and thyme, and settling into the varietal acidity that holds it all together. The Temè 2014 is a fresh-tasting, perky Pecorino with nicely paced acidity and floral hints.

● Montepulciano d'Abruzzo '12	❦❦ 6
○ Trebbiano d'Abruzzo '13	❦❦ 5
⊙ Montepulciano d'Abruzzo Cerasuolo '14	❦❦ 5
● Montepulciano d'Abruzzo '98	❦❦❦ 8
● Montepulciano d'Abruzzo '11	❦❦ 6
● Montepulciano d'Abruzzo '10	❦❦ 6
● Montepulciano d'Abruzzo '09	❦❦ 5
● Montepulciano d'Abruzzo '08	❦❦ 5
⊙ Montepulciano d'Abruzzo Cerasuolo '13	❦❦ 5
⊙ Montepulciano d'Abruzzo Cerasuolo '12	❦❦ 5
○ Trebbiano d'Abruzzo '12	❦❦ 5
○ Trebbiano d'Abruzzo '11	❦❦ 5
○ Trebbiano d'Abruzzo '10	❦❦ 6
○ Trebbiano d'Abruzzo '09	❦❦ 5

⊙ Montepulciano d'Abruzzo Cerasuolo Arboreo '14	❦❦ 2*
⊙ Montepulciano d'Abruzzo Cerasuolo Cerano '14	❦❦ 3
○ Pecorino Brut Temè '14	❦❦ 3
● Passito Rosso '11	❦ 4
○ Trebbiano d'Abruzzo Arboreo '14	❦ 1*
● Montepulciano d'Abruzzo Arboreo '11	❦❦ 2*
● Montepulciano d'Abruzzo Cerano '10	❦❦ 2*
● Montepulciano d'Abruzzo Cerano Ris. '10	❦❦ 3
● Montepulciano d'Abruzzo Cerano Ris. '09	❦❦ 3*
⊙ Montepulciano d'Abruzzo Cerasuolo Cerano '13	❦❦ 3
⊙ Montepulciano d'Abruzzo Sup. Cerasuolo Cerano '12	❦❦ 3*
○ Trebbiano d'Abruzzo Cerano '13	❦❦ 2*

San Lorenzo Vini

C.DA PLAVIGNANO, 2
64035 CASTILENTI [TE]
TEL. 0861999325
www.sanlorenzovini.com

CELLAR SALES
PRE-BOOKED VISITS
ANNUAL PRODUCTION 800,000 bottles
HECTARES UNDER VINE 150.00

For years this impressive and large winery
on the border between the provinces of
Teramo and Pescara has presented a
blend of modern style and determined
quality. The 100-plus hectares on the
big Castilenti estate turn out powerful,
very generous wines, often tamed by a
modern winemaking style to appeal to the
international markets. From the classic
native Abruzzo varieties to international
grapes and the richer Montepulciano
crus, the main features of San Lorenzo
wines are always their rich Mediterranean
body and pleasing flavour. The range
presented this year is particularly
well-stocked. The Casa Bianca 2013
is a mouthwatering Montepulciano that
undergoes spontaneous fermentation, with
a boisterous, generous but well-handled
flavour. The Escoll is an ambitious Colline
Teramane: the 2010 is more paced and
dynamic with Mediterranean flavour backed
up by varietal acidity.

● Montepulciano d'Abruzzo Casabianca '13	♟♟	2*
● Montepulciano d'Abruzzo Colline Teramane Escol Ris. '10	♟♟	5
○ Il Pecorino '14	♟♟	2*
● Montepulciano d'Abruzzo '13	♟♟	2*
● Montepulciano d'Abruzzo Colline Teramane Oinos '11	♟♟	4
● Montepulciano d'Abruzzo Sirio '13	♟♟	2*
○ Trebbiano d'Abruzzo Casabianca '14	♟♟	2*
○ La Passerina '14	♟	2
● Montepulciano d'Abruzzo Aldebaran '14	♟	2
● Montepulciano d'Abruzzo Antares '12	♟	2
● Montepulciano d'Abruzzo Zerosolfiti '14	♟	2
○ Trebbiano d'Abruzzo Sirio '14	♟	1*
● Montepulciano d'Abruzzo Antares '11	♟♟	2*
● Montepulciano d'Abruzzo Casabianca '12	♟♟	2*

Tiberio

C.DA LA VOTA
65020 CUGNOLI [PE]
TEL. 0858576744
www.tiberio.it

CELLAR SALES
PRE-BOOKED VISITS
ANNUAL PRODUCTION 90,000 bottles
HECTARES UNDER VINE 30.00

In a very few years this artisan winery has
skilfully carved itself a front-row spot with
personal, recognizable wines that offer a
good expression of the Colline Pescaresi
terroir. Cristiana Tiberio is particularly
sensitive to fresh, well-paced wines
showing balanced acidity. The 30-hectare
estate on the Cugnoli hills, directly below
Majella, enjoys a constant breeze from
sea to mountains and back again, with a
significant temperature variation moulding
the aromas and flavours. The cellar sticks
to minimal procedures, spontaneous
fermentation and artisan care. A pared-
down line-up presented by Tiberio this
year includes just a few wines but all very
impressive. The Montepulciano 2013 earns
a Tre Bicchieri, showing that this winery
makes more than whites. This excellent
red is made by spontaneous fermentation
and minimal winemaking techniques, with
clear-cut, multifaceted fruit. The Pecorino
is, as ever, one of the best and most
dynamic in the region, and will improve
further in bottle.

● Montepulciano d'Abruzzo '13	♟♟♟	2*
○ Pecorino '14	♟♟	3*
○ Pecorino FS '14	♟♟	3*
⊙ Montepulciano d'Abruzzo Cerasuolo '14	♟♟	2*
○ Trebbiano d'Abruzzo '14	♟♟	2*
○ Pecorino '13	♟♟♟	3*
○ Pecorino '12	♟♟♟	3*
○ Pecorino '11	♟♟♟	3*
○ Pecorino '10	♟♟♟	3
● Montepulciano d'Abruzzo '12	♟♟	2
⊙ Montepulciano d'Abruzzo Cerasuolo '13	♟♟	2*
○ Trebbiano d'Abruzzo '13	♟♟	2*
○ Trebbiano d'Abruzzo '12	♟♟	2*
○ Trebbiano d'Abruzzo Fonte Canale '13	♟♟	2*

ABRUZZO

Cantina Tollo

VIA GARIBALDI, 68
66010 TOLLO [CH]
TEL. 087196251
www.cantinatollo.it

CELLAR SALES
PRE-BOOKED VISITS
ANNUAL PRODUCTION 13,000,000 bottles
HECTARES UNDER VINE 3,200.00

This cooperative winery in the province of
Chieti has made Abruzzo wine famous on
the competitive international scene. With
3,500 hectares of vineyards, over 1,000
growers, and almost 13 million bottles
produced per year yet the cooperative has
never lost sight of quality. The wealth of
landscapes and terroirs where the growers
work contributes prime fruit, judiciously
transformed into a variety of wines in
the modern cellar. Ranging from fresh,
fragrant native varieties to traditional
Trebbianos and ambitious Montepulciano
d'Abruzzo crus, the array of labels is
always interesting, with both typical and
international styles. A significant tasting in
terms of both quantity and quality: the new
Montepulciano d'Abruzzo Mo Ris. 2011
impressed us all from the start with very
typical ash and lively fruit aromas and a
rounded, complex flavour, developing well
over focused tannins. The Montepulciano
Aldiano Riserva 2011 is full-bodied
and powerful with appealing husky,
varietal aromas and an approachable,
mouthwatering palate.

● Montepulciano d'Abruzzo Mo Ris. '11	♥♥♥ 2*
○ Cretico Chardonnay '13	♥♥ 4
● Montepulciano d'Abruzzo Aldiano Ris. '11	♥♥ 3
● Montepulciano d'Abruzzo Biologico '14	♥♥ 2*
⊙ Montepulciano d'Abruzzo Cerasuolo Hedòs '14	♥♥ 3
● Montepulciano d'Abruzzo Colle Secco Rubì '12	♥♥ 2*
● Montepulciano d'Abruzzo Heliko '14	♥♥ 3
○ Cococciola C '14	♥ 2
○ Pecorino '14	♥ 3
○ Trebbiano d'Abruzzo Aldiano '14	♥ 2
○ Trebbiano d'Abruzzo Biologico '14	♥ 2
● Montepulciano d'Abruzzo Cagiòlo Ris. '09	♥♥♥ 4*
○ Trebbiano d'Abruzzo C'Incanta '11	♥♥♥ 4*
○ Trebbiano d'Abruzzo C'Incanta '10	♥♥♥ 4*

Torre dei Beati

C.DA POGGIORAGONE, 56
65014 LORETO APRUTINO [PE]
TEL. 0854916069
www.torredeibeati.it

CELLAR SALES
PRE-BOOKED VISITS
ANNUAL PRODUCTION 100,000 bottles
HECTARES UNDER VINE 20.00
VITICULTURE METHOD Certified Organic
SUSTAINABLE WINERY

This impressive winery lies on the gentle
Pescara hills at Loreto Aprutino, between
the mountains and the Adriatic. Adriana
Galasso and Fausto Albanese, life and
business partners, set up this small artisan
winery which produces powerful, very
recognizable wines. The recipe is always
the same: a few well-tended hectares,
organically farmed; minimal, artisan cellar
techniques shaping a limited number
of bottles lavished with individual care.
The range includes fragrant whites and
powerful Montepulciano crus. A fully
impressive line-up of labels demonstrates
the state of health of this artisan Loreto
winery, placing it at the heights of Abruzzo
winemaking. The Cocciapazza 2012 is
a typical, old-school Montepulciano with
lovely fruity aromas and varietal spirit; it is
still too young but will unbend over time.
The Trebbiano 2013 reveals typical toasty
sensations and hints of freshly mown
grass, with a rounded, relaxed flavour.

⊙ Montepulciano d'Abruzzo Cerasuolo Rosa-ae '14	♥♥ 2*
● Montepulciano d'Abruzzo Mazzamurello '12	♥♥ 5
○ Trebbiano d'Abruzzo Bianchi Grilli per la Testa '13	♥♥ 4
○ Abruzzo Pecorino Giocheremo con i Fiori '14	♥♥ 3
● Montepulciano d'Abruzzo '13	♥♥ 2*
● Montepulciano d'Abruzzo Cocciapazza '12	♥♥ 5
● Montepulciano d'Abruzzo Cocciapazza '11	♥♥♥ 4*
● Montepulciano d'Abruzzo Cocciapazza '10	♥♥♥ 4*
● Montepulciano d'Abruzzo Cocciapazza '09	♥♥♥ 4*

Tenuta Ulisse

VIA SAN POLO, 40
66014 CRECCHIO [CH]
TEL. 0871407733
www.tenutaulisse.it

CELLAR SALES
PRE-BOOKED VISITS
ANNUAL PRODUCTION 550,000 bottles
HECTARES UNDER VINE 75.00

Generations of the Ulisse family have cultivated vineyards in the Crecchio area between Majella and the Adriatic, whose powerful, generous wines have made Montepulciano's fortune around the world. But this artisan cellar has taken a different path, with estates scattered across various parts of Chieti province yielding generous fruit tended traditionally and conversion in progress to organic farming. The grapes are processed in the lovely new cellar with an efficient blend of traditional and modern styles. Vinification in concrete and natural fermentation do the rest, producing wines that preserve the freshness of the fruit and the impetuous character of the variety. An impressive selection in quantity and quality from Ulisse. The Nativae 2014, a Montepulciano, undergoes spontaneous fermentation and vinification in concrete vats: its freshness and pacing earn it Tre Bicchieri for typical sooty hints on the nose alongside clear-cut fruit, and a multifaceted flavour supported by varietal edginess. The Montepulciano Amaranta 2013 is also very good.

● Montepulciano d'Abruzzo Nativae '14	▼▼▼	4*
○ Abruzzo Pecorino Nativae '14	▼▼	4
● Montepulciano d'Abruzzo Amaranta '13	▼▼	4
⊙ Montepulciano d'Abruzzo Cerasuolo Nativae '14	▼▼	3*
○ Cococciola Unico '14	▼▼	3
● Montepulciano d'Abruzzo Sogno di Ulisse '13	▼▼	2*
● Montepulciano d'Abruzzo Unico '13	▼▼	3
○ Passerina Unico '14	▼▼	3
○ Pecorino Brut Unico	▼▼	3
○ Pecorino Unico '14	▼▼	3
○ Trebbiano d'Abruzzo Nativae '14	▼▼	4
○ Trebbiano d'Abruzzo Unico '14	▼	3
○ Abruzzo Pecorino Nativae '13	♟♟♟	4*
● Montepulciano d'Abruzzo Nativae '12	♟♟♟	4*

La Valentina

VIA TORRETTA, 52
65010 SPOLTORE [PE]
TEL. 0854478158
www.lavalentina.it

CELLAR SALES
PRE-BOOKED VISITS
ANNUAL PRODUCTION 350,000 bottles
HECTARES UNDER VINE 40.00
VITICULTURE METHOD Certified Organic
SUSTAINABLE WINERY

Two estates, one on the gentle Pescara hills at Spoltore, opposite the Adriatic, and the other on the Pescara side of Majella. These are generous, potent, rugged mountainous lands which shape beautiful, powerful fruit with aromas sculpted by the temperature variations. The grapes are transformed at the modern Spoltore cellar to make interesting wines, the children of Abruzzo tradition as well as of newer, more restrained and less intrusive winemaking techniques. An exemplary tasting from La Valentina: the 2011 version of the Spelt earns it another Tre Bicchieri. This is a Montepulciano with boisterous aromas of morello cherries and medicinal herbs, a rounded, deep flavour, nicely tangy with acidic edge. The Bellovedere 2010 is also Montepulciano with rough, minerally aromas and a close-knit, dynamic palate. The edgy, food-friendly Trebbiano d'Abruzzo 2014 is remarkable.

● Montepulciano d'Abruzzo Spelt Ris. '11	▼▼▼	4*
● Montepulciano d'Abruzzo '13	▼▼	2*
● Montepulciano d'Abruzzo Bellovedere '10	▼▼	6
● Montepulciano d'Abruzzo Binomio Ris. '11	▼▼	5
⊙ Montepulciano d'Abruzzo Cerasuolo Sup. Binomio '14	▼▼	3
⊙ Montepulciano d'Abruzzo Cerasuolo Sup. Spelt '14	▼▼	3
○ Trebbiano d'Abruzzo '14	▼▼	2*
○ Trebbiano d'Abruzzo Sup. Spelt '14	▼▼	3
○ Fiano Bianco Colline Pescaresi '14	▼	3
○ Pecorino '14	▼	2
● Montepulciano d'Abruzzo Spelt '08	♟♟♟	3*
● Montepulciano d'Abruzzo Spelt '07	♟♟♟	3
● Montepulciano d'Abruzzo Spelt '05	♟♟♟	3
● Montepulciano d'Abruzzo Spelt Ris. '10	♟♟♟	3*

★★★Valentini

VIA DEL BAIO, 2
65014 LORETO APRUTINO [PE]
TEL. 0858291138

ANNUAL PRODUCTION 30,000 bottles
HECTARES UNDER VINE 60.00

These are important years for this famous
Loreto Aprutino winery. Francesco Paolo and
Elena, joined recently by their son Gabriele,
have reacted to a difficult period with the calm,
discreet style typical of Valentini, bringing a
new impetus to their business. Construction
is underway for a new, modern olive mill,
while the vineyards are being replanted. Over
the years, little has changed in the charming
old cellar in the town centre: vinification in
large oak barrels, and the watchful eye of
the artisan, tending and making decisions.
The 60 hectares of old Abruzzo pergola
vineyards yield as many as 30,000 bottles in
top years. Valentini presented the usual two
outstanding labels, while we await the return
of the Montepulciano, absent too long from
the ranks. The Trebbiano 2012 seduced us
again: a great wine, different every year in its
personal interpretation of the vintage, ready to
drink with a very appealing nose showing the
usual fermentative aromas and a series
of notes, from floral hints to medicinal herbs. A
complex and multifaceted white which
does justice to the grape variety. The
Cerasuolo 2014 is perky and sharp.

○ Trebbiano d'Abruzzo '12	♥♥♥	6
⊙ Montepulciano d'Abruzzo Cerasuolo '14	♥♥	6
● Montepulciano d'Abruzzo '06	♀♀♀	8
● Montepulciano d'Abruzzo '02	♀♀♀	8
● Montepulciano d'Abruzzo '01	♀♀♀	8
⊙ Montepulciano d'Abruzzo Cerasuolo '09	♀♀♀	6
⊙ Montepulciano d'Abruzzo Cerasuolo '08	♀♀♀	6
⊙ Montepulciano d'Abruzzo Cerasuolo '06	♀♀♀	6
○ Trebbiano d'Abruzzo '11	♀♀♀	6
○ Trebbiano d'Abruzzo '10	♀♀♀	6
○ Trebbiano d'Abruzzo '09	♀♀♀	6
○ Trebbiano d'Abruzzo '08	♀♀♀	6
○ Trebbiano d'Abruzzo '07	♀♀♀	6
○ Trebbiano d'Abruzzo '05	♀♀♀	6
○ Trebbiano d'Abruzzo '04	♀♀♀	6
○ Trebbiano d'Abruzzo '02	♀♀♀	6

★Valle Reale

LOC. SAN CALISTO
65026 POPOLI [PE]
TEL. 0859871039
www.vallereale.it

CELLAR SALES
PRE-BOOKED VISITS
ANNUAL PRODUCTION 250,000 bottles
HECTARES UNDER VINE 49.00
VITICULTURE METHOD Certified Organic
SUSTAINABLE WINERY

This winery produces mountain-style wines,
typical of the terrain and wide temperature
variation. One of the two estates is in
Popoli, near the attractive cellar, where
the Pescara hills become mountains,
in that strip of Majella leading up to the
perpetual snow. The other is near L'Aquila,
at Capestrano, just below the Calderone,
with organic vineyards now awaiting
biodynamic certification. The rest is down
to spontaneous fermentation and minimal
artisan winemaking techniques, producing
wines that show increasingly interesting,
recognizable identity. This year there is a
biodynamic vegetable garden too, to revive
old farming skills. A really memorable
tasting, demonstrating that this mountain
winery has reinvented itself in just a few
years. The 2013 version of the Vigneto di
Capestrano Trebbiano impressed us all with
complex aromas shaped by the landscape
and a vibrant, nuanced palate with flowers
and Alpine herbs. The uncomplicated
Montepulciano 2014 is very good: from
a tricky year in which the crus will not be
released, it has taken on a new complexity.

○ Trebbiano d'Abruzzo V. di Capestrano '13	♥♥♥	5
● Montepulciano d'Abruzzo '14	♥♥	2*
● Montepulciano d'Abruzzo San Calisto '12	♥♥	6
○ Trebbiano d'Abruzzo Vign. di Popoli '13	♥♥	5
⊙ Montepulciano d'Abruzzo Cerasuolo '14	♥♥	2*
○ Trebbiano d'Abruzzo '14	♥♥	2*
● Montepulciano d'Abruzzo		
San Calisto '08	♀♀♀	5
○ Trebbiano d'Abruzzo		
V. di Capestrano '12	♀♀♀	5
○ Trebbiano d'Abruzzo		
V. di Capestrano '11	♀♀♀	5
○ Trebbiano d'Abruzzo		
V. di Capestrano '10	♀♀♀	5
○ Trebbiano d'Abruzzo		
V. di Capestrano '08	♀♀♀	4

★Villa Medoro

C.DA MEDORO
64030 ATRI [TE]
TEL. 0858708142
www.villamedoro.it

CELLAR SALES
PRE-BOOKED VISITS
ACCOMMODATION
ANNUAL PRODUCTION 300,000 bottles
HECTARES UNDER VINE 100.00

The 100 hectares of vineyards are tended down to the tiniest details; a magnificent modern cellar, exquisitely clean-cut with its all-glass design, yet perfectly blended into the green hills overlooking the sea. The winery owned by bubbly Federica Morricone turns out modern, very well-made wines with the knack for appealing to market tastes and successfully blending tradition and modern style. The location is Atri, in the noble heart of the Teramo hills, which has always been real winegrowing terrain. A brilliant tasting from this winery, with contemporary, very well-made wines. The Adrano 2012 is an unexpectedly perky and well-paced Colline Teramane, with very tidy, clear fruit aromas and a tangy, edgy flavour despite the powerful texture. The Montepulciano 2013 demonstrates that Teramo can produce simple, dynamic Montepulcianos with astounding body for reds in this price range.

Ciccio Zaccagnini

C.DA POZZO
65020 BOLOGNANO [PE]
TEL. 0858880195
www.cantinazaccagnini.it

CELLAR SALES
PRE-BOOKED VISITS
ANNUAL PRODUCTION 1,500,000 bottles
HECTARES UNDER VINE 300.00

This venerable Bolognano winery has always been an Abruzzo leader. On the Pescara hills below Majella, it is no coincidence that Beuys held the Defence of Nature event here, founding his Land Art. Over time, the signs and links with art have been visible in the lovely, multifaceted cellar. The is stunning winegrowing terrain includes over 150 hectares of estate land and more rented, producing an impressive line-up of top labels every year. These range from the simple but striking basics to the more tailored, high-flying Montepulciano crus, all very well-made and powerful as they seek to blend typical Abruzzo features and international flavour. An impressive line-up of wines presented for tasting this year. The San Clemente is an ambitious, well-ordered Montepulciano which earns Tre Bicchieri thanks to its varietal typing and a stylish, focused palate. The No So2 is a sulphite-free wine: lively, perky, with powerful texture handled well by the varietal edginess.

● Montepulciano d'Abruzzo Colline Teramane Adrano '12	♥♥♥ 4*
● Montepulciano d'Abruzzo '13	♥♥ 2*
● Montepulciano d'Abruzzo Rosso del Duca '13	♥♥ 3*
⊙ Montepulciano d'Abruzzo Cerasuolo '14	♥♥ 2*
○ Passerina '14	♥♥ 2*
○ Pecorino '14	♥♥ 2*
○ Trebbiano d'Abruzzo '14	♥ 2
● Montepulciano d'Abruzzo '08	♥♥♥ 2*
● Montepulciano d'Abruzzo Colline Teramane Adrano '10	♥♥♥ 4*
● Montepulciano d'Abruzzo Colline Teramane Adrano '09	♥♥♥ 4*
● Montepulciano d'Abruzzo Colline Teramane Adrano '08	♥♥♥ 2*
● Montepulciano d'Abruzzo Rosso del Duca '12	♥♥♥ 3*

● Montepulciano d'Abruzzo S. Clemente Ris. '12	♥♥♥ 5
○ Abruzzo Pecorino Cuvèe dell'Abate '14	♥♥ 2*
○ Abruzzo Pecorino Yamada '14	♥♥ 3
○ Aster Extra Dry	♥♥ 3
⊙ Ibisco Rosa '14	♥♥ 2*
● Montepulciano d'Abruzzo Chronicon '12	♥♥ 3
● Montepulciano d'Abruzzo Cuvée dell'Abate '13	♥♥ 2*
● Montepulciano d'Abruzzo Il vino dal Tralcetto '13	♥♥ 2*
● Montepulciano d'Abruzzo NOSO2 '14	♥♥ 2*
○ Plaisir Bianco '14	♥♥ 4
○ Abruzzo Bianco S. Clemente '13	♥ 4
○ Bianco di Ciccio '14	♥ 2
○ Ispira '14	♥ 3
● Plaisir Rosso '14	♥ 4

Angelucci

C.DA VICENNE, 7
65020 CASTIGLIONE A CASAURIA [PE]
TEL. 0857998193
www.angeluccivini.it

CELLAR SALES
PRE-BOOKED VISITS
ANNUAL PRODUCTION 200,000 bottles
HECTARES UNDER VINE 30.00

⊙ Montepulciano d'Abruzzo Leonate '11	♟♟	3*
○ Leonate Pecorino '14	♟♟	3
○ Moscatello Travertine '14	♟♟	3

Bove

VIA ROMA, 216
67051 AVEZZANO [AQ]
TEL. 086333133
info@cantinebove.it

CELLAR SALES
PRE-BOOKED VISITS
ANNUAL PRODUCTION 1,200,000 bottles
HECTARES UNDER VINE 60.00

● Montepulciano d'Abruzzo Indio '12	♟♟	2*
● Montepulciano d'Abruzzo Poggio d'Albe '13	♟♟	2*
○ Safari Pecorino '14	♟♟	2*

Casal Thaulero

C.DA CUCULLO, 23
66026 ROSETO DEGLI ABRUZZI [TE]
TEL. 0859032537
www.casalthaulero.it

CELLAR SALES
PRE-BOOKED VISITS
ANNUAL PRODUCTION 1,300,000 bottles
HECTARES UNDER VINE 500.00
SUSTAINABLE WINERY

● Montepulciano d'Abruzzo Duca Thaulero '10	♟♟	3
● Montepulciano d'Abruzzo Orsetto Oro '12	♟♟	2*
● Montepulciano d'Abruzzo Prendimi '14	♟♟	1*
○ Pecorino Borgo Thaulero '14	♟♟	2*

Cerulli Spinozzi

LOC. CASALE 26
S.S. 150 DEL VOMANO KM 17,600
64020 CANZANO [TE]
TEL. 086157193
www.cerullispinozzi.it

CELLAR SALES
PRE-BOOKED VISITS
ACCOMMODATION AND RESTAURANT SERVICE
ANNUAL PRODUCTION 200,000 bottles
HECTARES UNDER VINE 53.00
VITICULTURE METHOD Certified Organic

⊙ Montepulciano d'Abruzzo Cerasuolo '14	♟♟	2*
● Montepulciano d'Abruzzo Colline Teramane Torre Migliori '10	♟♟	3
● Montepulciano d'Abruzzo '14	♟	2

Col del Mondo

C.DA CAMPOTINO, 35C
65010 COLLECORVINO [PE]
TEL. 0858207831
www.coldelmondo.com

CELLAR SALES
PRE-BOOKED VISITS
ANNUAL PRODUCTION 80,000 bottles
HECTARES UNDER VINE 12.00

○ Kerrias Pecorino '14	♟♟	2*
⊙ Montepulciano d'Abruzzo Cerasuolo '14	♟♟	2*
● Montepulciano d'Abruzzo Sunnae '13	♟♟	2*

Antonio Costantini

S.DA MIGLIORI, 20
65013 CITTÀ SANT'ANGELO [PE]
TEL. 0859699169
www.costantinivini.it

CELLAR SALES
PRE-BOOKED VISITS
ACCOMMODATION AND RESTAURANT SERVICE
ANNUAL PRODUCTION 450,000 bottles
HECTARES UNDER VINE 60.00

● Montepulciano d'Abruzzo '11	♟♟	3
○ Trebbiano d'Abruzzo '14	♟♟	2*
○ Abruzzo Pecorino Iolanda '13	♟	3
○ Pecorino '14	♟	3

Feudo Antico

VIA PERRUNA, 35
66010 TOLLO [CH]
TEL. 0871969128
www.feudoantico.it

CELLAR SALES
PRE-BOOKED VISITS
ANNUAL PRODUCTION 60,000 bottles
HECTARES UNDER VINE 20.00

○ Tullum Pecorino '14	♟♟ 3*
⊙ Rosato '14	♟♟ 2*
○ Tullum Brut	♟♟ 5
○ Tullum Passerina '14	♟♟ 3

Cantina Frentana

VIA PERAZZA, 32
66020 ROCCA SAN GIOVANNI [CH]
TEL. 087260152
www.cantinafrentana.it

CELLAR SALES
PRE-BOOKED VISITS
ACCOMMODATION
ANNUAL PRODUCTION 800,000 bottles
HECTARES UNDER VINE 22.00

○ Abruzzo Pecorino Coste del Mulino '14	♟♟ 1*
● Montepulciano d'Abruzzo '13	♟♟ 2*
● Montepulciano d'Abruzzo Rubesto '13	♟♟ 2*

Lidia e Amato

C.DA SAN BIAGIO, 2
64010 CONTROGUERRA [TE]
TEL. 0861817041
www.lidiaeamatoviticoltori.com

CELLAR SALES
PRE-BOOKED VISITS
ANNUAL PRODUCTION 50,000 bottles
HECTARES UNDER VINE 12.00

○ Controguerra Elena '14	♟♟ 2*
○ Controguerra Greta '14	♟ 3
○ Trebbiano d'Abruzzo Palù '14	♟ 2

Marchesi De' Cordano

C.DA CORDANO, 43
65014 LORETO APRUTINO [PE]
TEL. 0858289526
www.cordano.it

CELLAR SALES
PRE-BOOKED VISITS
ANNUAL PRODUCTION 180,000 bottles
HECTARES UNDER VINE 50.00
VITICULTURE METHOD Certified Organic

● Montepulciano d'Abruzzo Aida '12	♟♟ 2*
● Montepulciano d'Abruzzo Terra dei Vestini Santinum Ris. '09	♟♟ 5
○ Trebbiano d'Abruzzo Aida '14	♟ 2

Cantine Mucci

C.DA VALLONE DI NANNI, 65
66020 TORINO DI SANGRO [CH]
TEL. 0873913366
www.cantinemucci.com

CELLAR SALES
PRE-BOOKED VISITS
ANNUAL PRODUCTION 250,000 bottles
HECTARES UNDER VINE 24.00

○ Mucci Extra Dry '14	♟♟ 2*
● Montepulciano d'Abruzzo Valentino '14	♟ 2
○ Pecorino Valentino '14	♟ 2
○ Trebbiano d'Abruzzo Valentino '14	♟ 2

Praesidium

VIA GIOVANNUCCI, 24
67030 PREZZA [AQ]
TEL. 086445103
www.vinipraesidium.it

CELLAR SALES
PRE-BOOKED VISITS
ANNUAL PRODUCTION 26,000 bottles
HECTARES UNDER VINE 5.50

⊙ Montepulciano d'Abruzzo Cerasuolo '14	♟♟ 3
● Montepulciano d'Abruzzo Ris. '10	♟♟ 5

La Quercia

C.DA COLLE CROCE
64020 MORRO D'ORO [TE]
TEL. 0858959110
www.vinilaquercia.it

CELLAR SALES
PRE-BOOKED VISITS
ANNUAL PRODUCTION 200,000 bottles
HECTARES UNDER VINE 21.00

● Montepulciano d'Abruzzo Colline Teramane Mastrobono Ris. '07	♥♥ 5
● Montepulciano d'Abruzzo Primamadre '10	♥♥ 2*
● Montepulciano d'Abruzzo Peladi '14	♥ 1*

San Giacomo

C.DA NOVELLA, 36
66020 ROCCA SAN GIOVANNI [CH]
TEL. 0872620504
www.cantinasangiacomo.it

CELLAR SALES
PRE-BOOKED VISITS
ANNUAL PRODUCTION 20,000 bottles
HECTARES UNDER VINE 300.00
VITICULTURE METHOD Certified Organic

● Montepulciano d'Abruzzo Casino Murri 14 '13	♥♥ 2*
⊙ Montepulciano d'Abruzzo Cerasuolo Casino Murri '13	♥♥ 1*
○ Pecorino Casino Murri '14	♥♥ 1*

Talamonti

C.DA PALAZZO
65014 LORETO APRUTINO [PE]
TEL. 0858289039
www.cantinetalamonti.it

CELLAR SALES
PRE-BOOKED VISITS
ANNUAL PRODUCTION 420,000 bottles
HECTARES UNDER VINE 32.00

● Montepulciano d'Abruzzo Tre Saggi '13	♥♥ 2*
○ Trebbiano d'Abruzzo Trebì '14	♥♥ 2*
○ Pecorino Trabocchetto '14	♥ 2

Terzini

VIA ROMA, 52
65028 TOCCO DA CASAURIA [PE]
TEL. 0859158147
www.cantinaterzini.it

CELLAR SALES
ANNUAL PRODUCTION 200,000 bottles
HECTARES UNDER VINE 22.00

○ Abruzzo Pecorino '14	♥♥ 3
● Montepulciano d'Abruzzo '13	♥♥ 3
○ Trebbiano d'Abruzzo '14	♥ 3

Valori

VIA TORQUATO AL SALINELLO, 8
64027 SANT'OMERO [TE]
TEL. 087185241
www.mascirellidistribuzione.it/valori

PRE-BOOKED VISITS
ANNUAL PRODUCTION 150,000 bottles
HECTARES UNDER VINE 26.00
VITICULTURE METHOD Certified Organic
SUSTAINABLE WINERY

● Montepulciano d'Abruzzo Bio '14	♥♥ 2*
● Montepulciano d'Abruzzo V. Sant'Angelo '10	♥♥ 4
○ Trebbiano d'Abruzzo Bio '14	♥♥ 2*

Vigneti Radica

VIA PIANA MOZZONE, 4
66010 TOLLO [CH]
TEL. 0871962227
www.vignetiradica.it

CELLAR SALES
PRE-BOOKED VISITS
ACCOMMODATION
ANNUAL PRODUCTION 80,000 bottles
HECTARES UNDER VINE 14.00
SUSTAINABLE WINERY

● Montepulciano d'Abruzzo '14	♥♥ 2*
○ Pecorino '14	♥ 2

MOLISE

Green hills slope fast from the Apennines to the sea, seeming almost to have been forged deliberately for viticulture. The constant breezes mould the rhythmic, impetuous scents, and the rich soils are perfect for ensuring fullness in the grape. Sadly, however, the wines are often naive, and either far too rustic or aspire to too much modernity. The same varieties have always grown on this verdant and still pristine landscape. Viticulture has always been influenced by neighbouring regions, with cultivars imported to this border area dividing Abruzzo from Campania: captivating aglianico, lightweight falanghina, dense montepulciano, foody trebbiano. And tintilia, with its huge potential, Molise's true native red grape, with magical rustic hints and edgy fruit, making juicy, vital wines, but unfortunately all too often interpreted in a quest for weight and international hints of oak. The tastings this year suffered the influence of a difficult 2014, with fewer wineries entering samples, but there was a fine new entry to flank the old hands: Tenimenti Grieco. The cellar caught our attention immediately with modern, well-made wines, including an uncomplicated, very effective Tintilia that wasted no time in persuading us to send it on to the finals to reward its honest simplicity and fragrance. The Tre Bicchieri went to Don Luigi, an esteemed ambassador of Molise wines, coming up well, very tasty, close-knit and vigorous. The only regret is that a region with such potential and ancient traditions fails to find the right winemaking direction that its history and its landscape deserve. Here and there we see wines that go well beyond the international stereotype and we are sure that if Molise tries to meet demands from markets and consumers for more approachable, typical wines, it will open the door to a rosy and lengthy future.

MOLISE

Borgo di Colloredo

loc. Nuova Cliternia
via Colloredo, 15
86042 Campomarino [CB]
Tel. 087557453
www.borgodicolloredo.com

CELLAR SALES
PRE-BOOKED VISITS
ACCOMMODATION AND RESTAURANT SERVICE
ANNUAL PRODUCTION 200,000 bottles
HECTARES UNDER VINE 70.00

A large winery working with great enthusiasm in Campomarino, Molise's top wine country. The 60 hectares on the hills slope down from the Apennines to the Adriatic, where the Di Giulio family have been cultivating grapes for generations, vinified in their historic cellar, in a typical, slightly rustic style, for wines that are incisive, often offering sensational value for money. This year's somewhat scant line-up lacks the top wines, but the candidates held their own in terms of soundness and food-friendliness . The Girona 2008 Riserva is a close-knit, muscular red, with a well-defined fruity bouquet and plush, tamed overtones, while the mouth is acidic and lively despite its vintage. The uncomplicated yet vibrant Gironia 2014 rolls across the palate with aromas of strawberry and wild herbs, and an enjoyably consistent mouthfeel.

Claudio Cipressi

c.da Montagna, 5b
86030 San Felice del Molise [CB]
Tel. 0874874535
www.cantinecipressi.it

CELLAR SALES
PRE-BOOKED VISITS
ACCOMMODATION
ANNUAL PRODUCTION 50,000 bottles
HECTARES UNDER VINE 16.00
VITICULTURE METHOD Certified Organic

A winery that has focused on the rediscovery of tintilia, one of Molise's historic native red varietals. Just a few hectares, but managed with modern care and a craftsman's verve. The 16 certified organic hectares under vine produce top-quality raw material that Claudio interprets with a personal style respectful of tradition. Though small, the range submitted for this year's tasting is impressive. The Tintilias reign supreme, with their fresh, ever-challenging style typical of the varietal. The Settevigne 2014 has striking nuances of red berry and aromatic medicinal herbs, and an expansive and fresh-tasting palate, simple despite its conspicuous body. The uncomplicated Trebbiano Le Scoste 2013 captivated with fragrances characteristic of the varietal, combining hazelnut and wild flowers, expansive fruity palate, and brisk, tasty, sea-washed finale. Rather more demanding is the markedly aged Tintilia 2011 Macchiarossa.

○ Biferno Bianco Gironia '14	♈♈ 3
● Biferno Rosso Gironia Ris. '08	♈♈ 4
● Molise Rosso '12	♈♈ 2*
⊙ Biferno Rosato Gironia '14	♈ 3
○ Molise Falanghina '14	♈ 2
● Aglianico '10	♈♈♈ 3*
● Aglianico '07	♈♈ 2*
○ Biferno Bianco Gironia '13	♈♈ 2*
○ Biferno Bianco Gironia '12	♈♈ 2*
● Biferno Rosso Gironia '06	♈♈ 3
○ Greco '11	♈♈ 2*
○ Molise Falanghina '12	♈♈ 2*
○ Molise Falanghina '10	♈♈ 2*
○ Molise Falanghina '09	♈♈ 2*
● Molise Montepulciano '10	♈♈ 2*
● Molise Tintilia '08	♈♈ 5

● Molise Tintilia Settevigne '14	♈♈ 4
● Molise Tintilia Macchiarossa '11	♈♈ 4
○ Molise Trebbiano Le Scoste '13	♈♈ 3
● Molise Tintilia 66 '09	♈ 7
⊙ Molise Tintilia Collequinto '14	♈ 4
● Elkon Aglianico '08	♈♈ 3
○ Falanghina '12	♈♈ 2*
○ Falanghina Voira '13	♈♈ 3
● Molise Aglianico Elkon '06	♈♈ 2*
● Molise Rosso Mekan '07	♈♈ 2*
● Molise Rosso Mekan '06	♈♈ 3*
● Molise Rosso Rumen '09	♈♈ 2*
● Molise Tintilia Macchiarossa '10	♈♈ 4
● Molise Tintilia Macchiarossa '07	♈♈ 3
● Molise Tintilia Macchiarossa '06	♈♈ 4
● Molise Tintilia Macchiarossa '05	♈♈ 3

★Di Majo Norante

FRAZ. NUOVA CLITERNIA
VIA COLLE SAVINO, 6
86042 CAMPOMARINO [CB]
TEL. 087557208
www.dimajonorante.com

CELLAR SALES
PRE-BOOKED VISITS
ANNUAL PRODUCTION 800,000 bottles
HECTARES UNDER VINE 110.00
VITICULTURE METHOD Certified Organic

Few other companies are as synonymous of a region as Di Majo Norante is of Molise: a modern cellar producing wines that are always worthy, refreshing and very well-crafted. In Campomarino, over 100 hectares all tended with certified organic methods, the vineyards roll down the Apennine hills almost as far as the sea. Its well-defined cellar style is a big hit on the international and domestic markets. The Don Luigi red once again offers a blend of tradition and modernity. The 2012 impresses with its tight-knit, richly extracted bouquet, elegant woody notes, and typically fruit-driven montepulciano flavours with dark notes offered by a pinch of aglianico. The palate is full-flavoured and lingering, combining well-defined fruit and varietal acidity, despite its reckless ageing. The Contado 2013 has a soft yet incisive tannic weave that helps it slip down smoothly. We liked the simpler Falanghina 2014, initially fruit-driven, then becoming snappy with fresh-tasting grassy notes, food-friendly and easy-drinking.

Tenimenti Grieco

C.DA DIFENSOLA
86045 PORTOCANNONE [CB]
TEL. 0875590032
www.tenimentigrieco.it

CELLAR SALES
PRE-BOOKED VISITS
ANNUAL PRODUCTION 500,000 bottles
HECTARES UNDER VINE 85.00

A newly-established estate with very carefully crafted and attractive wines, in Larino, deep in the Molise hills overlooking the sea. As well as wine, the estate offers an agriturismo and a petting zoo, a form of cultural tourism that invests in the community. The wines this year were impressive and very carefully crafted, even down to the label, the reds more than the one-dimensional whites. The Tintilia, from the eponymous native grape is a keystone of production. The incisive 2014 swept into the final with its boisterous fragrances of brooding fruitiness and admirable Mediterranean nuances, its vibrant well-paced mouth, backed by nice freshness and well-defined cherry notes. Even the more ambitious Cupaia 2013, a Tintilia with a slightly closed bouquet, has a relaxed and attractive drinkability, despite its compactness.

Wine	Rating
● Molise Rosso Don Luigi Ris. '12	♥♥♥ 5
● Molise Aglianico Contado Ris. '13	♥♥ 3*
○ Molise Apianae '13	♥♥ 5
● Biferno Rosso Ramitello '13	♥♥ 3
● Moli Rosso '14	♥♥ 2*
○ Molise Falanghina '14	♥♥ 2*
○ Molise Greco '14	♥♥ 2*
● Sangiovese '14	♥♥ 2*
○ Moli Bianco '14	♥ 2
● Molise Aglianico Biorganic '13	♥ 2
○ Molise Falanghina Biorganic '14	♥ 2
● Molise Aglianico Biorganic '11	♥♥♥ 2*
● Molise Aglianico Contado Ris. '10	♥♥♥ 3*
● Molise Aglianico Contado Ris. '09	♥♥♥ 3*
● Molise Don Luigi Ris. '08	♥♥♥ 5
● Molise Rosso Don Luigi Ris. '11	♥♥♥ 5

Wine	Rating
● Molise Tintilia '14	♥♥ 2*
● Molise Monterosso '13	♥♥ 2*
⊙ Molise Rosato Passo alle Tremiti '14	♥♥ 2*
● Molise Tintilia Cupaia '13	♥♥ 3
● Biferno Sangue di Buoi '11	♥ 4
○ Falanghina Passo alle Tremiti '14	♥ 2
● Molise Rosso Passo alle Tremiti '13	♥ 2
● Cabernet Sauvignon '09	♥♥ 2
○ Falanghina '08	♥♥ 2
○ Falanghina '07	♥♥ 2*
● Molise Rosso Podere di Sot '08	♥♥ 2*
● Molise Rosso Podere di Sot '07	♥♥ 2*
○ Podere del Canneto '08	♥♥ 2*
○ Podere del Canneto '07	♥♥ 2*

Angelo D'Uva

C.DA MONTE ALTINO, 23A
86035 LARINO [CB]
TEL. 0874822320
www.cantineduva.com

CELLAR SALES
PRE-BOOKED VISITS
ACCOMMODATION AND RESTAURANT SERVICE
ANNUAL PRODUCTION 70,000 bottles
HECTARES UNDER VINE 20.00

○ Egò '09	♟♟ 5
○ Keres '14	♟♟ 2*
● Molise Tintilia Lagena '13	♟ 3
○ Molise Trebbiano Kantharos '14	♟ 2

Cantine Salvatore

C.DA VIGNE
86049 URURI [CB]
TEL. 0874830656
www.cantinesalvatore.it

CELLAR SALES
PRE-BOOKED VISITS
ANNUAL PRODUCTION 80,000 bottles
HECTARES UNDER VINE 15.00
SUSTAINABLE WINERY

● L'IndoVINO Rosso '13	♟♟ 2*
● Molise Rosso Don Donà '11	♟♟ 3
● Molise Tintilia Rutilia '13	♟ 3
⊙ Ros Is '14	♟ 2

Terresacre

C.DA MONTEBELLO
86036 MONTENERO DI BISACCIA [CB]
TEL. 0875960191
www.terresacre.net

CELLAR SALES
PRE-BOOKED VISITS
ACCOMMODATION AND RESTAURANT SERVICE
ANNUAL PRODUCTION 100,000 bottles
HECTARES UNDER VINE 35.00

● Molise Tintilia '12	♟♟ 5
○ Molise Falanghina '14	♟ 3
○ Molise Falanghina Oravera '12	♟ 4

CAMPANIA

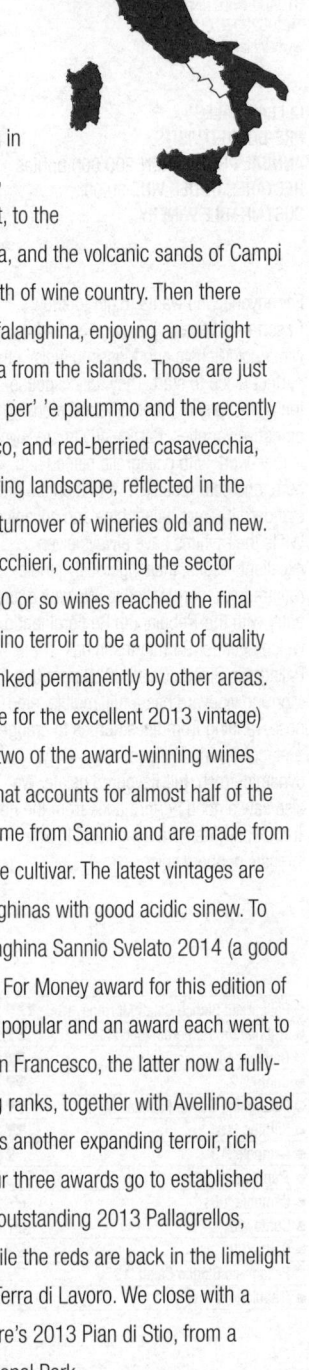

Another good year for Campania tastings. This region vaunts an amazing scenario and fascinating wealth of terroirs and native grape varieties, making it one of the most interesting in Italy. From vineyards at 700 metres in altitude, on the Apennines overlooking the Amalfi Coast, to the volcanic terroirs of Vesuvius and Roccamonfina, and the volcanic sands of Campi Flegrei, few other districts can offer this breadth of wine country. Then there are the grapes: aristocratic fiano; lush greco; falanghina, enjoying an outright revival; the Mediterranean charm of biancolella from the islands. Those are just the white varieties. The reds include aglianico; per' 'e palummo and the recently rediscovered pallagrello nero, pallagrello bianco, and red-berried casavecchia, all enjoying a renaissance in Caserta. An evolving landscape, reflected in the pages of the Guide, where we see a constant turnover of wineries old and new. This year a spectacular 20 took home a Tre Bicchieri, confirming the sector is now in its prime. A result to ponder is that 50 or so wines reached the final tastings. While in the past it was only the Avellino terroir to be a point of quality reference for regional production, it is now flanked permanently by other areas. Summing the four Tre Bicchieri (including three for the excellent 2013 vintage) for Fiano d'Avellino, four Greco di Tufo (again two of the award-winning wines are 2013s), and two Tre Bicchieri to Taurasi, that accounts for almost half of the prizes awarded. Four excellent white wines come from Sannio and are made from falanghina, Campania's most widespread white cultivar. The latest vintages are giving us excellent, tasty and affordable Falanghinas with good acidic sinew. To the point that one of these, the excellent Falanghina Sannio Svelato 2014 (a good vintage for Sannio whites) took the Best Value For Money award for this edition of the Guide. The Amalfi Coast wines are always popular and an award each went to Raffaele Palma, Marisa Cuomo and Tenuta San Francesco, the latter now a fully-fledged member of the Campania winemaking ranks, together with Avellino-based Fonzone and Sannio Torre a Oriente. Caserta is another expanding terroir, rich in developments and emerging operations. Our three awards go to established wineries: Terre del Principe and Alois, for two outstanding 2013 Pallagrellos, respectively Le Serole and Caiatì Morrone, while the reds are back in the limelight with an excellent 2013 vintage from Galardi: Terra di Lavoro. We close with a flourish with a fiano-based white, San Salvatore's 2013 Pian di Stio, from a vineyard at almost 600 metres, in Cilento National Park.

Alois

LOC. AUDELINO
VIA RAGAZZANO
81040 PONTELATONE [CE]
TEL. 0823876710
www.vinialois.it

CELLAR SALES
PRE-BOOKED VISITS
ANNUAL PRODUCTION 200,000 bottles
HECTARES UNDER VINE 30.00
SUSTAINABLE WINERY

For anyone who wants to get to know Caserta's complex viticultural area, the winery of Michele and Massimo Alois is the perfect place to start. They fully espouse the philosophy of monovarietals, focusing on native varieties. Particularly impressive is their work with pallagrello bianco and nero, and casavecchia, not to mention the standard bearers, falanghina and aglianico. While their whites have always given excellent results, their vigorously tannic reds require more patience. We saw a new entry with the Trebulanum Re Ferdinando, which ages for 24 months in oak. The Pallagrello Bianco Caiatì 2013 from the Morrone vineyard has a full, multifaceted nose, ranging from fines herbes to orange zest, combining fullness with a lively, dynamic, fresh, full-flavoured palate. We also saw a good performance from the new Trebulanum Re Ferdinando 2011, with intense, peppery spice.

○ Pallagrello Bianco Caiatì Morrone '13	♙♙♙	2*
● Trebulanum Re Ferdinando '11	♙♙	5
○ Caulino '14	♙♙	2*
● Cunto '12	♙♙	4
○ Falanghina Donna Paolina '14	♙♙	3
● Settimo '13	♙♙	3
● Campole '13	♙	3
● Trebulanum '10	♙♙♙	5
● Campole '08	♙♙	2*
● Cunto '10	♙♙	4
● Cunto '09	♙♙	4
○ Pallagrello Bianco Caiatì '13	♙♙	2*
● Trebulanum '11	♙♙	5

I Cacciagalli

FRAZ. AORIVOLA
VIA TEANO, 3
81059 TEANO [CE]
TEL. 0823875216
www.icacciagalli.it

CELLAR SALES
PRE-BOOKED VISITS
ACCOMMODATION
ANNUAL PRODUCTION 20,000 bottles
HECTARES UNDER VINE 9.00
VITICULTURE METHOD Certified Organic

Diano Iaccannone and Mario Basco's winery is certified organic, soon to be biodynamic, and uses maceration on the skins also for whites, and amphoras for vinification and ageing. On the basis of such a presentation, you could be forgiven for thinking they are dedicated followers of fashion, striving to keep up-to-date with the latest trends. Instead, it is precisely here, on the slopes of the Roccamonfina volcano in the Alto Casertano area, that we find some of the region's most original wines: expressive, pleasurable, playing on balances of unusual flavours, and offering superb drinkability even in macerated whites. Whilst awaiting the Zagreo 2014, which will be tasted for the next edition, the reds ruled the roost: the rich Lucno 2013, a complex Piedirosso showing juicy ripe blackcurrant offset by fresh juniper and pepper, is opulent but shows admirable grip and flavour. The Phos 2013, an Aglianico vinified in amphoras, boasts intense, vibrant balsamic notes of aniseed, leather and raspberries, over a lively, somewhat untidy but full-flavoured palate.

● Lucno '13	♙♙	4
● Phos '13	♙♙	4
● Sphaeranera '13	♙♙	4
○ Aorivola '14	♙	3
○ Aorivola '13	♙♙	4
● Basco '10	♙♙	3
● Masseria Cacciagalli '11	♙♙	4
○ Zagreo '13	♙♙	4

Antonio Caggiano

C.DA SALA
83030 TAURASI [AV]
TEL. 082774723
www.cantinecaggiano.it

CELLAR SALES
PRE-BOOKED VISITS
RESTAURANT SERVICE
ANNUAL PRODUCTION 155,000 bottles
HECTARES UNDER VINE 25.00

The wines produced by Antonio Caggiano, photographer, traveller, and innovator of Campanian winemaking, rest under arches, vaults and stone ceilings. The stunning underground cellar, designed in 1990, is decorated with photos from Antonio's travels around the world. With the support of his son Giuseppe, he works around 25 hectares of fine vineyards, some in excellent wine country at Contrada Sala, San Pietro, Coste and Piano di Montevergine. The results are the Vigna Macchia dei Goti, always one of the top Taurasis, and whites such as the Greco di Tufo Devon and the Fiano di Avellino Béchar. The Fiano di Avellino Bechar 2014 made our finals with its delicate notes of coffee, white peach and a velvety, creamy palate. Reflecting the vintage, and as always one of the best of its type, the Taurasi Vigna Macchia dei Goti 2011, showed ripe juicy cherry and blackberry and good stuffing, well sustained by acidity, with a touch of alcoholic warmth on the finish.

○ Fiano di Avellino Béchar '14	♥♥ 3*
● Irpinia Aglianico Taurì '13	♥♥ 2*
○ Mel	♥♥ 4
● Taurasi V. Macchia dei Goti '11	♥♥ 5
○ Fiagre '14	♥ 2
○ Greco di Tufo Devon '14	♥ 3
○ Fiano di Avellino Béchar '13	♥♥♥ 3*
● Taurasi V. Macchia dei Goti '08	♥♥♥ 5
● Taurasi V. Macchia dei Goti '04	♥♥♥ 5
○ Mel	♥♥ 5
○ Greco di Tufo Devon '13	♥♥ 3
● Irpinia Aglianico Taurì '12	♥♥ 2*
● Irpinia Campi Taurasini Salae Domini '11	♥♥ 5
● Taurasi V. Macchia dei Goti '10	♥♥ 5

Cantina del Taburno

VIA SALA, 16
82030 FOGLIANISE [BN]
TEL. 0824871338
www.cantinadeltaburno.it

CELLAR SALES
PRE-BOOKED VISITS
ANNUAL PRODUCTION 1,000,000 bottles
HECTARES UNDER VINE 600.00

Since 1901, Benevento's Consorzio Agrario Provinciale has been working to promote farming in the Sannio area. In 1972, the Cantina del Taburno was established, now with around 300 member-growers working over 600 hectares. At Foglianise, where the winery is based, Sannio's main varieties are vinified: aglianico, piedirosso, and falanghina, but also greco, fiano and coda di volpe. The wide range brings together pleasurable, drinkable labels as well as more structured, complex wines, released after long ageing, either in bottle or barrique, without forgetting raisin wines and sparklers. The Bue Apis 2011, which reached our finals, comes from century-old vines, and boasts impressive structure, rich fruit, smooth tannins and a long, spicy finish. Another finalist was the elegant Falanghina del Beneventano Cesco dell'Eremo 2013, brimming with fruit and spring flowers, citrus fruit and honey, underpinned by a good acid backbone. The rest of the range is solid.

○ Cesco dell'Eremo '13	♥♥ 2*
● Sannio Taburno Aglianico Bue Apis '11	♥♥ 8
● Coda di Volpe Amineo '14	♥♥ 2*
○ Fiano '14	♥♥ 2*
○ Greco '14	♥♥ 2*
● Sannio Aglianico Fidelis '11	♥♥ 2*
○ Sannio Taburno Falanghina '14	♥♥ 2*
⊙ Sannio Taburno Aglianico Rosato Albarosa '14	♥ 2
● Aglianico del Taburno Delius '09	♥♥♥ 4*
● Bue Apis '00	♥♥♥ 6
● Bue Apis '99	♥♥♥ 6
● Taburno Aglianico Bue Apis '04	♥♥♥ 8
● Aglianico del Taburno Bue Apis '08	♥♥ 7
● Aglianico del Taburno Delius '11	♥♥ 4
○ Falanghina del Sannio Taburno '13	♥♥ 2*

Cautiero

C.DA ARBUSTI
82030 FRASSO TELESINO [BN]
TEL. 3387640641
www.cautiero.it

CELLAR SALES
ACCOMMODATION
ANNUAL PRODUCTION 16,000 bottles
HECTARES UNDER VINE 4.00
VITICULTURE METHOD Certified Organic

Last year a whole series of accolades arrived, starting with the winery's first Tre Bicchieri, thanks to the vigorous Falanghina Fois 2013. Fulvio Cautiero is firmly in command of this boutique winery, in the western part of Sannio, embracing the Parco del Taburno. The winery only uses grapes from its own four hectares of vineyards, farmed by organic methods. Two aspects are worthy of note: the spontaneous, approachable character of the wines, always underpinned by refreshing acidity, and their excellent value for money. Once again, we were presented with an excellent range. The Falanghina Fois 2014 impressed as always, although lacking the expressive power of the last edition. Well-typed and lustrous, it showed fragrant hay, pennyroyal and a well-modulated palate with tangy citrus, leading to a long, refreshing finish. We were seduced by the grape skin and green tea notes of the Erba Bianca 2014, with its generous, incisive palate. The balsamic, savoury Aglianico 2012 also showed impressive depth on the nose.

○ Erba Bianca '14	♥♥ 2*
○ Sannio Falanghina Fois '14	♥♥ 2*
● Sannio Aglianico Fois '12	♥♥ 2*
○ Sannio Greco Trois '14	♥♥ 2*
● Piedirosso '14	♥ 2
○ Sannio Falanghina Fois '13	♥♥♥ 2*
● Piedirosso '13	♀♀ 2*
● Sannio Aglianico Donna Candida '10	♀♀ 4
● Sannio Aglianico Donna Candida '07	♀♀ 5
● Sannio Aglianico Fois Rosso '08	♀♀ 2*
○ Sannio Falanghina Fois '12	♀♀ 2*
○ Sannio Falanghina Fois '11	♀♀ 2*
○ Sannio Falanghina Fois '10	♀♀ 2*
○ Sannio Greco Trois '13	♀♀ 2*

Tenuta del Cavalier Pepe

VIA SANTA VARA
83050 SANT'ANGELO ALL'ESCA [AV]
TEL. 082773766
www.tenutapepe.it

CELLAR SALES
PRE-BOOKED VISITS
ACCOMMODATION AND RESTAURANT SERVICE
ANNUAL PRODUCTION 300,000 bottles
HECTARES UNDER VINE 50.00
SUSTAINABLE WINERY

The winery is located at Sant'Angelo all'Esca, in the Avellino area, with beautiful hillside vineyards. You could be forgiven for thinking this was France. The man behind it all is Angelo Pepe who became a successful restaurant owner in Belgium, returned to Italy, where he was made Cavaliere della Repubblica for his work promoting Italian food. In 2005 he was joined by his daughter Milena, an oenologist who studied in Belgium and France. Her determined work has brought the best out of Campania's native varieties, and has given the range a real boost in quality. The two versions of Taurasi proposed were both attractively nuanced, starting with the Opera Mia 2010, with its surefooted progression on the palate, showing notes of roasted coffee beans, nutmeg and dried fruits. The spicy profile of the Loggia del Cavaliere Riserva 2009 convinced us even more, with its nose of black pepper, blackberries and juniper, leading to a complex, deep, almost hot and spicy palate, with a long finish.

○ Fiano di Avellino Refiano '14	♥♥ 3
● Taurasi La Loggia del Cavaliere Ris. '09	♥♥ 6
● Taurasi Opera Mia '10	♥♥ 5
○ Fiano di Avellino Brancato '12	♥ 4
○ Greco di Tufo Grancare '13	♥ 4
○ Greco di Tufo Nestor '14	♥ 3
○ Irpinia Falanghina Lila '14	♥ 2
○ Irpinia Rosato del Varo '14	♥ 2
○ Fiano di Avellino Refiano '13	♀♀ 3
○ Greco di Tufo Nestor '12	♀♀ 3
● Irpinia Aglianico Terra del Varo '11	♀♀ 2*
● Irpinia Aglianico Terra del Varo '10	♀♀ 2*
○ Irpinia Coda di Volpe Bianco di Bellona '12	♀♀ 2*
● Taurasi La Loggia del Cavaliere Ris. '08	♀♀ 6
● Taurasi La Loggia del Cavaliere Ris. '07	♀♀ 6
● Taurasi Opera Mia '09	♀♀ 5

Colli di Castelfranci

C.DA BRAUDIANO
83040 CASTELFRANCI [AV]
TEL. 082772392
www.collidicastelfranci.com

CELLAR SALES
PRE-BOOKED VISITS
ACCOMMODATION AND RESTAURANT SERVICE
ANNUAL PRODUCTION 160,000 bottles
HECTARES UNDER VINE 25.00

Luciano Gregorio and Gerardo Colucci's winery, active since 2002, is a benchmark for Irpinia. The whites include supple, lean versions of Greco and Fiano matured in stainless steel, but there is also a brace of interesting reds from aglianico: the Taurasi Alta Valle and its Riserva. The winery is in northern Irpinia at Castelfranci, a small town at an altitude of around 450 metres at the heart of one of Campania's most interesting districts, whose slow, prolonged ripening cycles produce ageable wines with fresh acidity.   The Irpinia Greco Vallicelli 2013 shows the potential of the variety also in the northern Valle del Calore. A nose of moss, candied peel and white pepper paves the way for a juicy, creamy, dynamic palate, followed by slight smokiness and a finish of dried herbs. We also liked the mature, glycerine-rich Greco di Tufo Grotte 2014, the Mediterranean herbs of the Fiano di Avellino 2014, and the spirited Rosato Crote 2014.

○ Irpinia Greco Vallicelli '13	♟♟	4
○ Fiano di Avellino Pendino '14	♟♟	3
○ Greco di Tufo Grotte '14	♟♟	3
☉ Irpinia Aglianico Rosato Crote '14	♟♟	3
● Irpinia Campi Taurasini Candriano '11	♟	3
● Irpinia Campi Taurasini Vadantico '11	♟	3
○ Irpinia Fiano Paladino '13	♟	4
○ Sannio Falanghina Falangò '14	♟	2
● Taurasi Alta Valle '11	♟	5
○ Greco di Tufo Grotte '13	🏆🏆	3
○ Greco di Tufo Grotte '12	🏆🏆	3
● Irpinia Campi Taurasini Vadantico '10	🏆🏆	3
● Taurasi Alta Valle '10	🏆🏆	5
● Taurasi Alta Valle '09	🏆🏆	5

Colli di Lapio

VIA ARIANIELLO, 47
83030 LAPIO [AV]
TEL. 0825982184
www.collidilapio.it

CELLAR SALES
PRE-BOOKED VISITS
ANNUAL PRODUCTION 55,000 bottles
HECTARES UNDER VINE 8.00
VITICULTURE METHOD Certified Organic

Lapio is Fiano di Avellino's Grand Cru, and its clay-rich soils bring out the best in its flavour and aromatic breadth, resulting in authentic, complex expressions. We are at altitudes of around 600 metres, with a wide diurnal temperature range, giving wines driven by cutting acidity. The history of Colli di Lapio is linked to that of Clelia Romano, who together has been running the winery since 1994 with her husband Angelo and their children. They produce long-lived Fiano di Avellinos from vineyards in the small hamlet of Arianello, with other plots at Stazzone. The complicated 2014 growing year resulted in a kind of natural selection, but there was still room for great wines such as the Fiano di Avellino 2014. As usual, it opens shyly, reticently, with a restrained nose, then showing wonderful depth and flavour on the palate, with vibrant citrus and smoky notes, subtle but incredibly compact to the end. Stylistically different, but well-proportioned, the Greco di Tufo Alèxandros 2014 offers creamy ripe peach, candied peel and ginger.

○ Fiano di Avellino '14	♟♟♟	4*
○ Greco di Tufo Alèxandros '14	♟♟	3
● Taurasi V. Andrea '11	♟♟	5
● Irpinia Campi Taurasini Donna Chiara '12	♟	3
○ Fiano di Avellino '13	🏆🏆🏆	4*
○ Fiano di Avellino '10	🏆🏆🏆	4
○ Fiano di Avellino '09	🏆🏆🏆	4
○ Fiano di Avellino '08	🏆🏆🏆	4*
○ Fiano di Avellino '07	🏆🏆🏆	4
○ Fiano di Avellino '05	🏆🏆🏆	4
○ Fiano di Avellino '04	🏆🏆🏆	4
○ Fiano di Avellino '12	🏆🏆	4
○ Fiano di Avellino '11	🏆🏆	4
○ Greco di Tufo Alèxandros '13	🏆🏆	3
○ Greco di Tufo Alexandros '11	🏆🏆	4
● Taurasi V. Andrea '08	🏆🏆	5

Michele Contrada

C.DA TAVERNA, 31
83040 CANDIDA [AV]
TEL. 0825988434
www.vinicontrada.it

CELLAR SALES
PRE-BOOKED VISITS
ANNUAL PRODUCTION 60,000 bottles
HECTARES UNDER VINE 10.00

Michele Contrada's winery was established in 2003 after years working as a grower for a large operation. The ten hectares planted to Fiano di Avellino, Greco di Tufo and Taurasi provide around 60,000 bottles, dealt with by Gerardo, a humble grower with great experience and tenacity. Gerardo's desire to promote the vineyards in Candida territory persuaded him to organize a harvest festival with traditional dancing and grape pressing for the children on the last weekend of September. The venerable vineyards include Selvecorte, planted to fiano, that gives musky wines with focused floral aromas. The Fiano di Avellino Selvecorte 2013 offers broom, chamomile and citron on the nose, followed by great thrust in the mouth, for a leisurely finish with musky, salty notes. We suspect this will age well, like the marvellous 2003 we tasted again recently. We also enjoyed the Greco di Tufo Gaudioso 2013, brimming with toasted almond and orange blossom honey, with a leaner, smoky palate.

○ Fiano di Avellino Selvecorte '13	♈♈	3*
○ Greco di Tufo Gaudioso '13	♈♈	3
● Taurasi Hirpus '08	♈♈	5
○ Irpinia Coda di Volpe Taberna '14	♈	2
○ Fiano di Avellino Selvecorte '12	♈♈♈	3*
○ Fiano di Avellino '12	♈♈	3*
○ Fiano di Avellino Selvecorte '11	♈♈	3*
○ Greco di Tufo '12	♈♈	3
○ Greco di Tufo Gaudioso '12	♈♈	3
○ Greco di Tufo Gaudioso '07	♈♈	3*
○ Greco di Tufo Gaudioso '06	♈♈	3*
○ Irpinia Coda di Volpe Taberna '11	♈♈	2*

Contrade di Taurasi

VIA MUNICIPIO, 41
83030 TAURASI [AV]
TEL. 082774483
www.cantinelonardo.it

CELLAR SALES
PRE-BOOKED VISITS
ANNUAL PRODUCTION 25,000 bottles
HECTARES UNDER VINE 5.00
VITICULTURE METHOD Certified Organic

The Lonardo family has stubbornly earned itself a name as one of the most talented producers of Taurasi. Production figures are off-the-record, and farming techniques are organic, with five hectares planted to aglianico, giving two authentic, well-managed selections of Taurasi, the Coste and the Vigne d'Alto. These authoritative, territorial wines show impressive complexity, and are extremely drinkable despite their close-knit tannins. Although Taurasi rules the roost, Lonardo also produces a Grecomusc', a unique white with an original nose, from a native variety known locally as roviello. The Taurasi 2010 offers great drinkability and tautness, with aromas of juniper, black olives and crisp red berry fruit. This savoury, lean wine shows excellent progression, with a focused, perfectly nuanced finish. We saw another outstanding version of the Grecomusc': the unmissable 2013 has a Riesling edge to it, with its aromas of sage, thyme and hawthorn. In the mouth, salty notes accompany seductive, relaxed development.

● Taurasi '10	♈♈♈	6
○ Grecomusc' '13	♈♈	4
● Irpinia Aglianico '12	♈♈	3
● Taurasi Ris. '08	♈	6
○ Grecomusc' '12	♈♈♈	4*
○ Grecomusc' '10	♈♈♈	4*
● Taurasi '04	♈♈♈	6
● Taurasi Coste '08	♈♈♈	7
○ Grecomusc' '11	♈♈	4
● Taurasi Coste '09	♈♈	7
● Taurasi Coste '07	♈♈	7
● Taurasi Ris. '05	♈♈	6
● Taurasi Vigne d'Alto '09	♈♈	5
● Taurasi Vigne d'Alto '08	♈♈	7
● Taurasi Vigne d'Alto '07	♈♈	7

Marisa Cuomo

VIA G. B. LAMA, 16/18
84010 FURORE [SA]
TEL. 089830348
www.marisacuomo.com

CELLAR SALES
PRE-BOOKED VISITS
RESTAURANT SERVICE
ANNUAL PRODUCTION 109,000 bottles
HECTARES UNDER VINE 18.00

If we were in Norway, this would be a fjord. We are on the Amalfi Coast, a UNESCO heritage site, and specifically at Furore, a lovely town with fewer than 1,000 inhabitants on the clifftops moulded by the River Schiato. Here, fighting for survival among the rocks, we find plots planted to extremely rare varieties, such as fenile, ripoli, pepella, tintore, and sciascinoso. The wines, above all the whites, vinified exclusively in stainless steel, embody a uniquely Mediterranean energy and character. If the Amalfi Coast is also famous for its wines, this is thanks to the untiring work of Marisa Cuomo and Andrea Ferraioli, today assisted by their children Raffaele and Dora. The Furore Bianco 2014, an ethereal white with a nose of thyme and marjoram, ushers in a lively citrusy wake. On the fresh palate it shows surefooted, unfaltering progression. The Fiorduva 2014 offers summer flowers and orange zest. On the palate it shows juicier and more supple than other versions, with a long, fresh finish of toasted almonds and aniseed.

○ Costa d'Amalfi Furore Bianco Fiorduva '14	♟♟♟	7
○ Costa d'Amalfi Furore Bianco '14	♟♟	4
⊙ Costa d'Amalfi Rosato '14	♟♟	4
● Costa d'Amalfi Furore Rosso Ris. '12	♟♟	6
○ Costa d'Amalfi Ravello Bianco '14	♟♟	3
● Costa d'Amalfi Furore Rosso '14	♟	3
● Costa d'Amalfi Ravello Rosso Ris. '12	♟	5
○ Costa d'Amalfi Fiorduva '08	♟♟♟	6
○ Costa d'Amalfi Fiorduva '07	♟♟♟	6
○ Costa d'Amalfi Fiorduva '06	♟♟♟	6
○ Costa d'Amalfi Fiorduva '05	♟♟♟	6
○ Costa d'Amalfi Fiorduva '04	♟♟♟	6
○ Costa d'Amalfi Furore Bianco '10	♟♟♟	4
○ Costa d'Amalfi Furore Bianco Fiorduva '10	♟♟♟	6

D'Ambra Vini d'Ischia

FRAZ. PANZA
VIA MARIO D'AMBRA, 16
80077 FORIO [NA]
TEL. 081907210
www.dambravini.com

CELLAR SALES
PRE-BOOKED VISITS
ANNUAL PRODUCTION 450,000 bottles
HECTARES UNDER VINE 14.00

Tenuta Frassitelli is owned by the D'Ambra family, and has been producing wine since 1888. This is the perfect place to get to know the island of Ischia, and viewed from the sea, the terraced vineyards, with inclines of up to 60%, 600 metres of monorail, and the slopes of the extinct Epomeo volcano, are breathtaking. These vineyards require 1,500 hours of work per year per hectare, a Herculean task. Tenuta Frassitelli, a selection of biancolella, offers bright fruit and an unmistakable saltiness. The 2010 is on top form, while the 1990 was Campania's first white to win a Tre Bicchieri. Alongside biancolella there are varieties like forastera, guarnaccia and piedirosso. The Tenuta Frassitelli 2014 is still youthful, but shows promise for a brighter, more relaxed future, showing fresh citrus and a somewhat rigid palate, but bursting with salty energy and acid thrust. More immediate and expressive, the musky Forastera Euposia 2014 offers perfectly intact fruit, with good progression on the palate punctuated by intense, lingering hints of iodine.

○ Ischia Biancolella Tenuta Frassitelli '14	♟♟	3*
○ Ischia Forastera Euposia '14	♟♟	3
○ Ischia Bianco '14	♟	2
○ Ischia Biancolella '14	♟	3
○ Ischia Biancolella Tenuta Frassitelli '12	♟♟♟	3*
○ Ischia Biancolella Tenuta Frassitelli '90	♟♟♟	3*
○ Ischia Biancolella '12	♟♟	3
○ Ischia Biancolella Tenuta Frassitelli '13	♟♟	3*
○ Ischia Biancolella Tenuta Frassitelli '11	♟♟	3*
○ Ischia Forastera Euposia '13	♟♟	3
● Ischia Per' 'e Palummo '12	♟♟	3
● Ischia Per'e Palummo '13	♟♟	3
● Ischia Per'e Palummo La Vigna dei Mille Anni '12	♟♟	5
● Ischia Rosso Dedicato a Mario D'Ambra '11	♟♟	4

D'Antiche Terre

C.DA LO PIANO - SS 7 BIS
83030 MANOCALZATI [AV]
TEL. 0825675358
www.danticheterre.it

CELLAR SALES
PRE-BOOKED VISITS
ACCOMMODATION AND RESTAURANT SERVICE
ANNUAL PRODUCTION 420,000 bottles
HECTARES UNDER VINE 40.00
SUSTAINABLE WINERY

D'Antiche Terre is an historic name in Irpinian winemaking. Run by Gaetano Ciccarella, the Manocalzati winery boasts 40 hectares of vineyard holdings in some of the region's best wine country. The Greco comes from Tufo, Santa Paolina, Prata and Montefusco; Fiano from Pratola Serra and Manocalzati; and Aglianico from Pietradefusi and Torre le Nocelle. The result is a range of focused wines with a sense of place, showing particular consistency and drinkability this year. The Taurasi Il Vicario Riserva 2008 shows all the traits of a particularly good growing year, with perfectly ripe fruit and a nose played on fresh balsamic notes and dried fruit. The full, tangy, caressing palate is well sustained by perfectly integrated oak. We also loved the Fiano d'Avellino 2014, a white with an elegant, delicate nose, underpinned by aromatic herbs and white pepper, with a fresh, pleasurable palate. The Coriliano 2013 also impressed.

● Taurasi Il Vicario Ris. '08	♥♥ 5
● Coriliano '13	♥♥ 2*
○ Fiano di Avellino '14	♥♥ 3
○ Irpinia Falanghina '14	♥♥ 2*
○ Greco di Tufo '14	♥ 3
○ Irpinia Coda di Volpe '14	♥ 2
● Coriliano '11	♥♥ 2*
○ Fiano di Avellino '13	♥♥ 3
○ Fiano di Avellino '12	♥♥ 3*
○ Greco di Tufo '13	♥♥ 3
○ Greco di Tufo Vent'Anni '12	♥♥ 3
● Taurasi '08	♥♥ 5

Di Meo

C.DA COCCOVONI, 1
83050 SALZA IRPINA [AV]
TEL. 0825981419
www.dimeo.it

CELLAR SALES
PRE-BOOKED VISITS
RESTAURANT SERVICE
ANNUAL PRODUCTION 450,000 bottles
HECTARES UNDER VINE 30.00
SUSTAINABLE WINERY

The wines of Generoso and Roberto di Meo stand out for their essential, sober style, and require patience and long bottle ageing to express their full potential on the palate. It thus comes as no surprise that some of their Fianos are not released until ten years after harvest, and the extraordinary results prove that a variety still lacking international recognition can acquire complexity over time. The extensive range of this winery, which started out in 1986, is constantly developing. Among the reds, pride of place goes to the Taurasi, from grapes grown in plots at elevations of 650 metres in northern Montemarano. The Olmo vineyard is the highest plot in the area of Montemarano, and the Taurasi Riserva 2008 is its perfect interpretation. On the elegant nose, antique rose, freshly ground pepper and medicinal herbs combine with perfectly ripe, succulent fruit, followed by a graceful palate, where an assertive, full-flavoured attack combines with glossy tannins and extraordinary length.

● Taurasi V. Olmo Ris. '08	♥♥ 5
○ Falanghina '14	♥♥ 3
○ Fiano di Avellino F '12	♥♥ 3
○ Coda di Volpe '14	♥ 2
○ Fiano di Avellino '14	♥ 3
○ Greco di Tufo G '14	♥ 3
● Taurasi Ris. '06	♥♥♥ 5
● Aglianico '09	♥♥ 3
○ Fiano di Avellino Alessandra '10	♥♥ 3
○ Fiano di Avellino Alessandra '09	♥♥ 3
○ Fiano di Avellino Colle dei Cerri '10	♥♥ 4
○ Fiano di Avellino F Sel. Alessandra '11	♥♥ 3
○ Fiano di Avellino Sel. Erminia Di Meo '03	♥♥ 6
○ Greco di Tufo Sel. Roberto Di Meo '10	♥♥ 4

Di Prisco

C.DA ROTOLE, 27
83040 FONTANAROSA [AV]
TEL. 0825475738
www.cantinadiprisco.it

CELLAR SALES
PRE-BOOKED VISITS
ANNUAL PRODUCTION 100,000 bottles
HECTARES UNDER VINE 10.00

If we were at the Olympics, we would already have a triathlon winner, namely Pasqualino Di Prisco, a stubborn, unassuming grower with a deep respect for tradition. Di Prisco manages to achieve exciting results with all three of Irpinia's main DOC wines: Greco di Tufo, Fiano di Avellino and Taurasi. The Greco di Tufo Pietra Rosa is one of his champions, harking from the limestone soils of Fontanarosa, which give mineral notes and beautiful depth on the palate. Equally good are his Taurasi and a lustrous Fiano, offered at incredibly accessible prices. Among the wines presented, we were won over by the two versions of Greco di Tufo. The 2013 Greco boasts roasted hazelnut and elderflower, paving the way for chewy, dense, but not overpowering stuffing, with an attractively nuanced, long, tangy finish. A different style was found in the Greco di Tufo Pietra Rosa 2012, with its notes of hydrocarbons and white pepper. It displays almost aggressive minerality, salty progression and a deep, leisurely finish.

○ Greco di Tufo '13	♥♥ 3*
○ Greco di Tufo Pietra Rosa '12	♥♥ 3*
○ Irpinia Fiano Rotole '14	♥♥ 3
● Irpinia Campi Taurasini '11	♥ 3
○ Greco di Tufo '11	♥♥♥ 2*
● Taurasi '06	♥♥♥ 5
● Taurasi '05	♥♥♥ 5*
○ Fiano di Avellino '12	♥♥ 2*
○ Greco di Tufo '12	♥♥ 2*
○ Greco di Tufo Pietra Rosa '11	♥♥ 3*
○ Greco di Tufo Pietra Rosa '10	♥♥ 3*
● Irpinia Campi Taurasini '10	♥♥ 2*
● Taurasi '10	♥♥ 5

Donnachiara

LOC. PIETRACUPA
VIA STAZIONE
83030 MONTEFALCIONE [AV]
TEL. 0825977135
www.donnachiara.it

CELLAR SALES
PRE-BOOKED VISITS
RESTAURANT SERVICE
ANNUAL PRODUCTION 200,000 bottles
HECTARES UNDER VINE 27.00

Donnachiara is a byword for quality, and the range of wines proposed by Ilaria Petitto, lawyer and grower, never fails to astonish. She now runs the winery established by her father Umberto and mother Chiara, and travels around the world talking about her region and promoting the culture of Irpinia. The modern winery, overlooking beautiful vineyards, is at Montefalcione. There is also an elegant tasting room with views over the valley. The cellar, equipped with innovative technology, produces excellent expressions of Taurasi, Fiano di Avellino, Greco di Tufo and wines based on falanghina and coda di volpe. We recommend the Greco di Tufo 2014, with its sunny, summery character. The nose offers orange zest, bay leaf, and melon, leading to citrus freshness and a well-balanced, elegant finish. We also enjoyed the well-made Coda di Volpe and the Falanghina 2014, delighting with zesty lime and freshly cut grass. The rest of the range seemed a touch below par.

○ Falanghina '14	♥♥ 2*
○ Greco di Tufo '14	♥♥ 3
● Irpinia Coda di Volpe '14	♥♥ 3
○ Fiano di Avellino '14	♥ 3
● Taurasi '11	♥ 5
○ Falanghina del Beneventano '13	♀♀ 2*
○ Fiano di Avellino '13	♀♀ 3
○ Fiano di Avellino '12	♀♀ 3
● Irpinia Aglianico '10	♀♀ 3
● Irpinia Aglianico '09	♀♀ 3
● Irpinia Aglianico '08	♀♀ 3
● Taurasi '09	♀♀ 5
● Taurasi '08	♀♀ 5
● Taurasi Ris. '08	♀♀ 6
● Taurasi Ris. '07	♀♀ 6

I Favati

P.ZZA DI DONATO
83020 CESINALI [AV]
TEL. 0825666898
www.cantineifavati.it

CELLAR SALES
PRE-BOOKED VISITS
ANNUAL PRODUCTION 80,000 bottles
HECTARES UNDER VINE 10.00

In recent years, the winery run by Piersabino Favati, his brother Giancarlo and the latter's wife, Rossana Petrozziello, has clearly shifted up a gear, consistently achieving impressively high scores in our tastings, in particular with their Fiano. Specifically, the Pietramara comes from Atripalda, while the grapes for the Greco Terrantica come from Montefusco. We would prefer the extremely solid Etichetta Bianca range, produced only in the best vintages, to spend a couple more years ageing in the bottle before arriving on the market, especially the whites: tasted again after a couple of years, they are emblematic of how the variety can evolve over time. The range of whites suffered from the difficult 2014 harvest, but nevertheless confirmed the winery's excellent work. In particular, the Fiano di Avellino Pietramara 2014 offered an elegant, tidy weave, with fresh notes of aniseed and lemon zest, making way for toasted hazelnut. We also liked the two versions of Taurasi presented.

○ Fiano di Avellino Pietramara '14	♥♥ 3*
○ Greco di Tufo Terrantica '14	♥♥ 3
● Taurasi Terzo Tratto '09	♥♥ 5
● Taurasi Terzo Tratto Et. Bianca '08	♥♥ 7
○ Fiano di Avellino Pietramara '13	♥♥♥ 3*
○ Fiano di Avellino Pietramara '12	♥♥♥ 3*
○ Fiano di Avellino Pietramara Et. Bianca '13	♥♥ 5
○ Fiano di Avellino Pietramara Et. Bianca '12	♥♥ 5
○ Fiano di Avellino Pietramara Et. Bianca '11	♥♥ 5
○ Greco di Tufo Terrantica '13	♥♥ 3*
○ Greco di Tufo Terrantica '12	♥♥ 3
○ Greco di Tufo Terrantica Et. Bianca '13	♥♥ 5
○ Greco di Tufo Terrantica Et. Bianca '12	♥♥ 5
● Irpinia Campi Taurasini Cretarossa '11	♥♥ 3

Benito Ferrara

FRAZ. SAN PAOLO, 14A
83010 TUFO [AV]
TEL. 0825998194
www.benitoferrara.it

CELLAR SALES
PRE-BOOKED VISITS
ANNUAL PRODUCTION 50,000 bottles
HECTARES UNDER VINE 9.50

The renowned Vigna Cicogna vineyard has got all it takes. This cru of greco, covering under two hectares at San Paolo di Tufo, at an elevation of over 500 metres, has plants rooted in clay-rich, stony soils over a sulphurous substrate. At the helm of this artisanal operation we find Gabriella and her husband Sergio. The first vintage bottled was the 1991, and we are convinced that in recent years there has been a change in style, resulting in racier, fresher wines than the previous versions, which pursued complexity through concentration. The whole range, however, bears testimony to the quality of the work in the rows and cellar. Its musky tone and touch of smokiness, ranging from pencil lead to roasted hazelnut, gave away the Vigna Cicogna in our blind tastings. The 2014 vintage achieved extraordinary compactness considering the growing year, opening to citrus and sulphur on the nose. Slightly peaty notes distinguish the dynamic, vibrant finish.

○ Greco di Tufo V. Cicogna '14	♥♥♥ 4*
○ Fiano di Avellino '14	♥ 4
○ Greco di Tufo '14	♥ 3
○ Greco di Tufo V. Cicogna '13	♥♥♥ 5
○ Greco di Tufo V. Cicogna '12	♥♥♥ 4*
○ Greco di Tufo V. Cicogna '10	♥♥♥ 4
○ Greco di Tufo V. Cicogna '09	♥♥♥ 4
○ Fiano di Avellino '13	♥♥ 4
○ Fiano di Avellino '12	♥♥ 4
○ Greco di Tufo '13	♥♥ 4
○ Greco di Tufo '12	♥♥ 3*
○ Greco di Tufo V. Cicogna '11	♥♥ 4
● Taurasi V. Quattro Confini '10	♥♥ 6
● Taurasi V. Quattro Confini '08	♥♥ 5

★★Feudi di San Gregorio

LOC. CERZA GROSSA
83050 SORBO SERPICO [AV]
TEL. 0825986683
www.feudi.it

CELLAR SALES
PRE-BOOKED VISITS
RESTAURANT SERVICE
ANNUAL PRODUCTION 3,500,000 bottles
HECTARES UNDER VINE 250.00
VITICULTURE METHOD Certified Organic

Feudi di San Gregorio is already a case history, analysed on master's courses and at universities as a model of corporate development. It started out at Sorbo Serpico in 1986 and has seen exponential growth, giving a new lease of life to Campanian wine with innovative marketing and clear production policies. Today, it is one of the largest operations in southern Italy, with 250 hectares of its own land and annual production of 3.5 million bottles. Its range of products is consequently extremely varied, ranging from all the regional types to the increasingly convincing Dubl brand of classic method sparklers. We were very impressed by the Taurasi Piano di Montevergine Riserva 2010, with crisp fruit and roses. This taut, full-flavoured wine shows a beautifully nuanced palate and judiciously dosed oak. It was however the Fiano Pietracalda 2014 that took home a Tre Bicchieri, thanks to its seductive, delicate hint of smokiness.

○ Fiano di Avellino Pietracalda '14	♀♀ 4
● Taurasi Piano di Montevergine Ris. '10	♀♀ 6
○ Dubl + Brut '11	♀♀ 5
○ Greco di Tufo Cutizzi '14	♀♀ 4
○ Irpinia Fiano Passito Privilegio '13	♀♀ 6
⊙ Irpinia Ros'Aura '14	♀♀ 2*
● Piedirosso '14	♀♀ 3
○ Sannio Falanghina Serrociclo '14	♀♀ 3
⊙ Dubl Rosé Brut M. Cl.	♀ 5
○ Fiano di Avellino '14	♀ 3
● Irpinia Aglianico Dal Re '13	♀ 4
● Irpinia Aglianico Serpico '11	♀ 7
● Pàtrimo '12	♀ 8
○ Sannio Falanghina '14	♀ 3
○ Greco di Tufo Cutizzi '12	♀♀♀ 3*
● Taurasi Piano di Montevergine Ris. '07	♀♀♀ 6

Fontanavecchia

VIA FONTANAVECCHIA, 7
82030 TORRECUSO [BN]
TEL. 0824876275
www.fontanavecchia.info

CELLAR SALES
PRE-BOOKED VISITS
ACCOMMODATION AND RESTAURANT SERVICE
ANNUAL PRODUCTION 160,000 bottles
HECTARES UNDER VINE 16.00

The winery of Libero Rillo, who also dedicates his energies to heading the Sannio producers' consortium, is a benchmark for the Benevento area and its main variety, falanghina. Over the years, reduced yields have allowed it to shrug off its poor reputation and take its place among the region's best. The winery is located on the slopes of Mount Taburno, in the Sannio Valley, and boasts two main growing areas, in the Aglianico del Taburno and Sannio Falanghina DOC zones. The range, from 16 hectares of holdings at Torrecuso, Torrepalazzo and Foglianise, also includes Fiano, Greco and Piedirosso. For the third year in a row, the Falanghina del Sannio Taburno garnered a Tre Bicchieri. This white, with a delicately floral, fruit-infused nose, shows acidic sinew, good backbone and full flavour on the palate, leading to a long finish. This is one that will age well. The 2014 Fiano and Greco were interesting and well made, although slightly compromised by the disappointing growing year.

○ Falanghina del Sannio Taburno '14	♀♀♀ 2*
● Sannio Taburno Aglianico V. Cataratte Ris. '08	♀♀ 4
○ Nudo Eroico Extra Dry	♀ 3
⊙ Sannio Aglianico Taburno Rosato '14	♀ 3
○ Sannio Fiano '14	♀ 2
○ Sannio Greco '14	♀ 2
○ Taburno Falanghina '13	♀♀♀ 2*
○ Taburno Falanghina '12	♀♀♀ 2*
● Aglianico del Taburno '09	♀♀ 3
● Aglianico del Taburno V. Cataratte Ris. '07	♀♀ 4
○ Sannio Fiano '13	♀♀ 2*
○ Sannio Fiano '12	♀♀ 2*
● Sannio Piedirosso '12	♀♀ 2*

Fonzone

LOC. SCORZAGALLINE
83052 PATERNOPOLI [AV]
TEL. 08271730100
www.fonzone.it

CELLAR SALES
PRE-BOOKED VISITS
ANNUAL PRODUCTION 57,000 bottles
HECTARES UNDER VINE 22.00
SUSTAINABLE WINERY

The Fonzone Caccese family is reaping the fruits of its work ten years after beginning production. The winery, established at Paternopoli by Lorenzo, originally a surgeon, was a real revelation at the last round of regional tastings. The starting point is the 20-plus hectares of its own vineyards, around half in production, surrounded by olive groves and woodland. For years it has been applying integrated pest management, which means no weed killers, and constant cover cropping in the rows. The fragrant wines boast bright acidity and good length on the palate. It was the Greco di Tufo 2013 that earned the winery its first Tre Bicchieri. We were impressed with the perfectly intact fruit and aromatic focus. On the palate, it proved to be deep, incisive, and full-flavoured, brimming with citrus and fines herbes. This is a wine that has the flavour and grip to stand the test of time. The Fiano d'Avellino 2013 shows a focused nose and an intense, elegant touch of smoke.

○ Greco di Tufo '13	♛♛♛ 3*
○ Fiano di Avellino '13	♛♛ 3*
● Aglianico '12	♛♛ 3
○ Irpinia Fiano Sequoia '13	♛♛ 5
● Irpinia Campi Taurasini '12	♛ 3
○ Fiano di Avellino '12	♛♛ 3
○ Greco di Tufo '12	♛♛ 2*
● Irpinia Campi Taurasini '10	♛♛ 3

La Fortezza

LOC. TORA II, 20
82030 TORRECUSO [BN]
TEL. 0824886155
www.lafortezzasrl.it

CELLAR SALES
PRE-BOOKED VISITS
ANNUAL PRODUCTION 300,000 bottles
HECTARES UNDER VINE 50.00

La Fortezza is synonymous with Enzo Rillo, an entrepreneur who has tried his hand at everything from textiles to construction, road safety and, of course, winemaking. In 2006 he set up his winery at Torrecuso, purchasing 30 hectares of vineyards and renting a further 20. On the eastern side of the Parco Regionale del Taburno-Camposauro, the vineyards are typical of Sannio: aglianico, falanghina, greco and fiano, carefully selected in the rows to produce reliable, attractively-priced wines. Bright and well structured, the Sannio Taburno Falanghina 2014 opens to aromas of straw and citrus peel, over a firm, close-knit palate with well-balanced acidity and fruit, leading to a consistent finish. We found the Aglianico Riserva 2007 still lively and fragrant, almost ten years after harvest.

○ Sannio Taburno Falanghina '14	♛♛ 2*
● Beneventano Aglianico Noi Beviamo con la Testa '11	♛♛ 3
○ Beneventano Falanghina '14	♛♛ 2*
○ Sannio Taburno Aglianico Ris. '07	♛♛ 4
● Aglianico del Taburno '10	♛♛ 2
○ Sannio Fiano '14	♛ 2
○ Sannio Greco '14	♛ 2
○ Sannio Fiano '13	♛♛ 2*
○ Sannio Taburno Falanghina '13	♛♛ 2*

★Galardi

FRAZ. SAN CARLO
S.DA PROV.LE SESSA-MIGNANO
81037 SESSA AURUNCA [CE]
TEL. 08231440003
www.terradilavoro.com

CELLAR SALES
PRE-BOOKED VISITS
ANNUAL PRODUCTION 30,000 bottles
HECTARES UNDER VINE 10.00
VITICULTURE METHOD Certified Organic

Wineries that concentrate on a single wine
are few and far between. Galardi is one of
them, with an estate covering around ten
hectares at San Carlo di Sessa Aurunca, at
elevations of around 400 metres, on a
hilltop surrounded by old olive groves and
chestnut and oak woodland. Its volcanic,
deep alluvial soils are rich in limestone and
shale, and provide grapes for Campania's
most renowned blend of aglianico and
piedirosso, produced by Luisa Murena,
Arturo Celentano, Francesco and Dora
Catello. Terra di Lavoro returns to Tre
Bicchieri form with the 2013 vintage,
regaling us with sun-dried tomatoes, pencil
lead and black tea, over velvety, intact ripe
fruit. The full, fleshy palate is sustained by
soft, creamy tannins, and leads into a
darker finish with notes of black pepper
and roasted coffee beans.

● Terra di Lavoro '13	♟♟♟ 7
● Terra di Lavoro '11	♟♟♟ 7
● Terra di Lavoro '10	♟♟♟ 7
● Terra di Lavoro '09	♟♟♟ 7
● Terra di Lavoro '08	♟♟♟ 7
● Terra di Lavoro '07	♟♟♟ 7
● Terra di Lavoro '06	♟♟♟ 7
● Terra di Lavoro '05	♟♟♟ 7
● Terra di Lavoro '04	♟♟♟ 7
● Terra di Lavoro '03	♟♟♟ 6
● Terra di Lavoro '02	♟♟♟ 6
● Terra di Lavoro '01	♟♟ 6
● Terra di Lavoro '00	♟♟ 6

La Guardiense

C.DA SANTA LUCIA, 104/106
82034 GUARDIA SANFRAMONDI [BN]
TEL. 0824864034
www.laguardiense.it

CELLAR SALES
PRE-BOOKED VISITS
RESTAURANT SERVICE
ANNUAL PRODUCTION 3,700,000 bottles
HECTARES UNDER VINE 1,900.00

A top cooperative in southern Italy, boasting
impressive figures, with 50 years of history,
1,000 grower-members farming 1,900
hectares of vineyards, and annual
production of over 22,000 tonnes of grapes
for 3.7 million bottles. Domizio Pigna heads
this viticultural colossus, which has become
a benchmark for wineries in the Sannio
area in just a few years. Falanghina and
Aglianico are at the heart of a range well
distributed among basic products at very
fair prices and the Janare selections. There
are also forays into passitos and sparklers.
Once again, the Falanghina del Sannio Le
Janare earned a Tre Bicchieri, proving to be
one of the region's best whites. It shows a
modern, luscious style, with a bouquet of
yellow-fleshed tropical fruit, followed by
wild flowers and aromatic herbs. The tangy,
mineral, taut palate is brimming with fruit,
to end fresh and long on mineral notes. We
liked the rest of the range.

○ Falanghina del Sannio Janare '14	♟♟♟ 2*
● Sannio Aglianico I Mille per l'Aglianico '11	♟♟ 7
○ Sannio Fiano Janare '14	♟♟ 2*
● Sannio Piedirosso Janare '12	♟♟ 2*
○ Sannio Greco Janare '14	♟ 2
● Sannio Guardiolo Janare Ris. '12	♟ 2
○ Sannio Falanghina Janare '13	♟♟♟ 2*
● Sannio Aglianico Cantari Ris. '11	♟♟ 3
○ Sannio Falanghina Calvese '13	♟♟ 2*
○ Sannio Falanghina Le Janare Senete '12	♟♟ 2*
○ Sannio Fiano Colle di Tilio '13	♟♟ 3
○ Sannio Greco Pietralata '13	♟♟ 3
● Sannio Guardiolo Aglianico '11	♟♟ 2*

Luigi Maffini

FRAZ. SAN MARCO
LOC. CENITO
84048 CASTELLABATE [SA]
TEL. 0974966345
info@luigimaffini.it

CELLAR SALES
PRE-BOOKED VISITS
ANNUAL PRODUCTION 100,000 bottles
HECTARES UNDER VINE 15.00
VITICULTURE METHOD Certified Organic
SUSTAINABLE WINERY

Luigi Maffini has two production facilities
inside the Parco Nazionale del Cilento e
Vallo di Diano, both using organic farming
methods. The first is the historic coastal
plot at Castellabate, which dates back to
the 1970s; the second is a more recent
vineyard in the hills, with a new cellar. On
the latter the winery's Fianos and
Aglianicos benefit from limestone marl and
a fresher climate, translating on tasting into
greater tautness and vitality on the palate
compared to the winery's classic style. We
tasted three wines this year. The first is a
winery classic, the Cilento Fiano
Pietraincatenata 2013, which earned a
place in our finals with its nose of blossom
and Mediterranean scrub, leading to a
pervasive, generous, deep palate with good
progression, buttressed by a spirited acidic
vein that sustains the long finish. The
potent Kràtos offers a tangy, fruity, focused
palate. The 2012 version of the Klèos was
full of flavour.

○ Cilento Fiano Pietraincatenata '13	♥♥ 5	
● Klèos '12	♥♥ 3	
○ Kràtos '14	♥♥ 3	
● Cilento Aglianico Cenito '03	♥♥♥ 5	
○ Cilento Fiano Pietraincatenata '12	♥♥♥ 5	
○ Cilento Fiano Pietraincatenata '10	♥♥♥ 4*	
○ Pietraincatenata '07	♥♥♥ 4	
○ Pietraincatenata '04	♥♥♥ 4	
● Cilento Aglianico Cenito '10	♥♥ 5	
● Cilento Aglianico Cenito '09	♥♥ 5	
○ Cilento Fiano Pietraincatenata '11	♥♥ 5	
○ Kràtos '13	♥♥ 3	
○ Kràtos '12	♥♥ 3	
○ Kràtos '10	♥♥ 3	
○ Pietraincatenata '09	♥♥ 5	

Guido Marsella

VIA MARONE, 1
83010 SUMMONTE [AV]
TEL. 0825691005
www.guidomarsella.com

CELLAR SALES
PRE-BOOKED VISITS
ANNUAL PRODUCTION 25,000 bottles
HECTARES UNDER VINE 8.00
SUSTAINABLE WINERY

If Summonte now has a reputation as some
of the best wine country for Fiano di
Avellino, much of the merit goes to Guido
Marsella. In 1995 he decided to invest in
an area that was famous above all for the
production of chestnuts, and became one
of the first to hold back his wines, releasing
them over a year after harvest. His Fianos
are unmistakable even in blind tastings,
with their exuberant, typical, delicately
peaty nose, followed by faint lactic notes
and glycerine richness. Even when newly
released, they may sometimes seem
over-mature, only to undergo incredible
changes in terms of profile and progression
with bottle ageing, one of the beauties of
Fiano. The Fiano di Avellino 2012 opens up
slowly in the glass, at first seeming
over-evolved with a lack of dynamism on
the nose. Yet, for those prepared to wait, it
opens up to an intense profile of smoke
and blossom, with notes of curry plant,
chamomile and juicy peach. The zesty,
caressing mouth shows toasted hazelnut
and a long, flavoursome, spicy finish.

○ Fiano di Avellino '12	♥♥ 2*	
○ Fiano di Avellino '09	♥♥♥ 2*	
○ Fiano di Avellino '11	♥♥ 2*	
○ Fiano di Avellino '10	♥♥ 2*	
○ Fiano di Avellino '08	♥♥ 2*	
○ Fiano di Avellino '07	♥♥ 2*	
○ Fiano di Avellino '05	♥♥ 2*	
○ Fiano di Avellino '04	♥♥ 2*	
○ Fiano di Avellino '03	♥♥ 2*	
○ Greco di Tufo Poggi Reali '10	♥♥ 2*	

Masseria Felicia

FRAZ. CARANO
LOC. SAN TERENZANO
81037 SESSA AURUNCA [CE]
TEL. 0823935095
www.masseriafelicia.it

CELLAR SALES
PRE-BOOKED VISITS
ANNUAL PRODUCTION 25,000 bottles
HECTARES UNDER VINE 5.00

The vineyards of Masseria Felicia lie on loose soils rich in volcanic ash, on the north-western slopes of the Massico. This is the area the Romans called "ager falernus", a land that still gives us the wines made famous by authors like Pliny the Elder and Catullus. Felicia Brini and her father Alessandro run this boutique winery of around five hectares, planted solely to native Campanian varieties: falanghina for the whites, vinified in stainless steel; and aglianico and piedirosso for the reds, whose dense stuffing is attractively offset by full flavour and acidic verve. The Falerno del Massico Rosso Etichetta Bronzo 2011 made our finals. This inky-hued, dense wine shows good extraction and a nose of ripe blackcurrants and walnut over a smoky backdrop. The chewy, close-knit palate is well sustained by acidity, and just slightly restrained on the finish by clenched tannins. The Falerno del Massico Rosso 2012 offered succulent notes of blackberry jam and whiffs of balsam.

● Falerno del Massico Rosso Et. Bronzo '11	♟♟ 5
● Falerno del Massico Rosso '12	♟♟ 2*
○ Falerno del Massico Bianco Anthologia '14	♟ 3
● Falerno del Massico Rosso Ariapetrina '12	♟ 3
⊙ Rosalice '14	♟ 3
● Falerno del Massico Rosso Et. Bronzo '10	♟♟♟ 5
● Falerno del Massico Rosso Ariapetrina '11	♟♟ 3*
● Falerno del Massico Rosso Ariapetrina '08	♟♟ 3
● Falerno del Massico Rosso Et. Bronzo '11	♟♟ 5
● Falerno del Massico Rosso Et. Bronzo '09	♟♟ 5

★Mastroberardino

VIA MANFREDI, 75/81
83042 ATRIPALDA [AV]
TEL. 0825614111
www.mastroberardino.com

CELLAR SALES
PRE-BOOKED VISITS
ACCOMMODATION AND RESTAURANT SERVICE
ANNUAL PRODUCTION 2,000,000 bottles
HECTARES UNDER VINE 200.00
SUSTAINABLE WINERY

Mastroberardino represents the past and present of Campanian wine. It all began with the work of Antonio Mastroberardino, the father of viticulture in Irpinia, and has been continued by Piero Mastroberardino, increasingly dedicated to promoting the wines of Campania internationally. The family cellar is still home to bottles of Taurasi nearly a century old, and some we recently tasted from the 1960s left us spellbound. The grapes come from 200 hectares planted to vine in the best wine country of Irpinia. The cellar, meanwhile, is at Atripalda, but the winery also has the largest single plot planted to vine in the province, at Radici di Mirabella, which also boasts an experimental farm and resort. Although lacking the final thrust, we saw a long series of wines that achieved impressive scores, raising the average quality of the range. The Taurasi Radici 2011 offers ripe dark berry fruit, roasted coffee and a rounded palate, where fruit sweetness is well balanced by supporting acidity.

○ Fiano di Avellino Radici '14	♟♟ 3*
● Taurasi Naturalis Historia '08	♟♟ 6
● Taurasi Radici '11	♟♟ 5
○ Fiano di Avellino More Maiorum '11	♟♟ 4
○ Greco di Tufo Novaserra '14	♟♟ 3
● Irpinia Aglianico Redimore '13	♟♟ 2*
● Irpinia Falanghina Morabianca '14	♟♟ 3
⊙ Irpinia Rosato Lacrimarosa '14	♟ 2
○ Nerometà '13	♟ 3
● Taurasi Radici '08	♟♟♟ 5
● Taurasi Radici '07	♟♟♟ 5
● Taurasi Radici '06	♟♟♟ 5
● Taurasi Radici '05	♟♟♟ 5
● Taurasi Radici Ris. '07	♟♟♟ 5
● Taurasi Radici Ris. '04	♟♟♟ 5

Salvatore Molettieri

C.DA MUSANNI, 19B
83040 MONTEMARANO [AV]
TEL. 082763722
www.salvatoremolettieri.it

Montesole

LOC. SERRA DI MONTEFUSCO
VIA SERRA
83030 MONTEFUSCO [AV]
TEL. 0825963972
www.montesole.it

CELLAR SALES
PRE-BOOKED VISITS
ANNUAL PRODUCTION 65,000 bottles
HECTARES UNDER VINE 13.00

PRE-BOOKED VISITS
ANNUAL PRODUCTION 1,200,000 bottles
HECTARES UNDER VINE 120.00

Salvatore Molettieri is an artisan of wine, working the land himself, using traditional methods and farming experience, hand-in-hand with modern production technology. His pride is the vineyards at Montemarano at elevations of over 600 metres, where harvesting takes place in November. Long ripening cycles, an excellent diurnal temperature range and clay and limestone soils ensure well-typed Taurasis of great character. The Cinque Querce vineyard is one of the most renowned in the Taurasi DOC zone, also thanks to some extremely old pre-phylloxera vines. There are three Taurasis that deserve to be watched. Il Taurasi Vigna Cinque Querce Riserva 2008 is compromised by a certain variability from one bottle to the next, but retains a sense of place, as well as the flavour and thrust to age well. We found the Vigna Cinque Querce 2009 juicier with more stuffing, without losing any vitality even on the finish, ending to bitter chocolate and blood orange. The Taurasi Renonno 2010 boasts an intriguing Mediterranean, almost spicy profile.

Montesole is a large winery that maintains high levels of quality across its extensive range, while managing 120 hectares under vine. Michele D'Argenio personally supervises the entire production process, producing focused, often highly drinkable wines at competitive prices. The extremely diversified range takes in the various DOC wines of Irpinia and native varieties such as fiano, aglianico, greco and falanghina, as well as sparklers. The reds distinguish themselves for their well-managed tannins. The 2014 is without doubt one of the most successful versions of the Falanghina Vigna Zampino. Brilliant green highlights usher in fresh, airy aromas of aromatic herbs and citrus zest; on the palate, it is fresh, with mineral notes, and an elegantly focused fruity encore. With its long, elegantly spiced finish, among nuances of white pepper and dried herbs, the Fiano di Avellino Vigna Acquaviva 2014 shows incisive progression on the palate.

● Taurasi V. Cinque Querce '09	♟♟ 6
● Taurasi V. Cinque Querce Ris. '08	♟♟ 7
● Irpinia Aglianico Cinque Querce '11	♟♟ 3
● Taurasi Renonno '10	♟♟ 5
○ Fiano di Avellino Apianum '13	♟ 3
○ Greco di Tufo '13	♟ 3
● Irpinia Aglianico O'Calice Rosso '12	♟ 3
● Irpinia Rosso Ischia Piana '11	♟ 3
● Taurasi Renonno '08	♟♟♟ 5
● Taurasi V. Cinque Querce '05	♟♟♟ 6
● Taurasi V. Cinque Querce '04	♟♟♟ 6
● Taurasi V. Cinque Querce Ris. '05	♟♟♟ 7
● Taurasi V. Cinque Querce Ris. '04	♟♟♟ 7
● Taurasi V. Cinque Querce Ris. '01	♟♟♟ 7
● Aglianico Cinque Querce '10	♟♟ 4

○ Sannio Falanghina V. Zampino '14	♟♟ 3*
○ Fiano di Avellino '14	♟♟ 3
○ Fiano di Avellino V. Acquaviva '14	♟♟ 4
○ Grilae Brut	♟♟ 3
○ Greco di Tufo '14	♟ 3
○ Greco di Tufo V. Breccia '14	♟ 4
● Sairus '10	♟ 3
● Sannio Aglianico '11	♟ 2
○ Sannio Falanghina '14	♟ 3
○ Fiano di Avellino V. Acquaviva '13	♟♟ 4
● Sairus '08	♟♟ 3
● Taurasi '07	♟♟ 4
● Taurasi V. Vinieri '07	♟♟ 6
● Taurasi V. Vinieri '06	♟♟ 6

★Montevetrano

Loc. Nido
VIA Montevetrano, 3
84099 San Cipriano Picentino [SA]
Tel. 089882285
www.montevetrano.it

CELLAR SALES
PRE-BOOKED VISITS
ACCOMMODATION
ANNUAL PRODUCTION 25,000 bottles
HECTARES UNDER VINE 5.00

Modernity or tradition? Native or international varieties? When you taste the wines of the cultured, refined Silvia Imparato, these questions become irrelevant. It all started out in 1991 at San Cipriano Picentino, in the province of Salerno. Until very recently the only wine produced was Montevetrano, an extremely rare example of a successful blend of native Campanian varieties, specifically aglianico, with cabernet and merlot. This potent wine, concentrated but not overpowering, rich in contrasts and highly ageable, is an outright classic. In 2011 it was joined by Core, a monovarietal aglianico. The latest versions show that the Montevetrano is becoming slowly leaner, benefiting in terms of freshness and verve on the palate. The 2013 version shows balsamic tones and a hint of resin accompanied by forest fruits. The palate, whilst succulent, is also subtle and lean. Notes of black olives and blood orange distinguish the Core 2013, with its slightly mouth-drying finish.

Mustilli

VIA Caudina, 10
82019 Sant'Agata de' Goti [BN]
Tel. 0823718142
www.mustilli.com

CELLAR SALES
PRE-BOOKED VISITS
ACCOMMODATION AND RESTAURANT SERVICE
ANNUAL PRODUCTION 200,000 bottles
HECTARES UNDER VINE 21.00
VITICULTURE METHOD Certified Organic

Sannio's viticultural renaissance, and this winery's revival of falanghina as a quality variety, started here when Leonardo Mustilli made it his mission back in the 1960s. At the time, Mustilli had identified the most interesting biotypes, in Campi Flegrei and Bonea, and planted both in his new vineyards at Sant'Agata dei Goti, which became a successful DOC zone thanks to him. Today, his daughters Paola and Annachiara are at the helm of the winery with its 20-plus hectares of vineyards. The Falanghina 2014 is exemplary of its type. This spirited, vibrant white opens to citrus and Mediterranean herbs on the nose, leading to a fresh, lively acidic, mineral swathe in the mouth, exalting apple and pear fruit on the supple, pleasurable palate, and ensuring superb cellarability. The excellent Greco 2014 shows a rosemary nose and delicate smoky notes on the palate.

● Montevetrano '13	♈♈ 7
● Core '13	♈♈ 3
● Montevetrano '12	♈♈♈ 7
● Montevetrano '11	♈♈♈ 7
● Montevetrano '10	♈♈♈ 7
● Montevetrano '09	♈♈♈ 7
● Montevetrano '08	♈♈♈ 7
● Montevetrano '07	♈♈♈ 7
● Montevetrano '06	♈♈♈ 7
● Montevetrano '05	♈♈♈ 7
● Montevetrano '04	♈♈♈ 7
● Montevetrano '03	♈♈♈ 7
● Montevetrano '02	♈♈♈ 7
● Montevetrano '01	♈♈♈ 7

● Sannio Aglianico '12	♈♈ 4
○ Sannio Sant'Agata dei Goti Falanghina '14	♈♈ 2*
○ Sannio Sant'Agata dei Goti Greco '14	♈♈ 2*
● Sannio Sant'Agata dei Goti Piedirosso '14	♈ 3
● Sannio Aglianico Grifo di Rocca '09	♈♈ 3
○ Sannio Fiano '11	♈♈ 3
● Sannio Piedirosso '13	♈♈ 2*
● Sannio Piedirosso '12	♈♈ 3
● Sant'Agata dei Goti Aglianico Cesco di Nece '11	♈♈ 3
● Sant'Agata dei Goti Aglianico Cesco di Nece '10	♈♈ 3
○ Sant'Agata dei Goti Falanghina '13	♈♈ 2*
○ Sant'Agata dei Goti Falanghina '12	♈♈ 3

Nanni Copè

VIA TUFO, 3
81041 VITULAZIO [CE]
TEL. 330879815
www.nannicope.it

CELLAR SALES
PRE-BOOKED VISITS
ANNUAL PRODUCTION 7,500 bottles
HECTARES UNDER VINE 2.50
SUSTAINABLE WINERY

The winery of Giovanni Ascione, a food and wine journalist by profession, started out in 2007 with a small plot of two and a half hectares at Monticelli di Castel Campagnano, in the heart of the Colline Caiatine production area in the province of Caserta. It is here that he grows the grapes for the only wine produced, the Sabbie di Sopra il Bosco, from 90% pallagrello nero topped up with casavecchia and aglianico. The first vintage was in 2008, and production is limited, standing at a mere 7,500 bottles. This is one of the few wines that wine writers all agree on, and it has made leaps and bounds in quality. The 2013 vintage brings us a still youthful Sabbie di Sopra il Bosco, somewhat lacking consistency. A slightly herbaceous nose, with sun-dried tomatoes and a balsamic swathe, leads into good flavour and grip on the palate, although it is still held back by a tannic weave that requires time and patience.

Raffaele Palma

VIA ARSENALE, 8
84010 MAIORI [SA]
TEL. 3357601858
www.raffaelepalma.it

ANNUAL PRODUCTION 20,000 bottles
HECTARES UNDER VINE 6.00
VITICULTURE METHOD Certified Organic

It has been said before: but Maiori, on the Amalfi Coast, is a place of breathtaking beauty. The cliff-top vineyards are on old plots, many bush-trained, and rise up almost vertically to elevations of 450 metres. Here, in 2005, Raffaele Palma decided to renovate an old winery, entrusting the oenological side of operations to Vincenzo Mercurio, who opted for organic methods from the outset. The range includes a white, Puntacroce, from fenile, ripolo and pepella; a rosé and a red, both from piedirosso, aglianico and tintore. The only wine presented was the Costa d'Amalfi Bianco Puntacroce, a real revelation in last year's edition. The 2014 vintage is a lustrous white with an intense nose ranging from citrus to melon, and attractive chamomile. The generous, complex, succulent palate signs off to hints of bitter almond and is run through with notes of the sea. This is a wine with an unmistakable sense of place.

● Sabbie di Sopra il Bosco '13	♥♥ 5
● Sabbie di Sopra il Bosco '12	♔♔♔ 5
● Sabbie di Sopra il Bosco '11	♔♔♔ 5
● Sabbie di Sopra il Bosco '10	♔♔♔ 5
● Sabbie di Sopra il Bosco '09	♔♔♔ 5
● Sabbie di Sopra il Bosco '08	♔♔ 5

○ Costa d'Amalfi Bianco Puntacroce '14	♥♥♥ 6
○ Costa d'Amalfi Bianco Puntacroce '13	♔♔♔ 6

Perillo

C.DA VALLE, 19
83040 CASTELFRANCI [AV]
TEL. 082772252
cantinaperillo@libero.it

CELLAR SALES
PRE-BOOKED VISITS
ANNUAL PRODUCTION 20,000 bottles
HECTARES UNDER VINE 5.00

Michele Perillo is a guiding light for many lovers of Taurasi. His vineyards are distributed between Castelfranci and Montemarano at elevations of almost 700 metres, where the favourable aspect and ripening cycle of the grapes make it possible to harvest well into November. The feisty wines come from an aglianico, known here as coda di cavallo, its elongated cluster reminiscent of a horse's tail. The rest is down to the soils, rich in clay and silica; old vines and traditional vinification method. The richly extracted Taurasis have penetrating depth on the palate, and are always well-balanced by crunchy fruit, lively flavour, and good acidity. The gutsy Taurasi 2007 combines intense, rustic character with extraordinary energy and progression in the mouth. Black olive and sun-dried tomatoes pave the way for a juicy, racy palate, full of flavour and well-managed, but above all fabulously long, earning it a Tre Bicchieri. The Coda di Volpe 2012 alternates sulphurous notes with dried fruit.

● Taurasi '07	♟♟♟	6
○ Irpinia Coda di Volpe '12	♟♟	3
● Taurasi '05	♙♙♙	4
● Taurasi Ris. '06	♙♙♙	6
● Taurasi '04	♙♙	4*
● Taurasi '03	♙♙	5
● Taurasi Ris. '05	♙♙	5
● Taurasi Ris. '01	♙♙	5

Ciro Picariello

VIA MARRONI
83010 SUMMONTE [AV]
TEL. 082533848
www.ciropicariello.com

CELLAR SALES
PRE-BOOKED VISITS
ANNUAL PRODUCTION 50,000 bottles
HECTARES UNDER VINE 11.00

Summonte is a small town in Irpinia at an altitude of over 650 metres. Ciro Picariello and his Fianos confirm this subzone's vocation for white wines, although it is still one of the least densely planted in the Fiano di Avellino DOC zone. Summonte can be considered the grand cru of the zone, with its unique top layer of 30-40 centimetres of volcanic soil. His Fiano di Avellino combines grapes from Summonte and Montefredane, while the Fiano Ciro 906 is the expression of a plot at Summonte. After a past as a grower for Feudi di San Gregorio, in 2004 Ciro Picariello began earning a reputation for linear wines with vibrant, thrusting acidity. The racy Fiano di Avellino 2013 opens to a nose of mountain herbs, green tea and mint, over a tidy, fragrant palate. New this year was the full-bodied, summery Fiano di Avellino Ciro 906 2012, from a selection of Summonte, with intense smoky aromas and a long finish of medicinal herbs.

○ Fiano di Avellino Ciro 906 '12	♟♟	4
● Brut Contadino	♟♟	4
○ Fiano di Avellino '13	♟♟	4
○ Greco di Tufo '13	♟	3
● Irpinia Aglianico Zi Filicella '13	♟	3
○ Fiano di Avellino '10	♙♙♙	3*
○ Fiano di Avellino '08	♙♙♙	3*
○ Fiano di Avellino '11	♙♙	3*
○ Fiano di Avellino '09	♙♙	3
○ Fiano di Avellino '07	♙♙	3*

CAMPANIA

La Pietra di Tommasone

Via Provinciale Fango, 98
80076 Lacco Ameno [NA]
Tel. 0813330330
www.tommasonevini.it

CELLAR SALES
PRE-BOOKED VISITS
ANNUAL PRODUCTION 100,000 bottles
HECTARES UNDER VINE 11.00

Last year we saw a solid range on the way up, and this year's tastings confirmed our impression, leading to a debut in the main section of the Guide. The history of this cellar from Ischia is intertwined with the personal story of Antonio Monti, who in the 1980s left the island and moved to Germany to marry a local girl. In Cologne, a few years later, he opened the Osteria Centovini, a restaurant still going strong. In the late 1980s, on a trip back to the island, he decided to give a revive his family's viticultural heritage, and redeveloped a number of small plots. In 2005 this led to the birth of Pietra di Tommasone, which he now heads with his daughter Lucia, who has trained in both Germany and Italy. We particularly enjoyed the delicate, relaxed character of the salty Ischia Biancolella 2014, which opens slowly to notes of sage, aniseed and basil. The fragrant, subtle, yet savoury palate ends with delicious notes of sea breeze and salt.

○ Ischia Biancolella '14	♟♟	2*
○ Ischia Bianco Terradei '14	♟	2
○ Pithecusa Bianco '14	♟	3
○ Epomeo Bianco '13	♟♟	3
● Epomeo Rosso '11	♟♟	3
○ Ischia Biancolella '12	♟♟	2*
● Ischia Per' 'e Palummo '13	♟♟	3
● Pignanera '07	♟♟	6
● Pithecusa Rosso '08	♟♟	3
○ Terradei '13	♟♟	3
○ Terradei '08	♟♟	3*

★Pietracupa

C.da Vadiaperti, 17
83030 Montefredane [AV]
Tel. 0825607418
pietracupa@email.it

CELLAR SALES
PRE-BOOKED VISITS
ANNUAL PRODUCTION 50,000 bottles
HECTARES UNDER VINE 7.50

Sabino Loffredo is a unique, instinctive, self-taught producer. In 2006 he decided to work on his own style without a consultant oenologist. The winery, established by his father Giuseppe in 1990, has become a solid benchmark for enthusiasts looking for scintillating wines with acidic verve and full flavour. Focused, progressive and linear on the palate, these are wines that have northern character, but clearly reflect the mineral white soils of Montefredane for the fiano, and Tufo for the greco. If their commitment to whites persists, the r esults achieved in recent years with full-flavoured, racy reds risk falling by the wayside. This year it was the Greco di Tufo that brought home a Tre Bicchieri. The 2014 displays hints of sulphur, pollen and hazelnut, with lip-puckering acidity in the mouth but also full flavour and incredible length. The reds display increasing focus, with the Taurasi 2010 showing spectacular tautness and focused, complex aromas. Equally good was the Fiano di Avellino 2014, with pollen and bergamot on the nose, although slightly diluted on the finish.

○ Greco di Tufo '14	♟♟♟	3*
○ Fiano di Avellino '14	♟♟	3*
● Taurasi '10	♟♟	5
○ Cupo '10	♟♟♟	5
○ Cupo '08	♟♟♟	5
○ Cupo '05	♟♟♟	5
○ Cupo '03	♟♟♟	3*
○ Fiano di Avellino '13	♟♟♟	3*
○ Fiano di Avellino '12	♟♟♟	3*
○ Greco di Tufo '10	♟♟♟	3*
○ Greco di Tufo '09	♟♟♟	3*
○ Greco di Tufo '08	♟♟♟	3*
○ Greco di Tufo '07	♟♟♟	3*
○ Greco di Tufo '06	♟♟♟	3*
○ Greco di Tufo '13	♟♟	3*

Quintodecimo

VIA SAN LEONARDO, 27
83036 MIRABELLA ECLANO [AV]
TEL. 0825449321
www.quintodecimo.it

CELLAR SALES
PRE-BOOKED VISITS
ACCOMMODATION
ANNUAL PRODUCTION 53,000 bottles
HECTARES UNDER VINE 15.00
SUSTAINABLE WINERY

Luigi Moio, known to everybody as "o professore", grew up among the vineyards, and followed in the footsteps of his father Michele, who relaunched the Falerno zone for the production of high-quality reds. This was back in the 1950s, when Luigi Moio was little more than a boy. In the 1990s, he began to teach at the Department of Agriculture at the Federico II University in Naples, and since then his passion for winemaking has never abated. Today, Quintodecimo, near Mirabella Eclano, is run with the support of his wife Laura Di Marzio, who works with Luigi in the vineyards planted to aglianico at Mirabella Eclano, fiano at Lapio, greco at Tufo and falanghina, also at Mirabella. We saw a solid range, even though we remain convinced that more could be done to accentuate the wine's natural character, at times held back by the oak. The Greco di Tufo Giallo d'Arles 2013 combines notes of peach and melon over a backdrop of coffee and white pepper, melting together on the velvety, creamy palate. The Taurasi Vigna Quintodecimo Riserva 2010 showed excellent stuffing.

○ Greco di Tufo Giallo d'Arles '13	♟♟	6
○ Fiano di Avellino Exultet '13	♟♟	6
● Taurasi V. Quintodecimo Ris. '10	♟♟	8
● Irpinia Aglianico Terra d'Eclano '12	♟	6
○ Irpinia Falanghina Via del Campo '13	♟	5
○ Fiano di Avellino Exultet '09	♟♟♟	6
○ Fiano di Avellino Exultet '12	♟♟	6
○ Fiano di Avellino Exultet '08	♟♟	6
○ Greco di Tufo Giallo d'Arles '12	♟♟	6
● Irpinia Aglianico Terra d'Eclano '10	♟♟	6
● Taurasi V. Quintodecimo Ris. '07	♟♟	8
● Taurasi V. Quintodecimo Ris. '04	♟♟	8
○ Via del Campo Falanghina '07	♟♟	5

Fattoria La Rivolta

C.DA RIVOLTA
82030 TORRECUSO [BN]
TEL. 0824872921
info@fattorialarivolta.com

CELLAR SALES
PRE-BOOKED VISITS
ACCOMMODATION
ANNUAL PRODUCTION 150,000 bottles
HECTARES UNDER VINE 29.00
VITICULTURE METHOD Certified Organic

Contrada Rivolta, from which the winery takes its name, is at Torrecuso, in the Benevento area, and has always belonged to the Cotroneo family, since its launch in 1997. Paolo, a pharmacist by profession, decided to invest in the territory, and gradually renewed the vineyard and cellar. Today, he boasts around 30 hectares under vine, all farmed using organic methods. Greco, fiano, falanghina and coda di volpe dominate the range, but the reds are also impressive, with wines from piedirosso and two versions of Aglianico: an entry-level label aged in large oak and the Terra di Rivolta Riserva, in new barriques. The Terra di Rivolta Riserva 2012 made our finals again this year. Its dense ruby hue ushers in a dense, complex nose of red berry fruit, black tea and incense. In the mouth, it shows rich and well-extracted, although still clenched. The Fiano 2014 expresses attractive, fresh minerality, and its complex, full-flavoured palate finishes long to citrus notes, while the Greco delights with an iodine nose and complex honey aromas.

● Aglianico del Taburno Terra di Rivolta Ris. '12	♟♟	5
● Aglianico del Taburno '12	♟♟	3
○ Sannio Taburno Fiano '14	♟♟	2*
○ Sannio Taburno Greco '14	♟♟	3
☉ Aglianico del Taburno Rosato Le Mongolfiere a San Bruno '14	♟	2
○ Sannio Taburno Coda di Volpe '14	♟	2
○ Sannio Taburno Falanghina '14	♟	2
● Sannio Taburno Piedirosso '14	♟	2
● Aglianico del Taburno '10	♟♟♟	3*
● Aglianico del Taburno Terra di Rivolta Ris. '08	♟♟♟	5
● Aglianico del Taburno '11	♟♟	3
● Aglianico del Taburno Terra di Rivolta Ris. '11	♟♟	5
○ Sannio Taburno Greco '13	♟♟	3

Rocca del Principe

VIA ARIANIELLO, 9
83030 LAPIO [AV]
TEL. 08251728013
www.roccadelprincipe.it

CELLAR SALES
PRE-BOOKED VISITS
ANNUAL PRODUCTION 30,000 bottles
HECTARES UNDER VINE 6.50

The story of Rocca del Principe begins in 2004, when Ercole Zarella, his wife Aurelia Fabrizio and his brother Antonio, after working as growers for other wineries, decided to set up on their own, in under a decade becoming a benchmark for lovers of Fiano di Avellino. The peculiarity of their Fiano, the result of a careful selection of clay-rich soils in Lapio, is its late release on the market due to a lengthy stay on the fine lees. The wine shows intense, summery, and delicately smoky aromas, and marvellous complexity on the palate as it ages. We saw another success for Zarella's Fiano d'Avellino. The 2013 version won us over with seductive notes of hydrocarbons over a smoky backdrop, and complex aromas of summer flowers and spice. The full-flavoured palate manages to be at the same time both light and intense, in a crescendo of complex flavours. Once again, it took home a Tre Bicchieri.

○ Fiano di Avellino '13	▼▼▼	3*
● Taurasi Ris. '10	▼▼	5
○ Fiano di Avellino '12	♈♈♈	3*
○ Fiano di Avellino '08	♈♈♈	2*
○ Fiano di Avellino '07	♈♈♈	2*
○ Fiano di Avellino '11	♈♈	3*
○ Fiano di Avellino '09	♈♈	3*
○ Fiano di Avellino '06	♈♈	2*
● Irpinia Aglianico '11	♈♈	3*
● Taurasi Master Domini '07	♈♈	5
● Taurasi Mater Domini '09	♈♈	5
● Taurasi Mater Domini '08	♈♈	5

Tenuta San Francesco

FRAZ. CORSANO
VIA SOFILCIANO, 18
84010 TRAMONTI [SA]
TEL. 089876748
www.vinitenutasanfrancesco.com

CELLAR SALES
PRE-BOOKED VISITS
ACCOMMODATION
ANNUAL PRODUCTION 40,000 bottles
HECTARES UNDER VINE 10.00

The Amalfi Coast is the perfect destination for anyone seeking new sensations in the glass, and original, authentic flavours, impossible to find elsewhere. This is for various reasons: biodiversity, the influence of the sea and the extreme variety of soils and aspects on this stretch of coastline. Tenuta San Francesco opened in 2004 and has three hectares of its own property under vine and seven rented. The vines, many over a century old and ungrafted, are located in the subzone of Tramonti, in the heart of the Amalfi Coast. There are two whites vinified exclusively in stainless steel, alongside intense, Mediterranean reds such as the Quattrospine Riserva or the E' Iss Vigna Paradiso from tintore grapes. After having wines in the finals five times, top honours arrived with a Tre Bicchieri for the Costa d'Amalfi Bianco Per Eva 2013. This summery wine with delicately smoky charm showers mint and summer flowers over a full-flavoured, succulent palate that unbends with finesse into a full, deep finish. We also enjoyed the Rosato 2014.

○ Costa d'Amalfi Bianco Per Eva '13	▼▼▼	4*
○ Costa d'Amalfi Tramonti Bianco '14	▼▼	3
⊙ Costa d'Amalfi Tramonti Rosato '14	▼▼	3
● Costa d'Amalfi Tramonti Rosso Quattrospine Ris. '11	▼▼	5
● E' Iss '11	▼▼	5
● Costa d'Amalfi Tramonti Rosso '13	▼	3
○ Costa d'Amalfi Bianco Per Eva '12	♈♈	4
○ Costa d'Amalfi Tramonti Bianco '13	♈♈	3
○ Costa d'Amalfi Tramonti Bianco '12	♈♈	3*
○ Costa d'Amalfi Tramonti Bianco '11	♈♈	2*
● Costa d'Amalfi Tramonti Rosso '11	♈♈	3
● Costa d'Amalfi Tramonti Rosso Quattrospine Ris. '10	♈♈	5
● Costa d'Amalfi Tramonti Rosso Quattrospine Ris. '09	♈♈	5
● E' Iss V. Paradiso '10	♈♈	5

San Salvatore

VIA DIONISIO
84050 GIUNGANO [SA]
TEL. 08281990900
www.sansalvatore1988.it

CELLAR SALES
ACCOMMODATION AND RESTAURANT SERVICE
ANNUAL PRODUCTION 160,000 bottles
HECTARES UNDER VINE 23.00
VITICULTURE METHOD Certified Organic
SUSTAINABLE WINERY

All-round sustainability and organic production methods distinguish this winery, where even the fertilizer is produced on-site by the buffalos bred here, while the use of a photovoltaic system limits carbon dioxide emissions. The estate, which also has vegetable gardens and olive groves, is the brainchild of Giuseppe Pagano, who established this operation in 2004, with 23 hectares under vine distributed among the hills of Paestum, Stio and Giungano in the Parco del Cilento. The style of the wines, based on native varieties, is typically fragrant, for aromatic whites and velvety, richly-extracted reds. The Pian di Stio confirms its place as the winery's jewel. The 2014 version, with its brilliant green highlights, offers focused, fragrant white peach and Granny Smith apple, over a backdrop of fresh aromatic herbs, leading into an attractively profiled, taut, full-flavoured, racy palate with impressive length. A Tre Bicchieri was never in doubt. We also loved the Falanghina 2014, which manages to be at once creamy, zesty and racy, light yet intense.

○ Pian di Stio '14	▼▼▼ 4*
● Aglianico Corleto '13	▼▼ 3
○ Calpazio '14	▼▼ 3
○ Cecerale Senza Solfiti Aggiunti '14	▼▼ 3
○ Falanghina '14	▼▼ 3
⊙ Joi Brut Rosé '12	▼▼ 5
○ Trentenare '14	▼▼ 3
● Aglianico '14	▼ 3
○ Elea '13	▼ 3
○ Jungano '13	▼ 3
○ Pian di Stio '13	♀♀♀ 4*
○ Pian di Stio '12	♀♀♀ 3*
● Aglianico Gillo Dorfles '12	♀♀ 6
● Omaggio a Gillo Dorfles '10	♀♀ 6

Sanpaolo
Magistravini di Claudio Quarta

C.DA SAN PAOLO
83010 TORRIONI [AV]
TEL. 0832704398
www.magistravini.it

CELLAR SALES
PRE-BOOKED VISITS
ACCOMMODATION
ANNUAL PRODUCTION 250,000 bottles
HECTARES UNDER VINE 13.00

Claudio Quarta and his daughter Alessandra have begun one of the most dynamic and interesting winemaking projects in southern Italy. They have three wineries: two in Puglia's Salento area, and one in Irpinia, at Atripalda, halfway between Tufo and Torrioni. We have nothing but praise for their constant pursuit of sustainability, working with universities and participating in cutting-edge studies on biodiversity. This is reflected in the quality of the wines, with a clear change of gear in recent years. A case in point is the Greco di Tufo Claudio Quarta, released only in magnums. The 2013 version of the Greco di Tufo Selezione Claudio Quarta is different from last year's, but still earned a Tre Bicchieri. The nose is less summery and approachable, and therefore fuller and softer, but it is on the palate that we saw a change of gear, with a lean, vibrant profile of citron and grapefruit, and full flavour. This has a brilliant future ahead of it. The Taurasi Riserva 2009 showed a traditional profile of blood-rich meat and autumn leaves.

○ Greco di Tufo Claudio Quarta '13	▼▼▼ 6
● Taurasi Ris. '09	▼▼ 5
○ Falanghina '14	▼ 2
○ Fiano di Avellino '14	▼ 2
● Irpinia Aglianico '12	▼ 2
○ Greco di Tufo Claudio Quarta '12	♀♀♀ 6
○ Falanghina '13	♀♀ 2*
○ Fiano di Avellino '13	♀♀ 2*
○ Fiano di Avellino Lapio '12	♀♀ 3
○ Fiano di Avellino Montefredane '12	♀♀ 3
○ Greco di Tufo '13	♀♀ 2*
○ Greco di Tufo '12	♀♀ 2*
○ Greco di Tufo Montefusco '12	♀♀ 3
● Taurasi '08	♀♀ 5
● Taurasi Ris. '08	♀♀ 5

Tenuta Sarno 1860

C.DA SERRONI, 4B
83100 AVELLINO
TEL. 082526161
www.tenutasarno1860.it

ANNUAL PRODUCTION 15,000 bottles
HECTARES UNDER VINE 6.00

Maura Sarno produces a Fiano di Avellino
for real enthusiasts, with very low yields
and excellent quality. In the space of only a
few years this has made her one of the
most reliable producers of this Irpinia
classic. Her summery wine comes from a
single plot in the high land of Candida at
almost 550 metres in altitude. Here the
soils are rich in clay and limestone, and
benefit from unique day-night temperature
ranges, providing full-flavoured, bright
wines with intense fruit. Picking is by hand,
and vinification solely in stainless steel with
long maturation on the fine lees. What we
liked about the Fiano di Avellino 2014 was
precisely its expressive lightness, with
subtle complexity and a well-focused
palate. The nose brings together fresh
citron and dried fruit aromas, over a taut,
progressive palate, ending fresh,
well-rounded and focused.

○ Fiano di Avellino '14	♟♟ 3*
○ Fiano di Avellino '13	♀♀ 3*
○ Fiano di Avellino '12	♀♀ 3*
○ Fiano di Avellino '11	♀♀ 3
○ Fiano di Avellino '10	♀♀ 3*

La Sibilla

FRAZ. BAIA
VIA OTTAVIANO AUGUSTO, 19
80070 BACOLI [NA]
TEL. 0818688778
www.sibillavini.com

CELLAR SALES
PRE-BOOKED VISITS
ANNUAL PRODUCTION 70,000 bottles
HECTARES UNDER VINE 9.50

Few other areas in Italy can boast a terroir
as unique as the Campi Flegrei: volcanic
ash and lapilli soils near the sea, for
intriguing salty notes in the glass; a large
number of ungrafted vineyards; and a
wealth of biodiversity. It is here that we find
the winery of Vincenzo Di Meo, which has
been earning an increasingly important
reputation on Campania's winemaking
scene, producing wines that combine a
sense of place with a focused personal
style free from over-embellishment, based
on a light hand during vinification. This year
it was the Falanghina Cruna deLago that
got top marks, with its original profile. Rich
and concentrated, it delights with beeswax
and green tea on the nose, over a savoury
palate with hints of grape skin, whose
weight is perfectly sustained by its acidity.
Once again, we liked the Falanghina 2014,
with up-front citrus and pencil lead aromas.
The Piedirosso 2014 was lean but
delicious.

○ Campi Flegrei Falanghina Cruna deLago '13	♟♟ 4
○ Campi Flegrei Falanghina '14	♟♟ 3
● Campi Flegrei Piedirosso '14	♟♟ 4
○ Campi Flegrei Falanghina '13	♀♀♀ 2*
○ Campi Flegrei Falanghina Cruna deLago '12	♀♀ 4
○ Campi Flegrei Falanghina Cruna deLago '11	♀♀ 4
● Campi Flegrei Piedirosso '13	♀♀ 3*
● Campi Flegrei Piedirosso '12	♀♀ 3
● Campi Flegrei Piedirosso V. Madre '12	♀♀ 4
● Campi Flegrei Piedirosso Vigne Storiche '11	♀♀ 4
● Marsiliano '09	♀♀ 5

Luigi Tecce

C.DA TRINITÀ, 6
83052 PATERNOPOLI [AV]
TEL. 3492957565
ltecce@libero.it

PRE-BOOKED VISITS
ANNUAL PRODUCTION 10,000 bottles
HECTARES UNDER VINE 4.00

Luigi Tecce's wines are neither straightforward nor simple, and require time and a certain amount of knowledge of the Paternopoli terroir, which can give wines with unique character and evolution in the bottle. Luigi is not an oenologist or a businessman, but a vigneron to the core, who has given a strong identity to the whole range. He adjusts vinification every year on the basis of the harvest, passing from amphoras to chestnut barrels, and offers authentic, complex, multifaceted reds. Among the vineyards providing his excellent raw materials is a plot of old vines dating back to the 1930s. The Irpinia Campi Taurasini Satyricon 2012 proposes beautifully ripe dark fruit, over an original, complex palate ranging from black olives and capers, to oregano and blackcurrant. Dense with salty hints, it displays unpredictable progression on the palate. Notes of black tea and pencil lead distinguish the Taurasi Poliphemo 2011, with its spicy, mushroomy profile, that makes it seem more mature than the label declares.

● Irpinia Campi Taurasini Satyricon '12	♥♥	5
● Taurasi Poliphemo '11	♥♥	6
● Taurasi Poliphemo '08	♥♥♥	6
● Taurasi Poliphemo '07	♥♥♥	6
● Irpinia Campi Taurasini Satyricon '10	♥♥	5
● Irpinia Campi Taurasini Satyricon '09	♥♥	4
● Taurasi Poliphemo '10	♥♥	6
● Taurasi Poliphemo '09	♥♥	7
● Taurasi Poliphemo '06	♥♥	6
● Taurasi Poliphemo '05	♥♥	6

Terre del Principe

FRAZ. SQUILLE
S.DA 325 SS. GIOVANNI E PAOLO, 30
81010 CASTEL CAMPAGNANO [CE]
TEL. 0823867126
www.terredelprincipe.com

CELLAR SALES
PRE-BOOKED VISITS
ACCOMMODATION AND RESTAURANT SERVICE
ANNUAL PRODUCTION 50,000 bottles
HECTARES UNDER VINE 11.00
SUSTAINABLE WINERY

Some of the best wine country to the north of Caserta is found in the hills of Squille, a small town in the municipality of Castel Campagnano, surrounded by the Taburno and Matese mountains. Here, Peppe Mancini and Manuela Piancastelli decided to invest in native Campania varieties on their way to extinction. This means an abundance of pallagrello bianco and nero, and casavecchia, interpreted in a modern style. Ambruco, Centomoggia and Piancastelli age in small oak, while there are two selections of pallagrello bianco: Fontanavigna, vinified solely in stainless steel, and Le Sèrole, which spends three months in barriques. The Pallagrello Bianco Le Sèrole is one of the region's most interesting whites. The 2013 shows a complex bouquet of mountain flowers and herbs, peach and elegant nuances of balsam, leading to a full, complex, deep and assertive palate, finishing long to citrus and mineral notes. The elegantly tannic, well-structured Castello delle Femmine 2013 is from casavecchia and pallagrello nero.

○ Le Sèrole Pallagrello Bianco '13	♥♥♥	5
● Castello delle Femmine '13	♥♥	3
○ Pallagrello Bianco Fontanavigna '14	♥♥	3
⊙ Roseto del Volturno '14	♥♥	3
● Sasso di Riccardo '14	♥♥	5
● Casavecchia Centomoggia '12	♥	3
● Piancastelli '12	♥	6
● Casavecchia Centomoggia '11	♥♥♥	5
● Ambruco '12	♥♥	5
● Castello delle Femmine '12	♥♥	3
● Castello delle Femmine '10	♥♥	3*
○ Fontanavigna '12	♥♥	3
○ Le Sèrole '12	♥♥	5
○ Le Sèrole '11	♥♥	5
● Piancastelli '11	♥♥	6

Terre Stregate

loc. Santa Lucia
via Municipio, 105
82034 Guardia Sanframondi [BN]
Tel. 0824817857
www.terrestregate.it

CELLAR SALES
PRE-BOOKED VISITS
ANNUAL PRODUCTION 80,000 bottles
HECTARES UNDER VINE 22.00
SUSTAINABLE WINERY

After its debut in the main section of the Guide in the last edition, Terre Stregate confirmed that it was in fine fettle and one of the benchmarks for Sannio, thanks to its evident leap in quality over the last few years. Established in 1988 at Guardia Sanframondi, today the operation has a new winery which vinifies solely grapes from its own estate covering over 20 hectares of vineyards in this area near Benevento. Aglianico, Greco and Fiano accompany the Falanghina, the winery flagship, which comes in no fewer than three versions, each with its own distinctive character. Falanghina Svelato 2014 ran away with a Tre Bicchieri and looks set to become a classic not only locally but in Campania as a whole. Opening to a bright, greenish straw hue, it shows a concentrated, complex nose of rose, peach, spice and vanilla. The well-rounded, thrusting palate finishes long, fresh and vibrant with hints of citrus. A Tre Bicchieri for such an attractively priced wine earned it our Best Value for Money award.

○ Falanghina del Sannio Svelato '14	▼▼▼ 3*
● Sannio Aglianico Manent '13	▼▼ 3
○ Sannio Fiano Genius Loci '14	▼▼ 2*
○ Sannio Greco Aurora '14	▼ 2
○ Sannio Falanghina Svelato '13	♈♈♈ 2*
○ Falanghina del Beneventano Trama '13	♈♈ 2*
● Guardiolo Aglianico Scrypta '10	♈♈ 3
○ Sannio Falanghina Svelato '12	♈♈ 2*
○ Sannio Falanghina Svelato '07	♈♈ 2*
○ Sannio Falanghina Svelato Sur Lies '13	♈♈ 3*
○ Sannio Fiano Genius Loci '13	♈♈ 2*
○ Sannio Greco Aurora '12	♈♈ 2*

Terredora Di Paolo

via Serra
83030 Montefusco [AV]
Tel. 0825968215
www.terredora.com

CELLAR SALES
PRE-BOOKED VISITS
ACCOMMODATION
ANNUAL PRODUCTION 1,000,000 bottles
HECTARES UNDER VINE 200.00

This is one of the largest wineries in the province of Avellino, with 200 hectares under vine, and its strengths are to be found in a series of estates intelligently distributed over the whole of the Irpinia area, and in the constant commitment of Walter Mastroberardino and his children Daniela and Paolo at the helm. While Serra di Montefusco and Santa Paolina are planted to greco, at Lapio fiano and aglianico hold sway, while the Taurasi comes from Pietradefusi, in the Calore Valley. The wide, reliable range is divided into three lines: grand riservas, crus and classic labels. The characterful, full-flavoured Fiano di Avellino Campore 2012 showing peach, almond and hazelnut overtones, sustained by a glycerine-rich, dense, but not overly sumptuous profile, leading to a leisurely, balsamic finish. The two versions of Falanghina proposed were approachable and enjoyable.

○ Fiano di Avellino Campore '12	▼▼ 5
○ Falanghina '14	▼▼ 4
○ Irpinia Falanghina '14	▼▼ 4
○ Lacryma Christi del Vesuvio Bianco '14	▼▼ 4
○ Fiano di Avellino '14	▼ 3
○ Greco di Tufo Loggia della Serra '14	▼ 3
○ Greco di Tufo Terre degli Angeli '14	▼ 4
● Taurasi Fatica Contadina '08	♈♈♈ 5
● Aglianico '11	♈♈ 2*
○ Coda di Volpe '13	♈♈ 2*
○ Fiano di Avellino Campore '11	♈♈ 5
○ Greco di Tufo Loggia della Serra '13	♈♈ 3*
○ Lacryma Christi del Vesuvio Rosso '13	♈♈ 3
● Taurasi Fatica Contadina '09	♈♈ 5
● Taurasi Pago dei Fusi '08	♈♈ 5

Torre a Oriente

LOC. MERCURI I, 19
82030 TORRECUSO [BN]
TEL. 0824874376
www.torreaoriente.eu

CELLAR SALES
PRE-BOOKED VISITS
ACCOMMODATION AND RESTAURANT SERVICE
ANNUAL PRODUCTION 40,000 bottles
HECTARES UNDER VINE 10.00
SUSTAINABLE WINERY

Patrizia Iannella and Giorgio Gentilcore
share their life, their passions and their
land, and have created a brand of
excellence in farming. Their olive oil is also
extraordinary, but here we are interested in
their marvellous wines, from the rows
tended by Patrizia, on ten hectares in the
heart of Sannio, at Torrecuso. The land and
vineyards at Torre a Oriente are farmed
using organic methods. Falanghina del
Sannio Biancuzita 2012 was one of the
most interesting tasted this year and
romped off with a Tre Bicchieri. This
elegant, complex wine offers a full nose of
ripe melon, tropical fruit and aromatic
herbs. The generous palate shows full
flavour and tautness, accompanied by
fleshy fruit, elegance, balance and length.

Traerte

C.DA VADIAPERTI
83030 MONTEFREDANE [AV]
TEL. 0825607270
info@traerte.it

CELLAR SALES
PRE-BOOKED VISITS
ANNUAL PRODUCTION 81,000 bottles
HECTARES UNDER VINE 6.00

Vadiaperti has played a leading role on the
Irpinia wine scene. In 1984 Antonio Troisi,
previously a longstanding grower for a large
operation in Irpinia, decided to strike out on
his own. In 1993, his son Raffaele began to
give the winery a new lease of life and it
soon became a model for many small
producers, who followed his example and
established new wineries. In 2011 Raffaele,
with Giuseppe Pisano and Claudio Ciccone,
set up Traerte, maintaining the vineyards and
the Vadiaperti brand. The wines display
unique charm, but require time and
patience. The Aipierti and Tornante
selections are joined by Torama, a selection
of Coda di Volpe from Pietradefusi. The Coda
di Volpe Torama 2014 is undoubtedly the
best of its class tasted this year, showing a
crystalline profile and superbly fragrant nose
of mountain herbs over a palate of excellent
tautness and persistent freshness. Both the
Fiano di Avellino Aipierti 2014 and the Greco
di Tufo Tornante 2014 promise a great
future, and share a deep salty weave with
slowly revealed smoky notes.

Wine	Rating
○ Falanghina del Sannio Biancuzita '12	♟♟♟ 3*
● Sannio Aglianico Janico '10	♟♟ 2*
○ Taburno Falanghina Siriana '14	♟♟ 2*
● Taburno Aglianico U' Barone '09	♟ 3
○ Gioconda '13	♟♟ 2*
● Janico '10	♟♟ 2*
○ Sannio Falanghina Biancuzita '11	♟♟ 2*
○ Sannio Falanghina Biancuzita '10	♟♟ 2*
○ Sannio Falanghina Biancuzita '08	♟♟ 2*
● Taburno Aglianico U' Barone '08	♟♟ 3
● Taburno Aglianico U' Barone '07	♟♟ 3

Wine	Rating
○ Irpinia Coda di Volpe Torama '14	♟♟ 5
○ Fiano di Avellino '14	♟♟ 3
○ Fiano di Avellino Aipierti '14	♟♟ 5
○ Greco di Tufo Tornante '14	♟♟ 5
○ Greco di Tufo '14	♟ 3
○ Irpinia Coda di Volpe '14	♟ 2
○ Fiano di Avellino Aipierti '13	♟♟ 5
○ Fiano di Avellino Aipierti '12	♟♟ 5
○ Greco di Tufo '12	♟♟ 4
○ Greco di Tufo Tornante '13	♟♟ 5
○ Greco di Tufo Tornante '12	♟♟ 5
○ Irpinia Coda di Volpe Torama '13	♟♟ 5
○ Irpinia Coda di Volpe Torama '12	♟♟ 2*

Urciuolo

FRAZ. CELZI
VIA DUE PRINCIPATI, 9
83020 FORINO [AV]
TEL. 0825761649
www.fratelliurciuolo.it

CELLAR SALES
PRE-BOOKED VISITS
ANNUAL PRODUCTION 120,000 bottles
HECTARES UNDER VINE 22.00

The wines of the Urciuolo brothers, Ciro and Antonello, confirm the worth of their operation, launched in 1996 with seven hectares of its own and 15 rented. Taurasi, Greco di Tufo and Fiano di Avellino fuel the vast range, from solid, never overly-opulent aglianico-based reds, to well-extracted whites with summery aromas. The grapes for the Taurasi Riserva come from the Mirabella vineyard, while those for the entry-level wine are from Castelfranci. Nor should we forget their pricing policy, which over the years has proved to be extremely competitive. The Taurasi 2011 reflects the hot growing year in its ripe blackcurrant and morello cherry aromas. It shows a modern but well-modulated profile with notes of pennyroyal and leaf tobacco, and a juicy, satisfying palate. The classically-styled Fiano d'Avellino 2014 evolves in the glass, with hints of peach, hay and toasted almond. Whilst on first impact it may appear unexciting, it increases in intensity and flavour.

○ Fiano di Avellino '14	♟♟ 3
● Taurasi '11	♟♟ 4
○ Greco di Tufo '14	♟ 2
● Taurasi '10	♟♟♟ 4*
● Taurasi '07	♟♟♟ 5
● Taurasi '06	♟♟♟ 5*
● Taurasi '05	♟♟♟ 5
● Aglianico '10	♟♟ 2*
○ Fiano di Avellino '13	♟♟ 2*
○ Fiano di Avellino '12	♟♟ 2*
○ Fiano di Avellino '11	♟♟ 2*
○ Fiano di Avellino '10	♟♟ 2*
○ Greco di Tufo '13	♟♟ 2*
● Taurasi '09	♟♟ 4
● Taurasi '08	♟♟ 5

Villa Diamante

VIA TOPPOLE, 16
83030 MONTEFREDANE [AV]
TEL. 0825670014
www.villadiamante.eu

CELLAR SALES
PRE-BOOKED VISITS
ANNUAL PRODUCTION 15,000 bottles
HECTARES UNDER VINE 4.50
VITICULTURE METHOD Certified Organic

Our condolences go to Diamante Renna for the loss of Antoine Gaita, who passed away last January. Antoine was a real pioneer of Fiano di Avellino, even though the winery is actually based at Montefredane. He decided to harvest late and postpone release on the market, leaving the wine as long as possible on the fine lees in order to extract maximum complexity. He always believed in the potential of Fiano, and his Vigna della Congregazione has become a classic of its type: a highly ageable, constantly evolving wine, recently also beginning to benefit from work on spontaneous fermentation. The two versions of Fiano di Avellino 2013 presented were among the best expressions of the type. The Vigna della Congregazione showed classic character, while the Fiano di Avellino Clos d'Haut, in its first edition, further raised the bar, leaving us spellbound. Showing intense, unpredictable development, it is punctuated by blasts of peat, pepper and wild herbs, sustained by explosive, salty, seemingly endless energy on the palate.

○ Fiano di Avellino Clos d'Haut '13	♟♟♟ 5
○ Fiano di Avellino V. della Congregazione '13	♟♟ 5
● Taurasi Pater Nobilis Ris. '07	♟ 5
○ Fiano di Avellino V. della Congregazione '10	♟♟♟ 5
○ Fiano di Avellino V. della Congregazione '08	♟♟♟ 4
○ Fiano di Avellino V. della Congregazione '11	♟♟ 5
○ Fiano di Avellino V. della Congregazione '09	♟♟ 5
○ Fiano di Avellino V. della Congregazione '07	♟♟ 4
○ La Congregazione '12	♟♟ 5
● Taurasi Pater Nobilis '07	♟♟ 5

★Villa Matilde

s.s. Domitiana, 18
81030 Cellole [CE]
Tel. 0823932088
www.villamatilde.it

CELLAR SALES
PRE-BOOKED VISITS
ACCOMMODATION AND RESTAURANT SERVICE
ANNUAL PRODUCTION 700,000 bottles
HECTARES UNDER VINE 130.00
SUSTAINABLE WINERY

If today we can enjoy the wine praised in Horace's Odes, we owe this to Salvatore and Maria Ida Avallone, who have given a new lease of life to Falerno, continuing the work begun by their father Francesco. In 50 years of activity, the original winery at Massico has been joined by other estates: Tenuta Rocca dei Leoni in Sannio, and Tenute d'Altavilla in the heart of Irpinia. Almost 130 hectares of vineyards produce an extremely variegated range, led by the Caracci and Camarato selections from the slopes of the extinct Roccamonfina volcano. We should mention the latest addition, Pithos, the first Falerno del Massico vinified in amphoras. Our finals were graced by the close-knit, well-extracted Vigna Camarato Riserva 2010, combining balsam and orange zest with full body and a hazelnut finish. We loved the generous, tangy Falerno del Massico Bianco 2014, with its fragrant nose of meadow flowers and chamomile, sustained by acidic thrust and aromatic breadth.

Villa Raiano

loc. San Michele di Serino
via Bosco Satrano, 1
83020 Serino [AV]
Tel. 0825595663
www.villaraiano.com

CELLAR SALES
PRE-BOOKED VISITS
ANNUAL PRODUCTION 300,000 bottles
HECTARES UNDER VINE 30.00
VITICULTURE METHOD Certified Organic

Villa Raiano is an old village in the municipality of Serino where the family's oil production facility used to be located. In 1996 they opened Villa Raiano, but it was only in 2009 that the winery, which overlooks the valley running down to the River Sabato, was completed. The owners, Sabino and Simone Basso, and Paolo Sibillo, use organic farming methods with help from the local oenologist Fortunato Sebastiano. They have always focused on native varieties: fiano, greco, falanghina and aglianico. The range is divided into two lines, Classica and Vigne. In the latter, pride of place goes to the Fiano di Avellino 22, referring to the number of kilometres separating Lapio from the winery. A Tre Bicchieri was never in doubt for the 2013 Fiano di Avellino 22, with beautifully intact fruit, fragrant aromas, bright acidity and a solid, compact body leading to a leisurely mint and aniseed finish. It also has extraordinary ageing potential. The meaty, dynamic and elegantly spicy Taurasi 2011 was one of the year's best.

● Falerno del Massico Rosso V. Camarato Ris. '10	🍷🍷 7
● Aglianico Tenuta Rocca dei Leoni '12	🍷🍷 2*
○ Falerno del Massico Bianco '14	🍷🍷 3
● Falerno del Massico Rosso '11	🍷🍷 3
☉ Mata Brut M. Cl.	🍷🍷 4
○ Falanghina Rocca dei Leoni '14	🍷 2
○ Falanghina Roccamonfina '14	🍷 2
○ Fiano di Avellino Tenuta di Altavilla '14	🍷 3
○ Greco di Tufo Tenuta di Altavilla '14	🍷 3
☉ Terre Cerase Rosato '14	🍷 2
○ Falerno del Massico Bianco V. Caracci '08	🍷🍷🍷 3
● Falerno del Massico Camarato '05	🍷🍷🍷 6
● Falerno del Massico Camarato '04	🍷🍷🍷 5

○ Fiano di Avellino 22 '13	🍷🍷🍷 4*
● Taurasi '11	🍷🍷 5
○ Falanghina Beneventano '14	🍷 3
○ Fiano di Avellino '14	🍷 3
○ Fiano di Avellino Alimata '13	🍷 4
○ Fiano di Avellino Alimata '10	🍷🍷🍷 4
○ Fiano di Avellino '12	🍷🍷 3
○ Fiano di Avellino '11	🍷🍷 3
○ Fiano di Avellino 22 '12	🍷🍷 4
○ Fiano di Avellino 22 '11	🍷🍷 4
○ Fiano di Avellino 22 '10	🍷🍷 4
○ Greco di Tufo '12	🍷🍷 3
○ Greco di Tufo '11	🍷🍷 3
○ Greco di Tufo Contrada Marotta '11	🍷🍷 4
● Taurasi '10	🍷🍷 5
● Taurasi '09	🍷🍷 5

A Casa

LOC. PIANODARDINE
VIA FILANDE, 6
83100 AVELLINO
TEL. 0825626406
www.cantineacasa.it

CELLAR SALES
PRE-BOOKED VISITS
ANNUAL PRODUCTION 200,000 bottles
HECTARES UNDER VINE 40.00

○ Fiano di Avellino Oro del Passo '14	🍷 3
○ Greco di Tufo Bussi '14	🍷 3
● Irpinia Aglianico Vecchio Postale '10	🍷 4
○ Sannio Falanghina Cortenuda '14	🍷 3

Abbazia di Crapolla

LOC. AVIGLIANO
VIA SAN FILIPPO, 2
80069 VICO EQUENSE [NA]
TEL. 3383517280
www.abbaziadicrapolla.it

ANNUAL PRODUCTION 12,000 bottles
HECTARES UNDER VINE 2.00

● Sabato '12	🍷🍷 5
○ Sireo Bianco '13	🍷🍷 5

Agnanum

VIA VICINALE ABBANDONATA AGLI ASTRONI, 3
80125 NAPOLI
TEL. 3385315272
www.agnanum.it

CELLAR SALES
PRE-BOOKED VISITS
ANNUAL PRODUCTION 15,000 bottles
HECTARES UNDER VINE 6.50

● Campi Flegrei Piedirosso '13	🍷🍷 3*
● Campi Flegrei Piedirosso V. delle Volpi '12	🍷🍷 5
○ Campi Flegrei Falanghina '14	🍷 3

Aia dei Colombi

C.DA SAPENZIE
82034 GUARDIA SANFRAMONDI [BN]
TEL. 0824817139
www.aiadeicolombi.it

CELLAR SALES
PRE-BOOKED VISITS
ANNUAL PRODUCTION 60,000 bottles
HECTARES UNDER VINE 10.00

● Sannio Guardia Sanframondi Aglianico '12	🍷🍷 2*
○ Sannio Guardia Sanframondi Falanghina V. Suprema '13	🍷🍷 3

Albamarina

C.SO CARLO PISACANE, 28
84051 CENTOLA [SA]
TEL. 3495066001
www.fattorialbamarina.com

CELLAR SALES
PRE-BOOKED VISITS
ANNUAL PRODUCTION 20,000 bottles
HECTARES UNDER VINE 10.00

○ Cilento Fiano Valmezzana '14	🍷🍷 3
○ Cilento Fiano Valmezzana '13	🍷🍷 3
● Agriddi '12	🍷 3

Giuseppe Apicella

FRAZ. CAPITIGNANO
VIA CASTELLO SANTA MARIA, 1
84010 TRAMONTI [SA]
TEL. 089876075
www.giuseppeapicella.it

CELLAR SALES
PRE-BOOKED VISITS
ANNUAL PRODUCTION 60,000 bottles
HECTARES UNDER VINE 7.00
VITICULTURE METHOD Certified Organic

● Costa d'Amalfi Tramonti Rosso '12	🍷🍷 3
● Costa d'Amalfi Tramonti Rosso a' Scippata Ris. '10	🍷🍷 5
● Piedirosso '14	🍷🍷 2*

Cantine Astroni

FRAZ. ASTRONI
VIA SARTANIA, 48
80126 NAPOLI
TEL. 0815884182
www.cantineastroni.com

CELLAR SALES
PRE-BOOKED VISITS
RESTAURANT SERVICE
ANNUAL PRODUCTION 330,000 bottles
HECTARES UNDER VINE 25.00
VITICULTURE METHOD Certified Organic
SUSTAINABLE WINERY

○ Campi Flegrei Falanghina Colle Imperatrice '14	♟♟ 2*
○ Campi Flegrei Falanghina V. Astroni '13	♟♟ 3
○ Strione '10	♟♟ 4

Bambinuto

VIA CERRO
83030 SANTA PAOLINA [AV]
TEL. 0825964634
www.cantinabambinuto.com

PRE-BOOKED VISITS
ANNUAL PRODUCTION 25,000 bottles
HECTARES UNDER VINE 6.00

○ Greco di Tufo '13	♟♟ 3
○ Irpinia Falanghina Insania '14	♟ 2

Barone

VIA GIARDINO, 2
84070 RUTINO [SA]
TEL. 0974830463
www.cantinebarone.it

CELLAR SALES
PRE-BOOKED VISITS
ACCOMMODATION
ANNUAL PRODUCTION 100,000 bottles
HECTARES UNDER VINE 12.00
VITICULTURE METHOD Certified Organic

● Cilento Aglianico Miles '12	♟♟ 5
○ Cilento Fiano Una Mattina '14	♟♟ 3
⊙ Primula Rosa '14	♟♟ 2*

Bellaria

FRAZ. AREA PIP
LOC. CARRANI
83030 MONTEFALCIONE [AV]
TEL. 0825973467
www.agricolabellaria.it

CELLAR SALES
ANNUAL PRODUCTION 100,000 bottles
HECTARES UNDER VINE 15.00

○ Irpinia Falanghina '14	♟♟ 3
● Taurasi '09	♟♟ 6
○ Fiano di Avellino '14	♟ 3
○ Greco di Tufo Oltre '14	♟ 4

Boccella

VIA SANT'EUSTACHIO
83040 CASTELFRANCI [AV]
TEL. 082772574
www.boccellavini.it

CELLAR SALES
PRE-BOOKED VISITS
ANNUAL PRODUCTION 10,000 bottles
HECTARES UNDER VINE 5.00
VITICULTURE METHOD Certified Organic

● Irpinia Campi Taurasini Rasott '11	♟♟ 3
● Taurasi Sant'Eustachio '10	♟ 5

Borgodangelo

LOC. C.DA BOSCO DELLA SELVA
S.DA PROV.LE 52 KM 10
83050 SANT'ANGELO ALL'ESCA [AV]
TEL. 082773027
www.borgodangelo.it

CELLAR SALES
PRE-BOOKED VISITS
RESTAURANT SERVICE
ANNUAL PRODUCTION 30,000 bottles
HECTARES UNDER VINE 8.50
SUSTAINABLE WINERY

● Irpinia Aglianico '12	♟♟ 2*
○ Irpinia Rosato '14	♟♟ 3

Cantina Riccio

C.DA CAMPORE
83040 CHIUSANO DI SAN DOMENICO [AV]
TEL. 0825985631
www.cantinariccio.it

CELLAR SALES
PRE-BOOKED VISITS
ANNUAL PRODUCTION 50,000 bottles
HECTARES UNDER VINE 5.00

○ Falanghina I Vini di Janus '14	♥♥ 3
○ Fiano di Avellino '13	♥♥ 3
● Irpinia Aglianico '13	♥ 3

Cantine dell'Angelo

VIA SANTA LUCIA, 32
83010 TUFO [AV]
TEL. 3384512965
www.cantinedellangelo.com

CELLAR SALES
PRE-BOOKED VISITS
ANNUAL PRODUCTION 18,000 bottles
HECTARES UNDER VINE 5.00

○ Greco di Tufo Torrefavale '13	♥♥ 3*
○ Greco di Tufo '13	♥♥ 3

La Casa dell'Orco

FRAZ. SAN MICHELE
VIA LIMATURO, 52
83039 PRATOLA SERRA [AV]
TEL. 0825967038
www.lacasadellorco.it

CELLAR SALES
PRE-BOOKED VISITS
ANNUAL PRODUCTION 200,000 bottles
HECTARES UNDER VINE 30.00

○ Fiano di Avellino '14	♥♥ 3
● Taurasi '07	♥♥ 5
○ Greco di Tufo '14	♥ 3
● Irpinia Aglianico '11	♥ 2

Viticoltori del Casavecchia

VIA MADONNA DELLE GRAZIE, 28
81040 PONTELATONE [CE]
TEL. 3289726688
www.viticoltoridelcasavecchia.it

CELLAR SALES
PRE-BOOKED VISITS
ANNUAL PRODUCTION 16,000 bottles
HECTARES UNDER VINE 3.00

● Erta dei Ciliegi '13	♥♥ 2*
● Casavecchia Prea '12	♥ 4
○ Pallagrello Bianco '14	♥ 2

Casebianche

VIA CASE BIANCHE, 8
84076 TORCHIARA [SA]
TEL. 0974843244
www.casebianche.eu

CELLAR SALES
PRE-BOOKED VISITS
ANNUAL PRODUCTION 30,000 bottles
HECTARES UNDER VINE 5.50
VITICULTURE METHOD Certified Organic
SUSTAINABLE WINERY

● Cilento Aglianico Cupersito '12	♥♥ 3
○ La Matta Dosaggio Zero '14	♥♥ 3
○ Cilento Fiano Cumalè '14	♥ 2
● Cilento Rosso Delle More '13	♥ 2

Castello Ducale

VIA SAN NICOLA, 51
82031 AMOROSI [BN]
TEL. 0824970160
www.cantinacastelloducale.com

CELLAR SALES
PRE-BOOKED VISITS
ACCOMMODATION AND RESTAURANT SERVICE
ANNUAL PRODUCTION 800,000 bottles
HECTARES UNDER VINE 15.00
VITICULTURE METHOD Certified Organic

● Aglianico Contessa Ferrara '12	♥♥ 4
● Pallagrello Nero '13	♥♥ 3
○ Sannio Falanghina '14	♥♥ 2*

Casula Vinaria

via Mattinelle, 109
84022 Campagna [SA]
Tel. 3485437133
www.casulavinaria.com

CELLAR SALES
PRE-BOOKED VISITS
ANNUAL PRODUCTION 20,000 bottles
HECTARES UNDER VINE 3.00
VITICULTURE METHOD Certified Organic

● Brigante '13	🍷🍷 2*
○ Coccinella '12	🍷 3

Cenatiempo Vini d'Ischia

via Baldassarre Cossa, 84
80077 Ischia [NA]
Tel. 081981107
www.vinicenatiempo.it

CELLAR SALES
PRE-BOOKED VISITS
ANNUAL PRODUCTION 70,000 bottles
HECTARES UNDER VINE 4.00

○ Ischia Biancolella Kalimera '13	🍷🍷 4
● Ischia Per' 'e Palummo '14	🍷🍷 3
○ Ischia Forastera '14	🍷 4
⊙ Rosato '14	🍷 3

Colle di San Domenico

s.s. Ofantina km 7,500
83040 Chiusano di San Domenico [AV]
Tel. 0825985423
www.cantinecolledisandomenico.it

CELLAR SALES
PRE-BOOKED VISITS
ANNUAL PRODUCTION 100,000 bottles
HECTARES UNDER VINE 10.00

● Aglianico '13	🍷🍷 2*
○ Falanghina '14	🍷 2
● Irpinia Campi Taurasini Principe '12	🍷 3
● Taurasi Ris. '10	🍷 5

Contrada Salandra

fraz. Coste di Cuma
via Tre Piccioni, 40
80078 Pozzuoli [NA]
Tel. 0815265258
www.dolciqualita.com

CELLAR SALES
PRE-BOOKED VISITS
ANNUAL PRODUCTION 15,000 bottles
HECTARES UNDER VINE 4.00

● Campi Flegrei Piedirosso Ris. '11	🍷🍷 3
○ Campi Flegrei Falanghina '13	🍷 2

Terre D'Aione

fraz. San Paolo
83010 Tufo [AV]
Tel. 0825998353
www.terredaione.it

CELLAR SALES
PRE-BOOKED VISITS
ANNUAL PRODUCTION 75,000 bottles
HECTARES UNDER VINE 9.00

○ Greco di Tufo '14	🍷🍷 2*
● Taurasi '10	🍷🍷 4

Viticoltori De Conciliis

loc. Querce, 1
84060 Prignano Cilento [SA]
Tel. 0974831090
www.viticoltorideconciliis.it

CELLAR SALES
PRE-BOOKED VISITS
ANNUAL PRODUCTION 200,000 bottles
HECTARES UNDER VINE 21.00
VITICULTURE METHOD Certified Organic
SUSTAINABLE WINERY

○ Fiano Donnaluna '14	🍷🍷 3
○ Fiano Perella '12	🍷🍷 3
● Aglianico Donnaluna '13	🍷 3
○ Bacioilcielo Bianco '14	🍷 2

De Falco

VIA FIGLIOLA, 91
80040 SAN SEBASTIANO AL VESUVIO [NA]
TEL. 0817713755
www.defalco.it

CELLAR SALES
PRE-BOOKED VISITS
ANNUAL PRODUCTION 350,000 bottles
HECTARES UNDER VINE 8.00

○ Fiano di Avellino '14	♟♟ 3
● Vesuvio Lacryma Christi Rosso '14	♟♟ 2*
● Aglianico '13	♟ 2
○ Falanghina '14	♟ 2

Di Marzo

VIA GAETANO DI MARZO, 2
83010 TUFO [AV]
TEL. 0825998022
www.cantinedimarzo.it

CELLAR SALES
PRE-BOOKED VISITS
ANNUAL PRODUCTION 150,000 bottles
HECTARES UNDER VINE 23.00

○ Greco di Tufo Somnium Scipionis '13	♟♟ 5
○ Greco di Tufo Franciscus '14	♟ 3
● Taurasi Albertus '11	♟ 5

Cantina Farro

LOC. FUSARO
VIA VIRGILIO, 16/24
80070 BACOLI [NA]
TEL. 0818545555
www.cantinefarro.it

CELLAR SALES
PRE-BOOKED VISITS
ANNUAL PRODUCTION 207,000 bottles
HECTARES UNDER VINE 20.00

○ Campi Flegrei Falanghina '14	♟♟ 2*
● Campi Flegrei Piedirosso '14	♟ 2

Cantine Federiciane Monteleone

FRAZ. SAN ROCCO
VIA ANTICA CONSOLARE CAMPANA, 34
80016 MARANO DI NAPOLI [NA]
TEL. 0815764153
www.federiciane.it

CELLAR SALES
PRE-BOOKED VISITS
ANNUAL PRODUCTION 200,000 bottles
HECTARES UNDER VINE 15.00

○ Campi Flegrei Falanghina '14	♟♟ 2*
○ Campi Flegrei Falanghina Brut Flagreo	♟ 2
● Campi Flegrei Piedirosso '14	♟ 2
● Penisola Sorrentina Gragnano '14	♟ 2

Historia Antiqua

VIA VARIANTE EST SS 7BIS, 75
83030 MONOCALZATI [AV]
TEL. 0825675179
www.historiaantiqua.it

CELLAR SALES
PRE-BOOKED VISITS
ANNUAL PRODUCTION 90,000 bottles
HECTARES UNDER VINE 30.00

○ Fiano di Avellino '13	♟♟ 3*
○ Greco di Tufo '13	♟♟ 3
● Irpinia Aglianico '12	♟♟ 3
○ Irpinia Falanghina '14	♟♟ 3

Il Verro

LOC. ACQUAVALLE, LAUTONI
81040 FORMICOLA [CE]
TEL. 3456416200
www.ilverro.it

CELLAR SALES
ANNUAL PRODUCTION 20,000 bottles
HECTARES UNDER VINE 4.00

○ Pallagrello Bianco Verginiano '14	♟♟ 2*
○ Pallagrello Bianco Sheep '14	♟ 3

Lunarossa

VIA V. FORTUNATO LOTTO, 10
84095 GIFFONI VALLE PIANA [SA]
TEL. 0898021016
www.viniepassione.it

CELLAR SALES
PRE-BOOKED VISITS
ANNUAL PRODUCTION 50,000 bottles
HECTARES UNDER VINE 4.50

○ Costacielo Bianco '13	♀♀	3*
● Borgomastro '09	♀♀	6
○ Camporeale '14	♀♀	2*
● Marea Rosso '09	♀♀	3

Nativ

C.DA SAN NICOLA, 15
83052 PATERNOPOLI [AV]
TEL. 0825460611
www.winenativ.it

CELLAR SALES
PRE-BOOKED VISITS
ANNUAL PRODUCTION 250,000 bottles
HECTARES UNDER VINE 13.00

○ Falanghina Numero 99 Vico Riviera '13	♀♀	2*
● Irpinia Aglianico '13	♀♀	2*
● Irpinia Aglianico Blu Onice '12	♀♀	3
● Aglianico Rue dell'Inchiostro '13	♀	2

Pietratorcia

FRAZ. CUOTTO
VIA PROVINCIALE PANZA, 309
80075 FORIO [NA]
TEL. 081908206
www.pietratorcia.it

CELLAR SALES
PRE-BOOKED VISITS
ANNUAL PRODUCTION 130,000 bottles
HECTARES UNDER VINE 8.00

○ Ischia Bianco Sup. Tenute Chignole '14	♀♀	3
○ Ischia Bianco Sup. Tenuta Cuotto '14	♀	3

Manimurci

VIA CASALE, 9BIS
83052 PATERNOPOLI [AV]
TEL. 0827771012
www.cantinemanimurci.com

CELLAR SALES
PRE-BOOKED VISITS
ANNUAL PRODUCTION 300,000 bottles
HECTARES UNDER VINE 20.00

○ Greco di Tufo Zagreo '14	♀♀	2*
○ Puella '14	♀♀	1*
○ Fiano di Avellino Nepente '14	♀	2
○ Sannio Falanghina Falange '14	♀	2

Lorenzo Nifo Sarrapochiello

VIA PIANA, 62
82030 PONTE [BN]
TEL. 0824876450
www.nifo.eu

CELLAR SALES
PRE-BOOKED VISITS
ANNUAL PRODUCTION 70,000 bottles
HECTARES UNDER VINE 16.00
VITICULTURE METHOD Certified Organic

○ Sannio Fiano '14	♀♀	2*
● Sannio Taburno Aglianico '12	♀♀	3
● Aglianico del Taburno D'Erasmo Ris. '10	♀	5
○ Sannio Taburno Falanghina '14	♀	2

Porto di Mola

VIA RISIERA
81050 GALLUCCIO [CE]
TEL. 0823925801
www.portodimola.it

CELLAR SALES
PRE-BOOKED VISITS
ANNUAL PRODUCTION 250,000 bottles
HECTARES UNDER VINE 50.00

○ Montecamino '14	♀♀	2*
● Peppì '12	♀♀	2*
○ Collelepre '14	♀	2
● Galluccio Contra del Duca '11	♀	3

Quarto Miglio

VIA CESARE PAVESE, 19
80010 QUARTO [NA]
TEL. 0818760364
www.ilquartomiglio.it

CELLAR SALES
PRE-BOOKED VISITS
RESTAURANT SERVICE
ANNUAL PRODUCTION 70,000 bottles
HECTARES UNDER VINE 3.50
VITICULTURE METHOD Certified Organic

○ Campi Flegrei Falanghina '14	♛♛	2*
● Campi Flegrei Piedirosso '13	♛♛	2*

Andrea Reale

LOC. BORGO DI GETE
VIA CARDAMONE, 75
84010 TRAMONTI [SA]
TEL. 089856144
www.aziendaagricolareale.it

CELLAR SALES
PRE-BOOKED VISITS
ACCOMMODATION AND RESTAURANT SERVICE
ANNUAL PRODUCTION 12,000 bottles
HECTARES UNDER VINE 2.50
VITICULTURE METHOD Certified Organic

⊙ Costa d'Amalfi Tramonti Bianco Aliseo '14	♛♛	4
⊙ Costa d'Amalfi Tramonti Rosato Getis '14	♛♛	4
● Borgo di Gete '11	♛	6

Ettore Sammarco

VIA CIVITA, 9
84010 RAVELLO [SA]
TEL. 089872774
www.ettoresammarco.it

CELLAR SALES
PRE-BOOKED VISITS
ANNUAL PRODUCTION 60,000 bottles
HECTARES UNDER VINE 13.00

○ Costa d'Amalfi Bianco Terre Saracene '14	♛♛	3
● Costa d'Amalfi Ravello Rosso Selva delle Monache Ris. '10	♛♛	4

San Giovanni

C.DA TRESINO
84048 CASTELLABATE [SA]
TEL. 0974965136
www.agricolasangiovanni.it

CELLAR SALES
PRE-BOOKED VISITS
ACCOMMODATION
ANNUAL PRODUCTION 20,000 bottles
HECTARES UNDER VINE 4.00

○ Fiano Tresinus '14	♛♛	3
○ Paestum Bianco '14	♛♛	3
● Castellabate '13	♛	3
● Ficonera '13	♛	5

Sannino

VIA G. SEMMOLA, 146
80056 ERCOLANO [NA]
TEL. 0817394630
www.sanninovini.com

CELLAR SALES
PRE-BOOKED VISITS
ANNUAL PRODUCTION 200,000 bottles
HECTARES UNDER VINE 70.00

○ Falanghina '14	♛♛	2*
⊙ Vesuvio Lacryma Christi Rosato '14	♛♛	2*
● Aglianico '14	♛	2
● Vesuvio Lacryma Christi Rosso '14	♛	2

Santiquaranta

C.DA TORREPALAZZO
82030 TORRECUSO [BN]
TEL. 0824876128
www.santiquaranta.it

CELLAR SALES
PRE-BOOKED VISITS
ANNUAL PRODUCTION 45,000 bottles
HECTARES UNDER VINE 6.00
SUSTAINABLE WINERY

○ Sannio Falanghina '14	♛♛	2*
● Aglianico '09	♛	4

Setaro

LOC. PARCO NAZIONALE DEL VESUVIO
VIA BOSCO DEL MONACO, 34
80040 TRECASE [NA]
TEL. 0818628956
www.casasetaro.it

ANNUAL PRODUCTION 50,000 bottles
HECTARES UNDER VINE 10.00

● Terramatta '13	♟♟ 2*
○ Falanghina Campanelle '14	♟ 2
● Vesuvio Lacryma Christi Rosso Munazei '14	♟ 2

Sorrentino

VIA RIO, 26
80042 BOSCOTRECASE [NA]
TEL. 0818584963
www.sorrentinovini.com

CELLAR SALES
PRE-BOOKED VISITS
ACCOMMODATION AND RESTAURANT SERVICE
ANNUAL PRODUCTION 250,000 bottles
HECTARES UNDER VINE 30.00
VITICULTURE METHOD Certified Organic

● Vesuvio Lacryma Christi Rosso V. Lapillo '13	♟♟ 4
● Don Paolo '13	♟ 4
○ Latikadea '14	♟ 3

Telaro

LOC. CALABRITTO
VIA CINQUE PIETRE, 2
81045 GALLUCCIO [CE]
TEL. 0823925841
www.vinitelaro.it

CELLAR SALES
PRE-BOOKED VISITS
ANNUAL PRODUCTION 550,000 bottles
HECTARES UNDER VINE 70.00
VITICULTURE METHOD Certified Organic

● Galluccio Rosso Ara Mundi Ris. '12	♟♟ 3*
● Bariletta '14	♟♟ 2*
○ Galluccio Bianco Ripa Bianca '14	♟♟ 2*

Terra di Briganti

C.DA TACCETO, 6
82027 CASALDUNI [BN]
TEL. 0824856388
www.terradibriganti.it

CELLAR SALES
PRE-BOOKED VISITS
ACCOMMODATION AND RESTAURANT SERVICE
ANNUAL PRODUCTION 40,000 bottles
HECTARES UNDER VINE 12.00
VITICULTURE METHOD Certified
OrganicCertified Biodynamic

○ Sannio Coda di Volpe '14	♟♟ 2*
○ Sannio Falanghina '14	♟♟ 2*
● Sannio Sciascinoso '14	♟♟ 2*

Trabucco

VIA VITTORIO EMANUELE, 1
81030 CARINOLA [CE]
TEL. 3394791396
www.trabucconicola.it

CELLAR SALES
PRE-BOOKED VISITS
ANNUAL PRODUCTION 18,000 bottles
HECTARES UNDER VINE 2.80
SUSTAINABLE WINERY

● Falerno del Massico Rosso Érre '11	♟♟ 2*
○ Marì 1966 '14	♟♟ 2*
● Falerno del Massico Rosso Rapicano '11	♟ 4

Verrone Viticoltori

C.DA CANNETIELLO
84043 AGROPOLI [SA]
TEL. 089236306
www.verroneviticoltori.it

CELLAR SALES
PRE-BOOKED VISITS
RESTAURANT SERVICE
ANNUAL PRODUCTION 50,000 bottles
HECTARES UNDER VINE 18.00

● Cilento Aglianico V. Girapoggio '11	♟♟ 3
○ Cilento Fiano V. Girapoggio '14	♟♟ 3
○ Fiano '12	♟ 5
○ Rosato V. Girapoggio '14	♟ 3

Vestini Campagnano

FRAZ. SAN GIOVANNI E PAOLO
VIA BARRACCONE, 5
81013 CAIAZZO [CE]
TEL. 0823679087
www.vestinicampagnano.it

CELLAR SALES
PRE-BOOKED VISITS
ANNUAL PRODUCTION 80,000 bottles
HECTARES UNDER VINE 7.00
VITICULTURE METHOD Certified Organic

● Pallagrello Nero '12	♟♟ 5
● Kajanero '14	♟ 2
○ Pallagrello Bianco Le Ortole '13	♟ 4

Vigna Villae

C.DA PESANO
83030 TAURASI [AV]
TEL. 0815519396
www.vignavillae.it

CELLAR SALES
PRE-BOOKED VISITS
ANNUAL PRODUCTION 60,000 bottles
HECTARES UNDER VINE 5.50

○ Fiano di Avellino I Ricordi '14	♟♟ 2*
● Irpinia Aglianico Campi Taurasini Pezze de' Preti '10	♟♟ 3
○ Greco di Tufo I Ricordi '14	♟ 2

Vigne Guadagno

VIA TAGLIAMENTO, 237
83030 MONTEFREDANE [AV]
TEL. 08251686379
www.vigneguadagno.it

CELLAR SALES
PRE-BOOKED VISITS
ANNUAL PRODUCTION 47,000 bottles
HECTARES UNDER VINE 10.00

○ Greco di Tufo '14	♟♟ 3
○ Irpinia Falanghina '14	♟♟ 3
○ Fiano di Avellino '14	♟ 3

Vigne Sannite

LOC. SALELLA
82037 CASTELVENERE [BN]
TEL. 0824941494
www.cesas.it

CELLAR SALES
ANNUAL PRODUCTION 300,000 bottles
HECTARES UNDER VINE 150.00
VITICULTURE METHOD Certified Organic

○ Sannio Falanghina '14	♟♟ 2*
○ Beneventano Agostinella '12	♟ 3
● Sannio Aglianico '11	♟ 2
○ Sannio Fiano '14	♟ 2

Vitivinicola Cuomo
I Vini del Cavaliere

VIA FEUDO LA PILA, 16
84047 CAPACCIO [SA]
TEL. 0828725376
www.vinicuomo.com

CELLAR SALES
PRE-BOOKED VISITS
ANNUAL PRODUCTION 25,000 bottles
HECTARES UNDER VINE 4.00

● Primitivo Poseidon '14	♟♟ 2*
● Cilento Aglianico Granatum '13	♟ 2
○ Fiano Heraion '14	♟ 2

Votino

VIA FIZZO, 14
82013 BONEA [BN]
TEL. 0824834762
www.aziendavotino.com

CELLAR SALES
PRE-BOOKED VISITS
ANNUAL PRODUCTION 100,000 bottles
HECTARES UNDER VINE 5.00
SUSTAINABLE WINERY

● Sannio Taburno Aglianico Furius '10	♟♟ 2*
○ Sannio Taburno Falanghina Cocceius '14	♟♟ 2*
○ Sannio Fiano '14	♟ 2

BASILICATA

Basilicata is one of Italy's loveliest regions but one of the least known. It overlooks two seas, the Tyrrhenian and the Ionian, and is home to the Vulture massif, icon of the province of Potenza. The region is the location of Matera and its Sassi, a UNESCO World Heritage Site and European Capital of Culture for 2019. Greek, Roman and Byzantine relics are found everywhere, along with rock churches, castles and medieval monasteries, farmlands, vineyards and olive groves. The natural scenarios are breathtaking, overshadowed by the growing number of wind turbines that flaw some of the most beautiful Italian agricultural landscapes. A region whose fine foods and cuisine are some of the most interesting in the Mediterranean area. This is a portrait of Basilicata, a region with endless quality potential also in the wine industry. The great regional wine is Aglianico del Vulture, whose designation of origin has been protected since 1971, and which was elevated to DOCG in 2010 with the Aglianico Superiore label. The zone is in the northern part of the province of Potenza, a chain of 15 municipalities starting at Lavello and Venosa, ascending the slopes of Vulture, which reaches an altitude of 1,327 metres. For production reasons the winegrowers decided that all the wineries will debut together and release Aglianico Superiore Riserva 2011 for the next edition of the Guide. This year there are three Tre Bicchieri for Lucania, all three excellent versions of Aglianico del Vulture: Cantine del Notaio's Repertorio 2013; Elena Fucci's Titolo 2013; Terre degli Svevi's Serpara 2010. Three wines with different personalities, three expressions of three different terroirs of an area where this grape found its perfect habitat over 2,000 years ago, but sharing quality excellence. Of course not everything is rosy here and the enthusiasm of a decade ago, which had led to numerous new vineyards being planted, new wineries being opened, and lots of modern processing facilities being built, was followed by a time of stagnation, perhaps aggravated by the area's poor communication skills. Today the scenario may also be bogged down by the countless bottlers marketing this red at significantly lower prices and impacting the high-profile image that the new DOCG production protocol is helping to build. Nonetheless, we are entitled to expect more from the producers of Matera DOC, those of Grottino di Roccanova and of Terre dell'Alta Val d'Agri. Basilicata still has plenty of room to grow.

BASILICATA

Cantine del Notaio

VIA ROMA, 159
85028 RIONERO IN VULTURE [PZ]
TEL. 0972723689
www.cantinedelnotaio.com

CELLAR SALES
PRE-BOOKED VISITS
RESTAURANT SERVICE
ANNUAL PRODUCTION 250,000 bottles
HECTARES UNDER VINE 30.00
VITICULTURE METHOD Certified Organic

After falling in love with his land and with Aglianico, Gerardo Giuratrabocchetti has been enthusiastically running the estate dedicated to his father and his work since 1998. A trained agronomist, Gerardo gave up his job in research to tend 30 hectares of vines with organic and biodynamic methods. He has developed different expressions of Aglianico, including sparklers, rosés, off-the-skins, and passitos. Each label pays homage to the notarial world of deeds and seals, and the wines make this one of Southern Italy's most exciting cellars. The 2013 vintage of Il Repertorio confirms its quality status. We liked the generosity of its sun-drenched bouquet, the fresh-tasting integrity of its fruit, its succulent drinkability, and velvety tannins. Another deserving Tre Bicchieri. Also excellent was La Firma 2012, concentrated with complex oaky notes, while Il Sigillo 2011, from over-ripe grapes, is very sound.

● Aglianico del Vulture Il Repertorio '13	♟♟♟ 4*
● Aglianico del Vulture La Firma '12	♟♟ 6
● Aglianico del Vulture Il Sigillo '11	♟♟ 6
○ L'Autentica '13	♟♟ 5
○ Il Preliminare '14	♟ 3
⊙ Il Rogito '14	♟ 3
● L'Atto '14	♟ 3
○ La Raccolta '14	♟ 3
● Aglianico del Vulture Il Repertorio '12	♟♟♟ 4*
● Aglianico del Vulture La Firma '10	♟♟♟ 6
● Aglianico del Vulture La Firma '00	♟♟♟ 5
● Aglianico del Vulture Il Repertorio '08	♟♟ 4
● Aglianico del Vulture La Firma '11	♟♟ 6
● Aglianico del Vulture La Firma '06	♟♟ 6

Carbone

VIA NITTI, 48
85025 MELFI [PZ]
TEL. 0972237866
www.carbonevini.it

CELLAR SALES
PRE-BOOKED VISITS
ANNUAL PRODUCTION 45,000 bottles
HECTARES UNDER VINE 18.00

Siblings Luca and Sara Carbone have been running the 40-year-old Melfi-based family estate with passion since the early Noughties. With the active support of oenologist Sergio Paternoster, the Carbones work 20 hectares of well-aspected vineyards, in places like Monte Lapis and Piano dell'Incoronata, while ageing cellars for their wines have been excavated from the tufa in a historic building at the heart of Melfi. The Carbones keep environmental impact to a minimum, while their Braide cellar vaunts state-of-the-art equipment. Aglianico 400 Some is this winery's benchmark label. The 2013 reached the finals thanks to its full body, dense and juicy fruitiness, with hints of blackberry, morello cherry and blueberry, underpinned by spicy nuances, supported by velvety tannins and by a very pleasing tanginess. Also top-notch is Stupor Mundi 2012, with its attractive balsamic and liquorice tones, combining well with oaky notes, in an invitingly intact fruitiness.

● Aglianico del Vulture 400 Some '13	♟♟ 4
● Aglianico del Vulture Stupor Mundi '12	♟♟ 5
● Aglianico del Vulture Nero '13	♟ 2
○ Fiano '14	♟ 3
● Aglianico del Vulture 400 Some '11	♟♟ 4
● Aglianico del Vulture 400 Some '09	♟♟ 4
● Aglianico del Vulture 400 Some '08	♟♟ 4
● Aglianico del Vulture 400 Some '06	♟♟ 4
● Aglianico del Vulture Stupor Mundi '08	♟♟ 5
○ Fiano '12	♟♟ 3

Casa Maschito

VIA F. S. NITTI
85020 MASCHITO [PZ]
TEL. 097233101
www.casamaschito.it

CELLAR SALES
PRE-BOOKED VISITS
ACCOMMODATION AND RESTAURANT SERVICE
ANNUAL PRODUCTION 60,000 bottles
HECTARES UNDER VINE 10.00

Casa Maschito was set up by a group of 11 entrepreneurs and friends who shared a passion for wine. They bought up ten hectares of vineyards in the superb Vulture subzone of Maschito, at an altitude of 600 metres, on the volcanic soils that lend structure and elegance to aglianico grapes. Even though aglianico is the estate's mainstay, it also grows the other typical native varietals, which they vinify in their state-of-the-art cellar. Our favourite tipple this year was the Aglianico Portale Adduca 2012, with its inky hues, elegant nose of red berries, morello cherry and ripe plum to the fore stepping aside for more complex notes of spices and aromatic herbs. The full-flavoured and fresh-tasting palate, both firm and balanced, displays smooth tannins and an admirable fruity finish with balsamic notes. La Terrazza 2008 has a more mature character and outstanding concentration.

Casa Vinicola D'Angelo

VIA PADRE PIO, 8
85028 RIONERO IN VULTURE [PZ]
TEL. 0972721517
www.dangelowine.it

CELLAR SALES
PRE-BOOKED VISITS
ANNUAL PRODUCTION 300,000 bottles
HECTARES UNDER VINE 35.00

A venerable name in Basilicata winemaking. This 1930s' winery has now been using Basilica's history and traditions for some 80 years to showcase Aglianico del Vulture outside regional boundaries. Today it is owned by siblings Frminia and Rocco D'Angelo, successfully continuing the outfit's tradition of long periods of maceration and cask ageing. The D'Angelo family have over 40 hectares under vine in Rionero, Barile, Rapolla, and Ripacandida. Also worthy of mention are the firmly-structured Aglianico 2013, elegant and balanced, and a well-defined and fresh-tasting Villa dei Pini 2014, a Chardonnay with a pleasantly Mediterranean character. In the Tenuta del Portale range, the Aglianico Riserva 2010 and Le Vigne a Capanno 2012 displayed a more mature character, not without a certain charm.

● Aglianico del Vulture La Bottaia '12	▼▼ 3
● Aglianico del Vulture La Terrazza '08	▼▼ 6
● Aglianico del Vulture Portale Adduca '12	▼▼ 2*
● Aglianico del Vulture La Bottaia '11	♀♀ 3*
● Aglianico del Vulture Portale Adduca '09	♀♀ 2*
● Aglianico del Vulture Portale Adduca '08	♀♀ 2*
○ Malvasia Lucana '13	♀♀ 2*
○ Moscato Passito Majsor '11	♀♀ 3

● Aglianico del Vulture '13	▼▼ 3
● Aglianico del Vulture Le Vigne a Capanno Tenute del Portale '12	▼▼ 3
● Aglianico del Vulture Tenuta del Portale Ris. '10	▼▼ 4
○ Villa dei Pini '14	▼▼ 2*
● Aglianico del Vulture Tenuta del Portale '13	▼ 3
● Aglianico del Vulture V. Caselle Ris. '10	▼ 5
● Aglianico del Vulture Valle del Noce '13	▼ 5
● Aglianico del Vulture V. Caselle Ris. '01	♀♀♀ 3*
● Aglianico del Vulture Donato D'Angelo '01	♀♀ 3
● Aglianico del Vulture V. Caselle Ris. '04	♀♀ 4
● Aglianico del Vulture V. Caselle Ris. '03	♀♀ 4
● Aglianico del Vulture Valle del Noce '10	♀♀ 5
● Aglianico del Vulture Valle del Noce '05	♀♀ 5
● Aglianico del Vulture Valle del Noce '03	♀♀ 3

BASILICATA

★Elena Fucci

C.DA SOLAGNA DEL TITOLO
85022 BARILE [PZ]
TEL. 0972770736
www.elenafuccivini.com

CELLAR SALES
PRE-BOOKED VISITS
ANNUAL PRODUCTION 20,000 bottles
HECTARES UNDER VINE 6.70
SUSTAINABLE WINERY

The Fucci family saga continues unabated. In recent years, Aglianico del Vulture Titolo has become one of the mainstays of Basilicata winemaking, due in no small part to the whole family's passion in the vineyards and in the cellar, as well as to their vocation for almost seven hectares of estate, including some age-old vineyards in Solagna del Titolo, near Barile. The state-of-the-art cellar, surrounded by vineyards with perfect exposition at 600 metres, was inaugurated this year, and will no doubt enable Elena, the house oenologist, to enhance quality further. The 2013 vintage earned this splendid red its tenth Tre Bicchieri. With its rounded backbone, generous fruitiness and expansive elegance following through onto a concentrated and progressive palate, it has a long, satisfying finish. We also appreciated the elegance of the tannins and the judicious use of new oak barrels. Well done indeed!

● Aglianico del Vulture Titolo '13	♥♥♥	6
● Aglianico del Vulture Titolo '12	♀♀♀	5
● Aglianico del Vulture Titolo '11	♀♀♀	5
● Aglianico del Vulture Titolo '10	♀♀♀	5
● Aglianico del Vulture Titolo '09	♀♀♀	5
● Aglianico del Vulture Titolo '08	♀♀♀	6
● Aglianico del Vulture Titolo '07	♀♀♀	6
● Aglianico del Vulture Titolo '06	♀♀♀	5
● Aglianico del Vulture Titolo '05	♀♀♀	5
● Aglianico del Vulture Titolo '02	♀♀♀	5

Grifalco della Lucania

LOC. PIAN DI CAMERA
85029 VENOSA [PZ]
TEL. 097231002
grifalcodellalucania@email.it

CELLAR SALES
PRE-BOOKED VISITS
ANNUAL PRODUCTION 65,000 bottles
HECTARES UNDER VINE 15.00
VITICULTURE METHOD Certified Organic
SUSTAINABLE WINERY

After falling in love with the Vulture and having understood Aglianico's outstanding potential in this terroir, Fabrizio and Cecilia Piccin are putting their long experience of winemaking in the Tuscan city of Montepulciano to good use on these hills. Around a dozen years ago, they created this fine winery with 16 hectares of excellent organic vines in the area between Ginestra, Maschito, Rapolla, and Venosa. The mainstay of their exceptional labels is aglianico, of course, in all its various incarnations. Gricos, an admirably complex and full-bodied Aglianico del Vulture, once again lives up to its reputation. The brooding ruby 2013's stylish bouquet of red and black berries, particularly cherry, gives way to oaky and aromatic herb undertones. The palate is full-bodied, the tannins soft, with leisurely fruity undertones. The Daginestra 2011 is fleshy, well-orchestrated and balanced.

● Aglianico del Vulture Gricos '13	♥♥	3*
● Aglianico del Vulture Daginestra '11	♥♥	5
● Aglianico del Vulture Grifalco '13	♥♥	4
● Aglianico del Vulture Bosco del Falco '07	♀♀	4
● Aglianico del Vulture Damaschito '07	♀♀	3
● Aglianico del Vulture Gricos '12	♀♀	2*
● Aglianico del Vulture Gricos '11	♀♀	2*
● Aglianico del Vulture Grifalco '12	♀♀	3*
● Aglianico del Vulture Grifalco '11	♀♀	3
● Aglianico del Vulture Grifalco '09	♀♀	3
● Aglianico del Vulture Grifalco '06	♀♀	3*

Martino

VIA LA VISTA, 2A
85028 RIONERO IN VULTURE [PZ]
TEL. 0972721422
www.martinovini.com

CELLAR SALES
PRE-BOOKED VISITS
ANNUAL PRODUCTION 250,000 bottles
HECTARES UNDER VINE 50.00

Young Carolin Martino now helps her father Armando at the helm of this historic winery, dividing her time between the family estate and her role as President of the Aglianico del Vulture Consortium. They now have a state-of-the-art cellars in Rionero, and vineyards on the best-aspected hillsides in the production area, including the Bel Poggio estate in Ginestra. Roughly a third of their production comes from grapes grown in the estate-owned vineyards, with the remainder from the Vulture and Matera areas. As we await the débuts of the new DOCG bottlings, Martino features a good range, headed up by the Oraziano 2010, a darkly brooding ruby, with a rich nose of red berries and Mediterranean scrubland making way for well-defined oaky notes; the mouth is textured, delicate and balanced. Bel Poggio 2010 offers delicious hints of cherry and morello cherry to both nose and palate, where it is full-flavoured and lingering, closing on tones of liquorice.

● Aglianico del Vulture Bel Poggio '10	♟♟	2*
● Aglianico del Vulture Oraziano '10	♟♟	5
● Aglianico del Vulture '12	♟♟	2*
● Aglianico del Vulture Pretoriano '10	♟♟	5
● Aglianico del Vulture Bel Poggio '09	♀♀	2*
● Aglianico del Vulture Bel Poggio '05	♀♀	3
● Aglianico del Vulture Oraziano '09	♀♀	5
● Aglianico del Vulture Oraziano '06	♀♀	5
● Aglianico del Vulture Pretoriano '09	♀♀	5

Musto Carmelitano

VIA PIETRO NENNI, 23
85020 MASCHITO [PZ]
TEL. 097233312
www.mustocarmelitano.it

CELLAR SALES
PRE-BOOKED VISITS
ACCOMMODATION AND RESTAURANT SERVICE
ANNUAL PRODUCTION 20,000 bottles
HECTARES UNDER VINE 9.00
VITICULTURE METHOD Certified Organic

Elisabetta Musto Carmelitano combines enthusiasm and natural methods on her nine hectares of fine vines around Maschito. She has three different crus: the 80-year-old Pian del Moro; 45-year-old Serra del Prete; and the whippersnapper Vernavà aged just 25. They are vinified separately to produce an interesting range of labels. Cellar work is kept to a minimum, avoiding any stabilization or clarification and thus maintaining the charm and character of the various terroirs. The Aglianico Pian del Moro 2011 is a red of great attitude, that shone in our final tastings. It has rich extraction, compact chewy fruitiness, and is supported by a fresh-tasting swathe of acidity and very refined tannins. The Serra del Prete 2012 is on excellent form, with a well-defined balsamic vein but still somewhat lacking in drinkability.

● Aglianico del Vulture Pian del Moro '11	♟♟	4
● Aglianico del Vulture '13	♟♟	6
● Aglianico del Vulture Serra del Prete '12	♟♟	3
● Aglianico del Vulture Maschitano Rosso '13	♟	3
○ Maschitano Bianco '14	♟	3
● Aglianico del Vulture Serra del Prete '09	♀♀♀	2
● Aglianico del Vulture '12	♀♀	6
● Aglianico del Vulture Pian del Moro '10	♀♀	3
● Aglianico del Vulture Pian del Moro '09	♀♀	3
● Aglianico del Vulture Serra del Prete '10	♀♀	3*
● Pian del Moro '08	♀♀	3
● Serra del Prete '08	♀♀	3

Paternoster

C.DA VALLE DEL TITOLO
85022 BARILE [PZ]
TEL. 0972770224
www.paternostervini.it

CELLAR SALES
PRE-BOOKED VISITS
ANNUAL PRODUCTION 150,000 bottles
HECTARES UNDER VINE 20.00
VITICULTURE METHOD Certified Organic

Vito Paternoster and his siblings are about to celebrate 90 years of the family business. Grandfather Anselmo sold his first bottles of outstanding Aglianico way back in 1925 and Paternoster became a beacon for the DOC zone, with 20 hectares of excellent vines, all tended with organic methods on the best-aspected hillsides, such as Gelosia, Macarico and Valle del Titolo in the Barile subzone. The winery has a well-equipped, state-of-the-art cellar, and offers a line-up of prestigious labels. As we await the DOCG débuts of the major labels in the Don Anselmo and Rotondo selections, Vito Paternoster and oenologist Fabio Mecca have come up with a celebratory label, the 2011 Aglianico del Vulture Calibro 1919. A gutsy wine with plenty of personality, deep and complex, a tribute to the family's dedication to the territory. Alongside this, the usual array of excellent wines.

● Aglianico del Vulture Calibro 1919 '11	⬤⬤ 4
● Aglianico del Vulture Synthesi '12	⬤⬤ 3
● Barigliòtt '14	⬤ 2
○ Biancorte Fiano '14	⬤ 3
○ Klino '14	⬤ 2
● Aglianico del Vulture Don Anselmo '09	⬤⬤⬤ 6
● Aglianico del Vulture Don Anselmo '94	⬤⬤⬤ 6
● Aglianico del Vulture Don Anselmo Ris. '05	⬤⬤⬤ 6
● Aglianico del Vulture Rotondo '11	⬤⬤⬤ 5
● Aglianico del Vulture Rotondo '01	⬤⬤⬤ 5
● Aglianico del Vulture Rotondo '00	⬤⬤⬤ 5

Re Manfredi
Terre degli Svevi

LOC. PIAN DI CAMERA
85029 VENOSA [PZ]
TEL. 097231263
www.giv.it

CELLAR SALES
PRE-BOOKED VISITS
RESTAURANT SERVICE
ANNUAL PRODUCTION 220,000 bottles
HECTARES UNDER VINE 120.00

Gruppo Italiano Vini purchased Terre degli Svevi in 1988, and production has been of such consistent quality and quantity ever since that the winery has become one of the top outfits in the production area. Today they have 120 hectares under vine, mainly in the Venosa terroir, most being used for aglianico. There is also a good deal of white grape, mostly traminer and Müller Thurgau, used to make one of Basilicata's favourite whites. The 2010 Aglianico del Vulture Serpara is one of the best versions ever. Elegant, concentrated but also outstandingly balanced, it displays succulent red and black fruitiness, smooth tannins and elegantly complex notes of spice and mountain herbs. Tre Bicchieri. Also very successful is the Taglio del Tralcio 2013 selection, from grapes left to slightly over-ripen on the vine, which has a rich, chamois-soft structure yet is still fresh-tasting and drinkable.

● Aglianico del Vulture Serpara '10	⬤⬤⬤ 5
● Aglianico del Vulture Taglio del Tralcio '13	⬤⬤ 3*
● Aglianico del Vulture Re Manfredi '12	⬤⬤ 4
○ Re Manfredi Bianco '14	⬤⬤ 3
● Aglianico del Vulture Re Manfredi '11	⬤⬤⬤ 4*
● Aglianico del Vulture Re Manfredi '10	⬤⬤⬤ 4*
● Aglianico del Vulture Re Manfredi '05	⬤⬤⬤ 4*
● Aglianico del Vulture Re Manfredi '99	⬤⬤⬤ 4*
● Aglianico del Vulture Vign. Serpara '03	⬤⬤⬤ 4*

Taverna

C.DA TAVERNA, 15
75020 NOVA SIRI [MT]
TEL. 0835877083
www.aataverna.com

CELLAR SALES
PRE-BOOKED VISITS
ACCOMMODATION AND RESTAURANT SERVICE
ANNUAL PRODUCTION 150,000 bottles
HECTARES UNDER VINE 17.00

With some 280 hectares at its disposal around Nova Siri, on the Ionian coast, Taverna is one of the largest estates in Basilicata. Egidio Lunati, son of founder Pasquale, is a firm believer in native Basilicata cultivars like aglianico, greco and primitivo. The winery has almost 20 hectares under vine, spread across Matera province and the Vulture subzone, around Venosa, where aglianico is grown. Production figures are high, and in recent years there has been a marked improvement in quality. This year Taverna has come up with a great Syrah 2013, with delightful marked overtones of black and red berries both on the nose and palate, with a soft and pleasingly spicy finish. Aglianico Loukania remains a classy wine: the 2012 is generous, elegant, concentrated, with an admirable finish displaying fruitiness and bitter chocolate. The Matera Moro I Sassi 2013 is a full wine that flows across the palate, one of Matera's best reds.

● Aglianico del Vulture Loukania '12	♟♟	4
● Matera Moro I Sassi '13	♟♟	3
● Syrah '13	♟♟	3
● Il Lagarino di Dioniso '13	♟	4
● Primitivo '13	♟	2
● Aglianico del Vulture Loukania '11	♟♟	4
● Aglianico del Vulture Loukania '08	♟♟	2*
● Matera Moro I Sassi '11	♟♟	3*
○ Matera San Basile '12	♟♟	3
● Primitivo '12	♟♟	3*
● Syrah '12	♟♟	3

Cantina di Venosa

LOC. VIGNALI
VIA APPIA
85029 VENOSA [PZ]
TEL. 097236702
www.cantinadivenosa.it

CELLAR SALES
PRE-BOOKED VISITS
ANNUAL PRODUCTION 800,000 bottles
HECTARES UNDER VINE 800.00

Founded in 1957, Cantina di Venosa is the benchmark cooperative for the Vulture area. The 27 founder members have multiplied to over 500, with more than 900 hectares of vineyards, in Venosa, Ripacandida, Ginestra, and Maschito. The winery features a series of variations on the theme of Aglianico del Vulture, with various ripening times and styles. There are also plenty of whites, rosés and a fascinating Dry Muscat. Excellent value for money, as always. Another of this year's finalists is the Gesualdo da Venosa 2011, an Aglianico del Vulture with great character and texture, partly aged in new small oak. It has colour, backbone, richness of flavour and intact fruit, closing elegantly on spicy notes with a balsamic streak. The simpler, soft and succulent Vignali 2013 is also first-rate. Traditional and well-made, as ever, the Terre d'Orazio of the same vintage.

● Aglianico del Vulture Gesualdo da Venosa '11	♟♟	5
● Aglianico del Vulture Terre di Orazio '13	♟♟	4
● Aglianico del Vulture Vignali '13	♟♟	2*
● Aglianico del Vulture Bali'Aggio '12	♟	2
● D'Avalos di Gesualdo '14	♟	3
○ Dry Muscat Terre di Orazio '14	♟	3
⊙ Terre di Orazio Rosé '14	♟	3
● Aglianico del Vulture Carato Venusio '07	♟♟	4
● Aglianico del Vulture Terre di Orazio '12	♟♟	3*
● Aglianico del Vulture Terre di Orazio '11	♟♟	3*
● Aglianico del Vulture Vignali '07	♟♟	2*

Basilisco

VIA DELLE CANTINE, 22
85022 BARILE [PZ]
TEL. 0972771033
www.basiliscovini.it

CELLAR SALES
PRE-BOOKED VISITS
ACCOMMODATION
ANNUAL PRODUCTION 55,000 bottles
HECTARES UNDER VINE 27.00
VITICULTURE METHOD Certified Organic
SUSTAINABLE WINERY

● Aglianico del Vulture Teodosio '13		♛♛ 3*

Cantine Cerrolongo

C.DA CERROLONGO, 1
75020 NOVA SIRI [MT]
TEL. 0835536174
www.cerrolongo.it

CELLAR SALES
PRE-BOOKED VISITS
ANNUAL PRODUCTION 25,000 bottles
HECTARES UNDER VINE 25.00
SUSTAINABLE WINERY

○ Matera Greco Le Paglie '14		♛ 2
● Matera Moro Torre Bollita '12		♛ 2
● Matera Primitivo Akratos '13		♛ 2

Consorzio Viticoltori Associati del Vulture

S.S. 93
85022 BARILE [PZ]
TEL. 0972770386
conscoviv@tiscali.it

CELLAR SALES
PRE-BOOKED VISITS
ANNUAL PRODUCTION 130,000 bottles
HECTARES UNDER VINE 100.00

● Aglianico del Vulture Vetusto '08		♛♛ 7
○ Moscato Spumante		♛ 2

Donato D'Angelo di Filomena Ruppi

VIA PADRE PIO, 10
85028 RIONERO IN VULTURE [PZ]
TEL. 0972724602
www.agrida.it

CELLAR SALES
PRE-BOOKED VISITS
ANNUAL PRODUCTION 80,000 bottles
HECTARES UNDER VINE 20.00

● Aglianico del Vulture Donato D'Angelo '12		♛♛ 3*
● Balconara '12		♛ 4

Eleano

FRAZ. PIAN DELL'ALTARE
S.DA PROV.LE 8
85028 RIPACANDIDA [PZ]
TEL. 0972722273
www.eleano.it

CELLAR SALES
PRE-BOOKED VISITS
ACCOMMODATION
ANNUAL PRODUCTION 35,000 bottles
HECTARES UNDER VINE 7.50

● Aglianico del Vulture Eleano '12		♛♛ 5
○ Fedra '14		♛ 3
● Teseo '13		♛ 2

Cantine Graziano

VIA PONTE, 25
85036 ROCCANOVA [PZ]
TEL. 3406951612
www.cantinegraziano.com

CELLAR SALES
PRE-BOOKED VISITS
ANNUAL PRODUCTION 25,000 bottles
HECTARES UNDER VINE 6.00
VITICULTURE METHOD Certified Organic

○ Grottino di Roccanova Bianco Terre di Norce '14		♛♛ 2*
● Grottino di Roccanova Rosso Terre di Norce '13		♛ 2

Tenute Jacovazzo

VIA SARAGAT, 42
75100 MATERA
TEL. 3286696466
info@tenuteiacovazzo.it

CELLAR SALES
ANNUAL PRODUCTION 33,000 bottles
HECTARES UNDER VINE 31.00

⊙ Alba Rosa dei Sassi '14	♀2
○ Bianco d' Autore '14	♀3
○ Ityos dei Sassi '14	♀2
● Nettare d' Uva '13	♀2

Michele Laluce

VIA ROMA, 21
85020 GINESTRA [PZ]
TEL. 0972646145
www.vinilaluce.com

CELLAR SALES
PRE-BOOKED VISITS
ANNUAL PRODUCTION 40,000 bottles
HECTARES UNDER VINE 7.00

● Aglianico del Vulture Le Drude '12	♀♀5
○ Morbino Bianco '13	♀3

Masseria Lanzolla

LOC. MASSERIA LANZOLLA
75023 MONTALBANO JONICO [MT]
TEL. 0835691197
www.masserialanzolla.it

CELLAR SALES
PRE-BOOKED VISITS
ACCOMMODATION
ANNUAL PRODUCTION 100,000 bottles
HECTARES UNDER VINE 25.00
SUSTAINABLE WINERY

○ Chardonnay '14	♀1*
● Lucerio '14	♀1*
● Monade '10	♀2
⊙ Rosato '14	♀3

Macarico

VIA ROMA, 159
85028 RIONERO IN VULTURE [PZ]
TEL. 0972723689
www.macaricovini.it

CELLAR SALES
PRE-BOOKED VISITS
ANNUAL PRODUCTION 33,000 bottles
HECTARES UNDER VINE 7.00
VITICULTURE METHOD Certified Organic

● Aglianico del Vulture Macarì '13	♀♀3
● Aglianico del Vulture Macarico '12	♀♀5
○ Xjnestra '14	♀♀2*
○ Serra del Giglio '12	♀3

Cantine Madonna delle Grazie

LOC. VIGNALI
VIA APPIA
85029 VENOSA [PZ]
TEL. 097235704
www.cantinemadonnadellegrazie.it

CELLAR SALES
PRE-BOOKED VISITS
ANNUAL PRODUCTION 18,000 bottles
HECTARES UNDER VINE 8.00
VITICULTURE METHOD Certified Organic

● Aglianico del Vulture Bauccio '09	♀♀4
● Aglianico del Vulture Drogone d'Altavilla Ris. '07	♀♀4
● Aglianico del Vulture Liscone '10	♀3

Mastrodomenico

V. NAZIONALE PER RAPOLLA, 87
85022 BARILE [PZ]
TEL. 0972770108
www.vignemastrodomenico.com

CELLAR SALES
PRE-BOOKED VISITS
ANNUAL PRODUCTION 30,000 bottles
HECTARES UNDER VINE 8.00
VITICULTURE METHOD Certified Organic
SUSTAINABLE WINERY

● Aglianico del Vulture Likos '12	♀♀3
● Mòs '13	♀2

Ofanto - Tenuta I Gelsi

FRAZ. MONTICCHIO BAGNI
85020 RIONERO IN VULTURE [PZ]
TEL. 0972080289
www.ofantovini.it

CELLAR SALES
PRE-BOOKED VISITS
ANNUAL PRODUCTION 60,000 bottles
HECTARES UNDER VINE 10.00
SUSTAINABLE WINERY

● Aglianico del Vulture '11	♥♥ 5
⊙ Gelso Rosa '14	♥ 3
● Gelso Rosso '13	♥ 3

Regio Cantina

LOC. PIANO REGIO
85029 VENOSA [PZ]
TEL. 057754011
www.regiocantina.it

CELLAR SALES
PRE-BOOKED VISITS
ANNUAL PRODUCTION 100,000 bottles
HECTARES UNDER VINE 15.00

● Aglianico del Vulture Donpà '12	♥♥ 3
● Aglianico del Vulture Genesi '12	♥♥ 2*

San Martino

C.DA SAN MARTINO
85023 FORENZA [PZ]
TEL. 097231002
lorenzo.sanmartino@email.it

CELLAR SALES
PRE-BOOKED VISITS
ANNUAL PRODUCTION 25,000 bottles
HECTARES UNDER VINE 4.00

● Aglianico del Volture Arberesko '12	♥♥ 4
● Aglianico del Volture Siir '13	♥ 3
⊙ Neve Rosa '14	♥ 3

Tenute Serra del Prete

LOC. SERRA DEL PRETE
85020 MASCHITO [PZ]
TEL. 3341971231
www.tenuteserradelprete.it

ANNUAL PRODUCTION 8,000 bottles
HECTARES UNDER VINE 4.00

● Aglianico del Vulture Essenthia '12	♥♥ 3
● Aglianico del Vulture Narcisus '12	♥ 3

I Talenti - Padri Trinitari

P.ZZA DON BOSCO, 3
85029 VENOSA [PZ]
TEL. 097234221
www.trinitarivenosa.it

CELLAR SALES
PRE-BOOKED VISITS
ANNUAL PRODUCTION 6,000 bottles
HECTARES UNDER VINE 4.00
VITICULTURE METHOD Certified Organic

● Aglianico del Vulture Cripta Sant'Agostino '12	♥♥ 5

Vulcano & Vini

C.DA FINOCCHIARO
85024 LAVELLO [PZ]
TEL. 0972877033
www.vulcanoevini.com

CELLAR SALES
PRE-BOOKED VISITS
ANNUAL PRODUCTION 250,000 bottles
HECTARES UNDER VINE 45.00

● Aglianico del Vulture Gudarrà '12	♥♥ 3
● Aglianico del Vulture Terra di Vulcano '13	♥♥ 2*
○ Bosco delle Rose Chardonnay '14	♥ 3

PUGLIA

Despite some blackspots linked to the 2014 growing year, Puglia continues to grow. Happily, there are positive notes for at least two aspects: economic and qualitative. For the former, market success, especially abroad, is rolling along without mishap and two wines seem to be garnering more popularity than ever. The first is Primitivo, now a standard-bearer for the triumph of these fresh, fruit-rich wines with spicy overtones, the right amount of tannins, and rarely aged in oak; the second is the charmed Salento, which actually embraces all production in Grande Salento, a more extensive area than the classic district, encompassing the entire peninsular part of Puglia below the Bari-Taranto axis, regardless of grape variety and specific production area. In a context such as this a designation of origin progressively loses its raison d'être. Development of quality, on the other hand, is palpable in the DOC zones of Gioia del Colle and Manduria, which offer wines increasingly able to compete with the best of domestic and international production, buttressed by their Mediterranean typicity, the unmistakeable secret of their success. By contrast, Salice Salentino and Castel del Monte, the region's other two leading names, are struggling. The former is entrenched in an uphill process to rebuild a profile for the wine and the terroir, whose heritage bush-trained vines (the real secret weapon of Salento's quality production) have been seriously depleted over the past 20 years); the latter is prey to the confusion generated by its very structure and that linked to the area's best grape, nero di Troia, still striving to find its real identity. Then there are the hiccoughs in the production of whites and rosés. In this leading regional winemaking sector, above all for production of rosés, the issues raised by a year like 2014 were stickier than envisaged, and the wines produced were, quite frankly, below average compared to recent vintages. Lastly, we would like to return to the theme that closed last year's introduction: the problem of "over-heavy" bottles, which more producers are using for their flagship wines. What a waste and a choice going against the grain of sustainable agriculture, bringing no benefits and, indeed, irritating those consumers who are attentive to environmental issues . . . and to good taste.

PUGLIA

Cantina Albea

VIA DUE MACELLI, 8
70011 ALBEROBELLO [BA]
TEL. 0804323548
www.albeavini.com

CELLAR SALES
PRE-BOOKED VISITS
ANNUAL PRODUCTION 380,000 bottles
HECTARES UNDER VINE 40.00

Albea has been a benchmark for winemaking in Puglia for several years now. The Alberobello cellar can be found in an early-20th-century stone building, with vats carved out of the rock, in exactly the same way as water tanks in the trulli. The winery is committed to developing local native varieties, especially nero di Troia, and has various three different ranges: the Albea label for the high end, and Due Trulli and Terre del Sole for the other two price brackets. This monovarietal Nero di Troia Lui remains one of the best wines from this grape. Its nose of ripe dark berries with hints of aromatic herbs ushers in a consistent palate with good length and acid structure. The Raro 2013, a blend of 60% Negroamaro and Primitivo, with notes of plum and black damson, pleasingly juicy, is well crafted, as is the intense, spicy Primitivo Petranera 2013.

● Lui '13	♟♟ 5
● Petranera '13	♟♟ 3
● Raro '13	♟♟ 3
☉ Petrarosa '14	♟ 3
● Sol '13	♟ 3
● Lui '06	♟♟♟ 5
● Lui '05	♟♟♟ 5
● Lui '12	♟♟ 5
● Lui '10	♟♟ 5
● Lui '09	♟♟ 5
● Raro '08	♟♟ 3
● Riservato '10	♟♟ 3*

Cantele

S.DA PROV.LE SALICE SALENTINO-SAN DONACI KM 35,600
73010 GUAGNANO [LE]
TEL. 0832705010
www.cantele.it

CELLAR SALES
PRE-BOOKED VISITS
ANNUAL PRODUCTION 16,000,000 bottles
HECTARES UNDER VINE 150.00

Originally a bottling company launched in 1979, the Cantele family winery, now run by cousins Gianni, Paolo, Umberto, and Luisa, began purchasing vineyards back in the 1990s, creating their own labels and soon becoming one of the most consolidated wineries in Puglia. They now own 50 hectares under vine, between Guagnano, Montemesola and San Pietro Vernotico, on mainly terra rossa soils, and can also count on grapes from another 100 hectares grown by producers ably assisted by estate technicians. The Amativo remains the mainstay of the winery. The 2013 version of this wholly regional blend of 60% primitivo and negroamaro currently displays a touch too much oak, but on the whole it is balanced, with good stuffing and acid structure. The fresh-tasting, juicy Negroamaro Rosato 2014 is one of the year's best Puglia rosès, while the Primitivo 2013 and the Salice Salentino Rosso Riserva 2012 are both well crafted.

● Amativo '13	♟♟ 4
☉ Negroamaro Rosato '14	♟♟ 2*
● Primitivo '13	♟♟ 2*
● Salice Salentino Rosso Ris. '12	♟♟ 2*
☉ Rohesia '14	♟ 3
○ Teresa Manara Chardonnay '14	♟ 3
● Teresa Manara Negroamaro '13	♟ 3
● Amativo '07	♟♟♟ 4*
● Amativo '03	♟♟♟ 3*
● Salice Salentino Rosso Ris. '09	♟♟♟ 2*
● Amativo '12	♟♟ 4
☉ Negroamaro Rosato '12	♟♟ 2*
● Primitivo '11	♟♟ 2*
● Salice Salentino Rosso Ris. '10	♟♟ 2*
● Teresa Manara Negroamaro '12	♟♟ 3

Cantine San Marzano

VIA REGINA MARGHERITA, 149
74020 SAN MARZANO DI SAN GIUSEPPE [TA]
TEL. 0999576100
www.cantinesanmarzano.com

PRE-BOOKED VISITS
ANNUAL PRODUCTION 8,500,000 bottles
HECTARES UNDER VINE 1500.00
SUSTAINABLE WINERY

This cooperative, one of Salento's major viticultural concerns, vaunts 23 labels in various ranges, the result of vinifying grapes from over 1,200 growers, assisted by winery staff. Most of the vineyards are planted with ancient bush-trained vines, almost exclusively native varietals, located around San Marzano, Sava and Francavilla Fontana, predominantly on terra rossa soils. The winery's overall performance is quite superb, headed by the intense yet balanced Primitivo di Manduria Falò 2013, with its notes of ripe yet crisp black berry fruit, with a wonderfully fresh lengthy finale. Also very well-made is the juicy, dark fruit-heavy Collezione Cinquanta, an equal blend of negroamaro and primitivo, though it is still a tad too oaky.

Carvinea

LOC. PEZZA D'ARENA
VIA PER SERRANOVA
72012 CAROVIGNO [BR]
TEL. 0805862345
www.carvinea.com

CELLAR SALES
PRE-BOOKED VISITS
ACCOMMODATION AND RESTAURANT SERVICE
ANNUAL PRODUCTION 35,000 bottles
HECTARES UNDER VINE 12.00
VITICULTURE METHOD Certified Organic

In 2002, Beppe di Maria purchased Masseria Pezza d'Arena, outside Carovigno in the Upper Salento, surrounding it with nine hectares of vines, all on calcareous tufa soils. He originally went for non-traditional varieties, such as montepulciano, aglianico, fiano, and petit verdot, but later introduced some natives like primitivo and negroamaro, which soon took centre stage in a range which now features 11 different labels. Though only four labels were submitted this year, we should add that the conversion to native varietals has been completed, as shown by the results achieved, especially for the Negroamaro. The 2013 has earthy overtones of black berry fruit and sweet spices, while the palate is juicy, long and pleasing. We also enjoyed the fruit-laden Primitivo 2013, which flows across the palate, while the Merula Rosa from montepulciano and the Fiano Lucerna pay the price for the difficult 2014 growing year.

● Primitivo di Manduria Talò '13	♟♟♟ 3*
● Collezione Cinquanta	♟♟ 5
○ Estella Moscato '14	♟♟ 3
● Il Pumo Negroamaro '14	♟♟ 2*
● Il Pumo Primitivo '14	♟♟ 2*
● Il Pumo Rosso '14	♟♟ 2*
● Primitivo di Manduria Anniversario 62 Ris. '12	♟♟ 5
● Salice Salentino Rosso Talò '12	♟♟ 3
● Il Pumo Negroamaro '13	♟♟ 2*
● Il Pumo Rosso '13	♟♟ 2*
● Primitivo di Manduria Sessantanni '11	♟♟ 5
● Primitivo di Manduria Talò '12	♟♟ 3*

● Negroamaro '13	♟♟♟ 5
● Primitivo '13	♟♟ 5
○ Lucerna '14	♟ 2
⊙ Merula Rosa '14	♟ 2
● Frauma '08	♟♟♟ 4
● Merula '11	♟♟♟ 3*
● Negroamaro '11	♟♟♟ 3*
● Sierma '09	♟♟♟ 5
● Frauma '11	♟♟ 5
● Primitivo '11	♟♟ 3
● Sierma '12	♟♟ 5

Castello Monaci

LOC. C.DA DEI MONACI
VIA CASE SPARSE
73015 SALICE SALENTINO [LE]
TEL. 0831665700
www.castellomonaci.it

CELLAR SALES
PRE-BOOKED VISITS
RESTAURANT SERVICE
ANNUAL PRODUCTION 2,000,000 bottles
HECTARES UNDER VINE 150.00

The vineyards of Castello Monaci, owned by Gruppo Italiano Vini, are situated around the winery headquarters on the outskirts of Salice Salentino, enjoying a rich topsoil with a stonier, well-draining subsoil. The winery offers around 20 labels, in two ranges, Castello Monaci and Feudo Monaci, most of from native varietals, where territorial reds rule the roost, both from negroamaro and malvasia nera or primitivo. Despite the difficult growing year, Castello Monaci has come up with a successful 2014 range. The estate spearhead remains the Primitivo Artas, whose 2013 version is well-defined and fresh, with marked notes of black cherry and plum, with superb texture and length. Less ambitious, though still pleasing and fruity, is the other Primitivo, the Pilùna 2014, while the juicy drinkable Negroamaro Maru 2014 is a tad predictable.

Chiaromonte

VICO MURO SANT'ANGELO, 6
70021 ACQUAVIVA DELLE FONTI [BA]
TEL. 0803050432
www.tenutechiaromonte.com

CELLAR SALES
PRE-BOOKED VISITS
ANNUAL PRODUCTION 100,000 bottles
HECTARES UNDER VINE 27.00
VITICULTURE METHOD Certified Organic

Nicola Chiaromonte took over the family business in 1998. Since then, the winery has grown to become the undisputed star of regional viticulture. The astute acquisition policy pursued in recent years means most of the estate vineyards are made up of old bush-trained vines, aged from 60 to over 100 years old. Located in Acquaviva delle Fonti, at an elevation of over 300 metres, the vines enjoy mineral-rich limestone karst subsoils with thin topsoils of terra rossa and clay. The quite splendid Gioia del Colle Primitivo Muro Sant'Angelo Contrada Barbatto 2012 displays an intense nose of dark berry fruit with hints of Mediterranean scrub and a juicy, full-flavoured palate, outstandingly fresh with good balance and length. We adored the rich, spicy Gioia del Colle Primitivo Muro Sant'Angelo 2013 which also shows a crispy fruitiness.

● Artas '13	♟♟♟ 5
● Maru '14	♟♟ 2*
● Pilùna '14	♟♟ 2*
○ Acante '14	♟ 2
⊙ Kreos '14	♟ 2
○ Petraluce '14	♟ 2
● Salice Salentino Aiace Ris. '12	♟ 3
● Salice Salentino Liante '14	♟ 2
● Artas '12	♟♟ 5
● Maru '13	♟♟ 2*
● Maru '12	♟♟ 2*
● Médos '13	♟♟ 3
● Pilùna '12	♟♟ 2*
● Salice Salentino Aiace Ris. '11	♟♟ 3

● Gioia del Colle Primitivo Muro Sant'Angelo Contrada Barbatto '12	♟♟♟ 5
● Gioia del Colle Primitivo Muro Sant'Angelo '13	♟♟ 4
○ Kimìa '14	♟♟ 3
● Elè '13	♟ 3
● Gioia del Colle Primitivo Muro Sant'Angelo Contrada Barbatto '11	♟♟ 5
● Gioia del Colle Primitivo Muro Sant'Angelo Contrada Barbatto '10	♟♟ 7
● Gioia del Colle Primitivo Muro Sant'Angelo Contrada Barbatto '09	♟♟ 5
● Gioia del Colle Primitivo Muro Sant'Angelo Contrada Barbatto '08	♟♟ 5

Cantine Due Palme

VIA SAN MARCO, 130
72020 CELLINO SAN MARCO [BR]
TEL. 0831617865
www.cantineduepalme.it

CELLAR SALES
PRE-BOOKED VISITS
ACCOMMODATION AND RESTAURANT SERVICE
ANNUAL PRODUCTION 10,000,000 bottles
HECTARES UNDER VINE 2500.00
VITICULTURE METHOD Certified Organic
SUSTAINABLE WINERY

Founded by Angelo Maci in 1989, this
cooperative winery has grown to
encompass more than 1,200 members
tending about 2,500 hectares under vine.
The estate vineyards are 90% native red
grapes, with plenty of head-trained vines,
which were given protection in 2010 when
Maci set up the Accademia dell'Alberello
Pugliese along with other growers and local
institutions. The winery features 25
different labels, the most noteworthy being
the various versions of Salice Salentino.
The Salice Salentino Rosso Selvarossa
Riserva is once again the best of its type.
The 2012, with spicy hints of autumn
leaves and incense ushering in a generous,
juicy palate, has fruity, naturally sweet, ripe
overtones, as tradition would have it. We
very much liked the Serre 2014, a
particularly successful monovarietal
Susumaniello given the growing year:
crispy and fruity, fresh and highly drinkable.

● Salice Salentino Rosso Selvarossa Ris. '12	♛♛♛ 4*
● Serre '14	♛♛ 3*
○ Due Palme Brut M. Cl. millesimato '12	♛♛ 4
● Primitivo di Manduria Ettamiano Ris. '11	♛♛ 3
○ Selvaoro '12	♛♛ 6
○ Anthea '14	♛ 2
○ Canonico '14	♛ 2
☉ Corerosa '14	♛ 3
○ Salice Salentino Bianco Tinaia '14	♛ 3
○ Selvabianca '14	♛ 3
● Salice Salentino Rosso Selvarossa Ris. '11	♛♛♛ 4*
● Salice Salentino Rosso Selvarossa Ris. '10	♛♛♛ 4*
● Salice Salentino Rosso Selvarossa Ris. '09	♛♛♛ 4*

Tenute Eméra

C.DA PORVICA
74100 LIZZANO [TA]
TEL. 0832704398
www.tenuteemera.it

CELLAR SALES
PRE-BOOKED VISITS
ACCOMMODATION
ANNUAL PRODUCTION 370,000 bottles
HECTARES UNDER VINE 46.00
VITICULTURE METHOD Certified Organic

Tenute Eméra is the only Puglia-based
winery in Claudio Quarta's Gruppo
Magistravini. It covers around 80 hectares,
50 of which were planted in 2007
overlooking the Ionian coast. Its vineyards
lie on permeable calcareous tufa soils,
enhanced by a layer of debris and
calcareous-clay rock, and in addition to the
natives like primitivo, negroamaro and
fiano, they also grow internationals such as
syrah, merlot, cabernet sauvignon, and
chardonnay. This estate was extended in
2012 with the addition of the small-scale
Cantina Moros, which processes
negroamaro and malvasia nera grown in a
tiny one-hectare vineyard just outside
Guagnano. And it was the fruit-heavy, juicy
Salice Salentino Rosso Moros Riserva 2012
that impressed us most. Also well-crafted
were the Lizzano Negroamaro Superiore
Anima di Negroamaro 2013, with its fresh
red cherry notes and the Qu.Ale 2014, a
fresh red with berry fruit notes, best drunk
chilled.

● Lizzano Negroamaro Sup. Anima di Negroamaro '13	♛♛ 2*
● Salice Salentino Rosso Moros Ris. '12	♛♛ 4
○ Amure '14	♛ 2
● Primitivo di Manduria Anima di Primitivo '13	♛ 2
● Primitivo di Manduria Oro di Eméra '13	♛ 4
● Qu.Ale '14	♛ 2
● Salice Salentino Rosso '13	♛ 2
● Lizzano Negroamaro Sup. Anima di Negroamaro '12	♛♛ 2*
● Primitivo di Manduria '11	♛♛ 3
● Primitivo di Manduria Anima di Primitivo '12	♛♛ 2*
● Salice Salentino Rosso '11	♛♛ 2*
● Sud del Sud '13	♛♛ 3

Gianfranco Fino

via Piave, 12
74028 Sava [TA]
Tel. 0997773970
www.gianfrancofino.it

PRE-BOOKED VISITS
ANNUAL PRODUCTION 20,000 bottles
HECTARES UNDER VINE 16.00
SUSTAINABLE WINERY

A decade after setting up their winery, with great passion and enthusiasm Gianfranco and Simona Fino continue to offer top-quality wines. They have 12 plots between Manduria and Sava, all 50- to 90-year-old head-trained primitivo vines on terra rossa and limestone, with just a single hectare of negroamaro. There are now four estate labels, with the long-standing Primitivo di Manduria Es and the Negroamaro Jo joined by a sweet wine and a Metodo Classico sparkler. However, this year Simona and Gianfranco only submitted the Primitivo di Manduria Es, which was again very good but rather different from the style we had been used to. The 2013 seemed to hinge more on fruit and succulence, with its clear overtones of blackberry on both nose and palate, than on its usual close-knit complexity, for a more immediate and pleasant but somehow less charming Es.

Futura 14

via Senatore De Castris
73100 Salice Salentino [LE]
Tel. 063722120
ordini@futura14.it

ANNUAL PRODUCTION 40,000 bottles
HECTARES UNDER VINE 19.00
SUSTAINABLE WINERY

The Vespa family has co-owned a farmstead in Manduria for years, with 19 hectares under vine, and they lease another four hectares on clay and sandy clay. However, it was only recently that they decided to vinify and bottle their own grapes to produce their own labels, with expert advice from oenologist Riccardo Cotarella. Naturally production focuses on primitivo, together with a rosé sparkler from negroamaro, and a white from fiano. Tre Bicchieri for the winery flagship, the Primitivo di Manduria Riserva Raccontami 2013, with an interpretation mainly of alcoholic fullness and fruit, with sweet, smoky notes of charred oak, bramble jelly hints on the nose and a fleshy fullness on the palate. Also well-made is the fruit-forward Il Bruno dei Vespa 2014, with notes of oriental spices.

● Primitivo di Manduria Es '13	♥♥	7
● Primitivo di Manduria Es '12	♥♥♥	7
● Primitivo di Manduria Es '11	♥♥♥	7
● Primitivo di Manduria Es '10	♥♥♥	6
● Primitivo di Manduria Es '09	♥♥♥	6
● Primitivo di Manduria Es '08	♥♥♥	6
● Primitivo di Manduria Es '07	♥♥♥	6
● Primitivo di Manduria Es '06	♥♥♥	5
● Primitivo di Manduria Es '05	♥♥	5

● Primitivo di Manduria Raccontami '13	♥♥♥	5
⊙ Brut Noi Tre Rosé M. Cl. '11	♥♥	5
● Il Bruno dei Vespa '14	♥♥	2*
○ Il Bianco dei Vespa '14	♥	3
● Il Rosso dei Vespa '14	♥	3
● Il Bruno dei Vespa '13	♥♥	2*
● Primitivo di Manduria Raccontami '12	♥♥	5

Tenute Girolamo

VIA NOCI, 314
74015 MARTINA FRANCA [TA]
TEL. 0804402088
www.tenutegirolamo.it

CELLAR SALES
PRE-BOOKED VISITS
ANNUAL PRODUCTION 950,000 bottles
HECTARES UNDER VINE 50.00

Once again this year the Girolamo family
winery, one of the most interesting estates
in the Valle d'Itria, performed very well. The
estate has eight vineyards in all, at altitudes
of 350–400 metres, on limestone soils
mixed with terra rossa. The wines are
made both from native and international
cultivars, divided into several production
lines, headed by Monte dei Cocci. With its
intense nose of blackberry and damson,
coffee and chocolate, and a palate opening
with mild overtones of greenness, ushering
in fruit-laden notes and a full, lengthy finish,
Monte dei Cocci Negroamaro 2013 was
exceptionally convincing. Also well-crafted
was the Conte Giangirolamo 2012, a spicy
equal blend of negroamaro and primitivo
with hints of dark forest fruits on the nose,
and a cool, well-defined and very
pleasurable palate.

Vito Donato Giuliani

VIA GIOIA CANALE
070010 TURI [BA]
TEL. 0808915335
www.vitivinicolagiuliani.com

HECTARES UNDER VINE 20.00

This long-established Gioia del Colle estate
belonging to the Giuliani family, walks
straight into a full-length profile. Founded
some 70 years ago, it extends into the
district known as "sotto il canale", between
Turi and Gioia del Colle, near the Mount
Sannace archaeological site. This is the
heart of the Bari Murgia, on the area's
typical karst soils, made up of a thin terra
rossa topsoil over a complex, mineral-rich
stony subsoil. They produce around a
dozen labels but submitted only two, both
of which were of a very high standard. The
Gioia del Colle Primitivo Lavarossa 2012
strolled to our finals, with its intense nose
of black berry fruit and a smooth, graceful
palate that was brisk and tangy, lengthy
and fruity. The Gioia del Colle Primitivo
Baronaggio Riserva 2012 is fruity, with
quinine and red berry notes.

● Monte dei Cocci Negroamaro '13	♟♟	4
● Conte Giangirolamo '12	♟♟	6
○ Fiano La Voliera '14	♟	3
○ Monte dei Cocci Verdeca '14	♟	4
● Pizzo Rosso '12	♟	5
● Primitivo La Voliera '14	♟	3
● Conte Giangirolamo '10	♟♟	4
● Monte dei Cocci Negroamaro '12	♟♟	4
● Pétrakos '08	♟♟	3
● Pizzo Rosso '11	♟♟	2*
● Pizzo Rosso '09	♟♟	2*

● Gioia del Colle Primitivo Lavarossa '12	♟♟	3*
● Gioia del Colle Baronaggio Ris. '12	♟♟	5

PUGLIA

Paolo Leo

VIA TUTURANO, 21
72025 SAN DONACI [BR]
TEL. 0831635073
www.paololeo.it

CELLAR SALES
PRE-BOOKED VISITS
ANNUAL PRODUCTION 1,300,000 bottles
HECTARES UNDER VINE 35.00

The whole Leo family helps Paolo run this estate, founded in 1989 but with a workforce of four generations of winegrowers. The vineyards are mainly located on calcareous tufa soils around San Dònaci, with 15-year-old high-trained and 40-plus-year-old bush-trained vines. The main varieties grown are the classic Salento natives of negroamaro, malvasia nera di Lecce, malvasia bianca, and primitivo, alongside chardonnay and fiano. With over 20 labels in various lines, From the top of the range come a series of quality wines, such as the Negroamaro Taccorosso 2013, with its aromas of black berry fruit and Mediterranean scrub, with a balsamic edge, fresh, balanced, pleasantly lingering palate, or the spicy and juicy Primitivo Fiore di Vigna 2013, which despite slightly rough tannins remains close-focused with good staying power. The Negroamaro Orfeo 2013 and Negramante 2013 are also both well-made.

● Fiore di Vigna '13	♟♟	4
● Taccorosso '13	♟♟	3*
● Negramante '13	♟♟	3
● Orfeo '13	♟♟	4
○ Numen '14	♟	4
● Primitivo di Manduria Passo del Cardinale '13	♟	3
● Salice Salentino Rosso Ris. '10	♟	4
● Fiore di Vigna '12	♟♟	4
● Fiore di Vigna '10	♟♟	4
● Orfeo '11	♟♟	4
● Primitivo di Manduria '09	♟♟	3
● Salento Rosso '11	♟♟	2*

★Leone de Castris

VIA SENATORE DE CASTRIS, 26
73015 SALICE SALENTINO [LE]
TEL. 0832731112
www.leonedecastris.com

CELLAR SALES
PRE-BOOKED VISITS
ACCOMMODATION AND RESTAURANT SERVICE
ANNUAL PRODUCTION 2,500,000 bottles
HECTARES UNDER VINE 250.00
SUSTAINABLE WINERY

The venerable Leone de Castris winery, whose first traces as a wine producer date back to 1665, boasts Five Roses, Italy's first-ever bottled rosé, created in 1943, and currently offers a hugely diverse range of labels. The operation confirms its place as one of the region's leading estates and owns a number of different vineyards, located in Salice Salentino, Campi Salentino and Guagnano. The plots are planted with a multitude of varieties, both natives such as negroamaro and malvasia nera and internationals, 70% of which are gobelet-trained. The Salice Salentino Rosso Per Lui Riserva 2013 remains the best of its type. Spicy, with hints of dark stoned fruit, it is well-crafted, succulent and solidly built. The Primitivo Per Lui 2013 is more aggressive, but with good grip and length, while the Salice Salentino Rosso Riserva 2013 is balanced and shows good fruit. Despite the poor year, we liked both 2014 Five Roses, the base wine being bright and fresh, somewhat richer the 71¡ Anniversario.

● Salice Salentino Rosso Per Lui Ris. '13	♟♟♟	6
● Per Lui '13	♟♟	6
⊙ Five Roses '14	♟♟	3
⊙ Five Roses 71° Anniversario '14	♟♟	3
● Salice Salentino Rosso Ris. '13	♟♟	3
○ Messapia '14	♟	2
● Salice Salentino Brut Five Roses M. Cl. '12	♟	4
⊙ Salice Salentino Brut Five Roses M. Cl. Anniversario '11	♟	5
● Salice Salentino Rosso Donna Lisa Ris. '12	♟	5
● Salice Salentino Rosso Marlisa '13	♟	3
● Salice Salentino Rosso Per Lui Ris. '12	♟♟♟	6
● Per Lui '12	♟♟	6

Masseria Li Veli

S.DA PROV.LE CELLINO-CAMPI, KM 1
72020 CELLINO SAN MARCO [BR]
TEL. 0831618259
www.liveli.it

CELLAR SALES
PRE-BOOKED VISITS
ANNUAL PRODUCTION 350,000 bottles
HECTARES UNDER VINE 33.00
VITICULTURE METHOD Certified Organic

In 1999 the Falvo family moved from Tuscany to Puglia, acquiring and refounding Masseria Li Veli, a renowened Salento winery. The vineyards are located mainly on terra rossa and sandy soils, and are made up of 85% bush vines in septunx layout. The grape varieties are almost exclusively native, from negroamaro to primitivo, malvasia nera, susumaniello, aleatico, verdeca, and fiano minutolo, with the sole exception of a tiny amount of cabernet sauvignon. The MLV 2012, a blend of 60% negroamaro and cabernet sauvignon, once again expresses good qualities without finding the right balance. Its toasty spicy notes, with slight hints of dark berries on the nose, is followed by a very fruit-rich palate, but rather light of body and a finish lacking length. The remarkably terroir-true Susumaniello 2014 was pleasantly gutsy, while the Fiano 2014 was piquant and supple, with notes of white-fleshed fruit.

Morella

VIA PER UGGIANO, 147
74024 MANDURIA [TA]
TEL. 0999791482
www.morellavini.com

CELLAR SALES
PRE-BOOKED VISITS
ANNUAL PRODUCTION 26,000 bottles
HECTARES UNDER VINE 19.00

Old head-trained vines on terra rossa, particularly low yields per plant, rarely more than 20 quintals per hectare, and a lot of passion: this is the key to Lisa Gilbee and Gaetano Morella's winery. Primitivo, used for both estate crus, rules the roost, then there are negroamaro, international varietals and some fiano for the only white produced. The quest to express the terroir in all its authenticity means they intervene as little as possible in the cellar, where some unlined concrete vats were installed a couple of years ago. This year it was Old Vines' turn to stay in the cellar to soften out. The La Signora Primitivo 2011 displayed plenty of matière and generous fruit, but was rather lacking in freshness and gutsiness this time around. By contrast, this year's Negroamaro Primitivo Terre Rosse surpassed itself, with a 2012 swathed in black berry fruit, violet and liquorice, giving way to a tight-knit, juicy palate.

● MLV '12	♟♟	5
○ Fiano '14	♟♟	2*
● Susumaniello Askos '14	♟♟	3
● Malvasia Nera Askos '14	♟	3
● Orion '14	♟	2
● Primonero '14	♟	2
● Salice Salentino Rosso Passamante '14	♟	2
● Salice Salentino Rosso Pezzo Morgana Ris. '13	♟	4
● Masseria Li Veli '10	♟♟♟	5
● MLV '11	♟♟	5
● Salice Salentino Rosso Passamante '13	♟♟	2*
○ Verdeca Askos '13	♟♟	3

● Negroamaro Primitivo Terre Rosse '12	♟♟	4
● Primitivo La Signora '11	♟♟	6
○ Mezzogiorno '14	♟	3
● Primitivo La Signora '10	♟♟♟	6
● Primitivo Old Vines '09	♟♟♟	5
● Primitivo Old Vines '08	♟♟♟	5
● Old Vines Primitivo '10	♟♟	6
● Primitivo La Signora '09	♟♟	5
● Primitivo Old Vines '11	♟♟	6

Palamà

VIA A. DIAZ, 6
73020 CUTROFIANO [LE]
TEL. 0836542865
www.vinicolapalama.com

CELLAR SALES
PRE-BOOKED VISITS
ACCOMMODATION AND RESTAURANT SERVICE
ANNUAL PRODUCTION 200,000 bottles
HECTARES UNDER VINE 15.00

Only native vines for the Palamà family estate, founded in 1936. In 1990, owner Cosimo decided to begin bottling his own wine with a variety of labels in different lines. Negroamaro, primitivo, malvasia nera, malvasia bianca, and verdeca are the grapes grown in vineyards located around Cutrofiano and Matino, partly Puglia bush-trained and partly Guyot, planted mainly on moderately loose-packed, generally calcareous, soils. The Mavro 2013 is one of the best Negroamaros we have tried this year. Its mature plum nose with hints of wood resin gives way to a gutsy palate brimming over with black berry fruit notes and a long, succulent finale. The Albarossa range was well-made, both the spicy, fresh-tasting Primitivo 2013, and the complex, well-structured, though slightly grainy, Salice Salentino Rosso 2013. The Metiusco range, though, pays the price for the poor 2014 vintage, not quite up to past versions.

Pietraventosa

C.DA PARCO LARGO
70023 GIOIA DEL COLLE [BA]
TEL. 0805034436
www.pietraventosa.it

ANNUAL PRODUCTION 12,000 bottles
HECTARES UNDER VINE 5.40
VITICULTURE METHOD Certified Organic

Marianna Annio and Raffaele Leo's estate remains one of the finest wineries in Puglia. The vines are planted at an elevation of around 380 metres on a thin layer of terra rossa with rock less than a metre below the surface, with a mineral-rich limestone soil. They are divided into two plots, one planted with old head-trained vines from which the Primitivo Riserva comes and the other with young cordon-trained and spur-pruned vines. Without ever reaching dizzying heights, the Pietraventosa production is very reliable. We especially liked the new label, the Volere Volare 2012, a well-structured, fresh-tasting Primitivo brimming over with dark berry fruit and coffee. One of the year's best rosés, the lengthy and rather drinkable EstRosa 2014, from primitivo grapes, features a floral nose with hints of red berries. The only underperformer was the Gioia del Colle Primitivo Riserva 2011, a well-crafted wine but lacking the balance and thrust of past versions.

● Mavro '13	♟♟ 3*
● Albarossa Primitivo '13	♟♟ 2*
● Salice Salentino Rosso Albarossa '13	♟♟ 1*
☉ Metiusco Rosato '14	♟ 2
● Metiusco Rosso '14	♟ 2
● 75 Vendemmie '11	♟♟♟ 4*
● 75 Vendemmie '12	♟♟ 4
● Mavro '12	♟♟ 3*
● Mavro '09	♟♟ 3*
● Mavro '08	♟♟ 2*
● Mavro '07	♟♟ 2*
☉ Metiusco Rosato '13	♟♟ 2*
☉ Metiusco Rosato '12	♟♟ 2*

☉ EstRosa '14	♟♟ 3
● Gioia del Colle Primitivo Riserva di Pietraventosa '11	♟♟ 5
● Volere Volare '12	♟♟ 2*
● Gioia del Colle Primitivo Ris. '06	♟♟♟ 4
● Gioia del Colle Primitivo Allegoria '12	♟♟ 3*
● Gioia del Colle Primitivo Allegoria '08	♟♟ 3
● Gioia del Colle Primitivo Allegoria '07	♟♟ 3
● Gioia del Colle Primitivo Ris. '10	♟♟ 5
● Gioia del Colle Primitivo Riserva di Pietraventosa '08	♟♟ 5
● Gioia del Colle Primitivo Riserva di Pietraventosa '07	♟♟ 5
● Ossimoro '07	♟♟ 3

Plantamura

VIA SANTA CANDIDA, 1
70023 GIOIA DEL COLLE [BA]
TEL. 3474711027
www.viniplantamura.it

CELLAR SALES
PRE-BOOKED VISITS
ANNUAL PRODUCTION 45,000 bottles
HECTARES UNDER VINE 8.00
VITICULTURE METHOD Certified Organic
SUSTAINABLE WINERY

In just under ten years, Mariangela Plantamura and her husband Vincenzo have built their winery into one of the benchmarks of Puglia's viticulture. All production is based exclusively on the DOC Gioia del Colle Primitivo, with three labels from a few hectares under vine located deep in the Gioia countryside. At about 350 metres above sea level, typical soils of this area are a karst limestone topped by a thin layer of terra rossa and clay. Another good year for this small-scale winery. The Gioia del Colle Primitivo Contrada San Pietro 2013 is delicious, with a bouquet of wild berries and an attractively close-woven mouth which is at once gracefully contoured, brisk, long and supported by a good acid structure. Richer notes of chocolate and spices from the fresh-tasting, succulent Gioia del Colle Primitivo Parco Largo 2013, which just lacks a little more depth, while the Gioia del Colle Primitivo Riserva 2012 has grip to spare.

Polvanera

S.DA VICINALE LAMIE MARCHESANA, 601
70023 GIOIA DEL COLLE [BA]
TEL. 080758900
www.cantinepolvanera.it

CELLAR SALES
RESTAURANT SERVICE
ANNUAL PRODUCTION 280,000 bottles
HECTARES UNDER VINE 90.00
VITICULTURE METHOD Certified Organic

In 2003, Filippo Cassano purchased and began restoring an ancient farmstead outside Acquaviva delle Fonti, in Contrada Marchesana, with its cellar excavated down to eight metres into the bedrock. He set up Polvanera, which in little more than a decade has become one of Puglia's best-known and beloved wineries. The vineyards are located on the typical Murgia karst soils, with a thin layer of clay on a base of solid rock. Some have head-trained vines that are over the ripe old age of 60. The Gioia del Colle Primitivo17 Vigneto Montevella 2012 was yet again one of the finest Puglia wines we tasted. A coffee, chocolate and sour cherry bouquet are the prelude to a compact, richly textured palate, with good acidity. Though some brilliance has been lost, the Gioia del Colle Primitivo 16 Vigneto San Benedetto 2012 is still enfolding and rounded, while the Gioia del Colle Primitivo 14 Vigneto Marchesana 2012 is pleasantly fruit-heavy.

● Gioia del Colle Primitivo Et. Nera Contrada San Pietro '13	♟♟♟ 3*
● Gioia del Colle Primitivo Et. Rossa Parco Largo '13	♟♟ 3*
● Gioia del Colle Primitivo Ris. '12	♟♟ 3
● Gioia del Colle Primitivo Et. Nera Contrada San Pietro '12	♟♟♟ 3*
● Gioia del Colle Primitivo Et. Rossa '11	♟♟♟ 4*
● Gioia del Colle Primitivo Et. Bianca Ris. '11	♟♟ 3
● Gioia del Colle Primitivo Et. Nera '11	♟♟ 4
● Gioia del Colle Primitivo Et. Rossa '12	♟♟ 3
● Gioia del Colle Primitivo Ris. '10	♟♟ 5

● Gioia del Colle Primitivo 17 Vign. Montevella '12	♟♟♟ 6
● Gioia del Colle Primitivo 16 Vign. San Benedetto '12	♟♟ 5
● Gioia del Colle Primitivo 14 Vign. Marchesana '14	♟♟ 3
○ Minutolo '14	♟ 3
⊙ Rosato '14	♟ 2
● Gioia del Colle Primitivo 16 '07	♟♟♟ 2*
● Gioia del Colle Primitivo 17 '10	♟♟♟ 5
● Gioia del Colle Primitivo 17 '09	♟♟♟ 5
● Gioia del Colle Primitivo 17 '08	♟♟♟ 4*
● Gioia del Colle Primitivo 17 Vign. Montevella '11	♟♟♟ 6
● Gioia del Colle Primitivo 16 '11	♟♟ 6

Racemi

VIA XX SETTEMBRE, 75
74024 MANDURIA [TA]
TEL. 0999711660
www.racemi.it

CELLAR SALES
PRE-BOOKED VISITS
ANNUAL PRODUCTION 1,200,000 bottles
HECTARES UNDER VINE 60.00

Gregory Perrucci has brought together the various production units he runs, from Felline to Pervini, under the auspices of the Accademia dei Racemi project. For over 20 years Gregory has been working to safeguard Salento's winegrowing traditions, especially by helping smaller outfits both in the vineyard and in marketing their products, or by restoring the region's typical head-trained vines. Alongside the various Primitivos are other wines from such native cultivars as negroamaro, malvasia nera, ottavianello or susumaniello. The Primitivo di Manduria Zinfandel 2013 is once again a benchmark for the winery and for the DOC zone. The nose is fruity and balsamic, its mouthfeel full, fresh-tasting, very fruity, piquant and lingering. As ever the overall performance is particularly solid, with the Sum Torreguaceto 2013, a gutsy, thrusting Susumaniello and the Primitivo di Manduria Dunico Masseria Pepe 2013 with its pleasing notes of Mediterranean scrub standing out for us.

● Primitivo di Manduria Zinfandel Sinfarosa '13	♟♟♟ 3*
● Alberello '13	♟♟ 2*
● Primitivo di Manduria Dunico Masseria Pepe '13	♟♟ 5
● Primitivo di Manduria Giravolta Tenuta Pozzopalo '13	♟♟ 3
● Primitivo di Manduria Segnavento '14	♟♟ 2*
● Susumaniello Sum Torre Guaceto '13	♟♟ 4
⊙ Vigna Rosa '14	♟♟ 2*
● Anarkos '14	♟ 2
● Pietraluna Torre Guaceto '14	♟ 2
● Primitivo di Manduria Ris. '10	♟ 5
○ RuFiano '14	♟ 2
○ Vermentino '14	♟ 2

Rivera

LOC. C.DA RIVERA
S.DA PROV.LE 231 KM 60,500
76123 ANDRIA [BT]
TEL. 0883569510
www.rivera.it

CELLAR SALES
PRE-BOOKED VISITS
ANNUAL PRODUCTION 1,200,000 bottles
HECTARES UNDER VINE 75.00
SUSTAINABLE WINERY

For the last 60 years, the De Corato family winery has been one of the leading names in regional winegrowing, especially in the Castel del Monte zone. It relies on vineyards in two areas with rather different soil types: the Rivera, Torre di Bocca and Coppa estates, at elevations of 200-230 metres characterized by deep calcareous tufa soils; the Lama di Corvo estate, overlooking the sea and the Gargano peninsula, at an altitude of 350 metres, with rocky calcareous soils. Yet another good collective performance from Rivera. That means the Castel del Monte Rosso Il Falcone Riserva 2010, with its earthy notes of quinine and good fruit, a brilliant Moscato di Trani Piani di Tufara 2014, the best we tasted this year, balanced and fresh-tasting with overtones of candied orange peel, grapefruit and curry, and a rich Castel del Monte Nero di Troia Puer Apuliae 2010 with a finish lacking succulence.

● Castel del Monte Nero di Troia Puer Apuliae '10	♟♟ 5
● Castel del Monte Rosso Il Falcone Ris. '10	♟♟ 4
● Castel del Monte Rosso Rupicolo '13	♟♟ 2*
○ Moscato di Trani Piani di Tufara '14	♟♟ 2*
● Triusco '13	♟♟ 3
● Castel del Monte Aglianico Cappellaccio Ris. '09	♟ 2
⊙ Castel del Monte Bombino Nero Pungirosa '14	♟ 2
○ Castel del Monte Chardonnay Preludio n°1 '14	♟ 2
● Castel del Monte Nero di Troia Violante '13	♟ 2
⊙ Castel del Monte Rosé '14	♟ 2

Tenute Rubino

VIA E. FERMI, 50
72100 BRINDISI
TEL. 0831571955
www.tenuterubino.it

CELLAR SALES
PRE-BOOKED VISITS
ANNUAL PRODUCTION 1,200,000 bottles
HECTARES UNDER VINE 200.00

In just a few years, the Rubino family estate
has become one of Puglia's best-known
and loved wineries. They run four different
estates, from the Adriatic hills all the way
down to the plains behind Brindisi. They are
Jaddico, on limestone-based soils mixed
with plenty of sand; Marmorelle, which has
the youngest plantings; Uggìo, whose
calcareous soils feature a balanced mix of
sand and clay; and Punta Aquila, entirely
given over to growing primitivo. The
susumaniello project has been a constant
in the Rubino family winery since its
earliest days, and is now reaping the
rewards. The Torre Testa, a monovarietal
Susumaniello, wins its third consecutive Tre
Bicchieri with a balanced, full-bodied 2013
brimming with fruitiness, rounding off with
a fresh persistent finish. The best of the
rest are the two Primitivos, the piquant,
juicy Visellio 2013, with blackberry notes,
and the sweeter, fuller Punta Aquila 2013.

● Torre Testa '13	♥♥♥	6
● Oltremé '14	♥♥	2*
● Punta Aquila '13	♥♥	2*
● Visellio '13	♥♥	5
○ Marmorelle Bianco '14	♥	2
● Marmorelle Rosso '13	♥	2
● Miraglio '13	♥	2
⊙ Saturnino '14	♥	2
⊙ Sumarè Brut M. Cl. '12	♥	4
● Primitivo Visellio '01	♥♥♥	3*
● Torre Testa '12	♥♥♥	6
● Torre Testa '11	♥♥♥	6
● Torre Testa '11	♥♥♥	6
● Torre Testa '02	♥♥♥	5
● Torre Testa '01	♥♥♥	5
● Visellio '10	♥♥♥	4*
● Oltremé '13	♥♥	2*

Schola Sarmenti

VIA GENERALE CANTORE, 37
73048 NARDÒ [LE]
TEL. 0833567247
www.scholasarmenti.it

CELLAR SALES
PRE-BOOKED VISITS
ANNUAL PRODUCTION 240,000 bottles
HECTARES UNDER VINE 41.00
VITICULTURE METHOD Certified Organic

Luigi Carlo Marra and Benedetto Lorusso's
Schola Sarmenti is a point of reference for
an area undergoing great upheavals, such
as Nardò. In recent decades, hundreds of
hectares of old bush vines have been
uprooted in this area, but the estate
vineyards are a beacon, planted to 85%
head-trained native varietals, such as
negroamaro, primitivo and malvasia nera.
The winery is breaking new ground for
Primitivo, its version characterized not only
by great intensity and alcohol, with its 18
degrees declared by the name of the wine
itself, but also by freshness and drinkability.
The Diciotto 2013's tones of spices,
chocolate and dark berry fruit usher in a
fresh fruity palate and, despite rather rough
tannin, a lengthy, juicy finish. With its
typical and traditional sour cherry
sweetness, the Nardò Roccamora 2013 is
well-crafted.

● Diciotto '13	♥♥	8
● Nardò Rosso Roccamora '13	♥♥	2*
⊙ Nardò Rosato Masserei '14	♥	2
● Nauna '13	♥	5
● Cubardi '11	♥♥	3
● Cubardi '10	♥♥	3
● Diciotto '12	♥♥	7
● Diciotto '11	♥♥	7
● Nardò Nerìo Ris. '10	♥♥	3
● Nardò Nerìo Ris. '09	♥♥	3
● Nardò Rosso Roccamora '09	♥♥	2*

Cantine Soloperto

s.s. 7
74024 Manduria [TA]
Tel. 0999794286
www.soloperto.it

CELLAR SALES
PRE-BOOKED VISITS
ANNUAL PRODUCTION 2,000,000 bottles
HECTARES UNDER VINE 50.00

The long-established Soloperto family estate was a pioneer of the Primitivo di Manduria designation, and remains a figurehead on the Puglia wine scene. The estate vineyards are planted on both red and black soils, including 12 hectares of head-trained vines, from the age-old specimens in Contrada Bagnolo, to 40-year-olds in Contrada Spina and Contrada Schiavoni, as well as the recently planted cordon-trained and spur-pruned in Petrose. The Primitivo di Manduria Tenuta Bagnolo Centofuochi still takes pride of place. After presenting the 2013 last year, the winery submitted their 2012s this year. The wines were definitely readier, fresh-tasting and juicy with slightly smoky notes, and spicy, fruity hints. Also well-crafted were other Primitivo di Mandurias, such as the intense Mono 2011 displaying crunchy fruit, the Patriarca 2013 with its rougher tannic kick but good matière and length, and the pleasant, approachable Etichetta Rossa 2014.

● Primitivo di Manduria Centofuochi Tenuta Bagnolo '12	♟♟ 4
● Primitivo di Manduria Mono '11	♟♟ 3
● Primitivo di Manduria Patriarca '13	♟♟ 4
● Primitivo di Manduria Rubinum Et. Rossa '14	♟♟ 2*
● Primitivo di Manduria Dolce Naturale Nektare '13	♟ 3
⊙ Rosato Salento '14	♟ 2
● Vintia '12	♟ 3
● Primitivo di Manduria Centofuochi Tenuta Bagnolo '13	♟♟ 4
● Primitivo di Manduria Centofuochi Tenuta Bagnolo '11	♟♟ 4
● Primitivo di Manduria Rubinum 17 Et. Rossa '13	♟♟ 2*
⊙ Rosato Salento '13	♟♟ 2*

★Tormaresca

fraz. c.da Torre d'Isola
loc. Tofano
70055 Minervino Murge [BT]
Tel. 0883692631
www.tormaresca.it

CELLAR SALES
PRE-BOOKED VISITS
ACCOMMODATION
ANNUAL PRODUCTION 3,000,000 bottles
HECTARES UNDER VINE 380.00
VITICULTURE METHOD Certified Organic
SUSTAINABLE WINERY

This major winery in Puglia belonging to the Antinori family is made up of two estates, each with its own vinification and ageing facilities. The first, Bocca di Lupo is located in Alta Murgia, in the Castel del Monte designation, growing aglianico, nero di Troia, fiano pugliese, and moscato reale, as well as chardonnay and cabernet sauvignon. Masseria Maime, in the Upper Salento zone, not far from the Adriatic coast, focuses on negroamaro and primitivo. After a few years in the doldrums, the Negroamaro Masseria Maime is back to its best. The intense 2012 is rich and well-crafted, with earthy notes of black berry fruit. The Castel del Monte Rosso Trentangeli 2013, a blend of 70% aglianico and 20% cabernet sauvignon, topped up with syrah, shows hints of pencil lead and spices, fair fruitiness and good drinkability. The Bocca di Lupo was not presented, while the astringent and rather greenish Primitivo Torcicoda 2013 was off target.

● Masseria Maime '12	♟♟♟ 5
● Castel del Monte Rosso Trentangeli '13	♟♟ 3
⊙ Calafuria '14	♟ 3
● Fichimori '14	♟ 2
● Torcicoda '13	♟ 4
● Castel del Monte Rosso Trentangeli '11	♟♟♟ 3*
● Masseria Maime '08	♟♟♟ 5
● Masseria Maime '07	♟♟♟ 4
● Masseria Maime '06	♟♟♟ 4
● Masseria Maime '05	♟♟♟ 4*
● Masseria Maime '04	♟♟♟ 4*
● Masseria Maime '02	♟♟♟ 4
● Torcicoda '11	♟♟♟ 4*
● Torcicoda '10	♟♟♟ 3*
● Torcicoda '09	♟♟♟ 3
● Torcicoda '01	♟♟♟ 4*

Torrevento

LOC. CASTEL DEL MONTE
S.DA PROV.LE 234 KM 10,600
70033 CORATO [BA]
TEL. 0808980923
www.torrevento.it

CELLAR SALES
ACCOMMODATION AND RESTAURANT SERVICE
ANNUAL PRODUCTION 2,500,000 bottles
HECTARES UNDER VINE 450.00
VITICULTURE METHOD Certified Organic

In the Parco Rurale della Murgia, Francesco
Liantonio has made environmentally
sustainable winegrowing a cornerstone of
his cellars. A flagship for the Castel del
Monte designation, Torrevento's vineyards
are planted on the typically rocky limestone
soils of the Murgia karst plateau, as well as
on the red soils of the Valle d'Itria, and in
Salento, where it still has plenty of
head-trained vines. The estate's vast range
is produced almost exclusively from native
varieties, focusing mainly on nero di Troia.
The 2012 vintage saw the Castel del Monte
Rosso Vigna Pedale Riserva back at the top
of the range, with its berry-like notes,
autumn leaves on the nose, and a fruit-rich,
fresh-tasting, supple, juicy palate. An
excellent result from the earthy, austere
and lingering Matervitae Aglianico 2013,
with its hints of dark berry fruit and
rosemary. Of the rest, we especially liked
the juicy, pleasing 2013 version of Primitivo
Since 1913.

Cantine Tre Pini

VIA VECCHIA PER ALTAMURA SP 79 KM 16
70020 CASSANO DELLE MURGE [BA]
TEL. 080764911
www.agriturismotrepini.com

CELLAR SALES
PRE-BOOKED VISITS
ACCOMMODATION AND RESTAURANT SERVICE
ANNUAL PRODUCTION 30,000 bottles
HECTARES UNDER VINE 7.00
VITICULTURE METHOD Certified Organic

The Plantamura family runs this farm
estate and agriturismo in Alta Murgia
National Park with great passion and
skill. The primitivo used for the Gioia del
Colle range is grown next to the winery, in
Piscina delle Monache, outside Cassano
Murge. The single two-hectare south- to
south-east-facing vineyard is planted with
20-year-old head-trained vines at an
elevation of 450 metres, on mainly stony
soils. The malvasia bianca is grown at 400
metres above sea level, on south-east-
facing, moderately loose-packed soils.
With its fresh red berry fruit, violet and
plum aromas, and a palate which is
complex, leisurely and juicy, lip-smacking
and polished, laden with crunchy fruitiness,
the Gioia del Colle Primitivo Riserva 2012
missed the top award by a whisker. The
excellent Gioia Del Colle Primitivo 2011
comes out a year after the 2012, though it
has less finesse than the Riserva, but
with excellent thrust, and balsamic and
liquorice notes.

● Castel del Monte Rosso	
V. Pedale Ris. '12	♟♟♟ 3*
● Matervitae Aglianico '13	♟♟ 2*
● Salice Salentino Rosso	
Sine Nomine Ris. '13	♟♟ 3
● Since 1913 '13	♟♟ 3
☉ Castel del Monte Rosato Primaronda '14	♟ 2
● Castel del Monte Rosso Bolonero '13	♟ 2
● Matervitae Negroamaro '13	♟ 2
● Matervitae Primitivo '13	♟ 2
○ Matervitae Verdeca '13	♟ 2
● Salice Salentino Rosso Faneros '13	♟ 2
● Torre del Falco '13	♟ 2
● Castel del Monte Rosso Bolonero '12	♛♛♛ 2*
● Castel del Monte Rosso	
V. Pedale Ris. '10	♛♛♛ 3*
● Castel del Monte Rosso	
V. Pedale Ris. '09	♛♛♛ 3*

● Gioia del Colle Primitivo '11	♟♟ 4
● Gioia del Colle Primitivo Ris. '12	♟♟ 4
○ Donna Giovanna '14	♟ 2
○ Pinus Brut M. Cl.	♟ 3
● Gioia del Colle Primitivo	
Piscina delle Monache '12	♛♛ 3*

Vigne & Vini Varvaglione

C.DA SANTA LUCIA
74020 LEPORANO [TA]
TEL. 0995315370
www.vigneevini.it

CELLAR SALES
PRE-BOOKED VISITS
ANNUAL PRODUCTION 2,000,000 bottles
HECTARES UNDER VINE 155.00
VITICULTURE METHOD Certified Organic
SUSTAINABLE WINERY

Cosimo and Maria Teresa are the third generation of the Varvaglione family at the helm of the winery. The various production lines get their grapes from over 150 hectares of vineyards, thanks to the winery's affiliation with many local growers, mainly natives, particularly primitivo, negroamaro, malvasia and verdeca, although some well-known international grape varieties are also present. Without the sheen of last year, the Primitivo di Manduria Papale Linea Oro 2013 has good fruit but overly evident oak and is rather too sweet. One of Puglia's best whites of the difficult 2014 growing year was the slightly aromatic 12 e Mezzo Malvasia, with a nose of sage and citrus, and a fresh, close-focused, zesty palate, with a lovely citrussy finish. Also successful was the invitingly clean and drinkable Primitivo Tatù 2014, with its berry fruit and chocolate notes.

○ 12 e mezzo Malvasia '14	♀♀ 2*
● Primitivo di Manduria Papale Linea Oro '13	♀♀ 5
● Tatu '14	♀♀ 2*
● 12 e mezzo Negroamaro '14	♀ 2
● 12 e mezzo Primitivo '14	♀ 2
○ Marfi '14	♀ 2
● Passione '14	♀ 2
● Primitivo di Manduria Papale '14	♀ 3
● 12 e Mezzo Negroamaro '11	♀♀ 2*
● Primitivo di Manduria Papale Linea Oro '12	♀♀ 5
● Primitivo di Manduria Papale Linea Oro '11	♀♀ 5

Vecchia Torre

VIA MARCHE, 1
73045 LEVERANO [LE]
TEL. 0832925053
www.cantinavecchiatorre.it

CELLAR SALES
PRE-BOOKED VISITS
ANNUAL PRODUCTION 2,400,000 bottles
HECTARES UNDER VINE 1300.00

For over half a century this large cooperative winery has offered its members support in the vineyard and quality winegrowing services. From just 50 members in 1959 to today's 1,300-plus growers now supply Vecchia Torre with grapes, most of whom work within a few kilometres of Leverano. And it is the focus on territory, on maintaining Salento tradition of head-trained vines and native varieties, combined with a modern vinification process, in large steel or oak vats, that gives the wines great consistency and continuity year after year. This year we particularly enjoyed the spicy, well-textured 50° Anniversario 2012, an equal blend of negroamaro and syrah, with its fresh notes of Mediterranean scrub and black berry fruit, though all of the production displays excellence. Others we enjoyed were the traditionally plummy Salice Salentino Rosso 2013 and the clean, fresh-tasting Leverano Rosato 2014.

● 50° Anniversario '12	♀♀ 3*
● Arneide '11	♀♀ 3
⊙ Leverano Rosato '14	♀♀ 2*
● Leverano Rosso '13	♀♀ 2*
● Primitivo '13	♀♀ 2*
● Salice Salentino Rosso '13	♀♀ 2*
○ Vermentino '14	♀♀ 2*
● Leverano Rosso Ris. '10	♀ 2
● Malvasia Nera '13	♀ 2
● Negroamaro '13	♀ 2
● Salice Salentino Rosso Ris. '11	♀ 2
● Leverano Rosso '12	♀♀ 2*
● Negroamaro '11	♀♀ 2*
● Salice Salentino Rosso Ris. '09	♀♀ 2*

Tenuta Viglione

via Carlo Marx, 44p
70029 Santeramo in Colle [BA]
Tel. 0802123661
www.tenutaviglione.it

CELLAR SALES
PRE-BOOKED VISITS
ACCOMMODATION AND RESTAURANT SERVICE
ANNUAL PRODUCTION 200,000 bottles
HECTARES UNDER VINE 40.00
VITICULTURE METHOD Certified Organic
SUSTAINABLE WINERY

Giovanni Zullo's Tenuta Viglione has become one of the leading lights of the quality revolution enjoyed by the Gioia del Colle designation. The vineyards are located in the hills of the Bari Murgia, about 450 metres above sea level, at the highest point of the DOC zone, on a thin layer of terra rossa, containing chipped limestone and siliceous rock, lying on massive monolithic beds with a high marine fossil content. As well as primitivo, the cellar also grows aleatico, merlot, falanghina, trebbiano, and malvasia. This year, Giovanni Zullo's range featured an array of top-quality wines, starting with the Gioia del Colle Primitivo Marpione Riserva 2011, with its spicy bouquet with black berry fruit hints and its fresh-tasting, piquant, full mouthfeel, with a gutsy finish marked by notes of Mediterranean scrub. Slightly sweeter but still brilliant is the Gioia del Colle Primitivo 2012, while the blend of 50% aleatico and primitivo, the fruity Johe 2013, with its notes of ginger, is highly drinkable.

● Gioia del Colle Primitivo Marpione Ris. '11	▼▼▼ 3*
● Gioia del Colle Primitivo '12	▼▼ 2*
● Johe '13	▼▼ 2*
● Nisia '14	▼▼ 2*
● Gioia del Colle Primitivo Marpione Ris. '10	▽▽▽ 3*
● Gioia del Colle Pri-mit-ivo '11	▽▽ 5
● Gioia del Colle Primitivo '10	▽▽ 2*
● Gioia del Colle Rosso Marpione Ris. '09	▽▽ 3*
● Johe '12	▽▽ 2*
● Johe '11	▽▽ 2*
● Johe '11	▽▽ 2*

★Conti Zecca

via Cesarea
73045 Leverano [LE]
Tel. 0832925613
www.contizecca.it

CELLAR SALES
PRE-BOOKED VISITS
ANNUAL PRODUCTION 2,000,000 bottles
HECTARES UNDER VINE 320.00

The Conti Zecca have been cultivating large holdings in Leverano for over five centuries. The winery opened in 1935 and has since become a flagship for Puglia's wine industry. Its four estates are Saracena, Donna Marzia, Santo Stefano at Leverano, and Cantalupi at Salice Salentino, each with a wide range of labels, plus the Selezioni range, making up over thirty different wines, most from native vines. Although this venerable winery's selection is not quite up to previous years, it is nevertheless solid overall. We did love Terra 2012, from aglianico with a 15% negroamaro, with intense notes of dark berry fruit and liquorice. The Nero, the winery's established blend of 70% negroamaro and cabernet sauvignon, seemed rather too oaky to be succulent. Both the crunchy fruitiness of the Primitivo 2013 and the spicy, fluent Malvasia 2014, were a pleasure.

○ Malvasia Bianca '14	▼▼ 2*
● Nero '12	▼▼ 5
● Primitivo '13	▼▼ 3
● Terra '12	▼▼ 4
○ Fiano '14	▼ 2
● Primitivo Cantalupi '13	▼ 2
⊙ Venus '14	▼ 2
● Nero '09	▽▽▽ 5
● Nero '08	▽▽▽ 5
● Nero '07	▽▽▽ 5
● Nero '06	▽▽▽ 5
● Nero '03	▽▽▽ 5
● Nero '02	▽▽▽ 5
● Nero '01	▽▽▽ 5
● Nero '00	▽▽▽ 5
● Nero '99	▽▽▽ 5

A Mano

VIA SAN GIOVANNI, 41
70015 NOCI [BA]
TEL. 0803434872
www.amanowine.it

CELLAR SALES
PRE-BOOKED VISITS
ANNUAL PRODUCTION 390,000 bottles
VITICULTURE METHOD Certified Organic

● Negroamaro '13	▼▼ 2*
○ A Mano Bianco '14	▼ 2
⊙ A Mano Rosato '14	▼ 2

Masseria Altemura

S.DA PROV.LE 69 MESGANE
72028 TORRE SANTA SUSANNA [BR]
TEL. 0831740485
www.masseriaaltemura.it

CELLAR SALES
PRE-BOOKED VISITS
ACCOMMODATION
ANNUAL PRODUCTION 400,000 bottles
HECTARES UNDER VINE 150.00

○ Falanghina '14	▼▼ 3
● Sasseo '13	▼▼ 3
● Negroamaro '13	▼ 3
● Primitivo di Manduria Altemura '13	▼ 5

Antica Enotria

LOC. C.DA RISICATA
S.DA PROV.LE 65 KM 7
71042 CERIGNOLA [FG]
TEL. 0885418462
www.anticaenotria.it

CELLAR SALES
PRE-BOOKED VISITS
ANNUAL PRODUCTION 100,000 bottles
HECTARES UNDER VINE 13.00
VITICULTURE METHOD Certified Organic

⊙ Contessa Staffa '14	▼▼ 2*
● Puglia Rosso '13	▼ 2
● Vriccio '13	▼ 3

Antica Masseria Jorche

C.DA JORCHE
74020 TORRICELLA [TA]
TEL. 0999573232
www.jorche.it

CELLAR SALES
PRE-BOOKED VISITS
ACCOMMODATION AND RESTAURANT SERVICE
ANNUAL PRODUCTION 80,000 bottles
HECTARES UNDER VINE 30.00
SUSTAINABLE WINERY

● Primitivo di Manduria Dolce Naturale Lo Apu '14	▼▼ 5
● Caleido '11	▼ 2
● Primitivo di Manduria '11	▼ 4

Apollonio

VIA SAN PIETRO IN LAMA, 7
73047 MONTERONI DI LECCE [LE]
TEL. 0832327182
www.apolloniovini.it

CELLAR SALES
PRE-BOOKED VISITS
ANNUAL PRODUCTION 1,500,000 bottles
HECTARES UNDER VINE 20.00

● Elfo Negroamaro '14	▼▼ 2*
● Terragnolo Primitivo '11	▼▼ 4
⊙ Elfo Negroamaro Rosato '14	▼ 2
● Elfo Primitivo '14	▼ 2

Cantine Botromagno

VIA ARCHIMEDE, 24
70024 GRAVINA IN PUGLIA [BA]
TEL. 0803265865
www.botromagno.it

CELLAR SALES
PRE-BOOKED VISITS
ACCOMMODATION AND RESTAURANT SERVICE
ANNUAL PRODUCTION 350,000 bottles
HECTARES UNDER VINE 50.00

○ Fiano Poderi d'Agostino '14	▼▼ 3
● Gioia del Colle Primitivo Dedicato a Franco e Lucia Ris. '11	▼ 7
● Pier delle Vigne Et. Argento '11	▼ 4

I Buongiorno

c.so Vittorio Emanuele II, 71
72012 Carovigno [BR]
Tel. 0831996286
www.giasottolarco.it

ANNUAL PRODUCTION 50,000 bottles
HECTARES UNDER VINE 10.00

● Negramaro '13	♥♥	3
● Primitivo '13	♥♥	3
● Nicolaus '13	♥	3
⊙ Rosalento '14	♥	2

Francesco Cannito

c.da Parco Bizzarro
70025 Grumo Appula [BA]
Tel. 080623529
www.agricolacannito.it

CELLAR SALES
PRE-BOOKED VISITS
ANNUAL PRODUCTION 20,000 bottles
HECTARES UNDER VINE 4.00
VITICULTURE METHOD Certified Organic
SUSTAINABLE WINERY

● Gioia del Colle Primitivo Drùmon '11	♥♥	5
● Gioia del Colle Primitivo Drùmon Ris. '11	♥	8
⊙ Gioia del Colle Rosato Drùmon Rosé '14	♥	5

Cantolio Manduria

via per Lecce km 2,5
74024 Manduria [TA]
Tel. 0999796045
www.cantolio.it

CELLAR SALES
PRE-BOOKED VISITS
RESTAURANT SERVICE
ANNUAL PRODUCTION 500,000 bottles
HECTARES UNDER VINE 800.00
VITICULTURE METHOD Certified Organic

● Primitivo di Manduria Tema Ris. '11	♥♥	4
● Primitivo di Manduria Urceus '14	♥♥	2*
⊙ Arunte '14	♥	1*
⊙ L'Opis '13	♥	2

Giancarlo Ceci

c.da Sant'Agostino
76123 Andria [BT]
Tel. 0883565220
www.agrinatura.net

ANNUAL PRODUCTION 520,000 bottles
HECTARES UNDER VINE 70.00
VITICULTURE METHOD Certified Biodynamic

● Castel del Monte Nero di Troia Felice Ceci Ris. '12	♥♥	3*
● Castel del Monte Rosso Almagia '14	♥♥	2*
○ Castel del Monte Chardonnay '14	♥	2

Tenuta Coppadoro

via Tiberio Solis, 128
71016 San Severo [FG]
Tel. 0882223174
www.tenutacoppadoro.it

CELLAR SALES
PRE-BOOKED VISITS
ANNUAL PRODUCTION 360,000 bottles
HECTARES UNDER VINE 120.00

● Grifoni '14	♥♥	3
● Impavido '13	♥♥	3
● Pescorosso '14	♥♥	2*
● Brando '14	♥	2

Coppi

cir.ne sud - II tratto
70010 Turi [BA]
Tel. 0808915049
www.vinicoppi.it

CELLAR SALES
PRE-BOOKED VISITS
ANNUAL PRODUCTION 1,000,000 bottles
HECTARES UNDER VINE 10.00
VITICULTURE METHOD Certified Organic

● Gioia del Colle Primitivo Senatore '08	♥♥	3
● Negroamaro Pellirosso '12	♥♥	2*
● Gioia del Colle Primitivo Vanitoso Ris. '07	♥	3
● Primitivo Don Antonio '14	♥	1*

D'Alfonso del Sordo

C.DA SANT'ANTONINO
71016 SAN SEVERO [FG]
TEL. 0882221444
www.dalfonsodelsordo.it

CELLAR SALES
PRE-BOOKED VISITS
ACCOMMODATION
ANNUAL PRODUCTION 250,000 bottles
HECTARES UNDER VINE 45.00

● Guado San Leo '12	♛♛ 4
● Montero '12	♛♛ 2*
○ San Severo Bianco Posta Arignano '14	♛♛ 2*
● Casteldrione '13	♛ 2

De Falco

VIA MILANO, 25
73051 NOVOLI [LE]
TEL. 0832711597
www.cantinedefalco.it

CELLAR SALES
PRE-BOOKED VISITS
ACCOMMODATION
ANNUAL PRODUCTION 300,000 bottles
HECTARES UNDER VINE 20.00

● Artiglio Rosso '10	♛♛ 4
● Salice Salentino Rosso Salore '12	♛♛ 2*
● Salice Salentino Rosso Falconero Ris. '10	♛ 3
● Squinzano Rosso Serre di Sant'Elia '13	♛ 2

Ferri

VIA BARI, 347
70010 VALENZANO [BA]
TEL. 0804671753
www.cantineferri.it

CELLAR SALES
PRE-BOOKED VISITS
ANNUAL PRODUCTION 40,000 bottles
HECTARES UNDER VINE 5.00

● Ad Mira '09	♛♛ 5
● Purpureus '11	♛♛ 3
○ Duo Bianco '14	♛ 2
○ Sol di Cuti '14	♛ 2

Feudi di Guagnano

VIA CELLINO, 3
73010 GUAGNANO [LE]
TEL. 0832705422
www.feudiguagnano.com

CELLAR SALES
PRE-BOOKED VISITS
ANNUAL PRODUCTION 200,000 bottles
HECTARES UNDER VINE 15.00

● Salice Salentino Rosso Cupone Ris. '11	♛♛ 2*
● Diecianni Primitivo '14	♛ 2
● Nero di Velluto '11	♛ 4
● Pietrafinita '13	♛ 4

Feudi Salentini

FRAZ. LEPORANO
VIA AMENDOLA, 36
74020 TARANTO
TEL. 0995315370
www.feudisalentini.com

CELLAR SALES
PRE-BOOKED VISITS
ANNUAL PRODUCTION 300,000 bottles
HECTARES UNDER VINE 25.00

● Primitivo di Manduria Gocce '13	♛♛ 5
● Uno/Due/Cinque Primitivo '14	♛♛ 2*
● Re Sale '14	♛ 2
● Uno/Due/Cinque Negroamaro '14	♛ 2

Duca Carlo Guarini

L.GO FRISARI, 1
73020 SCORRANO [LE]
TEL. 0836460288
www.ducacarloguarini.it

CELLAR SALES
PRE-BOOKED VISITS
ACCOMMODATION AND RESTAURANT SERVICE
ANNUAL PRODUCTION 250,000 bottles
HECTARES UNDER VINE 70.00
VITICULTURE METHOD Certified Organic

● Piutri '12	♛♛ 2*
○ Ambra '13	♛ 4
● Nativo '13	♛ 3
● Vignevecchie Primitivo '12	♛ 3

Hiso Telaray
Libera Terra Puglia

VICO DEI CANTELMO, 1
72023 MESAGNE [BR]
TEL. 0831775981
www.hisotelaray.it

CELLAR SALES
ANNUAL PRODUCTION 120,000 bottles
HECTARES UNDER VINE 27.00
VITICULTURE METHOD Certified Organic
SUSTAINABLE WINERY

● Renata Fonte '13	♥♥ 3
● Filari di Sant'Antonii '14	♥ 2
● Primitivo Antò '13	♥ 3

Lucio Leuci

VIA VILLA BALDASSARRI, KM 1
73010 GUAGNANO [LE]
TEL. 0832706500
www.vinileuci.it

CELLAR SALES
PRE-BOOKED VISITS
ANNUAL PRODUCTION 200,000 bottles
HECTARES UNDER VINE 30.00

● Salice Salentino Rosso Terra Guaniani '13	♥♥ 2*
● Varale '13	♥♥ 3
● Altura '14	♥ 2

Alberto Longo

LOC. C.DA PADULECCHIA
S.DA PROV.LE 5 LUCERA-PIETRAMONTECORVINO KM 4
71036 LUCERA [FG]
TEL. 0881539057
www.albertolongo.it

CELLAR SALES
PRE-BOOKED VISITS
ANNUAL PRODUCTION 200,000 bottles
HECTARES UNDER VINE 35.00

● Cacc'e Mmitte di Lucera '13	♥♥ 3
⊙ Donnadele '14	♥ 3
○ Le Fossette '14	♥ 3

Produttori Vini Manduria

VIA FABIO MASSIMO, 19
74024 MANDURIA [TA]
TEL. 0999735332
www.cpvini.com

CELLAR SALES
PRE-BOOKED VISITS
ANNUAL PRODUCTION 700,000 bottles
HECTARES UNDER VINE 1000.00
SUSTAINABLE WINERY

● Primitivo di Manduria Elegia Ris. '11	♥♥ 4
● Primitivo di Manduria Sonetto Ris. '11	♥♥ 6
● Primitivo di Manduria Dolce Naturale Madrigale '12	♥ 3

Mocavero

VIA MALLACCA ZUMMARI
73010 ARNESANO [LE]
TEL. 0832327194
www.mocaverovini.it

CELLAR SALES
PRE-BOOKED VISITS
RESTAURANT SERVICE
ANNUAL PRODUCTION 600,000 bottles
HECTARES UNDER VINE 65.00

○ Curtirussi Verdeca '14	♥♥ 3
⊙ Sjre Negroamaro Rosato '14	♥♥ 2*
● Sjre Primitivo '13	♥♥ 2*
● Salice Salentino Rosso '13	♥ 3

Mottura Vini del Salento

P.ZZA MELICA, 4
73058 TUGLIE [LE]
TEL. 0833596601
www.motturavini.it

PRE-BOOKED VISITS
ANNUAL PRODUCTION 2,500,000 bottles
HECTARES UNDER VINE 200.00

● Negroamaro Le Pitre '13	♥♥ 5
● Primitivo Le Pitre '13	♥♥ 6
○ Fiano Le Pitre '14	♥ 5

Cantine Paradiso

VIA MANFREDONIA, 39
71042 CERIGNOLA [FG]
TEL. 0885428720
www.cantineparadiso.it

ANNUAL PRODUCTION 140,000 bottles
HECTARES UNDER VINE 16.00

● Podere Belmantello Darione '13	♥♥	3
⊙ Posta Piana Rosato '14	♥♥	2*
● Posta Piana Nero di Troia '13	♥	2
● Posta Piana Primitivo '13	♥	2

I Pastini - Carparelli

VIA ITALO BALBO, 22/24
70010 LOCOROTONDO [BA]
TEL. 0804313309
pastini@virgilio.it

CELLAR SALES
PRE-BOOKED VISITS
ANNUAL PRODUCTION 5,500 bottles
HECTARES UNDER VINE 14.00

○ Faraone '14	♥♥	2*
⊙ Le Rotaie Rosato '14	♥	3
○ Locorotondo Antico '14	♥	2
● Verso Sud '12	♥	2

Giovanni Petrelli

VIA VILLA CONVENTO, 33
73041 CARMIANO [LE]
TEL. 0832603051
www.cantinapetrelli.com

CELLAR SALES
PRE-BOOKED VISITS
ANNUAL PRODUCTION 100,000 bottles
HECTARES UNDER VINE 15.00

● Don Pepè '12	♥♥	4
● Primitivo P '14	♥♥	2*

Paolo Petrilli

LOC. MOTTA DELLA REGINA
71036 LUCERA [FG]
TEL. 0881523980
www.lamotticella.com

CELLAR SALES
PRE-BOOKED VISITS
ANNUAL PRODUCTION 15,000 bottles
HECTARES UNDER VINE 11.00

● Cacc'e Mmitte di Lucera Agramante '11	♥♥	3
● Fortuita '12	♥♥	2*
● Cacc'e Mmitte di Lucera Ferraù '10	♥	4

Pirro Varone

VIA SENATORE LACAITA, 90
74024 MANDURIA [TA]
TEL. 3397429098
www.pirrovarrone.eu

CELLAR SALES
PRE-BOOKED VISITS
ANNUAL PRODUCTION 90,000 bottles
HECTARES UNDER VINE 16.00
VITICULTURE METHOD Certified Organic

● Primitivo di Manduria Casa Vecchia '11	♥♥	4
● Primitivo di Manduria Ris. '10	♥♥	4
● Vigne Rare Rosso Grisola '10	♥♥	5
○ Vigne Rare Bianco '14	♥	5

Vigne di Rasciatano

FRAZ. C.DA RASCIATANO
S.S. 93, KM 13
76121 BARLETTA
TEL. 0883510999
www.rasciatano.com

CELLAR SALES
PRE-BOOKED VISITS
ANNUAL PRODUCTION 90,000 bottles
HECTARES UNDER VINE 18.00

● Rasciatano '12	♥♥	5
● Tenute Nero di Troia '12	♥♥	2*
○ Tenute Chardonnay '14	♥	2

Risveglio Agricolo

C.DA TORRE MOZZA
72100 BRINDISI
TEL. 0831519948
www.cantinerisveglio.it

CELLAR SALES
PRE-BOOKED VISITS
ANNUAL PRODUCTION 100,000 bottles
HECTARES UNDER VINE 44.00

● 72100 '13	♥♥ 2*
● Brindisi Rosso Simposio Ris. '10	♥♥ 2*

Rosa del Golfo

VIA GARIBALDI, 18
73011 ALEZIO [LE]
TEL. 0833281045
www.rosadelgolfo.com

CELLAR SALES
PRE-BOOKED VISITS
ANNUAL PRODUCTION 300,000 bottles
HECTARES UNDER VINE 40.00

⊙ Negroamaro Rosato 50° Vendemmia '14	♥♥ 3
● Primitivo '13	♥♥ 2*
● Scaliere '14	♥ 2

Conte Spagnoletti Zeuli

FRAZ. MONTEGROSSO
C.DA SAN DOMENICO, SP 231 KM 60,000
70031 ANDRIA [BT]
TEL. 0883569511
www.contespagnolettizeuli.it

CELLAR SALES
PRE-BOOKED VISITS
ANNUAL PRODUCTION 400,000 bottles
HECTARES UNDER VINE 120.00

● Castel del Monte Aglianico Ghiandara V. San Domenico '11	♥♥ 3
● Castel del Monte Nero di Troia Il Rinzacco Ris. '12	♥♥ 3

Spelonga

VIA MENOLA
71047 STORNARA [FG]
TEL. 0885431048
www.cantinespelonga.com

CELLAR SALES
PRE-BOOKED VISITS
ANNUAL PRODUCTION 40,000 bottles
HECTARES UNDER VINE 10.00
SUSTAINABLE WINERY

● Nero di Troia '14	♥♥ 3
● Donna Maria Franca Samà Rosso '14	♥ 2
⊙ Marilina Rosé '14	♥ 2

Cosimo Taurino

S.S. 365 KM 1,400
73010 GUAGNANO [LE]
TEL. 0832706490
www.taurinovini.it

CELLAR SALES
PRE-BOOKED VISITS
ANNUAL PRODUCTION 900,000 bottles
HECTARES UNDER VINE 90.00

● 64 A Cosimo Taurino '09	♥♥ 4
● Notarpanaro '10	♥♥ 3
○ Le Ricordanze Passito '12	♥ 5
⊙ Scaloti '14	♥ 2

Cantine Teanum

VIA CROCE SANTA, 48
71010 SAN SEVERO [FG]
TEL. 0882336332
www.teanum.it

CELLAR SALES
PRE-BOOKED VISITS
ANNUAL PRODUCTION 800,000 bottles
HECTARES UNDER VINE 150.00

● Gran Tiati Gold Vintage Nero di Troia '10	♥♥ 7
○ San Severo Bianco Favùgnë '14	♥ 2
● San Severo Rosso Canticum '14	♥ 2
○ Vento '13	♥ 3

Torre Quarto

C.DA QUARTO, 5
71042 CERIGNOLA [FG]
TEL. 0885418453
www.torrequarto.it

CELLAR SALES
PRE-BOOKED VISITS
ACCOMMODATION AND RESTAURANT SERVICE
ANNUAL PRODUCTION 500,000 bottles
HECTARES UNDER VINE 70.00

● Malvasia Nera '14	♥♥ 2*
● Rosso del Giudice '13	♥♥ 2*
● Rosso di Cerignola Quarto Ducale '13	♥ 3
● Sangue Blu '13	♥ 2

Agricole Vallone

VIA XXV LUGLIO, 5
73100 LECCE
TEL. 0832308041
www.agricolevallone.it

PRE-BOOKED VISITS
ANNUAL PRODUCTION 400,000 bottles
HECTARES UNDER VINE 161.00
VITICULTURE METHOD Certified Organic
SUSTAINABLE WINERY

● Vigna Castello '11	♥♥ 5
○ Tenuta Serranova '14	♥ 3

Vigneti Reale

VIA EGIDIO REALE, 55
73100 LECCE
TEL. 0832248433
www.vignetireale.it

PRE-BOOKED VISITS
ACCOMMODATION AND RESTAURANT SERVICE
ANNUAL PRODUCTION 100,000 bottles
HECTARES UNDER VINE 85.00
SUSTAINABLE WINERY

● Norie '13	♥♥ 2*
● Rudiae '13	♥♥ 3
● Salice Salentino Santa Croce Ris. '12	♥♥ 4
○ Malvasia '14	♥ 2

Valle dell'Asso

VIA GUIDANO, 18
73013 GALATINA [LE]
TEL. 0836561470
www.valleasso.it

CELLAR SALES
PRE-BOOKED VISITS
ACCOMMODATION
ANNUAL PRODUCTION 250,000 bottles
HECTARES UNDER VINE 75.00
VITICULTURE METHOD Certified Organic

● Piromàfo '10	♥♥ 4
● Terra San Giovanni '13	♥♥ 2*
● Il Macàro '05	♥ 3

Vetrere

FRAZ. VETRERE
S.DA PROV.LE MONTEIASI-MONTEMESOLA KM 16
74100 TARANTO
TEL. 0995661054
www.vetrere.it

CELLAR SALES
PRE-BOOKED VISITS
ACCOMMODATION AND RESTAURANT SERVICE
ANNUAL PRODUCTION 230,000 bottles
HECTARES UNDER VINE 37.00

⊙ Taranta '14	♥♥ 2*
● Tempio di Giano '14	♥♥ 2*
● Barone Pazzo '13	♥ 4
○ Finis '14	♥ 2

Vinicola Mediterranea

VIA MATERNITÀ E INFANZIA, 22
72027 SAN PIETRO VERNOTICO [BR]
TEL. 0831676323
www.vinicolamediterranea.it

CELLAR SALES
PRE-BOOKED VISITS
RESTAURANT SERVICE
ANNUAL PRODUCTION 500,000 bottles

● Negroamaro Il Nobile '14	♥♥ 3
● Negroamaro Il Primonobile '13	♥♥ 3
● Salice Salentino Rosso Il Barone '13	♥♥ 2*
● Primitivo di Manduria Primoduca '14	♥ 3

CALABRIA

Calabria was probably the first region in Italy to cultivate vines and produce wine in a modern way. In about the eighth century BC, colonizing Greeks introduced not only their vines (the most widespread white grape in the region is still called greco) but also bush-training in vineyards and use of fermentation vessels in the cellar. The vast range of varietals, with nearly 300 clones so far listed as native to Calabria, and sheer historical proof, suggest an important winemaking past but sadly, and conversely to other European regions, none of this has been sufficient inspiration for launching modern viticulture into a leading role today. So Calabria, despite its fascinating wine history, produces such low amounts that it brings up the rear among the Italian regions. Although recently much has been done, including in terms of quality, and despite having all the right land and climate credentials, the region continues to drag its heels. Again, this year, two of the three Tre Bicchieri wines come from the Cirò district, where wineries have been faster and more able in raising the quality bar of their production. We have Librandi's Magno Megonio 2013, an excellent pure Magliocco; iGreco's Masino 2013, a calabrese blend; and Ceraudo's white Grisara 2014, a native pecorello blend. Elsewhere in the region, performance is patchy, particularly in Cosenza, where in recent years many new wineries took steady first steps on the market. Unluckily, while offering wines of undisputed quality, many of these wineries are still tied to a style that leans more to concentration and weight than to elegance and finesse, and hence is no longer on trend. Viola's Moscato Passito 2014 once again flies the flag for the area. A positive note comes in the form of environmental sustainability: in recent years many wineries have turned their attention to their surroundings, not only converting to organic or biodynamic (a stronger trend in Calabria than in other regions) methods but also putting in place viable strategies in terms of renewable energy, as well as reducing emissions of greenhouse gases. Unfortunately, due to space constraints, we were unable to include several wineries that submitted admirable wines: Donnici 99, Masseria Falvo, La Pizzuta del Principe, Malaspina, and Termine Grosso. Look out for them in the near future.

Caparra & Siciliani

BIVIO SS 106
88811 CIRÒ MARINA [KR]
TEL. 0962373319
www.caparraesiciliani.com

CELLAR SALES
PRE-BOOKED VISITS
ANNUAL PRODUCTION 800,000 bottles
HECTARES UNDER VINE 180.00
VITICULTURE METHOD Certified Organic

Caparra & Siciliani was founded in 1963 when the two families decided to join forces to make a better attack on the market. The new winery was made up of Caparra family vineyards around Cirò Marina and nearby hilltop vines owned by the Sicilianis, for a total of around 180 hectares, which is still the case. There are now 19 grower-producers at Caparra & Siciliani, all heirs of the founders, whereas the vineyards have been divided up into 12 different holdings which work together to make sure that by the end of the season the best grapes are harvested. It is still the rule today that only wines made from member grapes can be bottled here. The Volvito 2012 made it to the finals. After a few minutes in the glass, this austere, traditional Riserva di Cirò Rosso Classico Superiore displays concentrated overtones of spices, mature red berry fruit and cakes on the nose, while the still-lively tannins are fresh-tasting and lingering on the palate.

● Cirò Rosso Cl. Sup. Volvito Ris. '12	♥♥ 3*
● Mastro Giurato '12	♥♥ 3
⊙ Cirò Rosato Le Formelle '14	♥ 2
● Cirò Rosso Cl. Sup. '12	♥ 2
● Cirò Solagi '13	♥ 2
○ Curiale '14	♥ 2
⊙ Insidia '14	♥ 2
● Cirò Rosso Cl. Sup. Volvito Ris. '11	♀♀ 3*
● Cirò Solagi '12	♀♀ 2*
○ Curiale '13	♀♀ 2*
⊙ Insidia '13	♀♀ 2*
● Mastrogiurato '10	♀♀ 3*

Roberto Ceraudo

LOC. MARINA DI STRONGOLI
C.DA DATTILO
88815 CROTONE
TEL. 0962865613
www.dattilo.it

CELLAR SALES
PRE-BOOKED VISITS
ACCOMMODATION AND RESTAURANT SERVICE
ANNUAL PRODUCTION 70,000 bottles
HECTARES UNDER VINE 20.00
VITICULTURE METHOD Certified Organic

Roberto Ceraudo, a true country gentleman, runs his lovely estate in Dattilo di Strongoli with unusual passion. Luckily he has passed that same passion on to his children, who have been running the winery with him for some time. The whole estate also produces quality citrus fruit and olive oil, and has always been farmed organically, whereas vineyard and cellar are subject to a biodynamic regime. Since the arrival of Caterina, Roberto's youngest daughter, the wines produced in Dattilo have revealed growing respect for the characteristics of the terroir and the original cultivar, as well as improving in terms of definition and style. A Tre Bicchieri went to the Grisara 2014, from pecorello, a native variety which had almost died out before the Ceraudo family stepped in to save it. Elegant Mediterranean bouquet of yellow-fleshed fruit, aromatic herbs, and salty, almost sea-breeze nuances, with a fresh-tasting and full-flavoured mouth of lively fragrant fruitiness.

○ Grisara '14	♥♥♥ 3*
● Petraro '11	♥♥ 5
● Dattilo '12	♥♥ 3
● Doro Bè '09	♥♥ 3
⊙ Grayasusi Et. Argento '14	♥♥ 4
⊙ Grayasusi Et. Rame '14	♥♥ 3
○ Petelia '14	♥♥ 3
⊙ Imyr '14	♥ 5
● Nanà '13	♥ 3
○ Grisara '13	♀♀♀ 3*
○ Grisara '12	♀♀♀ 3*

iGreco

LOC. SALICE
C.DA GUARDAPIEDI
87062 CARIATI [CS]
TEL. 0983969441
www.igreco.it

CELLAR SALES
PRE-BOOKED VISITS
ACCOMMODATION AND RESTAURANT SERVICE
ANNUAL PRODUCTION 250,000 bottles
HECTARES UNDER VINE 80.00
VITICULTURE METHOD Certified Organic
SUSTAINABLE WINERY

Although they all have day jobs, the seven
Greco siblings have an undeniable bond
with their native soil and the estate founded
by their father in Cariati, famous throughout
Italy for its exceptional EVO. About a
decade ago, encouraged by Giancarlo's
overriding passion, they decided to make
their own label wines, planting around 80
hectares of vine stock in Crotone's finest
soils. The estate's production stood out
from the outset for its extreme cleanness
and great drinkability, making modern
characterful wines with a strong local
identity. The Masino 2013 earned itself a
Tre Bicchieri. A monovarietal Calabrese,
balsamic, with a full nose profile of ripe
berry fruits, spices and Mediterranean
herbs, its palate is elegant, juicy and
lingering. We also liked both the Metodo
Classicos submitted, especially the elegant,
complex Gran Cuvée 2011, a Gaglioppo
rosé.

Ippolito 1845

VIA TIRONE, 118
88811 CIRÒ MARINA [KR]
TEL. 096231106
www.ippolito1845.it

CELLAR SALES
PRE-BOOKED VISITS
ANNUAL PRODUCTION 1,000,000 bottles
HECTARES UNDER VINE 100.00

Vincenzo and Gianluca Ippolito have
revolutionized their family estate, one
of the oldest to be found anywhere in
Calabria. The two brothers have traced out
a route aiming to maximize the potential
of indigenous grapes, working round the
clock both in the vineyard and in the cellar
to produce modern, highly-focused wines
without sacrificing local identity. To optimize
their environmental sustainability, Gianluca
and Vincenzo have drastically reduced
the weight of the bottles, rationalized
water consumption, banned the use of
all petrochemical products, and now use
crop rotation to enrich the soils so that
synthetic fertilizers are no longer needed.
Another prominent wine was the Cirò Colli
del Mancuso Riserva 2012, a pleasingly
drinkable Gaglioppo, offering a complex
nose combining fruitiness and spicy
balsamic undertones. Thumbs up also for
the Greco Passito Gemma del Sole 2014,
with its fruit-driven balsamic bouquet,
and fresh-tasting balance of acidity and
sweetness on the palate.

● Masino '13	♟♟ 5
● Catà '13	♟♟ 3
⊙ Gaglioppo Gran Cuvée Rosé '11	♟♟ 4
○ Greco Bianco Gran Cuvée '10	♟♟ 4
○ Filù '14	♟ 3
⊙ Savù '14	♟ 3
● Masino '12	♟♟♟ 5
● Masino '11	♟♟♟ 5
● Masino '10	♟♟♟ 5
○ Filù '13	♟♟ 2*

● Cirò Rosso Cl. Sup. Colli del Mancuso Ris. '12	♟♟ 3*
● 160 Anni '12	♟♟ 5
● Cirò Rosso Cl. Sup. Ripe del Falco Ris. '05	♟♟ 5
○ Gemma del Sole '11	♟♟ 4
○ Pecorello '14	♟♟ 2*
○ Cirò Bianco Res Dei '14	♟ 2
⊙ Cirò Rosato Mabilia '14	♟ 2
● I Mori '13	♟ 2
● 160 Anni '10	♟♟ 5
● Cirò Rosso Cl. Sup. Colli del Mancuso Ris. '11	♟♟ 3*

★Librandi

LOC. SAN GENNARO
S.S. JONICA 106
88811 CIRÒ MARINA [KR]
TEL. 096231518
www.librandi.it

CELLAR SALES
PRE-BOOKED VISITS
ANNUAL PRODUCTION 2,200,000 bottles
HECTARES UNDER VINE 232.00

Antonio and Nicodemo's foresight enabled
them to hand over a winery with huge
growth potential to the next generation
of Librandis, who have now completely
taken over at the helm of one of Southern
Italy's finest estates. Now it is up to them
to carry on the research into indigenous
Calabrian cultivars which has led to
such exceptional results with gaglioppo,
mantonico and magliocco, proving they
are on the right road. The wines describe
a company where quality is improving
year on year, and a range of wines that
even at entry level wines have proven to
be extremely reliable as well as modern,
elegant and exceptionally clean in style. Tre
Bicchieri to the Magno Megonio, a classy
elegant wine, with a strong local identity,
close-woven and fruity against a spicy,
balsamic background. We also appreciated
the pleasing Duca Sanfelice 2013, an
archetypal Cirò with Mediterranean
elegance, very fresh-tasting with a fruity
depth, and an admirably well-defined,
lingering finish.

Poderi Marini

LOC. SANT'AGATA
87069 SAN DEMETRIO CORONE [CS]
TEL. 0984947224
www.poderimarini.it

CELLAR SALES
ANNUAL PRODUCTION 42,000 bottles
HECTARES UNDER VINE 7.00
VITICULTURE METHOD Certified Organic

San Demetrio Corone, a beautiful medieval
township whose origins have been lost in
the mists of time, stands at 500 metres
among the foothills of the Sila massif,
a centre of the Arbëreshë community
whose language, customs and Byzantine
Greek rites it has kept alive to this day.
The Marini family have set aside over
300 hectares of their charming estate
for top-quality organic citrus and olive
groves. After moving into wine a dozen
or so years ago, thanks to Salvatore and
Maria Paola, in a bid to blend tradition and
modernity the latest generation now at the
helm began to produce elegant, complex
wines with a strong local identity. Another
finalist was the Basileus 2013, an elegant
close-woven Magliocco monovarietal with
a well-defined bouquet, all fruit-driven and
spicy overtones, with a full-bodied, complex
and tangy palate. The Collimarini 2014, a
passito made from sauvignon, chardonnay
and malvasia, with a citrusy lavender nose
and a fresh-tasting, invigorating flavour, is
extremely pleasing.

● Magno Megonio '13	♛♛♛ 4*
● Cirò Rosso Cl. Sup. Duca Sanfelice Ris. '13	♛♛ 3*
● Gravello '13	♛♛ 5
☉ Cirò Rosato '14	♛♛ 2*
○ Critone '14	♛♛ 2*
○ Efeso '14	♛♛ 4
☉ Rosaneti Brut Rosato M. Cl. '11	♛♛ 3
○ Cirò Bianco '14	♛ 2
● Cirò Rosso Cl. '14	♛ 2
● Melissa Asylia Rosso '14	♛ 2
● Cirò Rosso Cl. Sup. Duca Sanfelice Ris. '11	♛♛♛ 3*
● Cirò Rosso Duca Sanfelice Ris. '08	♛♛♛ 3*
● Gravello '10	♛♛♛ 5
● Gravello '09	♛♛♛ 5
● Magno Megonio '12	♛♛♛ 4*

● Basileus '13	♛♛ 5
○ Collimarini Passito '14	♛♛ 5
● Elaphe '13	♛♛ 4
☉ Brigantino Rosato '14	♛ 2
● Koronè '13	♛ 2
○ Sandolino '14	♛ 2
● Basileus '11	♛♛ 5
○ Collimarini Passito '13	♛♛ 5
● Elaphe '12	♛♛ 4
● Elaphe '11	♛♛ 4
● Koronè '11	♛♛ 2*

G.B. Odoardi

C.DA CAMPODORATO, 35
88047 NOCERA TERINESE [CZ]
TEL. 098429961
www.cantineodoardi.it

CELLAR SALES
ANNUAL PRODUCTION 120,000 bottles
HECTARES UNDER VINE 80.00

Gregorio Odoardi has outstanding support
from his wife Barbara who has been
helping him run the excellent family estate
for some years. This winery has been in
the Odoardi family for over five centuries,
covers around 80 hectares of hillside
close to the Savuto River, and benefits
from Tyrrhenian breezes. The vines, all
densely or very densely planted, even over
11,000 per hectare, run from sea level
all the way up to above 700 metres. This
cellar's uniquely original style is based on
bottling rich, broad-shouldered wines, with
compelling extractive weight and great
polyphenols. This year's tastings describe a
winery well on its way back to the excellent
standards we had come to expect. Though
a blue-ribbon candidate is still missing, the
whole range has proved very reliable, with
a truly pleasant GB Rosso 2013 that was
tight-knit, flavoursome and elegant.

○ Odoardi GB '14	♟♟	5
● Odoardi GB '13	♟♟	4
● Savuto '13	♟♟	2*
○ Terra Damia '14	♟♟	2*
● Scavigna V. Garrone '04	♟♟♟	5
● Scavigna V. Garrone '03	♟♟♟	5
○ Odoardi GB '13	♟♟	4
● Odoardi GB '11	♟♟	6
● Savuto '12	♟♟	2*
○ Scavigna Bianco '13	♟♟	2*
● Terra Damia '12	♟♟	3

Santa Venere

LOC. TENUTA VOLTA GRANDE
S.DA PROV.LE 04 KM 10,00
88813 CIRÒ [KR]
TEL. 096238519
www.santavenere.com

CELLAR SALES
PRE-BOOKED VISITS
ANNUAL PRODUCTION 125,000 bottles
HECTARES UNDER VINE 25.00
VITICULTURE METHOD Certified Organic

Records of the Scala family's presence in
Cirò date back to the 17th century when
they first took over the 150 hectares
that now form the Santa Venere estate.
The change of pace from landowners to
agricultural entrepreneurs took place as
late as 1960, when Federico Scala began
to rationalize the estate, starting from the
vineyards, identifying the most favourable
areas for planting. Federico passed the
running of the estate down to Giuseppe
Scala, soon to be joined by his son
Francesco, and they converted the whole
property to certified organic. Vineyard cover
was increased to 25 hectares while a
modern cellar was also installed. Top marks
once again for the outstanding qualities
of the production as a whole, which has
sought to combine a modern style with
elegance and drinkability rather than
aiming for firmness and extraction. The
Cirò Riserva 2012 Federico Scala, a fine
wine with a sun-drenched Mediterranean
sumptuousness, also reached the finals.

● Cirò Cl. Sup. Federico Scala Ris. '12	♟♟	5
● Cirò Rosso Cl. '13	♟♟	2*
● Speziale '14	♟♟	3
○ Vescovado '14	♟♟	3
○ Cirò Bianco '14	♟	2
⊙ Scassabarile '14	♟	3
⊙ Spumante Brut SP1 '13	♟	5
● Vurgadà '13	♟	3
● Cirò Rosso Cl. '11	♟♟	2*
● Cirò Rosso Cl. Sup. Federico Scala Ris. '11	♟♟	5

Senatore Vini

Loc. San Lorenzo
88811 Cirò Marina [KR]
Tel. 096232350
www.senatorevini.com

CELLAR SALES
PRE-BOOKED VISITS
ANNUAL PRODUCTION 280,000 bottles
HECTARES UNDER VINE 30.00

A large and very modern winery in
San Lorenzo with four different plots at
the heart of the Cirò district: these the
credentials of this fine estate run by
siblings Raffaele, Giuseppe, Franco, and
Salvatore Senatore. Whereas Giuseppe
and Franco followed in their ancestors'
footsteps, cultivating the grape from a
tender age, more recently Salvatore and
Raffaele's passion for the family winery
meant they jumped at the chance to give
up the medical profession and work here
instead. All of their production, ranging
from classic Ciròs to wines made from
pioneering blends, has now settled into a
top-quality reliable niche. Unfortunately,
even though there is clearly the potential
to go much further, this year's range again
lacked a wine capable of going the full
mile. The Nerello 2010 almost made it to
the finals, with its well-rounded snappy
bouquet of citrus and aromatic herbs,
tannin-heavy but well-balanced palate, and
leisurely finish.

○ Cirò Bianco Alaei '14	♥♥	2*
● Cirò Rosso Cl. Arcano '13	♥♥	2*
● Nerello '10	♥♥	4
○ Alikia '14	♥	3
⊙ Cirò Rosato Puntalice '14	♥	3
● Gaglioppo Merlot '11	♥	3
○ Alikia '13	♀♀	3
⊙ Cirò Rosato Puntalice '13	♀♀	3
● Cirò Rosso Cl. Arcano Ris. '10	♀♀	2*

Statti

c.da Lenti
88046 Lamezia Terme [CZ]
Tel. 0968456138
www.statti.com

CELLAR SALES
PRE-BOOKED VISITS
RESTAURANT SERVICE
ANNUAL PRODUCTION 300,000 bottles
HECTARES UNDER VINE 55.00

All 500 hectares of the Lenti estate, several
score of which are set aside for vines, have
belonged to the noble Statti family since
the 18th century. In addition to producing
wine and olive oil, much of the estate is
given over to prized breeds of cattle, whose
manure is used partly to fertilize the soil,
while the majority is combined with other
farm waste and fed into a modern power
station converting biogas into electricity,
enabling the whole estate to be self-
sufficient in energy terms. Although they
have yet to come up with a prize-winner,
all of their production has become cleaner,
more drinkable and authoritative in recent
years. The better reds included the layered
Gaglioppo Batasarro 2012, with its striking
tannin-heavy backbone, and complex
fruitiness, lacking that hint of finesse to
take it to the finals. Among the whites, the
Greco 2014 stood out, with its flavoursome
sweet fruitiness on the nose, and fresh-
tasting lingering palate.

● Arvino '12	♥♥	2*
● Batasarro '12	♥♥	4
● Gaglioppo '14	♥♥	2*
○ Greco '14	♥♥	2*
○ Mantonico '14	♥♥	3
○ Ferdinando 1938 Brut '11	♥	4
⊙ Ferdinando 1938 Brut Rosé '11	♥	4
● I Gelsi Bianco '14	♥	1*
⊙ I Gelsi Rosato '14	♥	2
● Arvino '11	♀♀	2*
○ Greco '13	♀♀	2*

Tenuta Terre Nobili

VIA CARIGLIALTO
87046 MONTALTO UFFUGO [CS]
TEL. 0984934005
www.tenutaterrenobili.it

CELLAR SALES
PRE-BOOKED VISITS
ACCOMMODATION
ANNUAL PRODUCTION 80,000 bottles
HECTARES UNDER VINE 15.00
VITICULTURE METHOD Certified Organic

Lidia Matera runs one of Cosenza province's biggest wineries. A great all-round winemaker, and an agronomist by trade, Lidia showed great intuition by investing in the potential of an area where, at the time, estates could be counted on the fingers of one hand. She was also the pioneer of organic methods, and native varieties, removing non-native cultivars and planting local types. The estate also produces outstanding olive oil, and is regarded as one of the best anywhere in Calabria. Its wines are a successful blend of tradition and modernity: fresh-tasting, firm and gutsy, though with a tendency to indulge extractive weight. We enjoyed the Teodora 2011, a blend of nerello and nerello cappuccio, with its gentle close-woven bouquet, refreshed by notes of mint and balsamic herbs. The Alarico 2013 also performed well, its layered bouquet combining fruitiness with balsamic hints of liquorice, and its full-flavoured tannic palate offset by a juicy, rich fruitiness.

● Alarico '13	♟♟	3
● Ipazia '13	♟♟	6
● Teodora '11	♟♟	5
⊙ Donn'Eleonò '14	♟	2
○ Santa Chiara '14	♟	2
● Alarico '12	♟♟	3
● Carilgio '13	♟♟	2*
● Cariglio '12	♟♟	2*
● Teodora '10	♟♟	5

Luigi Viola

VIA ROMA, 18
87010 SARACENA [CS]
TEL. 0981349099
www.cantineviola.it

CELLAR SALES
PRE-BOOKED VISITS
ANNUAL PRODUCTION 7,000 bottles
HECTARES UNDER VINE 3.00
VITICULTURE METHOD Certified Organic

Back in 1999, a primary school teacher in his hometown of Saracena, Luigi Viola, decided to breathe new life into an ancient passito known as Moscato di Saracena, which had been reduced to just a few litres for family use. So Luigi, with the help of his sons Roberto, Alessandro and Claudio, began to produce and sell this ancient wine, listed in the Enoteca Pontificia or papal wine cellar in the 16th century. Moscato di Saracena is still produced today with a long, complex hand-picking procedure involving the separate vinification of its three varietals, moscatello, guarnaccia and malvasia, which then undergo partial drying. We are delighted that Luigi Viola managed to achieve his dream of saving this noble wine from extinction. The 2014 is elegant, appealing, sweet and very lingering indeed.

○ Moscato Passito '14	♟♟♟	6
○ Moscato Passito '13	♟♟♟	6
○ Moscato Passito '12	♟♟♟	6
○ Moscato Passito '11	♟♟♟	6
○ Moscato Passito '10	♟♟♟	6
○ Moscato Passito '09	♟♟♟	6
○ Moscato Passito '08	♟♟♟	6

'A Vita

FRAZ. CIRÒ MARINA
S.S. 106 KM 279,800
88811 CROTONE
TEL. 3290732473
www.avitavini.it

CELLAR SALES
PRE-BOOKED VISITS
ANNUAL PRODUCTION 15,000 bottles
HECTARES UNDER VINE 8.00

⊙ Cirò Rosato '14	♟♟	2*
● Cirò Rosso Cl. '12	♟♟	2*
● Cirò Rosso Cl. Ris. '11	♟♟	4

Sergio Arcuri

VIA ROMA, 3
88811 CIRÒ MARINA [KR]
TEL. 3280250255
www.sergioarcuri.it

CELLAR SALES
PRE-BOOKED VISITS
ANNUAL PRODUCTION 10,000 bottles
HECTARES UNDER VINE 3.68

● Cirò Rosso Cl. Sup. Aris '12	♟♟	4
⊙ Il Marinetto '14	♟	3

Cataldo Calabretta

VIA MANDORLETO, 47
88811 CIRÒ MARINA [KR]
TEL. 3471866941
www.cataldocalabretta.it

CELLAR SALES
PRE-BOOKED VISITS
ANNUAL PRODUCTION 250,000 bottles
HECTARES UNDER VINE 13.50
VITICULTURE METHOD Certified Organic

○ Ansonica '14	♟♟	3
● Cirò Rosso Cl. '13	♟♟	3
○ Cirò Bianco '14	♟	3
⊙ Cirò Rosato '14	♟	3

Calacino Wines

VIA COLLE MANCO
87050 MARZI [CS]
TEL. 09841900252
www.colacino.it

CELLAR SALES
PRE-BOOKED VISITS
ANNUAL PRODUCTION 80,000 bottles
HECTARES UNDER VINE 21.00

● Amanzio '14	♟	2
○ Savuto Bianco '14	♟	2
● Savuto Sup. Britto '12	♟	4
● Savuto V. Colle Barabba '14	♟	3

Capoano

C.DA CERAMIDIO
88072 CIRÒ MARINA [KR]
TEL. 096235801
www.capoano.it

CELLAR SALES
ANNUAL PRODUCTION 100,000 bottles
HECTARES UNDER VINE 20.00

⊙ Cirò Rosato '14	♟♟	2*
○ Cirò Bianco Antea '14	♟	3
⊙ Cirò Rosato Don Angelo '14	♟	3
● Cirò Rosso Cl. Sup. Don Raffaele '10	♟	5

Chimento

C.DA GALLICE - VESCOVADO
87043 BISIGNANO [CS]
TEL. 3358258627
www.aziendachimento.it

CELLAR SALES
PRE-BOOKED VISITS
ACCOMMODATION AND RESTAURANT SERVICE
ANNUAL PRODUCTION 33,000 bottles
HECTARES UNDER VINE 7.00

● Terre di Cosenza Colline dei Crati Il Vescovado '13	♟♟	3
⊙ Gallice '13	♟	3
○ Matilde '14	♟	3

Cote de Franze

LOC. PIANA DI FRANZE
88811 CIRÒ MARINA [KR]
TEL. 3926911606
www.cotedifranze.it

CELLAR SALES
PRE-BOOKED VISITS
ANNUAL PRODUCTION 18,000 bottles
HECTARES UNDER VINE 9.00
VITICULTURE METHOD Certified Organic

○ Cirò Bianco '14	♥♥ 2*
● Cirò Rosso Cl. Sup. '12	♥♥ 3
☉ Cirò Rosato '14	♥ 2

Cantina Enotria

LOC. SAN GENNARO
S.S. JONICA 106
88811 CIRÒ MARINA [KR]
TEL. 0962371181
www.cantinaenotria.com

CELLAR SALES
PRE-BOOKED VISITS
ANNUAL PRODUCTION 1,000,000 bottles
HECTARES UNDER VINE 170.00

○ Cirò Bianco '14	♥♥ 2*
● Cirò Rosso Cl. '13	♥♥ 2*
● Cirò Rosso Cl. Sup. Piana delle Fate Ris. '12	♥ 3

Tenute Ferrocinto

C.DA FERROCINTO
87012 CASTROVILLARI [CS]
TEL. 0981415122
www.cantinecampoverde.it

CELLAR SALES
PRE-BOOKED VISITS
ANNUAL PRODUCTION 700,000 bottles
HECTARES UNDER VINE 45.00
VITICULTURE METHOD Certified Organic

● Terre di Cosenza Pollino Magliocco 24 Ris. '12	♥♥ 4
● Serra delle Ciavole '13	♥♥ 3
○ Terre di Cosenza Pollino Bianco '14	♥ 3

Feudo dei Sanseverino

VIA VITTORIO EMANUELE, 108/110
87010 SARACENA [CS]
TEL. 098121461
www.feudodeisanseverino.it

CELLAR SALES
PRE-BOOKED VISITS
ANNUAL PRODUCTION 20,000 bottles
HECTARES UNDER VINE 6.00
VITICULTURE METHOD Certified Organic
SUSTAINABLE WINERY

○ Mastro Terenzio '12	♥♥ 5
● Terre di Cosenza Lacrima Nera '12	♥ 3

Tenuta Iuzzolini

LOC. FRASSÀ
88811 CIRÒ MARINA [KR]
TEL. 0962371326
www.tenutaiuzzolini.it

CELLAR SALES
PRE-BOOKED VISITS
ANNUAL PRODUCTION 1,000,000 bottles
HECTARES UNDER VINE 65.00

● Cirò Rosso Cl. Maradea '11	♥♥ 3
○ Donna Giovanna '14	♥♥ 5
● Principe Spinelli '14	♥♥ 3
● Artino '13	♥ 4

Cantine Lento

VIA DEL PROGRESSO, 1
88046 LAMEZIA TERME [CZ]
TEL. 096828028
www.cantinelento.it

CELLAR SALES
PRE-BOOKED VISITS
ANNUAL PRODUCTION 500,000 bottles
HECTARES UNDER VINE 70.00

● Federico II '11	♥♥ 4
● Magliocco '11	♥♥ 5
○ Contessa Emburga '14	♥ 3
● Lamezia Rosso Salvatore Lento Ris. '11	♥ 4

Cantine Lucà

VIA MARCHESE, 34
89032 BIANCO [RC]
TEL. 09641903179
www.cantineluca.it

ANNUAL PRODUCTION 30,000 bottles
HECTARES UNDER VINE 15.00

○ Greco di Bianco '12	♟♟	4
○ Mantonico '12	♟♟	3

Malena

LOC. PETRARO
S.S. JONICA 106
88811 CIRÒ MARINA [KR]
TEL. 096231758
www.malena.it

CELLAR SALES
PRE-BOOKED VISITS
ANNUAL PRODUCTION 220,000 bottles
HECTARES UNDER VINE 16.00

⊙ Cirò Rosato '14	♟♟	2*
● Cirò Rosso Cl. '13	♟♟	2*
⊙ Bacco Rosato '14	♟	2
○ Cirò Bianco '14	♟	2

Fattoria San Francesco

LOC. QUATTROMANI
88813 CIRÒ [KR]
TEL. 096232228
www.fattoriasanfrancesco.it

CELLAR SALES
PRE-BOOKED VISITS
ANNUAL PRODUCTION 224,000 bottles
HECTARES UNDER VINE 40.00

○ Cirò Bianco '14	♟♟	2*
● Cirò Rosso Cl. Sup. Duca dell'Argillone Ris. '10	♟♟	4
⊙ Cirò Rosato '14	♟	2

Serracavallo

C.DA SERRACAVALLO
87043 BISIGNANO [CS]
TEL. 098421144
www.viniserracavallo.it

CELLAR SALES
PRE-BOOKED VISITS
RESTAURANT SERVICE
ANNUAL PRODUCTION 80,000 bottles
HECTARES UNDER VINE 32.00

○ Filì '14	♟♟	2*
● Terraccia '12	♟♟	3
● Vigna Savuco '11	♟♟	6
○ Besidiae '14	♟	2

Terre del Gufo - Muzzillo

FRAZ. DONNICI INFERIORE
C.DA ALBO SAN MARTINO
87100 COSENZA
TEL. 0984780364
www.terredelgufo.com

CELLAR SALES
ANNUAL PRODUCTION 27,000 bottles
HECTARES UNDER VINE 3.00

● Terre di Cosenza Portapiana '13	♟♟	3
● Timpamara '13	♟♟	5
⊙ Terre di Cosenza Chiaroscuro '14	♟	2
● Terre di Cosenza Kaulos '14	♟	3

Vinicola Zito

FRAZ. PUNTA ALICE
VIA SCALARETTO
88811 CIRÒ MARINA [KR]
TEL. 096231853
www.cantinezito.it

CELLAR SALES
PRE-BOOKED VISITS
ANNUAL PRODUCTION 800,000 bottles
HECTARES UNDER VINE 80.00
VITICULTURE METHOD Certified Organic

⊙ Cirò Rosato Imerio '14	♟♟	2*
● Cirò Rosso Cl. Sup. Krimisa '13	♟♟	3
● Cirò Rosso Cl. Sup. Ris. '12	♟♟	4
○ Cirò Bianco Nosside '13	♟	3

SICILY

The year's tastings confirm that the Sicilian wine
scenario is in a state of grace and its liveliness
can be seen in the results of the most established
brands and other cellars, including small and
medium-sized enterprises improving yearly with
their performances. We are also pleased to be able to
report a separate development, which is the emergence of numerous cooperative
wineries. These are still not in the public or critical eye but are announcing wines
that reveal a product quality perspective unthinkable not so long ago. The use of
the Sicilia DOC is also on the rise, able to characterize and give an immediate
identity to the island's labels on international markets. We awarded a Tre Bicchieri
to 20 wines for 2016, including Florio's splendid 2004 Marsala Superiore Riserva
Semisecco Targa Riserva 1840, a champion in its class. Truly elegant and
intriguing, Le Casematte's 2013 Faro makes its debut, showing a renewed
vitality of this remarkable DOC that had been on the brink of extinction. All boding
well for the future. Excellent sensorial profiles and expression of respective
terroirs from Firriato's Harmonium, Feudo Pricipi di Butera's Deliella, and Feudo
Maccari's Saia, three stellar products, all 2013 Nero d'Avolas. Memorable, and
also for its baggage of memories and history, we have Tasca d'Almerita's Riserva
del Conte 2010 on its first outing. Settesoli's Timperosse 2014 enchants and
Baglio di Pianetto's 2013 Ramione Baglio di Pianetto seduces. The soft,
persuasive Alliata Lorlando 2014 is a surprise and Feudi del Pisciotto's
Giambattista Valli 2011 Cerasuolo di Vittoria was the icing on the cake of the
entire class. Well-deserved recognition for Cusumano's refined 2013 Noà and the
exemplary Grillo Bianco Maggiore 2014 from Rallo, now a recognized icon of this
cultivar. Tre Bicchieri awards went again to Planeta's Cerasuolo di Vittoria
Classico Dorilli 2013, a territorial wine of considerable elegance. The satisfying
Tancredi 2001 was another worthy Tre Bicchieri, with strong character and plenty
of personality. Etna reaffirms its leading role with six great wines: Tenuta di
Fessina's 2013 Etna Bianco A' Puddara, and five Etna Rossos. Indeed, the deep,
elegant 2012 Vigna Barbagalli from Pietradolce is our Red of the Year. Alongside,
we placed Tenuta delle Terre Nere's persuasive Calderara Sottana 2013,
Cottanera's captivating Riserva Zottorinoto 2011, the unfailing Graci Arcuria 2013
Graci, and Russo's San Lorenzo 2013.

Abbazia Santa Anastasia

C.DA SANTA ANASTASIA
90013 CASTELBUONO [PA]
TEL. 091671959
www.abbaziasantanastasia.com

CELLAR SALES
PRE-BOOKED VISITS
ACCOMMODATION AND RESTAURANT SERVICE
ANNUAL PRODUCTION 250,000 bottles
HECTARES UNDER VINE 65.00
VITICULTURE METHOD Certified Biodynamic
SUSTAINABLE WINERY

Founded in 1100 by Roger I Hauteville, for 200 years the abbey from which the winery takes its name was an important centre in the Madonie Mountains, until the foundation of Castelbuono in 1316 and its subsequent progressive decline. In 1982, Franco Lena acquired around 300 hectares that were once part of the abbey's lands and on its ruins built the current complex, a charming Relais Château and cellar serving almost 70 hectares of vineyards, a labour of love that revived the area's cultural heritage. Also worthy of note is the commitment to reducing environmental impact, the use of renewable energy sources and the shift from organic to biodynamic farming methods. The biodynamic Nero d'Avola Sens(i)nverso 2012 only just missed the finals, with its intense varietal nose and rounded, fresh, soft fruit. The Montenero 2013, a blend of syrah and cabernet franc, offers an attractive touch of green and balsam, over a full-flavoured, dynamic palate, with up-front tannins.

● Montenero '13	♥♥	4
● Sens(i)nverso Cabernet Sauvignon '12	♥♥	4
● Sens(i)nverso Nero d'Avola '12	♥♥	4
○ Grillo '14	♥	2
● Nero d'Avola '14	♥	2
● Passomaggio '13	♥	3
○ Sens(i)nverso Chardonnay '13	♥	4
● Sinestesia '14	♥	3
● Litra '04	♥♥♥	6
● Litra '01	♥♥♥	7
● Litra '00	♥♥♥	7
● Montenero '04	♥♥♥	4
● Litra '11	♥♥	6
● Sens(i)nverso Nero d'Avola '11	♥♥	4
● Sens(i)nverso Nero d'Avola '08	♥♥	4

Alessandro di Camporeale

C.DA MANDRANOVA
90043 CAMPOREALE [PA]
TEL. 092437038
www.alessandrodicamporeale.it

CELLAR SALES
PRE-BOOKED VISITS
ANNUAL PRODUCTION 180,000 bottles
HECTARES UNDER VINE 35.00
VITICULTURE METHOD Certified Organic

The Camporeale area, also thanks to the beneficial day-night temperature range, is excellent wine country, and it is here that we find a family-run business with over a century of history, led with commitment and skill by Natale, Nino and Rosolino Alessandro. Today, the new generations are also on board, fresh from their studies in oenology, law and international marketing, and have given a new lease of life to an operation already much appreciated by wine lovers for its products of territorial character. The wines are the fruit of organic farming methods, and have earned a reputation on markets for their character, sensory profiles and attractive prices. The drinkable Syrah Kaid 2013 flew into the finals, with a rich, mature, leisurely palate well balanced by fresh acidity. The tantalizing, deep Kaid Vendemmia Tardiva 2014 is sweet and sensual. The dynamic Kaid Sauvignon Blanc 2014 offers aromatic herbs and peach. The Grillo Vigna di Mandranova 2014 is zesty and mineral.

● Kaid '13	♥♥	3*
● Kaid V. T. '14	♥♥	5
● Sicilia DonnaTà '14	♥♥	2*
○ Sicilia Grillo V. di Mandranova '14	♥♥	3
○ Sicilia Kaid Sauvignon Blanc '14	♥♥	3
○ Sicilia Benedè '14	♥	2
● DonnaTà '13	♥♥	2*
● DonnaTà '12	♥♥	2*
○ Grillo V. di Mandranova '12	♥♥	3
● Kaid '11	♥♥	3*
● Kaid '10	♥♥	3*
● Kaid '09	♥♥	3
● Kaid '08	♥♥	3*
● Kaid '07	♥♥	3
○ Kaid Sauvignon Blanc '13	♥♥	3
● Kaid Syrah '12	♥♥	3*

Alliata

VIA ARCHI 9
91100 TRAPANI
TEL. 0923547267
www.alliatavini.com

CELLAR SALES
ANNUAL PRODUCTION 75,000 bottles
HECTARES UNDER VINE 90.00

Claudia Alliata di Villafranca is heir to a long tradition dating back to her ancestor Giuseppe Alliata Moncada, Principe di Villafranca and Duca di Salaparuta, founder of Corvo at Casteldaccia in 1824, the first Sicilian winery conceived with modern business criteria, which was owned by the Alliata family up to 1959. The family's vocation for farming continued with Raimondo, Claudia's father, an agronomist and grower, and the inspiration behind the present operation, based in the hills near Trapani, in the municipality of Mazara del Vallo. The varieties grown include the native grillo, nero d'Avola and insolia, alongside chardonnay, merlot and syrah. The Nero d'Avola Lorlando 2014 romped off with a Tre Bicchieri thanks to its complex, deep, yet subtle nose, over a vibrant palate, with a focused fruit encore and good length. The Syrah Ruggiero 2014, with nice stuffing and fine-grained tannins, also nearly made the finals.

● Lorlando '14	♟♟♟	2*
● Baltasàr '12	♟♟♟	5
● Kaspàr '12	♟♟	4
● Melkior '12	♟♟	4
● Ruggiero '14	♟♟	2*
○ Taya '14	♟♟	4
○ Grillo '14	♟	2
○ Mommo '14	♟	2
● Baltasàr '11	♟♟	5
○ Daxia '11	♟♟	2*
● Kaspàr '11	♟♟	4
● Kaspàr '10	♟♟	4
● Lorlando '13	♟♟	2*
○ Mommo '13	♟♟	3
○ Taya '13	♟♟	4

Baglio del Cristo di Campobello

LOC. C.DA FAVAROTTA
S.S. 123 KM 19,200
92023 CAMPOBELLO DI LICATA [AG]
TEL. 0922 877709
www.cristodicampobello.it

CELLAR SALES
PRE-BOOKED VISITS
ANNUAL PRODUCTION 300,000 bottles
HECTARES UNDER VINE 30.00

The Bonetta family, Angelo and his sons Carmelo and Domenico, come from a long line of growers, custodians of a time-honoured tradition but also committed to the modern reality of communication, marketing strategies and the global market. Their skill lies in managing to reconcile these two apparently conflicting worlds, embodying a dynamic view of winegrowing in Sicily that preserves the essential values of its territory, the hills to the south of Campobello, near the sea of the gulf of Gela. The heart of the estate is the baglio, the historic enclosed farmstead, and the crucifix that gives the winery its name, which has always been the focus of popular worship. The Chardonnay Laudàri 2013 impressed, and walked into the finals thanks to its focused fruit and floral aromas, beautifully intertwined with vanilla notes, over a dynamic, velvety, leisurely palate. We liked the expressive, concentrated Syrah Lusirà 2013, while the red blend, C'D'C' 2014 is both invigorating and drinkable.

○ Sicilia Chardonnay Laudàri '13	♟♟	4
○ C'D'C' Bianco Cristo di Campobello '14	♟♟	2*
● C'D'C' Rosso Cristo di Campobello '14	♟♟	2*
○ Sicilia Bianco Adènzia '14	♟♟	3
○ Sicilia Grillo Lalùci '14	♟♟	3
● Sicilia Nero d'Avola Lu Patri '13	♟♟	5
● Sicilia Rosso Adènzia '13	♟♟	3
● Sicilia Syrah Lusirà '13	♟♟	5
⊙ C'D'C' Rosso Cristo di Campobello Rosato '14	♟	2
● Lu Patri '09	♟♟♟	5
● C'D'C' Rosso Cristo di Campobello '12	♟♟	2*
○ Laudàri '10	♟♟	4
● Lu Patri '12	♟♟	5
● Lu Patri '10	♟♟	5
● Lu Patri '08	♟♟	5

SICILY

Baglio di Pianetto

VIA FRANCIA
90030 SANTA CRISTINA GELA [PA]
TEL. 0918570002
www.bagliodipianetto.com

CELLAR SALES
PRE-BOOKED VISITS
ACCOMMODATION AND RESTAURANT SERVICE
ANNUAL PRODUCTION 550,000 bottles
HECTARES UNDER VINE 104.00
SUSTAINABLE WINERY

Paolo Marzotto and Sicily: a love story that began on the bends of the Targa Florio, during the golden age of car racing in the 1950s, when there were still "gentlemen drivers". In 1997, the bond between Conte Paolo and the island became tangible, with the opening of the winery. This old enclosed farmstead in the countryside near Santa Cristina Gela was transformed into a country hotel and agriturismo, alongside the cellar, which vinifies and ages grapes from the neighbouring vineyards and from Tenuta Baroni at Noto, the site of an initial vinification plant. We should mention the remarkable success of the B.D.P.Y line of pleasurable, easy-drinking wines. The Ramione 2013, a blend of Santa Cristina Gela Merlot and Nero d'Avola from Noto, earned a Tre Bicchieri with its complex, pervasive tertiary aromas of spice, nutmeg and blackberry jam, over a supple, close-knit palate with a long finish. The sweet Ra'is 2012 is summery and focused.

★Benanti

VIA G. GARIBALDI, 475
95029 VIAGRANDE [CT]
TEL. 0957893399
www.vinicolabenanti.it

CELLAR SALES
PRE-BOOKED VISITS
ANNUAL PRODUCTION 120,000 bottles
HECTARES UNDER VINE 45.00

With sons Antonio and Salvino, Cavalier Giuseppe Benanti pursues with passion the path that made the family business a top Etna producer. He laid the foundations for the rebirth of this territory, whose excellence for viticulture had waned by 1988, when the winery was established. Careful selection of terroirs resulted in 45 hectares of vineyards distributed among the best wine country, at Monte Serra, Guardiola, Rovittello, Caselle and Cavaliere. The picture is completed by two important outposts at Noto for nero d'Avola, and on Pantelleria for zibibbo. We saw a good performance from the Rosso di Verzella 2013, which made our finals, seducing us with its nose of pomegranate, spice and peach jam. The mineral, fruity palate shows breadth and silky finesse. The Monovitigno Nerello Mascalese 2012 shows a more austere nose yet great elegance.

● Sicilia Rosso Ramione '13	♈♈♈ 3*
○ Moscato di Noto Ra'is '12	♈♈ 5
○ Sicilia Bianco Ficiligno '14	♈♈ 4
● Sicilia Nero d'Avola Cembali '12	♈♈ 6
● Carduni '10	♈ 5
● Cembali '09	♈ 5
● Ramione '04	♈♈♈ 3*
● Carduni '11	♈♈ 5
● Cembali '11	♈♈ 5
● Chianu Carduni '05	♈♈ 6
○ Ficiligno '13	♈♈ 3
● Piana dei Salici '03	♈♈ 4
● Ramione '12	♈♈ 3
● Ramione '11	♈♈ 3*
● Salici '11	♈♈ 4

● Etna Rosso Rosso di Verzella '13	♈♈ 4
○ Etna Bianco Bianco di Caselle '13	♈♈ 3
○ Etna Bianco Sup. Pietramarina '11	♈♈ 5
● Nerello Mascalese Il Monovitigno '12	♈♈ 5
● Etna Rosso Rovittello '11	♈ 5
● Nerello Cappuccio Il Monovitigno '12	♈ 5
○ Etna Bianco Sup. Pietramarina '09	♈♈♈ 5
○ Etna Bianco Sup. Pietramarina '04	♈♈♈ 6
○ Etna Bianco Sup. Pietramarina '02	♈♈♈ 5
○ Etna Bianco Sup. Pietramarina '01	♈♈♈ 5
● Etna Rosso Serra della Contessa '06	♈♈♈ 7
● Etna Rosso Serra della Contessa '04	♈♈♈ 7
● Etna Rosso Serra della Contessa '03	♈♈♈ 7
● Il Drappo '04	♈♈♈ 5

Le Casematte

LOC. FARO SUPERIORE
C.DA CORSO
98163 MESSINA
TEL. 0906409427
www.lecasematte.it

CELLAR SALES
HECTARES UNDER VINE
VITICULTURE METHOD Certified Organic
SUSTAINABLE WINERY

A life's passion finally became a reality for
the footballer Andrea Barzagli and
accountant Gianfranco Sabbatino, two wine
lovers who joined forces to try and give
enhance the prestige of the Faro DOC zone,
on the verge of disappearing from the wine
scene not so long ago. The marvellous new
winery, recently opened, overlooks the
Straits of Messina and a splendid hillside
estate covering a few hectares, still the site
of three World War II pillboxes. The
scrupulous management of the operation
according to organic methods, and the
artisan style of the wines make this a
much- fêted boutique winery. The
formidable 2013 vintage of the Faro, from
nerello mascalese, cappuccio, nocera and
nero d'Avola, easily took a Tre Bicchieri.
This polished wine, with ripe aromas of
plum, cherry and black spice, seduces and
thrills with its lively, elegant freshness. The
other wines are also admirable.

● Faro '13	▼▼▼	5
○ Peloro Bianco '14	▼▼	3
● Peloro Rosso '13	▼▼	2*
☉ Rosematte '14	▼▼	3
● Faro Quattroenne '12	♀♀	5
● Faro Quattroenne '11	♀♀	5
● Faro Quattroenne '10	♀♀	5
● Faro Quattroenne '09	♀♀	5
● Figliodiennenne '12	♀♀	2*
● Figliodiennenne '11	♀♀	2*
● Figliodiennenne '10	♀♀	2*
● Figliodiennenne '09	♀♀	2
☉ Rosematte '13	♀♀	3

Centopassi

VIA PORTA PALERMO, 132
90048 SAN GIUSEPPE JATO [PA]
TEL. 0918577655
www.centopassisicilia.it

CELLAR SALES
PRE-BOOKED VISITS
ACCOMMODATION AND RESTAURANT SERVICE
ANNUAL PRODUCTION 500,000 bottles
HECTARES UNDER VINE 94.00
VITICULTURE METHOD Certified Organic
SUSTAINABLE WINERY

Centopassi is a combined effort of
cooperative wineries in the Alto Belice
Corleonese area, vinifying grapes from 90
hectares of vineyards confiscated from the
Mafia. This splendid operation has brought
development and jobs, giving a sense to
the concept of legality, exporting a different
image of Sicily, not the usual stereotype.
The San Giuseppe Jato cellars, also seized
from the Mafia, apply organic methods to
produce three lines: the entry-level
Centopassi, the Placido Rizzotto, and the
selections dedicated to those who lost their
lives in the struggle against the Mafia.
Since 2012 this has also been the Sicilian
headquarters of Simonit & Sirch's Scuola di
Potatura della Vite. The deep, minerally
Catarratto Terre Rosse di Giabbascio 2014
made the finals, with its complex,
full-flavoured fruit. We were also impressed
with the eloquent, varietal Nero d'Avola
Argille di Tagghia Via 2014, which showed
fresh and well-rounded. The two
Centopassi 2014s are well made: the
Rosso stylish and fragrant, the Bianco with
focused citrus aromas.

○ Terre Rosse di Giabbascio '14	▼▼	3*
● Argille di Tagghia Via '14	▼▼	3
○ Sicilia Bianco Centopassi '14	▼▼	2*
● Sicilia Rosso Centopassi '14	▼▼	2*
● Argille di Tagghia Via di Sutta '13	▼	3
● Marne di Saladino '13	▼	4
○ Rocce di Pietra Longa '14	▼	3
○ Tendoni di Trebbiano '13	▼	4
● Argille di Tagghia Via '13	♀♀	3*
● Argille di Tagghia Via '12	♀♀	3
● Argille di Tagghia Via di Sutta '11	♀♀	3
○ Catarratto Terre Rosse di Giabbascio '12	♀♀	3
○ Grillo Rocce di Pietra Longa '10	♀♀	3*
○ Tendoni di Trebbiano '11	♀♀	4

Frank Cornelissen

FRAZ. SOLICCHIATA
VIA NAZIONALE, 297
95012 CASTIGLIONE DI SICILIA [CT]
TEL. 0942986315
www.frankcornelissen.it

PRE-BOOKED VISITS
ANNUAL PRODUCTION 40,000 bottles
HECTARES UNDER VINE 12.00
VITICULTURE METHOD Certified Organic

Unfettered by the inflexible rules of biodynamic production and the technical dogma of organic farming, Frank Cornelissen is convinced that humanity's obsession for control can only partly appreciate the complexity of nature, that should be listened to and accommodated without affecting its delicate balance. His vineyards are located on the northern slopes of Etna at altitudes between 600 and 980 metres, and are all ungrafted bush vines, whose canes are used for the new plantings without rootstock. Frank's philosophy is also evident in the cellar, where he allows raw materials to express their primordial nature with spontaneous fermentation and long maceration. While awaiting the Magma, the Munjebel Rosso 2014 also made our finals, with its approachable, intense upfront fruit, interwoven with elegant notes of medicinal herbs, echoed on the lively, extremely pleasurable palate. Complex aromas of peach and citrus blossom distinguish the zesty, juicy Munjebel Bianco 2014.

○ Munjebel Bianco '14	♟♟	5
● Munjebel Rosso '14	♟♟	6
● Vino del Contadino '14	♟♟	4
● Contadino 10 '12	♟♟	4
● Magma Barbabecchi '10	♟♟	8
● Magma Decima Edizione '12	♟♟	8
○ Munjebel Bianco '13	♟♟	5
○ Munjebel Bianco 9 '12	♟♟	5
● Munjebel Chiusa Spagnola 9 '12	♟♟	7
● Munjebel Monte Colla '13	♟♟	7
● Munjebel Monte Colla 9 '12	♟♟	7
● Munjebel Rosso '13	♟♟	6
● Munjebel Rosso Chiusa Spagnola '13	♟♟	7
● Munjebel Rosso Le Vigne Alte '13	♟♟	7
● Munjebel Vigne Alte 9 '12	♟♟	7
☉ Susucaru '13	♟♟	4

Cottanera

LOC. IANNAZZO
S.DA PROV.LE 89
95030 CASTIGLIONE DI SICILIA [CT]
TEL. 0942963601
www.cottanera.it

CELLAR SALES
PRE-BOOKED VISITS
ANNUAL PRODUCTION 300,000 bottles
HECTARES UNDER VINE 65.00

Everything started in the early 1990s, when Guglielmo Cambria realized the potential of the family's land, at the time planted to fruit and hazelnut trees on the northern slopes of Etna. He converted the best aspected, most suitable plots into vineyards, which now cover 65 hectares out of a total of 100. His initial approach, focusing on international varieties, including the unheard-of mondeuse, gradually shifted towards the volcano's native varieties of nerello mascalese, nerello cappuccio and carricante. Guglielmo's work is now being continued with the same passion and dedication by his children Mariangela, Francesco and Emanuele, alongside their uncle Enzo. A Tre Bicchieri went to the Riserva Zottorinoto 2011, from 30-year-old vines at elevations of 800 metres. A sensual nose of sweet spice, leather and tobacco against a jammy backdrop returns on the palate with finesse and length. The Etna Bianco 2014 displays stylish notes of hydrocarbons and fresh, richly flavoured, juicy fruit.

● Etna Rosso Zottorinoto Ris. '11	♟♟♟	8
○ Etna Bianco '14	♟♟	3*
● Barbazzale Rosso '14	♟♟	2*
● Etna Rosso '12	♟♟	5
○ Sicilia Bianco Barbazzale '14	♟♟	2*
● Sicilia Cabernet Sauvignon Nume '12	♟♟	4
● Sicilia Merlot Grammonte '12	♟♟	4
● Sicilia Rosso Fatagione '12	♟♟	3
☉ Etna Rosato '14	♟	2
○ Etna Bianco '11	♟♟♟	3*
● Etna Rosso '11	♟♟♟	5
● Etna Rosso '07	♟♟♟	5
● Etna Rosso '06	♟♟♟	5
● Etna Rosso '05	♟♟♟	5
● Sole di Sesta '00	♟♟♟	5

★Cusumano

LOC. C.DA SAN CARLO
S.S. 13
90047 PARTINICO [PA]
TEL. 0918908713
www.cusumano.it

CELLAR SALES
PRE-BOOKED VISITS
ANNUAL PRODUCTION 2,500,000 bottles
HECTARES UNDER VINE 520.00
SUSTAINABLE WINERY

The vineyards of the Cusumano family are divided into no fewer than eight different plots at Piana degli Albanesi, Monreale, Butera and Pachino. At Partinico, their hometown, we find the beating heart of the winery, the beautiful, modern cellar within the historic enclosed farmstead dominated by the tower of San Carlo. A few years ago this was joined by the Alta Mora estate on Etna, an innovative cellar and 20 hectares under vine in the districts of Guardiola, Verzella, Porcaria and Pietramarina. This year Cusumano's wines are again modern in style, while reflecting perfectly the varietal traits and character of their terroirs. After a few years, top honours once more go to the Noà with the 2013 vintage, a blend of nero d'Avola, merlot and cabernet sauvignon. It opens to a focused, spicy, fruit-driven nose, echoed powerfully on the fresh, full flavoured palate, underpinned by close-knit, lean tannins. The other wines are also worthy of note.

● Sicilia Noà '13	♟♟♟ 4*
○ Etna Bianco Alta Mora '13	♟♟ 3*
● Sicilia Sàgana '13	♟♟ 4
○ Angimbé '14	♟♟ 2*
● Benuara '14	♟♟ 3
● Etna Rosso Alta Mora '13	♟♟ 4
○ Jalé '14	♟♟ 4
○ Shamaris '14	♟♟ 3
● Merlot '14	♟ 2
○ Moscato dello Zucco '10	♟♟♟ 5
● Noà '10	♟♟♟ 4*
● Sàgana '12	♟♟♟ 4*
● Sàgana '11	♟♟♟ 4*
● Sàgana '09	♟♟♟ 4
● Sàgana '08	♟♟♟ 4
● Sàgana '07	♟♟♟ 4

★Donnafugata

VIA SEBASTIANO LIPARI, 18
91025 MARSALA [TP]
TEL. 0923724200
www.donnafugata.it

CELLAR SALES
PRE-BOOKED VISITS
ANNUAL PRODUCTION 2,100,000 bottles
HECTARES UNDER VINE 270.00
SUSTAINABLE WINERY

One of the best-known Sicilian brands internationally, established by Giacomo and Gabriella Rallo, whose foresight and expertise soon made it synonymous with quality wine. Now run with enthusiasm and passion by their sons, Antonio and Josè, from the Marsala headquarters and historic cellars dating back to 1851. The estates are located at Contessa Entellina and Pantelleria, where both native and international varieties give their best, complying with a philosophy of environmental sustainability. This famous winery manages to combine tradition and modernity to perfection, promoting the territories of reference with effective, innovative marketing. Since the legendary Ben Ryé was left to rest in the cellar, it was another thoroughbred, the Tancredi 2011, from nero d'Avola and cabernet sauvignon, that reached the podium. Rich and elegant, with fragrant fruit and a sublime tannic weave, this is a wine of sheer class. The Chardonnay Chiarandà 2012 is also excellent.

● Tancredi '11	♟♟♟ 5
○ Contessa Entellina Chiarandà '12	♟♟ 5
● Contessa Entellina Milleunanotte '10	♟♟ 7
○ Lighea '14	♟♟ 3
● Sicilia Angheli '12	♟♟ 4
○ Sicilia Bianco V. di Gabri '13	♟♟ 3
● Sicilia Sherazade '14	♟♟ 2*
○ Sicilia Sursur '14	♟ 3
● Contessa Entellina Milleunanotte '06	♟♟♟ 7
● Contessa Entellina Milleunanotte '05	♟♟♟ 7
○ Passito di Pantelleria Ben Ryé '12	♟♟♟ 7
○ Passito di Pantelleria Ben Ryé '11	♟♟♟ 7
○ Passito di Pantelleria Ben Ryé '10	♟♟♟ 7
○ Passito di Pantelleria Ben Ryé '09	♟♟♟ 7
○ Passito di Pantelleria Ben Ryé '06	♟♟♟ 6
● Tancredi '07	♟♟♟ 4

Duca di Salaparuta

VIA NAZIONALE, S.S. 113
90014 CASTELDACCIA [PA]
TEL. 091945201
www.duca.it

PRE-BOOKED VISITS
ANNUAL PRODUCTION 9,000,000 bottles
HECTARES UNDER VINE 155.00

This winery of extraordinary prestige has
been known the world over since 1824,
when it was established by Giuseppe
Alliata, Principe di Villafranca, Principe del
Sacro Romano Impero, Grande di Spagna
and Duca di Salaparuta. It was acquired
with great foresight in 2001 by Augusto
Reina's ILLVA di Saronno, which over time
has exploited its potential through
innovative business strategies respecting
its various traditions and territories. The
operation includes three famous brands:
Florio, Corvo and, of course, Duca di
Salaparuta. The work done so far, with
admirable dedication and expertise, has
made it an international player of great
repute, authoritative and in step with the
times. The intense, deep monovarietal Nero
d'Avola, Duca Enrico 2011, flew into the
finals, with a nose of spice and black berry
fruit, over a dynamic, seductive palate with
appealing tannins. Equally good is the
elegant, fresh and inviting Vajasindi Làvico
Nerello Mascalese 2012. We loved the rest
of the range.

● Duca Enrico '11	♥♥	7
● Làvico Vajasindi '12	♥♥	3*
○ Bianca di Valguarnera '13	♥♥	6
● Corvo Irmana '14	♥♥	2*
○ Irmana Floris Corvo '14	♥♥	2*
● Passo delle Mule Tenuta Suor Marchesa '13	♥♥	2*
● Calanìca Nero d'Avola e Merlot '13	♥	3
○ Colomba Platino Risignolo '14	♥	4
● Duca Enrico '03	♥♥♥	6
● Duca Enrico '01	♥♥♥	6
● Duca Enrico '92	♥♥♥	6
● Duca Enrico '90	♥♥♥	6
● Duca Enrico '88	♥♥♥	6
● Duca Enrico '86	♥♥♥	6
● Duca Enrico '85	♥♥♥	6
● Duca Enrico '84	♥♥♥	6

Fazio Wines

FRAZ. FULGATORE
VIA CAPITAN RIZZO, 39
91010 ERICE [TP]
TEL. 0923811700
www.faziowines.com

ANNUAL PRODUCTION 750,000 bottles
HECTARES UNDER VINE 100.00
SUSTAINABLE WINERY

The fourth generation of the Fazio family is
now involved in winegrowing in the hills in
the north-west part of the province of
Trapani. The vineyards, covering an
impressive 100 hectares, fall within the
Erice DOC zone at elevations of between
250 and 600 metres. Farming methods
envisage an integrated approach with low
environmental impact, and the modern
vinification facilities are electrically
self-sufficient, thanks to a photovoltaic
system. The varieties grown include the
native nero d'Avola, catarratto, insolia and
grillo, alongside the main international
cultivars. There is a vast range of around
30 labels, including Erice DOC wines, those
labelled Sicilia, and IGTs. The Nero d'Avola
Torre dei Venti 2013 made the finals with
its complex, well-coordinated nose of
blossom, fruit and balsamic notes, paving
the way for a pleasurable, focused, chewy
palate of good length. The harmoniously
sweet late-harvest Zibibbo Ky 2009 shows
distinctive aromas of citrus and eucalyptus
honey.

● Erice Nero d'Avola Torre dei Venti '13	♥♥	4
○ Erice Grillo Aegades '14	♥♥	3
● Erice Pietra Sacra Ris. '09	♥♥	5
○ Erice V. T. Ky '09	♥♥	5
● Erice Cabernet Sauvignon Casa Santa '13	♥	4
○ Erice Catarratto Calebianche '14	♥	3
○ Erice Zibibbo Petali	♥	4
● Erice Cabernet Sauvignon Casa Santa '12	♥♥	4
○ Erice Catarratto Calebianche '13	♥♥	2*
○ Erice Catarratto Calebianche '12	♥♥	3*
○ Erice Grillo Aegades '13	♥♥	3
○ Erice Grillo Aegades '12	♥♥	3
○ Erice Grillo Aegades '11	♥♥	3
● Erice Pietra Sacra '06	♥♥	5
○ Pietra Sacra Bianco '12	♥♥	4

Tenuta di Fessina

LOC. C.DA ROVITTELLO
VIA NAZIONALE 120, 22
95012 CASTIGLIONE DI SICILIA [CT]
TEL. 0942395300
www.tenutadifessina.com

CELLAR SALES
PRE-BOOKED VISITS
ANNUAL PRODUCTION 70,000 bottles
HECTARES UNDER VINE 15.00
SUSTAINABLE WINERY

Lots of things have been happening at Silvia Maestrelli's winery: the 18th-century walled hamlet at Rovittello, with its old wine press and cellars hewn from lava stone, has been restored to provide accommodation and an excellent wine tourism centre. In the meantime, the technical management of Tenuta di Fessina has been assigned to the oenologist from Piedmont, Giandomenico Negro. Silvia has a deep-rooted attachment to her mountains, a magical place for those who appreciate wild, unpredictable beauty. The green heart of Fessina comprises seven hectares at an elevation of 670 metres, with century-old nerello mascalese bush vines sheltered by two lava flows from past eruptions. The fifth Tre Bicchieri for 'A Puddara came with the 2013 vintage, which seduces with its highly focused nose of white peaches, aromatic herbs and subtle mineral notes, echoed on a palate of fresh, green-fleshed fruit. The elegant Musmeci Riserva 2011 also made the finals.

○ Etna Bianco A' Puddara '13	▼▼▼ 5
● Etna Rosso Il Musmeci Ris. '11	▼▼ 6
○ Etna Bianco Erse '14	▼▼ 4
○ Etna Bianco Sup. Il Musmeci '13	▼▼ 5
● Etna Rosso Erse '14	▼▼ 4
● Laeneo '13	▼▼ 3
○ Etna Bianco A' Puddara '12	♀♀♀ 5
○ Etna Bianco A' Puddara '11	♀♀♀ 5
○ Etna Bianco A' Puddara '10	♀♀♀ 5
○ Etna Bianco A' Puddara '09	♀♀♀ 5
● Etna Rosso Musmeci '07	♀♀♀ 6
● Ero '13	♀♀ 3
○ Etna Bianco Erse '13	♀♀ 3
○ Etna Bianco Sup. Il Musmeci '12	♀♀ 5
● Etna Rosso Erse '13	♀♀ 4
● Etna Rosso Il Musmeci '10	♀♀ 6

Feudi del Pisciotto

C.DA PISCIOTTO
93015 NISCEMI [CL]
TEL. 09331930280
www.castellare.it

CELLAR SALES
PRE-BOOKED VISITS
ACCOMMODATION
ANNUAL PRODUCTION 200,000 bottles
HECTARES UNDER VINE 45.00

A visit to the impressive 18th-century wine press is a journey in time. With no fewer than eight vats, it is probably the largest in Sicily, and is situated at the heart of the old enclosed farmstead that dominates the Sicilian winery of Paolo Panerai, now been transformed into an elegant wine resort after admirable restoration work. A few steps lead down to the large, state-of-the-art underground cellar, where the technical staff work, headed by Alessandro Cellai. In the space of a few years, thanks above all to careful tending of the vineyards, he has managed to make Pisciotto one of the most consolidated and reliable wineries in Sicily. A Tre Bicchieri went to the elegant Cerasuolo di Vittoria Giambattista Valli Paris 2011, with its cherries, red berry fruit and attractive spicy swathe. The well-built palate is brimming with silky tannins, underpinned by an attractive acid backbone that accompanies the incredibly long finish. The rest of the range also impressed.

● Cerasuolo di Vittoria Giambattista Valli Paris '11	▼▼▼ 6
● Frappato Carolina Marengo Kisa '13	▼▼ 4
● L'Eterno '13	▼▼ 7
● Cabernet Sauvignon Missoni '13	▼▼ 4
○ Grillo Kisa '13	▼▼ 4
● Merlot Valentino '13	▼▼ 4
● Nero d'Avola Versace '13	▼▼ 4
○ Passito Gianfranco Ferrè '13	▼▼ 5
○ Tirsat Gurra di Mare '13	▼▼ 4
● Cerasuolo di Vittoria Giambattista Valli Paris '09	♀♀♀ 6
● Frappato Carolina Marengo '11	♀♀♀ 4*
● Nero d'Avola Versace '12	♀♀♀ 4*
● Nero d'Avola Versace '08	♀♀♀ 4*
● Nero d'Avola Versace '07	♀♀♀ 4*
○ Passito Gianfranco Ferrè '09	♀♀♀ 4

Feudo Arancio

C.DA PORTELLA MISILBESI
92017 SAMBUCA DI SICILIA [AG]
TEL. 0925579000
www.feudoarancio.it

CELLAR SALES
PRE-BOOKED VISITS
ANNUAL PRODUCTION 800,000 bottles
HECTARES UNDER VINE 690.00

Mezzacorona established its Sicilian winery at Sambuca, near Lake Arancio, 15 years ago. The 240 hectares of vineyards were joined in 2003 by another 450 near Acate, two zones sharing a particular vocation for quality viticulture. Expressing the potential of the area, using sustainable farming techniques and achieving impressive production figures are the key points of this successful project. The varieties grown range from the native nero d'Avola, grillo, inzolia and frappato to the international chardonnay, cabernet sauvignon, merlot, viognier and syrah. The range is divided into three lines, the monovarietal Feudo Arancio, the everyday Stemmari and the prestigious Selezioni. We appreciated the elegance, focused nose and rich fruit of the refreshing Inzolia 2014, and the attractive citrus notes of the fresh, pleasurable blend of grillo and viognier, the Dalila 2013. The mature, well balanced Cantadoro 2012, a blend of Nero d'Avola and Cabernet Sauvignon, shows mineral, smoky hints.

● Cantadoro '12	▼▼ 4
○ Dalila '13	▼▼ 4
○ Hekate Passito '12	▼▼ 5
○ Sicilia Grillo '14	▼▼ 3
○ Sicilia Inzolia '14	▼▼ 3
● Sicilia Syrah '13	▼ 4
● Cantadoro '11	♀♀ 3
○ Chardonnay '10	♀♀ 2*
○ Dalila '12	♀♀ 3
● Hedonis '07	♀♀ 4
○ Hekate Passito '11	♀♀ 5
○ Hekate Passito '09	♀♀ 4
○ Hekate Passito '08	♀♀ 4
● Nero d'Avola '13	♀♀ 2*

Feudo Maccari

LOC. C.DA MACCARI
S.DA PROV.LE PACHINO-NOTO KM 13,500
96017 NOTO [SR]
TEL. 0931596894
www.feudomaccari.it

CELLAR SALES
PRE-BOOKED VISITS
ANNUAL PRODUCTION 167,000 bottles
HECTARES UNDER VINE 50.00
SUSTAINABLE WINERY

Innovating while following tradition: this has always been the leitmotiv of Antonio Moretti's work in Sicily. This means bush vines, ideal for warm climates such as that of Noto. Equally traditional is the choice of varieties: nero d'Avola, but also grillo and moscato di Noto, alongside a small plot of syrah, planted only after long study by Gilbert Bouvet on the clones and rootstock best suited to the estate's volcanic soils. The rows are tended with painstaking care, in order to keep cellar intervention to a minimum, and the stylistically perfect wines are fine expressions of their variety and provenance. A Tre Bicchieri went to the Saia 2013, a monovarietal Nero d'Avola with marked territorial character, showing salty mineral notes, dried violets and a deep, spirited palate of rare length. Hot on its heels was the Mahâris 2013, an elegant, complex Syrah with intriguing Mediterranean nuances.

● Saia '13	▼▼▼ 4*
● Sicilia Mahâris '13	▼▼ 5
○ Grillo '14	▼▼ 2*
● Saia '12	♀♀♀ 4*
● Saia '11	♀♀♀ 4*
● Saia '10	♀♀♀ 4*
● Saia '08	♀♀♀ 4*
● Saia '07	♀♀♀ 4*
● Saia '06	♀♀♀ 4
○ Grillo '13	♀♀ 2*
○ Grillo '11	♀♀ 2*
● Mahâris '12	♀♀ 5
○ Moscato di Noto Sultana '10	♀♀ 5
● Nero d'Avola '12	♀♀ 2*
● Nero D'Avola '11	♀♀ 2*
○ Sultana '11	♀♀ 5

Feudo Principi di Butera

C.DA DELIELLA
93011 BUTERA [CL]
TEL. 0934347726
www.feudobutera.it

CELLAR SALES
PRE-BOOKED VISITS
ANNUAL PRODUCTION 900,000 bottles
HECTARES UNDER VINE 180.00
SUSTAINABLE WINERY

In the space of only four years, the new technical director, 32-year-old Claudio Galosi, has managed to take Gianni Zonin's estate to the top echelons of Sicilian wine, bringing the best out of Riesi's inhospitable territory, where the white limestone soils and high summer temperatures make it extremely difficult to tame the vigour of the vines. This means extensive work in the rows, which alone accounts for 70% of the winery's time, and short pruning to reduce yields, often not exceeding 45 quintals per hectare. In the winery, the use of new and small oak has been drastically reduced to preserve fruitiness and the terroir's classic mineral notes. The elegant, territorial Nero d'Avola Deliella took home a Tre Bicchieri, with an intense, complex nose and juicy, fresh, full-flavoured palate. The Bordeaux blend Symposio 2013 also made the finals, with its sweet nose of fruit and spice, and a full, succulent palate of rare length. The other wines also impressed.

● Sicilia Deliella '13	♔♔♔ 6	
● Symposio '13	♔♔ 5	
● Sicilia Cabernet Sauvignon '13	♔♔ 3	
○ Sicilia Chardonnay '14	♔♔ 3	
● Sicilia Nero d'Avola '13	♔♔ 3	
● Sicilia Riesi '13	♔♔ 3	
○ Sicilia Serò '14	♔♔ 5	
● Sicilia Syrah '13	♔♔ 3	
● Deliella '12	♕♕♕ 6	
● Deliella '05	♕♕♕ 6	
○ Chardonnay '13	♕♕ 3	
● Deliella '11	♕♕ 6	
● Nero d'Avola '11	♕♕ 3	
● Riesi '12	♕♕ 3	
● Symposio '12	♕♕ 5	
● Symposio '11	♕♕ 5	

★Firriato

VIA TRAPANI, 4
91027 PACECO [TP]
TEL. 0923882755
www.firriato.it

CELLAR SALES
PRE-BOOKED VISITS
ANNUAL PRODUCTION 4,250,000 bottles
HECTARES UNDER VINE 320.00
VITICULTURE METHOD Certified Organic

A perfect mix of entrepreneurial talent and love for the territory is the key to the success of the Di Gaetano family winery. Their judicious project has expanded to reach the two tips of Sicily, in an arch from Etna to Favignana, providing wines with an unmistakable style without sacrificing the personality of each terroir. The Firriato wine experience is completed by accommodation offered at the old Cavanera wine press, in Contrada Verzella, the airy apartments on Favignana, and above all the splendid Baglio Soria Resort, with a breathtaking view over the sea and the valley, set among the vineyards where Salvatore and Vinzia's adventure began. We saw a triumphant Harmonium 2013, a blend of three selections of nero d'Avola from the Trapani estate of Borgo Guarini. A complex nose of Mediterranean sensuality, opening to fruit and fresh herbs, exalts a palate of close-knit, elegant density. The Etna Rosso Cavanera 2013 and the Santagostino Rosso 2013 also made the finals.

● Harmonium '13	♔♔♔ 5	
● Etna Rosso Cavanera Rovo delle Coturnie '13	♔♔ 5	
● Santagostino Rosso Baglio Soria '13	♔♔ 4	
● Altavilla della Corte Syrah '13	♔♔ 3	
● Chiaramonte Nero d'Avola '13	♔♔ 2*	
○ Etna Bianco Le Sabbie dell'Etna '14	♔♔ 4	
● Etna Rosso Le Sabbie dell'Etna '12	♔♔ 4	
○ Jasmin Zibibbo '14	♔♔ 4	
○ Passito L'Ecrù '13	♔♔ 5	
● Quater Rosso '13	♔♔ 5	
● Ribeca '13	♔♔ 5	
○ Sicilia Bianco Santagostino Baglio Soria '14	♔♔ 3	
● Ribeca '10	♕♕♕ 5	
● Santagostino Rosso Baglio Soria '12	♕♕♕ 4*	
● Santagostino Rosso Baglio Soria '11	♕♕♕ 4*	

Cantine Florio

LOC. MARSALA
VIA VINCENZO FLORIO, 1
91025 MARSALA [TP]
TEL. 0923781111
www.duca.it/cantineflorio

CELLAR SALES
PRE-BOOKED VISITS
ANNUAL PRODUCTION 3,500,000 bottles
HECTARES UNDER VINE

Visiting the old, beautifully restored farmstead is like taking a trip back in time to the golden age of the Belle Époque, when the Florio family brought Palermo to centre stage, not only in Europe but perhaps the world. Crown princes, American magnates, and statesmen would seek invitations from the icon of the family, beautiful Donna Franca, to visit the splendid Villa Igea in Palermo, where it was not uncommon to spot the Kaiser or the Prince of Wales. After long restoration work, Baglio Florio has returned to its previous splendour, and production of Marsala proceed full steam, as does that of sipping wines such as Passito and Malvasia. Florio is back on Tre Bicchieri form with the spectacular 2004 vintage of the Marsala Superiore Riserva Semisecco Targa Riserva 1840. This ethery, intense wine, with a nose of spice, dried fruit, iodine and candied citrus peel, shows a generous, elegant, leisurely palate. The other wines also impressed.

○ Marsala Sup. Semisecco Targa 1840 Ris. '04	♥♥♥ 4*
○ Marsala Sup. Semisecco Ambra Donna Franca Ris.	♥♥ 6
○ Marsala Sup. Vecchio Florio '11	♥♥ 2*
○ Marsala Vergine Baglio Florio '02	♥♥ 5
○ Morsi di Luce '12	♥♥ 4
○ Passito di Pantelleria '12	♥♥ 6
○ Ambar	♥ 3
○ Oxydia	♥ 3
○ Malvasia delle Lipari Passito '07	♀♀ 6
○ Malvasia delle Lipari Passito '06	♀♀ 5
○ Marsala Sup. Targa 1840 Ris. '98	♀♀ 3
○ Marsala Targa 1840 Ris. '99	♀♀ 3
○ Marsala Terre Arse '99	♀♀ 3
○ Marsala Vergine Baglio Florio '97	♀♀ 5
○ Marsala Vergine Baglio Florio '94	♀♀ 5

Tenuta Gatti

C.DA CUPRANI
98064 LIBRIZZI [ME]
TEL. 0941368173
www.tenutagatti.com

CELLAR SALES
PRE-BOOKED VISITS
ANNUAL PRODUCTION 40,000 bottles
HECTARES UNDER VINE 15.00
VITICULTURE METHOD Certified Organic

The "rediscovered memory" of Nicolas Gatti Russo, back in his homeland after half a century of successful business in Argentina, resides in this splendid, organically farmed 217-hectare estate, owned by his family since 1825. We are at the foot of the Nebrodi mountains, among woodland, olive and hazelnut groves, at an altitude of over 350 metres, in a landscape of breathtaking beauty. There are 15 hectares under wine in total, scattered around the rolling hills, buffeted by the wind and breezes from the nearby coast. Here, Nicolas produces wines of great character from native and international varieties, with increasingly impressive results. Just missing a Tre Bicchieri, the original Nocera Sicè 2012, a wine with great character, shows sweet red berry fruit and spice, well balanced by enviable freshness. There was also a peerless performance from the mature, elegant, balsamic Mamertino Curpanè 2011, from nocera and nerello mascalese. We liked the rest of the range.

● Nocera Sicè '12	♥♥ 4
○ Mamertino Bianco Catalina '14	♥♥ 3
● Mamertino Rosso Curpanè '11	♥♥ 3
● Martiniano '11	♥♥ 3
● Martiniano '10	♥♥ 3
● Franco '10	♥ 3
○ Nocera Sicè '11	♀♀ 4

Graci

Loc. Passopisciaro
c.da Feudo di Mezzo
95012 Castiglione di Sicilia [CT]
Tel. 3487016773
www.graci.eu

CELLAR SALES
PRE-BOOKED VISITS
ANNUAL PRODUCTION 65,000 bottles
HECTARES UNDER VINE 18.00
VITICULTURE METHOD Certified Organic

The vineyards of this winery, undoubtedly
one of Etna's most representative, extend
to the districts of Arcuria, Feudo di Mezzo,
Barbabecchi, Moganazzi and Santo Spirito,
while the fine cellar, in a converted
19th-century wine press, is just outside the
town of Passopisciaro. Alberto and Elena
Graci believe a wine must be rooted in its
territory and reflect the character of the
vintage in full. It translates into painstaking
care in the rows to ensure healthy raw
materials, and oenological intervention kept
to a minimum. No barriques are used, only
large barrels and concrete tanks. Elegant
and territorial, the Etna Rosso Arcuria 2013
opens to spice, iron filings and ripe peach
on the nose, over a leisurely, fleshy palate,
well sustained by spirited tannins. The
refreshing, supple Etna Bianco 2014 shows
smoky, mineral notes.

Gulfi

c.da Patria
97012 Chiaramonte Gulfi [RG]
Tel. 0932921654
www.gulfi.it

CELLAR SALES
PRE-BOOKED VISITS
ACCOMMODATION AND RESTAURANT SERVICE
ANNUAL PRODUCTION 280,000 bottles
HECTARES UNDER VINE 70.00
VITICULTURE METHOD Certified Organic

Vito Catania should be given credit for
being one of the first in the Ragusa area to
bring the best out of nero d'Avola and the
terroir where he has always grown this
eclectic variety. Also committed to
environmental sustainability, right from the
outset Vito decided that all his estates
would be farmed using strictly organic
methods. The choice of bush vines as the
only type of training system is aimed at
producing wines as far as possible
consistent with the variety and terroir of
origin but an unmistakable expression of
the vintage. These, then, are wines full of
character, even if they sometimes require
long ageing to come into their own. The
Nero d'Avola Nerobufaleffj 2009 made our
finals, and played on its sense of place,
with an austere nose of red berry jam,
autumn leaves, aromatic herbs and spices.
The full-flavoured palate, bursting with
lively fruit, and underpinned by just slightly
husky tannins, showed impressive length.

● Etna Rosso Arcuria '13	♟♟♟ 6
○ Etna Bianco '14	♟♟ 3*
⊙ Etna Rosato '14	♟♟ 3
● Etna Rosso '13	♟♟ 3
○ Etna Bianco Arcuria '13	♟ 6
○ Etna Bianco '10	♟♟♟ 4*
○ Etna Bianco Arcuria '11	♟♟♟ 5
○ Etna Bianco Quota 600 '10	♟♟♟ 5
● Etna Rosso Arcuria '12	♟♟♟ 6
○ Etna Bianco '13	♟♟ 3
○ Etna Bianco Arcuria '12	♟♟ 6
⊙ Etna Rosato '13	♟♟ 3
● Etna Rosso '12	♟♟ 3
● Etna Rosso '11	♟♟ 3*
● Etna Rosso Quota 600 '11	♟♟ 5
● Etna Rosso Quota 600 '10	♟♟ 5

● Nerobufaleffj '09	♟♟ 6
○ Sicilia Carjcanti '12	♟♟ 5
● Nerojbleo '11	♟ 3
● Nerosanlorè '09	♟ 6
● Reseca '10	♟ 5
⊙ Sicilia Rosato Rosà '14	♟ 3
● Nerobufaleffj '07	♟♟♟ 5
● Neromàccarj '08	♟♟♟ 6
● Neromàccarj '07	♟♟♟ 5
● Neromàccarj '04	♟♟♟ 5
● Nerosanlorè '05	♟♟♟ 5
● Nerobaronj '10	♟♟ 5
● Neromàccarj '10	♟♟ 6
● Neromàccarj '09	♟♟ 6
○ Valcanzjria '13	♟♟ 3
○ Valcanzjria '12	♟♟ 3*

Hauner

LOC. SANTA MARIA
VIA G.GRILLO, 61
98123 MESSINA
TEL. 0906413029
www.hauner.it

CELLAR SALES
PRE-BOOKED VISITS
ANNUAL PRODUCTION 80,000 bottles
HECTARES UNDER VINE 18.00

A story of love and poetry ties Brescia artist
Carlo Hauner to the island of Salina and its
malvasia. It all started when he was on
holiday there in 1963, and it was love at
first sight, as the famous artist fell hook,
line and sinker for that marvellous volcanic
mountain emerging from the waters and for
the wine produced there. A decade later he
decided to move there for good and to
dedicate himself to promoting the
enchanting sweet grape he then introduced
to the rest of the world by modernizing
growing methods and vinification
techniques. Carlo Hauner Junior continues
in his footsteps with talent and enthusiasm,
together with manager Gianfranco
Sabbatino. The Malvasia delle Lipari Passito
Carlo Hauner 2012 boasts seductive hues
of deep gold and orange. This stylish wine
offers focused, intense nuances of dates,
almonds and prickly pear, over a creamy,
enfolding, silky palate with great depth and
length. We also liked the other wines.

○ Malvasia delle Lipari Passito Carlo Hauner '12	♀♀	6
● Hierà '13	♀♀	3
○ Malvasia delle Lipari Passito '13	♀♀	6
○ Malvasia delle Lipari '13	♀	5
○ Salina Bianco '14	♀	2
● Salina Rosso '13	♀	2
○ Malvasia delle Lipari Naturale '85	♀♀♀	8
○ Malvasia delle Lipari Ris. '11	♀♀♀	8
○ Malvasia delle Lipari Ris. '10	♀♀♀	8
○ Malvasia delle Lipari '12	♀♀	5
○ Malvasia delle Lipari Passito '12	♀♀	6
○ Malvasia delle Lipari Passito '11	♀♀	6
○ Malvasia Passito Carlo Hauner '09	♀♀	8
○ Malvasia Passito Carlo Hauner '08	♀♀	8
○ Malvasia Passito Carlo Hauner '06	♀♀	8
● Rosso Antonello '10	♀♀	4

Morgante

C.DA RACALMARE
92020 GROTTE [AG]
TEL. 0922945579
www.morgantevini.it

CELLAR SALES
PRE-BOOKED VISITS
ANNUAL PRODUCTION 310,000 bottles
HECTARES UNDER VINE 52.00

The Grotte countryside offers a stunning
landscape among hills cloaked with almond
and olive trees, wheat fields on the valley
floor, and abandoned sulphur mines,
bearing witness to a past of toil and
hardship. Here, the Morgante family have
been working the land for generations, and
here nero d'Avola has found a perfect
setting, on sites between 350 and 500
metres in altitude. The 50 hectares of
vineyards are distributed over an area of 30
kilometres around the town. The
calcareous-clay soils, benefiting from wide
temperature ranges, allow the sole variety
planted to express a great wealth of varietal
aromas and unmistakable Mediterranean
character. The Don Antonio 2013 is back on
Tre Bicchieri form, thanks to an
extraordinarily complex, well-focused,
elegant nose, paving the way for a polished,
harmonious palate with vibrant, chewy fruit.
Fragrant green notes of black cherry and
mulberry distinguish the refreshing, elegant,
velvety Nero d'Avola 2013.

● Sicilia Nero d'Avola Don Antonio '13	♀♀♀	5
○ Bianco di Morgante '14	♀♀	2*
● Sicilia Nero d'Avola '13	♀♀	2*
● Don Antonio '07	♀♀♀	4
● Don Antonio '06	♀♀♀	4
● Don Antonio '03	♀♀♀	4
● Don Antonio '02	♀♀♀	4
● Don Antonio '01	♀♀♀	4
● Don Antonio '00	♀♀♀	5
● Don Antonio '99	♀♀♀	5
● Don Antonio '98	♀♀♀	5

Cantine Nicosia

VIA LUIGI CAPUANA, 65
95039 TRECASTAGNI [CT]
TEL. 0957806767
www.cantinenicosia.it

CELLAR SALES
PRE-BOOKED VISITS
RESTAURANT SERVICE
ANNUAL PRODUCTION 1,800,000 bottles
HECTARES UNDER VINE 240.00
VITICULTURE METHOD Certified Organic
SUSTAINABLE WINERY

This family business, dating back to 1898, is now in the fifth generation. Over time it has become a modern operation committed to sustainable viticulture whose wines are a perfect expression of their respective territories. The hub of the operation is at Trecastagni, at an altitude of 700 metres, with its breath-taking views of Etna. The innovative 3,000-square-metre winery includes an atmospheric underground barrique cellar, and the Monte Gorna estate with its old vines planted on lava ston\e terraces. In the Ragusa district of Bonincontro there is the other vast estate with its ancient enclosed baglio farmstead and wine press. The intense, deep Nero d'Avola Sosta Tre Santi 2009 made our finals with its notes of topsoil, black cherry, spice and Mediterranean herbs, over a warm, graceful palate with attractive texture and elegant, velvety tannins. We also loved the elegant, pleasurable Fondo Filara Cerasuolo di Vittoria Classico 2012.

● Nero d'Avola Sosta Tre Santi '09	▼▼ 5
● Cerasuolo di Vittoria Cl. Fondo Filara '12	▼▼ 4
● Etna Rosso Fondo Filara '12	▼▼ 4
● Nerello Mascalese Sosta Tre Santi '10	▼▼ 5
● Sicilia Frappato '14	▼▼ 3
● Sicilia Nerello Mascalese Fondo Filara '13	▼▼ 3
○ Etna Bianco Fondo Filara '14	▼ 4
○ Etna Brut Collezione di Famiglia Sosta Tre Santi '12	▼ 5
○ Etna Bianco Fondo Filara '13	♀♀ 3
○ Etna Bianco Fondo Filara '12	♀♀ 3*
● Etna Rosso Fondo Filara '11	♀♀ 3
● Etna Rosso Fondo Filara '10	♀♀ 3
● Fondo Filara Sosta Tre Santi Nero d'Avola '09	♀♀ 6
○ Fondo Filara Viognier '11	♀♀ 2*
● Sosta Tre Santi '09	♀♀ 5

Occhipinti

S.DA PROV.LE 68 VITTORIA - PEDALINO KM 3,3
97019 VITTORIA [RG]
TEL. 09321865519
www.agricolaocchipinti.it

CELLAR SALES
PRE-BOOKED VISITS
ANNUAL PRODUCTION 130,000 bottles
HECTARES UNDER VINE 22.00
VITICULTURE METHOD Certified Organic
SUSTAINABLE WINERY

Including her latest plantings, Arianna Occhipinti now has 22 hectares under vine, distributed in small plots with traditional dry stone walls in the districts of Fosso di Lupo, Bombolieri, Bastonaca and Pettineo. Committed to biodiversity and environmental sustainability, Arianna uses only organic farming methods, and green manure alternated with grass between the rows. To safeguard in full the characteristics of the terroir and variety, intervention in the winery is kept to a minimum, and fermentation takes place in concrete tanks, while ageing is in large oak barrels, whose wood is curved by steam or undergoes extremely light toasting. The original Cerasuolo di Vittoria Grotte Alte 2010 made the finals, with its nose of aromatic herbs, berry fruit and Mediterranean forest floor, leading into a meaty palate, that remains supple despite slightly uneven tannins. The Frappato 2013 opens to a mineral nose brimming with red berry fruit, over a fresh, lingering palate.

● Cerasuolo di Vittoria Cl. Grotte Alte '10	▼▼ 7
● Il Frappato '13	▼▼ 6
● Siccagno '12	▼▼ 6
○ SP 68 Bianco '14	▼▼ 3
● SP 68 Rosso '14	▼▼ 3
● Il Frappato '12	♀♀♀ 5
● Il Frappato '11	♀♀♀ 5
● Il Frappato '10	♀♀ 4
● Siccagno '11	♀♀ 5
● Siccagno '09	♀♀ 5
● SP 68 '09	♀♀ 3*
○ SP 68 Bianco '13	♀♀ 4
○ SP 68 Bianco '12	♀♀ 4
● SP 68 Rosso '13	♀♀ 3
● SP 68 Rosso '12	♀♀ 3
● SP 68 Rosso '11	♀♀ 3

★Palari

LOC. SANTO STEFANO BRIGA
C.DA BARNA
98137 MESSINA
TEL. 090630194
www.palari.it

ANNUAL PRODUCTION 50,000 bottles
HECTARES UNDER VINE 7.00

In Sicily, the case of Palari is unique as no
other wine had managed to identify and
become the icon of a territory in . In 1989,
when Salvatore Geraci was still very young,
his friend Gino Veronelli encouraged him to
pursue his idea of saving the glorious,
time-honoured Faro DOC zone from
oblivion and extinction. Now it is safe and
can count on an extensive number of
producers. Hats off to Salvatore and his
brother Giampiero, even when they were
practically the only operation to do so on
the Straits of Messina, for all the friendship,
advice and expertise dispensed to anyone
who responded to the challenge of
producing this noble Messina wine. Turi
Geraci decided to leave the Palari 2012 to
rest a little longer in the cellar. His second
wine, the Rosso del Soprano 2013,
performed admirably, showing the same
austere elegance as its elder brother but
more approachable fruit and Mediterranean
character.

Passopisciaro

LOC. PASSOPISCIARO
C.DA GUARDIOLA
95030 CASTIGLIONE DI SICILIA [CT]
TEL. 0578267110
www.passopisciaro.com

CELLAR SALES
ANNUAL PRODUCTION 75,000 bottles
HECTARES UNDER VINE 26.00

Among the leaders of the nouvelle vague
which has changed the international profile
and perception of Etna wines, Tuscan
grower Andrea Franchetti, owner of Tenuta
di Trinoro, has the merit of having focused
the attention of wine writers and consumers
on the various districts that make up the
area around the volcano. These "contrade"
are at their various altitudes and have
different ages of lava and specific
microclimates, producing well-typed wines
of great variety, each with its own distinctive
personality, crus in the real sense of the
term. The small estate, at 550–1,000
metres, gives elegant, minerally wines,
benchmarks for high-altitude viticulture. The
Contrada C 2013, from nerello mascalese,
just missed top honours. This complex,
generous, intense wine, with focused notes
of cherry, Mediterranean herbs and spice,
shows an extremely elegant palate with
glossy tannins. Equally good is the stylish,
highly drinkable Contrada S 2013 from the
same grapes, boasting intact fruit.

● Rosso del Soprano '13	♟♟ 4
● Faro Palari '11	♟♟♟ 6
● Faro Palari '09	♟♟♟ 6
● Faro Palari '08	♟♟♟ 6
● Faro Palari '07	♟♟♟ 6
● Faro Palari '06	♟♟♟ 6
● Faro Palari '05	♟♟♟ 6*
● Faro Palari '04	♟♟♟ 7
● Faro Palari '03	♟♟♟ 6
● Faro Palari '02	♟♟♟ 6
● Faro Palari '01	♟♟♟ 6
● Faro Palari '00	♟♟♟ 6
● Faro Palari '98	♟♟♟ 6
● Rosso del Soprano '11	♟♟♟ 4*
● Rosso del Soprano '10	♟♟♟ 4*
● Rosso del Soprano '07	♟♟♟ 4

● Contrada C '13	♟♟ 6
● Contrada S '13	♟♟ 6
● Contrada P '13	♟♟ 7
● Contrada R '13	♟♟ 6
● Franchetti '13	♟♟ 8
● Passorosso '13	♟♟ 5
● Contrada G '11	♟♟♟ 8
● Contrada P '09	♟♟♟ 7
● Passopisciaro '04	♟♟♟ 5
● Contrada C '12	♟♟ 6
● Contrada C '11	♟♟ 6
● Contrada R '12	♟♟ 6
● Contrada R '11	♟♟ 6
● Contrada S '11	♟♟ 6
● Passopisciaro '11	♟♟ 5
● Passopisciaro '10	♟♟ 5

Carlo Pellegrino

VIA DEL FANTE, 39
91025 MARSALA [TP]
TEL. 0923719911
www.carlopellegrino.it

CELLAR SALES
PRE-BOOKED VISITS
ANNUAL PRODUCTION 6,900,000 bottles
HECTARES UNDER VINE 150.00
SUSTAINABLE WINERY

This operation vaunts a long history in wine, based on family ties and business wisdom, passed on for six generations. In fact, the fortunes of this historic winery in Marsala are still firmly in the hands of the descendants of its founder, Paolo Pellegrino, starting at the top, with Pietro Alagna and Benedetto Renda, respectively Chairman and CEO. The range of wines, which covers every market niche, is divided into the two brands Pellegrino and Duca di Castelmonte, the former reserved for Marsalas, Passito Nes and iconic labels such as Cent'Are and Traimari, the latter for more modern wines, offering excellence across the board. The magnificent series of Riservas continues with the Vergine 2000, with its intense, generous, ethery aromas, and great iodine finesse, encoring on the long finish. The Zibibbo Gibelè 2014 offers an aromatic, mineral nose, while the Catarratto Tripudium 2014 is juicy and pleasantly herbaceous.

○ Marsala Vergine Ris. '00	TT 6
○ Duca di Castelmonte Gibelè '14	TT 2*
○ Duca di Castelmonte Tripudium Bianco '14	TT 4
● Duca di Castelmonte Tripudium Rosso '12	TT 5
● Marsala Fine Rubino	TT 3
○ Passito di Pantelleria Nes '13	TT 7
○ Duca di Castelmonte Dinari del Duca Grillo '14	T 3
○ Marsala Sup. Ambra Semisecco Ris. '85	YYY 4*
○ Marsala Vergine Ris. '81	YYY 6
○ Passito di Pantelleria Nes '09	YYY 5
● Tripudium Rosso Duca di Castelmonte '09	YYY 4*

Pietradolce

FRAZ. SOLICCHIATA
C.DA RAMPANTE
95012 CASTIGLIONE DI SICILIA [CT]
TEL. 3484037792
www.pietradolce.it

ANNUAL PRODUCTION 24,000 bottles
HECTARES UNDER VINE 13.00

Despite their youth, brothers Mario and Michele Faro are two authoritative, reliable growers and in the space of only a few years have managed to turn a small, dynamic winery into one of the benchmarks of Etna territory. All their vineyard holdings, where the whites come from a century-old vineyard, are situated on the northern slopes of the volcano, in the districts of Zottorinoto, Barbagalli and Rampante, where they have just opened the functional new winery. Elegant, with masterfully dosed oak, and well-judged extraction, their wines, from nerello or carricante, are unmistakable products of Etna and vintage. A wine of extraordinary complexity and finesse, worthy of a Tre Bicchieri, the Vigna Barbagalli 2012 shows a complex, deep nose, played on red berry fruit, mineral notes, spice, tobacco and balsam, followed by a leisurely, focused palate, in which the fruit encores on the long finish in all its elegant sensuality.

● Etna Rosso V. Barbagalli '12	TTT 8
● Etna Rosso Archineri '13	TT 5
○ Etna Bianco Archineri '14	TT 5
○ Etna Bianco Pietradolce '14	TT 4
⊙ Etna Rosato Pietradolce '14	TT 3
● Etna Rosso Pietradolce '13	TT 4
● Etna Rosso Archineri '10	YYY 5
● Etna Rosso Archineri '08	YYY 3*
● Etna Rosso Archineri '07	YYY 3*
● Etna Rosso V. Barbagalli '11	YYY 8
● Etna Rosso V. Barbagalli '10	YYY 8
○ Etna Bianco Archineri '12	YY 5
● Etna Rosso Archineri '12	YY 5
● Etna Rosso Archineri '11	YY 5
● Etna Rosso Pietradolce '12	YY 5

★★Planeta

C.DA DISPENSA
92013 MENFI [AG]
TEL. 091327965
www.planeta.it

PRE-BOOKED VISITS
ACCOMMODATION AND RESTAURANT SERVICE
ANNUAL PRODUCTION 2,300,000 bottles
HECTARES UNDER VINE 370.00
SUSTAINABLE WINERY

With the Baronia winery at Capo Milazzo, Planeta has come full circle: there is now no zone in Sicily traditionally renowned for the production of wine where these enlightened entrepreneurs, deeply attached to their land, do not have a production facility. There are six different terroirs: Menfi, Sambuca, Noto, Vittoria, Etna, and Capo Milazzo, each with its own cellar and technical staff, producing the wines of the territory. We are not amazed so much by the quality and extraordinary elegance of the wines, since this is something Planeta has accustomed us to since the first bottlings, but by the fact that every bottle embodies the essence of its terroir and variety. The 2013 vintage of the Cerasuolo di Vittoria Dorilli earns another Tre Bicchieri, thanks to an intense, elegant nose, in which fruity mulberry, blackberry and raspberry fruit join forces with fresh balsam and Mediterranean herbs. The fresh, supple, deep palate boasts extraordinary length.

● Cerasuolo di Vittoria Cl. Dorilli '13	♟♟♟ 3*
○ Sicilia Carricante Eruzione 1614 '14	♟♟ 4
● Sicilia Merlot '12	♟♟ 4
○ Chardonnay '13	♟♟ 5
○ Cometa '14	♟♟ 5
○ Etna Bianco '14	♟♟ 3
○ Etna Rosso '14	♟♟ 3
● Noto Santa Cecilia '12	♟♟ 5
● Sicilia Nerello Mascalese Eruzione 1614 '13	♟♟ 4
● Sicilia Nero d'Avola Nocera '14	♟♟ 3
● Syrah Maroccoli '11	♟♟ 4
● Cerasuolo di Vittoria Cl. Dorilli '12	♟♟♟ 3*
○ Chardonnay '10	♟♟♟ 5
● Noto Santa Cecilia '10	♟♟♟ 5
● Plumbago '09	♟♟♟ 2*

Poggio di Bortolone

FRAZ. ROCCAZZO
VIA BORTOLONE, 19
97010 CHIARAMONTE GULFI [RG]
TEL. 0932921161
www.poggiodibortolone.it

CELLAR SALES
PRE-BOOKED VISITS
ACCOMMODATION AND RESTAURANT SERVICE
ANNUAL PRODUCTION 80,000 bottles
HECTARES UNDER VINE 15.00

The Cosenza family have been growing vines for over 200 years near Chiaramonte Gulfi, where the Para Para and Mazzarronello rivers meet. The winery began bottling 40 years ago, thanks to Ignazio, father of the current owner, Pierluigi, aka Pigi. A blend of syrah and cabernet sauvignon is dedicated to Ignazio but the heart of the 15 hectares of vineyards is planted to nero d'Avola and frappato used for Cerasuolo di Vittoria Classico, of which the Cosenzas are acknowledged to be the most faithful interpreters of local tradition. Top of the range is the selection Para Para, followed by Poggio di Bortolone and Contessa Costanza, using 50% frappato, slighting higher than is usual. The Cerasuolo Para Para 2011 offers well-typed aromas of focused black mulberry, caper and Mediterranean scrub notes, over a close-knit palate with fine-grained, velvety tannins and a long, slightly bitterish finish. We loved the intense, spicy Frappato 2014 with its fragrant fruit.

● Addamanera '13	♟♟ 2*
● Cerasuolo di Vittoria Cl. Contessa Costanza '12	♟♟ 3
● Cerasuolo di Vittoria Cl. Para Para '11	♟♟ 4
● Sicilia Rosso Pigi '13	♟♟ 5
● Vittoria Frappato '14	♟♟ 2*
● Cerasuolo di Vittoria Cl. Poggio di Bortolone '12	♟ 3
● Cerasuolo di Vittoria V. Para Para '05	♟♟♟ 4
● Addamanera '12	♀♀ 2*
● Cerasuolo di Vittoria Cl. Contessa Costanza '11	♀♀ 3
● Cerasuolo di Vittoria Cl. Poggio di Bortolone '11	♀♀ 2*
● Frappato '12	♀♀ 2*
● Pigi Rosso '06	♀♀ 5

Rallo

VIA VINCENZO FLORIO, 2
91025 MARSALA [TP]
TEL. 0923721633
www.cantinerallo.it

CELLAR SALES
PRE-BOOKED VISITS
ANNUAL PRODUCTION 450,000 bottles
HECTARES UNDER VINE 110.00
VITICULTURE METHOD Certified Organic

Andrea Vesco's winery is located on the Marsala seafront, looking towards the Egadi Islands. This solidly-built 19th-century enclosed farmstead was once entirely dedicated to the production of Marsala. Now, after extensive restoration, it houses the state-of-the-art winery, while the place where the Marsala used to mature with the solera method is now a large, functional barrique cellar. Andrea, who has always been committed to biodiversity and ecological sustainability, was one of the first to farm all his estates under certified organic methods. All the wines produced stand out for their finesse, drinkability, extreme cleanness and excellent value for money. A Tre Bicchieri went to the elegant Grillo Bianco Maggiore 2014, which stands out for its extremely clean nose, alternating mineral notes and peach, with lively hints of freshly-cut aromatic herbs. On the succulent palate, the fruit is sustained by a beautifully fresh, zesty acid swathe.

○ Sicilia Bianco Maggiore '14	♥♥♥ 3*
○ Alcamo Beleda '14	♥♥ 2*
○ Al Quasar Zibibbo '14	♥♥ 3
○ Sicilia Evrò '14	♥♥ 3
● Sicilia Il Principe '14	♥♥ 2*
● Sicilia Rujari '14	♥♥ 4
● Siocilia Il Manto '13	♥♥ 3
○ Sicilia Carta d'Oro '14	♥ 2
○ Alcamo Beleda '13	♀♀♀ 2*
○ Bianco Maggiore '12	♀♀♀ 3*
○ Al Qasar '13	♀♀ 3
○ Bianco Maggiore '13	♀♀ 3*
○ Carta d'Oro '13	♀♀ 2*
● Il Manto '12	♀♀ 3
● Il Principe '13	♀♀ 2*
○ Passito di Pantelleria Bugeber '10	♀♀ 5

Tenute Rapitalà

C.DA RAPITALÀ
90043 CAMPOREALE [PA]
TEL. 092437233
www.rapitala.it

CELLAR SALES
PRE-BOOKED VISITS
ANNUAL PRODUCTION 2,800,000 bottles
HECTARES UNDER VINE 175.00

This splendid estate covering 225 hectares on the hills between Camporeale and Alcamo, at elevations of 300 to 600 metres, stands on ideal farmland thanks to its clayey-sandy soils and wide diurnal temperature range. This land was brought fully to fruition with great passion by Gigi Guarrasi and Hugues Bernard de la Gatinais, a French aristocrat enamoured of Sicily. Their son Laurent is now at the helm of this famous, consolidated operation, pride of Gruppo Italiano Vini. He continues with enthusiasm and determination the work began over half a century ago by his parents. The extensive range, from both native and international varieties, fully reflects the terroir. There was a place in the finals for the intense, stylish Hugonis 2013, from cabernet sauvignon and nero d'Avola, with focused notes of black mulberries and Mediterranean herbs, plush palate and polished tannins, and for a very drinkable Syrah Solinero 2012, with its nose of mint, spice and chocolate.

● Hugonis '13	♥♥ 5
● Solinero '12	♥♥ 5
○ Alcamo Bianco '14	♥♥ 2*
○ Conte Hugues Bernard de la Gatinais Grand Cru '13	♥♥ 4
○ Sicilia Grillo '14	♥♥ 2*
● Sicilia Sire Nero '14	♥♥ 3
○ Alcamo Bianco V. Casalj '14	♥ 3
○ Bouquet '14	♥ 2
○ Conte Hugues Bernard de la Gatinais Grand Cru '10	♀♀♀ 4*
● Hugonis '01	♀♀♀ 6
● Solinero '03	♀♀♀ 5
○ Alcamo Bianco V. Casalj '13	♀♀ 3
● Hugonis '12	♀♀ 5
● Nuhar '12	♀♀ 3

Riofavara

C.DA FAVARA SP 49 ISPICA - PACHINO
97014 ISPICA [RG]
TEL. 0932705130
www.riofavara.it

CELLAR SALES
PRE-BOOKED VISITS
ACCOMMODATION
ANNUAL PRODUCTION 70,000 bottles
HECTARES UNDER VINE 16.00
VITICULTURE METHOD Certified Organic
SUSTAINABLE WINERY

The Padova family have been growing vines in Val di Noto since 1920. Massimo and Marianta, who set up the current winery 20 years ago, focused firmly on quality from the outset, adopting a sustainable production philosophy for environment and territory, both in the vineyards, farmed using organic methods, and in the cellar, where fermentation relies on ambient yeasts, and the only outside aid is temperature control. The 21 hectares under vine are distributed in six areas renowned for their viticultural credentials: the grapes for the Marzaiolo and the Notissimo come from Favarotta; the nero d'Avola for the reds from San Basilio, Favara-Biduri, Buonivini, and Sichilli. This year's best wine was the Nero d'Avola San Basilio 2013, whose deep, mature nose offers jam, over mineral, iodine notes, leading into a fine-grained, attractively solid palate with a captivating balsamic encore. The Eloro Sciavè 2012 is more evolved, but elegant and well-structured.

● Eloro Nero d'Avola Sciavè '12	♥♥	5
● Eloro Nero d'Avola Spaccaforno '12	♥♥	3
○ Marzaiolo '14	♥♥	3
● San Basilio '13	♥♥	2*
○ Moscato di Noto Mizzica '14	♥	3
● Eloro Nero d'Avola Sciavè '11	♥♥	5
● Eloro Nero d'Avola Sciavè '09	♥♥	4
● Eloro Nero d'Avola Sciavé '07	♥♥	4
○ Marzaiolo '13	♥♥	2*
○ Marzaiolo '12	♥♥	2*
○ Moscato di Noto Notissimo '12	♥♥	3
● San Basilio '12	♥♥	3
● San Basilio '11	♥♥	3

Girolamo Russo

LOC. PASSOPISCIARO
VIA REGINA MARGHERITA, 78
95012 CASTIGLIONE DI SICILIA [CT]
TEL. 3283840247
www.girolamorusso.it

CELLAR SALES
PRE-BOOKED VISITS
ANNUAL PRODUCTION 35,000 bottles
HECTARES UNDER VINE 15.00
VITICULTURE METHOD Certified Organic

Everyone who knows Giuseppe Russo, a pedigree Etna grower, appreciates his dry humour, manners, and pondered way of speaking. He is, in short, the exact opposite of his wines, which display a warm, spirited, at times restless soul, and an explosive character with incredible aromatic breadth and depth on the nose, thrusting acidity and untamed tannins that endow authoritativeness even when young, and great vitality over time. Nevertheless, these are not instinctive wines, but on the contrary, thought out right from pruning, which is never extreme, with fermentation aimed at moderate extraction, and a masterful use of oak that makes them absolute champions of the volcano. The focused, territorial Etna Rosso Feudo 2013 is an elegant, generous wine, showing a consistent encore of fruit on the palate. We also liked the other finalist, the Etna Rosso San Lorenzo 2013, with stylish mineral notes, peach and apricot, over an elegant, velvety, silky palate. The other wines are excellent.

● Etna Rosso San Lorenzo '13	♥♥♥	5
● Etna Rosso Feudo '13	♥♥	5
○ Etna Bianco Nerina '14	♥♥	6
⊙ Etna Rosato '14	♥♥	4
● Etna Rosso 'A Rina '13	♥♥	3
● Etna Rosso Feudo di Mezzo '13	♥♥	5
● Etna Rosso 'A Rina '12	♥♥♥	3*
● Etna Rosso Feudo '11	♥♥♥	5
● Etna Rosso Feudo '10	♥♥♥	5
● Etna Rosso Feudo '07	♥♥♥	5
● Etna Rosso San Lorenzo '09	♥♥♥	5
⊙ Etna Rosato Millemetri '13	♥♥	4
● Etna Rosso 'A Rina '11	♥♥	5
● Etna Rosso Feudo '12	♥♥	5
● Etna Rosso San Lorenzo '12	♥♥	5
● Etna Rosso San Lorenzo '11	♥♥	5

Emanuele Scammacca del Murgo

VIA ZAFFERANA, 13
95010 SANTA VENERINA [CT]
TEL. 095950520
www.murgo.it

CELLAR SALES
PRE-BOOKED VISITS
ACCOMMODATION AND RESTAURANT SERVICE
ANNUAL PRODUCTION 230,000 bottles
HECTARES UNDER VINE 35.00

This prestigious winery, which led the way for quality in Sicilian viticulture, dates back to 1860 and is owned by the aristocratic Scammacca del Murgo family. Its estates include San Michele, on the eastern slopes of Etna, at over 500 metres, which is the family headquarters, and also offers comfortable, elegant accommodation for visitors. This is joined by Gelso Bianco, and La Francescana, old estates converted with foresight into modern production facilities. It is worth remembering that this winery was the first in Sicily to produce Metodo Classico sparklers, exploiting the great potential of nerello mascalese. We loved the Etna Bianco 2014, with its greenish hue, elegantly grassy and mineral nose, and dynamic, long palate, boasting admirable freshness. Also excellent is the Murgo Extra Brut 2008, from nerello mascale vinified without maceration on the skins, that lives up to its reputation. The rest of the wines are good.

○ Arbiato '13	♀♀	4
○ Etna Bianco '14	♀♀	2*
● Etna Rosso Tenuta San Michele '12	♀♀	2*
○ Murgo Extra Brut '08	♀♀	5
● Tenuta San Michele Pinot Nero '12	♀♀	3
⊙ Etna Rosato '14	♀	2
○ Murgo Brut '11	♀	3
⊙ Murgo Brut Rosé '11	♀	4
○ Etna Bianco '13	♀♀	2*
● Etna Rosso '12	♀♀	2*
● Etna Rosso Tenuta San Michele '11	♀♀	2*
○ Murgo Brut '10	♀♀	3
● Pinot Nero Tenuta San Michele '11	♀♀	5

Settesoli

S.S. 115
92013 MENFI [AG]
TEL. 092577111
www.cantinesettesoli.it

CELLAR SALES
PRE-BOOKED VISITS
ANNUAL PRODUCTION 20,000,000 bottles
HECTARES UNDER VINE 6500.00

A European leader in wine production with over 6,000 hectares under vine, not to mention 2,000 grower-members, the winery produces 25 million bottles and brings in over 55 million euros. This socio-economic miracle involves in various ways 5,000 families, working together for the common good with amazing enthusiasm and dedication, focusing on quality and bringing the best out of their territory. The operation has been the subject of degree dissertations and is now a case history in MBA courses. At the helm of this exceptional winery, international manager Vito Varvaro, who enthusiastically took over the helm from Diego Planeta, the previous venerable chairman. A well-deserved Tre Bicchieri went to the Timperosse 2014, from petit verdot, a wine with an extraordinary aromatic profile, showing elegant nuances of bay leaf, black spice, Mediterranean herbs and red berry fruit, over a fresh, elegant, lively palate. Almost as good is the Urra di Mare 2014, from sauvignon blanc.

● Timperosse Mandrarossa '14	♀♀♀	3*
○ Sicilia Urra di Mare Mandrarossa '14	♀♀	2*
● Bonera Mandrarossa '14	♀♀	3
○ Santannella Mandrarossa '14	♀♀	3
● Sicilia Cartagho Mandrarossa '13	♀♀	3
● Sicilia V. Cinquanta '13	♀	4
● Cartagho Mandrarossa '09	♀♀♀	3*
● Cartagho Mandrarossa '08	♀♀♀	3*
● Cartagho Mandrarossa '06	♀♀♀	3
● Cartagho Mandrarossa '12	♀♀	3*
● Cavadiserpe Mandrarossa '13	♀♀	4
○ Santannella Mandrarossa '13	♀♀	3
● Seligo Rosso '13	♀♀	2*
● Timperosse Mandrarossa '13	♀♀	3
● V. Cinquanta '12	♀♀	4

Spadafora

C.DA VIRZI
90144 MONREALE [PA]
TEL. 091514952
www.spadafora.com

CELLAR SALES
PRE-BOOKED VISITS
RESTAURANT SERVICE
ANNUAL PRODUCTION 300,000 bottles
HECTARES UNDER VINE 95.00
VITICULTURE METHOD Certified Organic
SUSTAINABLE WINERY

Of the many places where wine is made, some are anonymous and impersonal, even if the facilities and vineyards display a certain formal beauty. Others, meanwhile, strike us because they bear the unmistakable hallmark of those who moulded them over time with dedication and hard work, and express personality and character. This is the case of Virzì, the largest estate of Francesco Spadafora, heir of an aristocratic family whose history can be traced as far back as 1230, where he found his spiritual home and workplace, in 1988, keeping pace with nature and the seasons. We saw good performance from the Alhambra Nero d'Avola 2013, showing an intense ruby hue with a violet rim, and offering a complex, inviting nose, with alternating black cherry, spice and Mediterranean herbs, over a fine-grained, velvety palate. The other wines presented were also enjoyable.

● Alhambra Nero d'Avola '13	♥♥ 2*
● Schietto Nero d'Avola '11	♥♥ 4
● Sole dei Padri '09	♥♥ 6
○ Alhambra Catarratto Inzolia '14	♥ 2
○ Don Pietro Bianco '14	♥ 3
● Don Pietro Rosso '12	♥ 3
○ Grillo '13	♥ 3
○ Schietto Chardonnay '12	♥ 4
● Alhambra Syrah '12	♀♀ 2*
○ Don Pietro Bianco '12	♀♀ 2*
● Don Pietro Rosso '11	♀♀ 3
● Don Pietro Rosso '09	♀♀ 3
● le jeux sont faits '13	♀♀ 2*
● Schietto Nero d'Avola '10	♀♀ 4
● Schietto Syrah '08	♀♀ 3

★★Tasca d'Almerita

C.DA REGALEALI
90129 SCLAFANI BAGNI [PA]
TEL. 0916459711
www.tascadalmerita.it

CELLAR SALES
PRE-BOOKED VISITS
ACCOMMODATION AND RESTAURANT SERVICE
ANNUAL PRODUCTION 3,000,000 bottles
HECTARES UNDER VINE 346.00

The Tasca d'Almerita family has made a mark on the viticultural and cultural history of Sicily in the last two centuries, and is now in its eighth generation. They have always managed to combine tradition and innovation impeccably, sensing and often anticipating the spirit of the times. This prestigious winery has five estates situated in strategic areas of Sicily, although the beautiful Regaleali estate, 520 hectares in the heart of Sicily, at elevations of between 450 and 900 metres, remains the pulsing heart of the operation. Production, which is territorial and elegant, fully reflects the philosophy and innovative spirit of Lucio Tasca and his sons Alberto and Giuseppe. Going forward sometimes means going back to one's roots, and a Tre Bicchieri goes to the memorable new Riserva del Conte 2010, from nero d'Avola and perricone. This deep, vibrant wine of exceptional finesse, elegance, and length, is aged in chestnut, as the unforgettable Conte Giuseppe used to do. The other wines are all excellent.

● Contea di Sclafani Riserva del Conte '10	♥♥♥ 8
● Contea di Sclafani Rosso del Conte '11	♥♥ 6
● Sicilia Contea di Sclafani Cabernet Sauvignon '12	♥♥ 5
○ Contea di Sclafani Chardonnay '13	♥♥ 5
○ Contea di Sclafani Nozze d'Oro '13	♥♥ 4
● Sicilia Lamùri '13	♥♥ 3
● Sicilia Tascante '12	♥♥ 3
○ Tasca d'Almerita Whitaker Grillo '14	♥♥ 3
● Cabernet Sauvignon '07	♀♀♀ 5
○ Chardonnay '06	♀♀♀ 5
● Contea di Sclafani Cabernet Sauvignon '10	♀♀♀ 5
● Contea di Sclafani Rosso del Conte '10	♀♀♀ 6
● Contea di Sclafani Rosso del Conte '07	♀♀♀ 6
● Contea di Sclafani Rosso del Conte '05	♀♀♀ 6
● Cygnus '10	♀♀♀ 4*

Tenuta delle Terre Nere

C.DA CALDERARA
95036 RANDAZZO [CT]
TEL. 095924002
www.tenutaterrenere.com

CELLAR SALES
PRE-BOOKED VISITS
ANNUAL PRODUCTION 200,000 bottles
HECTARES UNDER VINE 30.00
VITICULTURE METHOD Certified Organic

Marco De Grazia has the great merit of having produced a large number of Italian wines of international quality since the 1980s. Using his famous intuition, almost as if he were a wine clairvoyant, in 2002 he began to find particularly good plots with unusual characteristics in the marvellous area to the north of Etna, where he made purchases of almost 30 hectares. With a cru-based approach, he focused on the qualities and limitations of each individual plot, according to a personal interpretation of their diversity, to become one of the most appreciated producers in the area around the great volcano. A Tre Bicchieri was never in doubt for the 2013 vintage of the Etna Rosso Calderara Sottana, a wine of rare elegance, with focused nuances of spice, leather and tobacco, intact fruit and great drinkability. The complex, well-coordinated Etna Rosso Feudo di Mezzo Quadro delle Rose 2013 is also a wine of great class.

● Etna Rosso Calderara Sottana '13	♥♥♥ 6
● Etna Rosso Feudo di Mezzo Quadro delle Rose '13	♥♥ 6
○ Etna Bianco '14	♥♥ 4
○ Etna Bianco Le Vigne Niche '13	♥♥ 6
⊙ Etna Rosato '14	♥♥ 4
● Etna Rosso '13	♥♥ 4
● Etna Rosso Guardiola '13	♥♥ 6
● Etna Rosso Santo Spirito '13	♥♥ 6
● Etna Rosso Prephilloxera La V. di Don Peppino '07	♥♥♥ 8
● Etna Rosso Prephilloxera La V. di Don Peppino '06	♥♥♥ 8
● Etna Rosso Santo Spirito '12	♥♥♥ 6
● Etna Rosso Santo Spirito '11	♥♥♥ 6
● Etna Rosso Santo Spirito '10	♥♥♥ 6
● Etna Rosso Santo Spirito '08	♥♥♥ 6

Terrazze dell'Etna

C.DA BOCCA D'ORZO
95036 RANDAZZO [CT]
TEL. 0916236343
www.terrazzedelletna.it

CELLAR SALES
PRE-BOOKED VISITS
ANNUAL PRODUCTION 120,000 bottles
HECTARES UNDER VINE 38.00

This young yet already consolidated winery is the result of the love for wine and viticulture of Nino Bevilacqua, an engineer with an international reputation. He transformed a myriad of plots covered with thorns and weeds into a spectacular, well-tended estate, now jointly managed with the youthful enthusiasm by his daughter Alessia. We are in the heart of the Parco Naturale dell'Etna, near Randazzo, and the winery's holdings are located at elevations of 650 to 900 metres, in a natural setting of incredible beauty, with terraces, dry stone walls, and old wine presses. The products reflect the tradition of Etna with an attractively modern twist. Intense, elegant, and mineral, the Etna Rosso Cirneco 2012 easily made our finals, with its complex, inviting fruit aromas. The tangy, lively Ciuri 2014, from nerello mascalese vinified without maceration on the skins, and other native grapes, offers aromas of Mediterranean herbs.

● Etna Rosso Cirneco '12	♥♥ 6
○ Ciuri '14	♥♥ 3
○ Cuvée Brut '12	♥♥ 5
⊙ Rosé Brut '12	♥♥ 5
● Etna Rosso Carusu '13	♥ 4
● Etna Rosso Cirneco '09	♥♥♥ 6
● Etna Rosso Cirneco '08	♥♥♥ 5
○ Ciuri '12	♀♀ 3
● Cratere '11	♀♀ 4
● Etna Rosso Cirneco '11	♀♀ 6
● Etna Rosso Cirneco '10	♀♀ 6
⊙ Rosé Brut '11	♀♀ 5

Valle dell'Acate

C.DA BIDINI
97011 ACATE [RG]
TEL. 0932874166
www.valledellacate.it

CELLAR SALES
PRE-BOOKED VISITS
ANNUAL PRODUCTION 400,000 bottles
HECTARES UNDER VINE 100.00
SUSTAINABLE WINERY

Innovating while remaining true to tradition and without betraying the terroir: this has always been the philosophy of this consolidated winery, since it was taken over by Gaetana Jacono and Francesco Ferreri, the last generation of the families who shared its ownership. This also involved reorganizing the technical staff, now headed by Carlo Casavecchia, finally back in his beloved Sicily. There is no doubt that these changes have brought benefits: the wines of the last vintage are without doubt technically well-made, with more focused fruit, and crisp, varietal aromas. We are still at the beginning, but with this promising premise greater success will not be long in coming. The well-coordinated Cerasuolo di Vittoria 2012 missed out on a Tre Bicchieri by a hair's breadth, and showed intense fruit, in its most elegant version ever. The Frappato 2014 was extremely pleasurable, with its kaleidoscopic nose of red berry fruit, mineral notes, bay leaf, capers, spice and wildflowers, over an invigorating, fragrant palate.

● Cerasuolo di Vittoria Cl. '12	♥♥ 3*
○ Sicilia Bidis '13	♥♥ 4
● Sicilia Il Moro '12	♥♥ 3
● Vittoria Il Frappato '14	♥♥ 3
○ Sicilia Zagra '14	♥ 3
● Tanè '11	♥ 6
○ Bidis '09	♀♀ 3
● Cerasuolo di Vittoria Cl. '11	♀♀ 3
● Cerasuolo di Vittoria Cl. '10	♀♀ 3
● Il Moro '11	♀♀ 3
● Il Moro '10	♀♀ 3
● Il Moro '09	♀♀ 3
● Rusciano '11	♀♀ 4
● Tanè '10	♀♀ 5
● Vittoria Il Frappato '13	♀♀ 2*
● Vittoria Il Frappato '11	♀♀ 2*
○ Zagra '11	♀♀ 2*

Zisola

C.DA ZISOLA
96017 NOTO [SR]
TEL. 057773571
www.mazzei.it

CELLAR SALES
ANNUAL PRODUCTION 120,000 bottles
HECTARES UNDER VINE 21.00

The Mazzei family has been producing wine at the Fonterutoli estate in Chianti Classico for centuries, and more recently in Maremma, so it certainly did not come to Sicily with a colonizing spirit, interested only in a commercial operation. Right from the beginning, Filippo Mazzei, after persuading the family to buy the Zisola estate, tried to integrate himself with the utmost respect for tradition and local winegrowing history in a territory that has always been vineyard country. The winery's 21 hectares are all planted to bush vines, including syrah, as is the tradition here, and the estate is farmed without chemical products and with utmost respect for the environment. An attractive range of wines was presented this year. We liked the red berry fruit and spices of the fresh Petit Verdot Effe Emme 2012, well balanced by good structure and an elegant tannic weave. We loved the Azisa 2014, from grillo and catarratto, showing fresh and zesty but not without complexity.

● Sicilia Effe Emme '12	♥♥ 7
● Noto Zisola Doppiozeta '12	♥♥ 7
● Sicilia Zisola '13	♥♥ 4
○ Sicilia Zisola Azisa '14	♥♥ 4
● Doppiozeta '10	♀♀ 6
● Noto Doppiozeta '11	♀♀ 6
● Zisola '12	♀♀ 5
● Zisola Nero d'Avola '11	♀♀ 5

Avide

c.da Mastrella, 346
97013 Comiso [RG]
Tel. 0932967456
www.avide.it

CELLAR SALES
PRE-BOOKED VISITS
ANNUAL PRODUCTION 250,000 bottles
HECTARES UNDER VINE 68.00

● 1607 Frappato '14	♥♥ 4
○ Maria Stella Inzolia '14	♥♥ 4
● Cerasuolo di Vittoria Et. Nera '13	♥ 4
○ Vittoria Riflessi di Sole '12	♥ 4

Baglio Ingardia

c.da Porticalazzo
91027 Paceco [TP]
Tel. 0923882863
www.baglioingardia.com

CELLAR SALES
PRE-BOOKED VISITS
HECTARES UNDER VINE 2.00
VITICULTURE METHOD Certified Organic
SUSTAINABLE WINERY

○ Munir Catarratto '14	♥♥ 2*
● Ventu '10	♥♥ 3

Bentivegna

c.da Padre Vitale
95033 Biancavilla [CT]
Tel. 3486272615
www.cantinebentivegna.it

CELLAR SALES
ANNUAL PRODUCTION 10,000 bottles
HECTARES UNDER VINE 5.00
VITICULTURE METHOD Certified Organic

○ Etna Bianco Bianca di Navarra '14	♥♥ 3
⊙ Etna Rosato Bianca di Navarra '14	♥♥ 3
● Etna Rosso Bianca di Navarra '12	♥ 5

Biondi

c.so Sicilia, 20
95039 Trecastagni [CT]
Tel. 0957633933
www.levignebiondi.it

CELLAR SALES
PRE-BOOKED VISITS
ANNUAL PRODUCTION 22,000 bottles
HECTARES UNDER VINE 6.00

○ Etna Bianco Outis '14	♥♥ 4
● Etna Rosso Outis '13	♥♥ 5

Biscaris

via Maresciallo Giudice, 52
97011 Acate [RG]
Tel. 0932990762
www.biscaris.it

CELLAR SALES
ANNUAL PRODUCTION 50,000 bottles
HECTARES UNDER VINE 10.00
VITICULTURE METHOD Certified Biodynamic

● Cerasuolo di Vittoria Pricipuzzu '13	♥♥ 3
● Frappato Barunieddu '14	♥♥ 3
○ U' Duca '14	♥ 2

Alice Bonaccorsi

loc. Passopisciaro
c.da Croce Monaci
95036 Randazzo [CT]
Tel. 095337134
www.valcerasa.com

PRE-BOOKED VISITS
ANNUAL PRODUCTION 35,000 bottles
HECTARES UNDER VINE 14.00
VITICULTURE METHOD Certified Organic

○ Etna Bianco Valcerasa '13	♥♥ 3
● Etna Rosso Valcerasa '11	♥♥ 3

Bonavita

LOC. FARO SUPERIORE
C.DA CORSO
98158 MESSINA
TEL. 3471754983
www.bonavitafaro.it

PRE-BOOKED VISITS
ANNUAL PRODUCTION 5,000 bottles
HECTARES UNDER VINE 2.00

● Faro '13	♛♛ 5
⊙ Rosato '14	♛♛ 2*

Tenute Botticella

C.DA DIGERBATO, 236
91025 MARSALA [TP]
TEL. 0923714788
www.tenutebotticella.com

CELLAR SALES
PRE-BOOKED VISITS
ANNUAL PRODUCTION 20,000 bottles
HECTARES UNDER VINE 55.00

● Gilea Nero d'Avola '13	♛♛ 2*
○ Passito di Pantelleria Fuddrìa '10	♛♛ 6
● Don Diego Rosso '11	♛ 3
○ Gilea Inzolia Chardonnay '14	♛ 2

Calcagno

FRAZ. PASSOPISCIARO
C.DA VIA REGINA MARGHERITA
95012 CASTIGLIONE DI SICILIA [CT]
TEL. 3387772780
www.vinicalcagno.it

CELLAR SALES
PRE-BOOKED VISITS
ANNUAL PRODUCTION 13,000 bottles
HECTARES UNDER VINE 3.00

○ Etna Bianco '14	♛♛ 3
⊙ Etna Rosato Arcuria '14	♛♛ 3

Paolo Calì

LOC. C.DA SALAMÈ
VIA DEL FRAPPATO, 100
97019 VITTORIA [RG]
TEL. 0932510082
vinicali.weebly.com

CELLAR SALES
PRE-BOOKED VISITS
ANNUAL PRODUCTION 90,000 bottles
HECTARES UNDER VINE 15.00

● Vittoria Nero d'Avola Violino '12	♛♛ 3
● Cerasuolo di Vittoria Cl. Manene '13	♛ 4
● Jazz '14	♛ 2
⊙ Osa Frappato Rosato '14	♛ 4

Cantina Viticoltori Associati Canicattì

C.DA AQUILATA
92024 CANICATTÌ [AG]
TEL. 0922829371
www.cvacanicatti.it

CELLAR SALES
PRE-BOOKED VISITS
ANNUAL PRODUCTION 900,000 bottles
HECTARES UNDER VINE 1000.00

● Caliò '13	♛♛ 2*
● Scialo '12	♛♛ 3
● Aquilae Nero d'Avola '13	♛ 2
● Centouno '11	♛ 2

Caravaglio

LOC. MALFA SALINA
VIA NAZIONALE, 33
98050 MALFA [ME]
TEL. 3398115953
caravagliovini@virgilio.it

CELLAR SALES
PRE-BOOKED VISITS
ANNUAL PRODUCTION 40,000 bottles
HECTARES UNDER VINE 12.00

○ Infatata '14	♛♛ 3
○ Malvasia delle Lipari Passito '13	♛♛ 5
● Nero du Monti '14	♛♛ 3

Caruso & Minini

VIA SALEMI, 3
91025 MARSALA [TP]
TEL. 0923982356
www.carusoeminini.it

CELLAR SALES
PRE-BOOKED VISITS
ANNUAL PRODUCTION 1,200,000 bottles
HECTARES UNDER VINE 120.00

● Delia Nivolelli Terre di Giumara Cutaja '12	♥♥ 3
○ Sicilia Terre di Giumara Cusora Bianco '14	♥♥ 2*
○ Terre di Giumara Corte Ferro '14	♥ 3
○ Terre di Giumara Inzolia '14	♥ 2

Colomba Bianca

VIA GIOVANNI FALCONE, 72
91026 MAZARA DEL VALLO [TP]
TEL. 0923942747
www.cantinecolombabianca.it

HECTARES UNDER VINE 8,099.00

● Sicilia Nero d'Avola Kore '13	♥♥ 2*
○ Sicilia Grillo Kore '14	♥ 2

Cantine Colosi

VIA MILITARE RITIRO, 23
98152 MESSINA
TEL. 09053852
www.cantinecolosi.it

PRE-BOOKED VISITS
ANNUAL PRODUCTION 100,000 bottles
HECTARES UNDER VINE 10.00

○ Passito '10	♥♥ 4
○ Grillo '14	♥ 2
○ Malvasia delle Lipari Naturale '12	♥ 5
○ Malvasia delle Lipari Passito '09	♥ 5

Cossentino

VIA PRINCIPE UMBERTO, 241
90047 PARTINICO [PA]
TEL. 0918782569
www.cossentino.it

CELLAR SALES
PRE-BOOKED VISITS
ANNUAL PRODUCTION 70,000 bottles
HECTARES UNDER VINE 17.00
VITICULTURE METHOD Certified Organic

● Lioy '13	♥♥ 3
● Syrah '13	♥♥ 3
○ Gadì Chardonnay '14	♥ 2
● Nero d'Avola '13	♥ 4

Terra Costantino

VIA GARIBALDI, 417
95029 VIAGRANDE [CT]
TEL. 095434288
www.terracostantino.it

CELLAR SALES
PRE-BOOKED VISITS
HECTARES UNDER VINE 7.00

○ Etna Bianco Blandano '13	♥♥ 5
⊙ Etna Rosato de Aetna '14	♥♥ 3
● Etna Rosso de Aetna '13	♥♥ 3
○ Etna Bianco de Aetna '14	♥ 3

Tenuta Coste Ghirlanda

LOC. PIANA DI GHIRLANDA
91017 PANTELLERIA [TP]
TEL. 3388244649
www.costeghirlanda.it

ANNUAL PRODUCTION 10,500 bottles
HECTARES UNDER VINE 5.00

○ Jardinu Zibibbo '13	♥♥ 6
○ Silenzio '13	♥♥ 6

Curto

S.S. 115 ISPICA - ROSOLINI KM 358
97014 ISPICA [RG]
TEL. 0932950161
www.curto.it

CELLAR SALES
PRE-BOOKED VISITS
ANNUAL PRODUCTION 70,000 bottles
HECTARES UNDER VINE 30.00

| ● Eloro Nero d'Avola Fontanelle '10 | ♥♥ 4 |
| ● Ikano '11 | ♥ 3 |

I Custodi delle Vigne dell'Etna

C.DA MOGANAZZI
95012 CASTIGLIONE DI SICILIA [CT]
TEL. 3931898430
www.icustodi.it

CELLAR SALES
PRE-BOOKED VISITS
ANNUAL PRODUCTION 40,000 bottles
HECTARES UNDER VINE 12.50

⊙ Etna Rosato Alnus '13	♥♥ 3
● Etna Rosso Aetneus '09	♥♥ 4
○ Etna Bianco Ante '13	♥ 4
● Etna Rosso Pistus '13	♥ 3

Di Giovanna

C.DA SAN GIACOMO
92017 SAMBUCA DI SICILIA [AG]
TEL. 09251955675
www.di-giovanna.com

CELLAR SALES
PRE-BOOKED VISITS
ANNUAL PRODUCTION 250,000 bottles
HECTARES UNDER VINE 56.00
VITICULTURE METHOD Certified Organic

○ Grillo '14	♥♥ 2*
○ Helios Bianco '14	♥♥ 3
⊙ Gerbino Rosato Nerello Mascalese '14	♥ 2
● Nero d'Avola '13	♥ 3

Di Legami

VIA MARZABOTTO, 7
91014 CASTELLAMMARE DEL GOLFO [TP]
TEL. 3381749679
www.cantinedilegami.it

ANNUAL PRODUCTION 30,000 bottles
HECTARES UNDER VINE 45.00

● Zafaràna Nero d'Avola '13	♥♥ 3
○ Berlinghieri Grillo '14	♥ 3
○ Zafaràna Insolia '14	♥ 3
⊙ Zafaràna Rosato '14	♥ 3

Gaspare Di Prima

VIA G. GUASTO, 27
92017 SAMBUCA DI SICILIA [AG]
TEL. 0925941201
www.diprimavini.it

CELLAR SALES
PRE-BOOKED VISITS
ANNUAL PRODUCTION 50,000 bottles
HECTARES UNDER VINE 38.00
VITICULTURE METHOD Certified Organic

○ Grillo del Lago '14	♥♥ 2*
○ Janub '14	♥ 2
● Sicilia Pepita Rosso '13	♥ 2

Feudo Disisa

FRAZ. GRISÌ
C.DA DISISA
90046 MONREALE [PA]
TEL. 0919127109
www.vinidisisa.it

CELLAR SALES
PRE-BOOKED VISITS
ANNUAL PRODUCTION 150,000 bottles
HECTARES UNDER VINE 150.00
VITICULTURE METHOD Certified Organic

● Adhara '13	♥♥ 2*
○ Chara '14	♥♥ 2*
○ Sicilia Chardonnay Daliah '14	♥ 3
○ Sicilia Fiano Terra delle Fate '14	♥ 3

Cantine Ermes

C.DA SALINELLA
91029 SANTA NINFA [TP]
TEL. 092467153
www.cantineermes.it

CELLAR SALES
PRE-BOOKED VISITS
ANNUAL PRODUCTION 3,000,000 bottles
HECTARES UNDER VINE 4642.00
VITICULTURE METHOD Certified Organic
SUSTAINABLE WINERY

● Marchese Montefusco Nero d'Avola '14	♛♛ 1*
● Marchese Montefusco Syrah '14	♛♛ 1*
○ Vento di Mare Grillo Bio '14	♛ 2
● Vento di Mare Nero d'Avola '14	♛ 2

Ferreri

C.DA SALINELLA
91029 SANTA NINFA [TP]
TEL. 092461871
www.ferrerivini.it

CELLAR SALES
PRE-BOOKED VISITS
ANNUAL PRODUCTION 70,000 bottles
HECTARES UNDER VINE 30.00

● Cabernet Sauvignon '13	♛♛ 3
○ Zibibbo '14	♛♛ 3
○ Catarratto '14	♛ 3
○ Inzolia '14	♛ 3

Feudo Montoni

C.DA MONTONI VECCHI
90144 CAMMARATA [AG]
TEL. 091513106
www.feudomontoni.it

CELLAR SALES
PRE-BOOKED VISITS
ANNUAL PRODUCTION 205,000 bottles
HECTARES UNDER VINE 30.00
VITICULTURE METHOD Certified Organic
SUSTAINABLE WINERY

○ Sicilia Grillo V. della Timpa '14	♛♛ 3
● Sicilia Nero d'Avola V. Lagnusa '13	♛♛ 4
● Sicilia Perricone V. del Core '14	♛♛ 3
● Sicilia Rose di Adele '14	♛ 4

Feudo Ramaddini

FRAZ. MARZAMENI
C.DA LETTIERA
96018 PACHINO [SR]
TEL. 09311847100
www.feudoramaddini.com

CELLAR SALES
PRE-BOOKED VISITS
ANNUAL PRODUCTION 35,000 bottles
HECTARES UNDER VINE 17.00

○ Passito di Noto Al Hamen '14	♛♛ 5
● Sicilia Cabernet Note Nere '13	♛♛ 3
● Noto Nero d'Avola Patrono '12	♛ 5
○ Quattroventi Catarratto Chardonnay '14	♛ 4

Cantine Fina

C.DA BAUSA
91025 MARSALA [TP]
TEL. 0923733070
www.cantinefina.com

CELLAR SALES
PRE-BOOKED VISITS
ANNUAL PRODUCTION 150,000 bottles
HECTARES UNDER VINE 320.00
VITICULTURE METHOD Certified Organic

○ Kike '14	♛♛ 3
○ Sauvignon Blanc '14	♛♛ 3
● Bausa '12	♛ 3
○ Taif Zibibbo '14	♛ 3

Fischetti

LOC. CONTRADA MOSCAMENTO
FRAZ. ROVITTELLO
VIA NAZIONALE N. 2
95012 CASTIGLIONE DI SICILIA [CT]
TEL. 3341272527
www.fischettiwine.it

CELLAR SALES
PRE-BOOKED VISITS
ANNUAL PRODUCTION 8,000 bottles
HECTARES UNDER VINE 1.50

○ Etna Bianco Muscamento '14	♛♛ 4
○ Etna Rosato Muscamento '14	♛♛ 4
● Etna Rosso Muscamento '12	♛♛ 4

Fondo Antico

FRAZ. RILIEVO
VIA FIORAME, 54A
91100 TRAPANI
TEL. 0923864339
www.fondoantico.it

CELLAR SALES
PRE-BOOKED VISITS
ANNUAL PRODUCTION 350,000 bottles
HECTARES UNDER VINE 80.00

● Nero d'Avola '14	♟♟ 2*
☉ Aprile '14	♟ 2
○ Grillo Parlante '14	♟ 2
☉ Memorie '10	♟ 4

Tenute Galfano

VIA SALEMI 101
91025 MARSALA [TP]
TEL. 0923723311
www.galfano.it

PRE-BOOKED VISITS
ANNUAL PRODUCTION 120,000 bottles
HECTARES UNDER VINE 35.00

● Giuvà Alessà Nero d'Avola '11	♟♟ 6
○ Giuvà Carlotta '11	♟♟ 6
● Frappato '11	♟ 4
● Nero d'Avola '11	♟ 4

Geraci

VIA CORSICA, 18
90146 PALERMO
TEL. 0916154146
www.tarucco.com

CELLAR SALES
PRE-BOOKED VISITS
ANNUAL PRODUCTION 120,000 bottles
HECTARES UNDER VINE 15.00
VITICULTURE METHOD Certified Organic

○ Tarucco Chardonnay '14	♟♟ 3
● Tarucco Peralta '13	♟♟ 3
● Tarucco Alicante '14	♟ 3
● Tarucco Nero d'Avola '13	♟ 3

Giasira

C.DA RITILLINI
96019 ROSOLINI [SR]
TEL. 0931501700
www.lagiasira.it

CELLAR SALES
PRE-BOOKED VISITS
ANNUAL PRODUCTION 30,000 bottles
HECTARES UNDER VINE 7.00
VITICULTURE METHOD Certified Organic

○ Giasira Bianco '14	♟♟ 2*
● Morhum '13	♟♟ 3
● Giasira Rosso '13	♟ 3
○ Keration '14	♟ 5

Tenuta Gorghi Tondi

P.ZZA PIEMONTE E LOMBARDO, 13
91026 MARSALA [TP]
TEL. 0923719741
www.gorghitondi.com

CELLAR SALES
PRE-BOOKED VISITS
ACCOMMODATION AND RESTAURANT SERVICE
ANNUAL PRODUCTION 1,300,000 bottles
HECTARES UNDER VINE 130.00
VITICULTURE METHOD Certified Organic

○ Rajah '14	♟♟ 4
○ Sicilia Grillo Kheirè '14	♟♟ 4
○ Meridiano 12 Catarratto '14	♟ 2
● Meridiano 12 Syrah '14	♟ 3

Hibiscus

C.DA TRAMONTANA
90010 USTICA [PA]
TEL. 0918449543
www.agriturismohibiscus.com

CELLAR SALES
PRE-BOOKED VISITS
ACCOMMODATION
ANNUAL PRODUCTION 10,000 bottles
HECTARES UNDER VINE 3.00

○ Grotta dell'Oro '14	♟♟ 2*
○ Zhabib Passito '14	♟♟ 4
○ L'Isola Bianco '14	♟ 2
● L'Isola Rosso '14	♟ 2

Tenuta Enza La Fauci

C.DA MEZZANA-SPARTÀ
98163 MESSINA
TEL. 3476854318
www.tenutaenzalafauci.com

CELLAR SALES
ACCOMMODATION
ANNUAL PRODUCTION 14,000 bottles
HECTARES UNDER VINE 5.00

| ○ Case Bianche '14 | ♥♥ 4 |
| ● Faro Oblì '12 | ♥♥ 5 |

Tenuta La Favola

VIA PRINCIPE DI PIEMONTE, 39
96017 NOTO [SR]
TEL. 0931839216
www.tenutalafavola.it

CELLAR SALES
PRE-BOOKED VISITS
ANNUAL PRODUCTION 30,000 bottles
HECTARES UNDER VINE 10.00
VITICULTURE METHOD Certified Organic
SUSTAINABLE WINERY

● Eloro Pachino Nero d'Avola La Favola '13	♥♥ 3
○ Moscato di Noto Refosa '12	♥♥ 4
● Synà '12	♥♥ 2*
○ Grillo Catarratto '14	♥ 2

Maggiovini

S.DA COMUNALE MARANGIO, 35
97019 VITTORIA [RG]
TEL. 0932984771
www.maggiovini.it

CELLAR SALES
PRE-BOOKED VISITS
ACCOMMODATION
ANNUAL PRODUCTION 250,000 bottles
HECTARES UNDER VINE 45.00
VITICULTURE METHOD Certified Organic
SUSTAINABLE WINERY

● Amongae '12	♥♥ 3
● Cerasuolo di Vittoria Cl. V. di Pettineo '13	♥♥ 2*
● Vittoria Frappato V. di Pettineo '13	♥♥ 3
● Rasula Nero d'Avola '14	♥ 3

Marabino

LOC. C.DA BUONIVINI
S.DA PROV.LE ROSOLINI - PACHINO KM 8,5
97017 NOTO [SR]
TEL. 3355284101
www.marabino.it

CELLAR SALES
PRE-BOOKED VISITS
ACCOMMODATION AND RESTAURANT SERVICE
ANNUAL PRODUCTION 100,000 bottles
HECTARES UNDER VINE 30.00
VITICULTURE METHOD Certified Organic

○ Moscato di Noto Moscato della Torre '14	♥♥ 5
○ Moscato di Noto Muscatedda '14	♥♥ 3
◉ Eloro Rosa Nera '14	♥ 3
● Noto Nero d'Avola '13	♥ 2

Masseria del Feudo

C.DA GROTTAROSSA
93100 CALTANISSETTA
TEL. 0934569719
www.masseriadelfeudo.it

CELLAR SALES
PRE-BOOKED VISITS
ACCOMMODATION
ANNUAL PRODUCTION 800,000 bottles
HECTARES UNDER VINE 12.00
VITICULTURE METHOD Certified Organic

○ Sicilia Grillo '14	♥♥ 2*
○ Sicilia Haermosa '13	♥♥ 3
● Sicilia Rosso delle Rose '13	♥♥ 3
● Sicilia Il Giglio Nero d'Avola '14	♥ 2

Miceli

C.DA PIANA SCUNCHIPANI, 190
92019 SCIACCA [AG]
TEL. 092580188
www.miceli.net

PRE-BOOKED VISITS
ANNUAL PRODUCTION 350,000 bottles
HECTARES UNDER VINE 60.00

○ Passito di Pantelleria Nun '10	♥♥ 5
○ Baaria Grillo '14	♥ 2
○ Lliri '14	♥ 3
● Majo San Lorenzo '11	♥ 5

Cantina Modica
di San Giovanni

C.DA BUFALEFI
96017 NOTO [SR]
TEL. 09311805181
www.vinidinoto.it

CELLAR SALES
PRE-BOOKED VISITS
RESTAURANT SERVICE
ANNUAL PRODUCTION 80,000 bottles
HECTARES UNDER VINE 40.00
SUSTAINABLE WINERY

● Eloro Filinona '11	♟♟ 2*
⊙ Mamma Draja '14	♟♟ 2*
○ Moscato di Noto Dolcenoto '14	♟♟ 3
○ Lupara '14	♟ 2

Orestiadi

LOC. C.DA SALINELLA
V.LE SANTA NINFA
91029 GIBELLINA [TP]
TEL. 092469124
www.tenutaorestiadi.it

CELLAR SALES
PRE-BOOKED VISITS
ANNUAL PRODUCTION 1,000,000 bottles
HECTARES UNDER VINE 100.00
VITICULTURE METHOD Certified Organic
SUSTAINABLE WINERY

● Ludovico '10	♟♟ 5
● Molino a Vento Nero d'Avola '14	♟♟ 2*
○ Molino a Vento Grillo '14	♟ 2
● Molino a Vento Nerello Mascalese '14	♟ 2

Tenute dei Paladini

VIA PALESTRO, 23
91025 MARSALA [TP]
TEL. 3463513366
www.tenutedeipaladini.com

ANNUAL PRODUCTION 40,000 bottles
HECTARES UNDER VINE 45.00

○ Grillo Palatium '14	♟♟ 3
○ Cataratto - Chardonnay Palatium '14	♟ 3
● Nero d'Avola Palatium '14	♟ 3
● San Giorgio '14	♟ 3

Tenuta Palmeri

C.DA BOCHINI - FIUMARELLA
96012 AVOLA [SR]
TEL. 3345646866
www.cantinapalmeri.it

ANNUAL PRODUCTION 28,000 bottles
HECTARES UNDER VINE 11.00

● Celeste '14	♟ 4
○ Vintage Bianco '14	♟ 3

Cantine Paolini

C.DA GURGO 168A
91025 MARSALA [TP]
TEL. 0923967042
www.cantinapaolini.com

ANNUAL PRODUCTION 4,000,000 bottles
HECTARES UNDER VINE 2,739.00
VITICULTURE METHOD Certified Organic

○ Baronazzo Amafi '13	♟♟ 4
○ Gurgò Grillo '14	♟♟ 3
● Sicilia Frappato Syrah '12	♟ 3
● Sicilia Nero d'Avola Sicilien '13	♟ 2

Pupillo

C.DA LA TARGIA
96100 SIRACUSA
TEL. 0931494029
www.solacium.it

CELLAR SALES
PRE-BOOKED VISITS
ANNUAL PRODUCTION 100,000 bottles
HECTARES UNDER VINE 20.00

○ Moscato di Siracusa Solacium '14	♟♟ 5
○ Cyane '14	♟ 3
● Sicilia Rosso Baronessa di Canseria '13	♟ 3
⊙ Vignazza delle Monache '14	♟ 2

Rigoria

VIA CASSARO, 4
96010 FERLA [SR]
TEL. 0931870005
www.rigoria.it

CELLAR SALES
PRE-BOOKED VISITS
ANNUAL PRODUCTION 10,000 bottles
HECTARES UNDER VINE 2.50

● Il Canto delle Sirene '14	♥♥ 3
○ Moscato di Noto Siciliano '14	♥♥ 4
● Costantè '14	♥ 3

Sallier de la Tour

C.DA PERNICE
90144 MONREALE [PA]
TEL. 0916459711
www.tascadalmerita.it

PRE-BOOKED VISITS
ANNUAL PRODUCTION 250,000 bottles
HECTARES UNDER VINE 41.00

● La Monaca '12	♥♥ 5
● Sicilia Nero d'Avola '13	♥♥ 2*
● Sicilia Syrah '13	♥♥ 2*
○ Sicilia Inzolia '14	♥ 2

Barone di Serramarrocco

FRAZ. FULGATORE
VIA ALCIDE DE GASPERI, 15
91100 TRAPANI
TEL. 0923811266
www.baronediserramarrocco.com

CELLAR SALES
PRE-BOOKED VISITS
ANNUAL PRODUCTION 65,000 bottles
HECTARES UNDER VINE 20.00
SUSTAINABLE WINERY

● Nero d'Avola Baglio di Serramarrocco '14	♥♥ 3
○ Quojane di Serramarrocco '14	♥♥ 3
○ Grillo del Barone '14	♥ 2
● Nero di Serramarrocco '12	♥ 4

Solidea

C.DA KADDIUGGIA
91017 PANTELLERIA [TP]
TEL. 0923913016
www.solideavini.it

ANNUAL PRODUCTION 12,000 bottles
HECTARES UNDER VINE 1.80

○ Ilios '14	♥♥ 3
○ Passito di Pantelleria '14	♥♥ 5

Terre di Giurfo

VIA PALESTRO, 536
97019 VITTORIA [RG]
TEL. 0957221551
www.terredigiurfo.it

CELLAR SALES
PRE-BOOKED VISITS
ANNUAL PRODUCTION 100,000 bottles
HECTARES UNDER VINE 40.00

● Sicilia Nero d'Avola Kuntàri '13	♥♥ 3
● Sicilia Syrah Ronna '13	♥♥ 2*
● Cerasuolo di Vittoria Maskarìa '12	♥ 3
● Sicilia Nero d'Avola Kudyah '13	♥ 2

Terre di Shemir

LOC. GUARRATO
91100 TRAPANI
TEL. 0923865323
www.terredishemir.com

CELLAR SALES
PRE-BOOKED VISITS
ANNUAL PRODUCTION 40,000 bottles
HECTARES UNDER VINE 9.00

○ Noeli '14	♥♥ 3
● Pergiò '14	♥♥ 3
○ Haral '14	♥ 3
● Paradiso di Lara '13	♥ 4

Todaro

C.DA FEOTTO
90048 SAN GIUSEPPE JATO [PA]
TEL. 3461056393
www.todarowinery.com

PRE-BOOKED VISITS
ANNUAL PRODUCTION 80,000 bottles
HECTARES UNDER VINE 25.00
VITICULTURE METHOD Certified Organic

● 4 Elementa '11		♥♥ 3
○ Lybra '14		♥ 2
● Merlot di Turì Ginestra '12		♥ 3
○ Nihal '14		♥ 2

Girolamo Tola & C.

VIA GIACOMO MATEOTTI, 2
90047 PARTINICO [PA]
TEL. 0918781591
www.vinitola.it

ANNUAL PRODUCTION 180,000 bottles
HECTARES UNDER VINE 55.00

● Nero d'Avola '14		♥♥ 3
○ Catarratto Insolia '14		♥ 2
○ Grillo '14		♥ 3
● Nero d'Avola Black Label '12		♥ 3

Vaccaro

C.DA COMUNE
91020 SALAPARUTA [TP]
TEL. 092475151
www.vinivaccaro.it

CELLAR SALES
ANNUAL PRODUCTION 800,000 bottles
HECTARES UNDER VINE 40.00
VITICULTURE METHOD Certified Organic
SUSTAINABLE WINERY

○ Luna Grillo '14		♥♥ 1*
● Salaparuta Nero d'Avola Sofè '14		♥♥ 3
○ Catarratto - Zibibbo '14		♥ 2
○ Salaparuta Bianco Eycos '14		♥ 3

Le Vigne di Eli

C.DA CALDERARA
95036 RANDAZZO [CT]
TEL. 095924002
www.tenutaterrenere.com

CELLAR SALES
PRE-BOOKED VISITS
ANNUAL PRODUCTION 200,000 bottles
HECTARES UNDER VINE 30.00
VITICULTURE METHOD Certified Organic

○ Etna Bianco '14		♥♥ 6
● Etna Rosso '13		♥♥ 6
● Etna Rosso Moganazzi Voltasciara '13		♥♥ 6
● Etna Rosso Pignatuni '13		♥♥ 6

Virgona

VIA BANDIERA, 2
98050 MALFA [ME]
TEL. 0909844430
www.malvasiadellelipari.it

PRE-BOOKED VISITS
ANNUAL PRODUCTION 30,000 bottles
HECTARES UNDER VINE 5.00

○ Malvasia delle Lipari Passito '09		♥♥ 6
○ Salina Bianco '14		♥♥ 3
⊙ Salina Rosato '14		♥♥ 3

Vivera

LOC. C.DA MARTINELLA
S.DA PROV.LE 59 IV
95015 LINGUAGLOSSA [CT]
TEL. 095647942
www.vivera.it

PRE-BOOKED VISITS
ANNUAL PRODUCTION 150,000 bottles
HECTARES UNDER VINE 35.00
VITICULTURE METHOD Certified Organic

○ A'mami '12		♥♥ 3
⊙ Etna Rosato di Martinella '14		♥♥ 4
○ Altrove '14		♥ 2
● Terra dei Sogni '12		♥ 2

SARDINIA

Unlike various other Italian regions, 2014 was an
excellent year in Sardinia, above all for the whites,
although some early signals are also arriving from
districts better known for their reds, with vintage
labels now available. So it comes as no surprise
that Gallura has offered several perfectly balanced wines,
with measured alcohol but above all fresh, with scents that fully reflect the area of
provenance. Nonetheless, it is interesting to observe that not just the north-east of
the island is offering superb whites: some Vermentino di Sardegnas from different
terroirs can be typical and charming enough to bear comparison with the DOCGs.
Apart from Vermentino, we also find confirmation from Mogoro Semidanos,
Cagliari Nuragus and Oristano Vernaccias, the latter seeking to establish itself
thanks to different production methods. Not to mention the aromatic white grape
varieties, with Bosa malvasia and Cagliari nasco making all the difference although
it is always the same few usual suspects to believe in and cultivate these varieties.
Sterling work from producers of reds, with Cannonau di Sardegna confirmed as a
great Mediterranean wine, convincing both in younger versions and in the
Riservas, cask-aged for several years. For different reasons, the most interesting
come from Barbagia and Ogliastra. In this regard we can only emphasize the need
for a profound change to the production protocol, in order to make the most of
Sardinia's various Cannonau terroirs. Good news also from Sulcis, with the
Carignanos flying the flag for quality and consistency, while it would be ideal to
have more precise indications on other red grape varieties present on the island,
like bovale, muristellu, cagnulari, nieddera, and monica, especially from their best
vineyard country. Lastly, a word on the wines taking their first Tre Bicchieri. For the
reds: Cantina Dorgali's Cannonau di Sardegna Classico D53 2012, a true
expression of Ogliastra Cannonau. For the whites, Siddura's elegant, refined
Vermentino di Gallura Maia 2014 is fresh and so drinkable, while Cantina Gallura's
Vendemmia Tardiva 2014 is a limited edition of the famous Canayli, produced for
the first time precisely for this fortunate vintage; last, but not least, Pala's
Vermentino di Sardegna Stellato 2014 proves, as we have already said, that the
south can make great whites.

SARDINIA

★★Argiolas

VIA ROMA, 28
09040 SERDIANA [CA]
TEL. 070740606
www.argiolas.it

Capichera

S.S. ARZACHENA-SANT'ANTONIO, KM 4
07021 ARZACHENA [OT]
TEL. 078980612
www.capichera.it

CELLAR SALES
PRE-BOOKED VISITS
ANNUAL PRODUCTION 2,200,000 bottles
HECTARES UNDER VINE 230.00
SUSTAINABLE WINERY

CELLAR SALES
PRE-BOOKED VISITS
ANNUAL PRODUCTION 250,000 bottles
HECTARES UNDER VINE 50.00
SUSTAINABLE WINERY

Volumes have been written about Argiolas, the great Sardinian winery. This venerable cellar can produce over two million bottles and yet still maintain the quality of each one. It has a wide range of labels, all from native varietals planted exclusively in the most favourable production areas. Consequently, as well as its vineyards around Serdiana, it also has some plots in the Sulcis. This year sees two new arrivals: the Is Selis white and red labels, previously sold as IGTs, which have become two top DOC wines, proof of this winery's attention to its chosen area. The Turriga 2011 remains a thoroughbred and wins back the Tre Bicchieri. Compact, austere and displaying great complexity, it is a great Mediterranean red capable of astounding year after year. The 2012 vintage of the wholesome, well-typed Korem is also very good. Finally, the Cerdeña 2011, an excellent oak-aged white which maintains energy and freshness.

Capichera is without doubt synonymous of great Sardinian wine around the world, thanks to the efforts of the Ragnedda family, who have grown their business on quality, reliability and terroir over the decades. Of the whites, the Vermentino speaks for itself. Though the only DOCG is the Vign'angena, the other whites are also made from Gallura's most common grape. In recent years, the use of oak for selections has fallen by the wayside, and even longer-maturing wines have managed to maintain their typicity and authenticity. Rounding off the range are some interesting and very well-crafted reds. Once again the Capichera 2013 is the wine that impresses the most. It manages to combine structure and aromatic complexity with finesse and elegance. Tre Bicchieri to a wine showing a nose of peach and apricots, aromatic herbs, citrus peel, fresh almond and aniseed; a palate that is all supple freshness, and nicely savoury, with good length, despite its impressive breadth. In its first year, the young whippersnapper Albòri di Làmpata is without doubt a great Mediterranean red.

● Turriga '11	♛♛♛ 8
○ Angialis '12	♛♛ 6
○ Cerdeña '11	♛♛ 7
● Korem '12	♛♛ 5
● Antonio Argiolas 100 '11	♛♛ 6
● Cannonau di Sardegna Costera '13	♛♛ 3
● Is Solinas '12	♛♛ 4
● Monica di Sardegna Sup. Is Selis '13	♛♛ 3
○ Nasco di Cagliari Is Selis '14	♛♛ 3
● Monica di Sardegna Perdera '13	♛ 3
○ Nuragus di Cagliari S'Elegas '14	♛ 2
⊙ Serralori Rosato '14	♛ 2
○ Vermentino di Sardegna Costamolino '14	♛ 3
○ Vermentino di Sardegna Merì '14	♛ 3
● Turriga '09	♛♛♛ 8

○ Capichera '13	♛♛♛ 6
● Albòri di Làmpata '11	♛♛ 8
○ Santigaini '11	♛♛ 8
○ Capichera V.T. '13	♛♛ 8
● Mantenghja '10	♛ 6
● Assajè Rosso '12	♛ 6
○ Capichera '12	♛♛♛ 6
○ Capichera '11	♛♛♛ 6
○ Capichera '10	♛♛♛ 5
○ Vermentino di Gallura Vigna'ngena '10	♛♛♛ 5
● Assajè Rosso '11	♛♛ 6
○ Capichera V.T. '12	♛♛ 8
● Liànti '12	♛♛ 4
● Mantenghja '09	♛♛ 8
○ Santigaini '10	♛♛ 8
○ Vermentino di Gallura Vigna'ngena '13	♛♛ 5

Giovanni Maria Cherchi

LOC. SA PALA E SA CHESSA
07049 USINI [SS]
TEL. 079380273
www.vinicolacherchi.it

Chessa

VIA SAN GIORGIO
07049 USINI [SS]
TEL. 3283747069
www.cantinechessa.it

CELLAR SALES
PRE-BOOKED VISITS
ANNUAL PRODUCTION 170,000 bottles
HECTARES UNDER VINE 30.00

CELLAR SALES
PRE-BOOKED VISITS
ANNUAL PRODUCTION 43,000 bottles
HECTARES UNDER VINE 15.00

A lively family-run winery in the Usini district, Cherchi has been a regular entry in the Guide since the early editions. Producing both whites and reds, it has also come up with a Classic Method vermentino sparkler. Indeed, this is one of the best areas for what is Sardinia's iconic white grape variety. The leading red is Cagnulari, made from the grape of the same name, which Cherchi developed, and which is now grown all over the production zone. The star, as ever, is the Vermentino di Sardegna Tuvaoes 2014, with its well-typed aromas of almond and yellow-fleshed fruit. Never buttery, this is a stylish, fresh-tasting and highly drinkable wine. Of the reds, the Luzzana is without doubt in a class of its own. Cagnulari and other estate-owned grapes for hints of scrub and a soft, mouthfilling palate.

It is always a pleasure to find a woman at the helm of a winery, especially a tenacious and enthusiastic wine and vine lover like Giovanna Chessa. The winery can be found in the Usini winegrowing district of northern Sardinia. Despite having relatively few hectares at its disposal, the estate's quality is excellent, based on cagnulari, which has shown great promise in recent years. There is also a delightful, well-typed Vermentino di Sardegna and an IGT red, Lugherra, from Cannonau blended with a substantial base of oak-aged Cagnulari. In its 2012 version, the Lugherra displays brooding ripe red berry aromas, accompanied by spicy hints of tobacco and wood resin. The mouth is close-woven, soft and mouthfilling, shot through with a balsamic freshness that lengthens its clean, pleasant drinkability. No Cagnulari this year and the 2013 was scored last year, so we sampled the Mattariga, a full-flavoured Vermentino di Sardegna with almondy notes.

● Cagnulari '13	▼▼ 3
● Cannonau di Sardegna '13	▼▼ 3
● Luzzana '13	▼▼ 4
○ Vermentino di Sardegna Tuvaoes '14	▼▼ 3
○ Vermentino di Sardegna Filighe Brut '12	▼ 3
○ Vermentino di Sardegna Pigalva '14	▼ 2
● Billia Cagnulari '11	♀♀ 3
● Cagnulari '12	♀♀ 3
● Cagnulari '11	♀♀ 3
● Cagnulari Billia '12	♀♀ 3
● Cannonau di Sardegna '12	♀♀ 3
● Cannonau di Sardegna '11	♀♀ 3*
● Luzzana '12	♀♀ 4
● Luzzana '11	♀♀ 4
○ Vermentino di Sardegna Tuvaoes '13	♀♀ 3
○ Vermentino di Sardegna Tuvaoes '12	♀♀ 3

● Lugherra '12	▼▼ 5
○ Vermentino di Sardegna Mattariga '14	▼▼ 3
● Cagnulari '13	♀♀ 3
● Cagnulari '12	♀♀ 3
● Cagnulari '11	♀♀ 3
● Cagnulari '10	♀♀ 3*
● Cagnulari '09	♀♀ 3*
○ Kentàles	♀♀ 5
● Lugherra '10	♀♀ 5
● Lugherra '09	♀♀ 5
○ Vermentino di Sardegna Mattariga '13	♀♀ 3
○ Vermentino di Sardegna Mattariga '12	♀♀ 3
○ Vermentino di Sardegna Mattariga '10	♀♀ 3

Attilio Contini

VIA GENOVA, 48/50
09072 CABRAS [OR]
TEL. 0783290806
www.vinicontini.it

CELLAR SALES
PRE-BOOKED VISITS
ANNUAL PRODUCTION 800,000 bottles
HECTARES UNDER VINE 70.00
SUSTAINABLE WINERY

One of Sardinia's great private estates, not just in terms of production, but especially for its quality and history, Contini is located in Cabras, near Oristano, an area of unique wines, from the Vernaccia di Oristano all the way up to the Nieddera, a red from the traditional grape variety of the same name. Rounding off the range is a Vermentino, from the winery's Gallura vineyards; Cannonau; and a couple of simple, pleasant sparklers. It also produces several Vernaccias. From ancient vintage Riservas, to the passito, Soleras method, and fresh-tasting, easy-drinking standard-labels, which also have the task of preventing this outstanding varietal from falling into oblivion. The estate's flagship red is the Barrile 2012 from nieddera, combining spicy notes of Mediterranean scrubland, plum and dried roses. The palate is dense, with a good tannic weave, quite full-flavoured with great depth. The Antico Gregori, a non-vintage Vernaccia from Soleras, impresses yet again, while I Giganti is the latest of the whites: refreshing, savoury and sun-drenched.

● Barrile '12	♟♟ 7
○ Vernaccia di Oristano Antico Gregori	♟♟ 8
● Cannonau di Sardegna Inu Ris. '12	♟♟ 4
○ I Giganti - Quarant'anni '12	♟♟ 5
○ Karmis '14	♟♟ 3
○ Pontis '13	♟♟ 5
○ Vermentino di Gallura Elibaria '14	♟♟ 3
○ Vernaccia di Oristano Flor '04	♟♟ 3
○ Brut Attilio	♟ 3
⊙ Brut Attilio Rosé	♟ 3
● Cannonau di Sardegna Sartiglia '14	♟ 3
● Cannonau di Sardegna Tonaghe '14	♟ 2
⊙ Nieddera Rosato '14	♟ 2
● Nieddera Rosso '13	♟ 3
○ Vermentino di Sardegna Parìglia '14	♟ 2
○ Vermentino di Sardegna Tyrsos '14	♟ 2

Ferruccio Deiana

LOC. SU LEUNAXI
VIA GIALETO, 7
09040 SETTIMO SAN PIETRO [CA]
TEL. 070749117
www.ferrucciodeiana.it

CELLAR SALES
PRE-BOOKED VISITS
ANNUAL PRODUCTION 520,000 bottles
HECTARES UNDER VINE 94.00

Ferruccio Deiana is a talented grower and oenologist who runs almost 100 hectares of vineyard in southern Sardinia with passion and charisma. About half his production comes from the vineyards of Su Leunaxi in the municipality of Settimo San Pietro, while the rest comes from Sibiola, a town perfectly suited for wine production, a few miles from the main winery. A wide range of wines, all from traditional varieties planted to suit the characteristics of individual vineyards and to maximize the potential of each cultivar. The Ajana, a red from a blend of traditional varietals, is also very good. The 2012 vintage has come up with a summery wine with a nose of Mediterranean scrub and red berry, and a rich gutsy progression. The ever-excellent Sileno 2012 is a Cannonau di Sardegna Riserva with a nose of roses and wild berries. Of the whites, we liked the Vermentino di Sardegna Arvali 2014 and the sweet Oirad from over-ripe grapes.

● Ajana '12	♟♟ 6
● Cannonau di Sardegna Sileno '13	♟♟ 3
● Cannonau di Sardegna Sileno Ris. '12	♟♟ 4
○ Oirad '13	♟♟ 5
○ Vermentino di Sardegna Arvali '14	♟♟ 3
○ Vermentino di Sardegna Donnikalia '14	♟♟ 2*
⊙ Bellarosa '14	♟ 2
● Monica di Sardegna Karel '13	♟ 2
○ Pluminus '13	♟ 6
● Ajana '02	♟♟♟ 6
● Cannonau di Sardegna Sileno Ris. '10	♟♟♟ 3*
● Ajana '11	♟♟ 6
● Cannonau di Sardegna Sileno '12	♟♟ 3
● Cannonau di Sardegna Sileno Ris. '11	♟♟ 3
● Monica di Sardegna Karel '12	♟♟ 2*
○ Oirad '12	♟♟ 5

Cantine di Dolianova

LOC. SANT'ESU
S.S. 387 KM 17,150
09041 DOLIANOVA [CA]
TEL. 070744101
www.cantinedidolianova.it

CELLAR SALES
PRE-BOOKED VISITS
ANNUAL PRODUCTION 4,000,000 bottles
HECTARES UNDER VINE 1200.00

Cantina di Dolianova is one of Sardinia's
oldest cooperatives, just a few miles
outside Cagliari, in the middle of the
Parteolla area. In recent years, like many
Sardinian cooperative wineries, it has seen
impressive quality hikes, so that it can
produce great wines even bottling large
quantities. This has given the winery a vast
assortment of wines, all focused on
excellent value for money and all made
from native varietals, including the most
widespread aromatic types in the lower
Campidano area. Two different wines stood
out during our tastings. Both reds, one from
the barbera sarda variety, the other from
cannonau. Terresicci 2010 has a nose of
blackberry and autumn leaves, its mouth
stylish and supple. The Cannonau di
Sardegna Blasio Riserva 2010 is warm but
with a nice piquant balsamic freshness that
does not affect its drinkability.

Cantina Dorgali

VIA PIEMONTE, 11
08022 DORGALI [NU]
TEL. 078496143
www.cantinadorgali.com

CELLAR SALES
PRE-BOOKED VISITS
ANNUAL PRODUCTION 1,500,000 bottles
HECTARES UNDER VINE 600.00
SUSTAINABLE WINERY

Cantina Dorgali is one of Sardinia's most
venerable cooperatives. In recent years, to
its credit, it has undergone a remarkable
quality upgrade. After identifying their
growers' best vines, they began producing
top-quality wines which combine drinkability
with a profound attachment to the terroir.
One of the prime areas on the island for
cannonau, there is no lack of older stock
still planted to extremely low-yield bush
vines. Rounding off the range are
Vermentino di Sardegna and two fresh,
drinkable Charmat method sparklers. The
most impressive wine at the tastings could
not have been anything but a Cannonau.
Tre Bicchieri to the newly-denominated
Classico, the D53 '12, featuring alluring
aromas of blackberry, redcurrants and
roses. The palate is warm, mouthfilling and
soft, with a regal freshness that revives its
drinkability and ushers in a clean tangy
finish. We also liked the Hortos, a
cannonau-based IGT topped up with syrah.

Wine	Rating
● Cannonau di Sardegna Blasio Ris. '10	♟♟♟ 3*
● Terresicci '10	♟♟♟ 5
● Cannonau di Sardegna Anzenas '13	♟♟ 2*
● Falconaro '10	♟♟ 3
○ Montesicci '14	♟♟ 3
○ Nuragus di Cagliari Perlas '14	♟♟ 2*
⊙ Sibiola '13	♟ 2
○ Vermentino di Sardegna Naeli '14	♟ 2
○ Vermentino di Sardegna Prendas '14	♟ 2
● Cannonau di Sardegna Anzenas '12	♟♟ 2*
○ Montesicci '13	♟♟ 3
○ Moscato di Cagliari '11	♟♟ 3

Wine	Rating
● Cannonau di Sardegna Cl. D53 '12	♟♟♟ 4*
● Hortos '11	♟♟ 6
● Cannonau di Sardegna V. di Isalle '14	♟♟ 2*
● Cannonau di Sardegna Viniola Ris. '12	♟♟ 4
● Noriolo '12	♟♟ 4
● Bardia '14	♟ 2
● Cannonau di Sardegna Filieri '14	♟ 2
● Cannonau di Sardegna Tunila '14	♟ 2
○ Vermentino di Sardegna Filine '14	♟ 2
● Cannonau di Sardegna Viniola Ris. '10	♟♟♟ 4*
● Cannonau di Sardegna Viniola Ris. '07	♟♟♟ 3*
● Cannonau di Sardegna Viniola Ris. '06	♟♟♟ 3*
● Hortos '08	♟♟♟ 6
● Cannonau di Sardegna Viniola Ris. '11	♟♟ 4
● Hortos '10	♟♟ 6

Giuseppe Gabbas

VIA TRIESTE, 59
08100 NUORO
TEL. 078433745
www.gabbas.it

CELLAR SALES
PRE-BOOKED VISITS
ANNUAL PRODUCTION 70,000 bottles
HECTARES UNDER VINE 20.00

Giuseppe Gabbas is a true winegrower, who divides his time between his vineyards and his casks and bottles in the cellar. This meticulous craftsman has succeeded in producing some of the island's top Cannonau di Sardegna, faithful to the Barbagia tradition, but also highly drinkable, giving them finesse, elegance and great charm, just how Cannonaus should be. Apart from one white, a Manzanile from an area planted to vermentino, the rest is all for Cannonau. Grapes from the youngest vines are used for Lillové, a fresh-tasting wine made only in steel, whereas the older vines are used for Dule and Arbore, two true thoroughbreds. The Cannonau di Sardegna Classico Dule 2012 remains a thoroughbred. With its impeccable fresh acidity, it transmits all the characteristics of a great Mediterranean red, without sacrificing drinkability and finesse. Tre Bicchieri. The slightly more firmly structured Arbore 2012's best feature is its mouthfilling softness.

Cantina Gallura

VIA VAL DI COSSU, 9
07029 TEMPIO PAUSANIA
TEL. 079631241
www.cantinagallura.com

CELLAR SALES
PRE-BOOKED VISITS
ANNUAL PRODUCTION 1,300,000 bottles
HECTARES UNDER VINE 350.00

A veritable benchmark for the whole area, Cantina Gallura is Tempio Pausania's celebrated winery. Undisputed quality, territorial attachment and exceptional value for money throughout the range are the cornerstones of the success for this winery owned by oenologist Dino Addis. Vermentino takes pride of place, though there are also sparklers and sweet wines. The best of the reds are the Cannonau di Sardegna and the Nebbiolo, widespread in Gallura. The new arrival this year is the Canayli Vendemmia Tardiva, an ancient label for a dry, limited-edition wine of fine vintage, and now admitted to the appellation. And this was the wine which most impressed us during the tastings. Tre Bicchieri to the Vermentino di Gallura Canayli V.T. 2014, a white with a nose of almond and summer flowers, with hints of iodates and aromatic herbs leading to a full and caressing palate, warm but also full-flavoured and supple. We also loved the Genesi 2013, a selection of Gallura from one of the best estate vineyards.

● Cannonau di Sardegna Cl. Dule '12	♔♔♔ 4*
● Cannonau di Sardegna Cl. Arbòre '12	♔♔ 4
● Cannonau di Sardegna Lillové '14	♔♔ 2*
○ Vermentino di Sardegna Manzanile '14	♔♔ 3
● Cannonau di Sardegna Cl. Dule '11	♔♔♔ 4*
● Cannonau di Sardegna Dule Ris. '10	♔♔♔ 4*
● Cannonau di Sardegna Dule Ris. '09	♔♔♔ 3*
● Cannonau di Sardegna Dule Ris. '08	♔♔♔ 3*
● Cannonau di Sardegna Dule Ris. '07	♔♔♔ 3*
● Cannonau di Sardegna Dule Ris. '06	♔♔♔ 3*
● Cannonau di Sardegna Dule Ris. '05	♔♔♔ 3*
● Avra '10	♔♔ 5
● Cannonau di Sardegna Arbòre Ris. '10	♔♔ 4
● Cannonau di Sardegna Cl. Arbòre '11	♔♔ 4
● Cannonau di Sardegna Lillové '13	♔♔ 2*
○ Vermentino di Sardegna Manzanile '13	♔♔ 3

○ Vermentino di Gallura Canayli V. T. '14	♔♔♔ 4*
○ Vermentino di Gallura Sup. Genesi '13	♔♔ 5
● Karana '14	♔♔ 2*
○ Vermentino di Gallura Mavriana '14	♔♔ 2*
○ Vermentino di Gallura Piras '14	♔♔ 2*
○ Vermentino di Gallura Sup. Canayli '14	♔♔ 2*
☉ Campos '14	♔ 2
● Cannonau di Sardegna Templum '11	♔ 2
○ Moscato di Tempio Pausania	♔ 3
○ Vermentino di Gallura Brut Gallura '13	♔ 3
○ Vermentino di Gallura Gemellae '14	♔ 2
○ Vermentino di Gallura Sup. Genesi '10	♔♔♔ 5
○ Vermentino di Gallura Sup. Genesi '08	♔♔♔ 5

Cantina Giba - 6Mura

LOC. FUNATANONA
09010 GIBA [CI]
TEL. 0781689718
www.6mura.com

CELLAR SALES
ACCOMMODATION
ANNUAL PRODUCTION 100,000 bottles
HECTARES UNDER VINE 30.00

The corporate restructuring of Cantina Giba (once known as 6 Mura) has in no way damaged its pursuit of quality. On the contrary, it would seem that the winery is enjoying a new lease of life. Deep in Sulcis territory, the star performer here could be none other but the Carignano. It comes in two versions, the 6Mura is the selection from the older bush-trained vines, some of which are ungrafted, planted on sandy soil. The Giba is the simpler, fresher version, from younger vine stock. Rounding off the range are two Vermentino di Sardegnas. Once again 6Mura lives up to expectations. The Carignano del Sulcis 2011 is a fine example of a Mediterranean red, capable of bringing out hints of scrub and spices, red berry and noble wood resins. The mouth is warm yet balanced by sublime tannins and a balsamic acidity which refreshes the palate. The Carignano del Sulcis Giba is juicy and pleasant.

Antichi Poderi Jerzu

VIA UMBERTO I, 1
08044 JERZU [OG]
TEL. 078270028
www.jerzuantichipoderi.it

CELLAR SALES
PRE-BOOKED VISITS
ANNUAL PRODUCTION 1,500,000 bottles
HECTARES UNDER VINE 750.00

Antichi Poderi, the venerable Jerzu cooperative, has now passed the 1.5 million bottle landmark, with member vineyards now covering 750 hectares. Cannonau rules the roost and is found in each one of the reds (except for one Monica di Sardegna). For several years, due in no small part to a significant zoning project carried out by the cellar, the wines have become well-typed and extremely territorial, very much reflecting the conditions at harvest. The Riserva di Cannonaus, their top wines, always need a few years to express themselves fully. The Cannonau di Sardegna Jerzu Josto Miglior Riserva 2012 is the most interesting wine in the range. Red berry and spice aromas to the fore, accompanied by hints of scrub. The mouth is shot through with a balsamic freshness that makes it highly drinkable. The delicious Bantu is a fresh-tasting juicy version of Cannonau di Sardegna.

● Carignano del Sulcis 6Mura '11	♥♥ 5
● Carignano del Sulcis Giba '13	♥♥ 2*
○ Vermentino di Sardegna '14	♥♥ 4
○ Vermentino di Sardegna Giba '14	♥ 2
● Carignano del Sulcis 6Mura '10	♥♥♥ 5
● Carignano del Sulcis 6Mura '09	♥♥♥ 5
● Carignano del Sulcis 6Mura '08	♥♥ 5
● Carignano del Sulcis Giba '12	♥♥ 2*
● Carignano del Sulcis Giba '11	♥♥ 2*
● Carignano del Sulcis Giba '10	♥♥ 2*
● Carignano del Sulcis Giba '09	♥♥ 2*
○ Vermentino di Sardegna '12	♥♥ 4
○ Vermentino di Sardegna '11	♥♥ 4
○ Vermentino di Sardegna Giba '13	♥♥ 2*
○ Vermentino di Sardegna Giba '12	♥♥ 2*

● Cannonau di Sardegna Josto Miglior Ris. '12	♥♥ 5
● Akratos '11	♥♥ 5
● Cannonau di Sardegna Bantu '14	♥♥ 2*
● Cannonau di Sardegna Chuerra Ris. '12	♥♥ 5
● Cannonau di Sardegna Marghia '13	♥♥ 4
⊙ Cannonau di Sardegna Rosato Isara '14	♥ 2
● Monica di Sardegna Camalda '14	♥ 2
○ Vermentino di Sardegna Lucean Le Stelle '14	♥ 3
○ Vermentino di Sardegna Telavè '14	♥ 2
● Cannonau di Sardegna Josto Miglior Ris. '09	♥♥♥ 4*
● Cannonau di Sardegna Josto Miglior Ris. '05	♥♥♥ 4
● Radames '01	♥♥♥ 5

SARDINIA

Alberto Loi

s.s. 125 km 124,1
08040 Cardedu [OG]
Tel. 070240866
www.albertoloi.it

CELLAR SALES
PRE-BOOKED VISITS
ACCOMMODATION
ANNUAL PRODUCTION 250,000 bottles
HECTARES UNDER VINE 53.00

The Loi winery in Cardedu is one of the island's oldest, in a terroir with a strong vocation for Cannonau, embracing the Jerzu subzone. The wines are traditional, authentic and not without a touch of huskiness which very much brings out their origins. Large casks and lengthy ageing are the trademarks, which means the wines retain their charm sometimes for several years after harvest. The range is completed by a Monica di Sardegna, a Vermentino and by the almost unique Leila, a white Cannonau from grapes fermented off the skins. The Riserva Alberto Loi is the most impressive wine of the year. This 2011 wine offers a nose of blackberry, spices, eucalyptus and wood resins. Powerful in the mouth yet very fresh, with well-integrated, velvety tannins, and a clean finish. We also enjoyed the Sa Mola, a fresher, juicier Cannonau di Jerzu.

Masone Mannu

loc. Su Canale
s.s. 199 km 48
07020 Monti [SS]
Tel. 078947140
www.masonemannu.com

CELLAR SALES
PRE-BOOKED VISITS
ANNUAL PRODUCTION 100,000 bottles
HECTARES UNDER VINE 19.00

Despite the new ownership, the production philosophy that enabled Masone Mannu to stand out as one of the top cellars in Gallura and beyond, remains unchanged. While there has been a restyling of bottles and labels, some wine names have remained unaltered, and a few interesting new entries have arrived. The focus is on the Vermentino di Gallura, though there are some successful reds born on the unique granite-based subsoils. The soil here offers exceptional flavour and minerality, which is already clear in the selection of whites. All three Vermentino di Galluras did extremely well. The Superiore Costarenas 2014 was the most impressive, with its nose of aromatic herbs, flowers and white-fleshed fruit. Fresh-tasting and full-flavoured, it shows suppleness and outstanding drinkability. The Petrizza is a simpler wine, but still extremely well-made. Rather more unusual is the Roccaìa, cask-aged for a few months. The best of the reds is the Cannonau di Sardegna Zòjosu.

● Cannonau di Sardegna Jerzu Alberto Loi Ris. '11	▼▼ 3
● Cannonau di Sardegna Jerzu Cardedo Ris. '12	▼▼ 3
● Tuvara '11	▼▼ 5
● Cannonau di Sardegna Jerzu Sa Mola '13	▼ 2
○ Leila '13	▼ 4
○ Vermentino di Sardegna Theria '14	▼ 2
● Astangia '11	♀♀ 4
● Cannonau di Sardegna Jerzu Cardedo Ris. '11	♀♀ 3
○ Leila '12	♀♀ 4
● Loi Corona '10	♀♀ 5
● Tuvara '10	♀♀ 5

○ Vermentino di Gallura Sup. Costarenas '14	▼▼ 3*
● Cannonau di Sardegna Zòjosu '13	▼▼ 3
● Entu '12	▼▼ 5
○ Vermentino di Gallura Petrizza '14	▼▼ 3
● Zùrria '14	▼▼ 3
○ Vermentino di Gallura Sup. Roccaìa '13	▼ 5
⊙ Zeluiu '14	▼ 3
● Mannu '11	♀♀ 8
○ Vermentino di Gallura Petrizza '13	♀♀ 3
○ Zurria '13	♀♀ 2*

Meloni Vini

VIA GALLUS, 79
09047 SELARGIUS [CA]
TEL. 070852822
www.melonivini.com

CELLAR SALES
PRE-BOOKED VISITS
ANNUAL PRODUCTION 1,000,000 bottles
HECTARES UNDER VINE 200.00
VITICULTURE METHOD Certified Organic
SUSTAINABLE WINERY

Welcome back to the Meloni winery from Selargius among the full-length profiles. This outstanding old family-run winery boasts around 200 hectares under vine, all grown organically and dating back to well before the term "organic" became common in wine parlance. The updated image and labels coincide with a revamp of winemaking, going for the finest quality to uncovering the prime vine stock and areas for the production of traditional varieties. We especially liked the aromatic wines, especially those from the native nasco and giro varieties. The Cannonau di Sardegna Le Ghiaie 2009 is excellent, with its nose of dried roses and crushed wild berries and its fresh-tasting, menthol notes on a very deep palate. Both Vermentino di Sardegnas were excellent, especially the tangier, vibrant Le Sabbie 2014. Well-crafted and distinctive, the Frius is a cuve close sparkler from vermentino grapes.

● Cannonau di Sardegna Le Ghiaie Ris. '09	🏆🏆	4
○ Vermentino di Sardegna Le Sabbie '14	🏆🏆	3
○ Vermentino di Sardegna Frius	🏆	2
○ Vermentino di Sardegna Salike '14	🏆	2
● Cannonau di Sardegna Le Ghiaie Ris. '08	🏆🏆	3
● Cannonau di Sardegna Le Ghiaie Ris. '07	🏆🏆	4
● Cannonau di Sardegna Terreforru '10	🏆🏆	2*
● Cannonau di Sardegna Terreforru '09	🏆🏆	2*
● Girò di Cagliari Donna Jolanda '08	🏆🏆	3
○ Malvasia di Cagliari Donna Jolanda '11	🏆🏆	3
○ Moscato di Cagliari Donna Jolanda '09	🏆🏆	3
○ Moscato di Cagliari Donna Jolanda '08	🏆🏆	3
● Nue Rosso '11	🏆🏆	2*
○ Malvasia di Cagliari Donna Jolanda '08	🏆	3

Mesa

LOC. SU BARONI
09010 SANT'ANNA ARRESI [CA]
TEL. 0781965057
www.cantinamesa.it

CELLAR SALES
PRE-BOOKED VISITS
ANNUAL PRODUCTION 757,000 bottles
HECTARES UNDER VINE 43.00

Mesa is a Sulcis winery owned by the advertising guru Gavino Sanna. In recent years it has begun producing top-quality wines, perfectly rooted in the territory and with great cellarability. The Carignano del Sulcis is the most representative wine and is produced in various versions, from the fresher standard-labels, to the Riservas from the older vines, still bush-trained on sand. This year sees three new reds. A Riserva di Carignano named Gavino, a syrah (from Sulcis estate-owned vineyards), and a cagnulari from vines in the Usini area. The whites, by contrast, are all from vermentino. A fantastic performance this year for the Sant'Anna Arresi winery. All of the wines are well-typed, starting from the Buio Buio. A Tre Bicchieri goes to a Carignano del Sulcis Riserva with notes of ripe red berry fruit and Mediterranean scrubland. Crisp and plush on the palate, with textbook length. Other fine wines include the latest arrival, the Gavino, and the Opale Dopo, a vin de garde largely from vermentino.

● Carignano del Sulcis Buio Buio Ris. '12	🏆🏆🏆	5
● Carignano del Sulcis Gavino Ris. '11	🏆🏆	5
○ Opale Dopo '12	🏆🏆	5
● Brace Cagnulari '14	🏆🏆	4
● Brama Syrah '14	🏆🏆	4
○ Orodoro '13	🏆🏆	5
● Cannonau di Sardegna Moro '13	🏆	3
● Cannonau di Sardegna Primo Scuro '14	🏆	2
⊙ Carignano del Sulcis Rosa Grande '14	🏆	3
○ Vermentino di Sardegna Giunco '14	🏆	3
○ Vermentino di Sardegna Primo Bianco '14	🏆	2
● Buio Buio '10	🏆🏆🏆	4*

Cantina di Mogoro
Il Nuraghe

S.S. 131 KM 62
09095 MOGORO [OR]
TEL. 0783990285
www.cantinadimogoro.it

CELLAR SALES
PRE-BOOKED VISITS
ANNUAL PRODUCTION 850,000 bottles
HECTARES UNDER VINE 480.00

Cantina di Mogoro is located in upper Marmilla, in Oristano province, and owes its name to the nearby village and to the Cuccurada nuraghe, one of the most spectacular historical monuments in the area. Grapes have been grown here since time immemorial, especially semidano, native to the area and from which the Mogoro DOC is made, and bovale from the Alto Campidano. The winery has been focusing on the Semidano di Mogoro for some time, believing it to be a special white capable of defying the passage of time. The Puistèris 2012 is an exceptional Semidano di Mogoro Superiore, with its surprising notes of hedgerow flowers, fresh almond, aromatic herbs and lemon zest. Its complex palate is equally distinguished and the wine shows freshness and energy, vitality and a good supporting acidity even three years after harvest. A nice clean finish, long and very stylish.

Giovanni Montisci

VIA ASIAGO, 7B
08024 MAMOIADA [NU]
TEL. 0784569021
www.barrosu.it

CELLAR SALES
PRE-BOOKED VISITS
ANNUAL PRODUCTION 6,000 bottles
HECTARES UNDER VINE 2.00

Mamoiada, heart of Barbagia and of Cannonau di Sardegna production is a land of farmers and talented winegrowers. Without doubt one of these is Giovanni Montisci, a charismatic figure who does nothing to conceal his passion for vine and wine. Just a few hectares of gobelet-trained vines used for two Riserva di Cannonaus of which the Franzisca from the estate-owned century-old vine. Then we have the Rosato, also from cannonau, and a Moscato vinified with almost no residual sugar from a small vineyard in Mamoiada. The Cannonau di Sardegna Franzisca Riserva 2012 fully embodies the spirit of the Mamoiada terroir. With its nose of dried roses, myrtle, plum and blueberry, it has a stylish, supple progression despite its high alcohols which give it mouthfilling softness. It finishes with a balsamic note, with hints of wood resin, though sweet, ripe tannins prevent it from erring into edginess. A well-crafted and very charming wine. This year's Rosato was also excellent.

○ Semidano di Mogoro Sup. Puistèris '12	🍷🍷 4
● Cannonau di Sardegna Chio Ris. '11	🍷🍷 5
● Cannonau di Sardegna Vignaruja '13	🍷🍷 2*
● Terralba Bovale '12	🍷🍷 2*
● Terralba Bovale Tiernu '13	🍷🍷 2*
○ Anastasia Brut	🍷 3
● Cannonau di Sardegna Nero Sardo '13	🍷 2
● Monica di Sardegna San Bernardino '12	🍷 2
● Monica di Sardegna Sup. Nabui '11	🍷 5
☉ Rosé Frizzante '14	🍷 2
○ Semidano di Mogoro Anastasia '14	🍷 2
○ Vermentino di Sardegna Don Giovanni '14	🍷 2
○ Semidano di Mogoro Sup. Puistèris '10	🍷🍷🍷 4*
○ Semidano di Mogoro Sup. Puistèris '11	🍷🍷 4

● Cannonau di Sardegna Franzisca Ris. '12	🍷🍷 6
☉ Rosato '14	🍷🍷 2*
● Cannonau di Sardegna Barrosu Franzisca Ris. '11	🍷🍷🍷 6
● Cannonau di Sardegna Barrosu '09	🍷🍷 6
● Cannonau di Sardegna Barrosu Ris. '11	🍷🍷 6
● Cannonau di Sardegna Barrosu Ris. '10	🍷🍷 6
● Cannonau di Sardegna Barrosu Ris. '09	🍷🍷 6
● Cannonau di Sardegna Franzisca Ris. '10	🍷🍷 6
● Cannonau di Sardegna Rosato '12	🍷🍷 3

Mura

LOC. AZZANIDÒ, 1
07020 LOIRI PORTO SAN PAOLO [OT]
TEL. 078941070
www.vinimura.it

CELLAR SALES
PRE-BOOKED VISITS
RESTAURANT SERVICE
ANNUAL PRODUCTION 50,000 bottles
HECTARES UNDER VINE 12.00

Siblings Marianna and Salvatore Mura run their family winery with great dedication and passion. We are in Gallura, in a prime area for Vermentino, but also for several other of the island's traditional cultivars. In recent years, the winery has produced increasingly terroir-oriented wines, with great drinkability and a mineral backdrop forged by the weathering of the granite so typical of north-eastern Sardinia. This unique characteristic has helped Mura wines show delicacy, elegance, aromatic cleanliness and, in the best years, great ageworthiness. The Vermentino di Gallura Superiore Sienda 2014 is doubtless the most impressive of the line. With its nose of aromatic herbs, fresh almond, hedgerow and citrus hints, its vibrant drinkability flows across the palate. Acidity in the mouth ushers in a clean and full-flavoured finale. Also well made, the Vermentino di Gallura Cheremi and the Cortes 2014, a juicy fresh Cannonau.

Pala

VIA VERDI, 7
09040 SERDIANA [CA]
TEL. 070740284
www.pala.it

CELLAR SALES
PRE-BOOKED VISITS
ANNUAL PRODUCTION 490,000 bottles
HECTARES UNDER VINE 98.00

The Pala winery has become a benchmark for Sardinian winemaking. Not only for the undisputable quality of its wines but also for the entrepreneurial and managerial skills which have taken Pala labels around the world, and into leading restaurants and wine stores. This is all down to Mario Pala and family, who devote their lives to vine and wine. It has a wide range made from native cultivars grown in nearby vineyards and a few ungrafted vines on sandy plots around Oristano, mainly the bovale vine variety, which the winery has set great store by. The Cannonau di Sardegna Riserva 2013 was once again excellent, a great example of how this varietal manages to come up with fine, graceful wines. The Tre Bicchieri, though, went to the Stellato, a textbook Vermentino di Sardegna 2014, featuring savoury, salty notes and a lengthy palate.

○ Vermentino di Gallura Sup. Sienda '14	♟♟ 3*
● Cannonau di Sardegna Cortes '14	♟♟ 3
○ Vermentino di Gallura Cheremi '14	♟♟ 3
● Cannonau di Sardegna Prisma '14	♟ 2
○ Vermentino di Sardegna Prisma '14	♟ 2
○ Vermentino di Gallura Sup. Sienda '13	♟♟♟ 3*
● Baja '11	♟♟ 5
● Cannonau di Sardegna Cortes '10	♟♟ 2*
○ Vermentino di Gallura Cheremi '13	♟♟ 3
○ Vermentino di Gallura Cheremi '12	♟♟ 3
○ Vermentino di Gallura Cheremi '11	♟♟ 2*
○ Vermentino di Gallura Sup. Sienda '12	♟♟ 3*
○ Vermentino di Gallura Sup. Sienda '11	♟♟ 4
○ Vermentino di Gallura Sup. Sienda Il Decennio '11	♟♟ 3*
○ Vermentino di Sardegna Prisma '13	♟♟ 2*

○ Vermentino di Sardegna Stellato '14	♟♟♟ 3*
● Cannonau di Sardegna Ris. '13	♟♟ 3*
○ Assoluto '14	♟♟ 5
● Cannonau di Sardegna I Fiori '14	♟♟ 2*
○ Entemari '13	♟♟ 4
● Essentija '12	♟♟ 3
○ Nuragus di Cagliari I Fiori '14	♟♟ 2*
● S'Arai '12	♟♟ 5
⊙ Chiaro di Stelle '14	♟ 3
● Monica di Sardegna I Fiori '14	♟ 2
○ Silenzi Bianco '14	♟ 2
⊙ Silenzi Rosato '14	♟ 2
● Silenzi Rosso '14	♟ 2
● Siray '12	♟ 3
○ Vermentino di Sardegna I Fiori '14	♟ 2

Cantina Pedres

ZONA IND. SETTORE 7
07026 OLBIA
TEL. 0789595075
www.cantinapedres.it

CELLAR SALES
PRE-BOOKED VISITS
ANNUAL PRODUCTION 290,000 bottles
HECTARES UNDER VINE 40.00

The Pedres estate, headed up by Antonella Mancini, manages 40 hectares of vineyard in Gallura. Antonella is one of the Mancini family, who have been making wine on the island since the late 19th century. The estate's leading lights are the Vermentino di Gallura, vinified to obtain a highly refined, subtle, refreshing white, displaying the purity this variety offers in the Gallura terroir. The reds are also faithful exponents of the terroir: fresh and fragrant with an up-front vibrant fruitiness. Rounding off the range are some Charmat method sparklers, both dry and sweet, featuring a noteworthy Moscato di Tempio. The two most surprising wines during the tastings were the Vermentino di Gallura Superiore Thilibas 2014, one of the most focused in its category, with its flowery notes of aromatic herbs; and the delicious Cannonau di Sardegna Sulitài 2013 with its red berry aromas.

● Cannonau di Sardegna Sulitài '13	▼▼ 3
○ Moscato di Sardegna Spumante	▼▼ 3
○ Vermentino di Gallura Sup. Thilibas '14	▼▼ 4
⊙ Brut Rosé	▼ 3
○ Gaio Brut	▼ 3
○ Moscato di Sardegna Assolo	▼ 4
● Muros '14	▼ 4
○ Vermentino di Gallura Brino '14	▼ 3
○ Vermentino di Sardegna Colline '14	▼ 2
○ Vermentino di Gallura Sup. Thilibas '09	♀♀♀ 3*
○ Moscato di Sardegna	♀♀ 3
○ Vermentino di Gallura Brino '13	♀♀ 3

Agricola Punica

LOC. BARRUA
09010 SANTADI [CI]
TEL. 0781941012
www.agripunica.it

PRE-BOOKED VISITS
ANNUAL PRODUCTION 310,000 bottles
HECTARES UNDER VINE 70.00

It took Agricola Punica, this lovely Sulcis winery, just a few years to become one of the most impressive Sardinian winegrowers. Its wines, from carignano, the top Sulcis grape variety, and from various international varietals which have found a home here, have a modern though never banal outlook. They produce two Bordeaux-blend reds for the first and second label wines, and in recent years an interesting sunny, lip-smacking white too. The estate is still owned by the joint venture belonging to the Santadi winery and Tenuta San Guido. The Barrua did extremely well, cementing its place among the island's great reds. The 2012 vintage has aromas of myrtle, spices and a chewy red berry ushering in a slim-bodied palate, soft tannins and a long, clean finale. Tre Bicchieri. Another excellence from this year's crop is the simpler, drinkable Montessu 2013, with textbook aromatic complexity.

● Barrua '12	▼▼▼ 6
● Montessu '13	▼▼ 4
○ Samas '14	▼ 3
● Barrua '10	♀♀♀ 6
● Barrua '07	♀♀♀ 6
● Barrua '05	♀♀♀ 5
● Barrua '11	♀♀ 6
● Barrua '09	♀♀ 6
● Barrua '08	♀♀ 6
● Barrua '06	♀♀ 5
● Montessu '12	♀♀ 4
● Montessu '11	♀♀ 4
● Montessu '10	♀♀ 4
● Montessu '09	♀♀ 4

Santa Maria La Palma

LOC. SANTA MARIA LA PALMA
07041 ALGHERO [SS]
TEL. 079999008
www.santamarialapalma.it

CELLAR SALES
PRE-BOOKED VISITS
ANNUAL PRODUCTION 4,000,000 bottles
HECTARES UNDER VINE 700.00

An ancient Alghero-based cooperative winery, a few years ago Santa Maria La Palma embarked on a strategy that has led it to produce not only pleasing, well-made wines, but also champions that can compete with the best labels the island can offer. The credit goes to the non-stop experimentation on varieties and vines which is beginning to pay off. Just like any cooperative, the range of wines is truly vast, all characterized by exceptional value for money, pride of place going to the native varietals, together with a few international grapes that have managed to acclimatize to the Alghero area. The Cannonau di Sardegna Le Bombarde has a nose of myrtle, spices and dried roses. In the mouth it is fresh-tasting and easy-drinking with a characteristic savoury finish. Both the Vermentino di Sardegna I Papiri 2014 and the Aragosta 2014, the Italian DOC label with the highest number of bottles produced. The interesting Akenta, an Extra Dry sparkler from vermentino, has sweetish, fruit-driven notes.

● Cannonau di Sardegna Le Bombarde '14	♟♟ 2*
● Cannonau di Sardegna Valmell '14	♟♟ 2*
○ Vermentino di Sardegna Aragosta '14	♟♟ 2*
○ Vermentino di Sardegna I Papiri '14	♟♟ 3
⊙ Cannonau di Sardegna Punta Rosa '14	♟ 2
● Monica di Sardegna Sup. '13	♟ 2
○ Vermentino di Sardegna Blu '14	♟ 2
○ Vermentino di Sardegna Extra Dry Akenta	♟ 3
● Alghero Cagnulari '11	♟♟ 3
● Cannonau di Sardegna Le Bombarde '13	♟♟ 2*
● Cannonau di Sardegna R Ris. '10	♟♟ 4
● Cannonau di Sardegna Valmell '13	♟♟ 2*

★Cantina di Santadi

VIA CAGLIARI, 78
09010 SANTADI [CI]
TEL. 0781950127
www.cantinadisantadi.it

CELLAR SALES
PRE-BOOKED VISITS
ANNUAL PRODUCTION 1,700,000 bottles
HECTARES UNDER VINE 606.00

Santadi is one of the major cooperatives in Sardinia, not so much in terms of quantity but for the quality drive it has been on since the 1970s. This had encouraged quality growth at other cooperative wineries and private estates, which have wagered on traditional varieties, territory-dedicated wines and others capable of defying the passage of time. All credit should go to Antonello Pilloni, who was chairman for 40 years. This is Carignano country, and reds are based almost exclusively on this Sulcis grape. Several members tend the most beautiful vineyards on sand in the area, some centenarian and ungrafted, the secret behind the authenticity of labels such as Terre Brune or Rocca Rubia, a surprisingly affordable Riserva produced in tens of thousands of bottles. The thoroughbred remains the Terre Brune, which wins yet another Tre Bicchieri. The 2011 is a warm sun-drenched wine with hints of Mediterranean scrub and ripe berries. Also delicious is Shardana, a blend of carignano and other traditional varietals.

● Carignano del Sulcis Sup. Terre Brune '11	♟♟♟ 7
● Shardana '10	♟♟ 5
● Cannonau di Sardegna Noras '12	♟♟ 4
● Carignano del Sulcis Grotta Rossa '13	♟♟ 2*
● Carignano del Sulcis Rocca Rubia Ris. '12	♟♟ 4
○ Latinia '09	♟♟ 5
● Araja '13	♟ 3
⊙ Carignano del Sulcis Rosato Tre Torri '14	♟ 2
● Monica di Sardegna Antigua '14	♟ 2
○ Nuragus di Cagliari Pedraia '14	♟ 2
○ Solais Gran Cuvée	♟
○ Vermentino di Sardegna Cala Silente '14	♟ 3
○ Vermentino di Sardegna Villa Solais '14	♟ 2
○ Villa di Chiesa '13	♟ 5
● Carignano del Sulcis Sup. Terre Brune '10	♟♟♟ 7

SARDINIA

Sardus Pater

VIA RINASCITA, 46
09017 SANT'ANTIOCO [CI]
TEL. 0781800274
www.cantinesarduspater.com

CELLAR SALES
PRE-BOOKED VISITS
ANNUAL PRODUCTION 600,000 bottles
HECTARES UNDER VINE 295.00

Sardus Pater is a cooperative based in Sant'Antioco, a Sulcis outfit that brings together growers from all over the area, accounting for some 300 hectares of vines. These are ancient plots, some ungrafted and planted in sandy soils. The Carignano is the mainstay red, together with a few Vermentinos, a distinctive champagne method recently launched, and sweet wines from aromatic varieties. The flagships include the Carignano del Sulcis Superiore Arruga, the finest expression of the appellation, though we are going to wait till next year to taste the new vintage. We found the Carignano del Sulcis Is Arenas Riserva 2011 the most typical and complex wine in the range. Ripe fruit and bramble jelly on the nose are the prelude to a soft, mouthfilling palate. The Carignano del Sulcis Nur 2013 is a fresh-tasting, highly drinkable red. The other wines were also well-crafted.

Wine	Rating
● Carignano del Sulcis Is Arenas Ris. '11	♀♀ 4
● Carignano del Sulcis Nur '13	♀♀ 2*
○ Moscato di Cagliari Amentos '14	♀♀ 4
○ Vermentino di Sardegna Lugore '14	♀♀ 3
● Cannonau di Sardegna Foras '13	♀ 2
● Carignano del Sulcis Is Solus '12	♀ 2
⊙ Carignano del Sulcis Rosato Horus '14	♀ 2
● Monica di Sardegna Insula '14	♀ 2
○ Vermentino di Sardegna Terre Fenicie '14	♀ 2
● Carignano del Sulcis Is Arenas Ris. '09	♀♀♀ 4*
● Carignano del Sulcis Is Arenas Ris. '08	♀♀♀ 4*
● Carignano del Sulcis Sup. Arruga '09	♀♀♀ 6
● Carignano del Sulcis Sup. Arruga '07	♀♀♀ 5

Giuseppe Sedilesu

VIA VITTORIO EMANUELE II, 64
08024 MAMOIADA [NU]
TEL. 078456791
www.giuseppesedilesu.com

CELLAR SALES
PRE-BOOKED VISITS
ANNUAL PRODUCTION 120,000 bottles
HECTARES UNDER VINE 17.00

The Sedilesus are an important winemaking family based in Mamoiada, a Barbagia village where viticulture has been rooted for decades. The winery gave a strong impetus to viticulture in the area, producing well-crafted wines that express the terroir, but was also capable of building a good sales network to distribute its labels around Italy and the world. Here everything is cannonau di Sardegna, except for a white grape type, known locally as granazza, which produces a few bottles of a distinctive and semi-aromatic wine of which the Sulle Bucce version is well worth trying. Returning to the reds, the range is classified by vineyard age and soil type. Some Riservas are the product of older, bush-trained vines located at higher altitudes. The Cannonau di Sardegna Mamuthone 2012 embodies Sedilesu's thinking when it comes to this esteemed black grape. With its primary fragrance of rose, forest fruits and spices, it has an alcoholic mouthfeel, warm but never burning, and a nuanced balsamic acidity, slightly tangy with velvety tannins. It fully deserves its Tre Bicchieri.

Wine	Rating
● Cannonau di Sardegna Mamuthone '12	♀♀♀ 3*
● Cannonau di Sardegna Sartiu '12	♀♀ 3
○ Perda Pintà '13	♀♀ 5
● Cannonau di Sardegna Carnevale Ris. '11	♀ 5
⊙ Cannonau di Sardegna Erèssia '13	♀ 3
○ Perda Pintà Sulle Bucce '12	♀ 5
● Cannonau di Sardegna Mamuthone '11	♀♀♀ 3*
● Cannonau di Sardegna Mamuthone '08	♀♀♀ 3*
○ Perda Pintà '09	♀♀♀ 4
○ Perda Pintà '07	♀♀♀ 5
● Cannonau di Sardegna Ballu Tundu Ris. '10	♀♀ 6
● Cannonau di Sardegna Giuseppe Sedilesu Ris. '10	♀♀ 3*
● Cannonau di Sardegna Gràssia Ris. '11	♀♀ 3
● Cannonau di Sardegna Sartiu '09	♀♀ 3
○ Perda Pintà '12	♀♀ 5

★★Tenute Sella & Mosca

LOC. I PIANI
07041 ALGHERO [SS]
TEL. 079997700
www.sellaemosca.com

CELLAR SALES
PRE-BOOKED VISITS
ANNUAL PRODUCTION 6,700,000 bottles
HECTARES UNDER VINE 541.00

Sella & Mosca is without doubt the biggest Sardinian winery and among the largest in Italy. Established in the late 19th century, this estate is one of the brightest stars in the island's winemaking firmament, achieving excellent quality as well as quantity. Apart from a few hectares in Gallura and Sulcis, the main estate has over 500 hectares under vine on a single plot surrounding the winery, a few kilometres from Alghero. The winery grows traditional grape varieties, as well as international cultivars like cabernet sauvignon and sauvignon blanc which seem to have found their natural habitat here. This is also the only estate to grow torbato, a special white grape that produces intriguing, long-lived wines. Two wines stood out during the tastings. The Marchese di Villamarina 2010 is a great Mediterranean red, monovarietal cabernet sauvignon. Elegant and highly drinkable, it shows aromas of grass and Mediterranean scrub. The Monteoro, a Vermentino di Gallura 2014 with a citrussy floral nose, garnered a Tre Bicchieri for its outstanding complexity.

○ Vermentino di Gallura Sup. Monteoro '14	♥♥♥ 3*
● Alghero Marchese di Villamarina '10	♥♥ 6
○ Alghero Monteluce Passito '13	♥♥ 5
● Alghero Tanca Farrà Ris. '11	♥♥ 4
○ Alghero Torbato Terre Bianche Cuvée 161 '14	♥♥ 3
⊙ Alghero Oleandro '14	♥ 3
○ Alghero Thilion '14	♥ 4
○ Alghero Torbato Terre Bianche '14	♥ 3
● Cannonau di Sardegna Dimonios Ris. '11	♥ 3
● Monica di Sardegna Acino M '13	♥ 3
○ Vermentino di Sardegna Cala Reale '14	♥ 3
○ Vermentino di Sardegna La Cala '14	♥ 3
● Alghero Marchese di Villamarina '09	♥♥♥ 6

Siddùra

LOC. SIDDURA
07020 LUOGOSANTO [OT]
TEL. 0796513027
www.siddura.com

CELLAR SALES
PRE-BOOKED VISITS
ANNUAL PRODUCTION 90,000 bottles
HECTARES UNDER VINE 37.00

One of the most impressive wineries in recent years has been Siddura, based in Luogosanto. Focusing on developing its local territory, it began with the vineyards, beautiful plots on rolling promontories in the heart of Gallura, and then moved on to the technical facilities and hospitality areas. Everything here is crafted down to the nearest detail, as is clear from the wines. Extremely clean, fresh and invitingly drinkable, they never lose contact with their territory of origin, and this gives them a rather unique charm. In addition to the Vermentino di Galluras, there is also space for the reds, some of which come from estate-owned Gallura vineyards, with others from prime Sardinian subzones such as Usini, home to the cagnulari cultivar. Maìa, a Vermentino di Gallura Superiore 2014, is a white with a nose of white-fleshed fruit and citrus fruit, fresh almond and spring flowers. A lean palate underpinned by acidity and a delicate, piquant finale complete the flavours. It wins its first Tre Bicchieri. The Bèru 2013 is rather too anchored to its woody notes, while among the reds we appreciated the Bàcco, a monovarietal cagnulari.

○ Vermentino di Gallura Sup. Maìa '14	♥♥♥ 4*
● Bàcco Cagnulari '14	♥♥ 5
● Èrema '14	♥♥ 3
● Tiros '14	♥ 6
○ Vermentino di Gallura Sup. Bèru '13	♥ 6
● Bàcco Cagnulari '13	♀♀ 5
● Cannonau di Sardegna Fòla '13	♀♀ 3
● Èrema '13	♀♀ 3
● Tiros '12	♀♀ 6
○ Vermentino di Gallura Sup. Maìa '13	♀♀ 5

Tenute Soletta

LOC. SIGNOR'ANNA
07040 CODRONGIANOS [SS]
TEL. 079435067
www.tenutesoletta.it

CELLAR SALES
PRE-BOOKED VISITS
ANNUAL PRODUCTION 100,000 bottles
HECTARES UNDER VINE 15.00
VITICULTURE METHOD Certified Organic

The Soletta winery belongs to Umberto Soletta, a vigneron extraordinaire who has always produced wines emblematic of the terroir. We are in Codrongianus, a small village in Sassari province, on a prime hillside estate for viticulture. Production is based around native varietals, mainly cannonau, vermentino and moscato, and international cultivars with which Soletta has been experimenting for years. The wines have a firm backbone, while still showing freshness and drinkability. That explains why the Riserva di Cannonau di Sardegnas in particular withstand lengthy ageing, only reaching full pleasurableness several years after harvest. The Keramos is the most important Cannonau di Sardegna selection. This Riserva 2011 with its aromas of myrtle and ripe dark berries combining with spices, wood resin and autumn leaves. The mouth is muscular, stiff and warm, balanced with a fresh-tasting acidity ushering in lingering balsam notes. The Chimera 2014 and the Corona Majore 2012 were also excellent.

● Cannonau di Sardegna Corona Majore '12	♥♥ 4
● Cannonau di Sardegna Keramos Ris. '11	♥♥ 5
○ Vermentino di Sardegna Chimera '14	♥♥ 4
○ Hermes '07	♥ 4
⊙ Prius '14	♥ 3
○ Vermentino di Sardegna Sardo '14	♥ 3
● Cannonau di Sardegna Keramos Ris. '07	♥♥♥ 5
● Cannonau di Sardegna Keramos Ris. '04	♥♥♥ 4
● Cannonau di Sardegna Corona Majore '11	♥♥ 4
● Cannonau di Sardegna Keramos Ris. '10	♥♥ 5
○ Vermentino di Sardegna Chimera '13	♥♥ 4

Su Entu

S.DA PROV.LE KM 1,800
09025 SANLURI [CA]
TEL. 07093571200
www.cantinesuentu.com

CELLAR SALES
PRE-BOOKED VISITS
ANNUAL PRODUCTION 30,000 bottles
HECTARES UNDER VINE 32.00

Just an hour's drive from Cagliari, the wonderful inland Marmilla area used to be the cradle of wheat and a vast wine area. Although this has now changed, it is a pleasure to see local entrepreneurs investing in the area's agriculture, as in the case of Su Entu, a winery founded recently by Salvatore Pilloni, an entrepreneur from Sanluri. The aim is to breathe new life into the countryside by creating quality wines strongly expressive of their terroir. This was achieved by building a cutting-edge cellar with the finest technology, focusing in particular on environmental sustainability. Young vineyards and traditional varieties already offer highly drinkable wines and their future looks rosy indeed. The delicious Cannonau di Sardegna 2013 hinges around fresh-tasting varietal notes. Its aromas of rose, wild strawberry and spices are the prelude to a deep, juicy palate. The well-crafted Vermentino di Sardegna is simple, while a bright future beckons for the Bovale, with its rather impressive 2013 version.

● Bovale '13	♥♥ 3*
● Cannonau di Sardegna '13	♥♥ 3
○ Passito '13	♥♥ 5
○ Aromatico '14	♥ 3
○ Vermentino di Sardegna '14	♥ 3
○ Aromatico '13	♥♥ 3
● Cannonau di Sardegna '12	♥♥ 3
● Cannonau di Sardegna '11	♥♥ 3
○ Vermentino di Sardegna '13	♥♥ 3

Vigne Surrau

S.DA PROV.LE ARZACHENA - PORTO CERVO
07021 ARZACHENA [OT]
TEL. 078982933
www.vignesurrau.it

CELLAR SALES
PRE-BOOKED VISITS
ANNUAL PRODUCTION 300,000 bottles
HECTARES UNDER VINE 43.00
SUSTAINABLE WINERY

Surrau, just outside Arzachena in the heart
of Gallura, is a young estate and in just ten
years has built up an outstanding list of
labels, making territorial wines of the
highest quality, designed for ageing. On
top of all this they have built a superb
visitor centre, open all year round, hosting
exhibitions, events and tastings, in addition
to the vinification areas. From the
beginning the winery has focused on reds,
as well as on the Vermentino di Gallura, in
the belief that granite weathering would
also prove ideal for red varieties. Once
again, the most impressive wine in the
range was the Sciala, a Vermentino di
Gallura, which in this good vintage year
earned itself a Tre Bicchieri. With its nose
of fresh almond, and aniseed notes
ushering in hints of citrus, hedgerow and
aromatic herbs. Also outstanding was the
Barriu 2012, a blend of cannonau,
carignano, cabernet and muristellu.

○ Vermentino di Gallura Sup. Sciala '14	♟♟♟ 5
● Barriu '12	♟♟ 5
○ Vermentino di Gallura Sup. Sciala V.T. '14	♟♟ 5
● Cannonau di Sardegna Sincaru '13	♟♟ 5
● Rosso Surrau '13	♟♟ 4
○ Vermentino di Gallura Branu '14	♟♟ 3
● Surrau '09	♟♟♟ 4*
○ Vermentino di Gallura Sup. Sciala '13	♟♟♟ 5
○ Vermentino di Gallura Sup. Sciala '12	♟♟♟ 5
● Barriu '11	♟♟ 5
● Barriu '10	♟♟ 5
● Cannonau di Sardegna Sincaru '12	♟♟ 5
● Cannonau di Sardegna Sincaru '10	♟♟ 5
● Cannonau di Sardegna Sincaru Ris. '09	♟♟ 5
● Rosso Surrau '12	♟♟ 4
○ Vermentino di Gallura Sup. Sciala V.T. '12	♟♟ 5

Cantina Trexenta

V.LE PIEMONTE, 40
09040 SENORBÌ [CA]
TEL. 0709808863
www.cantinatrexenta.it

CELLAR SALES
PRE-BOOKED VISITS
ANNUAL PRODUCTION 1,000,000 bottles
HECTARES UNDER VINE 350.00

Cantina Trexenta is named after the area
where it operates and is a large
cooperative inaugurated in the 1950s.
With 200 working partners and about 350
hectares of vineyard, production reaches
one million bottles. The cooperative
produces a wide range of wines, all very
good value for money. Cannonau rules the
roost and is labelled in various versions
according to the quality of the grapes and
the vineyard they hail from. Overall we
found it to be the most complete and
authentic wine produced, a unique
southern Sardinian expression of the
varietal. Rounding off the range are
monica, nuragus, vermentino and a few
aromatic varieties. The Tanca su Conti is a
Cannonau di Sardegna Riserva 2010 with
Mediterranean scrub and spicy aromas
and a fresh, supple palate. Monica di
Sardegna Duca di Mandas 2012 is soft
and caressing, while the Nuragus di
Cagliari Tenute San Mauro 2014 is as
reliable as ever. The other wines were also
well-typed.

● Cannonau di Sardegna Corte Auda '13	♟♟ 2*
● Cannonau di Sardegna Tanca su Conti Ris. '10	♟♟ 4
● Monica di Sardegna Duca di Mandas '12	♟♟ 2*
○ Nuragus di Cagliari Tenute San Mauro '14	♟♟ 2*
● Cannonau di Sardegna Baione '13	♟ 2
● Cannonau di Sardegna Bingias '13	♟ 2
● Cannonau di Sardegna Goimajor '13	♟ 2
● Monica di Sardegna Bingias '12	♟ 2
○ Vermentino di Sardegna Bingias '14	♟ 2
○ Vermentino di Sardegna Contissa '14	♟ 2
○ Vermentino di Sardegna Donna Leonora '14	♟ 2
○ Vermentino di Sardegna Monteluna '14	♟ 2
● Cannonau di Sardegna Baione '12	♟♟ 2*

Tenuta Asinara

LOC. MARRITZA
GOLFO DELL'ASINARA
07037 SORSO [SS]
TEL. 0793402017
www.tenutaasinara.com

CELLAR SALES
PRE-BOOKED VISITS
ANNUAL PRODUCTION 70,000 bottles
HECTARES UNDER VINE 19.00

● Cannonau di Sardegna Indolente '13	♥♥ 2*
● Hassan '12	♥♥ 3
● Herculis '11	♥♥ 4
○ Vermentino di Sardegna Indolente '14	♥ 2

Poderi Atha Ruja

VIA EMILIA, 45
08022 DORGALI [NU]
TEL. 0784920516
www.atharuja.com

CELLAR SALES
PRE-BOOKED VISITS
ACCOMMODATION
ANNUAL PRODUCTION 25,000 bottles
HECTARES UNDER VINE 5.00

● Cannonau di Sardegna V. Sorella '13	♥♥ 3

Audarya

S.DA STATALE 466 KM 10,100
09040 SERDIANA [CA]
TEL. 070740437
www.audarya.it

CELLAR SALES
PRE-BOOKED VISITS
ANNUAL PRODUCTION 50,000 bottles
HECTARES UNDER VINE 35.00

● Cannonau di Sardegna '14	♥♥ 2*
○ Nuragus di Cagliari '14	♥♥ 2*
● Monica di Sardegnaa '14	♥ 2
○ Vermentino di Sardegna '14	♥ 2

Berritta

VIA KENNEDY, 108
08022 DORGALI [NU]
TEL. 078495372
www.cantinaberritta.it

ANNUAL PRODUCTION 5,000 bottles
HECTARES UNDER VINE 2.00

● Cannonau di Sardegna Nostranu '13	♥♥ 2*
● Cannonau di Sardegna Thurcalesu '13	♥♥ 2*
● Don Baddore '13	♥ 3
● Panzale '14	♥ 2

Cantina di Calasetta

VIA ROMA, 134
09011 CALASETTA [CI]
TEL. 078188413
www.cantinadicalasetta.it

CELLAR SALES
PRE-BOOKED VISITS
ANNUAL PRODUCTION 100,000 bottles
HECTARES UNDER VINE 300.00

● Carignano del Sulcis Tupei '12	♥♥ 2*
● Carignano del Sulcis Piede Franco '12	♥ 2
○ Vermentino di Sardegna Cala di Seta '14	♥ 2

Cantina delle Vigne Piero Mancini

LOC. CALA SACCAIA
VIA MADAGASCAR, 17
07026 OLBIA
TEL. 078950717
www.pieromancini.it

CELLAR SALES
PRE-BOOKED VISITS
ANNUAL PRODUCTION 1,500,000 bottles
HECTARES UNDER VINE 100.00

○ Vermentino di Gallura Sup. Cucaione '14	♥♥ 2*
○ Vermentino di Gallura Sup. Mancini Primo '14	♥♥ 4
● Cannonau di Sardegna Falcale '13	♥ 2

Silvio Carta

VIA ROMA, 2
09070 BARATILI SAN PIETRO [OR]
TEL. 0783410314
www.silviocarta.it

PRE-BOOKED VISITS
ANNUAL PRODUCTION 1,000,000 bottles
HECTARES UNDER VINE 90.00
VITICULTURE METHOD Certified Organic

○ Vernaccia di Oristano Ris. '03	♀♀	3
○ Vernaccia di Oristano Ris. '04	♀	3

Cantina di Castiadas

LOC. OLIA SPECIOSA
09040 CASTIADAS [CA]
TEL. 0709949004
www.cantinacastiadas.com

CELLAR SALES
PRE-BOOKED VISITS
ANNUAL PRODUCTION 120,000 bottles
HECTARES UNDER VINE 150.00

● Cannonau di Sardegna Capo Ferrato Rei '13	♀♀	2*
● Cannonau di Sardegna Capo Ferrato Ris. '11	♀♀	4

Columbu

VIA MARCONI, 1
08013 BOSA [OR]
TEL. 0785373380
www.vinibosa.com

CELLAR SALES
PRE-BOOKED VISITS
ANNUAL PRODUCTION 4,000 bottles
HECTARES UNDER VINE 3.40

○ Malvasia di Bosa '11	♀♀	5
○ Malvasia di Bosa Alvarèga '14	♀♀	2*

Consorzio San Michele

LOC. SAN MICHELE
07022 BERCHIDDA [OT]
TEL. 078923865
www.consorziosanmichele.com

CELLAR SALES
PRE-BOOKED VISITS
ANNUAL PRODUCTION 50,000 bottles
HECTARES UNDER VINE 10.00

○ Vermentino di Gallura Sinfonia Gallurese '14	♀♀	3
○ Vermentino di Gallura Sup. Superbia Gallurese '14	♀♀	4

Giovanni Luigi Deaddis

LOC. SAN PIETRO
VIA LEONARDO DA VINCI, 30
07035 SEDINI [SS]
TEL. 3481437765
www.cantinadeaddis.com

CELLAR SALES
PRE-BOOKED VISITS
ANNUAL PRODUCTION 35,000 bottles
HECTARES UNDER VINE 9.00

● Cannonau di Sardegna Capo Sardo '12	♀♀	3
● One Hundred '12	♀♀	3
● Ultana '12	♀♀	5
○ Vermentino di Sardegna Narami '14	♀	3

Vigne Deriu

LOC. SIGNORANNA
07040 CODRONGIANOS [SS]
TEL. 079435101
www.vignederiu.it

CELLAR SALES
PRE-BOOKED VISITS
ANNUAL PRODUCTION 35,000 bottles
HECTARES UNDER VINE 6.00

● Cannonau di Sardegna '13	♀♀	3
● Tiu Filippu '11	♀♀	5
○ Vermentino di Sardegna '14	♀	3

Fradiles

LOC. CRECCHERÌ
08030 ATZARA [NU]
TEL. 3331761683
www.fradiles.it

CELLAR SALES
PRE-BOOKED VISITS
ANNUAL PRODUCTION 20,000 bottles
HECTARES UNDER VINE 14.00
SUSTAINABLE WINERY

● Bagadiu '13		♟♟ 4
● Mandrolisai Azzara '13		♟♟ 2*
● Mandrolisai Fradiles '13		♟♟ 3

Cantina Giogantinu

VIA MILANO, 30
07022 BERCHIDDA [OT]
TEL. 079704163
www.giogantinu.it

CELLAR SALES
PRE-BOOKED VISITS
ANNUAL PRODUCTION 1,500,000 bottles
HECTARES UNDER VINE 320.00

○ Vermentino di Gallura Lunghente '14		♟♟ 3
○ Vermentino di Gallura Sup. Karenzia '13		♟♟ 4
○ Vermentino di Gallura Sup. Vigne Storiche '14		♟♟ 4

Gostolai

VIA FRIULI VENEZIA GIULIA, 24
08025 OLIENA [NU]
TEL. 0784288417
gostolai.arcadu@tiscali.it

CELLAR SALES
ANNUAL PRODUCTION 110,000 bottles
HECTARES UNDER VINE 20.00

● Cannonau di Sardegna Nepente di Oliena D'Annunzio Ris. '06		♟♟ 4
● Cannonau di Sardegna Nepente di Oliena Sos Usos de Una la Ris. '10		♟♟ 3

Jankara

VIA REGINA ELENA, 55
07030 SANT'ANTONIO DI GALLURA [OT]
TEL. 399 4381296
www.vinijankara.com

ANNUAL PRODUCTION 14,000 bottles
HECTARES UNDER VINE 5.00

○ Vermentino di Gallura Sup. '14		♟♟ 4
● Lu Nieddu '13		♟ 4

Tenuta l'Ariosa

LOC. PREDDA NIEDDA SUD
S.DA 15
07100 SASSARI
TEL. 079261905
www.lariosa.it

ANNUAL PRODUCTION 40,000 bottles
HECTARES UNDER VINE 9.00

● Pedrastella '13		♟♟ 4
● Sass'Antico Cagnulari '14		♟♟ 4
○ Vermentino di Sardegna Arenu '14		♟ 3
○ Vermentino di Sardegna Galatea '14		♟ 3

Andrea Ledda

VIA MUSIO, 13
07043 BONNANARO [SS]
TEL. 079845060
www.vitivinicolaledda.com

CELLAR SALES
PRE-BOOKED VISITS
ANNUAL PRODUCTION 25,000 bottles
HECTARES UNDER VINE 13.00

● Ebano '12		♟♟ 4
○ Moscato di Sardegna Passito Bagliori '11		♟♟ 4
○ Vermentino di Sardegna Acero '14		♟♟ 3

Li Duni

LOC. LI PARISI
07030 BADESI [OT]
TEL. 0799144480
www.cantinaliduni.com

CELLAR SALES
PRE-BOOKED VISITS
ANNUAL PRODUCTION 40,000 bottles
HECTARES UNDER VINE 25.00

● Nalboni '13	♥♥ 2*
○ Vermentino di Gallura Sup. Renabianca '14	♥♥ 3
● Tajanu '09	♥ 4

Pietro Lilliu

VIA SARDEGNA, 13
09020 USSARAMANNA [VS]
TEL. 3407591144
www.cantinalilliu.it

CELLAR SALES
PRE-BOOKED VISITS
ANNUAL PRODUCTION 20,000 bottles
HECTARES UNDER VINE 4.00
SUSTAINABLE WINERY

● Biazzu	♥♥ 3
⊙ Cannonau di Sardegna Pantumas '14	♥ 4

Cantina Sociale del Mandrolisai

C.SO IV NOVEMBRE, 20
08038 SORGONO [NU]
TEL. 078460113
www.mandrolisai.com

CELLAR SALES
PRE-BOOKED VISITS
ANNUAL PRODUCTION 200,000 bottles
HECTARES UNDER VINE 80.00

● Mandrolisai Rosso Sup. '11	♥♥ 2*
● Mandrolisai Sup. Kent'Annos '10	♥♥ 4
⊙ Granito	♥ 3
○ Ternura	♥ 3

Abele Melis

VIA SANTA SUINA, 3
09098 TERRALBA [OR]
TEL. 0783851090
melis.vini@tiscali.it

CELLAR SALES
PRE-BOOKED VISITS
ANNUAL PRODUCTION 100,000 bottles
HECTARES UNDER VINE 35.00

● Bovale '14	♥♥ 2*
● Terralba Bovale Dominariu '13	♥♥ 3
● Terralba Nabj Ris. '12	♥♥ 5
○ Vermentino di Sardegna localia '14	♥ 2

Mora&Memo

VIA CIUSA, 13
09040 SERDIANA [CA]
TEL. 3311972266
www.moraememo.it

CELLAR SALES
PRE-BOOKED VISITS
ANNUAL PRODUCTION 28,000 bottles
HECTARES UNDER VINE 30.00

● Cannonau di Sardegna Nau '14	♥♥ 3
● Nau&Co. '14	♥♥ 4
○ Vermentino di Sardegna Tino '14	♥ 3
○ Vermentino di Sardegna Tino Sur Lie '14	♥ 3

Murales

LOC. PILIEZZU, 1
07026 OLBIA
TEL. 078953174
www.vinimurales.com

CELLAR SALES
PRE-BOOKED VISITS
ACCOMMODATION AND RESTAURANT SERVICE
ANNUAL PRODUCTION 80,000 bottles
HECTARES UNDER VINE 20.00

○ Vermentino di Gallura Miradas '14	♥♥ 4
○ Sentenzia	♥ 4
○ Vermentino di Sardegna Tutti i Venti '14	♥ 3

Tenute Olbios

LOC. VENAFIORITA
VIA LOIRI, 83
07026 OLBIA
TEL. 0789641003
www.tenuteolbios.com

CELLAR SALES
PRE-BOOKED VISITS
ANNUAL PRODUCTION 65,000 bottles
HECTARES UNDER VINE 60.00

○ Vermentino di Gallura Sup. Lupus in Fabula '14	♥♥ 5

Olianas

LOC. PURRUDDU
09031 GERGEI [CA]
TEL. 0558300800
www.olianas.it

CELLAR SALES
PRE-BOOKED VISITS
ANNUAL PRODUCTION 50,000 bottles
HECTARES UNDER VINE 13.00
VITICULTURE METHOD Certified Organic

● Cannonau di Sardegna '14	♥♥ 3
⊙ Rosato '14	♥♥ 2*
○ Vernasco '14	♥♥ 2*
○ Vermentino di Sardegna '14	♥ 3

Cantina Cooperativa di Oliena

VIA NUORO, 112
08025 OLIENA [NU]
TEL. 0784287509
www.cantinasocialeoliena.it

ANNUAL PRODUCTION 300,000 bottles
HECTARES UNDER VINE 180.00

● Cannonau di Sardegna Cl. Nepente di Oliena Irilai '11	♥♥ 2*
● Cannonau di Sardegna Nepente di Oliena '13	♥♥ 2*

Cantine di Orgosolo

VIA ÌLOLE S. N.
08027 ORGOSOLO [NU]
TEL. 0784403096
www.cantinediorgosolo.it

CELLAR SALES
PRE-BOOKED VISITS
RESTAURANT SERVICE
ANNUAL PRODUCTION 17,000 bottles
HECTARES UNDER VINE 16.00
VITICULTURE METHOD Certified Organic

● Cannonau di Sardegna Soroi Cl. Ris. '11	♥♥ 5
● Cannonau di Sardegna Urùlu '13	♥♥ 4
● Locoe '12	♥ 3

Giampietro Puggioni

VIA NUORO, 11
08024 MAMOIADA [NU]
TEL. 0784203516
www.cantinagiampietropuggioni.it

CELLAR SALES
PRE-BOOKED VISITS
ANNUAL PRODUCTION 60,000 bottles
HECTARES UNDER VINE 15.00
VITICULTURE METHOD Certified Organic

● Cannonau di Sardegna Lakana '13	♥♥ 3
● Cannonau di Sardegna Mamuthone '13	♥♥ 3
● Babbu '14	♥ 3
● Cannonau di Sardegna Isula '13	♥ 3

Pusole

LOC. PERDA 'E CUBA
08040 LOTZORAI [OG]
TEL. 3334047219
roberto.pusole@gmail.com

CELLAR SALES
PRE-BOOKED VISITS
ACCOMMODATION
ANNUAL PRODUCTION 10,000 bottles
HECTARES UNDER VINE 7.50
SUSTAINABLE WINERY

● Cannonau di Sardegna '14	♥♥ 3*
⊙ Il Rosé di Pusole '14	♥♥ 3

Quartomoro di Sardegna

VIA DINO POLI, 33
09092 ARBOREA [OR]
TEL. 3467643552
www.quartomoro.it

CELLAR SALES
PRE-BOOKED VISITS
ANNUAL PRODUCTION 20,000 bottles
HECTARES UNDER VINE 2.50

● MAI Intrecci di Vite '12	♥♥ 6
● BVL '14	♥♥ 4
● CRG '14	♥♥ 4
○ Q Brut M. Cl. '12	♥ 4

U-Tabarka
Tanca Gioia Carloforte

VIA PIEMONTE, 16
09127 CAGLIARI
TEL. 3356359329
www.u-tabarka.com

CELLAR SALES
PRE-BOOKED VISITS
ANNUAL PRODUCTION 30,000 bottles
HECTARES UNDER VINE 7.00

● Carignano del Sulcis Roussou '13	♥♥ 3
● Ciù Roussou '14	♥♥ 3
○ Perdigiournou '14	♥ 3
○ Vermentino di Sardegna Ventou de Ma '14	♥ 3

Cantina del Vermentino

VIA SAN PAOLO, 2
07020 MONTI [SS]
TEL. 078944012
www.vermentinomonti.it

CELLAR SALES
PRE-BOOKED VISITS
ANNUAL PRODUCTION 2,000,000 bottles
HECTARES UNDER VINE 500.00

● Cannonau di Sardegna Kiri '14	♥♥ 2*
○ Vermentino di Gallura Funtanaliras '14	♥♥ 3
○ Vermentino di Gallura Sup. Arakena V.T. '14	♥♥ 4

Cantina Sociale
della Vernaccia

LOC. RIMEDIO
VIA ORISTANO, 6A
09170 ORISTANO
TEL. 078333383
www.vinovernaccia.com

CELLAR SALES
PRE-BOOKED VISITS
ANNUAL PRODUCTION 260,000 bottles
HECTARES UNDER VINE 120.00

● Cannonau di Sardegna Corash Ris. '12	♥♥ 3
○ Terresinis '14	♥♥ 2*
● Nieddera Montiprama '12	♥ 1*

Marco Zanatta

VIA SPIRITO SANTO
07026 OLBIA
TEL. 3926167907
bruno@vignetizanatta.it

CELLAR SALES
PRE-BOOKED VISITS
ANNUAL PRODUCTION 300,000 bottles
HECTARES UNDER VINE 80.00

○ Vermentino di Gallura Pilosdoro '14	♥♥ 3
● Cannonau di Sardegna Salana '13	♥ 2
○ Vermentino di Sardegna Orion '14	♥ 2

Zarelli Vini

VIA VITTORIO EMANUELE, 36
08010 MAGOMADAS [OR]
TEL. 078535311
www.zarellivini.it

CELLAR SALES
PRE-BOOKED VISITS
ANNUAL PRODUCTION 20,000 bottles
HECTARES UNDER VINE 7.00

● Ardesia	♥♥ 5
● Cannonau di Sardegna Sa Costa '12	♥♥ 2*
○ Inachis '14	♥ 3
○ Malvasia di Bosa Licoro '12	♥ 4

INDEXES
wineries in alphabetical order
wineries by region

WINERIES IN ALPHABETICAL ORDER

Luigi Cataldi Madonna	781		Damiano Ciolli	764
La Caudrina	82		Claudio Cipressi	800
Cautiero	806		La Cipriana	575
Cavalchina	348		Cirelli	781
Cavalier Bartolomeo	181		Tenute Cisa Asinari dei Marchesi di Grésy	85
Tenuta del Cavalier Pepe	806		Citari	260
Cavalieri	729		Citille di Sopra	576
Cavalleri	230		Codice Citra	782
Cantine Cavallotti	260		Ciù Ciù	703
F.lli Cavallotto – Tenuta Bricco Boschis	82		Il Civettaio	676
Cavazza	348		Podere della Civettaja	676
Cavicchioli U. & Figli	497		Civielle	260
Caviro	498		Cantina Clavesana	182
Cavit	275		Aldo Clerico	183
Le Cecche	181		Domenico Clerico	86
Simona Ceccherini	676		Cobelli	287
Giorgio Cecchetto	349		Tenuta Cocci Grifoni	704
Famiglia Cecchi	570		Coffele	350
Marco Cecchini	427		Elvio Cogno	86
Enrico Ceci	729		Tenuta Col d'Orcia	576
Giancarlo Ceci	869		Col dei Venti	183
Celler del Gat	676		Col del Mondo	796
Celli	498		Col di Bacche	577
Cembranidoc	287		Col di Corte	730
Cenatiempo Vini d'Ischia	835		Col Vetoraz	351
Cantina Cenci	742		Battista Cola	230
Giacomo Centanni	702		Antonello Coletti Conti	765
Centolani	570		Poderi Colla	87
Centopassi	889		Conte Collalto	407
Ceralti	571		Eugenio Collavini	427
Roberto Ceraudo	876		Fattoria Collazzi	577
La Cerbaiola	571		Cantina Colle Ciocco	758
Il Cerchio	676		Colle di Bordocheo	578
Ceretto	83		Colle di San Domenico	835
Cantine Cerrolongo	848		Colle Duga	428
Cerulli Spinozzi	796		Colle Manora	87
Cerutti	182		Colle Massari	578
Andrea Cervini	525		Colle Santa Mustiola	579
Cantina Sociale Cesanese del Piglio	773		Fattoria Colle Verde	579
Vincenzo Cesani	572		Fattoria Colleallodole	743
Gerardo Cesari	349		Collebello - Tenuta Terraviva	782
Umberto Cesari	499		Collefrisio	783
Cesarini Sforza	276		Collelceto	580
Italo Cescon	350		Collemattoni	676
Franco e Pierguido Ceste	182		Collestefano	704
Château Feuillet	26		Colli di Castelfranci	807
Cheo	200		Colli di Lapio	807
Giovanni Maria Cherchi	921		Colli di Poianis	486
Cherri d'Acquaviva	703		Colli di Serrapetrona	730
Chessa	921		Collina Serragrilli	183
Giovanni Chiappini	572		Colline della Stella	260
Cleto Chiarli Tenute Agricole	499		Le Colline di Sopra	580
Michele Chiarlo	83		Colline San Biagio	677
Chiaromonte	854		Tenuta di Collosorbo	677
Tenuta Chicccheri	406		Colmello di Grotta	428
Chimento	882		Cantina Cològnola - Tenuta Musone	705
Quinto Chionetti	84		Colognole	581
Chiorri	758		Colomba Bianca	911
Il Chiosso	182		Il Colombaio di Santa Chiara	581
Paride Chiovini	182		La Colombera	88
Le Chiuse	573		Colombera & Garella	183
Le Chiusure	260		Colombo - Cascina Pastori	183
Ciabot Berton	182		Colonnara	730
Cieck	84		Cantine Colosi	911
Cigliano	573		Fattoria Colsanto	743
F.lli Cigliuti	85		Cantina Produttori Colterenzio	296
Le Cimate	758		Le Colture	351
Fattoria di Cinciano	574		Columbu	937
Cincinnato	764		Gianpaolo Colutta	429
Le Cinciole	574		Giorgio Colutta - Bandut	429
Donatella Cinelli Colombini	575		Paolino Comelli	430
Cantina Cinque Terre	200		Cominium	773

Le Fraghe	359
La Fralluca	596
Francesco Moser	279
Paolo Francesconi	505
Frank & Serafico	596
Frascole	597
Frecciarossa	237
Cantina Frentana	797
Marchesi de' Frescobaldi	597
Fattoria di Fubbiano	679
Elena Fucci	844
Fuligni	598
La Fusina	185
Futura 14	856
Giuseppe Gabbas	924
Gabutti - Franco Boasso	101
Gaggino	102
Gaja	102
Galardi	815
Maria Galassi	505
Tenute Galfano	914
Gallegati	506
Filippo Gallino	103
Cantina Gallura	924
Garesio	185
Tenuta Garetto	103
Garlider - Christian Kerschbaumer	300
Gioacchino Garofoli	710
Cantine Garrone	185
Gattavecchi	598
Enrico Gatti	237
Marco Gatti	710
Tenuta Gatti	896
Gavioli	525
Generaj	104
Gentile	786
Geraci	914
La Gerla	679
Ettore Germano	104
I Gessi - Fabbio Defilippi	238
La Ghibellina	105
Attilio Ghisolfi	105
Tenuta di Ghizzano	599
Alberto Giacobbe	774
Giacomelli	201
Bruno Giacosa	106
Carlo Giacosa	106
F.lli Giacosa	107
Giorgio Gianatti	262
Donato Giangirolami	774
Giannoni Fabbri	679
Giasira	914
Cantina Giba - 6Mura	925
Adriano Gigante	437
Giovanni Battista Gillardi	107
La Ginestraia	202
Gini	359
Marchesi Ginori Lisci	599
Cantina Giogantinu	938
Giomi Zannoni	680
F.lli Giorgi	238
La Giribaldina	108
Cantina Girlan	300
Fattoria Giro di Vento	759
Tenute Girolamo	857
La Gironda	108
Giubertoni	262
Vito Donato Giuliani	857
I Giusti e Zanza	600
Giusti Wine	360
La Giustiniana	109
Glassierhof - Stefan Vaja	323
Glögglhof - Franz Gojer	301
Goretti	746
Tenuta Gorghi Tondi	914
Gorgo	408
Gori	437
Gostolai	938
Graci	897
Gradis'ciutta	438
Elio Grasso	109
Silvio Grasso	110
Podere Grattamacco	600
Gravner	438
Cantine Graziano	848
Podere Grecale	211
Podere Grecchi	774
Gregoletto	360
Griesbauerhof - Georg Mumelter	301
Grifalco della Lucania	844
Fattoria di Grignano	601
Grigoletti	279
Bruno Grigolli	288
Iole Grillo	439
Bruna Grimaldi	110
Giacomo Grimaldi	111
Sergio Grimaldi - Ca' du Sindic	111
F.lli Grosjean	32
La Grotta	526
Gruppo Cevico	506
Guado al Melo	601
Tenuta Guado al Tasso	602
Gualdo del Re	602
La Guardia	112
La Guardiense	815
Duca Carlo Guarini	870
Guido Guarini Matteucci	526
Clemente Guasti	112
Albano Guerra	488
Guerrieri Rizzardi	361
Guglierame	211
Tenute Guicciardini Strozzi	603
Guidi 1929	680
Gulfi	897
Gummerhof - Malojer	302
Gumphof - Markus Prackwieser	302
Franz Haas	303
Haderburg	303
Haidenhof	324
Hauner	898
Esther Hauser	731
Hibiscus	914
Hilberg - Pasquero	113
Hiso Telaray - Libera Terra Puglia	871
Historia Antiqua	836
Humar	488
Icardi	113
Icario	680
iGreco	877
Il Verro	836
Tenuta L' Illuminata	185
Dino Illuminati	787
Inama	361
Incisiana	185
Viticoltori Ingauni	211
Institut Agricole Régional	32
Ioppa	114
Ippolito 1845	877
Isimbarda	239
Isola Augusta	488
Isole e Olena	603
Istine	604
Tenuta Iuzzolini	883
Tenute Jacovazzo	849

WINERIES IN ALPHABETICAL ORDER

Torre Quarto	874	Marta Valpiani	530
Torre Rosazza	472	Cantina Valpolicella Negrar	395
Torre San Martino	518	Valturio	725
Torrevento	865	Vanzini	253
Torrevilla	269	Odino Vaona	395
Le Torri	662	Varramista	667
Marchesi Torrigiani	692	Vigne & Vini Varvaglione	866
Pietro Torti	269	La Vecchia Cantina	212
Trabucchi d'Illasi	393	Vecchia Cantina di Montepulciano	668
Trabucco	839	La Vecchia Posta	194
Traerte	829	Vecchia Torre	866
Cantina Tramin	319	Podere Vecciano	530
Trappolini	772	Alessandro Veglio	194
Giancarlo Travaglini	170	Mauro Veglio	171
Travaglino	252	Velenosi	726
Travignoli	662	Tenuta Le Velette	756
Tre Botti	776	Venica & Venica	474
Cantine Tre Pini	865	Cantina di Venosa	847
Trediberri	193	Ventolaio	693
Trerè	529	Roberto Venturi	726
Cantina Trexenta	935	Massimino Venturini	396
Triacca	269	Paolo Venturini	492
F.lli Trinchero	193	Venturini Baldini	519
Antonino Tringali - Casanuova	693	Bruno Verdi	253
Tenuta di Trinoro	663	Cantina del Vermentino	941
Tua Rita	663	Cantina Sociale della Vernaccia	941
Tudernum	755	I Veroni	668
La Tunella	473	Verrone Viticoltori	839
F.lli Turina	269	Vestini Campagnano	840
U-Tabarka Tanca Gioia Carloforte	941	Vetrere	874
Uberti	252	Maison Albert Vevey	32
Uccelliera	664	Francesco Vezzelli	519
Fattoria Uccelliera	693	Giuseppe Vezzoli	254
Tenuta dell' Ugolino	734	La Viarte	475
Tenuta Ulisse	793	Eraldo Viberti	194
Umani Ronchi	724	Giovanni Viberti	194
Thomas Unterhofer	326	Vicara	171
Untermoserhof - Georg Ramoser	326	Vicari	727
Tenuta Unterortl - Castel Juval	319	Agostino Vicentini	396
Urciuolo	830	Giacomo Vico	172
Urlari	693	Vidussi	475
Vaccaro	918	Vie di Romans	476
F.lli Vagnoni	664	Vietti	172
G. D. Vajra	170	Tenuta Viglione	867
Podere Val delle Corti	665	Tenuta La Vigna	270
Val di Suga - Bertani Domains	665	Vigna del Lauro	476
Val di Toro	693	Vigna Dorata	270
Valchiarò	473	Vigna Petrussa	477
Tenuta Valdipiatta	666	Vigna Roda	397
Valdiscalve	212	Vigna Traverso	477
Laura Valditerra	193	Vigna Villae	840
Spumanti Valdo	394	I Vignaioli di Santo Stefano	173
Valdonica	693	Vignale di Cecilia	397
La Valentina	793	Vignalta	398
Valentini	794	Vignamaggio	669
Valentini	666	Vignamato	727
Valfaccenda	194	Vigne dei Boschi	520
Tenuta di Valgiano	667	Vigne del Malina	478
Valla	530	Le Vigne di Eli	918
Vallarom	286	Le Vigne di Franca	734
La Valle	269	Le Vigne di San Pietro	398
Valle dell'Acate	908	Le Vigne di Zamò	478
Valle dell'Asso	874	Vigne Guadagno	840
Cantina Produttori Valle Isarco	320	Vigne Olcru	270
Valle Reale	794	Vigne Sannite	840
Valle Vermiglia	772	Vignedileo - Tre Castelli	728
Vallerosa Bonci	725	Vigneti Massa	173
Vallona	530	Vigneti Radica	798
Agricole Vallone	874	Vigneti Reale	874
Valori	798	Vigneti Valle Roncati	174
Valpanera	474	Vigneto Due Santi	399
Cantina Valpantena Verona	394	Villa Bellini	399

WINERIES BY REGION